# AP* Edition

# Literature

## An Introduction to Reading and Writing

**FOURTH EDITION**

### Edgar V. Roberts
*Lehman College*
*The City University of New York*

### Darlene Stock Stotler
*California State University, Bakersfield*

PEARSON

Prentice
Hall

*Upper Saddle River, New Jersey 07458*

Library of Congress Cataloging-in-Publication Data

Roberts, Edgar V.
    Literature: an introduction to reading and writing/Edgar V. Roberts.—
4th compact ed.
        p. cm.
    Includes bibliographical references and index.
    ISBN-13: 978-0-13-604433-8 (pbk.)    ISBN-10: 0-13-604433-6 (pbk.)
    1. Literature.   2. Exposition (Rhetoric)   3. Literature—Collections.
4. College readers.   5. Report writing.   I. Title.

PN45.R575 2008
808'.0668—dc22

                                                    2007050117

**Editorial Director:** Leah Jewell
**Editor-in-Chief:** Craig Campanella
**Senior Editor:** Vivian Garcia
**Assistant Editor:** Melissa Casciano
**Editorial Assistant:** Deborah Doyle
**Marketing Director:** Brandy Dawson
**Text Permission Specialist:** Mary Dalton
  Hoffman
**Senior Operations Supervisor:** Sherry Lewis
**Operations Specialist:** Christina Amato
**Project Manager:** Maureen Benicasa
**Senior Art Director:** Nancy Wells
**Interior Design:** ICC/Suzanne Duda
**Director, Image Resource Center:** Melinda Reo
**Manager, Cover Visual Research and**
  **Permissions:** Karen Sanatar

**Manager, Rights and Permissions:** Zina Arabia
**Manager, Visual Research:** Beth Brenzel
**Image Permission Cordinator:** Annette Linder
**Image Researcher:** Teri Stratford
**Cover Art Director:** Jayne Conte
**Cover Art Designer:** Bruce Kenselaar
**Cover Illustration/Photo:** New England Rural
  Images/Mark Klein
**Full-Service Production and Composition:** ICC
  Macmillan Inc.
**Full-Service Project Management:** Winifred
  Sanchez
**Printer/Binder:** Quad/Graphics- Taunton
**Cover Printer:** Phoenix Color Corp.
**Typeface:** 10/12 Palatino

Credits and acknowledgments borrowed from other sources and reproduced, with permission, in this textbook appear on appropriate page within text (or beginning on page 1607).

AP* and Advanced Placement Program are registered trademarks of The College Board, which was not involved in the production of, and does not endorse, this book

Pearson Education LTD., London
Pearson Education Singapore, Pte. Ltd
Pearson Education, Canada, Ltd
Pearson Education–Japan
Pearson Education Australia PTY, Limited

Pearson Education North Asia Ltd
Pearson Educación de Mexico, S.A. de C.V.
Pearson Education Malaysia, Pte. Ltd
Pearson Education, Upper Saddle River,
  New Jersey

10 9 8 7 6

ISBN-13 (AP* Edition):          978-0-13-604433-8
ISBN-10 (AP* Edition):          0-13-604433-6
ISBN-13 (College Edition):  978-0-13-223392-7
ISBN-10 (College Edition):  0-13-223392-7

# Contents

## 1 INTRODUCTION: THE PROCESS OF READING, RESPONDING TO, AND WRITING ABOUT LITERATURE     1

*What Is Literature, and Why Do We Study It?*   1   •   *Types of Literature: The Genres,*   2   •   *Reading Literature and Responding to It Actively,*   3

### ▪ Guy De Maupassant     The Necklace,   4

*To go to a ball, Mathilde Loisel borrows a necklace from a rich friend, but her rhapsodic evening has unforeseen consequences.*

*Reading and Responding by Computer or Notebook,*   11   •   *Writing Essays on Literary Topics,*   16   •   *Major Stages in Thinking and Writing: Discovering Ideas, Preparing to Write, Making Initial Drafts, and Completing the Essay,*   18   •   *Presenting an Argument,*   20   •   *Preparing to Write,*   23   •   *Making an Initial Draft of Your Essay,*   27   •   The Need for the Physical Process of Writing,   28   •   Verb Tenses in Literary Analysis,   30   •   Using the Names of Authors,   33   •   📄 *Illustrative Student Essay (First Draft): How Setting in "The Necklace" Is Related to the Character of Mathilde,*   34   •   *Completing the Essay: Developing and Strengthening through Revision,*   36   •   *Checking Your Development and Organization,*   39   •   *Using Exact, Comprehensive, and Forceful Language,*   41   •   📄 *Illustrative Student Essay (Improved Draft): How Maupassant Uses Setting in "The Necklace" to Show the Character of Mathilde,*   43   •   *A Summary of Guidelines,*   46   •   *Writing Topics: The Writing Process,*   46

## Reading and Writing About Fiction

## 3  Point of View: The Position of the Narrator or Speaker     107

## 4  Characters: The People in Fiction     151

# 6 STRUCTURE: THE ORGANIZATION OF STORIES 244

# 7 TONE AND STYLE: CONVEYING ATTITUDES IN FICTION 280

## 8   SYMBOLISM AND ALLEGORY: KEYS TO EXTENDED MEANING   321

## Reading and Writing About Poetry

## 12  WORDS: THE BUILDING BLOCKS OF POETRY    494

**14** FIGURES OF SPEECH, OR METAPHORICAL LANGUAGE: A SOURCE OF DEPTH AND RANGE IN POETRY                    **560**

**15** **TONE: THE CREATION OF ATTITUDE IN POETRY**    599

*Tone, Choice, and Response,*    599

*Tone and the Need for Control,*    601

*Tone and Common Grounds of Assent,*    602    •    *Tone in Conversation and Poetry,*    603    •    *Tone and Irony,*    603

*Tone and Satire,*    606

**16** FORM: THE SHAPE OF POEMS,    641

**19A** WRITING ABOUT LITERATURE WITH THE AID OF RESEARCH,
2—WRITING ESSAYS ON POETRY: USING EXTRA
RESOURCES FOR UNDERSTANDING                      **855**

*Topics to Discover in Research,   855   •   📄 Illustrative Student Essay Written
with the Aid of Research:"Beat! Beat! Drums!" and "I Hear America Singing": Two
Whitman Poems Spanning the Civil War,   857*

## Reading and Writing About Drama

**20** THE DRAMATIC VISION: AN OVERVIEW                      **862**

*Drama as Literature,   862   •   Performance: The Unique Aspect of Drama,   869
•   Drama from Ancient Times to Our Own: Tragedy, Comedy, and Additional
Forms,   873*

■ **Anonymous**       The Visit to the Sepulcher
(Visitatio Sepulchri),   875

*How does the news told by the angel cause the three Marys to react?*

Visualizing Plays,   879

PLAYS FOR STUDY,   883

■ **Edward Albee**       The Sandbox,   883

# Topical and Thematic Table of Contents

For analytical purposes, the following topical and thematic table of contents groups the selections into twenty-six separate subject categories. ("Reconciliation and Understanding" is a new category in the 4E, AP* Edition.) The idea is that the topics will facilitate a thematic and focused study and comparison of a number of works. Obviously each of the works brings out many other issues than are suggested by the topics. For comparison, however, the topics invite analyses based on specific issues. Thus, the category "Women" suggests that the listed works may profitably be examined for what they have to say about the lives and problems specifically of women, just as the category "Men" suggests a concentration on the lives and problems specifically of men. The subject headings are suggestive only; they are by no means intended to mandate interpretations or approaches. For emphasis, I will say that again, and underline it: <u>The subject headings are suggestive only; they are by no means intended to mandate interpretations or approaches.</u> I have accordingly assigned a number of works to two and often more categories. Ibsen's *A Dollhouse*, for example, is not easily classified within a single catgegory.

Because the topical and thematic table of contents is to be as brief as possible, we use only the last names of authors and artists, although for authors with the same last names (e.g., Phyllis Webb, Charles Harper Webb; Beth Henley, W. E. Henley; Flannery O'Connor, Frank O'Connor), I supply the complete name. In listing works I shorten a number of longer titles. Thus I refer to *A Certain Slant* (Dickinson), and to *That Time of Year* (Shakespeare) and so on, using recognizable short titles rather than the full titles that appear in the regular table of contents, in the text itself and in the index. Of course, some titles are brief, such as *Reconciliation* (Whitman), *Eating Poetry* (Strand), and *A Worn Path* (Welty). I include these in their entirety.

The 4E, AP* Edition includes references to works of art that are included in the plates. I hope that these will be usefully consulted for comparative purposes and that such comparisons will enhance the discussions of the various topics.

## YOUTH AND AGE

### Stories

### Poems

### Plays

### Art

# Preface to the 4E, AP* Edition

Most of the works anthologized in the 4E, AP* Edition are by American, British, and Canadian authors, but there are also a small number of ancient and medieval writers, along with later writers who lived in or came from France, Italy, Poland, Australia, Norway, and Russia, together with authors who represent the diverse backgrounds of African-American, American Indian, Latino, and Chinese cultures. In total, 237 authors are represented here, including five anonymous authors. Slightly more than 58 percent of the authors—142—were born after 1900. Of the 63 writers born since 1935, 32 are women, or just a bit higher than fifty percent. If one counts only the number of authors born since the ending of World War II (1945), the percentage of women writers rises to 62 percent.

The 4E, AP* Edition includes a total of 373 separate works–41 stories, 318 poems (including some portions of very long poems), and 14 plays. Each work is suitable for discussion either alone or in comparison with other works. For comparison, the works in two genres by five writers are included—specifically Hughes, Oates, Poe, Shakespeare, and Updike. In addition, there are two plays by Shakespeare—a tragedy and a comedy—and there are two or more poems by a number of poets. For intensive study, Chapter 18, *Four Major Poets*, contains 18 poems by Dickinson, 14 by Frost, 14 poems by Hughes, and 13 by Plath.

"Visualizing" sections on fiction, poetry, and drama, can be found in Chapters 2, 16, and 20. Commentators have often observed that today's students are more visually oriented than students of the past—most likely because of the ever-present influence of television in the home, and also because of the many other graphic forms in which the American public is introduced to facts and ideas. This aspect of our culture is often deplored, but it seems more fruitful to accept it as a fact of life and then go ahead to bring it to bear on the imaginative reading of literary works. What is important here is the development of the capacity

> to think,
> to follow through on ideas,
> and
> to imagine—

in short, to exercise the mind totally in the interpretation of literature, and in any intellectual endeavor which our students will ever undertake. The study of fiction in the 4E, AP* Edition is augmented by a discussion about the relationship between graphic narratives and verbal narratives. In poetry, the connection is made between traditional closed-form poetry, on the one hand, and visual poetry and prose poems, on the other. Of the three genres, the study of drama has traditionally been the most visual, for students can make connections between their own reading and the experiences they have had with plays on the stage or on film. The idea of these parallel sections is to provide students with an additional armament in their comprehension, their thought, and their emotional responses.

## A Brief Overview of the 4E, AP* Edition

The 4E, AP* Edition may be used for introduction-to-literature courses, genre courses, and both composition and composition-and-literature courses. Adaptability and flexibility are the keys to this variety. Teachers can use the book for classroom discussions, panel discussions, essay or paragraph-length writing and study assignments, and questions for special topics not covered in class.

**FICTION.**   The "Reading and Writing About Fiction" section, first in the book following the Introduction, consists of nine chapters. Chapter 2 presents a general introduction to fiction, and Chapters 3 through 9—the topical chapters central to each section of the book—introduce students to such important subjects as structure, character, point of view, symbolism, and idea. Chapter 10 contains four stories for additional enjoyment and study.

Following Chapter 10 is Chapter 10A, which is devoted to research connected to fiction. This chapter is devoted to research connected with fiction. Parallel discussions are Chapters 19A and 23A, which are about research in poetry and drama. These chapters reflect increased emphasis on research in the teaching of literature. Note that in Chapter 10A there is an extensive discussion of plagiarism and its avoidance. There has been great demand for this discussion on behalf of students, for as emphasis is placed on studying literature with the aid of research, comparable emphasis must also be placed on the judicious and ethical use of secondary sources.

**POETRY.**   The nine poetry chapters are arranged similarly to the fiction chapters. Chapter 11 is introductory. Chapters 12 through 17 deal with topics such as diction, imagery, tone, and symbolism. Chapter 18 presents the possibility of more intensive study of four major American poets, consisting of extensive selections by Dickinson, Frost, Hughes, and Plath. Chapter 19 contains 84 poems for additional enjoyment and study. Brief biographies of the anthologized poets are included in Appendix II.

Poetry selections range from poetry of late medieval times to poetry of the present, including poems published in the early years of the twenty-first century. Representative poets are the anonymous writer of "Sir Patrick Spens," Sir Thomas Wyatt, Queen Elizabeth I, Shakespeare, Donne, Dryden, Pope, Wordsworth, Keats, Tennyson, Hopkins, Pound, Yeats, Eliot, Layton, Amy Lowell, Nye, and Clifton. They represent a variety of poets, most of whom are widely recognized. Brewster, Edelman, Ginsberg, Henley, Housman, Hughes, Laux, Lazarus, Montale, Tate, Kenny, Kenyon, and Plath come readily to mind. Two of the poets included in the 4E, AP* Edition—Lincoln and

Carter—were American presidents. Another important poet is Micheal O'Siadhail, who has achieved distinction not only for his poetry but also for his governmental service in his native Ireland. Recent poets with many distinctions are Agüeros, Forché, Harjo, Hirshfield, Hospital, and Peacock. Of special note is the inclusion here of a number of nineteenth-century poets who were chosen for poems illustrating special aspects of American life. These are Bryant, Emerson, Ingham, Lincoln, Melville, and Whittier. (Please see the first category in the Topical and Thematic Table of Contents.)

**DRAMA.**   In the drama section, Chapter 20, which includes Albee's *The Sandbox*, is introductory. Chapters 21 and 22 deal with tragedy and comedy. Chapter 23 contains four full-length plays for additional enjoyment and study.

Longer plays are included in the 4E, AP* Edition because they are important and representative in an introductory study of drama (*Oedipus the King, Hamlet, A Midsummer Night's Dream, Death of a Salesman, Mulatto, A Dollhouse*). Among these is the important *Fences*, which has received great critical acclaim. These representative full plays make the 4E, AP* Edition useful as the basis for a discussion of the history of drama. In an anthology of this scope, the seven shorter plays (*The Sandbox, Am I Blue, The Bear, Before Breakfast, Tea Party, Visitatio Sepulchri, Trifles*) are valuable not only in themselves but also because they may be covered in no more than one or two classroom hours. The shorter plays may be enlivened by having parts read aloud and acted by students. Indeed, the anonymous *Visitatio Sepulchri* and Keller's *Tea Party* are brief enough to permit both classroom reading and discussion—or at least the beginning of a discussion—in a single period.

## Additional Features

**TABLE OF CONTENTS.**   The Table of Contents lists all the works and major chapter discussion heads in the book. A feature that has been well received are the sentences containing brief descriptions or impressions of the stories and the plays. It is hoped that these guiding sentences and questions will continue to interest students in approaching, anticipating, and reading the works.

**TOPICAL AND THEMATIC TABLE OF CONTENTS.**   To make the 4E, AP* Edition of *Literature: An Introduction to Reading and Writing* as flexible as possible, I have continued the Topical and Thematic Table of Contents. In this table, located immediately following the chapter-by-chapter Table of Contents, a number of topics are provided, such as *Hope and Renewal; Women; Men; Women and Men; Conformity and Rebellion; Endings and Beginnings; Innocence and Experience;* and *Race, Ethnicity, and Nationality*. Under these topics, generous numbers of stories, poems, and plays are listed (many in a number of categories), to aid in the creation and study of topical or thematic units.

A special word is in order for the category *America in Peace, War, and Tribulation*, which is included first in the Topical and Thematic Table of Contents. After the attacks on the United States on September 11, 2001, it is fitting that a category of uniquely American topics be included for student analysis and discussion. Obviously there cannot be a full and comprehensive examination of the background and thought to be considered in extensive courses in American Literature, but a selection of works that bear on American life and values seems now to be deeply important. Some works in the category reflect an idealized America, but many also shed light on problems and issues that the United States has faced in the past and is continuing to face today. A few of the works concern our country at its beginning; some reflect the life of the frontier and the Civil War; others introduce issues of minority culture; still others introduce subjects such as war, misfortune, personal anguish, regret, healing, relationships between parents and children, the symbolic value of work, nostalgia, love, prejudice, and reverence for the land. It is my hope that students will study the listed works broadly, as general human issues that also deal with the complexity of life in the United States today.

**QUESTIONS.** Following each anthologized selection in the detailed chapters are study questions designed to help students in their exploration and understanding of literature. Some of these questions are factual and may be answered quickly. Others provoke extended thought and classroom discussion, and may also serve for both in-class and out-of-class writing assignments. At the ends of twenty chapters I include a number of more general assignments, titled "Writing Topics About (Character, Symbolism, Tragedy, etc.)." Many of these are comparison-contrast topics, and a number of them—at least one in each chapter—are assignments requiring creative writing (for example, "Write a poem," or "Compose a short scene"). Unique about these topics is that students are asked not only to write creatively and argue cogently, but also to analyze their own creative processes.

**DATES.** To place the various works in historical context, I include the life dates for all authors. Along with the title of each anthologized work, I list the year of publication.

**NUMBERING.** For convenient reference, I have adopted a regular style of numbering the selections by fives:

| | |
|---|---|
| Stories: | *every fifth paragraph.* |
| Poems: | *every fifth line.* |
| Poetic plays: | *every fifth line, starting at 1 with each new scene and act.* |
| Prose plays: | *every fifth speech, starting at 1 with each new scene and act.* |

**GLOSSES AND EXPLANATORY FOOTNOTES.** For poetry and poetic plays, I provide brief marginal glosses wherever they are needed. When a fuller explanation is required—for stories, poems and plays—I supply explanatory footnotes. Words and phrases that are footnoted or glossed are highlighted by a raised degree sign (°). Footnotes are located according to line, paragraph, or speech numbers.

**GLOSSARY.** In the introductory discussions in the various chapters, significant terms and concepts are boldfaced. These are gathered alphabetically and explained briefly in the extensive glossary following the appendices, with references locating page numbers in the text where the terms are considered more fully. Although the glossary is based on the chapters of the 4E, AP* Edition, it is, in fact, comprehensive enough to be useful for general purposes.

**BOXED DISCUSSIONS WITHIN THE CHAPTERS.** In a number of chapters, separately boxed and shaded sections signal brief but essential discussions of a number of significant matters. The topics chosen for this treatment—such as the use of tenses in discussing a work, the use of authorial names, explanations of how to refer to parts of plays, and the concept of decorum—were based on the recommendations of teachers and students.

**SPECIAL WRITING TOPICS.** The 4E, AP* Edition includes a section titled "Special Writing Topics About Literature," which follows the drama section. These chapters are arranged for emphasis on recent critical theory together with practical guides for writing comparison-contrast essays on literature and writing examinations on literature.

**PHOTOGRAPHS AND ART REPRODUCTIONS.** To encourage the comparison of literary art and fine art and photography, a number of art reproductions and photographs are included, some within the chapters, and many in a full-colored insert. Most of these art works are considered directly in the introductions to the various chapters. I hope that the reproductions, together with others that instructors might wish to add during the course of teaching, will encourage comparison-and-contrast discussions and essays about the relationship of literature and art. As already noted, the "Topical and Thematic Table of Contents" lists relevant art works along with literary works.

**DRAMATIZATIONS ON VIDEOTAPE AND DVD.** To strengthen the connections between fiction and drama, a number of stories are included that are available on videocassettes and also DVDs, which can be used as teaching tools for support and interpretation. References to a number of the available dramatizations are included in the Instructor's Manual. In the introductions to many of the plays there is a listing of many of the cassette and DVD versions that can be brought into the classroom.

## Reading and Writing Now and in the Future

Many former students who have long since left our classrooms will often remember many works fondly because they once wrote essays about them in literature and composition classes. In fact, it is an article of faith, to adapt a well-known phrase of Joseph Joubert, that students learn twice when they write about literature, for as they develop their thinking and writing skills they also solidify their understanding of what they have read. Because writing is so major a mode of thinking, it is an essential reinforcement of analytical and critical reading. This interlocking approach is the bedrock idea of the 4E, AP* Edition of *Literature: An Introduction to Reading and Writing*.

Because writing so strongly reinforces reading, throughout the book I have included twenty-six illustrative essays, together with an additional twenty illustrative paragraphs, that demonstrate the strategies and methods brought out in the various chapters. These illustrative essays are intended as specimens to show what *might* be done (not what *must* be done) with a particular topic. Please emphasize this distinction. The essays have the goal of showing that the development of actual thinking does not take place until writers are able to fuse their reading responses with particular issues or topics (e.g., the symbolism in a poem, the main idea in a story, the use of stage directions in a play).

The illustrative essays are not as long as some teachers might assign (i.e., "write a 2,000-word essay"), but are relatively short, on the grounds that when responding to longer assignments, many writers inflate their papers with summary that is beside the point and therefore needless. It is clear that without a point, we don't have thinking, and that without thinking we cannot have a good essay. An unstructured summary of a work does not qualify as good writing.

Throughout the book, following each of the illustrative essays, there are analytical discussions of how the topics have brought out the thought. The format of underlining thesis and topic sentences in the illustrative essays is a graphic way of emphasizing the connections, and the format is thus a complementary way of fulfilling an essential aim of the book.

A logical extension (and a major hope) of the combined approach of topic and thought is that the techniques students acquire in studying literature as a reading and also a writing undertaking will help them in every course they may ever take, and in whatever professions or occupations they may eventually follow. Students will always *read*—if not the authors contained here, then other authors, and certainly newspapers, letters, legal documents, memoranda, directions, instructions, magazine articles, technical and non-technical reports, business proposals, Internet communications, and much more. Although students in their working years may never again need to write about topics such as setting, imagery, or symbolism, *they will certainly find a future need to express themselves and to write.*

Indeed, the more effectively students write about literature when taking their literature courses, the better they will be able to write later on—no matter what the topic. It is axiomatic that the power to analyze problems and make convincing written and oral presentations is a major characteristic of leadership and success in all fields. To acquire the skills of disciplined reading and strong writing is therefore the best possible preparation that students can make for the future, whatever it may hold.

While I stress the value of the 4E, AP* Edition as a teaching tool, I also emphasize that literature is to be enjoyed and loved. Sometimes we neglect the truth that study and delight are complementary, and that intellectual stimulation and emotional enjoyment develop not only from the immediate responses of pleasure, involvement, and sympathy, but also from the understanding, contemplation, and confidence generated by knowledge and developing skill. I therefore hope that the selections in the 4E, AP* Edition of *Literature: An Introduction to Reading and Writing* will teach students about humanity; about their own perceptions, feelings, and lives; and about the timeless patterns of human existence. I hope they will take delight in such discoveries and become enlarged as they make them. I see the book as a stepping-stone to lifelong understanding, future achievement, and never-ending joy in great literature.

## Features of the 4E, AP\* Edition

The new 4E, AP\* Edition features a host of resources specific to the AP course including:

**AP CORRELATION CHART.** A correlation chart is included that connects coverage in the book to AP course topics. This chart includes a list of required key skills that are used on the AP exam, a list of literary elements and terms, and a list of critical thinking skills, as well as where each may be found in the Roberts 4E, AP\* Edition text.

**AP PRACTICE ACTIVITIES.** AP practice activities include chapter-by-chapter review of all literary element chapters in Roberts 4E, AP\* Edition. These activities are based on a literary work from each chapter and relate directly to the literary element covered in that chapter. The activities are designed to help students master strategies they will need for the AP Literature and Composition Exam. Activities for each chapter include multiple choice questions and an answer key.

**MODEL AP TEST.** The 4E, AP\* Edition includes a model AP Literature and Composition Exam with multiple choice questions in AP exam format as well as essay-writing prompts. An annotated answer key explains each answer and sample model essays with commentary are provided as a study tool for students. This model exam uses works featured in Roberts AP\* 4th Edition.

**AP RELATED POINTERS AND STUDY STRATEGIES.** A general description of DOs and DON'Ts, as well as study pointers are provided to help students formulate test-taking strategies and prepare for the AP Exam.

**SUGGESTED AUTHORS AND READINGS.** A list of authors and readings that are recommended by the College Board are listed to provide students with additional resources for reading.

# SUPPLEMENTS

## Teacher Supplements

The following supplements are available to qualified adopters:

**INSTRUCTOR'S RESOURCE CENTER.** Most of the teacher supplements and resources for this book are available electronically for adoption preview and download on the IRC. Please go to www.pearsonschool.com/access _request and select "access to online instructor resources". You will be required to complete a one time registration subject to verification before being emailed access information for download materials.

**INSTRUCTOR'S MANUAL.** This comprehensive Instructor's Manual includes introductory remarks and interpretive comments about the works (stories, poems, plays) within each chapter of the book. Every page corresponds directly to the Roberts 4E, AP\* Edition. **ISBN: 0136033962**

**TEACHING LITERATURE ONLINE, 2/E.** Concise and practical, *Teaching Literature Online* provides instructors with strategies and advice for incorporating elements of computer technology into the literature classroom. Offering a range of information and examples, this manual provides ideas and activities for enhancing literature courses with the help of technology. **ISBN: 0321106180.**

**MYLITLAB.** This state-of-the art, interactive and instructive solution for use in literature courses provides Writing and Research; The Literary Elements; and Additional Literary Resources. This online resource also boasts Pearson author lectures, the Writers on Writing video series, and an extensive database of quizzes. For more information, go to www.mylitlab.com.

High school adopters should receive an access registration code with their textbook order. Directions on how to register for teacher and student access are available at www.pearsonschool.com/access_request by selecting "access for students and teachers to password-protected companion websites" and choosing the desired title from the pull-down menu. If a teacher does not receive an access registration card with the textbook order or would like to preview the website in advance of textbook adoption, he or she should contact the local Pearson sales representative or email PHwebaccess@pearsoned.com.

## Student Supplements

**COMPANION WEBSITE.** The text's open-access Companion Web site, www.prenhall.com/roberts, offers a multitude of resources including online quizzes, author Web links, writing activities, essay questions, Writing Workshops that show multiple drafts of student papers with commentary on each draft, and new research tutorials.

The following supplements are available for students to purchase:

**AUTHOR CASE STUDIES.** This case study features eight case studies focusing on eight different writers. Each case study features one work of literature and several critical pieces that explore the work and author in-depth. **ISBN: 0132369788**

**SHAKESPEARE SOURCEBOOKS.** These individual collections of Shakespearean plays include the entire text as well as a full reading of each play on an accompanying audio CD-ROM.

- Hamlet (from Sourcebooks, Inc.) ISBN: 0205505732
- Julius Caesar (from Sourcebooks, Inc.) Shakespeare & Ormsby ISBN: 0321436806
- King Lear (from Sourcebooks, Inc.) ISBN: 0205604684
- Macbeth (from Sourcebooks, Inc.) Shakespeare & Williams ISBN: 0321436784
- Midsummer Night's Dream, A (from Sourcebooks, Inc.) Shakespeare & Bourus ISBN: 0321436792
- Much Ado About Nothing (from Sourcebooks, Inc.) ISBN: 0205505724
- Othello (from Sourcebooks, Inc.) Shakespeare & Black ISBN: 0321436822
- Richard III (from Sourcebooks, Inc.) ISBN: 0205604676
- Romeo & Juliet (from Sourcebooks, Inc.) Shakespeare & Williams ISBN: 0321436814

**PRENTICE HALL POCKET READERS** The perfect writing companion for any writing course. Featured readers include:

- *Literature* **ISBN: 013134448X**
- *Argument* **ISBN: 0131895257**
- *Patterns* **ISBN: 0131443526**
- *Themes* **ISBN: 0131443550**
- *Writing Across the Curriculum* **ISBN: 0131942107**
- *Purposes* **ISBN: 0132281619**
- *Papers Across the Curriculum* **ISBN: 0131944819**

# Acknowledgments

As the book goes into the 4E, AP* Edition, I wish to acknowledge the many people who at various times have offered helpful advice, information, and suggestions. To name them, as Dryden says in *Absalom and Achitophel*, is to praise them. They are Professors Eileen Allman, Peggy Cole, David Bady, Andrew Brilliant, Rex Butt, Stanley Coberly, Betty L. Dixon, Elizabeth Keats Flores, Alice Griffin, Loren C. Gruber, Robert Halli, Leslie Healey, Rebecca Heintz, Karen Holt, Claudia Johnson, Matthew Marino, Edward Martin, Evan Matthews, Pearl McHaney, Ruth Milberg-Kaye, Nancy Miller, JoAnna Stephens Mink, Ervin Nieves, Glen Nygreen, Michael Paull, Norman Prinsky, Bonnie Ronson, Dan Rubey, Margaret Ellen Sherwood, Beverly J. Slaughter, Keith Walters, Chloe Warner, Scott Westrem, Mardi Valgemae, Matthew Winston, and Ruth Zerner, and also Christel Bell, Linda Bridgers, Catherine Davis, Jim Freund, Edward Hoeppner, Anna F. Jacobs, Eleanor Tubbs, Brooke Mitchell, April Roberts, David Roberts, Braden Welborn, and Eve Zarin. I give special recognition and thanks to Ann Marie Radaskiewicz. The skilled assistance of Jonathan Roberts has been essential and invaluable at every stage of all the editions.

A number of other people have provided sterling guidance for the preparation of the 4E, AP* Edition. They are Dan Bauer, Georgia College and State University; Carol Dabbs, Central Carolina Technical College; Billy Fontenot, Louisiana State University; Beverly Santillo, Georgia Perimeter College; Sonya Stephens, Cossatot Community College of the University of Arkansas; Rebecca Stewart, East Stroudsburg University; Bradley Waltman, Community College of Southern Nevada.

I wish especially to thank Vivian Garcia, Senior English Editor at Prentice Hall. She has been eminently cheerful, helpful, and obliging during the time we have worked together. I also thank Phil Miller, President, Humanities and Social Sciences; Leah Jewell, Editor in Chief, English; and Carrie Brandon, Maggie Barbieri, Nancy Perry, Alison Reeves, Kate Morgan Jackson, Bill Oliver, and Paul O'Connell, earlier Prentice Hall English editors, for their imagination and foresight, and also for their patience with me and support of me over the years. Of major importance was the work of Ray Mullaney, Editor-in-Chief, Development, for his pioneering work with the text and for his continued support. I am also grateful to Gina Sluss, Barbara Muller, Marlane Miriello, Viqi Wagner, and Anne Marie Welsh. To Kay Mallett, whose copy editing of the manuscript has been inestimably fine, I offer an extra salute of gratitude. Additional thanks are reserved for Winifred Sanchez, our Production Project Manager, who has devoted her knowledge, intelligence, diligence, good humor, and skill to the many tasks needed to bring a book of this size to fruition. Additional thanks are due to Mary Dalton-Hoffman for her superb work on securing permissions, and to Annette Linder/Teri Stratford for research into the various photographs and illustrations. I also extend my gratitude to Craig Campanella, Executive Managing Editor; Maureen Benicasa, Project Manager; Melissa Casciano, Assistant Editor; and Deborah Doyle, Editorial Assistant. Also, special thanks go to Professor Robert Zweig for his advice and contributions. Thank you to Darlene Stotler (California State University, Bakersfield) for creating the AP test materials featured in this edition.

Thank you to the reviewers of the AP* edition. They are Dee Schulten, AP* Consultant; Mary McDonald, Enid High School; Marcia Hilsabek, Round Rock High School; Linda Davey, Rio Rancho High School; and Shirley Counsil.

Special acknowledgement is due to my associate, Professor Henry E. Jacobs (1946–1986) of the University of Alabama. His energy and creativity were essential in planning, writing, and bringing out the first edition of *Literature: An Introduction to Reading and Writing*, but our working together on subsequent revisions was never to be. *Vale.*

—Edgar V. Roberts

*N.B.* The Prentice Hall Companion Web site offers many resources at <*www.prenhall. com/roberts*>. Here you will find a chapter-by-chapter guide through this text, as well as online quizzes that include instant scoring, a Syllabus Manager™ for instructors, and a message board where you may post questions or comments to a national audience. There is also an abundance of Web links to research specific authors, famous works written during numerous literary periods, and online literary journals.

# Chapter 1

# Introduction: The Process of Reading, Responding to, and Writing About Literature

The following chapters introduce a number of analytical approaches important in the study of literature, along with guidance for writing informative and well-focused essays based on these approaches. These chapters will help you fulfill two goals of composition and English courses: (1) to write good essays; and (2) to understand and assimilate great works of literature.

The premise of this book is that no educational process is complete until you can apply what you study. That is, you have not learned something—really *learned* it—*until you talk or write about it*. This does not mean that you retell a story, state an undeveloped opinion, or describe an author's life, but rather that you deal directly with topical and artistic issues about individual works. Writing requires you to strengthen your understanding and knowledge of material through recognizing where your original study might have fallen short. Thus, it is easy for you to read the chapter on point of view (Chapter 3), and it is also easy to read Shirley Jackson's story "The Lottery." Your grasp of point of view as a concept will not be complete, however, nor will your appreciation of the technical artistry of this story be complete, until you have prepared yourself to write about the technique. As you do so, you will need to reread parts of the work, study your notes, and apply your knowledge to the problem at hand; you must check facts, grasp relationships, develop insights, and try to express yourself with as much exactness and certainty as possible.

Primarily, then, this book aims to help you improve your writing skills through the use of literature as subject matter. After you have finished a number of essays derived from the following chapters, you will be able to approach just about any literary work with the confidence that you can understand it and write about it.

## What Is Literature, and Why Do We Study It?

We use the word **literature**, in a broad sense, to mean compositions that tell stories, dramatize situations, express emotions, and analyze and advocate ideas. Before the invention of writing thousands of years ago, literary works were necessarily spoken or sung, and they were retained only as long as living people continued to repeat them. In some societies, the oral tradition of literature still exists, with many poems and stories designed exclusively for spoken delivery. Even in our modern age of writing and printing, much literature is still heard aloud rather than read silently. Parents delight their children with stories and poems; poets and storywriters read their works before live audiences; plays and scripts are interpreted on stages and before movie and television cameras for the benefit of a vast public.

No matter how we assimilate literature, we gain much from it. In truth, readers often cannot explain why they enjoy reading, for goals and ideals are not easily articulated. There are, however, areas of general agreement about the value of systematic and extensive reading.

Literature helps us grow, both personally and intellectually. It opens doors for us. It stretches our minds. It develops our imagination, increases our understanding, and enlarges our power of sympathy. It helps us see beauty in the world around us. It links us with the cultural, philosophical, and spiritual world of which we are a part. It enables us to recognize human dreams and struggles in different places and times. It helps us develop mature sensibility and compassion for all living beings. It nurtures our ability to appreciate the beauty of order and arrangement—gifts that are also bestowed by a well-structured song, a beautifully painted canvas, or a well-chiseled piece of sculpture. It enables us to see worthiness in the aims of all people. It exercises our emotions through interest, concern, sympathy, tension, excitement, regret, fear, laughter, and hope. It encourages us to assist creative and talented people who need recognition and support. Through our cumulative experience in reading, literature shapes our goals and values by clarifying our own identities—both positively, through acceptance of the admirable in human beings, and negatively, through rejection of the sinister. It enables us to develop perspectives on events occurring locally and globally, and thereby it gives us understanding and control. It is one of the shaping influences of life. It makes us human.

## Types of Literature: The Genres

Literature may be classified into four categories or *genres:* (1) prose fiction, (2) poetry, (3) drama, and (4) nonfiction prose. The first three usually are classified as **imaginative literature**.

The genres of imaginative literature have much in common, but they also have distinguishing characteristics. **Prose fiction**, or **narrative fiction**, includes **myths**, **parables**, **romances**, **novels**, and **short stories**. Originally, *fiction* meant anything made up, crafted, or shaped, but today the word refers to prose stories based in the imaginations of authors. The essence of fiction is **narration**, the relating or recounting of a sequence of events or actions. Fictional works usually focus on one or a few major characters who change and grow (in their ability to make decisions, their awareness or insight, their attitude toward others, their sensitivity, and their moral capacity) as a result of how they deal with other characters and how they attempt to solve their problems. Although fiction, like all imaginative literature, can introduce true historical details, it is not real history, for its main purpose is to interest, stimulate, instruct, and divert, not to create a precise historical record.

While prose is expansive, **poetry** tends toward brevity. It offers us high points of emotion, reflection, thought, and feeling in what the English poet Wordsworth called "narrow room[s]." Yet in this context, it expresses the most powerful and deeply felt experiences of human beings, often awakening deep responses of welcome recognition: "Yes, I know what that's like. I would feel the same way. That's exactly right."

Poems make us think, make us reflect, and generally instruct us. They can also arouse our emotions, surprise us, make us laugh or cry, and inspire us. Many poems become lifelong friends, and we visit them again and again for insight, understanding, laughter, or the quiet reflection of joy or sorrow.

Poetry's power lies not only in its words and thoughts, but also in its music, using rhyme and a variety of rhythms to intensify its emotional impact. Although poems themselves vary widely in length, individual lines are often short because poets distill the greatest meaning and imaginative power from their words through rhetorical devices such as **imagery** and **metaphor**. Though poetry often requires many **formal** and **metrical** restrictions, it is paradoxically the very restrictiveness of poetry that provides poets with great freedom. Traditionally important poetic forms include the fourteen-line **sonnet**, **ballads**, **blank verse**, **couplets**, **elegies**, **epigrams**, **hymns**, **limericks**, **odes**, **quatrains**, **songs** or **lyrics**, **tercets** or **triplets**, **villanelles**, and the increasingly popular **haiku**. Many songs or lyrics have been set to music, and some were written expressly for that purpose. Some poems are long and **discursive**, such as many poems by the American poet Walt Whitman. **Epic** poems, such as those by Homer and Milton, contain thousands of lines. Since the time of Whitman, many poets have abandoned rhymes and regular rhythms in favor of **free verse**, a far-ranging type of poetry growing out of content and the natural rhythms of spoken language.

**Drama** is literature designed for stage or film presentation by people—actors—for the benefit and delight of other people—an audience. The essence of drama is the development of **character** and **situation** through **speech** and **action**. Like fiction, drama may focus on a single character or a small number of characters, and it enacts fictional (and sometimes historical) events as if they were happening right before our eyes. The audience therefore is a direct witness to the ways in which characters are influenced and changed by events and by other characters. Although most modern plays use prose **dialogue** (the conversation of two or more characters), on the principle that the language of drama should resemble the language of ordinary people as much as possible, many plays from the past, such as those of ancient Greece and Renaissance England, are in poetic form.

**Nonfiction prose** consists of news reports, feature articles, essays, editorials, textbooks, historical and biographical works, and the like, all of which describe or interpret facts and present judgments and opinions. The goal of nonfiction prose is to present truths and conclusions about the factual world. Imaginative literature, although also grounded in facts, is less concerned with the factual record than with the revelation of truths about life and human nature. Recently another genre has been emphasized within the category of nonfiction prose. This is **creative nonfiction**, a type of literature that is technically nonfiction, such as essays, articles, diaries, and journals, but that nevertheless introduces carefully structured form, vivid examples, relevant quotations, and highly creative and imaginative insights.

## Reading Literature and Responding to It Actively

Sometimes we find it difficult, after we have finished reading a work, to express our thoughts about it and to answer pointed questions about it. But more active and thoughtful reading gives us the understanding to develop well-considered answers.

Obviously, we need to follow the work and to understand its details, but just as importantly, we need to respond to the words, get at the ideas, and understand the implications of what is happening. We rely on our own fund of knowledge and experience to verify the accuracy and truth of situations and incidents, and we try to articulate our own emotional responses to the characters and their problems.

To illustrate such active responding, we examine "The Necklace" (1884), by the French writer Guy de Maupassant.[1] "The Necklace" is one of the best known of all stories, and it is included here with marginal notes such as those that any reader might make during original and follow-up readings. Many notes, particularly at the beginning, are *assimilative*; that is, they record details about the action. But as the story progresses, the marginal comments are more concerned with conclusions about the story's meaning. Toward the end, the comments are full rather than minimal; they result not only from first responses but also from considered thought. Here, then, is Maupassant's "The Necklace."

## GUY DE MAUPASSANT (1850–1893)

 ## The Necklace (1884)

*Translated by Edgar V. Roberts*

She was one of those pretty and charming women, born, as if by an error of destiny, into a family of clerks and copyists. She had no dowry, no prospects, no way of getting known, courted, loved, married by a rich and distinguished man. She finally settled for a marriage with a minor clerk in the Ministry of Education.

> "She" is pretty but poor, and has no chance in life unless she marries. Without connections, she has no entry into high society and marries an insignificant clerk. She is unhappy.

She was a simple person, without the money to dress well, but she was as unhappy as if she had gone through bankruptcy, for women have neither rank nor race. In place of high birth or important family connections, they can rely only on their beauty, their grace, and their charm. Their inborn finesse, their elegant taste, their engaging personalities, which are their only power, make working-class women the equals of the grandest ladies.

> A view of women who have no chance for an independent life and a career. In 1884, women had nothing more than this. Sad.

[1] Henri-René-Albert-Guy de Maupassant (1850–1893) is considered one of the major nineteenth-century French naturalist writers. Scion of an aristocratic Norman family, he received his baccalaureate degree from a lycée at Le Havre, after which he began studying law. When the Franco-Prussian War broke out he served in the French army, including battlefield duty. After leaving the military he became a minor bureaucrat, first in the Ministry of Marine and then in the Ministry of Education (also the workplace of Loisel, the husband of "The Necklace").

As a youth Maupassant was an energetic oarsman, swimmer, and boatman—a power that he also devoted to his career as a writer. During the 1870s in Paris he had regularly submitted his literary efforts to the novelist Gustave Flaubert (1821–1880), a family friend who regarded him as a son and whose criticism both improved and encouraged him. In Maupassant's thirties, after the death of his mentor Flaubert, his career flourished. His first published volume was a collection of poems (*Des Vers*, 1880), which he had to withdraw after it created a scandal and a lawsuit because of its sexual openness. After this time, until his death in 1893, he produced 30 volumes—novels, poems, articles, travel books, and three hundred short stories. In addition to "The Necklace," a few of his better-known stories are "The Ball of Fat," "Mademoiselle Fifi," and "A Piece of String."

Maupassant was a meticulous writer, devoting much attention to the reality of everyday existence (hence his status as a naturalist writer). A number of his stories are about events occurring during the Franco-Prussian War. Some are about life among bureaucrats, some about peasant life in Normandy, and a large number, including "The Necklace," about Parisian life. His major stories are characterized by strong irony; human beings are influenced by forces they cannot control, and their wishes are often frustrated by their own defects. Under such circumstances, Maupassant's characters exhibit varying degrees of weakness, hypocrisy, vanity, insensitivity, callousness, and even cruelty, but those who are victimized are viewed with understanding and sympathy.

She suffered constantly, feeling herself destined for all delicacies and luxuries. She suffered because of her grim apartment with its drab walls, threadbare furniture, ugly curtains. All such things, which most other women in her situation would not even have noticed, tortured her and filled her with despair. The sight of the young country girl who did her simple housework awakened in her only a sense of desolation and lost hopes. She daydreamed of large, silent anterooms, decorated with oriental tapestries and lighted by high bronze floor lamps, with two elegant valets in short culottes dozing in large armchairs under the effects of forced-air heaters. She imagined large drawing rooms draped in the most expensive silks, with fine end tables on which were placed knick-knacks of inestimable value. She dreamed of the perfume of dainty private rooms, which were designed only for intimate tête-à-têtes with the closest friends, who because of their achievements and fame would make her the envy of all other women.

*She suffers because of her cheap belongings, wanting expensive things. She dreams of wealth and of how other women would envy her if she could display finery. But such luxuries are unrealistic and unattainable for her.*

When she sat down to dinner at her round little table covered with a cloth that had not been washed for three days, in front of her husband who opened the kettle while declaring ecstatically, "Ah, good old beef stew! I don't know anything better," she dreamed of expensive banquets with shining place settings, and wall hangings portraying ancient heroes and exotic birds in an enchanted forest. She imagined a gourmet-prepared main course carried on the most exquisite trays and served on the most beautiful dishes, with whispered gallantries that she would hear with a sphinxlike smile as she dined on the pink meat of a trout or the delicate wing of a quail.

*Her husband's taste is for plain things, while she dreams of expensive gourmet food. He has adjusted to his status. She has not.*

5    She had no decent dresses, no jewels, nothing. And she loved nothing but these; she believed herself born only for these. She burned with the desire to please, to be envied, to be attractive and sought after.

*She lives for her unrealistic dreams, and these increase her frustration.*

She had a rich friend, a comrade from convent days, whom she did not want to see anymore because she suffered so much when she returned home. She would weep for the entire day afterward with sorrow, regret, despair, and misery.

*She even thinks of giving up a rich friend because she is so depressed after visiting her.*

Well, one evening, her husband came home glowing and carrying a large envelope.

*A new section in the story.*

"Here," he said, "this is something for you."

She quickly tore open the envelope and took out a card engraved with these words:

> *The* CHANCELLOR OF EDUCATION *and*
> MRS. GEORGE RAMPONNEAU
> *request that*
> MR. AND MRS. LOISEL
> *do them the honor of coming to dinner*
> *at the Ministry of Education*
> *on the evening of January 8.*

*An invitation to dinner at the Ministry of Education. A big plum.*

10      Instead of being delighted, as her husband had hoped, she      *It only upsets her.*
threw the invitation spitefully on the table, muttering:

"What do you expect me to do with this?"

"But honey, I thought you'd be glad. You never get to go out,      *Loisel really doesn't*
and this is a special occasion! I had a lot of trouble getting the invi-      *understand her. He can't*
tation. Everyone wants one. The demand is high and not many      *sympathize with her unhappiness.*
clerks get invited. Everyone important will be there."

She looked at him angrily and stated impatiently:      *She declares that she hasn't*

"What do you want me to wear to go there?"      *anything to wear.*

15      He had not thought of that. He stammered:      *He tries to persuade her that*

"But your theater dress. That seems nice to me . . . "      *her theater dress might do for*

He stopped, amazed and bewildered, as his wife began to cry.      *the occasion.*
Large tears fell slowly from the corners of her eyes to her mouth. He
said falteringly:

"What's wrong? What's the matter?"

But with a strong effort she had recovered, and she answered
calmly as she wiped her damp cheeks:

20      "Nothing, except that I have nothing to wear and therefore
can't go to the party. Give your invitation to someone else at the office whose wife will have nicer clothes than mine."

Distressed, he responded:      *Her name is Mathilde.*

"Well, all right, Mathilde. How much would a new dress
cost, something you could use at other times, but not anything
fancy?"

She thought for a few moments, adding things up and thinking      *He volunteers to pay for a new*
also of an amount that she could ask without getting an immediate      *dress.*
refusal and a frightened outcry from the frugal clerk.

Finally she responded tentatively:      *She is manipulating him.*

25      "I don't know exactly, but it seems to me that I could get by on
four hundred francs."

He blanched slightly at this, because he had set aside just that      *The dress will cost him his next*
amount to buy a shotgun for Sunday lark-hunts the next summer      *summer's vacation. (He*
with a few friends in the Plain of Nanterre.      *doesn't seem to have*

However, he said:      *included her in his plans.)*

"All right, you've got four hundred francs, but make it a pretty
dress."

As the day of the party drew near, Mrs. Loisel seemed sad, un-      *A new section, the third in the*
easy, anxious, even though her gown was all ready. One evening      *story. The day of the party is*
her husband said to her:      *near.*

30      "What's the matter? You've been acting funny for several
days."

She answered:

"It's awful, but I don't have any jewels to wear, not a single      *Now she complains that she*
gem, nothing to dress up my outfit. I'll look like a beggar. I'd almost      *doesn't have any nice jewelry.*
rather not go to the party."      *She is manipulating him again.*

He responded:

"You can wear a corsage of cut flowers. This year it's all the
rage. For only ten francs you can get two or three gorgeous roses."

35      She was not convinced.

"No . . . there's nothing more humiliating than looking shabby in the company of rich women."

But her husband exclaimed:

"God, but you're silly! Go to your friend Mrs. Forrestier, and ask her to lend you some jewelry. You know her well enough to do that."

She uttered a cry of joy:

40 "That's right. I hadn't thought of that."

The next day she went to her friend's house and described her problem.

Mrs. Forrestier went to her mirrored wardrobe, took out a large jewel box, opened it, and said to Mrs. Loisel:

"Choose, my dear."

She saw bracelets, then a pearl necklace, then a Venetian cross of finely worked gold and gems. She tried on the jewelry in front of a mirror, and hesitated, unable to make up her mind about each one. She kept asking:

45 "Do you have anything else?"

"Certainly. Look to your heart's content. I don't know what you'd like best."

Suddenly she found a superb diamond necklace in a black satin box, and her heart throbbed with desire for it. Her hands shook as she picked it up. She fastened it around her neck, watched it gleam at her throat, and looked at herself ecstatically.

Then she asked, haltingly and anxiously:

"Could you lend me this, nothing but this?"

50 "Why yes, certainly."

She jumped up, hugged her friend joyfully, then hurried away with her treasure.

The day of the party came. Mrs. Loisel was a success. She was prettier than anyone else, stylish, graceful, smiling and wild with joy. All the men saw her, asked her name, sought to be introduced. All the important administrators stood in line to waltz with her. The Chancellor himself eyed her.

She danced joyfully, passionately, intoxicated with pleasure, thinking of nothing but the moment, in the triumph of her beauty, in the glory of her success, on cloud nine with happiness made up of all the admiration, of all the aroused desire, of this victory so complete and so sweet to the heart of any woman.

She did not leave until four o'clock in the morning. Her husband, since midnight, had been sleeping in a little empty room with three other men whose wives had also been enjoying themselves.

55 He threw, over her shoulders, the shawl that he had brought for the trip home—a modest everyday wrap, the poverty of which contrasted sharply with the elegance of her evening gown. She felt it and hurried away to avoid being noticed by the other women who luxuriated in rich furs.

Loisel tried to hold her back:

"Wait a minute. You'll catch cold outdoors. I'll call a cab."

---

*She has a good point, but there seems to be no way out.*

*He proposes a solution: Borrow jewelry from Mrs. Forrestier, who is apparently the rich friend mentioned earlier.*

*Mathilde has her choice of her friend's jewels.*

*A "superb" diamond necklace. This is what the story has been building up to.*

*This is what she wants, just this.*

*She leaves with the "treasure." Things might be looking up for her.*

*A new section.*

*The party. Mathilde is a huge success.*

*Another judgment about women. Does the author mean that only women want to be admired? Don't men want admiration, too?*

*Loisel, with other husbands, is bored, while the wives are literally having a ball. Ashamed of her shabby everyday shawl, she rushes away to avoid being seen. She is forced back into the reality of her true situation. Her glamour is gone.*

But she paid no attention and hurried down the stairs. When they reached the street they found no carriages. They began to look for one, shouting at cabmen passing by at a distance.

They walked toward the Seine, desperate, shivering. Finally, on a quay, they found one of those old night-going buggies that are seen in Paris only after dark, as if they were ashamed of their wretched appearance in daylight.

*A comedown after the nice evening. They take a wretched-looking buggy home.*

60   It took them to their door, on the Street of Martyrs, and they sadly climbed the stairs to their flat. For her, it was finished. As for him, he could think only that he had to begin work at the Ministry of Education at ten o'clock.

*'Street of Martyrs.' Is this name significant? Loisel is down-to-earth.*

She took the shawl off her shoulders, in front of the mirror, to see herself once more in her glory. But suddenly she cried out. The necklace was no longer around her neck!

*SHE HAS LOST THE NECKLACE!*

Her husband, already half undressed, asked:

"What's wrong?"

She turned toward him frantically:

65   "I . . . I . . . I no longer have Mrs. Forrestier's necklace."

He stood up, bewildered:

"What! . . . How! . . . It's not possible!"

And they looked in the folds of the gown, in the folds of the shawl, in the pockets, everywhere. They found nothing.

*They can't find it.*

He asked:

70   "You're sure you still had it when you left the party?"

"Yes. I checked on it in the vestibule of the Ministry."

"But if you'd lost it in the street, we would've heard it fall. It must be in the cab."

"Yes, probably. Did you notice the number?"

"No. Did you see it?"

75   "No."

Overwhelmed, they looked at each other. Finally, Loisel got dressed again:

"I'm going out to retrace all our steps," he said, "to see if I can find the necklace that way."

And he went out. She stayed in her evening dress, without the energy to get ready for bed, stretched out in a chair, drained of strength and thought.

*He goes out to search for the necklace.*

Her husband came back at about seven o'clock. He had found nothing.

*But is unsuccessful.*

80   He went to Police Headquarters and to the newspapers to announce a reward. He went to the small cab companies, and finally he followed up even the slightest hopeful lead.

*He really tries. He's doing his best.*

She waited the entire day, in the same enervated state, in the face of this frightful disaster.

Loisel came back in the evening, his face pale and haggard. He had found nothing.

"You'll have to write to your friend," he said, "that you broke a clasp on her necklace and that you're having it fixed. That'll give us time to look around."

*Loisel's plan to explain delaying the return. He takes charge, is resourceful.*

She wrote as he dictated.

85   By the end of the week they had lost all hope.

*Things are hopeless.*

And Loisel, looking five years older, declared:
"We'll have to see about replacing the jewels."

The next day they took the case that had contained the necklace and went to the jeweler whose name was inside. He looked at his books:
"I wasn't the one, Madam, who sold the necklace. I only made the case."

90      Then they went from jeweler to jeweler, searching for a necklace like the other one, racking their memories, both of them sick with worry and anguish.

In a shop in the Palais-Royal, they found a necklace of diamonds that seemed to them exactly like the one they were looking for. It was priced at forty thousand francs. They could buy it for thirty-six thousand.

They got the jeweler to promise not to sell it for three days. And they made an agreement that he would buy it back for thirty-four thousand francs if the original were recovered before the end of February.

Loisel had saved eighteen thousand francs that his father had left him. He would have to borrow the rest.

He borrowed, asking a thousand francs from one, five hundred from another, five louis* here, three louis there. He wrote promissory notes, undertook ruinous obligations, did business with finance companies and the whole tribe of loan sharks. He compromised himself for the remainder of his days, risked his signature without knowing whether he would be able to honor it; and, terrified by anguish over the future, by the black misery that was about to descend on him, by the prospect of all kinds of physical deprivations and moral tortures, he went to get the new necklace, and put down thirty-six thousand francs on the jeweler's counter.

95      Mrs. Loisel took the necklace back to Mrs. Forrestier, who said with an offended tone:
"You should have brought it back sooner; I might have needed it."

She did not open the case, as her friend feared she might. If she had noticed the substitution, what would she have thought? What would she have said? Would she not have taken her for a thief?

Mrs. Loisel soon discovered the horrible life of the needy. She did her share, however, completely, heroically. That horrifying debt had to be paid. She would pay. They dismissed the maid; they changed their address; they rented an attic flat.

She learned to do the heavy housework, dirty kitchen jobs. She washed the dishes, wearing away her manicured fingernails on greasy pots and encrusted baking dishes. She handwashed dirty linen, shirts, and dish towels that she hung out on the line to dry. Each morning, she took the garbage down to the street, and she carried up water, stopping at each floor to catch her breath. And, dressed in cheap housedresses, she went to the fruit dealer,

---

*Side notes:*

*Note that Loisel does not even suggest that they explain things to Mrs. Forrestier. They hunt for a replacement.*

*A new diamond necklace will cost 36,000 francs, a monumental amount.*

*They make a deal with the jeweler. (Is Maupassant hinting that things might work out for them?)*

*It will take all of Loisel's inheritance . . .*

*. . . plus another 18,000 francs that must be borrowed at enormous rates of interest.*

*Mrs. Forrestier is offended and complains about Mathilde's delay. Is this enough justification for not telling the truth? It seems to be for the Loisels.*

*A new section, the fifth.*

*They suffer to repay their debts. Loisel works late at night. Mathilde accepts a cheap attic flat, and does all the heavy housework herself to save on domestic help.*

---

* *louis*: a gold coin worth twenty francs.

the grocer, the butchers, with her basket under her arms, haggling, insulting, defending her measly cash penny by penny.

100 They had to make installment payments every month, and, to buy more time, to refinance loans.

The husband worked evenings to make fair copies of tradesmen's accounts, and late into the night he made copies at five cents a page.

And this life lasted ten years.

At the end of ten years, they had paid back everything—everything—including the extra charges imposed by loan sharks and the accumulation of compound interest.

Mrs. Loisel looked old now. She had become the strong, hard, and rude woman of poor households. Her hair unkempt, with uneven skirts and rough, red hands, she spoke loudly, washed floors with large buckets of water. But sometimes, when her husband was at work, she sat down near the window, and she dreamed of that evening so long ago, of that party, where she had been so beautiful and so admired.

105 What would life have been like if she had not lost that necklace? Who knows? Who knows? Life is so peculiar, so uncertain. How little a thing it takes to destroy you or to save you!

Well, one Sunday, when she had gone for a stroll along the Champs-Elysées to relax from the cares of the week, she suddenly noticed a woman walking with a child. It was Mrs. Forrestier, still youthful, still beautiful, still attractive.

Mrs. Loisel felt moved. Would she speak to her? Yes, certainly. And now that she had paid, she could tell all. Why not?

She walked closer.

"Hello, Jeanne."

110 The other gave no sign of recognition and was astonished to be addressed so familiarly by this working-class woman. She stammered:

"But . . . Madam! . . . I don't know. . . . You must have made a mistake."

"No. I'm Mathilde Loisel."

Her friend cried out:

"Oh! . . . My poor Mathilde, you've changed so much."

115 "Yes. I've had some tough times since I saw you last; in fact hardships . . . and all because of you! . . ."

"Of me . . . how so?"

"You remember the diamond necklace that you lent me to go to the party at the Ministry of Education?"

"Yes. What then?"

"Well, I lost it."

120 "How, since you gave it back to me?"

"I returned another exactly like it. And for ten years we've been paying for it. You understand this wasn't easy for us, who have nothing. . . . Finally it's over, and I'm damned glad."

---

*Margin notes:*

She pinches pennies, and haggles with the local tradesmen.

They struggle to meet payments.

Mr. Loisel moonlights to make extra money.

For ten years they struggle, but they endure.

Another new section, the sixth of the story.

The Loisels have successfully paid back the loans. They have been quite virtuous.

Mrs. Loisel (why does the narrator not say "Mathilde"?) is roughened and aged by the work. But she has behaved "heroically" (¶ 98), and has shown her mettle.

A moral? Small, uncertain things shape our lives; we hang by a thread.

The seventh part of the story, a scene on the Champs-Elysées. Mathilde sees Jeanne Forrestier for the first time in the previous ten years.

Jeanne notes Mathilde's changed appearance.

Mathilde tells Jeanne everything.

Mrs. Forrestier stopped her.

"You say that you bought a diamond necklace to replace mine?"

"Yes, you didn't notice it, eh? It was exactly like yours."

125    And she smiled with proud and childish joy.

Mrs. Forrestier, deeply moved, took both her hands.

"Oh, my poor Mathilde! But mine was only costume jewelry. At most, it was worth only five hundred francs! . . ."

*SURPRISE! The lost necklace was not made of real diamonds, and the Loisels have slaved for no reason at all. But hard work and sacrifice probably brought out better qualities in Mathilde than she otherwise might have shown. Is this the moral of the story?*

## Reading and Responding by Computer or Notebook

The marginal comments printed with "The Necklace" demonstrate the active reading-responding process you should apply to everything you read. Use the margins in your text similarly to record your comments and questions, but plan also to record your more lengthy responses in a notebook, on note cards, on separate sheets of paper, or in a computer file. Be careful not to lose anything; keep all your notes. As you progress from work to work, you will find that your written or saved comments will be immensely important to you as your record, or journal, of your first impressions together with your more carefully considered and expanded thoughts.

In keeping your notebook, your objective should be to learn assigned works inside and out and then to say perceptive things about them. To achieve this goal, you need to read the work more than once. Develop a good note-taking system so that as you read, you will create a "memory bank" of your own knowledge. You can make withdrawals from this fund of ideas when you begin to write. As an aid in developing your own procedures for reading and "depositing" your ideas, you may wish to begin with the following *Guidelines for Reading*. Of course, you will want to modify these suggestions and add to them as you become a more experienced and disciplined reader.

### GUIDELINES FOR READING

1. **Observations for basic understanding**
   a. Explain words, situations, and concepts. Write down words that are new or not immediately clear. Use your dictionary, and record the relevant meanings in your notebook. Write down special difficulties so that you can ask your instructor about them.
   b. Determine what is happening in the work. For a story or play, where do the actions take place? What do they show? Who is involved? Who is the major figure? Why is he or she major? What relationships do the characters have with one another? What concerns do the characters have? What do they do? Who says what to whom? How do the speeches advance the action and reveal the characters? For a poem, what is the situation? Who is talking, and to whom? What does the speaker say about the situation? Why does the poem end as it does and where it does?

2. **Notes on first impressions**
   a. Make a record of your reactions and responses. What did you think was memorable, noteworthy, funny, or otherwise striking? Did you worry, get scared, laugh, smile, feel a thrill, learn a great deal, feel proud, find a lot to think about?
   b. Describe interesting characterizations, events, techniques, and ideas. If you like a character or an idea, explain what you like, and do the same for characters and ideas you don't like. Is there anything else in the work that you especially like or dislike? Are parts easy or difficult to understand? Why? Are there any surprises? What was your reaction to them? Be sure to use your own words when writing your explanations.

3. **Development of ideas and enlargement of responses**
   a. Trace developing patterns. Make an outline or a scheme: What conflicts appear? Do these conflicts exist between people, groups, or ideas? How are the conflicts resolved? Is one force, idea, or side the winner? How do you respond to the winner or to the loser?
   b. Write expanded notes about characters, situations, and actions. What explanations need to be made about the characters? What is the nature of the situations (e.g., young people discover a damaged boat, and themselves, in the spring; a prisoner tries to hide her baby from cruel guards; and so on)? What is the nature of the actions (e.g., a mother and daughter go shopping, a series of strangers intrude upon the celebration of a christening, a woman is told that her husband has been killed in a train wreck, a group of children are taken to a fashionable toy store, and so on)? What are the people like, and what are their habits and customs? What sort of language do they use?
   c. Memorize important, interesting, and well-written passages. Copy them in full on note cards, and keep these in your pocket or purse. When walking to class, riding public transportation, or otherwise not occupying your time, learn them by heart. Please take memorization seriously.
   d. Always write down questions that come up during your reading. You may raise these in class, and trying to write out your own answers will also aid your own study.

## Sample Notebook Entries on Maupassant's "The Necklace"

The following entries demonstrate how you can use the foregoing guidelines in your first thoughts about a work. You should try to develop enough observations and responses to be useful later, both for additional study and for developing essays. Notice that the entries contain not only comments but also questions.

> *Early in the story, Mathilde seems to be spoiled. She and her husband are not well off, but she is unable to face her own situation.*

She is a dreamer but seems harmless. Her daydreams about a fancy home, with all the expensive belongings, are not unusual. It would be unusual to find people who do not have such dreams.

She is embarrassed by her husband's taste for plain food. The storyteller contrasts her taste for trout and quail with Loisel's cheaper favorites.

When the Loisels get the invitation to the ball, Mathilde becomes difficult. Her wish for an expensive dress (the cost of Loisel's shotgun) creates a problem, and she creates another problem by wanting to wear fine jewelry.

Her change in character can be related to the places in the story: the Street of Martyrs, the dinner party scene, the attic flat. Also she fills the places she daydreams about with the most expensive things she can imagine.

Her success at the party shows that she has the charm the storyteller talks about in paragraph 2. She seems never to have had any other chance to exert her power.

The worst part of her personality is shown in rushing away from the party because she is ashamed of her shabby everyday shawl. It is Mathilde's unhappiness and unwillingness to adjust to her modest means that cause the financial downfall of the Loisels. This disaster is her fault.

Borrowing the money to replace the necklace shows that both Loisel and Mathilde have a strong sense of honor. Making up the loss is good, even if it destroys them financially.

There are some nice touches, like Loisel's seeming to be five years older (paragraph 86) and his staying with the other husbands of women enjoying themselves (paragraph 54). These are well done.

It's too bad that Loisel and Mathilde don't confess to Jeanne that the jewels are lost. Their pride or their honor stops them — or perhaps their fear of being accused of theft.

Their ten years of slavish work (paragraphs 98–102) show how they have come down in life. Mathilde does all her work by hand, so she really does pitch in and is, as the narrator says, heroic.

The attic flat is important. Mathilde becomes loud and frumpy when living there (paragraph 99), but she also develops strength. She does what she has to. The earlier apartment and the elegance of her imaginary rooms had brought out her limitations.

The setting of the Champs-Elysées also reflects her character, for she feels free there to tell Jeanne about the disastrous loss and sacrifice (paragraph 121), producing the surprise ending.

The narrator's statement "How little a thing it takes to destroy you or to save you!" (paragraph 105) is full of thought. The necklace is little, but it makes a huge problem. This creates the story's irony.

Questions: Is this story more about the surprise ending or about the character of Mathilde? Is she to be condemned or admired? Does the outcome stem from the little things that make us or break us, as the narrator suggests, or from the difficulty of rising above one's economic class, which seems true, or both? What do the speaker's remarks about women's status mean? (Remember, the story was published in 1884.) This probably isn't relevant, but wouldn't Jeanne, after hearing about the substitution, give the full value of the necklace to the Loisels, and wouldn't they then be pretty well off?

These are reasonable—and also fairly full—remarks and observations about "The Necklace." Use your notebook or journal similarly for all reading assignments. If your assignment is simply to learn about a work, general notes such as these should be enough. If you are preparing for a test, you might write pointed observations more in line with what is happening in your class, and also write and answer your own questions (see Chapter 26, "Taking Examinations on Literature"). If you have a writing assignment, observations like these can help you focus more closely on your topic—such as character, idea, or setting. Whatever your purpose, always take good notes, and put in as many details and responses as you can. The notes will be invaluable to you as a mind refresher and as a wellspring of thought.

## Writing Essays on Literary Topics

Finished writing is the sharpened, focused expression of thought and study. It begins with the search for something to say—an idea. Not all ideas are equal; some are better than others, and getting good ideas is an ability that you will develop the more you think and write. As you discover ideas and explain them in words, you will also improve your perceptions and increase your critical faculties.

In addition, because literature itself contains the subject material (though not in a systematic way) of philosophy, religion, psychology, sociology, and politics, learning to analyze literature and to write about it will also improve your capacity to deal with these and other disciplines.

### Writing Does Not Come Easily—for Anyone

A major purpose of your being in college, of which your composition and literature course is a vital part, is to develop your capacity to think and to express your thoughts clearly and fully. However, the process of creating a successfully argued essay—the actual process itself of writing—is not automatic. Writing begins in uncertainty and hesitation, and it becomes certain and confident—accomplished—only as a result of great care, applied thought, a certain amount of experimentation, the passage of time, and much effort. When you read complete, polished, well-formed pieces of writing, you might assume, as many of us do, that the writers wrote their successful versions the first time they tried and never needed to make changes and improvements. In an ideal world, perhaps, something like this could happen, but not in this one.

If you could see the early drafts of writing you admire, you would be startled—and also encouraged—to see that good writers are also human and that what they first write is often uncertain, vague, tangential, tentative, incomplete, and messy. Good writers do not always like their first drafts; nevertheless, they work with their efforts and build upon them. They reconsider their ideas and try to restate them, discard some details, add others, chop paragraphs in half and reassemble the parts elsewhere, throw out much (and then maybe recover some of it), revise or completely rewrite sentences, change words, correct misspellings, sharpen expressions, and add new material to tie all the parts together in a smooth, natural flow.

## The Goal of Writing: To Show a Process of Thought

As you approach the task of writing, you should constantly realize that your goal should always be to *explain* the work you are analyzing. You should never be satisfied simply to restate the events in the work. Too often students fall easily into a pattern of retelling a story or play, or of summarizing the details of a poem. But nothing could be further from what is expected of good writing. You need to demonstrate your thought. Thinking is an active process that does not happen accidentally. Thinking requires that you develop ideas, draw conclusions, exemplify them and support them with details, and connect everything in a coherent manner. Your goal should constantly be to explain the results of your thinking—your ideas, your play of mind over the materials of a work, your insights, your conclusions. This is the ideal.

Approach each writing assignment with the following thoughts in mind: You should consider your reader as a person who has read the work, just as you have done. This person knows what is in the work, and therefore does not need you to restate what she or he already knows. Instead, your reader wants to learn from you what to think about it. Therefore, always, your task as a writer is to explain something about the work, to describe the thoughts that you can develop about it. Let us consider the story we have just read, Maupassant's "The Necklace." We have recognized that the main character, Mathilde Loisel, is a young Parisian housewife who is married to a minor clerk in the Ministry of Education. We know this, but if we are reading an essay about the story we will want to learn more. Let us then suppose that a first goal of one of your paragraphs is to explain the deep dissatisfaction Mathilde feels in the early part of the story. Your paragraph might go as follows:

> In the early part of the story Maupassant establishes that Mathilde is deeply dissatisfied with her life. Her threadbare furniture and drab walls are a cause of her unhappiness. Under these circumstances her daydreams of beautiful rooms staffed by "elegant valets," together with a number of rooms for intimate conversations with friends, multiply her dissatisfaction. The meager meals that she shares with her husband make her imagine sumptuous banquets that she feels are rightfully hers by birth but that are denied her because of her circumstances. The emphasis in these early scenes of the story is always on Mathilde's discontentment and frustration.

Notice here that your paragraph ties the story's events to the idea of Mathilde's unhappiness. The events are there, but you are explaining to us, as readers, that the events are directly related Mathilde's unhappiness. The paragraph illustrates a process of thought. Here is another way in which you might use a thought to connect the same materials:

> In the early part of the story Maupassant emphasizes the economic difficulty of Mathilde's life. The threadbare furniture and ugly curtains, for example, highlight that there is no money to purchase better things. The same sparseness of existence is shown by the meager meals that she shares with her husband. With the capacity to appreciate better things, Mathilde is forced by circumstances to make do with worse. Her dreams of sumptuous banquets are therefore natural, given her level of frustration with the life around her. In short, her unhappiness is an understandable consequence of her aversion to her plain and drab apartment and the tightness of money.

Here the details are substantially the same as in our first paragraph, but they are unified by a different idea, namely the economic constraints of Mathilde's life. What is important is that neither paragraph tells only the details. Instead, the paragraphs illustrate the goal of writing with a purpose. Whenever you write, you should always be trying, as in these examples, to use a dominating thought or thoughts to shape the details in the work you are analyzing.

## Major Stages in Thinking and Writing: Discovering Ideas, Preparing to Write, Making Initial Drafts, and Completing the Essay

For practiced and beginning writers alike, there are three basic stages of composition, and in each of these there are characteristic activities. In the beginning stage, writers try to find the details and thoughts that seem to be right for eventual inclusion in what they are hoping to write. The next (or middle) stage is characterized by written drafts, or sketches—ideas, sentences, paragraphs. The final, or completion, stage is the forming and ordering of what has previously been done—the creation and determination of a final essay. Although these stages occur in a natural order, they are not separate and distinct, but merge with each other and in effect are fused together. Thus, when you are close to finishing your essay you may find that you need something else, something more, and something different. At this point you can easily re-create an earlier stage to discover new details and ideas. You might say that your work is always tentative until you regard it as finished or until you need to turn it in.

### Discovering Ideas ("Brainstorming")

With the foregoing general goal in mind, let us assume that you have read the work about which you are to write and have made notes and observations on which you are planning to base your thought. You are now ready to consider and plan what to include in your essay. This earliest stage of writing is unpredictable and somewhat frustrating because you are searching. You do not know quite what you want, for you are reaching out for ideas and you are not yet sure what they are and what you might say about them. This process of searching and discovery, sometimes also called brainstorming, requires you to examine any and every subject that your mind can produce.

Just as you are trying to reach for ideas, however, you also should try to introduce purpose and resolution into your thought. You have to zero in on something specific and develop your ideas through this process. Although what you first write may seem indefinite, the best way to help your thinking is to put your mind, figuratively, into specific channels or grooves, and then to confine your thoughts within these boundaries. What matters is to get your mind going on a particular topic and to get your thoughts down on paper or onto a computer screen. Once you can see your thoughts in front of you, you can work with them and develop them. The following drawing can be helpful to you as an illustration of the various facets of a literary work or ways of talking about it.

Consider the work you have read—story, poem, play—as the central circle, from which a number of points, like the rays of a star, shine out, some of them prominently, others less so. These points, or rays, are the various subjects, or topics, that you might decide to select in exploration, discovery, and discussion. Because some elements in a work may be more significant than others, the points are not all equal in size. Notice also that the points grow larger as they get nearer to the work, suggesting that once you select a point of discussion you may amplify that point with details and your own observations about the work.

You can consider literary works in many ways, but for now, as a way of getting started, you might choose to explore (1) the work's characters, (2) its historical period and background, (3) the social and economic conditions it depicts, (4) its major ideas, or (5) any of its artistic qualities.[2] These topics, of course, have many subtopics, but any one of them can help you in the concentration you will need for beginning your essay (and also for classroom discussion). All you need is one topic, just one; do not try everything at the same time. Let us see how our illustration can be revised to account for these topics. This time the number of points is reduced to illustrate the points or approaches we have just raised (with an additional and unnamed point to represent all the other approaches that might be used for other studies). These points represent your ways of discovering ideas about the work.

---

[2]Together with additional topics, these critical approaches are discussed in more detail in Chapter 24.

## Study the Characters in the Work

You do not need to be a professional psychologist to discuss the persons or characters that you find in a work (see also Chapter 4). You need only to raise issues about the characters and what they do and what they represent. What are the characters like at the work's beginning? What happens to them? Do they do anything that causes them to change, and how are they changed? Are the changes for good or for bad? Why do the characters do the things they do? What do they do correctly? What do they do incorrectly? Why? For example, is Mathilde wrong not to tell Jeanne about the lost necklace? Such an immediate admission of truth would save her and her husband 10 years of hardship and deprivation. But Mathilde does not tell the truth. Why not? What do we learn about her character because she avoids or ignores this admission? Is her avoidance understandable? Why?

---

## 🌿 PRESENTING AN ARGUMENT

As you write about literature, you should always try to connect your explanations to a specific argument; that is, you are writing about a specific work, but you are trying to prove—or argue—or demonstrate—a point or idea about it. This book provides you with a number of separate subjects relating to the study of literature. As you select one of these and begin writing, however, you are not to explain just that such-and-such a story has a character who changes and grows, or that such-and-such a poem contains the thought that nature creates great beauty. Rather, you should assert the importance of your topic to the work as a whole in relation to a specific point or argument. One example of an argument might be that a story's first-person point of view permits readers to draw their own conclusions about the speaker's character. Another argument might be that the poet's thought is shown in a poem's details about the bustling sounds and sights of animals in springtime.

Let us therefore repeat and stress that your writing *should always have an argumentative edge*—a goal of demonstrating the truth of your conclusions and clarifying and illuminating your idea about the topic and also about the work. It is here that the accuracy of your choices of details from the work, the soundness of your conclusions, and the cumulative weight of your evidence are essential. You cannot allow your main ideas to rest on one detail alone, but must support your conclusions by showing that the bulk of material leads to them and that they are linked in a reasonable chain of fact and logic. It is such clarification that is the goal of argumentation.

In discussing character, you might also wish to raise the issue of whether the people in the work do or do not do what might normally be expected from people in their circumstances. Do they correspond to type? The idea here is that certain attitudes and behaviors are typical of people at particular stages of life (e.g., children behaving like children, lovers dealing with their relationship, a young couple coping with difficult finances). Thus we might ask questions about whether the usual circumstances experienced by the characters affect them, either by limiting them in some way or by freeing them. What attitudes seem typical of the characters? How do these attitudes govern what the characters do, or don't do? For example, one of the most typical circumstances of life is marriage. According to the positive and ideal type of marriage, a husband and wife should be forthcoming with each other; they should tell each other things and should not conceal what is on their minds. If they have problems, they should discuss them and try to solve them together. In "The Necklace" we see that Mathilde and Loisel do not show these desired qualities, and their absence of communication can be seen as an element in their financial catastrophe. However, during their long years of trouble they work together, for they share a typical quality of honesty, and in this respect they fulfill their role, or type, as a married couple.

An analysis of typical attitudes themselves can also furnish you with material for discussion. For example, Mathilde, who is a member of the lower commercial class, has attitudes that are more appropriate to the upper or leisure class. She cannot bridge this gap, and her frustration causes her to nag her husband to give her enough money to live out her dream, if only for a moment.

## Determining the Work's Historical Period and Background

An obvious topic is the historical circumstances of the work. When was the work written? How well does it portray details about life at the time it appeared? What is historically unique about it? To what degree does it help you learn something about the past that you did not previously know? What actions in the work are like or unlike actions going on at the present time? What truthfulness to life do you discover in the work? In "The Necklace," for example, which was published more than a century ago, Mathilde's duty is to stay at home as a housewife—a traditional role—while her husband is the family breadwinner. After the loss of the necklace she can no longer afford domestic help, and she is compelled to do all her own housework and her own shopping. She has none of today's home conveniences such as a dishwasher, microwave, or car. Her husband, a clerk or secretary-copyist, spends his working day copying business records by hand, for at the period of the story there were no typewriters or word processors. Discussing matters such as these might also help you with works written during modern times, because our own assumptions, artifacts, and habits bear analysis and discussion.

## Describing the Economic and Social Conditions Depicted in the Work

Closely related to the historical period, an obvious topic to pursue in many works is the economic and social condition of the characters. To what level of life, economically, do the characters belong? How are events in the work related to their condition? How does their money, or lack of it, limit what they do? How do their economic circumstances either restrict or liberate their imaginations? How do their jobs and their apparent income determine their way of life? If we ask some of these questions about "The Necklace," as we have seen, we find that Mathilde and her husband are greatly burdened by their lack of money, and also that their obligation to repay their huge loan drives them into economic want and sacrifice.

An important part of the economic and social analysis of literature is the consideration of female characters and what it means to be a woman. This is the feminist analysis of literature, which asks questions such as: What role is Mathilde compelled to take as a result of her sex and family background? How does Jeanne's way of life contrast with that of Mathilde? What can Mathilde do with her life? To what degree is she limited by her role as a housewife? Does she have any chance of an occupation outside the home? How does her economic condition cause her to yearn for better things? What causes her to borrow the necklace? What is her contribution, as a woman, to the repayment of the loans? Should Mathilde's limited life in "The Necklace" be considered as a political argument for greater freedom for women? Once you start asking questions like these, you will find that your thinking is developing along with your ideas for writing.

The feminist approach to the interpretation of literature is well established, and it will usually provide you with a way to discuss a work. It is also possible, of course, to analyze what a work says about the condition of being a man, or being a child. Depending on the work, many of the questions important in a feminist approach are not dissimilar to those you might use if you are dealing with childhood or male adulthood.

One of the most important social and economic topics is that of race and ethnicity. What happens in the work that seems to occur mainly because of the race of the characters? Is the author pointing out any deprivations, any absence of opportunity, any oppression? What do the characters do under such circumstances? Do they succeed or not? Are they negative? Are they angry? Are they resolute and determined? Your aim in an inquiry of this type should be to concentrate on actions and ideas in the work that are clearly related to race.

## Explaining the Work's Major Ideas

One of the major ways of focusing on a work is to zero in on various ideas and values or issues to be discovered there. What ideas might we gain from the story of the lengthy but needless sacrifice and drudgery experienced by Mathilde and her husband? One obvious and acceptable idea is presented by the speaker, namely, that even the smallest, most accidental incident can cause immense consequences. This is an idea that we might expand and illustrate in an entire essay. Here are some other ideas that we also might pursue, all of them based on the story's actions.

- Many actions have unforeseeable and uncontrollable consequences.
- Lack of communication is a major cause of hardship.
- Adversity brings out a character's good qualities.
- Mutual effort enables people to overcome difficulties.

These ideas are all to be found in Maupassant's story. In other works, of course, we may find comparable ideas, in addition to other major ideas and issues.

## Learning About and Describing the Work's Artistic Qualities

A work's artistic qualities provide many possible topics for studying, but basically here you may consider matters such as the work's plan or organization and the author's narrative method, writing style, or poetic techniques. Thus, in "The Necklace," we observe that almost the entire story develops with Mathilde at the center (narrative method; see also Chapter 3, on point of view). At first, the story brings us close to Mathilde, for we are told of her dissatisfaction and impatience with her surroundings. As the story progresses, the storyteller/speaker presents her person and actions more objectively and also more distantly. Another artistic approach would be to determine the story's pattern of development—how, chronologically, the loss of the necklace brings financial misfortune to the Loisels. We might also look for the author's inclusion of symbols in the story, such as the name of the street where the Loisels originally live, their move to an attic flat, or the roughness of Mathilde's hands as a result of her continual housework. These are but a few of the ways to consider the formal aspects of a literary work.

## Preparing to Write

By this time you have been focusing on your topic and have assembled much that you can put into your essay. You should now aim to develop paragraphs and sketches of what you will eventually include. You should always keep in mind the point or argument you want to develop, but invariably digressions occur, together with other difficulties—false starts, dead ends, total cessation of thought, despair, hopelessness, and general frustration. Remember, however, that it is important just to start. Jump right in and start writing anything at all—no matter how unacceptable your first efforts may seem—and force yourself to deal with the materials. The writing down of ideas does not commit you. You should not think that these first ideas are untouchable and holy just because you have written them on paper or typed them into your computer screen. You can throw them out in favor of new ideas, you can make cross-outs and changes, and you can move paragraphs or even sections around as you wish. However, if you do not start writing, your first thoughts will remain locked in your mind and you will have nothing to work with. You must learn to accept the uncertainties in the writing process and make them work *for* you rather than *against* you.

## Building Ideas from Your Original Notes

When you begin writing, get your mind going by mining your notebook or computer file for useful things you have already written. Thus, let us use an observation in our original set of notes—"The attic flat is important," in reference to the poorer rooms where Mathilde and her husband live while they are paying back their creditors. With such a note as a start, you might develop a number of ideas to support an argument about Mathilde's character, as in the following:

> The attic flat is important. Early in the story, in her apartment, Mathilde is dreamy and impractical. She seems delicate, but after losing the necklace, she is delicate no longer. She becomes a worker after they move to the flat. She does a lot more when living there.
>
> In the flat, Mathilde has to sacrifice. She gives up her servant, washes greasy pots, climbs stairs carrying buckets of water, sloshes water around to clean floors, and does all the clothes washing by hand.
>
> When living in the flat she gets stronger, but she also becomes loud and common. She argues with shopkeepers to get the lowest prices. She stops caring for herself. There is a reversal here, from incapable and well groomed to capable but coarse.

In this way, even in an assertion as basic as "The attic flat is important," the process of putting together details is a form of concentrated thought that leads you creatively forward. You can express thoughts and conclusions that you could not express at the beginning. Such an exercise in stretching your mind leads you to put elements of the work together in ways that create ideas for good essays.

## Tracing Patterns of Action and Thought

You can also discover ideas by making a list or scheme for the story or main idea. What conflicts appear? Do these conflicts exist between people, groups, or ideas? How does the author resolve them? Is one force, idea, or side the winner? Why? How do you respond to the winner or to the loser? Using this method, you might make a list similar to this one:

> At the beginning, Mathilde is a fish out of water. She dreams of wealth, but her life is drab and her husband is dull.

Fantasies make her even more dissatisfied; she punishes herself by thinking of a wealthy life.

When the Loisels get the dinner invitation Mathilde pouts and whines. Her husband feels discomfort when she manipulates him into buying her an expensive party dress.

Her world of daydreams hurts her real life when her desire for wealth causes her to borrow the necklace. Losing the necklace is just plain bad luck.

These arguments all focus on Mathilde's character, but you may wish to trace other patterns you find in the story. If you start planning an essay about another pattern, be sure to account for all the actions and scenes that relate to your topic. Otherwise, you may miss a piece of evidence that could lead you to new conclusions.

## Raising and Answering Your Own Questions

A habit you should cultivate is to raise your own questions, and to try to answer them yourself as you consider your reading. The *Guidelines for Reading* will help you formulate questions (pp. 11–12), but you can raise additional questions such as these:

- What is happening as the work unfolds? How does an action at the work's beginning bring about the work's later actions and speeches?
- Who are the main characters? What seems unusual or different about what they do in the work?
- What conclusions can you draw about the work's actions, scenes, and situations? Explain these conclusions.
- What are the characters and speakers like? What do they do and say about themselves, their goals, the people around them, their families, their friends, their work, and the general circumstances of their lives?
- What kinds of words do the characters use: formal or informal words, slang or profanity?
- What literary conventions and devices have you discovered, and how do these affect the work? (When an author addresses readers directly, for example, that is a convention; when a comparison is used, that is a device, which might be either a metaphor or a simile.)

Of course, you can raise other questions as you reread the piece, or you can be left with one or two major questions that you decide to pursue.

## Putting Ideas Together Using the Plus–Minus, Pro–Con, or Either–Or Method

A common and very helpful method of discovering ideas is to develop a set of contrasts: plus–minus, pro–con, either–or. Let us suppose a plus–minus method of considering the following question about Mathilde: Should she be "admired" (plus) or "condemned" (minus)?

| PLUS: ADMIRED? | MINUS: CONDEMNED? |
|---|---|
| After she cries when they get the invitation, she recovers with a "strong effort"—maybe she doesn't want her husband to feel bad. | She wants to be envied and admired only for being attractive and intriguing, not for more important qualities. She seems spoiled and selfish. |
| She scores a great victory at the dance. She really does have the power to charm and captivate. | She wastes her time in daydreaming about things she can't have, and she whines because she is unhappy. |
| Once she loses the necklace, she and her husband become poor and deprived. But she does "her share . . . completely, heroically" (paragraph 98) to make up for the loss. | Even though the Loisels live poorly, Mathilde manipulates her husband into giving her more money than they can afford for a party dress. |
| Even when she is poor, she dreams about that marvelous, shining moment at the great ball. This is pathetic, because Mathilde gets worse than she deserves. | She assumes that her friend Jeanne would think her a thief if she admitted losing the necklace. Shouldn't she have had more confidence in Jeanne? |
| At the end, after everything is paid back, and her reputation is secure, Mathilde confesses the loss to Jeanne. | She becomes loud and coarse and haggles about pennies, thus undergoing a cheapening of her person and manner. |

By putting contrasting observations side by side in this way, you will find that ideas start to come naturally and will be helpful to you when you begin writing, regardless of how you finally organize your essay. It is possible, for example, that you might develop either column as the argumentative basis of an essay, or you might use your notes to support the idea that Mathilde is too complex to be either wholly admired or wholly condemned. You might also want to introduce an entirely new topic of development, such as that Mathilde should be pitied rather than condemned or admired. In short, arranging materials in the plus–minus pattern is a powerful way to discover ideas—a truly helpful habit of promoting thought—that can lead to ways of development that you do not at first realize.

## Originating and Developing Your Thoughts through Writing

You should always write down what you are thinking, for, as a principle, unwritten thought is incomplete thought. Make a practice of writing your observations about the work, in addition to any questions that occur to you. This is an exciting step in preliminary writing because it can be useful when you write later drafts. You will discover that looking at what you have written not only can enable you to correct and improve the writing you have done, but also can lead you to recognize that you need something more. The process goes like this: "Something needs to be added here— important details that my reader will not have noticed, new support for my argument, a new idea that has just occurred to me, a significant connection to link my thoughts." If you follow such a process, you can use your own written ideas to create new ideas. You can advance your own abilities as a thinker and writer.

The processes just described, of searching for ideas, or brainstorming, are useful for you at any stage of composition. Even when you are fairly close to finishing your essay, you might suddenly recognize that you need to add something (or subtract something you do not like). When that happens, you may return to the discovery or brainstorming process to initiate and develop new ideas and new arguments.

# Making an Initial Draft of Your Essay

As you use the brainstorming and focusing techniques, you are also, in fact, beginning your essay. You will need to revise your ideas as connections among them become clearer and as you reexamine the work to discover details to support the argument you are making. By this stage, however, you already have many of the raw materials you need for developing your topic.

## Basing Your Essay on a Central Idea, Argument, or Statement

By definition, an essay *is an organized, connected, and fully developed set of paragraphs that expand on a* **central idea**, **central argument**, or **central statement**. All parts of an essay should contribute to the reader's understanding of the idea. To achieve unity and completeness, each paragraph refers to the argument and demonstrates how selected details from the work relate to it and support it. The central idea helps you control and shape your essay, just as it also provides guidance for your reader.

A successful essay about literature is a brief but thorough (not exhaustive) examination of a literary work in light of topics like those we have already raised, such as character, background, economic conditions, circumstances of gender, major ideas, artistic qualities, or any additional topic such as point of view and symbolism. Central ideas or arguments might be (1) that a character is strong and tenacious, (2) that the story shows the unpredictability of action, (3) that the point of view makes the action seem "distant and objective," or (4) that a major symbol governs the actions and thoughts of the major characters. In essays on these topics, all materials must be tied to such central ideas or arguments. Thus, it is a fact that Mathilde in "The Necklace" endures 10 years of slavish work and sacrifice as she and her husband accumulate enough money to repay their monumental debt. This we know, but it is not relevant to an essay on her character unless you connect it by a central argument showing how it demonstrates one of her major traits—her growing strength and perseverance.

Look through all of your ideas for one or two that catch your eye for development. In all the early stages of preliminary writing, the chances are that you have already discovered at least a few ideas that are more thought provoking, or more important, than the others.

## THE NEED FOR THE PHYSICAL PROCESS OF WRITING

Thinking and writing are interdependent processes. If you do not get your thoughts into words that are visible to you on a paper or computer screen, your thinking will be impeded. It is therefore vital for you to use the writing process as the most significant means of developing your ideas. If you are doing an assignment in class—tests or impromptu essays—write your initial responses on a single side of your paper. This strategy enables you to spread your materials out to get an actual physical overview of them when you begin writing. Everything is open to you; none of your ideas are hidden on the other side of the paper.

Outside of class, however, when you are at home or otherwise able to use a computer/word processor, your machine is an indispensable tool for your writing. It helps you develop ideas, for it quickly enables you to eliminate unworkable thoughts and to replace them with others. You can move sentences and paragraphs into new contexts, test how they look, and move them somewhere else if you choose.

In addition, with the rapid printers now available, you can print even the initial and tentative stages of writing. Using the printed draft, you can make additional notes, corrections, and suggestions for further development. With the marked-up draft as a guide, you can go back to the word processor and fill in your changes and improvements, repeating this procedure as often as you can. This facility makes the machine an incentive for improvement, right up to your final draft.

Word processing also helps you in the final preparation of your essays. Studies have shown that errors and awkward sentences are frequently found at the bottoms of pages prepared by hand or with a conventional typewriter. The reason is that writers hesitate to make improvements when they get near the end of a page because they shun the dreariness of starting the page over. Word processors eliminate this difficulty completely. Changes can be made anywhere in the draft, at any time, without any ill effect on the final appearance of your essay.

Regardless of your writing method, you should always remember that unwritten thought is incomplete thought. You cannot lay everything out at once on the word processor's screen; you can see only a small part of what you are writing. Therefore, somewhere in your writing process, you need to prepare a complete draft of what you have written. A clean, readable draft permits you to gather everything together and to make even more improvements through revision.

Once you choose an idea you think you can work with, write it as a complete sentence that is essential to the argument of your essay. A simple phrase such as "setting and character" does not focus thought the way a sentence does. A sentence moves the topic toward new exploration and discovery because it combines a topic with an outcome, such as "The setting of 'The Necklace' reflects Mathilde's character." You can choose to be even more specific: "Mathilde's strengths and weaknesses are reflected in the real and imaginary places in 'The Necklace.'"

Now that you have phrased a single, central idea or argument for your essay, you also have established a guide by which you can accept, reject, rearrange, and change the ideas you have been planning to develop. You can now draft a few paragraphs (which you may base on some of the sketches you have already made; always use as much as you can of your early observations) to see whether your idea seems valid, or you can decide that it would be more helpful to make an outline or a list before you do more writing. In either case, you should use your notes for evidence to connect to your central idea. If you need to bolster your argument with more supporting details and ideas, go once again to the techniques of discovery and brainstorming.

Using the central idea that the changes in the story's settings reflect Mathilde's character might produce a paragraph such as the following, which presents an argument about her negative qualities:

> The original apartment in the Street of Martyrs and the dream world of wealthy places both show negative sides of Mathilde's character. The real-life apartment, though livable, is shabby. The furnishings all bring out her discontent. The shabbiness makes her think only of luxuriousness, and having one servant girl causes her to dream of having many servants. The luxury of her dream life heightens her unhappiness with what she actually has.

In such a preliminary draft, in which the purpose is to connect details and thoughts to the major idea, many details from the story are used in support. In the final draft, this kind of support is essential.

## Creating a Thesis Sentence as an Organizing Guide

With your central idea or argument as your focus, you can decide which of the earlier observations and ideas can be developed further. Your goal is to establish a number of major topics to support your argument and to express them in a **thesis sentence** or **thesis statement**—an organizing sentence that contains the major topics you plan to treat in your essay. Suppose you choose three ideas from your discovery stage of development. If you put the central idea at the left and the list of topics at the right, you have the shape of the thesis sentence. Note that the first two topics below are taken from the discovery paragraph.

| CENTRAL IDEA | TOPICS |
|---|---|
| The setting of "The Necklace" reflects Mathilde's character. | 1. First apartment |
| | 2. Dream-life mansion rooms |
| | 3. Attic flat |

This arrangement leads to the following thesis statement or thesis sentence.

> Mathilde's character growth is connected to her first apartment, her dream-life mansion rooms, and her attic flat.

You can revise the thesis sentence at any stage of the writing process if you find that you do not have enough evidence from the work to support it. Perhaps a new topic will occur to you, and you can include it, appropriately, as a part of your thesis sentence.

As we have seen, the central idea or central argument is the *glue* of the essay. The thesis sentence lists the parts to be fastened together—that is, the topics in which the central idea is to be demonstrated and argued. To alert your readers to your essay's structure, the thesis sentence is usually placed at the end of the introductory paragraph, just before the body of the essay.

## Writing a First Draft

To write a first draft, you support the points of your thesis sentence with your notes and discovery materials. You can alter, reject, and rearrange ideas and details as you wish, as long as you change your thesis sentence to account for the changes (a major reason why many writers write their introductions last). The thesis sentence just shown contains three topics (it could be two, or four, or more) to be used in forming the body of the essay.

## Begin Each Paragraph with a TOPIC SENTENCE

Just as the organization of the *entire essay* is based on the thesis, the form of each *paragraph* is based on its **topic sentence**. A topic sentence is an assertion about how a topic from the predicate of the thesis statement supports the argument contained or implied in the central idea. The first topic in our example is the relationship of Mathilde's character to her first apartment, and the resulting paragraph should emphasize this relationship. If your topic is the coarsening of her character during the ten-year travail, you can then form a topic sentence by connecting the trait with the location, as follows:

> The attic flat reflects the coarsening of Mathilde's character.

Beginning with this sentence, the paragraph will present details that argue how Mathilde's rough, heavy housework changes her behavior, appearance, and general outlook.

---

### ✿ VERB TENSES IN LITERARY ANALYSIS

Literary works spring into life with each and every reading. You may thus assume that everything happening takes place in the present, and when writing about literature you should use the *present tense of verbs*. It is correct to say, "Mathilde and her husband *work* and *economize* [not *worked* and *economized*] for 10 years to pay off the 18,000-franc loan they *take out* [not *took out*] to pay for the lost necklace."

When you consider an author's ideas, the present tense is also proper, on the principle that the words of an author are just as alive and current today (and tomorrow) as they were at the moment of writing, even if this same author might have been dead for hundreds or even thousands of years.

Because it is incorrect to shift tenses inappropriately, you may encounter a problem when you refer to actions that have occurred prior to the time of the main action. An instance is Bierce's "An Occurrence at Owl Creek Bridge" (Chapter 2), in which the main character, a Southern gentleman during the Civil War, is about to be hanged by Union soldiers because he tried to sabotage a strategically important bridge. The story emphasizes the relationship between cause (the attempted sabotage, occurring in the past) and effect (the punishment, occurring in the present). In discussing such a narrative it is important to keep details in order, and thus you can introduce the past tense as long as you make the relationship clear between past and present, as in this example: "Farquhar *is actually hanged* [present tense] by the Union soldiers. But his perceptions *turn him* [present tense] toward the past, and his final thoughts *dwell* [present tense] on the life and happiness he *knew* [past tense] at his own home with his dearest wife." This intermingling of past and present tenses is correct because it corresponds to the pattern of time brought out in the story.

A problem also arises when you introduce historical or biographical details about a work or author. It is appropriate to use the *past tense* for such details if they genuinely do belong to the past. Thus it is correct to state, "Shakespeare *lived* from 1564 to 1616," or that "Shakespeare *wrote* his tragedy *Hamlet* in about 1600–1601." It is also permissible to mix past and present tenses when you are treating historical facts about a literary work and are also considering it as a living text. Of prime importance is to keep things straight. Here is an example showing how past tenses (in bold) and present tenses (in italic) may be used when appropriate:

> Because *Hamlet* **was** first **performed** in about 1601, Shakespeare most probably **wrote** it shortly before this time. In the play, a tragedy, Shakespeare *treats* an act of vengeance, but more importantly he *demonstrates* the difficulty of ever learning the exact truth. The hero, Prince Hamlet, *is* the focus of this difficulty, for the task of revenge *is assigned* to him by the Ghost of his father. Though the Ghost *claims* that his brother, Claudius, *is* his murderer, Hamlet *is* not able to verify this claim.

Here, the historical details are in the past tense, while all details about the play *Hamlet*, including Shakespeare as the creating author whose ideas and words are still alive, are in the present.

As a general principle, you will be right most of the time if you use the present tense exclusively for literary details and the past tense for historical details. When in doubt, however, *consult your instructor.*

## Select Only One Topic—No More—for Each Paragraph

You should treat each separate topic in a single paragraph—one topic, one paragraph. However, if a topic seems especially difficult, long, and heavily detailed, you can divide it into two or more subtopics, each receiving a separate paragraph of its own—two or more subtopics, two or more separate paragraphs. Should you make this division, your topic is then a section, and each paragraph in the section should have its own topic sentence.

## Use Your Topic Sentence as the Basis of Your Paragraph Development

Once you choose a topic sentence, you can use it to focus your observations and conclusions. Let us see how our topic about the attic flat can be developed in a paragraph of argument:

> The attic flat reflects the coarsening of Mathilde's character. Maupassant emphasizes the burdens Mathilde endures to save money, such as mopping floors, cleaning greasy and encrusted pots and pans, taking out the garbage, and washing clothes and dishes by hand. This work makes her rough and coarse, an effect also shown by her giving up care of her hair and hands, wearing the cheapest dresses possible, haggling with the local shopkeepers, and becoming loud and penny-pinching. If at the beginning she is delicate and attractive, at the end she is unpleasant and coarse.

Here, details from the story are introduced to provide support for the topic sentence. All the subjects—the hard work, the lack of personal care, the wearing of cheap dresses, and the haggling with the shopkeepers—are introduced not to retell the story but rather to exemplify the argument the writer is making about Mathilde's character.

## Developing an Outline to Help Organize Your Essay

So far, we have been creating a de facto **outline**—that is, a skeletal plan of organization. Some writers never use any outline but prefer informal lists of ideas; others always rely on outlines. Still others insist that they cannot make an outline until they have finished writing. Regardless of your preference, your final essay should have a tight structure. Therefore, you should use a guiding outline to develop and shape your essay.

The outline we are concerned with here is the **analytical sentence outline**. This type is easier to create than it sounds. It consists of (1) an introduction, including the central idea and the thesis sentence, together with (2) topic sentences that are to be used in each paragraph of the body, followed by (3) a conclusion. When applied to the subject we have been developing, such an outline looks like this:

#### TITLE: SETTING IN "THE NECKLACE" IS CONNECTED TO MATHILDE'S CHARACTER

1. **Introduction**
   a. *Central idea*: Maupassant uses setting to show Mathilde's character.
   b. *Thesis statement*: Her character growth is brought out by her first apartment, her daydreams about elegant rooms in a mansion, and her attic flat.
2. **Body**: *Topic sentences* a, b, and c (and d, e, and f, if necessary)
   a. Details about her first apartment explain her dissatisfaction and depression.
   b. Her daydreams about mansion rooms are like the apartment because they too make her unhappy.
   c. The attic flat reflects the coarsening of her character.

3. **Conclusion**

*Topic sentence*: All details in the story, particularly the setting, are focused on the character of Mathilde.

The *conclusion* may be a summary of the body; it may evaluate the main idea; it may briefly suggest further points of discussion; or it may be a reflection on the details of the body.

## Using the Outline in Developing Your Essay

The illustrative essays included throughout this book are organized according to the principles of the analytical sentence outline. To emphasize the shaping effect of these outlines, all central ideas, thesis sentences, and topic sentences are underlined. In your own writing, you can underline or italicize these "skeletal" sentences as a check on your organization. Unless your instructor requires such markings, however, remove them in your final drafts.

---

### USING THE NAMES OF AUTHORS

For both men and women writers, you should regularly include the author's *full name* in the *first sentence* of your essay. Here are model first sentences.

Shirley Jackson's "The Lottery" is a story featuring both suspense and horror.

"The Lottery," by Shirley Jackson, is a story featuring both suspense and horror.

For all later references, use only last names, such as *Jackson, Maupassant, Lawrence,* or *Porter.* However, for the "giants" of literature, you should use the last names exclusively. In referring to writers like Shakespeare and Dickinson, for example, there is no need to include *William* or *Emily.*

In spite of today's informal standards, do not use an author's first name, as in "*Shirley* skillfully creates suspense and horror in 'The Lottery.'" Also, do not use a courtesy title before the names of dead authors, such as "*Ms.* Jackson's 'The Lottery' is a suspenseful horror story," or "*Mr.* Shakespeare's idea is that information is uncertain." Use the last names alone.

As with all conventions, of course, there are exceptions. If you are referring to a childhood work of a writer, the first name might be appropriate, but be sure to shift to the last name when referring to the writer's mature works. If your writer has a professional or a noble title, such as "*Lord* Byron" or "*Queen* Elizabeth," it is not improper to use the title. Even then, however, the titles are commonly omitted for males, so that most references to Lord Byron and Alfred, Lord Tennyson, should be simply to "Byron" and "Tennyson."

Referring to living authors is somewhat problematical. Some journals and newspapers often use the courtesy titles *Mr.* and *Ms.* in their reviews. However, scholarly journals, which are likely to remain on library shelves and Web sites for many decades, follow the general principle of beginning with the entire name and then using only the last name for later references.

## Illustrative Student Essay (First Draft)

The following illustrative essay is a first draft of the subject we have been developing. It follows our outline, and it includes details from the story in support of the various topics. It is by no means, however, as good a piece of writing as it could be. The draft omits a topic, some additional details, and some new insights that are included in the second draft, which follows (pp. 43–45). It therefore reveals the need to make improvements through additional brainstorming and discovery-prewriting techniques. The marginal comments, questions, and directions are those that might be written by an instructor who is reading and grading the essay as an assignment.

> Underlined sentences in this paper *do not* conform to MLA style and are used solely as teaching tools to emphasize the central idea, thesis sentence, and topic sentences throughout the paper.

Deal 1

James Deal

Professor Smith

English 102

16 April 2007

### How Setting in "The Necklace" Is Related to the Character of Mathilde

[1]    In "The Necklace" Guy de Maupassant does not give much detail about the setting. He does not even describe the necklace itself, which is the central object in his plot, but he says only that it is "superb" (paragraph 47). Rather, he uses the setting to reflect the character of the central figure, Mathilde Loisel.[*] All his details are presented to bring out her traits. Her character growth is related to her first apartment, her dream-life mansion rooms, and her attic flat.[†]

*Explain what setting is used for?*

*Does Mathilde's character grow or change?*

[2]    Details about her first apartment explain her dissatisfaction and depression. The walls are "drab," the furniture "threadbare," and the curtains "ugly" (paragraph 3). There is only a simple country girl to do the housework. The tablecloth is not changed daily, and the best dinner dish is beef stew. Mathilde has no evening clothes, only a theater dress that she does not like. These details show her dissatisfaction about her life with her low-salaried husband.

*More specific word needed*

*Explain her reaction to this*

*Dissatisfaction is with husband or her life?*

---
[*]Central idea
[†]Thesis sente3nce

Deal 2

[3]     Her dream-life images of wealth are like the apartment because they too make her unhappy. In her daydreams about life in a mansion, the rooms are large, filled with expensive furniture and bric-a-brac, and draped in silk. She imagines private rooms for intimate talks, and big dinners with delicacies like trout and quail. With dreams of such a rich home, she feels even more despair about her modest apartment on the Street of Martyrs in Paris.

*Be more specific what does she dream about?*

*Be more specific about her dream world*

*Quote from story?*

[4]     The attic flat reflects the coarsening of Mathilde's character. Maupassant emphasizes the burdens she endures to save money, such as mopping floors, cleaning greasy and encrusted pots and pans, taking out the garbage, and washing clothes and dishes by hand. This work makes her rough and coarse, a fact also shown by her giving up care of her hair and hands, wearing the cheapest dresses possible, haggling with local shop-keepers, and becoming loud and penny-pinching. If at the beginning she is delicate and attractive, at the end she is unpleasant and coarse.

*What else does the attic flat indicate about Mathilde? (Her work ethic?)*

[5]     Maupassant focuses everything in the story, including the setting, on the character of Mathilde. He does not add anything extra. Thus he says little about the big party scene, but emphasizes the necessary detail that Mathilde was a great "success" (paragraph 52). It is this detail that brings out some of her early attractiveness and charm, despite her more usual frustration and unhappiness. Thus in "The Necklace," Maupassant uses setting as a means to his end——the story of Mathilde and her unnecessary sacrifice.

*Perhaps a paragraph about her walk on the Champs-Elysées*

*Any other details that highlight Mathilde's character?*

Deal 3

**WORK CITED**

Maupassant, Guy de. "The Necklace." *Literature: An Introduction to Reading and Writing, Fourth Compact Edition*. Ed. Edgar V. Roberts. Upper Saddle River: Pearson Prentice Hall, 2008, 4–11.

*Good first draft. Work on more specific topic sentences and more details in body paragraphs. Make sure details in body paragraphs are related to topic sentences. You may wish to include another paragraph about the walk on the Champs-Elysées.*

# Completing the Essay: Developing and Strengthening through Revision

After finishing your first draft, like this one, you may wonder what more you can do. Your essay may seem to be complete as it is, and that's it. You have read the work several times, used discovery and brainstorming techniques to establish ideas to write about, made an outline of your ideas, and written a full draft. How can you do better?

The best way to begin is to observe that a major mistake writers make when writing about literature is to do no more than retell a story or summarize an idea. Retelling a story shows only that you have read it, not that you have thought about it. Writing a good essay requires you to arrange a pattern of argument and thought.

## Using Your Own Order of References

One way to escape the trap of summarizing stories and instead to set up a pattern of development is to stress your own order when referring to parts of a work. Rearrange details to suit your own central idea or argument. It is often important to write first about the conclusion or middle. Should you find that you have followed the chronological order of the work instead of stressing your own order, you can use one of the preliminary writing techniques to figure out new ways to connect your materials. The principle is that you should introduce details about the work *only* to support the points you wish to make. Details for the sake of detail are unnecessary.

## Using Literary Material as Evidence

When you write, you are like a detective using clues as evidence for building a case or a lawyer citing evidence to support an argument. Your goal is to convince your readers of your knowledge and the reasonableness of your conclusions. It is vital to use evidence convincingly so that your readers can follow your ideas. Let us look briefly at two drafts of a new example to see how writing can be improved by the pointed use of details. These are from drafts of an essay on the character of Mathilde.

**PARAGRAPH 1**

The major flaw of Mathilde's character is that she seems to be isolated, locked away from other people. She and her husband do not talk to each other much, except about external things. He speaks about his liking for beef stew, and she states that she cannot accept the big invitation because she has no nice dresses. Once she gets the dress, she complains because she has no jewelry. Even when borrowing the necklace from Jeanne Forrestier, she does not say much. When she and her husband discover that the necklace is lost, they simply

**PARAGRAPH 2**

The major flaw of Mathilde's character is that she is withdrawn and uncommunicative, apparently unwilling or unable to form an intimate relationship. For example, she and her husband do not talk to each other much, except about external things such as his taste for beef stew and her lack of a party dress and jewelry. With such an uncommunicative marriage, one might suppose that she would be more open with her close friend, Jeanne Forrestier, but Mathilde does not say much even to her. This flaw hurts

**PARAGRAPH 1 (Continued)**

go over the details, and Loisel dictates a letter of explanation, which Mathilde writes in her own hand. Even when she meets Jeanne on the Champs-Elysées, Mathilde does not say a great deal about her life but only goes through enough details about the loss and replacement of the necklace to make Jeanne exclaim about the needlessness of the 10-year sacrifice.

**PARAGRAPH 2 (Continued)**

her greatly, because if she were more open she might have explained the loss and avoided the horrible sacrifice. This lack of openness, along with her self-indulgent dreaminess, is her biggest defect.

A comparison of these paragraphs shows that the first has more words than the second (157 compared to 120 [computer count]) but that it is more appropriate for a rough than a final draft because the writer does little more than retell the story. Paragraph 1 is cluttered with details that do not support any conclusions. If you try to find what it says about Maupassant's use of Mathilde's solitary traits in "The Necklace," you will not succeed. The writer needs to revise the paragraph by eliminating details that do not support the central idea.

On the other hand, the details in paragraph 2 actually do support the declared topic. Phrases such as "for example," "with such," and "this lack" show that the writer of paragraph 2 has assumed that the audience knows the story and now wants to read an argument in support of a particular interpretation. Paragraph 2 therefore guides readers by connecting the details to the topic. It uses these details as evidence, *not* as a retelling of actions. By contrast, paragraph 1 recounts a number of relevant actions *but does not connect them to the topic*. More details, of course, could have been added to the second paragraph, but they are unnecessary because the paragraph develops the argument with the details used. Good writing has many qualities, but one of the most important is shown in a comparison of the two paragraphs: *In good writing, no details are included unless they are used as supporting evidence in a pattern of thought and argument.*

## Always Keep to Your Point; Stick to It Tenaciously

To show another distinction between first- and second-draft writing, let us consider a third example. The following unrevised paragraph, in which the writer assumes an audience that is interested in the relationship of economics to literature, is drawn from an essay about the idea of economic determinism in Maupassant's "The Necklace." In this paragraph the writer is trying to argue the point that economic circumstances underlie a number of incidents in the story. The idea is to assert that Mathilde's difficulties result not from her character traits but rather from her financial restrictions.

More important than chance in governing life is the idea that people are controlled by economic circumstances. Mathilde, as is shown at the story's opening, is born poor. Therefore she doesn't get the right doors opened for her, and she settles down to marriage with a minor clerk, Loisel. With a vivid imagination and a burning desire for luxury, seeming to be born only for a life of ease and wealth, she finds that her poor home brings out her daydreams of expensive surroundings. She taunts her husband when he brings the big invitation, because she does not have a suitable (that is, "expensive") dress. Once she gets the dress it is jewelry she lacks, and she borrows that and loses it. The loss of the necklace means great trouble because it forces the Loisels to borrow heavily and to struggle financially for ten years.

This paragraph begins with an effective topic sentence, indicating that the writer has a good plan. The remaining part, however, shows how easily writers can be diverted from their objective. The flaw is that the material of the paragraph, while accurate, is not clearly connected to the topic. Once the second sentence is under way, the paragraph gets lost in a retelling of events, and the promising topic sentence is forgotten. The paragraph therefore shows that the use of detail alone will not support an intended meaning or argument. *As a writer, you must do the connecting yourself, and make sure that all relationships are explicitly clear.* This point cannot be overemphasized.

Let us see how the problem can be treated. If the ideal paragraph can be schematized with line drawings, we might say that the paragraph's topic should be a straight line, moving toward and reaching a specific goal (the topic or argument of the paragraph), with an exemplifying line moving away from the straight line briefly to bring in evidence, but returning to the line to demonstrate the relevance of each new fact. Thus, the ideal scheme looks like this, with a straight line touched a number of times by an undulating line.

Notice that the exemplifying line, waving to illustrate how documentation or exemplification is to be used, always returns to the topic line. A scheme for the faulty paragraph on "The Necklace," however, looks like this, with the line never returning but flying out into space.

How might the faulty paragraph be improved? The best way is to remind the reader again and again of the topic and to use examples from the text in support.

As our model wavy-line diagram indicates, each time a topic is mentioned, the undulating line merges with the straight, or central-idea, line. This relationship of argument to illustrative examples should prevail no matter what subject you write about, and you have to be tenacious in forming these connecting relationships. If you are analyzing *point of view*, for example, you should keep connecting your material to the speaker, or narrator, and the same applies to topics such as character, idea, or setting. According to this principle, we might revise the paragraph on economic determinism in "The Necklace" as follows. (Parts of sentences stressing the relationship of the examples to the topic sentence are underlined.)

> *More important than chance in governing life is the idea that people are controlled by economic circumstances.* <u>As illustration</u>, the speaker begins by emphasizing that Mathilde, the main character, is born poor. Therefore she doesn't get the right doors opened for her, and she settles down to marriage with a minor clerk, Loisel. <u>In keeping with the idea</u>, her vivid imagination and burning desire for luxury feed on her weakness of character as she feels deep unhappiness and depression because of the contrast between her daydreams of expensive surroundings and the poor home she actually has. <u>These straitened economic circumstances</u> inhibit her relationship with her husband, and she taunts him when he brings the big invitation because she does not have a suitable (that is, "expensive") dress. As a merging of her unrealistic dream life with actual reality, <u>her borrowing of the necklace suggests the impossibility of overcoming economic restrictions</u>. In the context of the idea, the 10-year sacrifice to pay for the lost necklace <u>demonstrates that being poor keeps people down, destroying their dreams and their hopes for a better life.</u>

The paragraph now successfully develops the argument promised by the topic sentence. While it has also been lengthened, the length has been caused not by inessential detail but by phrases and sentences that give form and direction. You might object that if you lengthened all your paragraphs in this way, your essays would grow too bulky. The answer is to reduce the number of major points and paragraphs, on the theory that *it is better to develop a few topics pointedly than to develop many pointlessly*. Revising for the purpose of strengthening central and topic ideas requires that you either throw out some topics or else incorporate them as subpoints in the topics you keep. To control your writing in this way can result only in improvement.

## Checking Your Development and Organization

It bears repeating over and over again that the first requirement of a good essay is to introduce a central idea or argument and then stick to it. Another major step toward excellence is to make your central idea expand and grow. The word *growth* is a metaphor describing the disclosure of ideas that were not at first noticeable, together with the expression of original, new, and fresh interpretations.

### Be Original

In everything you write, now and in the future, you should always try to be original. You might claim that originality is impossible because you are writing about someone else's work. "The author has said everything," might be the argument, "and therefore I can do little more than follow the story." This claim rests on the mistaken assumption that you have no choice in selecting material and no opportunity to have individual thoughts and make original contributions.

But you do have choices and opportunities to be original. You really do. One obvious area of originality is the development and formulation of your central idea. For example, a natural first response to "The Necklace" is "The story is about a woman who loses a borrowed necklace and endures hardship to help pay for it." But this response does not promise an argument because it refers only to events in the story and not to any idea. You can point the sentence toward an argument, however, if you call the hardship "needless." Just this word alone demands that you explain the differences between needed and unneeded hardships, and your application of these differences to the heroine's plight would produce an original essay. Even better and more original insights could result if the topic of the budding essay were to connect the dreamy, withdrawn traits of the main character to her misfortunes. A resulting central idea might be "People create their own difficulties." Such an argument would require you to define not only the personal but also the representative nature of Mathilde's experiences, an avenue of exploration that could produce much in the way of a fresh, original essay about "The Necklace."

You can also develop your ability to treat your subject originally if you plan the body of the essay to build up to what you think is your most important and incisive idea. As examples of such planning, the following brief outline suggests how a central idea can be widened and expanded:

### ARGUMENT: MATHILDE GROWS AS A CHARACTER IN "THE NECKLACE"

1. She has normal daydreams about a better life.
2. In trying to make her daydreams seem real, she takes a risk but then loses.
3. She develops by facing her mistake and working hard to correct it.

The list shows how a subject can be enlarged if you treat your exemplifying details in an increasing order of importance. In this case, the order moves from Mathilde's habit of daydreaming to her growing strength of character. The pattern shows how you can meet two primary standards of excellence in writing—organization and growth.

Clearly, you should always try to develop your central idea or argument. Constantly adhere to your topic, and constantly develop it. Nurture it and make it grow. Admittedly, in a short essay you will be able to move only a short distance with an idea or argument, but you should never be satisfied to leave the idea exactly where you found it. To the degree that you can learn to develop your ideas, you will receive recognition for increasingly original writing.

## Writing with Your Audience in Mind

Whenever you write, you must decide how much detail to discuss. Usually you base this decision on your judgment of your readers. For example, if you assume that they have not read the work, you will need to include a short summary as background. Otherwise, they may not understand your argument.

Consider, too, whether your readers have any special interests or concerns. If they are particularly interested in politics, sociology, religion, or psychology, for example, you may need to select and develop your materials along one of these lines.

Your instructor will let you know who your audience is. Usually, it will be your instructor or your fellow students. They will be familiar with the work and will not expect you to retell a story or summarize an argument. Rather, they will want you to explain and interpret the work in the light of your main assertions about it. Thus, you can omit details that do not exemplify and support your argument, even if these details are important parts of the work. What you write should always be based on your developing idea and your assessment of your readers.

## Using Exact, Comprehensive, and Forceful Language

In addition to being original, organized, and well developed, the best writing is exact, comprehensive, and forceful. At any stage of the composition process, you should try to correct and improve your earliest sentences and paragraphs, which usually need to be rethought, reworded, and rearranged.

Try to make your sentences meaningful. First, ask yourself whether your sentences mean what you really intend, or whether you can make them more exact and therefore stronger. For example, consider these two sentences from essays about "The Necklace":

1. It seems as though the main character's dreams of luxury cause her to respond as she does in the story.
2. This incident, although it may seem trivial or unimportant, has substantial significance in the creation of the story; by this I mean the incident that occurred is essentially what the story is all about.

These sentences are inexact and vague and therefore are unhelpful. Neither of them goes anywhere. Sentence 1 is satisfactory up to the verb *cause*, but then it falls apart because the writer has lost sight of an argumentative or thematic purpose. It would be better to describe what the response *is* rather than to say nothing more than that some kind of response *exists*. To make the sentence more exact, we might try the following revision.

Mathilde's dreams of luxury make her dissatisfied with her own possessions, and therefore she goes beyond her financial means to attend the big party.

With this revision, the writer could readily go on to consider the relationship of the early part of the story to the later parts. Without the revision, it is not clear where the writer might go.

Sentence 2 is vague because the writer has lost all contact with the main thread of argument. If we adopt the principle of trying to be exact, however, we can create more meaning and more promise:

The accidental loss of the necklace, which is trivial though costly, supports the narrator's claim that major turns in life are produced not by earthshaking events but rather by minor ones.

In addition to working for exactness, try to make sentences—all sentences, but particularly thesis and topic sentences—complete and comprehensive. Consider the following sentence:

The idea in "The Necklace" is that Mathilde and her husband work hard to pay for the lost necklace.

Although this sentence promises to describe an idea, it does no more than state the story's major action. It needs additional rethinking and rephrasing to make it more comprehensive, as in these two revisions:

1. In "The Necklace" Maupassant brings out the importance of overcoming mistakes through hard work and responsibility.
2. Maupassant's surprise ending in "The Necklace" symbolizes the need for always being truthful.

Both new sentences are connected to the action described by the original phrasing, "Mathilde and her husband work hard to pay for the lost necklace," although they point toward differing treatments. The first sentence concerns the virtue shown by the Loisels in their sacrifice. Because the second sentence includes the word *symbolizes*, an essay stemming from it would stress the Loisels' mistake in not confessing the loss. In dealing with the symbolic meaning of their failure, an essay developed along the lines of the second sentence would focus on the negative sides of their characters, and an essay developed from the first sentence would stress their positive sides. Both of the revised sentences, therefore, are more comprehensive than the original sentence and thus would help a writer get on the track toward a thoughtful and analytical essay.

Of course, creating fine sentences is never easy, but as a mode of improvement, you might use some self-testing mechanisms:

- *For story materials.* Always relate the materials to a point or argument. Do not say simply, "Mathilde works constantly for 10 years to help pay off the debt." Instead, blend the material into a point, like this: "Mathilde's 10-year effort shows her resolution to overcome the horror of indebtedness," or "Mathilde's 10-year effort brings out her strength of character."
- *For responses and impressions.* Do not say simply, "The story's ending left me with a definite impression." What are you giving your readers with a sentence like this? They want to know what your impression is, and therefore you need to describe it, as in the following: "The story's ending surprised me and also made me sympathetic to the major character," or "The story's ending struck me with the idea that life is unpredictable and unfair."
- *For ideas.* Make the idea clear and direct. Do not say, "Mathilde lives in a poor household," but rather refer to the story to bring out an idea, as follows: "Mathilde's story shows that economic deprivation hurts a person's quality of life."
- *For critical commentary.* Do not be satisfied with a statement such as "I found 'The Necklace' interesting." All right, the story is interesting, but what does that tell us? Instead, try to describe *what* was interesting and *why* it was interesting, as in this sentence: "I found 'The Necklace' interesting because it shows how chance and bad luck may disrupt or even destroy people's lives."

Good writing begins with attempts, like these, to rephrase sentences to make them really say something. If you always name and pin down descriptions, responses, and judgments, no matter how difficult the task seems, your sentences can be strong and forceful because you will be making them exact and comprehensive.

## Illustrative Student Essay (Improved Draft)

If you refer again to the first draft of the essay about Maupassant's use of setting to illustrate Mathilde's character (pp. 34–35), you might notice that several parts of the draft need extensive reworking and revising. For example, paragraph 2 contains a series of short, unconnected comments, and the last sentence of that paragraph implies that Mathilde's dissatisfaction relates mainly to her husband rather than to her general circumstances. Paragraph 4 focuses too much on Mathilde's coarseness and not enough on her sacrifice and cooperation. The first draft also ignores the fact that the story ends in another location, the fashionable Parisian street the Champs-Elysées, where Maupassant continues to demonstrate the nature of Mathilde's character. Finally, there is not enough support in this draft for the contention (in paragraph 5) that everything in the story is related to the character of Mathilde.

To discover how these issues can be more fully considered, the following revision of the earlier draft creates more introductory detail, includes an additional paragraph, and reshapes each of the paragraphs to stress the relationship of the central idea or argument to the topics of the various paragraphs. Within the limits of a short assignment, the essay illustrates all the principles of organization and unity that we have been discussing here.

Underlined sentences in this paper *do not* conform to MLA style and are used solely as teaching tools to emphasize the central idea, thesis sentence, and topic sentences throughout the paper.

Deal 1

James Deal

Professor Smith

English 102

16 April 2007

### How Maupassant Uses Setting in "The Necklace" to Show the Character of Mathilde

[1]     In "The Necklace" Guy de Maupassant uses setting to reflect the character and development of the main character, Mathilde Loisel.[*] As a result, his setting is not particularly vivid or detailed. He does not even describe the ill-fated necklace—the central object in the story—but states only that it is "superb" (paragraph 47). In fact, he includes descriptions of setting only if they illuminate qualities about Mathilde. Her changing character can be connected to the first apartment, the dream-life mansion rooms, the attic flat, and a fashionable public street.[†]

[2]     Details about the modest apartment of the Loisels on the Street of Martyrs indicate Mathilde's peevish lack of adjustment to life. Though everything is serviceable, she is

---

[*]Central idea.
[†]Thesis sentence.

unhappy with the "drab" walls, "threadbare" furniture, and "ugly" curtains (paragraph 3). She has domestic help, but she wants more servants than the simple country girl who does the household chores in the apartment. Her embarrassment and dissatisfaction are shown by details of her irregularly cleaned tablecloth and the plain and inelegant beef stew that her husband adores. Even her best theater dress, which is appropriate for apartment life but which is inappropriate for more wealthy surroundings, makes her unhappy. All these details of the apartment establish that Mathilde's major trait at the story's beginning is maladjustment. She therefore seems unpleasant and unsympathetic.

[3]     Like the real-life apartment, the impossibly wealthy setting of her daydreams about owning a mansion strengthens her unhappiness and her avoidance of reality. All the rooms of her fantasies are large and expensive, draped in silk and filled with nothing but the best furniture and bric-a-brac. Maupassant gives us the following description of her dream world:

> She imagined a gourmet-prepared main course carried on the most exquisite trays and served on the most beautiful dishes, with whispered gallantries that she would hear with a sphinxlike smile as she dined on the pink meat of a trout or the delicate wing of a quail. (paragraph 4)

With such impossible dreams, her despair is complete. Ironically, this despair, together with her inability to live with reality, brings about her undoing. It makes her agree to borrow the necklace (which is just as unreal as her daydreams of wealth), and losing the necklace drives her into the reality of giving up her apartment and moving into the attic flat.

[4]     Also ironically, the attic flat is related to the coarsening of her character while at the same time it brings out her best qualities of hard work and honesty. Maupassant emphasizes the drudgery of the work Mathilde endures to maintain the flat, such as walking up many stairs, washing floors with large buckets of water, cleaning greasy and encrusted pots and pans, taking out the garbage, washing clothes by hand, and haggling loudly with local shopkeepers. All this reflects her coarsening and loss of sensibility, also shown by her giving up hair and hand care and by wearing cheap dresses. The work she performs, however, makes her heroic (paragraph 98). As she cooperates to help her husband pay back the loans, her dreams of a mansion fade, and all she has left is the memory of her triumphant appearance at the Minister of Education's party. Thus the attic flat brings out her physical change for the worse at the same time that it also brings out her psychological change for the better.

Deal 3

[5]     Her walk on the Champs-Elysées illustrates another combination of traits—self-indulgence and frankness. The Champs-Elysées is the most fashionable street in Paris, and her walk to it is similar to her earlier indulgences in her daydreams of upper-class wealth. But it is on this street where she meets Jeanne, and it is her frankness in confessing to Jeanne that makes her completely honest. While the walk thus serves as the occasion for the story's concluding surprise and irony, Mathilde's being on the Champs-Elysées is totally in character, in keeping with her earlier reveries about luxury.

[6]     Other details in the story also have a similar bearing on Mathilde's character. For example, the story presents little detail about the party scene beyond the statement that Mathilde is a great "success" (paragraph 52)—a judgment that shows her ability to shine if given the chance. After she and Loisel accept the fact that the necklace cannot be found, Maupassant includes details about the Parisian streets, about the visits to loan sharks, and about the jewelry shops in order to bring out Mathilde's sense of honesty and pride as she "heroically" prepares to live her new life of poverty. Thus, in "The Necklace," Maupassant uses setting to highlight Mathilde's maladjustment, her needless misfortune, her loss of youth and beauty, and finally her growth as a responsible human being.

**WORK CITED**

Deal 4

Maupassant, Guy de. "The Necklace." *Literature: An Introduction to Reading and Writing, Fourth Compact Edition.* Ed. Edgar V. Roberts. Upper Saddle River: Pearson Prentice Hall, 2008, 4–11.

## Commentary

Several improvements to the first draft are seen here. The language of paragraph 2 has been revised to show more clearly the inappropriateness of Mathilde's dissatisfaction. In paragraph 3, the irony of the story is brought out, and the writer has connected the details to the central idea in a richer pattern of ideas, showing the effects of Mathilde's despair. Paragraph 5—new in the improved draft—includes additional details about how Mathilde's walk on the Champs-Elysées is related to her character. In paragraph 6, the fact that Mathilde is able "to shine" at the dinner party is interpreted according to the central idea. Finally, the conclusion is now much more specific, summarizing the change in Mathilde's character rather than saying simply that the setting reveals "her needless misfortune." In short, the second draft reflects the complexity of "The Necklace" better than the first draft. Because the writer has revised the first-draft ideas about the story, the final essay is tightly structured, insightful, and forceful.

## Essay Commentaries

Throughout this book, the illustrative essays are followed by short commentaries that show how the essays embody the chapter instructions and guidelines. For each essay that has a number of possible approaches, the commentary points out which one is used, and when an essay uses two or more approaches, the commentary makes this fact clear. In addition, each commentary singles out one of the paragraphs for greater analysis of its argument and use of detail. The commentaries will hence help you develop the insights necessary to use the essays as aids in your own study and writing.

# A Summary of Guidelines

To sum up, follow these guidelines whenever you write about a story or any kind of literature:

- Never just retell the story or summarize the work. Bring in story materials only when you can use them as support for your central idea or argument.
- Throughout your essay, keep reminding your reader of your central idea.
- Within each paragraph, make sure that you stress your topic idea.
- Develop your subject. Make it bigger than it was when you began.
- Always make your statements exact, comprehensive, and forceful.
- And this bears repeating: Never just retell the story or summarize the work.

# Writing Topics: The Writing Process

1. Write a brainstorming paragraph on the topic of anything in a literary work that you find especially good or interesting. Write as the thoughts occur to you; do not slow yourself down in an effort to make your writing seem perfect. You can make corrections and improvements later.

2. Using marginal and notebook notations, together with any additional thoughts, describe the way in which the author of a particular work has expressed important ideas and difficulties.

3. Create a plus–minus table to list your responses about a character or ideas in a work.

4. Raise questions about the actions of characters in a story or play in order to determine the various customs and manners of the society out of which the work is derived.

5. Analyze and explain the way in which the conflicts in a story or play are developed. What pattern or patterns do you find? Determine the relationship of the conflicts to the work's development, and fashion your idea of this relationship as an argument for a potential essay.

6. Basing your ideas on your marginal and notebook notations, select an idea and develop a thesis sentence from it, using your idea and a list of possible topics for an argument or central idea for an essay.

7. Using the thesis sentence you write for exercise 6, develop a brief analytical sentence outline that could help you in writing a full essay.

# Chapter 1A

# A Short Guide to the Use of References and Quotations in Essays About Literature

In establishing evidence for the points you make in your essays and essay examinations, you constantly need to refer to various parts of stories, plays, and poems. You also need to include shorter and longer quotations and to keep the time sequences straight within the works you are writing about. In addition, you may need to refer to biographical and historical details that have a bearing on the work or works you are studying. So that your own writing may flow as accurately and naturally as possible, you must be able to integrate these references and distinctions of time clearly and easily.

## Integrating Passages and Ideas

Your essays should reflect your own thought as you study and analyze the characteristics, ideas, and qualities of an author's work. In a typical discussion of literature, you constantly need to introduce brief summaries, quotations, general interpretations, observations, and independent applications of everything you are discussing. It is not easy to keep these various elements integrated and to keep confusion from arising.

## Distinguishing Your Thoughts from Those of Your Author

Often a major problem is that it is hard for your reader to figure out when *your* ideas have stopped and your *author's* have begun. You must therefore arrange your sentences to make the distinctions clear, but you must also blend your materials so that your reader may follow you easily. Let us see an example of how such problems may be handled. Here, the writer being discussed is the Victorian poet Matthew Arnold (1822–1888). The passage moves from reference to Arnold's ideas to the essay writer's independent application of the ideas.

> [1] In his poem "Dover Beach," Arnold states that in past times religious faith was accepted as absolute truth. [2] To symbolize this idea he refers to the ocean, which surrounds all land, and the surf, which constantly rushes onto the earth's shores. [3] According to this symbolism, religious ideas are as vast as the ocean and as regular as the

surf, and these ideas at one time constantly and irresistibly replenished people's lives. [4] Arnold's symbol of the flowing ocean changes, however, to a symbol of the ebbing ocean, thus illustrating his idea that belief and religious certainty were falling away. [5] It is this personal sense of spiritual emptiness that Arnold is associating with his own times, because what he describes, in keeping with the symbolism, is that in the present time the "drear" shoreline has been left vacant by the "melancholy long withdrawing roar" of retreat and reduction (lines 25–27).

This specimen paragraph combines but also separates paraphrase, interpretation, and quotation, and it thereby eliminates any possible confusion about the origin of the ideas and also about who is saying what. In the first three sentences the writer uses the phrases "Arnold states," "To symbolize this idea," and "According to this symbolism," to show clearly that interpretation is to follow. Although the fourth sentence marks a new direction of Arnold's ideas, it continues to separate restatement from interpretation. The fifth sentence indicates, through the phrase "in keeping with the symbolism," to explain what seems to the writer to be the major idea of "Dover Beach."

## Integrating Material by Using Quotation Marks

It is often necessary, and also interesting, to use short quotations from your author to illustrate and reinforce your ideas and interpretations. Here the problem of separating your thoughts from the author's is solved by quotation marks. In such an internal quotation, you may treat prose and poetry in the same way. If a poetic quotation extends from the end of one line to the beginning of another, however, indicate the line break with a virgule (/), and use a capital letter to begin the next line, as in the following:

> In "Lines Written in Early Spring" Wordsworth describes a condition in which his speaker is united with the surrounding natural world. Nature is a combination of the "thousand blended notes" of joyful birds (line 1) and the sights of "budding twigs" (line 17) and the "periwinkle" (line 10). In the exact words of the speaker, these "fair works" form a direct "link" to "The human soul that through me ran" (lines 5 and 6).

## Blending Quotations into Your Own Sentences

The use of internal quotations still creates the problem of blending materials, however, for quotations should never be brought in unless you prepare your reader for them in some way. *Do not*, for example, use quotations in the following manner:

> Wordsworth states that his woodland grove is filled with the sounds of birds, the sights of flowers, and the feeling of the light wind, making for the thought that creatures of the natural world take pleasure in life. "The birds around me hopped and played."

This abrupt quotation throws the reader off balance because it is not blended into the previous sentence. It is necessary to prepare the reader to move from your discussion to the quotation, as in the following revision:

> Wordsworth claims that his woodland scene is made joyful by the surrounding flowers and the gentle breeze, causing his speaker, who states that "The birds around me hopped and played," to conclude that the natural world has resulted from a "holy plan" created by Nature.

Here the quotation is made an actual part of the sentence. This sort of blending is satisfactory, provided that the quotation is brief.

## Indenting and Using Block Style for Long Quotations

The standard for placing quotations should be not to quote within a sentence any passage longer than 20 or 25 words (but consult your instructor, for the allowable number of words may vary). Quotations of greater length demand so much separate attention that they interfere with your own sentence. It is possible but not desirable to conclude one of your sentences with a quotation, but you should never make an extensive quotation in the *middle* of a sentence. By the time you finish such an unwieldy sentence, your reader will have lost sight of how it began. When your quotation is long, you should make a point of introducing it and setting it off separately as a block.

## Block Quotations

The physical layout of block quotations should be this: Leave three blank lines between your own discourse and the quotation. Double-space the quotation (like the rest of your essay), and indent it five spaces from your left margin to distinguish it from your own writing. You might use fewer spaces for longer lines of poetry, but the standard should always be to create a balanced, neat page. After the quotation, leave a three-line space again, and resume your own discourse. Here is a specimen, from an essay about Wordsworth's "Lines Written in Early Spring":

> In "Lines Written in Early Spring" Wordsworth develops an idea that the world of nature is linked directly to the moral human consciousness. He speaks of no religious systems or books of moral values. Instead, he derives his ideas directly from his experience, assuming that the world was made for the joy of the living creatures in it, including human beings ("man"), and that anyone disturbing that power of joy is violating "Nature's holy plan" itself. Wordsworth's moral criticism, in other words, is derived from his faith in the integrity of creation:
>
>> If this belief from heaven be sent,
>> If such be Nature's holy plan,
>> Have I not reason to lament
>> What man has made of man?
>> (lines 21–24)

The concept that morality and life are joined is the most interesting and engaging aspect of the poem. It seems to encourage a live-and-let-live attitude toward others, however, not an active program of direct outreach and help.

When quoting lines of poetry, always remember to quote them *as lines*. Do not run them together as though they were continuous prose. When you create such block quotations, as in the preceding example, you do *not* need quotation marks.

Today, computer usage is becoming a more established means of preparing papers, and therefore computer styling has become prominent in the handling of the matters discussed here. If you have style features in your menu, such as "Poem Text" or "Quotation," each of which sets block quotations apart from "Normal" text, you may certainly make use of the features. Talk with your instructor, however, to make sure that you computer corresponds to the styles established for your class.

## Using Three Spaced Periods (an Ellipsis) to Show Omissions

Whether your quotation is long or short, you will often need to change some of the material in it to conform to your own sentence requirements. You might wish to omit something from the quotation that is not essential to your point or to the flow of your sentence. Indicate such omissions with three spaced periods, as follows (from an essay about Bierce's "An Occurrence at Owl Creek Bridge"):

> Under the immediate threat of death, Farquhar's perceptions are sharpened and heightened. In actuality there is "swirling water . . . racing madly beneath his feet," but it is his mind that is racing swiftly, and he accordingly perceives that a "piece of dancing driftwood . . . down the current" moves so slowly that he believes the stream is "sluggish."

If your quotation is very brief, however, do not use spaced periods, as they might be more distracting than helpful. For example, do not use the spaced periods in a quotation like this:

> Keats asserts that ". . . a thing of beauty . . ." always gives joy.

Instead, make your quotation without the ellipsis:

> Keats asserts that "a thing of beauty" always gives joy.

## Using Square Brackets to Enclose Words That You Add Within Quotations

If you add words of your own to integrate the quotation into your own train of discourse or to explain words that may seem obscure, put square brackets around these words, as in the following passage:

In "Lines Written in Early Spring," Wordsworth refers to a past experience of extreme happiness, in which Nature seemed to "link/The human soul that through . . . [him] ran." He is describing a state of mystical awareness in which "pleasant thoughts/Bring [him] sad thoughts," and make him "lament" moral and political cruelty (lines 2–8).

## Being Careful Not to Overquote

A word of caution: *Do not use too many quotations.* You will be judged on your own thought and on the continuity and development of your own essay. It is tempting to include many quotations on the theory that you need to use examples from the text to illustrate and support your ideas. Naturally, it is important to introduce examples, but realize that too many quotations can disturb the flow of your own thought. If your essay consists of many illustrations linked together by no more than your introductory sentences, how much thinking have you actually shown? Try, therefore, to create your own discussion, using appropriate examples to connect your thought to the text or texts you are analyzing.

## Preserving the Spellings in Your Source

Always reproduce your source exactly. The works of British authors may include words such as *tyre, defence, honour*, and *labour*. Duplicate these as you find them. Although most anthologies, such as this one, modernize the spelling of older writers, you may often encounter "old-spelling" editions in which all words—such as *entring, Shew, beautie, ore* (for "over"), *witte* (for "wit"), *specifick, 'twas, guaranty* (for "guarantee"), or *determin'd*—are spelled and capitalized exactly as they were centuries ago. Your principle should be *to duplicate everything exactly as you find it*, even if this means spelling words such as *achieve* as *atchieve, music* as *Musick,* or *joke* as *joak.* A student once changed the word *an* to "and" in the construction "an I were" in a Shakespeare play. The result was misleading, because in introductory clauses *an* really meant *if* (or *and if*) and not *and.* Difficulties such as this one are rare, but you can avoid them if you reproduce the text as you find it. Should you think that something is either misspelled or confusing as it stands, you may do one of two things:

**1.** Clarify or correct the confusing word or phrase within brackets, as in the following:

*In 1714, fencing was considered a "Gentlemany [i.e., gentlemanly] subject."*

**2.** Use the word *sic* (Latin for *thus*, meaning "It is this way in the text") in brackets immediately after the problematic word or obvious mistake:

*He was just "finning [sic] his way back to health" when the next disaster struck.*

# Reading and Writing
# about Fiction

# Chapter 2

## Fiction: An Overview

Fiction originally meant anything *made up* or *shaped*. As we understand the word today, it refers to *short or long prose stories*—and it has retained this meaning since 1599, the first year for which we have a record for the word in print. Fiction is distinguished from the works it imitates, such as *historical accounts, reports, biographies, autobiographies, letters,* and *personal memoirs* and *meditations.* Although fiction often resembles these forms, it has a separate identity because it may or may not originate in historical facts, but in either case, it then relies on the imaginative and creative powers of the author. Writers of fiction may include historically accurate details, but their overriding goal is to tell a story and say something significant about life.

The essence of fiction, as opposed to drama, is **narration**, the recounting or telling of a sequence of events or actions. The earliest works of fiction relied almost exclusively on narration, with speeches or dialogue being reported rather than quoted directly. Much recent fiction includes extended passages of dialogue, thereby becoming more like *drama* even though narration is still the work's primary mode.

Fiction is rooted in ancient legends and myths. Local priests told stories about their gods and heroes, as shown in some of the narratives of ancient Egypt. In the course of history, traveling storytellers appeared in a court or village to entertain listeners with tales of adventure in faraway countries. Although many of these were fictionalized accounts of events and people who may not ever have existed, they were largely accepted as fact or history. An especially long tale, an **epic**, was recited over a period of days. To aid their memories and to impress and entertain their listeners, the storytellers chanted their tales in poetry, often accompanying themselves on a stringed instrument.

Legends and epics also reinforced the local religious and legal power structures. Myths of gods such as Zeus and Athena (Greece), Jupiter and Minerva (Rome), and Baal and Ishtar (Mesopotamia) abounded, together with stories of famous men and women such as Oedipus, Helen of Troy, Hercules, Achilles, Odysseus, Penelope, Aeneas, Romulus and Remus, Utu-Napishtim, Joseph, David, and Ruth. The ancient Macedonian king and general Alexander the Great (356–323 BCE) developed many of his ideas about nobility and valor from *The Iliad,* Homer's epic about the Trojan War—and, we might add, from discussing the epic with his tutor, the philosopher Aristotle.

Perhaps nowhere is the moralistic-argumentative aspect of ancient storytelling better illustrated than in the **fables** of Aesop, a Greek who wrote in the sixth century BCE, and in the **parables** of Jesus as told in the Gospels of the New Testament (see

Chapter 8). In these works, a short narrative provides an illustration of a religious, philosophic, or psychological conclusion.

Starting about eight hundred years ago, storytelling in Western civilization was developed to a fine art by writers such as Marie de France, a Frenchwoman who wrote in England near the end of the twelfth century, Giovanni Boccaccio (Italian, 1313–1375), and Geoffrey Chaucer (English, ca. 1340–1400). William Shakespeare (1564–1616) drew heavily on history and legend for the stories and characters in his plays.

## Modern Fiction

**Fiction** as we understand the word today did not begin to flourish until the seventeenth and eighteenth centuries, when an alteration in the perception of human nature developed. For many centuries the idea had prevailed that human beings were in a fallen moral state, a state of "total depravity," and that they needed the controlling hands of church and monarchy to keep them pious, moral, and peaceful. Thinkers in the Renaissance, however, began to claim that humanity should be viewed within a perspective of greater and broader latitude. Some people were fallen, yes, but many others were not, and they could become moral through their own efforts without the control of moral and political authorities. It was this analysis that spurred the development of the democratic theory of government that has been accepted in much of modern society.

In literature, it thus became possible to view human beings of all social stations and ways of life as important literary topics. As one writer put it in 1709, human nature is by no means simple, for it is governed by many complex motives such as "passion, humor, caprice, zeal, faction, and a thousand other springs."[1] Observations such as this were the basis of the individual and psychological concerns that characterize fiction today. Indeed, fiction is strong because it is so real and personal. Characters have both first and last names; the countries and cities in which they live are visualized as real places, with real influences on the inhabitants; and their actions and interactions are like those which readers themselves have experienced, could experience, or could readily imagine themselves experiencing.

Along with attention to character, fiction is also concerned with the significance of place or environment on the lives of people. In the simplest sense, location is a backdrop or setting within which characters speak, move, and act. But more broadly, environment comprises the social, economic, and political conditions that affect the outcomes of people's lives. Fiction is primarily about the interactions among people, but it also involves these larger interactions—either directly or indirectly. Indeed, a typical work of fiction includes many forces, small and large, that influence the ways in which characters meet and deal with their problems.

The first true works of fiction in Europe, however, were less concerned with society or politics than adventure. These were the lengthy Spanish and French **romances**

---

[1]Anthony Ashley Cooper, Third Earl of Shaftesbury, "Sensus Communis," III, 3.

of the sixteenth and seventeenth centuries. In English the word **novel** was borrowed from French and Italian to describe these works and to distinguish them from medieval and classical romances as something that was *new* (the meaning of *novel*). In England the word **story** was used along with *novel* in reference to the new literary form.

The increased levels of education and literacy in the eighteenth century facilitated the development of fiction. During the times of Shakespeare (1564–1616) and John Dryden (1631–1700), the only way a writer could make a living from writing was to be a member of the nobility, have a subsidy from a member of the nobility, or have a play accepted at a theater and then receive either a direct payment for it or the proceeds of an "author's benefit." The paying audiences, however, were limited to people who lived within a short distance of the theater or who had the leisure and money to stay in town and attend the plays during the theater season.

Once great numbers of people could read for themselves, the paying audience for literature expanded. A writer could write a novel and receive money for it from a publisher, who could then profit from a wide sale. Readers could start reading the book when they wished, and they could finish it when it was convenient to do so. Reading a novel could even be a social event, for people would gather and read to each other as a means of sharing the reading experience. Quite often, as tastes for fiction developed, writers would publish monthly installments of their novels. When the mail brought these new episodes and chapters to readers, the principal activity quickly focused on forming circles of listeners, who would listen eagerly while an expressive reader brought the stories to life. Often these episodes extended for many months, and the fiction-consuming public discussed the latest experiences and speculated about what would happen next. With this wider audience of people whom authors never saw or knew, it became possible for writers to develop a legitimate career out of their trade. Lengthy fictional stories had arrived as a major genre of literature.

## The Short Story

Because novels were long, they took a long time to read—hours, days, even weeks. The early nineteenth-century American writer Edgar Allan Poe (1809–1849) addressed this problem and developed a theory of the short story, which he described in a review of Nathaniel Hawthorne's *Twice-Told Tales*. Poe was convinced that "worldly interests" prevented people from gaining the "totality" of comprehension and response that he believed reading should provide. A short, concentrated story (he called it "a brief prose tale" that could be read at a single sitting) was ideal for producing such a strong impression.

In the wake of the taste for short fiction after Poe, many writers have worked in the form. Today, stories are printed in many periodicals, such as *Harper's Magazine*, *The Atlantic Monthly*, and *Zoetrope*, and in many collections, such as *American Short Story Masterpieces*. Many of the better-established writers—William Faulkner, Ernest Hemingway, Shirley Jackson, Flannery O'Connor, Joyce Carol Oates, John Updike, Alice Walker, and Eudora Welty, to name only a small number—have published their stories in separate volumes.

# Elements of Fiction I: Verisimilitude and *Donnée*

Fiction, along with drama, has a basis in **realism** or **verisimilitude**. That is, the situations or characters, although they are the invention of writers, are similar to those that many human beings experience, know, or think. Even fantasy, the creation of events that are dreamlike or fantastic, is anchored in the real world, however remotely. This connection of art and life has led some critics to label fiction, and also drama, as an art of imitation. Shakespeare's Hamlet states that an actor attempts to portray real human beings in realistic situations (to "hold a mirror up to Nature").

The same may also be said about writers of fiction, with the provisos that reality is not easily defined and that authors can follow many paths in imitating it. What matters in fiction is the way in which authors establish the ground rules for their works, whether with realistic or nonrealistic characters, places, actions, or physical and chemical laws. The assumption that authors make about the nature of their story material is called a **postulate** or a **premise**—what the American novelist Henry James called a *donnée* (something given). The *donnée* of some stories is to resemble the everyday world as much as possible. Eudora Welty's "A Worn Path" is such a story. In it we follow the difficult walk of an elderly woman as she goes from home to a medical office in Natchez, and we also learn of the virtual futility of her mission. The events of the story are not uncommon; they could happen in life just as Welty presents them.

Once a *donnée* is established, it governs the directions in which the story moves. Jackson's "The Lottery" (Chapter 3), for example, contains a premise or *donnée* that may be phrased like this: "Suppose that a small, ordinary town held a lottery in which the prize was not something good but instead was something bad." Everything in Jackson's story follows from this premise. At first we seem to be reading about innocent actions in a rural American community. By the end, however, in accord with the premise, the story enters the realms of nightmare.

In such ways authors may lead us into remote, fanciful, and symbolic levels of reality, as in Charlotte Perkins Gilman's "The Yellow Wallpaper" (Chapter 9), in which we readers become drawn in to the disoriented world of a narrator who has totally lost her grip on the actuality of the situations around her. In Poe's "The Masque of the Red Death" (Chapter 5), the phantasmagoric *donnée* is that Death may assume a human but sinister shape. Literally nothing is out of bounds as long as the author makes clear the premise for the action.

Scenes and actions such as these, which are not realistic in our ordinary sense of the word, are normal in stories *as long as they follow the author's own stated or implied ground rules.* You may always judge a work by the standard of whether it is consistent with the premise, or the *donnée*, created by the writer.

In addition to referring to various levels of reality, the word *donnée* may also be taken more broadly. In *futuristic* and *science fiction*, for example, there is an assumption or *donnée* of certain situations and technological developments (e.g., interstellar space travel) that are not presently in existence. In a *love story*, the *donnée* is that two people meet and overcome an obstacle of some sort (usually not a serious one) on the way to fulfilling their love. Interesting variations of the love story are James Joyce's "Araby" (Chapter 5), D. H. Lawrence's "The Horse Dealer's Daughter" (Chapter 8), and Alice Munro's "The Found Boat" (Chapter 7).

There are of course other types. A *growth* or *apprenticeship story*, for example, is about the development of a major character, such as Jackie in Frank O'Connor's "First Confession" (Chapter 7). In the *detective story*, a mysterious event is posited, and then an individual draws conclusions from the available evidence, as in Susan Glaspell's short drama "Trifles" (Chapter 18), in which the correct detective work is done by two women, not by the legally authorized police investigators.

In addition to setting levels of reality and fictional types, authors may use other controls or springboards as their *données*. Sometimes an initial situation may be the springboard of the narrative, such as the orientation speech in Daniel Orozco's "Orientation" (Chapter 7). Or the key may be a pattern of behavior, such as the boy's reactions to the people around him in O'Connor's "First Confession" or the solution of a mystery about a community icon, as in Faulkner's "A Rose for Emily." A shaping force, or *donnée*, always guides the actions, and often a number of such controls operate at the same time.

# Elements of Fiction II: Character, Plot, Structure, and Idea or Theme

Works of fiction share a number of common elements. For reference here, the more significant ones are *character*, *plot*, *structure*, and *idea* or *theme*.

## CHARACTERS Bring Fiction to Life

Stories, like plays, are about characters, who are *not* real people but who are nevertheless *like* real people. A **character** may be defined as a reasonable facsimile of a human being, with all the good and bad traits of being human. Most stories are concerned with characters who are facing a major problem that develops from misunderstanding, misinformation, unfocused ideals and goals, difficult situations, troubled relationships, and generally challenging situations. The characters may win, lose, or tie. They may learn and be the better for the experience or may miss the point and be unchanged.

As we have stated, modern fiction has accompanied the development of a psychological interest in human beings. Psychology itself has grown out of the philosophical and religious idea that people have many inborn capacities—some of them good and others bad. People encounter many problems in their lives, and they make many mistakes; they expend much effort in coping and adjusting. But they nevertheless are important and interesting and are therefore worth writing about, whether male or female; young or old; white, black, tan, or yellow; rich or poor; worker or industrialist; traveler or resident; doctor, librarian, mother, daughter, homemaker, prince, ship captain, bartender, or army lieutenant.

The range of fictional characters is vast: A married couple struggling to repay an enormous debt, a young man learning about the nature of his desires, a woman recalling many conflicts with her mother, two close relatives speculating about the loss of their past, a woman surrounded by her insensitive and self-seeking brothers, a man making triumphs out of his blunders, an unmarried couple dealing with the serious issue of what to do about the possibility of childbirth, a woman feverishly recollecting her long experience without a man whom she had loved—all these, and more, may be found in fiction just as they may also be found in all levels and conditions of life. Because as human beings all of us share the same capacities for concern, involvement, sympathy, happiness, sorrow, exhilaration, and disappointment, we are able to find endless interest in such characters and their ways of coping with their circumstances.

## PLOT Is the Plan of Fiction

Fictional characters, who are drawn from life, go through a series of lifelike **actions** or **incidents**, which make up the story. In a well-done story, all the actions or incidents, speeches, thoughts, and observations are linked together to make up an entirety, sometimes called an **organic unity**. The essence of this unity is the development and resolution of a **conflict**—or conflicts—in which the **protagonist**, or central character, is engaged. The interactions of causes and effects as they develop **sequentially** or **chronologically** make up the story's **plot**. (See the section on writing following the selections in this chapter.) That is, a story's actions follow one another in time as the protagonist meets and tries to overcome opposing forces. Sometimes plot has been compared to a story's *map, scheme,* or *blueprint.*

Often the protagonist's struggle is directed against another character—an **antagonist**. Just as often, however, the struggle may occur between the protagonist and opposing groups, forces, ideas, and choices—all of which make up a collective antagonist. The conflict may be carried out wherever human beings spend their lives, such as a kitchen, a hotel, a railway station bar, a restaurant, a town square, a schoolroom, an ordinary living room, a church, an exclusive store, a vacation resort, a café, or a battlefield. The conflict may also take place internally, within the mind of the protagonist.

## STRUCTURE Is the Knitting Together of Fiction

**Structure** refers to the way a story is assembled. Chronologically, all stories are similar because they move from beginning to end in accord with the time needed for *causes* to produce *effects.* But authors choose many different ways to put their stories together. Some stories are told in straightforward sequential order, and a description of the plot of such stories is identical to a description of the structure. Other stories, however, may get pieced together through out-of-sequence and widely separated episodes, speeches, secondhand reports, vague recollections, accidental discoveries, dreams, nightmares, periods of delirium, fragments of letters, overheard conversations, and the like. In such stories, the plot and the structure diverge widely. Therefore, in dealing with the structure of stories, we emphasize not chronological order but the actual *arrangement* and *development* of the stories as they unfold, part by part. Usually we study an entire story, but we may also direct our attention toward the structure of a smaller aspect of arrangement such as an episode or passage of dialogue.

## IDEA or THEME Is the Vivifying Thought of Fiction

The word **idea** refers to the result or results of general and abstract thinking. Either directly or indirectly, fiction embodies ideas and themes that underlie and give life to stories and novels. The writers never need to state their ideas in specific words, but the strength of their works depends on the power with which they exemplify ideas and make them clear. Thus, writers of comic works are committed to the idea that human difficulties can be treated with humor. More serious works often show characters in the throes of difficult moral choices—the idea being that in a losing situation the only winners are those who maintain honor and self-respect. Mystery and suspense stories develop from the idea that problems have solutions, although the solutions at first may seem remote or impossible. Even stories written for entertainment alone, some of which may at first seem devoid of ideas, stem out of an idea or position that the work itself makes clear. Writers may deal with the triumphs and defeats of life, the admirable and the despicable, the humorous and the pathetic, but whatever their goal, they are always expressing ideas about human experience. We may therefore raise questions such as these as we look for ideas in fiction:

- *What does this mean?*
- *Why does the author include it?*
- *What idea or ideas does it show?*
- *Why is it significant?*

Many works can be discussed in terms of the *issues* that they raise. An **issue** may involve a work's characters in direct or implicit argument or opposition, and also may bring out crucially important moments of decision about matters of private or public concern. In addition to the issues that the characters face, the works themselves may be considered for their more general issues.

Fictional ideas can also be considered as major **themes** that tie individual works together. Often an author makes the theme obvious, as in the Aesop fable in which a man uses an ax to kill a fly on another man's forehead. The theme of this fable might loosely be expressed in the sentence "The cure should not be worse than the disease." A major theme in Maupassant's "The Necklace" (Chapter 1) is that people may be destroyed or saved by the most minor of unforeseeable but sometimes unlucky events.

The process of determining and describing the themes or ideas in stories is never complete; there is always another theme that we can discuss, another issue that may be explored. Thus, in Maupassant's "The Necklace," one might note the additional themes that adversity brings out worth, that telling the truth is better than concealing it, that envy often produces ill fortune, that people may build their lives on incorrect assumptions, and that good fortune is never recognized until it is lost. Indeed, one of the ways in which we judge stories is to determine the degree to which they embody a number of valid and important ideas.

# Elements of Fiction III: The Writer's Tools

## NARRATION Creates the Sequence and Logic of Fiction

Writers have a number of modes of presentation, or "tools," that they use in their stories. The principal tool (and the heart of fiction) is **narration**, the reporting of actions in sequential order. The object of narration is to *render* the story, to make it clear and to bring it alive to the reader's imagination through the movement of sentences through time. Unlike works of painting and sculpture, the reading and comprehension of a narration cannot be done in a single view. Jacques-Louis David's painting *The Death of Socrates* (I–7, Plate 2), for example, is like a narrative because it tells a story—an actual historical occurrence. As related by Plato in the dialogue *Phaedo*, Socrates takes the cup of hemlock, which he will drink as the means of carrying out his own execution. David includes details that tell the story visually. In the rear of the painting some of Socrates' friends have said good-bye and are sorrowfully mounting stairs to leave. Two of the remaining men hold their heads in grief, and two turn toward a wall in despair. The jailer avoids looking at Socrates as he offers him the cup of hemlock. Also, on the bed are the unlocked manacles that might have held Socrates, thus emphasizing that he was, all the time, free to walk away had he so chosen. In fact, however, it is only the moment just before Socrates drinks the hemlock that David is able to capture in his painting. As a contrast, the writer of a narrative may include details about the many events leading up to and following such a moment, for a narration moves in a continuous line, from word to word, scene to scene, action to action, and speech to speech. As a result of this chronological movement, the reader's comprehension must necessarily also be chronological.

---

**VISUALIZING FICTION**

## Cartoons, Graphic Narratives, Graphic Novels

---

David's painting is in the artistic tradition of "History Painting," which portrays a famous subject, such as *The Death of Socrates* (see I–7, Plate 2). A closely connected type of painting is "Genre Painting," which features scenes of ordinary life, such as Brueghel's *Peasant Dance* (see I–7, Plate 1). A modern popular development of such art is the single line-drawn cartoon together with a caption, brought to perfection by the many cartoonists who provided comic panels for *The New Yorker* and also the innumerable other publications that have flourished right up to the present time. The point about most of the cartoons is that they are based in narrative, just as in the history and genre painting traditions. In no more than a single picture drawing, clever cartoonists supply the graphic means by which viewers are able to infer how a situation has developed and how it will conclude.

Whereas the painting traditions featured realistic or semi-realistic visions of humanity, however, the cartoonists developed caricatures in their portrayal of their human and animal subjects. One of the many cartoons done for *The New Yorker* by Charles Addams (1912–1988), shows the Addams family, in their characteristically ghoulish garb and appearance, high on a terraced area of their ghostly house, preparing to pour boiling oil down on a group of Christmas choristers. One may easily imagine both the history and future of this event. The Addams cartoons, in this comically macabre vein, were so popular that a series of films and TV programs were successfully developed that dramatized various actions of the family. One of the most popular of modern cartoonists has been Gary Larson (b. 1950), who created thousands of panels for his "The Far Side," the title of the syndicated cartoons he drew to popular acclaim from 1980 to 1995. Many of Larson's devoted followers expressed great regret when he gave up these cartoons. As his narrative technique, Larson created a situation that is easily followed because of both various signs and also demonstrative actions of his characters, many of whom are not just caricatures of doughy and distorted human beings, but also of alien travelers, cows, ducks, dogs, snakes, spiders, ocean monsters, bears, deer, rhinoceroses, and comparable creatures. Even though there is no more than a single picture in the typical Larson cartoon, Larson skillfully supplies a comic caption and the artistic narrative details from which readers may easily infer both the beginning and the ending.

Closely connected to the single panel cartoon, another major popular mode of narrative presentation is the comic strip, which became a part of regular daily newspapers in the twentieth century. Usually the comics were printed in three or four panels during each day of the week, and then on Sundays there was a color strip, usually involving as many as a dozen narrative cartoon panels. Often there was a continuous story in these strips that held the interest of readers for a number of months. From 1933 until 1987, for example, a strip featuring "Brick Bradford" continued regularly. The story, mainly science fiction, was played out both on a global and universal scale. One interesting adventure involved Brick and company taking a trip in a uniquely compressing and expanding spaceship, which reduced them to such an infinitely small degree that they could engage in an adventure on one of the atoms within the eye of a Lincoln-head penny. Other extremely popular comics were "Dick Tracy," a prominent detective concerned with solving crimes and capturing criminals (still regularly published), and "Terry and the Pirates" (1934–1973), a strip that took its readers to those wars in Asia that led up to and included American involvement in the Pacific Theater of operations during World War II. So popular were these comic strips that quarterly publications were soon issued, in which crime fighters such as Superman, Batman, and The Specter would be the heroes of as many as four separate and complete adventure narratives.

Following World War II, many writers, collaborating with cartoonists, went beyond the traditional comic book limitations and started to adapt the comic book format for more serious and systematic novels. Well-known literary works first reached many readers through this medium, and many readers became so interested that they actually went on to read and appreciate the originals. In addition, many writers and cartoonists worked to create new graphically based works, often called "graphic novels." Perhaps the most famous of these is "Maus," by Art Spiegelman, the winner of a Special Pulitzer Prize award in 1992. "Maus" is a work in the comic/graphic format that describes the horror and brutality of the German concentration camps, as witnessed by his father, during the Second World War (see p. 65). The form has proliferated and has reached the level of its own narrative/dramatic type. A number of separate "Sin City yarns" by Frank Miller (b. 1957), for example, have been used as the basis for popular films. In 2007, a graphic novel originally by Miller, with Lynn Varley, was "300," which was made into a film dramatizing the story of the ancient battle between Greeks and Persians at Thermopylae.

**DAN PIRARO** (Born in the latter twentieth century in the northern hemisphere) Cartoon from Bizarro

Piraro is a multi-talented and prize-winning cartoonist who was born and educated in Oklahoma. He was especially artistic, and when working in the advertising department at Neiman-Marcus he would sketch out unique cartoons that fascinated and entertained his co-workers. With such material, he successfully began syndicating his work in 1985, just five years after Gary Larson first syndicated his The Far Side. Piraro named his cartoons Bizarro because of the closeness in sound to his own name, and also because of the obvious closeness to the Italian word bizzarro and our own word bizarre. His devoted followers, who look forward eagerly to his daily Bizarro cartoons, have termed his work as "surreal," "ascerbic," "oddball," and "off the wall." Piraro is not only a cartoonist, but he has also developed his skills as a speaker and a showman. He continues to do fine art, and to date has published eleven separate books, two of which are the recent The Three Little Pigs Buy the White House (2004) and Bizarro and Other Strange Manifestations of the Art of Dan Piraro (2006).

Dan Piraro. Bizarro cartoon strip of June 10, 2007.

## Questions

1. How does Piraro establish the narrative situation of this cartoon? On what very famous work of art does the drawing depend? What is the narrative in the original work? What is the narrative in Piraro's cartoon? How is the cartoon narrative particularly modern?

2. Why would the cartoon not be as funny as it is if we did not recognize the original from which the cartoon is derived?

3. On the basis of the contrast between the story in the cartoon and the story in the original to which it alludes, what principles of humor can you develop and describe?

## ART SPIEGELMAN (b. 1948) Sample page from Maus

Spiegelman was born in Sweden and came to the United States with his parents. When in high school, he became fascinated with the art of cartooning, and made that his profession. For more than 20 years he worked at designing popular products, including such things as candy wrappers. He also spent a number of years teaching at the School for Visual Arts in New York, and he founded a comics magazine, *Raw*. His most accomplished work is his graphic novel *Maus*, a page of which is included here as an illustration of subject and technique. Another of Spiegelman's honors was a Guggenheim Fellowship.

## Questions

1. Where are the places of action of this episode of *Maus* on this page of the story? At what time is the episode taking place?
2. What is the situation of the narrator, Spiegelman (the father of the author, Art Spiegelman)? As a prisoner, what is he doing to try to insure his survival? What happens to him during the period of the narration?
3. Describe the conflicts in this episode. What is the major conflict? What secondary conflict is shown in the sixth panel? How is this conflict related to the major conflict?
4. What is portrayed in the final two panels of the episode? What is illustrated by the smoke coming from the chimneys? In what ways are these two panels symbolic of circumstances in Germany and Poland during the Second World War?

## STYLE Is the Author's Skill in Bringing Language to Life

The medium of fiction and of all literature is language, and the manipulation of language—the **style**—is a primary skill of the writer. A mark of a good style is the use of active verbs and nouns that are **specific** and **concrete**. Even with the most active and graphic diction possible, writers can never render their incidents and scenes exactly, but they may be judged on how vividly they tell their stories.

## POINT OF VIEW Guides What We See and Understand in Fiction

One of the most important ways in which writers knit their stories together, and also an important way in which they try to interest and engage readers, is through the careful control of **point of view**. Point of view is the **voice** of the story, the speaker who does the narrating. It is the way the story establishes authenticity, either in reality or unreality. It may be regarded as the story's *focus*, the *angle of vision* from which things are not only seen and reported but also judged.

Basically, there are two kinds of points of view, but there are many, many variations, sometimes obvious and sometimes subtle. In the first, the **first-person point of view**, a fictitious observer tells us what he or she saw, heard, concluded, and thought. This viewpoint is characterized by the use of the pronoun *I* as the speaker refers to his or her position as an observer or commentator. The **speaker** or **narrator**—terms that are interchangeable—may sometimes seem to be the author speaking directly, using an **authorial voice**. More often, however, the speaker is an independent character—a **persona** with characteristics that separate her or him from the author.

In common with all narrators, the first-person narrator establishes a clearly defined relationship to the story's events. Some narrators are deeply engaged in the action; others are only minor participants or observers; still others have had nothing to

Art Spiegelman *Maus: A Survivor's Tale, II, And Here My Troubles Began New York: Pantheon Books, 1991*

do with the action but are transmitting the reports of others who were more fully involved. Sometimes the narrator uses the *we* pronoun if he or she is or has been part of a group that has witnessed the action or participated in it. Often, too, the narrator might use *we* when referring to ideas and interpretations shared with the reader or listener—the idea being to draw readers into the story as much as possible.

The second kind, the **third-person point of view**, uses third-person pronouns (*she, he, it, they, her, him, them,* etc.).[2] The third-person point of view may be (1) **limited**, with the focus being on one particular character and what he or she does, says, hears, thinks, and otherwise experiences; (2) **omniscient**, with the possibility that the activities and thoughts of all the characters are open and fully known by the speaker; or (3) **dramatic**, or **objective**, in which the story is confined *only* to the reporting of actions and speeches, with no commentary and no revelation of the thoughts of any of the characters unless the characters themselves express their thoughts dramatically.

Understanding point of view usually requires subtlety of perception—indeed, it may be one of the most difficult of all concepts in the study of fiction. In fuller perspective, therefore, we may think of it as the *total position* from which things are viewed, understood, and communicated. The position might be simply physical: *Where was the speaker located when the events occurred? Does the speaker give us a close or distant view of the events?* The position might also be personal or philosophical: *Do the events illustrate a personal opinion* (Maupassant's "The Necklace" [Chapter 1]), *embody a philosophical judgment* (Hawthorne's "Young Goodman Brown" [Chapter 8]), or *argue a theological principle* (St. Luke's "The Parable of the Prodigal Son" [Chapter 8])?

Point of view is one of the major ways by which authors make fiction vital. By controlling point of view, an author helps us make reasonable inferences about the story's actions. Authors use point of view to raise some of the same questions in fiction that perplex us in life. We need to evaluate what fictional narrators as well as real people tell us, for what they say is affected by their limitations, attitudes, opinions, and degree of candidness. The first-person narrator of James Joyce's "Araby," for example (Chapter 5), describes a series of boyhood incidents leading up to his memory that he had deceived himself with vain desires. In other words, he emphasizes what he considers to be his own shortcomings. But we might also realize that this narrator is unwittingly showing that it was not he who was at fault, but rather the religious and moral structure of which he was a part. For readers, the perception of a fictional point of view can be as complex as life itself, and it may be as difficult—in fiction as in life—to evaluate our sources of information.

## DESCRIPTION Creates the World of Fiction

Together with narration, a vital aspect of fiction is **description**, which is intended to cause readers to imagine or re-create the scenes and actions of the story. Description can be both physical (places and persons) and psychological (an emotion or a set of emotions). Because excessive description sometimes interrupts or postpones a story's actions, many writers include only as much as is necessary to provide locations for what is happening in the story.

---

[2]The possibilities of a second-person point of view are discussed in Chapter 3.

Mood and **atmosphere** are important aspects of descriptive writing, and to the degree that descriptions are evocative, they may reach the level of **metaphor** and **symbolism**. These characteristics of fiction are a property of all literature, and you will also encounter them whenever you read poems and plays.

## DIALOGUE Creates Interactions among Fictional Characters

Another major tool of the writer of fiction is **dialogue**. By definition, dialogue is the conversation of two people, but more than two characters may also participate. It is of course the major medium of the playwright, and it is one of the means by which fiction writers bring vividness and dramatic tension to their stories. Straight narration and description can do no more than make a secondhand assertion ("hearsay") that a character's thoughts and responses exist, but dialogue makes everything firsthand and real.

Dialogue is hence a means of *showing* or *actualizing* rather than *reporting*. If characters feel pain or declare love, their own words may be taken as the expression of what is on their minds. Some dialogue may be terse and minimal. Other dialogue may be expanded, depending on the situation, the personalities of the characters, and the author's intent. Dialogue may concern any topic, including everyday and practical matters, personal feelings, reactions to the past, future plans, changing thoughts, sudden realizations, and political, social, philosophical, and religious ideas.

The language of dialogue indicates the intelligence, articulateness, educational levels, or emotional states of the speakers. Hence the author might use *grammatical mistakes, faulty pronunciation*, or *slang* to show a character of limited or disadvantaged background or a character who is trying to be seen in that light. *Dialect* shows the region from which the speaker comes, just as *accent* indicates a place of national origin. *Jargon* and *cliché* suggest self-inflation or intellectual limitations—usually reasons for laughter. The use of *private or intimate expressions* clearly shows people who are close to each other emotionally. Speech that is interrupted by *voiced pauses* (e.g., "er," "ah," "um," "y' know") or speech characterized by *inappropriate words* might show a character who is unsure or not in control. There are many possibilities in dialogue, but no matter what qualities you find, writers include dialogue to enable you to know their characters better.

## TONE and IRONY Guide Our Perceptions of Fictional Works

In every story we may consider **tone**, that is, the ways in which authors convey attitudes toward readers and also toward the work's subjects. **Irony**, one of the major components of tone, refers to language and situations that seem to reverse normal expectations. *Word choice* is the characteristic of **verbal irony**, in which what is meant is usually the opposite of what is said, as when we *mean* that people are doing badly even though we *say* that they are doing well. Broader forms of irony are *situational* and *dramatic*. **Situational irony** refers to circumstances in which bad things happen to good people, or in which rewards are not earned because forces beyond human comprehension seem to be in control, making the world seem arbitrary and often absurd. In **dramatic irony** characters have only a nonexistent, partial, incorrect, or misguided understanding of what is happening to them, while both readers and other characters understand the situation more fully. Readers hence become concerned about the characters and hope that the characters will develop understanding quickly enough to avoid the problems bedeviling them and the pitfalls endangering them.

## SYMBOLISM and ALLEGORY Relate Fiction to the Larger World

In literature, even apparently ordinary things may acquire **symbolic** value; that is, everyday objects may be understood to have meanings that are beyond themselves, bigger than themselves. In fiction, many functional and essential incidents, objects, speeches, and characters may also be construed as symbols. Some symbols are widely recognized and therefore are considered as **cultural** or **universal**. Water, flowers, jewels, the sun, certain stars, the flag, altars, and minarets are examples of cultural symbols. Other symbols are **contextual**; that is, they take on symbolic meaning only in their individual works, as when in Maupassant's "The Necklace" (Chapter 1) Mathilde and her husband move into an attic flat, which may be taken as representative or symbolic of their loss of economic and social status.

When a complete story, in addition to maintaining its own narrative integrity, can be applied point by point to a parallel set of situations, it is an **allegory**. Many stories are not complete allegories, however, even though they may contain sections having allegorical parallels. For instance, the Loisels' long servitude in Maupassant's "The Necklace" is similar to the lives and activities of many people who perform tasks for mistaken or meaningless reasons. "The Necklace" therefore has allegorical overtones even though it is not, in totality, an allegory.

## COMMENTARY Provides Us with an Author's Thoughts

Writers may also include **commentary**, **analysis**, or **interpretation**, in the expectation that readers need insight into the characters and their actions. When fiction was new, authors often expressed such commentary directly. Henry Fielding (1707–1754) divided his novels into "books" and included a chapter of personal and philosophical commentary at the beginning of each of these. In the next century, George Eliot (1819–1880) included many extensive passages of commentary in her novels.

Later writers have kept commentary at a minimum, preferring instead to concentrate on direct action and dialogue, thereby allowing readers to draw their own conclusions about meaning. In first-person narrations, however, you may expect the narrators to make their own personal comments. Such observations may be accepted at face value, but you should recognize that anything the speakers say is also a mode of character disclosure and therefore just as much a part of the total story as the narrative incidents.

## The Elements Together

These, then, are the major tools of fiction, which authors usually employ simultaneously in their works. Thus, the story may be told by a character who is a witness, and thus it has a **first-person point of view**. The major **character**, the **protagonist**, goes through a series of **actions** as a result of a carefully arranged **plot**. Because of this plot, together with the author's chosen method of **narration**, the story will follow a certain kind of arrangement, or **structure**, such as a straightforward **sequence** or a disjointed series of **episodes**. The action may demonstrate the story's **theme** or **central idea**. The writer's **style** may be manifested in **ironic** expressions. The description of the character's actions may reveal **irony of situation**, while at the same time this situation is made vivid through **dialogue** in which the character is a participant. Because the plight of the character is like the plight of many persons in the world, it is an **allegory**, and the character herself or himself may be considered as a **symbol**.

Throughout each story we read, no matter what characteristics we are considering, it is most important to realize that a work of fiction is an entirety, a unity. Any reading of a story should be undertaken not to break things down into parts but to understand and assimilate the work *as a whole*. The separate analysis of various topics is thus a *means* to that end, *not* the end itself. The study of fiction, like the study of all literature, is designed to foster our growth and to increase our understanding of the human condition.

## Stories For Study

## AMBROSE BIERCE (1842–1914?)

Bierce was a native of Ohio, the youngest of nine children in the highly religious family of a poor farmer. When the Civil War began he enlisted in the Union army as a drummer boy and rose to the rank of major by the war's end. After the war he went to San Francisco to begin a career in journalism. At various times he reported, edited, and wrote reviews for papers such as the *San Francisco Examiner* and the *San Francisco News-Letter*. After he married he and his wife spent five years in England, but eventually she left him and their two children died—events that had an embittering effect on him. In 1913 he traveled to Mexico, and nothing further is known about him; he is presumed to have died in revolutionary fighting there in 1914. Bierce published his first story in 1871 and later published two volumes of stories: *In the Midst of Life* (1892, originally published in 1891 as *Tales of Soldiers and Civilians*, which included "An Occurrence at Owl Creek Bridge"), and *Can Such Things Be?* (1893). He is perhaps best known for his sometimes cynical *The Devil's Dictionary* (1911). He favored the short story as a form over the novel on much the same grounds as Poe, namely that the story could be designed to produce a single effect. He believed that fiction should be realistic and should build to concluding twists and surprises—goals that are seen in "An Occurrence at Owl Creek Bridge." His complete works, which he edited himself, appeared in twelve volumes from 1909 to 1912.

 ## An Occurrence at Owl Creek Bridge (1891)

A man stood upon a railroad bridge in northern Alabama, looking down into the swift water twenty feet below. The man's hands were behind his back, the wrists bound with a cord. A rope closely encircled his neck. It was attached to a stout cross-timber above his head and the slack fell to the level of his knees. Some loose boards laid upon the sleepers supporting the metals of the railway supplied a footing for him and his executioners—two private soldiers of the Federal army, directed by a sergeant who in civil life may have been a deputy sheriff. At a short remove upon the same temporary platform was an officer in the uniform of his rank, armed. He was a captain. A sentinel at each end of the bridge stood with his rifle in the position known as "support," that is to say, vertical in front of the left shoulder, the hammer resting on the forearm thrown straight across the chest—a formal and unnatural position, enforcing an erect carriage of the body. It did not appear to be the duty of these two men to know what was occurring at the center of the bridge; they merely blockaded the two ends of the foot planking that traversed it.

Beyond one of the sentinels nobody was in sight; the railroad ran straight away into a forest for a hundred yards, then, curving, was lost to view. Doubtless there was an outpost farther along. The other bank of the stream was open ground—a gentle acclivity topped with a stockade of vertical tree trunks, loopholed for rifles, with a single embrasure through which protruded the muzzle of a brass cannon commanding the bridge. Midway of the slope between the bridge and fort were the spectators—a single company of infantry in line, at "parade rest," the butts of the rifles on the ground, the barrels inclining slightly backward against the right shoulder, the hands crossed upon the stock. A lieutenant stood at the right of the line, the point of his sword upon the ground, his left hand resting upon his right. Excepting the group of four at the center of the bridge, not a man moved. The company faced the bridge, staring stonily, motionless. The sentinels, facing the banks of the stream, might have been statues to adorn the bridge. The captain stood with folded arms, silent, observing the work of his subordinates, but making no sign. Death is a dignitary who when he comes announced is to be received with formal manifestations of respect, even by those most familiar with him. In the code of military etiquette silence and fixity are forms of deference.

The man who was engaged in being hanged was apparently about thirty-five years of age. He was a civilian, if one might judge from his habit, which was that of a planter. His features were good—a straight nose, firm mouth, broad forehead, from which his long, dark hair was combed straight back, falling behind his ears to the collar of his well-fitting frock coat. He wore a mustache and pointed beard, but no whiskers; his eyes were large and dark gray, and had a kindly expression which one would hardly have expected in one whose neck was in the hemp. Evidently this was no vulgar assassin. The liberal military code makes provision for hanging many kinds of persons, and gentlemen are not excluded.

The preparations being complete, the two private soldiers stepped aside and each drew away the plank upon which he had been standing. The sergeant turned to the captain, saluted and placed himself immediately behind that officer, who in turn moved apart one pace. These movements left the condemned man and the sergeant standing on the two ends of the same plank, which spanned three of the cross-ties of the bridge. The end upon which the civilian stood almost, but not quite, reached a fourth. This plank had been held in place by the weight of the captain; it was now held by that of the sergeant. At a signal from the former the latter would step aside, the plank would tilt and the condemned man go down between two ties. The arrangement commended itself to his judgment as simple and effective. His face had not been covered nor his eyes bandaged. He looked a moment at his "unsteadfast footing," then let his gaze wander to the swirling water of the stream racing madly beneath his feet. A piece of dancing driftwood caught his attention and his eyes followed it down the current. How slowly it appeared to move! What a sluggish stream!

He closed his eyes in order to fix his last thoughts upon his wife and children. The water, touched to gold by the early sun, the brooding mists under the banks at some distance down the stream, the fort, the soldiers, the piece of driftwood—all had distracted him. And now he became conscious of a new disturbance. Striking through the thought of his dear ones was a sound which he could neither ignore nor understand, a sharp, distinct, metallic percussion like the stroke of a blacksmith's hammer upon the anvil; it had the same ringing quality. He wondered what it was, and whether immeasurably distant or near by—it seemed both. Its recurrence was regular, but as slow as the tolling of a death knell. He awaited each stroke with impatience and—he knew not why—apprehension. The intervals of silence grew progressively longer; the delays became maddening. With their greater infrequency the sounds increased in strength and sharpness. They hurt his ear like the thrust of a knife; he feared he would shriek. What he heard was the ticking of his watch.

He unclosed his eyes and saw again the water below him. "If I could free my hands," he thought, "I might throw off the noose and spring into the stream. By diving I could evade the bullets and, swimming vigorously, reach the bank, take to the woods and get away home. My home, thank God, is as yet outside their lines; my wife and little ones are still beyond the invader's farthest advance."

As these thoughts, which have here to be set down in words, were flashed into the doomed man's brain rather than evolved from it the captain nodded to the sergeant. The sergeant stepped aside.

## II

Peyton Farquhar was a well-to-do planter, of an old and highly respected Alabama family. Being a slave owner and like other slave owners a politician he was naturally an original secessionist and ardently devoted to the Southern cause. Circumstances of an imperious nature, which it is unnecessary to relate here, had prevented him from taking service with the gallant army that had fought the disastrous campaigns ending with the fall of Corinth,° and he chafed under the inglorious restraint, longing for the release of his energies, the larger life of the soldier, the opportunity for distinction. That opportunity, he felt, would come, as it comes to all in war time. Meanwhile he did what he could. No service was too humble for him to perform in aid of the South, no adventure too perilous for him to undertake if consistent with the character of a civilian who was at heart a soldier, and who in good faith and without too much qualification assented to at least a part of the frankly villainous dictum that all is fair in love and war.

One evening while Farquhar and his wife were sitting on a rustic bench near the entrance to his grounds, a gray-clad soldier rode up to the gate and asked for a drink of water.

---

Corinth: In the northeast corner of Mississippi, near the Alabama state line, Corinth was the site of a battle in 1862 won by the Union army.

Mrs. Farquhar was only too happy to serve him with her own white hands. While she was fetching the water her husband approached the dusty horseman and inquired eagerly for news from the front.

10      "The Yanks are repairing the railroads," said the man, "and are getting ready for another advance. They have reached the Owl Creek bridge, put it in order and built a stockade on the north bank. The commandant has issued an order, which is posted everywhere, declaring that any civilian caught interfering with the railroad, its bridges, tunnels or trains will be summarily hanged. I saw the order."

"How far is it to the Owl Creek bridge?" Farquhar asked.

"About thirty miles."

"Is there no force on this side of the creek?"

"Only a picket post half a mile out, on the railroad, and a single sentinel at this end of the bridge."

15      "Suppose a man—a civilian and student of hanging—should elude the picket post and perhaps get the better of the sentinel," said Farquhar, smiling, "what could he accomplish?"

The soldier reflected. "I was there a month ago," he replied, "I observed that the flood of last winter had lodged a great quantity of driftwood against the wooden pier at this end of the bridge. It is now dry and would burn like tow."

The lady had now brought the water, which the soldier drank. He thanked her ceremoniously, bowed to her husband and rode away. An hour later, after nightfall, he repassed the plantation, going northward in the direction from which he had come. He was a Federal scout.

### III

As Peyton Farquhar fell straight downward through the bridge he lost consciousness and was as one already dead. From this state he was awakened—ages later, it seemed to him—by the pain of a sharp pressure upon his throat, followed by a sense of suffocation. Keen, poignant agonies seemed to shoot from his neck downward through every fiber of his body and limbs. These pains appeared to flash along well-defined lines of ramification and to beat with an inconceivably rapid periodicity. They seemed like streams of pulsating fire heating him to an intolerable temperature. As to his head, he was conscious of nothing but a feeling of fulness—of congestion. These sensations were unaccompanied by thought. The intellectual part of his nature was already effaced; he had power only to feel, and feeling was torment. He was conscious of motion. Encompassed in a luminous cloud, of which he was now merely the fiery heart, without material substance, he swung through unthinkable arcs of oscillation, like a vast pendulum. Then all at once, with terrible suddenness, the light about him shot upward with the noise of a loud plash; a frightful roaring was in his ears, and all was cold and dark. The power of thought was restored; he knew that the rope had broken and he had fallen into the stream. There was no additional strangulation; the noose about his neck was already suffocating him and kept the water from his lungs. To die of hanging at the bottom of a river!—the idea seemed to him ludicrous. He opened his eyes in the darkness and saw above him a gleam of light, but how distant, how inaccessible! He was still sinking, for the light became fainter and fainter until it was a mere glimmer. Then it began to grow and brighten, and he knew that he was rising toward the surface—knew it with reluctance, for he was now very comfortable. "To be hanged and drowned," he thought, "that is not so bad; but I do not wish to be shot. No; I will not be shot; that is not fair."

He was not conscious of an effort, but a sharp pain in his wrist apprised him that he was trying to free his hands. He gave the struggle his attention, as an idler might observe the feat of a juggler, without interest in the outcome. What splendid effort—what magnificent, what superhuman strength! Ah, that was a fine endeavor! Bravo! The cord fell away; his arms parted and floated upward; the hands dimly seen on each side in the growing light. He watched them with a new interest as first one and then the other pounced upon the noose at his neck. They tore it away and thrust it fiercely aside, its undulations resembling those of a water snake. "Put it back, put it back!" He thought he shouted these words to his hands, for the undoing of the noose had been succeeded by the direst pang that he had yet experienced. His neck ached horribly; his brain was on fire; his heart, which had been fluttering faintly, gave a great leap, trying to force itself out at his mouth. His whole body was racked and wrenched with an insupportable anguish! But his disobedient hands gave no heed to the command. They beat the water vigorously with quick, downward strokes, forcing him to the surface. He felt his head emerge; his eyes were blinded by the sunlight; his chest expanded convulsively, and with a supreme and crowning agony his lungs engulfed a great draught of air, which instantly he expelled in a shriek!

He was now in full possession of his physical senses. They were indeed, preternaturally    20
keen and alert. Something in the awful disturbance of his organic system had so exalted and refined them that they made record of things never before perceived. He felt the ripples upon his face and heard their separate sounds as they struck. He looked at the forest on the bank of the stream, saw the individual trees, the leaves and the veining of each leaf—saw the very insects upon them: the locusts, the brilliant-bodied flies, the gray spiders stretching their webs from twig to twig. He noted the prismatic colors in all the dewdrops upon a million blades of grass. The humming of the gnats that danced above the eddies of the stream, the beating of the dragon flies' wings, the strokes of the water-spiders' legs, like oars which had lifted their boat—all these made audible music. A fish slid along beneath his eyes and he heard the rush of its body parting the water.

He had come to the surface facing down the stream; in a moment the visible world seemed to wheel slowly round, himself the pivotal point, and he saw the bridge, the fort, the soldiers upon the bridge, the captain, the sergeant, the two privates, his executioners. They were in silhouette against the blue sky. They shouted and gesticulated, pointing at him. The captain had drawn his pistol, but did not fire; the others were unarmed. Their movements were grotesque and horrible, their forms gigantic.

Suddenly he heard a sharp report and something struck the water smartly within a few inches of his head, spattering his face with spray. He heard a second report, and saw one of the sentinels with his rifle at his shoulder, a light cloud of blue smoke rising from the muzzle. The man in the water saw the eye of the man on the bridge gazing into his own through the sights of the rifle. He observed that it was a gray eye and remembered having read that gray eyes were keenest, and that all famous marksmen had them. Nevertheless, this one had missed.

A counter-swirl had caught Farquhar and turned him half round; he was again looking into the forest on the bank opposite the fort. The sound of a clear, high voice in a monotonous singsong now rang out behind him and came across the water with a distinctness that pierced and subdued all other sounds, even the beating of the ripples in his ears. Although no soldier, he had frequented camps enough to know the dread significance of that deliberate, drawling, aspirated chant; the lieutenant on shore was taking a part in the morning's work. How coldly and pitilessly—with what an even, calm intonation, presaging, and enforcing tranquility in the men—with what accurately measured intervals fell those cruel words:

"Attention, company! . . . Shoulder arms! . . . Ready! . . . Aim! . . . Fire!"

Farquhar dived—dived as deeply as he could. The water roared in his ears like the voice    25
of Niagara, yet he heard the dulled thunder of the volley and, rising again toward the surface, met shining bits of metal, singularly flattened, oscillating slowly downward. Some of them touched him on the face and hands, then fell away, continuing their descent. One lodged between his collar and neck; it was uncomfortably warm and he snatched it out.

As he rose to the surface, gasping for breath, he saw that he had been a long time under water; he was perceptibly farther down stream—nearer to safety. The soldiers had almost finished reloading; the metal ramrods flashed all at once in the sunshine as they were drawn from the barrels, turned in the air, and thrust into their sockets. The two sentinels fired again, independently and ineffectually.

The hunted man saw all this over his shoulder; he was now swimming vigorously with the current. His brain was as energetic as his arms and legs; he thought with the rapidity of lightning.

"The officer," he reasoned, "will not make that martinet's error a second time. It is as easy to dodge a volley as a single shot. He has probably already given the command to fire at will. God help me, I cannot dodge them all!"

An appalling plash within two yards of him was followed by a loud, rushing sound, *diminuendo*, which seemed to travel back through the air to the fort and died in an explosion which stirred the very river to its deeps! A rising sheet of water curved over him, fell down upon him, blinded him, strangled him! The cannon had taken a hand in the game. As he shook his head free from the commotion of the smitten water he heard the deflected shot humming through the air ahead, and in an instant it was cracking and smashing the branches in the forest beyond.

30       "They will not do that again," he thought; "the next time they will use a charge of grape. I must keep my eye upon the gun; the smoke will apprise me—the report arrives too late; it lags behind the missile. That is a good gun."

Suddenly he felt himself whirled round and round—spinning like a top. The water, the banks, the forests, the now distant bridge, fort and men—all were commingled and blurred. Objects were represented by their colors only; circular horizontal streaks of color—that was all he saw. He had been caught in a vortex and was being whirled on with a velocity of advance and gyration that made him giddy and sick. In a few moments he was flung upon the gravel at the foot of the left bank of the stream—the southern bank—and behind a projecting point which concealed him from his enemies. The sudden arrest of his motion, the abrasion of one of his hands on the gravel, restored him, and he wept with delight. He dug his fingers into the sand, threw it over himself in handfuls and audibly blessed it. It looked like diamonds, rubies, emeralds; he could think of nothing beautiful which it did not resemble. The trees upon the bank were giant garden plants; he noted a definite order in their arrangement, inhaled the fragrance of their blooms. A strange, roseate light shone through the spaces among their trunks and the wind made in their branches the music of Æolian harps. He had no wish to perfect his escape—was content to remain in that enchanting spot until retaken.

A whiz and rattle of grapeshot among the branches high above his head roused him from his dream. The baffled cannoneer had fired him a random farewell. He sprang to his feet, rushed up the sloping bank, and plunged into the forest.

All that day he traveled, laying his course by the rounding sun. The forest seemed interminable; nowhere did he discover a break in it, not even a woodman's road. He had not known that he lived in so wild a region. There was something uncanny in the revelation.

By nightfall he was fatigued, footsore, famishing. The thought of his wife and children urged him on. At last he found a road which led him in what he knew to be the right direction. It was as wide and straight as a city street, yet it seem untraveled. No fields bordered it, no dwelling anywhere. Not so much as the barking of a dog suggested human habitation. The black bodies of the trees formed a straight wall on both sides, terminating on the horizon in a point, like a diagram in a lesson in perspective. Overhead, as he looked up through this rift in the wood, shone great golden stars looking unfamiliar and grouped in strange constellations. He was sure they were arranged in some order which had a secret and malign significance. The wood on either side was full of singular noises, among which—once, twice, and again— he distinctly heard whispers in an unknown tongue.

His neck was in pain and lifting his hand to it found it horribly swollen. He knew that it 35 had a circle of black where the rope had bruised it. His eyes felt congested; he could no longer close them. His tongue was swollen with thirst; he relieved its fever by thrusting it forward from between his teeth into the cold air. How softly the turf had carpeted the untraveled avenue—he could no longer feel the roadway beneath his feet!

Doubtless, despite his suffering, he had fallen asleep while walking, for now he sees another scene—perhaps he has merely recovered from a delirium. He stands at the gate of his own home. All is as he left it, and all bright and beautiful in the morning sunshine. He must have traveled the entire night. As he pushes open the gate and passes up the wide white walk, he sees a flutter of female garments; his wife, looking fresh and cool and sweet, steps down from the veranda to meet him. At the bottom of the steps she stands waiting, with a smile of ineffable joy, an attitude of matchless grace and dignity. Ah, how beautiful she is! He springs forward with extended arms. As he is about to clasp her he feels a stunning blow upon the back of the neck; a blinding white light blazes all about him with a sound like the shock of a cannon—then all is darkness and silence!

Peyton Farquhar was dead; his body, with a broken neck, swung gently from side to side beneath the timbers of the Owl Creek bridge.

## Questions

1. What is the situation in the story? What did Farquhar do to deserve his execution?

2. Describe the various shifts in the story's point of view, particularly as indicated in paragraphs 5 and 37. How does Bierce make you aware of Farquhar's heightened consciousness?

3. According to Farquhar's perception of time, how long does it take him to get home after his escape (see paragraphs 33 and 36)?

4. What evidence can you find to indicate that Farquhar is experiencing great pain, despite his feelings that he is escaping?

5. What is the effect of the shift into the present tense in paragraph 36?

## WILLIAM FAULKNER (1897–1962)

Faulkner spent his childhood in Mississippi and became one of the foremost American novelists of the twentieth century. He twice received the Pulitzer Prize for Fiction (in 1955 and 1963), and he also received the Nobel Prize in Literature (in 1949). Throughout his extensive fiction about the special world that he named "Yoknapatawpha County," which is modeled on his own home area in Oxford, Mississippi, he treats life in the Southern United States as a symbol of humankind generally, emphasizing the decline of civilization and culture in the wake of the Civil War. Emily Grierson in "A Rose for Emily" is representative of this decline, for she maintains the appearances of status long after the substance is past. It is not unusual to find degraded, sullen, disturbed, and degenerate characters in Faulkner's fiction.

## 🌿 A Rose for Emily (1931)

I

When Miss Emily Grierson died, our whole town went to her funeral; the men through a sort of respectful affection for a fallen monument, the women mostly out of curiosity to see the inside of her house, which no one save an old manservant—a combined gardener and cook—had seen in at least ten years.

It was a big, squarish frame house that had once been white, decorated with cupolas and spires and scrolled balconies in the heavily lightsome style of the seventies, set on what had once been our most select street. But garages and cotton gins had encroached and obliterated even the august names of that neighborhood; only Miss Emily's house was left, lifting its stubborn and coquettish decay above the cotton wagons and the gasoline pumps—an eyesore among eyesores. And now Miss Emily had gone to join the representatives of those august names where they lay in the cedar-bemused cemetery among the ranked and anonymous graves of Union and Confederate soldiers who fell at the battle of Jefferson.

Alive, Miss Emily had been a tradition, a duty, and a care; a sort of hereditary obligation upon the town, dating from that day in 1894 when Colonel Sartoris, the mayor—he who fathered the edict that no Negro woman should appear on the streets without an apron—remitted her taxes, the dispensation dating from the death of her father on into perpetuity. Not that Miss Emily would have accepted charity. Colonel Sartoris invented an involved tale to the effect that Miss Emily's father had loaned money to the town, which the town, as a matter of business, preferred this way of repaying. Only a man of Colonel Sartoris' generation and thought could have invented it, and only a woman could have believed it.

When the next generation, with its more modern ideas, became mayors and aldermen, this arrangement created some little dissatisfaction. On the first of the year they mailed her a tax notice. February came, and there was no reply. They wrote her a formal letter, asking her to call at the sheriff's office at her convenience. A week later the mayor wrote her himself, offering to call or to send his car for her, and received in reply a note on paper of an archaic shape, in a thin, flowing calligraphy in faded ink, to the effect that she no longer went out at all. The tax notice was also enclosed, without comment.

5    They called a special meeting of the Board of Aldermen. A deputation waited upon her, knocked at the door through which no visitor had passed since she ceased giving china-painting lessons eight or ten years earlier. They were admitted by the old Negro into a dim hall from which a stairway mounted into still more shadow. It smelled of dust and disuse—a close, dank smell. The Negro led them into the parlor. It was furnished in heavy, leather-covered furniture. When the Negro opened the blinds of one window, they could see that the leather was cracked; and when they sat down, a faint dust rose sluggishly about their thighs, spinning with slow motes in the single sun-ray. On a tarnished gilt easel before the fireplace stood a crayon portrait of Miss Emily's father.

They rose when she entered—a small, fat woman in black, with a thin gold chain descending to her waist and vanishing into her belt, leaning on an ebony cane with a tarnished gold head. Her skeleton was small and spare; perhaps that was why what would have been merely plumpness in another was obesity in her. She looked bloated, like a body long submerged in motionless water, and of that pallid hue. Her eyes, lost in the fatty ridges of her face, looked like two small pieces of coal pressed into a lump of dough as they moved from one face to another while the visitors stated their errand.

She did not ask them to sit. She just stood in the door and listened quietly until the spokesman came to a stumbling halt. Then they could hear the invisible watch ticking at the end of the gold chain.

Her voice was dry and cold. "I have no taxes in Jefferson. Colonel Sartoris explained it to me. Perhaps one of you can gain access to the city records and satisfy yourselves."

"But we have. We are the city authorities, Miss Emily. Didn't you get a notice from the sheriff, signed by him?"

"I received a paper, yes," Miss Emily said. "Perhaps he considers himself the sheriff . . . I    10 have no taxes in Jefferson."

"But there is nothing on the books to show that, you see. We must go by the—"

"See Colonel Sartoris. I have no taxes in Jefferson."

"But, Miss Emily—"

"See Colonel Sartoris." (Colonel Sartoris had been dead almost ten years.) "I have no taxes in Jefferson. Tobe!" The Negro appeared. "Show these gentlemen out."


II

So she vanquished them, horse and foot, just as she had vanquished their fathers thirty years    15 before about the smell. That was two years after her father's death and a short time after her sweetheart—the one we believed would marry her—had deserted her. After her father's death she went out very little; after her sweetheart went away, people hardly saw her at all. A few of the ladies had the temerity to call, but were not received, and the only sign of life about the place was the Negro man—a young man then—going in and out with a market basket.

"Just as if a man—any man—could keep a kitchen properly," the ladies said; so they were not surprised when the smell developed. It was another link between the gross, teeming world and the high and mighty Griersons.

A neighbor, a woman, complained to the mayor, Judge Stevens, eighty years old.

"But what will you have me do about it, madam?" he said.

"Why, send her word to stop it," the woman said. "Isn't there a law?"

"I'm sure that won't be necessary," Judge Stevens said. "It's probably just a snake or a rat    20 that nigger of hers killed in the yard. I'll speak to him about it."

The next day he received two more complaints, one from a man who came in diffident deprecation. "We really must do something about it, Judge. I'd be the last one in the world to bother Miss Emily, but we've got to do something." That night the Board of Aldermen met— three graybeards and one younger man, a member of the rising generation.

"It's simple enough," he said. "Send her word to have her place cleaned up. Give her a certain time to do it in, and if she don't . . ."

"Dammit, sir," Judge Stevens said, "will you accuse a lady to her face of smelling bad?"

So the next night, after midnight, four men crossed Miss Emily's lawn and slunk about the house like burglars, sniffing along the base of the brickwork and at the cellar openings while one of them performed a regular sowing motion with his hand out of a sack slung from his shoulder. They broke open the cellar door and sprinkled lime there, and in all the outbuildings. As they recrossed the lawn, a window that had been dark was lighted and Miss Emily sat in it, the light behind her, and her upright torso motionlesss as that of an idol. They crept quietly across the lawn and into the shadow of the locusts that lined the street. After a week or two the smell went away.

That was when people had begun to feel really sorry for her. People in our town, remem-    25 bering how old lady Wyatt, her great-aunt, had gone completely crazy at last, believed that the Griersons held themselves a little too high for what they really were. None of the young men were quite good enough for Miss Emily and such. We had long thought of them as a tableau, Miss Emily a slender figure in white in the background, her father a spraddled silhouette in the foreground, his back to her and clutching a horsewhip, the two of them framed by the back flung front door. So when she got to be thirty and was still single, we were not pleased exactly, but vindicated; even with insanity in the family she wouldn't have turned down all of her chances if they had really materialized.

When her father died, it got about that the house was all that was left to her; and in a way, people were glad. At last they could pity Miss Emily. Being left alone, and a pauper, she had become humanized. Now she too would know the old thrill and the old despair of a penny more or less.

The day after his death all the ladies prepared to call at the house and offer condolence and aid, as is our custom. Miss Emily met them at the door, dressed as usual and with no trace of grief on her face. She told them that her father was not dead. She did that for three days, with the ministers calling on her, and the doctors, trying to persuade her to let them dispose of the body. Just as they were about to resort to law and force, she broke down, and they buried her father quickly.

We did not say she was crazy then. We believed she had to do that. We remembered all the young men her father had driven away, and we knew that with nothing left, she would have to cling to that which had robbed her, as people will.

**III**

She was sick for a long time. When we saw her again, her hair was cut short, making her look like a girl, with a vague resemblance to those angels in colored church windows—sort of tragic and serene.

30    The town had just let the contracts for paving the sidewalks, and in the summer after her father's death they began the work. The construction company came with niggers and mules and machinery, and a foreman named Homer Barron, a Yankee—a big, dark, ready man, with a big voice and eyes lighter than his face. The little boys would follow in groups to hear him cuss the niggers, and the niggers singing in time to the rise and fall of picks. Pretty soon he knew everybody in town. Whenever you heard a lot of laughing anywhere about the square, Homer Barron would be in the center of the group. Presently we began to see him and Miss Emily on Sunday afternoons driving in the yellow-wheeled buggy and the matched team of bays from the livery stable.

At first we were glad that Miss Emily would have an interest, because the ladies all said, "Of course a Grierson would not think seriously of a Northerner, a day laborer." But there were still others, older people, who said that even grief could not cause a real lady to forget *noblesse oblige*—without calling it *noblesse oblige*. They just said, "Poor Emily. Her kinsfolk should come to her." She had some kin in Alabama; but years ago her father had fallen out with them over the estate of old lady Wyatt, the crazy woman, and there was no communication between the two families. They had not even been represented at the funeral.

And as soon as the old people said, "Poor Emily," the whispering began. "Do you suppose it's really so?" they said to one another. "Of course it is. What else could. . . ." This behind their hands; rustling of craned silk and satin behind jalousies closed upon the sun of Sunday afternoon as the thin, swift clop-clop-clop of the matched team passed: "Poor Emily."

She carried her head high enough—even when we believed that she was fallen. It was as if she demanded more than ever the recognition of her dignity as the last Grierson; as if it had wanted that touch of earthiness to reaffirm her imperviousness. Like when she bought the rat poison, the arsenic. That was over a year after they had begun to say "Poor Emily," and while the two female cousins were visiting her.

"I want some poison," she said to the druggist. She was over thirty then, still a slight woman, though thinner than usual, with cold, haughty black eyes in a face the flesh of which was strained across the temples and about the eyesockets as you imagine a lighthouse-keeper's face ought to look. "I want some poison," she said.

"Yes, Miss Emily. What kind? For rats and such? I'd recom—"                                                35
"I want the best you have. I don't care what kind."

The druggist named several. "They'll kill anything up to an elephant. But what you want is—"

"Arsenic," Miss Emily said. "Is that a good one?"

"Is . . . arsenic? Yes, ma'am. But what you want—"

"I want arsenic."                                                                                         40

The druggist looked down at her. She looked back at him, erect, her face like a strained flag. "Why, of course," the druggist said. "If that's what you want. But the law requires you to tell what you are going to use it for."

Miss Emily just stared at him, her head tilted back in order to look him eye for eye, until he looked away and went and got the arsenic and wrapped it up. The Negro delivery boy brought her the package; the druggist didn't come back. When she opened the package at home there was written on the box, under the skull and bones: "For rats."

## IV

So the next day we all said, "She will kill herself"; and we said it would be the best thing. When she had first begun to be seen with Homer Barron, we had said, "She will marry him." Then we said, "She will persuade him yet," because Homer himself had remarked—he liked men, and it was known that he drank with the younger men in the Elks' Club—that he was not a marrying man. Later we said, "Poor Emily" behind the jalousies as they passed on Sunday afternoon in the glittering buggy, Miss Emily with her head high and Homer Barron with his hat cocked and a cigar in his teeth, reins and whip in a yellow glove.

Then some of the ladies began to say that it was a disgrace to the town and a bad example to the young people. The men did not want to interfere, but at last the ladies forced the Baptist minister—Miss Emily's people were Episcopal—to call upon her. He would never divulge what happened during that interview, but he refused to go back again. The next Sunday they again drove about the streets, and the following day the minister's wife wrote to Miss Emily's relations in Alabama.

So she had blood-kin under her roof again and we sat back to watch developments. At    45
first nothing happened. Then we were sure that they were to be married. We learned that Miss Emily had been to the jeweler's and ordered a man's toilet set in silver, with the letters H. B. on each piece Two days later we learned that she had bought a complete outfit of men's clothing, including a nightshirt, and we said, "They are married." We were really glad. We were glad because the two female cousins were even more Grierson than Miss Emily had ever been.

So we were not surprised when Homer Barron—the streets had been finished some time since—was gone. We were a little disappointed that there was not a public blowing-off, but we believed that he had gone on to prepare for Miss Emily's coming, or to give her a chance to get rid of the cousins. (By that time it was a cabal, and we were all Miss Emily's allies to help circumvent the cousins.) Sure enough, after another week they departed. And, as we had expected all along, within three days Homer Barron was back in town. A neighbor saw the Negro man admit him at the kitchen door at dusk one evening.

And that was the last we saw of Homer Barron. And of Miss Emily for some time. The Negro man went in and out with the market basket, but the front door remained closed. Now and then we would see her at a window for a moment, as the men did that night when they sprinkled the lime, but for almost six months she did not appear on the streets. Then we knew that this was to be expected too; as if that quality of her father which had thwarted her woman's life so many times had been too virulent and too furious to die.

When we next saw Miss Emily, she had grown fat and her hair was turning gray. During the next few years it grew grayer and grayer until it attained an even pepper-and-salt iron gray, when it ceased turning. Up to the day of her death at seventy-four it was still that vigorous iron-gray, like the hair of an active man.

From that time on her front door remained closed, save for a period of six or seven years, when she was about forty, during which she gave lessons in china-painting. She fitted up a studio in one of the downstairs rooms, where the daughters and granddaughters of Colonel Sartoris' contemporaries were sent to her with the same regularity and in the same spirit that they were sent to church on Sundays with a twenty-five-cent piece for the collection plate. Meanwhile her taxes had been remitted.

50  Then the newer generation became the backbone and the spirit of the town, and the painting pupils grew up and fell away and did not send their children to her with boxes of color and tedious brushes and pictures cut from the ladies' magazines. The front door closed upon the last one and remained closed for good. When the town got free postal delivery, Miss Emily alone refused to let them fasten the metal numbers above her door and attach a mailbox to it. She would not listen to them.

Daily, monthly, yearly we watched the Negro grow grayer and more stooped, going in and out with the market basket. Each December we sent her a tax notice, which would be returned by the post office a week later, unclaimed. Now and then we would see her in one of the downstairs windows—she had evidently shut up the top floor of the house—like the carven torso of an idol in a niche, looking or not looking at us, we could never tell which. Thus she passed from generation to generation—dear, inescapable, impervious, tranquil, and perverse.

And so she died. Fell ill in the house filled with dust and shadows, with only a doddering Negro man to wait on her. We did not even know she was sick; we had long since given up trying to get any information from the Negro. He talked to no one, probably not even to her, for his voice had grown harsh and rusty, as if from disuse.

She died in one of the downstairs rooms, in a heavy walnut bed with a curtain, her gray head propped on a pillow yellow and moldy with age and lack of sunlight.

V

The Negro met the first of the ladies at the front door and let them in, with their hushed, sibilant voices and their quick, curious glances, and then he disappeared. He walked right through the house and out the back and was not seen again.

55  The two female cousins came at once. They held the funeral on the second day, with the town coming to look at Miss Emily beneath a mass of bought flowers, with the crayon face of her father musing profoundly above the bier and the ladies sibilant and macabre; and the very old men—some in their brushed Confederate uniforms—on the porch and the lawn, talking of Miss Emily as if she had been a contemporary of theirs, believing that they had danced with her and courted her perhaps, confusing time with its mathematical progression, as the old do, to whom all the past is not a diminishing road but, instead, a huge meadow which no winter ever quite touches, divided from them now by the narrow bottle-neck of the most recent decade of years.

Already we knew that there was one room in that region above stairs which no one had seen in forty years, and which would have to be forced. They waited until Miss Emily was decently in the ground before they opened it.

The violence of breaking down the door seemed to fill this room with pervading dust. A thin, acrid pall as of the tomb seemed to lie everywhere upon this room decked and furnished as for a bridal: upon the valance curtains of faded rose color, upon the rose-shaded lights, upon the dressing table, upon the delicate array of crystal and the man's toilet things backed with tarnished silver, silver so tarnished that the monogram was obscured. Among them lay a collar and tie, as if they had just been removed, which, lifted, left upon the surface a pale crescent in the dust. Upon a chair hung the suit, carefully folded; beneath it the two mute shoes and the discarded socks.

The man himself lay in the bed.

For a long while we just stood there, looking down at the profound and fleshless grin. The body had apparently once lain in the attitude of an embrace, but now the long sleep that outlasts love, that conquers even the grimace of love, had cuckolded him. What was left of him, rotted beneath what was left of the nightshirt, had become inextricable from the bed in which he lay; and upon him and upon the pillow beside him lay that even coating of the patient and biding dust.

Then we noticed that in the second pillow was the indentation of a head. One of us lifted something from it, and leaning forward, that faint and invisible dust dry and acrid in the nostrils, we saw a long strand of iron-gray hair.    60

## Questions

1. Who is Emily Grierson? What was the former position of her family in the town? What has happened to Emily after her father died? What are her economic circumstances? How does the deputation of alderman from the town of Jefferson treat her?

2. How do we learn about Emily? How do reports and rumors about her create the narrative of her life?

3. What has happened between Emily and Homer Barron? What is the significance, if any, of the fact that Homer is from the North?

4. Describe the plot of "A Rose for Emily." What contrasts and oppositions are developed in the story?

5. How does Faulkner shape the story's events to make Emily mysterious or enigmatic? In what ways does the ending come as a surprise?

## TIM O'BRIEN (B. 1946)

William Timothy O'Brien was born in Minnesota and attended Macalester College in St. Paul. He saw duty in Vietnam during some of the more controversial times of that conflict, and after returning home he did graduate study, worked as a reporter, and became a writer. Among the works he has regularly published since the 1970s are *If I Die in a Combat Zone, Box Me Up and Ship Me Home* (1973); *Northern Lights* (1974); *Going After Cacciato* (1978); *The Things They Carried* (1990), and *July, July* (2002). In his stories, which interweave fiction and autobiography, he realistically treats both the horrors of the Vietnam War and the ways in which returning veterans and their loved ones adjust to life after returning home. Because he portrays the lives and feelings of combat soldiers so well, he has been called one of the best American writers about war.

**The Things They Carried**   (1990)

First Lieutenant Jimmy Cross carried letters from a girl named Martha, a junior at Mount Sebastian College in New Jersey. They were not love letters, but Lieutenant Cross was hoping, so he kept them folded in plastic at the bottom of his rucksack. In the late afternoon, after a day's march, he would dig his foxhole, wash his hands under a canteen, unwrap the letters, hold them with the tips of his fingers, and spend the last hour of light pretending. He would imagine romantic camping trips into the White Mountains in New Hampshire. He would sometimes taste the envelope flaps, knowing her tongue had been there. More than anything, he wanted Martha to love him as he loved her, but the letters were mostly chatty, elusive on the matter of love. She was a virgin, he was almost sure. She was an English major at Mount Sebastian, and she wrote beautifully about her professors and roommates and midterm exams, about her respect for Chaucer and her great affection for Virginia Woolf. She often quoted lines of poetry; she never mentioned the war, except to say, Jimmy, take care of yourself. The letters weighed 10 ounces. They were signed Love, Martha, but Lieutenant Cross understood that Love was only a way of signing and did not mean what he sometimes pretended it meant. At dusk, he would carefully return the letters to his rucksack. Slowly, a bit distracted, he would get up and move among his men, checking the perimeter, then at full dark he would return to his hole and watch the night and wonder if Martha was a virgin.

The things they carried were largely determined by necessity. Among the necessities or near-necessities were P-38 can openers, pocket knives, heat tabs, wristwatches, dog tags, mosquito repellent, chewing gum, candy, cigarettes, salt tablets, packets of Kool-Aid, lighters, matches, sewing kits, Military Payment Certificates, C rations, and two or three canteens of water. Together, these items weighed between 15 and 20 pounds, depending upon a man's habits or rate of metabolism. Henry Dobbins, who was a big man, carried extra rations; he was especially fond of canned peaches in heavy syrup over pound cake. Dave Jensen, who practiced field hygiene, carried a toothbrush, dental floss, and several hotel-sized bars of soap he'd stolen on R&R in Sydney, Australia. Ted Lavender, who was scared, carried tranquilizers until he was shot in the head outside the village of Than Khe in mid-April. By necessity, and because it was SOP, they all carried steel helmets that weighed 5 pounds including the liner and camouflage cover. They carried the standard fatigue jackets and trousers. Very few carried underwear. On their feet they carried jungle boots—2.1 pounds—and Dave Jensen carried three pairs of socks and a can of Dr. Scholl's foot powder as a precaution against trench foot. Until he was shot, Ted Lavender carried six or seven ounces of premium dope, which for him was a necessity. Mitchell Sanders, the RTO, carried condoms. Norman Bowker carried a diary. Rat Kiley carried comic books. Kiowa, a devout Baptist, carried an illustrated New Testament that had been presented to him by his father, who taught Sunday school in Oklahoma City, Oklahoma. As a hedge against bad times, however, Kiowa also carried his grandmother's distrust of the white man, his grandfather's old hunting hatchet. Necessity dictated. Because the land was mined and booby-trapped, it was SOP for each man to carry a steel-centered, nylon-covered flak jacket, which weighed 6.7 pounds, but which on hot days seemed much heavier. Because you could die so quickly, each man carried at least one large compress bandage, usually in the helmet band for easy access. Because the nights were cold, and because the monsoons were wet, each carried a green plastic poncho that could be used as a raincoat or groundsheet or makeshift tent. With its quilted liner, the poncho weighed almost two pounds, but it was worth every ounce. In April, for instance, when Ted Lavender was shot, they used his poncho to wrap him up, then to carry him across the paddy, then to lift him into the chopper that took him away.

They were called legs or grunts.

To carry something was to hump it, as when Lieutenant Jimmy Cross humped his love for Martha up the hills and through the swamps. In its intransitive form, to hump meant to walk, or to march, but it implied burdens far beyond the intransitive.

Almost everyone humped photographs. In his wallet, Lieutenant Cross carried two pho-   5
tographs of Martha. The first was a Kodacolor snapshot signed Love, though he knew better. She stood against a brick wall. Her eyes were gray and neutral, her lips slightly open as she stared straight-on at the camera. At night, sometimes, Lieutenant Cross wondered who had taken the picture, because he knew she had boyfriends, because he loved her so much, and because he could see the shadow of the picture-taker spreading out against the brick wall. The second photograph had been clipped from the 1968 Mount Sebastian yearbook. It was an action shot—women's volleyball—and Martha was bent horizontal to the floor, reaching, the palms of her hands in sharp focus, the tongue taut, the expression frank and competitive. There was no visible sweat. She wore white gym shorts. Her legs, he thought, were almost certainly the legs of a virgin, dry and without hair, the left knee cocked and carrying her entire weight, which was just over one hundred pounds. Lieutenant Cross remembered touching that left knee. A dark theater, he remembered, and the movie was *Bonnie and Clyde*, and Martha wore a tweed skirt, and during the final scene, when he touched her knee, she turned and looked at him in a sad, sober way that made him pull his hand back, but he would always remember the feel of the tweed skirt and the knee beneath it and the sound of the gunfire that killed Bonnie and Clyde, how embarrassing it was, how slow and oppressive. He remembered kissing her good night at the dorm door. Right then, he thought, he should've done something brave. He should've carried her up the stairs to her room and tied her to the bed and touched that left knee all night long. He should've risked it. Whenever he looked at the photographs, he thought of new things he should've done.

What they carried was partly a function of rank, partly of field specialty.

As a first lieutenant and platoon leader, Jimmy Cross carried a compass, maps, code books, binoculars, and a .45-caliber pistol that weighed 2.9 pounds fully loaded. He carried a strobe light and the responsibility for the lives of his men.

As an RTO, Mitchell Sanders carried the PRC-25 radio, a killer, 26 pounds with its battery.

As a medic, Rat Kiley carried a canvas satchel filled with morphine and plasma and malaria tablets and surgical tape and comic books and all the things a medic must carry, including M&M's for especially bad wounds, for a total weight of nearly 20 pounds.

As a big man, therefore a machine gunner, Henry Dobbins carried the M-60, which weighed   10
23 pounds unloaded, but which was almost always loaded. In addition, Dobbins carried between 10 and 15 pounds of ammunition draped in belts across his chest and shoulders.

As PFCs or Spec 4s, most of them were common grunts and carried the standard M-16 gas-operated assault rifle. The weapon weighed 7.5 pounds unloaded, 8.2 pounds with its full 20-round magazine. Depending on numerous factors, such as topography and psychology, the riflemen carried anywhere from 12 to 20 magazines, usually in cloth bandoliers, adding on another 8.4 pounds at minimum, 14 pounds at maximum. When it was available, they also carried M-16 maintenance gear—rods and steel brushes and swabs and tubes of LSA oil—all of which weighed about a pound. Among the grunts, some carried the M-79 grenade launcher, 5.9 pounds unloaded, a reasonably light weapon except for the ammunition, which was heavy. A single round weighed 10 ounces. The typical load was 25 rounds. But Ted Lavender, who was scared, carried 34 rounds when he was shot and killed outside Than Khe, and he went down under an exceptional burden, more than 20 pounds of ammunition, plus the flak jacket and helmet and rations and water and toilet paper and tranquilizers and all the rest, plus the unweighed fear. He was dead weight. There was no twitching or flopping. Kiowa, who saw it happen, said it was like watching a rock fall, or a big sandbag or something—just boom, then down—not like the movies where the dead guy rolls around and does fancy spins and goes ass over teakettle—not like that, Kiowa said, the poor bastard just flat-fuck fell. Boom. Down. Nothing else. It was a bright morning in mid-April. Lieutenant Cross felt the pain. He blamed himself. They stripped off Lavender's canteens and ammo, all the heavy things, and Rat Kiley said the obvious, the guy's dead, and Mitchell Sanders used his radio to report one U.S. KIA and to request a chopper. Then they wrapped Lavender in his poncho. They carried him out to a dry paddy, established security, and sat smoking the dead man's dope until the chopper came. Lieutenant Cross kept to himself. He pictured Martha's smooth young face, thinking he loved her more than anything, more than his men, and now Ted Lavender was dead because he loved her so much and could not stop thinking about her. When the dustoff arrived, they carried Lavender aboard. Afterward they burned Than Khe. They marched until dusk, then dug their holes, and that night Kiowa kept explaining how you had to be there, how fast it was, how the poor guy just dropped like so much concrete. Boom-down, he said. Like cement.

In addition to the three standard weapons—the M-60, M-16, and M-79—they carried whatever presented itself, or whatever seemed appropriate as a means of killing or staying alive. They carried catch-as-catch-can. At various times, in various situations, they carried M-14s and CAR-15s and Swedish Ks and grease guns and captured AK-47s and Chi-Coms and RPGs and Simonov carbines and black market Uzis and .38-caliber Smith & Wesson handguns and 66 mm LAWs and shotguns and silencers and blackjacks and bayonets and C-4 plastic explosives. Lee Strunk carried a slingshot; a weapon of last resort, he called it. Mitchell Sanders carried brass knuckles. Kiowa carried his grandfather's feathered hatchet. Every third or fourth man carried a Claymore antipersonnel mine—3.5 pounds with its firing device. They all carried fragmentation grenades—14 ounces each. They all carried at least one M-18 colored smoke grenade—24 ounces. Some carried CS or tear gas grenades. Some carried white phosphorus grenades. They carried all they could bear, and then some, including a silent awe for the terrible power of the things they carried.

In the first week of April, before Lavender died, Lieutenant Jimmy Cross received a good-luck charm from Martha. It was a simple pebble, an ounce at most. Smooth to the touch, it was a milky white color with flecks of orange and violet, oval-shaped, like a miniature egg. In the accompanying letter, Martha wrote that she had found the pebble on the Jersey shoreline, precisely where the land touched water at high tide, where things came together but also separated. It was this separate-but-together quality, she wrote, that had inspired her to pick up the pebble and to carry it in her breast pocket for several days, where it seemed weightless, and then to send it through the mail, by air, as a token of her truest feelings for him. Lieutenant Cross found this romantic. But he wondered what her truest feelings were, exactly, and what she meant by separate-but-together. He wondered how the tides and waves had come into play on that afternoon along the Jersey shoreline when Martha saw the pebble and bent down to rescue it from geology. He imagined bare feet. Martha was a poet, with the poet's sensibilities, and her feet would be brown and bare, the toenails unpainted, the eyes chilly and somber like the ocean in March, and though it was painful, he wondered who had been with her that afternoon. He imagined a pair of shadows moving along the strip of sand where things came together but also separated. It was phantom jealousy, he knew, but he couldn't help himself. He loved her so much. On the march, through the hot days of early April, he carried the pebble in his mouth, turning it with his tongue, tasting sea salt and moisture. His mind wandered. He had difficulty keeping his attention on the war. On occasion he would yell at his men to spread out the column, to keep their eyes open, but then he would slip away into daydreams, just pretending, walking barefoot along the Jersey shore, with Martha, carrying nothing. He would feel himself rising. Sun and waves and gentle winds, all love and lightness.

What they carried varied by mission.

When a mission took them to the mountains, they carried mosquito netting, machetes, 15 canvas tarps, and extra bug juice.

If a mission seemed especially hazardous, or if it involved a place they knew to be bad, they carried everything they could. In certain heavily mined AOs, where the land was dense with Toe Poppers and Bouncing Betties, they took turns humping a 28-pound mine detector. With its headphones and big sensing plate, the equipment was a stress on the lower back and shoulders, awkward to handle, often useless because of the shrapnel in the earth, but they carried it anyway, partly for safety, partly for the illusion of safety.

On ambush, or other night missions, they carried peculiar little odds and ends. Kiowa always took along his New Testament and a pair of moccasins for silence. Dave Jensen carried night-sight vitamins high in carotene. Lee Strunk carried his slingshot; ammo, he claimed, would never be a problem. Rat Kiley carried brandy and M&M's candy. Until he was shot, Ted Lavender carried the starlight scope, which weighed 6.3 pounds with its aluminum carrying case. Henry Dobbins carried his girlfriend's panty-hose wrapped around his neck as a comforter. They all carried ghosts. When dark came, they would move out single file across the meadows and paddies to their ambush coordinates, where they would quietly set up the Claymores and lie down and spend the night waiting.

Other missions were more complicated and required special equipment. In mid-April, it was their mission to search out and destroy the elaborate tunnel complexes in the Than Khe area south of Chu Lai. To blow the tunnels, they carried one-pound blocks of pentrite high explosives, four blocks to a man, 68 pounds in all. They carried wiring, detonators, and battery-powered clackers. Dave Jensen carried earplugs. Most often, before blowing the tunnels, they were ordered by higher command to search them, which was considered bad news, but by and large they just shrugged and carried out orders. Because he was a big man, Henry Dobbins was excused from tunnel duty. The others would draw numbers. Before Lavender died there were 17 men in the platoon, and whoever drew the number 17 would strip off his gear and crawl in headfirst with a flashlight and Lieutenant Cross's .45-caliber pistol. The rest of them would fan out as security. They would sit down or kneel, not facing the hole, listening to the ground beneath them, imagining cobwebs and ghosts, whatever was down there—the tunnel walls squeezing in—how the flashlight seemed impossibly heavy in the hand and how it was tunnel vision in the very strictest sense, compression in all ways, even time, and how you had to wiggle in—ass and elbows—a swallowed-up feeling—and how you found yourself worrying about odd things: Will your flashlight go dead? Do rats carry rabies? If you screamed, how far would the sound carry? Would your buddies hear it? Would they have the courage to drag you out? In some respects, though not many, the waiting was worse than the tunnel itself. Imagination was a killer.

On April 16, when Lee Strunk drew the number 17, he laughed and muttered something and went down quickly. The morning was hot and very still. Not good, Kiowa said. He looked at the tunnel opening, then out across a dry paddy toward the village of Than Khe. Nothing moved. No clouds or birds or people. As they waited, the men smoked and drank Kool-Aid, not talking much, feeling sympathy for Lee Strunk but also feeling the luck of the draw. You win some, you lose some, said Mitchell Sanders, and sometimes you settle for a rain check. It was a tired line and no one laughed.

Henry Dobbins ate a tropical chocolate bar. Ted Lavender popped a tranquilizer and went 20 off to pee.

After five minutes, Lieutenant Jimmy Cross moved to the tunnel, leaned down, and examined the darkness. Trouble, he thought—a cave-in maybe. And then suddenly, without willing it, he was thinking about Martha. The stresses and fractures, the quick collapse, the two of them buried alive under all that weight. Dense, crushing love. Kneeling, watching the hole, he tried to concentrate on Lee Strunk and the war, all the dangers, but his love was too much for him, he felt paralyzed, he wanted to sleep inside her lungs and breathe her blood and be smothered. He wanted her to be a virgin and not a virgin, all at once. He wanted to know her. Intimate secrets: Why poetry? Why so sad? Why that grayness in her eyes? Why so alone? Not lonely, just alone—riding her bike across campus or sitting off by herself in the cafeteria—even dancing, she danced alone—and it was the aloneness that filled him with love. He remembered telling her that one evening. How she nodded and looked away. And how, later, when he kissed her, she received the kiss without returning it, her eyes wide open, not afraid, not a virgin's eyes, just flat and uninvolved.

Lieutenant Cross gazed at the tunnel. But he was not there. He was buried with Martha under the white sand at the Jersey shore. They were pressed together, and the pebble in his mouth was her tongue. He was smiling. Vaguely, he was aware of how quiet the day was, the sullen paddies, yet he could not bring himself to worry about matters of security. He was beyond that. He was just a kid at war, in love. He was twenty-four years old. He couldn't help it.

A few moments later Lee Strunk crawled out of the tunnel. He came up grinning, filthy but alive. Lieutenant Cross nodded and closed his eyes while the others clapped Strunk on the back and made jokes about rising from the dead.

Worms, Rat Kiley said. Right out of the grave. Fuckin' zombie.

25     The men laughed. They all felt great relief.

Spook city, said Mitchell Sanders.

Lee Strunk made a funny ghost sound, a kind of moaning, yet very happy, and right then, when Strunk made that high happy moaning sound, when he went *Ahhooooo*, right then Ted Lavender was shot in the head on his way back from peeing. He lay with his mouth open. The teeth were broken. There was a swollen black bruise under his left eye. The cheekbone was gone. Oh shit, Rat Kiley said, the guy's dead. The guy's dead, he kept saying, which seemed profound—the guy's dead. I mean really.

The things they carried were determined to some extent by superstition. Lieutenant Cross carried his good-luck pebble. Dave Jensen carried a rabbit's foot. Norman Bowker, otherwise a very gentle person, carried a thumb that had been presented to him as a gift by Mitchell Sanders. The thumb was dark brown, rubbery to the touch, and weighed four ounces at most. It had been cut from a VC corpse, a boy of fifteen or sixteen. They'd found him at the bottom of an irrigation ditch, badly burned, flies in his mouth and eyes. The boy wore black shorts and sandals. At the time of his death he had been carrying a pouch of rice, a rifle and three magazines of ammunition.

You want my opinion, Mitchell Sanders said, there's a definite moral here.

30     He put his hand on the dead boy's wrist. He was quiet for a time, as if counting a pulse, then he patted the stomach, almost affectionately, and used Kiowa's hunting hatchet to remove the thumb.

Henry Dobbins asked what the moral was.

Moral?

You know. *Moral.*

Sanders wrapped the thumb in toilet paper and handed it across to Norman Bowker. There was no blood. Smiling, he kicked the boy's head, watched the flies scatter, and said, It's like with that old TV show—Paladin. Have gun, will travel.

35     Henry Dobbins thought about it.

Yeah, well, he finally said. I don't see no moral.

There it *is*, man.

Fuck off.

They carried USO stationery and pencils and pens. They carried Sterno, safety pins, trip flares, signal flares, spools of wire, razor blades, chewing tobacco, liberated joss sticks and statuettes of the smiling Buddha, candles, grease pencils, *The Stars and Stripes*, fingernail clippers, Psy Ops leaflets, bush hats, bolos, and much more. Twice a week, when the resupply choppers came in, they carried hot chow in green mermite cans and large canvas bags filled with iced beer and soda pop. They carried plastic water containers, each with a two-gallon capacity. Mitchell Sanders carried a set of starched tiger fatigues for special occasions. Henry Dobbins carried Black Flag insecticide. Dave Jensen carried empty sandbags that could be filled at night for added protection. Lee Strunk carried tanning lotion. Some things they carried in common. Taking turns, they carried the big PRC-77 scrambler radio, which weighed 30 pounds with its battery. They shared the weight of memory. They took up what others could no longer bear. Often, they carried each other, the wounded or weak. They carried infections. They carried chess sets, basketballs, Vietnamese-English dictionaries, insignia of rank, Bronze Stars and Purple Hearts, plastic cards imprinted with the Code of Conduct. They carried diseases, among them malaria and dysentery. They carried lice and ringworm and leeches and paddy algae and various rots and molds. They carried the land itself—Vietnam, the place, the soil—a powdery orange-red dust that covered their boots and fatigues and faces. They carried the sky. The whole atmosphere, they carried it, the humidity, the monsoons, the stink of fungus and decay, all of it, they carried gravity. They moved like mules. By daylight they took sniper fire, at night they were mortared, but it was not battle, it was just the endless march, village to village, without purpose, nothing won or lost. They marched for the sake of the march. They plodded along slowly, dumbly, leaning forward against the heat, unthinking, all blood and bone, simple grunts, soldiering with their legs, toiling up the hills and down into the paddies and across the rivers and up again and down, just humping, one step and then the next and then another, but no volition, no will, because it was automatic, it was anatomy, and the war was entirely a matter of posture and carriage, the hump was everything, a kind of inertia, a kind of emptiness, a dullness of desire and intellect and conscience and hope and human sensibility. Their principles were in their feet. Their calculations were biological. They had no sense of strategy or mission. They searched the villages without knowing what to look for, not caring, kicking over jars of rice, frisking children and old men, blowing tunnels, sometimes setting fires and sometimes not, then forming up and moving on to the next village, then other villages, where it would always be the same. They carried their own lives. The pressures were enormous. In the heat of early afternoon, they would remove their helmets and flak jackets, walking bare, which was dangerous but which helped ease the strain. They would often discard things along the route of march. Purely for comfort, they would throw away rations, blow their Claymores and grenades, no matter, because by nightfall the resupply choppers would arrive with more of the same, then a day or two later still more, fresh watermelons and crates of ammunition and sunglasses and woolen sweaters—the resources were stunning—sparklers for the Fourth of July, colored eggs for Easter—it was the great American war chest—the fruits of science, the smokestacks, the canneries, the arsenals at Hartford, the Minnesota forests, the machine shops, the vast fields of corn and wheat—they carried like freight trains; they carried it on their backs and shoulders—and for all the ambiguities of Vietnam, all the mysteries and unknowns, there was at least the single abiding certainty that they would never be at a loss for things to carry.

After the chopper took Lavender away, Lieutenant Jimmy Cross led his men into the village 40 of Than Khe. They burned everything. They shot chickens and dogs, they trashed the village well, they called in artillery and watched the wreckage, then they marched for several hours through the hot afternoon, and then at dusk, while Kiowa explained how Lavender died, Lieutenant Cross found himself trembling.

He tried not to cry. With his entrenching tool, which weighed five pounds, he began digging a hole in the earth.

He felt shame. He hated himself. He had loved Martha more than his men, and as a consequence Lavender was now dead, and this was something he would have to carry like a stone in his stomach for the rest of the war.

All he could do was dig. He used his entrenching tool like an ax, slashing, feeling both love and hate, and then later, when it was full dark, he sat at the bottom of his foxhole and wept. It went on for a long while. In part, he was grieving for Ted Lavender, but mostly it was for Martha, and for himself, because she belonged to another world, which was not quite real, and because she was a junior at Mount Sebastian College in New Jersey, a poet and a virgin and uninvolved, and because he realized she did not love him and never would.

Like cement, Kiowa whispered in the dark. I swear to God—boom, down. Not a word.

45    I've heard this, said Norman Bowker.

A pisser, you know? Still zipping himself up. Zapped while zipping.

All right, fine. That's enough.

Yeah, but you had to see it, the guy just—

I *heard*, man. Cement. So why not shut the fuck *up*?

50    Kiowa shook his head sadly and glanced over at the hole where Lieutenant Jimmy Cross sat watching the night. The air was thick and wet. A warm dense fog had settled over the paddies and there was the stillness that precedes rain.

After a time Kiowa sighed.

One thing for sure, he said. The lieutenant's in some deep hurt. I mean that crying jag—the way he was carrying on—it wasn't fake or anything, it was real heavy-duty hurt. The man cares.

Sure, Norman Bowker said.

Say what you want, the man does care.

55    We all got problems.

Not Lavender.

No, I guess not, Bowker said. Do me a favor, though.

Shut up?

That's a smart Indian. Shut up.

60    Shrugging, Kiowa pulled off his boots. He wanted to say more, just to lighten up his sleep, but instead he opened his New Testament and arranged it beneath his head as a pillow. The fog made things seem hollow and unattached. He tried not to think about Ted Lavender, but then he was thinking how fast it was, no drama, down and dead, and how it was hard to feel anything except surprise. It seemed unchristian. He wished he could find some great sadness, or even anger, but the emotion wasn't there and he couldn't make it happen. Mostly he felt pleased to be alive. He liked the smell of the New Testament under his cheek, the leather and ink and paper and glue, whatever the chemicals were. He liked hearing the sounds of night. Even his fatigue, it felt fine, the stiff muscles and the prickly awareness of his own body, a floating feeling. He enjoyed not being dead. Lying there, Kiowa admired Lieutenant Jimmy Cross's capacity for grief. He wanted to share the man's pain, he wanted to care as Jimmy Cross cared. And yet when he closed his eyes, all he could think was Boom-down, and all he could feel was the pleasure of having his boots off and the fog curling in around him and the damp soil and the Bible smells and the plush comfort of night.

After a moment Norman Bowker sat up in the dark.

What the hell, he said. You want to talk, *talk*. Tell it to me.

Forget it.

No, man, go on. One thing I hate, it's a silent Indian.

For the most part they carried themselves with poise, a kind of dignity. Now and then, however, there were times of panic, when they squealed or wanted to squeal but couldn't, when they twitched and made moaning sounds and covered their heads and said Dear Jesus and flopped around on the earth and fired their weapons blindly and cringed and sobbed and begged for the noise to stop and went wild and made stupid promises to themselves and to God and to their mothers and fathers, hoping not to die. In different ways, it happened to all of them. Afterward, when the firing ended, they would blink and peek up. They would touch their bodies, feeling shame, then quickly hiding it. They would force themselves to stand. As if in slow motion, frame by frame, the world would take on the old logic—absolute silence, then the wind, then sunlight, then voices. It was the burden of being alive. Awkwardly, the men would reassemble themselves, first in private, then in groups, becoming soldiers again. They would repair the leaks in their eyes. They would check for casualties, call in dust-offs, light cigarettes, try to smile, clear their throats and spit and begin cleaning their weapons. After a time someone would shake his head and say, No lie. I almost shit my pants, and someone else would laugh, which meant it was bad, yes, but the guy had obviously not shit his pants, it wasn't that bad, and in any case nobody would ever do such a thing and then go ahead and talk about it. They would squint into the dense, oppressive sunlight. For a few moments, perhaps, they would fall silent, lighting a joint and tracking its passage from man to man, inhaling, holding in the humiliation. Scary stuff, one of them might say. But then someone else would grin or flick his eyebrows and say, Roger-dodger, almost cut me a new asshole, *almost.*

There were numerous such poses. Some carried themselves with a sort of wistful resignation, others with pride or stiff soldierly discipline or good humor or macho zeal. They were afraid of dying but they were even more afraid to show it.

They found jokes to tell.

They used a hard vocabulary to contain the terrible softness. *Greased* they'd say. *Offed, lit up, zapped while zipping.* It wasn't cruelty, just stage presence. They were actors. When someone died, it wasn't quite dying, because in a curious way it seemed scripted, and because they had their lines mostly memorized, irony mixed with tragedy, and because they called it by other names, as if to encyst and destroy the reality of death itself. They kicked corpses. They cut off thumbs. They talked grunt lingo. They told stories about Ted Lavender's supply of tranquilizers, how the poor guy didn't feel a thing, how incredibly tranquil he was.

There's a moral here, said Mitchell Sanders.

They were waiting for Lavender's chopper, smoking the dead man's dope.

The moral's pretty obvious, Sanders said, and winked. Stay away from drugs. No joke, they'll ruin your day every time.

Cute, said Henry Dobbins.

Mind blower, get it? Talk about wiggy. Nothing left, just blood and brains.

They made themselves laugh.

There it is, they'd say. Over and over—there it is, my friend, there it is—as if the repetition itself were an act of poise, a balance between crazy and almost crazy, knowing without going, there it is, which meant be cool, let it ride, because Oh yeah, man, you can't change what can't be changed, there it is, there it absolutely and positively and fucking well *is.*

They were tough.

They carried all the emotional baggage of men who might die. Grief, terror, love, longing—these were intangibles, but the intangibles had their own mass and specific gravity, they had tangible weight. They carried shameful memories. They carried the common secret of cowardice barely restrained, the instinct to run or freeze or hide, and in many respects this was the heaviest burden of all, for it could never be put down, it required perfect balance and perfect posture. They carried their reputations. They carried the soldier's greatest fear, which was the fear of blushing. Men killed, and died, because they were embarrassed not to. It was what had brought them to the war in the first place, nothing positive, no dreams of glory or honor, just to avoid the blush of dishonor. They died so as not to die of embarrassment. They crawled into tunnels and walked point and advanced under fire. Each morning, despite the unknowns, they made their legs move. They endured. They kept humping. They did not submit to the obvious alternative, which was simply to close the eyes and fall. So easy, really. Go limp and tumble to the ground and let the muscles unwind and not speak and not budge until your buddies picked you up and lifted you into the chopper that would roar and dip its nose and carry you off to the world. A mere matter of falling, yet no one ever fell. It was not courage, exactly; the object was not valor. Rather, they were too frightened to be cowards.

By and large they carried these things inside, maintaining the masks of composure. They sneered at sick call. They spoke bitterly about guys who had found release by shooting off their own toes or fingers. Pussies, they'd say. Candy-asses. It was fierce, mocking talk, with only a trace of envy or awe, but even so the image played itself out behind their eyes.

They imagined the muzzle against flesh. So easy: squeeze the trigger and blow away a toe. They imagined it. They imagined the quick, sweet pain, then the evacuation to Japan, then a hospital with warm beds and cute geisha nurses.

80     And they dreamed of freedom birds.

At night, on guard, staring into the dark, they were carried away by jumbo jets. They felt the rush of takeoff. *Gone!* they yelled. And then velocity—wings and engines—a smiling stewardess—but it was more than a plane, it was a real bird, a big sleek silver bird with feathers and talons and high screeching. They were flying. The weights fell off; there was nothing to bear. They laughed and held on tight, feeling the cold slap of wind and altitude, soaring, thinking *It's over, I'm gone!*—they were naked, they were light and free—it was all lightness, bright and fast and buoyant, light as light, a helium buzz in the brain, a giddy bubbling in the lungs as they were taken up over the clouds and the war, beyond duty, beyond gravity and mortification and global entanglements—*Sin loi!* they yelled. *I'm sorry, motherfuckers, but I'm out of it, I'm goofed, I'm on a space cruise, I'm gone!*—and it was a restful, unencumbered sensation, just riding the light waves, sailing that big silver freedom bird over the mountains and oceans, over America, over the farms and great sleeping cities and cemeteries and highways and the golden arches of McDonald's, it was flight, a kind of fleeing, a kind of falling, falling higher and higher, spinning off the edge of the earth and beyond the sun and through the vast, silent vacuum where there were no burdens and where everything weighed exactly nothing—*Gone!* they screamed. *I'm sorry but I'm gone!*—and so at night, not quite dreaming, they gave themselves over to lightness, they were carried, they were purely borne.

On the morning after Ted Lavender died, First Lieutenant Jimmy Cross crouched at the bottom of his foxhole and burned Martha's letters. Then he burned the two photographs. There was a steady rain falling, which made it difficult, but he used heat tabs and Sterno to build a small fire, screening it with his body, holding the photographs over the tight blue flame with the tips of his fingers.

He realized it was only a gesture. Stupid, he thought. Sentimental, too, but mostly just stupid.

Lavender was dead. You couldn't burn the blame.

85     Besides, the letters were in his head. And even now, without photographs, Lieutenant Cross could see Martha playing volleyball in her white gym shorts and yellow T-shirt. He could see her moving in the rain.

When the fire died out, Lieutenant Cross pulled his poncho over his shoulders and ate breakfast from a can.

There was no great mystery, he decided.

In those burned letters Martha had never mentioned the war, except to say, Jimmy, take care of yourself. She wasn't involved. She signed the letters Love, but it wasn't love, and all the fine lines and technicalities did not matter. Virginity was no longer an issue. He hated her. Yes, he did. He hated her. Love, too, but it was a hard, hating kind of love.

The morning came up wet and blurry. Everything seemed part of everything else, the fog and Martha and the deepening rain.

He was a soldier, after all.

Half smiling, Lieutenant Jimmy Cross took out his maps. He shook his head hard, as if to clear it, then bent forward and began planning the day's march. In ten minutes, or maybe twenty, he would rouse the men and they would pack up and head west, where the maps showed the country to be green and inviting. They would do what they had always done. The rain might add some weight, but otherwise it would be one more day layered upon all the other days.

He was realistic about it. There was that new hardness in his stomach. He loved her but he hated her.

No more fantasies, he told himself.

Henceforth, when he thought about Martha, it would be only to think that she belonged elsewhere. He would shut down the daydreams. This was not Mount Sebastian, it was another world, where there were no pretty poems or midterm exams, a place where men died because of carelessness and gross stupidity. Kiowa was right. Boom-down, and you were dead, never partly dead.

Briefly, in the rain, Lieutenant Cross saw Martha's gray eyes gazing back at him.

He understood.

It was very sad, he thought. The things men carried inside. The things men did or felt they had to do.

He almost nodded at her, but didn't.

Instead he went back to his maps. He was now determined to perform his duties firmly and without negligence. It wouldn't help Lavender, he knew that, but from this point on he would comport himself as an officer. He would dispose of his good-luck pebble. Swallow it, maybe, or use Lee Strunk's slingshot, or just drop it along the trail. On the march he would impose strict field discipline. He would be careful to send out flank security, to prevent straggling or bunching up, to keep his troops moving at the proper pace and at the proper interval. He would insist on clean weapons. He would confiscate the remainder of Lavender's dope. Later in the day, perhaps, he would call the men together and speak to them plainly. He would accept the blame for what had happened to Ted Lavender. He would be a man about it. He would look them in the eyes, keeping his chin level, and he would issue the new SOPs in a calm, impersonal tone of voice, a lieutenant's voice, leaving no room for argument or discussion. Commencing immediately, he'd tell them, they would no longer abandon equipment along the route of march. They would police up their acts. They would get their shit together, and keep it together, and maintain it neatly and in good working order.

He would not tolerate laxity. He would show strength, distancing himself.

Among the men there would be grumbling, of course, and maybe worse, because their days would seem longer and their loads heavier, but Lieutenant Jimmy Cross reminded himself that his obligation was not to be loved but to lead. He would dispense with love; it was not now a factor. And if anyone quarreled or complained, he would simply tighten his lips and arrange his shoulders in the correct command posture. He might give a curt little nod. Or he might not. He might just shrug and say, Carry on, then they would saddle up and form into a column and move out toward the villages west of Than Khe.

## Questions

1. What do we learn about Lieutenant Jimmy Cross? How do we learn about him? Why does he blame himself for Lavender's death? How does Kiowa misinterpret his emotions? How do his concerns unify the story? What other unifying elements does the story contain?

2. What is the effect of the repetitions in the story (the constant descriptions of how much things weigh, the regular need to carry things, the way in which Lavender died)?

3. Why is Mitchell Sanders unable to put into words the moral of the dead man's thumb? How would you describe the moral?

4. Analyze paragraph 39. Discuss the various burdens the men of the platoon must carry. What bearing does this paragraph have upon other parts of the story?

## LUIGI PIRANDELLO (1867–1936)

Pirandello was born in southern Sicily into a wealthy family. At first he was home schooled, but eventually went to high school in Palermo, the capital of Sicily. Later he attended the University of Palermo and the University of Rome, but then he went to Bonn, in Germany (the birth city of Beethoven), where he gained a Doctorate in liberal studies in 1891. His resources failed because of a disastrous flood in the family's Sicilian sulfur mine, and he was left mainly to his own resources as a teacher and writer. His marriage, which produced three children, proved disastrous as his wife eventually was declared insane and had to be institutionalized. Pirandello's early years were taken up mainly with the writing of stories and dramas. One of his three sons fought in the First World War, and survived, unlike the son in the story "War." Eventually Pirandello developed a masterly career as a dramatist, his best known and highly original play being *Six Characters in Search of an Author* in 1921. With the support of Benito Mussolini, the Prime Minister and Dictator of Italy—support that many claimed was highly controversial because of Mussolini's later alliance with Adolf Hitler—Pirandello became well known internationally. In 1934, he was awarded the Nobel Prize for Literature.

## 🐦 War (1919)

The passengers who had left Rome by the night express had had to stop until dawn at the small station of Fabriano in order to continue their journey by the small old-fashioned local joining the main line with Sulmona.

At dawn, in a stuffy and smoky second-class carriage in which five people had already spent the night, a bulky woman in deep mourning was hoisted in—almost like a shapeless bundle. Behind her, puffing and moaning, followed her husband—a tiny man, thin and weakly, his face death-white, his eyes small and bright and looking shy and uneasy.

Having at last taken a seat he politely thanked the passengers who had helped his wife and who had made room for her; then he turned round to the woman trying top down the collar of her coat, and politely inquired:

"Are you all right, dear?"

5   The wife, instead of answering, pulled up her collar again to her eyes, so as to hide her face.

"Nasty world," muttered the husband with a sad smile.

And he felt it his duty to explain to his traveling companions that the poor woman was to be pitied, for the war was taking away from her only son, a boy of twenty to whom both had devoted their entire life, even breaking up their home at Sulmona to follow him to Rome, where he had to go as a student, then allowing him to volunteer for war with an assurance, however, that at least for six months he would not be sent to the front and now, all of a sudden, receiving a wire saying that he was due to leave in three days' time and asking them to go and see him off.

The woman under the big coat was twisting and wriggling, at times growling like a wild animal, feeling certain that all those explanations would not have aroused even a shadow of sympathy from those people who—most likely—were in the same plight as herself. One of them, who had been listening with particular attention, said:

"You should thank God that your son is only leaving now for the front. Mine has been sent there the first day of the war. He has already come back twice wounded and been sent back again to the front."

"What about me? I have two sons and three nephews at the front," said another passenger.    10

"Maybe, but in our case it is our only son," ventured the husband.

"What difference can it make? You may spoil your only son with excessive attentions, but you cannot love him more than you would all your other children if you had any. Paternal love is not like bread that can be broken into pieces and split amongst the children in equal shares. A father gives all his love to each one of his children without discrimination, whether it be one or ten, and if I am suffering now for my two sons, I am not suffering half for each of them but double."

"True . . . true . . . " sighed the embarrassed husband, "but suppose (of course we all hope it will never be your case) a father has two sons at the front and he loses one of them, there is still one left to console him . . . while . . ."

"Yes," answered the other, getting cross, "a son left to console him but also a son left for whom he must survive, while in the case of the father of an only son if the son dies the father can die too and put an end to his distress. Which of the two positions is the worse? Don't you see how my case would be worse than yours?"

"Nonsense," interrupted another traveler, a fat, red-faced man with bloodshot eyes of the    15
palest gray.

He was panting. From his bulging eyes seemed to spurt inner violence of an uncontrolled vitality which his weakened body could hardly contain.

"Nonsense," he repeated, trying to cover his mouth with his hand so as to hide the two missing front teeth. "Nonsense. Do we give life to our children for our own benefit?"

The other travelers stared at him in distress. The one who had had his son at the front since the first day of the war sighed: "You are right. Our children do not belong to us, they belong to the Country. . . ."

"Bosh," retorted the fat traveler. "Do we think of the Country when we give life to our children? Our sons are born because . . . well, because they must be born and when they come to life they take our own life with them. This is the truth. We belong to them but they never belong to us. And when they reach twenty they are exactly what we were at their age. We too had a father and mother, but there were so many other things as well . . . girls, cigarettes, illusions, new ties . . . and the Country, of course, whose call we would have answered—when we were twenty—even if father and mother had said no. Now at our age, the love of our Country is still great, of course, but stronger than it is the love for our children. Is there any one of us here who wouldn't gladly take his son's place at the front if he could?"

There was a silence all round, everybody nodding as to approve.    20

"Why then," continued the fat man, "shouldn't we consider the feelings of our children when they are twenty? Isn't it natural that at their age they should consider the love for their Country (I am speaking of decent boys, of course) even greater than the love for us? Isn't it natural that it should be so, as after all they must look upon us as upon old boys who cannot move any more and must stay at home? If Country exists, if Country is a natural necessity, like bread, of which each of us must eat in order not to die of hunger, somebody must go to defend it. And our sons go, when they are twenty, and they don't want tears, because if they die, they die inflamed and happy (I am speaking, of course, of decent boys). Now, if one dies young and happy, without having the ugly sides of life, the boredom of it, the pettiness, the bitterness of disillusion . . . what more can we ask for him? Everyone should stop crying; everyone should laugh, as I do . . . or at least thank God—as I do—because my son, before dying, sent me a message saying that he was dying satisfied at having ended his life in the best way he could have wished. That is why, as you see, I do not even wear mourning. . . ."

He shook his light fawn coat as to show it; his livid lip over his missing teeth was trembling, his eyes were watery and motionless, and soon after he ended with a shrill laugh which might well have been a sob.

"Quite so . . . quite so . . ." agreed the others.

The woman who, bundled in a corner under her coat, had been sitting and listening had—for the last three months—tried to find in the words of her husband and her friends something to console her in her deep sorrow, something that might show her how a mother should resign herself to send her son not even to death but to a probably dangerous life. Yet not a word had she found amongst the many which had been said . . . and her grief had been greater in seeing that nobody—as she thought—could share her feelings.

25 But now the words of the traveler amazed and almost stunned her. She suddenly realized that it wasn't the others who were wrong and could not understand her, but herself who could not rise up to the same height of those fathers and mothers willing to resign themselves, without crying, not only to the departure of their sons but even to their death.

She lifted her head, she bent over from her corner trying to listen with great attention to the details which the fat man was giving to his companions about the way his son had fallen as a hero, for his King and his Country, happy and without regrets. It seemed to her that she had stumbled into a world she had never dreamt of, a world so far unknown to her and she was so pleased to hear everyone joining in congratulating that brave father who could so stoically speak of his child's death.

Then suddenly, just as if she had heard nothing of what had been said and almost as if waking up from a dream, she turned to the old man, asking him:

"Then . . . is your son really dead?"

Everybody stared at her. The old man, too, turned to look at her, fixing his great, bulging, horribly watery light gray eyes, deep in her face. For some little time he tried to answer, but words failed him. He looked and looked at her, almost as if only then—at that silly, incongruous question—he had suddenly realized at last that his son was really dead—gone forever—forever. His face contracted, became horribly distorted, then he snatched in haste a handkerchief from his pocket and, to the amazement of everyone, broke into harrowing, heart-rending, uncontrollable sobs.

## Questions

1. Explain the means by which Pirandello develops the narrative structure of the story. Why does he include so much conversation? What might the story be like if it had been carried out exclusively through description?

2. Describe the thoughts about death expressed by the "fat, red-faced man with bloodshot eyes." How does this man seem to be defending the need for battlefield deaths? How do his true thoughts emerge in the story? How does he seem to be contradictory?

3. What do you think is the story's major idea, as it develops in the discussion by the passengers? Why does Pirandello choose the man who seems least appealing as the one to whom the ultimate sacrifice has happened?

**4.** In paragraph 28, why does the woman who is "bundled in a corner under her coat" ask the simple question of the fat man? Why is it she who asks the question, and not one of the other passengers?

## EUDORA WELTY° (1909–2001)

One of the major Southern writers, Welty was born in Jackson, Mississippi. She attended the Mississippi State College for Women and the University of Wisconsin, and she began her writing career during the Great Depression. By 1943 she had published two major story collections, *Curtain of Green* (1941, including "A Worn Path") and *The Wide Net* (1943). She is the author of many stories and was awarded the Pulitzer Prize in 1973 for her short novel *The Optimist's Daughter* (1972). "A Worn Path" received an O. Henry Award in 1941.

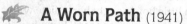

## A Worn Path (1941)

It was December—a bright frozen day in the early morning. Far out in the country there was an old Negro woman with her head tied in a red rag, coming along a path through the pinewoods. Her name was Phoenix Jackson. She was very old and small and she walked slowly in the dark pine shadows, moving a little from side to side in her steps, with the balanced heaviness and lightness of a pendulum in a grandfather clock. She carried a thin, small cane made from an umbrella, and with this she kept tapping the frozen earth in front of her. This made a grave and persistent noise in the still air, that seemed meditative like the chirping of a solitary little bird.

She wore a dark striped dress reaching down to her shoe tops, and an equally long apron of bleached sugar sacks, with a full pocket: all neat and tidy, but every time she took a step she might have fallen over her shoelaces, which dragged from her unlaced shoes. She looked straight ahead. Her eyes were blue with age. Her skin had a pattern all its own of numberless branching wrinkles and as though a whole little tree stood in the middle of her forehead, but a golden color ran underneath, and the two knobs of her cheeks were illuminated by a yellow burning under the dark. Under the rag her hair came down on her neck in the frailest of ringlets, still black, and with an odor like copper.

Now and then there was a quivering in the thicket. Old Phoenix said, "Out of my way, all you foxes, owls, beetles, jack rabbits, coons and wild animals! . . . Keep out from under these feet, little bob-whites. . . . Keep the big wild hogs out of my path. Don't let none of those come running my direction. I got a long way." Under her small black-freckled hand her cane, limber as a buggy whip, would switch at the brush as if to rouse up any hiding things.

On she went. The woods were deep and still. The sun made the pine needles almost too bright to look at, up where the wind rocked. The cones dropped as light as feathers. Down in the hollow was the mourning dove—it was not too late for him.

---

The path ran up a hill. "Seem like there is chains about my feet, time I get this far," she
said, in the voice of argument old people keep to use with themselves. "Something always
take a hold of me on this hill—pleads I should stay."

After she got to the top she turned and gave a full, severe look behind her where she had
come. "Up through pines," she said at length. "Now down through oaks."

Her eyes opened their widest, and she started down gently. But before she got to the bottom of the hill a bush caught her dress.

Her fingers were busy and intent, but her skirts were full and long, so that before she
could pull them free in one place they were caught in another. It was not possible to allow the
dress to tear. "I in the thorny bush," she said. "Thorns, you doing your appointed work. Never
want to let folks pass, no sir. Old eyes thought you was a pretty little *green* bush."

Finally, trembling all over, she stood free, and after a moment dared to stoop for her cane.

"Sun so high!" she cried, leaning back and looking, while the thick tears went over her
eyes. "The time getting all gone here."

At the foot of this hill was a place where a log was laid across the creek.

"Now comes the trial," said Phoenix.

Putting her right foot out, she mounted the log and shut her eyes. Lifting her skirt, level-
ing her cane fiercely before her, like a festival figure in some parade, she began to march
across. Then she opened her eyes and she was safe on the other side.

"I wasn't as old as I thought," she said.

But she sat down to rest. She spread her skirts on the bank around her and folded her
hands over her knees. Up above her was a tree in a pearly cloud of mistletoe. She did not dare
to close her eyes, and when a little boy brought her a plate with a slice of marble-cake on it she
spoke to him. "That would be acceptable," she said. But when she went to take it there was just
her own hand in the air.

So she left that tree, and had to go through a barbed-wire fence. There she had to creep
and crawl, spreading her knees and stretching her fingers like a baby trying to climb the
steps. But she talked loudly to herself: she could not let her dress be torn now, so late in
the day, and she could not pay for having her arm or leg sawed off if she got caught fast
where she was.

At last she was safe through the fence and risen up out in the clearing. Big dead trees, like
black men with one arm, were standing in the purple stalks of the withered cotton field. There
sat a buzzard.

"Who you watching?"

In the furrow she made her way along.

"Glad this is not the season for bulls," she said, looking sideways, "and the good Lord made
his snakes to curl up and sleep in the winter. A pleasure I don't see no two-headed snake coming
around that tree, where it come once. It took a while to get by him, back in the summer."

She passed through the old cotton and went into a field of dead corn. It whispered and
shook and was taller than her head. "Through the maze now," she said, for there was no
path.

Then there was something tall, black, and skinny there, moving before her.

At first she took it for a man. It could have been a man dancing in the field. But she stood
still and listened, and it did not make a sound. It was as silent as a ghost.

"Ghost," she said sharply, "who be you the ghost of? For I have heard of nary death close by."

But there was no answer—only the ragged dancing in the wind.

She shut her eyes, reached out her hand, and touched a sleeve. She found a coat and inside that an emptiness, cold as ice.

"You scarecrow," she said. Her face lighted. "I ought to be shut up for good," she said
with laughter. "My senses is gone. I too old, I the oldest people I ever know. Dance, old scarecrow," she said, "while I dancing with you."

She kicked her foot over the furrow, and with mouth drawn down, shook her head once or twice in a little strutting way. Some husks blew down and whirled in steamers about her skirts.

Then she went on, parting her way from side to side with the cane, through the whispering field. At last she came to the end, to a wagon track where the silver grass blew between the red ruts. The quail were walking around like pullets, seeming all dainty and unseen.

"Walk pretty," she said. "This is the easy place. This the easy going."                          30

She followed the track, swaying through the quiet bare fields, through the little strings of trees silver in their dead leaves, past cabins silver from weather, with the doors and windows boarded shut, all like old women under a spell sitting there. "I walking in their sleep," she said, nodding her head vigorously.

In a ravine she went where a spring was silently flowing through a hollow log. Old Phoenix bent and drank. "Sweet-gum makes the water sweet," she said, and drank more. "Nobody know who made this well, for it was here when I was born."

The track crossed a swampy part where the moss hung as white as lace from every limb. "Sleep on, alligators, and blow your bubbles." Then the track went into the road.

Deep, deep the road went down between the high green-colored banks. Overhead the live-oaks met, and it was as dark as a cave.

A black dog with a lolling tongue came up out of the weeds by the ditch. She was medi-  35 tating, and not ready, and when he came at her she only hit him a little with her cane. Over she went in the ditch, like a little puff of milkweed.

Down there, her sense drifted away. A dream visited her, and she reached her hand up, but nothing reached down and gave her a pull. So she lay there and presently went to talking. "Old woman," she said to herself, "that black dog come up out of the weeds to stall you off, and now there he sitting on his fine tail smiling at you."

A white man finally came along and found her—a hunter, a young man, with his dog on a chain.

"Well, Granny!" he laughed. "What are you doing there?"

"Lying on my back like a June-bug waiting to be turned over, mister," she said, reaching up her hand.

He lifted her up, gave her a swing in the air, and set her down. "Anything broken, Granny?"  40

"No sir, them old dead weeds is springy enough," said Phoenix, when she had got her breath. "I thank you for your trouble."

"Where do you live, Granny?" he asked, while the two dogs were growling at each other.

"Away back yonder, sir, behind the ridge. You can't even see it from here."

"On your way home?"

"No sir, I goin to town."                                                                         45

"Why, that's too far! That's as far as I walk when I come out myself, and I get something for my trouble." He patted the stuffed bag he carried, and there hung down a little closed claw. It was one of the bob-whites, with its beak hooked bitterly to show it was dead. "Now you go on home, Granny!"

"I bound to go to town, mister," said Phoenix. "The time come around."

He gave another laugh, filling the whole landscape. "I know you old colored people! Wouldn't miss going to town to see Santa Claus!"

But something held old Phoenix very still. The deep lines in her face went into a fierce and different radiation. Without warning, she had seen with her own eyes a flashing nickel fall out of the man's pocket onto the ground.

"How old are you, Granny?" he was saying.                                                        50

"There is no telling, mister," she said, "no telling."

Then she gave a little cry and clapped her hands and said, "Git on away from here, dog! Look! Look at that dog!" She laughed as if in admiration. "He ain't scared of nobody. He a big black dog." She whispered, "Sic him!"

"Watch me get rid of that cur," said the man. "Sic him, Pete! Sic him!"

Phoenix heard the dogs fighting, and heard the man running and throwing sticks. She even heard a gunshot. But she was slowly bending forward by that time, further and further forward, the lids stretched down over her eyes, as if she were doing this in her sleep. Her chin was lowered almost to her knees. The yellow palm of her hand came out from the fold of her apron. Her fingers slid down and along the ground under the piece of money with the grace and care they would have in lifting an egg from under a setting hen. Then she slowly straightened up, she stood erect, and the nickel was in her apron pocket. A bird flew by. Her lips moved. "God watching me the whole time. I come to stealing."

55 The man came back, and his own dog panted about them. "Well, I scared him off that time," he said, and then he laughed and lifted his gun and pointed it at Phoenix.

She stood straight and faced him.

"Doesn't the gun scare you?" he said, still pointing it.

"No sir. I seen plenty go off closer by, in my day, and for less than what I done," she said, holding utterly still.

He smiled, and shouldered the gun. "Well, Granny," he said, "you must be a hundred years old, and scared of nothing. I'd give you a dime if I had any money with me. But you take my advice and stay home, and nothing will happen to you."

60 "I bound to go on my way, mister," said Phoenix. She inclined her head in the red rag. Then they went in different directions, but she could hear the gun shooting again and again over the hill.

She walked on. The shadows hung from the oak trees to the road like curtains. Then she smelled wood-smoke, and smelled the river, and she saw a steeple and the cabins on their steep steps. Dozens of little black children whirled around her. There ahead was Natchez shining. Bells were ringing. She walked on.

In the paved city it was Christmas time. There were red and green electric lights strung and crisscrossed everywhere, and all turned on in the daytime. Old Phoenix would have been lost if she had not distrusted her eyesight and depended on her feet to know where to take her.

She paused quietly on the sidewalk where people were passing by. A lady came along in the crowd, carrying an armful of red-, green-, and silver-wrapped presents; she gave off perfume like the red roses in hot summer, and Phoenix stopped her.

"Please, missy, will you lace up my shoe?" She held up her foot.

65 "What do you want, Grandma?"

"See my shoe," said Phoenix. "Do all right for out in the country, but wouldn't look right to go in a big building."

"Stand still then, Grandma," said the lady. She put her packages down on the sidewalk beside her and laced and tied both shoes tightly.

"Can't lace 'em with a cane," said Phoenix. "Thank you, missy. I doesn't mind asking a nice lady to tie up my shoe, when I gets out on the street."

Moving slowly and from side to side, she went into the big building, and into a tower of steps, where she walked up and around and around until her feet knew to stop.

70 She entered a door, and there she saw nailed up on the wall the document that had been stamped with the gold seal and framed in the gold frame, which matched the dream that was hung up in her head.

"Here I be," she said. There was a fixed and ceremonial stiffness over her body.

"A charity case, I suppose," said an attendant who sat at the desk before her.

But Phoenix only looked above her head. There was sweat on her face, the wrinkles in her skin shone like a bright net.

"Speak up, Grandma," the woman said, "What's your name? We must have your history, you know. Have you been here before? What seems to be the trouble with you?"

Old Phoenix only gave a twitch to her face as if a fly were bothering her.    75

"Are you deaf?" cried the attendant.

But then the nurse came in.

"Oh, that's just old Aunt Phoenix," she said. "She doesn't come for herself—she has a little grandson. She makes these trips just as regular as clockwork. She lives away back off the Old Natchez Trace." She bent down. "Well, Aunt Phoenix, why don't you just take a seat? We won't keep you standing after your long trip." She pointed.

The old woman sat down, bolt upright in the chair.

"Now, how is the boy?" asked the nurse.    80

Old Phoenix did not speak.

"I said, how is the boy?"

But Phoenix only waited and stared straight ahead, her face very solemn and withdrawn into rigidity.

"Is his throat any better?" asked the nurse. "Aunt Phoenix, don't you hear me? Is your grandson's throat any better since the last time you came for the medicine?"

With her hands on her knees, the old woman waited, silent, erect, and motionless, just as    85
if she were in armor.

"You mustn't take up our time this way, Aunt Phoenix," the nurse said. "Tell us quickly about your grandson, and get it over. He isn't dead, is he?"

At last there came a flicker and then a flame of comprehension across her face, and she spoke.

"My grandson. It was my memory had left me. There I sat and forgot why I made my long trip."

"Forgot?" the nurse frowned. "After you came so far?"

Then Phoenix was like an old woman begging a dignified forgiveness for waking up    90
frightened in the night. "I never did go to school, I was too old at the Surrender," she said in a soft voice. "I'm an old woman without an education. It was my memory fail me. My little grandson, he is just the same, and I forgot it in the coming."

"Throat never heals, does it?" said the nurse, speaking in a loud, sure voice to old Phoenix. By now she had a card with something written on it, a little list. "Yes. Swallowed lye. When was it—January—two, three years ago—"

Phoenix spoke unasked now. "No missy, he not dead, he just the same. Every little while his throat begin to close up again, and he not able to swallow. He not get his breath. He not able to help himself. So the time come around, and I go on another trip for the soothing medicine."

"All right. The doctor said as long as you came to get it, you could have it," said the nurse. "But it's an obstinate case."

"My little grandson, he sit up there in the house all wrapped up, waiting by himself," Phoenix went on. "We is the only two left in the world. He suffer and it don't seem to put him back at all. He got a sweet look. He going to last. He wear a little patch quilt and peep out holding his mouth open like a little bird. I remembers so plain now. I not going to forget him again, no, the whole enduring time. I could tell him from all the others in creation."

"All right." The nurse was trying to hush her now. She brought her a bottle of medicine.    95
"Charity," she said, making a check mark in a book.

Old Phoenix held the bottle close to her eyes, and then carefully put it into her pocket.

"I thank you," she said.

"It's Christmas time, Grandma," said the attendant. "Could I give you a few pennies out of my purse?"

"Five pennies is a nickel," said Phoenix stiffly.

"Here's a nickel," said the attendant.

Phoenix rose carefully and held out her hand. She received the nickel and then fished the other nickel out of her pocket and laid it beside the new one. She stared at her palm closely, with her head on one side.

Then she gave a tap with her cane on the floor.

"This is what come to me to do," she said, "I going to the store and buy my child a little windmill they sells, made out of paper. He going to find it hard to believe there such a thing in the world. I'll march myself back where he waiting, holding it straight up in this hand."

She lifted her free hand, gave a little nod, turned around, and walked out of the doctor's office. Then her slow step began on the stairs, going down.

## Questions

1. From the description of Phoenix, what do you conclude about her economic condition? How do you know that she has taken the path through the woods before? Is she accustomed to being alone? What do you make of her speaking to animals, and of her imagining a boy offering her a piece of cake? What does her speech show about her education and background?

2. Describe the plot of the story. With Phoenix as the protagonist, what are the obstacles ranged against her? How might Phoenix be considered to be in the grip of large and indifferent social and political forces?

3. Comment on the meaning of this dialogue between Phoenix and the hunter:

   "Doesn't the gun scare you?" he said, still pointing it.
   "No, sir. I seen plenty go off closer by, in my day, and for less than what
   I done," she said, holding utterly still.

4. A number of responses might be made to this story, among them admiration for Phoenix, pity for her and her grandson and for the downtrodden generally, anger at her impoverished condition, and apprehension about her approaching senility. Do you share in any of these responses? Do you have any others?

## Plot: The Motivation and Causality of Fiction

Stories are made up mostly of **actions** or **incidents** that follow one another in chronological order. The same is also true of life, but there is a major difference, and that is that fiction must make sense even though life itself does not always seem to be rational. Finding a sequential or narrative order is therefore only a first step in our consideration of fiction. What we depend on for the sense or meaning of fiction is **plot**, or the elements governing the unfolding of the actions.

The English novelist E. M. Forster, in *Aspects of the Novel*, presents a memorable illustration of plot. To illustrate a bare set of actions, he proposes the following: "The king died, and then the queen died." Forster points out, however, that this sequence does not form a plot because it lacks *motivation* and *causation*; it's too much like life itself to be fictional. Thus he introduces motivation and causation in his next example: "The king died, and then the queen died of grief." The phrase "of grief" shows that one thing (grief) controls or overcomes another (the normal desire to live), and motivation and causation enter the sequence to form a plot. In a well-plotted story or play, one thing precedes or follows another not simply because time ticks away, but more importantly because *effects* follow *causes*. In a good work of fiction, nothing is irrelevant or accidental; everything is related and causative.

## Determining the Conflicts in a Story

The controlling impulse in a connected pattern of causes and effects is **conflict**, which refers to people or circumstances that a character must face and try to overcome. Conflicts bring out extremes of human energy, causing characters to engage in the decisions, actions, responses, and interactions that make up fictional literature.

In its most elemental form, a conflict is the opposition of two people. Their conflict may take the shape of anger, hatred, envy, argument, avoidance, political or moral opposition, gossip, lies, fighting, and many other actions and attitudes. Conflicts may also exist between groups, although conflicts between individuals are more identifiable and therefore more suitable for stories. Conflicts may also be abstract, such as when an individual opposes larger forces such as natural objects, ideas, modes of behavior, or public opinion. A difficult or even impossible *choice*—a **dilemma**—is a natural conflict for an individual person. A conflict may also be brought out in ideas and opinions that clash. In short, conflict shows itself in many ways.

**CONFLICT IS DIRECTLY RELATED TO DOUBT, TENSION, AND INTEREST.**    Conflict is the major element of plot because opposing forces arouse *curiosity*, cause *doubt*, create *tension*, and produce *interest*. The same responses are the lifeblood of athletic competition. Consider which kind of athletic event is more interesting: (1) One team gets so far ahead that the outcome is no longer in doubt, or (2) both teams are so evenly matched that the outcome is uncertain until the final seconds. Obviously, games are uninteresting—as games—unless they develop as contests between teams of comparable strength. The same principle applies to conflicts in stories and dramas. There should be uncertainty about a protagonist's success or failure. Unless there is doubt, there is no tension, and without tension there is no interest.

**FINDING THE CONFLICTS TO DETERMINE THE PLOT.**    To see a plot in operation, let us build on Forster's description. Here is a simple plot for a story of our own: "John and Jane meet, fall in love, and get married." This sentence contains a plot because it shows cause and effect (they get married *because* they fall in love), but with no conflict, the plot is not interesting. However, let us introduce conflicting elements into this common "boy meets girl" story:

John and Jane meet in college and fall in love. They go together for a number of years and plan to marry, but a problem arises. Jane first wants to establish herself in a career, and after marriage she wants to be an equal financial contributor to the family. John understands Jane's wishes for equality, but he wants to get married first and let her finish her studies and have her career after they have children. Jane believes that John's plan is unacceptable because she thinks of it as a trap from which she might not escape. As they discuss their options they find themselves increasingly more irritated and unhappy with each other. Finally, they bring their plans to an end, and they part in anger and sorrow. Their love is not dead, but both go on to marry someone else and build separate lives and careers. In their new lives, neither is totally happy even though they like and respect their spouses. The years pass, and, after children and grandchildren, Jane and John meet again. He is now divorced, and she is a widow. Because their earlier conflict is no longer a barrier, they rekindle their love, marry, and try to make up for the past. Even their new happiness, however, is tinged with regret and reproach because of their earlier conflicts, their unhappy decision to part, their lost years, and their increasing age.

Here we find a true plot because our original "boy meets girl" topic now contains a major conflict from which a number of related complications develop. These complications embody disagreements, choices, arguments, and ill feelings that produce tension, uncertainty, rupture, and regret. When we learn that John and Jane finally join together at the end we might still find the story painful to contemplate because it does not give us a "happily ever after" ending. Nevertheless, the story makes sense—as a story—because its plot brings out the plausible consequences of the understandable aims and hopes of John and Jane during their long relationship. It is the imposition of necessary causes and effects upon a series of events in time that creates the story's plot.

# Writing About Plot

An essay about plot is an analysis of the story's conflict and its developments. The organization of your essay should not be modeled on sequential sections and principal events, however, because these invite only a retelling of the story. Instead, the organization is to be developed from the important elements of conflict. As you look for ideas about plot, try to answer the following questions.

## Questions for Discovering Ideas

- Who are the major and minor characters, and how do their characteristics put them in conflict? How can you describe the conflict or conflicts?
- How does the story's action grow out of the major conflict?
- If the conflict stems from contrasting ideas or values, what are these, and how are they brought out?
- What problems do the major characters face? How do the characters deal with these problems?
- How do the major characters achieve (or not achieve) their major goal(s)? What obstacles do they overcome? What obstacles overcome them or alter them?
- At the end, are the characters successful or unsuccessful, happy or unhappy, satisfied or dissatisfied, changed or unchanged, enlightened or ignorant? How has the resolution of the major conflict produced these results?

## Strategies for Organizing Ideas

To keep your essay brief, you need to be selective. Rather than detailing everything a character does, for example, stress the major elements in his or her conflict. Such an essay on Eudora Welty's "A Worn Path" might emphasize Phoenix as she encounters the various obstacles both in the woods and in town. When there is a conflict between two major characters, the obvious approach is to focus equally on both. For brevity, however, emphasis might be placed on just one. Thus, an essay on the plot of "A Rose for Emily" might stress the details about Emily's life that make her the central participant in the story's conflict.

In addition, the plot may be analyzed more broadly in terms of impulses, goals, values, issues, and historical perspectives. Thus, you might emphasize the elements of chance working against Mathilde in Maupassant's "The Necklace" (Chapter 1) as a contrast to her dreams about wealth. A discussion of the plot of Poe's "The Masque of the Red Death" (Chapter 5) might stress the haughtiness of Prospero, the major character, because the plot could not develop without his egotism.

The conclusion may contain a brief summary of the points you have made. It is also a fitting location for a brief consideration of the effect or *impact* produced by the conflict. Additional ideas might focus on whether the author has arranged actions and dialogue to direct your favor toward one side or the other, or whether the plot is possible or impossible, serious or comic, fair or unfair, powerful or indifferent, and so on.

## Illustrative Student Essay

Underlined sentences in this paper *do not* conform to MLA style and are used solely as teaching tools to emphasize the central idea, thesis sentence, and topic sentences throughout the paper.

Getty 1

Beth Getty

Professor Farmer

English 214

12 March 2007

### The Plot of Eudora Welty's "A Worn Path" °

[1]      At first, the complexity of Eudora Welty's plot in "A Worn Path" is not clear. The main character is Phoenix Jackson, an old, poor, and frail woman; the story seems to be no more than a record of her walk to Natchez through the woods from her rural home. By the story's end, however, the plot is clear: <u>It consists of the brave attempts of a courageous, valiant woman to carry on against overwhelming forces.</u>* Her

---

° See page 95 for this story.

* Central idea.

Getty 2

determination despite the great odds against her gives the story its impact. <u>The powers ranged against her are old age, poverty, environment, and illness.</u>[†]

[2]     <u>Old age as a silent but overpowering antagonist is shown in signs of Phoenix's increasing senility.</u> Not her mind but her feet tell her where to find the medical office in Natchez. Despite her inner strength, she is unable to explain her errand when the nursing attendant asks her. Instead she sits dumbly and unknowingly for a time, until "a flame of comprehension" comes across her face (paragraph 87, p. 99). Against the power of advancing age, Phoenix is slowly losing. The implication is that soon she will lose entirely.

[3]     <u>An equally crushing opponent is her poverty.</u> She cannot afford to ride to town, but must walk. She has no money, and acquires her ten cents for the paper windmill by stealing and begging. The "soothing medicine" she gets for her grandson (paragraph 92, p. 99) is given to her out of charity. Despite the boy's need for advanced medical care, she has no money to provide it, and the story therefore shows that her guardianship is doomed.

[4]     <u>Closely connected to her poverty is the way through the woods, which during her walk seems to be an almost active opponent.</u> The long hill tires her, the thorn bush catches her clothes, the log endangers her balance as she crosses the creek, and the barbed-wire fence threatens to puncture her skin. Another danger on her way is the stray dog, which topples her over. Apparently not afraid, however, Phoenix carries on a cheerful monologue:

> "Out of my way, all you foxes, owls, beetles, jack rabbits, coons and wild animals! . . . Keep out from under these feet, little bob-whites. . . . Keep the big wild hogs out of my path. Don't let none of these come running my direction. I got a long way." (paragraph 3, p. 95)

She prevails for the moment as she enters Natchez, but all the hazards of her walk are still there, waiting for her to return.

[5]     <u>The force against Phoenix which shows her plight most clearly and pathetically is her grandson's incurable illness.</u> His condition highlights her helplessness, for she is his only support. Her difficulties would be enough for one person alone, but with the grandson the odds against her are doubled. Despite her care, there is nothing anyone can do for the grandson but take the long worn path to get something to help him endure his pain.

---

[†]Thesis sentence.

Getty 3

[6]    This brief description of the conflicts in "A Worn Path" only hints at the story's power. Welty layers the details to bring out the full range of the conditions against Phoenix, who cannot win despite her determination and devotion. The most hopeless fact, the condition of the invalid grandson, is not revealed until she reaches the medical office, and this delayed final revelation makes one's heart go out to her. <u>The plot is strong because it is so real, and Phoenix is a pathetic but memorable protagonist struggling against overwhelming odds</u>.

---

**WORK CITED**                                                                    Getty 4

Welty, Eudora. "A Worn Path." *Literature: An Introduction to Reading and Writing*. Ed. Edgar V. Roberts. 4th Compact Ed. Upper Saddle River: Prentice Hall, 2008, 95–100.

## Commentary

The strategy of this essay is to explain the elements of plot in "A Worn Path" selectively, without duplicating the story's narrative order. Thus the third aspect of conflict, the woods, might be introduced first if the story's narrative order were to be followed, but it is deferred while the more personal elements of old age and poverty are considered. It is important to note that the essay does not deal with the story's other characters as part of Phoenix's conflict. Rather, Phoenix's antagonist takes the shape of impersonal and unconquerable forces, like the grandson's illness.

Paragraph 1 briefly describes how one's first impressions are changed by the story's end. The thesis statement anticipates the body by listing the four topics about to be treated. Paragraph 2 concerns Phoenix's old age; paragraph 3 her poverty; paragraph 4 the woods; and paragraph 5, her grandson's illness. The concluding paragraph (6) points out that in this set of conflicts the protagonist cannot win, except as she lives out her duty and her devotion to help her grandson. Continuing the theme of the introduction, the last paragraph also accounts for the power of the plot: By building up to Phoenix's personal strength against unbeatable forces, the story evokes sympathy and admiration.

## Writing Topics About Plot in Fiction

1. Suppose that someone has told you that "The Things They Carried" is too detailed and realistic to be considered a story. Explain to this person why the assertion should be considered wrong. What elements of narrative, character, plot, point of view, idea, and description justify calling "The Things They Carried" a story?

2. Consider the illustrative essay on the plot of Welty's "A Worn Path." How well does the essay organize the details about the story's plot? Do you accept the arguments in the essay? What other details and arguments can you think of that might further explain Welty's plot?

3. In "War", by Pirandello, why is the father whose son is dead made so initially unappealing? What effect on the plot of the story is made plain by the apparent nature of his character?

4. How do the separate sections of "An Occurrence at Owl Creek Bridge" affect the story's plot? Why is the second section a "flashback" of events that occurred before the actual story is taking place? Why is this flashback necessary to your understanding of the plot?

5. Write contrasting paragraphs about a character (whom you know or about whom you have read). In the first, try to make your reader like the character. In the second, try to create a hostile response to the character. Write an additional paragraph explaining the ways in which you tried to create these opposite responses. How fair would it be for a reader to dislike your negative paragraph even though your hostile portrait is successful?

6. Write a brief episode or story that takes place in a historical period you believe you know well, being as factually accurate as you can. Introduce your own fictional characters as important "movers and shakers," and deal with their public or personal affairs or both. You may model your characters and episodes on historical persons, but you are free to exercise your imagination completely and construct your own characters.

# Chapter **3**

# Point of View: The Position of the Narrator or Speaker

The term "point of view" refers to the **speaker**, **narrator**, **persona**, or **voice** created by authors to tell stories, make observations, present arguments, and express personal attitudes and judgments. Literally, point of view deals with how action and dialogue have been seen and heard. How did the speaker learn about the situation? Was the speaker a participant in the situation, or no more than a witness, either close or distant? How close to the action was she? How much does the speaker know? How accurate and complete are his reports? Was she also involved in what happened? How thoroughly? Did he see everything, miss anything? How much did she understand? Point of view involves not only the speaker's actual position as an observer and recorder, but also the ways in which the speaker's social, political, and mental circumstances affect the narrative. For this reason, point of view is one of the most complex and subtle aspects of literary study.

The underlying issue of point of view is epistemological: How do we acquire information? How can we verify its authenticity? How can we trust those who explain the world to us? What is their authority? Are they partial or impartial? What is their interest in telling us things? How reliable are their explanations? What physical and psychological positions might affect, or even distort, what they are saying? Do they have anything to hide? When they speak, are they trying to justify themselves to any degree?

Bear in mind that authors try not only to make their works vital and interesting but also to bring their presentations alive. The presentation is similar to a dramatic performance: In a play, the actors are always themselves, but as they perform their roles they impersonate and temporarily become the characters they act. In fictional works, not only do authors impersonate or pretend to be characters who do the talking, but also they create these characters. One such character is Jackie, the narrator of Frank O'Connor's "First Confession" (Chapter 7), who is telling about events that occurred when he was a child. Because he is the subject as well as the narrator, he has firsthand knowledge of the actions, even though he also says things indicating that he, as an adult, has not fully assimilated his childhood experience. Another speaking character is Francie of Lorrie Moore's "How to Become a Writer." On the pretext of giving advice to a budding writer, Francie seems to be describing some of the more ironically comic and also serious episodes of her own writing career. Francie is the one we read and hear, but Moore is the one supplying the words because Francie is a literary creation. In Poe's "The Masque of the Red Death" (Chapter 5) we continually hear the speaker's voice and are influenced not only by his narration, but also by his attitudes.

Because of the ramifications of creating a narrative voice, point of view may also be considered as the centralizing or guiding intelligence in a work—the mind that filters the fictional experience and presents only the most important details to create the maximum impact. It may be compared to the perspectives utilized by painters. As we note in Chapter 6 (p. 244), Claude Lorrain's painting *Seaport at Sunset* (I–6, Plate 2) puts all the buildings, ships, landscape, and foreground figures into the perspective of the distant sun's mysterious glow. Comparable paintings are Renoir's *The Umbrellas* and Whistler's *The Little White Girl, Symphony in White*, both of which stress color—blue by Renoir and white by Whistler (I–8, Plate 1 and I–9, Plate 1). The girl and her white dress occupy half of Whistler's painting, just as Renoir's umbrellas direct our eyes to the bustling dark blue that unites the foreground figures with the hidden world beyond. Thus, Renoir and Whistler connect life with color, while Lorrain suggests that human activities are minor in the perspective of the vast universe. (His human figures are small, and some are distant; indeed, he often hired other painters to do his figures.) The way reality is presented in each of the paintings—the point of view or guiding intelligence of the painter—determines our understanding of artistic ideas. Similarly, the point of view fashioned by the author of a literary work determines how we read, respond, and understand.

## An Exercise in Point of View: Reporting an Accident

As an exercise to show that point of view is derived from lifelike situations, let us imagine that there has been an auto accident. Two cars, driven by Alice and Bill, have collided, and the after-crash scene is represented in the drawing. How might this accident be described? What would Alice say? What would Bill say?

Now, assume that Frank, who is Bill's best friend, and Mary, who knows neither Bill nor Alice, were witnesses. What might Frank say about who was responsible? What might Mary say? Additionally, assume that you are a reporter for a local newspaper and are sent to report on the accident. You know none of the people involved. How will your report differ from the other reports? Finally, to what degree are all the statements designed to persuade listeners and readers that the details and claims made in the respective reports are true?

The likely differences in the various reports may be explained by reference to point of view. Obviously, because both Alice and Bill are deeply involved—each of them is a major participant or what may be called a **major mover**—they will likely arrange their words to make themselves seem blameless. Frank, because he is Bill's best friend, will report things in Bill's favor. Mary will favor neither Alice nor Bill, but let us assume that she did not look up to see the colliding cars until she heard the crash. Thus, she did not see the accident happening but saw only the immediate aftereffects. Amid all this mixture of partial and impartial views of the action, to whom should we attribute the greatest reliability?

Each person's report will have the "hidden agenda" of making herself or himself seem honest, objective, intelligent, impartial, and thorough. Thus, although both Alice and Bill may be truthful to the best of their abilities, their reports will not be reliable because they both have something to gain from avoiding responsibility for the accident. Also, Frank may be questionable as a witness because he is Bill's friend and may report things to Bill's advantage. Mary could be reliable, but she did not see everything;

therefore, she is unreliable not because of motivation but rather because of her location as a witness. Most likely, your account as an impartial reporter will be the most reliable and objective of all, because your major interest is to learn all the details and to report the truth accurately, with no concern about the personal interests of either Alice or Bill.

As you can see, the ramifications of describing actions are far reaching, and the consideration of the various interests and situations is subtle. Indeed, of all the aspects of literature, point of view is the most complex because it is so much like life itself. On the one hand, point of view is intertwined with the many interests and wishes of humanity at large; on the other, it is linked to the enormous difficulty of uncovering and determining truth.

## Conditions That Affect Point of View

As this exercise in observation and expression demonstrates, point of view depends on two major factors. The first factor, as we have seen, is the physical situation of the narrator, or speaker, as an observer. How do the speaker's characteristics emerge from the narration? What are her qualifications or limitations as an observer? The second factor is the speaker's intellectual and emotional position. How might the speaker gain or lose from what takes place in the story? Are the speaker's observations and words colored by these interests? Does he have any persuasive purpose beyond being a straightforward recorder or observer? What values does the speaker impose upon the action?

In a story, as in many poems using narrative, authors take into account all these subtleties. For example, O'Connor's narrator, Jackie, in "First Confession" tells about boyhood family problems and his first experience with the sacrament of confession, but he has not yet fully separated himself from some of his youthful antagonisms. Whitecloud's speaker in "Blue Winds Dancing" (Chapter 6) is filled with misgivings about the life he leaves and relief about the life to which he is returning. These narrators show their own involvement and concern about the events they describe. The speaker in Jackson's "The Lottery," however, does not seem personally involved in the actions. This narrator listens, sees, and reports, but does not express deep involvement in the events of the story's country village. As readers, we need to develop our understanding of how such differing modes of presentation create the effects of these and all other stories and narrative poems.

## Point of View and Opinions

Because point of view is often popularly understood to mean ideas, opinions, or beliefs, it must be stressed that the term is not directly synonymous with any of these. Point of view refers to a work's mode of narration—comprising narrator, language, audience, and perceptions of events and characters—whereas opinions and beliefs are thoughts and ideas that may or may not have anything to do with a narration.

One may grant, however, that the position from which people see and understand things (e.g., established positions of political party, religion, social philosophy, and morality) has a most definite bearing on how they think and therefore on their opinions and beliefs. Opinions also affect how people view reality, and opinions affect, if not control, what they say about their perceptions of the world around them. Therefore, opinions stem out of point of view and at the same time have an influence on point of view. A four-star general and a buck private will have different things to say about what happens on a wartime battlefield.

For our purposes in this chapter, however, a discussion of point of view should emphasize how the narration and dramatic situation of a work create and shape the work. If ideas seem to be particularly important in a story, your objective should be not to analyze and discuss the ideas as ideas, but rather to consider whether and how these ideas affect what the narrator concludes and says about the story's actions and situations.

## Determining a Work's Point of View

In your reading you will encounter a wide variety of points of view. To begin your analysis of these views, first determine the work's grammatical voice (i.e., first, second, or third person). Then, study the ways in which the subject, characterization, dialogue, and form interact with the point of view.

## In the First-Person Point of View, the Narrator Tells about Events He or She Has Personally Witnessed

If the voice of the work is an "I," the author is using the **first-person point of view**—the impersonation of a fictional narrator or speaker who may be named or unnamed. In our hypothetical accident reports, both Alice and Bill are first-person speakers who are named. Similarly, the narrator of O'Connor's "First Confession," Jackie, is named and identified (Chapter 7). By contrast, the narrator of Poe's "The Masque of the Red Death" (Chapter 5) is an unnamed speaker. In Twain's "Luck" (Chapter 4), there are two unnamed first-person speakers (the first "I" introduces the second "I").

First-person speakers report events as though they have acquired their knowledge in a number of ways.

- What they themselves have done, said, heard, and thought (firsthand experience).
- What they have observed others doing and saying (firsthand witness).
- What others have said to them or otherwise communicated to them (secondhand testimony and hearsay).
- What they are able to infer or deduce from the information they have discovered (inferential information).
- What they are able to conjecture about how a character or characters might think and act, given their knowledge of a situation (conjectural, imaginative, or intuitive information).

**FIRST-PERSON SPEAKERS COME IN MANY VARIETIES.**  Of all the points of view, the first person is the most independent of the author, because the first-person speaker may have a unique identity, with name, job, and economic and social position—a life separated totally from that of the author. Often, however, the author creates a more anonymous but still independent first-person speaker, as with the unnamed speaker-narrator of Poe's "The Masque of the Red Death" (Chapter 5). There are also situations in which an "I" speaker is pluralized by "we" when the first person includes other characters. Such a first-person plural point of view lends reliability to the narrative, as in Ellison's "Battle Royal" (Chapter 6), because the characters included as "we," even if they are sometimes unidentified by the speaker, may be considered additional witnesses.

**FIRST-PERSON SPEAKERS CAN BE RELIABLE OR UNRELIABLE.**  When you encounter a first-person narrative (whether a story or narrative poem), determine the narrator's position and ability, prejudices or self-interest, and judgment of her readers or listeners. Most first-person speakers describing their own experiences are to be accepted as **reliable** and authoritative. But sometimes first-person speakers are **unreliable** because they may have interests or limitations that lead them to mislead, distort, or even lie. There is reason, for example, to question Jackie's reliability as the speaker of O'Connor's "First Confession" (Chapter 7). As an adult he is describing the events within his family and his after-school preparation sessions prior to his attending his first confession, but he is giving us his childhood memories, and he is not including the potential views of those in his family about the ways in which things happened.

Whether first-person speakers are reliable or unreliable, however, they are one of the means by which authors confer an authentic, lifelike aura to their works.

## In the Second-Person Point of View, the Narrator Is Speaking to Someone Else Who Is Addressed as "You"

The **second-person point of view**, the least common of the points of view, and the most difficult for authors to manage, offers two major possibilities. In the first, a narrator (almost necessarily a first-person speaker) tells a listener what he or she has done and said at a past time. The actions might be a simple retelling of events, as when a parent tells a child about something the child did during infancy, or when a doctor tells a patient with amnesia about events before the causative injury. Also, the actions might also be subject to dispute and interpretation, as when a prosecuting attorney describes a crime for which a defendant is on trial or when a spouse lists grievances against an alienated spouse in a custody or divorce case. Still another situation of the second-person point of view might occur when an angry person accuses the listener of a betrayal or some other wrong. In such instances, it is worth bearing in mind that the point of view may possibly be considered first person rather than second, for the speaker is likely to be speaking subjectively about his or her own perception or analysis of the listener's actions.

The second possibility is equally complex. Some narrators are obviously addressing a "you" but are instead referring mainly to themselves—and to listeners only tangentially—in preference to an "I." In addition, some narrators follow the usage—not uncommon in colloquial speech—of the indefinite "you." In this point of view, the "you" refers not only to a specific listener, who may or may not be present, but also to anyone at all, or maybe, and above all, to the speaker himself/herself. In this way the writer avoids the more formal use of such words as *one, a person, or people.* (Incidentally, the selection of *you* is non–gender-specific because it eliminates the need for the pronouns *he, she; she/he; he/she; or he or she.*) An ingenious employment of the second-person point of view is seen in Lorrie Moore's "How to Become a Writer." What we find on the pages is an informal, personal discussion in which the speaker uses "you" frequently, as though she is giving advice to any aspiring writers who hear her. More subtly, however, we infer that the speaker is masking personal experience, some of it painful, behind her jokes, puns, and sometimes flippant "advice."

## In the Third-Person Point of View, the Narrator Emphasizes the Actions and Speeches of Others

If events in the work are described in the third person (he, she, it, they), the author is using the **third-person point of view**. It is not always easy to characterize the voice in this point of view. Sometimes the speaker uses an "I," as in Poe's "The Masque of the Red Death" (Chapter 5), and this "I" may seemingly be identical with the author, but at other times the author creates a distinct **authorial voice** that may be included at times within the voice of the narrator, as in Hawthorne's "Young Goodman Brown" (Chapter 8). There are three variants of the third-person point of view: *dramatic or objective, omniscient,* and *limited omniscient.*

**1. THE DRAMATIC OR OBJECTIVE POINT OF VIEW IS THE BASIC METHOD OF NARRATION.** The most direct presentation of action and dialogue is the dramatic or objective point of view (also called third-person objective). It is the basic method of rendering action and speech that all the points of view share. The narrator of the dramatic point of view is an unidentified speaker who reports things in a way that is analogous to a hovering or tracking video camera or to what some critics have called "a fly on the wall (or tree)." Somehow, the narrator is always on the spot—in rooms, forests, village squares, moving vehicles, or even in outer space—to tell us what is happening and what is being said.

The dramatic presentation is limited only to what is said and what happens. The writer does not overtly draw conclusions or make interpretations, because the premise of the dramatic point of view is that readers, like a jury, can form their own interpretations if they are shown the right evidence. Jackson's "The Lottery"—a powerful example of the dramatic point of view—is an objective story about a bizarre public occasion in a small town. We, the readers, draw many conclusions about the story (such as that the people are tradition bound, insensitive, cruel, and so on), but because of the dramatic point of view Jackson does not state any of these conclusions for us.

**2. THE NARRATOR OF THE OMNISCIENT POINT OF VIEW CAN SEE ALL, KNOW ALL, AND POTENTIALLY DISCLOSE ALL.** The third-person point of view is **omniscient** (all-knowing) when the speaker not only presents action and dialogue but also, at times, reports the thoughts and reactions of the characters. In our everyday real world, we never know, nor can we ever know, what other people are thinking. For practical purposes, their minds are closed to us. However, we always make assumptions about the thoughts of others, and these assumptions are the basis of the omniscient point of view. Authors use it freely but judiciously to explain responses, thoughts, feelings, and plans—an additional dimension that aids in the development of character. For example, in Maupassant's "The Necklace" (Chapter 1) the speaker takes an omniscient stance to explain the responses and thoughts of the major character and also, though in just a short passage, of her husband. Even in an omniscient point of view story, however, relatively little description is actually devoted to the thoughts of the characters, for most of the narration must necessarily be taken up with dramatic third-person descriptions.

**3. THE NARRATOR IN THE LIMITED OR LIMITED-OMNISCIENT POINT OF VIEW FOCUSES ON THE THOUGHTS AND DEEDS OF A MAJOR CHARACTER.** More common than the omniscient and dramatic points of view is the **limited third person** or **limited omniscient third person**, in which the author concentrates on or limits the narration to the actions and thoughts of a major character. In our accident case (p. 108), Frank, being Bill's friend, would be sympathetic to Bill. Thus, Frank's report of the collision would likely be third-person limited, with Bill as the center of interest. Depending on whether a narration focuses on action or motivation, the limited third-person narrator may explore the mentality of the major character either lightly or in depth. The name given to the central figure on whom the third-person omniscient point of view is focused is the **point-of-view character**. Thus, Peyton Farquhar in "An Occurrence at

Owl Creek Bridge" (Chapter 2) and Miss Brill in Mansfield's "Miss Brill" (Chapter 4) are both point-of-view characters. Almost everything in these stories is there because the point-of-view characters see it, hear it, respond to it, think about it, imagine it entirely, do it or share in it, try to control it, or are controlled by it.

## Mingling Points of View

In some works, authors mingle points of view in order to imitate reality. For example, many first-person narrators use various types of the third-person point of view during much of their narration. Authors also vary points of view to sustain interest, create suspense, or put the burden of response entirely upon readers. For example, in "An Occurrence at Owl Creek Bridge" (Chapter 2) Bierce keeps our attention focused on the reactions of the major character, Peyton Farquhar, until the last paragraph of the story, when there is a shift to a dramatic point of view as Farquhar has been hanged from the bridge. This shift in point of view is an almost brutal pronouncement that none of Farquhar's hopes can ever come true. A comparable but contrasting change in point of view occurs at the end of Hawthorne's "Young Goodman Brown" (Chapter 8), where the narrator objectively summarizes Brown's loveless and bleak life after his nightmare about evil.

## Point of View and Verb Tense

As demonstrated in this chapter, point of view refers to the ways narrators and speakers perceive and report actions and speeches. In the broadest sense, however, point of view may be considered as a total way of rendering truth, and for this reason the tense chosen by the narrators is important. Most narratives rely on the past tense: The actions happened in the past, and they are now over.

The introduction of dialogue, however, even in a past-tense narration, dramatically brings the story into the present. Such dramatic rendering is accomplished by the dialogue concluding Maupassant's "The Necklace," for example, which emphasizes the irony of Mathilde's sacrifices during the previous 10 years.

The narrator of a past-tense narrative may also introduce present-tense commentary during the narration—a strong means of signifying the importance of past events. Examples are in O'Connor's "First Confession" (Chapter 7), in which the narrator Jackie makes personal comments about the events he is describing, and in Mark Twain's "Luck" (Chapter 4), where the second narrator expresses amazement over the mistakes of the main character. In addition, as noted in Chapter 8, the narrators of parables and fables use past-tense narratives as vehicles for teaching current lessons in philosophy and religion.

In recent years a number of writers have used the present tense as their principal time reference. With the present tense, the narrative story or poem is rendered as a virtual drama that is unfolded moment by moment, as in "Blue Winds Dancing" (Chapter 6), when Whitecloud uses the present tense to emphasize the immediate experience of the narrator as he returns home.

Some writers intermingle tenses to show how time itself can be blended within the human mind, because our consciousness never exists only in the present but instead is a composite made up of past memories cresting upon a never-ending wave carrying us into the future. Thus at the end of Bierce's "An Occurrence at Owl Creek Bridge" (Chapter 2), the past-tense narration shifts into the present tense to demonstrate the vividness of the main character's perceptions just before his death.

## Summary: Guidelines for Point of View

The following guidelines summarize and further classify the types of points of view. Use them to distinguish differences and shades of variation in stories and poems.

**1. First person (I, my, mine, me, and sometimes we, our, and us).** First-person speakers are involved to at least some degree in the actions of the work. Such narrators may have (1) complete understanding, (2) partial or incorrect understanding, (3) no understanding at all, or (4) complete understanding with the motive to mislead or lie. Although the narrators described in guidelines 1 through 3 are usually **reliable** and tell the truth, they may also sometimes be **unreliable**. The only way to tell is to study the story closely. Obviously, 4 is by nature unreliable, but nevertheless the mode might possibly be accepted (although critically) on matters of detail.

    a. *A Major Participant*
      i. Who tells his or her own story and thoughts as a major mover.
      ii. Who tells a story about others and also about herself or himself as one of the major movers.
      iii.Who tells a story mainly about others, and about himself or herself only tangentially.
    b. *A Minor Participant*, who tells a story about events experienced and witnessed.
    c. *A Nonparticipating but Identifiable Speaker*, who learns about events in other ways (e.g., listening to participants through direct conversation, overhearing conversation, examining documents, hearing news reports, imagining what might have occurred). The narrative of such a speaker is a combination of fact and conjectural reconstruction.

**2. Second person ("you," or possibly "thou").** A point of view that authors use often enough to justify our knowing about it. Its premise is that the speaker knows more about the actions of a character (the "you") than the character himself or herself. (a) It is used when the speaker (e.g., lawyer, spouse, friend, sports umpire, psychologist, parent, angry person) talks directly to the other person and explains that person's past actions and statements. More generally, and in a colloquial and informal style, the speaker may also use "you" to mean (b) himself or herself, (c) the reader, or (d) anyone at all.

**3. Third person (she, he, it, they).** The speaker is outside the action and is mainly a reporter of actions and speeches. Some speakers may have unique and distinguishing traits even though no separate identity is claimed for them ("the unnamed third-person narrator"). Other third-person speakers who are not separately identifiable may represent the words and views of the authors themselves ("the authorial voice").

a. *A Dramatic or Third-Person Objective Narrator*. The narrator reports only what can be seen and heard. The thoughts of characters are included only if they are spoken or written (dialogue, reported or overheard conversation, letters, reports, etc.).

b. *An Omniscient Narrator*. The omniscient speaker knows all, sees all, reports all, and when necessary, reveals the inner workings of the minds of any or all characters. Even an omniscient speaker, however, makes a mostly dramatic third-person presentation.

c. *A Limited, or Limited Omniscient Narrator*. The focus is on the actions, responses, thoughts, and feelings of a single major character. Although the narration may concentrate on the character's actions, it may simultaneously probe deep within the consciousness of the character.

### Stories for Study

## RAYMOND CARVER (1938–1988)

Originally from Oregon, Carver lived in Washington and spent much of his adult life in California. He studied at Chico State and at the Iowa Writers Workshop. After doing blue-collar jobs for a time he worked as an editor and then, finally, as a teacher. Some of his collections are *Will You Please Be Quiet, Please?* (1976) and *Cathedral* (1983). *Where I'm Calling From* (1988) collects earlier stories and adds a number of new ones. *Short Cuts* (1993) is a selection of ten stories that were woven together into a film (1993) by Robert Altman. Carver is considered a master of minimalism, that is, fiction that stresses only the essentials of action and description. Generally, his writing is economical, stripped to the bone. Many of his characters seem unusual if not odd or even cruel. For example, one of his brief stories, "Popular Mechanics," takes little more than a single page to depict how a couple breaking up is also about to break up (literally) their child. "Neighbors" is taken from *Where I'm Calling From*.

 **Neighbors** (1988)

Bill and Arlene Miller were a happy couple. But now and then they felt they alone among their circle had been passed by somehow, leaving Bill to attend to his bookkeeping duties and Arlene occupied with secretarial chores. They talked about it sometimes, mostly in comparison with the lives of their neighbors, Harriet and Jim Stone. It seemed to the Millers that the Stones lived a fuller and brighter life. The Stones were always going out for dinner, or entertaining at home, or traveling about the country somewhere in connection with Jim's work.

The Stones lived across the hall from the Millers. Jim was a salesman for a machine-parts firm and often managed to combine business with pleasure trips, and on this occasion the Stones would be away for ten days, first to Cheyenne, then on to St. Louis to visit relatives. In their absence, the Millers would look after the Stones' apartment, feed Kitty, and water the plants.

Bill and Jim shook hands beside the car. Harriet and Arlene held each other by the elbows and kissed lightly on the lips.

"Have fun," Bill said to Harriet.

"We will," said Harriet. "You kids have fun too."

Arlene nodded.

Jim winked at her. "Bye, Arlene. Take good care of the old man."

"I will," Arlene said.

"Have fun," Bill said.

"You bet," Jim said, clipping Bill lightly on the arm. "And thanks again, you guys."    10

The Stones waved as they drove away, and the Millers waved too.

"Well, I wish it was us," Bill said.

"God knows, we could use a vacation," Arlene said. She took his arm and put it around her waist as they climbed the stairs to their apartment.

After dinner Arlene said, "Don't forget. Kitty gets liver flavor the first night." She stood in the kitchen doorway folding the handmade tablecloth that Harriet had bought for her last year in Santa Fe.

Bill took a deep breath as he entered the Stones' apartment. The air was already heavy    15
and it was vaguely sweet. The sunburst clock over the television said half past eight. He remembered when Harriet had come home with the clock, how she had crossed the hall to show it to Arlene, cradling the brass case in her arms and talking to it through the tissue paper as if it were an infant.

Kitty rubbed her face against his slippers and then turned onto her side, but jumped up quickly as Bill moved to the kitchen and selected one of the stacked cans from the gleaming drainboard. Leaving the cat to pick at her food, he headed for the bathroom. He looked at himself in the mirror and then closed his eyes and then looked again. He opened the medicine chest. He found a container of pills and read the label—*Harriet Stone. One each day as directed*—and slipped it into his pocket. He went back to the kitchen, drew a pitcher of water, and returned to the living room. He finished watering, set the pitcher on the rug, and opened the liquor cabinet. He reached in back for the bottle of Chivas Regal. He took two drinks from the bottle, wiped his lips on his sleeve, and replaced the bottle in the cabinet.

Kitty was on the couch sleeping. He switched off the lights, slowly closing and checking the door. He had the feeling he had left something.

"What kept you?" Arlene said. She sat with her legs turned under her, watching television.

"Nothing. Playing with Kitty," he said, and went over to her and touched her breasts.

"Let's go to bed, honey," he said.    20

The next day Bill took only ten minutes of the twenty-minute break allotted for the afternoon and left at fifteen minutes before five. He parked the car in the lot just as Arlene hopped down from the bus. He waited until she entered the building, then ran up the stairs to catch her as she stepped out of the elevator.

"Bill! God, you scared me. You're early," she said.

He shrugged. "Nothing to do at work," he said.

She let him use her key to open the door. He looked at the door across the hall before following her inside.

25 "Let's go to bed," he said.

"Now? " She laughed. "What's gotten into you?"

"Nothing. Take your dress off." He grabbed for her awkwardly, and she said, "Good God, Bill."

He unfastened his belt.

Later they sent out for Chinese food, and when it arrived they ate hungrily, without speaking, and listened to records.

30 "Let's not forget to feed Kitty," she said.

"I was just thinking about that," he said. "I'll go right over."

* * *

He selected a can of fish flavor for the cat, then filled the pitcher and went to water. When he returned to the kitchen, the cat was scratching in her box. She looked at him steadily before she turned back to the litter. He opened all the cupboards and examined the canned goods, the cereals, the packaged foods, the cocktail and wine glasses, the china, the pots and pans. He opened the refrigerator. He sniffed some celery, took two bites of cheddar cheese, and chewed on an apple as he walked into the bedroom. The bed seemed enormous, with a fluffy white bedspread draped to the floor. He pulled out a nightstand drawer, found a half-empty package of cigarettes and stuffed them into his pocket. Then he stepped to the closet and was opening it when the knock sounded at the front door.

He stopped by the bathroom and flushed the toilet on his way.

"What's been keeping you?" Arlene said. "You've been over here more than an hour."

35 "Have I really?" he said.

"Yes, you have," she said.

"I had to go to the toilet," he said.

"You have your own toilet," she said.

"I couldn't wait," he said.

40 That night they made love again.

In the morning he had Arlene call in for him. He showered, dressed, and made a light breakfast. He tried to start a book. He went out for a walk and felt better. But after a while, hands still in his pockets, he returned to the apartment. He stopped at the Stones' door on the chance he might hear the cat moving about. Then he let himself in at his own door and went to the kitchen for the key.

Inside it seemed cooler than his apartment, and darker too. He wondered if the plants had something to do with the temperature of the air. He looked out the window, and then he moved slowly through each room considering everything that fell under his gaze, carefully, one object at a time. He saw ashtrays, items of furniture, kitchen utensils, the clock. He saw everything. At last he entered the bedroom, and the cat appeared at his feet. He stroked her once, carried her into the bathroom, and shut the door.

He lay down on the bed and stared at the ceiling. He lay for a while with his eyes closed, and then he moved his hand under his belt. He tried to recall what day it was. He tried to remember when the Stones were due back, and then he wondered if they would ever return. He could not remember their faces or the way they talked and dressed. He sighed and with effort rolled off the bed to lean over the dresser and look at himself in the mirror.

He opened the closet and selected a Hawaiian shirt. He looked until he found Bermudas, neatly pressed and hanging over a pair of brown twill slacks. He shed his own clothes and slipped into the shorts and the shirt. He looked in the mirror again. He went to the living room and poured himself a drink and sipped it on his way back to the bedroom. He put on a blue shirt, a dark suit, a blue and white tie, black wing-tip shoes. The glass was empty and he went for another drink.

In the bedroom again, he sat on a chair, crossed his legs, and smiled, observing himself in     45
the mirror. The telephone rang twice and fell silent. He finished the drink and took off the suit. He rummaged through the top drawers until he found a pair of panties and a brassiere. He stepped into the panties and fastened the brassiere, then looked through the closet for an out-fit. He put on a black and white checkered skirt and tried to zip it up. He put on a burgundy blouse that buttoned up the front. He considered her shoes, but understood they would not fit. For a long time he looked out the living-room window from behind the curtain. Then he re-turned to the bedroom and put everything away.

He was not hungry. She did not eat much, either. They looked at each other shyly and smiled. She got up from the table and checked that the key was on the shelf and then she quickly cleared the dishes.

He stood in the kitchen doorway and smoked a cigarette and watched her pick up the key.

"Make yourself comfortable while I go across the hall," she said. "Read the paper or something." She closed her fingers over the key. He was, she said, looking tired.

He tried to concentrate on the news. He read the paper and turned on the television. Finally he went across the hall. The door was locked.

"It's me. Are you still there, honey?" he called.     50

After a time the lock released and Arlene stepped outside and shut the door. "Was I gone so long?" she said.

"Well, you were," he said.

"Was I?" she said. "I guess I must have been playing with Kitty."

He studied her, and she looked away, her hand still resting on the doorknob.

"It's funny," she said. "You know—to go in someone's place like that."     55

He nodded, took her hand from the knob, and guided her toward their own door. He let them into their apartment.

"It *is* funny," he said.

He noticed white lint clinging to the back of her sweater, and the color was high in her cheeks. He began kissing her on the neck and hair and she turned and kissed him back.

"Oh, damn," she said. "Damn, damn," she sang, girlishly clapping her hands. "I just re-membered. I really and truly forgot to do what I went over there to do. I didn't feed Kitty or do any watering." She looked at him. "Isn't that stupid?"

"I don't think so," he said. "Just a minute. I'll get my cigarettes and go back with you."     60

She waited until he had closed and locked their door, and then she took his arm at the muscle and said, "I guess I should tell you. I found some pictures."

He stopped in the middle of the hall. "What kind of pictures?"

"You can see for yourself," she said, and she watched him.

"No kidding." He grinned. "Where?"

"In a drawer," she said.     65

"No kidding," he said.

And then she said, "Maybe they won't come back," and was at once astonished at her words.

"It could happen," he said. "Anything could happen."

"Or maybe they'll come back and . . ." but she did not finish.

They held hands for the short walk across the hall, and when he spoke she could barely     70
hear his voice.

"The key," he said. "Give it to me."

"What?" she said. She gazed at the door.

"The key," he said. "You have the key."

"My God," she said, "I left the key inside."

75 He tried the knob. It was locked. Then she tried the knob. It would not turn. Her lips were parted, and her breathing was hard, expectant. He opened his arms and she moved into them.

"Don't worry," he said into her ear. "For God's sake, don't worry."

They stayed there. They held each other. They leaned into the door as if against a wind, and braced themselves.

## Questions

1. Who is the speaker of "Neighbors"? On whom is the speaker's attention directed?
2. Who are the Millers? Do they seem normal at first? As the story progresses, do they seem to get odd? What happens to them?
3. Should the story be considered as realistic fiction, or would it be more appropriate to consider it as an illustration of life's absurdities?

## SHIRLEY JACKSON (1919–1965)

Jackson was a native of California. She graduated from Syracuse University in New York and lived much of her life in Vermont. Although her life was short, she was a successful writer of novels, short stories, biographies, and children's fiction. Her stories often depict unusual, unreal, or bizarre events in common settings, of which "The Lottery" is a major example. She wrote the story in only two hours and submitted it to *The New Yorker* without major revisions. When it was published many readers raised questions about how to interpret the conclusion. Jackson steadfastly refused to explain, leaving readers to decide for themselves.

 ## The Lottery (1948)

The morning of June 27th was clear and sunny, with the fresh warmth of a full summer day; the flowers were blossoming profusely and the grass was richly green. The people of the village began to gather in the square, between the post office and the bank, around ten o'clock; in some towns there were so many people that the lottery took two days and had to be started on June 26th, but in this village, where there were only about three hundred people, the whole lottery took less than two hours, so it could begin at ten o'clock in the morning and still be through in time to allow the villagers to get home for noon dinner.

The children assembled first, of course. School was recently over for the summer, and the feeling of liberty sat uneasily on most of them; they tended to gather together quietly for a while before they broke into boisterous play, and their talk was still of the classroom and the teacher, of books and reprimands. Bobby Martin had already stuffed his pockets full of stones, and the other boys soon followed his example, selecting the smoothest and roundest stones; Bobby and Harry Jones and Dickie Delacroix—the villagers pronounced this name "Dellacroy"—eventually made a great pile of stones in one corner of the square and guarded it against the raids of the other boys. The girls stood aside, talking among themselves, looking over their shoulders at the boys, and the very small children rolled in the dust or clung to the hands of their older brothers or sisters.

Soon the men began to gather, surveying their own children, speaking of planting and rain, tractors and taxes. They stood together, away from the pile of stones in the corner, and their jokes were quiet and they smiled rather than laughed. The women, wearing faded house dresses and sweaters, came shortly after their menfolk. They greeted one another and exchanged bits of gossip as they went to join their husbands. Soon the women, standing by their husbands, began to call to their children, and the children came reluctantly, having to be called four or five times. Bobby Martin ducked under his mother's grasping hand and ran, laughing, back to the pile of stones. His father spoke up sharply, and Bobby came quickly and took his place between his father and his oldest brother.

The lottery was conducted—as were the square dances, the teen-age club, the Halloween program—by Mr. Summers, who had time and energy to devote to civic activities. He was a round-faced, jovial man and he ran the coal business, and people were sorry for him, because he had no children and his wife was a scold. When he arrived in the square, carrying the black wooden box, there was a murmur of conversation among the villagers, and he waved and called, "Little late today, folks." The postmaster, Mr. Graves, followed him, carrying a three-legged stool, and the stool was put in the center of the square and Mr. Summers set the black box down on it. The villagers kept their distance, leaving a space between themselves and the stool, and when Mr. Summers said, "Some of you fellows want to give me a hand?" there was a hesitation before two men, Mr. Martin and his oldest son, Baxter, came forward to hold the box steady on the stool while Mr. Summers stirred up the papers inside it.

The original paraphernalia for the lottery had been lost long ago, and the black box now 5 resting on the stool had been put into use even before Old Man Warner, the oldest man in town, was born. Mr. Summers spoke frequently to the villagers about making a new box, but no one liked to upset even as much tradition as was represented by the black box. There was a story that the present box had been made with some pieces of the box that had preceded it, the one that had been constructed when the first people settled down to make a village here. Every year, after the lottery, Mr. Summers began talking again about a new box, but every year the subject was allowed to fade off without anything's being done. The black box grew shabbier each year; by now it was no longer completely black but splintered badly along one side to show the original wood color, and in some places faded or stained.

Mr. Martin and his oldest son, Baxter, held the black box securely on the stool until Mr. Summers had stirred the papers thoroughly with his hand. Because so much of the ritual had been forgotten or discarded, Mr. Summers had been successful in having slips of paper substituted for the chips of wood that had been used for generations. Chips of wood, Mr. Summers had argued, had been all very well when the village was tiny, but now that the population was more than three hundred and likely to keep on growing, it was necessary to use something that would fit more easily into the black box. The night before the lottery, Mr. Summers and Mr. Graves made up the slips of paper and put them in the box, and it was then taken to the safe of Mr. Summers' coal company and locked up until Mr. Summers was ready to take it to the square next morning. The rest of the year, the box was put away, sometimes one place, sometimes another; it had spent one year in Mr. Graves's barn and another year underfoot in the post office, and sometimes it was set on a shelf in the Martin grocery and left there.

There was a great deal of fussing to be done before Mr. Summers declared the lottery open. There were the lists to make up—of heads of families, heads of households in each family, members of each household in each family. There was the proper swearing-in of Mr. Summers by the postmaster, as the official of the lottery; at one time, some people remembered, there had been a recital of some sort, performed by the official of the lottery, a perfunctory, tuneless chant that had been rattled off duly each year; some people believed that the official of the lottery used to stand just so when he said or sang it, others believed that he was supposed to walk among the people, but years and years ago this part of the ritual had been allowed to lapse. There had been, also, a ritual salute, which the official of the lottery had had to use in addressing each person who came up to draw from the box, but this also had changed with time, until now it was felt necessary only for the official to speak to each person approaching. Mr. Summers was very good at all this; in his clean white shirt and blue jeans, with one hand resting carelessly on the black box, he seemed very proper and important as he talked interminably to Mr. Graves and the Martins.

Just as Mr. Summers finally left off talking and turned to the assembled villagers, Mrs. Hutchinson came hurriedly along the path to the square, her sweater thrown over her shoulders, and slid into place in the back of the crowd. "Clean forgot what day it was," she said to Mrs. Delacroix, who stood next to her, and they both laughed softly. "Thought my old man was out back stacking wood," Mrs. Hutchinson went on, "and then I looked out the window and the kids was gone, and then I remembered it was the twenty-seventh and came a-running." She dried her hands on her apron, and Mrs. Delacroix said, "You're in time, though. They're still talking away up there."

Mrs. Hutchinson craned her neck to see through the crowd and found her husband and children standing near the front. She tapped Mrs. Delacroix on the arm as a farewell and began to make her way through the crowd. The people separated good-humoredly to let her through; two or three people said, in voices just loud enough to be heard across the crowd, "Here comes your Missus, Hutchinson," and "Bill, she made it after all." Mrs. Hutchinson reached her husband, and Mr. Summers, who had been waiting, said cheerfully, "Thought we were going to have to get on without you, Tessie." Mrs. Hutchinson said, grinning, "Wouldn't have me leave m'dishes in the sink, now, would you, Joe?," and soft laughter ran through the crowd as the people stirred back into position after Mrs. Hutchinson's arrival.

10     "Well, now," Mr. Summers said soberly, "guess we better get started, get this over with, so's we can go back to work. Anybody ain't here?"

"Dunbar," several people said. "Dunbar, Dunbar."

Mr. Summers consulted his list. "Clyde Dunbar," he said. "That's right. He's broke his leg, hasn't he? Who's drawing for him?"

"Me, I guess," a woman said, and Mr. Summers turned to look at her. "Wife draws for her husband," Mr. Summers said. "Don't you have a grown boy to do it for you, Janey?" Although Mr. Summers and everyone else in the village knew the answer perfectly well, it was the business of the official of the lottery to ask such questions formally. Mr. Summers waited with an expression of polite interest while Mrs. Dunbar answered.

"Horace's not but sixteen yet," Mrs. Dunbar said regretfully. "Guess I gotta fill in for the old man this year."

15     "Right," Mr. Summers said. He made a note on the list he was holding. Then he asked, "Watson boy drawing this year?"

A tall boy in the crowd raised his hand. "Here," he said. "I'm drawing for m'mother and me." He blinked his eyes nervously and ducked his head as several voices in the crowd said things like "Good fellow, Jack," and "Glad to see your mother's got a man to do it."

"Well," Mr. Summers said, "guess that's everyone. Old Man Warner make it?"

"Here," a voice said, and Mr. Summers nodded.

A sudden hush fell on the crowd as Mr. Summers cleared his throat and looked at the list. "All ready?" he called. "Now, I'll read the names—heads of families first—and the men come up and take a paper out of the box. Keep the paper folded in your hand without looking at it until everyone has had a turn. Everything clear?"

The people had done it so many times that they only half listened to the directions; most of them were quiet, wetting their lips, not looking around. Then Mr. Summers raised one hand high and said, "Adams." A man disengaged himself from the crowd and came forward. "Hi, Steve," Mr. Summers said, and Mr. Adams said, "Hi, Joe." They grinned at one another humorlessly and nervously. Then Mr. Adams reached into the black box and took out a folded paper. He held it firmly by one corner as he turned and went hastily back to his place in the crowd, where he stood a little apart from his family, not looking down at his hand.

"Allen," Mr. Summers said. "Anderson. . . . Bentham."

"Seems like there's no time at all between lotteries any more," Mrs. Delacroix said to Mrs. Graves in the back row. "Seems like we got through with the last one only last week."

"Time sure goes fast," Mrs. Graves said.

"Clark . . . Delacroix."

"There goes my old man," Mrs. Delacroix said. She held her breath while her husband went forward.

"Dunbar," Mr. Summers said, and Mrs. Dunbar went steadily to the box while one of the women said, "Go on, Janey," and another said, "There she goes."

"We're next," Mrs. Graves said. She watched while Mr. Graves came around from the side of the box, greeted Mr. Summers gravely, and selected a slip of paper from the box. By now, all through the crowd there were men holding the small folded papers in their large hands, turning them over and over nervously. Mrs. Dunbar and her two sons stood together, Mrs. Dunbar holding the slip of paper.

"Harburt. . . . Hutchinson."

"Get up there, Bill," Mrs. Hutchinson said, and the people near her laughed.

"Jones."

"They do say," Mr. Adams said to Old Man Warner, who stood next to him, "that over in the north village they're talking of giving up the lottery."

Old Man Warner snorted. "Pack of crazy fools," he said. "Listening to the young folks, nothing's good enough for *them*. Next thing you know, they'll be wanting to go back to living in caves, nobody work any more, live *that* way for a while. Used to be a saying about 'Lottery in June, corn be heavy soon.' First thing you know, we'd all be eating stewed chickweed and acorns. There's *always* been a lottery," he added petulantly. "Bad enough to see young Joe Summers up there joking with everybody."

"Some places have already quit lotteries," Mrs. Adams said.

"Nothing but trouble in *that*," Old Man Warner said stoutly. "Pack of young fools."

"Martin." And Bobby Martin watched his father go forward. "Overdyke. . . . Percy."

"I wish they'd hurry," Mrs. Dunbar said to her older son. "I wish they'd hurry."

"They're almost through," her son said.

"You get ready to run tell Dad," Mrs. Dunbar said.

Mr. Summers called his own name and then stepped forward precisely and selected a slip from the box. Then he called, "Warner."

"Seventy-seventh year I been in the lottery," Old Man Warner said as he went through the crowd. "Seventy-seventh time."

"Watson." The tall boy came awkwardly through the crowd. Someone said, "Don't be nervous, Jack," and Mr. Summers said, "Take your time, son."

"Zanini."

After that, there was a long pause, a breathless pause, until Mr. Summers, holding his slip of paper in the air, said, "All right, fellows." For a minute, no one moved, and then all the slips of paper were opened. Suddenly, all the women began to speak at once, saying, "Who is it?" "Who's got it?" "Is it the Dunbars?" "Is it the Watsons?" Then the voices began to say, "It's Hutchinson. It's Bill," "Bill Hutchinson's got it."

"Go tell your father," Mrs. Dunbar said to her older son.

45 People began to look around to see the Hutchinsons. Bill Hutchinson was standing quiet, staring down at the paper in his hand. Suddenly, Tessie Hutchinson shouted to Mr. Summers, "You didn't give him time enough to take any paper he wanted. I saw you. It wasn't fair!"

"Be a good sport, Tessie," Mrs. Delacroix called, and Mrs. Graves said, "All of us took the same chance."

"Shut up, Tessie," Bill Hutchinson said.

"Well, everyone," Mr. Summers said, "that was done pretty fast, and now we've got to be hurrying a little more to get done in time." He consulted his next list. "Bill," he said, "you draw for the Hutchinson family. You got any other households in the Hutchinsons?"

"There's Don and Eva," Mrs. Hutchinson yelled. "Make *them* take their chance!"

50 "Daughters draw with their husbands' families, Tessie," Mr. Summers said gently. "You know that as well as anyone else."

"It wasn't *fair*," Tessie said.

"I guess not, Joe," Bill Hutchinson said regretfully. "My daughter draws with her husband's family, that's only fair. And I've got no other family except the kids."

"Then, as far as drawing for families is concerned, it's you," Mr. Summers said in explanation, "and as far as drawing for households is concerned, that's you, too. Right?"

"Right," Bill Hutchinson said.

55 "How many kids, Bill?" Mr. Summers asked formally.

"Three," Bill Hutchinson said. "There's Bill, Jr., and Nancy, and little Dave. And Tessie and me."

"All right, then," Mr. Summers said. "Harry, you got their tickets back?"

Mr. Graves nodded and held up the slips of paper. "Put them in the box, then," Mr. Summers directed. "Take Bill's and put it in."

"I think we ought to start over," Mrs. Hutchinson said, as quietly as she could. "I tell you it wasn't *fair*. You didn't give him time enough to choose. *Every*body saw that."

60 Mr. Graves had selected the five slips and put them in the box, and he dropped all the papers but those onto the ground, where the breeze caught them and lifted them off.

"Listen, everybody," Mrs. Hutchinson was saying to the people around her.

"Ready, Bill?" Mr. Summers asked, and Bill Hutchinson, with one quick glance around at his wife and children, nodded.

"Remember," Mr. Summers said, "take the slips and keep them folded until each person has taken one. Harry, you help little Dave." Mr. Graves took the hand of the little boy, who came willingly with him up to the box. "Take a paper out of the box, Davy," Mr. Summers said. Davy put his hand into the box and laughed. "Take just *one* paper," Mr. Summers said. "Harry, you hold it for him." Mr. Graves took the child's hand and removed the folded paper from the tight fist and held it while little Dave stood next to him and looked up at him wonderingly.

"Nancy next," Mr. Summers said. Nancy was twelve, and her school friends breathed heavily as she went forward, switching her skirt, and took a slip daintily from the box. "Bill, Jr.," Mr. Summers said, and Billy, his face red and his feet over-large, nearly knocked the box over as he got a paper out. "Tessie," Mr. Summers said. She hesitated for a minute, looking around defiantly, and then set her lips and went up to the box. She snatched a paper out and held it behind her.

65 "Bill," Mr. Summers said, and Bill Hutchinson reached into the box and felt around, bringing his hand out at last with the slip of paper in it.

The crowd was quiet. A girl whispered, "I hope it's not Nancy," and the sound of the whisper reached the edges of the crowd.

"It's not the way it used to be," Old Man Warner said clearly. "People ain't the way they used to be."

"All right," Mr. Summers said. "Open the papers. Harry, you open little Dave's."

Mr. Graves opened the slip of paper and there was a general sigh through the crowd as he held it up and everyone could see that it was blank. Nancy and Bill, Jr., opened theirs at the same time, and both beamed and laughed, turning around to the crowd and holding their slips of paper above their heads.

"Tessie," Mr. Summers said. There was a pause, and then Mr. Summers looked at Bill  70 Hutchinson, and Bill unfolded his paper and showed it. It was blank.

"It's Tessie," Mr. Summers said, and his voice was hushed. "Show us her paper, Bill."

Bill Hutchinson went over to his wife and forced the slip of paper out of her hand. It had a black spot on it, the black spot Mr. Summers had made the night before with the heavy pencil in the coal-company office. Bill Hutchinson held it up, and there was a stir in the crowd.

"All right, folks," Mr. Summers said. "Let's finish quickly."

Although the villagers had forgotten the ritual and lost the original black box, they still remembered to use stones. The pile of stones the boys had made earlier was ready; there were stones on the ground with the blowing scraps of paper that had come out of the box. Mrs. Delacroix selected a stone so large she had to pick it up with both hands and turned to Mrs. Dunbar. "Come on," she said. "Hurry up."

Mrs. Dunbar had small stones in both hands, and she said, gasping for breath, "I can't run  75 at all. You'll have to go ahead and I'll catch up with you."

The children had stones already, and someone gave little Davy Hutchinson a few pebbles.

Tessie Hutchinson was in the center of a cleared space by now, and she held her hands out desperately as the villagers moved in on her. "It isn't fair," she said. A stone hit her on the side of the head.

Old Man Warner was saying, "Come on, come on, everyone." Steve Adams was in the front of the crowd of villagers with Mrs. Graves beside him.

"It isn't fair, it isn't right," Mrs. Hutchinson screamed, and then they were upon her.

## Questions

1. Describe the point of view of the story. What seems to be the position from which the narrator sees and describes the events? How much extra information does the narrator provide?

2. What would the story be like if it were done with an omniscient point of view? With the first person? Could the story be as suspenseful as it is? In what other ways might the story be different with another point of view?

3. Does the conclusion of "The Lottery" seem to come as a surprise? In retrospect, what hints earlier in the story tell about what is to come?

4. A scapegoat, in the ritual of purification described in the Old Testament, was an actual goat that was released into the wilderness after having been ceremonially heaped with the "iniquities" of the people (Leviticus 16:22). What traces of such a ritual are suggested in "The Lottery"? Can you think of any other kinds of rituals that are retained today even though their purpose is now remote or even nonexistent?

5. Is "The Lottery" a horror story or a surprise story, or neither or both? Explain.

## **LORRIE MOORE** (b. 1957)

Lorrie Moore teaches at the University of Wisconsin. She was born in upstate New York and received a master of fine arts degree from Cornell. Following her first collection of stories, *Self-Help* (1985), from which "How to Become a Writer" is taken, she published her first novel, *Anagrams,* in 1986. A recent work is *Like Life* (1991), a collection of eight stories taking its title from the last story, a grim portrait of life in a polluted, deteriorating future. She has received awards from the National Endowment for the Humanities and the Rockefeller Foundation, and her book *Birds of America* was nominated for the 1999 National Book Critics Circle fiction prize. Her fiction has been heralded for its combination of wry humor, deep feeling, and impending tragedy.

 ## How to Become a Writer (1985)

First, try to be something, anything, else. A movie star/astronaut. A movie star/missionary. A movie star/kindergarten teacher. President of the World. Fail miserably. It is best if you fail at an early age—say, fourteen. Early, critical disillusionment is necessary so that at fifteen you can write long haiku sequences about thwarted desire. It is a pond, a cherry blossom, a wind brushing against sparrow wing leaving for mountain. Count the syllables. Show it to your mom. She is tough and practical. She has a son in Vietnam and a husband who may be having an affair. She believes in wearing brown because it hides spots. She'll look briefly at your writing, then back up at you with a face blank as a donut. She'll say: "How about emptying the dishwasher?" Look away. Shove the forks in the fork drawer. Accidentally break one of the freebie gas station glasses. This is the required pain and suffering. This is only for starters.

In your high school English class look only at Mr. Killian's face. Decide faces are important. Write a villanelle about pores. Struggle. Write a sonnet. Count the syllables: nine, ten, eleven, thirteen. Decide to experiment with fiction. Here you don't have to count syllables. Write a short story about an elderly man and woman who accidentally shoot each other in the head, the result of an inexplicable malfunction of a shotgun which appears mysteriously in their living room one night. Give it to Mr. Killian as your final project. When you get it back, he has written on it: "Some of your images are quite nice, but you have no sense of plot." When you are home, in the privacy of your own room, faintly scrawl in pencil beneath his black-inked comments: "Plots are for dead people, pore-face."

Take all the babysitting jobs you can get. You are great with kids. They love you. You tell them stories about old people who die idiot deaths. You sing them songs like "Blue Bells of Scotland," which is their favorite. And when they are in their pajamas and have finally stopped pinching each other, when they are fast asleep, you read every sex manual in the house, and wonder how on earth anyone could ever do those things with someone they truly loved. Fall asleep in a chair reading Mr. McMurphy's *Playboy.* When the McMurphys come home, they will tap you on the shoulder, look at the magazine in your lap, and grin. You will want to die. They will ask you if Tracey took her medicine all right. Explain, yes, she did, that you promised her a story if she would take it like a big girl and that seemed to work out just fine. "Oh, marvelous," they will exclaim.

Try to smile proudly.

5      Apply to college as a child psychology major.

As a child psychology major, you have some electives. You've always liked birds. Sign up for something called "The Ornithological Field Trip." It meets Tuesdays and Thursdays at two. When you arrive at Room 134 on the first day of class, everyone is sitting around a seminar table talking about metaphors. You've heard of these. After a short, excruciating while, raise your hand and say diffidently, "Excuse me, isn't this Bird-watching One-oh-one?" The class stops and turns to look at you. They seem to all have one face—giant and blank as a vandalized clock. Someone with a beard booms out, "No, this is Creative Writing." Say: "Oh—right," as if perhaps you knew all along. Look down at your schedule. Wonder how the hell you ended up here. The computer, apparently, has made an error. You start to get up to leave and then don't. The lines at the registrar this week are huge. Perhaps you should stick with this mistake. Perhaps your creative writing isn't all that bad. Perhaps it is fate. Perhaps this is what your dad meant when he said, "It's the age of computers, Francie, it's the age of computers."

Decide that you like college life. In your dorm you meet many nice people. Some are smarter than you. And some, you notice, are dumber than you. You will continue, unfortunately, to view the world in exactly these terms for the rest of your life.

The assignment this week in creative writing is to narrate a violent happening. Turn in a story about driving with your Uncle Gordon and another one about two old people who are accidentally electrocuted when they go to turn on a badly wired desk lamp. The teacher will hand them back to you with comments: "Much of your writing is smooth and energetic. You have, however, a ludicrous notion of plot." Write another story about a man and a woman who, in the very first paragraph, have their lower torsos accidentally blitzed away by dynamite. In the second paragraph, with the insurance money, they buy a frozen yogurt stand together. There are six more paragraphs. You read the whole thing out loud in class. No one likes it. They say your sense of plot is outrageous and incompetent. After class someone asks you if you are crazy.

Decide that perhaps you should stick to comedies. Start dating someone who is funny, someone who has what in high school you called a "really great sense of humor" and what now your creative writing class calls "self-contempt giving rise to comic form." Write down all of his jokes, but don't tell him you are doing this. Make up anagrams of his old girlfriend's name and name all of your socially handicapped characters with them. Tell him his old girlfriend is in all of your stories and then watch how funny he can be, see what a really great sense of humor he can have.

Your child psychology advisor tells you you are neglecting courses in your major. What you spend the most time on should be what you're majoring in. Say yes, you understand. 10

In creative writing seminars over the next two years, everyone continues to smoke cigarettes and ask the same things: "But does it work?" "Why should we care about this character?" "Have you earned this cliché?" These seem like important questions.

On days when it is your turn, you look at the class hopefully as they scour your mimeographs for a plot. They look back up at you, drag deeply, and then smile in a sweet sort of way.

You spend too much time slouched and demoralized. Your boyfriend suggests bicycling. Your roommate suggests a new boyfriend. You are said to be self-mutilating and losing weight, but you continue writing. The only happiness you have is writing something new, in the middle of the night, armpits damp, heart pounding, something no one has yet seen. You have only those brief, fragile, untested moments of exhilaration when you know: you are a genius. Understand what you must do. Switch majors. The kids in your nursery project will be disappointed, but you have a calling, an urge, a delusion, an unfortunate habit. You have, as your mother would say, fallen in with a bad crowd.

Why write? Where does writing come from? These are questions to ask yourself. They are like: Where does dust come from? Or: Why is there war? Or: If there's a God, then why is my brother now a cripple?

15    These are questions that you keep in your wallet, like calling cards. These are questions, your creative writing teacher says, that are good to address in your journals but rarely in your fiction.

The writing professor this fall is stressing the Power of the Imagination. Which means he doesn't want long descriptive stories about your camping trip last July. He wants you to start in a realistic context but then to alter it. Like recombinant DNA. He wants you to let your imagination sail, to let it grow big-bellied in the wind. This is a quote from Shakespeare.

Tell your roommate your great idea, your great exercise of imaginative power: a transformation of Melville to contemporary life. It will be about monomania and the fish-eat-fish world of life insurance in Rochester, New York. The first line will be "Call me Fishmeal," and it will feature a menopausal suburban husband named Richard, who because he is so depressed all the time is called "Mopey Dick" by his witty wife Elaine. Say to your roommate: "Mopey Dick, get it?" Your roommate looks at you, like a buddy, and puts an arm around your burdened shoulders. "Listen, Francie," she says, slow as speech therapy. "Let's go out and get a big beer."

The seminar doesn't like this one either. You suspect they are beginning to feel sorry for you. They say: "You have to think about what is happening. Where is the story here?"

The next semester the writing professor is obsessed with writing from personal experience. You must write from what you know, from what has happened to you. He wants deaths, he wants camping trips. Think about what has happened to you. In three years there have been three things: you lost your virginity; your parents got divorced; and your brother came home from a forest ten miles from the Cambodian border with only half a thigh, a permanent smirk nestled into one corner of his mouth.

20    About the first you write: "It created a new space, which hurt and cried in a voice that wasn't mine, 'I'm not the same anymore, but I'll be okay.'"

About the second you write an elaborate story of an old married couple who stumble upon an unknown land mine in their kitchen and accidentally blow themselves up. You call it: "For Better or for Liverwurst."

About the last you write nothing. There are no words for this. Your typewriter hums. You can find no words.

At undergraduate cocktail parties, people say, "Oh, you write? What do you write about?" Your roommate, who has consumed too much wine, too little cheese, and no crackers at all, blurts: "Oh, my god, she always writes about her dumb boyfriend."

Later on in life you will learn that writers are merely open, helpless texts with no real understanding of what they have written and therefore must half-believe anything and everything that is said of them. You, however, have not yet reached this stage of literary criticism. You stiffen and say, "I do not," the same way you said it when someone in the fourth grade accused you of really liking oboe lessons and your parents really weren't just making you take them.

25    Insist you are not very interested in any one subject at all, that you are interested in the music of language, that you are interested in—in—syllables, because they are the atoms of poetry, the cells of the mind, the breath of the soul. Begin to feel woozy. Stare into your plastic wine cup.

"Syllables?" you will hear someone ask, voice trailing off, as they glide slowly toward the reassuring white of the dip.

Begin to wonder what you do write about. Or if you have anything to say. Or if there even is such a thing as a thing to say. Limit these thoughts to no more than ten minutes a day; like sit-ups, they can make you thin.

You will read somewhere that all writing has to do with one's genitals. Don't dwell on this. It will make you nervous.

Your mother will come visit you. She will look at the circles under your eyes and hand you a brown book with a brown briefcase on the cover. It is entitled: *How to Become a Business Executive*. She has also brought the *Names for Baby* encyclopedia you asked for; one of your characters, the aging clown-school teacher, needs a new name. Your mother will shake her head and say: "Francie, Francie, remember when you were going to be a child psychology major?"

Say: "Mom, I like to write."

She'll say: "Sure you like to write. Of course. Sure you like to write."                                    30

Write a story about a confused music student and title it: "Schubert Was the One with the Glasses, Right?" It's not a big hit, although your roommate likes the part where the two violinists accidentally blow themselves up in a recital room. "I went out with a violinist once," she says, snapping her gum.

Thank god you are taking other courses. You can find sanctuary in nineteenth-century ontological snags and invertebrate courting rituals. Certain globular mollusks have what is called "Sex by the Arm." The male octopus, for instance, loses the end of one arm when placing it inside the female body during intercourse. Marine biologists call it "Seven Heaven." Be glad you know these things. Be glad you are not just a writer. Apply to law school.

From here on in, many things can happen. But the main one will be this: you decide not to go to law school after all, and, instead, you spend a good, big chunk of your adult life telling people how you decided not to go to law school after all. Somehow you end up writing again. Perhaps you go to graduate school. Perhaps you work odd jobs and take writing courses at night. Perhaps you are working on a novel and writing down all the clever remarks and intimate personal confessions you hear during the day. Perhaps you are losing your pals, your acquaintances, your balance.

You have broken up with your boyfriend. You now go out with men who, instead of whispering "I love you," shout: "Do it to me, baby." This is good for your writing.                           35

Sooner or later you have a finished manuscript more or less. People look at it in a vaguely troubled sort of way and say, "I'll bet becoming a writer was always a fantasy of yours, wasn't it?" Your lips dry to salt. Say that of all the fantasies possible in the world, you can't imagine being a writer even making the top twenty. Tell them you were going to be a child psychology major. "I bet," they always sigh, "you'd be great with kids." Scowl fiercely. Tell them you're a walking blade.

Quit classes. Quit jobs. Cash in old savings bonds. Now you have time like warts on your hands. Slowly copy all of your friends' addresses into a new address book.

Vacuum. Chew cough drops. Keep a folder full of fragments.

*An eyelid darkening sideways.*

*World as conspiracy.*

*Possible plot? A woman gets on a bus.*

*Suppose you threw a love affair and nobody came.*

At home drink a lot of coffee. At Howard Johnson's order the cole slaw. Consider how it looks like the soggy confetti of a map: where you've been, where you're going—"You Are Here," says the red star on the back of the menu.

40      Occasionally a date with a face blank as a sheet of paper asks you whether writers often become discouraged. Say that sometimes they do and sometimes they do. Say it's a lot like having polio.

"Interesting," smiles your date, and then he looks down at his arm hairs and starts to smooth them, all, always, in the same direction.

## Questions

1. To whom does the "you" in the story refer? How strong a case may be made that the "you" refers really to "I," and that Francie is actually telling a story about herself?
2. In light of the title, how adequate are Francie's "directions" for becoming a writer?
3. Describe some of the comic elements of the story. What serious ideas about the development of a writer's profession undergird the story's humor?

## JOYCE CAROL OATES (b. 1938)

A superabundantly productive and richly acclaimed author of more than thirty novels—some under pseudonyms—and many collections of stories, books of poems, and collections of criticism, Joyce Carol Oates attended a one-room school as a child, and went on to receive her higher education at Syracuse University and the University of Wisconsin. She began her teaching career at the University of Detroit and currently, in addition to various guest positions, is Distinguished Professor in the Humanities at Princeton University. Just a few of her many novels are *With Shuddering Fall* (1964), *Angel of Light* (1981), *Solstice* (1985), *Foxfire* (1993), *Middle Age: A Romance* (2001), *Missing Mom* (2005), and *Black Girl/White Girl* (2006). Recent story collections are *Faithless: Tales of Transgression* (2001), *I Am No One You Know* (2004), and *High Lonesome: Selected Stories, 1966–2006* (2006). Among her many awards and distinctions are a Guggenheim Fellowship, the Continuing Achievement Award of the O. Henry Award Prize Stories series, a National Book Award, and the Chicago Tribune Literary Prize, not to mention three nominations for the Pulitzer Prize.

## The Cousins (2004)

Lake Worth, Florida
September 14, 1998

Dear Professor Morgenstern,
      How badly I wish that I could address you as "Freyda"! But I don't have the right to such familiarity.

I have just read your memoir. I have reason to believe that we are cousins. My maiden name is "Schwart" (not my father's actual name, I think it was changed at Ellis Island in 1936),[1] but my mother's maiden name was "Morgenstern" and all her family was from Kaufbeuren as yours were. We were to meet in 1941 when we were small children, you and your parents and sister and brother were coming to live with my parents, my two brothers, and me in Milburn, New York. But the boat that was carrying you and other refugees, the *Marea*,[2] was turned back by U.S. Immigration at New York Harbor.

(In your memoir you speak so briefly of this. You seem to recall a name other than *Marea*. But I am sure that *Marea* was the name, for it seemed so beautiful to me like music. You were so young of course. So much would happen afterward, you would not remember this. By my calculation you were 6, and I was 5.)

All these years I had not known that you were living! I had not known that there were survivors in your family. It was told to us by my father that there were not. I am so happy for you and your success. To think that you were living in the U.S. since 1956 is a shock to me. That you were a college student in New York City while I was living (my first marriage, not a happy one) in upstate New York! Forgive me, I did not know of your previous books, though I would be intrigued by 'biological anthropology," I think! (I have nothing of your academic education, I'm so ashamed. Not only not college but I did not graduate from high school.)

Well, I am writing in the hope that we might meet. Oh very soon, Freyda! Before it's too late.

I am no longer your 5-year-old cousin dreaming of a new "sister" (as my mother promised) who would sleep with me in my bed and be with me always.

Your "lost" cousin,
Rebecca

Lake Worth, Florida
September 15, 1998

Dear Professor Morgenstern,

I wrote to you just the other day. Now I see to my embarrassment that I may have sent the letter to a wrong address. If you are "on sabbatical leave" from the University of Chicago, as it says on the dust jacket of your memoir. I will try again with this, care of your publisher.

I will enclose the same letter. Though I feel it is not adequate, to express what is in my heart.

Your "lost" cousin,
Rebecca

P.S. Of course I will come to you, wherever & whenever you wish, Freyda!

Lake Worth, Florida
October 2, 1998

Dear Professor Morgenstern,

I wrote to you last month but I'm afraid that my letters were misaddressed. I will enclose these letters here, now that I know you are at the "Institute for Advanced Research" at Stanford University, Palo Alto, California.

---

[1] *Ellis Island in 1936:* In actuality, the German liner S.S. *St Louis*, with 930 Jewish refugee passengers aboard, first reached Havana, Cuba, in May 1936, but only a few refugees were allowed entrance to Cuba. The *St. Louis* then went to New York, where no refugees at all were to be allowed. From Rebecca's description a little later we learn that she was born while the ship was anchored in the New York Harbor. We may infer that the birth of Rebecca, who, being born in the United States, was automatically a citizen, made it possible for her family to stay here, and we conclude that they went through immigration procedures at Ellis Island. But in early June 1936, the *St. Louis* was forced to return most of the refugees to Europe, where they were dispersed to a number of separate countries. Those who were sent to England survived, but the others eventually were sent to Nazi concentration and extermination camps.

[2] the *Marea:* This reference indicates that the *Marea* was turned back. The result was that it was not until 1956 that Freyda was allowed entry and citizenship in the United States.

It's possible that you have read my letters and were offended by them. I know, I am not a very good writer. I should not have said what I did about the Atlantic crossing in 1941, as if you would not know these facts for yourself. I did not mean to correct you, Professor Morgenstern, regarding the name of the very boat you and your family were on in that nightmare time!

In an interview with you reprinted in the Miami newspaper I was embarrassed to read that you have received so much mail from "relatives" since the memoir. I smiled to read where you said, "Where were all these relatives in America when they were needed?"

Truly we were here, Freyda! In Milburn, New York, on the Erie Canal.

Your cousin,
Rebecca

Palo Alto, CA
1 November 1998

Dear Rebecca Schward,

Thank you for your letter and for your response to my memoir. I have been deeply moved by the numerous letters I've received since the publication of *Back from the Dead: A Girlhood* both in the United States and abroad, and truly wish that I had time to reply to each of these individually and at length.

Sincerely,
FM
Freyda Morgenstern
Julius K. Tracey '48 Distinguished
Professor of Anthropology,
University of Chicago

Lake Worth, Florida
November 5, 1998

Dear Professor Morgenstern,

I'm very relieved now, I have the correct address! I hope that you will read this letter. I think you must have a secretary who opens your mail and sends back replies. I know, you are amused (annoyed?) by so many now claiming to be relatives of "Freyda Morgenstern." Especially since your television interviews. But I feel very strongly, I am your true cousin. For I was the (only) daughter of Anna Morgenstern. I believe that Anna Morgenstern was the (only) sister of your mother, Sara, a younger sister. For many weeks my mother spoke of her sister, Sara, coming to live with us, your father and your Elzbieta, who was older than you by 3 or 4 years, and your brother, Leon, who was also older than you, not by so much.

We had photographs of you. I remember so clearly how your hair was so neatly plaited and how pretty you were, a "frowning girl" my mother said of you, like me. We did look alike then, Freyda, though you were much prettier of course. Elzbieta was blonde with a plump face. Leon was looking happy in the photograph, a sweet-seeming boy of maybe 8. To read that your sister and brother died in such a terrible way in "Theresienstadt"[3] was so sad. My mother never recovered from the shock of that time, I think. She was so hoping to see her sister again. When the *Marea* was turned back in the harbor, she gave up hope. My father did not allow her to speak German, only English, but she could not speak English well, if anyone came to the house she would hide. She did not speak much afterward to any of us and was often sick. She died in May 1949.

Reading this letter I see that I am giving a wrong emphasis, really! I never think of these long-ago things.

---

[3] *Theresienstadt:* A Nazi concentration camp in what was then Czechoslovakia.

It was seeing your picture in the newspaper, Freyda! My husband was reading the *New York Times* & called me to him saying wasn't it strange, here was a woman looking enough like his wife to be a sister, though in fact you & I do not look so much alike, in my opinion, not any longer, but it was a shock to see your face, which is very like my mother's face as I remember it.

And then your name, *Freyda Morgenstern.*

At once I went out & purchased *Back from the Dead: A Girlhood.* I have not read any Holocaust memoirs out of a dread of what I would learn. Your memoir I read sitting in the car in the parking lot of the bookstore not knowing the time, how late it was, until my eyes could not see the pages. I thought, "It's Freyda! It's her! My sister I was promised." Now I am 62 years old, and so lonely in this place of retired wealthy people who look at me & think that I am one of them.

I am not one to cry. But I wept on many pages of your memoir though I know (from your interviews) you wish not to hear such reports from readers & have only contempt for "cheap American pity." I know, I would feel the same way. You are right to feel that way. In Milburn I resented the people who felt sorry for me as the "gravedigger's daughter" (my father's employment) more than the others who did not give a damn if the Schwarts lived or died.

I am enclosing my picture, taken when I was a girl of 16. It is all I have of those years. (I look very different now, I'm afraid!) How badly I wish I could send you a picture of my mother, Anna Morgenstern, but all were destroyed in 1949.

Your cousin,
Rebecca

Palo Alto, CA
16 November 1998

Dear Rebecca Schwart,

Sorry not to have replied earlier. I think yes it is quite possible that we are "cousins" but at such a remove it's really an abstraction, isn't it?

I am not traveling much this year, trying to complete a new book before my sabbatical ends. I am giving fewer "talks" and my book tour is over, thank God. (The venture into memoir was my first and will be my last effort at non-academic writing. It was far too easy, like opening a vein.) So I don't quite see how it would be feasible for us to meet at the present time.

Thank you for sending your photograph. I am returning it.

Sincerely,
FM

Lake Worth, Florida
November 20, 1998

Dear Freyda,

Yes, I am sure we are "cousins"! Though like you I don't know what "cousins" can mean.

I have no living relatives, I believe. My parents have been dead since 1949 & I know nothing of my brothers, whom I have not glimpsed in many years.

I think you despise me as your "American cousin." I wish you could forgive me for that. I am not sure how "American" I am, though I was not born in Kaufbeuren as you were but in New York Harbor in May 1936.[4] (The exact day is lost. There was no birth certificate or it was lost.) I mean, I was born on the refugee boat! In a place of terrible filth, I was told.

It was a different time then, 1936. The war had not begun & people of our kind were allowed to "emigrate" if they had money.

---

[4]*in May 1936:* This is the reference to the birth of Rebecca.

My brothers, Herschel & Augustus, were born in Kaufbeuren & of course both our parents. My father called himself "Jacob Schwart" in this country. (This is a name I have never spoken to anyone who knows me now. Not to my husband of course.) I knew little of my father except he had been a printer in the old world (as he called it with scorn) and at one time a math teacher in a boys' school. Until the Nazis forbade such people to teach. My mother, Anna Morgenstern, was married very young. She played piano, as a girl. We would listen to music on the radio sometime if Pa was not home. (The radio was Pa's.)

Forgive me, I know you are not interested in any of this. In your memoir you spoke of your mother as a record keeper for the Nazis, one of those Jewish "administrators" helping in the transport of Jews.[5] You are not sentimental about family. There is something so craven to it, isn't there. I respect the wishes of one who wrote *Back from the Dead*, which is so critical of your relatives & Jews & Jewish history & beliefs as of postwar "amnesia." I would not wish to dissuard you of such a true feeling, Freyda!

I have no true feelings myself, I mean that others can know.

Pa said you were all gone. Like cattle sent back to Hitler, Pa said. I remember his voice lifting, NINE HUNDRED SEVENTY-SIX REFUGEES, I am sick still hearing that voice.

Pa said for me to stop thinking about my cousins! They were not coming. They were *gone*.

Many pages of your memoir I have memorized, Freyda. And your letters to me. In your words, I can hear your voice. I love this voice so like my own. My secret voice I mean, that no one knows.

I will fly to California, Freyda. Will you give me permission? "Only say the word & my soul shall be healed."

> Your cousin,
> Rebecca

> Lake Worth, Florida
> November 21, 1998

Dear Freyda,

I am so ashamed, I mailed you a letter yesterday with a word misspelled: "dissuade." And I spoke of no living relatives, I meant no one remaining from the Schwart family. (I have a son from my first marriage, he is married with two children.)

I have bought other books of yours. *Biology: A History, Race and Racism: A History*. How impressed Jacob Schwart would be, the little girl in the photographs was never gone but has so very far surpassed him!

Will you let me come to see you in Palo Alto, Freyda? I could arrive for one day, we might have a meal together & I would depart the next morning. This is a promise.

> Your (lonely) cousin,
> Rebecca

> Lake Worth, Florida
> November 24, 1998

Dear Freyda,

An evening of your time is too much to ask, I think. An hour? An hour would not be too much, would it? Maybe you could talk to me of your work, anything in your voice would be precious to me. I would not wish to drag you into the cesspool of the past, as you speak of it so

---

[5] *helping in the transport of Jews:* In the Nazi concentration camps, a number of Jewish prisoners served the Germans in various administrative capacities. These were called "Kapos," and they were known for their arbitrariness and brutality. Freyda, in the letter dated September 23, indicates that her mother was not a Kapo.

strongly. A woman like yourself capable of such intellectual work & so highly regarded in your field has no time for maudlin sentiment, I agree.

I have been reading your books. Underlining & looking up words in the dictionary. (I love the dictionary, it's my friend.) So exciting to consider How does science demonstrate the genetic basis of behavior?

I have enclosed a card here for your reply. Forgive me I did not think of this earlier.

Your cousin,
Rebecca

Palo Alto, CA
24 November 1998

Dear Rebecca Schwart,

Your letters of Nov. 20 & 21 are interesting. But the name "Jacob Schwart" means nothing to me, I'm afraid. There are numerous "Morgensterns" surviving. Perhaps some of these are your cousins, too. You might seek them out if you are lonely.

As I believe I have explained, this is a very busy time for me. I work much of the day and am not feeling very sociable in the evening. "Loneliness" is a problem engendered primarily by the too-close proximity of others. One excellent remedy is work.

Sincerely,
FM

P.S. I believe you have left phone messages for me at the Institute. As my assistant has explained to you, I have no time to answer such calls.

Lake Worth, Florida
November 27, 1998

Dear Freyda,

Our letters crossed! We both wrote on Nov. 24, maybe it's a sign.

It was on impulse I telephoned. "If I could hear her voice"—the thought came to me.

You have hardened your heart against your "American cousin." It was courageous in the memoir to state so clearly how you had to harden your heart against so much, to survive. Americans believe that suffering makes saints of us, which is a joke. Still I realize you have no time for me in your life now. There is no "purpose" to me.

Even if you won't meet me at this time, will you allow me to write to you? I will accept it if you do not reply. I would only wish that you might read what I write, it would make me so happy (yes, less lonely!), for then I could speak to you in my thoughts as I did when we were girls.

Your cousin,
Rebecca

P.S. In your academic writing you refer so often to "adaptation of species to environment." If you saw me, your cousin, in Lake Worth, Florida, on the ocean just south of Palm Beach, so very far from Milburn, N.Y., and from the "old world," you would laugh.

Palo Alto, CA
1 December 1998

Dear Rebecca Schwart,

My tenacious American cousin! I'm afraid it is no sign of anything, not even "coincidence," that our letters were written on the same day and that they "crossed."

This card. I admit I am curious at the choice. It happens this is a card on my study wall. (Did I speak of this in the memoir? I don't think so.) How do you happen to come into possession of this reproduction of Caspar David Friedrich's *Sturzacker*—you have not been to the museum in Hamburg, have you?[6] It's rare that any American even knows the name of this artist much esteemed in Germany.

Sincerely,

FM

Lake Worth, Florida

4 December 1998

Dear Freyda,

The post card of Caspar David Friedrich was given to me, with other cards from the Hamburg museum, by someone who traveled there. (In fact my son, who is a pianist. His name would be known to you, it's nothing like my own.)

I chose a card to reflect your soul. As I perceive it in your words. Maybe it reflects mine also. I wonder what you will think of this new card, which is German also but uglier.

Your cousin,

Rebecca

Palo Alto, CA

10 December 1998

Dear Rebecca,

Yes I like this ugly Nolde.[7] Smoke black as pitch and the Elbe like molten lava. You see into my soul, don't you! Not that I have wished to disguise myself.

So I return *Towboat on the Elbe* to my tenacious American cousin. THANK YOU but please do not write again. And do not call. I have had enough of you.

FM

Palo Alto, CA

11 December 1998/2:00 A.M.

Dear "Cousin"!

Your 16-yr-old photo I made a copy of. I like that coarse mane of hair and the jaws so solid. Maybe the eyes were scared, but we know how to hide that, don't we cousin.

In the camp I learned to stand tall. I learned to be big. As animals make themselves bigger, it can be a trick to the eye that comes true. I guess you were a "big" girl, too.

I have always told the truth. I see no reason for subterfuge. I despise fantasizing. I have made enemies "among my kind" you can be sure. When you are "back from the dead" you do not give a damn for others' opinions & believe me, that has cost me in this so-called "profession" where advancement depends upon ass-kissing and its sexual variants not unlike the activities of our kindred primates.

Bad enough my failure to behave as a suppliant female through my career. In the memoir I take a laughing tone speaking of graduate studies at Columbia in the late 1950s. I did not laugh much then. Meeting my old enemies, who had wished to crush an impious female at the start of her career, not only female but a Jew & a refugee Jew from one of the camps, I looked them in the eye, I never flinched, but they flinched, the bastards. I took my revenge where & when I could. Now those generations are dying out, I am not pious about their memories. At conferences organized to revere them, Freyda Morgenstern is the "savagely witty" truth-teller.

---

[6] *Sturzacker:* Caspar David Friedrich (1774–1840), one of the best known German Romantic artists, painted the *Sturzacker* (a freshly plowed field) in 1825. It hangs in the Hamburg Kunsthalle, in Germany.

[7] *Nolde:* Emil Nolde (1867–1956, 1956), one of the best-known German Expressionists. His *Hamburg, Free Port* (1910) resembles the painting described here.

In Germany, where history was so long denied, *Back from the Dead* has been a bestseller for five months. Already it has been nominated for two major awards. Here is a joke, and a good one, yes?

In this country, no such reception. Maybe you saw the "good" reviews. Maybe you saw the one full-page ad my cheapskate publisher finally ran in the *New York Review of Books*. There have been plenty of attacks. Worse even than the stupid attacks to which I have become accustomed in my "profession."

In the Jewish publications, & in Jewish-slanted publications, such shock/dismay/disgust. A Jewish woman who writes so without sentiment of mother & other relatives who "perished" in Theresienstadt. A Jewish woman who speaks so coldly & "scientifically" of her "heritage." As if the so-called Holocaust is a "heritage." As if I have not earned my right to speak the truth as I see it and will continue to speak the truth, for I have no plans to retire from research, writing, teaching, & directing doctoral students for a long time. (I will take early retirement at Chicago, these very nice benefits, & set up shop elsewhere.)

This piety of the Holocaust! I laughed, you used that word so reverentially in one of your letters. I never use this word that slides off American tongues now like grease. One of the hatchet-reviewers called Morgenstern a traitor giving solace to the enemy (which enemy? there are many) by simply stating & restating, as I will each time I am asked, that the "holocaust" was an accident in history as all events in history are accidents. There is no purpose to history as to evolution, there is no goal or progress. Evolution is the term given to what is. The pious fantasizers wish to claim that the Nazis' genocidal campaign was a singular event in history, that it has elevated us above history. This is bullshit, I have said so & will continue to say so. There are many genocides, as long as there has been mankind. History is an invention of books. In biological anthropology we note that the wish to perceive "meaning" is one trait of our species among many. But that does not posit "meaning" in the world. If history did exist it is a great river/cesspool into which countless small streams & tributaries flow. In one direction. Unlike sewage it cannot back up. It cannot be "tested"—"demonstrated." It simply is. If the individual streams dry up, the river disappears. There is no "river-destiny." There are merely accidents in time. The scientist notes that without sentiment or regret.

Maybe I will send you these ravings, my tenacious American cousin. I'm drunk enough, in a festive mood!

Your (traitor) cousin,
FM

Lake Worth, Florida
15 December 1998

Dear Freyda,

How I loved your letter, that made my hands shake. I have not laughed in so long. I mean, in our special way.

It's the way of hatred. I love it. Though it eats you from the inside out. (I guess.)

It's a cold night here, a wind off the Atlantic. Florida is often wet-cold. Lake Worth/Palm Beach are very beautiful & very boring. I wish you might come here & visit, you could spend the rest of the winter, for it's often sunny of course.

I take your precious letters with me in the early morning walking on the beach. Though I have memorized your words. Until a year ago I would run, run, run for miles! At the rain-whipped edge of a hurricane I ran. To see me, my hard-muscled legs & straight back-bone, you would never guess I was not a young woman.

So strange that we are in our sixties, Freyda! Our baby-girl dolls have not aged a day.

(Do you hate it, growing old? Your photographs show such a vigorous woman. You tell yourself, "Every day I live was not meant to be" & there's happiness in this.)

Freyda, in our house of mostly glass facing the ocean you would have your own "wing." We have several cars, you would have your own car. No questions asked where you went. You would not have to meet my husband, you would be my precious secret.

Tell me you will come, Freyda! After the New Year would be a good time. When you finish your work each day we will go walking on the beach together. I promise we would not have to speak.

Your loving cousin,
Rebecca

Lake Worth, Florida
17 December 1998

Dear Freyda,

Forgive my letter of the other day, so pushy & familiar. Of course you would not wish to visit a stranger.

I must make myself remember: though we are cousins, we are strangers.

I was reading again *Back from the Dead*. The last section, in America. Your three marriages—"ill-advised experiments in intimacy/lunacy." You are very harsh & very funny, Freyda! Unsparing to others as to yourself.

My first marriage too was blind in love & I suppose "lunacy." Yet without it, I would not have my son.

In the memoir you have no regret for your "misbegotten fetuses" though for the "pain and humiliation" of the abortions illegal at the time. Poor Freyda! In 1957 in a filthy room in Manhattan you nearly bled to death, at that time I was a young mother so in love with my life. Yet I would have come to you, if I had known.

Though I know that you will not come here, yet I hold out hope that, suddenly yes you might! To visit, to stay as long as you wish. Your privacy would be protected.

I remain the tenacious cousin,
Rebecca

Lake Worth, Florida
New Year's Day 1999

Dear Freyda,

I don't hear from you, I wonder if you have gone away? But maybe you will see this. "If Freyda sees this even to toss away . . ."

I am feeling happy & hopeful. You are a scientist & of course you are right to scorn such feelings as "magical" & "primitive," but I think there can be a newness in the New Year. I am hoping this is so.

My father, Jacob Schwart, believed that in animal life the weak are quickly disposed of, we must hide our weakness always. You & I knew that as children. But there is so much more to us than just the animal, we know that, too.

Your loving cousin,
Rebecca

Palo Alto, CA
19 January 1999

Rebecca:

Yes I have been away. And I am going away again. What business is it of yours?

I was coming to think you must be an invention of mine. My worst weakness. But here on my windowsill propped up to stare at me is "Rebecca, 1952." The horse-mane hair & hungry eyes.

Cousin, you are so faithful! It makes me tired. I know I should be flattered, few others would wish to pursue "difficult" Professor Morgenstern now I'm an old woman. I toss your letters into a drawer, then in my weakness I open them. Once, rummaging through Dumpster trash I retrieved a letter of yours. Then in my weakness I opened it. You know how I hate weakness!

Cousin, no more.

FM

Lake Worth, Florida
23 January 1999

Dear Freyda,

I know! I am sorry.

I shouldn't be so greedy. I have no right. When I first discovered that you were living, last September, my thought was only "My cousin Freyda Morgenstern, my lost sister, she is alive! She doesn't need to love me or even know me or give a thought to me. It's enough to know that she did not perish and has lived her life."

Your loving cousin,
Rebecca

Palo Alto, CA
30 January 1999

Dear Rebecca,

We make ourselves ridiculous with emotions at our age, like showing our breasts. Spare us, please!

No more would I wish to meet you than I would wish to meet myself. Why would you imagine I might want a "cousin"—"sister"—at my age? I would like it that I have no living relatives any longer, for there is no obligation to think *Is he/she still living?*

Anyway, I'm going away. I will be traveling all spring. I hate it here. California suburban boring & without a soul. My "colleagues/friends" are shallow opportunists to whom I appear to be an opportunity.

I hate such words as "perish." Does a fly "perish," do rotting things "perish," does your enemy "perish"? Such exalted speech makes me tired.

Nobody "perished" in the camps. Many "died"—"were killed." That's all.

I wish I could forbid you to revere me. For your own good, dear cousin. I see that I am your weakness, too. Maybe I want to spare you.

If you were a graduate student of mine, though! I would set you right with a swift kick in the rear.

Suddenly there are awards & honors for Freyda Morgenstern. Not only the memoirist but the "distinguished anthropologist" too. So I will travel to receive them. All this comes too late of course. Yet like you I am a greedy person, Rebecca. Sometimes I think my soul is in my gut! I am one who stuffs herself without pleasure, to take food from others.

Spare yourself. No more emotion. No more letters!

FM

Chicago, IL
29 March 1999

Dear Rebecca Schwart,

Have been thinking of you lately. It has been a while since I've heard from you. Unpacking things here & came across your letters & photograph. How stark-eyed we all looked in black-and-white! Like x-rays of the soul. My hair was never so thick & splendid as yours, my American cousin.

I think I must have discouraged you. Now, to be frank, I miss you. It has been two months nearly since you wrote. These honors & awards are not so precious if no one cares. If no one hugs you in congratulations. Modesty is beside the point & I have too much pride to boast to strangers.

Of course, I should be pleased with myself: I sent you away. I know, I am a "difficult" woman. I would not like myself for a moment. I would not tolerate myself. I seem to have lost one or two of your letters, I'm not sure how many, vaguely I remember you saying you & your family lived in upstate New York, my parents had arranged to come stay with you? This was in 1941? You provided facts not in my memoir. But I do remember my mother speaking with such love of her younger sister, Anna. Your father changed his name to "Schwart" from—what? He was a math teacher in Kaufbeuren? My father was an esteemed doctor. He had many non-Jewish patients who revered him. As a young man he had served in the German army in the first war, he'd been awarded a Gold Medal for Bravery & it was promised that such a distinction would protect him while other Jews were being transported. My father disappeared so abruptly from our lives, immediately we were transported to that place, for years I believed he must have escaped & was alive somewhere & would contact us. I thought my mother had information she kept from me. She was not quite the Amazon-mother of *Back from the Dead* . . . Well, enough of this! Though evolutionary anthropology must scour the past relentlessly, human beings are not obliged to do so.

It's a blinding-bright day here in Chicago, from my aerie on the 52nd floor of my grand new apartment building I look out upon the vast inland sea Lake Michigan. Royalties from the memoir have helped me pay for this, a less "controversial" book would not have earned. Nothing more is needed, yes?

Your cousin,
Freyda

Lake Worth, Florida
April 3, 1999

Dear Freyda,

Your letter meant much to me. I'm so sorry not to answer sooner. I make no excuses. Seeing this card I thought, "For Freyda!"

Next time I will write more. Soon I promise.

Your cousin,
Rebecca

Chicago, IL
22 April 1999

Dear Rebecca,

Rec'd your card. Am not sure what I think of it. Americans are ga-ga for Joseph Cornell[8] as they are for Edward Hopper.[9] What is *Lanner Waltzes*? Two little-girl doll figures riding the crest of a wave & in the background an old-fashioned sailing ship with sails billowing? "Collage"? I hate riddle-art. Art is to see, not to *think*.

Is something wrong, Rebecca? The tone of your writing is altered, I think. I hope you are not playing coy, to take revenge for my chiding letter of January. I have a doctoral student, a bright young woman not quite so bright as she fancies herself, who plays such games with me at the present time, at her own risk! I hate games, too.

(Unless they are my own.)

Your cousin,
Freyda

---

[8]*Joseph Cornell:* (1903–72), American artist. His *Lanner Waltzes* hangs in the Smithsonian American Art Museum. *Lanner Waltzes* refers to waltz music by the Austrian composer Josef Lanner (1801–43), who in his day was as famous as Johann Strauss, Sr. (1804–49).

[9]*Edward Hopper:* (1882–1967), American realist painter. (See I–3, Plate 2).

Chicago, IL
6 May 1999

Dear Cousin:

Yes, I think you must be angry with me! Or you are not well.

I prefer to think that you are angry. That I did insult you in your American soft heart. If so, I am sorry. I have no copies of my letters to you & don't recall what I said. Maybe I was wrong. When I am coldly sober, I am likely to be wrong. When drunk, I am likely to be less wrong.

Enclosed here is a stamped addressed card. You need only check one of the boxes: [ ] angry [ ] not well.

Your cousin,
Freyda

P.S. This Joseph Cornell Pond reminded me of you, Rebecca. A doll-girl playing her fiddle beside a murky inlet.

Lake Worth, Florida
September 19, 1999

Dear Freyda,

How strong & beautiful you were, at the awards ceremony in Washington! I was there, in the audience at the Folger Library. I made the trip just for you.

All of the writers honored spoke very well. But none so witty & unexpected as "Freyda Morgenstern," who caused quite a stir.

I'm ashamed to say, I could not bring myself to speak to you. I waited in line with so many others for you to sign *Back from the Dead* & when my turn came you were beginning to tire. You hardly glanced at me, you were vexed at the girl assistant fumbling the book. I did no more than mumble, "Thank you," & hurried away.

I stayed just one night in Washington, then flew home. I tire easily now, it was a mad thing to do. My husband would have prevented me if he'd known where I was headed.

During the speeches you were restless onstage, I saw your eyes wandering. I saw your eyes on me. I was sitting in the third row of the theater. Such an old, beautiful little theater in the Folger Library. I think there must be so much beauty in the world we haven't seen. Now it is almost too late we yearn for it.

I was the gaunt-skull woman with the buzz cut. The heavy dark glasses covering half my face. Others in my condition wear gaudy turbans or gleaming wigs. Their faces are bravely made up. In Lake Worth/Palm Beach there are many of us. I don't mind my baldie head in warm weather & among strangers, for their eyes look through me as if I am invisible. You stared at me at first & then looked quickly away & afterward I could not bring myself to address you. It wasn't the right time, I had not prepared you for the sight of me. I shrink from pity & even sympathy is a burden. I had not known that I would make the reckless trip until that morning, for so much depends upon how I feel each morning, it's not predictable.

I had a present to give to you, I changed my mind & took away again feeling like a fool. Yet the trip was wonderful for me, I saw my cousin so close! Of course I regret my cowardice now it's too late.

You asked about my father. I will tell you no more than that I do not know my father's true name. "Jacob Schwart" was what he called himself & so I was "Rebecca Schwart," but that name was lost long ago. I have another more fitting American name, & I have also my husband's last name, only to you, my cousin, am I identified as "Rebecca Schwart."

Well, I will tell you one more thing: in May 1949 my father who was the gravedigger murdered your aunt Anna and wished to murder me but failed, he turned the shotgun onto himself

& killed himself when I was 13 struggling with him for the gun & my strongest memory of that time was his face in the last seconds & what remained of his face, his skull & brains & the warmth of his blood splattered onto me.

I have never told anyone this, Freyda. Please do not speak of it to me, if you write again.

Your cousin
Rebecca

(I did not intend to write such an ugly thing, when I began this letter.)

Chicago, IL
23 September 1999

Dear Rebecca,

I'm stunned. That you were so close to me—and didn't speak.

And what you tell me of—. What happened to you at age 13.

I don't know what to say. Except yes I am stunned. I am angry, & hurt. Not at you, I don't think I am angry at you but at myself.

I've tried to call you. There is no "Rebecca Schwart" in the Lake Worth phone directory. Of course, you've told me there is no "Rebecca Schwart." Why in hell have you never told me your married name? Why are you so coy? I hate games, I don't have time for games.

Yes I am angry with you. I am upset & angry you are not well. (You never returned my card. I waited & waited & you did not.)

Can I believe you about "Jacob Schwart"! We conclude that the ugliest things are likely to be true.

In my memoir that isn't so. When I wrote it, 54 yrs later it was a text I composed of words chosen for "effect." Yes there are true facts in *Back from the Dead*. But facts are not "true" unless explained. My memoir had to compete with other memoirs of its type & so had to be "original." I am accustomed to controversy, I know how to tweak noses. The memoir makes light of the narrator's pain & humiliation. It's true, I did not feel that I would be one of those to die; I was too young, & ignorant, & compared to others I was healthy. My big blonde sister Elzbieta the relatives so admired, looking like a German girl-doll, soon lost all that hair & her bowels turned to bloody suet. Leon died trampled to death, I would learn afterward. What I say of my mother, Sara Morgenstern, is truthful only at the start. She was not a kapo but one hoping to cooperate with the Nazis to help her family (of course) & other Jews. She was a good organizer & much trusted but never so strong as the memoir has her. She did not say those cruel things, I have no memory of anything anyone said to me except orders shouted by authorities. All the quiet spoken words, the very breath of our lives together, was lost. But a memoir must have spoken words, & a memoir must breathe life.

I am so famous now—infamous! In France this month I am a new bestseller. In the U.K. (where they are outspoken anti-Semites, which is refreshing!) my word is naturally doubted yet still the book sells.

Rebecca, I must speak with you. I will enclose my number here. I will wait for a call. Past 10:00 P.M. of any night is best, I am not so cold-sober & nasty.

Your cousin,
Freyda

P.S. Are you taking chemotherapy now? What is the status of your condition? Please answer.

Lake Worth, Florida
October 8

Dear Freyda,

Don't be angry with me, I have wanted to call you. There are reasons I could not but maybe I will be stronger soon & I promise, I will call.

It was important for me to see you, and hear you. I am so proud of you. It hurts me when you say harsh things about yourself, I wish you would not. "Spare us"—yes?

Half the time I am dreaming & very happy. Just now I was smelling snakeroot. Maybe you don't know what snakeroot is, you have lived always in cities. Behind the gravedigger's stone cottage in Milburn there was a marshy place where this tall plant grew. The wildflowers were as tall as five feet. They had many small white flowers that look like frost. Very powdery, with a strange strong smell. The flowers were alive with bees humming so loudly it seemed like a living thing. I was remembering how waiting for you to come from over the ocean I had two dolls—Maggie, who was the prettiest doll, for you, and my doll, Minnie, who was plain & battered but I loved her very much. (My brother Herschel found the dolls at the Milburn dump. We found many useful things at the dump!) For hours I played with Maggie & Minnie & you, Freyda. All of us chattering away. My brothers laughed at me. Last night I dreamt of the dolls that were so vivid to me I had not glimpsed in 57 yrs. But it was strange, Freyda, you were not in the dream. I was not, either.

I will write some other time. I love you.

Your cousin,
Rebecca

Chicago, IL
12 October

Dear Rebecca,

Now I am angry! You have not called me & you have not given me your telephone number & how can I reach you? I have your street address but only the name "Rebecca Schwart." I am so busy, this is a terrible time. I feel as if my head is being broken by a mallet. Oh I am very angry at you, cousin!

Yet I think I should come to Lake Worth, to see you.

Should I?

## Questions

1. Describe the nature of the narration in this story. Who are the speakers? How do you learn about them? What is the advantage, to the writer, of having each person describe aspects of the story?

2. To the best of your ability, describe the story that is actually being told here. What has happened? Who are the cousins? What sort of relationship have they had? How does Rebecca learn about her cousin Freyda? Why does she start the correspondence?

3. What sort of person is Freyda? How do we learn about her? What is she like, as a person? Is she "difficult," as she says of herself? Is she blunt? Is she unkind? What is happening to her life as she writes her letters over the year-long passage of time in the story? What changes does she undergo in the course of the story? Why are her final words so tentative, so unlike her earlier statements?

4. What sort of person is Rebecca? Why is she so sensitive? Is her self-assessment justified in the course of the story? What is happening to her during the time of the story? What positive aspects of her develop, as seen in her letters to her cousin?

5. Which character, Rebecca or Freyda, seems more fully portrayed in the story? Which seems more desirable, as a character? Why? What is the basis for your conclusions?

6. What do you learn, by Freyda's own words, about the nature of her book, *Back from the Dead*? Is everything in the book accurate? What reasons might Freyda have had for arranging truths in the book, and for introducing fictions?

## Writing About Point of View

In your essay on point of view, you should explain how point of view contributes to making the work exactly as it is. As you prepare to write, therefore, consider language, authority and opportunity for observation, the involvement or detachment of the speaker, the selection of detail, interpretive commentaries, and narrative development. The following questions will help you get started.

### Raising Questions to Discover Ideas

- How is the narration made to seem real or probable? Are the actions and speeches reported authentically, as they might be seen and reported in life?
- Is the narrator/speaker identifiable? What are the narrator's qualifications as an observer? How much of the story seems to result from the imaginative or creative powers of the narrator?
- How does the narrator/speaker perceive the time of the actions? If the predominant tense is the past, what relationship, if any, does the narrator establish between the past and the present (e.g., providing explanations, making conclusions)? If the tense is present, what effect does this tense have on your understanding of the story?
- To what extent does the point of view make the work interesting and effective?

#### FIRST-PERSON POINT OF VIEW

- What situation prompts the speaker to tell the story or explain the situation? What does the story tell us about the experience and interests of the narrator/speaker?
- Is the speaker talking to the reader, a listener, or herself? How does her audience affect what she is saying? Is the level of language appropriate to her and the situation? How much does she tell about herself?
- To what degree is the narrator involved in the action (i.e., as a major participant or major mover, minor participant, or nonparticipating observer)? Does he make himself the center of humor or admiration? How? Does he seem aware of changes he undergoes?
- Does the speaker criticize other characters? Why? Does she seem to report fairly and accurately what others have told her?
- How reliable is the speaker? Does the speaker seem to have anything to hide? Does it seem that he may be using the story for self-justification or exoneration? What effect does this complexity have on the story?

## SECOND-PERSON POINT OF VIEW

- What situation prompts the use of the second person? How does the speaker acquire the authority to explain things to the listener? How directly involved is the listener? What is the relationship between the speaker and listener? If the listener is indefinite, why does the speaker choose to use "you" as the basis of the narration?

## THIRD-PERSON POINT OF VIEW

- Does the author speak in an authorial voice, or does it seem that the author has adopted a special but unnamed voice for the work?
- What is the speaker's level of language (e.g., formal and grammatical, informal or intimate and ungrammatical)? Are actions, speeches, and explanations made fully or sparsely?
- From what apparent vantage point does the speaker report action and speeches? Does this vantage point make the characters seem distant or close? How much sympathy does the speaker express for the characters?
- To what degree is your interest centered on a particular character? Does the speaker give you thoughts and responses of this character (limited third person)?
- If the work is third-person omniscient, how extensive is this omniscience (e.g., all the characters or just a few)? Generally, what limitations or freedoms can be attributed to this point of view?
- What special kinds of knowledge does the narrator assume that the listeners or readers possess (e.g., familiarity with art, religion, politics, history, navigation, music, current or past social conditions)?
- How much dialogue is used in the story? Is the dialogue presented directly, as dramatic speech, or indirectly, as past-tense reports of speeches? What is your perception of the story's events as a result of the use of dialogue?

## TENSE

- What tense is used predominantly throughout the story? If a single tense is used throughout (e.g., present, past), what is the effect of this constant use of tense?
- Does the story demonstrate a mixture of tenses? Why are the tenses mixed? What purpose is served by these variations? What is the effect of this mixture?
- Is any special use made of the future tense? What is the effect of this use on the present and past circumstances of the characters?

# Organizing Your Essay About Point of View

Throughout your essay, you should develop your analysis of how the point of view determines such aspects as situation, form, general content, and language. The questions in the preceding section should help you decide how the point of view interacts with these other elements.

Begin by briefly stating the major influence of the point of view on the work. (Examples: "The omniscient point of view permits many insights into the major character," or "The first-person point of view makes the work seem like an exposé of backroom political deals.") How does the point of view make the work interesting and effective? How will your analysis support your central idea?

A fruitful and imaginative way to build your analysis and argument is to explore how changing the point of view might affect the presentation of the story. Let us consider Welty's "A Worn Path" (Chapter 2), which limits its third-person point of view to the circumstances of Phoenix Jackson, whose walk to Natchez is a mission of mercy for her invalid grandson. With the third-person limited focus as we have it, we derive just enough information about Phoenix to understand and sympathize deeply with her plight. If she herself were the narrator, however, we would get not an objective but rather a personalized view of her circumstances—and also perhaps a scattered and unfocused one—and the story would not be as powerful as it is. (Or it might become powerful through different means.) Two stories that would be vastly different if told from alternative perspectives are Carver's "Neighbors" and Tan's "Two Kinds." Just suppose—for a moment—that "Neighbors" were to have been written in the first person, not the third person, as though Bill or Arlene Miller were telling the story. Either speaker would likely dilute the narration and make himself or herself seem definitely limited intellectually when attempting to explain the unusual if not strange behavior once the Stones have departed. Or, suppose that "Two Kinds," which is the first-person narration of Jing-Mei, were rather to be told in the first person by Jing-Mei's mother. Certainly the mother would explain her ambitions for her daughter fully and reasonably, and Jing-Mei herself would not be as comprehensible to readers as she is in the story as we have it.

You can see that this alternative approach to point of view requires creative imagination, for to carry it out you must, as it were, invade the author's space and speculate about the results of a point of view that the author did not choose. Considering such hypothetical alternative points of view deeply, however, will greatly enhance your analytical and critical abilities.

In your conclusion, evaluate the success of the point of view. Is it consistent, effective, truthful? What does it contribute to the nature and quality of the story? What particular benefits does the writer gain or lose (if anything) as a result of the point of view?

## Illustrative Student Essay

Underlined sentences in this paper *do not* conform to MLA style and are used solely as teaching tools to emphasize the central idea, thesis sentence, and topic sentences throughout the paper.

Garcia 1

Ashley Garcia

Professor Sutton

English 220

21 November 2007

### Shirley Jackson's Dramatic Point of View in "The Lottery"°

[1]     The dramatic point of view in Shirley Jackson's "The Lottery" is essential to her success in rendering horror in the midst of the ordinary.* The story, however, is not only

°See pp. 120–25 for this story.
*Central idea.

about horror: It may also be called a surprise story, an allegory, or a portrayal of human insensitivity and cruelty. But the validity of all other claims for "The Lottery" hinges on the author's control over point of view to make the events develop out of a seemingly everyday, matter-of-fact situation—a control that could not be easily maintained with another point of view. <u>The success of Jackson's point of view is achieved through her characterization, selection of details, and diction.</u>[†]

[2] <u>Because of the dramatic point of view, Jackson succeeds in presenting the villagers as ordinary folks attending a normal, festive event—in contrast to the horror of their real purpose.</u> The contrast depends on Jackson's speaker, who is emotionally uninvolved and who tells only enough about the three hundred townsfolk and their customs to permit the conclusion that they are normal, common people. The principal character is a local housewife, Tessie Hutchinson, but the speaker tells little about her except that she is just like everyone else—an important characteristic when she, like any other person being singled out for punishment, objects not to the lottery itself but to the "unfairness" of the drawing. The same commonness applies also to the other characters, whose brief conversations are recorded but not analyzed. This detached, reportorial method of making the villagers seem common and one-dimensional is fundamental to Jackson's dramatic point of view, and the cruel twist of the ending depends on the method.

[3] <u>While there could be much description, Jackson's speaker omits some of the important details to conceal the lottery's horrifying purpose.</u> For example, the speaker presents enough information about the lottery to permit readers to understand its rules but does not disclose the grim prize for the "winner." The short saying "Lottery in June, corn be heavy soon" is mentioned as a remnant of a long-forgotten ritual, but the speaker does not explain anything more about this connection with scapegoatism and human sacrifice (paragraph 32). None of these references seems unusual as the narrator first presents them, and it is only the conclusion that reveals, in reconsideration, their shocking ghastliness.

[4] <u>Without doubt, a point of view other than the dramatic would spoil Jackson's concluding horror because it would require more explanatory detail.</u> A first-person speaker, for example, would not be credible without explaining the situation and revealing feelings that would give away the ending. Such an "I" speaker would need to

---

[†]Thesis sentence.

say something like "The little boys gathered rocks but seemed not to be thinking about their forthcoming use in the stoning." But how would such detail affect the reader's response to the terrifying conclusion? Similarly, an omniscient narrator would need to include details about people's reactions (how could he or she be omniscient otherwise?). A more suitable alternative might be a limited omniscient point of view confined to, say, a stranger in town or one of the local children. But any intelligent stranger would be asking "giveaway" questions, and any child but a tiny tot would know about the lottery's sinister outcome. Either hypothetical point-of-view character would therefore require revealing the information too soon. The only conclusion is that Jackson's point of view—the dramatic—is best for this story. Because it permits her naturally to hold back crucial details, it is essential for the suspenseful delay of horror.

[5]   <u>Appropriate both to the suspenseful ending and also to the simple character of the villagers is the speaker's language</u>. The words are accurate and descriptive but not elaborate. When Tessie Hutchinson appears, for example, she dries "her hands on her apron" (paragraph 8)—words that define her role as a housewife. Most of these simple, bare words may be seen as part of Jackson's technique of withholding detail to delay the reader's understanding. A prime example is the pile of stones, which is in truth a cruel preparation for the stoning, yet this conclusion cannot be drawn from the easy words describing it (120–21, paragraph 2):

> Bobby Martin had already stuffed his pockets full of stones, and the other boys soon
> followed his example, selecting the smoothest and roundest stones; Bobby and Harry Jones
> and Dickie Delacroix—the villagers pronounced this name "Dellacroy"—eventually made
> a great pile of stones in one corner of the square and guarded it against the raids of the
> other boys.

Both the nicknames and the connotation of boyhood games divert attention and obscure the horrible purpose of the stones. Even at the end, the speaker uses the word "pebbles" to describe the stones given to Tessie's son Davy (paragraph 76). The implication is that Davy is playing a game, not participating in the ritual stoning of his own mother!

[6]   Such masterly control over point of view is a major cause of Jackson's success in "The Lottery." Her narrative method is to establish the appearance of everyday, uneventful reality, which she maintains up to the beginning of the last scene. She is so successful that a reader's first response to the stoning is "Such an event could not take

Garcia 4

place among such common, earthy folks." Yet it is this reality that validates Jackson's

vision. Horror is not to be found on moors and in haunted castles but among everyday

people like Jackson's three hundred villagers. <u>Without her control of the dramatic point</u>

<u>of view, there could be little of this power of suggestion, and it would not be possible to</u>

<u>claim such success for the story</u>.

---

Garcia 5

**WORK CITED**

Jackson, Shirley. "The Lottery." *Literature: An Introduction to Reading and Writing.* Ed. Edgar V.
Roberts. 4th Compact Ed. Upper Saddle River: Prentice Hall, 2008, 120–25.

## Commentary

The strategy of this essay is to argue for the importance of Jackson's dramatic point
of view in building toward the shocking ending. Words of tribute throughout the
essay are "success," "control," "essential," "appropriate," and "masterly." The introductory paragraph sets out three areas for exploration in the body: character, detail,
and diction.

The body begins with paragraph 2, in which the aim is not to present a full character study (since the essay is not about character but point of view), but rather to
discuss the ways in which the dramatic point of view enables the characters to be
rendered. The argument of the paragraph is that the villagers are to be judged not as
complete human beings but as "ordinary folks."

The second part of the body (paragraphs 3 and 4) emphasizes that the sparseness
of detail permitted by the dramatic point of view aids Jackson in deferring conclusions about the horror of the drawing. Paragraph 4, which continues the topic of
paragraph 3, shows how talking about alternative points of view may aid understanding of the story's actual point of view (see pp. 147–49). The material for the
paragraph is derived from notes speculating about whether Jackson's technique of
withholding detail to build toward the concluding horror (the topic of paragraph 3)
could be maintained with differing points of view. A combination of analysis and
imagination is therefore at work in the paragraph.

The third section of the body (paragraph 5) emphasizes the idea that the flat, colorless diction defers awareness of what is happening; therefore the point of view is
vital in the story's surprise and horror. The concluding paragraph (6) emphasizes the
way in which general response to the story, and also its success, are conditioned by
the detached, dramatic point of view.

## Writing Topics About Point of View

1. Write a short narrative from the first-person point of view of one of these characters:
   a. Mathilde Loisel in "The Necklace" (Chapter 1): How I ruined 10 years of my life by not telling the truth.
   b. Old Man Warner in "The Lottery": People ain't the way they used to be.
   c. Faith in "Young Goodman Brown" (Chapter 8): I don't understand why my husband is so sour and sullen all the time.
   d. Bill Miller in "Neighbors": I am finding it fascinating to spend time in the apartment of the Stones.

3. Consider the narrative of "Neighbors" as an argument. How can you describe the argument? Is Carver arguing that people are civilized as long as they are being watched or instead that people, when unchecked, are irrational and uncivilized? What does the locked door signify in either argument?

4. How would Hawthorne's story "Young Goodman Brown" (Chapter 8) be affected if told by a narrator with different knowledge, different interests, and different purposes for telling the story, such as the narrators of "A Worn Path" (Chapter 6), Bierce's "An Occurrence at Owl Creek Bridge" (Chapter 2), and the second narrator of Mark Twain's "Luck" (Chapter 7)?

5. Recall a childhood occasion on which you were punished. Write an explanation of the punishment as though you were the adult who was in the position of punishing you. Be sure to consider your childhood self objectively, in the third person. Present things from the viewpoint of the adult, and try to determine how the adult would have learned about your action, judged it, and decided on your punishment.

6. Write an essay about the proposition that people often have something to gain when they speak and that therefore we need to be critical about what others tell us. Are they trying to change our judgments and opinions? Are they telling the truth? Are they leaving out any important details? Are they trying to sell us something? In your discussion, you may strengthen your ideas by referring to stories that you have been reading.

7. In the reference section of your library, find two books on literary terms and concepts. How completely and clearly do these works explain the concept of point of view? With the aid of these books, together with the materials in this chapter, describe the interests and views of the narrators in Moore's "How to Become a Writer," Bierce's "An Occurrence at Owl Creek Bridge," or another story of your choice.

# Chapter 4

# Characters: The People in Fiction

**W**riters of fiction create narratives that enhance and deepen our understanding of human character and human life. In our own day, under the influences of such pioneers as Freud (1856–1939), Jung (1875–1961), and Skinner (1904–1990), the science of psychology has influenced both the creation and the study of literature. It is well known that Freud buttressed some of his psychological conclusions by referring to literary works, especially plays by Shakespeare. Widely known classic films, such as *Spellbound* (1945) and *The Snake Pit* (1948), have popularized the relationships between literary character and psychology. Without doubt, the presentation and understanding of character is one of the major aims of fiction (and literature generally).

In literature, a **character** is a verbal representation of a human being. Through action, speech, description, and commentary, authors portray characters who are worth caring about, cheering for, and even loving, although there are also characters you may laugh at, dislike, or even hate.

In a story or play emphasizing a major character, you can expect that each action or speech, no matter how small, is part of a total presentation of the complex combination of both the inner and the outer self that constitutes a human being. Whereas in life things may "just happen," in literature all actions, interactions, speeches, and observations are deliberate. Thus, you read about important actions such as a long period of work and sacrifice (Maupassant's "The Necklace" [Chapter 1]), the uncertain relationship between a husband and wife (Carver's "Neighbors" [Chapter 3]), acts of defiance and retribution (Poe's "The Masque of the Red Death" [Chapter 5]), or a young man's poignant dream of freedom (Bierce's "An Occurrence at Owl Creek Bridge" [Chapter 2]). By making such actions interesting, authors help you understand and appreciate not only their major characters but also life itself.

## Character Traits

In studying a literary character, try to determine the character's outstanding *traits*. A **trait** is a quality of mind or habitual mode of behavior that is evident in both positive and negative ways, such as supplying moral support to friends and loved ones, being a person on whom people always rely, listening to the thoughts and problems of others, avoiding eye contact, never repaying borrowed money, taking the biggest portions, or always thinking oneself the center of attention. Similarly, artists utilize

"Bust of Lorenzo de Medici," Florentine, fifteenth or sixteenth century, probably after a model by Andrea del Verrocchio and O. Benintendi. *(Photograph © Board of Trustees, National Gallery of Art, Washington, D.C. Samuel H. Kress Collection.)*

elements such as facial characteristics and expressions to convey their judgments about the characteristics of their human subjects. If we study the facial expression of the bust of Lorenzo de' Medici by Andrea del Verrocchio (ca. 1435–1488), for example, we can see that Verrocchio is presenting a negative view of his subject. Lorenzo's firm mouth, his fixed stare, and his closely knit eyebrows suggest a high degree of pride and ruthlessness.

Sometimes, of course, the traits we encounter are minor and therefore negligible, but often a trait may be a person's *primary* characteristic (not only in fiction but also in life). Thus, characters may be ambitious or lazy, serene or anxious, aggressive or fearful, thoughtful or inconsiderate, open or secretive, confident or self-doubting, kind or cruel, quiet or noisy, visionary or practical, careful or careless, impartial or biased, straightforward or underhanded, "winners" or "losers," and so on.

With this sort of list, to which you may add at will, you can analyze and develop conclusions about character. For example, Mathilde in Maupassant's "The Necklace" (Chapter 1) indulges in thoughts of unattainable wealth and comfort, and is so swept up in her dreams that she scorns the comparatively good life she has with her reliable but dull husband. It is fair to say that this denial of reality is her major trait. It is also a major weakness, because Maupassant shows that her dream life harms her real life. Comparably, the character Miss Brill in Mansfield's "Miss Brill" is totally taken up by her overriding imaginary perceptions of her surroundings. All the actions she witnesses are filtered through these perceptions, and hence she seems disconnected from the true reality of her situation. A contrast between a mother's dreams and a daughter's realism is brought out by Amy Tan in "Two Kinds." By similarly analyzing the thoughts, actions, and speeches of the literary characters you encounter, you can also draw conclusions about their nature and their qualities.

## Distinguishing between Circumstances and Character Traits

When you study a fictional person, distinguish between circumstances and character, for circumstances have value *only if they demonstrate important traits*. Thus, if our friend Sam wins a lottery, let us congratulate him on his luck; but the win does not say much about his *character*—not much, that is, unless you also point out that for years he has been regularly spending hundreds of dollars each week for lottery tickets. In other words, making the effort to win a lottery *is* a character trait but winning (or losing) *is not*.

Or, let us suppose that an author stresses the neatness of one character and the sloppiness of another. If you accept the premise that people care for their appearance according to choice—and that choices develop from character—you can use these details to make conclusions about a person's self-esteem or the lack of it. In short, when reading about characters in literature, look beyond circumstances, actions, and appearances, and attempt to determine what these things show about character. Always try to get from the outside to the inside, for it is the internal qualities of character that determine external behavior.

# How Authors Disclose Character in Literature

Basically, authors rely on five ways of bringing characters to life. Remember that you must use your own knowledge and experience to make judgments about the qualities of the characters.

## The Actions of Characters Reveal Their Qualities

What characters *do* is our best clue to understanding what they *are*. For example, taking care of an apartment belonging to a neighbor who has gone on a trip is part of ordinary existence for most people who do it, and it shows little about their characters except a desire to be helpful (this, in itself, may be a significant trait). But when Bill and Arlene Miller of Carver's "Neighbors" (Chapter 3) agree to take care of the apartment of the Stones, their neighbors, they cease being ordinary but somewhat strange folks and begin indulging in all their incipient neuroses. By contrast, in Tan's "Two Kinds," the narrator Jing-Mei, after her turbulent childhood opposition to her mother's influences, reaches an emotional reconciliation when playing the piano her mother had bought for her and given to her.

Like ordinary people, fictional characters do not always understand why they do what they do, or think what they think. Nevertheless, their actions and thoughts reveal their characters. Miss Brill, of Mansfield's "Miss Brill" (this chapter), is alone on a Sunday afternoon, always alone, and she goes to a nearby public park to enjoy the passing crowds—her only weekly excitement. She eavesdrops on people sitting nearby, and draws silent conclusions about others, thus vicariously sharing in their lives. She even supposes that all those in the park are actors, along with her, performing in a massive drama of life. Her unrealistic daydreams reveal her habitual solitude and pathetic vulnerability.

Actions may also signal qualities such as naiveté, weakness, deceit, a scheming personality, strong inner conflicts, sudden comprehension, or other growth or change.

In Hardy's "The Three Strangers" (Chapter 6), the fact that the natives of Higher Crowstairs withhold their cooperation from the governmental forces trying to bring Timothy Summers to the gallows indicates a collective strength of character. The intellectual boy in the dentist's office in Gaines's "The Sky Is Gray" demonstrates an earnest commitment to ideas in which he believes. As he turns his cheek to permit the angry preacher to strike him a second time, he frustrates the preacher and emphatically asserts the value of his own intellect.

## The Author's Descriptions Tell Us About Characters

Appearance and environment reveal much about a character's social and economic status, and they also tell us about character traits. Although Mathilde's dreams in Maupassant's "The Necklace" (Chapter 1) are unrealizable and destructive, they also bring about her character strength that emerges in the story. A somewhat comparable situation occurs in Carver's "Neighbors" (Chapter 3). In this story the unusual actions that the Millers go through in the apartment of the Stones indicates their weak grip on their own characters. With nothing to inhibit them, they unconsciously take over their new but temporary quarters and begin living the lives of which they were formerly jealous.

## What Characters Say Reveals What They Are Like

Although the speeches of most characters are functional—essential to keeping the action moving along—they provide material from which you may draw conclusions. When the second traveler of Hawthorne's "Young Goodman Brown" (Chapter 8) speaks, for example, he reveals his devious and deceptive nature even though ostensibly he appears friendly. Jackie's parents and sister in "First Confession" (Chapter 7) speak angrily to Jackie, the intransigent child who is the story's narrator. Their anger suggests that they have little interest Jackie's thoughts or concerns, but view their world through nothing more than stultifyingly ordinary eyes. It is because of the unsympathetic nature of his family that Jackie is so refreshed by the priest, who shows enough interest in Jackie to listen to him.

Often, characters use speech to obscure their motives. The traveling pot mender in Steinbeck's "The Chrysanthemums" (Chapter 8) is deceptive and guileful. His sole aim is to have Elisa give him some work to do, and we may consequently believe nothing of what he says. The Federal scout in Bierce's "An Occurrence at Owl Creek Bridge" (Chapter 2) is masquerading as a Confederate soldier, and in speaking with the major character Farquhar, who is a landowner and a Confederate loyalist, he speaks confidentially but deceivingly. The result of the scout's lies is that Farquhar is fooled into believing that he will be safe if he sabotages the bridge at Owl Creek.

## What Others Say Tells Us About a Character

By studying what characters say about each other, you can enhance your understanding not only of the character being discussed, but also about the characters doing the talking. For example, the narrator's father in Chioles's "Before the Firing

Squad" speaks to his young son about not being too friendly with Fritz, who is still a teenager but who is also a member of the occupying German army. The father's summary is this: "He's the enemy." This oversimplified characterization of Fritz is belied at the story's end, when Fritz, at obvious personal risk, preserves the lives of the narrator, his family, and other villagers.

Ironically, speeches often indicate something other than what the speakers intend, perhaps because of prejudice, stupidity, or foolishness. Nora, in O'Connor's "First Confession" (Chapter 7), tells about Jackie's lashing out at her with a butter knife, but in effect she describes the boy's individuality just as she also discloses her own spitefulness.

## The Author, Speaking as a Storyteller or an Observer, May Present Judgments About Characters

What the author, speaking as a work's authorial voice, says about a character is usually accurate, and the authorial voice can be accepted factually. However, when the authorial voice interprets actions and characteristics, as in Hawthorne's "Young Goodman Brown" (Chapter 8), the author himself or herself assumes the role of a reader or critic, whose opinions are therefore open to question. For this reason, authors frequently avoid interpretations and devote their skill to arranging events and speeches so that readers can draw their own conclusions.

# Types of Characters: Round and Flat

No writer can present an entire life history of a protagonist, nor can each character in a story get "equal time" for development. Accordingly, some characters grow to be full and alive, while others remain shadowy. The British novelist and critic E. M. Forster, in *Aspects of the Novel*, calls the two major types "round" and "flat."

## Round Characters Are Three-Dimensional and Lifelike

The basic trait of **round** characters is that we are told enough about them to permit the conclusion that they are three-dimensional, rounded, authentic, memorable, original, and true to life. They are the centers of our attention in most works of fiction. Their roundness and fullness are characterized by both individuality and unpredictability. It is true that, like all human beings, round characters have inherent qualities that the circumstances of a story bring out, and therefore their full realization as characters is directly connected to the stories in which they live their lives. Mabel, of Lawrence's "The Horse Dealer's Daughter" (Chapter 9), is a round character. She has spent her life taking care of her father and his affairs, but following her father's death she sees no value in continuing to live. It is when she becomes aware of a favorable change in her life that she becomes restored. Along with her new direction, however, she also anticipates new complications, and it is this complexity of response that especially marks the roundness and fullness of her character.

A complementary quality about round characters is that they are **dynamic**. Dynamic characters *recognize, change with*, or *adjust to* circumstances. Such changes may be shown in (1) an action or actions, (2) the realization of new strength and therefore the affirmation of previous decisions, (3) the acceptance of new conditions and the need for making changes, (4) the discovery of unrecognized truths, or (5) the reconciliation of the character to adverse conditions. A case in point is Farquhar, of "An Occurrence at Owl Creek Bridge" (Chapter 2). Although he is a "well-to-do" Southern planter during the Civil War, for a number of reasons he has not been called to service in the Confederate Army. His life as a planter and slaveowner is stable, and would continue so, but when he learns about the possibility of dynamiting the bridge, he goes ahead and tries to do it. By this action he undergoes change and growth; he is dynamic.

This is not to say that only round characters are dynamic, for less significant characters in a story may also undergo alteration as their circumstances change, as with Carol, Eva's good friend, in Munro's "The Found Boat" (Chapter 7). Carol shares in Eva's developing growth as an adolescent approaching the point of becoming a woman. Usually, dynamic character growth is a good, but such growth, under some conditions, may bring a dynamic character to ruin—a situation, as we have just seen, experienced by Farquhar of "An Occurrence at Owl Creek Bridge."

Because a round character plays a major role in a story, he or she is often called the **hero** or **heroine**. Some round characters are not particularly heroic, however, so it is preferable to use the more neutral word **protagonist** (the "first actor"). The protagonist is central to the action, moves against an **antagonist** (the "opposing actor"), and exhibits the ability to adapt to new situations.

## Flat Characters Are One-Dimensional and Simple

Unlike round characters, **flat characters** are not complex, but are simple and one-dimensional. They may have no more than a single role to perform in a story, or they may be associated with no more than a single dominating idea. Most flat characters end pretty much where they begin, and for this reason we may think of them as **static**, not dynamic. Often their absence of growth or development results from lack of knowledge or understanding, or even from stupidity or insensitivity. Flat characters are not worthless in fiction, however, for they highlight the development of the round characters. In Joyce's "Araby" (Chapter 5), there is little if any growth in Mangan's sister, and yet her presence is the major reason for the narrator's attitudes, and he travels to the Saturday night Bazaar in order to please her.

Usually, flat characters are minor (e.g., relatives, acquaintances, functionaries), but not all minor characters are necessarily flat. Sometimes flat characters are prominent in certain types of literature, such as cowboy, police, and detective stories, where the focus is less on character than on performance. Such characters might be lively and engaging, even though they do not undergo significant change and development. They must be strong, tough, and clever enough to perform recurring tasks such as solving a crime, boxing with the major character, overcoming a villain, or finding a treasure. The term **stock character** is often used to describe characters in these repeating situations. To the degree that stock characters have many common traits, they are **representative** of their class or group. Such characters, with variations in names, ages, and sexes, have been constant in literature since the ancient Greeks. Some regular stock or representative characters are the insensitive father, the interfering mother, the sassy younger sister or brother, the greedy politician, the harassed boss, the resourceful cowboy or detective, the overbearing or henpecked husband, the submissive or nagging wife, the absent-minded professor, the angry police captain, the lovable drunk, and the town do-gooder.

Stock characters are usually also flat as long as they do no more than perform their roles and exhibit conventional and nonindividual traits. Because they possess no attitudes except those of their class, they are often called **stereotype** characters, or characters who all seem to have been cast in the same mold.

When authors bring characters into strong focus, however, no matter what roles they perform, the characters emerge from flatness and move into roundness. For example, Louise Mallard of Chopin's "The Story of an Hour" (Chapter 7) is a traditional housewife, and if she were no more than that she would be flat and stereotypical. After receiving the news that her husband has died, however, the roundness of her character emerges because of her sudden and unexpected exhilaration at the prospect of being widowed and free. A comparable character is Francie, the speaker of Lorrie Moore's "How to Become a Writer" (Chapter 3). Under the guise of giving instructions for undertaking the profession of writing, Francie demonstrates characteristic linguistic ability and wittiness. Of equal importance is that she also reveals a number of incidents in her personal and family life that have evoked both grief and disappointment. We may conclude that such experiences in effect have caused the adaptation and character growth that have made her the writer that she is. In sum, the ability to grow and develop and adjust to changing circumstances makes characters round and dynamic. Absence of these traits makes characters flat and static.

## Reality and Probability: Verisimilitude

Characters in fiction should be true to life. Therefore their actions, statements, and thoughts must all be what human beings are *likely* to do, say, and think under the conditions presented in the literary work. This is the standard of **verisimilitude**, **probability**, or **plausibility**. One may readily admit that there are people *in life* who perform tasks or exhibit characteristics that are difficult or seemingly impossible (such as always leading the team to victory, always getting A+'s on every test, always being cheerful and helpful, or always understanding the needs of others). However, such characters in fiction would not be true to life because they do not fit within normal or usual behavior.

You should therefore distinguish between what characters may *possibly* do and what they *most frequently* or *most usually* do. Thus, in Maupassant's "The Necklace" (Chapter 1) it is possible that Mathilde could be truthful and tell her friend Jeanne Forrestier about the lost necklace. In light of Mathilde's pride and concept of self-respect, however, it is more in character for her and her husband to hide the loss and borrow money for a replacement, even though they endure disastrous financial hardship for ten years. Granted the possibilities of the story (either self-sacrifice or the admission of fault or of a possible crime), the decision she makes with her husband is the more *probable* one.

Nevertheless, probability does not rule out surprise or even exaggeration. In Katherine Anne Porter's "The Jilting of Granny Weatherall" (Chapter 8) the accomplishments of Granny—such as fencing a hundred acres of farmland all by herself—do not seem impossible even if they do seem unlikely. But we learn that when she was young she became compulsively determined to overcome the ignominy of having been betrayed and jilted by her fiancé. It is therefore probable, or at least not improbable, that she would be capable of the heavy labor of building the fence.

Writers render probability of character in many ways. Works that attempt to mirror life—realistic, naturalistic, or "slice of life" stories such as Joyce's "Araby" (Chapter 5)—set up a pattern of ordinary, everyday probability. Less realistic conditions establish different frameworks of probability, in which characters are *expected* to be unusual, as in Hawthorne's "Young Goodman Brown" (Chapter 8). Because a major way of explaining this story is that Brown is having a nightmarish psychotic trance, his bizarre and unnatural responses are probable. Equally probable is the way the doctors explain Louise Mallard's sudden death at the end of Chopin's "The Story of an Hour" (Chapter 7) even though their smug analysis is totally and comically wrong.

You might also encounter works containing *supernatural* figures, such as the second traveler in "Young Goodman Brown" and the unannounced guest in Poe's "The Masque of the Red Death" (Chapter 5). You may wonder whether such characters are probable or improbable. Usually, gods and goddesses embody qualities of the best and most moral human beings, and devils such as Hawthorne's guide take on attributes of the worst. However, you might remember that the devil is often given dashing and engaging qualities so that he can deceive gullible sinners and then drag them screaming into the fiery pits of hell. The friendliness of Brown's guide is therefore not an improbable trait. In judging characters of this or any other type, your best criteria are probability, consistency, and believability.

## Stories for Study

## ERNEST J. GAINES (b. 1933)

A native of Louisiana, Gaines has spent much of his life in San Francisco. Since 1964, when he published his first novel, *Catherine Carmier,* he has written a number of novels chronicling the lives of Southern blacks, the best known of which is *The Autobiography of Miss Jane Pittman* (1971), which was translated into German in 1975. A recent novel is *A Lesson Before Dying* (1993). Two important recent publications featuring interviews with him are *Porch Talk with Ernest Gaines,* edited by Marcia Gau (1990), and *Conversations with Ernest Gaines,* edited by John Lowe (1995). "The Sky Is Gray" is selected from his 1968 collection of stories, *Bloodline.*

# 🖋 The Sky Is Gray (1968)

**1**

Go'n be coming in a few minutes. Coming round that bend down there full speed. And I'm go'n get out my handkerchief and wave it down, and we go'n get on it and go.

I keep on looking for it, but Mama don't look that way no more. She's looking down the road where we just come from. It's a long old road, and far's you can see you don't see nothing but gravel. You got dry weeds on both sides, and you got trees on both sides, and fences on both sides, too. And you got cows in the pastures and they standing close together. And when we was coming out here to catch the bus I seen the smoke coming out of the cows's noses.

I look at my mama and I know what she's thinking. I been with Mama so much, just me and her, I know what she's thinking all the time. Right now it's home—Auntie and them. She's thinking if they got enough wood—if she left enough there to keep them warm till we get back. She's thinking if it go'n rain and if any of them go'n have to go out in the rain. She's thinking 'bout the hog—if he go'n get out, and if Ty and Val be able to get him back in. She always worry like that when she leaves the house. She don't worry too much if she leave me there with the smaller ones, 'cause she know I'm go'n look after them and look after Auntie and everything else. I'm the oldest and she say I'm the man.

I look at my mama and I love my mama. She's wearing that black coat and that black hat and she's looking sad. I love my mama and I want put my arm round her and tell her. But I'm not supposed to do that. She say that's weakness and that's crybaby stuff, and she don't want no crybaby round her. She don't want you to be scared, either. 'Cause Ty's scared of ghosts and she's always whipping him. I'm scared of the dark, too, but I make 'tend I ain't. I make 'tend I ain't cause I'm the oldest, and I got to set a good sample for the rest. I can't ever be scared and I can't ever cry. And that's why I never said nothing 'bout my teeth. It's been hurting me and hurting me close to a month now, but I never said it. I didn't say it 'cause I didn't want act like a crybaby, and 'cause I know we didn't have enough money to go have it pulled. But, Lord, it been hurting me. And look like it wouldn't start till at night when you was trying to get yourself little sleep. Then soon 's you shut your eyes—ummm-ummm, Lord, look like it go right down to your heartstring.

"Hurting, hanh?" Ty'd say.

I'd shake my head, but I wouldn't open my mouth for nothing. You open your mouth and let that wind in, and it almost kill you.

I'd just lay there and listen to them snore. Ty there, right 'side me, and Auntie and Val over by the fireplace. Val younger than me and Ty, and he sleeps with Auntie. Mama sleeps round the other side with Louis and Walker.

I'd just lay there and listen to them, and listen to that wind out there, and listen to that fire in the fireplace. Sometimes it'd stop long enough to let me get little rest. Sometimes it just hurt, hurt, hurt. Lord, have mercy.

**2**

Auntie knowed it was hurting me. I didn't tell nobody but Ty, 'cause we buddies and he ain't go'n tell nobody. But some kind of way Auntie found out. When she asked me, I told her no, nothing was wrong. But she knowed it all the time. She told me to mash up a piece of aspirin and wrap it in some cotton and jugg it down in that hole. I did it, but it didn't do no good. It stopped for a little while, and started right back again. Auntie wanted to tell Mama, but I told her, "Uh-uh." 'Cause I knowed we didn't have any money, and it just was go'n make her mad again. So Auntie told Monsieur Bayonne, and Monsieur Bayonne came over to the house

5

and told me to kneel down 'side him on the fireplace. He put his finger in his mouth and made the Sign of the Cross on my jaw. The tip of Monsieur Bayonne's finger is some hard, 'cause he's always playing on that guitar. If we sit outside at night we can always hear Monsieur Bayonne playing on his guitar. Sometimes we leave him out there playing on the guitar.

10    Monsieur Bayonne made the Sign of the Cross over and over on my jaw, but that didn't do no good. Even when he prayed and told me to pray some, too, that tooth still hurt me.

"How you feeling?" he say.

"Same," I say.

He kept on praying and making the Sign of the Cross and I kept on praying, too.

"Still hurting?" he say.

15    "Yes, sir."

Monsieur Bayonne mashed harder and harder on my jaw. He mashed so hard he almost pushed me over on Ty. But then he stopped.

"What kind of prayers you praying, boy?" he say.

"Baptist," I say.

"Well, I'll be—no wonder that tooth still killing him. I'm going one way and he pulling the other. Boy, don't you know any Catholic prayers?"

20    "I know 'Hail Mary,'" I say.

"Then you better start saying it."

"Yes, sir."

He started mashing on my jaw again, and I could hear him praying at the same time. And, sure enough, after while it stopped hurting me.

Me and Ty went outside where Monsieur Bayonne's two hounds was and we started playing with them. "Let's go hunting," Ty say. "All right," I say; and we went on back in the pasture. Soon the hounds got on a trail, and me and Ty followed them all 'cross the pasture and then back in the woods, too. And then they cornered this little old rabbit and killed him, and me and Ty made them get back, and we picked up the rabbit and started on back home. But my tooth had started hurting me again. It was hurting me plenty now, but I wouldn't tell Monsieur Bayonne. That night I didn't sleep a bit, and first thing in the morning Auntie told me to go back and let Monsieur Bayonne pray over me some more. Monsieur Bayonne was in his kitchen making coffee when I got there. Soon 's he seen me he knowed what was wrong.

25    "All right, kneel down there 'side that stove," he say. "And this time make sure you pray Catholic. I don't know nothing 'bout that Baptist, and I don't want know nothing 'bout him."

**3**

Last night Mama say, "Tomorrow we going to town."

"It ain't hurting me no more," I say. "I can eat anything on it."

"Tomorrow we going to town," she say.

And after she finished eating, she got up and went to bed. She always go to bed early now. 'Fore Daddy went in the Army,° she used to stay up late. All of us sitting out on the gallery or round the fire. But now, look like soon 's she finish eating she go to bed.

30    This morning when I woke up, her and Auntie was standing 'fore the fireplace. She say: "Enough to get there and back. Dollar and a half to have it pulled. Twenty-five for me to go, twenty-five for him. Twenty-five for me to come back, twenty-five for him. Fifty cents left. Guess I get little piece of salt meat with that."

"Sure can use it," Auntie say. "White beans and no salt meat ain't white beans."

"I do the best I can," Mama say.

---

° *Daddy went in the Army*: The time of the story is about 1942, early in World War II, when millions of men were being drafted into the armed services.

They was quiet after that, and I made 'tend I was still asleep.

"James, hit the floor," Auntie say.

I still made 'tend I was asleep. I didn't want them to know I was listening.

"All right," Auntie say, shaking me by the shoulder. "Come on. Today's the day."

I pushed the cover down to get out, and Ty grabbed it and pulled it back.

"You, too, Ty," Auntie say.

"I ain't getting no teef pulled," Ty say.

"Don't mean it ain't time to get up," Auntie say. "Hit it, Ty."

Ty got up grumbling.

"James, you hurry up and get in your clothes and eat your food," Auntie say. "What time y'all coming back?" she say to Mama.

"That 'leven o'clock bus," Mama say. "Got to get back in that field this evening."

"Get a move on you, James," Auntie say.

I went in the kitchen and washed my face, then I ate my breakfast. I was having bread and syrup. The bread was warm and hard and lasted good. And I tried to make it last a long time.

Ty came back there grumbling and mad at me.

"Got to get up," he say. "I ain't having no teefes pulled. What I got to be getting up for?"

Ty poured some syrup in his pan and got a piece of bread. He didn't wash his hands, neither his face, and I could see that white stuff in his eyes.

"You the one getting your teef pulled," he say. "What I got to get up for. I bet if I was getting a teef pulled, you wouldn't be getting up. Shucks; syrup again. I'm getting tired of this old syrup. Syrup, syrup, syrup. I'm go'n take with the sugar diabetes. I want me some bacon sometime."

"Go out in the field and work and you can have your bacon," Auntie say. She stood in the middle door looking at Ty. "You better be glad you got syrup. Some people ain't got that—hard's time is."

"Shucks," Ty say. "How can I be strong."

"I don't know too much 'bout your strength," Auntie say; "but I know where you go'n be hot at, you keep that grumbling up. James, get a move on you; your mama waiting."

I ate my last piece of bread and went in the front room. Mama was standing 'fore the fireplace warming her hands. I put on my coat and my cap, and we left the house.

## 4

I look down there again, but it still ain't coming. I almost say, "It ain't coming yet," but I keep my mouth shut. 'Cause that's something else she don't like. She don't like for you to say something just for nothing. She can see it ain't coming. I can see it ain't coming, so why say it ain't coming. I don't say it, I turn and look at the river that's back of us. It's so cold the smoke's just raising up from the water. I see a bunch of pool-doos not too far out—just on the other side of the lilies. I'm wondering if you can eat pool-doos.° I ain't too sure, 'cause I ain't never ate none. But I done ate owls and blackbirds, and I done ate redbirds,° too. I didn't want kill the redbirds, but she made me kill them. They had two of them back there. One in my trap, one in Ty's trap. Me and Ty was go'n play with them and let them go, but she made me kill them 'cause we needed the food.

"I can't," I say. "I can't."

"Here," she say. "Take it."

---

° *pool-doos: Pool-doo* is a local Louisiana pronunciation of French *poule d'eau,* or "bird of water." It refers to a marsh hen, or bird of the rail family—most likely the American coot.
° *redbirds:* cardinals.

"I can't," I say. "I can't. I can't kill him, Mama, please."

"Here," she say. "Take this fork, James."

"Please, Mama, I can't kill him," I say.

60 I could tell she was go'n hit me. I jerked back, but I didn't jerk back soon enough.

"Take it," she say.

I took it and reached in for him, but he kept on hopping to the back.

"I can't, Mama," I say. The water just kept on running down my face. "I can't," I say.

"Get him out of there," she say.

65 I reached in for him and he kept on hopping to the back. Then I reached in farther, and he pecked me on the hand.

"I can't, Mama," I say.

She slapped me again.

I reached in again, but he kept on hopping out my way. Then he hopped to one side and I reached there. The fork got him on the leg and I heard his leg pop. I pulled my hand out 'cause I had hurt him.

"Give it here," she say, and jerked the fork out my hand.

70 She reached in and got the little bird right in the neck. I heard the fork go in his neck, and I heard it go in the ground. She brought him out and helt him right in front of me.

"That's one," she say. She shook him off and gived me the fork. "Get the other one."

"I can't, Mama," I say, "I'll do anything, but don't make me do that."

She went to the corner of the fence and broke the biggest switch over there she could find. I knelt 'side the trap, crying.

"Get him out of there," she say.

75 "I can't, Mama."

She started hitting me 'cross the back. I went down on the ground, crying.

"Get him," she say.

"Octavia?" Auntie say.

'Cause she had come out of the house and she was standing by the tree looking at us.

80 "Get him out of there," Mama say.

"Octavia," Auntie say, "explain to him. Explain to him. Just don't beat him. Explain to him."

But she hit me and hit me and hit me.

I'm still young—I ain't no more than eight; but I know now; I know why I had to do it. (They was so little, though. They was so little. I 'member how I picked the feathers off them and cleaned them and helt them over the fire. Then we all ate them. Ain't had but a little bitty piece each, but we all had a little bitty piece, and everybody just looked at me 'cause they was so proud.) Suppose she had to go away? That's why I had to do it. Suppose she had to go away like Daddy went away? Then who was go'n look after us? They had to be somebody left to carry on. I didn't know it then, but I know it now. Auntie and Monsieur Bayonne talked to me and made me see.

5

Time I see it I get out my handkerchief and start waving. It's still 'way down there, but I keep waving anyhow. Then it come up and stop and me and Mama get on. Mama tell me go sit in the back while she pay. I do like she say, and the people look at me. When I pass the little sign that say "White" and "Colored," I start looking for a seat. I just see one of them back there, but I don't take it, 'cause I want my mama to sit down herself. She comes in the back and sit down, and I lean on the seat. They got seats in the front, but I know I can't sit there, 'cause I have to sit back of the sign. Anyhow, I don't want sit there if my mama go'n sit back here.

They got a lady sitting 'side my mama and she looks at me and smiles little bit. I smile back, 85
but I don't open my mouth, 'cause the wind'll get in and make that tooth ache. The lady take out
a pack of gum and reach me a slice, but I shake my head. The lady just can't understand why a
little boy'll turn down gum, and she reach me a slice again. This time I point to my jaw. The lady
understands and smiles little bit, and I smile little bit, but I don't open my mouth, though.

They got a girl sitting 'cross from me. She got on a red overcoat and her hair's plaited in
one big plait. First, I make 'tend I don't see her over there, but then I start looking at her little
bit. She make 'tend she don't see me, either, but I catch her looking that way. She got a cold,
and every now and then she h'ist that little handkerchief to her nose. She ought to blow it, but
she don't. Must think she's too much a lady or something.

Every time she h'ist that little handkerchief, the lady 'side her say something in her ear.
She shakes her head and lays her hands in her lap again. Then I catch her kind of looking
where I'm at. I smile at her little bit. But think she'll smile back? Uh-uh. She just turn up her little old nose and turn her head. Well, I show her both of us can turn us head. I turn mine too
and look out at the river.

The river is gray. The sky is gray. They have pool-doos on the water. The water is wavy,
and the pool-doos go up and down. The bus go round a turn, and you got plenty trees hiding
the river. Then the bus go round another turn, and I can see the river again.

I look toward the front where all the white people sitting. Then I look at that little old gal
again. I don't look right at her, 'cause I don't want all them people to know I love her. I just
look at her little bit, like I'm looking out that window over there. But she knows I'm looking
that way, and she kind of look at me, too. The lady sitting 'side her catch her this time, and she
leans over and says something in her ear.

"I don't love him nothing," that little old gal says out loud. 90

Everybody back there hear her mouth, and all of them look at us and laugh.

"I don't love you, either," I say. "So you don't have to turn up your nose, Miss."

"You the one looking," she say.

"I wasn't looking at you," I say. "I was looking out that window, there."

"Out that window, my foot," she say. "I seen you. Everytime I turned round you was 95
looking at me."

"You must of been looking yourself if you seen me all them times," I say.

"Shucks," she say, "I got me all kind of boyfriends."

"I got girlfriends, too," I say.

"Well, I just don't want you getting your hopes up," she say.

I don't say no more to that little old gal 'cause I don't want have to bust her in the mouth. 100
I lean on the seat where Mama sitting, and I don't even look that way no more. When we get
to Bayonne, she jugg her little old tongue out at me. I make 'tend I'm go'n hit her, and she duck
down 'side her mama. And all the people laugh at us again.

**6**

Me and Mama get off and start walking in town. Bayonne is a little bitty town. Baton Rouge
is a hundred times bigger than Bayonne. I went to Baton Rouge once—me, Ty, Mama, and
Daddy. But that was 'way back yonder, 'fore Daddy went in the Army. I wonder when we
go'n see him again. I wonder when. Look like he ain't ever coming back home. . . . Even the
pavement all cracked in Bayonne. Got grass shooting right out the sidewalk. Got weeds in the
ditch, too; just like they got at home.

It's some cold in Bayonne. Look like it's colder than it is home. The wind blows in my
face, and I feel that stuff running down my nose. I sniff. Mama says use that handkerchief. I
blow my nose and put it back.

We pass a school and I see them white children playing in the yard. Big old red school, and them children just running and playing. Then we pass a café, and I see a bunch of people in there eating. I wish I was in there 'cause I'm cold. Mama tells me keep my eyes in front where they belong.

We pass stores that's got dummies, and we pass another café, and then we pass a shoe shop, and that bald-head man in there fixing on a shoe. I look at him and I butt into that white lady, and Mama jerks me in front and tells me stay there.

105    We come up to the courthouse, and I see the flag waving there. This flag ain't like the one we got at school. This one here ain't got but a handful of stars.° One at school got a big pile of stars—one for every state. We pass it and we turn and there it is—the dentist office. Me and Mama go in, and they got people sitting everywhere you look. They even got a little boy in there younger than me.

Me and Mama sit on that bench, and a white lady come in there and ask me what my name is. Mama tells her and the white lady goes on back. Then I hear somebody hollering in there. Soon's that little boy hear him hollering, he starts hollering, too. His mama pats him and pats him, trying to make him hush up, but he ain't thinking 'bout his mama.

The man that was hollering in there comes out holding his jaw. He is a big old man and he's wearing overalls and a jumper.

"Got it, hanh?" another man asks him.

The man shakes his head—don't want open his mouth.

110    "Man, I thought they was killing you in there," the other man says. "Hollering like a pig under a gate."

The man don't say nothing. He just heads for the door, and the other man follows him.

"John Lee," the white lady says. "John Lee Williams."

The little boy juggs his head down in his mama's lap and holler more now. His mama tells him go with the nurse, but he ain't thinking 'bout his mama. His mama tells him again, but he don't even hear her. His mama picks him up and takes him in there, and even when the white lady shuts the door I can still hear little old John Lee.

"I often wonder why the Lord let a child like that suffer," a lady says to my mama. The lady's sitting right in front of us on another bench. She's got on a white dress and a black sweater. She must be a nurse or something herself, I reckon.

115    "Not us to question," a man says.

"Sometimes I don't know if we shouldn't," the lady says.

"I know definitely we shouldn't," the man says. The man looks like a preacher. He's big and fat and he's got on a black suit. He's got a gold chain, too.

"Why?" the lady says.

"Why anything?" the preacher says.

120    "Yes," the lady says. "Why anything?"

"Not us to question," the preacher says.

The lady looks at the preacher a little while and looks at Mama again.

"And look like it's the poor who suffers the most," she says. "I don't understand it."

"Best not to even try," the preacher says. "He works in mysterious ways—wonders to perform"°

125    Right then little John Lee bust out hollering, and everybody turn they head to listen.

---

°*handful of stars*: The Confederate flag contains thirteen stars. At the time of the story, the American flag had forty-eight.

°*He works . . . perform*: an allusion to the well-known hymn "God moves in a mysterious way/His wonders to perform," by William Cowper (1731–1800).

"He's not a good dentist," the lady says. "Dr. Robillard is much better. But more expensive. That's why most of the colored people come here. The white people go to Dr. Robillard. Y'all from Bayonne?"

"Down the river," my mama says. And that's all she go'n say, 'cause she don't talk much. But the lady keeps on looking at her, and so she says, "Near Morgan."

"I see," the lady says.

## 7

"That's the trouble with the black people in this country today," somebody else says. This one here's sitting on the same side me and Mama's sitting, and he is kind of sitting in front of that preacher. He looks like a teacher or somebody that goes to college. He's got on a suit, and he's got a book that he's been reading. "We don't question is exactly our problem," he says. "We should question and question and question—question everything."

The preacher just looks at him a long time. He done put a toothpick or something in his 130
mouth, and he just keeps on turning it and turning it. You can see he don't like that boy with that book.

"Maybe you can explain what you mean," he says.

"I said what I meant," the boy says. "Question everything. Every stripe, every star, every word spoken. Everything."

"It 'pears to me that this young lady and I was talking 'bout God, young man," the preacher says.

"Question Him, too," the boy says.

"Wait," the preacher says. "Wait now."  135

"You heard me right," the boy says. "His existence as well as everything else. Everything."

The preacher just looks across the room at the boy. You can see he's getting madder and madder. But mad or no mad, the boy ain't thinking 'bout him. He looks at that preacher just 's hard 's the preacher looks at him.

"Is this what they coming to?" the preacher says. "Is this what we educating them for?"

"You're not educating me," the boy says. "I wash dishes at night so that I can go to school in the day. So even the words you spoke need questioning."  140

The preacher just looks at him and shakes his head.

"When I come in this room and seen you there with your book, I said to myself, 'There's an intelligent man.' How wrong a person can be."

"Show me one reason to believe in the existence of a God," the boy says.

"My heart tells me," the preacher says.

"'My heart tells me,'" the boy says. "'My heart tells me.' Sure, 'My heart tells me.' And as long as you listen to what your heart tells you, you will have only what the white man gives you and nothing more. Me, I don't listen to my heart. The purpose of the heart is to pump blood throughout the body, and nothing else."  145

"Who's your paw, boy?" the preacher says.

"Why?"

"Who is he?"

"He's dead."

"And you mom?"  150

"She's in Charity Hospital with pneumonia. Half killed herself, working for nothing."

"And 'cause he's dead and she's sick, you mad at the world?"

"I'm not mad at the world. I'm questioning the world. I'm questioning it with cold logic, sir. What do words like Freedom, Liberty, God, White, Colored mean? I want to know. That's why *you* are sending us to school, to read and to ask questions. And because we ask these questions, you call us mad. No sir, it is not us who are mad."

"You keep saying 'us'?"

"'Us.' Yes—us. I'm not alone."

155    The preacher just shakes his head. Then he looks at everybody in the room—everybody. Some of the people look down at the floor, keep from looking at him. I kind of look 'way myself, but soon 's I know he done turn his head, I look that way again.

"I'm sorry for you," he says to the boy.

"Why?" the boy says. "Why not be sorry for yourself? Why are you so much better off than I am? Why aren't you sorry for these other people in here? Why not be sorry for the lady who had to drag her child into the dentist office? Why not be sorry for the lady sitting on that bench over there? Be sorry for them. Not for me. Some way or the other I'm going to make it."

"No, I'm sorry for you," the preacher says.

"Of course, of course," the boy says, nodding his head. "You're sorry for me because I rock that pillar you're leaning on."

160    "You can't ever rock the pillar I'm leaning on, young man. It's stronger than anything man can ever do."

"You believe in God because a man told you to believe in God," the boy says. "A white man told you to believe in God. And why? To keep you ignorant so he can keep his feet on your neck."

"So now we the ignorant?" the preacher says.

"Yes," the boy says. "Yes." And he opens his book again.

The preacher just looks at him sitting there. The boy done forgot all about him. Everybody else make 'tend they done forgot the squabble, too.

165    Then I see that preacher getting up real slow. Preacher's a great big old man and he got to brace himself to get up. He comes over where the boy is sitting.

He just stands there a little while looking down at him, but the boy don't raise his head.

"Get up, boy," preacher says.

The boy looks up at him, then he shuts his book real slow and stands up. Preacher just hauls back and hit him in the face. The boy falls back 'gainst the wall, but he straightens himself up and looks right back at that preacher.

"You forgot the other cheek." he says.°

170    The preacher hauls back and hit him again on the other side. But this time the boy braces himself and don't fall.

"That hasn't changed a thing," he says.

The preacher just looks at the boy. The preacher's breathing real hard like he just run up a big hill. The boy sits down and opens his book again.

"I feel sorry for you," the preacher says. "I never felt so sorry for a man before."

The boy makes 'tend he don't even hear that preacher. He keeps on reading his book. The preacher goes back and gets his hat off the chair.

175    "Excuse me," he says to us. "I'll come back some other time. Y'all, please excuse me."

And he looks at the boy and goes out the room. The boy h'ist his hand up to his mouth one time to wipe 'way some blood. All the rest of the time he keeps on reading. And nobody else in there say a word.

---

° *other cheek*: Matthew 5:39.

8

Little John Lee and his mama come out the dentist office, and the nurse calls somebody else in. Then little bit later they come out, and the nurse calls another name. But fast's she calls somebody in there, somebody else comes in the place where we sitting, and the room stays full.

The people coming in now, all of them wearing big coats. One of them says something 'bout sleeting, another one says he hope not. Another one says he think it ain't nothing but rain. 'Cause, he says, rain can get awful cold this time of year.

All round the room they talking. Some of them talking to people right by them, some of them talking to people clear 'cross the room, some of them talking to anybody'll listen. It's a little bitty room, no bigger than us kitchen, and I can see everybody in there. The little old room's full of smoke, 'cause you got two old men smoking pipes over by that side door. I think I feel my tooth thumping me some, and I hold my breath and wait. I wait and wait, but it don't thump me no more. Thank God for that.

I feel like going to sleep, and I lean back 'gainst the wall. But I'm scared to go to sleep. 180 Scared 'cause the nurse might call my name and I won't hear her. And Mama might go to sleep, too, and she'll be mad if neither one of us heard the nurse.

I look up at Mama. I love my mama. I love my mama. And when cotton come I'm go'n get her a new coat. And I ain't go'n get a black one, either. I think I'm go'n get her a red one.

"They got some books over there," I say. "Want read one of them?"

Mama looks at the books, but she don't answer me.

"You got yourself a little man there," the lady says.

Mama don't say nothing to the lady, but she must've smiled, 'cause I seen the lady smil- 185 ing back. The lady looks at me a little while, like she's feeling sorry for me.

"You sure got that preacher out here in a hurry," she says to that boy.

The boy looks up at her and looks in his book again. When I grow up I want be just like him. I want clothes like that and I want keep a book with me, too.

"You really don't believe in God?" the lady says.

"No," he says.

"But why?" the lady says. 190

"Because the wind is pink," he says.

"What?" the lady says.

The boy don't answer her no more. He just reads in his book.

"Talking 'bout the wind is pink," that old lady says. She's sitting on the same bench with the boy and she's trying to look in his face. The boy makes 'tend the old lady ain't even there. He just keeps on reading. "Wind is pink," she says again. "Eh, Lord, what children go'n be saying next?"

The lady 'cross from us bust out laughing. 195

"That's a good one," she says. "The wind is pink. Yes sir, that's a good one."

"Don't you believe the wind is pink?" the boy says. He keeps his head down in the book.

"Course I believe it, honey," the lady says. "Course I do." She looks at us and winks her eye. "And what color is grass, honey?"

"Grass? Grass is black."

She bust out laughing again. The boy looks at her. 200

"Don't you believe grass is black?" he says.

The lady quits her laughing and looks at him. Everybody else looking at him, too. The place quiet, quiet.

"Grass is green, honey," the lady says. "It was green yesterday, it's green today, and it's go'n be green tomorrow."

"How do you know it's green?"

"I know because I know." 205

"You don't know it's green," the boy says. "You believe it's green because someone told you it was green. If someone had told you it was black you'd believe it was black."

"It's green," the lady says. "I know green when I see green."

"Prove it's green," the boy says.

"Sure, now," the lady says. "Don't tell me it's coming to that."

210    "It's coming to just that," the boy says. "Words mean nothing. One means no more than the other."

"That's what it all coming to?" that old lady says. That old lady got on a turban and she got on two sweaters. She got a green sweater under a black sweater. I can see the green sweater 'cause some of the buttons on the other sweater's missing.

"Yes, ma'am," the boy says. "Words mean nothing. Action is the only thing. Doing. That's the only thing."

"Other words, you want the Lord to come down here and show Hisself to you?" she says.

"Exactly, ma'am," he says.

215    "You don't mean that, I'm sure?" she says.

"I do, ma'am," he says.

"Done, Jesus," the old lady says, shaking her head.

"I didn't go 'long with that preacher at first," the other lady says; "but now—I don't know. When a person say the grass is black, he's either a lunatic or something's wrong."

"Prove to me that it's green," the boy says.

220    "It's green because the people say it's green."

"Those same people say we're citizens of these United States," the boy says.

"I think I'm a citizen," the lady says.

"Citizens have certain rights," the boy says. "Name me one right that you have. One right, granted by the Constitution, that you can exercise in Bayonne."

The lady don't answer him. She just looks at him like she don't know what he's talking 'bout. I know I don't.

225    "Things changing," she says.

"Things are changing because some black men have begun to think with their brains and not their hearts," the boy says.

"You trying to say these people don't believe in God?"

"I'm sure some of them do. Maybe most of them do. But they don't believe that God is going to touch these white people's hearts and change things tomorrow. Things change through action. By no other way."

Everybody sit quiet and look at the boy. Nobody says a thing. Then the lady 'cross the room from me and Mama just shakes her head.

230    "Let's hope that not all your generation feel the same way you do," she says.

"Think what you please, it doesn't matter," the boy says. "But it will be men who listen to their heads and not their hearts who will see that your children have a better chance than you had."

"Let's hope they ain't all like you, though," the old lady says. "Done forgot the heart absolutely."

"Yes ma'am, I hope they aren't all like me," the boy says. "Unfortunately, I was born too late to believe in your God. Let's hope that the ones who come after will have your faith—if not in your God, then in something else, something definitely that they can lean on. I haven't anything. For me, the wind is pink, the grass is black."

**9**

The nurse comes in the room where we all sitting and waiting and says the doctor won't take no more patients till one o'clock this evening.° My mama jumps up off the bench and goes up to the white lady.

---

°*evening*: local dialect for *afternoon*.

"Nurse, I have to go back in the field this evening," she says.                              235
"The doctor is treating his last patient now," the nurse says, "One o'clock this evening."
"Can I at least speak to the doctor?" my mama asks.
"I'm his nurse," the lady says.
"My little boy's sick," my mama says. "Right now his tooth almost killing him."
The nurse looks at me. She's trying to make up her mind if to let me come in. I look at     240
her real pitiful. The tooth ain't hurting me at all, but Mama say it is, so I make 'tend for her
sake.
"This evening," the nurse says, and goes on back in the office.
"Don't feel 'jected, honey," the lady says to Mama. "I been round them a long time—they
take you when they want to. If you was white, that's something else; but we the wrong color."
Mama don't say nothing to the lady, and me and her go outside and stand 'gainst the wall.
It's cold out there. I can feel that wind going through my coat. Some of the other people come
out of the room and go up the street. Me and Mama stand there a little while and we start
walking. I don't know where we going. When we come to the other street we just stand there.
"You don't have to make water, do you?" Mama says.
"No, ma'am," I say.                                                                          245
We go on up the street. Walking real slow. I can tell Mama don't know where she's going.
When we come to a store we stand there and look at the dummies. I look at a little boy wearing a brown overcoat. He's got on brown shoes, too. I look at my old shoes and look at his'n
again. You wait till summer, I say.
Me and Mama walk away. We come up to another store and we stop and look at them
dummies, too. Then we go on again. We pass a café where the white people in there eating.
Mama tells me keep my eyes in front where they belong, but I can't help from seeing them
people eat. My stomach starts to growling 'cause I'm hungry. When I see people eating, I get
hungry; when I see a coat, I get cold.
A man whistles at my mama when we go by a filling station. She makes 'tend she don't
even see him. I look back and I feel like hitting him in the mouth. If I was bigger, I say; if I was
bigger, you'd see.
We keep on going. I'm getting colder and colder, but I don't say nothing. I feel that stuff
running down my nose and I sniff.
"That rag," Mama says.                                                                       250
I get it out and wipe my nose. I'm getting cold all over now—my face, my hands, my feet,
everything. We pass another little café, but this'n for white people, too, and we can't go in there,
either. So we just walk. I'm so cold, now I'm 'bout ready to say it. If I knowed where we was
going I wouldn't be so cold, but I don't know where we going. We go, we go, we go. We walk
clean out of Bayonne. Then we cross the street and we come back. Same thing I seen when I got
off the bus this morning. Same old trees, same old walk, same old weeds, same old cracked
pave—same old everything.
I sniff again.
"That rag," Mama says.
I wipe my nose real fast and jugg that handkerchief back in my pocket 'fore my hand gets
too cold. I raise my head and I can see David's hardware store. When we come up to it, we go
in. I don't know why, but I'm glad.
It's warm in there. It's so warm in there you don't ever want to leave. I look for the heater,  255
and I see it over by them barrels. Three while men standing round the heater talking in Creole.°
One of them comes over to see what my mama want.

---

°*Creole*: the French Cajun dialect in Louisiana.

"Got any axe handles?" she says.

Me, Mama and the white man start to the back, but Mama stops me when we come up to the heater. She and the white man go on. I hold my hands over the heater and look at them. They go all the way to the back, and I see the white man pointing to the axe handles 'gainst the wall. Mama takes one of them and shakes it like she's trying to figure how much it weighs. Then she rubs her hand over it from one end to the other end. She turns it over and looks at the other side, then she shakes it again, and shakes her head and puts it back. She gets another one and she does it just like she did the first one, then she shakes her head. Then she gets a brown one and do it that, too. But she don't like this one, either. Then she gets another one, but 'fore she shakes it or anything, she looks at me. Look like she's trying to say something to me, but I don't know what it is. All I know is I done got warm now and I'm feeling right smart better. Mama shakes this axe handle just like she did the others, and shakes her head and says something to the white man. The white man just looks at his pile of axe handles, and when Mama pass him to come to the front, the white man just scratch his head and follows her. She tells me come on and we go on out and start walking again.

We walk and walk, and no time at all I'm cold again. Look like I'm colder now 'cause I can still remember how good it was back there. My stomach growls and I suck it in to keep Mama from hearing it. She's walking right 'side me, and it growls so loud you can hear it a mile. But Mama don't say a word.

**10**

When we come up to the courthouse, I look at the clock. It's got quarter to twelve. Mean we got another hour and a quarter to be out here in the cold. We go and stand 'side a building. Something hits my cap and I look up at the sky. Sleet's falling.

260        I look at Mama standing there. I want stand close 'side her, but she don't like that. She say that's crybaby stuff. She say you got to stand for yourself, by yourself.

"Let's go back to that office," she says.

We cross the street. When we get to the dentist office I try to open the door, but I can't. I twist and twist, but I can't. Mama pushes me to the side and she twist the knob, but she can't open the door, either. She turns 'way from the door. I look at her, but I don't move and I don't say nothing. I done seen her like this before and I'm scared of her.

"You hungry?" she says. She says it like she's made at me, like I'm the cause of everything.

"No, ma'am," I say.

265        "You want eat and walk back, or you rather don't eat and ride?"

"I ain't hungry," I say.

I ain't just hungry, but I'm cold, too. I'm so hungry and cold I want to cry. And look like I'm getting colder and colder. My feet done got numb. I try to work my toes, but I don't even feel them. Look like I'm go'n die. Look like I'm go'n stand right here and freeze to death. I think 'bout home. I think 'bout Val and Auntie and Ty and Louis and Walker. It's 'bout twelve o'clock and I know they eating dinner now. I can hear Ty making jokes. He done forgot 'bout getting up early this morning and right now he's probably making jokes. Always trying to make somebody laugh. I wish I was right there listening to him. Give anything in the world if I was home round the fire.

"Come on," Mama says.

We start walking again. My feet so numb I can't hardly feel them. We turn the corner and go on back up the street. The clock on the courthouse starts hitting for twelve.

270        The sleet's coming down plenty now. They hit the pave and bounce like rice. Oh, Lord; oh, Lord, I pray. Don't let me die, don't let me die, don't let me die, Lord.

**11**

Now I know where we going. We going back of town where the colored people eat. I don't care if I don't eat. I been hungry before. I can stand it. But I can't stand the cold.

I can see we go'n have a long walk. It's 'bout a mile down there. But I don't mind. I know when I get there I'm go'n warm myself. I think I can hold out. My hands numb in my pockets and my feet numb, too, but if keep moving I can hold out. Just don't stop no more, that's all.

The sky's gray. The sleet keeps on falling. Falling like rain now—plenty, plenty. You can hear it hitting the pave. You can see it bouncing. Sometimes it bounces two times 'fore it settles.

We keep on going. We don't say nothing. We just keep on going, keep on going.

I wonder what Mama's thinking. I hope she ain't mad at me. When summer come I'm 275 go'n pick plenty cotton and get her a coat. I'm go'n get her a red one.

I hope they'd make it summer all the time. I'd be glad if it was summer all the time—but it ain't. We got to have winter, too. Lord, I hate the winter. I guess everybody hate the winter.

I don't sniff this time. I get out my handkerchief and wipe my nose. My hand's so cold I can hardly hold the handkerchief.

I think we getting close, but we ain't there yet. I wonder where everybody is. Can't see a soul but us. Look like we the only two people moving round today. Must be too cold for the rest of the people to move round in.

I can hear my teeth. I hope they don't knock together too hard and make that bad one hurt. Lord, that's all I need, for that bad one to start off.

I hear a church bell somewhere. But today ain't Sunday. They must be ringing for a funeral 280 or something.

I wonder what they doing at home. They must be eating. Monsieur Bayonne might be there with his guitar. One day Ty played with Monsieur Bayonne's guitar and broke one of the strings. Monsieur Bayonne was some mad with Ty. He say Ty wasn't go'n ever 'mount to nothing. Ty can go just like Monsieur Bayonne when he ain't there. Ty can make everybody laugh when he starts to mocking Monsieur Bayonne.

I used to like to be with Mama and Daddy. We used to be happy. But they took him in the Army. Now, nobody happy no more. . . . I be glad when Daddy comes home.

Monsieur Bayonne say it wasn't fair for them to take Daddy and give Mama nothing and give us nothing. Auntie say, "Shhh, Etienne. Don't let them hear you talk like that." Monsieur Bayonne say, "It's God truth. What they giving his children? They have to walk three and a half miles to school hot or cold. That's anything to give for a paw? She's got to work in the field rain or shine just to make ends meet. That's anything to give for a husband?" Auntie say, "Shhh, Etienne, shhh." "Yes, you right," Monsieur Bayonne say. "Best don't say it in front of them now. But one day they go'n find out. One day." "Yes, I suppose so," Auntie say. "Then what, Rose Mary?" Monsieur Bayonne say. "I don't know, Etienne," Auntie say. "All we can do is us job, and leave everything else in His hand. . . ."

We getting closer, now. We getting closer. I can even see the railroad tracks.

We cross the tracks, and now I see the café. Just to get in there, I say. Just to get in there. 285 Already I'm starting to feel little better.

**12**

We go in. Ahh, it's good. I look for the heater; there 'gainst the wall. One of them little brown ones. I just stand there and hold my hands over it. I can't open my hands too wide 'cause they almost froze.

Mama's standing right 'side me. She done unbuttoned her coat. Smoke rises out of the coat, and the coat smells like a wet dog.

I move to the side so Mama can have more room. She opens out her hands and rubs them together. I rub mine together, too, 'cause this keeps them from hurting. If you let them warm too fast, they hurt you sure. But if you let them warm just little bit at a time, and you keep rubbing them, they be all right every time.

They got just two more people in the café. A lady back of the counter, and a man on this side the counter. They been watching us even since we come in.

290    Mama gets out the handkerchief and count up the money. Both of us know how much money she's got there. Three dollars. No, she ain't got three dollars, 'cause she had to pay us way up here. She ain't got but two dollars and a half left. Dollar and a half to get my tooth pulled, and fifty cents for us to go back on, and fifty cents worth of salt meat.

She stirs the money round with her finger. Most of the money is change 'cause I can hear it rubbing together. She stirs it and stirs it. Then she looks at the door. It's still sleeting. I can hear it hitting 'gainst the wall like rice.

"I ain't hungry, Mama." I say.

"Got to pay them something for they heat," she says.

She takes a quarter out the handkerchief and ties the handkerchief up again. She looks over her shoulder at the people, but she still don't move. I hope she don't spend the money. I don't want her spending it on me. I'm hungry, I'm almost starving I'm so hungry, but I don't want her spending the money on me.

295    She flips the quarter over like she's thinking. She's must be thinking 'bout us walking back home. Lord, I sure don't want walk home. If I thought it'd do any good to say something, I'd say it. But Mama makes up her own mind 'bout things.

She turns 'way from the heater right fast, like she better hurry up and spend the quarter 'fore she change her mind. I watch her go toward the counter. The man and the lady look at her, too. She tells the lady something and the lady walks away. The man keeps on looking at her. Her back's turned to the man, and she don't even know he's standing there.

The lady puts some cakes and a glass of milk on the counter. Then she pours a cup of coffee and sets it 'side me other stuff. Mama pays her for the things and comes on back where I'm standing. She tells me sit down at the table 'gainst the wall.

The milk and the cake's for me; the coffee's for Mama. I eat slow and I look at her. She's looking outside at the sleet. She's looking real sad. I say to myself, I'm go'n make all this up one day. You see, one day, I'm go'n make all this up. I want say it now; I want tell her how I feel right now; but Mama don't like for us to talk like that.

"I can't eat all this," I say.

300    They ain't got but just three little old cakes there. I'm so hungry right now, the Lord knows I can eat a hundred times three, but I want my mama to have one.

Mama don't even look my way. She knows I'm hungry, she knows I want it. I let it stay there a little while, then I get it and eat it. I eat just on my front teeth, though, 'cause if cake touch that back tooth I know what'll happen. Thank God it ain't hurt me at all today.

After I finish eating I see the man go to the juke box. He drops a nickel in it, then he just stand there a little while looking at the record: Mama tells me keep my eyes in front where they belong. I turn my head like she say, but then I hear the man coming toward us.

"Dance, pretty?" he says.

Mama gets up to dance with him. But 'fore you know it, she done grabbed the little man in the collar and done heaved him 'side the wall. He hit the wall so hard he stop the juke box from playing.

305    "Some pimp," the lady back of the counter says. "Some pimp."

The little man jumps up off the floor and starts toward my mama. 'Fore you know it, Mama done sprung open her knife and she's waiting for him.

"Come on," she says. "Come on. I'll gut you from your neighbo° to your throat. Come on."

I go up to the little man to hit him, but Mama makes me come and stand 'side her. The little man looks at me and Mama and goes on back to the counter.

"Some pimp," the lady back of the counter says. "Some pimp." She starts laughing and pointing at the little man. "Yes sir, you a pimp, all right. Yes sirree."

## 13

"Fasten that coat, let's go," Mama says.

"You don't have to leave," the lady says.

Mama don't answer the lady, and we right out in the cold again. I'm warm right now—my hands, my ears, my feet—but I know this ain't go'n last too long. It done sleet so much now you got ice everywhere you look.

We cross the railroad tracks, and soon's we do, I get cold. That wind goes through this little old coat like it ain't even there. I got on a shirt and a sweater under the coat, but that wind don't pay them no mind. I look up and I can see we got a long way to go. I wonder if we go'n make it 'fore I get too cold.

We cross over to walk on the sidewalk. They got just one sidewalk back here, and it's over there.

After we go just a little piece, I smell bread cooking. I look, then I see a baker shop. When we get closer, I can smell it more better. I shut my eyes and make 'tend I'm eating. But I keep them shut too long and I butt up 'gainst a telephone post. Mama grabs me and see if I'm hurt. I ain't bleeding or nothing and she turns me loose.

I can feel I'm getting colder and colder, and I look up to see how far we still got to go. Uptown is 'way up yonder. A half mile more, I reckon. I try to think of something. They say think and you won't get cold. I think of that poem, "Annabel Lee."° I ain't been to school in so long—this bad weather—I reckon they done passed "Annabel Lee" by now. But passed it or not, I'm sure Miss Walker go'n make me recite it when I get there. That woman don't never forget nothing. I ain't never seen nobody like that in my life.

I'm still getting cold. "Annabel Lee" or no "Annabel Lee," I'm still getting cold. But I can see we getting closer. We getting there gradually.

Soon's we turn the corner, I see a little old white lady up in front of us. She's the only lady on the street. She's all in black and she's got a long black rag over her head.

"Stop," she says.

Me and Mama stop and look at her. She must be crazy to be out in all this bad weather. Ain't got but a few other people out there, and all of them's men.

"Y'all done ate?" she says.

"Just finish," Mama says.

"Y'all must be cold then?" she says.

"We headed for the dentist," Mama says. "We'll warm up when we get there."

"What dentist?" the old lady says. "Mr. Bassett?"

"Yes, ma'am," Mama says.

"Come on in," the old lady says. "I'll telephone him and tell him y'all coming."

Me and Mama follow the old lady in the store. It's a little bitty store, and it don't have much in there. The old lady takes off her head rag and folds it up.

"Helena?" somebody calls from the back.

---

° *neighbo*: navel.

° *"Annabel Lee"*: poem (1849) by Edgar Allan Poe (1809–1849). See Chapter 19.

330      "Yes, Alnest?" the old lady says.

"Did you see them?"

"They're here. Standing beside me."

"Good. Now you can stay inside."

The old lady looks at Mama. Mama's waiting to hear what she brought us in here for. I'm waiting for that, too.

335      "I saw y'all each time you went by," she says. "I came out to catch you, but you were gone."

"We went back of town," Mama says.

"Did you eat?"

"Yes, ma'am."

The old lady looks at Mama a long time, like she's thinking Mama might be just saying that. Mama looks right back at her. The old lady looks at me to see what I have to say. I don't say nothing. I sure ain't going 'gainst my mama.

340      "There's food in the kitchen," she says to Mama. "I've been keeping it warm."

Mama turns right around and starts for the door.

"Just a minute," the old lady says. Mama stops. "The boy'll have to work for it. It isn't free."

"We don't take no handout," Mama says.

"I'm not handing out anything," the old lady says. "I need my garbage moved to the front. Ernest has a bad cold and can't go out there."

345      "James'll move it for you," Mama says.

"Not unless you eat," the old lady says. "I'm old, but I have my pride, too, you know."

Mama can see that she ain't go'n beat this old lady down, so she just shakes her head.

"All right," the old lady says. "Come into the kitchen."

She leads the way with that rag in her hand. The kitchen is a little bitty little old thing, too. The table and the stove just 'bout fill it up. They got a little room to the side. Somebody in there laying 'cross the bed—'cause I can see one of his feet. Must be the person she was talking to: Ernest or Alnest—something like that.

350      "Sit down," the old lady says to Mama. "Not you," she says to me. "You have to move the cans."

"Helena?" the man says in the other room.

"Yes, Alnest?" the old lady says.

"Are you going out there again?"

"I must show the boy where the garbage is, Alnest," the old lady says.

355      "Keep that shawl over your head," the old man says.

"You don't have to remind me, Alnest. Come, boy," the old lady says.

We go out in yard. Little old back yard ain't no bigger than the store or the kitchen. But it can sleet here just like it can sleet in any big back yard. And 'fore you know it, I'm trembling.

"There," the old lady says, pointing to the cans. I pick up one of the cans and set it right back down. The can's so light, I'm go'n see what's inside of it.

"Here," the old lady says. "Leave that can alone."

360      I look back at her standing there in the door. She's got that black rag wrapped round her shoulders, and she's pointing one of her little old fingers at me.

"Pick it up and carry it to the front," she says. I go by her with the can, and she's looking at me all the time. I'm sure the can's empty. I'm sure she could've carried it herself—maybe both of them at the same time. "Set it on the sidewalk by the door and come back for the other one," she says.

I go and come back, and Mama looks at me when I pass her. I get the other can and take it to the front. It don't feel a bit heavier than that first one. I tell myself I ain't go'n be nobody's fool, and I'm go'n look inside this can to see just what I been hauling. First, I look up the street, then down the street. Nobody coming. Then I look over my shoulder toward the door. That little old lady done slipped up there quiet 's mouse, watching me again. Look like she knowed what I was go'n do.

"Ehh, Lord," she says. "Children, children. Come in here, boy, and go wash your hands."

I follow her in the kitchen. She points toward the bathroom, and I go in there and wash up. Little bitty old bathroom, but it's clean, clean. I don't use any of her towels; I wipe my hands on my pants legs.

When I come back in the kitchen, the old lady done dished up the food. Rice, gravy, meat—and she even got some lettuce and tomato in a saucer. She even got a glass of milk and a piece of cake there, too. It looks so good, I almost start eating 'fore I say my blessing.

"Helena?" the old man says.

"Yes, Alnest?"

"Are they eating?"

"Yes," she says.

"Good," he says. "Now you'll stay inside."

The old lady goes in there where he is and I can hear them talking. I look at Mama. She's eating slow like she's thinking. I wonder what's the matter now. I reckon she's thinking 'bout home.

The old lady comes back in the kitchen.

"I talked to Dr. Bassett's nurse," she says. "Dr. Bassett will take you as soon as you get there."

"Thank you, ma'am," Mama says.

"Perfectly all right," the old lady says. "Which one is it?"

Mama nods toward me. The old lady looks at me real sad. I look sad, too.

"You're not afraid, are you?" she says.

"No, ma'am," I say.

"That's a good boy," the old lady says. "Nothing to be afraid of. Dr. Bassett will not hurt you."

When me and Mama get through eating, we thank the old lady again.

"Helena, are they leaving?" the old man says.

"Yes, Alnest."

"Tell them I say good-bye."

"They can hear you, Alnest."

"Good-bye both mother and son," the old man says. "And may God be with you."

Me and Mama tell the old man good-bye, and we follow the old lady in the front room. Mama opens the door to go out, but she stops and comes back in the store.

"You sell salt meat?" she says.

"Yes."

"Give me two bits worth."

"That isn't very much salt meat," the old lady says.

"That's all I have," Mama says.

The old lady goes back of the counter and cuts a big piece off the chunk. Then she wraps it up and puts it in a paper bag.

"Two bits," she says.

"That looks like awful lot of meat for a quarter," Mama says.

"Two bits," the old lady says. "I've been selling salt meat behind this counter twenty-five years. I think I know what I'm doing."

"You got a scale there," Mama says.

"What?" the old lady says.

"Weigh it," Mama says.

"What?" the old lady says. "Are you telling me how to run my business?"

400 "Thanks very much for the food," Mama says.

"Just a minute," the old lady says.

"James," Mama says to me. I move toward the door.

"Just one minute, I said," the old lady says.

Me and Mama stop again and look at her. The old lady takes the meat out of the bag and unwraps it and cuts 'bout half of it off. Then she wraps it up again and juggs it back in the bag and gives the bag to Mama. Mama lays the quarter on the counter.

405 "Your kindness will never be forgotten," she says. "James," she says to me.

We go out, and the old lady comes to the door to look at us. After we go a little piece I look back, and she's still there watching us.

The sleet's coming down heavy, heavy now, and I turn up my coat collar to keep my neck warm. My mama tells me turn it right back down.

"You not a bum," she says. "You a man."

## Questions

1. What does Gaines establish by using the eight-year-old boy, James, as the narrator who tells the story in the present tense and in his own dialect?

2. Why does James describe the family's need to kill and eat the small birds?

3. What is the major action in the story? What is the result of James and his mother Octavia taking the trip to the dentist? What is gained by the delays, which require the boy and his mother to wait in the office and then to walk out into the cold and sleet?

4. What is the significance of the discussions of suffering occasioned by the protesting child in the dentist's office? What ideas does the young man present (section 7)? When the minister hits him and reproaches him, what is demonstrated about the old and new ideas professed by African-Americans?

5. What values are represented by the elderly couple in the store? Why doesn't the woman phone Dr. Robillard, the "better" but "more expensive" dentist? Why doesn't Octavia accept the portion of salt meat the woman first offers her? What causes the woman to cut the salt meat in half?

## KATHERINE MANSFIELD (1888–1923)

"Katherine Mansfield" was the pen name of Kathleen Mansfield Beauchamp Murry. She was brought up in a prosperous household in New Zealand, and in the early years of the twentieth century she went to England to study at Queen's College. An accomplished cellist, she had been a serious student of music, but she was discouraged from that profession by her father. She then turned to writing. Before she was thirty she realized that she was afflicted with tuberculosis, and spent many of her remaining years desperately seeking a cure. Without the benefit of modern antibiotics, however, her doom was sealed, and she succumbed to the disease in her thirty-fifth year. During her lifetime her collections were *In a German Pension* (1911), *Bliss and Other Stories* (1920), and *The Garden Party and Other*

Stories (1922), which included "Miss Brill." Her posthumous collections were *The Dove's Nest* (1923) and *Something Childish* (1924). Her husband and literary executor, the critic John Middleton Murry, arranged for a number of other publications after her death, including her letters and selections from her journals.

## 🦅 Miss Brill (1920)

Although it was so brilliantly fine—the blue sky powdered with gold and great spots of light like white wine splashed over the Jardins Publiques°—Miss Brill° was glad that she had decided on her fur. The air was motionless, but when you opened your mouth there was just a faint chill, like a chill from a glass of iced water before you sip, and now and again a leaf came drifting—from nowhere, from the sky. Miss Brill put up her hand and touched her fur. Dear little thing! It was nice to feel it again. She had taken it out of its box that afternoon, shaken out the moth-powder, given it a good brush, and rubbed the life back into the dim little eyes. "What has been happening to me?" said the sad little eyes. Oh, how sweet it was to see them snap at her again from the red eiderdown! . . . But the nose, which was of some black composition, wasn't at all firm. It must have had a knock, somehow. Never mind—a little dab of black sealing-wax when the time came—when it was absolutely necessary. . . . Little rogue! Yes, she really felt like that about it. Little rogue biting its tail just by her left ear. She could have taken it off and laid it on her lap and stroked it. She felt a tingling in her hands and arms, but that came from walking, she supposed. And when she breathed, something light and sad—no, not sad, exactly—something gentle seemed to move in her bosom.

There were a number of people out this afternoon, far more than last Sunday. And the band sounded louder and gayer. That was because the Season had begun. For although the band played all the year round on Sundays, out of season it was never the same. It was like some one playing with only the family to listen; it didn't care how it played if there weren't any strangers present. Wasn't the conductor wearing a new coat, too? She was sure it was new. He scraped with his foot and flapped his arms like a rooster about to crow, and bandsmen sitting in the green rotunda blew out their cheeks and glared at the music. Now there came a little "flutey" bit—very pretty!—a little chain of bright drops. She was sure it would be repeated. It was; she lifted her head and smiled.

Only two people shared her "special" seat: a fine old man in a velvet coat, his hands clasped over a huge carved walking-stick, and a big old woman, sitting upright, with a roll of knitting on her embroidered apron. They did not speak. This was disappointing, for Miss Brill always looked forward to the conversation. She had become really quite expert, she thought, at listening as though she didn't listen, at sitting in other people's lives just for a minute while they talked round her.

She glanced, sideways, at the old couple. Perhaps they would go soon. Last Sunday, too, hadn't been as interesting as usual. An Englishman and his wife, he wearing a dreadful Panama hat and she button boots. And she'd gone on the whole time about how she ought to wear spectacles; she knew she needed them; but that it was no good getting any; they'd be sure to break and they'd never keep on. And he'd been so patient. He'd suggested everything—gold rims, the kind that curved round your ears, little pads inside the bridge. No, nothing would please her. "They'll always be sliding down my nose!" Miss Brill had wanted to shake her.

---

°*Jardins Publiques*: public gardens or park. The setting of the story is apparently a French seaside town.
°*Miss Brill*: Brill is the name of a common deep-sea flatfish.

5      The old people sat on the bench, still as statues. Never mind, there was always the crowd to watch. To and fro, in front of the flower-beds and the band rotunda, the couples and groups paraded, stopped to talk, to greet, to buy a handful of flowers from the old beggar who had his tray fixed to the railings. Little children ran among them, swooping and laughing; little boys with big white silk bows under their chins, little girls, little French dolls, dressed up in velvet and lace. And sometimes a tiny staggerer came suddenly rocking into the open from under the trees, stopped, stared, as suddenly sat down "flop," until its small high-stepping mother, like a young hen, rushed scolding to its rescue. Other people sat on the benches and green chairs, but they were nearly always the same, Sunday after Sunday, and—Miss Brill had often noticed—there was something funny about nearly all of them. They were odd, silent, nearly all old, and from the way they stared they looked as though they'd just come from dark little rooms or even—even cupboards!

Behind the rotunda the slender trees with yellow leaves down drooping and through them just a line of sea, and beyond the blue sky with gold-veined clouds.

Tum-tum-tum tiddle-um! tiddle-um! tum tiddle-um tum ta! blew the band.

Two young girls in red came by and two young soldiers in blue met them, and they laughed and paired and went off arm-in-arm. Two peasant women with funny straw hats passed, gravely, leading beautiful smoke-coloured donkeys. A cold, pale nun hurried by. A beautiful woman came along and dropped her bunch of violets, and a little boy ran after to hand them to her, and she took them and threw them away as if they'd been poisoned. Dear me! Miss Brill didn't know whether to admire that or not! And now an ermine toque° and a gentleman in grey met just in front of her. He was tall, stiff, dignified and she was wearing the ermine toque she'd bought when her hair was yellow. Now everything, her hair, her face, even her eyes, was the same colour as the shabby ermine, and her hand, in its cleaned glove, lifted to dab her lips, was a tiny yellowish paw. Oh, she was so pleased to see him—delighted! She rather thought they were going to meet that afternoon. She described where she'd been—everywhere, here, there, along by the sea. The day was so charming—didn't he agree? And wouldn't he, perhaps? . . . But he shook his head, lighted a cigarette, slowly breathed a great deep puff into her face, and, even while she was still talking and laughing, flicked the match away and walked on. The ermine toque was alone; she smiled more brightly than ever. But even the band seemed to know what she was feeling and played more softly, played tenderly, and the drum beat, "The Brute! The Brute!" over and over. What would she do? What was going to happen now? But as Miss Brill wondered, the ermine toque turned, raised her hand as though she'd seen some one else, much nicer, just over there, and pattered away. And the band changed again and played more quickly, more gaily than ever, and the old couple on Miss Brill's seat got up and marched away, and such a funny old man with long whiskers hobbled along in time to the music and was nearly knocked over by four girls walking abreast.

Oh, how fascinating it was! How she enjoyed it! How she loved sitting here, watching it all! It was like a play. It was exactly like a play. Who could believe the sky at the back wasn't painted? But it wasn't till a little brown dog trotted on solemn and then slowly trotted off, like a little "theatre" dog, a little dog that had been drugged, that Miss Brill discovered what it was that made it so exciting. They were all on the stage. They weren't only the audience, not only looking on; they were acting. Even she had a part and came every Sunday. No doubt somebody would have noticed if she hadn't been there; she was part of the performance after all. How strange she'd never thought of it like that before! And yet it explained why she made such a point of starting from home at just the same time each week—so as not to be late for the performance—and it also explained why she had quite a queer, shy feeling at telling her English pupils how she spent her Sunday afternoons. No wonder! Miss Brill nearly laughed out

---

°*ermine toque*: close-fitting hat made of the white fur of an ermine; here the phrase stands for the woman wearing the hat.

loud. She was on the stage. She thought of the old invalid gentleman to whom she read the newspaper four afternoons a week while he slept in the garden. She had got quite used to the frail head on the cotton pillow, the hollowed eyes, the open mouth and the high pinched nose. If he'd been dead she mightn't have noticed for weeks; she wouldn't have minded. But suddenly he knew he was having the paper read to him by an actress! "An actress!" The old head lifted; two points of light quivered in the old eyes. "An actress—are ye?" And Miss Brill smoothed the newspaper as though it were the manuscript of her part and said gently: "Yes, I have been an actress for a long time."

The band had been having a rest. Now they started again. And what they played was  10
warm, sunny, yet there was just a faint chill—a something, what was it?—not sadness—no, not sadness—a something that made you want to sing. The tune lifted, lifted, the light shone; and it seemed to Miss Brill that in another moment all of them, all the whole company, would begin singing. The young ones, the laughing ones who were moving together, they would begin, and the men's voices, very resolute and brave, would join them. And then she too, she too, and the others on the benches—they would come in with a kind of accompaniment—something low, that scarcely rose or fell, something so beautiful—moving. . . . And Miss Brill's eyes filled with tears and she looked smiling at all the other members of the company. Yes, we understand, we understand, she thought—though what they understood she didn't know.

Just at the moment a boy and girl came and sat down where the old couple had been. They were beautifully dressed; they were in love. The hero and heroine, of course, just arrived from his father's yacht. And still soundlessly singing, still with that trembling smile, Miss Brill prepared to listen.

"No, not now," said the girl, "Not here, I can't."

"But why? Because of that stupid old thing at the end there?" asked the boy. "Why does she come here at all—who wants her? Why doesn't she keep her silly old mug at home?"

"It's her fu-fur which is so funny," giggled the girl. "It's exactly like a fried whiting."

"Ah, be off with you!" said the boy in an angry whisper. Then: "Tell me, ma petite chérie—"  15
"No, not here," said the girl, "Not *yet*."

On her way home she usually bought a slice of honeycake at the baker's. It was her Sunday treat. Sometimes there was an almond in her slice, sometimes not. It made a great difference. If there was an almond it was like carrying home a tiny present—a surprise—something that might very well not have been there. She hurried on the almond Sundays and struck the match for the kettle in quite a dashing way.

But to-day she passed the baker's by, climbed the stairs, went into the little dark room—her room like a cupboard—and sat down on the red eiderdown. She sat there for a long time. The box that the fur came out of was on the bed. She unclasped the necklet quickly; quickly, without looking, laid it inside. But when she put the lid on she thought she heard something crying.

## Questions

1. Describe the scene in which the action of this story occurs.

2. What details about the life of Miss Brill do we learn from the story? What sort of life does she live? How often does she come to the park? How is her life comparable to the lives of the old people sitting on the benches as described in paragraph 5?

3. Miss Brill observes a number of people who are walking in the park, and she overhears some of their conversations. Why does Mansfield described these scenes, or vignettes, in so detailed a way?

4. What is the significance of the young couple near the story's end? What is Miss Brill's response to them? What is happening to Miss Brill as the story ends?

# AMY TAN (b. 1952)

Amy Tan was born in Oakland, California, several years after her parents had left their native China to settle in the San Francisco Bay Area. Early in her life she exhibited talent as a writer, winning a first prize for essay writing at the age of eight. Her family endured the untimely deaths of her father and brother in 1967 and 1968, and the remaining family spent time afterward in Switzerland. She attended a number of U.S. colleges, including San Jose State University, where she graduated with honors in 1972 and received an M.A. in 1973. After graduating she did free-lance business writing for companies such as IBM and Pacific Bell. By 1985 she had decided to devote herself to the writing of fiction, and she launched her career in 1986 with the publication of her first short story, "End Game." In 1989 her *The Joy Luck Club,* an interlinked collection of stories, was published and enjoyed forty weeks on the *New York Times* list of best-sellers. Her other major books are *The Kitchen God's Wife* (1991), *The Hundred Secret Senses* (1995), and *The Bonesetter's Daughter* (2001), which had been earlier excerpted for publication in *The New Yorker.* Tan has also written two children's books, *The Moon Lady* (1992) and *SAGWA The Chinese Siamese Cat* (1994). She collaborates with the novelist Stephen King and the humorist Dave Barry in a "literary garage band, the Rock Bottom Remainders," which raises money for literacy causes and also for groups devoted to First Amendment rights. "Two Kinds" is taken from *The Joy Luck Club.*

## Two Kinds (1989)

My mother believed you could be anything you wanted to be in America. You could open a restaurant. You could work for the government and get good retirement. You could buy a house with almost no money down. You could become rich. You could become instantly famous.

"Of course you can be prodigy, too," my mother told me when I was nine. "You can be best anything. What does Auntie Lindo know? Her daughter, she is only best tricky."

America was where all my mother's hopes lay. She had come here in 1949 after losing everything in China: her mother and father, her family home, her first husband, and two daughters, twin baby girls. But she never looked back with regret. There were so many ways for things to get better.

We didn't immediately pick the right kind of prodigy. At first my mother thought I could be a Chinese Shirley Temple. We'd watch Shirley's old movies on TV as though they were training films. My mother would poke my arm and say, "*Ni kan*"—You watch. And I would see Shirley tapping her feet, or singing a sailor song, or pursing her lips into a very round O while saying, "Oh my goodness."

5    "*Ni kan*," said my mother as Shirley's eyes flooded with tears. "You already know how. Don't need talent for crying!"

Soon after my mother got this idea about Shirley Temple, she took me to a beauty training school in the Mission district and put me in the hands of a student who could barely hold the scissors without shaking. Instead of getting big fat curls, I emerged with an uneven mass of crinkly black fuzz. My mother dragged me off to the bathroom and tried to wet down my hair.

"You look like Negro Chinese," she lamented, as if I had done this on purpose.

The instructor of the beauty training school had to lop off these soggy clumps to make my hair even again. "Peter Pan is very popular these days," the instructor assured my mother. I now had hair the length of a boy's, with straight-across bangs that hung at a slant two inches above my eyebrows. I liked the haircut and it made me actually look forward to my future fame.

In fact, in the beginning, I was just as excited as my mother, maybe even more so. I pictured this prodigy part of me as many different images, trying each one on for size. I was a dainty ballerina girl standing by the curtains, waiting to hear the right music that would send me floating on my tiptoes. I was like the Christ child lifted out of the straw manger, crying with holy indignity. I was Cinderella stepping from her pumpkin carriage with sparkly cartoon music filling the air.

In all of my imaginings, I was filled with a sense that I would soon become *perfect*. My mother and father would adore me. I would be beyond reproach. I would never feel the need to sulk for anything. 10

But sometimes the prodigy in me became impatient. "If you don't hurry up and get me out of here, I'm disappearing for good," it warned. "And then you'll always be nothing."

Every night after dinner, my mother and I would sit at the Formica kitchen table. She would present new tests, taking her examples from stories of amazing children she had read in *Ripley's Believe It or Not*, or *Good Housekeeping, Reader's Digest*, and a dozen other magazines she kept in a pile in our bathroom. My mother got these magazines from people whose houses she cleaned. And since she cleaned many houses each week, we had a great assortment. She would look through them all, searching for stories about remarkable children.

The first night she brought out a story about a three-year-old boy who knew the capitals of all the states and even most of the European countries. A teacher was quoted as saying the little boy could also pronounce the names of the foreign cities correctly.

"What's the capital of Finland?" my mother asked me, looking at the magazine story.

All I knew was the capital of California, because Sacramento was the name of the street we lived on in Chinatown. "Nairobi!" I guessed, saying the most foreign word I could think of. She checked to see if that was possibly one way to pronounce "Helsinki" before showing me the answer. 15

The tests got harder—multiplying numbers in my head, finding the queen of hearts in a deck of cards, trying to stand on my head without using my hands, predicting the daily temperatures in Los Angeles, New York, and London.

One night I had to look at a page from the Bible for three minutes and then report everything I could remember. "Now Jehoshaphat had riches° and honor in abundance and . . . that's all I remember, Ma," I said.

And after seeing my mother's disappointed face once again, something inside of me began to die. I hated the tests, the raised hopes and failed expectations. Before going to bed that night, I looked in the mirror above the bathroom sink and when I saw only my face staring back—and that it would always be this ordinary face—I began to cry. Such a sad, ugly girl! I made high-pitched noises like a crazed animal, trying to scratch out the face in the mirror.

And then I saw what seemed to be the prodigy side of me—because I had never seen that face before. I looked at my reflection, blinking so I could see more clearly. The girl staring back at me was angry, powerful. This girl and I were the same. I had new thoughts, willful thoughts,

---

°*Now Jehoshaphat had riches*: Jing-Mei had been told to report on the Hebrew monarch Jehoshaphat as narrated in the eighteenth chapter of II Chronicles.

or rather thoughts filled with lots of won'ts. I won't let her change me, I promised myself. I won't be what I'm not.

20     So now on nights when my mother presented her tests, I performed listlessly, my head propped on one arm. I pretended to be bored. And I was. I got so bored I started counting the bellows of the foghorns out on the bay while my mother drilled me in other areas. The sound was comforting and reminded me of the cow jumping over the moon. And the next day, I played a game with myself, seeing if my mother would give up on me before eight bellows. After a while I usually counted only one, maybe two bellows at most. At last she was beginning to give up hope.

    Two or three months had gone by without any mention of my being a prodigy again. And then one day my mother was watching *The Ed Sullivan Show*° on TV. The TV was old and the sound kept shorting out. Every time my mother got halfway up from the sofa to adjust the set, the sound would go back on and Ed would be talking. As soon as she sat down, Ed would go silent again. She got up, the TV broke into loud piano music. She sat down. Silence. Up and down, back and forth, quiet and loud. It was like a stiff embraceless dance between her and the TV set. Finally she stood by the set with her hand on the sound dial.

    She seemed entranced by the music, a little frenzied piano piece with this mesmerizing quality, sort of quick passages and then teasing lilting ones before it returned to the quick playful parts.

    "*Ni kan*," my mother said, calling me over with hurried hand gestures, "Look here."

    I could see why my mother was fascinated by the music. It was being pounded out by a little Chinese girl, about nine years old, with a Peter Pan haircut. The girl had the sauciness of a Shirley Temple. She was proudly modest like a proper Chinese child. And she also did this fancy sweep of a curtsy, so that the fluffy skirt of her white dress cascaded slowly to the floor like the petals of a large carnation.

25     In spite of these warning signs, I wasn't worried. Our family had no piano and we couldn't afford to buy one, let alone reams of sheet music and piano lessons. So I could be generous in my comments when my mother bad-mouthed the little girl on TV.

    "Play note right, but doesn't sound good! No singing sound," complained my mother.

    "What are you picking on her for?" I said carelessly. "She's pretty good. Maybe she's not the best, but she's trying hard." I knew almost immediately I would be sorry I said that.

    "Just like you," she said. "Not the best. Because you not trying." She gave a little huff as she let go of the sound dial and sat down on the sofa.

    The little Chinese girl sat down also to play an encore of "Anitra's Dance" by Grieg.° I remember the song, because later on I had to learn how to play it.

30     Three days after watching *The Ed Sullivan Show*, my mother told me what my schedule would be for piano lessons and piano practice. She had talked to Mr. Chong, who lived on the first floor of our apartment building. Mr. Chong was a retired piano teacher and my mother had traded housecleaning services for weekly lessons and a piano for me to practice on every day, two hours a day, from four until six.

    When my mother told me this, I felt as though I had been sent to hell. I whined and then kicked my foot a little when I couldn't stand it anymore.

    "Why don't you like me the way I am? I'm *not* a genius! I can't play the piano. And even if I could, I wouldn't go on TV if you paid me a million dollars!" I cried.

---

° *The Ed Sullivan Show*: Ed Sullivan (1902–1974), originally a newspaper columnist, hosted this popular variety television show from 1948 to 1971.
° "*Anitra's Dance*" *by Grieg*: a portion of the suite composed for Ibsen's *Peer Gynt* by Norwegian composer Edvard Grieg (1843–1907).

My mother slapped me. "Who ask you be genius?" she shouted. "Only ask you be your best. For you sake. You think I want you be genius? Hnnh! What for! Who ask you!"

"So ungrateful," I heard her mutter in Chinese. "If she had as much talent as she has temper, she would be famous now."

Mr. Chong, whom I secretly nicknamed Old Chong, was very strange, always tapping his fingers to the silent music of an invisible orchestra. He looked ancient in my eyes. He had lost most of the hair on top of his head and he wore thick glasses and had eyes that always looked tired and sleepy. But he must have been younger than I thought, since he lived with his mother and was not yet married.

I met Old Lady Chong once and that was enough. She had this peculiar smell like a baby that had done something in its pants. And her fingers felt like a dead person's, like an old peach I once found in the back of the refrigerator; the skin just slid off the meat when I picked it up.

I soon found out why Old Chong had retired from teaching piano. He was deaf. "Like Beethoven!" he shouted to me. "We're both listening only in our head!" And he would start to conduct his frantic silent sonatas.

Our lessons went like this. He would open the book and point to different things, explaining their purpose: "Key! Treble! Bass! No sharps or flats! So this is C major! Listen now and play after me!"

And then he would play the C scale a few times, a simple chord, and then, as if inspired by an old, unreachable itch, he gradually added more notes and running trills and a pounding bass until the music was really something quite grand.

I would play after him, the simple scale, the simple chord, and then I just played some nonsense that sounded like a cat running up and down on top of garbage cans. Old Chong smiled and applauded and then said, "Very good! But now you must learn to keep time!"

So that's how I discovered that Old Chong's eyes were too slow to keep up with the wrong notes I was playing. He went through the motions in half-time. To help me keep rhythm, he stood behind me, pushing down on my right shoulder for every beat. He balanced pennies on top of my wrists so I would keep them still as I slowly played scales and arpeggios. He had me curve my hand around an apple and keep that shape when playing chords. He marched stiffly to show me how to make each finger dance up and down, staccato like an obedient little soldier.

He taught me all these things, and that was how I also learned I could be lazy and get away with mistakes, lots of mistakes. If I hit the wrong notes because I hadn't practiced enough, I never corrected myself. I just kept playing in rhythm. And Old Chong kept conducting his own private reverie.

So maybe I never really gave myself a fair chance. I did pick up the basics pretty quickly, and I might have become a good pianist at that young age. But I was so determined not to try, not to be anybody different that I learned to play only the most earsplitting preludes, the most discordant hymns.

Over the next year, I practiced like this, dutifully in my own way. And then one day I heard my mother and her friend Lindo Jong both talking in a loud bragging tone of voice so others could hear. It was after church, and I was leaning against the brick wall wearing a dress with stiff white petticoats. Auntie Lindo's daughter, Waverly, who was about my age, was standing farther down the wall about five feet away. We had grown up together and shared all the closeness of two sisters squabbling over crayons and dolls. In other words, for the most part, we hated each other. I thought she was snotty. Waverly Jong had gained a certain amount of fame as "Chinatown's Littlest Chinese Chess Champion."

"She bring home too many trophy," lamented Auntie Lindo that Sunday. "All day she play chess. All day I have no time do nothing but dust off her winnings." She threw a scolding look at Waverly, who pretended not to see her.

"You lucky you don't have this problem," said Auntie Lindo with a sigh to my mother.

And my mother squared her shoulders and bragged: "Our problem worser than yours. If we ask Jing-Mei wash dish, she hear nothing but music. It's like you can't stop this natural talent."

And right then, I was determined to put a stop to her foolish pride.

A few weeks later, Old Chong and my mother conspired to have me play in a talent show which would be held in the church hall. By then, my parents had saved up enough to buy me a secondhand piano, a black Wurlitzer spinet with a scarred bench. It was the showpiece of our living room.

50   For the talent show, I was to play a piece called "Pleading Child" from Schumann's *Scenes from Childhood*.° It was a simple, moody piece that sounded more difficult than it was. I was supposed to memorize the whole thing, playing the repeat parts twice to make the piece sound longer. But I dawdled over it, playing a few bars and then cheating, looking up to see what notes followed. I never really listened to what I was playing. I daydreamed about being somewhere else, about being someone else.

The part I liked to practice best was the fancy curtsy: right foot out, touch the rose on the carpet with a pointed foot, sweep to the side, left leg bends, look up and smile.

My parents invited all the couples from the Joy Luck Club to witness my debut. Auntie Lindo and Uncle Tin were there. Waverly and her two older brothers had also come. The first two rows were filled with children both younger and older than I was. The littlest ones got to go first. They recited simple nursery rhymes, squawked out tunes on miniature violins, twirled Hula Hoops, pranced in pink ballet tutus, and when they bowed or curtsied, the audience would sigh in unison, "Awww," and then clap enthusiastically.

When my turn came, I was very confident. I remember my childish excitement. It was as if I knew, without a doubt, that the prodigy side of me really did exist. I had no fear whatsoever, no nervousness. I remember thinking to myself, This is it! This is it! I looked out over the audience, at my mother's blank face, my father's yawn. Auntie Lindo's stiff-lipped smile, Waverly's sulky expression. I had on a white dress layered with sheets of lace, and a pink bow in my Peter Pan haircut. As I sat down I envisioned people jumping to their feet and Ed Sullivan rushing up to introduce me to everyone on TV.

And I started to play. It was so beautiful. I was so caught up in how lovely I looked that at first I didn't worry how I would sound. So it was a surprise to me when I hit the first wrong note and I realized something didn't sound quite right. And then I hit another and another followed that. A chill started at the top of my head and began to trickle down. Yet I couldn't stop playing, as though my hands were bewitched. I kept thinking my fingers would adjust themselves back, like a train switching to the right track. I played this strange jumble through two repeats, the sour notes staying with me all the way to the end.

55   When I stood up, I discovered my legs were shaking. Maybe I had just been nervous and the audience, like Old Chong, had seen me go through the right motions and had not heard anything wrong at all. I swept my right foot out, went down on my knee, looked up and smiled. The room was quiet, except for Old Chong, who was beaming and shouting, "Bravo! Bravo! Well done!" But then I saw my mother's face, her stricken face. The audience clapped weakly, and as I walked back to my chair, with my whole face quivering as I tried not to cry, I heard a little boy whisper loudly to his mother, "That was awful," and the mother whispered back, "Well, she certainly tried."

And now I realized how many people were in the audience, the whole world it seemed. I was aware of eyes burning into my back. I felt the shame of my mother and father as they sat stiffly throughout the rest of the show.

---

° *Scenes from Childhood*: *Scenes from Childhood*, or *Kinderszenen* (1836), is one of the best-known works for piano by Robert Schumann (1810–1856).

We could have escaped during intermission. Pride and some strange sense of honor must have anchored my parents to their chairs. And so we watched it all: the eighteen-year-old boy with a fake mustache who did a magic show and juggled flaming hoops while riding a unicycle. The breasted girl with white makeup who sang from *Madama Butterfly*° and got honorable mention. And the eleven-year-old boy who won first prize playing a tricky violin song that sounded like a busy bee.°

After the show, the Hsus, the Jongs, and the St. Clairs from the Joy Luck Club came up to my mother and father.

"Lots of talented kids," Auntie Lindo said vaguely, smiling broadly.

"That was somethin' else," said my father, and I wondered if he was referring to me in a      60 humorous way, or whether he even remembered what I had done.

Waverly looked at me and shrugged her shoulders. "You aren't a genius like me," she said matter-of-factly. And if I hadn't felt so bad, I would have pulled her braids and punched her stomach.

But my mother's expression was what devastated me: a quiet, blank look that said she had lost everything. I felt the same way, and it seemed as if everybody were now coming up, like gawkers at the scene of an accident, to see what parts were actually missing. When we got on the bus to go home, my father was humming the busy-bee tune and my mother was silent. I kept thinking she wanted to wait until we got home before shouting at me. But when my father unlocked the door to our apartment, my mother walked in and then went to the back, into the bedroom. No accusations. No blame. And in a way, I felt disappointed. I had been waiting for her to start shouting, so I could shout back and cry and blame her for all my misery.

I assumed my talent-show fiasco meant I never had to play the piano again. But two days later, after school, my mother came out of the kitchen and saw me watching TV.

"Four clock," she reminded me as if it were any other day. I was stunned, as though she were asking me to go through the talent-show torture again. I wedged myself more tightly in front of the TV.

"Turn off TV," she called from the kitchen five minutes later.                                              65

I didn't budge. And then I decided. I didn't have to do what my mother said anymore. I wasn't her slave. This wasn't China. I had listened to her before and look what happened. She was the stupid one.

She came out from the kitchen and stood in the arched entryway of the living room. "Four clock," she said once again, louder.

"I'm not going to play anymore," I said nonchalantly. "Why should I? I'm not a genius."

She walked over and stood in front of the TV. I saw her chest was heaving up and down in an angry way.

"No!" I said, and I now felt stronger, as if my true self had finally emerged. So this was      70 what had been inside me all along.

"No! I won't!" I screamed.

She yanked me by the arm, pulled me off the floor, snapped off the TV. She was frighteningly strong, half pulling, half carrying me toward the piano as I kicked the throw rugs under my feet. She lifted me up and onto the hard bench. I was sobbing by now, looking at her bitterly. Her chest was heaving even more and her mouth was open, smiling crazily as if she were pleased I was crying.

---

° *Madama Butterfly*: The girl probably sang "Un Bel Di," the signature soprano aria from the opera *Madama Butterfly* by Giacomo Puccini (1858–1924).
° *busy bee*: probably the well-known "Flight of the Bumblebee" by Nikolay Rimsky-Korsakov (1844–1908).

"You want me to be someone that I'm not!" I sobbed. "I'll never be the kind of daughter you want me to be!"

"Only two kinds of daughters," she shouted in Chinese. "Those who are obedient and those who follow their own mind! Only one kind of daughter can live in this house. Obedient daughter!"

75 "Then I wish I wasn't your daughter. I wish you weren't my mother," I shouted. As I said these things I got scared. It felt like worms and toads and slimy things crawling out of my chest, but it also felt good, as if this awful side of me had surfaced, at last.

"Too late change this," said my mother shrilly.

And I could sense her anger rising to its breaking point. I wanted to see it spill over. And that's when I remembered the babies she had lost in China, the ones we never talked about. "Then I wish I'd never been born!" I shouted. "I wish I were dead! Like them."

It was as if I had said the magic words. Alakazam!—and her face went blank, her mouth closed, her arms went slack, and she backed out of the room, stunned, as if she were blowing away like a small brown leaf, thin, brittle, lifeless.

It was not the only disappointment my mother felt in me. In the years that followed, I failed her so many times, each time asserting my own will, my right to fall short of expectations. I didn't get straight As. I didn't become class president. I didn't get into Stanford. I dropped out of college.

80 For unlike my mother, I did not believe I could be anything I wanted to be. I could only be me.

And for all those years, we never talked about the disaster at the recital or my terrible accusations afterward at the piano bench. All that remained unchecked, like a betrayal that was now unspeakable. So I never found a way to ask her why she had hoped for something so large that failure was inevitable.

And even worse, I never asked her what frightened me the most: Why had she given up hope?

For after our struggle at the piano, she never mentioned my playing again. The lessons stopped. The lid to the piano was closed, shutting out the dust, my misery, and her dreams.

So she surprised me. A few years ago, she offered to give me the piano, for my thirtieth birthday. I had not played in all those years. I saw the offer as a sign of forgiveness, a tremendous burden removed.

85 "Are you sure?" I asked shyly. "I mean, won't you and Dad miss it?"

"No, this your piano," she said firmly. "Always your piano. You only one can play."

"Well, I probably can't play anymore," I said. "It's been years."

"You pick up fast," said my mother, as if she knew this was certain. "You have natural talent. You could been genius if you want to."

"No I couldn't."

90 "You just not trying," said my mother. And she was neither angry nor sad. She said it as if to announce a fact that could never be disproved. "Take it," she said.

But I didn't at first. It was enough that she had offered it to me. And after that, every time I saw it in my parents' living room, standing in front of the bay windows, it made me feel proud, as if it were a shiny trophy I had won back.

Last week I sent a tuner over to my parents' apartment and had the piano reconditioned, for purely sentimental reasons. My mother had died a few months before and I had been getting things in order for my father, a little bit at a time. I put the jewelry in special silk pouches. The sweaters she had knitted in yellow, pink, bright orange—all the colors I hated—I put those in moth-proof boxes. I found some old Chinese silk dresses, the kind with little slits up the sides. I rubbed the old silk against my skin, then wrapped them in tissue and decided to take them home with me.

After I had the piano tuned, I opened the lid and touched the keys. It sounded even richer than I remembered. Really, it was a very good piano. Inside the bench were the same exercise notes with handwritten scales, the same secondhand music books with their covers held together with yellow tape.

I opened up the Schumann book to the dark little piece I had played at the recital. It was on the left-hand side of the page, "Pleading Child." It looked more difficult than I remembered. I played a few bars, surprised at how easily the notes came back to me.

And for the first time, or so it seemed, I noticed the piece on the right-hand side. It was called "Perfectly Contented." I tried to play this one as well. It had a lighter melody but the same flowing rhythm and turned out to be quite easy. "Pleading Child" was shorter but slower; "Perfectly Contented" was longer, but faster. And after I played them both a few times, I realized they were two halves of the same song. 95

## Questions

1. What major characteristics about the narrator, Jing-Mei, are brought out in the story?
2. Describe the relationship between Jing-Mei and her mother. Why does Jing-Mei resist all efforts to develop her talents?
3. Characterize the mother. To what degree is she sympathetic? Unsympathetic? At the story's end, how does Jing-Mei feel about her mother?
4. What general details about the nature of first- and second-generation immigrants are presented in the story?

## MARK TWAIN (1835–1910)

Mark Twain (born Samuel Clemens) is one of the literary giants of nineteenth- and early-twentieth-century America. Largely because of his use of colloquial and regional English in *Huckleberry Finn*, he was acknowledged by Hemingway as a founder of American literature. He was born in Missouri and spent much of his youth as a Mississippi River pilot, Confederate soldier, journalist, and miner. In 1863 he adopted "Mark Twain" as his nom de plume. His most famous works are the novels *Tom Sawyer* (1876) and *Huckleberry Finn* (1884–1885). *Huckleberry Finn* is today the subject of controversy for characterizations some people consider racist, even though more than a century has passed since its publication. "Luck" is a brief story (Twain calls it a "sketch") illustrating Twain's art of comic debunking, a characteristic that he also shows in works such as *The Innocents Abroad* and the short critical essay "Fenimore Cooper's Literary Offenses." The technique in "Luck" is to present an inside, private view of a person of high reputation and in effect to show that "the emperor has no clothes."

# ✐ Luck[1] (1891)

It was at a banquet in London in honor of one of the two or three conspicuously illustrious English military names of this generation. For reasons which will presently appear, I will withhold his real name and titles and call him Lieutenant-General Lord Arthur Scoresby, Y.C., K.C.B., etc., etc. What a fascination there is in a renowned name! There sat the man, in actual flesh, whom I had heard of so many thousands of times since that day, thirty years before, when his name shot suddenly to the zenith from a Crimean battlefield,° to remain forever celebrated. It was food and drink to me to look, and look, and look at that demi-god; scanning, searching, noting: the quietness, the reserve, the noble gravity of his countenance; the simple honesty that expressed itself all over him; the sweet unconsciousness of his greatness—unconsciousness of the hundreds of admiring eyes fastened upon him, unconsciousness of the deep, loving, sincere worship welling out of the breasts of those people and flowing toward him.

The clergyman at my left was an old acquaintance of mine—clergyman now, but had spent the first half of his life in the camp and field and as an instructor in the military school at Woolwich. Just at the moment I have been talking about a veiled and singular light glimmered in his eyes and he leaned down and muttered confidentially to me—indicating the hero of the banquet with a gesture:

"Privately—he's an absolute fool."

This verdict was a great surprise to me. If its subject had been Napoleon, or Socrates, or Solomon, my astonishment could not have been greater. Two things I was well aware of: that the Reverend was a man of strict veracity and that his judgment of men was good. Therefore I knew, beyond doubt or question, that the world was mistaken about this hero: he *was* a fool. So I meant to find out, at a convenient moment, how the Reverend, all solitary and alone, had discovered the secret.

5      Some days later the opportunity came, and this is what the Reverend told me:

About forty years ago I was an instructor in the military academy at Woolwich. I was present in one of the sections when young Scoresby underwent his preliminary examination. I was touched to the quick with pity, for the rest of the class answered up brightly and handsomely, while he—why, dear me, he didn't know *anything*, so to speak. He was evidently good, and sweet, and lovable, and guileless; and so it was exceedingly painful to see him stand there, as serene as a graven image, and deliver himself of answers which were veritably miraculous for stupidity and ignorance. All the compassion in me was aroused in his behalf. I said to myself, when he comes to be examined again he will be flung over, of course; so it will be simply a harmless act of charity to ease his fall as much as I can. I took him aside and found that he knew a little of Caesar's history; and as he didn't know anything else, I went to work and drilled him like a galley-slave on a certain line of stock questions concerning Caesar which I knew would be used. If you'll believe me, he went through with flying colors on examination day! He went through on that purely superficial "cram," and got compliments too, while others, who knew a thousand times more than he, got plucked. By some strangely lucky accident—an accident not likely to happen twice in a century—he was asked no question outside of the narrow limits of his drill.

It was stupefying. Well, all through his course I stood by him, with something of the sentiment which a mother feels for a crippled child; and he always saved himself—just by miracle, apparently.

---

[1]This is not a fancy sketch. I got it from a clergyman who was an instructor at Woolwich forty years ago, and who vouched for its truth. [Twain's note.]

° *Crimean battlefield*: In the Crimean War (1853–1856), England was one of the allies that fought against Russia.

Now, of course, the thing that would expose him and kill him at last was mathematics. I resolved to make his death as easy as I could; so I drilled him and crammed him, and crammed him and drilled him, just on the line of questions which the examiners would be most likely to use, and then launched him on his fate. Well, sir, try to conceive of the result: to my consternation, he took the first prize! And with it he got a perfect ovation in the way of compliments.

Sleep? There was no more sleep for me for a week. My conscience tortured me day and night. What I had done I had done purely through charity, and only to ease the poor youth's fall. I never had dreamed of any such preposterous results as the thing that had happened. I felt as guilty and miserable as Frankenstein. Here was a wooden-head whom I had put in the way of glittering promotions and prodigious responsibilities, and but one thing could happen: he and his responsibilities would all go to ruin together at the first opportunity.

The Crimean War had just broken out. Of course there had to be a war, I said to myself. We couldn't have peace and give this donkey a chance to die before he is found out. I waited for the earthquake. It came. And it made me reel when it did come. He was actually gazetted to a captaincy in a marching regiment! Better men grow old and gray in the service before they climb to a sublimity like that. And who could ever have foreseen that they would go and put such a load of responsibility on such green and inadequate shoulders? I could just barely have stood it if they had made him a cornet; but a captain—think of it! I thought my hair would turn white. 10

Consider what I did—I who so loved repose and inaction. I said to myself, I am responsible to the country for this, and I must go along with him and protect the country against him as far as I can. So I took my poor little capital that I had saved up through years of work and grinding economy, and went with a sigh and bought a cornetcy in his regiment, and away we went to the field.

And there—oh, dear, it was awful. Blunders?—why he never did anything *but* blunder. But, you see, nobody was in the fellow's secret. Everybody had him focused wrong, and necessarily misinterpreted his performance every time. Consequently they took his idiotic blunders for inspirations of genius. They did, honestly! His mildest blunders were enough to make a man in his right mind cry; and they did make me cry—and rage and rave, too, privately. And the thing that kept me always in a sweat of apprehension was the fact that every fresh blunder he made increased the luster of his reputation! I kept saying to myself, he'll get so high that when discovery does finally come it will be like the sun falling out of the sky.

He went right along, up from grade to grade, over the dead bodies of his superiors, until at last, in the hottest moment of the battle of—down went our colonel, and my heart jumped into my mouth, for Scoresby was next in rank! Now for it, said I: we'll all land in Sheol in ten minutes, sure.

The battle was awfully hot; the allies were steadily giving way all over the field. Our regiment occupied a position that was vital; a blunder now must be destruction. At this crucial moment, what does this immortal fool do but detach the regiment from its place and order a charge over a neighboring hill where there wasn't a suggestion of an enemy! "There you go!" I said to myself; "this *is* the end at last."

And away we did go, and were over the shoulder of the hill before the insane movement could be discovered and stopped. And what did we find? An entire and unsuspected Russian army in reserve! And what happened? We were eaten up? That is necessarily what would have happened in ninety-nine cases out of a hundred. But no; those Russians argued that no single regiment would come browsing around there at such a time. It must be the entire English army, and that the sly Russian game was detected and blocked, so they turned tail, and away they went, pell-mell, over the hill and down into the field, in wild confusion, and we after them; they themselves broke the solid Russian center in the field, and tore through, and in no time there was the most tremendous rout you ever saw, and the defeat of the allies was turned into a sweeping and splendid victory! Marshall Canrobert looked on, dizzy with 15 astonishment, admiration, and delight; and sent right off for Scoresby, and hugged him, and decorated him on the field in presence of all the armies!

And what was Scoresby's blunder that time? Merely the mistaking his right hand for his left—that was all. An order had come to him to fall back and support our right; and, instead, he fell *forward* and went over the hill to the left. But the name he won that day as a marvelous military genius filled the world with his glory, and that glory will never fade while history books last.

He is just as good and sweet and lovable and unpretending as a man can be, but he doesn't know enough to come in when it rains. Now that is absolutely true. He is the supremest ass in the universe; and until half an hour ago nobody knew it but himself and me. He has been pursued, day by day and year by year, by a most phenomenal astonishing luckiness. He has been a shining soldier in all our wars for a generation; he has littered his whole military life with blunders, and yet has never committed one that didn't make him a knight or a baronet or a lord or something. Look at his breast; why, he is just clothed in domestic and foreign decorations. Well, sir, every one of them is the record of some shouting stupidity or other; and, taken together, they are proof that the very best thing in all this world that can befall a man is to be born lucky. I say again, as I said at the banquet, Scoresby's an absolute fool.

## Questions

1. Describe Twain's style as a writer of narrative prose. What kinds of detail does he present? Does he give you enough detail about the battle during the Crimean War, for example, to justify an assertion that he describes action vividly? Or does he confine his detail to illuminate the life of Scoresby?

2. What elements in the story are amusing? How does the development of humor depend on Twain's arrangement of words?

3. Study the first paragraph. What does Twain intend after the "look, and look, and look" phrase? Why do you think he begins the story with such a description, which might even be called heroic? Contrast this paragraph with paragraph 12, where the word *blunder* is repeated.

4. Who begins the story? Who finally tells it? How does the second narrator learn about Scoresby? How does he summarize Scoresby's career?

## WRITING ABOUT CHARACTER

When you write about characters, your topic usually will be a major character in a story or drama, although you might also study one or more minor characters. After your customary overview, begin taking notes. List as many traits as you can, and also determine how the author presents details about the character through actions, appearances, speeches, comments by others, or authorial explanations. If you discover unusual traits, determine what they show. The following suggestions and questions will help you get started.

### Questions for Discovering Ideas

- Who is the major character? What do you learn about this character from his or her actions and speeches? From the speeches and actions of other characters? How else do you learn about the character?

- How important is the character to the work's principal action? Which characters oppose the major character? How do the major character and the opposing character(s) interact? What effects do these interactions create?
- What actions bring out important traits of the main character? To what degree is the character creating events, or just responding to them?
- Describe the main character's actions: Are they good or bad, intelligent or stupid, deliberate or spontaneous? How do they help you understand her or him? What do they show about the character as a person?
- Describe and explain the traits, both major and minor, of the character you plan to discuss. To what extent do the traits permit you to judge the character? What is your judgment?
- What descriptions (if any) of how the character looks do you discover in the story? What does this appearance demonstrate about him or her?
- In what ways is the character's major trait a strength—or a weakness? As the story progresses, to what degree does the trait become more (or less) prominent?
- Is the character round and dynamic? How does the character recognize, change with, or adjust to circumstances?
- If the character you are analyzing is flat or static, what function does he or she perform in the story (for example, by doing a task or by bringing out qualities of the major character)?
- If the character is a stereotype, to what type does he or she belong? To what degree does the character stay in the stereotypical role or rise above it? How?
- What do any of the other characters do, say, or think to give you understanding of the character you are analyzing? What does the character say or think about himself or herself? What does the storyteller or narrator say? How valid are these comments and insights? How helpful are they in providing insights into the character?
- Is the character lifelike or unreal? Consistent or inconsistent? Believable or not believable?

## Strategies for Organizing Ideas

Sometimes when you have begun discussing a character you may find it easy to lapse into doing no more than presenting details of action without tying the actions to the character's traits and qualities. This is a trap to be avoided. Remember always to connect the actions and circumstances directly to characteristics—in other words to the *character* of the character. Do not be satisfied just to say what the character is doing, but tell your reader what the actions show about the character *as a person*—as a living, breathing individual with particular distinctness and unique identity. Always keep these thoughts in your mind when you discuss a literary character.

In your developing essay, identify the character you are studying, and refer to noteworthy problems in determining this character's qualities. Use your central idea and thesis statement to form for the body of your essay. Consider one of the following approaches to organize your ideas.

1. *Develop a central trait or major characteristic,* such as "a determination to preserve her children despite the constant threats around her" (Rosa of Ozick's "The Shawl" [Chapter 5]) or "the habit of remaking the world through one's own eyes alone" (Miss Brill of Mansfield's "Miss Brill"). This kind of structure should be organized to show how the work brings out the trait. For example, one story might use selected speeches and actions to bring the character to life (the Mother of Tan's "Two Kinds"). Another story might employ the character's speeches and actions alone (Tessie Hutchinson of Jackson's "The Lottery" [Chapter 3]). Studying the trait thus enables you to focus on the ways in which the author presents the character, and it also enables you to focus on separate parts of the work.

2. *Explain a character's growth or change.* This type of essay describes a character's traits at the work's beginning and then analyzes changes or developments. It is important to stress the actual alterations as they emerge, but at the same time to avoid retelling the story. Additionally, you should not only describe the changing traits but also analyze how they are brought out within the work (such as the dream of Goodman Brown [Chapter 8] or Mathilde Loisel's 10-year economic ordeal [Chapter 1]).

3. *Organize your essay around a number of important but separate characteristics.* Most major characters exhibit not just one but many separate traits and qualities. Thus, for example, Updike's Sammy of "A & P" (Chapter 7) appears at first to be just an ordinary young man. He seems lively, but does not show any more than ordinary interests and ordinary views on life. When a key incident occurs in the grocery store, however, he suddenly illustrates his capacity to make a significant moral gesture. His character might be studied on the basis of the separate characteristics he shows, provided, of course, that they are connected within the essay. (See the following illustrative essay for this type of development.)

4. *Organize your essay around central actions, objects, or quotations that reveal primary characteristics.* Key incidents may stand out (such as falling inadvertently into a ditch), along with objects closely associated with the character being analyzed (such as a falling hair ribbon). There may be important quotations spoken by the character or by someone else in the work. Show how such elements serve as signposts or guides to understanding the character.

5. *Develop qualities of a flat character or characters.* If the character is flat (such as Eva's friend in "The Found Boat," or Jackie's sister in "First Confession" [Chapter 7], or the nurses in the medical station in Welty's "A Worn Path" [Chapter 2]) you might develop topics such as the function and relative significance of the character, the group the character represents, the relationship of the flat character to the round ones, the importance of this relationship, and any additional qualities or traits. For a flat character, you should explain

the circumstances or characteristics that keep the character from seeming round and full, as well as the importance of these shortcomings in the author's presentation of character.

In your conclusion, show how the character's traits are related to the work as a whole. If the person was good but came to a bad end, does this misfortune make him or her seem especially worthy? If the person suffers, does the suffering suggest any attitudes about the class or type of which he or she is a part? Or does it illustrate the author's general view of human life? Or both? Do the characteristics explain why the person helps or hinders other characters? How does your essay help to clear up things that you did not understand on your first reading?

## Illustrative Student Essay

Underlined sentences in this paper *do not* conform to MLA style and are used solely as teaching tools to emphasize the central idea, thesis sentence, and topic sentences throughout the paper.

Zell 1

Joseph Zell

Professor Torres

English 32

5 October 2007

### The Character of the Narrator's Mother in Amy Tan's "Two Kinds"

[1]     The narrator of Tan's "Two Kinds" is Jing-Mei, a Chinese-American woman who tells the story as an adult looking back on her antagonism with her mother over a period of years in early adolescence, and it is through Jing-Mei's eyes alone that we learn of the mother. <u>The mother has been a displaced person, removed from her home in China in 1949; her powerful energies and strong will are devoted to the "raised hopes" of the United States.</u>* The story focuses on the mother-daughter conflicts resulting from the mother's wishes to make Jing-Mei excel in some activity or profession that will make her famous. <u>Through Jing-Mei's descriptions and quotations, we infer that the mother is a loving and proud person with strong optimism about her new land, a belief in the value of hard work, and an inability to comprehend her second-generation daughter.</u>†

---

*Central idea
†Thesis sentence

[2]      <u>The story makes clear, despite the narrator's frequent statements of childhood anger and dislike, that the mother is motivated by parental love, concern, and pride</u>. She wishes nothing so much as her daughter's success. For example, at the story's end her offer of the piano is an expression of love. As she says in her broken English: "Always your piano. You only one can play" (186, paragraph 86). At another point the mother brags about her daughter's "natural talent" in music (184, paragraph 47), even though Jing-Mei calls this "foolish pride" (184, paragraph 48). After the mother's death, some of her personal effects, most notably a number of hand-knitted sweaters, are put away by Jing-Mei. Although Jing-Mei even then cannot resist explaining that she hates the colors (186, paragraph 92), it is clear that the knitting is to be taken as a sign of the mother's love. With all the heated disputes and antagonisms now a thing of the past, Jing-Mei recognizes and accepts this love when she looks through the possessions, and also when she sits down to play the piano—her mother's gift—at which her mother pathetically wanted her to excel (187, paragraph 94).

[3]      <u>Related to this love is the mother's optimistic and hopeful nature</u>. In all the admittedly antagonistic mother-daughter interactions in this story, there is evidence of this hope. Jing-Mei tells us that her mother had come to America "after losing everything in China: her mother and father, her family home, her first husband, and two daughters, twin baby girls" (180, paragraph 3). Nevertheless, the mother does not brood on the past. No matter how much she might grieve privately, she accepts the optimistic idea that America, the new land, is a place of freedom from oppression where there are limitless opportunities for advancement. Success in business, a secure old age, home ownership, and national fame—all these are possibilities in which the mother, with her optimism about America, believes (180, paragraph 1).

[4]      <u>Closely connected with the mother's optimism is her strong conviction about the value of work</u>. By accepting America as the land of opportunity, she assumes that hard work is all one needs to be successful (180, paragraph 1). For herself, she is diligent in her work as a housecleaner, and in this way she practices her optimistic faith (181, paragraph 12). In the evenings she makes the same effort with Jing-Mei to nurture the girl's budding talents (181, paragraph 12). In trying to get Jing-Mei to learn mathematics, magic, weather prediction, geography, speed reading, and most importantly piano, the mother is acting on her faith that her daughter will find something in America that will turn her into a prodigy. It is this belief in the transforming power of work that leads to her

constant prodding of Jing-Mei, and that also leads her to reproach Jing-Mei for not working hard enough. With all the force of the mother's characteristic beliefs in work being put on the shoulders of her daughter, however, the hopes are not realized. Instead, Jing-Mei describes a childhood filled with resentment and anger against her mother's exhortations to work and perform (180, paragraph 2).

[5]     Despite the mother's positive qualities, her principal flaw is her inability to comprehend her daughter. Her imagination does not permit her to understand that her daughter's thoughts are "filled with lots of won'ts" (181, paragraph 19). Nor is the mother capable of understanding Jing-Mei's responses and feelings, for Jing-Mei tells us that "unlike my mother, I did not believe I could be anything I wanted to be. I could only be me" (186, paragraph 80). This conflict is one of personality, and it is also, likely, a difference in the culture of the two—a Chinese mother and an American daughter. As a parent, the mother demands the respect she believes children owe to older and wiser authority figures. In great anger after the disastrous recital, she declares her belief: "only two kinds of daughters. . . . Those who are obedient and those who follow their own mind!' " (186, paragraph 74)—and she insists on obedience from her own child. So strong is the mother's desire to have Jing-Mei yield to her parental wishes that she half pulls and half carries Jing-Mei to the piano to resume her regular practice. In extreme bitterness and anger against her mother's inability to sympathize with her, Jing-Mei cruelly uses her mother's past as a weapon when she says she wishes she were dead like her mother's twin girls (186, paragraph 77). Because of this outburst, the mother's illusion of American success is deflated. All her hopes of making up for her lost life in China, along with the optimism that she has centered in her daughter, are dashed, and she backs "out of the room, stunned, as if she were blowing away like a small brown leaf, thin, brittle, lifeless" (186, paragraph 78).

[6]     And so the mother quietly accepts new disappointment, even in her new land, because of her daughter. She has believed in renewal, and has thrown herself heart and soul into her dreams to make Jing-Mei a success. Obviously the mother's overriding character flaw, which she never recognizes, is that she fails to acknowledge her daughter's individuality. She is unable to deal with this fact despite all her love, hard work, optimism, and willingness to assist. The mother and daughter are of course "two kinds," which means that they are two totally different and inadaptable characters. The "two kinds" may also mean that they are both alike in their stubbornness and desire for

Zell 4

control. The result is that the daughter asserts herself even though she falls "short of expectations" (186, paragraph 79), while the mother silently retreats into resignation and disappointed hopes. Never do the mother and daughter discuss the breach that opens between them, and never does Jing-Mei hear her mother explain, "why she had hoped for something so large that failure was inevitable" (186, paragraph 81).

Zell 5

**WORK CITED**

Tan, Amy. "Two Kinds." *Literature: An Introduction to Reading and Writing*. Ed. Edgar V. Roberts. 4th Compact Ed. Upper Saddle River: Prentice Hall, 2009. 180–187.

## Commentary

The strategy of this essay is to use details from the story to bring out a number of the mother's separate traits, in this way illustrating strategy 3 (p. 191). Other plans of development could also have been chosen, such as the mother's belief in the value of work (strategy 1); the change in the mother after the outbursts of anger at the piano (strategy 2); or the mother's separate reproaches to her daughter for not trying hard enough (another way to use strategy 3).

A major function of paragraph 1 of this essay is to explain how all judgments about the mother are gained exclusively through the words of the daughter, the narrator. The essay thus highlights how Tan uses presentation method 4 (see p. 191) as the means of rendering the mother's character.

The essay's argument is developed through a number of the mother's characteristics, namely her parental love (paragraph 2), her optimistic nature (paragraph 3), her high valuation of work (paragraph 4), and her failure to recognize her daughter's desire for individuality (paragraph 5). The concluding paragraph (6) summarizes a number of these details, and it also considers the irreconcilable character differences between the "two kinds."

As a study in composition, paragraph 3 shows how discussion of a specific character trait, together with related details, contributes to the essay's development. The trait is the mother's optimistic nature (shown by her hope for a new life in America). Connecting details within the paragraph, selected from study notes, are the mother's belief in opportunity fueled by her uncritical understanding, through popular media, of some of the directions in which people might achieve success. The paragraph weaves together enough material to show the relationship between the mother's strong faith and her annoyance and reproachfulness, which lead to her emotional outburst against Jing-Mei—a climax producing the change that defines the mother as a round character.

# Writing Topics About Character

1. Compare the ways in which actions (or speeches, or the comments of others) are used to bring out the character traits of Jing-Mei in "Two Kinds," Jackie in "First Confession" (Chapter 7), and James in "The Sky Is Gray."

2. Compare the qualities and functions of two or more flat characters (e.g., Mangan's sister in Joyce's "Araby," (Chapter 5) the father and Old Chong in "Two Kinds," the hunter in "A Worn Path" [Chapter 2]). How do the flat characters bring out qualities of the major characters? What do you discover about their own character traits?

3. Using Scoresby (in Twain's "Luck"), the narrator of "Battle Royal" (Chapter 6), and Jing-Mei (in Tan's "Two Kinds") as examples, describe the effects of circumstance on character. Under the rubric "circumstance" you may consider elements such as education, family, economic and social status, cultural background, and geographic isolation.

4. Compare the parent-child relationships in "Two Kinds," "Fences" (Chapter 23), "The Sky Is Gray," and "First Confession" (Chapter 7).

5. Topics for argument or brief essays:
   a. It often seems that fictional characters are under stress and also that they lead lives of great difficulty. How true is this claim? To what degree do the difficulties that characters experience bring out either good or bad qualities, or both?

   b. Develop this argument: *To our friends and close relatives, we are round, but to ourselves and most other people, we are flat.*

6. Write a brief essay comparing the changes or developments of two major or round characters in stories included in this chapter. You might deal with issues such as what the characters are like at the beginning; what conflicts they confront, deal with, or avoid; what qualities are brought out that signal the characters' changes or developments; and so on.

7. Write a brief story about an important decision you have made (e.g., choosing a school, beginning or leaving a job, declaring a major, starting or ending a friendship). Show how your qualities of character (to the extent that you understand yourself), together with your experiences, have gone into the decision. You may write more comfortably if you give yourself another name and describe your actions in the third person.

# Chapter 5

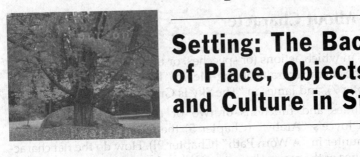

# Setting: The Background of Place, Objects, and Culture in Stories

Like all human beings, literary characters do not exist in isolation. Just as they become human by interacting with other characters, they gain identity because of their cultural and political allegiances, their possessions, their jobs, and where they live, move, and have their being. They are usually involved deeply with their environments, and their surroundings are causes of much of their motivation and many of their possible conflicts. Plays, stories, and narrative poems must therefore include descriptions of places, objects, and backgrounds—the **setting**.

## What Is Setting?

Setting is the natural, manufactured, political, cultural, and temporal environment, including everything that characters know, own, and otherwise experience. Characters may be either helped or hurt by their surroundings, and they may fight about possessions and goals. Further, as characters speak with each other, they reveal the degree to which they share the customs and ideas of their times.

### Authors Use Three Basic Types of Settings

PUBLIC AND PRIVATE PLACES, TOGETHER WITH VARIOUS POSSESSIONS, ARE IMPORTANT IN FICTION, AS IN LIFE.   To reveal or highlight qualities of character, and also to make literature lifelike, authors include many details about objects and places of human manufacture, construction, and maintenance. Houses, both interiors and exteriors, are common, as are streets, alleys, public parks, garden paths, fences, confessionals, park benches, terraces, cemeteries, railway cars, trolley cars, historical landmarks, grocery stores, recital rooms, bridges, and the like. In addition, writers include references to objects, such as walking sticks, baseballs, books, phonograph records, necklaces, money, guns, shawls, clocks, wallpaper, or hair ribbons. In Maupassant's "The Necklace" (Chapter 1), the loss of a comfortable home brings out the best in the major character by causing her to adjust to her economic reversal, whereas in Lawrence's "The Horse Dealer's Daughter" (Chapter 9), such a loss leads the major character to depression and attempted suicide.

Objects also enter directly into fictional action and character. The lives of the men in O'Brien's "The Things They Carried" (Chapter 2) depend on the myriad objects they must carry on their military missions. Trying on the neighbors' clothes is an indication of intense if not morbid peculiarity in Carver's "Neighbors" (Chapter 3). A falling hair ribbon reveals the inadequate relationship between Brown and Faith in Hawthorne's "Young Goodman Brown" (Chapter 8).

**OUTDOOR PLACES ARE SCENES OF MANY FICTIONAL ACTIONS.**   The natural world is an obvious location for the action of many narratives and plays. It is therefore important to note natural surroundings (hills, shorelines, valleys, mountains, meadows, fields, trees, lakes, streams), living creatures (birds, dogs, horses, snakes), and also the times, seasons, and conditions in which things happen (morning or night, summer or winter, sunlight or cloudiness, wind or calmness, rain or shine, sunlight or darkness, summer or winter, snowfall or blizzard, heat or cold)—any or all of which may influence and interact with character, motivation, and conduct.

**CULTURAL AND HISTORICAL CIRCUMSTANCES OFTEN FIGURE LARGELY IN FICTION.**   Just as physical setting influences characters, so do historical and cultural conditions and assumptions. The broad cultural setting of Jackson's "The Lottery" (Chapter 3) is built on the persistence of a primitive belief despite the sophistication of our own modern and scientific age. The brutal oppressiveness and obscene concentration-camp conditions in Ozick's "The Shawl" cause the major character to conceal a small child as the only way to keep that child alive (this chapter). In Mansfield's "Miss Brill" (Chapter 4), we see that the shabbiness of a favorite article of clothing suggests the isolation of the principal character.

## The Literary Uses of Setting

Authors use setting to create meaning, just as painters include backgrounds and objects to render ideas. The contrasting settings of François Boucher's portrait *Madame de Pompadour*, for example, and Edward Hopper's *Automat* demonstrate how the same subject—a single female figure—can show divergent views of human life, one elegant and pampered, the other ordinary and forlorn (I–8, Plate 2 and I–3, Plate 2).

Writers manipulate literary locations in a comparable way. For example, in Hawthorne's "Young Goodman Brown" (Chapter 8), a woodland path that is difficult to follow and filled with obstacles is a major topographical feature. The path is of course no more than ordinary, granted the time and circumstances of the story, but it also conveys the idea that life is difficult, unpredictable, treacherous, deceiving, and mysterious. Similarly, in O'Brien's "The Things They Carried" (Chapter 2), the constant attention to details indicates the exceedingly difficult and dangerous lives being led by American soldiers during the Vietnamese War.

### The Setting Is Usually Essential and Vital in the Story

To study the setting in a narrative (or play), discover the important details and then try to explain their function. Depending on the author's purpose, the amount of detail may vary. Poe provides many graphic and also impressionistic details in "The Masque of the Red Death," so that we can follow, almost visually, the bizarre action at the story's end. In some works the setting is so intensely present, like the various Dublin scenes in "Araby," that it is almost literally an additional participant in the action.

## Setting Augments a Work's Realism and Credibility

One of the major purposes of literary setting is to establish **realism,** or **verisimilitude.** As the description of location and objects becomes particular and detailed, the events of the work become more believable. Maupassant places "The Necklace" (Chapter 1) in real locations in late-nineteenth-century Paris, and for this reason the story has all the semblance of having actually happened. Even futuristic, symbolic, and fantastic stories, as well as ghost stories, seem more believable if they include places and objects from everyday experience. Hawthorne's "Young Goodman Brown" (Chapter 8) is such a story, as is Poe's "The Masque of the Red Death." Although these stories are by no means realistic, their credibility is enhanced because they take place in settings that have a basis in the world of reality.

## Setting May Accentuate Qualities of Character

Setting may intersect with character as a means by which authors underscore the influence of place, circumstance, and time on human growth and change. Whitecloud's progressive settings in "Blue Winds Dancing" (Chapter 6), from California to Wisconsin, explain the disillusionment and also the fear that possesses the narrator, and also help us understand why he longed so deeply for home and the comfort provided to him by once again being with his family. (A blending of setting and character as seen in Maupassant's "The Necklace" is explored in the two drafts of the illustrative essay in Chapter 1.)

The ways that characters respond and adjust to the world around them can reveal their qualities. Peyton Farquhar's scheme to escape from his fate, even when it is literally dangling in front of him, suggests that he is a character of great strength but also of powerful imagination (Bierce's "An Occurrence at Owl Creek Bridge" [Chapter 2]). In contrast, Goodman Brown's Calvinistic religious conviction that human beings are inclined to evil, which is confirmed to him by his nightmarish encounter, indicates the weakness and gullibility of his character (Hawthorne's "Young Goodman Brown.").

## Setting Is a Means by Which Authors Structure and Shape Their Works

Authors often use setting as one of the means of organizing their stories, as in Maupassant's "The Necklace." The story's final scene is believable because Mathilde leaves her impoverished home to take a nostalgic stroll on the Champs-Elysées, the most fashionable street in Paris. Without this change of setting, she could not have encountered Jeanne Forrestier again, for their usual ways of life would no longer bring them together. In short, the structure of the story depends on a normal and natural change of scene.

Another organizational application of place, time, and object is a **framing** or **enclosing setting**, when an author opens with a particular description and then returns to the same setting at the end. An example is Steinbeck's "The Chrysanthemums" (Chapter 8), which begins with the major character tending her flowers and ends with her seeing the destruction of some of these same flowers that she had given away. A comparable use of framing occurs in Welty's "A Worn Path" (Chapter 2), in which the walking trips taken by the main character open and close the story—to the town and then away from the town. By such means, framing creates a formal completeness, just as it may underscore the author's depiction of the human condition.

## Various Settings May Be Symbolic

If the scenes and materials of setting are highlighted or emphasized, they also may be taken as symbols through which the author expresses ideas. Such an emphasis is made in Ozick's "The Shawl," in which the shawl has the ordinary function of providing cover and warmth for a baby. Because it is so prominent, however, the shawl also symbolizes the attempt to preserve future generations, and because its loss also produces a human loss, it symbolizes the helplessness of the victims in Nazi extermination camps during World War II. In O'Brien's "The Things They Carried" (Chapter 2), the constant references to the weights of the objects symbolize how the men's lives depend on their own resources—their carried burdens.

## Setting Is Used in the Creation of Atmosphere and Mood

Most actions *require* no more than a functional description of setting. Thus, taking a walk in a forest needs just the statement that there are many, or few, trees. However, if you find descriptions of shapes, light and shadows, animals, wind, and sounds, you may be sure that the author is creating an **atmosphere** or **mood** for the action (as in Gilman's "The Yellow Wallpaper" [Chapter 10] and Joyce's "Araby"). There are many ways to develop moods. Descriptions of bright colors (red, orange, yellow) may contribute to a mood of happiness. The same colors in dim or eerie light, like the rooms in Poe's "The Masque of the Red Death," invoke gloom or augment hysteria. References to smells and sounds bring the setting to life further by asking additional sensory responses from the reader. The setting of a story in a small town or large city, in green or snow-covered fields, or in middle-class or lower-class residences may evoke responses to these places that contribute to the work's atmosphere.

## Setting May Underscore a Work's Irony

Just as setting may reinforce character and theme, so it may establish expectations that are the opposite of what occurs. At the beginning of "The Lottery" (Chapter 3), for example, Jackson describes the plainness and folksiness of the assembling townspeople—details that make the conclusion ironic, for it is these same everyday folks who bring about the final horror. Irony is also a motif in Chopin's "The Story of an Hour" inasmuch as the major characters in the story are unable to prevent the final outcome, even though their intentions aim toward the opposite result. The ironic use of setting is by no means limited only to fiction because it may also be significantly important in plays and poems. The case of dueling pistols in Chekhov's *The Bear* (Chapter 22) brings out the developing love between Smirnov and Mrs. Popov. Instead of separating these characters through death, the pistols actually bring them into intimate direct contact. Thomas Hardy creates a heavily ironic situation in the poem "Channel Firing" (Chapter 13) when the noise of large guns at sea "wakens" the skeletons buried in an English churchyard. The irony is that those engaged in the gunnery practice, if "red war" gets "yet redder," will soon be numbered among the skeletons in the graveyard.

## Stories for Study

## JOSEPH CONRAD (1857–1924)

Conrad (Teodor Jósef Konrad Korzeniowski), whose parents were Polish, was born in Ukraine. His parents died when he was quite young, and at the age of 16 he embarked on a career as a sailor, shipping aboard English sailing vessels. At this same time he began studying English, a learning task which occupied him for five years while he was plying his trade as a seaman. Ultimately he rose to become a ship's captain, and frequently traveled to many distant areas of the world, including the Far East, in the business of international trade. Throughout his life he spoke English with a Polish accent, but his command of written English, as readers of "The Secret Sharer" will quickly discover, was masterly. He maintained that he might never have become a writer if he had not been able to write in English. In ill health, he left the sailing profession in 1895, and at that point he took up an entirely new career as a writer in his adopted language, having published his first novel, *Almayer's Folly*. From this time until his death 29 years later, he regularly produced novels, as well as personal reminiscences and observations on "life and letters." His best-known novels are *Lord Jim* (1900) and *Nostromo* (1904). His best-known tale, or lengthy short story, is *Heart of Darkness* (1902). This work received great attention in the second half of the twentieth century because of Francis Ford Coppola's movie *Apocalypse Now* (1979), which is an adaptation of *Heart of Darkness* as the details of the story are applied to American involvement in the Vietnam War.

# The Secret Sharer (1912)

1

On my right hand there were lines of fishing stakes resembling a mysterious system of half-submerged bamboo fences, incomprehensible in its division of the domain of tropical fishes, and crazy of aspect as if abandoned forever by some nomad tribe of fishermen now gone to the other end of the ocean; for there was no sign of human habitation as far as the eye could reach. To the left a group of barren islets, suggesting ruins of stone walls, towers, and block-houses, had its foundations set in a blue sea that itself looked solid, so still and stable did it lie below my feet; even the track of light from the westering sun shone smoothly, without that animated glitter which tells of an imperceptible ripple. And when I turned my head to take a parting glance at the tug which had just left us anchored outside the bar, I saw the straight line of the flat shore joined to the stable sea, edge to edge, with a perfect and unmarked closeness, in one leveled floor half brown, half blue under the enormous dome of the sky. Corresponding in their insignificance to the islets of the sea, two small clumps of trees, one on each side of the only fault in the impeccable joint, marked the mouth of the river Meinam[1] we had just left on the first preparatory stage of our homeward journey; and, far back on the inland level, a larger and loftier mass, the grove surrounding the great Paknam pagoda, was the only thing on which the eye could rest from the vain task of exploring the monotonous sweep of the horizon. Here and there gleams as of a few scattered pieces of silver marked the windings of the great river; and on the nearest of them, just within the bar, the tug steaming right into the land became lost to my sight, hull and funnel and masts, as though the impassive earth had swallowed her up without an effort, without a tremor. My eye followed the light cloud of her smoke, now here, now there, above the plain, according to the devious curves of the stream, but always fainter and farther away, till I lost it at last behind the miter-shaped hill of the great pagoda. And then I was left alone with my ship, anchored at the head of the Gulf of Siam.

She floated at the starting point of a long journey, very still in an immense stillness, the shadows of her spars flung far to the eastward by the setting sun. At that moment I was alone on her decks. There was not a sound in her—and around us nothing moved, nothing lived, not a canoe on the water, not a bird in the air, not a cloud in the sky. In this breathless pause at the threshold of a long passage we seemed to be measuring our fitness for a long and arduous enterprise, the appointed task of both our existences to be carried out, far from all human eyes, with only sky and sea for spectators and for judges.

There must have been some glare in the air to interfere with one's sight, because it was only just before the sun left us that my roaming eyes made out beyond the highest ridge of the principal islet of the group something which did away with the solemnity of perfect solitude. The tide of darkness flowed on swiftly; and with tropical suddenness a swarm of stars came out above the shadowy earth, while I lingered yet, my hand resting lightly on my ship's rail as if on the shoulder of a trusted friend. But, with all that multitude of celestial bodies staring down at one, the comfort of quiet communion with her was gone for good. And there were also disturbing sounds by this time—voices, footsteps forward; the steward flitted along the main deck, a busily ministering spirit; a hand bell tinkled urgently under the poop deck. . . .

---

[1]The locations Conrad describes in the story are all real, although many have been renamed since his time. The river Meinam, or Mae Nam, is the Chao Phraya River, which empties into the Gulf of Siam (now the Gulf of Thailand), where the story's action begins. The "great Paknam" Pagoda is the Phra Samut Chedi Pagoda. The location of the ship at the story's end is near the island Kaôh Rŭng (Koh-ring), near Cambodia (Cambodje), many miles to the southeast of where the story begins (see paragraphs 295, 318).

I found my two officers waiting for me near the supper table, in the lighted cuddy.[2] We sat down at once, and as I helped the chief mate, I said:

5    "Are you aware that there is a ship anchored inside the islands? I saw her mastheads above the ridge as the sun went down."

He raised sharply his simple face, overcharged by a terrible growth of whisker, and emitted his usual ejaculations: "Bless my soul, sir! You don't say so!"

My second mate was a sound-cheeked, silent young man, grave beyond his years, I thought; but as our eyes happened to meet I detected a slight quiver on his lips. I looked down at once. It was not my part to encourage sneering on board my ship. It must be said, too, that I knew very little of my officers. In consequence of certain events of no particular significance, except to myself, I had been appointed to the command only a fortnight before. Neither did I know much of the hands forward. All these people had been together for eighteen months or so, and my position was that of the only stranger on board. I mention this because it has some bearing on what is to follow. But what I felt most was my being a stranger to the ship; and if truth must be told, I was somewhat of a stranger to myself. The youngest man on board (barring the second mate), and untried as yet by a position of the fullest responsibility, I was willing to take the adequacy of the others for granted. They had simply to be equal to their tasks: but I wondered how far I should turn out faithful to that ideal conception of one's own personality every man sets up for himself secretly.

Meantime the chief mate, with an almost visible effect of collaboration on the part of his round eyes and frightful whiskers, was trying to evolve a theory of the anchored ship. His dominant trait was to take all things into earnest consideration. He was of a painstaking turn of mind. As he used to say, he "liked to account to himself" for practically everything that came in his way, down to a miserable scorpion he had found in his cabin a week before. The why and the wherefore of that scorpion—how it got on board and came to select his room rather than the pantry (which was a dark place and more what a scorpion would be partial to), and how on earth it managed to drown itself in the inkwell of his writing desk—had exercised him infinitely. The ship within the islands was much more easily accounted for; and just as we were about to rise from the table he made his pronouncement. She was, he doubted not, a ship from home lately arrived. Probably she drew too much water to cross the bar except at the top of spring tides. Therefore she went into the natural harbor to wait for a few days in preference to remaining in an open roadstead.

"That's so," confirmed the second mate, suddenly, in his slightly hoarse voice. "She draws over twenty feet. She's the Liverpool ship *Sephora*[3] with a cargo of coal. Hundred and twenty-three days from Cardiff."

10    We looked at him in surprise.

"The tugboat skipper told me when he came on board for your letters, sir," explained the young man. "He expects to take her up the river the day after tomorrow."

After thus overwhelming us with the extent of his information he slipped out of the cabin. The mate observed regretfully that he "could not account for that young fellow's whims." What prevented him telling us all about it at once, he wanted to know.

I detained him as he was making a move. For the last two days the crew had had plenty of hard work, and the night before they had very little sleep. I felt painfully that I—a stranger— was doing something unusual when I directed him to let all hands turn in without setting an

---

[2] A small mess hall next to the ship's kitchen.

[3] *Sephora*: The Greek version of the Biblical name Zipporah, who was the wife of Moses. A puzzling story in Exodus (24–26) indicates that she saved her husband from the Lord's anger—the reason for which is not disclosed—by circumcising one of her sons. We may presume here that the ship had been named *Sephora* as a symbol of safety and good luck.

anchor. I proposed to keep on deck myself till one o'clock or thereabouts. I would get the second mate to relieve me at that hour.

"He will turn out the cook and the steward at four," I concluded, "and then give you a call. Of course at the lightest sign of any sort of wind we'll have the hands up and make a start at once."

He concealed his astonishment. "Very well, sir." Outside the cuddy he put his head in the 15 second mate's door to inform him of my unheard-of caprice to take a five hours' anchor watch on myself. I heard the other raise his voice incredulously:

"What? The captain himself?" Then a few more murmurs, a door closed, then another. A few moments later I went on deck.

My strangeness, which had made me sleepless, had prompted that unconventional arrangement, as if I had expected in those solitary hours of the night to get on terms with the ship of which I knew nothing, manned by men of whom I knew very little more. Fast alongside a wharf, littered like any ship in port with a tangle of unrelated things, invaded by unrelated shore people, I had hardly seen her yet properly. Now, as she lay cleared for sea, the stretch of her main deck seemed to me very fine under the stars. Very fine, very roomy for her size, and very inviting. I descended the poop and paced the waist, my mind picturing to myself the coming passage through the Malay Archipelago, down the Indian Ocean, and up the Atlantic. All its phases were familiar enough to me, every characteristic, all the alternatives which were likely to face me on the high seas—everything! . . . except the novel responsibility of command. But I took heart from the reasonable thought that the ship was like other ships, the men like other men, and that the sea was not likely to keep any special surprises expressly for my discomfiture.

Arrived at that comforting conclusion, I bethought myself of a cigar and went below to get it. All was still down there. Everybody at the after end of the ship was sleeping profoundly. I came out again on the quarter-deck, agreeably at ease in my sleeping suit on that warm breathless night, barefooted, a glowing cigar in my teeth, and, going forward, I was met by the profound silence of the fore end of the ship. Only as I passed the door of the forecastle I heard a deep, quiet, trustful sigh of some sleeper inside. And suddenly I rejoiced in the great security of the sea as compared with the unrest of the land, in my choice of that untempted life presenting no disquieting problems, invested with an elementary moral beauty by the absolute straightforwardness of its appeal and by the singleness of its purpose.

The riding light in the fore-rigging burned with a clear, untroubled, as if symbolic, flame, confident and bright in the mysterious shades of the night. Passing on my way aft along the other side of the ship, I observed that the rope side ladder, put over, no doubt, for the master of the tug when he came to fetch away our letters, had not been hauled in as it should have been. I became annoyed at this, for exactitude in small matters is the very soul of discipline. Then I reflected that I had myself peremptorily dismissed my officers from duty, and by my own act had prevented the anchor watch being formally set and things properly attended to. I asked myself whether it was wise ever to interfere with the established routine of duties even from the kindest of motives. My action might have made me appear eccentric. Goodness only knew how that absurdly whiskered mate would "account" for my conduct, and what the whole ship thought of that informality of their new captain. I was vexed with myself.

Not from compunction certainly, but, as it were mechanically, I proceeded to get the lad- 20 der in myself. Now a side ladder of that sort is a light affair and comes in easily, yet my vigorous tug, which should have brought it flying on board, merely recoiled upon my body in a totally unexpected jerk. What the devil! . . . I was so astounded by the immovableness of that ladder that I remained stock-still, trying to account for it to myself like that imbecile mate of mine. In the end, of course, I put my head over the rail.

The side of the ship made an opaque belt of shadow on the darkling glassy shimmer of the sea. But I saw at once something elongated and pale floating very close to the ladder. Before I could form a guess a faint flash of phosphorescent light, which seemed to issue suddenly from the naked body of a man, flickered in the sleeping water with the elusive, silent play of summer lightning in a night sky. With a gasp I saw revealed to my stare a pair of feet, the long legs, a broad livid back immersed right up to the neck in a greenish cadaverous glow. One hand, awash, clutched the bottom rung of the ladder. He was complete but for the head. A headless corpse! The cigar dropped out of my gaping mouth with a tiny plop and a short hiss quite audible in the absolute stillness of all things under heaven. At that I suppose he raised up his face, a dimly pale oval in the shadow of the ship's side. But even then I could only barely make out down there the shape of his black-haired head. However, it was enough for the horrid, frost-bound sensation which had gripped me about the chest to pass off. The moment of vain exclamations was past, too. I only climbed on the spare spar and leaned over the rail as far as I could, to bring my eyes nearer to that mystery floating alongside.

As he hung by the ladder, like a resting swimmer, the sea lightning played about his limbs at every stir; and he appeared in it ghastly, silvery, fishlike. He remained as mute as a fish, too. He made no motion to get out of the water, either. It was inconceivable that he should not attempt to come on board, and strangely troubling to suspect that perhaps he did not want to. And my first words were prompted by just that troubled incertitude.

"What's the matter?" I asked in my ordinary tone, speaking down to the face upturned exactly under mine.

"Cramp," it answered, no louder. Then slightly anxious, "I say, no need to call anyone."

25     "I was not going to," I said.

"Are you alone on deck?"

"Yes."

I had somehow the impression that he was on the point of letting go the ladder to swim away beyond my ken—mysterious as he came. But, for the moment, this being appearing as if he had risen from the bottom of the sea (it was certainly the nearest land to the ship) wanted only to know the time. I told him. And he, down there, tentatively:

"I suppose your captain's turned in?"

30     "I am sure he isn't," I said.

He seemed to struggle with himself, for I heard something like the low, bitter murmur of doubt. "What's the good?" His next words came out with a hesitating effort.

"Look here, my man. Could you call him out quietly?"

I thought the time had come to declare myself.

"I am the captain."

35     I heard a "By Jove!" whispered at the level of the water. The phosphorescence flashed in the swirl of the water all about his limbs, his other hand seized the ladder.

"My name's Leggatt."

The voice was calm and resolute. A good voice. The self-possession of that man had somehow induced a corresponding state in myself. It was very quietly that I remarked:

"You must be a good swimmer."

"Yes. I've been in the water practically since nine o'clock. The question for me now is whether I am to let go this ladder and go on swimming till I sink from exhaustion, or—to come on board here."

40     I felt this was no mere formula of desperate speech, but a real alternative in the view of a strong soul. I should have gathered from this that he was young; indeed, it is only the young who are ever confronted by such clear issues. But at this time it was pure intuition on my part. A mysterious communication was established already between us two—in the face of that silent darkened tropical sea. I was young, too; young enough to make no comment. The man

in the water began suddenly to climb up the ladder, and I hastened away from the rail to fetch some clothes.

Before entering the cabin I stood still, listening in the lobby at the foot of the stairs. A faint snore came through the closed door of the chief mate's room. The second mate's door was on the hook, but the darkness in there was absolutely soundless. He, too, was young and could sleep like a stone. Remained the steward, but he was not likely to wake up before he was called. I got a sleeping suit out of my room and, coming back on deck, saw the naked man from the sea sitting on the main hatch, glimmering white in the darkness, his elbows on his knees and his head in his hands. In a moment he had concealed his damp body in a sleeping suit of the same gray-stripe pattern as the one I was wearing and followed me like my double on the poop. Together we moved right aft, barefooted, silent.

"What is it?" I asked in a deadened voice, taking the lighted lamp out of the binnacle, and raising it to his face.

"An ugly business."

He had rather regular features; a good mouth; light eyes under somewhat heavy, dark eyebrows; a smooth, square forehead; no growth on his cheeks; a small, brown mustache, and a well-shaped, round chin. His expression was concentrated, meditative, under the inspecting light of the lamp I held up to his face; such as a man thinking hard in solitude might wear. My sleeping suit was just right for his size. A well-knit young fellow of twenty-five at most. He caught his lower lip with the edge of white, even teeth.

"Yes," I said, replacing the lamp in the binnacle. The warm, heavy tropical night closed    45
upon his head again.

"There's a ship over there," he murmured.

"Yes, I know. The *Sephora*. Did you know of us?"

"Hadn't the slightest idea. I am the mate of her—" He paused and corrected himself. "I should say I was."

"Aha! Something wrong?"

"Yes. Very wrong indeed. I've killed a man."

"What do you mean? Just now?"    50

"No, on the passage. Weeks ago. Thirty-nine south. When I say a man—"

"Fit of temper," I suggested, confidently.

The shadowy, dark head, like mine, seemed to nod imperceptibly above the ghostly gray of my sleeping suit. It was, in the night, as though I had been faced by my own reflection in the depths of a somber and immense mirror.

"A pretty thing to have to own up for a Conway boy,"[4] murmured my double, distinctly.    55

"You're a Conway boy?"

"I am," he said, as if startled. Then, slowly . . . "Perhaps you too—"

It was so; but being a couple of years older I had left before he joined. After a quick interchange of dates a silence fell; and I thought suddenly of my absurd mate with his terrific whiskers and the "Bless my soul—you don't say so" type of intellect. My double gave me an inkling of his thoughts by saying:

"My father's a parson in Norfolk. Do you see me before a judge and jury on that charge? For myself I can't see the necessity. There are fellows that an angel from heaven—And I am not that. He was one of those creatures that are just simmering all the time with a silly sort of wickedness. Miserable devils that have no business to live at all. He wouldn't do his duty and wouldn't let anybody else do theirs. But what's the good of talking! You know well enough the sort of ill-conditioned snarling cur—"

---

[4]A graduate of the Conway Merchant Marine Academy at Conway, in north Wales.

60   He appealed to me as if our experiences had been as identical as our clothes. And I knew well enough the pestiferous danger of such a character where there are no means of legal repression. And I knew well enough also that my double there was no homicidal ruffian. I did not think of asking him for details, and he told me the story roughly in brusque, disconnected sentences. I needed no more. I saw it all going on as though I were myself inside that other sleeping suit.

"It happened while we were setting a reefed foresail, at dusk. Reefed foresail! You understand the sort of weather. The only sail we had left to keep the ship running; so you may guess what it had been like for days. Anxious sort of job, that. He gave me some of his cursed insolence at the sheet. I tell you I was overdone with this terrific weather that seemed to have no end to it. Terrific, I tell you—and a deep ship. I believe the fellow himself was half crazed with funk. It was no time for gentlemanly reproof, so I turned round and felled him like an ox. He up and at me. We closed just as an awful sea made for the ship: All hands saw it coming and took to the rigging, but I had him by the throat, and went on shaking him like a rat, the men above us yelling, 'Look out! look out!' Then a crash as if the sky had fallen on my head. They say that for over ten minutes hardly anything was to be seen of the ship—just the three masts and a bit of the forecastle head and of the poop all awash driving along in a smother of foam. It was a miracle that they found us, jammed together behind the forebits. It's clear that I meant business, because I was holding him by the throat still when they picked us up. He was black in the face. It was too much for them. It seems they rushed us aft together, gripped as we were, screaming 'Murder!' like a lot of lunatics, and broke into the cuddy. And the ship running for her life, touch and go all the time, any minute her last in a sea fit to turn your hair gray only a-looking at it. I understand that the skipper, too, started raving like the rest of them. The man had been deprived of sleep for more than a week, and to have this sprung on him at the height of a furious gale nearly drove him out of his mind. I wonder they didn't fling me overboard after getting the carcass of their precious shipmate out of my fingers. They had rather a job to separate us, I've been told. A sufficiently fierce story to make an old judge and a respectable jury sit up a bit. The first thing I heard when I came to myself was the maddening howling of that endless gale, and on that the voice of the old man. He was hanging on to my bunk, staring into my face out of his sou'wester.

"'Mr. Leggatt, you have killed a man. You can act no longer as chief mate of this ship.'"

His care to subdue his voice made it sound monotonous. He rested a hand on the end of the skylight to steady himself with, and all that time did not stir a limb, so far as I could see. "Nice little tale for a quiet tea party," he concluded in the same tone.

One of my hands, too, rested on the end of the skylight; neither did I stir a limb, so far as I knew. We stood less than a foot from each other. It occurred to me that if old "Bless my soul—you don't say so" were to put his head up the companion and catch sight of us, he would think he was seeing double, or imagine himself come upon a scene of weird witchcraft; the strange captain having a quiet confabulation by the wheel with his own gray ghost. I became very much concerned to prevent anything of the sort. I heard the other's soothing undertone.

65   "My father's a parson in Norfolk," it said. Evidently he had forgotten he had told me this important fact before. Truly a nice little tale.

"You had better slip down into my stateroom now," I said, moving off stealthily. My double followed my movements; our bare feet made no sound; I let him in, closed the door with care, and, after giving a call to the second mate, returned on deck for my relief.

"Not much sign of any wind yet," I remarked when he approached.

"No, sir. Not much," he assented, sleepily, in his hoarse voice, with just enough deference, no more, and barely suppressing a yawn.

"Well, that's all you have to look out for. You have got your orders."

70   "Yes, sir."

I paced a turn or two on the poop and saw him take up his position face forward with his elbow in the rat-lines of the mizzen-rigging before I went below. The mate's faint snoring was still going on peacefully. The cuddy lamp was burning over the table on which stood a vase with flowers, a polite attention from the ships' provision merchant—the last flowers we should see for the next three months at the very least. Two bunches of bananas hung from the beam symmetrically, one on each side of the rudder casing. Everything was as before in the ship— except that two of her captain's sleeping suits were simultaneously in use, one motionless in the cuddy, the other keeping very still in the captain's stateroom.

It must be explained here that my cabin had the form of the capital letter L, the door being within the angle and opening into the short part of the letter. A couch was to the left, the bed-place to the right; my writing desk and the chronometers table faced the door. But anyone opening it, unless he stepped right inside, had no view of what I call the long (or vertical) part of the letter. It contained some lockers surmounted by a bookcase; and a few clothes, a thick jacket or two, caps, oilskin coat, and such like, hung on hooks. There was at the bottom of that part a door opening into my bathroom, which could be entered also directly from the saloon. But that way was never used.

The mysterious arrival had discovered the advantage of this particular shape. Entering my room, lighted strongly by a big bulkhead lamp swung on gimbals above my writing desk, I did not see him anywhere till he stepped out quietly from behind the coats hung in the re-cessed part.

"I heard somebody moving about, and went in there at once," he whispered.

I, too, spoke under my breath.

"Nobody is likely to come in here without knocking and getting permission." 75

He nodded. His face was thin and the sunburn faded, as though he had been ill. And no wonder. He had been, I heard presently, kept under arrest in his cabin for nearly seven weeks. But there was nothing sickly in his eyes or in his expression. He was not a bit like me, really; yet, as we stood leaning over my bed-place, whispering side by side, with our dark heads to-gether and our backs to the door, anybody bold enough to open it stealthily would have been treated to the uncanny sight of a double captain busy talking in whispers with his other self.

"But all this doesn't tell me how you came to hang on to our side ladder," I inquired, in the hardly audible murmurs we used, after he had told me something more of the proceedings on board the *Sephora* once the bad weather was over.

"When we sighted Java Head I had had time to think all those matters out several times over. I had six weeks of doing nothing else, and with only an hour or so every evening for a tramp on the quarter-deck."

He whispered, his arms folded on the side of my bed-place, staring through the open port. 80 And I could imagine perfectly the manner of this thinking out—a stubborn if not a steadfast operation; something of which I should have been perfectly incapable.

"I reckoned it would be dark before we closed with the land," he continued, so low that I had to strain my hearing, near as we were to each other, shoulder touching shoulder almost. "So I asked to speak to the old man. He always seemed very sick when he came to see me—as if he could not look me in the face. You know, that foresail saved the ship. She was too deep to have run long under bare poles. And it was I that managed to set it for him. Anyway, he came. When I had him in my cabin—he stood by the door looking at me as if I had the halter around my neck already—I asked him right away to leave my cabin door unlocked at night while the ship was going through Sunda Straits. There would be the Java coast within two or three miles, off Angier Point. I wanted nothing more. I've had a prize for swimming my second year in the Conway."

"I can believe it," I breathed out.

"God only knows why they locked me in every night. To see some of their faces you'd have thought they were afraid I'd go about at night strangling people. Am I a murdering brute? Do I look it? By Jove! if I had been he wouldn't have trusted himself like that into my room. You'll say I might have chucked him aside and bolted out, there and then—it was dark already. Well, no. And for the same reason I wouldn't think of trying to smash the door. There would have been a rush to stop me at the noise, and I did not mean to get into a confounded scrimmage. Somebody else might have got killed—for I would not have broken out only to get chucked back, and I did not want any more of that work. He refused, looking more sick than ever. He was afraid of the men, and also of that old second mate of his who had been sailing with him for years—a gray-headed old humbug; and his steward, too, had been with him devil knows how long—seventeen years or more—a dogmatic sort of loafer who hated me like poison, just because I was the chief mate. No chief mate ever made more than one voyage in the *Sephora*, you know. Those two old chaps ran the ship. Devil only knows what the skipper wasn't afraid of (all his nerve went to pieces altogether in that hellish spell of bad weather we had)—of what the law would do to him—of his wife, perhaps. Oh, yes! she's on board. Though I don't think she would have meddled. She would have been only too glad to have me out of the ship in any way. The 'brand of Cain' business, don't you see. That's all right. I was ready enough to go off wandering on the face of the earth—and that was price enough to pay for an Abel of that sort. Anyhow, he wouldn't listen to me. 'This thing must take its course. I represent the law here.' He was shaking like a leaf. 'So you won't?' 'No!' 'Then I hope you will be able to sleep on that,' I said, and turned my back on him. 'I wonder that you can,' cries he, and locks the door.

"Well, after that, I couldn't. Not very well. That was three weeks ago. We have had a slow passage through the Java Sea; drifted about Carimata for ten days. When we anchored here they thought, I suppose, it was all right. The nearest land (and that's five miles) is the ship's destination; the consul would soon set about catching me; and there would have been no object in bolting to these islets there. I don't suppose there's a drop of water on them. I don't know how it was, but tonight that steward, after bringing me my supper, went out to let me eat it, and left the door unlocked. And I ate it—all there was, too. After I had finished I strolled out on the quarter-deck. I don't know that I meant to do anything. A breath of fresh air was all I wanted, I believe. Then a sudden temptation came over me. I kicked off my slippers and was in the water before I had made up my mind fairly. Somebody heard the splash and they raised an awful hullabaloo. 'He's gone! Lower the boats! He's committed suicide! No, he's swimming.' Certainly I was swimming. It's not so easy for a swimmer like me to commit suicide by drowning. I landed on the nearest islet before the boat left the ship's side. I heard them pulling about in the dark, hailing, and so on, but after a bit they gave up. Everything quieted down and the anchorage became as still as death. I sat down on a stone and began to think. I felt certain they would start searching for me at daylight. There was no place to hide on those stony things—and if there had been, what would have been the good? But now I was clear of that ship, I was not going back. So after a while I took off my clothes, tied them up in a bundle with a stone inside, and dropped them in the deep water on the outer side of the islet. That was suicide enough for me. Let them think what they liked, but I didn't mean to drown myself. I meant to swim till I sank—but that's not the same thing. I struck out for another of these little islands, and it was from that one that I first saw your riding light. Something to swim for. I went on easily, and on the way I came upon a flat rock a foot or two above water. In the daytime, I dare say, you might make it out with a glass from your poop. I scrambled up on it and rested myself for a bit. Then I made another start. That last spell must have been over a mile."

85     His whisper was getting fainter and fainter, and all the time he stared straight out through the porthole, in which there was not even a star to be seen. I had not interrupted him. There was something that made comment impossible in his narrative, or perhaps in himself; a sort of feeling, a quality, which I can't find a name for. And when he ceased, all I found was a futile whisper. "So you swam for our light?"

"Yes—straight for it. It was something to swim for. I couldn't see any stars low down because the coast was in the way, and I couldn't see the land, either. The water was like glass. One might have been swimming in a confounded thousand feet deep cistern with no place for scrambling out anywhere; but what I didn't like was the notion of swimming round and round like a crazed bullock before I gave out; and as I didn't mean to go back . . . No. Do you see me being hauled back, stark naked, off one of these little islands by the scruff of the neck and fighting like a wild beast? Somebody would have got killed for certain, and I did not want any of that. So I went on. Then your ladder—"

"Why didn't you hail the ship?" I asked, a little louder.

He touched my shoulder lightly. Lazy footsteps came right over our heads and stopped. The second mate had crossed from the other side of the poop and might have been hanging over the rail, for all we knew.

"He couldn't hear us talking—could he?" My double breathed into my very ear, anxiously.

His anxiety was an answer, a sufficient answer, to the question I had put to him. An an-    90
swer containing all the difficulty of that situation. I closed the porthole quietly, to make sure. A louder word might have been overheard.

"Who's that?" he whispered then.

"My second mate. But I don't know much more of the fellow than you do."

And I told him a little about myself. I had been appointed to take charge while I least expected anything of the sort, not quite a fortnight ago. I didn't know either the ship or the people. Hadn't had the time in port to look about me or size anybody up. And as to the crew, all they knew was that I was appointed to take the ship home. For the rest, I was almost as much of a stranger on board as himself, I said. And at the moment I felt it most acutely. I felt that it would take very little to make me a suspect person in the eyes of the ship's company.

He had turned about meantime; and we, the two strangers in the ship, faced each other in identical attitudes.

"Your ladder—" he murmured, after a silence. "Who'd have thought of finding a ladder    95
hanging over at night in a ship anchored out here! I felt just then a very unpleasant faintness. After the life I've been leading for nine weeks, anybody would have got out of condition. I wasn't capable of swimming round as far as your rudder chains. And, lo and behold! there was a ladder to get hold of. After I gripped it I said to myself, 'What's the good?' When I saw a man's head looking over I thought I would swim away presently and leave him shouting—in whatever language it was. I didn't mind being looked at. I—I liked it. And then you speaking to me so quietly—as if you had expected me—made me hold on a little longer. It had been a confounded lonely time—I don't mean while swimming. I was glad to talk a little to somebody that didn't belong to the *Sephora*. As to asking for the captain, that was a mere impulse. It could have been no use, with all the ship knowing about me and the other people pretty certain to be round here in the morning. I don't know—I wanted to be seen, to talk with somebody, before I went on. I don't know what I would have said . . . 'Fine night, isn't it?' or something of the sort."

"Do you think they will be round here presently?" I asked with some incredulity.

"Quite likely," he said, faintly

He looked extremely haggard all of a sudden. His head rolled on his shoulders.

"H'm. We shall see then. Meantime get into that bed," I whispered. "Want help? There."

It was a rather high bed-place with a set of drawers underneath. This amazing swimmer re-    100
ally needed the lift I gave him by seizing his leg. He tumbled in, rolled over on his back, and flung one arm across his eyes. And then, with his face nearly hidden, he must have looked exactly as I used to look in that bed. I gazed upon my other self for a while before drawing across carefully the two green serge curtains which ran on a brass rod. I thought for a moment of pinning them together for greater safety, but I sat down on the couch, and once there I felt unwilling to

rise and hunt for a pin. I would do it in a moment. I was extremely tired, in a peculiarly intimate way, by the strain of stealthiness, by the effort of whispering and the general secrecy of this excitement. It was three o'clock by now and I had been on my feet since nine, but I was not sleepy; I could not have gone to sleep. I sat there, fagged out, looking at the curtains, trying to clear my mind of the confused sensation of being in two places at once, and greatly bothered by an exasperating knocking in my head. It was a relief to discover suddenly that it was not in my head at all, but on the outside of the door. Before I could collect myself the words "Come in" were out of my mouth, and the steward entered with a tray, bringing in my morning coffee. I had slept, after all, and I was so frightened that I shouted, "This way! I am here, steward," as though he had been miles away. He put down the tray on the table next the couch and only then said, very quietly, "I can see you are here, sir." I felt him give me a keen look, but I dared not meet his eyes just then. He must have wondered why I had drawn the curtains of my bed before going to sleep on the couch. He went out, hooking the door open as usual.

I heard the crew washing decks above me. I knew I would have been told at once if there had been any wind. Calm, I thought, and I was doubly vexed. Indeed, I felt dual more than ever. The steward reappeared suddenly in the doorway. I jumped up from the couch so quickly that he gave me a start.

"What do you want here?"

"Close your port, sir—they are washing decks."

"It is closed," I said, reddening.

105 "Very well, sir." But he did not move from the doorway and returned my stare in an extraordinary, equivocal manner for a time. Then his eyes wavered, all his expression changed, and in a voice unusually gentle, almost coaxingly:

"May I come in to take the empty cup away, sir?"

"Of course!" I turned my back on him while he popped in and out. Then I unhooked and closed the door and even pushed the bolt. This sort of thing could not go on very long. The cabin was as hot as an oven, too. I took a peep at my double, and discovered that he had not moved, his arm was still over his eyes; but his chest heaved; his hair was wet; his chin glistened with perspiration. I reached over him and opened the port.

"I must show myself on deck," I reflected.

Of course, theoretically, I could do what I liked, with no one to say nay to me within the whole circle of the horizon; but to lock my cabin door and take the key away I did not dare. Directly I put my head out of the companion I saw the group of my two officers, the second mate barefooted, the chief mate in long india-rubber boots, near the break of the poop, and the steward halfway down the poop ladder talking to them eagerly. He happened to catch sight of me and dived, the second ran down on the main deck shouting some order or other, and the chief mate came to meet me, touching his cap.

110 There was a sort of curiosity in his eye that I did not like. I don't know whether the steward had told them that I was "queer" only, or downright drunk, but I know the man meant to have a good look at me. I watched him coming with a smile which, as he got into point-blank range, took effect and froze his very whiskers. I did not give him time to open his lips.

"Square the yards by lifts and braces before the hands go to breakfast."

It was the first particular order I had given on board that ship; and I stayed on deck to see it executed, too. I had felt the need of asserting myself without loss of time. That sneering young cub got taken down a peg or two on that occasion, and I also seized the opportunity of having a good look at the face of every foremast man as they filed past me to go to the after braces. At breakfast time, eating nothing myself, I presided with such frigid dignity that the two mates were only too glad to escape from the cabin as soon as decency permitted; and all the time the dual working of my mind distracted me almost to the point of insanity. I was constantly watching myself, my secret self, as dependent on my actions as my own personality, sleeping in that bed, behind that door which faced me as I sat at the head of the table. It was very much like being mad, only it was worse because one was aware of it.

I had to shake him for a solid minute, but when at last he opened his eyes it was in the full possession of his senses, with an inquiring look.

"All's well so far," I whispered. "Now you must vanish into the bathroom."

He did so, as noiseless as a ghost, and I then rang for the steward, and facing him boldly, 115 directed him to tidy up my stateroom while I was having my bath— "and be quick about it." As my tone admitted of no excuses, he said, "Yes, sir," and ran off to fetch his dustpan and brushes. I took a bath and did most of my dressing, splashing, and whistling softly for the steward's edification, while the secret sharer of my life stood drawn up bolt upright in that little space, his face looking very sunken in daylight, his eyelids lowered under the stern, dark line of his eyebrows drawn together by a slight frown.

When I left him there to go back to my room the steward was finished dusting. I sent for the mate and engaged him in some insignificant conversation. It was, as it were, trifling with the terrific character of whiskers; but my object was to give him an opportunity for a good look at my cabin. And then I could at last shut, with a clear conscience, the door of my stateroom and get my double back into the recessed part. There was nothing else for it. He had to sit still on a small folding stool, half smothered by the heavy coats hanging there. We listened to the steward going into the bathroom out of the saloon, filling the water bottles there, scrubbing the bath, setting things to rights, whisk, bang, clatter—out again into the saloon—turn the key—click. Such was my scheme for keeping my second self invisible. Nothing better could be contrived under the circumstances. And there we sat; I at my writing desk ready to appear busy with some papers, he behind me, out of sight of the door. It would not have been prudent to talk in daytime; and I could not have stood the excitement of that queer sense of whispering to myself. Now and then, glancing over my shoulder, I saw him far back there, sitting rigidly on the low stool, his bare feet close together, his arms folded, his head hanging on his breast— and perfectly still. Anybody would have taken him for me.

I was fascinated by it myself. Every moment I had to glance over my shoulder. I was looking at him when a voice outside the door said:

"Beg pardon, sir."

"Well!" . . . I kept my eyes on him, and so, when the voice outside the door announced, "There's a ship's boat coming our way, sir," I saw him give a start—the first movement he had made for hours. But he did not raise his bowed head.

"All right. Get the ladder over." 120

I hesitated. Should I whisper something to him? But what? His immobility seemed to have been never disturbed. What could I tell him he did not know already? . . . Finally I went on deck.

**2**

The skipper of the *Sephora* had a thin red whisker all round his face, and the sort of complexion that goes with hair of that color; also the particular, rather smeary shade of blue in the eyes. He was not exactly a showy figure; his shoulders were high, his stature but middling—one leg slightly more bandy than the other. He shook hands, looking vaguely around. A spiritless tenacity was his main characteristic, I judged. I behaved with a politeness which seemed to disconcert him. Perhaps he was shy. He mumbled to me as if he were ashamed of what he was saying; gave his name (it was something like Archbold—but at this distance of years I hardly am sure), his ship's name, and a few other particulars of that sort, in the manner of a criminal making a reluctant and doleful confession. He had had terrible weather on the passage out— terrible—terrible—wife aboard, too.

By this time we were seated in the cabin and the steward brought in a tray with a bottle and glasses. "Thanks! No." Never took liquor. Would have some water, though. He drank two tumblerfuls. Terrible thirsty work. Ever since daylight had been exploring the islands round his ship.

"What was that for—fun?" I asked, with an appearance of polite interest.

125 "No!" He sighed. "Painful duty."

As he persisted in his mumbling and I wanted my double to hear every word, I hit upon the notion of informing him that I regretted to say I was hard of hearing.

"Such a young man, too!" he nodded, keeping his smeary blue, unintelligent eyes fastened upon me. What was the cause of it—some disease? he inquired, without the least sympathy and as if he thought that, if so, I'd got no more than I deserved.

"Yes; disease," I admitted in a cheerful tone which seemed to shock him. But my point was gained, because he had to raise his voice to give me his tale. It is not worth while to record that version. It was just over two months since all this had happened, and he had thought so much about it that he seemed completely muddled as to its bearings, but still immensely impressed.

"What would you think of such a thing happening on board your own ship? I've had the *Sephora* for these fifteen years. I am a well-known shipmaster."

130 He was densely distressed—and perhaps I should have sympathized with him if I had been able to detach my mental vision from the unsuspected sharer of my cabin as though he were my second self. There he was on the other side of the bulkhead, four or five feet from us, no more, as we sat in the saloon. I looked politely at Captain Archbold (if that was his name), but it was the other I saw, in a gray sleeping suit, seated on a low stool, his bare feet close together, his arms folded, and every word said between us falling into the ears of his dark head bowed on his chest.

"I have been at sea now, man and boy, for seven-and-thirty years, and I've never heard of such a thing happening in an English ship. And that it should be my ship. Wife on board, too."

I was hardly listening to him.

"Don't you think," I said, "that the heavy sea which, you told me, came aboard just then might have killed the man? I have seen the sheer weight of a sea kill a man very neatly, by simply breaking his neck."

"Good God!" he uttered, impressively, fixing his smeary blue eyes on me. "The sea! No man killed by the sea ever looked like that." He seemed positively scandalized at my suggestion. And as I gazed at him, certainly not prepared for anything original on his part, he advanced his head close to mine and thrust his tongue out at me so suddenly that I couldn't help starting back.

135 After scoring over my calmness in this graphic way he nodded wisely. If I had seen the sight, he assured me, I would never forget it as long as I lived. The weather was too bad to give the corpse a proper sea burial. So next day at dawn they took it up on the poop, covering its face with a bit of bunting; he read a short prayer, and then, just as it was, in its oilskins and long boots, they launched it amongst those mountainous seas that seemed ready every moment to swallow up the ship herself and the terrified lives on board of her.

"That reefed foresail saved you," I threw in.

"Under God—it did," he exclaimed fervently. "It was by a special mercy, I firmly believe, that it stood some of those hurricane squalls."

"It was the setting of that sail which—" I began.

"God's own hand in it," he interrupted me. "Nothing less could have done it. I don't mind telling you that I hardly dared give the order. It seemed impossible that we could touch anything without losing it, and then our last hope would have been gone."

140 The terror of that gale was on him yet. I let him go on for a bit, then said, casually—as if returning to a minor subject:

"You were very anxious to give up your mate to the shore people, I believe?"

He was. To the law. His obscure tenacity on that point had in it something incomprehensible and a little awful; something, as it were, mystical, quite apart from his anxiety that he should not be suspected of "countenancing any doings of that sort." Seven-and-thirty virtuous years at sea, of which over twenty of immaculate command, and the last fifteen in the *Sephora*, seemed to have laid him under some pitiless obligation.

"And you know," he went on, groping shamefacedly amongst his feelings, "I did not engage that young fellow. His people had some interest with my owners. I was in a way forced to take him on. He looked very smart, very gentlemanly, and all that. But do you know—I never liked him, somehow. I am a plain man. You see, he wasn't exactly the sort for the chief mate of a ship like the *Sephora*."

I had become so connected in thoughts and impressions with the secret sharer of my cabin that I felt as if I, personally, were being given to understand that I, too, was not the sort that would have done for the chief mate of a ship like the *Sephora*. I had no doubt of it in my mind.

"Not at all the style of man. You understand," he insisted, superfluously, looking hard 145 at me.

I smiled urbanely. He seemed at a loss for a while.

"I suppose I must report a suicide."

"Beg pardon?"

"Suicide! That's what I'll have to write to my owners directly I get in."

"Unless you manage to recover him before tomorrow," I assented, dispassionately. . . . "I 150 mean, alive."

He mumbled something which I really did not catch, and I turned my ear to him in a puzzled manner. He fairly bawled:

"The land—I say, the mainland is at least seven miles off my anchorage."

"About that."

My lack of excitement, of curiosity, of surprise, of any sort of pronounced interest, began to arouse his distrust. But except for the felicitous pretense of deafness I had not tried to pretend anything. I had felt utterly incapable of playing the part of ignorance properly, and therefore was afraid to try. It is also certain that he had brought some ready-made suspicions with him, and that he viewed my politeness as a strange and unnatural phenomenon. And yet how else could I have received him? Not heartily! That was impossible for psychological reasons, which I need not state here. My only object was to keep off his inquiries. Surlily? Yes, but surliness might have provoked a point-blank question. From its novelty to him and from its nature, punctilious courtesy was the manner best calculated to restrain the man. But there was the danger of his breaking through my defense bluntly. I could not, I think, have met him by a direct lie, also for psychological (not moral) reasons. If he had only known how afraid I was of his putting my feeling of identity with the other to the test! But, strangely enough—(I thought of it only afterward)—I believe that he was not a little disconcerted by the reverse side of that weird situation, by something in me that reminded him of the man he was seeking—suggested a mysterious similitude to the young fellow he had distrusted and disliked from the first.

However that might have been, the silence was not very prolonged. He took another 155 oblique step.

"I reckon I had no more than a two-mile pull to your ship. Not a bit more."

"And quite enough, too, in this awful heat," I said.

Another pause full of mistrust followed. Necessity, they say, is mother of invention, but fear, too, is not barren of ingenious suggestions. And I was afraid he would ask me point-blank for news of my other self.

"Nice little saloon, isn't it?" I remarked, as if noticing for the first time the way his eyes roamed from one closed door to the other. "And very well fitted out, too. Here, for instance," I continued reaching over the back of my seat negligently and flinging the door open, "is my bathroom."

160      He made an eager movement, but hardly gave it a glance. I got up, shut the door of the bathroom, and invited him to have a look round, as if I were very proud of my accommodation. He had to rise and be shown round, but he went through the business without any raptures whatever.

     "And now we'll have a look at my stateroom," I declared, in a voice as loud as I dared to make it, crossing the cabin to the starboard side with purposely heavy steps.

     He followed me in and gazed around. My intelligent double had vanished. I played my part.

     "Very convenient—isn't it?"

     "Very nice. Very comf. . . ." He didn't finish, and went out brusquely as if to escape from some unrighteous wiles of mine. But it was not to be. I had been too frightened not to feel vengeful; I felt I had him on the run, and I meant to keep him on the run. My polite insistence must have had something menacing in it, because he gave in suddenly. And I did not let him off a single item; mate's room, pantry, storerooms, the very sail locker which was also under the poop—he had to look into them all. When at last I showed him out on the quarter-deck he drew a long, spiritless sigh, and mumbled dismally that he must really be going back to his ship now. I desired my mate, who had joined us, to see to the captain's boat.

165      The man of whiskers gave a blast on the whistle which he used to wear hanging round his neck, and yelled, *"Sephora* away!" My double down there in my cabin must have heard, and certainly could not feel more relieved than I. Four fellows came running out from somewhere forward and went over the side, while my own men, appearing on deck too, lined the rail. I escorted my visitor to the gangway ceremoniously, and nearly overdid it. He was a tenacious beast. On the very ladder he lingered, and in that unique, guiltily conscientious manner of sticking to the point:

     "I say . . . you . . . you don't think that—"

     I covered his voice loudly:

     "Certainly not. . . . I am delighted. Good-by."

     I had an idea of what he meant to say, and just saved myself by the privilege of defective hearing. He was too shaken generally to insist, but my mate, close witness of that parting, looked mystified and his face took on a thoughtful cast. As I did not want to appear as if I wished to avoid all communication with my officers, he had the opportunity to address me.

170      "Seems a very nice man. His boat's crew told our chaps a very extraordinary story, if what I am told by the steward is true. I suppose you had it from the captain, sir?"

     "Yes. I had a story from the captain."

     "A very horrible affair—isn't it, sir?"

     "It is."

     "Beats all these tales we hear about murders in Yankee ships."

175      "I don't think it beats them. I don't think it resembles them in the least."

     "Bless my soul—you don't say so! But of course I've no acquaintance whatever with American ships, not I, so I couldn't go against your knowledge. It's horrible enough for me. . . . But the queerest part is that these fellows seemed to have some idea the man was hidden aboard here. They had really. Did you ever hear of such a thing?"

     "Preposterous—isn't it?"

     We were walking to and fro athwart the quarter-deck. No one of the crew forward could be seen (the day was Sunday), and the mate pursued:

     "There was some little dispute about it. Our chaps took offense. 'As if we would harbor a thing like that,' they said. 'Wouldn't you like to look for him in our coal hole?' Quite a tiff. But they made it up in the end. I suppose he did drown himself. Don't you, sir?"

"I don't suppose anything."

"You have no doubt in the matter, sir?"

"None whatever."

I left him suddenly. I felt I was producing a bad impression, but with my double down there it was most trying to be on deck. And it was almost as trying to be below. Altogether a nerve-trying situation. But on the whole I felt less torn in two when I was with him. There was no one in the whole ship whom I dared take into my confidence. Since the hands had got to know his story, it would have been impossible to pass him off for anyone else, and an accidental discovery was to be dreaded now more than ever. . . .

The steward being engaged in laying the table for dinner, we could talk only with our eyes when I first went down. Later in the afternoon we had a cautious try at whispering. The Sunday quietness of the ship was against us; the stillness of air and water around her was against us; the elements, the men were against us—everything was against us in our secret partnership; time itself—for this could not go on forever. The very trust in Providence was, I suppose, denied to his guilt. Shall I confess that this thought cast me down very much? And as to the chapter of accidents which counts for so much in the book of success, I could only hope that it was closed. For what favorable accident could be expected?

"Did you hear everything?" were my first words as soon as we took up our position side by side, leaning over my bed-place.

He had. And the proof of it was his earnest whisper, "The man told you he hardly dared to give the order."

I understood the reference to be to that saving foresail.

"Yes. He was afraid of it being lost in the setting."

"I assure you he never gave the order. He may think he did, but he never gave it. He stood there with me on the break of the poop after the maintopsail blew away, and whimpered about our last hope—positively whimpered about it and nothing else—and the night coming on! To hear one's skipper go on like that in such weather was enough to drive any fellow out of his mind. It worked me up into a sort of desperation. I just took it into my hands and went away from him, boiling, and—But what's the use telling you? *You* know! . . . Do you think that if I had not been pretty fierce with them I should have got the men to do anything? Not it! The bosun perhaps? Perhaps! It wasn't a heavy sea—it was a sea gone mad! I suppose the end of the world will be something like that; and a man may have the heart to see it coming once and be done with it—but to have to face it day after day—I don't blame anybody. I was precious little better than the rest. Only—I was an officer of that old coal-wagon, anyhow—"

"I quite understand," I conveyed that sincere assurance into his ear. He was out of breath with whispering; I could hear him pant slightly. It was all very simple. The same strung-up force which had given twenty-four men a chance, at least, for their lives, had, in a sort of recoil, crushed an unworthy mutinous existence.

But I had no leisure to weigh the merits of the matter—footsteps in the saloon, a heavy knock. "There's enough wind to get under way with, sir." Here was the call of a new claim upon my thoughts and even upon my feelings.

"Turn the hands up," I cried through the door. "I'll be on deck directly."

I was going out to make the acquaintance of my ship. Before I left the cabin our eyes met—the eyes of the only two strangers on board. I pointed to the recessed part where the little campstool awaited him and laid my finger on my lips. He made a gesture—somewhat vague—a little mysterious, accompanied by a faint smile, as if of regret.

This is not the place to enlarge upon the sensations of a man who feels for the first time a ship move under his feet to his own independent word. In my case they were not unalloyed. I was not wholly alone with my command; for there was that stranger in my cabin. Or rather, I was not completely and wholly with her. Part of me was absent. That mental feeling of being

180

185

190

in two places at once affected me physically as if the mood of secrecy had penetrated my very soul. Before an hour had elapsed since the ship had begun to move, having occasion to ask the mate (he stood by my side) to take a compass bearing of the Pagoda, I caught myself reaching up to his ear in whispers. I say I caught myself, but enough had escaped to startle the man. I can't describe it otherwise than by saying that he shied. A grave, preoccupied manner, as though he were in possession of some perplexing intelligence, did not leave him henceforth. A little later I moved away from the rail to look at the compass with such a stealthy gait that the helmsman noticed it—and I could not help noticing the unusual roundness of his eyes. These are trifling instances, though it's to no commander's advantage to be suspected of ludicrous eccentricities. But I was also more seriously affected. There are to a seaman certain words, gestures, that should in given conditions come as naturally, as instinctively as the winking of a menaced eye. A certain order should spring on to his lips without thinking; a certain sign should get itself made, so to speak, without reflection. But all unconscious alertness had abandoned me. I had to make an effort of will to recall myself back (from the cabin) to the conditions of the moment. I felt that I was appearing an irresolute commander to those people who were watching me more or less critically.

195 And, besides, there were the scares. On the second day out, for instance, coming off the deck in the afternoon (I had straw slippers on my bare feet) I stopped at the open pantry door and spoke to the steward. He was doing something there with his back to me. At the sound of my voice he nearly jumped out of his skin, as the saying is, and incidentally broke a cup.

"What on earth's the matter with you?" I asked, astonished.

He was extremely confused. "Beg your pardon, sir. I made sure you were in your cabin."

"You see I wasn't."

"No, sir. I could have sworn I had heard you moving in there not a moment ago. It's most extraordinary, very sorry, sir."

200 I passed on with an inward shudder. I was so identified with my secret double that I did not even mention the fact in those scanty, fearful whispers we exchanged. I suppose he had made some slight noise of some kind or other. It would have been miraculous if he hadn't at one time or another. And yet, haggard as he appeared, he looked always perfectly self-controlled, more than calm—almost invulnerable. On my suggestion he remained almost entirely in the bathroom, which, upon the whole, was the safest place. There could be really no shadow of an excuse for anyone ever wanting to go in there, once the steward had done with it. It was a very tiny place. Sometimes he reclined on the floor, his legs bent, his head sustained on one elbow. At others I would find him on the campstool, sitting in his gray sleeping suit and with his cropped dark hair like a patient, unmoved convict. At night I would smuggle him into my bed-place, and we would whisper together, with the regular footfalls of the officer of the watch passing and repassing over our heads. It was an infinitely miserable time. It was lucky that some tins of fine preserves were stowed in a locker in my stateroom; hard bread I could always get hold of; and so he lived on stewed chicken, paté de foie gras, asparagus, cooked oysters, sardines—on all sorts of abominable sham delicacies out of tins. My early morning coffee he always drank; and it was all I dared do for him in that respect.

Every day there was the horrible maneuvering to go through so that my room and then the bathroom should be done in the usual way. I came to hate the sight of the steward, to abhor the voice of that harmless man. I felt that it was he who would bring on the disaster of discovery. It hung like a sword over our heads.

The fourth day out, I think (we were working down the east side of the Gulf of Siam, tack for tack, in light winds and smooth water)—the fourth day, I say, of this miserable juggling with the unavoidable, as we sat at our evening meal, that man, whose slightest movement I dreaded, after putting down the dishes ran up on deck busily. This could not be dangerous. Presently he came down again; and then it appeared that he had remembered a coat of mine which I had thrown over a rail to dry after having been wetted in a shower which had passed over the ship in the afternoon. Sitting stolidly at the head of the table I became terrified at the sight of the garment on his arm. Of course he made for my door. There was no time to lose.

"Steward," I thundered. My nerves were so shaken that I could not govern my voice and conceal my agitation. This was the sort of thing that made my terrifically whiskered mate tap his forehead with his forefinger. I had detected him using that gesture while talking on deck with a confidential air to the carpenter. It was too far to hear a word, but I had no doubt that this pantomime could only refer to the strange new captain.

"Yes, sir," the pale-faced steward turned resignedly to me. It was this maddening course of being shouted at, checked without rhyme or reason, arbitrarily chased out of my cabin, suddenly called into it, sent flying out of his pantry on incomprehensible errands, that accounted for the growing wretchedness of his expression.

"Where are you going with that coat?"    205

"To your room, sir."

"Is there another shower coming?"

"I'm sure I don't know, sir. Shall I go up again and see, sir?"

"No! never mind."

My object was attained, as of course my other self in there would have heard everything    210
that passed. During this interlude my two officers never raised their eyes off their respective plates; but the lip of that confounded cub, the second mate, quivered visibly.

I expected the steward to hook my coat on and come out at once. He was very slow about it; but I dominated my nervousness sufficiently not to shout after him. Suddenly I became aware (it could be heard plainly enough) that the fellow for some reason or other was opening the door of the bathroom. It was the end. The place was literally not big enough to swing a cat in. My voice died in my throat and I went stony all over. I expected to hear a yell of surprise and terror, and made a movement, but had not the strength to get on my legs. Everything remained still. Had my second self taken the poor wretch by the throat? I don't know what I would have done next moment if I had not seen the steward come out of my room, close the door, and then stand quietly by the sideboard.

Saved, I thought. But, no! Lost! Gone! He was gone!

I laid my knife and fork down and leaned back in my chair. My head swam. After a while, when sufficiently recovered to speak in a steady voice, I instructed my mate to put the ship round at eight o'clock himself.

"I won't come on deck," I went on. "I think I'll turn in, and unless the wind shifts I don't want to be disturbed before midnight. I feel a bit seedy."

"You did look middling bad a little while ago," the chief mate remarked without showing    215
any great concern.

They both went out, and I stared at the steward clearing the table. There was nothing to be read on that wretched man's face. But why did he avoid my eyes I asked myself. Then I thought I should like to hear the sound of his voice.

"Steward!"

"Sir!" Startled as usual.

"Where did you hang up that coat?"

"In the bathroom, sir." The usual anxious tone. "It's not quite dry yet, sir."    220

For some time longer I sat in the cuddy. Had my double vanished as he had come? But of his coming there was an explanation, whereas his disappearance would be inexplicable. . . . I went slowly into my dark room, shut the door, lighted the lamp, and for a time dared not turn round. When at last I did I saw him standing bolt upright in the narrow recessed part. It would not be true to say I had a shock, but an irresistible doubt of his bodily existence flitted through my mind. Can it be, I asked myself, that he is not visible to other eyes than mine? It was like being haunted. Motionless, with a grave face, he raised his hands slightly at me in a gesture which meant clearly, "Heavens! what a narrow escape!" Narrow indeed. I think I had come creeping quietly as near insanity as any man who has not actually gone over the border. That gesture restrained me, so to speak.

The mate with the terrific whiskers was now putting the ship on the other tack. In the moment of profound silence which follows upon the hands going to their stations I heard on the poop his raised voice: "Hard alee!" and the distant shout of the order repeated on the main-deck. The sails, in that light breeze, made but a faint fluttering noise. It ceased. The ship was coming round slowly; I held my breath in the renewed stillness of expectation; one wouldn't have thought that there was a single living soul on her decks. A sudden brisk shout, "Mainsail haul!" broke the spell, and in the noisy cries and rush overhead of the men running away with the main brace we two, down in my cabin, came together in our usual position by the bed-place.

He did not wait for my question. "I heard him fumbling here and just managed to squat myself down in the bath," he whispered to me. "The fellow only opened the door and put his arm in to hang the coat up. All the same—"

"I never thought of that," I whispered back, even more appalled than before at the closeness of the shave, and marveling at that something unyielding in his character which was carrying him through so finely. There was no agitation in his whisper. Whoever was being driven distracted, it was not he. He was sane. And the proof of his sanity was continued when he took up the whispering again.

225     "It would never do for me to come to life again."

It was something that a ghost might have said. But what he was alluding to was his old captain's reluctant admission of the theory of suicide. It would obviously serve his turn—if I had understood at all the view which seemed to govern the unalterable purpose of his action.

"You must maroon me as soon as ever you can get amongst these islands off the Cambodje shore," he went on.

"Maroon you! We are not living in a boy's adventure tale," I protested. His scornful whispering took me up.

"We aren't indeed! There's nothing of a boy's tale in this. But there's nothing else for it. I want no more. You don't suppose I am afraid of what can be done to me? Prison or gallows or whatever they may please. But you don't see me coming back to explain such things to an old fellow in a wig and twelve respectable tradesmen, do you? What can they know whether I am guilty or not—or of *what* I am guilty, either? That's my affair. What does the Bible say? 'Driven off the face of the earth.'[5] Very well. I am off the face of the earth now. As I came at night so I shall go."

230     "Impossible!" I murmured. "You can't."

"Can't? . . . Not naked like a soul on the Day of Judgment. I shall freeze on to this sleeping suit. The Last Day is not yet—and, . . . you have understood thoroughly. Didn't you?"

I felt suddenly ashamed of myself. I may say truly that I understood—and my hesitation in letting that man swim away from my ship's side had been a mere sham sentiment, a sort of cowardice.

"It can't be done now till next night," I breathed out. "The ship is on the offshore tack and the wind may fail us."

"As long as I know that you understand," he whispered. "But of course you do. It's a great satisfaction to have got somebody to understand. You seem to have been there on purpose." And in the same whisper, as if we two whenever we talked had to say things to each other which were not fit for the world to hear, he added, "It's very wonderful."

235     We remained side by side talking in our secret way—but sometimes silent or just exchanging a whispered word or two at long intervals. And as usual he stared through the port.

---

[5] *face of the earth*: a common Biblical phrase; see Deuteronomy 6:15 or Jeremiah 28:16

A breath of wind came now and again into our faces. The ship might have been moored in dock, so gently and on an even keel she slipped through the water, that did not murmur even at our passage, shadowy and silent like a phantom sea.

At midnight I went on deck, and to my mate's great surprise put the ship round on the other tack. His terrible whiskers flitted round me in silent criticism. I certainly should not have done it if it had been only a question of getting out of that sleepy gulf as quickly as possible. I believe he told the second mate, who relieved him, that it was a great want of judgment. The other only yawned. That intolerable cub shuffled about so sleepily and lolled against the rails in such a slack, improper fashion that I came down on him sharply.

"Aren't you properly awake yet?"

"Yes, sir! I am awake."

"Well, then, be good enough to hold yourself as if you were. And keep a lookout. If there's any current we'll be closing with some islands before daylight."

The east side of the gulf is fringed with islands, some solitary, others in groups. On the 240 blue background of the high coast they seem to float on silvery patches of calm water, arid and gray, or dark green and rounded like clumps of evergreen bushes, with the larger ones, a mile or two long, showing the outlines of ridges, ribs of gray rock under the dark mantle of matted leafage. Unknown to trade, to travel, almost to geography, the manner of life they harbor is an unsolved secret. There must be villages—settlements of fishermen at least—on the largest of them, and some communication with the world is probably kept up by native craft. But all forenoon, as we headed for them, fanned along by the faintest of breezes, I saw no sign of man or canoe in the field of the telescope I kept on pointing at the scattered group.

At noon I gave no orders for a change of course, and the mate's whiskers became much concerned and seemed to be offering themselves unduly to my notice. At last I said:

"I am going to stand right in. Quite in—as far as I can take her."

The stare of extreme surprise imparted an air of ferocity also to his eyes, and he looked truly terrific for a moment.

"We're not doing well in the middle of the gulf," I continued, casually. "I am going to look for the land breezes tonight."

"Bless my soul! Do you mean, sir, in the dark amongst the lot of all them islands and reefs 245 and shoals?"

"Well—if there are any regular land breezes at all on this coast one must get close inshore to find them, mustn't one?"

"Bless my soul!" he exclaimed again under his breath. All that afternoon he wore a dreamy, contemplative appearance which in him was a mark of perplexity. After dinner I went into my stateroom as if I meant to take some rest. There we two bent our dark heads over a half-unrolled chart lying on my bed.

"There," I said. "It's got to be Koh-ring. I've been looking at it ever since sunrise. It has got two hills and a low point. It must be inhabited. And on the coast opposite there is what looks like the mouth of a biggish river—with some town, no doubt, not far up. It's the best chance for you that I can see."

"Anything. Koh-ring let it be."

He looked thoughtfully at the chart as if surveying chances and distances from a lofty 250 height—and following with his eyes his own figure wandering on the blank land of Cochin China, and then passing off that piece of paper clean out of sight into uncharted regions. And it was as if the ship had two captains to plan her course for her. I had been so worried and restless running up and down that I had not had the patience to dress that day. I had remained in my sleeping suit, with straw slippers and a soft floppy hat. The closeness of the heat in the gulf had been most oppressive, and the crew were used to see me wandering in that airy attire.

"She will clear the south point as she heads now," I whispered into his ear. "Goodness only knows when, though, but certainly after dark. I'll edge her in to half a mile, as far as I may be able to judge in the dark—"

"Be careful," he murmured, warningly—and I realized suddenly that all my future, the only future for which I was fit, would perhaps go irretrievably to pieces in any mishap to my first command.

I could not stop a moment longer in the room. I motioned him to get out of sight and made my way on the poop. That unplayful cub had the watch. I walked up and down for a while thinking things out, then beckoned him over.

"Send a couple of hands to open the two quarter-deck ports," I said, mildly.

255    He actually had the impudence, or else so forgot himself in his wonder at such an incomprehensible order, as to repeat:

"Open the quarter-deck ports! What for, sir?"

"The only reason you need concern yourself about is because I tell you to do so. Have them open wide and fastened properly"

He reddened and went off, but I believe made some jeering remark to the carpenter as to the sensible practice of ventilating a ship's quarter-deck. I know he popped into the mate's cabin to impart the fact to him because the whiskers came on deck, as it were by chance, and stole glances at me from below—for signs of lunacy or drunkenness, I suppose.

A little before supper, feeling more restless than ever, I rejoined, for a moment, my second self. And to find him sitting so quietly was surprising, like something against nature, inhuman.

260    I developed my plan in a hurried whisper.

"I shall stand in as close as I dare and then put her round. I shall presently find means to smuggle you out of here into the sail locker, which communicates with the lobby. But there is an opening, a sort of square for hauling the sails out, which gives straight on the quarter-deck and which is never closed in fine weather, so as to give air to the sails. When the ship's way is deadened in stays and all the hands are aft at the main braces you shall have a clear road to slip out and get overboard through the open quarter-deck port. I've had them both fastened up. Use a rope's end to lower yourself into the water so as to avoid a splash—you know. It could be heard and cause some beastly complication."

He kept silent for a while, then whispered, "I understand."

"I won't be there to see you go," I began with an effort. "The rest . . . I only hope I have understood, too."

"You have. From first to last," and for the first time there seemed to be a faltering, something strained in his whisper. He caught hold of my arm, but the ringing of the supper bell made me start. He didn't, though; he only released his grip.

265    After supper I didn't come below again till well past eight o'clock. The faint, steady breeze was loaded with dew; and the wet, darkened sails held all there was of propelling power in it. The night, clear and starry, sparkled darkly, and the opaque, lightless patches shifting slowly against the low stars were the drifting islets. On the port bow there was a big one more distant and shadowily imposing by the great space of sky it eclipsed.

On opening the door I had a back view of my very own self looking at a chart. He had come out of the recess and was standing near the table.

"Quite dark enough," I whispered.

He stepped back and leaned against my bed with a level, quiet glance. I sat on the couch. We had nothing to say to each other. Over our heads the officer of the watch moved here and there. Then I heard him move quickly. I knew what that meant. He was making for the companion; and presently his voice was outside my door.

"We are drawing in pretty fast, sir. Land looks rather close."

"Very well," I answered. "I am coming on deck directly." 270

I waited till he was gone out of the cuddy, then rose. My double moved too. The time had come to exchange our last whispers, for neither of us was ever to hear each other's natural voice.

"Look here!" I opened a drawer and took out three sovereigns.[6] "Take this, anyhow. I've got six and I'd give you the lot, only I must keep a little money to buy some fruit and vegetables for the crew from native boats as we go through Sunda Straits."

He shook his head.

"Take it," I urged him, whispering desperately. "No one can tell what—"

He smiled and slapped meaningly the only pocket of the sleeping jacket. It was not safe, 275 certainly. But I produced a large old silk handkerchief of mine, and tying the three pieces of gold in a corner, pressed it on him. He was touched, I suppose, because he took it at last and tied it quickly round his waist under the jacket, on his bare skin.

Our eyes met; several seconds elapsed, till, our glances still mingled, I extended my hand and turned the lamp out. Then I passed through the cuddy, leaving the door of my room wide open. "Steward!"

He was still lingering in the pantry in the greatness of his zeal, giving a rub-up to a plated cruet stand the last thing before going to bed. Being careful not to wake up the mate, whose room was opposite, I spoke in an undertone.

He looked round anxiously. "Sir!"

"Can you get me a little hot water from the galley?"

"I am afraid, sir, the galley fire's been out for some time now." 280

"Go and see."

He fled up the stairs.

"Now," I whispered, loudly, into the saloon—too loudly, perhaps, but I was afraid I couldn't make a sound. He was by my side in an instant—the double captain slipped past the stairs—through the tiny dark passage . . . a sliding door. We were in the sail locker, scrambling on our knees over the sails. A sudden thought struck me. I saw myself wandering barefooted, bareheaded, the sun beating on my dark poll. I snatched off my floppy hat and tried hurriedly in the dark to ram it on my other self. He dodged and fended off silently. I wonder what he thought had come to me before he understood and suddenly desisted. Our hands met gropingly, lingered united in a steady, motionless clasp for a second. . . . No word was breathed by either of us when they separated.

I was standing quietly by the pantry door when the steward returned.

"Sorry, sir. Kettle barely warm. Shall I light the spirit lamp?" 285

"Never mind."

I came out on deck slowly. It was not a matter of conscience to shave the land as close as possible—for now he must go overboard whenever the ship was put in stays. Must! There could be no going back for him. After a moment I walked over to leeward and my heart flew into my mouth at the nearness of the land on the bow. Under any other circumstances I would not have held on a minute longer. The second mate had followed me anxiously.

I looked on till I felt I could command my voice.

"She will weather," I said then in a quiet tone.

"Are you going to try that, sir?" he stammered out incredulously. 290

I took no notice of him and raised my tone just enough to be heard by the helmsman.

"Keep her good full."

"Good full, sir."

---

[6]Sovereigns: Gold coins worth a pound each.

The wind fanned my cheek, the sails slept, the world was silent. The strain of watching the dark loom of the land grow bigger and denser was too much for me. I had shut my eyes—because the ship must go closer. She must! The stillness was intolerable. Were we standing still?

295     When I opened my eyes the second view started my heart with a thump. The black southern hill of Koh-ring seemed to hang right over the ship like a towering fragment of the everlasting night. On that enormous mass of blackness there was not a gleam to be seen, not a sound to be heard. It was gliding irresistibly toward us and yet seemed already within reach of the hand. I saw the vague figures of the watch grouped in the waist, gazing in awed silence.

"Are you going on, sir?" inquired an unsteady voice at my elbow.

I ignored it. I had to go on.

"Keep her full. Don't check her way. That won't do now," I said warningly.

"I can't see the sails very well," the helmsman answered me, in strange, quavering tones.

300     Was she close enough? Already she was, I won't say in the shadow of the land, but in the very blackness of it, already swallowed up as it were, gone too close to be recalled, gone from me altogether.

"Give the mate a call," I said to the young man who stood at my elbow still as death. "And turn all hands up."

My tone had a borrowed loudness reverberated from the height of the land. Several voices cried out together. "We are all on deck, sir."

Then stillness again, with the great shadow gliding closer, towering higher, without a light, without a sound. Such a hush had fallen on the ship that she might have been a bark of the dead floating in slowly under the very gate of Erebus.

"My God! Where are we?"

305     It was the mate moaning at my elbow. He was thunderstruck, and as it were deprived of the moral support of his whiskers. He clapped his hands and absolutely cried out, "Lost!"

"Be quiet," I said sternly.

He lowered his tone, but I saw the shadowy gesture of his despair. "What are we doing here?"

"Looking for the land wind."

He made as if to tear his hair, and addressed me recklessly.

310     "She will never get out. You have done it, sir. I knew it'd end in something like this. She will never weather, and you are too close now to stay. She'll drift ashore before she's round. O my God!"

I caught his arm as he was raising it to batter his poor devoted head, and shook it violently.

"She's ashore already," he wailed, trying to tear himself away. "Is she? . . . Keep good full there!"

"Good full, sir," cried the helmsman in a frightened, thin, childlike voice.

I hadn't let go the mate's arm and went on shaking it. "Ready about, do you hear? You go forward"—shake—"and stop there"—shake—"and hold your noise"—shake—"and see these head sheets properly overhauled"—shake, shake—shake.

315     And all the time I dared not look toward the land lest my heart should fail me. I released my grip at last and he ran forward as if fleeing for dear life.

I wondered what my double there in the sail locker thought of this commotion. He was able to hear everything—and perhaps he was able to understand why, on my conscience, it had to be thus close—no less. My first order "Hard alee!" reechoed ominously under the towering shadow of Koh-ring as if I had shouted in a mountain gorge. And then I watched the land intently. In that smooth water and light wind it was impossible to feel the ship coming-to. No! I could not feel her. And my second self was making now ready to slip out and lower himself overboard. Perhaps he was gone already? . . .

The great black mass brooding over our very mastheads began to pivot away from the ship's side silently. And now I forgot the secret stranger ready to depart, and remembered only that I was a total stranger to the ship. I did not know her. Would she do it? How was she to be handled?

I swung the mainyard and waited helplessly. She was perhaps stopped, and her very fate hung in the balance, with the black mass of Koh-ring like the gate of the everlasting night towering over her taffrail. What would she do now? Had she way on her yet? I stepped to the side swiftly, and on the shadowy water I could see nothing except a faint phosphorescent flash revealing the glassy smoothness of the sleeping surface. It was impossible to tell—and I had not learned yet the feel of my ship. Was she moving? What I needed was something easily seen, a piece of paper, which I could throw overboard and watch. I had nothing on me. To run down for it I didn't dare. There was no time. All at once my strained, yearning stare distinguished a white object floating within a yard of the ship's side. White on the black water. A phosphorescent flash passed under it. What was that thing? . . . I recognized my own floppy hat. It must have fallen off his head . . . and he didn't bother. Now I had what I wanted—the saving mark for my eyes. But I hardly thought of my other self, now gone from the ship, to be hidden forever from all friendly faces, to be a fugitive and a vagabond on the earth, with no brand of the curse on his sane forehead to stay a slaying hand . . . too proud to explain.

And I watched the hat—the expression of my sudden pity for his mere flesh. It had been meant to save his homeless head from the dangers of the sun. And now—behold—it was saving the ship, by serving me for a mark to help out the ignorance of my strangeness. Ha! It was drifting forward, warning me just in time that the ship had gathered sternway.

"Shift the helm," I said in a low voice to the seaman standing still like a statue. 320

The man's eyes glistened wildly in the binnacle light as he jumped round to the other side and spun round the wheel.

I walked to the break of the poop. On the overshadowed deck all hands stood by the forebraces waiting for my order. The stars ahead seemed to be gliding from right to left. And all was so still in the world that I heard the quiet remark "She's round," passed in a tone of intense relief between two seamen.

"Let go and haul."

The foreyards ran round with a great noise, amidst cheery cries. And now the frightful whiskers made themselves heard giving various orders. Already the ship was drawing ahead. And I was alone with her. Nothing! no one in the world should stand now between us, throwing a shadow on the way of silent knowledge and mute affection, the perfect communion of a seaman with his first command.

Walking to the taffrail, I was in time to make out, on the very edge of a darkness thrown 325 by a towering black mass like the very gateway of Erebus—yes, I was in time to catch an evanescent glimpse of my white hat left behind to mark the spot where the secret sharer of my cabin and of my thoughts, as though he were my second self, had lowered himself into the water to take his punishment: a free man, a proud swimmer striking out for a new destiny.

## Questions

1. Analyze the first three paragraphs of the story. What is the purpose of all the details of setting? How might a person claim that Conrad's great attention to detail is overdone?

2. Who is the narrator? What sort of person is he? Why does he determine to help Leggatt? Why does the Captain constantly think of Leggatt as his double? What do the Captain and Leggatt have in common?

3. How do the details of the Captain's cabin enable the Captain to conceal Leggatt successfully?

4. What details does the story provide about the techniques of sailing and handling ships in a storm? Why do you think that Conrad provide these details?

5. What moral issue must the Captain deal with as he learns Leggatt's story and then decides to help Leggatt? Compare this issue with the issues confronted by Fritz in "Before the Firing Squad" (Chapter 10) and Sammy in "A & P" (Chapter 7). What possibilities of choice are available to the characters? How important are the consequences of those choices? Which character faces the most difficult decision?

## JAMES JOYCE (1882–1941)

Joyce, one of the greatest twentieth-century writers, was born in Ireland and received a vigorous and thorough education there. He left Ireland in 1902 and spent most of the rest of his life in Switzerland and France. His best-known works are *Dubliners* (1914), *A Portrait of the Artist as a Young Man* (1914–1915), *Ulysses* (1922), and *Finnegans Wake* (1939). Much of his work has been called "fictionalized autobiography," a quality shown in "Araby," which is selected from *Dubliners*. As a young child, Joyce had lived on North Richmond Street, just like the narrator of the story. The bazaar that the narrator visits actually did take place in Dublin, from May 14 to 19, 1894, when Joyce was the same age as the narrator. It was called "Araby in Dublin" and was advertised as a "Grand Oriental Fete."

 **Araby** (1914)

North Richmond Street,° being blind,° was a quiet street except at the hour when the Christian Brothers' School set the boys free. An uninhabited house of two storeys stood at the blind end, detached from its neighbours in a square ground. The other houses of the street, conscious of decent lives within them, gazed at one another with brown imperturbable faces.

The former tenant of our house, a priest, had died in the back drawing room. Air, musty from having long been enclosed, hung in all the rooms, and the waste room behind the kitchen was littered with old useless papers. Among these I found a few paper-covered books, the pages of which were curled and damp: *The Abbott*, by Walter Scott, *The Devout Communicant*° and *The Memoirs of Vidocq*.° I liked the last best because its leaves were yellow. The wild garden behind the house contained a central apple-tree and a few straggling bushes under one of which I found the late tenant's rusty bicycle-pump. He had been a very charitable priest; in his will he had left all his money to institutions and the furniture of his house to his sister.

When the short days of winter came dusk fell before we had well eaten our dinners. When we met in the street the houses had grown sombre. The space of sky above us was the colour of ever-changing violet and towards it the lamps of the street lifted their feeble lanterns. The cold air stung us and we played till our bodies glowed. Our shouts echoed in the silent street.

---

° *North Richmond Street*: name of a real street in Dublin on which Joyce lived as a boy.

° *blind*: dead-end street.

° *The Devout Communicant*: a book of meditations by Pacificus Baker, published 1873.

° *The Memoirs of Vidocq*: published 1829, the story of François Vidocq, a Parisian chief of detectives.

The career of our play brought us through the dark muddy lanes behind the houses where we ran the gauntlet of the rough tribes from the cottages, to the back doors of the dark dripping gardens where odours arose from the ashpits, to the dark odorous stables where a coachman smoothed and combed the horse or shook music from the buckled harness. When we returned to the street light from the kitchen windows had filled the areas. If my uncle was seen turning the corner we hid in the shadow until we had seen him safely housed. Or if Mangan's sister came out on the doorstep to call her brother in to his tea we watched her from our shadow peer up and down the street. We waited to see whether she would remain or go in and, if she remained, we left our shadow and walked up to Mangan's steps resignedly. She was waiting for us, her figure defined by the light from the half-opened door. Her brother always teased her before he obeyed and I stood by the railings looking at her. Her dress swung as she moved her body and the soft rope of her hair tossed from side to side.

Every morning I lay on the floor in the front parlor watching her door. The blind was pulled down within an inch of the sash so that I could not be seen. When she came out on the doorstep my heart leaped. I ran to the hall, seized my books and followed her. I kept her brown figure always in my eye and, when we came near the point at which our ways diverged, I quickened my pace and passed her. This happened morning after morning. I had never spoken to her, except for a few casual words, and yet her name was like a summons to all my foolish blood.

Her image accompanied me even in places the most hostile to romance. On Saturday evenings when my aunt went marketing I had to go to carry some of the parcels. We walked through the flaring street, jostled by drunken men and bargaining women, amid the curses of labourers, the shrill litanies of shop-boys who stood on guard by the barrels of pigs' cheeks, the nasal chanting of street singers, who sang a *come-all-you* about O'Donovan Rossa,° or a ballad about the troubles in our native land. These noises converged in a single sensation of life for me: I imagined that I bore my chalice safely through the throng of foes. Her name sprang to my lips at moments in strange prayers and praises which I myself did not understand. My eyes were often full of tears (I could not tell why) and at times a flood from my heart seemed to pour itself out into my bosom. I thought little of the future. I did not know whether I would ever speak to her or not or, if I spoke to her, how I could tell her of my confused adoration. But my body was like a harp and her words and gestures were like fingers running upon the wires.

One evening I went into the back drawing-room in which the priest had died. It was a dark rainy evening and there was no sound in the house. Through one of the broken panes I heard the rain impinge upon the earth, the fine incessant needles of water playing in the sodden beds. Some distant lamp or lighted window gleamed below me. I was thankful that I could see so little. All my senses seemed to desire to veil themselves and, feeling that I was about to slip from them, I pressed the palms of my hands together until they trembled, murmuring: *O love! O love!* many times.

At last she spoke to me. When she addressed the first words to me I was so confused that I did not know what to answer. She asked me was I going to *Araby.*° I forget whether I answered yes or no. It would be a splendid bazaar, she said; she would love to go.

—And why can't you? I asked.

While she spoke she turned a silver bracelet round and round her wrist. She could not go, she said, because there would be a retreat° that week in her convent. Her brother and two other boys were fighting for their caps and I was alone at the railings. She held one of the

5

---

°*O'Donovan Rossa*: popular ballad about Jeremiah O'Donovan (1831–1915), a leader in the movement to free Ireland from English control. He was called "Dynamite Rossa."

°*Araby*: the bazaar held in Dublin from May 14 to 19, 1894.

°*retreat*: a special time set aside for concentrated religious instruction, discussion, and prayer.

spikes, bowing her head towards me. The light from the lamp opposite our door caught the white curve of her neck, lit up her hair that rested there and, falling, lit up the hand upon the railing. It fell over one side of her dress and caught the white border of a petticoat, just visible as she stood at ease.

10       —It's well for you, she said.

—If I go, I said, I will bring you something.

What innumerable follies laid waste my waking and sleeping thoughts after that evening! I wished to annihilate the tedious intervening days. I chafed against the work of school. At night in my bedroom and by day in the classroom her image came between me and the page I strove to read. The syllables of the word *Araby* were called to me through the silence in which my soul luxuriated and cast an Eastern enchantment over me. I asked for leave to go to the bazaar on Saturday night. My aunt was surprised and hoped it was not some Freemason° affair. I answered few questions in class. I watched my master's face pass from amiability to sternness; he hoped I was not beginning to idle. I could not call my wandering thoughts together. I had hardly any patience with the serious work of life which, now that it stood between me and my desire, seemed to me child's play, ugly monotonous child's play.

On Saturday morning I reminded my uncle that I wished to go to the bazaar in the evening. He was fussing at the hall-stand, looking for the hatbrush, and answered me curtly:

—Yes, boy, I know.

15       As he was in the hall I could not go into the front parlour and lie at the window. I left the house in bad humour and walked slowly towards the school. The air was pitilessly raw and already my heart misgave me.

When I came home to dinner my uncle had not yet been home. Still, it was early. I sat staring at the clock for some time and, when its ticking began to irritate me, I left the room. I mounted the staircase and gained the upper part of the house. The high cold empty gloomy rooms liberated me and I went from room to room singing. From the front window I saw my companions playing below in the street. Their cries reached me weakened and indistinct and, leaning my forehead against the cool glass, I looked over at the dark house where she lived. I may have stood there for an hour, seeing nothing but the brown-clad figure cast by my imagination, touched discreetly by the lamplight at the curved neck, at the hand upon the railing and at the border below the dress.

When I came downstairs again I found Mrs. Mercer sitting at the fire. She was an old garrulous woman, a pawnbroker's widow, who collected used stamps for some pious purpose. I had to endure the gossip of the tea-table. The meal was prolonged beyond an hour and still my uncle did not come. Mrs. Mercer stood up to go: she was sorry she couldn't wait any longer, but it was after eight o'clock and she did not like to be out late, as the night air was bad for her. When she had gone I began to walk up and down the room, clenching my fists. My aunt said:

—I'm afraid you may put off your bazaar for this night of Our Lord.

At nine o'clock I heard my uncle's latchkey in the halldoor. I heard him talking to himself and heard the hall-stand rocking when it had received the weight of his overcoat. I could interpret these signs. When he was midway through his dinner I asked him to give me the money to go to the bazaar. He had forgotten.

20       —The people are in bed and after their first sleep now, he said.

I did not smile. My aunt said to him energetically:

—Can't you give him the money and let him go? You've kept him late enough as it is.

My uncle said he was very sorry he had forgotten. He said he believed in the old saying: *All work and no play makes Jack a dull boy.* He asked me where I was going and, when I had told

---

° *Freemason*: and therefore Protestant.

him a second time he asked me did I know *The Arab's Farewell to his Steed.*° When I left the kitchen he was about to recite the opening lines of the piece to my aunt.

I held a florin° tightly in my hand as I strode down Buckingham Street towards the station. The sight of the streets thronged with buyers and glaring with gas recalled to me the purpose of my journey. I took my seat in a third-class carriage of a deserted train. After an intolerable delay the train moved out of the station slowly. It crept onward among ruinous houses and over the twinkling river. At Westland Row Station a crowd of people pressed to the carriage doors; but the porters moved them back, saying that it was a special train for the bazaar. I remained alone in the bare carriage. In a few minutes the train drew up beside an improvised wooden platform. I passed out on to the road and saw by the lighted dial of a clock that it was ten minutes to ten. In front of me was a large building which displayed the magical name.

I could not find any sixpenny entrance and, fearing that the bazaar would be closed, I 25 passed in quickly through a turnstile, handing a shilling to a weary-looking man. I found myself in a big hall girdled at half its height by a gallery. Nearly all the stalls were closed and the greater part of the hall was in darkness. I recognized a silence like that which pervades a church after a service. I walked into the centre of the bazaar timidly. A few people were gathered about the stalls which were still open. Before a curtain, over which the words *Café Chantant* were written in coloured lamps, two men were counting money on a salver. I listened to the fall of the coins.

Remembering with difficulty why I had come I went over to one of the stalls and examined porcelain vases and flowered tea-sets. At the door of the stall a young lady was talking and laughing with two young gentlemen. I remarked their English accents and listened vaguely to their conversation.

—O, I never said such a thing!

—O, but you did!

—O, but I didn't!

—Didn't she say that?    30

—Yes I heard her.

—O, there's a . . . fib!

Observing me the young lady came over and asked me did I wish to buy anything. The tone in her voice was not encouraging; she seemed to have spoken to me out of a sense of duty. I looked humbly at the great jars that stood like eastern guards at either side of the dark entrance to the stall and murmured:

—No, thank you.

The young lady changed the position of one of the vases and went back to the two young 35 men. They began to talk of the same subject. Once or twice the young lady glanced at me over her shoulder.

I lingered before her stall, though I knew my stay was useless, to make my interest in her wares seem the more real. Then I turned away slowly and walked down the middle of the bazaar. I allowed the two pennies to fall against the sixpence in my pocket. I heard a voice call from one end of the gallery that the light was out. The upper part of the hall was now completely dark.

Gazing up into the darkness I saw myself as a creature driven and derided by vanity; and my eyes burned with anguish and anger.

---

° *The Arab's Farewell to his Steed*: poem by Caroline Norton (1808–1877).

° *florin*: a two-shilling coin in the 1890s (when the story takes place), worth perhaps twenty dollars in today's money.

## Questions

1. Describe what you consider to be the story's major idea.
2. How might the bazaar, "Araby," be considered symbolically in the story? To what extent does this symbol embody the story's central idea?
3. Consider the attitude of the speaker toward his home as indicated in the first paragraph. Why do you think the speaker uses the word *blind* to describe the dead-end street? What relationship exists between the speaker's pain at the end of the story to the ideas in the first paragraph?
4. Who is the narrator? About how old is he at the time of the story? About how old when he tells the story? What effect is produced by this difference in age between narrator-as-character and narrator-as-storyteller?

## CYNTHIA OZICK (b. 1928)

Ozick has published three novels, *Trust* (1966), *The Cannibal Galaxy* (1983), and *The Messiah of Stockholm* (1987); three short-story collections, *The Pagan Rabbi* (1971), *Bloodshed* (1976), and *Levitation* (1982); and frequent essays and reviews, among which is the collection *Fame and Folly* (1996). Among her many recognitions and awards, she serves on the Board of Advisers of the *American Poetry Review*. Her 1990 novella "Puttermesser Paired" was the first story featured in *Prize Stories 1992: The O. Henry Awards,* edited by William Abrahams. "The Shawl," first published in the *New Yorker* in 1980, was republished in *The Shawl* in 1989, with a companion story describing the heroine's experiences in the United States after surviving the death camp. Also, "The Shawl" was adapted as a play (1996).

##  The Shawl (1980)

Stella, cold, cold the coldness of hell. How they walked on the roads together, Rosa with Magda curled up between sore breasts, Magda wound up in the shawl. Sometimes Stella carried Magda. But she was jealous of Magda. A thin girl of fourteen, too small, with thin breasts of her own, Stella wanted to be wrapped in a shawl, hidden away, asleep, rocked by the march, a baby, a round infant in arms. Magda took Rosa's nipple, and Rosa never stopped walking, a walking cradle. There was not enough milk; sometimes Magda sucked air; then she screamed. Stella was ravenous. Her knees were tumors on sticks, her elbows chicken bones.

Rosa did not feel hunger; she felt light, not like someone walking but like someone in a faint, in trance, arrested in a fit, someone who is already a floating angel, alert and seeing everything, but in the air, not there, not touching the road. As if teetering on the tips of her fingernails. She looked into Magda's face through a gap in the shawl: a squirrel in a nest, safe, no one could reach her inside the little house of the shawl's windings. The face, very round, a pocket mirror of a face: but it was not Rosa's bleak complexion, dark like cholera, it was another kind of face altogether, eyes blue as air, smooth feathers of hair nearly as yellow as the Star sewn into Rosa's coat. You could think she was one of *their* babies.

Rosa, floating, dreamed of giving Magda away in one of the villages. She could leave the line for a minute and push Magda into the hands of any woman on the side of the road. But if she moved out of line they might shoot. And even if she fled the line for half a second and pushed the shawl-bundle at a stranger, would the woman take it? She might be surprised, or afraid; she might drop the shawl, and Magda would fall out and strike her head and die. The little round head. Such a good child, she gave up screaming, and sucked now only for the taste of the drying nipple itself. The neat grip of the tiny gums. One mite of a tooth tip sticking up in the bottom gum, how shining, an elfin tombstone of white marble gleaming there. Without complaining, Magda relinquished Rosa's teats, first the left, then the right; both were cracked, not a sniff of milk. The duct crevice extinct, a dead volcano, blind eye, chill hole, so Magda took the corner of the shawl and milked it instead. She sucked and sucked, flooding the threads with wetness. The shawl's good flavor, milk of linen.

It was a magic shawl, it could nourish an infant for three days and three nights. Magda did not die, she stayed alive, although very quiet. A peculiar smell, of cinnamon and almonds, lifted out of her mouth. She held her eyes open every moment, forgetting how to blink or nap, and Rosa and sometimes Stella studied their blueness. On the road they raised one burden of a leg after another and studied Magda's face. "Aryan," Stella said, in a voice grown as thin as a string; and Rosa thought how Stella gazed at Magda like a young cannibal. And the time that Stella said "Aryan," it sounded to Rosa as if Stella had really said "Let us devour her."

But Magda lived to walk. She lived that long, but she did not walk very well, partly be-    5
cause she was only fifteen months old, and partly because the spindles of her legs could not hold up her fat belly. It was fat with air, full and round. Rosa gave almost all her food to Magda, Stella gave nothing; Stella was ravenous, a growing child herself, but not growing much. Stella did not menstruate. Rosa did not menstruate. Rosa was ravenous, but also not; she learned from Magda how to drink the taste of a finger in one's mouth. They were in a place without pity, all pity was annihilated in Rosa, she looked at Stella's bones without pity. She was sure that Stella was waiting for Magda to die so she could put her teeth into the little thighs.

Rosa knew Magda was going to die very soon; she should have been dead already, but she had been buried away deep inside the magic shawl, mistaken there for the shivering mound of Rosa's breasts; Rosa clung to the shawl as if it covered only herself. No one took it away from her. Magda was mute. She never cried. Rosa hid her in the barracks, under the shawl, but she knew that one day someone would inform; or one day someone, not even Stella, would steal Magda to eat her. When Magda began to walk Rosa knew that Magda was going to die very soon, something would happen. She was afraid to fall asleep; she slept with the weight of her thigh on Magda's body; she was afraid she would smother Magda under her thigh. The weight of Rosa was becoming less and less; Rosa and Stella were slowly turning into air.

Magda was quiet, but her eyes were horribly alive, like blue tigers. She watched. Sometimes she laughed—it seemed a laugh, but how could it be? Magda had never seen anyone laugh. Still, Magda laughed at her shawl when the wind blew its corners, the bad wind with pieces of black in it, that made Stella's and Rosa's eyes tear. Magda's eyes were always clear and tearless. She watched like a tiger. She guarded her shawl. No one could touch it; only Rosa could touch it. Stella was not allowed. The shawl was Magda's own baby, her pet, her little sister. She tangled herself up in it and sucked on one of the corners when she wanted to be very still.

Then Stella took the shawl away and made Magda die.

Afterward Stella said: "I was cold."

And afterward she was always cold, always. The cold went into her heart: Rosa saw that    10
Stella's heart was cold. Magda flopped onward with her little pencil legs scribbling this way and that, in search of the shawl; the pencils faltered at the barracks opening, where the light began.

Rosa saw and pursued. But already Magda was in the square outside the barracks, in the jolly light. It was the roll-call arena. Every morning Rosa had to conceal Magda under the shawl against a wall of the barracks and go out and stand in the arena with Stella and hundreds of others, sometimes for hours, and Magda, deserted, was quiet under the shawl, sucking on her corner. Every day Magda was silent, and so she did not die. Rosa saw that today Magda was going to die, and at the same time a fearful joy ran into Rosa's two palms, her fingers were on fire, she was astonished, febrile: Magda, in the sunlight, swaying on her pencil legs, was howling. Ever since the drying up of Rosa's nipples, ever since Magda's last scream on the road, Magda had been devoid of any syllable; Magda was a mute. Rosa believed that something had gone wrong with her vocal cords, with her windpipe, with the cave of her larynx; Magda was defective, without a voice; perhaps she was deaf; there might be something amiss with her intelligence; Magda was dumb. Even the laugh that came when the ash-stippled wind made a clown out of Magda's shawl was only the air-blown showing of her teeth. Even when the lice, head lice and body lice, crazed her so that she became as wild as one of the big rats that plundered the barracks at daybreak looking for carrion, she rubbed and scratched and kicked and bit and rolled without a whimper. But now Magda's mouth was spilling a long viscous rope of clamor.

"Maaaa—"

It was the first noise Magda had ever sent out from her throat since the drying up of Rosa's nipples.

"Maaaa . . . aaa!"

Again! Magda was wavering in the perilous sunlight of the arena, scrabbling on such pitiful little bent shins. Rosa saw. She saw that Magda was grieving for the loss of her shawl, she saw that Magda was going to die. A tide of commands hammered in Rosa's nipples: Fetch, get, bring! But she did not know which to go after first, Magda or the shawl. If she jumped out into the arena to snatch Magda up, the howling would not stop, because Magda would still not have the shawl; but if she ran back into the barracks to find the shawl, and if she found it, and if she came after Magda holding it and shaking it, then she would get Magda back, Magda would put the shawl in her mouth and turn dumb again.

15      Rosa entered the dark. It was easy to discover the shawl. Stella was heaped under it, asleep in her thin bones. Rosa tore the shawl free and flew—she could fly, she was only air—into the arena. The sunheat murmured of another life, of butterflies in summer. The light was placid, mellow. On the other side of the steel fence, far away, there were green meadows speckled with dandelions and deep-colored violets; beyond them, even farther, innocent tiger lilies, tall, lifting their orange bonnets. In the barracks they spoke of "flowers," of "rain": excrement, thick turd-braids, and the slow stinking maroon waterfall that slunk down from the upper bunks, the stink mixed with a bitter fatty floating smoke that greased Rosa's skin. She stood for an instant at the margin of the arena. Sometimes the electricity inside the fence would seem to hum; even Stella said it was only an imagining, but Rosa heard real sounds in the wire: grainy sad voices. The farther she was from the fence, the more clearly the voices crowded at her. The lamenting voices strummed so convincingly, so passionately, it was impossible to suspect them of being phantoms. The voices told her to hold up the shawl, high; the voices told her to shake it, to whip with it, to unfurl it like a flag. Rosa lifted, shook, whipped, unfurled. Far off, very far, Magda leaned across her air-fed belly, reaching out with the rods of her arms. She was high up, elevated, riding someone's shoulder. But the shoulder that carried Magda was not coming toward Rosa and the shawl, it was drifting away, the speck of Magda was moving more and more into the smoky distance. Above the shoulder a helmet glinted. The light tapped the helmet and sparkled it into a goblet. Below the helmet a black body like a domino and a pair of black boots hurled themselves in the direction of the electrified fence. The electric voices began to chatter wildly. "Maa-maa, maaamaaa," they all hummed together. How far Magda was from Rosa now, across the whole square, past a dozen barracks, all the way on the other side! She was no bigger than a moth.

All at once Magda was swimming through the air. The whole of Magda traveled through loftiness. She looked like a butterfly touching a silver vine. And the moment Magda's feathered round head and her pencil legs and balloonish belly and zigzag arms splashed against the fence, the steel voices went mad in their growling, urging Rosa to run and run to the spot where Magda had fallen from her flight against the electrified fence; but of course Rosa did not obey them. She only stood, because if she ran they would shoot, and if she tried to pick up the sticks of Magda's body they would shoot, and if she let the wolf's screech ascending now through the ladder of her skeleton break out, they would shoot; so she took Magda's shawl and filled her own mouth with it, stuffed it in and stuffed it in, until she was swallowing up the wolf's screech and tasting the cinnamon and almond depth of Magda's saliva; and Rosa drank Magda's shawl until it dried.

## Questions

1. Describe how Ozick presents the setting. Why do you not receive a clear picture of how things look? Why does Ozick present the details as she does?

2. In paragraph 15, what is on the other side of the fence? Explain Ozick's description here. Why does Ozick include these details so close to the story's end?

3. What character is the center of interest in "The Shawl"? Why is she being treated as she is? What are her impressions of the conditions and circumstances around her? What are her responses to her hunger and deprivation?

4. Explain the function of the more unpleasant and brutal details. What do you need to know about the circumstances of the story to respond to these details?

## EDGAR ALLAN POE (1809–1849)

During his lifetime Poe experienced much adversity. He was born in Boston, and his parents separated before he was a year old. His mother, an actress, traveled from city to city to do her performances, and she took Poe, along with his two siblings, along with her. Before he was three, she died, but Poe was rescued from a childhood of poverty and neglect when he was taken into foster care by John and Francis Allan of Richmond, Virginia. In the care of the Allans, Poe was educated both in Virginia and England. For a brief time he was a cadet at West Point. He became alienated from Francis Allan (from whom he took his middle initial, "A," which he preferred to the name "Allan"), and began a lifelong struggle against poverty, alcohol addiction, and physical and psychological illness. To make a living, he worked at various editorships and produced a steady stream of poems, essays, and stories. "The Masque of the Red Death," for example, was one of his contributions in 1842 to *Graham's Magazine,* of which he was then the literary editor. Though he was constantly productive, he did not gain much fame beyond the great praise heaped upon his poem "The Raven" in 1845. His death in 1849 is still an unexplained mystery. He had been on a trip to Philadelphia, which he never completed, and when he was found in Baltimore he was delirious, and in dire condition. He may have consumed a lethal amount of alcohol, possibly because he was urged or forced to do so, or he may have succumbed to a severe neurological illness. As a belated recognition of his stature as a writer, he was selected to the Hall of Fame of American Authors in 1986.

##  The Masque of the Red Death (1842)

The "Red Death" had long devastated the country. No pestilence had ever been so fatal, or so hideous. Blood was its Avatar° and its seal—the redness and the horror of blood. There were sharp pains, and sudden dizziness, and then profuse bleeding at the pores, with dissolution. The scarlet stains upon the body and especially upon the face of the victim, were the pest ban which shut him out from the aid and from the sympathy of his fellow-men. And the whole seizure, progress, and termination of the disease, were the incidents of half an hour.

But the Prince Prospero° was happy and dauntless and sagacious. When his dominions were half depopulated, he summoned to his presence a thousand hale and light-hearted friends from among the knights and dames of his court, and with these retired to the deep seclusion of one of his castellated abbeys. This was an extensive and magnificent structure, the creation of the prince's own eccentric yet august taste. A strong and lofty wall girdled it in. This wall had gates of iron. The courtiers, having entered, brought furnaces and massy hammers and welded the bolts. They resolved to leave means neither of ingress nor egress to the sudden impulses of despair or of frenzy from within. The abbey was amply provisioned. With such precautions the courtiers might bid defiance to contagion. The external world could take care of itself. In the meantime it was folly to grieve, or to think. The prince had provided all the appliances of pleasure. There were buffoons, there were improvisatori, there were ballet-dancers, there were musicians, there was Beauty, there was wine. All these and security were within. Without was the "Red Death."

It was toward the close of the fifth or sixth month of his seclusion, and while the pestilence raged most furiously abroad, that the Prince Prospero entertained his thousand friends at a masked ball of the most unusual magnificence.

It was a voluptuous scene, that masquerade. But first let me tell of the rooms in which it was held. There were seven—an imperial suite. In many palaces, however, such suites form a long and straight vista, while the folding doors slide back nearly to the walls on either hand, so that the view of the whole extent is scarcely impeded. Here the case was very different; as might have been expected from the duke's love of the *bizarre*. The apartments were so irregularly disposed that the vision embraced but little more than one at a time. There was a sharp turn at every twenty or thirty yards, and at each turn a novel effect. To the right and left, in the middle of each wall, a tall and narrow Gothic window looked out upon a closed corridor which pursued the windings of the suite. These windows were of stained glass whose color varied in accordance with the prevailing hue of the decorations of the chamber into which it opened. That at the eastern extremity was hung, for example, in blue—and vividly blue were its windows. The second chamber was purple in its ornaments and tapestries, and here the panes were purple. The third was green throughout, and so were the casements. The fourth was furnished and lighted with orange—the fifth with white—the sixth with violet. The seventh apartment was closely shrouded in black velvet tapestries that hung all over the ceiling and down the walls, falling in heavy folds upon a carpet of the same material and hue. But in this chamber only, the color of the windows failed to correspond with the decorations. The panes here were scarlet—a deep blood color. Now in no one of the seven apartments was there any lamp or candelabrum, amid the profusion of golden ornaments that lay scattered to and

---

°*Avatar*: model, incarnation, manifestation.

°*Prospero*: that is, "prosperous." In Shakespeare's play *The Tempest*, the principal character is Prospero.

fro or depended from the roof. There was no light of any kind emanating from lamp or candle within the suite of chambers. But in the corridors that followed the suite, there stood, opposite to each window, a heavy tripod, bearing a brazier of fire, that projected its rays through the tinted glass and so glaringly illumined the room. And thus were produced a multitude of gaudy and fantastic appearances. But in the western or black chamber the effect of the fire-light that streamed upon the dark hangings through the blood-tinted panes was ghastly in the extreme, and produced so wild a look upon the countenances of those who entered, that there were few of the company bold enough to set foot within its precincts at all.

It was in this apartment, also, that there stood against the western wall, a gigantic clock of  5 ebony. Its pendulum swung to and fro with a dull, heavy, monotonous clang; and when the minute-hand made the circuit of the face, and the hour was to be stricken, there came from the brazen lungs of the clock a sound which was clear and loud and deep and exceedingly musical, but of so peculiar a note and emphasis that, at each lapse of an hour, the musicians of the orchestra were constrained to pause, momentarily, in their performance, to hearken to the sound; and thus the waltzers perforce ceased their evolutions; and there was a brief disconcert of the whole gay company; and, while the chimes of the clock yet rang, it was observed that the giddiest grew pale, and the more aged and sedate passed their hands over their brows as if in confused revery or meditation. But when the echoes had fully ceased, a light laughter at once pervaded the assembly; the musicians looked at each other and smiled as if at their own nervousness and folly, and made whispering vows, each to the other, that the next chiming of the clock should produce in them no similar emotion; and then, after the lapse of sixty minutes (which embrace three thousand and six hundred seconds of the Time that flies), there came yet another chiming of the clock, and then were the same disconcert and tremulousness and meditation as before.

But, in spite of these things, it was a gay and magnificent revel. The tastes of the duke were peculiar. He had a fine eye for colors and effects. He disregarded the *decora*° of mere fashion. His plans were bold and fiery, and his conceptions glowed with barbaric lustre. There are some who would have thought him mad. His followers felt that he was not. It was necessary to hear and see and touch him to be *sure* that he was not.

He had directed, in great part, the movable embellishments of the seven chambers, upon occasion of this great fête,° and it was his own guiding taste which had given character to the masqueraders. Be sure they were grotesque. There were much glare and glitter and piquancy and phantasm—much of what has been since seen in "Hernani."° There were arabesque figures with unsuited limbs and appointments. There were delirious fancies such as the madman fashions. There were much of the beautiful, much of the wanton, much of the *bizarre*, something of the terrible, and not a little of that which might have excited disgust. To and fro in the seven chambers there stalked, in fact, a multitude of dreams. And these—the dreams—writhed in and about, taking hue from the rooms, and causing the wild music of the orchestra to seem as the echo of their steps. And, anon, there strikes the ebony clock which stands in the hall of the velvet. And then, for a moment, all is still, and all is silent save the voice of the clock. The dreams are stiff-frozen as they stand. But the echoes of the chime die away—they have endured but an instant—and a light, half-subdued laughter floats after them as they depart. And now again the music swells, and the dreams live, and writhe to and fro more merrily than ever, taking hue from the many-tinted windows through which stream the rays from the tripods. But to the chamber which lies most westwardly of the seven there are now none of the maskers who venture; for the night is waning away; and there flows a ruddier light through

---

°*decora*: schemes, patterns.
°*fête*: party, revel.
°*Hernani*: tragedy by Victor Hugo (1802–1885), featuring elaborate scenes and costumes.

the blood-colored panes; and the blackness of the sable drapery appalls; and to him whose foot falls upon the sable carpet, there comes from the near clock of ebony a muffled peal more solemnly emphatic than any which reaches *their* ears who indulge in the more remote gaieties of the other apartments.

But these other apartments were densely crowded, and in them beat feverishly the heart of life. And the revel went whirlingly on, until at length there commenced the sounding of midnight upon the clock. And then the music ceased, as I have told; and the evolutions of the waltzers were quieted; and there was an uneasy cessation of all things as before. But now there were twelve strokes to be sounded by the bell of the clock; and thus it happened, perhaps that more of thought crept, with more of time, into the meditations of the thoughtful among those who revelled. And thus, too, it happened, perhaps, that before the last echoes of the last chime had utterly sunk into silence, there were many individuals in the crowd who had found leisure to become aware of the presence of a masked figure which had arrested the attention of no single individual before. And the rumor of this new presence having spread itself whisperingly around, there arose at length from the whole company a buzz, or murmur, expressive of disapprobation and surprise—then, finally, of terror, of horror, and of disgust.

In an assembly of phantasms such as I have painted, it may well be supposed that no ordinary appearance could have excited such sensation. In truth the masquerade license of the night was nearly unlimited; but the figure in question had out-Heroded Herod,° and gone beyond the bounds of even the prince's indefinite decorum. There are chords in the hearts of the most reckless which cannot be touched without emotion. Even with the utterly lost, to whom life and death are equally jests, there are matters of which no jest can be made. The whole company, indeed, seemed now deeply to feel that in the costume and bearing of the stranger neither wit nor propriety existed. The figure was tall and gaunt, and shrouded from head to foot in the habiliments of the grave. The mask which concealed the visage was made so nearly to resemble the countenance of a stiffened corpse that the closest scrutiny must have had difficulty in detecting the cheat. And yet all this might have been endured, if not approved, by the mad revellers around. But the mummer had gone so far as to assume the type of the Red Death. His vesture was dabbled in *blood*—and his broad brow, with all the features of the face, was besprinkled with the scarlet horror.

10    When the eyes of Prince Prospero fell upon this spectral image (which, with a slow and solemn movement, as if more fully to sustain its *rôle*, stalked to and fro among the waltzers) he was seen to be convulsed, in the first moment with a strong shudder either of terror or distaste; but, in the next, his brow reddened with rage.

"Who dares"—he demanded hoarsely of the courtiers who stood near him—"who dares insult us with this blasphemous mockery? Seize him and unmask him—that we may know whom we have to hang, at sunrise, from the battlements!"

It was in the eastern or blue chamber in which stood the Prince Prospero as he uttered these words. They rang throughout the seven rooms loudly and clearly, for the prince was a bold and robust man, and the music had become hushed at the waving of his hand.

It was in the blue room where stood the prince, with a group of pale courtiers by his side. At first, as he spoke, there was a slight rushing movement of this group in the direction of the intruder, who, at the moment was also near at hand, and now, with deliberate and stately step, made closer approach to the speaker. But from a certain nameless awe with which the mad assumptions of the mummer had inspired the whole party, there were found none who put forth hand to seize him; so that, unimpeded, he passed within a yard of the prince's person; and, while the vast assembly, as if with one impulse, shrank from the centres of the rooms to the walls, he made his way uninterruptedly, but with the same solemn and measured step which

---

°*out-Heroded Herod*: quoted from Shakespeare's *Hamlet*, Act 3, scene 2, line 13, in reference to extreme overacting.

had distinguished him from the first, through the blue chamber to the purple—through the purple to the green—through the green to the orange—through this again to the white—and even thence to the violet, ere a decided movement had been made to arrest him. It was then, however, that the Prince Prospero, maddening with rage and the shame of his own momentary cowardice, rushed hurriedly through the six chambers, while none followed him on account of a deadly terror that had seized upon all. He bore aloft a drawn dagger, and had approached, in rapid impetuosity, to within three or four feet of the retreating figure, when the latter, having attained the extremity of the velvet apartment, turned suddenly and confronted his pursuer. There was a sharp cry—and the dagger dropped gleaming upon the sable carpet, upon which, instantly afterward, fell prostrate in death the Prince Prospero. Then, summoning the wild courage of despair, a throng of the revellers at once threw themselves into the black apartment, and, seizing the mummer, whose tall figure stood erect and motionless within the shadow of the ebony clock, gasped in unutterable horror at finding the grave cerements and corpse-like mask, which they handled with so violent a rudeness, untenanted by any tangible form.

And now was acknowledged the presence of the Red Death. He had come like a thief in the night.° And one by one dropped the revellers in the blood-bedewed halls of their revel, and died each in the despairing posture of his fall. And the life of the ebony clock went out with that of the last of the gay. And the flames of the tripods expired. And Darkness and Decay and the Red Death held illimitable dominion over all.

## Questions

1. What is happening throughout the country in this story? What does the Prince's reaction to these events tell us about him?

2. How do the details of number, color, and lighting help create the atmosphere and mood of the story?

3. Why do the color and window of the last room disturb the revellers? To what extent does this last room reflect the plot and ideas of the story?

4. What single object is located in this last room? How is this object described? What effect does its sound have on the revellers? What do you think Poe is suggesting by this object and its effects?

5. How are the nobles dressed for the masquerade? Why is the "masked figure" remarkable? How does Prospero react to him?

---

° *thief in the night.* 2 Peter 3:10.

## WRITING ABOUT SETTING

In preparing to write about setting, determine the number and importance of locations, artifacts, and customs. Ask questions like the following:

- How extensive are the visual descriptions? Does the author provide such vivid and carefully arranged detail about surroundings that you could draw a map or plan? Or is the scenery vague and difficult for you to reconstruct imaginatively?

- What connections, if any, are apparent between locations and characters? Do the locations bring characters together, separate them, facilitate their privacy, make intimacy and conversation difficult?
- How fully are objects described? How vital are they to the action? How important are they in the development of the plot or idea? How are they connected to the mental states of the characters?
- How important to plot and character are shapes, colors, times of day, clouds, storms, light and sun, seasons of the year, and conditions of vegetation?
- Are the characters poor, moderately well off, or rich? How does their economic condition affect what happens to them, and how does it affect their actions and attitudes?
- What cultural, religious, and political conditions are brought out in the story? How do the characters accept and adjust to these conditions? How do the conditions affect the characters' judgments and actions?
- What is the state of houses, furniture, and objects (e.g., new and polished, old and worn, ragged and torn)? What connections can you find between these conditions and the outlook and behavior of the characters?
- How important are sounds or silences? To what degree is music or other sound important in the development of character and action?
- Do characters respect or mistreat the environment? If there is an environmental connection, how central is it to the story?
- What conclusions do you think the author expects you to draw as a result of the neighborhood, culture, and larger world of the story?

## Strategies for Organizing Ideas

Begin by making a brief description of the setting or scenes of the work, specifying the amount and importance of detail. Choosing one of the approaches in the following list, describe the approach you plan to develop. As you gather material for your essay, however, you may need to combine your major approach with one or more of the others. Whatever approach for development you choose, be sure to consider setting not as an end in itself but rather as illustration and evidence for claims you are making about the particular story.

1. *Setting and Action.* Explore the importance of setting in the work. How extensively is the setting described? Are locations essential or incidental to the actions? Does the setting serve as part of the action (e.g., places of flight or concealment; public places where people meet openly, or hidden places where they meet privately; natural or environmental conditions; seasonal conditions such as searing heat or numbing cold; customs and conventions)? Do any objects cause inspiration, difficulty, or conflict (for example, a bridge, a walking stick, a necklace, a fence, a hair ribbon, a frozen lake, a bizarre party, a hat floating in water)? How directly do these objects influence the action?

2. *Setting and Organization.* How is the setting connected to the various parts of the work? Does it undergo any changes as the action develops? Why are some parts of the setting more important than others? Is the setting used as a structural frame or enclosure for the story? How do objects, such as money, appliances, property, or physical location (e.g., a subway platform, a prison camp, a winter scene on a lake) influence the characters? How do descriptions made at the start become important in the action later on?

3. *Setting and Character.* (For examples of this approach, see the two drafts of the illustrative essay in Chapter 1.) Analyze the degree to which setting influences and interacts with character. Are the characters happy or unhappy where they live? Do they get into discussions or arguments about their home environments? Do they want to stay or leave? Do the economic, philosophical, religious, or ethnic aspects of the setting make the characters undergo changes? What jobs do the characters perform because of their ways of life? What freedoms or restraints do these jobs cause? How does the setting influence their decisions, transportation, speech habits, eating habits, attitudes about love and honor, and general behavior?

4. *Setting and Atmosphere.* To what extent does setting contribute to mood? Does the setting go beyond the minimum needed for action or character? How do descriptive words paint verbal pictures and evoke moods through references to colors, shapes, sounds, smells, or tastes? Does the setting establish a mood, say, of joy or hopelessness, plenty or scarcity? Do events happen in daylight or at night? Do the locations and activities of the characters suggest permanence or impermanence (such as returning home, creating figures out of mud, repairing a battered boat, perceiving ocean currents, being confined within a room)? Are things warm and pleasant, or cold and harsh? What connection do you find between the atmosphere and the author's expressed or apparent thoughts about existence?

5. *Setting and Other Aspects of the Story.* Does the setting reinforce the story's meaning? Does it establish irony about the circumstances and ideas in the story? If you choose this approach, consult the introductory paragraph in "The Literary Uses of Setting" earlier in this chapter. If you are interested in writing about the symbolic implications of a setting, consult Chapter 8.

To conclude, summarize your major points or write about related aspects of setting that you have not considered. Thus, if your essay treats the relationship of setting and action, your conclusion might mention connections of the setting with character or atmosphere. You might also point out whether your central idea about setting also applies to other major aspects of the story.

## Illustrative Student Essay

Underlined sentences in this paper *do not* conform to MLA style and are used solely as teaching tools to emphasize the central idea, thesis sentence, and topic sentences throughout the paper.

Doyle 1

Deborah Doyle

Professor Casciano

English 122

29 September 2007

### The Setting of Conrad's "The Secret Sharer"°

[1]      In "The Secret Sharer" Joseph Conrad makes his setting an integral and
inseparable part of his action and ideas.* The story is a sea story, which could not exist
without the many details about ocean, ships, currents, cabins, and men who sail. While
some of Conrad's ideas about guilt, human sympathies, and the connection of divinity
to human beings may be vague, the physical details about the setting are completely
realized. The integration of setting and story can be followed in details about the
Captain's cabin and the ocean itself and also in Conrad's suggestions that human affairs
are linked to large, cosmic forces.†

[2]      The Captain's cabin is essential to the story's main action because it enables the
Captain, the story's speaker, successfully to conceal Leggatt, the stowaway. The tension
resulting from the near-discoveries by the steward depends on Conrad's detailed
descriptions of the cabin (see, for example, paragraphs 72–73, p. 209). It is described
as having the shape of an *L*, with the door on "the short part of the letter" (paragraph
73). Because the "vertical" part is not visible to anyone entering, and because the
coats, the curtained bunk, and the bathroom all furnish concealment, Leggatt can avoid
the steward's searching eyes. Further, the noise made by sailors walking on the deck
above the cabin permits the Captain and Leggatt to speak together without being

---

°See pp. 203–26 for this story.

*Central idea.

†Thesis sentence.

overheard, and therefore the plans for the escape can be safely communicated between the two men.

[3]        While it is obvious that a sea story takes the presence of the ocean for granted, the ocean is, for the story's purposes, equally as important as the cabin. It was during a severe storm that Leggatt decided to "reef" the sail that saved his ship, the *Sephora*. It was the disobedient sailor's insults, probably brought about by fear of the storm, that enraged Leggatt and made him strangle this sailor. Thus the ocean itself produces both a good and a bad result, and it is the bad result that causes Leggatt to flee the *Sephora*. When he escapes he swims to the Captain's ship at night, thus connecting the two men, who otherwise would never have met. When Leggatt leaves the Captain's ship at the end of the story, he does so by going into the sea from a rope hung from the sail locker, and, because the Captain wishes to keep Leggatt as safe as possible, he steers too close to shore. Therefore the potential shallowness of the ocean becomes an immediate danger to the Captain, who risks his entire career (which could "go irretrievably to pieces") on the chance that he will not run around (paragraph 252, p. 222).

[4]        While the setting of ocean and cabin helps create the story's adventure and tension, the descriptions also form part of Conrad's religious and philosophic setting. At the beginning, for example, we read the Captain's words:

> In this breathless pause at the threshold of a long passage we seemed to be measuring our fitness for a long and arduous enterprise, the appointed task . . . to be carried out, far from all human eyes, with only sky and sea for spectators and for judges. (paragraph 2, p. 203)

When the captain of the *Sephora* agrees that Leggatt's reefing of the sail saved his ship, he asserts that "God's own hand" was "in it. . . . Nothing less could have done it" (paragraph 139, p. 214). In reflecting on Leggatt's both saving the *Sephora* and strangling the sailor, the Captain draws the following paradoxical conclusion:

> The same strung-up force which had given twenty-four men a chance, at least, for their lives, had, in a sort of recoil, crushed an unworthy mutinous existence. (paragraph 190, p. 217)

At the end of the story, when the Captain's hat floating on the water enables the Captain to save his ship by turning around (paragraph 319, p. 225), it is clear that the setting, through the currents of water, is intended to suggest cosmic approval of the Captain's decision to help Leggatt.

[5]      An additional merging of setting and story should be mentioned in conclusion. This concerns the character of the Captain, the unnamed narrator. In his role as narrator, the Captain's observations about the sea, the sky, and the things the ship will encounter on the way back to England all show him as a clear-sighted man who understands the sea and the forces that control it. It is his knowledge of the danger of the sea during storms that makes possible his own personal "verdict" acquitting Leggatt for having strangled the mutinous sailor. Conrad's setting in this instance is so vital to the story that it becomes the very material of the Captain's morality, and it is this morality that causes the central decision around which all the events in the story turn. Because of this and all the other details, it is no exaggeration to say that Conrad's setting and his story are totally integrated and intertwined.

**WORK CITED**

Conrad, Joseph. "The Secret Sharer." *Literature: An Introduction to Reading and Writing.* Ed. Edgar V. Roberts. 4th Compact Ed. Upper Saddle River: Prentice Hall, 2008, 203–226.

## Commentary on the Essay

This essay focuses on the connection between Conrad's setting and the action and ideas of the story. With this emphasis, the essay illustrates some of the aspects of strategy 1, described on page 239. In showing the connection between setting, character, and ideas, it illustrates strategies 1 and 3.

The introductory paragraph indicates the closeness of setting and story, and lays out the areas to be developed in the essay. Paragraph 2 is developed with details showing the importance of the Captain's cabin. Paragraph 3 presents details about the relationship of the ocean to the story: in storm as a cause of Leggatt's good and bad actions, in calm and night as a link between the Captain and Leggatt, and in shallow water as a means of safety for Leggatt but as a threat to the Captain and the ship. Paragraph 4 presents details about the larger, cosmic aspects of the setting, for Conrad's story is not only about physical details but about the unseen forces that control human beings. The concluding paragraph illustrates the significance that knowledge of the ocean plays in the moral decision—and hence in the character—of the Captain.

## Writing Topics: About Setting

1. How does Jackie respond to the setting of family and church in "First Confession" (Chapter 7)? In light of this story, together with knowledge you have gained elsewhere from your reading and experience, what can you conclude about the effects of home and religion on individual character?

2. Compare and contrast how details of setting establish qualities and traits of the following female characters: Stella of "The Shawl," Miss Brill of "Miss Brill" (Chapter 4), and the narrator of "The Yellow Wallpaper" (Chapter 10). To add to your comparison, you might discuss how the painters Boucher and Hopper portray background and dress to highlight the character of their female subjects (I–8, Plate 2 and I–3, Plate 2).

3. In what ways might we say that both "The Masque of the Red Death" and "The Shawl" are inseparable from their settings? To answer this question, consider the relationship of character to place and circumstance. How could the actions of the stories happen without the locations in which they occur?

4. Consider the significance of place and character in "A Rose for Emily" (Chapter 2) or "Araby."

5. Choose one story included in this chapter and rewrite a page or two, taking the characters out of their setting and placing them in an entirely new setting or in the setting of another story (you choose). Then write a brief analysis dealing with questions like these: How do you think your characters would be affected by their new settings? Do you make them change slowly or rapidly? Why? As a result of your rewriting, what can you conclude about the uses of setting in fiction?

6. Write a short narrative as though it is part of a story (which you may also wish to write for the assignment) using option *a* and/or *b*.
   a. Relate a natural setting or type of day to a mood—for example, a nice day to happiness and satisfaction, or a cold, cloudy, rainy day to sadness. Or create irony by relating the nice day to sadness or the rainy day to happiness.
   b. Indicate how an object or circumstance becomes the cause of conflict or reconciliation (such as the shawl in "The Shawl," or the newly tuned piano in "Two Kinds" [Chapter 4]).

7. In your library locate two books on the career of Edgar Allan Poe. On the basis of information you find in these sources, write a brief account of Poe's uses of setting and place to evoke atmosphere and to bring out qualities of human character.

# Chapter 6

# Structure: The Organization of Stories

Structure refers to the ways in which writers arrange materials in accord with the general ideas and purposes of their works. Unlike plot, which is focused on conflict or conflicts, structure defines the layouts of works—the ways the story, play, or poem is shaped. Structure is about matters such as placement, balance, recurring themes, true and misleading conclusions, suspense, and the imitation of models or forms such as reports, letters, conversations, or confessions. A work might be divided into numbered sections or parts, or it might begin in a countryside (or one state) and conclude in a city (or another state), or it might develop a relationship between two people from their first introduction to their falling in love.

The importance of structure may be seen graphically in the art of the painter. As an example, the painting *Seaport at Sunset* (I–6, Plate 2), by the French painter Claude Lorrain (1600–1682), pictures a lifelike scene comprising a harbor, ships, boats, buildings, and a shore on which people are working, chatting, transacting business, and fighting. Near the horizon, the distant and glowing sun bathes the scene in light and therefore the source of all the human activities. This structuring of figures and background brings out contrasts between human beings, between human artifacts and nature, and between human existence and the cosmos. Claude's painting suggests that, despite temporary human concerns, the source of life is like the sun—remote, vast, mysterious, and beautiful. In fiction, we find that organization and structure highlight many similar contrasts. To study structure is to study these arrangements and the purposes for which they are made.

## Formal Categories of Structure

Many aspects of structure are common to all genres of literature. Particularly for stories and plays, however, the following aspects form a skeleton, a pattern of development.

### The EXPOSITION Provides the Materials Necessary to Put the Plot into Operation

**Exposition** is the laying out, the putting forth, of the materials in the story—the main characters, their backgrounds, their characteristics, interests, goals, limitations, potentials, and basic assumptions. Exposition may not be limited to the beginning of the

244

work, where it is most expected, but may be found anywhere. Thus, intricacies, twists, turns, false leads, blind alleys, surprises, and other quirks may be introduced to interest, intrigue, perplex, mystify, and please readers. Whenever something new arises, to the degree that it is new it is a part of exposition.

## The COMPLICATION Marks the Beginning and the Growth of the Conflict

The **complication** is the onset and development of the major conflict—the plot. The major participants are the protagonist and antagonist, together with whatever ideas and values they represent, such as good or evil, freedom or oppression, independence or dependence, love or hate, intelligence or stupidity, and knowledge or ignorance.

## The CRISIS Marks the Decisions Made to End the Conflict

The **crisis** (Greek for judgment or separation—a separating, distinguishing, or turning point) marks that part of the action where the conflict reaches its greatest tension. During the crisis, a decision or an action is undertaken to resolve the complication or complications, and therefore the crisis is that point at which uncertainty and anxiety are greatest. Usually, the crisis is followed closely by the next stage, the *climax*. In fact, the two often occur so near each other that they are considered the same.

## The CLIMAX Is the Conclusion of the Conflict

Because the **climax** (Greek for *ladder*) is a consequence of the crisis, it is the story's *high point* (from the idea of a ladder) and may take the shape of an action, a decision, an affirmation or denial, or an illumination or realization. It is the logical conclusion of the preceding actions; no new major developments follow it. In most stories, the climax occurs at the end or close to it. For example, in Oates's "Cousins," the climax occurs when it becomes clear that the indifferent cousin has overcome her indifference. Previously in the story, it has seemed that she does not want of her cousin's letters, but the shift in her attitude is the story's high point, which demonstrates that her apparent annoyance has changed to her need to connect with her cousin.

## The RESOLUTION or DÉNOUEMENT Finishes the Work and Releases the Tension

The **resolution** (Latin for untying or releasing) or **dénouement** (French for untying or undoing) is the completing of the story or play after the climax, for once the climax has occurred, the work's tension and uncertainty are finished, and most authors conclude quickly to avoid losing their readers' interest. For instance, Poe ends "The Masque of the Red Death" (Chapter 5) by asserting that the "illimitable" power of the Red Death has overcome the earth and all its occupants. In other words, after the story's major conflicts are finished, the dénouement brings the work to its inevitable and rapid ending.

# Formal and Actual Structure

The structure just described is a *formal* one, an ideal pattern that moves directly from beginning to end. Few narratives and dramas follow this pattern exactly, however. A mystery story might hold back crucial details of exposition (because the goal is to mystify); a suspense story might keep the protagonist ignorant but provide readers with abundant details in order to maximize concern and tension about the outcome.

More realistic, less "artificial" stories might also contain structural variations. For example, Welty's "A Worn Path" (Chapter 2) produces a *double take* because of unique structuring. During most of the story the major character, Phoenix, seems to be in conflict with age, poverty, and environment. At the end, however, the story brings out an additional difficulty—a new conflict that enlarges our responses to include not just concern but also heartfelt anguish. "A Worn Path" is just one example of how a structural variation maximizes the impact of a work.

There are many other possible variants in structure. One of these is called **flashback**, or **selective recollection**, in which present circumstances are explained by the selective introduction of past events. The moment at which the flashback is introduced may be a part of the resolution of the plot, and the flashback might lead you into a moment of climax but then go from there to develop the details that are more properly part of the exposition. Let us again consider our brief story about John and Jane (above, p. 101) and use the flashback method of structuring the story:

> Jane is now old, and a noise outside causes her to remember the argument that forced her to part with John many years before. They were deeply in love, but their disagreement about her wishes for a career and equality split them apart. Then she pictures in her mind the years she and John have spent happily together after they married. She then contrasts her present happiness with her memory of her earlier, less happy marriage, and from there she recalls her youthful years of courtship with John before their disastrous conflict developed. Then she looks over at John, reading in a chair, and smiles. John smiles back, and the two embrace. Even then, Jane has tears on her cheeks.

In this structure the action begins and remains in the present. Important parts of the past flood the protagonist's memory in flashback, though not in the order in which they happened. Memory might be used structurally in other ways. An example is Porter's "The Jilting of Granny Weatherall," an intense story that is developed within the dying perceptions of an aged woman, Granny Weatherall (Chapter 8). As she passes in and out of delirium on her deathbed, we follow her recollection of major events in her life, such as being jilted on her wedding day, remarrying and bringing up her children, enduring her long widowhood, losing a favorite daughter, and retaining her lifelong obligation to her church. In short, this story builds its chronology through a series of apparently disconnected but closely unified flashbacks.

Each narrative or drama has its own unique structure. Some stories may be organized according to simple geography, as in Whitecloud's "Blue Winds Dancing" (a ride from California to Wisconsin [this chapter]) and Munro's "The Found Boat" (from a spring flood to an exploration on and beside a river [Chapter 7]). Parts or scenes might be carried on through conversations, as in Carver's "Neighbors," (Chapter 3) or through a period of dying fantasy, as in Bierce's "An Occurrence at Owl Creek Bridge" (Chapter 2). Additionally, parts of a work may be set out as fragments of conversation, as in St. Luke's "The Parable of the Prodigal Son" (Chapter 8), or as a ceremony, as in Hawthorne's "Young Goodman Brown" (Chapter 8), or as an announcement of a party, as in "The Necklace" (Chapter 1). The possible variations in literary structures are infinite.

## Stories for Study

## RALPH ELLISON (1914–1994)

Ellison was born in Oklahoma seven years after it became a state. As a youth he was attracted to music, particularly jazz, and at one point he planned on becoming a classical music composer, his ideal being Richard Wagner, the giant among nineteenth century German operatic composers. In 1933 Ellison went to Alabama's Tuskeegee Institute, but after three years he left for New York with a plan to become a sculptor. Once in New York, he met Richard Wright, and with Wright's encouragement and influence he began writing essays and stories for magazines such as *New Challenge* and *New Masses*. Before he published *Invisible Man* in 1952, his best known works were the stories "King of the Bingo Game" and "Flying Home." With *Invisible Man*, which won a National Book Award in 1953, his work became widely read and taught. In 1964 he published *Shadow and Act,* a collection of essays, and in 1985 he published *Going to the Territory*, a book of essays and interviews. In later years he held a chair in Humanities at New York University. His works published posthumously are *The Collected Essays of Ralph Ellison* (1995), *Flying Home and Other Stories* (1996), and the novel *Juneteenth* (1999).

 ## Battle Royal (1952)

It goes a long way back, some twenty years. All my life I had been looking for something, and everywhere I turned someone tried to tell me what it was. I accepted their answers too, though they were often in contradiction and even self-contradictory. I was naïve. I was looking for myself and asking everyone except myself questions which I, and only I, could answer. It took me a long time and much painful boomeranging of my expectations to achieve a realization everyone else appears to have been born with: That I am nobody but myself. But first I had to discover that I am an invisible man!

And yet I am no freak of nature, nor of history. I was in the cards, other things having been equal (or unequal) eighty-five years ago. I am not ashamed of my grandparents for having been slaves. I am only ashamed of myself for having at one time been ashamed. About eighty-five years ago they were told that they were free, united with others of our country in everything pertaining to the common good, and, in everything social, separate like the fingers of the hand.

And they believed it. They exulted in it. They stayed in their place, worked hard, and brought up my father to do the same. But my grandfather is the one. He was an odd old guy, my grandfather, and I am told I take after him. It was he who caused the trouble. On his deathbed he called my father to him and said, "Son, after I'm gone I want you to keep up the good fight. I never told you, but our life is a war and I have been a traitor all my born days, a spy in the enemy's country ever since I gave up my gun back in the Reconstruction. Live with your head in the lion's mouth. I want you to overcome 'em with yeses, undermine 'em with grins, agree 'em to death and destruction, let 'em swoller you till they vomit or bust wide open." They thought the old man had gone out of his mind. He had been the meekest of men. The younger children were rushed from the room, the shades drawn and the flame of the lamp turned so low that it sputtered on the wick like the old man's breathing. "Learn it to the younguns," he whispered fiercely; then he died.

But my folks were more alarmed over his last words than over his dying. It was as though he had not died at all, his words caused so much anxiety. I was warned emphatically to forget what he had said and, indeed, this is the first time it has been mentioned outside the family circle. It had a tremendous effect upon me, however. I could never be sure of what he meant. Grandfather had been a quiet old man who never made any trouble, yet on his deathbed he had called himself a traitor and a spy, and he had spoken of his meekness as a dangerous activity. It became a constant puzzle which lay unanswered in the back of my mind. And whenever things went well for me I remembered my grandfather and felt guilty and uncomfortable. It was as though I was carrying out his advice in spite of myself. And to make it worse, everyone loved me for it. I was praised by the most lily-white men of the town. I was considered an example of desirable conduct—just as my grandfather had been. And what puzzled me was that the old man had defined it as *treachery*. When I was praised for my conduct I felt a guilt that in some way I was doing something that was really against the wishes of the white folks, that if they had understood they would have desired me to act just the opposite, that I should have been sulky and mean, and that that really would have been what they wanted, even though they were fooled and thought they wanted me to act as I did. It made me afraid that some day they would look upon me as a traitor and I would be lost. Still I was more afraid to act any other way because they didn't like that at all. The old man's words were like a curse. On my graduation day I delivered an oration in which I showed that humility was the secret, indeed, the very essence of progress. (Not that I believed this—how could I, remembering my grandfather?—I only believed that it worked.) It was a great success. Everyone praised me and I was invited to give the speech at a gathering of the town's leading white citizens. It was a triumph for our whole community.

It was in the main ballroom of the leading hotel. When I got there I discovered that it was on the occasion of a smoker, and I was told that since I was to be there anyway I might as well take part in the battle royal to be fought by some of my schoolmates as part of the entertainment. The battle royal came first.

5    All of the town's big shots were there in their tuxedoes, wolfing down the buffet foods, drinking beer and whiskey and smoking black cigars. It was a large room with a high ceiling. Chairs were arranged in neat rows around three sides of a portable boxing ring. The fourth side was clear, revealing a gleaming space of polished floor. I had some misgivings over the battle royal, by the way. Not from a distaste for fighting, but because I didn't care too much for the other fellows who were to take part. They were tough guys who seemed to have no

grandfather's curse worrying their minds. No one could mistake their toughness. And besides, I suspected that fighting a battle royal might detract from the dignity of my speech. In those pre-invisible days I visualized myself as a potential Booker T. Washington.° But the other fellows didn't care too much for me either, and there were nine of them. I felt superior to them in my way, and I didn't like the manner in which we were all crowded together into the servants' elevator. Nor did they like my being there. In fact, as the warmly lighted floors flashed past the elevator we had words over the fact that I, by taking part in the fight, had knocked one of their friends out of a night's work.

We were led out of the elevator through a rococo hall into an anteroom and told to get into our fighting togs. Each of us was issued a pair of boxing gloves and ushered out into the big mirrored hall, which we entered looking cautiously about us and whispering, lest we might accidentally be heard above the noise of the room. It was foggy with cigar smoke. And already the whiskey was taking effect. I was shocked to see some of the most important men of the town quite tipsy. They were all there—bankers, lawyers, judges, doctors, fire chiefs, teachers, merchants. Even one of the more fashionable pastors. Something we could not see was going on up front. A clarinet was vibrating sensuously and the men were standing up and moving eagerly forward. We were a small tight group, clustered together, our bare upper bodies touching and shining with anticipatory sweat; while up front the big shots were becoming increasingly excited over something we still could not see. Suddenly I heard the school superintendent, who had told me to come, yell, "Bring up the shines gentlemen! Bring up the little shines!"

We were rushed up to the front of the ballroom, where it smelled even more strongly of tobacco and whiskey. Then we were pushed into place. I almost wet my pants. A sea of faces, some hostile, some amused, ringed around us, and in the center, facing us, stood a magnificent blonde—stark naked. There was dead silence. I felt a blast of cold air chill me. I tried to back away, but they were behind me and around me. Some of the boys stood with lowered heads, trembling. I felt a wave of irrational guilt and fear. My teeth chattered, my skin turned to goose flesh, my knees knocked. Yet I was strongly attracted and looked in spite of myself. Had the price of looking been blindness, I would have looked. The hair was yellow like that of a circus kewpie doll, the face heavily powdered and rouged, as though to form an abstract mask, the eyes hollow and smeared a cool blue, the color of a baboon's butt. I felt a desire to spit upon her as my eyes brushed slowly over her body. Her breasts were firm and round as the domes of East Indian temples, and I stood so close as to see the fine skin texture and beads of pearly perspiration glistening like dew around the pink and erected buds of her nipples. I wanted at one and the same time to run from the room, to sink through the floor, or go to her and cover her from my eyes and the eyes of the others with my body; to feel the soft thighs, to caress her and destroy her, to love her and murder her, to hide from her, and yet to stroke where below the small American flag tattooed upon her belly her thighs formed a capital V. I had a notion that of all in the room she saw only me with her impersonal eyes.

And then she began to dance, a slow sensuous movement; the smoke of a hundred cigars clinging to her like the thinnest of veils. She seemed like a fair bird-girl girdled in veils calling to me from the angry surface of some gray and threatening sea. I was transported. Then I became aware of the clarinet playing and the big shots yelling at us. Some threatened us if we looked and others if we did not. On my right I saw one boy faint. And now a man grabbed a silver pitcher from a table and stepped close as he dashed ice water upon him and stood him up and forced two of us to support him as his head hung and moans issued from his thick bluish lips. Another boy began to plead to go home. He was the largest of the group, wearing dark red fighting trunks much too small to conceal the erection which projected from him as

---

°Booker T. Washington (1856–1915) was born a slave, but after the Civil War he became widely recognized as an educator, and served as president of the Tuskeegee Institute.

though in answer to the insinuating low-registered moaning of the clarinet. He tried to hide himself with his boxing gloves.

And all the while the blonde continued dancing, smiling faintly at the big shots who watched her with fascination, and faintly smiling at our fear. I noticed a certain merchant who followed her hungrily, his lips loose and drooling. He was a large man who wore diamond studs in a shirtfront which swelled with the ample paunch underneath, and each time the blonde swayed her undulating hips he ran his hand through the thin hair of his bald head and, with his arms upheld, his posture clumsy like that of an intoxicated panda, wound his belly in a slow and obscene grind. This creature was completely hypnotized. The music had quickened. As the dancer flung herself about with a detached expression on her face, the men began reaching out to touch her. I could see their beefy fingers sink into her soft flesh. Some of the others tried to stop them and she began to move around the floor in graceful circles, as they gave chase, slipping and sliding over the polished floor. It was mad. Chairs went crashing, drinks were spilt, as they ran laughing and howling after her. They caught her just as she reached a door, raised her from the floor, and tossed her as college boys are tossed at a hazing, and above her red, fixed-smiling lips I saw the terror and disgust in her eyes, almost like my own terror and that which I saw in some of the other boys. As I watched, they tossed her twice and her soft breasts seemed to flatten against the air and her legs flung widely as she spun. Some of the more sober ones helped her to escape. And I started off the floor, heading for the anteroom with the rest of the boys.

10    Some were still crying and in hysteria. But as we tried to leave we were stopped and ordered to get into the ring. There was nothing to do but what we were told. All ten of us climbed under the ropes and allowed ourselves to be blindfolded with broad bands of white cloth. One of the men seemed to feel a bit sympathetic and tried to cheer us up as we stood with our backs against the ropes. Some of us tried to grin. "See that boy over there?" one of the men said. "I want you to run across at the bell and give it to him right in the belly. If you don't get him, I'm going to get you. I don't like his looks." Each of us was told the same. The blindfolds were put on. Yet even then I had been going over my speech. In my mind each word was as bright as flame. I felt the cloth pressed into place, and frowned so that it would be loosened when I relaxed.

But now I felt a sudden fit of blind terror. I was unused to darkness. It was as though I had suddenly found myself in a dark room filled with poisonous cottonmouths. I could hear the bleary voices yelling insistently for the battle royal to begin.

"Get going in there!"

"Let me at that big nigger!"

I strained to pick up the school superintendent's voice, as though to squeeze some security out of that slightly more familiar sound.

15    "Let me at those black sonsabitches!" someone yelled.

"No, Jackson, no!" another voice yelled. "Here, somebody, help me hold Jack."

"I want to get at that ginger-colored nigger. Tear him limb from limb," the first voice yelled.

I stood against the ropes trembling. For in those days I was what they called ginger-colored, and he sounded as though he might crunch me between his teeth like a crisp ginger cookie.

Quite a struggle was going on. Chairs were being kicked about and I could hear voices grunting as with a terrific effort. I wanted to see, to see more desperately than ever before. But the blindfold was as tight as a thick skinpuckering scab and when I raised my gloved hands to push the layers of white aside a voice yelled, "Oh, no you don't, black bastard! Leave that alone!"

20    "Ring the bell before Jackson kills him a coon!" someone boomed in the sudden silence. And I heard the bell clang and the sound of the feet scuffling forward.

A glove smacked against my head. I pivoted, striking out stiffly as someone went past, and felt the jar ripple along the length of my arm to my shoulder. Then it seemed as though all nine of the boys had turned upon me at once. Blows pounded me from all sides while I struck out as best I could. So many blows landed upon me that I wondered if I were not the only blindfolded fighter in the ring, or if the man called Jackson hadn't succeeded in getting me after all.

Blindfolded, I could no longer control my motions. I had no dignity. I stumbled about like a baby or a drunken man. The smoke had become thicker and with each new blow it seemed to sear and further restrict my lungs. My saliva became like hot bitter glue. A glove connected with my head, filling my mouth with warm blood. It was everywhere. I could not tell if the moisture I felt upon my body was sweat or blood. A blow landed hard against the nape of my neck. I felt myself going over, my head hitting the floor. Streaks of blue light filled the black world behind the blindfold. I lay prone, pretending that I was knocked out, but felt myself seized by hands and yanked to my feet. "Get going, black boy! Mix it up!" My arms were like lead, my head smarting from blows. I managed to feel my way to the ropes and held on, trying to catch my breath. A glove landed in my midsection and I went over again, feeling as though the smoke had become a knife jabbed into my guts. Pushed this way and that by the legs milling around me, I finally pulled erect and discovered that I could see the black, sweat-washed forms weaving in the smoky-blue atmosphere like drunken dancers weaving to the rapid drum-like thuds of blows.

Everyone fought hysterically. It was complete anarchy. Everybody fought everybody else. No group fought together for long. Two, three, four, fought one, then turned to fight each other, were themselves attacked. Blows landed below the belt and in the kidney, with the gloves open as well as closed, and with my eye partly opened now there was not so much terror. I moved carefully, avoiding blows, although not too many to attract attention, fighting from group to group. The boys groped about like blind, cautious crabs crouching to protect their midsections, their heads pulled in short against their shoulders, their arms stretched nervously before them, with their fists testing the smoke-filled air like the knobbed feelers of hypersensitive snails. In one corner I glimpsed a boy violently punching the air and heard him scream in pain as he smashed his hand against a ring post.

For a second I saw him bent over holding his hand, then going down as a blow caught his unprotected head. I played one group against the other, slipping in and throwing a punch then stepping out of range while pushing the others into the melee to take the blows blindly aimed at me. The smoke was agonizing and there were no rounds, no bells at three minute intervals to relieve our exhaustion. The room spun round me, a swirl of lights, smoke, seating bodies surrounded by tense white faces. I bled from both nose and mouth, the blood spattering upon my chest.

The men kept yelling, "Slug him, black boy! Knock his guts out!"

"Uppercut him! Kill him! Kill that big boy!"

Taking a fake fall, I saw a boy going down heavily beside me as though we were felled by a single blow, saw a sneaker-clad foot shoot into his groin as the two who had knocked him down stumbled upon him. I rolled out of range, feeling a twinge of nausea.

The harder we fought the more threatening the men became. And yet, I had begun to worry about my speech again. How would it go? Would they recognize my ability? What would they give me?

I was fighting automatically and suddenly I noticed that one after another of the boys was leaving the ring. I was surprised, filled with panic, as though I had been left alone with an unknown danger. Then I understood. The boys had arranged it among themselves. It was the custom for the two men left in the ring to slug it out for the winner's prize. I discovered this too late. When the bell sounded two men in tuxedoes leaped into the ring and removed the blindfold. I found myself facing Tatlock, the biggest of the gang. I felt sick at my stomach. Hardly had the bell stopped ringing in my ears than it clanged again and I saw him moving

25

swiftly toward me. Thinking of nothing else to do I hit him smash on the nose. He kept coming, bringing the rank sharp violence of stale sweat. His face was a black blank of a face, only his eyes alive—with hate of me and aglow with a feverish terror from what had happened to us all. I became anxious. I wanted to deliver my speech and he came at me as though he meant to beat it out of me. I smashed him again and again, taking his blows as they came. Then on a sudden impulse I struck him lightly and as we clinched, I whispered, "Fake like I knocked you out, you can have the prize."

30       "I'll break your behind," he whispered hoarsely.

"For *them?*"

"For *me*, sonofabitch!"

They were yelling for us to break it up and Tatlock spun me half around with a blow, and as a joggled camera sweeps in a reeling scene, I saw the howling red faces crouching tense beneath the cloud of blue-gray smoke. For a moment the world wavered, unraveled, flowed, then my head cleared and Tatlock bounced before me. That fluttering shadow before my eyes was his jabbing left hand. Then falling forward, my head against his damp shoulder, I whispered,

"I'll make it five dollars more."

35       "Go to hell!"

But his muscles relaxed a trifle beneath my pressure and I breathed, "Seven!"

"Give it to your ma," he said, ripping me beneath the heart.

And while I still held him I butted him and moved away. I felt myself bombarded with punches. I fought back with hopeless desperation. I wanted to deliver my speech more than anything else in the world, because I felt that only these men could judge truly my ability, and now this stupid clown was ruining my chances. I began fighting carefully now, moving in to punch him and out again with my greater speed. A lucky blow to his chin and I had him going too—until I heard a loud voice yell, "I got my money on the big boy."

Hearing this, I almost dropped my guard. I was confused: Should I try to win against the voice out there? Would not this go against my speech, and was not this a moment for humility, for nonresistance? A blow to my head as I danced about sent my right eye popping like a jack-in-the-box and settled my dilemma. The room went red as I fell. It was a dream fall, my body languid and fastidious as to where to land, until the floor became impatient and smashed up to meet me. A moment later I came to. An hypnotic voice said FIVE emphatically. And I lay there, hazily watching a dark red spot of my own blood shaping itself into a butterfly, glistening and soaking into the soiled gray world of the canvas.

40       When the voice drawled TEN I was lifted up and dragged to a chair. I sat dazed. My eye pained and swelled with each throb of my pounding heart and I wondered if now I would be allowed to speak. I was wringing wet, my mouth still bleeding. We were grouped along the wall now. The other boys ignored me as they congratulated Tatlock and speculated as to how much they would be paid. One boy whimpered over his smashed hand. Looking up front, I saw attendants in white jackets rolling the portable ring away and placing a small square rug in the vacant space surrounded by chairs. Perhaps, I thought, I will stand on the rug to deliver my speech.

Then the M.C. called to us, "Come on up here boys and get your money."

We ran forward to where the men laughed and talked in their chairs, waiting. Everyone seemed friendly now.

"There it is on the rug," the man said. I saw the rug covered with coins of all dimensions and a few crumpled bills. But what excited me, scattered here and there, were the gold pieces.

"Boys, it's all yours," the man said. "You get all you grab."

45       "That's right, Sambo," a blond man said, winking at me confidentially.

I trembled with excitement, forgetting my pain. I would get the gold and the bills, I thought. I would use both hands. I would throw my body against the boys nearest me to block them from the gold.

"Get down around the rug now," the man commanded, "and don't anyone touch it until I give the signal."

"This ought to be good," I heard.

As told, we got around the square rug on our knees. Slowly the man raised his freckled hand as we followed it upward with our eyes.

I heard, "These niggers look like they're about to pray!"                                                    50

Then, "Ready," the man said. "Go!"

I lunged for a yellow coin lying on the blue design of the carpet, touching it and sending a surprised shriek to join those rising around me. I tried frantically to remove my hand but could not let go. A hot, violent force tore through my body, shaking me like a wet rat. The rug was electrified. The hair bristled up on my head as I shook myself free. My muscles jumped, my nerves jangled, writhed. But I saw that this was not stopping the other boys. Laughing in fear and embarrassment, some were holding back and scooping up the coins knocked off by the painful contortions of the others. The men roared above us as we struggled.

"Pick it up, goddamnit, pick it up!" someone called like a bass-voiced parrot. "Go on, get it!"

I crawled rapidly around the floor, picking up the coins, trying to avoid the coppers and to get greenbacks and the gold. Ignoring the shock by laughing, as I brushed the coins off quickly, I discovered that I could contain the electricity—a contradiction, but it works. Then the men began to push us onto the rug. Laughing embarrassedly, we struggled out of their hands and kept after the coins. We were all wet and slippery and hard to hold. Suddenly I saw a boy lifted into the air, glistening with sweat like a circus seal, and dropped, his wet back landing flush upon the charged rug, heard him yell and saw him literally dance upon his back, his elbows beating a frenzied tattoo upon the floor, his muscles twitching like the flesh of a horse stung by many flies. When he finally rolled off, his face was gray and no one stopped him when he ran from the floor amid booming laughter.

"Get the money," the M.C. called. "That's good hard American cash!"                                         55

And we snatched and grabbed, snatched and grabbed. I was careful not to come too close to the rug now, and when I felt the hot whiskey breath descend upon me like a cloud of foul air I reached out and grabbed the leg of a chair. It was occupied and I held on desperately.

"Leggo, nigger! Leggo!"

The huge face wavered down to mine as he tried to push me free. But my body was slippery and he was too drunk. It was Mr. Colcord, who owned a chain of movie houses and "entertainment palaces." Each time he grabbed me I slipped out of his hands. It became a real struggle. I feared the rug more than I did the drunk, so I held on, surprising myself for a moment by trying to topple him upon the rug. It was such an enormous idea that I found myself actually carrying it out. I tried not to be obvious, yet when I grabbed his leg, trying to tumble him out of the chair, he raised up roaring with laughter, and, looking at me with soberness dead in the eye, kicked me viciously in the chest. The chair leg flew out of my hand. I felt myself going and rolled. It was as though I had rolled through a bed of hot coals. It seemed a whole century would pass before I would roll free, a century in which I was scared through the deepest levels of my body to the fearful breath within me and the breath seared and heated to the point of explosion. It'll all be over in a flash, I thought as I rolled clear. It'll all be over in a flash.

But not yet, the men on the other side were waiting, red faces swollen as though from apoplexy as they bent forward in their chairs. Seeing their fingers coming toward me I rolled away as a fumbled football rolls off the receiver's fingertips, back into the coals. That time I luckily sent the rug sliding out of place and heard the coins ringing against the floor and the boys scuffling to pick them up and the M.C. calling, "All right, boys, that's all. Go get dressed and get your money."

I was limp as a dish rag. My back felt as though it had been beaten with wires.                               60

When we had dressed the M.C. came in and gave us each five dollars, except Tatlock, who got ten for being last in the ring. Then he told us to leave. I was not to get a chance to deliver my speech, I thought. I was going out into the dim alley in despair when I was stopped and told to go back. I returned to the ballroom, where the men were pushing back their chairs and gathering in groups to talk.

The M.C. knocked on a table for quiet. "Gentlemen," he said, "we almost forgot an important part of the program. A most serious part, gentlemen. This boy was brought here to deliver a speech which he made at his graduation yesterday. . . ."

"Bravo!"

"I'm told that he is the smartest boy we've got out there in Greenwood. I'm told that he knows more big words than a pocket-sized dictionary."

65 Much applause and laughter.

"So now, gentlemen, I want you to give him your attention."

There was still laughter as I faced them, my mouth dry, my eye throbbing. I began slowly, but evidently my throat was tense, because they began shouting, "Louder! Louder!"

"We of the younger generation extol the wisdom of that great leader and educator," I shouted, "who first spoke these flaming words of wisdom: 'A ship lost at sea for many days suddenly sighted a friendly vessel. From the mast of the unfortunate vessel was seen a signal: "Water, water; we die of thirst!" The answer from the friendly vessel came back: "Cast down your bucket where you are." The captain of the distressed vessel, at last heeding the injunction, cast down his bucket, and it came up full of fresh sparkling water from the mouth of the Amazon River.' And like him I say, and in his words, 'To those of my race who depend upon bettering their condition in a foreign land, or who underestimate the importance of cultivating friendly relations with the Southern white man, who is his next-door neighbor, I would say: "Cast down your bucket where you are"—cast it down in making friends in every manly way of the people of all races by whom we are surrounded. . . ."

I spoke automatically and with such fervor that I did not realize that the men were still talking and laughing until my dry mouth, filling up with blood from the cut, almost strangled me. I coughed, wanting to stop and go to one of the tall brass, sand-filled spittoons to relieve myself, but a few of the men, especially the superintendent, were listening and I was afraid. So I gulped it down, blood, saliva and all, and continued. (What powers of endurance I had during those days! What enthusiasm! What a belief in the rightness of things!) I spoke even louder in spite of the pain. But still they talked and still they laughed, as though deaf with cotton in dirty ears. So I spoke with greater emotional emphasis. I closed my ears and swallowed blood until I was nauseated. The speech seemed a hundred times as long as before, but I could not leave out a single word. All had to be said, each memorized nuance considered, rendered. Nor was that all. Whenever I uttered a word of three or more syllables a group of voices would yell for me to repeat it. I used the phrase "social responsibility" and they yelled:

70 "What's the word you say, boy?"

"Social responsibility," I said.

"What?"

"Social . . . ."

"Louder."

75 ". . . responsibility."

"More!"

"Respon—"

"Repeat!"

"—sibility."

80 The room filled with the uproar of laughter until, no doubt, distracted by having to gulp down my blood, I made a mistake and yelled a phrase I had often seen denounced in newspaper editorials, heard debated in private.

"Social . . ."

"What?" they yelled.

". . . equality—"

The laughter hung smokelike in the sudden stillness. I opened my eyes, puzzled. Sounds of displeasure filled the room. The M.C. rushed forward. They shouted hostile phrases at me. But I did not understand.

A small dry mustached man in the front row blared out, "Say that slowly, son!"          85

"What sir?"

"What you just said!"

"Social responsibility, sir," I said.

"You weren't being smart, were you, boy?" he said, not unkindly.

"No, sir!"          90

"You sure that about 'equality' was a mistake?"

"Oh, yes, sir," I said. "I was swallowing blood."

"Well, you had better speak more slowly so we can understand. We mean to do right by you, but you've got to know your place at all times. All right, now, go on with your speech."

I was afraid. I wanted to leave but I wanted also to speak and I was afraid they'd snatch me down.

"Thank you, sir," I said, beginning where I had left off, and having them ignore me as before.   95

Yet when I finished there was a thunderous applause. I was surprised to see the superintendent come forth with a package wrapped in white tissue paper, and, gesturing for quiet, address the men.

"Gentlemen, you see that I did not overpraise this boy. He makes a good speech and some day he'll lead his people in the proper paths. And I don't have to tell you that that is important in these days and times. This is a good, smart boy, and so to encourage him in the right direction, in the name of the Board of Education I wish to present him a prize in the form of this . . ."

He paused, removing the tissue paper and revealing a gleaming calfskin brief case.

". . . in the form of this first-class article from Shad Whitmore's shop."

"Boy," he said, addressing me, "take this prize and keep it well. Consider it a badge of   100
office. Prize it. Keep developing as you are and some day it will be filled with important papers that will help shape the destiny of your people."

I was so moved that I could hardly express my thanks. A rope of bloody saliva forming a shape like an undiscovered continent drooled upon the leather and I wiped it quickly away. I felt an importance that I had never dreamed.

"Open it and see what's inside," I was told.

My fingers a-tremble, I complied, smelling the fresh leather and finding an official-looking document inside. It was a scholarship to the state college for Negroes. My eyes filled with tears and I ran awkwardly off the floor.

I was overjoyed; I did not even mind when I discovered that the gold pieces I had scrambled for were brass pocket tokens advertising a certain make of automobile.

When I reached home everyone was excited. Next day the neighbors came to congratulate   105
me. I even felt safe from grandfather, whose deathbed curse usually spoiled my triumphs. I stood beneath his photograph with my brief case in hand and smiled triumphantly into his stolid black peasant's face. It was a face that fascinated me. The eyes seemed to follow everywhere I went.

That night I dreamed I was at a circus with him and that he refused to laugh at the clowns no matter what they did. Then later he told me to open my brief case and read what was inside and I did, finding an official envelope stamped with the state seal; and inside the envelope I found another and another, endlessly, and I thought I would fall of weariness. "Them's years," he said. "Now open that one." And I did and in it I found an engraved document containing a short message in letters of gold. "Read it," my grandfather said. "Out loud."

"To Whom It May Concern," I intoned. "Keep This Nigger-Boy Running."

I awoke with the old man's laughter ringing in my ears.

(It was a dream I was to remember and dream again for many years after. But at the time I had no insight into its meaning. First I had to attend college.)

## Questions

1. Describe the narrator. How old is he? What are the circumstances that lead him to the "gathering of the town's leading white citizens"? What conclusions do you draw about the mental and moral qualities of these citizens?

2. What is the significance of the advice given by the narrator's grandfather? What is the connection between the narrator's dream and the grandfather's advice?

3. What is a battle royal? What is the narrator's attitude toward the battle in which he is to participate? Why does he have this attitude? To what indignities are the boys subjected as a result of their appearance before the assembled townsmen? In what way is the female dancer's plight like that of the boys?

4. Describe how the story's structure underlies the story's attack on racism.

5. What special indignities are imposed on the narrator? Why does he have difficulty in delivering his speech? Why is he reminded that "you've got to know your place at all times" (paragraph 93)?

## THOMAS HARDY (1840–1928)

Hardy was born in Dorsetshire, in southwest England, which he called "Wessex" in his novels and poems. He began a career as an architect but gave it up to become a novelist. In 1898, after he had published his stories and more than a dozen novels, including *Tess of the D'Urbervilles, The Return of the Native*, and *Jude the Obscure*, he gave up novels and devoted himself to poetry. Before his death in 1928, he had published eight volumes of verse, which were collected and published posthumously in 1931.

##  The Three Strangers (1888)

Among the few features of agricultural England which retain an appearance but little modified by the lapse of centuries may be reckoned the high, grassy and furzy downs, coombs, or ewe-leases, as they are indifferently called, that fill a large area of certain counties in the south and southwest. If any mark of human occupation is met with hereon, it usually takes the form of the solitary cottage of some shepherd.

Fifty years ago such a lonely cottage stood on such a down, and may possibly be standing there now. In spite of its loneliness, however, the spot, by actual measurement, was not more than five miles from a county-town. Yet that affected it little. Five miles of irregular upland, during the long inimical seasons, with their sleets, snows, rains, and mists, afford withdrawing space enough to isolate a Timon or a Nebuchadnezzar;° much less, in fair weather, to please that less repellent tribe, the poets, philosophers, artists, and others who "conceive and meditate of pleasant things."

Some old earthen camp or barrow, some clump of trees, at least some starved fragment of ancient hedge is usually taken advantage of in the erection of these forlorn dwellings. But, in the present case, such a kind of shelter had been disregarded. Higher Crowstairs, as the house was called, stood quite detached and undefended. The only reason for its precise situation seemed to be the crossing of two footpaths at right angles hard by, which may have crossed there and thus for a good five hundred years. Hence the house was exposed to the elements on all sides. But, though the wind up here blew unmistakably when it did blow, and the rain hit hard whenever it fell, the various weathers of the winter season were not quite so formidable on the coomb as they were imagined to be by dwellers on low ground. The raw rimes° were not so pernicious as in the hollows, and the frosts were scarcely so severe. When the shepherd and his family who tenanted the house were pitied for their sufferings from the exposure, they said that upon the whole they were less inconvenienced by "wuzzes and flames" (hoarses and phlegms) than when they had lived by the stream of a snug neighboring valley.

The night of March 28, 182–, was precisely one of the nights that were wont to call forth these expressions of commiseration. The level rainstorm smote walls, slopes, and hedges like the clothyard shafts of Senlac and Crécy.° Such sheep and outdoor animals as had no shelter stood with their buttocks to the winds; while the tails of little birds trying to roost on some scraggy thorn were blown inside-out like umbrellas. The gable-end of the cottage was stained with wet, and the eavesdroppings flapped against the wall. Yet never was commiseration for the shepherd more misplaced. For that cheerful rustic was entertaining a large party in glorification of the christening of his second girl.

The guests had arrived before the rain began to fall, and they were all now assembled in the chief or living room of the dwelling. A glance into the apartment at eight o'clock on this eventful evening would have resulted in the opinion that it was as cozy and comfortable a nook as could be wished for in boisterous weather. The calling of its inhabitant was proclaimed by a number of highly polished sheep crooks without stems that were hung ornamentally over the fireplace, the curl of each shining crook varying from the antiquated type engraved in the patriarchal pictures of old family Bibles to the most approved fashion of the last local sheep-fair. The room was lighted by half a dozen candles having wicks only a trifle smaller than the grease which enveloped them, in candlesticks that were never used but at high-days, holy-days, and family feasts. The lights were scattered about the room, two of them standing on the chimney piece. This position of candles was in itself significant. Candles on the chimney piece always meant a party.

On the hearth, in front of a back-brand to give substance, blazed a fire of thorns, that crackled "like the laughter of the fool."°

Nineteen persons were gathered here. Of these, five women, wearing gowns of various bright hues, sat in chairs along the wall; girls shy and not shy filled the window-bench; four men, including Charley Jake the hedge-carpenter, Elijah New the parish-clerk, and John Pitcher,

5

---

°Both Timon and Nebuchadnezzar were proverbial for their solitude. The ancient Greek Timon was disappointed because he did not receive the advancement he expected, and he therefore withdrew from society totally. Nebuchadnezzar was the Babylonian king who, suffering from the delusion that he was an ox, was driven away from society to eat with beasts (Daniel 4).

°Coatings of frost.

°"Clothyard shafts" were 36-inch arrows. Senlac and Crécy were battlefields in France where, in the middle ages, armies of English bowmen had defeated numerically superior French forces.

°Ecclesiastes 7:6.

a neighboring dairyman, the shepherd's father-in-law, lolled in the settle; a young man and maid, who were blushing over tentative *pourparlers* on a life-companionship,° sat beneath the corner-cupboard; and an elderly engaged man of fifty or upward moved restlessly about from spots where his betrothed was not to the spot where she was. Enjoyment was pretty general, and so much the more prevailed in being unhampered by conventional restrictions. Absolute confidence in each other's good opinion begat perfect ease, while the finishing stroke of manner, amounting to a truly princely serenity, was lent to the majority by the absence of any expression or trait denoting that they wished to get on in the world, enlarge their minds, or do any eclipsing thing whatever—which nowadays so generally nips the bloom and *bonhomie* of all except the two extremes of the social scale.

Shepherd Fennel had married well, his wife being a dairyman's daughter from a vale at a distance, who brought fifty guineas in her pocket and kept them there, till they should be required for ministering to the needs of a coming family. This frugal woman had been somewhat exercised as to the character that should be given to the gathering. A sit-still party had its advantages; but an undisturbed position of ease in chairs and settles was apt to lead on the men to such an unconscionable deal of toping that they would sometimes fairly drink the house dry. A dancing-party was the alternative; but this, while avoiding the foregoing objection on the score of good drink, had a counterbalancing disadvantage in the matter of good victuals, the ravenous appetites engendered by the exercise causing immense havoc in the buttery. Shepherdess Fennel fell back upon the intermediate plan of mingling short dances with short periods of talk and singing, so as to hinder any ungovernable rage in either. But this scheme was entirely confined to her own gentle mind: the shepherd himself was in the mood to exhibit the most reckless phases of hospitality.

The fiddler was a boy of those parts, about twelve years of age, who had a wonderful dexterity in jigs and reels, though his fingers were so small and short as to necessitate a constant shifting for the high notes, from which he scrambled back to the first position with sounds not of unmixed purity of tone. At seven the shrill tweedle-dee of this youngster had begun, accompanied by a booming ground-bass from Elijah New, the parish-clerk, who had thoughtfully brought with him his favorite musical instrument, the serpent. Dancing was instantaneous, Mrs. Fennel privately enjoining the players on no account to let the dance exceed the length of a quarter of an hour.

10    But Elijah and the boy, in the excitement of their position, quite forgot the injunction. Moreover, Oliver Giles, a man of seventeen, one of the dancers, who was enamored of his partner, a fair girl of thirty-three rolling years, had recklessly handed a new crown-piece to the musicians, as a bribe to keep going as long as they had muscle and wind. Mrs. Fennel, seeing the steam begin to generate on the countenances of her guests, crossed over and touched the fiddler's elbow and put her hand on the serpent's mouth. But they took no notice, and fearing she might lose her character of genial hostess if she were to interfere too markedly, she retired and sat down helpless. And so the dance whizzed on with cumulative fury, the performers moving in their planet-like courses, direct and retrograde, from apogee to perigee, till the hand of the well-kicked clock at the bottom of the room had traveled over the circumference of an hour.

While these cheerful events were in course of enactment within Fennel's pastoral dwelling, an incident having considerable bearing on the party had occurred in the gloomy night without. Mrs. Fennel's concern about the growing fierceness of the dance corresponded in point of time with the ascent of a human figure to the solitary hill of Higher Crowstairs from the direction of the distant town. This personage strode on through the rain without a pause, following the little-worn path which, further on in its course, skirted the shepherd's cottage.

---

°A pourparler is a conversation held prior to negotiation.

It was nearly the time of full moon, and on this account, though the sky was lined with a uniform sheet of dripping cloud, ordinary objects out of doors were readily visible. The sad, wan light revealed the lonely pedestrian to be a man of supple frame; his gait suggested that he had somewhat passed the period of perfect and instinctive agility, though not so far as to be otherwise than rapid of motion when occasion required. At a rough guess, he might have been about forty years of age. He appeared tall, but a recruiting sergeant, or other person accustomed to the judging of men's heights by the eye, would have discerned that this was chiefly owing to his gauntness, and that he was not more than five-feet eight or nine.

Notwithstanding the regularity of his tread, there was caution in it, as in that of one who mentally feels his way; and despite the fact that it was not a black coat nor a dark garment of any sort that he wore, there was something about him which suggested that he naturally belonged to the black-coated tribes of men. His clothes were of fustian,° and his boots hobnailed, yet in his progress he showed not the mud-accustomed bearing of hobnailed and fustianed peasantry.

By the time that he had arrived abreast of the shepherd's premises the rain came down, or rather came along, with yet more determined violence. The outskirts of the little settlement partially broke the force of wind and rain, and this induced him to stand still. The most salient of the shepherd's domestic erections was an empty sty at the forward corner of his hedgeless garden, for in these latitudes the principle of masking the homelier features of your establishment by a conventional frontage was unknown. The traveler's eye was attracted to this small building by the pallid shine of the wet slates that covered it. He turned aside, and, finding it empty, stood under the pent-roof for shelter.

While he stood, the boom of the serpent within the adjacent house, and the lesser strains of the fiddler, reached the spot as an accompaniment to the surging hiss of the flying rain on the sod, its louder beating on the cabbage-leaves of the garden, on the eight or ten beehives just discernible by the path, and its dripping from the eaves into a row of buckets and pans that had been placed under the walls of the cottage. For at Higher Crowstairs, as at all such elevated domiciles, the grand difficulty of housekeeping was an insufficiency of water; and a casual rainfall was utilized by turning out, as catchers, every utensil that the house contained. Some queer stories might be told of the contrivances for economy in suds and dishwaters that are absolutely necessitated in upland habitations during the droughts of summer. But at this season there were no such exigencies; a mere acceptance of what the skies bestowed was sufficient for an abundant store.

At last the notes of the serpent ceased and the house was silent. This cessation of activity aroused the solitary pedestrian from the reverie into which he had elapsed, and, emerging from the shed, with an apparently new intention, he walked up the path to the house-door. Arrived here, his first act was to kneel down on a large stone beside the row of vessels, and to drink a copious draught from one of them. Having quenched his thirst, he rose and lifted his hand to knock, but paused with his eye upon the panel. Since the dark surface of the wood revealed absolutely nothing, it was evident that he must be mentally looking through the door, as if he wished to measure thereby all the possibilities that a house of this sort might include, and how they might bear upon the question of his entry.

In his indecision he turned and surveyed the scene around. Not a soul was anywhere visible. The garden path stretched downward from his feet, gleaming like the track of a snail; the roof of the little well (mostly dry), the well-cover, the top rail of the garden-gate, were varnished with the same dull liquid glaze; while, far away in the vale, a faint whiteness of more than usual extent showed that the rivers were high in the meads. Beyond all this winked a few bleared lamplights through the beating drops—lights that denoted the situation of the county-town

15

---

°Fustian was a thick, coarse cloth.

from which he had appeared to come. The absence of all notes of life in that direction seemed to clinch his intentions, and he knocked at the door.

Within, a desultory chat had taken the place of movement and musical sound. The hedge-carpenter was suggesting a song to the company, which nobody just then was inclined to undertake, so that the knock afforded a not unwelcome diversion.

"Walk in!" said the shepherd, promptly.

20   The latch clicked upward, and out of the night our pedestrian appeared upon the door-mat. The shepherd arose, snuffed two of the nearest candles, and turned to look at him.

Their light disclosed that the stranger was dark in complexion and not unprepossessing as to feature. His hat, which for a moment he did not remove, hung low over his eyes, without concealing that they were large, open, and determined, moving with a flash rather than a glance round the room. He seemed pleased with his survey, and, baring his shaggy head, said, in a rich, deep voice: "The rain is so heavy friends, that I ask leave to come in and rest awhile."

"To be sure, Stranger," said the shepherd. "And faith, you've been lucky in choosing your time, for we are having a bit of a fling for a glad cause—though, to be sure, a man could hardly wish that glad cause to happen more than once a year."

"Nor less," spoke up a woman. "For 'tis best to get your family over and done with, as soon as you can, so as to be all the earlier out of the fag o't."

"And what may be this glad cause?" asked the stranger.

25   "A birth and christening," said the shepherd.

The stranger hoped his host might not be made unhappy either by too many or too few of such episodes and, being invited by a gesture to a pull at the mug, he readily acquiesced. His manner, which, before entering, had been so dubious, was now altogether that of a careless and candid man.

"Late to be traipsing athwart this coomb—hey?" said the engaged man of fifty. "Late it is, Master, as you say.—I'll take a seat in the chimney corner, if you have nothing to urge against it, Ma'am; for I am a little moist on the side that was next the rain."

Mrs. Shepherd Fennel assented, and made room for the self-invited comer, who, having got completely inside the chimney corner, stretched out his legs and arms with the expansiveness of a person quite at home.

"Yes, I am rather cracked in the vamp," he said freely, seeing that the eyes of the shepherd's wife fell upon his boots, "and I am not well fitted either. I have had some rough times lately, and have been forced to pick up what I can get in the way of wearing, but I must find a suit better fit for working-days when I reach home."

30   "One of hereabouts?" she inquired.

"Not quite that—further up the country."

"I thought so. And so be I; and by your tongue you come from my neighborhood."

"But you would hardly have heard of me," he said quickly. "My time would be long before yours, Ma'am, you see."

This testimony to the youthfulness of his hostess had the effect of stopping her cross-examination.

35   "There is only one thing more wanted to make me happy," continued the newcomer, "and that is a little baccy, which I am sorry to say I am out of."

"I'll fill your pipe," said the shepherd.

"I must ask you to lend me a pipe likewise."

"A smoker, and no pipe about 'ee?"

"I have dropped it somewhere on the road."

40   The shepherd filled and handed him a new clay pipe, saying, as he did so, "Hand me your baccy-box—I'll fill that too, now I am about it."

The man went through the movement of searching his pockets.

"Lost that too?" said his entertainer, with some surprise.

"I am afraid so," said the man with some confusion. "Give it to me in a screw of paper." Lighting his pipe at the candle with a suction that drew the whole flame into the bowl, he resettled himself in the corner and bent his looks upon the faint steam from his damp legs, as if he wished to say no more.

Meanwhile the general body of guests had been taking little notice of this visitor by reason of an absorbing discussion in which they were engaged with the band about a tune for the next dance. The matter being settled, they were about to stand up when an interruption came in the shape of another knock at the door.

At sound of the same the man in the chimney corner took up the poker and began stirring the brands as if doing it thoroughly were the one aim of his existence; and a second time the shepherd said, "Walk in!" In a moment another man stood upon the straw-woven door-mat. He too was a stranger.

45

This individual was one of a type radically different from the first. There was more of the commonplace in his manner, and a certain jovial cosmopolitanism sat upon his features. He was several years older than the first arrival, his hair being slightly frosted, his eyebrows bristly, and his whiskers cut back from his cheeks. His face was rather full and flabby, and yet it was not altogether a face without power. A few grog-blossoms marked the neighborhood of his nose. He flung back his long drab greatcoat, revealing that beneath it he wore a suit of cinder-gray shade throughout, large heavy seals, of some metal or other that would take a polish, dangling from his fob as his only personal ornament. Shaking the water drops from his low-crowned glazed hat, he said, "I must ask for a few minutes' shelter, comrades, or I shall be wetted to my skin before I get to Casterbridge."

"Make yourself at home, Master," said the shepherd, perhaps a trifle less heartily than on the first occasion. Not that Fennel had the least tinge of niggardliness in his composition; but the room was far from large, spare chairs were not numerous, and damp companions were not altogether desirable at close quarters for the women and girls in their bright-colored gowns.

However, the second comer, after taking off his greatcoat, and hanging his hat on a nail in one of the ceiling-beams as if he had been specially invited to put it there, advanced and sat down at the table. This had been pushed so closely into the chimney corner, to give all available room to the dancers, that its inner edge grazed the elbow of the man who had ensconced himself by the fire; and thus the two strangers were brought into close companionship. They nodded to each other by way of breaking the ice of unacquaintance, and the first stranger handed his neighbor the family mug—a huge vessel of brown ware, having its upper edge worn away like a threshold by the rub of whole generations of thirsty lips that had gone the way of all flesh, and bearing the following inscription burnt upon its rotund side in yellow letters:

THERE IS NO FUN
UNTIL i CUM

The other man, nothing loath, raised the mug to his lips, and drank on, and on, and on—till a curious blueness overspread the countenance of the shepherd's wife, who had regarded with no little surprise the first stranger's free offer to the second of what did not belong to him to dispense.

"I knew it!" said the toper to the shepherd with much satisfaction. "When I walked up your garden before coming in, and saw the hives all of a row, I said to myself, 'Where there's bees there's honey, and where there's honey there's mead.' But mead of such a truly comfortable sort as this I really didn't expect to meet in my older days." He took yet another pull at the mug, till it assumed an ominous elevation.

"Glad you enjoy it!" said the shepherd, warmly.

"It is goodish mead," assented Mrs. Fennel, with an absence of enthusiasm which seemed to say that it was possible to buy praise for one's cellar at too heavy a price. "It is trouble enough to make—and really I hardly think we shall make any more. For honey sells well, and

50

we ourselves can make shift with a drop o' small mead and metheglin for common use from the comb-washings."°

"Oh, but you'll never have the heart!" reproachfully cried the stranger in cinder-gray, after taking up the mug a third time and setting it down empty. "I love mead, when 'tis old like this, as I love to go to church o' Sundays, or to relieve the needy any day of the week."

"Ha, ha, ha!" said the man in the chimney corner, who, in spite of the taciturnity induced by the pipe of tobacco, could not or would not refrain from this slight testimony to his comrade's humor.

Now the old mead of those days, brewed of the purest first-year or maiden honey, four pounds to the gallon—with its due complement of white of eggs, cinnamon, ginger, cloves, mace, rosemary, yeast, and processes of working, bottling, and cellaring—tasted remarkably strong; but it did not taste so strong as it actually was. Hence, presently, the stranger in cinder-gray at the table, moved by its creeping influence, unbuttoned his waistcoat, threw himself back in his chair, spread his legs, and made his presence felt in various ways.

55 "Well, well, as I say," he resumed, "I am going to Casterbridge, and to Casterbridge I must go. I should have been almost there by this time; but the rain drove me into your dwelling, and I'm not sorry for it."

"You don't live in Casterbridge?" said the shepherd.

"Not as yet; though I shortly mean to move there."

"Going to set up in trade, perhaps?"

"No, no," said the shepherd's wife. "It is easy to see that the gentleman is rich, and don't want to work at anything."

60 The cinder-gray stranger paused, as if to consider whether he would accept that definition of himself. He presently rejected it by answering, "Rich is not quite the word for me, Dame. I do work, and I must work. And even if I only get to Casterbridge by midnight I must begin work there at eight tomorrow morning. Yes, heat or wet, blow or snow, famine or sword, my day's work tomorrow must be done."

"Poor man! Then, in spite o' seeming, you be worse off than we," replied the shepherd's wife.

"'Tis the nature of my trade, men and maidens. 'Tis the nature of my trade more than my poverty. . . . But really and truly I must up and off, or I shan't get a lodging in the town." However, the speaker did not move, and directly added, "There's time for one more draught of friendship before I go; and I'd perform it at once if the mug were not dry."

"Here's a mug o' small," said Mrs. Fennel. "Small, we call it, though to be sure 'tis only the first wash o' the combs."

"No," said the stranger, disdainfully. "I won't spoil your first kindness by partaking o' your second."

65 "Certainly not," broke in Fennel. "We don't increase and multiply every day, and I'll fill the mug again." He went away to the dark place under the stairs where the barrel stood. The shepherdess followed him.

"Why should you do this?" she said, reproachfully, as soon as they were alone. "He's emptied it once, though it held enough for ten people; and now he's not contented wi' the small, but must needs call for more o' the strong! And a stranger unbeknown to any of us. For my part, I don't like the look o' the man at all."

"But he's in the house, my honey; and 'tis a wet night, and a christening. Daze it, what's a cup of mead more or less? There'll be plenty more next bee-burning."

---

°Mead is an alcoholic drink made from honey. Metheglin was a cheaper drink made, with spices, from the water rinsed from the honeycomb after the better honey was extracted. See paragraph 54.

"Very well—this time, then," she answered, looking wistfully at the barrel. "But what is the man's calling, and where is he one of, that he should come in and join us like this?"

"I don't know. I'll ask him again."

The catastrophe of having the mug drained dry at one pull by the stranger in cinder-gray 70 was effectually guarded against this time by Mrs. Fennel. She poured out his allowance in a small cup, keeping the large one at a discreet distance from him. When he had tossed off his portion the shepherd renewed his inquiry about the stranger's occupation.

The latter did not immediately reply, and the man in the chimney corner, with sudden demonstrativeness, said, "Anybody may know my trade—I'm a wheelwright."

"A very good trade for these parts," said the shepherd.

"And anybody may know mine—if they've the sense the find it out," said the stranger in cinder-gray.

"You may generally tell what a man is by his claws," observed the hedge-carpenter, looking at his own hands. "My fingers be as full of thorns as an old pincushion is of pins."

The hands of the man in the chimney corner instinctively sought the shade, and he gazed 75 into the fire as he resumed his pipe. The man at the table took up the hedge-carpenter's remark, and added smartly, "True; but the oddity of my trade is that, instead of setting a mark upon me, it sets a mark upon my customers."

No observation being offered by anybody in elucidation of this enigma, the shepherd's wife once more called for a song. The same obstacles presented themselves as at the former time—one had no voice, another had forgotten the first verse. The stranger at the table, whose soul had now risen to a good working temperature, relieved the difficulty by exclaiming that, to start the company, he would sing himself. Thrusting one thumb into the armhold of his waistcoat, he waved the other hand in the air, and, with an extemporizing gaze at the shining sheepcrooks above the mantelpiece, began:

> O my trade it is the rarest one,
> > Simple shepherds all—
> My trade is a sight to see;
> For my customers I tie, and take them up on high,
> > And waft 'em to a far countree!

The room was silent when he had finished the verse—with one exception, that of the man in the chimney corner, who at the singer's word, "Chorus!" joined him in a deep bass voice of musical relish:

> And waft 'em to a far countree!

Oliver Giles, John Pitcher the dairyman, the parish-clerk, the engaged man of fifty, the row of young women against the wall, seemed lost in thought not of the gayest kind. The shepherd looked meditatively on the ground, the shepherdess gazed keenly at the singer, and with some suspicion; she was doubting whether this stranger were merely singing an old song from recollection, or was composing one there and then for the occasion. All were as perplexed at the obscure revelation as the guests at Belshazzar's Feast,° except the man in the chimney corner, who quietly said, "Second verse, stranger," and smoked on.

---

°The famous handwriting on the wall, predicting the downfall of the ancient Babylonian kingdom, happened at Belshazzar's Feast (Daniel 5).

The singer thoroughly moistened himself from his lips inward, and went on with the next stanza as requested:

> My tools are but common ones,
>                    Simple shepherds all—
> My tools are no sight to see:
> A little hempen string, and a post whereon to swing,
> Are implements enough for me!

Shepherd Fennel glanced round. There was no longer any doubt that the stranger was answering his question rhythmically. The guests one and all started back with suppressed exclamations. The young woman engaged to the man of fifty fainted halfway, and would have proceeded, but finding him wanting in alacrity for catching her she sat down trembling.

80    "Oh, he's the!" whispered the people in the background, mentioning the name of an ominous public officer. "He's come to do it! 'Tis to be at Casterbridge jail tomorrow—the man for sheep-stealing—the poor clockmaker we heard of, who used to live at Shottsford and had no work to do—Timothy Summers, whose family were astarving, and so he went out of Shottsford by the highroad, and took a sheep in open daylight, defying the farmer and the farmer's wife and the farmer's lad, and every man jack among 'em. He" (and they nodded toward the stranger of the deadly trade) "is come from up the country to do it because there's not enough to do in his own county-town, and he's got the place here now our own countyman's dead; he's going to live in the same cottage under the prison wall."

The stranger in cinder-gray took no notice of this whispered string of observations, but again wetted his lips. Seeing that his friend in the chimney corner was the only one who reciprocated his joviality in any way, he held out his cup toward that appreciative comrade, who also held out his own. They clinked together, the eyes of the rest of the room hanging upon the singer's actions. He parted his lips for the third verse; but at that moment another knock was audible upon the door. This time the knock was faint and hesitating.

The company seemed scared; the shepherd looked with consternation toward the entrance, and it was with some effort that he resisted his alarmed wife's deprecatory glance, and uttered for the third time the welcoming words, "Walk in!"

The door was gently opened, and another man stood upon the mat. He, like those who had preceded him, was a stranger. This time it was a short, small personage, of fair complexion, and dressed in a decent suit of dark clothes.

"Can you tell me the way to—?" he began: when, gazing round the room to observe the nature of the company among whom he had fallen, his eyes lighted on the stranger in cinder-gray. It was just at the instant when the latter, who had thrown his mind into his song with such a will that he scarcely heeded the interruption, silenced all whispers and inquiries by bursting into his third verse:

> Tomorrow is my working day,
>                    Simple shepherds all—
> Tomorrow is a working day for me:
> For the farmer's sheep is slain, and the lad who did it ta'en,
> And on his soul may God ha' merc-y!

The stranger in the chimney corner, waving cups with the singer so heartily that his mead splashed over on the hearth, repeated in his bass voice as before:

> And on his soul may God ha' merc-y!

All this time the third stranger had been standing in the doorway. Finding now that he 85
did not come forward or go on speaking, the guests particularly regarded him. They noticed to
their surprise that he stood before them the picture of abject terror—his knees trembling, his
hand shaking so violently that the door-latch by which he supported himself rattled audibly:
his white lips were parted, and his eyes fixed on the merry officer of justice in the middle of the
room. A moment more and he had turned, closed the door, and fled.

"What a man can it be?" said the shepherd.

The rest, between the awfulness of their late discovery and the odd conduct of this third
visitor, looked as if they knew not what to think, and said nothing. Instinctively they withdrew
further and further from the grim gentleman in their midst, whom some of them seemed to
take for the Prince of Darkness° himself, till they formed a remote circle, an empty space of
floor being left between them and him—

. . . circulas, cujus centrum diabolus.°

The room was so silent—though there were more than twenty people in it—that nothing could
be heard but the patter of the rain against the window-shutters, accompanied by the occasional
hiss of a stray drop that fell down the chimney into the fire, and the steady puffing of the man
in the corner, who had now resumed his pipe of long clay.

The stillness was unexpectedly broken. The distant sound of a gun reverberated through
the air—apparently from the direction of the county-town.

"Be jiggered!" cried the stranger who had sung the song, jumping up.

"What does that mean?" asked several. 90

"A prisoner escaped from the jail—that's what it means. "

All listened. The sound was repeated, and none of them spoke but the man in the chimney
corner, who said quietly, "I've often been told that in this county they fire a gun at such times;
but I never heard it till now."

"I wonder if it is *my* man?" murmured the personage in cinder-gray.

"Surely it is!" said the shepherd involuntarily. "And surely we've zeed him! That little
man who looked in at the door by now, and quivered like a leaf when he zeed ye and heard
your song!"

"His teeth chattered, and the breath went out of his body," said the dairyman. 95

"And his heart seemed to sink within him like a stone," said Oliver Giles.

"And he bolted as if he'd been shot at," said the hedge-carpenter.

"True—his teeth chattered, and his heart seemed to sink; and he bolted as if he'd been
shot at," slowly summed up the man in the chimney corner.

"I didn't notice it," remarked the hangman.

"We were all awondering what made him run off in such a fright," faltered one of the 100
women against the wall, "and now 'tis explained!"

The firing of the alarm-gun went on at intervals, low and sullenly, and their suspicions became a certainty. The sinister gentleman in cinder-gray roused himself. "Is there a constable
here?" he asked, in thick tones. "If so, let him step forward."

The engaged man of fifty stepped quavering out from the wall, his betrothed beginning to
sob on the back of the chair.

"You are a sworn constable?"

"I be, Sir."

---

°i.e., the Devil.

° . . . circles, whose center [is] the devil.

105     "Then pursue the criminal at once, with assistance, and bring him back here. He can't have gone far."

"I will, Sir, I will—when I've got my staff. I'll go home and get it, and come sharp here, and start in a body."

"Staff!—never mind your staff; the man'll be gone!"

"But I can't do nothing without my staff—can I, William, and John, and Charles Jake? No; for there's the king's royal crown apainted on en in yaller and gold, and the lion and the unicorn, so as when I raise en up and hit my prisoner, 'tis made a lawful blow thereby. I wouldn't 'tempt to take up a man without my staff—no, not I. If I hadn't the law to gie me courage, why, instead o' my taking up him he might take up me!"

"Now, I'm a king's man myself, and can give you authority enough for this," said the formidable officer in gray. "Now then, all of ye, be ready. Have ye any lanterns?"

110     "Yes—have ye any lanterns? I demand it!" said the constable.

"And the rest of you able-bodied—"

"Able-bodied men—yes—the rest of ye!" said the constable.

"Have you some good stout staves and pitchforks—"

"Staves and pitchforks—in the name o' the law! And take 'em in yer hands and go in quest, and do as we in authority tell ye!"

115     Thus aroused, the men prepared to give chase. The evidence was, indeed, though circumstantial, so convincing, that but little argument was needed to show the shepherd's guests that after what they had seen it would look very much like connivance if they did not instantly pursue the unhappy third stranger, who could not as yet have gone more than a few hundred yards over such uneven country.

A shepherd is always well provided with lanterns; and, lighting these hastily, and with hurdle-staves in their hands, they poured out of the door, taking a direction along the crest of the hill, away from the town, the rain having fortunately a little abated.

Disturbed by the noise, or possibly by unpleasant dreams of her baptism, the child who had been christened began to cry heart-brokenly in the room overhead. These notes of grief came down through the chinks of the floor to the ears of the women below, who jumped up one by one, and seemed glad of the excuse to ascend and comfort the baby, for the incidents of the last half-hour greatly oppressed them. Thus in the space of two or three minutes the room on the ground-floor was deserted quite.

But it was not for long. Hardly had the sound of footsteps died away when a man returned round the corner of the house from the direction the pursuers had taken. Peeping in at the door, and seeing nobody there, he entered leisurely. It was the stranger of the chimney corner, who had gone out with the rest. The motive of his return was shown by his helping himself to a cut piece of skimmer cake that lay on a ledge beside where he had sat, and which he had apparently forgotten to take with him. He also poured out half a cup more mead from the quantity that remained, ravenously eating and drinking these as he stood. He had not finished when another figure came in just as quietly—his friend in cinder-gray.

"Oh—you here?" said the latter, smiling. "I thought you had gone to help in the capture." And this speaker also revealed the object of his return by looking solicitously round for the fascinating mug of old mead.

120     "And I thought you had gone," said the other, continuing his skimmer-cake with some effort.

"Well, on second thoughts, I felt there were enough without me," said the first confidentially, "and such a night as it is, too. Besides, 'tis the business o' the Government to take care of its criminal—not mine."

"True; so it is. And I felt as you did, that there were enough without me."

"I don't want to break my limbs running over the humps and hollows of this wild country."

"Nor I neither, between you and me."

"These shepherd-people are used to it—simple-minded souls, you know, stirred up to 125
anything in a moment. They'll have him ready for me before the morning, and no trouble to
me at all."

"They'll have him, and we shall have saved ourselves all labor in the matter."

"True, true. Well, my way is to Casterbridge; and 'tis as much as my legs will do to take
me that far. Going the same way?"

"No, I am sorry to say! I have to get home over there" (he nodded indefinitely to the
right), "and I feel as you do, that it is quite enough for my legs to do before bedtime."

The other had by this time finished the mead in the mug, after which, shaking hands
heartily at the door, and wishing each other well, they went their several ways.

In the meantime the company of pursuers had reached the end of the hog's-back elevation 130
which dominated this part of the down. They had decided on no particular plan of action; and,
finding that the man of the baleful trade was no longer in their company, they seemed quite
unable to form any such plan now. They descended in all directions down the hill, and
straightway several of the party fell into the snare set by Nature for all misguided midnight
ramblers over this part of the cretaceous formation. The "lanchets," or flint slopes, which belted
the escarpment at intervals of a dozen yards, took the less cautious ones unawares, and losing
their footing on the rubbly steep they slid sharply downward, the lanterns rolling from their
hands to the bottom, and there lying on their sides till the horn was scorched through.

When they had again gathered themselves together, the shepherd, as the man who knew the
country best, took the lead, and guided them round these treacherous inclines. The lanterns,
which seemed rather to dazzle their eyes and warn the fugitive than to assist them in the exploration, were extinguished, due silence was observed; and in this more rational order they plunged
into the vale. It was a grassy, briery, moist defile, affording some shelter to any person who had
sought it; but the party perambulated it in vain, and ascended on the other side. Here they wandered apart, and after an interval closed together again to report progress. At the second time of
closing in they found themselves near a lonely ash, the single tree on this part of the coomb, probably sown there by a passing bird some fifty years before. And here, standing a little to one side of
the trunk, as motionless as the trunk itself appeared the man they were in quest of, his outline
being well defined against the sky beyond. The band noiselessly drew up and faced him.

"Your money or your life!" said the constable sternly to the still figure.

"No, no," whispered John Pitcher. "'Tisn't our side ought to say that. That's the doctrine
of vagabonds like him, and we be on the side of the law."

"Well, well," replied the constable, impatiently; "I must say something, mustn't I? and if
you had all the weight o' this undertaking upon your mind, perhaps you'd say the wrong
thing, too!—Prisoner at the bar, surrender in the name of the Father—the Crown, I mane!"

The man under the tree seemed now to notice them for the first time, and, giving them no 135
opportunity whatever for exhibiting their courage, he strolled slowly toward them. He was,
indeed, the little man, the third stranger; but his trepidation had in a great measure gone.

"Well, travelers," he said, "did I hear you speak to me?"

"You did; you've got to come and be our prisoner at once!" said the constable. "We arrest
'ee on the charge of not biding in Casterbridge jail in a decent proper manner to be hung tomorrow morning. Neighbors, do your duty, and seize the culprit!"

On hearing the charge, the man seemed enlightened, and, saying not another word, resigned himself with preternatural civility to the search-party, who, with their staves in their
hands, surrounded him on all sides, and marched him back toward the shepherd's cottage.

It was eleven o'clock by the time they arrived. The light shining from the open door, a
sound of men's voices within, proclaimed to them as they approached the house that some
new events had arisen in their absence. On entering they discovered the shepherd's living-
room to be invaded by two officers from Casterbridge jail, and a well-known magistrate

who lived at the nearest county-seat, intelligence of the escape having become generally circulated.

140   "Gentlemen," said the constable, "I have brought back your man—not without risk and danger; but everyone must do his duty! He is inside this circle of able-bodied persons, who have lent me useful aid, considering their ignorance of Crown work.—Men, bring forward your prisoner!" And the third stranger was led to the light.

"Who is this?" said one of the officials.

"The man," said the constable.

"Certainly not," said the turnkey; and the first corroborated his statement.

"But how can it be otherwise?" asked the constable. "Or why was he so terrified at sight o' the singing instrument of the law who sat there?" Here he related the strange behavior of the third stranger on entering the house during the hangman's song.

145   "Can't understand it," said the officer coolly. "All I know is that it is not the condemned man. He's quite a different character from this one; a gauntish fellow, with dark hair and eyes, rather good-looking, and with a musical bass voice that if you heard it once you'd never mistake as long as you lived."

"Why, souls—'twas the man in the chimney corner!"

"Hey—what?" said the magistrate, coming forward after inquiring particulars from the shepherd in the background. "Haven't you got the man after all?"

"Well, Sir," said the constable, "he's the man we were in search of, that's true; and yet he's not the man we were in search of. For the man we were in search of was not the man we wanted, Sir, if you understand my everyday way; for 'twas the man in the chimney corner!"

"A pretty kettle of fish altogether!" said the magistrate. "You had better start for the other man at once."

150   The prisoner now spoke for the first time. The mention of the man in the chimney corner seemed to have moved him as nothing else could do. "Sir," he said, stepping forward to the magistrate, "take no more trouble about me. The time is come when I may as well speak. I have done nothing; my crime is that the condemned man is my brother. Early this afternoon I left home at Shottsford to tramp it all the way to Casterbridge jail to bid him farewell. I was benighted, and called here to rest and ask the way. When I opened the door I saw before me the very man, my brother, that I thought to see in the condemned cell at Casterbridge. He was in this chimney corner; and jammed close to him, so that he could not have got out if he had tried, was the executioner who'd come to take his life, singing a song about it and not knowing that it was his victim who was close by, joining in to save appearances. My brother looked a glance of agony at me, and I know he meant, 'Don't reveal what you see; my life depends on it.' I was so terror-struck that I could hardly stand, and, not knowing what I did, I turned and hurried away."

The narrator's manner and tone had the stamp of truth, and his story made a great impression on all around. "And do you know where your brother is at the present time?" asked the magistrate.

"I do not. I have never seen him since I closed this door."

"I can testify to that, for we've been between ye ever since," said the constable.

"Where does he think to fly to?—what is his occupation?"

155   "He's a watch-and-clock-maker, Sir."

"'A said 'a was a wheelwright—a wicked rogue," said the constable.

"The wheels of clocks and watches he meant, no doubt," said Shepherd Fennel. "I thought his hands were palish for's trade."

"Well, it appears to me that nothing can be gained by retaining this poor man in custody," said the magistrate; "your business lies with the other, unquestionably."

And so the little man was released off-hand; but he looked nothing the less sad on that account, it being beyond the power of magistrate or constable to raze out the written troubles in his brain, for they concerned another whom he regarded with more solicitude than himself. When this was done, and the man had gone his way, the night was found to be so far advanced that it was deemed useless to renew the search before the next morning.

Next day, accordingly, the quest for the clever sheep-stealer became general and keen, to 160 all appearance at least. But the intended punishment was cruelly disproportioned to the transgression, and the sympathy of a great many country-folk in that district was strongly on the side of the fugitive. Moreover, his marvelous coolness and daring in hob-and-nobbing with the hangman, under the unprecedented circumstances of the shepherd's party, won their admiration. So that it may be questioned if all those who ostensibly made themselves so busy in exploring woods and fields and lanes were quite so thorough when it came to the private examination of their own lofts and outhouses. Stories were afloat of a mysterious figure being occasionally seen in some old overgrown trackway or other, remote from turnpike roads, but when a search was instituted in any of these suspected quarters nobody was found. Thus the days and weeks passed without tidings.

In brief, the bass-voiced man of the chimney corner was never recaptured. Some said that he went across the sea, others that he did not, but buried himself in the depths of a populous city. At any rate, the gentleman in cinder-gray never did his morning's work at Casterbridge, nor met anywhere at all, for business purposes, the genial comrade with whom he had passed an hour of relaxation in the lonely house on the coomb.

The grass has long been green on the graves of Shepherd Fennel and his frugal wife; the guests who made up the christening party have mainly followed their entertainers to the tomb; the baby in whose honor they all had met is a matron in the sere and yellow leaf. But the arrival of the three strangers at the shepherd's that night, and the details connected therewith, is a story as well-known as ever in the country about Higher Crowstairs.

## Questions

1. Describe the appearances of conflicts in this story. Which conflicts are real?
2. Describe the reasons for which the narrator tells so much about the people of Higher Crowstairs. How are these descriptions related to the story's major conflict?
3. Why does the author withhold the identities of the various strangers? How does this delay condition your attitudes toward the first stranger?
4. What kind of story might "The Three Strangers" be, structurally, if the first stranger were named and identified when he first enters the cottage, before the entrance of the other strangers?

## TOM WHITECLOUD (1914–1972)

Thomas St. Germain Whitecloud was born in New York City. However, he spent much of his youth on the Lac du Flambeau Indian Reservation near Woodruff, Wisconsin, the town mentioned in paragraph 20 of "Blue Winds Dancing." After attending colleges in New Mexico and California, he received his degree in medicine from Tulane University. He lived in Louisiana and Texas throughout his medical career, and at the time of his death he was a consultant for the Texas Commission on Alcoholism and Drug Abuse for Indians. "Blue Winds Dancing," which can be considered as either a story or a fictionalized autobiographical fragment, received a prize in 1938 from both *Scribner's Magazine*, in which it was published, and the Phi Beta Kappa National Honor Society.

## 🐦 Blue Winds Dancing (1938)

There is a moon out tonight. Moon and stars and clouds tipped with moonlight. And there is a fall wind blowing in my heart. Ever since this evening, when against a fading sky I saw geese wedge southward. They were going home. . . . Now I try to study, but against the pages I see them again, driving southward. Going home.

Across the valley there are heavy mountains holding up the night sky, and beyond the mountains there is home. Home, and peace, and the beat of drums, and blue winds dancing over snowfields. The Indian lodge will fill with my people, and our gods will come and sit among them. I should be there then. I should be at home.

But home is beyond the mountains, and I am here. Here where fall hides in the valleys, and winter never comes down from the mountains. Here where all the trees grow in rows; the palms stand stiffly by the roadsides, and in the groves the orange trees line in military rows, and endlessly bear fruit. Beautiful, yes: there is always beauty in order, in rows of growing things! But it is the beauty of captivity. A pine fighting for existence on a windy knoll is much more beautiful.

In my Wisconsin, the leaves change before the snows come. In the air there is the smell of wild rice and venison cooking; and when the winds come whispering through the forests, they carry the smell of rotting leaves. In the evenings, the loon calls, lonely; and birds sing their last songs before leaving. Bears dig roots and eat late fall berries, fattening for their long winter sleep. Later, when the first snows fall, one awakens in the morning to find the world white and beautiful and clean. Then one can look back over his trail and see the tracks following. In the woods there are tracks of deer and snowshoe rabbits, and long streaks where partridges slide to alight. Chipmunks make tiny footprints on the limbs and one can hear squirrels busy in hollow trees, sorting acorns. Soft lake waves wash the shores, and sunsets burst each evening over the lakes, and make them look as if they were afire.

5    That land which is my home! Beautiful, calm—where there is no hurry to get anywhere, no driving to keep up in a race that knows no ending and no goal. No classes where men talk and talk and then stop now and then to hear their own words come back to them from the students. No constant peering into the maelstrom of one's mind; no worries about grades and honors; no hysterical preparing for life until that life is half over; no anxiety about one's place in the thing they call Society.

I hear again the ring of axes in deep woods, the crunch of snow beneath my feet. I feel again the smooth velvet of ghost-birch bark. I hear the rhythm of the drums. . . . I am tired. I am weary of trying to keep up this bluff of being civilized. Being civilized means trying to do everything you don't want to, never doing anything you want to. It means dancing to the strings of custom and tradition; it means living in houses and never knowing or caring who is next door. These civilized white men want us to be like them—always dissatisfied—getting a hill and wanting a mountain.

Then again, maybe I am not tired. Maybe I'm licked. Maybe I am just not smart enough to grasp these things that go to make up civilization. Maybe I am just too lazy to think hard enough to keep up.

Still, I know my people have many things that civilization has taken from the whites. They know how to give; how to tear one's piece of meat in two and share it with one's brother. They know how to sing—how to make each man his own songs and sing them; for their music they do not have to listen to other men singing over a radio. They know how to make things with their hands, how to shape beads into design and make a thing of beauty from a piece of birch bark.

But we are inferior. It is terrible to have to feel inferior; to have to read reports of intelligence tests, and learn that one's race is behind. It is terrible to sit in classes and hear men tell you that your people worship sticks of wood—that your gods are all false, that the Manitou forgot your people and did not write them a book.

I am tired. I want to walk again among the ghost-birches. I want to see the leaves turn in   10
autumn, the smoke rise from the lodgehouses, and to feel the blue winds. I want to hear the
drums; I want to hear the drums and feel the blue whispering winds.

There is a train wailing into the night. The trains go across the mountains. It would be
easy to catch a freight. They will say he has gone back to the blanket; I don't care. The dance at
Christmas. . . .

A bunch of bums warming at a tiny fire talk politics and women and joke about the Relief
and the WPA and smoke cigarettes. These men in caps and overcoats and dirty overalls living on
the outskirts of civilization are free, but they pay the price of being free in civilization. They are
outcasts. I remember a sociology professor lecturing on adjustment to society; hobos and prostitutes and criminals are individuals who never adjusted, he said. He could learn a lot if he came
and listened to a bunch of bums talk. He would learn that work and a woman and a place to hang
his hat are all the ordinary man wants. These are all he wants, but other men are not content to let
him want only these. He must be taught to want radios and automobiles and a new suit every
spring. Progress would stop if he did not want these things. I listen to hear if there is any talk of
communism or socialism in the hobo jungles. There is none. At best there is a sort of disgusted
philosophy about life. They seem to think there should be a better distribution of wealth, or more
work, or something. But they are not rabid about it. The radicals live in the cities.

I find a fellow headed for Albuquerque, and talk road-talk with him. "It is hard to ride
fruit cars. Bums break in. Better to wait for a cattle car going back to the Middle West, and
ride that." We catch the next east-bound and walk the tops until we find a cattle car. Inside, we
crouch near the forward wall, huddle, and try to sleep. I feel peaceful and content at last. I am
going home. The cattle car rocks. I sleep.

Morning and the desert. Noon and the Salton Sea, lying more lifeless than a mirage under a
somber sun in a pale sky. Skeleton mountains rearing on the skyline, thrusting out of the desert
floor, all rock and shadow and edges. Desert. Good country for an Indian reservation. . . .

Yuma and the muddy Colorado. Night again, and I wait shivering for the dawn.   15

Phoenix. Pima country. Mountains that look like cardboard sets on a forgotten stage.
Tucson, Papago country. Giant cacti that look like petrified hitchhikers along the highways.
Apache country. At El Paso my road-buddy decides to go on to Houston. I leave him, and head
north to the mesa country. Las Cruces and the terrible Organ Mountains, jagged peaks that instill fear and wondering. Albuquerque. Pueblos along the Rio Grande. On the boardwalk there
are some Indian women in colored sashes selling bits of pottery. The stone age offering its art
to the twentieth century. They hold up a piece and fix the tourist with black eyes until, embarrassed, he buys or turns away. I feel suddenly angry that my people should have to do such
things for a living. . . .

Santa Fe trains are fast, and they keep them pretty clean of bums. I decide to hurry and
ride passenger coaltenders. Hide in the dark, judge the speed of the train as it leaves, and then
dash out, and catch it. I hug the cold steel wall of the tender and think of the roaring fire in the
engine ahead, and of the passengers back in the dining car reading their papers over hot coffee. Beneath me there is a blur of rails. Death would come quick if my hands should freeze and
I fall. Up over the Sangre De Cristo range, around cliffs and through canyons to Denver. Bitter
cold here, and I must watch out for Denver Bob. He is a railroad bull who has thrown bums
from fast freights. I miss him. It is too cold, I suppose. On north to the Sioux country.

Small towns lit for the coming Christmas. On the streets of one I see a beam-shouldered
young farmer gazing into a window filled with shining silver toasters. He is tall and wears a
blue shirt buttoned, with no tie. His young wife by his side looks at him hopefully. He wants
decorations for his place to hang his hat to please his woman. . . .

Northward again. Minnesota, and great white fields of snow; frozen lakes, and dawn
running into dusk without noon. Long forests wearing white. Bitter cold, and one night the
northern lights. I am nearing home.

20      I reach Woodruff at midnight. Suddenly I am afraid, now that I am but twenty miles from home. Afraid of what my father will say, afraid of being looked on as a stranger by my own people. I sit by a fire and think about myself and all other young Indians. We just don't seem to fit in anywhere—certainly not among the whites, and not among the older people. I think again about the learned sociology professor and his professing. So many things seem to be clear now that I am away from school and do not have to worry about some man's opinion of my ideas. It is easy to think while looking at dancing flames.

Morning, I spend the day cleaning up, and buying some presents for my family with what is left of my money. Nothing much, but a gift is a gift, if a man buys it with his last quarter. I wait until evening, then start up the track toward home.

Christmas Eve comes in on a north wind. Snow clouds hang over the pines, and the night comes early. Walking along the railroad bed, I feel the calm peace of snowbound forests on either side of me. I take my time; I am back in a world where time does not mean so much now. I am alone; alone but not nearly so lonely as I was back on the campus at school. Those are never lonely who love the snow and the pines; never lonely when the pines are wearing white shawls and snow crunches coldly underfoot. In the woods I know there are the tracks of deer and rabbit; I know that if I leave the rails and go into the woods I shall find them. I walk along feeling glad because my legs are light and my feet seem to know that they are home. A deer comes out of the woods ahead of me, and stands silhouetted on the rails. The North, I feel, has welcomed me home. I watch him and am glad that I do not wish for a gun. He goes into the woods quietly, leaving only the design of his tracks in the snow. I walk on. Now and then I pass a field, white under the night sky, with houses at the far end. Smoke comes from the chimneys of the houses, and I try to tell what sort of wood each is burning by the smoke; some burn pine, others aspen, others tamarack. There is one from which comes black coal smoke that rises lazily and drifts out over the tops of the trees. I like to watch houses and try to imagine what might be happening in them.

Just as a light snow begins to fall I cross the reservation boundary; somehow it seems as though I have stepped into another world. Deep woods in a white-and-black winter night. A faint trail leading to the village.

The railroad on which I stand comes from a city sprawled by a lake—a city with a million people who walk around without seeing one another; a city sucking the life from all the country around; a city with stores and police and intellectuals and criminals and movies and apartment houses; a city with its politics and libraries and zoos.

25      Laughing, I go into the woods. As I cross a frozen lake I begin to hear the drums. Soft in the night the drums beat. It is like the pulse beat of the world. The white line of the lake ends at a black forest, and above the trees the blue winds are dancing.

I come to the outlying houses of the village. Simple box houses, etched black in the night. From one or two windows soft lamplight falls on the snow. Christmas here, too, but it does not mean much; not much in the way of parties and presents. Joe Sky will get drunk. Alex Bodidash will buy his children red mittens and a new sled. Alex is a Carlisle man, and tries to keep his home up to white standards. White standards. Funny that my people should be ever falling farther behind. The more they try to imitate whites the more tragic the result. Yet they want us to be imitation white men. About all we imitate well are their vices.

The village is not a sight to instill pride, yet I am not ashamed; one can never be ashamed of his own people when he knows they have dreams as beautiful as white snow on a tall pine.

Father and my brother and sister are seated around the table as I walk in. Father stares at me for a moment, then I am in his arms, crying on his shoulder. I give them the presents I have brought, and my throat tightens as I watch my sister save carefully bits of red string from the packages. I hide my feelings by wrestling with my brother when he strikes my shoulder in token of affection. Father looks at me, and I know he has many questions, but he seems to know why I have come. He tells me to go alone to the lodge, and he will follow.

I walk along the trail to the lodge, watching the northern lights forming in the heavens. White waving ribbons that seem to pulsate with the rhythm of the drums. Clean snow creaks beneath my feet, and a soft wind sighs through the trees, singing to me. Everything seems to say, "Be happy! You are home now—you are free. You are among friends—we are your friends; we, the trees, and the snow, and the lights." I follow the trail to the lodge. My feet are light, my heart seems to sing to the music, and I hold my head high. Across white snow fields blue winds are dancing.

Before the lodge door I stop, afraid, I wonder if my people will remember me. I wonder— 30 "Am I Indian, or am I white?" I stand before the door a long time. I hear the ice groan on the lake, and remember the story of the old woman under the ice, trying to get out, so she can punish some runaway lovers. I think to myself, "If I am white I will not believe that story; If I am Indian, I will know that there is an old woman under the ice." I listen for a while, and I know that there is an old woman under the ice. I look again at the lights, and go in.

Inside the lodge there are many Indians. Some sit on benches around the walls, others dance in the center of the floor around a drum. Nobody seems to notice me. It seems as though I were among a people I have never seen before. Heavy women with long hair. Women with children on their knees—small children that watch with intent black eyes the movements of the dancers, whose small faces are solemn and serene. The faces of the old people are serene, too, and their eyes are merry and bright. I look at the old men. Straight, dressed in dark trousers and beaded velvet vests, wearing soft moccasins. Dark, lined faces intent on the music. I wonder if I am at all like them. They dance on, lifting their feet to the rhythm of the drums swaying lightly, looking upward. I look at their eyes, and am startled at the rapt attention to the rhythm of the music.

The dance stops. The men walk back to the walls, and talk in low tones or with their hands. There is little conversation, yet everyone seems to be sharing some secret. A woman looks at a small boy wandering away, and he comes back to her.

Strange, I think and then remember. These people are not sharing words—they are sharing a mood. Everyone is happy. I am so used to white people that it seems strange so many people could be together without someone talking. These Indians are happy because they are together, and because the night is beautiful outside, and the music is beautiful. I try hard to forget school and white people, and be one of these—my people. I try to forget everything but the night, and it is a part of me that I am one with my people and we are all a part of something universal. I watch eyes, and see now that the old people are speaking to me. They nod slightly, imperceptibly, and their eyes laugh into mine. I look around the room. All the eyes are friendly; they all laugh. No one questions my being here. The drums begin to beat again, and I catch the invitation in the eyes of the old men. My feet begin to lift to the rhythm, and I look out beyond the walls into the night and see the lights. I am happy. It is beautiful. I am home.

## Questions

1. Describe the first section of the story in terms of the structure. Could a case be made that this first section contains its own crisis and climax and that the rest of the story is really a resolution?

2. What do you learn in the first section about the conflict in the attitudes of the narrator? What is his attitude about "civilization"? What values make him think this way? If he is the protagonist, who or what is the antagonist?

**3.** What does the narrator mean by saying, "I am alone; alone but not nearly so lonely as I was back on the campus at school" (paragraph 22)?

**4.** What is meant by the dancing of the blue winds—what kind of wisdom? What is the place for such wisdom in a computerized, industrialized society?

## WRITING ABOUT STRUCTURE IN A STORY

Your essay should concern arrangement and shape. In form, the essay should not restate or summarize the part-by-part unfolding of the narrative or argument. Rather, it should explain why things are where they are: "Why is this here and not there?" is the fundamental question you need to answer. Thus it is possible to begin with a consideration of a work's crisis, and then to consider how the exposition and complication have built up to it. A vital piece of information, for example, might have been withheld in the story's earlier exposition (as in Bierce's "An Occurrence at Owl Creek Bridge" [Chapter 2] and Faulkner's "A Rose for Emily" [Chapter 2]) and introduced only at or near the conclusion. Therefore the crisis might be heightened because there would have been less suspense if the detail had been introduced earlier. Consider the following questions in planning to write about the story's structure.

### Questions for Discovering Ideas

- If spaces or numbers divide the story into sections or parts, what structural importance do these parts have?
- If there are no marked divisions, what major sections can you find? (You might make divisions according to places where actions occur, various times of day, changing weather, or increasingly important events.)
- If the story departs in major ways from the formal structure of exposition, complication, crisis, climax, and resolution, what purpose do these departures serve?
- What variations in chronological order, if any, appear in the story (for example, gaps in the time sequence; flashbacks or selective recollection)? What effects are achieved by these variations?
- Does the story delay any crucial details of exposition? Why? What effect is achieved by the delay?
- Where does an important action or a major section (such as the climax) begin? End? How is it related to the other formal structural elements, such as the crisis? Is the climax an action, a realization, or a decision? To what degree does it relieve the work's tension? What is the effect of the climax on your understanding of the characters involved in it? How is this effect related to the arrangement of the climax?

### Strategies for Organizing Ideas

Your essay should show why an entire story is arranged the way it is—to reveal the nature of a character's situation, to create surprise, or to evoke sympathy, reveal nobility (or depravity) of character, unravel apparently insoluble puzzles, express philosophical or political values, or bring out maximum humor. You might also, however, explain the structure of no more than a part of the story, such as the climax or the complication.

The essay is best developed in concert or agreement with what the work contains. The location of scenes is an obvious organizing element. Thus, essays on the structure of Hawthorne's "Young Goodman Brown" (Chapter 8) and Whitecloud's "Blue Winds Dancing" (this chapter) might be based on the fact that both take place outdoors (a dark forest for one and a series of railway locations and a winter scene for the other). Similarly, an essay might explore the structure of Maupassant's "The Necklace" (Chapter 1) by contrasting the story's indoor and outdoor locations.

Other ways to consider structure may be derived from a work's notable aspects, such as the growing suspense of Jackson's "The Lottery" or the revelations about the "sinfulness" of Goodman Brown's father and neighbors in Hawthorne's "Young Goodman Brown" (Chapter 8).

The conclusion should highlight the main parts of your essay. You may also deal briefly with the relationship of structure to the plot. If the work you have analyzed departs from chronological order, you might explain the causes and effects of this departure. Your aim should be to focus on the success of the work as it has been brought about by the author's choices in development.

## Illustrative Student Essay

Underlined sentences in this paper *do not* conform to MLA style and are used solely as teaching tools to emphasize the central idea, thesis sentence, and topic sentences throughout the paper.

Vasquez 1

Jose Vasquez

Professor Joseph

English 110

17 October 2007

### Conflict and Suspense in Hardy's "The Three Strangers"°

[1]     Thomas Hardy's "The Three Strangers" is a finely woven story of conflict and

suspense. The suspense is essential to the conflict, which builds from an opposition

of right and wrong when applied to criminal justice. <u>Hardy controls the structure to</u>

---

°See pp. 256–69 for this story.

develop this opposition, namely that the letter of the law is insignificant when compared with the spirit of the law.* The application of strict legality in Hardy's story is made to seem wrong, while understanding and forgiveness, even in an apparently illegal context, is made to seem right. As the basis of this idea, Hardy builds the story toward a major incident that presents a conflict for his Wessex shepherds between (1) duty toward law and (2) duty toward a human being who has been legally condemned but whose crime has been extenuated. Hardy develops his conflict and brings out his idea by showing the lives of his country people positively, by portraying his hangman negatively, and by creating suspense about his first stranger, who is the legally condemned "criminal."†

[2]       Although readers may not be aware of it during the early part of the story, Hardy arranges events to demonstrate a generous and broad view of right and wrong. The first one-sixth of the story is an exposition of the way of life of the natives of Higher Crowstairs, who are shown to be warm and human. But in the service of his idea, Hardy is actually building up one side of the conflict by demonstrating that his natives are such nice, ordinary peasant folk that their judgments on matters of life and death are to be trusted. This is the positive side of Hardy's narrative argument.

[3]       When Hardy does engage both sides of the conflict—a complication occurring about midway through the story—by introducing the second stranger (the hangman), he has already established the grounds for his case, but he solidifies his argument by negatively presenting this ghoulish figure as brash, selfish, and obnoxious. When the natives learn of the second stranger's identity as the hangman, they are startled "with suppressed exclamations" (paragraph 79, p. 265). The exclamations apparently take the form that if men such as the hangman are associated with the letter of the law, the natives—along with the reader—will prefer the spirit even if the spirit may lead people to support technically illegal actions. This reaction could not be sustained if the crime of the escaped criminal had been a violent one, but the "crime" was really the theft of a sheep to feed his starving family (paragraph 80, p. 265). One may grant that Hardy is mitigating the crime here, but the conflict is not between right when it is right and wrong when it is wrong, but rather between legality when it is wrong and illegality when it is right. As Hardy structures the events in the story, it is not possible to disagree

---

*Central idea.
†Thesis sentence.

with the consensus of the natives that the intended hanging of the thief "was cruelly disproportioned to the transgression" (paragraph 160, p. 270), for even if a reader wanted to disagree with Hardy's argument on legal grounds, the emotional thrust of the story leads toward extenuation.

[4]       Critical to this extenuation is Hardy's creation of suspense about the identity of the first stranger as Timothy Summers, the escaped prisoner. Because throughout the story readers have assented to the values and way of life of Shepherd Fennel and his guests, Hardy's crisis and climax forestall an exclusively legalistic reaction. Hardy puts Summers before the eyes of both country folk and readers as a brave and witty human being, not as a depraved fugitive who has just escaped hanging. The revelation at the end therefore causes a second view of Summers. In retrospect, readers join the natives in admiring this first stranger's "marvelous coolness and daring in hob-and-nobbing with the hangman" (paragraph 160, p. 270) and consequently would be indignant if such a person were actually to be hanged. As a result of Hardy's judicious withholding and disclosing of detail, he leads readers to deny the law when it is used unfairly.

[5]       Related to the major conflict in the story are a number of lesser but still important conflicts. At crucial points, for example, Hardy establishes that the natives living marginally "in the country about Higher Crowstairs" (paragraph 162, p. 270) are uneasy and fearful of the law. When they realize that the second stranger is the hangman, they are taken aback, and one of them begins trembling (paragraph 79, p. 265). Hardy invites readers to conclude that the natives view the conviction of Summers as a threat also to themselves. In a comic vein, Hardy contrasts the law with the ineptness of the shepherds who are called upon to enforce it (paragraphs 106–34, pp. 267–68). He makes the law so remote from their lives that when they actually make an arrest—of the third stranger— they use words more appropriate to criminals or to priests (paragraphs 132–34, p. 268). As an ironic dénouement of the story, Hardy tells us that the shepherds, resisting the legal but troubling hangman and magistrate, diligently search for Summers everywhere but where they know he can be found (paragraph 160, p. 270).

[6]       In addition, Hardy includes other little but human contrasts in order to develop sympathy for the folk and therefore to strengthen his argument. Although the Fennels have twenty guests in their home, Mrs. Fennel is alarmed about giving them too much food and drink, and she is disturbed when the hangman selfishly depletes her store of

Vasquez 4

mead. There is a small family disagreement on this score. Another minor and amusing conflict is set up by Hardy when Mrs. Fennel asks the musicians to stop playing, but they continue because they have been bribed by the amorous shepherd, Oliver Giles. There are also some noticeable contrasts in age among couples. Beyond these contrasts or opposites, which are vital to the story's structure, the technique of suspense is a conflict in itself, for it guides readers to consider and evaluate elements of the story a second time. These are all conflicts that Hardy employs in developing his major conflict between the right of the spirit of the law and the wrong of the letter of the law in "The Three Strangers."

Vasquez 5

**WORK CITED**

Hardy, Thomas. "The Three Strangers." *Literature: An Introduction to Reading and Writing.* Ed. Edgar V. Roberts. 4th Compact Ed. Upper Saddle River: Prentice Hall, 2008, 258–70.

## Commentary on the Essay

Essays about either plot (Chapter 2) or structure are concerned with the conflicts of the story, but the essay on plot concentrates on the opposing forces whereas the essay on structure focuses on the placement and arrangement of the story's details. Notice here that an essay on structure, like an essay on plot, does not simply retell the story event by event. That is not the concern of analytical writing. Instead, essays on both plot and structure explain the *conflict* (for plot) and the *arrangement and layout* (for structure). In both essays, the writer's assumption is that the reader has read the story, and therefore there is no need to retell it.

As expressed in paragraph 1, this essay focuses on how Hardy structures character and action in "The Three Strangers" to achieve a contrast between right and wrong. The discussion of all events leading to the people's exoneration of the fugitive as a right course of action is presented not simply in chronological order but rather as a part of Hardy's overarching instructive argument. To emphasize this aim, words and phrases are introduced, such as "arranges events," "engage both sides of the conflict," "structures the events," "creation of suspense," "establishes," and "in order to develop sympathy." All these expressions are intended as reminders that the subject of the essay is about the way in which Hardy structures the story.

In the body, paragraph 2 explains how Hardy introduces the natives and their guests at the Fennels' cottage to illustrate their qualities of warmth and humanity. Paragraph 3 stresses the negative reaction of the country folk when they learn that the second stranger is the hangman. Together, then, paragraphs 2 and 3 serve to explain the underlying causes of Hardy's arrangement of the narrative.

In paragraph 4 the essay explains Hardy's delay in identifying the fugitive. This delay allows Hardy to elaborate on his positive picture of the country folk and their values, and it also helps him in persuading readers of the story to concur in the decision for justice that the natives make. Paragraph 5 states that other conflicts in the story show that the natives are uneasy with the law and fearful of it—attitudes that reinforce their decision to favor the first stranger. The last paragraph argues that additional "but human" contrasts are placed so as to augment Hardy's favorable portraits of the Fennels and their guests.

## Writing Topics About Structure

1. What kind of story might Hardy's "The Three Strangers" be, structurally, if the first stranger were identified when he first appears, before the second stranger (the unnamed hangman) enters and starts to dominate the Christening party? What is gained, structurally, by the fact that the third stranger does not enter until late in the story?

2. Compare the structuring of the interior scenes in Conrad's "The Secret Sharer" (Chapter 5) and Hardy's "The Three Strangers." How do these scenes bring out the various conflicts of the stories? How does the presence of characters in the individual rooms contribute to the organization of the stories? What is the relationship of these characters to the major actions of the stories?

3. Compare Tan's "Two Kinds" (Chapter 4) and Whitecloud's "Blue Winds Dancing" as stories about clashing racial and social values. What are the comparative values? How do the narrators react to the values and ideas to which they object? How do the stories develop, structurally, as a result of their reactions?

4. Consider the surprises in Hardy's "The Three Strangers," Maupassant's "The Necklace" (Chapter 1), Faulkner's "A Rose for Emily" (Chapter 2), Bierce's "An Occurrence at Owl Creek Bridge" (Chapter 3), and Chopin's "The Story of an Hour" (Chapter 7). How much preparation is made in the stories, structurally, for these surprises? In retrospect, to what degree are the surprises not surprises at all but rather necessary outcomes of the preceding parts of the works?

5. Consider those aspects of Whitecloud's "Blue Winds Dancing" that seem socially and politically significant. You might consider questions about the ability of a young minority student to flourish when removed from the security he gained from his home, about the values that the narrator has questioned in the courses he has been taking, or about why he does not speak about any friendships he might have made at school. What are the implications of this story for minority assimilation into the country's dominant culture, even today, granted that the story was written in the late 1930s?

6. Select a circumstance in your life that caused you doubt, difficulty, and conflict. Making yourself anonymous (give yourself a fictitious name and put yourself in a fictitious location), write a brief story about the occasion, stressing how your conflict began, how it affected you, and how you resolved it. You might choose to begin your story in the present tense and introduce details in flashback.

# Chapter 7

# Tone and Style: Conveying Attitudes in Fiction

**T**one refers to the methods by which writers and speakers reveal attitudes or feelings—toward the material, toward their readers, and toward the general situation they are describing or analyzing. It is an aspect of all spoken and written statements, whether serious analyses of political campaigns, earnest declarations of love, requests to pass a dinner dish, descriptions of social or athletic events, letters from students asking parents for money, or official government notices threatening penalties if fines and taxes are not paid. The attitudes expressed in each of these situations are usually readily apparent. When we speak about tone here, we refer to a variety of similar and dissimilar attitudes, but, in addition, and more importantly, we stress those modes of expression that create and shape those attitudes.

Although tone is a vast subject that can involve large matters of action and situation, in this chapter we treat the interconnectedness of tone and style. **Style** refers to the ways in which writers assemble words to tell the story, to develop the argument, to dramatize the play, or to compose the poem. Sometimes style is distinguished from content, but actually style is best considered as the choice of words in the *service* of content. The written expression of an action or scene, in other words, cannot be separated from the action or scene itself, nor can it be separated from the impressions and attitudes it creates.

By reading a story carefully, we may deduce the author's attitude or attitudes toward the subject matter and toward readers. In "The Story of an Hour," for example, Kate Chopin sympathetically portrays a young wife's secret wishes for freedom, just as Chopin also sardonically reveals the unwitting smugness that often pervades men's relationships with women.

Words and subject matter may also indicate the writer's assessment of readers. When Hawthorne's woodland guide in "Young Goodman Brown" (Chapter 8) refers to "King Philip's War," for example, Hawthorne clearly assumes that his readers know that this war in seventeenth-century New England was notoriously cruel and inhumane. In this way he indicates respect for the knowledge of his readers, and he also assumes that they will assent to his interpretation. Authors always make such considerations about readers by implicitly complimenting them on their capacity to recognize and understand the ways in which materials are presented.

# Diction: The Writer's Choice and Control of Words

Control over style and tone is highly individual, because all authors put words uniquely together to fit the specific circumstances of specific works. We may therefore speak of the *style* of Ernest Hemingway and the *style* of Alice Munro, even though both writers adapt words to situations. An author may have a distinct style for narrative and descriptive passages, but a very different style for dialogue.

The essential aspect of style is **diction**, the writer's selection of words. First, words must be accurate and comprehensive, so that all actions, scenes, and ideas are absolutely understandable to readers. If a writer's work is effective—if it portrays an action graphically and clearly, explains ideas accurately, and indicates the conditions of human relationships among the major characters—we may confidently say that the words are right. Additionally, right words bear the burden of controlling the ways in which readers respond to the material. Thus, a passage of action should verbally create the action and the place or places in which things happen, and it should also cause readers to be interested and involved. Similarly, explanatory or reflective passages should be clear but should also pique the curiosity and satisfy the understanding of readers. In short, the writer should make all efforts to control the work's tone.

## Formal, Neutral, and Informal Diction Create Unique Effects

As a guide to the types of words authors use to control tone, a major classification of words can be made according to degrees of formality or informality. The choices of diction are **formal** or *high*, **neutral** or *middle*, and **informal** or *low*.

*Formal* or *high* diction confers major importance to the characters and actions being described. It consists of standard and also "elegant" words (frequently polysyllabic), correct word order, and the absence of contractions. The sentence "It is I," for example, is formal, for this expression is more "elegant" and grammatically correct than most American speakers normally now prefer. An example of formal diction may be seen in the narrative sections of Hawthorne's "Young Goodman Brown."

*Neutral* or *middle* diction is ordinary, everyday standard vocabulary, shunning longer words and using contractions when necessary. The sentence "It's me" is an example of what many American speakers naturally say in preference to the formal "It is I." Neutral words may be thought of as clear window glass, while words in the formal or high style are more decorative, like stained glass. Neutral diction is appropriate for stories about everyday, ordinary people going through situations they encounter or can imagine encountering in their lives. Generally, today's writers favor neutral diction as a means of putting their characters in a light that is normal and appropriate but also respectful. In Alice Munro's "The Found Boat" we see neutral, middle diction.

> Nobody said a word this time, they all bent and stripped themselves. Eva, naked first, started running across the field, and then all the others ran, all five of them running bare

through the knee-high hot grass, running towards the river. Not caring now about being caught but in fact leaping and yelling to call attention to themselves, if there was any-body to hear or see. They felt as if they were going to jump off a cliff and fly. They felt that something was happening to them different from anything that had happened be-fore, and it had to do with the boat, the water, the sunlight, the dark ruined station, and each other. They thought of each other now hardly as names or people, but as echoing shrieks, reflections, all bold and white and loud and scandalous, and as fast as arrows. They went running without a break into the cold water and when it came almost to the tops of their legs they fell on it and swam. It stopped their noise. Silence, amazement, came over them in a rush. They dipped and floated and separated, sleek as mink. (para-graph 87, p. 299)

The words of this passage are ordinary and easy. They are centered directly on the subject and do not draw attention to themselves. In an almost ritualistic way, the paragraph describes young people running impetuously toward a river and diving in. This action can be seen as sexually symbolic, but Munro's diction focuses on the experience itself, and the words are neither analytical nor clinical. If her inten-tion had been to create searching psychological scrutiny, she might have used for-mal or high words from the language of psychology (*libido, urge, sublimation,* and so on). Instead, she uses words that could have been in the vocabularies of the characters themselves, who would have used exactly such words to express their sensations. Hence they feel "as if they were going to jump off a cliff and fly" and in their excitement they think "that something was happening to them different from anything that had happened before." These neutral, middle words enable us to focus on the excitement of the situation rather than on deeper psychological sig-nificance. Munro therefore does not instruct us so much as she causes us to be amused and happy about the young people cavorting on the field and in the water.

*Informal* or *low* diction may range from *colloquial*—the language of relaxed, com-mon activities—to the level of *substandard* or *slang* expressions. A person speaking to a close friend uses diction that would not be appropriate in public and formal situa-tions and even in some social situations. Informal or low diction is thus appropriate for some narrative dialogue, depending, of course, on individual speakers. It is also a natural choice for stories told in the first-person point of view as though the speaker is talking directly to sympathetic and relaxed close friends—"pals." The fol-lowing sentence from Bambara's "The Lesson" (Chapter 9) illustrates informal, low diction.

And school suppose to let up in summer I heard, but she don't never let up.

Note the ungrammatical "don't never," a double negative often used in informal or low speech but frowned upon in writing. Note also that the *d* has been dropped in the participle "suppose," that "is" before "suppose" is omitted, and that "I heard" follows and does not precede the clause "And school suppose to let up in summer." The purpose of these substandard usages is clearly to establish the voice of the speaker, Sylvia, and to encourage us to listen attentively to her story.

## Authors Use Specific–General and Concrete–Abstract Language to Guide Readers

Another aspect of language is its degree of explicitness. **Specific** refers to words that bring to mind images from the real world. "My dog Teddie is barking" is specific. **General** statements refer to broad classes, such as "All people like pets" and "Dogs make good pets." There is an ascending order of generality from (1) very specific, to (2) less specific, to (3) general, as though the words themselves are climbing a ladder. Thus *peach* is a specific fruit. *Fruit* is specific but more general because it may also include apples, oranges, and all other fruits. *Dessert* is a still more general word, which can include all sweets, including fruits and peaches, and also other confections, such as ice cream. *Food* is more general yet, for it is a comprehensive word that describes everything we eat.

While *specific–general* refers to categories, *concrete–abstract* refers to qualities or conditions. **Concrete** words describe qualities of immediate perception. If you say, "Ice cream is cold," the word *cold* is concrete because it describes a condition that you can feel, just as you can taste ice cream's *sweetness* and feel its *creamy* texture in your mouth. **Abstract** words refer to broader, less palpable qualities; they may therefore apply to many separate things. If we describe ice cream as *good*, our word is abstract because *good* is far removed from ice cream itself and conveys no descriptive information about it. A vast number of things may be *good*, just as they may be *bad, fine,* "*cool*," *excellent*, and so on.

Usually, narrative and descriptive writing features specific and concrete words that are intended to help us visualize actions, scenes, and objects, for with more specificity and concreteness there is less ambiguity. Because exactness and vividness are goals of most fiction, specific and concrete words are the fiction writer's basic tools, with general and abstract words being used sparingly.

The point, however, is not that abstract and general words have no place at all, but rather that *words should be appropriate in the context*. Good writers control style in the interests of tone as well as description. Observe, for example, Hemingway's diction in "Hills Like White Elephants." This brief story takes place at a railway station in Spain, and it consists largely of conversation between the "American and the girl with him" as they are waiting for a train. The two speak idly about details of the day, the appearance of the nearby hills, and the drinks they are having as they wait. The language here is all quite specific, but at a certain point the specifics bring out an obvious issue of contention the two had been discussing before the story opens. About a third of the way through the story, the man speaks about an operation that is "not really an operation at all." It is clear that the operation he wants "Jig" (the woman's nickname) to have is an abortion. In the rest of the story, the dialogue takes a more negative turn. Even when he says that he doesn't want her to go through with it unless she wants it, she understands his words as an expression of the anger her refusal would cause. Her many questions about their relationship after such an operation indicate her apprehensiveness not only about the procedure but also her increasing disappointment in the American. The height of the American's generalized view of abortion is his claim to have known "lots of people that have done it." Her response, at the same level of generalization, but with cutting irony, marks the height of their dispute: "So have I," said the girl. "And afterward they were all so happy." Through such passages, mixing appropriate specific details with general observations, Hemingway skillfully points readers toward great understanding of the life these two characters have shared together.

## Authors Use Denotation and Connotation to Control Meaning and Suggestion

Another way to understand the connection of style and tone is to study the author's management of *denotation* and *connotation*. **Denotation** is a limiting term, referring to what a word means, and **connotation** is a broader word, referring to what the word suggests. For example, if a person in a social situation behaves in ways that are *friendly, warm, polite,* or *cordial,* these words are different in tone because they have different connotations. Similarly, both *cat* and *kitten* are close to each other denotatively, but *kitten* connotes more playfulness and cuteness than *cat.* Consider the connotations of words describing physical appearance. It is one thing to call a person *thin,* for example, but another to use such words as *skinny, gaunt, scrawny,* and *skeletal,* and still something else to say *fit, trim, svelte, slim,* and *slender.*

Through the careful choice of words, not only for denotation but also for connotation, writers control tone even though they might be describing similar or even identical situations. Let us look briefly at Cynthia Ozick's opening paragraph of "The Shawl" (Chapter 5).

> Stella, cold, cold the coldness of hell. How they walked on the roads together, Rosa with Magda curled up between sore breasts, Magda wound up in the shawl. Sometimes Stella carried Magda. But she was jealous of Magda. A thin girl of fourteen, too small, with thin breasts of her own, Stella wanted to be wrapped in a shawl, hidden away, asleep, rocked by the march, a baby, a round infant in arms. Magda took Rosa's nipple, and Rosa never stopped walking, a walking cradle. There was not enough milk; sometimes Magda sucked air; then she screamed. Stella was ravenous. Her knees were tumors on sticks, her elbows chicken bones.

This short but complex paragraph conveys a grisly close-up experience of horror during the enforced death marches of Nazi prisoners during the closing months of World War II. Many of the words here would be totally appropriate to the peaceful mothering and nurturing of an infant, but in the context of the paragraph these words dissolve into the bleakness and despair described in the passage. Stella, the thin 14-year-old girl who is forced to walk while carrying her infant sister, is "ravenous," a word suggesting her desperation for food, rather than "hungry," a word that connotes normal life in which meals are taken for granted. In addition, because of the march and her starved condition her knees have come to resemble "tumors on sticks" and her elbows are "chicken bones." Babies cry all the time, and the word *cry* would describe a baby under normal circumstances, but this paragraph conveys the unspeakably cruel treatment of innocent prisoners, and therefore Magda, Rosa's baby, "screamed." The brief discussion of these words shows how an author's skillful use of connotation shapes the tone of individual passages and, beyond that, of entire works.

# Tone, Irony, and Style

The capacity to have more than one attitude toward someone or something is a uniquely human trait. We know that people are not perfect, but we love a number of them anyway. Therefore we speak to them not only with love and praise, but also with banter and criticism. On occasion, you may have given mildly insulting greeting cards to your loved ones, not to affront them but to amuse them. You share smiles and laughs at these negative words on your cards, but at the same time you remind your loved ones of your affection.

The word **irony**, specifically **verbal irony**, describes such contradictory statements, in which one thing is said and the opposite is meant. There are important types of verbal irony. In **understatement** the expression does not fully describe the importance of a situation, and therefore makes its point by implication. For example, in Bierce's "An Occurrence at Owl Creek Bridge" (Chapter 2) the condemned man, Farquhar, contemplates the apparatus designed by the soldiers to hang him. After considering the method, Farquhar's response is described by the narrator: "The arrangement commended itself to his judgment as simple and effective" (paragraph 4). These words would be appropriate for ordinary machinery, perhaps, but because the apparatus is soon to cause Farquhar's death, the understated observation is ironic.

By contrast, in **hyperbole** or **overstatement**, the words are far in excess of the situation, and readers or listeners therefore understand that the true meaning is considerably less than what is said. An example is the priest's exaggerated dialogue with Jackie in "First Confession" (paragraphs 38–50, p. 304). Though the priest makes incongruously hyperbolic comments on Jackie's plans for slaughtering his grandmother, readers automatically know he means no such thing. The gulf between what is said and what is meant creates smiles and chuckles.

Often verbal irony is ambiguous, having double meaning or **double entendre**. Midway through "Young Goodman Brown" (Chapter 8), for example, the woodland guide leaves Brown alone while stating, "[W]hen you feel like moving again, there is my staff to help you along" (paragraph 40, p. 304). The word "staff" is ambiguous, for it refers to the staff that resembles a serpent (paragraph 13, p. 302). The word therefore suggests that the devilish guide is leaving Brown not only with a real staff but also with the spirit of evil (unlike the divine "staff" of Psalm 23:4 that gives comfort). Ambiguity of course may be used in relation to any topic. Quite often double-entendre is used in statements about sexuality, and on such occasions is intended for the amusement of listeners or readers.

# Tone, Humor, and Style

A major aspect of tone is humor and laughter. Everyone likes to laugh, and shared laughter is part of good human relationships. As common and enjoyable as laughter is, however, not many people can adequately explain why some things are funny. Even when reasons for laughter are analyzed and explained, it always seems that they do not answer all our questions. Explanation, however, is a goal worthy of pursuit. It seems that a common element in laughter is that it depends on our seeing something familiar in a new light, or in encountering something surprisingly new or unique. It also seems that whenever we laugh—perhaps in the company of our friends or as a result of our reading or looking at films and television shows—we likely find that laughter is most often unplanned, personal, idiosyncratic, and unpredictable.

A primary ingredient in humor is something to laugh at—a person, thing, situation, custom, habit of speech or dialect, or arrangement of words. But once we have this ingredient we must also have *disproportion* or *incongruity*; that is, something happens or is said that violates what we might normally expect. It is such jarring juxtapositions that provide the comic newness prompting the occasion of laughter. In O'Connor's "First Confession," we might expect that Mrs. Ryan's discourse about enduring the agonizing pain of hellfire for all eternity might have made Jackie, the narrator, fearful. But is this what happens? Let us look:

> She lit a candle, took out a new half-crown [a valuable coin], and offered it to the first boy who would hold one finger—only one finger!—in the flame for five minutes by the school clock. Being always very ambitious I was tempted to volunteer, but I thought it might look greedy. Then she asked were we afraid of holding one finger—only one finger!—in a little candle flame for five minutes and not afraid of burning all over in roasting hot furnaces for all eternity. "All eternity! Just think of that! A whole lifetime goes by and it's nothing, not even a drop in the ocean of your sufferings." The woman was really interesting about hell, but my attention was all fixed on the half-crown. . . . (paragraph 5, p. 301)

Jackie's response shows that Mrs. Ryan's challenge has not even dented his boyhood problems, which have nothing to do with eternal punishment. For him, punishment is a matter of things happening day by day: the "flaking" administered by his father and also the family disruptions caused by his grandmother. Eternity, for him as a little boy, is not even a remote concern. It is comparable incongruities in Jackie's responses that characterize the comic method in O'Connor's story. Situations producing laughter in most other works are not dissimilar to the situation of "First Confession," as in Orozco's "Orientation," in which a situation that we might expect to produce repulsion and alarm is treated by the speaker as though it is nothing extraordinary at all.

In addition, the language itself may be exploited for incongruity. A well-known example is the stand-up comedian's statement that "One day I was walking in the local shopping mall, and I turned into a drugstore." Here the comedian causes laughter through the ambiguous meaning of "turned into," thus verbally changing an ordinary walk into a miraculously comic event. Another verbal incongruity is this one: "Barking loudly, I was awakened by my dog." Here the humor depends on the juggling of grammar: the modifier "barking loudly" is misplaced, and the resulting sentence seems to say incongruously that the speaker, and not the dog, is barking. A real-life speaker, who will be nameless here, once stated that he had trouble understanding the "*congregation* of verbs," not quite catching up to the word *conjugation*. Here the inadvertent pun creates the humor of the sentence. We laugh *at* the pun, and we also laugh *at* the speaker whose verbal mistake has produced the pun. The same speaker also described the grammatical parts of speech as "nouns, verbs, and *proverbs*." We conclude that he intended to say (maybe) either *pronouns* or *adverbs*, but somehow his understanding slipped and he created a comic incongruity. If we discover such verbal errors in a story, the author is controlling tone by directing humor against the speaker and his or her language, for the amusement of both readers and author alike.

It is such flashes of insight, or sudden revelations like these, that create the newness and spontaneity underlying humor. Indeed, the task of the writer is to develop ordinary materials to that point when spontaneity brings us to the explosiveness of laughter. This is not to say that works that you already know are not spontaneous or new. You can read O'Connor's "First Confession" and laugh, and read it again and laugh again, because even though you know what happens, the story shapes your acceptance of how Jackie maintains his natural innocence despite the fact that the older people around him, except for the priest, are pushing him to accept their own fears and anxieties. Jackie's experience is and always will be comic—and new—because it is so incongruous and so spontaneous.

---

## Stories for Study

---

## KATE CHOPIN (1851–1904)

Born in St. Louis, Chopin lived in Louisiana from the time of her marriage until 1882. After her husband's death she returned to St. Louis and began to write. She published two collections of stories based on the life she had known back in Louisiana: *Bayou Folk* (1894) and *A Night in Acadie* (1897). However, she became best known for her major novel, *The Awakening* (1899), which aroused negative reactions because it mentioned taboo subjects like adultery and miscegenation. Indeed, the critical disapproval was so intense that Chopin published no further works, even though she was at the height of her literary power and lived five years after the controversy.

 ## The Story of an Hour (1894)

Knowing that Mrs. Mallard was afflicted with a heart trouble, great care was taken to break to her as gently as possible the news of her husband's death.

It was her sister Josephine who told her, in broken sentences: veiled hints that revealed in half concealing. Her husband's friend Richards was there, too, near her. It was he who had been in the newspaper office when intelligence of the railroad disaster was received, with Brently Mallard's name leading the list of "killed." He had only taken the time to assure himself of its truth by a second telegram, and had hastened to forestall any less careful, less tender friend in bearing the sad message.

She did not hear the story as many women have heard the same, with a paralyzed inability to accept its significance. She wept at once, with sudden, wild abandonment, in her sister's arms. When the storm of grief had spent itself she went away to her room alone. She would have no one follow her.

There stood, facing the open window, a comfortable, roomy armchair. Into this she sank, pressed down by a physical exhaustion that haunted her body and seemed to reach into her soul.

5      She could see in the open square before her house the tops of trees that were all aquiver with the new spring life. The delicious breath of rain was in the air. In the street below a peddler was crying his wares. The notes of a distant song which some one was singing reached her faintly, and countless sparrows were twittering in the eaves.

There were patches of blue sky showing here and there through the clouds that had met and piled one above the other in the west facing her window.

She sat with her head thrown back upon the cushion of the chair, quite motionless, except when a sob came up into her throat and shook her, as a child who has cried itself to sleep continues to sob in its dreams.

She was young, with a fair, calm face, whose lines bespoke repression and even a certain strength. But now there was a dull stare in her eyes, whose gaze was fixed away off yonder on one of those patches of blue sky. It was not a glance of reflection, but rather indicated a suspension of intelligent thought.

There was something coming to her and she was waiting for it, fearfully. What was it? She did not know; it was too subtle and elusive to name. But she felt it, creeping out of the sky, reaching toward her through the sounds, the scents, the color that filled the air.

10     Now her bosom rose and fell tumultuously. She was beginning to recognize this thing that was approaching to possess her, and she was striving to beat it back with her will—as powerless as her two white slender hands would have been.

When she abandoned herself a little whispered word escaped her slightly parted lips. She said it over and over under her breath: "free, free, free!" The vacant stare and the look of terror that had followed it went from her eyes. They stayed keen and bright. Her pulses beat fast, and the coursing blood warmed and relaxed every inch of her body.

She did not stop to ask if it were or were not a monstrous joy that held her. A clear and exalted perception enabled her to dismiss the suggestion as trivial.

She knew that she would weep again when she saw the kind, tender hands folded in death; the face that had never looked save with love upon her, fixed and gray and dead. But she saw beyond that bitter moment a long procession of years to come that would belong to her absolutely. And she opened and spread her arms out to them in welcome.

There would be no one to live for during those coming years; she would live for herself. There would be no powerful will bending hers in that blind persistence with which men and women believe they have a right to impose a private will upon a fellow-creature. A kind intention or a cruel intention made the act seem no less a crime as she looked upon it in that brief moment of illumination.

15     And yet she had loved him—sometimes. Often she had not. What did it matter! What could love, the unsolved mystery, count for in face of this possession of self-assertion which she suddenly recognized as the strongest impulse of her being!

"Free! Body and soul free!" she kept whispering.

Josephine was kneeling before the closed door with her lips to the keyhole, imploring for admission. "Louise, open the door! I beg; open the door—you will make yourself ill. What are you doing, Louise? For heaven's sake open the door."

"Go away. I am not making myself ill." No; she was drinking in a very elixir of life through that open window.

Her fancy was running riot along those days ahead of her. Spring days, and summer days, and all sorts of days that would be her own. She breathed a quick prayer that life might be long. It was only yesterday she had thought with a shudder that life might be long.

She arose at length and opened the door to her sister's importunities. There was a fever-     20
ish triumph in her eyes, and she carried herself unwittingly like a goddess of Victory. She clasped her sister's waist, and together they descended the stairs. Richards stood waiting for them at the bottom.

Some one was opening the front door with a latchkey. It was Brently Mallard who entered, a little travel-stained, composedly carrying his grip-sack and umbrella. He had been far from the scene of accident, and did not even know there had been one. He stood amazed at Josephine's piercing cry: at Richards' quick motion to screen him from the view of his wife.

But Richards was too late.

When the doctors came they said she had died of heart disease—of joy that kills.

## Questions

1. What do we learn about Louise's husband? How has he justified her responses? How are your judgments about him controlled by the context of the story?

2. Analyze the tone of paragraph 5. How is the imagery here (and in the following paragraphs) appropriate for her developing mood?

3. What is the apparent attitude of the narrator toward the institution of marriage, and what elements of tone make this apparent?

4. What do Louise's sister and Richards have in common? How do their attitudes contribute to the irony of the story?

5. Consider the tone of the last paragraph. What judgment is being made about how men view their importance to women?

## ERNEST HEMINGWAY° (1899–1961)

Hemingway was born in Illinois. During World War I he served in the Ambulance Corps in France, where he was wounded. In the 1920s he published *The Sun Also Rises* (1926) and *A Farewell to Arms* (1929), and the resulting critical fame made him a major literary celebrity. He developed a sparse style, in keeping with the elemental, stark lives of the characters he depicted. "Hills Like White Elephants," from the collection *Men Without Women* (1927), typifies that pared, annealed style. Of particular note in this story is the way in which Hemingway, by carefully controlling the various speeches of his two characters without providing any extra prose guidance, enables readers clearly to identify the speakers and to follow their interests about the topics of concern.

# Hills Like White Elephants (1927)

The hills across the valley of the Ebro[1] were long and white. On this side there was no shade and no trees and the station was between two lines of rails in the sun. Close against the side of the station there was the warm shadow of the building and a curtain, made of strings of bamboo beads, hung across the open door into the bar, to keep out flies. The American and the girl with him sat at a table in the shade, outside the building. It was very hot and the express from Barcelona would come in forty minutes. It stopped at this junction for two minutes and went on to Madrid.

"What should we drink?" the girl asked. She had taken off her hat and put it on the table.

"It's pretty hot," the man said.

"Let's drink beer."

5 "Dos cervezas," the man said into the curtain.

"Big ones?" a woman asked[2] from the doorway.

"Yes. Two big ones."

The woman brought two glasses of beer and two felt pads. She put the felt pads and the beer glasses on the table and looked at the man and the girl. The girl was looking off at the line of hills. They were white in the sun and the country was brown and dry.

"They look like white elephants," she said.

10 "I've never seen one," the man drank his beer.

"No, you wouldn't have."

"I might have," the man said. "Just because you say I wouldn't have doesn't prove anything."

The girl looked at the bead curtain. "They've painted something on it," she said. "What does it say?"

"Anis del Toro. It's a drink."

15 "Could we try it?"

The man called "Listen" through the curtain. The woman came out from the bar.

"Four reales."[3]

"We want two Anis del Toro."

"With water?"

20 "Do you want it with water?"

"I don't know," the girl said. "Is it good with water?"

"It's all right."

"You want them with water?" asked the woman.

"Yes, with water."

25 "It tastes like licorice," the girl said and put the glass down.

"That's the way with everything."

"Yes," said the girl. "Everything tastes of licorice. Especially all the things you've waited so long for, like absinthe."

"Oh, cut it out."

"You started it," the girl said. "I was being amused. I was having a fine time."

30 "Well, let's try and have a fine time."

---

[1] *Ebro*: A river in Spain.

[2] *a woman asked*: The waitress speaks in Spanish. The American man understands Spanish, but the girl does not. The man therefore translates for her throughout the story, when necessary.

[3] *reales*: A *real* was a silver Spanish coin.

"All right. I was trying. I said the mountains looked like white elephants. Wasn't that bright?"

"That was bright."

"I wanted to try this new drink. That's all we do, isn't it—look at things and try new drinks?"

"I guess so."

The girl looked across at the hills.                                                              35

"They're lovely hills," she said. "They don't really look like white elephants. I just meant the coloring of their skin through the trees."

"Should we have another drink?"

"All right."

The warm wind blew the bead curtain against the table.

"The beer's nice and cool," the man said.                                                      40

"It's lovely," the girl said.

"It's really an awfully simple operation, Jig," the man said. "It's not really an operation at all."

The girl looked at the ground the table legs rested on.

"I know you wouldn't mind it, Jig. It's really not anything. It's just to let the air in."

The girl did not say anything.                                                                 45

"I'll go with you and I'll stay with you all the time. They just let the air in and then it's all perfectly natural."

"Then what will we do afterward?"

"We'll be fine afterward. Just like we were before."

"What makes you think so?"

"That's the only thing that bothers us. It's the only thing that's made us unhappy."           50

The girl looked at the bead curtain, put her hand out and took hold of two of the strings of beads.

"And you think then we'll be all right and be happy."

"I know we will. You don't have to be afraid. I've known lots of people that have done it."

"So have I," said the girl. "And afterward they were all so happy."

"Well," the man said, "if you don't want to you don't have to. I wouldn't have you do it if   55
you didn't want to. But I know it's perfectly simple."

"And you really want to?"

"I think it's the best thing to do. But I don't want you to do it if you don't really want to."

"And if I do it you'll be happy and things will be like they were and you'll love me?"

"I love you now. You know I love you."

"I know. But if I do it, then it will be nice again if I say things are like white elephants, and  60
you'll like it?"

"I'll love it. I love it now but I just can't think about it. You know how I get when I worry."

"If I do it you won't ever worry?"

"I won't worry about that because it's perfectly simple."

"Then I'll do it. Because I don't care about me."

"What do you mean?"                                                                             65

"I don't care about me."

"Well, I care about you."

"Oh, yes. But I don't care about me. And I'll do it and then everything will be fine."

"I don't want you to do it if you feel that way."

The girl stood up and walked to the end of the station. Across, on the other side, were fields  70
of grain and trees along the banks of the Ebro. Far away, beyond the river, were mountains. The shadow of a cloud moved across the field of grain and she saw the river through the trees.

"And we could have all this," she said. "And we could have everything and every day we make it more impossible."

"What did you say?"

"I said we could have everything."

"We can have everything."

75   "No, we can't."

"We can have the whole world."

"No, we can't."

"We can go everywhere."

"No, we can't. It isn't ours any more."

80   "It's ours."

"No, it isn't. And once they take it away, you never get it back."

"But they haven't taken it away."

"We'll wait and see."

"Come on back in the shade," he said. "You mustn't feel that way."

85   "I don't feel any way," the girl said. "I just know things."

"I don't want you to do anything that you don't want to do—"

"Nor that isn't good for me," she said. "I know. Could we have another beer?"

"All right. But you've got to realize—"

"I realize," the girl said. "Can't we maybe stop talking?"

90   They sat down at the table and the girl looked across at the hills on the dry side of the valley and the man looked at her and at the table.

"You've got to realize," he said, "that I don't want you to do it if you don't want to. I'm perfectly willing to go through with it if it means anything to you."

"Doesn't it mean anything to you? We could get along."

"Of course it does. But I don't want anybody but you. I don't want any one else. And I know it's perfectly simple."

"Yes, you know it's perfectly simple."

95   "It's all right for you to say that, but I do know it."

"Would you do something for me now?"

"I'd do anything for you."

"Would you please please please please please please please stop talking?"

He did not say anything but looked at the bags against the wall of the station. There were labels on them from all the hotels where they had spent nights.

100   "But I don't want you to," he said, "I don't care anything about it."

"I'll scream," the girl said.

The woman came out through the curtains with two glasses of beer and put them down on the damp felt pads. "The train comes in five minutes," she said.

"What did she say?" asked the girl.

"That the train is coming in five minutes."

105   The girl smiled brightly at the woman, to thank her.

"I'd better take the bags over to the other side of the station," the man said. She smiled at him.

"All right. Then come back and we'll finish the beer."

He picked up the two heavy bags and carried them around the station to the other tracks. He looked up the tracks but could not see the train. Coming back, he walked through the barroom, where people waiting for the train were drinking. He drank an Anis at the bar and looked at the people. They were all waiting reasonably for the train. He went out through the bead curtain. She was sitting at the table and smiled at him.

"Do you feel better?" he asked.
"I feel fine," she said. "There's nothing wrong with me. I feel fine."    110

## Questions

**1.** Who are the major characters in this story? What is the principal problem that they are facing? What does "Jig" want to do? What does "the American" want her to do?

**2.** What are her responses to his wishes? In what ways can you determine what her wishes are? What is happening to her judgment about the American?

**3.** Describe Hemingway's handling of the dialogue. Stylistically, how does Hemingway make it plain who is speaking, without the many "he said" and "she said" statements that you might find in other stories?

**4.** Why does the American stop in the station barroom to have another Anis, to which "Jig" has voiced what seems to be an objection?

**5.** What evidence do you find in the dialogue about the relationship between the American and "Jig" before the story has opened? Explain Hemingway's use of irony in Jig's speeches after speech 53. How do the speeches of Jig and the American let you know about their attitudes toward the future of their relationship? How does Jig seem to be growing psychologically as the story unfolds? How believable is her final statement, that she "feels fine"?

## ALICE MUNRO (b. 1931)

Munro, who is a writer almost exclusively of short stories, grew up in Western Ontario, twenty miles east of Lake Huron—the approximate geographic locale of "The Found Boat." She received her higher education at the University of Western Ontario, after which she married and moved to British Columbia, where she began her writing career. Her first collection was *Dance of the Happy Shades* (1968), followed three years later by the novelistic *Lives of Girls and Women*. Later volumes are *Something I've Been Meaning to Tell You* (1974), *The Beggar Maid* (1978), *The Moons of Jupiter* (1982), *The Progress of Love* (1986), *Friend of My Youth* (1990), *Open Secrets* (1995), *Selected Stories* (1997), *The Love of a Good Woman* (1998), *Hateship, Friendship, Courtship, Loveship, Marriage: Stories* (2002), and *Runaway* (2004). Her stories are mainly regional and have a realistic basis in her own experiences. The stories are not autobiographical, however; her characters and their actions develop out of her powerful imagination and strong sympathy and compassion. Recipient of Canada's Governor-General's Award for her very first work, she has merited additional honors throughout her full and distinguished career. Among her honors is the 1999 National Book Critics Circle Fiction Prize for *The Love of a Good Woman*. In 2004 *The New York Times* named *Runaway* one of the ten best books of 2004. In 2005 *Time Magazine* named her one of the world's most influential people.

## 🦅 The Found Boat (1974)

At the end of Bell Street, McKay Street, Mayo Street, there was the Flood. It was the Wawanash River, which every spring overflowed its banks. Some springs, say one in every five, it covered the roads on that side of town and washed over the fields, creating a shallow choppy lake. Light reflected off the water made everything bright and cold, as it is in a lakeside town, and woke or revived in people certain vague hopes of disaster. Mostly during the late afternoon and early evening, there were people straggling out to look at it, and discuss whether it was still rising, and whether this time it might invade the town. In general, those under fifteen and over sixty-five were most certain that it would.

Eva and Carol rode out on their bicycles. They left the road—it was the end of Mayo Street, past any houses—and rode right into a field, over a wire fence entirely flattened by the weight of the winter's snow. They coasted a little way before the long grass stopped them, then left their bicycles lying down and went to the water.

"We have to find a log and ride on it," Eva said.

"Jesus, we'll freeze our legs off."

5    "Jesus, we'll freeze our legs off!" said one of the boys who were there too at the water's edge. He spoke in a sour whine, the way boys imitated girls although it was nothing like the way girls talked. These boys—there were three of them—were all in the same class as Eva and Carol at school and were known to them by name (their names being Frank, Bud and Clayton), but Eva and Carol, who had seen and recognized them from the road, had not spoken to them or looked at them or, even yet, given any sign of knowing they were there. The boys seemed to be trying to make a raft, from lumber they had salvaged from the water.

Eva and Carol took off their shoes and socks and waded in. The water was so cold it sent pain up their legs, like blue electric sparks shooting through their veins, but they went on, pulling their skirts high, tight behind and bunched so they could hold them in front.

"Look at the fat-assed ducks in wading."

"Fat-assed fucks."

Eva and Carol, of course, gave no sign of hearing this. They laid hold of a log and climbed on, taking a couple of boards floating in the water for paddles. There were always things floating around in the Flood—branches, fence-rails, logs, road signs, old lumber; sometimes boilers, washtubs, pots and pans, or even a car seat or stuffed chair, as if somewhere the Flood had got into a dump.

10    They paddled away from shore, heading out into the cold lake. The water was perfectly clear, they could see the brown grass swimming along the bottom. Suppose it was the sea, thought Eva. She thought of drowned cities and countries. Atlantis. Suppose they were riding in a Viking boat—Viking boats on the Atlantic were more frail and narrow than this log on the Flood—and they had miles of clear sea beneath them, then a spired city, intact as a jewel irretrievable on the ocean floor.

"This is a Viking boat," she said. "I am the carving on the front." She stuck her chest out and stretched her neck, trying to make a curve, and she made a face, putting out her tongue. Then she turned and for the first time took notice of the boys.

"Hey, you sucks!" she yelled at them. "You'd be scared to come out here, this water is ten feet deep!"

"Liar," they answered without interest, and she was.

They steered the log around a row of trees, avoiding floating barbed wire, and got into a little bay created by a natural hollow of the land. Where the bay was now, there would be a pond full of frogs later in the spring, and by the middle of summer there would be no water visible at all, just a low tangle of reeds and bushes, green, to show that mud was still wet around their roots. Larger bushes, willows, grew around the steep bank of this pond and were still partly out of the water. Eva and Carol let the log ride in. They saw a place where something was caught.

It was a boat, or part of one. An old rowboat with most of one side ripped out, the board 15 that had been the seat just dangling. It was pushed up among the branches, lying on what would have been its side, if it had a side, the prow caught high.

Their idea came to them without consultation, at the same time:

"You guys! Hey, you guys!"

"We found you a boat!"

"Stop building your stupid raft and come and look at the boat!"

What surprised them in the first place was that the boys really did come, scrambling over- 20 land, half running, half sliding down the bank, wanting to see.

"Hey, where?"

"Where is it. I don't see no boat."

What surprised them in the second place was that when the boys did actually see what boat was meant, this old flood-smashed wreck held up in the branches, they did not understand that they had been fooled, that a joke had been played on them. They did not show a moment's disappointment, but seemed as pleased at the discovery as if the boat had been whole and new. They were already barefoot, because they had been wading in the water to get lumber, and they waded in here without a stop, surrounding the boat and appraising it and paying no attention even of an insulting kind to Eva and Carol who bobbed up and down on their log. Eva and Carol had to call to them.

"How do you think you're going to get it off?"

"It won't float anyway." 25

"What makes you think it will float?"

"It'll sink. Glub-blub-blub, you'll all be drowned."

The boys did not answer, because they were too busy walking around the boat, pulling at it in a testing way to see how it could be got off with the least possible damage. Frank, who was the most literate, talkative and inept of the three, began referring to the boat as *she*, an affectation which Eva and Carol acknowledged with fish-mouths of contempt.

"She's caught two places. You got to be careful not to tear a hole in her bottom. She's heavier than you'd think."

It was Clayton who climbed up and freed the boat, and Bud, a tall fat boy, who got the 30 weight of it on his back to turn it into the water so that they could half float, half carry it to shore. All this took some time. Eva and Carol abandoned their log and waded out of the water. They walked overland to get their shoes and socks and bicycles. They did not need to come back this way but they came. They stood at the top of the hill, leaning on their bicycles. They did not go on home, but they did not sit down and frankly watch, either. They stood more or less facing each other, but glancing down at the water and at the boys struggling with the boat, as if they had just halted for a moment out of curiosity, and staying longer than they intended, to see what came of this unpromising project.

About nine o'clock, or when it was nearly dark—dark to people inside the houses, but not quite dark outside—they all returned to town, going along Mayo Street in a sort of procession. Frank and Bud and Clayton came carrying the boat, upside-down, and Eva and Carol walked behind, wheeling their bicycles. The boys' heads were almost hidden in the darkness of the overturned boat, with its smell of soaked wood, cold swampy water. The girls could look ahead and see the street lights in their tin reflectors, a necklace of lights climbing Mayo Street, reaching all the way up to the standpipe. They turned onto Burns Street heading for Clayton's house, the nearest house belonging to any of them. This was not the way home for Eva or for Carol either, but they followed along. The boys were perhaps too busy carrying the boat to tell them to go away. Some younger children were still out playing, playing hopscotch on the sidewalk though they could hardly see. At this time of year the bare sidewalk was still such a novelty and delight. These children cleared out of the way and watched the boat go by with unwilling respect; they shouted questions after it, wanting to know where it came from and what was going to be done with it. No one answered them. Eva and Carol as well as the boys refused to answer or even look at them.

The five of them entered Clayton's yard. The boys shifted weight, as if they were going to put the boat down.

"You better take it round to the back where nobody can see it," Carol said. That was the first thing any of them had said since they came into town.

The boys said nothing but went on, following a mud path between Clayton's house and a leaning board fence. They let the boat down in the back yard.

35     "It's a stolen boat, you know," said Eva, mainly for the effect. "It must've belonged to somebody. You stole it."

"You was the ones who stole it then," Bud said, short of breath. "It was you seen it first."

"It was you took it."

"It was all of us then. If one of us gets in trouble then all of us does."

"Are you going to tell anybody on them?" said Carol as she and Eva rode home, along the streets which were dark between the lights now and potholed from winter.

40     "It's up to you, I won't if you won't."

"I won't if you won't."

They rode in silence, relinquishing something, but not discontented.

The board fence in Clayton's back yard had every so often a post which supported it, or tried to, and it was on these posts that Eva and Carol spent several evenings sitting, jauntily but not very comfortably. Or else they just leaned against the fence while the boys worked on the boat. During the first couple of evenings neighborhood children attracted by the sound of hammering tried to get into the yard to see what was going on, but Eva and Carol blocked their way.

"Who said you could come in here?"

45     "Just us can come in this yard."

These evenings were getting longer, the air milder. Skipping was starting on the sidewalks. Further along the street there was a row of hard maples that had been tapped. Children drank the sap as fast as it could drip into the buckets. The old man and woman who owned the trees, and who hoped to make syrup, came running out of the house making noises as if they were trying to scare away crows. Finally, every spring, the old man would come out on his porch and fire his shotgun into the air, and then the thieving would stop.

None of those working on the boat bothered about stealing sap, though all had done so last year.

The lumber to repair the boat was picked up here and there, along back lanes. At this time of year things were lying around—old boards and branches, sodden mitts, spoons flung out with the dishwater, lids of pudding pots that had been set in the snow to cool, all the debris that can sift through and survive winter. The tools came from Clayton's cellar—left over, presumably, from the time when his father was alive—and though they had nobody to advise them the boys seemed to figure out more or less the manner in which boats are built, or rebuilt. Frank was the one who showed up with diagrams from books and *Popular Mechanics* magazines. Clayton looked at these diagrams and listened to Frank read the instructions and then went ahead and decided in his own way what was to be done. Bud was best at sawing. Eva and Carol watched everything from the fence and offered criticism and thought up names. The names for the boat that they thought of were: Water Lily, Sea Horse, Flood Queen, and

Caro-Eve, after them because they had found it. The boys did not say which, if any, of these names they found satisfactory.

The boat had to be tarred. Clayton heated up a pot of tar on the kitchen stove and brought it out and painted slowly, his thorough way, sitting astride the overturned boat. The other boys were sawing a board to make a new seat. As Clayton worked, the tar cooled and thickened so that finally he could not move the brush any more. He turned to Eva and held out the pot and said, "You can go in and heat this on the stove."

Eva took the pot and went up the back steps. The kitchen seemed black after outside, but it must be light enough to see in, because there was Clayton's mother standing at the ironing board, ironing. She did that for a living, took in wash and ironing.

"Please may I put the tar pot on the stove?" said Eva, who had been brought up to talk politely to parents, even wash-and-iron ladies, and who for some reason especially wanted to make a good impression on Clayton's mother.

"You'll have to poke up the fire then," said Clayton's mother, as if she doubted whether Eva would know how to do that. But Eva could see now, and she picked up the lid with the stove-lifter, and took the poker and poked up a flame. She stirred the tar as it softened. She felt privileged. Then and later. Before she went to sleep a picture of Clayton came to her mind; she saw him sitting astride the boat, tar-painting, with such concentration, delicacy, absorption. She thought of him speaking to her, out of his isolation, in such an ordinary peaceful taking-for-granted voice.

On the twenty-fourth of May, a school holiday in the middle of the week, the boat was carried out of town, a long way now, off the road over fields and fences that had been repaired, to where the river flowed between its normal banks. Eva and Carol, as well as the boys, took turns carrying it. It was launched in the water from a cow-trampled spot between willow bushes that were fresh out in leaf. The boys went first. They yelled with triumph when the boat did float, when it rode amazingly down the river current. The boat was painted black, and green inside, with yellow seats, and a strip of yellow all the way around the outside. There was no name on it, after all. The boys could not imagine that it needed any name to keep it separate from the other boats in the world.

Eva and Carol ran along the bank, carrying bags full of peanut butter-and-jam sandwiches, pickles, bananas, chocolate cake, potato chips, graham crackers stuck together with corn syrup and five bottles of pop to be cooled in the river water. The bottles bumped against their legs. They yelled for a turn.

"If they don't let us they're bastards," Carol said, and they yelled together. "We found it! We found it!"

The boys did not answer, but after a while they brought the boat in, and Carol and Eva came crashing, panting down the bank.

"Does it leak?"

"It don't leak yet."

"We forgot a bailing can," wailed Carol, but nevertheless she got in, with Eva, and Frank pushed them off, crying. "Here's to a Watery Grave!"

And the thing about being in a boat was that it was not solidly bobbing, like a log, but was cupped in the water, so that riding in it was not like being on something in the water, but like being in the water itself. Soon they were all going out in the boat in mixed-up turns, two boys and a girl, two girls and a boy, a girl and a boy, until things were so confused it was impossible to tell whose turn came next, and nobody cared anyway. They went down the river—those who weren't riding, running along the bank to keep up. They passed under two bridges, one iron, one cement. Once they saw a big carp just resting, it seemed to smile at them, in the bridge-shaded water. They did not know how far they had gone on the river, but things had changed—the water had got shallower, and the land flatter. Across an open field they saw a building that looked like a house, abandoned. They dragged the boat up on the bank and tied it and set out across the field.

"That's the old station," Frank said. "That's Pedder Station." The others had heard this name but he was the one who knew, because his father was the station agent in town. He said that this was a station on a branch line that had been torn up, and that there had been a sawmill here, but a long time ago.

Inside the station it was dark, cool. All the windows were broken. Glass lay in shards and in fairly big pieces on the floor. They walked around finding the larger pieces of glass and tramping on them, smashing them, it was like cracking ice on puddles. Some partitions were still in place, you could see where the ticket window had been. There was a bench lying on its side. People had been here, it looked as if people came here all the time, though it was so far from anywhere. Beer bottles and pop bottles were lying around, also cigarette packages, gum and candy wrappers, the paper from a loaf of bread. The walls were covered with dim and fresh pencil and chalk writings and carved with knives.

I LOVE RONNIE COLES
I WANT TO FUCK
KILROY WAS HERE
RONNIE COLES IS AN ASS-HOLE
WHAT ARE YOU DOING HERE?
WAITING FOR A TRAIN
DAWNA MARY-LOU BARBARA JOANNE

It was exciting to be inside this large, dark, empty place, with the loud noise of breaking glass and their voices ringing back from the underside of the roof. They tipped the old beer bottles against their mouths. That reminded them that they were hungry and thirsty and they cleared a place in the middle of the floor and sat down and ate the lunch. They drank the pop just as it was, lukewarm. They ate everything there was and licked the smears of peanut butter and jam off the bread-paper in which the sandwiches had been wrapped.

They played Truth or Dare.

65      "I dare you to write on the wall, I am a Stupid Ass, and sign your name."

"Tell the truth—what is the worst lie you ever told?"

"Did you ever wet the bed?"

"Did you ever dream you were walking down the street without any clothes on?"

"I dare you to go outside and pee on the railway sign."

70      It was Frank who had to do that. They could not see him, even his back, but they knew he did it, they heard the hissing sound of his pee. They all sat still, amazed, unable to think of what the next dare would be.

"I dare everybody," said Frank from the doorway. "I dare—Everybody."

"What?"

"Take off all our clothes."

Eva and Carol screamed.

75      "Anybody who won't do it has to walk—has to *crawl*—around this floor on their hands and knees."

They were all quiet, till Eva said, almost complacently, "What first?"

"Shoes and socks."

"Then we have to go outside, there's too much glass here."

They pulled off their shoes and socks in the doorway, in the sudden blinding sun. The field before them was bright as water. They ran across where the tracks used to go.

80      "That's enough, that's enough," said Carol. "Watch out for thistles!"

"Tops! Everybody take off their tops!"

"I won't! We won't, will we, Eva?"

But Eva was whirling round and round in the sun where the track used to be. "I don't care, I don't care! Truth or Dare! Truth or Dare!"

She unbuttoned her blouse as she whirled, as if she didn't know what her hand was doing, she flung it off.

Carol took off hers. "I wouldn't have done it, if you hadn't!"

"Bottoms!"

Nobody said a word this time, they all bent and stripped themselves. Eva, naked first, started running across the field, and then all the others ran, all five of them running bare through the knee-high hot grass, running towards the river. Not caring now about being caught but in fact leaping and yelling to call attention to themselves, if there was anybody to hear or see. They felt as if they were going to jump off a cliff and fly. They felt that something was happening to them different from anything that had happened before, and it had to do with the boat, the water, the sunlight, the dark ruined station, and each other. They thought of each other now hardly as names or people, but as echoing shrieks, reflections, all bold and white and loud and scandalous, and as fast as arrows. They went running without a break into the cold water and when it came almost to the tops of their legs they fell on it and swam. It stopped their noise. Silence, amazement, came over them in a rush. They dipped and floated and separated, sleek as mink.

Eva stood up in the water her hair dripping, water running down her face. She was waist deep. She stood on smooth stones, her feet fairly wide apart, water flowing between her legs. About a yard away from her Clayton also stood up, and they were blinking the water out of their eyes, looking at each other. Eva did not turn or try to hide; she was quivering from the cold of the water, but also with pride, shame, boldness, and exhilaration.

Clayton shook his head violently, as if he wanted to bang something out of it, then bent over and took a mouthful of river water. He stood up with his cheeks full and made a tight hole of his mouth and shot the water at her as if it was coming out of a hose, hitting her exactly, first one breast and then the other. Water from his mouth ran down her body. He hooted to see it, a loud self-conscious sound that nobody would have expected, from him. The others looked up from wherever they were in the water and closed in to see.

Eva crouched down and slid into the water, letting her head go right under. She swam, and when she let her head out, downstream, Carol was coming after her and the boys were already on the bank, already running into the grass, showing their skinny backs, their white, flat buttocks. They were laughing and saying things to each other but she couldn't hear, for the water in her ears.

"What did he do?" said Carol.

"Nothing."

They crept in to shore. "Let's stay in the bushes till they go," said Eva. "I hate them anyway. I really do. Don't you hate them?"

"Sure," said Carol, and they waited, not very long, until they heard the boys still noisy and excited coming down to the place a bit upriver where they had left the boat. They heard them jump in and start rowing.

"They've got all the hard part, going back," said Eva, hugging herself and shivering violently. "Who cares? Anyway. It never was our boat."

"What if they tell?" said Carol.

"We'll say it's all a lie."

Eva hadn't thought of this solution until she said it, but as soon as she did she felt almost light-hearted again. The ease and scornfulness of it did make them both giggle, and slapping themselves and splashing out of the water they set about developing one of those fits of laughter

85

90

95

in which, as soon as one showed signs of exhaustion, the other would snort and start up again, and they would make helpless—soon genuinely helpless—faces at each other and bend over and grab themselves as if they had the worst pain.

## Questions

1. Consider the details used in passages of description in the story. What kinds of details are included?
2. What is the level of diction in the dialogue of the story? From the dialogue, what do you learn about the various speakers?
3. Study paragraph 10. What does the paragraph tell you about Eva as a limited-point-of-view center of interest? How?
4. Consider the last paragraph in the story as a paragraph of action. What verbs are used, and how well do they help you visualize and imagine the sounds of the scene? What is the effect of the verb "snort"?
5. From the lifestyle and artifacts mentioned, what do you learn about the time of the events and the economic level of the town? What is the effect of the facts that it is early spring-time, that the water is still cold, but that in May the water is swimmable? What are the implications for summer?

## FRANK O'CONNOR (1903–1966)

Frank O'Connor, the nom de plume of Michael O'Donovan, was an only child of poor parents in County Cork, Ireland. He began writing when young, and for a time he was a director of Ireland's national theater. His output as a writer was considerable, with sixty-seven stories appearing in the posthumous *Collected Stories* of 1981. A meticulous writer, he was constantly revising his work. "First Confession," for example, went through a number of stages before the final version included here.

 ## First Confession (1951)

All the trouble began when my grandfather died and my grandmother—my father's mother—came to live with us. Relations in the one house are a strain at the best of times, but, to make matters worse, my grandmother was a real old countrywoman and quite unsuited to the life in town. She had a fat, wrinkled old face, and, to Mother's great indignation, went round the house in bare feet—the boots had her crippled, she said. For dinner she had a jug of porter° and a pot of potatoes with—sometimes—a bit of salt fish, and she poured out the potatoes on the table and ate them slowly, with great relish, using her fingers by way of a fork.

Now, girls are supposed to be fastidious, but I was the one who suffered most from this. Nora, my sister, just sucked up to the old woman for the penny she got every Friday out of the old-age pension, a thing I could not do. I was too honest, that was my trouble; and when I was playing with Bill Connell, the sergeant-major's son, and saw my grandmother steering up the

---

°*porter*: a dark-brown beer.

path with the jug of porter sticking out from beneath her shawl I was mortified. I made excuses not to let him come into the house, because I could never be sure what she would be up to when we went in.

When Mother was at work and my grandmother made the dinner I wouldn't touch it. Nora once tried to make me, but I hid under the table from her and took the bread-knife with me for protection. Nora let on to be very indignant (she wasn't, of course, but she knew Mother saw through her, so she sided with Gran) and came after me. I lashed out at her with the bread-knife, and after that she left me alone. I stayed there till Mother came in from work and made my dinner, but when Father came in later Nora said in a shocked voice: "Oh, Dadda, do you know what Jackie did at dinner-time?" Then, of course, it all came out; Father gave me a flaking; Mother interfered, and for days after that he didn't speak to me and Mother barely spoke to Nora. And all because of that old woman! God knows, I was heart-scalded.

Then, to crown my misfortune, I had to make my first confession and communion. It was an old woman called Ryan who prepared us for these. She was about the one age with Gran; she was well-to-do, lived in a big house on Montenotte, wore a black cloak and bonnet, and came every day to school at three o'clock when we should have been going home, and talked to us of hell. She may have mentioned the other place as well, but that could only have been by accident, for hell had the first place in her heart.

She lit a candle, took out a new half-crown, and offered it to the first boy who would hold one finger—only one finger!—in the flame for five minutes by the school clock. Being always very ambitious I was tempted to volunteer, but I thought it might look greedy. Then she asked were we afraid of holding one finger—only one finger!—in a little candle flame for five minutes and not afraid of burning all over in roasting hot furnaces for all eternity. "All eternity! Just think of that! A whole lifetime goes by and it's nothing, not even a drop in the ocean of your sufferings." The woman was really interesting about hell, but my attention was all fixed on the half-crown. At the end of the lesson she put it back in her purse. It was a great disappointment; a religious woman like that, you wouldn't think she'd bother about a thing like a half-crown.

Another day she said she knew a priest who woke one night to find a fellow he didn't recognize leaning over the end of his bed. The priest was a bit frightened—naturally enough—but he asked the fellow what he wanted, and the fellow said in a deep, husky voice that he wanted to go to confession. The priest said it was an awkward time and wouldn't it do in the morning, but the fellow said that last time he went to confession, there was one sin he kept back, being ashamed to mention it, and now it was always on his mind. Then the priest knew it was a bad case, because the fellow was after making a bad confession and committing a mortal sin. He got up to dress, and just then the cock crew in the yard outside, and—lo and behold!—when the priest looked round there was no sign of the fellow, only a smell of burning timber, and when the priest looked at his bed didn't he see the print of two hands burned in it? That was because the fellow had made a bad confession. This story made a shocking impression on me.

But the worst of all was when she showed us how to examine our conscience. Did we take the name of the Lord, our God, in vain? Did we honour our father and our mother? (I asked her did this include grandmothers and she said it did.) Did we love our neighbours as ourselves? Did we covet our neighbour's goods? (I thought of the way I felt about the penny that Nora got every Friday.) I decided that, between one thing and another, I must have broken the whole ten commandments, all on account of that old woman, and so far as I could see, so long as she remained in the house I had no hope of ever doing anything else.

I was scared to death of confession. The day the whole class went I let on to have a toothache, hoping my absence wouldn't be noticed; but at three o'clock, just as I was feeling safe, along comes a chap with a message from Mrs. Ryan that I was to go to confession myself

5

on Saturday and be at the chapel for communion with the rest. To make it worse, Mother couldn't come with me and sent Nora instead.

Now, that girl had ways of tormenting me that Mother never knew of. She held my hand as we went down the hill, smiling sadly and saying how sorry she was for me, as if she were bringing me to the hospital for an operation.

10     "Oh, God help us!" she moaned. "Isn't it a terrible pity you weren't a good boy? Oh, Jackie, my heart bleeds for you! How will you ever think of all your sins? Don't forget you have to tell him about the time you kicked Gran on the shin."

"Lemme go!" I said, trying to drag myself free of her. "I don't want to go to confession at all."

"But sure, you'll have to go to confession, Jackie," she replied in the same regretful tone. "Sure, if you didn't the parish priest would be up to the house, looking for you.'Tisn't, God knows, that I'm not sorry for you. Do you remember the time you tried to kill me with the bread-knife under the table? And the language you used to me? I don't know what he'll do with you at all, Jackie. He might have to send you up to the bishop."

I remember thinking bitterly that she didn't know the half of what I had to tell—if I told it. I knew I couldn't tell it, and understood perfectly why the fellow in Mrs. Ryan's story made a bad confession; it seemed to me a great shame that people wouldn't stop criticizing him. I remember that steep hill down to the church, and the sunlit hillsides beyond the valley of the river, which I saw in the gaps between the houses like Adam's last glimpse of Paradise.°

Then, when she had manœuvered me down the long flight of steps to the chapel yard, Nora suddenly changed her tone. She became the raging malicious devil she really was.

15     "There you are!" she said with a yelp of triumph, hurling me through the church door. "And I hope he'll give you the penitential psalms, you dirty little caffler."

I knew then I was lost, given up to eternal justice. The door with the coloured-glass panels swung shut behind me, the sunlight went out and gave place to deep shadow, and the wind whistled outside so that the silence within seemed to crackle like ice under my feet. Nora sat in front of me by the confession box. There were a couple of old women ahead of her, and then a miserable-looking poor devil came and wedged me in at the other side, so that I couldn't escape even if I had the courage. He joined his hands and rolled his eyes in the direction of the roof, muttering aspirations in an anguished tone, and I wondered had he a grandmother too. Only a grandmother could account for a fellow behaving in that heartbroken way, but he was better off than I, for he at least could go and confess his sins; while I would make a bad confession and then die in the night and be continually coming back and burning people's furniture.

Nora's turn came, and I heard the sound of something slamming, and then her voice as if butter wouldn't melt in her mouth, and then another slam, and out she came. God, the hypocrisy of women! Her eyes were lowered, her head was bowed, and her hands were joined very low down on her stomach, and she walked up the aisle to the side altar looking like a saint. You never saw such an exhibition of devotion, and I remembered the devilish malice with which she had tormented me all the way from our door, and wondered were all religious people like that, really. It was my turn now. With the fear of damnation in my soul I went in, and the confessional door closed of itself behind me.

It was pitch-dark and I couldn't see the priest or anything else. Then I really began to be frightened. In the darkness it was a matter between God and me, and He had all the odds. He knew what my intentions were before I even started; I had no chance. All I had ever been told about confession got mixed up in my mind, and I knelt to one wall and said: "Bless me, father, for I have sinned; this is my first confession." I waited for a few minutes, but nothing happened, so I tried it on the other wall. Nothing happened there either. He had me spotted all right.

---

° *Adam's last glimpse of Paradise:* Genesis 3:23–24.

It must have been then that I noticed the shelf at about one height with my head. It was really a place for grown-up people to rest their elbows, but in my distracted state I thought it was probably the place you were supposed to kneel. Of course, it was on the high side and not very deep, but I was always good at climbing and managed to get up all right. Staying up was the trouble. There was room only for my knees, and nothing you could get a grip on but a sort of wooden moulding a bit above it. I held on to the moulding and repeated the words a little louder, and this time something happened all right. A slide was slammed back; a little light entered the box, and a man's voice said: "Who's there?"

"'Tis me, father," I said for fear he mightn't see me and go away again. I couldn't see him      20
at all. The place the voice came from was under the moulding, about level with my knees, so I took a good grip of the moulding and swung myself down till I saw the astonished face of a young priest looking up at me. He had to put his head on one side to see me, and I had to put mine on one side to see him, so we were more or less talking to one another upside-down. It struck me as a queer way of hearing confessions, but I didn't feel it my place to criticize.

"Bless me, father, for I have sinned; this is my first confession," I rattled off all in one breath, and swung myself down the least shade more to make it easier for him.

"What are you doing up there?" he shouted in an angry voice, and the strain the politeness was putting on my hold of the moulding, and the shock of being addressed in such an uncivil tone, were too much for me. I lost my grip, tumbled, and hit the door an unmerciful wallop before I found myself flat on my back in the middle of the aisle. The people who had been waiting stood up with their mouths open. The priest opened the door of the middle box and came out, pushing his biretta back from his forehead; he looked something terrible. Then Nora came scampering down the aisle.

"Oh, you dirty little caffler!" she said. "I might have known you'd do it. I might have known you'd disgrace me. I can't leave you out of my sight for one minute."

Before I could even get to my feet to defend myself she bent down and gave me a clip across the ear. This reminded me that I was so stunned I had even forgotten to cry, so that people might think I wasn't hurt at all, when in fact I was probably maimed for life. I gave a roar out of me.

"What's all this about?" the priest hissed, getting angrier than ever and pushing Nora off      25
me. "How dare you hit the child like that, you little vixen?"

"But I can't do my penance with him, father," Nora cried, cocking an outraged eye up to him.

"Well, go and do it, or I'll give you some more to do," he said, giving me a hand up. "Was it coming to confession you were, my poor man?" he asked me.

"'Twas, father," said I with a sob.

"Oh," he said respectfully, "a big hefty fellow like you must have terrible sins. Is this your first?"

"'Tis, father," said I.                                                                                      30

"Worse and worse," he said gloomily. "The crimes of a lifetime. I don't know will I get rid of you at all today. You'd better wait now till I'm finished with these old ones. You can see by the looks of them they haven't much to tell."

"I will, father," I said with something approaching joy.

The relief of it was really enormous. Nora stuck out her tongue at me from behind his back, but I couldn't even be bothered retorting. I knew from the very moment that man opened his mouth that he was intelligent above the ordinary. When I had time to think, I saw how right I was. It only stood to reason that a fellow confessing after seven years would have more to tell than people that went every week. The crimes of a lifetime, exactly as he said. It was only what he expected, and the rest was the cackle of old women and girls with their talk of hell, the bishop, and the penitential psalms. That was all they knew. I started to make my examination of conscience, and barring the one bad business of my grandmother it didn't seem so bad.

The next time, the priest steered me into the confession box himself and left the shutter back the way I could see him get in and sit down at the further side of the grille from me.

35    "Well, now," he said, "what do they call you?"

"Jackie, father," said I.

"And what's a-trouble to you, Jackie?"

"Father," I said, feeling I might as well get it over while I had him in good humour, "I had it all arranged to kill my grandmother."

He seemed a bit shaken by that, all right, because he said nothing for quite a while.

40    "My goodness," he said at last, "that'd be a shocking thing to do. What put that into your head?"

"Father," I said, feeling very sorry for myself, "she's an awful woman."

"Is she?" he asked. "What way is she awful?"

"She takes porter, father," I said, knowing well from the way Mother talked of it that this was a mortal sin, and hoping it would make the priest take a more favourable view of my case.

"Oh, my!" he said, and I could see he was impressed.

45    "And snuff, father," said I.

"That's a bad case, sure enough, Jackie," he said.

"And she goes round in her bare feet, father," I went on in a rush of self-pity, "and she knows I don't like her, and she gives pennies to Nora and none to me, and my da sides with her and flakes me, and one night I was so heart-scalded I made up my mind I'd have to kill her."

"And what would you do with the body?" he asked with great interest.

"I was thinking I could chop that up and carry it away in a barrow I have," I said.

50    "Begor, Jackie," he said, "do you know you're a terrible child?"

"I know, father," I said, for I was just thinking the same thing myself. "I tried to kill Nora too with a bread-knife under the table, only I missed her."

"Is that the little girl that was beating you just now?" he asked.

"'Tis, father."

"Someone will go for her with a bread-knife one day, and he won't miss her," he said rather cryptically. "You must have great courage. Between ourselves, there's a lot of people I'd like to do the same to but I'd never have the nerve. Hanging is an awful death."

55    "Is it, father?" I asked with the deepest interest—I was always very keen on hanging. "Did you ever see a fellow hanged?"

"Dozens of them," he said solemnly. "And they all died roaring."

"Jay!" I said.

"Oh, a horrible death!" he said with great satisfaction. "Lots of fellows I saw killed their grandmothers too, but they all said 'twas never worth it."

He had me there for a full ten minutes talking, and then walked out the chapel yard with me. I was genuinely sorry to part with him, because he was the most entertaining character I'd ever met in the religious line. Outside, after the shadow of the church, the sunlight was like the roaring of waves on a beach; it dazzled me; and when the frozen silence melted and I heard the screech of trams on the road my heart soared. I knew now I wouldn't die in the night and come back, leaving marks on my mother's furniture. It would be a great worry to her, and the poor soul had enough.

60    Nora was sitting on the railing, waiting for me, and she put on a very sour puss when she saw the priest with me. She was made jealous because a priest had never come out of the church with her.

"Well," she asked coldly, after he left me, "what did he give you?"

"Three Hail Marys," I said.

"Three Hail Marys," she repeated incredulously. "You mustn't have told him anything."

"I told him everything," I said confidently.

"About Gran and all?" 65

"About Gran and all."

(All she wanted was to be able to go home and say I'd made a bad confession.)

"Did you tell him you went for me with the bread-knife?" she asked with a frown.

"I did to be sure."

"And he only gave you three Hail Marys?" 70

"That's all."

She slowly got down from the railing with a baffled air. Clearly, this was beyond her. As we mounted the steps back to the main road she looked at me suspiciously.

"What are you sucking?" she asked.

"Bullseyes."

"Was it the priest gave them to you?" 75

"'Twas."

"Lord God," she wailed bitterly, "some people have all the luck! 'Tis no advantage to anybody trying to be good. I might just as well be a sinner like you."

## Questions

1. Describe Jackie as a narrator. What is the level of his language? To whom does he seem to be speaking or writing? What elements of language do you find in the story that seem characteristically Irish?

2. Describe Jackie's character. How old do you think he is at the time of the narration? Is there evidence that he has grown as a person since the time of the story's events? Do you think his attitudes have changed about his grandmother? His parents? His sister? Mrs. Ryan? The priest?

3. Is Jackie's confession a "good" one? Whose religion seems more appealing, Mrs. Ryan's or the priest's?

4. To what degree do the relationships within Jackie's family seem either ordinary or unusual?

5. "First Confession" is a funny story. What contributions are made to the humor by the situations? The language?

## DANIEL OROZCO (b. ca. 1957)

Orozco is a native of San Francisco. He studied at the University of Washington, where he earned a Master's Degree in Fine Arts. He also studied at Stanford University, where he was a Scowcroft and L'Heureux Fiction Fellow, and also a Jones Lecturer in Fiction in the Creative Writing Program. In 2005 he was a MacDowell Colony Fellow. He has become a prolific writer of stories, having published in collections such as *The Best American Short Stories, The Best American Mystery Stories*, the *Pushcart Prize Anthology* of 2005, *Harper's Magazine, Zoetrope: All Story, Story Quarterly*, and *McSweeney's*. His story "Samoza's Dream" was one of the finalists in the competition for a 2006 National Magazine Award in fiction. He currently teaches creative writing at the University of Idaho. "Orientation," one of his best-known stories, first appeared in *The Seattle Review*. It was chosen by Jane Smiley for *The Best American Short Stories, 1995* (Boston: Houghton Mifflin, 1995).

## 🐦 Orientation (1994)

Those are the offices and these are the cubicles. That's my cubicle there, and this is your cubicle. This is your phone. Never answer your phone. Let the Voicemail System answer it. This is your Voicemail System Manual. There are no personal phone calls allowed. We do, however, allow for emergencies. If you must make an emergency phone call, ask your supervisor first. If you can't find your supervisor, ask Phillip Spiers, who sits over there. He'll check with Clarissa Nicks, who sits over there. If you make an emergency phone call without asking, you may be let go.

These are your IN and OUT boxes. All the forms in your IN box must be logged in by the date shown in the upper left-hand corner, initialed by you in the upper right-hand corner, and distributed to the Processing Analyst whose name is numerically coded in the lower left-hand corner. The lower right-hand corner is left blank. Here's your Processing Analyst Numerical Code Index. And here's your Forms Processing Procedures Manual.

You must pace your work. What do I mean? I'm glad you asked that. We pace our work according to the eight-hour workday. If you have twelve hours of work in your IN box, for example, you must compress that work into the eight-hour day. If you have one hour of work in your IN box, you must expand that work to fill the eight hour day. That was a good question. Feel free to ask questions. Ask too many questions, however, and you may be let go.

That is our receptionist. She is a temp. We go through receptionists here. They quit with alarming frequency. Be polite and civil to the temps. Learn their names, and invite them to lunch occasionally. But don't get close to them, as it only makes it more difficult when they leave. And they always leave. You can be sure of that.

5   The men's room is over there. The women's room is over there. John LaFountaine, who sits over there, uses the women's room occasionally. He says it is accidental. We know better, but we let it pass. John LaFountaine is harmless, his forays into the forbidden territory of the women's room simply a benign thrill, a faint blip on the dull flat line of his life.

Russell Nash, who sits in the cubicle to your left, is in love with Amanda Pierce, who sits in the cubicle to your right. They ride the same bus together after work. For Amanda Pierce, it is just a tedious bus ride made less tedious by the idle nattering of Russell Nash. But for Russell Nash, it is the highlight of his day. It is the highlight of his life. Russell Nash has put on forty pounds, and grows fatter with each passing month, nibbling on chips and cookies while peeking glumly over the partitions at Amanda Pierce, and gorging himself at home on cold pizza and ice cream while watching adult videos on TV.

Amanda Pierce, in the cubicle to your right, has a six-year-old son named Jamie, who is autistic. Her cubicle is plastered from top to bottom with the boy's crayon artwork—sheet after sheet of precisely drawn concentric circles and ellipses, in black and yellow. She rotates them every other Friday. Be sure to comment on them. Amanda Pierce also has a husband, who is a lawyer. He subjects her to an escalating array of painful and humiliating sex games, to which Amanda Pierce reluctantly submits. She comes to work exhausted and freshly wounded each morning, wincing from the abrasions on her breasts, or the bruises on her abdomen, or the second-degree burns on the backs of her thighs.

But we're not supposed to know any of this. Do not let on. If you let on, you may be let go.

Amanda Pierce, who tolerates Russell Nash, is in love with Albert Bosch, whose office is over there. Albert Bosch, who only dimly registers Amanda Pierce's existence, has eyes only for Ellie Tapper, who sits over there. Ellie Tapper, who hates Albert Bosch, would walk through fire for Curtis Lance. But Curtis Lance hates Ellie Tapper. Isn't the world a funny place? Not in the ha-ha sense, of course.

Anika Bloom sits in that cubicle. Last year, while reviewing quarterly reports in a meeting     10
with Barry Hacker, Anika Bloom's left palm began to bleed. She fell into a trance, stared into
her hand, and told Barry Hacker when and how his wife would die. We laughed it off. She
was, after all, a new employee. But Barry Hacker's wife is dead. So unless you want to know
exactly when and how you'll die, never talk to Anika Bloom.

Cohn Heavey sits in that cubicle over there. He was new once, just like you. We warned
him about Anika Bloom. But at last year's Christmas Potluck, he felt sorry for her when he saw
that no one was talking to her. Cohn Heavey brought her a drink. He hasn't been himself since.
Cohn Heavey is doomed. There's nothing he can do about it, and we are powerless to help
him. Stay away from Cohn Heavey. Never give any of your work to him. If he asks to do something, tell him you have to check with me. If he asks again, tell him I haven't gotten back
to you.

This is the Fire Exit. There are several on this floor, and they are marked accordingly. We
have a Floor Evacuation Review every three months, and an Escape Route Quiz once a month.
We have our Biannual Fire Drill twice a year, and our Annual Earthquake Drill once a year.
These are precautions only. These things never happen.

For your information, we have a comprehensive health plan. Any catastrophic illness, any
unforeseen tragedy is completely covered. All dependents are completely covered. Larry
Bagdikian, who sits over there, has six daughters. If anything were to happen to any of his
girls, or to all of them, if all six were to simultaneously fall victim to illness or injury—stricken
with a hideous degenerative muscle disease or some rare toxic blood disorder, sprayed with
semiautomatic gunfire while on a class field trip, or attacked in their bunk beds by some
prowling nocturnal lunatic—if any of this were to pass, Larry's girls would all be taken care of.
Larry Bagdikian would not have to pay one dime. He would have nothing to worry about.

We also have a generous vacation and sick leave policy. We have an excellent disability insurance plan. We have a stable and profitable pension fund. We get group discounts for the
symphony, and block seating at the ballpark. We get commuter ticket books for the bridge. We
have Direct Deposit. We are all members of Costco.

This is our kitchenette. And this, this is our Mr. Coffee. We have a coffee pool, into which     15
we each pay two dollars a week for coffee, filters, sugar, and CoffeeMate. If you prefer Cremora
or half-and-half to CoffeeMate, there is a special pool for three dollars a week. If you prefer
Sweet'n Low to sugar, there is a special pool for two-fifty a week. We do not do decaf. You are
allowed to join the coffee pool of your choice, but you are not allowed to touch the Mr. Coffee.

This is the microwave oven. You are allowed to heat food in the microwave oven. You are
not, however, allowed to cook food in the microwave oven.

We get one hour for lunch. We also get one fifteen-minute break in the morning, and one
fifteen-minute break in the afternoon. Always take your breaks, if you skip a break, it is gone
forever. For your information, your break is a privilege, not a right. If you abuse the break policy, we are authorized to rescind your breaks. Lunch, however, is a right, not a privilege. If you
abuse the lunch policy, our hands will be tied, and we will be forced to look the other way. We
will not enjoy that.

This is the refrigerator. You may put your lunch in it. Barry Hacker, who sits over there,
steals food from this refrigerator. His petty theft is an outlet for his grief. Last New Year's Eve,
while kissing his wife, a blood vessel burst in her brain. Barry Hacker's wife was two months
pregnant at the time, and lingered in a coma for half a year before dying. It was a tragic loss for
Barry Hacker. He hasn't been himself since. Barry Hacker's wife was a beautiful woman. She
was also completely covered. Barry Hacker did not have to pay one dime. But his dead wife
haunts him. She haunts all of us. We have seen her, reflected in the monitors of our computers,
moving past our cubicles. We have seen the dim shadow of her face in our photocopies. She

pencils herself in in the receptionist's appointment book, with the notation: To see Barry Hacker. She has left messages in the receptionist's Voicemail box, messages garbled by the electronic chirrups and buzzes in the phone line, her voice echoing from an immense distance within the ambient hum. But the voice is hers. And beneath her voice, beneath the tidal whoosh of static and hiss, the gurgling and crying of a baby can be heard.

In any case, if you bring a lunch, put a little something extra in the bag for Barry Hacker. We have four Barrys in this office. Isn't that a coincidence?

20   This is Matthew Payne's office. He is our Unit Manager, and his door is always closed. We have never seen him, and you will never see him. But he is here. You can be sure of that. He is all around us.

This is the Custodian's Closet. You have no business in the Custodian's Closet.

And this, this is our Supplies Cabinet. If you need supplies, see Curtis Lance. He will log you in on the Supplies Cabinet Authorization Log, then give you a Supplies Authorization Slip. Present your pink copy of the Supplies Authorization Slip to Ellie Tapper. She will log you in on the Supplies Cabinet Key Log, then give you the key. Because the Supplies Cabinet is located outside the Unit Manager's office, you must be very quiet. Gather your supplies quietly. The Supplies Cabinet is divided into four sections. Section One contains letterhead stationery, blank paper and envelopes, memo and note pads, and so on. Section Two contains pens and pencils and typewriter and printer ribbons, and the like. In Section Three we have erasers, correction fluids, transparent tapes, glue sticks, et cetera. And in Section Four we have paper clips and push pins and scissors and razor blades. And here are the spare blades for the shredder. Do not touch the shredder, which is located over there. The shredder is of no concern to you.

Gwendolyn Stich sits in that office there. She is crazy about penguins, and collects penguin knickknacks: penguin posters and coffee mugs and stationery, penguin stuffed animals, penguin jewelry, penguin sweaters and T-shirts and socks. She has a pair of penguin fuzzy slippers she wears when working late at the office. She has a tape cassette of penguin sounds which she listens to for relaxation. Her favorite colors are black and white. She has personalized license plates that read PEN GWEN. Every morning, she passes through all the cubicles to wish each of us a good morning. She brings Danish on Wednesdays for Hump Day morning break, and doughnuts on Fridays for TGIF afternoon break. She organizes the Annual Christmas Potluck, and is in charge of the Birthday List. Gwendolyn Stich's door is always open to all of us. She will always lend an ear, and put in a good word for you; she will always give you a hand, or the shirt off her back, or a shoulder to cry on. Because her door is always open, she hides and cries in a stall in the women's room. And John LaFountaine—who, enthralled when a woman enters, sits quietly in his stall with his knees to his chest—John LaFountaine has heard her vomiting in there. We have come upon Gwendolyn Stich huddled in the stairwell, shivering in the updraft, sipping a Diet Mr. Pibb and hugging her knees. She does not let any of this interfere with her work. If it interfered with her work, she might have to be let go.

Kevin Howard sits in that cubicle over there. He is a serial killer, the one they call the Carpet Cutter, responsible for the mutilations across town. We're not supposed to know that, so do not let on. Don't worry. His compulsion inflicts itself on strangers only, and the routine established is elaborate and unwavering. The victim must be a white male, a young adult no older than thirty, heavyset, with dark hair and eyes, and the like. The victim must be chosen at random, before sunset, from a public place; the victim is followed home, and must put up a struggle; et cetera. The carnage inflicted is precise: the angle and direction of the incisions; the layering of skin and muscle tissue; the rearrangement of the visceral organs; and so on. Kevin Howard does not let any of this interfere with his work. He is, in fact, our fastest typist. He types as if he were on fire. He has a secret crush on Gwendolyn Stich, and leaves a red-foil-wrapped Hershey's Kiss on her desk every afternoon. But he hates Anika Bloom, and keeps well away from her. In his presence, she has uncontrollable fits of shaking and trembling. Her left palm does not stop bleeding.

25    In any case, when Kevin Howard gets caught, act surprised. Say that he seemed like a nice person, a bit of a loner, perhaps, but always quiet and polite.

This is the photocopier room. And this, this is our view. It faces southwest. West is down there, toward the water. North is back there. Because we are on the seventeenth floor, we are afforded a magnificent view. Isn't it beautiful? It overlooks the park, where the tops of those trees are. You can see a segment of the bay between those two buildings there. You can see the sun set in the gap between those two buildings over there. You can see this building reflected in the glass panels of that building across the way. There. See? That's you, waving. And look there. There's Anika Bloom in the kitchenette, waving back.

Enjoy this view while photocopying. If you have problems with the photocopier, see Russell Nash. If you have any questions, ask your supervisor. If you can't find your supervisor, ask Phillip Spiers. He sits over there. He'll check with Clarissa Nicks. She sits over there. If you can't find them, feel free to ask me. That's my cubicle. I sit in there.

## Questions  *i don't belong here, i'm not smart enough*

1. What is the situation throughout this story? Who is talking? To whom is he talking? Does the listener have any chance to comment on the speaker's discourse?

2. In the first four paragraphs, is there anything unusual about the speaker's language? What does Orozco have the speaker say in paragraph 5 that alerts you to the unusual nature of the persons in the office?

3. Is there anything funny about the situations of fellow employees in the office? If not, how does one account for the fact that the story is comic? How do the speaker's controlled descriptions of the plights of the various office workers contribute to the story's comic tone?

4. Why is Kevin Howard the last one to be described by the speaker? Of what is Kevin guilty? What might the story be like if Kevin Howard had been mentioned first? Describe the comic technique of paragraph 25.

## JOHN UPDIKE (b. 1932)

Updike was born and reared in Pennsylvania during the Great Depression. His parents were diligent about his education, and in 1950 he received a scholarship for study at Harvard, graduating in 1954. He worked for *The New Yorker* for two years before deciding to devote himself exclusively to his own writing, but since then he has remained a frequent contributor of stories and poems to that magazine. In 1959, he published his first story collection, *The Same Door*, and his first novel, *The Poorhouse Fair*. In 1960, with *Rabbit, Run*, he began his extensive *Rabbit* chronicles. In 1981 he received the Pulitzer Prize for *Rabbit Is Rich*. His collected poems were published in 1993, and he is continually productive in writing new stories and poems. Today he is considered one of the best of America's major writers of fiction and poetry.

# 🦅 A & P° (1961)

In walks these three girls in nothing but bathing suits. I'm in the third checkout slot, with my back to the door, so I don't see them until they're over by the bread. The one that caught my eye first was the one in the plaid green two-piece. She was a chunky kid, with a good tan and a sweet broad soft-looking can with those two crescents of white just under it, where the sun never seems to hit, at the top of the backs of her legs. I stood there with my hand on a box of HiHo crackers trying to remember if I rang it up or not. I ring it up again and the customer starts giving me hell. She's one of these cash-register-watchers, a witch about fifty with rouge on her cheekbones and no eyebrows, and I know it made her day to trip me up. She'd been watching cash registers for fifty years and probably never seen a mistake before.

By the time I got her feathers smoothed and her goodies into a bag—she gives me a little snort in passing, if she'd been born at the right time they would have burned her over in Salem—by the time I get her on her way the girls had circled around the bread and were coming back, without a pushcart, back my way along the counters, in the aisle between the checkouts and the Special bins. They didn't even have shoes on. There was this chunky one, with the two-piece—it was bright green and the seams on the bra were still sharp and her belly was still pretty pale so I guessed she just got it (the suit)—there was this one, with one of those chubby berry-faces, the lips all bunched together under her nose, this one, and a tall one, with black hair that hadn't quite frizzed right, and one of these sunburns right across under the eyes, and a chin that was too long—you know, the kind of girl other girls think is very "striking" and "attractive" but never quite makes it, as they very well know, which is why they like her so much—and then the third one, that wasn't quite so tall. She was the queen. She kind of led them, the other two peeking around and making their shoulders round. She didn't look around, not this queen, she just walked straight on slowly, on these long white prima-donna legs. She came down a little hard on her heels, as if she didn't walk in her bare feet that much, putting down her heels and then letting the weight move along to her toes as if she was testing the floor with every step, putting a little deliberate extra action into it. You never know for sure how girls' minds work (do you really think it's a mind in there or just a little buzz like a bee in a glass jar?) but you got the idea she had talked the other two into coming in here with her, and now she was showing them how to do it, walk slow and hold yourself straight.

She had on a kind of dirty-pink—beige, maybe, I don't know—bathing suit with a little nubble all over it and, what got me, the straps were down. They were off her shoulders looped loose around the cool tops of her arms, and I guess as a result the suit had slipped a little on her, so all around the top of the cloth there was this shining rim. If it hadn't been there you wouldn't have known there could have been anything whiter than those shoulders. With the straps pushed off, there was nothing between the top of the suit and the top of her head except just *her*, this clean bare plane of the top of her chest down from the shoulder bones like a dented sheet of metal tilted in the light. I mean, it was more than pretty.

She had sort of oaky hair that the sun and salt had bleached, done up in a bun that was unraveling, and a kind of prim face. Walking into the A & P with your straps down, I suppose it's the only kind of face you *can* have. She held her head so high her neck, coming up out of those white shoulders, looked kind of stretched, but I didn't mind. The longer her neck was, the more of her there was.

5      She must have felt in the corner of her eye me and over my shoulder Stokesie in the second slot watching, but she didn't tip. Not this queen. She kept her eyes moving across the racks, and

---

°*A & P*: the Great Atlantic and Pacific Tea Company, a large grocery chain established in 1859 and still flourishing in 18 states, with more than 800 A & P stores in the United States and 200 in Canada.

stopped, and turned so slow it made my stomach rub the inside of my apron, and buzzed to the other two, who kind of huddled against her for relief, and then they all three of them went up the cat-and-dog-food-breakfast-cereal-macaroni-rice-raisins-seasonings-spreads-spaghetti soft-drinks-crackers-and-cookies aisle. From the third slot I look straight up this aisle to the meat counter, and I watched them all the way. The fat one with the tan sort of fumbled with the cookies, but on second thought she put the package back. The sheep pushing their carts down the aisle—the girls were walking against the usual traffic (not that we have one-way signs or anything)—were pretty hilarious. You could see them, when Queenie's white shoulders dawned on them, kind of jerk, or hop, or hiccup, but their eyes snapped back to their own baskets and on they pushed. I bet you could set off dynamite in an A & P and the people would by and large keep reaching and checking oatmeal off their lists and muttering "Let me see, there was a third thing, began with A, asparagus, no ah, yes, applesauce!" or whatever it is they do mutter. But there was no doubt, this jiggled them. A few houseslaves in pin curlers even looked around after pushing their carts past to make sure what they had seen was correct.

You know, it's one thing to have a girl in a bathing suit down on the beach, where what with the glare nobody can look at each other much anyway, and another thing in the cool of the A & P, under the fluorescent lights, against all those stacked packages, with her feet paddling along naked over our checkerboard green-and-cream rubber-tile floor.

"Oh Daddy," Stokesie said beside me. "I feel so faint."

"Darling," I said. "Hold me tight." Stokesie's married, with two babies chalked up on his fuselage already, but as far as I can tell that's the only difference. He's twenty-two, and I was nineteen this April.

"Is it done?" he asks, the responsible married man finding his voice. I forgot to say he thinks he's going to be manager some sunny day, maybe in 1990 when it's called the Great Alexandrov and Petrooshki° Tea Company or something.

What he meant was, our town is five miles from the beach, with a big summer colony out on the Point, but we're right in the middle of town, and the women generally put on a shirt or shorts or something before they get out of the car into the street. And anyway these are usually women with six children and varicose veins mapping their legs and nobody, including them could care less. As I say, we're right in the middle of town, and if you stand at our front doors you can see two banks and the Congregational church and the newspaper store and three real-estate offices and about twenty-seven old freeloaders tearing up Central Street because the sewer broke again. It's not as if we're on the Cape,° we're north of Boston and there's people in this town haven't seen the ocean for twenty years.

The girls had reached the meat counter and were asking McMahon something. He pointed, they pointed, and they shuffled out of sight behind a pyramid of Diet Delight peaches. All that was left for us to see was old McMahon patting his mouth and looking after them sizing up their joints. Poor kids, I began to feel sorry for them, they couldn't help it.

Now here comes the sad part of the story, at least my family says it's sad, but I don't think it's so sad myself. The store's pretty empty, it being Thursday afternoon, so there was nothing much to do except lean on the register and wait for the girls to show up again. The whole store was like a pinball machine and I didn't know which tunnel they'd come out of. After a while they come around out of the far aisle, around the light bulbs, records at discount of the Caribbean Six or Tony Martin Sings or some such gunk you wonder they waste the wax on, sixpacks of candy bars, and plastic toys done up in cellophane that fall apart when a kid looks at them anyway. Around they come, Queenie still leading the way, and holding a little gray jar in her hand. Slots Three through Seven are unmanned and I could see her wondering between Stokes and me, but Stokesie with

10

---

° *Great Alexandrov and Petrooshki:* apparently a reference to the possibility that someday Russia might rule the United States.
° *the Cape:* Cape Cod, the southeastern area of Massachusetts, a place of many resorts and beaches.

his usual luck draws an old party in baggy gray pants who stumbles up with four giant cans of pineapple juice (what do these bums *do* with all that pineapple juice? I've often asked myself) so the girls come to me. Queenie puts down the jar and I take it into my fingers icy cold. Kingfish Fancy Herring Snacks in Pure Sour Cream: 49¢. Now her hands are empty, not a ring or a bracelet, bare as God made them, and I wonder where the money's coming from. Still with that prim look she lifts a folded dollar bill out of the hollow at the center of her nubbed pink top. The jar went heavy in my hand. Really, I thought that was so cute.

Then everybody's luck begins to run out. Lengel comes in from haggling with a truck full of cabbages on the lot and is about to scuttle into that door marked MANAGER behind which he hides all day when the girls touch his eye. Lengel's pretty dreary, teaches Sunday school and the rest, but he doesn't miss that much. He comes over and says, "Girls, this isn't the beach."

Queenie blushes, though maybe it's just a brush of sunburn I was noticing for the first time, now that she was so close. "My mother asked me to pick up a jar of herring snacks." Her voice kind of startled me, the way voices do when you see the people first, coming out so flat and dumb yet kind of tony, too, the way it ticked over "pick up" and "snacks." All of a sudden I slid right down her voice into her living room. Her father and the other men were standing around in ice-cream coats and bow ties and the women were in sandals picking up herring snacks on toothpicks off a big glass plate and they were all holding drinks the color of water with olives and sprigs of mint in them. When my parents have somebody over they get lemonade and if it's a real racy affair Schlitz in tall glasses with "They'll Do It Every Time"° cartoons stenciled on.

15 "That's all right," Lengel said. "But this isn't the beach." His repeating this struck me as funny, as if it had just occurred to him, and he had been thinking all these years the A & P was a great big dune and he was the head lifeguard. He didn't like my smiling—as I say he doesn't miss much—but he concentrates on giving the girls that sad Sunday-school-superintendent stare.

Queenie's blush is no sunburn now, and the plump one in plaid, that I liked better from the back—a really sweet can—pipes up, "We weren't doing any shopping. We just came in for the one thing."

"That makes no difference," Lengel tells her, and I could see from the way his eyes went that he hadn't noticed she was wearing a two-piece before. "We want you decently dressed when you come in here."

"We *are* decent," Queenie says suddenly, her lower lip pushing, getting sore now that she remembers her place, a place from which the crowd that runs the A & P must look pretty crummy. Fancy Herring Snacks flashed in her very blue eyes.

"Girls, I don't want to argue with you. After this come in here with your shoulders covered. It's our policy." He turns his back. That's policy for you. Policy is what the kingpins want. What the others want is juvenile delinquency.

20 All this while, the customers had been showing up with their carts but, you know, sheep, seeing a scene, they had all bunched up on Stokesie, who shook open a paper bag as gently as peeling a peach, not wanting to miss a word. I could feel in the silence everybody getting nervous, most of all Lengel, who asks me, "Sammy, have you rung up their purchase?"

I thought and said "No" but it wasn't about that I was thinking. I go through the punches, 4, 9, GROC, TOT—it's more complicated than you think, and after you do it often enough, it begins to make a little song, that you hear words to, in my case "Hello (*bing*) there, you (*gung*) hap-py *pee*-pul (*splat*)!"—the *splat* being the drawer flying out. I uncrease the bill, tenderly as you may imagine, it just having come from between the two smoothest scoops of vanilla I had ever known were there, and pass a half and a penny into her narrow pink palm, and nestle the herrings in a bag and twist its neck and hand it over, all the time thinking.

The girls, and who'd blame them, are in a hurry to get out, so I say "I quit" to Lengel quick enough for them to hear, hoping they'll stop and watch me, their unsuspected hero.

---

° *They'll Do It Every Time*: syndicated daily and Sunday cartoon created by Jimmy Hatlo.

They keep right on going, into the electric eye; the door flies open and they flicker across the lot to their car, Queenie and Plaid and Big Tall Goony-Goony (not that as raw material she was so bad), leaving me with Lengel and a kink in his eyebrow.

"Did you say something, Sammy?"

"I said I quit."

"I thought you did."                                                                                      25

"You didn't have to embarrass them."

"It was they who were embarrassing us."

I started to say something that came out "Fiddle-de-doo." It's a saying of my grand-mother's, and I know she would have been pleased.

"I don't think you know what you're saying," Lengel said.

"I know you don't," I said. "But I do." I pull the bow at the back of my apron and start    30
shrugging it off my shoulders. A couple customers that had been heading for my slot begin to knock against each other, like scared pigs in a chute.

Lengel sighs and begins to look very patient and old and gray. He's been a friend of my parents for years. "Sammy, you don't want to do this to your Mom and Dad," he tells me. It's true, I don't. But it seems to me that once you begin a gesture it's fatal not to go through with it. I fold the apron, "Sammy" stitched in red on the pocket, and put it on the counter, and drop the bow tie on top of it. The bow tie is theirs, if you've ever wondered. "You'll feel this for the rest of your life," Lengel says, and I know that's true, too, but remembering how he made that pretty girl blush makes me so scrunchy inside I punch the No Sale tab and the machine whirs "pee-pul" and the drawer splats out. One advantage to this scene taking place in summer, I can follow this up with a clean exit, there's no fumbling around getting your coat and galoshes, I just saunter into the electric eye in my white shirt that my mother ironed the night before, and the door heaves itself open, and outside the sunshine is skating around on the asphalt.

I look around for my girls, but they're gone, of course. There wasn't anybody but some young married screaming with her children about some candy they didn't get by the door of a powder-blue Falcon° station wagon. Looking back in the big windows, over the bags of peat moss and aluminum lawn furniture stacked on the pavement, I could see Lengel in my place in the slot, checking the sheep through. His face was dark gray and his back stiff, as if he'd just had an injection of iron, and my stomach kind of fell as I felt how hard the world was going to be to me hereafter.

## Questions

1. From Sammy's language, what do you learn about his view of himself? About his educational and class level? The first sentence, for example, is grammatically incorrect in standard English but not uncommon in colloquial English. Point out and explain similar passages.

2. Consider the first eleven paragraphs as exposition, in which you learn about the location, the issues, and the participants in the story's conflict. Is there anything inessential in this section? Do you learn enough to understand the story? How might someone other than Sammy present the material?

3. How do you learn that Sammy is an experienced "girl watcher"? What does *he think* he thinks about most girls? To what degree is this estimate inconsistent with what he finally does after the girls leave?

4. Why does Sammy say "I quit" so abruptly? What does he mean when he says that the world is going to be hard to him after his experience at the A & P?

---

°*Falcon*: small car that had recently been introduced by the Ford Motor Company.

## WRITING ABOUT TONE AND STYLE

The task of writing about tone and style is to identify attitudes that you find in the work and then to explain how attitudes are made obvious by the author's style. How do words describing characters, scenes, thoughts, and actions indicate attitude? In Poe's "The Masque of the Red Death" (Chapter 5), for example, do the descriptions of the dimly lit rooms evoke fear or tension, or do they seem exaggerated? Depending on the story, your devising and answering such questions will help you understand an author's control over tone.

### Questions for Discovering Ideas

- Use a dictionary to discover the meaning of any words you do not immediately know. Are there any unusual words? Any especially difficult or uncommon ones? Do any of the words distract you as you read?
- How strongly do you respond to the story? What words bring out your interest, concern, indignation, fearfulness, anguish, amusement, or sense of affirmation?
- Does the diction seem unusual or noteworthy, such as words in dialect, polysyllabic words, or foreign words or phrases that the author assumes you know? Are there any especially connotative or emotive words? What do these words suggest concerning the author's apparent assumptions about readers?
- Can you easily visualize and imagine the situations described by the words? If you find it easy, or hard, to what degree does your success or difficulty stem from the level of diction?
- For passages describing action, how vivid are the words? How do they help you picture the action? How do they hold your attention?
- For passages describing exterior or interior scenes, how specific are the words? How much detail does the writer provide? Should there be more or fewer words? How vivid are the descriptions? How successfully does the author locate scenes spatially? How many words are devoted to colors, shapes, sizes, and so on? What is the effect of such passages?
- For passages of dialogue, what does the level of speech indicate about the characters? How do a person's speeches help to establish her or his character? For what purposes does the author use formal or informal diction? How much slang (low or informal language) do you find? Why is it there? How does dialogue shape your responses to the characters and to the actions?
- What role does the narrator/speaker play in your attitudes toward the story material? Does the speaker seem intelligent/stupid, friendly/unfriendly, sane/insane, or idealistic/pragmatic?
- What verbal irony do you find in the story? How is the irony connected to philosophies of marriage, family, society, politics, religion, or morality? How do you think you are expected to respond to the irony?
- Did anything in the story make you laugh? What placement of words brought out the humor? Explain how the word arrangement caused your laughter.

## Strategies for Organizing Ideas

Begin with a careful reading, noting particularly those elements of language that convey attitudes. How does the author establish the dominant moods of the story (e.g., the humor of "First Confession," the tension in "Hills Like White Elephants")? Some possibilities are the use or misuse of language, the exposé of a pretentious speaker, the use of exact and specific descriptions, the isolation of a major character, the failure of plans, and the continuance of naiveté in a disillusioned world.

Here are some of the things to discuss.

1. *How Is the Work's Tone Affected by Situation, Characters, Action, and Audience?* Does the speaker directly address any person or group? What attitude is expressed (love, respect, condescension, confidentiality, confidence, etc.)? What is the basic situation in the story? Do you find instances of verbal irony? What do these show (optimism or pessimism, for example)? How is the situation of the story controlled to shape your responses? That is, can actions, situations, or characters be seen as expressions of attitude, or as embodiments of certain favorable or unfavorable ideas or positions? What sort of person is the narrator or persona? Why does the narrator speak exactly as he or she does? How is the narrator's character manipulated to show apparent authorial attitude and to elicit reader response? Does the story promote respect, admiration, dislike, or other feelings about character or situation? How?

2. *What Do Diction and Descriptions Contribute to the Tone?* Your concern here is not to analyze descriptions or diction for themselves alone, but to relate these matters to attitude. *For descriptions*: Do descriptions of natural scenery and conditions (snowstorms, cold, rain, ice, intense sunlight) complement or oppose the circumstances of the characters? Are there any systematic references to colors, sounds, or noises that collectively reflect an attitude? *For diction*: Do connotative meanings of words control response in any way? Does the diction require readers to have a large or technical vocabulary? Do speech patterns or the use of dialect evoke attitudes about speakers or their condition of life? Is the level of diction formal, middle, or informal? Do you find any substandard or slang expressions? What effect do these create? Are there unusual or particularly noteworthy expressions? If so, what attitudes do these show?

3. *To What Degree Does the Story Contain Humor?* Is the story funny? How funny, how intense? How is the humor achieved? How does the language bring out the incongruity of funny situations? Are the objects of laughter still respected or loved even though the story's treatment of them causes amusement?

4. *How Does the Expression of Ideas Shape the Work's Tone?* Are any ideas advocated, defended mildly, or attacked? How does the author clarify his or her attitude toward these ideas—directly, by statement, or indirectly, through understatement, overstatement, or a character's speeches? In what ways does the story assume agreement between author and readers? What common religious views can you find? What political views, moral and behavioral standards, and so on?

In concluding, first summarize your main points and then go on to definitions, explanations, or afterthoughts, together with ideas reinforcing earlier points. To what extent has your analysis increased or reinforced your appreciation of the author's technique? Does the passage take on added importance as a result of your study? Is there anything else in the work comparable to the content, words, or ideas you have discussed in the passage?

## Numbering Your Passage for Easy Reference

To focus on specifics of style and tone, the assignment visualized here is to analyze a passage—either short or long—from a story. After you have selected a passage, include a copy at the beginning of your essay, as in the example. For your reader's convenience, number the sentences in the passage, and use these numbers when you refer to them. To focus your essay, either single out one aspect of style and tone, or discuss everything, depending on the length of the assignment. Be sure to consider relationships that you can discover between tone and *levels of diction, specific and general words, concrete and abstract words, denotation and connotation, irony,* and *humor.*

## Illustrative Student Essay

Underlined sentences in this paper *do not* conform to MLA style and are used solely as teaching tools to emphasize the central idea, thesis sentence, and topic sentences throughout the paper.

Torres 1

Elizabeth Torres

Professor Moorehouse

English 210

15 November 2007

**Frank O'Connor's Control of Tone and Style in "First Confession"\***

[1] Nora's turn came, and I heard the sound of something slamming, and then her voice as if butter wouldn't melt in her mouth, and then another slam, and out she came. [2] God, the hypocrisy of women! [3] Her eyes were lowered, her head was bowed, and her hands were joined very low down on her stomach, and she walked up the aisle to the side altar looking like a saint. [4] You never saw such an exhibition of devotion, and I remembered the devilish malice with which she had tormented me all the way from our door, and wondered were all

---

\*See pp. 300–05 for this story.

religious people like that, really. [5] It was my turn now. [6] With the fear of damnation in my soul I went in, and the confessional door closed of itself behind me.

[1] This paragraph from O'Connor's "First Confession" appears midway in the story. It is transitional, coming between Jackie's "heartscalded" memories of family troubles and his happier memory of the confession itself. Though mainly narrative, the passage is punctuated by Jackie's recollections of disgust with his sister and fear of eternal punishment for his childhood "sins." It is the controlled contrast of these attitudes that creates the humor of the passage.[+] In all respects—brevity, word level, concreteness, and grammatical control—the passage is typical of the story's humor.[#]

[2] The actions and responses of the paragraph are described briefly and accurately. The first four sentences convey Jackie's exaggerated reactions to Nora's confession. Sentence 1 describes his recollections of her voice in the confessional, and the tone of sentence 3 makes his judgment clear about the hypocrisy of her pious appearance when she leaves for the altar. Each of these descriptive sentences is followed by Jackie's angry reactions, at which readers smile if not laugh. This depth of feeling is transformed to "fear of damnation" at the beginning of sentence 6, which describes Jackie's own entry into the confessional, with the closing door suggesting that he is being shut off from the world and thrown into hell. In other words, the paragraph succinctly presents the sounds, reactions, sights, and confusion of the scene itself, all of which furnish readers with a brief and comic drama.

[3] The humorous action of the passage is augmented by O'Connor's neutral level of diction, which enables readers to concentrate fully on Jackie's responses. For the most part, Jackie is recalling unpleasant childhood memories, and the neutral, middle diction enables readers both to sympathize with him and to be amused by him. His words are neither unusual nor difficult. What could be more ordinary, for example, than "butter," "slam," "out," "hands," "joined," "low," "people," and "closed"? Even Jackie's moral and religious words fall within the vocabulary of ordinary discussions about sin and punishment: "hypocrisy," "exhibition," "devilish," "malice," "tormented," and "damnation." In the passage, therefore, the diction accurately conveys Jackie's vision of

---

[+] Central idea.
[#] Thesis sentence.

the oppressive religious forces which he dislikes, and which he also exaggerates. Readers follow these words easily and with amusement.

[4]    Additionally, the words of the paragraph are appropriate to Jackie's boyhood anger because they are specific and concrete. When he tells about Nora going into the confessional, he says specifically that he "heard the sound of something slamming," followed by the sound of Nora's "voice," "another slam," and then her appearance as "she came" out of the confessional. Equally specific, and equally comic, is his description of Nora's appearance as she leaves. Readers can easily visualize her "bowed" head, her "lowered" eyes, and her prayerful hands, and are amused by the scene just as Jackie is annoyed by it. In addition to these specific descriptions, sentences 2 and 4 contain Jackie's angry responses, which also provoke amusement. Sentence 4 presents the greater number of connotative abstractions—first the "exhibition of devotion," and second the "devilish malice with which she had tormented me." But these define Jackie's childhood conclusions about his sister, not his adult ones, and their incongruity furnishes readers with a realistic basis for laughter.

[5]    A major element contributing to Jackie's remembrance of his boyhood attitudes is the control over grammar that O'Connor gives to him. At the time of the narrative Jackie is presumably no longer angry, even though as a child he felt misunderstood and unfairly treated. He therefore does not need to recall his story in angry outbursts, despite his exclamation about the "hypocrisy of women," but rather he presents details in correct and grammatical—controlled—sentences. The very first sentence, for example, contains three parallel grammatical direct objects ("sound," "voice," "slam"), thereby using a minimal number of words while still detailing the major sounds of Nora's confession. The grammar of the third sentence illustrates the swiftness and sparseness of O'Connor's (and Jackie's) narrative style. The first three parallel clauses are each made up of four words ("her eyes were lowered," "her head was bowed," and "her hands were joined"). These clauses give Jackie the opportunity to introduce his sarcastic and amusing phrase "looking like a saint" at the end to express his disgust over his sister's "hypocrisy." This control shapes the developing comedy of the paragraph.

[6]    In all respects, the passage shows the right use of words and exactly the right tone. Jackie's accurate descriptions are mixed with his expressions of childhood emotions— all important aspects of O'Connor's good humor. In retrospect, Jackie's anger and

Torres 4

disgust were unnecessary, but they were important to him as a child—so much so that his exaggerations make him the center of the story's comedy. The words that O'Connor skillfully puts in Jackie's mouth (or on his page) enable readers to share this particular experience of a first confession but to do so while smiling. <u>Jackie's bittersweet memories are successfully rendered and made comic through O'Connor's control over style.</u>

Torres 5

**WORK CITED**

O'Connor, Frank. "First Confession." *Literature: An Introduction to Reading and Writing.* Ed. Edgar V. Roberts. 4th Compact Ed. Upper Saddle River: Prentice Hall, 2008, 300–05.

## Commentary on the Essay

Paragraph 1 demonstrates how a passage being studied may be related to the entire work of which it is a part. The central idea connects the story's comic tone to O'Connor's control over situation and diction. Throughout the essay, the connection of style and humor are emphasized. The thesis sentence presents four topics that the essay will develop. Any one of these topics, if necessary, could also be treated separately.

In the body of the essay, the writer stresses the way O'Connor creates the story's tone by the careful manipulation of words and expressions. Paragraph 2 indicates O'Connor's verbal economy in describing the actions and reactions of the passage. Paragraph 3 deals with the level of diction, noting that the words are appropriate both to the action and to Jackie's anger when recollecting it. In paragraph 4 the topic is O'Connor's use of specific and concrete diction, a quality that makes for easy visualization of the details. This paragraph also considers the small number of abstract and general words that appear in O'Connor's sentences 2 and 4.

Paragraph 5 connects O'Connor's grammatical control with the speaker's recollected boyhood anger. Examples of parallelism are three direct objects in sentence 1 and the first three clauses in sentence 3. Paragraph 6, the conclusion of the essay, summarizes the means by which O'Connor uses style to create the comedy of Jackie and his recollected feelings.

# Writing Topics About Tone and Style

**1.** In "First Confession" the adult narrator is describing events that happened to him as a child. To what degree has this narrator, Jackie, separated himself from his childish emotions? What does he say that might be considered residual childhood responses? What effect, if any, do such comments create? For an additional dimension to this topic you might compare Jackie as a narrator with the unnamed narrator of Joyce's "Araby" (Chapter 5).

2. Munro's "The Found Boat" and Gilman's "The Yellow Wallpaper" (Chapter 10) probe the psychological makeup of the major characters. Write an essay about the nature and effect of the language of character depiction in these stories.

3. In "Hills Like White Elephants," how does Hemingway's style shape your responses to the two main characters? How much description do you find in the story? How much dialogue?

4. Consider a short story in which the narrator is the central character (for example, "The Lesson" [Chapter 9], "First Confession," "How to Become a Writer" [Chapter 3], and "Blue Winds Dancing" [Chapter 6]). Write an essay showing how the language of the narrator affects your attitudes toward him or her (that is, your sympathy for the narrator, your interest in the narrative, your feelings toward the other characters and what they do). Be sure to emphasize the relationship between the language of the narrators and the attitudes they demonstrate and elicit.

5. How does Chopin convey attitudes toward the marital role of women and men in "The Story of an Hour"? Consider Louise's reactions to the news that her husband has been killed, and also consider Josephine's responses.

6. Write two brief character sketches, or a description of an action, to be included in a longer story of your own. Make the first favorable, and the second negative. Analyze your word choices in the contrasting accounts: What kinds of words do you select, and on what principles do you select them? What kinds of words might you select if you wanted to create a neutral account? On the basis of your answers, what can you conclude about the development of a fiction writer's style?

7. In your school library, consult the most recent copy of the *MLA International Bibliography of Books and Articles on the Modern Languages and Literatures,* and make a short list of books and articles on Kate Chopin, Ernest Hemingway, Alice Munro, Frank O'Connor, or Mark Twain (just one, not all). Consult at least two of the works, and with these, together with your own insights, write a short description of the writer's irony (comic or serious) and social criticism.

# Chapter 8

# Symbolism and Allegory: Keys to Extended Meaning

**S**ymbolism and allegory, like metaphors and similes (see Chapter 15), are modes that expand meaning. They are literary devices developed from the connections that real-life people make between their own existence and particular objects, places, or occurrences, through experience or reading: A young woman might recall a number of childhood difficulties with her mother, but realize that her mother acted out of love. A college student might remember the quiet satisfaction of returning home after a turbulent time spent away at a distant university. A war veteran might recall the crushing burdens that he and his fellow soldiers carried in combat. An elderly woman on her deathbed might consider the value of her life even though she sustained a crushing disappointment when she was young. The significance of details such as these can be meaningful not just at a single moment but also throughout an entire lifetime. Merely bringing them to mind or speaking about them unlocks their meanings, implications, and consequences. It is as though the reference alone can be the equivalent of pages of explanation and analysis.

From this principle, both symbolism and allegory are derived. By highlighting details as *symbols*, and stories or parts of stories as *allegories*, writers expand their meaning while keeping their works within reasonable lengths.

## Symbolism

The words **symbol** and **symbolism** are derived from the Greek word meaning "to throw together" (*syn*, "together," and *ballein*, "to throw"). A symbol creates a direct meaningful equation between (1) a specific object, scene, character, or action and (2) ideas, values, persons, or ways of life. In effect, a symbol is a *substitute* for the elements being signified, much as the flag stands for the ideals of the nation.

In painting and sculpture, symbols are easily recognized, for to tell a story visually, the artist must make every object count. In the anonymous fresco *Hercules and the Infant Telephus* from ancient Herculaneum, for example, the painter has depicted a crucial event in the life of the mythical hero Hercules—the choice he had to make early in his life between pleasure or toil (I–10, Plate 1). By symbolically turning his head away from the seated figure representing Pleasure, Hercules is rejecting the life of ease that she symbolizes. Instead, his life will be one of work, hardship, battle, victory, and glory, as symbolized by the lion, the eagle, and the sheaf of arrows. The image of his child, Telephus, whom he later abandons and who is being suckled by a donkey, symbolizes Hercules' insensitivity, verging on cruelty, which became a part of his single-minded existence as a warrior and hero.

When we first encounter a symbol in a story (also in poems and plays), it may seem to carry no more weight than its surface or obvious meaning. It can be a description of a character, an object, a place, an action, or a situation, and it may function normally and usefully in this capacity. What makes a symbol symbolic, however, is its capacity to signify additional levels of meaning—major ideas, simple or complex emotions, or philosophical or religious qualities or values. There are two types of symbols—*cultural* and *contextual*.

## Cultural Symbols Are Derived from Our Cultural and Historical Heritage

Many symbols are *generally* or *universally* recognized and are therefore **cultural** (also called **universal**). They embody ideas and emotions that writers and readers share as heirs of the same historical and cultural tradition. When using cultural symbols, a writer assumes that readers already know what the symbols represent. An example is the character Sisyphus of ancient Greek myth. As a punishment for trying to overcome death not just once but twice, Sisyphus is doomed by the underworld gods to roll a large boulder up a high hill forever. Just as he gets the boulder to the top, it rolls down, and then he is fated to roll it up again—and again—and again—because the boulder always rolls back. The plight of Sisyphus has been interpreted as a symbol of the human condition: In spite of constant struggle, a person rarely if ever completes anything. Work must always be done over and over from day to day and from generation to generation, and the same problems confront humanity throughout all time. Because of such fruitless effort, life seems to have little or no meaning. Nevertheless, there is hope: People who confront their tasks, as Sisyphus does, stay involved and active, and their tasks make their lives meaningful. A writer referring to Sisyphus would expect us to understand that this ancient mythological figure symbolizes these conditions.

Similarly, ordinary water, because living creatures cannot live without it, is recognized as a symbol of life. It has this meaning in the ceremony of baptism, and it conveys this meaning and dimension in a variety of literary contexts. Thus, a spouting fountain might symbolize optimism (as upwelling, bubbling life), and a stagnant pool might symbolize the pollution and diminution of life. Water is also a universal symbol of sexuality, and its condition or state can symbolize various romantic relationships. For instance, stories in which lovers meet near a turbulent stream, a roaring waterfall, a mud puddle, a beach with high breakers, a stormy sea, a calm lake, or a wide and gently flowing river symbolically represent love relationships that range from uncertainty to serenity.

## Contextual Symbols Apply Only to the Work in Which They Appear

Objects and descriptions that are not universal symbols can be symbols *only if they are made so within individual works*. These are **contextual**, **private**, or **authorial** symbols. Unlike cultural symbols, contextual symbols derive their meanings from the context and circumstances of individual works. For example, the standing clock in Poe's "The Masque of the Red Death" (Chapter 5) is a large timepiece that in the story symbolizes not only the passage of time but also the sinister forces of death. Similarly, Elisa's chrysanthemums in Steinbeck's "The Chrysanthemums" seem at first nothing more than prized flowers. As the story progresses, however, they gain symbolic significance. The traveling tinsmith's apparent interest in them is the wedge he uses to wheedle a small mending job from Elisa. Her description of the care needed in planting and tending them suggests that they symbolize her kindness, love, orderliness, femininity, and motherliness.

Like Poe's clock, Steinbeck's chrysanthemums are a major contextual symbol. But there is not necessarily any carryover of symbolic meaning. In other stories, clocks and flowers are not symbolic unless the authors of these stories deliberately give them a symbolic charge. Further, if they are symbolic, they can be given different meanings than in the Poe and Steinbeck stories.

## Determining What Is Symbolic

In determining whether a particular object, action, or character is a symbol, you need to judge the importance that the author gives to it. If the element is prominent and also maintains a constancy of meaning, you can justify interpreting it as a symbol. In Coleman's "Unfinished Masterpieces" we are told about how as a child, Dora Johns made things "out of mud." These little figures—"dolls and toys, flying birds and trotting horses, frisking dogs and playing kittens"—are remembered by the narrator as "drying in the sun," but they are intensely fragile. When wet, their shapes can be destroyed by a touch, and when dry they can fall and break. Although these figures are made of ordinary mud, they symbolize the suppressing of talent among minorities. It is the importance that Coleman gives to Dora's shaped figures that invests them with symbolic meaning. Importance is therefore a key to the determination of symbolism, as at the end of Welty's "A Worn Path" (Chapter 2). Phoenix, Welty's major character, plans to spend all her money—10 cents—for a toy windmill for her sick grandson. Readers will note that the windmill is small and fragile, like Phoenix's life and that of her grandson, but that she wants to give the boy a little happiness despite their poor and hopeless circumstances. For these reasons the windmill is a contextual or authorial symbol of Phoenix's loving character, bravery, generous nature, and pathetic existence.

## Allegory

An **allegory** is like a symbol because it transfers and broadens meaning. The term is derived from the Greek word *allegorein*, which means "to say something beyond what is commonly understood" (from *allos*, "other" and *agoreuein*, "to speak in public"). Allegory, however, is more sustained than symbolism. An allegory is to a symbol as a motion picture is to a still picture. In form, an allegory is a complete and self-sufficient narrative, but it also signifies another series of conditions or events. Although some stories are allegories from beginning to end, many stories that are not allegories nevertheless contain brief sections or episodes that are *allegorical*. Allegories are often concerned with morality and especially with religion, but we may also find political and social allegories. To the degree that literary works are true not only because of the lives of their main characters, but also because of life generally, one might maintain that much literature may be considered allegorical even though the authors did not plan their works as allegories.

## Understanding the Applications and Meaning of Allegory

Allegories and the allegorical method are more than literary exercises. Without question, readers and listeners learn and memorize stories and tales more easily than moral lessons, and therefore allegory is a favorite method of teaching morality. In addition, thought and expression have not always been free and safe, as we hope they are today in the United States. At times in other nations, under sometimes repressive political systems, the threat of censorship and the danger of political or economic reprisal have prompted authors to express their views indirectly in the form of allegory rather than to name names and write openly, thereby risking political prosecution, accusations of libel, or even bodily harm. Hence, the double meanings of many allegories are based not just in the literary form but also in the reality of circumstances in our difficult world.

In studying allegory, determine whether all or part of a work can have an extended, allegorical meaning. The popularity of George Lucas's film *Star Wars* and its sequels (in videotape and newly refurbished re-releases) and also its "prequels" (*The Phantom Menace*, *Attack of the Clones*, and *Revenge of the Sith*), for example, is attributable at least partly to its being an allegory about the conflict between good and evil. Obi Wan Kenobi (intelligence) assists Luke Skywalker (heroism, boldness) and instructs him in "the Force" (moral or religious faith). Thus armed and guided, Skywalker opposes the powers of Darth Vader (evil) to rescue the Princess Leia (purity and goodness) with the aid of the latest spaceships and weaponry (technology). The story has produced a set of popular adventure films, accompanied by dramatic music and ingenious visual and sound effects. With the obvious allegorical overtones, however, it stands for any person's quest for self-fulfillment.

To apply a part of the allegory more specifically, consider that for a time the evil Vader imprisons Skywalker and that Skywalker must exert all his skill and strength to get free and overcome Vader. In the allegorical application of the episode, this imprisonment signifies those moments of doubt, discouragement, and depression that people experience while trying to better themselves through education, work, self-improvement, friendship, marriage, and so on.

Almost from the beginning of recorded literature, similar heroic deeds have been represented in allegorical forms. From ancient Greece, the allegorical hero Jason sails the *Argo* to distant lands to gain the Golden Fleece (those who take risks are rewarded). From Anglo-Saxon England, the hero Beowulf saves King Hrothgar's throne by killing the monster Grendel and his even more monstrous mother (victory comes to those who rely on the forces of good). From seventeenth-century England, Bunyan's *The Pilgrim's Progress* tells how the hero Christian overcomes difficulties and temptations while traveling from this world to the next (belief, perseverance, and resistance to temptation save the faithful). As long as the parallel connections are close and consistent, such as those mentioned here, an allegorical interpretation is valid.

## Fable, Parable, and Myth

Closely related to symbolism and allegory in the ability to extend and expand meaning are three additional forms—*fable*, *parable*, and *myth*.

### A Fable Is a Short Tale with a Pointed Moral

The **fable** (from Latin *fabula*, a story or narration) is an old, brief, and popular form. Often but not always, fables are about animals that possess human traits (such fables are called **beast fables**). Past collectors and editors of fables have attached "morals" or explanations to the brief stories, as is the case with Aesop, the most enduringly popular of fable writers. Tradition has it that Aesop was a slave who composed fables in ancient Greece. His fable "The Fox and the Grapes" signifies the trait of belittling things we cannot have. More recent popular contributions to the fable tradition include Walt Disney's "Mickey Mouse," Walt Kelly's "Pogo," and Berke Breathed's "Bloom County." The adjective *fabulous* refers to the collective body of fables of all sorts, even though the word is often used as little more than a vague term of approval.

### A Parable Is a Short Narrative Illustrating a Religious Concept

A **parable** (from Greek *parabolé*, a "setting beside" or comparison) is a short, simple story with a moral or religious bent. Parables are most often associated with Jesus, who used them to embody unique religious insights and truths. For example, his parables "The Prodigal Son" and "The Good Samaritan," as recorded by Luke, are interpreted to show God's understanding, forgiveness, concern, and love.

### A Myth Is a Tale with Social, Political, Religious, or Philosophical Meanings

A **myth** (from Greek *muthos*, a "story" or "plot") is a traditional story that embodies and codifies the religious, philosophical, and cultural values of the civilization in which it is composed. Usually the central figures of mythical stories are heroes, gods, and demigods, such as the ancient figures Zeus, Hera, Prometheus, Athena, Dionysus, Sisyphus, Oedipus, Atalanta, Hercules, Venus, and Aeneas. Most myths are of course fictional, but some are based in historical truth. They are by no means confined to the past, for the word *myth* can also refer to abstractions and ideas that people today hold collectively, such as the concept of never-ending economic growth or the idea that the earth can endlessly sustain all human exploitation and activities with no adverse effects. Sometimes the words *myth* and *mythical* are used with the meaning "fanciful" or "untrue." Such disparagement is misleading because the truths of mythology are not to be found literally in the myths themselves but rather in their symbolic and allegorical interpretations.

## Allusion in Symbolism and Allegory

Cultural or universal symbols and allegories often **allude** to other works from our cultural heritage, such as the Bible, ancient history and literature, and works of the British and American traditions. Sometimes understanding a story may require knowledge of history and current politics.

If the meaning of a symbol is not immediately clear to you, you will need a dictionary or other reference work. The scope of your college dictionary will surprise you. If you cannot find an entry there, however, try one of the major encyclopedias, or ask your reference librarian, who can direct you to shelves loaded with helpful books. A few excellent guides are *The Oxford Companion to Classical Liteture* (ed. M. C. Howatson and Ian Chilvers), *The Oxford Companion to English Literature* (ed. Margaret Drabble), William Rose Benét's *The Reader's Encyclopedia*, Timothy Gantz's *Early Greek Myth: A Guide to Literary and Artistic Sources*, and Richmond Y. Hathorn's *Greek Mythology*.

Useful aids in finding biblical references are *Cruden's Complete Concordance*, which in various editions has been a reliable guide since 1737, and *Strong's Exhaustive Concordance of the Bible*, which has been revised and expanded regularly—and renamed as *The Strongest Strong's Exhaustive Concordance of the Bible*—since it was first published in 1890. These concordances list all the major words used in the Bible (King James version), so you can easily locate the chapter and verse of any and all biblical passages. If you still have trouble after using sources like these, be sure to see your instructor.

### Stories for Study

From a painting by Diego
Velasquez (1599–1660)

### AESOP (ca. 620 B.C.E.–560 B.C.E.)

Not much is known about the ancient fabulist Aesop. According to tradition, he was a freed slave who lived from about 620 to 560 B.C.E. Aristotle claimed that he had been a public defender, but there is no other evidence that he existed at all. In fact, versions of some of the fables were known a millennium before his time. Aesop might therefore be considered as much a collector as a creator of fables.

## The Fox and the Grapes (ca. 6th C. B.C.E.)

A hungry Fox came into a vineyard where there hung delicious clusters of ripe Grapes; his mouth watered to be at them; but they were nailed up to a trellis so high, that with all his springing and leaping he could not reach a single bunch. At last, growing tired and disappointed, "Let who will take them!" says he, "they are but green and sour; so I'll e'en let them alone."

## Questions

1. How much do you learn about the characteristics of the fox? How are these characteristics related to the moral or message of the fable?
2. What is the conflict in the fable? What is the resolution?
3. In your own words, explain the meaning of the fable. Is the "sour grapes" explanation a satisfactory excuse, or is it a rationalization for failure?
4. From your reading of "The Fox and the Grapes," explain the characteristics of the fable as a type of literature.

## THE MYTH OF ATALANTA

The story of Atalanta is an anonymous myth that was known throughout both the ancient Greek and Roman worlds. Because communication in ancient times was uncertain, there were variations in some of the details of the story, such as the names of Atalanta's father and her suitors. However, there was general agreement about the details of her story, which was told by many different writers, such as Apollodorus, Aelian, and Pacuvius. The best-known ancient text of the story appears in Ovid's *Metamorphoses*. The story included here is slightly adapted from the brief but comprehensive version by Richmond Y. Hathorn (*Greek Mythology*, 1977).

## Atalanta (5th–1st C. B.C.E.)

There was once a man from Arcadia, in southern Greece, who hoped very much for a son, and when his wife gave birth to a daughter, he abandoned the child in the woods. A she-bear that lived there suckled the baby, until some hunters chanced on the child and reared it, calling it Atalanta [i.e., "the invincible one"]. Atalanta grew up to be a true daughter of the wilderness, an incomparable hunter, being instructed by the Goddess of the Hunt, Artemis, herself. Atalanta was a runner who could outrace any man, and a skillful wrestler, on one occasion defeating the hero Peleus at Pelias' funeral games. She tried also to go on the expedition with the Argonauts to recover the Golden Fleece, but she was turned away by Jason, who was afraid of the trouble a beautiful young woman might cause in a crew of young men.

Then Atalanta took part in the hunting of the Calydonian Boar, falling in love with the Calydonian Prince Meleager and being loved in return. But as this love brought about Meleager's death and as Atalanta was already inclined toward celibacy because of her allegiance to Artemis, she resolved on leading a solitary manless life henceforth, especially because the oracle at Delphi warned her that marriage would cause her whole nature to be changed. So when she gave birth to Meleager's child on her way back from Calydon to Arcadia, she kept it a secret and exposed the baby boy on Mount Parthenion. This child, called Parthenopaeous, was found by the same shepherds who had found and reared Telephus (the son of Hercules and the Princess Auge), and he grew up to be Telephus' companion in early adventures. Eventually Parthenopaeous met his death in the war of the Seven against Thebes.

Meanwhile Atalanta had returned to her old hunting haunts, fighting off attacks of satyrs and discouraging the proposals of mortal men by stipulating that each suitor should complete with her in a race, in which she would be armed with a spear. The condition was that if she overtook her opponent she might stab him to death. And in this way she had disposed of three suitors, cutting off their heads and displaying them beside the racecourse.

There was a young Arcadian named Milanion, who hated women as much as Atalanta hated men, and who was as fond of the chase as she was. He encountered Atalanta frequently during his hunts, and imperceptibly he fell in love with her. More and more he put himself in her way, until he was faithfully following her around, carrying her hunting-nets and enduring her endless disdain. Once when a centaur, Hylaeus, whom Atalanta had rejected, attacked her in anger, Milanion intervened, receiving the blows of the centaur's club and even being wounded by one of the centaur's arrows while protecting Atalanta with his body. Atalanta killed the man-beast, and then nursed the injured Milanion back to health, her feeling for him growing warmer all the while.

5      Still there was no way of winning Atalanta short of defeating her in the footrace; so in spite of all her discouragements Milanion challenged her. But before the day of the race he prayed to Aphrodite, the Goddess of Love, for aid, and the Goddess plucked three golden apples from the Garden of the Hesperides and instructed him in their use. When the race had begun and Atalanta was drawing near, Milanion dropped one golden apple and the young woman stopped to pick it up. Again she drew near, and again he dropped an apple, the Goddess causing them to weigh heavily in Atalanta's bosom. So when the third apple was dropped and picked up, Milanion was able to reach the goal unscathed and to claim Atalanta as his bride.

But in the flush of his victory and her willing defeat they both forgot to give thanks to Aphrodite. The Goddess punished them by inflicting a rage of lust on both of them, so that they lost all control of themselves. Passing by a sanctuary of Cybele, the Great Mother of Gods, they fell immediately to lovemaking in the holy grotto near the holy temple. They behaved with such abandon that the very statues averted their eyes. The Great Mother was incensed and thought of killing them at once, but instead she changed Milanion into a Lion and Atalanta into a lioness and made them the team that draws her chariot.

## Questions

1. What abilities does Atalanta have? How does she try to preserve her independence?
2. Why does Atalanta vow to shun men? What causes her to change her mind? What finally happens to her?
3. Consider the symbolic significance of Atalanta's name, the golden apples, the chopping off of the heads of slow-running suitors, the father's abandonment of Atalanta, the exposure of the infant Parthenopaeus, the battle with the centaur, the way in which Atalanta loses the race, and the lovemaking in the holy grotto of the Great Mother of Gods.

## ANITA SCOTT COLEMAN (1890–1960)

Coleman, a writer of stories, poems, and essays, was born in Mexico and educated in New Mexico. Her mother had been a slave who had been bought out of slavery by her father. She published mainly in magazines. "Unfinished Masterpieces," for example, was published in *Crisis: A Record of the Darker Races,* the magazine begun in 1910 that heralded the development of the Harlem Renaissance.

## 🦅 Unfinished Masterpieces (1927)

There are days which stand out clearly like limpid pools beside the dusty road; when your thoughts, crystal clear as water, are pinioned in loveliness like star-points. Solitary days, which come often, if you are given to browsing in fields of past adventure; or rarely, if you are seldom retrospective; and not at all, if you are too greatly concerned with rushing onward to a nebulous future. Days whereupon your experiences glimmer before you waveringly like motion-pictures and the people you have known stroll through the lanes of memory, arrayed in vari-colored splendor or in amusing disarray. Days like these are to be revered, for they have their humors and their whimsicalities. Hurry your thoughts and the gathering imageries take flight. Perplexity but makes the lens of introspection blur. And of annoyance beware, for it is an evil vapor that disseminates and drowns the visions in the sea of grim realities. Such days must be cultivated. Scenes for their reception must be set. Cushions perhaps, and warmth of fire. Above all, the warmth of sweet content. Ease and comfort, comfort and ease and moods of receptivity. Then hither, come hither the places and the people we have known, the associations that withstand time's effacements. Backward ho, through the mazes of the past.

STOP! "Why howdy, Dora Johns." Darling playmate of my child-years. With wooly hair a length too short for even pigtails. Mud-spatters upon your funny black face. Mud-spatters all over your dress and your little black hands mud-spattered too.

Why? What? Come on and see. And lo! I am a child again.

Hand in hand, unmindful of her muddy ones, we skip around the old ramshackle house, back to the furthest corner of an unkempt yard, impervious to the tin cans, the ash-heap, the litter, the clutter that impedes our way, our eyes upon, our thoughts bent upon one small clean-swept corner, where there is mud. More mud and water in a battered tin can. And row after row of mud. No, not mud—not merely mud, but things made out of mud. Row on row, drying in the sun.

Carefully, I sit down, doubling up, to be as small as possible, for only this corner where mud things are drying is clean and corners are seldom, if ever, quite large enough. Besides, I must not touch the things made out of mud. If the dried ones fall, they break. If the moist ones are molested, be it with ever so gentle a finger, they lose their shape. Moreover I must not disturb Dora.

Her little hands are busied with the mud. Little moulder's fingers are deftly plying their skill. Her child's face is alight. What has splashed her grave child's face with such a light? I wondered. I wonder now. The glitter of brittle talent, a gleam of sterling genius or the glow from artistic fires burning within the soul of a little black child?

Little Dora shaping figures out of mud. Vases and urns, dolls and toys, flying birds and trotting horses, frisking dogs and playing kittens, marvelous things out of mud. Crying aloud as though dealt a blow if one of the dried mud-figures is broken. Working in mud for endless hours, while the neighbor children play. Their hilarious merriment dropping like bombs into the quiet of our clean-swept corner. Deadly missiles seeking to find a mark. The insistent halloes of futile mirth forever bubbling on the other side of a highboard fence. The dividing fence and upon one side the clean-swept corner and the row on row of mud things drying in the sun. And Dora seeming not to heed the seething bubbles upon the other side, shaping, shaping marvelous things out of mud.

Yet, Oh Dora, now that the day is ours, will you not say, "When did the bombs of futile mirth strike their target? When did the tin-cans and the rags and the old ash-heap crowd you out from your clean-swept corner? What rude hand caused the dried mud shapes to fall and break? Who set a ruthless foot in the midst of your damp mud things?" Or were you too

5

plastic, as plastic as your mud? You dare not tell. Only this you can whisper into the mists of our today. You are one of the Master's unfinished shapes which He will some day gather to mould anew into the finished masterpiece.

A lump of mud. Now, there is a sobriquet for you—you funny, funny man. Mr. William Williams. I saw you but once. We chanced to meet in the home of a mutual friend. I thought you so very funny then. Uncouth and very boorish, but ever, when these pageants of the past, these dumb shows of inarticulate folks arise before me upon retrospective days, you appear garbed in the tatters of pathos.

10      "I am fifty-one years old," you kept repeating. How pitiful those fifty-one years are. You wear a child's simplicity, the sort that is so sad to see upon a man. Fifty-one and penniless. Fifty-one and possessed of naught else but the clothing you wore. Fifty-one and no place on earth you might call home. You confessed to being a vagabond though "bum" was the term you used and you were very proud of your one accomplishment, an ability to avoid all labour.

"I've given no man a full day's honest work in all my fifty-one years," you boasted. "I gambles. I ain't no cotton-pickin' nigger." Your one and only boast after holding life, the fathomless fountain of eternal possibilities, in your possession for fifty-one priceless years.

Nevertheless you have lived and so intensely. You held us against our will. Clustered around you, listening to you talk. Relating clippings as it were from the scrap-book of your life.

Tales of the road, of the only places you knew. Roads leading away from plantations where the cotton waited to be picked by numberless "cotton-pickin' niggers." Roads leading to pool halls and gambling dens. Roads beginning and roads ending in "riding the roads," carrying backward and forward, here and yon through the weird goblin land of the South's black belt.

With a hardened casualness you told stories that revolted and at the same time cheered us with an all sufficing glow of thankfulness that life had spared us the sordidness of yours. Offhandily, you gave us humorous skits that tempered our laughter with wishes that we might know at least a bit of such a droll existence as had been yours. With magical words you painted pictures so sharply they cut scars upon our hearts. You drew others so filled with rollicking delight their gladsomeness was contagious. With the nonchalance of a player shuffling cards you flipped your characters before us, drawn directly from the cesspool of your contacts, and spellbound we listened.

15      Someone remarked how wonderful you talked and you replied, "Once, I sorter wanted to write books. Once, I uster read a heaps. See times when I was broke and nobody would stake me for a game. I'd lay around and read. I've read the Bible through and through and every Police Gazette I could lay my hands on. Yes, suh, I've read a heap. And I've wished a lot'er times I'd sense enough to write a book."

Lump of mud. Containing the you, the splendid artist in you, the soul of you, the unfinished you in the ungainly lump of you, awaiting the gathering-up to be molded anew into the finished masterpiece.

What a day! Here is my friend at whose fire-side I have lingered beholding Mr. William Williams, great lump of mud. To be sure, she also is an unfinished production. Though it is apparent that the Master had all but done when she slipped from his hands and dropped to earth to lie groping like the rest of us thereon.

Let us sit here together, friend, and enjoy this day.

I shall try to discover what recent gift you have given to the poor the while you are quietly stitching upon the garments, linens and scarlet, with which to clothe your household. Sit here and smile with the welcoming light in your eyes, knowing that your door is open to such as William Williams and Dora Johns, the Dora who is become as the mud beneath one's feet. Kind mistress of the widely opened door where white and black, rich and poor, of whatever caste or creed may enter and find comfort and ease and food and drink.

## Questions

**1.** What talents do Dora and William possess? Why have they not lived up to their talents? What has kept them down? Why are they "unfinished masterpieces"?

**2.** How may Dora and William be seen as symbols? What do they symbolize?

**3.** Characterize the narrator. What attitude does she exhibit toward the lack of fulfillment of the major characters (see particularly paragraph 19)? How might the story have been different if the narrator had shown hostility, for example, or extreme bitterness?

## NATHANIEL HAWTHORNE (1804–1864)

Hawthorne, a friend and associate of the fourteenth president of the United States, Franklin Pierce, is one of the great American writers of the nineteenth century. His most famous work is *The Scarlet Letter* (1850), the sale of which gave him a degree of independence. During the administration of President Pierce (1853–1857), Hawthorne served as American consul in Liverpool, England, and this opportunity enabled him to travel extensively in Europe. Throughout his writing there runs a conflict between freedom and conventionality, with those choosing freedom sometimes suffering from the guilt that their choice brings. "Young Goodman Brown," which is one of the early stories that he included in *Twice-Told Tales* (1837, 1842), embodies this conflict.

 **Young Goodman Brown** (1835)

Young Goodman Brown came forth at sunset, into the street of Salem village,° but put his head back, after crossing the threshold, to exchange a parting kiss with his young wife. And Faith, as the wife was aptly named, thrust her own pretty head into the street, letting the wind play with the pink ribbons of her cap, while she called to Goodman Brown.

"Dearest heart," whispered she, softly and rather sadly, when her lips were close to his ear, "prithee, put off your journey until sunrise, and sleep in your own bed tonight. A lone woman is troubled with such dreams and such thoughts, that she's afeared of herself, sometimes. Pray, tarry with me this night, dear husband, of all nights in the year!"

"My love and my Faith," replied young Goodman Brown, "of all nights in the year, this one night must I tarry away from thee. My journey, as thou callest it, forth and back again, must needs be done 'twixt now and sunrise. What, my sweet, pretty wife, dost thou doubt me already, and we but three months married!"

"Then God bless you!" said Faith with the pink ribbons, "and may you find all well, when you come back."

"Amen!" cried Goodman Brown. "Say thy prayers, dear Faith, and go to bed at dusk, and    5
no harm will come to thee."

---

°*Salem village:* in Massachusetts, about fifteen miles north of Boston. The time of the story is the late seventeenth or early eighteenth century.

So they parted; and the young man pursued his way, until, being about to turn the corner by the meeting-house, he looked back and saw the head of Faith still peeping after him, with a melancholy air, in spite of her pink ribbons.

"Poor little Faith!" thought he, for his heart smote him. "What a wretch am I, to leave her on such an errand! She talks of dreams, too. Methought, as she spoke, there was trouble in her face, as if a dream had warned her what work is to be done tonight. But no, no! 't would kill her to think it. Well; she's a blessed angel on earth; and after this one night, I'll cling to her skirts and follow her to Heaven."

With this excellent resolve for the future, Goodman Brown felt himself justified in making more haste on his present evil purpose. He had taken a dreary road, darkened by all the gloomiest trees of the forest, which barely stood aside to let the narrow path creep through, and closed immediately behind. It was all as lonely as could be; and there is this peculiarity in such a solitude, that the traveller knows not who may be concealed by the innumerable trunks and the thick boughs overhead; so that, with lonely footsteps, he may yet be passing through an unseen multitude.

"There may be a devilish Indian behind every tree," said Goodman Brown to himself; and he glanced fearfully behind him, as he added, "What if the devil himself should be at my very elbow!"

10   His head being turned back, he passed a crook of the road, and looking forward again, beheld the figure of a man, in grave and decent attire, seated at the foot of an old tree. He arose at Goodman Brown's approach, and walked onward, side by side with him.

"You are late, Goodman Brown," said he. "The clock of the Old South° was striking, as I came through Boston; and that is full fifteen minutes agone."

"Faith kept me back awhile," replied the young man, with a tremor in his voice, caused by the sudden appearance of his companion, though not wholly unexpected.

It was now deep dusk in the forest, and deepest in that part of it where these two were journeying. As nearly as could be discerned, the second traveller was about fifty years old, apparently in the same rank of life as Goodman Brown, and bearing a considerable resemblance to him, though perhaps more in expression than features. Still, they might have been taken for father and son. And yet, though the elder person was as simply clad as the younger, and as simple in manner too, he had an indescribable air of one who knew the world, and would not have felt abashed at the governor's dinner-table, or in King William's° court, were it possible that his affairs should call him thither. But the only thing about him that could be fixed upon as remarkable, was his staff, which bore the likeness of a great black snake, so curiously wrought, that it might almost be seen to twist and wriggle itself like a living serpent. This, of course, must have been an ocular deception, assisted by the uncertain light.

"Come, Goodman Brown!" cried his fellow-traveller, "this is a dull pace for the beginning of a journey. Take my staff, if you are so soon weary."

15   "Friend," said the other, exchanging his slow pace for a full stop, "having kept covenant by meeting thee here, it is my purpose now to return whence I came. I have scruples, touching the matter thou wot'st of.°"

"Sayest thou so?" replied he of the serpent, smiling apart. "Let us walk on, nevertheless, reasoning as we go, and if I convince thee not, thou shalt turn back. We are but a little way in the forest, yet."

"Too far, too far!" exclaimed the goodman, unconsciously resuming his walk. "My father never went into the woods on such an errand, nor his father before him. We have been a race

---

°*Old South*: The Old South Church, in Boston, is still there.
°*King William*: William III was king of England from 1688 to 1701 (the time of the story). William IV was king from 1830 to 1837 (the period when Hawthorne wrote the story).
°*thou wot'st*: you know.

of honest men and good Christians, since the days of the martyrs.° And shall I be the first of the name of Brown that ever took this path and kept—"

"Such company, thou wouldst say," observed the elder person, interrupting his pause. "Well said, Goodman Brown! I have been as well acquainted with your family as ever a one among the Puritans; and that's no trifle to say. I helped your grandfather, the constable, when he lashed the Quaker woman so smartly through the streets of Salem. And it was I that brought your father a pitch-pine knot, kindled at my own hearth, to set fire to an Indian village, in King Philip's war.° They were my good friends, both; and many a pleasant walk have we had along this path, and returned merrily after midnight. I would fain be friends with you, for their sake."

"If it be as thou sayest," replied Goodman Brown, "I marvel they never spoke of these matters. Or, verily, I marvel not, seeing that the least rumor of the sort would have driven them from New England. We are a people of prayer, and good works to boot, and abide no such wickedness."

"Wickedness or not," said the traveller with twisted staff, "I have a very general acquaintance here in New England. The deacons of many a church have drunk the communion wine with me; the selectmen, of divers towns, make me their chairman; and a majority of the Great and General Court are firm supporters of my interest. The governor and I, too—but these are state secrets." 20

"Can this be so!" cried Goodman Brown, with a stare of amazement at his undisturbed companion. "Howbeit, I have nothing to do with the governor and council; they have their own ways, and are no rule for a simple husbandman like me. But, were I to go on with thee, how should I meet the eye of that good old man, our minister, at Salem village? Oh, his voice would make me tremble, both Sabbath-day and lecture-day!"°

Thus far, the elder traveller had listened with due gravity, but now burst into a fit of irrepressible mirth, shaking himself so violently, that his snakelike staff actually seemed to wriggle in sympathy.

"Ha! ha! ha!" shouted he, again and again; then composing himself, "Well, go on, Goodman Brown, go on; but, prithee, don't kill me with laughing!"

"Well, then, to end the matter at once," said Goodman Brown, considerably nettled, "there is my wife, Faith. It would break her dear little heart; and I'd rather break my own!"

"Nay, if that be the case," answered the other, "e'en go thy ways, Goodman Brown. I would not, for twenty old women like the one hobbling before us, that Faith should come to any harm." 25

As he spoke, he pointed his staff at a female figure on the path, in whom Goodman Brown recognized a very pious and exemplary dame, who had taught him his catechism in youth, and was still his moral and spiritual adviser, jointly with the minister and Deacon Gookin.

"A marvel, truly, that Goody° Cloyse should be so far in the wilderness, at nightfall!" said he. "But, with your leave, friend, I shall take a cut through the woods, until we have left this Christian woman behind. Being a stranger to you, she might ask whom I was consorting with, and whither I was going."

"Be it so," said his fellow-traveller. "Betake you to the woods, and let me keep the path."

---

°*days of the martyrs*: the martyrdoms of Protestants in England during the reign of Queen Mary (1553–1558).

°*King Philip's war*: This war (1675–1676), infamous for the atrocities committed by the New England settlers, resulted in the suppression of Indian tribal life and prepared the way for unlimited settlement of New England by European immigrants. "Philip" was the English name of Chief Metacomet of the Wampanoag tribe.

°*Sabbath-day and lecture-day*: "Sabbath-day" is Sunday. "Lecture-day" refers to Thursday lectures on Biblical and moral topics.

°*Goody*: shortened form of "goodwife," a respectful name for a married woman of low rank. A "Goody Cloyse" was one of the women sentenced to execution by Hawthorne's great-grandfather, Judge John Hathorne.

Accordingly, the young man turned aside, but took care to watch his companion, who advanced softly along the road, until he had come within a staff's length of the old dame. She, meanwhile, was making the best of her way, with singular speed for so aged a woman, and mumbling some indistinct words, a prayer, doubtless, as she went. The traveller put forth his staff, and touched her withered neck with what seemed the serpent's tail.

30    "The devil!" screamed the pious old lady.

"Then Goody Cloyse knows her old friend?" observed the traveller, confronting her, and leaning on his writhing stick.

"Ah, forsooth, and is it your worship, indeed?" cried the good dame. "Yea, truly is it, and in the very image of my old gossip,° Goodman Brown, the grandfather of the silly fellow that now is. But, would your worship believe it? My broomstick hath strangely disappeared, stolen, as I suspect, by that unhanged witch, Goody Cory,° and that, too, when I was all anointed with the juice of smallage and cinquefoil and wolf's-bane—"°

"Mingled with fine wheat and the fat of a new-born babe," said the shape of old Goodman Brown.

"Ah, your worship knows the recipe," cried the old lady, cackling aloud. "So, as I was saying, being all ready for the meeting, and no horse to ride on, I made up my mind to foot it; for they tell me there is a nice young man to be taken into communion tonight. But now your good worship will lend me your arm, and we shall be there in a twinkling."

35    "That can hardly be," answered her friend. "I will not spare you my arm, Goody Cloyse, but here is my staff, if you will."

So saying, he threw it down at her feet, where, perhaps, it assumed life, being one of the rods which its owner had formerly lent to the Egyptian Magi.° Of this fact, however, Goodman Brown could not take cognizance. He had cast up his eyes in astonishment, and looking down again, beheld neither Goody Cloyse nor the serpentine staff, but his fellow-traveller alone, who waited for him as calmly as if nothing had happened.

"That old woman taught me my catechism!" said the young man; and there was a world of meaning in this simple comment.

They continued to walk onward, while the elder traveller exhorted his companion to make good speed and persevere in the path, discoursing so aptly, that his arguments seemed rather to spring up in the bosom of his auditor, than to be suggested by himself. As they went he plucked a branch of maple, to serve for a walking-stick, and began to strip it of the twigs and little boughs, which were wet with evening dew. The moment his fingers touched them, they became strangely withered and dried up, as with a week's sunshine. Thus the pair proceeded, at a good free pace, until suddenly, in a gloomy hollow of the road, Goodman Brown sat himself down on the stump of a tree, and refused to go any farther.

"Friend," said he, stubbornly, "my mind is made up. Not another step will I budge on this errand. What if a wretched old woman do choose to go to the devil, when I thought she was going to Heaven! Is that any reason why I should quit my dear Faith, and go after her?"

40    "You will think better of this by and by," said his acquaintance, composedly. "Sit here and rest yourself a while; and when you feel like moving again, there is my staff to help you along."

Without more words, he threw his companion the maple stick, and was as speedily out of sight as if he had vanished into the deepening gloom. The young man sat a few moments by the roadside, applauding himself greatly, and thinking with how clear a conscience he should meet the minister, in his morning walk, nor shrink from the eye of good old Deacon Gookin.

---

°*gossip*: from "good sib" or "good relative."

°*Goody Cory*: name of a woman who was also sent to execution by Judge Hathorne.

°*smallage and cinquefoil and wolf's-bane*: plants commonly used by witches in making ointments.

°*lent to the Egyptian Magi*: See Exodus 7:10–12.

And what calm sleep would be his, that very night, which was to have been spent so wickedly, but purely and sweetly now, in the arms of Faith! Amidst these pleasant and praiseworthy meditations, Goodman Brown heard the tramp of horses along the road, and deemed it advisable to conceal himself within the verge of the forest, conscious of the guilty purpose that had brought him thither, though now so happily turned from it.

On came the hoof-tramps and the voices of the riders, two grave old voices, conversing soberly as they drew near. These mingled sounds appeared to pass along the road, within a few yards of the young man's hiding-place; but owing, doubtless, to the depth of the gloom, at that particular spot, neither the travellers nor their steeds were visible. Though their figures brushed the small boughs by the wayside, it could not be seen that they intercepted, even for a moment, the faint gleam from the strip of bright sky, athwart which they must have passed. Goodman Brown alternately crouched and stood on tiptoe, pulling aside the branches, and thrusting forth his head as far as he durst, without discerning so much as a shadow. It vexed him the more, because he could have sworn, were such a thing possible, that he recognized the voices of the minister and Deacon Gookin, jogging° along quietly, as they were wont to do, when bound to some ordination or ecclesiastical council. While yet within hearing, one of the riders stopped to pluck a switch.

"Of the two, reverend Sir," said the voice like the deacon's, "I had rather miss an ordination dinner than to-night's meeting. They tell me that some of our community are to be here from Falmouth and beyond, and others from Connecticut and Rhode Island; besides several of the Indian powwows,° who, after their fashion, know almost as much deviltry as the best of us. Moreover, there is a goodly young woman to be taken into communion."

"Mighty well, Deacon Gookin!" replied the solemn old tones of the minister. "Spur up, or we shall be late. Nothing can be done, you know, until I get on the ground."

The hoofs clattered again, and the voices, talking so strangely in the empty air, passed on through the forest, where no church had ever been gathered, nor solitary Christian prayed. Whither, then, could these holy men be journeying, so deep into the heathen wilderness? Young Goodman Brown caught hold of a tree, for support, being ready to sink down on the ground, faint and over-burthened with the heavy sickness of his heart. He looked up to the sky, doubting whether there really was a Heaven above him. Yet, there was the blue arch, and the stars brightening in it.  45

"With Heaven above, and Faith below, I will yet stand firm against the devil!" cried Goodman Brown.

While he still gazed upward, into the deep arch of the firmament, and had lifted his hands to pray, a cloud, though no wind was stirring, hurried across the zenith, and hid the brightening stars. The blue sky was still visible, except directly overhead, where this black mass of cloud was sweeping swiftly northward. Aloft in the air, as if from the depths of the cloud, came a confused and doubtful sound of voices. Once, the listener fancied that he could distinguish the accents of town's people of his own, men and women, both pious and ungodly, many of whom he had met at the communion-table, and had seen others rioting at the tavern. The next moment, so indistinct were the sounds, he doubted whether he had heard aught but the murmur of the old forest, whispering without a wind. Then came a stronger swell of those familiar tones, heard daily in the sunshine, at Salem village, but never, until now, from a cloud at night. There was one voice, of a young woman, uttering lamentations, yet with an uncertain sorrow, and entreating for some favor, which, perhaps, it would grieve her to obtain. And all the unseen multitude, both saints and sinners, seemed to encourage her onward.

---

°*jogging*: riding a horse at a slow trot.

°*powwow*: a Narragansett Indian word describing a priest or cult leader who led ritual ceremonies of dance, incantation, and magic.

"Faith!" shouted Goodman Brown, in a voice of agony and desperation; and the echoes of the forest mocked him, crying—"Faith! Faith!" as if bewildered wretches were seeking her, all through the wilderness.

The cry of grief, rage, and terror was yet piercing the night, when the unhappy husband held his breath for a response. There was a scream, drowned immediately in a louder murmur of voices fading into far-off laughter, as the dark cloud swept away, leaving the clear and silent sky above Goodman Brown. But something fluttered lightly down through the air, and caught on the branch of a tree. The young man seized it and beheld a pink ribbon.

50    "My Faith is gone!" cried he, after one stupefied moment. "There is no good on earth, and sin is but a name. Come, devil! for to thee is this world given."

And maddened with despair, so that he laughed loud and long, did Goodman Brown grasp his staff and set forth again, at such a rate, that he seemed to fly along the forest path, rather than to walk or run. The road grew wilder and drearier, and more faintly traced, and vanished at length, leaving him in the heart of the dark wilderness, still rushing onward, with the instinct that guides mortal man to evil. The whole forest was peopled with frightful sounds; the creaking of the trees, the howling of wild beasts, and the yell of Indians; while, sometimes, the wind tolled like a distant church bell, and sometimes gave a broad roar around the traveller, as if all Nature were laughing him to scorn. But he was himself the chief horror of the scene, and shrank not from its other horrors.

"Ha! ha! ha!" roared Goodman Brown, when the wind laughed at him. "Let us hear which will laugh loudest! Think not to frighten me with your deviltry! Come witch, come wizard, come Indian powwow, come devil himself! and here comes Goodman Brown. You may as well fear him as he fear you!"

In truth, all through the haunted forest, there could be nothing more frightful than the figure of Goodman Brown. On he flew, among the black pines, brandishing his staff with frenzied gestures, now giving vent to an inspiration of horrid blasphemy, and now shouting forth such laughter, as set all the echoes of the forest laughing like demons around him. The fiend in his own shape is less hideous than when he rages in the breast of man. Thus sped the demoniac on his course, until, quivering among the trees, he saw a red light before him, as when the felled trunks and branches of a clearing have been set on fire, and throw up their lurid blaze against the sky, at the hour of midnight. He paused, in a lull of the tempest that had driven him onward, and heard the swell of what seemed a hymn, rolling solemnly from a distance, with the weight of many voices. He knew the tune. It was a familiar one in the choir of the village meeting-house. The verse died heavily away, and was lengthened by a chorus, not of human voices, but of all the sounds of the benighted wilderness, pealing in awful harmony together. Goodman Brown cried out; and his cry was lost to his own ear, by its unison with the cry of the desert.

In the interval of silence, he stole forward, until the light glared full upon his eyes. At one extremity of an open space, hemmed in by the dark wall of the forest, arose a rock, bearing some rude, natural resemblance either to an altar or a pulpit, and surrounded by four blazing pines, their tops aflame, their stems untouched, like candles at an evening meeting. The mass of foliage, that had overgrown the summit of the rock, was all on fire, blazing high into the night, and fitfully illuminating the whole field. Each pendent twig and leafy festoon was in a blaze. As the red light arose and fell, a numerous congregation alternately shone forth, then disappeared in shadow, and again grew, as it were, out of the darkness, peopling the heart of the solitary woods at once.

55    "A grave and dark-clad company!" quoth Goodman Brown.

In truth, they were such. Among them, quivering to-and-fro, between gloom and splendor, appeared faces that would be seen, next day, at the council-board of the province, and others which, Sabbath after Sabbath, looked devoutly heavenward, and benignantly over the crowded pews, from the holiest pulpits in the land. Some affirm that the lady of the governor was there. At least, there were high dames well known to her, and wives of honored husbands, and widows a great multitude, and ancient maidens, all of excellent repute, and fair young girls, who trembled lest their mothers should espy them. Either the sudden gleams of light, flashing over the obscure field, bedazzled Goodman Brown, or he recognized a score of the church members of Salem village, famous for their especial sanctity. Good old Deacon Gookin had arrived, and waited at the skirts of that venerable saint, his reverend pastor. But, irreverently consorting with these grave, reputable, and pious people, these elders of the church, these chaste dames and dewy virgins, there were men of dissolute lives and women of spotted fame, wretches given over to all mean and filthy vice, and suspected even of horrid crimes. It was strange to see, that the good shrank not from the wicked, nor were the sinners abashed by the saints. Scattered, also, among their pale-faced enemies, were the Indian priests, or powwows, who had often scared their native forest with more hideous incantations than any known to English witchcraft.

"But, where is Faith?" thought Goodman Brown; and, as hope came into his heart, he trembled.

Another verse of the hymn arose, a slow and mournful strain, such as the pious love, but joined to words which expressed all that our nature can conceive of sin, and darkly hinted at far more. Unfathomable to mere mortals is the lore of fiends. Verse after verse was sung, and still the chorus of the desert swelled between, like the deepest tone of a mighty organ. And, with the final peal of that dreadful anthem, there came a sound, as if the roaring wind, the rushing streams, the howling beasts, and every other voice of the unconverted wilderness were mingling and according with the voice of guilty man, in homage to the prince of all. The four blazing pines threw up a loftier flame, and obscurely discovered shapes and visages of horror on the smoke-wreaths, above the impious assembly. At the same moment, the fire on the rock shot redly forth, and formed a glowing arch above its base, where now appeared a figure. With reverence be it spoken, the apparition bore no slight similitude, both in garb and manner, to some grave divine of the New England churches.

"Bring forth the converts!" cried a voice, that echoed through the field and rolled into the forest.

At the word, Goodman Brown stepped forth from the shadow of the trees, and approached the congregation, with whom he felt a loathful brotherhood, by the sympathy of all that was wicked in his heart. He could have well-nigh sworn, that the shape of his own dead father beckoned him to advance, looking downward from a smoke-wreath, while a woman, with dim features of despair, threw out her hand to warn him back. Was it his mother? But he had no power to retreat one step, nor to resist, even in thought, when the minister and good old Deacon Gookin seized his arms, and led him to the blazing rock. Thither came also the slender form of a veiled female, led between Goody Cloyse, that pious teacher of the catechism, and Martha Carrier, who had received the devil's promise to be queen of hell. A rampant hag was she! And there stood the proselytes, beneath the canopy of fire.

"Welcome, my children," said the dark figure, "to the communion of your race! Ye have found, thus young, your nature and your destiny. My children, look behind you!"

They turned; and flashing forth, as it were, in a sheet of flame, the fiend-worshippers were seen; the smile of welcome gleamed darkly on every visage.

"There," resumed the sable form, "are all whom ye have reverenced from youth. Ye deemed them holier than yourselves, and shrank from your own sin, contrasting it with their lives of righteousness and prayerful aspirations heavenward. Yet, here are they all, in my worshipping assembly! This night it shall be granted you to know their secret deeds; how hoary-bearded elders of the church have whispered wanton words to the young maids of their households; how many a woman, eager for widow's weeds, has given her husband a drink at bedtime, and let him sleep his last sleep in her bosom; how beardless youths have made haste to inherit their father's wealth; and how fair damsels—blush not, sweet ones!—have dug little graves in the garden, and bidden me, the sole guest, to an infant's funeral. By the sympathy of your human hearts for sin, ye shall scent out all the places—whether in church, bed-chamber, street, field, or forest—where crime has been committed, and shall exult to behold the whole earth one stain of guilt, one mighty blood-spot. Far more than this! It shall be yours to penetrate, in every bosom, the deep mystery of sin, the fountain of all wicked arts, and which inexhaustibly supplies more evil impulses than human power—than my power, at its utmost!—can make manifest in deeds. And now, my children, look upon each other."

They did so; and, by the blaze of the hell-kindled torches, the wretched man beheld his Faith, and the wife her husband, trembling before that unhallowed altar.

65   "Lo! there ye stand, my children," said the figure, in a deep and solemn tone, almost sad, with its despairing awfulness, as if his once angelic nature° could yet mourn for our miserable race. "Depending upon one another's hearts, ye had still hoped that virtue were not all a dream! Now are ye undeceived!—Evil is the nature of mankind. Evil must be your only happiness. Welcome, again, my children, to the communion of your race!"

"Welcome!" repeated the fiend-worshippers, in one cry of despair and triumph.

And there they stood, the only pair, as it seemed, who were yet hesitating on the verge of wickedness, in this dark world. A basin was hollowed, naturally, in the rock. Did it contain water, reddened by the lurid light? or was it blood? or, perchance, a liquid flame? Herein did the Shape of Evil dip his hand, and prepare to lay the mark of baptism upon their foreheads, that they might be partakers of the mystery of sin, more conscious of the secret guilt of others, both in deed and thought, than they could now be of their own. The husband cast one look at his pale wife, and Faith at him. What polluted wretches would the next glance show them to each other, shuddering alike at what they disclosed and what they saw!

"Faith! Faith!" cried the husband. "Look up to Heaven, and resist the Wicked One!"

Whether Faith obeyed, he knew not. Hardly had he spoken, when he found himself amid calm night and solitude, listening to a roar of the wind, which died heavily away through the forest. He staggered against the rock, and felt it chill and damp, while a hanging twig, that had been all on fire, besprinkled his cheek with the coldest dew.

70   The next morning, young Goodman Brown came slowly into the street of Salem village staring around him like a bewildered man. The good old minister was taking a walk along the grave-yard, to get an appetite for breakfast and meditate his sermon, and bestowed a blessing, as he passed, on Goodman Brown. He shrank from the venerable saint, as if to avoid an anathema. Old Deacon Gookin was at domestic worship, and the holy words of his prayer were heard through the open window. "What God doth the wizard pray to?" quoth Goodman Brown. Goody Cloyse, that excellent old Christian, stood in the early sunshine, at her own lattice, catechising a little girl, who had brought her a pint of morning's milk. Goodman Brown snatched away the child, as from the grasp of the fiend himself. Turning the corner by the meetinghouse, he spied the head of Faith, with the pink ribbons, gazing anxiously forth, and bursting into such joy at the sight of him that she skipt along the street, and almost kissed her husband before the whole village. But Goodman Brown looked sternly and sadly into her face, and passed on without a greeting.

Had Goodman Brown fallen asleep in the forest, and only dreamed a wild dream of a witch-meeting?

---

°*once angelic nature:* Lucifer ("light bearer"), another name for the Devil, led the traditional revolt of the angels and was thrown into hell as his punishment. See Isaiah 14:12–15.

Be it so, if you will. But, alas! it was a dream of evil omen for young Goodman Brown. A stern, a sad, a darkly meditative, a distrustful, if not a desperate man did he become, from the night of that fearful dream. On the Sabbath day, when the congregation were singing a holy psalm, he could not listen, because an anthem of sin rushed loudly upon his ear, and drowned all the blessed strain. When the minister spoke from the pulpit, with power and fervid eloquence, and with his hand on the open Bible, of the sacred truths of our religion, and of saint-like lives and triumphant deaths, and of future bliss or misery unutterable, then did Goodman Brown turn pale, dreading lest the roof should thunder down upon the gray blasphemer and his hearers. Often, awaking suddenly at midnight, he shrank from the bosom of Faith, and at morning or eventide, when the family knelt down in prayer, he scowled, and muttered to himself, and gazed sternly at his wife, and turned away. And when he had lived long, and was borne to his grave, a hoary corpse, followed by Faith, an aged woman, and children and grandchildren, a goodly procession, besides neighbors not a few, they carved no hopeful verse upon his tombstone; for his dying hour was gloom.

## Questions

1. Near the end of the story the narrator asks the following: "Had Goodman Brown fallen asleep in the forest, and only dreamed a wild dream of a witch-meeting?" What is the answer? If Goodman Brown's visions come out of his own dreams (mind, subconscious), what do they tell us about him?

2. Is Goodman Brown round or flat? To what extent is he a symbolic "everyman" or representative of humankind?

3. Consider Hawthorne's use of symbolism, such as sunset and night, the walking sticks, the witches' sabbath, the marriage to Faith, and the vague shadows amid the darkness, together with other symbols that you may find.

4. What details establish the two settings? What characterizes Salem? The woods? Why might we be justified in seeing the forest as a symbolic setting?

5. To what extent are the people, objects, and events in Goodman Brown's adventure invested with enough *consistent* symbolic resonance to justify calling his episode in the woods an allegory? Consider Brown's wife, Faith, as an allegorical figure. What do you make of Brown's statements "I'll cling to her skirts and follow her to Heaven" (paragraph 7) and "Faith kept me back awhile" (paragraph 12)? In this same light, consider the other characters Brown meets in the forest, the sunset, the walk into the forest, and the staff "which bore the likeness of a great black snake" (paragraph 13).

## ST. LUKE (1st c. c.e.)

Although little is known about St. Luke, evidence in Colossians, Philemon, and 2 Timothy indicates that a man named Luke was the "beloved physician" and traveling companion of the apostle Paul, who journeyed in the Mediterranean area during the middle of the first century c.e. Scholars indicate that Luke built his gospel from the Gospel of St. Mark and also from written sources known as "Q," some of which were also used by St. Matthew. Luke also relied on other sources that were available only to him. In addition to his gospel, Luke is also accepted as the author of the Acts of the Apostles.

## 🕊 The Parable of the Prodigal Son
### (Luke 15:11–32) (ca. 90 C.E.)

¹¹ And he [Jesus] said, A certain man had two sons:

¹²And the younger of them said to *his* father, Father, give me the portion of goods that falleth *to me*. And he divided unto them *his* living.°

¹³And not many days after the younger son gathered all together, and took his journey into a far country,° and there wasted his substance with riotous living.

¹⁴ And when he had spent all, there arose a mighty famine in that land; and he began to be in want.

¹⁵ And he went and joined himself to a citizen of that country; and he sent him into his fields to feed swine.°

¹⁶ And he would fain have filled his belly with the husks° that the swine did eat: and no man gave unto him.

¹⁷ And when he came to himself, he said, How many hired servants of my father's have bread enough and to spare, and I perish with hunger!

¹⁸ I will arise and go to my father, and will say unto him, Father, I have sinned against heaven, and before thee.

¹⁹ And am no more worthy to be called thy son: make me as one of thy hired servants.

²⁰ And he arose, and came to his father. But when he was yet a great way off, his father saw him, and had compassion, and ran, and fell on his neck, and kissed him.

²¹ And the son said unto him, Father, I have sinned against heaven, and in thy sight, and am no more worthy to be called thy son.

²² But the father said to his servants, Bring forth the best robe, and put *it* on him; and put a ring on his hand, and shoes on *his* feet:

²³ And bring hither the fatted calf,° and kill *it*; and let us eat, and be merry:

²⁴ For this my son was dead, and is alive again; he was lost, and is found. And they began to be merry.

²⁵ Now his elder son was in the field: and as he came and drew nigh to the house, he heard music and dancing.

²⁶ And he called one of the servants, and asked what these things meant.

²⁷ And he said unto him, Thy brother is come; and thy father hath killed the fatted calf, because he hath received him safe and sound.

²⁸ And he was angry, and would not go in: therefore came his father out, and intreated him.

²⁹ And he answering said to *his* father, Lo, these many years do I serve thee, neither transgressed I at any time thy commandment: and yet thou never gavest me a kid, that I might make merry with my friends:

³⁰ But as soon as this thy son was come, which hath devoured thy living with harlots, thou hast killed for him the fatted calf.

³¹ And he said unto him, Son, thou art ever with me, and all that I have is thine.

³² It was meet° that we should make merry, and be glad: for this thy brother was dead, and is alive again: and was lost, and is found.

---

°*divided . . . his living*: one-third of the father's estate; the son had to renounce all further claim.

°*far country*: countries of the Jewish dispersal, or diaspora, in the areas bordering the Mediterranean Sea.

°*feed swine*: In Jewish custom, pigs were unclean.

°*husks*: pods of the carob tree, the eating of which was thought to be penitential.

°*fatted calf*: grain-fed calf.

°*meet*: appropriate.

## Questions

1. Describe the character of the Prodigal Son. Is he flat or round, representative or individual? Why is it necessary that the character be considered representatively, even though he has individual characteristics?

2. What is the plot? What is the antagonism against which the Prodigal Son contends? Why is it necessary that the brother resent the brother's return?

3. What is the resolution of the parable? Why is there no "they lived happily ever after" ending?

4. Using verse numbers, analyze the structure of the parable. What determines your division of the parts? Do these parts coincide with the development of the plot? Describe the relationship of plot to structure in the parable.

5. What is the point of view here? How does the emphasis shift with verse 22?

6. On the basis of the fact that there are many characteristics here of many stories you have read, write a description of the parable as a type of literature.

## KATHERINE ANNE PORTER (1890–1980)

Porter was a native of Texas but made her home in many places during her life, spending considerable time in Mexico and Germany. She established her reputation with her early collections *Flowering Judas* (1930) and *Pale Horse, Pale Rider* (1939), which gained praise for her analyses and insights into human character. A later collection of stories was *The Leaning Tower* (1944). Her major novel, *Ship of Fools,* appeared in 1962 and was made into a motion picture. She was awarded the Pulitzer Prize for fiction and also the National Book Award in 1966 for her *The Collected Stories.* "The Jilting of Granny Weatherall" first appeared in *Flowering Judas.*

 ## The Jilting of Granny Weatherall (1930)

She flicked her wrist neatly out of Doctor Harry's pudgy careful fingers and pulled the sheet up to her chin. The brat ought to be in knee breeches. Doctoring around the country with spectacles on his nose! "Get along now, take your schoolbooks and go. There's nothing wrong with me."

Doctor Harry spread a warm paw like a cushion on her forehead where the forked green vein danced and made her eyelids twitch. "Now, now, be a good girl, and we'll have you up in no time."

"That's no way to speak to a woman nearly eighty years old just because she's down. I'd have you respect your elders, young man."

"Well, Missy, excuse me." Doctor Harry patted her cheek. "But I've got to warn you, haven't I? You're a marvel, but you must be careful or you're going to be good and sorry."

"Don't tell me what I'm going to be. I'm on my feet now, morally speaking. It's Cornelia. I had to go to bed to get rid of her."          5

Her bones felt loose, and floated around in her skin, and Doctor Harry floated like a balloon around the foot of the bed. He floated and pulled down his waistcoat and swung his glasses on a cord. "Well, stay where you are, it certainly can't hurt you."

"Get along and doctor your sick," said Granny Weatherall. "Leave a well woman alone. I'll call for you when I want you. . . . Where were you forty years ago when I pulled through milk-leg and double pneumonia? You weren't even born. Don't let Cornelia lead you on," she shouted, because Doctor Harry appeared to float up to the ceiling and out. "I pay my own bills, and I don't throw my money away on nonsense!"

She meant to wave good-by, but it was too much trouble. Her eyes closed of themselves, it was like a dark curtain drawn around the bed. The pillow rose and floated under her, pleasant as a hammock in a light wind. She listened to the leaves rustling outside the window. No, somebody was swishing newspapers: no, Cornelia and Doctor Harry were whispering together. She leaped broad awake, thinking they whispered in her ear.

"She was never like this, *never* like this!" "Well, what can we expect?" "Yes, eighty years old. . . ."

10   Well, and what if she was? She still had ears. It was like Cornelia to whisper around doors. She always kept things secret in such a public way. She was always being tactful and kind. Cornelia was dutiful; that was the trouble with her. Dutiful and good: "So good and dutiful," said Granny, "that I'd like to spank her." She saw herself spanking Cornelia and making a fine job of it.

"What'd you say, Mother?"

Granny felt her face tying up in hard knots.

"Can't a body think, I'd like to know?"

"I thought you might want something."

15   "I do. I want a lot of things. First off, go away and don't whisper."

She lay and drowsed, hoping in her sleep that the children would keep out and let her rest a minute. It had been a long day. Not that she was tired. It was always pleasant to snatch a minute now and then. There was always so much to be done, let me see: tomorrow.

Tomorrow was far away and there was nothing to trouble about. Things were finished somehow when the time came; thank God there was always a little margin over for peace: then a person could spread out the plan of life and tuck in the edges orderly. It was good to have everything clean and folded away, with the hair brushes and tonic bottles sitting straight on the white embroidered linen: the day started without fuss and the pantry shelves laid out with rows of jelly glasses and brown jugs and white stone-china jars with blue whirligigs and words painted on them: coffee, tea, sugar, ginger, cinnamon, allspice: and the bronze clock with the lion on top nicely dusted off. The dust that lion could collect in twenty-four hours! The box in the attic with all those letters tied up, well she'd have to go through that tomorrow. All those letters—George's letters and John's letters and her letters to them both—lying around for the children to find afterwards made her uneasy. Yes, that would be tomorrow's business. No use to let them know how silly she had been once.

While she was rummaging around she found death in her mind and it felt clammy and unfamiliar. She had spent so much time preparing for death there was no need for bringing it up again. Let it take care of itself now. When she was sixty she had felt very old, finished, and went around making farewell trips to see her children and grandchildren, with a secret in her mind: This is the very last of your mother, children! Then she made her will and came down with a long fever. That was all just a notion like a lot of other things, but it was lucky too, for she had once for all got over the idea of dying for a long time. Now she couldn't be worried. She hoped she had better sense now. Her father had lived to be one hundred and two years old and had drunk a noggin of strong hot toddy on his last birthday. He told the reporters it was his daily habit, and he owed his long life to that. He had made quite a scandal and was very pleased about it. She believed she'd just plague Cornelia a little.

"Cornelia! Cornelia!" No footsteps, but a sudden hand on her cheek. "Bless you, where have you been?"

"Here, mother."

"Well, Cornelia, I want a noggin of hot toddy."

"Are you cold, darling?"

"I'm chilly, Cornelia. Lying in bed stops the circulation. I must have told you that a thousand times."

Well, she could just hear Cornelia telling her husband that Mother was getting childish and they'd have to humor her. The thing that most annoyed her was that Cornelia thought she was deaf, dumb, and blind. Little hasty glances and tiny gestures tossed around her and over her head saying, "Don't cross her, let her have her way, she's eighty years old," and she sitting there as if she lived in a thin glass cage. Sometimes Granny almost made up her mind to pack up and move back to her own house where nobody could remind her every minute that she was old. Wait, wait, Cornelia, till your own children whisper behind your back!

In her day she had kept a better house and had got more work done. She wasn't too old yet for Lydia to be driving eighty miles for advice when one of the children jumped the track, and Jimmy still dropped in and talked things over: "Now, Mammy, you've a good business head, I want to know what you think of this? . . ." Old Cornelia couldn't change the furniture around without asking. Little things, little things! They had been so sweet when they were little. Granny wished the old days were back again with the children young and everything to be done over. It had been a hard pull, but not too much for her. When she thought of all the food she had cooked, and all the clothes she had cut and sewed, and all the gardens she had made—well, the children showed it. There they were, made out of her, and they couldn't get away from that. Sometimes she wanted to see John again and point to them and say, Well, I didn't do so badly, did I? But that would have to wait. That was for tomorrow. She used to think of him as a man, but now all the children were older than their father, and he would be a child beside her if she saw him now. It seemed strange and there was something wrong in the idea. Why, he couldn't possibly recognize her. She had fenced in a hundred acres once, digging the post holes herself and clamping the wires with just a negro boy to help. That changed a woman. John would be looking for a young woman with the peaked Spanish comb in her hair and the painted fan. Digging post holes changed a woman. Riding country roads in the winter when women had their babies was another thing: sitting up nights with sick horses and sick negroes and sick children and hardly ever losing one. John, I hardly ever lost one of them! John would see that in a minute, that would be something he could understand, she wouldn't have to explain anything!

It made her feel like rolling up her sleeves and putting the whole place to rights again. No matter if Cornelia was determined to be everywhere at once, there were a great many things left undone on this place. She would start tomorrow and do them. It was good to be strong enough for everything, even if all you made melted and changed and slipped under your hands, so that by the time you finished you almost forgot what you were working for. What was it I set out to do? she asked herself intently, but she could not remember. A fog rose over the valley, she saw it marching across the creek swallowing the trees and moving up the hill like an army of ghosts. Soon it would be at the near edge of the orchard, and then it was time to go in and light the lamps. Come in children, don't stay out in the night air.

Lighting the lamps had been beautiful. The children huddled up to her and breathed like little calves waiting at the bars in the twilight. Their eyes followed the match and watched the flame rise and settle in a blue curve, then they moved away from her. The lamp was lit, they didn't have to be scared and hang on to mother any more. Never, never, never more. God, for all my life I thank Thee. Without Thee, my God, I could never have done it. Hail, Mary, full of grace.

I want you to pick all the fruit this year and see that nothing is wasted. There's always someone who can use it. Don't let good things rot for want of using. You waste life when you waste good food. Don't let things get lost. It's bitter to lose things. Now, don't let me get to thinking, not when I am tired and taking a little nap before supper. . . .

The pillow rose about her shoulders and pressed against her heart and the memory was being squeezed out of it: oh, push down the pillow, somebody: it would smother her if she tried to hold it. Such a fresh breeze blowing and such a green day with no threats in it. But he had not come, just the same. What does a woman do when she has put on the white veil and set out the white cake for a man and he doesn't come? She tried to remember. No, I swear he never harmed me but in that. He never harmed me but in that . . . and what if he did? There was the day, the day, but a whirl of dark smoke rose and covered it, crept up and over into the bright field where everything was planted so carefully in orderly rows. That was hell, she knew hell when she saw it. For sixty years she had prayed against remembering him and against losing her soul in the deep pit of hell, and now the two things were mingled in one and the thought of him was a smoky cloud from hell that moved and crept in her head when she had just got rid of Doctor Harry and was trying to rest a minute. Wounded vanity, Ellen, said a sharp voice in the top of her mind. Don't let your wounded vanity get the upper hand of you. Plenty of girls get jilted. You were jilted, weren't you. Then stand up to it. Her eyelids wavered and let in streamers of blue-gray light like tissue paper over her eyes. She must get up and pull the shades down or she'd never sleep. She was in bed again and the shades were not down. How could that happen? Better turn over, hide from the light, sleeping in the light gave you nightmares. "Mother, how do you feel now?" and a stinging wetness on her forehead. But I don't like having my face washed in cold water!

30     Hapsy? George? Lydia? Jimmy? No, Cornelia, and her features were swollen and full of little puddles. "They're coming, darling, they'll all be here soon." Go wash your face, child, you look funny.

Instead of obeying, Cornelia knelt down and put her head on the pillow. She seemed to be talking but there was no sound. "Well, are you tongue-tied? Whose birthday is it? Are you going to give a party?"

Cornelia's mouth moved urgently in strange shapes. "Don't do that, you bother me, daughter."

"Oh, no, Mother, Oh, no . . ."

Nonsense. It was strange about children. They disputed your every word. "No what, Cornelia?"

35     "Here's Doctor Harry."

"I won't see that boy again. He just left five minutes ago."

"That was this morning, Mother. It's night now. Here's the nurse."

"This is Doctor Harry, Mrs. Weatherall. I never saw you look so young and happy!"

"Ah, I'll never be young again—but I'd be happy if they'd let me lie in peace and get rested."

40     She thought she spoke up loudly, but no one answered. A warm weight on her forehead, a warm bracelet on her wrist, and a breeze went on whispering, trying to tell her something. A shuffle of leaves in the everlasting hand of God. He blew on them and they danced and rattled. "Mother, don't mind, we're going to give you a little hypodermic." "Look here, daughter, how do ants get in this bed? I saw sugar ants yesterday." Did you send for Hapsy too?

It was Hapsy she really wanted. She had to go a long way back through a great many rooms to find Hapsy standing with a baby on her arm. She seemed to herself to be Hapsy also, and the baby on Hapsy's arm was Hapsy and himself and herself, all at once, and there was no surprise in the meeting. Then Hapsy melted from within and turned flimsy as gray gauze and the baby was a gauzy shadow, and Hapsy came up close and said, "I thought you'd never come," and looked at her very searchingly and said, "You haven't changed a bit!" They leaned forward to kiss, when Cornelia began whispering from a long way off, "Oh, is there anything you want to tell me? Is there anything I can do for you?"

Yes, she had changed her mind after sixty years and she would like to see George. I want you to find George. Find him and be sure to tell him I forgot him. I want him to know I had my husband just the same and my children and my house like any other woman. A good house too and a good husband that I loved and fine children out of him. Better than I hoped for even. Tell him I was given back everything he took away and more. Oh, no, oh, God, no, there was something else besides the house and the man and the children. Oh, surely they were not all? What was it? Something not given back. . . . Her breath crowded down under her ribs and grew into a monstrous frightening shape with cutting edges; it bored up into her head, and the agony was unbelievable: Yes, John, get the doctor now, no more talk, my time has come.

When this one was born it should be the last. The last. It should have been born first, for it was the one she had truly wanted. Everything came in good time. Nothing left out, left over. She was strong, in three days she would be as well as ever. Better. A woman needed milk in her to have her full health.

"Mother, do you hear me?"

"I've been telling you—"

"Mother, Father Connolly's here." 45

"I went to Holy Communion only last week. Tell him I'm not so sinful as all that."

"Father just wants to speak to you."

He could speak as much as he pleased. It was like him to drop in and inquire about her soul as if it were a teething baby, and then stay on for a cup of tea and a round of cards and gossip. He always had a funny story of some sort, usually about an Irishman who made his little mistakes and confessed them, and the point lay in some absurd thing he would blurt out in the confessional showing his struggles between native piety and original sin. Granny felt easy about her soul. Cornelia, where are your manners? Give Father Connolly a chair. She had her secret comfortable understanding with a few favorite saints who cleared a straight road to God for her. All as surely signed and sealed as the papers for the new Forty Acres. Forever . . . heirs and assigns forever. Since the day the wedding cake was not cut, but thrown out and wasted. The whole bottom dropped out of the world, and there she was blind and sweating with nothing under her feet and the walls falling away. His hand had caught her under the breast, she had not fallen, there was the freshly polished floor with the green rug on it, just as before. He had cursed like a sailor's parrot and said, "I'll kill him for you." Don't lay a hand on him, for my sake leave something to God. "Now, Ellen, you must believe what I tell you . . ."

So there was nothing, nothing to worry about any more, except sometimes in the night 50 one of the children screamed in a nightmare, and they both hustled out shaking and hunting for the matches and calling, "There, wait a minute, here we are!" John, get the doctor now. Hapsy's time has come. But there was Hapsy standing by the bed in a white cap. "Cornelia, tell Hapsy to take off her cap. I can't see her plain."

Her eyes opened very wide and the room stood out like a picture she had seen somewhere. Dark colors with the shadow rising towards the ceiling in long angles. The tall black dresser gleamed with nothing on it but John's picture, enlarged from a little one, with John's eyes very black when they should have been blue. You never saw him, so how do you know how he looked? But the man insisted the copy was perfect, it was very rich and handsome. For a picture, yes, but it's not my husband. The table by the bed had a linen cover and a candle and a crucifix. The light was blue from Cornelia's silk lampshades. No sort of light at all, just frippery. You had to live forty years with kerosene lamps to appreciate honest electricity. She felt very strong and she saw Doctor Harry with a rosy nimbus around him.

"You look like a saint, Doctor Harry, and I vow that's as near as you'll ever come to it."

"She's saying something."

"I heard you, Cornelia. What's all this carrying-on?"

55    "Father Connolly's saying—"

Cornelia's voice staggered and bumped like a cart in a bad road. It rounded corners and turned back again and arrived nowhere. Granny stepped up in the cart very lightly and reached for the reins, but a man sat beside her and she knew him by his hands, driving the cart. She did not look in his face, for she knew without seeing, but looked instead down the road where the trees leaned over and bowed to each other and a thousand birds were singing a Mass. She felt like singing too, but she put her hand in the bosom of her dress and pulled out a rosary, and Father Connolly murmured Latin in a very solemn voice and tickled her feet. My God, will you stop that nonsense? I'm a married woman. What if he did run away and leave me to face the priest by myself? I found another a whole world better. I wouldn't have exchanged my husband for anybody except St. Michael himself, and you may tell him that for me with a thank you in the bargain.

Light flashed on her closed eyelids, and a deep roaring shook her. Cornelia, is that lightning? I hear thunder. There's going to be a storm. Close all the windows. Call the children in . . . "Mother, here we are, all of us." "Is that you, Hapsy?" "Oh, no, I'm Lydia. We drove as fast as we could." Their faces drifted above her, drifted away. The rosary fell out of her hands and Lydia put it back. Jimmy tried to help, their hands fumbled together, and Granny closed two fingers around Jimmy's thumb. Beads wouldn't do, it must be something alive. She was so amazed her thoughts ran round and round. So, my dear Lord, this is my death and I wasn't even thinking about it. My children have come to see me die. But I can't, it's not time. Oh, I always hated surprises. I wanted to give Cornelia the amethyst set—Cornelia, you're to have the amethyst set, but Hapsy's to wear it when she wants, and, Doctor Harry, do shut up. Nobody sent for you. Oh, my dear Lord, do wait a minute. I meant to do something about the Forty Acres, Jimmy doesn't need it and Lydia will later on with that worthless husband of hers. I meant to finish the altar cloth and send six bottles of wine to Sister Borgia for her dyspepsia. I want to send six bottles of wine to Sister Borgia, Father Connolly, now don't let me forget.

Cornelia's voice made short turns and tilted over and crashed. "Oh, Mother, oh, Mother, oh, Mother. . . ."

"I'm not going, Cornelia. I'm taken by surprise. I can't go."

60    You'll see Hapsy again. What about her? "I thought you'd never come." Granny made a long journey outward, looking for Hapsy. What if I don't find her? What then? Her heart sank down and down, there was no bottom to death, she couldn't come to the end of it. The blue light from Cornelia's lampshade drew into a tiny point in the center of her brain, it flickered and winked like an eye, quietly it fluttered and dwindled. Granny lay curled down within herself, amazed and watchful, staring at the point of light that was herself; her body was now only a deeper mass of shadow in an endless darkness and this darkness would curl around the light and swallow it up. God, give a sign!

For the second time there was no sign. Again no bridegroom and the priest in the house. She could not remember any other sorrow because this grief wiped them all away. Oh, no, there's nothing more cruel than this—I'll never forgive it. She stretched herself with a deep breath and blew out the light.

## Questions

1. What are Granny's circumstances in the story? What is happening to her? How do we learn about her and her past life? What evidence do you see in the story that Granny is hallucinating and becoming delirious?

2. What sort of person is Granny? Would you call her admirable? Why or why not? In what way is light symbolic in the story? In what ways is Granny associated with light? Would it be fair to claim that Granny has been a giver of light during her life?

3. What is the meaning of "jilting" as it applies to Granny? To what degree does Granny feel "jilted" at the end of her life? How has jilting colored and symbolized her life? How has she lived to overcome it?

4. Explain the story's point of view. (See also Chapter 3.) To what degree does the narrator enter Granny's mind to explain what is happening to her?

5. Who is Hapsy? What is the significance of Hapsy to Granny? What has apparently happened to Hapsy?

## JOHN STEINBECK (1902–1968)

Steinbeck was born in Salinas, California, and for a time attended Stanford University. In the 1920s, while working at jobs such as surveying, picking fruit, and hatching trout, he began his writing career. A number of stories and novels preceded his best-known novel, *The Grapes of Wrath* (1939), for which he was awarded the Pulitzer Prize in 1940. He received the Nobel Prize in literature in 1962. His fiction, often set in rural areas, features a realistic and pessimistic view of life. A number of his novels have been made into films, the best known of which is *The Grapes of Wrath*. His home in Salinas is open to the visiting public.

##  The Chrysanthemums (1937)

The high grey-flannel fog of winter closed off the Salinas Valley° from the sky and from all the rest of the world. On every side it sat like a lid on the mountains and made of the great valley a closed pot. On the broad, level land floor the gang plows bit deep and left the black earth shining like metal where the shares had cut. On the foothill ranches across the Salinas River, the yellow stubble fields seemed to be bathed in pale cold sunshine, but there was no sunshine in the valley now in December. The thick willow scrub along the river flamed with sharp and positive yellow leaves.

It was a time of quiet and of waiting. The air was cold and tender. A light wind blew up from the southwest so that the farmers were mildly hopeful of a good rain before long; but fog and rain do not go together.

Across the river, on Henry Allen's foothill ranch there was little work to be done, for the hay was cut and stored and the orchards were plowed up to receive the rain deeply when it should come. The cattle on the higher slopes were becoming shaggy and rough-coated.

°*Salinas Valley*: in Monterey County, California, about 50 miles south of San Jose.

Elisa Allen, working in her flower garden, looked down across the yard and saw Henry, her husband, talking to two men in business suits. The three of them stood by the tractor shed, each man with one foot on the side of the little Fordson.° They smoked cigarettes and studied the machines as they talked.

5     Elisa watched them for a moment and then went back to her work. She was thirty-five. Her face was lean and strong and her eyes were as clear as water. Her figure looked blocked and heavy in her gardening costume, a man's black hat pulled low down over her eyes, clod-hopper shoes, a figured print dress almost completely covered by a big corduroy apron with four big pockets to hold the snips, the trowel and scratcher, the seeds and the knife she worked with. She wore heavy leather gloves to protect her hands while she worked.

She was cutting down the old year's chrysanthemum stalks with a pair of short and pow-erful scissors. She looked down toward the men by the tractor shed now and then. Her face was eager and mature and handsome; even her work with the scissors was over-eager, over-powerful. The chrysanthemum stems seemed too small and easy for her energy.

She brushed a cloud of hair out of her eyes with the back of her glove, and left a smudge of earth on the cheek in doing it. Behind her stood the neat white farm house with red gerani-ums close-banked around it as high as the windows. It was a hard-swept looking little house, with hard-polished windows, and a clean mud-mat on the front steps.

Elisa cast another glance toward the tractor shed. The strangers were getting into their Ford coupe. She took off a glove and put her strong fingers down into the forest of new green chrysanthemum sprouts that were growing around the old roots. She spread the leaves and looked down among the close-growing stems. No aphids were there, no sowbugs or snails or cutworms. Her terrier fingers destroyed such pests before they could get started.

Elisa started at the sound of her husband's voice. He had come near quietly, and he leaned over the wire fence that protected her flower garden from cattle and dogs and chickens.

10     "At it again," he said. "You've got a strong new crop coming."

Elisa straightened her back and pulled on the gardening glove again. "Yes. They'll be strong this coming year." In her tone and on her face there was a little smugness.

"You've got a gift with things," Henry observed. "Some of those yellow chrysanthemums you had this year were ten inches across. I wish you'd work out in the orchard and raise some apples that big."

Her eyes sharpened. "Maybe I could do it, too. I've a gift with things, all right. My mother had it. She could stick anything in the ground and make it grow. She said it was having planters' hands that knew how to do it."

"Well, it sure works with flowers," he said.

15     "Henry, who were those men you were talking to?"

"Why, sure, that's what I came to tell you. They were from the Western Meat Company. I sold those thirty head of three-year-old steers. Got nearly my own price, too."

"Good," she said. "Good for you."

"And I thought," he continued, "I thought how it's Saturday afternoon, and we might go to Salinas for dinner at a restaurant, and then to a picture show—to celebrate, you see."

"Good," she repeated. "Oh, yes. That will be good."

20     Henry put on his joking tone. "There's fights tonight. How'd you like to go to the fights?"

"Oh, no," she said breathlessly. "No, I wouldn't like fights."

"Just fooling, Elisa. We'll go to a movie. Let's see. It's two now. I'm going to take Scotty and bring down those steers from the hill. It'll take us maybe two hours. We'll go in town about five and have dinner at the Cominos Hotel. Like that?"

---

°*Fordson*: a tractor manufactured by the Ford Motor Company, with large steel-lugged rear wheels.

"Of course I'll like it. It's good to eat away from home."

"All right, then. I'll go get up a couple of horses."

She said, "I'll have plenty of time to transplant some of these sets, I guess."        25

She heard her husband calling Scotty down by the barn. And a little later she saw the two men ride up the pale yellow hillside in search of the steers.

There was a little square sandy bed kept for rooting the chrysanthemums. With her trowel she turned the soil over and over, and smoothed it and patted it firm. Then she dug ten parallel trenches to receive the sets. Back at the chrysanthemum bed she pulled out the little crisp shoots, trimmed off the leaves of each one with her scissors and laid it on a small orderly pile.

A squeak of wheels and plod of hoofs came from the road. Elisa looked up. The country road ran along the dense bank of willows and cottonwoods that bordered the river, and up this road came a curious vehicle, curiously drawn. It was an old springwagon, with a round canvas top on it like the cover of a prairie schooner. It was drawn by an old bay horse and a little grey-and-white burro. A big stubble-bearded man sat between the cover flaps and drove the crawling team. Underneath the wagon, between the hind wheels, a lean and rangy mongrel dog walked sedately. Words were painted on the canvas in clumsy, crooked letters. "Pots, pans, knives, sisors, lawn mores. Fixed." Two rows of articles and the triumphantly definitive "Fixed" below. The black paint had run down in little sharp points beneath each letter.

Elisa, squatting on the ground, watched to see the crazy, loose-jointed wagon pass by. But it didn't pass. It turned into the farm road in front of her house, crooked old wheels skirling and squeaking. The rangy dog darted from between the wheels and ran ahead. Instantly the two ranch shepherds flew out at him. Then all three stopped, and with stiff and quivering tails, with taut straight legs, with ambassadorial dignity, they slowly circled, sniffing daintily. The caravan pulled up to Elisa's wire fence and stopped. Now the newcomer dog, feeling outnumbered, lowered his tail and retired under the wagon with raised hackles and bared teeth.

The man on the wagon seat called out. "That's a bad dog in a fight when he gets started."        30

Elisa laughed. "I see he is. How soon does he generally get started?"

The man caught up her laughter and echoed it heartily. "Sometimes not for weeks and weeks," he said. He climbed stiffly down, over the wheel. The horse and the donkey dropped like unwatered flowers.

Elisa saw that he was a very big man. Although his hair and beard were greying, he did not look old. His worn black suit was wrinkled and spotted with grease. The laughter had disappeared from his face and eyes the moment his laughing voice ceased. His eyes were dark and they were full of the brooding that gets in the eyes of teamsters and of sailors. The calloused hands he rested on the wire fence were cracked, and every crack was a black line. He took off his battered hat.

"I'm off my general road, ma'am," he said. "Does this dirt road cut over across the river to the Los Angeles highway?"

Elisa stood up and shoved the thick scissors in her apron pocket. "Well, yes, it does, but        35 it winds around and then fords the river. I don't think your team could pull through the sand."

He replied with some asperity, "It might surprise you what them beasts can pull through."

"When they get started?" she asked.

He smiled for a second. "Yes. When they get started."

"Well," said Elisa, "I think you'll save time if you go back to the Salinas road and pick up the highway there."

40  He drew a big finger down the chicken wire and made it sing. "I ain't in any hurry, ma'am. I go from Seattle to San Diego and back every year. Takes all my time. About six months each way. I aim to follow nice weather."

Elisa took off her gloves and stuffed them in the apron pocket with the scissors. She touched the under edge of her man's hat, searching for fugitive hairs. "That sounds like a nice kind of a way to live," she said.

He leaned confidentially over the fence. "Maybe you noticed the writing on my wagon. I mend pots and sharpen knives and scissors. You got any of them things to do?"

"Oh, no," she said quickly. "Nothing like that." Her eyes hardened with resistance.

"Scissors is the worst thing," he explained. "Most people just ruin scissors trying to sharpen 'em, but I know how. I got a special tool. It's a little bobbit kind of thing, and patented. But it sure does the trick."

45  "No. My scissors are all sharp."

"All right, then. Take a pot," he continued earnestly, "a bent pot, or a pot with a hole. I can make it like new so you don't have to buy no new ones. That's saving for you."

"No," she said shortly. "I tell you I have nothing like that for you to do."

His face fell to an exaggerated sadness. His voice took on a whining undertone. "I ain't had a thing to do today. Maybe I won't have no supper tonight. You see I'm off my regular road. I know folks on the highway clear from Seattle to San Diego. They save their things for me to sharpen up because they know I do it so good and save them money."

"I'm sorry," Elisa said irritably. "I haven't anything for you to do."

50  His eyes left her face and fell to searching the ground. They roamed about until they came to the chrysanthemum bed where she had been working. "What's them plants, ma'am?"

The irritation and resistance melted from Elisa's face. "Oh, those are chrysanthemums, giant whites and yellows. I raise them every year, bigger than anybody around here."

"Kind of a long-stemmed flower? Looks like a quick puff of colored smoke?" he asked.

"That's it. What a nice way to describe them."

"They smell kind of nasty till you get used to them," he said.

55  "It's a good bitter smell," she retorted, "not nasty at all."

He changed his tone quickly. "I like the smell myself."

"I had ten-inch blooms this year," she said.

The man leaned farther over the fence. "Look. I know a lady down the road a piece, has got the nicest garden you ever seen. Got nearly every kind of flower but no chrysantheums. Last time I was mending a copper-bottom washtub for her (that's hard job but I do it good), she said to me, 'If you ever run acrost some nice chrysantheums I wish you'd try to get me a few seeds.' That's what she told me."

Elisa's eyes grew alert and eager. "She couldn't have known much about chrysanthemums. You can raise them from seed, but it's much easier to root the little sprouts you see there."

60  "Oh," he said. "I s'pose I can't take none to her, then."

"Why yes you can," Elisa cried. "I can put some in damp sand, and you can carry them right along with you. They'll take root in the pot if you keep them damp. And then she can transplant them."

"She'd sure like to have some, ma'am. You say they're nice ones?"

"Beautiful," she said. "Oh, beautiful." Her eyes shone. She tore off the battered hat and shook out her dark pretty hair. "I'll put them in a flower pot, and you can take them right with you. Come into the yard."

While the man came through the picket gate Elisa ran excitedly along the geranium-bordered path to the back of the house. And she returned carrying a big red flower pot. The gloves were forgotten now. She kneeled on the ground by the starting bed and dug up the sandy soil with her fingers and scooped it into the bright new flower pot. Then she picked up the little pile of shoots she had prepared. With her strong fingers she pressed them into the sand and tamped around them with her knuckles. The man stood over her. "I'll tell you what to do," she said. "You remember so you can tell the lady."

"Yes, I'll try to remember."

"Well, look. These will take root in about a month. Then she must set them out, about a foot apart in good rich earth like this, see?" She lifted a handful of dark soil for him to look at. "They'll grow fast and tall. Now remember this. In July tell her to cut them down, about eight inches from the ground."

"Before they bloom?" he asked.

"Yes, before they bloom." Her face was tight with eagerness. "They'll grow right up again. About the last of September the buds will start."

She stopped and seemed perplexed. "It's the budding that takes the most care," she said hesitantly. "I don't know how to tell you." She looked deep into his eyes, searchingly. Her mouth opened a little, and she seemed to be listening. "I'll try to tell you," she said. "Did you ever hear of planting hands?"

"Can't say I have, ma'am."

"Well, I can only tell you what it feels like. It's when you're picking off the buds you don't want. Everything goes right down into your fingertips. You watch your fingers work. They do it themselves. You can feel how it is. They pick and pick the buds. They never make a mistake. They're with the plant. Do you see? Your fingers and the plant. You can feel that, right up your arm. They know. They never make a mistake. You can feel it. When you're like that you can't do anything wrong. Do you see that? Can you understand that?"

She was kneeling on the ground looking up at him. Her breast swelled passionately.

The man's eyes narrowed. He looked away self-consciously. "Maybe I know," he said. "Sometimes in the night in the wagon there—"

Elisa's voice grew husky. She broke in on him. "I've never lived as you do, but I know what you mean. When the night is dark—why, the stars are sharp-pointed, and there's quiet. Why, you rise up and up! Every pointed star gets driven into your body. It's like that. Hot and sharp and—lovely."

Kneeling there, her hand went out toward his legs in the greasy black trousers. Her hesitant fingers almost touched the cloth. Then her hand dropped to the ground. She crouched low like a fawning dog.

He said, "It's nice, just like you say. Only when you don't have no dinner, it ain't."

She stood up then, very straight, and her face was ashamed. She held the flower pot out to him and placed it gently in his arms. "Here. Put it in your wagon, on the seat, where you can watch it. Maybe I can find something for you to do."

At the back of the house she dug in the can pile and found two old and battered aluminum saucepans. She carried them back and gave them to him. "Here, maybe you can fix these."

His manner changed. He became professional. "Good as new I can fix them." At the back of his wagon he set a little anvil, and out of an oily tool box dug a small machine hammer. Elisa came through the gate to watch him while he pounded out the dents in the kettles. His mouth grew sure and knowing. At a difficult part of the work he sucked his under-lip.

"You sleep right in the wagon?" Elisa asked.

"Right in the wagon, ma'am. Rain or shine. I'm dry as a cow in there."

"It must be nice," she said. "It must be very nice. I wish women could do such things."

"It ain't the right kind of a life for a woman."

Her upper lip raised a little, showing her teeth. "How do you know? How can you tell?" she said.

85    "I don't know ma'am," he protested. "Of course I don't know. Now here's your kettles, done. You don't have to buy no new ones."

"How much?"

"Oh, fifty cents'll do. I keep my prices down and my work good. That's why I have all them satisfied customers up and down the highway."

Elisa brought him a fifty-cent piece from the house and dropped it in his hand. "You might be surprised to have a rival some time. I can sharpen scissors, too. And I can beat the dents out of little pots. I could show you what a woman might do."

He put his hammer back in the oily box and shoved the little anvil out of sight. "It would be a lonely life for a woman, ma'am, and a scarey life, too, with animals creeping under the wagon all night." He climbed over the single-tree, steadying himself with a hand on the burro's white rump. He settled himself in the seat, picked up the lines. "Thank you kindly, ma'am," he said. "I'll do like you told me; I'll go back and catch the Salinas road."

90    "Mind," she called, "if you're long in getting there, keep the sand damp."

"Sand, ma'am? . . . Sand? Oh, sure. You mean round the chrysantheums. Sure I will." He clucked his tongue. The beasts leaned luxuriously into their collars. The mongrel dog took his place between the back wheels. The wagon turned and crawled out the entrance road and back the way it had come, along the river.

Elisa stood in front of her wire fence watching the slow progress of the caravan. Her shoulders were straight, her head thrown back, her eyes half-closed, so that the scene came vaguely into them. Her lips moved silently, forming the words "Good-bye—good-bye." Then she whispered, "That's a bright direction. There's a glowing there." The sound of her whisper startled her. She shook herself free and looked about to see whether anyone had been listening. Only the dogs had heard. They lifted their heads toward her from their sleeping in the dust, and then stretched out their chins and settled asleep again. Elisa turned and ran hurriedly into the house.

In the kitchen she reached behind the stove and felt the water tank. It was full of hot water from the noonday cooking. In the bathroom she tore off her soiled clothes and flung them into the corner. And then she scrubbed herself with a little block of pumice, legs and thighs, loins and chest and arms, until her skin was scratched and red. When she had dried herself she stood in front of a mirror in her bedroom and looked at her body. She tightened her stomach and threw out her chest. She turned and looked over her shoulder at her back.

After a while she began to dress, slowly. She put on her newest under-clothing and her nicest stockings and the dress which was the symbol of her prettiness. She worked carefully on her hair, pencilled her eyebrows and rouged her lips.

95    Before she was finished she heard the little thunder of hoofs and the shouts of Henry and his helper as they drove the red steers into the corral. She heard the gate bang shut and set herself for Henry's arrival.

His step sounded on the porch. He entered the house calling "Elisa, where are you?"

"In my room, dressing. I'm not ready. There's hot water for your bath. Hurry up. It's getting late."

When she heard him splashing in the tub, Elisa laid his dark suit on the bed, and shirt and socks and tie beside it. She stood his polished shoes on the floor beside the bed. Then she went to the porch and sat primly and stiffly down. She looked toward the river road where the willow-line was still yellow with frosted leaves so that under the high grey fog they seemed a thin band of sunshine. This was the only color in the grey afternoon. She sat unmoving for a long time. Her eyes blinked rarely.

Henry came banging out of the door, shoving his tie inside his vest as he came. Elisa stiffened and her face grew tight. Henry stopped short and looked at her. "Why—why, Elisa. You look so nice!"

100    "Nice? You think I look nice? What do you mean by 'nice'?"

Henry blundered on. "I don't know. I mean you look different, strong and happy."

"I am strong? Yes, strong. What do you mean 'strong'?"

He looked bewildered. "You're playing some kind of a game," he said helplessly. "It's a kind of a play. You look strong enough to break a calf over your knee, happy enough to eat it like watermelon."

For a second she lost her rigidity. "Henry! Don't talk like that. You didn't know what you said." She grew complete again. "I'm strong," she boasted. "I never knew before how strong."

Henry looked down toward the tractor shed, and when he brought his eyes back to her, 105 they were his own again. "I'll get out the car. You can put on your coat while I'm starting."

Elisa went into the house. She heard him drive to the gate and idle down his motor, and then she took a long time to put on her hat. She pulled it here and pressed it there. When Henry turned the motor off she slipped into her coat and went out.

The little roadster bounced along on the dirt road by the river, raising the birds and driving the rabbits into the brush. Two cranes flapped heavily over the willow-line and dropped into the river-bed.

Far ahead on the road Elisa saw a dark speck. She knew.

She tried not to look as they passed it, but her eyes would not obey. She whispered to herself sadly. "He might have thrown them off the road. That wouldn't have been much trouble, not very much. But he kept the pot," she explained. "He had to keep the pot. That's why he couldn't get them off the road."

The roadster turned a bend and she saw the caravan ahead. She swung full around to- 110 ward her husband so she could not see the little covered wagon and the mismatched team as the car passed them.

In a moment it was over. The thing was done. She did not look back. She said loudly, to be heard above the motor, "It will be good, tonight, a good dinner."

"Now you're changed again," Henry complained. He took one hand from the wheel and patted her knee. "I ought to take you in to dinner oftener. It would be good for both of us. We get so heavy out on the ranch."

"Henry," she asked, "could we have wine at dinner?"

"Sure we could. Say! That will be fine."

She was silent for a little while; then she said, "Henry, at those prize fights, do the men 115 hurt each other very much?"

"Sometimes a little, not often. Why?"

"Well, I've read how they break noses, and blood runs down their chests. I've read how the fighting gloves get heavy and soggy with blood."

He looked around at her. "What's the matter, Elisa? I didn't know you read things like that." He brought the car to a stop, then turned to the right over the Salinas River bridge.

"Do any women ever go to the fights?" she asked.

"Oh, sure, some. What's the matter, Elisa? Do you want to go? I don't think you'd like it, 120 but I'll take you if you really want to go."

She relaxed limply in the seat. "Oh, no. No. I don't want to go. I'm sure I don't." Her face was turned away from him. "It will be enough if we can have wine. It will be plenty." She turned up her coat collar so he could not see that she was crying weakly—like an old woman.

## Questions

1. What point of view is used in the story? What are the advantages of this point of view?

2. Consider the symbolism of the setting in this story with respect to the Salinas Valley, the time of year, and the description of the Allen house. What do these things tell us about Elisa Allen and her world?

3. To what extent is Steinbeck's description of Elisa in paragraphs 5 and 6 symbolic? What is she wearing? What do her clothes hide or suppress?

4. What do the chrysanthemums symbolize for Elisa? What do they symbolize *about* her? What role do these flowers play in her life?

5. How does Elisa's character or sense of self change during the episode in which she washes and dresses for dinner? To what extent is this washing-dressing episode symbolic? How would you explain the symbolism?

6. Consider the symbolic impact of Elisa's seeing the chrysanthemum sprouts at the roadside. What does her reaction tell us about her values?

## WRITING ABOUT SYMBOLISM OR ALLEGORY

To discover possible parallels that determine the presence of symbolism or allegory, consider the following questions.

### Questions for Discovering Ideas

#### A. SYMBOLISM

- What cultural or universal symbols can you discover in names, objects, places, situations, or actions in a work (e.g., the character Faith, the woods, and the walking stick in "Young Goodman Brown"; the lumps of mud in "Unfinished Masterpieces"; the bleakness of the weather in "The Chrysanthemums"; or the straying son in "The Parable of the Prodigal Son")?
- What contextual symbolism can be found in a work? What makes you think it is symbolic? What is being symbolized? How definite or direct is the symbolism? How systematically is it used? How necessary to the work is it? To what degree does it strengthen the work? How strongly does the work stand on its own without the reading for symbolism?
- Is it possible to make parallel lists to show how qualities of a particular symbol match the qualities of a character or action? Here is such a list for the toy windmill in Welty's "A Worn Path" (Chapter 2):

| QUALITIES OF THE WINDMILL | COMPARABLE QUALITIES IN PHOENIX AND HER LIFE |
|---|---|
| 1. Cheap | 1. Poor, but she gives all her money for the windmill |
| 2. Breakable | 2. Old, and not far from death |
| 3. A gift | 3. Generous |
| 4. Not practical | 4. Needs relief from reality and practicality |
| 5. Colorful | 5. Needs something new and cheerful |

#### B. ALLEGORY

- How clearly does the author point you toward an allegorical reading (i.e., through names and allusions, consistency of narrative, literary context)?

- How consistent is the allegorical application? Does the entire work, or only a part, embody the allegory? On what basis do you draw these conclusions?
- How complete is the allegorical reading? How might the allegory yield to a diagram such as the following one on Hawthorne's "Young Goodman Brown," which shows how characters, actions, objects, and ideas correspond allegorically?

| Young Goodman Brown | Brown Himself | Citizens of the Village | The Forest Figure (Father), the Devil | Faith | The Forest Meeting | Retreat into Suspicion and Distrust |
|---|---|---|---|---|---|---|
| **Allegorical application to morality and faith** | Potential for good | Culture and religious reinforcement | Forces of evil and deceit | Salvation and love; ideals to be rescued and preserved | Attack on ideals; incentive to disillusionment | Destruction of faith; doubt, spiritual negligence, loss of certainty, increase of gloom and suspicion |
| **Allegorical application to personal and general concerns** | Individual in pursuit of goals | External support for personal strength and growth | Obstacles to overcome, or by which to be overcome | Personal involvement, steadiness, happiness, religious conviction | Susceptibility to deceit, lack of conviction, misunderstanding, misinterpretation of others | Failure, depression, discouragement, disappointment, bitterness |

## C. OTHER FORMS

- What enables you to identify the story as a parable or fable? What lesson or moral is either clearly stated or implicit?
- What mythological identification is established in the work? What do you find in the story (names, situations, etc.) that enables you to determine its mythological significance? How is the myth to be understood? What symbolic value does the myth have? What current and timeless application does it have?

## Strategies for Organizing Ideas

Relate the central idea of your essay to the meaning of the major symbols or allegorical thrust of the story. An idea about "Young Goodman Brown," for example, is that fanaticism darkens and limits the human soul. An early incident in the story provides symbolic support for this idea. Specifically, when Goodman Brown enters the woods, he resolves "to stand firm against the devil," and he then looks up toward "Heaven above him." As he looks, a "black mass of cloud" appears to hide the "brightening stars" (paragraph 47). Within the limits of our central idea, the cloud can be seen as a symbol, just like the widening path or the night walk itself. Look for ways to make solid connections like this when you designate something as a symbol or allegory.

Also, your essay will need to include justifications for your symbols or allegorical parallels. In Poe's "The Masque of the Red Death" (Chapter 5), for example, Prince Prospero's seemingly impregnable "castellated abbey" is a line of defense against the plague. But the Red Death in a human shape easily invades the castle and conquers Prospero and his ill-fated guests. If you treat the abbey as a symbol, it is important to apply it to measures that people take (medicine, escapist activity, etc.) to keep death distant and remote. In the same way, in describing the allegorical elements in "Young Goodman Brown," you need to establish a comprehensive statement such as the following: People lose ideals and forsake principles not because they are evil but because they misunderstand the people around them (see the second illustrative essay that follows).

For the body of your essay there are a number of strategies for discussing symbolism and allegory. You might use one exclusively or a combination.

SYMBOLISM. If you want to write about symbolism, you might consider the following points.

1. *The meaning of a major symbol.* Identify the symbol and what it stands for. Then answer questions such as these: Is the symbol cultural or contextual? How do you decide? How do you derive your interpretation of the symbolic meaning? What is the extent of the meaning? Does the symbol undergo modification or new applications if it reappears in the work? How does the symbol affect your understanding of the work? Does the symbol bring out any ironies? How does the symbol add strength and depth to the work?

2. *The development and relationship of symbols.* For two or more symbols, consider issues such as these: How do the symbols connect with each other (like night and the cloud in "Young Goodman Brown" as symbols of a darkening mind)? What additional meanings do the symbols provide? (The windmill and the medicine in "A Worn Path," for example, are ironic because the windmill suggests cheer while the medicine suggests hopelessness.) Do the symbols control the form of the work? How? (For example, at the beginning of Steinbeck's "The Chrysanthemums," the barren wintry countryside is compared to a "closed pot," and at the ending Elisa learns that the tinsmith has dumped the earth out of the flower pot that she had given to him as a gift. In a similar vein, Joyce's "Araby" [Chapter 5] begins with the "blind" or dead-end street and ends with the darkness of the closed bazaar.) Can these comparable objects and conditions be viewed symbolically in relationship to the development of the two stories? Other issues are whether the symbols fit naturally or artificially into the context of the story or whether and how the writer's symbols create unique quality or excellence.

ALLEGORY. When writing about allegory, you might use one of the following approaches.

1. *The application and meaning of the allegory.* What is the subject of the story (allegory, fable, parable, myth)? How can it be more generally applied to ideas or to qualities of human character, not only of its own time but also of our

own? What other versions of the story do you know, if any? Does it illustrate, either closely or loosely, particular philosophies or religious views? If so, what are these? How do you know?

2. *The consistency of the allegory.* Is the allegory used consistently throughout the story, or is it used intermittently? Explain and illustrate this use. Would it be correct to call your story allegorical rather than an allegory? Can you determine how parts of the story are introduced for their allegorical importance? Examples are the increasingly dark pathway leading to home in Bierce's "An Occurrence at Owl Creek Bridge" (Chapter 2), which indicates the weakening hold that Farquhar has on life, the shabby fur muff in Mansfield's "Miss Brill" (Chapter 4), which suggest the comparably dismal circumstances of Miss Brill herself, and the Champs Elysées, the fashionable Parisian street in Maupassant's "The Necklace" (Chapter 1), which corresponds to Mathilde's constant temptation to live beyond her means.

In concluding, you might summarize main points, describe general impressions, explain the impact of the symbolic or allegorical methods, indicate personal responses, or suggest further lines of thought and application. You might also assess the quality and appropriateness of the symbolism or allegory (such as Hawthorne's "Young Goodman Brown" opening in darkness and closing in gloom).

## Illustrative Student Essay (Symbolism)

Underlined sentences in this paper *do not* conform to MLA style and are used solely as teaching tools to emphasize the central idea, thesis sentence, and topic sentences throughout the paper.

Raj 1

Michael Raj

Professor Thomas

English 320

27 September 2007

### Symbols of Light and Darkness in Porter's "The Jilting of Granny Weatherall"°

[1]     In Katherine Anne Porter's "The Jilting of Granny Weatherall," Ellen Weatherall— Granny Weatherall—is lying on her deathbed, and things in the story are described as they are being filtered through her conscious and unconscious mind. For 60 of her

---

°See pp. 341–46 for this story.

Raj 2

80 years Granny has been a tower of strength to those around her, but now she is succumbing to powerful strokes, climaxed by the "deep roaring" of the terminal, killing stroke (346, paragraph 57). As she gets closer and closer to her last moments she fades in and out of awareness, and she finally loses contact with her adult children who are keeping vigil around her. Near the end, as she receives extreme unction from her priest, she does not understand what is happening to her (346, paragraph 56). While she sometimes makes contact with those around her, her mind wanders and touches base with her lifelong beliefs, hopes, plans, fears, embarrassments, sorrows, intentions, and convictions. <u>Her mental associations reveal her personality as a valiant and triumphant woman who has met and overcome the major obstacles and challenges of her life.</u>

[2]      She has been constant in her religious duties, and religious concerns are never far from her mind. For example, one of her last thoughts is that she wants to send six bottles of wine to a Sister Borgia (358, paragraph 57). In her delirium her thoughts touch on her gratefulness for her life of hard work and service, and also on her love for her children, even including a child, Hapsy, whom she apparently lost in childbirth but whom she imagines as having lived to adulthood (Hapsy seems to be the "something not given back" that she tries to remember [358, paragraph 42]). <u>Significantly, as Granny's thoughts "spread out the plan of life and tuck in the edges orderly" (358, paragraph 17), her memories are dominated by biblical symbols of light and darkness.</u>\* <u>The symbols of light crystallize her convictions and ideals, while the symbols of darkness express her lifelong fears and anxieties.</u>†

[3]      <u>Light, whiteness, and brightness symbolize the security and inner peace that Granny has sought but not always found.</u> Several times she recalls that during her lifetime she made a ceremony out of lighting the household lamps to dispel the darkness, thus acting out many actions reminiscent of the Bible, such as the books of Genesis and Exodus. She remembers that when fog began to move toward her house, "marching across the creek swallowing the trees and moving up the hill like an army of ghosts," her regular reaction was "to go in and light the lamps" (345, paragraph 26). She also remembers that "lighting the lamps had been beautiful" when her children were small (342, paragraph 27). After the rooms had been illuminated, the children would no longer be frightened: "they didn't

---

\*Central idea.
†Thesis sentence.

have to be scared and hang on to mother any more. Never, never, never more" (343, paragraph 27). Furthermore, when Granny contemplates having chased the darkness of their fears away with light, she associates the light with divine protection and guidance. She likes strong, bright light, not the blue light shining from her daughter Cornelia's silk lampshades, which she believes are "[no] sort of light at all, just frippery" (345, paragraph 51). Although darkness has always loomed near her, Granny constantly found comfort in light and brightness, symbols that reflect her need for order and peace of mind.

[4]        In contrast, images of darkness, smoke, and fog suggest the fear, doubt, and instability that Granny associates with uncertainty and abandonment. We learn that at the age of twenty she experienced the most crushing event of her life. On the day of her intended marriage, her fiancé, George, jilted her at the altar. She was inconsolable; and "The whole bottom dropped out of the world, and there she was blind and sweating and nothing under her feet and the walls falling away" (345, paragraph 49). When she recalls this betrayal, dark images flow into her mind—disturbing symbols of horror and rejection: "There was the day, the day, but a whirl of dark smoke rose and covered it, crept up and over into the bright field. [. . .] That was hell, she knew hell when she saw it" (344, paragraph 29). Even her marriage with John, who died young and left her as a widow to rear their children, has not lessened her pain and regret. On her deathbed, after 60 years of "pray[ing] against remembering him [George] and against losing her soul in the deep pit of hell" (344, paragraph 29), another symbol of darkness indicates that she has never truly recovered from being rejected: "the thought of him was a smoky cloud from hell that moved and crept in her head" (344, paragraph 29). These symbols of darkness bring out the shattering anguish of Granny's memory.

[5]        At the end of the story, the combination of references to light and dark symbolizes the second "jilting" that Granny experiences. After Porter establishes that darkness symbolizes doubt and despair and that light symbolizes safety and security, she uses both symbols to show Granny's state of mind during her final moments. Granny visualizes a "point of light that was herself," which is being consumed by darkness (346, paragraph 60). Through repetition, Porter stresses the negative symbolism of darkness, for Granny's "body was now only a deeper mass of shadow in an endless darkness and this darkness would curl around the light and swallow it up" (346, paragraph 60). As the darkness overwhelms her, she cries out to God to give her a saving and healing sign

of divine presence. But "[f]or the second time there was no sign" (346, paragraph 61)—
a direct echo of Matthew 12:39 ("there shall no sign be given"). It is safe to assume that
Granny feels the despair of darkness as she dies, for her thoughts of George as
bridegroom merge with her thoughts of God as bridegroom, and she feels jilted by the
second just as by the first. Despite her despair, however, the true status of her soul is
demonstrated by what we have learned throughout the story about the energy and
devotion of her life. Her achievement as the center of her family is summed up by her
brief prayer as she remembers lighting the lamps, which is to her the symbol of divine
love: "God, for all my life I thank thee. Without Thee, my God, I could never have done
it" (343, paragraph 27).

[6]      The symbols are of course not only symbols, but they also have a basis in the
actual reality of light and darkness. Thus at one point Granny remarks that she should
"hide from the light" and that "sleeping in the light gave you nightmares" (344,
paragraph 29). It appears that here, at least, reality is more significant than symbolism.
When Granny approaches the very end of the "hard pull" of her life, she despairs
because of the "cruel" realization that she has received no divine sign. The last words
of the story describe her last moment: "She stretched herself with a deep breath and
blew out the light." This ending is final, and at first we might think that Granny's light
is gone and that the darkness she feared has overcome her. Another Biblical quotation,
however, may put the two symbols into additional perspective, for we learn in Isaiah
that in the long run both light and darkness are divine, for God says, "I form the light,
and create darkness" (Isaiah 45:7). <u>This is a dimension of Granny's life that goes</u>
<u>beyond symbolism.</u>

---

Raj 5

**WORK CITED**

Porter, Katherine Anne. "The Jilting of Granny Weatherall." *Literature: An Introduction to Reading and
Writing.* Ed. Edgar V. Roberts. 4th Compact Ed. Upper Saddle River: Prentice Hall, 2008, 341–46.

## Commentary

This essay illustrates the principles of analysis described in the second part of the guide
for considering symbolism. Connection within the essay may be seen in the continuity
of topic from paragraph 1 to paragraph 2, and also from paragraph 4 to paragraph 5.

Additionally, some of the individual words and phrases providing continuity are "in contrast," "another," "despite," "however," and "not only . . . but also."

Paragraph 1 establishes the nature of the story and also the qualities of the major character, Granny Weatherall. Paragraph 2 introduces her religious outlook, and it also contains the central idea, about the significance of symbolic light and darkness in the story. The concluding thesis sentence indicates that the body of the essay will treat the meanings of both symbols.

In the body, paragraph 3 introduces the idea that both symbols are common in the Bible, and that therefore they are a natural function of Granny's religiosity. Paragraph 4 is in contrast to paragraph 3 because it explains that Granny was jilted at age 20 and that she has always associated this horrible memory with darkness. Paragraph 5 emphasizes that to Granny, the darkness seems to be victorious as she assumes that God has deserted her just as she had been jilted when she was young. Paragraph 6 concludes the essay by (1) treating the reality of light and dark in the story, thereby pointing out that the symbols are not consistently used symbolically, and (2) introducing the biblical idea that Granny is in divine hands, whether in lightness or darkness.

## Illustrative Student Essay (Allegory)

Underlined sentences in this paper *do not* conform to MLA style and are used solely as teaching tools to emphasize the central idea, thesis sentence, and topic sentences throughout the paper.

Murphy 1

Heather Murphy

Professor Thomas

English 2B

5 February 2007

### The Allegory of Hawthorne's "Young Goodman Brown"°

[1]     Nathaniel Hawthorne's "Young Goodman Brown" is a nightmarish narrative. It allegorizes the process by which something good—religion—becomes a justification for intolerance and prejudice. The major character, Young Goodman Brown of colonial Salem, begins as a pious and holy person, but he takes a walk into a nearby darkening forest of suspicion. The process is portrayed by Hawthorne as something created by the devil himself, who leads Goodman Brown into the increasingly evil and sinful night. By

---

°See pp. 331–39 for this story.

the end of the allegory, Brown is transformed into an unforgiving, antisocial, dour, and dreary misanthrope.

[2]     Hawthorne's choice of the story's location reminds us that it was in Salem, in the late seventeenth century, that religious zealousness became so extreme that a number of witch trials and public hangings took place solely on the basis of suspicion and false accusation. This setting indicates that Hawthorne's immediate allegorical target is the overzealous pursuit of religious principles. And so Goodman Brown's trip not only takes him into the gloom of night, but also marks a descent into the darkest dungeons of his soul.*

[3]     While the story presents Brown's embarkation into religious zealotry, Hawthorne's allegory may also be applied generally to the ways in which people uncritically follow *any* ideal that leads them to distrust and suspect others. The allegory thus applies to those who swallow political slogans, who believe in their own racial or ethnic superiority, or who justify super-patriotism and super-nationalism. Thus convinced of their own supremacy, people ignore the greater need for love, understanding, toleration, cooperation, and forgiveness. Hawthorne's allegory is a realistic portrait of how people get into such a mental state, with Goodman Brown as the major example. Such people push ahead even against their own good nature and background, and they become prejudiced through delusion and suspicion.†

[4]     Young Goodman Brown's pathway into the night is not a direct plunge, but first Hawthorne shows that Brown does not begin without good nature. Many times early in the story we learn that Brown has doubts about the "evil purpose" of his allegorical walk. At the very beginning, Faith calls him back and pleads with him to stay with her (331, paragraph 2), but even so, he leaves her. As he walks away he thinks of himself as "a wretch" for doing so (332, paragraph 7). He excuses himself with a promise that once the evening is over he will stick with Faith forever after—an "excellent resolve for the future," as the narrator ironically states (332, paragraph 8). When Goodman Brown is reproached by the devil for being late he gives the excuse "Faith kept me back a while" (332, paragraph 12), a sentence of ironic double meaning. Once he has kept his appointment with the devil, he states his intention to go no farther because he has "scruples" that remind him that "it is my purpose now to return whence I came" (332, paragraph 15). When he refers to his family's proud and virtuous heritage, the devil is

---

*Central idea.
†Thesis sentence.

amused by his naivety. Even when Brown is standing before the altar of profanation deep within the forest, he appeals to Faith, "Look up to Heaven, and resist the Wicked One!" (338, paragraph 68). All this hesitation represents a true conscience in Goodman Brown even though he ignores it as he progresses deeper into the forest of sin. His failure—and failure it is—is his inability or unwillingness to persist in making his own insight and conscience his guides of conduct.

[5]      It is important to remember that Goodman Brown is favored by his background, which should have kept him on a true path of goodness. Almost as a claim of entitlement he cries out, "With Heaven above, and Faith below, I will yet stand firm against the devil" (335, paragraph 46). He also cries out for Faith even when he hears a voice resembling hers that is "uttering lamentations" within the darkening woods (335, paragraph 47). When he sees Faith's pink ribbon fluttering down, he exclaims, "My Faith is gone!" (336, paragraph 50). These instances show allegorically that Goodman Brown's previous way of life has given him proper spiritual guidance. Even as he is tempted before the "unhallowed altar" (338, paragraph 64), he asks the question "But, where is Faith?" as though he could reclaim his previous innocence (337, paragraph 57). Just as he ignores his conscience, he also ignores the power of his background, and it is this neglect that fuels his change into the "demoniac" who abandons himself to "the instinct that guides mortal man to evil" (336, paragraph 51).

[6]      Another major element in Goodman Brown's allegorical path to darkness is that he persuades himself that virtually all the people he knows have yielded their lives to sin. In the grips of this distorted view of others, he believes not what he sees but what he thinks he is seeing. Thus he witnesses the encounter between the devil and Goody Cloyse shortly after he enters the forest, but what he sees is not the good woman who taught him his catechism but rather a witch who is bent on evil and who is friendly with the devil. He ignores the fact that he too is friendly with the devil (the image of his own father) and therefore, while ignoring the log in his own eye, he condemns Goody Cloyse for the speck in hers. After his transformation, when he walks back into his village from his allegorical walk into evil, he "snatche[s] away" a child from Goody as though she were preaching the words of the devil (338, paragraph 70). He cannot believe that others possess goodness as long he is convinced by the devil's words that "the whole earth [is] one stain of guilt, one mighty blood-spot" (338, paragraph 63). For this reason he

condemns both his minister and Deacon Gookin, whose conspiratorial voices he imagines that he overhears on the pathway through the forest. In short, the process of Hawthorne's allegory about the growth of harmful pietism demonstrates that travelers on the pathway to prejudice accept suspicion and mistrust without trying to get at the whole truth and without recognizing that judgment is not in human but rather in divine hands.

[7]    <u>As Hawthorne allegorizes the development of religious discrimination he makes clear that mistrust and suspicion form its basis</u>. Certainly, as the devil claims, human beings commit many criminal and depraved sins (337–38, paragraph 63), but this does not mean that all human beings are equally at fault, and that they are beyond love and redemption. The key for Goodman Brown is that he exceeds his judgmental role and condemns others solely on his own hasty conclusions. As long as he has faith he will not falter, but when he leaves his faith, or believes that he has lost his faith, he is adrift and will see only evil wherever he looks. For this reason he permits suspicion and loathing to distort his previous love for his wife and neighbors, and he becomes harsh and desperate. Hawthorne devotes the concluding paragraph of the story to a brief summary of Brown's life after the fateful night. This conclusion completes the allegorical cycle beginning with Brown's initiation into evil and extending to his "dying hour" of "gloom" and his unhopeful tombstone (339, paragraph 72).

[8]    <u>Hawthorne's "Young Goodman Brown" allegorizes the paradox of how noble beliefs become ignoble</u>. Goodman Brown dies in gloom because he believes that his wrong vision is true. His form of evil is the hardest to stop because wrongdoers who are convinced of their own goodness are beyond reach. In view of such self-righteous evil, whether cloaked in the apparent virtues of Puritanism or of some other blindly rigorous doctrine, Hawthorne writes, "the fiend in his own shape is less hideous than when he rages in the breast of man" (336, paragraph 53). Young Goodman Brown is one of the many who create darkness but are convinced that they alone walk in light.

**WORK CITED**

Hawthorne, Nathaniel. "Young Goodman Brown." *Literature: An Introduction to Reading and Writing.* Ed. Edgar V. Roberts. 4th Compact Ed. Upper Saddle River: Prentice Hall, 2008, 331–39.

## Commentary

This essay deals with a major idea in "Young Goodman Brown," and it therefore illustrates the first approach described earlier (p. 356). Unity in the essay is achieved by a number of means. For example, paragraph 2 extends a topic in paragraph 1. Also, a phrase in sentence 2 of paragraph 1 is echoed in sentence 1 of paragraph 8. Making additional connections within the essay are individual words such as "another," "while," "therefore," and the repetition of words throughout the essay that are contained in the thesis sentence.

The first three paragraphs of the essay constitute an extended introduction to the topics of paragraphs 4 through 8, for they establish "Young Goodman Brown" as an allegory. Paragraph 1 briefly treats the allegorical nature of the narrative. Paragraph 2 relates the historical basis of the topic to Hawthorne's purpose in writing the story, and it concludes with the essay's central idea. Paragraph 3 broadens the scope of Hawthorne's allegory by showing that it includes zealousness wherever it might appear. Paragraph 3 also concludes with the essay's thesis sentence.

Paragraph 4, the first in the body, deals with an important aspect of the allegory, and one that makes it particularly relevant and timely even today—namely, that people of goodwill may become evil under the pretense of goodness. Similarly, paragraph 5 points out that such people usually come from good backgrounds and have benefited from good influences during their lives.

Paragraphs 6 and 7 locate the origins of evil in two major human qualities—first, the belief in one's own delusions; and second, the mental confusion that results from the conviction that appearance is more real and believable than reality itself. Paragraph 8 concludes the essay on the note that the finished "product"—a person who has become suspicious and misguided—demonstrates how good ideas, when pushed to the extreme by false imagination, can backfire.

## Writing Topics: Symbolism and Allegory

1. Compare and contrast the symbolism in Munro's "The Found Boat" (Chapter 7), Porter's "The Jilting of Granny Weatherall," Coleman's "Unfinished Masterpieces," and Steinbeck's "The Chrysanthemums." To what degree do the stories rely on contextual symbols? On universal symbols? On the basis of your comparison, what is the case for asserting that realism and fantasy are directly related to the nature of the symbolism employed by the writer?

2. Why do writers who advocate moral, philosophical, or religious issues frequently use symbolism or allegory? In treating this question, you might introduce references from "The Parable of the Prodigal Son," and Hawthorne's "Young Goodman Brown."

3. Write an essay on the allegorical method of one or more of the parables included in the Gospel of St. Luke, such as "The Bridegroom" (5:34–35), "The Garments and the Wineskins" (5:36–39), "The Sower" (8:4–15), "The Good Samaritan" (10:25–37), "The Prodigal Son" (15:11–32), "The Ox in the Well" (14:5–6), "The Watering of Animals on the Sabbath" (13:15–17), "The Rich Fool" (12:16–21),

"Lazarus" (16:19–31), "The Widow and the Judge" (18:1–8), and "The Pharisee and the Publican" (18:9–14).

4. Write your own brief story using a widely recognized cultural symbol such as the flag (patriotism, love of country, a certain type of politics), water (life, sexuality, regeneration), or the population explosion (the end of life on earth). By arranging actions and dialogue, make clear the issues conveyed by your symbol, and also try to resolve conflicts the symbol might raise among your characters.

5. Write a brief story in which you develop your own contextual symbol. You might, for example, demonstrate how holding a job brings out character strengths that are not at first apparent or how neglecting to care for the inside or outside of a house indicates a character's decline. The principle is to take something that can at first seem normal and ordinary, then to make that thing symbolic as you develop your story.

6. Using the catalogue system of your library, discover a recent critical-biographical book or books about Hawthorne. Explain what the book says about Hawthorne's uses of symbolism. To what extent does the book relate Hawthorne's symbolism to his religious and family heritage?

# Chapter 9

# Idea or Theme: The Meaning and Message in Fiction

The word **idea** refers to the result or results of general and abstract thinking. Synonymous words are *concept*, *thought*, *opinion*, and *principle*. In literary study the consideration of ideas relates to *meaning*, *interpretation*, *explanation*, and *significance*. Although ideas are usually extensive and complex, separate ideas can be described by individual words such as *right*, *good*, *love*, *piety*, *liberty*, *causation*, *wilderness*, and, not surprisingly, *idea* itself.

## Ideas And Assertions

Although single words alone can name ideas, we must put these words into operation in *sentences* or *assertions* before they can advance our understanding. Good operational sentences about ideas are not the same as ordinary conversational statements such as "It's a nice day." An observation of this sort may be true (depending on the weather), but it gives us no ideas and does not stimulate our minds. Rather, a sentence asserting an idea about a nice day should initiate a thought or argument about the day's quality, such as "A nice day requires light breezes, blue sky, a warm sun, and relaxation." Because this sentence makes an assertion about the word *nice*, it allows us to consider and develop the idea of a nice day.

In studying literature, always express ideas as assertions. For example, you might state that an idea in Lawrence's "The Horse Dealer's Daughter" is "love," but it would be difficult to discuss anything more unless you make an assertion that promises an argument, such as "This story demonstrates the idea that love is irresistible and irrational." This assertion would lead you to explain the unlikely love that bursts out in the story. Similarly, for Welty's "A Worn Path" (Chapter 2) an assertion like the following would advance further argument: "Phoenix embodies the idea that caring for others gives no reward but the continuation of the duty itself."

Although we have noted only one idea in these two works, most stories contain many ideas. When one of the ideas seems to be the major one, it is called the **theme**. In practice, the words *theme* and *major idea* are the same.

## Ideas and Issues

A word that is often used as an equivalent to idea is **issue**, which may be defined as an open and unsettled point or concern about which there may be argument or contention. On political matters, issues are usually about what courses of action to take, such as whether a new bridge should be built, or whether more money should be spent on schools. Often, however, the issues revolve about the theoretical basis on which to proceed. To this extent, issues are identical with ideas. The nature of issue as a concept—because issues develop out of situations—is particularly helpful in the study of literature. Sometimes issues are not stated and we as readers make inferences from the work or works we are discussing. What do we find there? What do we take away from that work? Have we understood the issue properly? How do we define the issue as an idea? The answers to such questions frequently lead us directly into discussions of ideas. Chopin's "The Story of an Hour" (Chapter 7) deals with a woman's unexpected thoughts when she is (mistakenly) told that her husband has died, and through her thoughts the story raises the issue of what a woman's role should be in marriage. In Bambara's "The Lesson" we find the issue of economic inequality and political injustice. Here the idea is that economic inequality results in an unacceptably high human cost. (See the illustrative essay at the end of this chapter.)

## Ideas and Values

Literature embodies **values** along with ideas. *Value*, of course, commonly refers to the price of something, but in the realm of ideas and principles, it is a standard of what is desired, sought, esteemed, and treasured. For example, *democracy* refers to our political system, but it is also a complex idea of representative government that we esteem most highly, and so also do we esteem concepts such as honor, cooperation, generosity, and love. A vital idea/value is *justice*, which, put most simply, involves equality before the law and also the fair evaluation of conduct that is deemed unacceptable or illegal. Literature embodies **values** along with ideas. This means that ideas imply that certain conditions and standards should be—or should not be— highly esteemed. For example, the idea of *justice* may be considered abstractly and broadly, as Plato does in his *Republic* when developing his concept of a just government. In comparison, justice is also a subject of Ernest J. Gaines in "The Sky Is Gray" (Chapter 4), but Gaines is not general and speculative, like Plato. Rather, he is personal, and makes his idea clear through the personal interactions of the various characters. Gaines's idea is that human beings are equal regardless of race, and he asserts the need for equal treatment by showing that the narrator, the young boy James, has pains, needs, difficulties, and fears that are the same as those of all human beings, regardless of race. In short, the idea of justice underlying Gaines's "The Sky Is Gray" also involves a deeply held value.

A graphic connection of ideas and values is seen in Pablo Picasso's massive painting *Guernica* (I–6, Plate 1). The painting superbly illustrates the agony of Guernica, the

Spanish town bombed by Nazi planes in 1937. The agonized horse and the screaming man, the disembodied head and arms, the mother holding her dead infant—all convey the idea that war is an unspeakable crime against humanity. Picasso's condemnation of war and the man responsible for the slaughter at Guernica, Francisco Franco (1892–1975), is also clear. That Picasso wanted his values to be understood is confirmed by his instruction that the painting was not to be displayed in Spain until after Franco died.

# The Place of Ideas in Literature

Because writers of poems, plays, and stories are usually not systematic philosophers, it is not appropriate to go "message hunting" as though their works contained nothing but ideas. Indeed, there is great benefit and pleasure to be derived from just savoring a work—getting engrossed in the story, following the patterns of narrative and conflict, getting to like the characters, understanding the work's implications and suggestions, and listening to the sounds of the author's words—to name only a few of the reasons for which literature is treasured.

Nevertheless, ideas are vital to understanding and appreciating not just fiction, but all literature. Writers have ideas and want to communicate them to you. For example, in "The Horse Dealer's Daughter," Lawrence tells the story of a man and a woman who fall impetuously and unpredictably in love. This love is unlikely but real, and the story is therefore effective, but the story is also provocative because it develops the idea that love has the power to override all other personal emotions and decisions. Paredes's narrator in "The Hammon and the Beans" tells the story of a little Mexican girl, with great potential but no opportunities at all, who dies from an undisclosed illness caused by medical neglect and her family's impoverishment. Through this event the story conveys the idea that massive humanitarian damage is a major result of economic deprivation. In these works, the ideas of the authors both underlie and connect the various narrative details.

## Distinguishing between Ideas and Actions

As you analyze works for ideas, it is important to avoid the trap of confusing ideas and actions. Such a trap is contained in the following sentence about O'Connor's "First Confession" (Chapter 7): "The major character, Jackie, misbehaves at home and tries to stab his sister with a bread knife." This sentence successfully describes a major action in the story, but it does not express an *idea* that connects characters and events, and for this reason it obstructs understanding. Some possible connections might be achieved with sentences such as these: "'First Confession' illustrates the idea that family life may produce anger and potential violence" or "'First Confession' shows that compelling children to accept authority may produce effects that are the opposite of adult intentions." A study based on these connecting formulations could be focused on ideas and would not be sidetracked into doing no more than retelling O'Connor's story.

## Distinguishing between Ideas and Situations

You should also distinguish between ideas and situations. For example, in Joyce's "Araby" (Chapter 5), the narrator describes his frustration and embarrassment when he arrives late at the Araby bazaar in Dublin. This is a *situation*, but it is not the *idea* brought out by the situation. Joyce's idea here is rather that immature love causes unreal dreams and hopes that result in disappointment and self-reproach. If you are able to distinguish a story's various situations from the writer's major idea or ideas, you will be able to focus on ideas and therefore sharpen your own thinking.

# How to Find Ideas

Ideas are not as obvious as characters or setting. To determine an idea, you need to consider the meaning of what you read and then to develop explanatory and comprehensive assertions. Your assertions need not be the same as those that others might make. People notice different things, and individual formulations vary. In Chopin's "The Story of an Hour" (Chapter 7), for example, an initial expression of some of the story's ideas might take any of the following forms: (1) Partners in even a good marriage can have ambivalent feelings about their lives together. (2) An accident can lead a wife to think negative but previously unrecognized thoughts. (3) Even those closest to a person may never realize that person's innermost feelings. Although any one of these choices could be a basic idea in the study of "The Story of an Hour," they have in common the main character's surprising feelings of release when she is told that her husband has been killed. In discovering ideas, you should follow a similar process—making a number of formulations for an idea and then selecting one for further development.

As you read, be alert to the different ways in which authors convey ideas. One author might prefer an indirect way through a character's speeches, whereas another may prefer direct statements. In practice, authors can employ any or all the following methods.

**1. Study the Authorial Voice.** Although authors mainly render action, dialogue, and situation, they sometimes state ideas to guide us and deepen our understanding. In the second paragraph of Maupassant's "The Necklace" (Chapter 1), for example, the authorial voice presents the idea that women have only charm and beauty to get on in the world. Ironically, Maupassant uses the story to show that for the major character Mathilde, nothing is effective, for her charm cannot prevent disaster. Hawthorne, in "Young Goodman Brown" (Chapter 8), expresses this powerful idea: "The fiend in his own shape is less hideous than when he rages in the breast of man" (paragraph 53). The narrator makes this statement just when the major character, Goodman Brown, is speeding through "the benighted wilderness" on his way to the satanic ritual. Although the idea is complex and will sustain extensive discussion, its essential aspect is that the causes of evil originate within human beings themselves, and the implication is that we alone are responsible for all our actions, whether good or evil.

**2. Study the First-Person Speaker.** First-person narrators or speakers frequently express ideas along with their depiction of actions and situations, and they also make statements from which you can make inferences about ideas. (See also Chapter 3, on point of view.) Because what they say is part of a dramatic presentation, they can be right or wrong, well-considered or thoughtless, good or bad, or brilliant or half-baked, depending on the speaker. A somewhat half-baked speaker, yet an interesting one, is Sammy, the narrator of Updike's "A & P" (Chapter 7), who seems engulfed in intellectual commonplaces, particularly in his insinuation about the intelligence of women. In his defense, however, Sammy *acts* on the worthy idea that people have private rights. If the speaker seems to possess limited understanding or inadequate consideration of what he or she is saying, like Jackie, sometimes, in Frank O'Connor's "First Confession" (Chapter 7), you may nevertheless still study and evaluate such a speaker's ideas. Jackie, for example, maintains some of his childhood attitudes even though at the time of the narration he is an older and presumably mature narrator. An especially mature narrator is the unnamed speaker of Whitecloud's "Blue Winds Dancing" (Chapter 6), who is honestly discouraged by his experiences at a large Western university, and he is deeply distressed by the ideas he has heard from his professor about the inferiority of Native American culture. The first-person narrator of Gilman's "The Yellow Wallpaper" (Chapter 10) is increasingly delusional, yet an idea we can derive from her speech and circumstances is that people with her illness need less harsh and more humane treatment. In Tan's "Two Kinds" (Chapter 4), the narrator describes the negative behavior that stemmed from her childhood conflicts with her mother. An idea that may be taken from this narration is that adult composure is reached only through tortuous childhood paths. If the speaker seems to possess incomplete or limited understanding of what he or she is saying, you may nevertheless still study and evaluate this speaker's ideas. In Bambara's "The Lesson," for example, the narrator Sylvia is a child who speaks the language of the streets but who nevertheless exhibits natural analytical skills befitting an astute and committed political scientist.

**3. Study the Statements Made by Characters.** In many stories, characters express their own views, which can be right or wrong, admirable or contemptible. When you consider such dramatic speeches, you must do considerable interpreting and evaluating yourself. The Second Stranger, the hangman, in Hardy's "The Three Strangers" (Chapter 6) expresses ideas about crime and punishment that are inflexibly unenlightened and unjust. It is clear that the peasant folk of Higher Crowstairs hold kinder and more humane ideas. Old Man Warner in Jackson's "The Lottery" (Chapter 3) states that the lottery is valuable even though we learn from the narrator that the beliefs underlying it have long been forgotten. Because Warner is a zealous and insistent person, however, his words show that outdated ideas continue to do harm even when there is strong reason to reevaluate and abandon them.

**4. Study the Work's Figurative Language.** Figurative language is one of the major components of poetry, but it also abounds in prose fiction (see also Chapter 12). In Joyce's "Araby," for example (Chapter 5), the narrator uses a beautiful comparison to describe his youthful admiration for his friend Mangan's sister. He says that his body "was like a harp and her words and gestures were like fingers running upon the wires" (paragraph 5). A less complimentary figure is seen in D. H. Lawrence's

"The Horse Dealer's Daughter." Lawrence develops the comparison through the Pervin family. Joe Pervin, one of Mabel's brothers, is demeaning himself by accepting his future role as no more than a subordinate worker for his future father-in-law. Lawrence's idea is that financial security alone involves the sacrifice of personal freedom, and so the comparison shows that Joe is no different from the great draft horses on the Pervin estate: "He [Joe] would marry and go into harness. His life was over, he would be a subject animal now" (paragraph 7).

**5. Study How Characters Stand for Ideas.** Characters and their actions can often be equated with certain ideas and values. The power of Mathilde's story in Maupassant's "The Necklace" (Chapter 1) emphasizes the idea is that unrealizable dreams can invade and damage the real world. Two diverse or opposed characters can embody contrasting ideas, as with Louise and Josephine of Chopin's "The Story of an Hour" (Chapter 7). Each woman can be taken to represent differing views about the role of women in marriage. In effect, characters who stand for ideas can assume symbolic status, as in Hawthorne's "Young Goodman Brown" (Chapter 8) where the protagonist symbolizes the alienation accompanying zealousness, or in Ozick's "The Shawl" (Chapter 5), where the small child Magda embodies the vulnerability and helplessness of human beings in the face of dehumanizing state brutality. Such characters can be equated directly with particular ideas, and to talk about them is a shorthand way of talking about the ideas.

**6. Study the Work Itself as an Embodiment of Ideas.** One of the most important ways in which authors express ideas is to interlock them within all parts and aspects of the work. The art of painting is instructive here, for a painting can be taken in with a single view that comprehends all the aspects of color, form, action, and expression, which can also be considered separately. Thus, we may again refer to the broken and distorted figures in Picasso's *Guernica* (1–6, Plate 1), which can be viewed together, and which emphasize the idea that war is not noble, for it creates unspeakable horror and suffering for human beings, animals, and the earth itself. In the same way, when a work is considered in its totality, the various parts collectively can embody major ideas, as in Bierce's "An Occurrence at Owl Creek Bridge" (Chapter 2), where Bierce dramatizes the idea that under great stress the human mind operates with lightning speed. Most works represent ideas in a similar way. Even "escape literature," which ostensibly enables readers to forget immediate problems, contains conflicts between good and evil, love and hate, good spies and bad, earthlings and aliens, and so on. Thereby, such works *do* embody ideas, even though their avowed intention is not to make readers think but rather to help them forget.

## Stories for Study ←

## TONI CADE BAMBARA (1939–1995)

Bambara (an African tribal name that Toni Cade appropriated from an old manuscript) was brought up in Harlem and Bedford Stuyvesant in New York. She received a B.A. from Queens College and an M.A. in American Studies from the City College of New York. For a time she was a social worker, and later she taught at many schools, including Rutgers, Duke, and the Scribe Video Center in Philadelphia. She also collaborated in the writing of television documentaries, including a life of W. E. B. Du Bois. In her fiction she treats the subjects of the black and also the female experience. She avoids using this material for political purposes, however, even though the subjects could easily fall within the political realm. Instead, she deals with her characters on the human level, trying to offer her readers "nourishment." Story collections are *Gorilla, My Love* (1972), from which "The Lesson" is taken, and *The Sea Birds Are Still Alive* (1977). Her novels are *The Salt Eaters* (1980) and *If Blessing Comes* (1987).

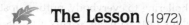 **The Lesson** (1972)

Back in the days when everyone was old and stupid or young and foolish and me and Sugar were the only ones just right, this lady moved on our block with nappy hair and proper speech and no makeup. And quite naturally we laughed at her, laughed the way we did at the junk man who went about his business like he was some big-time president and his sorry-ass horse his secretary. And we kinda hated her too, hated the way we did the winos who cluttered up our parks and pissed on our handball walls and stank up our hallways and stairs so you couldn't halfway play hide-and-seek without a goddamn gas mask. Miss Moore was her name. The only woman on the block with no first name. And she was black as hell, cept for her feet, which were fish-white and spooky. And she was always planning these boring-ass things for us to do, us being my cousin, mostly, who lived on the block cause we all moved North the same time and to the same apartment then spread out gradual to breathe. And our parents would yank our heads into some kinda shape and crisp up our clothes so we'd be presentable for travel with Miss Moore, who always looked like she was going to church, though she never did. Which is just one of the things the grownups talked about when they talked behind her back like a dog. But when she came calling with some sachet she'd sewed up or some gingerbread she'd made or some book, why then they'd all be too embarrassed to turn her down and we'd get handed over all spruced up. She'd been to college and said it was only right that she should take responsibility for the young ones education, and she not even related by marriage or blood. So they'd go for it. Specially Aunt Gretchen. She was the main gofer in the family. You got some ole dumb shit foolishness you want somebody to go for, you send for Aunt Gretchen. She been screwed into the go-along for so long, it's a blood-deep natural thing with her. Which is how she got saddled with me and Sugar and Junior in the first place while our mothers were in a la-de-da apartment up the block having a good ole time.

So this one day Miss Moore rounds us all up at the mailbox and it's purdee° hot and she's knockin herself out about arithmetic. And school suppose to let up in summer I heard, but she

°*purdee*: pretty.

don't never let up. And the starch in my pinafore scratching the shit outta me and I'm really hating this nappy-head bitch and her goddamn college degree. I'd much rather go to the pool or to the show where it's cool. So me and Sugar leaning on the mailbox being surly, which is a Miss Moore word. And Flyboy checking out what everybody brought for lunch. And Fat Butt already wasting his peanut-butter-and-jelly sandwich like the pig he is. And Junebug punchin on Q.T.'s arm for potato chips. And Rosie Giraffe shifting from one hip to the other waiting for somebody to step on her foot or ask her if she from Georgia so she can kick ass, preferably Mercedes'. And Miss Moore asking us do we know what money is, like we a bunch of retards. I mean real money, she say, like it's only poker chips or Monopoly papers we lay on the grocer. So right away I'm tired of this and say so. And would much rather snatch Sugar and go to the Sunset and terrorize the West Indian kids and take their hair ribbons and their money too. And Miss Moore files that remark away for next week's lesson on brotherhood, I can tell. And finally I say we oughta get to the subway cause it's cooler and besides we might meet some cute boys. Sugar done swiped her mama's lipstick, so we ready.

So we heading down the street and she's boring us silly about what things cost and what our parents make and how much goes for rent and how money ain't divided up right in this country. And then she gets to the part about we all poor and live in the slums, which I don't feature. And I'm ready to speak on that, but she steps out in the street and hails two cabs just like that. Then she hustles half the crew in with her and hands me a five-dollar bill and tells me to calculate 10 percent tip for the driver. And we're off. Me and Sugar and Junebug and Flyboy hangin out the window and hollering to everybody, putting lipstick on each other cause Flyboy a faggot anyway, and making farts with our sweaty armpits. But I'm mostly trying to figure how to spend this money. But they all fascinated with the meter ticking and Junebug starts laying bets as to how much it'll read when Flyboy can't hold his breath no more. Then Sugar lays bets as to how much it'll be when we get there. So I'm stuck. Don't nobody want to go for my plan, which is to jump out at the next light and run off to the first bar-b-que we can find. Then the driver tells us to get the hell out cause we there already. And the meter reads eighty-five cents. And I'm stalling to figure out the tip and Sugar say give him a dime. And I decide he don't need it bad as I do, so later for him. But then he tries to take off with Junebug foot still in the door so we talk about his mama something ferocious. Then we check out that we on Fifth Avenue and everybody dressed up in stockings. One lady in a fur coat, hot as it is. White folks crazy.

"This is the place," Miss Moore say, presenting it to us in the voice she uses at the museum. "Let's look in the windows before we go in."

5    "Can we steal?" Sugar asks very serious like she's getting the ground rules squared away before she plays. "I beg your pardon," say Miss Moore, and we fall out. So she leads us around the windows of the toy store and me and Sugar screamin, "This is mine, that's mine, I gotta have that, that was made for me, I was born for that," till Big Butt drowns us out.

"Hey, I'm going to buy that there."

"That there? You don't even know what it is, stupid."

"I do so," he say punchin on Rosie Giraffe. "It's a microscope."

"Whatcha gonna do with a microscope, fool?"

10    "Look at things."

"Like what, Ronald?" ask Miss Moore. And Big Butt ain't got the first notion. So here go Miss Moore gabbing about the thousands of bacteria in a drop of water and the somethin-orother in a speck of blood and the million and one living things in the air around us is invisible to the naked eye. And what she say that for? Junebug go to town on that "naked" and we rolling. Then Miss Moore ask what it cost. So we all jam into the window smudgin it up and the price tag say $300. So then she ask how long'd take for Big Butt and Junebug to save up their allowances. "Too long," I say. "Yeh," adds Sugar, "outgrown it by that time." And Miss Moore say no, you never outgrow learning instruments. "Why, even medical students and interns and," blah, blah, blah. And we ready to choke Big Butt for bringing it up in the first damn place.

"This here costs four hundred eighty dollars," say Rosie Giraffe. So we pile up all over her to see what she pointin out. My eyes tell me it's a chunk of glass cracked with something heavy, and different-color inks dripped into the splits, then the whole thing put into a oven or something. But for $480 it don't make sense.

"That's a paperweight made of semi-precious stones fused together under tremendous pressure," she explains slowly, with her hands doing the mining and all the factory work.

"So what's a paperweight?" asks Rosie Giraffe.

"To weigh paper with, dumbbell," say Flyboy, the wise man from the East.                    15

"Not exactly," say Miss Moore, which is what she say when you warm or way off too. "It's to weigh paper down so it won't scatter and make your desk untidy." So right away me and Sugar curtsy to each other and then to Mercedes who is more the tidy type.

"We don't keep paper on top of the desk in my class," say Junebug, figuring Miss Moore crazy or lyin one.

"At home, then," she say. "Don't you have a calendar and a pencil case and a blotter and a letter-opener on your desk at home where you do your homework?" And she know damn well what our homes look like cause she nosys around in them every chance she gets.

"I don't even have a desk," say Junebug. "Do we?"

"No. And I don't get no homework neither," says Big Butt.                                      20

"And I don't even have a home," say Flyboy like he do at school to keep the white folks off his back and sorry for him. Send this poor kid to camp posters, is his specialty.

"I do," says Mercedes. "I have a box of stationery on my desk and a picture of my cat. My godmother bought the stationery and the desk. There's a big rose on each sheet and the envelopes smell like roses."

"Who wants to know about your smelly-ass stationery," say Rosie Giraffe fore I can get my two cents in.

"It's important to have a work area all your own so that. . . ."

"Will you look at this sailboat, please," say Flyboy, cuttin her off and pointin to the thing     25
like it was his. So once again we tumble all over each other to gaze at this magnificent thing in the toy store which is just big enough to maybe sail two kittens across the pond if you strap them to the posts tight. We all start reciting the price tag like we in assembly. "Handcrafted sailboat of fiberglass at one thousand one hundred ninety-five dollars."

"Unbelievable," I hear myself say and am really stunned. I read it again for myself just in case the group recitation put me in a trance. Same thing. For some reason this pisses me off. We look at Miss Moore and she lookin at us, waiting for I dunno what.

"Who'd pay all that when you can buy a sailboat set for a quarter at Pop's, a tube of glue for a dime, and a ball of string for eight cents? It must have a motor and a whole lot else besides," I say. "My sailboat cost me about fifty cents."

"But will it take water?" say Mercedes with her smart ass.

"Took mine to Alley Pond Park once," say Flyboy. "String broke. Lost it. Pity."

"Sailed mine in Central Park and it keeled over and sank. Had to ask my father for     30
another dollar."

"And you got the strap," laugh Big Butt. "The jerk didn't even have a string on it. My old man wailed on his behind."

Little Q.T. was staring hard at the sailboat and you could see he wanted it bad. But he too little and somebodyd just take it from him. So what the hell. "This boat for kids, Miss Moore?"

"Parents silly to buy something like that just to get all broke up," say Rosie Giraffe.

"That much money it should last forever," I figure.

35 "My father'd buy it for me if I wanted it."

"Your father, my ass," say Rosie Giraffe getting a chance to finally push Mercedes.

"Must be rich people shop here," say Q.T.

"You are a very bright boy," say Flyboy. "What was your first clue?" And he rap him on the head with the back of his knuckles, since Q.T. the only one he could get away with. Though Q.T. liable to come up behind you years later and get his licks in when you half expect it.

"What I want to know is," I says to Miss Moore though I never talk to her, I wouldn't give the bitch that satisfaction, "is how much a real boat costs? I figure a thousand'd get you a yacht any day."

40 "Why don't you check that out," she says, "and report back to the group?" Which really pains my ass. If you gonna mess up a perfectly good swim day least you could do is have some answers. "Let's go in," she say like she got something up her sleeve. Only she don't lead the way. So me and Sugar turn the corner to where the entrance is, but when we get there I kinda hang back. Not that I'm scared, what's there to be afraid of, just a toy store. But I feel funny, shame. But what I got to be shamed about? Got as much right to go in as anybody. But somehow I can't seem to get hold of the door, so I step away from Sugar to lead. But she hangs back too. And I look at her and she looks at me and this is ridiculous. I mean, damn, I have never ever been shy about doing nothing or going nowhere. But then Mercedes steps up and then Rosie Giraffe and Big Butt crowd in behind and shove, and next thing we all stuffed into the doorway with only Mercedes squeezing past us, smoothing out her jumper and walking right down the aisle. Then the rest of us tumble in like a glued-together jigsaw done all wrong. And people lookin at us. And it's like the time me and Sugar crashed into the Catholic church on a dare. But once we got in there and everything so hushed and holy and the candles and the bowin and the handkerchiefs on all the drooping heads, I just couldn't go through with the plan. Which was for me to run up to the altar and do a tap dance while Sugar played the nose flute and messed around in the holy water. And Sugar kept givin me the elbow. Then later teased me so bad I tied her up in the shower and turned it on and locked her in. And she'd be there till this day if Aunt Gretchen hadn't finally figured I was lyin about the boarder takin a shower.

Same thing in the store. We all walkin on tiptoe and hardly touchin the games and puzzles and things. And I watched Miss Moore who is steady watchin us like she waitin for a sign. Like Mama Drewery watches the sky and sniffs the air and takes note of just how much slant is in the bird formation. Then me and Sugar bump smack into each other, so busy gazing at the toys, 'specially the sailboat. But we don't laugh and go into our fat-lady bump-stomach routine. We just stare at that price tag. Then Sugar run a finger over the whole boat. And I'm jealous and want to hit her. Maybe not her, but I sure want to punch somebody in the mouth.

"Whatcha bring us here for, Miss Moore?"

"You sound angry, Sylvia. Are you mad about something?" Givin me one of them grins like she tellin a grown-up joke that never turns out to be funny. And she's lookin very closely at me like maybe she plannin to do my portrait from memory. I'm mad, but I won't give her that satisfaction. So I slouch around the store bein very bored and say, "Let's go."

Me and Sugar at the back of the train watchin the tracks whizzin by large then small then gettin gobbled up in the dark. I'm thinking about this tricky toy I saw in the store. A clown that somersaults on a bar then does chin-ups just cause you yank lightly at his leg. Cost $35. I could see me askin my mother for a $35 birthday clown. "You wanna who that costs what?" she'd say, cocking her head to the side to get a better view of the hole in my head. Thirty-five dollars could buy new bunk beds for Junior and Gretchen's boy. Thirty-five dollars and the whole household could go visit Granddaddy Nelson in the country. Thirty-five dollars would pay for the rent and the piano bill too. Who are these people that spend that much for performing clowns and $1000 for toy sailboats? What kinda work they do and how they live and how come we ain't in on it? Where we are is who we are. Miss Moore always pointin out. But it don't necessarily have to be that way, she always adds then waits for somebody to say that poor people have to wake up and demand their share of the pie and don't none of us know what kind of pie she talking about in the first damn place. But she ain't so smart cause I still got her four dollars from the taxi and she sure ain't gettin it. Messin up my day with this shit. Sugar nudges me in my pocket and winks.

Miss Moore lines us up in front of the mailbox where we started from, seem like years    45
ago, and I got a headache for thinkin so hard. And we lean all over each other so we can hold up under the draggy-ass lecture she always finishes us off with at the end before we thank her for borin us to tears. But she just looks at us like she readin tea leaves. Finally she say, "Well, what did you think of F.A.O. Schwarz?"

Rosie Giraffe mumbles, "White folks crazy."

"I'd like to go there again when I get my birthday money," says Mercedes, and we shove her out the pack so she has to lean on the mailbox by herself.

"I'd like a shower. Tiring day," say Flyboy.

Then Sugar surprises me by sayin, "You know, Miss Moore, I don't think all of us here put together eat in a year what that sailboat costs." And Miss Moore lights up like somebody goosed her. "And?" she say, urging Sugar on. Only I'm standin on her foot so she don't continue.

"Imagine for a minute what kind of society it is in which some people can spend on a toy    50
what it would cost to feed a family of six or seven. What do you think?"

"I think," say Sugar pushing me off her feet like she never done before, cause I whip her ass in a minute, "that this is not much of a democracy if you ask me. Equal chance to pursue happiness means an equal crack at the dough, don't it?" Miss Moore is besides herself and I am disgusted with Sugar's treachery. So I stand on her foot one more time to see if she'll shove me. She shuts up, and Miss Moore looks at me, sorrowfully I'm thinkin. And somethin weird is goin on, I can feel it in my chest.

"Anybody else learn anything today?" lookin dead at me. I walk away and Sugar has to run to catch up and don't even seem to notice when I shrug her arm off my shoulder.

"Well, we got four dollars anyway," she says.

"Uh hunh."

"We could go to Hascombs and get half a chocolate layer and then go to the Sunset and    55
still have plenty money for potato chips and ice cream sodas."

"Uh hunh."

"Race you to Hascombs," she say.

We start down the block and she gets ahead which is O.K. by me cause I'm going to the West End and then over to the Drive to think this day through. She can run if she want to and even run faster. But ain't nobody gonna beat me at nuthin.

## Questions

1. Who is Miss Moore? Why does she take an interest in the neighborhood children? Where does she take them? How does she attempt to teach them?

2. Describe Sylvia, the narrator, as a character. Why does she keep $4 of the five-dollar bill given her by Miss Moore? What does she mean by "ain't nobody gonna beat me at nuthin" in the story's final paragraph?

3. Describe the level of language of the narrator. Is she writing the story or speaking it? How do you know?

4. Consider paragraphs 44–50. What ideas about equality and inequality are brought out in the story? Do you think the children will remember the "lesson" or that they will forget it? Why?

## D. H. LAWRENCE (1885–1930)

Lawrence was born in an English mining community, but he received a sufficient education to enable him to become a teacher and writer. He fictionalized the early years of his life in the novel *Sons and Lovers* (1913). His most controversial work, *Lady Chatterley's Lover,* was printed privately in Italy in 1928 but was not published in an uncut version in the United States until the 1960s. He shocked his contemporaries with his emphasis on the importance of sexuality, an idea that is central to "The Horse Dealer's Daughter." He was afflicted with tuberculosis and lived in a number of warm, sunny places, including Italy, New Zealand, and New Mexico, in an attempt to restore his health. Nevertheless, his illness claimed him in 1930, when he was only forty-five years old.

## The Horse Dealer's Daughter (1922)

"Well, Mabel, and what are you going to do with yourself?" asked Joe, with foolish flippancy. He felt quite safe himself. Without listening for an answer, he turned aside, worked a grain of tobacco to the tip of his tongue, and spat it out. He did not care about anything, since he felt safe himself.

The three brothers and the sister sat round the desolate breakfast table, attempting some sort of desultory consultation. The morning's post had given the final tap to the family fortunes, and all was over. The dreary dining-room itself, with its heavy mahogany furniture, looked as it were waiting to be done away with.

But the consultation amounted to nothing. There was a strange air of ineffectuality about the three men, as they sprawled at table, smoking and reflecting vaguely on their own condition. The girl was alone, a rather short, sullen-looking young woman of twenty-seven. She did not share the same life as her brothers. She would have been good-looking, save for the impassive fixity of her face, "bulldog," as her brothers called it.

There was a confused tramping of horses' feet outside. The three men all sprawled round in their chairs to watch. Beyond the dark holly-bushes that separated the strip of lawn from the high-road, they could see a cavalcade of shire horses swinging out of their own yard, being taken for exercise. This was the last time. These were the last horses that would go through their hands. The young men watched with critical, callous look. They were all frightened at the collapse of their lives, and the sense of disaster in which they were involved left them no inner freedom.

5      Yet they were three fine, well-set fellows enough. Joe, the eldest, was a man of thirty-three, broad and handsome in a hot, flushed way. His face was red, he twisted his black

moustache over a thick finger, his eyes were shallow and restless. He had a sensual way of uncovering his teeth when he laughed, and his bearing was stupid. Now he watched the horses with a glazed look of helplessness in his eyes, a certain stupor of downfall.

The great draught-horses swung past. They were tied head to tail, four of them, and they heaved along to where a lane branched off from the highroad, planting their great hoofs floutingly in the fine black mud, swinging their great rounded haunches sumptuously, and trotting a few sudden steps as they were led into the lane, round the corner. Every movement showed a massive, slumbrous strength, and a stupidity which held them in subjection. The groom at the head looked back, jerking the leading rope. And the cavalcade moved out of sight up the lane, the tail of the last horse, bobbed up tight and stiff, held out taut from the swinging great haunches as they rocked behind the hedges in a motionlike sleep.

Joe watched with glazed hopeless eyes. The horses were almost like his own body to him. He felt he was done for now. Luckily, he was engaged to a woman as old as himself, and therefore her father, who was steward of a neighbouring estate, would provide him with a job. He would marry and go into harness. His life was over, he would be a subject animal now.

He turned uneasily aside, the retreating steps of the horses echoing in his ears. Then, with foolish restlessness, he reached for the scraps of bacon-rind from the plates, and making a faint whistling sound, flung them to the terrier that lay against the fender. He watched the dog swallow them, and waited till the creature looked into his eyes. Then a faint grin came on his face, and in a high, foolish voice he said:

"You won't get much more bacon, shall you, you little b—?"

The dog faintly and dismally wagged its tail, then lowered its haunches, circled round, and lay down again.   10

There was another helpless silence at the table. Joe sprawled uneasily in his seat, not willing to go till the family conclave was dissolved. Fred Henry, the second brother, was erect, clean-limbed, alert. He had watched the passing of the horses with more *sang-froid*.° If he was an animal, like Joe, he was an animal which controls, not one which is controlled. He was master of any horse, and he carried himself with a well-tempered air of mastery. But he was not master of the situations of life. He pushed his coarse brown moustache upwards, off his lip, and glanced irritably at his sister, who sat impassive and inscrutable.

"You'll go and stop with Lucy for a bit, shan't you?" he asked. The girl did not answer.

"I don't see what else you can do," persisted Fred Henry.

"Go as a skivvy,"° Joe interpolated laconically.

The girl did not move a muscle.   15

"If I was her, I should go in for training for a nurse," said Malcolm, the youngest of them all. He was the baby of the family, a young man of twenty-two, with a fresh, jaunty *museau*.°

But Mabel did not take any notice of him. They had talked at her and round her for so many years, that she hardly heard them at all.

The marble clock on the mantel-piece softly chimed the half-hour, the dog rose uneasily from the hearthrug and looked at the party at the breakfast table. But still they sat on in ineffectual conclave.

"Oh, all right," said Joe suddenly, *à propos* of nothing. "I'll get a move on."

He pushed back his chair, straddled his knees with a downward jerk, to get them free, in   20 horsey fashion, and went to the fire. Still he did not go out of the room; he was curious to

---

°*sang-froid*: unconcern (literally, cold blood).

°*skivvy*: British slang for housemaid.

°*museau*: French for nose, snout (muzzle).

know what the others would do or say. He began to charge his pipe, looking down at the dog and saying, in a high, affected voice:

"Going wi' me? Going wi' me are ter? Tha'rt goin' further than tha counts on just now, dost hear?"

The dog faintly wagged its tail, the man stuck out his jaw and covered his pipe with his hands, and puffed intently, losing himself in the tobacco, looking down all the while at the dog, with an absent brown eye. The dog looked up at him in mournful distrust. Joe stood with his knees stuck out, in real horsey fashion.

"Have you had a letter from Lucy?" Fred Henry asked of his sister.

"Last week," came the neutral reply.

25     "And what does she say?"

There was no answer.

"Does she *ask* you to go and stop there?" persisted Fred Henry.

"She says I can if I like."

"Well, then, you'd better. Tell her you'll come on Monday."

30     This was received in silence.

"That's what you'll do then, is it?" said Fred Henry, in some exasperation.

But she made no answer. There was a silence of futility and irritation in the room. Malcolm grinned fatuously.

"You'll have to make up your mind between now and next Wednesday," said Joe loudly, "or else find yourself lodgings on the kerbstone."

The face of the young woman darkened, but she sat on immutable.

35     "Here's Jack Fergusson!" exclaimed Malcolm, who was looking aimlessly out of the window.

"Where?" exclaimed Joe, loudly.

"Just gone past."

"Coming in?"

Malcolm craned his neck to see the gate.

40     "Yes," he said.

There was a silence. Mabel sat on like one condemned, at the head of the table. Then a whistle was heard from the kitchen. The dog got up and barked sharply. Joe opened the door and shouted:

"Come on."

After a moment, a young man entered. He was muffled up in overcoat and a purple woolen scarf, and his tweed cap, which he did not remove, was pulled down on his head. He was of medium height, his face was rather long and pale, his eyes looked tired.

"Hello, Jack! Well, Jack!" exclaimed Malcolm and Joe. Fred Henry merely said "Jack!"

45     "What's doing?" asked the newcomer, evidently addressing Fred Henry.

"Same. We've got to be out by Wednesday—Got a cold?"

"I have—got it bad, too."

"Why don't you stop in?"

"*Me* stop in? When I can't stand on my legs, perhaps I shall have a chance." The young man spoke huskily. He had a slight Scotch accent.

50     "It's a knock-out, isn't it," said Joe boisterously, "if a doctor goes round croaking with a cold. Looks bad for the patients, doesn't it?"

The young doctor looked at him slowly.

"Anything the matter with *you*, then?" he asked, sarcastically.

"Not as I know of. Damn your eyes, I hope not. Why?"

"I thought you were very concerned about the patients, wondered if you might be one yourself."

"Damn it, no, I've never been patient to no flaming doctor, and hope I never shall be,"    55
returned Joe.

At this point Mabel rose from the table, and they all seemed to become aware of her
existence. She began putting the dishes together. The young doctor looked at her, but did not
address her. He had not greeted her. She went out of the room with the tray, her face impassive
and unchanged.

"When are you off then, all of you?" asked the doctor.

"I'm catching the eleven-forty," replied Malcolm. "Are you goin' down wi' th' trap,°
Joe?"

"Yes, I've told you I'm going down wi' th' trap, haven't I?"

"We'd better be getting her in then.—So long, Jack, if I don't see you before I go," said    60
Malcolm, shaking hands.

He went out, followed by Joe, who seemed to have his tail between his legs.

"Well, this is the devil's own," exclaimed the doctor, when he was left alone with Fred
Henry. "Going before Wednesday, are you?"

"That's the orders," replied the other.

"Where, to Northampton?"

"That's it."

"The devil!" exclaimed Fergusson, with quiet chagrin.    65

And there was silence between the two.

"All settled up, are you?" asked Fergusson.

"About."

There was another pause.

"Well, I shall miss yer, Freddy boy," said the young doctor.    70

"And I shall miss thee, Jack," returned the other.

"Miss you like hell," mused the doctor.

Fred Henry turned aside. There was nothing to say. Mabel came in again, to finish clearing the table.

"What are *you* going to do then, Miss Pervin?" asked Fergusson. "Going to your sister's,    75
are you?"

Mabel looked at him with her steady, dangerous eyes, that always made him uncomfortable, unsettling his superficial ease.

"No," she said.

"Well, what in the name of fortune *are* you going to do? Say what you *mean* to do," cried
Fred Henry, with futile intensity.

But she only averted her head, and continued her work. She folded the white table-cloth,
and put on the chenille cloth.

"The sulkiest bitch that ever trod!" muttered her brother.

But she finished her task with perfectly impassive face, the young doctor watching her    80
interestedly all the while. Then she went out.

Fred Henry stared after her, clenching his lips, his blue eyes fixing in sharp antagonism, as
he made a grimace of sour exasperation.

"You could bray her into bits, and that's all you'd get out of her," he said, in a small,
narrowed tone.

The doctor smiled faintly.

"What's she *going* to do then?" he asked.

"Strike me if *I* know!" returned the other.    85

There was a pause. Then the doctor stirred.

---

°*trap*: small wagon.

"I'll be seeing you to-night, shall I?" he said to his friend.

"Ay—where's it to be? Are we going over to Jessdale?"

90   "I don't know. I've got such a cold on me. I'll come round to the Moon and Stars, anyway."

"Let Lizzie and May miss their night for once, eh?"

"That's it—if I feel as I do now."

"All's one—"

The two young men went through the passage and down to the back door together. The house was large, but it was servantless now, and desolate. At the back was a small bricked house-yard, and beyond that a big square, gravelled fine and red, and having stables on two sides. Sloping, dank, winter-dark fields stretched away on the open sides.

95   But the stables were empty. Joseph Pervin, the father of the family, had been a man of no education, who had become a fairly large horse dealer. The stables had been full of horses, there was a great turmoil and come-and-go of horses and of dealers and grooms. Then the kitchen was full of servants. But of late things had declined. The old man had married a second time, to retrieve his fortunes. Now he was dead and everything was gone to the dogs, there was nothing but debt and threatening.

For months, Mabel had been servantless in the big house, keeping the home together in penury for her ineffectual brothers. She had kept house for ten years. But previously, it was with unstinted means. Then, however brutal and coarse everything was, the sense of money had kept her proud, confident. The men might be foul-mouthed, the women in the kitchen might have bad reputations, her brothers might have illegitimate children. But so long as there was money, the girl felt herself established, and brutally proud, reserved.

No company came to the house, save dealers and coarse men. Mabel had no associates of her own sex, after her sister went away. But she did not mind. She went regularly to church, she attended to her father. And she lived in the memory of her mother, who had died when she was fourteen, and whom she had loved. She had loved her father, too, in a different way, depending upon him, and feeling secure in him, until at the age of fifty-four he married again. And then she had set hard against him. Now he had died and left them all hopelessly in debt.

She had suffered badly during the period of poverty. Nothing, however, could shake the curious sullen, animal pride that dominated each member of the family. Now, for Mabel, the end had come. Still she would not cast about her. She would follow her own way just the same. She would always hold the keys of her own situation. Mindless and persistent, she endured from day to day. Why should she think? Why should she answer anybody? It was enough that this was the end, and there was no way out. She need not pass any more darkly along the main street of the small town, avoiding every eye. She need not demean herself any more, going into the shops and buying the cheapest food. This was at an end. She thought of nobody, not even of herself. Mindless and persistent, she seemed in a sort of ecstasy to be coming nearer to her fulfilment, her own glorification, approaching her dead mother, who was glorified.°

In the afternoon she took a little bag, with shears and sponge and a small scrubbing brush, and went out. It was a grey, wintry day, with saddened, dark-green fields and an atmosphere blackened by the smoke of foundries not far off. She went quickly, darkly along the causeway, heeding nobody, through the town to the churchyard.

100   There she always felt secure, as if no one could see her, although as a matter of fact she was exposed to the stare of everyone who passed along under the churchyard wall. Nevertheless, once under the shadow of the great looming church, among the graves, she felt immune from the world, reserved within the thick churchyard wall as in another country.

---

°*who was glorified*: See Romans 8:17, 30.

Carefully she clipped the grass from the grave, and arranged the pinky-white, small chrysanthemums in the tin cross. When this was done, she took an empty jar from a neighbouring grave, brought water, and carefully, most scrupulously sponged the marble headstone and the coping-stone.

It gave her sincere satisfaction to do this. She felt in immediate contact with the world of her mother. She took minute pains, went through the park in a state bordering on pure happiness, as if in performing this task she came into a subtle, intimate connection with her mother. For the life she followed here in the world was far less real than the world of death she inherited from her mother.

The doctor's house was just by the church. Fergusson, being a mere hired assistant, was slave to the countryside. As he hurried now to attend to the outpatients in the surgery, glancing across the graveyard with his quick eye, he saw the girl at her task at the grave. She seemed so intent and remote, it was like looking into another world. Some mystical element was touched in him. He slowed down as he walked, watching her as if spell-bound.

She lifted her eyes, feeling him looking. Their eyes met. And each looked again at once, each feeling, in some way, found out by the other. He lifted his cap and passed on down the road. There remained distinct in his consciousness, like a vision, the memory of her face, lifted from the tombstone in the churchyard, and looking at him with slow, large, portentous eyes. It *was* portentous, her face. It seemed to mesmerise him. There was a heavy power in her eyes which laid hold of his whole being, as if he had drunk some powerful drug. He had been feeling weak and done before. Now the life came back into him, he felt delivered from his own fretted, daily self.

He finished his duties at the surgery as quickly as might be, hastily filling up the bottles of the waiting people with cheap drugs. Then, in perpetual haste, he set off again to visit several cases in another part of his round, before teatime. At all times he preferred to walk, if he could, but particularly when he was not well. He fancied the motion restored him.

The afternoon was falling. It was grey, deadened, and wintry, with a slow, moist, heavy coldness sinking in and deadening all the faculties. But why should he think or notice? He hastily climbed the hill and turned across the dark-green fields, following the black cinder-track. In the distance, across a shallow dip in the country, the small town was clustered like smouldering ash, a tower, a spire, a heap of low, raw, extinct houses. And on the nearest fringe of the town, sloping into the dip, was Oldmeadow, the Pervins' house. He could see the stables and the outbuildings distinctly, as they lay towards him on the slope. Well, he would not go there many more times! Another resource would be lost to him, another place gone: the only company he cared for in the alien, ugly little town he was losing. Nothing but work, drudgery, constant hastening from dwelling to dwelling among the colliers and the iron-workers. It wore him out, but at the same time he had a craving for it. It was a stimulant to him to be in the homes of the working people, moving as it were through the innermost body of their life. His nerves were excited and gratified. He could come so near, into the very lives of the rough, inarticulate, powerfully emotional men and women. He grumbled, he said he hated the hellish hole. But as a matter of fact it excited him, the contact with the rough, strongly-feeling people was a stimulant applied direct to his nerves.

Below Oldmeadow, in the green, shallow, soddened hollow of fields, lay a square, deep pond. Roving across the landscape, the doctor's quick eye detected a figure in black passing through the gate of the field, down towards the pond. He looked again. It would be Mabel Pervin. His mind suddenly became alive and attentive.

Why was she going down there? He pulled up on the path on the slope above, and stood staring. He could just make sure of the small black figure moving in the hollow of the failing day. He seemed to see her in the midst of such obscurity, that he was like a clairvoyant, seeing rather with the mind's eye than with ordinary sight. Yet he could see her positively enough, whilst he kept his eye attentive. He felt, if he looked away from her, in the thick, ugly falling dusk, he would lose her altogether.

He followed her minutely as she moved, direct and intent, like something transmitted rather than stirring in voluntary activity, straight down the field towards the pond. There she stood on the bank for a moment. She never raised her head. Then she waded slowly into the water.

110 He stood motionless as the small black figure walked slowly and deliberately towards the centre of the pond, very slowly, gradually moving deeper into the motionless water, and still moving forward as the water got up to her breast. Then he could see her no more in the dusk of the dead afternoon.

"There!" he exclaimed. "Would you believe it?"

And he hastened straight down, running over the wet, soddened fields, pushing through the hedges, down into the depression of callous wintry obscurity. It took him several minutes to come to the pond. He stood on the bank, breathing heavily. He could see nothing. His eyes seemed to penetrate the dead water. Yes, perhaps that was the dark shadow of her black clothing beneath the surface of the water.

He slowly ventured into the pond. The bottom was deep, soft clay, he sank in, and the water clasped dead cold round his legs. As he stirred he could smell the cold, rotten clay that fouled up into the water. It was objectionable in his lungs. Still, repelled and yet not heeding, he moved deeper into the pond. The cold water rose over his thighs, over his loins, upon his abdomen. The lower part of his body was all sunk in the hideous cold element. And the bottom was so deeply soft and uncertain, he was afraid of pitching with his mouth underneath. He could not swim, and was afraid.

He crouched a little, spreading his hands under the water and moving them round, trying to feel for her. The dead cold pond swayed upon his chest. He moved again, a little deeper, and again, with his hands underneath, he felt all around under the water. And he touched her clothing. But it evaded his fingers. He made a desperate effort to grasp it.

115 And so doing he lost his balance and went under, horribly, suffocating in the foul earthy water, struggling madly for a few moments. At last, after what seemed an eternity, he got his footing, rose again into the air and looked around. He gasped, and knew he was in the world. Then he looked at the water. She had risen near him. He grasped her clothing, and drawing her nearer, turned to take his way to land again.

He went very slowly, carefully, absorbed in the slow progress. He rose higher, climbing out of the pond. The water was not only about his legs; he was thankful, full of relief to be out of the clutches of the pond. He lifted her and staggered on to the bank, out of the horror of wet, grey clay.

He laid her down on the bank. She was quite unconscious and running with water. He made the water come from her mouth, he worked to restore her. He did not have to work very long before he could feel the breathing begin again in her; she was breathing naturally. He worked a little longer. He could feel her live beneath his hands; she was coming back. He wiped her face, wrapped her in his overcoat, looked round into the dim, dark-grey world, then lifted her and staggered down the bank and across the fields.

It seemed an unthinkably long way, and his burden so heavy he felt he would never get to the house. But at last he was in the stable-yard, and then in the house-yard. He opened the door and went into the house. In the kitchen he laid her down on the hearthrug, and called. The house was empty. But the fire was burning in the grate.

Then again he kneeled to attend to her. She was breathing regularly, her eyes were wide open as if conscious, but there seemed something missing in her look. She was conscious in herself, but unconscious of her surroundings.

120 He ran upstairs, took blankets from a bed, and put them before the fire to warm. Then he removed her saturated, earthy-smelling clothing, rubbed her dry with a towel, and wrapped

her naked in the blankets. Then he went into the dining-room, to look for spirits. There was a little whiskey. He drank a gulp himself, and put some into her mouth.

The effect was instantaneous. She looked full into his face, as if she had been seeing him for some time, and yet had only just become conscious of him.

"Dr. Fergusson?" she said.

"What?" he answered.

He was divesting himself of his coat, intending to find some dry clothing upstairs. He could not bear the smell of the dead, clayey water, and he was mortally afraid for his own health.

"What did I do?" she asked. 125

"Walked into the pond," he replied. He had begun to shudder like one sick, and could hardly attend to her. Her eyes remained full on him, he seemed to be going dark in his mind, looking back at her helplessly. The shuddering became quieter in him, his life came back in him, dark and unknowing, but strong again.

"Was I out of my mind?" she asked, while her eyes were fixed on him all the time.

"Maybe, for the moment," he replied. He felt quiet, because his strength had come back. The strange fretful strain had left him.

"Am I out of my mind now?" she asked.

"Are you?" he reflected a moment. "No," he answered truthfully, "I don't see that you 130 are." He turned his face aside. He was afraid, now, because he felt dazed, and felt dimly that her power was stronger than his, in this issue. And she continued to look at him fixedly all the time. "Can you tell me where I shall find some dry things to put on?" he asked.

"Did you dive into the pond for me?" she asked.

"No," he answered. "I walked in. But I went in overhead as well."

There was silence for a moment. He hesitated. He very much wanted to go upstairs to get into dry clothing. But there was another desire in him. And she seemed to hold him. His will seemed to have gone to sleep, and left him, standing there slack before her. But he felt warm inside himself. He did not shudder at all, though his clothes were sodden on him.

"Why did you?" she asked.

"Because I didn't want you to do such a foolish thing," he said. 135

"It wasn't foolish," she said, still gazing at him as she lay on the floor, with a sofa cushion under her head. "It was the right thing to do. *I* knew best, then."

"I'll go and shift these wet things," he said. But still he had not the power to move out of her presence, until she sent him. It was as if she had the life of his body in her hands, and he could not extricate himself. Or perhaps he did not want to.

Suddenly she sat up. Then she became aware of her own immediate condition. She felt the blankets about her, she knew her own limbs. For a moment it seemed as if her reason were going. She looked round, with wild eye, as if seeking something. He stood still with fear. She saw her clothing lying scattered.

"Who undressed me?" she asked, her eyes resting full and inevitable on his face.

"I did," he replied, "to bring you round." 140

For some moments she sat and gazed at him awfully, her lips parted.

"Do you love me then?" she asked.

He only stood and stared at her, fascinated. His soul seemed to melt.

She shuffled forward on her knees, and put her arms round him, round his legs, as he stood there, pressing her breasts against his knees and thighs, clutching him with strange, convulsive certainty, pressing his thighs against her, drawing him to her face, her throat, as she looked up at him with flaring, humble eyes of transfiguration, triumphant in first possession.

"You love me," she murmured, in strange transport, yearning and triumphant and confi- 145 dent. "You love me. I know you love me, I know."

And she was passionately kissing his knees, through the wet clothing, passionately and indiscriminately kissing his knees, his legs, as if unaware of everything.

He looked down at the tangled wet hair, the wild, bare, animal shoulders. He was amazed, bewildered, and afraid. He had never thought of loving her. He had never wanted to love her. When he rescued her and restored her, he was a doctor, and she was a patient. He had had no single personal thought of her. Nay, this introduction of the personal element was very distasteful to him, a violation of his professional honour. It was horrible to have her there embracing his knees. It was horrible. He revolted from it, violently. And yet—and yet—he had not the power to break away.

She looked at him again, with the same supplication of powerful love, and that same transcendent, frightening light of triumph. In view of the delicate flame which seemed to come from her face like a light, he was powerless. And yet he had never intended to love her. He had never intended. And something stubborn in him could not give way.

"You love me," she repeated, in a murmur of deep, rhapsodic assurance. "You love me."

150    Her hands were drawing him, drawing him down to her. He was afraid, even a little horrified. For he had, really, no intention of loving her. Yet her hands were drawing him towards her. He put out his hand quickly to steady himself, and grasped her bare shoulder. A flame seemed to burn the hand that grasped her soft shoulder. He had no intention of loving her: his whole will was against his yielding. It was horrible—And yet wonderful was the touch of her shoulder, beautiful the shining of her face. Was she perhaps mad? He had a horror of yielding to her. Yet something in him ached also.

He had been staring away at the door, away from her. But his hand remained on her shoulder. She had gone suddenly very still. He looked down at her. Her eyes were now wide with fear, with doubt, the light was dying from her face, a shadow of terrible greyness was returning. He could not bear the touch of her eyes' question upon him, and the look of death behind the question.

With an inward groan he gave way, and let his heart yield towards her. A sudden gentle smile came on his face. And her eyes, which never left his face, slowly, slowly filled with tears. He watched the strange water rise in her eyes, like some slow fountain coming up. And his heart seemed to burn and melt away in his breast.

He could not bear to look at her any more. He dropped on his knees and caught her head with his arms and pressed her face against his throat. She was very still. His heart, which seemed to have broken, was burning with a kind of agony in his breast. And he felt her slow, hot tears wetting his throat. But he could not move.

He felt the hot tears wet his neck and the hollows of his neck, and he remained motionless, suspended through one of man's eternities. Only now it had become indispensable to him to have her face pressed close to him; he could never let her go again. He could never let her head go away from the close clutch of his arm. He wanted to remain like that for ever, with his heart hurting him in a pain that was also life to him. Without knowing, he was looking down on her damp, soft brown hair.

155    Then, as it were suddenly, he smelt the horrid stagnant smell of the water. And at the same moment she drew away from him and looked at him. Her eyes were wistful and unfathomable. He was afraid of them, and he fell to kissing her, not knowing what he was doing. He wanted her eyes not to have that terrible, wistful, unfathomable look.

When she turned her face to him again, a faint delicate flush was glowing, and there was again dawning that terrible shining of joy in her eyes, which really terrified him, and yet which he now wanted to see, because he feared the look of doubt still more.

"You love me?" she said, rather faltering.

"Yes." The word cost him a painful effort. Not because it wasn't true. But because it was too newly true, the *saying* seemed to tear open again his newly-torn heart. And he hardly wanted it to be true, even now.

She lifted her face to him, and he bent forward and kissed her on the mouth gently, with the one kiss that is an eternal pledge. And as he kissed her his heart strained again in his breast. He never intended to love her. But now it was over. He had crossed over the gulf to her, and all that he had left behind had shrivelled and become void.

After the kiss, her eyes again slowly filled with tears. She sat still, away from him, with 160 her face drooped aside, and her hands folded in her lap. The tears fell very slowly. There was complete silence. He too sat there motionless and silent on the hearthrug. The strange pain of his heart that was broken seemed to consume him. That he should love her? That this was love! That he should be ripped open in this way!—Him, a doctor!—How they would all jeer if they knew!—It was agony to him to think they might know.

In the curious naked pain of the thought he looked again to her. She was sitting there drooped into a muse. He saw a tear fall, and his heart flared hot. He saw for the first time that one of her shoulders was quite uncovered, one arm bare, he could see one of her small breasts; dimly, because it had become almost dark in the room.

"Why are you crying?" he asked, in an altered voice.

She looked up at him, and behind her tears the consciousness of her situation for the first time brought a dark look of shame to her eyes.

"I'm not crying, really," she said, watching him half frightened.

He reached his hand, and softly closed it on her bare arm.                                        165

"I love you! I love you!" he said in a soft, low vibrating voice, unlike himself.

She shrank, and dropped her head. The soft, penetrating grip of his hand on her arm distressed her. She looked up at him.

"I want to go," she said. "I want to go and get you some dry things."

"Why?" he said. "I'm all right."

"But I want to go," she said. "And I want you to change your things."                            170

He released her arm, and she wrapped herself in the blanket, looking at him rather frightened. And still she did not rise.

"Kiss me," she said wistfully.

He kissed her, but briefly, half in anger.

Then, after a second, she rose nervously, all mixed up in the blanket. He watched her in her confusion, as she tried to extricate herself and wrap herself up so that she could walk. He watched her relentlessly, as she knew.

And as she went, the blanket trailing, and as he saw a glimpse of her feet and her white 175 leg, he tried to remember her as she was when he had wrapped her in the blanket. But then he didn't want to remember, because she had been nothing to him then, and his nature revolted from remembering her as she was when she was nothing to him.

A tumbling muffled noise from within the dark house startled him. Then he heard her voice:—"There are clothes." He rose and went to the foot of the stairs, and gathered up the garments she had thrown down. Then he came back to the fire, to rub himself down and dress. He grinned at his own appearance, when he had finished.

The fire was sinking, so he put on coal. The house was now quite dark, save for the light of a street-lamp that shone in faintly from beyond the holly trees. He lit the gas with matches he found on the mantel-piece. Then he emptied the pockets of his own clothes, and threw all his wet things in a heap into the scullery. After which he gathered up her sodden clothes, gently, and put them in a separate heap on the copper-top in the scullery.

It was six o'clock on the clock. His own watch had stopped. He ought to be back to the surgery. He waited, and still she did not come down. So he went to the foot of the stairs and called:

"I shall have to go."

Almost immediately he heard her coming down. She had on her best dress of black voile, 180 and her hair was tidy, but still damp. She looked at him—and in spite of herself, smiled.

"I don't like you in those clothes," she said.

"Do I look a sight?" he answered.

They were shy of one another.

"I'll make you some tea," she said.

185    "No, I must go."

"Must you?" And she looked at him again with the wide, strained, doubtful eyes. And again, from the pain of his breast, he knew how he loved her. He went and bent to kiss her, gently, passionately, with his heart's painful kiss.

"And my hair smells so horrible," she murmured in distraction. "And I'm so awful, I'm so awful! Oh, no, I'm too awful." And she broke into bitter, heartbroken sobbing. "You can't want to love me, I'm horrible."

"Don't be silly, don't be silly," he said, trying to comfort her, kissing her, holding her in his arms. "I want you, I want to marry you, we're going to be married, quickly, quickly—to-morrow if I can."

But she only sobbed terribly, and cried.

190    "I feel awful. I feel awful. I feel I'm horrible to you."

"No, I want you, I want you," was all he answered blindly, with that terrible intonation which frightened her almost more than her horror lest he should *not* want her.

## Questions

1. What idea is Lawrence illustrating by the breakup of the Pervin household?
2. What does the comparison of Joe Pervin and the draft horses mean with regard specifically to Joe, and generally to people without love?
3. What kind of person is Mabel? How do her brothers treat her? How does she feel about her brothers? What dilemma does she face as the story begins?
4. What effect does Mabel have on Fergusson as he watches her in her home, in the church-yard, and at the pond? What does this effect contribute to Lawrence's ideas about love?
5. What do Mabel and Fergusson realize as he revives and warms her? How do their responses signify their growth as characters?
6. Why does the narrator tell us at the story's end that Fergusson "had no intention of loving" Mabel? What idea does this repeated assertion convey?
7. In this story, there is an extensive exploration of the ambiguous feelings of both Fergusson and Mabel after they realize their love. Why does Lawrence explore these feelings so extensively?

## AMÉRICO PAREDES (1915–1999)

Paredes was a Mexican-American storyteller, folklorist, essayist, and poet, closely identified with Mexican-Americans living in Texas, his native state. He received his Ph.D. at the University of Texas in 1956 and also taught there for many years. His dissertation was published in 1958 as *With His Pistol in His Hand*, a study of an early-twentieth-century popular ballad about a fugitive, Gregorio Cortés. Deeply interested in the culture of the "lower border," he was one of the leaders of the Chicano movement in cultural-literary studies. He edited the *Journal of American Folklore* and also edited *Folklore and Culture on the Texas-Mexican Border* (1993). Among his honors was a Guggenheim Fellowship in 1962 and the Aztec Eagle medal from the Mexican government in 1991.

"The Hammon and the Beans" was first published in the *Texas Observer* in 1963 and was republished in *The Hammon and the Beans and Other Stories* in 1994.

# The Hammon and the Beans (1963)

Once we lived in one of my grandfather's houses near Fort Jones.° It was just a block from the parade grounds, a big frame house painted a dirty yellow. My mother hated it, especially because of the pigeons that cooed all day about the eaves. They had fleas, she said. But it was a quiet neighborhood at least, too far from the center of town for automobiles and too near for musical, night-roaming drunks.

At this time Jonesville-on-the-Grande was not the thriving little city that it is today. We told off our days by the routine on the post. At six sharp the flag was raised on the parade grounds to the cackling of the bugles, and a field piece thundered out a salute. The sound of the shot bounced away through the morning mist until its echoes worked their way into every corner of town. Jonesville-on-the-Grande woke to the cannon's roar, as if to battle, and the day began.

At eight the whistle from the post laundry sent us children off to school. The whole town stopped for lunch with the noon whistle, and after lunch everybody went back to work when the post laundry said that it was one o'clock, except for those who could afford to be old-fashioned and took the siesta. The post was the town's clock, you might have said, or like some insistent elder person who was always there to tell you it was time.

At six the flag came down, and we went to watch through the high wire fence that divided the post from the town. Sometimes we joined in the ceremony, standing at salute until the sound of the cannon made us jump. That must have been when we had just studied about George Washington in school, or recited "The Song of Marion's Men"° about Marion the Fox and the British cavalry that chased him up and down the broad Santee. But at other times we stuck out our tongues and jeered at the soldiers. Perhaps the night before we had hung at the edges of a group of old men and listened to tales about Aniceto Pizaña and the "border troubles,"° as the local paper still called them when it referred to them gingerly in passing.

It was because of the border troubles, ten years or so before, that the soldiers had come back    5
to old Fort Jones. But we did not hate them for that; we admired them even, at least sometimes. But when we were thinking about the border troubles instead of Marion the Fox we hooted them and the flag they were lowering, which for the moment was theirs alone, just as we would have jeered an opposing ball team, in a friendly sort of way. On these occasions even Chonita would join in the mockery, though she usually ran home at the stroke of six. But whether we taunted or saluted, the distant men in khaki uniforms went about their motions without noticing us at all.

The last word from the post came in the night when a distant bugle blew. At nine it was all right because all the lights were on. But sometimes I heard it at eleven when everything was dark and still, and it made me feel that I was all alone in the world. I would even doubt that I was me, and that put me in such a fright that I felt like yelling out just to make sure I was really there. But next morning the sun shone and life began all over again. With its whistles and cannon shots and bugles blowing. And so we lived, we and the post, side by side with the wire fence in between.

---

°*Fort Jones*: The setting of Fort Jones and Jonesville-on-the-Grande in Texas is fictional. The story takes place in the mid-1920s, one of the most turbulent periods of Mexican history and only a few years after the deaths of two of the greatest heroes of the Mexican revolution—Pancho Villa (1877–1923) and Emiliano Zapata (ca. 1879–1919).

° *"Song of Marion's Men"*: a poem by William Cullen Bryant (1794–1878) about Colonel Francis Marion (ca. 1732–1795), who was a leader of irregular guerrilla forces in South Carolina during the Revolutionary War. Because of his hit-and-run tactics, involving his hiding in the swamps near the "broad Santee" river in South Carolina, Marion was nicknamed the "Swamp Fox."

°*border troubles*: The most serious border incidents occurred in 1916, when Pancho Villa was responsible for deaths of Americans on both sides of the border. He made repeated raids into New Mexico and Texas.

The wandering soldiers whom the bugle called home at night did not wander in our neighborhood, and none of us ever went into Fort Jones. None except Chonita. Every evening when the flag came down she would leave off playing and go down towards what was known as the "lower" gate of the post, the one that opened not on Main Street but against the poorest part of town. She went into the grounds and to the mess halls and pressed her nose against the screens and watched the soldiers eat. They sat at long tables calling to each other through food-stuffed mouths.

"Hey bud, pass the coffee!"

"Give me the ham!"

10     "Yeah, give me the beans!"

After the soldiers were through the cooks came out and scolded Chonita, and then they gave her packages with things to eat.

Chonita's mother did our washing, in gratefulness—as my mother put it— for the use of a vacant lot of my grandfather's which was a couple of blocks down the street. On the lot was an old one-room shack which had been a shed long ago, and this Chonita's father had patched up with flattened-out pieces of tin. He was a laborer. Ever since the end of the border troubles there had been a development boom in the Valley, and Chonita's father was getting his share of the good times. Clearing brush and building irrigation ditches he sometimes pulled down as much as six dollars a week. He drank a good deal of it up, it was true. But corn was just a few cents a bushel in those days. He was the breadwinner, you might say, while Chonita furnished the luxuries.

Chonita was a poet too. I had just moved into the neighborhood when a boy came up to me and said, "Come on! Let's go hear Chonita make a speech."

She was already on top of the alley fence when we got there, a scrawny little girl of about nine, her bare dirty feet clinging to the fence almost like hands. A dozen other kids were there below her, waiting. Some were boys I knew at school; five or six were her younger brothers and sisters.

15     "Speech! Speech!" they all cried. "Let Chonita make a speech! Talk in English, Chonita!"

They were grinning and nudging each other except for her brothers and sisters, who looked up at her with proud serious faces. She gazed out beyond us all with a grand, distant air and then she spoke.

"Give me the hammon and the beans!" she yelled. "Give me the hammon and the beans!"

She leaped off the fence and everybody cheered and told her how good it was and how she could talk English better than the teachers at the grammar school.

I thought it was a pretty poor joke. Every evening almost, they would make her get up on the fence and yell, "Give me the hammon and the beans!" And everybody would cheer and make her think she was talking English. As for me, I would wait there until she got it over with so we could play at something else. I wondered how long it would be before they got tired of it all. I never did find out because just about that time I got the chills and fever, and when I got up and around Chonita wasn't there anymore.

20     In later years I thought of her a lot, especially during the thirties when I was growing up. Those years would have been just made for her. Many's the time I have seen her in my mind's eyes, in the picket lines demanding not bread, not cake, but the hammon and the beans. But it didn't work out that way.

One night Doctor Zapata came into our kitchen through the back door. He set his bag on the table and said to my father, who had opened the door for him, "Well, she is dead."

My father flinched. "What was it?" he asked.

The doctor had gone to the window and he stood with his back to us, looking out toward the light of Fort Jones. "Pneumonia, flu, malnutrition, worms, the evil eye," he said without turning around. "What the hell difference does it make?"

"I wish I had known how sick she was," my father said in a very mild tone. "Not that it's really my affair, but I wish I had."

The doctor snorted and shook his head.

My mother came in and I asked her who was dead. She told me. It made me feel strange but I did not cry. My mother put her arm around my shoulders. "She is in Heaven now," she said. "She is happy."

I shrugged her arm away and sat down in one of the kitchen chairs.

"They're like animals," the doctor was saying. He turned round suddenly and his eyes glistened in the light. "Do you know what that brute of a father was doing when I left? He was laughing! Drinking and laughing with his friends."

"There's no telling what the poor man feels," my mother said.

My father made a deprecatory gesture. "It wasn't his daughter anyway."

"No?" the doctor said. He sounded interested.

"This is the woman's second husband," my father explained. "First one died before the girl was born, shot and hanged from a mesquite limb. He was working too close to the tracks the day the Olmito train was derailed."

"You know what?" the doctor said. "In classical times they did things better. Take Troy, for instance. After they stormed the city they grabbed the babies by the heels and dashed them against the wall. That was more humane."

My father smiled. "You sound very radical. You sound just like your relative down there in Morelos."°

"No relative of mine," the doctor said. "I'm a conservative, the son of a conservative, and you know that I wouldn't be here except for that little detail."

"Habit," my father said. "Pure habit, pure tradition. You're a radical at heart."

"It depends on how you define radicalism," the doctor answered. "People tend to use words too loosely. A dentist could be called a radical, I suppose. He pulls up things by the roots."

My father chuckled.

"Any bandit in Mexico nowadays can give himself a political label," the doctor went on, "and that makes him respectable. He's a leader of the people."

"Take Villa, now—" my father began.

"Villa was a different type of man," the doctor broke in.

"I don't see any difference."

The doctor came over to the table and sat down. "Now look at it this way," he began, his finger in front of my father's face. My father threw back his head and laughed.

"You'd better go to bed and rest," my mother told me. "You're not completely well, you know."

So I went to bed, but I didn't go to sleep, not right away. I lay there for a long time while behind my darkened eyelids Emiliano Zapata's cavalry charged down to the broad Santee, where there were grave men with hoary hairs.° I was still awake at eleven when the cold voice of the bugle went gliding in and out of the dark like something that couldn't find its way back to wherever it had been. I thought of Chonita in Heaven, and I saw her in her torn and dirty dress, with a pair of bright wings attached, flying round and round like a butterfly shouting, "Give me the hammon and the beans!"

Then I cried. And whether it was the bugle, or whether it was Chonita or what, to this day I do not know. But cry I did, and I felt much better after that.

---

°*Morelos*: the home state of Zapata.
°*grave men with hoary hairs*: Cf. lines 49–52 of Bryant's "Song of Marion's Men":

Grave men there are by broad Santee,
    Grave men with hoary hairs;
Their hearts are all with Marion,
    For Marion are their prayers.

## Questions

1. How does Paredes establish the setting of the story? What is the significance of the fort? Of the "dirty yellow" paint? Of the vacant lot and the shack?

2. Is Chonita a round or flat character? To what extent does the author make her symbolic and representative?

3. What is the tone of the story (some possibilities: ironic, cynical, resigned, bitter, resentful)? What techniques does Paredes use to control the tone?

4. How does Doctor Zapata's attitude toward Chonita's death, and the words he uses to announce it, help to control the tone?

5. How does the tale of Chonita's brief life and her death fit into the political, social, and broadly human framework of the story?

6. Near the end of Bryant's "Song of Marion's Men" (lines 53–56) the following four lines appear:

> And lovely ladies greet our band [i.e., of soldiers]
> With kindliest welcoming,
> And smiles like those of summer,
> And tears like those of spring.

Contrast these lines with the narrator's vision of Chonita in heaven.

## WRITING ABOUT MAJOR IDEAS

Most likely you will write about a major idea or theme, but you may also get interested in one of your story's other ideas. As you begin brainstorming and developing your first drafts, consider questions such as the following:

### Questions for Discovering Ideas

#### GENERAL IDEAS

- What ideas do you discover in the work? How do you discover them (through action, character description, scenes, figurative language)?
- To what do the ideas pertain? To individuals themselves? To individuals and society? To religion? To social, political, or economic circumstances? To fairness? To inequality? To justice?
- How balanced are the ideas? If a particular idea is strongly presented, what conditions and qualifications are also presented (if any)? What contradictory ideas are presented?
- Are the ideas limited to members of any groups represented by the characters (age, race, nationality, personal status)? Or are the ideas applicable to general conditions of life? Explain.
- Which characters in their own right represent or embody ideas? How do their actions and speeches bring out these ideas?
- If characters state ideas directly, how persuasive is their expression, how intelligent and well considered? How germane are the ideas to the work? How germane to more general conditions?

- With children, young adults, or the old, how do the circumstances express or embody an idea?

### A SPECIFIC IDEA

- What idea seems particularly important in the work? Why? How is it presented? Is it asserted directly, indirectly, dramatically, ironically? Does any one method predominate? Why?
- How pervasive in the work is the idea (throughout or intermittent)? To what degree is it associated with a major character or action? How does the structure of the work affect or shape your understanding of the idea?
- What value or values are embodied in the idea? Of what importance are the values to the work's meaning?
- How compelling is the idea? How could the work be appreciated without reference to any idea at all?

## Strategies for Organizing Ideas

Narrative and dramatic elements have a strong bearing on ideas in well-written stories, poems, and plays. In this sense, an idea is like a key in music or like a continuous thread tying together actions, characters, statements, symbols, and dialogue. As readers, we can trace such threads throughout the entire fabric of the work.

As you write about ideas, you may find yourself relying most heavily on the direct statements of the authorial voice or on a combination of these and your interpretation of characters and action. Or you might focus exclusively on a first-person speaker and use his or her ideas to develop your analysis. Always make clear the sources of your details and distinguish the sources from your own commentary.

In your essay, your general goal is to describe an idea and show its importance in the story. Each separate work will invite its own approach, but here are a number of strategies you might use to organize your essay:

1. *Analyze the idea as it applies to character. Example*: "Chonita embodies the idea that life amid poverty leads to the loss of dignity and opportunity, and also to the loss of health and even to death itself" ("The Hammon and the Beans").

2. *Show how actions bring out the idea. Example*: "That Mabel and Dr. Fergusson fall in love rather than go their separate ways indicates Lawrence's idea that love literally rescues human lives."

3. *Show how dialogue and separate speeches bring out the idea. Example*: "The priest's responses to Jackie's confession embody the idea that kindness and understanding are the best means to encourage religious and philosophical commitment" ("First Confession" [Chapter 7]).

4. *Show how the story's structure is determined by the idea. Example*: "The idea that horror can exist in ordinary things leads to a structure in which Jackson (in 'The Lottery,' Chapter 3) introduces seemingly commonplace people, builds suspense about an impending misfortune, and develops a conclusion of mob insensitivity and cruelty."

5.  *Treat variations or differing manifestations of the idea. Example*: "The idea that zealousness leads to harm is shown in Brown's nightmarish distortion of reality, his rejection of others, and his dying gloom" ("Young Goodman Brown" [Chapter 8]).

6.  *Deal with a combination of these (together with any other significant aspect). Example*: "The idea in 'Araby' (Chapter 5) that devotion is complex and contradictory is shown in the narrator's romantic mission as a carrier of parcels, his outcries to love in the back room of his house, and his self-reproach and shame at the story's end." (Here the idea is traced through both speech and action.)

Your conclusion might begin with a summary, together with your evaluation of the validity or force of the idea. If you have been convinced by the author's ideas, you might say that the author has expressed the idea forcefully and convincingly, or else you might show the relevance of the idea to current conditions. If you are not persuaded by the idea, you should demonstrate its shortcomings or limitations. If you wish to mention a related idea, whether in the story you have studied or in some other story, you might introduce that here, but be sure to stress the connections.

## Illustrative Student Essay

Underlined sentences in this paper *do not* conform to MLA style and are used solely as teaching tools to emphasize the central idea, thesis sentence, and topic sentences throughout the paper.

Reyes 1

Oscar de los Reyes

Professor Garcia

English 112

7 October 2007

### D. H. Lawrence's "The Horse Dealer's Daughter" as an Expression of the Idea That

### Loving Commitment Is Essential in Life.°

[1]     Lawrence's "The Horse Dealer's Daughter" is an unusual love story. We learn that

the lovers—Mabel Pervin (the "Horse Dealer's Daughter") and Dr. Jack Fergusson—

have known each other for many years but have never thought of themselves as lovers. It

is not until after a potentially disastrous event that the two recognize that they love each

other. Lawrence makes clear that this new love is about to bring new meaning and new

---

°See pp. 378–88 for this story.

Reyes 2

direction to their lives. <u>Most important about this love is that it fulfills Lawrence's idea that it is dedicated commitment that gives life meaning.</u>* Lawrence brings out this idea first by showing characters with no sense of love or commitment and then by developing the two major characters whose lives are to be fulfilled by commitment.†

[2]      <u>Negatively, Lawrence introduces his idea through the Pervin brothers, who have no sense of service or commitment and who therefore are leading obtuse, insensitive, somewhat cruel, and basically "ineffectual" lives</u> (382, paragraph 96). It is true that Joe, the oldest brother, is planning to marry, and, one might assume, is also undertaking the promises and commitments that marriage brings. But Joe is seeking marriage only to receive a job from his future father-in-law. His only duty is to himself, in other words, and even though that is a commitment of sorts, it is only a limited one. In line with Lawrence's idea, Joe's life therefore has little if any meaning. Lawrence's speaker dismisses him with the cutting words that he is not much better than the large draft horses on the Pervin farm, whose "stupidity . . . [holds] them in subjection" (379, paragraph 6).

[3]      <u>Lawrence's first use of his major characters, Mabel Pervin and Dr. Jack Fergusson, also embodies the negative aspect of his idea that lack of service and commitment to others leaves people weak and sick.</u> When Jack first enters the story his eyes look "tired" (380, paragraph 43), and he is suffering from a severe cold. His social life seems to be confined to spending time at a nearby pub and drinking with one of the Pervin brothers, Fred Henry, and two women named "Lizzie and May" (382, paragraphs 90–91). These outward signs of illness and aimlessness suggest an inner lack of conviction and commitment. Nevertheless, Jack is a good doctor. He may sometimes think of himself as a "slave" to his patients (383, paragraph 103), but he is dedicated to his work and finds excitement in it (383, paragraph 106). Therefore he declares that he cannot take a brief rest from serving his patients even to overcome his cold (paragraph 49). Clearly he is committed to his profession, but the commitment that comes from love is lacking in his life. When he goes into the pond to rescue Mabel, it is as a professional, not as a committed lover. His action, however, will change him and point him in the path of completeness.

[4]      <u>Mabel is in a similar position.</u> Lawrence introduces her as "a rather ⸱ⁱ looking young woman" with an "impassive fixity of her face" (378

---

*Central idea.
†Thesis sentence.

brothers all seem to dislike her. Like Jack, she is living only half a life, even though she has gained some little meaning through service, of a sort, to others. In the past she has been "keeping the home together" for her father and her brothers as the family fortunes declined. As long as the family had had money, her life was adequate, even if the household to which she was committed was "brutal and coarse" in many ways (paragraph 96). But with the family now "hopelessly in debt," requiring the breakup of the household, her duties are vanishing, and this loss also brings the loss of the meaning that her service has brought to her (382, paragraphs 97–98).

[5]      In line with the idea, Lawrence makes plain that Mabel's developing despair will end her existence and that Jack's rootlessness, if unchanged, will keep him incomplete. Mabel's situation is, of course, the more critical. After completing her chores at home she sets about to care for the grave of her dead mother, to whom her commitment has been complete (383, paragraphs 98–101). Once she finishes this last loving task, she has nowhere to go, nothing more to do, and she therefore walks purposefully to the nearby pond and enters it in an attempt to drown herself (384, paragraph 109). One can read her attempted suicide as a symbol of Lawrence's idea that once a person's commitments end, meaning is gone and life is, in effect, over.

[6]      The paragraphs devoted by Lawrence to the interchanges of Mabel and Jack after he has rescued her from the pond demonstrate the interconnectedness of love and commitment. When he brings her to the shore, he works "to restore her" (384, paragraph 117). After he carries her home—a long and difficult task—he disrobes her and wraps her in blankets to bring back warmth and life to her. At this point his commitment to her, however, is not to a loved one but to a victim. But when Mabel recovers, her first thought is to associate her nakedness with a newly discovered love for her. She asks him "Do you love me then?" (paragraph 142). Once she has extracted a declaration of love, her first wishes are an enactment of Lawrence's idea of the power of commitment. She wants to get him "dry things" and then to make him some tea (387, 388, paragraphs 170, 184). She has been awakened to a new life by a man who suddenly appears in a totally new light, and her response is immediately to begin the simple tasks that follow naturally from commitment. For his part, Jack demonstrates his newly found commitment by stating that he wants the two of them "to be married" (388, paragraph 188). The idea is that love is for the moment, but commitment is for the long term.

Reyes 4

[7]     The major and most truthful aspect of Lawrence's idea is that the transformation to loving commitment and responsibility is not easy but is both tentative and complex. Lawrence demonstrates this complexity by showing that both Mabel and Jack are uneasy and uncertain, for neither one can easily give up the past (even though Mabel was willing to give up everything by killing herself). When Jack expresses love for Mabel it is in a voice that is "unlike himself" (paragraph 166), and her response is to say "I feel I'm horrible to you" (paragraph 190). Difficult and fearful as the change to their new commitment is, however, it is leading them into the lives they have been designed for. Generally, people who evade such a change, like the Pervin brothers, may find life easy, but they are permanently incomplete because they lack the bravery of commitment shown by Mabel and Jack. Thus, Lawrence's idea in "The Horse Dealer's Daughter" emphasizes that a full life requires love and commitment, no matter how difficult, and that without such commitment lives can be lived only in the shadows.

Reyes 5

**WORK CITED**

Lawrence, D. H. "The Horse Dealer's Daughter." *Literature: An Introduction to Reading and Writing*. Ed. Edgar V. Roberts. 4th Compact Ed. Upper Saddle River: Prentice Hall, 2008, 378–88.

## Commentary

This essay follows strategy 6 (p. 394) by showing how separate components of the story exhibit the idea's pervasiveness. Throughout, citations of characters, actions, and speeches, together with observations about the story's organization, are used as evidence for the various conclusions. Transitions between paragraphs are effected by phrases like "introduces," "similar," "after he has rescued her," and "the major and most truthful aspect," all of which emphasize the continuity of the topic.

The first paragraph asserts that the story's major action—the development of love between the major characters—brings out the Lawrence's idea that commitment gives meaning to life. The idea is to be developed as it applies to characters without commitment and then to those who find it.

The argument of paragraphs 2 through 4 is to show how Lawrence brings out his idea negatively by demonstrating the shortcomings of characters, including the story's two major characters, who are living without commitment. The essay thus asserts that Joe is following a path of stupidity, Jack a life of rootlessness, and Mabel an action of suicide. These details are brought out in support of the essay's central idea or argument. Paragraphs 5 and 6 treat the positive aspects of the main idea, focusing on the renewing effect of commitment for both Jack and Mabel. The last paragraph pays tribute to Lawrence's idea by demonstrating that it is realistic and true to life because both Jack and Mabel discover that their new commitments are not made easily but require profound and disturbing changes in their lives.

## Writing Topics: Major Ideas

1. Compare two stories containing similar themes. *Examples*: Joyce's "Araby" and Lawrence's "The Horse Dealer's Daughter," Ozick's "The Shawl" (Chapter 5) and Chioles's "Before the Firing Squad" (Chapter 10), Chopin's "The Story of an Hour" (Chapter 7) and Gilman's "The Yellow Wallpaper" (Chapter 10). For help in developing your essay, consult Chapter 25 on the technique of comparison-contrast.

2. Write an essay criticizing the ideas in a story in this anthology that you dislike or to which you are indifferent. With what statements in the story do you disagree? What actions? What characters? How do your own beliefs and values cause you to disagree with the story's ideas? How might the story be changed to illustrate ideas with which you would agree?

3. Select an idea that particularly interests you, and write a story showing how characters may or may not live up to the idea. If you have difficulty getting started, try one of these possible ideas:

   a. Interest and enthusiasm are hard to maintain for long.

   b. People always want more than they have or need.

   c. The concerns of adults are different from those of children.

   d. Confronting another person about a grievance is awkward.

   e. Making a romantic or career decision is hard because it requires a change in life's directions.

4. Using books that you discover through the retrieval system in your college or local library, search for discussions of only one of the following topics, and write a brief report on what you find.

   a. D. H. Lawrence on the power of the working classes.

   b. James Joyce on the limitations of religious ideas.

   c. Cynthia Ozick on the Holocaust.

   d. Ernest Hemingway on individualism and self-realization.

   e. The ideas underlying Poe's concept of the short story as a form.

   f. Nathaniel Hawthorne on the nature of religious ideas, good or bad.

# Chapter **10**

# Four Stories for Additional Enjoyment and Study

## JOHN CHIOLES (b. 1940)

Chioles, a Greek American, is a Professor of Comparative Literature at New York University. He spends half of his time in New
York, and half in Athens. He is known for his *Literary Theory*
(1996) and *Aeschylus: Mythic Theater, Political Voice* (1995). He
has translated a number of Greek writers, including Taktsis,
Siotis, and Cavafy. With Dinos Siotis, he translated *Twenty Contemporary Greek Poets* (1979). He also wrote a description of the
history, art, and architecture of Athens titled *Athens, Capital City*
(1985). In the early 1990s, with Alexander Damianikos, he developed audio cassettes on *Arab and Islam, Hellenism,* and *Refor-
mation*. His moving story "Before the Firing Squad" was included
in *The Available Press/PEN Short Story Collection,* with an introduction by Anne Tyler
(1985).

The time of "Before the Firing Squad" is World War II, about 1944, during the closing
days of the German occupation of Greece. The physical setting is an area of the Peloponnesus (i.e., Southern Greece) not far from the site of ancient Sparta. Chioles mentions the
Arkadian Mountains and also the area of Mani to the south (paragraph 2). Mani is the middle of the three peninsulas forming the southern part of the Peloponnesus. (The historical
ancient Sparta, also in the Peloponnesus, was known for the discipline and ferocity of its
armies and for the fact that in the Peloponnesian War in the fifth century B.C.E. it defeated
the forces of Athens.)

##  Before the Firing Squad (1985)

The sound at first was a low moan, and you knew the momentum would build as soon a
hand-cranked siren, managed by teenaged boys, would pick up speed. No matter where
my knees turned to jelly, my pulse quickened, instinctively I would look up the hill to

tower of the church feeling betrayed that I could not be up there; at least there, watching the crank turn, the sound didn't frighten me. But the watch at the bell tower was for the older boys. You had to be at least twelve. From atop, where the giant bell hung, the boys kept a lookout for movement of vehicles; on a clear day they could see seven kilometers in the distance, beyond the bend.

Their convoys came from the main road. The moment they turned the bend that brings you full face with the town, their approach would echo against the side of the mountain. A hollow reverberation. The siren had by then stopped, to be replaced now by the rumbling of their trucks and heavy artillery. A moan of a different kind. The boys would run from the bell tower down the narrow streets to their homes. In no time, the dissonance of the enemy, something as ugly, efficient, and foreign to these parts as the unclean death they brought, appeared and disappeared, taking away the sun, leaving behind clouds of dust. They rarely stopped. But if they did, it could only bring down the reign of terror on all our heads. Mostly, though, they rode through on their way to Mani, where they would embark on ships bound for North Africa. To that end, they would ride roughshod over the Arkadian Mountains. What interested them most was to make sure they passed through the towns and hamlets without incident or delay, ready to crush any attempt at interference.

Their garrison of twelve soldiers stationed in the town wore mustard-colored uniforms, not the sinister black kind worn by the ones in the convoys.° These soldiers seemed very young and curiously happy. Everyone said they spoke a softer kind of German, without the harsh sounds of those northern peoples; most of them knew ancient Greek even, and liked the lilting songs of Homer. Their weapons were limited and not always in evidence. The whole town was ready to swear that these youths had never fought even a skirmish, let alone been in a war. My father used to call them Hitler's boy-soldiers, sent to promote a peaceful occupation, playing on the conscience of the partisans, counting on their decency. And, a curious thing, these young soldiers were never ambushed; none of them died in the everyday activity along these mountains, the daily sabotaging of the main artery, the only asphalt road leading down to the sea. While killing was the order of the day during that spring–ten townspeople executed for the death of one dark-uniformed German—these twelve had become practically the mascots of the town.

"I don't want you talking to this Fritz so much," Father said one day. "Everybody treats him like one of us. It isn't right." All the nice Germans we called Fritz and all the mean ones Ludwig; except that Fritz was really the name of my friend.

5        "He's harmless," I said. "And sometimes he brings his ration of chocolate and biscuits to share."

"He's the enemy," Father retorted the way he did when he would have no more discussion.

But the siren prevented any further talk. They came late in the afternoon of that day. My father was caught unawares. One convoy had already passed earlier, and he had run to the mountain and back again. They rarely had more than one a day. His reflexes were so swift that he practically knocked me over when he jumped to his feet.

"Put your warm sweater on and let's go." He had never taken me with him before. Women and children never ran to the mountain. The siren was for the men, whether they were part of the road sabotage teams or not. My father often stayed in the mountains for days; we never knew what he did there. "Hurry, we have no time. We'll take the back way so Fritz will not spot us. Your mother will know I've taken you with me."

The small garrison, our German mascots, lived across the street from us. They had requisitioned the best two-storied house, using the ground floor as offices and the second floor as

---

°*mustard colored . . . black kind*: The mustard-colored uniforms are those of the regular German army. The black uniforms belong to the Waffen SS, ˙se members were infamous for their cruelty.

living quarters. They were fully aware of the siren, but they pretended it came from the partisan stronghold in the mountain. Some said they even welcomed it; it gave them time to put on battle outfits, grab their guns, and move, a fierce-looking patrol, along the road. They never asked about the men of each household; their frequent absences from home they were content to believe had to do with working in the fields and vineyards. So Fritz had never asked about my father. Much like any of my friends, he was shy in his presence and avoided passing by whenever it was obvious Father was at home. Often he would come over to show us photos of his parents and his sisters, tell my mother how homesick he was, express joy or sadness whenever he would receive mail from home. And always my mother would find something to give him by way of comfort, a bunch of grapes or chestnuts or a few raisins. But whenever Father was at home it was understood he would never come over. He seemed no more than a boy and was treated much like the rest of us.

"Run faster! They're getting greedy today, and they could be mean." As we ran through    10
brush foliage I would scrape my legs and thought how nice it will be when I get to wear long trousers in another year or so.

"When we get on top I'll pick some wild tea leaves and chamomile buds for Mother. We don't have to come right back, do we?"

"We'll stay as long as we have to. Till they're gone." My father's furrowed brow told me this was not a usual run. The enemy was changing its routine; that meant everything would become unpredictable.

"Whoever is not alert, and doesn't expect the worst, will never know the unexpected when it comes his way," my father was saying to his friends when we reached the thick forest of pines. Below us, like ants in the distance, carefully covered heavy artillery rolled along the asphalt road. The atmosphere was highly charged. An unusually large number of people had taken to the mountain. The mood had changed as the sun went away and a cold mid-afternoon chill set in. All the world turned dark green and it smelled of rain, even the canvas covering the moving guns and trucks below took on the color of running oil in the absence of the sun.

"It's best to do nothing for a couple of days. They'll have patrols everywhere," one of the older men was saying to Father.

"We could've blown the far bridge yesterday. We should have been warned about this."    15

"Maybe this is only the beginning of moving out their heavy stuff. It's up to us."

My presence in this adult conversation went unnoticed. Yet I knew I should not be hearing what was being said. So I slipped away quietly. Nearby, some goats beat their grazing rhythm on the bushes; they made the acanthus bob up and down. I had no time to wonder why the goats seemed so nervous. Just then I stepped on a dried branch which flew up at me, my feet got tangled, and I came tumbling a good ten meters down the slope. Though I was stunned, I felt hardly any pain. But the fear was real, for I heard the pounding of a machine-gun and felt the whistle of bullets flying above my head. I stayed down, hardly breathing. The machine-gun, rattling but unable to pin down movement in the vast forest, moved on along a horizontal line, then stopped.

As the moan of the convoy became more distant, I felt my father's hand lifting me up. I was more ashamed than hurting. Not until I stood upright did I see the blood running down my leg and a whole patch of skin from my knee hanging upside down.

"It's nothing" my father said, and quickly used his handkerchief to patch it up.

"It doesn't hurt any," I said.    20

"It will. Why did you come this far? Didn't we say we never come into full view of the road?"

"I fell down."

"You'll be all right. I'm going to have to send you home with your cousins. Your mother should take care of that knee."

I said nothing but followed sheepishly the downward path, my father's handkerchief tied behind my left knee. He had made the knot too tight and I felt a numbing pain but did not let on to my older cousins. Father had whispered something to them, that they should take care of me, I guessed, so I did not want to show I needed looking after.

25  At home there was commotion; our window was open. Mother had been putting my baby sister to sleep; she had lit the oil lamp. Across the way, the German soldiers were playing phonograph records, their usual sad music. (Only, Fritz had told me many times that their music was not at all funereal as the townspeople thought—it was happy and exultant, he'd say; still, it sounded sad to me.) Nobody got wind that I limped into the house at dusk. Stealth was always my strong point.

When Mother saw me, there was an uproar and a lot to answer for. I explained quickly, and, seeing that my wound was still bleeding, she softened her tone as to the mystery of my whereabouts all afternoon.

"Here, sit down. Let's have a look."

I clenched my teeth while she cleaned the whole knee with a sponge. It stung good and sharp now.

"You must be starved, too. Fritz has brought you a surprise. Uncover that bowl on the table. It's all for you."

30  A bowl of food, rice with bits of chicken, cubed chunks of meat in a thick white soup. Never had I eaten anything so tasty before. It came from a fancy tin that my friend received on special occasions. If each of us had to cherish one memory of food that would make our taste buds water, Fritz's bowl of chicken with rice on that evening would be mine. I felt no pain from the leg while I ate to my heart's content, nor did I notice that he had come to the window, looking in, and already my mother had silently shown him my knee. In no time, he returned with a first-aid kit and set about to dress the wound. He spoke admonishingly to me in German, but also found the right phrases in Greek to let me know he was unhappy with me.

"Children don't become partisans, you know." But his smile gave him away. He only meant I should be careful. Then he became serious again. Whenever he looked serious his eyebrows went from the straw color of his hair to a darker shade and he looked older. Even his eyes did not keep their blue but went dark like the sea.

It seemed a cloud hung over the fate of the twelve German soldiers of our town. They would be transferred soon. They might be taken to the front lines. Everything was becoming very unpredictable, he was telling my mother. I had never seen Fritz so sad before. He hung his head low as he pulled out of his trouser pocket a letter he had just received from his mother. She lived, he told us, in a big city in his country that was being bombed constantly now, and they had even less to eat than we did.

"I do not know if I will see them again."

"You will, you will. All this will soon be over and you'll get to go home. You'll see," my mother consoled as best she could.

35  The next morning the news was out. The whole town became concerned. If they left, would they be replaced by the black-uniformed ones? What would be in store for us? The neighborhood around us began to treat them like departing friends; they offered them sweets, dried fruits and nuts, and whatever parting hospitality they could. In their turn, the boy-soldiers responded with moist eyes, uncertain, and very scared of the weeks ahead. My mother always said, remembering those last few hours, not one of them looked a day over sixteen.

An old philosopher who dwelled along the dusty plains of Asia Minor once said there will come a Great Year whose summer will be a World Conflagration. That's just what happened to us that summer. On the very day they came to collect their soldiers and depart for good, they also set fire to nearly every house in the town.

Activity along the mountains had been fierce lately. The far bridge had been blown up; so had the narrow pass beyond. The siren howled urgently at full speed on that day. When they turned the bend they began to slow down, rolling into town at a snail's pace to cover for their foot soldiers, who darted off the road, torches in hand, setting fire to every house, every barn, every haystack in sight. That way they took a long time to get to us who lived near the square; but we had seen the smoke and the flames and we knew what was in store for us.

My mother refused to run away, hoping, with children in hand, she might at least save the house. But as the confusion around us got worse, the shooting in all directions, the trails of smoke, the terror-filled sounds of homes bursting open under the flame—no one could possibly be reasoned with, no one caught up in such careening panic. Every black Ludwig looked like a madman in passionate play with fire. During these terrible moments Fritz was nowhere to be seen.

We stood at the door of our house and watched the commotion all around us, until a burst from an automatic hit near our feet and we were routed and shown the way to the open space in the middle of the square. While she held the baby and I held on to her sleeve, my mother shuffled us to the gathering place. We never looked behind. But we knew. All around the square the trucks were moving slowly, never at rest, making a terrible din, which drowned out the cries of the dozen or so women and children huddled in the middle. We were shoved against them, and for the first time I saw a number of our town mascots, the boy-soldiers, armed to the teeth, some guarding us, some being given stern orders by an officer while others were already jumping onto the moving trucks with all their gear.

The officer pointed in our direction and began to scream an order to his subordinates. 40 Three of them rushed over to our group and kneaded us all into a straight line. I saw to my horror that Fritz was one of them. His eyes were dark and furious, hardly anyone recognized him; his whole body and movements had taken on a different shape. I felt a crushing disappointment. He looked old now like the others.

Their mission accomplished, the three ran back to the officer. He gave them what seemed final instructions and climbed into the cab of his moving truck. The three raced to set up just ahead of us a machine-gun with tripod at the front of the barrel. One of them brought the ammunition, and I saw Fritz reach into the box and bring out a magazine, which he loaded onto the gun. Just then, whistles began blowing, those piercing kind they use at train platforms to signal an imminent departure. They didn't want to remain sitting targets for the partisans, so they had to make haste.

Suddenly the motors got louder; speed was only seconds away. Fritz, now arguing with the other two soldiers, appeared even more fierce. They were pushing to get behind the machine-gun, but he seemed to win out. While they rushed to jump on the trucks, he fell on his belly and hugged the gun, groping for the trigger. We were all frozen with fear. I searched for his eyes in utter disbelief. Time fled and backtracked toward me again. I was aware only that the trucks were moving faster, that Fritz was frozen in his place, his right hand now on the ground, too far from the latch of the trigger. Then in a flash he jumped up, lifted the gun from its tripod, and let it sing half across the sky, while in the same motion he chased the last truck, leaping headfirst into it. His torso, writhing wildly to get his weight into the truck, was the last thing I saw of Fritz, who had in those last dancerlike movements transformed his body once more into the boy that he really was, waving good-bye at us with his legs.

## Questions

1. Describe the historical period and the time of action of "The Firing Squad."
2. What aspects of the story may be categorized as realistic?
3. Who is the narrator of the story? How old is he? How much does he understand? In what ways is he a contact between the Greek and the German forces?

**4.** Explain the irony in this story. What is the irony of the family's knowing Fritz, particularly in view of the story's conclusion?

**5.** What is the nature of the crisis and climax of this story?

## ANDRE DUBUS (1936–1999)

Dubus was born in Louisiana and received degrees from McNeese State College and the University of Iowa. He taught at Bradford College in Massachusetts before he was struck and disabled by a speeding automobile. He lived northwest of Boston near the Merrimack River, an area he often employed as the setting in his ficiton. The stories in his *Selected Stories* (1988), from which "The Curse" is taken, touch the darker areas of human existence, but nevertheless have a compelling force. In "They Now Live in Texas," for example, a woman sees a horror ghost movie on her VCR and then awaits her own demons. In another story, "Townies," a drifting, purposeless young man kills his girlfriend and then achieves a curious serenity as he waits for the police. Dubus's last short story collection was *Dancing After Hours* (1996). He also worked in the longer form of the novella and published several novellas in *We Don't Live Here Anymore* (1984). He gained many honors, among them a Guggenheim Fellowship and a MacArthur Fellowship.

 **The Curse** (1988)

Mitchell Hayes was forty-nine years old, but when the cops left him in the bar with Bob, the manager, he felt much older. He did not know what it was like to be very old, a shrunken and wrinkled man, but he assumed it was like this: fatigue beyond relieving by rest, by sleep. He also was not a small man: his weight moved up and down in the hundred and seventies and he was five feet, ten inches tall. But now his body seemed short and thin. Both stood at one end of the bar; he was a large blackhaired man, and there was nothing in front of him but an ash tray he was using. He looked at Mitchell at the cash register and said: "Forget it. You heard what Smitty said."

Mitchell looked away, at the front door. He had put the chairs upside down on the table. He looked from the door past Bob to the empty space of floor at the rear; sometimes people danced there, to the jukebox. Opposite Bob, on the wall behind the bar, was a telephone; Mitchell looked at it. He had told Smitty there were five guys and when he moved to the phone one of them stepped around the corner of the bar and shoved him: one hand against Mitchell's chest, and it pushed him backward; he nearly fell. That was when they were getting rough with her at the bar. When they took her to the floor Mitchell looked once at her sounds, then looked down at the duckboard he stood on, or at the belly or chest of a young man in front of him.

He knew they were not drunk. They had been drinking before they came to his place, a loud popping of motorcycles outside, then walking into the empty bar, young and sunburned and carrying helmets and wearing thick leather jackets in August. They stood in front of Mitchell and drank drafts. When he took their first order he thought they were on drugs and later, watching them, he was certain. They were not relaxed, in the way of most drinkers near closing time. Their eyes were quick, alert as wary animals, and they spoke loudly, with passion, but their passion was strange and disturbing, because they were only chatting, bantering. Mitchell knew nothing of the effects of drugs, so could not guess what was in their blood. He feared and hated drugs because of his work and because he was the stepfather of teenagers: a boy and a girl. He gave last call and served them and leaned against the counter behind him.

Then the door opened and the girl walked in from the night, a girl he had never seen, and she crossed the floor toward Mitchell. He stepped forward to tell her she had missed last call, but before he spoke she asked for change for the cigarette machine. She was young, he guessed nineteen to twenty-one, and deeply tanned and had dark hair. She was sober and wore jeans and a dark blue tee shirt. He gave her the quarters but she was standing between two of the men and she did not get to the machine.

When it was over and she lay crying on the cleared circle of floor, he left the bar and    5
picked up the jeans and tee shirt beside her and crouched and handed them to her. She did not look at him. She lay the clothes across her breasts and what Mitchell thought of now as her wound. He left her and dialed 911, then Bob's number. He woke up Bob. Then he picked up her sneakers from the floor and placed them beside her and squatted near her face, her crying. He wanted to speak to her and touch her, hold a hand or press her brow, but he could not.

The cruiser was there quickly, the siren coming east from town, then slowing and deepening as the car stopped outside. He was glad Smitty was one of them; he had gone to high school with Smitty. The other was Dave, and Mitchell knew him because it was a small town. When they saw the girl Dave went out to the cruiser to call for an ambulance, and when he came back he said two other cruisers had those scumbags and were taking them in. The girl was still crying and could not talk to Smitty and Dave. She was crying when a man and woman lifted her onto a stretcher and rolled her out the door and she vanished forever in a siren.

Bob came in while Smitty and Dave were sitting at the bar drinking coffee and Smitty was writing his report; Mitchell stood behind the bar. Bob sat next to Dave as Mitchell said: "I could have stopped them, Smitty."

"That's our job," Smitty said. "You want to be in the hospital now?"

Mitchell did not answer. When Smitty and Dave left, he got a glass of Coke from the cobra and had a cigarette with Bob. They did not talk. Then Mitchell washed his glass and Bob's cup and they left, turning off the lights. Outside Mitchell locked the front door, feeling the sudden night air after almost ten hours of air conditioning. When he had come to work the day had been very hot, and now he thought it would not have happened in winter. They had stopped for a beer on their way somewhere from the beach; he had heard them say that. But the beach was not the reason. He did not know the reason, but he knew it would not have happened in winter. The night was cool and now he could smell trees. He turned and looked at the road in front of the bar. Bob stood beside him on the small porch.

"If the regulars had been here," Bob said.    10

He turned and with his hand resting on the wooden rail he walked down the ramp to the ground. At his car he stopped and looked over its roof at Mitchell.

"You take it easy," he said.

Mitchell nodded. When Bob got in his car and left, he went down the ramp and drove home to his house on a street that he thought was neither good nor bad. The houses were small and there were old large houses used now as apartments for families. Most of the people had work, most of the mothers cared for their children, and most of the children were clean and looked like they lived in homes, not caves like some he saw in town. He worried about the older kids, one group of them anyway. They were idle. When he was a boy in a town farther up the Merrimack River, he and his friends committed every mischievous act he could recall on afternoons and nights when they were idle. His stepchildren were not part of that group. They had friends from the high school. The front porch light was on for him and one in the kitchen at the rear of the house. He went in the front door and switched off the porch light and walked through the living and dining rooms to the kitchen. He got a can of beer from the refrigerator, turned out the light, and sat at the table. When he could see, he took a cigarette from Susan's pack in front of him.

Down the hall he heard Susan move on the bed then get up and he hoped it wasn't for the bathroom but for him. He had met her eight years ago when he had given up on ever marrying and having kids, then one night she came into the bar with two of her girl friends from work. She made six dollars an hour going to homes of invalids, mostly what she called her little old ladies, and bathing them. She got the house from her marriage, and child support the guy paid for a few months till he left town and went south. She came barefoot down the hall and stood in the kitchen doorway and said: "Are you all right?"

15      "No."

She sat across from him, and he told her. Very soon she held his hand. She was good. He knew if he had fought all five of them and was lying in pieces in a hospital bed she would tell him he had done the right thing, as she was telling him now. He liked her strong hand on his. It was a professional hand and he wanted from her something he had never wanted before: to lie in bed while she bathed him. When they went to bed he did not think he would be able to sleep, but she kneeled beside him and massaged his shoulders and rubbed his temples and pressed her hands on his forehead. He woke to the voices of Marty and Joyce in the kitchen. They had summer jobs, and always when they woke him he went back to sleep till noon, but now he got up and dressed and went to the kitchen door. Susan was at the stove, her back to him, and Marty and Joyce were talking and smoking. He said good morning, and stepped into the room.

"What are you doing up?" Joyce said.

She was a pretty girl with her mother's wide cheekbones and Marty was a tall good-looking boy, and Mitchell felt as old as he had before he slept. Susan was watching him. Then she poured him a cup of coffee and put it at his place and he sat, Marty said: "You getting up for the day?"

"Something happened last night. At the bar." They tried to conceal their excitement, but he saw it in their eyes. "I should have stopped it. I think I *could* have stopped it. That's the point. There were these five guys. They were on motorcycles but they weren't bikers. Just punks. They came in late, when everybody else had gone home. It was a slow night anyway. Everybody was at the beach."

20      "They rob you?" Marty said.

"No. A girl came in. Young. Nice looking. You know: just a girl, minding her business." They nodded, and their eyes were apprehensive.

"She wanted cigarette change, that's all. Those guys were on dope. Coke or something. You know: they were flying in place."

"Did they rape her?" Joyce said.

25      "Yes, honey."

"The *fuckers*."

Susan opened her mouth then closed it and Joyce reached quickly for Susan's pack of cigarettes. Mitchell held his lighter for her and said: "When they started getting rough with her at the bar I went for the phone. One of them stopped me. He shoved me, that's all. I should have hit him with a bottle."

Marty reached over the table with his big hand and held Mitchell's shoulder.

"No, Mitch. Five guys that mean. And coked up or whatever. No way. You wouldn't be here this morning."

30      "I don't know. There was always a guy with me. But just one guy, taking turns."

"Great," Joyce said. Marty's hand was on Mitchell's left shoulder; she put hers on his right hand.

"They took her to the hospital," he said. "The guys are in jail."

"They are?" Joyce said.

"I called the cops. When they left."

"You'll be a good witness," Joyce said.

He looked at her proud face.

"At the trial," she said.

The day was hot but that night most of the regulars came to the bar. Some of the younger ones came on motorcycles. They were a good crowd: they all worked, except the retired ones and no one ever bothered the women, not even the young ones with their summer tans. Everyone talked about it: some had read the newspaper story, some had heard the story in town, and they wanted to hear it from Mitchell. He told it as often as they asked but he did not finish it because he was working hard and could not stay with any group of customers long enough.

He watched their faces. Not one of them, even the women, looked at him as if he had not cared enough for the girl, or was a coward. Many of them even appeared sympathetic, making him feel for moments that he was a survivor of something horrible, and when that feeling left him he was ashamed. He felt tired and old, making drinks and change, moving and talking up and down the bar. At the stool at the far end Bob drank coffee and whenever Mitchell looked at him he smiled or nodded and once raised his right fist, with the thumb up.

Reggie was drinking too much. He did that two or three times a month and Mitchell had to shut him off and Reggie always took it humbly. He was a big gentle man with a long brown beard. But tonight shutting off Reggie demanded from Mitchell an act of will, and when the eleven o'clock news came on the television and Reggie ordered another shot and a draft, Mitchell pretended not to hear him. He served the customers at the other end of the bar, where Bob was. He could hear Reggie calling: Hey Mitch; shot and a draft, Mitch. Mitchell was close to Bob now. Bob said softly: "He's had enough."

Mitchell nodded and went to Reggie, leaned closer to him so he could speak quietly, and said: "Sorry, Reggie. Time for coffee. I don't want you dead out there."

Reggie blinked at him.

"Okay, Mitch." He pulled some bills from his pocket and put them on the bar. Mitchell glanced at them and saw at least a ten dollar tip. When he rang up Reggie's tab the change was sixteen dollars and fifty cents, and he dropped the coins and shoved the bills into the beer mug beside the cash register. The mug was full of bills, as it was on most nights, and he kept his hand in there, pressing Reggie's into the others, and saw the sunburned young men holding her down on the floor and one kneeling between her legs, spread and held, and he heard their cheering voices and her screaming and groaning and finally weeping and weeping and weeping, until she was the siren crying then fading into the night. From the floor behind him, far across the room, he felt her pain and terror and grief, then her curse upon him. The curse moved into his back and spread down and up his spine, into his stomach and legs and arms and shoulders until he quivered with it. He wished he were alone so he could kneel to receive it.

## Questions

1. What kind of violence occurs in "The Curse"? What is your response to the violence? What issues are brought out by the violent action?

2. What is Mitchell's attitude toward the reality that he was able to do nothing to prevent the violence? What do his friends tell him? How right are they about what he might have done? How justifiable is Mitchell's sense of guilt at the incident?

3. What is Mitchell's dilemma? Why does he think about things as he does at the story's end?

4. In what ways does it seem that Mitchell has been changed by his experiences in the story? How is such change justifiable? Inevitable?

## CHARLOTTE PERKINS GILMAN (1860–1935)

Born in 1860, Gilman did not begin writing seriously until after the birth of her daughter in the 1880s, which was followed by her "nervous breakdown." Attempting to establish her independence, she left her husband in 1890 and went to California, where she launched what was to become a distinguished career as an advocate for women's rights. For many decades she lectured and wrote extensively, her touchstone work being *Women and Economics* (1898), in which she championed the need for women's financial independence. Among her many writings were *Concerning Children* (1900), *Human Work* (1904), and *His Religion and Hers* (1923). In the 1930s she became incurably ill, and with death facing her, she took her own life in 1935.

## The Yellow Wallpaper° (1892)

It is very seldom that mere ordinary people like John and myself secure ancestral halls for the summer.

A colonial mansion, a hereditary estate, I would say a haunted house and reach the height of romantic felicity—but that would be asking too much of fate!

Still I will proudly declare that there is something queer about it.

Else, why should it be let so cheaply? And why have stood so long untenanted?

5    John laughs at me, of course, but one expects that.

John is practical in the extreme. He has no patience with faith, an intense horror of superstition, and he scoffs openly at any talk of things not to be felt and seen and put down in figures.

John is a physician, and *perhaps*—(I would not say it to a living soul, of course, but this is dead paper and a great relief to my mind)—*perhaps* that is one reason I do not get well faster.

You see, he does not believe I am sick! And what can one do?

If a physician of high standing, and one's own husband, assures friends and relatives that there is really nothing the matter with one but temporary nervous depression—a slight hysterical tendency—what is one to do?

10    My brother is also a physician, and also of high standing, and he says the same thing.

So I take phosphates or phosphites—whichever it is—and tonics, and air and exercise, and journeys, and am absolutely forbidden to "work" until I am well again.

---

°*The Yellow Wallpaper*: The story is based on the "rest cure" developed after the Civil War by the famous Philadelphia physician S. Weir Mitchell (1829–1914); see paragraph 83. The Mitchell treatment required confining the patient to a hospital, hotel, or some other remote residence. Once isolated, the patient was to have complete bed rest, increased food intake, iron supplements, exercise, and sometimes massage and electric shock therapy. Gilman had experienced Mitchell's "cure," and sent a copy of this story to him as criticism. After receiving the story Mitchell modified his methods.

Personally, I disagree with their ideas.

Personally, I believe that congenial work, with excitement and change, would do me good.

But what is one to do?

I did write for a while in spite of them; but it *does* exhaust me a good deal—having to be   15
so sly about it, or else meet with heavy opposition.

I sometimes fancy that in my condition, if I had less opposition and more society and stimulus—but John says the very worst thing I can do is to think about my condition, and I confess it always makes me feel bad.

So I will let it alone and talk about the house.

The most beautiful place! It is quite alone, standing well back from the road, quite three miles from the village. It makes me think of English places that you read about, for there are hedges and walls and gates that lock, and lots of separate little houses for the gardeners and people.

There is a *delicious* garden! I never saw such a garden—large and shady, full of box-bordered paths, and lined with long grape-covered arbors with seats under them.

There were greenhouses, but they are all broken now.   20

There was some legal trouble, I believe, something about the heirs and co-heirs; anyhow, the place has been empty for years.

That spoils my ghostliness, I am afraid, but I don't care—there is something strange about the house—I can feel it.

I even said so to John one moonlight evening, but he said what I felt was a draught, and shut the window.

I get unreasonably angry with John sometimes. I'm sure I never used to be so sensitive. I think it is due to this nervous condition.

But John says if I feel so I shall neglect proper self-control; so I take pains to control   25
myself—before him, at least, and that makes me very tired.

I don't like our room a bit. I wanted one downstairs that opened onto the piazza and had roses all over the window, and such pretty old-fashioned chintz hangings! But John would not hear of it.

He said there was only one window and not room for two beds, and no near room for him if he took another.

He is very careful and loving, and hardly lets me stir without special direction.

I have a schedule prescription for each hour in the day; he takes all care from me, and so I feel basely ungrateful not to value it more.

He said he came here solely on my account, that I was to have perfect rest and all the air I   30
could get. "Your exercise depends on your strength, my dear," said he, "and your food some-what on your appetite; but air you can absorb all the time." So we took the nursery at the top of the house.

It is a big, airy room, the whole floor nearly, with windows that look all ways, and air and sunshine galore. It was nursery first, and then playroom and gymnasium, I should judge, for the windows are barred for little children, and there are rings and things in the walls.

The paint and paper look as if a boys' school had used it. It is stripped off—the paper—in great patches all around the head of my bed, about as far as I can reach, and in a great place on the other side of the room low down. I never saw a worse paper in my life. One of those sprawling, flamboyant patterns committing every artistic sin.

It is dull enough to confuse the eye in following, pronounced enough constantly to irritate and provoke study, and when you follow the lame uncertain curves for a little distance they suddenly commit suicide—plunge off at outrageous angles, destroy themselves in unheard-of contradictions.

The color is repellent, almost revolting: a smouldering unclean yellow, strangely faded by the slow-turning sunlight. It is a dull yet lurid orange in some places, a sickly sulphur tint in others.

35 No wonder the children hated it! I should hate it myself if I had to live in this room long.

There comes John, and I must put this away—he hates to have me write a word.

We have been here two weeks, and I haven't felt like writing before, since that first day.

I am sitting by the window now, up in this atrocious nursery, and there is nothing to hinder my writing as much as I please, save lack of strength.

John is away all day, and even some nights when his cases are serious.

40 I am glad my case is not serious!

But these nervous troubles are dreadfully depressing.

John does not know how much I really suffer. He knows there is no reason to suffer, and that satisfies him.

Of course it is only nervousness. It does weigh on me so not to do my duty in any way!

I meant to be such a help to John, such a real rest and comfort, and here I am a comparative burden already!

45 Nobody would believe what an effort it is to do what little I am able—to dress and entertain, and order things.

It is fortunate Mary is so good with the baby. Such a dear baby!

And yet I *cannot* be with him, it makes me so nervous.

I suppose John never was nervous in his life. He laughs at me so about this wallpaper!

At first he meant to repaper the room, but afterward he said that I was letting it get the better of me, and that nothing was worse for a nervous patient than to give way to such fancies.

50 He said that after the wallpaper was changed it would be the heavy bedstead, and then the barred windows, and then that gate at the head of the stairs, and so on.

"You know the place is doing you good," he said, "and really, dear, I don't care to renovate the house just for a three months' rental."

"Then do let us go downstairs," I said. "There are such pretty rooms there."

Then he took me in his arms and called me a blessed little goose, and said he would go down to the cellar, if I wished, and have it whitewashed into the bargain.

But he is right enough about the beds and windows and things.

55 It is as airy and comfortable a room as anyone need wish, and, of course, I would not be so silly as to make him uncomfortable just for a whim.

I'm really getting quite fond of the big room, all but that horrid paper.

Out of one window I can see the garden—those mysterious deep-shaded arbors, the riotous old-fashioned flowers, and bushes and gnarly trees.

Out of another I get a lovely view of the bay and a little private wharf belonging to the estate. There is a beautiful shaded lane that runs down there from the house. I always fancy I see people walking in these numerous paths and arbors, but John has cautioned me not to give way to fancy in the least. He says that with my imaginative power and habit of story-making, a nervous weakness like mine is sure to lead to all manner of excited fancies, and that I ought to use my will and good sense to check the tendency. So I try.

I think sometimes that if I were only well enough to write a little it would relieve the press of ideas and rest me.

60 But I find I get pretty tired when I try.

It is so discouraging not to have any advice and companionship about my work. When I get really well, John says we will ask Cousin Henry and Julia down for a long visit; but he says he would as soon put fireworks in my pillow-case as to let me have those stimulating people about now.

I wish I could get well faster.

But I must not think about that. This paper looks to me as if it *knew* what a vicious influence it had!

There is a recurrent spot where the pattern lolls like a broken neck and two bulbous eyes stare at you upside down.

I get positively angry with the impertinence of it and the everlastingness. Up and down and sideways they crawl, and those absurd unblinking eyes are everywhere. There is one place where two breadths didn't match, and the eyes go all up and down the line, one a little higher than the other.

I never saw so much expression in an inanimate thing before, and we all know how much expression they have! I used to lie awake as a child and get more entertainment and terror out of blank walls and plain furniture than most children could find in a toy-store.

I remember what a kindly wink the knobs of our big old bureau used to have, and there was one chair that always seemed like a strong friend.

I used to feel that if any of the other things looked too fierce I could always hop into that chair and be safe.

The furniture in this room is no worse than inharmonious, however, for we had to bring it all from downstairs. I suppose when this was used as a playroom they had to take the nursery things out, and no wonder! I never saw such ravages as the children have made here.

The wallpaper, as I said before, is torn off in spots, and it sticketh closer than a brother°— they must have had perseverance as well as hatred.

Then the floor is scratched and gouged and splintered, the plaster itself is dug out here and there, and this great heavy bed, which is all we found in the room, looks as if it had been through the wars.

But I don't mind it a bit—only the paper.

There comes John's sister. Such a dear girl as she is, and careful of me! I must not let her find me writing.

She is a perfect and enthusiastic housekeeper, and hopes for no better profession. I verily believe she thinks it is the writing which made me sick!

But I can write when she is out, and see her a long way off from these windows.

There is one that commands the road, a lovely shaded winding road, and one that just looks off over the country. A lovely country, too, full of great elms and velvet meadows.

This wallpaper has a kind of sub-pattern in a different shade, a particularly irritating one, for you can only see it in certain lights, and not clearly then.

But in the places where it isn't faded and where the sun is just so—I can see a strange, provoking, formless sort of figure that seems to skulk about behind that silly and conspicuous front design.

There's sister on the stairs!

Well, the Fourth of July is over! The people are all gone, and I am tired out. John thought it might do me good to see a little company, so we just had Mother and Nellie and the children down for a week.

Of course I didn't do a thing. Jennie sees to everything now.

But it tired me all the same.

John says if I don't pick up faster he shall send me to Weir Mitchell° in the fall.

But I don't want to go there at all. I had a friend who was in his hands once, and she says he is just like John and my brother, only more so!

Besides, it is such an undertaking to go so far.

---

°*sticketh closer than a brother*: Proverbs 18:24.
°*Weir Mitchell*: See note on page 408.

I don't feel as if it was worthwhile to turn my hand over for anything, and I'm getting dreadfully fretful and querulous.

I cry at nothing, and cry most of the time.

Of course I don't when John is here, or anybody else, but when I am alone.

And I am alone a good deal just now. John is kept in town very often by serious cases, and Jennie is good and lets me alone when I want her to.

So I walk a little in the garden or down that lovely lane, sit on the porch under the roses, and lie down up here a good deal.

I'm getting really fond of the room in spite of the wallpaper. Perhaps *because* of the wallpaper.

It dwells in my mind so!

I lie here on this great immovable bed—it is nailed down, I believe—and follow that pattern about by the hour. It is as good as gymnastics, I assure you. I start, we'll say, at the bottom, down in the corner over there where it has not been touched, and I determine for the thousandth time that I *will* follow that pointless pattern to some sort of a conclusion.

I know a little of the principle of design, and I know this thing was not arranged on any laws of radiation, or alternation, or repetition, or symmetry, or anything else that I ever heard of.

It is repeated, of course, by the breadths, but not otherwise.

Looked at in one way, each breadth stands alone; the bloated curves and flourishes—a kind of "debased Romanesque" with delirium tremens—go waddling up and down in isolated columns of fatuity.

But, on the other hand, they connect diagonally, and the sprawling outlines run off in great slanting waves of optic horror, like a lot of wallowing sea-weeds in full chase.

The whole thing goes horizontally, too, at least it seems so, and I exhaust myself trying to distinguish the order of its going in that direction.

They have used a horizontal breadth for a frieze, and that adds wonderfully to the confusion.

There is one end of the room where it is almost intact, and there, when the crosslights fade and the low sun shines directly upon it, I can almost fancy radiation after all—the interminable grotesque seems to form around a common center and rush off in headlong plunges of equal distraction.

It makes me tired to follow it. I will take a nap, I guess.

I don't know why I should write this.

I don't want to.

I don't feel able.

And I know John would think it absurd. But I *must* say what I feel and think in some way—it is such a relief!

But the effort is getting to be greater than the relief.

Half the time now I am awfully lazy, and lie down ever so much. John says I mustn't lose my strength, and has me take cod liver oil and lots of tonics and things, to say nothing of ale and wine and rare meat.

Dear John! He loves me very dearly, and hates to have me sick. I tried to have a real earnest reasonable talk with him the other day, and tell him how I wish he would let me go and make a visit to Cousin Henry and Julia.

But he said I wasn't able to go, nor able to stand it after I got there; and I did not make out a very good case for myself, for I was crying before I had finished.

It is getting to be a great effort for me to think straight. Just this nervous weakness, I suppose.

And dear John gathered me up in his arms, and just carried me upstairs and laid me on the bed, and sat by me and read to me till it tired my head.

He said I was his darling and his comfort and all he had, and that I must take care of myself for his sake, and keep well.

He says no one but myself can help me out of it, that I must use my will and self-control and not let any silly fancies run away with me.

There's one comfort—the baby is well and happy, and does not have to occupy this nursery with the horrid wallpaper.

If we had not used it, that blessed child would have! What a fortunate escape! Why, I 115 wouldn't have a child of mine, an impressionable little thing, live in such a room for worlds.

I never thought of it before, but it is lucky that John kept me here after all; I can stand it so much easier than a baby, you see.

Of course I never mention it to them any more—I am too wise—but I keep watch for it all the same.

There are things in that wallpaper that nobody knows about but me, or ever will.

Behind that outside pattern the dim shapes get clearer every day.

It is always the same shape, only very numerous. 120

And it is like a woman stooping down and creeping about behind that pattern. I don't like it a bit. I wonder—I begin to think—I wish John would take me away from here!

It is so hard to talk with John about my case, because he is so wise, and because he loves me so.

But I tried it last night.

It was moonlight. The moon shines in all around just as the sun does.

I hate to see it sometimes, it creeps so slowly, and always comes in by one window or 125 another.

John was asleep and I hated to waken him, so I kept still and watched the moonlight on that undulating wallpaper till I felt creepy.

The faint figure behind seemed to shake the pattern, just as if she wanted to get out.

I got up softly and went to feel and see if the paper *did* move, and when I came back John was awake.

"What is it, little girl?" he said. "Don't go walking about like that—you'll get cold."

I thought it was a good time to talk, so I told him that I really was not gaining here, and 130 that I wished he would take me away.

"Why, darling!" said he. "Our lease will be up in three weeks, and I can't see how to leave before.

"The repairs are not done at home, and I cannot possibly leave town just now. Of course, if you were in any danger, I could and would, but you really are better, dear, whether you can see it or not. I am a doctor, dear, and I know. You are gaining flesh and color, your appetite is better, I feel really much easier about you."

"I don't weigh a bit more," said I, "nor as much; and my appetite may be better in the evening when you are here but it is worse in the morning when you are away!"

"Bless her little heart!" said he with a big hug. "She shall be as sick as she pleases! But now let's improve the shining hours by going to sleep, and talk about it in the morning!"

"And you won't go away?" I asked gloomily. 135

"Why, how can I, dear? It is only three weeks more and then we will take a nice little trip of a few days while Jennie is getting the house ready. Really, dear, you are better!"

"Better in body perhaps—" I began, and stopped short, for he sat up straight and looked at me with such a stern, reproachful look that I could not say another word.

"My darling," said he, "I beg of you, for my sake and for our child's sake, as well as for your own, that you will never for one instant let that idea enter your mind! There is nothing so dangerous, so fascinating, to a temperament like yours. It is a false and foolish fancy. Can you not trust me as a physician when I tell you so?"

So of course I said no more on that score, and we went to sleep before long. He thought I was asleep first, but I wasn't, and lay there for hours trying to decide whether that front pattern and the back pattern really did move together or separately.

140     On a pattern like this, by daylight, there is a lack of sequence, a defiance of law, that is a constant irritant to a normal mind.

The color is hideous enough, and unreliable enough, and infuriating enough, but the pattern is torturing.

You think you have mastered it, but just as you get well under way in following, it turns a back-somersault and there you are. It slaps you in the face, knocks you down, and tramples upon you. It is like a bad dream.

The outside pattern is a florid arabesque, reminding one of a fungus. If you can imagine a toadstool in joints an interminable string of toadstools, budding and sprouting in endless convolutions—why, that is something like it.

That is, sometimes!

145     There is one marked peculiarity about this paper, a thing nobody seems to notice but myself, and that is that it changes as the light changes.

When the sun shoots in through the east window—I always watch for that first long, straight ray—it changes so quickly than I never can quite believe it.

That is why I watch it always.

By moonlight—the moon shines in all night when there is a moon—I wouldn't know it was the same paper.

At night in any kind of light, in twilight, candlelight, lamplight, and worst of all by moonlight, it becomes bars! The outside pattern, I mean, and the woman behind it is as plain as can be.

150     I didn't realize for a long time what the thing was that showed behind, that dim sub-pattern, but now I am quite sure it is a woman.

By daylight she is subdued, quiet. I fancy it is the pattern that keeps her so still. It is so puzzling. It keeps me quiet by the hour.

I lie down ever so much now. John says it is good for me, and to sleep all I can.

Indeed he started the habit by making me lie down for an hour after each meal.

It is a very bad habit, I am convinced, for you see, I don't sleep.

155     And that cultivates deceit, for I don't tell them I'm awake—oh, no!

The fact is I am getting a little afraid of John.

He seems very queer sometimes, and even Jennie has an inexplicable look.

It strikes me occasionally, just as a scientific hypothesis, that perhaps it is the paper!

I have watched John when he did not know I was looking, and come into the room suddenly on the most innocent excuses, and I've caught him several times *looking at the paper*! And Jennie too. I caught Jennie with her hand on it once.

160     She didn't know I was in the room, and when I asked her in a quiet, a very quiet voice, with the most restrained manner possible, what she was doing with the paper, she turned around as if she had been caught stealing, and looked quite angry—asked me why I should frighten her so!

Then she said that the paper stained everything it touched, that she had found yellow smooches on all my clothes and John's and she wished we would be more careful!

Did not that sound innocent? But I know she was studying that pattern, and I am determined that nobody shall find it out but myself.

Life is very much more exciting now than it used to be. You see, I have something more to expect, to look forward to, to watch. I really do eat better, and am more quiet than I was.

John is so pleased to see me improve! He laughed a little the other day, and said I seemed to be flourishing in spite of my wallpaper.

I turned it off with a laugh. I had no intention of telling him it was *because* of the 165
wallpaper—he would make fun of me. He might even want to take me away.

I don't want to leave now until I have found it out. There is a week more, and I think that
will be enough.

I'm feeling so much better!

I don't sleep much at night, for it is so interesting to watch developments; but sleep a
good deal during the daytime.

In the daytime it is tiresome and perplexing.

There are always new shoots on the fungus, and new shades of yellow all over it. I cannot 170
keep count of them, though I have tried conscientiously.

It is the strangest yellow, that wallpaper! It makes me think of all the yellow things I ever
saw—not beautiful ones like buttercups, but old, foul, bad yellow things.

But there is something else about that paper—the smell! I noticed it the moment we came
into the room, but with so much air and sun it was not bad. Now we have had a week of fog
and rain, and whether the windows are open or not, the smell is here.

It creeps all over the house.

I find it hovering in the dining-room, skulking in the parlor, hiding in the hall, lying in
wait for me on the stairs.

It gets into my hair.                                                                    175

Even when I go to ride, if I turn my head suddenly and surprise it—there is that smell!

Such a peculiar odor, too! I have spent hours in trying to analyze it, to find what it smelled
like.

It is not bad—at first—and very gentle, but quite the subtlest, most enduring odor I ever
met.

In this damp weather it is awful. I wake up in the night and find it hanging over me.

It used to disturb me at first. I thought seriously of burning the house—to reach the 180
smell.

But now I am used to it. The only thing I can think of that it is like is the *color* of the paper!
A yellow smell.

There is a very funny mark on this wall, low down, near the mopboard. A streak that runs
round the room. It goes behind every piece of furniture, except the bed, a long, straight, even
*smooch*, as if it had been rubbed over and over.

I wonder how it was done and who did it, and what they did it for. Round and round and
round—round and round and round—it makes me dizzy!

I really have discovered something at last.

Through watching so much at night, when it changes so, I have finally found out.        185

The front pattern *does* move—and no wonder! The woman behind shakes it!

Sometimes I think there are a great many women behind, and sometimes only one, and
she crawls around fast, and her crawling shakes it all over.

Then in the very bright spots she keeps still, and in the very shady spots she just takes
hold of the bars and shakes them hard.

And she is all the time trying to climb through. But nobody could climb through that
pattern—it strangles so; I think that is why it has so many heads.

They get through and then the pattern strangles them off and turns them upside down, 190
and makes their eyes white!

If those heads were covered or taken off it would not be half so bad.

I think that woman gets out in the daytime!

And I'll tell you why—privately—I've seen her!

I can see her out of every one of my windows!

It is the same woman, I know, for she is always creeping, and most women do not creep 195
by daylight.

I see her in that long shaded lane, creeping up and down. I see her in those dark grape arbors, creeping all around the garden.

I see her on that long road under the trees, creeping along, and when a carriage comes she hides under the blackberry vines.

I don't blame her a bit. It must be very humiliating to be caught creeping by daylight!

I always lock the door when I creep by daylight. I can't do it at night, for I know John would suspect something at once.

200 And John is so queer now that I don't want to irritate him. I wish he would take another room! Besides, I don't want anybody to get that woman out at night but myself.

I often wonder if I could see her out of all the windows at once.

But, turn as fast as I can, I can only see out of one at a time.

And though I always see her, she *may* be able to creep faster than I can turn! I have watched her sometimes away off in the open country, creeping as fast as a cloud shadow in a wind.

If only that top pattern could be gotten off from the under one! I mean to try it, little by little.

205 I have found out another funny thing, but I shan't tell it this time! It does not do to trust people too much.

There are only two more days to get this paper off, and I believe John is beginning to notice. I don't like the look in his eyes.

And I heard him ask Jennie a lot of professional questions about me. She had a very good report to give.

She said I slept a good deal in the daytime.

John knows I don't sleep very well at night, for all I'm so quiet!

210 He asked me all sorts of questions, too, and pretended to be very loving and kind.

As if I couldn't see through him!

Still, I don't wonder he acts so, sleeping under this paper for three months.

It only interests me, but I feel sure John and Jennie are affected by it.

Hurrah! This is the last day, but it is enough. John is to stay in town over night, and won't be out until this evening.

215 Jennie wanted to sleep with me—the sly thing; but I told her I should undoubtedly rest better for a night all alone.

That was clever, for really I wasn't alone a bit! As soon as it was moonlight and that poor thing began to crawl and shake the pattern, I got up and ran to help her.

I pulled and she shook. I shook and she pulled, and before morning we had peeled off yards of that paper.

A strip about as high as my head and half around the room.

And then when the sun came and that awful pattern began to laugh at me, I declared I would finish it today!

220 We go away tomorrow, and they are moving all my furniture down again to leave things as they were before.

Jennie looked at the wall in amazement, but I told her merrily that I did it out of pure spite at the vicious thing.

She laughed and said she wouldn't mind doing it herself, but I must not get tired.

How she betrayed herself that time!

But I am here, and no person touches this paper but Me—not *alive*!

225 She tried to get me out of the room—it was too patent! But I said it was so quiet and empty and clean now that I believed I would lie down again and sleep all I could, and not to wake me even for dinner—I would call when I woke.

So now she is gone, and the servants are gone, and the things are gone, and there is nothing left but that great bedstead nailed down, with the canvas mattress we found on it.

We shall sleep downstairs tonight, and take the boat home tomorrow.

I quite enjoy the room, now it is bare again.

How those children did tear about here!

This bedstead is fairly gnawed!

But I must get to work.

I have locked the door and thrown the key down into the front path.

I don't want to go out, and I don't want to have anybody come in, till John comes.

I want to astonish him.

I've got a rope up here that even Jennie did not find. If that woman does get out, and tries to get away, I can tie her!

But I forgot I could not reach far without anything to stand on!

This bed will *not* move!

I tried to lift and push it until I was lame, and then I got so angry I bit off a little piece at one corner—but it hurt my teeth.

Then I peeled off all the paper I could reach standing on the floor. It sticks horribly and the pattern just enjoys it! All those strangled heads and bulbous eyes and waddling fungus growths just shriek with derision!

I am getting angry enough to do something desperate. To jump out of the window would be admirable exercise, but the bars are too strong even to try.

Besides I wouldn't do it. Of course not. I know well enough that a step like that is improper and might be misconstrued.

I don't like to *look* out of the windows even—there are so many of those creeping women, and they creep so fast.

I wonder if they all came out of that wallpaper as I did?

But I am securely fastened now by my well-hidden rope—you don't get *me* out in the road there!

I suppose I shall have to get back behind the pattern when it comes night, and that is hard!

It is so pleasant to be out in this great room and creep around as I please!

I don't want to go outside. I won't, even if Jennie asks me to.

For outside you have to creep on the ground, and everything is green instead of yellow.

But here I can creep smoothly on the floor, and my shoulder just fits in that long smooch around the wall, so I cannot lose my way.

Why, there's John at the door!

It is no use, young man, you can't open it!

How he does call and pound!

Now he's crying to Jennie for an axe.

It would be a shame to break down that beautiful door!

"John, dear!" said I in the gentlest voice. "The key is down by the front steps, under a plantain leaf!"

That silenced him for a few moments.

Then he said, very quietly indeed, "Open the door, my darling!"

"I can't," said I. "The key is down by the front door under a plantain leaf!" And then I said it again, several times, very gently and slowly, and said it so often that he had to go and see, and he got it of course, and came in. He stopped short by the door.

"What is the matter?" he cried. "For God's sake, what are you doing!"

I kept on creeping just the same, but I looked at him over my shoulder.

"I've got out at last," said I, "in spite of you and Jane. And I've pulled off most of the paper, so you can't put me back!"

Now why should that man have fainted? But he did, and right across my path by the wall, so that I had to creep over him every time!

## Questions

1. Describe the point of view of "The Yellow Wallpaper." How consistent is the point of view? How is the story told? To whom does the narrator seem to be speaking? How does the narrator change as the story progresses?

2. How much time elapses in the story? How well does this passage of time explain what is happening to the narrator?

3. What is the narrator's connection to the room's wallpaper? What has she obviously been doing in the course of the story? What does this show about her mental condition?

4. How effectively can a case be made that the "treatment" the narrator receives is actually the cause of her mental disturbance, which is so evident at the story's end?

## FLANNERY O'CONNOR (1925–1964)

Mary Flannery O'Connor, a Georgia native, graduated from the Women's College of Georgia and received a master of fine arts degree from the University of Iowa in 1947. She contracted lupus, a disorder of the immune system, and was an invalid for the last ten years of her life. Despite her illness, she wrote extensively, publishing two novels and many short stories. Her first collection was *A Good Man Is Hard to Find*, in 1955. A posthumous collection, *Everything That Rises Must Converge*, was published in 1965, and *Complete Stories* appeared in 1971. Her works combine flat realism with grotesque situations; violence occurs without apparent reason or preparation. Many of her characters are odd, eccentric, and bizarre. Others, such as the Misfit in "A Good Man Is Hard to Find," are gratuitously cruel. Ironically, however, their cold and depraved actions highlight the need for religious awakening because they enable some of the characters, such as the grandmother in the following story, to achieve spiritual elevation.

##  A Good Man Is Hard to Find (1955)

The grandmother didn't want to go to Florida. She wanted to visit some of her connections in east Tennessee and she was seizing at every chance to change Bailey's mind. Bailey was the son she lived with, her only son. He was sitting on the edge of his chair at the table, bent over the orange sports section of the *Journal*. "Now look here, Bailey," she said, "see here, read this," and she stood with one hand on her thin hip and the other rattling the newspaper at his bald head. "Here this fellow that calls himself The Misfit is aloose from the Federal Pen and headed toward Florida and you read here what it says he did to these people. Just you read it I wouldn't take my children in any direction with a criminal like that aloose in it. I couldn't answer to my conscience if I did."

Bailey didn't look up from his reading so she wheeled around then and faced the children's mother, a young woman in slacks, whose face was as broad and innocent as a cabbage and was tied round with a green head-kerchief that had two points on the top like rabbit's ears. She was sitting on the sofa, feeding the baby his apricots out of a jar. "The children have been to Florida before," the old lady said. "You all ought to take them somewhere else for a change so they would see different parts of the world and be broad. They never have been to east Tennessee."

The children's mother didn't seem to hear her but the eight-year-old boy, John Wesley, a stocky child with glasses, said, "If you don't want to go to Florida, why dontcha stay at home?" He and the little girl, June Star, were reading the funny papers on the floor.

"She wouldn't stay at home to be queen for a day," June Star said without raising her yellow head.

"Yes and what would you do if this fellow, The Misfit, caught you?" the grandmother asked.                                                                                            5

"I'd smack his face," John Wesley said.

"She wouldn't stay at home for a million bucks." June Star said. "Afraid she'd miss something. She has to go everywhere we go."

"All right, Miss," the grandmother said. "Just remember that the next time you want me to curl your hair."

June Star said her hair was naturally curly.

The next morning the grandmother was the first one in the car, ready to go. She had her   10
big black valise that looked like the head of a hippopotamus in one corner, and underneath it she was hiding a basket with Pitty Sing, the cat, in it. She didn't intend for the cat to be left alone in the house for three days because he would miss her too much and she was afraid he might brush against one of the gas burners and accidentally asphyxiate himself. Her son, Bailey, didn't like to arrive at a motel with a cat.

She sat in the middle of the back seat with John Wesley and June Star on either side of her. Bailey and the children's mother and the baby sat in the front and they left Atlanta at eight forty-five with the mileage on the car at 55890. The grandmother wrote this down because she thought it would be interesting to say how many miles they had been when they got back. It took them twenty minutes to reach the outskirts of the city.

The old lady settled herself comfortably, removing her white cotton gloves and putting them up with her purse on the shelf in front of the back window. The children's mother still had on slacks and still had her head tied up in a green kerchief, but the grandmother had on a navy blue straw sailor hat with a bunch of white violets on the brim and a navy blue dress with a small white dot in the print. Her collar and cuffs were white organdy trimmed with lace and at her neckline she had pinned a purple spray of cloth violets containing a sachet. In case of an accident, anyone seeing her dead on the highway would know at once that she was a lady.

She said she thought it was going to be a good day for driving, neither too hot nor too cold, and she cautioned Bailey that the speed limit was fifty-five miles an hour and that the patrolmen hid themselves behind billboards and small clumps of trees and sped out after you before you had a chance to slow down. She pointed out interesting details of the scenery: Stone Mountain; the blue granite that in some places came up to both sides of the highway; the brilliant red clay banks slightly streaked with purple; and the various crops that made rows of green lacework on the ground. The trees were full of silver-white sunlight and the meanest of them sparkled. The children were reading comic magazines and their mother had gone back to sleep.

"Let's go through Georgia fast so we won't have to look at it much," John Wesley said.

"If I were a little boy," said the grandmother. "I wouldn't talk about my native state that   15
way. Tennessee has the mountains and Georgia has the hills."

"Tennessee is just a hillbilly dumping ground," John Wesley said, "and Georgia is a lousy state too."

"You said it," June Star said.

"In my time," said the grandmother, folding her thin veined fingers, "children were more respectful of their native states and their parents and everything else. People did right then. Oh look at the cute little pickaninny!" she said and pointed to a Negro child standing in the door of a shack. "Wouldn't that make a picture, now?" she asked and they all turned and looked at the little Negro out of the back window. He waved.

"He didn't have any britches on," June said.

20    "He probably didn't have any," the grandmother explained. "Little niggers in the country don't have things like we do. If I could paint, I'd paint that picture," she said.

The children exchanged comic books.

The grandmother offered to hold the baby and the children's mother passed him over the front seat to her. She set him on her knee and bounced him and told him about the things they were passing. She rolled her eyes and screwed up her mouth and stuck her leathery thin face into his smooth bland one. Occasionally he gave her a faraway smile. They passed a large cotton field with five or six graves fenced in the middle of it, like a small island. "Look at the graveyard!" the grandmother said, pointing it out. "That was the old family burying ground. That belonged to the plantation."

"Where's the plantation?" John Wesley asked.

"Gone With the Wind," said the grandmother. "Ha. Ha."

25    When the children finished all the comic books they had brought, they opened the lunch and ate it. The grandmother ate a peanut butter sandwich and an olive and would not let the children throw the box and the paper napkins out the window. When there was nothing else to do they played a game by choosing a cloud and making the other two guess what shape it suggested. John Wesley took one the shape of a cow and June Star guessed a cow and John Wesley said, no, an automobile, and June Star said he didn't play fair, and they began to slap each other over the grandmother.

The grandmother said she would tell them a story if they would keep quiet. When she told a story, she rolled her eyes and waved her head and was very dramatic. She said once when she was a maiden lady she had been courted by a Mr. Edgar Atkins Teagarden from Jasper, Georgia. She said he was a very good-looking man and a gentleman and that he brought her a watermelon every Saturday afternoon with his initials cut in it, E. A. T. Well, one Saturday, she said, Mr. Teagarden brought the watermelon and there was nobody at home and he left it on the front porch and returned in his buggy to Jasper, but she never got the watermelon, she said, because a nigger boy ate it when he saw the initials, E. A. T.! This story tickled John Wesley's funny bone and he giggled and giggled but June Star didn't think it was any good. She said she wouldn't marry a man that just brought her a watermelon on Saturday. The grandmother said she would have done well to marry Mr. Teagarden because he was a gentleman and had bought Coca-Cola stock when it first came out and that he had died only a few years ago, a very wealthy man.

They stopped at The Tower for barbecued sandwiches. The Tower was a part stucco and part wood filling station and dance hall set in a clearing outside of Timothy. A fat man named Red Sammy Butts ran it and there were signs stuck here and there on the building and for miles up and down the highway saying, TRY RED SAMMY'S FAMOUS BARBECUE. NONE LIKE FAMOUS RED SAMMY'S! RED SAM! THE FAT BOY WITH THE HAPPY LAUGH A VETERAN! SAMMY'S YOUR MAN!

Red Sammy was lying on the bare ground outside The Tower with his head under a truck while a gray monkey about a foot high, chained to a small chinaberry tree, chattered nearby. The monkey sprang back into the tree and got on the highest limb as soon as he saw the children jump out of the car and run toward him.

Inside, The Tower was a long dark room with a counter at one end and tables at the other and dancing space in the middle. They all sat down at a broad table next to the nickelodeon and Red Sam's wife, a tall burnt-brown woman with hair and eyes lighter than her skin, came and took their order. The children's mother put a dime in the machine and played "The Tennessee Waltz," and the grandmother said the tune always made her want to dance. She asked Bailey if he would like to dance but he only glared at her. He didn't have a naturally sunny disposition like she did and trips made him nervous. The grandmother's brown eyes were very bright. She swayed her head from side to side and pretended she was dancing in her chair. June Star said play something she could tap to so the children's mother put in another dime and played a fast number and June Star stepped out onto the dance floor and did her up routine.

"Ain't she cute?" Red Sam's wife said, leaning over the counter. "Would you like to come 30 be my little girl?"

"No I certainly wouldn't," June Star said. "I wouldn't live in a broken-down place like this for a million bucks!" and she ran back to the table.

"Ain't she cute?" the woman repeated, stretching her mouth politely.

"Aren't you ashamed?" hissed her grandmother.

Red Sam came in and told his wife to quit lounging on the counter and hurry with these people's order. His khaki trousers reached just to his hip bones and his stomach hung over them like a sack of meal swaying under his shirt. He came over and sat down at a table nearby and let out a combination sigh and yodel, "You can't win," he said. "You can't win," and he wiped his sweating red face with a gray handkerchief. "These days you don't know who to trust," he said. "Ain't that the truth?"

"People are certainly not nice like they used to be," said the grandmother. 35

"Two fellers come in here last week," Red Sammy said, "driving a Chrysler. It was a old beat-up car but it was a good one and these boys looked all right to me. Said they worked at the mill and you know I let them fellers charge the gas they bought? Now why did I do that?"

"Because you're a good man!" the grandmother said at once.

"Yes'm, I suppose so," Red Sam said as if he were struck with the answer.

His wife brought the orders, carrying the five plates all at once without a tray, two in each hand and one balanced on her arm. "It isn't a soul in this green world of God's that you can trust," she said. "And I don't count anybody out of that, not nobody," she repeated, looking at Red Sammy.

"Did you read about that criminal, The Misfit, that's escaped?" asked the grandmother. 40

"I wouldn't be a bit surprised if he didn't attack this place right here," said the woman. "If he hears about it being here, I wouldn't be none surprised to see him. If he hears it's two cent in the cash register, I wouldn't be a tall surprised if he . . ."

"That'll do," Red Sam said, "Go bring these people their Co'Colas," and the woman went off to get the rest of the order.

"A good man is hard to find." Red Sammy said. "Everything is getting terrible. I remember the day you could go off and leave your screen door unlatched. Not no more."

He and the grandmother discussed better times. The old lady said that in her opinion Europe was entirely to blame for the way things were now. She said the way Europe acted you would think we were made of money and Red Sam said it was no use talking about it, she was exactly right. The children ran outside into the white sunlight and looked at the monkey in the lacy chinaberry tree. He was busy catching fleas on himself and biting each one carefully between his teeth as if it were a delicacy.

They drove off again into the hot afternoon. The grandmother took cat naps and woke up 45 every few minutes with her own snoring. Outside of Toombsboro she woke up and recalled an old plantation that she had visited in this neighborhood once when she was a young lady. She said the house had six white columns across the front and that there was an avenue of oaks leading up to it and two little wooden trellis arbors on either side in front where you sat down with your suitor after a stroll in the garden. She recalled exactly which road to turn off to get to it. She knew that Bailey would not be willing to lose any time looking at an old house, but the more she talked about it, the more she wanted to see it once again and find out if the little twin arbors were still standing. "There was a secret panel in this house," she said craftily, not telling the truth but wishing that she were, "and the story went that all the family silver was hidden in it when Sherman° came through but it was never found . . ."

"Hey!" John Wesley said, "Let's go see it! We'll find it! We'll poke all the woodwork and find it! Who lives there? Where do you turn off at? Hey Pop, can't we turn off there?"

---

°*Sherman*: William Tecumseh Sherman (1820–1892), Union general during the Civil War.

"We never have seen a house with a secret panel!" June Star shrieked, "Let's go to the house with the secret panel! Hey, Pop, can't we go see the house with the secret panel!"

"It's not far from here, I know," the grandmother said. "It wouldn't take over twenty minutes."

Bailey was looking straight ahead. His jaw was as rigid as a horseshoe. "No," he said.

50    The children began to yell and scream that they wanted to see the house with the secret panel. John Wesley kicked the back of the front seat and June Star hung over her mother's shoulder and whined desperately into her ear that they never had any fun even on their vacation, and that they could never do what THEY wanted to do. The baby began to scream and John Wesley kicked the back of the seat so hard that his father could feel the blows in his kidney.

"All right!" he shouted, and drew the car to a stop at the side of the road. "Will you all shut up? Will you all just shut up for one second? If you don't shut up, we won't go anywhere."

"It would be very educational for them," the grandmother murmured.

"All right," Bailey said, "but get this: this is the only time we're going to stop for anything like this. This is the one and only time."

"The dirt road that you have to turn down is about a mile back," the grandmother directed. "I marked it when we passed."

55    "A dirt road," Bailey groaned.

After they had turned around and were headed toward the dirt road, the grandmother recalled other points about the house, the beautiful glass over the front doorway and the candlelamp in the hall. John Wesley said that the secret panel was probably in the fireplace.

"You can't go inside this house," Bailey said. "You don't know who lives there."

"While you all talk to the people in front, I'll run around behind and get in a window," John Wesley suggested.

"We'll all stay in the car," his mother said.

60    They turned onto the dirt road and the car raced roughly along in swirl of pink dust. The grandmother recalled the times when there were no paved roads and thirty miles was a day's journey. The dirt road was hilly and there were sudden washes in it and sharp curves on dangerous embankments. All at once they would be on a hill, looking down over the blue tops of trees for miles around, then the next minute, they would be in a red depression with the dust-coated trees looking down on them.

"This place had better turn up in a minute," Bailey said, "or I'm going to turn around."

The road looked as if no one had traveled on it in months.

"It's not much farther," the grandmother said and just as she said it, a horrible thought came to her. The thought was so embarrassing that she turned red in the face and her eyes dilated and her feet jumped up, upsetting her valise in the corner. The instant the valise moved, the newspaper top she had over the basket under it rose with a smart and Pitty Sing, the cat, sprang onto Bailey's shoulder.

The children were thrown to the floor and their mother, clutching the baby, was thrown out the door onto the ground; the old lady was thrown into the front seat. The car turned over once and landed right-side-up in a gulch on the side of the road. Bailey remained in the driver's seat with the cat—gray-striped with a broad white face and an orange nose—clinging to his neck like a caterpillar.

65    As soon as the children saw they could move their arms and legs, they scrambled out of the car, shouting, "We've had an ACCIDENT!" The grandmother was curled up under the dashboard, hoping she was injured so that Bailey's wrath would not come down on her all at once. The horrible thought she had had before the accident was that the house she had remembered so vividly was not in Georgia but in Tennessee.

Bailey removed the cat from his neck with both hands and flung it out the window against the side of a pine tree. Then he got out of the car and started looking for the children's mother. She was sitting against the side of the red gutted ditch, holding the screaming baby, but she only had a cut down her face and a broken shoulder. "We've had an ACCIDENT!" the children screamed in a frenzy of delight.

"But nobody's killed," June Star said with disappointment as the grandmother limped out of the car, her hat still pinned to her head but the broken front brim standing up at a jaunty angle and the violet spray hanging off the side. They all sat down in the ditch, except the children, to recover from the shock. They were all shaking.

"Maybe a car will come along," said the children's mother hoarsely.

"I believe I have injured an organ," said the grandmother, pressing her side, but no one answered her. Bailey's teeth were clattering. He had on a yellow sport shirt with bright blue parrots designed in it and his face was as yellow as the shirt. The grandmother decided that she would not mention that the house was in Tennessee.

The road was about ten feet above and they could see only the tops of the trees on the    70
other side of it. Behind the ditch they were sitting in there were more woods, tall and dark and deep. In a few minutes they saw a car some distance away on top of a hill, coming slowly as if the occupants were watching them. The grandmother stood up and waved both arms dramatically to attract their attention. The car continued to come on slowly, disappeared around a bend and appeared again, moving even slower, on top of the hill they had gone over. It was a big black battered hearse-like automobile. There were three men in it.

It came to a stop just over them and for some minutes, the driver looked down with a steady expressionless gaze to where they were sitting, and didn't speak. Then he turned his head and muttered something to the other two and they got out. One was a fat boy in black trousers and a red sweat shirt with a silver stallion embossed on the front of it. He moved around on the right side of them and stood staring, his mouth partly open in a kind of loose grin. The other had on khaki pants and a blue striped coat and a gray hat pulled down very low, hiding most of his face. He came around slowly on the left side. Neither spoke.

The driver got out of the car and stood by the side of it, looking down at them. He was an older man than the other two. His hair was just beginning to gray and he wore silver-rimmed spectacles that gave him a scholarly look. He had a long creased face and didn't have on any shirt or undershirt. He had on blue jeans that were too tight for him and was holding a black hat and a gun. The two boys also had guns.

"We've had an ACCIDENT!" the children screamed.

The grandmother had the peculiar feeling that the bespectacled man was someone she knew. His face was as familiar to her as if she had known him all her life but she could not recall who he was. He moved away from the car and began to come down the embankment, placing his feet carefully so that he wouldn't slip. He had on tan and white shoes and no socks, and his ankles were red and thin. "Good afternoon," he said. "I see you all had a little spill."

"We turned over twice!" said the grandmother.    75

"Oncet," he corrected. "We seen it happen. Try their car and see will it run, Hiram," he said quietly to the boy with the gray hat.

"What you got that gun for?" John Wesley asked. "Whatcha gonna do with that gun?"

"Lady," the man said to the children's mother, "would you mind calling them children to sit down by you? Children make me nervous. I want all you all to set down right together there where you're at."

"What are you telling us what to do for?" June Star asked.

Behind them the line of woods gaped like a dark, open mouth. "Come here," said their    80
mother.

"Look here now," Bailey began suddenly, "we're in a predicament! We're in . . ."

The grandmother shrieked. She scrambled to her feet and stood staring. "You're The Misfit!" she said. "I recognized you at once."

"Yes'm," the man said, smiling slightly at if he were pleased in spite of himself to be known, "but it would have been better for all of you, lady, if you hadn't reckernized me."

Bailey turned his head sharply and said something to his mother that shocked even the children. The old lady began to cry and The Misfit reddened.

85   "Lady," he said, "don't you get upset: Sometimes a man says things he don't mean. I don't reckon he meant to talk to you thataway."

"You wouldn't shoot a lady, would you?" the grandmother said and removed a clean handkerchief from her cuff and began to slap at her eyes with it.

The Misfit pointed the toe of his shoe into the ground and made a little hole and then covered it up again. "I would hate to have to," he said.

"Listen," the grandmother almost screamed, "I know you're a good man. You don't look a bit like you have common blood. I know you must come from nice people!"

"Yes mam," he said, "finest people in the world." When he smiled he showed a row of strong white teeth. "God never made a finer woman than my mother and my daddy's heart was pure gold," he said. The boy with the red sweat shirt had come around behind them and was standing with his gun at his hip. The Misfit squatted down on the ground. "Watch them children, Bobby Lee," he said. "You know they make me nervous." He looked at the six of them huddled together in front of him and he seemed to be embarrassed as it he couldn't think if anything to say. "Ain't a cloud in the sky," he remarked, looking up at it. "Don't see no sun but don't see no cloud neither."

90   "Yes, it's a beautiful day," said the grandmother. "Listen," she said, "you shouldn't call yourself The Misfit because I know you're a good man at heart. I can just look at you and tell."

"Hush!" Bailey yelled. "Hush! Everybody shut up and let me handle this!" He was squatting in the position of a runner about to sprint forward but he didn't move.

"I pre-chate that, lady," The Misfit said and drew a little circle in the ground with the butt of his gun.

"It'll take a half a hour to fix this here car," Hiram called, looking over the raised hood of it.

"Well, first you and Bobby Lee get him and that little boy to step over yonder with you," The Misfit said, pointing to Bailey and John Wesley. "The boys want to ask you something," he said to Bailey. "Would you mind stepping back in them woods there with them?"

95   "Listen," Bailey began, "we're in a terrible predicament. Nobody realizes what this is," and his voice cracked. His eyes were as blue and intense as the parrots in his shirt and he remained perfectly still.

The grandmother reached up to adjust her hat brim as if she were going to the woods with him but it came off in her hand. She stood staring at it and after a second she let it fall to the ground. Hiram pulled Bailey up by the arm as if he were assisting an old man. John Wesley caught hold of his father's hand and Bobby Lee followed. They went off toward the woods and just as they reached the dark edge. Bailey turned and supporting himself against a gray naked pine trunk, he shouted, "I'll be back in a minute, Mamma, wait on me!"

"Come back this instant!" his mother shrilled but they all disappeared into the woods.

"Bailey Boy!" the grandmother called in a tragic voice but she found she was looking at The Misfit squatting on the ground in front of her. "I just know you're a good man," she said desperately. "You're not a bit common!"

"Nome, I ain't a good man," The Misfit said after a second as if he had considered her statement carefully, "but I ain't the worst in the world neither. My daddy said I was different breed of dog from my brothers and sisters. 'You know,' Daddy said, 'it's some that can live their whole life out without asking about it and it's others has to know why it is, and this boy is one of the latters. He's going to be into everything!'" He put on his black hat and looked up suddenly and then away deep into the woods as if he were embarrassed again. "I'm sorry I don't have on a shirt before you ladies," he said, hunching his shoulders slightly. "We buried our clothes that we had on when we escaped and we're just making do until we can get better. We borrowed these from some folks we met," he explained.

"That's perfectly all right," the grandmother said. "Maybe Bailey has an extra shirt in his suitcase." 100

"I'll look and see terrectly," the Misfit said.

"Where are they taking him?" the children's mother screamed.

"Daddy was a card himself," the Misfit said. "You couldn't put anything over on him. He never got in trouble with the Authorities though. Just had the knack of handling them."

"You could be honest too if you'd only try," said the grandmother. "Think how wonderful it would be to settle down and live a comfortable life and not have to think about somebody chasing you all the time."

The Misfit kept scratching in the ground with the butt of his gun as if he were thinking 105 about it. "Yes'm, somebody is always after you," he murmured.

The grandmother noticed how thin his shoulder blades were just behind his hat because she was standing up looking down on him. "Do you ever pray?" she asked.

He shook his head. All she saw was the black hat wiggle between his shoulder blades. "Nome," he said.

There was a pistol shot from the woods, followed closely by another. Then silence. The old lady's head jerked around. She could hear the wind move through the tree tops like a long satisfied insuck of breath. "Bailey Boy!" she called.

"I was a gospel singer for a while," The Misfit said. "I been most everything. Been in the arm service, both land and sea, at home and abroad, been twicet married, been an undertaker, been with the railroads, plowed Mother Earth, been in a tornado, seen a man burnt alive oncet," and he looked up at the children's mother and the little girl who were sitting close together, their faces white and their eyes glassy; "I even seen a woman flogged," he said.

"Pray, pray," the grandmother began, "pray, pray . . ." 110

"I never was a bad boy that I remember of," The Misfit said in an almost dreamy voice, "but somewheres along the line I done something wrong and got sent to the penitentiary. I was buried alive," and he looked up and held her attention to him by a steady stare.

"That's when you should have started to pray," she said. "What did you do to get sent to the penitentiary that first time?"

"Turn to the right, it was a wall," The Misfit said, looking up again at the cloudless sky. "Turn to the left, it was a wall. Look up it was a ceiling, look down it was a floor. I forgot what I done, lady. I set there and set there, trying to remember what it was I done and I ain't recalled it to this day. Oncet in a while, I would think it was coming to me, but it never come."

"Maybe they put you in by mistake," the old lady said vaguely.

"Nome," he said. "It wasn't no mistake. They had the papers on me." 115

"You must have stolen something," she said.

The Misfit sneered slightly. "Nobody had nothing I wanted," he said. "It was a head-doctor at the penitentiary said what I had done was kill my daddy but I know that for a lie. My daddy died in nineteen ought nineteen of the epidemic flu and I never had a thing to do with it. He was buried in the Mount Hopewell Baptist churchyard and you can go there and see for yourself."

"If you would pray," the old lady said, "Jesus would help you."

"That's right," The Misfit said.

"Well then, why don't you pray?" she asked trembling with delight suddenly. 120

"I don't want no hep," he said. "I'm doing all right by myself."

Bobby Lee and Hiram came ambling back from the woods. Bobby Lee was dragging a yellow shirt with bright blue parrots in it.

"Throw me that shirt, Bobby Lee," The Misfit said. The shirt came flying at him and landed on his shoulder and he put it on. The grandmother couldn't name what the shirt reminded her of. "No, lady," The Misfit said while he was buttoning it up. "I found out the crime don't matter. You can do one thing or you can do another, kill a man or take a tire off his car, because sooner or later you're going to forget what it was you done and just be punished for it."

The children's mother had begun to make heaving noises as if she couldn't get her breath. "Lady," he asked, "would you and that little girl like to step off yonder with Bobby Lee and Hiram and join your husband?"

125     "Yes, thank you," the mother said faintly. Her left arm dangled helplessly and she was holding the baby, who had gone to sleep, in the other. "Hep that lady up, Hiram," The Misfit said as she struggled to climb out of the ditch, "and Bobby Lee, you hold onto that little girl's hand."

"I don't want to hold hands with him," June Star said. "He reminds me of a pig."

The fat boy blushed and laughed and caught her by the arm and pulled her off into the woods after Hiram and her mother.

Alone with The Misfit, the grandmother found that she had lost her voice. There was not a cloud in the sky nor any sun. There was nothing around her but woods. She wanted to tell him that he must pray. She opened and closed her mouth several times before anything came out. Finally she found herself saying, "Jesus, Jesus," meaning Jesus will help you, but the way she was saying it, it sounded as if she might be cursing.

"Yes'm," The Misfit said as if he agreed. "Jesus thown everything off balance. It was the same case with Him as with me except He hadn't committed any crime and they could prove I had committed one because they had the papers on me. Of course," he said, "they never shown me any papers. That's why I sign myself now. I said long ago, you get you a signature and sign everything you do and keep a copy of it. Then you'll know what you done and you can hold up the crime to the punishment and see do they match and in the end you'll have something to prove you ain't been treated right. I call myself The Misfit," he said, "because I can't make what all I done wrong fit what all I gone through in punishment."

130     There was a piercing scream from the woods, followed closely by a pistol report. "Does it seem right to you, lady, that one is punished a heap and another ain't punished at all?"

"Jesus!" the old lady cried. "You've got good blood! I know you wouldn't shoot a lady! I know you come from nice people! Pray! Jesus, you ought not to shoot a lady: I'll give you all the money I've got!"

"Lady," The Misfit said, looking beyond her far into the woods, "there never was a body that give the undertaker a tip."

There were two more pistol reports and the grandmother raised her head like a parched old turkey hen crying for water and called, "Bailey Boy, Bailey Boy!" as if her heart would break.

"Jesus was the only One that ever raised the dead," The Misfit continued, "and He shouldn't have done it. He thown everything off balance. If He did what He said then it's nothing for you to do but thow away everything and follow Him, and if He didn't, then it's nothing for you to do but enjoy the few minutes you got left the best way you can—by killing somebody or burning down his house or doing some other meanness to him. No pleasure but meanness," he said and his voice had become almost a snarl.

135     "Maybe He didn't raise the dead," the old lady mumbled, not knowing what she was saying and feeling so dizzy that she sank down in the ditch with her legs twisted under her.

"I wasn't there so I can't say He didn't." The Misfit said, "I wisht I had of been there," he said, hitting the ground with his fist. "It ain't right I wasn't there because if I had of been there

I would of known. Listen lady," he said in a high voice, "if I had of been there I would of known and I wouldn't be like I am now." His voice seemed about to crack and the grandmother's head cleared for an instant. She saw the man's face twisted close to her own as if he were going to cry and she murmured, "Why you're one of my babies. You're one of my own children!" She reached out and touched him on the shoulder. The Misfit sprang back as if a snake had bitten him and shot her three times through the chest. Then he put his gun down on the ground and took off his glasses, and began to clean them.

Hiram and Bobby Lee returned from the woods and stood over the ditch, looking down at the grandmother who half sat and half lay in a puddle of blood with her legs crossed under her like a child's and her face smiling up at the cloudless sky.

Without his glasses, The Misfit's eyes were red-rimmed and pale and defenseless-looking. "Take her off and thow her where you thown the others," he said, picking up the cat that was rubbing itself against his leg.

"She was a talker, wasn't she?" Bobby Lee said, sliding down the ditch with a yodel.

"She would of been a good woman," The Misfit said, "if it had been somebody there to 140 shoot her every minute of her life."

"Some fun!" Bobby Lee said.

"Shut up, Bobby Lee," The Misfit said. "It's no real pleasure in life."

## Questions

1. Describe the story's point of view. On whom is the story focused? How appealing is this character as a focal point of attention?

2. What is the function of chance in the story's development? Describe some of the chances, or unlikelihoods, in the story? Why does O'Connor develop the story through the unfolding of these unlikelihoods?

3. Who is the Misfit? Why is he given this name? To what degree is he symbolic? What might he symbolize?

4. Some have called this story a religious allegory. How might it be considered allegorical? What might the story's violence be seen to symbolize?

# Chapter **10A**

# Writing and Documenting the Research Essay: Using Extra Resources for Understanding

**B**roadly, *research* is systematic investigation, examination, and experimentation. It is the basic tool of intellectual inquiry for anyone working in any discipline—physics, chemistry, biology, psychology, anthropology, history, and literature, to name just a few disciplines. With research, and with the breakthroughs of knowledge that research brings, our understanding and our civilization grow; without research, they languish.

The major assumption of doing research is that the researcher is reaching out to find and master new areas of knowledge. With each assignment the researcher acquires not only the knowledge gained from the particular task but also the skills needed to undertake further research and thereby to gain further knowledge. Some research tasks are elementary, such as using a dictionary to discover the meaning of a word and thereby aiding the understanding of an important passage. Many people would not even call that research. More detailed research uses an array of resources: critical studies, biographies, introductions, bibliographies, and histories. When you begin a research task you usually have little or no knowledge about your topic, but with such resources you can acquire expert knowledge in a relatively short time.

Although research is the animating spark of all disciplines, our topic here is **literary research**—the systematic use of primary and secondary sources in studying a literary problem. In doing literary research, you consult not only individual works themselves (primary sources) but many other works that shed light on them and interpret them (secondary sources). Typical research tasks are to learn important facts about a work and about the period in which it was written; to learn about the lives, careers, and other works of authors; to discover and apply the comments and judgments of modern or earlier critics; to learn details that help explain the meaning of works; and to learn about critical and artistic taste.

## Selecting a Topic

In most instances, your instructor assigns a research essay on a specific topic. Sometimes, however, the choice of a topic will be left in your hands. For such assignments, it is helpful to know the types of research essays you might find most congenial. Here are some possibilities:

428

1. **A particular work.** This type is probably the most common one, as shown in the illustrative essay. You might treat character (for example, "The Character of Louise in Chopin's 'The Story of an Hour'" or "The Question of Whether Young Goodman Brown Is a Hero or a Dupe in Hawthorne's 'Young Goodman Brown'") or tone and style, ideas, structure, form, and the like. A research paper on a single work is similar to an essay on the same work, except that the research paper takes into account more views and facts than those you are likely to have without the research.

2. **A particular author.** A project might focus on an idea or some facet of style, imagery, setting, or tone of the author, tracing the origins and development of the topic through a number of different stories, poems, or plays. Examples are "Hardy's Treatment of Local Country Folkways in His Short Stories" and "Faulkner's Use of the Yoknapatawpha Environment in His Stories." This type of essay is suitable for a number of shorter works, although it is also applicable for a single major work, such as a longer story, novel, or play.

3. **Comparison and contrast** (see Chapter 25). There are two types.
   a. *An idea or quality common to two or more authors.* Here you show points of similarity or contrast, or else you show how one author's work can be taken to criticize another's. A possible subject is "Contrasting Uses of Dialogue in Ellison's 'Battle Royal' and Tan's 'Two Kinds,'" or "The Theme of Love and Sexuality in Faulkner's 'A Rose for Emily,' Munro's 'The Found Boat,' and Joyce's 'Araby.'"
   b. *Different critical views of a particular work or body of works.* Sometimes much is to be gained from an examination of differing critical opinions on topics such as "The Meaning of Poe's 'The Masque of the Red Death'" or "Various Views of Hawthorne's 'Young Goodman Brown.'" Such a study would attempt to determine the critical opinion and taste to which a work did or did not appeal, and it might also aim at conclusions about whether the work was in the advance or rear guard of its time.

4. **The influence of an idea, author, philosophy, political situation, or artistic movement on specific works.** An essay on influences can be specific and to the point, as in "Details of Twentieth-Century Native American Life as Reflected in Whitecloud's 'Blue Winds Dancing,'" or else it can be more abstract and critical, as in "The Influence of Traditional Religion on Hawthorne's 'Young Goodman Brown.'"

5. **The origin of a particular work or type of work.** Such an essay might examine an author's biography to discover the germination and development of a work—for example, "Poe's 'The Masque of the Red Death' and Poe's Theory of the Short Story."

If you consider these types, an idea of what to write may come to you. Perhaps you have particularly liked one author or several authors. If so, you might start to think along the lines of types 1, 2, or 3. If you are interested in influences or origins, then type 4 or 5 may suit you better.

If you still cannot decide on a topic after rereading the works you have liked, then you should carry your search for a topic into your school library. Look up your author or authors in the library's retrieval system. Your first goal should be to find a relatively recent book-length critical study published by a university press. Look for a title indicating that the book is a general one dealing with the author's major works rather than just one work. Study those chapters relevant to the work or works you have chosen. Most writers of critical studies describe their purpose and plan in their introductions or first chapters, so begin with the first part of the book. If there is no separate chapter on your primary text, use the index as your guide to the relevant pages. Reading in this way will give you enough knowledge about the issues and ideas raised by the work to enable you to select a promising topic. Once you make your decision, you are ready to develop a working bibliography.

## Setting Up a Bibliography

The best way to develop a working bibliography of books and articles is to begin by finding major critical studies of the writer or writers. Again, use a book or books published by university presses-maybe the books you used to determine your topic. Such books will contain comprehensive bibliographies. Be careful to read the chapters on your primary work or works and to look for the footnotes or endnotes, for often you can save time if you record the names of books and articles listed in these notes. Then refer to the bibliographies included at the ends of the books, and select likely looking titles. Now, look at the dates of publication of the scholarly books. Let us suppose that you have found three books, published in 1999, 2004, and 2006. Unless you are planning an extensive research assignment, you can safely assume that the writers of critical works will have done the selecting for you of important works published before the date of publication. These bibliographies will be reliable, and you can use them with confidence. Thus, the bibliography in a book published in 2004 will be complete up through about 2003, for the writer will have finished the manuscript a year or so before the book was published. But such bibliographies will not go up to the present. For that, you will need to search for works published after the most recent of the books.

### Consult Bibliographical Guides

Fortunately for students doing literary research, the Modern Language Association (MLA) of America has been providing a complete bibliography of literary studies for years, not only in English and American literatures but also in the literatures of many foreign languages. This is the *MLA International Bibliography of Books and Articles on the Modern Languages and Literatures* ("*MLA Bibliography*"). The *MLA Bibliography* started achieving completeness in the late 1950s. By 1969 the project had grown so huge that it was published in many parts, which are bound together in library editions. In the latest volume, dated 2005, this comprehensive bibliography lists 20,425 books and articles that were published in the year 2005. In addition, following these numbered listings there is a second half of the bibliography, 964 pages long, containing a detailed subject and author index. University and college libraries have sets of the *MLA Bibliography* on open shelves or tables. The bibliography is also published on CD-ROM and on the Internet—formats accessible to you through your college library services. You will need to consult a librarian about Internet access.

In the traditional book format, the *MLA Bibliography* is conveniently organized by period and author. Should you be doing research about James Joyce, look him up in *Volume I* under the category "Irish literature/1900–1999," where there are 191 entries of works about him. In this same volume you will also find references to most other authors of works in English, such as Shakespeare (drama, poetry), Wordsworth (poetry), and Arnold (poetry). You will find most books and articles listed under the author's last name. Journal references are abbreviated, but a lengthy list explaining abbreviations appears at the beginning of the volume. Using the *MLA Bibliography* in the book format, begin with the most recent one and then go backward to your stopping point. If your library has machines dedicated to electronic versions of the bibliography, you can search by typing in the name of your author or subject. By whatever means you gain access to the bibliography, be sure to get the complete information—especially volume numbers and years of publication—for each article and book.

There are many other bibliographies useful for students doing literary research, such as the *Essay and General Literature Index*, the *Reader's Guide to Periodical Literature*, and various specific indexes. The *MLA Bibliography* contains far in excess of abundance, however, for your present research purposes. Remember that as you progress in your reading, the notes and bibliographies in the works you consult will also constitute an unfolding selective bibliography. For the illustrative research essay in this chapter, a number of entries were discovered not from bibliographies like those just listed but from the reference lists in critical books.

Your list will make up a fairly comprehensive search bibliography, which you can use when you physically enter the library to begin collecting and using materials. An additional convenience is that many associated libraries, such as state colleges and urban public libraries, have pooled their resources. Thus, if you use the services of a network of nearby county libraries, you can go to another library to use materials that are not accessible at your own college or branch. If distances are great, however, and your own library does not have a book that you think is important to your project, you can ask a librarian to get the book for you through the Interlibrary Loan Service. Usually, given time, the libraries will accommodate as many of your needs as they can.

You are now ready to find your sources and take notes. Make the maximum use of your college library. Call out the books themselves, the kind you can hold in your hands, and the relevant journals containing the articles in which you are interested. Read them, and make the best use you can of them.

## Online Library Services

Through computer access, many college and university libraries are constantly connected to a vast array of local, national, and even international libraries, so that by using various online services, you can extend your research far beyond the capacities of your own library. You can use one of the computers in your library, or your own personal computer, to gain access to the catalogues of large research libraries, provided that you punch in the correct entry information, are able and willing to follow the program codes, and are patient and persistent.

**ACCESSING RESOURCES VIA THE INTERNET.**   At one time, many smaller schools did not have copies of all the books and scholarly periodicals containing the results and reports of research. Many students were therefore frustrated in their attempts to find all the works that they had listed on their working bibliographies. Times, however, have changed. You may now gain access to many sources that are not in your library, for many of the works you want to read, which are not in your school's library, are now directly available to you through computer, page by page. A major source is *Questia*, an electronic depository of books and articles which is likely available to you through your college library. In total, *Questia* contains 67,000 "full-text" books, and more than 1.5 million articles. For students doing research on Hawthorne's short stories, for example, Questia claims to have more than 6,000 books and more than 1,300 scholarly articles.

Another major electronic source is *Jstor* (i.e., *Journal Storage*), the "Scholarly Journal Archive." Most college and university libraries, and many high schools, subscribe to this service, and it is available to you as a registered student. It includes computerized copies of complete sets of more than 600 scholarly journals in the field of Arts and Sciences. By gaining the proper credentials available to you as a student, you will have access to virtually any item you have listed in your bibliography.

Still another vital source is <scholar.google.com>. Scholar Google is in the process of duplicating the pages of many thousands of scholarly works. The service is available, like *Questia* and *Jstor*, through your college library. In other words, these electronic book and article services are available right now to provide you with abundant materials that previously were not readily available to most students at American colleges and universities.

## IMPORTANT CONSIDERATIONS FOR COMPUTER RESEARCH

You must always remind yourself that online catalogues, such as those you might select from other colleges and universities, and from private organizations, can give you only what has been entered into them. If one university library classifies a work under "criticism and interpretation" and another classifies it under "characters," a search of "criticism and interpretation" at the first library will find the work but the same search at the second will not. Sometimes the inclusion of an author's life dates immediately following the name might throw off your search. Typographic errors in the system will cause additional search problems, although many programs try to forestall such difficulties by providing "nearby" entries to enable you to determine whether incorrectly entered topics may in fact be helpful to you.

Also, if you use online services, be careful to determine the year when the computerization began. Many libraries have a recent commencement date—1978, for example, or 1985. For completeness, therefore, you would need assistance in finding catalogue entries for items published before these years.

It is particularly important *to avoid the many and varied so-called "free essays" on literary topics that fill a number of today's extremely popular search engines*. These essays are written largely by people who are themselves just beginning, not by scholars who have studied particular topics for many years and who have become experts in their analyses. The reason for using books and articles approved by scholarly publishers is that the works have been *refereed* by authorities in the particular field. If these authorities, or referees, have recommended publication, you are entitled to expect that the breadth and depth of the critical analyses will be well considered and reliable. That is not the case with the innumerable "free essays" that you might find in more general and unrefereed entries in the search engine.

Just a few years ago, the broadness of scope that electronic searches provide for most undergraduate students doing research assignments was not possible; today, it is commonplace. Even with the astounding possibilities of electronic resources, however, it is still necessary to take out actual books and articles—and read them and take notes on them—before you can begin and complete a research essay. These days, electronic services can supply you with actual copies of many of the materials you are seeking, but they cannot do your reading, note taking, and writing. All that is still up to you, as it always has been for all students doing research.

## Taking Notes and Paraphrasing Material

There are many ways of taking notes, but a few things are clear. Because your notes should facilitate, not hinder, your writing of the final research essay, you will need a systematic way of handling your notes. Notes should not be taken helter skelter. Nor should notes be taken front and back in a notebook, with only one side showing and the other side being out of your sight. The best way is to develop a method whereby you will be able to see all your notes together, laid out on a table in front of you. You might type your notes into your computer—leaving space between them, printing them out, and then, after cutting the separate items on your printout, laying these notes side by side and group by group. If you are taking handwritten notes, you can achieve simultaneous viewability by using note cards. If you have never used cards before, you might profit from consulting any one of a number of handbooks and special workbooks on research.[1] The principal advantage of cards is the ease with which you can see them at a glance when you lay them out on a desk or other large surface. Cards are also sturdy, and maintain their physical integrity as you handle them and assign them to their relevant piles. As a result, cards—or notes taken from printouts from your computer—may be easily classified; they may be numbered and renumbered; shuffled; tried out in one place, rejected, and then used in another place (or thrown away); and arranged in order when you start to write.

---

[1]See Muriel Harris, *Prentice Hall Reference Guide to Grammar and Usage*. 5th ed. (Upper Saddle River: Prentice Hall, 2003), 283–301.

## Taking Complete and Accurate Notes

**RECORD THE SOURCE OF EACH NOTE YOU TAKE.**  Be especially diligent about writing the source of your information on each card or computer note. This may seem bothersome, but it is easier than going back to the library to locate the correct source after you have begun your essay. You can save time if you take the complete data on one card or computer file—a "master card" for that source—and then create an abbreviation for the separate notes you take from the source. Here is an example, which also includes the location where the reference was originally found (e.g., card or computer catalogue, computer search, bibliography in a book, the *MLA Bibliography*, etc.). Observe that the author's last name goes first.

> DONOVAN, JOSEPHINE, ED. <u>FEMINIST</u>    PN
>
>    *Literary Criticism: Explorations*    98
>
>    *in Theory.* 2nd ed. Lexington:    W64
>
> UP of Kentucky. 1989    F4
>
> DONOVAN
>
>    *Card Catalogue, "Women"*

If you take many notes from this book, the name "Donovan" will serve as identification. Be sure not to lose your master group of references because you will need them when you prepare your list of works cited. If you are working with a computer, record the complete bibliographical data in a computer file.

**RECORD THE PAGE NUMBER FOR EACH NOTE.**  It would be hard to guess how much exasperation has been caused by the failure to record page numbers in notes. Be sure to write the page number down first, before you begin to take your note, and, to be doubly sure, write the page number again at the end of your note. If the detail goes from one page to the next in your source, record the exact spot where the page changes, as in this example.

> HEILBRUN AND STIMSON, IN DONOVAN, pp. 63–64
>
> [63]*After the raising of the feminist consciousness it is necessary to develop/*[64] *"the growth of moral perception" through anger and the "amelioration of social inequities."*

The reason for such care is that you may wish to use only a part of a note you have taken, and when there are two pages you will need to be accurate in locating what goes where.

**RECORD ONLY ONE FACT OR OPINION ON A CARD OR COMPUTER ENTRY.**  Record only one major detail for each of your notes—one quotation, one paraphrase, one observation—never two or more. You might be tempted to fill up the entire note with many separate but unrelated details, but such a try at economy often gets you in trouble because you might want to use some of the details in other places. If you have only one entry per note, you will avoid such problems and also retain the freedom you need.

**USE QUOTATION MARKS FOR ALL QUOTED MATERIAL.**   In taking notes it is extremely important—vitally important, urgently important—to distinguish copied material from your own words. Always put quotation marks around every direct quotation you copy verbatim from a source. Make the quotation marks immediately, before you forget, so that you will always know that the words of your notes within quotation marks are the words of another writer.

Often, as you write your notes, you may use some of your own words and some of the words from your source. In cases like this you should be even more cautious. *Put quotation marks around every word that you take directly from the source, even if your note looks like a picket fence.* Later, when you begin writing your essay, your memory of what is yours and not yours will be dim, and if you use another's words in your own essay without proper acknowledgment, you are risking the charge of plagiarism. Much of the time, plagiarism is caused not by deliberate deception but rather by sloppy note taking.[2]

**FOR LONGER SOURCES, MAKE A BRIEF AND ACCURATE PARAPHRASE.**   When you take notes, it is best to paraphrase the sources. A paraphrase is a restatement in your own words, and because of this it is actually a first step in the writing of your essay. A big problem in paraphrasing is to capture the idea in the source without copying the words in the source. The best way is to read and reread the passage you are noting. Turn over the book or journal, and write out the idea in your own words as accurately as you can. Once you have completed this note, compare it with the original and make corrections to improve your thought and emphasis. Add a short quotation if you believe it is needed, but be sure to use quotation marks. If your paraphrase is too close to the original, throw out the note and write another one. This effort may have its own reward because often you may be able to transfer some or even all of your note, word for word, directly to the appropriate place in your research essay.

To see the problems of paraphrasing, let us look at a paragraph of criticism and then see how a student doing research might take notes on it. The paragraph is by Richard F. Peterson, from an essay entitled "The Circle of Truth: The Stories of Katherine Mansfield and Mary Lavin," published in *Modern Fiction Studies* 24 (1978): 383–394. In the passage to be quoted, Peterson is considering the structures of two Mansfield stories, "Bliss" and "Miss Brill":

> "Bliss" and "Miss Brill" are flawed stories, but not because the truth they reveal about their protagonists is too brutal or painful for the tastes of the common reader. In each story, the climax of the narrative suggests an arranged reality that leaves a lasting impression, not of life, but of the author's cleverness. This strategy of arrangement for dramatic effect or revelation, unfortunately, is common in Katherine Mansfield's fiction.

---

[2]See p. 446 for a further discussion of plagiarism.

> Too often in her stories a dropped remark at the right or wrong moment, a chance meeting or discovery, an intrusive figure in the shape of a fat man at a ball or in the Café de Madrid, a convenient death of a hired man or a stranger dying aboard a ship, or a *deus ex machina* in the form of two doves, a dill pickle, or a fly plays too much of a role in/[386] creating a character's dilemma or deciding the outcome of the narrative. 385–386

Because taking notes forces a shortening of this or any criticism, it also requires you to discriminate, judge, interpret, and select; good note taking is not easy. There are some things to guide you, however, when you go through the many sources you uncover.

**THINK ABOUT THE PURPOSE OF YOUR RESEARCH.**    You may not know exactly what you are "fishing for" when you start to take notes, for you cannot prejudge what your essay will contain. Research is a form of discovery. But soon you will notice subjects and issues that your sources constantly explore. If you can accept one of these as your major topic, or focus of interest, you can use that as your guide in all further note taking.

For example, suppose you start to take notes on criticism about Katherine Mansfield's "Miss Brill," and after a certain amount of reading, you decide to focus on the story's structure. This decision guides your further research and note taking. Thus, for example, Richard Peterson criticizes Mansfield's technique of arranging climaxes in her stories. With your topic being structure, it would therefore be appropriate to take a note on Peterson's judgment. The following note is adequate as a brief reminder of the content in the passage:

> Peterson 385                                                 structure: negative
>
> Peterson claims that Mansfield creates climaxes that are too artificial, too unlifelike, giving the impression not of reality but of Mansfield's own "cleverness." 385

Let us now suppose that you want a fuller note, in the expectation that you need to deal not only with Peterson's general idea but also some of his supporting detail. Such a note might look like this:

> Peterson 385                                                 structure: negative
>
> Peterson thinks that "Bliss" and "Miss Brill" are "flawed" because they have contrived endings that give the impression "not of life but of" Mansfield's "cleverness." She arranges things artificially, according to Peterson, to cause the endings in many other stories. Some of these things are chance remarks, discoveries, or meetings, together with other unexpected or chance incidents and objects. These contrivances make their stories imperfect. 385

In an actual research essay, any part of this note would be useful. The words are almost all the note taker's own, and the few quotations are within quotation marks. Note that Peterson, the critic, is properly recognized as the source of the criticism, so you could adapt the note easily when you are doing your writing. The key here is that your note taking should be guided by your developing plan for your essay.

Note taking is part of your thinking and composing process. You may not always know whether you will be able to use each note that you take, and you will always exclude many notes when you write your essay. You will always find, however, that taking notes is easier once you have determined your purpose.

**GIVE YOUR NOTES TITLES.**   To help plan and develop the various parts of your essay, write a title for each of your notes, as in the examples in this chapter. This practice is a form of outlining. Let us continue discussing the structure of Mansfield's "Miss Brill," the actual subject of the illustrative research essay (page 447). As you do your research, you discover that there is a divergence of critical thought about how the ending of the story should be understood. Here is a note about one of the diverging interpretations:

---

Daly 90                                                    Last sentence of the story

Miss Brill's "complete" "identification" with the shabby fur piece at the very end may
cause readers to conclude that she is the one in tears but bravely does not recognize
this fact, and also to conclude that she may never use the fur in public again because
of her complete defeat. Everything may be for "perhaps the very last time." 90

---

Notice that the title classifies the topic of the note. If you use such classifications, a number of like-titled cards or computer notes could form the basis for a section in your essay about how to understand the conclusion of "Miss Brill." Whether you use this note or not—and very often you may not, for it may not fit into your final plan for your essay—the topic itself will guide you in further study and note-taking.

**RECORD YOUR ORIGINAL THOUGHTS, AND MAKE SURE TO MARK THEM AS YOUR OWN.**
As you take notes, you will be acquiring your own observations and thoughts. Do not push these aside in your mind, on the chance of remembering them later, *but write them down immediately*. Often you may notice a detail that your source does not mention, or you may get a hint for an idea that the critic does not develop. Often, too, you may get thoughts that can serve as "bridges" between details in your notes or as introductions or concluding observations. Be sure to title your comments and also to mark them as your own thought. Here is such a note, which is about Katherine Mansfield's emphasis on the impoverished existence of her heroine, Miss Brill, and the many people inhabiting the park where the action of the story takes place:

---

My Own                                         About Miss Brill's "cupboard"

Mansfield's speaker avoids taking us to the homes of the other people in the park, as
she does when we follow Miss Brill into her living quarters. Instead, she lets us know
that the silent couple, the complaining wife and suffering husband, the unseen man
rejected by the young woman dumping the flowers, the "ermine toque," and the funny
gentleman, not to mention the many people resembling statues in the park, all return
to loneliness and personal pain.

---

Observe that the substance of this note (also most of the language) is used as the basis for much of paragraph 10 in the illustrative essay. The point here is that as you make your own observations while doing your research, you are also free to develop materials that can go directly into your final essay.

**CLASSIFYING YOUR CARDS OR COMPUTER NOTES, AND GROUPING THEM.** If you do a careful and thorough job of taking notes, your essay will already have been forming in your mind. The titles of your notes and cards will suggest areas to be developed as you do your planning and initial drafting. Once you have assembled a stack of materials derived from a reasonable number of sources (your instructor may have assigned an approximate number or a minimum number), you can sort them into groups according to the topics and titles. For the illustrative research essay, after some shuffling and retitling, the cards were assembled in the following groups:

---

GENERAL STRUCTURE

*Specific structures: season, time of day, levels of cruelty, Miss Brill's own "hierarchies" of unreality*

*The concluding paragraphs, especially the last sentence*

---

If you look at the major sections of the illustrative essay, you will see that the topics are closely adapted from these groups of cards. In other words, the arrangement of the cards is an effective means of outlining and organizing a research essay. Be smart; do it this way.

**MAKING LOGICAL ARRANGEMENTS OF THE NOTES AND CARDS IN EACH GROUP.** There is still much to do with each group of cards or printed notes. You cannot use the details as they happen to fall randomly in your stack. You need to decide which notes are relevant. You might also need to retitle some cards and use them elsewhere. Those that remain will have to be arranged in a logical order for you to find use for them in your essay.

Once you have your notes or cards in order, you can write whatever comments or transitions are needed to move from detail to detail. Write this material directly on the cards and be sure to use a different color ink so that you can distinguish later between the original note and what you add. Here is an example of such a "developed" note:

---

Magalaner 39                                                        Structure, general

Magalaner, using "Miss Brill" as an example, speaks of Mansfield's weaving "a myriad of threads into a rigidly patterned whole" in her stories. (39)

---

Some of these "threads" are the fall season, the time of day, examples of unkindness, the park bench sitters from the cupboards, and Miss Brill's stages of unreality. Each of these is separate, but all work together structurally to unify the story.

By adding such commentary to your notes, you are also simplifying the writing of your first draft. In many instances, the note and whatever comments you make may be moved directly into the paper with minor adjustments (some of the content of this note appears in paragraph 6 of the illustrative essay, and almost all the topics introduced here are developed in paragraphs 9 to 14).

## Be Creative and Original Even Though You Are Doing Research

You will not always transfer your notes directly into your essay. The major trap to avoid in a research paper is that your use of sources can become an end in itself and therefore a shortcut for your own thinking and writing. Often, students make the mistake of introducing details the way a master of ceremonies introduces performers in a variety show. This is unfortunate because it is the student whose essay will be judged, even though the sources, like the performers, do all the work. Thus, it is important to be creative and original in a research essay and to do your own thinking and writing, even though you are relying heavily on your sources. Here are five ways in which research essays may be original.

**Your selection of material is original with you.** In each major part of your essay you will include many details from your sources. To be creative you should select different but related details and avoid overlapping or repetition. Your completed essay will be judged on the basis of the thoroughness with which you make your points with different details (which in turn will represent the completeness of your research). Even though you are relying on published materials and cannot be original on that score, your selection can be original because you bring these materials together for the first time, and because you emphasize some details and minimize others. Inevitably, your assemblage of details from your sources will be unique and therefore original.

**Your development of your essay is yours alone.** Your arrangement of your various points is an obvious area of originality: One detail seems naturally to precede another, and certain conclusions stem from certain details. As you present the details, conclusions, and arguments from your sources, you can also add an original stamp by introducing supporting details different from those in the source material. You can also add your own emphasis to particular points–an emphasis that you do not find in your sources.

**Your words are yours and yours alone.** Naturally, the words that you use will be original because they are yours. Your topic sentences, for example, will all be your own. As you introduce details and conclusions, you will need to write "bridges" to get yourself from point to point. These can be introductory remarks or transitions. In other words, as you write, you are not just stringing your notes together, but rather you are actively assembling and arranging your thoughts, based on your notes, in creative and unique ways.

**Explaining and contrasting controversial views is an original presentation of material.** Closely related to your selection is that in your research you may have found conflicting or differing views on a topic. If you make a point to describe and distinguish these views, and explain the reasons for the differences, you are presenting material originally. To see how differing views can be handled, see paragraphs 19 through 21 of the illustrative essay.

**Your insights and positions are yours and yours alone.** There are three possibilities here, all related to how well you have learned the primary texts on which your research in secondary sources is based.

*Weave your own interpretations and ideas into your essay.* An important part of taking notes is to make your own points precisely when they occur to you. Often you can expand these as truly original parts of your essay. Your originality does not need to be extensive; it may consist of no more than a single insight. Here is such a card, which was written during research on the structure of "Miss Brill."

---

My Own                                                          Miss Brill's unreality

In light of this hierarchical structure of unrealities, it is ironic that the boy and girl sit down next to her just when she is at the height of her fancy about her own importance. When she hears the girl's insults, the couple introduces objective reality to her with a vengeance, and she is plunged from rapture to pain.

---

The originality here is built around the contrast between Miss Brill's exhilaration and her rapid and cruel deflation. This observation is not unusual or startling, but it nevertheless represents original thought about the story. When modified and adapted (and put into full sentences with proper punctuation), the material of the card supplies much of paragraph 13 of the illustrative essay. You can see that your development of a "My Own" note card is an important part of the prewriting stage of a research essay.

*Filling gaps in the sources enables you to present original thoughts and insights.* As you read your secondary sources, you may realize that an obvious conclusion is not being made or that an important detail is not being stressed. Here is an area that you can develop on your own. Your conclusions may involve a particular interpretation or major point of comparison, or they may rest on a particularly important but understressed word or fact. For example, paragraphs 10 to 13 in the illustrative essay form an argument based on observations that critics have overlooked, or have not stressed, about the attitudes of the heroine of "Miss Brill." In your research, whenever you find such a critical "vacuum" (assuming that you cannot read all the articles about some of your topics, where your discovery may already have been made a number of times), it is right to include whatever is necessary to fill it.

*By disputing your sources with your own arguments, you are being original.* The originality of your disagreement is that you will be using details in a different way from that of the critic or critics whom you are disputing, and your conclusions will be your own. This area of originality is similar to the laying out of controversial critical views, except that you furnish one of the opposing views yourself. The approach is limited because it is difficult to find many substantive points of interpretation on which there are not already clearly delineated opposing views. Paragraph 13 of the illustrative research essay shows how a disagreement can lead to a different, if not original, interpretation.

# Documenting Your Work

It is necessary and essential to acknowledge—to *document*—all sources from which you have quoted or paraphrased factual and interpretive information. Because of the need to avoid being challenged for plagiarism, this point cannot be overemphasized. As the means of documentation, various reference systems use parenthetical references, footnotes, or endnotes. Whatever system is used, documentation almost always includes a carefully prepared bibliography, or list of works cited.

We will first discuss the list of works cited and then review the two major reference systems for use in a research paper. Parenthetical references, preferred by the Modern Language Association (MLA) since 1984, are described in Joseph Gibaldi, *MLA Handbook for Writers of Research Papers*, 6th ed., 2003. Footnotes or endnotes, recommended by the MLA before 1984, are still required by many instructors.

## A List of Works Cited (Bibliography) Contains All the Sources You Have Used

The key to any reference system is a carefully prepared list of works cited that is included at the end of the essay. "Works cited" means exactly that; the list should include just those books and articles you have actually used in your essay. If, however, your instructor requires that you use footnotes or endnotes, you can extend your concluding list to be a complete bibliography both of works cited and also of works consulted but not actually used. Always, always, always, follow your instructor's directions.

The list of works cited should include the following information, in each entry, in the form indicated. If you are using a word processor with the capacity to make italics, you can italicize book and article titles rather than underline them.

### FOR A BOOK

The author's name: last name first, followed by first name and middle name or initial. Period.

The title, italicized or underlined. Period.

The city of publication (not state or nation), colon; publisher (easily recognized abbreviations or key words can be used unless they seem awkward or strange; see the *MLA Handbook*, pp. 272–74), comma; year of publication. Period.

### FOR AN ARTICLE

The author's name: last name first, followed by first name and middle name or initial. Period.

The title of the article in quotation marks. Period.

The title of the journal or periodical, italicized or underlined, followed by the volume number in Arabic (not Roman) numbers with no punctuation, then the year of publication within parentheses. Colon. For a daily paper or weekly magazine, omit the parentheses and cite the date in the British style followed by a colon (day, month, year, as in 2 Feb. 2007). Inclusive page numbers (without any preceding p. or pp.). Period.

The works you are citing should be listed alphabetically according to the last names of authors, with unsigned articles included in the list alphabetically by titles. Bibliographical lists are begun at the left margin, with subsequent lines in hanging indentation, so that the key locating word—the author's last name or the first title word of an unsigned article—can be easily seen. Many unpredictable and complex combinations, including ways to describe works of art, musical or other performances, and films, are detailed extensively in the *MLA Handbook* (142–235). Here are two model entries.

## BOOK

Alpers, Antony. *The Life of Katherine Mansfield*. New York: Viking, 1980.

## ARTICLE:

Hankin, Cheryl. "Fantasy and the Sense of an Ending in the Work of Katherine Mansfield." *Modern Fiction Studies* 24 (1978): 465–74.

## Refer to Works Parenthetically as You Draw Details from Them

Within the text of your research essay, use parentheses in referring to works from which you are using facts and conclusions. This parenthetical citation system is recommended in the *MLA Handbook* (238–60), and its guiding principle is to provide documentation without asking readers to interrupt their reading to find footnotes or endnotes. Readers wanting to see the complete reference can easily find it in your list of works cited. With this system, you incorporate the author's last name and the relevant page number or numbers directly, whenever possible, into the body of your essay. If the author's name is mentioned in your discussion, you need to give only the page number or numbers in parentheses. Here are two examples, from a critical study of another author, the eighteenth-century poet Alexander Pope:

> Alexander Pope believed in the idea that the universe is a whole, a totally unified body, which provides a "viable benevolent system for the salvation of everyone who does good" (Kallich 24).

> Martin Kallich draws attention to Alexander Pope's belief in the idea that the universe is a whole, a totally unified body, which provides a "viable benevolent system for the salvation of everyone who does good" (24).

## Footnotes and Endnotes Are Formal and Traditional Reference Formats

The most formal system of documentation still widely used is that of footnotes (references at the bottom of each page) or endnotes (references listed numerically at the end of the essay). If your instructor wants you to use one of these formats, do the following: Make a note the first time you quote or refer to a source, with the details ordered as outlined below.

## FOR A BOOK

The author's name: first name or initials first, followed by middle name or initial, then last name. Comma.

The title, underlined or italicized for a book, no punctuation. If you are referring to a work in a collection (article, story, poem) use quotation marks for that, but italicize or underline the title of the book. No punctuation, but use a comma after the title if an editor, translator, or edition number follows.

The name of the editor or translator, if relevant. Abbreviate "editor" or "edited by" as ed., "editors" as eds. Use trans. for "translator" or "translated by." No punctuation, but use a comma if an edition number follows.

The edition (if indicated), abbreviated thus: 2nd ed., 3rd ed., and so on. No punctuation.

The publication facts, within parentheses, without any preceding or following punctuation, in the following order:

City (but not the state or nation) of publication, colon.

Publisher (clear abbreviations are acceptable and desirable), comma.

Year of publication.

The page number(s) with no p. or pp., for example, 5, 6–10, 15–19, 295–307, 311–16. Period. If you are referring to longer works, such as novels or longer stories with division or chapter numbers, include these numbers for readers who may be using an edition different from yours.

## FOR A JOURNAL OR MAGAZINE ARTICLE

The author: first name or initials first, followed by middle name or initial, then last name. Comma.

The title of the article, in quotation marks. Comma.

The name of the journal, italicized or underlined. No punctuation.

The volume number, in Arabic letters. No punctuation.

The year of publication within parentheses. Colon. For newspaper and journal articles, omit the parentheses, and include day, month, and year (in the British style: 21 May 2005). Colon.

The page number(s) with no p. or pp.: 5, 6–10, 34–36, 98–102, 345–47. Period.

For later notes to the same work, use the last name of the author as the reference unless you are referring to two or more works by the same author. Thus, if you refer to only one work by, say, Thomas Hardy, the name Hardy will be enough for all later references. Should you be referring to other works by Hardy, however, you will also need to make a short reference to the specific works to distinguish them, such as Hardy, "The Three Strangers," and Hardy, "The Man He Killed."

Footnotes are placed at the bottom of each page, and endnotes are included on separate page(s) at the end of the essay. The first lines of both footnotes and endnotes should be paragraph indented, and continuing lines should be flush with the left margin. Both endnote and footnote numbers are set in a smaller font and positioned slightly above the line (as superior numbers) like this: [12]. You can single-space footnotes and endnotes and leave a line of space between them. *Most computer programs have specially designed and consecutively numbered footnote formats. These are generally acceptable, but be sure to consult your instructor.* (For more detailed coverage of footnoting practices, see the *MLA Handbook*, 298–313.)

## Sample Footnotes

In the examples below, book titles and periodicals are shown italicized, as they would be in an essay prepared on the computer. If the essay is typewritten or handwritten, these titles should be <u>underlined</u>.

> Blanche H. Gelfant, *Women Writing in America: Voices in Collage* (Hanover: UP of New England, for Dartmouth College, 1984) 110.
>
> Günter Grass, "Losses," *Granta* 42 (Winter 1992): 99.
>
> John O'Meara, "Hamlet and the Fortunes of Sorrowful Imagination: A Reexamination of the Genesis and Fate of the Ghost," *Cahiers Elisabéthains* 35 (1989): 21.
>
> Grass 104.
>
> Gelfant 141.
>
> O'Meara 17.

As a principle, you do not need to repeat in a footnote or endnote any material you have already mentioned in your own discourse. For example, if you recognize the author and title of your source, then the footnote or endnote should give no more than the data about publication. Here is an example:

---

In *The Fiction of Katherine Mansfield*, Marvin Magalaner points out that Mansfield was as skillful in the development of epiphanies (that is, the use of highly significant though perhaps unobtrusive actions or statements to reveal the depths of a particular character) as James Joyce himself, the "inventor" of the technique.

---

[9] (Carbondale: Southern Illinois UP, 1971) 130.

---

## Many Academic Disciplines Set Their Own Requirements for Documentation

Other reference systems and style manuals have been adopted by various disciplines (e.g., mathematics, medicine, psychology) to serve their own special needs. If you receive no instructions from your instructors in other courses, you can adapt the systems described here. If you need to use the documentation methods of other fields, however, use the *MLA Handbook*, pages 316–17 for guidance about which style manual to select.

## When in Doubt, Consult Your Instructor

As long as all you want from a reference is the page number of a quotation or para-phrase, the parenthetical system described briefly here—and detailed fully in the *MLA Handbook*—is the most suitable and convenient one you can use. However, you may wish to use footnotes or endnotes if you need to add more details, provide addi-tional explanations, or refer your readers to other materials that you are not using. Whatever method you follow, you must always acknowledge sources properly. Remember that whenever you begin to write and cite references, you might forget a number of specific details about documentation, and you will certainly discover that you have many questions. Be sure, then, to ask your instructor, who is your final authority.

## Strategies for Organizing Ideas in Your Research Essay

**INTRODUCTION.** In your research essay you may wish to expand your introduction more than usual because of the need to relate the problem of research to your topic. You may wish to bring in relevant historical or biographical information. You may also wish to summarize critical opinion or describe critical problems about your topic. The idea is to lead your reader into your topic by providing interesting and sig-nificant materials that you have found.

Because of the length of many research essays, some instructors require a topic outline, which is in effect a brief table of contents. Because the inclusion of an outline is a matter of the instructor's choice, be sure to learn whether your instructor re-quires it.

**BODY AND CONCLUSION.** As you write the body and conclusion of your research essay, your development will be governed by your choice of topic. Consult the rele-vant chapters in this book about what to include for whatever approach or approaches you select (setting, ideas, point of view, character, tone, or any other).

In length, the research essay can be anywhere from as few as two or three or as many as fifteen or thirty or more pages, depending on your instructor's assignment. Obviously, an essay on a single work will be shorter than one based on several. If you narrow the scope of your topic, as suggested in the approaches described at the beginning of this chapter, you can readily keep your essay within the assigned length. The following illustrative research essay, for example, illustrates approach 1 (page 429) by being limited to only one character in one story. Were you to write on characters in a number of other stories by Mansfield or any other writer (approach 2), you could limit your total number of pages by stressing comparative treatments and by avoiding excessive detail about problems pertaining to only one work.

Although you limit your topic yourself in consultation with your instructor, you may encounter problems because you will deal not with one source alone but with many. Naturally, the sources will provide you with details and also trigger many of your ideas. The problem is to handle the many strands without piling on too many details, and also without being led into digressions. It is important therefore to keep your central idea foremost; the constant stressing of your central idea will help you both to select relevant materials and to reject irrelevant ones.

## Plagiarism: A Danger to Avoid

When you are using sources as the substance of many of the details in your essay, *plagiarism* is a great danger. Plagiarism means that a writer uses the words and ideas of other writers without their consent and without acknowledgement. Recognizing the source means being clear about the identity of other authors, together with the name or names of the works from which one gets details and ideas. When there is no recognition, readers, and the intellectual world generally, are deceived. They assume that the material they are reading is the original work and the intellectual possession of the writer. When there is no recognition, the plagiarizing author is committing intellectual theft.

This is no small matter. In the world of publications, many people who have committed plagiarism have suffered irreparable damage to their credibility and reputations as writers and authorities. Some well-known writers have found it hard if not impossible to continue their careers, and all because of the wide knowledge of their plagiarism. It does not end there. A plagiarist might be open to legal actions, and might, if the situation is grave enough, be required to supply financial restitution to the author or authors whose work has been illegally appropriated. In schools and colleges, students who plagiarize may face academic discipline. Often the discipline is a failure for the course, but it might also include suspension and expulsion. It is not possible to predict all the ill consequences of committing an act of plagiarism.

It therefore bears constant awareness and emphasis that you need to distinguish between the sources you are using and your own work. Your readers will assume that everything you write is your own unless you indicate otherwise. Therefore, when blending your words with the ideas from sources, **be clear about proper acknowledgments**. Most commonly, if you are simply presenting details and facts, you can write straightforwardly and let parenthetical references suffice as your authority, as in the following sentence from the illustrative research essay:

> Marvin Magalaner, using "Miss Brill" as an example, speaks of Mansfield's weaving of "a myriad of threads into a rigidly patterned whole" (39). Also noting Mansfield's control over form, Cheryl Hankin suggests that Mansfield's structuring is perhaps more "instinctive" than deliberate (474).

Here there can be no question about plagiarism, for the names of the authors of the critical sources are fully acknowledged, the page numbers are specific, and the quotation marks clearly distinguish the words of the critics from the words of the essay writer. If you grant recognition as recommended here, no confusion can result about the authority underlying your essay. The linking words obviously belong to the writer of the essay, but the parenthetical references clearly indicate that the sentence is based on two sources.

If you use an interpretation unique to a particular writer, or if you rely on a significant quotation from your source, you should make your acknowledgment an essential part of your discussion, as in this sentence.

Saralyn Daly, referring to Miss Brill as one of Mansfield's "isolatoes"—that is, solitary persons cut off from normal human contacts—fears that the couple's callous insults have caused Miss Brill to face the outside world with her fur piece "perhaps for the very last time" (88, 90).

Here the idea of the critic is singled out for special acknowledgment. If you recognize your sources in this way, no confusion can arise about how you have used them.

Please, always keep foremost in your mind that *the purpose of research is to acquire knowledge and details from which to advance your own thoughts and interpretations*. You should consider your research discoveries as a kind of springboard, from which you can launch yourself into your own written work. In this way, research should be creative. A test of how you use research is to determine how well you move from the details you are using to the development of your own ideas. Once you have gone forth in this way, you are using research correctly and creatively. Plagiarism will then no more be even a remote issue for you.

# Illustrative Student Essay Using Research

Underlined sentences in this paper do not conform to MLA style and are used solely as teaching tools to emphasize the central idea, thesis sentence, and topic sentences throughout the paper.

## Outline

I. Introduction. The parallel structures of "Miss Brill"

Use 1/2 inch top margin, 1 inch bottom and side margin; double space throughout.

II. Season and time as structure

III. Insensitive or cruel actions as structure

IV. Miss Brill's "hierarchy of unrealities" as structure

V. The story's conclusion

VI. Conclusion

Delgado 1

Simone Delgado

Professor Leeshock

Composition 102

30 January, 2007

### The Structure of Katherine Mansfield's "Miss Brill" °

[1]     In the story "Miss Brill," Mansfield creates an aging and emotionally vulnerable character, Miss Brill, whose good feelings are dashed when she overhears some cruel and shattering personal insults. In accord with Miss Brill's emotional deflation, the story is developed through a parallel number of structures.* This parallelling demonstrates Mansfield's power generally over tight narrative control. Marvin Magalaner, using "Miss Brill" as an example, speaks of Mansfield's weaving "a myriad of threads into a rigidly patterned whole" (39). Also noting Mansfield's control over form, Cheryl Hankin suggests that Mansfield's structuring is perhaps more "instinctive" than deliberate (474). Either of these observations is great praise for Mansfield. The complementary parallels, threads, stages, or "levels" of "unequal length" (Harmat uses the terms "niveaux" and "longueur inégale," 49, 51) are the fall season, the time of day, insensitive or cruel actions, Miss Brill's own unreal perceptions, and the final section or dénouement.†

[2]     An important aspect of structure in "Miss Brill" is Mansfield's use of the season of the year. Autumn, with its propulsion toward winter, is integral to the deteriorating life of the heroine. In the first paragraph, we learn that there is a "faint chill" in the air (is the word "chill" chosen to rhyme with "Brill"?), and this phrase is repeated in paragraph 10 (179). Thus the author establishes autumn and the approaching year's end as the beginning of the downward movement toward dashed hopes. This seasonal reference is also carried out when we read that "yellow leaves" are "down drooping" in the local *Jardins Publiques* (178, paragraph 6) and that leaves are drifting "now and again" from almost "nowhere, from the sky" (paragraph 1). It is the

°See pages 176–79 for this story.
*Central idea
†Thesis sentence

autumn cold that has caused Miss Brill to wear her shabby fur piece, which later the young girl considers the object of contempt. The chill, together with the fur, forms a structural setting for both the action and the mood of the story. Sewell notes that "Miss Brill" both begins and ends with the fur, which is the direct cause of the heroine's deep hurt at the conclusion (25).

[3]      Like the seasonal structuring, the times of day parallel Miss Brill's darkening existence. At the beginning, the speaker points out that the day is "brilliantly fine—the blue sky powdered with gold," and that the light is "like white wine." This figurative language suggests the brightness and crispness of full sunlight. In paragraph 6 (178), where we also learn of the yellow leaves, "the blue sky with gold-veined clouds" indicates that time has been passing as clouds accumulate during late afternoon. By the story's end, Miss Brill has returned in sadness to her "little dark room" (179, paragraph 18). In other words, the time moves from day to evening, from light to darkness, as a virtual accompaniment to Miss Brill's emotional pain.

[4]      Mansfield's most significant structural device, which is not emphasized by critics, is the introduction of insensitive or cruel actions. It is as though the hurt felt by Miss Brill on the bright Sunday afternoon is also being felt by many others. Because she is the spectator who is closely related to Mansfield's narrative voice, Miss Brill is the filter through whom these negative examples reach the reader. Considering the patterns that emerge, one may conclude that Mansfield intends that the beauty of the day and the joyousness of the band be taken as an ironic contrast to the pettiness and insensitivity of the people in the park.

[5]      The first of these people are the silent couple on Miss Brill's bench (177, paragraph 3) and the incompatible couple of the week before (177, paragraph 4). Because these seem no more than ordinary, they do not at first appear to be part of the story's pattern of cruelty and rejection. But their incompatibility, suggested by their silence and one-way complaining, establishes a structural parallel with the young and insensitive couple who later insult Miss Brill. Thus the first two couples prepare the way for the third, and all show increasing insensitivity and cruelty.

[6]      Almost unnoticed as a second level of negation is the vast group of "odd, silent, nearly all old" people filling "the benches and green chairs" (178, paragraph 5). They seem to be no more than a normal part of the Sunday afternoon landscape. But these

Delgado 3

people are significant structurally because the "dark little rooms—or even cupboards" that Miss Brill associates with them also, ironically, describe the place where she lives (178, 179, paragraphs 5, 18). The reader may conclude from Miss Brill's quiet eavesdropping that she herself is one of these nameless and faceless ones who lead similarly dreary lives.

[7]     After Mansfield sets these levels for her heroine, she introduces characters experiencing additional rejection and cruelty. The beautiful woman who throws down the bunch of violets is the first of these (178, paragraph 8). The story does not explain the causes of this woman's scorn, and Miss Brill does not know what to make of the incident; but the woman's actions suggest that she has been involved in a relationship that has ended in anger and bitterness.

[8]     The major figure involved in rejection, who is important enough to be considered a structural double of Miss Brill, is the woman wearing the ermine toque (178, paragraph 8). It is clear that she, like Miss Brill, is one of "the lonely and isolated women in a hostile world" that Mansfield is so skillful in portraying (Gordon 6). This woman tries to please the "gentleman in grey," but this man insults her by blowing smoke in her face. It could be, as Peter Thorpe observes, that she is "obviously a prostitute" (661). But it is more likely that the "ermine toque" has had a broken relationship with the gentleman, or perhaps even no relationship. Being familiar with his Sunday habits, she comes to the park to meet him, as though by accident, to attempt to renew contact. After her rejection, her hurrying off to meet someone "much nicer" (there is no such person, for Mansfield uses the phrase "as though" to introduce "ermine toque's" departure) is her way of masking her hurt. Regardless of the exact situation, however, Mansfield makes it plain that the encounter demonstrates vulnerability, unkindness, and pathos, but also a certain amount of self defense.

> In MLA style, put author and page number in parentheses when the author is not named in the sentence.

[9]     Once Mansfield establishes this major incident, she introduces two additional examples of insensitivity. At the end of paragraph 8 (178), the hobbling old man "with long whiskers" is nearly knocked over by the group of four girls, who show arrogance if not contempt toward him. The final examples involve Miss Brill herself. These are her recollections of the apparent indifference Of her students and of the old invalid "who habitually sleeps" when she reads to him.

Delgado 4

[10]    Although "Miss Brill" is a brief story, Mansfield creates a large number of structural parallels to the sudden climax brought about by the boorishly insensitive young couple. The boy and girl do not appear until the very end, in other words (179, paragraph 11), but extreme insults like theirs have been fully anticipated in the story's earlier parts. Mansfield's speaker does not take us to the homes of the other people in the park, as she does when we follow Miss Brill to her wretched room. Instead, the narrative invites us to conclude that the silent couple, the complaining wife and long-suffering husband, the unseen man rejected by the young woman, the "ermine toque," and the funny gentleman, not to mention the many silent and withdrawn people sitting like statues in the park, all return to loneliness and personal pain that are comparable to the feelings of Miss Brill.

[11]    The intricacy of the structure of "Miss Brill" does not end here. Of great importance is the structural development of the protagonist herself. Peter Thorpe notes a "hierarchy of unrealities" which govern the reader's increasing awareness of Miss Brill's plight (661). By this measure, the story's actions progressively bring out Miss Brill's failures of perception and understanding—failures that in this respect make her like her namesake fish, the lowly brill (Gargano).

[12]    These unrealities begin with Miss Brill's fanciful but harmless imaginings about her shabby fur piece. This beginning sets up the pattern of her pathetic inner life. When she imagines that the park band is a "single, responsive, and very sensitive creature" (Thorpe 661), we realize that she is unrealistically making too much out of a mediocre band of ordinary musicians. Although she cannot interpret the actions of the beautiful young woman with the violets, she does see the encounter between the "ermine toque" and the gentleman in grey as a vision of rejection. Her response is correct, but then her belief that the band's drumbeats are sounding out "The Brute! The Brute!" indicates her vivid overdramatization of the incident. The "top of the hierarchy of unrealities" (Thorpe 661) is her fancy that Miss Brill is an actor with a vital part in a gigantic drama played by all the people in the park. The most poignant aspect of this daydream is her unreal thought that someone would miss her if she were to be absent.

[13]    In light of this hierarchical structure of unrealities, it is ironic that the boy and girl sit down next to her just when she is at the height of her fancy about her own

> **Quotation marks around phrases show that they appeared separately in the source.**

Delgado 5

importance. <u>When she hears the girl's insults, the couple has introduced objective reality to her with a vengeance, and she is plunged from rapture to pain.</u> The concluding two paragraphs of "Miss Brill" hence form a rapid dénouement to reflect her loneliness and solitude.

[14]     <u>Of unique importance in the structure of "Miss Brill" are these final two paragraphs, in which Miss Brill, all alone, returns to her wretched little room.</u> Saralyn Daly, referring to Miss Brill as one of Mansfield's "isolatoes"—that is, solitary persons cut off from normal human contacts—fears that the couple's callous insults have caused Miss Brill to face the outside world with her fur piece "perhaps for the very last time" (88, 90). Sydney Kaplan adds a political dimension to Miss Brill's defeat, asserting that here and in other stories Mansfield is expressing "outrage" against "a society in which privilege is . . . marked by indifference" to situations like those of Miss Brill (192).

[15]     <u>It is clear that Mansfield is asking readers to consider not only Miss Brill alone, but also her similarity to the many park inhabitants who are like her.</u> Miss Brill's grim existence exemplifies a common personal pattern in which the old are destroyed "by loneliness and sickness, by fear of death, by the thoughtless energy of the younger world around them" (Zinman 457). More generally, Mansfield herself considered such negative situations as "the snail under the leaf," which implies that a gnawing fate is waiting for everyone, not just those who are old (Meyers, 213). With such a crushing experience for the major character, "Miss Brill" may be fitted to the structuring of Mansfield's stories described by André Maurois: "moments of beauty suddenly broken by contact with ugliness, cruelty, or death" (342–43).

Delgado 6

**WORKS CITED**

Daly, Saralyn R. *Katherine Mansfield*. New York: Twayne, 1965.

Gargano, James W. "Mansfield's Miss Brill." *Explicator* 19. 2 (1960): item 10 (one page, unnumbered).

Gordon, Ian A. "Katherine Mansfield: Overview." D. L. Kirkpatrick, ed., *Reference Guide to English Literature*, 2nd ed., St. James Press, 1991 (found at <www.galenet.com>).

In MLA style, the list of sources, called the works cited, begins a new page. Double space throughout.

Delgado 7

Hankin, Cheryl. "Fantasy and the Sense of an Ending in the Work of Katherine Mansfield." *Modern Fiction Studies* 24 (1978): 465–74.

Harmat, Andrée-Marie. "Essai D'Analyse Structurale d'une Nouvelle Lyrique Anglaise: 'Miss Brill' de Katherine Mansfield." *Les Cahiers de la Nouvelle* 1 (1983): 49–74.

Kaplan, Sydney Janet. *Katherine Mansfield and the Origins of Modernist Fiction*. Ithaca and London: Cornell UP, 1991.

McLaughlin, Ann L. "The Same Job: The Shared Writing Aims of Katherine Mansfield and Virginia Woolf." *Modern Fiction Studies* 24 (1978): 369–82.

Magalaner, Marvin. *The Fiction of Katherine Mansfield*. Carbondale: Southern Illinois UP, 1971.

——————. *The Short Stories of Katherine Mansfield*. New York: Knopf, 1967.

Mansfield, Katherine. "Miss Brill." *Literature: An Introduction to Reading and Writing*. Ed. Edgar V. Roberts. 4th Compact Ed. Upper Saddle River: Prentice Hall, 2009. 176–79. Parenthetical page numbers to "Miss Brill" refer to pages in this text.

Maurois, André. *Points of View from Kipling to Graham Greene*. 1935. New York: Ungar, 1968.

Meyers, Jeffrey. *Katherine Mansfield: A Darker View*. 1978. New York: Cooper Square Press, 2002.

Sewell, Arthur. *Katherine Mansfield: A Critical Essay*. Auckland: Unicorn, 1936.

Thorpe, Peter. "Teaching 'Miss Brill.'" *College English* 23 (1962): 661-63.

Zinman, Toby Silverman. "The Snail Under the Leaf: Katherine Mansfield's Imagery." *Modern Fiction Studies* 24 (1978): 457–64

**List sources in alphabetical order.**

## Commentary on the Essay

This essay fulfills an assignment of 1500-2000 words, with ten to fifteen sources. (There are actually fifteen, not counting a dictionary reference.) The bibliography was developed from a college library computer catalogue, references in books of criticism (Magalaner, Daly); the *MLA International Bibliography*; the *Essay and General Literature Index*, and the Literature Resource Center available through Netscape and a county library system (<www.wls.lib.ny.us>). The sources themselves were found in a college library with selective holdings, in a local public library, and in online resources. There is only one rare source, an article (Harmat) obtained in photocopy through interlibrary loan from one of only two United States libraries holding the journal in which it appears. The location was made through the national OCLC library service ("Online Computer Library Center"). For most semester-long or quarter-long courses, you will probably not have time to add to your sources by such a method, but the article in question refers specifically to "Miss Brill," and it was therefore desirable to examine it.

The sources consist of books, articles, and chapters or portions of books. One article (Sewell) has been published as a separate short monograph. Also, one of the sources is the story "Miss Brill" itself (with locations made by paragraph number), together with a collection of her stories. The sources are used for facts, interpretations, reinforcement of conclusions, and general guidance and authority.

All necessary thematic devices, including overall organization and transitions, are unique to the illustrative essay. The essay also contains passages taking issue with certain conclusions in a few of the sources. Additional particulars about the handling of sources and developing a research essay are included in the discussion of note taking and related matters in this chapter.

The central idea of the essay (paragraph 1) is built out of this idea, explaining that the movement of emotions in the story is accompanied by an intricate and complementary set of structures. Paragraphs 2 through 13 examine various elements of the story for their structural relationship to Miss Brill's emotions.

Paragraphs 2 and 3 detail the structural uses of the settings of autumn and times of day, pointing out how they parallel her experiences.

The longest part, paragraphs 4 through 10, is based on an idea not found in the sources—that a number of characters are experiencing difficulties and cruelties such as those that befall Miss Brill. Paragraph 5 cites the three couples of the story, paragraph 6 the silent old people, and paragraph 7 the scornful woman with violets. Paragraph 8 is developed in disagreement with one of the sources, showing how an essay involving research may be original even though the sources form the basis of discussion. Paragraph 9 contains additional examples of insensitivity—two of them involving Miss Brill herself. Paragraph 10 summarizes the story's instances of insensitivity and cruelty, once again emphasizing parallels to Miss Brill's situation.

Paragraphs 11 through 13 of the essay are based on ideas about the story's structure found in one of the sources (Thorpe). It is hence more derivative than paragraphs 4 through 10. Paragraphs 14 and 15, the concluding paragraphs of the essay, are devoted to the story's dénouement and to the broader application of the story: Miss Brill is to be considered an example of the anonymous "isolatoes" who inhabit the park. Because they are comparable to Miss Brill, their lives are just as sad and anguishing as hers is.

The list of "Works Cited" is the basis of all references in the essay, in accord with the *MLA Handbook for Writers of Research Papers*, 6th ed. By locating these references, a reader might readily examine, verify, and study any of the ideas and details drawn from the sources and developed in the essay.

## Writing Topics: How to Undertake Research Essays

In beginning research on any of the following topics, follow the steps in research described in this chapter.

1. Common themes in a number of stories by Hawthorne, Poe, Hardy, or Mansfield (just one, not all).
2. Various critical views of a Hemingway story.
3. Hawthorne's use of religious and moral topic material.
4. Porter's exemplification of Granny Weatherall's strength of character.
5. Views about women in Chopin, Welty, Mansfield, or Steinbeck.
6. Poe's view of the short story as represented in "The Masque of the Red Death."

# Reading and Writing
# about Poetry

# Chapter 11

# Meeting Poetry:
# An Overview

**O**ur words *poem* and *poetry* are derived from the Greek word *poiein,* "to create or make," the idea being that poetry is a created artifact, a structure that develops from the human imagination and that is expressed rhythmically in words. Although the word **poet** originally meant the writer of any kind of literature, we now use the word exclusively to mean a person who writes poems. *Poetry* and *poem* describe a wide variety of spoken and written forms, styles, and patterns, and also a wide variety of subjects. In light of this variety, we believe that the best way to understand poetry is to experience it—read it, study it, savor it, think about it, dream about it, learn it, memorize it, mull it over, talk about it with others, ask questions about it, enjoy it, love it. The more experience with poetry you have, the more you will develop your own ideas and definitions of just what poetry is, and the deeper will be your understanding and the greater your appreciation.

## The Nature of Poetry

We begin with a poem based in the lives of students and teachers alike.

### BILLY COLLINS (b. 1941)

###  Schoolsville (1985)

Glancing over my shoulder at the past,
I realize the number of students I have taught
is enough to populate a small town.

I can see it nestled in a paper landscape,
5    chalk dust flurrying down in winter,
nights dark as a blackboard.

The population ages but never graduates.
On hot afternoons they sweat the final in the park
and when it's cold they shiver around stoves
10   reading disorganized essays out loud.

A bell rings on the hour and everybody zigzags
in the streets with their books.

I forgot all their last names first and their
first names last in alphabetical order.
But the boy who always had his hand up                                   15
is an alderman and owns the haberdashery.
The girl who signed her papers in lipstick
leans against the drugstore, smoking,
brushing her hair like a machine.

Their grades are sewn into their clothes                                 20
like references to Hawthorne.°                          i.e., *The Scarlet Letter*
The A's stroll along with other A's.
The D's honk whenever they pass another D.

All the creative writing students recline
on the courthouse lawn and play the lute.                                25
Wherever they go, they form a big circle.

Needless to say, I am the mayor.
I live in the white colonial at Maple and Main.
I rarely leave the house. The car deflates
in the driveway. Vines twirl around the porchswing.                      30

Once in a while a student knocks on the door
with a term paper fifteen years late
or a question about Yeats or double-spacing.
And sometimes one will appear in a window pane
to watch me lecturing the wall paper,                                    35
quizzing the chandelier, reprimanding the air.

## Questions

1. What recognizable school experiences does the poem mention? Why is "Schoolsville" the title?

2. Describe the speaker. How does he indicate affection for students?

3. What details indicate that the poem is fantasy and not reality? To what degree is the poem humorous?

4. Compare the details of this poem with those in Roethke's "Dolor" (Chapter 14). What similarities do you find in the choice and appropriateness of detail? What differences?

5. Each poem you read may help you understand, and therefore define, poetry. How might this poem help you begin making a definition?

"Schoolsville" reveals the variety and freedom of poetry. Unlike poems that are set out in strict line lengths, rhythms, and rhymes, "Schoolsville," though arranged in lines, does not follow measured rhythmical or rhyming patterns. The language is not difficult, the descriptions are straightforward, and the scenes seem both real and amusing, though fanciful. Many details—such as the "chalk dust flurrying down" like snow, "the girl who signed her papers in lipstick," and the students forming a circle when they meet—are outrightly funny. But the poem moves from apparent reality to something beyond reality. Unifying the poem is the idea that school life is, like life generally, at once comical, serious, memorable, and poignant.

We may contrast "Schoolsville" with the following poem, "Hope," by Lisel Mueller, which deals with a topic—hope—that is common to us all, a topic that governs both our present and future behavior. What is unique, however, is that the poet provides us with thoughts about the nature of hope that might never have occurred to us. In this sense the poem fulfills the creative goal of poetry to lead us and guide us.

## LISEL MUELLER (b. 1924)

 **Hope** (1976)

It hovers in dark corners
before the lights are turned on,
   it shakes sleep from its eyes
   and drops from mushroom gills,
5       it explodes in the starry heads
      of dandelions turned sages,
         it sticks to the wings of green angels
         that sail from the tops of maples.

It sprouts in each occluded° eye                    *closed, blind*
10 of the many-eyed potato,
   it lives in each earthworm segment
   surviving cruelty,
      it is the motion that runs
      from the eyes to the tail of a dog,
15       it is the mouth that inflates the lungs
      of the child that has just been born.

It is the singular gift
we cannot destroy in ourselves,
the argument that refutes death,
20 the genius that invents the future,
all we know of God.

It is the serum which makes us swear
not to betray one another;
it is in this poem, trying to speak.

## Questions

1. How does the poem illustrate the meaning of hope? How true or adequate are the specific locations where hope may be found? How do these locations provide the grounds for a broadened understanding of hope?

2. What does the poet mean by saying that hope is a "singular gift/we cannot destroy in ourselves" and that hope is a "serum" that prevents people from betraying each other?

3. According to the illustrations in the poem, how strong is the connection between hope and life? Can anything or anyone exist without hope?

4. Why does the poet write "trying to speak" rather than "speaking" in the final line?

"Hope" demonstrates that poetry is inseparable from life and living. We regularly hope for fine weather, good luck, happier times, love, successful academic and athletic performance, more money, more and better friendships, successful and rewarding careers, and so on. But Mueller leads us on a new and unexpected trip. Her speaker reminds us that hope exists in common things around us where we have never even imagined it might be, such as the fluttering seeds ("angels") of maple trees, the expanding lungs of a newborn baby, and "the genius that invents the future." Hope may even be found in the blind eyes of a potato which, when planted in lowly garden dirt, possess an indomitable impulse for growth. The poem makes these ordinary things extraordinary. Mueller even leaves us with a speculative and unusual conclusion, giving life to hope by stating that hope speaks simultaneously with poetry itself. All these connections, which Mueller naturally and easily creates for us, cause us to say yes, to agree that hope exists in every obscure and out-of-the-way part of existence. Like all good poetry, "Hope" leads us into thoughts which we have not only not considered, but which we have never even dreamed about.

We should always recognize that good poems, regardless of their topic, have similar power. To see this, let us look at another poem, by the seventeenth-century English poet Robert Herrick.

## ROBERT HERRICK (1591–1664)

 ## Here a Pretty Baby Lies (1648)

Here a pretty baby lies
Sung asleep with lullabies:
Pray be silent, and not stir
Th'easy earth that covers her.

## Questions

1. What situation is described in this poem? To what degree is this situation either ordinary or unusual?

2. How does the final line change your perception of the first three lines? How does it change your response to the poem?

3. Consider the double meanings of the following words and phrases: "Here . . . lies"; "Sung asleep"; "lullabies"; "stir."

Nothing in the first three lines of this short poem seems anything other than ordinary. A scene is described that takes place over and over again everywhere in the world. A baby is sleeping quietly, and we are told to make no sounds that would awaken her. But the last line hits us with a hammer, making us realize that nothing in the poem is what we understood at first. We immediately change our initial impressions and realize that the baby is not just sleeping but dead, lying not in a cradle but in a coffin; that the lullabies are not the lullabies sung by a loving mother but the religious songs sung at a funeral ceremony; and that the stirring is not just making noise but disturbing the still-loose earth that has just been shoveled onto the baby's grave. The effect of this very simple poem has been called overwhelming; it was overwhelming when it was first written in the seventeenth century, and it is still overwhelming.

The three poems we have just seen have much in common; they are serious, engaging, original, and powerful. The first, however, is amusing and slightly perplexing; the second is serious and thought provoking; the third is sad and deeply moving. There are no other poems like them. Once we have read them, we will never forget them. Even if we never read them again (but we should), they will echo in our minds as time passes, sometimes with great power and impact, sometimes with less. In reading them again we may rediscover our original responses, and often we may have entirely new responses to them. In short, these poems live, and as long as we too live, they will be a permanent part of our minds.

## Preliminary Ideas About Poetry Can Help Understanding

As "Schoolsville," "Hope," and "Here a Pretty Baby Lies" demonstrate, all good poems are unique, and all good poems broaden our comprehension and add layers to our understandings. Like living itself, the experience of poetry is a growing process, but nevertheless, it is possible to offer a number of preliminary statements as a guide to understanding. To begin with, poems are imaginative works expressed in words that are used with the utmost compression, force, and economy. Unlike prose, which is expansive if not exhaustive, many poems are brief. But poetry is also comprehensive, offering us high points of thought, feeling, reflection, and resolution. Poems may be formed in just about any coherent and developed shape, from a line of a single word to lines of 20, 30, or more words; and these lines may be organized into any number of repeating or nonrepeating patterns. Some poems make us think, give us new and unexpected insights, and generally instruct us. Other poems arouse our emotions, surprise us, amuse us, and inspire us. Ideally, reading and understanding poetry should prompt us to reexamine, reinforce, and reshape our ideas, our attitudes, our feelings, and our lives. Let us hear what Robert Frost concluded about poetry: "Read it a hundred times: it will forever keep its freshness as a metal keeps its fragrance. It can never lose its sense of a meaning that once unfolded by surprise as it went."[1] Always be prepared for surprise, and be delighted when it appears.

---

[1]"The Figure a Poem Makes," in *Complete Poems of Robert Frost 1949* (New York: Holt, 1949), p. viii.

## Poetry of the English Language

Today, most nations of the world have their own literatures, including poetry, with their own unique histories and characteristics. In this anthology, however, we are concerned primarily, but not exclusively, with poetry in our own language by American, British, and Canadian poets.

The earliest poems in English date back to the period of *Old English* (450–1100). Many of these early English poems reflect the influence of Christianity. Indeed, the most famous poem, the epic *Beowulf,* was probably interpreted as a Christian allegory even though it concerns the secular themes of adventure, courage, and war. Ever since the *Middle English* period (1100–1500), poets have written about many other subjects, although religious themes have remained important. Today, we find poetry on virtually all topics, including worship, music, love, society, sports, individuality, strong drink, sexuality, warfare, government, and politics; some poems treat special and unusual topics such as fishing, machines, buildings, computers, exotic birds, and car crashes.

In short, poetry is in a flourishing condition in all its many forms. Commonly held moral principles are instilled by the use of well-known brief poems, epigrams, rhymes, and jingles, such as "Work./Don't shirk," "A good beginning/Is half the winning," and "A stitch in time/Saves nine." Many people, such as poets themselves and teachers, read poetry or parts of poems aloud in front of audiences of students, friends, families, and general audiences. Many others read poetry silently in private for their own benefit. Nursery rhymes are one of the important means by which children learn the vocabulary and rhythms of our language. Poems that are set to music and sung aloud are especially powerful. Francis Scott Key's "The Star-Spangled Banner," which he wrote during the Battle of Fort McHenry in the War of 1812, is our national anthem and is sung before sports competitions and many other events. More recently, musical groups such as the Beatles and U2, along with singer Bruce Springsteen, have given poetic expression to ideas that huge masses of people have taken to heart. Ever since the 1960s, people devoted to civil rights have been unified and strengthened by the simple lyrics of "We Shall Overcome," not only in the United States but throughout the world. During the national crisis following the attacks on the World Trade Center and the Pentagon in 2001, many people turned to "America the Beautiful" and "God Bless America" as songs that stir the heart. The strength and vitality of poetry could be similarly documented time and time again.

## How to Read a Poem

With poetry, as with any other literary form, the more effort we put into understanding, the greater will be our reward. Poems are often about subjects that we have never experienced directly. We have never met the poet, never had his or her exact experiences, and never thought about things in exactly the same way. To recapture the experience of the poem, we need to understand the language, ideas, attitudes, and frames of reference that bring the poem to life.

We must therefore read all poems carefully, thoughtfully, sympathetically. The economy and compression of poetry mean that every part of the poem must carry some of the impact and meaning, and thus every part repays careful attention. Try to interact with the poem. Do not expect the poem (or the poet) to do all the work. The poem contributes its language, imagery, rhythms, ideas, and all the other aspects that make it poetry, but you, the reader, will need to open your mind and your heart to the poem's impact. You have to use your imagination and let it happen.

There is no single technique for reading, absorbing, and appreciating poetry. In Chapter 1 we offer a number of guidelines for studying any work of literature (pp. 11–12). In addition to following the guidelines, read each poem more than once and keep in mind these objectives.

1. **Read straight through to get a general sense of the poem.** In this first reading, do not stop to puzzle out hard passages or obscure words; just read through from beginning to end. The poem is probably not as hard as you might at first think.

2. **Try to understand the poem's meaning and organization.** As you read and reread the poem, study these elements.

   • *The title.* The title is almost always informative. The title of Collins's "Schoolsville" suggests that the poem will contain a flippant treatment of school life. The title of Frost's "Stopping by Woods on a Snowy Evening" suggests that the poem will present ideas derived from a natural scene of cold and darkness.

   • *The speaker.* Poems are dramatic, having points of view just like prose fiction. First-person speakers talk from the "inside" because they are directly involved in the action (such as the speaker in Collins's "Schoolsville"). Other speakers are "outside" observers demonstrating the third-person limited and omniscient points of view, as in the anonymous "Sir Patrick Spens" (see also Chapter 3).

   • *The meanings of all words, whether familiar or unfamiliar.* The words in many poems are immediately clear, as in Herrick's "Here a Pretty Baby Lies," but other poems may contain unfamiliar words and references that need looking up. You will need to consult dictionaries, encyclopedias, and other sources until you get a firm grasp of the poem's content. If you have difficulty with meanings even after using your sources, ask your instructor.

   • *The poem's setting and situation.* Some poems establish their settings and circumstances vividly. Frost's "Stopping by Woods on a Snowy Evening" describes an evening scene in which the speaker stops his sleigh by a woods so that he can watch snow falling amid the trees. Although not all poems are so clear, you should learn as much as you can about setting and situation in every poem you read.

   • *The poem's basic form and development.* Some poems, like the anonymous "Sir Patrick Spens," are narratives; others, like Northrup's "Ogichidag," are personal statements; still others may be speeches to another person, such as Herrick's "Here a Pretty Baby Lies." The poems may be laid out in a sonnet form or may develop in two-line sequences (couplets). They may contain stanzas, as in Mueller's "Hope," each unified by a particular action or thought.

Try to determine the form and to trace the way in which the poem unfolds, part by part.

- *The poem's subject and theme.* The **subject** indicates the general or specific topic, while the **theme** refers to the idea or ideas that the poem explores. Jarrell's "The Death of the Ball Turret Gunner" announces its subject in the title. However, you must usually make inferences about the theme. Jarrell's theme is the repulsive ugliness of war, the poignancy of untimely death, the callousness of the living toward the dead, and the suddenness with which war forces young people to face cruelty and horror.

3. **Read the poem aloud, sounding each word clearly.** Although this step may seem unnecessary, reading aloud will enable you to judge the effect of sound, rhythm, and rhyme. If you read Jarrell's "The Death of the Ball Turret Gunner" aloud, for example, you will notice the impact of rhyming *froze* with *hose* and the suggestion of the percussive sounds of cannon fire in the repeated and rhyming *l*, *a*, and *k* sounds of *black flak*. (For a more detailed consideration of sounds in poetry, see Chapter 15.)

4. **Prepare a paraphrase of the poem, and make an explication of the ideas and themes.** A paraphrase (discussed later in this chapter) is a restatement of the poem in your own words which helps crystallize your understanding (see also Chapter 2, pp. 101–103). An explication, which is both explanation and interpretation, goes beyond paraphrase to consider significance—either of brief passages or of the entire poem.

## Studying Poetry

Let us now look in detail at a poem, in this case one that tells a story. It was composed as a song, or ballad, sometime during the late Middle Ages or early Renaissance, when most people got information about the outside world from strolling balladeers who sang the news to them (there were no newspapers way back then, and besides, few people could read). It tells a story that was probably true, or at least that was based on a real event.

### ANONYMOUS

 **Sir Patrick Spens** (Fifteenth century)

The king sits in Dumferline° town,
   Drinking the blood-red wine:
"O where will I get a good sailor
   To sail this ship of mine?"

---

°SIR PATRICK SPENS. 1 *Dumferline*: a town on the Firth of Forth, in Scotland.

5  Up and spoke an eldern° knight                      *old, senior*
   Sat° at the king's right knee:                  *who sat*
  "Sir Patrick Spens is the best sailor
   That sails upon the sea."

  The king has written a braid° letter           *large, commanding*
10    And signed it wi'° his hand,                 *with*
  And sent it to Sir Patrick Spens,
   Was° walking on the sand.                     *who was*

  The first line that Sir Patrick read,
   A loud laugh laughèd he;
15  The next line that Sir Patrick read,
   A tear blinded his eye.

  "O who is this has° done this deed,              *who has*
   This ill deed done to me,
  To send me out this time o'° the year,          *of*
20    To sail upon the sea?

  "Make haste, make haste, my merry men all,
   Our good ship sails the morn."°                *in the morning*
  "O say not so, my master dear,
   For I fear a deadly storm.

25  Late late yestere'en° I saw the new moon          *yesterday evening*
   With the old moon in her arm,
  And I fear, I fear, my dear master,
   That we will come to harm."

  O our Scots nobles were right loath
30    To wet their cork-heeled shoon,°             *shoes*
  But long ere a'° the play were played           *all*
   Their hats they swam aboon.°                  *about [in the water]*

  O long, long may their ladies sit
   Wi' their fans into their hand,
35  Or e'er they see Sir Patrick Spens
   Come sailing to the land.

  O long, long may the ladies stand,
   Wi' their gold combs in their hair,
  Waiting for their own dear lords,
40    For they'll see them no more.

  Half o'er, half o'er to Aberdour°                *
   It's fifty fathom deep,
  And there lies good Sir Patrick Spens,
   Wi' the Scots lords at his feet.

---

°41 *Aberdour*: Aberdeen, on the east coast of Scotland on the North Sea, about 80 miles north of Dumferline.

## Questions

1. What action does the poem describe? Who are the principal individual figures? What groups of people are involved with and concerned about the action?
2. What do you learn about the principal figure, Sir Patrick Spens? Why does he follow the king's orders rather than his own judgment?
3. What conflicts do you find in the poem? Do they seem personal or political?
4. What emotions are conveyed in the last two stanzas? Since the poem does not explain why the king sends Sir Patrick and his men to sea, how might the emotions have been expressed more strongly?
5. Describe the poem's use of dialogue. How many people speak? How do the speeches assist in conveying the poem's action?

"Sir Patrick Spens" is a **narrative ballad**. A narrative tells a story, and the term *ballad* defines the poem's shape or form, which was originally a song for dancing. The first two stanzas set up the situation: The king needs a captain and crew to undertake a vital mission, and an old knight—one of the king's close advisers—suggests Sir Patrick Spens, who is obviously distinguished and reliable. The rest of the poem focuses on the feelings and eventual death of Sir Patrick and his men. The third stanza provides a transition from the king to Sir Patrick. The king orders Sir Patrick to embark on an important sea voyage, and Sir Patrick reads the order. At first he laughs—probably sardonically, because Sir Patrick's response is that an order to go to sea during an obvious time of danger is a grim joke. But when he realizes that the order is real, he foresees disaster. Our sense of impending calamity is increased when we learn that Sir Patrick's crewmen are also frightened (lines 23–28).

The shipwreck, described in the eighth stanza, is presented with ironic understatement. There is no description of the storm or of the crew's panic, nor does the speaker describe the masts splitting or the ship sinking under the waves. Although these horrors are omitted, the floating hats are grim evidence of destruction and death. The remainder of the poem continues in this vein of understatement. In the ninth and tenth stanzas the focus shifts back to the land, and to the ladies who will wait a "long, long" time (forever) for Sir Patrick and his men to return. The poem ends with a vision of Sir Patrick and the "Scots lords" lying "fifty fathom deep."

On first reflection, "Sir Patrick Spens" tells a sad tale without complications. The subject seems to describe no more than Sir Patrick's drowning, along with his crew and the Scots noblemen. One might therefore claim that the poem does not have a clear theme. Even the irony of the floating hats and the waiting ladies is straightforward and unambiguous.

However, you might consider how the poem appeals to our imaginations through its suggestions of the contradictions and conflicts between authority and individuals. Sir Patrick knows the danger, yet he still obeys the king. In addition, in lines 5, 17 to 20, and 31 there is a suggestion of political infighting. The "eldern knight" is in effect responsible for dooming the ship. Moreover, the "play" being "played" suggests that a political game is happening beyond the grim game of the men caught in the deadly storm (if Sir Patrick knows the danger, would not the knight also know it, and would not this knight also know the consequences of choosing Sir Patrick?). These political motives are not spelled out, but they are implied. Thus the poem is not only a sad tale but also a stark dramatization of how power operates, of how a loyal person responds to a tragic dilemma, and of the pitiful consequences of that response.

In reading poetry, then, let the poem be your guide. Get all the words, try to understand dramatic situations, follow the emotional cues the poet gives you, and try to explain everything that is happening. Let the poem trigger your imagination. If you find implications that you believe are important, as with the political overtones of "Sir Patrick Spens," use details from the poem to support your observations. Resist the temptation to "uncover" unusual or far-fetched elements in the poem (such as that hope is a tiny spirit that inhabits human beings, trees, and vegetables, or that the "man he killed" was literally the speaker's brother). Draw only those conclusions that the poem itself supports.

## Poems for Study ◄

## ELIZABETH BREWSTER (b. 1922)

 ## Where I Come From (1994)

People are made of places. They carry with them
hints of jungles or mountains, a tropic grace
or the cool eyes of sea-gazers. Atmosphere of cities
how different drops from them, like the smell of smog
or the almost-not-smell of tulips in the spring,          5
nature tidily plotted in little squares
with a fountain in the centre; museum smell,
art also tidily plotted with a guidebook;
or the smell of work, glue factories maybe,
chromium-plated offices; smell of subways          10
crowded at rush hours.

                  Where I come from, people
carry woods in their minds, acres of pine woods;
blueberry patches in the burned-out bush;
wooden farmhouses, old, in need of paint,          15
with yards where hens and chickens circle about,
clucking aimlessly; battered schoolhouses
behind which violets grow. Spring and winter
are the mind's chief seasons: ice and the breaking of ice.

A door in the mind blows open, and there blows          20
a frosty wind from fields of snow.

## Questions

1. In what sense are people "made of places" (line 1)? What kinds of places does the poet describe in the first eleven lines?
2. How does the poem shift at the middle of line eleven? Does it seem that the speaker presents a more favorable view of the area "Where I come from" than of the area described in the first eleven lines?
3. What is the sense of the final two lines? How are these lines connected to the earlier parts of the poem? What sense of self-criticism is apparent in these last two lines?

## WILLIAM COWPER (1731–1800)

 ## The Poplar Field (1782)

The poplars are felled,° farewell to the shade          *cut down*
And the whispering sound of the cool colonnade.
The winds play no longer, and sing in the leaves,
Nor Ouse° on his bosom their image receives.

---

°4 *Ouse*: river in northern England, near which Cowper lived.

5   Twelve years have elapsed since I last took a view
    Of my favourite field and the bank where they grew,
    And now in the grass behold they are laid,
    And the tree is my seat that once lent me a shade.

    The blackbird has fled to another retreat
10  Where the hazels afford him a screen from the heat,
    And the scene where his melody charmed me before,
    Resounds with his sweet-flowing ditty no more.

    My fugitive years are all hasting away,
    And I must ere long lie as lowly as they,
15  With a turf on my breast, and a stone at my head,
    Ere another such grove shall arise in its stead.

    'Tis a sight to engage me, if any thing can,
    To muse on the perishing pleasures of man;
    Though his life be a dream, his enjoyments, I see,
20  Have a being less durable even than he.

## Questions

1. What situation does the speaker describe? How has the scene changed from what he knew twelve years before? Why does the speaker refer to the passage of time? What kind of person is he?

2. How has the situation affected the blackbird? Why does the speaker care?

3. How does the scene affect the speaker? What idea does he express about what has occurred?

## EMILY DICKINSON (1830–1886)

*For a photo, see Chapter 18, page 734.*

# Because I Could Not Stop for Death (J712, F479) (1890 (ca. 1863))

    Because I could not stop for Death—
    He kindly stopped for me—
    The Carriage held but just Ourselves—
    And Immortality.

5   We slowly drove—He knew no haste
    And I had put away
    My labor and my leisure too,
    For His Civility—

We passed the School, where Children strove
At Recess—in the Ring— 10
We passed the Fields of Gazing Grain—
We passed the Setting Sun—

Or rather—He passed Us—
The Dews drew quivering and chill—
For only Gossamer,° my Gown— *thin fabric* 15
My Tippet°—only Tulle°— *cape, scarf; thin silk*

We passed before a House that seemed
A Swelling of the Ground—
The Roof was scarcely visible—
The Cornice—in the Ground— 20

Since then—tis Centuries—and yet
Feels shorter than the Day
I first surmised the Horses' Heads
Were toward Eternity—

## Questions

1. Who is the speaker, and what is she like? Why couldn't she stop for Death? What perspective does her present position give the poem?
2. In what unusual ways does the poem characterize death?
3. What does the carriage represent? Where is it headed? Who are the riders? What is meant by the things the carriage passes?
4. What is represented by the house in line 17? Why does the poet use the word "House" in preference to some other word?

## ROBERT FRANCIS (1901–1987)

 ## Catch (1950)

Two boys uncoached are tossing a poem together,
Overhand, underhand, backhand, sleight of hand, every hand,
Teasing with attitudes, latitudes, interludes, altitudes,
High, make him fly off the ground for it, low, make him stoop,
Make him scoop it up, make him as-almost-as-possible miss it, 5
Fast, let him sting from it, now, fool him slowly,
Anything, everything tricky, risky, nonchalant,
Anything under the sun to outwit the prosy,
Over the tree and the long sweet cadence down,
Over his head, make him scramble to pick up the meaning, 10
And now, like a posy, a pretty one plump in his hands.

## Questions

1. Describe the language of "Catch." How does the poet establish that there are two meanings to most of the words in the game of catch played by the "boys"?

2. How accurately does the poem describe a game of ordinary catch in which the participants are throwing a baseball? How interesting would a game of catch be if the participants stood still and merely threw the ball back and forth to each other? How interesting would poetry be if the poet did not create variety just as the catch players vary their throws?

3. How well does the analogy of the game of catch explain why poetry sometimes requires extra efforts of understanding?

## ROBERT FROST (1874–1963)

*For a photo, see Chapter 18, page 748.*

 ## Stopping by Woods on a Snowy Evening (1923)

Whose woods these are I think I know.
His house is in the village though;
He will not see me stopping here
To watch his woods fill up with snow.

5  My little horse must think it queer
To stop without a farmhouse near
Between the woods and frozen lake
The darkest evening of the year.

He gives his harness bells a shake
10  To ask if there is some mistake.
The only other sound's the sweep
Of easy wind and downy flake.

The woods are lovely, dark and deep,
But I have promises to keep,
15  And miles to go before I sleep,
And miles to go before I sleep.

## Questions

1. What do we learn about the speaker? Where is he? What is he doing?
2. What is the setting (place, weather, time) of this poem?
3. Why does the speaker want to watch the "woods fill up with snow"?
4. What evidence suggests that the speaker is embarrassed or self-conscious about stopping? Consider the words "though" in line 2 and "must" in line 5.
5. The last stanza offers two alternative attitudes and courses of action. What are they? Which does the speaker choose?

**6.** To what extent do the sound and rhyme of this poem contribute to its impact? Note especially the *s* sounds in line 11 and the *w* sounds in line 12.

## JOHN HAINES (b. 1936)

 ## Little Cosmic Dust Poem (1985)

Out of the debris of dying stars,
this rain of particles
that waters the waste with brightness;
the sea-wave of atoms hurrying home,
collapse of the giant,
unstable guest who cannot stay;                                                    5

the sun's heart reddens and expands,
his mighty aspiration is lasting,
as the shell of his substance
one day will be white with frost.                                                   10

In the radiant field of Orion°
great hordes of stars are forming,
just as we see every night,
fiery and faithful to the end.

Out of the cold and fleeing dust                                                    15
that is never and always,
the silence and waste to come—
this arm, this hand,
my voice, your face, this love.

---

°11 *Orion*: a prominent winter constellation. Recent observations have led scientists to conclude that stars are being formed in the nebulous area in the "sword" of the constellation.

## THOMAS HARDY (1840–1928)

 ## The Man He Killed (1902)

"Had he and I but met
By some old ancient inn,
We should have sat us down to wet
Right many a nipperkin!°                                 *half-pint cup*

"But ranged as infantry,                                                            5
And staring face to face,
I shot at him as he at me,
And killed him in his place.

"I shot him dead because—
10     Because he was my foe.
Just so: my foe of course he was;
     That's clear enough; although

"He thought he'd 'list,° perhaps,                                    *enlist*
Off-hand like—just as I—
15 Was out of work—had sold his traps°—                            *possessions*
No other reason why.

"Yes; quaint and curious war is!
You shoot a fellow down
You'd treat if met where any bar is,
20     Or help to half-a-crown."°

─────────────
°20 *half a crown*: at the time, the equivalent of $20 or $30.

## Questions

1. Who and what is the speaker? What do you learn about him from his language?
2. What situation and event is the speaker recalling and relating?
3. What is the effect produced by repeating the word "because" in lines 9 and 10 and using the word "although" in line 12?
4. What is the speaker's attitude toward his "foe" and toward what he has done?
5. What point, if any, does this poem make about war? How are this poem and Jarrell's "The Death of the Ball Turret Gunner" similar and different?

## JOY HARJO (b. 1951)

 ### Eagle Poem (1990)

To pray you open your whole self
To sky, to earth, to sun, to moon
To one whole voice that is you.
And know there is more
5 That you can't see, can't hear,
Can't know except in moments
Steadily growing, and in languages
That aren't always sound but other
Circles of motion.
10 Like eagle that Sunday morning
Over Salt River. Circled in blue sky
In wind, swept our hearts clean
With sacred wings.
We see you, see ourselves and know
15 That we must take the utmost care
And kindness in all things.

Breathe in, knowing we are made of
All this, and breathe, knowing
We are truly blessed because we
Were born, and die soon within a                                                    20
True circle of motion,
Like eagle rounding out the morning
Inside us.
We pray that it will be done
In beauty.                                                                                      25
In beauty.

## Questions

1. What is meant by the requirement that "to pray you open your whole self/To sky, to earth, to sun, to moon"? What is the meaning of lines 4–9?
2. Why is the eagle significant to the speaker? Of what importance is the figure that the eagle makes?
3. Why does the poet repeat the phrase "In beauty" at the poem's end?

# RANDALL JARRELL (1914–1965)

 ## The Death of the Ball Turret Gunner° (1945)

From my mother's sleep I fell into the State
And I hunched in its belly till my wet fur froze.°
Six miles from earth, loosed from its dream of life,
I woke to black flak° and the nightmare fighters.
When I died they washed me out of the turret with a hose.        5

---

°BALL TURRET GUNNER: High-altitude bombers in World War II (1941–1945) contained a revolvable gun turret both at the top and at the bottom, from which a machine-gunner could shoot at attacking fighter planes. Gunners in these turrets were sometimes mutilated by the gunfire of attacking planes. 2 froze: The stratospheric below-zero temperatures caused the moisture in the gunner's breath to freeze as it contacted the collar of his flight jacket. 4 flak: the round, black explosions of antiaircraft shells fired at bombers from the ground, an acronym of the German word Fliegerabwehrkanone.

## Questions

1. Who is the speaker? Where has he been, and what has he been doing? What has happened to him?
2. In the first line, what is the poet saying about the age of the speaker and the opportunities he had for living before he was killed? How may this line be read politically and polemically?
3. What is a turret? What is your response to the last line?

**DORIANNE LAUX** (b. 1952)

 ## The Life of Trees (2003)

The pines rub their great noise
Into the spangled dark.
They scratch their itchy boughs
Against the house and the mystery
5  of that moan translates
into drudgery of ownership: time
to drag the ladder from the shed,
climb onto the roof with a saw
between my teeth, cut those suckers down.
10 What's reality if not a long exhaustive
cringe from the blade,
the teeth. I want to sleep
and dream the life of trees, beings
from the muted world who care nothing
15 for Money, Politics, Power,
Will or Right, who want little from the night
but a few dead stars going dim, a white owl
lifting from their limbs, who want only
to sink their roots into the wet ground
20 and terrify the worms or shake
their bleary heads like fashion models
or old hippies. If they could speak,
they wouldn't, only hum some low
green note, roll their pinecones
25 down the empty streets and blame it,
with a shrug, on the cold wind.
During the day they sleep inside
their furry bark, clouds shredding
like ancient lace above their crowns.
30 Sun. Rain. Snow. Wind. They fear
Nothing but the Hurricane, and Fire,
that whipped bully who rises up
and becomes his own dead father.
Then the young ones bend and bend
35 and the old know they may not make it,
go down with the power lines sparking,
broken at the trunk. They fling
their branches, forked sacrifice
to the beaten earth. They do not pray.
40 If they make a sound it's eaten
by the wind. And though the stars
return they do not offer thanks,
only ooze a sticky sap from their roundish
concentric wounds, clap the water
45 from their needles, straighten their spines
and breathe, and breathe again.

## Questions

1.  What contrast does the poem develop between human and sylvan or arboreal life? In general terms, what kind of existence do trees represent? How accurately does the poem describe this existence?

2.  In what way does the speaker seem to idealize the cares and interests of trees, in contrast to the tasks and duties of human beings? How does the final line, "breathe, and breathe again," represent a goal or duty from which human beings may benefit?

3.  Why does the speaker say "What's reality if not a long exhaustive/cringe from the blade,/the teeth"? How does this description fit an idea of the reality facing human beings?

## EMMA LAZARUS (1849–1887)

 ## The New Colossus (1883)

Not like the brazen giant of Greek fame,°
With conquering limbs astride from land to land;
Here at our sea-washed, sunset gates shall stand
A might woman with a torch, whose flame
Is the imprisoned lightning, and her name                                 5
Mother of Exiles. From her beacon-hand
Glows world-wide welcome; her mild eyes command
The air-bridged harbor that twin cities frame.
    "Keep, ancient lands, your storied pomp!" cries she
With silent lips. "Give me your tired, your poor,                          10
Your huddled masses yearning to breathe free,
The wretched refuse of your teeming shore.
Send these, the homeless, tempest-tossed to me,
I lift my lamp beside the golden door!"

---

1 *brazen giant of Greek fame*: the statue of Apollo that stood at the harbor of ancient Rhodes, an island in the Aegean Sea. Known as the "Colossus," it was sheathed in copper, and it was one of the seven wonders of the ancient world. 8 *The air-bridged harbor that twin cities frame*: "The air-bridged harbor that is framed by the twin cities [of New York and Newark, New Jersey]."

## Questions

1.  Why does the poem open with the word "Not"? What argument is introduced by the use of this word and its contrast with the Statue of Liberty? How is this argument brought out throughout the sonnet? Why is this poem always associated with the Statue of Liberty?

2.  What does "golden door" mean about the United States? Why does the poet use the name "Mother of Exiles" in reference to the statue? How is "golden" (line 14) to be contrasted with "brazen" (line 1)?

3.  What is meant by the "New Colossus"? How does the poem present an optimistic view for the "huddled masses" that will come to the United States to "breathe free"?

## LOUIS MACNEICE (1907–1963)

 **Snow** (1935)

The room was suddenly rich and the great bay-window was
Spawning snow and pink roses against it
Soundlessly collateral and incompatible:
World is suddener than we fancy it.

5   World is crazier and more of it than we think,
Incorrigibly plural. I peel and portion
A tangerine and spit the pips and feel
The drunkenness of things being various.

And the fire flames with a bubbling sound for world
10  Is more spiteful and gay than one supposes—
On the tongue on the eyes on the ears in the palms of one's hands—
There is more than glass between the snow and the huge roses.

### Questions

1.  Where is the speaker at the time of the poem? What is the contrast between the roses and the snow? Why is this contrast important?
2.  What words describe snow in lines 1–3? What words in lines 4, 5, 6, 8, 10 describe the world generally? Why does the speaker choose these words rather than more descriptive ones?
3.  What does the last line suggest?
4.  What similarities and differences do you find between "Snow" (p. 474) and Frost's "Stopping by Woods on a Snowy Evening" (p. 474)?

## EUGENIO MONTALE (1896–1981)

 **English Horn (Corno Inglese)** (1916–20)

*Translated by Robert Zweig*

The intent wind that plays tonight
—recalling a strong slashing of blades—
the instrument of dense trees and sweeps
the horizon of copper
5   where streaks of light are stretching,
like roaring kites in the sky
(Moving clouds, clear kingdoms
above!  High Eldorados'
partly shut doors!)
10  and the angry sea, which scale by scale,
changes color

launches a twisted horn
of spume towards land;
The wind that is born and dies
in the hour that slowly goes black—
if only, tonight, it could play you too
dissonant instrument,
heart.

15

## Questions

1. What does the wind do in this poem? Why do you think the speaker wishes the wind to "play" her heart?
2. What are the images of the earth? What are the images of the sky? How are they different?
3. What lines indicate that the speaker is either satisfied or dissatisfied with with her life? What images help you to understand her feelings about herself?
4. What does the speaker mean by referring to Eldorados' doors as "partly shut"?
5. What is the meaning of the title, "Engish Horn (Corno Inglese)"?

## JIM NORTHRUP (b. 1943)

 Ogichidag° (1993)

I was born in war, WW Two.
Listened as the old men told stories
of getting gassed in the trenches, WW One.
Saw my uncles come back from
Guadalcanal, North Africa,                                    5
and the Battle of the Bulge.
Memorized the war stories
my cousins told of Korea.
Felt the fear in their voices.
Finally it was my turn,                                       10
my brothers too.
Joined the marines in time
for the Cuban Missile Crisis.
Heard the crack of rifles
in the rice paddies south of Da Nang.                         15
Watched my friends die there
then tasted the bitterness of
the only war America ever lost.
My son is now a warrior.
Will I listen to his war stories                              20
or cry into his open grave?

---

°The title "Ogichidag" is the Ojibway word for "warriors."

## Questions

1. What battles are mentioned in the poem, and over what period of time do these battles extend?
2. How does the speaker state that he learned about the battles? Why is this method of gaining knowledge important? What experience has the speaker had with war?
3. Why does the speaker finish the poem by referring to his son? In relationship to the poem's structure, why is the concluding question important?

## NAOMI SHIHAB NYE (b. 1952)

 ### Where Children Live (1982)

Homes where children live exude a pleasant rumpledness,
like a bed made by a child, or a yard littered with balloons.

To be a child again one would need to shed details
till the heart found itself dressed in the coat with a hood.
5   Now the heart has taken on gloves and mufflers,
the heart never goes outside to find something to "do."
And the house takes on a new face, dignified.
No lost shoes blooming under bushes.
No chipped trucks in the drive.
10  Grown-ups like swings, leafy plants, slow-motion back and forth.
While the yard of a child is strewn with the corpses
of bottle-rockets and whistles,
anything whizzing and spectacular, brilliantly short-lived.

Trees in children's yards speak in clearer tongues.
15  Ants have more hope. Squirrels dance as well as hide.
The fence has a reason to be there, so children can go in and out.
Even when the children are at school, the yards glow
with the leftovers of their affection,
the roots of the tiniest grasses curl toward one another
20  like secret smiles.

## Questions

1. How accurately does the poem present the "pleasant rumpledness" of children?
2. What is the speaker's view of the comparative dependence or independence of children? What does the speaker think of children?
3. Sometimes poems about children can be overly sentimental. How well does this poem present sentiment about children? Does it go too far, or is it about right?

# JOYCE CAROL OATES (b. 1938)

 **Loving** (1970)

A balloon of gauze around us,
sheerest gauze: it is a balloon of skin
around us, fine light-riddled skin,
invisible.

If we reach out to pinch its walls it floats from us—    5
it eludes us wetly, this sac.

It is warmed by a network of veins
fine as hairs and invisible.
The veins pulsate and expand to the width
of eyelashes.    10
In them blood floats weightless as color.
The warm walls sink upon us when we love
each other, and are blinded by the heavier skin
that closes over our eyes.

We are in here together.    15
Outside, people are walking in a landscape—
it is a city landscape, it is theirs.
Their shouts and laughter come to us in broken sounds.
Their strides take them everywhere in daylight.
If they turn suddenly toward us we draw back—    20
the skin shudders wetly, finely—
will  we be torn into two people?

The balloon will grow up around us again
as if  breathed out of us, moist and sticky and light
as skin, more perfect than our own skin,    25
invisible.

## Questions

1. What does the speaker mean by a "balloon of gauze around us"? How does she define this balloon? What does she mean by "We are in here together" (line 15)?

2. Why does the speaker refer to veins and blood and "warm walls" in discussing the subject of loving? How common are these references to love? How appropriate is the language?

3. How would you characterize the speaker's attitudes about love? To what does the final stanza refer?

## MOLLY PEACOCK (b. 1947)

 ### Desire (1984)

It doesn't speak and it isn't schooled,
like a small foetal animal with wettened fur.
It is the blind instinct for life unruled,
visceral frankincense and animal myrrh.
5   It is what babies bring to kings,
an eyes-shut, ears-shut medicine of the heart
that smells and touches endings and beginnings
without the details of time's experienced *part-
fit-into-part-fit-into-part*. Like a paw,
10  it is blunt; like a pet who knows you
and nudges your knee with its snout—but more raw
and blinder and younger and more divine, too,
than the tamed wild—it's the drive for what is real,
deeper than the brain's detail: the drive to feel.

### Questions

1.  In line 4, what is the meaning of the references to frankincense and myrrh? Why does line 5 introduce a reference to "what babies bring to kings"? What ideas about desire does the poet seem to be suggesting by using these references?

2.  What thoughts about desire does the poet introduce in the poem's last six lines, particularly the concluding couplet? Why is desire compared to "a pet who knows you"?

3.  In view of the poem's topic, what reason can you give to explain why the poet does not begin every line with a capital letter?

## WILLIAM SHAKESPEARE (1564–1616)

*For a portraite, see Chapter 21, page 981.*

 ### Sonnet 55: Not Marble, Nor the Gilded Monuments (1609)

Not marble, nor the gilded monuments
Of princes, shall outlive this powerful rhyme;
But you shall shine more bright in these contents
Than unswept stone, besmeared with sluttish time.
5   When wasteful war shall statues overturn,
And broils root out the work of masonry,
Nor° Mars his° sword nor war's quick fire shall burn          *Neither; Mars's*
The living record of your memory.
'Gainst death and all-oblivious enmity
10  Shall you pace forth; your praise shall still find room
Even in the eyes of all posterity

That wear this world out to the ending doom.°                                   *Judgment Day*
So, till the judgment that yourself arise,
You live in this, and dwell in lovers' eyes.

## Questions

1. Who is the speaker of the poem, and who is being addressed?
2. What powers of destruction does the speaker mention? What, according to the speaker, will survive these powers?
3. What does "the living record of your memory" (line 8) mean?
4. What is the poem's subject? Theme?

## PERCY BYSSHE SHELLEY (1792–1822)

 ## To—— ("Music, When Soft Voices Die") (1824)

Music, when soft voices die,
Vibrates in the memory;
Odors, when sweet violets sicken,
Live within the sense they quicken.°                                   *make vibrantly alive*

Rose leaves, when the rose is dead,                                              5
Are heaped for the belovèd's bed;
And so thy thoughts,° when thou art gone,                    *this shall also happen to thy thoughts*
Love itself shall slumber on.

## Questions

1. What is the topic of this poem? What view of reality is the poet describing? What is the purpose of the words *die*, *sicken*, *dead*, and *art gone*? If music, odors, roses, and thoughts are no longer alive in actuality, in what sense do they continue to live?
2. What is meant by the phrase "shall slumber on" (line 8)? How can love slumber on, but not die? What is the connection between love slumbering and the memory of music, the sense of the odors of violets, and the heaping of rose leaves on the marriage bed?
3. In what way does the speaker praise the thoughts of the listener?

## ELAINE TERRANOVA (b. 1939)

 ## Rush Hour (1995)

Odd, the baby's scabbed face peeking over
the woman's shoulder. The little girl
at her side with her arm in a cast,
wearing a plain taffeta party dress.
The woman herself who is in shorts and sunglasses                                5
among commuters in the underground station. Her body
that sags and tenses at the same time.

The little girl has not once moved
to touch her or to be touched.
10 Even on the train, she never turns and says,
"Mommy." Sunlight bobs over her blond head
inclining toward the window. The baby
is excited now. "Loo, loo, loo, loo,"
he calls, a wet crescendo. "He's pulling
15 my hair," the little girl at last cries out.

A kind man comes up the aisle to see
the baby. He stares at those rosettes of blood
and wants to know what's wrong with him.
The woman says a dog bit him. "It must have been
20 a big dog, then." "Oh, no. A neighbor's little dog."
The man says, "I hope they put that dog to sleep."
The woman is nearly pleading. "It was an accident. He didn't
mean to do it." The conductor, taking tickets,

25 asks the little girl how she broke her arm.
But the child looks out to the big, shaded houses.
The woman says, "She doesn't like to talk
about that." No one has seen what is behind
her own dark glasses. She pulls the children to her.
30 Maybe she is thinking of the arm raised over them,
Its motion that would begin like a blessing.

## Questions

1. What clues early in the poem indicate that the woman and her children are victims of domestic abuse?

2. Why does the mother not appeal for help when the two men, the "kind man" and the conductor, inquire about the injuries of the children? What is the irony of the raised arm in the last two lines? What is the pathos of the mother's situation?

3. Describe the attitude of the speaker telling the story of the poem. Why does the speaker do no more than describe details, and not actually rail against domestic abuse?

## WILLIAM WORDSWORTH (1770–1850)

 ## Lines Composed a Few Miles Above Tintern Abbey on Revisiting the Banks of the Wye During a Tour, June 13, 1798° (1798)

Five years have past; five summers, with the length
Of five long winters! and again I hear
These waters, rolling from their mountain-springs
With a soft inland murmur.—Once again
5 Do I behold these steep and lofty cliffs,

---

°Wordsworth first visited the valley of the Wye in southwest England in August 1793 at age twenty-three. On this second visit he was accompanied by his sister Dorothy (the "Friend" in line 115).

That on a wild secluded scene impress
Thoughts of more deep seclusion, and connect
The landscape with the quiet of the sky.
The day is come when I again repose

Here, under this dark sycamore, and view                    10
These plots of cottage-ground, these orchard-tufts,
Which at this season, with their unripe fruits,
Are clad in one green hue, and lose themselves
'Mid groves and copses. Once again I see
These hedge-rows, hardly hedge-rows, little lines          15
Of sportive wood run wild; these pastoral farms,
Green to the very door; and wreaths of smoke
Sent up, in silence, from among the trees!
With some uncertain notice, as might seem
Of vagrant dwellers in the houseless woods,                20
Or of some Hermit's cave, where by his fire
The Hermit sits alone.
                                These beauteous forms,
Through a long absence, have not been to me
As is a landscape to a blind man's eye:
But oft, in lonely rooms, and 'mid the din                 25
Of towns and cities, I have owed to them
In hours of weariness, sensations sweet,
Felt in the blood, and felt along the heart;
And passing even into my purer mind,                       30
With tranquil restoration:—feelings too
Of unremembered pleasure: such, perhaps,
As have no slight or trivial influence
On that best portion of a good man's life,
His little, nameless, unremembered acts                    35
Of kindness and of love. Nor less, I trust,
To them I may have owed another gift,
Of aspect more sublime; that blessed mood,
In which the burden of the mystery,
In which the heavy and the weary weight                    40
Of all this unintelligible world,
Is lightened:—that serene and blessed mood,
In which the affections gently lead us on,—
Until, the breath of this corporeal frame
And even the motion of our human blood                     45
Almost suspended, we are laid asleep
In body, and become a living soul:
While with an eye made quiet by the power
Of harmony, and the deep power of joy,
We see into the life of things.                            50
                                If this
Be but a vain belief, yet, oh!—how oft—
In darkness and amid the many shapes
Of joyless daylight; when the fretful stir
Unprofitable, and the fever of the world,                  55

Have hung upon the beatings of my heart—
How oft, in spirit, have I turned to thee,
O sylvan Wye! thou wanderer thro' the woods,
How often has my spirit turned to thee!
60     And now, with gleams of half extinguished thought,
With many recognitions dim and faint,
And somewhat of a sad perplexity,
The picture of the mind revives again:
While here I stand, not only with the sense
65   Of present pleasure, but with pleasing thoughts
That in this moment there is life and food
For future years. And so I dare to hope,
Though changed, no doubt, from what I was when first
I came among these hills; when like a roe
70   I bounded o'er the mountains, by the sides
Of the deep rivers, and the lonely streams,
Wherever nature led: more like a man
Flying from something that he dreads, than one
Who sought the thing he loved. For nature then
75   (The coarser pleasures of my boyish days,
And their glad animal movements all gone by)
To me was all in all.—I cannot paint
What then I was. The sounding cataract
Haunted me like a passion: the tall rock,
80   The mountain, and the deep and gloomy wood,
Their colours, and their forms, were then to me
An appetite; a feeling and a love,
That had no need of a remoter charm,
By thought supplied, nor any interest
85   Unborrowed from the eye.—That time is past,
And all its aching joys are now no more,
And all its dizzy raptures. Not for this
Faint I, nor mourn nor murmur; other gifts
Have followed; for such loss, I would believe,
90   Abundant recompense. For I have learned
To look on nature, not as in the hour
Of thoughtless youth; but hearing oftentimes
The still, sad music of humanity,
Nor harsh nor grating, though of ample power
95   To chasten and subdue. And I have felt
A presence that disturbs me with the joy
Of elevated thoughts; a sense sublime
Of something far more deeply interfused,
Whose dwelling is the light of setting suns,
100  And the round ocean, and the living air,
And the blue sky, and in the mind of man;
A motion and a spirit, that impels
All thinking things, all objects of all thought,
And rolls through all things. Therefore am I still
105  A lover of the meadows and the woods,

And mountains; and of all that we behold
From this green earth; of all the mighty world
Of eye, and ear,—both what they half create,
And what perceive; well pleased to recognize
In nature and the language of the sense,             110
The anchor of my purest thoughts, the nurse,
The guide, the guardian of my heart, and soul
Of all my moral being.
                       Nor perchance,
If I were not thus taught, should I the more       115
Suffer my genial spirits to decay:
For thou art with me here upon the banks
Of this fair river; thou my dearest Friend,
My dear, dear Friend; and in thy voice I catch
The language of my former heart, and read        120
My former pleasures in the shooting lights
Of thy wild eyes. Oh! yet a little while
May I behold in thee what I was once,
My dear, dear Sister! and this prayer I make,
Knowing that Nature never did betray            125
The heart that loved her; 'tis her privilege,
Through all the years of this our life, to lead
From joy to joy: for she can so inform
The mind that is within us, so impress
With quietness and beauty, and so feed          130
With lofty thoughts, that neither evil tongues,
Rash judgments, nor the sneers of selfish men,
Nor greetings where no kindness is, nor all
The dreary intercourse of daily life,
Shall e'er prevail against us, or disturb         135
Our cheerful faith that all which we behold
Is full of blessings. Therefore let the moon
Shine on thee in thy solitary walk;
And let the misty mountain-winds be free
To blow against thee: and, in after years,        140
When these wild ecstasies shall be matured
Into a sober pleasure; when thy mind
Shall be a mansion for all lovely forms,
Thy memory be as a dwelling-place
For all sweet sounds and harmonies; oh! then,   145
If solitude, or fear, or pain, or grief,
Should be thy portion, with what healing thoughts
Of tender joy wilt thou remember me,
And these my exhortations! Nor, perchance—
If I should be where I no more can hear        150
Thy voice, nor catch from thy wild eyes these gleams
Of past existence—wilt thou then forget
That on the banks of this delightful stream
We stood together; and that I, so long
A worshipper of Nature, hither came

155 Unwearied in that service: rather say
    With warmer love—oh! with far deeper zeal
    Of holier love. Nor wilt thou then forget,
    That after many wanderings, many years
    Of absence, these steep woods and lofty cliffs,
160 And this green pastoral landscape, were to me
    More dear, both for themselves and for thy sake!

# Writing a Paraphrase of a Poem

**Paraphrasing** is especially useful in the study of poetry. It fixes both the general shape and the details of a poem in your mind, and it also reveals the poetic devices at work. A comparison of the original poem with the paraphrase highlights the techniques and the language that make the poem effective.

To paraphrase a poem, rewrite it in prose, in your own words. Decide what details to include—a number that you determine partly by the length of the poem and partly by the total length of your paraphrase. When you deal with lyrics, sonnets, and other short poems, you may include all the details, and thus your paraphrase may be as long as the work, or longer. Paraphrases of long poems, however, will be shorter than the originals because some details must be summarized briefly while others may be cut entirely.

It is vital to make your paraphrase accurate and also to use *only your own words*. To make sure that your words are all your own, read through the poem several times. Then, put the poem out of sight and write your paraphrase. Once you've finished, check yourself both for accuracy and vocabulary. If you find that you've borrowed too many of the poem's words, choose other words that convey the same meaning, or else use quotation marks to set off the original words (but do not overuse quotations).

Above all, remain faithful to the poem, but *avoid drawing conclusions and giving unnecessary explanations*. It would be wrong in a paraphrase of Jarrell's "The Death of the Ball Turret Gunner," for example, to state, "This poem makes a forceful argument against the brutal and wasteful deaths caused by war." This assertion states the poem's *theme*, but it *does not* describe the poem's actual content.

## Organizing Your Paraphrase

The organization of your paraphrase should reflect the poem's form or development. Include material in the order in which it occurs. With short poems, organize your paraphrase to reflect the poem's development line by line or stanza by stanza. In paraphrasing Shakespeare's "Not Marble, Nor the Gilded Monuments," for example, you should deal with each four-line group in sequence and then consider the final couplet. With longer poems, look for natural divisions such as groups of related stanzas, verse paragraphs, or other possible organizational units. In every situation, the poem's shape should determine the form of your paraphrase.

# Illustrative Student Paraphrase

---

**A Paraphrase of Thomas Hardy's "The Man He Killed"°**

[1]     If the man I killed had met me in a bar, we would have sat down together and had many drinks. But because we belonged to armies of warring foot soldiers lined up on a battlefield, we shot at each other, and my shot killed him.

[2]     The reason I killed him, I think, was that he and I were enemies—just that. But as I think of it, I realize that he had enlisted exactly as I did. Maybe he did it on a whim, or maybe he had lost his job and sold everything he owned. There was no other reason to enlist.

[3]     Being at war is unusual and strange. Instead of buying a man a drink, or helping him out with a little money, you have to kill him.

---

°See p. 475 for this poem.

## Commentary on the Paraphrase

Because Hardy's poem is short, the paraphrase attempts to include all its details. The organization closely follows the poem's development. Paragraph 1, for example, restates the contents of the first two stanzas. Paragraph 2 restates the third and fourth stanzas. Finally, the last paragraph separately paraphrases the last stanza, which contains the reflections made by the poem's "I" speaker. This paragraph concludes the paraphrase just as the last stanza concludes the poem.

Notice that the essay does not abstract details from the poem, such as "The dead man might have become a good friend in peacetime" in paraphrasing stanza 5; nor does it extend details, such as "We would have gotten acquainted, had drinks together, told many stories, and done quite a bit of laughing" for stanza 1 (both stanzas, however, actually do suggest these details). Although the paraphrase reflects the poem's strong antiwar sentiments, an interpretive sentence such as "By his very directness, the narrator brings out the senselessness and brutality of warfare" would be out of place. What is needed is a short restatement of the poem to demonstrate the essay writer's understanding of the poem's content, and no more.

## WRITING A GENERAL EXPLICATION OF A POEM

**Explication** goes beyond the assimilation required for a paraphrase and thus provides you with the opportunity to show your understanding. But there is no need to explain everything in the poem. A complete, or total, explication would theoretically require you to explain the meaning and implications of each word and every line—a technique that obviously would be exhaustive (and exhausting). It would also be self-defeating, for explicating everything would prohibit you from using your judgment and deciding what is important.

A more manageable and desirable technique is therefore the **general explication**, which devotes attention to the meaning of individual parts in relationship to the entire work, as in the discussion of "Sir Patrick Spens" (p. 469). You might think of a general explication as your explanation or "reading" of the poem. Because it does not require you to go into exhaustive detail, you will need to be selective and to consider only those details that are significant in themselves and vital to your own thematic development.

## Questions for Discovering Ideas

- What does the title contribute to the reader's understanding?
- Who is speaking? Where is the speaker when the poem is happening?
- What is the situation? What has happened in the past, or what is happening in the present, that has brought about the speech?
- What difficult, special, or unusual words does the poem contain? What references need explaining? How does an explanation assist in the understanding of the poem?
- How does the poem develop? Is it a personal statement? Is it a story?
- What is the main idea of the poem? What details make possible the formulation of the main idea?

## Strategies for Organizing Ideas

Your general explication demonstrates your ability to (1) follow the essential details of the poem (the same as in a paraphrase), (2) understand the issues and the meaning the poem reveals, (3) explain some of the relationships of content to technique, and (4) note and discuss especially important or unique aspects of the poem.

In your introduction, use your central idea to express a general view of the poem, which your essay will bear out. The discussion of the anonymous "Sir Patrick Spens" (p. 469) suggests some possible central ideas, namely that (1) the poem highlights a conflict between self-preservation and obedience to authority, and (2) innocent people may be caught in political infighting. In the following illustrative student essay explicating Hardy's "The Man He Killed," the central idea is that war is senseless.

In the body of your essay, first explain the poem's content—not with a paraphrase but with a description of the poem's major organizing elements. Hence, if the speaker of the poem is "inside" the poem as a first-person involved "I," you do not need to reproduce this voice yourself in your description. Instead, *describe* the poem in your own words, with whatever brief introductory phrases you find necessary, as in the second paragraph of the following illustrative essay.

Next, explicate the poem in relation to your central idea. Choose *your own* order of discussion, depending on your topics. You should, however, re-emphasize your central idea with each new topic. Thus, you might wish to follow your description by discussing the poem's meaning, or even by presenting two or more possible interpretations.

You might also wish to refer to significant techniques. For example, in the anonymous "Sir Patrick Spens" a noteworthy technique is the unintroduced quotations (i.e., quotations appearing without any "he said" or "quoth he" phrases) as the ballad writer's means of dramatizing the commands and responses of Sir Patrick and his doomed crew. You might also introduce special topics, such as the crewman who explains that there will be bad luck because the new moon has "the old moon in her arm" (line 26). Such a reference to superstition might include the explanation of the crewman's assumptions, the relationship of his uneasiness to the remainder of the poem, and also how the ballad writer keeps the narrative brief. In short, discuss those aspects of meaning and technique that bear upon your central idea.

In your conclusion, you may repeat your major idea to reinforce the thematic structure of your essay. Because your essay is a general and not a complete explication, there will parts of the poem that you will not have discussed. You might therefore mention what might be gained from an exhaustive discussion of various parts of the poem (do not, however, begin to exhaust any subject in the conclusion of your essay). The last stanza of Hardy's "The Man He Killed," for example, contains the words "quaint and curious" in reference to war. These words are unusual, particularly because the speaker might have chosen *hateful, senseless, destructive,* or other similarly descriptive words. Why did Hardy have his speaker make such a choice? With brief attention to such a problem, you may conclude your essay.

## Illustrative Student Explication

Underlined sentences in this paper *do not* conform to MLA style and are used solely as teaching tools to emphasize the central idea, thesis sentence, and topic sentences throughout the paper.

Lagerstrom 1

Steven Lagerstrom

Professor Bonner

English 110

22 September 2007

**An Explication of Thomas Hardy's "The Man He Killed"°**

[1]     Hardy's "The Man He Killed" deals with the senselessness of war.* It does this

through a silent contrast between the needs of ordinary people, as represented by a young

---

°See p. 475 for this poem.

*Central idea.

man—the speaker—who has killed an enemy soldier in battle, and the antihuman and unnatural deaths of war. <u>Of major note in this contrast are the speaker's circumstances, his language, his sense of identity with the dead man, and his concerns and wishes.</u>[†]

[2]     <u>The speaker begins by contrasting the circumstances of warfare with those of peace.</u> He does not identify himself, but his speech reveals that he is common and ordinary—a person who enjoys drinking in a bar and who prefers friendship and helpfulness to violence. If he and the man he killed had met in an inn, he says, they would have shared many drinks, but because they met on a battlefield they shot at each other, and he killed the other man. The speaker tries to justify the killing but can produce no good reason except that the dead man was his "foe." Once he states this reason, he again thinks of the similarities between himself and the dead man, and then he concludes that warfare is "quaint and curious" (line 17) because it forces a man to kill another man who could have been a friend if they had met during peacetime.

[3]     <u>To make the irony of warfare clear, the poem uses easy, everyday language to bring out the speaker's ordinary qualities.</u> His manner of speech is conversational, as in "We should have sat us down" (line 3), "'list" (for "enlist," line 13), and his use of "you" in the last stanza. Also, his word choices, shown in words like "nipperkin," "traps," and "fellow" (lines 4, 15, and 18), are common and informal, at least in British usage. This language is important because it establishes that the speaker is an average man whom war has thrown into an unnatural role.

[4]     <u>As another means of stressing the stupidity of war, the poem makes clear that the two men—the live soldier who killed and the dead soldier who was killed—were so alike that they could have been brothers or even twins.</u> They had similar ways of life, similar economic troubles, similar wishes to help other people, and similar motives in enlisting in the army. Symbolically, the "man he killed" is the speaker himself, and hence the killing may be considered a form of suicide. The poem thus raises the question of why two people who are almost identical should try to kill each other. This question is rhetorical, for the obvious answer is that there is no good reason.

[5]     <u>Because the speaker (and also, very likely, the dead man) is shown as a person embodying the virtues of friendliness and helpfulness, Hardy's poem is a strong disapproval of war.</u> Clearly, political reasons for violence as policy are irrelevant to the

---

[†]Thesis sentence.

characters and concerns of the men who fight. They, like the speaker, would prefer to follow their own needs rather than remote and meaningless ideals. The failure of complex but irrelevant political explanations is brought out most clearly in the third stanza, in which the speaker tries to give a reason for shooting the other man. Hardy's use of punctuation—the dashes—stresses the fact that the speaker has no commitment to the cause he served when killing. Thus the speaker stops at the word "because—" and gropes for a reason (line 9). Not being articulate, he can say only "Because he was my foe./Just so: my foe of course he was;/That's clear enough" (lines 10–12). These short bursts of words indicate that he cannot explain things to himself or to anyone else except in the most obvious and trite terms, and in apparent embarrassment he inserts "of course" as a way of emphasizing hostility even though he clearly felt none toward the man he killed.

[6]     A reading thus shows the power of the poem's dramatic argument. Hardy does not establish closely detailed reasons against war as a policy but rather dramatizes the idea that all political arguments are unimportant in view of the central and glaring brutality of war—killing. Hardy's speaker is not able to express deep feelings; rather he is confused because he is an average sort who wants only to live and let live and to enjoy a drink in a bar with friends. But this very commonness stresses the point that everyone is victimized by war—both those who die and those who kill. The poem is a powerful argument for peace and reconciliation.

**WORK CITED**

Hardy, Thomas. "The Man He Killed." *Literature: An Introduction to Reading and Writing.* Ed. Edgar V. Roberts. Compact 4th ed. Upper Saddle River: Prentice Hall, 2009, 475.

## Commentary on the Explication

This explication begins by stating a central idea about "The Man He Killed," then indicates the topics to follow that will develop the idea. Although nowhere does the speaker state that war is senseless, the illustrative essay takes the position that the poem embodies this idea. A more detailed examination of the poem's themes might develop the idea by discussing the ways in which individuals are caught up in social and political forces, or the contrast between individuality and the state. In this essay, however, the simple statement of the idea is enough.

Paragraph 2 describes the major details of the poem, with guiding phrases like "The speaker begins," "he says," and "he again thinks." Thus, the paragraph goes over the poem, like a paraphrase, but explains how things occur, as is appropriate for an explication. Paragraph 3 is devoted to the speaker's words and idioms, with the idea that his conversational manner is part of the poem's contrasting method of argument. If these brief references to style were more detailed, this topic could be more fully developed as an aspect of Hardy's implied argument against war.

Paragraph 4 extends paragraph 3 inasmuch as it points out the similarities of the speaker and the man he killed. If the situation were reversed, the dead man might say exactly the same things about the present speaker. This affinity underscores the suicidal nature of war. Paragraph 5 treats the style of the poem's fourth stanza. In this context, the treatment is brief. The last paragraph reiterates the main idea and concludes with a tribute to the poem as an argument.

The entire explication therefore represents a reading and explanation of the poem's high points. It stresses a particular interpretation and briefly shows how various aspects of the poem bear it out.

## Writing Topics About the Nature of Poetry

1. Skim the titles of poems listed in the table of contents of this book. Judging by the subjects of these poems, describe and discuss the possible range of subject matter for poetry. What topics seem most suitable? Why? Do any topics seem to be ruled out? Why? What additional subject matter would you suggest as possible topics for poems?

2. How accurate is the proposition that poetry is a particularly compressed form of expression? To support your position, you might refer to poems such as Dickinson's "Because I Could Not Stop for Death," Francis's "Catch," Frost's "Stopping by Woods on a Snowy Evening," Shelley's "Music, When Soft Voices Die," and Terranova's "Rush Hour."

3. Consider the subject of war as brought out in Jarrell's "The Death of the Ball Turret Gunner," Hardy's "The Man He Killed," and Northrop's "Ogichidag." What ideas are common to the poems? What ideas are distinct and unique? On the basis of your comparison, consider the use of poetry as a vehicle for the expression of moral and political ideas.

4. Write two poems of your own about your future plans. In one, assume that the world is stable and will go on forever. In the other, assume that a large asteroid is on a direct path toward a collision with earth. It is moving at great speed, and when it hits earth a year from now it will bring untold destruction, and may even end life on earth. After composing your poems, write a brief explanation of how and why they differ in terms of language, references, and attitudes toward friends, family, country, religion, and so on.

5. Consult the brief section on reader-response criticism in Chapter 24. Then write an essay about your responses to one poem, or a number of poems, in this chapter. Assume that your own experiences are valuable guides for your judgment. In the poems that you have read, what has had a bearing on your experiences? What in your own experiences has given you insights into the poems? Try to avoid being anecdotal; instead, try to find a relationship between your experiences and the poetry.

6. In the reference section of your library, find two books (anthologies, encyclopedias, introductions, dictionaries of literary terms) about the general subject of poetry. On the basis of how these two sources define and explain poetry, together with your own experiences, write a brief essay telling a person younger than you what to expect from the reading of poems.

# Chapter 12

# Words: The Building Blocks of Poetry

**W**ords are the spoken and written signifiers of thoughts, objects, and actions. They are also the building blocks of both poetry and prose, but poetry is unique because by its nature it uses words with the utmost economy. The words of poetry create rhythm, rhyme, meter, and form. They define the poem's speaker, the characters, the setting, and the situation, and they also carry its ideas and emotions. For this reason, each poet searches for perfect and indispensable words, words that convey all the compressed meanings, overtones, and emotions that each poem requires, and also the words that sound right and look right.

Life—and poetry—might be simpler (but less interesting) if there were an exact, one-to-one correspondence between words and the objects or ideas they signify. Such close correspondences exist in artificial language systems such as chemical equations and computer languages. This identical correlation, however, is not characteristic of English or any other natural language. Instead, words have the independent and glorious habit of attracting and expressing a vast array of different meanings.

Even if we have not thought much about language, most of us know that words are sometimes ambiguous, and that much literature is built on ambiguity. For instance, in Shakespeare's *Romeo and Juliet*, when Mercutio says, "Seek for me tomorrow and you shall find me a grave man," the joke works because *grave* has two separate meanings, both of which come into play. In reading poetry, we recognize that poets rejoice in this shifting and elusive but also rich nature of language.

## Choice of Diction: Specific and Concrete, General and Abstract

Because poets always try to use only the exactly right words, they constantly make conscious and subconscious decisions about diction. One of the major categories of their choice is diction that is either specific and concrete or general and abstract.

**Specific** language refers to objects or conditions that can be perceived or imagined, and **general** language signifies broad classes of persons, objects, and phenomena. **Concrete** diction describes conditions or qualities that are exact and particular; **abstract** diction refers to qualities that are rarefied and theoretical. In practice, poems using specific and concrete words tend to be visual, familiar, and compelling. By

**494**

contrast, poems that use general and abstract words tend to be detached and cerebral, and they often deal with universal questions or emotions.

These distinctions become clear when we compare Housman's "Loveliest of Trees" and Eberhart's "The Fury of Aerial Bombardment." Many of the terms and images that Housman uses, such as "cherry . . . /hung with bloom" and "threescore years and ten," are specific and concrete; they evoke exact time and clear visualization. By contrast, Eberhart's terms, such as "infinite spaces" and "eternal truth," are general and abstract, and it is therefore hard to define them with clarity and exactness. This contrast, which by no means implies that Housman's poem is superior to Eberhart's, reflects differences in word choices for different objectives.

Most poets employ mixtures of words in these categories because in many poems they draw general observations and abstract conclusions from specific situations and concrete responses. They therefore interweave their words to fit their situations and ideas, as in Roethke's "Dolor," which uses specific and concrete words to define a series of abstract emotional states.

# Levels of Diction

Like ordinary speakers and writers of prose, poets choose words from the category of the three levels of diction: high or formal, middle or neutral, and low or informal. Often, the high and middle levels are considered standard or "right" while low language is dismissed as substandard or "wrong." In poetry, however, none of the classes is more correct than any other, for what counts is that they all function according to the poet's wishes, from broadly formal and intellectual to ordinary and popular.

## High or Formal Diction Is Elevated and Elaborate

**High** or **formal diction** exactly follows the rules of syntax, seeking accuracy of expression even if unusually elevated or complex words are brought into play. Beyond "correctness," formal language is characterized by complex words and a lofty tone. In general, formal diction freely introduces words of French, Latin, and Greek derivation, some of which are quite long, so some people might think that formal language is "difficult." Graves uses formal diction in "The Naked and the Nude" when the speaker asserts that the terms in the title are "By lexicographers construed/As synonyms that should express/The same deficiency of dress." The Latinate words stiffen and generalize the passage: We find *lexicographers* instead of *dictionary writers*, *construed* (from Latin) instead of *thought* (native English), *express* (from Latin) instead of *say* or *show* (native English), and *deficiency* (Latin) instead of *lack* (English). It is simply a fact that our language contains thousands of words that have descended to our language from French, Latin, or Greek and that many of these are long and abstract. But not all words of this sort are necessarily long, nor are they abstract and stiff. Many of our short words, for example, are French in origin, such as *class, face, fort, paint, bat, tend, gain, cap, trace, order,* and *very*. A college-level dictionary contains brief descriptions of word origins, or etymologies; as an exercise, you might trace the origins of a number of words in a poem.

## Middle or Neutral Diction Stresses Simplicity

**Middle** or **neutral diction** maintains the correct language and word order of formal diction but avoids elaborate words and elevated tone just as it avoids idioms, colloquialisms, contractions, slang, jargon, and fads of speech. For example, Emily Dickinson's "Because I Could Not Stop for Death" (Chapter 13) is almost entirely in middle diction.

## Low or Informal Diction Is the Language of Common, Everyday Use

**Low** or **informal diction** is relaxed and unself-conscious, the language of people buying groceries, gasoline, and pizza, and of people who may just be "hanging out." Poems using informal diction include common and simple words, idiomatic expressions, substandard expressions, foreign expressions, slang, "swearwords" or "cusswords," grammatical "errors," and contractions. Informal diction is seen in Hardy's "The Man He Killed" (Chapter 13), in which the speaker uses words and phrases like "many a nipperkin," "He thought he'd 'list," and "off-hand like."

# Special Types of Diction

Depending on their subjects and purposes, poets (and writers of prose) may wish to introduce four special types of diction into their poems: *idiom, dialect, slang,* and *jargon.*

## Idiom Refers to Unique Forms of Diction and Word Order

The words **idiom** and **idioms**, originally meaning "making one's own," refer to words, phrases, and expressions that are common and acceptable in a particular language, even though they might, upon analysis, seem peculiar or illogical. Standard English idioms are so ingrained into our thought that we do not notice them. Poems automatically reflect these idioms. Thus, for example, a poet may "think *of*" an idea, speak of "living *in*" a house, talk of "going *out* to play," or describe a woman "lovely *as* chandeliers." Poets hardly have choices about such idioms as long as they are using standard English. Real choice occurs when poets select idioms that are unusual or even ungrammatical, as in phrases such as "had he and I but met," "we was happy," and "except that You than He" (this last phrase is by Emily Dickinson). Idioms such as these enable poets to achieve levels of ordinary and colloquial diction, depending on their purposes.

## Dialect Refers to Regional and Group Usage and Pronunciation

Although we recognize English as a common language, in practice the language is made up of many habits of speech or **dialects** that are characteristic of many groups, regions, and nations. In addition to "general American," we can recognize many common dialects such as Southern, Midwestern, New England, Brooklynese, American Black English, Yiddish English, and Texan, together with "upper" British, Cockney, Scottish, and Australian English. Dialect is concerned with whether we refer to a *pail* (general American) or a *bucket* (Southern); or sit down on a *sofa* (Eastern) or a *couch* (general American) or *davenport* (Midwestern); or drink *soda* (Eastern), *pop* (Midwestern), *soda pop* (a confused Midwesterner living in the East, or a confused Easterner living in the Midwest), or *tonic* (Bostonian). Burns's "Green Grow the Rashes, O" and Hardy's "The Ruined Maid" illustrate the poetic use of dialect.

## Slang Refers to Informal and Substandard Vocabulary and Idiom

Much of the language that people use every day is **slang**. Sometimes slang is impermanent, appearing among certain speakers and then vanishing. The use of the word *bad* to mean "good" illustrates how a new slang meaning can develop, and even stay for a time. This is not to say that slang is not persistent, for some of it is a significant part of our language. There is a continuous word stock of substandard or "impolite" words, some of which are so-called "four-letter" words, that everyone knows but speaks only privately. There are also innumerable slang expressions. For example, we have many slang phrases describing dying, such as *kick the bucket, croak, be wasted, sleep with the fishes, buy the farm, be disappeared, be whacked,* and *be offed.* A nonnative speaker of English, unfamiliar with our slang, would have difficulty understanding that a person who "kicked the bucket," "bought the farm," "croaked," or "was offed" had actually died.

Even though slang is a permanent part of our language, it is usually confined to colloquial or conversational levels. (Interestingly, people with perfect command of standard English regularly use slang in private among their friends and acquaintances.) If slang is introduced into a standard context, therefore, it mars and jars, as in Cummings's "Buffalo Bill's Defunct" (Chapter 14), where the speaker refers to Buffalo Bill as a "blueeyed boy." Because the poem deals with the universality of death, the phrase, which usually refers to a young man on the make, ironically underscores this intention.

## Jargon Is the Special Language and Terminology of Groups

Particular groups develop **jargon**—specialized words and expressions that are usually employed by members of specific professions or trades, such as astronauts, doctors, lawyers, computer experts, plumbers, and football players. Without an initiation, people ordinarily cannot understand the special meanings. Although jargon at its worst befuddles rather than informs, it is significant when it becomes part of mainstream English or is used in literature. Poets may introduce jargon for special effects. For example, Paul Zimmer, in "The Day Zimmer Lost Religion" (Chapter 19), wryly uses the phrase "ready for Him now," a boxing expression that describes a fighter in top condition. Linda Pastan uses "gives me an A" and "I'm dropping out," both phrases from school life, to create comic effects in "Marks" (Chapter 19). Another poem employing jargon is Eberhart's "The Fury of Aerial Bombardment," which uses technical terms for firearms to establish the authenticity of the poem's references and therefore to reinforce the poem's judgments about warfare.

## ◆ DECORUM: THE MATCHING OF SUBJECT AND WORD

A vital literary concept is **decorum** ("beautiful," "appropriate"); that is, words and subjects should be in perfect accord—formal words for serious subjects, and informal words for low subjects and comedy. In Shakespeare's *A Midsummer Night's Dream*, for example, the nobles usually speak poetry and the "mechanicals" speak prose (Chapter 22). When the nobility are relaxed and in the forest, however, they also speak prose. Decorum governs such choices of language.

In the eighteenth century, English writers aimed to make their language as dignified as ancient Latin, which was the international language of discourse. They therefore asserted that only formal diction was appropriate for poetry; common life and colloquial language were excluded except in drama and popular ballads. These rules of decorum required standard and elevated language rather than common words and phrases. The development of scientific terminology during the eighteenth century also influenced language. In the scientific mode, poets of the time used descriptive phrases such as "lowing herd" for cattle (Thomas Gray) and "finny prey" for fish (Alexander Pope). In this vein, Thomas Gray observed the dependence of color on light in the line "cheerful fields resume their green attire" from the "Sonnet on the Death of Richard West."

Pope, one of the greatest eighteenth-century poets, maintained these rules of decorum—and also made fun of them—in his mock-epic poem *The Rape of the Lock*, and more fully in the mock-critical work *Peri Bathous, or The Art of Sinking in Poetry*. In *The Rape of the Lock*, he refers to a scissors as a "glittering forfex." Similarly, in the following couplet he elevates the simple act of pouring coffee.

> From silver spouts the grateful liquors glide,
> While China's earth receives the smoking tide.

Since Wordsworth transformed poetic diction early in the nineteenth century, the topics and language of people of all classes, with a special stress on common folk, have become a feature of poetry. Poets have continued to follow rules of decorum, however, inasmuch as the use of colloquial diction and even slang is a necessary consequence of popular subject matter.

## Syntax

**Syntax** refers to word order and sentence structure. Normal English word order is fixed in a *subject-verb-object* sequence. At the simplest level, we say, "A dog (*subject*) bites (*verb*) a man (*object*)." This order is so central to our communication that any change significantly affects meaning: "A dog bites a man" is not the same as "A man bites a dog."

Much of the time, poets follow normal word order, as in "The Lamb," where Blake creates a simple, easy order in keeping with the poem's purpose of presenting a childlike praise of God. Many modern poets, such as Mark Strand, go out of their way to create ordinary, everyday syntax, on the theory that a poem's sentence structures should not get in the way of the reader's perceptions.

Yet, just as poets always explore the limits of ideas, so also do they sometimes explore the many possibilities of syntax, as in line 7 of Donne's "Batter My Heart": "Reason, Your viceroy in me, me should defend." In prose, this sentence would read "Reason, who is Your viceroy in me, should defend me." But note that Donne drops the "who is," and that he also puts the direct object "me" before and not after the verb. The resulting emphasis on the pronoun *me* is appropriate to the personal-divine relationship that is the topic of the sonnet. The alteration also meets the demand of the poem's rhyme scheme. A set of particularly noteworthy syntactic variations occurs in Roethke's "Dolor." The poet uses an irregular and idiosyncratic combination of objects, phrases, and appositives to create ambiguity and uncertainty, underscoring the idea that school and office routines are aimless and depressing.

Some of the other means by which poets shape word order to create emphasis are an aspect of **rhetoric**. **Parallelism** is the most easily recognized rhetorical device. A simple form of parallelism is **repetition**, as with the phrase "who made thee" in Blake's "The Lamb." Through the use of the same grammatical forms, though in different words, parallelism produces lines or portions of lines that impress our minds strongly, as in this passage from Robinson's "Richard Cory," in which there are four parallel past-tense verbs (italicized here).

> So on we *worked*, and *waited* for the light,
> And *went* without the meat, and *cursed* the bread;

The final two lines of this poem demonstrate how parallelism may embody **antithesis**—a contrasting situation or idea that brings out surprise and climax:

> And Richard Cory, one calm summer night,
> *Went* home and *put* a bullet through his head.

A major quality of parallelism is the packing of words (the *economy* and *compression* of poetry), for by using a parallel structure the poet makes a single word or phrase function a number of times, with no need for repetition. The opening verb phrase "have known" in Roethke's "Dolor," though used once, controls six parallel direct objects. At the end of Donne's "Batter My Heart," parallelism (along with antithesis) permits Donne to omit the italicized words added and bracketed in the last line here.

for I,

> Except° You enthrall° me, never shall be free,                    *unless; enslave*
> Nor [*shall I*] ever [*be*] chaste, except You ravish me.

Note also that parallelism and antithesis make possible the unique *a b b a* ordering of these two lines, with the pattern "enthrall" (verb) "free" (adjective) "chaste" (adjective) "ravish" (verb). This rhetorical pattern is called **antimetabole** or **chiasmus** and is a common pattern of creating emphasis.

# Denotation and Connotation

To achieve the maximum impact, poets depend not just on the simplest, most essential meanings of words but also on the suggestions and associations that words bring to us. For this reason, control over denotation and connotation (see also Chapter 7) is so important that it has been called the very soul of the poet's art.

## Denotation Refers to Standard, Most Commonly Recognized Meanings

The ordinary dictionary meaning of a word—**denotation**—indicates conventional correspondences between words and objects or ideas. Although we might expect denotation to be straightforward, most English words have multiple denotations. The noun *house*, for example, can refer to a *building*, a *family*, a *branch of Congress*, a *theater*, a *theater audience*, a *sorority* or *fraternity*, an *astrological classification*, or a *brothel*. Although context usually makes the denotation of *house* more specific, the various meanings confer a built-in ambiguity in this simple word.

Denotation presents problems because with the passing of time new meanings emerge and old ones are shed. In poems written in the eighteenth century and earlier, there are many words that have changed so completely that a modern dictionary is not much help. In Marvell's "To His Coy Mistress" (Chapter 17), for example, the speaker asserts that his "vegetable love should grow/Vaster than empires, and more slow." At first reading, "vegetable" may seem to refer to something like a giant, loving turnip. When we turn to a current dictionary, we discover that *vegetable* is an adjective meaning "plantlike," but *plantlike love* does not get us much beyond *vegetable love*. A reference to the *Oxford English Dictionary (OED)*, however, tells us that *vegetable* was used as an adjective in the seventeenth century to mean "living or growing like a plant." Thus we find out that "vegetable love" means love that grows slowly but steadily larger.

## Connotation Refers to a Word's Emotional, Psychological, Social, and Historical Overtones

The life of language, and the most difficult to control, is a result of **connotation**. Almost no word is without it. For instance, according to the dictionary, the words *childish* and *childlike* denote the state of being like a child. Nevertheless, they connote or imply different sets of characteristics. *Childish* suggests a person who is bratty, stubborn, immature, silly, and petulant, whereas *childlike* suggests that a person may be innocent, charming, and unaffected. These different meanings are based entirely on connotations, for the denotations make little distinction.

Connotation affects us in almost everything we hear and read. We constantly encounter the manipulation of connotation in advertising, for example, which could not exist without the controlled management of meaning. Such manipulation may be as simple as calling a *used car* a *pre-owned car* to avoid the negative connotations of *used*. On the other hand, the manipulation may be as sophisticated as the current use of the word *lite* or *light* to describe foods and drinks. In all such products, *lite* denotes "dietetic," "low-calorie," or even "weak." The distinction—and the selling point—is found in connotation. Imagine how difficult it would be to sell a drink called "dietetic beer" or "weak beer." *Light* and *lite*, however, carry none of the negative connotations and, instead, suggest products that are pleasant, sparkling, bright, and healthy.

Poets always try to make individual words carry as many appropriate and effective denotations and connotations as possible. Put another way, poets use *packed* or *loaded* words that carry a broad range of meaning and association. With this in mind, read the following poem by Robert Graves.

## ROBERT GRAVES (1895–1985)

 ## The Naked and the Nude (1957)

For me, the naked and the nude
(By lexicographers° construed
As synonyms that should express
The same deficiency of dress
Or shelter) stand as wide apart          5
As love from lies, or truth from art.
Lovers without reproach will gaze
On bodies naked and ablaze;
The Hippocratic° eye will see
In nakedness, anatomy;                    10
And naked shines the Goddess when
She mounts her lion among men.

The nude are bold, the nude are sly
To hold each treasonable eye.
While draping by a showman's trick        15
Their dishabille° in rhetoric,
They grin a mock-religious grin
Of scorn at those of naked skin.

The naked, therefore, who compete
Against the nude may know defeat;         20
Yet when they both together tread
The briary pastures of the dead,
By Gorgons° with long whips pursued,
How naked go the sometime nude!

---

°THE NAKED AND THE NUDE. 2 *lexicographers*: writers of dictionaries. 9 *Hippocratic*: medical; the adjective derives from Hippocrates (ca. 460–377 B.C.E.), the ancient Greek who is considered the "father of medicine." 16 *dishabille*: being carelessly or partly dressed. 23 *Gorgons*: mythological female monsters with snakes for hair.

## Questions

1. How does the speaker explain the denotations and connotations of "naked" and "nude" in the first stanza? What is indicated by the fact that the word *naked* is derived from Old English *nacod* while *nude* comes from Latin *nudus*?
2. What examples of "the naked" and "the nude" do the second and third stanzas provide? What do the examples have in common?
3. How do the connotations of words like "sly," "draping," "dishabille," "rhetoric," and "grin" contribute to the poem's ideas about "the nude"?
4. What does "briary pastures of the dead" mean in line 22?

This poem explores the connotative distinctions between the title words, *naked* and *nude*, which share a common denotation. The title also suggests that the poem is about human customs, for if the speaker were considering the words alone, he would say "naked" and "nude" instead of "*the* naked and *the* nude." The speaker's use of *the* signifies a double focus on both language and human perspectives. In the first five lines the poem establishes that the two key words should be "synonyms that should express/The same deficiency of dress" (lines 3–4). By introducing elevated and complex words such as "lexicographers" and "construed," however, Graves implies that the connection between "the naked" and "the nude" is sophisticated and artificial.

In the rest of the poem, Graves develops this distinction, linking the word *naked* to virtues of love, truth, innocence, and honesty, while connecting *nude* to artifice, hypocrisy, and deceit. At the end, he visualizes a classical underworld in which all pretentiousness will disappear, and the nude will lose their sophistication and become merged with the naked. The implication is that artifice will vanish in the face of eternal reality. A thorough study of the words in the poem bears out the consistency of Graves's idea, not only about the two words in the title, but also about the accumulated layers of history, usage, and philosophy that weigh upon human life and thought.

## Poems for Study ⟵

# WILLIAM BLAKE (1757–1827)

## The Lamb (1789)

Little Lamb, who made thee?
  Dost thou know who made thee?
Gave thee life & bid thee feed,
By the stream & o'er the mead;
Gave thee clothing of delight,               5
Softest clothing wooly bright;
Gave thee such a tender voice,
Making all the vales rejoice!
  Little Lamb who made thee?
  Dost thou know who made thee?          10
  Little Lamb I'll tell thee,
  Little Lamb I'll tell thee!

He is called by thy name,
For he calls himself a Lamb:
He is meek & he is mild,                   15
He became a little child:
I a child & thou a lamb,
We are called by his name.
  Little Lamb God bless thee.
  Little Lamb God bless thee.           20

## Questions

1. Who or what is the speaker in this poem? The listener? How are they related?
2. What is the effect of repetition in the poem?
3. How would you characterize the diction in this poem? High, middle, or low? Abstract or concrete? How is it consistent with the speaker?
4. What are the connotations of "softest," "bright," "tender," "meek," and "mild"? What do these words imply about the Creator?
5. Describe the characteristics of God imagined in this poem. Contrast the image here with the image of God in Donne's "Batter My Heart."

## ROBERT BURNS (1759–1796)

### 🖋 Green Grow the Rashes, O (1787)

**1**

There's naught but care on ev'ry han',°                                 *hand*
    In every hour that passes, O;
What signifies the life o'° man                                          *of*
    An' 'twere na° for the lasses, O?                                    *if it were not*
Chorus:
Green grow the rashes,° O;                                              *rushes*
5   Green grow the rashes, O;
The sweetest hours that e'er I spend
    Are spent among the lasses, O!

**2**

The war'ly° race may riches chase,                                      *worldly*
10    An' riches still may fly them, O;
An' tho' at last they catch them fast,
    Their hearts can ne'er enjoy them, O.
Chorus.

**3**

But gie me a cannie° hour at e'en,°                                     *give me a happy; evening*
    My arms about my dearie, O,
15  An' war'ly cares an war'ly men
    May a' gae tapsalteerie,° O!                                        *all go topsy-turvy*
Chorus.

**4**

For you sae douce° ye sneer at this,                                    *so sober, so straitlaced*
    Ye're naught but senseless asses, O;
The wisest man the warl' e'er° saw,                                     *world ever*
20    He dearly loved the lasses, O.
Chorus.

**5**

Auld Nature swears the lovely dears
    Her noblest work she classes, O;
Her prentice han'° she tried on man,                                    *apprentice hand*
    An' then she made the lasses, O.
Chorus.

# Questions

**1.** Who is the speaker? What is he like? What is his highest value? How seriously do you take his pronouncements?

**2.** How does the speaker justify his feelings? How does he compare his interests with those of other people?

**3.** What is the speaker's explanation of the origins of men and women? How might this explanation have been received in 1787, the year of publication, when most people accepted the creation story as told in Genesis?

## LEWIS CARROLL (1832–1898)

 **Jabberwocky°** (1871)

'Twas brillig, and the slithy toves
  Did gyre and gimble in the wabe;
All mimsy were the borogoves,
  And the mome raths outgrabe.

"Beware the Jabberwock, my son!                 5
  The jaws that bite, the claws that catch!
Beware the Jubjub bird, and shun
  The frumious Bandersnatch!"

He took his vorpal sword in hand;
  Long time the manxome foe he sought—        10
So rested he by the Tumtum tree,
  And stood awhile in thought.

And, as in uffish thought he stood,
  The Jabberwock, with eyes of flame,
Came whiffling through the tulgey wood,        15
  And burbled as it came!

One, two! One, two! And through and through
  The vorpal blade went snicker-snack!
He left it dead, and with its head
  He went galumphing back.                     20

---

°The poem "Jabberwocky," which appears in the first chapter of *Through the Looking Glass*, is full of nonsense words that Carroll made up with the sound (rather than the sense) in mind. Alice admits that the poem makes some sense even though she does not know the words: "It seems very pretty . . . but it's rather hard to understand! . . . Somehow it seems to fill my head with ideas—only I don't exactly know what they are!"

"And hast thou slain the Jabberwock?
    Come to my arms, my beamish boy!
O frabjous day! Callooh! Callay!"
    He chortled in his joy.

25   'Twas brillig, and the slithy toves
    Did gyre and gimble in the wabe;
All mimsy were the borogoves,
    And the mome raths outgrabe.

## Questions

1. Summarize in your own words the story that this poem tells.
2. Humpty Dumpty begins to explain or explicate this poem for Alice in Chapter 6 of *Through the Looking Glass*. He explains that "'brillig' means four o'clock in the afternoon—the time when you begin *broiling* things for dinner." He also explains that "'slithy' means 'lithe' and 'slimy.' 'Lithe' is the same as 'active.' You see it's like a portmanteau—there are two meanings packed into one word." Go through the poem and determine what combinations of words are packed into these portmanteau words. *Brillig*, for example, might be seen as a combination of *broiling, brilliant,* and *light*.

### HAYDEN CARRUTH (b. 1921)

 **An Apology for Using the Word "Heart"**
**in Too Many Poems** (1959)

      What does it mean? Lord knows; least of all I.
         Faced with it, schoolboys are shy,
      And grown-ups speak it at moments of excess
         Which later seem more or less
5       Unfeasible. It is equivocal, sentimental,
         Debatable, really a sort of lentil—
      Neither pea nor bean. Sometimes it's a muscle,
         Sometimes courage or at least hustle,
      Sometimes a core or center, but mostly it's
10          A sound that slushily fits
      The meters of popular songwriters without
         Meaning anything. It is stout,
Leonine, chicken, great, hot, warm, cold,
    Broken, whole, tender, bold,
15 Stony, soft, green, blue, red, white,
    Faint, true, heavy, light,
Open, down, shallow, etc. No wonder
    Our superiors thunder
Against it. And yet in spite of a million abuses
20     The word survives; its uses

Are such that it remains virtually indispensable
   And, I think, defensible.
The Freudian terminology is awkward or worse,
   And suggests so many perverse
Etiologies that it is useless; but "heart" covers            25
   The whole business, lovers
To monks, i.e., the capacity to love in the fullest
   Sense. Not even the dullest
Reader misapprehends it, although locating
   It is a matter awaiting                                   30
Someone more ingenious than I. But given
   This definition, driven
Though it is out of a poet's necessity, isn't
   The word needed at present
As much as ever, if it is well written and said,           35
   With the heart and the head?

## Questions

1. How much attention is given in this poem to the meanings of the word "heart"? How accurate are the definitions? Why does the poet title the poem "An Apology. . . ."?

2. Would it be fair to describe some of the definitions as "flippant"? Why? How do we know that the poet is being serious?

3. Why does Carruth say, "Not even the dullest/Reader misapprehends it" (i.e., the word "heart")? How true is this claim?

## E. E. CUMMINGS (1894–1962)

# next to of course god america i (1926)

"next to of course god america i
love you land of the pilgrims' and so forth oh
say can you see by the dawn's early my
country 'tis of centuries come and go
and are no more what of it we should worry
in every language even deafanddumb                          5
thy sons acclaim your glorious name by gorry
by jingo by gee by gosh by gum
why talk of beauty what could be more beautiful than these heroic happy dead
who rushed like lions to the roaring slaughter              10
they did not stop to think they died instead
then shall the voice of liberty be mute?"

He spoke.   And drank rapidly a glass of water

## Questions

1. What is the form of this poem? What is the rhyme scheme? What does Cummings achieve by not using capitalization and punctuation?

2. Who is the speaker? What characteristics and capacities does he show? How do you respond to him?

3. What ideas does the poem bring out? In what ways does the speaker parody the speakers that one is likely to hear on the Fourth of July throughout the United States? What is Cummings saying not only about the speakers but also about the crowds that listen to such speeches?

## JOHN DONNE (1572–1631)

## Holy Sonnet 14: Batter My Heart, Three-Personed God (1633)

Batter my heart, three-personed God; for You
As yet but knock, breathe, shine, and seek to mend;
That I may rise and stand, o'erthrow me, and bend
Your force to break, blow, burn and make me new.
I, like an usurped° town, to another due,
Labor to admit You, but Oh, to no end;
Reason, Your viceroy in me, me should defend,
But is captived, and proves weak or untrue.
Yet dearly I love You, and would be loved fain.°
But am betrothed unto Your enemy.
Divorce me, untie or break that knot again;
Take me to You, imprison me, for I,
Except You enthrall me, never shall be free,
Nor ever chaste, except you ravish me.

## Questions

1. What kind of God is suggested by the words "batter," "knock," "overthrow," and "break"? What does "three-personed God" mean?

2. With which person of God might the verbs "knock" and "break" be associated? The verbs "breathe" and "blow"? The verbs "shine" and "burn"?

3. What is the effect of the altered word order at the ends of lines 7 and 9?

4. Explain the words "enthrall" (line 13) and "ravish" (line 14) to resolve the apparent paradox or contradiction in the last two lines.

# RICHARD EBERHART (1904–2005)

 ## The Fury of Aerial Bombardment (1947)

You would think the fury of aerial bombardment
Would rouse God to relent; the infinite spaces
Are still silent. He looks on shock-pried faces.
History, even, does not know what is meant.

You would feel that after so many centuries          5
God would give man to repent; yet he can kill
As Cain could, but with multitudinous will,
No farther advanced than in his ancient furies.

Was man made stupid to see his own stupidity?
Is God by definition indifferent, beyond us all?     10
Is the eternal truth man's fighting soul
Wherein the Beast ravens in its own avidity?

Of Van Wettering I speak, and Averill,
Names on a list, whose faces I do not recall
But they are gone to early death, who late in school  15
Distinguished the belt feed lever from the belt holding pawl.

## Questions

1. Who or what is the speaker in this poem? What does the last stanza tell you about him? (Eberhart was a gunnery instructor during World War II.)
2. What type and level of diction predominates in lines 1–12? What observations about God are made in these lines? Compare the image of God presented here with the one found in Donne's "Batter My Heart, Three-Personed God" and Blake's "The Lamb." What similarities or differences do you find?
3. How does the level and type of diction change in the last stanza? What is the effect of these changes? How is jargon used here?
4. Compare this poem with Thomas Hardy's "Channel Firing" (Chapter 13). How are the ideas in the poems similar?

# BART EDELMAN (b. 1951)

 ## Chemistry Experiment (2001)

We listened intently to the professor,
Followed each one of her instructions,
Read through the textbook twice,
Wore lab coats and safety goggles,
Mixed the perfect chemical combinations          5
In the proper amounts and order.
It was all progressing smoothly;

We thought we were a complete success.
And then the flash of light,
10　The loud, perplexing explosion,
The black rope of smoke,
Rising freely above our singed hair.
Someone in another lab down the hallway
Phoned the local fire department
15　Which arrived lickety-split
With the hazardous waste crew,
And they assessed the accident,
Deciding we were out of danger.
It was the talk of the campus
20　For many weeks afterwards.
We, however, became so disillusioned
That we immediately dropped the course
And slowly retreated from each other.
The very idea we could have done
25　More damage than we actually did—
Blown up ourselves and the building
From the base of its foundation—
Shook us, like nothing had before.
And even now, years later,
30　When anyone still asks about you,
I get this sick feeling in my stomach
And wonder what really happened
To all that elementary matter.

## Questions

1. What events are recounted in this poem? How may the narrative be placed into sections? Who is the listener or implied reader of the poem?

2. What level of language is contained here? Study lines 13–18. How does the diction change here? Why?

3. Why does the poem end as it does? What connection does this conclusion have with the previous parts of the poem? Why might this incident have caused the participants to have lost contact with each other?

## THOMAS GRAY (1716–1771)

 ### Sonnet on the Death of Richard West ((1742) 1775)

In vain to me the smiling mornings shine,
　　And redd'ning Phoebus° lifts his golden fire;
The birds in vain their amorous descant° join,　　　　　song
　　Or cheerful fields resume their green attire;°

°2 *Phoebus:* Apollo, the Sun God  4 *resume their green attire:* During the darkness of night, the "cheerful fields" have no color, but in the light of the morning sun they become green again.

These ears, alas! for other notes repine;
   A different object do these eyes require.
My lonely anguish melts no heart but mine.                    5
   And in my breast the imperfect joys expire.
Yet morning smiles the busy race to cheer,
   And new-born pleasure brings to happier men;
The fields to all their wonted tribute bear;°               10
   To warm their little loves the birds complain;°
I fruitless mourn to him that cannot hear,
   And weep the more because I weep in vain.

°11 *The fields . . . bear*: The fields contribute their customary harvest to benefit all creation. 12 *complain*: sing love songs.

## Questions

1. What is the poem's subject, the speaker or the dead friend? How effective is the poem as a lament or dirge?

2. Describe the poem's level of diction. Why does the speaker use phrases like "smiling mornings" (line 1), "redd'ning Phoebus" (2), "golden fire" (2), "resume their green attire" (4), and "notes" (5)? How common are these phrases? What is their effect?

3. Consider the syntax in lines 5, 6, 9, 10, 11, and 12. What is unusual about the word order in these lines? What is the effect of this word order?

4. In the 1800 Preface to *Lyrical Ballads*, William Wordsworth printed this poem. He italicized lines 6–8 and 13 and 14 and wrote, "It will easily be perceived, that the only part of this Sonnet which is of any value is the lines printed in Italics; it is equally obvious, that . . . the language of these lines does in no respect differ from that of prose." What does Wordsworth's criticism mean? To what degree is it justified?

## THOMAS HARDY (1840–1928)

*For a photo, see Chapter 11 page 471.*

### The Ruined Maid (1866)

"O 'melia,° my dear, this does everything crown!°;           *i.e., Amelia*
Who could have supposed I should meet you in Town?
And whence such fair garments, such prosperi-ty"—
"O didn't you know I'd been ruined," said she.

—"You left us in tatters, without shoes or socks,                5
Tired of digging potatoes, and spudding up docks;°         *digging up weeds*
And now you've gay bracelets and bright feathers three!"
"Yes: that's how we dress when we're ruined," said she.

—"At home in the barton° you said 'thee' and 'thou,'
And 'thik oon,' and 'theäs oon,' and t'other';° but now          10
Your talking quite fits 'ee° for high compa-ny!"—             *thee*
"Some polish is gained with one's ruin," said she.

°1 *does everything crown*: crowns everything; is a great surprise. 9 *At home in the barton*: when you lived at home on the farm. 9–10 *'thee' . . . 't'other'*: i.e., you spoke familiarly in the country dialect (using the second-person pronoun), saying "thik oon" for "that one" and "theäs oon" for "this one."

—"Your hands were like paws then, your face blue and bleak
But now I'm bewitched by your delicate cheek,
15   And your little gloves fit as on any la-dy!"—
"We never do work when we're ruined," said she.

—"You used to call home-life a hag ridden dream.
And you'd sigh, and you'd sock°; but at present you seem       *moan, groan*
To know not of megrims° or melancho-ly!"—       *migraine headaches*
20   "True. One's pretty lively when ruined," said she.

—"I wish I had feathers, a fine sweeping gown,
And a delicate face, and could strut about Town!"—
"My dear—a raw country girl, such as you be,
Cannot quite expect that. You ain't ruined," said she.

## Questions

1. Who are the two speakers? How have they come together? What are their present economic circumstances? Who is 'melia (Amelia)? Does she seem to be bragging to the first speaker? Why has not the first speaker learned about 'melia earlier, before their encounter in town?

2. How aware of her situation is 'melia? Is she happy or unhappy about it? How completely has she shed her country habits of speech?

3. What double meaning does the word "ruined" have in this poem? To what extent does Hardy use the poem to challenge conventional moral judgments?

## JANE HIRSHFIELD (b. 1953)

 **The Lives of the Heart** (1997)

Are ligneous,° muscular, chemical.
Wear birch-colored feathers,
green tunnels of horse-tail reed.
Wear calcified spirals, Fibonnacian spheres.°
5   Are edible; are glassy; are clay; blue schist.°
Can be burned as tallow, as coal,
can be skinned for garnets, for shoes.
Cast shadows or light;
shuffle; snort; cry out in passion.
10   Are salt, are bitter,
tear sweet grass with their teeth.
Step silently into blue needle-fall at dawn.
Thrash in the net until hit.
Rise up as cities, as serpentined magma, as maples,
15   hiss lava-red into the sea.

---

°1 *Ligneous*: woody, and therefore easily ignited.   4 *Fibonnacian spheres*: after Leonardo Fibonnaci (d. 1250), who described a sequence of numbers in which each new number is the sum of the previous two numbers. This pattern of numbers is found as a basic structure in many plants.   5 *schist*: a metamorphic, heavily layered rock.

Leave the strange kiss of their bodies
in Burgess Shale. Can be found, can be lost
can be carried, broken, sung.
Lie dormant until they are opened by ice,
by drought. Go blind in the service of lace.
Are starving, are sated, indifferent, curious, mad.                    20
Are stamped out in plastic, in tin.
Are stubborn, are careful, are slipshod,
are strong on the blue backs of flies
on the black backs of cows.
Wander the vacant whale-roads,° the white thickets                     25
heavy with slaughter.
Wander the fragrant carpets of alpine flowers.
Not one is not held in the arms of the rest, to blossom.
Not one is not given to ecstasy's lions.
Not one does not grieve.                                                30
Each of them opens and closes, closes and opens
the heavy gate—violent, serene, consenting, suffering it all.

---

°26 *whale-roads*: a figurative phrase in Old English poetry referring to the sea.

## Questions

1. Describe the attributes of the lives of the heart as brought out through the language of the first five lines.

2. Is there anywhere that lives of the heart are not to be found on earth? What is meant by lines such as "Not one is not given to ecstasy's lions" and "Go blind in the service of lace"?

3. How does the repetitiveness in this poem affect your perception of the lives of the heart? Explain the effect of the many repetitions of words and phrases like "are," "can be," "Not one," and the repetitions of verbs like "step," "thrash," "rise up," "hiss," lie, "wander," and "opens and closes."

4. Do you find this poem easy or difficult? Why?

5. Contrast this poem with Carruth's "An Apology for Using the Word 'Heart' in Too Many Poems."

## A. E. HOUSMAN (1859–1936)

 ## Loveliest of Trees, the Cherry Now (1896)

Loveliest of trees, the cherry now
Is hung with bloom along the bough,
And stands about the woodland ride°                    *path*
Wearing white for Eastertide.

Now, of my threescore years and ten,                               5
Twenty will not come again,
And take from seventy springs a score,
It only leaves me fifty more.

And since to look at things in bloom
10  Fifty springs are little room,
About the woodland I will go
To see the cherry hung with snow.

## Questions

1. How old is the speaker? How can you tell? Why does he assume he will live seventy years ("threescore years and ten")?

2. How would you describe the speaker's perception or sense of time? What is the effect of the words "only" (line 8) and "little" (line 10)?

3. What ideas about time, beauty, and life does this poem explore? What does it suggest about the way we should live?

## CAROLYN KIZER (b. 1925)

# Night Sounds (1984)

*imitated from the Chinese*

The moonlight on my bed keeps me awake;
Living alone now, aware of the voices of evening,
A child weeping at nightmares, the faint love-cries of a woman,
Everything tinged by terror or nostalgia.

5   No heavy, impassive back to nudge with one foot
While coaxing, "Wake up and hold me,"
When the moon's creamy beauty is transformed
Into a map of impersonal desolation.

But, restless in this mock dawn of moonlight
10  That so chills the spirit, I alter our history;
You were never able to lie quite peacefully at my side,
Not the night through. Always withholding something.

Awake before morning, restless and uneasy,
Trying not to disturb me, you would leave my bed
15  While I lay there rigidly, feigning sleep.
Still—the night was nearly over, the light not as cold
As a full cup of moonlight.

And there were the lovely times when, to the skies' cold *No*
You cried to me, *Yes!* Impaled me with affirmation.
20  Now when I call out in fear, not in love, there is no answer.

Nothing speaks in the dark but the distant voices,
A child with the moon in his face, a dog's hollow cadence.

## Questions

1. To what degree may this poem be considered confessional? What is being confessed?

2. Who is the "you" of the poem? What has happened between the speaker and the "you"? With what contrasts does the speaker conclude the poem? How are these contrasts related to the relationship between the speaker and the "you"?

3. What situation and impressions are brought about by these words in the first stanza: "moonlight," "weeping," "nightmares," "tinged," "terror," "nostalgia"?

4. What is the effect of the participles in stanzas 1–4 ("living," "coaxing," "withholding," "trying," "feigning")?

## DENISE LEVERTOV (1923–1997)

 **Of Being** (1997)

I know this happiness
Is provisional:

> the looming presences—
> great suffering, great fear—

> withdraw only
> into peripheral vision:

but ineluctable this shimmering
of wind in the blue leaves:

this flood of stillness
widening the lake of sky:

this need to dance,
this need to kneel:
          this mystery:

## Questions

1. What is meant by "this happiness/Is provisional"?

2. What is it that withdraws (line 5)? How does the poet connect withdrawing with the poem's title?

3. What do the words "peripheral vision," "ineluctable," "blue leaves," "flood of stillness," and "lake of sky" contribute to your understanding of the "mystery" with which the poem closes? What is noteworthy about these words?

4. Why does the poet end the poem with a colon rather than a period?

## HENRY REED (1914–1986)

 **Naming of Parts** (1946)

To-day we have naming of parts. Yesterday,
We had daily cleaning. And to-morrow morning,
We shall have what to do after firing. But to-day,
To-day we have naming of parts. Japonica
5   Glistens like coral in all of the neighboring gardens,
    And to-day we have naming of parts.

This is the lower sling swivel. And this
Is the upper sling swivel, whose use you will see,
When you are given your slings. And this is the piling swivel,
10  Which in your case you have not got. The branches
Hold in the gardens their silent, eloquent gestures,
    Which in our case we have not got.

This is the safety-catch, which is always released
With an easy flick of the thumb. And please do not let me
15  See anyone using his finger. You can do it quite easy
If you have any strength in your thumb. The blossoms
Are fragile and motionless, never letting anyone see
    Any of them using their finger.

And this you can see is the bolt. The purpose of this
20  Is to open the breech, as you see. We can slide it
Rapidly backwards and forwards: we call this
Easing the spring. And rapidly backwards and forwards
The early bees are assaulting and fumbling the flowers:
    They call it easing the Spring.

25  They call it easing the Spring: it is perfectly easy
If you have any strength in your thumb: like the bolt,
And the breech, and the cocking-piece, and the point of balance,
Which in our case we have not got; and the almond-blossom
Silent in all of the gardens and the bees going backwards and forwards,
30      For to-day we have naming of parts.

## Questions

1. There may be two speakers in this poem, or one speaker repeating the words of another and adding his own thoughts. What two voices do you hear?
2. What is the setting? The situation? How do these affect the speaker?
3. How and why is jargon used in the poem? With what set of "parts" is the jargon initially associated? How does this change?
4. How are phrases like "easing the spring" (lines 22, 24, 25) and "point of balance" (27) used ambiguously? What is the effect of repetition?

# EDWIN ARLINGTON ROBINSON (1869–1935)

 ## Richard Cory (1897)

Whenever Richard Cory went down town,
We people on the pavement looked at him:
He was a gentleman from sole to crown,
Clean favored, and imperially slim.

And he was always quietly arrayed,                                      5
And he was always human when he talked;
But still he fluttered pulses when he said,
'Good-morning,' and he glittered when he walked.

And he was rich—yes, richer than a king—
And admirably schooled in every grace:                                  10
In fine, we thought that he was everything
To make us wish that we were in his place.

So on we worked, and waited for the light,
And went without the meat, and cursed the bread;
And Richard Cory, one calm summer night,                                15
Went home and put a bullet through his head.

## Questions

1. What is the effect of using "down town," "pavement," "meat," and "bread" in connection with the people who admire Richard Cory?
2. What are the connotations and implications of the name "Richard Cory"? Of the word "gentleman"?
3. Why does the poet use "sole to crown" instead of "head to toe" and "imperially slim" instead of "very thin" to describe Cory?
4. What effect does repetition produce in this poem? Consider especially the six lines that begin with "And."
5. What positive characteristic does Richard Cory possess (at least from the perspective of the speaker) besides wealth?

# THEODORE ROETHKE (1908–1963)

 ## Dolor (1943)

I have known the inexorable sadness of pencils,
Neat in their boxes, dolor of pad and paper-weight,
All the misery of manila folders and mucilage,
Desolation in immaculate public places,
Lonely reception room, lavatory, switchboard,                           5
The unalterable pathos of basin and pitcher,

Ritual of multigraph, paper-clip, comma,
Endless duplication of lives and objects.
And I have seen dust from the walls of institutions,
10   Finer than flour, alive, more dangerous than silica,
Sift, almost invisible, through long afternoons of tedium,
Dropping a fine film on nails and delicate eyebrows,
Glazing the pale hair, the duplicate grey standard faces.

## Questions

1. What does "dolor" mean? What words objectify the concept?
2. Why does "Dolor" not contain the fourteen lines usual in a sonnet?
3. What institutions, conditions, and places does the speaker associate with "dolor"? What do these have in common?
4. Describe the relationships of sentence structures and lines in "Dolor."

## STEPHEN SPENDER (1909–1995)

 ## I Think Continually of Those Who Were Truly Great (1934)

I think continually of those who were truly great.
Who, from the womb, remembered the soul's history
Through corridors of light where the hours are suns,
Endless and singing. Whose lovely ambition
5   Was that their lips, still touched with fire,
Should tell of the spirit clothed from head to foot in song.
And who hoarded from the spring branches
The desires falling across their bodies like blossoms.

What is precious is never to forget
10   The delight of the blood drawn from ageless springs
Breaking through rocks in worlds before our earth;
Never to deny its pleasure in the simple morning light,
Nor its grave evening demand for love;
Never to allow gradually the traffic to smother
15   With noise and fog the flowering of the spirit.

## Questions

1. How does this poem cause you to reconsider what is usually understood by the word "great"? What are the principal characteristics of people "who were truly great"?
2. Why does Spender use the words "were great" rather than "are great"? What difference, if any, does this distinction make to Spender's definition of greatness?
3. What is the meaning of phrases like "delight of the blood," "in worlds before our earth," "hours are suns," "still touched with fire"? What other phrases need similar thought and explanation?
4. How practical is the advice of the poem in the light of its definitions of "great" and "precious"? Why should the practicality or impracticality of these definitions probably not be considered in your judgment of the poem?

## WALLACE STEVENS (1879–1955)

 ## Disillusionment of Ten O'Clock (1923)

The houses are haunted
By white night-gowns.
None are green,
Or purple with green rings,
Or green with yellow rings,     5
Or yellow with blue rings.
None of them are strange,
With socks of lace
And beaded ceintures.°     *belts*
People are not going     10
To dream of baboons and periwinkles.
Only, here and there, an old sailor,
Drunk and asleep in his boots,
Catches tigers
In red weather.     15

## Questions

1. Is the "O'Clock" here morning or night? How can you tell?
2. What do "haunted" and "white night-gowns" suggest about the poeple who live in the houses? What do the negative images in lines 3–9 suggest?
3. To whom are these people contrasted in lines 12–15?
4. What are the connotations of "socks with lace" and "beaded ceintures"? With which character in the poem would you associate these things?
5. What is the effect of using words and images like "baboons," "periwinkles," "tigers," and "red weather" in lines 11–15? Who will dream of these things?
6. Explain the term "disillusionment" and explore its relation to the point that this poem makes about dreams, images, and imagination.

## MARK STRAND (b. 1934)

 ## Eating Poetry (1968)

Ink runs from the corners of my mouth.
There is no happiness like mine.
I have been eating poetry.

The librarian does not believe what she sees.
Her eyes are sad     5
and she walks with her hands in her dress.

The poems are gone.
The light is dim.
The dogs are on the basement stairs and coming up.

10  Their eyeballs roll,
their blond legs burn like brush.
The poor librarian begins to stamp her feet and weep.

She does not understand.
When I get on my knees and lick her hand,
15  She screams.

I am a new man.
I snarl at her and bark.
I romp with joy in the bookish dark.

## Questions

1. In the first three lines, which words tell you the poem is not to be taken literally?
2. What is the serious topic of the poem? What words indicate its serious intent?
3. What is the comic topic? Which words tell you that the poem's action is comic?

## WILLIAM WORDSWORTH (1770–1850)

 ### Daffodils (I Wandered Lonely as a Cloud) (1807 (1804))

I wandered lonely as a cloud
That floats on high o'er vales and hills,
When all at once I saw a crowd,
A host, of golden daffodils;
5  Beside the lake, beneath the trees,
Fluttering and dancing in the breeze.

Continuous as the stars that shine
And twinkle on the milky way,
They stretched in never-ending line
10  Along the margin of a bay:
Ten thousand saw I at a glance,
Tossing their heads in sprightly dance.

The waves beside them danced; but they
Out-did the sparkling waves in glee:
15  A poet could not but be gay,
In such a jocund° company:                           *cheerful, merry*
I gazed—and gazed—but little thought
What wealth the show to me had brought:

For oft, when on my couch I lie
In vacant or in pensive mood,
They flash upon that inward eye
Which is the bliss of solitude;
And then my heart with pleasure fills,
And dances with the daffodils.

20

---

Wordsworth's note: "Written at Town-end, Grasmere. Daffodils grew and still grow on the margin of Ullswater and probably may be seen to this day as beautiful in the month of March, nodding their golden heads beside the dancing and foaming waves." Wordsworth also pointed out that lines 21 and 22, the "best lines," were by his wife, Mary.

## JAMES WRIGHT (1927–1980)

## A Blessing (1963)

Just off the highway to Rochester, Minnesota,
Twilight bounds softly forth on the grass.
And the eyes of those two Indian ponies
Darken with kindness.
They have come gladly out of the willows          5
To welcome my friend and me.
We step over the barbed wire into the pasture
Where they have been grazing all day, alone.
They ripple tensely, they can hardly contain their happiness
That we have come.                                  10
They bow shyly as wet swans. They love each other.
There is no loneliness like theirs.
At home once more,
They begin munching the young tufts of spring in the darkness.
I would like to hold the slenderer one in my arms.  15
For she has walked over to me
And nuzzled my left hand.
She is black and white,
Her mane falls wild on her forehead.
And the light breeze moves me to caress her long ear. 20
That is delicate as the skin over a girl's wrist.
Suddenly I realize
That if I stepped out of my body I would break
Into blossom.

## Questions

1. What has happened just before the poem opens? Because the action of the poem has obviously happened in the past, account for the speaker's use of the present tense in his descriptions.

2. Are the descriptions in the poem general or specific? What happens as the poem progresses? What specific actions does the speaker describe up through line 21?

3. What realization overtakes the speaker? How does this realization constitute a "blessing"? What does this realization show about the speaker's character?

# WRITING ABOUT DICTION AND SYNTAX IN POETRY

Study your poem carefully, line by line, to gain a general sense of its meaning. Try to establish how diction and syntax may be connected to elements such as tone, character, and idea. As you develop your ideas, look for effective and consistent patterns of word choice, connotation, repetition, and syntactic patterns that help create and reinforce the conclusions you have drawn about the poem. Ask questions like these:

## Questions for Discovering Ideas

- Who is the speaker? What is the speaker's profession or way of life? How does the speaker's background affect his or her power of observation? How does the background affect his or her level of speech?
- Who is the listener? How does the listener affect what the speaker says?
- What other characters are in the poem? How are their actions described? How accurate and fair do you think these descriptions are?
- Is the level of diction in the poem elevated, neutral, or informal, and how does this level affect your perception of the speaker, subject, and main idea or ideas?
- What patterns of diction or syntax do you discover in the poem? (*Example:* Consider words related to situation, action, setting, or particular characters.) How ordinary or unusual are these words? Which, if any, are unusual enough to warrant further examination?
- Does the poem contain many "loaded" or connotative words in connection with any single element, such as setting, speaker, or theme?
- Does the poem contain a large number of general and abstract or specific and concrete words? What is the effect of these choices?
- Does the poem contain dialect? Colloquialisms? Jargon? If so, how does this special diction shape your response to the poem?
- What is the nature of the poem's syntax? Is there any unusual word order? What seems to be the purpose or effect of syntactic variations?
- Has the poet used any striking patterns of sentence structure such as parallelism or repetition? If so, what is the effect?

## Strategies for Organizing Ideas

When you narrow your examination to one or two specific areas of diction or syntax, you should list important words, phrases, and sentences. Begin grouping examples that work in similar ways or produce similar effects. Investigate the full range of meaning and effect that the examples produce. Eventually, you may be able to develop the related examples as units or sections for your essay.

Your central idea should emerge from your investigation of the diction or syntax that you find most fruitful and interesting. Let the poem be your guide. Because diction and syntax contribute to the poem's impact and meaning, try to connect your thesis and examples to your other conclusions. If you are writing about Stevens's "Disillusionment of Ten O'Clock," for example, your central idea might assert that Stevens uses words describing colors (i.e., "white," "green," "purple," "yellow," "blue," "red") to contrast life's visual reality with the psychological "disillusionment" of the "houses," "People," and "old sailor." Such a formulation makes a clear connection of diction to meaning.

There are many different ways to organize your material. If you deal with only one aspect of diction, such as connotative words, you might treat these in the order in which they appear in the poem. When you deal with two or three different aspects of diction and syntax, however, you might devote a series of paragraphs to related examples of multiple denotation, then connotation, and finally jargon (assuming the presence of jargon in the poem). In such an instance, your organization would be controlled by the types of material under consideration rather than by the order in which the words occur.

Alternatively, you might deal with the impact of diction or syntax on a series of other elements, such as character, setting, or situation. Such an essay would focus on a single type of lexical or syntactic device (described earlier in this chapter) as it relates to these different elements in sequence. Thus, you might discuss the link between connotation and situation, character, and the basic situation of the poem. Whatever organization you select, keep in mind that each poem will suggest its own avenues of exploration and strategies of organization.

In your conclusion summarize your ideas about the impact of the poem's diction or syntax. You might also consider the larger implications of your ideas in connection with the thoughts and emotions evoked by your reading.

## Illustrative Student Essay

Underlined sentences in this paper *do not* conform to MLA style and are used solely as teaching tools to emphasize the central idea, thesis sentence, and topic sentences throughout the paper.

Fitzpatrick 1

Lionel Fitzpatrick

Professor Allen

English 1B

20 October 2007

**Diction and Character in Robinson's "Richard Cory"°**

[1]        In "Richard Corey," Edwin Arlington Robinson dramatizes the idea that nothing

can guarantee happiness. He explores this idea by focusing on a central character—

---

°See p. 521 for this poem.

Richard Cory—who apparently has everything: wealth, status, dignity, taste, and respect. Cory's suicide, however, reveals that these qualities do not necessarily make people happy. By creating a gulf between Cory and the people of the town who admire and envy him, Robinson sets us up for the surprising suicide described in the last two lines. The distinction is produced through the words that Robinson uses to demean the general populace and elevate the central character.* The speaker and his or her fellow townspeople are associated with words that indicate their common lot, while Richard Cory is described in terms of nobility and privilege.†

[2]    For the most part, the poem focuses on Richard Cory as perceived by the townspeople, who wish that they "were in his place" (line 12). Robinson skillfully employs words about these common folk to suggest their poverty and low status. In the first line, for example, the speaker places himself or herself and these other people "down town." The phrase refers to a central business district, but here it also carries the negative connotation of the word *down*. The word implies that Cory's journey to town seems to be a descent, and that the people constantly live in this "down" condition. A similar instance of connotative diction is *pavement* (line 2), which can mean "sidewalk," but can also mean "street" or "roadbed." The net effect of the word *pavement* rather than *sidewalk* is to place the "people" even lower than Richard Cory— literally on the street.

[3]    In contrast to these few words suggesting the people's lowness, the poem contains many words that connote Cory's elevation. Many words and phrases suggest nobility or royalty. These implications begin with the title of the poem and the name "Richard Cory." That the word *rich* is contained within *Richard* implies Cory's wealth and privilege. It is also the name of a number of English kings, most notably Richard the Lion Hearted ("*Richard Coeur de Lion*"). The name *Cory* is equally connotative. It clearly suggests the "Coeur" of the famous king, and it also reminds us of *core*, the central or innermost part of anything. The name thus points toward Cory's singular position and significance. Through sound, *Cory* also suggest the English word *court*—that is, a place for kings and courtiers. The name "Richard Cory" thus begins an association through sound and implication that links the central character to kingship and elegance.

---

*Central Idea.
†Thesis Sentence.

[4]    <u>There are other similar words in the poem's first stanza</u>. The speaker describes Richard Cory as "a gentleman from sole to crown" (line 3). *Gentleman* refers to a civilized and well-mannered individual, but it originally also meant a man of "high" or "noble" birth. The phrase "from sole to crown" is another way of saying "from head to toe," but it connotes a great deal more. *Sole* means both "the bottom of a shoe or foot" and "alone" or "singular." Thus, the word suggests Cory's isolation and separation from the common folk. The word is also a pun (and homophone) on *soul*, implying that Cory's gentility is inward as well as outward. The final touch is the word *crown*. In context, the term denotes the top of the head, but it also has aristocratic and royal connotations.

[5]    <u>The speaker also describes Cory as "clean favored" and "imperially slim"</u> (line 4). The word *imperially*, like *crown*, makes an explicit connection between Cory and emperors. "Clean favored," instead of the more common *good-looking*, connotes crisp and untouched features. More to the point, the term *favored* also means "preferred," "elevated," "honored," and "privileged." "Imperially slim," instead of *thin*, is equally connotative of wealth and status. While both terms denote the same physical condition, *slim* suggests elegance, wealth, and choice, whereas *thin* suggests poverty and necessity.

[6]    <u>Although this type of diction is mostly in the first stanza, Robinson sustains the link between Cory and royalty by using similar terms in the rest of the poem</u>. In stanza two, for example, he uses "quietly arrayed" and "glittered." Both carry elevated and imperial connotations. *Arrayed* means "dressed," but it is also a word in the King James Bible that suggests elegant and heavenly clothing (see Matthew 6:29; Acts 12:21, Revelation 7:13). *Quietly* also suggests solitude and introversion. *Glittered* complements *quietly*; it connotes richness of dress and manner, suggesting that the man himself is golden. In the third stanza, the deliberate cliché "richer than a king" again clearly links Richard Cory to royalty. The speaker also notes that Cory was "schooled in every grace" (line 10). The phrase means that Cory was trained in manners and social niceties, but *grace* connotes privilege and nobility ("Your Grace") and also the idea of heavenly love and forgiveness ("God's Grace").

[7]    It is clear, then, that Robinson uses the effects of connotation to lower the common folk and elevate the central character. The words linked to the speaker and the

other townspeople have demeaning and negative implications. At the same time, the

poet uses words and phrases about Cory that connote royalty and privilege. This careful

manipulation of diction widens the gulf between Cory and the town. It also heightens

our sense that Cory has aristocratic looks, manners, taste, and breeding. <u>The network of</u>

<u>associations built through this skillful diction makes the poem's ending powerfully</u>

<u>shocking, and reinforces the poem's idea that appearance, wealth, and high status</u>

<u>cannot necessarily produce happiness.</u>

**WORK CITED**

Robinson, Edwin Arlington. "Richard Cory." *Literature: An Introduction to Reading and Writing*. Ed.
    Edgar V. Roberts. 4th Compact ed. Upper Saddle River: Prentice Hall, 2008, 521.

## Commentary on the Essay

This essay deals with the Robinson's use of connotative words to elevate the central
character and demean the townspeople. The opening paragraph makes a general assertion about the poem's theme, connects character to this assertion, and argues that
Robinson controls diction to make his distinctions.

The body of the essay, in five paragraphs, deals with the effects of a number of
examples of word choice. The examples of connotative words are arranged to reflect
partly the characters they define and partly the order in which they appear in the
poem. Thus, paragraph 2 discusses the common people and the speaker in connection with two highly connotative terms: *down town* and *pavement*.

The next four paragraphs (3–6) focus on Richard Cory and words or phrases that
suggest royalty and privilege. The examples or diction examined here are taken up in
the order in which they appear in the poem. Thus, paragraph 3 considers Cory's
name, and the fourth explores the effects of *gentleman* and *sole to crown*. Paragraphs 5
and 6 continue this process, examining instances of diction that sustain the association between Cory and nobility. Taken together, the four paragraphs devoted to this
central character illustrate Robinson's consistent manipulation of diction both to en-
noble and isolate Cory.

The conclusion reasserts that Robinson's diction not only contributes to Cory's
isolation, but also adds to the impact of his mysterious suicide. In this way, the words
and phrases examined in the essay are linked to the poem's exploration of ideas
about the human condition.

# Writing Topics: About the Words of Poetry

1. Using Eberhart's "The Fury of Aerial Bombardment" in this chapter, together with poems by Jarrell (Chapter 11) and Owen (Chapters 13, 15), study the words that these poets use to indicate the weapons and actions of warfare. In an essay, consider these questions: What shared details make the poems similar? What separate details make them different? How do the poets use word choices to make their points about war as action, tragedy, and horror?

2. Write an essay considering the sound qualities of the invented words in "Jabberwocky." Some obvious choices are "brillig," "frumious," "vorpal," and "manxome," but you are free to choose any or all of them. What is the relationship between the sound and apparent meaning of these words? What effect do the surrounding normal words and normal word order have on the special words? How does Carroll succeed in creating a narrative "structure" even though the key words are, on the surface, nonsense?

3. Compare and contrast Hirshfield's "The Lives of the Heart" and Carruth's "An Apology for Using the Word 'Heart' in Too Many Poems." What common idea about love do the poems share? What differences? How does each poet use the comparable topics to develop ideas unique to each poem?

4. Write a brief essay discussing the use of connotation in Cummings's "next to of course god america i," Hirshfield's "The Lives of the Heart," Levertov's "Of Being," Plath's "Tulips" (Chapter 18), and Roethke's "Dolor." What particularities of meaning do the poets introduce? How does their control of connotation contribute to the various ideas you discover in the poems?

5. Compare the words describing natural scenes in Gray's "Sonnet on the Death of Richard West" and Wordsworth's "Daffodils." Which poem seems more specific and direct in its depiction of Nature?

6. Write a short poem describing a violent crime and commenting on it. Then, assume that you are the "alleged perpetrator" of the crime, and write another poem on the same topic. Even though you describe the same situation, how do your words differ, and why have you made these different choices? Explain the other different word choices you have made. You might also discuss words that you considered using but rejected.

7. Find a book or books in your library about the works of Gray, Roethke, Robinson, Wordsworth, or another poet represented in this chapter. How fully do these sources discuss the style of these poets? Write a brief report explaining how the writers of the book or books deal with poetic diction.

# Chapter 13

# Imagery: The Poem's Link to the Senses

In literature, **imagery** refers to words that trigger your imagination to recall and recombine images—memories or mental pictures of sights, sounds, tastes, smells, sensations of touch, and motions. The process is active and even vigorous, for when words or descriptions produce images, you are using your personal experiences with life and language to help you understand the works you are reading. In effect, you are recreating the work *in your own way* through the controlled stimulation produced by the writer's words. Imagery is therefore one of the strongest modes of literary expression because it provides a channel to your active imagination, and along this channel, writers bring their works directly to you and into your consciousness.

For example, reading the word *lake* may bring to your mind your literal memory of a particular lake. Your mental picture—or image—may be a distant view of calm waters reflecting blue sky, a nearby view of gentle waves rippling in the wind, a close-up view of the sandy lake bottom from a boat, or an overhead view of a sun-drenched shoreline. Similarly, the words *rose, apple, hot dog, malted milk,* and *pizza* all cause you to recollect these objects, and, in addition, may cause you to recall their smells and tastes. Active and graphic words such as *row, swim,* and *dive* stimulate you to picture moving images of someone performing these actions.

## Responses and the Writer's Use of Detail

In studying imagery, we try to comprehend and explain our imaginative reconstruction of the pictures and impressions evoked by the work's images. We let the poet's words simmer and percolate in our minds. To get our imaginations stirring, we might follow a description by Samuel Taylor Coleridge in lines 37–41 of "Kubla Khan."

> A damsel with a dulcimer
> In a vision once I saw:
> It was an Abyssinian maid,
> And on her dulcimer she played
> Singing of Mount Abora.

We do not read about the color of the young woman's clothing or learn anything else about her appearance except that she is playing a stringed instrument, a dulcimer, and that she is singing a song about a mountain in a foreign, remote land. But Coleridge's image is enough. From it we can visualize a vivid, exotic picture of a young woman from a distant land singing, together with impressions of the loveliness of her song (even though we never hear it or understand it). The image lives.

## The Relationship of Imagery to Ideas and Attitudes

Images do more than elicit impressions. By the *authenticating* effects of the vision and perceptions underlying them, they give you new ways of seeing the world and of strengthening your old ways of seeing it. Shakespeare, in Sonnet 116: "Let Me Not to the Marriage of True Minds" (Chapter 16), develops the idea that love provides people with consistency of purpose in their lives. Rather than stating the idea directly, he uses images of a landmark or lighthouse and also of a fixed star—sights with which we as his readers are familiar.

> . . . it [love] is an ever fixéd mark
> That looks on tempests and is never shaken;
> It is the star to every wandering bark°                    *boat, ship*
> Whose worth's unknown, although his° height be taken.        *its*

These images form a link with readers that is clear and also verifiable by observation. Such uses of imagery comprise one of the strongest means by which writers reinforce ideas.

In addition, as you form mental pictures and impressions from a poet's images, you respond with appropriate attitudes and feelings. Thus the phrase "Beside the lake, beneath the trees," from Wordsworth's poem "Daffodils" (Chapter 12) prompts both the visualization of a wooded lakeshore and the related pleasantness of outdoor relaxation and happiness. A contrasting visualization is to be found in Hubert von Herkomer's painting *Hard Times* (I–5, Plate 1), in which all the images—the tired faces, the heavy load, the tools, the bleak road, the leafless trees—point toward the harsh life of the worker and his family, causing a response of sadness and sympathy. Imagery used in a more negative way is found in Ray Durem's "I Know I'm Not Sufficiently Obscure," which triggers disturbing responses through images of blood, lynching, and "cold Korean mud." By using such imagery, artists and poets create sensory vividness, and they also influence and control our attitudes as readers.

## Types of Imagery

### Visual Imagery Is the Language of Sight

Human beings are visual. Sight is the most significant of our senses, for it is the key to our remembrance of other sense impressions. Therefore, the most frequently occurring literary imagery is to things we can visualize either exactly or approximately—**visual**

**images**. In the three-stanza poem "Cargoes," John Masefield creates mental pictures or images of oceangoing merchant vessels from three periods of human history.

## JOHN MASEFIELD (1878–1967)

 **Cargoes** (1902)

Quinquereme° of Nineveh° from distant Ophir,°
Rowing home to haven in sunny Palestine,
With a cargo of ivory,
And apes and peacocks,°
5  Sandalwood, cedarwood,° and sweet white wine.

Stately Spanish galleon coming from the Isthmus,°
Dipping through the Tropics by the palm-green shores,
With a cargo of diamonds,
Emeralds, amethysts,
10  Topazes, and cinnamon, and gold moidores.°

Dirty British coaster with a salt-caked smoke-stack,
Butting through the Channel in the mad March days,
With a cargo of Tyne coal,°
Road-rails, pig-lead,
15  Firewood, iron-ware, and cheap tin trays.

---

°CARGOES. 1 *quinquereme*: the largest of the ancient ships. It was powered by three tiers of oars and was named "quinquereme" because five men apparently operated each vertical oar station. The top two oars were each taken by two men, while one man alone took the bottom oar. 1 *Nineveh*: the capital of ancient Assyria, and an "exceeding great city" (Jonah 3:3). 1 *Ophir*: Ophir probably was in Africa and was known for its gold (1 Kings 10:22; 1 Chron. 29:4). Masefield quotes from some of the biblical verses in his first stanza. 4 *apes and peacocks*: 1 Kings 10:22, and 2 Chron. 9:21. 5 *cedarwood*: 1 Kings 9:11. 6 *Isthmus*: the Isthmus of Panama. 10 *moidores*: coins used in Portugal and Brazil at the time the New World was being explored. 13 *Tyne coal*: coal from Newcastle upon Tyne, in northern England, renowned for its coal production.

## Questions

1. Consider the images of life during three periods of history: ancient Israel at the time of Solomon (ca. 950 B.C.E.), sixteenth-century Spain, and modern England. What do these images tell you about Masefield's interpretation of modern commercial life?
2. To what senses do most of the images refer (e.g., sight, taste)?
3. The poem contains no complete sentences. Why do you think Masefield included only verbals ("rowing," "dipping," "butting") to begin the second line of each stanza, rather than finite verbs?
4. In historical reality, the quinquereme was likely rowed by slaves, and the Spanish galleon likely carried riches stolen from Central American natives. How might these unpleasant details affect the impressions otherwise achieved in the first two stanzas?

Masefield's images are vivid as they stand and need no further amplification. For us to reconstruct them imaginatively, we do not need ever to have seen the ancient biblical lands or waters, or ever to have seen or handled the cheap commodities on a modern merchant ship. We have seen enough in our lives to *imagine* places and objects like these, and hence Masefield is successful in fixing his visual images in our minds.

## Auditory Imagery Is the Language of Sound

**Auditory images** trigger our experiences with sound. For such images, let us consider Wilfred Owen's "Anthem for Doomed Youth," which is about the death of soldiers in warfare and the sorrow of their loved ones.

### WILFRED OWEN (1893–1918)

 ### Anthem for Doomed Youth (1920)

What passing-bells° for these who die as cattle?
Only the monstrous anger of the guns.
Only the stuttering rifles' rapid rattle
Can patter out their hasty orisons.°                                             prayers
No mockeries for them from prayers or bells,                                           5
Nor any voice of mourning save the choirs—
The shrill, demented choirs of wailing shells;
And bugles calling for them from sad shires.°

What candles may be held to speed them all?
Not in the hands of boys, but in their eyes                                           10
Shall shine the holy glimmers of good-byes.
The pallor of girls' brows shall be their pall;
Their flowers the tenderness of patient minds,
And each slow dusk a drawing-down of blinds.

---

°ANTHEM FOR DOOMED YOUTH. 1 *passing-bells*: church bells tolling upon the entry of a funeral cortege into a church cemetery.   8 *shires*: British counties.

## Questions

1. What type of imagery predominates in the first eight lines? How does the imagery change in the last six lines?

2. Contrast the images of death at home and death on the battlefield. How does this contrast affect your experience and understanding of the poem?

3. Consider these images: "holy glimmers of good-byes," "pallor of girls' brows," "patient minds," "drawing-down of blinds." What relationship do the people defined by these images have to the doomed youth?

The poem begins with the question of "What passing-bells" may be tolled "for these who die as cattle." Owen's speaker is referring to the traditional tolling of a church bell to announce a burial. The images of these ceremonial sounds suggest a period of peace and order, when there is time to pay respect to the dead. But the poem points out that the only sound for those who have fallen in battle is the "rapid rattle" of "stuttering" rifles—not the solemn, dignified sounds of peace but the horrifying noises of war. Owen's auditory images evoke corresponding sounds in our imaginations, and they help us to experience the poem and to hate the uncivilized depravity of war.

## Olfactory, Gustatory, and Tactile Imagery Refers to Smell, Taste, and Touch

In addition to sight and sound, you will find images from the other senses: smell, taste, and touch. Shakespeare includes an olfactory image of sweet perfumes in Sonnet 130: "My Mistress' Eyes Are Nothing Like the Sun," and the odor of roses is suggested in Burns's "A Red, Red Rose" (Chapter 14) and in Shelley's "Music, when Soft Voices Die" (Chapter 11).

Gustatory images are also common, though less frequent than those referring to sight and sound. Lines 5 and 10 of Masefield's "Cargoes," for example, include images of "sweet white wine" and "cinnamon." Although the poem refers to these commodities as cargoes, the words themselves also register in our minds as gustatory images because they evoke our sense of taste.

Images of touch and texture are not as common because touch is difficult to render except in terms of effects. The speaker of Amy Lowell's "Patterns" (Chapter 19), for example, uses tactile imagery when imagining a never-to-happen embrace with her fiancé, who we learn has been killed on a wartime battlefield. Her imagery in lines 51–52 records the effect of the embrace ("bruised"), whereas her internalized feelings are expressed in metaphors ("aching, melting"):

> And the buttons of his waistcoat bruised my body as he clasped me
> *Aching, melting, unafraid.*

Tactile images are not uncommon in love poetry, where references to touch and feeling are natural.

## Kinetic and Kinesthetic Imagery Refers to Motion and Activity

References to movement are also images. Images of general motion are **kinetic** (remember that *motion pictures* may be called "cinema"; note the closeness of *kine* in *kinetic* and *cine* in *cinema*), whereas the term **kinesthetic** is applied to human or animal movement. Imagery of motion is closely related to visual images, for motion is most often seen. Masefield's "British coaster" is a visual image, but when it goes "Butting through the channel," this reference to motion makes it also kinetic. When Hardy's skeletons sit upright at the beginning of "Channel Firing," the image is kinesthetic, as is the action of Lowell's speaker in "Patterns" walking in the garden after hearing about her fiancé's death. Both types are seen at the conclusion of the following poem, Elizabeth Bishop's "The Fish."

# ELIZABETH BISHOP (1911–1979)

 ## The Fish (1946)

I caught a tremendous fish
and held him beside the boat
half out of water, with my hook
fast in a corner of his mouth.
He didn't fight.                                                             5
He hadn't fought at all.
He hung a grunting weight,
battered and venerable
and homely. Here and there
his brown skin hung in strips                                                10
like ancient wallpaper,
and its pattern of darker brown
was like wallpaper:
shapes like full-blown roses
stained and lost through age.                                               15
He was speckled with barnacles,
fine rosettes of lime,
and infested
with tiny white sea-lice,
and underneath two or three                                                 20
rags of green weed hung down.
While his gills were breathing in
the terrible oxygen
—the frightening gills,
fresh and crisp with blood,                                                 25
that can cut so badly—
I thought of the coarse white flesh
packed in like feathers,
the big bones and the little bones,
the dramatic reds and blacks                                                30
of his shiny entrails,
and the pink swim-bladder
like a big peony.
I looked into his eyes
which were far larger than mine                                             35
but shallower, and yellowed,
the irises backed and packed
with tarnished tinfoil
seen through the lenses
of old scratched isinglass.°            *a thin sheet of mica*             40
They shifted a little, but not
to return my stare.
—It was more like the tipping
of an object toward the light.
I admired his sullen face,                                                  45

the mechanism of his jaw,
and then I saw
that from his lower lip
—if you could call it a lip—
50  grim, wet, and weaponlike,
hung five old pieces of fish-line,    → idea that humans
or four and a wire leader        did this to the fish
with the swivel still attached,
with all their five big hooks
55  grown firmly in his mouth.
A green line, frayed at the end
where he broke it, two heavier lines,
and a fine black thread
still crimped from the strain and snap
60  when it broke and he got away.
Like medals with their ribbons
frayed and wavering,
a five-haired beard of wisdom
trailing from his aching jaw.
65  I stared and stared
and victory filled up
the little rented boat,
from the pool of bilge
where oil had spread a rainbow
70  around the rusted engine
to the bailer rusted orange,
the sun-cracked thwarts,
the oarlocks on their strings,
the gunnels—until everything
75  was rainbow, rainbow, rainbow!
And I let the fish go.

## Questions

1. Describe the poem's images of action. What is unusual about them?
2. What impression does the fish make upon the speaker? Is the fish beautiful? ugly? Why is the fish described in such detail?
3. What do the "five old pieces of fish-line" indicate?
4. How is the rainbow formed around the boat's engine? Why does the speaker refer to the "pool of bilge"? What does the rainbow mean to the speaker?
5. What right does the speaker have to keep the fish? Why does she choose to relinquish this right?

The kinetic images at the end of "The Fish" are those of victory filling the boat (difficult to visualize) and the oil spreading to make a rainbow in the bilgewater (easy to visualize). The kinesthetic images are readily imagined—the speaker's staring, observing, and letting the fish go—and they are vivid and real. The final gesture is the necessary outcome of the observed contrast between the deteriorating artifacts of human beings and the natural world of the fish, and it is a vivid expression of the right of the natural world to exist without human intervention. In short, Bishop's kinetic and kinesthetic images are designed to objectivize the need for freedom not only for human beings but for all the earth and animated Nature.

The areas from which kinetic and kinesthetic imagery can be derived are too varied and unpredictable to describe. Occupations, trades, professions, businesses, recreational activities—all these might furnish images. One poet introduces references from gardening, another from money and banking, another from modern real estate developments, another from the falling of leaves in autumn, another from life in the jungle, another from life in the home. The freshness, newness, and surprise of much poetry result from the many and varied areas from which writers draw their images.

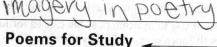
imagery in poetry

## Poems for Study

## ♥ ELIZABETH BARRETT BROWNING (1806–1861)

 ### Sonnets from the Portuguese, Number 14:
### If Thou Must Love Me (1850)

If thou must love me, let it be for nought
Except for love's sake only. Do not say
"I love her for her smile—her look—her way
Of speaking gently—for a trick of thought
That falls in well with mine, and certes° brought

A sense of pleasant ease on such a day"—
For these things in themselves, Belovèd, may
Be changed, or change for thee,—and love, so wrought,°    *created*
May be unwrought so. Neither love me for
10  Thine own dear pity's wiping my cheeks dry,—
A creature might forget to weep, who bore
Thy comfort long, and lost thy love thereby!
But love me for love's sake, that evermore
Thou mayst love on, through love's eternity.

## Questions

1. Who is the speaker of this poem? Why might you conclude that the speaker is female?
2. What images does the speaker use to indicate possible causes for loving? What kinds of images are they? How does the speaker explain why they should be rejected?
3. How does the idea of lines 1, 13, and 14 build upon the ideas in the rest of the poem?

## SAMUEL TAYLOR COLERIDGE (1772–1834)

 ### Kubla Khan (1816)

In Xanadu did Kubla Khan
A stately pleasure dome decree:
Where Alph,° the sacred river, ran
Through caverns measureless to man
5        Down to a sunless sea.
So twice five miles of fertile ground
With walls and towers were girdled round:
And there were gardens bright with sinuous rills,
Where blossomed many an incense-bearing tree;
10  And here were forests ancient as the hills,
Enfolding sunny spots of greenery.
But oh! that deep romantic chasm which slanted
Down the green hill athwart a cedarn cover!
A savage place! as holy and enchanted
15  As e'er beneath a waning moon was haunted
By woman wailing for her demon lover!
And from this chasm, with ceaseless turmoil seething,
As if this earth in fast thick pants were breathing.
A mighty fountain momently was forced:
20  Amid whose swift half-intermitted burst
Huge fragments vaulted like rebounding hail,

---

°3 *Alph:* possibly a reference to the river Alpheus in Greece, as described by the ancient writers Virgil and Pausanias.

Or chaffy grain beneath the thresher's flail;
And 'mid these dancing rocks at once and ever
It flung up momently the sacred river.
Five miles meandering with a mazy motion                    25
Through wood and dale the sacred river ran,
Then reached the caverns measureless to man,
And sank in tumult to a lifeless ocean:
And 'mid this tumult Kubla heard from far
Ancestral voices prophesying war!                           30
The shadow of the dome of pleasure
Floated midway on the waves;
Where was heard the mingled measure
From the fountain and the caves.
It was a miracle of rare device,                            35
A sunny pleasure dome with caves of ice!

    A damsel with a dulcimer
    In a vision once I saw:
    It was an Abyssinian maid,
    And on her dulcimer she played                      40
    Singing of Mount Abora.°
Could I revive within me
Her symphony and song,
To such a deep delight 'twould win me,
That with music loud and long,                              45
I would build that dome in air,
That sunny dome! those caves of ice!
And all who heard should see them there,
And all should cry, Beware! Beware!
His flashing eyes, his floating hair!                       50
Weave a circle round him thrice,
And close your eyes with holy dread,
For he on honeydew hath fed,
And drunk the milk of Paradise.

---

°41 *Mount Abora*: a mountain of Coleridge's imagination. But see John Milton's *Paradise Lost*, IV. 268–84.

## Questions

1. How many of the poem's images might be sketched or visualized? Which ones would be panoramic landscapes? Which might be close-ups?

2. What is the effect of auditory images such as "wailing," "fast thick pants," "tumult," "ancestral voices prophesying war," and "mingled measure"?

3. When Coleridge was writing this poem, he was recalling it from a dream. At line 54 he was interrupted, and when he resumed he could write no more. How might an argument be made that the poem is finished?

**4.** How do lines 35–36 establish the pleasure dome as a place of mysterious oddity? What is the effect of the words "miracle" and "rare"? The effect of combining the images "sunny" and "caves of ice"?

**5.** Why does the speaker yearn for the power of the singing Abyssinian maid? What kinesthetic images end the poem? How are these images important in the speaker's desire to reconstruct the vision of the pleasure dome?

**RAY DUREM** (1915–1963)

 **I Know I'm Not Sufficiently Obscure** (1962)

I know I'm not sufficiently obscure
to please the critics—nor devious enough.
Imagery escapes me.
I cannot find those mild and gracious words
5   To clothe the carnage.
Blood is blood and murder's murder.
What's a lavender word for lynch?
Come, you pale poets, wan, refined and dreamy:
Here is a black woman working out her guts
10   in a white man's kitchen
for little money and no glory.
How should I tell that story?
There is a black boy, blacker still from death,
face down in the cold Korean mud.
15   Come on with your effervescent jive
explain to him why he ain't alive.
Reword our specific discontent
into some plaintive melody,
a little whine, a little whimper,
20   not too much—and no rebellion!
God, no! Rebellion's much too corny.
You deal with finer feelings,
very subtle—an autumn leaf
hanging from a tree—I see a body!

## Questions

**1.** Who is the "you" listener addressed by the speaker (lines 8, 15, 22)? Why does the speaker admit that he is "not sufficiently obscure"? What issue is he dealing with by this admission?

**2.** In line 3 the speaker says, "Imagery escapes me." How does the rest of the poem contradict this statement?

**3.** Consider the images in lines 7, 13, and 23–24. To what degree are these images timely? Dated?

# T. S. ELIOT (1888–1965)

 ## Preludes (1910)

I

The winter evening settles down
With smell of steaks in passageways.
Six o'clock.
The burnt-out ends of smoky days.
And now a gusty shower wraps                    5
The grimy scraps
Of withered leaves about your feet
And newspapers from vacant lots;
The showers beat
On broken blinds and chimney-pots,              10
And at the corner of the street
A lonely cab-horse steams and stamps.
And then the lighting of the lamps.


II

The morning comes to consciousness
Of faint stale smells of beer                   15
From the sawdust-trampled street
With all its muddy feet that press
To early coffee-stands.
With the other masquerades
That time resumes,                              20
One thinks of all the hands
That are raising dingy shades
In a thousand furnished rooms.


III

You tossed a blanket from the bed,
You lay upon your back, and waited;             25
You dozed, and watched the night revealing
The thousand sordid images
Of which your soul was constituted;
They flickered against the ceiling.
And when all the world came back                30
And the light crept up between the shutters
And you heard the sparrows in the gutters,
You had such a vision of the street,
As the street hardly understands;
Sitting along the bed's edge, where             35
You curled the papers from your hair,
Or clasped the yellow soles of feet
In the palms of both soiled hands.

*personification*

IV

His soul stretched tight across the skies
40 That fade behind a city block,
Or trampled by insistent feet
At four and five and six o'clock;
And short square fingers stuffing pipes,
And evening newspapers, and eyes
45 Assured of certain certainties,
The conscience of a blackened street
Impatient to assume the world.

*↑ visual*
*↓ personification*

 I am moved by fancies that are curled
Around these images, and cling:
50 The notion of some infinitely gentle
Infinitely suffering thing.

 Wipe your hand across your mouth, and laugh;
The worlds revolve like ancient women
Gathering fuel in vacant lots.

## Questions

1. From what locations are the images in the first stanza derived? How do the images shift in the second stanza? What is the connection between the images in the second and third stanzas?

2. Who is the "you" in the third stanza? What images are associated with this listener?

3. Who is the "His" of the fourth stanza? How do the images develop in this stanza? What is meant particularly in the images of lines 46–47?

4. What is the nature of the bodily imagery in the poem? The urban imagery? What impressions do these images cause?

5. In lines 48–51, what does the speaker conclude? How do the last two unnumbered stanzas constitute a contrast of attitude?

## SUSAN GRIFFIN (b. 1943)

### Love Should Grow Up Like a Wild Iris in the Fields (1972)

Love should grow up like a wild iris in the fields,
unexpected, after a terrible storm, opening a purple
mouth to the rain, with not a thought to the future,
ignorant of the grass and the graveyard of leaves
5 around, forgetting its own beginning. Love should
grow like a wild iris
but does not.
Love more often is to be found in kitchens at the dinner hour,
tired out and hungry, lingers over tables in houses where

the walls record movements; while the cook is probably angry,                10
and the ingredients of the meal are budgeted, while
a child cries feed me now and her mother not quite
hysterical says over and over, wait just a bit, just a bit.
Love should grow up in the fields like a wild iris
but never does                                                               15
really startle anyone, was to be expected, was to be
predicted, is almost absurd, goes on from day to day, not quite
blindly, gets taken to the cleaners every fall, sings old
songs over and over, and falls on the same piece of rug that
never gets tacked down, gives up, wants to hide, is not            20
brave, knows too much, is not like an
iris growing wild but more like
staring into space
in the street
not quite sure                                                               25
which door it was, annoyed about the sidewalk being
slippery, trying all the doors, thinking
if love wished the world to be well, it would be well.
Love should
grow up like a wild iris, but doesn't, it comes from          30
the midst of everything else, sees like the iris
of an eye, when the light is right,
feels in blindness and when there is nothing else is
tender, blinks, and opens
face up to the skies.                                                        35

## Questions

1. Contrast the locations of the images in the first seven lines and in the next eight. How do the ideas of the poet depend on this contrast in locations?

2. Note the difference in the mood of the verbs, from the "should" clause in the first six lines to the declarative present verb in line 7. Also, note the present tense verbs from lines 8–13, and then the "should" again in line 14. What is the effect of this differing use of verbs?

3. Trace the image of the wild iris throughout the poem. Why is the iris wild, and not cultivated? How does the iris grow? What is the effect of the change in the image of the iris from the flower to the eye (line 32)?

4. How is the sentence in lines 30–31 ("it comes from/the midst of everything else") related to the ideas and images in the rest of the poem?

## THOMAS HARDY (1840–1928)

*For a photo, see Chapter 6, page 252.*

 **Channel Firing** (1914)

That night your great guns, unawares,
Shook all our coffins° as we lay,

_____

°2 *Coffins:* It has been common practice in England for hundreds of years to bury people in the floors or basements of churches.

And broke the chancel window-squares,
We thought it was the Judgment Day

5    And sat upright. While drearisome
Arose the howl of wakened hounds;
The mouse let fall the altar-crumb,
The worms drew back into the mounds,

The glebe° cow drooled. Till God called, "No;
10    It's gunnery practice out at sea
Just as before you went below;
The world is as it used to be:

"All nations striving strong to make
Red war yet redder. Mad as hatters
15    They do no more for Christés sake
Than you who are helpless in such matters.

"That this is not the judgment hour
For some of them's a blessed thing,
For if it were they'd have to scour
20    Hell's floor for so much threatening. . . .

"Ha, ha. It will be warmer when
I blow the trumpet (if indeed
I ever do; for you are men,
And rest eternal sorely need)."

25    So down we lay again. "I wonder,
Will the world ever saner be,"
Said one, "than when He sent us under
In our indifferent century!"

And many a skeleton shook his head.
30    "Instead of preaching forty year,"
My neighbor Parson Thirdly said,
"I wish I had stuck to pipes and beer."

Again the guns disturbed the hour,
Roaring their readiness to avenge,
35    As far inland as Stourton Tower,°
And Camelot,° and starlit Stonehenge.°

---

°9 *glebe*: a parcel of land adjoining and belonging to a church. Cows were grazed there to keep the grass short.  35 *Stourton Tower*: tower commemorating King Alfred the Great's defeat of the Danes in C.E. 879.  36 *Camelot*: legendary seat of King Arthur's court. *Stonehenge*: group of standing stones on Salisbury Plain, probably built as a place of worship before 1000 B.C.E. Stonehenge today is one of England's most famous landmarks.

## Questions

1. Who is the speaker in this poem? What is the setting? The situation?
2. To whom does the "your" in line 1 refer? The "our" in line 2?

3. What has awakened the speaker and his companions? What mistake have they made?
4. What three other voices are heard in the poem? How are their traits revealed?
5. What ideas about war and the nature of humanity does this poem explore?

## GEORGE HERBERT (1593–1633)

 **The Pulley** (1633)

When God at first made man,
Having a glass of blessings standing by,
　"Let us," said he, "pour on him all we can.
Let the world's riches, which dispersed lie,
　　Contract into a span."°                                            5

　So strength first made a way;
Then beauty flowed, then wisdom, honor, pleasure.
　When almost all was out, God made a stay,
Perceiving that, alone of all his treasure,
　　Rest° in the bottom lay.                                          10

　"For if I should," said he,
"Bestow this jewel also on my creature,
　He would adore my gifts instead of me.
And rest in Nature, not the God of Nature;
　　So both should losers be.                                         15

　"Yet let him keep the rest,
But keep them with repining restlessness.
　Let him be rich and weary, that at least,
If goodness lead him not, yet weariness
　　May toss him to my breast."                                       20

---

°4 *into a span*: that is, within the control of human beings. 10 *rest*: (1) repose, security; (2) all that remains.

## Questions

1. Describe the dramatic scene of the poem. Who is doing what?
2. What are the particular "blessings" that God confers on humanity, according to the speaker? Why should these be considered blessings?
3. Consider the image of the pulley as the means, or device (through "repining restlessness"), by which God compels people to become worshipful.
4. Analyze and discuss the meaning of the kinetic images signified by the words "pour," "flowed," "rest," and "toss."

## GERARD MANLEY HOPKINS (1844–1889)

 ## Spring (1877)

Nothing is so beautiful as Spring—
　　When weeds, in wheels, shoot long and lovely and lush;
　　Thrush's eggs look little low heavens, and thrush
Through the echoing timber does so rinse and wring
5　The ear, it strikes like lightnings to hear him sing;
　　The glassy peartree leaves and blooms, they brush
　　The descending blue; that blue is all in a rush
With richness; the racing lambs too have fair their fling.

　　What is all this juice and all this joy?
10　　A strain of the earth's sweet being in the beginning
In Eden garden.—Have, get, before it cloy,
　Before it cloud, Christ, lord, and sour with sinning,
Innocent mind and Mayday in girl and boy,
　Most, O maid's child, thy choice and worthy the winning.

## Questions

1. What images does the speaker mention as support for his first line, "Nothing is so beautiful as Spring"? Are these images those that you would normally expect? To what degree do they seem to be new or unusual?

2. What images of motion and activity do you find in the poem? Are these mainly static or dynamic? What do these suggest about the speaker's view of spring?

3. What is the relationship between "Eden garden" in line 11 and the scene described in lines 1–8? To what extent are spring and "Innocent mind and Mayday" a glimpse of the Garden of Eden?

4. Christ is mentioned in lines 12 and 14 (as "maid's child"). Do these references seal the poem off from readers who are not Christian? Why or why not?

## A. E. HOUSMAN (1859–1936)

 ## On Wenlock Edge (1887)

On Wenlock Edge° the wood's in trouble;
His forest fleece the Wrekin° heaves;
The gale, it plies the saplings double,
And thick on Severn° snow the leaves.

---

°1 *Wenlock Edge*: A range of high hills in western England, south of Birmingham.  2 *the Wrekin*: a volcano (now extinct) northwest of Birmingham. Housman suggests that the volcano is erupting, just one of the natural disturbances he describes in the first two stanzas.  4 *Severn*: a major river winding southward through the area toward Bristol.

'Twould° blow like this through holt and hanger°       5
When Uricon° the city stood;
'Tis the old wind in the old anger,
But then it threshed another wood.

Then, 'twas before my time, the Roman
At yonder heaving hill would stare;       10
The blood that warms an English yeoman,°
The thoughts that hurt him, they were there.

There, like the wind through woods in riot,
Through him the gale of life blew high;
The tree of man was never quiet—       15
Then 'twas the Roman, now 'tis I.

The gale, it plies the saplings double;
It blows so hard, 'twill soon be gone.
Today the Roman and his trouble
Are ashes under Uricon.       20

---

°5 'Twould: it would [back in Roman times]. 5 holt and hanger: woods and thick underbrush along a hillside or mountainside. 6 Uricon: Uriconium, a regional capital in western England during the Roman occupation from the first to the fifth centuries C.E. 11 yeoman: a medieval English farmer who owned the land he farmed.

## Questions

1. How extensively does the speaker stress the images of natural disturbances that are taking place on Wenlock Edge, with the wind, for example, plying the saplings double? Why does Housman repeat this line (line 3) in line 17?
2. What concerns of the ancient Roman in England are continued in the feelings of the speaker, who is inhabiting the same location as the Roman?
3. What is the view of history that the speaker develops in this poem? Is it a usual view of what we ordinarily think of as history? Why or why not? On what idea does the poem conclude?

## DENISE LEVERTOV (1923–1997)

*For a photo, see Chapter 12, page 515.*

 **A Time Past** (1975)

The old wooden steps to the front door
where I was sitting that fall morning
when you came downstairs, just awake,
and my joy at sight of you (emerging
into golden day—       5
             the dew almost frost)
pulled me to my feet to tell you
how much I loved you:

those wooden steps
10 are gone now, decayed
replaced with granite,
hard, gray, and handsome.
The old steps live
only in me;
15 my feet and thighs
remember them, and my hands
still feel their splinters.
Everything else about and around that house
brings memories of others—of marriage,
20 of my son. And the steps do too: I recall
sitting there with my friend and her little son who died,
or was it the second one who lives and thrives?
And sitting there 'in my life,' often, alone or with my husband.
Yet that one instant,
25 your cheerful, unafraid, youthful, 'I love you too,'
the quiet broken by no bird, no cricket, gold leaves
spinning in silence down without
any breeze to blow them,
                     is what twines itself
30 in my head and body across those slabs of wood
that were warm, ancient, and now
wait somewhere to be burnt.

## Questions

1. Describe the visual imagery of the poem. What tactile imagery is associated with the steps? What other images are part of the speaker's memory?

2. How is the image of the "old wooden steps" developed in the poem? What has happened to the wooden steps? What meaning may be derived from their having been replaced by the granite steps? How are these steps tied to the speaker's "time past"?

3. Why do you think the speaker expressly denies the recollection of any sounds of bird or cricket?

**THOMAS LUX** (b. 1946)

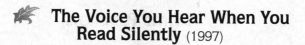 **The Voice You Hear When You Read Silently** (1997)

THE VOICE YOU HEAR WHEN YOU READ SILENTLY
is not silent, it is a speaking-
out-loud voice in your head: it is *spoken*,
a voice is *saying* it
5 as you read. It's the writer's words,
of course, in a literary sense
his or her "voice" but the sound

of that voice is the sound of *your* voice.
Not the sound your friends know
or the sound of a tape played back                                    10
but your voice
caught in the dark cathedral
of your skull, your voice heard
by an internal ear informed by internal abstracts
and what you know by feeling,                                         15
having felt. It is your voice
saying, for example, the word "barn"
that the writer wrote
but the "barn" you say
is a barn you know or knew. The voice                                 20
in your head, speaking as you read,
never says anything neutrally—some people
hated the barn they knew,
some people love the barn they know
so you hear the word loaded                                           25
and a sensory constellation
is lit: horse-gnawed stalls,
hayloft, black heat tape wrapping
a water pipe, a slippery
spilled *chirrr* of oats from a split sack,                          30
the bony, filthy haunches of cows. . . .
And "barn" is only a noun—no verb
or subject has entered into the sentence yet!
The voice you hear when you read to yourself
is the clearest voice: you speak it                                   35
speaking to you.

## Questions

1. What is meant by the "constellation" being lit when the reader reads a word, in this case "barn"? How does "constellation" explain the development of the barn image in lines 26–30?

2. Why is the "voice you hear when you read silently/. . . not silent"?

3. Describe the meaning and associations of "the dark cathedral/of your skull" in lines 11–12. What is particularly significant about the use of "cathedral" in these lines?

## EUGENIO MONTALE (1896–1981)

 ## Buffalo (Buffalo) (1929)

### *Translated by Robert Zweig*

Gusting, a sweet inferno channeled
crowds of every color
in the loop of blaring megaphones.
The buses gushed out
into the evening.                                                     5

On the churning gulf, heat evaporated
into smoke; down below, a shining arc
etched a current and the crowd was ready
at the passage. A black man
10 slumbered inside a ray of light
that cut the darkness; in a box, loose, easy women awaited
the ferry's landing. I said to myself:
Buffalo! – and the name worked.
               I fell
15 into the limbo of the deafening voices of the blood where flashes
burn the sight like flickers of mirror.
I heard the dry crashes, and all around me
saw the curved, striped backs whirling
on the track.

---

°BUFFALO (BUFFALO).  The Vélodrome Buffalo, a Parisian cycling racetrack, was the site of many world cycling records from 1893 until World War I, when it was replaced by an airplane factory. The Buffalo was named after Buffalo Bill Cody, whose Wild West show was performed there during the first year of its existence.

## Questions

**1.** The setting of *Buffalo* is an indoor bicycle racetrack. Why do you think Montale chose this setting?

**2.** Is the description of this bicycle race is objective or subjective? Which images can you cite to support your conclusion?

**3.** In Dante's *Inferno*, a medieval Italian poem that greatly influenced Montale, a ferry takes Dante across a river into "hell." Might the ferry that the "loose, easy women" wait for be such a ferry? If so, how does that image help you to understand *Buffalo*?

**4.** What do you think is meant when the speaker says that uttering the word "Buffalo" worked? What did uttering that word do?

## MICHEAL O'SIADHAIL (b. 1947)

 ## Abundance (1995)

*(for Marie)*

To be there, childlike, when it happens.
Nothing I've ever earned or achieved.
Delight. Sudden quivers of abundance.

A whole glorious day with a friend.
5 Brunch. This honeyed bread. Talk.
All the time in the world to spend.

Those icy stings and a gladdened vein,
an autumn swim tingling my nape,
dousing pleasure on a sleepy brain.

Watching children on a bandstand floor;
some irrepressible urge to celebrate,
squealing, tramping, pleasing for more.                          10

November birches with leaves of apricot,
After a long walk in the frosty air,
to warm our palms around a coffee-pot.

Waves and moments of energy released.                           15
I hoard them. A child with sweets and cakes
chortles at prospects of a midnight feast.

So much is that might never have been.

## Questions

1. Describe the images that the speaker equates with abundance. What is the location of these images? From the images, what idea about abundance does the speaker convey?
2. What types of images are developed in the poem? What tactile images does the speaker introduce? What gustatory images?
3. Why does the poet describe images of autumn scenes and activities, rather than images from spring days?
4. What is the meaning of the poem's last line? In what way does the line stem out of the preceding six stanzas?

**EZRA POUND** (1885–1972)

 **In a Station of the Metro°** (1916)

The apparition of these faces in the crowd;
Petals on a wet, black bough.

―――――――――――――

°*Metro*: the Paris subway.

## Questions

1. Is the image of the wet, black bough happy or sad? If the petals were on a tree in the sunlight, what would be the effect?
2. What is the meaning of the image suggested by "apparition"? Does it suggest a positive or negative view of human life?
3. This poem contains only two lines. Is it proper to consider it as a poem nevertheless? If it is not a poem, what is it?

## FRIEDRICH RÜCKERT (1788–1866)

### If You Love for the Sake of Beauty (1823)

*Anonymous Translator*

If you love for the sake of beauty, O never love me!
Love the sun, which has bright golden hair.
If you love for the sake of youth, O never love me!
Love the spring, which is reborn each year.
5  If you love for the sake of wealth, O never love me!
Love the mermaid, whose pearls are rich and clear.
If you love for the sake of love alone, O yes then, love me!
Love me as I love you—forever!

## Questions

1. What is the poem's situation? Who is speaking? Who is the listener?
2. How do the images in lines 2, 4, and 6 exemplify the abstract concepts in lines 1, 3, and 5? How does the speaker use these images to reinforce his or her negative requests?
3. How may the final two lines be considered a climax of the poem?

## WILLIAM SHAKESPEARE (1564–1616)

*For a portrait, see Chapter 21, page 981.*

### Sonnet 130: My Mistress' Eyes Are Nothing Like the Sun (1609)

My mistress' eyes are nothing like the sun;
Coral is far more red than her lips' red;
If snow be white, why then her breasts are dun;
If hairs be wires, black wires grow on her head.
5  I have seen roses damasked,° red and white,
But no such roses see I in her cheeks;
And in some perfumes is there more delight
Than in the breath that from my mistress reeks.
I love to hear her speak, yet well I know
10 That music hath a far more pleasing sound;
I grant I never saw a goddess go;
My mistress, when she walks, treads on the ground.
And yet, by heaven, I think my love as rare
As any she belied with false compare.

*set in an elaborate bouquet*

## Questions

1. To what does the speaker negatively compare his mistress's eyes? Lips? Breasts? Hair? Cheeks? Breath? Voice? Walk? What kinds of images are created in these negative comparisons?

2. What conventional images does this poem ridicule? What sort of poem is Shakespeare mocking by using the negative images in lines 1–12?

3. In the light of the last two lines, do you think the speaker intends the images as insults? If not as insults, how should they be taken?

4. Are most of the images auditory, olfactory, visual, or kinesthetic? Explain.

5. What point does this poem make about love poetry? About human relationships? How does the imagery contribute to the development of both points?

## JAMES TATE (b. 1943)

 **Dream On** 1998

Some people go their whole lives
without ever writing a single poem.
Extraordinary people who don't hesitate
to cut somebody's heart or skull open.
They go to baseball games with the greatest of ease          5
and play a few rounds of golf as if it were nothing.
These same people stroll into a church
as if that were a natural part of life.
Investing money is second nature to them.
They contribute to political campaigns                        10
that have absolutely no poetry in them
and promise none for the future.
They sit around the dinner table at night
and pretend as though nothing is missing.
Their children get caught shoplifting at the mall            15
and no one admits that it is poetry they are missing.
The family dog howls all night,
lonely and starving for more poetry in his life.
Why is it so difficult for them to see
that, without poetry, their lives are effluvial.             20
Sure, they have their banquets, their celebrations,
croquet, fox hunts, their seashores and sunsets,
their cocktails on the balcony, dog races,
and all that kissing and hugging, and don't
forget the good deeds, the charity work,                     25
nursing the baby squirrels all through the night,
filling the birdfeeders all winter,
helping the stranger change her tire.
Still, there's that disagreeable exhalation
from decaying matter, subtle but ever present                30
They walk around erect like champions.
They are smooth-spoken, urbane and witty.
When alone, rare occasion, they stare
into the mirror for hours, bewildered.
There was something they meant to say, but didn't:           35
"And if we put the statue of the rhinoceros

next to the tweezers, and walk around the room three
times
learn to yodel, shave our heads, call
40 our ancestors back from the dead—"
poetrywise it's still a bust, bankrupt.
You haven't scribbled a syllable of it.
You're a nowhere man misfiring
the very essence of your life, flustering
45 nothing from nothing and back again.
The hereafter may not last all that long.
Radiant childhood sweetheart,
secret code of everlasting joy and sorrow,
fanciful pen strokes beneath the eyelids:
50 all day, all night meditation, knot of hope,
kernel of desire, pure ordinariness of life,
seeking, through poetry, a benediction
or a bed to lie down on, to connect, reveal,
explore, to imbue meaning on the day's extravagant labor.
55 And yet it's cruel to expect too much.
It's a rare species of bird
That refuses to be categorized.
Its song is barely audible.
It is like a dragonfly in a dream—
60 Here, then there, then here again,
Low-flying amber-wing darting upward
and then out of sight.
And the dream has a pain in its heart
the wonders of which are manifold,
65 or so the story is told.

## Questions

1. Characterize the images from lines 3 to 20. What types of images, for the most part, are these? What part do they play in the poem's argument?

2. In lines 36–42 there is a different unit of imagery. What are the characteristics and purpose of these?

3. How does the speaker use images to characterize poetry from lines 55 through 64 (if we take the repetition of "it" in lines 55, 56, 58, and 59 as descriptions of poetry). How true is the idea that poetry is a dream with a pain in its heart (line 63)? What is the effect of the final line?

## WRITING ABOUT IMAGERY

### Questions for Discovering Ideas

In preparing to write, you should develop a set of thoughtful notes dealing with issues such as the following:

- What type or types of images prevail in the work? Visual (shapes, colors)? Auditory (sounds)? Olfactory (smells)? Tactile (touch and texture)?

Gustatory (taste)? Kinetic or kinesthetic (motion)? Or is the imagery a combination?

- To what degree do the images reflect either the poet's actual observation or the poet's reading and knowledge of fields such as science or history?
- How well do the images stand out? How vivid are they? How does the poet make the images vivid?
- Within a group of images, say, visual or auditory, do the images pertain to one location or area rather than another (e.g., natural scenes rather than interiors, snowy scenes rather than grassy ones, loud and harsh sounds rather than quiet and soothing ones)?
- What explanation is needed for the images? (Images might be derived from the classics or the Bible, the Vietnam War or World War II, the behaviors of four-footed creatures or birds or fish, and so on.)
- What effect do the circumstances described in the poem (e.g., conditions of brightness or darkness, warmth or cold) have on your responses to the images? What purpose do you think the poet achieves by controlling these responses?
- How well are the images integrated within the poem's argument or development?

Answering questions like these will provide you with a sizable body of ready-made material that you can convert directly to your essay.

## Strategies for Organizing Ideas

Connect a brief overview of the poem to your plan for the body of your essay, noting perhaps that the writer uses images to strengthen ideas about war, character, or love or that the writer relies predominantly on images of sight, sound, and action. You might deal with just one of the following aspects, or you may combine your approaches, as you wish.

1. *Images suggesting ideas and/or moods.* Such an essay should emphasize the effects of the imagery. What ideas or moods are evoked by the images? (The auditory images beginning Owen's "Anthem for Doomed Youth," for example, all point toward a condemnation of the brutality of war. The visual images in "Spring," by Hopkins, all point toward a sense of earthly and also divine growth and lushness.) Do the images promote approval or disapproval? Cheerfulness? Melancholy? Are the images drab, exciting, vivid? How? Why? Are they conducive to humor or surprise? How does the writer achieve these effects? Are the images consistent, or are they ambiguous? (The images in Masefield's "Cargoes" indicate first approval and then disapproval, with no ambiguity. By contrast, Shakespeare's images in "My Mistress' Eyes" might be construed as insults, but in context, they are really compliments.)

2. *The types of images.* Here the emphasis is on the categories of images themselves. Is there a predominance of a particular type of image (e.g., visual or auditory) or is there a blending? Is there a bunching of types at particular points in the poem or story? If so, why? Is there any shifting as the work

develops (for example, in Owen's "Anthem for Doomed Youth" the auditory images first suggest loudness and harshness, but later images describe quietness and sorrow)? Are the images appropriate, granted the nature and apparent intent of the work? Do they assist in making the ideas seem convincing? If any images seem inappropriate, is the inappropriateness intentional or inadvertent? What is the effect of the inappropriate imagery?

3. *Systems of images.* Here the emphasis should be on the areas from which the images are drawn. This is another way of considering the appropriateness of the imagery: Is there a pattern of similar or consistent images, such as dark and dreary urban scenes (Eliot's "Preludes") or color and activity (Hopkins's "Spring")? Do all the images adhere consistently to a particular frame of reference, such as a sunlit garden (Lowell's "Patterns" [Chapter 19]), an extensive recreational forest and garden (Coleridge's "Kubla Khan"), a front stair (Levertov's "A Time Past"), or a forest at night (Blake's "The Tyger" [Chapter 14])? What is unusual or unique about the set of images? What unexpected or new responses do they produce?

Your conclusion, in addition to restating your major points, is the place for additional insights. It would not be proper to go too far in new directions here, but you might briefly take up one or more of the ideas that you have not developed in the body. In short, what have you learned from your study of imagery in the poem?

## Illustrative Student Essay

Underlined sentences in this paper *do not* conform to MLA style and are used solely as teaching tools to emphasize the central idea, thesis sentence, and topic sentences throughout the paper.

Mike Pugh

Professor Skaggs

English 101

14 January 2007

### Imagery in T. S. Eliot's "Preludes"°

[1]    T. S. Eliot's poem "Preludes" offers a series of generally depressing images of

inhabitants of modern cities.* The first stanza sets the scene by describing a wet, wintry

urban street scene. The second stanza moves indoors to describe the actions of the

_____

°See p. 539 for this poem.
*Central idea.

residents "in a thousand furnished rooms" (line 23). The third stanza zooms in even closer to focus on one particular "you" (lines 24–38). Then the fourth stanza expands outward again to the action on the street. This alternation of images from outside to inside and then back to outside follows Eliot's use of specific images to communicate pessimistic ideas about modern urban life. <u>Four types of images suggest Eliot's view that modern city dwellers are spiritually impoverished and that they suffer from a sense of meaninglessness.</u>[†]

[2]       <u>Numerous images of the human body focus on the commonness and antiheroism of most modern human beings.</u> Eliot's speaker refers to human feet four different times (lines 7, 17, 37, and 41)—not the mind, not the soul, but the feet. In the third stanza, the soles of a woman's feet are described as "yellow" (line 37), a color suggesting not health but sickness. And throughout the poem these feet are not marching heroically to a stirring martial tune, nor do they carry runners to victory, dance brilliantly to happy music, walk purposefully with children in tow, or carry a political leader to a podium to deliver an important speech. No, these feet trudge through city streets as though they are just going through the motions: they "press" to "coffee-stands," presumably at lunch and break times (lines 17–18) and their only insistence occurs "At four and five and six o'clock" (line 42) when business closes for the day and people are in a rush to leave their purposeless jobs and get home to their equally purposeless lives. The feet are also destructive, for they not only trample the sawdust in the street (line 16), but in the fourth stanza they might somehow be thought to be trampling on a soul (lines 39–41).

[3]       <u>Eliot's speaker zooms in on other specific parts of the body, too, including hands, fingers, eyes, and a mouth.</u> The hands and fingers, like the feet, seem to be just going through the motions of raising shades or stuffing pipes (lines 21–22 and 43). The eyes are "Assured of certain certainties" (line 45), a phrase which suggests that they focus only on the concrete and tangible world and avoid the consideration of faith and mystery. The mouth needs to be wiped (line 52) as though it is dirty—or perhaps foamy from beer. Such bodily images indicate that modern-day people are immersed in the physical world, and they also suggest that this focus amounts to a destructive anomie that is dulling their souls and making their lives meaningless.

---

[†]Thesis sentence.

[4]     While the bodily images suggest modern antiheroism, comparable images of dirt and squalor indicate that the world of cities is soiled and impoverished. Tree leaves are not fresh and green, but they are fallen and have become "grimy scraps" (line 6), blown by the wind, together with the pages of discarded newspapers of mindless headlines and news articles (line 8). The urban streets are "muddy" (line 17) and the shades in people's homes are "dingy" (line 22). The hands of a woman described in the third stanza are "soiled" (line 38). People wake up in the morning to the "faint stale smells of beer" (line 15) from the previous night's bingeing. All these images indicate a lack of cleanliness, and others stem from deterioration and neglect: The window blinds are "broken" (line 10), and even the songs of sparrows come from "the gutters" (line 32). In this dirty, squalid world, individual souls seem to have nowhere to go but down.

[5]     Not only is this environment filthy and tawdry, but also it is gloomy and unenlightened, and the city-dwellers' spiritual void is reflected in images of darkness. The first stanza begins in the darkness of an early winter evening (line 1), but even the relatively short days are described as "smoky" (line 4). Morning comes in the second and third stanzas, but in the third stanza the woman who rises from bed is disconcerted by the "thousand sordid images" (line 27) that have "flickered against the ceiling" during the night (line 29). The light of day has to creep "up between the shutters" (line 31), an image that suggests it is uninvited and unwelcome.

[6]     A final set of images suggests that, in addition to being dirty, cheap, and dark, this urban world—both natural and human—is one of spiritual bankruptcy and enervation. The poem is set in winter (line 1), a cold, lifeless, and colorless season when the leaves have fallen from the branches to be blown about aimlessly on the streets and sidewalks. Evenings are described as the "burnt-out ends of smoky days" (line 4)—an image suggesting that human effort, day by day, amounts to no more than a foul-smelling cigarette butt. Twice, Eliot's speaker mentions vacant lots (lines 8, 54), an image conveying the idea that the outside world consists of both emptiness and wasted space scattered with undifferentiated litter. Such images of disuse and depletion are consistent with the poem's emphasis on spiritual stagnation.

[7]     These images are gloomy and hopeless, but the poem also contains slight signs— glimmers—of something more positive. In lines 46 and 47 the speaker introduces the image of the "conscience of a blackened street" which is "Impatient to assume the

world." These lines do not make up a complete sentence, but rather form a fragment, and therefore the potentially positive associations and implications are tentative and maybe even illusory. Even so, the word "conscience" suggests something spiritual that may survive and even emerge despite the image of the "blackened street" on which people live. In addition, in the final stanza, Eliot's speaker explains, "I am moved by fancies that are curled/Around these images, and cling" (48–49). Specifically, they put him in mind of "some infinitely gentle/Infinitely suffering thing" (50–51). Something better, then, may be present, and may be redemptive through infinite gentleness in the face of all the tawdriness of modern humanity. But the poet's final words reflect the idea that his speaker has been given no more than a fleeting image of a better world, and so the poem's negative images prevail. All we can do, we are told, is to take what comes and not to expect too much, for the world has always been like this, even from ancient times, revolving in its orbit while people go about their tasks of daily survival and drudgery.

**WORK CITED**

Eliot, T. S. "Preludes." *Literature: An Introduction to Reading and Writing.* Ed. Edgar V. Roberts. 4th Compact ed. Upper Saddle River: Prentice Hall, 2008, 539.

## Commentary on the Essay

This essay illustrates the third strategy for writing about imagery (p. 552), referring to the various locations that make up sets of images developed by Eliot in "Preludes." This method permits the introduction of imagery drawn from identifiable visual classes, specifically, negative images of the human body and negative images of street life and the time of day. The introductory paragraph of the essay presents the central idea that Eliot uses his images to emphasize a gloomy view of modern urban life. The thesis sentence indicates that the essay will discuss four different types of images.

Paragraphs 2, 3, and 4 form a connected group stressing Eliot's use of images which focus on various parts of the human body. In particular, paragraph 2 uses the words "sickness," "trudge," "purposeless," and "destructive" to characterize the negative mental pictures prompted by the images. Although the paragraph indicates downside responses to the images, it does not go beyond the limits of the images themselves. The idea is that Eliot invites these responses.

Paragraph 5 stresses a second type of image in the poem, namely, images that refer to darkness and connect it to the psychological darkness and sordidness of individuals inhabiting the modern city.

The sixth paragraph demonstrates an additional class of image that denotes a whittling away of the human spirit. Here the images of winter, deciduous leaf fall, evening, and vacant lots are cited for the ways in which they cumulatively bring out this impression. The last paragraph deals with the images and thoughts about redemption brought out in the poem. The idea of the paragraph is that the images are so fleeting that they do not counterbalance the prevailing negative images of the rest of the poem.

# Special Writing Topics About Imagery in Poetry

1. Compare the images of war in Owen's "Anthem for Doomed Youth" and Hardy's "Channel Firing." Describe the differing effects of the images. How are the images used? How effectively do these images aid in the development of the attitudes toward war expressed in each poem?

2. Basing your work on the poems in this chapter by Blake, Coleridge, Griffin, Hopkins, and O'Siadhail, write an essay discussing the poetic use of images drawn from the natural world. What sorts of references do the poets make? What attitudes do they express about the details they select? What is the relationship between the images and religious views? What judgments about topics such as Nature, God, humanity, and friendship do the poets show by their images?

3. Considering the imagery of Tate's "Dream On," write an essay explaining the nature and use of imagery in poetry. As you develop your thoughts, be sure to consider the different characteristics of Tate's images and to account for the impressions and ideas that they create. You may also wish to introduce references to images from other poems that are relevant to your points.

4. Write a comparison of the imagery in Elizabeth Browning's "If Thou Must Love Me" and Rückert's "If You Love for the Sake of Beauty." Even though the poems are on virtually identical subjects, how does the selection of images contribute toward making each poem distinct?

5. Write a poem describing one of these:
   a. Athletes who have just completed an exhausting run.
   b. Children getting out of school for the day.
   c. Your recollection of having been lost as a child.
   d. A cat that always sits down right on your schoolwork.
   e. A particularly good meal you had recently.
   f. The best concert you ever attended.
   g. Driving to work or school on a rainy or snowy day.

   Then, write an analysis of the images you selected for your poem, and explain your choices. What details stand out in your mind? What do you recall best—

sight, smell, sound, action? What is the relationship between your images and the ideas you express in your poem?

6. Study the reproduction of Herkomer's painting *Hard Times* (I–5, Plate 1). Then write an essay comparing and contrasting Herkomer's artistic techniques with Hopkins's poem "Spring" and Pound's "In a Station of the Metro," along with other poems that you may wish to include. What similarities and differences do you find in subject matter, treatment, arrangement, and general idea? On the basis of your comparison, what relationships do you perceive between poetic and painterly technique?

7. Use the retrieval system in your library to research the topic of imagery in Shakespeare (see *imagery* or *style and imagery*). How many titles do you find? Over how many years have these works been published? Take one of the books out, and write a brief report on one of the chapters. What topics are discussed? What types of imagery are introduced? What relationship does the author make between imagery and content?

# Chapter **14**

# Figures of Speech, or Metaphorical Language: A Source of Depth and Range in Poetry

**F**_igures of speech_, **metaphorical language, figurative language, figurative devices**, and **rhetorical figures** are terms describing organized patterns of comparison that deepen, broaden, extend, illuminate, and emphasize meaning. First and foremost, the use of figures of speech is a major characteristic by which great literature provides us with fresh and original ways of thinking, feeling, and understanding. Although figurative language is sometimes called "ornate," as though it were unnecessarily decorative, it is not uncommon in conversational speech, and it is essential in literary thought and expression. Unlike the writing of the social and "hard" sciences, imaginative literature is not direct and unambiguous, offering exact correspondences of words and things. Yes, literature presents specific and accurate descriptions and explanations, but it also moves in areas of implication and suggestiveness through the use of **figurative language**, which enables writers to amplify their ideas while still employing relatively small numbers of words. Such language is therefore a sine qua non in imaginative literature, particularly poetry, where it compresses thought, deepens understanding, and shapes response.

The two most important figures of speech, and the most easily recognized, are _metaphors_ and _similes_. There are also many other metaphorical figures, some of which are _paradox, anaphora, apostrophe, personification, synecdoche_ and _metonymy, pun_ (or _paronomasia_), _synesthesia, overstatement_, and _understatement_. All these figures are modes of comparison, and they may be expressed in single words, phrases, clauses, or entire structures.

## Metaphors and Similes: The Major Figures of Speech

### A Metaphor Shows That Something Unknown Is Identical to Something Known

A **metaphor** (a "carrying out a change") equates known objects or actions with something that is unknown or to be explained (e.g., "Your words are music to my ears," "You are the sunshine of my life," "My life is a squirrel cage"). The equation of the metaphor not only explains and illuminates the thing—let us choose Judith Minty's concept of marital inseparability in "Conjoined"—but also offers distinctive and original and often startling ways of seeing it and thinking about it. Thus, Minty draws her metaphor of a married couple from the joining of two onions under one

**560**

onion skin. Here the metaphor is unique and surprising, and yet on examination it is right and natural, and also somewhat comic.

Metaphors are inseparable from language. In a heavy storm, for example, trees may be said to *bow* constantly as the wind blows against them. *Bow* is a metaphor because the word usually refers to performers' bending forward to acknowledge the applause of an audience and to indicate their gratitude for the audience's approval. The metaphor therefore asks us to equate our knowledge of theater life (something known) to a weather occurrence (something to be explained). A comparable reference to theater life creates one of the best-known metaphors to appear in Shakespeare's plays: "All the world's a stage,/And all the men and women merely players." Here, Shakespeare's character Jacques (JAY-queez) from Act 2, scene 7 of *As You Like It*, identifies human life exactly with stage life. In other words, the things said and done by stage actors are also said and done by living people in real life. It is important to recognize that Shakespeare's metaphor does not state that the world is *like* a stage but that it literally *is* a stage.

## A Simile Shows That Something Unknown Is Similar to Something Known

A **simile** (a "showing of likeness or resemblance") illustrates the similarity or comparability of the known to something unknown or to be explained. Whereas a metaphor merges identities, a simile focuses on resemblances (e.g., "Your words are like music to me," "You are like sunshine in my life," "I feel like a squirrel in a cage"). Similes are distinguishable from metaphors because they are introduced by *like* with nouns and *as* (also "as if" and "as though") with clauses. If Minty had written that a married couple is like "The onion in my cupboard," her comparison would have been a simile.

Let us consider one of the best-known similes in poetry, from "A Valediction: Forbidding Mourning" by Renaissance poet John Donne. This is a dramatic poem spoken by a lover about to go on a trip. His loved one is sorrowful, and he attempts to console her by claiming that even when he is gone, he will remain with her in spirit. The following stanza contains the famous simile embodying this idea.

> Our two souls therefore, which are one,
>     Though I must go, endure not yet
> A breach,° but an expansion                                       *break, separation*
>     Like gold to airy thinness beat.

The simile compares the souls of the speaker and his loved one to gold, a metal both valuable and malleable. By the simile, the speaker asserts that the impending departure will not be a separation but rather a thinning out, so that the relationship of the lovers will remain constant and rich even as the distance between them increases. Because the comparison is introduced by *like*, the emphasis of the figurative language is on the similarity of the lovers' love to gold (which is always gold even when it is thinned out by the goldsmith's hammer), not on the identification of the two.

## Characteristics of Metaphorical Language

In language, the words **image** and **imagery** define words that stimulate the imagination and recall memories (images) of sights, sounds, tastes, smells, sensations of touch, and motions. Metaphors and similes go beyond literal imagery to introduce perceptions and comparisons that can be unusual, unpredictable, and surprising, as in Donne's simile comparing the lovers' relationship to gold. The comparison emphasizes the bond between the two lovers; the reference to gold shows how valuable the bond is; the unusual and original comparison is one of the elements that make the poem striking and memorable.

To see metaphorical language in further operation, let us take a commonly described condition—happiness. In everyday speech, we might use the sentence "She was happy" to state that a particular character was experiencing joy and excitement. The sentence is of course accurate, but it is not interesting. A more vivid way of saying the same thing is to use an image of action, such as "She jumped for joy." But another and better way of communicating joy is the following simile: "She felt as if she had just won the lottery." Because readers easily understand the disbelief, excitement, exhilaration, and delight that such an event would bring, they also understand—and feel—the character's happiness. It is the simile that evokes this perception and enables each reader to personalize the experience, for no simple description could help a reader comprehend the same degree of emotion.

As a parallel poetic example, let us look at John Keats's sonnet "On First Looking into Chapman's Homer," which Keats wrote soon after reading the translation of Homer's great epics *The Iliad* and *The Odyssey* by the Renaissance poet George Chapman. Keats, one of the greatest of all poets himself, describes his enthusiasm about Chapman's successful and exciting work.

### ✒ **JOHN KEATS** (1795–1821)

## On First Looking into Chapman's Homer (1816)

|   | | |
|---|---|---|
| | Much have I travell'd in the realms of gold,° | *the world of great art* |
| | And many goodly states and kingdoms seen: | |
| | Round many western islands° have I been | *much ancient literature* |
| | Which bards in fealty to Apollo° hold. | |
| 5 | Oft of one wide expanse° had I been told | *epic poetry* |
| | That deep-brow'd Homer ruled as his demesne°; | *realm, estate* |
| | Yet did I never breathe its pure serene° | |
| | Till I heard Chapman speak out loud and bold: | |
| | Then felt I like some watcher of the skies | |
| 10 | When a new planet swims into his ken°; | *his range of vision* |

°ON FIRST LOOKING INTO CHAPMAN'S HOMER. George Chapman (c. 1560–1634) published his translations of Homer's *Iliad* in 1612 and *Odyssey* in 1614–15.  4 *bards . . . Apollo*: writers who are sworn subjects of Apollo, the Greek god of light, music, poetry, prophecy, and the sun.  7 *serene*: a clear expanse of air; also grandeur, clarity; rulers were also sometimes called "serene majesty."

Or like stout Cortez° when with eagle eyes
  He star'd at the Pacific—and all his men
Look'd at each other with a wild surmise°—
  Silent, upon a peak in Darien.

*conjecture, supposition*

°11 *Cortez*: Hernando Cortès (1485–1547), a Spanish general and the conqueror of Mexico. Keats confuses him with Vasco de Balboa (c. 1475–1519), the first European to see the Pacific Ocean (in 1510) from Darien, an early name for the Isthmus of Panama.

As a first step in understanding the power of metaphorical language, we can briefly paraphrase the sonnet's content.

> I have enjoyed much art and read much poetry, and I have been told that Homer is the best writer of all. However, I did not appreciate his works until I first read them in Chapman's clear and forceful translation. This discovery was exciting and awe-inspiring.

If all Keats had written had been a paragraph like this one, we would pay little attention to it, for it conveys no excitement or wonder. But the last six lines of the sonnet contain two memorable similes ("like some watcher of the skies" and "like stout Cortez") that stand out and demand a special effort of imagination. To appreciate these similes fully, we need to imagine what it would be like to be an astronomer as he or she discovers a previously unknown planet, and what it would have been like to be one of the first European explorers to see the Pacific Ocean. As we imagine ourselves in these roles, we get a sense of the amazement, excitement, exhilaration, and joy that would accompany such discoveries. With that experience comes the realization that the world is far bigger and more astonishing than we had ever dreamed. Metaphorical language therefore makes strong demands on our creative imaginations. It bears repeating that as we develop our own mental pictures under the stimulation of metaphors and similes, we also develop appropriately associated attitudes and feelings. Let us consider once more Keats's metaphor "realms of gold," which invites us both to imagine brilliant and shining kingdoms and also to join Keats in valuing and loving not just poetry but all literature. The metaphorical "realms of gold" act upon our minds, liberating our imaginations, directing our understanding, and evoking our feelings. In such a way, reading and responding to the works of writers like Keats produces both mental and

## VEHICLE AND TENOR

To describe the relationship between a writer's ideas and the metaphors and similes chosen to objectify them, two useful terms have been coined by I. A. Richards (in *The Philosophy of Rhetoric* [1929]). First is the **vehicle,** or the specific words of the metaphor or simile. Second is the **tenor,** which is the totality of ideas and attitudes not only of the literary speaker but also of the author. For example, the tenor of Donne's simile in "A Valediction: Forbidding Mourning" is the inseparable love and unbreakable connection of the two lovers; the vehicle is the hammering of gold "to airy thinness." Similarly, the tenor of the similes in the sestet of Keats's sonnet "On First Looking into Chapman's Homer" is awe and wonder; the vehicle is the description of astronomical and geographical discovery.

emotional experiences that were previously hidden to us. Poets continually give us something new, and they increase our power to think and know. They enlarge us.

# Other Figures of Speech

## A Paradox Uses an Apparent Error or Contradiction to Reveal Truth

A **paradox** is "a thought beyond a thought," a figurative device through which something apparently wrong or contradictory is shown to be truthful and noncontradictory. The phrase "I, a child, very old" in Whitman's "Facing West from California's Shores" is a paradox. The obvious contradiction is that no one can be old and young at the same time, but this contradiction can be reconciled if we realize that even as people get older they still retain many of the qualities of children (such as enthusiasm and hope). Thus Whitman's contradiction is not contradictory (is this clause a paradox?) and the speaker may genuinely be "a child, very old." The second line of Sir Thomas Wyatt's sonnet "I Find No Peace" embodies two paradoxes. One opposes fear with hope, the other fire with ice: "I fear and hope, I burn and freeze like ice." These paradoxes reflect the contradictory states of people in love—wanting love ("hope," "burn") but also being uncertain and unsure about the relationship ("fear," "freeze"). The paradoxes thus highlight the truth that love is a complex and often unsettling emotion.

## Anaphora Provides Weight and Emphasis Through Repetition

**Anaphora** ("to carry again or repeat") is the repetition of the same word or phrase throughout a work or a section of a work in order to lend weight and emphasis. An example occurs in Blake's "The Tyger," when the interrogative word "what" is used five times to emphasize the mystery of evil (italics added).

> *What* the hammer? *what* the chain?
> In *what* furnace was thy brain?
> *What* the anvil? *what* dread grasp
> Dare its deadly terrors clasp?

Anaphora is the most obvious feature of Muriel Rukeyser's "Looking at Each Other," where the word *yes* begins each of the poem's 25 lines.

## Apostrophe Creates the Drama of a Speaker Addressing an Audience

In an **apostrophe** (a "turning away," or redirection of attention) a speaker addresses a real or imagined listener who is not present. It is like a public speech, with readers as audience, and it therefore makes a poem dramatic. An apostrophe enables the speaker to develop ideas that might arise naturally on a public occasion, as in Wordsworth's sonnet "London, 1802," which is addressed to the long dead English poet Milton. In the following sonnet by Keats, "Bright Star," the speaker addresses a distant and inanimate star, yet through apostrophe he speaks as though the star has human understanding and divine power.

# JOHN KEATS (1795–1822)

 Bright Star (1838 (1819))

Bright star! would I were steadfast as thou art—
  Not in lone splendor hung aloft the night,
And watching, with eternal lids apart,
  Like Nature's patient, sleepless eremite,° *hermit, a holy presence*
The moving waters at their priestlike task    5
  Of pure ablution round earth's human shores,
Or gazing on the new soft-fallen mask
  Of snow upon the mountains and the moors;
No—yet still steadfast, still unchangeable,
  Pillowed upon my fair love's ripening breast,    10
To feel forever its soft fall and swell,
  Awake forever in a sweet unrest,
    Still, still to hear her tender-taken breath,
    And so live ever—or else swoon to death.

## Questions

1. With what topic is the speaker concerned in this sonnet? How does he compare himself with the distant star?
2. What qualities does the speaker attribute specifically to the star? What role does he seem to assign to it? In light of this role, and the qualities needed to serve in it, how might the star be compared to a divine and benign presence?
3. In light of the emphasis on the words "forever" and "ever" in lines 11–14, how appropriate is the choice of the star as the subject of the apostrophe in the poem?

In this sonnet the speaker addresses the star as though it is a person or god, an object of adoration, and the poem is therefore like a petitional prayer. The star is idealized with qualities that the speaker wishes to establish in himself, namely, steadfastness, eternal watchfulness, and fidelity. The point of the apostrophe is thus to dramatize the speaker's yearning and to stress the permanence of space and eternity as contrasted with earthly impermanence.

## Personification Is the Attribution of Human Traits to Abstractions or to Nonhuman Objects

A close neighbor of apostrophe is **personification**, another dramatic figurative device through which poets explore relationships to environment, ideals, and inner lives. In "Bright Star," as we have just seen, Keats personifies the star addressed by the speaker. Shakespeare's speaker in Sonnet 146, "Poor Soul, the Center of My Sinful Earth" (Chapter 19), personifies his own soul as he speaks of earthly and heavenly concerns. Other important uses of personification are seen in Keats's "To Autumn" (this chapter) and "Ode on a Grecian Urn" (Chapter 19).

## Synecdoche and Metonymy Transfer Meanings by Parts and Associations

These figures are close in purpose and effect. **Synecdoche** ("taking one thing out of another") is a device in which a part stands for the whole or a whole for a part, like the expression "all hands aboard," which describes the whole of a ship's crew by their hands, that part of them that performs work. **Metonymy** (a "transfer of name") substitutes one thing for another with which it is closely identified, as when "Hollywood" is used to mean the movie industry, or when "the White House" signifies the policies and activities of the president. The purpose of both figures of speech is the creation of new insights and ideas, just like metaphors and similes.

Synecdoche is seen in Keats's "To Autumn," where the gourd and hazel shells, which are single instances of ripe produce, stand for the entire autumnal harvest. In Wordsworth's "London, 1802," the phrase "thy heart" (line 13) is a synecdoche in which a part—the heart—refers to the complete person. Metonymy is seen again in Keats's "To Autumn," when the "granary floor" (line 14), the place where grain is stored, bears the transferred meaning of the entire autumnal harvest.

## Pun, or Paronomasia, Shows That Words with Similar or Identical Sounds Have Different Meanings

A pun ("a point or a puncture") or paronomasia ("[something] beside a name") is wordplay stemming from the fact that words with different meanings have surprisingly similar or even identical sounds and that some individual words have surprisingly differing and even contradictory meanings. Because puns are sometimes considered outrageous and often require a little bit of thinking, people may groan when they hear them (even while they enjoy them). Also, because many puns seem to play only with sound, they have not always enjoyed critical acclaim. Good puns can always be relished because they work with sounds to reveal ideas. John Gay, for example, creates clever puns in the following song, sung chorally by the gang of thieves in *The Beggar's Opera* (1728), a play that, incidentally, marked the beginning of the modern musical comedy tradition.

### JOHN GAY (1685–1732)

 **Let Us Take the Road** (1728)

Let us take the road.
   Hark! I hear the sound of coaches!
   The hour of attack approaches,
To your arms, brave boys, and load.
5    See the ball I hold!          *[holding up a bullet]*
   Let the chemists° toil like asses,      *alchemists*
   Our fire their fire surpasses,°   *Our [gun]fire is better than their [forge] fire.*
    And turns all our lead to gold.

## Questions

1. What traits are shown by the singers of this poem? Why do they not seem frightening, despite their admission that they are holdup men?
2. Describe the puns in the poem. What kind of knowledge is needed to explain them fully? How many puns are there? How are they connected? Why do the puns seem both witty and outrageous?

Here "fire," "lead," and "gold" are puns. Lead was the "base" or "low" metal that the medieval alchemists ("chemists") tried to transform into ingots of gold, using the heat from their fires. The puns develop because the gang of cutthroats singing the song is about to go out to rob travelers at gunpoint. Hence their bullets are their lead, that they plan to transform into the gold coins they steal. Their fire is not the fire of alchemists, but rather pistol fire. Through these puns, Gay's villains charm us by their wit and delight in their villainy, even though in real life they would scare us to death.

## Synesthesia Demonstrates the Oneness or Unity of Feelings

In **synesthesia** (the "bringing together of feelings") a poet describes a feeling or perception with words that usually refer to different or even opposite feelings or perceptions. Keats uses synesthesia extensively, as, for example, in the "Ode to a Nightingale" (Chapter 16), where a plot of ground is "melodious," a draught of wine tastes of "Dance, and Provençal song, and sunburnt mirth," and beaded bubbles are "winking at the brim" of a wine glass.

## Overstatement and Understatement Are Means of Creating Emphasis

Two important devices creating emphasis are overstatement (or hyperbole), and understatement. **Overstatement**, also called the **overreacher**, is exaggeration for effect. In "London, 1802," for example, Wordsworth declares that England "is a fen/Of stagnant waters." That is, the country and its people collectively make up a stinking, polluted marsh, a muddy dump. What Wordsworth establishes by this overstatement is his judgment that England in 1802 was so morally and politically rotten that it needed a writer like Milton to unite the people around noble ideas.

In contrast with overstatement, **understatement** is the deliberate underplaying or undervaluing of a thing. One of the most famous poetic understatements is in Marvell's "To His Coy Mistress" (Chapter 17).

> The grave's a fine and private place,
> But none, I think, do there embrace.

Here Marvell, through understatement, wittily and grimly emphasizes the eternity of death by contrasting the motionless privacy of the grave with the active privacy of a trysting place.

## Poems for Study

## JACK AGÜEROS (b. 1934)

 ## Sonnet for You, Familiar Famine (1996)

Nobody's waiting for any apocalypse to meet you, Famine!

We know you. There isn't a corner of our round world
where you don't politely accompany someone to bed each
night. In some families, you're the only one sitting
5   at the table when the dinner bell tolls. "He's not so
bad," say people who have plenty and easily tolerate you.
They argue that small portions are good for us, and
are just what we deserve. There's an activist side to
you, Famine. You've been known to bring down governments,
10  yet you never get any credit for your political reforms.

Don't make the mistake I used to make of thinking fat
people are immune to Famine. Famine has this other ugly

side. Famine knows that the more you eat the more you
long. That side bears his other frightening name, Emptiness.

## Questions

1. What figure of speech does the poet use in this poem? What situation does the poem
address?

2. What is the purpose of using this figure for the poem rather than a more direct analysis of
the causes and effects of hunger?

3. What powers does the speaker attribute to Famine? How correct is his assessment of these
powers?

## WILLIAM BLAKE (1757–1827)

*For a drawing, see Chapter 12, page 503.*

 **The Tyger°** (1794)

Tyger! Tyger! burning bright
In the forests of the night,
What immortal hand or eye
Could frame thy fearful symmetry?

In what distant deeps or skies                                                 5
Burnt the fire of thine eyes?
On what wings dare he aspire?
What the hand, dare seize the fire?

And what shoulder, & what art,
Could twist the sinews of thy heart?                                          10
And when thy heart began to beat,
What dread hand? & what dread feet?

What the hammer? what the chain?
In what furnace was thy brain?
What the anvil? what dread grasp                                             15
Dare its deadly terrors clasp?

When the stars threw down their spears,
And water'd heaven with their tears,
Did he smile his work to see?
Did he who made the Lamb make thee?                                          20

Tyger! Tyger! burning bright
In the forests of the night,
What immortal hand or eye
Dare frame thy fearful symmetry?

_____

°"Tyger" refers not only to a tiger but also to any large, wild, ferocious cat.

## Questions

1. What do the associations of the image of "burning" suggest? Why is the burning done at night rather than day? What does night suggest?

2. Describe the kinesthetic images of lines 5–20. What ideas is Blake's speaker representing by these images? What attributes does the speaker suggest may belong to the blacksmith-type initiator of these actions?

3. Line 20 presents the kinesthetic image of a creator. What is implied about the mixture of good and evil in the world? What answer does the poem offer? Why does Blake phrase this line as a question rather than an assertion?

4. The sixth stanza repeats the first stanza with only one change of imagery of action. Contrast these stanzas, stressing the difference between "could" (line 4) and "dare" (24).

## ROBERT BURNS (1759–1796)

*For a portrait, see Chapter 12, page 504.*

 ### A Red, Red Rose (1796)

O my Luve's like a red, red rose,
    That's newly sprung in June:
O my Luve's like the melodie
    That's sweetly play'd in tune.

5    As fair art thou, my bonnie lass,
    So deep in luve am I;
And I will luve thee still, my Dear,
    Till a'° the seas gang° dry.                                   *all; go*

Till a' the seas gang dry, my Dear,
10    And the rocks melt wi'° the sun:                              *with*
And I will luve thee still, my Dear,
    While the sands o'° life shall run.                            *of*

And fare thee weel, my only Luve!
    And fare thee weel, awhile!
15 And I will come again, my Luve,
    Tho' it were ten thousand mile!

## Questions

1. In the light of the character and background of the speaker, do the two opening similes seem common or unusual? If they are just ordinary, does that fact diminish their value? How and why?

2. Describe the shift of listener envisioned after the first stanza. How are the last three stanzas related to the first?

3. Consider the metaphors concerning time and travel. How do the metaphors assist you in comprehending the speaker's character?

**JOHN DONNE** (1572–1631)

*For a portrait, see Chapter 12, page 508.*

 ## A Valediction: Forbidding Mourning (1633)

As virtuous men pass mildly away,
   And whisper to their souls to go,
Whilst some of their sad friends do say
   The breath goes now, and some say, No;

So let us melt, and make no noise,                                              5
   No tear-floods, nor sigh-tempests move,
'Twere profanation of our joys
   To tell the laity° our love.

Moving of th'earth° brings harm and fears,                        *earthquakes*
   Men reckon what it did and meant:                               10
But trepidation° of the spheres,
   Though greater far, is innocent.

Dull sublunary lovers' love
   (Whose soul is sense°) cannot admit
Absence, because it doth remove
   Those things which elemented it.                                15

But we by a love so much refined
   That our selves know not what it is,
Inter-assured of the mind,
   Care less, eyes, lips, and hands to miss.                        20

Our two souls therefore, which are one,
   Though I must go, endure not yet
A breach, but an expansion
   Like gold to airy thinness beat.°

If they be two, they are two so                                    25
   As stiff twin compasses° are two;
Thy soul, the fixt foot, makes no show
   To move, but doth, if th'other do.

And though it in the center sit,
   Yet when the other far doth roam,                                30

---

°7, 8 *profanation . . . laity*: as though the lovers are priests of love, whose love is a mystery. 11 *trepidation*: Before Sir Isaac Newton explained the precession of the equinoxes. it was assumed that the positions of heavenly bodies should be constant and perfectly circular. The clearly observable irregularities (caused by the slow wobbling of the earth's axis) were explained by the concept of *trepidation*, or a trembling or oscillation that occurred in the outermost of the spheres surrounding the earth. 14 *soul is sense*: lovers whose attraction is totally physical. 24 *gold to airy thinness beat*: a reference to the malleability of gold. 26 *compasses*: a compass used for drawing circles.

It leans and harkens after it,
   And grows erect, as that comes home.

Such wilt thou be to me, who must
   Like th'other foot, obliquely run;
35 Thy firmness draws my circle just,°
   And makes me end where I begun.

---

°35 *just*: perfectly round.

## Questions

1. What is the situation envisioned as the occasion for the poem? Who is talking to whom? What is their relationship?
2. What is the intention of the first two stanzas? What is the effect of the phrases "tear-floods" and "sigh-tempests"?
3. Describe the effect of the opening simile about men on their deathbeds.
4. What is the metaphor of the third stanza (lines 9–12)? In what sense might the "trepidation of the spheres" be less harmful than the parting of the lovers?
5. In lines 13–20 there is a comparison making the love of the speaker and his sweetheart superior to the love of average lovers. What is the basis for the speaker's claim?
6. What is the comparison begun by the word "refined" in line 17 and continued by the simile in line 24?

## JOHN DRYDEN (1631–1700)

## A Song for St. Cecilia's Day° (1687)

I

From harmony, from heavenly harmony
   This universal frame began:
   When Nature underneath a heap
     Of jarring atoms lay,
5     And could not heave her head,
The tuneful voice was heard from high,
   "Arise, ye more than dead."
Then cold, and hot, and moist, and dry°
In order to their stations leap,
10     And Music's pow'r obey.
From harmony, from heavenly harmony

---

° *St. Cecilia*: St. Cecilia, the patron saint of music, was traditionally considered the creator of the pipe organ. In London after 1683, she was celebrated annually on November 22 by the performance of a poem set to orchestral and choral music. Dryden wrote two poems for the occasion: this one in 1687, and the longer "Alexander's Feast" in 1697. The best-known choral and orchestral version of the "Song for St. Cecilia's Day" is by Georg Frederic Handel. 8 *cold . . . dry*: Before the modern classification of elements, it was supposed that there were four "elements" having four primary qualities: earth = cold, fire = hot, water = moist, and air = dry.

This universal frame began:
From harmony to harmony
Through all the compass of the notes it ran,
The diapason° closing full in Man.°          15

## II

What passion cannot Music raise and quell!
   When Jubal° struck the corded shell,
   His listening brethren stood around,
   And, wondering, on their faces fell
   To worship that celestial sound:
Less than a god they thought there could not dwell          20
   Within the hollow of that shell,
   That spoke so sweetly and so well.
What passion cannot Music raise and quell!

## III

The trumpet's loud clangor
   Excites us to arms          25
With shrill notes of anger
   And mortal alarms.
The double double double beat
   Of the thundering drum
Cries, "Hark! the foes come;          30
Charge, charge, 'tis too late to retreat."

## IV

The soft complaining flute
   In dying notes discovers
   The woes of hopeless lovers,
Whose dirge is whispered by the warbling lute.          35

## V

Sharp violins proclaim
Their jealous pangs, and desperation,
Fury, frantic indignation,
Depth of pains, and height of passion
   For the fair, disdainful dame.          40

---

°15 *diapason*: the organ stop determining keys and chords; thus, metaphorically, the quality that created and shaped humankind. 15 *Man*: the human race. 17 *Jubal*: "the father of all such as handle the harp and organ" (Genesis 4:21).

VI

But O! what art can teach,
What human voice can reach
The sacred organ's praise?
45    Notes inspiring holy love,
Notes that wing their heavenly ways
To mend the choirs above.

VII

Orpheus° could lead the savage race
And trees unrooted left their place,
50    Sequacious of the lyre;
But bright Cecilia raised the wonder higher:
When to her organ vocal breath was given,
An angel heard, and straight appeared,
Mistaking earth for heaven.

GRAND CHORUS

55   As from the power of sacred lays
The spheres began to move,
And sung the great Creator's praise
To all the blessed above;
So, when the last and dreadful hour
60   This crumbling pageant shall devour
The trumpet shall be heard on high,
The dead shall live, the living die,
And Music shall untune the sky.°

---

°48 *Orpheus*: in Greek myth, the greatest of all musicians. His playing tamed wild animals, and trees uprooted themselves to go to hear him. 63
*And Music shall untune the sky*: The harmony of the sky (i.e., heavenly harmony) will be replaced eternally by musical harmony.

## Questions

1. What is the central idea of "A Song for St. Cecilia's Day"? In light of this idea, what is the major attribute of the creator God (whom Dryden does not specifically mention)? Why does the angel mistake earth for heaven (stanza VII)? How is this example related to the poem's major idea?

2. Through what attribute is music related to the created universal order? How is music analogous to the ordering principles of creation? How long will music continue to exist? Why?

3. What powers are attributed to the various instruments? When is vocal music introduced? What is its effect?

4. Should Dryden's ideas in the poem be considered outdated? To what degree are the ideas still important and valid?

## ABBIE HUSTON EVANS (1881–1983)

 ## The Iceberg Seven-Eighths Under (1961)

Under the sky at night, stunned by our guesses,
We know incredibly much and incredibly little.
Wrapped in the envelope of gossamer air,
A clinging mote whirled round in a blizzard of stars,
A chaff-cloud of great suns that has not settled,          5
By the barn's black shoulder where the gibbous moon
Hangs low, no other light making a glimmer
In the dark country, hearing the breathing of cattle—
I do not need that anyone should tell me
Most real goes secret, sunken, nigh-submerged:            10
Yet does it dazzle with its least part showing,
Like the iceberg seven-eighths under.

### Questions

1. How does the simile of the "iceberg seven-eighths under" explain the "Most real" that "goes secret"? In what way is this simile, together with line 11, an extension of the idea in line 2?
2. What metaphors does the poet use to describe the earth and the people ("We") on it?
3. Explain the contrast between the metaphors of night and darkness (lines 1, 6, 8) and the use of the word "dazzle" in line 11. How does the poem express awe about the visible universe?

## THOMAS HARDY (1840–1928)

*For a photo, see Chapters 6 and 11, pages 256 and 471.*

 ## The Convergence of the Twain (1912)

#### Lines on the Loss of the "Titanic"°

I

>      In a solitude of the sea
>      Deep from human vanity,
> And the Pride of Life that planned her, stilly couches she.

II

>      Steel chambers, late the pyres
>      Of her salamandrine fires,°
> Cold Currents thrid,° and turn to rhythmic tidal lyres.          5

*thread, instrumental strings*

---

°The *Titanic*, the largest passenger ship in existence at the time, and considered unsinkable, was sunk after a collision with an iceberg on its maiden voyage in April 1912. The loss was particularly notable because some of the passengers were among the world's social elite, and 1,500 people were lost because there were not enough lifeboats for everyone. In 1985 the wreck of the ship was discovered on the ocean floor 13,000 feet down, and some of the ship's artifacts have been recovered. The loss of the *Titanic* has become legendary. 4–5 *Steel chambers . . . salamandrine fires*: The idea here is that the "steel chambers" of the ship's furnaces were built to resist the high heat of the coal fires, much like the salamander of ancient myth, which could live through fire.

III

      Over the mirrors meant
      To glass the opulent
The sea-worm crawls—grotesque, slimed, dumb, indifferent.

IV

10      Jewels in joy designed
      To ravish the sensuous mind
Lie lightless, all their sparkles bleared and black and blind.

V

      Dim moon-eyed fishes near
      Gaze at the gilded gear
15  And query: "What does this vaingloriousness down here?"

VI

      Well: while was fashioning
      This creature of cleaving wing,
The Immanent Will that stirs and urges everything

VII

20      Prepared a sinister mate
      For her—so gaily great—
A Shape of Ice, for the time far and dissociate.

VIII

      And as the smart ship grew
      In stature, grace, and hue,
In shadowy silent distance grew the Iceberg too.

IX

25      Alien they seemed to be:
      No mortal eye could see
The intimate welding of their later history.

X

      Or sign that they were bent
      By paths coincident
30  On being anon twin halves of one august event.

XI

Till the Spinner of the Years
Said "Now!" And each one hears,
And consummation comes, and jars two hemispheres.

## Questions

1. What human attributes does Hardy ascribe to the *Titanic*? What pronoun does he regularly use in reference to the ship? What is the name of this figure of speech?

2. What are the meanings of "vanity" (line 2), "Pride of Life" (line 3), and "vaingloriousness" (line 15) in relation to the speaker's judgment of the meaning of the *Titanic*?

3. Why does Hardy introduce the phrases "Spinner of the Years" (line 31) and "Immanent Will" (line 18)?

4. What is the idea of calling the iceberg the "sinister mate" of the *Titanic* (line 19)? What irony results from this phrase, and from the word "consummation" in line 33?

# JOY HARJO (b. 1951)

*For a photo, see Chapter 11, page 472.*

 # Remember (1983)

Remember the sky that you were born under,
know each of the star's stories.
Remember the moon, know who she is. I met her
in a bar once in Iowa City.
Remember the sun's birth at dawn, that is the                                    5
strongest point of time. Remember sundown
and the giving away to night.
Remember your birth, how your mother struggled
to give you form and breath. You are evidence of
her life, and her mother's, and hers.                                            10
Remember your father. He is your life, also.
Remember the earth whose skin you are:
red earth, black earth, yellow earth, white earth
brown earth, we are earth.
Remember the plants, trees, animal life who all have their                       15
tribes, their families, their histories, too. Talk to them,
listen to them. They are alive poems.
Remember the wind. Remember her voice. She knows the
origin of this universe. I heard her singing Kiowa war
dance songs at the corner of Fourth and Central once.                            20
Remember that you are all people and that all people
are you.
Remember that you are this universe and that this
universe is you.

25  Remember that all is in motion, is growing, is you.
Remember that language comes from this.
Remember the dance that language is, that life is.
Remember.

## Questions

1. How many times is the word "remember" repeated in this poem? What is the name of this figure of speech? What is the effect of the repetitions?

2. Who is the speaker, and who is the listener? What is the apparent purpose of stating all the things that the listener is being asked to remember? What is the implication of the word "remember," inasmuch as many of the things designated for remembrance happened before the listener was alive or was old enough to have a memory?

3. What is meant by "the earth whose skin you are" in line 12? Explain the paradox of "you are all people and . . . all people/are you" in lines 21–22.

## JOHN KEATS (1795–1821)

*For a portrait, see page 562.*

 **To Autumn** (1820)

Season of mists and mellow fruitfulness!
  Close bosom-friend of the maturing sun;
Conspiring with him to load and bless
  With fruit the vines that round the thatch-eaves run;
5  To bend with apples the mossed cottage-trees,
  And fill all fruit with ripeness to the core;
    To swell the gourd, and plump the hazel shells
With a sweet kernel; to set budding more,
  And still more, later flowers for the bees,
10  Until they think warm days will never cease,
    For Summer has o'erbrimmed their clammy cells.

Who hath not seen thee oft amid thy store?
  Sometimes whoever seeks abroad may find
Thee sitting careless on a granary floor,
15  Thy hair soft-lifted by the winnowing wind,
Or on a half-reaped furrow sound asleep,
  Drowsed with the fume of poppies, while thy hook
    Spares the next swath and all its twinèd flowers;
And sometimes like a gleaner thou dost keep
20  Steady thy laden head across a brook;
    Or by a cider-press, with patient look,
  Thou watchest the last oozings hours by hours.

Where are the songs of Spring? Ay, where are they?
  Think not of them, thou hast thy music too,—

While barrèd clouds bloom the soft-dying day,
    And touch the stubble-plains with rosy hue;
Then in a wailful choir the small gnats mourn
    Among the river sallows, borne aloft
        Or sinking as the light wind lives or dies;
And full-grown lambs loud bleat from hilly bourn;                            30
    Hedge-crickets sing; and now with treble soft
    The redbreast whistles from a garden-croft;
        And gathering swallows twitter in the skies.

*25* (at line 25)

## Questions

1. How is personification used in the first stanza? How does it change in the second? What is the effect of such personification?

2. How does Keats structure the poem to accord with his apostrophe to autumn? That is, in what ways can the stanzas be distinguished by the type of discourse addressed to the season?

3. Analyze Keats's metonymy in the first stanza and synecdoche in the second. What effects does he achieve with these devices?

4. How, through the use of images, does Keats develop his idea that autumn is a season of "mellow fruitfulness"?

## MAURICE KENNY (b. 1929)

 **Legacy** (1984)

my face is grass
    color of April rain;
arms, legs are the limbs
    of birch, cedar;
my thoughts are winds
    which blow;                              5
pictures are in my mind
    are the climb uphill
    to dream in the sun;
    hawk feathers, and quills
    of porcupine running                      10
    the edge of the stream
which reflects stories
    of my many mornings
    and the dark faces of night
    mingled with victories                  15
    of dawn and tomorrow;
corn of the fields and squash . . .
    the daughters of my mother
    who collect honey
    and all the fruits;                      20

meadow and sky are the end of my day
    the stretch of my night
    yet the birth of my dust;
25  my wind is the breath of a fawn
    the cry of the cub
    the trot of the wolf
    whose print covers
    the tracks of my feet;
30  my word, my word,
    loaned
legacy, the obligation I hand
    to the blood of my flesh
    the sinew of the loins
35  to hold to the sun
and the moon
which direct the river
    that carries my song
    and the beat of the drum
40  to the fires of the village
    which endures.

## Questions

1. Describe some of the paradoxes that Kenny explores in this poem. What do the paradoxes contribute to the speaker's explanation of his identity?

2. How can it be said that "meadow and sky are the end of my day / the stretch of my night / yet the birth of my dust"?

3. What is the speaker's legacy? How does it differ from what is usually thought of as a legacy?

4. Describe the content of the use of phrases and clauses beginning with "which" in this poem. What is the name of this repetitive usage? What is the effect in this poem?

## JANE KENYON (1947–1995)

 ### Let Evening Come (1990)

Let the light of late afternoon
shine through chinks in the barn, moving
up the bales as the sun moves down.

Let the cricket take up chafing
5  as a woman takes up her needles
and her yarn. Let evening come.

Let dew collect on the hoe abandoned
in long grass. Let the stars appear
and the moon disclose her silver horn.

Let the fox go back to its sandy den.
Let the wind die down. Let the shed
go black inside. Let evening come.                                    10

To the bottle in the ditch, to the scoop
in the oats, to air in the lung
let evening come.                                                    15

Let it come as it will, and don't
be afraid.° God does not leave us
comfortless,° so let evening come.

Matthew 28:10<br>John 14:18

## Questions

**1.** This poem features the repetition of phrases beginning with the word "let." What is this pattern called? How many such phrases does the poem contain? How does the pattern furnish strength to the poem?

**2.** What sorts of activities does the speaker associate with day? With night? How are these activities connected?

**3.** Describe the shift of topic in the last stanza. Does this shift occur logically or illogically from the earlier topic material of the poem? How does the final stanza seem to be an ordinary and necessary part of the activities described in the first five stanzas?

## HENRY KING (1592–1669)

## Sic Vita° (1657)

Like to the falling of a star,
Or as the flights of eagles are,
Or like the fresh spring's gaudy hue,
Or silver drops of morning dew,
Or like a wind that chafes the flood,
Or bubbles which on water stood:                                     5
Even such is man, whose borrowed light
Is straight called in, and paid to night.
    The wind blows out, the bubble dies;
    The spring entombed in autumn lies:
    The dew dries up, the star is shot;                              10
    The flight is past, and man forgot.

---

°*Sic vita* (Latin): Such is life.

## Questions

**1.** How many similes do you find in lines 1–6? Describe the range of references; that is, from what sources are the similes derived? What do all these similes (and references) have in common?

2. Explain the two metaphors in lines 7–8. (One is brought out by the words "borrowed," "called in," and "paid," the other by "light" and "night.")

3. Explain the continuation in lines 9–12 of the similes in 1–6. Do you think that these last four lines are essential, or might the poem have been successfully concluded with line 8? Explain.

4. What point does this poem make about humanity? In what ways do the similes in the poem help explore these ideas and bring them to life?

## JUDITH MINTY (b. 1937)

 **Conjoined** (1981)

*a marriage poem*

The onion in my cupboard, a monster, actually
two joined under one transparent skin:
each half-round, then flat and deformed
where it pressed and grew against the other.

5   An accident, like the two-headed calf rooted
in one body, fighting to suck at its mother's teats;
or like those other freaks, Chang and Eng,° twins
joined at the chest by skin and muscle, doomed
to live, even make love, together for sixty years.

10  Do you feel the skin that binds us
together as we move, heavy in this house?
To sever the muscle could free one,
but might kill the other. Ah, but men
don't slice onions in the kitchen, seldom see
15  what is invisible. We cannot escape each other.

---

°7 *Chang and Eng:* born in 1811, the original and most famous Siamese twins. Although they were never separated, they nevertheless fathered twenty-two children. They died in 1874.

## Questions

1. What are the two things—the "us" and "we" of lines 10 and 11—that are conjoined? Since this is "a marriage poem," might they be the man and the woman? Why might they also be considered as the body and soul of the speaker; or the desire to be married and subordinated, on the one hand, and to be free and in control of destiny, on the other?

2. Explore the metaphor of the onion and the similes of the two-headed calf and the Siamese twins. Why do you think the poet introduces the words "monster," "accident," and

"freaks" into these figures in lines 1, 5, and 7? In what sense do you believe that these words are applicable to the nature and plight of women?

3. Is it true that *all* "men/don't slice onions in the kitchen, seldom see/what is invisible"? Explain.

# MARGE PIERCY (b. 1934)

 ## A Work of Artifice (1973)

The bonsai tree
in the attractive pot
could have grown eighty feet tall
on the side of a mountain
till split by lightning.                                    5
But a gardener
carefully pruned it.
It is nine inches high.
Every day as he
whittles back the branches                                10
the gardener croons,

It is your nature
to be small and cozy,
domestic and weak;
how lucky, little tree,                                    15
to have a pot to grow in.
With living creatures
one must begin very early
to dwarf their growth:
the bound feet,                                           20
the crippled brain,
the hair in curlers,
the hands you
love to touch.

## Questions

1. What is a bonsai tree? In what ways is it an apt metaphor for women? The tree "could have grown eighty feet tall." What would be the comparable growth and development of a woman?

2. What do you make of the gardener's song (lines 12–16)? If the bonsai tree were able to respond, would it accept the gardener's consolation? What conclusions about women's lives are implied by the metaphor of the tree?

3. How does the poem shift at line 17? To what extent do the next images (lines 20–24) embody women's lives? How are the images metaphorical?

## MURIEL RUKEYSER (1913–1980)

### Looking at Each Other (1978)

Yes, we were looking at each other
Yes, we knew each other very well
Yes, we had made love with each other many times
Yes, we had heard music together
5   Yes, we had gone to the sea together
Yes, we had cooked and eaten together
Yes, we had laughed often day and night
Yes, we fought violence and knew violence
Yes, we hated the inner and outer oppression
10  Yes, that day we were looking at each other
Yes, we saw the sunlight pouring down
Yes, the corner of the table was between us
Yes, bread and flowers were on the table
Yes, our eyes saw each other's eyes
15  Yes, our mouths saw each other's mouth
Yes, our breasts saw each other's breasts
Yes, our bodies entire saw each other
Yes, it was beginning in each
Yes, it threw waves across our lives
20  Yes, the pulses were becoming very strong
Yes, the beating became very delicate
Yes, the calling the arousal
Yes, the arriving the coming
Yes, there it was for both entire
25  Yes, we were looking at each other

## Questions

1. What is the dramatic situation of the poem? What sort of listener is the speaker addressing?
2. Describe the rhetorical device at work here. How many different words are being repeated?
3. What is the effect of the repetitions? What is their relationship to the emotions and experiences that the speaker is describing?

## WILLIAM SHAKESPEARE (1564–1616)

*For a portrait, see Chapter 21, page 979.*

### Sonnet 18: Shall I Compare Thee to a Summer's Day? (1609)

Shall I compare thee to a summer's day?
Thou art more lovely and more temperate:
Rough winds do shake the darling° buds of May,                    *dear, cherished*

And summer's lease hath all too short a date:
Sometime too hot the eye of heaven° shines                    *the sun*   5
And often is his° gold complexion dimmed;                     *its*
And every fair from fair sometime declines,
By chance, or nature's changing course, untrimmed;
But thy eternal summer shall not fade,
Nor lose possession of that fair thou owest;°               *own, possess*   10
Nor shall Death brag thou wand'rest in his shade,
When in eternal lines to time thou growest:
   So long as men can breathe, or eyes can see,
   So long lives this, and this gives life to thee.

## Questions

1. What is the dramatic situation of the poem? Who is speaking to whom?
2. What do the metaphors in lines 1–8 assert? Why does the speaker emphasize life's brevity?
3. Describe the shift in topic beginning in line 9. How do these lines both deny and echo the subject of lines 1–8?
4. What relationship do the last two lines have to the rest of the poem? What is the meaning of "this" (line 14)? What sort of immortality does Shakespeare exalt in the sonnet?

## WILLIAM SHAKESPEARE (1564–1616)

*For a portrait, see Chapter 21, page 979.*

## Sonnet 30: When to the Sessions of Sweet Silent Thought (1609)

When to the sessions° of sweet silent thought                *holding of court*
I summon° up remembrance of things past,
I sigh the lack of many a thing I sought,
And with old woes new wail my dear time's waste:°
Then can I drown an eye (un-used to flow)                                    5
For precious friends hid in death's dateless° night,        *endless*
And weep afresh love's long since canceled° woe,            *paid in full*
And moan th'expense° of many a vanished sight.              *cost, loss*
Then can I grieve at grievances foregone,
And heavily° from woe to woe tell° o'er                      *sadly; count*   10
The sad account of fore-bemoanèd moan,
Which I new pay, as if not paid before.
   But if the while I think on thee (dear friend)
   All losses are restored, and sorrows end.

---

°2 *summon:* to issue a summons to appear at a legal hearing. 4 *old woes . . . waste:* revive old sorrows about lost opportunities and express sorrow for them again.

## Questions

1. Explain the metaphor of "sessions" and "summon" in lines 1–2. Where are the "sessions" being held? What is a "summons" for remembrance?

2. What is the metaphor brought out by the word "canceled" in line 7? In what sense might a "woe" of love be canceled? Explain the metaphor of "expense" in line 8.

3. What type of transaction does Shakespeare refer to in the metaphor of lines 9–12? What understanding does the metaphor provide about the sadness and regret that a person feels about past mistakes and sorrows?

4. What role does the speaker assign to the "dear friend" of line 13 in relation to the metaphors of the poem?

## ELIZABETH TUDOR, QUEEN ELIZABETH I (1533–1603)

 **On Monsieur's Departure** (ca. 1560 (1964))

I grieve° and dare not show my discontent,                              *I am unhappy*
I love and yet am forced to seem to hate,
I do, yet dare not say I ever meant,
I seem stark mute but inwardly do prate.°                              *chatter endlessly*
5    I am and not, I freeze and yet am burned,
     Since from myself another self I turned.

My care° is like my shadow in the sun,                                  *loved one*
Follows me flying, flies when I pursue it,
Stands and lies by me, doth what I have done.
10   His too familiar care° doth make me rue it.                        *alternativeness, love*
     No means I find to rid him from my breast,
     Till by the end of things it be supprest.

Some gentler passion slide into my mind,
For I am soft and made of melting snow;
15   Or be more cruel, love, and so be kind.
Let me or float or sink, be high or low.
     Or let me live with some more sweet content.
     Or die and so forget what love ere meant.

## Questions

1. What is the significance of "Monsieur's Departure"? How does this detail prompt the patterns of thought in the poem?

2. Explain the speaker's use of antithesis in the poem to explain her ambivalent situation. How seriously should we take the ideas in lines 12 and 18? Assuming that this is a deeply personal and private lyric, why, granted the speaker's royal status, does she express such contradictory feelings?

3. What is the meaning of the shadow simile in lines 7–10? How well does this comparison reveal her situation?

4. What is explained by the paradoxes in lines 5 and 15?

## MONA VAN DUYN (b. 1921)

 ## Earth Tremors Felt in Missouri (1964)

The quake last night was nothing personal,
you told me this morning. I think one always wonders,
unless, of course, something is visible: tremors
that take us, private and willy-nilly, are usual.

But the earth said last night that what I feel,          5
you feel; what secretly moves you, moves me.
One small, sensuous catastrophe
makes inklings letters, spelled in a worldly tremble.

The earth, with others on it, turns in its course
as we turn toward each other, less than ourselves, gross,     10
mindless, more than we were. Pebbles, we swell
to planets, nearing the universal roll,
in our conceit even comprehending the sun,
whose bright ordeal leaves cool men woebegone.

## Questions

1. In what ways is this poem intensely personal, a "confessional" poem? How does the poem develop materials that might be considered less personal and more public?
2. Why does the speaker equate herself and her listener with the earth? Granted that this metaphor is apt, what is then meant by "earth tremors," "quake last night," "Pebbles, we swell/to planets," and "comprehending the sun"?
3. What feelings are brought out in the last line through the words "ordeal" and "woebegone"?
4. Compare the use of the earth/person metaphor as it is used in this poem and in Donne's "The Good Morrow" (Chapter 19).

## WALT WHITMAN (1819–1892)

 ## Facing West from California's Shores (1860)

Facing west from California's shores,
Inquiring, tireless, seeking what is yet unfound,
I, a child, very old, over waves, towards the house of maternity,°
    the land of migrations, look afar.
Look off the shores of my Western sea, the circle almost circled;
For starting westward from Hindustan,° from the vales of Kashmir,     5

---

°3 *house of maternity*: Asia, then considered the cradle of human civilization. 5 *Hindustan*: India.

From Asia, from the north, from the God, the sage, and the hero,
From the south, from the flowery peninsulas° and the spice islands.°
Long having wandered since, round the earth having wandered
Now I face home again, very pleased and joyous.
10  (But where is what I started for so long ago?
And why is it yet unfound?)

---

°7 *flowery peninsulas*: south India, south Burma, and the Maylay peninsula.  7 *spice islands*: the Molucca Islands of Indonesia.

## Questions

1. What major paradox, or apparently contradictory situation, is described in this poem? How does the poet bring out this paradox? What has the speaker been seeking? Where has he looked for it?

2. Describe the meaning of the phrase "a child, very old"; "where is what I started for"; "the circle almost circled." In what ways are these phrases paradoxical?

3. Why does the speaker twice use the word "unfound" (lines 2, 11)? How might the word be considered a theme of the poem?

# WILLIAM WORDSWORTH (1770–1850)

##  London, 1802 (1807 (1802))

Milton! thou should'st be living at this hour:
England hath need of thee: she is a fen°        bog, marsh
Of stagnant waters: altar, sword, and pen,
Fireside, the heroic wealth of hall and bower,
Have forfeited their ancient English dower°         widow's
5    Of inward happiness. We are selfish men;          inheritance
Oh! raise us up, return to us again;
And give us manners,° virtue, freedom, power.
Thy soul was like a star, and dwelt apart:
Thou hadst a voice whose sound was like the sea:
10    Pure as the naked heavens, majestic, free,
So didst thou travel on life's common way,
In cheerful godliness; and yet thy heart
The lowliest duties on herself did lay.

---

°8 *manners*: customs, moral codes of social and political conduct.

## Questions

1. What is the effect of Wordsworth's apostrophe to Milton? What elements of Milton's career as a writer does Wordsworth emphasize?

2. In lines 3 and 4, the device of metonymy is used. How does Wordsworth judge the respective institutions represented by the details?

3. Consider the use of overstatement, or hyperbole, from lines 2–6. What effect does Wordsworth achieve by using the device as extensively as he does here?

4. What effect does Wordsworth make through his use of overstatement in his praise of Milton in lines 9–14? What does he mean by the metonymic references to "soul" (line 9) and "heart" (line 13)?

## SIR THOMAS WYATT (1503–1542)

 **I Find No Peace** (1557)

I find no peace, and all my war is done,
  I fear and hope, I burn and freeze like ice;
  I fly above the wind yet can I not arise;
  And naught I have and all the world I season.
That looseth nor locketh holdeth me in prison,°                       5
  And holdeth me not, yet I can scape° nowise;                 *escape*
  Nor letteth me live nor die at my devise,°                   *choice*
  And yet of death it giveth none occasion.
Without eyen° I see, and without tongue I plain;°             *eyes*
  I desire to perish, and yet I ask health;                          10
  I love another, and thus I hate myself;
I feed me in sorrow, and laugh in all my pain.
  Likewise displeaseth me both death and life°
  And my delight is causer of this strife.

---

I FIND NO PEACE. 5 *that . . . prison:* that is, "that which neither lets me go nor contains me holds me in prison." At the time of Wyatt, *-eth* was used for the third person singular present tense. 9 *plain:* express desires about love. 13 *Likewise . . . life:* literally, "it is displeasing to me, in the same way, both death and life." That is, "both death and life are equally distasteful to me."

## Questions

1. What situation is the speaker reflecting upon? What metaphors and similes express his feelings? How successful are these figures?

2. How many paradoxes are in the poem? What is their cumulative effect? What is the topic of the paradoxes in lines 1–4? In lines 5–8? Why does the speaker declare that hating himself is a consequence of loving another? Why is it ironic that his "delight" is the "causer of this strife"?

3. To what extent do you think the paradoxes express the feelings of a person in love, particularly because in the sixteenth century, the free and unchaperoned meetings of lovers were not easily arranged?

## WRITING ABOUT FIGURES OF SPEECH

Begin by determining the use, line by line, of metaphors, similes, or other rhetorical figures. Obviously, similes are the easiest figures to recognize because they introduce comparisons with the word *like* or *as*. Metaphors can be recognized because the topics are discussed not as themselves but as other topics. If the poems speak of falling leaves or law courts, but the subjects involve memory or increasing age, you are looking at metaphors. Similarly, if the poet is addressing an absent person or a natural object, or if you find clear double meanings in words, you may have apostrophe, personification, or puns.

### Questions for Discovering Ideas

- What figures of speech does the work contain? Where do they occur? Under what circumstances? How extensive are they?
- How do you recognize them? Are they signaled by a single word or phrase, such as "desert places" in Frost's "Desert Places" (Chapter 16), or are they more extensively detailed, as in Shakespeare's Sonnet 30, "When to the Sessions of Sweet Silent Thought"?
- How vivid are the figures? How obvious? How unusual? What kind of effort is needed to understand them in context?
- Structurally, how are the figures developed? How do they rise out of the situation envisioned in the poem? To what degree are the figures integrated into the poem's development of ideas? How do they relate to other aspects of the poem?
- Is one type of figure used in a particular section while another type predominates in another section? Why?
- If you have discovered a number of figures, what relationships can you find among them (such as the judicial and financial connections in Shakespeare's "When to the Sessions of Sweet Silent Thought")?
- How do the figures of speech broaden, deepen, or otherwise assist in making the ideas in the poem forceful?
- In general, how appropriate and meaningful are the figures of speech in the poem? What effect do the figures have on the poem's tone, and on your understanding and appreciation of the poem?

### Strategies for Organizing Ideas

For this essay, two types of compositions are possible. One is a full-scale essay. The other, because some rhetorical figures may occupy only a small part of the poem, is a single paragraph. Let us consider the single paragraph first.

**1.** A PARAGRAPH. For a single paragraph you need only one topic, such as the hyperbole used in the opening of "London, 1802." The goal is to deal with the single figure and its relationship to the poem's main idea. Thus the essay should describe the figure and discuss its meaning and implications. It is important to begin with a comprehensive topic sentence, such as one that explains the cleverness of the puns in Gay's "Let Us Take the Road" or the use of paradox in Wyatt's "I Find No Peace."

**2. A FULL-LENGTH ESSAY.** One type of essay might examine just one figure, if the figure is pervasive enough in the poem to justify a full treatment. Most often, the poet's use of metaphors and similes is suitable for extensive discussion. A second type of essay might explore the meaning and effect of two or more figures, with the various parts of the body of the essay being taken up with each figure. The unity of this second kind of essay is achieved by the linking of a series of two or three different rhetorical devices to a single idea or emotion.

In the introduction, relate the quality of the figures to the general nature of the work. Thus, metaphors and similes of suffering might be appropriate to a religious, redemptive work, while those of sunshine and cheer might be right for a romantic one. If there is any discrepancy between the metaphorical language and the topic, you could consider that contrast as a possible central idea, for it would clearly indicate the writer's ironic perspective. Suppose that the topic of the poem is love, but the figures put you in mind of darkness and cold: What might the poet be saying about the quality of love? You should also try to justify any claims that you make about the figures. For example, one of the similes in Coleridge's "Kubla Khan" (Chapter 13) compares the sounds of a "mighty fountain" to the breathing of the earth in "fast thick pants." How is this simile to be taken? As a reference to the animality of the earth? As a suggestion that the fountain, and the earth, are dangerous? Or simply as a comparison suggesting immense, forceful noise? How do you explain your answer or answers? Your introduction is the place to establish ideas and justifications of this sort.

The following approaches for discussing rhetorical figures are not mutually exclusive, and you may combine them as you wish. Most likely, your essay will bring in most of the following classifications.

1. *Interpret the meaning and effect of the figures.* Here you explain how the figures enable you to make an interpretation. In the second stanza of "A Valediction: Forbidding Mourning," for example, the following metaphor introduces church hierarchy and religious mystery to explain lovers and their love.

> 'Twere profanation of our joys
> To tell the laity our love.

Here Donne emphasizes the mystical relationship of two lovers, drawing the metaphor from the religious tradition whereby any popular explanation of religious mysteries is considered a desecration. A directly explanatory approach, such as this, requires that metaphors, similes, or other figures be expanded and interpreted, including the explanation of necessary references and allusions.

2. *Analyze the frames of reference and their appropriateness to the subject matter.* Here you classify and locate the sources and types of the references and determine the appropriateness of these to the poem's subject matter. Ask questions similar to those you might ask in a study of imagery: Does the writer refer extensively to nature, science, warfare, politics, business, reading (e.g., Shakespeare's metaphor equating personal reverie with courtroom proceedings)? Does the metaphor seem appropriate? How? Why?

3. *Focus on the interests and sensibilities of the poet.* In a way this approach is like strategy 2, but the emphasis here is on what the selectivity of the writer might show about his or her vision and interests. You might begin by listing the figures in the poem and then determining the sources, just as you would do in discussing the sources of images generally. But then you should raise questions like the following: Does the writer use figures derived from one sense rather than another (i.e., sight, hearing, taste, smell, touch)? Does he or she record color, brightness, shadow, shape, depth, height, number, size, slowness, speed, emptiness, fullness, richness, drabness? Has the writer relied on the associations of figures of sense? Do metaphors and similes referring to green plants and trees, to red roses, or to rich fabrics, for example, suggest that life is full and beautiful, or do references to touch suggest amorous warmth? This approach is designed to help you draw conclusions about the author's taste or sensibility.

4. *Examine the effect of one figure on the other figures and ideas of the poem.* The assumption of this approach is that each literary work is unified and organically whole, so that each part is closely related and inseparable from everything else. Usually it is best to pick a figure that occurs at the beginning of the poem and then determine how this figure influences your perception of the rest of the poem. Your aim is to consider the relationship of part to parts and part to whole. The beginning of Donne's "A Valediction: Forbidding Mourning," for example, contains a simile comparing the parting of the speaker and his listener to the quiet dying of "virtuous men." What is the effect of this comparison upon the poem? To help you with questions like this, you might substitute a totally different detail, such as, here, the violent death of a condemned criminal, or the slaughter of a domestic animal, rather than the deaths of "virtuous men." Such suppositions, that would clearly be out of place, may help you understand and then explain the poet's figures of speech.

In your conclusion, summarize your main points, describe your general impressions, try to describe the impact of the figures, indicate your personal responses, or show what might further be done along the lines you have been developing. If you know other works by the same writer, or other works by other writers who use comparable or contrasting figures, you might explain the relationship of the other work or works to your present analysis.

# Illustrative Student Paragraph

**Wordsworth's Use of Overstatement in "London, 1802"°**

<u>Through overstatement in "London, 1802," Wordsworth emphasizes his tribute to Milton as a master of idealistic thought.</u>* The speaker's claim that England is "a fen/Of stagnant waters" (lines 2–3) is overstated, as is the implication that people ("We") in England have no "manners, virtue, freedom, power" (lines 6, 8). With the overstatements, however, Wordsworth implies that the nation's well-being depends on the constant flow of creative thoughts by persons of great ideas. Because Milton was clearly the greatest of these, in the view of Wordsworth's speaker, the overstatements stress the need for leadership. Milton is the model, and the overstated criticism lays the foundation in the real political and moral world for the rebirth of another Milton. Thus, through overstatement, Wordsworth emphasizes Milton's importance and in this way pays tribute to him.

°See p. 588 for this poem.
*Central idea.

## Commentary on the Paragraph

This paragraph deals with a single rhetorical figure, in this case Wordsworth's overstatements in "London, 1802." Although most often the figure of speech will be fairly obvious, as this one in "London, 1802" is, prominence is not a requirement. In addition, there is no need to write an excessively long paragraph. The goal here is not to describe all the details of Wordsworth's overstatement, but to show how the figure affects his tribute to Milton. For this reason the paragraph illustrates clear and direct support of the major point.

## Illustrative Student Essay

Underlined sentences in this paper *do not* conform to MLA style and are used solely as teaching tools to emphasize the central idea, thesis sentence, and topic sentences throughout the paper.

Kerri Scott

Professor Kyritz

English 111

16 April 2007

### Personification in Hardy's "The Convergence of the Twain"°

[1]       Shortly after the luxury ocean liner *Titanic* sank in 1912, killing more than 1,500 people, Thomas Hardy wrote "The Convergence of the Twain." This poem, which is subtitled "Lines on the Loss of the Titanic," does not try to describe the sinking but focuses instead on the ship when at the bottom, on the building of the ship, and on the iceberg, the ship's "sinister mate" (line 19) that "grew" at the same time the ship was being built. Hardy does not refer to the fashionable passengers who died, nor does he mention the members of the crew who were killed. Interestingly, though, the poem still includes, through the personification of inanimate and nonhuman objects, many human characteristics.* By the use of personification Hardy develops the idea that the sinking of the Titanic is cause for pondering the immense power of the universe and also the ridiculousness of human pride and vanity.†

[2]       Both the *Titanic* and the iceberg that it struck are personified in the poem. Hardy gives the ship the attributes of a woman by referring to it with the feminine pronouns "she" and "her" (lines 3, 5, 20), thus following the traditional custom of referring to large ships as female. He adds elegance to the personification by describing the *Titanic* as "gaily great" (line 20) with "stature" and "grace" (line 23). After the ship sinks, she "couches" on the ocean floor (line 3), a word that normally describes the human action of reclining or lying down.

---

°See p. 575 for this poem.
*Central idea.
†Thesis sentence.

[3]     Ironically, the iceberg is also personified, but as the *Titanic*'s "sinister mate" (line 19) and not as a fashionably acceptable husband. Hardy continues to develop the human attributes of both ship and iceberg by describing them, even though they seem "alien" to one another (line 25), as "twin halves" (line 30). Both display the human ability to hear (line 32), and Hardy ironically describes their collision as the disastrous "consummation" of their union (line 33). By thus personifying the ship and the iceberg, Hardy introduces the metaphor that the convergence of ship and natural object formed a bizarre marriage. The personification also emphasizes the major roles of the ship and the iceberg in a cosmic event that "jars two hemispheres" (i.e., earth and heaven, line 33). The implication of the "consummation" is that while human beings plan and create, their power is futile when compared to immense and uncontrollable universal power that has somehow brought the two together.

[4]     The exact nature of universal power is not made clear in the poem, for Hardy does not provide explanations with names like "God," or "Fate," or "Destiny" to describe them. In fact, Hardy speaks ironically if not jestingly of divine power. He refers to "The Immanent Will" (line 18), a vague term for divinity, and "the Spinner of the Years" (line 31), which is almost flippant. Hardy's use of capitalization for these personifications indicates that they are names for a superior force or being, but the names themselves lead more to puzzlement than to definiteness. "The Immanent Will," Hardy's speaker states, is a personification "that stirs and urges everything" (line 18), even though events affecting human life are mysterious. So is it also with the "Spinner of the Years" (line 31), a personification reminiscent of Lachesis, the ancient Greek Fate who spun out the threads of life for all living beings. However, this power has a "will," like a human being, and it "spins," a human action. Furthermore, it acts as another character in the drama, one operating in secrecy, outside the scope of human awareness, who arranges for the other characters to be brought together. It is this "Will" that has "prepared" the iceberg and then left it to grow (line 24), and it is the "Spinner of the Years" that says the word "Now!" (line 32) to cause the collision of ship and iceberg as though the two had been drawing together throughout all time. Clearly, by using personification to characterize mysteries beyond human comprehension, Hardy suggests that this "convergence of the twain" was somehow destined to happen.

Scott 3

[5]     But why does the universal power create this destiny? <u>Two other instances of personification in the poem suggest the reason.</u> First of all, although the sunken *Titanic* is now "Deep from human vanity" (line 2), the third line of the poem refers to the "Pride of Life that planned" the ship. Thus, human pride is personified as the builders of a ship supposedly so grand and advanced that it could not sink. But the ship did sink, and the personified "fishes" in the fifth stanza make the observation that the product of pride is now meaningless and vain. These fish perform the human actions of gazing "at the gilded gear" of the shipwreck and then of asking the question "What does this vaingloriousness down here?" (lines 14–15). The fishes' question leads readers to the inescapable conclusion that even the proudest human efforts are nothing much more than rusting scrap metal in the scale of the larger universe.

[6]     <u>It seems that Hardy's personifications in this poem are functional and appropriate in light of the disastrous sinking of the</u> *Titanic*. As a matter of historical record, there were a number of causes, such as the ship's high speed at night even though it was traveling through waters known to contain icebergs, and such as the builders' miscalculations about the ship's hull design, but the ultimate causes of the calamity itself cannot be known. Even the obvious religious and philosophical answers are not satisfying. It would have been possible for Hardy to develop the idea that Divinity rules human affairs, or that the many deaths were tragic, or that the wreck served some purpose of punishment for the human pride that led to the original building of the ship. But Hardy introduces the poem's personifications to explain the mystery in human terms, and he only hints at the traditional answers. To do anything else would have made the poem more positive, perhaps, but it would have implied that explanations are available even though they really are not.

Scott 4

**WORK CITED**

Hardy, Thomas. "The Convergence of the Twain." *Literature: An Introduction to Reading and Writing.* 7th ed. Ed. Edgar V. Roberts. 4th Compact ed. Upper Saddle River: Prentice Hall, 2008, 575.

## Commentary on the Essay

This essay begins with a treatment of Hardy's personification of the ship and the iceberg that sank her. The goal of the essay is to explain how the personifications enable Hardy to treat the topic fully but also ironically. The essay therefore illustrates strategy 1 described on page 590.

In addition to providing a brief description of the poem, the introduction brings out the central idea and the thesis sentence. Paragraph 2 deals with the personification of the ship. The iceberg is explained as a personification in paragraph 3. Paragraph 3 also demonstrates that the personifications of ship and iceberg permit Hardy to introduce the metaphor of a marriage between the two. Paragraph 4 considers the more perplexing personifications of divinity and fate, which underlay the sinking according to Hardy's interpretation of the disaster. Paragraph 5 discusses two additional personifications. The first is human pride, which caused the makers to believe that *Titanic* was unsinkable. The second is the fish that swim around the wreck as witnesses to the folly of such pride. Paragraph 6 deals with the issues of Hardy's use of personification. The idea is that this figure of speech, pursued throughout the poem, permits the poet to deal with the disaster in human terms, inasmuch as any other explanation is not possible.

Throughout the essay, transitions are brought about by linking words and phrases. In paragraph 3, for example, the words "also personified" and "but as" move the reader from paragraph 2 to the new content. In paragraph 4, the phrase effecting the transition is the repetition of "universal power." The opening sentence of paragraph 6 is a summarizing sentence that extends the topic by treating the effect of the personifications throughout the poem.

# Writing Topics About Figures of Speech in Poetry

1. Study the simile of the "stiff twin compasses" in Donne's "A Valediction: Forbidding Mourning." Using such a compass or a drawing of one, write an essay that demonstrates the accuracy, or lack of it, of Donne's descriptions. What light does the simile shed on the relationship of two lovers? How does it emphasize any or all of these aspects of love: closeness, immediacy, extent, importance, duration, intensity?

2. Consider some of the metaphors and similes in the poems included in this chapter. Write an essay that answers the following questions. How effective are the figures you select? (Examples: the bonsai tree [Piercy], the Siamese twins [Minty], the court sessions [Shakespeare], the summer's day [Shakespeare].) What insights do the figures provide within the contexts of their respective poems? How appropriate are they? Might they be expanded more fully, and if they were, what would be the effect?

3. Consider some of the other rhetorical figures in the poems of this chapter. Write an essay describing the importance of figures of speech in creating emphasis and in extending and deepening the ideas of poetry. Here are some possible topics:

    a. Paradox in Wyatt's "I Find No Peace" or Whitman's "Facing West from California's Shores."

    b. Paradox and apparent contradiction in Kenny's "Legacy."

    c. Metaphor in Minty's "Conjoined" or Piercy's "A Work of Artifice."

    d. Metaphor and simile in Evans's "The Iceberg Seven-Eighths Under" or in Hardy's "The Convergence of the Twain."

    e. Anaphora in Rukeyser's "Looking at Each Other," Harjo's "Remember," or Kenyon's "Let Evening Come."

    f. A comparison of contrasts and paradoxes in Elizabeth I's "On Monsieur's Departure" and Wyatt's "I Find No Peace."

    g. Similes in King's "Sic Vita" or Hughes's "Harlem." Personification in the poems by Wordsworth, Keats, or Agüeros. Metonymy in Keats's "To Autumn."

**4.** Write a poem in which you create a governing metaphor or simile. Examples: "My girlfriend/boyfriend is like (a) an opening flower, (b) a difficult book, (c) an insoluble mathematical problem, (d) a bill that cannot be paid, (e) a slow-moving chess game." "Teaching a person how to do a particular job is like (a) shoveling heavy snow, (b) climbing a mountain during a landslide, (c) having someone force you underwater when you're gasping for breath." When you finish, describe the relationship between your comparison and the development and structure of your poem.

**5.** In your library's reference section, find the third edition of J. A. Cuddon's *A Dictionary of Literary Terms and Literary Theory* (1991) or some other dictionary of literary terms. Study the entries for *metaphysical* and *conceit*, and write a brief report on these sections. You might attempt to answer questions like these: What is meant by the word *conceit*? What are some of the kinds of conceit the reference work discusses? What is a metaphysical conceit? Who are some of the writers considered metaphysical? In the "metaphysical" entry, of what importance is John Donne?

# Chapter 15

# Tone: The Creation of Attitude in Poetry

**T**one, a term derived from the phrase *tone of voice*, describes the shaping of attitudes in poetry (see also Chapter 7, on style and tone in fiction). Each poet's choice of words governs the reader's responses, as do the participants and situations in the poem. In addition, the poet shapes responses through denotation and connotation, seriousness or humor, irony, metaphors, similes, understatement, overstatement, and other figures of speech (see Chapter 14). Of major importance is the poem's speaker. How much self-awareness does the speaker show? What is his or her background? What relationship does the speaker establish with listeners and readers? What does the speaker assume about the readers and about their knowledge? How do these assumptions affect the ideas and the diction?

To compare poetic tone with artistic tone, see the reproduction of Fernand Léger's painting *The City* (I–3, Plate 1). A viewer's response to the painting depends on the relationships of the various shapes to Léger's arrangement and color. The signs, stairs, pole, and human figures in the painting are all common in modern cities. By cutting them up or leaving them partially hidden, Léger creates an atmosphere suggesting that contemporary urban life is truncated, sinister, and even threatening.

The same control applies to poetic expression. The sentences must be just long enough to achieve the poet's intended effect—no shorter and no longer. In a conversational style there should be no formal words, just as in a formal style there should be no slang, no rollicking rhythms, and no frivolous rhymes—that is, unless the poet deliberately wants readers to be startled or shocked. In all the features that contribute to a poem's tone, the poet's consistency of intention is primary. Any unintentional deviations will cause the poem to sink and the poet to fail.

## Tone, Choice, and Response

Remember that a major objective of poets is to stimulate, enrich, and inspire readers. Poets may begin their poems with a brief idea, a vague feeling, or a fleeting impression. Then, in the light of their developing design, they *choose* what to say—the form of their material and the words and phrases to express their ideas. The poem "Theme for English B" by Langston Hughes illustrates this process in almost outline form. Hughes's speaker lays out many interests that he shares with his intended reader, his English teacher, for the poem is imagined to be a response to a classroom assignment.

In this way, Hughes encourages all readers to accept his ideas of human equality (see the illustrative student essay, p. 636).

In the long run, readers might not accept all the ideas in any poem, but the successful poem gains agreement—at least for a time—because the poet's control over tone is right. Each poem attempts to evoke total responses, which might be destroyed by any lapses in tone. Let us look at a poem in which the tone misses, and misses badly.

## CORNELIUS WHUR (1782–1853)

 ## The First-Rate Wife (1837)

This brief effusion I indite,
 And my vast wishes send,
That thou mayst be directed right,
And have ere long within thy sight
5    A most *enchanting* friend!

The *maiden* should have *lovely face*,
 And be of *genteel mien*;
If not, within thy dwelling place,
There may be vestige of disgrace,
10    Not much admired—when seen.

Nor will thy dearest be complete
 Without *domestic* care;
If otherwise, howe'er discreet,
Thine eyes will very often meet
15    What none desire to share!

And further still—thy future *dear*,
 Should have some *mental ray*;
If not, thou mayest drop a tear,
Because no *real sense* is there
20    To charm life's dreary day!

## Questions

1. What kind of person is the poem's speaker? The listener? What is the situation? What requirements does the speaker create for the "first-rate wife"?

2. Describe the poem's tone. How does the speaker's character influence the tone? In light of the tone, to what degree can the poem be considered insulting?

3. How might lines 14 and 15 be interpreted as a possible threat if the woman as a wife does not keep the house clean and straight?

In this poem, the speaker is talking to a friend or associate and is explaining his requirements for a "first-rate wife." From his tone, he clearly regards getting married as little more than hiring a pretty housekeeper. In the phrase "some *mental ray*," for example, the word *some* does not mean "a great deal" but is more like "*at least* some," as though nothing more could be expected of a woman. Even allowing for the fact that the poem was written early in the nineteenth century and represents a benighted view of women and marriage, "The First-Rate Wife" offends most readers. Do you wonder why you've never heard of Cornelius Whur before?

## Tone and the Need for Control

"The First-Rate Wife" demonstrates the need for the poet to be in control over all facets of the poem. The speaker must be aware of his or her situation and should not, like Whur's speaker, demonstrate any smugness or insensitivity, unless the poet is deliberately revealing the shortcomings of the speaker by dramatizing them for the reader's amusement, as E. E. Cummings does in the poem "next to of course god america i" (Chapter 12). In a poem with well-controlled tone, details and situations should be factually correct; observations should be logical and fair, and also comprehensive and generally applicable. The following poem, based on battlefield conditions in World War I, illustrates a masterly control over tone.

### WILFRED OWEN (1893–1918)

### Dulce et Decorum Est° (1920)

Bent double, like old beggars under sacks,
Knock-kneed, coughing like hags, we cursed through sludge,
Till on the haunting flares we turned our backs
And towards our distant rest began to trudge.
Men marched asleep. Many had lost their boots                              5
But limped on, blood-shod. All went lame; all blind;
Drunk with fatigue; deaf even to the hoots
Of tired, outstripped Five-Nines° that dropped behind.

Gas!° GAS! Quick, boys!—An ecstasy of fumbling,
Fitting the clumsy helmets° just in time;                                   10
But someone still was yelling out and stumbling
And flound'ring like a man in fire or lime . . .
Dim, through the misty panes and thick green° light,
As under a green sea, I saw him drowning.

In all my dreams, before my helpless sight,                                 15
He plunges at me, guttering, choking, drowning.

---

°DULCE ET DECORUM EST.  The Latin title is taken from Horace's *Odes*, Book 3, line  13: *Dulce et decorum est pro patria mori* ("It is sweet and honorable to die for the fatherland").  8 *Five-Nines*: A "five-nine" was a 5.9 caliber German high-explosive artillery shell that made a hooting sound before landing.  9 *Gas*: Chlorine gas was used as an antipersonnel weapon in 1915 by the Germans at Ypres, in Belgium.  10 *helmets*: Soldiers carried gas masks as normal battle equipment.  13 *thick green*: The deadly chlorine gas used in gas attacks has a greenish-yellow color.

If in some smothering dreams you too could pace
Behind the wagon that we flung him in.
And watch the white eyes writhing in his face,
20   His hanging face, like a devil's sick of sin;
If you could hear, at every jolt, the blood
Come gargling from the froth-corrupted lungs,
Obscene as cancer, bitter as the cud
Of vile, incurable sores on innocent tongues.—
25   My friend, you would not tell with such high zest
To children ardent for some desperate glory,
The old Lie: Dulce et decorum est
Pro patria mori.

## Questions

1. What is the scene described in lines 1–8? What expressions does the speaker use to indicate his attitude toward the conditions?

2. What does the title of the poem mean? What attitude or conviction does it embody?

3. Does the speaker really mean "my friend" in line 25? In what tone of voice might this phrase be spoken?

4. What is the tonal relationship between the patriotic fervor of the Latin phrase and the images of the poem? How does the tonal contrast create the dominant tone of the poem?

The tone of "Dulce et Decorum Est" never lapses. The poet intends the description to evoke a response of horror and shock, for he contrasts the strategic goals of warfare with the speaker's personal experience of terror in battle. The speaker's language skillfully emphasizes first the dreariness and fatigue of warfare (with words like "sludge," "trudge," "lame," and "blind") and second the agony of violent death from chlorine gas (embodied in the participles "guttering," "choking," "drowning," "smothering," and "writhing"). With these details established, the concluding attack against the "glory" of war is difficult to refute, even if warfare is undertaken to defend or preserve one's country. Although the details about the agonized death may distress or discomfort a sensitive reader, they are not designed to do that alone but instead are integral to the poem's argument. Ultimately, it is the contrast between the high ideals of the Latin phrase and the ugliness of battlefield death that creates the dominant tone of the poem. The Latin phrase treats war and death in the abstract; the poem makes images of battle and death vividly real. The resultant tone is that of controlled bitterness and irony.

## Tone and Common Grounds of Assent

Not all those reading Owen's poem will deny that war is sometimes necessary; the issues of politics and warfare are far too complex for that. But the poem does show another important aspect of tone—namely, the degree to which the poet judges and tries to control responses through the establishment of a *common ground of assent*. An appeal to a bond of commonly held interests, concerns, and assumptions is essential if a poet is to maintain an effective tone. Owen, for example, does not create arguments against the necessity of a just war. Instead, he bases the poem on realistic details about the choking, writhing, spastic death suffered by the speaker's comrade, and he appeals to emotions that everyone, pacifist and militarist alike, would feel—horror at the contemplation of violent death. Even assuming a widely divergent audience, in other words, the *tone* of the poem is successful because it is based on commonly acknowledged facts and commonly felt emotions. Knowing a poem like this one, even advocates of a strong military would need to defend their ideas on the grounds of *preventing* just such needless, ugly deaths. Owen carefully considers the responses of his readers, and he regulates speaker, situation, detail, and argument in order to make the poem acceptable for the broadest possible spectrum of opinion.

---

## 🌿 TONE IN CONVERSATION AND POETRY

Many readers think that tone is a subtle and difficult subject, but it is nevertheless true that in ordinary situations we master tone easily and expertly (see Chapter 7). We constantly use standard questions and statements that deal with tone, such as "What do you mean by that?" "What I'm saying is this . . . ," and "Did I hear you correctly?" together with other comments that extend to humor and, sometimes, to hostility. In poetry we do not have everyday speech situations; we have only the poems themselves and are guided by the materials they provide us. Some poems are straightforward and unambiguous, but in other poems feeling and mood are essential to our understanding. In Hardy's "The Workbox" (p. 604), for example, the husband's handmade gift to his wife indicates not love but suspicion. Also, the husband's relentless linking of the dead man's coffin to the gift reveals his anger. Pope, in the passage from the "Epilogue to the Satires" included in this chapter, satirically describes deplorable habits and customs of his English contemporaries in the 1730s. His concluding lines (of the passage and also of the poem) emphasize his scorn.

> Yet may this verse (if such a verse remain)
> Show there was one who held it in disdain.

Poems, of course, may also reveal respect and wonder, as shown in the last six lines of Keats's "On First Looking into Chapman's Homer" (Chapter 14). By attending carefully to the details of such poems, you can draw conclusions about poetic tone that are as accurate as those you draw in normal speech situations.

---

## Tone and Irony

Irony is a mode of indirection, a means of making a point by emphasizing a discrepancy or opposite (see also Chapter 7). Thus, Owen uses the title "Dulce et Decorum Est" to emphasize that death in warfare is not sweet and honorable but rather demeaning and horrible. The title ironically reminds us of eloquent holiday speeches at the tombs of unknown soldiers, but as we have seen, it also reminds us of the reality of the agonized death of Owen's soldier. As an aspect of tone, therefore, irony is a powerful way of conveying attitudes, for it draws your attention to at least two ways of seeing a situation, enabling you not only to *understand* but also to *experience*. Poetry shares with fiction the various kinds of ironies that afflict human beings. These are *verbal irony*, *situational irony*, and *dramatic irony*.

## Verbal Irony, through Word Selection, Emphasizes Ambiguities and Discrepancies

At almost any point in a poem, a poet may introduce the ironic effects of language itself—**verbal irony**. The poem "she being Brand/-new," by E. E. Cummings, is built on the double meanings derived from the procedures of breaking in a new car. Indeed, the entire poem is a virtuoso piece of double entendre. Another example of verbal irony occurs in Theodore Roethke's "My Papa's Waltz," in which the speaker uses the name of this graceful and stately dance to describe his childhood memories of his father's whirling him around the kitchen in wild, boisterous drunkenness.

## Life's Anomalies and Uncertainties Underlie Situational Irony

**Situational irony** is derived from the discrepancies between the ideal and the actual. People would like to live their lives in terms of a standard of love, friendship, honor, success, and general excellence, but the irony is that the reality of their lives often falls far short of such standards. Whereas in fiction ironic situations emerge from extended narrative, in poetry such situations are usually at a high point or climax, and we must infer the narrative circumstances that have gone on before. Thomas Hardy, in "The Workbox," skillfully exploits an ironic situation between a husband and a wife.

### THOMAS HARDY (1840–1928)

### The Workbox (1914)

"See, here's the workbox, little wife,
  That I made of polished oak."
He was a joiner,° of village° life;             *cabinetmaker*
  She came of borough° folk.

5  He holds the present up to her
    As with a smile she nears
And answers to the profferer,
  "'Twill last all my sewing years!"

---

°THE WORKBOX. 3, 4 *village, borough*: An English village was small and rustic; a borough was larger and more sophisticated.

"I warrant it will. And longer too.
  'Tis a scantling° that I got
Off poor John Wayward's coffin, who
  Died of they knew not what.                                    10

"The shingled pattern that seems to cease
  Against your box's rim
Continues right on in the piece
  That's underground with him.                                   15

"And while I worked it made me think
  Of timber's varied doom:
One inch where people eat and drink,
  The next inch in a tomb.                                       20

"But why do you look so white, my dear,
  And turn aside your face?
You knew not that good lad, I fear,
  Though he came from your native place?"

"How could I know that good young man,                           25
  Though he came from my native town,
When he must have left far earlier than
  I was a woman grown?"

"Ah, no. I should have understood!
  It shocked you that I gave                                     30
To you one end of a piece of wood
  Whose other is in a grave?"

"Don't, dear, despise my intellect.
  Mere accidental things
Of that sort never have effect                                   35
  On my imaginings."

Yet still her lips were limp and wan,
  Her face still held aside,
As if she had known not only John,
  But known of what he died.                                     40

---

°10 *scantling*: a small leftover piece of wood.

# Questions

1. Who does most of the speaking here? What does the speaker's tone show about the characters of the husband and the wife? What does the tone indicate about the poet's attitude toward them?

2. What do lines 21–40 indicate about the wife's knowledge of John and about her earlier relationship with him? Why does she deny such knowledge? What does the last stanza show about her? Why is John's death kept a mystery?

3. In lines 17–20, what irony is suggested by the fact that the wood was used both for John's coffin and the workbox?

4. Why is the husband's irony more complex than he realizes? What do his words and actions show about his character?

5. The narrator, or poet, speaks only in lines 3–7 and 37–40. How much of his explanation is essential? How much shows his attitude? How might the poem have been more effectively concluded?

"The Workbox" is a domestic drama of deception, cruelty, and sadness. The complex details are evidence of situational irony, that is, an awareness that human beings do not control their lives but are rather controlled by powerful forces—in this case by both death and earlier feelings and commitments. Beyond this domestic irony, Hardy also emphasizes symbolically the direct connection that death has with the living. As a result of the husband's gift made of the wood with which he has also made a coffin for the dead man, the wife will never escape being reminded of this man. Within the existence imagined in the poem, she will have to live with regret and the constant need to deny her true emotions, and her situation is therefore endlessly ironic.

## Dramatic Irony Is Built on the Ignorance of Characters and the Greater Knowledge of Readers

In addition to the situational irony of "The Workbox," the wife's deception reveals that the husband is in a situation of **dramatic irony**. He does not know the circumstances of his wife's past, and he does not actually *know*—though he suspects—that his wife is not being truthful about her earlier relationship with the dead man, but the poem is sufficient to enable readers to draw the right conclusions. By emphasizing the wood, the husband is apparently trying to make his wife uncomfortable, even to the point of extracting a confession from her, but he has only his suspicions, and he therefore remains unsure of the truth and also of his wife's feelings. Because of these uncertainties, Hardy has deftly used dramatic irony to create a poem of great complexity and pathos.

# Tone and Satire

**Satire**, a vital genre in the study of tone, is designed to expose human follies and vices. In method, a satiric poem may be bitter and vituperative, but often it employs humor and irony, on the grounds that anger turns readers away while a comic tone more easily wins interest and agreement. The speaker of a satiric poem may either attack folly and vice directly, or may dramatically embody the folly or vice himself or herself and thus serve as an illustration of the satiric subject. An example of the first type is the following short poem by Alexander Pope, in which the speaker directly attacks a listener who has claimed to be a poet but whom the speaker considers a fool. The speaker cleverly uses insult as the method of attack.

## ALEXANDER POPE (1688–1744)

 ## Epigram from the French (1732)

Sir, I admit your general rule
That every poet is a fool:
But you yourself may serve to show it,
That every fool is not a poet.

### Questions

1. What has the listener said before the poem begins? How does the speaker build on the listener's previous comment?
2. Considering this poem as a brief satire, describe the nature of satiric attack and the corresponding tone of attack.
3. Look at the pattern "poet," "fool," "fool," "poet." This is a rhetorical pattern (a, b, b, a) called *chiasmus* or *antimetabole*. What does the pattern contribute to the poem's effectiveness?

An example of the second type of satiric poem is another of Pope's epigrams, in which the speaker is an actual embodiment of the subject being attacked.

## ALEXANDER POPE (1688–1744)

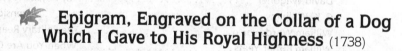 ## Epigram, Engraved on the Collar of a Dog Which I Gave to His Royal Highness (1738)

I am his Highness' dog at Kew:°                                    *the royal palace near London*
Pray tell me sir, whose dog are you?

### Questions

1. Who or what is the subject of the satiric attack?
2. What attitude is expressed toward social pretentiousness?

Here the speaker is, comically, the king's dog, and the listener is an unknown dog. Pope's satire is directed not against canines, however, but against human beings who overemphasize the significance of social class. The first line ridicules those who claim social status that is derived, not earned. The second implies an unwillingness to recognize the listener until the question of rank is resolved. Pope, by using the dog as a speaker, reduces such snobbishness to an absurdity. A similar satiric poem attacking pretentiousness is "next to of course god america i" by E. E. Cummings (Chapter 12). In this poem, the speaker voices a set of patriotic platitudes, and in doing so illustrates Cummings's satiric point that most speeches of this sort are empty-headed. Satiric tone may thus range widely, being sometimes objective, comic, and distant; sometimes deeply concerned and scornful; and sometimes dramatic, ingenuous, and revelatory. Always, however, the satiric mode aims toward confrontation and exposé.

## Poems for Study

## WILLIAM BLAKE (1757–1827)

## On Another's Sorrow (1789)

Can I see another's woe,
And not be in sorrow too.
Can I see another's grief,
And not seek for kind relief.

5   Can I see a falling tear,
And not feel my sorrows share,
Can a father see his child
Weep, nor be with sorrow filled.

Can a mother sit and hear,
10  An infant groan an infant fear—
No never can it be.
Never never can it be.

And can he who smiles on all
Hear the wren with sorrows small,
Hear the small birds grief & care
Hear the woes that infants bear— 15

And not sit beside the nest
Pouring pity in their breast,
And not sit the cradle near
Weeping tear on infants tear. 20

And not sit both night & day,
Wiping all our tears away.
O! no never can it be.
Never never can it be.

He doth give his joy to all. 25
He becomes an infant small.
He becomes a man of woe
He doth feel the sorrow too.

Think not, thou canst sigh a sigh,
And thy maker is not by. 30
Think not, thou canst weep a tear,
And thy maker is not near.

O! he gives to us his joy,
That our grief he may destroy
Till our grief is fled & gone 35
He doth sit by us and moan.

## Questions

1. Describe the character of this poem's speaker. What is he like? What are the circumstances of the persons in need of sympathy?
2. Describe the tone of the poem. What connection with human suffering does the speaker establish with human sympathy and with the divine "maker"?
3. Why do you think Blake uses the word "maker" (line 32) rather than God? According to the poem, what are the continuing roles of the maker among human beings? What assurances do people in sorrow have from their belief in divinity?

# ROBERT BROWNING (1812–1889)

 # My Last Duchess° (1842)

### Ferrara

That's my last Duchess painted on the wall,
Looking as if she was alive. I call

---

°The poem "My Last Duchess" is based on incidents in the life of Alfonso II, duke of Ferrara, whose first wife died in 1561. Some claimed she was poisoned. The duke negotiated his second marriage to the daughter of the count of Tyrol through an agent.  3 *Frà Pandolf*: an imaginary painter who is also a monk.

That piece a wonder, now: Frà Pandolf's° hands
Worked busily a day, and there she stands.
5   Will't please you sit and look at her? I said
"Frà Pandolf" by design, for never read
Strangers like you that pictured countenance,
The depth and passion of its earnest glance,
But to myself they turned (since none puts by
10   The curtain I have drawn for you, but I)
And seemed as they would ask me, if they durst,°                                    *dared*
How such a glance came there; so, not the first
Are you to turn and ask thus. Sir, 'twas not
Her husband's presence only, called that spot
15   Of joy into the Duchess' cheek: perhaps
Frà Pandolf chanced to say "Her mantle laps
Over my lady's wrist too much," or "Paint
Must never hope to reproduce the faint
Half-flush that dies along her throat": such stuff
20   Was courtesy, she thought, and cause enough
For calling up that spot of joy. She had
A heart—how shall I say?—too soon made glad,
Too easily impressed; she liked whate'er
She looked on, and her looks went everywhere.
25   Sir, 'twas all one! My favor at her breast,
The dropping of the daylight in the West,
The bough of cherries some officious fool
Broke in the orchard for her, the white mule
She rode with round the terrace—all and each
30   Would draw from her alike the approving speech,
Or blush, at least. She thanked men—good! but thanked
Somehow—I know not how—as if she ranked
My gift of a nine-hundred-years-old name
With anybody's gift. Who'd stoop to blame
35   This sort of trifling? Even had you skill
In speech—(which I have not)—to make your will
Quite clear to such a one, and say, "Just this
Or that in you disgusts me; here you miss,
Or there exceed the mark"—and if she let
40   Herself be lessoned so, nor plainly set
Her wits to yours, forsooth, and made excuse
—E'en then would be some stooping; and I choose
Never to stoop. Oh sir, she smiled, no doubt,
Whene'er I passed her; but who passed without
45   Much the same smile? This grew; I gave commands;
Then all smiles stopped together. There she stands
As if alive. Will't please you rise? We'll meet
The company below, then. I repeat,
The Count your master's known munificence
50   Is ample warrant that no just pretense
Of mine for dowry will be disallowed;
Though his fair daughter's self, as I avowed

At starting, is my object. Nay, we'll go
Together down, sir. Notice Neptune,° though,
Taming a sea horse, thought a rarity,                                      55
Which Claus of Innsbruck° cast in bronze for me!

---

°54 *Neptune*: Roman god of the sea.  56 *Claus of Innsbruck*: an imaginary sculptor.

## Questions

1. Who dominates the conversation in this poem? Who is the listener? What is the purpose of the "conversation"? Why does the speaker avoid dealing with the purpose until near the poem's end?

2. What third character does the speaker describe? In what ways are his descriptions accurate or inaccurate? What judgment do you think Browning wants you to make of the speaker? Why?

3. How does the speaker's language illustrate his attitude toward his own power? In light of this attitude, what do you think Browning's point is in the poem?

## JIMMY CARTER (b. 1924)

 ## I Wanted to Share My Father's World (1995)

This is a pain I mostly hide,
but ties of blood, or seed, endure,
and even now I feel inside
the hunger for his outstretched hand,
a man's embrace to take me in,                                            5
the need for just a word of praise.

I despised the discipline
he used to shape what I should be,
not owning up that he might feel
his own pain when he punished me.                                         10

I didn't show my need to him,
since his response to an appeal
would not have meant as much to me,
or been as real.

From those rare times when we did cross                                   15
the bridge between us, the pure joy
survives.
            I never put aside
the past resentments of the boy
until, with my own sons, I shared
his final hours, and came to see                                          20

what he'd become, or always was—
the father who will never cease to be
alive in me.

## Questions

1. This poem is about the remembered attitudes of President Carter's speaker toward his father. What is the nature of these attitudes? To what degree are these attitudes of sons to fathers either usual or unusual? Why does the speaker state in line 1, "This is a pain I mostly hide"?

2. Why does the speaker use the words "despised" (line 7) and "resentments" (line 18)? Why does he mention "those rare times" in line 15?

3. What is the tone of the last stanza? Why does the speaker refer to going with his own sons to share the "final hours" of his father? What is the tone of the final two lines?

## LUCILLE CLIFTON (b. 1936)

 ## homage to my hips (1987)

these hips are big hips
they need space to
move around in.
they don't fit into little
5  petty places, these hips
are free hips.
they don't like to be held back.
these hips have never been enslaved.
they go where they want to go.
10  they do what they want to do.
these hips are mighty hips.
these hips are magic hips.
i have known them
to put a spell on a man and
15  spin him like a top!

## Questions

1. What is unusual about the subject matter? Considering that some people are embarrassed to mention their hips, what attitudes does the speaker express here?

2. How do the words "enslaved," "want to go," "want to do," "mighty," and "spell" define the poem's ideas about the relationship between mentality and physicality?

3. To what degree is this a comic poem? What about the subject and the diction makes the poem funny?

## BILLY COLLINS (b. 1941)

*For a photo, see Chapter 11, page 456.*

 ## The Names° (2002)

Yesterday, I lay awake in the palm of the night.
A fine rain stole in, unhelped by any breeze,
And when I saw the silver glaze on the windows,
I started with A, with Ackerman, as it happened,
Then Baxter and Calabro,                                              5
Davis and Eberling, names falling into place
As droplets fell through the dark.

Names printed on the ceiling of the night.
Names slipping around a watery bend.
Twenty-six willows on the banks of a stream.                         10

In the morning, I walked out barefoot
Among thousands of flowers
Heavy with dew like the eyes of tears,
And each had a name—
Fiori inscribed on a yellow petal                                    15
Then Gonzalez and Han, Ishikawa and Jenkins.

Names written in the air
And stitched into the cloth of the day.
A name under a photograph taped to a mailbox.
Monogram on a torn shirt,                                            20
I see you spelled out on storefront windows
And on the bright unfurled awnings of this city.
I say the syllables as I turn a corner—
Kelly and Lee,
Medina, Nardella, and O'Connor.                                      25
When I peer into the woods,
I see a thick tangle where letters are hidden
As in a puzzle concocted for children.
Parker and Quigley in the twigs of an ash,
Rizzo, Schubert, Torres, and Upton,                                  30
Secrets in the boughs of an ancient maple.

Names written in the pale sky.
Names rising in the updraft amid buildings.

Names silent in stone
Or cried out behind a door.                                          35
Names blown over the earth and out to sea.

---

°This poem was read by Professor Collins before a joint session of the U.S. Congress held in New York City on September 6, 2002. It was first published earlier that day in the *New York Times*.

In the evening—weakening light, the last swallows.
A boy on a lake lifts his oars.
A woman by a window puts a match to a candle,
40 And the names are outlined on the rose clouds—
Vanacore and Wallace,
(let X stand, if it can, for the ones unfound)
Then Young and Ziminsky, the final jolt of Z.

Names etched on the head of a pin.
45 One name spanning a bridge, another undergoing a tunnel.
A blue name needled into the skin.
Names of citizens, workers, mothers and fathers,
The bright-eyed daughter, the quick son.
Alphabet of names in green rows in a field.
50 Names in the small tracks of birds.
Names lifted from a hat
Or balanced on the tip of the tongue.
Names wheeled into the dim warehouse of memory.
So many names, there is barely room on the walls of the heart.°

---

°N.B. In light of the topic of this poem, questions seem superfluous.

## E. E. CUMMINGS (1894–1962)

*For a photo, see Chapter 12, page 507.*

 ### she being Brand / -new (1926)

she being Brand

-new;and you
know consequently a
little stiff i was
5 careful of her and (having

thoroughly oiled the universal
joint tested my gas felt of
her radiator made sure her springs were O.

K.)i went right to it flooded-the-carburetor cranked her

10 up, slipped the
clutch (and then somehow got into reverse she
kicked what

the hell) next
minute i was back in neutral tried and

again slo-wly;bare,ly nudg. ing (my          15

lev-er Right-
oh and her gears being in

A 1 shape passed
from low through
second-in-to-high like          20
greasedlightning) just as we turned the corner of Divinity

avenue i touched the accelerator and give

her the juice,good

        (it

was the first ride and believe i we was          25
happy to see how nice she acted right up to
the last minute coming back down by the Public
Gardens i slammed on

the
internalexpanding          30
&
externalcontracting
brakes Bothatonce and

brought allofher tremB
-ling          35
to a:dead.

stand-
;Still)

## Questions

1. How extensive is the verbal irony, the double entendre, in this poem? This poem is considered comic. Do you agree? Why or why not? This poem might also be considered sexist. Do you agree? Why or why not?

2. How do the spacing and alignment affect your reading of the poem? How does the unexpected and sometimes absent punctuation—such as in line 15, "again slo-wly;bare,ly nudg. ing (my"—contribute to the humor?

3. Can this poem in any respect be called off-color or bawdy? How might you refute such charges in light of the tone the speaker uses to equate a first sexual experience with the breaking in of a new car?

## BART EDELMAN (b. 1951)

 **Trouble** (2005)

Everything pointed to trouble;
Danger and distress pranced
Topless on my wooden roof.
Misfortune grew in the garden
5    I tended day and night
I was afflicted by the urge
To do myself in,
But I was so out of it
I failed to plan ahead.
10   I eased into my hardship
Like a pair of black loafers,
Suddenly two sizes too small.
Soon I began to pity
My big, fat, flat feet.
15   Woe became my middle name,
I suffered from the heebie-jeebies
And Saint Vitus left the order
When he saw me dance;
Alas, it wasn't a pretty picture.
20   I found my meager little life
Lost any sense of decency.
I could smell disaster in the wind—
Hot air breathing down my back.
In other words . . .
25   I was hopelessly unable
To shoulder the burden I bore.
Then I simply gave up,
Drove to the hardware store,
Bought a gallon of Dutch Boy #157,
30   And painted myself into a corner,
Where I now live, rather comfortably,
Monopolizing every moment
I choose to spend with myself;
No more a victim of boredom—
35   A teller of tall tales.

## Questions

   **1.** How serious is this poem? How funny is it? Can it be both serious and funny? What does
   the diction contribute to the tone, particularly well-worn phrases such as "out of it" and
   "heebie jeebies"?

   **2.** What situation is the speaker describing when he says at the beginning that "everything
   pointed to trouble" (i.e., he was suffering from malaise or maybe depression)? What is the
   tone of the descriptions in the poem?

**3.** On what situation does the poem close? What does the speaker mean by "painted myself into a corner"? How has the speaker solved his problems and ended his trouble?

## MARI EVANS (b. 1923)

 ## I Am a Black Woman (1970)

I am a black woman
the music of my song
some sweet arpeggio of tears
is written in a minor key
and I
can be heard humming in the night          5
Can be heard
   humming
in the night

I saw my mate leap screaming to the sea          10
and I/with these hands/cupped the lifebreath
from my issue in the canebreak
I lost Nat's swinging body° in a rain of tears

and heard my son scream all the way from Anzio°
for Peace he never knew . . . I          15

learned Da Nang° and Pork Chop Hill°
in anguish
Now my nostrils know the gas
and these trigger tire/d fingers
seek the softness in my warrior's beard          20
I
am a black woman
tall as a cypress
strong
beyond all definition still          25
defying place
and time
and circumstance
   assailed
      impervious          30
         indestructible

Look
   on me and be
renewed

---

°13 *Nat's swinging body*: Nat Turner was hanged in 1831 for leading a slave revolt in Southampton, Virginia.  14 *Anzio*: seacoast town in Italy, the scene of fierce fighting between the Allies and the Germans in 1943 during World War II.  16 *Da Nang*: major American military base in South Vietnam, frequently attacked during the Vietnam War. *Pork Chop Hill*: site of a bloody battle between UN and Communist forces during the Korean War (1950–1953).

## Questions

1. What attitude is indicated by the phrase "sweet arpeggio of tears"? How does "in a minor key" complete both the idea and the comparison?

2. What phrases and descriptions does the speaker use to indicate her attitudes of anguish, despair, pain, and indignation?

3. In the last fourteen lines, what contrasting attitude is expressed? How does the speaker make this attitude clear? On balance, is the poem optimistic or pessimistic? Why?

## SEAMUS HEANEY (b. 1939)

 **Mid-Term Break** (1966)

I sat all morning in the college sick bay
Counting bells knelling classes to a close.
At two o'clock our neighbors drove me home.

In the porch I met my father crying—
5   He had always taken funerals in his stride—
And Big Jim Evans saying it was a hard blow.

The baby cooed and laughed and rocked the pram
When I came in, and I was embarrassed
By old men standing up to shake my hand

10   And tell me they were "sorry for my trouble,"
Whispers informed strangers I was the eldest,
Away at school, as my mother held my hand

In hers and coughed out angry tearless sighs.
At ten o'clock the ambulance arrived
15   With the corpse, stanched and bandaged by the nurses.

Next morning I went up into the room. Snowdrops
And candles soothed the bedside; I saw him
For the first time in six weeks. Paler now,

Wearing a poppy bruise on his left temple,
20   He lay in the four foot box as in his cot.
No gaudy scars, the bumper knocked him clear.

A four foot box, a foot for every year.

## Questions

1. What is the situation of the poem? Who is the speaker? Why has he been called home? What are his responses to the circumstances at home?

2. How old was the speaker's brother at the time of the accident? How do you know? When you read line 19, what do you at first make of the "poppy bruise"?

**3.** Describe your responses to the last four lines of the poem the first time you read them. What clues in the earlier part of the poem prepare you for these final three lines? Do they sufficiently prepare you, or does the final line come as a surprise? Why is the poem unrhymed until the final two lines?

## WILLIAM ERNEST HENLEY (1849–1903)

 ## When You Are Old (1888)

When you are old, and I am passed away—
Passed, and your face, your golden face, is gray—
I think whate'er the end, this dream of mine,
Comforting you, a friendly star will shine
Down the dim slope where still you stumble and stray.        5
So may it be: that so dead Yesterday,
No sad-eyed ghost but generous and gay,
May serve you memories like almighty wine,
     When you are old!
Dear Heart, it shall be so. Under the sway                   10
Of death the past's enormous disarray
Lies hushed and dark. Yet though there come no sign,
Live on well pleased; immortal and divine
Love shall still tend you, as God's angels may,
     When you are old.                15

## Questions

**1.** Describe the organization of thought as it is affected by time. How much attention is given to a visualization of the old age of the listener? What does the speaker imagine will have happened to him? What consolation does the speaker believe the listener will have in this future period?

**2.** What comfort does the speaker say will justify the listener's living on "well pleased" (line 13)? What "shall still tend" the listener? Why does the speaker say "God's angels may" rather than "God's angels will"?

## LANGSTON HUGHES (1902–1967)

*For a photo, see Chapter 18, page 761.*

 ## Theme for English B (1959)

The instructor said,

  Go home and write
  a page tonight.
  And let that page come out of you—
  Then, it will be true.                                    5

I wonder if it's that simple?

I am twenty-two, colored, born in Winston-Salem.
I went to school there, then Durham, then here
to this college on the hill above Harlem.°
10   I am the only colored student in my class.
The steps from the hill lead down to Harlem,
through a park, then I cross St. Nicholas,
Eighth Avenue, Seventh, and I come to the Y,
the Harlem Branch Y, where I take the elevator
15   up to my room, sit down, and write this page:

It's not easy to know what is true for you or me
at twenty-two, my age. But I guess I'm what
I feel and see and hear. Harlem, I hear you:
hear you, hear me—we two—you, me talk on this page.
20   (I hear New York, too.) Me—who?

Well, I like to eat, sleep, drink, and be in love.
I like to work, read, learn, and understand life.
I like a pipe for a Christmas present,
or records—Bessie,° bop,° or Bach.°

25   I guess being colored doesn't make me not like
the same things other folks like who are other races.
So will my page be colored that I write?
Being me, it will not be white.
But it will be
30   a part of you, instructor.
You are white—
yet a part of me, as I am a part of you.
That's American.

Sometimes perhaps you don't want to be a part of me.
35   Nor do I often want to be a part of you.
But we are, that's true!
As I learn from you,
I guess you learn from me—
although you're older—and white—
40   and somewhat more free.

This is my page for English B.

°9 *college . . . Harlem*: a reference to Columbia University in the Columbia Heights section of New York City. The other streets and buildings mentioned in lines 11–14 refer to specific places in the same vicinity.   24 *Bessie*: Bessie Smith (ca. 1898–1937), American jazz singer, famed as the "Empress of the Blues." *bop*: a type of popular music that was in vogue in the 1940s through the 1960s. *Bach*: Johann Sebastian Bach (1685–1750), German composer, considered the master of the baroque style of music.

## Questions

1. What is the tone of the speaker's self-assessment? What does the tone indicate about his feelings toward the situation in the class and at the Y?

**2.** What tone is implicit in the fact that the speaker, in response to a theme assignment, has composed a poem rather than a prose essay?

**3.** What is the tone of lines 21–24, where the speaker indicates his likes? In what way may the characteristics brought out in these lines serve as an argument for social and political equality?

**4.** How does the tone in lines 27–40, particularly lines 34–36, prevent the statements of the speaker from becoming overly assertive or strident?

## ABRAHAM LINCOLN (1809–1865)

 My Childhood's Home° (1844)

My childhood's home I see again,
  And sadden with the view;
And still, as memory crowds my brain,
  There's pleasure in it too.

O Memory! thou midway world      5
  'Twixt earth and paradise,
Where things decayed and loved ones lost
  In dreamy shadows rise,

And, freed from all that's earthly vile,
  Seem hallowed, pure, and bright,      10
Like scenes in some enchanted isle
  All bathed in liquid light.

As dusky mountains please the eye
  When twilight chases day;
As bugle-notes that, passing by,      15
  In distance die away.

As leaving some grand waterfall,
  We, lingering, list its roar—
So memory will hallow all
  We've known, but know no more.      20

Near twenty years have passed away
  Since here I bid farewell
To woods and fields, and scenes of play,
  And playmates loved so well.

Where many were, but few remain      25
  Of old familiar things;
But seeing them, to mind again
  The lost and absent brings.

---

°In 1844, while on a political campaign in Indiana, Lincoln visited the home where he had been raised and where his mother and sister were buried. The occasion prompted him to write this poem.

The friends I left the parting day,
30    How changed, as time has sped!
Young childhood grown, strong manhood gray,
    And half of all are dead.

I hear the loved survivors tell
    How nought from death could save
35   Till every sound appears a knell,
    And every spot a grave.

I range the fields with pensive tread
    And pace the hollow rooms,
And feel (companion of the dead)
40   I'm living in the tombs.

## Questions

1.  How does Lincoln's speaker explain the importance of memory? How is the sentence "So memory will hallow all/We've known, but know no more" (lines 19–20) related to the descriptions and ideas that follow?
2.  Do stanzas 6 and 7 seem exaggerated, self-indulgent, or sentimental? What seems to forestall this criticism of the ideas here?
3.  What leads the speaker to the conclusion he makes in the last two lines?

## SHARON OLDS (b. 1942)

### 🖋 The Planned Child (1996)

I hated the fact that they had planned me, she had taken
a cardboard out of his shirt from the laundry
as if sliding the backbone up out of his body,
and made a chart of the month and put
5   her temperature on it, rising and falling
to know the day to make me—I would have
liked to have been conceived in heat,
in haste, by mistake, in love, in sex,
not on cardboard, the little x on the
10   rising line that did not fall again.

But when a friend was pouring wine
and said that I seem to have been a child who had been wanted,
I took the wine against my lips
as if my mouth were moving along
15   that valved wall in my mother's body, she was
bearing down, and then breathing from the mask, and then
bearing down, pressing me out into
the world that was not enough for her without me in it,

not the moon, the sun, Orion
cartwheeling across the dark, not
the earth, the sea—none of it
was enough, for her, without me.                                    20

## Questions

1. Who is the speaker? What is she like? What is she talking about? Why does she begin the poem talking about something she hated?
2. What change of attitudes is described by the poem? Why does the poem seem to require such a change?
3. What attitude is expressed in the concluding global, planetary, solar, and stellar references? Why does the speaker state that, to her mother, she has more value than this image?
4. What unique qualities of perception and expression does the speaker exhibit? Have you ever read a poem before in which details about conception and childbirth have been so prominent? Why are these details included in this poem?

## ROBERT PINSKY (b. 1940)

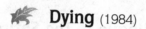 **Dying** (1984)

Nothing to be said about it, and everything—
The change of changes, closer or further away:
The Golden Retriever next door, Gussie, is dead,

Like Sandy, the Cocker Spaniel from three doors down
Who died when I was small; and every day                            5
Things that were in my memory fade and die.

Phrases die out: first, everyone forgets
What doornails are; then after certain decades
As a dead metaphor, *"dead as a doornail"* flickers

And fades away. But someone I know is dying—                        10
And though one might say glibly, "everyone is,"
The different pace makes the difference absolute.

The tiny invisible spores in the air we breathe,
That settle harmlessly on our drinking water
And on our skin, happen to come together,                           15

With certain conditions on the forest floor,
Or even a shady corner of the lawn—
And overnight the fleshy, pale stalks gather,

The colorless growth without a leaf or flower;
And around the stalks, the summer grass keeps growing               20
With steady pressure, like the insistent whiskers

That grow between shaves on a face, the nails
Growing and dying from the toes and fingers
At their own humble pace, oblivious

25  As the nerveless moths, that live their night or two—
Though like a moth a bright soul keeps on beating,
Bored and impatient in the monster's mouth.

## Questions

1. What details about death does the poem introduce? How are they connected in the poem's development? What is the effect of these details on the tone of the poem?

2. What is meant by line 12, "The different pace makes the difference absolute"? How strongly does this statement counter the phrase "everyone is" in line 11?

3. Up until line 25 this poem can be considered negative or even despairing. What is the effect of lines 26 and 27 on this negative tone? What is the meaning of the phrase "monster's mouth" in these last two lines?

## ALEXANDER POPE (1685–1744)

### From Epilogue to the Satires, Dialogue I, Lines 137–72 (1738)

Virtue may choose the high or low degree,
'Tis just alike to Virtue, and to me;
Dwell in a monk, or light upon a king,
She's still the same, beloved, contented thing.
140  Vice is undone, if she forgets her birth,
And stoops from angels to the dregs of earth:
But 'tis the Fall degrades her to a whore;
Let Greatness own her, and she's mean no more:°
Her birth, her beauty, crowds and courts confess,°
145  Chaste matrons praise her, and grave bishops bless:
In golden chains the willing world she draws,
And hers the gospel is, and hers the laws:
Mounts the tribunal, lifts her scarlet head,
And sees pale Virtue carted° in her stead!
150  Lo! at the wheels of her triumphal car,°                                  carriage
Old England's genius, rough with many a scar,
Dragged in the dust! his arms hang idly round,
His flag inverted trails along the ground!°
Our youth, all liveried o'er with foreign gold,
155  Before her dance; behind her crawl the old!
See thronging millions to the pagod° run,
And offer country, parent, wife, or son!
Hear her black trumpet through the land proclaim,
That "not to be corrupted is the shame."
160  In soldier, churchman, patriot, man in power,
'Tis avarice all, ambition is no more!

See, all our nobles begging to be slaves!
See, all our fools aspiring to be knaves!
The wit of cheats, the courage of a whore,
Are what ten thousand envy and adore. 165
All, all look up, with reverential awe,
On crimes that scape,° or triumph o'er the law: *escape*
While truth, worth, wisdom, daily they decry—
"Nothing is sacred now but villainy."
   Yet may this verse (if such a verse remain)
Show there was one who held it in disdain.

---

°144 *mean no more*: i.e., if the rich and powerful follow vice, vice is no longer low but fashionable. 145 *Her birth . . . confess*: i.e., under the dictates of fashion, both crowds and courts claim that Vice is both high-born and beautiful. 150 *carted*: It was an eighteenth-century punishment to display prostitutes in a cart; in addition, condemned criminals were carried in a cart from prison to Tyburn, in London, where they were hanged. 152–154 *Old England's genius . . . along the ground*: i.e., the spirit of England is humiliated by being tied to Vice's triumphal carriage and then dragged along the ground. The idea is that corrupt politicians have sacrificed England's defensive power for their own gain. 157 *pagod*: i.e., a pagoda, a symbol of how people have forsaken their own religion and adopted foreign religions.

## Questions

1. The entire poem is in the form of a dialogue, in which these concluding lines are identified as being spoken by "P" (Pope). Should readers therefore take these lines as an expression of Pope's own ideas? In your answer, pay special attention to the final couplet.

2. Explain this poem as social satire. What is attacked? What evidence does the speaker advance to support his case that society has deserted virtue and religion?

3. Describe the poem's tone. What specific charges does the speaker make against the prevailing sociopolitical structure?

4. How timely is the poem? To what degree might such charges be advanced in our society today?

## SALVATORE QUASÍMODO (1901–1968)

 **Auschwitz°** (1983)

### Translated by Jack Bevan

Far from the Vistula,° along the northern plain,
love, in a death-camp there at Auschwitz:
on the pole's rust and tangled fencing, rain
funeral cold.
No tree, no birds in the grey air 5
or above our thought, but limp
pain that memory leaves
to its silence without irony or anger.

---

°*Auschwitz* is the German name for the town of Oswiecim in southern Poland, site of the most notorious of the German concentration-extermination camps in World War II. There were two major camps—Auschwitz itself, a former Polish army camp, and nearby Birkenau, which contained many temporary barracks for worker-prisoners, together with gas chambers and crematoria for the extermination of hundreds of thousands of victims. 1 *Vistula*: The Vistula River rises in the northern Carpathian Mountains, south of Auschwitz.

You ask no elegies or idylls: only
10  the meaning of our destiny, you, here,
hurt by the mind's war,
uncertain at the clear
presence of life. For life is here
in every No that seems a certainty:
15  here we shall hear the angel weep, the monster, hear
our future time
beating the hereafter that is here, forever
in motion, not an image
of dreams, of possible pity.
20  Here are the myths, the metamorphoses.
Lacking the name of symbols or a god,
they are history, earth places,
they are Auschwitz, love. How suddenly
the dear forms of Alpheus and Arethusa°
25  changed into shadow-smoke!

Out of that hell hung with a white
inscription "work will make you free"°
there came the endless smoke
of many thousand women thrust at dawn
30  out of the kennels up to the firing-wall,
or, screaming for mercy to water, choked,
their skeleton mouths under the jets of gas.

You, soldier, will find them in your annals
taking the forms of animals and rivers,
35  or are you too, now, ash of Auschwitz,
medal of silence?
Long tresses in glass urns can still be seen
bound up with charms, and an infinity
of ghostly little shoes and shawls of Jews:°
40  relics of a time of wisdom,
of man whose knowledge takes the shape of arms,
they are the myths, our metamorphoses.
Over the plains where love and sorrow
and pity rotted, there in the rain
45  a No inside us beat;
a No to death that died at Auschwitz
never from the pit of ashes
to show itself again.

---

°24 *Alpheus and Arethusa*: a river and fountain in Greece. In ancient mythology, Alpheus, who loved Arethusa, was transformed into the river (bearing his name) to be united with Arethusa, who was transformed into the fountain (bearing her name). 27 *work will make you free*: a translation of the large metal sign *Arbeit macht frei*, which crested the main gate of Auschwitz and is still on display there. A copy of the sign is displayed in the Holocaust Museum in Washington, D.C. 37–39 *Long tresses . . . shawls of Jews*: Today the barracks at Auschwitz house permanent displays that include the hair, shoes, eyeglasses, luggage, and clothing of thousands of the victims.

## Questions

1. Compare the tone of the first ten lines with that of the last six. What differences do you notice? How does the idea of the last three lines answer the question posed in lines 9 and 10?
2. Even though the speaker is referring to the deadliest of all the camps, what does he mean by "For life is here/in every No that seems a certainty" (lines 13–14)?
3. In line 20 the speaker mentions ancient myths about metamorphoses or transformations. What type of metamorphosis is linked to the death camps in lines 26–42? What attitudes are brought out by this linkage?

### ANNE RIDLER (1912–2001)

 **Nothing Is Lost** (1994)

Nothing is lost.
We are too sad to know that, or too blind;
Only in visited moments do we understand:
   It is not that the dead return—
     They are about us always, though unguessed.     5

   This penciled Latin verse
You dying wrote me, ten years past and more,
Brings you as much alive to me as the self you wrote it for,
   Dear father, as I read your words
     With no word but Alas.     10

   Lines in a letter, lines in a face
Are faithful currents of life: the boy has written
His parents across his forehead, and as we burn
   Our bodies up each seven years,
     His own past self has left no plainer trace.     15

   Nothing dies.
The cells pass on their secrets, we betray them
Unknowingly: in a freckle, in the way
   We walk, recall some ancestor,
     And Adam in the color of our eyes.     20

   Yes, on the face of the new born,
Before the soul has taken full possession,
There pass, as over a screen, in succession
   The images of other beings:
     Face after face looks out, and then is gone.     25

   Nothing is lost, for all in love survive.
I lay my cheek against his sleeping limbs

To feel if he is warm, and touch in him
30   Those children whom no shawl could warm,
      No arms, no grief, no longing could revive.

      Thus what we see, or know,
Is only a tiny portion, at the best,
Of the life in which we share; an iceberg's crest
35   Our sunlit present, our partial sense,
      With deep supporting multitudes below.

## Questions

1. What is unusual about the phrase "nothing dies" (line 16)? How successfully does the poet explain and exemplify the idea?

2. In what ways does the "face of the new born" reflect the "images of other beings" (lines 21–24)? How might the "color of our eyes" demonstrate that we are descended from Adam (line 20)? How true is it that "all in love survive" (line 26)?

3. In what ways might this poem offer comfort to readers who believe strongly in the concept of their own uniqueness and originality?

## THEODORE ROETHKE (1907–1963)

*For a photo, see Chapter 12, page 517.*

 **My Papa's Waltz** (1942)

The whiskey on your breath
Could make a small boy dizzy;
But I hung on like death:
Such waltzing was not easy.

5   We romped until the pans
Slid from the kitchen shelf;
My mother's countenance
Could not unfrown itself.

The hand that held my wrist
10  Was battered on one knuckle;
At every step you missed
My right ear scraped a buckle.

You beat time on my head
With a palm caked hard by dirt,
15  Then waltzed me off to bed
Still clinging to your shirt.

## Questions

**1.** What is the tone of the speaker's opening description of his father? What is the tone of the phrases "like death" and "such waltzing"?

**2.** What is the "waltz" the speaker describes? What is the tone of his words describing it in lines 5–15?

**3.** What does the reference to his "mother's countenance" contribute to the tone? What situation is suggested by the selection of the word "unfrown"?

**4.** What does the tone of the physical descriptions of the father contribute to your understanding of the speaker's attitude toward his childhood experiences as his father's dancing partner?

## JANE SHORE (b. 1947)

 A Letter Sent to Summer (1977)

Oh summer if you would only come
with your big baskets of flowers,
dropping by like an old friend
just passing through the neighborhood!

If you came to my door disguised                                       5
as a thirsty biblical angel
I'd buy all your hairbrushes and magazines!
I'd be more hospitable
than any ancient king.

I'd personally carry your luggage in,                                  10
Your monsoons. Your squadrons of bugs,
Your plums and lovely melons.
Let the rose let out its long long sigh
And Desire return to the hapless rabbit.

This request is also in my own behalf.                                 15
Inside my head it is always snowing,
even when I sleep. When I wake up,
and still you have not arrived,
I curl back into my blizzard of linens.

Not like winter's buckets of whitewash.                                20
Please wallpaper my bedroom
with leafy vegetables and farms.
If you knocked right now,
I would not interfere.
Start near the window.                                                 25
Start right here.

## Questions

1. Describe the speaker. What do you learn about her and how she is responding to the time of year?

2. Describe what summer means to the speaker. What attributes does she give to summer? What contrasts are brought out by references to "bugs" and "monsoons" in addition to "plums" and "the rose"?

3. What does the phrase "always snowing" contribute to your understanding of the speaker's yearning for summer?

## JONATHAN SWIFT (1667–1745)

# A Description of the Morning (1709)

Now hardly here and there a hackney-coach
Appearing, showed the ruddy morn's approach.
Now Betty from her master's bed had flown,
And softly stole to discompose her own.
5  The slip-shod 'prentice from his master's door
Had pared the dirt, and sprinkled round the floor.
Now Moll had whirled her mop with dextrous airs,
Prepared to scrub the entry and the stairs.
The youth with broomy stumps began to trace
10  The kennel's edge,° where wheels had worn the place.
The small-coal man° was heard with cadence deep,     *charcoal seller*
Till drowned in shriller notes of chimney-sweep.
Duns° at his lordship's gate began to meet;     *bill collectors*
And brickdust Moll had screamed through half the street.
15  The turnkey° now his flock returning sees,
Duly let out a-nights to steal for fees.
The watchful bailiffs take their silent stands,
And schoolboys lag° with satchels in their hands.

---

°10 *kennel's edge*: that is, the edge of the gutter. Swift annotated this line "To find old Nails." 15 *turnkey*: an entrepreneur, operating a jail for profit, who allowed prisoners to go free at night so that they might bring him a night's booty to pay for the necessities provided them in jail. 18 *schoolboys lag*: cf. Shakespeare's *As You Like It*, 2.7.145–47.

## Questions

1. What images of life in early-eighteenth-century London are presented in this poem? Who is "Betty"? Why is she discomposing her bed? Are such images to be considered ordinary, heroic, or antiheroic? Why?

2. Why does Swift conclude with the reference to "schoolboys" lagging "with satchels in their hands"? Why would it not have been preferable to conclude with reference to adult behavior?

3. How do you know that Swift's poem is satiric? What is being satirized?

## DAVID WAGONER (b. 1926)

 ## My Physics Teacher (1981)

He tried to convince us, but his billiard ball
Fell faster than his pingpong ball and thumped
To the floor first, in spite of Galileo.°
The rainbows from his prism skidded off-screen
Before we could tell an infra from an ultra.                                    5
His hand-cranked generator refused to spit
Sparks and settled for smoke. The dangling pith
Ignored the attractions of his amber wand,
No matter how much static he rubbed and dubbed
From the seat of his pants, and the housebrick                                10
He lowered into a tub of water weighed
(Eureka!) more than the overflow.°

He believed in a World of Laws, where problems had answers,
Where tangible objects and intangible forces
Acting thereon could be lettered, numbered, and crammed                       15
Through our tough skulls for lifetimes of homework.
But his only uncontestable demonstration
Came with our last class: he broke his chalk
On a formula, stooped to catch it, knocked his forehead
On the eraser-gutter, staggered slewfoot, and stuck                           20
One foot forever into the wastebasket.

---

°3–12 *Galileo . . . overflow*: These lines describe classic classroom demonstrations in physics. Galileo first formulated the law of uniform falling bodies. Newton explained that a prism divides light into the colors of the rainbow. ("Infra" refers to infrared light; "ultra" to ultraviolet.) Sparks leaping across the space between two wires graphically demonstrate electrical generation and power. The motion of dried pith toward a charged piece of amber demonstrates the magnetic power of static electricity. Archimedes explained how the weight of a floating object is the same as the weight of water it displaces, and also how the volume of an immersed object (not the weight) is the same as the volume of displaced water. The physics teacher did not understand this distinction. (According to legend, Archimedes made this discovery when taking a bath, and then shouted *"Eureka!"* ["I have found it"].)

## Questions

1. What idea underlies the physics teacher's use of classroom demonstrations? What is the speaker's apparent response to this idea?
2. What happens to these demonstrations? Why are these failures comic and farcical? What effect do the poem's farcical actions have upon the validity of the teacher's ideas?

## C. K. WILLIAMS (b. 1936)

 ## Dimensions (1969)

There is a world somewhere else that is unendurable.
Those who live in it are helpless in the hands of the elements,
they are like branches in the deep woods in wind

that whip their leaves off and slice the heart of the night
5  and sob. They are like boats bleating wearily in fog.

But here, no matter what, we know where we stand.
We know more or less what comes next. We hold out.
Sometimes a dream will shake us like little dogs, a fever
hang on so we're not ourselves or love wring us out,
10  but we prevail, we certify and make sure, we go on.

There is a world that uses its soldiers and widows
for flour, its orphans for building stone, its legs for pens.
In that place, eyes are softened and harmless like God's
and all blend in the traffic of their tragedy and pass by
15  like people. And sometimes one of us, losing the way,
will drift over the border and see them there, dying,
laughing, being revived. When we come home, we are half way.
Our screams heal the torn silence. We are like scars.

## Questions

1. Why should this poem be called ironic? Should the irony be called situational? Cosmic? Why?

2. What is intended by the poem's title? What is the implication of the first line? What irony does the line bring out? Describe the irony of the second stanza (lines 6–10).

3. What is meant by "losing the way" and drifting "over the border" (lines 15–16)? What is the meaning and the irony of the last three lines? What does it mean to be "like scars" (line 18)?

## WILLIAM WORDSWORTH (1770–1850)

 **The Solitary Reaper** (1807)

Behold her, single in the field,
Yon solitary Highland Lass!
Reaping and singing by herself;
Stop here, or gently pass!

5  Alone she cuts and binds the grain,
And sings a melancholy strain;
O listen! for the Vale profound
Is overflowing with the sound.

No Nightingale did ever chaunt
10  More welcome notes to weary bands
Of travelers in some shady haunt,
Among Arabian sands;
A voice so thrilling ne'er was heard
In springtime from the Cuckoo bird,

Breaking the silence of the seas
Among the farthest Hebrides.°                                                            15

Will no one tell me what she sings?°
Perhaps the plaintive numbers flow
For old, unhappy, far-off things,
And battles long ago;                                                                    20
Or is it some more humble lay,
Familiar matter of today?
Some natural sorrow, loss, or pain,
That has been, and may be again?

Whate'er the theme, the Maiden sang                                                      25
As if her song could have no ending;
I saw her singing at her work,
And o'er the sickle bending—

I listened, motionless and still;
And, as I mounted up the hill,                                                           30
The music in my heart I bore,
Long after it was heard no more.

---

°16 *Hebrides:* a group of islands off the west coast of Scotland.  17 *Will . . . sings:* The speaker does not understand Scots Gaelic, the language in which the woman sings.

## Questions

1. What is the scene described in the poem? Where is the speaker? What actions does he describe?
2. Why does the poet shift from present tense to the past tense at line 25? What is gained by this shift?
3. What speculations does the speaker make about the meaning of the woman's song? What conclusions does he make? What do you conclude from his observations?

## WILLIAM BUTLER YEATS (1865–1939)

### When You Are Old (1893)

When you are old and grey and full of sleep,
And nodding by the fire, take down this book,
And slowly read, and dream of the soft look
Your eyes had once, and of their shadows deep;

How many loved your moments of glad grace,                                               5
And loved your beauty with love false or true,
But one man loved the pilgrim soul in you,
And loved the sorrows of your changing face;

And bending down beside the glowing bars,
10 Murmur, a little sadly, how Love fled
And paced upon the mountains overhead
And hid his face amid a crowd of stars.

## Questions

1. What is the speaker of this poem like? How does the speaker describe himself?
2. To whom is the speaker speaking? What are you asked to conclude about the past relationship between the speaker and the listener?
3. Describe the dominant attitudes expressed by the speaker. What words might describe the poem's tone?
4. Compare the tone of this poem with that of Henley's "When You Are Old" (p. 619).?

## WRITING ABOUT TONE IN POETRY

Be careful to note those elements of the work that touch particularly on attitudes or authorial consideration. For example, you may be studying Hughes's "Theme for English B," where it is necessary to consider the force of the poet's claim for equality. How serious is the claim? Does the speaker's apparent matter-of-factness make him seem less than enthusiastic? Or does this tone indicate that equality is so fundamental a right that its realization should be an everyday part of life? Devising and answering such questions can help you understand the degree to which authors show control of tone. Similar questions apply when you study internal qualities such as style and characterization.

### Questions for Discovering Ideas

- What is the speaker like? Is he or she intelligent, observant, friendly, idealistic, realistic, trustworthy? How do you think you should respond to the speaker's characteristics?
- Do all the speeches seem right for the speaker and situation? Are all descriptions appropriate, all actions believable?
- If the work is comic, at what is the comedy directed? At situations? At characters? At the speaker himself or herself? What is the poet's apparent attitude toward the comic objects?
- Does the writer ask you to (1) sympathize with those in misfortune, (2) rejoice with those who have found happiness, (3) lament the human condition, (4) become angry against unfairness and inequality, (5) admire examples of noble human behavior, or (6) have another appropriate emotional response?
- Do any words seem unusual or especially noteworthy, such as dialect, polysyllabic words, foreign words or phrases that the author assumes you know, or especially connotative words? What is the effect of such words on the poem's tone?

## Strategies for Organizing Ideas

The goal of your essay is to examine all aspects bearing on the tone. Consider the following topics.

1. *The audience, situation, and characters.* Is any person or group directly addressed by the speaker? What attitude is expressed (love, respect, condescension, confidentiality, confidence, etc.)? What is the basic situation in the work? What is the nature of the speaker or persona? What is the relationship of the speaker to the material? What is the basis of the speaker's authority? Does the speaker give you the whole truth? Is he or she trying to withhold anything? Why? How is the speaker's character manipulated to show apparent authorial attitude and to stimulate responses? Do you find any of the various sorts of irony? If so, what does the irony show (optimism or pessimism, for example)? How is the situation controlled to shape your responses? That is, can actions, situations, or characters be seen as expressions of attitude or as embodiments of certain favorable or unfavorable ideas or positions? How does the work promote respect, admiration, dislike, or other feelings about character or situation?

2. *Descriptions and diction.* Your concern here is to relate attitudes to the poet's use of language and description. Are there any systematic references, such as to colors, sounds, noises, natural scenes, and so on, that collectively reflect an attitude? Do connotative meanings of words control response in any way? Is any special knowledge of references or unusual words expected of readers? What is the extent of this knowledge? Do speech or dialect patterns indicate attitudes about speakers or their condition of life? Are speech patterns normal and standard or slang and substandard? What is the effect of these patterns? Are there unusual or particularly noteworthy expressions? If so, what attitudes do these show? Does the author use verbal irony? To what effect?

3. *Humor.* Is the work funny? How funny, how intense? How is the humor achieved? Does the humor develop out of incongruous situations or language, or both? Is there an underlying basis of attack in the humor, or are the objects of laughter still respected or even loved despite having humor directed against them?

4. *Ideas.* Ideas may be advocated, defended mildly, attacked, or ridiculed. Which attitude is present in the work you have been studying? How does the poet make his or her attitude clear—directly, by statement, or indirectly, through understatement, overstatement, or the language of a character? In what ways does the work assume a common ground of assent between author and reader? That is, are there apparently common assumptions about religious views, political ideas, moral and behavioral standards, and so on? Are these common ideas readily acceptable, or is any concession needed by the reader to approach the work? For example, a major subject of Arnold's "Dover Beach" (Chapter 19) is that absolute belief in the truth of organized

religion has been lost. This subject may not be important to everyone, but even an irreligious reader or a follower of another faith may find common ground in the poem's psychological situation or in the desire to learn as much as possible about so important an institution as religion.

5. *Unique characteristics.* Each work has unique properties that contribute to the tone. For example, Roethke's "My Papa's Waltz" is a brief narrative in which the speaker's recollected feelings about his father's boisterously drunken behavior must be inferred from understatement. Hardy's "Channel Firing" (Chapter 13) develops from the comic but also absurd idea that the sounds of cannons being fired from ships at sea are so loud they could waken the dead. Be alert for such special circumstances in the poem you are considering, and as you plan and develop your essay, take them into account.

Your conclusion may summarize your main points and from there go on to any needed definitions, explanations, or afterthoughts, together with ideas reinforcing earlier points. If you have changed your mind or have made new realizations, briefly explain these. Finally, you might mention some other major aspect of the work's tone that you did not develop in the body.

## Illustrative Student Essay

Underlined sentences in this paper *do not* conform to MLA style and are used solely as teaching tools to emphasize the central idea, thesis sentence, and topic sentences throughout the paper.

Bergen 1

Delia Bergen

Professor Capton

English 112

18 May 2007

### The Tone of Confidence in "Theme for English B" by Langston Hughes°

[1]    "Theme for English B" grows from the situational irony of racial differences as seen by the speaker, an African American college student. This situation might easily produce bitterness, anger, outrage, or vengefulness. However, the poem contains none of these. It is not angry or indignant; it is not an appeal for revenge or revolution. It is rather a declaration of personal independence and individuality. The tone is that of daring

---

°See p. 619 for this poem.

and occasional playfulness, but above all, of confidence.* These attitudes are made plain in the speaker's situation, the ideas, the poetic form, the diction, and the expressions.†

[2]    Hughes's poetic treatment is objective, factual, and personal, not emotional or political. The poem contains a number of factual details: The speaker is black in an otherwise all-white College English class. He has come from North Carolina, and is now living alone at the Harlem YMCA, away from family and roots. He is also, at 22, an "older" student in the first-year classroom. All this is evidence of disadvantage, yet the speaker does no more than present the facts objectively, without comment.

[3]    Hughes's thoughts about equality—the idea underlying the poem—are presented in the same objective, cool manner. The speaker writes to his instructor as an equal, not as an inferior. His idea is that all people are the same, regardless of race or background. In defining himself, therefore, he does not deal in abstractions, but emphasizes that he, like everyone else, has ordinary likes and needs, and that his abilities and activities are like those of everyone else. By causing the speaker to avoid emotionalism and controversy, Hughes makes counterarguments difficult if not impossible.

[4]    The argument for equality is carried out even in Hughes's actual use of the poetic form. The title here is the key, for it does not promise the most exciting of topics. Normally, in fact, one would expect no more than a short prose essay or theme in response to an English assignment, but a poem is unexpected and therefore daring and original, particularly one like this that touches on the topic of equality and identity. The wit, originality, and skill of the speaker's use of the form itself demonstrate the self-confidence and self-sufficiency that underlie the theoretical claim for equality.

[5]    Hughes's diction is also in keeping with the poem's confidence and daring. Almost all the words are short and simple—of no more than one or two syllables—showing the speaker's confidence in the truth and power of his ideas. This high proportion of short words reflects a conscious attempt to keep the diction clear and direct. A result is that Hughes avoids any possible ambiguities, as the following words show:

> Well, I like to eat, sleep, drink, and be in love.
> I like to work, read, learn, and understand life.
> I like a pipe for a Christmas present,
> or records—Bessie, bop, or Bach. (lines 21–24)

---

*Central idea.
†Thesis sentence.

Bergen 3

With the exception of what it means to "understand life," these words are free of emotional overtones. They reflect the speaker's confident belief that equality should replace inequality and prejudice.

[6]  A number of the speaker's phrases and expressions also show this same confidence. Although most of the language is simple and descriptive, it is also playful and ironic. In lines 18–20, there seems to be a deliberate use of confusing language to bring about a verbal merging of the identities of the speaker, the instructor, Harlem, and the greater New York area:

> Harlem, I hear you:
> hear you, hear me—we two—you, me talk on this page.
> (I hear New York, too.) Me—who? (lines 18–20)

One may also find a certain whimsy in the way in which the speaker treats the irony of the black-white situation:

> So will my page be colored that I write? (line 27)

Underlying this last expression is an awareness that, despite the claim that people are equal and are tied to each other by common humanity, there are also strong differences among individuals. The speaker is confidently asserting grounds for independence as well as equality.

[7]  Thus, an examination of "Theme for English B" reveals vitality and confidence. The poem is a statement of trust and an almost open challenge on the personal level to the unachieved ideal of equality. Hughes makes this point through the deliberate simplicity of the speaker's words and descriptions. Yet the poem definitely includes irony, particularly at the end, where the speaker mentions that the instructor is "somewhat more free" than he is. "Theme for English B" is complex and engaging. It shows the speaker's confidence through daring and playfulness.

Bergen 4

### WORK CITED

Hughes, Langston. "Theme for English B." *Literature: An Introduction to Reading and Writing*. Ed. Edgar V. Roberts. 4th Compact ed. Upper Saddle River: Prentice Hall, 2008, 619–620.

## Commentary on the Essay

Because this essay embodies a number of approaches by which tone may be studied in any work (situation, common ground, diction, special characteristics), it is typical of many essays that use a combined, eclectic approach. The central idea is that the dominant attitude in "Theme for English B" is the speaker's confidence, and that this confidence is shown in the similar but separable attitudes of objectivity, daring, and playfulness.

Paragraph 2 deals with situational irony in relation to the social and political circumstance of racial discrimination (see approach 1, p. 635). Paragraph 3 considers the objectivity with which Hughes considers the idea of equality (approach 4).

Paragraph 4 shows how a topic that might ordinarily be taken for granted, in this case the basic form or genre of expression, can be seen as a unique feature of tone (approach 5). The paragraph contrasts the *expected* student response (no more than a brief prose essay) with the *actual* response (the poem itself, with its interesting twists and turns). Since the primary tone of the poem is that of self-confidence, which is the unspoken basis for the speaker's assertion of independence and equality, the paragraph stresses that the form itself embodies this attitude.

Paragraphs 5 and 6 consider how Hughes's word choices exhibit his attempts at clarity, objectivity, playfulness, and confidence (approach 2). The attention given in these paragraphs to Hughes's simple, direct diction is justified by its importance in the poem's tone.

The concluding paragraph stresses again the attitude of confidence in the poem and also notes additional attitudes of trust, challenge, irony, daring, and playfulness.

## Writing Topics About Tone in Poetry

1. Consider "homage to my hips," "she being Brand/-new," "The Workbox," "The First-Rate Wife," and Henley's "When You Are Old" as poems about love. What similarities do you find? That is, do the poets state that love creates joy, satisfaction, distress, embarrassment, trouble? How does the tone of each of the poems enable you to draw your conclusions? What differences do you find in the ways the poets either control or do not control tone?

2. Consider these same poems from a feminist viewpoint (see Chapter 24). What importance and value do the poems give to women? How do they view women's actions? Generally, what praise or blame do the poems deserve because of their treatment of women?

3. a. Consider the tone of Roethke's "My Papa's Waltz." Some readers have concluded that the speaker is expressing fond memories of his childhood experiences with his father. Others believe that the speaker is ambiguous about the father and that he suppresses childhood pain as he describes the father's boisterousness in the kitchen. Basing your conclusion on the tone of the poem alone, how should the poem be interpreted?

    b. In your library, find two critical biographies about Theodore Roethke published by university presses. What do these books disclose about Roethke's childhood and his family, particularly his father? On the basis of what you learn, should your interpretation of the tone of "My Papa's Waltz" be changed or unchanged? Why?

4. Write a poem about a person or occasion that has made you either glad or angry. Try to create the same feelings in your reader, but create these feelings through your rendering of situation and your choices of the right words. (*Possible topics:* a social injustice, an unfair grade, a compliment you have received on a task well done, the landing of a good job, the winning of a game, a rise in the price of gasoline, a good book or movie, and so on.)

5. What judgments about modern city life do you think Léger conveys in his painting *The City* (I–3, Plate 1)? If the tone of paintings can be considered similar to poetic tone, in what ways is *The City* comparable to the presentation of detail in Eliot's "Preludes" (Chapter 13), Blake's "London" (Chapter 19), Sandburg's "Chicago" (Chapter 19), and Swift's "A Description of the Morning"(this chapter)—together with any other poems you wish to include?

6. How does Edelman establish a friendly relationship between the speaker and the reader in "Trouble"? In what way does this relationship establish the tone of the poem?

7. Explain how the details and ideas in Ridler's "Nothing Is Lost" shape the poem's tone. What is the effect of the stanzaic pattern and the rhymes on your understanding and on your responses to the poem's ideas? In terms of ideas and tone, how does this poem compare with Pinsky's "Dying"?

8. Quasímodo's "Auschwitz" concerns one of the twentieth century's central evils, the most abhorrent of the Nazi death camps, about which people have expressed anger, horror, indignation, outrage, disgust, hatred, and vengefulness (see p. 625). To what degree do you find these attitudes in Quasímodo's poem? How do such attitudes, or others, govern the poem's tone?

# Chapter 16

# Form: The Shape of Poems

**B**ecause poetry is compressed and highly rhythmical, it always exists under self-imposed restrictions, or conventions. Traditionally, many poets have chosen a variety of clearly recognizable shapes or forms—*closed-form* poetry. Since the middle of the nineteenth century, however, many poets have rejected the more regular patterns in favor of poems that appear more free and spontaneous—*open form* poetry. These terms refer to the structure and technique of the poems, not to content or ideas.

## Closed-Form Poetry

The poetic **line** is, loosely, the equivalent of the prose sentence. Individual lines may coincide exactly with sentences, but sentences often stretch out over two lines and beyond. Closed-form lines contain specific numbers of syllables measured out according to comparative loudness (**heavy stress**) and softness (**light stress**). The units of loud and soft syllables are **feet**, and the measures are referred to as **meter**.

The major poetic feet are the **iamb** (light heavy), **trochee** (heavy light), **spondee** (heavy heavy), **pyrrhic** (light light), **anapest** (light light heavy), **dactyl** (heavy light light), and **imperfect** (a single light or a single heavy). There are also a number of other feet that were used particularly by nineteenth-century poets, but many poems can be **scanned** (studied and described) with reference to the feet listed here. The analysis of poetic rhythm is called **metrics, prosody**, or **versification**.

The characteristic of closed-form lines is the repetition of feet according to a designated number, so that an entire poem may contain lines of five feet (**pentameter**), four feet (**tetrameter**), three feet (**trimeter**), two feet (**dimeter**), and even one foot (**monometer**). Also, however, poets intersperse lines of varying length (e.g., a trimeter or dimeter line following a pentameter or tetrameter line). Usually these variations are regular and predictable.

The poetic equivalent of the prose paragraph is the **stanza** (adj. **stanzaic**). Stanzas are connected internally by the development of a subject, idea, or feeling. Usually stanzas in the same poem have identical appearance on the page because they contain repeating patterns of lines with the same number of feet.

In addition to metrical rhythm and patterning of stanzas, **rhyme** is a major characteristic of closed-form poetry. Rhyme is the systematic use of words with identical or closely related or similar terminating sounds, usually at the ends of lines, such as *gold, told; thought, sought; seasons, reasons; show it, poet; ever, never, river;* and *pattering, chattering, clattering.* Rhymes are laid out in a prescribed pattern. Thus, every two lines of a poem may conclude with a rhyme, or the first and fourth lines, or the second and third, and so on. There are many separate schemes, and some poets may even include rhymes within lines (**internal rhyme**), as Poe does in "Annabel Lee" (Chapter 19). In the discussion of rhyme, alphabetical letters are used. Thus *a a* indicates two successive rhyming lines, and *a b a b* indicates a rhyming sound concluding lines 1 and 3 and a different rhyming sound concluding lines 2 and 4.

Similar to rhyme in both closed-form and open-form poetry is the use of words occurring together or near each other that contain the same sounds. **Alliteration** is the duplication of a consonant sound, most often at the beginnings of words but also of internal syllables, as in *long love, chance* or *Nature's changing course,* and *somewhere safe to sea.* **Assonance** is the duplication of a vowel sound, usually within words, as in *sings hymns, old woes, precious friends,* and *break of day.*

The alternation of heavy and light stresses required by the feet of lines permits the reading and recitation of poetry to become more rhythmical and emphatic than the utterances of prose and of everyday speech. In addition, the repetitions of sounds in rhymes and also in assonance and alliteration encourage readers to dwell on particular words and therefore on the ideas and feelings these words bring out. Such characteristics are part of the **music of poetry**, which is present not only in the closed form but also in the open form. It is the music of poetry that makes the speaking and hearing of poetry dramatic, exciting, and inspiring.

## Types of Closed Forms

Over the centuries English and American poets have appropriated and developed many closed forms. Among the most important of these are *blank verse,* the *couplet,* the *tercet* or *triplet, terza rima,* the *villanelle,* the *quatrain,* the *sonnet,* the *song* or *lyric,* the *ode,* the *ballad,* the *elegy,* and *common measure* or the *hymnal stanza,* together with forms such as *haiku,* the *epigram,* the *epitaph,* the *limerick,* the *clerihew,* and the *double dactyl.*

## Blank Verse Consists of Five Unrhymed Iambic Lines

One of the most common closed forms in English is **blank verse**, or unrhymed iambic pentameter, which represents the adaptation and fusion of sentences to poetic form. The great advantage of blank verse is that it resembles normal speech but at the same time it maintains poetic identity. It is suitable for relatively short poems, but it may also extend for hundreds or even thousands of lines. It is the most adaptable line of English poetry. The master of blank verse is Shakespeare, who used it extensively in his plays. Since Shakespeare, poets of English have used blank verse again and again. Milton used it in his masterly epic *Paradise Lost*. Wordsworth was fond of blank verse and used it in some of his best-known poems. Let us look at a passage from his autobiographical poem *The Prelude* (1850) to see some of his blank verse—which has been praised as "conversational," "flexible," and "majestic"—in action.

> Wisdom and Spirit of the universe!
> Thou Soul that art the eternity of thought,
> That givest to forms and images a breath
> And everlasting motion, not in vain
> By day or star-light thus from my first dawn
> Of childhood didst thou intertwine for me
> The passions that build up our human soul;
> Not with the mean and vulgar works of man,
> But with high objects, with enduring things—
> With life and nature, purifying thus
> The elements of feeling and of thought,
> And sanctifying, by such discipline,
> Both pain and fear, until we recognize
> A grandeur in the beatings of the heart. (Book I, lines 401–414)

The development of these lines takes place through a simultaneous blending of line lengths and grammatical coherence. Wordsworth expresses his ideas enthusiastically within his chosen iambic rhythm, which is both restricting and liberating, and by this means he brings about the "majestic" elevation that is characteristic of his poetry.

## The Couplet Consists of Two Lines Connected by Thought and Rhyme

The **couplet** contains two rhyming lines and is the shortest distinct closed form. The two lines are usually identical in length and meter. Some couplets are short. Even lines in monometer (one major stress), such as "I sing/Each spring," can make up a couplet. However, most English couplets are in iambic tetrameter (four stresses) or iambic pentameter (five stresses), and they have been a regular feature of English poetry since Chaucer used them in the fourteenth century. In the seventeenth and eighteenth centuries, the iambic-pentameter couplet was considered appropriate for epic, or heroic, poetry. For this reason it is often called the **heroic couplet**. Because these centuries are considered the "neoclassic" age of literature, the form is also called the **neoclassic couplet**. It was used with consummate skill by John Dryden (1631–1700) and Alexander Pope (1688–1744).

Usually, the heroic couplet expresses a complete idea and is grammatically self-sufficient. It thrives on the rhetorical strategies of **parallelism** and **antithesis**. Look, for example, at these two couplets from "The Rape of the Lock," Pope's well-known mock-epic poem (1711).

Here Britain's statesmen oft the fall foredoom
Of foreign tyrants, and of nymphs at home;
Here thou, great Anna! whom three realms obey,
Dost sometimes counsel take—and sometimes tea.

These lines describe activities at Hampton Court, the royal palace and residence of Queen Anne (reigned 1701–1714). Notice that the first couplet allows Pope to link "Britain's statesmen" with two parallel but also antithetical events: the fall of nations and the "fall" of young women. Similarly, the second heroic couplet allows for the parallel and comic linking of royal meetings of state ("counsel") and teatime (in the early eighteenth century, *tea* was pronounced "tay"). The example thus demonstrates how the heroic couplet may contrast amusing and ironic actions and situations.

## The Tercet or Triplet Consists of Three Lines

A three-line stanza is called a **tercet** or **triplet**. Tercets may be written in any uniform line length or meter and most commonly contain three rhymes (*a a a, b b b,* and so on), which are, in effect, short stanzas. The following poem by Tennyson is in iambic-tetrameter triplets.

### ALFRED, LORD TENNYSON (1809–1892)

 **The Eagle** (1851)

He clasps the crag with crooked hands;
Close to the sun in lonely lands,
Ring'd with the azure world, he stands.

5  The wrinkled sea beneath him crawls;
He watches from his mountain walls,
And like a thunderbolt he falls.

In the first tercet, we view the eagle as though at a distance. In the second, the perspective shifts, and we see through the eagle's eyes and follow his actions. In this tercet the verbs are active: the sea "crawls" and the eagle "falls." While the two tercets and the shift in perspective divide the poem, alliteration pulls things back together. This is especially true of the *k* sound in "clasps," "crag," "crooked," "close," and "crawls" and the *w* sound in "with," "world," "watches," and "walls."

**TERZA RIMA.** There are two important variations on the tercet pattern, each requiring a high degree of ingenuity and control. The first tercet variation is **terza rima**, in which stanzas are interlocked through a pattern that requires the center termination in one tercet to be rhymed twice in the next: *a b a, b c b, c d c, d e d,* and so on.

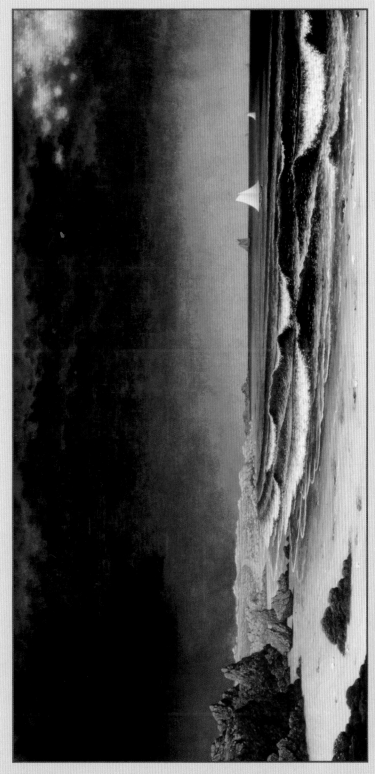

❧ Martin Johnson Heade (American, 1819-1904), *Approaching Storm: Beach Near Newport*, c. 1861-1862. Oil on canvas, 28 X 58 3/8 in./71.12 X 148.27 cm. Courtesy Museum of Fine Arts, Boston. Gift of Maxim Karolik for the M. and M. Karolik Collection of American Paintings, 1815–1865. 45.889. Reproduced with permission. (© 2003 Museum of Fine Arts, Boston. All rights reserved.)

**Heade's treatment of the ocean and shore may be compared with Arnold's "Dover Beach" (p. 793) and Longfellow's "The Sound of the Sea" (p. 824).**

Joseph Mallord William Turner (1775-1851), *Keelmen Heaving in Coals by Moonlight*, 1942. Oil on Canvas, 36 1/4" X 48 1/4". National Gallery of Art, Washington, D.C., Widener Collection.

Note the virtual blending of sea and sky in this painting. Compare with Chapter 3, on Point of View, esp. pp. 107-110, and also pp. 868 ff. Compare with Picasso's Guernica (Plate I-6) and Claude's Harbor at Sunset (Plate I-6). Compare also with Gilman's story "The Yellow Wallpaper" (pp. 408 ff.), and Dickinson's poems "There's a Certain Slant of Light" (p. 746) and "I Dwell in Possibility" (p. 741).

Regrettably, we have not been permitted to include Henri Matisse's "Harmony in Red" in this version of *Literature: An Introduction to Reading and Writing*, Fourth Edition.

❧ Fernand Leger (1881-1955), *The City*, 1919. Oil on canvas, 91 X 177 1/2 in. The Philadelphia Museum of Art, Philadelphia. A. E. Gallatin Collection. (© 2004 Artists Rights Society [ARS], New York/ADAGP, Paris)

**The City** is discussed in Chapter 15 (p. 599). Compare with Frost's "The Tuft of Flowers" (p. 752) and Sandburg's "Chicago" (p. 837).

❧ Edward Hopper (1882-1967), *Automat*, 1927. Oil on canvas, 28 1/8 X 35 in. Des Moines Art Center Permanent Collections; purchased with funds from the Edmundson Art Foundation, Inc. 1958.2. (Photograph by Michael Tropea, Chicago)

**These two paintings are discussed in Chapter 5 (p. 199). Compare with Frost's "The Silken Tent" (p. 759), Joyce's "Araby" (p. 226), Browning's "My Last Duchess" (p. 609), and Whur's "The First-Rate Wife" (p. 600). See also Boucher's *Madame de Pompadour*.**

Thomas Cole (1801-1848), *View from Mount Holyoke, Northampton, Massachusetts, After a Thunderstorm (The Oxbow)*, 1836. Oil on canvas, 51 1/2 in. high X 76 in. wide/130.8 X 193 cm. Signed and dated: T. Cole 1836 (lower left). The Metropolitan Museum of Art, New York. Gift of Mrs. Russell Sage, 1908 (08.228). (Photograph © 1995 The Metropolitan Museum of Art)

**This painting may be compared with Evans, "The Iceberg Seven-Eighths Under" (p. 575) and Bryant's "To Cole, the Painter" (p. 799).**

Albert Bierstadt (1830-1902), *Among the Sierra Nevada Mountains, California*, 1868. Oil on canvas, 71 X 120 in./183 X 305 cm. (© Smithsonian American Art Museum, Washington, DC/Art Resource, New York)

**Compare with Wordsworth's "Tintern Abbey Lines" (p. 484) and Chief Dan George's "The Beauty of the Trees" (p. 811).**

Sir Hubert von Herkomer (1849-1914), *Hard Times, 1885*. (© Manchester City Art Gallery) (p. 495)

**This painting is discussed in Chapter 13 (p. 531). Compare with Cowper's "The Poplar Field" (p. 469) and Whitecloud's "Blue Winds Dancing" (p. 269).**

Pieter Brueghel the Elder (c. 1525-1569), *Landscape with the Fall of Icarus*, c. 1554-1555. Musées Royaux des Beaux-Arts, Brussels. (© Scala/Art Resource, New York)

**Compare with Bierce's "An Occurrence at Owl Creek Bridge" (p. 70), Auden's "The Unknown Citizen" (p. 794).**

Pablo Picasso (1881-1973), *Guernica*, 1937. Oil on canvas, 350 X 782 cm.  Museo Nacional Centro de Arte Reina Sofia, Madrid.  (© Estate of Pablo Picasso/Artists Rights Society [ARS], New York)

**Guernica is discussed in Chapter 9 (p. 368). Compare with Pirandello's "War" (p. 92), Crane's "Do Not Weep" (p. 802), and Forché's "The Colonel" (p. 659).**

Claude Lorrain (1600-1682), *Harbour at Sunset (Seaport at Sunset)*, 1639.  Oil on canvas.  Louvre, Paris. (© Erich Lessing/Art Resource, New York)

**Claude's *Harbor at Sunset* is discussed in Chapter 3 (p. 108). Compare with Lynn Emanuel's "Like God" (p. 809) and Plath's "Song for a Summer's Day" (p. 788).**

Pieter Brueghel the Elder (c. 1525-1569), *Peasants' Dance*, 1568. Oil on oak wood, 114 X 164 cm. Kunsthistorisches Museum, Vienna. (© Erich Lessing/Art Resource, New York).
**Compare with William Carlos Williams's "The Dance" (p. 683) and Hardy's "The Three Strangers" (p. 256).**

Jacques-Louis David (1748-1825), *The Death of Socrates*, 1787. Oil on canvas, 51 X 77.25 in./129.5 X 196.2 cm. Signed and dated: L. David (on bench at right); L.D./MDCCLXXXVII (lower left). The Metropolitan Museum of Art, New York. Catherine Lorillard Wolfe Collection, Wolfe Fund, 1931. 31.45. (Photograph © 1995 The Metropolitan Museum of Art)
*The Death of Socrates* is discussed in Chapter 2 (p. 61). **Compare with Hardy's "The Convergence of the Twain" (p. 575) and Thomas's "Do Not Go Gentle" (p. 681).**

François Boucher (1703-1770), *Madame de Pompadour.* Paper on canvas, 60 X 45.5 cm. Louvre, Paris. (© Erich Lessing/Art Resource, New York)

**See also Hopper's *Automat.***

August Renoir (1841-1919), *The Umbrellas (Les Parapluies)*, c. 1881-1886. National Gallery, London. (© Art Resource, New York)

*The Umbrellas* shows a Parisian scene crowded with people. It may almost be considered an illustration of Maupassant's "The Necklace" (p. 4). Compare with Maupassant, and also with Nye's "Where Children Live " (p. 480).

Francisco de Goya y Lucientes (1746-1828), *The Colossus*, 1808-1810. Oil on canvas, 116 X 105 cm. Museo del Prado, Madrid. (© Erich Lessing/Art Resource, New York)

*The Colossus* may be compared with "The New Colossus" by Emma Lazarus, Whitman's "Dirge for Two Veterans" (p. 851) and Eberhart's "The Fury of Aerial Bombardment" (p. 511).

James Abbott McNeill Whistler (1834-1903), *The Little White Girl, Symphony in White, No. 2*, 1864. Oil on canvas, 76.5 X 51.1 cm. (© Tate Gallery, London/Art Resource, New York)

Compare with Joyce's "Araby" (p. 226) and Ransom's "Bells for John Whiteside's Daughter" (p. 835).

∞ *Hercules and the Infant Telephus.* A Roman fresco from
Herculaneum. Museo Archeologico Nazionale, Naples. (©
Scala/Art Resource, New York)

This anonymous fresco from ancient Herculaneum is
discussed in Chapter 8 (p. 319). Compare with Coleman's
"Unfinished Masterpieces" (p. 327), Larkin's "Next, Please"
(p. 718), and Graham's "The Geese" (p. 709).

∞ *Theatre of Dionysus,* fourth century B.C.E. Athens.

Ancient Greek theaters are discussed in Chapter 21
(pp. 932–34).

&#x2767; *Interior of the Globe Theatre.* London. (Photograph by April Roberts)

**Theaters of Shakespeare's day, particularly the Globe, are discussed in Chapter 21 (pp. 976–79).**

&#x2767; *Exterior of the Globe Theatre.* London. (Photograph by April Roberts)

**Authentic reconstruction based on sixteenth-century drawings and archaeological research, opening 1996 (p. 976-79).**

❧ *Stage of the Globe Theater.* London. (Photograph by April Roberts)

**THE VILLANELLE.**   The most complex variation of the tercet pattern is the **villanelle**, a nineteen-line form containing six tercets, rhymed *a b a*, and concluded by four lines. The first and third lines of the first tercet are repeated alternately in subsequent tercets as a refrain, and also are used in the concluding four lines. For examples see Elizabeth Bishop's "One Art," Theodore Roethke's "The Waking," and Dylan Thomas's "Do Not Go Gentle into That Good Night."

## The Quatrain Is a Unit of Four Lines

The most common and adaptable stanzaic building block is the four-line **quatrain**. This stanza has been popular for hundreds of years and has lent itself to many variations. Like couplets and tercets, quatrains may be written in any line length and meter; even the line lengths within a quatrain may vary. The determining factor is the rhyme scheme, and even that is variable, depending on the form and the poet's aims. Quatrains may be rhymed *a a a a*, but they can also be rhymed *a b a b*, *a b b a*, *a a b a*, or even *a b c b*. Quatrains are basic components of many traditional closed forms, most notably ballads and sonnets, and they are significant in many religious hymns.

## The Sonnet Is a Versatile Poem of Fourteen Lines

The **sonnet**, consisting of 14 lines, is one of the most popular and durable closed poetic forms. Initially it was an Italian form (*sonnetto* means "little song") created by the medieval Italian poet Petrarch (1304–1374), who wrote collections or *cycles* of sonnets. The sonnet form as made famous by Petrarch is called the **Italian sonnet** or **Petrarchan sonnet** in Petrarch's honor. The form and style of Petrarchan sonnets were adapted to English poetry in the early sixteenth century, and with variations they have been used ever since. As a form, the Petrarchan sonnet is in iambic pentameter, and it contains two quatrains (the **octave**) and two tercets (the **sestet**). In structure and meaning, the octave presents a problem or situation that is resolved in the sestet, as in Milton's "On His Blindness." The rhyme scheme of the Petrarchan octave is fixed in an *a b b a, a b b a* pattern. The sestet offers a number of different rhyming possibilities, including *c d c, c d c* and *c d e, c d e*.

**THE SHAKESPEAREAN SONNET.**   Shakespeare was the most original adapter of the sonnet tradition. Recognizing that there are fewer rhyming words in English than in Italian, he developed the **Shakespearean sonnet** or **English sonnet**, based on seven rhymes (in the pattern *a b a b, c d c d, e f e f, g g*) rather than the five rhymes of the Italian sonnet. As indicated by the rhyme scheme, the Shakespearean sonnet contains three quatrains and a concluding couplet. The pattern of thought therefore shifts from the octave-sestet organization of the Italian sonnet to a four-part argument on a single thought or emotion. Each Shakespearean quatrain contains a separate development of the sonnet's central idea or problem, and the couplet provides a climax and resolution.

## The Song or Lyric Is a Stanzaic Poem of Variable Measure and Length

The **song** or **lyric** is a stanzaic form that was originally designed to be sung to a repeating melody, although few lyrics today are written specifically for music. Even so, the line lengths and rhyme schemes of the first stanza are duplicated in subsequent stanzas, as though for repeated singing to the same tune. The stanzas of a lyric may be built from any combination of single lines, couplets, triplets, and quatrains. The line lengths may shift, and a great deal of metrical variation is common.

The lyric is one of the most adaptable and variable of all verse forms at the present time. In fact, the lyric is one of the forms most commonly used by contemporary poets. The form may be personal, public, philosophical, religious, and political, in addition to its use as a vehicle to express love and other emotions. There is theoretically no limit to the number of stanzas in a lyric, although there are usually no more than five or six. A. E. Housman's "Loveliest of Trees" (Chapter 12), for example, is a lyric made up of three quatrains containing two couplets each. It is in iambic tetrameter and rhymes *a a b b*. The second and third stanzas repeat the same pattern of rhyme, *c c d d, e e f f*. Lyrics often feature quite complex and ingenious stanzaic structures. Donne's "The Canonization" (Chapter 17) for instance, contains five stanzas that repeat the following pattern: *iambic: 5a 4b 5b 5a 4c 4c 4c 4a 3a*. This nine-line stanza contains three different rhymes and three different line lengths. Nevertheless, the same intricate pattern is repeated in each of the five stanzas.

## The Ode Is a Complex and Extensive Stanzaic Poem

The **ode** is a more variable stanzaic form than the lyric, with varying line lengths and intricate rhyme schemes. Usually the topics of odes are meditative and philosophical, but there is no set topic material, just as there is no set form. Some odes have repeating patterns, while others offer no duplication and introduce a new structure in each stanza. Poets have developed their own structures according to their needs. Keats's great odes were particularly congenial to his ideas, as in "Ode to a Nightingale," which consists of eight stanzas in iambic pentameter with the repeating form *a b a b c d e 3c d e*. Although many odes have been set to music, most do not fit repeating melodies.

## The Elegy Is a Poem About Death and Its Meaning for the Living

The **elegy** ("lament," or "mournful song") has had a long and rich history in other languages, extending back to ancient times, and it has defined a number of topics, but for our purposes it is a poem of lamentation. Usually the topic is the death of a specific person, but it is also generally concerned with mortality and the negative and tragic aspects of life. In English, the most notable elegy is Milton's "Lycidas" (1638), which he wrote in observance of the death by drowning of a "learned friend" with whom he had gone to school. Milton also composed this poem as a **pastoral**, that is, a poem describing rural lives and concerns, with direct allegorical implications for the lives of urban city-dwellers. So that you may get a sense of this poem, here are the opening twenty-four lines.

Yet once more, O ye laurels, and once more
Ye myrtles brown, with ivy never sere,°                                                      *dry, withered*
I come to pluck your berries° harsh and crude,                                      *to write this poem*
And with forced fingers rude,
Shatter your leaves before the mellowing year.                                                          5
Bitter constraint, and sad occasion dear,
Compels me to disturb your season due;
For Lycidas is dead, dead ere his prime,
Young Lycidas, and hath° not left his peer:                                                       *who hath*
Who would not sing for Lycidas? he knew                                                             10
Himself to sing, and build the lofty rhyme.
He must not float upon his watery bier
Unwept, and welter to the parching wind,
Without the meed° of some melodious tear.                                                    *gift, honor*
    Begin then, sisters° of the sacred well,                                                  *the muses*  15
That from beneath the seat of Jove° doth spring,                                        *God (Jupiter)*
Begin, and somewhat loudly sweep the string.
Hence with denial vain, and coy excuse,
So may some gentle muse
With lucky° words favor my destined urn,                                      *providential, inspired*  20
And as he passes turn,
And bid fair peace be to my sable shroud.
For we were nursed upon the self-same hill,
Fed the same flock; by fountain, shade, and rill.°                      *i.e., we went to the same school*

Today few people think of the traditional formalities of elegiac writing, and prefer to understand poems as elegies if they concern death, mortality, and grief. Thus, Collins's "The Names" (Chapter 15), Dryden's "To the Memory of Mr. Oldham" (this chapter), Pinsky's "Dying" (Chapter 15), Ransom's "Bells for John Whiteside's Daughter" (Chapter 19), Cummings' "Buffalo Bill's Defunct" (this chapter), and Dickinson's "The Bustle in a House" (Chapter 18), to name just a few poems in this book, might, broadly, all be considered elegies.

## Ballads Consist of Many Narrative Quatrains

The **ballad**, which fuses narrative description with dramatic dialogue, originated in folk literature and is one of the oldest closed forms in English poetry. Ballads consist of many quatrains in which lines of iambic tetrameter alternate with iambic trimeter. Normally, only the second and fourth lines of each stanza rhyme, in the pattern *x a x a*, *x b x b*, *x c x c*, and so on. The ballad was designed for singing, like the anonymous "Sir Patrick Spens" (Chapter 11). Popular ballad tunes were used over and over again by later balladeers, often as many as forty and fifty times, and many of the tunes have survived to the present day and are still well known—for example, the anonymous "Lord Randal."

## Common Measure, or The Hymnal Stanza, Is a Poem Consisting of a Number of Quatrains

**Common measure**, a quatrain form, is similar to the ballad stanza. It shares with the ballad the alternation of four-beat and three-beat iambic lines but adds a second rhyme to the first and third lines of each quatrain: *a b a b, c d c d*, and so on. Because the measure is often used in hymns, it is sometimes called the **hymnal stanza**. Many of Emily Dickinson's poems, including "Because I Could Not Stop for Death" (Chapter 11), are in common measure.

## The Haiku Is a Complete Poem of Seventeen Syllables

The **haiku** originated in Japan, where it has been a favorite genre for hundreds of years. It traditionally imposes strict rules on the writer: (1) There should be three lines (a tercet) of five, seven, and five syllables per line, for a total of seventeen syllables. (2) The topic should be derived from nature. (3) The poem should embody a unique observation or insight. Today, English-language poets have adapted the haiku but have taken liberties with the subject matter and have often reduced the syllable count. Whether the traditional pattern is varied or not, however, the haiku must be short, simple, objective, clear, and (often) symbolic. The following anonymous haiku illustrates some of these qualities.

*Spun in High, Dark Clouds*

Spun in high, dark clouds,
Snow forms vast webs of white flakes
And drifts lightly down.

In the tradition of haiku, the subject is derived from nature, and the syllable pattern is 5–7–5. The central metaphor equates gathering snow with the webs of silkworms or spiders. To supply tension, the lines contrast "high" with "down" and "dark" with "white." Because of the enforced brevity, the diction is simple and, except for the word "forms," of English derivation (the word *form* was originally French). In addition, most of the words are monosyllabic, and through this means the poem fills the 17-syllable form with 16 words.

## There Are Additional but Less Significant Closed-Form Types

Many other closed forms have enjoyed long popularity. One of these, the **epigram**, is a short and witty poem that usually makes a humorous or satiric point. Epigrams are two to four lines long and are often written in couplets. The form was developed by the Roman poet Martial (ca. 40–103 C.E.) and has always been popular. Humorous and sometimes irreverent **epitaphs**, brief poems composed to mark the death of someone, can also be epigrams.

Another popular type is the **limerick**, a five-line form popularized by the English artist and humorist Edward Lear (1812–1888). Like the epigram, limericks are comic, their humor being reinforced by falling rhymes. Usually, they are bawdy.

Comic closed forms continue to be devised by enterprising writers. The **clerihew**, a two-couplet form invented in the late nineteenth century by Edmund Clerihew Bentley (1875–1956), is related to the epigram. A final illustration of closed-form humor is the **double dactyl**, devised in the 1960s by Anthony Hecht and Paul Pascal. The form is related to the epigram, limerick, and clerihew, and it has rules that govern the meter, line length, and specific topic material.

## Poets Use the Closed Form to Shape and Polish Meaning

Although many contemporary poets consider closed forms restrictive and even stultifying, the closed form has always provided both a framework and a challenge for poets to express new and fresh ideas, attitudes, and feelings. Let us look at the way Shakespeare uses the sonnet form to shape thoughts and emotions.

### WILLIAM SHAKESPEARE (1564–1616)

 ### Sonnet 116: Let Me Not to the Marriage of True Minds (1609)

Let me not to the marriage of true minds
Admit impediments.° Love is not love
Which alters when it alteration finds,
Or bends with the remover to remove:
Oh, no! it is an ever-fixéd mark,             5
That looks on tempests and is never shaken;
It is the star to every wandering bark,
Whose worth's unknown, although his height° be taken   *its altitude*
Love's not Time's fool,° though rosy lips and cheeks     *slave*
Within his° bending sickle's compass come;      *Time's* 10
Love alters not with his brief hours and weeks,
But bears it out even to the edge of doom.°    *the Last Judgment*
If this be error and upon me proved,
I never writ, nor no man ever loved.

---

°SONNET 116. 2 *impediments*: a reference to "The Order of Solemnization of Matrimony" in the Anglican Church's *Book of Common Prayer*: "I require that if either of you know of any impediment why ye may not be lawfully joined together in Matrimony, ye do now confess it."

## Questions

1. Describe the restrictions of this closed form. How is the poem's argument structured by the form?

**2.** What is the poem's meter? Rhyme scheme? Structure?

**3.** Describe the varying ideas about love explored in the three quatrains.

**4.** What does the concluding couplet contribute to the poem's argument about love?

Even if we did not know that the poem is Shakespeare's, we would recognize it as a Shakespearean sonnet. It is in iambic pentameter and contains three quatrains and a concluding couplet, rhyming *a b a b, c d c d, e f e f, g g*. The sonnet form provides the organization for the poem's argument—that real love is a "marriage of true minds" existing independent of earthly time and change. Each quatrain advances a new perspective on this idea.

This is not to say that Shakespeare exhausts the subject or that he wants to. The ideas in the third quatrain, for example, about how love transcends time, could be greatly expanded. A philosophical analysis of the topic might deal extensively with Platonic ideas about reality—whether it exists in *particulars* or *universals*. Similarly, the poem's very last line, if it were to become the topic of a prose discourse, might include the introduction of evidence about the poet's own writing, and also about many examples of human love. But the two lines are enough, granted the restrictions of the form, and more would be superfluous. One might add that most readers find Shakespeare's poem interesting and vital, while extensive philosophical discourses often drop into laps as readers fall asleep.

The closed poetic form therefore may be viewed as a complex consequence of poetic compression. No matter what form a poet chooses—couplet, sonnet, song, ballad, ode—that form imposes restrictions, and it therefore challenges and shapes the poet's thought. The poet of the closed form shares with all writers the need to make ideas seem logical and well supported, but the challenge of the form is to make all this happen *within the form itself.* The thought must be developed clearly and also fully, and there should be no lingering doubts once the poem is completed. The words must be the most fitting and exact ones that could be selected. When we look at good poems in the closed form, in short, we may be sure that they represent the ultimate degree of poetic thought, discipline, and skill.

## Open-Form Poetry

Among the closed forms, as we have seen, the ode is the form that gives poets great opportunity for variability and expansion. The ode is thus the closed form that is most nearly related, in spirit, to **open-form poetry**, but the open form eliminates the restrictions of the closed form. Each open-form poem is unique and unpredictable. Poetry of this type was once termed **free verse** (from the French *vers libre*) to signify its liberation from regular metrics and its embrace of spoken rhythms. But open-form poetry is not therefore disorganized or chaotic. Open-form poets have instead created new and original ways to arrange words and lines—new ways to express thoughts and feelings, and new ways to order poetic experience.

Poets writing in the open form attempt to fuse form and content by stressing speechlike rhythms, creating a natural and easy-flowing word order, altering and varying line lengths according to the importance of ideas, and creating emphasis through the control of shorter and longer pauses. They often isolate individual words, phrases, and clauses as single lines, freely emphasize their ideas through the manipulation of spaces separating words and sentences, and sometimes even break up individual words in separate lines to highlight their importance. Sometimes they create poems that look exactly like prose and that are printed in blocks and paragraphs instead of stanzas or lines, as with "Museum" by Robert Hass. Such **prose poems** rely on a progression of images and the cadences of language.

## Open-Form Poetry Is Free in Form and Variable in Content

An early example of open-form poetry is Walt Whitman's "Reconciliation." This poem was included in *Drum Taps*, a collection of 53 poems about the poet's reactions to Civil War battles in Virginia.

## WALT WHITMAN (1819–1892)

 ## Reconciliation (1865, 1881)

Word over all, beautiful as the sky,
Beautiful that war and all its deeds of carnage must in time be utterly lost,
That the hands of the sisters Death and Night incessantly softly wash again, and ever again,
    this soiled world;
For my enemy is dead, a man divine as myself is dead,
I look where he lies white-faced and still in the coffin—I draw near, 5
Bend down and touch lightly with my lips the white face in the coffin.

## Questions

1. How do individual lines, varying line lengths, punctuation, pauses, and cadences create rhythm and organize the images and ideas in this poem?
2. How do alliteration, assonance, and the repetition of words unify the poem and reinforce its content?
3. What is the "word" referred to in line 1? What does the speaker find "beautiful" about this "word" and the passage of time?
4. What instances of personification can you find? What do these personified figures do? What does the speaker do in lines 5–6? Why does he do this?

"Reconciliation" shows the power of open-form poetry. There is no dominant meter, rhyme scheme, or stanza pattern. Instead, Whitman uses individual lines and varying line lengths to organize and emphasize the images, ideas, and emotions. He also uses repetition, alliteration, and assonance to make internal line connections.

Without going into every aspect of the poem, one may note the unifying elements in the first few lines. The "word over all" (i.e., reconciliation, peace) is linked to the second line by the repetition of the words "beautiful" and "all," while "beautiful" is grammatically complemented by the clauses "that . . . lost" (line 2) and "That . . . world" (line 3). The reconciling word is thus connected to the image of the two personified figures, Death and Night, who "wash" war and carnage (bloodshed) out of "this soiled world."

In the third line, unity and emphasis are created through the repetition of "again" and the alliteration on the *ly* sound of "incessant*ly*" and "soft*ly*," the *s* sound in "*s*isters," "incessantly," "*s*oftly," and "*s*oil'd," and the *d* sound in "han*d*s," "*D*eath," "soil'*d*," and "Worl*d*." One may also note the unifying assonance patterns of *ih* in "*i*ts," "*i*n," "s*i*sters," "*i*ncessantly," and "th*i*s;" and *ay* in "sk*y*," "t*i*me," and "*Ni*ght." The pauses, or junctures, of the line create internal rhythms that coincide with the thought, "That the hands // of the sisters // Death and Night // incessantly softly // wash again and ever again // this soiled world."

This selective analysis demonstrates that open-form poetry creates its own unity. While some of the unifying elements, such as alliteration and assonance, are also a property of closed-form poetry, many are unique to poetry of the open form, such as the repetitions, the reliance on grammatical structures, and the control of rhythms. The concept of the open form is that the topic itself shapes the number of lines, the line lengths, and the physical appearance on the page. Unity is there—development is there—but the open form demands that there be as many shapes and forms as there are topics.

---

**VISUALIZING POETRY**

## Poetry and Artistic Expression: Visual Poetry, Concrete Poetry, and Prose Poems

---

Along with the fact that many poets have rejected traditional closed form patterns, they have moved in new directions with the open form. The idea has been to free poetry to follow a wide range of poetic shapes, including areas of experimentation. Poets have continued to express ideas about the topics we usually associate with poetry—which really means just about everything—but in addition, they have imaginatively invented new looks for their poems on the actual page. Some poets may indulge in creative playfulness by fashioning visual surprises, thus focusing on the medium itself, in which each poem starts its life, waiting patiently for readers. In fact, some poets give almost as much attention to their visual arrangement of letters, words, lines, and white space as they do to the content of their poems. To draw attention to particular thoughts, many poets may deliberately alter the spellings of certain words; or they may run a number of words together, without spaces between them, to set them apart; or they may abandon the traditional capitalization of each new line; or, for that matter, they may simply reject some or all capitalization. We may see some of these characteristics in E. E. Cummings's poem "Buffalo Bill's Defunct," in which Cummings uses stretched-out lines in contrast with shorter lines, runs successive words together, and varies the placement of line beginnings, all as the means of guiding readers to see, hear, and comprehend the poem in accordance with his wishes.

# E. E. CUMMINGS (1894–1962)

*For a photo, see Chapter 12, page 507 .*

 ## Buffalo Bill's Defunct° (1923)

Buffalo Bill's
defunct
  who used to
  ride a watersmooth-silver
     stallion               5
and break onetwothreefourfive pigeonsjustlikethat
         Jesus

he was a handsome man
      and what i want to know is
how do you like your blueeyed boy        10
Mister Death

---

°The poem has no title; it is usually referred to as "Portrait" or by its first two lines. Buffalo Bill (William F. Cody, 1846–1917) was an American plains-man, hunter, army scout, sharpshooter, and showman whose Wild West show began touring the world in 1883; he became a symbol of the Wild West.

## Questions

1. What is the effect of devoting a whole line to "Buffalo Bill's" (line 1), "defunct" (line 2), "stallion" (line 5), "Jesus" (line 7), and "Mister Death" (line 11)? How does this technique reflect and emphasize the content of the poem?

2. How does the typographical arrangement of line 6 contribute to the fusion of sound and sense? What other examples of this technique do you find?

3. Explain the denotations and connotations of *defunct*. What would be lost (or gained) by using the term *dead* or *deceased* instead?

4. To what extent is this poem a "portrait" of Buffalo Bill? What do we learn about him? Is the portrait respectful, mocking, or something in between?

A traditional aspect of poetry is **visual poetry**, also called **shaped verse** and, sometimes, **picture poetry**. In such a form, poets not only emphasize the idea and emotion of their subjects, but they also fashion their poems into a generalized or pictorial shape on the page. Poets can create visual poems that are pictures built up with words, lines, and spaces. Such visual poetry is not a recent development. The Chinese have been producing it for many generations, and there are surviving examples from ancient Greece. In the English Renaissance, many poets fashioned the lines of their poems to represent wings, altars, squares, triangles, stars, and the like. This type of poetry was often quite ingenious, and the figures were graphic extensions of traditional poetic images and symbols.

In reading visual and concrete poems, you should seek correspondences between images and poetic ideas. Describe the shape of the poem and the figures it resembles. Determine how varying line lengths, the placement of individual words and phrases, and the use of space all contribute to the visual effect. A superb example of traditional visual poetry is "Easter Wings," by the seventeenth-century poet George Herbert. "Easter Wings" is a religious poem that can be visualized as two differing but complementary shapes.

## GEORGE HERBERT (1593–1633)

### Easter Wings (1633)

Lord, who createdst man in wealth and store,°　　　　　　　　　*abundance*
　　Though foolishly he lost the same,
　　　　Decaying more and more
　　　　　　Till he became
5　　　　　　　Most poor:
　　　　　　With thee
　　　　　O let me rise
　　　As larks, harmoniously,
　　And sing this day thy victories:
10　Then shall the fall° further the flight in me.

My tender age in sorrow did I begin:
　　And still° with sicknesses and shame　　　　　　*always, constantly*
　　　　Thou didst so punish sin,
　　　　　That I became
15　　　　　　Most thin.
　　　　　　With thee
　　　　　Let me combine,
　　　And feel this day thy victory;°
　　For, if I imp° my wing on thine,
20　Affliction shall advance the flight in me.

---

°EASTER WINGS. 2, 10 *foolishly he lost; fall*: two references to the biblical account of how sin and death were introduced as a punishment for humankind after Adam and Eve disobeyed God in the Garden of Eden. 18 *victory*: I Corinthians 15:54–57. 19 *imp*: to repair a falcon's wing or tail by grafting on feathers.

## Questions

1. What does the poem look like when viewed straight on? When viewed sideways, with the left side at the top? How do these two images echo and emphasize the poem's content?
2. How does the typographical arrangement echo the sense? In lines 5 and 15, for example, how are typography, shape, and meaning fused?
3. What do lines 1–5 tell you about humanity's spiritual history, according to Herbert? What do lines 11–15 tell you about the speaker's spiritual state? How are these parallel?

In our own time, many poets have followed Herbert's precedent by creating shaped verse in which the visual image and the poetic meaning merge as separate aspects of one major idea. A unique shape for a recent poem is Charles Harper Webb's "The Shape of History." Let us see how Webb controls the lengths of lines to build his geometrical figure:

## CHARLES HARPER WEBB (b. 1952)

 **The Shape of History** (1995)

*Turning and turning in the widening gyre . . .°*

Today's paper is crammed full of news: pages and pages on the Somalia
Famine, the Balkan Wars, Gays in the Military. On this date a year ago,
only 1/365 of "The Year's Top Stories" happened. *Time* magazine fits a
decade into one thin retrospective. Barely enough occurred a century
ago to fill one sub-chapter in a high school text. 500 years ago, one                      5
or two things happened every 50 years. 5000 years ago, a city
was founded, a grain cultivated, a civilization toppled every
other century. Still farther back, the years march by in
groups like graduates at a big state university: 10,000 to
20,000 BC; 50,000–100,000 BC; 1–10 million BC.                                             10
Before that, things happened once an Era: Mam-
mals in the Cenozoic, Dinosaurs in the Meso-
zoic, Forests in the Paleozoic, Protozoans in
the Pre-Cambrian. Below that, at the
very base of time's twisting gyre, its                                                    15
cornucopia, its ram's-horn trum-
pet, its tornado tracking across
eternity, came what Christians call Creation, astro-
physicists call the Big                                                                  20
Bang. Then, for tril-
lions of years,
nothing at
all.

---

°*Turning . . . gyre*: See line 1 of Yeats's "The Second Coming," page 727.

## Questions

1. What shape does the poet give to history? How accurate is this shape?
2. How do the lengths of the first and final two lines graphically show how civilization has grown? What "top stories" are mentioned in the first few lines? How representative of modern news are these stories? How long will it take for such stories to be replaced by new, similar stories?
3. In the light of the epigraph by Yeats, what does the speaker apparently think will happen in the future?
4. Considering the content and the diminishing shape of the poem's twenty-four lines, what do you think is meant by "nothing at/all"?

A comparable visual poem is John Hollander's "Swan and Shadow." Notice that Hollander, in order to compose the top image and the bottom reflection he seeks, develops a creative pattern of lines and individual words. The pattern coheres grammatically, and it also functions constructively to create the visual picture, which is also dimensional. The connections here are skilful, and the finished poem shows a command over both poetic and graphic art.

## JOHN HOLLANDER (b. 1929)

 ### Swan and Shadow (1969)

```
                    Dusk
                  Above the
               water hang the
                           loud
5                           flies
                          Here
                         O so
                        gray
                       then
10            What                      A pale signal will appear
              When                      Soon before its shadow fades
              Where                     Here in this pool of opened eye
              In us          No Upon us As at the very edges
                  of where we take shape in the dark air
15                  this object bares its image awakening
                    ripples of recognition that will
                      brush darkness up into light
  even after this bird this hour both drift by atop the perfect sad instant now
                      already passing out of sight
20                  toward yet-untroubled reflection
                    this image bears its object darkening
                    into memorial shades Scattered bits of
                light           No of water Or something across
                water           Breaking up No Being regathered
25              soon              Yet by then a swan will have
                gone               Yes out of mind into what
                   vast
                    pale
                     hush
30                    of a
                       place
                        past
              sudden dark as
                 if a swan
35                 sang
```

## Questions

1. How effectively and consistently does the shape image reinforce the meaning?

2. What specific words, phrases, and lines are emphasized by the typographical arrangement? To what extent does this effect give added impact to the poem?

3. How well does the structure echo the verbal images of the poem?

**4.** Do you find Hollander's experiment with shaped verse as successful as Herbert's in "Easter Wings" (p. 654)? If so, demonstrate how it succeeds. If not, explain why.

Many patterns of visual form may be variable and, sometimes, surprising. William Heyen creates a unique form in his poem "Mantle," about his reflections about the brilliant professional career of Mickey Mantle, who is fondly remembered by sports fans as one of the superior home run sluggers in baseball history. Many students experience a great joy of discovery when they recognize the shape that Heyen is simulating here with his poetic stanzas.

## WILLIAM HEYEN (b. 1940)

 ### Mantle° (1980)

> Mantle ran so hard, they said,
> he tore his legs to pieces,
> What is this but spirit?
>
> 52 homers in '56, the triple crown.
> I was a high school junior, batting          5
> fourth behind him in a dream.
>
> I prayed for him to quit, before
> his lifetime dropped below .300.
> But he didn't, and it did.
>
> He makes Brylcreem commercials now,          10
> models with open mouths draped around him
> as they never were in Commerce, Oklahoma,
>
> where the sandy-haired, wide-shouldered boy
> stood up against his barn,
> lefty for an hour (Ruth, Gehrig),          15
>
> then righty (DiMaggio),
> as his father winged them in,
> and the future blew toward him,
>
> now a fastball, now a slow
> curve hanging          20
> like a model's smile.

---

°Mickey Mantle (1931–1995), a Yankee outfielder from 1951–1968. A switch hitter, he hit eighteen World Series home runs (a record) and 536 career home runs. He was the American League's most valuable player in 1956, the year he won the triple crown (line 4).

## Questions

**1.** Describe the shape of the poem, being careful to study the last stanza. Why is this shape appropriate for a famous baseball player?

**2.** How does the poet use Mantle as a symbol in this poem?

**3.** Who are Ruth, Gehrig, and DiMaggio? In what ways are they like Mantle?

Just as some visual art is abstract and suggestive, rather than pictorial, so also may be the forms created by writers of visual poems. Such a poem is May Swenson's "Women," which is suggestive of feminine rhythm and movement. It is almost as though the poem itself is a dancing and gently swaying figure.

### MAY SWENSON (1919–1989)

 **Women** (1968)

```
Women                    Or they
    should be                should be
        pedestals                little horses
            moving                   those wooden
 5              pedestals                sweet
                moving                   oldfashioned
                to the                   painted
                motions                  rocking
                of men                   horses
10              the gladdest things in the toyroom
                The                          feelingly
                pegs                         and then
                of their                     unfeelingly
                ears                         To be
15              so familiar                  joyfully
                and dear                     ridden
                to the trusting              rockingly
                fists                        ridden until
            To be chafed        the restored
20          egos dismount and the legs stride away
            Immobile                willing
                sweetlipped              to be set
                sturdy                   into motion
                and smiling              Women
25              women                    should be
                should always            pedestals
                be waiting               to men
```

## Questions

**1.** Is this poem an instance of closed-form, open-form, or visual poetry? In what different ways or sequences can it be read? How do the different sequences change the meaning?

**2.** How well does the image of the poem reinforce its meaning? Would the effect be different if the columns of words were straight instead of undulating?

**3.** To what extent do repetition and alliteration help to organize the poem and underscore its sense? Note especially *w, m, f, r,* and *s* sounds.

**4.** What does this poem *say* that women should be? Does it mean what it says? How are men characterized? In what way is this poem ironic?

Another and less graphic type of free verse is called the "prose poem." This phrase may seem like a contradiction in terms, but the idea that poets can write poems in the shape of prose is not surprising, granted that many modern poets are committed to principles of poetic freedom.[1] Some topics might possibly be more suitable to a prose form because they may seem less connected to poetry than to local or international news events, or they may involve the poet in reflections about politics, or about moral or religious matters. "Museum," by Robert Hass, is such a poem, in which the speaker lays out a tranquil scene and draws an optimistic conclusion. But sometimes the subject may seem problematic, and therefore more appropriate for a less formal treatment than poetry might offer. Above all, however, the major characteristic of the prose poem is that it should have the compactness and intensity of poetry, even though on the page, from a distance, it may at first seem just like any ordinary prose paragraph. Carolyn Forché creates such poetic intensity in her prose poem "The Colonel."

## CAROLYN FORCHÉ (b. 1950)

 ## The Colonel (1978)

What you have heard is true. I was in his house. His wife carried a tray of coffee and sugar. His daughter filed her nails, his son went out for the night. There were daily papers, pet dogs, a pistol on the cushion beside him. The moon swung bare on its black cord over the house. On the television was a cop show. It was in English. Broken bottles were embedded in the walls around the house to scoop the kneecaps from a man's legs or cut his hands to lace. On the windows there ⁵ were gratings like those in liquor stores. We had dinner, rack of lamb, good wine, a gold bell was on the table for calling the maid. The maid brought green mangoes, salt, a type of bread. I was asked how I enjoyed the country. There was a brief commercial in Spanish. His wife took everything away. There was some talk then of how difficult it had become to govern. The parrot said hello on the terrace. The colonel told it to shut up, and pushed himself from the table. My friend ¹⁰ said to me with eyes: say nothing. The colonel returned with a sack used to bring groceries home. He spilled many human ears on the table. They were like dried peach halves. There is no other way to say this. He took one of them in his hands, shook it in our faces, dropped it into a water glass. It came alive there. I am tired of fooling around he said. As for the rights of anyone, tell your people they can go fuck themselves. He swept the ears to the floor with his arm and ¹⁵ held the last of his wine in the air. Something for your poetry, no? he said. Some of the ears on the floor caught this scrap of his voice. Some of the ears on the floor were pressed to the ground.

## Questions

**1.** Why does the poet use the prose poem form for this poem?
**2.** What is the character of the colonel? How can he be gracious, and then abusive, at the same time? What atrocities has he committed or ordered committed?

---

[1]See David Lehman, ed., *Great American Prose Poems: From Poe to the Present* (New York: Scribner, 2003).

**3.** Why does the speaker include details about the walls about the house? What do the walls show about the mentality of those within the walls? Explain the meaning of the last sentence.

As you explore modern poems, you will regularly encounter many different forms. Most poems will appear to be no more than slight variations of traditional poetic lines, but many will stretch and alter normal and expected linear patterns. And some will aim at fusing words and pictures, such as those we have examined briefly here. Modern writers seek to explore ideas and to blend their new thoughts with the poetic medium of new and original patterns of development. In addition to the poets mentioned here, many other modern poets have worked similarly with free forms. Some of these poets, included elsewhere in this volume, are Allan Ginsberg, Robinson Jeffers, Marge Piercy, Alberto Rios, Sonya Sanchez, and C. K. Williams.

### Poems for Study

# ELIZABETH BISHOP (1911–1979)

 **One Art** (1976)

The art of losing isn't hard to master;
so many things seem filled with the intent
to be lost that their loss is no disaster.

Lose something every day. Accept the fluster
of lost door keys, the hour badly spent.                    5
The art of losing isn't hard to master.

Then practice losing farther, losing faster;
places, and names, and where it was you meant
to travel. None of these will bring disaster.

I lost my mother's watch. And look! my last, or          10
next-to-last, of three loved houses went.
The art of losing isn't hard to master.

I lost two cities, lovely ones. And, vaster,
some realms I owned, two rivers, a continent.
I miss them, but it wasn't a disaster.                       15

—Even losing you (the joking voice, a gesture
I love) I shan't have lied. It's evident
the art of losing's not too hard to master
though it may look like (*Write* it!) like disaster.

## Questions

1. This poem is written in a traditional closed form called the villanelle (originally an Italian peasant song), which was developed in France during the Middle Ages. A villanelle is nineteen lines long. Fairly strict rules govern the length and structure of stanzas, the rhyme scheme, and the repetition of complete lines. Try to formulate these rules. For comparison, see Roethke's "The Waking" and Thomas's "Do Not Go Gentle into That Good Night."

2. On what idea is the poem based? What evidence does the speaker produce about losing? What feelings does she express about her losses?

3. How could the speaker have lost "two cities"? What other things has she lost that justify her claim that "the art of losing isn't hard to master"? What might she mean by having lost the "you" to whom the poem is addressed?

## BILLY COLLINS (b. 1941)

*For a photo, see Chapter 11, page 456.*

## Sonnet (1999)

All we need is fourteen lines, well, thirteen now,
and after this next one just a dozen
to launch a little ship on love's storm-tossed seas,
then only ten more left like rows of beans.
5    How easily it goes unless you get Elizabethan
and insist the iambic bongos must be played
and rhymes positioned at the ends of lines,
one for every station of the cross.
But hang on here while we make the turn
10   into the final six where all will be resolved,
where longing and heartache will find an end,
where Laura will tell Petrarch to put down his pen,
take off those crazy medieval tights,
blow out the lights, and come at last to bed.

### Questions

1. Why is this poem amusing? What makes it amusing?
2. What is the effect of lines 6 and 7? Why does the speaker refer to "every station of the cross" in line 8?
3. What is the "little ship" that is to be launched on "love's storm-tossed seas"? To what tradition of the sonnet form is this a reference?
4. Why does the poet conclude the poem with a description of a scene between Petrarch and Laura?

## JOHN DRYDEN (1631–1700)

## To the Memory of Mr. Oldham° (1684)

Farewell, too little and too lately known,
Whom I began to think and call my own:
For sure our souls were near allied, and thine
Cast in the same poetic mold with mine.
5    One common note on either lyre did strike,
And knaves and fools we both abhorred alike.
To the same goal did both our studies drive;
The last set out the soonest did arrive.
Thus Nisus° fell upon the slipp'ry place,

---

°John Oldham (1653–1683) was a young poet whom Dryden admired.  9 *Nisus*: a character in Virgil's *Aeneid* who slipped in a pool of blood while running a race, thus allowing his best friend to win.

While his young friend performed and won the race. 10
O early ripe! to thy abundant store
What could advancing age have added more?
It might (what nature never gives the young)
Have taught the numbers of thy native tongue.
But satire needs not those, and wit will shine 15
Through the harsh cadence of a rugged line;
A noble error, and but seldom made,
When poets are by too much force betrayed.
Thy gen'rous fruits, though gathered ere their prime,
Still showed a quickness; and maturing time 20
But mellows what we write to the dull sweets of rhyme.
Once more, hail and farewell;° farewell, thou young.
But ah too short, Marcellus° of our tongue;
Thy brows with ivy and with laurels° bound;
But fate and gloomy night encompass thee around. 25

°22 *hail and farewell*: an echo of the Latin phrase "ave atque vale" spoken by gladiators about to fight. 23 *Marcellus*: a Roman general who was adopted by the Emperor Augustus as his successor but died at the age of twenty. 24 *laurels*: a plant sacred to Apollo, the Greek god of poetry; the traditional prize given to poets is a wreath of laurel.

## Questions

1. What is the meter of this poem? Rhyme scheme? Closed form? How does the form control the tempo? Why is this tempo appropriate?

2. What does the speaker reveal about himself in lines 1–10? About Oldham? About his relationship with Oldham? What did the two have in common?

3. What is the effect of Dryden's frequent classical allusions? What pairs of rhyming words most effectively clinch ideas?

### T. S. ELIOT (1888–1965)

*For a photo, see Chapter 13, page 539.*

 **Macavity: The Mystery Cat** (1939)

Macavity's a Mystery Cat: he's called the Hidden Paw—
For he's the master criminal who can defy the Law.
He's the bafflement of Scotland Yard, the Flying Squad's despair:
For when they reach the scene of the crime—*Macavity's not there!*

Macavity, Macavity, there's no one like Macavity, 5
He's broken every human law, he breaks the law of gravity.
His powers of levitation would make a fakir stare,
And when you reach the scene of crime—*Macavity's not there!*
You may seek him in the basement, you may look up in the air—
But I tell you once and once again, *Macavity's not there!* 10

Macavity's a ginger cat, he's very tall and thin;
You would know him if you saw him, for his eyes are sunken in.
His brow is deeply lined with thought, his head is highly domed;
His coat is dusty from neglect, his whiskers are uncombed.
15  He sways his head from side to side, with movements like a snake;
And when you think he's half asleep, he's always wide awake.

Macavity, Macavity, there's no one like Macavity,
For he's a fiend in feline shape, a monster of depravity.
You may meet him in a by-street, you may see him in the square—
20  But when a crime's discovered, then *Macavity's not there!*

He's outwardly respectable. (They say he cheats at cards.)
And his footprints are not found in any file of Scotland Yard's.
And when the larder's looted, or the jewel-case is rifled,
Or when the milk is missing, or another Peke's been stifled,°
25  Or the greenhouse glass is broken, and the trellis past repair—
Ay, there's the wonder of the thing! *Macavity's not there!*

And when the Foreign Office find a Treaty's gone astray,
Or the Admiralty lose some plans and drawings by the way,
There may be a scrap of paper in the hall or on the stair—
30  But it's useless to investigate—*Macavity's not there!*

And when the loss has been disclosed, the Secret Service say:
"It *must* have been Macavity!"—but he's a mile away.
You'll be sure to find him resting, or a-licking of his thumbs,
Or engaging in doing complicated long division sums.

35  Macavity, Macavity, there's no one like Macavity,
There never was a Cat of such deceitfulness and suavity.
He always has an alibi, and one or two to spare:
At whatever time the deed took place—MACAVITY WASN'T THERE!
And they say that all the Cats whose wicked deeds are widely known
40  (I might mention Mungojerrie, I might mention Griddlebone)
Are nothing more than agents for the Cat who all the time
Just controls their operations: the Napoleon of Crime!

---

°24 *Peke's been stifled*: A Pekinese dog (a small animal, with silky hair) has been found dead.

## Questions

1. What are some of Macavity's major "crimes" as a master criminal and "mystery cat"? How, if the "crimes" had been attributed to a human being, would they be grievous wrongs? Since they are attributed to a cat, how do they add to the comic qualities of the poem?

2. What is the basic metrical foot of the poem? How many feet are contained in each of the lines? What is the norm?

3. Once you begin reading and getting into the lines, what new kind of pattern emerges? How many major stresses appear in each line? In light of the nature of the poem. how is the dipodic rhythm appropriate?

## ROBERT FROST (1874–1963)

*For a photo, see Chapter 18, page 748.*

 ## Desert Places (1936)

Snow falling and night falling fast, oh, fast
In a field I looked into going past,
And the ground almost covered smooth in snow,
But a few weeds and stubble showing last.

The woods around it have it—it is theirs.                                    5
All animals are smothered in their lairs.
I am too absent-spirited to count;
The loneliness includes me unawares.

And lonely as it is that loneliness
Will be more lonely ere it will be less—                                     10
A blanker whiteness of benighted snow
With no expression, nothing to express.

They cannot scare me with their empty spaces
Between stars—on stars where no human race is.
I have it in me so much nearer home                                          15
To scare myself with my own desert places.

## Questions

1. What is the meter? The rhyme scheme? The form?

2. What setting and situation are established in lines 1–4? What does the snow affect here? What does it affect in lines 5–8? In lines 9–12?

3. What different kinds of "desert places" is this poem about? Which kind is the most important? Most frightening?

4. How does the type of rhyme (rising or falling) change in the last stanza? How does this change affect the tone and impact of the poem?

5. How does the stanzaic pattern of this poem organize the progression of the speaker's thoughts, feelings, and conclusions?

## ALLEN GINSBERG (1926–1997)

 ## A Supermarket in California (1955)

What thoughts I have of you tonight, Walt Whitman,° for
I walked down the sidestreets under the trees with a headache
self-conscious looking at the full moon.
    In my hungry fatigue, and shopping for images, I went
into the neon fruit supermarket, dreaming of your
5       enumerations!°
    What peaches and what penumbras! Whole families
shopping at night! Aisles full of husbands! Wives in the
avocados, babies in the tomatoes!—and you, Garcia Lorca,° what
were you doing down by the watermelons?

10   I saw you, Walt Whitman, childless, lonely old grubber,
poking among the meats in the refrigerator and eyeing the grocery boys.
    I heard you asking questions of each: Who killed the pork
chops? What price bananas? Are you my Angel?
    I wandered in and out of the brilliant stacks of cans
15 following you, and followed in my imagination by the store detective.
    We strode down the open corridors together in our solitary
fancy tasting artichokes, possessing every frozen delicacy, and
never passing the cashier.

    Where are we going, Walt Whitman? The doors close in
20 an hour. Which way does your beard point tonight?
    (I touch your book and dream of our odyssey in the supermarket
and feel absurd.)
    Will we walk all night through solitary streets? The trees
add shade to shade, lights out in the houses, we'll both be lonely.

25   Will we stroll dreaming of the lost America of love past blue
automobiles in driveways, home to our silent cottage?
    Ah, dear father, graybeard, lonely old courage-teacher,
what America did you have when Charon° quit poling his ferry
and you got out on a smoking bank and stood watching the
30 boat disappear on the black waters of Lethe?°

---

°1 *Walt Whitman*: American poet (1819–1892) who experimented with open forms and significantly influenced the development of twentieth-century poetry. 5 *enumerations*: Many of Whitman's poems contain long lists. 8 *Garcia Lorca*: Spanish surrealist poet and playwright (1896–1936) whose later poetry became progressively more like prose. 28 *Charon*: boatman in Greek mythology who ferried the souls of the dead across the river Styx into Hades, the underworld. 30 *Lethe*: the river of forgetfulness in Hades. The dead drank from this river and forgot their former lives.

## Questions

1. Where is the speaker? What is he doing? What is his condition?
2. What effect is produced by placing Whitman and Lorca in the market?

3. To what extent do we find Whitman-like enumerations in this work? What is the effect of such enumerations?
4. Why is this a poem? What poetic devices are employed here? To what extent might it make more sense to consider this prose rather than poetry?

# NIKKI GIOVANNI (b. 1943)

## Nikki-Rosa (1968)

childhood remembrances are always a drag
if you're Black
you always remember things like living in Woodlawn°
with no inside toilet
and if you become famous or something                                    5
they never talk about how happy you were to have your mother
all to yourself and
how good the water felt when you got your bath from one of those
big tubs that folk in chicago barbecue in
and somehow when you talk about home                                    10
it never gets across how much you
understood their feelings
as the whole family attended meetings about Hollydale
and even though you remember
your biographers never understand                                      15
your father's pain as he sells his stock
and another dream goes
and though you're poor it isn't poverty that
concerns you
and though they fought a lot                                           20
it isn't your father's drinking that makes any difference
but only that everybody is together and you
and your sister have happy birthdays and very good christmasses
and I really hope no white person ever has cause to write about me
because they never understand Black love is Black wealth and they'll   25
probably talk about my hard childhood and never understand that
all the while I was quite happy

---

°3 *Woodlawn*: a predominantly black suburb of Cincinnati, Ohio.

## Questions

1. To what extent do individual lines, caesurae, and cadences create a rhythm and reinforce the sense of this poem?
2. What points does the speaker make about childhood in general, the childhoods of blacks, and her own childhood?
3. What ideas about the ways in which whites understand or misunderstand blacks does this poem explore?

## ROBERT HASS (b. 1941)

## Museum (1989)

On the morning of the Käthe Kollwitz° exhibit, a young man and woman come into the museum restaurant. She is carrying a baby; he carries the air-freight edition of the Sunday *New York Times*. She sits in a high-backed wicker chair, cradling the infant in her arms. He fills a tray with fresh fruit, rolls, and coffee in white cups and brings it to the table. His hair is tousled, her
5  eyes are puffy. They look like they were thrown down into sleep and then yanked out of it like divers coming up for air. He holds the baby. She drinks coffee, scans the front page, butters a roll and eats it in their little corner in the sun. After a while, she holds the baby. He reads the *Book Review* and eats some fruit. Then he holds the baby while she finds the section of the paper she wants and eats fruit and smokes. They've hardly exchanged a look. Meanwhile, I
10  have fallen in love with this equitable arrangement, and with the baby who cooperates by sleeping. All around them are faces Käthe Kollwitz carved in wood of people with no talent or capacity for suffering who are suffering the numbest kinds of pain: hunger, helpless terror. But this young couple is reading the Sunday paper in the sun, the baby is sleeping, the green has begun to emerge from the rind of the cantaloupe, and everything seems possible.

---

°1 *Käthe Kollwitz*: Kollwitz (1867–1945) was a German artist well known for her sculptures and engravings portraying the misery of poverty and war.

## Questions

1. Does this poem contain material that you ordinarily think of as poetic? What seems "poetic"? "Unpoetic"? Why?

2. Why does Hass not present the poem in lines? On what principle (topical, grammatical) might you set it up in line form? How might its being in lines change the way you read it as well as see it?

3. How does the poem contrast the young couple and their baby with the art of Käthe Kollwitz?

4. In the light of this poem, how seriously should we take the final statement ("and everything seems possible")?

## GEORGE HERBERT (1593–1633)

## Virtue° (1633)

Sweet day, so cool, so calm, so bright,
The bridal of the earth and sky:
The dew shall weep thy fall tonight;
　　For thou must die.

5  Sweet rose, whose hue, angry° and brave,°　　　　　　　　　*red; splendid*
Bids the rash° gazer wipe his eye:
Thy root is ever in its grave,
　　And thou must die.

---

°The title can allude to (*a*) divine Power operating both outside and inside an individual; (*b*) a characteristic quality or property; (*c*) conformity to divine and moral laws.  6 *rash*: eager or sympathetic.

Sweet spring, full of sweet days and roses,
10  A box where sweets° compacted lie:  *perfumes*  10
My music shows ye have your closes, °
    And all must die.

Only a sweet and virtuous soul,
Like seasoned timber, never gives;°
15  But though the whole world turn to coal,°  15
    Then chiefly lives.

---

°11 *closes*: A *close* is the conclusion of a musical composition. 14 *never gives*: i.e., never gives in, never deteriorates and collapses (like rotted timber). 15 *turn to coal*: the burned-out residue of the earth and universe after the universal fire on Judgment Day.

## Questions

1. What is the rhyme scheme of this poem? The meter? The form?
2. What points does the speaker make about the day, the rose, spring, and the "sweet and virtuous soul"?

## GERARD MANLEY HOPKINS (1844–1889)

*For a photo, see Chapter 13, page 544.*

##  God's Grandeur (1877)

The world is charged with the grandeur of God.
    It will flame out, like shining from shook foil;
    It gathers to a greatness, like the ooze of oil
Crushed. Why do men then now not reck his rod?°
Generations have trod, have trod, have trod;  5
    And all is seared with trade; bleared, smeared with toil;
    And wears man's smudge and shares man's smell: the soil
Is bare now, nor can foot feel, being shod.
And for all this, nature is never spent;
    There lives the dearest freshness deep down things;  10
And though the last lights off the black West went
    Oh, morning, at the brown brink eastward, springs—
Because the Holy Ghost over the bent
    World broods with warm breast and with ah! bright wings.

---

°4 *reck his rod*: God as king holds a scepter, making official laws through scriptures which people ("men") disobey.

## Questions

1. What is the contrast between the assertions in lines 1–4 and 5–8 (the octave)? How do lines 9–14 (the sestet) develop out of this contrast?
2. Analyze Hopkins's use of alliteration. What alliterative patterns occur? How do these affect meter and emphasis? On the basis of your analysis, describe "sprung rhythm" as used by Hopkins.
3. What instances of assonance, repetitions, and internal rhyme do you find?

**JOHN HALL INGHAM** (1860–CA. 1931)

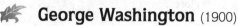 George Washington (1900)

This was the man God gave us when the hour
Proclaimed the dawn of Liberty begun;
Who dared a deed and died when it was done
Patient in triumph, temperate in power,—
5    Not striving like the Corsican° to tower
To heaven, nor like great Philip's greater son°
To win the world and weep for worlds unwon,
Or lose the star to revel in the flower.
The lives that serve the eternal verities
10   Alone do mold mankind. Pleasure and pride
Sparkle awhile and perish, as the spray
Smoking across the crests of cavernous seas
Is impotent to hasten or delay
The everlasting surges of the tide.

---

°5 *Corsican*: Napoleon I (1769–1821), General and Emperor of France from 1804–1814. 7 *great Philip's greater son*: Alexander the Great, King of Macedonia (356–323 B.C.E.), who conquered all the known world in the short years of his reign. There was a tradition, derived from Plutarch's *Life*, that Alexander wept because there were no more worlds for him to conquer.

## Questions

1. For what reasons does the poet extoll Washington? Explain the symbolism of line 8, "Or lose the star to revel in the flower." What is the sense of the simile in the last five lines of the poem?

2. Trace the patterning of alliteration and assonance in the poem. How effectively does the poet use these devices? Are they appropriate, or might some think they are overly obvious?

3. In line 3 there occurs a pattern called *consonance*, in which words have the same beginning and ending consonant sounds ("*dared* a *deed* and *died*"). Why do you think the poet includes this pattern here?

**JOHN KEATS** (1795–1821)

*For a portrait, see Chapter 14, page 562.*

 Ode to a Nightingale (1819)

1

My heart aches, and a drowsy numbness pains
    My sense, as though of hemlock° I had drunk,                    *a poisonous herb*
Or emptied some dull opiate to the drains
    One minute past, and Lethe-wards° had sunk:

---

°4 *Lethe-wards*: toward the river of forgetfulness in Hades, the underworld of Greek mythology.

'Tis not through envy of thy happy lot,          5
   But being too happy in thine happiness,—
      That thou, light-winged Dryad° of the trees,
         In some melodious plot
      Of beechen green, and shadows numberless,
   Singest of summer in full-throated ease.          10


2

O, for a draught of vintage! that hath been
   Cool'd a long age in the deep-delved earth,
Tasting of Flora° and the country green,
   Dance, and Provençal song, and sunburnt mirth!
O for a beaker full of the warm South,          15
   Full of the true, the blushful Hippocrene,°
      With beaded bubbles winking at the brim,
         And purple-stainèd mouth;
      That I might drink, and leave the world unseen,
   And with thee fade away into the forest dim:          20


3

Fade far away, dissolve, and quite forget
   What thou among the leaves hast never known,
The weariness, the fever, and the fret
   Here, where men sit and hear each other groan;
Where palsy shakes a few, sad, last gray hairs,          25
   Where youth grows pale, and spectre-thin, and dies;
      Where but to think is to be full of sorrow
         And leaden-eyed despairs,
      Where Beauty cannot keep her lustrous eyes,
   Or new Love pine at them beyond to-morrow.          30


4

Away! away! for I will fly to thee,
   Not charioted by Bacchus° and his pards,°          *leopards*
But on the viewless wings of Poesy,°          *poetry*
   Though the dull brain perplexes and retards:
Already with thee! tender is the night,          35
   And haply the Queen-Moon is on her throne,
      Cluster'd around by all her starry Fays;°          *fairies*
         But here there is no light,
      Save what from heaven is with the breezes blown
   Through verdurous glooms and winding mossy ways.          40

°7 *Dryad*: in Greek mythology, a semidivine tree spirit. 13 *Flora*: the Roman goddess of flowers. 16 *Hippocrene*: the fountain of the Muses on Mt. Helicon in Greek mythology; the phrase thus refers to both the waters of poetic inspiration and a cup of wine. 32 *Bacchus*: the Greek god of wine. See Chapter 21.

**5**

I cannot see what flowers are at my feet,
   Nor what soft incense hangs upon the boughs,
But, in embalmed° darkness, guess each sweet                    *fragrant*
   Wherewith the seasonable month endows
45  The grass, the thicket, and the fruit-tree wild;
     White hawthorn, and the pastoral eglantine;°            *honeysuckle*
       Fast fading violets cover'd up in leaves;
          And mid-May's eldest child,
       The coming musk-rose, full of dewy wine,
50  The murmurous haunt of flies on summer eves.

**6**

Darkling° I listen; and, for many a time                *in the dark*
   I have been half in love with easeful Death,
Call'd him soft names in many a musèd rhyme,
   To take into the air my quiet breath;
55  Now more than ever seems it rich to die,
   To cease upon the midnight with no pain,
     While thou art pouring forth thy soul abroad
       In such an ecstasy!
     Still wouldst thou sing, and I have ears in vain—
60     To thy high requiem become a sod.

**7**

Thou wast not born for death, immortal Bird!
   No hungry generations tread thee down;
The voice I hear this passing night was heard
   In ancient days by emperor and clown:
65  Perhaps the self-same song that found a path
   Through the sad heart of Ruth,° when, sick for home,
     She stood in tears amid the alien corn;°        *wheat, grain*
       The same that oft-times hath
     Charm'd magic casements, opening on the foam
70     Of perilous seas, in faery lands forlorn.

**8**

Forlorn! the very word is like a bell
   To toll me back from thee to my sole self!
Adieu! the fancy° cannot cheat so well              *imagination*
   As she is fam'd to do, deceiving elf.
75  Adieu! adieu! thy plaintive anthem fades
   Past the near meadows, over the still stream,
     Up the hill-side; and now 'tis buried deep
       In the next valley-glades:
     Was it a vision, or a waking dream?
80     Fled is that music:—Do I wake or sleep?

---

°66 *Ruth*: the widow of Boaz in the biblical Book of Ruth.

## Questions

1. Formulate the structure (meter of each line and rhyme scheme) of the stanzas. What traditional form is employed here?
2. What is the speaker's mental and emotional state in stanza 1? What similes are employed to describe this condition?
3. What does the speaker want in stanza 2? Whom does he want to join? Why? From what aspects of the world (stanza 3) does he want to escape?
4. How do the speaker's mood and perspective change in stanza 4? How does he achieve this transition? What characterizes the world that the speaker enters in stanza 5? What senses are employed to describe this world?
5. What does the speaker establish about the nightingale's song in stanza 7? What does the song come to symbolize?

## CLAUDE McKAY (1890–1948)

 **In Bondage** (1922)

I would be wandering in distant fields
Where man, and bird, and beast, live leisurely,
And the old earth is kind, and ever yields
Her goodly gifts to all her children free;
Where life is fairer, lighter, less demanding,
And boys and girls have time and space for play
Before they come to years of understanding—
Somewhere I would be singing, far away.
For life is greater than the thousand wars
Men wage for it in their insatiate lust,
And will remain like the eternal stars,
When all that shines to-day is drift and dust.

But I am bound with you in your mean graves,
O black men, simple slaves of ruthless slaves.

## Questions

1. What is the meter of this poem? The rhyme scheme? The form? To what extent does the form organize the speaker's thoughts?
2. Lines 1–8 present a conditional (rather than actual) situation that the speaker desires. What word signals this nature? What is the speaker's wish?
3. What point does the speaker make about life in lines 9–12?
4. How does the couplet undermine the rest of the poem? What single word conveys this reversal? How effectively do the rhymes clinch the poem's meaning? What is the speaker telling us about the lives of African Americans?

## HERMAN MELVILLE (1819–1891)

 ### Shiloh: A Requiem° (1862)

Skimming lightly, wheeling still,
    The swallows fly low
Over the field in clouded days,
    The forest field of Shiloh—
5  Over the field where April rain
Solaced the parched one stretched in pain
Through the pause of night
That followed the Sunday fight
    Around the church of Shiloh—
10  The church so lone, the log-built one,
That echoed to many a parting groan
    And natural prayer
Of dying foemen mingled there—
Foemen at morn, but friends at eve—
15  Fame or country least their care:
(What like a bullet can undeceive!)
    But now they lie low,
While over them the swallows skim,
    And all is hushed at Shiloh.

°One of the earliest major battles of the Civil War, the Battle of Shiloh, in southwestern Tennessee, also called the Battle of Pittsburg Landing, took place in April 1862. It was a remarkably bloody but substantially indecisive conflict, with 10,000 casualties on each side.

## Questions

1. Why is it difficult to determine the dominant meter in this poem? What do you think the dominant meter is? What types of metrical feet can you find here?

2. What connection can you make between the indeterminate meter and Melville's subject?

3. What rhymes does Melville create for "Shiloh"? What is the effect of these rhymes? What other rhymes does Melville introduce? How do these rhymes link together his ideas?

4. What irony is expressed in line 14: "Foemen at morn, but friends at eve"?

## JOHN MILTON (1608–1674)

 ### On His Blindness (When I Consider How My Light Is Spent)° (1655)

When I consider how my light is spent
    Ere half my days, in this dark world and wide,
    And that one talent° which is death to hide,

°Milton began to go blind in the late 1640s and was completely blind by 1651. 3 *talent*: both a skill and a reference to the talents discussed in the parable in Matthew 25:14–30.

Lodged with me useless, though my soul more bent
To serve therewith my Maker, and present                                    5
  My true account, lest he returning chide;
  "Doth God exact day-labor, light denied?"
  I fondly° ask; but Patience to prevent°              *foolishly; forestall*
That murmur, soon replies, "God doth not need
  Either man's work or his own gifts; who best           10
  Bear his mild yoke, they serve him best. His state
Is kingly. Thousands at his bidding speed
  And post o'er land and ocean without rest;
  They also serve who only stand and wait."

## Questions

1. What is the meter of this poem? The rhyme scheme? The closed form?
2. To what extent do the two major divisions of this form organize the poem's ideas?
3. What problem is raised in the octave? What are the speaker's complaints? Who is the speaker in the sestet? How are the earlier conflicts resolved?
4. Explore the word *talent* and relate its various meanings to the poem as a whole.

## ALEXANDER POPE (1685–1744)

## From An Essay on Man, Epistle I, Lines 17–90 (1734)

  I. Say first, of God above, or man° below,                    *men; humanity*
What can we reason but from what we know?
Of man, what see we but his station here,
From which to reason, or to which refer?
Through worlds unnumbered though the God be known,        5
'Tis ours to trace him° only in our own.                                *God*
He who through vast immensity can pierce,
See worlds on worlds compose one universe,
Observe how system into system runs,
What other planets circle other suns,                         10
What varied being peoples every star,
May tell why Heaven has made us as we are.
But of this frame the bearings and the ties,
The strong connections, nice dependencies,
Gradations just, has thy pervading soul                       15
Looked through? or can a part contain the whole?
  Is the great chain that draws all to agree,
And drawn supports, upheld by God, or thee?
  II. Presumptuous man! the reason wouldst thou find,
Why formed so weak, so little, and so blind?                  20
First, if thou canst, the harder reason guess,
Why formed no weaker, blinder, and no less!
Ask of thy mother earth, why oaks are made
Taller or stronger than the weeds they shade!

25 Or ask of yonder argent fields above,
Why Jove's satellites are less than Jove!
   Of systems possible, if 'tis confessed
That wisdom infinite must form the best,
Where all must full or not coherent be,
30 And all that rises, rise in due degree;
Then, in the scale of reasoning life, 'tis plain,
There must be, somewhere, such a rank as man:
And all the question (wrangle e'er so long)
Is only this, if God has placed him wrong.
35    Respecting man, whatever wrong we call,
May, must be right, as relative to all.
In human works, though labored on with pain,
A thousand movements scarce one purpose gain;
In God's, one single can its end produce;
40 Yet serves to second too some other use.
So man, who here seems principal alone,
Perhaps acts second to some sphere unknown,
Touches some wheel, or verges to some goal;
'Tis but a part we see, and not a whole.
45    When the proud steed shall know why man restrains
His fiery course, or drives him o'er the plains:
When the dull ox, why now he breaks the clod,
Is now a victim, and now Egypt's god:
Then shall man's pride and dullness comprehend
50 His actions', passions', being's, use and end;
Why doing, suffering, checked, impelled; and why
This hour a slave, the next a deity.
   Then say not man's imperfect, Heaven in fault;
Say rather, man's as perfect as he ought:
55 His knowledge measured to his state and place;
His time a moment, and a point his space.
If to be perfect in a certain sphere,
What matter, soon or late, or here or there?
The blessed today is as completely so,
60 As who began a thousand years ago.
   III. Heaven from all creatures hides the book of fate,
All but the page prescribed, their present state;
From brutes what men, from men what spirits know,
Or who could suffer being here below?
65 The lamb thy riot dooms to bleed today,
Had he thy reason, would he skip and play?
Pleased to the last, he crops the flowery food,
And licks the hand just raised to shed his blood.
Oh blindness to the future! kindly given,
70 That each may fill the circle marked by Heaven:
Who sees with equal eye, as God of all,
A hero perish, or a sparrow fall,
Atoms or systems into ruin hurled,
And now a bubble burst, and now a world.

## Questions

1. What is the topic of the passage? How appropriate is it to present such material in the form of couplets? How does Pope use the couplet to develop his thought in the poem?

2. Analyze five or six of the couplets. On the basis of your study, what principles of the couplet does Pope follow? You might consider the average lengths of words and the use of iambs, caesurae, and end-stopped lines.

3. Describe Pope's use of rhyme. What types of words does he rhyme? How helpful are the rhymes in the emphasis of Pope's ideas?

## DUDLEY RANDALL (1914–2000)

 ## Ballad of Birmingham° (1966)

*(On the bombing of a church in Birmingham, Alabama, 1963)*

"Mother dear, may I go downtown
Instead of out to play,
And march the streets of Birmingham
In a Freedom March today?"

"No, baby, no, you may not go,                                      5
For the dogs are fierce and wild,
And clubs and hoses, guns and jails
Aren't good for a little child."

"But, mother, I won't be alone.
Other children will go with me,                                    10
And march the streets of Birmingham
To make our country free."

"No, baby, no, you may not go,
For I fear those guns will fire.
But you may go to church instead                                   15
And sing in the children's choir."

She has combed and brushed her night-dark hair,
And bathed rose petal sweet,
And drawn white gloves on her small brown hands,
And white shoes on her feet.                                       20

The mother smiled to know her child
Was in the sacred place,
But that smile was the last smile
To come upon her face.

---

°Four black children were killed when the 16th Street Baptist Church in Birmingham, Alabama, was bombed in 1963. A man was finally indicted for the murders in 1977 and convicted in 1982. There was an additional conviction in 2002.

25  For when she heard the explosion,
     Her eyes grew wet and wild.
     She raced through the streets of Birmingham
     Calling for her child.

     She clawed through bits of glass and brick,
30  Then lifted out a shoe
     "Oh, here's the shoe my baby wore,
     But, baby, where are you?"

## Questions

1. Formulate the structure (meter, rhyme scheme, stanza form) of this poem. What traditional closed form is employed here?

2. Who is the speaker in stanzas 1 and 3? In stanzas 2 and 4? How are quotation and repetition employed to create tension?

3. What ironies do you find in the mother's assumptions? In the poem as a whole? In the society pictured in the poem?

4. Compare the poem to "Sir Patrick Spens" (p. 463). How are the structures of all three alike? To what extent do all three deal with the same type of subject matter?

## THEODORE ROETHKE (1908–1963)

*For a photo, see Chapter 12, page 517.*

 ## The Waking (1953)

     I wake to sleep, and take my waking slow.
     I feel my fate in what I cannot fear.
     I learn by going where I have to go.

     We think by feeling. What is there to know?
5  I hear my being dance from ear to ear.
     I wake to sleep, and take my waking slow.

     Of those so close beside me, which are you?
     God bless the Ground! I shall walk softly there,
     And learn by going where I have to go.

10  Light takes the Tree; but who can tell us how?
     The lowly worm climbs up a winding stair;
     I wake to sleep, and take my waking slow.

     Great Nature has another thing to do
     To you and me; so take the lively air,
15  And, lovely, learn by going where to go.

This shaking keeps me steady. I should know.
What falls away is always. And is near.
I wake to sleep, and take my waking slow.
I learn by going where I have to go.

## Questions

1. Compare the form of this poem with the poems by Bishop and Thomas in this chapter.
2. In what way or ways does the speaker "wake to sleep"? What other apparent contradictions does the speaker develop in this poem? Why might a reader conclude that the poem is positive rather than negative?
3. What does the speaker mean by saying that he learns "by going where I have to go"? In what way does "always" fall away (line 17)?

## GEORGE WILLIAM RUSSELL ("Æ") (1867–1935)

 **Continuity** (1897)

No sign is made while empires pass.
The flowers and stars are still His care.
The constellations hid in grass,
The golden miracles in air.

Life in an instant will be rent                                                    5
Where death is glittering blind and wild—
The Heavenly Brooding is intent
To that last instant on Its child.

It breathes the glow in brain and heart,
Life is made magical. Until                                                       10
Body and spirit are apart
The Everlasting works Its will.

In that wild orchid that your feet
In their next falling shall destroy,
Minute and passionate and sweet                                                   15
The Mighty Master holds His joy.

Though the crushed jewels droop and fade
The artist's labors will not cease,
And of the ruins shall be made
Some yet more lovely masterpiece.                                                 20

## Questions

1. Describe the form of this poem, including the number of stanzas, the regularity of the meter, and the variations that you find.

2. What is the nature of the topic matter of this poem? Is it more appropriate for a song or for a hymn? Would you consider the poem personal, or public?

3. What is the conceptualization of "The Mighty Master" in this poem? In particular, consider the ideas in lines 2, 12, 16, and 18.

4. Compare this poem with Hardy's "In Time of 'The Breaking of Nations'" (Chapter 21). What comparable ideas do you find in the two poems? What differing ideas?

## WILLIAM SHAKESPEARE (1564–1616)

*For a portrait, see Chapter 21, page 979.*

###  Sonnet 73: That Time of Year Thou May'st in Me Behold (1609)

That time of year thou may'st in me behold
When yellow leaves, or none, or few, do hang
Upon those boughs which shake against the cold,
Bare ruined choirs,° where late the sweet birds sang.
5  In me thou see'st the twilight of such day
As after sunset fadeth in the west;
Which by and by black night doth take away,
Death's second self,° that seals up all in rest.
In me thou see'st the glowing of such fire,
10  That on the ashes of his° youth doth lie,                          *its*
As the death-bed whereon it must expire,
Consumed with that which it was nourished by.°
This thou perceivest, which makes thy love more strong,
To love that well which thou must leave ere long.

---

°4 *choirs:* the part of a church just in front of the altar.  8 *Death's . . . self:* That is, night is a mirror image of death inasmuch as it brings the sleep of rest just as death brings the sleep of actual death.  12 *Consumed . . . by:* That is, the ashes of the fuel burned at the fire's height now prevent the fire from continuing, and in fact extinguish it.

## Questions

1. Describe the content of lines 1–4, 5–8, and 9–12. What connects these three sections? How does the concluding couplet relate to the first twelve lines?

2. Analyze the iambic pentameter of the poem. Consider the spondees in lines 2 ("do hang"), 4 ("bare ru-" and "birds sang"), 5 ("such day"), 7 ("black night"), 8 ("death's sec-"), 9 ("such fire"), 10 ("doth lie"), 11 ("death-bed"), 13 ("more strong"), and 14 ("ere long"). What is the effect of these substitutions on the poem's ideas?

3. How does the enjambment of lines 1–3 and 5–6 permit these lines to seem to conclude *as lines* even though grammatically they carry over to form sentences?

4. In lines 2, 5, 6, and 9, where does Shakespeare place the caesurae? What relationship is there between the rhythms produced by these caesurae and the content of lines 1–12? In lines 13 and 14, how do the rising stressed caesurae relate to the content?

## PERCY BYSSHE SHELLEY (1792–1822)

 ### Ozymandias (1818)

I met a traveller from an antique land,
Who said—"Two vast and trunkless legs of stone
Stand in the desert. . . . Near them, on the sand,
Half sunk, a shattered visage lies, whose frown,
And wrinkled lip, and sneer of cold command,     5
Tell that its sculptor well those passions read
Which yet survive, stamped on these lifeless things,
The hand that mocked them, and the heart that fed;
And on the pedestal, these words appear;
'My name is Ozymandias, King of Kings,     10
Look on my Works, ye Mighty, and despair!'
Nothing beside remains. Round the decay
Of that colossal Wreck, boundless and bare
The lone and level sands stretch far away."

## Questions

1. What is the meter of this poem? The rhyme scheme? What traditional closed form is modified here? How do the modifications affect the poem?
2. To what extent are content and meaning shaped by the closed form? What is described in the octave? In the sestet?
3. Characterize Ozymandias (thought to be Ramses II, pharaoh of Egypt, who died in 1225 B.C.E.) from the way he is portrayed in this poem.

## DYLAN THOMAS (1914–1953)

 ## Do Not Go Gentle into That Good Night (1951)

Do not go gentle into that good night,
Old age should burn and rave at close of day;
Rage, rage against the dying of the light.

Though wise men at their end know dark is right,
Because their words had forked no lightning they     5
Do not go gentle into that good night.

Good men, the last wave by, crying how bright
Their frail deeds might have danced in a green bay,
Rage, rage against the dying of the light.

10 Wild men who caught and sang the sun in flight,
And learn, too late, they grieved it on its way,
Do not go gentle into that good night.

Grave men, near death, who see with blinding sight
Blind eyes could blaze like meteors and be gay,
15 Rage, rage against the dying of the light.

And you, my father, there on the sad height,
Curse, bless, me now with your fierce tears, I pray.
Do not go gentle into that good night.
Rage, rage against the dying of the light.

## Questions

1. What conclusions do you make about the poem's speaker, listener, and situation?

2. What connotative words do you find here? Consider "dying," the "good" of "good night," "gentle," "Curse, bless, me now with your fierce tears, I pray," and "grave."

3. What five different kinds of men does the speaker discuss in stanzas 2–5? What do they have in common? Of what value are they to the speaker's father (line 16)?

4. Compare the form of this poem with the poems by Bishop and Roethke in this chapter.

## JEAN TOOMER (1894–1967)

 **Reapers** (1923)

Black reapers with the sound of steel on stones
Are sharpening scythes. I see them place the hones
In their hip-pockets as a thing that's done,
And start their silent swinging, one by one.
5 Black horses drive a mower through the weeds,
And there, a field rat, startled, squealing bleeds,
His belly close to ground. I see the blade,
Blood-stained, continue cutting weeds and shade.

## Questions

1. What is the poem's meter? The rhyme scheme? The form? What is the difference between Toomer's use of the form and Dryden's?

2. How do the images of this poem relate to each other? How does the image of the bleeding field rat and the "blood-stained" blade heighten the impact?

3. How does alliteration unify this poem and make sound echo sense? Note especially the *s* and *b* sounds and the phrase "silent swinging."

## **PHYLLIS WEBB** (b. 1927)

 ## Poetics Against the Angel of Death° (1962)

I am sorry to speak of death again
(some say I'll have a long life)
but last night Wordsworth's 'Prelude' °
suddenly made sense—I mean the measure,
the elevated tone, the attitude                                      5
of private Man speaking to public men.
Last night I thought I would not wake again
but now with this June morning I run ragged to elude
the Great Iambic Pentameter
who is the Hound of Heaven° in our stress                           10
because I want to die
writing Haiku
or, better,
long lines, clean and syllabic as knotted bamboo. Yes!

---

°*Angel of Death*: See Byron's "The Destruction of Sennacherib," stanza 3 (Chapter 25).  3 *Wordsworth's 'Prelude'*: See Chapter 24.  10 *Hound of Heaven (The)*: a long poem (1893) by Francis Thompson (1859–1907) about attempting to evade God's love.

### Questions

1. In the poem itself, what is meant by the "Angel of Death"?
2. What attitude does the speaker express about iambic pentameter? How does the speaker explain this attitude? How defensible is the attitude?
3. For what poetic forms does the speaker express a preference? Why? How does the form of this poem bear out the preference?

## **WILLIAM CARLOS WILLIAMS** (1883–1963)

 ## The Dance (1944)

In Brueghel's° great picture, The Kermess,
the dancers go round, they go round and
around, the squeal and the blare and the
tweedle of bagpipes, a bugle and fiddles
tipping their bellies (round as the thick-sided                     5
glasses whose wash they impound)
their hips and their bellies off balance
to turn them. Kicking and rolling about
the Fair Grounds, swinging their butts, those
shanks must be sound to bear up under such                          10
rollicking measures, prance as the dance
in Brueghel's great picture, The Kermess.

---

°1 *Brueghel's*: Pieter Brueghel (ca. 1525–1569), a Flemish painter. *Peasants' Dance (The Kermess)* shows peasants dancing in celebration of the anniversary of the founding of a church *(church mass)*. See l–7, Plate 1.

## Questions

1. What effect is produced by repeating the first line as the last line?

2. How do repetition, alliteration, assonance, onomatopoeia, and internal rhyme affect the tempo, feeling, and meaning of the poem? How do the numerous participles (like "tipping," "kicking," "rolling") make sound echo sense?

3. What words are capitalized? What effect is produced by omitting the capital letters at the beginning of each line? How does this typographical choice reinforce the sound and the sense of the poem?

4. Most of the lines of this poem are run-on rather than end-stopped, and many of them end with fairly weak words such as *and*, *the*, *about*, and *such*. What effect is produced through these techniques?

5. How successful is Williams in making the words and sentence rhythms echo the visual rhythms in Brueghel's painting? Why is this open form more appropriate to the images of the poem than any closed form could be?

## WRITING ABOUT FORM IN POETRY

An essay about form in poetry should demonstrate a relationship between a poem's sense and its form. Do not discuss form or shape in isolation, for such an essay would be no more than a detailed description. The first thing to do as you go about determining what you want to say is to examine the poem's main ideas. Consider the various elements that contribute to the poem's impact and effectiveness: the speaker, listener, setting, situation, diction, imagery, and rhetorical devices. Once you understand these, it will be easier to establish a connection between form and content.

You will find it helpful to prepare a work sheet that highlights the elements you are deciding that you wish to discuss. For closed forms, these elements will be rhyme scheme, meter, line lengths, and stanzaic patterns. They may also include significant words and phrases that connect stanzas. The work sheet for an open-form poem should indicate variables such as rhythm and phrases; the use of pauses; significant words that are isolated or emphasized through typography; and patterns of repeated sounds, words, phrases, and images.

### Questions for Discovering Ideas

#### CLOSED FORM

- What is the principal meter? Line length? Rhyme scheme? To what extent do these establish and/or reinforce the form?

- What is the form of each stanza or unit? How many stanzas or divisions does the poem contain? How does the poem establish a pattern? How does the pattern control the poem's developing content?

- What is the form of the poem (e.g., couplet, tercet, ballad, villanelle, sonnet)? In what ways is the poem traditional, and what variations does it introduce? What is the effect of the variations?

- How effectively does the structure create or reinforce the poem's internal logic? What topical, logical, or thematic progressions unite the various parts of the poem?
- To what extent does the form organize the images of the poem? Are key images developed within single units or stanzas? Do images recur in more than one section?
- To what extent does the form organize and bring out the poem's ideas or emotions?

## OPEN FORM

- What does the poem look like on the page? What is the relationship of its shape to its meaning?
- How does the poet use variable line lengths, spaces, punctuation, capitalization, and the like to shape the poem? How do these variables contribute to the poem's sense and impact?
- What rhythms are built into the poem through language or typography? How are these relevant to the poem's content?
- What is the poem's progression of ideas, images, and/or emotions? How is the logic created and what does it contribute?
- How does form or typography isolate or unite, and thus emphasize, various words and phrases? What is the effect of such emphasis?
- What patterns do you discover of words and sounds? To what degree do the patterns create order and structure? How are they related to the sense of the poem?

## Strategies for Organizing Ideas

In developing your central idea, you should illustrate the connections between form and meaning. For example, in planning an essay on Randall's "Ballad of Birmingham," you might develop your ideas according to the speeches that are a normal feature of the ballad form. The poem's first part is a dialogue between mother and child about the hazard of the local streets and the safety of the local church. In the second part, after the explosion, the mother runs toward the church and calls for her child, who, ironically, will never again engage with her in dialogue. Another plan is needed for an essay on Williams's "The Dance"; such a plan might link the lively, bustling movement of the dancers pictured in Brueghel's painting (I–7, Plate 1) to the rhythms, repetitions, and run-on lines of the poem. Still another plan would be needed for a discussion of Heyen's "Mantle," the form of which requires enough stanzas of approximately equal length to make up the pattern of a pitched ball (what is this pattern?).

Your introduction may contain general remarks about the poem, but it should focus on the connection between form and substance. Describe the ways in which structure and content interact together, with a brief listing of your specific topics.

Early in the body, describe the formal characteristics of your poem, using schemes and numbers (as in paragraph 2 of the illustrative student essay). With closed forms, your description should detail such standard features as the traditional form, meter, rhyme scheme, stanzaic structure, and number of stanzas. With open-form poetry, you should focus on the most striking and significant features of the verse (as in the brief discussion of Whitman's "Reconciliation" on p. 653).

Be sure to integrate your discussion of both form and content. It may be that you have uncovered a good deal of information about technical features such as alliteration or rhyme, or you may wish to stress that words, phrases, and clauses develop a pattern of ideas. Remember that you are not making a paraphrase or a general explication, but instead are showing how the poet uses form—either an open or a closed one—in the service of meaning. The order in which you deal with your topics is entirely your decision.

The conclusion of your essay might contain additional relevant observations about shape or structure. It might also summarize your argument. Here, as in all essays about literature, make sure to reach an actual conclusion rather than simply a stopping point.

## Illustrative Student Essay

Underlined sentences in this paper *do not* conform to MLA style and are used solely as teaching tools to emphasize the central idea, thesis sentence, and topic sentences throughout the paper.

Kimberley Adams

Professor Patter

English 114

20 February 2007

### Form and Meaning in George Herbert's "Virtue"°

[1]      Herbert's devotional four-stanza poem "Virtue" (1633) contrasts the mortality of

worldly things with the immortality of the "virtuous soul." This is not an uncommon

topic in religious poetry and hymns, and there is nothing unusual about this contrast.

What is unusual, however, is the simplicity and directness of Herbert's expressions and

the way in which he integrates his ideas within his stanzaic song pattern. Each part of

---

°See p. 668 for this poem.

Adams 2

the poem organizes the images logically and underscores the supremacy of life over death.[*] Through control over line and stanza groupings, rhyme scheme, and repeated sounds and words, Herbert's stanzas create a structural and visual distinction between the "sweet" soul and the rest of creation.[†]

[2]    Herbert's control over lines within the stanzas is particularly strong. Each stanza follows the same *a b a b* rhyme scheme. Because some rhyme sounds and words are repeated throughout the first three stanzas, however, the structure of the poem can be formulated as *4a 4b 4a 2b; 4c 4b 4c 2b; 4d 4b 4d 2b; 4e 4f 4e 2f.* Each stanza thus contains three lines of iambic tetrameter with a final line of iambic dimeter—an unusual pattern that creates a unique emphasis. In the first three stanzas, the dimeter lines repeat the phrase "must die," while in the last stanza the contrast is made on the words "Then chiefly lives." These rhythms require a sensitive reading, and they powerfully underscore Herbert's idea that death is conquered by eternal life.

[3]    Like individual lines, Herbert's stanzaic structure provides the poem's pattern of organization and logic. The first stanza focuses on the image of the "Sweet day," comparing the day to "The bridal of the earth and sky" (line 2) and asserting that the day inevitably "must die." Similarly, the second stanza focuses on the image of a "Sweet rose" and asserts that it too "must die." The third stanza shifts to the image of "Sweet spring." Here, the poet blends the images of the first two stanzas into the third by noting that the "Sweet spring" is "full of sweet days and roses" (line 9). The stanza concludes with the summarizing claim that "all must die." In this way, the third stanza is the climax of Herbert's imagery of beauty and mortality. The last stanza introduces a new image—"a sweet and virtuous soul"—and an assertion that is the opposite of the ideas expressed in the previous three stanzas. Although the day, the rose, and the spring "must die," the soul "never" deteriorates, but "chiefly lives" even "though the whole world turn to coal" (line 15). With its key image of the "virtuous soul," this last stanza marks the logical conclusion of Herbert's argument. His pattern of organization allows this key image of permanence to be separated structurally from the images of impermanence.

[4]    This structural organization of images and ideas is repeated and reinforced by other techniques. Herbert's rhyme scheme, for example, links the first three stanzas while isolating the fourth. That the b rhyme is repeated at the ends of the second and fourth lines

---

[*]Central idea.
[†]Thesis sentence.

of each of the first three stanzas makes these stanzas into a complete unit. The fourth stanza, however is different in both content and rhyme. The stanza introduces the concept of immortality, and it also introduces entirely new rhymes, replacing the <u>b</u> rhyme with an <u>f</u> rhyme. Thus the rhyme scheme, by sound alone, parallels the poem's imagery and logic.

[5]     <u>As a complement to the rhyming sounds, the poem also demonstrates organizing patterns of assonance.</u> Most notable is the <u>oo</u> sound, which is repeated throughout the first three stanzas in the words "c<u>oo</u>l," "d<u>ew</u>," "wh<u>o</u>se," "h<u>ue</u>," "r<u>oo</u>t," and "m<u>u</u>sic." In Herbert's time, the sound might still have been prominent in the word "thou," so that in the first three stanzas the <u>oo</u>, which is not unlike a moan (certainly appropriate to things that die), is repeated eight times. In the last stanza there is a stress on the <u>o</u> sound, in "<u>o</u>nly," "s<u>ou</u>l," "th<u>o</u>ugh" "wh<u>o</u>le," and "c<u>o</u>al." While <u>oh</u> may also be a moan, in this context it is more like an exclamation, in keeping with the triumph contained in the final line.

[6]     <u>Herbert's repetition of key words and phrases also distinguishes the first three stanzas from the last stanza.</u> Each of the first three stanzas begins with "sweet" and ends with "must die." These repetitions stress both the beauty and the mortality of worldly things. In the last stanza, however, this repetition is abandoned, just as the stress on immortality transcends mortality. The "Sweet" that begins each of the first three stanzas is replaced by "Only" (line 13). Similarly, "must die" is replaced with "chiefly lives." Both substitutions separate this final stanza from the three previous stanzas. More importantly, the shift in the verbal pattern emphasizes the transition from death to the virtuous soul's immortality.

[7]     The lyric form of Herbert's "Virtue" provides an organizational pattern for the poem's images and ideas. At the same time, the stanzaic pattern and the rhyme scheme allow the poet to draw a strong distinction between the corruptible world and the immortal soul. <u>The closed form of this poem is not arbitrary or incidental; it is an integral way of asserting the importance of the key image, the "sweet and virtuous soul."</u>

**WORK CITED**

George Herbert, "Virtue." *Literature: An Introduction to Reading and Writing.* 4th Compact edition. ed. Edgar V. Roberts. Upper Saddle River: Prentice Hall, 2008, 668.

## Commentary on the Essay

The introductory paragraph establishes the groundwork of the essay—the treatment of form in relationship to content. The main idea is that each part of the poem represents a complete blending of image, logic, and meaning.

Paragraph 2, the first in the body, demonstrates how the poem's schematic formulation is integrated into Herbert's contrast of death and life. In this respect, the paragraph demonstrates how a formal enumeration can be integrated within an essay's thematic development.

The focus of paragraph 3 is the organization of both images and ideas from stanza to stanza. Paragraph 4 begins with a transitional sentence that repeats part of the essay's central idea and, at the same time, connects it to paragraph 3. In the same way, paragraph 4 is closely tied to both paragraphs 1 and 3. The main topic here, the rhyme scheme of "Virtue," is introduced in the second sentence. This paragraph also asserts that rhythm also reinforces the division between mortality and immortality. On much the same topic, paragraph 5 introduces Herbert's use of assonance, which can be seen as integral in the poem's blending of form and content.

Paragraph 6 takes up the last structural element described in the introduction—repeated key words and phrases. The idea is that these repetitions emphasize the distinction in the poem between mortality and immortality.

Paragraph 7, the conclusion, provides a brief overview and summation of the essay's argument. In addition, it concludes that form in "Virtue" is neither arbitrary nor incidental but rather an integral part of the poem's meaning.

# Writing Topics About Poetic Form

1. Describe the use of the ode form as exemplified by Shelley's "Ode to the West Wind" and Keats's "Ode to a Nightingale." What patterns of regularity do you find? What differences do you find in the form and content of the poems? How do you account for these differences?

2. How do Cummings, Dryden, Randall, and Thomas use different forms to consider the subject of death (in "Buffalo Bill's Defunct," "To the Memory of Mr. Oldham," "Ballad of Birmingham," and "Do Not Go Gentle into That Good Night")? What differences in form and treatment do you find? What similarities do you find, despite these differences?

3. Consider the structural arrangement and shaping of the following works: Brueghel's painting *La Kermesse* (I–7, Plate 7), Hass's "Museum," Heyen's "Mantle," Hollander's "Swan and Shadow," Charles Harper Webb's "The Shape of History," and Williams's "The Dance." How do painter and poets utilize topic, arrangement, shape, and space to draw attention to their main ideas? How do the shaped and prose poems (Hass, Heyen, Hollander, and Webb) blend poetic and artistic techniques?

4. Compare and contrast the use of the villanelle by Bishop ("One Art"), Roethke ("The Waking"), and Thomas ("Do Not Go Gentle into That Good Night"). What

topics do the poets develop? Why do the poets choose the villanelle as their poetic form? What lines do they repeat? What is the effect of this repetition?

5. Compare Keats's "Ode to a Nightingale" and Hopkins's "God's Grandeur." How do these poems sound when read aloud? What can you say about each poet's use of strong stresses in order to achieve emphasis?

6. Compare the sonnets in this chapter by Shakespeare, Shelley, Milton, and Collins. In what ways are the poetic forms of Shakespeare, Milton, and Shelley similar? Different? How may Collins's poem be read as a commentary on the sonnet forms of the other poets?

7. Write a visual poem, and explain the principles on which you develop your lines. Here are some possible topics (just to get you started): a telephone, a cat, a dog, a car, a football, a snow shovel, a giraffe. After finishing your poem, write a short essay that considers these questions: What are the strengths and limitations of the visual form, according to your experience? How does the form help make your poem serious or comic? How does it encourage creative language and original development of ideas?

8. Write a haiku. Be sure to fit your poem to the 5–7–5 pattern of syllables. What challenges and problems do you encounter in this form? Once you have completed your haiku (which, to be traditional, should be on a topic concerned with nature), try to cut the number of syllables to 4–5–4. Explain how you establish the first haiku pattern, and also explain how you go about cutting the total number of syllables. Be sure to explain what kinds of words you use (length, choice of diction, etc.).

9. Using a computer reference system or regular card catalogue, depending on availability in your college library, look up one of the following topics: "ballads, England," "concrete poetry," or "blank verse." How many references are included under these listings? What sorts of topics are included under the basic topic?

# Chapter 17

# Symbolism and Allusion: Windows to Wide Expanses of Meaning

**S**ymbolism refers to the use of symbols in works of art and in all other forms of expression. As we note in Chapter 8, a **symbol** has meaning in and of itself, but it is also understood to represent something else, such as the flag for the country or the school song for the school. Symbols occur in stories as well as in poems, but poetry relies more heavily on symbols because it is more concise and because it comprises more forms than fiction, which is restricted to narratives.

Most of the words we use every day are symbols, for they stand for various objects without actually being those objects. When we say *horse*, for example, or *tree*, or *run*, these words are symbols of horses and trees and people who are running. They direct our minds to real horses, real trees, and real actions in the real world that we have seen and can therefore easily imagine. In literature, however, symbolism implies a special relationship that expands our ordinary understanding of words, descriptions, and arguments.

## Symbolism and Meanings

Symbolism goes beyond the close referral of word to thing; it is more like a window through which one can glimpse the extensive world outside. Because poetry is compact, its descriptions and portrayals of experience are brief. Symbolism is therefore one of its primary characteristics. It is a shorthand way of referring to extensive ideas or attitudes that otherwise would be inappropriate to include in the brief format of a poem. Thus, Philip Larkin, in "Next, Please," uses the word "armada" as a symbol that is both apt and original. His thought is that we do not find fulfillment in the present, but rather we look to the symbolic "armada of promises" and expectations that we constantly and habitually dream about for a better future. Like the Spanish Armada that attempted to overthrow the English government in 1588, Larkin's armada seems tiny and far removed from present reality, but as a symbol it suggests that human beings neglect the opportunities they have at the moment in favor of fixing their hopes on the promise of better things to happen—things that are defeated or that never even materialize. This idea could easily be developed through many more observations about the futility of unreal hope, but Larkin is more concerned to symbolize the idea than to amplify it.

## Symbolism Extends Meaning Beyond Normal Connotation

The use of symbols is a way of moving outward, a means of extending and crystalliz-ing information and ideas. For example, at the time of William Blake (1757–1827), the word *tiger* meant both a large, wild cat and also the specific animal we know today as a tiger. The word's connotation therefore links it with wildness and predation. As a symbol in "The Tyger" (Chapter 14), however, Blake uses the animal as a stand-in for what he considers cosmic negativism—the savage, wild forces that undermine the progress of civilization. Thus, the tiger as a symbol is more meaningful than either the denotation or the connotation of the word would indicate. A visual comparison can be made with Francisco Goya's painting *The Colossus* (I–9, Plate 2), in which the giant pugilistic figure above the tiny figures in the landscape represents the combi-nation of anger, defiance, and ruthlessness that is unleashed and unchecked during times of war.

## Cultural or Universal Symbols Are Widely Recognized

Many symbols, wherever they are used, possess a ready-made, clearly agreed upon meaning. These are **cultural** or **universal symbols** (also discussed in Chapter 8). Many such symbols, such as the tiger, are drawn directly from nature. Other natural universal symbols are springtime and morning, which signify beginnings, growth, hope, optimism, and love. If such symbols were to be introduced into a poem about the suddenness and irrevocability of death, however, they would be ironic, for their presence would emphasize the contrast between death and life.

Cultural symbols are drawn from history and custom, such as the many Judeo-Christian religious symbols that appear in poetry. References to the lamb, Eden, Egyptian bondage, shepherds, exile, the Temple, blood, water, bread, the cross, and wine—all Jewish and/or Christian symbols—occur over and over again. Sometimes these symbols are prominent in a purely devotional context. In other contexts, how-ever, they may be contrasted with symbols of warfare and corruption to show how extensively people neglect their moral and religious obligations.

## Contextual, Private, or Authorial Symbols Are Operative as Symbols Only within Individual Works

Symbols that are not widely or universally recognized are termed **contextual**, **private**, or **authorial symbols** (also discussed in Chapter 8). Some of these have a natural relationship with the objects and ideas being symbolized. Let us consider snow, which is cold and white and covers everything when it falls. A poet can exploit this quality and make snow a symbol. At the beginning of the long poem "The Waste Land," T. S. Eliot does exactly that; he refers to snow as a symbol of retreat from life, a withdrawal into an intellectual and moral hibernation. Another poem symbolizing snow is the following one. Here, the poet refers to snow as a both a literal and figura-tive link between the living and the dead.

# VIRGINIA SCOTT (b. 1938)

 Snow (1977)

A doe stands at the roadside,
spirit of those who have lived here
and passed known through our memory.
The doe stands at the edge of the icy road,
then darts back into the woods.                                    5

Snow falling,
mother-spirit hovering,
white on the drops in the road and fields,
light from the windows
of the old house                                                  10
brightening the snow.

Presences: mother,
grandmother,
here in their place
at the foot of *ben lomond*,                                      15
green trees black in the hemlock night.

The doe stands at the edge of the icy road,
then darts back into the woods.

*Golden Grove, New Brunswick, Canada*
*January 5, 1977*

## Questions

1. How is snow described in the poem? How and where is it seen? As a symbol, what does it signify in relationship to the doe, the memory of other people, the mother-spirit, the old house, the light, the presences, the mountains, and the trees?

2. Explain the structural purpose for which the doe is mentioned three times in the poem, with lines 17 and 18 repeating 4 and 5. As a symbol, what do you think the doe signifies?

3. What are the relationships described in the poem between memory of the past and existence in the present? What does the symbolism contribute to your understanding of these relationships?

This poem describes a real circumstance at a real place at a real time; the poet has even provided an actual location and date, just as we do when writing a letter. We can therefore presume that the snow is real snow, falling in the evening just as lights go on in the nearby houses. This detail by itself would be sufficient as a realistic image, but as Scott develops the poem, the snow symbolizes the link between the speaker's memory of the past and perception of the present. The reality of the moment is suffused with the memory of the people—"mother,/grandmother"—who "lived here." The poet is meditating on the idea that individuals, though they may often be by themselves, like the speaker, are never alone as long as they have a vivid memory of the past. Symbolically, the past and present are always connected, just as the snow covers the scene.

At the poem's conclusion, the doe darting into the woods suggests a linking of present and future (i.e., as long as there are woods, does will dart into them). Both the snow and the deer are private and contextual symbols, for they are established and developed within the poem, and they do not have the same symbolic value elsewhere. Through the symbolism, therefore, the poet has converted a private moment into an idea of general significance.

Similarly, references to other ordinary materials may be symbolic if the poet emphasizes them sufficiently, as in Keats's "La Belle Dame Sans Merci," which opens and closes with the image of withered sedge, or grass. What might seem like nothing more than a natural detail becomes additionally important because it can be understood to symbolize the loss and bewilderment felt by people when loved ones seem to be faithless and destructive rather than loyal and supportive.

The meanings of symbols may be placed on a continuum of qualities from good to bad, high to low, favorable to unfavorable. For example, the sea-washed shore in Clampitt's "Beach Glass" is on the positive end, symbolizing the regular and eternal relationship of ocean and land. Outright horror is suggested by the symbol of the rough beast slouching toward Bethlehem in Yeats's "The Second Coming." Although this mythical beast shares the same birthplace with Jesus, the commonality is ironic because the beast represents the extremes of anger, hatred, and brutality that in Yeats's judgment were dominant in modern politics.

## The Function of Symbolism in Poetry

Poets do not simply jam symbols into a poem artificially and arbitrarily. Rather, symbols are structurally important and meaningful first and are secondarily symbolic. We therefore find symbols in single words, and also in actions, scenes and settings, characters and characterizations, and various situations.

### Many Words Are Automatically Symbolic

With general and universal symbols, a single word is often sufficient, as with references to the lamb, shepherd, cross, blood, bread, and wine; or to summer and winter; or to drought and flood, morning and night, heat and shade, storm and calm, or feast and famine. One of the most famous of all birds, the nightingale, is an example of a single word being instantly symbolic. Because of this bird's beautiful song, it symbolizes natural, unspoiled beauty as contrasted with the contrived attempts by human beings to create beauty. Keats refers to the bird in this way in his "Ode to a Nightingale" (Chapter 16), and his speaker compares human mortality with the virtually eternal beauty of this singer.

Another word also referring to a species of bird as a symbol is *geese*. Because migratory Canada geese fly south in the fall, they symbolize the loss of summer abundance, seasonal change, alteration, and loss, with accompanying feelings of regret and sorrow. Because they return north in the spring, however, they also symbolize regeneration, newness, anticipation, and hope. These contrasting symbolic values are important in Jorie Graham's "The Geese" and Mary Oliver's "Wild Geese." Graham emphasizes that the geese are "crossing" overhead but nevertheless that human affairs of "the everyday" continue despite the changes symbolized by the geese. In contrast, Oliver emphasizes geese as symbols of renewal, for the geese returning in spring suggest that "the world offers itself to your imagination."

## Symbolism Is to Be Seen in Actions

Not only words but also actions may be presented as symbols. In Scott's "Snow," as we have just observed, the doe darting into the darkening woods symbolizes renewal and the mystery of life. In Hardy's "In Time of 'The Breaking of Nations,'" the action of the man plowing a field symbolizes the continued life and vitality of the folk, the people, despite the political wrangling and endless brutality that are constantly occurring in the world.

## Symbolism Is to Be Seen in Settings and Scenes

While settings and scenes may be no more than just that—settings and scenes—the poet may develop them as symbols. We may note a symbolic setting in Wilbur's "Year's End." Wilbur draws our attention to a little dog, curled up as if sleeping, and its (presumable) owners, all of whom were killed by falling lava when the eruption of Mount Vesuvius destroyed Pompeii, the ancient Roman town in southern Italy, in 79 C.E. In the poem's context, this scene symbolizes the incompleteness of human achievements, a condition not only of present life but also of ancient life. Keats, in "La Belle Dame Sans Merci," introduces the "elfin grot" (grotto) of the "lady in the meads." This grotto is an unreal, magical, womblike location symbolizing both the allure and the disappointment that on occasions characterize sexual attraction.

## Symbolism Is to Be Seen in Characters

Poets also devise characters or people as symbols of ideas or values, like the speaker in Herbert's "The Collar." This speaker describes his fierce reluctance against committing himself to God's service, but his anger vanishes when he thinks he hears a soothingly divine voice calling "Child." In this way he becomes a symbol of devoted obedience. In Keats's "La Belle Dame Sans Merci," the "fairy's child" is a symbol of the mystery of love. The figures in Hardy's "In Time of 'The Breaking of Nations'" symbolize the power of average, ordinary people to endure even "Though Dynasties pass."

## Symbolism Is to Be Seen in Situations

A poem's situations, circumstances, and conditions may also be symbolic. The position of the young gunner in the World War II bomber, six miles above the earth

(Jarrell's "The Death of the Ball Turret Gunner" [Chapter 11]), makes him vulnerable and helpless, and his death symbolizes the condition of humankind in the modern age of fear and anxiety, when life is threatened by global war and technologically expert destructiveness. In "she being Brand/-new" (Chapter 15) Cummings cleverly uses the situation of the speaker's breaking in a new automobile as the symbol of another kind of encounter involving the speaker.

# Allusions and Meaning

Just as symbolism enriches meaning, so also do **allusions** (see also Chapter 8), that take the form of (1) unacknowledged brief quotations from other works and (2) references to historical events and any aspect of human culture—art, music, literature, and so on. The use of allusions is a means of connecting new literary works with the broader cultural tradition of which the works are a part. In addition, allusions presuppose a common bond of knowledge between the poet and the reader. On the one hand, poets making allusions compliment the past, and on the other, they salute readers able to discover how the meanings of the allusions are transformed in the new context.

## Allusions Add Dimension to Poetry

An allusion carries with it the entire context of the work from which it is drawn. Perhaps the richest sources of references and stories are the King James Bible and the plays of Shakespeare. Keats introduces a biblical allusion in "Ode to a Nightingale" (Chapter 16), where he refers to the story of Ruth, who was "sick for home" while standing "in tears amid the alien corn." This allusion is particularly rich, because Ruth became the mother of Jesse. According to the Gospel of Matthew, it was from the line of Jesse that King David was born, and it was from the house of David that Jesus was born. Thus Keats's nightingale is not only a symbol of natural beauty, but through the biblical allusion it symbolizes regeneration and redemption, much in keeping with Keats's assertion that the bird is "not born for death." In Yeats's "The Second Coming," we encounter an allusion to Shakespeare's *Macbeth*. Yeats uses the phrase "blood-dimmed tide," which refers to Macbeth's soliloquy in the second act of *Macbeth*. In the play, after murdering Duncan, Macbeth asks if there is enough water in Neptune's ocean to wash the blood from his hands. His immediate, guilt-ridden response is that Duncan's blood will instead turn the green water to red (2.2.63–66). This image of crime being bloody enough to stain the ocean's water is thus the allusive context of Yeats's "blood-dimmed tide."

Once works become well known, as with the Bible and the plays of Shakespeare, they may in turn become a source of allusions for subsequent writers. Such a well-known work is Frost's "Stopping by Woods on a Snowy Evening" (Chapter 11), which contains an oft-quoted last line: "And miles to go before I sleep." This line is so universally recognized that it has become a symbol of completing tasks and fulfilling responsibilities.

Allusions may be discovered in no more than a single word or phrase in a poem, provided that the expression is unusual enough or associative enough to bear the weight of the reference. Scott's "Snow," for example, speaks of "green trees black in the hemlock night." Of course, the word *hemlock* refers to a common evergreen tree observed by the speaker, but a distillation of hemlock was also the poison drunk by Socrates when the ancient Athenians executed him, as described in Plato's dialogue *Phaedo*.[1] Because of this association, any use of the word *hemlock* can be construed as an allusion to the death of Socrates and the abuse of legal authority. Another allusion to hemlock occurs in the beginning lines of "Ode to a Nightingale," in which Keats refers to hemlock. His speaker declares that a "drowsy numbness" has overtaken him "as though of hemlock . . . [he] had drunk." As the poem continues, we realize that Keats's allusion refers to the way in which death might open a new plane of existence for the speaker—a life of immortal beauty. Thus Keats builds the single-word allusion into new speculation about the possible nature of life and death.

Phrases and also descriptions and situations may also signal allusions, as in Josephine Jacobsen's "Tears," where the following sentence occurs: "Yet the globe is salt/with that savor." This is an allusion to the book of Matthew, 5:13: "Ye are the salt of the earth: but if the salt have lost his savour, wherewith shall it be salted?" This biblical passage refers to the need for believers to retain their faith, for without such faith they are "good for nothing, but to be cast out." However, Jacobsen is discussing something different, namely the endlessness of grief as a condition of life, with the continuing facts of sorrow remaining on the earth as a silent legacy. By making this allusion, Jacobsen adds to her idea the implication that, throughout human history, sorrow and tears have been a result of the loss of faith and love in human relationships.

Allusions are therefore an important means by which poets broaden context and deepen meaning. The issues a poet raises in a new poem, in other words, are important not only there but are linked through allusion to issues raised earlier by other thinkers or brought out by previous events, places, or persons. With connections made through allusions, poets clarify their own ideas. Allusion is hence not literary "theft" but is rather a means of enrichment.

## Studying for Symbols and Allusions

As you study poetry, remember that symbols and allusions do not come marked with special notice and fanfare. Your decision to call something symbolic must be based on the circumstances of the poem. Let us say that the poet introduces a major item of importance at a climactic part of the poem, or that the poet introduces a description that is unusual or noteworthy, such as the connection between "stony sleep" and the "rough beast" in Yeats's "The Second Coming." When such a connection occurs, the element may no longer be taken literally but should be read as a symbol.

---

[1] To see Jacque-Louis David's painting of this scene, see I–7, Plate 2.

Even after you have found a connection such as this, however, you will need to discover and understand symbolic meaning. For instance, in the context of Yeats's "The Second Coming," the phrase "rough beast" might refer to the person or persons hinted at in traditional interpretations of the New Testament as the "Antichrist." In a secular frame of reference, the associations of blankness and pitilessness suggest brutality and suppression. Still further, however, if the last hundred years had not been a period in which millions of people were persecuted and exterminated in military and secret police operations, even these associations might make the "rough beast" quizzical but not necessarily symbolic. But because of the rightness of the application, together with the traditional biblical associations, the figure clearly should be construed as a symbol of heartless persecution and brutality.

As you can see, the interpretation of a symbol requires that you consider, in some depth, the person, object, situation, or action being considered as symbolic. If the element can be seen as general and representative—characteristic of the condition of a large number of human beings—it assumes symbolic significance. As a rule, the more ideas that you can associate with the element, the more likely it is to be a symbol.

As for allusions, the identification of an allusion is usually simple. A word, situation, or phrase either is an allusion or it is not, and hence the matter is easily settled once a source is located. The problem comes in determining how the allusion affects the context of the poem you are reading. Thus we understand that in the poem "Snow," Scott alludes to Frost's "Desert Places" (Chapter 16) by borrowing Frost's phrase "Snow falling." Once this allusion is established, its purpose must still be learned. Thus, on the one hand, the allusion might mean that the situation in "Snow" is the same as in Frost's poem, namely, that the speaker is making observations about interior blankness—the "desert places" of the mind, or soul. On the other hand, the poet may be using the allusion in a new sense, and such is indeed the case. Whereas Frost uses the falling snow to suggest coldness of spirit, Scott uses it, more warmly, to connect the natural scene to the memory of family. In other words, once the presence of an allusion is established, the challenge of reading and understanding still continues.

## Poems for Study

# EMILY BRONTË (1818–1848)

 ## No Coward Soul Is Mine (1850 (1846))

No coward soul is mine,
No trembler in the world's storm-troubled sphere:
   I see Heaven's glories shine,
And faith shines equal, arming me from fear.

   O God within my breast,                                   5
Almighty, ever-present Deity!
   Life—that in me has rest,
As I—undying Life—have power in Thee!

   Vain are the thousand creeds
That move men's hearts, unutterably vain,                     10
   Worthless as withered weeds,
Or idle froth amid the boundless main,°           *i.e., oceans throughout the world*

   To waken doubt in one
Holding so fast by Thine infinity;
   So surely anchored on                                        15
The steadfast rock of immortality.

   With wide-embracing love
Thy spirit animates eternal years,
   Pervades and broods above,
Changes, sustains, dissolves, creates, and rears.         20

   Though earth and man were gone,
And suns and universes ceased to be,
   And Thou wert left alone,°     *If Thou were to be left [totally] alone*
Every existence would exist in Thee.

25    There is not room for Death,
Nor atom that his might could render void:
Thou—THOU art Being and Breath,
And what THOU art may never be destroyed.

## Questions

1. Why does the speaker assert in the first stanza that "No coward soul in mine"? Why does she raise this issue? Why might someone consider a soul like hers cowardly? Does the speaker make a convincing argument for the poem's first line?

2. Who is "God within my breast" of the poem? What connection or lack of connection does this "Thee/THOU/THY" have with the "thousand creeds/That move men's hearts" of lines 9 and 10?

3. In general, what is the breadth and scope of the symbolic references in this poem? Compare the symbolism of the "storm-troubled sphere" in stanza one, and of the vanished world, suns, universes, and even humanity in stanza six.

4. What is the meaning and connection of the symbols "withered weeds" (line 11) and "idle froth" (line 12)? To what extent does the speaker, in lines 9–12, seem to be denigrating conventional religious faiths? How does the grammatical connection between stanzas three and four help in the understanding of these stanzas?

5. What does the speaker apparently mean, in lines 23–24, by the statement "And Thou wert left alone,/Every existence would exist in Thee"?

6. Describe the symbolism implied in the word "arming" in the first stanza. Against what does the speaker need arming? Who or what is arming her soul? What do "infinity" (line 14) and "immortality" (line 16) contribute to her expressed sense of her own personal strength?

## AMY CLAMPITT (1920–1994)

 **Beach Glass** (1983)

While you walk the water's edge,
turning over concepts
I can't envision, the honking buoy
serves notice that at any time
5    the wind may change,
the reef-bell clatters
its treble monotone, deaf as Cassandra°
to any note but warning. The ocean,
cumbered by no business more urgent
10    than keeping open old accounts
that never balanced,
goes on shuffling its millenniums
of quartz, granite, basalt.

---

°*7 Cassandra:* mythical Trojan prophetess who accurately foretold future disasters but whom no one believed.

It behaves
toward the permutations of novelty—
driftwood and shipwreck, last night's
beer cans, spilt oil, the coughed-up
residue of plastic—with random
impartiality, playing catch or tag
or touch-last like a terrier,
turning the same thing over and over,
over and over. For the ocean, nothing
is beneath consideration.

    The houses
of so many mussels and periwinkles
have been abandoned here, it's hopeless
to know which to salvage. Instead
I keep a lookout for beach glass—
amber of Budweiser, chrysoprase°
of Almadén and Gallo, lapis
by way of (no getting around it,
I'm afraid) Phillips'
Milk of Magnesia, with now and then a rare
translucent turquoise or blurred amethyst
of no known origin.

    The process
goes on forever: they came from sand,
they go back to gravel,
along with the treasuries
of Murano,° the buttressed
astonishments of Chartres,°
which even now are readying
for being turned over and over as gravely
and gradually as an intellect
engaged in the hazardous
redefinitions of structures
no one has yet looked at.

15

20

25

30

35

40

45

---

°29 *chrysoprase*: a gold-green gemstone. 40 *Murano*: a Venetian island famous for its glass. 41 *Chartres*: the medieval cathedral of Chartres, France, which is unique because of the incredible beauty of its stained glass windows.

# Questions

1. What is the symbolic idea of the poet's description of the buoy near the shore? How does the reference to Cassandra support the poem's meaning?

2. What life forms, now jetsam, does the speaker observe on the shore? What human artifacts have been cast ashore? Why does she choose to collect some of these artifacts?

Why does she use words like "chrysoprase," "lapis," and "amethyst" in reference to these objects?

**3.** What is the meaning of the last stanza? What is the purpose of the poem's symbolic contrast between the beach glass and the glass from Murano and Chartres? What do these objects symbolize?

## ARTHUR HUGH CLOUGH (1819–1861)

 ### Say Not the Struggle Nought Availeth (1849)

Say not the struggle nought availeth,
  The labour and the wounds are vain,
The enemy faints not, nor faileth,°                               *See Isaiah 40:28–31*
  And as things have been they remain.°

5  If hopes were dupes, fears may be liars;°
  It may be, in yon smoke concealed,
Your comrades chase e'en now the fliers,°                     *soldiers in retreat*
  And, but for you, possess the field.°            *have control over the battlefield*

For while the tired waves, vainly breaking,
10  Seem here no painful inch to gain,
Far back, through creeks and inlets making,
  Comes silent, flooding in, the main.°                      *i.e., the ocean*

And not by eastern windows only,
  When daylight comes, comes in the light,
15  In front, the sun climbs slow, how slowly,
  But westward, look, the land is bright.

---

°1–4 *Say . . . remain*: In more direct syntax, the title sentence may be construed as "Do not say that the struggle [of life] is of no value." Lines 2, 3, and 4 are each direct objects of the opening verb "Say not." 5 *If hopes . . . liars*: i.e., If one grants that hope is unreal and therefore deceptive, one may also grant that fear is unreal and therefore equally deceptive.

## Questions

**1.** How many separate symbols are there in this poem? From what topics are they drawn? Why does Clough allude to some of the words in Isaiah?

**2.** Consider this poem as a persuasive argument against feelings of personal depression and desolation. How does Clough use symbols as the basis of his argument that the listener should overcome his/her despair?

**3.** Why does Clough end the poem, in line 16, with the observation that the sun shining in the East illuminates the West? Why does Clough draw attention to the slowness of the ascendant sun? Additionally, to what degree might "westward" be considered as a symbol of immortality because it is the location of the setting sun?

# PETER DAVISON (b. 1928)

## Delphi° (1964)

The crackle of parched grass bent by wind
Is the only music in the grove
Except the gush of the Pierian Spring.°
Eagles are often seen, but through a glass
Their naked necks declare them to be vultures.                                5
The place is sacred with a sanctity
Now faded, like a kerchief washed too often.
There lies the crevice where the priestesses
Hid in the crypt and drugged themselves and spoke
Until in later years the ruling powers                                        10
Bribed them to prophesy what was desired.
Till then the Greeks took pride in hopelessness
And, though they sometimes wrestled with their gods,°
They never won a blessing or a name
But only knowledge.                                                           15
                I shall never know myself
Enough to know what things I half believe
And, half believing, only half deny.

---

°In ancient Greece, Delphi was the location of the Temple of Apollo, the home of the famous oracle. Fumes issuing from an underground opening, around which the temple was built, would overcome the priestess, always named Pythia, and she would then deliver prophecies to priests, who would then pass them on, in prose, to inquiring people who wished to know the future. These people of course would have previously made an offering to the Temple. 3 *Pierian Spring*: A famous spring near Delphi, on the western slope of Mount Olympus, sacred to the Muses. Consider Alexander Pope's lines from *An Essay on Criticism*: "A little learning is a dangerous thing;/Drink deep, or taste not, the Pierian Spring." 13 *wrestled with their gods*: See Genesis 32:24–32.

## Questions

1. What is the topic of this poem? Why is the poem titled "Delphi"?
2. What is the meaning of the final three lines? How do they relate to the previous part of the poem? Why does the speaker include them?
3. Explain the allusions to Delphi, the "crevice where the priestesses/Hid in the crypt," and the reference to Genesis in lines 13–15.

# JOHN DONNE (1572–1631)

*For a portrait, see Chapter 12, page 508.*

## The Canonization° (1633)

For Godsake hold your tongue, and let me love,
  Or chide my palsy, or my gout,
My five gray hairs, or ruin'd fortune flout,

---

°*The Canonization*: the making of saints.

With wealth your state, your mind with Arts improve,°
5      Take you a course,° get you a place,°
       Observe His Honor,° or his grace,°
Or the King's real, or his stampèd face
Contemplate,° what you will, approve,°
       So you will let me love.

10  Alas, alas, who's injured by my love?
       What merchant's ships have my sighs drown'd?
Who says my tears have overflow'd his ground?
       When did my colds a forward spring° remove?
       When did the heats which my veins fill°
15      Add one more to the plaguy Bill?°
Soldiers find wars, and Lawyers find out still
       Litigious men, which quarrels move,
       Though she and I do love.

Call us what you will, we are made such by love;
20      Call her one, me another fly,°
We'are Tapers° too, and at our own cost die,°                         *candles*
       And we in us find the Eagle and the Dove.°
       The Phoenix riddle° hath more wit
       By us, we two, being one, are it.
25  So, to one neutral thing both sexes fit,
       We die and rise the same, and prove
       Mysterious° by this love.

We can die by it, if not live by love,
       And if unfit for tombs and hearse
30  Our legend be, it will be fit for verse;
       And if no piece of Chronicle we prove,
          We'll build in sonnets pretty rooms;
          As well a well wrought run becomes
The greatest ashes, as half-acre tombs,
35      And by these hymns, all shall approve
       Us *Canoniz'd* for love:°

---

°4 *With wealth . . . improve*: i.e., Improve your state with wealth and your mind with arts. 5 *Take you a course*: take up a career. *place*: a political appointment. 6 *His Honor*: any important courtier. *his grace*: a person of greatest eminence, such as a bishop or the king. 7, 8 *Or . . . contemplate*: i.e., Or contemplate either the king's real face (at court) or stamped face (on coins). 8 *What . . . approve*: Try anything you like (i.e., "Mind your own business"). 13 a *forward spring*: an early spring (season). 14 *the heats . . . fill*: i.e., "the heats (fevers) that fill my veins." Donne apparently wrote this line before the discovery of blood circulation was announced by William Harvey in 1616. 15 *plaguy Bill*: a regularly published list of deaths caused by the plague. 20 *fly*: a butterfly or moth (and apparently superficial and light-headed). 21 *at . . . die*: It was supposed that sexual climax shortened life. 22 *the Eagle and the Dove*: masculine and feminine symbols. 23 *Phoenix riddle*: In ancient times the phoenix, a mythical bird that lived for a thousand years, was supposed to die and rise five hundred years later from its own ashes; hence the phoenix symbolized immortality and the renewal of life and desire. 27 *Mysterious*: unknowable to anyone but God, and therefore quintessentially holy. 35, 36 *by these hymns . . . Canoniz'd for love*: The idea is that later generations will remember the lovers and elevate them to the sainthood of a religion of love. Because the lovers' love is recorded so powerfully in the speaker's poems ("sonnets" in line 33), these later generations will use the poems as hymns in their worship of love.

And thus invoke° us; "You whom reverend love                *pray to saints*
  Made one another's hermitage;°
You, to whom love was peace, that now is rage;
  Who did the whole world's soul extract, and drove           40
    Into the glasses of your eyes
    So made such mirrors, and such spies,
That they did all to you epitomize,°
  Countries, towns, courts: Beg from above
  A pattern of your love!"                               45

---

°38 *Made . . . hermitage*: made a religious retreat for each other. 40–43 *Who did . . . epitomize*: An allusion to reputed alchemical processes, and therefore to be understood approximately like this: "Who extracted the whole world's soul and, through your eyes, assimilated this soul into yours, so that you, whose eyes saw and reflected each other, embodied the love and desire felt by all human beings."

## Questions

1. What is the situation of the poem? Whom is the speaker addressing? Why does he begin as he does? How does he defend his love?

2. What symbols do you find in the poem? What are the symbols? What is being symbolized?

3. What mythic and religious mysteries are linked with sexual love in the third stanza? What does "canonization" mean? What canonizes and immortalizes the lovers? How does the "canonization" symbolize the poem's idea about the nature of love?

4. What will future lovers ask of these saints of love? Of what use will the speaker's poem be at that time? What do you think of the speaker's claim about love?

## STEPHEN DUNN (b. 1939)

 # Hawk (1989)

What a needy, desperate thing
to claim what's wild for oneself,
yet the hawk circling above the pines
looks like the same one I thought

might become mine after it crashed            5
into the large window and lay
one wing spread, the other loosely
tucked, then no, not dead, got up

dazed, and in minutes was gone.
Now once again                       10
this is its sky, this its woods.
The tasty small birds it loves

have seen their God and know
the suddenness of such love
as we know lightning or flash flood.           15
If hawks can learn, this hawk learned

what's clear can be hard
down where the humans live,
and that the hunting isn't good
20    where the air is such a lie.

It glides above the pines and I
turn back into the room, the hawk book
open on the cluttered table
to Cooper's Hawk

25    and the unwritten caption
that to be wild
means nothing you do or have done
needs to be explained.

## Questions

1. Why does the speaker consider the issue of owning or not owning the hawk that crashed into his window?
2. In what way is the hawk significant? How can a reader justify considering it as a symbol? What does the bird symbolize?
3. What is the meaning of the final four lines? How true are the lines? If "to be wild" needs no explanation, what does it mean, in contrast, to be civilized?

## ISABELLA GARDNER (1915–1981)

 ### Collage of Echoes (1979)

I have no promises to keep
Nor miles to go before I sleep,°
For miles of years I have made promises
and (mostly) kept them.
5        It's time I slept.
Now I lay me down to sleep°
With no promises to keep.
        My sleaves are ravelled°
        I have travelled.°

---

°2 *miles to go before I sleep*: See Robert Frost, "Stopping by Woods on a Snowy Evening" (page 470), lines 13–16.  6 *Now I lay me down to sleep*: from the child's prayer: Now I lay me down to sleep;/I pray the Lord my soul to keep./If I should die before I wake,/I pray the Lord my soul to take  8 *My sleaves are ravelled*: *See Macbeth*, 11.2.37: "Sleep that knits up the ravelled sleave of care."  9 *I have travelled*: See Keats, "On First Looking into Chapman's Homer" (page 562).

## Questions

1. Given the allusions in the poem, what do you conclude about the speaker's judgment of the reader's knowledge of literature?
2. How reliant is "Collage of Echoes" upon the contexts being echoed? How do the echoes assist in enabling enjoyment and appreciation of the poem?
3. In relation to the speaker's character as demonstrated in the poem, consider the phrases "(mostly) kept them," "With no promises to keep," and "My sleaves are ravelled." What do they show about the speaker's self-assessment? In what way might these phrases be considered comic?

## RALPH WALDO EMERSON (1803–1882)

 ### Concord Hymn (1837)

*Sung at the completion of the Battle Monument, July 4, 1837*

By the rude bridge that arched the flood,
   Their flag to April's breeze unfurled,
Here once the embattled farmers stood,
   And fired the shot heard round the world.

The foe long since in silence slept;                 5
   Alike the conqueror silent sleeps;
And Time the ruined bridge has swept
   Down the dark stream which seaward creeps.

On the green bank, by this soft stream,
   We set to-day a votive stone;
That memory may their deed redeem,
   When, like our sires, our sons are gone.           10

Spirit, that made those spirits dare
   To die, and leave their children free,
Bid Time and Nature gently spare
   The shaft we raise to them and thee.           15

## Questions

1. Line 4 is one of the best-known lines of American poetry. Why is it so well known? Discuss the rhythm of the line. Where are the heavy accents? What complication occurs in the phrase "heard round"?
2. Discuss line 7. What does Emerson do grammatically to get his idea across and also to create the verbal "swept" to rhyme with "slept"?
3. Describe the symbolism of the "votive stone" that Emerson speaks about in line 10.

# LOUISE GLÜCK (b. 1943)

## 🖋 Celestial Music (1990)

I have a friend who still believes in heaven.
Not a stupid person, yet with all she knows, she literally talks to god,
she thinks someone listens in heaven.
On earth, she's unusually competent.
5    Brave, too, able to face unpleasantness.

We found a caterpillar dying in the dirt, greedy ants crawling over it.
I'm always moved by weakness, by disaster, always eager to oppose vitality.
But timid, also, quick to shut my eyes.
Whereas my friend was able to watch, to let events play out
10   according to nature. For my sake, she intervened,
brushing a few ants off the torn thing, and set it down across the road.

My friend says I shut my eyes to god, that nothing else explains
my aversion to reality. She says I'm like the child who buries her head in the pillow
so as not to see, the child who tells herself
that light causes sadness—
15   My friend is like the mother. Patient, urging me
to wake up an adult like herself, a courageous person—

In my dreams, my friend reproaches me. We're walking
on the same road, except it's winter now;
20   she's telling me that when you love the world you hear celestial music:
look up, she says. When I look up, nothing.
Only clouds, snow, a white business in the trees
like brides leaping to a great height—
Then I'm afraid for her; I see her
25   caught in a net deliberately cast over the earth—

In reality, we sit by the side of the road, watching the sun set;
from time to time, the silence pierced by a birdcall.
It's this moment we're both trying to explain, the fact
that we're at ease with death, with solitude.
30   My friend draws a circle in the dirt; inside, the caterpillar doesn't move.

She's always trying to make something whole, something beautiful, an image
capable of life apart from her.
We're very quiet. It's peaceful sitting here, not speaking, the composition
fixed, the road turning suddenly dark, the air
35   going, cool, here and there the rocks shining and glittering—
it's this stillness that we both love.
The love of form is a love of endings.

## Questions

1. What is the significance of the caterpillar at the poem's beginning? How might the caterpillar be taken as a symbol? What might it symbolize? What does the "celestial music" of line 20 signify? Why does the speaker not seem to hear it?

2. Why does the speaker describe the character of her friend? How does the speaker assert the differences she has with her friend? What does the setting sun symbolize in lines 26–37? How might it be symbolic that the speaker and her friend are sitting at the same side of the road?

3. Explain the poem's final line. What is the form that the speaker describes? Why might not the "love of endings" be the love of beginnings? Why is it necessary to love endings?

## JORIE GRAHAM (b. 1954)

 ### The Geese (1980)

Today as I hang out the wash I see them again, a code
as urgent as elegant,
tapering with goals.
For days they have been crossing. We live beneath these geese

as if beneath the passage of time, or a most perfect heading.                              5
Sometimes I fear their relevance.
Closest at hand,
between the lines,

the spiders imitate the paths the geese won't stray from,
imitate them endlessly to no avail:                                                         10
things will not remain connected,
will not heal,

and the world thickens with texture instead of history,
texture instead of place.
Yet the small fear of the spiders                                                           15
binds and binds

the pins to the lines, the line to the eaves, to the pincushion bush,
as if, at any time, things could fall further apart
and nothing could help them
recover their meaning. And if these spiders had their way,                                  20

chainlink over the visible world,
would we be in or out? I turn to go back in.
There is a feeling the body gives the mind
of having missed something, a bedrock poverty, like falling

without the sense that you are passing through one world,                                   25
that you could reach another

anytime. Instead the real
is crossing you,

your body an arrival
30  you know is false but can't outrun. And somewhere in between
these geese forever entering and
these spiders turning back

this astonishing delay, the everyday, takes place.

## Questions

1. What is the dominant tense of the poem? What effect does this tense have on the speaker's conclusions?

2. What action does the speaker perform in the course of the poem? What is the relationship between this action and the final lines?

3. What do the geese symbolize? What do the spiders symbolize? How are these symbols contrasted?

4. The first half of this poem, particularly lines 11 and 18, is reminiscent of Yeats's "The Second Coming" (page 727). In your judgment, what use does Graham make of this allusion?

## THOMAS HARDY (1840–1928)

*For a photo, see Chapter 6, page 256.*

 ## In Time of "The Breaking of Nations"° (1916 (1915))

Only a man harrowing clods
   In a slow silent walk,
With an old horse that stumbles and nods
   Half asleep as they stalk.

5  Only thin smoke without flame
   From the heaps of couch grass:°                          *quack grass*
Yet this will go onward the same
   Though Dynasties pass.

Yonder a maid and her wight°                               *fellow*
10   Come whispering by;
War's annals will fade into night
   Ere their story die.

─────────────
°See Jeremiah 51:20, "with you I break nations in pieces."

## Questions

1. What does Hardy symbolize by the man, horse, smoke and couple? How realistic and vivid are these symbols? Are they universal or contextual?

2. How does Hardy show that the phrase "breaking of nations" is to be taken symbolically? What meaning is gained by the biblical allusion of this phrase?

3. Contrast the structure of stanza 1 with that of stanzas 2 and 3. How does the form of stanzas 2 and 3 enable Hardy to emphasize the main idea?

4. How does the speaker show his evaluation of the life of the common people? You might consider that at the time (1915), World War I was raging in Europe.

## GEORGE HERBERT (1593–1633)

 **The Collar°** (1633)

I struck the board, and cry'd "No more;
    I will abroad!
What? shall I ever sigh and pine?
My lines and life are free; free as the road,
  Loose as the wind, as large as store,          5
    Shall I be still in suit? °
  Have I no harvest but a thorn °
To let me blood, and not restore
What I have lost with cordial fruit?
    Sure there was wine          10
  Before my sighs did dry it: there was corn
    Before my tears did drown it.
  Is the year only lost to me?
    Have I no bays° to crown it?
No flowers, no garlands gay? all blasted?          15
    All wasted?
  Not so, my heart: but there is fruit,
    And thou hast hands.
  Recover all thy sight-blown age
On double pleasures: leave thy cold dispute          20
Of what is fit, and not; forsake thy cage;
    Thy rope of sands,
Which petty thoughts have made, and made to thee
  Good cable, to enforce and draw,
    And be thy law,          25
  While thou didst wink and wouldst not see.
    Away; take heed:
    I will abroad.
Call in thy death's head there: tie up thy fears.
    He that forbears          30
To suit° and serve his need,          *follow*
    Deserves his load."
But as I rav'd and grew more fierce and wild
    At every word,
  Me thought I heard one calling, "Child:"          35
    And I replied, "*My Lord.*"

---

°*collar*: (a) the collar worn by a member of the clergy; (b) the collar of the harness of a draft animal such as a horse; (c) a restraint placed on prisoners; (d) a pun on *choler* (yellow bile), a bodily substance that was thought to cause quick rages. 6 *in suit*: waiting upon a person of power to gain favor or position. 7 *thorn*: See Mark 15:17. 14 *bays*: laurel crowns to signify victory and honor.

## Questions

1. What is the opening situation? Why is the speaker angry? Against what role in life is he complaining?
2. In light of the many possible meanings of *collar* (see note), explain the title as a symbol in the poem.
3. Explain the symbolism of the thorn (line 7), blood (line 8), wine (line 10), bays (line 14), flowers and garlands (line 15), cage (line 27), rope of sands (line 22), death's head (line 29), and the dialogue in lines 35 and 36.

## JOSEPHINE JACOBSEN (b. 1908)

 **Tears** (1981)

Tears leave no mark on the soil
or pavement; certainly not in sand
or in any known rain forest;
never a mark on stone.
5   One would think that no one in Persepolis°
or Ur° ever wept.

You would assume that, like Alice,°
we would all be swimming, buffeted
in a tide of tears.
10   But they disappear. Their heat goes.
Yet the globe is salt
with that savor.°

The animals want no part in this.
The hare both screams and weeps
15   at her death, one poet says.
The stag, at death, rolls round drops
down his muzzle; but, he is in
Shakespeare's forest.°

These cases are mythically rare.
20   No, it is the human being who persistently
weeps, in some countries, openly, in others, not.
Children who, even when frightened, weep most hopefully;
women, licensed weepers.°
Men, in secret, or childishly; or nobly.

---

°5, 6 *Persepolis . . . Ur*: Persepolis was the capital city of ancient Persia (now Iran). Ur, on the Persian Gulf, was the capital city of the ancient Sumerian Empire. Today, both cities survive only in ruins. The Hebrew patriarch Abraham traveled from "Ur of the Chaldees" to settle in the land of Canaan, the "promised land." 7 *Alice*: in Lewis Carroll's *Alice in Wonderland* (Ch. 2), Alice sheds tears, and then is reduced in size and almost drowns in her own teardrops. 11–12 *Yet . . . Savor*: Matthew 5:13. 14–18 *The hare . . . forest*: In the poem *Autumn* by James Thomson (1700–1748), lines 401–57, a cruel hunt of the hare and the stag is described. It is the stag who sheds "big round tears" and "groans in anguish" when dying. Jacobsen's allusion to Shakespeare—to whom Thomson is also alluding—is *As You Like It*, 2.1.29–43. 23 *licensed weepers*: In certain countries, such as Greece, professional "weepers" weep and cry aloud at funerals.

Could tears not make a sea of their mass?                                    25
It could be salt and wild enough;
it could rouse storms and sink ships,
erode, erode its shores:
tears of rage, of love, of torture,
of loss. Of loss.                                                             30

Must we see the future
in order to weep? Or the past?
Is that why the animals
refuse to shed tears?
But what of the present, the tears of the present?                           35
The awful relief, like breath

after strangling? The generosity
of the verb "to shed"?
They are a classless possession
yet are not found in the museum                                               40
of even our greatest city.
Sometimes what was human, turns
into an animal, dry-eyed.

## Questions

1. What does the poem's major symbol, tears, mean? What significance does the poem attribute to tears? Why are tears sometimes disregarded?
2. How does the poem apply the symbol to various cultures and conditions?
3. How do tears differentiate human beings from animals? What is the symbolic value of this difference? In light of the contrast, what is the meaning of the last two lines?
4. Explain the poem's use of allusions (i.e., Persepolis, Ur, the New Testament, *Alice in Wonderland*, professional mourners, Shakespeare).

## ROBINSON JEFFERS (1887–1962)

 ### The Purse-Seine (1937)

1

Our sardine fishermen work at night in the dark of the moon;
        daylight or moonlight
They could not tell where to spread the net, unable to see the
        phosphorescence of the shoals of fish.
They work northward from Monterey, coasting Santa Cruz;
        off New Year's Point or off Pigeon Point
The look-out man will see some lakes of milk-color light on the seas's
        night-purple; he points, and the helmsman

Turns the dark prow, the motorboat circles the gleaming shoal and drifts out
5      her seine-net. They close the circle
And purse the bottom of the net, then with great labor haul it in.

2

                                      I cannot tell you
How beautiful the scene is, and a little terrible, then, when the crowded fish
Know they are caught, and wildly beat from one wall to the other of their closing destiny
      the phosphorescent
Water to a pool of flame, each beautiful slender body sheeted with flame, like a
10      live rocket
A comet's tail wake of clear yellow flame; while outside the narrowing
Floats and cordage of the net great sea-lions come up to watch, sighing in the dark; the
      vast walls of night
Stand erect to the stars.

3

                         Lately I was looking from a night mountain-top
On a wide city, the colored splendor, galaxies of light; how could I help but recall the
15      seine-net
Gathering the luminous fish? I cannot tell you how beautiful the city appeared, and a
      little terrible.
I thought, We have geared the machines and locked all together into interdependence;
      we have built the great cities; now
There is no escape. We have gathered vast populations incapable of free survival,
      insulated
From the strong earth, each person in himself helpless, on all dependent. The circle is
      closed, and the net
Is being hauled in. They hardly feel the cords drawing, yet they shine already. The
20      inevitable mass-disasters
Will not come in our time nor in our children's, but we and our children
Must watch the net draw narrower, government take all powers—or revolution, and
      the new government
Take more than all, add to kept bodies kept souls—or anarchy, the mass-disasters.

4

                     These things are Progress;
Do you marvel our verse is troubled or frowning, while it keeps its reason? Or it lets go,
25      lets the mood flow
In the manner of the recent young men into mere hysteria, splintered gleams, crackled
      laughter. But they are quite wrong.
There is no reason for amazement; surely one always knew that cultures decay, and life's
      end is death.

## Questions

1. Describe how the purse-seine is used to haul in the sardines. What is the speaker's reaction to the scene as described in stanza 2?

**2.** How does the speaker explain that the purse-seine is a symbol? What does it symbolize? What do the sardines symbolize?

**3.** Compare the ideas of Jeffers with those of Yeats in "The Second Coming." Are the ideas of Jeffers more or less methodical?

**4.** Is the statement at the end to be taken as a fact or as a resigned acceptance of that fact? Does the poem offer any solution to the problem?

**5.** How can the sea-lions of line 12, and their sighs, be construed as a symbol?

## JOHN KEATS (1795–1821)

*For a portrait, see Chapter 14, page 562.*

 ## La Belle Dame Sans Merci: A Ballad° (1820 (1819))

1

O what can ail thee, knight at arms,
    Alone and palely loitering?
The sedge has wither'd from the lake,
    And no birds sing.


2

O what can ail thee, knight at arms,                                                      5
    So haggard and so woe-begone?
The squirrel's granary is full,
    And the harvest's done.


3

I see a lily on thy brow
    With anguish moist and fever dew,                                          10
And on dry cheeks a fading rose
    Fast withereth too.


4

I met a lady in the meads,°                                                      *meadows*
    Full beautiful, a fairy's child;
Her hair was long, her foot was light,                                                   15
    And her eyes were wild.

---

°"La Belle Dame Sans Merci" is French for "The beautiful lady without pity" (that is, "The heartless woman"). "La Belle Dame Sans Merci" is the title of a medieval poem by Alain Chartier; Keats's poem bears no other relationship to the medieval poem, which was thought at the time to have been by Chaucer.

**5**

I made a garland for her head,
　　And bracelets too, and fragrant zone;° _belt_
She look'd at me as she did love,
20　　And made sweet moan.

**6**

I set her on my pacing steed,
　　And nothing else saw all day long,
For sidelong would she bend, and sing
　　A fairy's song.

**7**

25　She found me roots of relish° sweet, _magical potion_
　　And honey wild, and manna° dew, _see Exodus 16:14–36_
And sure in language strange she said—
　　I love thee true.

**8**

She took me to her elfin grot,° _grotto_
30　　And there she wept, and sigh'd full sore,
And there I shut her wild wild eyes
　　With kisses four.

**9**

And there she lullèd me asleep,
　　And there I dream'd—Ah! woe betide!
35　The latest° dream I ever dream'd _last_
　　On the cold hill's side.

**10**

I saw pale kings, and princes too,
　　Pale warriors, death pale were they all;
They cried—"La belle dame sans merci
40　　Hath thee in thrall!"° _slavery_

**11**

I saw their starv'd lips in the gloam
　　With horrid warning gapèd wide,
And I awoke and found me here
　　On the cold hill's side.

12

And this is why I sojourn here,     45
    Alone and palely loitering,
Though the sedge is wither'd from the lake,
    And no birds sing.

## Questions

1. Who is the speaker of stanzas 1–3? Who speaks after that?
2. In light of the dreamlike content of the poem, how can the knight's experience be viewed as symbolic? What is being symbolized?
3. Consider "relish" (line 25), "honey" (line 26), and "manna" (line 26) as symbols. Are they realistic or mythical? What does the allusion to manna signify? What is symbolized by the "pale kings, and princes too" and "Pale warriors" (lines 37–38)?
4. Consider the poem's setting as symbols of the knight's state of mind.

## X. J. KENNEDY (b. 1929)

 ## Old Men Pitching Horseshoes (1985)

Back in a yard where ringers groove a ditch,
These four in shirtsleeves congregate to pitch
Dirt-burnished iron. With appraising eye,
One sizes up a peg, hoists and lets fly—
A clang resounds as though a smith had struck     5
Fire from a forge. His first blow, out of luck,
Rattles in circles. Hitching up his face,
He swings, and weight once more inhabits space,
Thumbles as gently as a new-laid egg.
Extended iron arms surround their peg     10
Like one come home to greet a long-lost brother.
Shouts from one outpost. Mutters from the other.
Now changing sides, each withered pitcher moves
As his considered dignity behooves
Down the worn path of earth where August flies     15
And sheaves of air in warm distortions rise.
To stand ground, fling, kick dust with all the force
Of shoes still hammered to a living horse.

## Questions

1. How does the poet indicate that the pitching of horseshoes is symbolic? As symbols, why are old men chosen rather than young men?
2. Discuss the effects of the words "congregate," "outpost," "withered," "sheaves," "kick dust," and "force." What do these words contribute to the poem's symbolism?
3. Compare the topic of this poem with the concluding lines of T. S. Eliot's "Preludes" (page 539), especially the last two lines. How is the symbolism of these poems similar? Different?

## TED KOOSER (b. 1939)

###  Year's End (1985)

Now the seasons are closing their files
on each of us, the heavy drawers
full of certificates rolling back
into the tree trunks, a few old papers
5   flocking away. Someone we loved
has fallen from our thoughts,
making a little, glittering splash
like a bicycle pushed by a breeze.
Otherwise, not much has happened;
10  we fell in love again, finding
that one red feather in the wind.

## Questions

1. What is the occasion of the poem? Why does the speaker use the pronouns "us," "we," "our," and "we" as references? Does the mean only himself? Does he mean others beside himself?

2. How might certificates roll back into tree trunks? What is the meaning of the speaker's mention of papers "flocking away"?

3. In line 10 the speaker says that "We fell in love again." In what way does the "one red feather in the wind" symbolize this action? Why doesn't the speaker talk sooner in the poem about falling in love?

4. Compare this poem with Wilbur's "Year's End" and Roethke's "Dolor" (Chapter 12). What do the poems have in common? In what ways is Kooser's "Year's End" unique?

## PHILIP LARKIN (1922–1985)

###  Next, Please (1955)

Always too eager for the future, we
Pick up bad habits of expectancy.
Something is always approaching; every day
*Till then* we say,

5   Watching from a bluff the tiny, clear,
Sparkling armada of promises draw near.
How slow they are! And how much time they waste,
Refusing to make haste!

Yet still they leave us holding wretched stalks
10  Of disappointment, for, though nothing balks
Each big approach, leaning with brasswork prinked,°          adorned
Each rope distinct.

Flagged, and the figurehead with golden tits
Arching our way, it never anchors; it's
No sooner present than it turns to past.                    15
Right to the last

We think each one will heave to and unload
All good into our lives, all we are owed
For waiting so devoutly and so long.
But we are wrong:                                           20

Only one ship is seeking us, a black-
Sailed unfamiliar, towing at her back
A huge and birdless silence. In her wake
No waters breed or break.

## Questions

1. What is the subject of the poem? The theme? What point does it make about time, expectation, human nature, and the way we live our lives?

2. What cliché does the extended metaphor that begins in the second stanza ironically revi-
   talize and reverse? How does this metaphor make the total meaning of the poem clearer
   and more palpable?

3. How do meter, rhyme, and diction help create meaning? Consider, for example, the metrical variation in the fourth line of each stanza, rhyming pairs such as "waste-haste" and
   "wake-break," or words such as "bluff" and "armada."

4. Compare this poem to Marvell's "To His Coy Mistress." To what extent is "Next, Please"
   a *carpe diem* poem?

## DAVID LEHMAN (b. 1948)

 **Venice Is Sinking** (2002)

In New York we defy
everything but gravity
but we're not sinking
unlike Venice we're level
though encircled with water                                 5
we travel underground in
trains going through tunnels
our grandparents built
in a way it's a miracle
when you think of any of                                    10
the ways any of us could
die in a day if some
apparatus we rely on
unthinkingly,
the elevator or the subway                                  15

or the good faith of motorists,
should fail—
think of it—
what are the odds
20  that we'd still be here
as we are

## Questions

1. Why is the poem titled "Venice Is Sinking." In light of the title, why does the poet discuss New York throughout the poem? In what way can Venice be considered symbolic of New York, and also, generally, of all big cities?

2. Why does the poet discuss the "miracle" of New York? To what degree might New York symbolize the precariousness of existence? How is it significant that pedestrians are dependent on the "good faith of motorists"? Is it only the faith of motorists on whom we rely for our continued existence?

3. Why do you think the poet largely avoids punctuation and capitalization? How could this lack illustrate any ideas about the nature of modern life?

## ANDREW MARVELL (1621–1678)

 ## To His Coy Mistress (1681)

Had we but world enough, and time,
This coyness, lady, were no crime.
We would sit down, and think which way
To walk, and pass our long love's day.

5   Thou by the Indian Ganges° side
Shouldst rubies find; I by the tide
Of Humber° would complain. I would
Love you ten years before the flood,°                    *Noah's flood*
And you should, if you please, refuse
10  Till the conversion of the Jews.°
My vegetable love should grow
Vaster than empires and more slow;
An hundred years should go to praise
Thine eyes, and on thy forehead gaze;
15  Two hundred to adore each breast,
But thirty thousand to the rest;
An age at least to every part,
And the last age should show your heart.
For, lady, you deserve this state,
20  Nor would I love at lower rate.
     But at my back I always hear

---

°5 *Ganges*: a large river than runs across most of India.  7 *Humber*: a small river that runs through the north of England to the North Sea.  10 *Jews*: Traditionally, this conversion is supposed to occur just before the Last Judgment.

Time's wingéd chariot hurrying near;
And yonder all before us lie
Deserts of vast eternity.
Thy beauty shall no more be found,                                                  25
Nor, in thy marble vault, shall sound
My echoing song, then worms shall try
That long-preserved virginity,
And your quaint honor turn to dust,
And into ashes all my lust;                                                         30
The grave's a fine and private place,
But none, I think, do there embrace.
   Now therefore, while the youthful hue
Sits on thy skin like morning dew,
And while thy willing soul transpires                                               35
At every pore with instant fires,
Now let us sport us while we may,
And now, like amorous birds of prey,
Rather at once our time devour
Than languish in his slow-chapped° power.                    *slow-jawed*    40
Let us roll all our strength and all
Our sweetness up into one ball,
And tear our pleasures with rough stife
Thorough° the iron gates of life:                              *through*
Thus, though we cannot make our sun                                                45
Stand still, yet we will make him run.

## Questions

1. In lines 1–20 the speaker sets up a hypothetical situation and the first part of a pseudolog-
   ical proof: If *A* then *B*. What specific words indicate the logic of this section? What hypothetical situation is established?

2. How do geographic and biblical allusions affect our sense of time and place?

3. In lines 21–32 the speaker refutes the hypothetical condition set up in the first twenty
   lines. What word indicates that this is a refutation? How do symbols of death create and
   reinforce meaning here?

4. The last part of the poem (lines 33–46) presents the speaker's "logical" conclusion. What
   words indicate that this is a conclusion? What is the conclusion?

**MARY OLIVER** (b. 1935)

 **Wild Geese** (1986)

You do not have to be good.
You do not have to walk on your knees
for a hundred miles through the desert, repenting
You only have to let the soft animal of your body
   love what it loves.
Tell me about despair, yours, and I will tell you mine.                             5

Meanwhile the world goes on.
Meanwhile the sun and the clear pebbles of the rain
are moving across the landscapes,
10   over the prairies and the deep trees,
the mountains and the rivers.
Meanwhile the wild geese, high in the clean blue air,
are heading home again.
Whoever you are, no matter how lonely,
15   the world offers itself to your imagination,
calls to you like the wild geese, harsh and exciting—
over and over announcing your place
in the family of things.

## Questions

1. What idea is contained in the first five lines? What ideas are expressed in lines 6–12? In what ways are lines 13–17 a climax of the poem? How does this last section build on the poem's earlier parts?

2. What is symbolized by the references to "the sun and the clear pebbles of the rain," and so on, in lines 7–10? Do these symbols suggest futility or hope?

3. What do the wild geese symbolize (lines 11–12, 15)? How is the symbol of the geese a response to the poem's first six lines? How well would the words *acceptance, self-knowledge,* or *adjustment* describe the poem's ideas? What other words would be better or more suitable? Why?

## JUDITH VIORST (b. 1931)

 ## A Wedding Sonnet for the Next Generation (2000)

He might compare you to a summer's day,°
Declaring you're far fairer in his eyes.
She might, with depth and breadth and many sighs,
Count all the ways she loves you, way by way.°

5   He might say when you're old and full of sleep,
He'll cherish still the Pilgrim soul in you.°
She might—oh, there are poems so fine, so true,
To help you speak of love and vows to keep.

10   Words help. And you are writing your own poem.
It doesn't always scan or always rhyme.
It mingles images of the sublime
With plainer words: Respect. Trust. Comfort. Home.

How very rich is love's vocabulary
When friends, dear friends, best friends decide to marry.

---

°1 *summer's day*: See Shakespeare, "Shall I Compare Thee to a Summer's Day?" (Chapter 14). 3, 4 *She might . . . way by way*: See Elizabeth Barrett Browning, "How Do I Love Thee" (Chapter 19). 5, 6 *He might say . . . Pilgrim soul in you*: See Yeats, "When You Are Old" (Chapter 15).

## Questions

1. Why does the poem speak of "the Next Generation" in the title? What is the form of the poem? Why do the first lines alternate between "he" and "she"?

2. What is the meaning and effect of the allusions in lines 1–6? Why does Viorst introduce these allusions? What assumptions does she make about her audience for this poem?

3. How does the poem change in the last six lines? How does the language shift in these lines?

4. What does it mean to say "you are writing your own poem"? How are the final two lines related to the previous parts of the poem?

## WALT WHITMAN (1819–1892)

*For a photo, see Chapter 14, page 587.*

 ## A Noiseless Patient Spider (1868)

A noiseless patient spider,
I marked where on a little promontory it stood isolated,
Marked how to explore the vacant vast surrounding,
It launched forth filament, filament, filament out of itself,
Ever unreeling them, ever tirelessly speeding them.                    5

And you O my soul where you stand,
Surrounded, detached, in measureless oceans of space,
Ceaselessly musing, venturing, throwing, seeking the spheres
    to connect them,
Till the bridge you will need be formed, till the ductile anchor hold,
Till the gossamer thread you fling catch somewhere, O my soul.         10

## Questions

1. The subject of the second stanza is seemingly unrelated to the subject of the first. How are these stanzas related?

2. In what way does the spider's web symbolize the soul and the poet's view of the isolation of human beings? How does the web symbolize the soul's ceaseless "musing . . . seeking" and the attempt "to connect"?

3. Explain why the second stanza is not a complete sentence. How might this grammatical feature be related to the spider's web? To the poet's idea that life requires striving but does not offer completeness?

 ## RICHARD WILBUR (b. 1921)

 ## Year's End (1950)

Now winter downs the dying of the year,
And Night is all a settlement of snow;
From the soft street the rooms of houses show
A gathered light, a shapen atmosphere,

5  Like frozen-over lakes whose ice is thin
And still allows some stirring down within.

I've known the wind by water banks to shake
The late leaves down, which frozen where they fell
And held in ice as dancers in a spell
10  Fluttered all winter long into a lake;
Graved on the dark in gestures of descent,
They seemed their own most perfect monument.

There was perfection in the death of ferns
Which laid their fragile cheeks against the stone
15  A million years. Great mammoths overthrown
Composedly have made their long sojourns,
Like palaces of patience, in the gray
And changeless lands of ice. And at Pompeii°

The little dog lay curled and did not rise
20  But slept the deeper as the ashes rose
And found the people incomplete, and froze
The random hands, the loose unready eyes
Of men expecting yet another sun
To do the shapely thing they had not done.

25  These sudden ends of time must give us pause.
We fray into the future, rarely wrought
Save in the tapestries of afterthought.
More time, more time. Barrages of applause
Come muffled from a buried radio.
30  The New-year bells are wrangling with the snow.

---

°18 *Pompeii*: the southern Italian Roman city covered by lava during the eruption of Mount Vesuvius in 79 C.E. Many people and animals died trying to escape the lava flow and were covered over where they fell. Modern excavators created statues of these fallen figures by using plaster to fill in cavities left by their bodies. One of these was the "little dog" mentioned in line 19.

## Questions

1. What natural and historical symbols does Wilbur introduce in the poem? What ideas do the symbols present about time and the use people make of time?

2. Describe Wilbur's use of two-word groups united by assonance and consonance in the poem (e.g., "People incomplete," downs the dying," "still . . . stirring"). How effective are these groups in drawing your attention to Wilbur's meaning?

3. Describe the symbols in the final stanza ("fray into the future," "tapestries of afterthought," "muffled from a buried radio"). Why does the poem conclude with the symbols of "New-year bells" and "snow"?

4. Consider the meaning of line 25. How can this line be interpreted so that the poem may have either positive or negative views of human activity?

# WILLIAM BUTLER YEATS (1865–1939)

 ## The Second Coming° (1920 (1919))

Turning and turning in the widening gyre°
The falcon cannot hear the falconer;
Things fall apart; the center cannot hold;
Mere anarchy is loosed upon the world,
The blood-dimmed tide° is loosed, and everywhere          5
The ceremony of innocence is drowned;
The best lack all conviction, while the worst
Are full of passionate intensity.
Surely some revelation is at hand;
Surely the Second Coming is at hand.                     10
The Second Coming! Hardly are those words out
When a vast image out of *Spiritus Mundi*°
Troubles my sight; somewhere in sands of the desert
A shape with lion body and the head of a man,°
A gaze blank and pitiless as the sun,                    15
Is moving its slow thighs, while all about it
Reel shadows of the indignant desert birds.
The darkness drops again; but now I know
That twenty centuries of stony sleep
Were vexed to nightmare by a rocking cradle,             20
And what rough beast, its hour come round at last,
Slouches towards Bethlehem to be born?

---

°The phrase "second coming" has been traditionally used to refer to expectations of the return of Jesus for the salvation of believers, as described in the New Testament. The prophecies foretold that Christ's return would be preceded by famine, epidemics, wars between nations, and general civil disturbance. Yeats believed that human history could be measured in cycles of approximately 2,000 years (see line 19, "twenty centuries"). According to this system, the birth of Jesus ended the Greco-Roman cycle and in 1919, when Yeats wrote "The Second Coming," it appeared to him that the Christian period was ending and a new era was about to take its place. The New Testament expectation was that Jesus would reappear. Yeats, by contrast, holds that the disruptions of the twentieth century were preceding a takeover by the forces of evil. 1 *gyre*: a radiating spiral, cone, or vortex. Yeats used the intersecting of two of these shapes as a visual symbol of his cyclic theory. As one gyre spiraled and widened out, to become dissipated, one period of history would end; at the same time a new gyre, closer to the center, would begin and spiral in a reverse direction to the starting point of the old gyre. A drawing of this plan looks like this:

The falcon of line 2 is at the broadest, centrifugal point of one gyre, symbolically illustrating the end of a cycle. The "indignant desert birds" of line 17 "reel" in a tighter circle, symbolizing the beginning of the new age in the new gyre. 5 *blood-dimmed tide*: quotation from Shakespeare's *Macbeth*, II.2.60–63. 12 *Spiritus Mundi*: literally, the spirit of the world, a collective human consciousness that furnished writers and thinkers with a common fund of images and symbols. Yeats referred to this collective repository as "a great memory passing on from generation to generation." 14 *lion body and the head of a man*: that is, the Sphinx, which in ancient Egypt symbolized the pharaoh as a spirit of the sun. Because of this pre-Christian origin, the reincarnation of a sphinx could therefore represent qualities associated in New Testament books like Revelation (11, 13, 17), Mark (13:14–20), and 2 Thessalonians (2:1–12) with a monstrous, superhuman, satanic figure.

## Questions

1. Consider the following as symbols: the "gyre," the "falcon," the "blood-dimmed tide," the "ceremony of innocence," the "worst" who are "full of passionate intensity." What ideas and values do these symbolize in the poem?

2. Why does Yeats capitalize the phrase "Second Coming"? To what does this phrase refer? Explain the irony of Yeats's use of the phrase in this poem.

3. Contrast the symbols of the falcon of line 2 and the desert birds of line 17. Considering that these are realistically presented, how does the realism contribute to their identity as symbols?

4. What is symbolized by the sphinx being revealed as a "rough beast"? What is the significance of the beast's going "towards Bethlehem to be born"?

## WRITING ABOUT SYMBOLISM AND ALLUSION IN POETRY

As you read the assigned poem, take careful and accurate notes, and make all the observations you can about the presence of symbols or allusions or both. Explanatory notes will help you establish basic information, but you also need to explain meanings and create interpretations in your own words. Use a dictionary for understanding words or phrases that require further study. For allusions, you might check out original sources to determine original contexts. Use the footnotes that your text supplies, and ask your instructor. Try to determine the ways in which your poem is similar to, or different from, the original work or source, and then determine the purpose served by the allusion.

### Questions for Discovering Ideas

#### CULTURAL OR UNIVERSAL SYMBOLS

- What symbols that you can characterize as cultural or universal can you discover in names, objects, places, situations, or actions in the poem (e.g., nightingales, hemlock, a thorn, two lovers, Bethlehem)?
- How are these symbols used? What do they mean, both specifically, in the poem, and universally, in a broader context? What would the poem be like without the symbolic meaning?

#### CONTEXTUAL SYMBOLS

- What contextual symbols can you locate in the poem (e.g., withered sedge, a flock of birds, a doe running into a woods)? How are these symbols used specifically in the poem? What would the poem be like if the contextual symbol were not taken to be symbolic?
- What causes you to conclude that the symbols are truly symbolic? What is being symbolized? What do the symbols mean? How definite or direct is the symbolism?

- Is the symbolism used systematically throughout the poem, or is it used only once? How does the symbolism affect the poem's ideas or emotions?

## ALLUSIONS

- Granted your knowledge of literature, science, geography, television, the Bible, film, popular culture, and other fields of knowledge, what allusions do you recognize?
- Do you find other references in these or other categories? What do the allusions mean in their original context? What do they mean within the poem?
- Do you see any possible allusions that you are not sure about? What help do you find in the explanatory notes in the text you are using? Consult a dictionary, such as *The Oxford Dictionary of Allusions*, or another reference work to discover the nature of these allusions. If you have questions, be sure to ask your reference librarian for assistance.

## Strategies for Organizing Ideas

Begin with a brief description of the poem and of the symbolism or allusions in it. A symbol might be central to the poem, or an allusion might be introduced at a particularly important point. Your central idea might take you in a number of directions: You might conclude that the symbolism is based on objects like flowers and natural scenes, or that it stems out of an action or set of actions, or that it is developed from an initial situation such as a time of the day or year. The symbols may be universal or contextual; they may be applicable particularly to personal life or to political or social life. Allusions may emphasize the differences between your poem and the work or event to which the allusion refers, or they may highlight the circumstances of your poem. In addition, you might make a point that the symbols and/or allusions make the poem seem optimistic, or pessimistic, and so on.

Here are some possible approaches for your essay, which may be combined as need arises.

1. *The meaning of symbols or allusions.* This approach is the most natural one to take for an essay on symbolism or allusion. If you have discovered a symbol or symbols, or allusions, explain the meaning as best you can. What is the poem's major idea? How do you know that your interpretation is valid? How do the poem's symbols and allusions contribute to your interpretation? How pervasive, how applicable, are these devices? If you have discovered many symbols and allusions, which ones predominate? What do they mean? Why are some more important than others? What connects them with each

other and with the poem's main ideas? How are you able to make conclusions about all this?

2.  *The effect of symbols or allusions on the poem's form.* Here the goal is to determine how symbolism or allusion is related to the poetic structure. Where does the symbol occur? If it is early in the poem, how do the subsequent parts relate to the ideas borne by the symbol? What logical or chronological function does the symbol serve in the poem's development? Is the symbol repeated, and if so, to what effect? If the symbol is introduced later, has it been anticipated earlier? How do you know? Can the symbol be considered climactic? What might the structure of the poem have been like if the symbolism had not been used? (Answering this question can help you judge how the symbol influences the poem's structure.) Many of these same questions might also be applied to an allusion or allusions. In addition, for an allusion, it is important to compare the contexts of the work you are studying and the original to determine how the poet uses the allusion as a part of the poem's form or structure.

3.  *The relationship between the literal and the symbolic.* The object here is to describe the literal nature of the symbols, and then to determine their appropriateness to the poem's context. If the symbol is part of a narrative, what is its literal function? If the symbol is a person, object, or setting, what physical aspects are described? Are colors included? Shapes? Sizes? Sounds? In light of this description, how applicable is the symbol to the ideas it embodies? How appropriate is the literal condition to the symbolic condition? The answers to questions like these should lead not so much to a detailed account of the meaning of the symbols but rather to an account of their appropriateness to the topics and ideas of the poem.

4.  *The implications and resonances of symbols and allusions.* This type of essay is more personal than the others, for it is devoted to the suggestions and associations—the "implications and resonances"—that the poem's symbols and allusions bring out. The object of the essay is to describe your own responses or chain of thinking that the poem sets in motion. You are therefore free to move in your own direction as long as you base your discussion on the symbols and allusions in the poem. If the poet is speaking in general terms about the end of an era, for example, as with the symbol of the "rough beast" in Yeats's "The Second Coming" and the giant fishnets in Jeffers's "The Purse-Seine," then you could apply these symbols to your own thinking.

Your conclusion might contain a summary of your main points. If your poem is rich in symbols or allusions, you might also consider some of the elements that you have not discussed in the body and try to tie these together with those you have already discussed. It would also be appropriate to introduce any new ideas you developed as a result of your study.

# Illustrative Student Essay

Jani 1

Sonal Jani

Professor Barack

English 212

20 March 2007

**Symbolism in Oliver's "Wild Geese"°**

[1]     Mary Oliver's "Wild Geese" can be understood as an extended answer to the issue raised in its first line. This idea, to be refuted, is unusual—one might almost say startling—because it is stated so baldly: "You do not have to be good." It does not seem that many poems begin with a line like that. The rest of the poem is developed through a series of symbols asserting the idea that there is a more significant kind of goodness.* Oliver's argument is to shun traditional habits of contrition and repentance, and instead to embrace the idea that goodness is to be realized through the animal and human spirit to be found within oneself and to be seen and heard everywhere in Nature. She demonstrates this idea first through a traditional but negative symbol, and second through a series of positive symbols of the natural world.†

[2]     The first symbol in the poem negatively symbolizes traditional but ineffective approaches to creating goodness within oneself. The picture is that of a hermit-like person actively suffering for contrition's sake:

> You do not have to walk on your knees
> for a hundred miles through the desert, repenting. (lines 2–3)

The notion of "repenting" symbolizes the tradition that human beings must endure punishment in atonement for their guilt and sinfulness. The vision of knees in the desert thus symbolizes the deeply ingrained idea that self-denial and suffering are necessary for goodness and inner peace.

---

° See p. 721 for this poem.
\* Central idea.
† Thesis sentence.

Jani 2

[3]     Before going on with the more detailed symbolism of the poem, Oliver introduces

another element of the conversation the speaker is having with the listener who has

spoken before the poem begins, but who now just listens. The idea is that goodness can

be found within "the soft animal of your body":

> You only have to let the soft animal of your body
> love what it loves. (lines 4, 5)

It is not clear just what sort of animal is described, but the word "animal" is based on

the action of breathing, the essential characteristic of living beings. The essence of life

is therefore the "soft animal" (not a vicious animal) of the self, which here symbolizes

the ethics that are a consequence of love.

[4]     A second part of the poem begins with the seventh line, "Meanwhile the world

goes on." The idea here is that there is a larger existence than the one that is defined by

human concepts of goodness or repentance, guilt or despair. The speaker's argument is

carried out with a cumulative set of symbols derived from the natural world. These are

"the sun and the clear pebbles of the rain" which are visualized as "moving across"

the world—over "prairies," "deep trees," "mountains," and "rivers" (lines 8–11), all

of which suggest vast expanses of land and wilderness. Because of their virtual

infiniteness, these natural objects make human concerns seem small and insignificant.

Thus, as symbols, they signify the need for a larger perspective and a more broad

dedication than human beings have usually made.

[5]     In this context the poet introduces the symbol of "the wild geese, high in the clean

blue air" (line 12). The geese, part of the general symbol of the world going on, are

migrating homeward. The idea seems mystical, but nevertheless the symbolism provides

a clear analogy for human beings living in our modern troubled and troubling civilization.

We are part of the universe, the world. We live here and belong here, just as the wild

geese do. We tend to forget our place here, however, as we lose perspective and become

enmeshed in cultural concerns which lead us only to guilt and loneliness (line 14). The

need is to listen to the inner animal, the outer world, which has a strong pull on us if

only we will let it consume our imaginations, just as the wild geese symbolize a natural

power that restores the world's creatures to home and to a sense of belonging.

[6]     The "world," in the symbolic fabric of the poem, is an active participant in the

process. It "offers itself to your imagination,/calls to you like the wild geese, harsh and

exciting—" (lines 15, 16). The idea of the symbol is that we, like the wild geese, need to let our imaginations follow the call. While people are traditionally preoccupied with despair, the sentient and nonsentient elements of nature are simply <u>being</u>. We could be like that if only we could perceive the symbolic meaning of the world around us. If we pay attention to the trees and the sun and the rain, we too will experience the strength of being a part of nature, and our morality will follow as a matter of course because we in fact have a definite place "in the family of things" (line 18) just as the geese return home to lead their lives in the landscapes of the world.

**WORK CITED**

Oliver, Mary. "Wild Geese." *Literature: An Introduction to Reading and Writing.* Ed. Edgar V. Roberts. 4th Compact ed. Upper Saddle River: Prentice Hall, 2008, 721.

## Commentary on the Essay

This essay conforms to the first strategy for writing about symbolism (p. 727) inasmuch as it involves a concentrated explanation of the symbolism in Oliver's "Wild Geese"—symbolism that is mainly drawn from the world of Nature.

The introduction briefly characterizes Oliver's confrontational opening line and goes on to assert that the rest of the poem is developed through a succession of symbols. The central idea is responsive to the opening line, namely, that the poem is to introduce symbols of "a more significant kind of goodness," and the thesis sentence states that in the body there will be a discussion of a negative symbol and a set of more positive symbols.

Paragraphs 3 through 6 consider the meanings of the poem's three major symbols—the "soft animal" (3); rain, land, and wilderness (4); and the "wild geese" (5). The final paragraph, 6, deals with the issue of goodness and the different kind of "good" brought out in the poem's symbolism (that is, being part of the "family of things").

# Special Writing Topics for Symbolism and Allusions in Poetry

1. Analyze the ways in which Keats, Herbert, and Jeffers use symbols to convey the fact and idea of capture and thralldom ("La Belle Dame Sans Merci," "The Collar," and "The Purse-Seine"). What major symbols do the three poets use? How appropriate is each symbol in its respective poem? How do the poets use the symbols to focus on the problems they present in their poems?

2. Describe the differences in the ways in which Graham, Viorst, and Yeats use allusions in "The Geese," "A Wedding Sonnet for the Next Generation," and "The Second Coming." How completely can we understand these poems without an explanation of the allusions? How extensive should explanations be? To what extent does the allusiveness make the poems difficult? Challenging? Interesting? Enriching?

3. Compare the use of religious symbols in Donne's "The Canonization" and Herbert's "The Collar." What are the locations from which the poets draw their symbols? How do the symbols figure into the major ideas and arguments of the poems?

4. Describe the nature of the symbols in Bronte's "No Coward Soul is Mine," Hardy's "In Time of 'The Breaking of Nations,'" and Whitman's "A Noiseless Patient Spider." What parallels in general topic matter do you discover? How do the poets make the poems diverge, despite the common qualities of the symbols?

5. Write a poem in which you develop a major symbol, as Jeffers does in "The Purse-Seine" and Cowper does in "The Poplar Field" (Chapter 11). To get yourself started, you might consider symbols like these:

   - A littered street or sidewalk
   - A new SUV, or an all-terrain vehicle
   - Coffee-hour after religious services
   - An athletic competition
   - A computer
   - The checkout counter at the neighborhood supermarket
   - The family dog looking out a front window as the children leave for school
   - A handgun

   Write an essay describing the process of your creation. How do you begin? How much detail is necessary? How many conclusions do you need to bring out about your symbol? When do you think you have said enough? Too much? How do you decide?

6. Write a poem in which you make your own allusions to your own experiences, such as attending school, participating in an activity, joining a team, reading a book, identifying with a movie character, recalling a passage from a popular song or a poem or story you have read, or going to a recent artistic or political event. What assumptions do you make about your reader when you bring out your allusions? How do you make the allusion (i.e., by a quotation, a name, a title, an indirect reference)? How does your allusion deepen your meaning? How does your allusion increase your own power of expression?

7. Write an essay describing the use of animals and birds as symbols in this chapter's poems by Graham, Jeffers, Oliver, and Whitman. How do the poets show the symbolic connection of the animals to human affairs? How faithfully do they consider the animals as animals?

8. From your library, take out a university press study of Yeats or Jeffers. How much detail is devoted in the study to either poet's use of symbols? How pervasively is symbolism employed by the poet? How does the poet use symbolism to express ideas about science or nationalism? What other use or uses does the poet make of symbolism?

# Chapter 18

## Four Major American Poets: Emily Dickinson, Robert Frost, Langston Hughes, and Sylvia Plath

In Chapters 11 through 17, we consider poetry in terms of its elements and effects. In this chapter we present collections of poems by four major American poets: Emily Dickinson (1830–1886), Robert Frost (1874–1963), Langston Hughes (1902–1967), and Sylvia Plath (1932–1963). As both history and chance would have it, Dickinson, Frost, and Plath were New Englanders, although Plath spent four of her last six years living in England. Hughes was born and raised in the Midwest, but came to New York as an adult, and stayed. Dickinson is one of the most prominent poetic voices of the nineteenth century. Both Frost and Hughes are recognized as poetic giants of the twentieth century. Plath's poetic career was unfortunately cut short, but the posthumous edition of her poems was honored by a Pulitzer Prize when it was published in 1982, almost 20 years after her death.

Although the poems included here comprise only a small part of the work of these poets, our hope is that there are enough poems to illustrate the typical concerns and major characteristics that are to be found in the study of their poetic careers.

## EMILY DICKINSON (1830–1886)

 ## Life and Work

Emily Elizabeth Dickinson, who is acknowledged as one of America's greatest poets, was born on December 10, 1830. She was raised in Amherst, Massachusetts, which in the nineteenth century was a small and tradition-bound town. Dominating the Dickinson family was Emily's father, Edward, a lawyer, a legislator, and a rigorous Calvinist, whose concept of life was stern religious observance and obedience to God's laws as expressed in the Bible. Emily was taken to Sunday School, but late in her teens she declined to pronounce herself a believing Christian. She spent a number of years at primary school and eventually studied classics at Amherst Academy. She also enrolled at the South Hadley Seminary for Women

Emily Dickinson

(now Mount Holyoke College), but her parents withdrew her after a year because of ill health.[1]

During these years of childhood and youth, she led a normally active life. She saw many people, liked school and her teachers, wrote essays, acquired a number of good friends, gossiped, sang at the piano to her own accompaniment, treasured spring flowers, amused her friends with impromptu stories, studied theology, read Pope's *An Essay on Man*, and planned to become the "Belle of Amherst" at the age of 17. She also began writing poetry, which consisted mainly of occasional verses and Valentines.

After leaving school she returned home. She was to spend the rest of her life there, sharing in family and household duties. In 1856 she won a second prize at the local fair for her recipe for Rye and Indian bread. She took occasional trips, including long stays in Boston in 1864 and 1865 to be treated for an undisclosed eye ailment. Eventually, however, she stopped traveling altogether.

Although Dickinson had written poems since her school days, she did not devote herself to poetry until her late twenties—beginning in about 1858. After this time her poetic output expanded, almost miraculously. Many of her poems are quite short, consisting of no more than a single stanza, but some are much longer. No more

---

[1]It would appear that there are four reliable likenesses of Emily Dickinson. The first is a painting of her and her brother and sister, done by Otis A. Bullard in about 1840, showing Emily at the age of about nine. There is a silhouette of her at the age of about 14. The first and most reliable photo is a daguerreotype taken of her at her at about the age of 16. This is the photo that is always duplicated. Still another photograph has come to light that may show Dickinson at the age of about 30 to 35. As yet the photo, an albumen print with Dickinson's name on the back, has not been authenticated, but it is fair to say that its resemblance to the authentic photo is uncanny. See *The New Yorker*, May 22, 2000, pp. 30–31. This photo is included in Alfred Habegger, *My Wars Are Laid Away in Books* (2001), where all the likenesses are included. Habegger believes that the photo is authentic. Richard B. Sewall includes a photograph of a young woman as the frontispiece to the second volume of his *The Life of Emily Dickinson* (1974), and he duplicates this same photo on page 752 of the one-volume *Life* of 1980. On the back of the original is written "Emily Dickenson [sic] 1860" in an unknown hand, and the features of the portrayed woman are consistent with those in the daguerreotype of Dickinson at 16. Although it is tempting to consider this photograph genuine, the attribution has not been validated.

than ten of them were published during her lifetime, mostly against her wishes. Instead, her "publication" consisted of making fair copies of the poems in handwriting that is quite difficult to read. In the privacy of her own room she put numbers of poems together in "fascicles," which consist of folded sheets of stationery bound with thread. These handwritten copies were for her eyes only, although she frequently sent copies in letters and also sent batches of poems to friends. The poems she didn't prepare carefully for her fascicles were kept in little packets. She locked away all these private literary treasures, which were discovered only after her death.

In total, 1,775 to 1,789 of her poems have been recovered. The figure 1,775 is the number of poems included by Thomas H. Johnson in *The Complete Poems of Emily Dickinson* (1955), the first major complete edition of Dickinson's poetry. The figure 1,789 is the number included by Ralph W. Franklin in *The Poems of Emily Dickinson: Variorum Edition* (1998). Both editions are based on exhaustive studies of all the documentary evidence available at the times when the editors were doing their research. Beyond these major scholarly editions, a number of brief poems have been mined from Dickinson's letters, and these were published, in 1993, as 498 new poems, on the theory that parts of the letters reach a succinctness and rhythm more characteristic of poetry than prose. These poems are short, some being no more than two lines long. If one accepts them as additional Dickinson poems, they bring the total count above 2,280.

Although a surprising amount of biographical information is available about Dickinson, the connections between events in her life and her poems are missing. For example, it seems obvious that a real and powerful sadness underlies the poignant conclusion of "I Cannot Live with You," just as a sense of personal inadequacy or reproach may have caused her to write "I Felt a Funeral in My Brain." We can only guess, however, about the specific situations, if any, that led her to write such poems.

Nevertheless, the general occasions inspiring some of her poems are clear. The world she lived in was small, and she found subjects in her surroundings: house, garden, yard, and village. A lowly snake is the topic of one of her poems—one of the few published when she was alive—as are butterflies, a singing oriole, and a vibrating hummingbird. She even wrote a poem about the railroad locomotives servicing her home town of Amherst. Sometimes no more than a recollection, a single word, a concept, or a paradox that arose from her own interior monologue enabled her to originate poems. Such inspirations account for topics such as a haunted mind, a memory, a state of solitude, the nature of truth and beauty, the condition of self-reliance, the angle of winter light. For one of the poems, "My Triumph Lasted Till the Drums," one may postulate a connection with her thoughts about the Civil War. She was at the height of her poetic power during this time, and she expresses feelings about the horrors of the war in these ironic lines: "A Bayonet's contrition/Is nothing to the Dead."

Dickinson's poems on death and dying probably had occasional sources also, even though these sources may be far removed from the time and circumstance of the poems. One of Dickinson's dearest childhood friends was Sophia Holland, who died in 1844. Perhaps the loss of Sophia was one of her memories when she wrote "I Never Lost as Much But Twice," and "The Bustle in a House," together with her other poems on death.

Much of her other poetry may have a similar if remote occasional origin. She wrote poems about love and the psychology of personal relationships, even though she never married or had a love affair that we know about. We may therefore wonder about the internal necessity that caused her to write poems like "Wild Nights—Wild Nights!" and "I Cannot Live with You," which portray states of sexual ecstasy and final renunciation. And what sorts of personal experience and introspection underlay such poems as "After Great Pain, a Formal Feeling Comes," "The Soul Selects Her Own Society," and "I Dwell in Possibility"?

In the absence of specific details linking her life to her poetry, therefore, the occasions of her poems must remain no more than peripherally relevant—themselves unseen, though in the effects they remain. We are left to conclude that her inspiration rose from within herself. She is a contemplative and personal poet, whether she herself is the omnipresent "I" of her poems or whether the "I" is an objective speaker to whom she assigns all the strength of her imagination and her dreams. This speaker possesses bright wit, clever and engaging playfulness, acute powers of observation, deep sensitivity, intense introspection, and tender responsiveness. She is alive, quick, and inventive. She enjoys riddles. She leads readers into new and unexplored regions of thought and feeling.

All these characteristics are to be discovered everywhere in her poetry. Her speaker expresses a vital joy and delirious energy in the quizzical poem "I Taste a Liquor Never Brewed," an insouciant bluffness in "Some Keep the Sabbath Going to Church," and overwhelming tenderness and regret at the end of "The Bustle in a House." In the last stanza of "I Cannot Live with You," she captures the deep anguish of a relationship that is ending.

> So We must meet apart -
> You there - I - here -
> With just the Door ajar
> That Oceans are - and Prayer -
> And that White Sustenance -
> Despair -

She is also reverent, and a number of poems introduce the topics of God, immortality, scripture, and the final judgment. But she is sometimes saucy and flippant about religion. Going to church on Sunday, for example, was expected of the dutiful Christian, but she explains why she prefers staying home with "a Bobolink for a Chorister."

> So instead of getting to Heaven, at last -
> I'm going, all along.

Undeniably, Dickinson's external daily life was uneventful. Her inner life was anything but uneventful, however, for she was always reflecting and thinking. What we know about her is that her inquiring and restless mind was the source of her compulsive poetic strength, and that her poetry expresses the vital personal feelings and psychological insights that emerged from her thoughts about life, love, death, Nature, and God. It is not possible to read her poems without revering her as a person and as a poet.

After Emily Dickinson died, in 1886, her sister, Lavinia, was astonished to find the many fascicles and packets of poems that she had left. Lavinia recognized the significance of this work and eventually turned much of it over to Thomas Higginson and Mabel L. Todd for editing and publication. They published three separate volumes of Dickinson's verse (in 1890, 1891, and 1896), each containing about a hundred poems. In these volumes, the editors eliminated slant rhymes, smoothed out the meter, revised those metaphors that struck them as outrageous, and regularized the punctuation.

These well-intentioned editorial "adjustments" remained intact until 1955, when the Harvard University Press published Thomas H. Johnson's three-volume complete edition. Johnson also published a single-volume edition of the poems in 1961 and, in addition, a paperback selection titled *Final Harvest: Emily Dickinson's Poems* (1961). Johnson's pioneering edition has been followed by the ambitious and comprehensive *The Poems of Emily Dickinson: Variorum Edition* in three volumes (Cambridge: Harvard UP, 1998), edited by Ralph W. Franklin, who also edited the facsimile edition of the handwritten poems, *The Manuscript Books of Emily Dickinson* (Cambridge: Harvard UP, 1981). Franklin's edition has also been published in one volume as *The Poems of Emily Dickinson: Reading Edition* (Cambridge: Harvard UP, 1999). The poems that have been extracted from Dickinson's letters were edited by William H. Shurr, with Anna Dunlap and Emily Grey Shurr, as *New Poems of Emily Dickinson* (Chapel Hill: U of North Carolina P, 1993).

Definitive biographies of Dickinson are Richard B. Sewall, *The Life of Emily Dickinson* (New York: Farrar, 1974; rpt. [Harvard UP] 1980; rpt. 1994); Alfred Habegger, *My Wars Are Laid Away in Books: The Life of Emily Dickinson* (New York: Random House, 2001); and Cynthia Griffin Wolff, *Emily Dickinson* (New York: Knopf, 1986). A useful book containing biographical, critical, and many other details is Jane Donahue Eberwein, ed., *An Emily Dickinson Encyclopedia* (Westport: Greenwood, 1998). The numbers of important critical studies are legion. Some of these are Albert J. Gelpi, *Emily Dickinson: The Mind of the Poet* (Cambridge: Harvard UP, 1966); Joanne F. Diehl, *Dickinson and the Romantic Imagination* (Princeton: Princeton UP, 1981); David Porter, *Dickinson, the Modern Idiom* (Cambridge: Harvard UP, 1981); Susan Juhasz, *The Undiscovered Continent: Emily Dickinson and the Space of the Mind* (Bloomington: U of Indiana P, 1983); Donna Dickenson, *Emily Dickinson* (Leamington Spa: Berg, 1985); Sharon Leder and Andrea Abbott, *The Language of Exclusion: The Poetry of Emily Dickinson and Christina Rossetti* (New York: Greenwood, 1987); Cristanne Miller, *Emily Dickinson: A Poet's Grammar* (Cambridge: Harvard UP, 1987); Joanne Dobson, *Dickinson and the Strategies of Reticence* (Bloomington: U of Indiana P, 1989); Paula Bennett, *Emily Dickinson: Woman Poet* (Iowa City: U of Iowa P, 1990); Gary Lee Stonum, *The Dickinson Sublime* (Madison: U of Wisconsin P, 1990); Joan Kirkby, *Emily Dickinson* (New York: St. Martin's, 1991); Judith Farr, *The Passion of Emily Dickinson* (Cambridge: Harvard UP, 1992); Claudia Ottlinger, *The Death-Motif in the Poetry of Emily Dickinson and Christina Rossetti* (Frankfurt: Lang, 1996); and Paul Crumbley, *Inflections of the Pen: Dash and Voice in Emily Dickinson* (Lexington: U of Kentucky P, 1996).

Collections of essays on Dickinson are Paul J. Ferlazzo, ed., *Critical Essays on Emily Dickinson* (Boston: Hall, 1958, a historical collection); Richard B. Sewall, ed., *Emily Dickinson: A Collection of Critical Essays* (Englewood Cliffs: Prentice Hall, 1963); Judith Farr, ed., *Emily Dickinson: A Collection of Critical Essays* (Upper Saddle River: Prentice Hall, 1996); and Gudrun Grabher et al., eds., *The Emily Dickinson Handbook* (Amherst: U of Massachusetts P, 1998). One of the hour-long programs in the PBS *Voices and Visions* series (1987) features Dickinson's work.

## Writing Topics About the Poetry of Emily Dickinson

1. Dickinson's characteristic brevity in the explanation of situations and the expression of ideas.

2. Dickinson's use of personal but not totally disclosed subject matter.

3. Dickinson's use of imagery and symbolism: sources, types, meanings. Her humor and irony.

4. Dickinson's ideas about love, separation, personal pain, war, death, faith, religion, science, the soul.

5. Dickinson's power as a poet.

6. Dickinson's poems as they appear on the page: the relationship of meaning to lines, stanzas, capitalization, punctuation, the use of the dash.

7. The structuring of a number of Dickinson's poems: subject, development, conclusions.

8. The character of the speaker in a number of Dickinson's poems: personality, things noticed, accuracy of conclusions. If there appears to be a listener in the poems, what effect does this listener have on the speaker?

9. Dickinson's verse forms and use of rhymes.

10. Themes of exhilaration, sorrow, pity, triumph, and regret in Dickinson.

## Poems by Emily Dickinson, Alphabetically Arranged

For ease in locating the selections included here, the poems are arranged alphabetically by the first significant words in first lines. There are two numbers following the title of each poem. The first number (e.g., J501) refers to the poem numbers in Thomas H. Johnson's *The Complete Poems of Emily Dickinson*. Critics since Johnson's edition have unanimously employed these numbers. The second number (e.g., F373) refers to the new numbering in Ralph W. Franklin's *The Poems of Emily Dickinson: Variorum Edition*. It would appear that future Dickinson criticism will need to include both numbers if the poem under discussion is to be properly identified, as with the following title: *After Great Pain, a Formal Feeling Comes (J341, F372)*.

Typographically, we have treated the dash as it is presented in Franklin's edition, as in the following line, *After great pain, a formal feeling comes -*. Many past editions have utilized a longer dash, as in *After great pain, a formal feeling comes—*.

## After Great Pain, a Formal Feeling Comes (J341, F372) (1929 (ca. 1862))

After great pain, a formal feeling comes -
The Nerves sit ceremonious, like Tombs -
The Stiff Heart questions 'was it He, that bore,'
And 'Yesterday, or Centuries before'?

The Feet, mechanical, go round -                                                    5
A Wooden way
Of Ground, or Air, or Ought° -                                    *anything, nothing*
Regardless grown,
A Quartz contentment, like a stone -

This is the Hour of Lead -                                                          10
Remembered, if outlived,
As Freezing persons, recollect the Snow -
First - Chill - then Stupor - then the letting go -

 ## Because I Could not Stop for Death (J712, F479) (Included in Chapter 11, p. 468)

 ## The Bustle in a House (J1078, F1108) (1890 (ca. 1865))

The Bustle in a House
The Morning after Death
Is solemnest of industries
Enacted upon Earth -

The Sweeping up the Heart                                                            5
And putting Love away
We shall not want to use again
Until Eternity -

## I Cannot Live with You (J640, F706) (1890 (ca. 1863))

I cannot live with You -
It would be Life -
And Life is over there -
Behind the Shelf

5  The Sexton keeps the Key to -
Putting up
Our Life - His Porcelain -
Like a Cup -

Discarded of the Housewife -
10 Quaint - or Broke -
A newer Sevres° pleases -                                *a fine French porcelain*
Old Ones crack -

I could not die - with You -
For One must wait
15 To shut the Other's Gaze down -
You - could not -

And I - Could I stand by
And see You - freeze -
Without my Right of Frost -
20 Death's privilege?

Nor could I rise - with You -
Because Your Face
Would put out Jesus' -
That New Grace

25 Glow plain - and foreign
On my homesick eye -
Except that You than He
Shone closer by -

They'd judge Us - How -
30 For You - served Heaven - You know,
Or sought to -
I could not -

Because You saturated sight -
And I had no more eyes
35 For sordid excellence
As Paradise

And were You lost, I would be -
Though my name
Rang loudest
40 On the Heavenly fame -

And were You - saved -
And I - condemned to be
Where You were not
That self - were Hell to Me -

So We must meet apart -                                    45
You there - I - here -
With just the Door ajar
That Oceans are - and Prayer -
And that White Sustenance -
Despair -                                                 50

##  I Dwell in Possibility (F466, J657) (1929 (ca. 1862))

I dwell in Possibility -
A fairer House than Prose -
More numerous of Windows -
Superior - for Doors -

Of Chambers as the Cedars -                               5
Impregnable of eye -
And for an everlasting Roof
The Gambrels of the Sky -

Of Visitors - the fairest -
For Occupation - This -                                   10
The spreading wide my narrow Hands
To gather Paradise -

##  I Felt a Funeral in My Brain (J280, F340) (1896 (ca. 1862))

I felt a Funeral, in my Brain,
And Mourners to and fro
Kept treading - treading - till it seemed
That Sense was breaking through -

And when they all were seated,                            5
A Service, like a Drum -
Kept beating - beating - till I thought
My mind was going numb -

And then I heard them lift a Box
And creak across my Soul                                  10
With those same Boots of Lead, again,
Then Space - began to toll,

As all the Heavens were a Bell,
And Being, but an Ear,
15 And I, and Silence, some strange Race
Wrecked, solitary, here -

And then a Plank in Reason, broke,
And I dropped down, and down -
And hit a World, at every plunge,
20 And Finished knowing - then -

 ## I Heard a Fly Buzz - When I Died (J465, F591) (1896 (ca. 1863))

I heard a Fly buzz - when I died -
The Stillness in the Room
Was like the Stillness in the Air -
Between the Heaves of Storm -

5 The Eyes around - had wrung them dry -
And Breaths were gathering firm
For that last Onset - when the King
Be witnessed - in the Room -

I willed my Keepsakes - Signed away
10 What portion of me be
Assignable - and then it was
There interposed a Fly -

With Blue - uncertain - stumbling Buzz -
Between the light - and me -
And then the Windows failed - and then
15 I could not see to see -

## I Like to See It Lap the Miles (J585, F383) (1891 (ca. 1862))

I like to see it lap the Miles -
And lick the Valleys up -
And stop to feed itself at Tanks -
And then - prodigious step

5 Around a Pile of Mountains -
And supercilious peer
In Shanties - by the sides of Roads -
And then a Quarry pare

To fit it's sides
10 And crawl between
Complaining all the while
In horrid - hooting stanza -
Then chase itself down Hill -

And neigh like Boanerges° -
Then - prompter than a Star
Stop - docile and omnipotent
At it's own stable door -

15

---

°I LIKE TO SEE IT LAP THE MILES.  14 *Boanerges*: a surname meaning "the sons of thunder" that appears in Mark 3:17.

 ## I Never Lost as Much But Twice (J49, F39) (1890 (ca. 1858))

I never lost as much but twice -
And that was in the sod.
Twice have I stood a beggar
Before the door of God!

Angels - twice descending
Reimbursed my store -
Burglar! Banker - Father!
I am poor once more!

5

## I Taste a Liquor Never Brewed
## (J214, F207) (1861, 1890 (ca. 1860))

I taste a liquor never brewed -
From Tankards scooped in Pearl -
Not all the Frankfort Berries°                    *grapes*
Yield such an Alcohol!

Inebriate of Air - am I -                          5
And Debauchee of Dew -
Reeling - thro endless summer days -
From inns of Molten Blue -

When "Landlords" turn the drunken Bee
Out of the Foxglove's door -
When Butterflies - renounce their "drams" -       10
I shall but drink the more!

Till Seraphs swing their Snowy Hats -
And Saints - to windows run -
To see the little Tippler
From Manzanilla° come!                             15

---

°I TASTE A LIQUOR NEVER BREWED.  16 *Manzanilla*: a pale sherry from Spain. Dickinson may also have been thinking of Manzanillo, a Cuban city known for rum.

## Much Madness Is Divinest Sense
### (J435, F620) (1890 (ca. 1863))

Much Madness is divinest Sense -
To a discerning Eye -
Much Sense - the starkest Madness -
'Tis the Majority
5   In this, as all, prevail -
Assent - and you are sane -
Demur - you're straightway dangerous -
And handled with a Chain -

## My Life Closed Twice Before Its Close
### (J1732, F1773) (1896)

My life closed twice before it's close;
It yet remains to see
If Immortality unveil
A third event to me,

5   So huge, so hopeless to conceive
As these that twice befell.
Parting is all we know of heaven,
And all we need of hell.

## My Triumph Lasted Till the Drums
### (J1227, F1212) (1935 (ca. 1871))

My Triumph lasted till the Drums
Had left the Dead alone
And then I dropped my Victory
And chastened stole along
5   To where the finished Faces
Conclusion turned on me
And then I hated Glory
And wished myself were They.

What is to be is best descried
10  When it has also been -
Could Prospect taste of Retrospect
The Tyrannies of Men
Were Tenderer, diviner
The Transitive toward -
15  A Bayonet's contrition
Is nothing to the Dead.

## Safe in Their Alabaster Chambers
## (J216, F124) (1862 (ca. 1859))

Safe in their Alabaster Chambers -
Untouched by Morning -
And untouched by Noon -
Lie the meek members of the Resurrection -
Rafter of Satin - and Roof of Stone!                                    5

Grand go the Years - in the Crescent - above them -
Worlds scoop their Arcs -
And Firmaments - row -
Diadems - drop - and Doges° - surrender -
Soundless as dots - on a Disc of snow -                                10

°SAFE IN THEIR ALABASTER CHAMBERS. 9 *Doges*: Rulers of Venice and Genoa, Italian city-states during the Renaissance.

 ## Some Keep the Sabbath Going to Church
## (J324, F236) (1864 (ca. 1861))

Some keep the Sabbath going to Church -
I keep it, staying at Home -
With a Bobolink for a Chorister -
And an Orchard, for a Dome -

Some keep the Sabbath in Surplice -                                    5
I, just wear my Wings -
And instead of tolling the Bell, for Church,
Our little Sexton - sings.

God preaches, a noted Clergyman -
And the sermon is never long.                                         10
So instead of getting to Heaven, at last -
I'm going, all along.

 ## The Soul Selects Her Own Society
## (J303, F409) (1890 (ca. 1862))

The Soul selects her own Society -
Then - shuts the Door -
To her divine Majority -
Present no more -

Unmoved - she notes the Chariots - pausing -                          5
At her low Gate -
Unmoved - an Emperor be kneeling
Opon° her Mat -                                            °*upon*

I've known her - from an ample nation -
10   Choose One -
Then - close the Valves of her attention -
Like Stone -

## Success Is Counted Sweetest
### (J67, F112) (1864 (ca. 1859))

Success is counted sweetest
By those who ne'er succeed.
To comprehend a nectar
Requires sorest need.

5   Not one of all the purple Host
Who took the Flag today
Can tell the definition
So clear of Victory

As he defeated - dying -
10   On whose forbidden ear
The distant strains of triumph
Burst agonized and clear!

## There's a Certain Slant of Light
### (J258, F320) (1890 (ca. 1862))

There's a certain Slant of light,
Winter Afternoons -
That oppresses, like the Heft
Of Cathedral Tunes -

5   Heavenly Hurt, it gives us -
We can find no scar,
But internal difference -
Where the Meanings, are -

None may teach it - Any -
10   'Tis the Seal Despair -
An imperial affliction
Sent us of the Air -

When it comes, the Landscape listens -
Shadows - hold their breath -
15   When it goes, 'tis like the Distance
On the look of Death -

**Wild Nights - Wild Nights! (J249, F269)** (1891 (ca. 1861))

Wild Nights - Wild Nights!
Were I with thee
Wild Nights should be
Our luxury!

Futile - the winds -                                                                                      5
To a Heart in port -
Done with the Compass -
Done with the Chart!

Rowing in Eden -
Ah - the Sea!                                                                                              10
Might I but moor - tonight -
In thee!

## ROBERT FROST (1874–1963)

Robert Lee Frost published his first book of poems, *A Boy's Will*, when he was living in England in 1913. At this time he was unrecognized and unknown in the United States. Ezra Pound wrote that "it is a sinister thing that so American . . . a talent . . . should have to be exported before it can find due encouragement and recognition." Time, of course, made Frost the most visible and admired American poet of his day. He eventually received twenty-five honorary degrees and four Pulitzer Prizes. Although there was no officially recognized national poet until the 1980s, when the Poet Laureateships were established through the Library of Congress, he came as close as possible to being America's official poet when he read "The Gift Outright" at the inauguration of President John F. Kennedy in January 1961. Writing in 1999, Joyce Carol Oates stated, "Frost's influence is so pervasive in American poetry, like Whitman's, as to be beyond assessment."[2] His collected poetic works continue to earn him this recognition.

Although in his person, and in his poetry, Frost presented himself as the quintessential New Englander, he was born on March 26, 1874, in California, where he spent his first 10 years of life. His father, William Frost, had gone to San Francisco to take a job with the *San Francisco Bulletin*, and he and his wife Belle had their two children there. When William died in 1885, Frost's mother returned east to Lawrence, Massachusetts, where Frost attended high school, studied classics, and began writing poetry. He graduated in 1892 as co-valedictorian with Elinor White, whom he married in 1895. After high school he attended Dartmouth College for seven weeks and then turned to newspaper work and teaching school. Two years after his marriage, he enrolled at Harvard (1897–1899), aiming at a specialty in classical literature. He had hoped to take courses with William James, but he was disappointed because James was on leave during the years of Frost's attendance. However, Frost was able to take a class taught by the famous philosopher George Santayana. Personal reasons,

---

Robert Frost

including an unwillingness to submit to rigorous academic discipline, led him to end his student days at Harvard without a degree.

The image that one gains of Frost at this time is that he had enormous capability, powerful energy, much anxiety and self-doubt, and uncertain focus. In later years he stated that his early interests inclined him toward a number of separate careers: archaeology, astronomy, farming, or teaching Latin. It does not seem that he had any vision of himself as the poet and man of letters he was to become. Even at the height of his fame, he minimized his poetic achievement by telling an audience at Amherst College that all he ever wanted from his poetic career was to be successful in writing "a few little poems it'd be hard to get rid of. That's all I ask."[3]

Much of Frost's early uncertainty resulted from his need to support his growing family. He gravitated toward farming as a way of life that would take up his physical energies and also give him the chance to think and to write. Fortunately, he had a supportive grandfather, William Frost, Sr., who backed up his grandfatherly affection with financial support. In 1900, William Senior gave Robert a farm in Derry, New Hampshire, and for the next 12 years the poet lived in Derry, raised chickens and apples, wrote poetry, and taught English (from 1906 to 1911) at Pinkerton Academy in Derry. His life was hard but satisfying, but, as he later said, he was "not much of a farmer." He preferred to sit up late at night reading and studying, and then sleeping until noon. He did not see it as his obligation to get up with the sun and then go about the endless tasks needed for successful farming. He was also an unusual farmer because he had been acquiring an immense amount of erudition, including the study of Latin and Greek poets and large numbers of Shakespeare's sonnets. It was during this time in Derry, in the first decade of the twentieth century, that he wrote many of his most famous poems, either in completed form or in draft. He sent many of these poems to magazines, but he got no publications and many rejection slips.

---

[3]*Amherst Alumni News* (April 1954), quoted in Jay Parini, *Robert Frost: A Life* (New York: Holt, 1999), p. 391.

By 1912, he was aching to devote himself to writing but was extremely discouraged with the way things were going. According to the terms of Grandfather Frost's gift, however, he was permitted to sell the farm and use the money for his own purposes. Because he believed that he might make a better start abroad, he decided to move to England, one of the many moves he was to make in his life. He also told the joke that he might live in poverty abroad without embarrassing his relatives and friends. Once he landed in England, his poetic career was energized. He found a publisher who liked his poems and put him under contract. Almost overnight he emerged from obscurity through the publication of his first two poetic volumes, *A Boy's Will* (1913) and *North of Boston* (1914), which were favorably reviewed and which started to earn him acclaim in the United States. He also met a number of emerging and established poets, including Pound, Eliot, and Yeats.

Just as in 1913 he had been anxious to move abroad, early in 1915 he was anxious to return home. In 1914, World War I had been declared, and he believed life would be better and safer in the United States. Once he got back he took up residence on a farm near Franconia, New Hampshire. His life after this time was one of increasing professional success together with a heavy burden of personal anxiety and grief. He and his wife had already lost two of their children in infancy. In addition, their daughter Marjorie died in 1934, and their son Carol, who suffered severe bouts of depression, committed suicide in 1940. Elinor herself died in 1938. In addition, Frost was constantly stretching his finances to help his remaining adult children as they attempted to create their own lives. There is no question that Frost, who was becoming the most successful poet of his generation, suffered intensely in private.

But it must be emphasized that his career as a poet flourished beyond his early hopes. In 1916 he published *Mountain Interval*, a book containing "The Road Not Taken," "Birches," and "Out, Out—." He soon was in constant demand as a teacher and speaker. Amherst College created the position of poet-in-residence for him, an honor that would continue for much of his life. He also regularly lectured at Michigan, Harvard, Yale, and Dartmouth. Stories abound about his brilliance in front of audiences, both large and small. Seminars that he began teaching in the afternoon would stretch late into the evening as he captivated his students with his insights and his immense knowledge. Moreover, when television blossomed as a medium after 1950, he enthusiastically widened his national audience. With his memorably rumpled appearance, white hair, and cultivated New England voice, he was interviewed on many early television shows, and as a result he became perhaps the most widely recognizable poet in the history of literature.

As he gained all these successes as a teacher and lecturer, his poetic output remained constant and regular. In 1923 he published *Selected Poems* and *New Hampshire*. *New Hampshire*, for which he won a Pulitzer Prize, contains some of his best-known work: "Stopping by Woods on a Snowy Evening," "Fire and Ice," and "Nothing Gold Can Stay." Throughout his career there were many additional collections. *West Running Brook* appeared in 1928, *Collected Poems* in 1930. Additional collections were *A Further Range* (1936), *A Witness Tree* (1942), *Steeple Bush* (1947), *Complete Poems* (1949), *Aforesaid* (1954), and *In the Clearing* (1962).

Early in his career and throughout his long public experience as a speaker and lecturer, Frost cultivated his persona as a philosophical, wry, and wise country poet. This is the friendly, avuncular voice we most regularly hear, the one that expresses knowledge and concern for the land, history, and human nature. Even with this genial persona, however, there are complicated undertones of wit and irony. There is also what Randall Jarrell called "The Other Frost," the often agonized and troubled spirit whose voice is heard in poems such as "Acquainted with the Night," "Desert Places," and "Fire and Ice."

Regardless of the voice we hear, Frost preferred traditional poetic forms and rhythms, and he disapproved of free verse so strongly that he once asserted that writing it was like playing tennis without a net. He possessed complete knowledge of traditional forms (he knew much Latin poetry by heart). We therefore find, in much of his poetry, that he uses conventional rhyme schemes and clear meters with traditional metrical substitutions, together with closed forms such as couplets, sonnets (with interesting varying rhyme patterns), terza rima, quatrains, stanzas, and blank verse (see Chapter 16). Tension in the poems is created through the contrast of traditional form and Frost's characteristic conversational style. His diction is informal, plain, and colloquial, and his phrases are simple and direct. He uses and refines the natural speech patterns and rhythms of New England, polishing the language of everyday life and blending speech and formal patterns into a compact and unique poetic texture.

Structurally, Frost's poems typically move in a smooth, uninterrupted flow from an event or an object, through a metaphor, to an idea. Within this pattern, he usually describes a complete event rather than a single vision. The heart of the process is image or metaphor. Frost's metaphors are sparse and careful; they are brought sharply into focus and skillfully interwoven within each poem. Frost himself saw metaphors as the beginning of the process. In *Education by Poetry* (1931) he states, "poetry begins in trivial metaphors, pretty metaphors, 'grace' metaphors, and goes on to the profoundest thinking that we have. Poetry provides the one permissible way of saying one thing and meaning another." In "The Figure a Poem Makes," a brief essay that he wrote as the Preface to *The Complete Poems of Robert Frost* of 1949, he goes on further to describe what to him was the poetic process: "The figure a poem makes. It begins in delight and ends in wisdom. The figure is the same as for love. No one can really hold that the ecstasy should be static and stand still in one place. It begins in delight, it inclines to the impulse, it assumes direction with the first line laid down, it runs a course of lucky events, and ends in a clarification of life—not necessarily a great clarification, such as sects and cults are founded on, but in a momentary stay against confusion."

Frost's poems are usually based in everyday life and rural settings. Poems are occasioned by flowers, stone fences, rain, snow, birch trees, falling leaves, a spider, a tree branch, birds, a hired man, a garden, children, wood chopping, apple picking, piano playing, sleigh riding, and hay cutting, to name just a few of the topics. However, the Frostian poetic structure always moves from such subjects toward philosophical generalizations about life and death, survival and responsibility, and nature and humanity. As he said in "The Figure a Poem Makes," the "delight" of poetry "is in the surprise of remembering something I didn't know I knew."

One of Frost's major appeals is that his poems are easily accessible. They are by no means simplistic, however, but run deep, as may be seen in such poems as "The Road Not Taken" and "Misgiving." They are often complex and ambiguous, as in "Mending Wall," in which the philosophies of the speaker and his fence-repairing neighbor are memorably presented and contrasted. Readers often conclude that the speaker's wish to remove barriers is this poem's major idea, but the neighbor's argument for maintaining them is equally strong. Further, in "Desert Places" (Chapter 16) we are presented with a chilling view of the infinite desert within the human spirit. In "Acquainted with the Night," Frost's sophisticated urban speaker tells us of the night of the city and also presents hints about the dark night of the soul.

Frost's complete works are in Richard Poirier and Mark Richardson, eds., *Robert Frost: Collected Poems, Prose, & Plays* (1995), and in Edward Connery Lathem, ed., *The Poetry of Robert Frost: The Collected Poems* (1969, frequently reprinted), which is also available in a paperback edition (2002). Of great use is Edward Connery Lathem's *A Concordance to the Poetry of Robert Frost* (rpt. 1994). Twelve of Frost's lectures have been preserved in Reginald Cook, *Robert Frost, A Living Voice* (Amherst: U of Massachusetts P, 1974). The standard biography, although often hostile, is by Lawrance Thompson, in three volumes: *Robert Frost: The Early Years; The Years of Triumph;* and *The Later Years* (New York: Holt Rinehart, 1966–1977). The last volume was completed after Thompson's death by Roy H. Winnick. An excellent biography is Jay Parini, *Robert Frost: A Life* (New York: Holt, 1999).

Useful criticism includes George Nitchie, *Human Values in the Poetry of Robert Frost* (Durham: Duke UP, 1960); Reuben Brower, *The Poetry of Robert Frost: Constellations of Intention* (New York: Oxford UP, 1963); Philip L. Gerber, *Robert Frost* (Boston: Twayne, 1966, rpt. 1982); Richard Poirier, *Robert Frost: The Work of Knowing* (Palo Alto: Stanford UP, 1990); John Kemp, *Robert Frost and New England: The Poet as Regionalist* (Princeton: Princeton UP, 1979); Richard Wakefield, *Robert Frost and the Opposing Lights of the Hour* (New York: Lang, 1985); James Potter, *A Robert Frost Handbook* (University Park: Pennsylvania State UP, 1980); Harold Bloom, ed., *Robert Frost,* Bloom's Modern Critical Views (New York: Chelsea House, 2003; a collection of critical essays); George Monteiro, *Robert Frost and the New England Renaissance* (Lexington: U of Kentucky P, 1988); Judith Oster, *Toward Robert Frost: The Reader and the Poet* (Athens: U of Georgia P, 1991); George F. Bagby, *Frost and the Book of Nature* (Knoxville: U of Tennessee P, 1993); and Katherine Kearns, *Robert Frost and a Poetics of Appetite* (New York: Cambridge UP, 1994). One of the hour-long programs in the PBS *Voices and Visions* series (1987) features his work.

## Writing Topics About the Poetry of Robert Frost

1. The nature of Frost's topics (situations, scenes, actions) and his use of them for observation, narration, and metaphor.

2. Frost's assessment of the human situation: work, love, death, choices, diminution of life, stoicism, keeping or not keeping boundaries.

3. Frost's speaker: character, experiences, recollections, and reflections. In developing his subjects, to what degree does the speaker take a possible listener into account?

4. Frost as a poet of ideas. His vision of the way things are or should be.

5. Frost as a "confessional" poet: misgivings, the admission of personal error and personal fears.

6. Frost's use of narration and description in his poetry.

7. The structuring of Frost's poems: situation, observation, and generalization.

8. Frost's poetic diction: level and relationship to topic; conversational style.

9. Poetic forms in Frost: rhythm, meter, rhyme, and line and stanza patterns.

10. Frost's wry humor.

## Poems By Robert Frost (Chronologically Arranged)

 ## The Tuft of Flowers (1913)

I went to turn the grass once after one
Who mowed it in the dew before the sun.

The dew was gone that made his blade so keen
Before I came to view the leveled scene

5   I looked for him behind an isle of trees;
I listened for his whetstone on the breeze.

But he had gone his way, the grass all mown,
And I must be, as he had been,—alone.

"As all must be," I said within my heart,
10  "Whether they work together or apart."

But as I said it, swift there passed me by
On noiseless wing a bewildered butterfly,

Seeking with memories grown dim o'er night
Some resting flower of yesterday's delight.

And once I marked his flight go round and round, 15
As where some flower lay withering on the ground.

And then he flew as far as eye could see,
And then on tremulous wing came back to me.

I thought of questions that have no reply,
And would have turned to toss the grass to dry. 20

But he turned first, and led my eye to look
At a tall tuft of flowers beside a brook,

A leaping tongue of bloom the scythe had spared
Beside a reedy brook the scythe had bared.

The mower in the dew had loved them thus, 25
By leaving them to flourish, not for us,

Nor yet to draw one thought of ours to him,
But from sheer morning gladness at the brim.

The butterfly and I had lit upon,
Nevertheless, a message from the dawn, 30

That made me hear the wakening birds around,
And hear his long scythe whispering to the ground,

And feel a spirit kindred to my own;
So that henceforth I worked no more alone;

But glad with him, I worked as with his aid, 35
And weary, sought at noon with him the shade.

And dreaming, as it were, held brotherly speech
With one whose thought I had not hoped to reach.

"Men work together," I told him from the heart,
"Whether they work together or apart." 40

 # Mending Wall (1914)

Something there is that doesn't love a wall,
That sends the frozen-ground-swell under it,
And spills the upper boulders in the sun;
And makes gaps even two can pass abreast.
The work of hunters is another thing: 5
I have come after them and made repair
Where they have left not one stone on a stone,
But they would have the rabbit out of hiding,
To please the yelping dogs. The gaps I mean,
No one has seen them made or heard them made, 10
But at spring mending-time we find them there.

I let my neighbor know beyond the hill;
And on a day we meet to walk the line
And set the wall between us once again.
15   We keep the wall between us as we go.
To each the boulders that have fallen to each.
And some are loaves and some so nearly balls
We have to use a spell to make them balance:
'Stay where you are until our backs are turned!'
20   We wear our fingers rough with handling them.
Oh, just another kind of outdoor game,
One on a side. It comes to little more;
There where it is we do not need the wall;
He is all pine and I am apple orchard.
25   My apple trees will never get across
And eat the cones under his pines, I tell him.
He only says "Good fences make good neighbors."
Spring is the mischief in me, and I wonder
If I could put a notion in his head;
30   "*Why* do they make good neighbors? Isn't it
Where there are cows? But here there are no cows."
Before I built a wall I'd ask to know
What I was walling in or walling out,
And to whom I was like to give offense.
35   Something there is that doesn't love a wall,
That wants it down. I could say "Elves" to him,
But it's not elves exactly, and I'd rather
He said it for himself. I see him there
Bringing a stone grasped firmly by the top
40   In each hand, like an old-stone savage armed.
He moves in darkness as it seems to me,
Not of woods only and the shade of trees.
He will not go behind his father's saying,
And he likes having thought of it so well
45   He says again, "Good fences make good neighbors."

## Birches (1915)

When I see birches bend to left and right
Across the lines of straighter darker trees,
I like to think some boy's been swinging them.
But swinging doesn't bend them down to stay
5   As ice-storms do. Often you must have seen them
Loaded with ice a sunny winter morning
After a rain. They click upon themselves
As the breeze rises, and turn many-colored
As the stir cracks and crazes their enamel.
10   Soon the sun's warmth makes them shed crystal shells

Shattering and avalanching on the snow-crust—
Such heaps of broken glass to sweep away
You'd think the inner dome of heaven had fallen.
They are dragged to the withered bracken by the load,
And they seem not to break; though once they are bowed     15
So low for long, they never right themselves:
You may see their trunks arching in the woods
Years afterwards, trailing their leaves on the ground
Like girls on hands and knees that throw their hair
Before them over their heads to dry in the sun.     20
But I was going to say when Truth broke in
With all her matter-of-fact about the ice-storm
I should prefer to have some boy bend them
As he went out and in to fetch the cows—
Some boy too far from town to learn baseball,     25
Whose only play was what he found himself,
Summer or winter, and could play alone.
One by one he subdued his father's trees
By riding them down over and over again
Until he took the stiffness out of them,     30
And not one but hung limp, not one was left
For him to conquer. He learned all there was
To learn about not launching out too soon
And so not carrying the tree away
Clear to the ground. He always kept his poise     35
To the top branches, climbing carefully
With the same pains you use to fill a cup
Up to the brim, and even above the brim.
Then he flung outward, feet first, with a swish,
Kicking his way down through the air to the ground.     40
So was I once myself a swinger of birches.
And so I dream of going back to be.
It's when I'm weary of considerations,
And life is too much like a pathless wood
Where your face burns and tickles with the cobwebs     45
Broken across it, and one eye is weeping
From a twig's having lashed across it open.
I'd like to get away from earth awhile
And then come back to it and begin over.
May no fate willfully misunderstand me     50
And half grant what I wish and snatch me away
Not to return. Earth's the right place for love:
I don't know where it's likely to go better.
I'd like to go by climbing a birch tree,
And climb black branches up a snow-white trunk     55
*Toward* Heaven, till the tree could bear no more,
But dipped its top and set me down again.
That would be good both going and coming back.
One could do worse than be a swinger of birches.

## The Road Not Taken (1915)

Two roads diverged in a yellow wood,
And sorry I could not travel both
And be one traveler, long I stood
And looked down one as far as I could
5  To where it bent in the undergrowth;

Then took the other, as just as fair,
And having perhaps the better claim,
Because it was grassy and wanted wear;
Though as for that the passing there
10  Had worn them really about the same,

And both that morning equally lay
In leaves no step had trodden black.
Oh, I kept the first for another day!
Yet knowing how way leads on to way,
15  I doubted if I should ever come back.

I shall be telling this with a sigh
Somewhere ages and ages hence;
Two roads diverged in a wood, and I—
I took the one less traveled by,
20  And that has made all the difference.

 ## "Out, Out—" (1916)

The buzz saw snarled and rattled in the yard
And made dust and dropped stove-length sticks of wood,
Sweet-scented stuff when the breeze drew across it.
And from there those that lifted eyes could count
5  Five mountain ranges one behind the other
Under the sunset far into Vermont,
And the saw snarled and rattled, snarled and rattled,
As it ran light, or had to bear a load.
And nothing happened: day was all but done.
10  Call it a day, I wish they might have said
To please the boy by giving him the half hour
That a boy counts so much when saved from work.
His sister stood beside them in her apron
To tell them "Supper." At the word, the saw,
15  As if to prove saws knew what supper meant,
Leaped out at the boy's hand, or seemed to leap—
He must have given the hand. However it was,
Neither refused the meeting. But the hand!
The boy's first outcry was rueful laugh,
20  As he swung toward them holding up the hand

Half in appeal, but half as if to keep
The life from spilling. Then the boy saw all—
Since he was old enough to know, big boy
Doing a man's work, though a child at heart—
He saw all spoiled. "Don't let him cut my hand off—    25
The doctor, when he comes. Don't let him, sister!"
So. But the hand was gone already.
The doctor put him in the dark of ether.
He lay and puffed his lips out with his breath.
And then—the watcher at his pulse took fright.    30
No one believed. They listened at his heart.
Little—less—nothing!—and that ended it.
No more to build on there. And they, since they
Were not the one dead, turned to their affairs.

 **Fire and Ice** (1920)

Some say the world will end in fire,
Some say in ice.
From what I've tasted of desire
I hold with those who favor fire.
But if it had to perish twice,    5
I think I know enough of hate
To say that for destruction ice
Is also great
And would suffice.

 **Stopping by Woods on a Snowy Evening (1923)
(Included in Chapter 11, p. 470.)**

 **Misgiving** (1923)

All crying, "We will go with you, O Wind!"
The foliage follow him, leaf and stem;
But a sleep oppresses them as they go,
And they end by bidding him stay with them.

Since ever they flung abroad in spring    5
The leaves had promised themselves this flight,
Who now would fain seek sheltering wall,
Or thicket, or hollow place for the night.

And now they answer his summoning blast
With an ever vaguer and vaguer stir,    10
Or at utmost a little reluctant whirl
That drops them no further than where they were.

I only hope that when I am free
As they are free to go in quest
15  Of the knowledge beyond the bounds of life
It may not seem better to me to rest.

 ## Nothing Gold Can Stay (1923)

Nature's first green is gold,
Her hardest hue to hold.
Her early leaf's a flower;
But only so an hour.
5  Then leaf subsides to leaf.
So Eden sank to grief,
So dawn goes down to day.
Nothing gold can stay.

 ## Acquainted with the Night (1928)

I have been one acquainted with the night.
I have walked out in rain—and back in rain.
I have outwalked the furthest city light.

I have looked down the saddest city lane.
5  I have passed by the watchman on his beat
And dropped my eyes, unwilling to explain.

I have stood still and stopped the sound of feet
When far away an interrupted cry
Came over houses from another street,

10  But not to call me back or say good-by,
And further still at an unearthly height,
One luminary clock against the sky

Proclaimed the time was neither wrong nor right.
I have been one acquainted with the night.

 ## Desert Places (1936) (Included in Chapter 16, p. 665.)

 ## Design (1936)

I found a dimpled spider, fat and white,
On a white heal-all,° holding up a moth
Like a white piece of rigid satin cloth—

---

°2 *heal-all*: a flower, usually blue, thought to have healing powers.

Assorted characters of death and blight
Mixed ready to begin the morning right,                              5
Like the ingredients of a witches' broth—
A snow-drop spider, a flower like a froth,
And dead wings carried like a paper kite.

What had that flower to do with being white,                         10
The wayside blue and innocent heal-all?
What brought the kindred spider to that height,
Then steered the white moth thither in the night?
What but design of darkness to appall?—
If design govern in a thing so small.

 ## The Silken Tent (1936)

She is as in a field a silken tent
At midday when a sunny summer breeze
Has dried the dew and all its ropes relent,
So that in guys it gently sways at ease,
And its supporting central cedar pole,                               5
That is its pinnacle to heavenward
And signifies the sureness of the soul,
Seems to owe naught to any single cord,
But strictly held by none, is loosely bound
By countless silken ties of love and thought                        10
To everything on earth the compass round,
And only by one's going slightly taut
In the capriciousness of summer air
Is of the slightest bondage made aware.

 ## The Gift Outright (1941)

The land was ours before we were the land's.
She was our land more than a hundred years
Before we were her people. She was ours
In Massachusetts, in Virginia,
But we were England's, still colonials,                              5
Possessing what we still were unpossessed by,
Possessed by what we now no more possessed.
Something we were withholding made us weak
Until we found out that it was ourselves
We were withholding from our land of living,                        10
And forthwith found salvation in surrender.
Such as we were we gave ourselves outright
(The deed of gift was many deeds of war)
To the land vaguely realizing westward,
But still unstoried, artless, unenhanced,                           15
Such as she was, such as she would become.

## A Considerable Speck (1942)

*(Microscopic)*

A speck that would have been beneath my sight
On any but a paper sheet so white
Set off across what I had written there.
And I had idly poised my pen in air
5   To stop it with a period of ink
When something strange about it made me think.
This was no dust speck by my breathing blown,
But unmistakably a living mite
With inclinations it could call its own.
10  It paused as with suspicion of my pen,
And then came racing wildly on again
To where my manuscript was not yet dry;
Then paused again and either drank or smelt—
With loathing, for again it turned to fly.
15  Plainly with an intelligence I dealt.
It seemed too tiny to have room for feet,
Yet must have had a set of them complete
To express how much it didn't want to die.
It ran with terror and with cunning crept.
20  It faltered: I could see it hesitate;
Then in the middle of the open sheet
Cower down in desperation to accept
Whatever I accorded it of fate.
I have none of the tenderer-than-thou
25  Collectivistic regimenting love
With which the modern world is being swept
But this poor microscopic item now!
Since it was nothing I knew evil of
I let it lie there till I hope it slept.
30  I have a mind myself and recognize
Mind when I meet with it in any guise.
No one can know how glad I am to find
On any sheet the least display of mind.

## Take Something Like a Star° (1943)

O Star (the fairest one in sight),
We grant your loftiness the right
To some obscurity of cloud—
It will not do to say of night,
5   Since dark is what brings out your light.
Some mystery becomes the proud.

---

°Earlier versions of this poem used the title "Choose Something Like a Star."

But to be wholly taciturn
In your reserve is not allowed.
Say something to us we can learn
By heart and when alone repeat.                                    10
Say something! And it says, "I burn,"
But say with what degree of heat.
Talk Fahrenheit, talk Centigrade.
Use language we can comprehend.
Tell us what elements you blend.                                   15
It gives us strangely little aid,
But does tell something in the end.
And steadfast as Keats' Eremite,
Not even stooping from its sphere,
It asks a little of us here.                                       20
It asks of us a certain height,
So when at times the mob is swayed
To carry praise or blame too far,
We may take something like a star
To stay our minds on and be staid.                                 25

# LANGSTON HUGHES (1902–1967)

James Mercer Langston Hughes was born in Missouri in 1902. His childhood was characterized by uncertainty and instability. When his parents became estranged he was cared for by his maternal grandmother, but he also lived with friends of his parents, and was moved, among other places, to Kansas, Illinois, and Ohio, where he received his primary and secondary schooling. He began writing early, and while in grade school in Lincoln, Illinois, he was declared class poet. Upon graduation from high school in Ohio, he lived for a year in Mexico. His father supported him when he promised to study engineering at Columbia, but he left after a year because he objected to the racism he perceived there. For a time after that he went from job to job without much purpose. At one point he was a seaman, then a cook in a nightclub in Paris, then a bouncer, and then a busboy in a Washington hotel. During those Washington years, Hughes worked for a brief time as an assistant to Dr. Carter G. Woodson, known today as the "father" of Black History, and the founder, in 1926, of what has become Black History Week, celebrated each year. It was in Washington that he submitted his earliest poems to the poet Vachel Lindsay (1879–1931), who was a resident of the hotel. Lindsay quickly became a champion of the increasing body of Hughes's poetry, and introduced the young man to various publishers. One of the earliest major results of this association was the publication of Hughes's first poetic collection, *The Weary Blues*, in 1926, which included "The Negro Speaks of Rivers."

With such encouragement Hughes went back to school in earnest, graduating in 1929 from Lincoln University in Pennsylvania, from which he later received an honorary doctorate. In the wake of the Stock Market Crash in 1929, the United States sank into the Depression. During this time Hughes was hard put to make his living as a thinker and writer. It was also during this time that he became radicalized. He visited Haiti and Cuba, and as a result of his experiences there he attacked what he considered to be American imperialist foreign policy in the Caribbean area. He also translated the poetry of a number of Cuban and Haitian writers. He was able to spend a year in Soviet Russia, assisting in the preparation of a film exposing racial prejudice in the United States. He continued to write and publish, and soon he became recognized as one of the leading figures of the Harlem Renaissance—that energetic burst of African-American literary creativity that also included Claude McKay and Jean Toomer. It has been observed that Hughes was the first African-American to make his living as a writer. Make his living he did, but he was not a recipient of the public acclaim that created opulence for many subsequent writers.

During the following 40 years of his writing career, Hughes was to write in every major literary genre, including translations, regular newspaper columns, and, in the late thirties, reports on the Spanish Civil War. He published a total of 35 books. Along with other early works were poems that he published in *Crisis*, the official journal of the National Association for the Advancement of Colored People. In his first collection of stories, *The Ways of White Folks* (1934), he fictionalized his disaffection with the condition of both Southern and Northern African Americans. One of the stories in this collection was "Father and Son," a version of the material that he turned into the two-act play *Mulatto*, which was produced at the Vanderbilt Theater in New York in October 1935. The play had a run of 373 performances, the record at that time for a Broadway play by an African American dramatist (see Chapter 23).

Hughes's own description of his calling as an author was to write about "Negro life in America." In addition to three short-story collections, he eventually published 16 books of poems and 2 novels, together with 20 plays and texts for musical plays. He also edited a number of anthologies of the works of other African-American writers, in addition to his constant production of articles and reviews. His total output was indeed voluminous. A few of his poetry collections, after *The Weary Blues* in 1926, were *The Dream Keeper* (1932), *Montage of a Dream Deferred* (1951), *The First Book of Jazz* (1955), and *Selected Poems* (1959). He published more than 860 poems during his lifetime.

His poetry develops from the idea of observing and celebrating Negro life in America. To achieve this goal, Hughes adopts a number of voices—not one voice, as in most of the poems of Dickinson and Frost, but a number of voices. His diction therefore is characterized by variety. Sometimes the words are straightforward and eloquent, as in "Let America Be America Again." We also encounter varieties of speech, from that of Hughes's beloved Harlem to the words to be found in the blues that Hughes also loved so dearly. In the poem "125th Street," he deals with the potentiality of blacks, who are both beautiful and capable. The underlying idea is that the American Dream has not been fulfilled for blacks, and that America, as a nation dedicated to equality, therefore remains unfulfilled and incomplete.

It is from such thinking that Hughes employs poetry, and literature generally, as a medium for political criticism. In "Negro" (1958), for example, Hughes asserts that Negroes, from the very beginnings of human history, have been enslaved and economically handicapped, and have suffered from all the cruelty that slavery and inequality have entailed. Thus, in the days of ancient Egypt, and Rome, the speaker's forbears were enslaved. In America, George Washington, the father of the country, kept slaves at Mount Vernon, just as Caesar had kept slaves on his estate in the first century B.C.E, and just as blacks, in inferior positions of heavy labor, made mortar so that the men who constructed the Woolworth Building in New York might practice their skills of craftsmanship, which they gained because of their racial privilege. In the nineteenth century, the age of colonialism, the men who exploited the Belgian Congo for profit also cruelly subjugated and exploited their slaves, just as in the twentieth-century agrarian South there was violent and cruel racial suppression—a topic Hughes more fully considers in the play *Mulatto* (see Chapter 23). Hughes fills his poetry with the voices of modern African Americans who are the living heirs of this age-old inequality and prejudice. Thus the speaker of "The Weary Blues" is tired of life, and the speaker of "Po' Boy Blues" claims that "I's so weary/I wish I'd never been born." A more violent avenue of response is seen in the legendarily famous poem "Harlem," in which the speaker considers the possibility that a "raisin in the sun" might "explode" (in violence against the cumulative suppression of centuries). A more subdued but ultimately more powerful response is that of education, which Hughes considers in "Theme for Engish B." Here, the speaker is a black who is obviously successful in the sphere of education. Even though this speaker recognizes his lack of equality, he is prepared to compete equally in the society which is producing resignation and possible violence among others of his race.

In looking at Hughes's poetry, then, one may discover the many aspects of the life of being black in America. There are expressions of religious renunciation, feelings of personal unease, rationalizations for personal cruelty, observations about funerals (i.e., the death of a "cool bop daddy" [or "re-bop daddy"]), descriptions of the depraved horror of lynchings, anticipation of a future of equality, uneasiness about being castigated by angry parents, the irony of naming a movie theater after Lincoln but not after John Brown, the irony of uncontrolled population growth, a sense of personal loneliness, the excitement of Harlem night life, the beauties of juke box love songs, and the difficulty of being both loving and nurturing. In short, in the poetry of Hughes, one may find the reflections about life that he believed represented not only the voice but also the soul of his people.

The complete poems of Langston Hughes are contained in Arnold Rampersad, ed., *The Collected Poems of Langston Hughes* (New York: Knopf, 1994). Rampersad's 18 volume set of *The Collected Works of Langston Hughes* (Columbia, Mo.: Missouri UP) is currently still in progress. Hughes himself was involved in selecting the works for inclusion in *The Langston Hughes Reader: The Selected Writings of Langston Hughes* (New York: Braziller, 1958). (In this volume, selected poems are included from pp. 87 to 164. The volume is unique because it contains much introductory and explanatory commentary by Hughes.) Biographies of Hughes are Milton Meltzer, *Langston Hughes* (New York: Crowell, 1968); and Arnold Rampersad, *The Life of Langston Hughes*, 2 vols. (Oxford: Oxford UP, 2002). Works of poetry criticism are Onwuchekwa Jemie, *Langston Hughes: An Introduction to the Poetry* (New York: Columbia, 1976); Steven C. Tracy, *Langston Hughes and the Blues* (Urbana: U of Illinois P, 1988, rpt 2001); and Harold Bloom, *Langston Hughes*, Bloom's Biocritiques (New York: Chelsea House, 2002). More general books of criticism of Hughes are Henry L. Gates, *Langston Hughes: Critical Perspectives Past and Present* (New York: Amistad, 1993); Harold Bloom, *Langston Hughes: Comprehensive Research and Study Guide*, Bloom's Major Poets (New York: Chelsea House, 1999); Harold Bloom, *Langston Hughes*, Bloom's Modern Critical

Views (New York: Chelsea House, 2007), and Steven C. Tracy, ed., *A Historical Guide to Langston Hughes* (Oxford: Oxford UP, 2004). (This last volume contains a short biography of Hughes by R. Baxter Miller.)

## Topics for Writing About the Poetry of Langston Hughes

1. Direct and indirect political implications in Hughes's poetry: social and political protest. Many of Hughes' poems reflect his concern with injustice in America and make reference to historical events. For instance, *The Negro Speaks of Rivers* makes reference to Abraham Lincoln's visit to New Orleans that influenced his decision to end slavery. Do you think that reading one of Hughes' poems may have an effect on how people think about this issue?

2. The dramatic use of speakers in the poems. Different individuals, different concerns, different voices, one poet.

3. Hughes's use of geographical place and religionalism in the poetry.

4. Hughes's diction in the poems: levels of diction, standard and substandard speech. Hughes often uses everyday speech, common words, and slang. In which poems do you find this characteristic most predominant? How might the poems be different if they were written in standard English?

5. The treatment of racial cruelty in the poems. (For comparison on this topic, you might also want to consider Hughes's play *Mulatto*, in Chapter 23.)

6. The connection of the blues to the content and to the points of view in the poems. Following the pattern of songs, such as blues patterns in "Po' Boy Blues," many of the poems repeat lines, sometimes with slight variation. What is the effect of these repetitions? How are the lyrics of songs and poems different or the same?

7. "Weariness" and resignation as a recurring topic in the poems.

8. Hughes's ideas about what should be and what really exists. The ideal vs. the actual in the poems.

9. The sense of humor in the poems. Laughing to keep from crying. (The title of a collection of Hughes's stories published in 1952.)

### Selected Poems of Langston Hughes (Alphabetically Arranged)

## Bad Man (1927)

I'm a bad, bad man
Cause everybody tells me so.
I'm a bad, bad man.
Everybody tells me so.
I takes my meanness and ma licker                    5
Everywhere I go.

I beats my wife an'
I beats ma side fall too.
Beats my wife an'
Beats my side gall too.                               10
Don't know why I do it but
It keeps me from feelin' blue.

I'm so bad I
Don't even want to be good.
So bad, bad, bad I                                    15
Don't even want to be good.
I'm goin' to da devil an'
I wouldn't go to heaven if I could.

## Cross (1925, 1926)

My old man's a white old man
And my old mother's black.
If ever I cursed my white old man
I take my curses back.
If ever I cursed my black old mother                 5
And wished she were in hell,
I'm sorry for that evil wish
And now I wish her well.
My old man died in a fine big house.
My ma died in a shack.                               10
I wonder where I'm going to die,
Being neither white nor black.

## Dead in There (1951)

Sometimes
A night funeral
Going by
Carries home
5   A cool bop daddy.

Hearse and flowers
Guarantee
He'll never hype
Another paddy.

10  It's hard to believe,
But dead in there,
He'll never lay a
Hype nowhere!

He's my ace-boy,
15  Gone away.
Wake up and live!
He used to say.

Squares
Who couldn't dig him,
20  Plant him now—
Out where it makes
No diff' no how.

## Dream Variations (1924, 1926)

To fling my arms wide
In some place of the sun,
To whirl and to dance
Till the white day is done.
5  Then rest at cool evening
Beneath a tall tree
While night comes on gently,
    Dark like me—
This is my dream!
10  To fling my arms wide
In the face of the sun,
Dance! Whirl! Whirl!
Till the quick day is done.
Rest at pale evening . . .
15  A tall, slim tree . . .
Night coming tenderly
    Black like me.

## Harlem (1951)

What happens to a dream deferred?
Does it dry up
like a raisin in the sun?
Or fester like a sore—
And then run?                                                    5
Does it stink like rotten meat?
Or crust and sugar over—
like a syrupy sweet?

Maybe it just sags
like a heavy load.                                               10

Or does it explode?

## Let America Be America Again (1936)

Let America be America again.
Let it be the dream it used to be.
Let it be the pioneer on the plain
Seeking a home where he himself is free.

(America never was America to me.)                               5

Let America be the dream the dreamers dreamed—
Let it be that great strong land of love
Where never kings connive nor tyrants scheme
That any man be crushed by one above.

(It never was America to me.)                                    10

O, let my land be a land where Liberty
Is crowned with no false patriotic wreath,
But opportunity is real, and life is free,
Equality is in the air we breathe.

(There's never been equality for me,                             15
Nor freedom in this "homeland of the free.")

*Say who are you that mumbles in the dark?*
And who are you that draws your veil across the stars?
I am the poor white, fooled and pushed apart,
I am the Negro bearing slavery's scars.
I am the red man driven from the land,                           20
I am the immigrant clutching the hope I seek—
And finding only the same old stupid plan
Of dog eat dog, of mighty crush the weak.

25   I am the young man, full of strength and hope,
      Tangled in that ancient endless chain
      Of profit, power, gain, of grab the land!
      Of grab the gold! Of grab the ways of satisfying need!
      Of work the men! Of take the pay!
30   Of owning everything for one's own greed!

      I am the farmer, bondsman to the soil.
      I am the worker sold to the machine.
      I am the Negro, servant to you all.
      I am the people, worried, hungry, mean—
35   Hungry yet today despite the dream.
      Beaten yet today—O, Pioneers!
      I am the man who never got ahead,
      The poorest worker bartered through the years.

      Yet I'm the one who dreamt our basic dream
40   In the Old World while still a serf of kings,
      Who dreamt a dream so strong, so brave, so true,
      That even yet its mighty daring sings
      In every brick and stone, in every furrow turned
      That's made America the land it has become.
45   O, I'm the man who sailed those early seas
      In search of what I meant to be my home—
      For I'm the one who left dark Ireland's shore,
      And Poland's plain, and England's grassy lea,
      And torn from Black Africa's strand I came
50   To build a "homeland of the free."
      The free?

      A dream—
      Still beckoning to me!

      O, let America be America again—
55   The land that never has been yet—
      And yet must be—
      The land where *every* man is free.
      The land that's mine—
      The poor man's, Indian's, Negro's, ME—
60   Who made America,
      Whose sweat and blood, whose faith and pain,
      Whose hand at the foundry, whose plow in the rain,
      Must bring back our mighty dream again.
      Sure, call me any ugly name you choose—
65   The steel of freedom does not stain.
      From those who live like leeches on the people's lives,
      We must take back our land again,
      America!

      O, yes;
70   I say it plain,
      America never was America to me,
      And yet I swear this oath—

America will be!
An ever-living seed,
Its dream                                                                    75
Lies deep in the heart of me.

We, the people, must redeem
Our land, the mines, the plants, the rivers,
The mountains and the endless plain—
All, all the stretch of these great green states—        80
And make America again!

 ## Madam and Her Madam (1943, 1949)

I worked for a woman,
She wasn't mean—
But she had a twelve-room
House to clean.

Had to get breakfast,                                                         5
Dinner, and supper, too—
Then take care of her children
When I got through.

Wash, iron, and scrub,
Walk the dog around—                                                         10
It was too much,
Nearly broke me down.

I said, Madam,
Can it be
You trying to make a                                                         15
Pack-horse out of me?

She opened her mouth.
She cried, Oh, no!
You know, Alberta,
I love you so!                                                               20

I said, Madam,
That may be true—
But I'll be dogged
If I love you!

## Negro (1958)

I am a Negro:
    Black as the night is black,
    Black like the depths of my Africa.

I've been a slave:
5      Caesar told me to keep his door-steps clean.
       I brushed the boots of Washington.

I've been a worker:
       Under my hand the pyramids arose.
       I made mortar for the Woolworth Building.

10  I've been a singer:
       All the way from Africa to Georgia
       I carried my sorrow songs.
       I made ragtime.

I've been a victim:
15     The Belgians cut off my hands in the Congo.
       They lynch me still in Mississippi.

I am a Negro:
       Black as the night is black,
       Black like the depths of my Africa.

##  The Negro Speaks of Rivers (1926)

I've known rivers:
I've known rivers ancient as the world and older than the flow of human blood in
       human veins.

My soul has grown deep like the rivers.

I bathed in the Euphrates when dawns were young.
5  I built my hut near the Congo and it lulled me to sleep.

I looked upon the Nile and raised the pyraminds above it.
I heard the singing of the Mississippi when Abe Lincoln went down to New Orleans,
       and I've seen its muddy bosom turn all golden in the sunset.

I've known rivers:
Ancient, dusky rivers.

10  My soul has grown deep kike the rivers.

##  125th Street (1951)

Face like a chocolate bar
Full of nuts and sweet.

Face like a jack-o'-lantern,
Candle inside.

5  Face like slice of melon
Grin that wide.
                    (1950, 1951)

## Po' Boy Blues (1926, 1927)

When I was home de
Sunshine seemed like gold.
When I was home de
Sunshine seemed like gold.
Since I come up North de                                                5
Whole damn world's turned cold.

I was a good boy,
Never done no wrong.
Yes, I was a good boy,
Never done no wrong,                                                    10
But this world is weary
An' de road is hard an' long.

I fell in love with
A gal I thought was kind.
Fell in love with                                                      15
A gal I thought was kind.
She made me lose ma money
An' almost lose ma mind.

Weary, weary,
Weary early in de morn.                                                 20
Weary, weary,
Early, early in de morn.
I's so weary
I wish I'd never been born.

 ## Silhouette (1936)

Southern gentle lady,
   Do not swoon.
They've just hung a black man
   In the dark of the moon.

They've hung a black man                                                5
   To a roadside tree
In the dark of the moon
   For the world to see
   How Dixie protects
   Its white womanhood.                                                10

Southern gentle lady
      Be good!
      Be good!

## Subway Rush Hour (1951)

Mingled
breath and smell
so close
mingled
5   black and white
so near
no room for fear.

## Theme for English B (1959) (Included in Chapter 15, p. 619)

## The Weary Blues (1923, 1926)

Droning a drowsy syncopated tune,
Rocking back and forth to a mellow croon,
    I heard a Negro play.
Down on Lenox Avenue the other night
5   By the pale dull pallor of an old gas light
        He did a lazy sway . . .
        He did a lazy sway . . .
To the tune o' those Weary Blues.
With his ebony hands on each ivory key
10  He made that poor piano moan with melody.
        O Blues!
Swaying to and fro on his rickety stool
He played that sad raggy tune like a musical fool.
        Sweet Blues!
15  Coming from a black man's soul.
        O Blues!
In a deep song voice with a melancholy tone
I heard that Negro sing, that old piano moan—
    "Ain't got nobody in all this world,
20      Ain't got nobody but ma self.
    I's gwine to quit ma frownin'
    And put ma troubles on the shelf."
Thump, thump, thump, went his foot on the floor.
He played a few chords then he sang some more—
25      "I got the Weary Blues
    And I can't be satisfied.
    Got the Weary Blues
    And can't be satisfied—
    I ain't happy no mo'
    And I wish that I had died."
30  And far into the night he crooned that tune.
The stars went out and so did the moon.

The singer stopped playing and went to bed
While the Weary Blues echoed through his head.
He slept like a rock or a man that's dead.                    35

## SYLVIA PLATH (1932–1963)

Sylvia Plath is one of those poets about whom the life facts are integrally connected to her works. She is considered a "confessional" poet, the basis of whose work lies in her own personal experiences, with all their difficulties, uncertainties, and personal pain. Her confessions, however, are not intended as expressions of complaint or as descriptions of intimate details. Instead, she is confessional in that she attempts to demonstrate her relationship to the many unique and often adverse situations she encountered in life. In historical comparison, the *Confessions* of St. Augustine (354–430) were composed to reveal the power and beneficence of God. John Bunyan (1628–88) wrote his *Grace Abounding to the Chief of Sinners* as testimony of the bountiful forgiveness of God. Jean-Jacques Rousseau (1712–78) wrote his autobiographical *Confessions,* perhaps partially to shock readers, but also to show the particular links that together make up the whole person. One might add that in "Sonnet 146" (1609), Shakespeare's speaker considers the defects of his own soul, and urges rededication to spiritual pursuits (p. 841).

In all these instances of confessional literature, confession itself is based in the admission of some sorts of transgression—usually in the form of self-indulgence—but the confession is also put in a wider context. As a twentieth-century confessional poet, Plath is ranked with fellow American poets Robert Lowell (one of Plath's teachers), Anne Sexton (a friend and confidante of Plath, and a fellow student in Lowell's class), D. W. Snodgrass, and John Berryman. Plath was a tormented soul, tortured at times, but she was a poet of great ability and brilliance, of extremes of happiness and depression—alternatively charming and blunt, but never dull. That her poems were not unrelievedly concerned with the negative aspects of confession may be seen in her "Song for a Summer's Day" and "Metaphors"—poems which would not seem unusual or special in the work of any other lyric poet. But in the poems Plath wrote during the final years of her life, one can see evidence of deeper discontent and anger. At times she refers to direct autobiographical details, or else she presents inferences based on such details. As a result, events of her brief life and lamentable death are definitely relevant to her poetry.

Sylvia Plath was born in 1932. Her father, Otto Plath, was a naturalized citizen whose native country was Germany. He was a professor at Boston University, an entomologist, and an authority on bees. Her mother, Aurelia Schober, was much younger than Otto, and was from Austria. She also eventually taught at Boston University. Plath's father was diabetic, but was in denial about his affliction. In 1940 he was hospitalized for a foot infection. The foot was amputated, but the infection was rampant. It metastasized and caused his death when Sylvia was just eight years old. It then fell to her mother, Aurelia, to take over the management of her household and children—Sylvia and her brother, Warren.

Sylvia was deeply grieved by her father's death, and upon being told of it, swore that she could no longer believe in God. One of her first responses was an unsuccessful and perhaps accidental suicide attempt when she was 10, using a razor blade to gash her throat. Her adolescent responses were less destructive, but there can be no doubt the loss of her father afflicted her deeply for the rest of her brief life. Her later experiences with insomnia, her frequent respiratory infections, and her depression perhaps had their own etiology, but the loss of her father was always there, undermining her struggle for normality. She compensated for her loss by becoming an exceedingly fine student, regularly receiving A's in her courses. As she achieved academic excellence and advancement, she also, at an early age, began sending her writings, primarily poems, to various publications, hoping for the national acceptance that would demonstrate that others recognized her precociousness. Throughout her school years she continued the arduous process of submission and publication, and by the time she matriculated at Smith College in 1952, she had developed an impressive list of academic prizes and local publications. She was tops in her high school graduating class, and she published essays, stories, and poems in publications like *Mademoiselle* and *The Christian Science Monitor*. Eventually, she signed a contract with *The New Yorker*, agreeing that she would give that magazine the right of first submission for any and all of her new poems.

Despite such successes, however, she regularly received rejection slips—not at all uncommon for beginning writers—and these weighed heavily upon her self-image. She became so despondent that she once again attempted suicide. In 1953, she hid herself in the crawl space under her mother's house and swallowed almost the entire contents of a bottle of sleeping pills, many of which she fortunately regurgitated. She was, however, rendered unconscious. Everyone thought she had been abducted, and her disappearance made headlines in the Boston area. After a few days, her brother heard her groaning under the house, and she was taken to the hospital for treatment and recovery. After that she underwent electric shock therapy, which in the 1950s was a standard medical treatment for depression and attempted suicide. She describes this experience in her well-received *The Bell Jar* early in 1963, and she also alludes to it in her poem "Lady Lazarus," which she wrote just four months before her actual suicide in February, 1963:

> Dying
> Is an art, like everything else,
> I do it exceptionally well.
> > lines 43–45

She recovered, took heart, and went on to graduate from Smith *summa cum laude*. In 1955, as a new graduate, she applied for a Fulbright Scholarship for study in England. She won the award, and matriculated at Newnham College, Cambridge, for the year 1955–56, which was extended to 1956–57. The winning of a Fulbright was an inestimable honor for those who received it, but the allowances were quite low— just about $1,450 for all the living expenses of an entire year. Needless to say, Sylvia was regularly hurting for money.

During her days at Cambridge, Plath met Ted Hughes, then a striving poet, who later became English Poet Laureate (1984–98). It was at this point that she decided to try achieving excellence through marriage and children. The two married in 1956, and their marriage continued for six years, two of which they spent in the United States after Sylvia had finished the period of her Fulbright Scholarship. When she became pregnant, the couple returned to England, where childbirth was paid for by the English National Health Service. Although the Hugheses had two children, born in 1960 and 1962, and although there were long periods of peace, tenderness, and constructive and peaceful cooperation between the two, their relationship also generated conflict and bitterness. Indeed, they once came to blows and inflicted scratches on each other. They separated in 1962. Sylvia became guardian of the children, and took up residence in rooms in a London house where William Butler Yeats had one time lived. Although she was encouraged by the connection with Yeats, she became unconquerably depressed during the bitterly cold winter of 1962–63. Early in the morning of February 11, 1963, in the throes of deep and final anguish, she sealed the cracks in the doors of the bedroom of her sleeping children, to protect them, and left milk and cookies for them. She went to her kitchen, and turned on the gas. Despite her intellectual power and desire to excel, she had never been able to escape the demon of depression. She died at the age of 30—her life cut regrettably short, her full potential never to be realized or recognized.

When she died, Sylvia Plath had not yet gained a major reputation. Just a few weeks before her death, her novel *The Bell Jar* appeared. Although the work was well received, she had written it under a *nom de plume* ("Victoria Lucas") and she had not yet received the public recognition that was to follow. Ever since the 1960s, however, her reputation has been elevated posthumously to the point where some critics have called her one of the greatest poets of the twentieth century. The story of her life has also made her a *cause célèbre* of the feminist movement. The idea is that during her last years her star was falling just as the star of her husband was rising. And as she necessarily became enmeshed in the endless tasks of caring for her baby and her toddler, he looked elsewhere for companionship. After Plath's suicide, there were people who accused him of having brought about her death. On her gravestone, her married name, "Hughes," was chiseled out, and then was chiseled out again when a new stone was reinstalled over the grave. When Hughes, even as Poet Laureate, would have a speaking engagement in the 35 years after her death, hecklers would sometimes try to drown him out. He was never able to live down the circumstances of Plath's suicide.

Plath's poems, grounded as they are in her own experiences, do not necessarily make for easy reading, because they frequently describe reactions to specific details known by the speaker, but unknown by the reader. The result is that some of the poems seem obscure. Let us take the opening three lines from "Ariel," the poem that Plath wrote on her birthday, October 27, 1962: "Stasis in darkness./Then the substanceless blue/Pour of tor and distances." As readers we accept these details as meaningful, even though the process of mind that produced the lines is not known. "Tor" is a venerable English word for a high hill, probably borrowed from the Celts, who lived in the land before the Angles and the Saxons took the country over militarily in the fifth century. "Pour" suggests figuratively how the hill emerges in the landscape of early morning as though it is being poured out to the viewer's eye. A further probe seems in order. A biographical detail is that "Ariel," the poem's title, was the name of a horse that Plath had ridden frequently in 1957, during the earlier and happier years of her marriage. It would appear that riding had given her a sense of freedom and fulfillment. In addition, Ariel is a spirit/fairy that serves Prospero in Shakespeare's *The Tempest* (1611). At the play's end, when Prospero is bidding farewell to his magical powers, he gives Ariel his freedom. We may therefore conclude that the reference to Ariel is Plath's dominating image of a desire for release from restrictions and a wish for the freedom of rolling hills, far distances, and the endless blue of the air. Somewhere, one can find a better existence than the one we know here on earth, although, from the poem's last line, it could also be a "cauldron" that creates difficulty and causes other problems. And so "Ariel" the poem may be taken as an expression of yearning and not unmixed hope.

Comparably, one of Plath's best known confessional poems is "Daddy." It was only natural that she could not ever have totally overcome her grief at losing her father, despite all her compensating excellences during her adolescent and college years. When she and Ted Hughes became parents themselves, she became "Mommy" and he "Daddy." Most young parents, in delight at having their own children, rejoice in using these names for each other. It would therefore appear that when Plath wrote "Daddy," she was thinking of both Daddies together. She never was given the time to know her own father well, and may even have subconsciously condemned him for the neglect of his own illness and his consequent culpability for deserting the Plath family. Such a response is not unusual among survivors of a family loss. In addition to this grievance, she had profoundly loved and admired her children's Daddy, but he had caused her extreme anger, grief, and bitterness. She wrote the poem "Daddy" on October 12, 1962, just at the time when she and Hughes were undergoing what was appearing to be their final separation. In the poem, Plath's speaker castigates the Daddy virtually as a persecuting Nazi. Nothing even remotely like this was true, of course, but nevertheless the speaker talks of her anguish as though the details about Nazism were factual. Thus, this major detail of the poem is fictional, but Plath's mental anguish was real, and her anger was real. It is for the power and the expression of such personal insights that Plath is today valued so highly as a lyric and confessional poet.

The most comprehensive edition of Plath's poems is Ted Hughes, ed., *The Collected Poems: Sylvia Plath* (Cambridge: Harper & Row, 1981). The appearance of this volume in 1981 posthumously earned Plath the Pulitzer Prize for Poetry in 1982. Before she died, Plath planned a volume of "Ariel" poems. Her intended collection is included in *Ariel: The Restored Edition. A Facsimile of Plath's Manuscript, Reinstating Her Original Selection and Arrangements* (New York: Harper, 2005). Susan R. Van Dine's *Revising Life: Sylvia Plath's Ariel Poems* (Chapel Hill, U of North Carolina P, 1994) considers these poems. Plath's journals are published in *The Unabridged Journals of Sylvia Plath*, Karen V. Kukil, ed. (New York: Anchor Books, 2000), a lengthy volume. Well-detailed biographies of Plath are Linda Wagner-Martin, *Sylvia Plath: A Biography* (New York: St. Martin's, 1988), and Anne Stevenson, *Bitter Fame: A Life of Sylvia Plath* (Boston: Houghton Mifflin, 1990). A blending of biography and criticism is Wagner-Martin's *Sylvia Plath: A Literary Life* (New York: Palgrave McMillan, 2003). Critical works are Tim Kendall, *Sylvia Plath: A Critical Study* (London: Faber, 2001), and Lynda K. Bundtzen, *The Other Ariel* (Amhurst: U of Massachusetts P, 2001). A significant number of critical essays are included in Jo Gill, ed., *The Cambridge Companion to Sylvia Plath,* Cambridge Companions to Literature (Cambridge: Cambridge UP,

2006). A detailed review of criticism on Plath is Claire Brennan, ed., *The Poetry of Sylvia Plath*, Columbia Critical Guides (New York: Columbia UP, 2001).

## Topics for Writing About the Poetry of Sylvia Plath

1. Plath as a "confessional" poet. What is she confessing? How much is personal? How much seems objective description and discussion? What problems and concerns does she confess?

2. Plath's references to death in her poems. What is her attitude toward her own suicide attempts? What is the relationship of "Cut" to "Last Words" and to "Lady Lazarus"?

3. The problems of "Daddy." Who is the Daddy whom she addresses? What objective criticism does she make of Daddy? What do you make of the concluding lines? Why does Plath introduce references to Nazi cruelties, here and in "Lady Lazarus"?

4. Plath's use of comparisons. How expected are her comparisons? What causes the uniqueness and surprise of her best comparisons?

5. Plath's poetic rhythms. What use does she make of adjoining heavy accents (spondees)? What is the relationship of her rhythms to her ideas?

6. Her use of rhymes, assonance, and alliteration. How do these rhythms and sounds undergird her ideas?

7. Write an explication of any one of Plath's poems.

8. The meaning of "Mirror." Explain the concluding image.

9. Plath's more cheerful poems ("Metaphors," "Song for a Summer's Day"). What do these poems suggest about her thoughts about what most people probably think of about happiness?

### Selected Poems of Sylvia Plath (Arranged Alphabetically)

N.B. The numbers beginning each of the following Plath poems refer to the numbering made by Ted Hughes for *The Collected Poems: Sylvia Plath* (Cambridge: Harper & Row, 1981). The dates following some of the poems indicate the dates on which Plath either wrote the poems, or completed them.

## Ariel (1962)

194
Stasis in darkness.
Then the substanceless blue
Pour of tor and distances.

God's lioness,
5   How one we grow,
Pivot of heels and knees!—The furrow

Splits and passes, sister to
The brown arc
Of the neck I cannot catch,

10  Nigger-eye
Berries cast dark
Hooks—

Black sweet blood mouthfuls,
Shadows.
15  Something else

Hauls me through air—
Thighs, hair;
Flakes from my heels.

White
20  Godiva, I unpeel—
Dead hands, dead stringencies.

And now I
Foam to wheat, a glitter of seas.
The child's cry

25  Melts in the wall.
And I
Am the arrow,

The dew that flies
Suicidal, at one with the drive
30  Into the red

Eye, the cauldron of morning.
                    *27 October 1962*

## 🪶 **The Colossus** (1959)

117
I shall never get you put together entirely,
Pieced, glued, and properly jointed.
Mule-bray, pig-grunt and bawdy cackles
Proceed from your great lips.
It's worse than a barnyard.                                                          5

Perhaps you consider yourself an oracle,
Mouthpiece of the dead, or of some god or other.
Thirty years now I have labored
To dredge the silt from your throat.
I am none the wiser.                                                                 10

Scaling little ladders with gluepots and pails of lysol
I crawl like an ant in mourning
Over the weedy acres of your brow
To mend the immense skull-plates and clear
The bald, white tumuli° of your eyes.                                *grave mounds*    15

A blue sky out of the Oresteia
Arches above us. O father, all by yourself
You are pithy and historical as the Roman Forum
I open my lunch on a hill of black cypress.
Your fluted bones and acanthine hair° are littered                                    20

In their old anarchy to the horizon-line.
It would take more than a lightning-stroke
To create such a ruin.
Nights, I squat in the cornucopia
Of your left ear, out of the wind.                                                    25

Counting the red stars and those of plum-color.
The sun rises under the pillar of your tongue.
My hours are married to shadow.
No longer do I listen for the scrape of a keel
On the blank stones of the landing.                                                   30

---

°THE COLOSSUS. At the harbor of the Aegean island of Rhodes, the ancient Rhodians erected a gigantic statue of Apollo, the "Colossus," which was considered one of the seven wonders of the ancient world. When earthquakes later hit the city, the Colossus was destroyed. Modern marine archaeologists have discovered fragments of the statue in the harbor waters.  20 *fluted bones and acanthine hair:* The design of ancient temple columns was not smooth, but rather fluted. In the Corinthian style, the most elaborate columnar design, capitals atop the fluted columns were modeled on the acanthus plant.

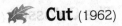

# Cut (1962)

### For Susan O'Neill Roe

191
What a thrill—
My thumb instead of an onion.
The top quite gone
Except for a sort of a hinge

Of skin,
A flap like a hat,
Dead white.
Then that red plush.

Little pilgrim,
10 The Indian's axed your scalp.
Your turky wattle
Carpet rolls

Straight from the heart.
I step on it,
15 Clutching my bottle
Of pink fizz.

A celebration, this is.
Out of a gap
A million soldiers run,
20 Redcoats, every one.

Whose side are they on?
O my
Homunculus,° I am ill.                                   *a tiny human being*
I have taken a pill to kill

25 The thin
Papery feeling.
Saboteur,
Kamikaze man—

The stain on your
30 Gauze Ku Klux Klan
Babushka
Darkens and tarnishes and when

The balled
Pulp of your heart
35 Confronts its small
Mill of silence

How you jump—
Trepanned° veteran,    *i.e., trephined, usually the result of an operation opening skull bone*
Dirty girl,
Thumb stump.                                                                                    40
                    *24 October 1962*

 **Daddy** (1962)

183
You do not do, you do not do
Any more, black shoe
In which I have lived like a foot
For thirty years, poor and white
Barely daring to breathe or Achoo.                                                                5

Daddy, I have had to kill you.
You died before I had time—
Marble-heavy, a bag full of God,
Ghastly statue with one gray toe
Big as a Frisco seal                                                                             10

And a head in the freakish Atlantic
Where it pours bean green over blue
In the waters off beautiful Nauset.
I used to pray to recover you.
Ach, du.                                                                                        15

In the German tongue, in the Polish town
Scraped flat by the roller
Of wars, wars, wars.
But the name of the town is common.
My Polack friend                                                                                 20

Says there are a dozen or two.
So I never could tell where you
Put your foot, your root,
I never could talk to you.
The tongue stuck in my jaw.                                                                      25

It stuck in a barb wire snare.
Ich, ich, ich, ich,
I could hardly speak.
I thought every German was you.
And the language obscene                                                                         30

An engine, an engine
Chuffing me off like a Jew.
A Jew to Dachau, Auschwitz, Belsen.
I began to talk like a Jew.
I think I may well be a Jew.                                                                     35

The snows of the Tyrol, the clear beer of Vienna
Are not very pure or true.
With my gipsy ancestress and my weird luck
And my Taroc pack and my Taroc pack
40  I may be a bit of a Jew.

I have always been scared of *you*,
With your Luftwaffe, your gobbledygoo.
And your neat mustache
And your Aryan eye, bright blue.
45  Panzer-man, panzer-man, O You—

Not God but a swastika
So black no sky could squeak through.
Every woman adores a Fascist,
The boot in the face, the brute
50  Brute heart of a brute like you.

You stand at the blackboard, daddy,
In the picture I have of you,
A cleft in your chin instead of your foot
But no less a devil for that, no not
55  Any less the black man who

Bit my pretty red heart in two.
I was ten when they buried you.
At twenty I tried to die
And get back, back, back to you.
60  I thought even the bones would do.

But they pulled me out of the sack,
And they stuck me together with glue.
And then I knew what to do.
I made a model of you,
65  A man in black with a Meinkampf look

And a love of the rack and the screw.
And I said I do, I do.
So daddy, I'm finally through.
The black telephone's off at the root,
70  The voices just can't worm through.

If I've killed one man, I've killed two—
The vampire who said he was you
And drank my blood for a year,
Seven years, if you want to know.
75  Daddy, you can lie back now.

There's a stake in your fat black heart
And the villagers never liked you.

They are dancing and stamping on you.
They always *knew* it was you.
Daddy, daddy, you bastard, I'm through.                          80

*12 October 1962*

 **Edge** (1963)

224
The woman is perfected.
Her dead

Body wears the smile of accomplishment,
The illusion of a Greek necessity

Flows in the scrolls of her toga,                                5
Her bare

Feet seem to be saying:
We have come so far, it is over.

Each dead child coiled, a white serpent,
One at each little                                               10

Pitcher of milk, now empty.
She has folded

Them back into her body as petals
Of a rose close when the garden

Stiffens and odors bleed                                         15
From the sweet, deep throats of the night flower.

The moon has nothing to be sad about,
Staring from her hood of bone.

She is used to this sort of thing.
Her blacks crackle and drag.                                     20

*5 February 1963*

 **The Hanging Man** (1960)

123
By the roots of my hair some god got hold of me.
I sizzled in his blue volts like a desert prophet.

The nights snapped out of sight like a lizard's eyelid:
A world of bald white days in a shadeless socket.

5   A vulturous boredom pinned me in this tree.
    If he were I, he would do what I did.

*27 June 1960*

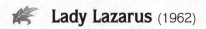

## Lady Lazarus (1962)

198
I have done it again.
One year in every ten
I manage it—

A sort of walking miracle, my skin
5   Bright as a Nazi lampshade,
My right foot

A paperweight,
My face a featureless, fine
Jew linen.

10  Peel off the napkin
O my enemy.
Do I terrify?—

The nose, the eye pits, the full set of teeth?
The sour breath
15  Will vanish in a day.

Soon, soon the flesh
The grave cave ate will be
At home on me

And I a smiling woman.
20  I am only thirty.
And like the cat I have nine times to die.

This is Number Three.
What a trash
To annihilate each decade.

25  What a million filaments.
The peanut-crunching crowd
Shoves in to see

Them unwrap me hand and foot
The big strip tease.
30  Gentlemen, ladies

These are my hands
My knees.
I may be skin and bone,

Nevertheless, I am the same, identical woman.
The first time it happened I was ten.
It was an accident.                                                        35

The second time I meant
To last it out and not come back at all.
I rocked shut

As a seashell.
They had to call and call                                                  40
And pick the worms off me like sticky pearls.

Dying
Is an art, like everything else,
I do it exceptionally well.                                                45

I do it so it feels like hell.
I do it so it feels real.
I guess you could say I've a call.

It's easy enough to do it in a cell.
It's easy enough to do it and stay put.                                    50
It's the theatrical

Comeback in broad day
To the same place, the same face, the same brute
Amused shout:

"A miracle!"                                                               55
That knocks me out.
There is a charge

For the eyeing of my scars, there is a charge
For the hearing of my heart—
It really goes.                                                            60

And there is a charge, a very large charge
For a word or a touch
Or a bit of blood

Or a piece of my hair or my clothes.
So, so, Herr Doktor.                                                       65
So, Herr Enemy.

I am your opus,
I am your valuable,
The pure gold baby

That melts to a shriek.                                                    70
I turn and burn.
Do not think I underestimate your great concern.

Ash, ash—
You poke and stir.
Flesh, bone, there is nothing there—

A cake of soap,
A wedding ring,
A gold filling.

Herr God, Herr Lucifer
Beware
Beware.

Out of the ash
I rise with my red hair
And I eat men like air.

23–29 October 1962

 ## Last Words (1961)

152
I do not want a plain box, I want a sarcophagus
With tigery stripes, and a face on it
Round as the moon, to stare up.
I want to be looking at them when they come
Picking among the dumb minerals, the roots
I see them already—the pale, star-distance faces.
Now they are nothing, they are not even babies.
Imagine them without fathers or mothers, like the first gods.
They will wonder if I was important.
I should sugar and preserve my days like fruit!
My mirror is clouding over—
A few more breaths, and it will reflect nothing at all.
The flowers and the faces whiten to a sheet.

I do not trust the spirit. It escapes like steam
In dreams, through mouth-hole or eye-hole. I can't stop it.
One day it won't come back. Things aren't like that.
They stay, their little particular lusters
Warmed by much handling. They almost purr.
When the soles of my feet grow cold,
The blue eye of my turquoise will comfort me.
Let me have my copper cooking pots, let my rouge pots
Bloom about me like night flowers, with a good smell.
They will roll me up in bandages, they will store my heart
Under my feet in a neat parcel.
I shall hardly know myself. It will be dark,
And the shine of these small things sweeter than the face of Ishtar.°

21 October, 1961

---

°LAST WORDS. 26 *Ishtar*. In ancient Babylonian and Assyrian mythology, the principal goddess of fertility, love, and war.

## Metaphors (1959)

102

I'm a riddle in nine syllables,
An elephant, a ponderous house,
A melon strolling on two tendrils.
O red fruit, ivory, fine timbers!
This loaf's big with its yeasty rising.          5
Money's new-minted in this fat purse.
I'm a means, a stage, a cow in calf.
I've eaten a bag of green apples,
Boarded the train there's no getting off.

*20 March 1959*

## Mirror (1961)

154

I am silver and exact. I have no preconceptions.
Whatever I see, I swallow immediately.
Just as it is, unmisted by love or dislike
I am not cruel, only truthful—
The eye of a little god, four-cornered.          5
Most of the time I meditate on the opposite wall.
It is pink, with speckles. I have looked at it so long
I think it is a part of my heart. But it flickers.
Faces and darkness separate us over and over.

Now I am a lake. A woman bends over me.
Searching my reaches for what she really is.          10
Then she turns to those liars, the candles or the moon.
I see her back, and reflect it faithfully
She rewards me with tears and an agitation of hands.
I am important to her. She comes and goes.
Each morning it is her face that replaces the darkness.          15
In me she has drowned a young girl, and in me an old woman
Rises toward her day after day, like a terrible fish.

*23 October 1961*

## The Rival (1961)

147

If the moon smiled, she would resemble you.
You leave the same impression
Of something beautiful, but annihilating.
Both of you are great light borrowers.
Her O-mouth grieves at the world; yours is unaffected,          5

And your first gift is making stone out of everything.
I wake to a mausoleum; you are here,
Ticking your fingers on the marble table, looking for cigarettes,
Spiteful as a woman, but not so nervous,
And dying to say something unanswerable.

The moon, too, abases her subjects,
But in the daytime she is ridiculous.
Your dissatisfactions, on the other hand,
Arrive through the mailslot with loving regularity,
White and blank, expansive as carbon monoxide.

No day is safe from news of you,
Walking about in Africa maybe, but thinking of me.

*July 1961*

##  Song for a Summer's Day (1956)

12
Through fen and farmland walking
With my own country love
I saw slow flocked cows move
White hulks on their day's cruising;
Sweet grass sprang for their grazing.

The air was bright for looking:
Most far in blue, aloft,
Clouds steered a burnished drift;
Larks' nip and tuck arising
Came in for my love's praising.

Sheen of the noon sun striking
Took my heart as if
It were a green-tipped leaf
Kindled by my love's pleasing
Into an ardent blazing.

And so, together, talking,
Through Sunday's honey-air
We walked (and still walk there—
Out of the sun's bruising)
Till the night mists came rising.

## Tulips (1961)

142
The tulips are too excitable, it is winter here.
Look how white everything is, how quiet, how snowed-in.

I am learning peacefulness, lying by myself quietly
As the light lies on these white walls, this bed, these hands.
I am nobody; I have nothing to do with explosions.    5
I have given my name and my day-clothes up to the nurses
And my history to the anesthetist and my body to surgeons.

They have propped my head between the pillow and the sheet-cuff
Like an eye between two white lids that will not shut.
Stupid pupil, it has to take everything in.    10
The nurses pass and pass, they are no trouble,
They pass the way gulls pass inland in their white caps,
Doing things with their hands, one just the same as another,
So it is impossible to tell how many there are.

My body is a pebble to them, they tend it as water    15
Tends to the pebbles it must run over, smoothing them gently.
They bring me numbness in their bright needles, they bring me sleep.
Now I have lost myself I am sick of baggage—
My patent leather overnight case like a black pillbox,
My husband and child smiling out of the family photo;    20
Their smiles catch onto my skin, little smiling hooks.

I have let things slip, a thirty-year-old cargo boat
Stubbornly hanging on to my name and address.
They have swabbed me clear of my loving associations.
Scared and bare on the green plastic-pillowed trolley    25
I watched my tea set, my bureaus of linen, my books
Sink out of sight, and the water went over my head.
I am a nun now, I have never been so pure.

I didn't want any flowers, I only wanted
To lie with my hands turned up and be utterly empty.    30
How free it is, you have no idea how free–
The peacefulness is so big it dazes you,
And it asks nothing, a name tag, a few trinkets.
It is what the dead close on, finally; I imagine them
Shutting their mouths on it, like a Communion tablet.    35

The tulips are too red in the first place, they hurt me.
Even through the gift paper I could hear them breathe
Lightly, through their white swaddlings, like an awful baby.
Their redness talks to my wound, it corresponds.
They are subtle: they seem to float, though they weigh me down,    40
Upsetting me with their sudden tongues and their color,
A dozen red lead sinkers round my neck.

Nobody watched me before, now I am watched.
The tulips turn to me, and the window behind me
Where once a day the light slowly widens and slowly thins,    45
And I see myself, flat, ridiculous, a cut-paper shadow

Between the eye of the sun and the eyes of the tulips,
And I have no face, I have wanted to efface myself.
The vivid tulips eat my oxygen.

50  Before they came the air was calm enough,
Coming and going, breath by breath, without any fuss.
Then the tulips filled it up like a loud noise.
Now the air snags and eddies round them the way a river
Snags and eddies round a sunken rust-red engine.
55  They concentrate my attention, that was happy
Playing and resting without committing itself.

The walls, also, seem to be warming themselves.
The tulips should be behind bars like dangerous animals;
They are opening like the mouth of some great African cat,
60  And I am aware of my heart: it opens and closes
Its bowl of red blooms out of sheer love of me.
The water I taste is warm and salt, like the sea,
And comes from a country far away as health.

*18 March 1961*

# Chapter 19

## Eighty-Four Poems for Additional Enjoyment and Study

## ANONYMOUS (NAVAJO)

 ## Healing Prayer from the Beautyway Chant (Traditional)

Out of the East, Beauty has come home,
Out of the South, Beauty has come home,
Out of the West, Beauty has come home,
Out of the North, Beauty has come home,
Out of the highest heavens and the lowest lands,      5
    Beauty has come home.
    Everywhere around us, Beauty has come home.
As we live each day, everything evil will leave us.
    We will be entirely healed,
    Our bodies will exult in the fresh winds,      10
    Our steps will be firm.
As we live each day,
    Everything before us will be Beautiful;
    Everything behind us will be Beautiful;
    Everything above us will be Beautiful;      15
    Everything below us will be Beautiful;
    Everything around us will be Beautiful;
    All our thoughts will be Beautiful;
    All our words will be Beautiful;
    All our dreams will be Beautiful.      20
We will be forever restored, forever whole.
All things will be Beautiful forever.

 ### MATTHEW ARNOLD (1822–1888)

 ## Dover Beach (1867 (1849))

The sea is calm tonight.
The tide is full, the moon lies fair
Upon the straits—on the French coast the light
Gleams and is gone; the cliffs of England stand,
Glimmering and vast, out in the tranquil bay.      5

Come to the window, sweet is the night air!
Only, from the long line of spray
Where the sea meets the moon-blanched land,
Listen! you hear the grating roar
10 Of pebbles which the waves draw back, and fling,
At their return, up the high strand,
Begin, and cease, and then again begin,
With tremulous cadence slow, and bring
The eternal note of sadness in.

15 Sophocles long ago
Heard it on the Aegean, and it brought
Into his mind the turbid ebb and flow
Of human misery; we
Find also in the sound a thought,
20 Hearing it by this distant northern sea.

The Sea of Faith
Was once, too, at the full, and round earth's shore
Lay like the folds of a bright girdle furled.
But now I only hear
25 Its melancholy, long, withdrawing roar,
Retreating, to the breath
Of the night wind, down the vast edges drear
And naked shingles° of the world.                    beaches

Ah, love, let us be true
30 To one another! for the world, which seems
To lie before us like a land of dreams,
So various, so beautiful, so new,
Hath really neither joy, nor love, nor light,
Nor certitude, nor peace, nor help for pain;
35 And we are here as on a darkling plain
Swept with confused alarms of struggle and flight,
Where ignorant armies clash by night.


## W. H. AUDEN (1907–1973)

## The Unknown Citizen (1940)

*(To JS/07/M/378*
*This Marble Monument*
*Is Erected by the State)*

He was found by the Bureau of Statistics to be
One against whom there was no official complaint,

And all the reports on his conduct agree
That, in the modern sense of an old-fashioned word, he was a saint,
For in everything he did he served the Greater Community.                    5

Except for the War till the day he retired
He worked in a factory and never got fired,
But satisfied his employers, Fudge Motors Inc.
Yet he wasn't a scab° or odd in his views.                          *strikebreaker*
For his Union reports that he paid his dues,                                10
(Our report on his Union shows it was sound)
And our Social Psychology workers found
That he was popular with his mates° and liked a drink.              *co-workers*
The Press are convinced that he bought a paper every day
And that his reactions to advertisements were normal in every way.          15
Policies taken out in his name prove that he was fully insured,
And his Health-card shows he was once in hospital but left it cured.
Both Producers Research and High-Grade Living declare
He was fully sensible to the advantages of the Installment Plan
And had everything necessary to the Modern Man,                             20
A phonograph, a radio, a car and a frigidaire.
Our researchers into Public Opinion are content
That he held the proper opinions for the time of year;
When there was peace, he was for peace; when there was war, he went.
He was married and added five children to the population,                   25
Which our Eugenist says was the right number for a parent of his generation,
And our teachers report that he never interfered with their education.
Was he free? Was he happy? The question is absurd:
Had anything been wrong, we should certainly have heard.

# WENDELL BERRY (b. 1934)

 ## Another Descent (1985)

Through the weeks of deep snow
we walked above the ground
on fallen sky, as though we did
not come of root and leaf, as though
we had only air and weather                                                 5
for our difficult home.
                    But now
as March warms, and the rivulets
run like birdsong on the slopes,
and the branches of light sing in the hills,                               10
slowly we return to earth.

## WILLIAM BLAKE (1757–1827)

*For a portrait, see Chapter 12, page 503.*

## London (1794)

I wander thro' each charter'd° street,
Near where the charter'd Thames does flow,
And mark in every face I meet
Marks of weakness, marks of woe.

5　In every cry of every Man,
In every Infant's cry of fear,
In every voice, in every ban,°　　　　　　　　*public pronouncement*
The mind-forg'd manacles I hear.

How the Chimney-sweeper's cry
10　Every blackning Church appalls;°
And the hapless Soldier's sigh
Runs in blood down Palace walls.

But most thro' midnight streets I hear
How the youthful Harlot's curse
15　Blasts the new-born Infant's tear,
And blights with plagues the Marriage hearse.

———————————————

°1 *charter'd*: privileged, licensed, authorized.　10 *appalls*: weakens, makes pale, shocks.

## LOUISE BOGAN (1897–1970)

## Women (1923)

Women have no wilderness in them,
They are provident instead,
Content in the tight hot cell of their hearts
To eat dusty bread.

5　They do not see cattle cropping red winter grass,
They do not hear
Snow water going down under culverts
Shallow and clear.

They wait, when they should turn to journeys,
10　They stiffen, when they should bend.
They use against themselves that benevolence
To which no man is friend.

They cannot think of so many crops to a field
Or of clean wood cleft by an axe.
Their love is an eager meaninglessness                    15
Too tense, or too lax.

They hear in every whisper that speaks to them
A shout and a cry.
As like as not, when they take life over their door-sills
They should let it go by.                                  20

## ARNA BONTEMPS (1902–1973)

### A Black Man Talks of Reaping (1940)

I have sown beside all waters in my day.
I planted deep, within my heart the fear
that wind or fowl would take the grain away.
I planted safe against this stark, lean year.

I scattered seed enough to plant the land          5
in rows from Canada to Mexico
but for my reaping only what the hand
can hold at once is all that I can show.

Yet what I sowed and what the orchard yields
my brother's sons are gathering stalk and root;    10
small wonder then my children glean in fields
they have not sown, and feed on bitter fruit.

## ELIZABETH BARRETT BROWNING (1806–1861)

### Sonnets from the Portuguese: Number 43, How Do I Love Thee? (1850)

How do I love thee? Let me count the ways.
I love thee to the depth and breadth and height
My soul can reach, when feeling out of sight
For the ends of Being and ideal Grace.
I love thee to the level of every day's             5
Most quiet need, by sun and candlelight.
I love thee freely, as men strive for Right;
I love thee purely, as they turn from Praise.
I love thee with the passion put to use
In my old griefs, and with my childhood's faith.    10
I love thee with a love I seemed to lose
With my lost saints,—I love thee with the breath,
Smiles, tears, of all my life!—and, if God choose,
I shall but love thee better after death.

## ROBERT BROWNING (1812–1889)

*For a photo, see Chapter 15, page 609.*

 ## Porphyria's Lover° (1836)

The Rain set early in to-night,
   The sullen wind was soon awake,
It tore the elm-tops down for spite,
   And did its worst to vex the lake:
5     I listened with heart fit to break.
When glided in Porphyria; straight
   She shut the cold out and the storm,
And kneeled and made the cheerless grate
   Blaze up, and all the cottage warm;
10    Which done, she rose, and from her form
Withdrew the dripping cloak and shawl,
   And laid her soiled gloves by, untied
Her hat and let the damp hair fall,
   And, last, she sat down by my side
15    And called me. When no voice replied,
She put my arm about her waist,
   And made her smooth white shoulder bare,
And all her yellow hair displaced,
   And, stooping, made my cheek lie there,
20    And spread, o'er all, her yellow hair.
Murmuring how she loved me—she
   Too weak, for all her heart's endeavor,
To set its struggling passion free
   From pride, and vainer ties dissever,
25    And give herself to me forever,
But passion sometimes would prevail,
   Nor could to-night's gay feast restrain
A sudden thought of one so pale
   For love of her, and all in vain:
30    So, she was come through wind and rain.
Be sure I looked up at her eyes
   Happy and proud; at last I knew
Porphyria worshipped me: surprise
   Made my heart swell, and still it grew
35    While I debated what to do.
That moment she was mine, mine, fair,
   Perfectly pure and good: I found
A thing to do, and all her hair
   In one long yellow string I wound

---

°When Browning published "Porphyria's Lover" in his *Dramatic Lyrics* of 1842, he grouped it with another poem under the title "Madhouse Cells."

Three times her little throat around 40
And strangled her. No pain felt she;
   I am quite sure she felt no pain.
As a shut bud that holds a bee,
   I warily oped her lids: again
   Laughed the blue eyes without a stain. 45
And I untightened next the tress
   About her neck; her cheek once more
Blushed bright beneath my burning kiss:
   I propped her head up as before
   Only, this time my shoulder bore 50
Her head, which droops upon it still:
   The smiling rosy little head,
So glad it has its utmost will,
   That all it scorned at once is fled,
   And I, its love, am gained instead! 55
Porphyria's love: she guessed not how
   Her darling one wish would be heard.
And thus we sit together now,
   And all night long we have not stirred,
   And yet God has not said a word! 60

# WILLIAM CULLEN BRYANT (1794–1878)

 ## To Cole,° the Painter, Departing for Europe (1829)

Thine eyes shall see the light of distant skies;
   Yet, Cole! thy heart shall bear to Europe's strand
   A living image of our own bright land,
Such as upon thy glorious canvas lies;
Lone lakes—savannas where the bison roves— 5
   Rocks rich with summer garlands—solemn streams—
   Skies where the desert eagle wheels and screams—
Spring bloom and autumn blaze of boundless groves.

Fair scenes shall greet thee where thou goest—fair,
   But different—everywhere the trace of men, 10
   Paths, homes, graves, ruins, from the lowest glen
To where life shrinks from the fierce Alpine air.
   Gaze on them, till the tears shall dim thy sight,
   But keep that earlier, wilder image bright.

---

°*Cole:* see I–4, Plate 1 for a painting by Thomas Cole (1801–1848).

## LEONARD COHEN (b. 1934)

 ## "The killers that run . . ." (1972)

The killers that run
      the other countries
are trying to get us
to overthrow the killers
      that run our own
I for one
prefer the rule
      of our native killers
I am convinced
      the foreign killer
will kill more of us
than the old familiar killer does
      Frankly I don't believe
anyone out there
really wants us to solve
our social problems
      I base this all on how I feel
about the man next door
I just hope he doesn't
      get any uglier
Therefore I am a patriot
I don't like to see
      a burning flag
because it excites
the killers on either side
to unfortunate excess
which goes on gaily
      quite unchecked
until everyone is dead

## BILLY COLLINS (b. 1941)

*For a photo, see Chapter 11, page 456.*

 ## Days (1995)

Each one *is* a gift, no doubt.
mysteriously placed in your waking hand
or set upon your forehead
moments before you open your eyes.

5   Today begins cold and bright,
the ground heavy with snow
and the thick masonry of ice.
the sun glinting off the turrets of clouds.

Through the calm eye of the window
everything is in its place    10
but so precariously
this day might be resting somehow

on the one before it,
all the days of the past stacked high    15
like the impossible tower of dishes
entertainers used to build on stage.

No wonder you find yourself
perched on the top of a tall ladder
hoping to add one more.
Just another Wednesday    20

you whisper,
then holding your breath,
place this cup on yesterday's saucer
without the slightest clink.

## FRANCES CORNFORD (1886–1960)

 ## From a Letter to America on a Visit to Sussex: Spring 1942 (1942)

How simply violent things
Happen, is strange.
How strange it was to see
In the soft Cambridge sky our Squadron's wings,
And hear the huge hum in the familiar grey.    5
And it was odd today
On Ashdown Forest that will never change,
To find a gunner in the gorse, flung down,
Well-camouflaged, and bored and lion-brown.
A little further by those twisted trees    10
(As if it rose on humped preposterous seas
Out of a Book of Hours) up a bank
Like a large dragon, purposeful though drunk,
Heavily lolloped, swayed and sunk,
A tank.    15
All this because manoeuvres had begun.
But now, but soon,
At home on any usual afternoon,
High overhead
May come the Erinyes° winging    *the furies in Greek mythology*    20
Or here the boy may lie beside his gun,
His mud-brown tunic gently staining red,
While larks get on with their old job of singing.

## STEPHEN CRANE (1871–1900)

 ## Do Not Weep, Maiden, for War Is Kind (1896, 1899 (1895))

Do not weep, maiden, for war is kind.
Because your lover threw wild hands toward the sky
And the affrighted steed ran on alone,
Do not weep.
5  War is kind.

      Hoarse, booming drums of the regiment
      Little souls who thirst for fight,
      These men were born to drill and die
      The unexplained glory flies above them
10      Great is the battle-god, great, and his kingdom—
      A field where a thousand corpses lie.

Do not weep, babe, for war is kind.
Because your father tumbled in the yellow trenches,
Raged at his breast, gulped and died,
15  Do not weep.
War is kind.

      Swift, blazing flag of the regiment
      Eagle with crest of red and gold,
      These men were born to drill and die
20      Point for them the virtue of slaughter
      Make plain to them the excellence of killing
      And a field where a thousand corpses lie.

Mother whose head hung humble as a button
On the bright splendid shroud of your son,
25  Do not weep.
War is kind.

## ROBERT CREELEY (b. 1926–2005)

 ## "Do you think . . ." (1972)

Do you think that if
you once do what you want
to do you will want not to do it.

Do you think that if
5  there's an apple on the table
and somebody eats it, it
won't be there anymore.

Do you think that if
two people are in love with one another,
one or the other has got to be
less in love than the other at
some point in the otherwise happy relationship.

Do you think that if
you once take a breath, you're by
that committed to taking the next one
and so on until the very process of
breathing's an endlessly expanding need
almost of its own necessity forever.

Do you think that if
no one knows then whatever
it is, no one will know and
that will be the case, like
they say, for an indefinite
period of time if such time
can have a qualification of such time.

Do you know anyone,
really. Have you been, really,
much alone. Are you lonely,
now, for example. Does anything
really matter to you, really, or
has anything mattered. Does each
thing tend to be there, and then not
to be there, just as if that were it.

Do you think that if
I said, *I love you*, or anyone
said it, or you did. Do you
think that if you had all
such decisions to make and could
make them. Do you think that
if you did. That you really
would have to think it all into
reality, that world, each time, new.

10

15

20

25

30

35

40

# E. E. CUMMINGS (1894–1962)

*For a photo, see Chapter 12, page 507.*

##  if there are any heavens (1931)

if there are any heavens my mother will (all by herself) have
one.     It will not be a pansy heaven nor
a fragile heaven of lilies-of-the-valley but
it will be a heaven of blackred roses

5   my father will be (deep like a rose
    tall like a rose)

    standing near my

    swaying over her
    (silent)
10  with eyes which are really petals and see

    nothing with the face of a poet really which
    is a flower and not a face with
    hands
    which whisper
15  This is my beloved my

                (suddenly in sunlight

    he will bow,

    & the whole garden will bow)

## CARL DENNIS (b. 1939)

 ## The God Who Loves You (2001)

    It must be troubling for the god who loves you
    To ponder how much happier you'd be today
    Had you been able to glimpse your many futures.
    It must be painful for him to watch you on Friday evenings
5   Driving home from the office, content with your week—
    Three fine houses sold to deserving families—
    Knowing as he does exactly what would have happened
    Had you gone to your second choice for college,
    Knowing the roommate you'd have been allotted
10  Whose ardent opinions on painting and music
    Would have kindled in you a lifelong passion.
    A life thirty points above the life you're living
    On any scale of satisfaction. And every point
    A thorn in the side of the god who loves you.
15  You don't want that, a large-souled man like you
    Who tries to withhold from your wife the day's disappointments
    So she can save her empathy for the children.
    And would you want this god to compare your wife
    With the woman you were destined to meet on the other campus?
20  It hurts you to think of him ranking the conversation
    You'd have enjoyed over there higher in insight
    Than the conversation you're used to.
    And think how this loving god would feel

Knowing that the man next in line for your wife
Would have pleased her more than you ever will            25
Even on your best days, when you really try.
Can you sleep at night believing a god like that
Is pacing his cloudy bedroom, harassed by alternatives
You're spared by ignorance? The difference between what is
And what could have been will remain alive for him        30
Even after you cease existing, after you catch a chill
Running out in the snow for the morning paper,
Losing eleven years that the god who loves you
Will feel compelled to imagine scene by scene
Unless you come to the rescue by imagining him            35
No wiser than you are, no god at all, only a friend
No closer than the actual friend you made at college,
The one you haven't written in months. Sit down tonight
And write him about the life you can talk about
With a claim to authority, the life you've witnessed,      40
Which for all you know is the life you've chosen.

# JAMES DICKEY (1923–1997)

 ## Kudzu (1964)

Japan invades. Far Eastern vines
Run from the clay banks they are

Supposed to keep from eroding,
Up telephone poles,
Which rear, half out of leafage,                          5
As though they would shriek,
Like things smothered by their own
Green, mindless, unkillable ghosts.
In Georgia, the legend says
That you must close your windows                          10

At night to keep it out of the house.
The glass is tinged with green, even so,

As the tendrils crawl over the fields.
The night the kudzu has
Your pasture, you sleep like the dead.                    15
Silence has grown Oriental
And you cannot step upon ground:
Your leg plunges somewhere
It should not, it never should be,
Disappears, and waits to be struck                        20

Anywhere between sole and kneecap:
For when the kudzu comes,

The snakes do, and weave themselves
Among its lengthening vines,
25 Their spade heads resting on leaves,
Growing also, in earthly power
And the huge circumstance of concealment.
One by one the cows stumble in,
Drooling a hot green froth,
30 And die, seeing the wood of their stalls

Strain to break into leaf.
In your closed house, with the vine

Tapping your window like lightning,
You remember what tactics to use.
35 In the wrong yellow fog-light of dawn
You herd them in, the hogs,
Head down in their hairy fat,
The meaty troops, to the pasture.
The leaves of the kudzu quake
40 With the serpents' fear, inside

The meadow ringed with men
Holding sticks, on the country roads.

The hogs disappear in the leaves.
The sound is intense, subhuman,
45 Nearly human with purposive rage.
There is no terror
Sound from the snakes.
No one can see the desperate, futile
Striking under the leaf heads.
50 Now and then, the flash of a long

Living vine, a cold belly,
Leaps up, torn apart, then falls
Under the tussling surface.
You have won, and wait for frost,
55 When, at the merest touch
Of cold, the kudzu turns
Black, withers inward and dies,
Leaving a mass of brown strings
Like the wires of a gigantic switchboard.
60 You open your windows,

With the lightning restored to the sky
And no leaves rising to bury

You alive inside your frail house,
And you think, in the opened cold,
65 Of the surface of things and its terrors,
And of the mistaken, mortal

Arrogance of the snakes
As the vines, growing insanely sent
Great powers into their bodies
And the freedom to strike without warning:                          70

From them, though they killed
Your cattle, such energy also flowed

To you from the knee-high meadow
(It was as though you had
A green sword twined among                                          75
The veins of your growing right arm—
Such strength as you would not believe
If you stood alone in a proper
Shaved field among your safe cows—):
Came in through your closed                                         80

Leafy windows and almighty sleep
And prospered, till rooted out.

## JOHN DONNE (1572–1631)

*For a portrait, see Chapter 12, page 508.*

 ## The Good Morrow (1633)

I wonder, by my troth, what thou and I
Did, till we loved! Were we not weaned till then,
But sucked on country pleasures, childishly?
Or snorted we in the seven sleepers' den?°
T'was so; But this, all pleasures fancies be.                       5
If ever any beauty I did see,
Which I desired, and got, t'was but a dream of thee.

And now good morrow to our waking souls,
Which watch not one another out of fear;
For love all love of other sights controls,°                       10
And makes one little room an everywhere.
Let sea-discoverers to new worlds have gone,
Let maps to other, worlds on worls have shown,°
Let us possess one world; each hath one, and is one.

---

°4 *seven sleepers' den*: a reference to the miraculous legend of the Seven Sleepers of Ephesus, in Asia Minor. Seven young nobles fled Ephesus to avoid religious persecution by the Emperor Decius (ca. 250 c.e.). They took refuge in a cave and were sealed inside. They then slept for either 230 or 309 years, and they emerged praising God. After they died, their remains were taken to St. Victor's Church in Marseilles, France, where they were encrypted. 10 *For love . . . controls*: i.e., Love is so powerful that it eliminates fear and makes everything in the world worthy of love. 13, 14 *let sea-discoverers . . . shown*: i.e., let sea-explorers discover new worlds, and let maps show other new worlds to other discoverers.

My face in thine eye, thine in mine appears,°
And true plain hearts do in the faces rest;
Where can we find two better hemispheres
Without sharp North, without declining West?
Whatever dies was not mixed equally;
If our two loves be one, or thou and I
Love so alike, that none do slacken, none can die.°

---

°15 *My face . . . appears*: Each face is reflected in the pupils of the other lover's eyes. 19–21 *Whatever . . . can die*: Scholastic philosophy argued that elements that are united in perfect balance will never change or decay; hence, such a mixture cannot die. Donne's analogy suggests—humorously—that the love of the lovers is too pure to die, and that they may therefore go on making love forever.

## JOHN DONNE (1572–1631)

 ## Holy Sonnet 10: Death Be Not Proud (1633)

Death, be not proud, though some have callèd thee
Mighty and dreadful, for thou art not so;
For those whom thou think'st thou dost overthrow
Die not, poor Death, nor yet canst thou kill me.
From rest and sleep, which but thy pictures° be,      *imitations*
Much pleasure; then from thee much more must flow,
And soonest our best men with thee do go,
Rest of their bones, and soul's delivery.
Thou art slave to fate, chance, kings, and desperate men,
10  And dost with poison, war, and sickness dwell,
And poppy° or charms can make us sleep as well      *opium*
And better than thy stroke; why swell'st° thou then?      *puff up with pride*
One short sleep past, we wake eternally°      *i.e., we will live eternally*
And death shall be no more; Death, thou shalt die.

## PAUL LAURENCE DUNBAR (1872–1906)

 ## Sympathy (1895)

I know what the caged bird feels, alas!
When the sun is bright on the upland slopes;
When the wind stirs soft through the springing grass
And the river flows like a stream of glass;
5  When the first bird sings and the first bud opes,
And the faint perfume from its chalice steals—
I know what the caged bird feels!

I know why the caged bird beats his wing
Till its blood is red on the cruel bars;
For he must fly back to his perch and cling    10
When he fain would be on the bough a-swing;
And a pain still throbs in the old, old scars
And they pulse again with a keener sting—
I know why he beats his wing!

I know why the caged bird sings, ah me,    15
When his wing is bruised and his bosom sore,
When he beats his bars and would be free;
It is not a carol of joy or glee,
But a prayer that he sends from his heart's deep core,
But a plea, that upward to Heaven he flings—    20
I know why the caged bird sings!

## JAMES EMANUEL (b. 1921)

 ## The Negro (1968)

Never saw him.
Never can.
Hypothetical,
Haunting man:

Eyes a-saucer,    5
Yessir bossir,
Dice a-clicking,
Razor flicking.

The-ness froze him
In a dance.    10
A-ness never
Had a chance.

## LYNN EMANUEL (b. 1949)

 ## Like God (1998)

you hover above the page staring
down on a small town. By its roads
some scenery loafs in a hammock of
sleepy prose and here is a mongrel
loping and here is a train pulling into    5
a station in three long sentences and
here are the people in galoshes waiting.

But you know this story and it is not
about those travelers and their galoshes,
10  but about your life, so, like a diver
climbing over the side of a boat and
down into the ocean, you climb, sentence
by sentence, into this story on this page.

You have been expecting yourself
15  as the woman who purrs by in a dress
by Patou, and a porter manacled to
the luggage, and a matron bulky as
the *Britannia*, and there, haunting
her ankles like a piece of ectoplasm
20  that barks is, once again, that small
white dog from chapter twenty.
These are your fellow travelers and
you become part of their logjam of
images of hats and umbrellas and
25  Vuitton luggage, you are a face
behind or inside these faces, a
heartbeat in the volley of these
heartbeats, as you choose, out of all
the passengers, the journey of a man
30  with a mustache scented faintly with
*Prince Albert*. "He must be a secret
sensualist," you think and your awareness
drifts to his trench coat, worn, softened,
and flabby, a coat with a lobotomy, just
35  as the train arrives at a destination.

No, you would prefer another stop
in a later chapter where the climate is
affable and sleek. But most of
the passengers are disembarking, and
40  you did not choose to be in the story
of the white dress. You did not choose
the story of the matron whose bosom
is like the prow of a ship and who is
launched toward lunch at The Hotel Pierre,
45  or even the story of the dog-on-a-leash,
even though this is now your story:
the story of the man-who-had-to-
take-the-train and walk the dark road
described hurriedly by someone sitting
50  at the café so you could discover it,
although you knew all along it would
be there, you, who have been hovering
above this page, holding the book in
your hands, like God, reading.

## CHIEF DAN GEORGE (1899–1981)

 ## The Beauty of the Trees (1974)

The beauty of the trees,
the softness of the air,
the fragrance of the grass,
 speaks to me.

The summit of the mountain,
the thunder of the sky,
the rhythm of the sea,
 speaks to me.

The faintness of the stars,
the freshness of the morning,
the dewdrop on the flower,
 speaks to me.

The strength of fire,
the taste of salmon,
the trail of the sun,
and the life that never goes away,
 they speak to me.

And my heart soars.

            5

            10

            15

## NIKKI GIOVANNI (b. 1943)

 ## Woman (1978)

she wanted to be a blade
of grass amid the fields
but he wouldn't agree
to be the dandelion

she wanted to be a robin singing
through the leaves
but he refused to be
her tree

she spun herself into a web
 and looking for a place to rest
turned to him
but he stood straight
declining to be her corner

            5

            10

    she tried to be a book
15   but he wouldn't read
    she turned herself into a bulb
    but he wouldn't let her grow

    she decided to become
    a woman
20   and though he still refused
    to be a man
    she decided it was all
    right

## LOUISE GLÜCK (b. 1943)

 Snowdrops (1992)

Do you know what I was, how I lived? You know
what despair is; then
winter should have meaning for you.

I did not expect to survive,
5   earth suppressing me, I didn't expect
to waken again, to feel
in damp earth my body
able to respond again, remembering
after so long how to open again
10  in the cold light
of earliest spring—

afraid, yes, but among you again
crying yes risk joy

in the raw wind of the new world.

## MARILYN HACKER (b. 1942)

 Sonnet Ending with a Film Subtitle (1979)

**For Judith Landry**

Life has its nauseating ironies:
The good die young, as often has been shown;
Chaste spouses catch Venereal Disease;
And feminists sit by the telephone.
5   Last night was rather bleak, tonight is starker.
I may stare at the wall till half-past-one.
My friends are all convinced Dorothy Parker
Lives, but is not well, in Marylebone.°

                                      *a district in London*

I wish that I could imitate my betters
And fortify my rhetoric with guns.                                    10
Some day we women all will break our fetters
And raise our daughters to be Lesbians.
(I wonder if the bastard kept my letters?)
Here follow untranslatable French puns.

## DANIEL HALPERN (b. 1945)

 ## Snapshot of Hué (1982)

### For Robert Stone

They are riding bicycles on the other side
of the Perfume River.

A few months ago the bridges were down
and there was no one on the streets.

There were the telling piles on corners,                              5
debris that contained a little of everything.

There was nothing not under cover—
even the sky remained impenetrable

day after day. And if you were seen
on the riverbank you were knocked down.                               10

It is clear today. The litter in the streets
has been swept away. It couldn't have been

that bad, one of us said, the river barely moving,
the bicycles barely moving, the sun posted above.

## H. S. (SAM) HAMOD (b. 1936)

 ## Leaves (1973)

### For Sally

Tonight, Sally and I are making stuffed
grapeleaves, we get out a package, it's
drying out, I've been saving it in the freezer, it's
one of the last things my father ever picked in this
life—they're over five years old                                     5
and up to now
we just kept finding packages of them in the
freezer, as if he were still picking them
somewhere packing them
carefully to send to us                                               10
making sure they didn't break into pieces.

\* \* \*

"To my Dar Garnchildn
Davd and Lura
from Thr Jido"
15  twisted on tablet paper
between the lines
in this English lettering
hard for him even to print,
I keep this small torn record,
20  this piece of paper stays in the upstairs storage,
one of the few pieces of American
my father ever wrote. We find his Arabic letters
all over the place, even in the files we find
letters to him in English, one I found from Charles Atlas
25  telling him, in 1932,
"Of course, Mr. Hamod, you too can build
your muscles like mine . . . "

\* \* \*

Last week my mother told me, when I was
asking why I became a poet, "But don't you remember,
30  your father made up poems, don't you remember him
singing in the car as we drove—those were poems."
Even now, at night, I sometimes
get out the Arabic grammar book
though it seems so late.

## FRANCES E. W. HARPER (1825–1911)

 **She's Free!** (1854)

How say that by law we may torture and chase
A woman whose crime is the hue of her face?—
With her step on the ice, and her arm on her child,
The danger was fearful, the pathway was wild. . . .
5  But she's free! yes, free from the land where the slave,
From the hand of oppression, must rest in the grave;
Where bondage and blood, where scourges and chains,
Have placed on our banner indelible stains. . . .

The bloodhounds have miss'd the scent of her way,
10  The hunter is rifled and foiled of his prey,
The cursing of men and clanking of chains
Make sounds of strange discord on Liberty's plains. . . .
Oh! poverty, danger and death she can brave,
For the child of her love is no longer a slave.

**ROBERT HASS** (b. 1941)

### Spring Rain (1989)

Now the rain is falling, freshly, in the intervals between sunlight,

a Pacific squall started no one knows where, drawn east as the drifts of
warm air make a channel;

it moves its own way, like water or the mind,

and spills this rain passing over. The Sierras will catch it as last snow    5
flurries before summer, observed only by the wakened marmots at ten
thousand feet,

and we will come across it again as larkspur and penstemon sprouting
along a creek above Sonora Pass next August,

where the snowmelt will have trickled into Dead Man's Creek and the    10
creek spilled into the Stanislaus and the Stanislaus into the San Joaquin
and the San Joaquin into the slow salt marshes of the bay.

That's not the end of it: the gray jays of the mountains eat larkspur seeds,
which cannot propagate otherwise.

To simulate the process, you have to soak gathered seeds all night in the    15
acids of coffee

and then score them gently with a very sharp knife before you plant them
in the garden.

**ROBERT HAYDEN** (1913–1980)

### Those Winter Sundays (1962)

Sundays too my father got up early
and put his clothes on in the blueblack cold,
then with cracked hands that ached
from labor in the weekday weather made
banked fires blaze. No one ever thanked him.    5
I'd wake and hear the cold splintering, breaking,
When the rooms were warm, he'd call,
and slowly I would rise and dress,
fearing the chronic angers of that house,

Speaking indifferently to him,    10
who had driven out the cold
and polished my good shoes as well.
What did I know, what did I know
of love's austere and lonely offices?

## WILLIAM HEYEN (b. 1940)

 ## The Hair: Jacob Korman's Story (1980)

Ten kilometers from Warsaw,
I arrived in Rembertow where
hundreds of Jews had lived
until the wheel turned: *Judenrein.*°                              *cleansed, rid of Jews*

5   You think they let themselves be taken?
They would not fill the trucks.
Men were shot trying to pull guns
from the guards' hands.

and hands of dead women
10  clutched hair, hair of SS guards
blood-patched hair everywhere,
a *velt mit hor*, a field of hair.

## A. D. HOPE (1907–2000)

 ## Advice to Young Ladies (1970)

A.U.C.° 334: about this date
For a sexual misdemeanor, which she denied,
The vestal virgin Postumia was tried.
Livy records it among affairs of state.

5   They let her off: it seems she was perfectly pure;
The charge arose because some thought her talk
Too witty for a young girl, her ways, her walk
Too lively, her clothes too smart to be demure.

The Pontifex Maximus, summing up the case,
10  Warned her in future to abstain from jokes,
To wear less modish and more pious frocks.
She left the court reprieved, but in disgrace.

What then? With her the annalist is less
Concerned than what the men achieved that year;
15  Plots, quarrels, crimes, with oratory to spare!
I see Postumia with her dowdy dress,

Stiff mouth and listless step; I see her strive
To give dull answers. She had to knuckle down.

---

°1 *A.U.C.*: A.U.C. stands for *ab urbe condita,* "from the founding of the city." A.U.C. 334 therefore means 334 years after the founding of ancient Rome.

A vestal virgin who scandalized that town
Had fair trial, then they buried her alive.                          20

Alive, bricked up in suffocating dark,
A ration of bread, a pitcher if she was dry
Preserved the body they did not wish to die
Until her mind was quenched to the last spark.

How many the black maw has swallowed in its time!                   25
Spirited girls who would not know their place.
Talented girls who found that the disgrace
Of being a woman made genius a crime;

How many others, who would not kiss the rod
Domestic bullying broke, or public shame?                           30
Pagan or Christian, it was much the same:
Husbands, Saint Paul declared, rank next to God.

Livy and Paul, it may be, never knew
That Rome was doomed; each spoke of her with pride.
Tacitus, writing after both had died,                               35
Showed that whole fabric rotten through and through.

Historians spend their lives and lavish ink
Explaining how great commonwealths collapse
From great defects of policy—perhaps
The cause is sometimes simpler than they think.                     40

It may not seem so grave an act to break
Postumia's spirit as Galileo's, to gag
Hypatia as crush Socrates, or drag
Joan as Giordano Bruno to the stake.

Can we be sure: Have more states perished, then,                    45
For having shackled the enquiring mind,
Than those who, in their folly not less blind,
Trusted the servile womb to breed free men?

## CAROLINA HOSPITAL (b. 1957)

 **Dear Tia** (1988)

I do not write.
The years have frightened me away.
My life in a land so familiarly foreign,
a denial of your presence.
Your name is mine.                                                  5
One black and white photograph of your youth,
all I hold on to.
One story of your past.

The pain comes not from nostalgia.
10  I do not miss your voice urging me in play,
    your smile,
    or your pride when others called you my mother.
    I cannot close my eyes and feel your soft skin;
    listen to your laughter;
15  smell the sweetness of your bath
    I write because I cannot remember at all.

## ROBINSON JEFFERS (1887–1962)

*For a photo, see Chapter 17, page 713.*

## The Answer (1937)

Then what is the answer?—Not to be deluded by dreams.
To know that great civilizations have broken down into violence, and their tyrants come,
    many times before.
When open violence appears, to avoid it with honor or choose the least ugly faction;
    these evils are essential.
To keep one's own integrity, be merciful and uncorrupted and not wish for evil; and not
    be duped
5  By dreams of universal justice or happiness. These dreams will not be fulfilled.
To know this, and know that however ugly the parts appear the whole remains beautiful.
    A severed hand
Is an ugly thing, and man dissevered from the earth and stars and his history . . . for
    contemplation or in fact . . .

Often appears atrociously ugly. Integrity is wholeness, the greatest beauty is
Organic wholeness, the wholeness of life and things, the divine beauty of the universe.
    Love that, not man
10  Apart from that, or else you will share man's pitiful confusions, or drown in despair
    when his days darken.

## JOHN KEATS (1795–1821)

*For a portrait, see Chapter 14, page 562.*

## Ode on a Grecian Urn° (1820 (1819))

**1**

Thou still unravish'd bride of quietness,
    Thou foster-child of silence and slow time,

---

°The imaginary Grecian urn to which the poem is addressed combines design motifs from many different existing urns. This imaginary one is decorated with a border of leaves and trees, men (or gods) chasing women, a young musician sitting under a tree, lovers, and a priest and congregation
leading a heifer to sacrifice.

"The Krater of Thanagra," fourth century B.C.E., showing a wedding procession and musicians. National Museum, Athens, Greece. Alinari/Art Resource, New York, NY.

Sylvan historian, who canst thus express
A flowery tale more sweetly than our rhyme:
What leaf-fring'd legend° haunts about thy shape    *border and tale*    5
   Of deities or mortals, or of both,
     In Tempe° or the dales of Arcady?°
What men or gods are these? What maidens loth?
What mad pursuit? What struggle to escape?
     What pipes and timbrels? What wild ecstasy?    10

2

Heard melodies are sweet, but those unheard
   Are sweeter; therefore, ye soft pipes, play on;
Not to the sensual ear, but, more endear'd,

---

°7 *Tempe*: a beautiful rustic valley in Greece. *Arcady*: refers to the valleys of Arcadia, a state in ancient Greece known for its beauty and peacefulness.

Pipe to the spirit ditties of no tone:

15  Fair youth, beneath the trees, thou canst not leave
    Thy song, nor ever can those trees be bare;
       Bold lover, never, never canst thou kiss,
Though winning near the goal—yet, do not grieve;
       She cannot fade, though thou hast not thy bliss,

20  For ever wilt thou love, and she be fair!


  3

Ah, happy, happy boughs! that cannot shed
    Your leaves, nor ever bid the spring adieu;
And, happy melodist, unwearied,
    For ever piping songs for ever new;

25  More happy love! more happy, happy love!
    For ever warm and still to be enjoy'd,
       For ever panting, and for ever young;
All breathing human passion far above,
    That leaves a heart high-sorrowful and cloy'd,

30         A burning forehead, and a parching tongue.


  4

Who are these coming to the sacrifice?
    To what green altar, O mysterious priest,
Lead'st thou that heifer lowing at the skies,
    And all her silken flanks with garlands drest?

35  What little town by river or sea shore,
    Or mountain-built° with peaceful citadel,      *built on a mountain*
       Is emptied of this folk, this pious morn?
And, little town, thy streets for evermore
    Will silent be; and not a soul to tell

40         Why thou art desolate, can e'er return.


  5

O Attic shape! Fair attitude! with brede°      *braid, pattern*
    Of marble men and maidens overwrought,°      *ornamented*
With forest branches and the trodden weed;
    Thou, silent form, dost tease us out of thought

45  As doth eternity: Cold Pastoral!
    When old age shall this generation waste,
       Thou shalt remain, in midst of other woe
Than ours, a friend to man, to whom thou say'st,
"Beauty is truth, truth beauty,"—that is all

50         Ye know on earth, and all ye need to know.

## GALWAY KINNELL (b. 1927)

 ## After Making Love We Hear Footsteps (1980)

For I can snore like a bullhorn
or play loud music
or sit up talking with any reasonably sober Irishman
and Fergus will only sink deeper
into his dreamless sleep, which goes by all in one flash, 5
but let there be that heavy breathing
or a stifled come-cry anywhere in the house
and he will wrench himself awake
and make for it on the run—as now, we lie together,
after making love, quiet, touching along the length of our bodies, 10
familiar touch of the long-married,
and he appears—in his baseball pajamas, it happens,
the neck opening so small
he has to screw them on, which one day may make him wonder
about the mental capacity of baseball players— 15
and flops down between us and hugs us and snuggles himself to sleep,
his face gleaming with satisfaction at being this very child.

In the half darkness we look at each other
and smile
and touch arms across his little, startlingly muscled body— 20
this one whom habit of memory propels to the ground of his making,
sleeper only the mortal sounds can sing awake,
this blessing love gives again into our arms.

## IRVING LAYTON (b. 1912–2006)

 ## Rhine Boat Trip° (1977)

The castles on the Rhine
are all haunted
by the ghosts of Jewish mothers
looking for their ghostly children

And the clusters of grapes 5
in the sloping vineyards
are myriads of blinded eyes
staring at the blind sun

---

°The title refers to the Rhine River, which flows through Germany.

The tireless Lorelei:°
10   can never comb from their hair
    the crimson beards
    of murdered rabbis

However sweetly they sing
one hears only
15   the low wailing of cattle-cars°
    moving invisibly across the land

---

°9. *Lorelei*: legendary seductive nymphs who lived in the cliffs overlooking the Rhine, and whose singing lured sailors to shipwreck.   15 *cattle-cars*: railroad cars designed to transport cattle but used by the Nazis to transport Jews from the cities of Europe to extermination camps.

## ALAN P. LIGHTMAN (b. 1948)

## In Computers (1982 (1981))

In the magnets of computers will
    be stored

Blend of sunset over wheat
    fields.
5   Low thunder of gazelle.
Light, sweet wind on high
    ground.
Vacuum stillness spreading from
    a thick snowfall.

10   Men will sit in rooms
upon the smooth, scrubbed earth
or stand in tunnels on the moon
and instruct themselves in how it
    was.
15   Nothing will be lost.
Nothing will be lost.

## LIZ LOCHHEAD (b. 1947)

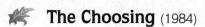

## The Choosing (1984)

We were first equal Mary and I
with same coloured ribbons in mouse-coloured hair
and with equal shyness,
we curtseyed to the lady councillor

for copies of Collins' Children's Classics.                                    5
First equal, equally proud.


Best friends too Mary and I
a common bond in being cleverest (equal)
in our small school's small class.
I remember                                                                     10
the competition for top desk
or to read aloud the lesson
at school service.
And my terrible fear
of her superiority at sums.                                                     15
I remember the housing scheme
where we both stayed.
The same houses, different homes,
where the choices were made.


I don't know exactly why they moved,                                           20
but anyway they went.
Something about a three-apartment
and a cheaper rent.
But from the top deck of the high-school bus
I'd glimpse among the others on the corner                                      25
Mary's father, mufflered, contrasting strangely
with the elegant greyhounds by his side.
He didn't believe in high school education,
especially for girls,
or in forking out for uniforms.                                                30


Ten years later on a Saturday—
I am coming from the library—
sitting near me on the bus,
Mary
with a husband who is tall,                                                     35
curly haired, has eyes
for no one else but Mary.
Her arms are round the full-shaped vase
that is her body.
Oh, you can see where the attraction lies                                       40
in Mary's life—
not that I envy her, really.


And I am coming from the library
with my arms full of books.
I think of those prizes that were ours for the taking                           45
and wonder when the choices got made
we don't remember making.

## HENRY WADSWORTH LONGFELLOW (1807–1882)

 ## The Sound of the Sea (1875)

The sea awoke at midnight from its sleep,
   And round the pebbly beaches far and wide
   I heard the first wave of the rising tide
Rush onward with uninterrupted sweep;
5  A voice out of the silence of the deep,
   A sound mysteriously multiplied
   As of a cataract from the mountain's side,
Or roar of winds upon a wooded steep.
   So comes to us at times, from the unknown
10    And inaccessible solitudes of being,
     The rushing of the sea-tides of the soul;
And inspirations, that we deem our own,
    Are some divine foreshadowing and foreseeing
     Of things beyond our reason or control.

## AUDRE LORDE (1934–1992)

 ## Every Traveler Has One Vermont Poem (1986)

Spikes of lavender aster under Route 91
hide a longing or confession
"I remember when air was invisible"
from Chamberlin Hill down to Lord's Creek
5  tree mosses point the way home.

Two nights of frost
and already the hills are turning
curved green against the astonished morning
sneeze-weed and ox-eye daisies
10  nor caring I am a stranger
making a living choice.

Tanned boys I do not know
on their first proud harvest
wave from their father's tractor
15  one smiles as we drive past
the other hollers
nigger
into cropped and fragrant air.

# AMY LOWELL (1874–1925)

## Patterns (1916)

I walk down the garden paths,
And all the daffodils
Are blowing, and the bright blue squills.
I walk down the patterned garden-paths
In my stiff, brocaded gown.                                    5
With my powdered hair and jewelled fan,
I too am a rare
Pattern. As I wander down
The garden paths.
My dress is richly figured,                                    10
And the train
Makes a pink and silver stain
On the gravel, and the thrift
Of the borders.
Just a plate of current fashion                                15
Tripping by in high-heeled, ribboned shoes.
Not a softness anywhere about me,
Only whalebone° and brocade.
And I sink on a seat in the shade
Of a lime tree. For my passion                                 20
Wars against the stiff brocade.
The daffodils and squills
Flutter in the breeze
As they please.
And I weep;                                                    25
For the lime-tree is in blossom
And one small flower has dropped upon my bosom.

And the plashing of waterdrops
In the marble fountain
Comes down the garden-paths.                                   30
The dripping never stops.
Underneath my stiffened gown
Is the softness of a woman bathing in a marble basin,
A basin in the midst of hedges grown
So thick, she cannot see her lover hiding,                     35
But she guesses he is near,
And the sliding of the water
Seems the stroking of a dear
Hand upon her.
What is Summer in a fine brocaded gown!                        40
I should like to see it lying in a heap upon the ground.
All the pink and silver crumpled up on the ground.

---

°18 *whalebone*: Baleen from whales was used to make corsets for women because it was strong and flexible, like an early plastic.

I would be the pink and silver as I ran along the paths,
And he would stumble after,
45  Bewildered by my laughter.
I should see the sun flashing from his sword-hilt and buckles on his shoes.
I would choose
To lead him in a maze along the patterned paths,
A bright and laughing maze for my heavy-booted lover.
50  Till he caught me in the shade,
And the buttons of his waistcoat bruised my body as he clasped me,
Aching, melting, unafraid.
With the shadows of the leaves and the sundrops,
And the plopping of the waterdrops,
55  All about us in the open afternoon—
I am very like to swoon
With the weight of this brocade,
For the sun sifts through the shade.

Underneath the fallen blossom
60  In my bosom,
Is a letter I have hid.
It was brought to me this morning by a rider from the Duke.
Madam, we regret to inform you that Lord Hartwell
Died in action Thursday se'nnight.°
65  As I read it in the white, morning sunlight,
The letters squirmed like snakes.
"Any answer, Madam," said my footman.
"No," I told him.
"See that the messenger takes some refreshment.

70  No, no answer."
And I walked into the garden,
Up and down the patterned paths,
In my stiff, correct brocade.
The blue and yellow flowers stood up proudly in the sun,
75  Each one.
I stood upright too,
Held rigid to the pattern
By the stiffness of my gown.
Up and down I walked.
80  Up and down.

In a month he would have been my husband.
In a month, here, underneath this lime,
We would have broken the pattern;
He for me, and I for him,
85  He as Colonel, I as Lady,
On this shady seat.
He had a whim

---

°64 *se'nnight*: seven nights, hence a week ago.

That sunlight carried blessing.
And I answered, "It shall be as you have said."
Now he is dead.                                                    90

In Summer and In Winter I shall walk
Up and down
The patterned garden-paths
In my stiff, brocaded gown.
The squills and daffodils                                          95
Will give peace to pillared roses, and to asters, and to snow.
I shall go
Up and down,
In my gown.
Gorgeously arrayed,                                                100
Boned and stayed.
And the softness of my body will be guarded from embrace
By each button, hook, and lace.
For the man who should loose me is dead,
Fighting with the Duke in Flanders,°                               105
In a pattern called a war.
Christ! What are patterns for?

---

°105 *Flanders*: a place of frequent warfare in Belgium. The speaker's clothing (lines 5, 6) suggests the time of the Duke of Marlborough's Flanders campaigns of 1702–1710. The Battle of Waterloo (1815) was also fought nearby under the Duke of Wellington. During World War I, fierce fighting against the Germans occurred in Flanders in 1914 and 1915, with great loss of life.

## CLAUDE McKAY (1890–1948)

 ## The White City (1922)

I will not toy with it nor bend an inch.
Deep in the secret chambers of my heart
I muse my life-long hate, and without flinch
I bear it nobly as I live my part.
My being would be a skeleton, a shell,                            5
If this dark Passion that fills my every mood,
And makes my heaven in the white world's hell,
Did not forever feed me vital blood.
I see the mighty city through a mist—
The strident trains that speed the goaded mass,                   10
The poles and spires and towers vapor-kissed,
The fortressed port through which the great ships pass,
The tides, the wharves, the dens I contemplate,
Are sweet like wanton loves because I hate.

## W. S. MERWIN (b. 1927)

### Listen (1988)

Listen
with the night falling we are saying thank you
we are stopping on the bridges to bow from the railings
we are running out of the glass rooms
5  with our mouths full of food to look at the sky
and say thank you
we are standing by the water looking out
in different directions

back from a series of hospitals back from a mugging
10  after funerals we are saying thank you
after the news of the dead
whether or not we knew them we are saying thank you
looking up from tables we are saying thank you
in a culture up to its chin in shame
15  living in the stench it has chosen we are saying thank you
over telephones we are saying thank you
in doorways and in the backs of cars and in elevators
remembering wars and the police at the back door
and the beatings on stairs we are saying thank you
20  in the banks that use us we are saying thank you

with the animals dying around us
our lost feelings we are saying thank you
with the forests falling faster than the minutes
of our lives we are saying thank you
25  with the words going out like cells of a brain
with the cities growing over us like the earth
we are saying thank you faster and faster
with nobody listening we are saying thank you
we are saying thank you and waving
30  dark though it is

## N. SCOTT MOMADAY (b. 1934)

### The Bear (1992)

What ruse of vision,
escarping the wall of leaves,
    rending incision
into countless surfaces,

would cull and color
his somnolence, whose old age
   has outworn valor,
all but the fact of courage?                                          5

  Seen, he does not come,
move, but seems forever there,
   dimensionless, dumb
in the windless noon's hot glare.                                    10

  More scarred than others
these years since the trap maimed him,
   pain slants his withers,
drawing up the crooked limb.                                         15

  Then he is gone, whole,
without urgency, from sight,
   as buzzards control,
imperceptibly, their flight.                                         20

## HOWARD NEMEROV (1920–1991)

## Life Cycle of Common Man (1960)

Roughly figured, this man of moderate habits,
This average consumer of the middle class,
Consumed in the course of his average life span
Just under half a million cigarettes,
Four thousand fifths of gin and about                                5
A quarter as much vermouth; he drank
Maybe a hundred thousand cups of coffee,
And counting his parents' share it cost
Something like half a million dollars
To put him through life. How many beasts                            10
Died to provide him with meat, belt and shoes
Cannot be certainly said.

         But anyhow,
It is in this way that a man travels through time,
Leaving behind him a lengthening trail
Of empty bottles and bones, of broken shoes,                        15
Frayed collars and worn out or outgrown
Diapers and dinnerjackets, silk ties and slickers.

Given the energy and security thus achieved,
He did . . .? What? The usual things, of course,
The eating, dreaming, drinking and begetting,                       20

And he worked for the money which was to pay
For the eating, et cetera, which were necessary
If he were to go on working for the money, et cetera,
25  But chiefly he talked. As the bottles and bones
Accumulated behind him, the words proceeded
Steadily from the front of his face as he
Advanced into the silence and made it verbal.
Who can tally the tale of his words? A lifetime
30  Would barely suffice for their repetition;
If you merely printed all his commas the result
Would be a very large volume, and the number of times
He said "thank you" or "very little sugar, please,"
Would stagger the imagination. There were also
35  Witticisms, platitudes, and statements beginning
"It seems to me" or "As I always say."
Consider the courage in all that, and behold the man
Walking into deep silence, with the ectoplastic
Cartoon's balloon of speech proceeding
40  Steadily out of the front of his face, the words
Borne along on the breath which is his spirit
Telling the numberless tale of his untold Word
Which makes the world his apple, and forces him to eat.

# JIM NORTHRUP (b. 1943)

 ## wahbegan° (1993)

Didja ever hear a sound
smell something
taste something
that brought you back
5  to Vietnam, instantly?
Didja ever wonder
when it would end?
It ended for my brother.
He died in the war
10  but didn't fall down
for fifteen tortured years.
His flashbacks are over,
another casualty whose name
will never be on the Wall.
15  Some can find peace
only in death.
The sound of his
family crying hurt.
The smell of the flowers

°The title "wahbegan" is an Ojibway name.

didn't comfort us.
The bitter taste
in my mouth
still sours me.                                        20
How about a memorial
for those who made it
through the war
but still died                                        25
before their time?


# MARY OLIVER (b. 1935)

 ## Ghosts (1983)

**1**

*Have you noticed?*


**2**

Where so many millions of powerful bawling beasts
lay down on the earth and died
it's hard to tell now
what's bone, and what merely
was once.                                             5

The golden eagle, for instance,
has a bit of heaviness in him;
moreover the huge barns
seem ready, sometimes, to ramble off
toward deeper grass.                                  10


**3**

1805
near the Bitterroot Mountains:
a man named Lewis kneels down
on the prairie watching
a sparrow's nest cleverly concealed in the wild hyssop    15
and lined with buffalo hair. The chicks,
not more than a day hatched, lean
quietly into the thick wool as if
content, after all,
to have left the perfect world and fallen,            20
helpless and blind
into the flowered fields and the perils
of this one.

**4**

25  In the book of the earth it is written:
*nothing can die.*

In the book of the Sioux it is written:
*they have gone away into the earth to hide.*
*Nothing will coax them out again*
30  *but the people dancing.*

**5**

Said the old-timers:
the tongue
is the sweetest meat.

Passengers shooting from train windows
35  could hardly miss, they were
that many.
Afterward the carcasses
stank unbelievably, and sang with flies, ribboned
with slopes of white fat,
40  black ropes of blood—hellhunks
in the prairie heat.

**6**

*Have you noticed?* how the rain
falls soft as the fall
of moccasins. *Have you noticed?*
45  how the immense circles still,
stubbornly, after a hundred years,
mark the grass where the rich droppings
from the roaring bulls
fell to the earth as the herd stood
50  day after day, moon after moon
in their tribal circle, outwaiting
the packs of yellow-eyed wolves that are also
*have you noticed?* gone now.

**7**

Once only, and then in a dream,
55  I watched while, secretly
and with the tenderness of any caring woman,
a cow gave birth
to a red calf, tongued him dry and nursed him
in a warm corner
60  of the clear night
in the fragrant grass
in the wild domains
of the prairie spring, and I asked them,
in my dream I knelt down and asked them
65  to make room for me.

## LINDA PASTAN (b. 1932)

 ## Marks (1978)

My husband gives me an A
for last night's supper,
an incomplete for my ironing,
a B plus in bed.
My son says I am average,                                    5
an average mother, but if
I put my mind to it
I could improve.
My daughter believes
in Pass/Fail and tells me                                    10
I pass. Wait 'til they learn
I'm dropping out.

## MARGE PIERCY (b. 1936)

*For a photo, see Chapter 14, page 583.*

 ## The Secretary Chant (1973)

My hips are a desk.
From my ears hang
chains of paper clips.
Rubber bands form my hair.
My breasts are wells of mimeograph ink.                      5
My feet bear casters.
Buzz. Click.
My head is a badly organized file.
My head is a switchboard
where crossed lines crackle.                                 10
Press my fingers
and in my eyes appear
credit and debit.
Zing. Tinkle.
My navel is a reject button.                                 15
From my mouth issue canceled reams.
Swollen, heavy, rectangular
I am about to be delivered
of a baby
Xerox machine.                                               20
File me under W
because I wonce
was
a woman.

## EDGAR ALLAN POE (1809–1849)

*For a photo, see Chapter 5, page 233.*

 **Annabel Lee** (1849)

It was many and many a year ago,
   In a kingdom by the sea,
That a maiden there lived whom you may know
   By the name of Annabel Lee;
5  And this maiden she lived with no other thought
   Than to love and be loved by me.

*She* was a child and *I* was a child,
   In this kingdom by the sea,
But we loved with a love that was more than love—
10   I and my Annabel Lee—
With a love that the wingèd seraphs of Heaven
   Coveted her and me.

And this was the reason that, long ago,
   In this kingdom by the sea,
15  A wind blew out of a cloud by night
   Chilling my Annabel Lee;
So that her high-born kinsmen came
   And bore her away from me,
To shut her up in a sepulchre
20   In this kingdom by the sea.

The angels, not half so happy in Heaven,
   Went envying her and me:—
Yes! that was the reason (as all men know,
   In this kingdom by the sea)
25  That the wind came out of the cloud chilling
   And killing my Annabel Lee.

But our love it was stronger by far than the love
   Of those who were older than we—
   Of many far wiser than we—
30  And neither the angels in Heaven above
   Nor the demons down under the sea
Can ever dissever my soul from the soul
   Of the beautiful Annabel Lee:—

For the moon never beams without bringing me dreams
35   Of the beautiful Annabel Lee;
And the stars never rise but I feel the bright eyes
   Of the beautiful Annabel Lee:
And so all the night-tide, I lie down by the side

Of my darling, my darling, my life and my bride
  In her sepulchre there by the sea—
  In her tomb by the side of the sea.     40

## JOHN CROWE RANSOM (1888–1974)

 ## Bells for John Whiteside's Daughter (1924)

There was such speed in her little body,
And such lightness in her footfall,
It is no wonder her brown study
Astonishes us all.

Her wars were bruited in our high window.     5
We looked among orchard trees and beyond
Where she took arms against her shadow,
Or harried unto the pond.

The lazy geese, like a snow cloud
Dripping their snow on the green grass,     10
Tricking and stopping, sleepy and proud,
Who cried in goose, Alas,

For the tireless heart within the little
Lady with rod that made them rise
From their noon apple-dreams and scuttle     15
Goose-fashion under the skies!

But now go the bells, and we are ready,
In one house we are sternly stopped
To say we are vexed at her brown study,
Lying so primly propped.     20

## JOHN RAVEN (b. 1936)

 ## Assailant (1969)

He jumped me while I was asleep.
He was big and fat.
I been in many fights before,
but never one like that.
The only way I could survive,
was to get my hat . . .     5
His *name?*
Officers, I ain't talkin' 'bout no man;
I'm talkin' 'bout a rat!

# LUIS OMAR SALINAS (b. 1937)

 ## In a Farmhouse (1973)

Fifteen miles
out of Robstown
with the Texas sun
fading in the distance
5  I sit in the bedroom
profoundly,
animated by the day's work
in the cottonfields.

I made two dollars and
10  thirty cents today
I am eight years old
and I wonder
how the rest of the Mestizos°
do not go hungry
15  and if one were to die
of hunger
what an odd way
to leave for heaven.

---

°13 *Mestizos*: persons of mixed Spanish and Amerindian ancestry.

# SONIA SANCHEZ (b. 1934)

 ## rite on: white america (1970)

this country might have
been a pio
   neer land
once.
5    but,    there ain't
no mo
    indians    blowing
custer's° mind
     with a different
10  image of america.
            this country
might have
      needed shoot/
outs/ daily/

---

°8 *custer's*: General George Armstrong Custer (1839–1876) was killed in his "last stand" at the Little Bighorn in Montana during a battle with Sioux
Indians.

once.
        but there ain't                                               15
no mo real/ white/    allamerican
                  bad/guys.
just
    u & me.
             blk/ and un/armed.                            20
this country might have
been a pion
             eer land.          once.
                       and it still is.
check out                                               25
            the falling
gun/shells        on our blk/tomorrows.

# CARL SANDBURG (1878–1967)

##  Chicago (1916)

Hog Butcher for the World,
Tool Maker, Stacker of Wheat,
Player with Railroads and the Nation's Freight Handler;
Stormy, husky, brawling,
City of the Big Shoulders:                          5

They tell me you are wicked and I believe them, for I have
    seen your painted women under the gas lamps luring
    the farm boys.
And they tell me you are crooked and I answer: Yes, it is true I have seen the gunman
    kill and go free to kill again.
And they tell me you are brutal and my reply is: On the faces of women and children I
    have seen the marks of wanton hunger.
And having answered so I turn once more to those who sneer at this my city, and I give
    them back the sneer and say to them:
Come and show me another city with lifted head singing so proud to be alive and coarse and
    strong and cunning.                                  10
Flinging magnetic curses amid the toil of piling job on job, here is a tall bold slugger set vivid
    against the little soft cities;
Fierce as a dog with tongue lapping for action, cunning as a savage pitted against the
    wilderness,
    Bareheaded,
    Shoveling,
    Wrecking,                                                 15
    Planning,
    Building, breaking, rebuilding,
Under the smoke, dust all over his mouth, laughing with white teeth,
Under the terrible burden of destiny laughing as a young man laughs,
Laughing even as an ignorant fighter laughs who has never lost a battle,             20

Bragging and laughing that under his wrist is the pulse, and under his ribs the heart of
    the people,
        Laughing!
Laughing the stormy, husky, brawling laughter of Youth, half-naked, sweating, proud to
    be Hog Butcher, Tool Maker, Stacker of Wheat, Player with Railroads and Freight
    Handler to the Nation.

## SIEGFRIED SASSOON (1886–1967)

 ## Dreamers (1918)

Soldiers are citizens of death's grey land,
    Drawing no dividend from time's to-morrows.
In the great hour of destiny they stand,
    Each with his feuds, and jealousies, and sorrows.

5    Soldiers are sworn to action; they must win
    Some flaming, fatal climax with their lives.
Soldiers are dreamers; when the guns begin
    They think of firelit homes, clean beds, and wives.

I see them in foul dug-outs, gnawed by rats,
10    And in the ruined trenches, lashed with rain,
Dreaming of things they did with balls and bats,
    And mocked by hopeless longing to regain
Bank-holidays,° and picture shows, and spats,
    And going to the office in the train.

---

°13 *Bank-holidays*: legal holidays in Great Britain.

## GJERTRUD SCHNACKENBERG (b. 1953)

 ## The Paperweight (1982)

The scene within the paperweight is calm,
A small white house, a laughing man and wife,
Deep snow. I turn it over in my palm
And watch it snowing in another life,

5    Another world, and from this scene learn what
It is to stand apart: she serves him tea
Once and forever, dressed from head to foot
As she is always dressed. In this toy, history

Sifts down through the glass like snow, and we
Wonder if her single deed tells much
Or little of the way she loves, and whether he      10
Sees shadows in the sky. Beyond our touch,

Beyond our lives, they laugh, and drink their tea.
We look at them just as the winter night
With its vast empty spaces bends to see
Our isolated little world of light,      15

Covered with snow, and snow in clouds above it,
And drifts and swirls too deep to understand.
Still I must try to think a little of it,
With so much winter in my head and hand.      20

## ALAN SEEGER (1888–1916)

 ## I Have a Rendezvous with Death (1916)

I have a rendezvous with Death
At some disputed barricade,
When Spring comes back with rustling shade
And apple blossoms fill the air—
I have a rendezvous with Death
When Spring brings back blue days and fair.      5

It may be he shall take my hand
And lead me into his dark land
And close my eyes and quench my breath—
It may be I shall pass him still.      10

I have a rendezvous with Death
On some scarred slope of battered hill,
When Spring comes round again this year
And the first meadow flowers appear.

God knows 'twere better to be deep
Pillowed in silk and scented down,      15
Where Love throbs out in blissful sleep,
Pulse nigh to pulse and breath to breath,
Where hushed awakenings are dear. . . .
But I've a rendezvous with Death
At midnight in some flaming town,      20
When Spring trips north again this year,
And I to my pledged word am true,
I shall not fail that rendezvous.

## BRENDA SEROTTE (b. 1946)

 **My Mother's Face** (1991)

Dressing for work
I glanced in the mirror
startled to see my mother's face
white, with the mouth turned down
5   her red frizzled hair
wild in all directions.
She turned sideways
to study my dress
standing tiptoe like I do
10  craning her long neck
in a futile attempt to see my feet.
Then without warning, the tears
rolling from the outer corners down
past slightly pitted cheeks
15  past that inverted smile
into the cave of her bosom
which heaved a sigh so forlorn
so weighted with loss
that had I not been standing silent
20  I would have surely thought it was me.

## WILLIAM SHAKESPEARE (1564–1616)

*For a portrait, see Chapter 21, page 979.*

 **Sonnet 29: When in Disgrace with Fortune and Men's Eyes** (1609)

When, in disgrace with Fortune and men's eyes,
I all alone beweep my outcast state,
And trouble deaf heaven with my bootless° cries,          *futile, useless*
And look upon myself and curse my fate,
5   Wishing me like to one more rich in hope,
Featured like him, like him with friends possessed,
Desiring this man's art and that man's scope,
With what I most enjoy contented least;
Yet in these thoughts myself almost despising,
10  Haply I think on thee, and then my state,
(Like to the lark at break of day arising)
From sullen earth sings hymns at heaven's gate,
For thy sweet love remembered such wealth brings
That then I scorn to change my state with kings.

# WILLIAM SHAKESPEARE (1564–1616)

 ## Sonnet 146: Poor Soul, the Center of My Sinful Earth (1609)

Poor soul, the center of my sinful earth,
Thrall° to these rebel powers that thee array,°             *captive*
Why dost thou pine within and suffer dearth
Painting thy outward walls so costly gay?
Why so large cost having so short a lease,               5
Dost thou upon thy fading mansion spend?
Shall worms, inheritors of this excess,
Eat up thy charge? Is this thy body's end?
Then, soul, live thou upon thy servant's loss,°
And let that pine to aggravate thy store;°              10
Buy terms° divine in selling hours of dross°         *periods; refuse*
Within be fed, without be rich no more:
So shalt thou feed on Death, that feeds on men,
And Death once dead, there's no more dying then.

---

°2 *array*: surround or dress out, as in a military formation. 9 *thy servant's loss*: the loss of the body. 10 *let . . . store*: let the body ("that") dwindle ("pine") to increase ("aggravate") the riches ("store") of the soul.

# KARL SHAPIRO (1913–2000)

 ## Auto Wreck (1941)

Its quick soft silver bell beating, beating,
And down the dark one ruby flare
Pulsing out red light like an artery,
The ambulance at top speed floating down
Past beacons and illuminated clocks              5
Wings in a heavy curve, dips down,
And brakes speed, entering the crowd.
The doors leap open, emptying light;
Stretchers are laid out, the mangled lifted
And stowed into the little hospital.              10
Then the bell, breaking the hush, tolls once,
And the ambulance with its terrible cargo
Rocking, slightly rocking, moves away,
As the doors, an afterthought, are closed.
We are deranged, walking among the cops            15
Who sweep glass and are large and composed.
One is still making notes under the light.
One with a bucket douches ponds of blood
Into the street and gutter.
One hangs lanterns on the wrecks that cling,         20

Empty husks of locusts, to iron poles.
Our throats were tight as tourniquets,
Our feet were bound with splints, but now,
Like convalescents intimate and gauche,
25  We speak through sickly smiles and warn
With the stubborn saw of common sense,
The grim joke and the banal resolution.
The traffic moves around with care,
But we remain, touching a wound
30  That opens to our richest horror.
Already old, the question Who shall die?
Becomes unspoken Who is innocent?
For death in war is done by hands;
Suicide has cause and stillbirth, logic;
35  And cancer, simple as a flower, blooms.
But this invites the occult mind,
Cancels our physics with a sneer,
And spatters all we knew of dénouement
Across the expedient and wicked stones.

## LESLIE MARMON SILKO (b. 1948)

 ## Where Mountain Lion Lay Down with Deer (1974)

I climb the black rock mountain
   stepping from day to day
                silently.
I smell the wind for my ancestors
5     pale blue leaves
     crushed wild mountain smell.
Returning
   up the gray stone cliff
   where I descended
10      a thousand years ago.

Returning to faded black stone
   where mountain lion lay down with deer.
It is better to stay up here

               watching wind's reflection
15              in tall yellow flowers.
The old ones who remember me are gone
     the old songs are all forgotten
and the story of my birth.
How I danced in snow-frost moonlight
20     distant stars to the end of the Earth,

<pre>
How I swam away
                in freezing mountain water
                narrow mossy canyon tumbling down
                            out of the mountain
                                out of the deep canyon stone          25

             down
                     the memory
                              spilling out
                              into the world.
</pre>

## STEVIE SMITH (1902–1971)

###  Not Waving But Drowning (1957)

Nobody heard him, the dead man,
But still he lay moaning:
I was much further out than you thought
And not waving but drowning.

Poor chap, he always loved larking                                    5
And now he's dead
It must have been too cold for him his heart gave way,
They said.

Oh, no no no, it was too cold always
(Still the dead one lay moaning)                                      10
I was much too far out all my life
And not waving but drowning.

## WILLIAM STAFFORD (1914–1993)

###  Traveling Through the Dark (1960)

Traveling through the dark I found a deer
dead on the edge of the Wilson River road.
It is usually best to roll them into the canyon:
that road is narrow; to swerve might make more dead.

By glow of the tail-light I stumbled back of the car                  5
and stood by the heap, a doe, a recent killing;
she had stiffened already, almost cold.
I dragged her off; she was large in the belly.

My fingers touching her side brought me the reason—
her side was warm; her fawn lay there waiting,                        10

alive, still, never to be born.
Beside that mountain road I hesitated.

The car aimed ahead its lowered parking lights;
under the hood purred the steady engine.
15  I stood in the glare of the warm exhaust turning red;
around our group I could hear the wilderness listen.
I thought hard for us all—my only swerving—,
then pushed her over the edge into the river.

## GERALD STERN (b. 1925)

 ## Burying an Animal on the Way to New York (1977)

Don't flinch when you come across a dead animal lying on the road;
you are being shown the secret of life.
Drive slowly over the brown flesh;
you are helping to bury it.
5  If you are the last mourner there will be no caress
at all from the crushed limbs
and you will have to slide over the dark spot imagining
the first suffering all by yourself
Shreds of spirit and little ghost fragments will be spread out
10  for two miles above the white highway.
Slow down with your radio off and your window open
to hear the twittering as you go by.

## WALLACE STEVENS (1879–1955)

*For a photo, see Chapter 12, page 519.*

 ## The Emperor of Ice-Cream (1923)

Call the roller of big cigars,
The muscular one, and bid him whip
In kitchen cups concupiscent curds.
Let the wenches dawdle in such dress
5  As they are used to wear, and let the boys
Bring flowers in last month's newspapers.
Let be be finale° of seem.
The only emperor is the emperor of ice-cream.
Take from the dresser of deal,°
10  Lacking the three glass knobs, that sheet
On which she embroidered fantails° once

---

°7 *finale*: the grand conclusion.  9 *deal*: unfinished pine or fir used to make cheap furniture.  11 *fantails*: fantail pigeons.

And spread it so as to cover her face.
If her horny feet protrude, they come
To show how cold she is, and dumb.
Let the lamp affix its beam.                                        15
The only emperor is the emperor of ice-cream.

## MAY SWENSON (1919–1989)

 ## Question (1978)

Body my house
my horse my hound
what will I do
when you are fallen

Where will I sleep                                                  5
How will I ride
What will I hunt

Where can I go
without my mount
all eager and quick                                                10
How will I know
in thicket ahead
is danger or treasure
when Body my good
bright dog is dead                                                 15

How will it be
to lie in the sky
without roof or door
and wind for an eye

With cloud for shift                                               20
how will I hide?

## DYLAN THOMAS (1914–1953)

*For a photo, see Chapter 16, page 681.*

 ## A Refusal to Mourn the Death, by Fire, of a Child in London (1946)

Never until the mankind making
Bird beast and flower
Fathering and all humbling darkness

Tells with silence the last light breaking
5    And the still hour
Is come of the sea tumbling in harness

And I must enter again the round
Zion of the water bead
And the synagogue of the ear of corn
10   Shall I let pray the shadow of a sound
Or sow my salt seed
In the least valley of sackcloth to mourn

The majesty and burning of the child's death.
I shall not murder
15   The mankind of her going with a grave truth
Nor blaspheme down the stations of the breath
With any further
Elegy of innocence and youth.

Deep with the first dead lies London's daughter,
20   Robed in the long friends,
The grains beyond age, the dark veins of her mother,
Secret by the unmourning water
Of the riding Thames.°
After the first death, there is no other.

---

°23 *Thames*: the River Thames, which flows through London.

# JOHN UPDIKE (b. 1932)

*For a photo, see Chapter 7, page 309.*

## Perfection Wasted (1990)

And another regrettable thing about death
is the ceasing of your own brand of magic,
which took a whole life to develop and market—
the quips, the witticisms, the slant
5    adjusted to a few, those loved ones nearest
the lip of the stage, their soft faces blanched
in the footlight glow, their laughter close to tears,
their tears confused with their diamond earrings,
their warm pooled breath in and out with your heartbeat,
10   their response and your performance twinned.
The jokes over the phone. The memories packed
in the rapid-access file. The whole act.
Who will do it again? That's it: no one;
imitators and descendants aren't the same.

## SHELLY WAGNER (b. ca. 1950)

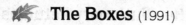 ### The Boxes (1991)

When I told the police I couldn't find you,
they began a search that included everything—
even the boxes in the house;
the footlockers of clothes in the attic,
the hamper in the bathroom,                                            5
and the Chinese lacquered trunk by the sofa.
They made me raise every lid.
I told them you would never stay in a box,
not with all the commotion.
You would have jumped out,                                             10
found your flashlight
and joined the search.

Poor Thomas, taking these men
who don't know us
through our neighbors' garages                                         15
where you never played,
hoping they were right
and we were wrong
and he would find you and
snatch you home by the hand                                            20

so the police cars could
get out of our driveway
and the divers would
get out of our river
because it was certainly                                               25
past our bedtime.
We would double-bolt our doors
like always,
say longer prayers than usual
and go to bed. But during the night                                    30
I would have sat till morning
beside my sleeping boys.
But that's not what happened.
Thomas is still here, now older.
I still go to his room                                                 35
when he is sleeping
just to look at him.
I still visit the cemetery,
not as often,
but the urge is the same:                                             40
to lie down on the grass,
put my arm around the hump of ground
and tell you, "Get out of this box!
Put a stop to this commotion. Come home.
You should be in bed."                                                45

## ALICE WALKER (b. 1944)

 ## Revolutionary Petunias (1972)

Sammy Lou of Rue
sent to his reward
the exact creature who
murdered her husband,
5  using a cultivator's hoe
with verve and skill;
and laughed fit to kill
in disbelief
at the angry, militant
10  pictures of herself
the Sonneteers quickly drew:
not any of them people that
she knew.
A backwoods woman
15  her house was papered with
funeral home calendars and
faces appropriate for a Mississippi
Sunday School. She raised a George,
a Martha, a Jackie and a Kennedy. Also
20  a John Wesley Junior.°
"Always respect the word of God,"
she said on her way to she didn't
know where, except it would be by
electric chair, and she continued
25  "Don't yall forget to *water*
my purple petunias."

---

°18–20 *George . . . Junior*: The children are named after George and Martha Washington, Jackie and John Fitzgerald Kennedy (1917–1963, thirty-fifth U.S. president), and John Wesley (1703–1791), English evangelical preacher who founded Methodism.

## EDMUND WALLER (1606–1687)

 ## Go, Lovely Rose (1645)

Go, lovely rose!
Tell her that wastes her time and me
  That now she knows,
When I resemble° her to thee,
5  How sweet and fair she seems to be.

Tell her that's young,
And shuns to have her graces spied,
  That hadst thou sprung

*compare*

In deserts, where no men abide,
Thou must have uncommended died.

   Small is the worth
Of beauty from the light retired;
   Bid her come forth,
Suffer herself to be desired,
And not blush so to be admired.

   Then die! that she
The common fate of all things rare
   May read in thee;
How small a part of time they share
That are so wondrous sweet and fair.

10

15

20

# **BRUCE WEIGL** (b. 1949)

 ## **Song of Napalm** (1985)

### *For My Wife*

After the storm, after the rain stopped pounding,
We stood in the doorway watching horses
Walk off lazily across the pasture's hill.
We stared through the black screen,
Our vision altered by the distance
So I thought I saw a mist
Kicked up around their hooves when they faded
Like cut-out horses
Away from us.
The grass was never more blue in that light, more
Scarlet; beyond the pasture
Trees scraped their voices in the wind, branches
Criss-crossed the sky like barbed-wire
But you said they were only branches.

Okay. The storm stopped pounding.
I am trying to say this straight: for once
I was sane enough to pause and breathe
Outside my wild plans and after the hard rain
I turned my back on the old curses, I believed
They swung finally away from me . . .

But still the branches are wire
And thunder is the pounding mortar,
Still I close my eyes and see the girl
Running from her village, napalm
Stuck to her dress like jelly,

5

10

15

20

25

Her hands reaching for the no one
Who waits in waves of heat before her.

So I can keep on living,
So I can stay here beside you,
30  I try to imagine she runs down the road and wings
Beat inside her until she rises
Above the stinking jungle and her pain
Eases, and your pain, and mine.
But the lie swings back again.
35  The lie works only as long as it takes to speak
And the girl runs only so far
As the napalm allows
Until her burning tendons and crackling
Muscles draw her up
40  Into that final position
Burning bodies so perfectly assume. Nothing
Can change that; she is burned behind my eyes
And not your good love and not the rain-swept air
And not the jungle green
45  Pasture unfolding before us can deny it.

# WALT WHITMAN (1819–1892)

*For a photo, see Chapter 14, page 587.*

## 🐦 Beat! Beat! Drums! (1861)

Beat! beat! drums!—blow! bugles! blow!
Through the windows—through doors—burst like a ruthless force,
Into the solemn church, and scatter the congregation,
Into the school where the scholar is studying;
5   Leave not the bridegroom quiet—no happiness must he have now with his bride,
Nor the peaceful farmer any peace, plowing his field or gathering his grain,
So fierce you whir and pound you drums—so shrill you bugles blow.

Beat! beat! drums!—blow! bugles! blow!
Over the traffic of cities—over the rumble of wheels in the streets;
10  Are beds prepared for sleepers at night in the houses? no sleepers must sleep in those beds,
No bargainers' bargains by day—no brokers or speculators—would they continue?
Would the talkers be talking? would the singer attempt to sing?
Would the lawyer rise in the court to state his case before the judge?
Beat! beat! drums—blow! bugles! blow!
15  Then rattle quicker, heavier drums—you bugles wilder blow.
Make no parley—stop for no expostulation,
Mind not the timid—mind not the weeper or prayer,
Mind not the old man beseeching the young man,
Let not the child's voice be heard, nor the mother's entreaties,
20  Make even the trestles to shake the dead where they lie awaiting the hearses,
So strong you thump O terrible drums—so loud you bugles blow.

# WALT WHITMAN (1819–1892)

 ## Dirge for Two Veterans (1865)

The last sunbeam
Lightly falls from the finished Sabbath,
On the pavement here, and there beyond it is looking,
    Down a new-made double grave.


    Lo, the moon ascending,    5
Up from the east the silvery round moon,
Beautiful over the house-tops, ghastly, phantom moon,
    Immense and silent moon.


    I see a sad procession,
And I hear the sound of coming full-keyed bugles,    10
All the channels of the city streets they're flooding,
    As with voices and with tears.


    I hear the great drums pounding
And the small drums steady whirring,
And every blow of the great convulsive drums,    15
    Strikes me through and through.


    For the son is brought with the father,
(In the foremost ranks of the fierce assault they fell,
Two veterans son and father dropped together,
    And the double grave awaits them.)    20


    Now nearer blow the bugles,
And the drums strike more convulsive,
And the daylight o'er the pavement quite has faded,
    And the strong dead-march enwraps me.


    In the eastern sky up-buoying,    25
The sorrowful vast phantom moves illumined,
('Tis some mother's large transparent face,
    In heaven brighter growing.)


    O strong dead-march you please me!
O moon immense with your silvery face you soothe me!    30
O my soldiers twain! O my veterans passing to burial!
    What I have I also give you.


    The moon gives you light,
And the bugles and the drums give you music,
And my heart, O my soldiers, my veterans,    35
    My heart gives you love.

## WALT WHITMAN (1819–1892)

 ## Full of Life Now (1857)

Full of life now, compact, visible,
I, forty years old the eighty-third year of the States,
To one a century hence or any number of centuries hence,
To you yet unborn these, seeking you.

5   When you read these I that was visible am become invisible,
Now it is you, compact, visible, realizing my poems, seeking me,
Fancying how happy you were if I could be with you and become your comrade;
Be it as if I were with you. (Be not too certain but I am now with you.)

## WALT WHITMAN (1819–1892)

 ## I Hear America Singing (1867)

I hear America singing, the varied carols I hear;
Those of mechanics—each one singing his, as it should be, blithe and strong;
The carpenter singing his, as he measures his plank or beam,
The mason singing his, as he makes ready for work, or leaves off work;
5   The boatman singing what belongs to him in his boat—the deckhand singing on the
        steamboat deck;
The shoemaker singing as he sits on his bench—the hatter singing as he stands;
The wood cutter's song—the ploughboy's on his way in the morning, or at noon
        intermissions, or at sundown;
The delicious singing of the mother—or of the young wife at work—or of the girl sewing or
        washing—
Each singing what belongs to him or her and to none else;
10  The day what belongs to the day—at night, the part of young fellows, robust, friendly,
Singing, with open mouths, their strong melodious songs.

## JOHN GREENLEAF WHITTIER (1807–1892)

 ## The Bartholdi Statue° (1886)

The land, that, from the rule of kings,
    In freeing us, itself made free,
Our Old World Sister, to us brings
    Her sculptured Dream of Liberty;

---

°The Statue of Liberty, by Frédéric Auguste Bartholdi (1834–1904) was dedicated in October, 1886. The Compte de Rochambeau (1725–1807) was a general commanding the French forces at Yorktown in 1781, and his efforts were helpful and decisive in defeating the English (see line 12).

Unlike the shapes on Egypt's sands
   Uplifted by the toil-worn slave,
On Freedom's soil with freemen's hands
   We rear the symbol free hands gave.

O France, the beautiful! to thee
   Once more a debt of love we owe;                   10
In peace beneath thy Colors three,
   We hail a later Rochambeau!

Rise, stately Symbol! holding forth
   Thy light and hope to all who sit
In chains and darkness! Belt the earth           15
   With watch-fires from thy torch uplit!

Reveal the primal mandate still
   Which Chaos heard and ceased to be,
Trace on mid-air th'Eternal Will
   In signs of fire: "Let Man be free!"           20

Shine far, shine free, a guiding light
   To Reason's ways and Virtue's aim,
A lightning-flash the wretch to smite
   Who shields his licence with thy name!

## RICHARD WILBUR (b. 1921)

*For a photo, see Chapter 17, page 723.*

 ## April 5, 1974 (1976)

The air was soft, the ground still cold.
In the dull pasture where I strolled
Was something I could not believe.
Dead grass appeared to slide and heave,
Though still too frozen-flat to stir,           5
And rocks to twitch, and all to blur.
What was this rippling of the land?
Was matter getting out of hand
And making free with natural law?
I stopped and blinked, and then I saw      10
A fact as eerie as a dream.
There was a subtle flood of steam
Moving upon the face of things.
It came from standing pools and springs
And what of snow was still around;       15
It came of winter's giving ground

So that the freeze was coming out,
As when a set mind, blessed by doubt,
Relaxes into mother-wit.
20  Flowers, I said, will come of it.

**PAUL ZIMMER** (b. 1934)

 ## The Day Zimmer Lost Religion (1973)

The first Sunday I missed Mass on purpose
I waited all day for Christ to climb down
Like a wiry flyweight° from the cross and
Club me on my irreverent teeth, to wade into
5  My blasphemous gut and drop me like a
Red hot thurible,° the devil roaring in
Reserved seats until he got the hiccups.

It was a long cold way from the old days
When cassocked and surpliced° I mumbled Latin
10  At the old priest and rang his obscure bell.
A long way from the dirty wind that blew
The soot like venial sins° across the schoolyard
Where God reigned as a threatening,
One-eyed triangle high in the fleecy sky.

15  The first Sunday I missed Mass on purpose
I waited all day for Christ to climb down
Like the playground bully, the cuts and mice
Upon his face agleam, and pound me
Till my irreligious tongue hung out.
20  But of course He never came, knowing that
I was grown up and ready for Him now.

---

3 *flyweight*: a boxer weighing less than 112 pounds.  6 *thurible*: a censer, a container in which incense is burned.  9 *cassocked and surpliced*: wearing the traditional garb of an altar boy during Mass.  12 *venial sins*: minor inadvertent sins.

# Chapter 19A

## WRITING ABOUT LITERATURE WITH THE AID OF RESEARCH, 2

# Writing Essays on Poetry: Using Extra Resources for Understanding

The end of the fiction section of this book, Chapter 10A (p. 428), contains a chapter on the use of research as the basis of an essay of term-paper length on fiction. Because the objects and goals of research are general, most of the materials in Chapter 10A are also essential for research projects in all the genres. It is therefore necessary to consult Chapter 10A for many relevant ways to engage in detailed research, which you can apply not only to writing about fiction, but also to writing about both poetry and drama.

Here, however, our concern is to suggest a more limited use of research for the development of essays on the topic of poetry. Any of the essay assignments on poetry described in Chapters 11 to 16 can serve as the basic topic for the introduction of helpful research materials. Because of the general nature of research, the use of research for writing about poetry is not essentially different from research used in writing about fiction and drama.

## Topics to Discover in Research

There are some general objectives in the use of research, but your goal should always be to discover materials that have a meaningful bearing on the poem or poems about which you are writing. Some things to look for might be some of these:

- *The period of time when the poem or poems were written, together with significan-tevents*. In this current chapter, 19A, the illustrative essay about Whitman cites the American Civil War (1861–65) as the dominating national event occurring at the time of the poems. Comparably, Hardy's "The Convergence of the Twain" was written as a commentary on the sinking of the British liner *Titanic* in 1912. Emerson's "Concord Hymn" was written for a ceremonial occasion 60 years after the Revolutionary War events described in the poem.

- *Social, natural, and/or political circumstances at the time of the poem or poems.* What was the dominant political situation at the time? Who were the sorts of persons in political power? What attitudes were prevalent at the time with regard to the circumstances of nature? Wordsworth, for example, often creates an implicit comparison between the natural world at peace and negative human activities that are at odds with it. Pope, in the "Epilogue to the Satires," cites a general condition of moral laxity that he perceived in the social and political structure of England of his day.

- *Biographical details about a poet.* At what time in his/her life did the poet write a particular poem, or poems? What kind of work was he/she doing at the time, and which of his/her particular concerns might be relevant to our understanding of the poem/poems? Did the poet write anything about the poem/poems in his/her personal correspondence? What was this? Are there any results of interviews with the poet that might be introduced to explain the poem/poems? What were the poet's aims in creating the particular poem or poems?

- *Specific or general thoughts by the poet that are relevant to the poem/poems.* Sometimes there might be details about a poet's thoughts on the thinking and reading he/she was doing, or on works of art he/she had seen, or on religious or philosophical musings in which he/she might have been engaged. Langston Hughes was deeply concerned about the circumstances of African Americans in the United States, and wrote many poems on this topic. Elaine Terranova was equally concerned with the condition of women and families, and her "Rush Hour" is an expression of this deep concern.

In planning your essay, you should aim at a normal type of essay for the poem or poems you have chosen. Thus, your topic may be the nature of the poem's speaker, such as "The Character of Frosts Speaker in 'A Considerable Speck,'" or "Cummings's Use of the Speaker to Control Tone in 'if there are any heavens.'" Or it may be the poet's use of images, or metaphors, or symbols, such as "Shakespeare's Widely Varied Imagery in His Sonnets." Or you may want to write about the poet's use of allusions, or his/her use of mythical materials. A rich field for discussion might be the comparison of poems or poets, such as "Uses of Description in Schnackenberg's 'The Paperweight' and Lynn Emanuel's 'Like God'" or "The Topic of Death in Frost's 'Out, Out—' and Sassoon's 'Dreamers,'" or "The Treatment of Love and Sexuality by Peacock in 'Desire' and Donne in 'The Sun Rising.'" The possibilities are legion. Of even greater significance than your choice of topic—which should be basically the same whether you are using or not using research—is your integration of research discoveries into the development of your essay.

# Illustrative Student Essay Written with the Aid of Research

Underlined sentences in this paper *do not* conform to MLA style and are used solely as teaching tools to emphasize the central idea, thesis sentence, and topic sentences throughout the paper.

Zweig 1

Put identifying information in upper left corner, double space.

Micol Zweig

Professor Melvin

English 112 25

April 2007

Use 1/2 inch top margin, 1 inch bottom and side margin; double space throughout.

Center title one double space below identifying information.

### "Beat! Beat! Drums!" and "I Hear America Singing:"

### Two Whitman Poems Spanning the Civil War°

[1]     Comparing two of Walt Whitman's poems, "Beat! Beat! Drums!" and "I Hear America Singing," alongside the historical background informing his writing, helps in the understanding of both poems.* Walt Whitman was born in 1819, when American democracy was in its infancy. He held many jobs as a young man; at various times he worked as a printer, editor, and teacher, and in 1840 he even campaigned for future President Martin Van Buren (Callow 365).

[2]     As a keen observer, Whitman took many notes about what he saw. He started to write in celebration of America's potential. He wrote many poems about the people and places of his immediate environment, and these poems gave birth to his famous collection, *Leaves of Grass* (1855). Many critics have pointed out that Whitman was uncertain about his poetic skills before he began this collection. One critic remarks that "Whitman was not really a poet at all, but a man of the people with his eyes open and his senses hungry for experience" (Zweig 113). By the time of the Civil War in 1861, he had written many of his best known poems, but the experience of war was to transform him.

In MLA style, put author and page number in parentheses when author is not named in the sentence.

[3]     His "Beat! Beat! Drums!" was written in 1861 at the beginning of the Civil War. In this poem, Whitman expresses his disfavor of the war, claiming that the pounding of the

°See pages 850 and 852 for these poems.
*Central idea.

drums, which represents the fierceness of war itself, is an egregious disruption of
ordinary American life. His 1860 poem, "I Hear America Singing"—also published
again in <u>Leaves of Grass</u> after the war had ended—serves as a sharp contrast to "Beat!
Beat! Drums!" In this more tranquil poem, music is transformed to symbolize peace.
Both poems serve as examples of how similar motifs may be used to exemplify very
different moods and tones. <u>Whitman's tone and his use of musical imagery demonstrate
the difference between America at peace and America at war.</u>[†]

[4]        Whitman's attitude towards the war was complex. <u>As the war developed, he saw it as
an opportunity for America to develop its own identity, but he also feared impending
horrors of combat.</u> "Beat! Beat! Drums" reflects both the ominous nature of war and also
the "patriotic fervor which swept the North" (Allen 75). In contrast, "I Hear America
Singing" reflects the optimism in Whitman's poetry both before and after his many
disturbing experiences during the war. "From the time Whitman visited his wounded
brother George in Virginia in the spring of 1862 until the end of the war . . . he visited
thousands of soldiers in army hospitals" (Allen 84). On these visits he sometimes saw people
dying right in front of him, and he also saw piles of amputated limbs that were decaying in
the sun. "Beat! Beat! Drums!" describes the high-pitched "ruthless force" (line 2) that he
had perceived. "I Hear America Singing," although first written before the war, was
republished at a time when Whitman's best work was behind him, when "there was not
silence but sporadic effort, sparse and diminished" (Zweig 345). Seen in this light, "I Hear
America Singing" can be seen as a looking back to earlier times in its vision of a whole
nation singing as individuals—yet as one—and a looking forward to a hopeful future.

[5]        <u>Though references to music form recurring images of sound in both poems, they
are used in each to symbolize different states.</u> In "Beat! Beat! Drums!", the blowing of
the bugles and the beating of the drums are a warning of the terrible and all-
encompassing aspects of war. In this poem, the speaker commands the fierce and
pounding noises invoking the startling sound of drums and bugles to serve as a warning
of impending war. "Beat! Beat! drums!—blow! bugles! blow!" (Lines 1, 8, 14) is
repeated every six to seven lines, punctuating the flow of disturbing imagery in the lines
surrounding them. These repeated lines, with the exception of one word ("bugles") all
have one syllable, making the lines themselves sound like the military rhythm of a snare
drum which is a sharp contrast to the "varied carols" that each American possesses in "I

*In MLA style, the header has the student's last name and page number.*

*When citing poetry in MLA style, cite the line number for the poem.*

---

[†]Thesis sentence.

Hear America Singing." While the sounds of "Beat! Beat! Drums!" attempt to unite and alert different people to the oncoming conflict, the music in "I Hear America Singing" focuses on the idea that differences are both the strength and hallmark of America. The speaker's admonition in "Beat! Beat! Drums!" to increase the intensity of sound—"Then rattle quicker, heavier drums—you bugles wilder blow" (line 15)—may be contrasted with the varied rhythms of "I Hear America Singing," which come together as "strong melodious songs" (line 11). This harmonious resolution of diverse songs sets a very different tone from the one at the end of "Beat! Beat! Drums!," when the speaker's command has been realized: "So strong you thump O terrible drums—so loud you bugles blow" (line 21). The symbolic sounds of both poems convey contrasting states of mind.

[6]      In each of the Whitman poems, images of sound emphasize tone and mood. "Beat! Beat! Drums!" conveys a tone of serious urgency. Where life had been going on peacefully before the outbreak of war, the drums and bugles "burst like a ruthless force" (line 2) through doors and windows, now rendering a peaceful existence impossible. These jarring sounds disrupt the studying scholar and "scatter the congregation" of "the solemn church" (line 3). The mood of the poem conveys hopelessness as the speaker wonders if life will be able to continue amidst the din. He asks, "would the talkers be talking? would the singer attempt to sing?" (line 13). "I hear America Singing" conveys the opposite tone, one of peaceful contentment and proud patriotism as the poet becomes an approving listener of the harmonies around him. There is a predominant feeling of optimism in this poem as the mechanics, carpenters, masons, and all others sing their respective songs. The reader gets a sense of America's strength and hope, unlike the lives of Americans during the disruption and strife of war, as all different types of people cheerfully sing "what belongs to him or her and none else" (line 9), and then at night these same people gather to sing melodiously together. "I Hear America Singing" stresses the individualism and optimism of a country emerging from the all-encompassing strife indicated by the incessant beating drums and blaring bugles of "Beat! Beat! Drums!"

[7]      As the "poet of American democracy" (Dutton 104) Whitman wrote about the great events of his time. "Beat! Beat! Drums!" paints a disturbing picture for the reader, the image of an unstoppable army playing the shrieking music of destruction that affects everything in its path, leaving the bridegroom unhappy and the "peaceful farmer" without "any peace" (line 6). "I Hear America Singing" announces the significance of

the individual—the "I" that is part of the melody of a large and prosperous nation at peace. In Walt Whitman's most famous and ambitious poem, "Song of Myself," the symbolic singing of "myself" announces the pride and exuberant presence of the speaker's ego amidst the diversity of a democratic nation. In "Beat! Beat! Drums!" and "I Hear America Singing" the images of sound are used to convey very different aspects of American life. While to some critics "Whitman's art as a poet" may be a matter of mystery (Van Doren xxiii) there is little doubt of his intense feelings about the Civil War and what he wrote about it. Reading the poems together, along with knowing about Whitman's life, brings greater meaning to each poem.

Zweig 5

**WORKS CITED**

Allen, Gay Wilson. *A Reader's Guide to Walt Whitman*. New York: Farrar, Straus, and Giroux. 1970.

Callow, Philip. *From Noon to Starry Night; A Life of Walt Whitman*. Chicago: Ivan R. Dee. 1992.

Doren, Mark Van, ed. *The Portable Walt Whitman*. New York: Viking. 1973.

Whitman, Walt. "Beat! Beat! Drums!" "I Hear America Singing." *Literature: An Introduction to Reading and Writing*. Ed. Edgar V. Roberts. 4th compact ed. Upper Saddle River: Prentice Hall, 2009, 850, 852.

Zweig, Paul. *Walt Whitman; The Making of the Poet*. New York: Basic. 1984.

> In MLA style, the list of sources, called the works cited, begins a new page. Double space throughout.
>
> List sources in alphabetical order.

## Commentary on the Essay

The research objective of this essay is the introduction of biographical details as informational support for the topic of comparison and contrast. The opening paragraph, citing one research reference, places the two poems in the context of Whitman's life. In paragraph 2, the writer connects the poems to Whitman's unique qualities as an observer, citing a research reference in support of this capacity. In paragraph 3, the writer locates the poems in the time of the American Civil War, pointing out how the poems deal with opposites of American life. Paragraph 4 introduces three research references that support the details of Whitman's actual Civil War experiences. Paragraphs 5 and 6, based on the texts of the two poems themselves, grow out of paragraph 4, for they deal with the opposing music of harshness, on the one hand, and "peaceful contentment and proud patriotism," on the other. In the final paragraph, 7, the writer introduces two additional research references, while stressing Whitman's intense feelings about the subject matter of the two poems.

# Reading and Writing
## about Drama

# Chapter **20**

# The Dramatic Vision:
# An Overview

**D**rama has much in common with the other genres of literature. Like fiction, drama focuses on one or a few major characters who enjoy success or endure failure as they face challenges and deal with other characters. Many plays are written in prose, as is fiction, on the principle that the language of drama should resemble the language of life as much as possible. Drama is also like poetry because both genres develop situations through speech and action. Indeed, a great number of plays, particularly those of past ages, exist as poetry. The dramatists of ancient Athens employed intricate poetic forms in their plays. Many European plays from the Renaissance through the nineteenth century were written in blank verse or rhymed couplets, a tradition of poetic drama preserved by twentieth-century dramatists such as Christopher Fry and T. S. Eliot.

As separate genres, however, there are, necessarily, major differences among drama, fiction, and poetry. Fiction is distinguished from drama because the essence of fiction is narration—the making known or relating or recounting of a sequence of events or actions, the actual telling of a story. Poetry is unlike both drama and fiction because it exists in many formal and informal shapes, and it is the shortest of the genres. Although we usually read poetry silently and alone, it is also frequently read aloud before groups. Unlike both fiction and poetry, drama is literature designed for impersonation by people— actors—for the benefit and delight of other people—an audience.

## Drama as Literature

Drama is a unique genre because it can be presented and discussed both as literature— drama itself—and as performance—the production of plays in the theater. The major literary aspects of drama are the *text, language, characters, plot, structure, point of view, tone, symbolism*, and *theme or meaning*. All these elements have remained constant throughout the history of drama. In addition, drama written in poetic forms, such as Shakespeare's *Hamlet* (Chapter 21) and *A Midsummer Night's Dream* (Chapter 22), includes elements such as meter and rhyme.

### The Text Is the Printed (or Handwritten) Play

The text of a play is a plan for bringing the play into action on the stage. The most notable features of the text are *dialogue, monologue*, and *stage directions*. **Dialogue** is the conversation of two or more characters. A **monologue** is spoken by a single character who is usually alone onstage. **Stage directions** are the playwright's instructions about facial and vocal expression, movement and action, gesture and "body language," stage appearance, lighting, and similar matters. In addition, some dramatists, such as George Bernard Shaw and Tennessee Williams, provide introductions and explanations for their plays. Such material may be considered additional directions for interpretation and staging.

## Language, Imagery, and Style Bring the Play to Life

What we learn about characters, relationships, and conflicts is conveyed in dramatic language. Through dialogue, and sometimes through soliloquy and aside, characters use language to reveal intimate details about their lives and their deepest thoughts—their loves, hatreds, hopes, and plans.

To bring such revelations before the audience, dramatists employ words that have wide-ranging connotations and that acquire many layers of meaning. Such is the case with the variations of the phrase "well liked" in Arthur Miller's *Death of a Salesman* (Chapter 23). Similarly, playwrights can introduce metaphors and symbols that contribute significantly to the play's meaning and impact. Again in *Death of a Salesman*, the abandoned auto trip and the imminence of an auto accident are central symbols.

Dramatists also make sure that the words of their characters fit the circumstances, the time, and the place of the play. Miller's Willy Loman speaks the language of modern America, and Shakespeare's Hamlet speaks Elizabethan blank verse, almost academic prose, and "one-liner" remarks. In addition, dramatists employ accents, dialects, idiom, jargon, and clichés to indicate character traits. The gravediggers in *Hamlet* speak in a Renaissance English lower-class dialect that distinguishes them from the aristocratic characters in the play.

## Characters Talk Themselves Alive Through Speech and Action

Drama necessarily focuses on its **characters**, who are persons the playwright creates to embody the play's actions, ideas, and attitudes. Of course characters are characters, no matter where we find them, and many of the character types that populate drama are also inhabitants of fiction. The major quality of characters in drama, however, is that they come alive through their speeches and actions. To understand them we must listen to their words and watch and interpret how they react both to their circumstances and to the characters around them. They are also sometimes described and discussed by other characters, but primarily they are rendered dramatically.

Drama is not designed to present the full life stories of its characters. Rather, the plots of drama bring out intense and highly focused oppositions or conflicts in which the characters are engaged. In accord with such conflicts, most major dramatic characters are considered as *protagonists* and *antagonists*. The **protagonist** (the first or leading struggler or actor), usually the central character, is opposed by the **antagonist** (the one who struggles against). A classic conflict is seen in Shakespeare's *Hamlet*, in which Prince Hamlet, the protagonist, tries first to confirm and then to punish the crime committed by King Claudius, his uncle and the play's antagonist.

Just as in fiction, drama presents us with both *round* and *flat* characters. A **round, dynamic, developing,** and **growing character**, such as Shakespeare's Hamlet and Ibsen's Nora, possesses great **motivation**. The round character profits from experience and undergoes a development in awareness, insight, understanding, moral capacity, and the ability to make decisions. A **flat, static, fixed,** and **unchanging character**, such as Daddy in Albee's *The Sandbox*, does not undergo any change or growth. There is no rule, however, that flat characters must be dull. They can be charming, vibrant, entertaining, and funny, but even if they are memorable in these ways, they remain fixed and static.

Dramatic characters can also be considered as *realistic, nonrealistic, stereotyped* (or *stock*), *ancillary*, and *symbolic*. **Realistic characters** are designed to seem like individualized women and men; the dramatist gives them thoughts, desires, motives, personalities, and lives of their own. **Nonrealistic characters** are often undeveloped and symbolic. An interesting example is Torvald Helmer of Ibsen's *A Dollhouse* (Chapter 23). In terms of his assumptions and expectations, he is nonrealistic for most of the play, but he becomes sadly realistic when he recognizes the disastrous effects of his previous outlook on life and marriage. He is unique because he does not so much grow as undergo an almost instant change.

Throughout the ages, drama and other types of literature have relied on **stereotype** or **stock characters**, that is, unindividualized characters whose actions and speeches make them seem to have been taken from a mold. The general types developed in the comedy of ancient Athens and Rome, and in the drama of the Renaissance, are the *stubborn father*, the *romantic hero* and *heroine*, the *clever male servant*, the *saucy maidservant*, the *braggart soldier*, the *bumpkin*, the *trickster*, the *victim*, the *insensitive husband*, the *shrewish wife*, and the *lusty youth*. Modern drama continues these stereotypes, and it has also invented many of its own, such as the *private eye*, the *stupid bureaucrat*, the *corrupt politician*, the *independent pioneer*, the *kindly prostitute*, the *loner cowboy*, and the *town sheriff who never loses the draw in a showdown*.

There are also **ancillary characters** who set off or highlight the protagonist and who provide insight into the action. The first type, the **foil**, has been a feature of drama since its beginnings in ancient Athens. The foil is a character who is to be compared and contrasted with the protagonist. Laertes and Fortinbras are foils in *Hamlet*. Because of the play's circumstances, Laertes is swept into destruction along with Hamlet, whereas Fortinbras picks up the pieces and gets life moving again after the final death scene. The second type is the **choric figure**, who is loosely connected to the choruses of ancient drama. Usually the choric figure is a single character, often a confidant of the protagonist, such as Hamlet's friend Horatio. When the choric figure expresses ideas about the play's major issues and actions, he or she is called a **raisonneur** (the French word meaning "reasoner") or **commentator**.

Any of the foregoing types of characters can also be **symbolic** in the context of individual plays. They can symbolize ideas, moral values, religious concepts, ways of life, or some other abstraction. For instance, Linda in *Death of a Salesman* symbolizes helplessness before destructive forces, whereas Fred Higgins in *Mulatto* (Chapter 23) symbolizes the cynicism, indifference, cruelty, and misuse of responsibility that accompany the concept of racial supremacy.

## Action, Conflict, and Plot Make Up a Play's Development

Plays are made up of a series of sequential and related **actions** or **incidents**. The actions are connected by **chronology**—the logic of time—and the term given to the principles underlying this ordered chain of actions and reactions is **plot**, which is a connected plan or pattern of causation. The impulse controlling the connections is **conflict**, which refers to people or circumstances—the antagonist—that the protagonist tries to overcome. Most dramatic conflicts are vividly apparent because the clashes of wills and characters take place onstage, right in front of our eyes. Conflicts can also exist between groups, although conflicts between individuals are more identifiable and therefore more common in plays.

Dramatic plots can be simplified and schematized, but most of them are as complicated as life itself. Special complications result from a **double** or **multiple plot**—two or more different but related lines of action. Usually one of these plots is the **main plot**, but the **subplot** can be independently important and sometimes even more interesting. Such a situation occurs in *A Midsummer Night's Dream*, where the exploits of Bottom and the "mechanicals," which form just one of the four strands of plot, are so funny that they often steal the show in productions of the play.

## Structure Is the Play's Pattern of Organization

The way a play is arranged or laid out is its **structure**. With variations, many traditional plays contain elements that constitute a structure of *five stages*: (1) *exposition* or *introduction*, (2) *complication* and *development*, (3) *crisis* or *climax*, (4) *falling action*, and (5) *dénouement, resolution,* or *catastrophe*. In the nineteenth century, the German novelist and critic Gustav Freytag (1816–1895) visualized this pattern as a pyramid (though he used six elements rather than five). In the so-called "**Freytag pyramid**," the exposition and complication lead up to a high point of tension—the crisis or climax—followed by the falling action and the catastrophe.

THE FREYTAG PYRAMID

1. Exposition or Introduction
2. Complication and Development
3. Crisis or Climax
4. Falling Action
5. Dénouement, Resolution, or Catastrophe

This pyramidal pattern of organization can be observed to greater or lesser degrees throughout many plays. Some plays follow the pattern closely, but often there is uncertainty about when one phase of the structure ends and the next one begins. In addition, words defining some of the stages are variable. Even though students of drama agree about the meaning of the first two stages, the terms for the final three are not used with precision. With these reservations, the Freytag pyramid is valuable in the analysis of dramatic plot structure.

**1.** *The exposition or introduction brings out everything we need to know to understand and follow what is to happen in the play.* In the first part of a drama, the dramatist introduces the play's background, characters, situations, and conflicts. Although exposition is occasionally presented through direct statements to the audience, the better method is to render it dramatically. Both major and minor characters thus perform the task of exposition through dramatic dialogue—describing situations, actions, and plans, and also explaining the traits and motives of other characters. In such a way, Sophocles in *Oedipus the King* (Chapter 21) provides expository material in the prologue featuring Oedipus, the Priest, and Creon. Eugene O'Neill in *Before Breakfast* dramatizes the exposition in the early actions and speeches of the major character, Mrs. Rowland. In *Hamlet*, Horatio's explanations to Barnardo and Marcellus provide vital information about circumstances in the Danish court.

**2.** *The complication and development mark the onset of the play's major conflicts.* In this second stage, also called the **rising action**, we see the beginning of difficulties that seem overwhelming and insoluble, as in *Hamlet*, where we learn in the exposition that the death of the king has occurred before the play opens. Complication develops as the characters try to learn answers to some of the following perplexing questions: Was the death a murder? If so, who did it? How was it done? How can the murderer be identified? Is the man suspected of the murder truly guilty? What should be done about the murder? What punishment should there be? In *A Midsummer Night's Dream*, less serious complications result from the development of issues like these: Can young lovers overcome parental opposition? Can a bumbling group of amateur actors successfully perform a play before the highest social group in the nation? Can a squabble among supernatural beings be brought to a peaceful conclusion?

**3.** *The crisis or climax is the culmination of the play's conflicts and complications—the intense moments of decision.* The uncertainty and anxiety of the complication lead to the third stage, the **crisis** ("turning point") or **climax** ("high point"). In this third stage, all the converging circumstances compel the hero or heroine to recognize what needs to be done to resolve the play's major conflict. Another way of considering the crisis or climax is to define it as that point in the play when uncertainty ends and inevitability begins, as when Hamlet vows vengeance after drawing conclusions about the king's reaction to the player scene.

**4.** *The falling action is a time of avoidance and delay.* The downward slope of the pyramid is the **falling action**, which contains complicating elements deferring the play's conclusion. In *Hamlet*, for example, a number of scenes make up the falling action: Hamlet's decision not to kill Claudius at prayer, Hamlet's departure for

England, the gravedigger scene and the conflicts at Ophelia's grave, and the murderous conspiracy of Claudius and Laertes. In *Oedipus the King*, Oedipus continues to seek confirming evidence about the death of his father, although by the end of Episode 3—the climax—he has all the information he needs to determine that he himself is the murderer.

**5.** *The dénouement is the end, the logical outcome of what has gone before.* In the **dénouement** ("unraveling") or **resolution** ("untying"), also called the **catastrophe** ("overturning"), all tragic protagonists undergo suffering or death, all mysteries are explained, all conflicts are resolved, all mistakes are corrected, all dastardly schemes are defeated, all long-lost children are identified, all obstacles to love are overcome, all deserving characters are rewarded, and the play ends. In short, the function of the dénouement is to end complications and conflicts, not to create new ones. It is important to observe that the word *catastrophe* for the final dramatic stage should not necessarily be construed in the sense of a calamity, even though most tragic catastrophes are calamitous. It is probably best, however, to use the words *dénouement* and *resolution* as general descriptions of a play's final stage and to reserve *catastrophe* for tragedies.

Of great significance is that the various points of the pyramid define an abstract model that is applicable to most plays—tragedy, comedy, and tragicomedy alike. Since the time of Shakespeare, however, most dramatists writing in English have been concerned less with dramatic form than with dramatic effect. As a result, many plays in English do not perfectly follow the pattern charted in the Freytag pyramid. You should therefore be prepared for plays that conceal or delay essential parts of the exposition; create a number of separate crises and climaxes; confine the climax, falling action, and dénouement into a short space at the play's end; or modify the formal pattern in other significant ways.

## Point of View Focuses on a Play's Major Character (or Characters) and Ideas

In fiction, **point of view** refers to the narrative *voice* of the story, the speaker or guiding intelligence through which the characters and actions are presented (see Chapter 3). In drama, the term refers generally to a play's **perspective** or focus—the ways in which dramatists direct attention to the play's characters and their concerns. In the theater, dramatists govern our responses visually by putting major characters onstage and keeping them there. That these characters are always speaking and moving before our eyes makes us devote our attention to them, become involved with them, and see things pretty much as they see things. For example, once the opening speeches of *Hamlet* are over, the play focuses directly on Hamlet and never wavers, even after he lies dead on the stage in the last act. In O'Neill's *Before Breakfast*, the entire play is a monologue spoken by Mrs. Rowland, and we therefore see things from her perspective even though we recognize her limitations and shortcomings.

The dramatist can also keep characters and issues in our minds by causing other characters to speak about them. Thus, most of the speeches in Glaspell's *Trifles* are designed to shape our understanding of what Minnie Wright did to her husband on the lonely Wright farm, and why she did it. Because everyone is always talking about Minnie and her boorish but recently murdered husband, the play makes this perspective inescapable.

## Tone or Atmosphere Creates Mood and Attitude

Authors of plays have unique ways of conveying **tone** or **atmosphere** beyond those used by poets and fiction writers (see Chapter 7). Some of these are vocal ranges and stage gestures (such as rolling one's eyes, throwing up one's hands, staring at another character, holding one's forehead in despair, jumping for joy, making side remarks, and staggering in grief). Even silence, intensive stares, and shifting glances can be effective means for creating moods and controlling attitudes.

Whereas the voices and actions of actors establish mood on the stage, we do not have these guides in reading. There are written guides, however, to dramatic tone: Sometimes a playwright uses stage directions as an indication of tone, as Ibsen does in *A Dollhouse*, directing the inflections of a speaker's voice with the stage direction that she is shaking her head when speaking. Similarly, Hughes suggests the mood of one of his characters in *Mulatto* with the direction that he "runs" to his mother and hugs her "teasingly."

When such directions are absent—and usually they are—we need to take the diction, tempo, imagery, and context as clues to the tone of specific speeches and whole plays. In the opening scene of *Hamlet*, Shakespeare uses short and rapidly delivered sentences to create a mood of fearfulness, anxiety, and apprehensiveness. This opening passage anticipates the Ghost's forthcoming charge of murder against Claudius, and it also prepares us for the ominous events to come in the rest of the play.

One of the most common methods playwrights employ to control the tone of the play is **dramatic irony**. This type of **situational** (as opposed to **verbal**) irony refers to circumstances in which characters have only a partial, incorrect, or misguided understanding of what is happening, while both readers and other characters understand the situation completely. Readers hence become concerned about the characters and hope that they will develop understanding quickly enough to avoid the problems bedeviling them and the threats endangering them. The classic example of dramatic irony occurs in Sophocles's *Oedipus the King*: As Oedipus condemns the murderer of his father, he also unwittingly condemns himself.

## Dramatists Frequently Introduce Symbolism and Allegory

In drama, as in fiction and poetry, the meaning of a **symbol** extends beyond its surface meaning (see Chapters 8 and 17). Dramatic symbols, which can be characters, settings, objects, actions, situations, or statements, can be either cultural or contextual. **Cultural** or **universal symbols**—such as crosses, flags, snakes, and flowers—are generally understood by the audience or reader regardless of the context in which they appear. In Act 5 of *Hamlet*, for example, we readily accept Yorick's skull as a symbol of death. **Contextual** or **private symbols** develop their impact only within the context of a specific play or even a particular scene. We often don't realize at first that such objects or actions are symbolic; they acquire symbolic meaning only through context and continued action. In the living room setting of Hughes's *Mulatto*, for instance, there is a vestibule "leading to the porch." There is nothing unusual about this location, but as the play develops we realize that it symbolizes that the rights and privileges of whites on the plantation are denied to the African Americans who work there.

When a play offers consistent and sustained symbols that refer to general human experiences, that play can be construed as an **allegory**, or at least as being **allegorical**. For example, Ibsen's *A Dollhouse* can be considered allegorically as an expression of the shortcomings of any way of life in which a grown person is infantilized and therefore is prevented from realizing the mature and independent life that she is entitled to seek as an adult.

## Subject and Theme Are the Complex of Ideas Presented by the Dramatist

Most playwrights do not aim to propagandize their audience, but nevertheless they do embody ideas in their plays. The aspects of humanity a playwright explores constitute the play's **subject**. Plays can be *about* love, religion, hatred, war, ambition, death, envy, or anything else that is part of the human condition.

The ideas that the play dramatizes make up the play's **theme** or meaning. A play might explore the idea that love will always find a way or that marriage can be destructive, that pride always leads to disaster, or that grief can be conquered through strength and a commitment to life. Full, evening-long plays can contain many thematic strands. Ibsen creates such complexity in *A Dollhouse*, in which he deals with themes of selfless devotion, egotism, pompousness, hypocrisy, betrayal, and women's self-determination. Even short plays can have complex themes, as in O'Neill's *Before Breakfast*, which explores the themes that anger can be stronger than love, that deceit is a consequence of alienation, and that despair and fear can conquer the normal wish to live.

# Performance: The Unique Aspect of Drama

As we read and talk about drama, we should always remind ourselves that *plays are meant to be acted*. It is **performance** that makes a play immediate, exciting, and powerful. The elements of performance are the *actors*, the *director* and the *producer*, the *stage*, *sets* or *scenery*, *lighting*, *costumes* and *makeup*, and the *audience*.

## Actors Bring the Play to Our Eyes and Ears

Good **actors** are trained and have the experience to exert their intelligence, emotions, imaginations, voices, and bodies to make their characters real to us. Actors speak as they imagine the characters might speak—earnestly, eagerly, calmly, excitedly, prayerfully, exultantly, sorrowfully, or angrily. When they respond, they respond as they imagine the characters might respond—with surprise, expectation, approval, happiness, irony, acceptance, rejection, resignation, or resolution. When they move about the stage according to patterns called **blocking**, they move as they imagine the characters might move—slowly, swiftly, smoothly, hesitatingly, furtively, stealthily, or clumsily, and gesturing broadly or subtly. Actors also frequently engage in **stage business**—gestures or movements that make the play dynamic, spontaneous, and often funny.

## The Director and the Producer Create and Support the Play's Production

In the theater, all aspects of performance are shaped and supervised by the **director** and the **producer**. The producer, the one with the money, is responsible for financing and arranging the production. Working closely with the producer is the director, who is the most significant member of the entire dramatic production. The director cooperates closely with the actors and guides them in speaking, responding, standing, and moving in ways that are consistent with his or her vision of the play. When a play calls for special effects (for example, the Ghost in *Hamlet*) both the producer and the director work with specialists such as musicians, choreographers, and sound and lighting technicians to enhance and enliven the performance.

## The Stage Is the Location of Both Speech and Action

Most modern theaters feature an interior **proscenium stage**—a picture-frame stage that is like a room with one wall missing so that the audience can look in on the action. In most proscenium stages, a large curtain representing the missing wall is usually opened and closed to indicate the beginning and ending of acts. Members of the audience who are seated centrally before the stage are close to the action, but people seated at the sides, to the rear, behind a tall person, or in the balcony are to greater or lesser degrees removed from the vital and up-close involvement that is desirable in good theater. There is no question that such remoteness is a built-in disadvantage of many proscenium stages.

Modern theater designers have therefore experimented with stage designs inspired by theaters of the past. One notable success has been to revive the shape of the ancient Greek amphitheater (with seats rising from the stage in an expanding half-circle), a structure employed in theaters like the Tyrone Guthrie in Minneapolis and at the Shakespeare Festival Theatre in Ashland, Oregon. Because seats for the audience ascend in semicircular tiers around three sides of the stage, most of the audience is closer to the action—and better able to see—than in a theater with a proscenium stage. The audience is also, therefore, more closely involved in the dramatic action.

Like many other modern theaters, these theaters feature a **thrust stage** or **apron stage** (such as the **platform stage** used in the time of Shakespeare), which enlarges the proscenium stage with an acting area projecting into the audience by 20 or more feet. It is on this apron that a good deal of the acting occurs. Closely related to the apron stage is **theater-in-the-round**, a stage open on all sides like a boxing ring, surrounded by the audience. Productions for both types of stages are especially lively because the actors usually enter and leave through the same doorways and aisles used by the audience.

## Sets (Scenery) Create the Play's Location and Appearance

Most productions use **sets** (derived from the phrase "set scenes," i.e., fixed scenes) or **scenery** to establish the action in place and time, to underscore the ideas of the director, and to determine the level of reality of the production. Sets are constructed and decorated to indicate a specific place (a living room, a kitchen, a throne room, a forest, a graveyard) or a detached and indeterminate place with a specific atmosphere (an open plain, a vanished past, a nightmarish future). When we first see the stage at the beginning of a performance, it is the scenery that we see, bringing the play to life through walls, windows, stairways, furniture, furnishings, and painted locations.

In most proscenium stages, the sets establish a permanent location or **scene** resembling a framed picture. All characters enter this setting, and they leave once they have achieved their immediate purpose. Such a fixed scene is established in *Oedipus the King*, which is set entirely in front of the royal palace of ancient Thebes, and in *Before Breakfast*, set in the dreary kitchen of a New York apartment. Generally, one-act plays rely on a single setting and a short imagined time of action. Many full-length plays also confine the action to a single setting despite the longer imagined time during which the action takes place.

Because sets are usually elaborate and costly, many producers use single fixed-scene sets that are flexible and easily changed. Some productions employ a single, neutral set throughout the play and then mark scene changes with the physical introduction of movable **properties** (or **props**)—chairs, tables, beds, flower vases, hospital curtain-enclosures, trees, shovels, skulls, and so on. The use of props to mark separate scenes is a necessity in modern productions of plays that require constant scene changes, like *Hamlet*. Interestingly, many productions make scene changes an integral part of the drama by having costumed stagehands, or even the actors themselves, carry props on and off the stage. In a 1995 New York production of *Hamlet*, for example, Hamlet himself (performed by Ralph Fiennes) carried in the chairs needed for the spectators of the player scene.

The constant changing of scenery is sometimes avoided by the use of a **unit set**—a series of platforms, rooms, stairs, and exits that form the locations for all the play's actions, as in Miller's *Death of a Salesman*. The movement of the characters from place to place within the unit set marks the shifting scenes and changing topics.

Like characters, the setting can be realistic or nonrealistic. A **realistic setting**, sometimes called a **naturalistic setting**, requires extensive construction and properties, for the object is to create as lifelike a stage as possible. In O'Neill's *Before Breakfast*, for example, the setting is a realistic copy of a tacky early–twentieth-century apartment kitchen. By contrast, a **nonrealistic setting** is nonrepresentational and often symbolic, as in the beach scene established in Albee's *The Sandbox*. Sometimes a realistic play can be made suggestive and expressive through the use of a nonrealistic setting.

## Lighting Creates Clarity, Emphasis, and Mood

In ancient and medieval times, plays were performed in daylight, and hence no artificial illumination was required. With the advent of indoor theaters and evening performances, **lighting** became a necessity. At first, artificial lighting was provided by lanterns, candelabras, sconces, and torches (yes, some theaters burned down), and indirect lighting was achieved by reflectors and valances—all of which were used with great ingenuity and effect. Later, gaslight and limelight lamps replaced the earlier open flames.

The evolution of theater lighting reached its climax with the development of electric lights in the nineteenth century. Today, dramatic performances are enhanced by virtually all the technical features of our electronic age—including specialized lamps, color filters, spotlights, dimmers, and simulated fires. This dazzling technology, which employs hundreds or even thousands of lights of varying intensity in unlimited combination, is used to highlight individual characters, to isolate and emphasize various parts of the stage, to establish times, and generally to shape the moods of individual scenes. Lighting can also divide the stage or a unit set into different acting areas simply through the illumination of one section and the darkening of the rest, as in productions of plays such as Albee's *The Sandbox*. The result is that lighting has become an integral element of set design, especially when the dramatist uses a *scrim* (a curtain that becomes transparent when illuminated from behind), which permits great variety in the portrayal of scenes and great rapidity in scene changes. In our day it is a rare stage indeed that does not contain an elaborate, computerized, and complicated (and expensive) lighting system.

## Costumes and Makeup Establish the Nature and Appearance of the Actors

Actors make plays vivid by wearing **costumes** and using **makeup**, which help the audience understand a play's time period together with the occupations, mental outlooks, and socioeconomic conditions of the characters. Costumes, which include not only dress but also items such as jewelry, good-luck charms, swords, firearms, and canes, can be used realistically (farm women in plain clothes, a salesman in a business suit, a king in rich robes) or symbolically (a depressed character wearing black). Makeup usually enhances an actor's facial features, just as it can fix the illusion of youth or age or emphasize a character's joy or sorrow.

## The Audience Responds to the Performance and Helps to Shape It

To be complete, plays require an interaction of actors and **audience**. Drama enacts fictional or historical events as if they were happening in the present, and members of the audience—whether spectators or readers—are direct witnesses to the dramatic action from start to finish. The audience most definitely has a creative impact on theatrical performances. Although audiences are made up of people who otherwise do not know each other, they have a common bond of interest in the play. Therefore, even though they are isolated by the darkness of the theater in which they sit, they respond communally. Their reactions (e.g., laughter, gasps, applause) provide instant feedback to the actors and thus continually influence the delivery and pace of the performance. For this reason, drama *in the theater* is the most immediate and accessible of the literary arts. There is no intermediary between the audience and the stage action—no narrator, as in prose fiction, and no speaker, as in poetry.

## Drama from Ancient Times to Our Own: Tragedy, Comedy, and Additional Forms

Today, people interested in drama have more options than at any other time in human history. There is professional live theater in many major cities, and touring theatrical troupes reach areas with smaller populations. Many cities and towns have amateur community theaters, and so also do many schools and churches. Movie theaters and multiplexes are flourishing. Television has brought film versions of plays to the home screen, together with innumerable situation comedies ("sitcoms"), continuous narrative dramas (including soap operas), made-for-TV films, documentary dramas ("docudramas"), short skits on comedy shows, and many other types. All these different genres ultimately spring from the drama that was developed twenty-six hundred years ago in Athens, the leading ancient Greek city-state. Although subsequent centuries have produced many variations, the types the Athenians created are still as important today as they were then. They are tragedy and comedy.[1]

### Tragedy and Comedy Originated in Ancient Greece

During the sixth century B.C.E., drama first arose from choral presentations the Athenians held during religious festivals celebrating Dionysus, the god of wine, conviviality, sexual vitality, ecstasy, fertility, and freedom. The choruses were made up of young men who sang or chanted lengthy songs that the Athenians called **dithyrambs**; the choruses also performed interpretive dance movements during the presentations. The dithyrambs were not dramatizations but rather recitations, which became dramatic when a member of the chorus was designated to step forward and impersonate—*act*—one of the heroes. Soon, additional men from the choruses took acting roles, and the focus of the performances shifted from the choral group to individual actors. Greek **tragedy** as we know it had come into being. It was this pattern of drama that during the fifth century B.C.E. produced a golden age of tragedy. Most of the tragedies have been lost, and only a small but very significant number of plays by the three greatest Athenian dramatists—Aeschylus, Sophocles, and Euripides—have survived.

Not long after the emergence of tragedy, **comedy** became an additional feature of the festivals. Because the ancient Athenians encouraged free speech, at least

---

[1]Fuller discussions of tragedy and comedy are presented in Chapters 21 and 22.

for males, the comedy writers created a boisterous, lewd, and freely critical type of burlesque comedy that later critics called **Old Comedy**. The 11 surviving plays of the comic dramatist Aristophanes represent this tradition. In the fourth century B.C.E., after Athenian power and freedom had declined because of the debilitating Peloponnesian War at the end of the fifth century, this type of comedy was replaced by **Middle Comedy**, a more social, discreet, and international drama, and then by **New Comedy**, a type of play featuring the development of situation, plot, and character. The best-known writer of New Comedy was Menander, whose plays for centuries were thought to be totally lost. In the last hundred years, however, a number of fragments of his work have been discovered, including one play in its entirety.

Both of these Greek dramatic types have proved long lasting. The introduction of subject matter about loss in the earliest tragedies has led to today's common understanding that tragedy dramatizes an individual's fall from a secure and elevated position to social or personal defeat. Likewise, what we usually consider typical comedies are directly linked to the pattern of ancient New Comedy: plays that dramatize the regeneration of individuals who begin in insecurity and end with their overcoming troubles and anticipating happiness.

## Tragedy and Comedy Were of Less Significance in Ancient Rome

The two Athenian dramatic forms were adopted by the Romans during the periods of the Republic (before 29 B.C.E.) and the Empire (after 29 B.C.E.). Although Republican Rome produced writers of note who created comedies (Plautus, ca. 254–184 B.C.E., and Terence, ca. 195 or 185–159 B.C.E.), the only significant playwright of imperial times was the tragedian Seneca (4 B.C.E.–65 C.E.), who wrote "closet dramas"—that is, plays designed to be read in private, household rooms, but not performed in public.

## Ancient Drama Faded along with the Breakup of the Western Roman Empire

As the Roman Empire in Western Europe disintegrated in the fifth century C.E., many of its institutions, including the theater, disintegrated with it. In the next five centuries, often called the "Dark Ages," Europe fell into feudalism, characterized by political decentralization and social fragmentation. The intellectuals of the period—most of them clergy—were creating Christian theology and establishing the growing church while abandoning the memories and records of the past, of which drama was a major element. As far as we know, there were no public theaters, no patrons able or willing to support public performances, no popular audiences with the money to pay for admission, no official permission by secular and religious authorities to perform plays, and no practicing dramatists—in short, there was no organized theater. It is hard to believe, however, that the human need for stories and fantasies did not remain. Tales and songs were unquestionably passed on from parents to children and community to community throughout these otherwise gloomy centuries.

## Medieval Drama Developed as a Part of Church Services

When drama emerged hundreds of years after the fall of Rome, it had little to do with the Greek and Roman dramatic tradition because it was a creation of the Christian church. It was at some point in the tenth century—approximately when the medieval period or Middle Ages were emerging from the Dark Ages—that the clergy started to realize the potential of dramatic presentations within the mass. It was then that dramatic **tropes** (short interludes performed in conjunction with the mass, either with or without musical accompaniment) developed in the churches. These tropes were not considered as separate dramas, however, but became an integral part of regular services.

The earliest tropes were written for Easter rituals. The prototype of the Easter trope, which is included here, represented the discovery of the empty tomb as evidence of Christ's resurrection. This is the *Visitatio Sepulchri*, or *The Visit to the Sepulcher*, often known as the *Quem Quaeritis* ("Whom are you seeking") trope. This is considered the first European drama, from which all later medieval, Renaissance, and modern dramas have developed. Authored by persons who are unknown and forever unknowable, the trope was in Latin and was chanted not for the people but for cloistered monks and priests. It was enacted many times both on the continent and the British Isles, and in later centuries it became a regular feature of Easter worship. It has survived in a variety of forms in medieval manuscripts. Some versions contain detailed directions about performance, and some are cast in a question-and-answer format.

Although the *Quem Quaeritis* trope was a part of ritual, it clearly involved impersonation—and therefore drama—to the degree that priests and monks represented the persons and scenes contained in the gospel accounts of the resurrection. The heart of the trope is that the Angel at the tomb announces the resurrection to the three Marys, who then leave to proclaim the news.

## ANONYMOUS

# The Visit to the Sepulcher (Visitatio Sepulchri)

Tenth Century C.E.

[CAST OF CHARACTERS]

[The Angel at the Tomb]

[Mary the Mother of James and Joses]

[Mary Magdalen]

[Mary of Bethany, the Sister of Martha and Lazarus°]

---

°Although gospel accounts are in accord about the first two Marys, there is no agreement about the third woman, who is named Salome by Mark and Joanna by Luke. Neither of the gospel accounts of the Resurrection indicates that Mary of Bethany was the third Mary. Nevertheless, medieval tradition had it that there was a third Mary, and that she was Mary the sister of Lazarus and Martha, most likely on the authority of John 12:7, where Jesus implies that this Mary will be one of those to anoint his dead body.

[*Scene: The Sepulcher in which Christ was entombed after the Crucifixion. The Angel, dressed in white and holding a palm leaf, enters and sits beside a location curtained off to represent the tomb. Behind the curtain is a table or other surface representing a burial slab on which there is a linen sheet (i.e., the burial shroud supplied by Joseph of Aramathea). The three Marys enter, carrying vessels (thuribles) as though they are intending to anoint Christ's body with aromatic oils and spices. At first they do not see the tomb, and they wander about until they do. Then they stop in front of the Angel.*]

Angel: Whom are you seeking in this Sepulcher, O followers of Christ?

The Three Holy Women: [*Speaking together.*] Jesus of Nazareth, who was crucified, O heavenly one.

Angel: [*Pulling back the curtain to show the empty tomb.*] He is not here. He has been resurrected, as was predicted. Go forth. Tell everyone that he is risen. Spread the news!

The Three Holy Women: [*Kneeling and singing.*] Alleluia! Today Christ the Lord, the Son of God, the Mighty Lion, has been resurrected! Thanks be to God! Tell it to all the world!

5   Angel: Come and see the place where the Lord was laid.

[*The Three Holy Women examine the empty tomb and, with the Angel, display the burial shroud.*]

Angel: Alleluia! Alleluia! Hurry, tell the disciples that the Lord has risen! Alleluia! Alleluia!
   [*He exits, singing alleluias.*]

The Three Holy Women: [*Rejoicing, and singing in unison.*] The Lord, who hung on the tree for us, has risen from the grave! Alleluia!

[*They exit, joyfully repeating these lines.*]

## Questions

1. What dramatic characteristics, as opposed to the obvious theology, do you find in this brief play?

2. Describe the play's dramatic actions. What sorts of movement would have been carried out? How extensive might have been the use of properties?

3. How do you imagine this play would have affected people attending the service in which it was performed?

## Comparable Dramatic Ceremonies Followed the *Visitatio Sepulchri*

During the eleventh and twelfth centuries, the *Visit to the Sepulcher* ceremony became more elaborate, with additional characters and actions such as the race by Peter and John to the tomb and Mary Magdalen's recognition of the risen Christ after having first confused him for a gardener. Some of the ceremonies, which were eventually performed before congregations, became extensive enough to require a lengthy performance. Historians of drama observe that this Easter ceremony was *dramatic liturgy* rather than *liturgical drama*, but any congregations present would likely have ignored this distinction. Instead, they would have welcomed the ceremony as something totally new, dramatic, vital, and exciting.

In addition to the Easter pageantry, the church also developed special Christmas ceremonies such as those for the Three Wise Men, the Shepherds, the scene at the stable, the ranting Herod, and the Slaughter of the Innocents (Innocents Day was December 28). These ceremonies were observed as regular parts of Easter and Christmas rituals for hundreds of years after their beginnings in the tenth century.

## A New Kind of Drama, the Corpus Christi Play, Grew Independently of the Church

Growing out of the religious dramatic tradition, a full-blown religious and civic drama developed in the fourteenth century. This was the Corpus Christi (i.e., "Body of Christ") play, which evolved just as the drama of ancient Athens had developed out of religious festivals for the god Dionysus in the sixth century B.C.E.[2] The major expression of the new religious drama came during the celebration of Corpus Christi Day, a celebration of the doctrine of transubstantiation (i.e., during mass, Eucharistic bread and wine are said to become transformed miraculously into the real body and blood of Christ). The Corpus Christi feast is observed on the first Thursday after Trinity Sunday, which itself is the first Sunday after Pentecost.

Corpus Christi Day regularly featured local processions devoted to the worship of the Eucharist, and in this way it brought religious celebration into the streets and before the public. Because the feast occurred at the end of the liturgical year, it coincided with the beginning of good weather. The winter and spring rains abated, daylight hours lengthened, short trips from country villages to nearby towns became possible, and people could spend an entire day outside and still be comfortable.

The goal of the new plays was to create a complete **cycle** dramatizing the biblical accounts of world history from the Creation to Judgment Day. The plays were produced by local craft guilds, the members of which were master tradesmen. Hence the plays were also known as *mysteries*, or *mystery plays*. Naturally, the guild masters wanted to boost the prestige of their towns and their own wealth and power. They therefore welcomed the customers and patrons who thronged to these annual religious celebrations. Although there were as yet no professional acting companies such as the one that Shakespeare was to join in the late sixteenth century, the annual staging of the Corpus Christi plays required many participants. The planning by the local guilds was therefore complex and challenging; the result was an engaging and inspiring drama.

As the Corpus Christi feasts grew in importance, the plays became a highlight of town life in the early summer. By the fifteenth century as many as 40 towns had their own cycles. Some were large and elaborate; some—probably those performed in the smaller towns—were modest. Often the performances took place not only on Corpus Christi Thursday but also on Friday and Saturday, thus creating an extensive religious and secular celebration. Although the texts of most of these plays have been lost, cycles from four towns have been preserved. These cycles, named after the towns that presented them, contain more than 150 plays.

---

[2]See p. 873.

## English Replaced Latin as the Language of the Corpus Christi Plays

A major influence on the Corpus Christi drama—with profound implications for later drama—was the increasing importance of the English language at this time. During the two centuries following the Norman Conquest in 1066, the ruling and intellectual languages of England had been French and Latin. By the fourteenth century, however, things were changing: English had been enriched with close to 10,000 French words (a huge number of which we still retain) and was reasserting its role as the major language of England. More and more, the governing classes were committed to England—having a centuries-long tradition there—and used English as the language of intellectual and political discourse. Native writers began looking with increased favor on English as a literary language. A new literature in English—including drama—was ripe for development.

## Other Religious Dramas Originated after the Corpus Christi Plays

In the course of time, additional types of religious dramas were developed. One of these was the **miracle play**, a devotional dramatization of the lives of saints. In addition, the **morality play** was developed as a genre instructing the faithful in the proper way to lead a devotional life. The most famous of these, in about 1500, was *Everyman*, which even today retains a good deal of interest and power.

## In the Renaissance, Ancient and Medieval Traditions Fused to Create a New Secular Drama

In the sixteenth century, drama became liberated from these religious foundations and began rendering the twists and turns of more secular human conflicts. It was also at this time that the drama of ancient Greece and Rome was rediscovered. Therefore, the performing tradition growing out of the medieval church was combined with the surviving ancient tragedies and comedies to create an entirely new drama that quickly reached its highest point in the plays of Shakespeare. In this way, tragedy and comedy, the forms originated by the Athenians, had a revival during the Renaissance in Europe.[3]

## New Types of Drama Have Developed Since the Renaissance

Renaissance drama was by no means a copy of ancient forms, however, even though a number of sixteenth- and seventeenth-century playwrights, including Shakespeare, reworked many of the ancient plays. The plays of Renaissance England, and later the plays of the United States, offer mixtures of tragedy and comedy. For example, some of Shakespeare's comedies treat disturbing and potentially destructive topics, just as

---

[3]The Renaissance revival of drama also transformed the theater into a business. Earlier drama had been a product of the church and religious life, but during the Renaissance, actors and theater people found that they could make a living in the theater. Although at first there was little money in acting and in writing plays, some of the theater managers were able to do quite well. Shakespeare himself was a theater manager as well as a dramatist and minor actor. He earned enough from his shares in the Globe Theatre to retire in 1611 and leave London to spend his remaining days in his native Stratford-upon-Avon.

many of his tragedies include scenes that are farcical, witty, and ironic. When the patterns and emotions are truly mixed, the play is called a **tragicomedy**, a term first used by the Roman playwright Plautus. In many ways tragicomedy is the dominant form of twentieth-century drama.

Additional types of drama that evolved from tragedy and comedy include farce, melodrama, and social drama. The major purpose of **farce**, which was also a strong element in the Athenian Old Comedy, is to make audiences laugh. Typically, it is crammed full of extravagant dialogue, stage business, and slapstick, with exaggerated emotions and rapid extremes of action. The "mechanicals" in Shakespeare's *A Midsummer Night's Dream* offer us good examples of farcical action and speech.

Resembling tragedy but stepping back from tragic outcomes is **melodrama**, a form in which most situations and characters are so exaggerated that they seem ridiculous. In its pure form, melodrama brings characters to the brink of ruin but saves them through the superhuman resources of a hero who always arrives just in time to pay the mortgage, save the business, and rescue the heroine, while the grumbling villain flees the stage muttering "Curses, foiled again," or words, believe it or not, to this effect.

The nineteenth century saw the creation of a form of topical drama known as **social drama** (sometimes called **problem drama**), a type that still exists as serious drama today. This type of play explores social problems and the individual's place in society. The plays can be tragic, comic, or mixed. Examples of social drama are Ibsen's *A Dollhouse,* Hughes's *Mullato,* and Miller's *Death of a Salesman.*

Despite all these terms and types, keep in mind that classification is not the goal of reading or seeing plays. It is less important to identify the melodramatic elements in O'Neill's *Before Breakfast* or the absurdist elements in Albee's *The Sandbox* than it is to understand and share the experiences and ideas that each play offers.

## VISUALIZING PLAYS

As we have noted, drama relies heavily on actors and directors to bring it to life. You might therefore ask why we bother to read plays without seeing them performed. The most obvious answer is that we may never get the chance actually to *see* a professional or amateur performance of a particular play. But we also read plays to familiarize ourselves with important literature. Plays are not simply maps to theatrical production; they are a significant and valuable part of our literary heritage. Dramas like Sophocles's *Oedipus the King*, Shakespeare's *Hamlet*, and Miller's *Death of a Salesman* have become cultural touchstones. Finally, we read plays in order to have the time to study and understand them. Only through reading do we have the opportunity to look at the parts that make up the whole and to determine how they fit together to create a moving and meaningful experience.

Reading a play, as opposed to attending a performance, carries both advantages and disadvantages. The major disadvantage is that we lack the immediacy of live theater. We do not see a majestic palace or a run-down living room, the rich robes of a king or the pathetic rags of a beggar, a vital and smiling young person or a tired and tearful old person. We do not hear the lovers flirting, the servants complaining, the soldiers boasting, the opponents threatening, the conspirators plotting; nor do we hear fanfares of trumpets or the sounds of a wedding ceremony or a funeral procession.

The primary advantage of reading is that we can consider each element in the play at length, and we can "stage" the play in our imagination and do our best to visualize it. Here are some major things for you to consider: In the theater, the action proceeds at the director's pace. You have no opportunity to turn back to an interesting scene or to reconsider an important speech. In addition, a performance always represents someone else's interpretation. The director and the actors have made choices that emphasize certain avenues of exploration, and thereby they have cut off others. Reading a play lets us avoid these drawbacks—provided that we read attentively and with understanding. We can read at our own tempo, turn back and reread a particular speech or scene, or explore those implications or ideas that strike us as interesting.

Nevertheless, of the three types of imaginative literature, *drama is most particularly suited for your visual imagination*. Aids in visualization are often available to help you in your study. At the present time there are many versions of plays that have been acted and recorded on tape and on DVD. You may look at such commercial versions to stimulate your imagination and give you almost a director's view of how a play might be presented onstage. There are professional interpretations of *Oedipus the King*, *A Dollhouse*, *Fences*, and *Death of a Salesman* that you might consult. In addition, there are a great many versions of *Hamlet* on DVD. Looking at selected scenes from any of these performances will give you a sense of the choices made by various directors, and therefore you can achieve a heightened awareness of how you yourself might want the plays to look, and to sound.

As a specimen scene, we might consider Shakespeare's *Hamlet* 1.5, in which Hamlet sees and hears the Ghost for the first time as the Ghost describes his murder at the hand of Claudius—his brother and Hamlet's uncle. In addition, the Ghost charges Hamlet to avenge the murder. This scene is most crucial, and it might be called Hamlet's principal information scene, for it deeply affects Hamlet's understanding and objectives. When he first appears in Act 1, Scene 2, he is quite sad and depressed as a result of his father's death and the quick remarriage of his mother with Claudius. But after the scene with the Ghost, who provides seemingly truthful testimony that Claudius is a murderer, Hamlet becomes a person consumed with the intention of gaining revenge. So the scene is pivotal, and you, or any reader, would want the scene to seem authentic and believable.

It's important to begin with a thought. Always begin with a thought: How do you think you yourself might demonstrate the scene's importance? How would you make the scenery look? How complete should everything in the scene be made to appear? That is, should the Ghost be totally visible, or should he perhaps be somewhat obscured, or should he be seen through a haze, in order to emphasize his ghostliness? What sorts of costumes would you use? How would you make the Elsinore walls and battlements seem like a place where significant truth is to be expressed? How would you show Hamlet's agitation when he first sees the Ghost? How would you show the ways in which Hamlet's encounter with the Ghost affect him? After the encounter, when Hamlet's companions rejoin him, how should he behave? How would you demonstrate his comments about the Ghost's voice under the stage? What do his words show about his mental state, and how should the actor doing the role of Hamlet deliver these words?

For brief illustration here, about how the Ghost's scene may be visualized, we might refer to five different DVD versions of the scene in productions featuring Ethan Hawke, Derek Jacobi, Kevin Kline, Laurence Olivier, and Campbell Scott.[1] Perhaps the most traditional setting of our scene is in the Olivier version of 1948, in black and white, that shows many stone walls and stairs, in which a good deal of smoke and fog obscures the scene and also surrounds the Ghost when the camera is focused on him. The Jacobi version, in color, uses a staging that is similar to this. Fog is also present in the Campbell Scott color version, in which the confrontation of Hamlet and the Ghost takes place on an ocean shore, with a mild surf, rather than high on the parapets of Elsinore. When Hamlet tells his companions that the Ghost can tunnel under the earth very rapidly, the Scott version realistically confirms this action, for the Ghost's hands actually appear at various places coming out of the beach sand, most startlingly when the hand grabs the sword on which all Hamlet's companions have sworn silence. The Ethan Hawke version is different from these—and all the others—because the action takes place within Hamlet's room in a New York apartment. When we first see the Ghost (acted by Sam Shepard), he is outside, on a terrace, appearing to be an ordinary businessman and looking out at the city. It is then that Hamlet lets him in through the door to his computer room. There is nothing ghostly here, as in the other versions, but all seems ordinary, and the room actually seems rather cluttered. Things are so ordinary, in fact, that the TV set in the room is on, and is showing a picture. Is the state of this messy computer room meant to suggest anything about Hamlet's mind?

The point here is that you can boost your own imaginative reconstruction of the scene, and any other scene in any other play, by considering what others have done. The key is your own reading and thinking. What were other viewers trying to do, and to show? How might you want to do things differently? What other effects might be achieved? You will need to figure out what stage effects might be needed. What sorts of lighting would best bring out the scene? What would be the significance of spotlighting, if you were to use it? Think. What scenes might best be done in close-up? What sorts of stage movement might there be? A particularly tension-filled moment is created in the Jacobi version of the Ghost scene, for example, when Hamlet falls dangerously backward from a high stairway, seemingly heading toward severe injury, but his companions catch him and save him. What does that production gain by this action, which is not called for in the text of the play? Another question you might deal with concerns how the characters interact with each other, as when Hamlet, after returning from his encounter with the Ghost, tells his friends that "There's ne'er a villain dwelling in all Denmark/But he's

---

[1] *Hamlet*, starring Ethan Hawke et al. Adapted by Michael Almereyda. Directed by Michael Almereyda. Produced by Andrew Fierberg and Amy Hobby. Burbank: Buena Vista Home Entertainment, 2000.

    *Hamlet* (The Dramatic Works of William Shakespeare), starring Derek Jacobi et al. New York: Ambrose Video Publishing, Inc., BBX & Time-Life Films, 1980.

    *William Shakespeare's Hamlet*, starring Kevin Kline et al. Kevin Kline and Kirk Browning, directors. Kimberly Myers and Iris Merlis, producers. Chatsworth, CA: Educational Broadcasting Corp, 1990.

    *Laurence Olivier's Hamlet*, starring Laurence Olivier, et al. Laurence Olivier, director. Two Cities Film Ltd., 1948. The Criterion Collection 82, 2000.

    *Hamlet*, starring Campbell Scott et al. Campbell Scott and Eric Simonson, adapters and directors. Robert Halmi Jr., executive producer. Santa Monica, CA: Artisan Entertainment, 2000.

an arrant knave" (1.5.124–25). Should Horatio's response be spoken seriously, or comically? Other questions you can raise might concern whether some of the action, from *Hamlet* or any other play, should be cut for production.

You might also think about questions of costuming. One might expect to see a *Hamlet* production done in clothing that was customary at the time of Shakespeare, as in the Olivier and Jacobi versions. What is the effect of more recent clothing, as in the Scott version, or ordinary late twentieth-century clothing, as in the Hawke version? And you should also consider the modes of speech, and their effect on your imaginary production. The Olivier Ghost, for example, speaks as we might expect a ghost to speak, in deep tones, slowly. This is not so in the Jacobi version, in which this Ghost, who is angry, speaks rapidly and forcefully about the circumstances of his death. He is not happy, and he clearly wants Hamlet not to be happy either. The Ghost in the Hawke version is more quietly conversational, in keeping with the interior in which the action takes place, and before he leaves he embraces Hamlet, his son, even if he is a Ghost and therefore non-substantial at the time of the action. Indeed, this ghost looks very substantial and very realistic.

In a word, try to use the advantages of reading and study, together with your own imagination. You have the time and freedom to read carefully, reflect deeply, and follow your thoughts. Think. Rely on whatever experiences you can gain from theatrical productions, movies, and recorded productions to enhance your reading.

(Scene from Olivier's *Hamlet*): The costuming of Sir Laurence Olivier's *Hamlet*, shown above is traditionally Shakespearean.

(Scene from Hawke's *Hamlet*): As seen in this production still, late twentieth-century costumes were used in Ethan Hawke's version of *Hamlet*.

Stage the play as fully as you can in the theater of your mind. Become the director, producer, set designer, lighting technician, and costume designer, and pretend that you control all the actors. Build whatever mental presentations you like, dress your actors as you see fit, and move the characters across the stage of your mind. Enjoy.

## Plays for Study

## EDWARD ALBEE (b. 1928)

Edward Albee, one of the leading American playwrights of the last half of the twentieth century, began life with many personal and educational handicaps. He was an adopted child whose adoptive mother alienated and eventually disowned him. As a boy he was moved in and out of various schools. Eventually, he studied at Trinity College in Hartford, Connecticut, but he left without a degree even though in 1997 the "alumni, faculty, students, and friends" of Trinity "proudly" congratulated him on having received the Kennedy Center Honors of 1996.

After leaving Trinity, Albee worked for many years at a variety of odd jobs, including three years delivering telegrams, but at the urging of the Pulitzer Prize winning playwright Thornton Wilder (1897–1975), he turned his talent to writing plays. He has been constantly productive ever since. His first play was *The Zoo Story* (1958), a brief play that was premiered in 1959 in Berlin and published in 1960. This was followed by *The Sandbox* (1960), *The Death of Bessie Smith* (1960), and *The American Dream* (1961). His best-known play, *Who's Afraid of Virginia Woolf?*, appeared in 1962 and marks the pinnacle of his career. After a long and successful run in New York, it was awarded the 1963 Tony Award as best play. In 1966 it was made into a successful film featuring Richard Burton and Elizabeth Taylor, who won an Academy Award for her performance.

Albee's work after *Who's Afraid of Virginia Woolf* has met with mixed reactions. *Tiny Alice* (1964) was declared confusing and derivative, but *A Delicate Balance* (1966) and *Seascape* (1975) both won Pulitzer Prizes. *Listening*, which appeared in 1977, is unique in Albee's work because it was intended for radio, not the stage. Some of his later plays and adaptations had short lives in the theater. *The Lady from Dubuque* (1980) survived only twelve performances on Broadway, and negative reviews forced *The Man Who Had Three Arms* off the Broadway stage in 1983.

Some of his more recent work has achieved more favorable recognition. In 1993–1994, the Signature Theater Company of New York presented a season-long set of Albee performances. One of them featured *The Sandbox* as one of three one-act "sand plays," the others being *Box* (1968) and *Finding the Sun* (1983). Additionally, two of his other plays, *Three Tall Women* (1991, Pulitzer Prize in Drama for 1994) and *Fragments* (1994), were performed to great acclaim. In the last several years he has written *The Play about the Baby* (2001) and *The Occupant* (2002). He continues to write, and states that he has no plans to stop doing so.

He claims that his plays are about "closings down"; that is, about how dreams never reach fulfillment, and how happiness—our greatest dream and our constant pursuit—is constantly beyond our grasp. Other descriptions of his work might include a pervasive sense of alienation, loss, uneasiness, fear, and uncertainty, mixed with a certain degree of humor. Although Albee is not easily categorized, he has introduced elements of the theater of the absurd into his work. His first play, *The Zoo Story*, is in the absurdist manner, which is characterized by the stripping away of the conventions of behavior and accidents of personality. The idea is that life is, at bottom, irrational and meaningless. The title of one of his plays, *A Delicate Balance*, symbolizes the Albee view of existence: Any stability that we are lucky enough to achieve in life is no more than a stage of delicate balance, which can be toppled by distrust, bitterness, reproach, and anger that can strike with hurricane force at almost any time. If life seems happy, that happiness is only temporary, and to think otherwise is superficial and untrue.

*The Sandbox*, written in 1959 and first performed in New York in 1960, represents Albee's critique of the American family as an institution that is not constructive but destructive. His vacationing family consists of characters whom he presents in an absurdist frame of reference. Grandma, the protagonist, is in conflict with society, her family, and death. Only the last of these conflicts is resolved at the conclusion. Mommy and Daddy represent Albee's vision of the American family reduced to a bare-bones form. Plot, character, setting, and symbol all convey the judgment that modern lives and values are drab and, basically, dull and average. Albee provides his characters with absurd, banal, sometimes childish, and idiomatic speeches that are filled with specific and concrete words interspersed with clichés that bring the play to the level of ordinary life or, perhaps, somewhat below it. In effect, the characters dramatize their own bleak lives through their own words. Although the number of characters is small and the scene is restricted, there is a surprising amount of activity, which culminates in the unusual but surprisingly tender conclusion.

## The Sandbox (1959)

### THE PLAYERS

**The Young Man, 25,** a good-looking, well-built boy in a bathing suit

**Mommy, 55,** a well-dressed, imposing woman

**Daddy, 60,** a small man; gray, thin

**Grandma, 86,** a tiny, wizened woman with bright eyes

**The Musician,** no particular age, but young would be nice

*Note: When, in the course of the play, MOMMY and DADDY call each other by these names, there should be no suggestion of regionalism. These names are of empty affection and point up the presenility and vacuity of their characters.*          0.1

*The Scene: A bare stage, with only the following: Near the footlights, far stage-right, two simple chairs set side by side, facing the audience; near the footlights, far stage-left, a chair facing stage-right with a music stand before it; farther back, and stage-center, slightly elevated and raked, a large child's sandbox with a toy pail and shovel; the background is the sky, which alters from brightest day to deepest night.*          0.2

*At the beginning, it is brightest day; the YOUNG MAN is alone on stage, to the rear of the sandbox, and to one side. He is doing calisthenics until quite at the very end of the play. These calisthenics, employing the arms only, should suggest the beating and fluttering of wings. The YOUNG MAN is, after all, the Angel of Death.*          0.3

*MOMMY and DADDY enter from stage-left, MOMMY first.*

MOMMY: [*Motioning to DADDY.*] Well, here we are; this is the beach.

DADDY: [*Whining.*] I'm cold.

MOMMY: [*Dismissing him with a little laugh.*] Don't be silly; it's as warm as toast. Look at that nice young man over there: *he* doesn't think it's cold. [*Waves to the YOUNG MAN.*] Hello.

YOUNG MAN: [*With an endearing smile.*] Hi!

MOMMY: [*Looking about.*] This will do perfectly . . . don't you think so, Daddy? There's sand there . . . and the water beyond. What do you think, Daddy?          5

DADDY: [*Vaguely.*] Whatever you say, Mommy.

MOMMY: [*With the same little laugh.*] Well, of course . . . whatever I say. Then, it's settled, is it?

DADDY: [*Shrugs.*] She's *your* mother, not mine.

MOMMY: *I* know she's my mother. What do you take me for? [*A pause.*] All right, now; let's get on with it. [*She shouts into the wings, stage-left.*] You! Out there! You can come in now.

*The MUSICIAN enters, seats himself in the chair, stage-left, places music on the music stand, is ready to play. MOMMY nods approvingly.*

10   MOMMY:  Very nice; very nice. Are you ready, Daddy? Let's go get Grandma.
      DADDY:  Whatever you say, Mommy.
      MOMMY:  [*Leading the way out, stage-left.*] Of course, whatever I say. [*To the MUSICIAN.*] You can
           begin now. [*The MUSICIAN begins playing; MOMMY and DADDY exit; the MUSICIAN, all the while
           playing, nods to the YOUNG MAN.*]
      YOUNG MAN:  [*With the same endearing smile.*] Hi!

*After a moment, MOMMY and DADDY re-enter, carrying GRANDMA. She is borne in by their hands under her armpits; she is quite rigid; her legs are drawn up; her feet do not touch the ground; the expression on her ancient face is that of puzzlement and fear.*

      DADDY:  Where do we put her?
15   MOMMY:  [*The same little laugh.*] Wherever I say, of course. Let me see . . . well . . . all right,
           over there . . . in the sandbox. [*Pause.*] Well, what are you waiting for, Daddy? . . . The
           sandbox!

*Together they carry GRANDMA over to the sandbox and more or less dump her in.*

      GRANDMA:  [*Righting herself to a sitting position; her voice a cross between a baby's laugh and cry.*]
           Ahhhhhh! Graaaaa!
      DADDY:  [*Dusting himself.*] What do we do now?
      MOMMY:  [*To the MUSICIAN.*] You can stop now.

*The MUSICIAN stops.*

      [*Back to DADDY.*] What do you mean, what do we do now? We go over there and sit down, of
           course. [*To the YOUNG MAN.*] Hello there.
      YOUNG MAN:  [*Again smiling.*] Hi!

*MOMMY and DADDY move to the chairs, stage-right, and sit down. A pause.*

20   GRANDMA:  [*Same as before.*] Ahhhhhh! Ah-haaaaaa! Graaaaaa!
      DADDY:  Do you think . . . do you think she's . . . comfortable?
      MOMMY:  [*Impatiently.*] How would I know?
      DADDY:  [*Pause.*] What do we do now?
      MOMMY:  [*As if remembering.*] We . . . wait. We . . . sit here . . . and we wait . . . that's what we do.
25   DADDY:  [*After a pause.*] Shall we talk to each other?
      MOMMY:  [*With that little laugh; picking something off her dress.*] Well, you *can* talk, if you want
           to . . . if you can think of anything to *say* . . . if you can think of anything *new*.
      DADDY:  [*Thinks.*] No . . . I suppose not.
      MOMMY:  [*With a triumphant laugh.*] Of course not!
      GRANDMA:  [*Banging the toy shovel against the pail.*] Haaaaaa! Ah-haaaaaa!
30   MOMMY:  [*Out over the audience.*] Be quiet, Grandma . . . just be quiet, and wait.

*GRANDMA throws a shovelful of sand at MOMMY.*

      MOMMY:  [*Still out over the audience.*] She's throwing sand at me! You stop that, Grandma; you
           stop throwing sand at Mommy! [*To DADDY.*] She's throwing sand at me.

*DADDY looks around at GRANDMA, who screams at him.*

GRANDMA: GRAAAAAA!

MOMMY: Don't look at her. Just . . . sit here . . . be very still . . . and wait. [*To the MUSICIAN.*] You . . . uh . . . you go ahead and do whatever it is you do.

*The MUSICIAN plays.*

*MOMMY and DADDY are fixed, staring out beyond the audience. GRANDMA looks at them, looks at the MUSICIAN, looks at the sandbox, throws down the shovel.*

GRANDMA: Ah-haaaaaa! Graaaaaa! [*Looks for reaction; gets none. Now . . . directly to the audience.*] Honestly! What a way to treat an old woman! Drag her out of the house . . . stick her in a car . . . bring her out here from the city . . . dump her in a pile of sand . . . and leave her to set. I'm eighty-six years old! I was married when I was seventeen. To a farmer. He died when I was thirty. [*To the MUSICIAN.*] Will you stop that, please?

*The MUSICIAN stops playing.*

I'm a feeble old woman . . . how do you expect anybody to hear me over that peep! Peep! Peep! [*To herself.*] There's no respect around here. [*To the YOUNG MAN.*] There's no respect around here!

YOUNG MAN: [*Same smile.*] Hi!                                                               35

GRANDMA: [*After a pause, a mild double-take, continues, to the audience.*] My husband died when I was thirty [*indicates Mommy*], and I had to raise that big cow over there all by my lonesome. You can imagine what *that* was like. Lordy! [*To the YOUNG MAN.*] Where'd they get *you*?

YOUNG MAN: Oh . . . I've been around for a while.

GRANDMA: I'll bet you have! Heh, heh, heh. Will you look at you!

YOUNG MAN: [*Flexing his muscles.*] Isn't that something? [*Continues his calisthenics.*]

GRANDMA: Boy, oh boy; I'll say. Pretty good.                                                 40

YOUNG MAN: [*Sweetly.*] I'll say.

GRANDMA: Where ya from?

YOUNG MAN: Southern California.

GRANDMA: [*Nodding.*] Figgers; figgers. What's your name, honey?

YOUNG MAN: I don't know. . . .                                                               45

GRANDMA: [*To the audience.*] Bright, too!

YOUNG MAN: I mean . . . I mean, they haven't given me one yet . . . the studio . . .

GRANDMA: [*Giving him the once-over.*] You don't say . . . you don't say. Well . . . uh, I've got to talk some more . . . don't you go 'way.

YOUNG MAN: Oh, no.

GRANDMA: [*Turning her attention back to the audience.*] Fine; fine. [*Then, once more, back to the* YOUNG MAN.] You're . . . you're an actor, hunh?                                      50

YOUNG MAN: [*Beaming.*] Yes. I am.

GRANDMA: [*To the audience again; shrugs.*] I'm smart that way. *Anyhow,* I had to raise . . . *that* over there all by my lonesome; and what's next to her there . . . . that's what she married. Rich? I tell you . . . money, money, money. They took me off the *farm* . . . which was real decent of them . . . and they moved me into the big town house with *them* . . . fixed a nice place for me under the stove . . . gave me an army blanket . . . and my own dish . . . my very own dish! So, what have I got to complain about? Nothing, of course. I'm not complaining. [*She looks up at the sky, shouts to someone off-stage.*] Shouldn't it be getting dark now, dear?

*The lights dim; night comes on. The* MUSICIAN *begins to play; it becomes deepest night. There are spots on all the players, including the* YOUNG MAN, *who is, of course, continuing his calisthenics.*

DADDY: [*Stirring.*] It's nighttime.

MOMMY: Shhhh. Be still . . . wait.

55  DADDY: [*Whining.*] It's so hot.

MOMMY: Shhhh. Be still . . . wait.

GRANDMA: [*To herself.*] That's better. Night. [*To the* MUSICIAN.] Honey, do you play all through
    this part?

*The* MUSICIAN *nods.*

Well, keep it nice and soft; that's a good boy.

*The* MUSICIAN *nods again; plays softly.*

That's nice.

*There is an off-stage rumble.*

DADDY: [*Starting.*] What was that?

MOMMY: [*Beginning to weep.*] It was nothing.

60  DADDY: It was . . . it was . . . thunder . . . or a wave breaking . . . or something.

MOMMY: [*Whispering, through her tears.*] It was an off-stage rumble . . . and you know what *that*
    means.

DADDY: I forget. . . .

MOMMY: [*Barely able to talk.*] It means the time has come for poor Grandma . . . and I can't bear it!

DADDY: [*Vacantly.*] I . . . I suppose you've got to be brave.

65  GRANDMA: [*Mocking.*] That's right, kid; be brave. You'll bear up; you'll get over it.

*Another off-stage rumble . . . louder.*

MOMMY: Ohhhhhhhhhh . . . poor Grandma . . . poor Grandma. . . .

GRANDMA: [*To* MOMMY.] I'm fine! I'm all right! It hasn't happened yet!

*A violent off-stage rumble. All the lights go out, save the spot on the YOUNG MAN; the* MUSICIAN
*stops playing.*

MOMMY: Ohhhhhhhhhh . . . Ohhhhhhhhhh. . . .

GRANDMA: Don't put the lights up yet. . . . I'm not ready; I'm not quite ready. [*Silence.*] All
    right, dear . . . I'm about done.

*The lights come up again, to brightest day; the* MUSICIAN *begins to play.* GRANDMA *is discovered, still in the
sandbox, lying on her side, propped up on an elbow, half covered, busily shoveling sand over herself.*

70  GRANDMA: I don't know how I'm supposed to do anything with this goddam toy shovel. . . .

DADDY: Mommy! It's daylight!

MOMMY: [*Brightly.*] So it is! Well! Our long night is over. We must put away our tears, take off
    our mourning . . . and face the future. It's our duty.

GRANDMA: [*Still shoveling; mimicking*] . . . take off our mourning . . . face the future. . . . Lordy!

MOMMY *and* DADDY *rise, stretch.* MOMMY *waves to the* YOUNG MAN.

YOUNG MAN: [*With that smile.*] Hi!

GRANDMA *plays dead.* (!) MOMMY *and* DADDY *go over to look at her; she is a little more than half buried in the sand; the toy shovel is in her hands, which are crossed on her breast.*

MOMMY: [*Before the sandbox; shaking her head.*] Lovely! It's . . . it's hard to be sad . . . she looks . . . 75
so happy. [*With pride and conviction.*] It pays to do things well. [*To the* MUSICIAN.] All right,
you can stop now, if you want to. I mean, stay around for a swim, or something; it's all
right with us. [*She sighs heavily.*] Well Daddy . . . off we go.
DADDY: Brave Mommy!
MOMMY: Brave Daddy! [*They exit, stage-left.*]

GRANDMA: [*After they leave; lying quite still.*] It pays to do things well. . . . Boy, oh boy! [*She tries
to sit up.*] . . . Well, kids . . . [*But she finds she can't.*] . . . I . . . I can't get up. I . . . can't move.

*The* YOUNG MAN *stops his calisthenics, nods to the* MUSICIAN, *walks over to* GRANDMA, *kneels down by the sandbox.*

GRANDMA: I . . . can't move. . . .
YOUNG MAN: Shhhhh . . . be very still. . . .                                                           80
GRANDMA: I . . . I can't move. . . .
YOUNG MAN: Uh . . . ma'am; I . . . I have a line here.
GRANDMA: Oh, I'm sorry, sweetie; you go right ahead.
YOUNG MAN: I am . . . uh . . .
GRANDMA: Take your time, dear.                                                                         85
YOUNG MAN: [*Prepares; delivers the line like a real amateur.*] I am the Angel of Death. I am . . .
uh . . . I am come for you.
GRANDMA: What . . . wha . . . [*Then, with resignation.*] . . . ohhh . . . ohhhh, I see.

*The* YOUNG MAN *bends over, kisses* GRANDMA *gently on the forehead.*

GRANDMA: [*Her eyes closed, her hands folded on her breast again, the shovel between her hands, a
sweet smile on her face.*] Well . . . that was very nice, dear. . . .
YOUNG MAN: [*Still kneeling.*] Shhhhhh . . . be still. . . .
GRANDMA: What I meant was . . . you did that very well, dear. . . .                                    90
YOUNG MAN: [*Blushing.*] . . . oh . . .
GRANDMA: No; I mean it. You've got that . . . you've got a quality.
YOUNG MAN: [*With his endearing smile.*] Oh . . . thank you; thank you very much . . . ma'am.
GRANDMA: [*Slowly; softly—as the* YOUNG MAN *puts his hands on top of* GRANDMA'S.] You're . . .
you're welcome . . . dear.

*Tableau. The* MUSICIAN *continues to play as the curtain slowly comes down.*

*CURTAIN*

## Questions

1. Why does Mommy say, "This is the beach" (line 1)? What are the characters waiting for
there?

2. Why does Albee indicate that Daddy is whining? What is the effect of Daddy's repetition of "Whatever you say, Mommy"?

3. How does Grandma "speak" to Mommy and Daddy? How does she speak to the audience and the Young Man? How do you account for this difference?

4. At the end of the play, just as in the opening scene directions (0.3 S.D.), Albee identifies the Young Man as the Angel of Death (speech 86). What else does the Young Man symbolize or represent? What does Grandma apparently think of him? How does he treat her?

5. What do the off-stage rumbles signify (57.1 S.D., 65.1 S.D., 67.1 S.D.)?

6. How do Mommy and Daddy react to Grandma's "death"? How would you characterize their language, both here and throughout the play?

7. How does Grandma react to the comments of Mommy and Daddy about her death? What does Grandma reveal about the way Mommy and Daddy deal with death?

## General Questions

1. How does the setting, described at the play's beginning (0.2–3 S.D.) illustrate the play's level of reality? What props are realistic? Symbolic? Why is the play titled *The Sandbox*? What does the sandbox represent? What is your reaction when you realize what the sandbox is to be used for?

2. What is the realistic/nonrealistic effect of speeches such as Mommy's telling the Musician "You can come in now" (speech 9), Grandma's cueing of the lighting technician (speech 69), and the Young Man's statement that he has "a line here" (speech 82)?

3. Are the characters in the play interesting as characters? Why does Albee not give them names? What does each character symbolize?

4. *The Sandbox* is full of repetition. Characters repeat words and even whole lines two and sometimes three times. How does this repetition affect your understanding of character, meaning, and level of reality?

5. Is there anything unusual about the diction spoken by the characters? Do any of the characters voice any original thoughts? Why or why not? How would you describe the nature of their vocabulary?

6. How many different generations are presented in *The Sandbox*? Which characters represent each generation? Why does Grandma inveigh against Mommy? How does Grandma illustrate her feelings about how she has been treated in the home of Mommy and Daddy?

7. Almost every speech in this play is preceded by a stage direction, and stage directions are included within a number of speeches. What is the purpose of these directions? What might the play be like without them?

8. A student observed that *The Sandbox* at first seems strange and absurd but nevertheless that the concluding speeches are deeply moving. Is your reaction different or the same? Explain the growth or change of your responses to the play.

9. Compare the treatment of Death in this play with the treatments you find in Dickinson's "Because I Could Not Stop for Death" (p. 468), Pinsky's "Dying" (p. 623), Frost's "Out, Out—" (p. 756), Porter's "The Jilting of Granny Weatherall" (p. 341), and any other relevant work of your choice in this book.

# SUSAN GLASPELL (1882–1948)

Susan Glaspell, a writer of both plays and fiction, was a native of Iowa. She was educated at Drake University and the University of Chicago. In her thirties she moved to the Northeast and became interested in theater. Along with her husband, George Cook, she was a founder and director of the Provincetown Players of Cape Cod in 1914. The organization encouraged lesser-known young dramatists and was often experimental, but nevertheless it became successful enough to justify the opening of a second theater in New York. The first offerings of the theater were many one-act plays, featuring the earlier works of Glaspell herself, Eugene O'Neill, Edna Ferber, Edmund Wilson, and Edna St. Vincent Millay.

Glaspell wrote or coauthored over ten plays for the Provincetown Players, including *Suppressed Desires* (1914), *Close the Book* (1917), *Women's Honor* (1918), *Tickless Time* (1918), *Bernice* (1919, her first full-length play), *The Inheritors* (1921), and *The Verge* (1921). After 1922, however, she gave up the theater and turned almost exclusively to fiction. The exception was *Alison's House* (1930), a play loosely based on the life and family of Emily Dickinson, for which she won a Pulitzer Prize.

Glaspell deals with diverse topics in her drama, including misunderstood parentage, the effects of psychoanalysis, rejection of the machine age, the function and importance of honor, the tensions between political conservatives and liberals, and the onset of psychosis. Running through much of her work are strongly feminist ideas, based on a critique of the power—personal, social, and political—that men possess and that women are denied. Usually, Glaspell focuses on the negative and destructive effects that male–female relationships have on women, but she also stresses the ways in which women cope with their circumstances. To maintain character integrity and to preserve their domestic strength, they are forced into roles that are characterized not by direct but by indirect action.

*Trifles*, Glaspell's best-known drama, displays these characteristics. She wrote it in ten days for the Provincetown Players, who produced the play in 1916. Its inspiration was a murder trial she had covered while working as a reporter for a Des Moines newspaper before moving to the Northeast. In 1917 she refashioned the material for the short story "A Jury of Her Peers," with which *Trifles* can be compared. Although Glaspell preserves a considerable amount of dramatic dialogue in the story, the additions and changes she makes are indicative of the differences between drama and fiction.

*Trifles* concerns a murder investigation, but the play is not a mystery. Soon after the characters enter and go about their business, the two women characters begin to uncover the circumstances that reveal the killer and the nature of the crime. Once the facts are established, however, the action focuses on the significant details of motive. Indeed, the heart of the play consists of the contrasting ways in which the men and the women attempt to uncover and understand the motive. The men—the county attorney and the sheriff, accompanied by Hale—look for signs of violent rage, and they move onstage and offstage throughout the house in their search. The women—Mrs. Hale and Mrs. Peters—stay onstage and draw their conclusions from the ordinary, everyday details of a farm woman's kitchen. It is finally the women, not the men, who realize the true power that comes from understanding. Their realization—as well as their strength—leads them to their final decisions about how to judge the killer and treat the evidence.

The language that Glaspell gives to her characters is in keeping with the plain and simple lives the characters lead: simple, specific, and unadorned. Of the two groups, the women are more direct in the expression of their ideas. Once they realize the gravity of the situation they are exploring, however, they become indirect, but only because they fear to speak the words that describe the truths they have discovered. By contrast, the men usually talk convivially and smugly about the crime and their own roles in life, patronizingly among themselves about the women, and almost scornfully to the women about womanly concerns.

## Trifles (1916)

### CAST OF CHARACTERS

**George Henderson,** county attorney
**Henry Peters,** sheriff
**Lewis Hale,** a neighboring farmer
**Mrs. Peters**
**Mrs. Hale**

SCENE: *The kitchen in the now abandoned farmhouse of* JOHN WRIGHT, *a gloomy kitchen, and left without having been put in order—unwashed pans under the sink, a loaf of bread outside the bread-box, a dish-towel on the table—other signs of incompleted work. At the rear the outer door opens and the* SHERIFF *comes in followed by the* COUNTY ATTORNEY *and* HALE. *The* SHERIFF *and* HALE *are men in middle life, the County Attorney is a young man; all are much bundled up and go at once to the stove. They are followed by the two women—the* SHERIFF'S *wife first; she is a slight wiry woman, a thin nervous face.* MRS. HALE *is larger and would ordinarily be called more comfortable looking, but she is disturbed now and looks fearfully about as she enters. The women have come in slowly, and stand close together near the door.*

COUNTY ATTORNEY: [*Rubbing his hands.*] This feels good. Come up to the fire, ladies.
MRS. PETERS: [*After taking a step forward.*] I'm not—cold.
SHERIFF: [*Unbuttoning his overcoat and stepping away from the stove as if to mark the beginning of official business.*] Now, Mr. Hale, before we move things about, you explain to Mr. Henderson just what you saw when you came here yesterday morning.
COUNTY ATTORNEY: By the way, has anything been moved? Are things just as you left them yesterday?

The five principal actors arrive in the cold and bleak kitchen of the Wright farm at the beginning of Glaspell's *Trifles* in the original 1916 production, featuring Marjorie Vonnegut, Elinor M. Cox, John Kind, Arthur Hohl, and T. W. Gibson.

SHERIFF: [*Looking about.*] It's just the same. When it dropped below zero last night I thought    5
   I'd better send Frank out this morning to make a fire for us—no use getting pneumonia
   with a big case on, but I told him not to touch anything except the stove—and you know
   Frank.
COUNTY ATTORNEY: Somebody should have been left here yesterday.
SHERIFF: Oh—yesterday. When I had to send Frank to Morris Center for that man who went
   crazy—I want you to know I had my hands full yesterday. I knew you could get back
   from Omaha by today and as long as I went over everything here myself—
COUNTY ATTORNEY: Well, Mr. Hale, tell just what happened when you came here yesterday
   morning.
HALE: Harry and I had started to town with a load of potatoes. We came along the road from
   my place and as I got here I said, "I'm going to see if I can't get John Wright to go in with
   me on a party telephone." I spoke to Wright about it once before and he put me off, saying
   folks talked too much anyway, and all he asked was peace and quiet—I guess you know
   about how much he talked himself; but I thought maybe if I went to the house and talked
   about it before his wife, though I said to Harry that I didn't know as what his wife wanted
   made much difference to John—
COUNTY ATTORNEY: Let's talk about that later, Mr. Hale. I do want to talk about that, but tell    10
   now just what happened when you got to the house.
HALE: I didn't hear or see anything; I knocked at the door, and still it was all quiet inside. I
   knew they must be up, it was past eight o'clock. So I knocked again, and I thought I heard
   somebody say, "Come in." I wasn't sure, I'm not sure yet, but I opened. the door—this
   door [*Indicating the door by which the two women are still standing.*] and there in that rocker—
   [*Pointing to it.*] sat Mrs. Wright.

[*They all look at the rocker.*]

COUNTY ATTORNEY: What—was she doing?

HALE: She was rockin' back and forth. She had her apron in her hand and was kind of—pleating it.

COUNTY ATTORNEY: And how did she—look?

15 HALE: Well, she looked queer.

COUNTY ATTORNEY: How do you mean—queer?

HALE: Well, as if she didn't know what she was going to do next. And kind of done up.

COUNTY ATTORNEY: How did she seem to feel about your coming?

HALE: Why, I don't think she minded—one way or other. She didn't pay much attention. I said, "How do, Mrs. Wright, it's cold, ain't it?" And she said, "Is it?"—and went on kind of pleating at her apron. Well, I was surprised; she didn't ask me to come up to the stove, or to set down, but just sat there, not even looking at me, so I said, "I want to see John." And then she—laughed. I guess you would call it a laugh. I thought of Harry and the team outside, so I said a little sharp: "Can't I see John?" "No," she says, kind o' dull like. "Ain't he home?" says I. "Yes," says she, "he's home." "Then why can't I see him?" I asked her, out of patience. "Cause he's dead," says she. "*Dead*?" says I. She just nodded her head, not getting a bit excited, but rockin' back and forth. "Why—where is he?" says I, not knowing what to say. She just pointed upstairs—like that. [*Himself pointing to the room above.*] I got up, with the idea of going up there. I walked from there to here—then I says, "Why, what did he die of?" "He died of a rope round his neck," says she, and just went on pleatin' at her apron. Well, I went out and called Harry. I thought I might—need help. We went upstairs and there he was lyin'—

20 COUNTY ATTORNEY: I think I'd rather have you go into that upstairs, where you can point it all out. Just go on now with the rest of the story.

HALE: Well, my first thought was to get that rope off. It looked . . . [*Stops, his face twitches.*] . . . but Harry, he went up to him, and he said, "No, he's dead all right, and we'd better not touch anything." So we went back downstairs. She was still sitting that same way. "Has anybody been notified?" I asked. "No," says she, unconcerned. "Who did this, Mrs. Wright?" said Harry. He said it businesslike—and she stopped pleatin' of her apron. "I don't know," she says. "You don't *know*?" says Harry. "No," says she. "Weren't you sleepin' in the bed with him?" says Harry. "Yes," says she, "but I was on the inside." "Somebody slipped a rope round his neck and strangled him and you didn't wake up?" says Harry. "I didn't wake up," she said after him. We must 'a looked as if we didn't see how that could be, for after a minute she said, "I sleep sound." Harry was going to ask her more questions but I said maybe we ought to let her tell her story first to the coroner, or the sheriff, so Harry went fast as he could to Rivers' place, where there's a telephone.

COUNTY ATTORNEY: And what did Mrs. Wright do when she knew that you had gone for the coroner?

HALE: She moved from that chair to this one over here [*Pointing to a small chair in the corner.*] and just sat there with her hands held together and looking down. I got a feeling that I ought to make some conversation, so I said I had come in to see if John wanted to put in a telephone, and at that she started to laugh, and then she stopped and looked at me—scared. [*The COUNTY ATTORNEY, who has had his notebook out, makes a note.*] I dunno, maybe it wasn't scared. I wouldn't like to say it was. Soon Harry got back, and then Dr. Lloyd came, and you, Mr. Peters, and so I guess that's all I know that you don't.

COUNTY ATTORNEY: [*Looking around.*] I guess we'll go upstairs first—and then out to the barn and around there. [*To the SHERIFF.*] You're convinced that there was nothing important here—nothing that would point to any motive.

SHERIFF:  Nothing here but kitchen things.　　25

[*The* COUNTY ATTORNEY, *after again looking around the kitchen, opens the door of a cupboard closet. He gets up on a chair and looks on a shelf. Pulls his hand away, sticky.*]

COUNTY ATTORNEY:  Here's a nice mess.

[*The women draw nearer.*]

MRS. PETERS:  [*To the other woman.*] Oh, her fruit; it did freeze. [*To the* LAWYER.] She worried about that when it turned so cold. She said the fire'd go out and her jars would break.

SHERIFF:  Well, can you beat the women! Held for murder and worryin' about her preserves.

COUNTY ATTORNEY:  I guess before we're through she may have something more serious than preserves to worry about.

HALE:  Well, women are used to worrying over trifles.　　30

[*The two women move a little closer together.*]

COUNTY ATTORNEY:  [*With the gallantry of a young politician.*] And yet, for all their worries, what would we do without the ladies? [*The women do not unbend. He goes to the sink, takes a dipperful of water from the pail and pouring it into a basin, washes his hands. Starts to wipe them on the roller towel, turns it for a cleaner place.*] Dirty towels! [*Kicks his foot against the pans under the sink.*] Not much of a housekeeper, would you say, ladies?

MRS HALE:  [*Stiffly.*] There's a great deal of work to be done on a farm.

COUNTY ATTORNEY:  To be sure. And yet [*With a little bow to her.*] I know there are some Dickson county farmhouses which do not have such roller towels.

[*He gives it a pull to expose its full length again.*]

MRS HALE:  Those towels get dirty awful quick. Men's hands aren't always as clean as they might be.

COUNTY ATTORNEY:  Ah, loyal to your sex, I see. But you and Mrs. Wright were neighbors. I　35 suppose you were friends, too.

MRS HALE:  [*Shaking her head.*] I've not seen much of her of late years. I've not been in this house—it's more than a year.

COUNTY ATTORNEY:  And why was that? You didn't like her?

MRS HALE:  I liked her all well enough. Farmers' wives have their hands full, Mr. Henderson. And then—

COUNTY ATTORNEY:  Yes—?

MRS HALE:  [*Looking about.*] It never seemed a very cheerful place.　　40

COUNTY ATTORNEY:  No—it's not cheerful. I shouldn't say she had the homemaking instinct.

MRS HALE:  Well. I don't know as Wright had, either.

COUNTY ATTORNEY:  You mean that they didn't get on very well?

MRS HALE:  No, I don't mean anything. But I don't think a place'd be any cheerfuller for John Wright's being in it.

COUNTY ATTORNEY:  I'd like to talk more of that a little later. I want to get the lay of things up-　45 stairs now.

[*He goes to the left, where three steps lead to a stair door.*]

SHERIFF:  I suppose anything Mrs. Peters does'll be all right. She was to take in some clothes for her, you know, and a few little things. We left in such a hurry yesterday.

County Attorney: Yes, but I would like to see what you take, Mrs. Peters, and keep an eye out for anything that might be of use to us.

Mrs. Peters: Yes, Mr. Henderson.

[*The women listen to the men's steps on the stairs, then look about the kitchen.*]

Mrs Hale: I'd hate to have men coming into my kitchen, snooping around and criticising.

[*She arranges the pans under the sink which the Lawyer had shoved out of place.*]

50    Mrs. Peters: Of course it's no more than their duty.

Mrs Hale: Duty's all right, but I guess that deputy sheriff that came out to make the fire might have got a little of this on. [*Gives the roller towel a pull.*] Wish I'd thought of that sooner. Seems mean to talk about her for not having things slicked up when she had to come away in such a hurry.

Mrs. Peters: [*Who had gone to a small table in the left rear corner of the room, and lifted one end of a towel that covers a pan.*] She had bread set.

[*Stands still.*]

Mrs. Hale: [*Eyes fixed on a loaf of bread beside the breadbox, which is on a low shelf at the other side of the room. Moves slowly toward it.*] She was going to put this in there. [*Picks up loaf, then abruptly drops it. In a manner of returning to familiar things.*] It's a shame about her fruit. I wonder if it's all gone. [*Gets up on the chair and looks.*] I think there's some here that's all right, Mrs. Peters. Yes—here; [*Holding it toward the window.*] this is cherries, too. [*Looking again.*] I declare I believe that's the only one. [*Gets down, bottle in her hand. Goes to the sink and wipes it off on the outside.*] She'll feel awful bad after all her hard work in the hot weather. I remember the afternoon I put up my cherries last summer.

[*She puts the bottle on the big kitchen table, center of the room. With a sigh, is about to sit down in the rocking-chair. Before she is seated realizes what chair it is; with a slow look at it, steps back. The chair which she has touched rocks back and forth.*]

Mrs. Peters: Well, I must get those things from the front room closet. [*She goes to the door at the right, but after looking into the other room, steps back.*] You coming with me, Mrs. Hale? You could help me carry them.

[*They go in the other room; reappear, Mrs. Peters carrying a dress and skirt, Mrs. Hale following with a pair of shoes.*]

55    Mrs. Peters: My, it's cold in there.

[*She puts the clothes on the big table and hurries to the stove.*]

Mrs. Hale: [*Examining the skirt.*] Wright was close. I think maybe that's why she kept so much to herself. She didn't even belong to the Ladies Aid. I suppose she felt she couldn't do her part, and then you don't enjoy things when you feel shabby. She used to wear pretty clothes and be lively, when she was Minnie Foster, one of the town girls singing in the choir. But that—oh, that was thirty years ago. This all you was to take in?

Mrs. Peters: She said she wanted an apron. Funny thing to want, for there isn't much to get you dirty in jail, goodness knows. But I suppose just to make her feel more natural. She said they was in the top drawer in this cupboard. Yes, here. And then her little shawl that always hung behind the door. [*Opens stair door and looks.*] Yes, here it is.

[*Quickly shuts door leading upstairs.*]

MRS. HALE: [*Abruptly moving toward her.*] Mrs. Peters?

MRS. PETERS: Yes, Mrs. Hale?

MRS. HALE: Do you think she did it?

MRS. PETERS: [*In a frightened voice.*] Oh, I don't know.    60

MRS. HALE: Well, I don't think she did. Asking for an apron and her little shawl. Worrying about her fruit.

MRS. PETERS: [*Starts to speak, glances up, where footsteps are heard in the room above. In a low voice.*] Mr. Peters says it looks bad for her. Mr. Henderson is awful sarcastic in a speech and he'll make fun of her sayin' she didn't wake up.

MRS. HALE: Well, I guess John Wright didn't wake when they was slipping that rope under his neck.

MRS. PETERS: No, it's strange. It must have been done awful crafty and still. They say it was    65 such a—funny way to kill a man, rigging it all up like that.

MRS. HALE: That's just what Mr. Hale said. There was a gun in the house. He says that's what he can't understand.

MRS. PETERS: Mr. Henderson said coming out that what was needed for the case was a motive; something to show anger, or—sudden feeling.

MRS. HALE: [*Who is standing by the table.*] Well, I don't see any signs of anger around here. [*She puts her hand on the dish towel which lies on the table, stands looking down at table, one half of which is clean, the other half messy.*] It's wiped to here. [*Makes a move as if to finish work, then turns and looks at loaf of bread outside the breadbox. Drops towel. In that voice of coming back to familiar things.*] Wonder how they are finding things upstairs. I hope she had it a little more redd-up° up there. You know, it seems kind of *sneaking*. Locking her up in town and then coming out here and trying to get her own house to turn against her!

MRS. PETERS: But Mrs. Hale, the law is the law.

MRS. HALE: I s'pose 'tis. [*Unbuttoning her coat.*] Better loosen up your things,    70

MRS. PETERS: You won't feel them when you go out.

[*Mrs. Peters takes off her fur tippet,° goes to hang it on hook at back of room, stands looking at the under part of the small corner table.*]

MRS. PETERS: She was piecing a quilt.

[*She brings the large sewing basket and they look at the bright pieces.*]

MRS. HALE: It's log cabin pattern. Pretty, isn't it? I wonder if she was goin' to quilt it or just knot it?

[*Footsteps have been heard coming down the stairs. The SHERIFF enters followed by HALE and the COUNTY ATTORNEY.*]

SHERIFF: They wonder if she was going to quilt it or just knot it!

[*The men laugh; the women look abashed.*]

COUNTY ATTORNEY: [*Rubbing his hands over the stove.*] Frank's fire didn't do much up there, did    75 it? Well, let's go out to the barn and get that cleared up.

[*The men go outside.*]

---

°68 *redd-up*: neat, arranged in order.  71 S.D. *tippet*: scarf-like garment of fur or wool for the neck and shoulders.

Mrs. Hale: [*Resentfully.*] I don't know as there's anything so strange, our takin' up our time with little things while we're waiting for them to get the evidence. [*She sits down at the big table smoothing out a block with decision.*] I don't see as it's anything to laugh about.

Mrs. Peters: [*Apologetically.*] Of course they've got awful important things on their minds.

[*Pulls up a chair and joins Mrs. Hale at the table.*]

Mrs. Hale: [*Examining another block.*] Mrs. Peters, look at this one. Here, this is the one she was working on, and look at the sewing! All the rest of it has been so nice and even. And look at this! It's all over the place! Why, it looks as if she didn't know what she was about!

[*After she has said this they look at each other, then start to glance back at the door. After an instant Mrs. Hale: has pulled at a knot and ripped the sewing.*]

Mrs. Peters: Oh, what are you doing, Mrs. Hale?

80 Mrs. Hale: [*Mildly.*] Just pulling out a stitch or two that's not sewed very good. [*Threading a needle.*] Bad sewing always made me fidgety.

Mrs. Peters: [*Nervously.*] I don't think we ought to touch things.

Mrs. Hale: I'll just finish up this end. [*Suddenly stopping and leaning forward.*] Mrs. Peters?

Mrs. Peters: Yes, Mrs. Hale?

Mrs. Hale: What do you suppose she was so nervous about?

85 Mrs. Peters: Oh—I don't know. I don't know as she was nervous. I sometimes sew awful queer when I'm just tired. [*Mrs. Hale starts to say something, looks at Mrs. Peters, then goes on sewing.*] Well I must get these things wrapped up. They may be through sooner than we think. [*Putting apron and other things together.*] I wonder where I can find a piece of paper, and string.

Mrs. Hale: In that cupboard, maybe.

Mrs. Peters: [*Looking in cupboard.*] Why, here's a bird-cage. [*Holds it up.*] Did she have a bird, Mrs. Hale?

Mrs. Hale: Why, I don't know whether she did or not—I've not been here for so long. There was a man around last year selling canaries cheap, but I don't know as she took one; maybe she did. She used to sing real pretty herself.

Mrs. Peters: [*Glancing around.*] Seems funny to think of a bird here. But she must have had one, or why would she have a cage? I wonder what happened to it?

90 Mrs. Hale: I s'pose maybe the cat got it.

Mrs. Peters: No, she didn't have a cat. She's got that feeling some people have about cats—being afraid of them. My cat got in her room and she was real upset and asked me to take it out.

Mrs. Hale: My sister Bessie was like that. Queer, ain't it?

Mrs. Peters: [*Examining the cage.*] Why, look at this door. It's broke. One hinge is pulled apart.

Mrs. Hale: [*Looking too.*] Looks as if someone must have been rough with it.

95 Mrs. Peters: Why, yes.

[*She brings the cage forward and puts it on the table.*]

Mrs. Hale: I wish if they're going to find any evidence they'd be about it. I don't like this place.

Mrs. Peters: But I'm awful glad you came with me, Mrs. Hale. It would be lonesome for me sitting here alone.

MRS. HALE: It would, wouldn't it? [*Dropping her sewing.*] But I tell you what I do wish, Mrs. Peters. I wish I had come over sometimes when she was here. I—[*Looking around the room.*]—wish I had.

MRS. PETERS: But of course you were awful busy, Mrs. Hale—your house and your children.

MRS. HALE: I could've come. I stayed away because it weren't cheerful—and that's why I 100 ought to have come. I—I've never liked this place. Maybe because it's down in a hollow and you don't see the road. I dunno what it is, but it's a lonesome place and always was. I wish I had come over to see Minnie Foster sometimes. I can see now—

[*Shakes her head.*]

MRS. PETERS: Well, you mustn't reproach yourself, Mrs. Hale. Somehow we just don't see how it is with other folks until—something comes up.

MRS. HALE: Not having children makes less work—but it makes a quiet house, and Wright out to work all day, and no company when he did come in. Did you know John Wright, Mrs. Peters?

MRS. PETERS: Not to know him; I've seen him in town. They say he was a good man.

MRS. HALE: Yes—good; he didn't drink, and kept his word as well as most, I guess, and paid his debts. But he was a hard man, Mrs. Peters. Just to pass the time of day with him— [*Shivers.*] Like a raw wind that gets to the bone. [*Pauses, her eye falling on the cage.*] I should think she would 'a wanted a bird. But what do you suppose went with it?

MRS. PETERS: I don't know, unless it got sick and died. 105

[*She reaches over and swings the broken door, swings it again, both women watch it.*]

MRS. HALE: You weren't raised round here, were you? [*MRS. PETERS shakes her head.*] You didn't know—her?

MRS. PETERS: Not till they brought her yesterday.

MRS. HALE: She—come to think of it, she was kind of like a bird herself—real sweet and pretty, but kind of timid and—fluttery. How—she—did—change. [*Silence; then as if struck by a happy thought and relieved to get back to everyday things.*] Tell you what, Mrs. Peters, why don't you take the quilt in with you? It might take up her mind.

MRS. PETERS: Why, I think that's a real nice idea, Mrs. Hale. There couldn't possibly be any objection to it, could there? Now, just what would I take? I wonder if her patches are in here—and her things.

[*They look in the sewing basket.*]

MRS. HALE: Here's some red. I expect this has got sewing things in it. [*Brings out a fancy box.*] 110 What a pretty box. Looks like something somebody would give you. Maybe her scissors are in here. [*Opens box. Suddenly puts her hand to her nose.*] Why— [*MRS. PETERS bends nearer, then turns her face away.*] There's something wrapped up in this piece of silk.

MRS. PETERS: Why, this isn't her scissors.

MRS. HALE: [*Lifting the silk.*] Oh, Mrs. Peters—it's—

[*Mrs. Peters bends closer.*]

MRS. PETERS: It's the bird.

MRS. HALE: [*Jumping up.*] But, Mrs. Peters—look at it! Its neck! Look at its neck! It's all—other side to.

MRS. PETERS: Somebody—wrung—its—neck. 115

[*Their eyes meet. A look of growing comprehension, of horror. Steps are heard outside.* Mrs. Hale *slips box under quilt pieces, and sinks into her chair. Enter* Sheriff *and* County Attorney. Mrs. Peters *rises.*]

County Attorney: [*As one turning from serious things to little pleasantries.*] Well, ladies, have you decided whether she was going to quilt it or knot it?

Mrs. Peters: We think she was going to—knot it.

County Attorney: Well, that's interesting, I'm sure. [*Seeing the bird-cage.*] Has the bird flown?

Mrs. Hale: [*Putting more quilt pieces over the box.*] We think the—cat got it.

120   County Attorney: [*Preoccupied.*] Is there a cat?

[Mrs. Hale *glances in a quick covert way at* Mrs. Peters.]

Mrs. Peters: Well, not *now.* They're superstitious, you know. They leave.

County Attorney: [*To* Sheriff Peters, *continuing an interrupted conversation.*] No sign at all of anyone having come from the outside. Their own rope. Now let's go up again and go over it piece by piece. [*They start upstairs.*] It would have to have been someone who knew just the—

[Mrs. Peters *sits down. The two women sit there not looking at one another, but as if peering into something and at the same time holding back. When they talk now it is in the manner of feeling their way over strange ground, as if afraid of what they are saying, but as if they cannot help saying it.*]

Mrs. Hale: She liked the bird. She was going to bury it in that pretty box.

Mrs. Peters: [*In a whisper.*] When I was a girl—my kitten—there was a boy took a hatchet, and before my eyes—and before I could get there—[*Covers her face an instant.*] If they hadn't held me back I would have—[*Catches herself, looks upstairs where steps are heard, falters weakly.*]—hurt him.

125   Mrs. Hale: [*With a slow look around her.*] I wonder how it would seem never to have had any children around. [*Pause.*] No, Wright wouldn't like the bird—a thing that sang. She used to sing. He killed that, too.

Mrs. Peters: [*Moving uneasily.*] We don't know who killed the bird.

Mrs. Hale: I knew John Wright.

Mrs. Peters: It was an awful thing was done in this house that night, Mrs. Hale. Killing a man while he slept, slipping a rope around his neck that choked the life out of him.

Mrs. Hale: His neck. Choked the life out of him.

[*Her hand goes out and rests on the bird-cage.*]

130   Mrs. Peters: [*With rising voice.*] We don't know who killed him. We don't know.

Mrs. Hale: [*Her own feeling not interrupted.*] If there'd been years and years of nothing, then a bird to sing to you, it would be awful—still, after the bird was still.

Mrs. Peters: [*Something within her speaking.*] I know what stillness is. When we homesteaded in Dakota, and my first baby died—after he was two years old, and me with no other then—

Mrs. Hale: [*Moving.*] How soon do you suppose they'll be through, looking for the evidence?

Mrs. Peters: I know what stillness is. [*Pulling herself back.*] The law has got to punish crime, Mrs. Hale.

135   Mrs. Hale: [*Not as if answering that.*] I *wish* you'd seen Minnie Foster when she wore a white dress with blue ribbons and stood up there in the choir and sang. [*A look around the room.*]

Oh, I wish I'd come over here once in a while! That was a crime! That was a crime! Who's going to punish that?

MRS. PETERS: [*Looking upstairs.*] We mustn't—take on.

MRS. HALE: I might have known she needed help! I know how things can be— for women. I tell you, it's queer, Mrs. Peters. We live close together and we live far apart. We all go through the same things—it's all just a different kind of the same thing. [*Brushes her eyes, noticing the bottle of fruit, reaches out for it.*] If I was you I wouldn't tell her her fruit was gone. Tell her it *ain't*. Tell her it's all right. Take this in to prove it to her. She—she may never know whether it was broke or not.

MRS. PETERS: [*Takes the bottle, looks about for something to wrap it in; takes petticoat from the clothes brought from the other room, very nervously begins winding this around the bottle. In a false voice.*] My, it's a good thing the men couldn't hear us. Wouldn't they just laugh! Getting all stirred up over a little thing like a—dead canary. As if that could have anything to do with—with—wouldn't they *laugh*!

[*The men are heard coming down stairs.*]

MRS. HALE: [*Under her breath.*] Maybe they would—maybe they wouldn't.

COUNTY ATTORNEY: No, Peters, it's all perfectly clear except a reason for doing it. But you know 140 juries when it comes to women. If there was some definite thing. Something to show— something to make a story about—a thing that would connect up with this strange way of doing it—

[*The women's eyes meet for an instant. Enter HALE from outer door.*]

HALE: Well, I've got the team° around. Pretty cold out there.

COUNTY ATTORNEY: I'm going to stay here a while by myself. [*To the SHERIFF.*] You can send Frank out for me, can't you? I want to go over everything. I'm not satisfied that we can't do better.

SHERIFF: Do you want to see what Mrs. Peters is going to take in?

[*The COUNTY ATTORNEY goes to the table, picks up the apron, laughs.*]

COUNTY ATTORNEY: Oh, I guess they're not very dangerous things the ladies have picked out. [*Moves a few things about, disturbing the quilt pieces which cover the box. Steps back.*] No, Mrs. Peters doesn't need supervising. For that matter, a sheriff's wife is married to the law. Ever think of it that way, Mrs. Peters?

MRS. PETERS: Not—just that way.                                                          145

SHERIFF: [*Chuckling.*] Married to the law. [*Moves toward the other room.*] I just want you to come in here a minute, George. We ought to take a look at these windows.

COUNTY ATTORNEY: [*Scoffingly.*] Oh, windows!

SHERIFF: We'll be right out, Mr. Hale.

[*HALE goes outside. The SHERIFF follows the COUNTY ATTORNEY into the other room. Then MRS. HALE rises, hands tight together, looking intensely at MRS. PETERS, whose eyes make a slow turn, finally meeting MRS. HALE's. A moment MRS. HALE holds her, then her own eyes point the way to where the box is concealed. Suddenly MRS. PETERS throws back quilt pieces and tries to put the box in the bag she is*

---

°141 *team*: team of horses drawing a wagon.

*wearing. It is too big. She opens box, starts to take bird out, cannot touch it, goes to pieces, stands there helpless. Sound of a knob turning in the other room. MRS. HALE snatches the box and puts it in the pocket of her big coat. Enter COUNTY ATTORNEY and SHERIFF.*]

COUNTY ATTORNEY: [*Facetiously.*] Well, Henry, at least we found out that she was not going to quilt it. She was going to—what is it you call it, ladies?

150 MRS. HALE: [*Her hand against her pocket.*] We call it—knot it, Mr. Henderson.

*CURTAIN*

## Questions

1. How does the first entrance of the characters establish a distinction between the men and women in the play? What is suggested by the different reactions of the men and women to the frozen preserves?

2. What does Mr. Hale report to the County Attorney in his extended narrative? How observant is he? How accurate?

3. What is needed for a strong legal case against Minnie? What does the Sheriff conclude about the kitchen? What do his conclusions tell you about the men?

4. What are the women's conclusions about the bad sewing? What does Mrs. Hale do about it? At this point, what might she be thinking about the murder?

5. Of what importance are Mrs. Hale's descriptions (a) of Minnie as a young woman and (b) of the Wrights' marriage?

6. What do the women deduce from the broken birdcage and the dead bird? How are these symbolic, and what do they symbolize?

7. How did Minnie Wright murder her husband? What hints lead you to this solution? What information permits the women to make the right inferences about the crime and the method of strangulation?

8. What does Mrs. Hale do with the "trifles" of evidence? Why? How is her reaction to the evidence different from that of Mrs. Peters? What conflict develops between these women? How is it resolved?

9. Why does Mrs. Hale feel guilty about her relationship with Minnie Wright? To what degree does her guilt shape her decisions and actions?

## General Questions

1. To what does the title of this play refer? How does this irony of the word trifles help shape the play's meaning?

2. What are the men like? Are they round characters or flat? How observant are they? What is their attitude toward their jobs? Toward their own importance? Toward the women and "kitchen things"?

3. What is Mrs. Hale like? How observant is she? What is her attitude toward the men and their work, and toward herself?

4. Some critics argue that Minnie is the play's most important character, even though she never appears onstage. Do you agree? Why do you think Glaspell did not make Minnie a speaking character?

**5.** How is symbolism employed to establish and underscore the play's meaning? Consider especially the birdcage, the dead bird, and the repeated assertion that Mrs. Wright was going to "knot" (tie) rather than "quilt" (sew) the quilt.

## BETTY KELLER (b. 1930)

Betty Keller, a Canadian, has brought a wide variety of experience to her work for the theater, including such unlikely jobs as insurance adjuster, farmer, photographer's assistant, and prison matron. She served as a teacher for many theatrical workshops in Vancouver, including four years with *Playhouse Holiday*. She taught drama and theater at the Windsor Secondary School in North Vancouver until 1974, the year she published *Improvisations in Creative Drama,* the collection of short plays and sketches from which *Tea Party* is selected. She also taught at Simon Fraser University and the University of British Columbia. She was the founder/producer of the western Canadian writers festival and workshop program *The Festival of the Written Arts* from 1983 to 1994. In addition to her work in drama, she has written biographical and historical works, including *Pauline: A Biography of Pauline Johnson* (1982); *Black Wolf: The Life of Ernest Thompson Seton* (1984); *On the Shady Side: Vancouver 1886–1914* (1986); *Sea Silver: Inside British Columbia's Salmon Farming Industry* (1996); *Bright Seas and Pioneer Spirits: The Sunshine Coast* (1996). *Better the Devil You Know* (2001); and *A Stain upon the Sea: West Coast Salmon Farming* (2004).

Brief as *Tea Party* is, it illustrates the power of drama to depict character and situation and to convey emotion. The main characters are two lonely elderly sisters who have outlived their friends and relatives and have no one except the people who occasionally come to their house to perform various services, such as delivering the paper and reading the meters. The sketch presents their plight deftly and succinctly, touching with great tenderness on the pathos of their loneliness.

*Tea Party* is too short to present difficult choices for the characters, and hence they hardly get the opportunity to go through the responses and changes that are found in full-length plays. Both Alma and Hester are individualized, however, as they carry on a minor controversy about names and dates from their long-vanished past. Beyond this, in Alma's last speech, which ends the dramatic sketch, one might find a hint of the awareness and recognition that we expect of round, developed characters. Even though the paperboy is not a speaking part, his unkindness to the sisters is shown clearly, and in this way Keller dramatizes the poignant situation of persons whom life has passed by. It is difficult to find a play that conveys so much of life and feeling in so short a span of time and action.

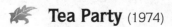 ## Tea Party (1974)

### CHARACTERS

**Alma Evans:** *seventy-five years old, small and spare framed. Her clothing is simple but not outdated, her grey hair cut short and neat. She walks with the aid of a cane, although she would not be classed as a cripple.*

**Hester Evans:** *seventy-nine years old. There is little to distinguish her physically from her sister, except perhaps a face a little more pinched and pain-worn. She sits in a wheelchair; but although her legs may be crippled, her mind certainly is not.*

**The Boy:** *in his early teens, seen only fleetingly.*

SCENE: *The sitting room of the Evans sisters' home. The door to the street is on the rear wall Upstage Left,° a large window faces the street Upstage Center. On the right wall is the door to the kitchen; on the left, a door to the remainder of the house. Downstage Left is an easy chair, Upstage Right a sofa, Downstage Right a tea trolley. The room is crowded with the knickknacks gathered by its inhabitants in three-quarters of a century of living.*

[*At rise,* ALMA *is positioning* HESTER'S *wheelchair Upstage Left.* ALMA'S *cane is on* HESTER'S *lap.*]

HESTER: That's it.

[ALMA *takes her cane from* HESTER. *They both survey the room.*]

ALMA: I think I'll sit on the sofa . . . at the far end.
HESTER: Yes. That will be cosy. Then he can sit on this end between us.

[ALMA *sits on the Downstage Right end of the sofa. They both study the effect.*]

ALMA: But then he's too close to the door, Hester!

[HESTER *nods, absorbed in the problem.*]

5    ALMA: [*Moving to the Upstage Left end of sofa.*] Then I'd better sit here.
HESTER: But now he's too far away from me, Alma.

[*Alma stands; both of them study the room again.*]

ALMA: But if I push the tea trolley in front of you, he'll have to come to you, won't he?
HESTER: Oh, all right, Alma. You're sure it's today?
ALMA: [*Pushing the tea trolley laden with cups and napkins, etc. to Hester.*] The first Thursday of the month.
10   HESTER: You haven't forgotten the chocolate biscuits?°
ALMA: No dear, they're on the plate. I'll bring them in with the tea. [*Goes to the window, peering up the street to the Right.*]
HESTER: And cocoa?
ALMA: I remembered.
HESTER: You didn't remember for Charlie's visit.
15   ALMA: Charlie drinks tea, Hester. I didn't make cocoa for him because he drinks tea.
HESTER: Oh, He didn't stay last time anyway.
ALMA: It was a busy day. . . .
HESTER: Rushing in and out like that. I was going to tell him about father and the *Bainbridge* . . . and he didn't stay.

---

°*Upstage Left*: To visualize stage locations, assume that the stage directions are described from the viewpoint of an actor facing the audience. Thus "Right" is actually to the left of the audience, and "Left" is right. "Downstage" refers to the front of the stage, whereas "Upstage" is the back. The terms down and up were established at a time when stages were tilted toward the audience, so that spectators at floor level could have as complete a view as possible of the entire stage.  10 *chocolate biscuits*: chocolate cookies.

Alma (standing) and Hester (in the wheelchair) discuss what they will do if their newsboy comes in for some tea in Keller's *Tea Party*. The actors are Fran Burnside and Sandie McGinnis in the production by the Driftwood Players in February 1987.

ALMA: What about the *Bainbridge*?

HESTER: Her maiden voyage out of Liverpool . . . when father was gone three months and we    20
thought he'd gone down with her.

ALMA: That wasn't the *Bainbridge*.

HESTER: Yes, it was. It was the *Bainbridge*. I remember standing on the dock in the snow when
she finally came in. That was the year I'd begun first form, and I could spell out the letters
on her side.

ALMA: It was her sister ship, the *Heddingham*.

HESTER: The *Bainbridge*. You were too young to remember. Let's see, the year was . . .

ALMA: Mother often told the story. It was the *Heddingham* and her engine broke down off Cape    25
Wrath beyond the Hebrides.

HESTER: It was 1902 and you were just four years old.

ALMA: The *Heddingham*, and she limped into port on January the fifth.

HESTER: January the fourth just after nine in the morning, and we stood in the snow and
watched the *Bainbridge* nudge the pier, and I cried and the tears froze on my cheeks.

ALMA: The *Heddingham.*

30 HESTER: Alma, mother didn't cry, you know. I don't think she ever cried. My memory of names and places is sharp so that I don't confuse them as some others I could mention, but sometimes I can't remember things like how people reacted. But I remember that day. There were tears frozen on my cheeks but mother didn't cry.

ALMA: [*Nodding.*] She said he didn't offer a word of explanation. Just marched home beside her.

HESTER: [*Smiling.*] He never did say much. . . . Is he coming yet?

ALMA: No, can't be much longer though. Almost half past four.

HESTER: Perhaps you'd better bring in the tea. Then it will seem natural.

35 ALMA: Yes dear, I know. [*Exits out door Upstage Right.*] Everything's ready.

HESTER: What will you talk about?

ALMA: [*Re-entering with the teapot.*] I thought perhaps . . . [*Carefully putting down the teapot.*] . . . perhaps brother George!

HESTER: And the torpedo? No, Alma, he's not old enough for that story!

ALMA: He's old enough to know about courage. I thought I'd show him the medal, too. [*She goes to the window, peers both ways worriedly, then carries on towards the kitchen.*]

40 HESTER: Not yet? He's late to-night. You're sure it's today?

ALMA: He'll come. It's the first Thursday. [*Exit.*]

HESTER: You have his money?

ALMA: [*Returning with the plate of biscuits.*] I've got a twenty dollar bill, Hester.

HESTER: Alma!

45 ALMA: Well, we haven't used that one on him. It was Dennis, the last one, who always had change. We could get two visits this way, Hester.

HESTER: Maybe Dennis warned him to carry change for a twenty.

ALMA: It seemed worth a try. [*Goes to the window again.*] Are you going to tell him about the *Heddingham?*

HESTER: The *Bainbridge.* Maybe . . . or maybe I'll tell him about the day the Great War ended. Remember, Alma, all the noise, the paper streamers . . .

ALMA: And father sitting silent in his chair.

50 HESTER: It wasn't the same for him with George gone. Is he coming yet?

ALMA: No dear, maybe he's stopped to talk somewhere. [*Looking to the right.*] . . . No . . . no, there he is, on the Davis' porch now!

HESTER: I'll pour then. You get the cocoa, Alma.

ALMA: [*Going out.*] It's all ready, I just have to add hot water.

HESTER: Don't forget the marshmallows!

55 ALMA: [*Reappearing.*] Oh, Hester, what if he comes in and just sits down closest to the door? He'll never stay!

HESTER: You'll have to prod him along. For goodness sakes, Alma, get his cocoa!

[*Alma disappears.*]

HESTER: He must be nearly here. He doesn't go to the Leschynskis, and the Blackburns don't get home till after six.

ALMA: [*Returning with the cocoa.*] Here we are! Just in . . .

[*The Boy passes the window. There is a slapping sound as the newspaper lands on the porch.*]
[*Alma and Hester look at the door and wait, hoping to hear a knock, but they both know the truth. Finally, Alma goes to the door, opens it and looks down at the newspaper.*]

ALMA: He's gone on by.

60 HESTER: You must have had the day wrong.

ALMA: No, he collected at the Davis'.

HESTER: [*After a long pause.*] He couldn't have forgotten us.

ALMA: [*Still holding the cocoa, she turns from the door.*] He's collecting at the Kerighan's now. [*She closes the door and stands forlornly.*]

HESTER: Well, don't stand there with that cocoa! You look silly. [*Alma brings the cocoa to the tea trolley.*] Here's your tea. [*Alma takes the cup, sits on the Upstage Left end of the sofa. There is a long silence.*]

HESTER: I think I'll save that story for the meter man. 65

ALMA: The *Heddingham*?

HESTER: The *Bainbridge*.

ALMA: [*After a pause.*] They don't read the meters for two more weeks.

*Slow Blackout*

## Questions

1. What is the play's major conflict? The minor conflict?

2. Why do the two sisters discuss their seating arrangements for the paperboy? How do we learn that they have made these arrangements before?

3. What does Alma's plan for the twenty-dollar bill show about her? What does the discussion about both the money and the paperboys indicate about their own self-awareness?

4. How does controversy about the names *Bainbridge* and *Heddingham* help you understand the two sisters?

## General Questions

1. How does Keller's description of the sets aid you in understanding the action? The normal tasks of the women? From the setting of this play, what are your conclusions about the relationship of objects and spatial arrangements to the action and development of drama?

2. Consider the women, particularly with regard to their age. In the light of their health and their isolation, how does *Tea Party* present the circumstances of the aged? How can the play be constructed as a sociological/political argument, with the elderly as the focus?

## EUGENE O'NEILL (1888–1953)

Eugene O'Neill is one of America's great playwrights. He wrote more than forty plays and won three Pulitzer Prizes. He is still the only U.S. dramatist to have received the Nobel Prize for literature (1936).

O'Neill was born in New York, the son of a well-known actor, and was educated sporadically as his parents traveled from city to city on theatrical tours. Eventually he studied at Princeton, but he left to go to work, first in a mail-order house and then in Honduras, where he engaged in prospecting. He then began a brief career as a seaman, traveling on both sides of the Atlantic. He contracted tuberculosis in about 1912, and while in a sanitarium he began to write plays. Upon release he studied playwriting at Harvard, but by 1916 he had left to try his luck as a playwright with the Provincetown Players, the same company that Susan Glaspell had helped found and where she began her writing career. It was in 1916, the same year that Glaspell wrote *Trifles,* that the Provincetown Players produced O'Neill's first drama, *Bound East for Cardiff.*

O'Neill maintained a close connection with the Provincetown Players for several years, providing them with ten one-act plays between 1916 and 1920. Among these were *Thirst* (1916), *Before Breakfast* (1916), *Fog* (1917), *The Long Voyage Home* (1917), *Ile* (1917), and *The Rope* (1917). His later (and longer) works include *The Emperor Jones* (1920), *Anna Christie* (1921), *Desire Under the Elms* (1924), *Strange Interlude* (1928), *Mourning Becomes Electra* (1931), and *The Iceman Cometh* (1946). O'Neill also wrote an autobiographical play, *Long Day's Journey into Night* (1936), that at his request was withheld until after his death. Staged on Broadway in 1956, it received the Pulitzer Prize in drama (O'Neill's third Pulitzer); it was later made into a film starring Katherine Hepburn.

*Before Breakfast,* though one of O'Neill's earliest plays, shows his characteristic control of point of view, conflict, character, and setting. The play was first staged in December 1916 by the Provincetown Players in New York City's Greenwich Village (where Christopher Street, the address of the Rowlands' apartment, is located). The play contains little action, and yet it is charged with conflict. The plot is simple and straightforward—a wife onstage berates her offstage husband for twenty minutes. The conflict between them is long-standing and bitter, and it is resolved in the play's horrifying conclusion.

Above all, *Before Breakfast* illustrates O'Neill's skillful control over the dramatic point of view. By giving Mrs. Rowland every word spoken on the stage, O'Neill causes the audience to understand everything as it is filtered through her mind. Indeed, the play is a bravura piece for a gifted actress. Because Mrs. Rowland dominates the stage so completely, it is tempting to see her character as one of constantly nagging spitefulness. It is to O'Neill's credit, however, that she is not without basic strength, and that her bitterness is not without cause. Alfred, the unseen and unheard offstage husband, has contributed to their estranged relationship.

Of particular note in indicating the impasse that the characters have reached are O'Neill's extensive stage directions describing the setting. We learn that the Rowlands' flat is in Greenwich Village, the traditional New York home of artists, poets, and actors. On the one hand, therefore, the flat suggests Alfred's artistic aspirations, but on the other, the poverty of the surroundings indicates the sad truth that such dreams cannot be sustained unless someone pays the rent.

The language of Mrs. Rowland, the only speaking character in the play, indicates both her lack of education and her intense dissatisfaction. Phrases such as "I got," "like I was," "liable" for "likely," and "sewing my fingers off" suggest that her knowledge of language has not been derived from education and study. Her speech also suggests the social gulf that originally separated her from Alfred, a gulf that they tried to bridge in their marriage but which now has opened up irretrievably. A number of other phrases embody the taunts that Mrs. Rowland directs at Alfred ("pawn, pawn, pawn," "like a man," "a fine life," "in trouble," etc.).

# Before Breakfast (1916)

## CHARACTERS

**Mrs. Rowland,** the wife

**Mr. Alfred Rowland,** the husband

SCENE. *A small room serving both as kitchen and dining room in a flat on Christopher Street,* 0.1
*New York City. In the rear, to the right, a door leading to the outer hallway. On the left of the*
*doorway, a sink, and a two-burner gas stove. Over the stove, and extending to the left wall, a*
*wooden closet for dishes, etc. On the left, two windows looking out on a fire escape where several*
*potted plants are dying of neglect. Before the windows, a table covered with oilcloth. Two cane-*
*bottomed chairs are placed by the table. Another stands against the wall to the right of door in*
*rear. In the right wall, rear, a doorway leading into a bedroom. Farther forward, different articles*
*of a man's and a woman's clothing are hung on pegs. A clothes line is strung from the left corner,*
*rear, to the right wall, forward.*

*It is about eight thirty in the morning of a fine, sunshiny day in the early fall.* 0.2

MRS. ROWLAND *enters from the bedroom, yawning, her hands still busy putting the finishing* 0.3
*touches on a slovenly toilet by sticking hairpins into her hair which is bunched up in a drab-colored*
*mass on top of her round head. She is of medium height and inclined to a shapeless stoutness, accen-*
*tuated by her formless blue dress, shabby and worn. Her face is characterless, with small regular fea-*
*tures and eyes of a nondescript blue. There is a pinched expression about her eyes and nose and her*
*weak, spiteful mouth. She is in her early twenties but looks much older.*

*She comes to the middle of the room and yawns, stretching her arms to their full length. Her* 0.4
*drowsy eyes stare about the room with the irritated look of one to whom a long sleep has not been a*
*long rest. She goes wearily to the clothes hanging on the right and takes an apron from a hook. She*
*ties it about her waist, giving vent to an exasperated "damn" when the knot fails to obey her clumsy*
*fingers. Finally gets it tied and goes slowly to the gas stove and lights one burner. She fills the coffee*
*pot at the sink and sets it over the flame. Then slumps down into a chair by the table and puts a hand*
*over her forehead as if she were suffering from headache. Suddenly her face brightens as though she*
*had remembered something, and she casts a quick glance at the dish closet; then looks sharply at the*
*bedroom door and listens intently for a moment or so.*

MRS. ROWLAND. [*In a low voice.*] Alfred! Alfred! [*There is no answer from the next room and she*
 *continues suspiciously in a louder tone.*] You needn't pretend you're asleep. [*There is no reply*
 *to this from the bedroom, and, reassured, she gets up from her chair and tiptoes cautiously to the*
 *dish closet. She slowly opens one door, taking great care to make no noise, and slides out, from their*
 *hiding place behind the dishes, a bottle of Gordon gin and a glass. In doing so she disturbs the top*
 *dish, which rattles a little. At this sound she starts guiltily and looks with sulky defiance at the*
 *doorway to the next room.*]

[*Her voice trembling.*] Alfred!

[*After a pause, during which she listens for any sound, she takes the glass and pours out a large drink*
*and gulps it down; then hastily returns the bottle and glass to their hiding place. She closes the closet*
*door with the same care as she had opened it, and, heaving a great sigh of relief, sinks down into her chair*
*again. The large dose of alcohol she has taken has an almost immediate effect. Her features become more*
*animated, she seems to gather energy, and she looks at the bedroom door with a hard, vindictive smile on*
*her lips. Her eyes glance quickly about the room and are fixed on a man's coat and vest which hang from*
*a hook at right. She moves stealthily over to the open doorway and stands there, out of sight of anyone*
*inside, listening for any movement.*]

Mrs. Rowland (Lona Leigh) attends to the coffee in the 2001 Provincetown, Playhouse, New York City, production of *Before Breakfast*, directed by Stephen Kennedy Murphy, lights by Matthew E. Adelson, and sets by Roger Hanna.

[*Calling in a half-whisper.*] Alfred!

[*Again there is no reply. With a swift movement she takes the coat and vest from the hook and returns with them to her chair. She sits down and takes the various articles out of each pocket but quickly puts them back again. At last, in the inside pocket of the vest, she finds a letter.*]

[*Looking at the handwriting—slowly to herself.*] Hmm! I knew it.

[*She opens the letter and reads it. At first her expression is one of hatred and rage, but as she goes on to the end it changes to one of triumphant malignity. She remains in deep thought for a moment, staring before her, the letter in her hands, a cruel smile on her lips. Then she puts the letter back in the pocket of the vest, and still careful not to awaken the sleeper, hangs the clothes up again on the same hook, and goes to the bedroom door and looks in.*]

5    [*In a loud, shrill voice.*] Alfred! [*Still louder.*] Alfred! [*There is a muffled, yawning groan from the next room.*] Don't you think it's about time you got up? Do you want to stay in bed all day? [*Turning around and coming back to her chair.*] Not that I've got any doubts about your being lazy enough to stay in bed forever. [*She sits down and looks out of the window, irritably.*] Goodness knows what time it is. We haven't even got any way of telling the time since you pawned your watch like a fool. The last valuable thing we had, and you knew it. It's been nothing but pawn, pawn, pawn, with you— anything to put off getting a job, anything to get out of going to work like a man.

[*She taps the floor with her foot nervously, biting her lips.*]

[*After a short pause.*] Alfred! Get up, do you hear me? I want to make that bed before I go out. I'm sick of having this place in a continual muss on your account. [*With a certain vindictive satisfaction.*] Not that we'll be here long unless you manage to get some money some place. Heaven knows I do my part—and more—going out to sew every day while you play the gentleman and loaf around bar rooms with that good-for-nothing lot of artists from the Square.°

6 *Square:* Washington Square, at the center of Greenwich Village in New York.

[*A short pause during which she plays nervously with a cup and saucer on the table.*]

And where are you going to get money, I'd like to know? The rent's due this week and you know what the landlord is. He won't let us stay a minute over our time. You say you *can't* get a job. That's a lie and you know it. You never even look for one. All you do is moon around all day writing silly poetry and stories that no one will buy—and no wonder they won't. I notice I can always get a position, such as it is; and it's only that which keeps us from starving to death.

[*Gets up and goes over to the stove—looks into the coffee pot to see if the water is boiling; then comes back and sits down again.*]

You'll have to get money to-day some place. I can't do it all, and I won't do it all. You've got to come to your senses. You've got to beg, borrow, or steal it somewheres. [*With a contemptuous laugh.*] But where, I'd like to know? You're too proud to beg, and you've borrowed the limit, and you haven't the nerve to steal.

[*After a pause—getting up angrily.*] Aren't you up yet, for heaven's sake? It's just like you to go to sleep again, or pretend to. [*She goes to the bedroom door and looks in.*] Oh, you are up. Well, it's about time. You needn't look at me like that. Your airs don't fool me a bit any more. I know you too well—better than you think I do—you and your goings-on. [*Turning away from the door—meaningly.*] I know a lot of things, my dear. Never mind what I know, now. I'll tell you before I go, you needn't worry. [*She comes to the middle of the room and stands there, frowning.*]

[*Irritably.*] Hmm! I suppose I might as well get breakfast ready—not that there's anything much to get. [*Questioningly.*] Unless you have some money? [*She pauses for an answer from the next room which does not come.*] Foolish question! [*She gives a short, hard laugh.*] I ought to know you better than that by this time. When you left here in such a huff last night I knew what would happen. You can't be trusted for a second. A nice condition you came home in! The fight we had was only an excuse for you to make a beast of yourself. What was the use pawning your watch if all you wanted with the money was to waste it in buying drink? 10

[*Goes over to the dish closet and takes out plates, cups, etc., while she is talking.*]

Hurry up! It don't take long to get breakfast these days, thanks to you. All we got this morning is bread and butter and coffee; and you wouldn't even have that if it wasn't for me sewing my fingers off. [*She slams the loaf of bread on the table with a bang.*]

The bread's stale. I hope you'll like it. *You* don't deserve any better, but I don't see why *I* should suffer.

[*Going over to the stove.*] The coffee'll be ready in a minute, and you needn't expect me to wait for you.

[*Suddenly with great anger.*] What on earth are you doing all this time? [*She goes over to the door and looks in.*] Well, you're *almost* dressed at any rate. I expected to find you back in bed. That'd be just like you. How awful you look this morning! For heaven's sake, shave! You're disgusting! You look like a tramp. No wonder no one will give you a job. I don't blame them—when you don't even look halfway decent. [*She goes to the stove.*] There's plenty of hot water right here. You've got no excuse. [*Gets a bowl and pours some of the water from the coffee pot into it.*] Here.

[*He reaches his hand into the room for it. It is a sensitive hand with slender fingers. It trembles and some of the water spills on the floor.*]

[*Tauntingly.*] Look at your hand tremble! You'd better give up drinking. You can't stand it. It's just your kind that get the D.T.'s. *That would be* the last straw! [*Looking down at the floor.*] 15 Look at the mess you've made of this floor—cigarette butts and ashes all over the place. Why can't you put them on a plate? No, you wouldn't be considerate enough to do that. You never think of me. You don't have to sweep the room and that's all you care about.

[*Takes the broom and commences to sweep viciously, raising a cloud of dust. From the inner room comes the sound of a razor being stropped.*]°

[*Sweeping.*] Hurry up! It must be nearly time for me to go. If I'm late I'm liable to lose my position, and then I couldn't support you any longer. [*As an afterthought she adds sarcastically.*] And then you'd have to go to work or something dreadful like that. [*Sweeping under the table.*] What I want to know is whether you're going to look for a job to-day or not. You know your family won't help us any more. They've had enough of you, too. [*After a moment's silent sweeping.*] I'm about sick of all this life. I've a good notion to go home, if I wasn't too proud to let them know what a failure you've been—you, the millionaire Rowland's only son, the Harvard graduate, the poet, the catch of the town—Huh! [*With bitterness.*] There wouldn't be many of them now envy my catch if they knew the truth. What has our marriage been, I'd like to know? Even before your *millionaire* father died owing everyone in the world money, you certainly never wasted any of your time on your wife. I suppose you thought I'd ought to be glad you were *honorable* enough to marry me—after getting me into trouble. You were ashamed of me with your fine friends because my father's only a grocer, that's what you were. At least he's honest, which is more than any one could say about yours. [*She is sweeping steadily toward the door. Leans on her broom for a moment.*]

You hoped every one'd think you'd been forced to marry me, and pity you, didn't you? You didn't hesitate much about telling me you loved me, and making me believe your lies, before it happened, did you? You made me think you didn't want your father to buy me off as he tried to do. I know better now. I haven't lived with you all this time for nothing. [*Somberly.*] It's lucky the poor thing was born dead, after all. What a father you'd have been!

[*Is silent, brooding moodily for a moment—then she continues with a sort of savage joy.*]

But I'm not the only one who's got you to thank for being unhappy. There's one other, at least, and *she* can't hope to marry you now. [*She puts her head into the next room.*] How about Helen? [*She starts back from the doorway, half frightened.*]

Don't look at me that way! Yes, I read her letter. What about it? I got a right to. I'm your wife. And I know all there is to know, so don't lie. You needn't stare at me so. You can't bully me with your superior airs any longer. Only for me you'd be going without breakfast this very morning. [*She sets the broom back in the corner—whiningly.*] You never did have any gratitude for what I've done. [*She comes to the stove and puts the coffee into the pot.*] The coffee's ready. I'm not going to wait for you. [*She sits down in her chair again.*]

20 [*After a pause—puts her hand to her head—fretfully.*] My head aches so this morning. It's a shame I've got to go to work in a stuffy room all day in my condition. And I wouldn't if you were half a man. By rights I ought to be lying on my back instead of you. You know how sick I've been this last year; and yet you object when I take a little something to keep up my spirits. You even didn't want me to take that tonic I got at the drug store. [*With a hard laugh.*] I know you'd be glad to have me dead and out of your way; then you'd be free to run after all these silly girls that think you're such a wonderful, misunderstood person—this Helen and the others. [*There is a sharp exclamation of pain from the next room.*]

[*With satisfaction.*] There! I knew you'd cut yourself. It'll be a lesson to you. You know you oughtn't to be running around nights drinking with your nerves in such an awful shape. [*She goes to the door and looks in.*]

What makes you so pale? What are you staring at yourself in the mirror that way for? For goodness sake, wipe that blood off your face! [*With a shudder.*] It's horrible. [*In relieved tones.*] There, that's better. I never could stand the sight of blood. [*She shrinks back from the door a little.*] You better give up trying and go to a barber shop. Your hand shakes dreadfully. Why do you stare at me like

---

°15. *S.D. stropped:* alfred is using a leather strap to sharpen a straight razor, the kind barbers still use, with a very sharp steel blade that is hinged to a handle.

that? [*She turns away from the door.*] Are you still mad at me about that letter? [*Defiantly.*] Well, I had a right to read it. I'm your wife. [*She comes to the chair and sits down again. After a pause.*]

I knew all the time you were running around with someone. Your lame excuses about spending the time at the library didn't fool me. Who is this Helen, anyway? One of those artists? Or does she write poetry, too? Her letter sounds that way. I'll bet she told you your things were the best ever, and you believed her, like a fool. Is she young and pretty? I was young and pretty, too, when you fooled me with your fine, poetic talk; but life with you would soon wear anyone down. What I've been through!

[*Goes over and takes the coffee off the stove.*] Breakfast is ready. [*With a contemptuous glance.*] Breakfast! [*Pours out a cup of coffee for herself and puts the pot on the table.*] Your coffee'll be cold. What are you doing—still shaving, for heaven's sake? You'd better give it up. One of these mornings you'll give yourself a serious cut. [*She cuts off bread and butters it. During the following speeches she eats and sips her coffee.*]

I'll have to run as soon as I've finished eating. One of us has got to work. [*Angrily.*] Are 25 you going to look for a job to-day or aren't you? I should think some of your fine friends would help you, if they really think you're so much. But I guess they just like to hear you talk. [*Sits in silence for a moment.*]

I'm sorry for this Helen, whoever she is. Haven't you got any feelings for other people? What will her family say? I see she mentions them in her letter. What is she going to do—have the child—or go to one of those doctors? That's a nice thing, I must say. Where can she get the money? Is she rich? [*She waits for some answer to this volley of questions.*]

Hmm! You won't tell me anything about her, will you? Much I care. Come to think of it, I'm not so sorry for her after all. She knew what she was doing. She isn't any schoolgirl, like I was, from the looks of her letter. Does she know you're married? Of course, she must. All your friends know about your unhappy marriage. I know they pity you, but they don't know my side of it. They'd talk different if they did.

[*Too busy eating to go on for a second or so.*]

This Helen must be a fine one, if she knew you were married. What does she expect, then? That I'll divorce you and let her marry you? Does she think I'm crazy enough for that—after all you've made me go through? I guess not! And you can't get a divorce from me and you know it. No one can say *I've* ever done anything wrong. [*Drinks the last of her cup of coffee.*]

She deserves to suffer, that's all I can say. I'll tell you what I think; I think your Helen is no better than a common street-walker, that's what I think. [*There is a stifled groan of pain from the next room.*]

Did you cut yourself again? Serves you right. [*Gets up and takes off her apron.*] Well, I've got 30 to run along. [*Peevishly.*] This is a fine life for me to be leading! I won't stand for your loafing any longer. [*Something catches her ear and she pauses and listens intently.*] There! You've over-turned the water all over everything. Don't say you haven't. I can hear it dripping on the floor. [*A vague expression of fear comes over her face.*] Alfred! Why don't you answer me?

[*She moves slowly toward the room. There is the noise of a chair being overturned and something crashes heavily to the floor. She stands, trembling with fright.*]

Alfred! Alfred! Answer me! What is it you knocked over? Are you still drunk? [*Unable to stand the tension a second longer she rushes to the door of the bedroom.*]
Alfred!

[*She stands in the doorway looking down at the floor of the inner room, transfixed with horror. Then she shrieks wildly and runs to the other door, unlocks it and frenziedly pulls it open, and runs shrieking madly into the outer hallway.*]

[*The curtain falls.*]

## Questions

1. What does the setting tell you about the Rowlands?

2. How is Mrs. Rowland described in the opening stage directions? How does O'Neill use adjectives to shape your initial response to her? How does the rest of the play sustain or alter this image?

3. How does Mrs. Rowland speak to Alfred? What does she complain about? What does she accuse Alfred of being and doing?

4. What happened during Mrs. Rowland's premarital affair with Alfred? Why didn't she let Alfred's father "buy her off"?

5. Where is the play's crisis? Which character comes to a crisis? What leads you to conclude that the character and play have reached a crisis?

6. Mrs. Rowland precipitates the climax by discussing Alfred's affair. What do we learn about Helen? What pushes Alfred over the edge?

## General Questions

1. How does the setting define the characters, their relationship, and their life? What details of setting are most significant?

2. Is Mrs. Rowland flat or round? Static or dynamic? Individualized or stereotyped? Why does she have no first name?

3. Why is Alfred Rowland kept off stage (except for his hand) and given no dialogue? How does this affect the play?

4. Alfred is presented from his wife's point of view. How accurate is this portrait? To what degree does Alfred justify his wife's accusations?

5. Why does O'Neill present the history of Alfred's family and his relationship with Mrs. Rowland out of chronological order? What is the effect of this method of presentation?

## WRITING ABOUT THE ELEMENTS OF DRAMA

Although some aspects of drama, such as lighting and stage movement, are purely theatrical, drama shares a number of elements with fiction and poetry. The planning and the writing processes for essays about drama are therefore similar to those used for essays on the other genres. As you plan, select a play and an appropriate element or series of elements. It would be inappropriate, for example, to attempt an essay about character development in *Tea Party* (p. 903) because this play is too short to probe the two characters deeply.

Once you select the play, choose a focus, which will be your central idea. For example, you might argue that a character is flat, static, nonrealistic, or symbolic of good or evil. Or, to assert relationships among elements, you might claim that a play's meaning is shaped and emphasized through setting or through conflict.

## Topics for Discovering Ideas

PLOT, ACTION, CONFLICT. (See also Chapter 2.) In planning an essay on plot or structure, demonstrate how actions and conflicts unfold. In addition, link this concern to other dramatic elements, such as tone or theme. In general, this topic breaks down into three areas—conflict, plot, and structure. For conflict, determine what the conflicts are, which one is central, and how it is resolved. What kind of conflict is it? Does it suggest any general behavioral patterns? For plot, determine the separate stages of development. What is the climax? The dénouement? How are they anticipated or foreshadowed? In examining plot structures and patterns, determine whether the play has a subplot or second plot. If so, how is it related to the main plot? Is a significant pattern of action repeated? If so, what is the effect? To what extent do these parallel or repetitive patterns influence theme and meaning? How do they control your responses?

CHARACTERS. (See also Chapter 4.) Focus on a significant figure and formulate a central idea about his or her personality, function, or meaning. Is the character round or flat? Static or dynamic? Individualized or stereotyped? Realistic or nonrealistic? Symbolic? How is the character described in the stage directions? By other characters? By himself or herself? What does he or she do, think, say? What is the character's attitude toward the environment? The action? Other characters? Himself or herself? To what extent does he or she articulate and/or embody key ideas in the play?

POINT OF VIEW AND PERSPECTIVE. (See also Chapter 3.) In many plays, such as *Hamlet* (Chapter 21) and *Before Breakfast,* the playwright presents the action from the perspective of an individual character. The audience therefore sees things as this character sees the same things, influences them, and is influenced by them. When you deal with such a technique, consider how the perspective affects the play's structure and meaning. Why is this point of view useful or striking? What does it suggest about character? Theme? To what extent does your reaction to the play correspond with or diverge from this perspective?

Another feature of perspective is that characters may speak directly to the audience, in a *soliloquy,* or indirectly, in a *monologue.* In dealing with these perspectives, consider whether you sympathize with the character doing the speaking. What information does the character convey? What is he or she trying to prove? What is the tone of the speech? What do these devices contribute to your response? Generally, what does the perspective contribute to your understanding of the play?

SETTING, SETS, AND PROPS. (See also Chapter 5.) Normally, you will not write about setting and properties in isolation; such an essay would simply produce a detailed description of the setting(s) and objects. Instead, a discussion of setting in drama should be linked to another element, such as character, mood, or meaning. Such an essay will demonstrate the ways in which setting(s) and objects help establish the play's time, place, characters, lifestyle, values, or ideas.

When dealing with a single setting, pay close attention to the opening stage directions and any other directions or dialogue that describe the environment or objects. In plays with multiple settings, you will normally select one or two for examination. Ask yourself whether the setting is realistic or nonrealistic and to what extent it may be symbolic. What details and objects are specified? What do these tell you about the time, the place, and the characters and their way of life and values? To what extent does the setting contribute to the play's tone, atmosphere, impact, and meaning?

**DICTION, IMAGERY, AND STYLE.** (See also Chapters 7, 12, and 13.) As with setting, try to connect the devices of language to some other element such as tone, character, or meaning. Investigate the play's levels of diction and types of dialect, jargon, slang, or clichés. To what extent do these techniques define the characters and support or undercut their ideas? What connotative words or phrases are repeated? Which are spoken at particularly significant moments? What striking or consistent threads of imagery, metaphor, tone, or meaning do you find? How do all these aspects of language shape your reaction?

**TONE AND ATMOSPHERE.** (See also Chapters 7, 12, and 13.) Try to deal with *how* the tone is established and *what* impact it has on the play's meaning. Seek those devices the playwright employs to control your attitudes toward individual characters, situations, and outcomes. Look for clues in stage directions, diction, imagery, rhetorical devices, tempo, and context. Is tone articulated directly? Or indirectly, through irony? Also try to establish the presence of dramatic irony: To what extent do you (as a reader or spectator) know more than many of the onstage characters?

**SYMBOLISM AND ALLEGORY.** (See also Chapters 8 and 17.) Try to determine the characters, objects, settings, situations, actions, words or phrases, and/or costumes that seem to be symbolic. What do they symbolize, and how do you know that they are symbolic? Are they universal or contextual? Is the symbolism extensive and consistent enough to form an allegorical system? If so, what are the two levels of meaning addressed by the allegory? To what extent does the symbolism or allegory shape the play's meaning and your responses to it?

**THEME.** (See also Chapter 9.) The questions and areas of concern listed above should help you in discussing theme. Try to connect theme with various other aspects of the play such as character, conflict, action, setting, language, or symbolism. What key ideas does the play explore, and what aspects of the play convey these ideas most emphatically? In dealing with each topic and question, isolate the elements and devices that have the strongest impact on meaning.

## 🍃 REFERRING TO PLAYS AND PARTS OF PLAYS

*Italicize* or <u>underline</u> the titles of plays as you would do for book titles. In referring to speeches, assume that your reader may have a text different from yours. Therefore, provide the information necessary for finding the exact location, regardless of text.

**In the body of your essay**, for a play with act, scene, and line or speech numbers, refer to *Act* (Arabic numeral), *scene* (Arabic numeral), and *line* or *speech* number (Arabic numeral), separated by commas. For clarity, spell out these words: *Hamlet accuses his mother of offenses against his father in Act 3, scene 4, line 9,* or *Claudius defends his own status as king in Act 4, scene 5, lines 120–23.*

**In direct quotations**, including block quotations (set apart from your own writing), write the Arabic numbers in parentheses following the quotation, as in (*3.1.33*). Use periods to separate these numbers. When no word precedes the last number, this number is understood to refer to a line in a poetic play. If you are referring to speeches, however, it is best for you to make this fact clear. Thus, if you write "(*2.2.speech 38*)," you will leave no doubt in your reader's mind that you are referring to the second act, the second scene, and the thirty-eighth speech. The principle you should always follow is that your reference should leave no doubts in your reader's mind about what the numbers mean.

When a play is divided into acts but not scenes, or if the play contains only one act, spell out the details completely. Thus, in a play like *Death of a Salesman*, which contains two acts and an epilogue, you may refer to *Act 1, speech 348* or *Epilogue, speech 5*. If the play contains no act numbers but only numbered scenes, spell things out similarly: *scene 1, speech 29*. When referring to a one-act play like *Tea Party*, use the speech number; e.g., *speech 60, speech 22*.

**For stage directions**, use the line or speech number immediately preceding the direction, and abbreviate *stage direction* as *S.D.*, as in *scene 1, speech 16 S.D.* Your reader will then know that you are referring to the stage direction following speech 16 in scene 1. If there are stage directions at the opening of the play before the speeches begin (as in *Before Breakfast*), use a zero and then a decimal point followed by an Arabic numeral to refer to the paragraph of directions. Thus, *0.3 S.D.* refers to the third paragraph of directions at the play's beginning.

**For prefaces, scene directions, and casts of characters**. Not all of the plays have prefatory material, but if there is a preface, refer to it as though you are considering a stage direction, as in *Miller reminds us to be "aware of towering angular shapes" in the introductory remarks to Act 1 (0.2 S.D.).*

For scene directions at the beginning of acts or scenes, use the most specific style to make the circumstances clear: *The scene directions for Act 1 of Ibsen's* A Dollhouse *describe the comfortable home of the Helmer family*; or *In the section marked "The Setting" beginning Act 1 of* Mulatto, *Hughes states that Colonel Norwood's living room is "long outdated" (0.2 S.D.).*

For the cast of characters, the same principle applies. Spell out what you mean, such as the *cast of characters*, the *Characters* list, or the *Dramatis Personae*, as in "*In the 'Cast of Characters' list of* Mulatto, *Hughes indicates that Colonel Norwood is a 'commanding' person.*" The important thing about referring to parts of plays is that you be clear and exact. The guidance offered here will cover most situations, but complications and exceptions will occur. When they do, always ask your instructor what to do and what systems of reference to use.

## Strategies for Organizing Ideas

For an essay on drama, you might choose from a number of strategies. If you are writing about loneliness and frustration in Keller's *Tea Party*, for example, you might select a number of objects or occurrences as the launching point for your discussion. Some of these might be the tea trolley and the sofa, the bringing in of the cocoa, or the paperboy's rapid movement past the window. In discussing the crimes of Claudius in Shakespeare's *Hamlet*, you might choose (1) the testimony of the Ghost to Hamlet, (2) Claudius's reaction to the players' scene, (3) his speech as he is praying, and (4) his poisoning of the cup, showing how these actions convincingly establish his villainy. For such essays, you might devote separate paragraphs to each element, or you might use two or more paragraphs for each element as you develop your ideas further.

Similar strategies can be found for every possible type of essay on drama. In dealing with character in Keller's *Tea Party*, for example, you might claim that a number of symbolic props help to establish and reinforce the characters of the two aged sisters and their loneliness. You might then use separate paragraphs to discuss these related symbols, such as Hester's wheelchair, the arrangement of the furniture, the preparation for serving tea. Similarly, in writing about language in plays like Anton Chekhov's *The Bear* (Chapter 22), you would establish how the particular play connects qualities of speech to revelations about topics such as character and idea. Thus, Smirnov's constant use of exclamations, shouts, and profanity, at least until shortly before the play's end, establish his irascibility.

# Illustrative Student Essay

Underlined sentences in this paper *do not* conform to MLA style and are used solely as teaching tools to emphasize the central idea, thesis sentence, and topic sentences throughout the paper.

Cooper 1

Cameron Cooper

Professor Ortiz

English 129

6 April 2007

**Eugene O'Neill's Use of Negative Descriptions and Stage Directions**

**in Before Breakfast° as a Means of Revealing Character**

[1]        In the one-act play <u>Before Breakfast</u>, O'Neill dramatizes the suicidal crisis and

climax of a worsening husband-wife relationship. The story of the marriage is clear.

°See pp. 909–913 for this play.

Mrs. Rowland, when still a young girl, was naive and opportunistic. She seduced and then married Alfred Rowland, who she thought was the heir of his father's millions. Her resulting pregnancy ended in stillbirth. As if this were not enough, Alfred's father died not a millionaire, but a pauper. <u>During the years of these disappointments, Mrs. Rowland has lost whatever pleasantness she once possessed and has descended into a state of personal neglect, alcoholism, and selfishness.</u>[*] <u>To bring out these traits early in the play, O'Neill relies on negative descriptions and stage directions.</u>[†]

[2]        <u>The descriptions of Mrs. Rowland's personal neglect emphasize her loss of self-esteem.</u> The directions indicate that she has allowed her figure to become "a shapeless stoutness," and that she has piled her hair into a "drab-colored mass." This neglect of her physical person is capped off, according to O'Neill's description, by her blue dress, which is "shabby and worn" and "formless" (0.1 S.D.). Clearly, the shabbiness and excessive wear may result from poverty and thus show little about her character, but the formlessness of the dress indicates a characteristic lack of concern about appearance, also shown by her stoutness and her hair. This slovenliness shows how she wants to appear in public, because she is dressed and ready to go to work for the day. O'Neill's negative descriptions thus define her lack of self-respect.

[3]        <u>Similarly uncomplimentary, O'Neill's directions about her sneakiness reveal her dependence on alcohol.</u> A serious sign of distress, even though it might also be funny onstage, is the direction indicating that she takes out a bottle of gin that she keeps hidden in a "dish closet" (speech 1 S.D.). With this stage direction O'Neill symbolizes the weakest trait of the secret drinker, which he also shows in the direction that Mrs. Rowland brightens up once she has taken a stiff jolt of gin:

> The large dose of alcohol she has taken has an almost immediate effect. Her features become more animated, she seems to gather energy, and she looks at the bedroom with a hard, vindictive smile on her lips. (speech 1 S.D.)

It is safe to assume that these stage directions, on the morning of the play's action, would also have applied to her behavior on many previous mornings. In short, O'Neill is telling us that Mrs. Rowland is a secret alcoholic.

[4]        <u>The furtiveness of her drinking also shows up in her search of Alfred's clothing, which also shows her selfishness and bitterness.</u> When she methodically empties his

---

[*]Central idea.

[†]Thesis sentence.

Cooper 3

pockets and uncovers the letter that we soon learn is from his mistress, the stage directions show that she unhesitatingly reads the letter. Then O'Neill directs the actress to form "a cruel smile on her lips" as she thinks about what to do with this new information (speech 4 S.D.). As with the drinking, we see Mrs. Rowland rifling through Alfred's things only this once, but the action suggests that this secretive prying is a regular feature of her life. However, it is her discovery on <u>this</u> morning—before breakfast—that is the key to the action, because her extensive monologue against her husband, which constitutes most of the play, allows her to vent all her hatred by reproaching him about his lack of work, his neglect of her, the time he spends with friends, and his love affair.

[5]    <u>While O'Neill uses these stage directions and descriptions to convey</u> <u>Mrs. Rowland's unpleasantness, he provides balance in her speeches and additional</u> <u>actions.</u> He makes her a master of harangue, but there is nothing either in the directions or in her speeches to indicate that she wants to drive Alfred to suicide. Indeed, her horror at his suicide is genuine—just as it concludes the play with an incredible shock. In addition, on the positive side, her speeches show that despite her alcoholism and anger she is actually functioning in the outside world—as a seamstress—and that it is she who provides the meager money on which the couple is living (910, speech 6). In addition, she is working despite the fact that she has been feeling ill for a period of time (912, speech 20). She also has enough concern for Alfred to bring him hot water for shaving (911, speech 14 S.D.).

[6]    It is clear that O'Neill wants us to conclude that if Mrs. Rowland were a supportive person, Alfred might not be the nervous alcoholic who cuts his throat in the bathroom. However, the play does not make clear that he ever could have been better, even with the maximum support of a perfect wife. Certainly, Mrs. Rowland is not supportive. The stage directions and speeches show that she is limited by her weakness and bitterness. With such defects of character, she has unquestionably never given Alfred any support at all, and probably never could. <u>Everything that O'Neill tells us about her indicates that</u> <u>she is petty and selfish, and that she originally married Alfred expecting to receive and</u> <u>not to give.</u>

[7]    As things stand at the beginning of the play, then, Alfred is at the brink of despair, and Mrs. Rowland's bitter and reproachful speeches drive him to self destruction.

Cooper 4

Despite all the malice that O'Neill attributes to her character through the stage
descriptions and directions, however, it is not possible to say that she is the sole cause
of Alfred's suicide. <u>O'Neill shows that Mrs. Rowland is an unpleasant, spiteful, and
messy whiner, but it is not possible to reach any further conclusions</u>.

Cooper 5

**WORK CITED**

Eugene O'Neill, *Before Breakfast. Literature: An Introduction to Reading and Writing*. Ed. Edgar V.
Roberts. 4th Compact ed. Upper Saddle River: Prentice Hall, 2008, 909–913.

## Commentary on the Essay

This essay shows how dramatic conventions can be considered in reference to the
analysis of character. Although the essay refers briefly to Mrs. Rowland's speeches, it
stresses those descriptions and directions that O'Neill designs specifically for the actress performing the role. The essay thus indicates one way to discuss a play, as distinguished from a story or poem.

The introductory paragraph contains enough of the story about Mrs. Rowland
and her husband to help the reader make sense of the subsequent material about the
stage directions and descriptions. Throughout the essay, paragraph transitions are effected by words such as *similarly, also, while*, and *then*.

Paragraph 2, the first of the body, deals with O'Neill's stage directions concerning Mrs. Rowland's slovenly appearance and personal care. Paragraphs 3 and 4 are
concerned with directions about her behavior—first her drinking and then her
search of Alfred's clothing. Paragraph 5 briefly attempts to consider how O'Neill
uses Mrs. Rowland's speeches and other actions to balance the totally negative portrait he builds up through the negative stage directions.

Paragraphs 6 and 7 close the essay. Paragraph 6 considers how the stage directions lead no further than the conclusion that the Rowland's marriage is a terrible
one. Paragraph 7 continues the argument of paragraph 6, with the additional
thought that O'Neill's stage directions do not justify concluding that Mrs. Rowland's
spiteful character is the cause of her husband's suicide.

# Writing About the Elements of Drama

**1.** *Tea Party* might be considered sentimental, on the grounds that the two elderly
characters are presented to evoke sympathy and anguish, not to resemble the life
of real persons. Write an essay defending the play against this judgment, being

sure to make references to Keller's characterizations and her development of character.

2. *Before Breakfast* is set in an apartment in Greenwich Village in lower Manhattan around 1916. It was performed in Greenwich Village in December 1916. Write an essay that deals with the following questions.

   a. What do you make of this convergence of settings—artistic and realistic?
   b. What do you think O'Neill assumed about his original audience's reaction to the setting?

3. Write an essay on one of the following topics. Before you begin writing, you might read Chapter 24 for suggestions on how to proceed.

   a. The viewpoint of the men in *Trifles*.
   b. A feminist analysis of Mrs. Rowland in *Before Breakfast*.
   c. The two sisters as archetypal old people in *Tea Party*.
   d. The economic situation of the characters in *The Sandbox*.

5. On the basis of the plays included in this chapter, write an essay dealing with the characteristics of the dramatic form. Consider topics such as dialogue, monologue, soliloquy, action, vocal ranges, staging, comparative lengths of plays, pauses in speech, stage directions, laughter, seriousness, and the means by which the dramatists engage the audience in characters and situations.

6. Using the catalogue in your library, look up the category *Drama—Criticism* or *Drama—History and Criticism*, whichever title your library uses. You will find a number of categories, such as the relationship of drama to (a) elements, (b) history, (c) origin, (d) philosophy, (e) production, (f) religion, (g) stagecraft, and (h) themes. Develop a short bibliography on one of these topics and take out two or three of the relevant books. Describe them briefly, and explain—and criticize if possible—the principal ideas in one of the chapters.

# Chapter 21

# The Tragic Vision: Affirmation Through Loss

**Tragedy** is drama in which a major character undergoes a loss but also achieves illumination or a new perspective. It is considered the most elevated literary form because it concentrates affirmatively on the religious and cosmic implications of its major character's misfortunes. In ancient Greece, it originated as a key element in Athenian religious festivals during the decades before Athens became a major military, economic, and cultural power during the fifth century B.C.E.

Tragedy, however, was not religious in a sectarian sense. It did not dramatize religious doctrines and did not present a consistent religious view. To the Athenians, religion connected the past with the present and with the gods, and through this connection it served to enrich individuals, society, and the state.

Originally, tragedy in Athens was associated with the worship of one of the twelve principal gods—Dionysus—who, it was thought, transformed human personality, freed people from care and grief, ensured their fertility, and provided them with joy. To elevate this god in the eyes of his fellow Athenians, the Athenian tyrant Peisistratus (ruled 560–527 B.C.E.) added the worship of Dionysus to the regular religious festivals that the Athenians held in honor of their gods.[1]

## The Origins of Tragedy

From the standpoint of drama, the most significant of these Dionysian festivals were the Lenaia and the Great or City Dionysia. The **Lenaia** was a short celebration held in January (the Greek month *Gamelion*), and the **City Dionysia** (or Great Dionysia) was a weeklong event in March–April (*Elaphebolion*, the month of stags). In the sixth century

---

[1] Ancient religion is difficult for us to comprehend fully because of our completely different religious traditions and the passage of 2,500 years of history. In its origins, Greek religion was local in nature—a by-product of the geographic isolation of the various Greek city-states. Collective public worship of a single god within centrally located religious buildings—like the churches, temples, and mosques we know today—did not then exist. Instead, the Greeks believed in many gods with varying powers and interests who could travel invisibly and at will from place to place within their dominions. Consequently the Greeks erected many separate local shrines and sanctuaries for their gods, which were considered holy to particular gods and where people might place offerings and say prayers (see Acts, 17:24, for a reference to such shrines). Throughout the Greek world there were apparently more than 300 shrines dedicated to Asclepius, the God of Healing and Medicine, where worshipers could pray individually for their ailments to be cured. In important city-states like Athens and Corinth, large temples were dedicated to gods, such as Zeus, Athena, and Apollo, whom leading citizens especially revered. Even then, the temples were not designed for mass worship, but rather were considered resident sanctuaries for the gods themselves. Therefore, the major space in the temples was a holy-of-holies reserved only for the god. To make public this essentially private worship, the Greek city-states held religious festivals such as the Athenian celebrations of Dionysus and Athena.

B.C.E., ceremonies held during the festival of the City Dionysia began to include tragedy, although not in the form that has been transmitted to us. The philosopher and critic Aristotle (384–322 B.C.E.), writing almost two hundred years after these events, claimed that the first tragedies developed from a choral ode called a **dithyramb**—an ode or a song that was sung or chanted and also danced by large choruses of men at the festivals.[2] According to Aristotle, the first tragedies were choral improvisations originating with "the authors of the Dithyramb" (*Poetics* IV.12, p. 19).

## The Stories of Tragedy Were Drawn from Tales of Prehistoric Times

From Aristotle's claim, we can conclude that tragedy soon took on the characteristics and conventions that elevated it. For subject matter, writers turned to well-known stories, or myths, or legends, about the heroes and demigods of the prehistoric period between the vanished age of bronze and the living age of iron. These myths described individual adventures and achievements, including epic explorations and battles that had taken place principally during the time of the Trojan War. Like the stories that we know from the Bible, the Greek myths illustrated divine-human relationships and also served as examples or models of heroic behavior. With few exceptions, these myths became the fixed tragic subject matter. Indeed, Aristotle called them the "received legends" that by his time in the fourth century B.C.E. had become the "usual subjects of tragedy" (*Poetics* IX.8, p. 37).

The mythical heroes—many of whom were objects of cult worship—were kings, queens, princes, and princesses. They engaged in conflicts; they suffered; and, often, they died. Though great and noble, they were nevertheless human, and a common critical judgment is that they were dominated by **hubris** or **hybris** (arrogant pride, insolence, contemptuous violence), which was manifested in destructive actions such as deceit, subterfuge, lying, betrayal, revenge, cruelty, murder, suicide, patricide, infanticide, and self-mutilation. By truthfully demonstrating the faults of these heroes along with their greatness, the writers of tragedy also invoked philosophical and religious issues that provided meaning and value in the face of misfortune and suffering.

## The Word *Tragedy* Underwent an Elevation in Meaning

One of the genuine puzzles about tragedy is the word itself, which combines the Greek words *tragos* ("goat") and *oide* ("ode" or "song")—a "goat ode" or "goat song." This meaning raises the question of how so unlikely a word is linked to the tragic form. One often-repeated answer is that the word was first applied to choral ceremonials performed at the ritual sacrifice of a goat. Another is that the word described a choral competition in which a goat was the prize.

---

[2]S. H. Butcher, *Aristotle's Theory of Poetry and Fine Art*, 4th ed. (New York: Dover, 1951), p. 19 (VI.12). All parenthetical references to Aristotle are from this edition, but see also Stephen Halliwell, *The Poetics of Aristotle: Translation and Commentary* (Chapel Hill: U of North Carolina P, 1987). The origin of the word *dithyramb* is obscure. Some ancient etymologists claimed that the word was derived from the legendary "double birth" of Dionysus. This derivation is based on the idea that dithyramb is a compound (*dis*, "two," and *thyra*, "door") referring to the myth that Zeus removed Dionysus from the womb of his mother, Semele, and then placed the fetus within his thigh. When Zeus removed Dionysus, the god had "come through the door" of birth twice. This derivation, however, has been disputed. For a description of the origin of comedy during the festivals for Dionysus, see Chapter 22.

A more persuasive recent answer is that the word *tragedy* stemmed from the word *tragoidoi*, or "billy goat singers," which was applied pejoratively to the young men (*ephebes*) in the choruses.[3] The ephebes were military trainees between the ages of eighteen and twenty, and those trainees who were best at close-order drill were selected for their ability as chorus members to carry out precision dance movements. Because of their youth, however, they were still likened to young goats.[4] Indeed, tragedy was originally not called *tragodia* (tragedy) at all, but rather *tragoidoi*, as though the chorus members were more important than the speeches they recited. This explanation is consistent with the improvisatory origins of tragedy as explained by Aristotle. In the decades following its beginnings, the genre grew in importance, quality, and stature, and the word *tragedy* underwent the accompanying elevation that it still possesses.

## Tragedy Evolved from a Choral Form to a Dramatic Form

Because the surviving Athenian plays are dominated by acting parts, modern readers sometimes conclude that the chorus parts annoyingly interrupt the main action. It may be surprising to recognize that in the beginning there were no individual actors at all, only choruses. The introduction of actors—and their eventual domination—was one of the improvisations that Aristotle associates with the evolution of tragedy. We can surmise that during a festival performance of a now unknown choral ode, the chorus leader stepped forward to deliver lines introducing and linking the choral speeches. Because of this special function, the new speaker—called a **hypocrites** (hip-POCK-rih-tayss), which became the word for actor—was soon separated and distinguished from the chorus.

The next essential step was impersonation, or the assuming of a dramatic role. The *hypocrites* would represent a hero, and the chorus would represent groups such as townspeople, worshipers, youths, or elders. With the commencement of such role-playing, genuine drama had begun. According to tradition, the first *hypocrites* or actor—and therefore the acknowledged founder of the acting profession—was the writer and choral leader Thespis, in about 536–533 B.C.E., during the reign of Peisistratus.

---

### THE ORIGIN OF TRAGEDY IN BRIEF

In the sixth century B.C.E., tragedy originated in Athens at the time of the City Dionysia, one of the major religious festivals held to celebrate Dionysus, a liberating god and one of the 12 major gods of the city. As a genre, tragedy first featured improvisations on a type of choral ode called a *dithyramb*. It then evolved, as

---

[3]For this argument, see John J. Winkler, "The Ephebes' Song: *Tragodia* and *Polis*," in John J. Winkler and Froma I. Zeitlin, eds., *Nothing to Do with Dionysos? Athenian Drama in Its Social Context* (Princeton: Princeton UP, 1990), pp. 20–62. For a discussion of the military nature of the ancient Greek city-state, see Paul Rahe, "The Martial Republics of Classical Greece," *The Wilson Quarterly*, vol. 17, no. 1 (Winter 1993): 58–70.

[4]There is nothing unusual about this comparison. In English a common everyday word for a child is *kid*, which is the standard word (along with *kit*) for a young goat and also other young animals.

Aristotle says, "by slow degrees" (*Poetics* IV.12, p. 19), developing new elements as they seemed appropriate and necessary.

One of the vital new elements was an emphasis on the misfortune or death of a major character.* This emphasis resulted not from a preconceived theoretical design, however, but rather from the reality of suffering in the lives of the heroic subjects. As writers of tragedy developed the cosmic and religious implications of such adversity, performances offered philosophic, religious, moral, and civic benefits, and therefore, presumably, simply attending the performance of a tragedy came to be regarded as the fulfillment of a religious obligation.

Because tragedy was originally linked to the choral dithyrambs, it is important to stress that *tragedy began as a dramatic form for choruses, not for actors.* Even after actors became dominant in the plays, the chorus was important enough for Aristotle to state that "the chorus should be regarded as one of the actors" (XVIII.7, p. 69).

---

*Although the tragic protagonist often dies at the play's end, the extant Athenian tragedies do not follow this pattern rigidly. It is true that the major figures suffer, and sometimes they die, but often they escape punishment entirely, and they may even receive divine pardon.

# The Ancient Competitions in Tragedy

Once Thespis set the pattern of action involving actor and chorus, the writing of tragedies as a competition within the Dionysian festivals became institutionalized.

## The Tragic Dramatists Competed for the Honor of Having Their Plays Performed

Early each summer, a number of dramatists vied for the honor of having their plays performed at the next City Dionysia, to be held the following spring. They prepared three tragedies (a **trilogy**)[5] together with a **satyr** play (a boisterous burlesque) and submitted the four works to the Eponymous Archon, one of the city's two principal magistrates and the man for whom the year was named. The three best submissions were approved, or "given a chorus," for performance at the festival. On the last day of the festival, after the performances were over, the Archon awarded a prize to the tragic playwright voted best for that year. There was also a prize for the best writer of a comedy. The winner's prize was not money, but rather a crown of ivy and the glory of triumph.

---

[5]In the earliest dramas, the trilogies shared a common subject, as may be seen in the *Oresteia* of Aeschylus, which is a cycle of three plays on the subject of the royal house of Agamemnon. But by the time of Sophocles and Euripides, connected trilogies were no longer required. Sophocles' *Oedipus the King* and *Oedipus at Colonus*, for example, were submitted at widely different times.

## The Three Greatest Athenian Tragic Playwrights Were Aeschylus, Sophocles, and Euripides

To gain the honor of victory during the centuries of the competitions, many writers of tragedy composed and submitted many plays. The total number must have been exceedingly large, certainly in the high hundreds and likely in the thousands. Most of these have long since vanished because there were no more than a few copies of each play, all handwritten on perishable papyrus scrolls, and because there was no systematic and secure way of preserving the copies.

A small number of works by three tragic playwrights, however, have survived. These dramatists are **Aeschylus** (525–456 B.C.E.), who added a second actor; **Sophocles** (ca. 496–406/5 B.C.E.), who added a third actor, created scene design, and enlarged the chorus from 12 to 15; and **Euripides** (ca. 484–406 B.C.E.). Although these three playwrights did not win prizes every time they entered the competitions, a consensus grew that they were the best, and by the middle of the fourth century B.C.E., their works were recognized as classics. Although tragedies seem to have been originally intended for only one performance—at the festival for which they competed—an exception was made for these three dramatists, whose tragedies were then performed repeatedly both in Athens and elsewhere in the Greek-speaking world.

The combined output of the three classic playwrights was slightly more than three hundred plays, of which three-fourths were tragedies and one-fourth were satyr plays. As many as eight hundred years after the end of the fifth century B.C.E., these plays, together with many other Greek tragedies, satyr plays, and comedies, were available to readers who could afford to buy copies or to pay scribes to copy them.[6] However, with the increasing dominance of Christianity, the plays fell into neglect because they were considered pagan and also because vellum or parchment, which made up the pages of the books (*codexes* or *codices*) that replaced papyrus scrolls, was enormously expensive and was reserved for Christian works. Most of the unique and priceless copies of Athenian plays were subsequently forgotten, burned, or thrown out with the garbage.

## Thirty-Three Tragedies by the Three Great Athenian Tragedians Have Survived to the Present Day

The Greek dramatic tradition might have vanished entirely had it not been for the efforts of Byzantine scholars during the ninth century C.E., when Constantinople became the center of a revival of interest in classical Greek language and literature. A primary characteristic of this revival was the copying and preservation of important texts—including those of the major Greek writers. We may conclude that the scholars and scribes copied as many of the plays as they could locate, and that they tried to shelter their copies in the supposedly secure monastery libraries.

---

[6]In the third century B.C.E., a complete hand-copied set of Greek plays was apparently deposited in the Egyptian Royal Library that formed a part of the Ptolemaic museum and palace of Alexandria, but at some point all the holdings were lost, thrown away, or destroyed, just as the palace and museum were destroyed. In modern Alexandria, the location of the ancient library is not exactly known. Recent underwater explorations in the harbor of Alexandria may yet result, however, in increased knowledge about the location of the library. See Luciano Canfora, *The Vanished Library: A Wonder of the Ancient World* (Berkeley: U of California P, 1990).

However, security was impossible to maintain during those centuries. Fire, neglect, time, political destabilization, and pillage (such as the sack of Constantinople by Christian Crusaders in 1204) took an enormous toll on the Byzantine manuscript collections. Even so, seven tragedies by Aeschylus, seven by Sophocles, and ten by Euripides somehow were saved from destruction.[7] Additionally, in the fourteenth century, a scholar named Demetrius Triclinius made a lucky find of scrolls containing nine more plays by Euripides (part of what was once a complete set), bringing the total of Euripidean plays to 19. Therefore, of all the hundreds upon hundreds of plays written by all the Greek tragic playwrights, only 33 still survive intact. These plays make up the complete Greek tragedy as we know it.[8]

There is, however, just a little more: Many ancient writers often quoted brief passages from plays that were not otherwise preserved, and these portions therefore still exist. Moreover, many collectors living in the ancient world owned copies of the plays, and not everything from these collections was lost. In recent centuries, papyrus and vellum fragments—some quite extensive—have been recovered by archaeologists from such unlikely locations as ancient Egyptian rubbish dumps, tombs, and the linings of coffins.[9]

## Aristotle and the Nature of Tragedy

Because Aristotle's *Poetics* (*Peri Poietikes*), the first section of his major critical work, survives substantially intact from antiquity, he is in effect the Western world's first critic and aesthetician. From him, later critics derived the various "rules" of tragic composition. He also wrote a second part of the *Poetics* concerning comedy. This second work is lost, but enough fragments and summaries survive to permit a partial hypothetical reconstruction.[10] Aristotle also considered aspects of literature in parts of other philosophical works, principally the *Ethics* and the *Politics*. In addition he, along with his students, assembled a complete catalogue of Greek tragedy from its beginnings to his own time (the *Didaskaliae*). He was therefore able to base his

---

[7]Many standard reference works contain the assertion that these twenty-four plays were selected by an unnamed Byzantine schoolmaster for use in the Byzantine schools, and that this anthology was widely adopted and exclusively used thereafter. This claim would explain why the anthologized plays were preserved while unanthologized plays were lost. L. D. Reynolds and N. G. Wilson, in their authoritative *Scribes and Scholars: A Guide to the Transmission of Greek and Latin Literature*, 3rd ed. (Oxford UP, 1991), question this hypothesis. They point out that there is no historical record that such an anthology was ever made, that modern scholars are in truth ignorant "of the origin of the selection," and that therefore "it is perhaps best to abandon the idea that a conscious act of selection by an individual was a primary factor in determining the survival of texts" (p. 54).

[8]The survival of Greek drama was under constant threat until the first printed editions were published at the beginning of the sixteenth century.

[9]There are some interesting leads that may yet yield additional copies of ancient texts. The finds from the excavations at Oxyrrhynchus, in Egypt, have been deposited in boxes stored at the University of Oxford. Because they have been considered unreadable, they have lain neglected for more than a hundred years. The recent use of special ultraviolet light, however, has now made it possible for the first time to read and record the texts of the documents. It is possible that copies of ancient plays may be among the finds. In addition, a private library at the Villa of the Papyri in Herculaneum, in Italy, has been unrecoverable ever since 79 B.C.E., when it was buried beneath the pyroclastic flow from Vesuvius during the disastrous eruption that covered Pompeii and Herculaneum. Recent efforts have suggested that diligent archaeological work might yet produce copies of ancient manuscripts, possibly including copies of Greek plays. All this is yet for the future.

[10]See Richard Janko, trans., *Aristotle, Poetics I with the Tractatus Coislinianus, A Hypothetical Reconstruction of Poetics II, the Fragments of the On Poets* (Indianapolis: Hackett, 1987), pp. 47–55.

criticism on virtually the entire body of Greek tragedy, including written copies of many plays, since lost, that he had probably never seen performed. No one before or after Aristotle has had more firsthand knowledge of Greek tragedy. His criticism is therefore especially valuable because it rests not only on his acute powers of observation, but also on his unique and encyclopedic knowledge.

As we have seen, Aristotle states that tragedy grew out of improvisations related to dithyrambic choral odes. He adds that once tragedy reached its "natural" or ideal form it stopped evolving (*Poetics* IV.12, p. 19). His observations are designed to explain the ideal characteristics of tragedy. Throughout the *Poetics* he stresses concepts of exactitude, proportion, appropriateness, and control. His famous definition of tragedy is in accord with these concepts. In the sixth chapter of the *Poetics*, he states that tragedy is "an imitation of an action that is serious, complete, and of a certain magnitude; in language embellished with each kind of artistic ornament, the several kinds being found in separate parts of the play; in the form of action, not of narrative; through pity and fear effecting the proper purgation of these emotions" (VI.2, p. 23).

## To Aristotle, the Key to Tragedy Is the Concept of Catharsis

The last part of this definition—that purgation or **catharsis** is the end or goal of tragedy—crystallizes the earlier parts. In Aristotle's view, tragedy arouses the powerful emotions of pity and fear (*eleos* and *phobos*), and, through the experience of the drama, brings about a "proper purgation" or purification of these emotions. Originally, the word *catharsis* was a medical term, and therefore many interpreters argue that tragedy produces a therapeutic effect through an actual purging or "vomiting" of emotions—a sympathetic release of feelings that produces emotional relief and encourages psychological health. In other words, tragedy heals.

A complementary and compelling view is that tragic catharsis has a larger public and moral purpose. In this sense, Aristotle's description of tragedy is an implicit argument defending literature itself against the strong disapproval of his teacher, Plato.[11] Both master and pupil accepted the premise that human beings behave thoughtlessly and stupidly as a result of uncontrolled emotion. While in the grip of deep feelings, people cannot be virtuous and can do no good for others because they make bad decisions that produce bad personal, social, political, military, and moral results. Consequently, if individual temperance and public justice are to prevail, there is a universal need to moderate and regulate the emotions. Because Plato states that the emotionalism of literature is untrue, undignified, and unreasonable, he denies that literature can address this need.

But in the *Poetics* and in relevant parts of other works, Aristotle asserts that tragedy does indeed address the need, and does so through the process of catharsis. By arousing our dominant feelings of pity and fear, tragedy trains our emotions and *habituates* us to measure, shape, channel, and control our passions. Through catharsis, we develop a condition of poise and balance among emotional forces, and we achieve this balanced state harmlessly because the artistic context of tragedy gives us immunity from the personal damage that our deepest passions might produce in our

---

[11] See Janko, especially pp. xvi–xx, and Butcher's discussion on pp. 245–251 of *Aristotle's Theory of Poetry and Fine Art.*

actual lives. It is the habitual compassion for the plights of others that makes us part of our civic and national communities and that ultimately develops our greater humanity. Tragedy therefore is vital in the growth of personal and collective virtue, for people who regularly experience the emotional catharsis or regulation of tragedy will be led to measure and direct their loves and their hates, to pledge their loyalties sensibly, and to make balanced decisions and take balanced actions, both for themselves and for the public.

It is important to stress that Aristotle states that catharsis is also brought about by other literary genres, especially comedy and epic, and, in addition, by music. In other words, artistic works have in common that they cleanse or purify the emotions. It is through the continuous and renewed shaping and regulating of feelings—catharsis—that tragedy, like literature and art broadly, encourages moral virtue, and therefore on philosophical, religious, and political grounds it is defensible and necessary.

## The Tragic Plot Is Structured to Arouse and Shape Emotions

In the light of the concept of catharsis, Aristotle's description of the formal aspects and characteristics of tragedy can be seen as an outline of the ways in which these characteristics first arouse the emotions and then shape them.

**THE TRAGIC PLOT REQUIRES THE REPRESENTATION OF A SINGLE MAJOR ACTION.** Aristotle concedes that tragedy is not true in the sense that history is true. He therefore stresses that a tragic plot, or *muthos*, is not an exact imitation or duplication of life, but rather a **representation** or *mimesis*. The concept of representation acknowledges both the moral role of the writer and the artistic freedom needed to create works conducive to proper responses. A tragic plot therefore consists of a self-contained and concentrated single action. Anything outside this action, such as unrelated incidents in the life of the major character, is not to be contained in the play. The action of *Oedipus the King*, for example, is focused on Oedipus's determination as king of Thebes to free his city from the pestilence that is destroying it. Although other aspects of his life are introduced in the play's dialogue because they are relevant to the action, they are reported rather than dramatized. Only those incidents integral to the action are included in the play.

**TRAGIC RESPONSES ARE BROUGHT TO A HEAD THROUGH REVERSAL, RECOGNITION, AND SUFFERING.** Aristotle's discussion of the three major elements of tragic plot is particularly significant. The elements all appear near the conclusion of a tragic play because they are the probable and inevitable results of the early elements of exposition and complication. First is the **"reversal** of the situation" (*peripeteia*) from apparent good to bad, or a "change [usually also a surprise] by which the action veers round to its opposite," as in *Oedipus the King*, where the outcome is the reverse of what Oedipus intends and expects (XI.1, p. 41). Even if the outcome is unhappy—especially if it is unhappy—it is "the right ending" (XIII.6, p. 47) because it is the most tragic; that is, it evokes the greatest degree of pity and fear.

Second is "a change from ignorance to knowledge, producing love or hate between the persons destined by the poet for good or bad fortune." Aristotle calls this change *anagnorisis* or **recognition** (XI.2, p. 41). In the best and most powerful tragedies, according to him, the reversal and the recognition occur together and create surprise. Aristotle considers recognition to be the discovery of the true identity and involvement of persons, the establishment of guilt or innocence, and the revelation of previously unknown details, for "it is upon such situations that the issues of good or bad fortune will depend" (XI.4, p. 41). One might add that recognition is of major importance because ideally, upon discovering the truth, the protagonist acknowledges errors and accepts responsibility. In *Oedipus the King*, Oedipus finally recognizes his own guilt even though during most of the play he has been trying to escape it. He then becomes the agent of his own punishment. Because such recognition illustrates that human beings have the strength to preserve their integrity even in adversity, it is one of the elements making tragedy the highest of all literary forms.

Aristotle describes the third part of plot as a "scene of suffering" (*pathos*) that he defines as "a destructive or painful action, such as death on the stage, bodily agony, wounds, and the like" (XI.6, p. 43). He stresses that the destructive or painful action, including death, should be caused by "those who are near or dear to one another" (XIV.4, pp. 49–50). That is, violence should occur within a royal household or family rather than against a hostile foe. Because the trust, love, and protectiveness that one hopes for in a family is replaced by treachery, hate, and mayhem, the suffering of the tragic protagonist is one of the major ways in which tragedy arouses fear and pity.

## Additional Aristotelian Tragic Requirements Are Seriousness, Completeness, and Artistic Balance

The first part of Aristotle's definition, asserting that a tragedy is "serious, complete, and of a certain magnitude," can be seen as a vital aspect of his analysis of how tragedy shapes responses. The term **serious**, or noble or elevated, concerns the play's tone and level of life, in contrast with the boisterousness and ribaldry of Athenian comedies. While comedy represents human character as less serious than it is, tragedy shows it as more serious (II.4, p. 13). Seriousness is also a consequence of the political and cosmological dimensions of the issues in which the heroic characters are engaged. By **complete**, we understand that a tragedy must be shaped and perfected into a logical and finished whole. The beginning, the middle, and the ending must be so perfectly placed that changing or removing any part would spoil the work's integrity (VII.2–3, p. 31). By stating that a tragedy should be of a "certain" or proportional **magnitude**, Aristotle refers to a balance of length and subject matter. The play should be short enough to "be easily embraced by the memory" and long enough to "admit of a change . . . from good fortune to bad" (VII.5–7, p. 33). In other words, everything is artistically balanced; nothing superfluous is included, and nothing essential is omitted.

## For Aristotle, Appropriate Diction and Song Are Necessary in Tragedy

For modern readers, Aristotle's description of tragic structure is more easily understood than his discussion of tragic language. His statement about tragic poetry—that it is the "mere metrical arrangement of the words" (VI.4, p. 25)—is clear as far as it goes, for the plays themselves show that the tragic playwrights used poetic forms deliberately and exactly. As for **song** (*melos*), Aristotle's claim that it is "a term whose sense everyone understands" (VI.4, p. 25) is not illuminating. What is therefore significant about his discussion of verse and song is his statement that the "several kinds of artistic ornament are to be found in separate parts of the play" (VI.2, p. 23). That is, where verse is appropriate, the tragic playwrights include poetry as a means of elevating the drama; where music and song are appropriate, they include these to increase beauty and intensify the drama. As with the other aspects of tragedy, therefore, the most fitting standards of judgment are placement, balance, and appropriateness.

## The Tragedy's Hero Is the Focus of Sympathetic Tragic Emotions

Aristotle's description of the tragic protagonist or hero, though not included in his definition of tragedy, is integral to the concept of catharsis and therefore to his description of tragedy. As with the other parts of his analysis, he demonstrates the exact effects and limits of the topic—the perfected balance of form necessary to bring about proper tragic responses. To this end, he states that we, as normally imperfect human beings, are able to sympathize with a "highly renowned and prosperous" protagonist because that protagonist is also imperfect—a person who exists between extremes, just "like ourselves" (XIII.2, p. 45). The misfortunes of this noble protagonist are caused not by "vice" or "depravity" but rather by "some great error or frailty" (XIII.4, p. 47). Aristotle's word for such shortcomings is *hamartia*, which is often translated as **tragic flaw**, and it is this flaw that makes the protagonist human—neither a saint nor a villain. If the protagonist were a saint (one who is "eminently good and just"), his or her suffering would be undeserved and unfair, and our pity would be overwhelmed by indignation and anger—not a proper tragic reaction. Nor could we pity a villain enduring adversity and pain, for we would judge the suffering to be deserved, and our primary response would then be satisfaction— also not a proper reaction. Therefore, an ideal tragedy is fine-tuned to control our emotions exactly, producing horror and fear because the suffering protagonist is a person like ourselves, and pity because the suffering far exceeds what the protagonist deserves.

---

### ARISTOTLE'S VIEW OF TRAGEDY IN BRIEF

Aristotle's definition of tragedy hinges on his idea that tragedy, as a dramatic form, is designed to evoke powerful emotions and thereby, through catharsis, to serve a salutary political, moral, and ethical purpose. The tragic incidents and plot must be artistically constructed to produce the "essential tragic effect" (VI.12, p. 27). Therefore Aristotle stresses that plot and incidents, arranged for this effect, form the end or goal—the "chief thing of all"—of tragedy (VI.10, p. 27).

# Irony in Tragedy

Implicit in the excessiveness of tragic suffering is the idea that the universe is mysterious and often unfair and that unseen but powerful forces—fate, fortune, circumstances, and the gods—directly intervene in human life. Ancient Athenian belief was that the gods give rewards or punishments to suit their own purposes, which mortals cannot bring about, prevent, or understand. For example, in *Prometheus Bound* (attributed to Aeschylus), the god Hephaestus binds Prometheus to a rock in the Scythian Mountains as punishment for having given fire and technology to humankind. (A good deed produces suffering.) Conversely, in *Medea*, Euripides shows that the god Apollo permits Medea to escape after killing her own children. (An evil deed produces reward.)

## Situational and Cosmic Irony Are Essential in Tragedy

These examples illustrate the pervasiveness of situational and cosmic irony in tragedy. Characters find themselves in unforeseeable difficulties that are caused by others or that they themselves unwittingly cause. When they try to try to resolve these difficulties responsibly and nobly, their actions do not produce the desired results—this is consistent with Aristotle's idea of reversal—and usually things come out badly. For example, Oedipus brings suffering on himself just when he succeeds—and *because* he succeeds—in rescuing his city. Whether on the personal or cosmic level, therefore, there is no escape—no way to evade responsibility, and no way to change the unalterable laws that thrust human beings into such situations.

Situational and cosmic irony is not confined to ancient tragedies. Shakespeare's tragic hero Hamlet speaks about the "divinity that shapes our ends," thus expressing the unpredictability of hopes, plans, and achievements, and also the wisdom of resignation. In *Death of a Salesman* (Chapter 23), Miller's hero, Willy Loman, is gripped not so much by divine power as by time—the agent of destruction being the inexorable force of economic circumstances.

## The Tragic Dilemma Confronts the Problem of Free Will vs. Fate

These ironies are connected to what is called the **tragic dilemma**—a situation that forces the tragic protagonist to make a difficult choice. The tragic dilemma has also been called a "lose-lose" situation. Thus, Oedipus cannot shirk his duty as king of Thebes because that would be ruinous. He therefore tries to eliminate his city's affliction, but that course is also ruinous. In other words, the choices posed in a tragic dilemma seemingly permit freedom of will, but the consequences of any choice demonstrate the inescapable fact that powerful forces, perhaps even fate or inevitability, baffle even the most reasonable and noble intentions. As Shakespeare's Hamlet states, "O cursèd spite, / That ever I was born to set it right" (1.5.188–89).

## Dramatic Irony Focuses Attention on the Tragic Limitations of Human Vision and Knowledge

It is from a perspective of something like divinity that we as readers or spectators perceive the action of tragedies. We are like the gods because we always know more than the characters. Such dramatic irony permits us, for example, to know what Oedipus does not know: In defensive rage he killed his real father, and he himself is therefore his city's bane. Similar dramatic irony can be found in *Hamlet*, for we realize that Claudius murdered Hamlet's father while Hamlet himself has only unconfirmable accusations of this truth. The underlying basis of dramatic irony in real life is of course that no one can know the future, and few if any can anticipate accident, illness, and all the social, economic, political, and military adversity that may invade and destroy our way of life.

## The Ancient Athenian Audience and Theater

Athenian audiences of the fifth century B.C.E., predominantly free men but also a small number of women, took their theater seriously. Indeed, as young men many citizens had taken active parts in the parades and choruses. Admission was charged for those able to pay, but subsidies allowed poorer people to attend as well. Rich Athenians, as a duty (*liturgeia*) to the state, underwrote the costs of the productions—except for three professional actors who were paid by the government. Each wealthy man, for his contribution, was known as a *choragos*, or choral sponsor. To gain public recognition, the choragos sometimes performed as the leader of the chorus.

### Ancient Athenian Theater Originated in the Marketplace, or *Agora*

In the beginning, tragic performances were given specially designated space in the Athenian *agora*, or marketplace. In the center of the performing area was an altar dedicated to Dionysus, around which the choruses danced and chanted. Apparently, wooden risers must have been set up for the spectators around the performers.

### Ancient Greek Plays Were Performed in the Athenian Theater of Dionysus

By the early fifth century B.C.E., a half-circular outdoor theater (*theatron*, or "place for seeing") was constructed at the base of the southern hill of the Acropolis in the area sacred to Dionysus (see the photograph, I–10, Plate 2). All later performances of Athenian tragedies were held at this **Theater of Dionysus**, which held as many as fourteen thousand people (the comic dramatist Aristophanes indicated that thirteen thousand were in attendance at one of his plays). In the earliest days of the theater, most spectators sat on the sloping ground, but eventually wooden and then stone benches were constructed in the rising semicircle, with more elegant seating for dignitaries in front. Although the Theater was outdoors, the acoustics were sufficiently good to permit audiences to hear both the chorus and the actors, provided that the audience remained reasonably quiet during performances.

**THE *ORCHESTRA* WAS THE FOCAL POINT OF BOTH SIGHT AND SOUND.**   Centered at the base of the hill—the focus of attention—was a round area modeled on the space that had been used in the agora. This was the *orchestra* (or-KESS-tra) or "dancing place," which was about 65 feet in diameter. Here, each chorus sang its odes and performed its dance movements to the rhythm of a double-piped flute (*aulos*), an instrument that was also used to mark the step in military drill. In the center was a permanent altar.

**THE SKENE WAS A VERSATILE BUILDING USED FOR BOTH ACTION AND ENTRANCES.** Behind the *orchestra* was a building for actors, costumes, and props called the *skene* (SKAY-nay, "tent"), from which is derived our modern word *scene*. Originally a tent or hut, the *skene* was later made of wood and decorated to provide backdrops for the various plays. Some theater historians argue that the stage itself was a wooden platform (*proskenion* [pro-SKAY-nee-on] or proscenium) in front of the *skene* to elevate the actors and set them off from the chorus. At the center of the *skene* a double door for entrances and exits opened out to the stage and the *orchestra*. Through this door a large platform (*ekkyklyma* [eck-KEEK-lee-mah]) could be rolled out to show interior scenes. There was no curtain.

The roof of the *skene* was sometimes used as a place of action (as in Aeschylus's *Agamemnon*). A *mechane* (may-KAH-nay), or crane, was also located there so that actors playing gods could be swung up, down, and around as a mark of divine power. It was this crane that inspired Menander to coin the phrase *theos apo mechanes*, or, in Latin, *deus ex machina* ("a god out of the machine"), terms that refer to an artificial and/or illogical action or device introduced at a play's end to bring otherwise impossible conflicts to a satisfactory solution.

**THE ACTORS PERFORMED IN ALL STAGE AND ORCHESTRA AREAS, AND THE CHORUS PERFORMED IN THE ORCHESTRA.**   The performing space for the actors was mainly in front of the *skene*. The space for the chorus was the entire *orchestra*. The chorus entered the *orchestra*—and left it at the end of the play—along the aisles between the retaining wall of the hillside seats and the front of the *skene*. Each of these lateral walkways was known as a *parados* ("way in"), the name also given to the chorus's entry scene. The actors often used the *skene* for entrances and exits, but they were also free to use either of the walkways.

**THE THEATER WAS REPAIRED AND RESTORED A NUMBER OF TIMES IN ANTIQUITY.**   In the centuries after it was built, the Theater of Dionysus was remodeled and restored a number of times. Aeschylus' trilogy the *Oresteia* was performed in 458 B.C.E., for example, not long after a renovation. The ruins existing on the south slope of the Acropolis today are not those of the theater known by Sophocles, but rather those of a Roman restoration. A better sense of how the theater looked during the time of Sophocles can be gained from the Theater of Epidaurus, which has been preserved in excellent condition (see the photographs, p. 936) and which even in antiquity was considered one of the best Greek theaters.

Ancient theater at Epidaurus, Greece.

View of modern production of Sophocles' Oedipus at Colonus at the Theater of Epidaurus. Note the size of the orchestra, the formation and gestures of the chorus (fifteen members, in masks, together with the choral leader), the central altar, the reconstructed skene, and the single actor on the proscenium.

## Ancient Greek Tragic Actors and Their Costumes

The task of the three competing playwrights who had been "given a chorus" by the archon to stage their works during the City Dionysia (and later during the Lenaia) was to plan, choreograph, and direct the productions, usually with the aid of professionals.

By performance time, the dramatists would already have spent many months preparing the three assigned actors and fifteen choristers. They also would have directed rehearsals for a small number of auxiliary chorus members and other silent extras taking roles such as servants and soldiers.

## Costumes Distinguished the Actors from the Chorus

All these participants needed costumes. The chorus members were lightly clad, for ease of movement, and were apparently barefoot. The main actors wore the identifying costumes of tragedy, namely, sleeved robes, boots, and masks. Their robes were heavily decorated and embroidered. Their calf-high leather boots, called *kothornoi* or, in English, **buskins**, were like the elegant boots worn by the patron god Dionysus in painting and statuary. During the following centuries, the buskins became elevator shoes that made the tragic actors taller, in keeping with their heroic stature.

## Masks Worn by Chorus and Actors Helped the Audience Recognize and Distinguish the Characters

A vital aspect of ancient tragic costuming was the use of conventionalized plaster and linen masks, which were designed to identify and delineate characters. These were of particular help for those in the audience who sat at increasing distances away and up from the orchestra and stage, and who therefore would have had trouble seeing facial expressions. As many as 28 different kinds of masks were in use for the tragic productions. Each mask portrayed a distinct facial type and expression (e.g., king, queen, young woman or man, old woman or man, servant, shepherd). The choristers wore identical masks for their group roles. Apparently the masks covered the entire head, except for openings for seeing, breathing, and speaking. They included a high headdress and, when necessary, a beard.

The masks, along with costume changes, gave the actors great versatility. Each actor could assume a number of different roles simply by entering the *skene*, changing mask and costume, and reentering as a new character. Thus, in *Oedipus the King* a single actor could represent the seer Tiresias and later reappear as the Messenger. The masks even made it possible for two actors, or even all three, to perform as the same character in separate parts of the play if the need arose.

# Performance and the Formal Organization of Greek Tragedy

On performance days, the competing playwrights staged their plays from morning to afternoon, first the tragedies, then the satyr plays (and after these, comedies by other writers). Because plays were performed with a minimum of scenery and props, dramatists used dialogue to establish times and locations. Each tragedy was performed in the order of the formally designated sections that modern editors have marked in the printed texts. It is therefore possible to describe the production of a play in terms of these structural divisions.

## The First Part Was the Prologue, the Play's Exposition

There was considerable variety in the performance of the **prologue**. Sometimes it was given by a single actor, speaking as either a mortal or a god. In *Oedipus the King*, Sophocles used all three actors for the prologue (Oedipus, the Priest, and Creon), speaking to themselves and also to the extras acting as the Theban populace.

## The Second Part Was the Parados, the Entry of the Chorus into the Orchestra

Once the chorus members entered the orchestra, they remained there until the play's end. Because they were required to project their voices to spectators in the top seats, they both sang and chanted their lines. They also moved rhythmically in a number of stanzaic *strophes* (turns), *antistrophes* (counterturns), and *epodes* (units following the songs). These dance movements, regulated by the rhythm of the *aulos* or flute as in military drill, were done in straight-line formations of five or three, but we do not know whether the chorus stopped or continued moving when delivering their lines. After the *parados*, the choristers would necessarily have knelt or sat at attention, in this way focusing on the activities of the actors and, when necessary, responding as a group.

## The Play's Principal Action Consisted of Four Episodes and Stasimons

With the chorus as a model audience, the drama itself was developed in four full sections or acting units. The major part of each section was the **episode**. Each episode featured the actors, who presented both action and speech, including swift one-line interchanges known as **stichomythy**.

When the episode ended, the actors withdrew.[12] The following second part of the acting section was called a *stasimon* (plural *stasima*), performed by the chorus in the *orchestra*. Like the *parados*, the *stasima* required dance movements, along with the chanting and singing of strophes, antistrophes, and epodes. The topics concerned the play's developing action, although over time the *stasima* became more general and therefore less integral to the play.

## The Play Concluded with the Exodos

When the last of the four episode-*stasimon* sections had been completed, the *exodos* (literally, "a way out"), or the final section, commenced. It contained the resolution of the drama, the exit of the actors, and the last pronouncements, dance movements, and exit of the chorus.

---

[12]For example, at the end of the first episode of *Oedipus the King*, Oedipus goes into the *skene*—the palace—while a servant leads Tiresias off along the *parados*, thus indicating that he is leaving Thebes entirely.

## The Role of the Chorus Was Diminished as Greek Tragedy Evolved

We know little about tragic structure at the very beginning of the form, but Athenian tragedies of the fifth century B.C.E. followed the pattern just described. Aeschylus, whose works are the earliest surviving Athenian tragedies, lengthened the episodes, thus emphasizing the actors and diminishing "the importance of the Chorus" (*Poetics* IV.13, p. 19). Sophocles made the chorus even less important. Euripides, Sophocles's younger contemporary, concentrated on the episodes, making the chorus almost incidental. In later centuries, dramatists dropped the choral sections completely, establishing the pattern for the five-act structure adopted by Roman dramatists and later by Renaissance dramatists.

### Plays for Study ◀

## SOPHOCLES (ca. 496–406 B.C.E)

Sophocles was born between 500 and 494 B.C.E. into an affluent Athenian family. He began acting and singing early, and he served as a choral leader in the celebrations for the defeat of the Persians at Marathon in 480 B.C.E. In 468 he won highest festival honors for the first play he submitted for competition, *Triptolemos.* He wrote at least 120 plays, approximately 90 of them tragedies, and he won the prize a record 24 times. He was also an active citizen. He was twice elected general of his tribe, and he served as a priest in the cult of Asclepius, the god of healing. Because of his dramatic and public achievements, he was venerated during his lifetime, and after his death in 406–405 B.C.E., a cult was established in his honor.

When *Oedipus the King* was first performed between 430 and 425 B.C.E., most of the audience would have known the general outlines of the story inasmuch as it was one of the "received legends" of tragedy: the antagonism of the gods Hephaestus and Hera toward Cadmus of Thebes (of whom Oedipus was a descendant); the prophecy that the Theban king Laius would be killed by his own son; the exposure of the newly born Oedipus on a mountainside; his rescue by a well-meaning shepherd; his youth spent as the adopted son of King Polybus and Queen Merope of Corinth; his trip to Delphi to learn his origins; his impetuous murder of Laius (a stranger to him); his solution of the Sphinx's riddle; his ascension as king of Thebes and his marriage to Queen Jocasta, his mother; his reign as king; the plague that afflicted Thebes; his attempts at restoration; and Jocasta's suicide when the truth of Oedipus's past is revealed.

Although these details were commonly known, there was disagreement about the outcome of Oedipus's life. One version told that he remarried, had four children with his new wife, reigned long and successfully, died in battle, and was finally worshiped as a hero. Sophocles, however, dramatizes a version—either borrowed or of his own creation—that tells of Oedipus's self-imposed punishment.

As we have said, Aristotle prized *Oedipus the King* so highly that he used it to illustrate many of his principles of tragedy. Of particular interest is that the play embodies the so-called three **unities**, which are implicit in the *Poetics* although Aristotle does not stress them. Sophocles creates *unity of place* by using the front of the royal palace of Thebes as the location for the entire action. He creates *unity of action* by dramatizing only those activities leading to Oedipus's recognition of the true scourge of the city. Finally, he creates *unity of time* because the stage or action time coincides with real-life time. In fact, the play's time is considerably shorter than the "single revolution of the sun" (*sic*) that Aristotle recommends as the proper period for a complete tragic action (V.4, p. 23). Above all, *Oedipus the King* meets Aristotle's requirements for one of the very best plays because of the skill with which Sophocles makes Oedipus's recognition of his guilt coincide exactly with the disastrous reversal of his fortunes (XI.2, p. 41).

# Oedipus the King (430–425 B.C.E.)

## *Translated by Thomas Gould*

### CHARACTERS

**Oedipus,**° The King of Thebes

**Priest of Zeus,** Leader of the Suppliants

**Creon,** Oedipus's Brother-in-law

**Chorus,** a Group of Theban Elders

**Choragos,** Spokesman of the Chorus

**Tiresias,** a blind Seer or Prophet

**Jocasta,** The Queen of Thebes

**Messenger,** from Corinth, once a Shepherd

**Herdsman,** once a Servant of Laius

**Second Messenger,** a Servant of Oedipus

### MUTES

**Suppliants,** Thebans seeking Oedipus's help

**Attendants,** for the Royal Family

**Servants,** to lead Tiresias and Oedipus

**Antigone,** Daughter of Oedipus and Jocasta

**Ismene,** Daughter of Oedipus and Jocasta

[*The action takes place during the day in front of the royal palace in Thebes. There are two altars (left and right) on the Proscenium and several steps leading down to the Orchestra. As the play opens, Thebans of various ages who have come to beg Oedipus for help are sitting on these steps and in part of the Orchestra. These suppliants are holding branches of laurel or olive which have strips of wool*° *wrapped around them. Oedipus enters from the palace (the central door of the Skene).*]

---

°*Oedipus:* The name means "swollen foot." It refers to the mutilation of Oedipus's feet by his father, Laius, before the infant was sent to Mount Cithaeron to be put to death by exposure.

°0.1 S.D. *wool:* Branches wrapped with wool are traditional symbols of prayer or supplication.

## PROLOGUE

OEDIPUS: My children, ancient Cadmus'° newest care,
    why have you hurried to those seats, your boughs
    wound with the emblems of the suppliant?
    The city is weighed down with fragrant smoke,
    with hymns to the Healer° and the cries of mourners.    5
    I thought it wrong, my sons, to hear your words
    through emissaries, and have come out myself,
    I, Oedipus, a name that all men know.

[OEDIPUS *addresses the* PRIEST.]

    Old man—for it is fitting that you speak
    for all—what is your mood as you entreat me,    10
    fear or trust? You may be confident
    that I'll do anything. How hard of heart
    if an appeal like this did not rouse my pity!
PRIEST: You, Oedipus, who hold the power here,
    you see our several ages, we who sit    15
    before your altars—some not strong enough
    to take long flight, some heavy in old age,
    the priests, as I of Zeus,° and from our youths
    a chosen band. The rest sit with their windings
    in the markets, at the twin shrines of Pallas,°    20
    and the prophetic embers of Ismēnos.°
    Our city, as you see yourself, is tossed
    too much, and can no longer lift its head
    above the troughs of billows red with death.
    It dies in the fruitful flowers of the soil,    25
    it dies in its pastured herds, and in its women's
    barren pangs. And the fire-bearing god°
    has swooped upon the city, hateful plague,
    and he has left the house of Cadmus empty.
    Black Hades° is made rich with moans and weeping.    30
    Not judging you an equal of the gods,
    do I and the children sit here at your hearth,
    but as the first of men, in troubled times
    and in encounters with divinities.
    You came to Cadmus' city and unbound    35
    the tax we had to pay to the harsh singer,°

---

°1 *Cadmus*: Oedipus's great-great-grandfather (although he does not know this) and the founder of Thebes. 5 *Healer*: Apollo, god of prophecy, light, healing, justice, purification, and destruction. 18 *Zeus*: father and king of the gods. 20 *Pallas*: Athena, goddess of wisdom, arts, crafts, and war. 21 *Ismēnos*: a reference to the temple of Apollo near the river Ismenos in Thebes. Prophecies were made here by "reading" the ashes of the altar fires. 27 *fire-bearing god*: contagious fever viewed as a god. 30 *Black Hades*: refers to both the underworld, where the spirits of the dead go, and the god of the underworld. 36 *harsh singer*: the Sphinx, a monster with a woman's head, a lion's body, and wings. The "tax" that Oedipus freed Thebes from was the destruction of all the young men who failed to solve the Sphinx's riddle and were subsequently devoured. The Sphinx always asked the same riddle: "What goes on four legs in the morning, two legs at noon, and three legs in the evening, and yet is weakest when supported by the largest number of feet?" Oedipus discovered the correct answer—man, who crawls in infancy, walks in his prime, and uses a stick in old age—and thus ended the Sphinx's reign of terror. The Sphinx destroyed herself when Oedipus answered the riddle. Oedipus's reward for freeing Thebes of the Sphinx was the throne and the hand of the recently widowed Jocasta.

did it without a helpful word from us,
with no instruction; with a god's assistance
you raised up our life, so we believe.
40  Again now Oedipus, our greatest power,
we plead with you, as suppliants, all of us,
to find us strength, whether from a god's response,
or learned in some way from another man.
I know that the experienced among men
45  give counsels that will prosper best of all.
Noblest of men, lift up our land again!
Think also of yourself; since now the land
calls you its Savior for your zeal of old,
oh let us never look back at your rule
50  as men helped up only to fall again!
Do not stumble! Put our land on firm feet!
The bird of omen was auspicious then,
when you brought that luck; be that same man again!
The power is yours; if you will rule our country,
55  rule over men, not in an empty land.
A towered city or a ship is nothing
if desolate and no man lives within.
OEDIPUS:  Pitiable children, oh I know, I know
the yearnings that have brought you. Yes, I know
60  that you are sick. And yet, though you are sick,
there is not one of you so sick as I.
For your affliction comes to each alone,
for him and no one else, but my soul mourns
for me and for you, too, and for the city.
65  You do not waken me as from a sleep,
for I have wept, bitterly and long,
tried many paths in the wanderings of thought,
and the single cure I found by careful search
I've acted on: I sent Menoeceus' son,
70  Creon, brother of my wife, to the Pythian
halls of Phoebus,° so that I might learn
what I must do or say to save this city.
Already, when I think what day this is,
I wonder anxiously what he is doing.
75  Too long, more than is right, he's been away.
But when he comes, then I shall be a traitor
if I do not do all that the god reveals.
PRIEST:  Welcome words! But look, those men have signaled
that it is Creon who is now approaching!
80  OEDIPUS:  Lord Apollo! May he bring Savior Luck,
a Luck as brilliant as his eyes are now!
PRIEST:  His news is happy, it appears. He comes,
forehead crowned with thickly berried laurel.°

---

°70–71 *Pythian . . . Phoebus*: the temple of Phoebus Apollo's oracle or prophet at Delphi. 83 *laurel*: Creon is wearing a garland of laurel leaves, sacred to Apollo.

OEDIPUS: We'll know, for he is near enough to hear us.

[*Enter* CREON *along one of the Parados.*]

Lord, brother in marriage, son of Menoeceus! 85
What is the god's pronouncement that you bring?
CREON: It's good. For even troubles, if they chance
to turn out well, I always count as lucky.
OEDIPUS: But what was the response? You seem to say
I'm not to fear—but not to take heart either. 90
CREON: If you will hear me with these men present,
I'm ready to report—or go inside.

[CREON *moves up the steps toward the palace.*]

OEDIPUS: Speak out to all! The grief that burdens me
concerns these men more than it does my life.
CREON: Then I shall tell you what I heard from the god. 95
The task Lord Phoebus sets for us is clear:
drive out pollution sheltered in our land,
and do not shelter what is incurable.
OEDIPUS: What is our trouble? How shall we cleanse ourselves?
CREON: We must banish or murder to free ourselves 100
from a murder that blows storms through the city.
OEDIPUS: What man's bad luck does he accuse in this?
CREON: My Lord, a king named Laius ruled our land
before you came to steer the city straight.
OEDIPUS: I know. So I was told—I never saw him. 105
CREON: Since he was murdered, you must raise your hand
against the men who killed him with their hands.
OEDIPUS: Where are they now? And how can we ever find
the track of ancient guilt now hard to read?
CREON: In our own land, he said. What we pursue, 110
that can be caught; but not what we neglect.
OEDIPUS: Was Laius home, or in the countryside—
or was he murdered in some foreign land?
CREON: He left to see a sacred rite, he said;
He left, but never came home from his journey. 115
OEDIPUS: Did none of his party see it and report—
someone we might profitably question?
CREON: They were all killed but one, who fled in fear,
and he could tell us only one clear fact.
OEDIPUS: What fact? One thing could lead us on to more 120
if we could get a small start on our hope.
CREON: He said that bandits chanced on them and killed him—
with the force of many hands, not one alone.
OEDIPUS: How could a bandit dare so great an act—
unless this was a plot paid off from here! 125
CREON: We thought of that, but when Laius was killed,
we had no one to help us in our troubles.
OEDIPUS: It was your very kingship that was killed!
What kind of trouble blocked you from a search?

130  CREON: The subtle-singing Sphinx asked us to turn
              from the obscure to what lay at our feet.
      OEDIPUS: Then I shall begin again and make it plain.
              It was quite worthy of Phoebus, and worthy of you,
              to turn our thoughts back to the murdered man,
135           and right that you should see me join the battle
              for justice to our land and to the god.
              Not on behalf of any distant kinships,
              it's for myself I will dispel this stain.
              Whoever murdered him may also wish
140           to punish me—and with the selfsame hand.
              In helping him I also serve myself.
              Now quickly, children: up from the altar steps,
              and raise the branches of the suppliant!
              Let someone go and summon Cadmus' people:
              say I'll do anything.

> [*Exit an* ATTENDANT *along one of the Parados.*]

145                          Our luck will prosper
              if the god is with us, or we have already fallen.
      PRIEST: Rise, my children; that for which we came,
              he has himself proclaimed he will accomplish.
              May Phoebus, who announced this, also come
150           as Savior and reliever from the plague.

> [*Exit* OEDIPUS *and* CREON *into the Palace. The* PRIEST *and the* SUPPLIANTS *exit left and right along the Parados. After a brief pause, the* CHORUS *(including the* CHORAGOS*) enters the Orchestra from the Parados.*]

## PARADOS

### Strophe 1°

      CHORUS: Voice from Zeus,° sweetly spoken, what are you
              that have arrived from golden
              Pytho° to our shining
              Thebes? I am on the rack, terror
155           shakes my soul.
              Delian Healer,° summoned by "iē!"
              I await in holy dread what obligation, something new
              or something back once more with the revolving years,
                  you'll bring about for me.
160           Oh tell me, child of golden Hope,
                  deathless Response!

---

°151 *Strophe:* Strophe and antistrophe (line 162) are stanzaic units referring to movements, countermovements, and gestures that the Chorus performed while singing or chanting in the orchestra. See p. 938.  151 *Voice from Zeus:* a reference to Apollo's prophecy. Zeus taught Apollo how to prophesy.  153 *Pytho:* Delphi.  156 *Delian Healer:* Apollo.

## Antistrophe 1

I appeal to you first, daughter of Zeus,
    deathless Athena,
    and to your sister who protects this land,
    Artemis,° whose famous throne is the whole circle
    of the marketplace,        165
and Phoebus, who shoots from afar: iō!
Three-fold defenders against death, appear!
If ever in the past, to stop blind ruin
    sent against the city,
you banished utterly the fires of suffering,    170
    come now again!

## Strophe 2

Ah! Ah! Unnumbered are the miseries
I bear. The plague claims all
our comrades. Nor has thought found yet a spear
by which a man shall be protected. What our glorious    175
earth gives birth to does not grow. Without a birth
from cries of labor
    do the women rise.
One person after another
    you may see, like flying birds,    180
faster than indomitable fire, sped
to the shore of the god that is the sunset.°

## Antistrophe 2

And with their deaths unnumbered dies the city.
Her children lie unpitied on the ground,
spreading death, unmourned.    185
Meanwhile young wives, and gray-haired mothers with them,
on the shores of the altars, from this side and that,
suppliants from mournful trouble,
    cry out their grief.
A hymn to the Healer shines,    190
the flute a mourner's voice.
Against which, golden goddess, daughter of Zeus,
    send lovely Strength.

## Strophe 3

Cause raging Ares°—who,
    armed now with no shield of bronze,    195
burns me, coming on amid loud cries—
to turn his back and run from my land,

---

°165 *Artemis:* goddess of virginity, childbirth, and hunting. 183 *god . . . sunset:* Hades, god of the underworld. 195 *Ares:* god of war and destruction.

with a fair wind behind, to the great
200        hall of Amphitritē,°
or to the anchorage that welcomes no one,
Thrace's troubled sea!
If night lets something get away at last,
        it comes by day.
205   Fire-bearing god . . .
        you who dispense the might of lightning,
Zeus! Father! Destroy him with your thunderbolt!

[*Enter Oedipus from the palace.*]

## Antistrophe 3

Lycēan Lord!° From your looped
        bowstring, twisted gold,
210   I wish indomitable missiles might be scattered
and stand forward, our protectors; also fire-bearing
radiance of Artemis, with which
        she darts across the Lycian mountains.
I call the god whose head is bound in gold,
215   with whom this country shares its name,
Bacchus,° wine-flushed, summoned by "euoi!,"
        Maenads' comrade,
to approach ablaze
        with gleaming . . . . . .
220   pine, opposed to that god-hated god.

## EPISODE 1

OEDIPUS:  I hear your prayer. Submit to what I say
and to the labors that the plague demands
and you'll get help and a relief from evils.
I'll make the proclamation, though a stranger
225   to the report and to the deed. Alone,
had I no key, I would soon lose the track.
Since it was only later that I joined you,
to all the sons of Cadmus I say this:
whoever has clear knowledge of the man
230   who murdered Laius, son of Labdacus,
I command him to reveal it all to me—
nor fear if, to remove the charge, he must
accuse himself: his fate will not be cruel—
he will depart unstumbling into exile.
235   But if you know another, or a stranger,
to be the one whose hand is guilty, speak:
I shall reward you and remember you.
But if you keep your peace because of fear,
and shield yourself or kin from my command,

---

°**200** *Amphitritē*: the Atlantic Ocean.  **208** *Lycēan Lord*: Apollo.  **216** *Bacchus*: Dionysus, god of fertility and wine.

hear you what I shall do in that event:                                                240
I charge all in this land where I have throne
and power, shut out that man—no matter who—
both from your shelter and all spoken words,
nor in your prayers or sacrifices make
him partner, not allot him lustral° water.                                             245
All men shall drive him from their homes: for he
is the pollution that the god-sent Pythian
response has only now revealed to me.
In this way I ally myself in war
with the divinity and the deceased.°                                                   250
And this curse, too, against the one who did it,
whether alone in secrecy, or with others:
may he wear out his life unblest and evil!
I pray this, too: if he is at my hearth
and in my home, and I have knowledge of him,                                           255
may the curse pronounced on others come to me.
All this I lay to you to execute,
for my sake, for the god's, and for this land
now ruined, barren, abandoned by the gods.
Even if no god had driven you to it,                                                    260
you ought not to have left this stain uncleansed,
the murdered man a nobleman, a king!
You should have looked! But now, since, as it happens,
It's I who have the power that he had once,
and have his bed, and a wife who shares our seed,                                       265
and common bond had we had common children
(had not his hope of offspring had back luck—
but as it happened, luck lunged at his head);
because of this, as if for my own father,
I'll fight for him, I'll leave no means untried,                                        270
to catch the one who did it with his hand,
for the son of Labdacus, of Polydôrus,
of Cadmus before him, and of Agênor.°
This prayer against all those who disobey:
the gods send out no harvest from their soil,                                           275
nor children from their wives. Oh, let them die
victims of this plague, or of something worse.
Yet for the rest of us, people of Cadmus,
we the obedient, may Justice, our ally,
and all the gods, be always on our side!                                               280
CHORAGOS:  I speak because I feel the grip of your curse:
    the killer is not *I*. Nor can I point
    to him. The one who set us to this search,
    Phoebus, should also name the guilty man.
OEDIPUS:  Quite right, but to compel unwilling gods—                                    285
    no man has ever had that kind of power.

---

°245 *lustral*: purifying. 250 *the deceased*: Laius. 272–73 *son . . . Agênor*: refers to Laius by citing his genealogy.

CHORAGOS:  May I suggest to you a second way?
OEDIPUS:  A second or a third—pass over nothing!
CHORAGOS:  I know of no one who sees more of what
290       Lord Phoebus sees than Lord Tiresias.
          My Lord, one might learn brilliantly from him.
OEDIPUS:  Nor is this something I have been slow to do.
          At Creon's word I sent an escort—twice now!
          I am astonished that he has not come.
295 CHORAGOS:  The old account is useless. It told us nothing.
OEDIPUS:  But tell it to me. I'll scrutinize all stories.
CHORAGOS:  He is said to have been killed by travelers.
OEDIPUS:  I have heard, but the one who did it no one sees.
CHORAGOS:  If there is any fear in him at all,
300       he won't stay here once he has heard that curse.
OEDIPUS:  He won't fear words: he had no fear when he did it.

[*Enter* TIRESIAS *from the right, led by a* SERVANT *and two of Oedipus's* ATTENDANTS.]

CHORAGOS:  Look there! There is the man who will convict him!
          It's the god's prophet they are leading here.
          one gifted with the truth as no one else.
305 OEDIPUS:  Tiresias, master of all omens—
          public and secret, in the sky and on the earth—
          your mind, if not your eyes, sees how the city
          lives with a plague, against which Thebes can find
          no Saviour or protector, Lord, but you.
310       For Phoebus, as the attendants surely told you,
          returned this answer to us: liberation
          from the disease would never come unless
          we learned without a doubt who murdered Laius—
          put them to death, or sent them into exile.
315       Do not begrudge us what you may learn from birds
          or any other prophet's path you know!
          Care for yourself, the city, care for me,
          care for the whole pollution of the dead!
          We're in your hands. To do all that he can
320       to help another is man's noblest labor.
TIRESIAS:  How terrible to understand and get
          no profit from the knowledge! I knew this,
          but I forgot, or I had never come.
OEDIPUS:  What's this? You've come with very little zeal.
325 TIRESIAS:  Let me go home! If you will listen to me,
          You will endure your troubles better—and I mine.
OEDIPUS:  A strange request, not very kind to the land
          that cared for you—to hold back this oracle!
TIRESIAS:  I see your understanding comes to you
330       inopportunely. So that won't happen to me . . . .
OEDIPUS:  Oh, by the gods, if you understand about this,
          don't turn away! We're on our knees to you.
TIRESIAS:  None of you understands! I'll never bring
          my grief to light—will not speak of yours.

OEDIPUS:  You know and won't declare it! Is your purpose                    335
    to betray us and to destroy this land?
TIRESIAS:  I will grieve neither of us. Stop this futile
    cross-examination. I'll tell you nothing!
OEDIPUS:  Nothing? You vile traitor! You could provoke
    a stone to anger! You still refuse to tell?                          340
    Can nothing soften you, nothing convince you?
TIRESIAS:  You blamed anger in me—you haven't seen.
    Can nothing soften you, nothing convince you?
OEDIPUS:  Who wouldn't fill with anger, listening
    to words like yours which now disgrace this city?                    345
TIRESIAS:  It will come, even if my silence hides it.
OEDIPUS:  If it will come, then why won't you declare it?
TIRESIAS:  I'd rather say no more. Now if you wish,
    respond to that will all your fiercest anger!
OEDIPUS:  Now I am angry enough to come right out                           350
    with this conjecture: you, I think, helped plot
    the deed; you did it—even if your hand
    cannot have struck the blow. If you could see,
    I should have said the deed was yours alone.
TIRESIAS:  Is that right! Then I charge you to abide                        355
    by the decree you have announced: from this day
    say no word to either these or me,
    for you are the vile polluter of this land!
OEDIPUS:  Aren't you appalled to let a charge like that
    come bounding forth? How will you get away?                         360
TIRESIAS:  You cannot catch me. I have the strength of truth.
OEDIPUS:  Who taught you this? Not your prophetic craft!
TIRESIAS:  You did. You made me say it. I didn't want to.
OEDIPUS:  Say what? Repeat it so I'll understand.
TIRESIAS:  I made no sense? Or are you trying me?                           365
OEDIPUS:  No sense I understood. Say it again!
TIRESIAS:  I say you are the murderer you seek.
OEDIPUS:  Again that horror! You'll wish you hadn't said that.
TIRESIAS:  Shall I say more, and raise your anger higher?
OEDIPUS:  Anything you like! Your words are powerless.                      370
TIRESIAS:  You live, unknowing, with those nearest to you
    in the greatest shame. You do not see the evil.
OEDIPUS:  You won't go on like that and never pay!
TIRESIAS:  I can if there is any strength in truth.
OEDIPUS:  In truth, but not in you! You have no strength,                   375
    blind in your ears, your reason, and your eyes.
TIRESIAS:  Unhappy man! Those jeers you hurl at me
    before long all these men will hurl at you.
OEDIPUS:  You are the child of endless night; it's not
    for me or anyone who sees to hurt you.                              380
TIRESIAS:  It's not my fate to be struck down by you.
    Apollo is enough. That's his concern.
OEDIPUS:  Are these inventions Creon's or your own?
TIRESIAS:  No, your affliction is yourself, not Creon.

385 OEDIPUS: Oh success!—in wealth, kingship, artistry,
     in any life that wins much admiration—
     the envious ill will stored up for you!
     to get at my command, a gift I did not
     seek, which the city put into my hands,
390      my loyal Creon, colleague from the start,
     longs to sneak up in secret and dethrone me.
     So he's suborned this fortuneteller—schemer!
     deceitful beggar-priest!—who has good eyes
     for gains alone, though in his craft he's blind.
395      Where were your prophet's powers ever proved?
     Why, when the dog who chanted verse° was here,
     did you not speak and liberate this city?
     Her riddle wasn't for a man chancing by
     to interpret; prophetic art was needed,
400      but you had none, it seems—learned from birds
     or from a god. I came along, yes I,
     Oedipus the ignorant, and stopped her—
     by using thought, not augury from birds.
     And it is I whom you may wish to banish,
405      so you'll be close to the Creontian throne.
     You—and the plot's concocter—will drive out
     pollution to your grief; you look quite old
     or you would be the victim of that plot!
CHORAGOS: It seems to us that this man's words were said
410      in anger, Oedipus, and yours as well.
     Insight, not angry words, is what we need,
     the best solution to the god's response.
TIRESIAS: You are the king, and yet I am your equal
     in my right to speak. In that I too am Lord,
415      for I belong to Loxias,° not you.
     I am not Creon's man. He's nothing to me.
     Hear this, since you have thrown my blindness at me:
     Your eyes can't see the evil to which you've come,
     nor where you live, nor who is in your house.
420      Do you know your parents? Now knowing, you are
     their enemy, in the underworld and here.
     A mother's and a father's double-lashing
     terrible-footed curse will soon drive you out.
     Now you can see, then you will stare into darkness.
425      What place will not be harbor to your cry,
     or what Cithaeron° not reverberate
     when you have heard the bride-song in your palace
     to which you sailed? Fair wind to evil harbor!
     Nor do you see how many other woes
430      will level you to yourself and to your children.
     So, at my message, and at Creon, too,

---

°396 *dog . . . verse*: the Sphinx. 415 *Loxias*: Apollo. 426 *Cithaeron*: reference to the mountain on which Oedipus was to be exposed as an infant.

splatter muck! There will never be a man
ground into wretchedness as you will be.
OEDIPUS: Am I to listen to such things from him!
   May you be damned! Get out of here at once!                    435
   Go! Leave my palace! Turn around and go!

[*TIRESIAS begins to move away from OEDIPUS.*]

TIRESIAS: I wouldn't have come had you not sent for me.
OEDIPUS: I did not know you'd talk stupidity,
   or I wouldn't have rushed to bring you to my house.
TIRESIAS: Stupid I seem to you, yet to your parents                           440
   who gave you natural birth I seemed quite shrewd.
OEDIPUS: Who? Wait! Who is the one who gave me birth?
TIRESIAS: This day will give you birth,° and ruin too.
OEDIPUS: What murky, riddling things you always say!
TIRESIAS: Don't you surpass us all at finding out?                            445
OEDIPUS: You sneer at what you'll find has brought me greatness.
TIRESIAS: And that's the very luck that ruined you.
OEDIPUS: I wouldn't care, just so I saved the city.
TIRESIAS: In that case I shall go. Boy, lead the way!
OEDIPUS: Yes, let him lead you off. Here, underfoot,                          450
   you irk me. Gone, you'll cause no further pain.
TIRESIAS: I'll go when I have said what I was sent for.
   Your face won't scare me. You can't ruin me.
   I say to you, the man whom you have looked for
   as you pronounced your curses, your decrees                         455
   on the bloody death of Laius—he is here!
   A seeming stranger, he shall be shown to be
   a Theban born, though he'll take no delight
   in that solution. Blind, who once could see,
   a beggar who was rich, through foreign lands                        460
   he'll go and point before him with a stick.
   To his beloved children, he'll be shown
   a father who is also brother; to the one
   who bore him, son and husband; to his father,
   his seed-fellow and killer. Go in                                   465
   and think this out; and if you find I've lied,
   say then I have no prophet's understanding!

[*Exit TIRESIAS, led by a SERVANT. OEDIPUS exits into the palace with his ATTENDANTS.*]

## STASIMON 1

### Strophe 1

CHORUS: Who is the man of whom the inspired
     rock of Delphi° said
   he has committed the unspeakable                                     470
     with blood-stained hands?

---

°443 *give you birth*: that is, identify your parents.  469 *rock of Delphi*: Apollo's oracle at Delphi.

Time for him to ply a foot
mightier than those of the horses
    of the storm in his escape;
475    upon him mounts and plunges the weaponed
son of Zeus,° with fire and thunderbolts,
and in his train the dreaded goddesses
of Death, who never miss.

### Antistrophe 1

The message has just blazed,
480        gleaming from the snows
of Mount Parnassus: we must track
    everywhere the unseen man.
He wanders, hidden by wild
forests, up through caves
485        and rocks, like a bull,
anxious, with an anxious foot, forlorn.
He puts away from him the mantic° words come from earth's
navel,° at its center, yet these live
forever and still hover round him.

### Strophe 2

490    Terribly he troubles me,
    the skilled interpreter of birds!°
I can't assent, nor speak against him.
    Both paths are closed to me.
I hover on the wings of doubt,
495        not seeing what is here nor what's to come.
What quarrel started in the house of Labdacus°
or in the house of Polybus,°
    either ever in the past
    or now, I never
500    heard, so that . . . with this fact for my touchstone
I could attack the public
    fame of Oedipus, by the side of the Labdaceans
an ally, against the dark assassination.

### Antistrophe 2

No, Zeus and Apollo
505        understand and know things
mortal; but that another man
    can do more as a prophet than I can—
for that there is no certain test,
    though, skill to skill,
510    one man might overtake another.

---

°476 *son of Zeus*: Apollo. 487 *mantic*: prophetic. 487–488 *earth's navel*: Delphi. 491 *interpreter of birds*: Tiresias. The Chorus is troubled by his accusations. 496 *house of Labdacus*: the line of Laius. 497 *Polybus*: Oedipus's foster father.

No, never, not until
    I see the charges proved,
when someone blames him shall I nod assent.
For once, as we all saw, the winged maiden° came
against him: he was seen then to be skilled,                      515
    proved, by that touchstone, dear to the people. So,
never will my mind convict him of the evil.

## EPISODE 2

[*Enter* CREON *from the right door of the skene and speaks to the* CHORUS.]

CREON:  Citizens, I hear that a fearful charge
    is made against me by King Oedipus!
    I had to come. If, in this crisis,                           520
    he thinks that he has suffered injury
    from anything that I have said or done,
    I have no appetite for a long life—
    bearing a blame like that! It's no slight blow,
    the punishment I'd take from what he said:            525
    it's the ultimate hurt to be called traitor
    by the city, by you, by my own people!
CHORAGOS:  The thing that forced that accusation out
    could have been anger, not the power of thought.
CREON:  But who persuaded him that thoughts of mine      530
    had led the prophet into telling lies?
CHORAGOS:  I do not know the thought behind his words.
CREON:  But did he look straight at you? Was his mind right
    when he said that I was guilty of this charge?
CHORAGOS:  I have no eyes to see what rulers do.              535
    But here he comes himself out of the house.

[*Enter* OEDIPUS *from the palace.*]

OEDIPUS:  What? You here? And can you really have
    the face and daring to approach my house
    when you're exposed as its master's murderer
    and caught, too, as the robber of my kingship?     540
    Did you see cowardice in me, by the gods,
    or foolishness, when you began this plot?
    Did you suppose that I would not detect
    your stealthy moves, or that I'd not fight back?
    It's your attempt that's folly, isn't it—            545
    tracking without followers or connections,
    kingship which is caught with wealth and numbers?
CREON:  Now wait! Give me as long to answer back!
    Judge me for yourself when you have heard me!
OEDIPUS:  You're eloquent, but I'd be slow to learn      550
    from you, now that I've seen your malice toward me.

---

°514 *winged maiden:* the Sphinx.

CREON:  That I deny. Hear what I have to say.

OEDIPUS:  Don't you deny it! You are the traitor here!

CREON:  If you consider mindless willfulness

555       a prized possession, you are not thinking sense.

OEDIPUS:  If you think you can wrong a relative
          and get off free, you are not thinking sense.

CREON:  Perfectly just, I won't say no. And yet
          what is this injury you say I did you?

560 OEDIPUS:  Did you persuade me, yes or no, to send
          someone to bring that solemn prophet here?

CREON:  And I still hold to the advice I gave.

OEDIPUS:  How many years ago did your King Laius . . .

CREON:  Laius! Do what? Now I don't understand.

565 OEDIPUS:  Vanish—victim of a murderous violence?

CREON:  That is a long count back into the past.

OEDIPUS:  Well, was this seer then practicing his art?

CREON:  Yes, skilled and honored just as he is today.

OEDIPUS:  Did he, back then, ever refer to me?

570 CREON:  He did not do so in my presence ever.

OEDIPUS:  You did inquire into the murder then.

CREON:  We had to, surely, though we discovered nothing.

OEDIPUS:  But the "skilled" one did not say this then? Why not?

CREON:  I never talk when I am ignorant.

575 OEDIPUS:  But you're not ignorant of your own part.

CREON:  What do you mean? I'll tell you if I know.

OEDIPUS:  Just this: if he had not conferred with you
          he'd not have told about my murdering Laius.

CREON:  If he said that, you are the one who knows.

580       But now it's fair that you should answer me.

OEDIPUS:  Ask on! You won't convict me as the killer.

CREON:  Well then, answer. My sister is your wife?

OEDIPUS:  Now there's a statement that I can't deny.

CREON:  You two have equal power in this country?

585 OEDIPUS:  She gets from me whatever she desires.

CREON:  And I'm a third? The three of us are equals?

OEDIPUS:  That's where you're treacherous to your kinship!

CREON:  But think about this rationally, as I do.
          First look at this: do you think anyone

590       prefers the anxieties of being king
          to untroubled sleep—if he has equal power?
          I'm not the kind of man who falls in love
          with kingship. I am content with a king's power.
          And so would any man who's wise and prudent.

595       I get all things from you, with no distress;
          as king I would have onerous duties, too.
          How could the kingship bring me more delight
          than this untroubled power and influence?
          I'm not misguided yet to such a point

600       that profitable honors aren't enough.
          As it is, all wish me well and all salute;

those begging you for something have me summoned,
for their success depends on that alone.
Why should I lose all this to become king?
A prudent mind is never traitorous.                                                    605
Treason's a thought I'm not enamored of;
nor could I join a man who acted so.
In proof of this, first go yourself to Pytho°
and ask if I brought back the true response.
Then, if you find I plotted with that portent                                          610
reader,° don't have me put to death by your vote
only—I'll vote myself for my conviction.
Don't let an unsupported thought convict me!
It's not right mindlessly to take the bad
for good or to suppose the good are traitors.                                           615
Rejecting a relation who is loyal
is like rejecting life, our greatest love.
In time you'll know securely without stumbling,
for time alone can prove a just man just,
though you can know a bad man in a day.                                                 620

CHORAGOS:  Well said, to one who's anxious not to fall.
    Swift thinkers, Lord, are never safe from stumbling.

OEDIPUS:  But when a swift and secret plotter moves
    against me, I must make swift counterplot.
    If I lie quiet and await his move,                                                  625
    he'll have achieved his aims and I'll have missed.

CREON:  You surely cannot mean you want me exiled!

OEDIPUS:  Not exiled, no. Your death is what I want!

CREON:  If you would first define what envy is . . .

OEDIPUS:  Are you still stubborn! Still disobedient?                                    630

CREON:  I see you cannot think!

OEDIPUS:                     For me I can.

CREON:  You should for me as well!

OEDIPUS:                          But you're a traitor!

CREON:  What if you're wrong?

OEDIPUS:                      Authority must be maintained.

CREON:  Not if the ruler's evil.

OEDIPUS:                        Hear that, Thebes!

CREON:  It is my city too, not yours alone!                                             635

CHORAGOS:  Please don't, my Lords! Ah, just in time, I see
    Jocasta there, coming from the palace.
    With her help you must settle your quarrel.

[*Enter* JOCASTA *from the Palace.*]

JOCASTA:  Wretched men! What has provoked this ill-
    advised dispute? Have you no sense of shame,                                        640
    with Thebes so sick, to stir up private troubles?
    Now go inside! And Creon, you go home!
    Don't make a general anguish out of nothing!

---

°608 *Pytho*: Delphi. 610–611 *portent reader*: Apollo's oracle or prophet.

CREON: My sister, Oedipus your husband here
645    sees fit to do one of two hideous things:
   to have me banished from the land—or killed!
OEDIPUS: That's right: I caught him, Lady, plotting harm
   against my person—with a malignant science.
CREON: May my life fail, may I die cursed, if I
650    did any of the things you said I did!
JOCASTA: Believe his words, for the god's sake, Oedipus,
   in deference above all to his oath
   to the gods. Also for me, and for these men!

## KOMMOS°

### Strophe 1

CHORUS: Consent, with will and mind,
655    my king, I beg of you!
OEDIPUS: What do you wish me to surrender?
CHORUS: Show deference to him who was not feeble in time past
   and is now great in the power of his oath!
OEDIPUS: Do you know what you're asking?
CHORUS:                       Yes.
OEDIPUS:                           Tell me then.
660 CHORUS: Never to cast into dishonored guilt, with an unproved
   assumption, a kinsman who has bound himself by curse.
OEDIPUS: Now you must understand, when you ask this,
   you ask my death or banishment from the land.

### Strophe 2

CHORUS: No, by the god who is the foremost of all gods,
665    the Sun! No! Godless,
      friendless, whatever death is worst of all,
   let that be my destruction, if this
      thought ever moved me!
   But my ill-fated soul
670       this dying land
   wears out—the more if to these older troubles
   she adds new troubles from the two of you!
OEDIPUS: Then let him go, though it must mean my death,
   or else disgrace and exile from the land.
675    My pity is moved by your words, not by his—
   he'll only have my hate, wherever he goes.
CREON: You're sullen as you yield; you'll be depressed
   when you've passed through this anger. Natures like yours
   are hardest on themselves. That's as it should be.
OEDIPUS: Then won't you go and let me be?
680 CREON:                         I'll go.
   Though you're unreasonable, they know I'm righteous.

                                                  *[Exit CREON.]*

---

°654 *Kommos*: a dirge or lament sung by the Chorus and one or more of the chief characters.

## Antistrophe 1

CHORUS: Why are you waiting, Lady?
    Conduct him back into the palace!
JOCASTA: I will, when I have heard what chanced.
CHORUS: Conjectures—words alone, and nothing based on thought.    685
    But even an injustice can devour a man.
JOCASTA: Did the words come from both sides?
CHORUS:                               Yes.
JOCASTA: What was said?
CHORUS: To me it seems enough! enough! the land already troubled,
    that this should rest where it has stopped.    690
OEDIPUS: See what you've come to in your honest thought,
    in seeking to relax and blunt my heart?

## Antistrophe 2

CHORUS: I have not said this only once, my Lord.
    That I had lost my sanity,
        without a path in thinking—    695
    be sure this would be clear
        if I put you away
    who, when my cherished land
        wandered crazed
    with suffering, brought her back on course.    700
    Now, too, be a lucky helmsman!
JOCASTA: Please, for the god's sake, Lord, explain to me
    the reason why you have conceived this wrath?
OEDIPUS: I honor you, not them,° and I'll explain
    to you how Creon has conspired against me.    705
JOCASTA: All right, if that will explain how the quarrel started.
OEDIPUS: He says I am the murderer of Laius!
JOCASTA: Did he claim knowledge or that someone told him?
OEDIPUS: Here's what he did: he sent that vicious seer
    so he could keep his own mouth innocent.    710
JOCASTA: Ah then, absolve yourself of what he charges!
    Listen to this and you'll agree, no mortal
    is ever given skill in prophecy.
    I'll prove this quickly with one incident.
    It was foretold to Laius—I shall not say    715
    by Phoebus himself, but by his ministers—
    that when his fate arrived he would be killed
    by a son who would be born to him and me.
    And yet, so it is told, foreign robbers
    murdered him, at a place where three roads meet.    720
    As for the child I bore him, not three days passed
    before he yoked the ball-joints of its feet,°

---

°704 *them*: the Chorus.  722 *ball-joints of its feet*: the ankles.

then cast it, by others' hands, on a trackless mountain.
That time Apollo did not make our child

725    a patricide, or bring about what Laius
feared, that he be killed by his own son.
That's how prophetic words determined things!
Forget them. The things a god must track
he will himself painlessly reveal.

730 OEDIPUS: Just now, as I was listening to you, Lady,
what a profound distraction seized my mind!

JOCASTA: What made you turn around so anxiously?

OEDIPUS: I thought you said that Laius was attacked
and butchered at a place where three roads meet.

735 JOCASTA: That is the story, and it is told so still.

OEDIPUS: Where is the place where this was done to him?

JOCASTA: The land's called Phocis, where a two-forked road
comes in from Delphi and from Daulia.

OEDIPUS: And how much time has passed since these events?

740 JOCASTA: Just prior to your presentation here
as king this news was published to the city.

OEDIPUS: Oh, Zeus, what have you willed to do to me?

JOCASTA: Oedipus, what makes your heart so heavy?

OEDIPUS: No, tell me first of Laius' appearance,

745    what peak of youthful vigor he had reached.

JOCASTA: A tall man, showing his first growth of white.
He had a figure not unlike your own.

OEDIPUS: Alas! It seems that in my ignorance
I laid those fearful curses on myself.

750 JOCASTA: What is it, Lord? I flinch to see your face.

OEDIPUS: I'm dreadfully afraid the prophet sees.
But I'll know better with one more detail.

JOCASTA: I'm frightened too. But ask: I'll answer you.

OEDIPUS: Was his retinue small, or did he travel

755    with a great troop, as would befit a prince?

JOCASTA: There were just five in all, one a herald.
There was a carriage, too, bearing Laius.

OEDIPUS: Alas! Now I see it! But who was it,
Lady, who told you what you know about this?

760 JOCASTA: A servant who alone was saved unharmed.

OEDIPUS: By chance, could he be now in the palace?

JOCASTA: No, he is not. When he returned and saw
you had the power of the murdered Laius,
he touched my hand and begged me formally

765    to send him to the fields and to the pastures,
so he'd be out of sight, far from the city.
I did. Although a slave, he well deserved
to win this favor, and indeed far more.

OEDIPUS: Let's have him called back in immediately.

770 JOCASTA: That can be done, but why do you desire it?

OEDIPUS: I fear, Lady, I have already said
too much. That's why I wish to see him now.

JOCASTA:  Then he shall come; but it is right somehow
    that I, too, Lord, should know what troubles you.

OEDIPUS:  I've gone so deep into the things I feared          775
    I'll tell you everything. Who has a right
    greater than yours, while I cross through this chance?
    Polybus of Corinth was my father,
    my mother was the Dorian Meropē.
    I was first citizen, until this chance          780
    attacked me—striking enough, to be sure,
    but not worth all the gravity I gave it.
    This: at a feast a man who'd drunk too much
    denied, at the wine, I was my father's son.
    I was depressed and all that day I barely          785
    held it in. Next day I put the question
    to my mother and father. They were enraged
    at the man who'd let this fiction fly at me.
    I was much cheered by them. And yet it kept
    grinding into me. His words kept coming back.          790
    Without my mother's or my father's knowledge
    I went to Pytho. But Phoebus sent me away
    dishonoring my demand. Instead, other
    wretched horrors he flashed forth in speech.
    He said that I would be my mother's lover,          795
    show offspring to mankind they could not look at,
    and be his murderer whose seed I am.°
    When I heard this, and ever since, I gauged
    the way to Corinth by the stars alone,
    running to a place where I would never see          800
    the disgrace in the oracle's words come true.
    But I soon came to the exact location
    where, as you tell of it, the king was killed.
    Lady, here is the truth. As I went on,
    when I was just approaching those three roads,          805
    a herald and a man like him you spoke of
    came on, riding a carriage drawn by colts.
    Both the man out front and the old man himself°
    tried violently to force me off the road.
    The driver, when he tried to push me off,          810
    I struck in anger. The old man saw this, watched
    me approach, then leaned out and lunged down
    with twin prongs° at the middle of my head!
    He got more than he gave. Abruptly—struck
    once by the staff in this my hand—he tumbled          815
    out, head first, from the middle of the carriage.
    And then I killed them all. But if there is
    a kinship between Laius and this stranger,

---

°797 *be . . . am*: that is, murder my father. 808 *old man himself*: Laius. 812–813 *lunged . . . prongs*: Laius strikes Oedipus with a two-pronged horse goad or whip.

who is more wretched than the man you see?
820  Who was there born more hated by the gods?
For neither citizen nor foreigner
may take me in his home or speak to me.
No, they must drive me off. And it is I
who have pronounced these curses on myself!
825  I stain the dead man's bed with these my hands,
by which he died. Is not my nature vile?
Unclean?—if I am banished and even
in exile I may not see my own parents,
or set foot in my homeland, or else be yoked
830  in marriage to my mother, and kill my father,
Polybus, who raised me and gave me birth?
If someone judged a cruel divinity
did this to me, would he not speak the truth?
You pure and awful gods, may I not ever
835  see that day, may I be swept away
from men before I see so great and so
calamitous a stain fixed on my person!
CHORAGOS:  These things seem fearful to us, Lord, and yet,
until you hear it from the witness, keep hope!
840 OEDIPUS:  That is the single hope that's left to me,
to wait for him, that herdsman—until he comes.
JOCASTA:  When he appears, what are you eager for?
OEDIPUS:  Just this: if his account agrees with yours
then I shall have escaped this misery.
845 JOCASTA:  But what was it that struck you in my story?
OEDIPUS:  You said he spoke of robbers as the ones
who killed him. Now: if he continues still
to speak of many, then I could not have killed him.
One man and many men just do not jibe.
850  But if he says one belted man, the doubt
is gone. The balance tips toward me. I did it.
JOCASTA:  No! He told it as I told you. Be certain.
He can't reject that and reverse himself.
The city heard these things, not I alone.
855  But even if he swerves from what he said,
he'll never show that Laius' murder, Lord,
occurred just as predicted. For Loxias
expressly said my son was doomed to kill him.
The boy—poor boy—he never had a chance
860  to cut him down, for he was cut down first.
Never again, just for some oracle
will I shoot frightened glances right and left.
OEDIPUS:  That's full of sense. Nonetheless, send a man
to bring that farm hand here. Will you do it?
865 JOCASTA:  I'll send one right away. But let's go in.
Would I do anything against your wishes?

[*Exit* OEDIPUS *and* JOCASTA *through the central door into the palace.*]

## STASIMON 2

### Strophe 1

CHORUS:  May there accompany me
    the fate to keep a reverential purity in what I say,
    in all I do, for which the laws have been set forth
    and walk on high, born to traverse the brightest,                    870
    highest upper air; Olympus° only
    is their father, nor was it
    mortal nature
    that fathered them, and never will
    oblivion lull them into sleep;                                       875
    the god in them is great and never ages.

### Antistrophe 1

    The will to violate, seed of the tyrant,
    if it has drunk mindlessly of wealth and power,
    without a sense of time or true advantage,
    mounts to a peak, then                                               880
    plunges to an abrupt . . . destiny,
    where the useful foot
    is of no use. But the kind
    of struggling that is good for the city
    I ask the god never to abolish.                                      885
    The god is my protector: never will I give that up.

### Strophe 2

    But if a man proceeds disdainfully
        in deeds of hand or word
    and has no fear of Justice
        or reverence for shrines of the divinities                          890
    (may a bad fate catch him
        for his luckless wantonness!),
    if he'll not gain what he gains with justice
    and deny himself what is unholy,
    or if he clings, in foolishness, to the untouchable                  895
    (what man, finally, in such an action, will have strength
    enough to fend off passion's arrows from his soul?),
    if, I say, this kind of
        deed is held in honor—
    why should I join the sacred dance?                                  900

### Antistrophe 2

    No longer shall I visit and revere
        Earth's navel° the untouchable,
    nor visit Abae's° temple,
        or Olympia,°

---

°871 *Olympus*: Mount Olympus, home of the gods, treated as a god.  902 *Earth's navel*: Delphi.  903 *Abae*: a town in Phocis where there was another oracle of Apollo.  904 *Olympia*: site of the oracle of Zeus.

905    if the prophecies are not matched by events
      for all the world to point to.
   No, you who hold the power, if you are rightly called
   Zeus the king of all, let this matter not escape you
   and your ever-deathless rule,
910    for the prophecies to Laius fade . . .
   and men already disregard them;
   nor is Apollo anywhere
      glorified with honors.
   Religion slips away.

## EPISODE 3

[*Enter* JOCASTA *from the palace carrying a branch wound with wool and a jar of incense. She is attended by two women.*]

915 JOCASTA: Lords of the realm, the thought has come to me
   to visit shrines of the divinities
   with suppliant's branch in hand and fragrant smoke.
   For Oedipus excites his soul too much
   with alarms of all kinds. He will not judge
920    the present by the past, like a man of sense.
   He's at the mercy of all terror-mongers.

[*JOCASTA approaches the altar on the right and kneels.*]

   Since I can do no good by counseling,
   Apollo the Lycēan!—you are the closest—
   I come a suppliant, with these my vows,
925    for a cleansing that will not pollute him.
   For when we see him shaken we are all
   afraid, like people looking at their helmsman.

[*Enter a* MESSENGER *along one of the Parados. He sees* JOCASTA *at the altar and then addresses the* CHORUS.]

MESSENGER: I would be pleased if you would help me, stranger.
   Where is the palace of King Oedipus?
930    Or tell me where he is himself, if you know.
CHORUS: This is his house, stranger. He is within.
   This is his wife and mother of his children.
MESSENGER: May she and her family find prosperity,
   if, as you say, her marriage is fulfilled.
935 JOCASTA: You also, stranger, for you deserve as much
   for your gracious words. But tell me why you've come.
   What do you wish? Or what have you to tell us?
MESSENGER: Good news, my Lady, both for your house and
   husband.
940 JOCASTA: What is your news? And who has sent you to us?
MESSENGER: I come from Corinth. When you have heard my
     news
   you will rejoice, I'm sure—and grieve perhaps.

JOCASTA: What is it? How can it have this double power?
MESSENGER: They will establish him their king, so say                              945
    the people of the land of Isthmia°
JOCASTA: But is old Polybus not still in power?
MESSENGER: He's not, for death has clasped him in the tomb.
JOCASTA: What's this? Has Oedipus' father died?
MESSENGER: If I have lied then I deserve to die.                                  950
JOCASTA: Attendant! Go quickly to your master,
    and tell him this.

                                     *[Exit an ATTENDANT into the palace.]*

              Oracles of the gods!
Where are you now? The man whom Oedipus
fled long ago, for fear that he should kill him—
he's been destroyed by chance and not by him!                                    955

*[Enter OEDIPUS from the palace.]*

OEDIPUS: Darling Jocasta, my beloved wife,
    Why have you called me from the palace?
JOCASTA: First hear what this man has to say. Then see
    what the god's grave oracle has come to now!
OEDIPUS: Where is he from? What is this news he brings me?                        960
JOCASTA: From Corinth. He brings news about your father:
    that Polybus is no more! that he is dead!
OEDIPUS: What's this, old man? I want to hear you say it.
MESSENGER: If this is what must first be clarified,
    please be assured that he is dead and gone.                           965
OEDIPUS: By treachery or by the touch of sickness?
MESSENGER: Light pressures tip agéd frames into their sleep.
OEDIPUS: You mean the poor man died of some disease.
MESSENGER: And of the length of years that he had tallied.
OEDIPUS: Aha! Then why should we look to Pytho's vapors,°                         970
    or to the birds that scream above our heads?°
    If we could really take those things for guides,
    I would have killed my father. But he's dead!
    He is beneath the earth, and here am I,
    who never touched a spear. Unless he died                            975
    of longing for me and I "killed" him that way!
    No, in this case, Polybus, by dying, took
    the worthless oracle to Hades with him.
JOCASTA: And wasn't I telling you that just now?
OEDIPUS: You were indeed. I was misled by fear.                                  980
JOCASTA: You should not care about this anymore.
OEDIPUS: I must care. I must stay clear of my mother's bed.
JOCASTA: What's there for man to fear? The realm of chance
    prevails. True foresight isn't possible.
    His life is best who lives without a plan.                           985

---

°946 *land of Isthmia*: Corinth, which is on an isthmus.  970 *Pytho's vapors*: the prophecies of the oracle at Delphi.  971 *birds . . . heads*: the prophecies derived from interpreting the flights of birds.

This marriage with your mother—don't fear it.
How many times have men in dreams, too, slept
with their own mothers! Those who believe such things
mean nothing endure their lives most easily.

990 OEDIPUS: A fine, bold speech, and you are right, perhaps,
except that my mother is still living,
so I must fear her, however well you argue.

JOCASTA: And yet your father's tomb is a great eye.

OEDIPUS: Illuminating, yes. But I still fear the living.

995 MESSENGER: Who is the woman who inspires this fear?

OEDIPUS: Merope, Polybus' wife, old man.

MESSENGER: And what is there about her that alarms you?

OEDIPUS: An oracle, god-sent and fearful, stranger.

MESSENGER: Is it permitted that another know?

1000 OEDIPUS: It is. Loxias once said to me
I must have intercourse with my own mother
and take my father's blood with these my hands.
So I have long lived far away from Corinth.
This has indeed brought much good luck, and yet,

1005 to see one's parents' eyes is happiest.

MESSENGER: Was it for this that you have lived in exile?

OEDIPUS: So I'd not be my father's killer, sir.

MESSENGER: Had I not better free you from this fear,
my Lord? That's why I came—to do you service.

1010 OEDIPUS: Indeed, what a reward you'd get for that!

MESSENGER: Indeed, this is the main point of my trip,
to be rewarded when you get back home.

OEDIPUS: I'll never rejoin the givers of my seed!°

MESSENGER: My son, clearly you don't know what you're doing.

1015 OEDIPUS: But how is that, old man? For the gods' sake, tell me!

MESSENGER: If it's because of them you won't go home.

OEDIPUS: I fear that Phoebus will have told the truth.

MESSENGER: Pollution from the ones who gave you seed?

OEDIPUS: That is the thing, old man, I always fear.

1020 MESSENGER: Your fear is groundless. Understand that.

OEDIPUS: Groundless? Not if I was born their son.

MESSENGER: But Polybus is not related to you.

OEDIPUS: Do you mean Polybus was not my father?

MESSENGER: No more than I. We're both the same to you.

1025 OEDIPUS: Same? One who begot me and one who didn't?

MESSENGER: He didn't beget you any more than I did.

OEDIPUS: But then, why did he say I was his son?

MESSENGER: He got you as a gift from my own hands.

OEDIPUS: He loved me so, though from another's hands?

1030 MESSENGER: His former childlessness persuaded him.

OEDIPUS: But had you bought me, or begotten me?

MESSENGER: Found you. In the forest hallows of Cithaeron.

OEDIPUS: What were you doing traveling in that region?

---

°1013 *givers of my seed*: that is, my parents. Oedipus still thinks Meropē and Polybus are his parents.

MESSENGER: I was in charge of flocks which grazed those mountains.
OEDIPUS: A wanderer who worked the flocks for hire?                    1035
MESSENGER: Ah, but that day. I was your savior, son.
OEDIPUS: From what? What was my trouble when you took me?
MESSENGER: The ball-joints of your feet might testify.
OEDIPUS: What's that? What makes you name that ancient trouble?
MESSENGER: Your feet were pierced and I am your rescuer.              1040
OEDIPUS: A fearful rebuke those tokens left for me!
MESSENGER: That was the chance that names you who you are.
OEDIPUS: By the gods, did my mother or my father do this?
MESSENGER: That I don't know. He might who gave you to me.
OEDIPUS: From someone else? You didn't chance on me?                  1045
MESSENGER: Another shepherd handed you to me.
OEDIPUS: Who was he? Do you know? Will you explain!
MESSENGER: They called him one of the men of—was it Laius?
OEDIPUS: The one who once was king here long ago?
MESSENGER: That is the one! The man was shepherd to him.             1050
OEDIPUS: And is he still alive so I can see him?
MESSENGER: But you who live here ought to know that best.
OEDIPUS: Does any one of you now present know
    about the shepherd whom this man has named?
    Have you seen him in town or in the fields? Speak out!     1055
    The time has come for the discovery!
CHORAGOS: The man he speaks of, I believe, is the same
    as the field hand you have already asked to see.
    But it's Jocasta who would know this best.
OEDIPUS: Lady, do you remember the man we just                        1060
    now sent for—is that the man he speaks of?
JOCASTA: What? The man he spoke of? Pay no attention!
    His words are not worth thinking about. It's nothing.
OEDIPUS: With clues like this within my grasp, give up?
    Fail to solve the mystery of my birth?                         1065
JOCASTA: For the love of the gods, and if you love your life,
    give up this search! My sickness is enough.
OEDIPUS: Come! Though my mothers for three generations
    were in slavery, you'd not be lowborn!
JOCASTA: No, listen to me! Please! Don't do this thing!              1070
OEDIPUS: I will not listen; I will search out the truth.
JOCASTA: My thinking is for you—it would be best.
OEDIPUS: This "best" of yours is starting to annoy me.
JOCASTA: Doomed man! Never find out who you are!
OEDIPUS: Will someone go and bring that shepherd here?               1075
    Leave her to glory in her wealthy birth!
JOCASTA: Man of misery! No other name
    shall I address you by, ever again.

[*Exit* JOCASTA *into the palace after a long pause.*]

CHORAGOS: Why has your lady left, Oedipus,
    hurled by a savage grief? I am afraid                          1080
    disaster will come bursting from this silence.

OEDIPUS: Let it burst forth! However low this seed
    of mine may be, yet I desire to see it.
    She, perhaps—she has a woman's pride—
1085    is mortified by my base origins.
    But I who count myself the child of Chance,
    the giver of good, shall never know dishonor.
    She is my mother,° and the months my brothers
    who first marked out my lowness, then my greatness.
1090    I shall not prove untrue to such a nature
    by giving up the search for my own birth.

## STASIMON 3

### Strophe

CHORUS: If I have mantic power
    and excellence in thought,
    by Olympus,
1095        you shall not, Cithaeron, at tomorrow's
    full moon,
    fail to hear us celebrate you as the countryman
    of Oedipus, his nurse and mother,
    or fail to be the subject of our dance,
1100        since you have given pleasure
    to our king.
Phoebus, whom we summon by "iē!,"
may this be pleasing to you!

### Antistrophe

Who was your mother, son?
1105    which of the long-lived nymphs
    after lying with Pan,°
        the mountain roaming . . . Or was it a bride
    of Loxias?°
    For dear to him are all the upland pastures.
1110    Or was it Mount Cyllēnē's lord,°
    or the Bacchic god,°
        dweller of the mountain peaks,
    who received you as a joyous find
    from one of the nymphs of Helicon,
1115    the favorite sharers of his sport?

## EPISODE 4

OEDIPUS: If someone like myself, who never met him,
    may calculate—elders, I think I see
    the very herdsman we've been waiting for.
    His many years would fit that man's age,

---

°1088 *She . . . mother*: Chance is my mother. 1106 *Pan*: god of shepherds and woodlands, half man and half goat. 1108 *Loxias*: Apollo. 1110 *Mount Cyllēnē's lord*: Hermes, messenger of the gods. 1111 *Bacchic god*: Dionysus.

and those who bring him on, if I am right,                                              1120
are my own men. And yet, in real knowledge,
you can outstrip me, surely: you've seen him.

[*Enter the old* HERDSMAN *escorted by two of Oedipus's* ATTENDANTS. *At first, the* HERDSMAN *will not look at* OEDIPUS.]

CHORAGOS:  I know him, yes, a man of the house of Laius,
    a trusty herdsman if he ever had one.
OEDIPUS:  I ask you first, the stranger come from Corinth:                               1125
    is this the man you spoke of?
MESSENGER:                            That's he you see.
OEDIPUS:  Then you, old man. First look at me! Now answer:
    did you belong to Laius' household once?
HERDSMAN:  I did. Not a purchased slave but raised in the palace.
OEDIPUS:  How have you spent your life? What is your work?                               1130
HERDSMAN:  Most of my life now I have tended sheep.
OEDIPUS:  Where is the usual place you stay with them?
HERDSMAN:  On Mount Cithaeron. Or in that district.
OEDIPUS:  Do you recall observing this man there?
HERDSMAN:  Doing what? Which is the man you mean?                                        1135
OEDIPUS:  This man right here. Have you had dealings with him?
HERDSMAN:  I can't say right away. I don't remember.
MESSENGER:  No wonder, master. I'll bring clear memory
    to his ignorance. I'm absolutely sure
    he can recall it, the district was Cithaeron,                                1140
    he with a double flock, and I, with one,
    lived close to him, for three entire seasons,
    six months long, from spring right to Arcturus.°
    Then for the winter I'd drive mine to my fold,
    and he'd drive his to Laius' pen again.                                       1145
    Did any of the things I say take place?
HERDSMAN:  You speak the truth, though it's from long ago.
MESSENGER:  Do you remember giving me, back then,
    a boy I was to care for as my own?
HERDSMAN:  What are you saying? Why do you ask me that?                                  1150
MESSENGER:  There, sir, is the man who was that boy!
HERDSMAN:  Damn you! Shut your mouth! Keep your silence!
OEDIPUS:  Stop! Don't you rebuke his words.
    Your words ask for rebuke far more than his.
HERDSMAN:  But what have I done wrong, most royal master?                                1155
OEDIPUS:  Not telling of the boy of whom he asked.
HERDSMAN:  He's ignorant and blundering toward ruin.
OEDIPUS:  Tell it willingly—or under torture.
HERDSMAN:  Oh god! Don't—I am old—don't torture me!
OEDIPUS:  Here! Someone put his hands behind his back!                                  1160
HERDSMAN:  But why? What else would you find out, poor man?
OEDIPUS:  Did you give him the child he asks about?

---

°1143 *from spring right to Arcturus*: that is, from spring to early fall, when the summer star Arcturus (in the constellation Boötes) is no longer visible in the early evening sky. It does not rise at night again until the following spring.

HERDSMAN: I did. I wish that I had died that day!

OEDIPUS: You'll come to that if you don't speak the truth.

1165 HERDSMAN: It's if I speak that I shall be destroyed.

OEDIPUS: I think this fellow struggles for delay.

HERDSMAN: No, no! I said already that I gave him.

OEDIPUS: From your own home, or got from someone else?

HERDSMAN: Not from my own. I got him from another.

1170 OEDIPUS: Which of these citizens? What sort of house?

HERDSMAN: Don't—by the gods!—don't, master, ask me more!

OEDIPUS: It means your death if I must ask again.

HERDSMAN: One of the children of the house of Laius.

OEDIPUS: A slave—or born into the family?

1175 HERDSMAN: I have come to the dreaded thing, and I shall say it.

OEDIPUS: And I to hearing it, but hear I must.

HERDSMAN: He was reported to have been—his son.

    Your lady in the house could tell you best.

OEDIPUS: Because she gave him to you?

HERDSMAN:                    Yes, my lord.

OEDIPUS: What was her purpose?

1180 HERDSMAN:                   I was to kill the boy.

OEDIPUS: The child she bore?

HERDSMAN:              She dreaded prophecies.

OEDIPUS: What were they?

HERDSMAN:            The word was that he'd kill his parents.

OEDIPUS: Then why did you give him up to this old man?

HERDSMAN: In pity, master—so he would take him home,

1185     to another land. But what he did was save him

    for this supreme disaster. If you are the one

    he speaks of—know your evil birth and fate!

OEDIPUS: Ah! All of it was destined to be true!

    Oh light, now may I look my last upon you,

1190     shown monstrous in my birth, in marriage monstrous,

    a murderer monstrous in those I killed.

                    [*Exit* OEDIPUS, *running into the palace.*]

## STASIMON 4

### Strophe 1

CHORUS: Oh generations of mortal men,

    while you are living, I will

        appraise your lives at zero!

1195     What man

    comes closer to seizing lasting blessedness

    than merely to seize its semblance,

    and after living in this semblance, to plunge?

    With your example before us,

1200     with your destiny, yours,

        suffering Oedipus, no mortal

    can I judge fortunate.

## Antistrophe 1

For he,° outranging everybody,
shot his arrow° and became the lord
    of wide prosperity and blessedness,                    1205
oh Zeus, after destroying
the virgin with the crooked talons,°
singer of oracles; and against death,
in my land, he arose a tower of defense.
From which time you were called my king                       1210
and granted privileges supreme—in mighty
Thebes the ruling lord.

## Strophe 2

But now—whose story is more sorrowful than yours?
Who is more intimate with fierce calamities,
with labors, now that your life is altered?                   1215
Alas, my Oedipus, whom all men know:
one great harbor.°—
one alone sufficed for you,
as son and father,
when you tumbled,° plowman° of the woman's chamber.          1220
How, how could your paternal
    furrows, wretched man,
endure you silently so long.

## Antistrophe 2

Time, all-seeing, surprised you living an unwilled life
and sits from of old in judgment on the marriage, not a marriage,    1225
where the begetter is the begot as well.
Ah, son of Laius . . . ,
would that—oh, would that
I had never seen you!
I wail, my scream climbing beyond itself                      1230
from my whole power of voice. To say it straight:
    from you I got new breath—
but I also lulled my eye to sleep.°

## EXODOS

[*Enter the* SECOND MESSENGER *from the palace.*]

SECOND MESSENGER: You who are first among the citizens,
    what deeds you are about to hear and see!                1235
What grief you'll carry, if, true to your birth,
you still respect the house of Labdacus!
Neither the Ister nor the Phasis river

---

°1203 *he*: Oedipus. 1204 *shot his arrow*: took his chances; made a guess at the Sphinx's riddle. 1207 *virgin . . . talons*: the Sphinx. 1217 *one great harbor*: metaphorical allusion to Jocasta's body. 1220 *tumbled*: were born and had sex. *plowman*: Plowing is used here as a sexual metaphor. 1233 *I . . . sleep*: I failed to see the corruption you brought.

could purify this house, such suffering
1240    does it conceal, or soon must bring to light—
willed this time, not unwilled. Griefs hurt worst
which we perceive to be self-chosen ones.
CHORAGOS:  They were sufficient, the things we knew before,
to make us grieve. What can you add to those?
1245 SECOND MESSENGER:  The thing that's quickest said and quickest heard:
our own, our royal one, Jocasta's dead.
CHORAGOS:  Unhappy queen! What was responsible?
SECOND MESSENGER:  Herself. The bitterest of these events
is not for you, you were not there to see,
1250    but yet, exactly as I can recall it,
you'll hear what happened to that wretched lady.
She came in anger through the outer hall,
and then she ran straight to her marriage bed,
tearing her hair with the fingers of both hands.
1255    Then, slamming shut the doors when she was in,
she called to Laius, dead so many years,
remembering the ancient seed which caused
his death, leaving the mother to the son
to breed again an ill-born progeny.
1260    She mourned the bed where she, alas, bred double—
husband by husband, children by her child.
From this point on I don't know how she died,
for Oedipus then burst in with a cry,
and did not let us watch her final evil.
1265    Our eyes were fixed on him. Wildly he ran
to each of us, asking for his spear
and for his wife—no wife: where he might find
the double mother-field, his and his children's.
He raved, and some divinity then showed him—
1270    for none of us did so who stood close by.
With a dreadful shout—as if some guide were leading—
he lunged through the double doors; he bent the hollow
bolts from the sockets, burst into the room,
and there we saw her, hanging from above,
1275    entangled in some twisted hanging strands.
He saw, was stricken, and with a wild roar
ripped down the dangling noose. When she, poor woman,
lay on the ground, there came a fearful sight:
he snatched the pins of worked gold from her dress,
1280    with which her clothes were fastened: these he raised
and struck into the ball-joints of his eyes.°
He shouted that they would no longer see
the evils he had suffered or had done,
see in the dark those he should not have seen,
1285    and know no more those he once sought to know.
While chanting this, not once but many times

---

°1281 *ball-joints of his eyes*: his eyeballs. Oedipus blinds himself in both eyes at the same time.

he raised his hand and struck into his eyes.
Blood from his wounded eyes poured down his chin,
not freed in moistening drops, but all at once
a stormy rain of black blood burst like hail.
These evils, coupling them, making them one,                           1295
have broken loose upon both man and wife.
The old prosperity that they had once
was true prosperity, and yet today,
mourning, ruin, death, disgrace, and every
evil you could name—not one is absent.                                 1299

CHORAGOS: Has he allowed himself some peace from all this grief?
SECOND MESSENGER: He shouts that someone slide the bolts and show
    to all the Cadmeians the patricide,
    his mother's—I can't say it, it's unholy—                          1300
    so he can cast himself out of the land,
    not stay and curse his house by his own curse.
    He lacks the strength, though, and he needs a guide,
    for his is a sickness that's too great to bear.
    Now you yourself will see: the bolts of the doors                  1305
    are opening. You are about to see
    a vision even one who hates must pity.

[*Enter the blinded* OEDIPUS *from the palace, led in by a household* SERVANT.]

CHORAGOS: This suffering sends terror through men's eyes,
    terrible beyond any suffering
    my eyes have touched. Oh man of pain,
    what madness reached you? Which god from far off,                  1310
    surpassing in range his longest spring,
        struck hard against your god-abandoned fate?
    Oh man of pain,
    I cannot look upon you—though there's so much
    I would ask you, so much to hear,                                  1315
    so much that holds my eyes—
        so awesome the convulsions you send through me.

OEDIPUS: Ah! Ah! I am a man of misery.
    Where am I carried? Pity me! Where
    is my voice scattered abroad on wings?                             1320
        Divinity, where has your lunge transported me?

CHORAGOS: To something horrible, not to be heard or seen.

## KOMMOS

### Strophe 1

OEDIPUS: Oh, my cloud
    of darkness, abominable, unspeakable as it attacks me,             1325
    not to be turned away, brought by an evil wind!
    Alas!
    Again alas! Both enter me at once:
    the sting of the prongs,° the memory of evils!

---

°1329 *prongs*: refers to both the whip that Laius used and the two gold pins Oedipus used to blind himself.

1330 CHORUS: I do not marvel that in these afflictions
        you carry double griefs and double evils.

### Antistrophe 1

OEDIPUS: Ah, friend,
        so you at least are there, resolute servant!
        Still with a heart to care for me, the blind man.
1335   Oh! Oh!
        I know that you are there. I recognize
        even inside my darkness, that voice of yours.
CHORUS: Doer of horror, how did you bear to quench
        your vision? What divinity raised your hand?

### Strophe 2

1340 OEDIPUS: It was Apollo there, Apollo, friends,
        who brought my sorrows, vile sorrows to their perfection,
                these evils that were done to me.
        But the one who struck them with his hand,
                that one was none but I, in wretchedness.
1345   For why was I to see
        when nothing I could see would bring me joy?
CHORUS: Yes, that is how it was.
OEDIPUS: What could I see, indeed,
        or what enjoy—what greeting
1350   is there I could hear with pleasure, friends?
        Conduct me out of the land
                as quickly as you can!
        Conduct me out, my friends,
                the man utterly ruined,
1355   supremely cursed,
                the man who is by gods
        the most detested of all men!
CHORUS: Wretched in disaster and in knowledge:
        oh, I could wish you'd never come to know!

### Antistrophe 2

1360 OEDIPUS: May he be destroyed, whoever freed the savage shackles
        from my feet when I'd been sent to the wild pasture,
                whoever rescued me from murder
        and became my savior—
                a bitter gift:
1365           if I had died then,
        I'd not have been such grief to self and kin.
CHORUS: I also would have had it so.
OEDIPUS: I'd not have returned to be my father's
        murderer; I'd not be called by men
1370   my mother's bridegroom.
        Now I'm without a god,
                child of a polluted parent,

fellow progenitor with him
 who gave me birth in misery.
If there's an evil that
 surpasses evils, that
has fallen to the lot of Oedipus.         1375
CHORAGOS: How can I say that you have counseled well?
 Better not to be than live a blind man.
OEDIPUS: That this was not the best thing I could do—   1380
 don't tell me that, or advise me any more!
 Should I descend to Hades and endure
 to see my father with these eyes? Or see
 my poor unhappy mother? For I have done,
 to both of these, things too great for hanging.    1385
 Or is the sight of children to be yearned for,
 to see new shoots that sprouted as these did?
 Never, never with these eyes of mine!
 Nor city, nor tower, nor holy images
 of the divinities! For I, all-wretched,       1390
 most nobly raised—as no one else in Thebes—
 deprived myself of these when I ordained
 that all expel the impious one—god-shown
 to be polluted, and the dead king's son!°
 Once I exposed this great stain upon me,     1395
 could I have looked on these with steady eyes?
 No! No! And if there were a way to block
 the source of hearing in my ears, I'd gladly
 have locked up my pitiable body,
 so I'd be blind and deaf. Evils shut out—    1400
 that way my mind could live in sweetness.
 Alas, Cithaeron,° why did you receive me?
 Or when you had me, not killed me instantly?
 I'd not have had to show my birth to mankind.
 Polybus, Corinth, halls—ancestral,       1405
 they told me—how beautiful was your ward,
 a scar that held back festering disease!
 Evil my nature, evil my origin.
 You, three roads, and you, secret ravine,
 you oak grove, narrow place of those three paths   1410
 that drank my blood° from these my hands, from him
 who fathered me, do you remember still
 the things I did to you? When I'd come here,
 what I then did once more? Oh marriages! Marriages!
 You gave us life and when you'd planted us    1415
 you sent the same seed up, and then revealed
 fathers, brothers, sons, and kinsman's blood,
 and brides, and wives, and mothers, all the most
 atrocious things that happen to mankind!

---

°1392–94 *I . . . son*: Oedipus refers to his own curse against the murderer as well as his sins of patricide and incest. 1402 *Cithaeron*: the mountain on which the infant Oedipus was exposed. 1411 *my blood*: i.e., the blood of my father, Laius, and therefore my family's blood.

1420    One should not name what never should have been.
        Somewhere out there, then, quickly, by the gods,
        cover me up, or murder me, or throw me
        to the ocean where you will never see me more!

[OEDIPUS *moves toward the* CHORUS *and they back away from him.*]

        Come! Don't shrink to touch this wretched man!
1425    Believe me, do not be frightened! I alone
        of all mankind can carry these afflictions.

[*Enter* CREON *from the palace with* ATTENDANTS.]

CHORAGOS:  Tell Creon what you wish for. Just when we need him
        he's here. He can act, he can advise you.
        He's now the land's sole guardian in your place.
1430  OEDIPUS:  Ah! Are there words that I can speak to him?
        What ground for trust can I present? It's proved
        that I was false to him in everything.
CREON:  I have not come to mock you, Oedipus,
        nor to reproach you for your former falseness.
1435    You men, if you have no respect for sons
        of mortals, let your awe for the all-feeding
        flames of lordly Hēlius° prevent
        your showing unconcealed so great a stain,
        abhorred by earth and sacred rain and light.
1440    Escort him quickly back into the house!
        If blood kin only see and hear their own
        afflictions, we'll have no impious defilement.
OEDIPUS:  By the gods, you've freed me from one terrible fear,
        so nobly meeting my unworthiness:
1445    grant me something—not for me; for you!
CREON:  What do you want that you should beg me so?
OEDIPUS:  To drive me from the land at once, to a place
        where there will be no man to speak to me!
CREON:  I would have done just that—had I not wished
1450    to ask first of the god what I should do.
OEDIPUS:  His answer was revealed in full—that I,
        the patricide, unholy, be destroyed.
CREON:  He said that, but our need is so extreme,
        it's best to have sure knowledge what must be done.
1455  OEDIPUS:  You'll ask about a wretched man like me?
CREON:  Is it not time you put your trust in the god?
OEDIPUS:  But I bid you as well, and shall entreat you.
        Give her who is within what burial
        you will—you'll give your own her proper rites;
1460    but me—do not condemn my fathers' land
        to have me dwelling here while I'm alive,
        but let me live on mountains—on Cithaeron
        famed as mine, for my mother and my father,

---

°1437 *Hēlius*: the sun.

while they yet lived, made it my destined tomb,
and I'll be killed by those who wished my ruin!
And yet I know: no sickness will destroy me,                    1465
nothing will: I'd never have been saved
when left to die unless for some dread evil.
Then let my fate continue where it will!
As for my children, Creon, take no pains                        1470
for my sons—they're men and they will never lack
the means to live, wherever they may be—
but my two wretched, pitiable girls,
who never ate but at my table, never
were without me—everything that I                               1475
would touch, they'd always have a share of it—
please care for them! Above all, let me touch
them with my hands and weep aloud my woes!
Please, my Lord!
Please, noble heart! Touching with my hands,                    1480
I'd think I held them as when I could see.

[*Enter* ANTIGONE *and* ISMENE *from the palace with* ATTENDANTS.]

What's this?
Oh gods! Do I hear, somewhere, my two dear ones
sobbing? Has Creon really pitied me
and sent to me my dearest ones, my children?                    1485
Is that it?
CREON:  Yes, I prepared this for you, for I knew
you'd feel this joy, as you have always done.
OEDIPUS:  Good fortune, then, and, for your care, be guarded
far better by divinity than I was!                              1490
Where are you, children? Come to me! Come here
to these my hands, hands of your brother, hands
of him who gave you seed, hands that made
these once bright eyes to see now in this fashion.

[OEDIPUS *embraces his daughters.*]

He, children, seeing nothing, knowing nothing,                  1495
he fathered you where his own seed was plowed.
I weep for you as well, though I can't see you,
imagining your bitter life to come,
the life you will be forced by men to live.
What gatherings of townsmen will you join,                      1500
what festivals, without returning home
in tears instead of watching holy rites?
And when you've reached the time for marrying,
where, children, is the man who'll run the risk
of taking on himself the infamy                                 1505
that will wound you as it did my parents?
What evil is not here? Your father killed
his father, plowed the one who gave him birth,
and from the place where he was sown, from there

1510    he got you, from the place he too was born.
        These are the wounds: then who will marry you?
        No man, my children. No, it's clear that you
        must wither in dry barrenness, unmarried.

[OEDIPUS *addresses* CREON.]

        Son of Menoeceus! You are the only father
1515    left to them—we two who gave them seed
        are both destroyed: watch that they don't become
        poor, wanderers, unmarried—they are your kin.
        Let not my ruin be their ruin, too!
        No, pity them! You see how young they are,
1520    bereft of everyone, except for you.
        Consent, kind heart, and touch me with your hand!

[CREON *grasps* OEDIPUS'S *right hand.*]

        You, children, if you had reached an age of sense,
        I would have counseled much. Now, pray you may live
        always where it's allowed, finding a life
1525    better than his was, who gave you seed.
        CREON: Stop this now. Quiet your weeping. Move away, into the house.
        OEDIPUS: Bitter words, but I obey them.
        CREON:                          There's an end to all things.
        OEDIPUS: I have first this request.
        CREON:                          I will hear it.
        OEDIPUS: Banish me from my homeland.
        CREON:                          You must ask that of the god.
        OEDIPUS: But I am the gods' most hated man!
1530    CREON:                          Then you will soon get what you want.
        OEDIPUS: Do you consent?
        CREON:                          I never promise when, as now, I'm ignorant.
        OEDIPUS: Then lead me in.
        CREON:                          Come. But let your hold fall from your children.
        OEDIPUS: Do not take them from me, ever!
        CREON:                          Do not wish to keep all of the
        power. You had power, but that power did not follow you through life.

[OEDIPUS'S *daughters are taken from him and led into the palace by* ATTENDANTS. OEDIPUS *is led into
the palace by a* SERVANT. CREON *and the other* ATTENDANTS *follow. Only the* CHORUS *remains.*]

1535    CHORUS: People of Thebes, my country, see: here is that Oedipus—
        he who "knew" the famous riddle, and attained the highest power,
        whom all citizens admired, even envying his luck!
        See the billows of wild troubles which he has entered now!
        Here is the truth of each man's life: we must wait, and see his end,
1540    scrutinize his dying day, and refuse to call him happy
        till he has crossed the border of his life without pain.

[*Exit the* CHORUS *along each of the Parados.*]

## Questions

1. *Prologue and Parados*. What is the situation in Thebes as the play begins? Why does Oedipus want to discover the murderer of Laius?

2. *Episode 1 and Stasimon 1*. When Tiresias refuses to speak, how is the reaction of Oedipus characteristic of him? What other examples of this behavior can you find?

3. When Tiresias does speak, he speaks the truth. Why doesn't Oedipus accept the story that Tiresias tells?

4. *Episode 2 and Stasimon 2*. Of what does Oedipus accuse Creon, and how does Creon defend himself? Why or why not is Creon convincing?

5. What does Jocasta have to say about oracles and prophecy? Why do you think she expresses this attitude? How do her views differ from those of the Chorus?

6. When does Oedipus begin to think that he himself is the murderer? What details lead him to this conclusion?

7. *Episode 3 and Stasimon 3*. Why does the news from the Messenger from Corinth at first seem good? How is the situation reversed?

8. *Episode 4 and Stasimon 4*. What do you make of the coincidences that the same Herdsman (a) saved the infant Oedipus from death, (b) was the lone survivor of the attack on Laius and also the sole witness to the attack, and (c) will provide testimony that will destroy Oedipus?

9. What moral does the Chorus express about the life and downfall of Oedipus?

## General Questions

1. In *Oedipus the King*, the peripeteia, anagnorisis, and catastrophe all occur at the same moment. When is this moment? Who is most severely affected by it?

2. Sophocles describes Oedipus's life piecemeal, out of chronological order. Put the details into chronological order, and consider how you might dramatize them. Why does Sophocles's ordering of events make for an effective play? Be sure to emphasize some of the coincidences in the life and career of Oedipus.

3. What is the major conflict in the play? What other conflicts does Sophocles bring out? How is the complexity of the conflicts brought out by Sophocles?

4. In the light of your understanding of tragedy and the tragic hero, describe *Oedipus the King* as a tragedy.

5. Describe Sophocles's use of dramatic irony in the play.

6. Describe the functions of the Chorus and the Choragos. Explain the relationship of the choral odes to the play's actions.

## Renaissance Drama and Shakespeare's Theater

In the early years of the English Renaissance, there was a flourishing native tradition of theater that had developed first within the church and then with the cooperation of the church.[13] The bridge from religious drama to the drama of the Renaissance was created in a number of ways. Of great importance was the growth of traveling

---

[13]For an account of the medieval dramatic tradition, see Ch. 20, pp. 877–880.

dramatic professional companies, who performed their plays in local innyards—square or quadrangular spaces surrounded by the rooms of the inn. In addition, plays were performed at court, in the great rooms of aristocratic houses, in the law courts, and at universities.

Aside from the performing tradition, the immediate influence on the creation of a new drama was the development of a taste for dramatic topics drawn from non-religious sources. The earliest of such plays in the sixteenth century was the so-called **Tudor interlude**, named after the monarchs of the Tudor family who ruled England from 1485 to 1603. *Interlude* is a misnomer, for the plays were often quite long. The interludes, supported by the nobility, were tragedies, comedies, or historical plays that were performed by both professional actors and students. They sometimes featured abstract and allegorical characters and provided opportunities for both music and farcical action.

After the middle of the sixteenth century, the revival of ancient drama and culture came increasingly to the fore. The dominating influence was the Roman dramatist Seneca (4 B.C.E.–65 C.E.), eight of whose tragedies, derived from Greek tragedy, had survived from antiquity. A vital quality of the Senecan tragedies was that they were violent and bloody, and thus they gave a classical precedent for the revenge and murder that were to be featured in the Elizabethan drama. Seneca became important not so much because he had written great works but rather because he had written in Latin. He could therefore be readily understood by a generation of new dramatists who had been schooled in Roman history, culture, language, and literature.

## Shakespeare Became a Theatrical Entrepreneur as Well as a Writer

The first group of these Elizabethan playwrights included Christopher Marlowe, Thomas Kyd, Robert Greene, George Peele, Thomas Lodge, and John Lyly. These were the men whose plays William Shakespeare watched and acted in when he first arrived in London from Stratford-upon-Avon in the late 1580s. By 1594 he had joined the Lord Chamberlain's Men, the most popular of the London acting companies. He rose swiftly as both an actor and dramatist, and by 1599 he had become an active partner with the company (called the "King's Men" after the accession of James I in 1603) in a venture to construct a new theater, the Globe, within a stone's throw of the earlier theater, the Rose. It was for exclusive production at the Globe that Shakespeare wrote some of his greatest plays (including *Hamlet*) from 1599 to 1608, when the company began playing alternately at the outdoor Globe and the indoor Blackfriars (formerly a part of a monastery that had been adapted for theatrical presentations).

## The Globe Was a Small but Versatile Theater That Strongly Influenced the Nature of Shakespeare's Plays

Compared with the massive Greek outdoor amphitheaters, the Globe was small. Some theater historians have calculated that it could have held an audience of as many as two to three thousand, although this estimate seems excessive, for half that number would have been extremely large. Moreover, we need not suppose that the theater was always filled to squeezing room only.

**THE GLOBE WAS A "RING"-TYPE THEATER OPEN TO THE SKY.**   Recent archaeological excavations of the site of the Globe, together with a complete reconstruction based on the knowledge newly gained, show that it was a twenty-sided building. For practical purposes it was round—as it is shown in a contemporary drawing—and its outer diameter was approximately a hundred feet. From above, it would have resembled a ring, or, as Shakespeare called the type in *Henry V*, a "wooden O." Its central yard was open to the sky, a detail that it had appropriated from the confined areas of the inns. The platform stage, covered by a roof, was built thirty feet into the yard at the building's south side. Because of the uncertainty and capriciousness of English weather, the acting season extended from spring through fall. During the wettest and coldest months, the theater was empty.

**THE GLOBE PROVIDED A NUMBER OF ACTING AREAS.**   This thrust stage was close to five feet high—probably lower in front (*downstage*) and higher in back (*upstage*). Actors could move anywhere on this stage to speak their lines. On the second level above the stage was a gallery for spectators, musicians, and actors (as in the balcony scene in Shakespeare's *Romeo and Juliet*). Actors might enter this gallery to deliver lines, and then they might also descend from there to the main stage. The area below the stage was called the *hell*. At center stage there was a trapdoor to the hell that was used for the entrances and exits of devils, monsters, and ghosts such as the Ghost of Hamlet's father. Downstage, holding up the protective roof, there were two columns. The ceiling of this roof, called the *heavens*, was decorated with colorful paintings. A hut on the roof itself contained machinery for lowering and raising actors who took the roles of fairies, witches, and gods. Behind the upstage area, which could be curtained off for interior scenes, there was a small and cramped *tiring house* and storage area where actors changed their costumes and waited for their cues. Two or three doors opened outward from the tiring house to the stage.

**THERE WERE THREE LOCATIONS FOR THE AUDIENCE.**   The admission price permitted spectators into the ground area. Those who remained there stood during the entire performance and crowded as close as they could to the stage. These people, who were patronizingly called the *groundlings*, often endured rain and cold in addition to the discomfort of their need to stand. For additional charges, spectators could get out of bad weather by sitting in one of the three seating levels within the roofed galleries (part of the "O"). Those who could afford it paid still another charge for seats directly on the stage—a custom that continued in English theaters until the time of David Garrick in the eighteenth century.

**THE GLOBE, LIKE OTHER ELIZABETHAN THEATERS, MANDATED ITS OWN PRODUCTION AND STAGE CONVENTIONS.**   Just as in the Athenian theater, there was no artificial lighting, and performances therefore took place in the afternoon. The plays were performed rapidly, without intermissions or indications of act and scene changes except for occasional rhymed couplets. With no curtain and no scenery, the exits and entrances of the actors indicated shifts in scene. This type of scene division produced swift changes in time and place and made for great fluidity and fast pacing.

The conditions of performance and the physical shape of the theater resulted in a number of theatrical conventions. The two columns supporting the stage roof, for example, were versatile. Sometimes they represented trees or the sides of buildings, and conventionally they were used as places of concealment and for eavesdropping. Time, place, and circumstances of weather were established through dialogue, as in the opening scene of *Hamlet* when Horatio speaks of "the morn, in russet mantle clad" (line 166), or in *As You Like It*, when Rosalind says, "This is the forest of Arden" (2.4.15).

The Globe's relatively small size and its thrust stage made for intimate performances. There was little separation of audience and actors, unlike the *orchestra* in Greek theaters that widened the distance between actors and spectators, or with the proscenium and curtain of many modern theaters. The groundlings surrounding the thrust stage at a typical Elizabethan performance were extremely close to the actors at all times. The close proximity of the groundlings and of those spectators who had paid to sit on the stage itself encouraged much interaction between actors and audience. This closeness led to two unique stage conventions. One of these, the **aside**, permitted a character to make brief remarks directly to the audience or to another character without the rest of the characters' hearing the words. In the other, the **soliloquy**, a character alone onstage described his or her thoughts or plans directly to the audience. For example, when Hamlet delivers his second soliloquy, he criticizes his emotional detachment from his father's murder and explains how he plans to test Claudius's guilt (2.2.524–580). Under such circumstances, members of the Elizabethan audience almost literally became additional members of the cast.

**THE ACTORS FOLLOWED ESTABLISHED CONVENTIONS IN GESTURE AND COSTUME.** The actors in Shakespeare's day were legally bound to the company of which they were members. Without the protection of the company, they were considered "rogues and vagabonds." In England, the actors were male, with adolescent boys performing the women's roles because women were excluded from the stage. The actors used no masks. Instead, they developed expressions and gestures that would seem to us, today, excessively stylized. The acting mannerisms sometimes seemed excessive to Shakespeare, too, as is indicated by Hamlet's instructions to the traveling actors. He tells them not to "saw the air too much with your hand" and not to "tear a passion to tatters, to very rags" (3.2.4–9).

The actors wore elaborate costumes to demonstrate the nature and status of the characters. Thus kings always wore robes and crowns, and they carried orbs and scepters. A fool (a type of comic and ironic commentator) wore a multicolored or *motley* costume, and clowns and "mechanicals" wore the common clothing of the humble classes, as with the "hempen homespuns" of *A Midsummer Night's Dream*. Ragged clothing indicated a reduction in circumstances, as in *King Lear*, and Ophelia's description of Hamlet's disordered clothing in the second act of *Hamlet* indicates the prince's disturbed mental condition (2.1.74–82). Whenever characters took on a disguise, as in *As You Like It*, this disguise was impenetrable to the other characters.

## The New Globe Theater Has Been Built Near the Site of Shakespeare's Globe

Shakespeare's Globe burned in 1613, and the Globe that replaced it was torn down by the Puritans under Oliver Cromwell in 1644. From then on the location was variously occupied by tenements, breweries, other buildings, and a road. In the late 1980s, however, archaeological excavations took place at the sites of both the Globe and the nearby Rose Theater, and the subsequent discoveries have provided exciting new information about theaters and theatergoing in Shakespeare's day. A reconstruction of the Globe was undertaken and is now complete—not at the original location, but close by. The original site could not be used because it was preempted by a protected building and a vital street leading to Southwark Bridge. Theatergoers in London are now able to attend performances of Shakespeare's plays in this new theater under conditions almost identical to those that Shakespeare's audiences and acting company knew, including, for the "groundlings," rain, wind, cold, and the discomfort of standing (see the photograph of the reconstruction of the Globe stage, I–11, I–12).[14]

## WILLIAM SHAKESPEARE (1564–1616)

Shakespeare was born in 1564 in Stratford-upon-Avon, in western England. He attended the Stratford grammar school; he married in 1582, and he and his wife had three children. He left his family and moved to London sometime between 1585 and 1592. During this period he became a professional actor, and he also began writing plays and poems. Because the London theaters were closed during the plague years 1592–1594, he apparently worked at other jobs, about which we know nothing. By 1595, however, he was recognized as a major writer of comedies and tragedies. He soon became a member of the Lord Chamberlain's Men, the leading theatrical company, and, as we have seen, he became a shareholder in the new Globe Theatre in 1599. Fortunately, he realized good returns from the business venture and also from his plays, and he became moderately wealthy. He stopped writing for the stage in 1611, having written a total of thirty-seven plays, of which eleven were tragedies. He also collaborated in writing a few other plays. During his retirement he lived in his native Stratford. He died in 1616 and is buried next to the altar of Stratford's Trinity Church, beneath a bust and an inscribed gravestone.

When the Lord Chamberlain's Men first staged *Hamlet* in 1602 at the Globe, it was not the first time the story had been dramatized on the London stage. There is evidence that a play based on the Hamlet story, now lost, had been performed before 1589. Therefore, at least some of the theatergoers might have known the story.

Even if none of them knew the story, however, they would have known the tradition of **revenge tragedy**. The Elizabethans had been introduced to the drama of vengeance through the English translations of Seneca's tragedies during the 1570s and early 1580s. Another important precedent was Thomas Kyd's *Spanish Tragedy* (ca. 1587), the first English play in the revenge tradition, which featured a hero who commits suicide. The major conventions of the genre were a ghost who calls for vengeance and a revenger who pretends to be insane at least part of the time. Above all, the tradition required that the revenger would also die, no matter how good a person or how just his cause.

Although Elizabethan audiences were prepared for *Hamlet* by the revenge formula, they could have anticipated neither a protagonist of Hamlet's likeableness and complexity

---

[14]See J. R. Mulryne and Margaret Shewring, eds., *Shakespeare's Globe Rebuilt* (Cambridge: Cambridge UP, 1997). Further information about the Globe Theatre may be found at the Shakespeare Globe Center, USA, <www.sgc.umd.edu>.

nor a play of such profundity. The earlier revengers were flat characters with a single fix-
ation on righting wrongs through personal vengeance. Hamlet, however, is acutely
aware of the political and moral corruption of the Danish court, and he reflects on the
fallen state of humanity. Experiencing despair and guilt, he even contemplates suicide.
He learns from his experiences and meditations, discovering that he must look beyond
reason and philosophy for ways of coping with the world. He also develops patience
and learns to trust in Providence, the "divinity that shapes our ends" (5.2.10).

The play itself demonstrates the far-reaching effects of evil, which branches inex-
orably outward from Claudius's initial act of murder. The evil ensnares innocent and
guilty alike. Hamlet, the avenger, becomes the direct and indirect cause of deaths, and
as a result, he in turn also becomes an object of revenge. By the play's end, all the major
and two of the minor characters are dead: Polonius, Ophelia, Rosencrantz, Guildenstern,
Gertrude, Claudius, Laertes, and, finally, Hamlet himself. The play's crowning irony is
that Hamlet does not complete his vengeance because of the murder of his father, King
Hamlet, as he originally sets out to do. Rather, he kills Claudius immediately upon learning
that the king has murdered Gertrude, his mother.

In the centuries since Shakespeare wrote *Hamlet*, the play has remained among the
most popular, most moving, and most effective plays in the world. It has been translated
into scores of languages. Major actors from Shakespeare's day to ours—including
Richard Burbage as the first Hamlet, and John Barrymore, Kenneth Branagh, Ralph
Fiennes, Mel Gibson, Ethan Hawke, Derek Jacoby, Kevin Kline, Laurence Olivier, and
Nicol Williamson—have starred in the role. Beyond the play's stage popularity, *Hamlet*
has become one of the central documents of Western civilization. Somehow, most people know about Hamlet and are familiar with passages like "To be or not to be," "The
play's the thing," and "The undiscovered country, from whose bourn/No traveler returns" even if they have never read the play or seen a live or filmed performance.

# The Tragedy of Hamlet, Prince of Denmark (ca. 1602)

### *Edited by Alice Griffin**

**CHARACTERS**

**Claudius,** King of Denmark

**Hamlet,** Son to the former, and nephew to the present King

**Polonius,** Lord Chamberlain

**Horatio,** Friend to Hamlet

**Laertes,** Son to Polonius

**Valtemand**

**Cornelius**

**Rosencrantz** ⎱ Courtiers

**Guildenstern**

**Osric**

**A Gentleman**

**A Priest**

*Professor Griffin's text for *Hamlet* was the Second Quarto (edition) published in 1604, with modifications based on the First Folio, published in 1623.
Stage directions in those editions are printed here without brackets; added stage directions are printed within brackets. We have edited Griffin's
notes for this text.

| Marcellus | ⎫ | Officers |
| Barnardo | ⎬ | |

**Francisco,** a Soldier

**Reynaldo,** Servant to Polonius

**Players**

**Two Clowns,** gravediggers

**Fortinbras,** Prince of Norway

**A Norwegian Captain**

**English Ambassadors**

**Gertrude,** Queen of Denmark, mother to Hamlet

**Ophelia,** Daughter to Polonius

**Ghost of Hamlet's Father**

**Lords, Ladies, Officers, Soldiers, Sailors, Messengers, Attendants**

[SCENE: *Elsinore*]

## Act 1

## Scene 1. [A platform on the battlements of the castle]

*Enter* BARNARDO *and* FRANCISCO, *two Sentinels.*

BARNARDO: Who's there?

FRANCISCO: Nay, answer me. Stand and unfold° yourself.

BARNARDO: Long live the king.

FRANCISCO: Barnardo?

BARNARDO: He.                                                                                  5

FRANCISCO: You come most carefully upon your hour.

BARNARDO: 'Tis now struck twelve, get thee to bed Francisco.

FRANCISCO: For this relief much thanks, 'tis bitter cold, And I am sick at heart.

BARNARDO: Have you had quiet guard?

FRANCISCO:                                               Not a mouse stirring.

BARNARDO: Well, good night:                                                                10

If you do meet Horatio and Marcellus,

The rivals° of my watch, bid them make haste.

*Enter* HORATIO *and* MARCELLUS.

FRANCISCO: I think I hear them. Stand ho, who is there?

HORATIO: Friends to this ground.

MARCELLUS:                                      And liegemen° to the Dane°

FRANCISCO: Give you good night.

MARCELLUS:                                    O, farewell honest soldier,                      15

Who hath relieved you?

FRANCISCO:                              Barnardo hath my place;

Give you good night.                                                          *Exit Francisco.*

MARCELLUS:                     Holla, Barnardo!

BARNARDO:                                          Say,

What, is Horatio there?

HORATIO:                              A piece of him.

°2 *unfold*: reveal. 12 *rivals*: partners. 14 *liegemen*: subjects. *Dane*: King of Denmark.

BARNARDO:  Welcome Horatio, welcome good Marcellus.

20 HORATIO:  What, has this thing appeared again tonight?

BARNARDO:  I have seen nothing.

MARCELLUS:  Horatio says 'tis but our fantasy,°
    And will not let belief take hold of him,
    Touching this dreaded sight twice seen of us,
25     Therefore I have entreated him along
    With us to watch the minutes of this night,
    That if again this apparition come,
    He may approve° our eyes and speak to it.

HORATIO:  Tush, tush, 'twill not appear.

BARNARDO:                  Sit down awhile,
30     And let us once again assail your ears,
    That are so fortified against our story,
    What we have two nights seen.

HORATIO:               Well, sit we down,
    And let us hear Barnardo speak of this,

BARNARDO:  Last night of all,
35     When yon same star that's westward from the pole°
    Had made his course t'illume that part of heaven
    Where now it burns, Marcellus and myself,
    The bell then beating one—

*Enter* GHOST.

MARCELLUS:  Peace, break thee off, look where it comes again.
40 BARNARDO:  In the same figure like the king that's dead.

MARCELLUS:  Thou art a scholar, speak to it Horatio.

BARNARDO:  Looks a' not like the king? mark it Horatio.

HORATIO:  Most like, it harrows me with fear and wonder.

BARNARDO:  It would be spoke to.

MARCELLUS:             Question it Horatio.
45 HORATIO:  What art thou that usurp'st° this time of night,
    Together with that fair and warlike form,
    In which the majesty of buried Denmark°
    Did sometimes° march? by heaven I charge thee speak.

MARCELLUS:  It is offended.

BARNARDO:             See, it stalks away.
50 HORATIO:  Stay, speak, speak, I charge thee speak.           *Exit* GHOST.

MARCELLUS:  'Tis gone and will not answer.

BARNARDO:  How now Horatio, you tremble and look pale,
    Is not this something more than fantasy?
    What think you on't?
55 HORATIO:  Before my God I might not this believe,
    Without the sensible and true avouch°
    Of mine own eyes.

MARCELLUS:            Is it not like the king?

---

°22 *fantasy*: imagination.  28 *approve*: prove reliable.  35 *pole*: North Star.  45 *usurp'st*: wrongfully occupy (both the time and the shape of the dead king).  47 *buried Denmark*: the buried King of Denmark.  48 *Sometimes*: formerly.  56 *sensible . . . avouch*: assurance of the truth of the senses.

HORATIO:  As thou art to thyself.
    Such was the very armour he had on,
    When he the ambitious Norway° combated:
    So frowned he once, when in an angry parle°       60
    He smote the sledded Polacks° on the ice.
    'Tis strange.
MARCELLUS:  Thus twice before, and jump° at this dead hour,
    With martial stalk hath he gone by our watch.
HORATIO:  In what particular thought to work, I know not,      65
    But in the gross and scope° of mine opinion,
    This bodes some strange eruption to our state.
MARCELLUS:  Good now sit down, and tell me he that knows,
    Why this same strict and most observant watch      70
    So nightly toils the subject° of the land,
    And why such daily cast of brazen cannon
    And foreign mart,° for implements of war,
    Why such impress° of shipwrights, whose sore° task
    Does not divide the Sunday from the week,      75
    What might be toward° that this sweaty haste
    Doth make the night joint-labourer with the day,
    Who is't that can inform me?
HORATIO:                That can I.
    At least the whisper goes so; our last king,
    Whose image even but now appeared to us,
    Was as you know by Fortinbras of Norway,      80
    Thereto pricked on by a most emulate° pride,
    Dared to the combat; in which our valiant Hamlet
    (For so this side of our known world esteemed him)
    Did slay this Fortinbras, who by a sealed compact,°
    Well ratified by law and heraldy,°      85
    Did forfeit (with his life) all those his lands
    Which he stood seized° of, to the conqueror:
    Against the which a moiety competent°
    Was gagèd° by our King, which had returned      90
    To the inheritance of Fortinbras,
    Had he been vanquisher; as by the same co-mart,°
    And carriage of the article designed,°
    His fell to Hamlet; now sir, young Fortinbras,
    Of unimprovèd mettle° hot and full,      95
    Hath in the skirts° of Norway here and there
    Sharked up° a list of lawless resolutes°
    For food and diet to some enterprise
    That hath a stomach° in't, which is no other,

---

°60 *Norway*: King of Norway. 61 *Parle*: Parley, verbal battle. 62 *sledded Polacks*: Polish soldiers on sleds. 64 *jump*: just. 67 *gross and scope*: general view. 71 *toils the subject*: makes the subjects toil. 73 *mart*: trade. 74 *impress*: conscription. *sore*: difficult. 76 *toward*: forthcoming. 82 *emulate*: rivaling. 85 *compact*: treaty. 86 *law and heraldy*: heraldic law regulating combats. 88 *seized*: possessed. 89 *moiety competent*: equal amount. 90 *gagèd*: pledged. 92 *co-mart*: joint bargain. 93 *carriage . . . designed*: intent of the treaty drawn up. 95 *unimproved mettle*: untested (1) metal (2) spirit. 96 *skirts*: outskirts. 97 *Sharked up*: gathered up indiscriminately (as a shark preys). *lawless resolutes*: determined outlaws. 99 *stomach*: show of courage.

100   As it doth well appear unto our state,
      But to recover of us by strong hand
      And terms compulsatory, those foresaid lands
      So by his father lost; and this I take it,
      Is the main motive of our preparations,
105   The source of this our watch, and the chief head°
      Of this post-haste and romage° in the land.
    BARNARDO:  I think it be no other, but e'en so;
      Well may it sort° that this portentous figure
      Comes armèd through our watch so like the king
110   That was and is the question of these wars.
    HORATIO:  A mote it is to trouble the mind's eye:
      In the most high and palmy° state of Rome,
      A little ere the mightest Julius fell,
      The graves stood tenantless, and the sheeted dead
115   Did squeak and gibber in the Roman Streets,
      As stars with trains of fire,° and dews of blood,
      Disasters° in the sun; and the moist star,°
      Upon whose influence Neptune's empire stands,
      Was sick almost to doomsday with eclipse.
120   And even the like precurse° of feared events,
      As harbingers preceding still° the fates
      And prologue to the omen° coming on,
      Have heaven and earth together demonstrated
      Unto our climatures° and countrymen.

    *Enter* GHOST.

125   But soft, behold, lo where it comes again.
      I'll cross° it though it blast me:                              *Spreads his arms.*
                              stay illusion,
      If thou hast any sound or use of voice,
      Speak to me.
      If there be any good thing to be done
130   That may to thee do ease, and grace° to me,
      Speak to me.
      If thou art privy° to thy country's fate
      Which happily° foreknowing may avoid,
      O speak:
135   Or if thou hast uphoarded in thy life
      Extorted treasure in the womb of earth,
      For which they say you spirits oft walk in death,        *The cock crows.*

      Speak of it, stay and speak. Stop it Marcellus.
    MARCELLUS:  Shall I strike it with my partisan?°

---

°105 *head*: fountainhead. 106 *romage*: bustle (rummage). 108 *sort*: turn out. 112 *palmy*: triumphant. 116 *stars . . . fire*: meteors. 117 *Disasters*: unfavorable portents. *moist star*: moon. 120 *precurse*: portent. 121 *still*: always. 122 *omen*: disaster. 124 *climatures*: regions. 126 *cross*: (1) cross its path (2) spread my arms to make a cross of my body (to ward against evil). 130 *grace*: (1) honor (2) blessedness. 132 *art privy*: know secretly of. 133 *happily*: perhaps. 139 *partisan*: spear.

HORATIO:  Do, if it will not stand
BARNARDO:                                      'Tis here.
HORATIO:                                                'Tis here.                                    140
MARCELLUS: 'Tis gone.                                                      *Exit GHOST.*
    We do it wrong being so majestical,
    To offer it the show of violence,
    For it is as the air, invulnerable,
    And our vain blows malicious mockery.°                              145
BARNARDO: It was about to speak when the cock crew.°
HORATIO:  And then it started like a guilty thing,
    Upon a fearful summons; I have heard,
    The cock that is the trumpet to the morn,
    Doth with his lofty and shrill-sounding throat                      150
    Awake the god of day, and at his warning
    Whether in sea or fire, in earth or air,°
    Th'extravagant and erring° spirit hies°
    To his confine, and of the truth herein
    This present object made probation.°                                155
MARCELLUS: It faded on the crowing of the cock.
    Some say that ever 'gainst° that season comes
    Wherein our Saviour's birth is celebrated
    This bird of dawning singeth all night long,
    And then they say no spirit dare stir abroad,                      160
    The nights are wholesome,° then no planets strike,°
    No fairy takes,° nor witch hath power to charm,
    So hallowed, and so gracious is that time.
HORATIO:  So have I heard and do in part believe it.
    But look, the morn in russet° mantle clad                          165
    Walks o'er the dew of yon high eastward hill:
    Break we our watch up and by my advice
    Let us impart what we have seen tonight
    Unto young Hamlet, for upon my life
    This spirit dumb to us, will speak to him:                         170
    Do you consent we shall acquaint him with it,
    As needful in our loves,° fitting our duty?
MARCELLUS: Let's do't I pray, and I this morning know
    Where we shall find him most convenient.                            *Exeunt.°*

## Scene 2. [A room of state in the castle]

*Flourish.° Enter* CLAUDIUS *King of Denmark,* GERTRUDE *the Queen,* [*members of the*] *Council: as*
POLONIUS; *and his son* LAERTES, HAMLET, [VALTEMAND *and* CORNELIUS] *cum aliis.°*

KING:  Though yet of Hamlet our dear brother's death
    The memory be green, and that it us befitted

---

°145 *malicious mockery*: mockery because they only imitate harm. 146 *cock crew*: (traditional signal for ghosts to return to their confines).
152 *sea . . . air*: the four elements (inhabited by spirits, each indigenous to a particular element). 153 *extravagant and erring*: going beyond its
bounds (vagrant) and wandering. *hies*: hastens. 155 *made probation*: gave proof. 157 *'gainst*: just before. 161 *wholesome*: healthy (night air was
considered unhealthy). *strike*: exert evil influence. 162 *takes*: bewitches. 165 *russet*: reddish. 172 *needful . . . loves*: urged by our friendship.
174 S.D.: *Exeunt*: all exit. 0.1 S.D.: *Flourish*: fanfare or trumpets. *cum aliis*: with others.

To bear our hearts in grief, and our whole kingdom
To be contracted in one brow of woe,
5   Yet so far hath discretion fought with nature,°
That we° with wisest sorrow think on him
Together with remembrance of ourselves:°
Therefore our sometime° sister,° now our queen,
Th'imperial jointress° to this warlike state,
10  Have we as 'twere with a defeated joy,
With an auspicious, and a dropping eye,°
With mirth in funeral, and with dirge in marriage,
In equal scale weighing delight and dole,
Taken to wife: nor have we herein barred
15  Your better wisdoms,° which have freely gone
With this affair along—for all, our thanks.
Now follows that you know, young Fortinbras,
Holding a weak supposal of our worth°
Or thinking by our late dear brother's death
20  Our state to be disjoint and out of frame,°
Colleaguèd° with this dream of his advantage,°
He hath not failed to pester us with message
Importing the surrender of those lands
Lost by his father, with all bands° of law,
25  To our most valiant brother—so much for him:
Now for ourself, and for this time of meeting,
Thus much the business is. We have here writ
To Norway, uncle of young Fortinbras—
Who impotent and bed-rid scarcely hears
30  Of this his nephew's purpose—to suppress
His further gait° herein, in that the levies,
The lists, and full proportions are all made
Out of his subject.° and we here dispatch
You good Cornelius, and you Valtemand,
35  For bearers of this greeting to old Norway,
Giving to you no further personal power
To business with the king, more than the scope
Of these delated° articles allow:
Farewell, and let your haste commend your duty.°
40  CORNELIUS, VALTEMAND:  In that, and all things, will we show our duty.
KING:  We doubt it nothing, heartily farewell.

*EXEUNT VALTEMAND and CORNELIUS.*

And now Laertes what's the news with you?
You told us to some suit, what is't Laertes?
You cannot speak of reason to the Dane

---

°5 *nature*: natural impulse (of grief). 6 *we*: royal plural. The King speaks not only for himself, but for his entire government. 7 *remembrance of ourselves*: reminder of our duties. 8 *sometime*: former. *sister*: sister-in-law. 9 *jointress*: widow who inherits the estate. 11 *auspicious . . . eye*: one eye happy, the other tearful. 14–15 *barred . . . wisdoms*: failed to seek and abide by your good advice. 18 *weak . . . worth*: low opinion of my ability in office. 20 *out of frame*: tottering. 21 *Colleaguèd*: supported. *advantage*: superiority. 24 *bands*: bonds. 31 *gait*: progress. 31–33 *levies . . . subject*: Taxes, conscriptions, and supplies are all obtained from his subjects. 38 *delated*: prescribed; defined. 39 *haste . . . duty*: prompt departure signify your respect.

And lose your voice;° what wouldst thou beg, Laertes, 45
That shall not be my offer, not thy asking?°
The head is not more native° to the heart,
The hand more instrumental to the mouth,
Than is the throne of Denmark to thy father.
What wouldst thou have, Laertes?

LAERTES:                              My dread lord, 50
Your leave and favour° to return to France,
From whence, though willingly I came to Denmark
To show my duty in your coronation,
Yet now I must confess, that duty done,
My thoughts and wishes bend again toward France, 55
And bow them to your gracious leave and pardon.°

KING: Have you your father's leave? What says Polonius?
POLONIUS: He hath my lord wrung from me my slow leave
    By laboursome petition, and at last
    Upon his will I sealed my hard consent.° 60
    I do beseech you give him leave to go.
KING: Take thy fair hour Laertes, time be thine,
    And thy best graces spend it at thy will.
    But now my cousin° Hamlet, and my son—
HAMLET: [Aside.] A little more than kin,° and less than kind.° 65
KING: How is it that the clouds still hang on you?
HAMLET: Not so my lord, I am too much in the sun.°
QUEEN: Good Hamlet cast thy nighted colour° off
    And let thine eye look like a friend on Denmark,°
    Do not for ever with thy vailèd° lids 70
    Seek for thy noble father in the dust,
    Thou know'st 'tis common, all that lives must die,
    Passing through nature to eternity.
HAMLET: Ay madam, it is common.°
QUEEN:                        If it be,
    Why seems it so particular with thee? 75
HAMLET: Seems, madam? nay it is, I know not "seems."
    'Tis not alone my inky cloak, good mother,
    Nor customary suits of solemn black,
    Nor windy suspiration of forced breath,
    No, nor the fruitful river in the eye,° 80
    Nor the dejected haviour° of the visage,
    Together with all forms, moods, shapes of grief,
    That can denote me truly: these indeed seem,
    For they are actions that a man might play,°

---

°45 *lose your voice*: speak in vain. 46 *offer . . . asking*: grant even before requested. 47 *native*: related. 51 *leave and favour*: kind permission.
56 *pardon*: allowance. 60 *Upon . . . consent*: (1) At his request, I gave my grudging consent. (2) On the soft sealing wax of his (legal) will, I stamped
my approval. 64 *cousin*: kinsman (used for relatives outside the immediate family). 65 *more than kin*: too much of a kinsman, being both uncle and
stepfather. *less than kind*: (1) unkind because of being a kin (proverbial) and taking the throne from the former king's son (2) unnatural (as it was considered incest to marry the wife of one's dead brother). 67 *in the sun*: (1) in presence of the king (often associated metaphorically with the sun)
(2) proverbial: "out of heaven's blessing into the warm sun" (3) of a "son." 68 *nighted colour*: black. 69 *Denmark*: the King of Denmark. 70 *vailèd*:
downcast. 74 *common*: (1) general (2) vulgar. 79–80 *windy . . . eye*: (hyperbole used to describe exaggerated sighs and tears). 81 *haviour*: behavior.
84 *play*: act.

<br>

85     But I have that within which passes show,
       These but the trappings and the suits of woe.°
    KING: 'Tis sweet and commendable in your nature Hamlet,
       To give these mourning duties to your father:
       But you must know your father lost a father,
90     That father lost, lost his, and the survivor bound
       In filial obligation for some term
       To do obsequious sorrow:° but to persever
       In obstinate condolement,° is a course
       Of impious stubbornness, 'tis unmanly grief,
95     It shows a will most incorrect to heaven,
       A heart unfortified, a mind impatient,
       An understanding simple and unschooled:
       For what we know must be, and is as common
       As any the most vulgar thing to sense,°
100    Why should we in our peevish opposition
       Take it to heart? Fie, 'tis a fault to heaven,
       A fault against the dead, a fault to nature,
       To reason most absurd, whose common theme
       Is death of fathers, and who still° hath cried
105    From the first corse,° till he that died today,
       "This must be so." We pray you throw to earth
       This unprevailing° woe, and think of us
       As of a father, for let the world take note
       You are the most immediate° to our throne,
110    And with no less nobility of love
       Than that which dearest father bears his son,
       Do I impart toward you. For your intent
       In going back to school in Wittenberg,
       It is most retrograde° to our desire,
115    And we beseech you, bend you° to remain
       Here in the cheer and comfort of our eye,
       Our chiefest courtier, cousin, and our son.
    QUEEN: Let not thy mother lose her prayers Hamlet,
       I pray thee stay with us, go not to Wittenberg.
120 HAMLET: I shall in all my best obey you madam.
    KING: Why 'tis a loving and a fair reply,
       Be as ourself in Denmark. Madam come,
       This gentle and unforced accord of Hamlet
       Sits smiling to my heart, in grace whereof,
125    No jocund health that Denmark drinks today,
       But the great cannon to the clouds shall tell,
       And the king's rouse° the heaven shall bruit° again,
       Re-speaking earthly thunder; come away.

*Flourish: Exeunt all but* HAMLET.

---

°86 *trappings . . . woe*: outward, superficial costumes of mourning. 92 *do obsequious sorrow*: express sorrow befitting obsequies or funerals. 93 *condolement*: grief. 99 *As any . . . sense*: as the most ordinary thing the senses can perceive. 104 *still*: always. 105 *corse*: corpse (of Abel, also, ironically, the first fratricide). 107 *unprevailing*: useless. 109 *most immediate*: next in succession (though Danish kings were elected by the council, an Elizabethan audience might feel that Hamlet, not Claudius, should be king). 114 *retrograde*: movement (of planets) in a reverse direction. 115 *beseech . . . you*: hope you will be inclined. 127 *rouse*: toast that empties the wine cup. *bruit*: sound.

HAMLET: O that this too too sullied° flesh would melt,
  Thaw and resolve itself into a dew,          130
  Or that the Everlasting had not fixed
  His canon° 'gainst self-slaughter. O God, God,
  How weary, stale, flat, and unprofitable
  Seem to me all the uses of this world!
  Fie on't, ah fie, 'tis an unweeded garden       135
  That grows to seed, things rank° and gross in nature
  Possess it merely.° That it should come to this,
  But two months dead, nay not so much, not two,
  So excellent a king, that was to this
  Hyperion° to a satyr,° so loving to my mother,     140
  That he might not beteem° the winds of heaven
  Visit her face too roughly—heaven and earth,
  Must I remember? why, she would hang on him
  As if increase of appetite had grown
  By what it fed on,° and yet within a month—     145
  Let me not think on't: Frailty, thy name is woman—
  A little month or ere those shoes were old
  With which she followed my poor father's body
  Like Niobe° all tears, why she, even she—
  O God, a beast that wants° discourse of reason     150
  Would have mourned longer—married with my uncle,
  My father's brother, but no more like my father
  Than I to Hercules: within a month,
  Ere yet the salt of most unrighteous° tears
  Had left the flushing° in her gallèd° eyes,      155
  She married. O most wicked speed, to post°
  With such dexterity to incestuous° sheets:
  It is not, nor it cannot come to good,
  But break my heart, for I must hold my tongue.

*Enter* HORATIO, MARCELLUS *and* BARNARDO.

HORATIO: Hail to your lordship.
HAMLET:       I am glad to see you well;    160
  Horatio, or I do forget my self.
HORATIO: The same my lord, and your poor servant ever.
HAMLET: Sir my good friend, I'll change° that name with you:
  And what make you from Wittenberg, Horatio?
  Marcellus.               165
MARCELLUS: My good lord.
HAMLET: I am very glad to see you: good even, sir.
  But what in faith make you from Wittenberg?
HORATIO: A truant disposition, good my lord.
HAMLET: I would not hear your enemy say so,     170

---

°129 *sullied*: tainted. 132 *canon*: divine edict. 136 *rank*: (1) luxuriant, excessive (2) bad-smelling. 137 *merely*: entirely. 140 *Hyperion*: god of the sun. *satyr*: part-goat, part-man woodland deity (noted for lust). 141 *beteem*: allow. 144–145 *As if . . . on*: as if the more she fed, the more her appetite increased. 149 *Niobe*: (who boasted of her children before Leto and was punished by their destruction; Zeus changed the weeping mother to a stone dropping continual tears). 150 *wants*: lacks. 154 *unrighteous*: (because untrue). 155 *flushing*: redness. *gallèd*: rubbed sore. 156 *post*: rush. 157 *incestuous*: (the church forbade marriage to one's brother's widow). 163 *change*: exchange (and be called your friend).

Nor shall you do mine ear that violence
To make it truster of your own report
Against yourself. I know you are no truant,
But what is your affair in Elsinore?

175    We'll teach you to drink deep ere you depart.

HORATIO:  My Lord, I came to see your father's funeral.

HAMLET:  I prithee do not mock me, fellow student,
I think it was to see my mother's wedding.

HORATIO:  Indeed my lord it followed hard upon.

180  HAMLET:  Thrift, thrift, Horatio, the funeral baked meats°
Did coldly° furnish forth the marriage tables.
Would I had met my dearest° foe in heaven
Or ever I had seen that day Horatio.
My father, methinks I see my father.

HORATIO:  Where my lord?

185  HAMLET:                              In my mind's eye Horatio.

HORATIO:  I saw him once, a' was a goodly° king.

HAMLET:  A' was a man, take him for all in all,
I shall not look upon his like again.

HORATIO:  My lord, I think I saw him yesternight.

190  HAMLET:  Saw? Who?

HORATIO:  My lord, the king your father.

HAMLET:                                    The king my father?

HORATIO:  Season your admiration° for a while
With an attent ear till I may deliver
Upon the witness of these gentlemen
This marvel to you.

195  HAMLET:                              For God's love let me hear!

HORATIO:  Two nights together had these gentlemen,
Marcellus and Barnardo, on their watch
In the dead waste and middle of the night,
Been thus encountered. A figure like your father

200    Armed at point exactly, cap-a-pe,°
Appears before them, and with solemn march,
Goes slow and stately by them; thrice he walked
By their oppressed° and fear-surprisèd eyes
Within his truncheon's° length, whilst they distilled°

205    Almost to jelly with the act of fear,
Stand dumb and speak not to him; this to me
In dreadful secrecy° impart they did,
And I with them the third night kept the watch,
Where as they had delivered, both in time,

210    Form of the thing, each word made true and good,
The apparition comes: I knew your father,
These hands are not more like.

HAMLET:                              But where was this?

---

°180 *funeral baked meats*: food prepared for the funeral. 181 *coldly*: when cold. 182 *dearest*: direst. 186 *goodly*: handsome. 192 *Season your admiration*: control your wonder. 200 *at point . . . cap-a-pe*: in every detail, head to foot. 203 *oppressed*: overcome by horror. 204 *truncheon*: staff (of office). *distilled*: dissolved. 207 *in dreadful secrecy*: as a dread secret.

Marcellus: My lord upon the platform where we watch.

Hamlet: Did you not speak to it?

Horatio:                                        My lord I did,
    But answer made it none, yet once methought                              215
    It lifted up it° head, and did address
    Itself to motion° like as it would speak:
    But even then the morning cock crew loud,
    And at the sound it shrunk in haste away
    And vanished from our sight.

Hamlet:                                        'Tis very strange.                        220

Horatio: As I do live my honoured lord 'tis true,
    And we did think it writ down in our duty
    To let you know of it.

Hamlet: Indeed indeed sirs, but this troubles me.
    Hold you the watch tonight?

All:                                        We do my lord.                              225

Hamlet: Armed say you?

All: Armed my lord.

Hamlet: From top to toe?

All:                                        My lord from head to foot.

Hamlet: Then saw you not his face.

Horatio: O yes my lord, he wore his beaver° up.                                      230

Hamlet: What, looked he frowningly?

Horatio: A countenance more in sorrow than in anger.

Hamlet: Pale, or red?

Horatio: Nay, very pale.

Hamlet:                                        And fixed his eyes upon you?

Horatio: Most constantly.

Hamlet:                                        I would I had been there.                  235

Horatio: It would have much amazed you.

Hamlet: Very like, very like, stayed it long?

Horatio: While one with moderate haste might tell° a hundred.

Marcellus, Barnardo: Longer, longer.

Horatio: Not when I saw't.

Hamlet:                                        His beard was grizzled,° no?              240

Horatio: It was as I have seen it in his life,
    A sable silvered.°

Hamlet:                        I will watch tonight;
    Perchance 'twill walk again.

Horatio:                                        I warr'nt it will.

Hamlet: If it assume my noble father's person,
    I'll speak to it though hell itself should gape                               245
    And bid me hold my peace;° I pray you all
    If you have hitherto concealed this sight
    Let it be tenable° in your silence still,
    And whatsoever else shall hap tonight,

---

°216 *it*: its. 216–217 *address . . . motion*: start to move. 230 *beaver*: visor. 238 *tell*: count. 240 *grizzled*: grey. 242 *A sable silvered*: black flecked with gray. 245–246 *though hell . . . peace*: despite the risk of hell (for speaking to a demon) warning me to be silent. 248 *tenable*: held, kept.

250      Give it an understanding but no tongue.
         I will requite your loves, so fare you well:
         Upon the platform 'twixt eleven and twelve
         I'll visit you.
ALL:                 Our duty to your honour.
HAMLET: Your loves, as mine to you:° farewell.               *Exeunt. [Hamlet remains.]*
255      My father's spirit (in arms) all is not well,
         I doubt° some foul play, would the night were come;
         Till then sit still my soul. Foul deeds will rise,
         Though all the earth o'erwhelm them to men's eyes.                           *Exit.*

## Scene 3. [Polonius's chambers]

*Enter* LAERTES *and* OPHELIA *his sister.*

LAERTES:  My necessaries are embarked, farewell,
          And sister, as the winds give benefit
          And convoy° is assistant, do not sleep
          But let me hear from you.
OPHELIA:                 Do you doubt that?
5   LAERTES: For Hamlet, and the trifling of his favour,
          Hold it a fashion, and a toy in blood,°
          A violet in the youth of primy nature,°
          Forward,° not permanent, sweet, not lasting,
          The perfume and suppliance of° a minute,
          No more.
OPHELIA:      No more but so?
10  LAERTES:                 Think it no more.
          For nature crescent° does not grow alone
          In thews and bulk,° but as this temple waxes°
          The inward service of the mind and soul
          Grows wide withal.° Perhaps he loves you now,
15        And now no soil nor cautel° doth besmirch
          The virtue of his will:° but you must fear,
          His greatness weighed,° his will is not his own,
          For he himself is subject to his birth:
          He may not as unvalued persons° do,
20        Carve° for himself, for on his choice depends
          The sanctity and health of this whole state,
          And therefore must his choice be circumscribed
          Unto the voice and yielding° of that body
          Whereof he is the head. Then if he says he loves you,
25        It fits your wisdom so far to believe it
          As he in his particular act and place
          May give his saying deed,° which is no further

---

°254 *Your loves . . . you*: offer your friendship (rather than duty) in exchange for mine. 256 *doubt*: fear. 3 *convoy*: conveyance. 6 *toy in blood*: whim of the passions. 7 *youth of primy nature*: early spring. 8 *Forward*: premature. 9 *suppliance of*: supplying diversion for. 11 *nature crescent*: man as he grows. 12 *thews and bulk*: sinews and body. *temple waxes*: body grows (1 Cor. 6:19). 14 *withal*: at the same time. 15 *cautel*: deceit. 16 *will*: desire. 17 *weighed*: considered. 19 *unvalued persons*: common people. 20 *Carve*: choose (as does the one who carves the food). 23 *voice and yielding*: approving vote. 26–27 *in his . . . deed*: limited by personal responsibilities and rank, may perform what he promises.

Than the main voice of Denmark goes withal.
Then weigh what loss your honour may sustain
If with too credent° ear you list° his songs,                                           30
Or lose your heart, or your chaste treasure open
To his unmast'red importunity.°
Fear it Ophelia, fear it my dear sister,
And keep you in the rear of your affection,
Out of the shot and danger of desire.                                                  35
The chariest° maid is prodigal enough
If she unmask her beauty to the moon.
Virtue itself 'scapes not calumnious strokes.
The canker galls the infants° of the spring
Too oft before their buttons° be disclosed,                                            40
And in the morn and liquid dew of youth
Contagious blastments° are most imminent.
Be wary then, best safety lies in fear,
Youth to itself rebels,° though none else near.

OPHELIA: I shall the effect° of this good lesson keep                                  45
        As watchman to my heart: but good my brother,
        Do not as some ungracious° pastors do,
        Show me the steep and thorny way to heaven,
        Whiles like a puffed and reckless libertine
        Himself the primrose path of dalliance treads,                                 50
        And recks not his own rede.°

*Enter* POLONIUS.

LAERTES:                          O fear me not,°
        I stay too long, but here my father comes:
        A double blessing is a double grace,
        Occasion smiles upon a second leave.°

POLONIUS: Yet here Laertes? aboard, aboard for shame,                                  55
        The wind sits in the shoulder of your sail,
        And you are stayed for: there, my blessing with thee,
        And these few precepts in thy memory
        Look thou character.° Give thy thoughts no tongue,
        Nor any unproportioned thought his act:                                        60
        Be thou familiar, but by no means vulgar;°
        Those friends thou hast, and their adoption tried,°
        Grapple them unto thy soul with hoops of steel,
        But do not dull° thy palm with entertainment
        Of each new-hatched unfledged° comrade. Beware                                 65
        Of entrance to a quarrel, but being in,
        Bear't that th'opposèd may beware of thee.
        Give every man thy ear, but few thy voice:

---

30 *credent*: credulous. *list*: listen to. 31–32 *your chaste . . . importunity*: lose your virginity to his uncontrolled persistence. 36 *chariest*: most cautious. 39 *canker . . . infants*: cankerworm or caterpillar harms the young plants. 40 *buttons*: buds. 42 *blastments*: blights. 44 *to itself rebels*: lusts by nature. 45 *effect*: moral. 47 *ungracious*: lacking God's grace. 51 *recks . . . rede*: does not follow his own advice. *fear me not*: Don't worry about me. 54 *Occasion . . . leave*: opportunity favors a second leave-taking. 59 *character*: write, impress, imprint. 61 *vulgar*: indiscriminately friendly. 62 *adoption tried*: loyalty proved. 64 *dull*: get callouses on. 65 *new-hatched unfledged*: new and untested.

Take each man's censure,° but reserve thy judgment.
70   Costly thy habit° as thy purse can buy,
But not expressed in fancy,° rich, not gaudy,
For the apparel oft proclaims the man,
And they in France of the best rank and station,
Are of a most select and generous chief° in that:
75   Neither a borrower nor a lender be,
For loan oft loses both itself and friend,
And borrowing dulls the edge of husbandry;°
This above all, to thine own self be true
And it must follow as the night the day,
80   Thou canst not then be false to any man.
Farewell, my blessing season° this in thee.
LAERTES:  Most humbly do I take my leave my lord.
POLONIUS:  The time invites you, go, your servants tend.°
LAERTES:  Farewell Ophelia, and remember well
What I have said to you.
85   OPHELIA:                                'Tis in my memory locked,
And you yourself shall keep the key of it.
LAERTES:  Farewell.                                                            *Exit* LAERTES.
POLONIUS:  What is't Ophelia he hath said to you?
OPHELIA:  So please you, something touching the Lord Hamlet.
90   POLONIUS:  Marry,° well bethought:
'Tis told me he hath very oft of late
Given private time to you, and you yourself
Have of your audience been most free and bounteous.
If it be so, as so 'tis put on me,
95   And that in way of caution, I must tell you,
You do not understand yourself so clearly
As it behooves my daughter, and your honour.
What is between you? give me up the truth.
OPHELIA:  He hath my lord of late made many tenders°
100      Of his affection to me.
POLONIUS:  Affection, puh, you speak like a green girl
Unsifted° in such perilous circumstance.
Do you believe his tenders as you call them?
OPHELIA:  I do not know my lord what I should think.
105  POLONIUS:  Marry, I will teach you; think yourself a baby
That you have ta'en these tenders° for true pay
Which are not sterling.° Tender yourself more dearly,°
Or (not to crack the wind of the poor phrase,
Running it thus°) you'll tender me a fool.°
110  OPHELIA:  My lord he hath importuned me with love
In honourable fashion.
POLONIUS:  Ay, fashion you may call it, go to, go to.

---

°69 *censure*: opinion. 70 *habit*: clothing. 71 *expressed in fancy*: so fantastic as to be ridiculous. 74 *select . . . chief*: judicious and noble eminence. 77 *husbandry*: thrift. 81 *season*: bring to maturity. 83 *tend*: attend, wait. 90 *Marry*: (a mild oath, from "By the Virgin Mary"). 99 *tenders*:
offers (see lines 106–9). 102 *Unsifted*: untested. 106 *tenders*: offers (of money). 107 *sterling*: genuine (currency). *Tender . . . dearly*: hold yourself
at a higher value. 108–9 *crack . . . thus*: make the phrase lose its breath. 109 *tender . . . fool*: (1) make me look foolish (2) present me with a baby.

OPHELIA:  And hath given countenance° to his speech, my lord,
    With almost all the holy vows of heaven.
POLONIUS:  Ay, springes° to catch woodcocks.° I do know             115
    When the blood burns, how prodigal the soul
    Lends the tongue vows: these blazes daughter,
    Giving more light than heat, extinct in both,
    Even in their promise, as it is a-making,°
    You must not take for fire. From this time             120
    Be something scanter of your maiden presence,
    Set your entreatments at a higher rate
    Than a command to parle;° for Lord Hamlet,
    Believe so much in him that he is young,
    And with a larger tether may he walk             125
    Than may be given you: in few° Ophelia,
    Do not believe his vows, for they are brokers°
    Not of that dye which their investments° show,
    But mere implorators° of unholy suits,
    Breathing° like sanctified and pious bonds,°            130
    The better to beguile. This is for all,
    I would not in plain terms from this time forth
    Have you so slander any moment leisure
    As to give words or talk with the Lord Hamlet.
    Look to't I charge you, come your ways.°            135
OPHELIA:  I shall obey, my lord.                              *[Exeunt.]*

## Scene 4. [The platform on the battlements]

*Enter HAMLET, HORATIO and MARCELLUS.*

HAMLET:  The air bites shrewdly,° it is very cold.
HORATIO:  It is a nipping and an eager° air.
HAMLET:  What hour now?
HORATIO:  I think it lacks of twelve.
MARCELLUS:  No, it is struck.
HORATIO:  Indeed? I heard it not: it then draws near the season°      5
    Wherein the spirit held his wont to walk.

          *A flourish of trumpets, and two pieces [of ordnance] go off.*

    What does this mean my lord?
HAMLET:  The king doth wake° tonight and takes his rouse,°      10
    Keeps wassail° and the swagg'ring up-spring° reels:
    And as he drains his draughts of Rhenish° down,
    The kettle-drum and trumpet thus bray out
    The triumph of his pledge.°

---

°113 *countenance*: confirmation. 115 *springes*: snares. *woodcocks*: snipelike birds (believed to be stupid and therefore easily trapped). 118–19 *extinct . . . a-making*: losing both appearance, because of brevity, and substance, because of broken promises. 122–23 *Set . . . parle*: Don't rush to negotiate a surrender as soon as the besieger asks for a discussion of terms. 126 *few*: short. 127 *brokers*: (1) business agents (2) procurers. 128 *investments*: (1) business ventures (2) clothing. 129 *implorators*: solicitors. 130 *Breathing*: speaking softly. *bonds*: pledges. 135 *come your ways*: come along. 1 *shrewdly*: fiercely. 2 *eager*: sharp. 6 *season*: time, period. 9 *wake*: stay awake. *rouse*: drinks that empty the cup. 10 *Keeps wassail*: holds drinking bouts. *up-spring*: a vigorous German dance. 11 *Rhenish*: Rhine wine. 13 *triumph . . . pledge*: victory of emptying the cup with one draught.

HORATIO:                              Is it a custom?
HAMLET:  Ay marry is't,
15      But to my mind, though I am native here
        And to the manner born,° it is a custom
        More honoured in the breach than the observance.°
        This heavy-headed revel east and west
        Makes us traduced and taxed of° other nations:
20      They clepe° us drunkards, and with swinish phrase
        Soil our addition,° and indeed it takes
        From our achievements, though performed at height,°
        The pith and marrow of our attribute.°
        So oft it chances in particular men,
25      That for some vicious mole of nature° in them,
        As in their birth, wherein they are not guilty
        (Since nature cannot choose his origin),
        By the o'ergrowth of some complexion,°
        Oft breaking down the pales° and forts of reason,
30      Or by some habit, that too much o'er-leavens°
        The form of plausive° manners—that these men,
        Carrying I say the stamp of one defect,
        Being nature's livery,° or fortune's star,°
        His virtues else be they as pure as grace,
35      As infinite as man may undergo,
        Shall in the general censure° take corruption
        From that particular fault: the dram of evil
        Doth all the noble substance often doubt,
        To his own scandal.°

*Enter GHOST.*

HORATIO:                              Look my lord, it comes.
40  HAMLET:  Angels and ministers of grace defend us:
        Be thou a spirit of health, or goblin damned,°
        Bring with thee airs from heaven, or blasts from hell,
        Be thy intents wicked, or charitable,
        Thou com'st in such a questionable° shape,
45      That I will speak to thee. I'll call thee Hamlet,
        King, father, royal Dane. O answer me,
        Let me not burst in ignorance, but tell
        Why thy canonized° bones hearsèd° in death
        Have burst their cerements°? why the sepulchre,
50      Wherein we saw thee quietly interred

---

°16 *to . . . born*: accustomed to the practice since birth. 17 *More . . . observance*: better to break than to observe. 19 *traduced and taxed of*: defamed and taken to task by. 20 *clepe*: call. 20–21 *with swinish . . . addition*: blemish our reputation by comparing us to swine. 22 *at height*: to the maximum. 23 *attribute*: reputation. 25 *mole of nature*: natural blemish. 28 *o'er growth . . . complexion*: overbalance of one of the body's four humors or fluids believed to determine temperament. 29 *pales*: defensive enclosures. 30 *too much o'er-leavens*: excessively modifies (like too much leaven in bread). 31 *plausive*: pleasing. 33 *nature's livery*: marked by nature. *fortune's star*: destined by chance. 36 *general censure*: public opinion. 37–39 *the dram . . . scandal*: the minute quantity of evil often casts doubt upon his noble nature, to his shame. 41 *spirit . . . damned*: true ghost or demon from hell. 44 *questionable*: question-raising. 48 *canonized*: buried in accordance with church edict. *hearsèd*: entombed. 49 *cerements*: waxed cloth wrappings.

Hath oped his ponderous and marble jaws,
To cast thee up again? What may this mean
That thou, dead corse, again in complete steel
Revisits thus the glimpses of the moon,
Making night hideous, and we fools of nature°                                    55
So horridly to shake our disposition
With thoughts beyond the reaches of our souls,
Say why is this? wherefore? what should we do?                  *GHOST beckons HAMLET.*

HORATIO:  It beckons you to go away with it,
  As if it some impartment did desire°                                           60
  To you alone.

MARCELLUS:          Look with what courteous action
  It waves you to a more removèd ground,
  But do not go with it.

HORATIO:                  No, by no means.

HAMLET:  It will not speak, then I will follow it.

HORATIO:  Do not my lord.

HAMLET:                  Why what should be the fear?                            65
  I do not set my life at a pin's fee,°
  And for my soul, what can it do to that
  Being a thing immortal as itself;
  It waves me forth again, I'll follow it.

HORATIO:  What if it tempt you toward the flood my lord,                         70
  Or to the dreadful summit of the cliff
  That beetles o'er° his base into the sea,
  And there assume some other horrible form
  Which might deprive your sovereignty of reason,°
  And draw you into madness? think of it,                                        75
  The very place puts toys of desperation,°
  Without more motive, into every brain
  That looks so many fathoms to the sea
  And hears it roar beneath.

HAMLET:                  It waves me still:
  Go on, I'll follow thee.                                                       80

MARCELLUS:  You shall not go my lord.

HAMLET:                  Hold off your hands.

HORATIO:  Be ruled, you shall not go.

HAMLET:                  My fate cries out,
  And makes each petty artire° in this body
  As hardy as the Nemean lion's° nerve;°
  Still am I called, unhand me gentlemen,                                        85
  By heaven I'll make a ghost of him that lets° me:
  I say away; go on, I'll follow thee.                          *Exeunt Ghost and Hamlet.*

HORATIO:  He waxes desperate° with imagination.

MARCELLUS:  Let's follow, 'tis not fit thus to obey him.

---

°55 *fools of nature*: mocked by our natural limitations when faced with the supernatural. 60 *some . . . desire*: desired to impart something. 66 *fee*: value. 72 *beetles o'er*: overhangs. 74 *deprive . . . reason*: dethrone your reason from its sovereignty. 76 *toys of desperation*: desperate whims. 83 *artire*: ligament. 84 *Nemean lion*: (killed by Hercules as one of his twelve labors). *nerve*: sinew. 86 *lets*: prevents. 88 *waxes desperate*: grows frantic.

90  HORATIO: Have after—to what issue will this come?
    MARCELLUS: Something is rotten in the state of Denmark.
    HORATIO: Heaven will direct it.
    MARCELLUS:                    Nay, let's follow him.                    *Exeunt.*

### Scene 5. [Another part of the platform]

*Enter GHOST and HAMLET.*

    HAMLET: Whither wilt thou lead me? Speak, I'll go no further.
    GHOST: Mark me.
    HAMLET:            I will.
    GHOST:                    My hour is almost come
        When I to sulphurous and tormenting flames
        Must render up myself.
    HAMLET:                    Alas poor ghost.
5   GHOST: Pity me not, but lend thy serious hearing
        To what I shall unfold.
    HAMLET: Speak, I am bound° to hear.
    GHOST: So art thou to revenge, when thou shalt hear.
    HAMLET: What?
    GHOST:        I am thy father's spirit,
10      Doomed for a certain term to walk the night,
        And for the day confined to fast in fires,
        Till the foul crimes done in my days of nature°
        Are burnt and purged away: but that I am forbid
        To tell the secrets of my prison-house,
15      I could a tale unfold whose lightest word
        Would harrow up thy soul, freeze thy young blood,
        Make thy two eyes like stars start from their spheres,°
        Thy knotted and combinèd locks to part,
        And each particular hair to stand an° end,
20      Like quills upon the fretful porpentine:°
        But this eternal blazon° must not be
        To ears of flesh and blood; list, list, O list:
        If thou didst ever thy dear father love—
    HAMLET: O God!
25  GHOST: Revenge his foul and most unnatural murder.
    HAMLET: Murder?
    GHOST: Murder most foul, as in the best it is,
        But this most foul, strange and unnatural.
    HAMLET: Haste me to know't, that I with wings as swift
30      As meditation or the thoughts of love,
        May sweep to my revenge.
    GHOST: I find thee apt,°
        And duller shouldst thou be than the fat° weed

---

°6 *bound*: obliged by duty.  12 *crimes . . . nature*: sins committed during my life on earth.  17 *spheres*: (1) orbits (according to Ptolemy, each planet was confined to a sphere revolving around the earth) (2) sockets.  19 *an*: on.  20 *fretful porpentine*: angry porcupine.  21 *eternal blazon*: revelation about eternity.  31 *apt*: ready.  32 *fat*: slimy.

That rots itself in ease on Lethe wharf,°
Wouldst thou not stir in this; now Hamlet hear,
'Tis given out, that sleeping in my orchard,°                              35
A serpent stung me, so the whole ear of Denmark
Is by a forgèd process° of my death
Rankly abused:° but know thou noble youth,
The serpent that did sting thy father's life
Now wears his crown.

HAMLET:                              O my prophetic soul!                   40
    My uncle?

GHOST: Ay, that incestuous, that adulterate° beast,
    With witchcraft of his wit, with traitorous gifts,
    O wicked wit and gifts, that have the power
    So to seduce; won to his shameful lust                                 45
    The will of my most seeming-virtuous queen;
    O Hamlet, what a falling-off was there,
    From me whose love was of that dignity
    That it went hand in hand, even with the vow
    I made to her in marriage, and to decline                              50
    Upon° a wretch whose natural gifts were poor
    To° those of mine;
    But virtue, as it never will be moved,
    Though lewdness court it in a shape of heaven,°
    So lust, though to a radiant angle linked,                            55
    Will sate itself in a celestial bed
    And prey on garbage.
    But soft, methinks I scent the morning air,
    Brief let me be; sleeping within my orchard,
    My custom always of the afternoon,                                     60
    Upon my secure° hour thy uncle stole
    With juice of cursèd hebona° in a vial,
    And in the porches of my ears did pour
    The leperous° distilment, whose effect
    Holds such an enmity with blood of man,                                65
    That swift as quicksilver it courses through
    The natural gates and alleys of the body,
    And with a sudden vigour it doth posset°
    And curd, like eager° droppings into milk,
    The thin and wholesome° blood; so did it mine,                        70
    And a most instant tetter° barked about°
    Most lazar°-like with vile and loathsome crust
    All my smooth body.
    Thus was I sleeping by a brother's hand,
    Of life, of crown, of queen at once dispatched,                        75

---

°33 *Lethe wharf*: the banks of Lethe (river in Hades from which spirits drank to forget their past lives). 35 *orchard*: garden. 37 *process*: account. 38 *abused*: deceived. 42 *adulterate*: adulterous. 50–51 *decline Upon*: descend to. 52 *To*: compared to. 54 *shape of heaven*: angelic appearance. 61 *secure*: unsuspecting. 62 *hebona*: poisonous sap of the ebony or henbane. 64 *leperous*: leprosy-causing. 68 *posset*: curdle. 69 *eager*: sour. 70 *wholesome*: healthy. 71 *tetter*: skin eruption. *barked about*: covered (like bark on a tree). 72 *lazar*: leper.

Cut off even in the blossoms of my sin,
Unhouseled, disappointed, unaneled,°
No reck'ning° made, but sent to my account°
With all my imperfections on my head;
80      O horrible, O horrible, most horrible!
If thou hast nature in thee bear it not,
Let not the royal bed of Denmark be
A couch for luxury° and damnèd incest.
But howsoever thou pursues this act,
85      Taint not thy mind, nor let thy soul contrive
Against thy mother aught,° leave her to heaven,
And to those thorns that in her bosom lodge
To prick and sting her. Fare thee well at once,
The glow-worm shows the matin° to be near
90      And 'gins to pale this uneffectual fire:°
Adieu, adieu, adieu, remember me.                                    *Exit.*
Hamlet:  O all you host of heaven! O earth! what else?
And shall I couple° hell? O fie! Hold, hold my heart,
And you my sinews, grow not instant old,
95      But bear me stiffly up; remember thee?
Ay thou poor ghost, while memory holds a seat
In this distracted globe.° Remember thee?
Yea, from the table° of my memory
I'll wipe away all trivial fond° records,
100     All saws of books,° all forms, all pressures° past
That youth and observation copied there,
And thy commandment all alone shall live
Within the book and volume of my brain,
Unmixed with baser matter, yes by heaven:
105     O most pernicious woman!
O villain, villain, smiling damnèd villain!
My tables,° meet° it is I set it down
That one may smile, and smile, and be a villain,
At least I am sure it may be so in Denmark.
110     So uncle, there you are: now to my word,°
It is 'Adieu, adieu, remember me.'
I have sworn't.

*Enter Horatio and Marcellus.*

Horatio:  My lord, my lord!
Marcellus:                    Lord Hamlet!
Horatio:                                    Heaven secure° him.
Hamlet:  So be it.
115 Marcellus:  Illo, ho, ho, my lord!

---

°77 *Unhouseled . . . unaneled*: without final sacrament, unprepared (without confession) and lacking extreme unction (anointing). 78 *reck'ning*:
(1) accounting (2) payment of my bill (3) confession and absolution. *account*: judgment. 83 *luxury*: lust. 86 *aught*: anything. 89 *matin*: dawn.
90 *'gins . . . fire*: his light becomes ineffective, made pale by day. 93 *couple*: engage in a contest against. 97 *distracted globe*: (his head).
98 *table*: tablet, "table-book." 99 *fond*: foolish. 100 *saws of books*: maxims (sayings) copied from books. *forms, all pressures*: ideas, impressions,
meditations, etc. 107 *tables*: tablet; notepad. *meet*: fitting. 110 *word*: motto (to guide my actions). 113 *secure*: protect.

HAMLET: Hillo, ho, ho, boy, come° bird, come.
MARCELLUS: How is't my noble lord?
HORATIO:                               What news my lord?
HAMLET: O, wonderful!
HORATIO:                  Good my lord, tell it.
HAMLET: No, you will reveal it.
HORATIO: Not I my lord, by heaven.
MARCELLUS:                        Nor I my lord.                              120
HAMLET: How say you then, would heart of man once think it?
    But you'll be secret?
BOTH:                        Ay, by heaven, my lord.
HAMLET: There's ne'er a villain dwelling in all Denmark
    But he's an arrant° knave.
HORATIO: There needs no ghost my lord, come from the grave     125
    To tell us this.
HAMLET:            Why right, you are in the right,
    And so without more circumstance° at all
    I hold it fit that we shake hands and part,
    You, as your business and desire shall point you,
    For every man hath business and desire             130
    Such as it is, and for my own poor part,
    Look you, I will go pray.
HORATIO: These are but wild and whirling words my lord.
HAMLET: I am sorry they offend you, heartily,
    Yes faith, heartily.
HORATIO:            There's no offence my lord.                   135
HAMLET: Yes by Saint Patrick, but there is Horatio,
    And much offence too: touching this vision here,
    It is an honest° ghost, that let me tell you:
    For your desire to know what is between us,
    O'ermaster't as you may. And now good friends,      140
    As you are friends, scholars, and soldiers,
    Give me one poor request.
HORATIO: What is't, my lord? we will.
HAMLET: Never make known what you have seen tonight.
BOTH: My lord we will not.
HAMLET:                  Nay, but swear't.
HORATIO:                          In faith                        145
    My lord, not I.
MARCELLUS:      Nor I my lord, in faith.
HAMLET: Upon my sword.
MARCELLUS:            We have sworn my lord already.
HAMLET: Indeed, upon my sword,° indeed.
GHOST: Swear.                              *Ghost cries under the stage.*
HAMLET: Ha, ha, boy, say'st thou so, art thou there, truepenny°?     150
    Come on, you hear this fellow in the cellarage,
    Consent to swear.
HORATIO:            Propose the oath my lord.

---

°116 *Hillo . . . come*: falconer's cry with which Hamlet replies to their calls.  124 *arrant*: thoroughgoing.  127 *circumstance*: ceremony.  138 *honest*: true (not a devil in disguise).  148 *sword*: (the cross-shaped hilt).  150 *truepenny*: old pal.

HAMLET:  Never to speak of this that you have seen.
    Swear by my sword.
155 GHOST:  [*Beneath.*] Swear.
HAMLET:  Hic et ubique?° then we'll shift our ground:
    Come hither gentlemen,
    And lay your hands again upon my sword,
    Swear by my sword
160     Never to speak of this that you have heard.
GHOST:  [*Beneath.*] Swear by his sword.
HAMLET:  Well said old mole, canst work i'th' earth so fast?
    A worthy pioner°—once more remove;° good friends.
HORATIO:  O day and night, but this is wondrous strange.
165 HAMLET:  And therefore as a stranger give it welcome.
    There are more things in heaven and earth Horatio,
    Than are dreamt of in your philosophy.
    But come,
    Here as before, never so help you mercy,
170     How strange or odd some'er I bear myself,
    (As I perchance hereafter shall think meet
    To put an antic disposition on°)
    That you at such times seeing me, never shall
    With arms encumbere° thus, or this head-shake,
175     Or by pronouncing of some doubtful phrase,
    As "Well, well, we know," or "We could an if we would,"
    Or "If we list° to speak," or "There be and if they might,"
    Or such ambiguous giving out, to note
    That you know aught of me; this do swear,
180     So grace and mercy at your need help you.
GHOST:  [*Beneath.*] Swear. [*They swear.*]
HAMLET:  Rest, rest, perturbed spirit: so gentlemen,
    With all my love I do commend me to you,°
    And what so poor a man as Hamlet is,
185     May do t'express his love and friending to you
    God willing shall not lack: let us go in together,
    And still° your fingers on your lips I pray.
    The time is out of joint: O cursèd spite,
    That ever I was born to set it right.
190     Nay come, let's go together.
                                         *Exeunt.*

## ACT 2

### Scene 1. [Polonius's chambers]

*Enter old POLONIUS with his man REYNALDO.*

POLONIUS:  Give him this money, and these notes Reynaldo.
REYNALDO:  I will my lord.

---

°156 *Hic et ubique*: here and everywhere.  163 *pioner*: digger (army trencher).  *remove*: move elsewhere.  172 *put . . . on*: assume a mad or grotesque behavior.  174 *encumbered*: folded.  177 *list*: please.  183 *commend . . . you*: put myself in your hands.  187 *still*: always.

POLONIUS: You shall do marvellous° wisely, good Reynaldo,
    Before you visit him, to make inquire
    Of his behaviour.
REYNALDO:          My lord, I did intend it.
POLONIUS: Marry, well said, very well said; look you sir,        5
    Inquire me first what Danskers° are in Paris,
    And how, and who, what means, and where they keep,°
    What company, at what expense, and finding
    By this encompassment° and drift of question        10
    That they do know my son, come you more nearer
    Than your particular demands° will touch it,
    Take you as 'twere some distant knowledge of him,
    As thus, "I know his father, and his friends,
    And in part him"—do you mark this, Reynaldo?        15
REYNALDO: Ay, very well my lord.
POLONIUS: "And in part him, but," you may say, "not well,
    But if't be he I mean, he's very wild,
    Addicted so and so;" and there put on him
    What forgeries° you please, marry none so rank°        20
    As may dishonour him, take heed of that,
    But sir, such wanton, wild, and usual slips,
    As are companions noted and most known
    To youth and liberty.
REYNALDO:          As gaming my lord.
POLONIUS: Ay, or drinking, fencing, swearing,        25
    Quarrelling, drabbing°—you may go so far.
REYNALDO: My lord, that would dishonour him.
POLONIUS: Faith no, as you may season it in the charge.°
    You must not put another scandal on him,
    That he is open to incontinency,°        30
    That's not my meaning, but breathe his faults so quaintly°
    That they may seem the taints of° liberty,
    The flash and outbreak of a fiery mind,
    A savageness in unreclaimèd blood,°
    Of general assault.°        35
REYNALDO:        But my good lord—
POLONIUS: Wherefore° should you do this?
REYNALDO:                Ay my lord,
    I would know that.
POLONIUS: Marry sir, here's my drift,
    And I believe it is a fetch of warrant:°
    You laying these slight sullies on my son,
    As 'twere a thing a little soiled i'th' working,°        40
    Mark you, your party in converse, him you would sound,

---

°3 *marvellous*: wonderfully. 7 *Danskers*: Danes. 8 *keep*: lodge. 10 *encompassment*: roundabout way. 12 *particular demands*: specific questions. 20 *forgeries*: inventions. *rank*: excessive. 26 *drabbing*: whoring. 28 *season . . . charge*: temper the charge as you make it. 30 *incontinency*: uncontrolled lechery. 31 *quaintly*: delicately. 32 *taints of*: blemishes due to. 34 *unreclaimèd blood*: unbridled passion. 35 *general assault*: attacking all (young men). 36 *Wherefore*: why. 39 *fetch of warrant*: trick guaranteed to succeed. 41 *working*: handling.

Having ever seen° in the prenominate crimes°
The youth you breathe of guilty, be assured
45    He closes with you in this consequence,°
"Good sir," or so, or "friend," or "gentleman,"
According to the phrase, or the addition°
Of man and country.

REYNALDO:                     Very good my lord.

POLONIUS: And then sir, does a'° this, a' does, what was I
50    about to say?
By the mass I was about to say something,
Where did I leave?

REYNALDO:                At "closes in the consequence,"
At "friend, or so, and gentleman."

POLONIUS: At "closes in the consequence," ay marry,
55    He closes thus, "I know the gentleman,
I saw him yesterday, or th'other day,
Or then, or then, with such or such, and as you say,
There was a' gaming, there o'ertook in's rouse,°
There falling out at tennis," or perchance
60    "I saw him enter such a house of sale,"
Videlicet,° a brothel, or so forth. See you now,
Your bait of falsehood takes this carp of truth,
And thus do we of wisdom, and of reach,°
With windlasses,° and with assays of bias,°
65    By indirections find directions out:
So by my former lecture and advice
Shall you my son; you have me, have you not?

REYNALDO: My lord I have.

POLONIUS:                     God bye ye, fare ye well.

REYNALDO: Good my lord.

70  POLONIUS: Observe his inclination in yourself.°

REYNALDO: I shall my lord.

POLONIUS: And let him ply° his music.

REYNALDO:                     Well my lord.

POLONIUS: Farewell.

*Exit REYNALDO.*

*Enter OPHELIA.*

              How now Ophelia, what's the matter?

OPHELIA: O my lord, my lord, I have been so affrighted.

75  POLONIUS: With what, i'th'name of God?

OPHELIA: My lord, as I was sewing in my closet,°
Lord Hamlet with his doublet all unbraced,°
No hat upon his head, his stockings fouled,

---

°43 *Having ever seen:* if he has ever seen. *prenominate crimes:* aforenamed sins. 45 *closes . . . consequence:* comes to terms with you as follows. 47 *addition:* title, form of address. 49 *a':* he. 58 *o'ertook in's rouse:* overcome by drunkenness. 61 *Videlicet:* namely. 63 *reach:* far-reaching knowledge. 64 *windlasses:* roundabout approaches. *assays of bias:* indirect attempts. 70 *in yourself:* personally. 72 *ply:* practice. 76 *closet:* private room. 77 *doublet all unbraced:* jacket all unfastened.

Ungart'red, and down-gyvèd° to his ankle,
Pale as his shirt, his knees knocking each other,                        80
And with a look so piteous in purport°
As if he had been loosèd out of hell
To speak of horrors, he comes before me.
POLONIUS: Mad for thy love?
OPHELIA:                    My lord I do not know,
But truly I do fear it.
POLONIUS:                What said he?                                    85
OPHELIA: He took me by the wrist, and held me hard,
Then goes he to the length of all his arm,°
And with his other hand thus o'er his brow,
He falls to such perusal of my face
As° a' would draw it; long stayed he so,                                 90
At last, a little shaking of mine arm,
And thrice his head thus waving up and down,
He raised a sigh so piteous and profound
As it did seem to shatter all his bulk,°
And end his being; that done, he lets me go,                            95
And with his head over his shoulder turned
He seemed to find his way without his eyes,
For out adoors he went without their helps,
And to the last bended their light on me.
POLONIUS: Come, go with me, I will go seek the king,                   100
This is the very ecstasy° of love,
Whose violent property fordoes itself,°
And leads the will to desperate undertakings
As oft as any passion under heaven
That does afflict our natures: I am sorry.                              105
What, have you given him any hard words of late?
OPHELIA: No my good lord, but as you did command
I did repel his letters, and denied
His access to me.
POLONIUS:            That hath made him mad.
I am sorry that with better heed and judgment                          110
I had not quoted° him. I feared he did but trifle
And meant to wrack° thee, but beshrew my jealousy.°
By heaven it is as proper to our age
To cast beyond ourselves in our opinions,°
As it is common for the younger sort                                    115
To lack discretion; come, go we to the king,
This must be known, which being kept close, might move
More grief to hide, than hate to utter love.°                   [*Exeunt.*]

---

°79 *down-gyvèd*: down around his ankles (like prisoners' fetters or gyves). 81 *purport*: expression. 87 *goes . . . arm*: holds me at arm's length. 90 *As*: as if. 94 *bulk*: body. 101 *ecstasy*: madness. 102 *Whose . . . itself*: that, by its violent nature, destroys the lover. 111 *quoted*: observed. 112 *wrack*: ruin. *beshrew my jealousy*: curse my suspicion. 113–14 *proper . . . opinions*: natural for old people to read more into something than is actually there. 117–18 *being kept . . . love*: if kept secret, might cause more grief than if we risked the king's displeasure.

**Scene 2. [A room in the castle]**

*Flourish. Enter* King *and* Queen, Rosencrantz *and* Guildenstern, *cum aliis.*

King: Welcome dear Rosencrantz and Guildenstern.
      Moreover° that we much did long to see you,
      The need we have to use you did provoke
      Our hasty sending. Something have you heard
5    Of Hamlet's transformation—so call it.
      Sith° nor th'exterior nor the inward man
      Resembles that it was. What it should be,
      More than his father's death, that thus hath put him
      So much from th'understanding of himself,
10   I cannot dream of: I entreat you both,
      That being of so young days° brought up with him,
      And sith so neighboured to his youth and haviour,
      That you vouchsafe your rest° here in our court
      Some little time, so by your companies
15   To draw him on to pleasures, and to gather
      So much as from occasion you may glean,
      Whether aught to us unknown afflicts him thus,
      That opened° lies within our remedy.
Queen: Good gentlemen, he hath much talked of you,
20   And sure I am, two men there are not living
      To whom he more adheres. If it will please you
      To show us so much gentry° and good will,
      As to expend your time with us awhile,
      For the supply and profit of our hope,
25   Your visitation shall receive such thanks
      As fits a king's remembrance.
Rosencrantz:                    Both your majesties
      Might by the sovereign power you have of us,
      Put your dread pleasures more into command
      Than to entreaty.
Guildenstern:      But we both obey,
30   And here give up ourselves in the full bent,°
      To lay our service freely at your feet
      To be commanded.
King: Thanks Rosencrantz, and gentle Guildenstern.
Queen: Thanks Guildenstern, and gentle Rosencrantz.
35   And I beseech you instantly to visit
      My too much changèd son. Go some of you
      And bring these gentlemen where Hamlet is.
Guildenstern: Heavens make our presence and our practices°
      Pleasant and helpful to him.
Queen:                    Ay, amen.

                              *Exeunt* Rosencrantz *and* Guildenstern.

---

°2 *Moreover*: in addition to the fact.  6 *Sith*: since.  11 *of . . . days*: from your early days.  13 *vouchsafe your rest*: agree to stay.  18 *opened*: discovered.
22 *gentry*: courtesy.  30 *in the full bent*: to the utmost (in archery, bending the bow).  38 *practices*: (1) actions (2) plots.

*Enter* POLONIUS.

POLONIUS:  Th'ambassadors from Norway my good lord,                    40
    Are joyfully returned.
KING:  Thou still° hast been the father of good news.
POLONIUS:  Have I, my lord? Assure you, my good liege,
    I hold my duty as I hold my soul,
    Both to my God and to my gracious king;                          45
    And I do think, or else this brain of mine
    Hunts not the trail of policy° so sure
    As it hath used to do, that I have found
    The very cause of Hamlet's lunacy.
KING:  O speak of that, that do I long to hear.                        50
POLONIUS:  Give first admittance to th'ambassadors,
    My news shall be the fruit° to that great feast.
KING:  Thyself do grace to them, and bring them in.              [*Exit* POLONIUS.]
    He tells me my dear Gertrude, he hath found
    The head and source of all your son's distemper.                 55
QUEEN:  I doubt° it is no other but the main,
    His father's death and our o'erhasty marriage.
KING:  Well, we shall sift him.

*Enter* POLONIUS, VALTEMAND, *and* CORNELIUS.

                Welcome, my good friends.
    Say Valtemand, what from our brother Norway?
VALTEMAND:  Most fair return of greetings and desires;                 60
    Upon our first,° he sent out to suppress
    His nephew's levies, which to him appeared
    To be a preparation 'gainst the Polack,
    But better looked into, he truly found
    It was against your highness, whereat grieved                     65
    That so his sickness, age, and impotence
    Was falsely borne in hand,° sends out arrests
    On Fortinbras, which he in brief obeys,
    Receives rebuke from Norway, and in fine,°
    Makes vow before his uncle never more                             70
    To give th'assay° of arms against your majesty:
    Whereon old Norway, overcome with joy,
    Gives him threescore thousand crowns in annual fee,
    And his commission to employ those soldiers
    So levied (as before) against the Polack,                        75
    With an entreaty herein further shown,
    That it might please you to give quiet pass°
    Through your dominions for this enterprise,
    On such regards of safety and allowance
    As therein are set down.
KING:                     It likes° us well,                    [*Giving a paper.*]  80
    And at our more considered time° we'll read,

---

°42 *still*: always. 47 *policy*: (1) politics (2) plots. 52 *fruit*: dessert. 56 *doubt*: suspect. 61 *first*: first presentation. 67 *borne in hand*: deceived. 69 *fine*: finishing. 71 *assay*: test. 77 *pass*: passage. 80 *likes*: pleases. 81 *at . . . time*: when time is available for consideration.

Answer, and think upon this business:
Meantime, we thank you for your well-took labour,
Go to your rest, at night we'll feast together.
Most welcome home.                                    *Exeunt* AMBASSADORS.

85  POLONIUS:                    This business is well ended.
My liege and madam, to expostulate°
What majesty should be, what duty is,
Why day is day, night night, and time is time,
Were nothing but to waste night, day, and time.

90  Therefore since brevity is the soul of wit,°
And tediousness the limbs and outward flourishes,°
I will be brief. Your noble son is mad:
Mad call I it, for to define true madness,
What is't but to be nothing else but mad?
But let that go.

95  QUEEN:                More matter, with less art.
POLONIUS: Madam, I swear I use no art at all:
That he is mad 'tis true: 'tis true, 'tis pity,
And pity 'tis 'tis true: a foolish figure,°
But farewell it, for I will use no art.

100  Mad let us grant him then, and now remains
That we find out the cause of this effect,
Or rather say, the cause of this defect,
For this effect defective comes by cause:
Thus it remains, and the remainder thus.

105  Perpend.°
I have a daughter, have while she is mine,
Who in her duty and obedience, mark,
Hath given me this, now gather and surmise.
[*Reads.*] "To the celestial, and my soul's idol, the most

110  beautified° Ophelia,"—
That's an ill phrase, a vile phrase, "beautified" is a vile
phrase, but you shall hear. Thus:                    [*Reads.*]
        "In her excellent white bosom, these," &c.—
QUEEN: Came this from Hamlet to her?

115  POLONIUS: Good madam stay awhile, I will be faithful.        [*Reads.*]
        "Doubt thou the stars are fire,
            Doubt that the sun doth move,°
        Doubt° truth to be a liar,
            But never doubt I love.

120  O dear Ophelia, I am ill at these numbers, I have not
art to reckon° my groans, but that I love thee best, O
most best, believe it. Adieu.
        Thine evermore, most dear lady, whilst
        this machine° is to° him, Hamlet."

125  This in obedience hath my daughter shown me,
And more above hath his solicitings,

---

°86 *expostulate*: discuss. 90 *wit*: understanding. 91 *tediousness . . . flourishes*: embellishments and flourishes cause tedium. 98 *figure*: rhetorical figure. 105 *Perpend*: consider. 110 *beautified*: beautiful. 117 *move*: (as it was believed to do, around the earth). 118 *Doubt*: suspect. 121 *reckon*: express in meter. 124 *machine*: body. *to*: attached to.

As they fell out by time, by means, and place,
All given to mine ear.
KING:                  But how hath she
Received his love?
POLONIUS:            What do you think of me?
KING:  As of a man faithful and honourable.                     130
POLONIUS:  I would fain prove so. But what might you think
  When I had seen this hot love on the wing,
  As I perceived it (I must tell you that)
  Before my daughter told me, what might you,
  Or my dear majesty your queen here think,              135
  If I had played the desk or table-book,°
  Or given my heart a winking° mute and dumb,
  Or looked upon this love with idle° sight,
  What might you think? No, I went round to work,
  And my young mistress this I did bespeak,             140
  "Lord Hamlet is a prince out of thy star,°
  This must not be:" and then I prescripts° gave her
  That she should lock herself from his resort,°
  Admit no messengers, receive no tokens:
  Which done, she took the fruits of my advice,          145
  And he repellèd, a short tale to make,
  Fell into a sadness, then into a fast,
  Thence to a watch,° thence into a weakness,
  Thence to a lightness,° and by this declension,
  Into the madness wherein now he raves,             150
  And all we mourn for.
KING:                Do you think 'tis this?
QUEEN:  It may be, very like.
POLONIUS:  Hath there been such a time, I would fain know that,
  That I have positively said "'Tis so,"
  When it proved otherwise?
KING:             Not that I know.            155
POLONIUS:  Take this, from this, if this be otherwise;

[*Points to his head and shoulder.*]

  If circumstances lead me, I will find
  Where truth is hid, though it were hid indeed
  Within the center.
KING:              How may we try° it further?
POLONIUS:  You know sometimes he walks four hours together   160
  Here in the lobby.
QUEEN:           So he does indeed.
POLONIUS:  At such a time, I'll loose° my daughter to him.
  Be you and I behind an arras° then,
  Mark the encounter: if he love her not,
  And be not from his reason fall'n thereon,
  Let me be no assistant for a state,°               165

---

°136 *played . . . book*: kept it concealed as in a desk or personal notebook. 137 *given . . . winking*: had my heart shut its eyes to the matter. 138 *idle*: unseeing. 141 *out . . . star*: out of your sphere (above you in station). 142 *prescripts*: orders. 143 *resort*: company. 148 *watch*: sleeplessness. 149 *lightness*: lightheadedness. 159 *try*: test. 162 *loose*: (1) release (2) turn loose. 163 *arras*: hanging tapestry. 166 *assistant . . . state*: state official.

But keep a farm and carters.

KING:                                   We will try it.

*Enter* HAMLET *reading on a book.*

QUEEN: But look where sadly the poor wretch comes reading.

POLONIUS: Away, I do beseech you both away,

170   I'll board him presently,° O give me leave.                *Exeunt* KING *and* QUEEN.
      How does my good Lord Hamlet?

HAMLET: Well, God-a-mercy.

POLONIUS: Do you know me, my lord?

HAMLET: Excellent well, you are a fishmonger.°

175 POLONIUS: Not I my lord.

HAMLET: Then I would you were so honest a man.

POLONIUS: Honest, my lord?

HAMLET: Ay sir, to be honest as this world goes, is to be one
      man picked out of ten thousand.

180 POLONIUS: That's very true, my lord.

HAMLET: For if the sun breed maggots° in a dead dog, being a good
      kissing carrion°—have you a daughter?

POLONIUS: I have my lord.

HAMLET: Let her not walk i'th'sun:° conception° is a blessing, but as

185   your daughter may conceive, friend look to'it.

POLONIUS: [*Aside.*] How say you by that? Still harping on my daughter,
      yet he knew me not at first, a' said I was a fishmonger.
      A' is far gone, far gone, and truly in my youth, I suffered
      much extremity for love, very near this. I'll speak to him

190   again. What do you read my lord?

HAMLET: Words, words, words.

POLONIUS: What is the matter my lord?

HAMLET: Between who?

POLONIUS: I mean the matter° that you read, my lord.

195 HAMLET: Slanders sir; for the satirical rogue says here, that old men
      have grey beards, that their faces are wrinkled, their eyes
      purging thick amber and plum-tree gum,° and that they
      have a plentiful lack of wit, together with most weak
      hams. All which sir, though I most powerfully and

200   potently believe, yet I hold it not honesty° to have it thus set
      down, for yourself sir shall grow old as I am: if like a crab
      you could go backward.

POLONIUS: [*Aside.*] Though this be madness, yet there is method
      in't.

205   Will you walk out of the air° my lord?

HAMLET: Into my grave.

---

°170 *board him presently*: approach him immediately. 174 *fishmonger*: (1) fish dealer (2) pimp. 181 *breed maggots*: (in the belief that the rays of the sun caused maggots to breed in dead flesh). 182 *kissing carrion*: piece of flesh for kissing. 184 *Let . . . sun*: (1) (proverbial: "out of God's blessing, into the warm sun") (2) because the sun is a breeder (3) don't let her go near me (with a pun on "sun" and "son"). *conception*: (1) understanding (2) pregnancy. 194 *matter*: (1) content (Polonius's meaning) (2) cause of a quarrel (Hamlet's interpretation). 197–98 *purging . . . gum*: exuding a viscous yellowish discharge. 200 *honesty*: decency. 205 *out . . . air*: (in the belief that fresh air was bad for the sick).

POLONIUS: [*Aside.*] Indeed that's out of the air; how pregnant°
    sometimes his replies are, a happiness° that often
    madness hits on, which reason and sanity could not so
    prosperously° be delivered of. I will leave him, and                          210
    suddenly contrive the means of meeting between him
    and my daughter. My honourable lord, I will most
    humbly take leave of you.
HAMLET: You cannot sir take from me anything that I will more
    willingly part withal: except my life, except my life,                         215
    except my life.
POLONIUS: Fare you well my lord.
HAMLET: These tedious old fools.

*Enter* ROSENCRANTZ *and* GUILDENSTERN.

POLONIUS: You go to seek the Lord Hamlet, there he is.
ROSENCRANTZ: [*To* POLONIUS.] God save you sir.                    [*Exit* POLONIUS.] 220
GUILDENSTERN: My honoured lord.
ROSENCRANTZ: My most dear lord.
HAMLET: My excellent good friends, how dost thou Guildenstern?
    Ah Rosencrantz, good lads, how do you both?
ROSENCRANTZ: As the indifferent° children of the earth.                             225
GUILDENSTERN: Happy, in that we are not over-happy:
    On Fortune's cap we are not the very button.°
HAMLET: Nor the soles of her shoe?
ROSENCRANTZ: Neither my lord.
HAMLET: Then you live about her waist, or in the middle of her                     230
    favours?
GUILDENSTERN: Faith, her privates° we.
HAMLET: In the secret parts of Fortune? O most true, she is a
    strumpet.° What news?
ROSENCRANTZ: None my lord, but that the world's grown honest.                       235
HAMLET: Then is doomsday near: but your news is not true. Let me
    question more in particular: what have you my good
    friends, deserved at the hands of Fortune, that she sends
    you to prison hither?
GUILDENSTERN: Prison, my lord?                                                      240
HAMLET: Denmark's a prison.
ROSENCRANTZ: Then is the world one.
HAMLET: A goodly one, in which there are many confines, wards,°
    and dungeons; Denmark being one o'th'worst.
ROSENCRANTZ: We think not so my lord.                                               245
HAMLET: Why then 'tis none to you; for there is nothing either good
    or bad, but thinking makes it so: to me it is a prison.
ROSENCRANTZ: Why then your ambition makes it one: 'tis too narrow for
    your mind.

---

°207 *pregnant*: full of meaning. 208 *happiness*: aptness. 210 *prosperously*: successfully. 225 *indifferent*: ordinary. 227 *On Fortune's . . . button*: we are not at the height of our fortunes. 232 *privates*: (1) intimate friend (2) private parts. 234 *strumpet*: inconstant woman, giving favor to many. 243 *wards*: cells.

250 HAMLET: O God, I could be bounded in a nutshell, and count
      myself a king of infinite space; were it not that I have bad
      dreams.
   GUILDENSTERN: Which dreams indeed are ambition: for the very substance
      of the ambitious, is merely the shadow of a dream.
255 HAMLET: A dream itself is but a shadow.
   ROSENCRANTZ: Truly, and I hold ambition of so airy and light a quality,
      that it is but a shadow's shadow.
   HAMLET: Then are our beggars bodies, and our monarchs and
      outstretched heroes the beggars' shadows:° shall we to th'
260   court? for by my fay,° I cannot reason.
   BOTH: We'll wait upon° you.
   HAMLET: No such matter. I will not sort° you with the rest of my
      servants: for to speak to you like an honest man, I am most
      dreadfully attended. But in the beaten way of friendship,
265   what make you at Elsinore?
   ROSENCRANTZ: To visit you my lord, no other occasion.
   HAMLET: Beggar that I am, I am even poor in thanks, but I thank
      you, and sure dear friends, my thanks are too dear a
      halfpenny:° were you not sent for? is it your own inclining?
270   is it a free° visitation? come, come, deal justly with me,
      come, come, nay speak.
   GUILDENSTERN: What should we say my lord?
   HAMLET: Anything but to th'purpose: you were sent for, and there
      is a kind of confession in your looks, which your modesties
275   have not craft enough to colour: I know the good king and
      queen have sent for you.
   ROSENCRANTZ: To what end my lord?
   HAMLET: That you must teach me: but let me conjure° you, by the
      rights of our fellowship, by the consonancy of our youth,°
280   by the obligation of our ever-preserved love, and by what
      more dear a better proposer can charge you withal,° be
      even and direct with me whether you were sent for or no.
   ROSENCRANTZ: [*Aside to Guildenstern.*] What say you?
   HAMLET: Nay then, I have an eye of° you: If you love me,
285   hold not off.
   GUILDENSTERN: My lord, we were sent for.
   HAMLET: I will tell you why, so shall my anticipation prevent° your
      discovery,° and your secrecy to the king and queen moult
      no feather.° I have of late, but wherefore I know not, lost all
290   my mirth, forgone all custom of exercises: and indeed it
      goes so heavily with my disposition, that this goodly
      frame the earth, seems to me a sterile promontory, this
      most excellent canopy the air, look you, this brave°
      o'erhanging firmament, this majestical roof fretted° with

---

°258–59 *Then are . . . shadows*: then beggars are the true substance and ambitious kings and heroes the elongated shadows of beggars' bodies (for only a real substance can cast a shadow). 260 *fay*: faith. 261 *wait upon*: attend. 262 *sort*: class. 268–69 *too dear a halfpenny*: worth not even a halfpenny (as I have no influence). 270 *free*: voluntary. 278 *conjure*: appeal to. 279 *consonancy . . . youth*: agreement in our ages. 281 *withal*: with. 284 *of*: on. 287 *prevent*: forestall. 288 *discovery*: disclosure. 288–89 *moult no feather*: change in no way. 293 *brave*: splendid. 294 *fretted*: ornamented with fretwork.

golden fire,° why it appeareth nothing to me but a foul and                         295
pestilent congregation of vapours.° What a piece of work is
a man! How noble in reason, how infinite in faculties,° in
form and moving, how express° and admirable in action,
how like an angel in apprehension, how like a god: the
beauty of the world; the paragon of animals; and yet to              300
me, what is this quintessence of dust? Man delights not
me, no, nor woman neither, though by your smiling, you
seem to say so.

ROSENCRANTZ:  My lord, there was no such stuff in my thoughts.

HAMLET:  Why did ye laugh then, when I said 'man delights not me'?       305

ROSENCRANTZ:  To think, my lord, if you delight not in man, what lenten
      entertainment° the players shall receive from you: we coted°
      them on the way, and hither are they coming to offer you
      service.

HAMLET:  He that plays the king shall be welcome, his majesty shall       310
      have tribute of me, the adventurous knight° shall use his
      foil and target,° the lover shall not sigh gratis,° the humorous
      man° shall end his part in peace,° the clown shall make
      those laugh whose lungs are tickle o'th'sere,° and the lady
      shall say her mind freely: or the blank verse shall halt° for't.       315
      What players are they?

ROSENCRANTZ:  Even those you were wont to take such delight in, the
      tragedians of the city.

HAMLET:  How chances it they travel? Their residence° both in
      reputation and profit was better both ways.       320

ROSENCRANTZ:  I think their inhibition comes by the means of the late
      innovation.°

HAMLET:  Do they hold the same estimation they did when I was in
      the city; are they so followed?

ROSENCRANTZ:  No indeed are they not.       325

HAMLET:  How comes it? Do they grow rusty?

ROSENCRANTZ:  Nay, their endeavour keeps in the wonted pace; but there
      is sir an aery° of children, like eyases,° that cry out on the
      top of question,° and are most tyrannically° clapped for't:
      these are now the fashion, and so berattle° the common       330
      stages° (so they call them) that many wearing rapiers° are
      afraid of goose-quills,° and dare scarce come thither.

HAMLET:  What, are they children? Who maintains 'em? How are

---

°295 *golden fire*: stars. 296 *pestilent . . . vapours*: (clouds were believed to carry contagion). 297 *faculties*: physical powers. 298 *express*: well framed. 306–7 *lenten entertainment*: meager treatment. 307 *coted*: passed. 311 *adventurous knight*: knight errant (a popular stage character). 312 *foil and target*: sword blunted for stage fighting, and small shield. 312 *gratis*: (without applause). 312–13 *humorous man*: eccentric character with a dominant trait, caused by an excess of one of the four humors, or bodily fluids. 313 *in peace*: without interruption. 314 *tickle o'th'sere*: attuned to respond to laughter, as the finely adjusted gunlock responds to the touch of the trigger (fr. hunting). 315 *halt*: limp (if she adds her own opinions and spoils the meter). 319 *residence*: i.e., in a city theatre. 321–22 *inhibition . . . innovation*: i.e., they were forced out of town by a more popular theatrical fashion. The following speeches allude to the "War of the Theatres" (1601–1602) between the child and adult acting companies. 328 *aery*: nest. *eyases*: young hawks. 328–29 *that cry . . . question*: whose shrill voices can be heard above all others. 329 *tyrannically*: strongly. 330 *berattle*: berate. 330–31 *common stages*: public playhouses (the children's companies performed in private theatres). 331 *wearing rapiers*: (worn by gentlemen). 332 *goose-quills*: pens (of satirical dramatists who wrote for the children).

they escoted°? Will they pursue the quality no longer than
335    they can sing°? Will they not say afterwards if they should
grow themselves to common players (as it is most like, if
their means are not better) their writers do them wrong, to
make them exclaim against their own succession°?

ROSENCRANTZ: Faith, there has been much to-do on both sides: and the
340    nation holds it no sin to tarre° them to controversy. There
was for a while, no money bid for argument,° unless the
poet and the player went to cuffs in the question.°

HAMLET: Is't possible?

GUILDENSTERN: O there has been much throwing about of brains.

345 HAMLET: Do the boys carry it away°?

ROSENCRANTZ: Ay, that they do my lord, Hercules and his load too.°

HAMLET: It is not very strange, for my uncle is king of Denmark,
and those that would make mows° at him while my father
lived, give twenty, forty, fifty, a hundred ducats apiece
350    for his picture in little.° 'Sblood,° there is something in this
more than natural, if philosophy° could find it out.

*A flourish for the Players.*

GUILDENSTERN: There are the players.

HAMLET: Gentlemen, you are welcome to Elsinore: your hands,
come then, th'appurtenance° of welcome is fashion and
355    ceremony; let me comply with you in this garb,° lest my
extent° to the players, which I tell you must show fairly
outwards, should more appear like entertainment than
yours.° You are welcome: but my uncle-father, and aunt-mother,
are deceived.

360 GUILDENSTERN: In what my dear lord?

HAMLET: I am but mad north-north-west; when the wind is southerly,
I know a hawk from a handsaw.°

*Enter POLONIUS.*

POLONIUS: Well be with you, gentlemen.

HAMLET: Hark you Guildenstern, and you too, at each ear a hearer:
365    that great baby you see there is not yet out of his swaddling
clouts.°

ROSENCRANTZ: Happily° he is the second time come to them, for they say
an old man is twice a child.

HAMLET: I will prophesy, he comes to tell me of the players, mark
370    it.—You say right sir, a Monday morning, 'twas then
indeed.

---

°334 *escoted*: supported.  334–35 *pursue . . . sing*: continue acting only until their voices change.  338 *succession*: inheritance.  340 *tarre*: provoke.
341 *bid for argument*: paid for the plot of a proposed play.  342 *went . . . question*: came to blows on the subject.  345 *carry it away*: carry off the
prize.  346 *Hercules . . . too*: (Shakespeare's own company at the Globe Theater, whose sign was Hercules carrying the globe of the world).
348 *mows*: mouths, grimaces.  350 *little*: a miniature.  *'Sblood*: by God's blood.  351 *philosophy*: science.  354 *appurtenance*: accessory.
355 *comply . . . garb*: observe the formalities with you in this style.  356 *extent*: i.e., of welcome.  357–58 *should . . . yours*: should appear more
hospitable than yours.  362 *I know . . . handsaw*: I can tell the difference between two things that are unlike ("hawk" = [1] bird of prey [2] mattock,
pickaxe; "handsaw" = [1] hernshaw or heron bird [2] small saw).  365–66 *swaddling clouts*: strips of cloth binding a newborn baby.  367 *Happily*:
perhaps.

Polonius: My lord, I have news to tell you.

Hamlet: My lord, I have news to tell you. When Roscius° was an
actor in Rome—

Polonius: The actors are come hither, my lord                            375

Hamlet: Buz, buz.°

Polonius: Upon my honour.

Hamlet: Then came each actor on his ass—

Polonius: The best actors in the world, either for tragedy, comedy,
history, pastoral, pastoral-comical, historical-pastoral,              380
tragical-historical, tragical-comical-historical-pastoral,
scene individable,° or poem unlimited.° Seneca cannot be
too heavy, nor Plautus° too light for the law of writ, and the
liberty:° these are the only men.

Hamlet: O Jephthah,° judge of Israel, what a treasure hadst thou      385

Polonius: What a treasure had he, my lord?

Hamlet: Why

'One fair daughter and no more,
    The which he lovèd passing° well.'

Polonius: [Aside.] Still on my daughter                                390

Hamlet: Am I not i'th' right, old Jephthah?

Polonius: If you call me Jephthah my lord, I have a daughter that I
love passing well.

Hamlet: Nay, that follows not.

Polonius: What follows then, my lord?                                   395

Hamlet: Why

"As by lot, God wot,"
and then you know
        "It came to pass, as most like° it was:"
the first row° of the pious chanson will show you more, for    400
look where my abridgement° comes.

*Enter four or five* Players.

You are welcome masters, welcome all. I am glad to see
thee well: welcome, good friends. O my old friend, why
thy face is valanced° since I saw thee last, com'st thou to
beard me in Denmark? What, my young lady° and             405
mistress? by'r lady, your ladyship is nearer to heaven than
when I saw you last, by the altitude of a chopine.° Pray
God your voice, like a piece of uncurrent° gold, be not
cracked within the ring.° Masters, you are all welcome:
we'll e'en to't like French falconers, fly at any thing we see:°   410
we'll have a speech straight. Come give us a taste of your
quality: come, a passionate speech.

1. Player: What speech, my good lord?

---

°373 *Roscius*: famous Roman actor. 376 *Buz, buz*: (contemptuous). 382 *scene individable*: play observing the unities (time, place, action). *poem unlimited*:
play ignoring the unities. 382–83 *Seneca, Plautus*: Roman writers of tragedy and comedy, respectively. 383–84 *law . . . liberty*: "rules" regarding the unities and those exercising freedom from the unities. 385 *Jephthah*: (who was forced to sacrifice his only daughter because of a rash promise: Judges
11:29–39). 389 *passing*: surpassingly. 399 *like*: likely. 400 *row*: stanza. 401 *abridgement*: (the players who will cut short my song). 404 *valanced*:
fringed with a beard. 405 *lady*: boy playing women's role. 407 *chopine*: thick-soled shoe. 408 *uncurrent*: not legal tender. 409 *ring*: (1) ring enclosing the
design on a gold coin (to crack it within the ring [to steal the gold] made it "uncurrent") (2) sound. 410 *fly . . . see*: undertake any difficulty.

HAMLET: I heard thee speak me a speech once, but it was never
415       acted, or if it was, not above once, for the play I remember
          pleased not the million, 'twas caviary to the general,° but it
          was (as I received it, and others, whose judgments in such
          matters cried in the top of mine°) an excellent play, well
          digested in the scenes, set down with as much modesty as
420       cunning.° I remember one said there were no sallets.° In the
          lines, to make the matter savoury, nor no matter in the
          phrase that might indict the author of° affection, but called
          it an honest method, as wholesome as sweet, and by very
          much more handsome than fine:° one speech in't I chiefly
425       loved, 'twas Aeneas' tale to Dido, and thereabout of it
          especially where he speaks of Priam's slaughter.° If it live in
          your memory begin at this line, let me see, let me see:
                "The rugged Pyrrhus,° like th'Hyrcanian beast'°—
          'tis not so: it begins with Pyrrhus—
430             "The rugged Pyrrhus, he whose sable° arms,
          Black as his purpose, did the night resemble
          When he lay couched in th'ominous horse,°
          Hath now this dread and black complexion smeared
          With heraldy more dismal: head to foot
435       Now is he total gules,° horridly tricked°
          With blood of fathers, mothers, daughters, sons,
          Baked and impasted° with the parching° streets,
          That lend a tyrannous and damnèd light
          To their lord's murder. Roasted in wrath and fire,
440       And thus o'er-sizèd° with coagulate gore,
          With eyes like carbuncles,° the hellish Pyrrhus
          Old grandsire Priam seeks;"
          So proceed you.
POLONIUS: 'Fore God, my lord, well spoken, with good accent and
445       good discretion.°
1. PLAYER: "Anon he finds him,
          Striking too short at Greeks, his antique° sword,
          Rebellious to his arm, lies where it falls,
          Repugnant to command,° unequal matched,
450       Pyrrhus at Priam drives, in rage strikes wide,
          But with the whiff and wind of his fell° sword,
          Th'unnervèd father falls: then senseless Ilium,°
          Seeming to feel this blow, with flaming top

---

°416 *caviary . . . general*: like caviar, too rich for the general public. 418 *cried . . . mine*: spoke with more authority than mine. 419–20 *modesty as cunning*: moderation as skill. 420 *sallets*: spicy bits. 422 *indict . . . of*: charge . . . with. 424 *handsome than fine*: dignified than finely wrought. 426 *Priam's slaughter*: the murder of the King of Troy (as told in the Aeneid). 428 *Pyrrhus*: son of Achilles. *Hyrcanian beast*: tiger noted for fierceness. 430 *sable*: black. 432 *horse*: the hollow wooden horse used by the Greeks to enter Troy. 435 *gules*: red. *horridly tricked*: horribly decorated. 437 *impasted*: coagulated. *parching*: (because the city was on fire). 440 *o'er-sizèd*: covered over. 441 *carbuncles*: red gems. 445 *discretion*: interpretation. 447 *antique*: ancient. 449 *Repugnant to command*: refusing to obey its commander. 451 *fell*: savage. 452 *senseless Ilium*: unfeeling Troy.

Stoops to his base; and with a hideous crash
Takes prisoner Pyrrhus' ear. For lo, his sword
Which was declining on the milky head                                  455
Of reverend Priam, seemed i'th'air to stick;
So as a painted° tyrant Pyrrhus stood,
And like a neutral to his will and matter,°
Did nothing:
But as we often see, against° some storm,                             460
A silence in the heavens, the rack° stand still,
The bold winds speechless, and the orb° below
As hush as death, anon the dreadful thunder
Doth rend the region, so after Pyrrhus' pause,
A rousèd vengeance sets him new awork,                                 465
And never did the Cyclops'° hammers fall
On Mars's armour, forged for proof eterne,°
With less remorse than Pyrrhus' bleeding sword
Now falls on Priam.
Out, out, thou strumpet Fortune: all you gods,                        470
In general synod° take away her power,
Break all the spokes and fellies from her wheel,°
And bowl the round nave° down the hill of heaven
As low as to the fiends."°
POLONIUS: This is too long.                                           475
HAMLET: It shall to the barber's with your beard; prithee say on: he's
    for a jig, or a tale of bawdry, or he sleeps. Say on, come to
    Hecuba.
1. PLAYER: "But who, ah woe, had seen the mobled° queen—"
HAMLET: "The mobled queen"?                                           480
POLONIUS: That's good, "mobled queen" is good.
1. PLAYER: "Run barefoot up and down, threat'ning the flames
    With bissom rheum,° a clout° upon that head
    Where late the diadem stood, and for a robe,
    About her lank and all o'er-teemèd° loins,                        485
    A blanket in the alarm of fear caught up—
    Who this had seen, with tongue in venom steeped,
    'Gainst Fortune's state° would treason have pronounced;
    But if the gods themselves did see her then,
    When she saw Pyrrhus make malicious sport                         490
    In mincing with his sword her husband's limbs,
    The instant burst of clamour that she made,
    Unless things mortal move them not at all,
    Would have made milch° the burning eyes of heaven,
    And passion in the gods."                                         495

---

°458 *painted*: pictured. 459 *like . . . matter*: unmoved by either his purpose or its achievement. 461 *against*: before. 462 *rack*: clouds. 463 *orb*: earth. 467 *Cyclops*: workmen of Vulcan, armorer of the gods. 468 *for proof eterne*: to be eternally invincible. 472 *synod*: assembly. 473 *fellies . . . wheel*: curved pieces of the rim of the wheel that fortune turns, representing a man's fortunes. 474 *nave*: hub. 475 *fiends*: i.e., of hell. 480 *mobled*: muffled in a scarf. 484 *bissom rheum*: binding tears. *clout*: cloth. 486 *o'er-teemed*: worn out by excessive childbearing. 489 *state*: reign. 495 *milch*: milky, moist.

POLONIUS: Look where° he has not turned° his colour, and has tears in's
    eyes, prithee no more.
HAMLET: 'Tis well, I'll have thee speak out the rest of this soon.
500      Good my lord, will you see the players well bestowed,° do
    you hear, let them be well used, for they are the abstract°
    and brief chronicles° of the time; after your death you were
    better have a bad epitaph than their ill report while you
    live.
505 POLONIUS: My lord, I will use them according to their desert.°
HAMLET: God's bodkin° man, much better. Use every man after° his
    desert, and who shall 'scape whipping? Use them after
    you own honour and dignity: the less they deserve, the
    more merit is in your bounty. Take them in.
510 POLONIUS: Come sirs.                 *Exeunt* POLONIUS *and* PLAYERS.
HAMLET: Follow him friends, we'll hear a play tomorrow; [*Stops the*
    FIRST PLAYER.] dost thou hear me, old friend, can you play
    The Murder of Gonzago?
1. PLAYER: Ay my lord.
515 HAMLET: We'll ha't tomorrow night. You could for a need° study a
    speech of some dozen or sixteen lines, which I would set
    down and insert in't, could you not?
1. PLAYER: Ay my lord.
HAMLET: Very well, follow that lord, and look you mock him not.

                                                         [*Exit* FIRST PLAYER.]

520      [*To Rosencrantz and Guildenstern.*] My good friends, I'll
    leave you till night, you are welcome to Elsinore.
ROSENCRANTZ: Good my lord.        [*Exeunt* ROSENCRANTZ *and* GUILDENSTERN.]
HAMLET: Ay so, God bye to you.—Now I am alone.
    O what a rogue and peasant slave am I.
525    Is it not monstrous that this player here,
    But in a fiction, in a dream of passion,°
    Could force his soul so to his own conceit°
    That from her working all his visage wanned,°
    Tears in his eyes, distraction in his aspect,
530    A broken voice, and his whole function° suiting
    With forms° to his conceit; and all for nothing,
    For Hecuba!
    What's Hecuba to him, or he to Hecuba,
    That he should weep for her? what would he do,
535    Had he the motive and the cue for passion
    That I have? he would drown the stage with tears,
    And cleave the general ear° with horrid speech,
    Make mad the guilty and appal the free,°

---

°497 *where*: whether. *turned*: changed. 500 *bestowed*: lodged. 501 *abstract*: summary (noun). 502 *brief chronicles*: history in brief. 505 *desert*: merit. 506 *God's bodkin*: God's little body, the communion wafer (an oath). *after*: according to. 515 *for a need*: if necessary. 526 *dream of passion*: portrayal of emotion. 527 *conceit*: imagination. 528 *wanned*: grew pale. 530 *function*: bearing. 531 *With forms*: in appearance. 537 *general ear*: ears of all in the audience. 538 *free*: innocent.

Confound° the ignorant, and amaze indeed
The very faculties of eyes and ears; yet I,                                    540
A dull and muddy-mettled° rascal, peak°
Like John-a-dreams, unpregnant of° my cause,
And can say nothing; no, not for a king,
Upon whose property and most dear life,
A damned defeat was made: am I a coward?                                       545
Who calls me villain, breaks my pate° across,
Plucks off my beard° and blows it in my face,
Tweaks me by the nose, gives me the lie i'th'throat
As deep as to the lungs,° who does me this?
Ha, 'swounds,° I should take it; for it cannot be                              550
But I am pigeon-livered,° and lack gall
To make oppression bitter, or ere this
I should ha' fatted all the region kites°
With this slave's offal: bloody, bawdy villain,
Remorseless, treacherous, lecherous, kindless° villain!                       555
O vengeance!
Why what an ass am I, this is most brave,°
That I, the son of a dear father murdered,
Prompted to my revenge by heaven and hell,
Must like a whore unpack my heart with words,                                 560
And fall a-cursing like a very drab,°
A scullion,° fie upon't, foh.
About, my brains; hum, I have heard,
That guilty creatures sitting at a play,
Have by the very cunning of the scene                                         565
Been struck so to the soul, that presently°
They have proclaimed their malefactions:
For murder, though it have no tongue, will speak
With most miraculous organ: I'll have these players
Play something like the murder of my father                                   570
Before mine uncle, I'll observe his looks,
I'll tent° him to the quick, if a' do blench°
I know my course. The spirit that I have seen
May be a devil, and the devil hath power
T'assume a pleasing shape, yea, and perhaps                                   575
Out of my weakness, and my melancholy,
As he is very potent with such spirits,
Abuses me to damn me; I'll have grounds
More relative than this: the play's the thing
Wherein I'll catch the conscience of the king.                     *Exit.* 580

---

°539 *Confound*: confuse. 541 *muddy-mettled*: dull-spirited. *peak*: pine, mope. 542 *John-a-dreams*: a daydreaming fellow. *unpregnant of*: unstirred by. 546 *pate*: head. 547 *Plucks . . . beard*: (a way of giving insult). 548–49 *gives . . . lungs*: insults me by calling me a liar of the worst kind (the lungs being deeper than the throat). 550 *'swounds*: God's wounds. 551 *pigeon-livered*: meek and uncouraged. 553 *region kites*: vultures of the upper air. 555 *kindless*: unnatural. 557 *brave*: fine. 561 *drab*: whore. 562 *scullion*: kitchen wench. 566 *presently*: immediately. 572 *tent*: probe. *blench*: flinch.

## ACT 3

### Scene 1. [A room in the castle]

*Enter* King, Queen, Polonius, Ophelia, Rosencrantz, Guildenstern, Lords.

King:  And can you by no drift of conference°
    Get from him why he puts on this confusion,°
    Grating so harshly all his days of quiet
    With turbulent and dangerous lunacy?
5  Rosencrantz:  He does confess he feels himself distracted,
    But from what cause, a' will by no means speak.
  Guildenstern:  Nor do we find him forward to be sounded,°
    But with a crafty madness keeps aloof
    When we would bring him on to some confession
    Of his true state.
10  Queen:             Did he receive you well?
  Rosencrantz:  Most like a gentleman.
  Guildenstern:  But with much forcing of his disposition.°
  Rosencrantz:  Niggard of question,° but of our demands
    Most free in his reply.
  Queen:             Did you assay° him
15  To any pastime?
  Rosencrantz:  Madam, it so fell out that certain players
    We o'er-raught° on the way: of these we told him,
    And there did seem in him a kind of joy
    To hear of it: they are here about the court,
20    And as I think, they have already order
    This night to play before him.
  Polonius:  'Tis most true,
    And he beseeched me to entreat your majesties
    To hear and see the matter.°
25  King:  With all my heart, and it doth much content me
    To hear him so inclined.
    Good gentlemen, give him a further edge,°
    And drive his purpose into these delights.
  Rosencrantz:  We shall my lord.        *Exeunt* Rosencrantz *and* Guildenstern.
  King:             Sweet Gertrude, leave us too,
30  For we have closely° sent for Hamlet hither,
    That he, as 'twere by accident, may here
    Affront° Ophelia;
    Her father and myself, lawful espials,°
    Will so bestow° ourselves, that seeing unseen,
35  We may of their encounter frankly° judge,

---

°1 *drift of conference*: turn of conversation. 2 *puts . . . confusion*: seems so distracted ("puts on" indicates the king's private suspicion that Hamlet is playing mad). 7 *forward . . . sounded*: disposed to be sounded out. 12 *forcing . . . disposition*: forcing himself to be so. 13 *Niggard of question*: unwilling to talk. 14 *assay*: tempt. 17 *o'er-raught*: overtook. 24 *matter*: i.e., of the play. 27 *give . . . edge*: encourage his keen interest. 30 *closely*: secretly. 32 *Affront*: meet face to face with. 33 *espials*: spies. 34, 45 *bestow*: place. 35 *frankly*: freely.

And gather by him as he is behaved,
If't be th'affliction of his love or no
That thus he suffers for.
QUEEN:                             I shall obey you.
And for your part Ophelia, I do wish
That your good beauties be the happy cause                                    40
Of Hamlet's wildness, so shall I hope your virtues
Will bring him to his wonted° way again,
To both your honours.
OPHELIA:                             Madam, I wish it may.                    [*Exit* QUEEN.]
POLONIUS: Ophelia, walk you here—Gracious,° so please you,
We will bestow ourselves—read on this book,°                                 45
That show of such an exercise° may colour°
Your loneliness; we are oft to blame in this,
'Tis too much proved,° that with devotion's visage
And pious action, we do sugar o'er
The devil himself.
KING:                             [*Aside.*] O 'tis too true,°                50
How smart a lash that speech doth give my conscience.
The harlot's cheek, beautied with plast'ring art,
Is not more ugly to° the thing that helps it,
Than is my deed to my most painted word:°
O heavy burden!                                                              55
POLONIUS: I hear him coming, let's withdraw my lord.

                                                            *Exeunt.*


*Enter* HAMLET.

HAMLET: To be, or not to be, that is the question,
Whether 'tis nobler in the mind° to suffer
The slings and arrows of outrageous fortune,
Or to take arms against a sea of troubles,                                  60
And by opposing, end them: to die, to sleep,
No more; and by a sleep, to say we end
The heart-ache, and the thousand natural shocks
That flesh is heir to; 'tis a consummation
Devoutly to be wished. To die, to sleep,                                    65
To sleep, perchance to dream, ay there's the rub,°
For in that sleep of death what dreams may come
When we have shuffled off this mortal coil°
Must give us pause—there's the respect°
That makes calamity of so long life:°                                       70

---

°42 *wonted*: customary. 44 *Gracious*: i.e., Your Grace. 45 *book*: (of prayer). 46 *exercise*: religious exercise. *colour*: make plausible. 48 *'Tis . . . proved*: it is all too apparent. 50 *'tis too true*: (the king's first indication that he is guilty). 53 *to*: compared to. 52–54 *harlot's cheek . . . word*: just as the harlot's cheek is even uglier by contrast to the makeup that tries to beautify it, so my deed is uglier by contrast to the hypocritical words under which I hide it. 58 *nobler in the mind*: best, according to "sovereign" reason. 66 *rub*: obstacle. 68 *mortal coil*: (1) turmoil of mortal life (2) coil of flesh encircling the body. 69 *respect*: consideration. 70 *makes calamity of so long life*: makes living long a calamity.

For who would bear the whips and scorns of time,
Th'oppressor's wrong, the proud man's contumely,°
The pangs of disprized love, the law's delay,°
The insolence of office,° and the spurns
75 That patient merit of th'unworthy takes,
When he himself might his quietus° make
With a bare bodkin;° who would fardels° bear,
To grunt and sweat under a weary life,
But that the dread of something after death,
80 The undiscovered° country, from whose bourn°
No traveler returns, puzzles the will,
And makes us rather bear those ills we have,
Than fly to others that we know not of.
Thus conscience does make cowards of us all,
85 And thus the native hue° of resolution
Is sicklied o'er with the pale cast of thought,
And enterprises of great pitch° and moment,°
With this regard° their currents turn awry,°
And lose the name of action. Soft you now,
90 The fair Ophelia—Nymph, in thy orisons°
Be all my sins remembered.

OPHELIA:                        Good my lord,
How does your honour for this many a day.°

HAMLET: I humbly thank you: well, well, well.

OPHELIA: My lord, I have remembrances of yours
95 That I have longèd long to re-deliver,
I pray you now receive them.

HAMLET:                        No, not I,
I never gave you aught.

OPHELIA: My honoured lord, you know right well you did,
And with them words of so sweet breath° composed
100 As made the things more rich: their perfume lost,
Take these again, for to the noble mind
Rich gifts wax° poor when givers prove unkind.
There my lord.

HAMLET: Ha, ha, are you honest°?

105 OPHELIA: My lord.

HAMLET: Are you fair°?

OPHELIA: What means your lordship?

HAMLET: That if you be honest and fair, your honesty should admit
no discourse to your beauty.°

---

°72 *contumely*: contempt. 73 *law's delay*: longevity of lawsuits. 74 *office*: officials. 76 *quietus*: settlement of his debt. 77 *bare bodkin*: mere dagger. *fardels*: burdens. 78 *undiscovered*: unknown, unexplored. *bourn*: boundary. 85 *native hue*: natural complexion. 87 *pitch*: height, excellence. *moment*: importance. 88 *regard*: consideration. *their currents turn awry*: change their course. 90 *orisons*: prayers (referring to her prayer book). 92 *this . . . day*: all these days. 99 *breath*: speech. 102 *wax*: grow. 104 *honest*: (1) chaste (2) truthful. 106 *fair*: (1) beautiful (2) honorable. 108–9 *admit . . . beauty*: (1) not allow communication with your beauty (2) not allow your beauty to be used as a trap (Hamlet may have overheard the Polonius–Claudius plot or spotted their movement behind the arras).

OPHELIA: Could beauty my lord, have better commerce than with          110
    honesty?
HAMLET: Ay truly, for the power of beauty will sooner transform
    honesty° from what it is to a bawd,° than the force of
    honesty can translate beauty into his likeness. This was
    sometime° a paradox, but now the time gives it proof. I did          115
    love you once.
OPHELIA: Indeed my lord, you made me believe so.
HAMLET: You should not have believed me, for virtue cannot so
    inoculate our old stock, but we shall relish of it.° I loved
    you not.
OPHELIA: I was the more deceived.          120
HAMLET: Get thee to a nunnery,° why wouldst thou be a breeder of
    sinners? I am myself indifferent honest,° but yet I could
    accuse me of such things, that it were better my mother
    had not borne me: I am very proud, revengeful, ambitious,
    with more offences at my beck,° than I have thoughts          125
    to put them in, imagination to give them shape, or time to
    act them in: what should such fellows as I do, crawling
    between earth and heaven? we are arrant° knaves all,
    believe none of us, go thy ways to a nunnery. Where's
    your father?          130
OPHELIA: At home my lord.
HAMLET: Let the doors be shut upon him, that he may play the fool
    nowhere but in's own house. Farewell.
OPHELIA: O help him, you sweet heavens.
HAMLET: If thou dost marry, I'll give thee this plague° for thy dowry:          135
    be thou as chaste as ice, as pure as snow, thou shalt not
    escape calumny; get thee to a nunnery, go, farewell. Or if
    thou wilt needs marry, marry a fool, for wise men know
    well enough what monsters° you make of them: to a nunnery
    go, and quickly too, farewell.          140
OPHELIA: O heavenly powers, restore him.
HAMLET: I have heard of your paintings too, well enough. God hath
    given you one face, and you make yourselves another: you
    jig,° you amble, and you lisp,° you nick-name God's
    creatures, and make your wantonness your ignorance,° go to,          145
    I'll no more on't, it hath made me mad. I say we will have
    no moe° marriage. Those that are married already, all but
    one shall live, the rest shall keep as they are: to a nunnery,
    go.

*Exit* HAMLET. 150

---

°113 *honesty*: chastity. *bawd*: procurer, pimp. 115 *sometime*: once. 119 *inoculate . . . it*: change our sinful nature (as a tree is grafted to improve it) but we will keep our old taste (as will the fruit of the grafted tree). 122 *nunnery*: (1) cloister (2) slang for "brothel" (cf. "bawd" above). 123 *indifferent honest*: reasonably virtuous. 126 *beck*: beckoning. 129 *arrant*: absolute. 136 *plague*: curse. 140 *monsters*: horned cuckolds (men whose wives were unfaithful). 145 *jig*: walk in a mincing way. *lisp*: put on affected speech. 146 *make your . . . ignorance*: excuse your caprices as being due to ignorance. 148 *moe*: more.

OPHELIA: O what a noble mind is here o'erthrown!
        The courtier's, soldier's, scholar's, eye, tongue, sword,
        Th'expectancy and rose° of the fair state,
        The glass° of fashion, and the mould of form,°
155     Th'observed of all observers, quite quite down,
        And I of ladies most deject and wretched,
        That sucked the honey of his music vows,
        Now see that noble and most sovereign° reason
        Like sweet bells jangled, out of tune and harsh,
160     That unmatched form and feature° of blown° youth
        Blasted with ecstasy,° O woe is me,
        T'have seen what I have seen, see what I see.

        *Enter* KING *and* POLONIUS.

KING:   Love? his affections° do not that way tend,
        Nor what he spake, though it lacked form a little,
165     Was not like madness. There's something in his soul
        O'er which his melancholy sits on brood,
        And I do doubt,° the hatch and the disclose°
        Will be some danger; which for to prevent,
        I have in quick determination
170     Thus set it down: he shall with speed to England,
        For the demand of our neglected° tribute:
        Haply° the seas, and countries different,
        With variable° objects, shall expel
        This something°-settled matter in his heart,
175     Whereon his brains still beating puts him thus
        From fashion of himself.° What think you on't?

POLONIUS: It shall do well. But yet do I believe
        The origin and commencement of his grief
        Sprung from neglected° love. How now Ophelia?
180     You need not tell us what Lord Hamlet said,
        We heard it all. My lord, do as you please,
        But if you hold it fit, after the play,
        Let his queen-mother all alone entreat him
        To show his grief, let her be round° with him,
185     And I'll be placed (so please you) in the ear
        Of° all their conference. If she find° him not,
        To England send him: or confine him where
        Your wisdom best shall think.

KING:                          It shall be so,
        Madness in great ones must not unwatched go.                *Exeunt.*

---

°153 *expectancy and rose:* fair hope. 154 *glass:* mirror. *mould of form:* model of manners. 158 *sovereign:* (because it should rule). 160 *feature:*
external appearance. *blown:* flowering. 161 *Blasted with ecstasy:* blighted by madness. 163 *affections:* emotions, afflictions. 167 *doubt:* fear.
166–67 *on brood . . . hatch . . . disclose:* (metaphor of a hen sitting on eggs). 171 *neglected:* (being unpaid). 172 *Haply:* perhaps. 173 *variable:*
varied. 174 *something:* somewhat-. 176 *fashion of himself:* his usual self. 179 *neglected:* unrequited. 184 *round:* direct. 185–86 *in the ear Of:* so
as to overhear. 186 *find:* find out.

## Scene 2 [A hall in the castle]

*Enter* HAMLET *and three of the* PLAYERS.

HAMLET: Speak the speech° I pray you as I pronounced it to you,
　　trippingly on the tongue, but if you mouth it° as many of
　　your players do, I had as lief the town-crier spoke my
　　lines. Nor do not saw the air too much with your hand
　　thus, but use all gently, for in the very torrent, tempest,　　　　　　5
　　and as I may say, whirlwind of your passion, you must
　　acquire and beget° a temperance that may give it smoothness.
　　O it offends me to the soul, to hear a robustious°
　　periwig-pated° fellow tear a passion to tatters, to very rags,
　　to split the ears of the groundlings,° who for the most part　　　10
　　are capable of° nothing but inexplicable dumb shows° and
　　noise: I would have such a fellow whipped for o'erdoing
　　Termagant.° It out-herods Herod,° pray you avoid it.
1. PLAYER: I warrant you honour.
HAMLET: Be not too tame neither, but let your own discretion be
　　your tutor, suit the action to the word, the word to the　　　　　15
　　action, with this special observance, that you o'erstep not
　　the modesty° of nature: for any thing so o'erdone, is from°
　　the purpose of playing, whose end both at the first, and
　　now, was and is, to hold as 'twere the mirror up to nature,
　　to show virtue her own feature, scorn° her own image, and　　　20
　　the very age and body of the time his form and pressure.°
　　Now this overdone, or come tardy off,° though it make the
　　unskilful° laugh, cannot but make the judicious grieve, the
　　censure of the which one,° must in your allowance°
　　o'erweigh a whole theatre of others. O there be players　　　　　25
　　that I have seen play, and heard others praise, and that
　　highly (not to speak it profanely) that neither having
　　th'accent of Christians, nor the gait of Christian, pagan,
　　nor man, have so strutted and bellowed, that I have
　　thought some of nature's journeymen° had made men, and　　　30
　　not made them well, they imitated humanity so
　　abominably.
1. PLAYER: I hope we have reformed that indifferently° with us, sir.
HAMLET: O reform it altogether, and let those that play your clowns
　　speak no more than is set down for them,° for there be of　　　35
　　them that will themselves laugh, to set on some quantity
　　of barren° spectators to laugh too, though in the meantime,

---

°1 *the speech*: i.e., that Hamlet has inserted. 2 *mouth it*: deliver it slowly and overdramatically. 7 *acquire and beget*: achieve for yourself and instill in other actors. 8 *robustious*: boisterous. 9 *periwig-pated*: wig-wearing. 10 *groundlings*: audience who paid least and stood on the ground floor. 11 *capable of*: able to understand. *dumb shows*: pantomimed synopses of the action to follow. 13 *Termagant*: violent, ranting character in the guild or mystery plays. *out-herods Herod*: outdoes even Herod, King of Judea, who commanded the slaughter of the Innocents and who was a ranting tyrant in the Corpus Christi plays. See p. 879. 18 *modesty*: moderation. *from*: away from. 21 *scorn*: that which should be scorned. 22 *age . . . pressure*: shape of the times in its accurate impression. 23 *come tardy off*: understated, underdone. 24 *unskilful*: unsophisticated. 25 *one*: the judicious. *allowance*: estimation. 31 *journeymen*: artisans working for others and not yet masters of their trades. 34 *indifferently*: reasonably well. 36 *speak no more . . . them*: stick to their lines. 38 *barren*: witless.

some necessary question° of the play be then to be considered:
40    that's villainous, and shows a most pitiful ambition
in the fool that uses it. Go make you ready.                    *Exeunt* PLAYERS.

*Enter* POLONIUS, ROSENCRANTZ, *and* GUILDENSTERN.

How now my lord, will the king hear this piece of work?
POLONIUS:  And the queen too, and that presently.
HAMLET:  Bid the players make haste.                            *Exit* POLONIUS.
45    Will you two help to hasten them?
ROSENCRANTZ:  Ay my lord.                                       *Exeunt they two.*
HAMLET:  What ho, Horatio!

*Enter* HORATIO.

HORATIO:  Here sweet lord, at your service.
HAMLET:  Horatio, thou art e'en as just° a man
50    As e'er my conversation coped withal.°
HORATIO:  O my dear lord.
HAMLET:                              Nay, do not think I flatter,
For what advancement may I hope from thee,
That no revenue hast but thy good spirits
To feed and clothe thee? Why should the poor be flattered?
55    No, let the candied° tongue lick° absurd pomp,
And crook the pregnant° hinges of the knee
Where thrift may follow fawning.° Dost thou hear,
Since my dear soul was mistress of her choice,
And could of men distinguish her election,°
60    Sh'hath sealed° thee for herself, for thou hast been
As one in suff'ring all that suffers nothing,
A man that Fortune's buffets° and rewards
Hast ta'en with equal thanks; and blest are those
Whose blood° and judgment are so well co-mingled,
65    That they are not a pipe for Fortune's finger
To sound what stop° she please.° give me that man
That is not passion's slave, and I will wear him
In my heart's core, ay in my heart of heart,
As I do thee. Something too much of this.
70    There is a play tonight before the king,
One scene of it comes near the circumstance
Which I have told thee of my father's death.
I prithee when thou seest that act afoot,
Even with the very comment° of thy soul
75    Observe my uncle: if his occulted° guilt
Do not itself unkennel° in one speech,

---

°39 *question*: dialogue. 49 *just*: well balanced. 50 *coped withal*: had to do with. 55–57 *candied . . . fawning*: (metaphor of a dog licking and fawning for candy). 55 *candied*: flattering. *lick* pay court to. 56–57 *crook . . . fawning*: obsequiously kneel when personal profit may ensue.
56 *pregnant*: quick in motion. 59 *election*: choice. 60 *sealed*: confirmed. 62 *buffets*: blows. 64 *blood*: passions. 66 *sound . . . please*: play whatever tune she likes. *stop*: finger hole in wind instrument for varying the sound. 74 *very comment*: acutest observation. 75 *occulted*: hidden.
76 *unkennel*: force from hiding.

It is a damnèd ghost° that we have seen,
And my imaginations are as foul
As Vulcan's stithy,° give him heedful note,
For I mine eyes will rivet to his face,                                                          80
And after we will both our judgments join
In censure of his seeming.°
HORATIO:                                    Well my lord,
If a' steal aught the whilst this play is playing,
And 'scape detecting, I will pay° the theft.                        *Sound a flourish.*
HAMLET:  They are coming to the play. I must be idle,°                                     85
Get you a place.

*Enter Trumpets and Kettledrums, KING, QUEEN, POLONIUS, OPHELIA, ROSENCRANTZ, GUILDENSTERN,*
*and other LORDS attendant, with his GUARD carrying torches. Danish March.*

KING:  How fares° our cousin Hamlet?
HAMLET:  Excellent i'faith, of the chameleon's dish: I eat the air,°
   promise-crammed, you cannot feed capons so.°
KING:  I have nothing with° this answer Hamlet, these words are                           90
   not mine.°
HAMLET:  No, nor mine now. [*To Polonius.*] My lord, you played
   once i'th'university you say?
POLONIUS:  That did I my lord, and was accounted a good actor.
HAMLET:  What did you enact?                                                              95
POLONIUS:  I did enact Julius Caesar, I was killed i'th'Capitol, Brutus
   killed me.
HAMLET:  It was a brute part of him to kill so capital a calf there. Be
   the players ready?
ROSENCRANTZ:  Ay my lord, they stay upon your patience.°                                 100
QUEEN:  Come hither my dear Hamlet, sit by me.
HAMLET:  No, good mother, here's metal more attractive.°
POLONIUS:  [*To the King.*] O ho, do you mark that?
HAMLET:  Lady, shall I lie in your lap?
OPHELIA:  No my lord.                                                                    105
HAMLET:  I mean, my head upon your lap?
OPHELIA:  Ay my lord.
HAMLET:  Do you think I meant country° matters?
OPHELIA:  I think nothing my lord.
HAMLET:  That's a fair thought to lie between maids' legs.                               110
OPHELIA:  What is, my lord?
HAMLET:  Nothing.

---

°77 *damnèd ghost*: devil (not the ghost of my father). 79 *Vulcan's stithy*: the forge of the blacksmith of the gods. 82 *censure . . . seeming*: (1) judgment of his appearance (2) disapproval of his pretending. 84 *pay*: i.e., for. 85 *be idle*: act mad. 87 *fares*: does, but Hamlet takes it to mean "eats" or "dines." 88 *eat the air*: the chamelion supposedly ate air, but Hamlet also puns on "heir." 89 *you cannot . . . so*: (1) even a capon cannot feed on air and your promises (2) like a capon stuffed with food before being killed, I am stuffed (fed up) with your promises. 90 *nothing with*: nothing to do with. 91 *not mine*: not in answer to my question. 100 *stay . . . patience*: await your permission. 102 *metal more attractive*: (1) iron more magnetic (2) stuff ("mettle") more beautiful. 108 *country*: rustic, sexual (with a pun on a slang word for the female sexual organ).

Hamlet (played by Kevin Kline), Queen Gertrude (played by Dana Ivy), and Ophelia (played by Diane Venora) in the New York Shakespeare Festival production of *Hamlet* (1990), directed by Mr. Kline for the Public Broadcasting System.

OPHELIA:  You are merry my lord.

HAMLET:  Who, I?

115  OPHELIA:  Ay my lord.

HAMLET:  O God, your only jig-maker: what should a man do but be
merry, for look you how cheerfully my mother looks, and
my father died within's two hours.

OPHELIA:  Nay, 'tis twice two months my lord.

120  HAMLET:  So long? Nay then let the devil wear black, for I'll have a
suit of sables,° O heavens, die two months ago, and not
forgotten yet? Then there's hope a great man's memory

---

°121 *sables*: (1) rich fur (2) black mourning garb.

may outlive his life half a year, but by'r lady° a' must build
churches then, or else shall a' suffer not thinking on,° with
the hobby-horse,° whose epitaph is "For O, for O, the
hobby-horse is forgot." 125

*The trumpets sound. Dumb Show° follows. Enter a King and a Queen, very lovingly, the Queen embracing him, and he her. She kneels and makes show of protestation unto him. He takes her up, and declines his head upon her neck. He lies him down upon a bank of flowers; she seeing him asleep leaves him: anon comes in another man, takes off his crown, kisses it, pours poison in the sleeper's ears, and leaves him: the Queen returns, finds the King dead, and makes passionate action. The poisoner with some three or four mutes° comes in again, seeming to condole with her. The dead body is carried away. The poisoner wooes the Queen with gifts: she seems harsh and unwilling awhile, but in the end accepts his love.*

*Exeunt.*

OPHELIA: What means this, my lord?
HAMLET: Marry, this is miching mallecho,° it means mischief.
OPHELIA: Belike this show imports the argument° of the play.

*Enter* PROLOGUE.

HAMLET: We shall know by this fellow: the players cannot keep
counsel,° they'll tell all. 130
OPHELIA: Will a' tell us what this show meant?
HAMLET: Ay, or any show that you will show him. Be not you
ashamed to show, he'll not shame to tell you what it
means. 135
OPHELIA: You are naught,° you are naught, I'll mark the play.
PROLOGUE: For us and for our tragedy,
Here stooping to your clemency,
We beg your hearing patiently. *[Exit.]*
HAMLET: Is this a prologue, or the posy° of a ring? 140
OPHELIA: 'Tis brief, my lord.
HAMLET: As woman's love.

*Enter* PLAYER KING *and* QUEEN.

PLAYER KING: Full thirty times hath Phoebus' cart° gone round
Neptune's salt wash,° and Tellus' orbèd ground,°
And thirty dozen moons with borrowed sheen
About the world have times twelve thirties been, 145
Since love our hearts, and Hymen° did our hands
Unite commutual,° in most sacred bands.
PLAYER QUEEN: So many journeys may the sun and moon
Make us again count o'er ere love be done, 150

---

°123 *by'r lady*: by Our Lady (the Virgin Mary). 124 *not thinking on*: being forgotten. 125 *hobby-horse*: (1) character in the May games (2) slang for "prostitute." 126 S.D.: *Dumb Show*: pantomimed synopsis of the action to follow. 126 S.D.: *mutes*: actors without speaking parts. 128 *miching mallecho*: skulking mischief. 129 *imports the argument*: signifies the plot. 131 *counsel*: a secret. 136 *naught*: naughty, lewd. 140 *posy*: motto (engraved in a ring). 143 *Phoebus' cart*: chariot of the sun. 144 *wash*: sea. *Tellus . . . ground*: the earth (Tellus was a Roman earth goddess). 147 *Hymen*: Roman god of marriage. 148 *commutual*: mutually.

But woe is me, you are so sick of late,
So far from cheer, and from your former state,
That I distrust you:° yet though I distrust,
Discomfort you, my lord, it nothing must.
155   For women fear too much, even as they love,
And women's fear and love hold quantity,°
In neither aught, or in extremity:°
Now what my love is, proof° hath made you know,
And as my love is sized, my fear is so.
160   Where love is great, the littlest doubts are fear,
Where little fears grow great, great love grows there.
PLAYER KING:  Faith, I must leave thee love, and shortly too,
My operant° powers their functions leave° to do,
And thou shalt live in this fair world behind,
165   Honoured, beloved, and haply° one as kind
For husband shalt thou—.
PLAYER QUEEN:                    O confound the rest:
Such love must needs be treason in my breast.
In second husband let me be accurst,
None wed the second, but who killed the first.
170 HAMLET:  [Aside.] That's wormwood,° wormwood.
PLAYER QUEEN:  The instances° that second marriage move°
Are base respects of thrift,° but none of love.
A second time I kill my husband dead,
When second husband kisses me in bed.
175 PLAYER KING:  I do believe you think what now you speak,
But what we do determine, oft we break:
Purpose is but the slave to memory
Of violent birth but poor validity.°
Which now like fruit unripe sticks on the tree,
180   But fall unshaken when they mellow be.
Most necessary 'tis that we forget
To pay ourselves what to ourselves is debt.°
What to ourselves in passion we propose,
The passion ending, doth the purpose lose.
185   The violence of either grief or joy
Their own enactures° with themselves destroy:
Where joy most revels, grief doth most lament;
Grief joys, joy grieves, on slender accident.
This world is not for aye,° nor 'tis not strange
190   That even our loves should with our fortunes change:
For 'tis a question left us yet to prove,
Whether love lead fortune, or else fortune love.°

---

°153 *distrust you*: am worried about you. 156 *quantity*: proportion. 157 *In neither . . . extremity*: their love and fear are either absent or excessive.
158 *proof*: experience. 163 *operant*: vital. *leave*: cease. 165 *haply*: perhaps. 170 *wormwood*: bitter (like the herb). 171 *instances*: causes.
*move*: motivate. 172 *respects of thrift*: consideration of profit. 178 *validity*: strength. 181–82 *Most . . . debt*: we are easy creditors to ourselves
and forget our former promises (debts). 186 *enactures*: fulfillments. 189 *aye*: ever. 192 *fortune love*: fortune lead love.

The great man down, you mark his favourite flies,
The poor advanced, makes friends of enemies:
And hitherto doth love on fortune tend,                                             195
For who not needs, shall never lack a friend,
And who in want a hollow friend doth try,
Directly seasons him° his enemy.
But orderly to end where I begun,
Our wills and fates do so contrary run,                                             200
That our devices still° are overthrown,
Our thoughts are ours, their ends none of our own.
So think thou wilt no second husband wed,
But die thy thoughts when thy first lord is dead.

PLAYER QUEEN:  Nor earth to me give food, nor heaven light,       205
Sport and repose lock from me day and night,
To desperation turn my trust and hope,
An anchor's° cheer in prison be my scope,
Each opposite that blanks° the face of joy,
Meet what I would have well, and it destroy,                                        210
Both here and hence° pursue me lasting strife,
If once a widow, ever I be wife.

HAMLET:  If she should break it now.

PLAYER KING:  'Tis deeply sworn: sweet, leave me here awhile,
My spirits grow dull, and fain° I would beguile                                      215
The tedious day with sleep.                                                *Sleeps.*

PLAYER QUEEN:                              Sleep rock thy brain.
And never come mischance between us twain.                                  *Exit.*

HAMLET:  Madam, how like you this play?

QUEEN:  The lady doth protest too much methinks.

HAMLET:  O but she'll keep her word.                                                220

KING:  Have you heard the argument°? Is there no offence in't?

HAMLET:  No, no, they do but jest, poison in jest, no offence
    i'th'world.

KING:  What do you call the play?

HAMLET:  The Mouse-trap. Marry, how? Tropically:° this play is the          225
    image of a murder done in Vienna: Gonzago is the duke's
    name, his wife Baptista, you shall see anon, 'tis a knavish
    piece of work, but what of that? Your majesty, and we
    that have free° souls, it touches us not: let the galled jade
    winch,° our withers are unwrung.°                                               230

*Enter LUCIANUS.*

This is one Lucianus, nephew to the king.

OPHELIA:  You are as good as a chorus,° my lord.

---

°198 *seasons him*: causes him to become. 201 *devices still*: plans always. 208 *anchor's*: hermit's. 209 *opposite that blanks*: contrary event that pales. 211 *here and hence*: in this world and the next. 215 *fain*: gladly. 221 *argument*: plot. 225 *Tropically*: figuratively. 229 *free*: innocent. 229–30 *galled jade winch*: chafed old horse wince (from its sores). 230 *withers are unwrung*: (1) shoulders are unchafed (2) consciences are clear. 232 *chorus*: actor who introduced the action.

HAMLET: I could interpret between you and your love, if I could see
the puppets dallying.

235 OPHELIA: You are keen my lord, you are keen.°

HAMLET: It would cost you a groaning to take off mine edge.

OPHELIA: Still better and worse.°

HAMLET: So you mistake° your husbands. Begin, murderer. Pox,°
leave thy damnable faces° and begin. Come, the croaking
240    raven doth bellow for revenge.

LUCIANUS: Thoughts black, hands apt, drugs fit, and time agreeing,
Confederate season, else no creature seeing,°
Thou mixture rank, of midnight weeds collected,
With Hecate's° ban° thrice blasted, thrice infected,
245    Thy natural magic, and dire property,
On wholesome° life usurps immediately.        *Pours the poison in his ears.*

HAMLET: A' poisons him i'th'garden for's estate, his name's Gonzago,
the story is extant, and written in very choice
Italian, you shall see anon how the murderer gets the love
250    of Gonzago's wife.

OPHELIA: The king rises.

HAMLET: What, frighted with false fire°?

QUEEN: How fares my lord?

POLONIUS: Give o'er the play.

255 KING: Give me some light. Away!        *Exeunt all but* HAMLET *and* HORATIO.

ALL: Lights, lights, lights!

HAMLET: Why, let the stricken deer go weep,
The hart ungallèd° play,°
For some must watch while some must sleep,
260            Thus runs the world away.
Would not this° sir, and a forest of feathers,° if the rest of my
fortunes turn Turk with° me, with two Provincial roses° on
my razed° shoes, get me a fellowship° in a cry° of players?

HORATIO: Half a share.°

265 HAMLET: A whole one, I.
For thou dost know, O Damon° dear,
This realm dismantled was
Of Jove° himself, and now reigns here
A very very—pajock.°

270 HORATIO: You might have rhymed.°

HAMLET: O good Horatio, I'll take the ghost's word for a thousand
pound. Didst perceive?

---

°235 *keen*: (1) sharp (Ophelia's meaning) (2) sexually excited (Hamlet's interpretation). 237 *better and worse*: better wit but a worse meaning, with a pun on "better" and "bitter." 238 *mistake*: mis-take. *Pox*: a plague on it. 239 *faces*: exaggerated facial expressions. 242 *Confederate . . . seeing*: no one seeing me except time, my confederate. 244 *Hecate*: goddess of witchcraft. *ban*: evil spell. 246 *wholesome*: healthy. 252 *false fire*: discharge of blanks (not gunpowder). 257–58 *deer . . . play*: (the belief that a wounded deer wept, abandoned by the others). 258 *ungallèd*: unhurt. 261 *this*: i.e., sample (of my theatrical talent). *feathers*: plumes (worn by actors). 262 *turn Turk with*: cruelly turn against. *Provincial roses*: rosettes named for Provins, France. 263 *razed*: slashed, decorated with cutouts. *fellowship*: partnership. *cry*: pack, troupe. 264 *share*: divisions of profits among members of a theatrical production company. 266 *Damon*: legendary ideal friend to Pythias. 268 *Jove*: (Hamlet's father). 269 *pajock*: peacock (associated with lechery). 270 *rhymed*: (used "ass" instead of "pajock").

HORATIO:  Very well my lord.
HAMLET:  Upon the talk of the poisoning?
HORATIO:  I did very well note him.                                              275

*Enter ROSENCRANTZ and GUILDENSTERN.*

HAMLET:  Ah ha, come, some music. Come, the recorders.°
　　For if the king like not the comedy,
　　Why then belike he likes it not, perdy.°
　　Come, some music.
GUILDENSTERN:  Good my lord, vouchsafe me a word with you.          280
HAMLET:  Sir, a whole history.
GUILDENSTERN:  The king, sir—
HAMLET:  Ay sir, what of him?
GUILDENSTERN:  Is in his retirement, marvellous distempered.
HAMLET:  With drink sir?                                                         285
GUILDENSTERN:  No my lord, with choler.°
HAMLET:  Your wisdom should show itself more richer to signify
　　this to the doctor: for, for me to put him to his purgation,°
　　would perhaps plunge him into more choler.
GUILDENSTERN:  Good my lord, put your discourse into some frame,° and    290
　　start not so wildly from my affair.
HAMLET:  I am tame sir, pronounce.
GUILDENSTERN:  The queen your mother, in most great affliction of spirit,
　　hath sent me to you.
HAMLET:  You are welcome.                                                        295
GUILDENSTERN:  Nay good my lord, this courtesy is not of the right breed.°
　　If it shall please you to make me a wholesome° answer, I
　　will do your mother's commandment: if not, your pardon°
　　and my return shall be the end of my business.
HAMLET:  Sir I cannot.                                                           300
ROSENCRANTZ:  What, my lord?
HAMLET:  Make you a wholesome answer: my wit's diseased. But
　　sir, such answer as I can make, you shall command, or
　　rather as you say, my mother: therefore no more, but to
　　the matter. My mother you say.                                              305
ROSENCRANTZ:  Then thus she says, your behaviour hath struck her into
　　amazement and admiration.°
HAMLET:  O wonderful son that can so 'stonish a mother. But is there
　　no sequel at the heels of this mother's admiration? Impart.
ROSENCRANTZ:  She desires to speak with you in her closet°                       310
　　ere you go to bed.
HAMLET:  We shall obey, were she ten times our mother. Have you
　　any further trade with us?
ROSENCRANTZ:  My lord, you once did love me.

---

°276 *recorders*: soft-toned woodwind instruments, similar to flutes.  278 *perdy*: by God (*pardieu*).  286 *choler*: anger.  288 *purgation*: (1) purging of excessive bile (2) judicial investigations (3) purgatory.  290 *frame*: order.  296 *breed*: (1) species (2) manners.  297 *wholesome*: reasonable. 298 *pardon*: permission to depart.  307 *admiration*: wonder.  310 *closet*: private room, bedroom.

315 HAMLET:  And do still, by these pickers and stealers.°
   ROSENCRANTZ:  Good my lord, what is your cause of distemper? You do
      surely bar the door upon your own liberty, if you deny
      your griefs to your friend.°
   HAMLET:  Sir, I lack advancement.
320 ROSENCRANTZ:  How can that be, when you have the voice° of the king
      himself for your succession in Denmark?
   HAMLET:  Ay sir, but 'while the grass grows'°—the proverb is
      something musty. °

*Enter the* PLAYERS *with recorders.*

      O the recorders, let me see one. To withdraw° with you,
325   why do you go about to recover the wind of me,° as if you
      would drive me into a toil°?
   GUILDENSTERN:  O my lord, if my duty be too bold, my love is too
      unmannerly.°
   HAMLET:  I do not well understand that. Will you play
330   upon this pipe°?
   GUILDENSTERN:  My lord I cannot.
   HAMLET:  I pray you.
   GUILDENSTERN:  Believe me. I cannot.
   HAMLET:  I do beseech you.
335 GUILDENSTERN:  I know no touch of it° my lord.
   HAMLET:  It is as easy as lying; govern these ventages° with your
      fingers and thumb, give it breath with your mouth, and it
      will discourse most eloquent music. Look you, these are
      the stops.
340 GUILDENSTERN:  But these cannot I command to any utt'rance of harmony,
      I have not the skill.
   HAMLET:  Why look you now how unworthy a thing you make of
      me: you would play upon me, you would seem to know
      my stops, you would pluck out the heart of my mystery,
345   you would sound me from my lowest note to the top of my
      compass.° and there is much music, excellent voice in this
      little organ,° yet cannot you make it speak. 'Sblood, do you
      think I am easier to be played on than a pipe? Call me what
      instrument you will, though you can fret° me, you cannot
350   play upon me.

*Enter* POLONIUS.

      God bless you sir.
   POLONIUS:  My lord, the queen would speak with you, and presently.

---

°315 *pickers and stealers* : hands (from the prayer, "Keep my hands from picking and stealing"). 317–818 *deny . . . friend* : refuse to let your friend know the cause of your suffering. 320 *voice* : vote. 322 *while . . . grows* : (the proverb ends: "the horse starves"). 323 *something musty* : somewhat too old and trite (to finish). 324 *withdraw* : speak privately. 325 *recover . . . me* : drive me toward the wind, as with a prey, to avoid its scenting the hunter. 326 *toil* : snare. 327–28 *is too unmannerly* : makes me forget my good manners. 330 *pipe* : recorder. 335 *know . . . it* : have no skill at fingering it. 336 *ventages* : holes, stops. 346 *compass* : range. 347 *organ* : musical instrument. 349 *fret* : (1) irritate (2) play an instrument that has "frets" or bars to guide the fingering.

HAMLET:  Do you see yonder cloud that's almost in shape of a camel?
POLONIUS:  By th'mass and 'tis, like a camel indeed.
HAMLET:  Methinks it is like a weasel.
POLONIUS:  It is backed like a weasel.                                                                      355
HAMLET:  Or like a whale?
POLONIUS:  Very like a whale.
HAMLET:  Then I will come to my mother by and by.°
   [*Aside.*] They fool me to the top of my bent.°
   I will come by and by.                                                                      360
POLONIUS:  I will say so. *Exit.*
HAMLET:  "By and by" is easily said.
   Leave me, friends.
   'Tis now the very witching time of night.                    [*Exeunt all but* HAMLET.]
   When churchyards yawn,° and hell itself breathes out                          365
   Contagion° to this world: now could I drink hot blood,
   And do such bitter business as the day
   Would quake to look on: soft, now to my mother—
   O heart, lose not thy nature,° let not ever                                       370
   The soul of Nero° enter this firm bosom,
   Let me be cruel, not unnatural.
   I will speak daggers to her, but use none:
   My tongue and soul in this be hypocrites,°
   How in my words somever she be shent,°                                            375
   To give them seals,° never my soul consent. *Exit.*

## Scene 3. [A room in the castle]

*Enter* KING, ROSENCRANTZ, *and* GUILDENSTERN.

KING:  I like him not, nor stands it safe with us
   To let his madness range. Therefore prepare you,
   I your commission will forthwith dispatch,°
   And he to England shall along with you:
   The terms of our estate° may not endure                                           5
   Hazard so near's° as doth hourly grow
   Out of his brows.°
GUILDENSTERN:         We will ourselves provide:°
   Most holy and religious fear it is
   To keep those many many bodies safe
   That live and feed upon your majesty.
ROSENCRANTZ:  The single and peculiar° life is bound                                      10
   With all the strength and armour of the mind
   To keep itself from noyance,° but much more

---

°359 *by and by*: very soon. 360 *fool me . . . bent*: force me to play the fool to my utmost. 366 *churchyards yawn*: graves open. 367 *Contagion*: (1) evil (2) diseases. 370 *nature*: natural affection. 371 *Nero*: (who killed his mother). 374 *My tongue . . . hypocrites*: I will speak cruelly but intend no harm. 375 *shent*: chastised. 376 *give them seals*: confirm them with action (as a legal "deed" is confirmed with a "seal"). 3 *forthwith dispatch*: immediately have prepared. 5 *terms . . . estate*: circumstances of my royal office. 6 *near's*: near us. 7 *brows*: effronteries. *provide*: prepare. 11 *peculiar*: individual. 13 *noyance*: harm.

That spirit, upon whose weal° depends and rests
15   The lives of many; the cess° of majesty
Dies not alone, but like a gulf° doth draw
What's near it, with it. O 'tis a massy wheel
Fixed on the summit of the highest mount,
To whose huge spokes, ten thousand lesser things
20   Are mortised° and adjoined, which when it falls,
Each small annexment, petty consequence,
Attends° the boist'rous ruin. Never alone
Did the king sigh, but with a general groan.
KING:   Arm° you I pray you, to this speedy voyage,
25   For we will fetters put about this fear,
Which now goes too free-footed.
ROSENCRANTZ:                    We will haste us.

                    *Exeunt* [ROSENCRANTZ *and* GUILDENSTERN.]

*Enter* POLONIUS.

POLONIUS:   My lord, he's going to his mother's closet:
Behind the arras I'll convey myself
To hear the process.° I'll warrant she'll tax him home,
30   And as you said, and wisely was it said,
'Tis meet° that some more audience than a mother,
Since nature makes them partial, should o'erhear
The speech of vantage,° fare you well my liege,°
I'll call upon you ere you go to bed,
And tell you what I know.
35   KING:                    Thanks, dear my lord.                    *Exit* [POLONIUS.]
O my offence is rank, it smells to heaven,
It hath the primal eldest curse° upon't,
A brother's murder. Pray can I not,
Though inclination be as sharp as will.°
40   My stronger guilt defeats my strong intent,
And like a man to double business bound,
I stand in pause where I shall first begin,
And both neglect; what if this cursèd hand
Were thicker than itself with brother's blood,
45   Is there not rain enough in the sweet heavens
To wash it white as snow? Whereto serves mercy
But to confront the visage of offence°?
And what's in prayer but this two-fold force,
To be forestallèd° ere we come to fall,
50   Or pardoned being down? Then I'll look up,
My fault is past. But O what form of prayer

---

°14 *weal:* well-being. 15 *cess:* cessation, death. 16 *gulf:* whirlpool. 20 *mortised:* securely fitted. 22 *Attends:* accompanies. 24 *Arm:* prepare. 29 *the process:* what proceeds. 31 *meet:* fitting. 33 *of vantage:* from an advantageous position. *liege:* lord. 37 *primal . . . curse:* curse of Cain. 39 *inclination . . . will:* my desire to pray is as strong as my determination to do so. 47 *confront . . . offence:* plead in man's behalf against sin (at the Last Judgment). 49 *forestallèd:* prevented.

Can serve my turn? "Forgive me my foul murder":
That cannot be, since I am still possessed
Of those effects° for which I did the murder:
My crown, mine own ambition, and my queen.                                55
May one be pardoned and retain th'offence?
In the corrupted currents of this world,
Offence's gilded hand may shove by justice,
And oft 'tis seen the wicked prize itself
Buys out the law;° but 'tis not so above,                                 60
There is no shuffling,° there the action lies
In his true nature,° and we ourselves compelled
Even to the teeth and forehead of our faults°
To give in evidence. What then? What rests°?
Try what repentance can. What can it not?                                 65
Yet what can it, when one can not repent?
O wretched state? O bosom black as death!
O limèd soul, that struggling to be free,
Art more engaged;° help, angels, make assay:°
Bow stubborn knees, and heart with strings of steel,                     70
Be soft as sinews of the new-born babe,
All may be well.                                                    [*He kneels.*]

*Enter* HAMLET.

HAMLET:   Now might I do it pat,° now a' is a-praying,
And now I'll do't, [*Draws his sword.*] and so a' goes to heaven,
And so am I revenged: that would be scanned:°                            75
A villain kills my father, and for that,
I his sole son, do this same villain send
To heaven.
Why, this is hire and salary, not revenge.
A' took my father grossly,° full of bread,°                              80
With all his crimes° broad blown,° as flush° as May,
And how his audit° stands who knows save heaven,
But in our circumstance and course of thought,
'Tis heavy° with him: and am I then revenged
To take him in the purging of his soul,                                  85
when he is fit and seasoned° for his passage?
No.                                                            [*Sheathes his sword.*]
Up sword, and know thou a more horrid hent,°
When he is drunk asleep, or in his rage,
Or in th'incestuous pleasure of his bed,                                 90

---

°54 *effects*: results. 59–60 *wicked . . . law*: fruits of the crime bribe the judge. 61 *shuffling*: evasion. 61–62 *action . . . nature*: (1) deed is seen in its true nature (2) legal action is sustained according to the truth. 63 *to the teeth . . . faults*: meeting our sins face to face. 64 *rests*: remains. 68–69 *limèd . . . engaged*: like a bird caught in lime (a sticky substance spread on twigs as a snare), the soul in its struggle to clear itself only becomes more entangled. 69 *make assay*: I'll make an attempt. 73 *pat*: opportunely. 75 *would be scanned*: needs closer examination. 80 *grossly*: unpurified (by final rites). *bread*: self-indulgence. 81 *crimes*: sins. *broad blown*: in full flower. *flush*: lusty. 82 *audit*: account. 84 *heavy*: grievous. 86 *seasoned*: ready (prepared). 88 *horrid hent*: horrible opportunity ("hint") for seizure ("hent") by me.

At game, a-swearing, or about some act
That has no relish° of salvation in't,
Then trip him that his heels may kick at heaven,
And that his soul may be as damned and black
95   As hell whereto it goes; my mother stays,
This physic° but prolongs thy sickly days              *Exit.*

KING: [*Rises.*] My words fly up, my thoughts remain below,
Words without thoughts never to heaven go.             *Exit.*


## Scene 4. [The queen's closet]

*Enter* QUEEN *and* POLONIUS.

POLONIUS: A' will come straight, look you lay home° to him,
Tell him his pranks have been too broad° to bear with,
And that your grace hath screened and stood between
Much heat° and him. I'll silence me° even here:
5   Pray you be round with him.
HAMLET: [*Within.*] Mother, mother, mother.
QUEEN:                                  I'll war'nt you,
Fear me not. Withdraw, I hear him coming. [POLONIUS *hides behind the arras.*]

*Enter* HAMLET.

HAMLET: Now mother, what's the matter?
QUEEN: Hamlet, thou hast thy father much offended.
10   HAMLET: Mother, you have my father much offended.
QUEEN: Come, come, you answer with an idle° tongue.
HAMLET: Go, go, you question with a wicked tongue.
QUEEN: Why, how now Hamlet?
HAMLET:                              What's the matter now?
QUEEN: Have you forgot me?
HAMLET:                              No by the rood,° not so,
15   You are the queen, your husband's brother's wife,
And would it were not so, you are my mother.
QUEEN: Nay, then I'll set those to you that can speak.°
HAMLET: Come, come, and sit you down, you shall not budge,
You go not till I set you up a glass°
20   Where you may see the inmost part of you.
QUEEN: What wilt thou do? Thou wilt not murder me?
Help, help, ho!
POLONIUS: [*Behind the arras.*] What ho! help, help, help!
HAMLET: How now, a rat? dead for a ducat,° dead.          *Kills* POLONIUS [*through the arras.*]

25   POLONIUS: O I am slain!

---

°92 *relish:* taste. 96 *physic:* (1) medicine (2) purgation of your soul by prayer. 1 *lay home:* thrust home; speak sharply. 2 *broad:* unrestrained.
4 *heat:* anger. *silence me:* hide in silence. 11 *idle:* foolish. 14 *rood:* cross. 17 *speak:* i.e., to you as you should be spoken to. 19 *glass:* looking
glass. 24 *for a ducat:* I wager a ducat (an Italian gold coin).

QUEEN: O me, what hast thou done?
HAMLET:                              Nay I know not,
   Is it the king?
QUEEN: O what a rash and bloody deed is this!
HAMLET: A bloody deed, almost as bad, good mother,
   As kill a king, and marry with his brother.                          30
QUEEN: As kill a king?
HAMLET: Ay lady, it was my word.
   [*To Polonius.*] Thou wretched, rash, intruding fool, farewell,
   I took thee for thy better,° take thy fortune,
   Thou find'st to be too busy is some danger.                          35
   [*To the Queen.*] Leave wringing of your hands, peace, sit you down,
   And let me wring your heart, for so I shall
   If it be made of penetrable stuff,
   If damnèd custom° have not brazed° it so,
   That it be proof° and bulwark against sense.°                        40
QUEEN: What have I done, that thou dar'st wag thy tongue
   In noise so rude against me?
HAMLET:                              Such an act
   That blurs the grace and blush of modesty,
   Calls virtue hypocrite, takes off the rose°
   From the fair forehead of an innocent love                          45
   And sets a blister there,° makes marriage vows
   As false as dicers' oaths, O such a deed,
   As from the body of contraction° plucks
   The very soul and sweet religion makes
   A rhapsody° of words; heaven's face does glow,°                      50
   Yea this solidity and compound mass°
   With heated visage, as against the doom,°
   Is thought-sick at the act.
QUEEN:                              Ay me, what act,
   That roars so loud, and thunders in the index°?
HAMLET: Look here upon this picture, and on this,                       55
   The counterfeit presentment° of two brothers:
   See what a grace was seated on this brow,
   Hyperion's curls, the front° of Jove himself,
   An eye like Mars, to threaten and command,
   A station° like the herald Mercury,                                  60
   New-lighted on a heaven-kissing hill,
   A combination and a form indeed,
   Where every god did seem to set his seal
   To give the world assurance of a man.

---

°34 *thy better*: the king. 39 *custom*: habit. *brazed*: brass-plated (brazened). 40 *proof*: armor. *sense*: sensibility. 44 *rose*: (symbol of perfection and innocence). 46 *blister there*: (whores were punished by being branded on the forehead). 48 *body of contraction*: marriage contract. 50 *rhapsody*: (meaningless) mixture. *glow*: blush. 51 *solidity . . . mass*: solid earth, compounded of the four elements. 52 *against the doom*: expecting Judgment Day. 54 *index*: (1) table of contents (2) prologue. 56 *counterfeit presentment*: painted likeness. 58 *Hyperion*: Greek sun god. *front*: forehead. 60 *station*: bearing.

65     This was your husband. Look you now what follows.
    Here is your husband, like a mildewed ear,°
    Blasting° his wholesome brother. Have you eyes?
    Could you on this fair mountain leave to feed,°
    And batten° on this moor? Ha! Have you eyes?
70     You cannot call it love, for at your age
    The hey-day in the blood° is tame, it's humble,
    And waits upon the judgment, and what judgment
    Would step from this to this? Sense° sure you have
    Else could you not have motion,° but sure that sense
75     Is apoplexed,° for madness would not err,
    Nor sense to ecstasy was ne'er so thralled°
    But it reserved some quantity of choice
    To serve in such a difference.° What devil was't
    That thus hath cozened you at hoodman-blind°?
80     Eyes without feeling, feeling without sight,
    Ears without hands or eyes, smelling sans all,°
    Or but a sickly part of one true sense
    Could not so mope:° O shame, where is thy blush?
    Rebellious hell,
85     If thou canst mutine° in a matron's bones,
    To flaming youth let virtue be as wax
    And melt in her own fire. Proclaim no shame
    When the compulsive° ardour gives the charge,°
    Since frost itself as actively doth burn,
    And reason panders will.°
90 QUEEN:             O Hamlet, speak no more,
    Thou turn'st my eyes into my very soul,
    And there I see such black and grainèd° spots
    As will not leave their tinct.°
HAMLET:           Nay, but to live
    In the rank sweat of an enseamèd° bed,
95     Stewed in corruption, honeying, and making love
    Over the nasty sty.
QUEEN:            O speak to me no more,
    These words like daggers enter in mine ears,
    No more, sweet Hamlet.
HAMLET:           A murderer and a villain,
    A slave that is not twentieth part the tithe°
100     Of your precedent lord, a vice° of kings,
    A cutpurse° of the empire and the rule,
    That from a shelf the precious diadem stole
    And put it in his pocket.

---

°66 *ear.* i.e., of grain. 67 *Blasting*: blighting. 68 *leave to feed*: leave off feeding. 69 *batten*: gorge yourself. 70 *hey-day in the blood*: youthful passion. 73 *Sense*: perception by the senses. 74 *motion*: impulse. 75 *apoplexed*: paralyzed. 76 *sense . . . thralled*: sensibility was never so enslaved by madness. 78 *in . . . difference*: where the difference was so great. 79 *cozened . . . blind*: cheated you at blindman's bluff. 81 *sans all*: without the other senses. 83 *so mope*: be so dull. 85 *mutine*: rebel, mutiny. 88 *compulsive*: compelling. *gives the charge*: attacks. 90 *panders will*: pimps for lust. 92 *grainèd*: dyed in grain, unfading. 93 *leave their tinct*: lose their color. 94 *enseamèd*: greasy. 99 *tithe*: one-tenth part. 100 *vice*: buffoon (like the character of Vice in the morality plays). 101 *cutpurse*: pickpocket.

QUEEN:                                 No more.
HAMLET:   A king of shreds and patches—

*Enter the* GHOST *in his night-gown.*°

    Save me and hover o'er me with your wings,                                                                      105
    You heavenly guards. What would your gracious figure?
QUEEN: Alas, he's mad.
HAMLET:   Do you not come your tardy son to chide,
    That lapsed in time and passion° lets go by
    Th'important acting of your dread command?                                                                      110
    O say!
GHOST:   Do not forget: this visitation
    Is but to whet thy almost blunted purpose.
    But look, amazement on thy mother sits,
    O step between her and her fighting soul,
    Conceit° in weakest bodies strongest works,                                                                      115
    Speak to her Hamlet.
HAMLET:                                 How is it with you lady?
QUEEN: Alas, how is't with you,
    That you do bend your eye on vacancy,°
    And with th'incorporal° air do hold discourse?                                                                      120
    Forth at your eyes your spirits° wildly peep,
    And as the sleeping soldiers in th'alarm,
    Your bedded° hairs, like life in excrements,°
    Start up and stand an° end. O gentle son,
    Upon the heat and flame of thy distemper                                                                      125
    sprinkle cool patience. Whereon do you look?
HAMLET:   On him, on him, look you how pale he glares,
    His form and cause conjoined, preaching to stones,
    Would make them capable.° Do not look upon me,
    Lest with this piteous action you convert                                                                      130
    My stern effects,° then what I have to do
    Will want° true colour,° tears perchance for blood.
QUEEN: To whom do you speak this?
HAMLET:                                 Do you see nothing there?
QUEEN: Nothing at all, yet all that is I see.
HAMLET:   Nor did you nothing hear?
QUEEN:                                 No, nothing but ourselves.                                                                      135
HAMLET:   Why look you there, look how it steals away,
    My father in his habit as he lived,°
    Look where he goes, even now out at the portal.

                                                             *Exit* [GHOST.]

---

°104.1 S.D.: *night-gown*: dressing gown. 109 *lapsed . . . passion*: having let time elapse and passion cool. 116 *Conceit*: imagination. 119 *vacancy*: (she cannot see the ghost). 120 *incorporal*: bodiless. 121 *spirits*: vital forces. 123 *bedded*: lying flat. *excrements*: outgrowths (of the body). 124 *an*: on. 129 *capable*: i.e., of feeling pity. 130–31 *convert . . . effects*: transform my outward signs of sternness. 132 *want*: lack. *colour*: (1) complexion (2) motivation. 137 *habit . . . lived*: clothing he wore when alive.

QUEEN:  This is the very coinage of your brain,
140     This bodiless creation ecstasy
    Is very cunning in.°

HAMLET:            Ecstasy?
    My pulse as yours doth temperately keep time,
    And makes as healthful music. It is not madness
    That I have uttered; bring me to the test
145     And I the matter will re-word, which madness
    Would gambol° from. Mother, for love of grace,
    Lay not that flattering unction° to your soul,
    That not your trespass but my madness speaks,
    It will but skin and film the ulcerous place,
150     Whiles rank corruption mining° all within,
    Infects unseen. Confess yourself to heaven,
    Repent what's past, avoid what is to come,
    And do not spread the compost° on the weeds
    To make them ranker. Forgive me this my virtue,°
155     For in the fatness° of these pursy° times
    Virtue itself of vice must pardon beg,
    Yea curb and woo° for leave to do him° good.

QUEEN:  O Hamlet, thou hast cleft my heart in twain.

HAMLET:  O throw away the worser part of it,
160     And live the purer with the other half.
    Good night, but go not to my uncle's bed,
    Assume° a virtue if you have it not.
    That monster custom, who all sense doth eat
    Of habits evil,° is angel yet in this,
165     That to the use° of actions fair and good,
    He likewise gives a frock or livery
    That aptly° is put on. Refrain tonight,
    And that shall lend a kind of easiness
    To the next abstinence, the next more easy:
170     For use° almost can change the stamp° of nature,
    And either . . . the° devil, or throw him out
    With wondrous potency: once more good night,
    And when you are desirous to be blessed,
    I'll blessing beg of you. For this same lord,°
175     I do repent; but heaven hath pleased it so
    To punish me with this, and this with me,
    That I must be their scourge and minister.°
    I will bestow° him and will answer well
    The death I gave him; so again good night.
180     I must be cruel only to be kind;

---

°140– 41 *bodiless . . . cunning in:* madness (ecstasy) is very skillful in causing an affected person to hallucinate. 146 *gambol:* leap. 147 *unction:* salve. 150 *mining:* undermining. 153 *compost:* manure. 154 *virtue:* sermon on virtue. 155 *fatness:* grossness. *pursy:* flabby. 157 *curb and woo:* bow and plead. *him:* vice. 162 *Assume:* put on the guise of. 163–164 *all sense . . . evil:* confuses the sense of right and wrong in a habitué. 165 *use:* habit. 167 *aptly:* readily. 170 *use:* habit. *stamp:* form. 171 *either . . . the:* (word omitted, for which "tame," "curl," "lodge," and "quell" have been suggested). 173 *lord:* Polonius. 177 *their . . . minister:* heaven's punishment and agent of retribution. 178 *bestow:* stow away. *answer well:* assume full responsibility for.

This bad begins, and worse remains behind.°
One word more, good lady.

QUEEN:               What shall I do?

HAMLET:  Not this by no means that I bid you do:
    Let the bloat° king tempt you again to bed,
    Pinch wanton on your cheek, call you his mouse,         185
    And let him for a pair of reechy° kisses,
    Or paddling in your neck with his damned fingers,
    Make you to ravel° all this matter out
    That I essentially am not in madness,
    But mad in craft. 'Twere good you let him know,         190
    For who that's but a queen, fair, sober, wise,
    Would from a paddock, from a bat, a gib,°
    Such dear concernings hide? who would do so?
    No, in despite of sense and secrecy,
    Unpeg the basket on the house's top,         195
    Let the birds fly, and like the famous ape,
    To try conclusions° in the basket creep,
    And break your own neck down.°

QUEEN:  Be thou assured, if words be made of breath,
    And breath of life, I have no life to breathe         200
    What thou hast said to me.

HAMLET:  I must to England, you know that.

QUEEN:                    Alack,
    I had forgot: 'tis so concluded on.

HAMLET:  There's letters sealed, and my two school-fellows,
    Whom I will trust as I will adders fanged,         205
    They bear the mandate, they must sweep my way
    And marshal me to knavery:° let it work,
    For 'tis the sport to have the enginer°
    Hoist with his own petar,° and't shall go hard
    But I will delve one yard below their mines,         210
    And blow them at the moon: O 'tis most sweet
    When in one line two crafts directly meet.°
    This man shall set me packing,°
    I'll lug the guts into the neighbour room;
    Mother good night indeed. This counsellor         215
    Is now most still, most secret, and most grave,
    Who was in life a foolish prating knave.
    Come sir, to draw toward an end with you.
    Good night mother.

                        *Exit* HAMLET *tugging in* POLONIUS.

---

°181 *bad . . . behind*: is a bad beginning to a worse end to come. 184 *bloat*: bloated with dissipation. 186 *reechy*: filthy. 188 *ravel*: unravel. 192 *paddock, bat, gib*: toad, bat, tomcat ("familiars" or demons in animal shape that attend on witches). 195–198 *Unpeg . . . down*: (the story refers to an ape that climbs to the top of a house and opens a basket of birds; when the birds fly away, the ape crawls into the basket, tries to fly, and breaks his neck. The point is that if she gives away Hamlet's secret, she harms herself). 197 *try conclusions*: experiment. 206–7 *sweep . . . knavery*: (like the marshal who went before a royal procession, clearing the way, so Rosencrantz and Guildenstern clear Hamlet's path to some unknown evil). 208 *enginer*: maker of war engines. 209 *Hoist . . . betar*: blown up by his own bomb. 212 *in one . . . meet*: the digger of the mine and the digger of the countermine meet halfway in their tunnels. 213 *packing*: (1) i.e., my bags (2) rushing away (3) plotting.

## ACT 4

### Scene 1. [A room in the castle]

*Enter KING and QUEEN with ROSENCRANTZ and GUILDENSTERN.*

KING: There's matter in these sighs, these profound heaves,
You must translate, 'tis fit we understand them.
Where is your son?
QUEEN: Bestow this place on us° a little while.

*Exeunt ROSENCRANTZ and GUILDENSTERN.*

5          Ah mine own lord, what have I seen tonight!
KING: What, Gertrude? How does Hamlet?
QUEEN: Mad as the sea and wind when both contend
Which is the mightier, in his lawless fit,
Behind the arras hearing something stir,
10         Whips out his rapier, cries "A rat, a rat,"
And in this brainish apprehension° kills
The unseen good old man.
KING:                              O heavy deed!
It had been so with us° had we been there:
His liberty is full of threats to all,
15         To you yourself, to us, to every one.
Alas, how shall this bloody deed be answered?
It will be laid to us,° whose providence°
Should have kept short,° restrained, and out of haunt°
This mad young man; but so much was our love,
20         We would not understand what was most fit,
But like the owner of a foul disease,
To keep it from divulging,° let it feed
Even on the pith of life: where is he gone?
QUEEN: To draw apart the body he hath killed,
25         O'er whom his very madness, like some ore
Among a mineral of metals base,°
Shows itself pure: a' weeps for what is done.
KING: O Gertrude, come away:
The sun no sooner shall the mountains touch,
30         But we will ship him hence and this vile deed
We must with all our majesty and skill
Both countenance° and excuse. Ho Guildenstern!

*Enter ROSENCRANTZ and GUILDENSTERN.*

Friends both, go join you with some further aid;
Hamlet in madness hath Polonius slain,

---

°4 *Bestow . . . us: us:* leave us. 11 *brainish apprehension:* insane delusion. 13 *us:* me (royal plural). 17 *laid to us:* blamed on me. *providence:* foresight. 18 *short:* tethered by a short leash. *out of haunt:* away from others. 22 *divulging:* being divulged. 25–26 *ore . . . base:* pure ore (such as gold) in a mine of base metal. 32 *countenance:* defend.

And from his mother's closet hath he dragged him. 35
Go seek him out, speak fair, and bring the body
Into the chapel; I pray you haste in this. [*Exeunt Gentlemen.*]
Come Gertrude, we'll call up our wisest friends,
And let them know both what we mean to do
And what's untimely done: [so haply slander,] 40
Whose whisper o'er the world's diameter,
As level° as the cannon to his blank°
Transports his ° poisoned shot, may miss our name,
And hit the woundless° air. O come away,
My soul is full of discord and dismay. *Exeunt.* 45

## Scene 2. [Another room in the castle]

*Enter* HAMLET.

HAMLET: Safely stowed.
    *Gentlemen within:* Hamlet, Lord Hamlet!
    But soft, what noise, who calls on Hamlet?
    O here they come.

*Enter* ROSENCRANTZ *and* GUILDENSTERN.

ROSENCRANTZ: What have you done my lord with the dead body? 5
HAMLET: Compounded it with dust whereto 'tis kin.
ROSENCRANTZ: Tell us where 'tis that we may take it thence,
    And bear it to the chapel.
HAMLET: Do not believe it.
ROSENCRANTZ: Believe what? 10
HAMLET: That I can keep your counsel° and not mine own.° Besides,
    to be demanded of° a sponge, what replication° should be
    made by the son of a king?
ROSENCRANTZ: Take you me for a sponge, my lord?
HAMLET: Ay sir, that soaks up the king's countenance,° his rewards, 15
    his authorities. But such officers do the king best service in
    the end; he keeps them like an apple in the corner of his
    jaw, first mouthed to be last swallowed: when he needs
    what you have gleaned, it is but squeezing you, and
    sponge, you shall be dry again. 20
ROSENCRANTZ: I understand you not my lord.
HAMLET: I am glad of it: a knavish speech sleeps in° a foolish ear.
ROSENCRANTZ: My lord, you must tell us where the body is, and go with
    us to the king.
HAMLET: The body is with the king, but the king° is not with the 25
    body. The king is a thing—

---

°42 *As level*: with a straight aim. *blank*: white bull's-eye at the target's center. 43 *his*: slander's. 44 *woundless*: invulnerable. 11 *counsel*: (1) advice (2) secret. *keep . . . own*: follow your advice and not keep my own secret. 12 *demanded of*: questioned by. *replication*: reply to a charge. 14 *countenance*: favor. 22 *sleeps in*: means nothing to. 25 *king . . . king*: Hamlet's father . . . Claudius.

GUILDENSTERN:  A thing my lord?

HAMLET:  Of nothing, bring me to him. Hide fox, and all after.° *Exeunt.*

### Scene 3. [Another room in the castle]

*Enter* KING *and two or three.*

KING:  I have sent to seek him, and to find the body:
How dangerous is it that this man goes loose,
Yet must not we put the strong law on him,
He's loved of the distracted multitude,°
5      Who like not in° their judgment, but their eyes,
And where 'tis so, th'offender's scourge° is weighed
But never the offence: to bear all° smooth and even,
This sudden sending him away must seem
Deliberate pause° diseases desperate grown,
10     By desperate appliance° are relieved,
Or not at all.

*Enter* ROSENCRANTZ *and all the rest.*

       How now, what hath befallen?

ROSENCRANTZ:  Where the dead body is bestowed my lord,
We cannot get from him.

KING:                      But where is he?

ROSENCRANTZ:  Without, my lord, guarded,° to know your pleasure.

KING:  Bring him before us.

15     ROSENCRANTZ:            Ho, bring in the lord.

*Enter* HAMLET *(guarded) and* GUILDENSTERN.

KING:  Now Hamlet, where's Polonius?

HAMLET:  At supper.

KING:  At supper? where?

HAMLET:  Not where he eats, but where a' is eaten: a certain
20     convocation of politic° worms are e'en° at him. Your worm is your
only emperor for diet, we fat all creatures else to fat us,
and we fat ourselves for maggots. Your fat king and your
lean beggar is but variable service,° two dishes but to one
table, that's the end.

25     KING:  Alas, alas.

HAMLET:  A man may fish with the worm that hath eat of a king, and
eat of the fish that hath fed of that worm.

KING:  What dost thou mean by this?

HAMLET:  Nothing but to show you how a king may go a progress°
30     through the guts of a beggar.

KING:  Where is Polonius?

HAMLET:  In heaven, send thither to see. If your messenger find him
not there, seek him i'th'other place yourself: but if indeed

---

°28 *Hide fox . . . after.* (cry in a children's game, like hide-and-seek).  4 *distracted multitude:* confused mob.  5 *in:* according to.  6 *scourge:* punishment.  7 *bear all:* carry out everything.  9 *Deliberate pause:* considered delay.  10 *appliance:* remedy.  14 *guarded:* (Hamlet is under guard until he boards the ship).  20 *politic:* (1) statesmanlike (2) crafty.  *e'en:* even now.  23 *variable service:* different types of food.  29 *go a progress:* make a splendid royal journey from one part of the country to another.

you find him not within this month, you shall nose him as
you go up the stairs into the lobby.

KING: [*To* ATTENDANTS.] Go seek him there.                                    35

HAMLET: A' will stay till you come.                                    [*Exeunt.*]

KING: Hamlet, this deed, for thine especial safety—
Which we do tender,° as we dearly grieve
For that which thou hast done—must send thee hence                     40
With fiery quickness. Therefore prepare thyself,
The bark is ready, and the wind at help,°
Th'associates tend,° and every thing is bent
For England.

HAMLET:                For England.

KING:                                    Ay Hamlet.

HAMLET:                                            Good.

KING: So is it if thou knew'st our purposes.                           45

HAMLET: I see a cherub° that sees them: but come, for England.
Farewell dear mother.

KING: Thy loving father, Hamlet.

HAMLET: My mother: father and mother is man and wife, man and
wife is one flesh, and so my mother: come, for England.        *Exit.*  50

KING: [*To* ROSENCRANTZ *and* GUILDENSTERN.]
Follow him at foot,° tempt him with speed aboard,
Delay it not, I'll have him hence tonight.
Away, for every thing is sealed and done
That else leans on° th'affair, pray you make haste.               [*Exeunt.*]
And England,° if my love thou hold'st at aught°—                       55
As my great power thereof may give thee sense,
Since yet thy cicatrice° looks raw and red
After the Danish sword, and thy free awe
Pays homage° to us—thou mayst not coldly set°
Our sovereign process,° which imports at full                          60
By letters congruing° to that effect,
The present° death of Hamlet. Do it England,
For like the hectic° in my blood he rages,
And thou must cure me; till I know 'tis done,
Howe'er my haps,° my joys were ne'er begun.                    *Exit.*  65

## Scene 4. [A plain in Denmark]

*Enter* FORTINBRAS *with his army over the stage.*

FORTINBRAS: Go captain, from me greet the Danish king,
Tell him that by his license, Fortinbras
Craves the conveyance° of a promised march
Over his kingdom. You know the rendezvous:

---

°39 *tender*: cherish.  42 *at help*: helpful.  43 *tend*: wait.  46 *cherub*: (considered the watchmen of heaven).  51 *at foot*: at his heels.  54 *leans on*: relates to.  55 *England*: King of England.  *my love . . . aught*: you place any value on my favor.  57 *cicatrice*: scar.  58–59 *free . . . homage*: awe which you, though free, still show by paying homage.  59 *coldly set*: lightly estimate.  60 *process*: command.  61 *congruing*: agreeing.  62 *present*: immediate.  63 *hectic*: fever.  65 *haps*: fortunes  3 *conveyance of*: escort for.

5      If that his majesty would aught with us,
       We shall express our duty in his eye,°
       And let him know so.

CAPTAIN:             I will do't, my lord.

FORTINBRAS:  Go softly° on.                        *Exit.*

*Enter* HAMLET, ROSENCRANTZ, [GUILDENSTERN,] *etc.*

HAMLET:  Good sir whose powers° are these?

10  CAPTAIN:  They are of Norway sir.

HAMLET:  How purposed sir I pray you?

CAPTAIN:  Against some part of Poland.

HAMLET:  Who commands them sir?

CAPTAIN:  The nephew to old Norway, Fortinbras.

15  HAMLET:  Goes it against the main° of Poland sir,
       Or for some frontier?

CAPTAIN:  Truly to speak, and with no addition,
       We go to gain a little patch of ground
       That hath in it no profit but the name.°

20       To pay five ducats, five, I would not farm it;
       Nor will it yield to Norway or the Pole
       A ranker° rate, should it be sold in fee.°

HAMLET:  Why then the Polack never will defend it.

CAPTAIN:  Yes, it is already garrisoned.

25  HAMLET:  Two thousand souls, and twenty thousand ducats
       Will not debate the question of° this straw:°
       This is th'imposthume of much wealth and peace,°
       That inward breaks, and shows no cause without
       Why the man dies. I humbly thank you sir.

CAPTAIN:  God bye you sir.                    *[Exit.]*

30  ROSENCRANTZ:         Will't please you go my lord?

HAMLET:  I'll be with you straight, go a little before.

                                  *[Exeunt all but Hamlet.]*

       How all occasions do inform against me,
       And spur my dull revenge. What is a man
       If his chief good and market° of his time

35       Be but to sleep and feed? a beast, no more:
       Sure he that made us with such large discourse,°
       Looking before and after,° gave us not
       That capability and god-like reason
       To fust° in us unused. Now whether it be

40       Bestial oblivion,° or some craven° scruple
       Of thinking too precisely on th'event°—

---

°6 *in his eye:* face to face. 8 *softly:* slowly. 9 *powers:* troops. 15 *main:* body. 19 *name:* glory. 22 *ranker:* higher (as annual interest on the total). *in fee:* outright. 26 *debate . . . of:* settle the dispute over. *straw:* triviality. 27 *imposthume . . . peace:* swelling discontent (inner abscess) resulting from too much wealth and peace. 34 *market:* profit. 36 *discourse:* power of reasoning. 37 *Looking . . . after:* seeing causes and effects. 39 *fust:* grow moldy. 40 *Bestial oblivion:* forgetfulness, as a beast forgets its parents. *craven:* cowardly. 41 *event:* outcome.

A thought which quartered hath but one part wisdom,
And ever three parts coward—I do not know
Why yet I live to say "This thing's to do,"
Sith I have cause, and will, and strength, and means
To do't; examples gross° as earth exhort me:                              45
Witness this army of such mass and charge,°
Led by a delicate and tender° prince,
Whose spirit with divine ambition puffed,
Makes mouths° at the invisible event,°
Exposing what is mortal, and unsure,                                      50
To all that fortune, death, and danger dare,
Even for an egg-shell. Rightly to be great,
Is not to stir without great argument,
But greatly to find quarrel in a straw
When honour's at the stake.° How stand I then                            55
That have a father killed, a mother stained,
Excitements° of my reason, and my blood,
And let all sleep, while to my shame I see
The imminent death of twenty thousand men,
That for a fantasy and trick° of fame                                     60
Go to their graves like beds, fight for a plot
Whereon the numbers cannot try the cause,°
Which is not tomb enough and continent°
To hide the slain. O from this time forth,
My thoughts be bloody, or be nothing worth.                              65
                                                              *Exit.*

## Scene 5. [A room in the castle]

*Enter* QUEEN, HORATIO *and a* GENTLEMAN.

QUEEN:  I will not speak with her.
GENTLEMAN:  She is importunate, indeed distract,°
    Her mood will needs be° pitied.
QUEEN:                              What would she have?
GENTLEMAN:  She speaks much of her father, says she hears
    There's tricks i'th'world, and hems,° and beats her heart,           5
    Spurns enviously at straws,° speaks things in doubt°
    That carry but half sense: her speech is nothing,
    Yet the unshapèd use of it doth move
    The hearers to collection;° they aim° at it,
    And botch° the words up fit to their own thoughts,                   10

---

°46 *gross*: obvious. 47 *charge*: expense. 48 *delicate and tender*: gentle and young. 50 *mouths*: faces. *event*: outcome. 53–56 *Rightly . . . stake*: the truly great do not fight without just cause ("argument"), but it is nobly ("greatly") done to fight even for a trifle if honor is at stake. 58 *Excitements*: incentives. 61 *fantasy and trick*: illusion and trifle. 63 *Whereon . . . cause*: too small to accommodate all the troops fighting for it. 64 *continent*: container. 2 *distract*: insane. 3 *will needs be*: needs to be. 5 *hems*: coughs. 6 *Spurns . . . straws*: reacts maliciously to trifles. *in doubt*: ambiguous. 9 *collection*: inference. *aim*: guess. 10 *botch*: patch.

Which as her winks, and nods, and gestures yield them,
Indeed would make one think there might be thought,
Though nothing sure, yet much unhappily.
HORATIO: 'Twere good she were spoken with, for she may strew
15      Dangerous conjectures in ill-breeding minds.
QUEEN: Let her come in.                                    *Exit Gentleman.*
        [*Aside.*] To my sick soul, as sin's true nature is;°
        Each toy° seems prologue to some great amiss,°
        So full of artless jealousy° is guilt,
20      It spills itself, in fearing to be spilt.

*Enter* OPHELIA, *distracted.*°

OPHELIA: Where is the beauteous majesty of Denmark?
QUEEN: How now Ophelia?
OPHELIA: [*Sings.*] How should I your true love know
                        From another one?
25                   By his cockle hat and staff,°
                        And his sandal shoon.°

QUEEN: Alas sweet lady, what imports this song?
OPHELIA: Say you? nay, pray you mark.
        [*Sings.*] He is dead and gone, lady,
30                   He is dead and gone,
                        At his head a grass-green turf,
                        At his heels a stone.
            O ho.
QUEEN: Nay but Ophelia—
OPHELIA:                      Pray you mark.
35      [*Sings.*] White his shroud as the mountain snow—

*Enter* KING.

QUEEN: Alas, look here my lord,
OPHELIA: [*Sings.*] Larded° all with sweet flowers,
                Which bewept to the ground did not go,
                With true-love showers.
40  KING: How do you, pretty lady?
OPHELIA: Well, God 'ild° you. They say the owl was a baker's
        daughter.° Lord, we know what we are, but know not what
        we may be. God be at your table.°
KING: Conceit° upon her father.

---

°17 *as sin's . . . is:* as is natural for the guilty. 18 *toy:* trifle.*amiss:* disaster. 19 *artless jealousy:* uncontrollable suspicion. 20 S.D.: *distracted:* insane. 25 *cockle hat and staff.* (marks of the pilgrim, the cockle shell symbolizing his journey to the shrine of St. James; the pilgrim was a common metaphor for the lover). 26 *shoon:* shoes. 37 *Larded:* trimmed. 41 *God 'ild:* God yield (reward). 41–42 *owl . . . daughter.* (in a medieval legend, a baker's daughter was turned into an owl because she gave Jesus short weight on a loaf of bread). 43 *God . . . table:* (a blessing at dinner). 44 *Conceit:* thinking.

OPHELIA:  Pray you let's have no words of this, but when they ask    45
    you what it means, say you this:

    [*Sings.*] Tomorrow is Saint Valentine's day,
        All in the morning betime,°
    And I a maid at your window
        To be your Valentine.    50
    Then up he rose, and donned his clo'es,
        And dupped° the chamber door,
    Let in the maid, that out a maid,
        Never departed more.
KING:  Pretty Ophelia.    55
OPHELIA:  Indeed, la, without an oath I'll make an end on't.

    [*Sings.*] By Gis° and by Saint Charity,
        Alack and fie for shame,
    Young men will do't, if they come to't,
        By Cock° they are to blame.    60
    Quoth she, Before you tumbled me,
        You promised me to wed.
    He answers. So would I ha' done, by yonder sun,
        An° thou hadst not come to my bed.
KING:  How long hath she been thus?    65
OPHELIA:  I hope all will be well. We must be patient, but I cannot
    choose but weep to think they would lay him i'th' cold
    ground. My brother shall know of it, and so I thank you
    for your good counsel. Come, my coach: good night
    ladies, good night. Sweet ladies, good night, good night.    [*Exit Ophelia.*]    70
KING:  Follow her close, give her good watch I pray you.    [*Exit Horatio.*]
    O this is the poison of deep grief, it springs
    All from her father's death, and now behold:
    O Gertrude, Gertrude,
    When sorrows come, they come not single spies,    75
    But in battalions: first her father slain,
    Next, your son gone, and he most violent author
    Of his own just remove, the people muddied,°
    Thick and unwholesome in their thoughts and whispers
    For good Polonius' death: and we have done but greenly°    80
    In hugger-mugger° to inter him: poor Ophelia
    Divided from herself and her fair judgment,
    Without the which we are pictures or mere beasts,
    Last, and as much containing° as all these,
    Her brother is in secret come from France,    85
    Feeds on his wonder,° keeps himself in clouds,°
    And wants not buzzers° to infect his ear

---

°48 *betime*: early (because the first woman a man saw on Valentine's Day would be his true love). 52 *dupped*: opened. 57 *Gis*: contraction of "Jesus." 60 *Cock*: (vulgarization of "God" in oaths). 64 *An*: if. 78 *muddied*: stirred up. 80 *done but greenly*: acted like amateurs. 81 *hugger-mugger*: secret haste. 84 *containing*: i.e., cause for sorrow. 86 *Feeds . . . wonder*: sustains himself by wondering about his father's death. *clouds*: gloom, obscurity. 87 *wants not buzzers*: lacks not whispering gossips.

With pestilent speeches of his father's death,
Wherein necessity, of matter beggared,
90    Will nothing stick our person to arraign°
In ear and ear:° O my dear Gertrude, this
Like to a murdering-piece° in many places
Gives me superfluous death.                         *A noise within.*
QUEEN:                              Alack, what noise is this?
KING:  Attend!      *Enter a* MESSENGER.
95    Where are my Switzers°. Let them guard the door.
What is the matter?
MESSENGER.                   Save yourself, my lord.
The ocean, overpeering of his list,°
Eats not the flats° with more impiteous haste
Than young Laertes in a riotous head°
100   O'erbears your officers: the rabble call him lord,
And as the world were now but to begin,
Antiquity forgot, custom not known,
The ratifiers and props of every word,
They cry "Choose we, Laertes shall be king!"
105   Caps, hands, and tongues applaud it to the clouds,
"Laertes shall be king, Laertes king!"                *A noise within.*
QUEEN:  How cheerfully on the false trail they cry.
O this is counter,° you false Danish dogs.
KING:  The doors are broke.

*Enter* LAERTES *with others.*

110   LAERTES:  Where is this king? Sirs, stand you all without.°
DANES:  No, let's come in.
LAERTES:                        I pray you give me leave.°
DANES:  We will, we will.                              *[They retire.]*
LAERTES:  I thank you, keep the door. O thou vile king,
Give me my father.
QUEEN:                        Calmly, good Laertes.
115   LAERTES:  That drop of blood that's calm proclaims me bastard,
Cries cuckold° to my father, brands° the harlot
Even here between the chaste unsmirchèd brows
Of my true mother.
KING:                        What is the cause Laertes,
That thy rebellion looks so giant-like?
120   Let him go Gertrude, do not fear° our person,
There's such divinity° doth hedge a king,
That treason can but peep to° what it would,

---

°89–90 *Wherein . . . arraign*: in which the tellers, lacking facts, will not hesitate to accuse me.  91 *In ear and ear*: whispering from one ear to another.
92 *murdering-piece*: small cannon shooting shrapnel, to inflict numerous wounds.  95 *Switzers*: Swiss guards.  97 *overpeering . . . list*: rising above
its usual limits.  98 *flats*: lowlands.  99 *head*: armed force.  108 *counter*: following the scent backward.  110 *without*: outside.  111 *leave*: i.e., to
enter alone.  116 *cuckold*: betrayed husband.  *brands*: (so harlots were punished).  120 *fear*: i.e., for.  121 *divinity*: divine protection.  122 *peep to*:
strain to see.

Acts little of his° will. Tell me Laertes,
Why thou art this incensed. Let him go Gertrude.
Speak man.

LAERTES: Where is my father?

KING:                              Dead.

QUEEN:                                        But not by him.

KING: Let him demand his fill.

LAERTES: How came he dead? I'll not be juggled with.
To hell allegiance, vows to the blackest devil,
Conscience and grace, to the profoundest pit.
I dare damnation: to this point I stand,
That both the worlds I give to negligence,°
Let come what comes, only I'll be revenged
Most throughly for my father.

KING:                              Who shall stay you?

LAERTES: My will, not all the world's:°
And for my means, I'll husband° them so well,
They shall go far with little.

KING:                              Good Laertes,
If you desire to know the certainty
Of your dear father, is't writ in your revenge
That swoopstake,° you will draw both friend and foe,
Winner and loser?

LAERTES: None but his enemies.

KING:                              Will you know them then?

LAERTES: To his good friends thus wide I'll ope my arms,
And like the kind life-rend'ring pelican,°
Repast them with my blood.

KING:                              Why now you speak
Like a good child, and a true gentleman.
That I am guiltless of your father's death,
And am most sensibly° in grief for it,
It shall as level° to your judgment 'pear
As day does to your eye.

[*A noise within.*]

[*Crowd shouts.*] Let her come in.

LAERTES: How now, what noise is that?

*Enter OPHELIA.*

O heat, dry up my brains, tears seven time salt,
Burn out the sense and virtue° of mine eye!
By heaven, thy madness shall be paid with weight,°
Till our scale turn the beam,° O rose of May,
Dear maid, kind sister, sweet Ophelia:

125

130

135

140

145

150

155

---

°123 *his*: treason's. 132 *both . . . negligence*: I care nothing for this world or the next. 135 *world's*: i.e., will. 136 *husband*: economize. 140 *swoop-stake*: sweeping in all the stakes in a game, both of winner and loser. 144 *pelican*: (the mother pelican was believed to nourish her young with blood pecked from her own breast). 148 *sensibly*: feelingly. 149 *level*: plain. 154 *sense and virtue*: feeling and power. 155 *with weight*: with equal weight. 156 *turn the beam*: outweigh the other side.

     O heavens, is't possible a young maid's wits
     Should be as mortal as an old man's life?
160     Nature is fine in love, and where 'tis fine,
     It sends some previous instance of itself
     after the thing it loves.°
OPHELIA: [*Sings.*] They bore him barefaced on the bier,
          Hey non nonny, nonny, hey nonny:
165          And in his grave rained many a tear—
        Fare you well my dove.
LAERTES: Hadst thou thy wits, and didst persuade revenge,
     It could not move thus.
OPHELIA: You must sing "adown adown," and you call him adown-a.
170     O how the wheel becomes it.° It is the false steward that
     stole his master's daughter.
LAERTES: This nothing's more than matter.°
OPHELIA: There's rosemary,° that's for remembrance, pray you love
     remember: and there is pansies, that's for thoughts.
175 LAERTES: A document° in madness, thoughts and remembrance
     fitted.°
OPHELIA: There's fennel for you, and columbines.° There's rue° for
     you, and here's some for me, we may call it herb of grace°
     o'Sundays: O, you must wear your rue with a difference.°
180     There's daisy,° I would give you some violets,° but they
     withered all when my father died: they say a' made a good
     end;
        [*Sings.*] For bonny sweet Robin is all my joy.
LAERTES: Thought and affliction, passion, hell itself,
185     She turns to favour and to prettiness.
OPHELIA: [*Sings.*] And will a' not come again,
          And will a' not come again?
          No, no, he is dead,
          Go to thy death-bed,
190          He never will come again.
          His beard was as white as snow,
          All flaxen was his poll,°
          He is gone, he is gone,
          And we cast away moan,
195          God ha' mercy on his soul.
    And of all Christian souls, I pray God. God bye you.

                                                       *Exit Ophelia.*

LAERTES: Do you see this, O God?

---

°160–62 *Nature . . . loves:* filial love that is so refined and pure sends some precious token (her wits) after the beloved dead. 170 *wheel becomes it:* refrain ("adown") suits the subject (Polonius's fall). 172 *more than matter:* more eloquent than sane speech. 173 *There's rosemary:* (given to Laertes; she may be distributing imaginary or real flowers). 175 *document:* lesson. 175–76 *thoughts . . . fitted:* thoughts of revenge matched with remembrance of Polonius. 177 *fennel . . . columbines:* (given to the king, symbolizing flattery and ingratitude). *rue:* (given to the queen, symbolizing sorrow or repentance). 178 *herb of grace:* (because it symbolizes repentance). 179 *with a difference:* for a different reason (Ophelia's is for sorrow and the queen's for repentance). 180 *daisy:* (symbolizing dissembling). *violets:* (symbolizing faithfulness). 192 *flaxen . . . poll:* white was his head.

KING: Laertes, I must commune with your grief,
    Or you deny me right: go but apart,
    Make choice of whom your wisest friends you will,          200
    And they shall hear and judge 'twixt you and me;
    If by direct or by collateral° hand
    They find us touched,° we will our kingdom give,
    Our crown, our life, and all that we call ours
    To you in satisfaction; but if not,          205
    Be you content to lend your patience to us,
    And we shall jointly labour with your soul
    To give it due content.
LAERTES:             Let this be so.
    His means of death, his obscure funeral,
    No trophy,° sword, nor hatchment° o'er his bones,          210
    No noble rite, nor formal ostentation,°
    Cry° to be heard as 'twere from heaven to earth,
    That I must call't in question.
KING:               So you shall,
    And where th'offence is, let the great axe fall.
    I pray you go with me.          [*Exeunt.*] 215

## Scene 6. [Another room in the castle]

*Enter* HORATIO *and others.*

HORATIO: What are they that would speak with me?
GENTLEMAN: Seafaring men sir, they say they have letters for you.
HORATIO: Let them come in.          [*Exit* ATTENDANT.]
    I do not know from what part of the world
    I should be greeted, if not from Lord Hamlet.          5

*Enter* SAILORS.

SAILOR: God bless you sir.
HORATIO: Let him bless thee too.
SAILOR: A'shall sir, an't please him. There's a letter for you sir, it
    came from th'ambassador that was bound for England, if
    your name be Horatio, as I am let to know it is.          10
HORATIO: [*Reads the letter.*] "Horatio, when thou shalt have
    overlooked° this, give these fellows some means to the king,
    they have letters for him. Ere we were two days old at sea,
    a pirate of very warlike appointment° gave us chase.
    Finding ourselves too slow of sail, we put on a compelled          15
    valour, and in the grapple° I boarded them. On the instant
    they got clear of our ship, so I alone became their prisoner.
    They have dealt with me like thieves of mercy,° but they
    knew what they did. I am to do a good turn for them. Let
    the king have the letters I have sent, and repair° thou to me          20

---

°202 *collateral*: indirect. 203 *touched*: tainted with guilt. 210 *trophy*: memorial. *hatchment*: tablet displaying coat of arms. 211 *ostentation*: ceremony. 212 *Cry*: cry out. 12 *overlooked*: read over. 14 *appointment*: equipment. 16 *in the grapple*: when the pirate ship hooked onto ours. 18 *of mercy*: merciful. 20 *repair*: come.

with as much speed as thou wouldst fly death. I have
words to speak in thine ear will make thee dumb, yet are
they much too light for the bore° of the matter. These good
fellows will bring thee where I am. Rosencrantz and
25 Guildenstern hold their course for England. Of them I
have much to tell thee. Farewell.

                       He that thou knowest thine, Hamlet."
Come, I will give you way° for these your letters,
And do't the speedier that you may direct me
30 To him from whom you brought them.                            *Exeunt.*

## Scene 7. [Another room in the castle]

*Enter* KING *and* LAERTES.

KING:  Now must your conscience my acquittance seal,°
     And you must put me in your heart for friend,
     Sith you have heard and with a knowing ear,
     That he which hath your noble father slain
     Pursued my life.
5 LAERTES:              It well appears: but tell me
     Why you proceeded not against these feats
     So crimeful and so capital in nature,
     As by your safety, greatness, wisdom, all things else,
     You mainly were stirred up.°
KING:                   O for two special reasons,
10     Which may to you perhaps seem much unsinewed,°
     But yet to me they're strong. The queen his mother
     Lives almost by his looks, and for myself,
     My virtue or my plague, be it either which,
     She's so conjunctive° to my life and soul,
15     That as the star moves not but in his sphere,°
     I could not but by her. The other motive,
     Why to a public count° I might not go,
     Is the great love the general gender° bear him,
     Who dipping all his faults in their affection,
20     Would like the spring that turneth wood to stone,°
     Convert his gyves to graces,° so that my arrows,
     Too slightly timbered° for so loud a wind,
     Would have reverted to my bow again,
     And not where I had aimed them.

---

°23 *bore*: size, caliber. 28 *way*: access (to the king). 1 *my acquittance seal*: confirm my acquittal. 9 *mainly . . . up*: were strongly urged. 10 *much unsinewed*: very weak. 14 *conjunctive*: closely allied. 15 *in his sphere*: (referring to the Ptolemaic belief that each planet, fixed in its own sphere, revolved around the earth). 17 *count*: accounting. 18 *general gender*: common people. 20 *the spring . . . stone*: (the baths of King's Newnham in Warwickshire were described as being able to turn wood to stone because of their high concentrations of lime). 21 *Convert . . . graces*: regard his fetters (had he been imprisoned) as honors. 22 *slightly timbered*: light-shafted.

LAERTES:  And so have I a noble father lost,                                          25
  A sister driven into desperate terms,°
  Whose worth, if praises may go back° again,
  Stood challenger on mount of all the age
  For her perfections.° But my revenge will come.
KING:  Break not your sleeps for that, you must not think                             30
  That we are made of stuff so flat and dull,
  That we can let our beard be shook with danger,
  And think it pastime. You shortly shall hear more,
  I loved your father, and we love ourself,
  And that I hope will teach you to imagine—                                          35

*Enter a* MESSENGER *with letters.*

  How now. What news?
MESSENGER:                    Letters my lord, from Hamlet.
  These to your majesty, this to the queen.
KING:  From Hamlet? Who brought them?
MESSENGER:  Sailors my lord they say, I saw them not:
  They were given me by Claudio, he received them                                     40
  Of him that brought them.
KING:                      Laertes you shall hear them:
  Leave us.                                               *Exit* [MESSENGER]
  [*Reads*] "High and mighty, you shall know I am set naked° on
  your kingdom. Tomorrow shall I beg leave to see your kingly
  eyes, when I shall, first asking your pardon° thereunto,                            45
  recount the occasion of my sudden and more strange return.
                                        Hamlet."
  What should this mean? Are all the rest come back?
  Or is it some abuse,° and no such thing?
LAERTES:  Know you the hand?
KING:                        'Tis Hamlet's character.° "Naked,"                        50
  And in a postscript here he says "alone."
  Can you devise° me?
LAERTES:  I am lost in it my lord, but let him come,
  It warms the very sickness in my heart
  That I shall live and tell him to his teeth,                                        55
  "Thus didest thou."
KING:                  If it be so Laertes—
  As how should it be so? how otherwise?—
  Will you be ruled by me?
LAERTES:                   Ay my lord,
  So you will not o'errule me to a peace.

---

°26 *desperate terms*: madness. 27 *go back*: i.e., before her madness. 28–29 *challenger . . . perfections*: like a challenger on horseback, ready to
defend against the world her claim to perfection. 43 *naked*: without resources. 45 *pardon*: permission. 49 *abuse*: deception. 50 *character*:
handwriting. 52 *devise me*: explain it.

60 KING: To thine own peace: if he be now returned,
As checking at° his voyage, and that he means
No more to undertake it, I will work him
To an exploit, now ripe in my device,°
Under the which he shall not choose but fall:
65 And for his death no wind of blame shall breathe,
But even his mother shall uncharge the practice,°
And call it accident.
LAERTES:                    My lord, I will be ruled,
The rather if you could devise it so
That I might be the organ.°
KING:                              It falls right.
70 You have been talked of since your travel much,
And that in Hamlet's hearing, for a quality
Wherein they say you shine: your sum of parts°
Did not together pluck such envy from him
As did that one, and that in my regard
Of the unworthiest siege.°
75 LAERTES:                    What part is that my lord?
KING: A very riband° in the cap of youth,
Yet needful too, for youth no less becomes°
The light and careless livery° that it wears,
Than settled age his sables° and his weeds°
80 Importing health and graveness; two months since,°
Here was a gentleman of Normandy—
I have seen myself, and served against the French,
And they can° well on horseback—but this gallant
Had witchcraft in't, he grew unto his seat,
85 And to such wondrous doing brought his horse,
As had he been incorpsed and demi-natured°
With the brave beast. So far he topped my thought,
That I in forgery of° shapes and tricks
Come short of what he did.
LAERTES:                    A Norman was't?
90 KING: A Norman.
LAERTES: Upon my life, Lamord.°
KING:                              The very same.
LAERTES: I know him well, he is the brooch° indeed
And gem of all the nation.
KING: He made confession° of you,
95     And gave you such a masterly report

---

°61 *checking at:* altering the course of (when the falcon forsakes one quarry for another). 63 *ripe in my device:* already planned by me. 66 *uncharge the practice:* acquit the plot (of treachery). 69 *organ:* instrument. 72 *your sum of parts:* all your accomplishments. 75 *siege:* rank. 76 *riband:* decoration. 77 *becomes:* befits. 78 *livery:* clothing (denoting rank or occupation). 79 *sables:* fur-trimmed gowns. *weeds:* garments. 80 *since:* ago. 83 *can:* can do. 86 *incorpsed . . . natured:* made into one body, sharing half its nature. 88 *in forgery of:* imagining. 91 *Lamord:* a name meaning "death" in French. 92 *brooch:* ornament. 94 *confession:* report.

For art and exercise in your defence,
And for your rapier most especial,
That he cried out 'twould be a sight indeed
If one could match you; the scrimers° of their nation
He swore had neither motion, guard, nor eye, 100
If you opposed them; sir this report of his
Did Hamlet so envenom° with his envy,
That he could nothing do but wish and beg
Your sudden coming o'er to play with him.
Now out of this— 
LAERTES:          What out of this, my lord? 105
KING: Laertes, was your father dear to you?
Or are you like the painting of a sorrow,
A face without a heart?
LAERTES:          Why ask you this?
KING: Not that I think you did not love your father.
But that I know love is begun by time, 110
And that I see in passages of proof,°
Time qualifies° the spark and fire of it:
There lives within the very flame of love
A kind of wick or snuff that will abate it,°
And nothing is at a like goodness still,° 115
For goodness growing to a plurisy,°
Dies in his own too-much. That we would do
We should do when we would: for this "would"° changes,
And hath abatements and delays as many
As there are tongues, are hands, are accidents, 120
And then this "should"° is like a spendthrift sigh,
That hurts by easing,° but to the quick° of th'ulcer:
Hamlet comes back, what would you undertake
To show yourself in deed your father's son
More than in words?
LAERTES:          To cut his throat i'th'church. 125
KING: No place indeed should murder sanctuarize,°
Revenge should have no bounds: but good Laertes,
Will you do this, keep close within your chamber:
Hamlet returned shall know you are come home,
We'll put on° those shall praise your excellence, 130
And set a double varnish on the fame
The Frenchman gave you, bring you in fine° together,
And wager on your heads; he being remiss,°
Most generous, and free from all contriving,
Will not peruse the foils, so that with ease, 135

---

°99 *scrimers*: fencers. 102 *envenom*: poison. 111 *passages of proof*: examples drawn from experience. 112 *qualifies*: weakens. 114 *snuff . . . it*: charred end of the wick that will diminish the flame. 115 *still*: always. 116 *plurisy*: excess. 118 *"would"*: will to act. 121 *"should"*: reminder of one's duty. 121–22 *spendthrift . . . easing*: A sigh which, though giving temporary relief, wastes life, as each sigh draws a drop of blood away from the heart (a common Elizabethan belief). 122 *quick*: most sensitive spot. 126 *murder sanctuarize*: give sanctuary to murder. 130 *put on*: incite. 132 *in fine*: finally. 133 *remiss*: easy-going.

Or with a little shuffling, you may choose
A sword unbated,° and in a pass of practice°
Requite him for your father.

LAERTES:                               I will do't,
And for the purpose, I'll anoint my sword.
140   I bought an unction° of a mountebank°
So mortal,° that but dip a knife in it,
Where it draws blood, no cataplasm° so rare,
Collected from all simples° that have virtue°
Under the moon,° can save the thing from death
145   That is but scratched withal: I'll touch my point
With this contagion, that if I gall° him slightly,
It may be death.

KING:                     Let's further think of this,
Weigh what convenience both of time and means
May fit us to our shape;° if this should fail,
150   And that our drift° look through° our bad performance,
'Twere better not assayed; therefore this project
Should have a back or second that might hold
If this did blast in proof,° soft, let me see,
We'll make a solemn wager on your cunning°—
155   I ha't:
When in your motion you are hot and dry,
As make your bouts more violent to that end,
And that he calls for drink, I'll have prepared him
A chalice for the nonce,° whereon but sipping,
160   If he by chance escape your venomed stuck,°
Our purpose may hold there; but stay, what noise?

*Enter* QUEEN.

How, sweet queen?
QUEEN: One woe doth tread upon another's heel,
So fast they follow; your sister's drowned, Laertes.
165   LAERTES: Drowned! O where?
QUEEN: There is a willow grows aslant a brook,
That shows his hoar° leaves in the glassy stream,
There with fantastic garlands did she make
Of crow-flowers,° nettles, daisies, and long purples,°
170   That liberal° shepherds give a grosser name,
But our cold° maids do dead men's fingers call them.
There on the pendent boughs her coronet weeds°

---

°137 *unbated:* not blunted (the edges and points were blunted for fencing). *pass of practice:* (1) match for exercise (2) treacherous thrust. 140 *unc-tion:* ointment. *mountebank:* quack doctor, medicine man. 141 *mortal:* deadly. 142 *cataplasm:* poultice. 143 *simples:* herbs. *virtue:* power (of healing). 144 *Under the moon:* (when herbs were supposed to be collected to be most effective). 146 *gall:* scratch. 149 *shape:* plan. 150 *drift:* aim. *look through:* be exposed by. 153 *blast in proof:* fail when tested (as a bursting cannon). 154 *cunnings:* skills. 159 *nonce:* occasion. 160 *stuck:* thrust. 167 *hoar:* grey (on the underside). 169 *crow-flowers:* buttercups. *long purples:* spike-like early orchid. 170 *liberal:* libertine. 171 *cold:* chaste. 172 *coronet weeds:* garland of weeds.

Clamb'ring to hang, an envious sliver° broke,
When down her weedy trophies and herself
Fell in the weeping brook: her clothes spread wide,                                        175
And mermaid-like awhile they bore her up,
Which time she chanted snatches of old tunes,
As one incapable of° her own distress,
Or like a creature native and induced
Unto° that element: but long it could not be                                              180
Till that her garments, heavy with their drink,
Pulled the poor wretch from her melodious lay
To muddy death.
LAERTES:                Alas, then she is drowned?
QUEEN:  Drowned, drowned.
LAERTES:  Too much of water hast thou, poor Ophelia,                                      185
And therefore I forbid my tears; but yet
It is our trick, nature her custom holds,
Let shame say what it will; when these° are gone,
The woman will be out.° Adieu my lord,
I have a speech o'fire that fain would blaze,                                             190
But that this folly douts it.°                                                *Exit.*
KING:                        Let's follow, Gertrude,
How much I had to do to calm his rage;
Now fear I this will give it start again,
Therefore let's follow.                                                      *Exeunt.*

## ACT 5

### Scene 1. [A churchyard]

*Enter two CLOWNS°*

1. CLOWN:  Is she to be buried in Christian burial,° when she wilfully
   seeks her own salvation?°
2. CLOWN:  I tell thee she is, therefore make her grave straight.° The
   crowner hath sat on her,° and finds it Christian burial.
1. CLOWN:  How can that be, unless she drowned herself in her own                          5
   defence?°
2. CLOWN:  Why, 'tis found so.
1. CLOWN:  It must be "se offendendo,"° it cannot be else: for here lies
   the point: if I drown myself wittingly, it argues an act,
   and an act hath three branches, it is to act, to do, and to                            10
   perform; argal,° she drowned herself wittingly.

---

°173 *envious sliver*: malicious branch  178 *incapable of*: unable to understand.  179–180 *induced Unto*: endowed by nature to exist in.  188 *these*:
i.e., tears.  189 *woman . . . out*: womanly habits will be out of me.  191 *folly douts it*: tears put it out.  0.2 S.D.: *clowns*: rustics.  1 *Christian burial*:
consecrated ground within a churchyard (where suicides were not allowed burial).  2 *salvation*: i.e., "damnation." The gravediggers make a number
of such "mistakes," later termed "malapropisms."  3 *straight*: straightaway, at once.  4 *crowner . . . her*: coroner has ruled on her case.  5–6 *her
own defence*: (as self-defense justifies homicide, so may it justify suicide).  8 *"se offendendo"*: (he means "se defendendo," in self-defense).  11
*argal*: (corruption of "ergo" = therefore).

    2. CLOWN: Nay, but hear you, Goodman Delver.

    1. CLOWN: Give me leave: here lies the water, good. Here stands the
        man, good. If the man go to this water and drown himself,

15         it is, will he nill he,° he goes, mark you that. But if the
        water come to him, and drown him, he drowns not
        himself. Argal, he that is not guilty of his own death, shortens not his own
        life.

    2. CLOWN: But is this law?

20   1. CLOWN: Ay marry is't, crowner's quest° law.

    2. CLOWN: Will you ha' the truth on't? If this had not been a
        gentlewoman, she would have been buried out o'Christian
        burial.

    1. CLOWN: Why there thou say'st, and the more pity that great folk

25         should have countenance° in this world to drown or hang
        themselves more than their even-Christen.° Come, my
        spade; there is no ancient gentlemen but gardeners,
        ditchers and grave-makers; they hold up Adam's profession.

    2. CLOWN: Was he a gentleman?

30   1. CLOWN: A' was the first that ever bore arms.°

    2. CLOWN: Why, he had none.

    1. CLOWN: What, art a heathen? How dost thou understand the
        Scripture? The Scripture says Adam digged; could he dig
        without arms? I'll put another question to thee; if thou

35         answerest me not to the purpose, confess thyself—

    2. CLOWN: Go to.

    1. CLOWN: What is he that builds stronger than either the mason, the
        shipwright, or the carpenter?

    2. CLOWN: The gallows-maker, for that frame outlives a thousand

40         tenants.

    1. CLOWN: I like thy wit well in good faith, the gallows does well, but
        how does it well? It does well to those that do ill. Now
        thou dost ill to say the gallows is built stronger than the
        church. Argal, the gallows may do well to thee.° To't

45         again, come.

    2. CLOWN: "Who builds stronger than a mason, a shipwright, or a
        carpenter?"

    1. CLOWN: Ay, tell me that, and unyoke.°

    2. CLOWN: Marry, now I can tell.

50   1. CLOWN: To't.

    2. CLOWN: Mass,° I cannot tell.

    1. CLOWN: Cudgel thy brains no more about it, for your dull ass will
        not mend his pace with beating, and when you are asked
        this question next, say "a grave-maker:" the houses he

55         makes last till doomsday. Go get thee to Yaughan,° and
        fetch me a stoup° of liquor.                *[Exit 2. Clown.]*

---

°15 *will he nill he*: will he or will he not (willy nilly). 20 *quest*: inquest. 25 *countenance*: privilege. 26 *even-Christen*: fellow Christian. 30 *arms*: (with a pun on "coat of arms"). 44 *to thee*: i.e., by hanging you. 48 *unyoke*: unharness (your wits, after this exertion). 51 *Mass*: by the mass. 55 *Yaughan*: probably a local innkeeper. 56 *stoup*: stein, drinking mug.

*Enter HAMLET and HORATIO afar off.*

1. CLOWN:  [*Sings.*] In youth when I did love, did love,
              Methought it was very sweet,
              To contract oh the time for a° my behove,°
              O methought there a was nothing a meet.°                          60

HAMLET:  Has this fellow no feeling of his business, that a'sings in
    grave-making?

HORATIO:  Custom hath made it in him a property of easiness.°

HAMLET:  'Tis e'en so, the hand of little employment hath the
    daintier sense.°                                                             65

1. CLOWN:  [*Sings.*] But age with his stealing steps
              Hath clawed me in his clutch,
              And hath shipped me intil° the land,
              As if I had never been such.                    [*Throws up a skull.*]

HAMLET:  That skull had a tongue in it, and could sing once: how the          70
    knave jowls° it to the ground, as if'twere Cain's jaw-bone,°
    that did the first murder. This might be the pate of a
    politician, which this ass now o'erreaches;° one that
    would circumvent° God, might it not?

HORATIO:  It might my lord.                                                      75

HAMLET:  Or of a courtier, which could say "Good morrow sweet
    lord, how dost thou good lord?" This might be my lord
    such-a-one, that praised my lord such-a-one's horse, when
    a'meant to beg it, might it not?

HORATIO:  It might my lord.                                                      80

HAMLET:  Why e'en so, and now my Lady Worm's, chopless,° and
    knocked about the mazzard° with a sexton's spade; here's
    fine revolution an° we had the trick° to see't. Did these
    bones cost no more the breeding, but to play at loggets°
    with them? Mine ache to think on't.                                         85

1. CLOWN:  [*Sings.*] A pick-axe and a spade, a spade,
              For and a shrouding sheet,
              O a pit of clay for to be made
              For such a guest is meet.°              [*Throws up another skull.*]
                                                                                 90

HAMLET:  There's another: why may not that be the skull of a
    lawyer? Where be his quiddities° now, his quillets,° his
    cases, his tenures,° and his tricks? Why does he suffer this
    rude knave now to knock him about the sconce° with a
    dirty shovel, and will not tell him of his action of battery?

---

°59 *oh, a:* (he grunts as he works). *behove:* benefit. 60 *meet:* suitable. 63 *Custom . . . easiness:* being accustomed to it has made him indifferent. 65 *daintier sense:* finer sensibility (being uncalloused). 68 *intil:* into. 71 *jowls:* casts (with obvious pun). *Cain's jaw-bone:* the jawbone of an ass with which Cain murdered Abel. 73 *o'erreaches:* (1) reaches over (2) gets the better of. 74 *would circumvent:* tried to outwit. 81 *chopless:* lacking the lower jaw. 82 *mazzard:* head. 83 *an:* if. *trick:* knack. 84 *loggets:* game in which small pieces of wood were thrown at fixed stakes. 89 *meet:* fitting. 91 *quiddities:* subtle definition. *quillets:* minute distinctions. 92 *tenures:* property holdings. 93 *sconce:* head.

95     Hum, this fellow might be in's time a great buyer of land,
       with his statutes,° his recognizances,° his fines,° his double
       vouchers,° his recoveries:° is this the fine° of his fines, and
       the recovery° of his recoveries, to have his fine pate full of
       fine dirt? Will his vouchers vouch him no more of his
100    purchases, and double ones too, than the length and
       breadth of a pair of indentures?° The very conveyances° of
       his lands will scarcely lie in this box,° and must th'inheritor°
       himself have no more, ha?
   HORATIO:  Not a jot more my lord.
105  HAMLET:  Is not parchment made of sheep-skins?
   HORATIO:  Ay my lord, and of calves'-skins too.
   HAMLET:  They are sheep and calves which seek out assurance° in
       that. I will speak to this fellow. Whose grave's this, sirrah?
   1. CLOWN:  Mine sir:
110       [*Sings.*] O a pit of clay for to be made
             For such a guest is meet.
   HAMLET:  I think it be thine indeed, for thou liest in't.
   1. CLOWN:  You lie out on't° sir, and therefore 'tis not yours; for my
       part I do not lie in't, and yet it is mine.
115  HAMLET:  Thou dost lie in't, to be in't and say it is thine: 'tis for the
       dead, not for the quick,° therefore thou liest.
   1. CLOWN:  'Tis a quick lie sir, 'twill away again from me to you.
   HAMLET:  What man dost thou dig it for?
   1. CLOWN:  For no man sir.
120  HAMLET:  What woman then?
   1. CLOWN:  For none neither.
   HAMLET:  Who is to be buried in't?
   1. CLOWN:  One that was a woman sir, but rest her soul she's dead.
   HAMLET:  How absolute° the knave is, we must speak by the card,° or
125     equivocation° will undo us. By the lord, Horatio, this
       three years I have took note of it, the age is grown so
       picked,° that the toe of the peasant comes so near the heel of
       the courtier, he galls his kibe.° How long hast thou been
       grave-maker?
130  1. CLOWN:  Of all the days i'th'year I came to't that day that our last
       king Hamlet overcame Fortinbras.
   HAMLET:  How long is that since?
   1. CLOWN:  Cannot you tell that? Every fool can tell that. It was the very
       day that young Hamlet was born: he that is mad and
135     sent into England.

---

°96 *statutes*: mortgages. *recognizances*: promissory bonds. 96–97 *fines, recoveries*: legal processes for transferring real estate. 97 *vouchers*: persons who vouched for a title to real estate. *fine*: end. 98 *recovery*: attainment. 100–101 *length . . . indentures*: contracts in duplicate, which spread out, would just cover his grave. 101 *conveyances*: deeds. 102 *box*: the grave. *inheritor*: owner. 107 *assurance*: (1) security (2) transfer of land. 113 *on*: of. 116 *quick*: living. 124 *absolute*: precise. *by the card*: exactly to the point (card on which compass points are marked). 125 *equivocation*: ambiguity. 127 *picked*: fastidious ("picky"). 128 *galls his kibe*: chafes the sore on the courtier's heel.

HAMLET: Ay marry, why was he sent into England?
1. CLOWN: Why because a' was mad: a' shall recover his wits there, or
    if a' do not, 'tis no great matter there.
HAMLET: Why?
1. CLOWN: 'Twill not be seen in him there, there the men are as mad        140
    as he.
HAMLET: How came he mad?
1. CLOWN: Very strangely they say.
HAMLET: How strangely?
1. CLOWN: Faith, e'en with losing his wits.        145
HAMLET: Upon what ground?
1. CLOWN: Why here in Denmark: I have been sexton here man and
    boy thirty years.
HAMLET: How long will a man lie i'th'earth ere he rot?
1. CLOWN: Faith, if a' be not rotten before a' die, as we have many       150
    pocky° corses nowadays that will scarce hold the laying in,
    a' will last you some eight year, or nine year. A tanner will
    last you nine year.
HAMLET: Why he more than another?
1. CLOWN: Why sir, his hide is so tanned with his trade, that a' will       155
    keep out water a great while; and your water is a sore°
    decayer of your whoreson dead body. Here's a skull now:
    this skull hath lain you i'th'earth three-and-twenty years.
HAMLET: Whose was it?
1. CLOWN: A whoreson mad fellow's it was, whose do you think it       160
    was?
HAMLET: Nay, I know not.
1. CLOWN: A pestilence on him for a mad rogue, a' poured a flagon of
    Rhenish° on my head once; this same skull sir, was sir,
    Yorick's skull, the king's jester.       165
HAMLET: This?
1. CLOWN: E'en that.
HAMLET: Let me see. [*Takes the skull.*] Alas poor Yorick, I knew him
    Horatio, a fellow of infinite jest, of most excellent fancy,°
    he hath borne me on his back a thousand times: and now       170
    how abhorred in my imagination it is: my gorge rises at it.
    Here hung those lips that I have kissed I know not how
    oft. Where be your gibes now? your gambols, your songs,
    your flashes of merriment, that were wont to set the table
    on a roar?° not one now to mock your own grinning? quite       175
    chop-fallen?° Now get you to my lady's chamber, and tell
    her, let her paint an inch thick, to this favour° she must
    come. Make her laugh at that. Prithee Horatio, tell me one
    thing.
HORATIO: What's that, my lord?       180

---

°151 *pocky*: rotten (with venereal disease). 156 *sore*: grievous. 164 *Rhenish*: Rhine wine. 169 *fancy*: imagination. 175 *on a roar*: roaring with laughter. 176 *chop-fallen*: (a) lacking a lower jaw (2) dejected, "down in the mouth." 177 *favour*: appearance.

HAMLET: Dost thou think Alexander looked o' this fashion
    i'th'earth?

HORATIO: E'en so.

HAMLET: And smelt so? pah.                 *[Puts down the skull.]*

185 HORATIO: E'en so my lord.

HAMLET: To what base uses we may return, Horatio. Why may not
    imagination trace the noble dust of Alexander, til a'find it
    stopping a bung-hole?°

HORATIO: 'Twere to consider too curiously,° to consider so.

190 HAMLET: No faith, not a jot, but to follow him thither with modesty°
    enough, and likelihood to lead it; as thus: Alexander died,
    Alexander was buried, Alexander returneth to dust, the
    dust is earth, of earth we make loam,° and why of that loam
    whereto he was converted, might they not stop a
195     beer-barrel?

        Imperious Caesar, dead and turned to clay,
        Might stop a hole to keep the wind away.
        O that that earth which kept the world in awe,
        Should patch a wall t'expel the winter's flaw.°

200     But soft, but soft awhile, here comes the king,
    The queen, the courtiers.

*Enter KING, QUEEN, LAERTES, [Doctor of Divinity], and a coffin, with Lords attendant.*

                         Who is this they follow?
    And with such maimèd° rites? This doth betoken
    The corse they follow did with desp'rate hand
    Fordo it° own life; 'twas of some estate.°
    Couch° we awhile, and mark.                 *[They retire.]*

205 HAMLET:                 That is Laertes,
    A very noble youth: mark.

LAERTES: What ceremony else?

DOCTOR: Her obsequies have been as far enlarged
    As we have warranty: her death was doubtful,°
210     And but that great command o'ersways the order,
    She should in ground unsanctified have lodged
    Til the last trumpet: for charitable prayers,
    Shards,° flints and pebbles should be thrown on her:
    Yet here she is allowed her virgin crants,°
215     Her maiden strewments,° and the bringing home
    Of° bell and burial.

LAERTES: Must there no more be done?

DOCTOR:                  No more be done:
    We should profane the service of the dead,

---

°188 *bung-hole*: hole in a cask. 189 *curiously*: minutely. 190 *modesty*: moderation. 193 *loam*: a clay mixture used as plaster. 199 *flaw*: windy gusts. 202 *maimèd*: abbreviated. 204 *Fordo it*: destroy its. *estate*: social rank. 205 *Couch*: hide. 209 *doubtful*: suspicious. 213 *Shards*: bits of broken pottery. 214 *crants*: garland. 215 *strewments*: flowers strewn on the grave. 215–16 *bringing home Of*: laying to rest with.

To sing sage requiem° and such rest to her
As to peace-parted souls.
LAERTES:                         Lay her i'th'earth,                        220
And from her fair and unpolluted flesh
May violets spring: I tell thee churlish priest,
A minist'ring angel shall my sister be,
When thou liest howling.
HAMLET:                         What, the fair Ophelia?
QUEEN: [*Scattering flowers.*] Sweets to the sweet, farewell.        225
I hoped thou shouldst have been my Hamlet's wife:
I thought thy bride-bed to have decked, sweet maid,
And not have strewed thy grave.
LAERTES:                         O treble woe
Fall ten times treble on that cursèd head
Whose wicked deed thy most ingenious sense °                        230
Deprived thee of. Hold off the earth awhile,
Till I have caught her once more in mine arms;        *Leaps in the grave.*
Now pile your dust upon the quick° and dead,
Till of this flat a mountain you have made
T'o'ertop old Pelion,° or the skyish head                        235
Of blue Olympus.
HAMLET: [*Comes forward.*] What is he whose grief
Bears such an emphasis? whose phrase of sorrow
Conjures the wand'ring stars,° and makes them stand
Like wonder-wounded hearers? This is I,                        240
Hamlet the Dane.                         *HAMLET leaps in after LAERTES.*
LAERTES: [*Grapples with him.*] The devil take thy soul.
HAMLET: Thou pray'st not well,
I prithee take thy fingers from my throat,
For though I am not splenitive° and rash,                        245
Yet have I in me something dangerous,
Which let thy wiseness fear; hold off thy hand.
KING: Pluck them asunder.
QUEEN:                         Hamlet, Hamlet!
ALL: Gentlemen!
HORATIO:        Good my lord, be quiet.
                         [*ATTENDANTS part them, and they come out of the grave.*]
HAMLET: Why, I will fight with him upon this theme                        250
Until my eyelids will no longer wag.
QUEEN: O my son, what theme?
HAMLET: I loved Ophelia, forty thousand brothers
Could not with all their quantity of love
Make up my sum. What wilt thou do for her?                        255
KING: O he is mad, Laertes.
QUEEN: For love of God, forbear° him.

---

°219 *sage requiem*: solemn dirge.   230 *sense*: mind.   233 *quick*: live.   235 *Pelion*: mountain (on which the Titans placed Mt. Ossa, to scale Mt. Olympus and reach the gods).   239 *Conjures . . . stars*: casts a spell over the planets.   245 *splenitive*: quick-tempered (anger was thought to originate in the spleen).   257 *forbear*: be patient with.

HAMLET: 'Swounds,° show me what thou't do:
　　Woo't° weep? woo't fight? woo't fast? woo't tear thyself?
260　Woo't drink up eisel?° eat a crocodile?°
　　I'll do't. Dost thou come here to whine?
　　To outface me with leaping in her grave?
　　Be buried quick with her, and so will I.
　　And if thou prate of mountains, let them throw
265　Millions of acres on us, till our ground,
　　Singeing his pate against the burning zone,°
　　Make Ossa° like a wart. Nay, an thou'lt mouth,
　　I'll rant as well as thou.
QUEEN:　　　　　　　　This is mere° madness,
　　And thus awhile the fit will work on him:
270　Anon as patient as the female dove
　　When that her golden couplets° are disclosed,
　　His silence will sit drooping.
HAMLET:　　　　　　　　Hear you sir,
　　What is the reason that you use me thus?
　　I loved you ever; but it is no matter.
275　Let Hercules himself do what he may,
　　The cat will mew, and dog will have his day.
KING:　I pray thee good Horatio, wait upon him.　　　　　*Exit* HAMLET.
　　[*Aside to Laertes.*] Strengthen your patience in our last night's speech,　　[HORATIO *follows.*]
　　We'll put the matter to the present push°—
280　Good Gertrude, set some watch over your son—
　　This grave shall have a living monument.°
　　An hour of quiet shortly shall we see,
　　Till then, in patience our proceeding be.　　　　　　*Exeunt.*

## Scene 2. [A hall in the castle]

*Enter* HAMLET *and* HORATIO.

HAMLET:　So much for this sir, now shall you see the other;
　　You do remember all the circumstance.
HORATIO:　Remember it my lord!
HAMLET:　Sir, in my heart there was a kind of fighting
5　That would not let me sleep; methought I lay
　　Worse than the mutines in the bilboes.° Rashly—
　　And praised be rashness for it: let us know,
　　Our indiscretion sometimes serves us well
　　When our deep plots do pall,° and that should learn us
10　There's a divinity that shapes our ends,
　　Rough-hew them how we will—

---

°258 *'Swounds:* corruption of "God's wounds." 259 *Woo't:* wilt thou. 260 *eisel:* vinegar (thought to reduce anger and encourage melancholy). *crocodile:* (associated with hypocritical tears). 266 *burning zone:* sun's sphere. 267 *Ossa:* see p. 1069, line 235n. 268 *mere:* absolute. 271 *golden couplets:* fuzzy yellow twin fledglings. 279 *present push:* immediate test. 281 *living monument:* (1) lasting tombstone (2) living sacrifice (Hamlet) to memorialize it. 6 *mutines . . . bilboes:* mutineers in shackles. 9 *pall:* fail.

HORATIO:                                   That is most certain.
HAMLET:  Up from my cabin,
    My sea-gown° scarfed about me, in the dark
    Groped I to find out them, had my desire,
    Fingered° their packet, and in fine° withdrew                                    15
    To mine own room again, making so bold,
    My fears forgetting manners, to unseal
    Their grand commission; where I found, Horatio—
    Ah royal knavery—an exact command,
    Larded° with many several sorts of reasons,                                    20
    Importing Denmark's health, and England's too,
    With ho, such bugs and goblins in my life,°
    That on the supervise,° no leisure bated,°
    No, not to stay° the grinding of the axe,
    My head should be struck off.
HORATIO:                                   Is't possible?
HAMLET:  Here's the commission, read it at more leisure.                            25
    But wilt thou hear now how I did proceed?
HORATIO:  I beseech you.
HAMLET:  Being thus be-netted round with villainies,
    Ere I could make a prologue to my brains,                                       30
    They had begun the play.° I sat me down,
    Devised a new commission, wrote it fair°—
    I once did hold it, as our statists° do,
    A baseness° to write fair, and laboured much
    How to forget that learning, but sir now                                        35
    It did me yeoman's° service: wilt thou know
    Th'effect of what I wrote?
HORATIO:                                   Ay, good my lord.
HAMLET:  An earnest conjuration° from the king,
    As England was his faithful tributary,
    As love between them like the palm might flourish,                             40
    As peace should still her wheaten garland wear
    And stand a comma° 'tween their amities,
    And many such like "as'es"° of great charge,°
    That on the view and know of these contents,
    Without debatement further, more or less,                                       45
    He should those bearers put to sudden death,
    Not shriving° time allowed.
HORATIO:                                   How was this sealed?

---

°13 *sea-gown*: short-sleeved knee-length gown worn by seamen. 15 *Fingered*: got my fingers on. *in fine*: to finish. 20 *Larded*: embellished. 22 *bugs . . . life*: imaginary evils attributed to me, like imaginary goblins ("bugs") meant to frighten children. 23 *supervise*: looking over (the commission). *leisure bated*: delay excepted. 24 *stay*: await. 30–31 *Ere . . . play*: Before I could outline the action in my mind, my brains started to play their part. 32 *wrote it fair*: wrote a finished (neat) copy, a "fair copy." 33 *statists*: statesmen. 34 *baseness*: mark of humble status. 36 *yeoman's*: (in the sense of "faithful"). 38 *conjuration*: entreaty (he parodies the rhetoric of such documents). 42 *comma*: connection. 43 *as'es*: (1) the "as" clauses in the commission (2) asses. *charge*: (1) weight (in the clauses) (2) burdens (on the asses). 47 *shriving*: confession and absolution.

HAMLET:  Why even in that was heaven ordinant,°
    I had my father's signet° in my purse,
50    Which was the model° of that Danish seal:
    Folded the writ up in the form of th'other,
    Subscribed° it, gave't th'impression,° placed it safely,
    The changeling° never known: now the next day
    Was our sea-fight, and what to this was sequent
55    Thou knowest already.
HORATIO:  So Guildenstern and Rosencrantz go to't.
HAMLET:  Why man, they did make love to this employment,°
    They are not near my conscience, their defeat
    Does by their own insinuation° grow:
60    'Tis dangerous when the baser nature comes
    Between the pass° and fell° incensed points
    Of mighty opposites.
HORATIO:                  Why, what a king is this!
HAMLET:  Does it not, think thee, stand me now upon°—
    He that hath killed my king, and whored my mother,
65    Popped in between th'election° and my hopes,
    Thrown out his angle° for my proper° life,
    And with such cozenage°—is't not perfect conscience
    To quit° him with this arm? And isn't not to be damned,
    To let this canker of our nature° come
70    In further evil?
HORATIO:  It must be shortly known to him from England
    What is the issue of the business there.
HAMLET:  It will be short, the interim is mine,
    And a man's life's no more than to say "One."°
75    But I am very sorry good Horatio,
    That to Laertes I forgot myself;
    For by the image of my cause, I see
    The portraiture of his;° I'll court his favours:
    But sure the bravery° of his grief did put me
    Into a towering passion.
80  HORATIO:              Peace, who comes here?

*Enter young* OSRIC.

OSRIC:  Your lordship is right welcome back to Denmark.
HAMLET:  I humbly thank you sir. [*Aside to Horatio.*] Dost know this
    water-fly?
HORATIO:  No my good lord.

---

°48 *was heaven ordinant*: it was divinely ordained. 49 *signet*: seal. 50 *model*: replica. 52 *Subscribed*: signed. *impression*: i.e., of the seal. 53 *changeling*: substitute (baby imp left when an infant was spirited away). 57 *did . . . employment*: asked for it. 59 *insinuation*: intrusion. 61 *pass*: thrust. *fell*: fierce. 63 *stand . . . upon*: become incumbent upon me now. 65 *election*: (the Danish king was so chosen). 66 *angle*: fishing hook. *proper*: very own. 67 *cozenage*: deception. 68 *quit*: repay, requite. 69 *canker of our nature*: cancer of humanity. 74 *to say "One"*: to score one hit in fencing. 77–78 *by the image . . . his*: in the depiction of my situation, I see the reflection of his. 79 *bravery*: ostentation.

HAMLET: Thy state is the more gracious,° for 'tis a vice to know him:  85
    he hath much land, and fertile: let a beast be lord of beasts,
    and his crib shall stand at the king's mess;° 'tis a chough,°
    but as I say, spacious in the possession of dirt.
OSRIC: Sweet lord, if you lordship were at leisure, I should
    impart a thing to you from his majesty.  90
HAMLET: I will receive it sir, with all diligence of spirit; put your
    bonnet° to his right use, 'tis for the head.
OSRIC: I thank your lordship, it is very hot.
HAMLET: No, believe me 'tis very cold, the wind is northerly.
OSRIC: It is indifferent° cold my lord indeed.  95
HAMLET: But yet methinks it is very sultry and hot for my
    complexion.°
OSRIC: Exceedingly, my lord, it is very sultry, as 'twere, I cannot
    tell how: but my lord, his majesty bade me signify to you
    that a' has laid a great wager on your head. Sir, this is the  100
    matter—
HAMLET: [*Moves him to put on his hat.*] I beseech you remember—
OSRIC: Nay good my lord, for mine ease,° in good faith. Sir, here
    is newly come to court Laertes, believe me, an absolute
    gentleman, full of most excellent differences,° of very soft  105
    society, and great showing: indeed to speak feelingly of
    him, he is the card° or calendar of gentry: for you shall find
    in him the continent of what part a gentleman would see.°
HAMLET: Sir, his definement° suffers no perdition° in you, though I
    know to divide him inventorially would dozy°  110
    th'arithmetic of memory, and yet but yaw neither, in
    respect of his quick sail,° but in the verity of extolment,° I
    take him to be a soul of great article,° and his infusion° of
    such dearth and rareness, as to make true diction of him,
    his semblable° is his mirror, and who else would trace° him,  115
    his umbrage,° nothing more.°
OSRIC: Your lordship speaks most infallibly of him.
HAMLET: The concernancy° sir? why do we wrap the gentleman in
    our more rawer breath?°
OSRIC: Sir?  120
HORATIO: Is't not possible to understand in another tongue?° You
    will do't sir, really.

---

°85 *gracious:* favorable. 86–87 *let a beast . . . mess:* An ass who owns enough property can eat with the king. 87 *chough:* chattering bird, jackdaw. 92 *bonnet:* hat. 95 *indifferent:* reasonably. 97 *complexion:* temperament. 103 *for mine ease:* for my own comfort. 105 *differences:* accomplishments. 107 *card:* shipman's compass card. 108 *continent . . . see:* (continuing the marine metaphor) (1) geographical continent (2) all the qualities a gentleman would look for. 109–16 *Sir . . . more:* (Hamlet outdoes Osric in affected speech). 109 *definement:* description. *perdition:* loss. 110 *dozy:* dizzy. 111–12 *yaw . . . sail:* (1) moving in an unsteady course (as another boat would do, trying to catch up with Laertes "quick sail") (2) staggering to one trying to list his accomplishments. 112 *in . . . extolment:* to praise him truthfully. 113 *article:* scope. *infusion:* essence. 114–16 *as to make . . . more:* to describe him truly I would have to employ his mirror to depict his only equal—himself, and who would follow him is only a shadow. 115 *semblable:* equal. *trace:* (1) describe (2) follow. 116 *umbrage:* shadow. 118 *concernancy:* relevance. 119 *rawer breath:* crude speech. 121 *Is't not . . . tongue:* Cannot Osric understand his own way of speaking when used by another?

HAMLET: What imports the nomination° of this gentleman?

OSRIC: Of Laertes?

125 HORATIO: His purse is empty already, all's golden words are spent.

HAMLET: Of him, sir.

OSRIC: I know you are not ignorant—

HAMLET: I would you did sir, yet in faith if you did, it would not
much approve me.° Well, sir.

130 OSRIC: You are not ignorant of what excellence Laertes is—

HAMLET: I dare not confess that, lest I should compare with him in
excellence, but to know a man well were to know himself.°

OSRIC: I mean sir for his weapon, but in the imputation° laid on
him by them in his meed,° he's unfellowed.°

135 HAMLET: What's his weapon?

OSRIC: Rapier and dagger.

HAMLET: That's two of his weapons—but well.

OSRIC: The king sir, hath wagered with him six Barbary horses,
against which he has impawned,° as I take it, six French

140 rapiers and poniards,° with their assigns,° as girdle, hangers,°
and so. Three of the carriages° in faith are very dear to
fancy,° very responsive to the hilts, most delicate carriages,
and of very liberal conceit.°

HAMLET: What call you the carriages?

145 HORATIO: I knew you must be edified by the margent° ere you had
done.

OSRIC: The carriages sir, are the hangers.

HAMLET: The phrase would be more germane to the matter, if we
could carry a cannon by our sides: I would it might be

150 hangers till then, but on: six Barbary horses against six
French swords, their assigns, and three liberal-conceited
carriages—that's the French bet against the Danish. Why
is this all "impawned" as you call it?

OSRIC: The king sir, hath laid sir, that in a dozen passes between

155 yourself and him, he shall not exceed you three hits°; he
hath laid on twelve for nine, and it would come to
immediate trial, if your lordship would vouchsafe the
answer.°

HAMLET: How if I answer no?

160 OSRIC: I mean my lord, the opposition of your person in trial.

HAMLET: Sir, I will walk here in the hall; if it please his majesty, it is
the breathing time° of day with me; let the foils be brought,
the gentleman willing, and the king hold his purpose, I
will win for him an I can, if not, I will gain nothing but my

165 shame and the odd hits.

---

°123 *nomination:* naming. 128–129 *if you did . . . me:* If you found me to be "not ignorant," it would prove little (as you are no judge of ignorance).
132 *to know . . . himself:* to know a man well, one must first know oneself. 133 *imputation:* repute. 134 *meed:* worth. *unfellowed:* unequaled.
139 *impawned:* staked. 140 *poniards:* daggers. *assigns:* accessories. *girdle, hangers:* belt, straps attached thereto, from which swords were
hung. 141 *carriages:* hangers. 141–42 *dear to fancy:* rare in design. 143 *liberal conceit:* elaborate conception. 145 *margent:* marginal note.
154–55 *laid . . . three hits:* wagered that in twelve bouts Laertes must win three more than Hamlet. 158 *answer:* acceptance of the challenge (Hamlet interprets as "reply"). 162 *breathing time:* exercise period.

OSRIC: Shall I re-deliver you° e'en so?

HAMLET: To this effect sir, after what flourish your nature will.°

OSRIC: I commend° my duty to your lordship.

HAMLET: Yours, yours.                    [*Exit* OSRIC.]
    He does well to commend it himself, there are no tongues           170
    else for's turn.°

HORATIO: This lapwing° runs away with the shell on his head.

HAMLET: A' did comply° sir, with his dug° before a' sucked it: thus
    has he—and many more of the same bevy that I know the
    drossy° age dotes on—only got the tune of the time, and           175
    out of an habit of encounter,° a kind of yeasty collection,°
    which carries them through and through the most fond
    and winnowed° opinions; and do but blow them to their
    trial, and bubbles are out.°

*Enter a* LORD.

LORD: My lord, his majesty commended him to you by young           180
    Osric, who brings back to him that you attend him in
    the hall. He sends to know if your pleasure hold to play
    with Laertes, or that you will take longer time.

HAMLET: I am constant to my purposes, they follow the king's
    pleasure, if his fitness speaks,° mine is ready: now or           185
    whensoever, provided I be so able as now.

LORD: The king, and queen, and all are coming down.

HAMLET: In happy time.

LORD: The queen desires you to use some gentle entertainment°
    to Laertes, before you fall to play.           190

HAMLET: She well instructs me.                    [*Exit* LORD.]

HORATIO: You will lose this wager, my lord.

HAMLET: I do not think so, since we went into France, I have been in
    continual practice, I shall win at the odds; but thou
    wouldst not think how ill all's here about my heart: but it           195
    is no matter.

HORATIO: Nay good my lord—

HAMLET: It is but a foolery, but it is such a kind of gaingiving° as
    would perhaps trouble a woman.

HORATIO: If your mind dislike any thing, obey it. I will forestall their           200
    repair° hither, and say you are not fit.

HAMLET: Not a whit, we defy augury;° there is a special providence
    in the fall of a sparrow.° If it be now, 'tis not to come:

---

°166 *re-deliver you*: take back your answer. 167 *after . . . will*: embellished as you wish. 168 *commend*: offer (Hamlet interprets as "praise"). 170–71 *no tongues . . . turn*: no others who would. 172 *lapwing*: (reported to be so precocious that it ran as soon as hatched). 173 *comply*: observe the formalities of courtesy. *dug*: mother's breast. 175 *drossy*: frivolous. 176 *habit of encounter*: habitual association (with others as frivolous). *yeasty collection*: frothy assortment of phrases. 177–78 *fond and winnowed*: trivial and considered. 178–79 *blow . . . out*: blow on them to test them and they are gone. 185 *his fitness speaks*: it agrees with his convenience. 189 *gentle entertainment*: friendly treatment. 198 *gaingiving*: misgiving 201 *repair*: coming. 202 *augury*: omens. 202–3 *special . . . sparrow*: ("Are not two sparrows sold for a farthing? and one of them shall not fall on the ground without your Father": Matthew 10:29).

205

if it be not to come, it will be now; if it be not now,
yet it will come—the readiness is all. Since no man has
aught of what he leaves, what is't to leave betimes?° let
be.

*A table prepared. Trumpets, Drums, and officers with cushions. Enter* KING, QUEEN, *and all the state,*
[OSRIC], *foils, daggers, and* LAERTES.

KING:  Come Hamlet, come and take this hand from me.
    [*Puts Laertes' hand into Hamlet's.*]

210

HAMLET:  Give me your pardon sir, I have done you wrong,
    But pardon't as you are a gentleman.
    This presence knows, and you must needs have heard,
    How I am punished with a sore distraction.°
    What I have done
    That might your nature, honour, and exception°

215

    Roughly awake, I here proclaim was madness:
    Was't Hamlet wronged Laertes? never Hamlet.
    If Hamlet from himself be ta'en away,
    And when he's not himself, does wrong Laertes,
    Then Hamlet does it not, Hamlet denies it:

220

    Who does it then? his madness. If't be so,
    Hamlet is of the faction that is wronged,
    His madness is poor Hamlet's enemy.
    Sir, in this audience,
    Let my disclaiming from a purposed evil,

225

    Free me so far in your most generous thoughts,
    That I have shot my arrow o'er the house
    And hurt my brother.°

LAERTES:              I am satisfied in nature,
    Whose motive in this case should stir me most
    To my revenge, but in my terms of honour

230

    I stand aloof, and will no reconcilement,
    Till by some elder masters of known honour
    I have a voice and precedent° of peace
    To keep my name ungored:° but till that time,
    I do receive your offered love, like love,
    And will not wrong it.

235 HAMLET:            I embrace it freely,
    And will this brother's wager frankly° play.
    Give us the foils: come on.

LAERTES:             Come, one for me.

HAMLET:  I'll be your foil° Laertes, in mine ignorance
    Your skill shall like a star i'th' darkest night
    Stick fiery off° indeed.

---

°206 *betimes*: early (before one's time).  212 *sore distraction*: grievous madness.  214 *exception*: disapproval.  226–27 *That I have . . . brother.* (that
it was accidental).  232 *voice and precedent*: opinion based on precedent.  233 *name ungored*: reputation uninjured. Laertes says that he cannot accept Hamlet's apology formally until he is assured that his acceptance will not harm his honor or damage his reputation.  236 *frankly*: freely.  238 *foil*:
(1) the blunted sword with which they fence (2) leaf of metal set under a jewel to make it shine more brilliantly.  240 *Stick fiery off*: show in shining
contrast.

| | | |
|---|---|---|
| LAERTES: | You mock me sir. | 240 |

HAMLET:  No, by this hand.

KING:  Give them the foils young Osric. Cousin° Hamlet,
    You know the wager.

HAMLET:                      Very well my lord.
    Your grace has laid the odds o'th'weaker side.

KING:  I do not fear it, I have seen you both,                245
    But since he is bettered,° we have therefore odds.

LAERTES:  This is too heavy: let me see another.°

HAMLET:  This likes° me well, these foils have all a° length?

OSRIC:  Ay my good lord.                                *Prepare to play.*

KING:  Set me the stoups° of wine upon that table:         250
    If Hamlet give the first or second hit,
    Or quit in answer of° the third exchange,
    Let all the battlements their ordnance fire.
    The king shall drink to Hamlet's better breath,
    And in the cup an union° shall he throw,             255
    Richer than that which four successive kings
    In Denmark's crown have worn: give me the cups,
    And let the kettle° to the trumpet speak,
    The trumpet to the cannoneer without,
    The cannons to the heavens, the heaven to earth,    260
    "Now the king drinks to Hamlet." Come begin.
    And you the judges bear a wary eye.              *Trumpets the while.*

HAMLET:  Come on sir.

LAERTES:             Come my lord.                   *They play.*

HAMLET:                    One.

LAERTES:                    No.

HAMLET:                  Judgment.

OSRIC:  A hit, a very palpable hit.

                         *Flourish. Drum, trumpets and shot. A piece° goes off.*

LAERTES:             Well, again.

KING:  Stay, give me drink. Hamlet, this pearl is thine.    265
    Here's to thy health: give him the cup.

HAMLET:  I'll play this bout first, set it by a while.
    Come.                                      *[They play.]*
         Another hit. What say you?

LAERTES:  A touch, a touch, I do confess't.

KING:  Our son shall win.                               270

QUEEN:            He's fat° and scant of breath.
    Here Hamlet, take my napkin,° rub thy brows.    *[She takes HAMLET's cup.]*
    The queen carouses° to thy fortune, Hamlet.

HAMLET:  Good madam.

KING:             Gertrude, do not drink.

QUEEN:  I will my lord, I pray you pardon me.

---

°242 *Cousin:* kinsman.  246 *bettered:* either (a) judged to be better, or (b) better trained.  247 *another:* (the unbated and poisoned sword).  248 *likes:* pleases. *all a:* all the same.  250 *stoups:* goblets.  252 *quit in answer of:* score a draw in.  255 *union:* large pearl.  258 *kettle:* kettledrum.  264.1 S.D.: *piece:* i.e., a cannon.  270 *fat:* sweating (sweat was thought to be melted body fat).  271 *napkin:* handkerchief.  272 *carouses:* drinks.

275  KING: [*Aside.*] It is the poisoned cup, it is too late.
HAMLET: I dare not drink yet madam: by and by.
QUEEN: Come, let me wipe thy face.
LAERTES: [*To the King.*] My lord, I'll hit him now.
KING:                                    I do not think't.
LAERTES: [*Aside.*] And yet 'tis almost 'gainst my conscience.
280  HAMLET: Come for the third Laertes, you do but dally,
      I pray you pass° with your best violence,
      I am afeard you make a wanton of me.°
LAERTES: Say you so? Come on.                                    *Play.*
OSRIC: Nothing neither way                              [*They break off.*]
LAERTES: Have at you now.°                              [*Wounds Hamlet.*]

                                    *In scuffling they change rapiers.*

285  KING:                    Part them, they are incensed.
HAMLET: Nay, come again.                              [*The* QUEEN *falls.*]
OSRIC:                    Look to the queen there, ho!

                                    [HAMLET *wounds* LAERTES.]

HORATIO: They bleed on both side. How is it, my lord?
OSRIC: How is't, Laertes?
LAERTES: Why as a woodcock° to my own springe,° Osric,
290      I am justly killed with mine own treachery.
HAMLET: How does the queen?
KING:                    She sounds° to see them bleed.
QUEEN: No, no, the drink, the drink, O my dear Hamlet,
      The drink, the drink, I am poisoned.                    [*Dies.*]
HAMLET: O villainy! ho! let the door be locked,
295      Treachery, seek it out!
LAERTES: It is here Hamlet. Hamlet, thou art slain,
      No medicine in the world can do thee good,
      In thee there is not half an hour of life,
      The treacherous instrument is in thy hand,
300      Unbated° and envenomed. The foul practice°
      Hath turned itself on me, lo, here I lie
      Never to rise again: thy mother's poisoned:
      I can no more: the king, the king's to blame.
HAMLET: The point envenomed too:
305      Then venom, to thy work.                    *Hurts the* KING.
ALL: Treason! treason!
KING: O yet defend me friends, I am but hurt.°
HAMLET: Here, thou incestuous, murderous, damnèd Dane,
      Drink off this potion: is thy union here?
      Follow my mother.                              KING *dies.*
310  LAERTES:          He is justly served,
      It is a poison tempered° by himself:

---

°281 *pass:* thrust. 282 *make a wanton of me:* are indulging me like a spoiled child. 285 *Have . . . now:* (the bout is over when Laertes attacks Hamlet and catches him off guard). 289 *woodcock:* snipe-like bird (believed to be foolish and therefore easily trapped). *springe:* trap. 291 *sounds:* swoons. 300 *Unbated:* not blunted. *practice:* plot. 307 *but hurt:* only wounded. 311 *tempered:* mixed.

Exchange forgiveness with me, noble Hamlet,
Mine and my father's death come not upon thee,°
Nor thine on me.                                                                              *Dies.*
HAMLET:  Heaven make thee free° of it, I follow thee.                             315
I am dead, Horatio; wretched queen, adieu.
You that look pale, and tremble at this chance,
That are but mutes,° or audience to this act,
Had I but time, as this fell sergeant° Death
Is strict in his arrest, O I could tell you—                                           320
But let it be; Horatio, I am dead,
Thou livest, report me and my cause aright
To the unsatisfied.°
HORATIO:  Never believe it;
I am more an antique Roman° than a Dane:                                          325
Here's yet some liquor left.
HAMLET:                                    As thou'rt a man,
Give me the cup, let go, by heaven I'll ha't.
O God, Horatio, what a wounded name,
Things standing thus unknown, shall live behind me.
If thou didst ever hold me in thy heart,                                               330
Absènt thee from felicity awhile,
And in this harsh world draw thy breath in pain
To tell my story.                                *A march afar off, and shot within.*
                              What warlike noise is this?
OSRIC:  Young Fortinbras with conquest come from Poland,
To th'ambassadors of England gives                                                    335
This warlike volley.
HAMLET:                              O I die Horatio,
The potent poison quite o'er-crows° my spirit,
I cannot live to hear the news from England,
But I do prophesy th'election° lights
On Fortinbras, he has my dying voice,°                                               340
So tell him, with th'occurrents more and less °
Which have solicited°—the rest is silence.                                         *Dies.*
HORATIO:  Now cracks a noble heart: good night sweet prince,
And flights of angels sing thee to thy rest.
Why does the drum come hither?                                                       345

*Enter FORTINBRAS and English Ambassadors, with drum, colours, and attendants.*

FORTINBRAS:  Where is this sight?
HORATIO:                                        What is it you would see?
If aught of woe, or wonder, cease your search.
FORTINBRAS:  This quarry cries on havoc.° O proud death,
What feast is toward° in thine eternal cell,

---

°313 *come . . . thee:* are not to be blamed on you. 315 *free:* guiltless. 318 *mutes:* actors without speaking parts. 319 *fell sergeant:* cruel sheriff's officer. 323 *unsatisfied:* uninformed. 325 *antique Roman:* ancient Roman (who considered suicide honorable). 337 *o'er-crows:* overpowers, conquers. 339 *election:* (for king of Denmark). 340 *voice:* vote. 341 *occurrents more and less:* events great and small. 342 *solicited:* incited me. 348 *quarry . . . havoc:* heap of dead bodies proclaims slaughter done here. 349 *toward:* in preparation.

350        That thou so many princes at a shot
            So bloodily hast struck?
       AMBASSADOR:                The sight is dismal,
            And our affairs from England come too late;
            The ears° are senseless that should give us hearing,
            To tell him his commandment is fulfilled,
355        That Rosencrantz and Guildenstern are dead:
            Where should we have our thanks?
       HORATIO:                     Not from his mouth,
            Had it th'ability of life to thank you;
            He never gave commandment for their death;
            But since so jump° upon this bloody question,
360        You from the Polack wars, and you from England
            Are here arrived, give order that these bodies
            High on a stage be placèd to the view,
            And let me speak to th'yet unknowing world
            How these things came about; so shall you hear
365        Of carnal, bloody and unnatural acts,
            Of accidental judgments, casual° slaughters,
            Of deaths put on° by cunning and forced cause, °
            And in this upshot, purposes mistook,
            Fall'n on th'inventors' heads:° all this can I
            Truly deliver.
370 FORTINBRAS:        Let us haste to hear it,
            And call the noblest to the audience.
            For me, with sorrow I embrace my fortune;
            I have some rights of memory° in this kingdom,
            Which now to claim my vantage° doth invite me.
375 HORATIO:  Of that I shall have also cause to speak,
            And from his mouth whose voice will draw on more: °
            But let this same° be presently performed,
            Even while men's minds are wild,° lest more mischance
            On° plots and errors happen.
       FORTINBRAS:                Let four captains
380        Bear Hamlet like a soldier to the stage,
            For he was likely, had he been put on,°
            To have proved most royal; and for his passage,°
            The soldiers' music and the rite of war
            Speak loudly for him:
385        Take up the bodies, such a sight as this,
            Becomes the field, but here shows much amiss.
            Go bid the soldiers shoot.

*Exeunt marching: after the which a peal of ordnance are shot off.*

---

°353 *ears*: (of Claudius). 359 *jump*: opportunely. 366 *casual*: unpremeditated. 367 *put on*: prompted by. *forced cause*: being forced to act in self-defense. 368–369 *purposes . . . heads*: plots gone wrong and destroying their inventors. 373 *of memory*: remembered. 374 *vantage*: advantageous position. 376 *draw on more*: influence more (votes). 377 *this same*: this telling of the story. 378 *wild*: upset. 379 *On*: on top of. 381 *put on*: i.e., put on the throne. 382 *passage*: i.e., to the next world.

## Questions

1. *Act 1.* How do you learn in the first scene that something is wrong in Denmark?
2. In scene 2, how does Claudius appear? Does he seem rational? Good? A good administrator? A competent ruler? A loving husband and uncle?
3. What does Hamlet reveal about his own mental and psychological state in his first soliloquy?
4. Why do both Laertes and Polonius caution Ophelia about Hamlet's interest in her?
5. What does the Ghost tell Hamlet to do and not to do? Why does Hamlet believe he needs independent proof about the validity of the Ghost?
6. *Act 2.* Who is Polonius? What is his analysis of Hamlet's "madness"? What do his speeches show us about him?
7. Describe Hamlet's self-accusation in the "O What a Rogue" soliloquy (2.2.524–80). To what degree is his accusation justified?
8. *Act 3.* How do you react to Hamlet's treatment of Ophelia in Act 3, Scene 1? What evidence suggests that he knows he is being watched by Claudius and Polonius?
9. What does Hamlet think of Claudius's reaction to "The Murder of Gonzago"? Why does Claudius not react to the dumb-show before the play-within-a-play?
10. Why does Hamlet not kill Claudius when the King is at prayer?
11. Describe Hamlet's treatment of Gertrude during their confrontation in her private room? Is Hamlet justified in his treatment? Why does the Ghost appear here?
12. *Act 4.* How are Laertes's wishes for revenge like Hamlet's wishes for revenge?
13. How does Claudius plan to use Laertes's desire for vengeance against Hamlet? To what extent does Laertes allow himself to be used?
14. *Act 5.* Comic relief is a humorous episode designed to ease tension. How does the scene of the gravediggers qualify as comic relief? Why is comic relief appropriate at this point of the play? How does the scene broaden the play's themes?
15. Describe the lessons that Hamlet tells Horatio he has learned about life. How does this understanding show that Hamlet has changed? Why is it ironic?
16. How is Gertrude killed? Hamlet? Laertes? Claudius? Why does Hamlet insist that Horatio not commit suicide?

## General Questions

1. Describe Claudius. Is he purely evil, or is he merely a flawed human being? Could the play also be called "The Tragedy of Claudius, King of Denmark"?
2. Characterize Horatio. Why does Hamlet trust and admire him? How is he different from Rosencrantz and Guildenstern? Are these characters round or flat? How can one justify Hamlet's arrangement for the deaths of R & G?
3. *Hamlet* is full of conflicts that oppose people to other people, to society, and to themselves. List all the conflicts you can find in the play. Decide which of these is the central conflict, and explain your choice.
4. What is the crisis of *Hamlet*? When does it occur? Whom does it affect? What is the catastrophe? The Resolution?
5. In Act 4, Claudius notes that "sorrows come . . . in battalions." By the end of the play these sorrows include the deaths of all the major characters except Horatio. To what degree can Claudius be held responsible for all the sorrows of the play? Which sorrows may be particularly traced to Hamlet?

6. How does Shakespeare demonstrate that *Hamlet* is a tragedy of the state as well as the individual? Is the condition of Denmark better or worse at the end of the play than at the beginning?

## WRITING ABOUT TRAGEDY

As you plan and write an essay about tragedy, keep in mind all the elements of drama. A full discussion of traditional approaches to these elements—plot, character, point of view, setting, language, tone, symbol, and theme—is found in Chapter 20. Review this material before you begin your essay.

Although the basic elements remain consistent in tragedy, the form requires a few special considerations. In planning to write about plot and conflict, you might explore the crisis or climax—that point at which the downfall becomes inevitable. Similarly, you might consider the degree to which the conflicts shape or accelerate the tragic action. With character, pay special attention to the tragic protagonist and the major antagonists: What is the connection between the protagonist's strengths and weaknesses? To what extent does the protagonist bring about or cooperate with his or her own destruction? What key characteristics and behavior patterns ensure both the protagonist's heroic stature and fall? In dealing with tone, consider the degree to which the play is ironic. Do you know more about what is going on than the protagonist? Than most of the characters? If so, how does your knowledge affect your understanding of the play?

Along with these considerations, all the traditional elements of drama can provide fruitful essays about tragic drama. Here, however, we introduce an additional way of writing about literature: an examination of a problem. This approach can be employed to write about prose fiction, poetry, or any type of dramatic literature. Our discussion will naturally focus on tragedy—specifically *Hamlet*—and the plays in which problem solving can generate effective essays about tragic drama.

### An Essay About a Problem

A **problem** is any question put before you that you cannot answer easily and correctly. The question "Who is the major character in *Hamlet*?" is not a problem, because the obvious answer is Hamlet. Let us, however, ask another question: "Why is it *correct* to say that Hamlet is the major character?" This question is not as easy as the first, and for this reason it creates a problem. It requires that we think about our answer, even though we do not need to search very far. Hamlet is the title character. He is involved in most of the actions of the play. He is so much the center of our liking and concern that his death causes sadness and regret. To "solve" this problem has required a set of responses, all of which provide answers to the question "Why?"

More complex, however, and more typical of most problems, are questions like these: "Why does Hamlet talk of suicide in his first soliloquy?" "Why does he treat Ophelia so coarsely in the 'nunnery' scene?" "Why does he delay in avenging his father's death?" "Why does he so immediately and uncritically accept Laertes's challenge to the concluding duel?" Essays on a problem are normally concerned with such questions, because they require a good deal of thought, together with a number of interpretations knitted together into a whole essay. More broadly, dealing with problems is one of the major tasks of the intellectual, scientific, social, and political disciplines. Being able to advance and then explain solutions is therefore one of the most important techniques that you can acquire.

## Strategies for Organizing Ideas

Your first purpose is to convince your reader that your solution is a good one. This you do by making sound conclusions from supporting evidence. In nonscientific subjects such as literature, you rarely find absolute proofs, so your conclusions will not be *proved* in the way you prove triangles congruent in geometry. But your organization, your use of facts from the text, your interpretations, and your application of general or specific knowledge should all make your conclusions convincing. Thus your basic strategy is *persuasion*.

1. *Demonstrate that conditions for a solution are fulfilled.* This type of development is the most basic in writing—namely, illustration. You first explain that certain conditions need to exist for your solution to be plausible. Your central idea—really a brief answer to the question—is that the conditions do indeed exist. Your development is to show how the conditions can be found in the work.

   Suppose that you are writing on the problem of why Hamlet delays revenge against Claudius. Suppose also that you make the point that Hamlet delays because he is never sure that Claudius is guilty. This is your "solution" to the problem. In your essay you support your answer by challenging the credibility of the information Hamlet receives about the crime (i.e., the two visits from the Ghost and Claudius's distress at the play within the play). Once you have "attacked" these sources of data on the grounds that they are unreliable, you have succeeded because your solution is consistent with the details of the play.

2. *Analyze words in the phrasing of the problem.* Your object in this approach is to clarify important words in the statement of the problem, then to decide how applicable they are. This kind of attention to words, in fact, might give you enough material for all or part of your essay. Thus, an essay on the problem of Hamlet's delay might focus in part on a treatment of the word *delay*: What, really, does *delay* mean? For Hamlet, is there a difference between delay that is reasonable and delay that is unreasonable? Does Hamlet delay unreasonably? Is his delay the result of a psychological fault? Would speedy revenge

be more or less reasonable than the delay? By the time you have answered such pointed questions, you will also have sufficient material for your full essay.

3. *Refer to literary conventions or expectations.* With this strategy, the argument is to establish that the problem can be solved by reference to the literary mode or conventions of a work, or to the limitations of the work itself. In other words, what appears to be a problem is really no more than a normal characteristic. A problem about the artificiality of the choruses in *Oedipus the King,* for example, might be resolved by reference to the fact that choruses were a normal feature of Greek drama. In a similar manner, the knowledge that delay is a convention of all revenge tragedy might provide a key to the problem of Hamlet's apparent procrastination.

4. *Argue against possible objections.* With this strategy, you raise your own objections and then argue against them. Called **procatalepsis** or **anticipation**, this approach helps you sharpen your arguments, because *anticipating* and dealing with objections forces you to make analyses and use facts that you might otherwise overlook. Although procatalepsis can be used point by point throughout your essay, you may find it most useful at the end.

The situation to imagine is that someone is raising objections to your solution to the problem. It is then your task to show that the objections (1) are not accurate or valid, (2) are not strong or convincing, or (3) are based on unusual rather than usual conditions (on an exception and not the rule). Here are some examples of these approaches.

1. *The objection is not accurate or valid.* You reject this objection by showing that either the interpretation or the conclusions are wrong and also by emphasizing that the evidence supports your solution.

> Although Hamlet's delay is reasonable, the claim might be made that his duty is to kill Claudius in revenge immediately after the Ghost's accusations. This claim is not persuasive because it assumes that Hamlet knows everything the audience knows. The audience accepts the Ghost's word that Claudius is guilty, but Hamlet has no certain reason to believe the Ghost. Would it not seem insane for Hamlet to kill Claudius, who reigns legally, and then to claim he did it because of the Ghost's words? The argument for speedy revenge is not good because it is based on an incorrect view of Hamlet's situation.

2. *The objection is not strong or convincing.* You *concede* that the objection has some truth or validity, but you then try to show that it is weak and that your own solution is stronger.

> One might claim that Claudius's distress at the play within the play is evidence for his guilt and that therefore Hamlet should carry out his revenge right away. This argument has merit, and Hamlet's speech after Claudius has fled the scene ("I'll take the Ghost's word for a thousand pound") shows that the "conscience of the king" has been

caught. But the king's guilty behavior is not a strong cause for killing him. Hamlet could justifiably ask for an investigation of his father's death on these grounds, but he could not justify a revenge killing. Claudius could not be convicted in any court on the testimony that he was disturbed at seeing *The Murder of Gonzago*. Even after the play within the play, the reasons for delay are stronger than for action.

3. *The objection depends on unusual rather than usual conditions.* You reject the objection on the grounds that it could be valid only if normal conditions were suspended. The objection depends on an exception, not a rule.

> The case for quick action is simple: Hamlet should kill Claudius right after seeing the Ghost (1.3) or else after seeing the King's reaction to the stage murder of Gonzago (3.2) or else after seeing the Ghost again (3.4). Redress under these circumstances, goes the argument, must be both personal and extralegal. This argument wrongly assumes that due process does not exist in the Denmark of Hamlet and Claudius. Nothing in the play indicates that the Danes, even though they carouse a bit, do not value legality and the rules of evidence. Thus Hamlet cannot rush out to kill Claudius because he knows that the king has not had anything close to due process. The argument for quick action is poor because it rests on an exception being made from civilized law.

Remember that writing an essay on a problem requires you to argue a position: Either there is a solution or there is not. To develop your position requires that you show the steps to your conclusion. Your general thematic form is thus (1) to describe the conditions that need to be met for the solution you propose, and then (2) to demonstrate that these conditions exist. If you assert that there is no solution, then your form would be the same for the first part, but your second part—the development—would show that these conditions have *not* been met.

In developing your response, use one or more of the strategies described in this chapter. These are, again, (1) to demonstrate that conditions for a solution are fulfilled, (2) to analyze the words in the phrasing of the problem, (3) to refer to literary conventions or expectations, and (4) to argue against possible objections. You might combine these. Thus, if we assume that your argument is that Hamlet's delay is reasonable, you might first consider the word *delay* (strategy 2). Then you might use strategy 1 to explain the reasons for Hamlet's delay. Finally, to answer objections to your argument, you might show that Hamlet acts promptly when he believes he is justified (strategy 4). Whatever your topic, the important thing is to use the method or methods that best help you make a good argument for your solution.

In your conclusion, try to affirm the validity of your solution in view of the supporting evidence. You might do this by reemphasizing your strongest points, or you might simply present a brief summary. Or you might think of your argument as still continuing and thus use the strategy of procatalepsis or anticipation to raise and answer possible objections to your solution, as in the last paragraph of the following illustrative essay.

## Illustrative Student Essay

Underlined sentences in this paper *do not* conform to MLA style and are used solely as teaching tools to emphasize the central idea, thesis sentence, and topic sentences throughout the paper.

Rezik 1

Antonio Rezik

Professor Tomaiuolo

English 312

1 November 2007

### The Problem of Hamlet's Apparent Delay°

[1]     Many readers and spectators of Shakespeare's Hamlet have been puzzled by the prince's apparent failure to kill Claudius quickly. Early in the play, the Ghost calls on his son to "Revenge his foul and most unnatural murder" (1.5.25). Hamlet, however, delays his vengeance until the end of the play. The problem results from why does he not act sooner. The answer is that there is no unjustified delay and that in fact Hamlet acts as quickly as possible.* This becomes evident when we examine the conventions of revenge tragedy, the actual "call to revenge," and the steps that Hamlet takes to achieve vengeance.†

[2]     Revenge tragedy obviously requires that vengeance be delayed until the closing moments of the play. Given this limitation, Shakespeare must justify the wide gap of time between the call to revenge in Act 1 and the killing of Claudius in Act 5. We find such justification in the unreliability of the ghost's initial accusation, Hamlet's need for additional evidence, and the events that occur after this evidence is obtained.

[3]     The Ghost's accusations and demands are straightforward: he accuses his brother of murdering him and he calls on his son for vengeance. Shakespeare is careful, however, to establish that this testimony is doubtful. Horatio questions the Ghost's truthfulness and motives, and he warns Hamlet that the spirit might "assume some other horrible form / Which might deprive your sovereignty of reason, / And draw you into madness" (1.4.72–74). Hamlet himself expresses doubt about the ghost (2.2.573–79):

---

°see pp. 982–1080 for this play.

*Central idea.

†Thesis sentence.

> The spirit that I have seen
> May be a devil, and the devil hath power
> T'assume a pleasing shape, yea, and perhaps
> Out of my weakness, and my melancholy,
> As he is very potent with such spirits,
> Abuses me to damn me; I'll have grounds
> More relative than this.

The prince thus cannot act on the unsupported word of the Ghost; he needs more evidence.

[4]     There is no delay at this point in the play, because Hamlet quickly begins developing a plan of action. Immediately after speaking with the Ghost, he decides to cover himself under an "antic disposition" while he gathers information. He swears his companions to silence and warns them not to react knowingly if he should seem to behave strangely or insanely (1.5.169–79). His idea is that this pose will make him less a subject of suspicion and will therefore make others less careful.

[5]     Once Hamlet has begun his plan, he takes advantage of every opportunity to carry out his vengeance. When the players come to Elsinore, he adroitly plans to test Claudius by making him publicly view a play, The Murder of Gonzago, which shows a murder just like Claudius's murder of Hamlet's father. Hamlet states that Claudius's appearance will give him the clue he needs to confirm the Ghost's information (2.2.571–573).

> I'll observe his looks,
> I'll tent him to the quick, if a' do blench°        if he flinches
> I know my course.

Once the king breaks up the performance in great agitation, which Hamlet correctly interprets as an admission of guilt, Hamlet declares confidence in the Ghost ("I'll take the ghost's word for a thousand pound" [3.2.271–272]). Moreover, he is psychologically ready to act against the king, for he asserts that he could "drink hot blood, / And do such bitter business as the day / Would quake to look on" (3.2.367–369). Without doubt, Hamlet is only a prayer away from stabbing Claudius, for when he sees the king kneeling, his opportunity has merged with his desire and also with his promise to the Ghost. He tells the audience, "Now might I do it pat, now a' is a-praying, / And now I'll do't" (3.3.73–74).

[6]      But he does not "do't," and for this reason he is open to the accusation that he cannot act. <u>Again, however, Shakespeare carefully justifies this hesitation</u>. The prince does not want to send Claudius's soul to heaven by killing him at prayer. This reason is not simply an excuse for delay. Rather, Hamlet wants his revenge to match Claudius's treacherous murder of old King Hamlet, who died without the chance to pray and repent (3.3.88–95):

> Up sword, and know thou a more horrid hent,
> When he is drunk asleep, or in his rage,
> Or in th'incestuous pleasure of his bed,
> At game, a-swearing, or about some act
> That has no relish of salvation in't,
> Then trip him that his heels may kick at heaven,
> And that his soul may be as damned and black
> As hell whereto it goes.

This deferral is in keeping with the code of personal blood vengeance, whereby the revenge must match or exceed the original crime. There is no question of Hamlet's incapacity to act, because his putting up his sword is reasonable and justifiable.

[7]      <u>From this point on, Hamlet acts or reacts to every situation as the opportunity presents itself</u>. After he kills Polonius, Claudius initiates a counterplot to send Hamlet off to England and execution. Clearly, Hamlet's chances to kill the king are thus reduced to zero. It is not until Act 5 that Hamlet gets back to Denmark, after having decisively thwarted Claudius's murderous instructions by turning them against Rosencrantz and Guildenstern. He makes it clear to Horatio, however, that he will take the earliest opportunity, and that "the readiness is all" (5.2.205). Once the rigged fencing match is under way, the opportunity finally comes. Claudius, Hamlet learns, has not only killed his father but has poisoned his mother, and he himself is about to die from Laertes's poisoned sword. Upon such certain information, Hamlet immediately kills Claudius. When the revenge is complete, the Ghost, who began the cry for vengeance, is nowhere to be heard or seen, and four bodies lie on the stage.

[8]      <u>Thus, we see that the problem of Hamlet's delay—and the vengeance does take four acts to carry out—is really not a problem</u>. The prince acts in accordance with the code of revenge as quickly as circumstances permit. Although the text of the play supports this solution, critics might still argue that procrastination is an issue because

Rezik 4

Hamlet twice accuses himself of delay. This objection does not take into consideration that Hamlet's perception of time and action is distorted by his eagerness for vengeance.

From Hamlet's subjective point of view, any break in activity is delay. From our objective viewpoint, however, delay is not a true issue.

---

Rezik 5

**WORK CITED**

William Shakespeare, *Hamlet. Literature: An Introduction to Reading and Writing.* Ed. Edgar V. Roberts. 4th Compact ed. Upper Saddle River: Prentice Hall, 2008, 982–1083.

## Commentary on the Essay

The structure of the essay illustrates strategy 1 (p. 1083). Paragraph 2, however, makes brief use of strategy 3 in its reference to the conventions of revenge tragedy. In both paragraphs 6 and 8, the argument is carried on by use of procatalepsis, or strategy 4, whereby a counterargument is raised and then answered.

The introductory paragraph raises the problem of Hamlet's apparent delay and offers a brief statement of the solution (the central idea). This plan is developed in paragraphs 2–7 in exactly the same order in which the issues are raised in the introduction. Paragraph 2 deals with the meaning and requirements of revenge, and paragraph 3 takes up the issue of the Ghost's reliability. Paragraphs 4 and 5 deal with Hamlet's attempts to corroborate the Ghost's accusations, and paragraphs 6 and 7 consider the subsequent action. Note that each paragraph in the argument grows naturally out of the one that precedes it, just as all the paragraphs are linked to the introductory paragraph.

The concluding paragraph asserts that the original problem is solved; the paragraph then summarizes the steps of the solution. It also continues the argument by raising and then dealing with a possible objection.

# Writing About Tragedy

1. Much has been made of the contrast in *Oedipus the King* between vision and blindness. Write an essay that considers this contrast as it is related to the character of Oedipus. How are blindness and seeing reversed, with regard to his understanding about the curse on the city, his attempts to ferret out the guilty ones, his awakening perceptions of his own responsibility and guilt, and his self-blinding? How can Tiresias be compared and contrasted with Oedipus?

2. Develop an argument for one of these assertions.
   a. Oedipus's fall is the result of fate, predestination, and the gods, and it would happen no matter what kind of person he is.
   b. Oedipus's fall is the result only of his character and has nothing to do with fate or the gods.

3. Write an essay considering the degree to which Gertrude and Ophelia in *Hamlet* justify Hamlet's assertion "Frailty, thy name is woman" (1.2.146). Questions you might take into account concern the status of these women, their power to exert their own individuality and to make their own decisions, Gertrude as a royal queen and Ophelia as an aristocratic daughter, their capacity to undergo the pain of bereavement, Hamlet's own feelings about the death of his father, and so on.

4. Hamlet, Laertes, and Fortinbras are young men whose fathers have been killed and who set out to avenge these deaths. Their courses of action, however, are different. In an essay, consider these three as typical or archetypal sons. What characteristics do they share? What, in turn, makes them individual and distinct? Compare and contrast how each character deals with his father's death. Which approach seems most reasonable to you? Most emotional? Most effective? For additional directions in handling comparison and contrast, consult Chapter 25.

5. Considering *Oedipus the King* and *Hamlet,* write an essay defining and explaining tragedy. Include references to the nature of the tragic protagonists, the situations they face, their solutions to their problems, their responses to the consequences of their actions, and their worthiness of character. Be sure to compare and contrast the actions and speeches of the characters in the plays as evidence.

6. Use your library or the Internet to locate books on tragedy. Some general topics might be *ancient and modern tragedy, definitions, emotions, heroes, passions, problems,* and *questions.* You might also wish to locate specific books on Aristotle and tragedy or on *Oedipus the King* or *Hamlet.* Write a brief report on one of the books, being careful to consider topics such as the author's definitions of tragedy and the author's application of the topic to various specific plays. Try also to consider the completeness of the author's presentation of material and the persuasiveness of the author's arguments.

# Chapter 22

# The Comic Vision: Restoring the Balance

**C**omedy is the fraternal twin of tragedy. As a form was it was first created in the ancient Greek world, like tragedy, and the two forms bear many family resemblances.[1] Comedy is often filled with tragic potential, and tragedy sometimes is built on a story that is potentially comic. Indeed, tragedy can be seen as an abortive or incomplete comedy in which affairs turn into disaster, and comedy can be considered a tragedy in which the truth is discovered (or covered up), the hero saves the day, the villain is overcome, the hero and heroine are united, and equilibrium and balance are restored. The major difference is that tragedy moves toward despair or death, whereas comedy moves toward success, happiness, and marriage. Tragic diction is elevated and heroic. Comic diction can be elevated too, but often it is common or colloquial, and although it is frequently witty, it is also sometimes witless and bawdy. The mask of tragedy despairs, grieves, and weeps, whereas the mask of comedy rejoices, smiles, and laughs.

## The Origins of Comedy

In the *Poetics*, Aristotle states that he knows less about the origin of Athenian comedy than of tragedy because comedy "was not at first treated seriously" (V.2, p. 21). He does say, however, that comedy developed as an improvisatory form (IV.12, p. 19), just as tragedy did. Most comic improvisations were an outgrowth of "phallic songs," which were bacchanalian processions that took place during the **Lenaia**, the Athenian religious festival held in January–February each year in *Gamelion*, the month of weddings, just following the winter solstice.

The word *comedy* is consistent with this explanation, for as "a *komos* song" its Greek meaning is "a song of revels" or "a song sung by merrymakers." The revels, like the tragedies, were religious in ways that the Greeks considered meaningful but that seem secular to us today. During parades or processions at the Lenaia, the merrymakers expressed their joy boisterously, traded bawdy and obscene remarks with spectators, lampooned public persons, wore ceremonial phalluses, and dressed in paunchy costumes suggesting feasting, fatness, friskiness, fertility, frolic, and fun. We may conclude that these *komos* processions were supported officially in the belief

---

[1]For a more detailed discussion of how tragedy developed within the ancient Athenian religious festivals, see Chapter 21, pp. 923–928.

and hope that human ceremonies would encourage divine favor and bring about prosperity and happiness. As the form developing out of such processions, comedy began with many of these characteristics and has retained them to the present day. If one briefly may generalize about subsequent comedies—even those that are cold sober rather than boisterous—it is clear that love, marriage, and ritualized celebrations of a happy future are usually major concerns.

## The Athenians Held Competitions for Comedy, Just as for Tragedy

Tragedy originated in Athens, but the same does not appear to be true of comedy. Rather, comedy coexisted in the areas surrounding Greece called *Magna Graecia* ("Greater Greece"). Aristotle himself admitted that it was "late" when comic performances were separated from the phallic songs (V.2, p. 21); that is, comedy followed tragedy by many years. The earliest certain date for the existence of Athenian comedy is 486 B.C.E., when a writer named Chionides won a state-sponsored comedy competition. Although the earliest comedies apparently consisted of little more than loosely connected lampoons, they were highly enough regarded to justify regular competitions. Comedies were scheduled on each day of the festivals, following the tragedies and satyr plays.

According to Aristotle, the first writer to transform comedy by creating a thematic plot development was Crates, who won the first of his three prizes in about the mid-fifth century B.C.E. (V.3, p. 21). It was at this time that comedies became popular enough to justify an additional state comedy competition, which was instituted in about 440 B.C.E. For the remainder of the century, writers of comedy as well as tragedy tried to win prizes for their new plays at both the Lenaia and the City Dionysia.

## The Earliest Greek Comedy Is Called "Old Comedy"

The comedies of the fifth century B.C.E., called **Old Comedy** or **Old Attic Comedy** by later historians, followed intricate structural patterns and displayed complex poetic conventions. Nevertheless, they bore the marks of their origins in the bacchanalian *komos* processions. The actors (three or four men) and the members of the chorus (24 men), each dressed in a distortingly padded costume, wore a character-defining mask and displayed a ceremonial phallus. The role of the chorus usually dictated the comedy's title (e.g., *The Frogs, The Wasps*). Customarily, the plot was fantastic and impossible, and the dialogue was farcical and bawdy. In the tradition of satires and tirades associated with the phallic songs and with early comedy, the comic dramatists freely lashed public persons (usually but not always without legal reprisal).

Although the most successful comedy writer of the fifth century B.C.E. was Magnes (flourished 475–450 B.C.E.), who won 11 times, the only writer whose works survive is Aristophanes (ca. 450–385 B.C.E.), who won four times. His plays constitute our principal firsthand knowledge of Greek Old Comedy. He wrote at least 32 comedies. Fortunately, 11 have survived, along with fragments of some of his other plays. His plots and actions are outrageous, his characters are funny, and his language is satirical, bawdy, and biting.

## Middle Comedy Became Prominent after Aristophanes

Aristophanes lived into the next period of Greek comedy, called **Middle Comedy**. His plays *Ecclesiazusae* (*The Women at the Assembly*, ca. 392 B.C.E.) and *Plutus* (*Plutus, the God of Riches*, 388 B.C.E.) presaged Middle Comedy. All the Middle Comedy plays by other authors are lost, although there are many extant fragments. Middle Comedy eliminated some of the complex patterns of Old Comedy and treated more broadly international and less narrowly Athenian topics. Political criticism was abandoned, and character types such as the braggart soldier were introduced. The role of the chorus was diminished or eliminated (as with tragedy), and the exaggerated costumes were eliminated.

## New Comedy, a Type of Romantic Comedy, Flourished after Middle Comedy

By the end of the fourth century B.C.E., Middle Comedy was supplanted by **New Comedy**. The most important of the New Comedy dramatists was Menander (342–292 B.C.E.), who was heralded in ancient times as the greatest comic writer of them all. Everyone knows quotations from Menander, such as "I call a fig a fig, a spade a spade," "The gods first make mad those they intend to destroy," and "He who fights and runs away lives to fight another day." St. Paul quotes him in 1 Corinthians 15:33 ("Be not deceived: evil communications corrupt good manners"), but after the fifth century CE, copies of Menander's plays were no longer available and for the next fourteen centuries were presumed totally lost. In the last hundred years, however, many Menandrian manuscripts have been discovered, mostly in the sands of Egypt. We now have Menander's *Dyscolus* (*The Grouch*) in its entirety, and near-complete versions of some of his other comedies, together with numerous fragments and passages.[2] In total, the titles of close to one hundred of his plays are known. His comedies, which are romantic rather than satirical, employ such stock characters as young lovers, stubborn fathers, clever slaves, and long-separated relatives.

## Roman Comedy Was Composed Largely in the Third and Second Centuries B.C.E.

After Menander, Greek power in the Mediterranean waned and was replaced by the might of Rome. In the third century B.C.E., Roman comedy began and flourished, largely through the translation and adaptation of Greek New Comedies. The significant Roman writers were Plautus (ca. 254–184 B.C.E.), with 20 surviving comedies, and Terence (ca. 186–159 B.C.E.), whose six comedies still exist. Briefly, the comedies of Plautus are brisk, and those of Terence are more restrained. The central issue in most of the Roman comedies is the overcoming of a **blocking agent**, or obstruction to true love, which could be almost anyone or anything—a rival lover, an angry father, a family feud, an old law, a previously arranged marriage, or differences in social class.

---

[2]See David R. Slavitt and Palmer Bovie, eds., *Menander: The Grouch, Desperately Seeking Justice, Closely Cropped Locks, The Girl from Samos, The Shield* (Philadelphia: U of Pennsylvania P, 1998).

The pattern of action, traditionally called the **plot of intrigue**, stems from the strategems that young lovers undertake to overcome the blocking agent, so that the outcome frequently heralds the victory of youth over age and the passing of control from one generation to the next.

## Comedy from Roman Times to the Renaissance

By the time the Roman Empire was established in 29 B.C.E., the writing of comedy had largely disappeared because pantomime entertainments and public spectacles such as gladiatorial combat had preempted Roman dramatic creativity. Comedy thus accompanied tragedy into fifteen hundred years of obscurity—a period when the Roman Empire rose and fell, the Dark Ages descended, and the medieval period emerged. Although many comic and farcical scenes were included in the mystery cycles of late medieval times,[3] comedy as a form was not established again until the Renaissance.

Once reintroduced, comedy grew rapidly. By 1500 the six plays of Terence had been discovered and were achieving wide recognition, followed by the twenty surviving plays of Plautus. When English dramatists began writing comedies, they followed Roman conventions. The English plays of the mid-sixteenth century contained five acts and observed the unities of time, place, and action, thus justifying the claim that they were "regular" (i.e., following the rules or "regulations"). Character types from the Roman comedies, such as the intriguing couple, the fussing father, and the bragging soldier, initially predominated. Soon, more specifically English types appeared, anticipating the roisterers of Shakespeare's *Henry IV* plays and the "hempen homespuns" of *A Midsummer Night's Dream*. By the end of the sixteenth century, when Shakespeare had completed many of his comedies, English comedy was in full bloom. It has often been observed that this comedy was Latin in structure but English in character.

When the sixteenth century began, the chief obstacle to a wide public assimilation of drama had been the absence of institutionalized theaters. London authorities, maintaining that attending plays was a sinful public nuisance, banned theaters within the city itself. Builders therefore had to construct theaters outside the London city limits. For example, the Rose and the Globe, where Shakespeare saw his plays produced from the mid-1590s to 1611, were built in Southwark across the Thames. We should realize that many people in Shakespeare's audiences got to the theater by walking over London Bridge or by being ferried across the river, and that they returned home the same way.

## The Patterns, Characters, and Language of Comedy

Dictionaries sometimes give *funny* as a synonym for *comic*, but the two terms are not identical. Words like *funny, amusing, comical,* or *humorous* define our emotional conditioning to incidents, and our reactions always depend on context. We usually think it

---

[3]For a description of the medieval mystery or Corpus Christi plays, see Chapter 20, p. 879.

is funny or comical to see an actor in a slapstick routine falling down, being hit in the face with a cream pie, or being struck with a paddle. We laugh because we know that everything is staged and that no real harm is being done. But if we leave the theater and see some of the same things occurring on the streets, we are horrified to recognize that someone is enduring real harm and real pain. Street violence occurs randomly, with no apparent purpose, and there is nothing funny or comic about it. But onstage all actions occur as part of a governing pattern or plan leading to a satisfying outcome. It is the context that makes the difference.

## Comedy Implies a Complete Narrative Pattern of Humorous Action

Comedy as a genre involves patterns of humorous or comic situations and actions that make up a complete and coherent story. Often the situations are simply ordinary; sometimes they are fantastic; sometimes they are even bizarre. But they are always resolvable and correctable (unless we are dealing with the special genre of problem comedy). The patterns grow out of character and situation, and they reach a resolution in a logical or at least an understandable pattern of development. In considering comic patterns, we perceive most dialogue and activity—even serious problems and dangerous situations—as amusing, entertaining, and usually instructive.

**COMEDY INVOLVES A PATTERN OF EDUCATION AND CHANGE.**   In many comedies the principal characters benefit from learning about themselves and their commitments, about living well and loving deeply, about getting along with the people around them, and about finding their place in the world. This "education," which they receive in the play, enables them to improve, and the process of their learning reaches its height in crucial moments of illumination and change. The characters realize their past errors, are ready to amend them, and also are human and humble enough to ask forgiveness which, according to the comic pattern, is promptly granted. In many comedies, particularly those that touch on significant social and political problems, the audience is also educated, and the play's implication is that improvement should occur in the world just as it has occurred on the stage.

**COMIC PROBLEMS FLOURISH AMID CHAOS AND POTENTIAL DISASTER.**   Before the moments of change leading to the comic conclusion, however, comedy must introduce many of the problems and complications that could, in real life, lead not to happiness but to unhappiness and even to calamity. These problems can be personal, social, political, economic, or military; in short, they may enter every arena of human affairs. A man wants to find a place in the world and to gain his fortune, and he also wants to find love. A woman wants to find love also, but must be reserved and somewhat aloof when meeting suitors. A number of people want to succeed in a business venture. A politician is accused of corruption and thus needs help in exonerating himself. A man and woman in love become angry or disenchanted because others tell them lies about each other. Another man and woman need to overcome family hostility so that they may successfully begin their lives together with the approval of everyone around them. Still another man and woman, upon meeting for the first time, become so angry they threaten to murder each other. Failure, though it is to be always overcome in comedy, is never far away; it lurks over the horizon, around corners, in business rooms, in malicious telephone calls, and on the Internet, waiting to emerge and scatter uncertainty, indecisiveness, and distress.

All such situations, which might possibly lead to ruin, are the stuff of comedy. The worse things seem, and the more apparently chaotic, the better. In a good comic complication, the problems are constantly being fueled by misunderstanding, mistaken identity, misdirection, misinformed speech, errors in judgment, faults in intelligence, excessive or unreasonable behavior, and coincidences that stretch credulity.

**THE COMIC CLIMAX IS THE PEAK OF CONFUSION.**   Such complications lead ultimately to the comic climax, which is that moment or moments in the play when everything reaches the peak of confusion and when no good solution seems in sight. Misunderstanding is dominant, pressure is at a high point, and choices must be made even though solutions seem impossible. The catastrophe—the changing or turning point—is frequently launched by a sudden revelation in which a new fact, a misunderstood event, or a previously hidden identity is explained to characters and audience at the same time, and then things undergo a turnaround and start rushing toward improvement.

**THE COMIC DÉNOUEMENT RESTORES SANITY AND CALM.**   In most comedies, the events of the dénouement resolve the initial difficulties and allow for the comic resolution, which dramatizes how things are set right at every level of action. Errors are explained, personal lives are straightened out, people at odds with each other are reconciled, promises are made for the future, new families are formed through marriage, and a stable social order is reestablished.

## Comic Characters Are More Limited Than Characters in Tragedy

Comic characters are relatively limited because they are almost necessarily common and representative rather than individual and heroic. Characters with breadth or individuality are therefore not typical of comedy. Instead, comedy gives us stock characters who represent classes, types, and generations. In Shakespeare's *A Midsummer Night's Dream* many of the characters are representative and stock figures. Egeus is a conventionally indignant and unreasonable father, and Hermia and Lysander are typical young lovers (along with Helena and Demetrius). In Henley's *Am I Blue*, Ashbe and John Polk are young people who are trying to find themselves under confusing circumstances. Their meeting provides them with a stay against their own personal difficulties, but they do not reach any elevated insights.

## Comic Language Is a Vital Vehicle of Humor

As in other types of literature, comic dramatists use language to delineate character, to establish tone and mood, and to express ideas and feelings. In comedy, however, language is also one of the most important vehicles for humor. Some comedies are characterized by elegant and witty language, others by puns and bawdy jokes.

Characters in comedy tend either to be masters of language or to be mastered by it. Those who are skillful with language can use a witty phrase to satirize their foes and friends alike. Those who are unskilled with language, like Bottom in *A Midsummer Night's Dream*, bungle their speeches because they misuse words and stumble into inadvertent puns. Both types of characters are amusing; we smile a knowing smile with the wits and laugh aloud at the would-be wits and the bunglers.

## Types of Comedy

Differences in comic style, content, and intent that have evolved over the centuries make it possible to divide comedy into various types. The broadest of these divisions, based on both style and content, separates comic literature into *high comedy* and *low comedy*.

### High Comedy Develops Mainly from Character

Ideally, **high comedy** (a term coined by George Meredith in 1877 in *The Idea of Comedy*) is witty, graceful, and sophisticated. The problems and complications are more closely related to character than to situation, even though, admittedly, they develop out of situations. The appeal of high comedy is to the intellect, for the comic resolution must come about because the characters learn enough to accept adjustments and changes in their lives. A simple change of situation alone will not do for high comedy.

1. *Romantic comedy focuses on problems of youthful love.* One of the major kinds of high comedy is **romantic comedy**, which views action and character from the standpoint of earnest young lovers like Hermia and Lysander in *A Midsummer Night's Dream*. Ultimately derived from Roman comedy, this kind of play is built on a plot of intrigue featuring lovers who try to overcome opposition (such as Egeus) to achieve a successful union. The aim of such plays is amusement and entertainment rather than ridicule and reform. Although vice and folly may be exposed in romantic comedy, especially the follies of the antagonists blocking the young lovers, the dominant impulse is toleration and amused indulgence.

2. *Comedy of manners tests the strength of social customs and assumptions.* Related to romantic comedy is the **comedy of manners**, an important type from the seventeenth century to our own times. The comedy of manners examines and satirizes attitudes and customs in the light of high intellectual and moral standards. The dialogue is witty and sophisticated, and characters are often measured according to their linguistic and intellectual powers. The love plots are serious and real, even though they share with romantic comedy the need to create intrigues to overcome opposition and impediments. The realism and seriousness in some of the manners comedies written in Restoration England (1660–1700) in fact are so great that one might consider them not only as plays of manners but also as plays of social and personal problems.

3. *Satiric comedy, like all satire, ridicules vices and follies.* Midway between high and low comedy is **satiric comedy**, which is based in a comic attack on foolishness and/or viciousness. The playwright of satiric comedy assumes the perspective of

a rational and moderate observer measuring human life against a moderate norm that is represented by high and serious characters. Members of the audience are invited to share this viewpoint as they, along with the dramatist, heap scorn upon the vicious and laugh loudly at the eccentric and the foolish.

## Low Comedy Dwells Amid the Silly and the Bumbling

In **low comedy**, emphasis is on funny remarks and outrageous circumstances. Complications develop from situation and plot rather than from character. Plays of this type are by definition full of physical humor and stage business—a character rounds his forefinger and thumb to imitate a hole in a wall, through which other characters speak; an irascible man constantly breaks furniture; a character masquerading as a doctor takes the pulse of a father to determine his daughter's medical condition; characters who have just declared their love are visited by people to whom they formerly swore love.

The quintessential type of low comedy is **farce** (a word derived from the Latin word *farsus*, meaning "stuffed"), the aim of which, in the words of Henry Fielding, "is but to make you laugh." A farce is an outlandish physical comedy overflowing with silly characters, unlikely happenings, wild clowning, improbable pratfalls, extravagant language, and bawdy jokes.

Another type of farce is the *commedia dell'arte*, a prototypical comic drama that developed among traveling companies in Italy and France in the sixteenth and seventeenth centuries. The broadly humorous characters of *commedia dell'arte* recurred from play to play with consistent names and characteristics. The action usually involved a plot of intrigue. The lovers were the permanently youthful and glowing *Inamorato* and *Inamorata*, who were aided by Inamorata's clever servant, the *soubrette*, to overcome *Pantaloon*, the foolish and presuming old man. The servant characters were *Harlequin* (who was invisible) and *Columbine* (his sweetheart, also invisible), who were joined in highjinks by *Pierrot* (a clown lover) and *Scaramouche* (the soldier). Other stock characters, most of whom were derived from Greek New Comedy by way of Roman comedy, have in turn become constant features of much subsequent comedy.

With characters of low comedy, of course, there is much tomfoolery and improvisation—the major qualities of the extreme form of farce, **slapstick**, which is named after the double paddles ("slap sticks") that made loud cracking noises when actors in the *commedia dell'arte* used them for striking each other. Slapstick depends heavily on exaggerated actions, poses, and facial expressions. In slapstick there is constant onstage business with objects such as paddles, pies, pails, paint, paste, or toilet paper, along with wild and silly actions such as squirming, hiding, stumbling, tripping, tumbling, falling, and flopping.

## Other Kinds of Comedy Emphasize Complexity and Absurdity

Other types of modern and contemporary comedy include **ironic comedy**, **realistic comedy**, and **comedy of the absurd**. All of these shun the happy endings of traditional comedy. Often the blocking agents are successful, the protagonists are defeated, and the initial problem—either a realistic or an absurdist dilemma—remains unresolved.

Such comedies, which began to appear in the late nineteenth century, illustrate the complexities and absurdities of modern life and the funny but futile efforts that people make when coming to grips with existence.

Many of the types of comedy just discussed still flourish. Romantic comedies, comedies of manners, and farces can be found on innumerable stages and movie screens. They revolve about a central situation that might be quite ordinary. (Will Hank get along with a visiting lodge member? Will Sue be accepted by schoolmates at her new school? Will Jim get a date for the prom?) Such situations find their ways into the huge numbers of **sitcoms** (situation comedies) that occupy prime-time television programming.

In view of the variety of comedy, it is most important to recognize that comedy is rarely a pure and discrete form. High comedies might include crude physical humor, especially with characters to be disapproved. Low comedies can sometimes contain wit and elegance. Satiric comedies might deal with successful young lovers. Romantic comedies can mock the vices and follies of weird and eccentric characters. Farce and slapstick can contain satire on social values and conventions.

## Plays for Study

## WILLIAM SHAKESPEARE (1564–1616)

*For a brief biography and portrait, see Chapter 21, p. 981.*

*A Midsummer Night's Dream* was written early in Shakespeare's career, in 1594 or 1595.[4] It is a romantic comedy dramatizing the idea that "the course of true love never did run smooth." This central line of action, which owes much to Roman comedy, involves blocked love, a journey of circumvention and education that takes the lovers from the world of laws and problems into an imaginary world of chaos and transformations, and an ultimate victory back in the world of daylight and order.

The subject of *A Midsummer Night's Dream* is love. Shakespeare skillfully interweaves this topic in the play's four separate plots, four groups of characters, and four styles of language. Each plot explores the nature of love, the madness of irrational love, and the harmony needed for regenerative love.

In the *overplot*—the action that establishes the time for the play—the relationship is between the rulers, Theseus and Hippolyta, who have undergone a change from irrational war to rational peace. As such, they represent the dynastic continuity of the state, the order of the daylight world of Athens, and the rigor of law. These characters are the rulers, and they speak predominantly in blank verse (unrhymed iambic pentameter; see Chapter 16).

---

[4]See Chapter 21, pages 977–982, for a description of Shakespeare's theater and career as a dramatist.

The two connected *middle love plots* concern the adventures of the four lovers and the actions of Oberon and Titania. The four lovers, embodying the most passionate and insistent phase of love, are from the upper class, and they speak mainly in rhymed couplets. During their long night of illusion in the woods, conjured by Oberon and his servant, Puck, their adventures drive them toward rationality, and they recognize and accept the need for faithfulness and constancy. The parallel middle plot involves the conflict between Oberon and Titania, the king and queen of the fairies, because of their mutually exclusive wishes to control a "changeling" child. Oberon is "jealous" and wants the child as an attendant, but Titania wants to keep him in her service because his mother had been Titania's attendant, friend, and confidante. With great power over Titania, Oberon humbles her, and she then reacknowledges his superiority—the proper attitude of a wife, according to Elizabethan males. Oberon and Titania, of course, are supernatural forces. Although they and the other fairies speak in both blank verse and rhymed couplets, the fairies are the only singing characters and also the only characters to speak in iambic tetrameter.

The examination of love in the subplot occurs partly in Titania's relationship with Bottom—the most hilarious instance of love's madness in the play—and partly in the play-within-a-play about Pyramus and Thisby. This play, filled with "very tragical mirth" echoes the central plot of *A Midsummer Night's Dream* and demonstrates, again, the pitfalls and unpredictability of love. It also emphasizes the happy and harmonious marriages and rapprochements that occur in both the overplot and the middle plots.

While *A Midsummer Night's Dream* is chiefly about love, it is equally concerned with the complicated relationship of perception, imagination, passion, art, and illusion. In Act 5 Theseus asserts that "The lunatic, the lover, and the poet" are alike because they all try to make reality conform with their own imaginations and desires (1.7–22). It would seem that chaos is therefore a normal human state, but, as Hippolyta concludes in response to Theseus, order and certainty somehow prevail, "howsoever" extraordinary and almost miraculous this result may seem (lines 23–27). The movement of the play is governed by these ideas that, along with the brilliant language and comic actions, are directly attributable to the genius of Shakespeare.

 # A Midsummer Night's Dream (1600 (ca. 1594))

### *Edited by Alice Griffin***

#### THE NAMES OF THE ACTORS

**Theseus,** Duke of Athens

**Egeus,** father of Hermia

**Lysander,** beloved of Hermia

**Demetrius,** in love with Hermia, favoured by Egeus

**Philostrate,** Master of the Revels to Theseus

**Peter Quince,** a carpenter (Prologue)*

**Nick Bottom,** a weaver (Pyramus)*

**Francis Flute,** a bellows-mender (Thisby)*

**Tom Snout,** a tinker (Wall)*

**Snug,** a joiner (Lion)*

---

**Professor Griffin's text for *A Midsummer Night's Dream* is the First Quarto (edition) published in 1600, with modifications based on the Quarto edition of 1619 and the First Folio, published in 1623. Stage directions in those editions are printed here without brackets; added stage directions are printed within brackets. We have edited Griffin's notes for this text.

*Characters who play in the interlude.

**Robin Starveling,** a tailor (Moonshine)*

**Hippolyta,** Queen of the Amazons, betrothed to Theseus

**Hermia,** daughter of Egeus, in love with Lysander

**Helena,** in love with Demetrius

**Oberon,** King of the Fairies

**Titania,** Queen of the Fairies

**Puck,** or **Robin** Goodfellow

**Peaseblossom**

**Cobweb**

**Moth**        } Fairies

**Mustardseed**

*Other Fairies attending Oberon and Titania. Attendants on Theseus and Hippolyta.*

SCENE. *Athens, and a wood nearby*

## ACT 1

## [Scene 1. Athens. The palace of Theseus]

*Enter* THESEUS, HIPPOLYTA,° [PHILOSTRATE,] *with others.*

THESEUS:  Now fair Hippolyta, our nuptial hour
    Draws on apace: four happy days bring in
    Another moon: but O, methinks how slow
    This old moon wanes! she lingers° my desires,
    Like to a stepdame or a dowager,°                                    5
    Long withering out° a young man's revenue.
HIPPOLYTA:  Four days will quickly steep themselves in night:
    Four nights will quickly dream away the time:
    And then the moon, like to a silver bow
    New-bent in heaven, shall behold the night              10
    Of our solemnities.
THESEUS:               Go Philostrate,
    Stir up the Athenian youth to merriments,
    Awake the pert° and nimble spirit of mirth,
    Turn melancholy forth to funerals:
    The pale companion° is not for our pomp.        *[Exit* PHILOSTRATE*]*  15
    Hippolyta, I wooed thee with my sword,
    And won thy love doing thee injuries;
    But I will wed thee in another key,
    With pomp, with triumph,° and with revelling.

*Enter* EGEUS *and his daughter* HERMIA, LYSANDER *and* DEMETRIUS.

EGEUS:  Happy be Theseus, our renownèd duke.                           20
THESEUS:  Thanks good Egeus:° what's the news with thee?

---

°0.3 S.D.: *Theseus, Hippolyta*: In Greek legend, Theseus captured the Amazon Queen Hippolyta and brought her to Athens where they were married.
4 *lingers*: delays the fulfillment of.  5 *dowager*: a widow supported by her dead husband's heirs.  6 *withering out*: (1) depleting (2) growing withered.
13 *pert*: lively.  15 *companion*: fellow (contemptuous).  19 *triumph*: public festival.  21 *Egeus*: (trisyllabic).

EGEUS:  Full of vexation come I, with complaint
    Against my child, my daughter Hermia.
    Stand forth Demetrius. My noble lord,
25     This man hath my consent to marry her.
    Stand forth Lysander. And my gracious duke,
    This man hath bewitched the bosom of my child.
    Thou, thou Lysander, thou hast given her rhymes,
    And interchanged love tokens with my child:
30     Thou hast by moonlight at her window sung,
    With feigning voice, verses of feigning° love,
    And stol'n the impression of her fantasy°
    With bracelets of thy hair, rings, gauds° conceits,°
    Knacks,° trifles, nosegays, sweetmeats—messengers
35     Of strong prevailment in unhardened youth.
    With cunning hast thou filched my daughter's heart,
    Turned her obedience, which is due to me,
    To stubborn harshness. And my gracious duke,
    Be it so° she will not here before your grace
40     Consent to marry with Demetrius,
    I beg the ancient privilege of Athens:
    As she is mine, I may dispose of her:
        Which shall be, either to this gentleman,
        Or to her death, according to our law
45         Immediately° provided in that case.
THESEUS:  What say you, Hermia? Be advised, fair maid.
    To you your father should be as a god:
    One that composed your beauties: yea and one
    To whom you are but as a form in wax
50     By him imprinted, and within his power
    To leave the figure, or disfigure it:
    Demetrius is a worthy gentleman.
HERMIA:  So is Lysander.
THESEUS:             In himself he is:
    But in this kind, wanting your father's voice,°
55     The other must be held the worthier.
HERMIA:  I would my father looked but with my eyes.
THESEUS:  Rather your eyes must with his judgment look.
HERMIA:  I do entreat your grace to pardon me.
    I know not by what power I am made bold,
60     Nor how it may concern my modesty,
    In such a presence, here to plead my thoughts:
    But I beseech your grace that I may know
    The worst that may befall me in this case,
    If I refuse to wed Demetrius.
65 THESEUS:  Either to die the death, or to abjure
    For ever the society of men.

---

°31 *feigning*: (1) deceptive (2) desirous ("faining"). 32 *stol'n . . . fantasy*: stealthily imprinted your image upon her fancy. 33 *gauds*: trinkets. *conceits*: either (a) love poetry, or (b) love tokens. 34 *Knacks*: knick-knacks. 39 *Be it so*: if it be that. 45 *Immediately*: precisely. 54 *in . . . voice*: in this respect, lacking your father's approval.

Therefore fair Hermia, question your desires,
Know of your youth,° examine well your blood,°
Whether, if you yield not to your father's choice,
You can endure the livery° of a nun,    70
For aye° to be in shady cloister mewed,°
To live a barren sister all your life,
Chanting faint hymns to the cold fruitless moon.°
Thrice blessèd they that master so their blood,
To undergo such maiden pilgrimage:    75
But earthlier happy° is the rose distilled,°
Than that which, withering on the virgin thorn,
Grows, lives, and dies, in single blessedness.

HERMIA: So will I grow, so live, so die my lord,
Ere I will yield my virgin patent° up    80
Unto his lordship, whose unwishèd yoke
My soul consents not to give sovereignty.

THESEUS: Take time to pause, and by the next moon,
The sealing day betwixt my love and me,
For everlasting bond of fellowship,    85
Upon that day either prepare to die
For disobedience to your father's will,
Or else to wed Demetrius, as he would,
Or on Diana's altar to protest°
For aye, austerity and single life.    90

DEMETRIUS: Relent, sweet Hermia, and Lysander, yield
Thy crazèd° title to my certain right.

LYSANDER: You have her father's love, Demetrius:
Let me have Hermia's: do you marry him.

EGEUS: Scornful Lysander, true, he hath my love:    95
And what is mine, my love shall render him.
And she is mine, and all my right of her
I do estate° unto Demetrius.

LYSANDER: I am, my lord, as well derived° as he,
As well possessed;° my love is more than his:    100
My fortunes every way as fairly ranked
(If not with vantage) as° Demetrius':
And, which is more than all these boasts can be,
I am beloved of beauteous Hermia.
Why should not I then prosecute my right?    105
Demetrius, I'll avouch it to his head,°
Made love to Nedar's daughter, Helena,
And won her soul: and she, sweet lady, dotes,
Devoutly dotes, dotes in idolatry,
Upon this spotted° and inconstant man.    110

---

°68 *Know . . . youth*: ask yourself as a young person. 68 *blood*: passions. 70 *livery*: habit. 71 *aye*: ever. *mewed*: shut up. 73 *moon*: (the moon goddess Diana represented unmarried chastity). 76 *earthlier happy*: more happy on earth. *distilled*: i.e., into perfume (thus its essence is passed on, as to a child). 80 *patent*: privilege. 89 *protest*: vow. 92 *crazèd*: flawed. 98 *estate*: transfer. 99 *well derived*: well born. 100 *well possessed*: wealthy. 102 *with vantage, as*: better, than. 106 *avouch . . . head*: prove it to his face. 110 *spotted*: stained.

THESEUS:  I must confess that I have heard so much,
    And with Demetrius thought to have spoke thereof:
    But being over-full of self-affairs,
    My mind did lose it. But Demetrius come,
115    And come Egeus, you shall go with me:
    I have some private schooling for you both.
    For you fair Hermia, look you arm yourself,
    To fit your fancies to your father's will;
    Or else the law of Athens yields you up
120    (Which by no means we may extenuate)
    To death or to a vow of single life.
    Come my Hippolyta, what cheer my love?
    Demetrius and Egeus, go along:
    I must employ you in some business
125    Against° our nuptial, and confer with you
    Of something nearly° that concerns yourselves.
EGEUS:  With duty and desire we follow you.

                          *Exeunt.° Manent° LYSANDER and HERMIA.*

LYSANDER:  How now my love? Why is your cheek so pale?
    How chance the roses there do fade so fast?
130 HERMIA:  Belike° for want of rain, which I could well
    Beteem° them from the tempest of my eyes,
LYSANDER:  Ay me, for aught that I could ever read,
    Could ever hear by tale or history,
    The course of true love never did run smooth;
135    But either it was different in blood—
HERMIA:  O cross! too high° to be enthralled to low.°
LYSANDER:  Or else misgraffed° in respect of years—
HERMIA:  O spite! too old to be engaged to young.
LYSANDER:  Or else it stood upon the choice of friends—
140 HERMIA:  O hell! to choose love by another's eyes.
LYSANDER:  Or if there were a sympathy in choice,
    War, death, or sickness did lay siege to it;
    Making it momentany° as a sound,
    Swift as a shadow, short as any dream,
145    Brief as the lightning in the collied° night,
    That, in a spleen,° unfolds both heaven and earth;
    And ere a man hath power to say "Behold,"
    The jaws of darkness do devour it up:
    So quick bright things come to confusion.
150 HERMIA:  If then true lovers have been ever crossed,°
    It stands as an edict in destiny:
    Then let us teach our trial patience,°
    Because it is a customary cross,

---

°125 *Against*: in preparation for. 126 *nearly*: closely. 127 S.D.: *Exeunt*: they exit. *Manent*: they remain. 130 *Belike*: likely. 131 *Beteem*: (1) pour out on (2) allow. 136 *high*: highborn. *enthralled to low*: made a slave to one of low birth. 137 *misgraffed*: badly joined. 143 *momentany*: momentary. 145 *collied*: black as coal. 146 *in a spleen*: impulsively, in a sudden outburst. 150 *ever crossed*: evermore thwarted. 152 *teach . . . patience*: teach ourselves to be patient.

As due to love as thoughts and dreams and sighs,
Wishes and tears; poor Fancy's° followers.                                             155
LYSANDER:  A good persuasion: therefore hear me, Hermia:
    I have a widow aunt, a dowager,
    Of great revenue, and she hath no child:
    From Athens is her house remote seven leagues,
    And she respects° me as her only son:                                               160
    There gentle Hermia, may I marry thee,
    And to that place the sharp Athenian law
    Cannot pursue us. If thou lov'st me then,
    Steal forth thy father's house tomorrow night:
    And in the wood, a league without the town,                                         165
    Where I did meet thee once with Helena
    To do observance to a morn of May,°
    There will I stay° for thee.
HERMIA:                          My good Lysander,
    I swear to thee, by Cupid's strongest bow,
    By his best arrow, with the golden head,°                                           170
    By the simplicity of Venus' doves,
    By that which knitteth souls and prospers loves,
    And by that fire which burned the Carthage queen,
    When the false Troyan° under sail was seen,
    By all the vows that ever men have broke,                                           175
    (In number more than ever women spoke)
    In that same place thou hast appointed me,
    Tomorrow truly will I meet with thee.
LYSANDER:  Keep promise love: look, here comes Helena.

*Enter* HELENA.

HERMIA:  God speed fair Helena: whither away?                                           180
HELENA:  Call you me fair? That fair again unsay.
    Demetrius loves your fair:° O happy fair!
    Your eyes are lodestars,° and your tongue's sweet air°
    More tuneable than lark to shepherd's ear,
    When wheat is green, when hawthorn buds appear.                                     185
    Sickness is catching: O were favour° so,
    Yours would I catch, fair Hermia, ere I go,
    My ear should catch your voice,° my eye your eye,°
    My tongue should catch your tongue's sweet melody.
    Were the world mine, Demetrius being bated,°                                        190
    The rest I'd give to be to you translated.°
    O teach me how you look, and with what art
    You sway the motion of Demetrius' heart.
HERMIA:  I frown upon him; yet he loves me still.
HELENA:  O that your frowns would teach my smiles such skill.                           195

---

°155 *Fancy*: love (sometimes infatuation). 160 *respects*: regards. 167 *do . . . May*: celebrate May Day. 168 *stay*: wait. 170 *golden head*: (The arrow with the gold Head causes love). 173–74 *Carthage Queen . . . false Troyan*: Dido, who burned herself to death on a funeral pyre when Trojan Aeneas deserted her. 182 *your fair*: i.e., beauty. 183 *lodestars*: guiding stars. *air*: music. 186 *favour*: appearance. 188 *My ear . . . voice*: my ear should catch the tone of your voice. *my eye your eye*: my eye should catch the way you glance. 190 *bated*: subtracted, excepted. 191 *translated*: transformed.

HERMIA:  I give him curses; yet he gives me love.

HELENA:  O that my prayers could such affection move.

HERMIA:  The more I hate, the more he follows me.

HELENA:  The more I love, the more he hateth me.

200 HERMIA:  His folly, Helena, is no fault of mine.

HERMIA:  None but your beauty; would that fault were mine.

HERMIA:  Take comfort: he no more shall see my face:

    Lysander and myself will fly this place.

    Before the time I did Lysander see,

205     Seemed Athens as a paradise to me:

    O then, what graces in my love do dwell,

    That he hath turned a heaven unto a hell!

LYSANDER:  Helen, to you our minds we will unfold:

    Tomorrow night, when Phoebe° doth behold

210     Her silver visage in the wat'ry glass,°

    Decking with liquid pearl the bladed grass

    (A time that lovers' flights doth still° conceal)

    Through Athens gates have we devised to steal.

HERMIA:  And in the wood, where often you and I

215     Upon faint primrose beds were wont to lie,

    Emptying our bosoms of their counsel° sweet,

    There my Lysander and myself shall meet,

    And thence from Athens turn away our eyes,

    To see new friends and stranger companies.°

220     Farewell, sweet playfellow: pray thou for us:

    And good luck grant thee thy Demetrius.

    Keep word Lysander: we must starve our sight

    From lovers' food,° till morrow deep midnight.

LYSANDER:  I will my Hermia.                                         *Exit* HERMIA.

             Helena adieu:

225     As you on him, Demetrius dote on you.°               *Exit* LYSANDER.

HELENA:  How happy some, o'er other some, can be!

    Through Athens I am thought as fair as she.

    But what of that? Demetrius thinks not so:

    He will not know what all but he do know.

230     And as he errs, doting on Hermia's eyes,

    So I, admiring of his qualities.

    Things base and vile, holding no quantity.°

    Love can transpose to form and dignity.

    Love looks not with the eyes, but with the mind:

235     And therefore is winged Cupid painted blind.

    Nor hath Love's mind of any judgment taste:

    Wings, and no eyes, figure° unheedy haste.

    And therefore is Love said to be a child:

    Because in choice he is so oft beguiled.

240     As waggish boys in game themselves forswear:

---

°209 *Phoebe*: Diana, the moon.  210 *wat'ry glass*: mirror of the water.  212 *still*: always.  216 *counsel*: secrets.  219 *stranger companies*: the companionship of strangers.  223 *lovers' food*: the sight of the loved one.  225 *As . . . you*: As you dote on Demetrius, so may Demetrius also dote on you.  232 *holding no quantity*: out of proportion.  237 *figure*: symbolize.

So the boy Love is perjured everywhere.
For ere Demetrius looked on Hermia's eyne,°
He hailed down oaths that he was only mine.
And when this hail some heat from Hermia felt,
So he dissolved, and show'rs of oaths did melt.                                         245
I will go tell him of fair Hermia's flight:
Then to the wood will he tomorrow night
Pursue her: and for this intelligence,°
If I have thanks, it is a dear expense.°
But herein mean I to enrich my pain,                                                    250
To have his sight° thither and back again.                                    *Exit.*

## [Scene 2. Quince's house]

*Enter* QUINCE *the Carpenter; and* SNUG *the Joiner; and* BOTTOM *the Weaver; and* FLUTE *the Bellows-mender; and* SNOUT *the Tinker; and* STARVELING *the Tailor.*°

QUINCE:  Is all our company here?
BOTTOM:  You were the best to call them generally,° man by man,
    according to the scrip.
QUINCE:  Here is the scroll of every man's name which is thought
    fit, through all Athens, to play in our interlude° before                            5
    the duke and the duchess, on his wedding-day at night.
BOTTOM:  First good Peter Quince, say what the play treats on,
    then read the names of the actors: and so grow to a point.
QUINCE:  Marry,° our play is "The most lamentable comedy, and
    most cruel death of Pyramus and Thisby."                                             10
BOTTOM:  A very good piece of work I assure you, and a merry. Now
    good Peter Quince, call forth your actors by the scroll.
    Masters, spread yourselves.
QUINCE:  Answer as I call you. Nick Bottom the weaver?
BOTTOM:  Ready: name what part I am for, and proceed.                                    15
QUINCE:  You, Nick Bottom, are set down for Pyramus.
BOTTOM:  What is Pyramus? A lover, or a tyrant?
QUINCE:  A lover that kills himself, most gallant, for love.
BOTTOM:  That will ask some tears in the true performing of it. If I
    do it, let the audience look to their eyes: I will move                              20
    storms: I will condole° in some measure. To the rest—
    yet my chief humour° is for a tyrant. I could play Ercles°
    rarely, or a part to tear a cat in, to make all split.°
        The raging rocks
        And shivering shocks,                                                            25
        Shall break the locks

---

°242 *eyne*: eyes. 248 *intelligence*: information. 249 *dear expense*: costly outlay (on Demetrius' part). 250–51 *But . . . sight*: but I will be rewarded just by the sight of him. 0.2 S.D.: the low characters' names describe their work: *Quince*: quoins, wooden wedges used in building. *Snug*: fitting snugly, suiting a joiner of furniture. *Bottom*: bobbin or core on which yarn is wound. *Flute*: mender of fluted church organs and bellows. *Snout*: spout (of the kettles he mends). *Starveling*: (tailors being traditionally thin). 2 *generally*: Bottom often uses the wrong word; here he means the opposite: "severally, one by one." 5 *interlude*: short play. 9 *Marry*: indeed (mild oath, corruption of "by the Virgin Mary"). 21 *condole*: lament. 22 *humour*: inclination. *Ercles*: Hercules (typified by ranting). 23 *tear . . . split*: (terms for ranting and raging on the stage).

     Of prison gates,
     And Phibbus' car°
     Shall shine from far,
30    And make and mar
      The foolish Fates.
  This was lofty. Now name the rest of the players. This is
  Ercles' vein, a tyrant's vein: a lover is more condoling.

QUINCE: Francis Flute, the bellows-mender?

35 FLUTE: Here Peter Quince.

QUINCE: Flute, you must take Thisby on you.

FLUTE: What is Thisby? A wand'ring knight?

QUINCE: It is the lady that Pyramus must love.

FLUTE: Nay faith, let not me play a woman: I have a beard
40  coming.

QUINCE: That's all one:° you shall play it in a mask, and you may
  speak as small° as you will.

BOTTOM: And° I may hide my face, let me play Thisby too: I'll speak
  in a monstrous little voice; "Thisne, Thisne," "Ah
45  Pyramus, my lover dear, thy Thisby dear, and lady
  dear."

QUINCE: No, no, you must play Pyramus: and Flute, you Thisby.

BOTTOM: Well, proceed.

QUINCE: Robin Starveling, the tailor?

50 STARVELING: Here Peter Quince.

QUINCE: Robin Starveling, you must play Thisby's mother. Tom
  Snout, the tinker?

SNOUT: Here Peter Quince.

QUINCE: You, Pyramus' father; myself, Thisby's father; Snug the
55  joiner, you the lion's part: and I hope here is a play.
  fitted.°

SNUG: Have you the lion's part written? Pray you, if it be, give
  it me: for I am slow of study.

QUINCE: You may do it extempore: for it is nothing but roaring.

60 BOTTOM: Let me play the lion too. I will roar, that° I will do any
  man's heart good to hear me. I will roar, that I will make
  the duke say "Let him roar again: let him roar again."

QUINCE: And you should do it too terribly, you would fright the
  duchess and the ladies, that they would shriek: and
65  that were enough to hang us all.

ALL: That would hang us, every mother's son.

BOTTOM: I grant you, friends, if you should fright the ladies out of
  their wits, they would have no more discretion but to
  hang us: but I will aggravate° my voice so, that I will roar
70  you as gently as any sucking dove: I will roar you and
  'twere° any nightingale.

QUINCE: You can play no part but Pyramus: for Pyramus is a
  sweet-faced man; a proper° man as one shall see in a

---

°28 *Phibbus' car*: Phoebus Apollo's chariot. 41 *That's all one*: never mind. 42 *small*: softly. 43 *And*: if. 56 *fitted*: cast. 60 *that*: so that.
69 *aggravate*: (he means "moderate"). 70–71 *and 'twere*: as if it were. 73 *proper*: handsome.

summer's day; a most lovely gentleman-like man: therefore
you must needs play Pyramus.                                                        75
BOTTOM: Well: I will undertake it. What beard were I best to play
it in?
QUINCE: Why, what you will.
BOTTOM: I will discharge it in either your straw-colour beard, your
orange-tawny beard, your purple-in-grain° beard, or your                            80
French-crown-colour° beard, your perfit yellow.
QUINCE: Some of your French crowns° have no hair at all; and
then you will play barefaced. But masters here are your
parts, and I am to entreat you, request you, and desire
you, to con° them by tomorrow night: and meet me in the                             85
palace wood, a mile without the town, by moonlight;
there will we rehearse: for if we meet in the city, we
shall be dogged with company, and our devices° known.
In the meantime, I will draw a bill of properties,° such
as our play wants. I pray you fail me not.                                          90
BOTTOM: We will meet, and there we may rehearse most obscenely°
and courageously. Take pain, be perfit: adieu.
QUINCE: At the duke's oak we meet.
BOTTOM: Enough: hold, or cut bow-strings.°                          *Exeunt.*

# ACT 2

## [Scene 1. A wood near Athens]

*Enter a* FAIRY *at one door, and* ROBIN GOODFELLOW [PUCK] *at another.*

PUCK: How now spirit, whither wander you?
FAIRY: Over hill, over dale,
Thorough bush, thorough brier,
Over park, over pale,°
  Thorough flood, thorough fire:                                                    5
I do wander everywhere,
Swifter than the moon's sphere:
And I serve the Fairy Queen,
To dew° her orbs° upon the green.
The cowslips° tall her pensioners° be,                                              10
In their gold coats, spots you see:
Those be rubies, fairy favours.°
In those freckles live their savours.°
I must go seek some dewdrops here,
And hang a pearl in every cowslip's ear.                                            15
Farewell thou lob° of spirits: I'll be gone,
Our queen and all her elves come here anon.

---

°80 *purple-in-grain*: dyed permanently purple. 81 *French-crown-colour*: golden, like French crowns (gold coins). 82 *French crowns*: bald heads believed to be caused by syphilis, the "French" disease. 85 *con*: learn by heart. 88 *devices*: plans. 89 *bill of properties*: list of stage props. 91 *obscenely*: (he may mean "fittingly" or "obscurely"). 94 *hold, or cut bow-strings*: (meaning uncertain, but equivalent to "fish, or cut bait"). 4 *pale*: enclosure. 9 *dew*: bedew. *orbs*: fairy rings (circles of high grass). 10 *cowslips*: primroses. *pensioners*: royal bodyguards. 12 *favours*: gifts. 13 *savours*: perfumes. 16 *lob*: lout, lubber.

PUCK:  The king doth keep his revels here tonight.
    Take heed the queen come not within his sight.
20    For Oberon is passing fell° and wrath,
    Because that she, as her attendant, hath
    A lovely boy, stol'n from an Indian king:
    She never had so sweet a changeling.°
    And jealous Oberon would have the child
25    Knight of his train, to trace° the forests wild.
    But she, perforce,° withholds the lovèd boy,
    Crowns him with flowers, and makes him all her joy.
    And now, they never meet in grove or green,
    By fountain clear, or spangled starlight sheen,
30    But they do square,° that all their elves for fear
    Creep into acorn cups, and hide them there.
FAIRY:  Either I mistake your shape and making quite,
    Or else you are that shrewd and knavish sprite
    Called Robin Goodfellow. Are not you he
35    That frights the maidens of the villagery,
    Skim milk,° and sometimes labour in the quern,°
    And bootless° make the breathless housewife churn,
    And sometime make the drink to bear no barm,°
    Mislead night-wanderers, laughing at their harm?
40    Those that Hobgoblin call you, and sweet Puck,
    You do their work, and they shall have good luck.
    Are not you he?
PUCK:            Thou speakest aright;
    I am that merry wanderer of the night.
    I jest to Oberon, and make him smile,
45    When I a fat and bean-fed horse beguile,
    Neighing in likeness of a filly foal;
    And sometime lurk I in a gossip's° bowl,
    In very likeness of a roasted crab,°
    And when she drinks, against her lips I bob,
50    And on her withered dewlap° pour the ale.
    The wisest aunt, telling the saddest tale,
    Sometime for three-foot stool mistaketh me:
    Then slip I from her bum, down topples she,
    And "tailor"° cries, and falls into a cough;
55    And then the whole quire° hold their hips and laugh,
    And waxen° in their mirth, and neeze,° and swear
    A merrier hour was never wasted° there.
    But room° fairy: here comes Oberon.
FAIRY:  And here, my mistress. Would that he were gone.

---

°20 *passing fell*: surpassingly fierce. 23 *changeling*: creature exchanged by fairies for a stolen baby (among the fairies, the stolen child). 25 *trace*: traverse. 26 *perforce*: by force. 30 *square*: quarrel. 36 *Skim milk*: steals the cream off the milk. *quern*: handmill for grinding grain. 37 *bootless*: without result. 38 *barm*: foamy head (therefore the drink was flat). 47 *gossip's*: old woman's. 48 *crab*: crabapple (often put into ale). 50 *dewlap*: loose skin hanging about the throat. 54 *"tailor"*: (variously explained: perhaps the squatting position of the tailor, or "tailard"—one with a tail). 55 *quire*: choir, group. 56 *waxen*: increase. *neeze*: sneeze. 57 *wasted*: spent. 58 *room*: make room.

*Enter [OBERON] the King of Fairies, at one door with his TRAIN, and the QUEEN [TITANIA], at another, with hers.*

OBERON:  Ill met by moonlight, proud Titania.                                60
QUEEN:  What, jealous Oberon? Fairy, skip hence.
    I have forsworn his bed and company.
OBERON:  Tarry, rash wanton,° Am not I thy lord?
QUEEN:  Then I must be thy lady; but I know
    When thou hast stol'n away from fairyland,                       65
    And in the shape of Corin° sat all day,
    Playing on pipes of corn,° and versing love
    To amorous Phillida.° Why art thou here
    Come from the farthest steep of India?
    But that, forsooth, the bouncing Amazon,°                        70
    Your buskined° mistress and your warrior love,
    To Theseus must be wedded; and you come,
    To give their bed joy and prosperity.
OBERON:  How canst thou thus, for shame, Titania,
    Glance at my credit with° Hippolyta,                             75
    Knowing I know thy love to Theseus?
    Didst thou not lead him through the glimmering night,
    From Perigenia, whom he ravishèd?
    And make him with fair Aegles break his faith,
    With Ariadne, and Antiopa°?                                      80
QUEEN:  These are the forgeries of jealousy:
    And never, since the middle summer's spring,°
    Met we on hill, in dale, forest, or mead,
    By pavèd° fountain, or by rushy brook,
    Or in the beachèd margent° of the sea,                           85
    To dance our ringlets to the whistling wind,
    But with thy brawls° thou hast disturbed our sport.
    Therefore° the winds, piping to us in vain,
    As in revenge, have sucked up from the sea
    Contagious° fogs: which falling in the land,                     90
    Hath every pelting° river made so proud,
    That they have overborne their continents.°
    The ox hath therefore stretched his yoke in vain,
    The ploughman lost his sweat, and the green corn°
    Hath rotted, ere his youth attained a beard:°                    95
    The fold° stands empty in the drownèd field,
    And crows are fatted with the murrion° flock.

---

°63 *Tarry, rash wanton*: wait, headstrong one. 66–68 *Corin, Phillida*: (traditional names in pastoral literature for a shepherd and his loved one, respectively). 67 *corn*: wheat straws. 70 *Amazon*: Hippolyta. 71 *buskined*: wearing boots. 75 *Glance . . . credit with*: hint at my favors from. 78–80 *Perigenia . . . Antiopa*: women that Theseus supposedly loved and deserted. 82 *middle . . . spring*: beginning of midsummer. 84 *pavèd*: with a pebbly bottom. 85 *margent*: margin, shore. 87 *brawls*: A brawl was a group dance—*branle* in French—obviously accompanied by noisy shouting and clapping. 88–117 *Therefore . . . original*: (the disturbance in nature reflects the discord between Oberon and Titania). 90 *Contagious*: spreading pestilence. 91 *pelting*: paltry. 92 *overborne their continents*: overflown the banks which contain them. 94 *corn*: grain. 95 *beard*: the tassels on ripened grain. 96 *fold*: enclosure for livestock. 97 *murrion*: dead from murrain, a cattle disease.

The nine men's morris° is filled up with mud;
And the quaint mazes° in the wanton green,°
100    For lack of tread, are undistinguishable.
The human mortals want° their winter here,
No night is now with hymn or carol blest;
Therefore the moon, the governess of floods,
Pale in her anger, washes all the air,
105    That rheumatic diseases do abound.
And thorough this distemperature,° we see
The seasons alter: hoary-headed frosts
Fall in the fresh lap of the crimson rose,
And on old Hiems'° thin and icy crown,
110    An odorous chaplet° of sweet summer buds
Is, as in mockery, set. The spring, the summer,
The childing° autumn, angry winter change
Their wonted liveries:° and the mazèd° world,
By their increase, now knows not which is which:
115    And this same progeny of evils comes
From our debate, from our dissension:
We are their parents and original.
OBERON:  Do you amend it then: it lies in you.
Why should Titania cross her Oberon?
120    I do but beg a little changeling boy,
To be my henchman.°
QUEEN:                         Set your heart at rest.
The fairy land buys not the child of me.
His mother was a vot'ress° of my order:
And in the spicèd Indian air, by night,
125    Full often hath she gossiped by my side.
And sat with me on Neptune's yellow sands,
Marking th' embarkèd traders° on the flood:
When we have laughed to see the sails conceive,
And grow big-bellied with the wanton° wind:
130    Which she, with pretty and with swimming gait,
Following (her womb then rich with my young squire)
Would imitate, and sail upon the land,
To fetch me trifles, and return again,
As from a voyage, rich with merchandise.
135    But she, being mortal, of that boy did die,
And for her sake, do I rear up her boy:
And for her sake, I will not part with him.
OBERON:  How long within this wood intend you stay?
QUEEN:  Perchance till after Theseus' wedding day.
140    If you will patiently dance in our round,°
And see our moonlight revels, go with us:

---

°98 *nine men's morris*: game played on squares cut in the grass on which stones or disks are moved.    99 *quaint mazes*: intricate paths.    *wanton green*: luxuriant grass.    101 *want*: lack.    106 *distemperature*: upset in nature.    109 *Hiems*: god of winter.    110 *odorous chaplet*: sweet-smelling wreath. 112 *childing*: fruitful.    113 *wonted liveries*: accustomed dress.    *mazèd*: amazed.    121 *henchman*: attendant.    123 *vot'ress*: vowed and devoted follower. 127 *traders*: merchant ships.    129 *wanton*: sportive.    140 *round*: round dance.

    If not, shun me, and I will spare° your haunts.
OBERON:  Give me that boy, and I will go with thee.
QUEEN:  Not for thy fairy kingdom. Fairies away
    We shall chide downright, if I longer stay.          145

                                   *Exeunt* [TITANIA *and her* TRAIN.]
OBERON:  Well, go thy way. Thou shalt not from this grove,
    Till I torment thee for this injury.
    My gentle Puck come hither: thou rememb'rest,
    Since° once I sat upon a promontory,
    And heard a mermaid, on a dolphin's back,          150
    Uttering such dulcet and harmonious breath,
    That the rude° sea grew civil° at her song,
    And certain stars shot madly from their spheres,
    To hear the sea-maid's music.
PUCK:                   I remember.
OBERON:  That very time, I saw (but thou couldst not)    155
    Flying between the cold moon and the earth,
    Cupid, all armed: a certain aim he took
    At a fair Vestal,° thronèd by the west,
    And loosed his love-shaft smartly from his bow,
    As it should pierce a hundred thousand hearts:    160
    But I might see young Cupid's fiery shaft
    Quenched in the chaste beams of the wat'ry moon:
    And the imperial vot'ress° passèd on,
    In maiden meditation, fancy-free.°
    Yet marked I where the bolt° of Cupid fell.    165
    It fell upon a little western flower;
    Before, milk-white; now purple with love's wound,
    And maidens call it love-in-idleness.°
    Fetch me that flow'r: the herb I showed thee once.
    The juice of it, on sleeping eyelids laid,    170
    Will make or man or woman madly dote
    Upon the next live creature that it sees.
    Fetch me this herb, and be thou here again
    Ere the leviathan° can swim a league.
PUCK:  I'll put a girdle round about the earth,    175
    In forty minutes.                           *[Exit.]*
OBERON:  Having once this juice,
    I'll watch Titania when she is asleep,
    And drop the liquor of it in her eyes:
    The next thing then she waking looks upon,
    (Be it on lion, bear, or wolf, or bull,    180
    On meddling monkey, or on busy° ape)
    She shall pursue it, with the soul of love.
    And ere I take this charm from off her sight

---

°142 *spare*: shun.  149 *Since*: when.  152 *rude*: rough.  *civil*: calm.  158 *Vestal*: virgin, probable reference to Queen Elizabeth.  163 *imperial vot'ress*: royal devotee (Queen Elizabeth) of Diana.  164 *fancy-free*: free from love.  165 *bolt*: arrow.  168 *love-in-idleness*: pansy.  174 *leviathan*: whale. 182 *busy*: mischievous.

185 (As I can take it with another herb)
 I'll make her render up her page to me.
 But who comes here? I am invisible,
 And I will overhear their conference.

*Enter DEMETRIUS, HELENA following him.*

 DEMETRIUS: I love thee not: therefore pursue me not.
190 Where is Lysander and fair Hermia?
 The one I'll slay: the other slayeth me.
 Thou told'st me they were stol'n unto this wood:
 And here am I, and wood° within this wood:
 Because I cannot meet my Hermia.
195 Hence, get thee gone, and follow me no more.
 HELENA: You draw me, you hard-hearted adamant:°
 But yet you draw not iron, for my heart
 Is true as steel. Leave you your power to draw,
 And I shall have no power to follow you.
200 DEMETRIUS: Do I entice you? Do I speak you fair°?
 Or rather do I not in plainest truth
 Tell you I do not, nor I cannot love you?
 HELENA: And even for that, do I love you the more:
 I am your spaniel: and Demetrius,
205 The more you beat me, I will fawn on you.
 Use me but as your spaniel: spurn me, strike me,
 Neglect me, lose me: only give me leave,
 Unworthy as I am, to follow you.
 What worser place can I beg in your love
210 (And yet a place of high respect with me)
 Than to be usèd as you use your dog.
 DEMETRIUS: Tempt not too much the hatred of my spirit,
 For I am sick, when I do look on thee.
 HELENA: And I am sick, when I look not on you.
215 DEMETRIUS: You do impeach° your modesty too much,
 To leave the city and commit yourself
 Into the hands of one that loves you not,
 To trust the opportunity of night,
 And the ill counsel of a desert° place,
220 With the rich worth of your virginity.
 HELENA: Your virtue is my privilege:° for that°
 It is not night, when I do see your face,
 Therefore I think I am not in the night.
 Nor doth this wood lack worlds of company,
225 For you, in my respect,° are all the world.
 Then how can it be said I am alone,
 When all the world is here to look on me?

---

°193 *wood*: crazy. 196 *adamant*: (1) magnet (2) impenetrably hard lodestone. 200 *speak you fair*: speak to you in a kindly way. 215 *impeach*: discredit. 219 *desert*: deserted. 221 *Your . . . privilege*: your attraction is my excuse (for coming). *for that*: because. 225 *respect*: regard.

DEMETRIUS:  I'll run from thee and hide me in the brakes,°
    And leave thee to the mercy of wild beasts.
HELENA:  The wildest hath not such a heart as you.                  230
    Run when you will: the story shall be changed;
    Apollo flies, and Daphne° holds the chase:
    The dove pursues the griffin:° the mild hind°
    Makes speed to catch the tiger. Bootless° speed,
    When cowardice pursues, and valour flies.              235
DEMETRIUS:  I will not stay° thy questions. Let me go:
    Or if thou follow me, do not believe
    But I shall do thee mischief in the wood.           [*Exit* DEMETRIUS.]
HELENA:  Ay, in the temple, in the town, the field,
    You do me mischief. Fie Demetrius,              240
    Your wrongs do set a scandal on my sex:
    We cannot fight for love, as men may do:
    We should be wooed, and were not made to woo.
    I'll follow thee and make a heaven of hell,
    To die upon the hand I love so well.           *Exit.* 245
OBERON:  Fare thee well nymph. Ere he do leave this grove,
    Thou shalt fly him, and he shall seek thy love.

*Enter* PUCK.

    Hast thou the flower there? Welcome wanderer.
PUCK:  Ay, there it is.
OBERON:              I pray thee give it me.
    I know a bank where the wild thyme blows,         250
    Where oxlips and the nodding violet grows,
    Quite over-canopied with luscious woodbine,
    With sweet musk-roses, and with eglantine:
    There sleeps Titania, sometime of the night,
    Lulled in these flowers, with dances and delight:     255
    And there the snake throws° her enamelled skin,
    Weed° wide enough to wrap a fairy in.
    And with the juice of this, I'll streak her eyes,
    And make her full of hateful fantasies.
    Take thou some of it, and seek through this grove:    260
    A sweet Athenian lady is in love
    With a disdainful youth: anoint his eyes.
    But do it when the next thing he espies
    May be the lady. Thou shalt know the man
    By the Athenian garments he hath on.          265
    Effect it with some care, that he may prove
    More fond° on her, than she upon her love:
    And look thou meet me ere the first cock crow.
PUCK:  Fear not my lord: your servant shall do so.        *Exeunt.*

---

°228 *brakes*: thickets.  232 *Apollo . . . Daphne*: (in Ovid, Apollo pursues Daphne, who turns into a laurel tree).  233 *griffin*: legendary beast with the head of an eagle and the body of a lion.  *hind*: doe.  234 *Bootless*: useless.  236 *stay*: wait for.  256 *throws*: casts off.  257 *weed*: garment.  267 *fond*: doting, madly in love.

## [Scene 2. Another part of the wood]

*Enter* TITANIA *Queen of Fairies with her train.*

QUEEN:  Come, now a roundel° and a fairy song:
    Then, for the third part of a minute, hence—
    Some to kill cankers in the musk-rose buds,
    Some war with reremice° for their leathren wings,
5    To make my small elves coats, and some keep back
    The clamorous owl, that nightly hoots and wonders
    At our quaint° spirits. Sing me now asleep:
    Then to your offices,° and let me rest.

*Fairies sing.*

    You spotted snakes with double° tongue,
10      Thorny hedgehogs be not seen,
    Newts and blind-worms,° do no wrong,
      Come not near our Fairy Queen.
      Philomele,° with melody,
      Sing in our sweet lullaby,
15    Lulla, lulla, lullaby, lulla, lulla, lullaby.
      Never harm,
      Nor spell, nor charm,
    Come our lovely lady nigh.
    So good night, with lullaby.

20 1. FAIRY:  Weaving spiders come not here:
      Hence you long-legged spinners, hence:
    Beetles black approach not near:
    Worm nor snail do no offence.
    Philomele, with melody, &c.
25 2. FAIRY:  Hence away: now all is well:            *She sleeps.*
    One aloof stand sentinel.                 *[Exeunt fairies.]*

*Enter* OBERON *[and applies the flower juice to* TITANIA'S *eyelids.]*

OBERON:  What thou seest, when thou dost wake,
    Do it for thy true love take:
    Love and languish for his sake.
30    Be it ounce,° or cat, or bear,
    Pard,° or boar with bristled hair,
    In thy eye that shall appear,
    When thou wak'st, it is thy dear:
    Wake when some vile thing is near.           *[Exit.]*

*Enter* LYSANDER *and* HERMIA.

35 LYSANDER:  Fair love, you faint with wand'ring in the wood:
    And to speak troth° I have forgot our way.
    We'll rest us Hermia, if you think it good,
    And tarry for the comfort of the day.

---

°1 *roundel*: dance in a ring.  4 *reremice*: bats.  7 *quaint*: dainty.  8 *offices*: duties.  9 *double*: forked.  11 *blind-worms*: legless lizards.  13 *Philomele*: the nightingale.  30 *ounce*: lynx.  31 *Pard*: leopard.  36 *troth*: truth.

HERMIA:  Be't so Lysander: find you out a bed:
   For I upon this bank will rest my head.
LYSANDER:  One turf shall serve as pillow for us both,       40
   One heart, one bed, two bosoms, and one troth.°
HERMIA:  Nay good Lysander: for my sake, my dear,
   Lie further off yet; do not lie so near.
LYSANDER:  O take the sense, sweet, of my innocence.°
   Love takes the meaning in love's conference.°       45
   I mean that my heart unto yours is knit,
   So that but one heart we can make of it:
   Two bosoms interchainèd with an oath,
   So then two bosoms and a single troth.
   Then by your side no bed-room me deny:       50
   For lying so, Hermia, I do not lie.
HERMIA:  Lysander riddles very prettily.
   Now much beshrew° my manners and my pride,
   If Hermia meant to say Lysander lied.
   But gentle friend, for love and courtesy,       55
   Lie further off, in human modesty:
   Such separation as may well be said
   Becomes a virtuous bachelor and a maid,
   So far be distant, and good night sweet friend:
   Thy love ne'er alter till thy sweet life end.       60
LYSANDER:  Amen, amen, to that fair prayer say I,
   And then end life, when I end loyalty.
   Here is my bed: sleep give thee all his rest.
HERMIA:  With half that wish, the wisher's eyes be pressed.°       65

*Enter* PUCK.                                    *They sleep.*

PUCK:  Through the forest have I gone,
   But Athenian found I none,
   On whose eyes I might approve°
   This flower's force in stirring love.
   Night and silence. Who is here?       70
   Weeds° of Athens he doth wear:
   This is he (my master said)
   Despisèd the Athenian maid:
   And here the maiden, sleeping sound,
   On the dank and dirty ground.       75
   Pretty soul, she durst not lie
   Near this lack-love, this kill-courtesy.
   Churl, upon thy eyes I throw
   All the power this charm doth owe.°
   When thou wak'st, let love forbid       80
   Sleep his seat on thy eyelid.°

---

°42 *troth*: true love.  45 *take . . . innocence*: understand the innocence of my remark.  46 *Love . . . conference*: Love enables lovers to understand each other when they converse.  54 *beshrew*: curse.  65 *pressed*: i.e., by sleep.  68 *approve*: test.  71 *Weeds*: garments.  79 *owe*: own.  80–81 *forbid . . . eyelid*: make you sleepless (with love).

So awake when I am gone:
For I must now to Oberon.                                           *Exit.*

*Enter* Demetrius *and* Helena *running.*

Helena:  Stay, thou kill me, sweet Demetrius.
85    Demetrius:  I charge thee hence, and do not haunt me thus.
Helena:  O, wilt thou darkling° leave me? Do not so.
Demetrius:  Stay on thy peril: I alone will go.              *Exit* Demetrius.
Helena:  O, I am out of breath in this fond° chase:
      The more my prayer, the lesser is my grace.°
90    Happy is Hermia, wheresoe'er she lies:
      For she hath blessèd and attractive eyes.
      How came her eyes so bright? Not with salt tears:
      If so, my eyes are oft'ner washed than hers.
      No, no: I am as ugly as a bear:
95    For beasts that meet me run away for fear.
      Therefore no marvel, though Demetrius
      Do as a monster, fly my presence thus.
      What wicked and dissembling glass° of mine,
      Made me compare with Hermia's sphery eyne°!
100   But who is here? Lysander, on the ground?
      Dead, or asleep? I see no blood, no wound.
      Lysander, if you live, good sir awake.
Lysander:  [*Wakes.*] And run through fire, I will for thy sweet sake.
      Transparent° Helena, nature shows art,
105   That through thy bosom, makes me see thy heart.
      Where is Demetrius? O how fit a word
      Is that vile name to perish on my sword!
Helena:  Do not say so, Lysander, say not so.
      What though he love your Hermia? Lord, what though?
110   Yet Hermia still loves you: then be content.
Lysander:  Content with Hermia? No: I do repent
      The tedious minutes I with her have spent.
      Not Hermia, but Helena I love.
      Who will not change a raven for a dove?
115   The will of man is by his reason swayed:°
      And reason says you are the worthier maid.
      Things growing are not ripe until their season:
      So I, being young, till now ripe° not to reason.
      And touching now the point° of human skill,°
120   Reason becomes the marshal to my will,
      And leads me to your eyes; where I o'erlook
      Love's stories, written in love's richest book.
Helena:  Wherefore° was I to this keen mockery born?
      When at your hands did I deserve this scorn?
125   Is't not enough, is't not enough, young man,

---

°86 *darkling*: in the dark. 88 *fond*: foolishly doting. 89 *my grace*: favor shown to me. 98 *glass*: looking glass. 99 *sphery eyne*: starry eyes. 104 *Transparent*: radiant. 115 *swayed*: ruled. 118 *ripe*: mature. 119 *point*: peak. *skill*: knowledge. 123 *Wherefore*: why.

That I did never, no, nor never can,
Deserve a sweet look from Demetrius' eye,
But you must flout° my insufficiency?
Good troth you do me wrong, good sooth you do,
In such disdainful manner me to woo.
But fare you well: perforce I must confess, 130
I thought you lord of more true gentleness.°
O, that a lady, of one man refused,
Should of another, therefore be abused!                                    *Exit.*

LYSANDER:  She sees not Hermia. Hermia, sleep thou there, 135
And never mayst thou come Lysander near.
For, as a surfeit of the sweetest things
The deepest loathing to the stomach brings:
Or as the heresies that men do leave,
Are hated most of those they did deceive: 140
So thou, my surfeit and my heresy,
Of all be hated; but the most, of me:
And all my powers, address your love and might,
To honour Helen, and to be her knight.                                    *Exit.*

HERMIA:  [*Wakes.*] Help me Lysander, help me: do thy best 145
To pluck this crawling serpent from my breast.
Ay me, for pity. What a dream was here?
Lysander, look how I do quake with fear.
Methought a serpent eat my heart away,
And you sat smiling at his cruel prey.° 150
Lysander: what, removed? Lysander, lord!
What, out of hearing, gone? No sound, no word?
Alack, where are you? Speak, and if you hear:
Speak, of° all loves. I swoon almost with fear.
No? Then I well perceive you are not nigh: 155
Either death, or you, I'll find immediately.                              *Exit.*

## ACT 3

### [Scene 1. The wood]

*Enter the* CLOWNS [QUINCE, SNUG, BOTTOM, FLUTE, SNOUT, *and* STARVELING.]

BOTTOM:  Are we all met?
QUINCE:  Pat, pat: and here's a marvellous convenient place for
our rehearsal. This green plot shall be our stage, this
hawthorn brake° our tiring-house,° and we will do it in
action, as we will do it before the duke.
BOTTOM:  Peter Quince? 5
QUINCE:  What sayest thou, bully° Bottom?

---

°128 *flout:* mock. 132 *lord . . . gentleness:* more of a gentleman. 150 *prey:* preying. 154 *of:* for the sake of. 4 *brake:* thicket. *tiring-house:* dressing
room. 7 *bully:* "old pal."

BOTTOM:  There are things in this Comedy of Pyramus and Thisby
    that will never please. First, Pyramus must draw a sword
10    to kill himself; which the ladies cannot abide. How
    answer you that?

SNOUT:  By'r lakin,° a parlous° fear.

STARVELING:  I believe we must leave the killing out, when all is done.

BOTTOM:  Not a whit: I have a device to make all well. Write me
15    a prologue, and let the prologue seem to say, we will
    do no harm with our swords, and that Pyramus is not
    killed indeed: and for the more better assurance, tell
    them that I Pyramus am not Pyramus, but Bottom the
    weaver: this will put them out of fear.

20 QUINCE:  Well, we will have such a prologue, and it shall be
    written in eight and six.°

BOTTOM:  No, make it two more: let it be written in eight and
    eight.

SNOUT:  Will not the ladies be afeared of the lion?

25 STARVELING:  I fear it, I promise you.

BOTTOM:  Masters, you ought to consider with yourselves, to bring
    in (God shield us) a lion among ladies, is a most dreadful
    thing. For there is not a more fearful wild-fowl than
    your lion living: and we ought to look to't.

30 SNOUT:  Therefore another prologue must tell he is not a lion.

BOTTOM:  Nay, you must name his name, and half his face must be
    seen through the lion's neck, and he himself must speak
    through, saying thus, or to the same defect:° "Ladies,"
    or "Fair ladies—I would wish you," or "I would request
35    you," or "I would entreat you, not to fear,
    not to tremble: my life for yours. If you think I come
    hither as a lion, it were pity of my life. No, I am no
    such thing: I am a man as other men are." And there
    indeed let him name his name, and tell them plainly he
40    is Snug the joiner.

QUINCE:  Well, it shall be so, but there is two hard things: that is,
    to bring the moonlight into a chamber: for you know,
    Pyramus and Thisby meet by moonlight.

SNOUT:  Doth the moon shine that night we play our play?

45 BOTTOM:  A calendar, a calendar: look in the almanac: find out
    moonshine, find out moonshine.

QUINCE:  Yes, it doth shine that night.

BOTTOM:  Why then may you leave a casement of the great
    chamber window, where we play, open; and the moon may
50    shine in at the casement.

QUINCE:  Ay, or else one must come in with a bush of thorns° and
    a lantern, and say he comes to disfigure,° or to present,
    the person of Moonshine. Then, there is another thing;

---

°12 *By'r lakin*: mild oath, "by Our Lady." *parlous*: awful, perilous.  21 *eight and six*: alternate lines of eight and six syllables (the ballad meter).
33 *defect*: (he means "effect").  51 *bush of thorns*: bundle of firewood (the man in the moon was supposed to have been placed there as a punishment for gathering wood on Sundays).  52 *disfigure*: (he means "figure," symbolize).

we must have a wall in the great chamber: for Pyramus
and Thisby, says the story, did talk through the chink 55
of a wall.

SNOUT: You can never bring in a wall. What say you, Bottom?

BOTTOM: Some man or other must present wall: and let him have
some plaster, or some loam, or some rough-cast° about
him, to signify wall; and let him hold his fingers thus: 60
and through that cranny, shall Pyramus and Thisby whisper.

QUINCE: If that may be, then all is well. Come, sit down every
mother's son, and rehearse your parts. Pyramus, you
begin: when you have spoken your speech, enter into that
brake, and so every one according to his cue. 65

*Enter* PUCK.

PUCK: What hempen homespuns° have we swagg'ring here,
So near the cradle of the Fairy Queen?
What, a play toward°? I'll be an auditor,
An actor too perhaps, if I see cause.

QUINCE: Speak Pyramus. Thisby stand forth. 70

PYRAMUS: Thisby, the flowers of odious savours sweet—

QUINCE: "Odorous, odorous."

PYRAMUS: —odours savours sweet,
So hath thy breath, my dearest Thisby dear.
But hark, a voice: stay thou but here awhile, 75
And by and by I will to thee appear. *Exit* PYRAMUS
[*Exit.*]

PUCK: A stranger Pyramus than e'er played here.

THISBY: Must I speak now?

QUINCE: Ay marry must you. For you must understand he goes
but to see a noise that he heard, and is to come again. 80

THISBY: Most radiant Pyramus, most lily-white of hue,
Of colour like the red rose, on triumphant brier,
Most brisky juvenal,° and eke most lovely Jew,°
As true as truest horse, that yet would never tire,
I'll meet thee Pyramus, at Ninny's tomb. 85

QUINCE: "Ninus' tomb,"° man: why, you must not speak that yet.
That you answer to Pyramus. You speak all your part
at once, cues and all. Pyramus, enter; your cue is past:
it is "never tire."

THISBY: O—As true as truest horse, that yet would never tire. 90

*Enter* PYRAMUS *with the ass-head* [*followed by* PUCK].

PYRAMUS: If I were fair, Thisby, I were only thine.

QUINCE: O monstrous! O strange! We are haunted. Pray masters,
fly masters. Help! *The clowns all exeunt.*

PUCK: I'll follow you: I'll lead you about a round,°
Through bog, through bush, through brake, through brier. 95

---

°59 *rough-cast*: coarse plaster of lime and gravel. 66 *hempen homespuns*: wearers of clothing spun at home from hemp. 68 *toward*: in preparation.
83 *brisky juvenal*: lively youth. *Jew*: diminutive of either "juvenal" or "jewel." 86 *Ninus' tomb*: (tomb of the founder of Nineveh, and meeting place
of the lovers in Ovid's version of the Pyramus story). 94 *about a round*: in circles, like a round dance (round about).

Sometime a horse I'll be, sometime a hound,
   A hog, a headless bear, sometime a fire,
And neigh, and bark, and grunt, and roar, and burn,
Like horse, hound, hog, bear, fire, at every turn.         *Exit.*

100 BOTTOM: Why do they run away? This is a knavery of them to
   make me afeared.

*Enter* SNOUT.

SNOUT: O Bottom, thou art changed. What do I see on thee?
BOTTOM: What do you see? You see an ass-head of your own, do
   you?                                    [*Exit* SNOUT.]

*Enter* QUINCE.

105 QUINCE: Bless thee Bottom, bless thee. Thou art translated.°      *Exit.*
BOTTOM: I see their knavery. This is to make an ass of me, to
   fright me if they could: but I will not stir from this
   place, do what they can. I will walk up and down here,
   and will sing that they shall hear I am not afraid.
110       [*Sings.*] The woose° cock, so black of hue,
           With orange tawny bill,
        The throstle,° with his note so true,
           The wren, with little quill.°
TITANIA: What angel wakes me from my flow'ry bed?
115 BOTTOM: [*Sings.*] The finch, the sparrow, and the lark,
           The plain-song° cuckoo gray:
        Whose note full many a man doth mark,
           And dares not answer, nay.
   For indeed, who would set his wit to° so foolish a bird?
120    Who would give a bird the lie,° though he cry "cuckoo"°
   never so°?
TITANIA: I pray thee, gentle mortal, sing again.
   Mine ear is much enamoured of thy note:
   So is mine eye enthrallèd to thy shape
125    And thy fair virtue's force (perforce°) doth move me,
   On the first view to say, to swear, I love thee.
BOTTOM: Methinks mistress, you should have little reason for
   that. And yet, to say the truth, reason and love keep
   little company together now-a-days. The more the pity,
130    That some honest neighbours will not make them friends.
   Nay, I can gleek° upon occasion.
TITANIA: Thou art as wise as thou art beautiful.
BOTTOM: Not so neither: but if I had wit enough to get out of
   this wood, I have enough to serve mine own turn.
135 TITANIA: Out of this wood do not desire to go:
   Thou shalt remain here, whether thou wilt or no.
   I am a spirit of no common rate:°

---

°105 *translated*: transformed. 110 *woose*: ousel, blackbird. 112 *throstle*: thrush. 113 *quill*: piping note. 116 *plain-song*: sounding a simple unvaried note. 119 *set . . . to*: match his wit against. 120 *Who . . . lie*: who could call a bird a liar. *"cuckoo"*: (which sounded like "cuckold" = a deceived husband). 121 *never so*: i.e., often. 125 *perforce*: by force. 131 *gleek*: joke satirically. 137 *rate*: rank, value.

The summer still doth tend upon my state,°
And I do love thee: therefore go with me.
I'll give thee fairies to attend on thee:                                         140
And they shall fetch thee jewels from the deep,
And sing, while thou on pressèd flowers dost sleep:
And I will purge thy mortal grossness so,
That thou shalt like an airy spirit go.
Peaseblossom, Cobweb, Moth,° and Mustardseed!                      145

*Enter four* FAIRIES.

PEASEBLOSSOM: Ready.
COBWEB: And I.
MOTH:            And I.
MUSTARDSEED:         And I.
ALL:                              Where shall we go?
TITANIA: Be kind and courteous to this gentleman,
   Hop in his walks and gambol in° his eyes,
   Feed him with apricocks° and dewberries,°                              150
   With purple grapes, green figs, and mulberries.
   The honey-bags steal from the humblebees,°
   And for night-tapers, crop° their waxen thighs,
   And light them at the fiery glow-worm's eyes,
   To have my love to bed and to arise:                                         155
   And pluck the wings from painted butterflies,
   To fan the moonbeams from his sleeping eyes.
   Nod to him elves, and do him courtesies.
PEASEBLOSSOM: Hail, mortal.
COBWEB: Hail.
MOTH: Hail.                                                                                    160
MUSTARDSEED: Hail.
BOTTOM: I cry your worships mercy,° heartily: I beseech your
   worship's name.
COBWEB: Cobweb.
BOTTOM: I shall desire you of more acquaintance, good Master     165
   Cobweb: if I cut my finger,° I shall make bold with you.
   Your name, honest gentleman?
PEASEBLOSSOM: Peaseblossom.
BOTTOM: I pray you commend me° to Mistress Squash,° your mother,   170
   and to Master Peascod,° your father. Good Master Peaseblossom,
   I shall desire you of more acquaintance, too.
   Your name I beseech you sir?
MUSTARDSEED: Mustardseed.
BOTTOM: Good Master Mustardseed, I know your patience well.        175
   That same cowardly giant-like ox beef hath devoured
   many a gentleman of your house. I promise you, your

---

°138 *still . . . state*: always serves as an attendant in my royal train.  145 *Moth*: mote (so pronounced), tiny speck.  149 *gambol in*: caper before.
150 *apricocks*: apricots.  *dewberries*: blackberries.  152 *humblebees*: bumblebees.  153 *crop*: clip.  163 *I . . . mercy*: I respectfully beg your pardons.
167 *cut my finger*: (cobwebs were used to stop bleeding).  170 *commend me*: offer my respects.  *Squash*: unripe peapod.  171 *Peascod*: ripe peapod.

kindred hath made my eyes water ere now. I desire you
of more acquaintance, good Master Mustardseed.
TITANIA:  Come wait upon him: lead him to my bower.
          The moon methinks looks with a wat'ry eye:
          And when she weeps, weeps every little flower,
          Lamenting some enforcèd° chastity.
          Tie up my lover's tongue, bring him silently.                                 *Exeunt.*

## [Scene 2. Another part of the wood]

*Enter [OBERON,] King of Fairies, solus.°*

OBERON:  I wonder if Titania be awakèd;
          Then what it was that next came in her eye,
          Which she must dote on in extremity.

*Enter PUCK.*

          Here comes my messenger. How now, mad spirit?
          What night-rule° now about this haunted grove?
PUCK:  My mistress with a monster is in love.
          Near to her close and consecrated bower,
          While she was in her dull° and sleeping hour,
          A crew of patches,° rude mechanicals,°
          That work for bread upon Athenian stalls,°
          Were met together to rehearse a play,
          Intended for great Theseus' nuptial day:
          The shallowest thickskin of that barren sort,°
          Who Pyramus presented in their sport,
          Forsook his scene and entered in a brake:
          When I did him at this advantage take,
          An ass's nole° I fixèd on his head.
          Anon° his Thisby must be answerèd,
          And forth my mimic° comes. When they him spy,
          As wild geese, that the creeping fowler° eye,
          Or russet-pated choughs,° many in sort,°
          Rising and cawing at the gun's report,
          Sever themselves and madly sweep the sky,
          So at his sight away his fellows fly:
          And at our stamp, here o'er and o'er one falls:
          He murder cries, and help from Athens calls.
          Their sense thus weak, lost with their fears thus strong,
          Made senseless things begin to do them wrong.
          For briers and thorns at their apparel snatch:
          Some° sleeves, some hats; from yielders, all things catch°
          I led them on in this distracted° fear,

---

°183 *enforced*: violated. S.D.: *solus*: alone. 5 *night-rule*: diversion ("misrule") in the night. 8 *dull*: drowsy. 9 *patches*: fools. *mechanicals*: workers. 10 *stalls*: shops. 13 *barren sort*: stupid crew. 17 *nole*: head, noodle. 18 *Anon*: presently. 19 *mimic*: actor. 20 *fowler*: hunter of fowl. 21 *russet-pated choughs*: grey-headed jackdaws. *sort*: a flock. 30 *Some*: i.e., snatch. *from yielders . . . catch*: (everything joins in to harm the weak). 31 *distracted*: maddened.

And left sweet Pyramus translated there:
When in that moment (so it came to pass)
Titania waked, and straightway loved an ass.
OBERON:  This falls out better than I could devise.                    35
    But has thou yet latched° the Athenian's eyes
    With the love-juice, as I did bid thee do?
PUCK:  I took him sleeping (that is finished too)
    And the Athenian woman by his side;
    That when he waked, of force° she must be eyed.                    40

*Enter DEMETRIUS and HERMIA.*

OBERON:  Stand close:° this is the same Athenian.
PUCK:  This is the woman: but not this the man.
DEMETRIUS:  O why rebuke you him that loves you so?
    Lay breath so bitter on your bitter foe.
HERMIA:  Now I but chide: but I should use thee worse,                 45
    For thou, I fear, hast given me cause to curse.
    If thou hast slain Lysander in his sleep,
    Being o'er shoes in blood, plunge in the deep,
    And kill me too.
    The sun was not so true unto the day,                             50
    As he to me. Would he have stolen away
    From sleeping Hermia? I'll believe as soon
    This whole° earth may be bored,° and that the moon
    May through the center creep, and so displease
    Her brother's noontide with th' Antipodes.°                       55
    It cannot be but thou hast murdered him.
    So should a murderer look; so dead,° so grim.
DEMETRIUS:  So should the murdered look, and so should I,
    Pierced through the heart with your stern cruelty.
    Yet you, the murderer, look as bright, as clear                   60
    As yonder Venus in her glimmering sphere.°
HERMIA:  What's this to my Lysander? Where is he?
    Ah good Demetrius, wilt thou give him me?
DEMETRIUS:  I had rather give his carcass to my hounds.
HERMIA:  Out dog, out cur! Thou driv'st me past the bounds           65
    Of maiden's patience. Hast thou slain him then?
    Henceforth be never numbered among men.
    O, once tell true: tell true, even for my sake:
    Durst thou have looked upon him, being awake?
    And hast thou killed him sleeping? O brave touch°!                70
    Could not a worm,° an adder, do so much?
    An adder did it: for with doubler tongue°
    Than thine, thou serpent, never adder stung.

---

°36 *latched*: moistened. 40 *of force*: by necessity. 41 *close*: hidden. 53 *whole*: solid. *be bored*: have a hole bored through it. 55 *Her brother's . . . Antipodes*: the noon of her brother sun, by appearing among the Antipodes (the people on the other side of the earth). 57 *dead*: deadly. 61 *sphere*: (in the Ptolemaic system, each planet moved in its own sphere around the earth). 70 *brave touch*: splendid stroke (ironic). 71 *worm*: snake. 72 *doubler tongue*: (1) tongue more forked (2) more deceitful speech.

DEMETRIUS: You spend your passion on a misprised mood°
    I am not guilty of Lysander's blood:
    Nor is he dead, for aught that I can tell.
HERMIA: I pray thee, tell me then that he is well.
DEMETRIUS: And if I could, what should I get therefore?
HERMIA: A privilege never to see me more:
    And from thy hated presence part I so:
    See me no more, whether he be dead or no.        *Exit.*
DEMETRIUS: There is no following her in this fierce vein.
    Here therefore for a while I will remain.
    So sorrow's heaviness doth heavier grow
    For debt that bankrout sleep doth sorrow owe:°
    Which now in some slight measure it will pay,
    If for his tender° here I make some stay.°      *Lies down.*
OBERON: What hast thou done? Thou hast mistaken quite,
    And laid the love-juice on some true-love's sight.
    Of thy misprision° must perforce° ensue
    Some true love turned, and not a false turned true.
PUCK: Then fate o'errules, that one man holding troth,
    A million fail, confounding° oath on oath.°
OBERON: About the wood, go swifter than the wind,
    And Helena of Athens look thou find.
    All fancy-sick° she is, and pale of cheer,°
    With sighs of love, that costs the fresh blood dear.
    By some illusion see thou bring her here:
    I'll charm his eyes against she do appear.°
PUCK: I go, I go, look how I go.
    Swifter than arrow from the Tartar's bow.°     *Exit.*
OBERON: Flower of this purple dye,
    Hit with Cupid's archery,
    Sink in apple of his eye:
    When his love he doth espy,
    Let her shine as gloriously
    As the Venus of the sky.
    When thou wak'st, if she be by,
    Beg of her for remedy.

*Enter PUCK.*

PUCK: Captain of our fairy band,
    Helena is here at hand,
    And the youth, mistook by me,
    Pleading for a lover's fee.°
    Shall we their fond pageant° see?
    Lord, what fools these mortals be!

---

°74 *on . . . mood*: in mistaken anger. 85 *For debt . . . owe*: because sleep cannot pay the debt of repose he owes the man who is kept awake by sorrow. 87 *tender*: offer. *stay*: pause. 90 *misprision*: mistake. *perforce*: of necessity. 93 *confounding*: destroying. *oath on oath*: one oath after another. 96 *fancy-sick*: lovesick. *cheer*: face. 99 *against . . . appear*: in preparation for her appearance. 101 *Tartar's bow*: (the Tartars, who used powerful Oriental bows, were famed as archers). 113 *fee*: reward. 114 *fond pageant*: foolish spectacle.

OBERON:  Stand aside. The noise they make
         Will cause Demetrius to awake.
PUCK:  Then will two at once woo one:
       That must needs be sport alone.°
       And those things do best please me                          120
       That befall prepost'rously.

*Enter LYSANDER and HELENA.*

LYSANDER:  Why should you think that I should woo in scorn?
           Scorn and derision never come in tears.
           Look when I vow, I weep: and vows so born,
           In their nativity all truth appears.°                    125
           How can these things in me seem scorn to you,
           Bearing the badge° of faith to prove them true?
HELENA:  You do advance your cunning more and more.
         When truth kills truth,° O devilish-holy fray!
         These vows are Hermia's. Will you give her o'er?          130
         Weigh oath with oath, and you will nothing weigh.
         Your vows to her and me, put in two scales,
         Will even weigh: and both as light as tales.
LYSANDER:  I had no judgment, when to her I swore.
HELENA:  Nor none, in my mind, now you give her o'er.              135
LYSANDER:  Demetrius loves her: and he loves not you.
DEMETRIUS:  [*Awakes.*] O Helen, goddess, nymph, perfect, divine,
            To what, my love, shall I compare thine eyne!
            Crystal is muddy. O, how ripe in show,
            Thy lips, those kissing cherries, tempting grow!       140
            That pure congealèd white, high Taurus'° snow,
            Fanned with the eastern wind, turns to a crow,
            When thou hold'st up thy hand. O let me kiss
            This princess of pure white,° this seal of bliss.
HELENA:  O spite! O hell! I see you all are bent                   145
         To set against me, for your merriment.
         If you were civil,° and knew courtesy,
         You would not do me thus much injury.
         Can you not hate me, as I know you do,
         But you must join in souls° to mock me too?               150
         If you were men, as men you are in show,
         You would not use a gentle lady so;
         To vow, and swear, and superpraise my parts,°
         When I am sure you hate me with your hearts.
         You both are rivals, and love Hermia:                     155
         And now both rivals, to mock Helena.
         A trim° exploit, a manly enterprise,
         To conjure tears up in a poor maid's eyes

---

°119 *alone*: unique. 124–25 *vows . . . appears*: vows born in weeping must be true ones. 127 *badge*: (1) outward signs (2) family crest. 129 *truth kills truth*: Former true love is killed by vows of present true love. 141 *Taurus*: mountain range in Asia Minor. 144 *princess . . . white*: sovereign example of whiteness (her hand). 147 *civil*: well behaved. 150 *join in souls*: agree in spirit. 153 *parts*: qualities. 157 *trim*: fine (ironic).

With your derision. None of noble sort
160     Would so offend a virgin, and extort°
A poor soul's patience, all to make you sport.
LYSANDER: You are unkind, Demetrius: be not so.
For you love Hermia: this you know I know.
And here, with all good will, with all my heart,
165     In Hermia's love I yield you up my part:
And yours of Helena to be bequeath,
Whom I do love, and will do to my death.
HELENA: Never did mockers waste more idle breath.
DEMETRIUS: Lysander, keep thy Hermia: I will none,°
170     If e'er I loved her, all that love is gone.
My heart to her but as guest-wise sojourned:°
And now to Helen is it home returned,
There to remain.
LYSANDER:            Helen, it is not so.
DEMETRIUS: Disparage not the faith thou dost not know,
175     Lest to thy peril thou aby it dear.°
Look where thy love comes: yonder is thy dear.

*Enter* HERMIA.

HERMIA: Dark night, that from the eye his function takes,
The ear more quick of apprehension makes.
Wherein it doth impair the seeing sense,
180     It pays the hearing double recompense.
Thou art not by mine eye, Lysander, found:
Mine ear, I thank it, brought me to thy sound.
But why unkindly didst thou leave me so?
LYSANDER: Why should he stay, whom love doth press to go?
185 HERMIA: What love could press Lysander from my side?
LYSANDER: Lysander's love, that would not let him bide—
Fair Helena: who more engilds the night
Than all your fiery oes and eyes of light.°
Why seek'st thou me? Could not this make thee know,
190     The hate I bare thee made me leave thee so?
HERMIA: You speak not as you think: it cannot be.
HELENA: Lo: She is one of this confederacy.
Now I perceive they have conjoined all three,
To fashion this false sport in spite of° me.
195     Injurious° Hermia, most ungrateful maid,
Have you conspired, have you with these contrived
To bait° me with this foul derision?
Is all the counsel° that we two have shared,
The sisters' vows, the hours that we have spent,
200     When we have chid the hasty-footed time
For parting us; O, is all forgot?

---

°160 *extort*: wring. 169 *none*: have none of her. 171 *to her . . . sojourned*: visited her only as a guest. 175 *aby it dear*: buy it at a high price. 188 *oes . . . light*: stars. 194 *in spite of*: to spite. 195 *Injurious*: insulting. 197 *bait*: attack. 198 *counsel*: secrets.

All schooldays' friendship, childhood innocence?
We Hermia, like two artificial° gods,
Have with our needles created both one flower,
Both on one sampler,° sitting on one cushion,                     205
Both warbling of one song, both in one key;
As if our hands, our sides, voices, and minds
Had been incorporate.° So we grew together,
Like to a double cherry, seeming parted,
But yet an union in partition,                                    210
Two lovely berries moulded on one stem:
So with two seeming bodies, but one heart,
Two of the first, like coats in heraldry,
Due but to one, and crownèd with one crest.°
And will you rent° our ancient love asunder,                      215
To join with men in scorning your poor friend?
It is not friendly, 'tis not maidenly.
Our sex, as well as I, may chide you for it;
Though I alone do feel the injury.

HERMIA:  I am amazèd at your passionate words:                    220
I scorn you not. It seems that you scorn me.

HELENA:  Have you not set Lysander, as in scorn,
To follow me, and praise my eyes and face?
And made your other love, Demetrius
(Who even but now did spurn° me with his foot)                    225
To call me goddess, nymph, divine, and rare,
Precious, celestial? Wherefore speaks he this
To her he hates? And wherefore doth Lysander
Deny your love, so rich within his soul,
And tender° me (forsooth) affection,                              230
But by your setting on, by your consent?
What though I be not so in grace° as you,
So hung upon with love, so fortunate,
But miserable most, to love unloved?
This you should pity, rather than despise.                        235

HERMIA:  I understand not what you mean by this.

HELENA:  Ay, do. Persèver, counterfeit sad° looks:
Make mouths upon° me when I turn my back:
Wink each at other, hold the sweet jest up.
This sport well carried, shall be chronicled.°                    240
If you have any pity, grace, or manners,
You would not make me such an argument.°
But fare ye well: 'tis partly my own fault:
Which death or absence soon shall remedy.

LYSANDER:  Stay, gentle Helena: hear my excuse,                   245
My love, my life, my soul, fair Helena.

---

°203 *artificial*: skilled in art. 205 *sampler*: work of embroidery. 208 *incorporate*: in one body. 213–14 *Two . . . crest*: (the two bodies being) like double coats of arms joined under one crest (with one heart). 215 *rent*: rend, tear. 225 *spurn*: kick. 230 *tender*: offer. 232 *in grace*: favored. 237 *sad*: serious. 238 *mouths upon*: faces at. 240 *chronicled*: written down in the history books. 242 *argument*: subject (of your mockery).

HELENA: O excellent!

HERMIA:                    Sweet, do not scorn her so.

DEMETRIUS: If she cannot entreat,° I can compel.

LYSANDER: Thou canst compel no more than she entreat.

      Thy threats have no more strength than her weak prayers.
      Helen, I love thee, by my life I do:
      I swear by that which I will lose for thee.
      To prove° him false that says I love thee not.

DEMETRIUS: I say I love thee more than he can do.

5  LYSANDER: If thou say so, withdraw, and prove° it too.

DEMETRIUS: Quick, Come.

HERMIA:                    Lysander, whereto tends all this?

LYSANDER: Away, you Ethiope.°

DEMETRIUS:                    No, no, sir,

      Seem to break loose: take on as you would follow;
      But yet come not.° You are a tame man, go.

0  LYSANDER: Hang off,° thou cat, thou burr: vile thing, let loose;
      Or I will shake thee from me like a serpent.

HERMIA: Why are you grown so rude? What change is this,
      Sweet love?

LYSANDER: Thy love? Out, tawny Tartar, out;
      Out, loathèd med'cine: O hated potion, hence!

HERMIA: Do you not jest?

55  HELENA:                    Yes sooth: and so do you.

LYSANDER: Demetrius, I will keep my word° with thee.

DEMETRIUS: I would I had your bond.° For I perceive
      A weak bond holds you. I'll not trust your word.

LYSANDER: What? Should I hurt her, strike her, kill her dead?

70      Although I hate her, I'll not harm her so.

HERMIA: What? Can you do me greater harm than hate?
      Hate me, wherefore°? O me, what news,° my love?
      Am not I Hermia? Are not you Lysander?
      I am as fair now, as I was erewhile.°

75      Since night, you loved me; yet since night, you left me.
      Why then, you left me—O, the gods forbid—
      In earnest, shall I say?

LYSANDER:                    Ay, by my life:
      And never did desire to see thee more.
      Therefore be out of hope, of question, of doubt:

80      Be certain: nothing truer: 'tis no jest
      That I do hate thee, and love Helena.

HERMIA: O me, you juggler,° you canker blossom,°
      You thief of love: what, have you come by night,
      And stol'n my love's heart from him?

---

°248 *entreat*: sway you by entreaty. 253, 255 *prove*: i.e., by a duel. 257 *Ethiope*: (because she is a brunette). 258–59 *Seem . . . not*: You only seem to break loose from Hermia and pretend to follow me to a duel, but you actually hold back. 260 *Hang off*: let go. 266 *keep my word*: i.e., to duel. 267 *bond*: written agreement. 272 *wherefore*: why. *what news*: what's the matter. 274 *erewhile*: a short while ago. 282 *juggler*: deceiver. *canker blossom*: worm that causes canker in blossoms.

HELENA:                              Fine, i' faith.                                    285
   Have you no modesty, no maiden shame,
   No touch of bashfulness? What, will you tear
   Impatient answers from my gentle tongue?
   Fie, fie, you counterfeit, you puppet,° you.
HERMIA:  Puppet? Why so—ay, that way goes the game.
   Now I perceive that she hath made compare                      290
   Between our statures, she hath urged her height,
   And with her personage, her tall personage,
   Her height (forsooth) she hath prevailed with him.
   And are you grown so high in his esteem.
   Because I am so dwarfish and so low?                            295
   How low am I, thou painted maypole? Speak:
   How low am I? I am not yet so low,
   But that my nails can reach unto thine eyes.
HELENA:  I pray you, though you mock me, gentlemen,
   Let her not hurt me. I was never curst:°                        300
   I have no gift at all in shrewishness:
   I am a right maid for my cowardice:°
   Let her not strike me. You perhaps may think,
   Because she is something lower than myself,
   That I can match her.                                          305
HERMIA:                    Lower? Hark again.
HELENA:  Good Hermia, do not be so bitter with me,
   I evermore did love you Hermia.
   Did ever keep your counsels, never wronged you;
   Save that in love unto Demetrius,
   I told him of your stealth unto this wood.
   He followed you: for love I followed him.                      310
   But he hath chid me hence, and threatened me
   To strike me, spurn me, nay to kill me too;
   And now, so° you will let me quiet go,
   To Athens will I bear my folly back,
   And follow you no further. Let me go.                          315
   You see how simple and how fond° I am.
HERMIA:  Why, get you gone. Who is't that hinders you?
HELENA:  A foolish heart, that I leave here behind.
HERMIA:  What, with Lysander?
HELENA:                    With Demetrius.
LYSANDER:  Be not afraid: she shall not harm thee Helena.         320
DEMETRIUS:  No sir: she shall not, though you take her part.
HELENA:  O when she's angry, she is keen and shrewd.°
   She was a vixen when she went to school:
   And though she be but little, she is fierce.
HERMIA:  "Little" again? Nothing but "low" and "little"?          325
   Why will you suffer her to flout° me thus?
   Let me come to her.

---

°288 *puppet*: (Hermia is short and Helena tall). 300 *curst*: bad-tempered. 302 *right . . . cowardice*: true woman in being cowardly. 314 *so*: if. 317 *fond*: foolish. 323 *keen and shrewd*: sharp and malicious. 327 *flout*: mock.

LYSANDER:                    Get you gone, you dwarf;
       You minimus,° of hind'ring knot-grass° made;
       You bead, you acorn.
330 DEMETRIUS:                    You are too officious
       In her behalf that scorns your services.
       Let her alone: speak not of Helena,
       Take not her part. For if thou dost intend°
       Never so little show of love to her,
335    Thou shalt aby it.°
LYSANDER:                    Now she holds me not:
       Now follow, if thou dar'st, to try whose right,
       Of thine or mine, is most in Helena.°
DEMETRIUS: Follow? Nay, I'll go with thee, cheek by jowl.

                                        *Exeunt* LYSANDER *and* DEMETRIUS.

HERMIA: You, mistress, all this coil is long of° you.
       Nay, go not back.
340 HELENA:                    I will not trust you, I,
       Nor longer stay in your curst company
       Your hands than mine are quicker for a fray:
       My legs are longer though, to run away.                    [*Exit.*]
HERMIA: I am amazed,° and know not what to say.                    *Exit.*
345 OBERON: This is thy negligence: still thou mistak'st,
       Or else commit'st thy knaveries wilfully.
PUCK: Believe me, king of shadows, I mistook.
       Did not you tell me I should know the man
       By the Athenian garments he had on?
350    And so far blameless proves my enterprise,
       That I have 'nointed an Athenian's eyes:
       And so far am I glad it so did sort,°
       As this their jangling I esteem a sport.
OBERON: Thou seest these lovers seek a place to fight;
355    Hie therefore Robin, overcast the night,
       The starry welkin° cover thou anon
       With drooping fog as black as Acheron,°
       And lead these testy° rivals so astray,
       As° one come not within another's way.
360    Like to Lysander sometime frame thy tongue:
       Then stir Demetrius up with bitter wrong:°
       And sometime rail thou like Demetrius:
       And from each other look thou lead them thus;
       Till o'er their brows death-counterfeiting sleep
365    With leaden legs and batty wings doth creep:
       Then crush this herb into Lysander's eye;
       Whose liquor hath this virtuous° property,
       To take from thence all error with his might,

---

°329 *minimus*: smallest of creatures. *knot-grass*: weed believed to stunt the growth if eaten. 333 *intend*: extend. 335 *aby it*: buy it dearly.
336–37 *try . . . Helena*: prove by fighting which of us has most right to Helena. 339 *coil is long of*: turmoil is because of. 344 *amazed*: confused.
352 *sort*: turn out. 356 *welkin*: sky. 357 *Acheron*: one of the four rivers in the underworld. 358 *testy*: irritable. 359 *As*: so that. 361 *wrong*: insult.
367 *virtuous*: potent.

And make his eyeballs roll with wonted° sight.
When they next wake, all this derision°                                                    370
Shall seem a dream, and fruitless vision,
And back to Athens shall the lovers wend,
With league whose date° till death shall never end.
Whiles I in this affair do thee employ,
I'll to my queen and beg her Indian boy:                                                  375
And then I will her charmèd eye release
From monster's view, and all things shall be peace.
PUCK:  My fairy lord, this must be done with haste,
For night's swift dragons cut the clouds full fast:
And yonder shines Aurora's harbinger,°                                                    380
At whose approach, ghosts wand'ring here and there,
Troop home to churchyards: damnèd spirits all,
That in crossways° and floods° have burial,
Already to their wormy beds are gone:
For fear lest day should look their shames upon,                                          385
They wilfully themselves exile from light,
And must for aye consort° with black-browed night.
OBERON:  But we are spirits of another sort.
I with the morning's love have oft made sport,°
And like a forester, the groves may tread                                                 390
Even till the eastern gate all fiery red,
Opening on Neptune, with fair blessèd beams,
Turns into yellow gold his salt green streams.
But notwithstanding, haste, make no delay:
We may effect this business yet ere day.                                    [*Exit.*] 395
PUCK:  Up and down, up and down,
I will lead them up and down.
I am feared in field and town.
Goblin, lead them up and down.
Here comes one.                                                                           400

*Enter* LYSANDER.

LYSANDER:  Where art thou, proud Demetrius? Speak thou now.
PUCK:  Here villain, drawn° and ready. Where art thou?
LYSANDER:  I will be with thee straight.
PUCK:                                    Follow me then
To plainer° ground.
                                                                      [*Exit* LYSANDER.]

*Enter* DEMETRIUS.

DEMETRIUS:                    Lysander, speak again.
Thou runaway, thou coward, art thou fled?                                                 405
Speak:  in some bush? Where dost thou hide thy head?

---

°369 *wonted*: (previously) accustomed.  370 *derision*: laughable interlude.  373 *date*: term.  380 *Aurora's harbinger*: the morning star heralding Aurora, the dawn.  383 *crossways*: cross-roads, where suicides were buried. *floods*: those who drowned.  387 *aye consort*: ever associate.  389 *morning's . . . sport*: hunted with Cephalus (beloved of Aurora and himself devoted to his wife Procris, whom he killed by accident; "sport" also = "amorous dalliance," and "love" = Aurora's love for Oberon).  402 *drawn*: with sword drawn.  404 *plainer*: more level.

PUCK:  Thou coward, art thou bragging to the stars,
    Telling the bushes that thou look'st for wars,
    And wilt not come? Come recreant,° come thou child,
410    I'll whip thee with a rod. He is defiled
    That draws a sword on thee.
DEMETRIUS:                  Yea, art thou there?
PUCK:  Follow my voice: we'll try no manhood° here.          *Exeunt.*

[*Enter* LYSANDER.]

LYSANDER:  He goes before me and still dares me on:
    When I come where he calls, then he is gone
415    The villain is much lighter-heeled than I;
    I followed fast: but faster he did fly,
    That fallen am I in dark uneven way,
    And here will rest me. [*Lie down.*] Come thou gentle day,
    For if but once thou show me thy grey light.
420    I'll find Demetrius and revenge this spite.        [*Sleeps.*]

*Enter* PUCK *and* DEMETRIUS.

PUCK:  Ho, ho, ho! Coward, why com'st thou not?
DEMETRIUS:  Abide° me, if thou dar'st, for well I wot°
    Thou run'st before me, shifting every place,
    And dar'st not stand, nor look me in the face.
    Where art thou now?
425 PUCK:              Come hither: I am here.
DEMETRIUS:  Nay then thou mock'st me. Thou shalt buy this dear,°
    If ever I thy face by daylight see.
    Now go thy way. Faintness constraineth me
    To measure out my length on this cold bed.
430    By day's approach look to be visited.    [*Lies down and sleeps.*]

*Enter* HELENA.

HELENA:  O weary night, O long and tedious night,
    Abate° thy hours; shine comforts° from the east,
    That I may back to Athens by daylight,
    From these that my poor company detest:
435    And sleep, that sometimes shuts up sorrow's eye.
    Steal me awhile from mine own company.      *Sleeps.*
PUCK:  Yet but three? Come one more,
    Two of both kinds makes up four.
    Here she comes, curst° and sad.
440    Cupid is a knavish lad,
    Thus to make poor females mad.

*Enter* HERMIA.

HERMIA:  Never so weary, never so in woe,
        Bedabbled with the dew, and torn with briers:

---

°409 *recreant*: oath-breaker, coward. 412 *try no manhood*: test no valor. 422 *Abide*: wait for. *wot*: know. 426 *buy this dear*: pay dearly for this.
432 *Abate*: shorten. *shine comforts*: may strength, power shine. 439 *curst*: cross.

> I can no further crawl, no further go:
>> My legs can keep no pace with my desires.
> Here will I rest me till the break of day.                                                    445
> Heavens shield Lysander, if they mean a fray.                    *[Lies down and sleeps.]*
PUCK: On the ground,
>> Sleep sound:
>> I'll apply
>> To your eye,                                                                                    450
>> Gentle lover, remedy.                          *[Squeezes the love-juice on LYSANDER's eyelids.]*
>> When thou wak'st,
>> Thou tak'st
>> True delight                                                                                    455
>> In the sight
> Of thy former lady's eye:
> And the country proverb known,
> That every man should take his own,
> In your waking shall be shown.                                                                  460
>> Jack shall have Jill:
>> Naught shall go ill:
> The man shall have his mare again, and all shall be well.

> *[Exit PUCK. The lovers remain asleep on stage.]*

## ACT 4

### [Scene 1. The Wood]

*Enter [TITANIA] QUEEN OF FAIRIES, and [BOTTOM] THE CLOWN, and FAIRIES, and the KING [OBERON]
behind them [unseen].*

TITANIA:  Come sit thee down upon this flow'ry bed,
>> While I thy amiable° cheeks do coy,°
> And stick musk-roses in thy sleek smooth head,
>> And kiss thy fair large ears, my gentle joy.
BOTTOM:  Where's Peaseblossom?                                                                    5
PEASEBLOSSOM:  Ready.
BOTTOM:  Scratch my head, Peaseblossom. Where's Mounsieur
    Cobweb?
COBWEB:  Ready.
BOTTOM:  Mounsieur Cobweb, good mounsieur, get you your weapons              10
    in your hand, and kill me a red-hipped humblebee on
    the top of a thistle: and good mounsieur, bring me the
    honey-bag. Do not fret yourself too much in the action,
    mounsieur: and good mounsieur have a care the honey-
    bag break not, I would be loath to have you overflowen             15
    with a honey bag, signior. Where's Mounsieur
    Mustardseed?
MUSTARDSEED:  Ready.
BOTTOM:  Give me your neaf,° Mounsieur Mustardseed. Pray you
    leave your curtsy,° good mounsieur.                                                         20

---

°2 *amiable:* lovely.  *coy:* caress.  19 *neaf:* fist.  20 *leave your curtsy:* either (a) stop bowing, or (b) replace your hat.

Titania, Queen of the Fairies (Juliet Mills) is entranced by the ass's-eared Bottom (Paul Hardwick) in the Royal Shakespeare Company production of *A Midsummer Night's Dream* (1959–1962) at the Aldwych Theatre, London—director, Peter Hall.

MUSTARDSEED:  What's your will?

BOTTOM:  Nothing, good mounsieur, but to help Cavalery° Cobweb
    to scratch. I must to the barber's mounsieur, for
    methinks I am marvellous hairy about the face. And I am
25    such a tender ass, if my hair do but tickle me, I must
    scratch.

TITANIA:  What, will thou hear some music, my sweet love?

BOTTOM:  I have a reasonable good ear in music. Let's have the tongs°
    and the bones.°

30 TITANIA:  Or say, sweet love, what thou desirest to eat.

BOTTOM:  Truly, a peck of provender. I could munch your good
    dry oats. Methinks I have a great desire to a bottle° of hay.
    Good hay, sweet hay, hath no fellow.

TITANIA:  I have a venturous fairy that shall seek
35    The squirrel's hoard, and fetch thee new nuts.

BOTTOM:  I had rather have a handful or two of dried pease. But
    I pray you, let none of your people stir me: I have an
    exposition of° sleep come upon me.

TITANIA:  Sleep thou, and I will wind thee in my arms.
40    Fairies, be gone, and be all ways° away.               [*Exeunt* FAIRIES.]
    So doth the woodbine the sweet honeysuckle
    Gently entwist: the female ivy so

---

°22 *Cavalery*: (he means "cavalier"). **28** *tongs*: crude music made by striking tongs with a piece of metal. **29** *bones*: pieces of bone held between the fingers and clapped together rhythmically. **32** *bottle*: bundle. **38** *exposition of*: (he means "disposition to"). **40** *all ways*: in every direction.

Enrings the barky fingers of the elm.
O how I love thee! how I dote on thee!　　　　　　　　　　　　　*[They sleep.]*

*Enter* ROBIN GOODFELLOW *[*PUCK.*]*

OBERON: *[Advances.]* Welcome good Robin. Seest thou this sweet sight?　　　45
　Her dotage now I do begin to pity.
　For meeting her of late behind the wood,
　Seeking sweet favours° for this hateful fool,
　I did upbraid her and fall out with her.
　For she his hairy temples then had rounded　　　　　　　　　　　　50
　With coronet of fresh and fragrant flowers
　And that same dew which sometime° on the buds
　Was wont to° swell like round and orient° pearls,
　Stood now within the pretty flowerets' eyes,
　Like tears that did their own disgrace bewail.　　　　　　　　　　55
　When I had at my pleasure taunted her,
　And she in mild terms begged my patience,
　I then did ask of her her changeling child:
　Which straight she gave me, and her fairy sent
　To bear him to my bower in fairy land.　　　　　　　　　　　　60
　And now I have the boy, I will undo
　This hateful imperfection of her eyes.
　And gentle Puck, take this transformèd scalp
　From off the head of this Athenian swain;
　That he awaking when the other do,　　　　　　　　　　　　　65
　May all to Athens back again repair,°
　And think no more of this night's accidents,°
　But as the fierce vexation of a dream.
　But first I will release the Fairy Queen.
　　Be as thou wast wont to be:　　　　　　　　　　　　　　　70
　　See, as thou wast wont to see.
　　Dian's bud o'er Cupid's flower°
　　Hath such force and blessèd power.
　Now my Titania, wake you, my sweet queen.
TITANIA: My Oberon, what visions have I seen!　　　　　　　　　　75
　Methought I was enamoured of an ass.
OBERON: There lies your love.
TITANIA:　　　　　　　　How came these things to pass?
　O, how mine eyes do loathe his visage now!
OBERON: Silence awhile Robin, take off this head:
　Titania, music call, and strike more dead
　Than common sleep of all these five the sense.°　　　　　　　　80
TITANIA: Music, ho music! such as charmeth sleep.
PUCK: Now, when thou wak'st, with thine own fools' eyes peep.
OBERON: Sound music:
　　　　　　　　　　　　　　　　　　　　　　　　*Music still.°*
　　Come my queen, take hands with me,

---

°48 *favours*: bouquets as love tokens. 52 *sometime*: formerly. 53 *Was wont to*: used to. *orient*: (where the most beautiful pearls came from).
66 *repair*: return. 67 *accidents*: incidents. 72 *Dian's bud . . . flower*: (Diana's bud counteracts the effects of love-in-idleness, the pansy).
80–81 *strike . . . sense*: Make these five (the lovers and Bottom) sleep more soundly. 84.1 S.D.: *still*: continuously.

85    And rock the ground whereon these sleepers be.                    [*Dance.*]
      Now thou and I are new in amity,
      And will tomorrow midnight solemnly
      Dance in Duke Theseus' house triumphantly,°
      And bless it to all fair prosperity.
90    There shall the pairs of faithful lovers be
      Wedded, with Theseus, all in jollity.
PUCK:  Fairy King, attend and mark:
          I do hear the morning lark.
OBERON:  Then my queen, in silence sad,°
95        Trip we after the night's shade:
          We the globe can compass soon,
          Swifter than the wand'ring moon.
TITANIA:  Come my lord, and in our flight,
          Tell me how it came this night,
100       That I sleeping here was found,
          With these mortals on the ground.                    *Exeunt*

*Wind° horns. Enter* THESEUS, HIPPOLYTA, EGEUS *and all his train.*

THESEUS:  Go one of you, find out the forester:
          For now our observation° is performed.
          And since we have the vaward° of the day,
105       My love shall hear the music of my hounds.
          Uncouple° in the western valley, let them go:
          Dispatch I say, and find the forester.          [*Exit an* ATTENDANT.]
          We will, fair queen, up to the mountain's top,
          And mark the musical confusion
110       Of hounds and echo in conjunction.
HIPPOLYTA:  I was with Hercules and Cadmus° once,
          When in a wood of Crete they bayed the bear,°
          With hounds of Sparta;° never did I hear
          Such gallant chiding. For besides the groves,
115       The skies, the fountains, every region near
          Seemed all one mutual cry. I never heard
          So musical a discord, such sweet thunder.
THESEUS:  My hounds are bred out of the Spartan kind:
          So flewed, so sanded.° and their heads are hung
120       With ears that sweep away the morning dew,
          Crook-kneed, and dewlapped° like Thessalian bulls:
          Slow in pursuit; but matched in mouth like bells,
          Each under each.° A cry° more tuneable
          Was never holloa'd to, nor cheered with horn,
125       In Crete, in Sparta, nor in Thessaly.
          Judge when you hear. But soft.° What nymphs are these?

---

°88 *triumphantly*: in celebration.  94 *sad*: serious.  101.1 S.D.: *wind*: blow, sound.  103 *observation*: observance of the May Day rites.  104 *vaward*: vanguard, earliest part.  106 *Uncouple*: unleash (the dogs).  111 *Cadmus*: mythical builder of Thebes.  112 *bayed the bear*: brought the bear to bay, to its last stand.  113 *hounds of Sparta*: (a breed famous for their swiftness and quick scent).  119 *flewed, so sanded*: with hanging cheeks, so sand-colored.  121 *dewlapped*: with skin hanging from the chin.  122–23 *matched . . . each*: with each voice matched for harmony with the next in pitch, like bells in a chime.  123 *cry*: pack of dogs.  126 *soft*: wait.

EGEUS: My lord, this is my daughter here asleep,
    And this Lysander, this Demetrius is,
    This Helena, old Nedar's Helena.
    I wonder of their being here together.
THESEUS: No doubt they rose up early to observe     130
    The rite of May: and hearing our intent,
    Came here in grace° of our solemnity.
    But speak Egeus, is not this the day
    That Hermia should give answer of her choice?     135
EGEUS: It is, my lord.
THESEUS: Go bid the huntsmen wake them with their horns.

*Shout within: wind horns. They all start up.*

    Good morrow, friends. Saint Valentine is past.
    Begin these wood-birds but to couple now?°
LYSANDER: Pardon, my lord.
                             *[They kneel.]*
THESEUS:                I pray you all, stand up.     140
    I know you two are rival enemies.
    How comes this gentle concord in the world,
    That hatred is so far from jealousy,°
    To sleep by hate° and fear no enmity?
LYSANDER: My lord, I shall reply amazedly,     145
    Half sleep, half waking. But as yet, I swear,
    I cannot truly say how I came here.
    But as I think—for truly would I speak,
    And now I do bethink me, so it is—
    I came with Hermia hither. Our intent     150
    Was to be gone from Athens, where we might,
    Without° the peril of the Athenian law—
EGEUS: Enough, enough, my lord: you have enough.
    I beg the law, the law upon his head:
    They would have stol'n away, they would, Demetrius,     155
    Thereby to have defeated you and me:
    You of your wife, and me of my consent:
    Of my consent that she should be your wife.
DEMETRIUS: My lord, fair Helen told me of their stealth,
    Of this their purpose hither, to this wood,     160
    And I in fury hither followed them;
    Fair Helena in fancy° following me.
    But my good lord, I wot not by what power
    (But by some power it is) my love to Hermia,
    Melted as the snow, seems to me now     165
    As the remembrance of an idle gaud,°
    Which in my childhood I did dote upon:
    And all the faith, the virtue of my heart,
    The object and the pleasure of mine eye,

---

°133 *grace:* honor. 138–39 *Saint . . . now:* (birds traditionally chose their mates on St. Valentine's Day). 143 *jealousy:* suspicion. 144 *hate:* one it hates. 152 *Without:* beyond. 162 *in fancy:* out of doting love. 166 *idle gaud:* trifling toy.

170        Is only Helena. To her, my lord,
            Was I betrothed ere I saw Hermia:
            But like a sickness,° did I loathe this food.
            But as in health, come° to my natural taste,
            Now I do wish it, love it, long for it.

175        And will for evermore be true to it.
      THESEUS:  Fair lovers, you are fortunately met.
            Of this discourse we more will hear anon.
            Egeus, I will overbear your will:
            For in the temple, by and by,° with us,

180        These couples shall eternally be knit.
            And for the morning now is something worn,°
            Our purposed hunting shall be set aside.
            Away with us to Athens. Three and three,
            We'll hold a feast in great solemnity.

185        Come Hippolyta.

                             *Exeunt Duke [HIPPOLYTA, EGEUS] and Lords.*

      DEMETRIUS:  These things seem small and undistinguishable,
            Like far-off mountains turned into clouds.
      HERMIA:  Methinks I see these things with parted° eye,
             When everything seems double.
      HELENA:                     So methinks:

190        And I have found Demetrius, like a jewel,
            Mine own, and not mine own.°
      DEMETRIUS:                Are you sure
            That we are awake? It seems to me,
            That yet we sleep, we dream. Do not you think
            The duke was here, and bid us follow him?

195 HERMIA:  Yea, and my father.
      HELENA:               And Hippolyta.
      LYSANDER:  And he did bid us follow to the temple.
      DEMETRIUS:  Why then, we are awake: let's follow him,
            And by the way let us recount our dreams.       *Exeunt Lovers.*
      BOTTOM.  [*Wakes.*] When my cue comes, call me, and I will answer.

200        My next is "Most fair Pyramus." Hey ho. Peter Quince?
            Flute the bellows-mender? Snout the tinker? Starveling?
            God's my life! Stol'n hence, and left me asleep? I have
            had a most rare vision. I have had a dream, past the wit
            of man to say what dream it was. Man is but an ass, if he

205        go about° to expound this dream. Methought I was—
            there is no man can tell what. Methought I was, and
            methought I had—but man is but a patched fool,° if he
            will offer to say what methought I had. The eye of man
            hath not heard, the ear of man hath not seen, man's hand is

210        not able to taste, his tongue to conceive, nor his

---

°172 *sickness*: sick person. 173 *come*: i.e., back. 179 *by and by*: immediately. 181 *something worn*: somewhat worn on. 188 *parted*: divided (each eye seeing a separate image). 190–91 *like . . . own*: like a person who finds a jewel: the finder is the owner, but insecurely so. 205 *go about*: attempt. 207 *patched fool*: fool dressed in motley.

heart to report, what my dream was. I will get Peter
Quince to write a ballad of this dream: it shall be called
Bottom's Dream; because it hath no bottom: and I
will sing it in the latter end of our play, before the duke.
Peradventure, to make it the more gracious, I shall sing
it at her° death.                                                                              215

*Exit.*

## [Scene 2. Athens, Quince's house]

*Enter QUINCE, FLUTE, SNOUT, and STARVELING.*

QUINCE:  Have you sent to Bottom's house? Is he come home yet?
STARVELING:  He cannot be heard of. Out of doubt he is transported.°
FLUTE:  If he come not, then the play is marred. It goes not forward,
    doth it?
QUINCE:  It is not possible. You have not a man in all Athens able
    to discharge° Pyramus but he.                                                           5
FLUTE:  No, he hath simply the best wit of any handicraft man in Athens.
QUINCE:  Yea, and the best person too, and he is a very paramour
    for a sweet voice.
FLUTE:  You must say "paragon." A paramour is (God bless us)
    a thing of naught.°                                                                       10

*Enter SNUG THE JOINER.*

SNUG:  Masters, the duke is coming from the temple, and there
    is two or three lords and ladies more married. If our
    sport had gone forward, we had all been made men.°
FLUTE:  O sweet bully Bottom. Thus hath he lost sixpence a day°                               15
    during his life: he could not have 'scaped sixpence a day.
    And the duke had not given him sixpence a day for playing
    Pyramus, I'll be hanged. He would have deserved it.
    Sixpence a day in Pyramus, or nothing.

*Enter BOTTOM.*

BOTTOM:  Where are these lads? Where are these hearts?
QUINCE:  Bottom! O most courageous° day! O most happy hour!                                   20
BOTTOM:  Masters, I am to discourse wonders: but ask me not what.
    For if I tell you, I am not true Athenian. I will tell you
    everything, right as it fell out.
QUINCE:  Let us hear, sweet Bottom.
BOTTOM:  Not a word of me. All that I will tell you is, that the                              25
    duke hath dined. Get your apparel together, good
    strings to your beards, new ribbands to your pumps, meet
    presently° at the palace, every man look o'er his part: for
    the short and the long is, our play is preferred.° In any
    case, let Thisby have clean linen: and let not him that                                   30

---

°216 *her*: Thisby's. 2 *transported*: carried away (by spirits). 6 *discharge*: portray. 11 *of naught*: wicked, naughty. 14 *made men*: men made rich. 15 *sixpence a day*: i.e., as a pension. 21 *courageous*: (he may mean "auspicious"). 29 *presently*: immediately. 30 *preferred*: recommended (for presentation).

plays the lion pare his nails, for they shall hang out for
the lion's claws. And most dear actors, eat no onions nor
garlic, for we are to utter sweet breath: and I do not
35    doubt but to hear them say it is a sweet comedy. No more
words: away, go away.

                                     *Exeunt.*

## ACT 5

### [Scene 1. The palace of Theseus]

*Enter* THESEUS, HIPPOLYTA, *and* PHILOSTRATE, *and his* LORDS.

HIPPOLYTA: 'Tis strange, my Theseus, that these lovers speak of.
THESEUS: More strange than true. I never may believe
    These antick° fables, nor these fairy toys.°
    Lovers and madmen have such seething brains,
5    Such shaping fantasies,° that apprehend
    More than cool reason ever comprehends.
    The lunatic, the lover, and the poet,
    Are of imagination all compact.°
    One sees more devils than vast hell can hold:
10    That is the madman. The lover, all as frantic,
    Sees Helen's beauty in a brow of Egypt.°
    The poet's eye, in a fine frenzy rolling,
    Doth glance from heaven to earth, from earth to heaven.
    And as imagination bodies forth
15    The forms of things unknown, the poet's pen
    Turns them to shapes, and gives to airy nothing,
    A local habitation and a name.
    Such tricks hath strong imagination,
    That if it would but apprehend some joy,
20    It comprehends° some bringer of that joy.
    Or in the night, imagining some fear,
    How easy is a bush supposed a bear.
HIPPOLYTA:  But all the story of the night told over,
    And all their minds transfigured so together,
25    More witnesseth than fancy's images,°
    And grows to something of great constancy:°
    But howsoever, strange and admirable.°

*Enter* LOVERS: LYSANDER, DEMETRIUS, HERMIA, *and* HELENA.

THESEUS: Here come the lovers, full of joy and mirth.
    Joy, gentle friends, joy and fresh days of love
    Accompany your hearts.
30  LYSANDER:               More° than to us
    Wait in your royal walks, your board, your bed.

---

°3 *antick*: fantastic. *fairy toys*: trivial fairy stories. 5 *fantasies*: imaginations. 8 *of . . . compact*: totally composed of imagination. 11 *a brow of Egypt*: the swarthy face of a gypsy (believed to come from Egypt). 20 *comprehends*: includes. 25 *More . . . images*: testifies that it is more than just imagination. 26 *constancy*: certainty. 27 *admirable*: to be wondered at. 30 *More*: even more (joy and love).

THESEUS: Come now, what masques,° what dances shall we have,
    To wear away this long age of three hours
    Between our after-supper° and bed-time?
    Where is our usual manager of mirth?
    What revels are in hand? Is there no play,           35
    To ease the anguish of a torturing hour?
    Call Philostrate.
PHILOSTRATE:          Here, mighty Theseus.
THESEUS: Say, what abridgment° have you for this evening?
    What masque,° what music? How shall we beguile       40
    The lazy time, if not with some delight?
PHILOSTRATE: There is a brief° how many sports are ripe.°
    Make choice of which your highness will see first.

[*Gives a paper.*]

THESEUS: "The battle with the Centaurs, to be sung
    By an Athenian eunuch to the harp."            45
    We'll none of that. That have I told my love
    In glory of my kinsman Hercules.
    "The riot of the tipsy Bacchanals,
    Tearing the Thracian singer in their rage."°
    That is an old device: and it was played         50
    When I from Thebes came last a conqueror.
    "The thrice three Muses mourning for the death
    Of Learning, late deceased in beggary."
    That is some satire keen and critical,
    Not sorting with° a nuptial ceremony.         55
    "A tedious brief scene of young Pyramus
    And his love Thisby; very tragical mirth."
    Merry and tragical? Tedious and brief?
    That is hot ice and wondrous strange snow.
    How shall we find the concord of this discord?
PHILOSTRATE: A play there is, my lord, some ten words long,   60
    Which is as brief as I have known a play:
    But by ten words, my lord, it is too long,
    Which makes it tedious: for in all the play
    There is not one word apt, one player fitted.°
    And tragical, my noble lord, it is:         65
    For Pyramus therein doth kill himself.
    Which when I saw rehearsed, I must confess,
    Made mine eyes water; but more merry tears
    The passion of loud laughter never shed.
THESEUS: What are they that do play it?         70

---

°32, 40 *masques*: lavish courtly entertainments combining song and dance. 34 *after-supper*: late supper. 39 *abridgment*: either (a) diversion to make the hours seem shorter or (b) short entertainment. 40 *masque*: a light musical or non-musical drama, usually allegorical or mythological in subject, with many dances and pantomime actions. Often the actors wore masks. 42 *brief*: list. *ripe*: ready. 48–49 *riot . . . rage*: (The singer Orpheus of Thrace was torn limb from limb by the Maenads, frenzied female priests of Bacchus). 55 *sorting with*: befitting. 65 *fitted*: (well) cast.

PHILOSTRATE: Hard-handed men, that work in Athens here,
    Which never laboured in their minds till now:
    And now have toiled their unbreathed° memories
75    With this same play, against° your nuptial.
THESEUS: And we will hear it.
PHILOSTRATE:               No, my noble lord,
    It is not for you. I have heard it over,
    And it is nothing, nothing in the world;
    Unless you can find sport in their intents,
80    Extremely stretched and conned° with cruel pain.
    To do your service.
THESEUS:            I will hear that play.
    For never anything can be amiss,
    When simpleness and duty tender° it.
    Go bring them in, and take your places, ladies.          *[Exit PHILOSTRATE.]*
85 HIPPOLYTA: I love not to see wretchedness o'ercharged,°
    And duty in his service perishing.
THESEUS: Why, gentle sweet, you shall see no such thing.
HIPPOLYTA: He says they can do nothing in this kind.°
THESEUS: The kinder we, to give them thanks for nothing.
90    Our sport shall be to take what they mistake.
    And what poor duty cannot do, noble respect
    Takes it in might, not merit.°
    Where I have come, great clerks° have purposèd
    To greet me with premeditated welcomes;
95    Where I have seen them shiver and look pale,
    Make periods in the midst of sentences,
    Throttle° their practised accent in their fears,
    And in conclusion dumbly have broke off,
    Not paying me a welcome. Trust me, sweet,
100    Out of this silence yet I picked a welcome:
    And in the modesty of fearful duty°
    I read as much as from the rattling tongue
    Of saucy and audacious eloquence.
    Love, therefore, and tongue-tied simplicity,
105    In° least, speak most, to my capacity.°

*[Enter PHILOSTRATE.]*

PHILOSTRATE: So please your grace, the Prologue is addressed.°
THESEUS: Let him approach.

*Flourish trumpets. Enter the PROLOGUE [QUINCE].*

PROLOGUE: If we offend, it is with our good will.
    That you should think, we come not to offend,

---

°74 *unbreathed*: unpracticed, unexercised. 75 *against*: in preparation for. 80 *stretched and conned*: strained and memorized. 83 *tender*: offer.
85 *wretchedness o'ercharged*: poor fellows taxing themselves too much. 88 *in this kind*: of this sort. 91–92 *noble . . . merit*: a noble nature considers the sincerity of effort rather than the skill of execution. 93 *clerks*: scholars. 97 *Throttle*: choke on. 101 *fearful duty*: subjects whose devotions
gave them stage fright. 105 *In*: i.e., saying. *capacity*: way of thinking. 106 *addressed*: ready.

But with good will. To show our simple skill,                                    110
    That is the true beginning of our end.
Consider then, we come but in despite.°
    We do not come, as minding to content you,
Our true intent is. All for your delight,
    We are not here. That you should here repent you,                            115
The actors are at hand: and by their show,
You shall know all, that you are like to know.°
THESEUS: This fellow doth not stand upon points.°
LYSANDER: He hath rid his prologue like a rough colt: he knows
    not the stop.° A good moral my lord: it is not enough                        120
    to speak; but to speak true.
HIPPOLYTA: Indeed he hath played on his prologue like a child on a
    recorder:° a sound, but not in government.°
THESUS: His speech was like a tangled chain: nothing impaired, but
    all disordered. Who is next?                                                 125

*Enter PYRAMUS and THISBY, WALL, MOONSHINE, and LION.*

PROLOGUE: Gentles, perchance you wonder at this show,
    But wonder on, till truth make all things plain.
This man is Pyramus, if you would know:
    This beauteous lady, Thisby is certain.
This man, with lime and rough-cast,° doth present                                130
    Wall, that vile wall which did these lovers sunder:
And through Wall's chink, poor souls, they are content
    To whisper. At the which, let no man wonder.
This man, with lantern, dog, and bush of thorn,
    Presenteth Moonshine. For if you will know,                                  135
By moonshine did these lovers think no scorn
    To meet at Ninus' tomb, there, there to woo:
This grisly beast (which Lion hight° by name)
    The trusty Thisby, coming first by night,
Did scare away, or rather did affright:                                          140
    And as she fled, her mantle she did fall:°
Which Lion vile with bloody mouth did stain.
    Anon comes Pyramus, sweet youth and tall,°
    And finds his trusty Thisby's mantle slain:
Whereat, with blade, with bloody blameful blade,                                 145
    He bravely broached° his boiling bloody breast.
And Thisby, tarrying in mulberry shade,
    His dagger drew, and died. For all the rest,
Let Lion, Moonshine, Wall, and lovers twain.
    At large° discourse, while here they do remain.                              150

°108–17 *If . . . know*: (Quince's blunders in punctuation exactly reverse the meaning). 112 *despite*: malice. 118 *stand upon points*: (1) pay attention to punctuation (2) bother about the niceties (of expression). 120 *stop*: (1) halt (2) period. 123 *recorder*: flutelike wind instrument. *in government*: well managed. 130 *rough-cast*: rough plaster made of lime and gravel. 138 *hight*: is called. 141 *fall*: let fall. 143 *tall*: brave. 146 *broached*: opened (Shakespeare parodies the overuse of alliteration in the earlier bombastic Elizabethan plays). 150 *At large*: in full.

THESEUS:  I wonder if the lion be to speak.

DEMETRIUS:  No wonder, my lord: one lion may, when many asses do.

*Exeunt [PROLOGUE, PYRAMUS,] LION, THISBY, MOONSHINE.*

WALL:  In this same interlude° it doth befall

That I, one Snout by name, present a wall:

155    And such a wall, as I would have you think,

That had in it a crannied hole or chink:

Through which the lovers, Pyramus and Thisby,

Did whisper often, very secretly.

This loam, this rough-cast, and this stone doth show

160    That I am that same wall: the truth is so.

And this the cranny is, right and sinister,°

Through which the fearful lovers are to whisper.

THESEUS:  Would you desire lime and hair to speak better?

DEMETRIUS:  It is the wittiest° partition° that ever I heard discourse,

165    my lord.

*Enter PYRAMUS.*

THESEUS:  Pyramus draws near the wall: silence.

PYRAMUS:  O grim-looked night, O night with hue so black,

O night, which ever art when day is not:

O night, O night, alack, alack, alack,

170    I fear my Thisby's promise is forgot.

And thou O wall, O sweet, O lovely wall,

That stand'st between her father's ground and mine,

Thou wall, O wall, O sweet and lovely wall,

Show me thy chink, to blink through with mine eyne.°

*[WALL holds up his fingers.]*

175    Thanks, courteous wall. Jove shield thee well for this.

But what see I? No Thisby do I see.

O wicked wall, through whom I see no bliss,

Cursed be thy stones for thus deceiving me.

THESEUS:  The wall methinks being sensible,° should curse again.°

180  PYRAMUS:  No in truth sir, he should not. "Deceiving me" is

Thisby's cue: she is to enter now, and I am to spy her

through the wall. You shall see it will fall pat° as I told you:

yonder she comes.

*Enter THISBY.*

THISBY:  O wall, full often hast thou heard my moans,

185    For parting my fair Pyramus and me.

My cherry lips have often kissed thy stones;

Thy stones with lime and hair knit up in thee.

PYRAMUS:  I see a voice: now will I to the chink,

To spy and I can hear my Thisby's face.

190    Thisby?

---

°153 *interlude*: short play. 161 *right and sinister*: from right to left (he probably uses the fingers of his right and left hands to form the cranny). 164 *wittiest*: most intelligent. *partition*: (1) wall (2) section of a learned book or speech. 174 *eyne*: eyes. 179 *sensible*: capable of feelings and perception. *again*: back. 182 *pat*: exactly.

THISBY:  My love thou art, my love I think.
PYRAMUS:  Think what thou wilt, I am thy lover's grace:
　　And, like Limander,° am I trusty still.
THISBY:  And I like Helen, ° till the Fates me kill.
PYRAMUS:  Not Shafalus to Procrus,° was so true.　　　　　　　　　　　195
THISBY:  As Shafalus to Procrus, I to you.
PYRAMUS:  O kiss me through the hole of this vile wall.
THISBY:  I kiss the wall's hole, not your lips at all.
PYRAMUS:  Wilt thou at Ninny's° tomb meet me straightway?
THISBY:  Tide° life, tide death, I come without delay.　　　　　　　　200

　　　　　　　　　　　　　　　　　[*Exeunt* PYRAMUS *and* THISBY.]

WALL:  Thus have I, Wall, my part dischargèd so;
　　And being done, thus Wall away doth go.　　　　　　　　　　*Exit.*
THESEUS:  Now is the mural° down between the two neighbours.
DEMETRIUS:  No remedy my lord, when walls are so wilful to hear
　　without warning.°　　　　　　　　　　　　　　　　　　205
HIPPOLYTA:  This is the silliest stuff that ever I heard.
THESEUS:  The best in this kind are but shadows,° and the worst are
　　no worse, if imagination amend them.
HIPPOLYTA:  It must be your imagination then, and not theirs.
THESEUS:  If we imagine no worse of them than they of themselves,　210
　　they may pass for excellent men. Here come two noble
　　beasts in, a man and a lion.

*Enter* LION *and* MOONSHINE.

LION:  You ladies, you, whose gentle hearts do fear
　　The smallest monstrous mouse that creeps on floor,
　　May now perchance both quake and tremble here.　　　　　　215
　　When lion rough in wildest rage doth roar.
　　Then know that I, as Snug the joiner am
　　A lion fell,° nor else no lion's dam:°
　　For if I should as lion come in strife
　　Into this place, 'twere pity on my life.　　　　　　　　　　220
THESEUS:  A very gentle beast, and of a good conscience.
DEMETRIUS:  The very best at a beast,° my lord, that e'er I saw.
LYSANDER:  This lion is a very fox for his valour.
THESEUS:  True: and a goose for his discretion.
DEMETRIUS:  Not so my lord: for his valour cannot carry his discretion,　225
　　and the fox carries the goose.
THESEUS:  His discretion, I am sure, cannot carry his valour: for the
　　goose carries not the fox. It is well: leave it to his discretion,
　　and let us listen to the moon.
MOONSHINE:  This lanthorn° doth the hornèd moon present—　　　230
DEMETRIUS:  He should have worn the horns on his head.°

---

°193 *Limander*: (he means "Leander"). 194 *Helen*: (he means "Hero"). 195 *Shafalus to Procrus*: (he means "Cephalus" and "Procris" [see 3.2.389 n., p. 1133]). 199 *Ninny*: fool (he means "Ninus"). 200 *Tide*: come, betide. 203 *mural*: wall. 205 *without warning*: either (a) without warning the parents or (b) unexpectedly. 207 *in . . . shadows*: of this sort are only plays (or only actors). 218 *fell*: fierce. *nor . . . dam*: and not a lioness. 222 *best, beast*: (pronounced similarly). 230 *lanthorn*: lantern (once made of horn). 230–31 *hornèd . . . head*: (referring to the cuckold or deceived husband, who supposedly grew horns).

THESEUS:  He is no crescent, and his horns are invisible within the
    circumference.
MOONSHINE:  This lanthorn doth the hornèd moon present,
235    Myself, the man i' th' moon do seem to be.
THESEUS:  This is the greatest error of all the rest; the man should
    be put into the lanthorn. How is it else the man i'th'
    moon?
DEMETRIUS:  He dares not come there for the candle; for you see, it
240    is already in snuff.°
HIPPOLYTA:  I am aweary of this moon. Would he would change.
THESEUS:  It appears, by his small light of discretion, that he is in
    the wane: but yet in courtesy, in all reason, we must stay °
    the time.
245 LYSANDER:  Proceed, Moon.
MOONSHINE:  All that I have to say, is to tell you that the lanthorn is
    the moon, I the man i' th' moon, this thornbush my
    thornbush, and this dog my dog.
DEMETRIUS:  Why, all these should be in the lanthorn: for all these are
250    in the moon. But silence: here comes Thisby.

*Enter* THISBY.

THISBY.  This is old Ninny's tomb. Where is my love?
LION:  Oh!                                       *The* LION *roars.* THISBY *runs off.*
DEMETRIUS:  Well roared, Lion.
THESEUS:  Well run, Thisby.
255 HIPPOLYTA:  Well shone, Moon. Truly, the moon shines with a good
    grace.

[*The* LION *shakes* THISBY'S *mantle.*]

THESEUS:  Well moused,° Lion.
DEMETRIUS:  And then came Pyramus.

*Enter* PYRAMUS. [*Exit* LION.]

LYSANDER:  And so the lion vanished.
260 PYRAMUS:  Sweet moon, I thank thee for thy sunny beams,
        I thank thee, moon, for shining now so bright.
        For by thy gracious, golden, glittering gleams,
        I trust to take of truest Thisby sight.
        But stay: O spite!
265        But mark, poor knight,
        What dreadful dole° is here?
            Eyes, do you see!
            How can it be!
        O dainty duck, O dear!
270            Thy mantle good,
            What, stained with blood?

---

°240 *in snuff*: (1) in need of snuffing (having a long, burnt-out wick or snuff) (2) in a temper.  243 *stay*: await.  257 *moused*: shaken, as a cat shakes
a mouse.  266 *dole*: grief.

        Approach, ye Furies° fell:
          O Fates!° come, come:
          Cut thread and thrum.°
        Quail,° crush, conclude, and quell.°         275
THESEUS: This passion, and the death of a dear friend, would go
    near to make a man look sad.
HIPPOLYTA: Beshrew° my heart, but I pity the man.
PYRAMUS. O wherefore Nature, didst thou lions frame?
        Since lion vile hath here deflowered my dear.       280
        Which is—no, no—which was the fairest dame
          That lived, that loved, that liked, that looked with cheer.
          Come tears, confound:
            Out sword, and wound
          The pap° of Pyramus:         285
            Ay, that left pap,
            Where heart doth hop. [*Stabs himself.*]
          Thus die, I, thus, thus, thus.
            Now am I dead,
            Now am I fled,         290
          My soul is in the sky.
          Tongue lose thy light,
            Moon° take thy flight,     [*Exit* MOONSHINE.]
          Now die, die, die, die, die.        [*Dies.*]
DEMETRIUS: No die,° but an ace° for him. For he is but one.    295
LYSANDER: Less than an ace, man. For he is dead, he is nothing.
THESEUS: With the help of a surgeon, he might yet recover, and
    prove an ass.
HIPPOLYTA: How chance Moonshine is gone before Thisby comes
    back and finds her lover?         300

*Enter* THISBY.

THESEUS: She will find him by starlight. Here she comes, and her
    passion ends the play.
HIPPOLYTA: Methinks she should not use a long one for such a
Pyramus: I hope she will be brief.
DEMETRIUS: A mote will turn the balance, which Pyramus, which   305
    Thisby, is the better: he for a man. God warr'nt° us;
    she for a woman, God bless us.
LYSANDER: She hath spied him already with those sweet eyes.
DEMETRIUS: And thus she means,° videlicet°—
THISBY: Asleep my love?
        What, dead, my dove?         310
      O Pyramus, arise,
        Speak, speak. Quite dumb?
        Dead, dead? A tomb
      Must cover thy sweet eyes.         315

---

°272 *Furies*: classical spirits of the underworld who avenged murder. 273 *Fates*: three sisters who spun the thread of human destiny, which at will was cut with a shears. 274 *thrum*: fringelike end of the warp in weaving. 275 *Quail*: subdue. *quell*: kill. 278 *Beshrew*: curse (meant lightly). 285 *pap*: breast. 292–93 *Tongue . . . Moon*: (he reverses the two subjects). 295 *die*: (singular of "dice"). *ace*: a throw of one at dice. 306 *warr'nt*: warrant, protect. 309 *means*: laments. 309 *videlicet*: namely.

    These lily lips,
    This cherry nose,
   These yellow cowslip° cheeks,
    Are gone, are gone:
320    Lovers, make moan:
   His eyes were green as leeks.
    O Sisters Three,°
    Come, come to me,
   With hands as pale as milk,
325    Lay them in gore,
    Since you have shore
   With shears his thread of silk.
    Tongue, not a word:
    Come trusty sword,
330   Come blade, my breast imbrue°         *[Stabs herself.]*
    And farewell friends:
    Thus Thisby ends:
   Adieu, adieu, adieu.           *[Dies.]*
THESEUS: Moonshine and Lion are left to bury the dead.
335 DEMETRIUS: Ay, and Wall too.
BOTTOM: *[Starts up.]* No, I assure you, the wall is down that parted
   their fathers. Will it please you to see the Epilogue, or
   to hear a Bergomask° dance between two of our company?
THESEUS: No epilogue, I pray you; for your play needs no excuse.
340   Never excuse: for when the players are all dead, there
   need none to be blamed. Marry, if he that writ it had
   played Pyramus and hanged himself in Thisby's garter,
   it would have been a fine tragedy: and so it is truly, and
   very notably discharged. But come, your Bergomask:
345   let your Epilogue alone.          *[A dance.]*
   The iron tongue° of midnight hath told° twelve.
   Lovers, to bed, 'tis almost fairy time.°
   I fear we shall outsleep the coming morn,
   As much as we this night have overwatched.
350   This palpable gross° play hath well beguiled
   The heavy gait of night. Sweet friends, to bed.
   A fortnight hold we this solemnity,
   In nightly revels, and new jollity.        *Exeunt.*

*Enter* PUCK *[with a broom].*

PUCK: Now the hungry lion roars,
355    And the wolf behowls the moon;
   Whilst the heavy° ploughman snores,
    All with weary task fordone.°
   Now the wasted brands° do glow,

---

°318 *cowslip*: yellow primrose. 322 *Sisters Three*: the Fates. 330 *imbrue*: stain with gore. 338 *Bergomask*: exaggerated country dance. 346 *iron tongue*: i.e., of the bell. 346 *told*: counted, tolled. 347 *fairy time*: (from midnight to daybreak). 350 *palpable gross*: obvious and crude. 356 *heavy*: sleepy. 357 *fordone*: worn out, "done in." 358 *wasted brands*: burnt logs.

> Whilst the screech-owl, screeching loud,
>   Puts the wretch that lies in woe°
> In remembrance of a shroud.                              360
>   Now it is the time of night,
> That the graves, all gaping wide,
>   Every one lets forth his sprite, °
> In the church-way paths to glide.
>   And we fairies, that do run                            365
> By the triple Hecate's° team,°
>   From the presence of the sun,
> Following darkness like a dream,
>   Now are frolic:° not a mouse
> Shall disturb this hallowed house.                       370
> I am sent with broom before,
> To sweep the dust° behind° the door.

*Enter KING and QUEEN OF FAIRIES, with all their train.*

OBERON:  Through the house give glimmering light,
>   By the dead and drowsy fire,
> Every elf and fairy sprite,                              375
>   Hop as light as bird from brier,
> And this ditty after me,
>   Sing, and dance it trippingly.

TITANIA:  First rehearse your song by rote,
> To each word a warbling note.                            380
> Hand in hand, with fairy grace,
> Will we sing and bless this place.

OBERON:  Now, until the break of day,
> Through this house each fairy stray.                     [*Song and dance.*]
> To the best bride-bed will we,                           385
> Which by us shall blessèd be:
> And the issue° there create,°
> Ever shall be fortunate:
> So shall all the couples three
> Ever true in loving be:                                  390
> And the blots of Nature's hand °
> Shall not in their issue stand.
> Never mole, harelip, nor scar,
> Nor mark prodigious,° such as are
> Despisèd in nativity,                                    395
> Shall upon their children be.
> With this field-dew consecrate.
> Every fairy take his gait,°
> And each several° chamber bless,                         400

---

°360 *wretch . . . woe*: sick person. 364 *sprite*: spirit, ghost. 367 *triple Hecate*: the moon goddess, identified as Cynthia in heaven, Diana on earth, and Hecate in hell. *team*: dragons that pull the chariot of the night moon. 370 *frolic*: frolicsome. 373 *To sweep the dust*: (Puck often helped with household chores). *behind*: from behind. 388 *issue*: children. 388 *create*: created. 392 *blots . . . hand*: birth defects. 395 *mark prodigious*: unnatural birthmark. 399 *take his gait*: proceed. 400 *several*: separate.

Through this palace, with sweet peace;
And the owner of its blest,
Ever shall in safety rest.
Trip away: make no stay:
405     Meet me all by break of day.

PUCK:  If we shadows have offended,
Think but this, and all is mended,
That you have but slumbered here,
While these visions did appear.
410     And this weak and idle° theme,
No more yielding but° a dream,
Gentles, do not reprehend.
If you pardon, we will mend.°
And as I am an honest Puck,
415     If we have unearnèd luck,
Now to scape the serpent's tongue,°
We will make amends, ere long:
Else the Puck a liar call.
So, good night unto you all.
420     Give me your hands,° if we be friends;
And Robin shall restore amends.°

*Exeunt [all but* PUCK*].*

[*Exit.*]

## Questions

### ACT 1

1. Describe the relationship between Theseus and Hippolyta. What does each of them represent? How does Shakespeare show us that they have different attitudes toward their marriage?

2. Characterize Hermia and Lysander. What blocks their relationship? How do they plan to circumvent these obstructions?

3. What are Helena's feelings about herself? About Hermia? About Demetrius? How might you account for her self-image?

4. Why have the mechanicals gathered at Quince's house? How does Shakespeare show us that Bottom is eager, ill-educated, energetic, and funny?

### ACT 2

5. What is Puck's job? What do you find out about his personality, habits, and pastimes in his first conversation?

6. Why are Titania and Oberon fighting with each other, and what are the specific consequences of their conflict?

7. What does Oberon plan to do to Titania? Why? What is "love-in-idleness"? What power does it have? What does it symbolize?

8. Why are Demetrius and Helena in the woods? What does Oberon decide to do to them? What error occurs? What happens to Lysander when Helena awakens him?

---

°410 *idle*: foolish. 411 *No . . . but*: yielding nothing more than. 413 *mend*: improve. 416 *serpent's tongue*: hissing of the audience. 420 *hands*: applause. 421 *restore amends*: do better in the future.

## ACT 3

9. How and why does Puck change Bottom? How is this transformation appropriate? What happens when Bottom awakens Titania? Why?

10. What does Oberon decide to do when he realizes that Puck has made a mistake? What is Puck's attitude toward the confusion he has created?

11. What happens when Helena awakens Demetrius? How does this situation reverse the one that began the play? Explain Helena's reaction to the behavior of Demetrius and Lysander.

12. What real dangers (tragic potential) do the lovers face in Act 3? How do Oberon and Puck deal with these dangers? What is their plan? How successful is it?

## ACT 4

13. Why does Oberon cure Titania of her infatuation with Bottom? How does the relationship between Oberon and Titania change? How is this change symbolized? Why is it significant?

14. How are the relationships among the four lovers straightened out? How does each explain his or her feelings? What does Theseus decide about the couples? Why is this significant?

## ACT 5

15. What momentous event occurs offstage and is briefly reported in Act 5?

16. Describe Pyramus and Thisby. What blocks their relationship? How do they plan to circumvent these obstructions? What happens to them?

17. What is the significance of the fairy masque (a combination of poetry, music, dance, and drama) that ends the play?

18. What does Puck's epilogue suggest about you as a reader or spectator? How does it reinforce the connections among dreaming, imagination, illusion, and drama?

## General Questions

1. To what extent are the characters in this play conventional and representative types? What is the effect of Shakespeare's style of characterization?

2. Are any of the characters symbolic? If so, what do they symbolize? How does such symbolism reinforce the themes of the play?

3. How does Shakespeare employ language, imagery, and poetic form to define the characters in this play and differentiate among the various groups of characters?

4. To what extent do the two settings—city and woods—structure the play? Where does exposition occur? Complication and catastrophe? The comic resolution? How complete is the resolution? Why is the round-trip journey from one setting to the other necessary for the lovers? The rulers? The "hempen homespuns"?

5. What are the similarities or parallels in plot and theme between *A Midsummer Night's Dream* and "Pyramus and Thisby"? To what degree are they versions of the same play with different endings? Why do you think Shakespeare included the play-within-the-play in *A Midsummer Night's Dream*?

6. In the first soliloquy of the play, Helena discusses love. What kind of love is she talking about? What are its qualities and characteristics? How far do the relationships in the play bear out her ideas about love?

7. How well do the mechanicals understand the nature of dramatic illusion? What sorts of production problems concern them? How do they solve these?

8. What ideas about drama and the ways in which audiences respond to it does *A Midsummer Night's Dream* explore?

9. Compare the play-within-a-play in *A Midsummer Night's Dream* to the one in Act 3 of *Hamlet*. How are the internal plays and situations similar? Different? What parallels do you see in the connections between each play-within-a-play and the larger play in which each occurs?

## Comedy after Shakespeare

The subject of comedy in the centuries from Shakespeare to the present is vast. In all the major European countries, and eventually in the United States, there were many comic dramatists. Some of them were successful in their time but are neglected today, such as Eugène Scribe in France, and some, such as Anton Chekhov in Russia, are known not only for their comedy but also for other works (such as Chekhov's tragicomedies and stories).

The acknowledged master of comedy in the years following Shakespeare was Molière, the pen name of Jean Baptiste Poquelin (1622–1673). He wrote 29 comedies, ranging from broad farce to satirical comedies of manners. Generally he drew his plots from Roman comedy, Italian *commedia dell'arte*, and French farce, all of which schooled him in comic character, tempo, and situation. He elevated comedy to the seriousness of tragedy, as in his satiric comedies *The Ridiculous Dilettantes* (*Les Précieuses Ridicules*, 1659), *The Misanthrope* (1666), *The Miser* (1668), and *Tartuffe* (1669). His plays advocate a balance or norm of behavior, and from this standpoint they mock and expose greed, snobbery, personal rigidity, religious posturing, and professional hypocrisy.

This is not to say that comedy was not flourishing in other nations. In England in the seventeenth century, dramatists such as William Wycherley (1640–1716) and William Congreve (1670–1729) created a sophisticated type of drama in the comedy-of-manners tradition that is termed "Restoration comedy" because it developed after King Charles II was reestablished on the English throne in 1660. The Restoration comedies combined and contrasted elegant and boisterous manners, and they often dealt with serious social and sexual problems. In the first part of the eighteenth century dramatists created "sentimental" drama. Sentimental comedies showed individuals who verge on behavioral excesses but who eventually conform to morality because their goodness of heart overcomes their personal interests, feelings, and self-indulgence—hence the term "sentimental."

The first half of the eighteenth century saw the popularity of other forms such as the musical play and the burlesque play. The musical play was first known as **ballad opera,** and later it was called **comic opera** and **musical comedy.** The characteristic of the musical play was the combination of spoken dialogue and brief songs. The first such play was *The Beggar's Opera* (1728) by John Gay (1685–1732).[4] *The Beggar's Opera*

---

[4]See p. 566 for a song from *The Beggar's Opera*.

was also a burlesque that satirized the Italian operas so popular in the early eighteenth century. Henry Fielding (1707–1754), best known for his later novels, wrote the best of English burlesque plays, *Tom Thumb* (1730, 1731), and, in addition, he wrote at least nine ballad operas in the manner of *The Beggar's Opera*. Also unique in Fielding's comic writing were a number of five-act plays dealing with serious social situations. The comic opera reached its high point in the nineteenth century with the Savoy Operas of William Gilbert (1836–1911) and Arthur Sullivan (1842–1900). The Gilbert and Sullivan operas, such as *H.M.S. Pinafore* (1878) and *The Mikado* (1885), are regularly performed today by both professionals and amateurs. In the United States during the twentieth century, the musical comedy form became a major force, as with the plays of Richard Rodgers (1902–1979) and Oscar Hammerstein II (1895–1960), and Alan Jay Lerner (1918–1986) and Frederick Loewe (1901–1988).

At the turn of the nineteenth century the major comic dramatists in addition to Chekhov were Oscar Wilde (1854–1900) and George Bernard Shaw (1856–1950), most of whose plays are still regularly revived and well attended. The twentieth century marked the appearance of numbers of important comic dramatists, including many, like Eugene O'Neill, who are better known for more serious plays. A number of writers divided their time between theater and film, as with George Kaufman (1889–1961), whose *The Man Who Came to Dinner* (1939) was successful both on stage and on the screen. For a time, Kaufman also wrote film scripts for some of the early film comedies of the Marx Brothers. Many other comic playwrights experimented with comedy. Such a writer is Arthur Kopit (b. 1937), whose *Oh Dad, Poor Dad, Mamma's Hung You in the Closet and I'm Feelin' so Sad* (1961) created a great stir when it was first performed. Of particular note is the development of the "theater of the absurd." Some significant plays in this tradition are *Waiting for Godot* (1953) by Samuel Beckett (1906–1989), *Rhinocéros* (1960) by Jean Genet (1910–1986), and *The Homecoming* (1960) by Harold Pinter (b. 1930).

The technology of the twentieth century has had a great influence on the development of comedy. With the growth of radio in the 1930s, a number of short radio comic dramas developed that were broadcast regionally and nationally on a daily basis, such as "Vic and Sade," written by Paul Rhymer, and "Ma Perkins," both of which were heard by millions who sat regularly beside their radios. With the growth of television in the 1950s there was a virtual explosion of so-called "soap operas," or "soaps," and situation comedies, or sitcoms, in the tradition of the earlier radio shows. Some of the more prominent sitcoms among the many were *I Love Lucy*, the *Jackie Gleason* show, *Frasier*, and *Friends*. Athough the shorter radio comedies were performed daily, the longer television sitcoms, because of greater and more elaborate production requirements, were performed weekly.

Comedy today is characterized by great variety. All the types described earlier (see pp. 1097–1099) are regularly being presented. Serious plays may contain comic and farcical elements. Farcical and comic plays may introduce serious sequences and also may contain strong elements of satire. Satirical plays may contain songs to complement the onstage action and also to divert and entertain. Writers at the beginning of the twenty-first century clearly were continuing to combine the various comic forms that were brought into prominence by Shakespeare and the comic dramatists in the centuries that followed him.

## ANTON CHEKHOV (1860–1904)

Anton Chekhov was born in Taganrog in southern Russia in 1860, the son of a merchant and grandson of a serf. He entered medical school in Moscow in 1879, graduating in 1884. While a student he was also obligated to help support his family, and he turned to writing stories, jokes, and potboilers for pay under a variety of pen names, one of which was "The Doctor Without Patients." *The Bear* belongs to the end of this early period, ten years before Chekhov's association with the Moscow Art Theater at the end of the century.

Chekhov downplayed *The Bear*, referring to it as a "joke" and a "vaudeville"—both words suggesting a farcical work with little form or substance. Nevertheless the play was greatly acclaimed and financially successful, to the author's amazement and delight. Three months after its first performance in 1888, he likened *The Bear* to a "milk cow" ("cash cow") because, to his happiness, it earned him a steady income.

*The Bear* is a farce, a dramatic form designed preeminently to evoke laughter, and it therefore contains extravagant language and boisterous and sudden action. But there is also an underlying seriousness that sustains the humor. In their way, both Smirnov and Mrs. Popov have been failures; they could conceivably sink into lives of depression and futility, and both are walking a very fine wire as the play begins. Chekhov makes clear that Mrs. Popov is filled with resentment at her unfaithful and now dead husband, and also that she is chafing under her self-imposed resolution to lead a life of mourning and self-denial in his memory. Smirnov is having difficulty with creditors, and he admits that his relationships with the many women he has known have ended unhappily. He is therefore both cynical and angry.

The climax of the play is the improbable and preposterous challenge to a duel that Smirnov offers Mrs. Popov, resolved by the equally preposterous outcome. Despite the improbabilities of the play, however, the actions are not impossible because they manifest the true internal needs of the main characters. Chekhov's friend Leo Tolstoy, who criticized some of Chekhov's late plays, laughed heartily at *The Bear*, and countless audiences and readers since then have joined him in laughter.

 ## The Bear, A Joke in One Act (1900)

### CAST OF CHARACTERS

**Mrs. Popov.** A widow of seven months, Mrs. Popov is small and pretty, with dimples. She is a landowner. At the start of the play, she is pining away in memory of her dead husband.

**Grigory Stepanovich Smirnov.** Easily angered and loud, Smirnov is older. He is a landowner, too, and a man of substance.

**Luka.** Luka is Mrs. Popov's footman (a servant whose main tasks were to wait table and attend the carriages, in addition to general duties). He is old enough to feel secure in telling Mrs. Popov what he thinks.

**Gardener, Coachman, Workmen,** who enter at the end.

SCENE. *The drawing room of* MRS. POPOV'S *country home.*

[MRS. POPOV, *in deep mourning, does not remove her eyes from a photograph.*]

LUKA: It isn't right, madam . . . you're only destroying yourself. . . . The chambermaid and the cook have gone off berry picking; every living being is rejoicing; even the cat knows how to be content, walking around the yard catching birds, and you sit in your room all day as if it were a convent, and you don't take pleasure in anything. Yes, really! Almost a year has passed since you've gone out of the house!

MRS. POPOV: And I shall never go out. . . . What for? My life is already ended. He lies in his grave; I have buried myself in these four walls . . . we are both dead.

LUKA: There you go again! Your husband is dead, that's as it was meant to be, it's the will of God, may he rest in peace. . . . You've done your mourning and that will do. You can't go on weeping and mourning forever. My wife died when her time came, too. . . . Well? I grieved, I wept for a month, and that was enough for her; the old lady wasn't worth a second more. [*Sighs.*] You've forgotten all your neighbors. You don't go anywhere or accept any calls. We live, so to speak, like spiders. We never see the light. The mice have eaten my uniform. It isn't as if there weren't any nice neighbors—the district is full of them . . . there's a regiment stationed at Riblov, such officers—they're like candy—you'll never get your fill of them! And in the barracks, never a Friday goes by without a dance; and, if you please, the military band plays music every day. . . . Yes, madam, my dear lady: you're young, beautiful, in the full bloom of youth—if only you took a little pleasure in life . . . beauty doesn't last forever, you know! In ten years' time, you'll be wanting to wave your fanny in front of the officers—and it will be too late.

MRS. POPOV: [*Determined.*] I must ask you never to talk to me like that! You know that when Mr. Popov died, life lost all its salt for me. It may seem to you that I am alive, but that's only conjecture! I vowed to wear mourning to my grave and not to see the light of day. . . . Do you hear me? May his departed spirit see how much I love him. . . . Yes, I know, it's no mystery to you that he was often mean to me, cruel . . . and even unfaithful, but I shall remain true to the grave and show him I know how to love. There, beyond the grave, he will see me as I was before his death. . . .

LUKA: Instead of talking like that, you should be taking a walk in the garden or have Toby or 　5
Giant harnessed and go visit some of the neighbors. . . .

MRS. POPOV: Ai! [*She weeps.*]

LUKA: Madam! Dear lady! What's the matter with you! Christ be with you!

MRS. POPOV: Oh, how he loved Toby! He always used to ride on him to visit the Korchagins or the Vlasovs. How wonderfully he rode! How graceful he was when he pulled at the reins with all his strength! Do you remember? Toby, Toby! Tell them to give him an extra bag of oats today.

LUKA: Yes, madam.

[*Sound of loud ringing.*]

MRS. POPOV: [*Shudders.*] Who's that? Tell them I'm not at home! 　10

LUKA: Of course, madam. [*He exits.*]

MRS. POPOV: [*Alone. Looks at the photograph.*] You will see, Nikolai, how much I can love and forgive . . . my love will die only when I do, when my poor heart stops beating. [*Laughing through her tears.*] Have you no shame? I'm a good girl, a virtuous little wife. I've locked myself in and I'll be true to you to the grave, and you . . . aren't you ashamed, you chubby cheeks? You deceived me, you made scenes, for weeks on end you left me alone . . .

LUKA: [*Enters, alarmed.*] Madam, somebody is asking for you. He wants to see you. . . .

MRS. POPOV: But didn't you tell them that since the death of my husband, I don't see anybody?

LUKA: I did, but he didn't want to listen; he spoke about some very important business. 　15

MRS. POPOV: I am *not at home!*

LUKA: That's what I told him . . . but . . . the devil . . . he cursed and pushed past me right into the room . . . he's in the dining room right now.

MRS. POPOV: [*Losing her temper.*] Very well, let him come in . . . such manners! [*LUKA goes out.*] How difficult these people are! What does he want from me? Why should he disturb my peace? [*Sighs.*] But it's obvious I'll have to go live in a convent. . . . [*Thoughtfully.*] Yes, a convent. . . .

SMIRNOV: [*Enters while speaking to LUKA.*] You idiot, you talk too much. . . . Ass! [*Sees Mrs. Popov and changes to dignified speech.*] Madam, may I introduce myself: retired lieutenant of the artillery and landowner, Grigory Stepanovich Smirnov! I feel the necessity of troubling you about a highly important matter. . . .

20 MRS. POPOV: [*Refusing her hand.*] What do you want?

SMIRNOV: Your late husband, whom I had the pleasure of knowing, has remained in my debt for two twelve-hundred-ruble notes. Since I must pay the interest at the agricultural bank tomorrow, I have come to ask you, madam, to pay me the money today.

MRS. POPOV: One thousand two hundred. . . . And why was my husband in debt to you?

SMIRNOV: He used to buy oats from me.

MRS. POPOV: [*Sighing, to LUKA.*] So, Luka, don't you forget to tell them to give Toby an extra bag of oats.

[*LUKA goes out.*]

[*To SMIRNOV.*] If Nikolai, my husband, was in debt to you, then it goes without saying that I'll pay; but please excuse me today. I haven't any spare cash. The day after tomorrow, my steward will be back from town and I will give him instructions to pay you what is owed; until then I cannot comply with your wishes. . . . Besides, today is the anniversary—exactly seven months ago my husband died, and I'm in such a mood that I'm not quite disposed to occupy myself with money matters.

25 SMIRNOV: And I'm in such a mood that if I don't pay the interest tomorrow, I'll be owing so much that my troubles will drown me. They'll take away my estate!

MRS. POPOV: You'll receive your money the day after tomorrow.

SMIRNOV: I don't want the money the day after tomorrow. I want it today.

MRS. POPOV: You must excuse me. I can't pay you today.

SMIRNOV: And I can't wait until after tomorrow.

30 MRS. POPOV: What can I do, if I don't have it now?

SMIRNOV: You mean to say you can't pay?

MRS. POPOV: I can't pay. . . .

SMIRNOV: Hm! Is that your last word?

MRS. POPOV: That is my last word.

35 SMIRNOV: Positively the last?

MRS. POPOV: Positively.

SMIRNOV: Thank you very much. We'll make a note of that. [*Shrugs his shoulders.*] And people want me to be calm and collected! Just now, on the way here, I met a tax officer and he asked me: why are you always so angry, Grigory Stepanovich? Goodness' sake, how can I be anything but angry? I need money desperately . . . I rode out yesterday early in the morning, at daybreak, and went to see all my debtors; and if only one of them had paid his debt . . . I was dog-tired, spent the night God knows where—a Jewish tavern beside a barrel of vodka. . . . Finally I got here, fifty miles from home, hoping to be paid, and you treat me to a "mood." How can I help being angry?

MRS. POPOV: It seems to me that I clearly said: My steward will return from the country and then you will be paid.

SMIRNOV: I didn't come to your steward, but to you! What the hell, if you'll pardon the expression, would I do with your steward?

MRS. POPOV: Excuse me, my dear sir, I am not accustomed to such profane expressions nor to 40 such a tone. I'm not listening to you any more. [*Goes out quickly.*]

SMIRNOV: [*Alone.*] Well, how do you like that? "A mood." . . . "Husband died seven months ago"! Must I pay the interest or mustn't I? I ask you: Must I pay, or must I not? So, your husband's dead, and you're in a mood and all that finicky stuff . . . and your steward's away somewhere; may he drop dead. What do you want me to do? Do you think I can fly away from my creditors in a balloon or something? Or should I run and bash my head against the wall? I go to Gruzdev—and he's not at home; Yaroshevich is hiding, with Kuritsin it's a quarrel to the death and I almost throw him out the window; Mazutov has diarrhea, and this one is in a "mood." Not one of these swine wants to pay me! And all because I'm too nice to them. I'm a sniveling idiot, I'm spineless, I'm an old lady! I'm too delicate with them! So, just you wait! You'll find out what I'm like! I won't let you play around with me, you devils! I'll stay and stick it out until she pays. Rrr! . . . How furious I am today, how furious! I'm shaking inside from rage and I can hardly catch my breath. . . . Damn it! My God, I even feel sick! [*He shouts.*] Hey, you!

LUKA: [*Enters.*] What do you want?

SMIRNOV: Give me some beer or some water! [*LUKA exits.*] What logic is there in this! A man needs money desperately, it's like a noose around his neck—and she won't pay because, you see, she's not disposed to occupy herself with money matters! . . . That's the logic of a woman! That's why I never did like and do not like to talk to women. I'd rather sit on a keg of gunpowder than talk to a woman. Brr! . . . I even have goose pimples, this broad has put me in such a rage! All I have to do is see one of those spoiled bitches from a distance, and I get so angry it gives me a cramp in the leg. I just want to shout for help.

LUKA: [*Entering with water.*] Madam is sick and won't see anyone.

SMIRNOV: Get out! [*LUKA goes.*] Sick and won't see anyone! No need to see me . . . I'll stay and sit 45 here until you give me the money. You can stay sick for a week, and I'll stay for a week . . . if you're sick for a year, I'll stay a year. . . . I'll get my own back, dear lady! You can't impress me with your widow's weeds and your dimpled cheeks . . . we know all about those dimples! [*Shouts through the window.*] Semyon, unharness the horses! We're not going away quite yet! I'm staying here! Tell them in the stable to give the horses some oats! You brute, you let the horse on the left side get all tangled up in the reins again! [*Teasing.*] "Never mind" . . . I'll give you a never mind! [*Goes away from the window.*] Shit! The heat is unbearable and nobody pays up. I slept badly last night and on top of everything else this broad in mourning is "in a mood" . . . my head aches . . . [*Drinks, and grimaces.*] Shit! This is water! What I need is a drink! [*Shouts.*] Hey, you!

LUKA: [*Enters.*] What is it?

SMIRNOV: Give me a glass of vodka. [*LUKA goes out.*] Oaf! [*Sits down and examines himself.*] Nobody would say I was looking well! Dusty all over, boots dirty, unwashed, unkempt, straw on my waistcoat. . . . The dear lady probably took me for a robber. [*Yawns.*] It's not very polite to present myself in a drawing room looking like this; oh well, who cares? . . . I'm not here as a visitor but as a creditor, and there's no official costume for creditors. . . .

LUKA: [*Enters with vodka.*] You're taking liberties, my good man. . . .

SMIRNOV: [*Angrily.*] What?

LUKA: I . . . nothing . . . I only . . . 50

SMIRNOV: Who are you talking to? Shut up!

LUKA: [*Aside.*] The devil sent this leech. An ill wind brought him. . . . [*LUKA goes out.*]

SMIRNOV: Oh how furious I am! I'm so mad I could crush the whole world into a powder! I even feel faint! [*Shouts.*] Hey, you!

MRS. POPOV: [*Enters, eyes downcast.*] My dear sir, in my solitude, I have long ago grown unaccustomed to the masculine voice and I cannot bear shouting. I must request you not to disturb my peace and quiet!

55 SMIRNOV: Pay me my money and I'll go.

MRS. POPOV: I told you in plain language: I haven't any spare cash now; wait until the day after tomorrow.

SMIRNOV: And I also told you respectfully, in plain language: I don't need the money the day after tomorrow, but today. If you don't pay me today, then tomorrow I'll have to hang myself.

MRS. POPOV: But what can I do if I don't have the money? You're so strange!

SMIRNOV: Then you won't pay me now? No?

60 MRS. POPOV: I can't. . . .

SMIRNOV: In that case, I can stay here and wait until you pay. . . . [*Sits down.*] You'll pay the day after tomorrow? Excellent! In that case I'll stay here until the day after tomorrow. I'll sit here all that time . . . [*Jumps up.*] I ask you: Have I got to pay the interest tomorrow, or not? Or do you think I'm joking?

MRS. POPOV: My dear sir, I ask you not to shout! This isn't a stable!

SMIRNOV: I wasn't asking you about a stable but about this: Do I have to pay the interest tomorrow or not?

MRS. POPOV: You don't know how to behave in the company of a lady!

65 SMIRNOV: No, I don't know how to behave in the company of a lady!

MRS. POPOV: No, you don't! You are an ill-bred, rude man! Respectable people don't talk to a woman like that!

SMIRNOV: Ach, it's astonishing! How would you like me to talk to you? In French, perhaps? [*Lisps in anger.*] *Madame, je vous prie°* . . . how happy I am that you're not paying me the money. . . . Ah, pardon, I've made you uneasy! Such lovely weather we're having today! And you look so becoming in your mourning dress. [*Bows and scrapes.*]

MRS. POPOV: That's rude and not very clever!

SMIRNOV: [*Teasing.*] Rude and not very clever! I don't know how to behave in the company of ladies. Madam, in my time I've seen far more women than you've seen sparrows. Three times I've fought duels over women; I've jilted twelve women, nine have jilted me! Yes! There was a time when I played the fool; I became sentimental over women, used honeyed words, fawned on them, bowed and scraped. . . . I loved, suffered, sighed at the moon; I became limp, melted, shivered . . . I loved passionately, madly, every which way, devil take me, I chattered away like a magpie about the emancipation of women, ran through half my fortune as a result of my tender feelings; but now, if you will excuse me, I'm on to your ways! I've had enough! Dark eyes, passionate eyes, ruby lips, dimpled cheeks; the moon, whispers, bated breath—for all that I wouldn't give a good goddamn. Present company excepted, of course, but all women, young and old alike, are affected clowns, gossips, hateful, consummate liars to the marrow of their bones, vain, trivial, ruthless, outrageously illogical, and as far as this is concerned [*taps on his forehead.*], well, excuse my frankness, any sparrow could give pointers to a philosopher in petticoats! Look at one of those romantic creatures: muslin, ethereal demigoddess, a thousand raptures, and you look into her soul—a common crocodile! [*Grips the back of a chair; the chair cracks and breaks.*] But the most revolting part of it all is that this crocodile imagines that she has, above everything, her own privilege, a monopoly on tender feelings. The hell with it—you can hang

---

°67 *Madame, je vous prie*: I beg you, Madam.

me upside down by that nail if a woman is capable of loving anything besides a lapdog. All she can do when she's in love is slobber! While the man suffers and sacrifices, all her love is expressed in playing with her skirt and trying to lead him around firmly by the nose. You have the misfortune of being a woman, you know yourself what the nature of a woman is like. Tell me honestly: Have you ever in your life seen a woman who is sincere, faithful, and constant? You never have! Only old and ugly ladies are faithful and constant! You're more liable to meet a horned cat or a white woodcock than a faithful woman!

MRS. POPOV:  Pardon me, but in your opinion, who is faithful and constant in love? The man?

SMIRNOV:  Yes, the man!    70

MRS. POPOV:  The man! [*Malicious laugh.*] Men are faithful and constant in love! That's news! [*Heatedly.*] What right have you to say that? Men are faithful and constant! For that matter, as far as I know, of all the men I have known and now know, my late husband was the best. . . . I loved him passionately, with all my being, as only a young intellectual woman can love; I gave him my youth, my happiness, my life, my fortune; he was my life's breath; I worshiped him as if I were a heathen, and . . . and, what good did it do—this best of men himself deceived me shamelessly at every step of the way. After his death, I found his desk full of love letters; and when he was alive—it's terrible to remember—he used to leave me alone for weeks at a time, and before my eyes he flirted with other women and deceived me. He squandered my money, made a mockery of my feelings . . . and, in spite of all that, I loved him and was true to him . . . and besides, now that he is dead, I am still faithful and constant. I have shut myself up in these four walls forever and I won't remove these widow's weeds until my dying day. . . .

SMIRNOV:  [*Laughs contemptuously.*] Widow's weeds . . . I don't know what you take me for! As if I didn't know why you wear that black outfit and bury yourself in these four walls! Well, well! It's no secret, so romantic! When some fool of a poet passes by this country house, he'll look up at your window and think: "Here lives the mysterious Tamara, who, for the love of her husband, buried herself in these four walls." We know these tricks!

MRS. POPOV:  [*Flaring.*] What? How dare you say that to me?

SMIRNOV:  You may have buried yourself alive, but you haven't forgotten to powder yourself!

MRS. POPOV:  How dare you use such expressions with me?    75

SMIRNOV:  Please don't shout. I'm not your steward! You must allow me to call a spade a spade. I'm not a woman and I'm used to saying what's on my mind! Don't you shout at me!

MRS. POPOV:  I'm not shouting, you are! Please leave me in peace!

SMIRNOV:  Pay me my money and I'll go.

MRS. POPOV:  I won't give you any money!

SMIRNOV:  Yes, you will.    80

MRS. POPOV:  To spite you, I won't pay you anything. You can leave me in peace!

SMIRNOV:  I don't have the pleasure of being either your husband or your fiancé, so please don't make scenes! [*Sits down.*] I don't like it.

MRS. POPOV:  [*Choking with rage.*] You're sitting down?

SMIRNOV:  Yes, I am.

MRS. POPOV:  I ask you to get out!

SMIRNOV:  Give me my money . . . [*Aside.*] Oh, I'm so furious! Furious!    85

MRS. POPOV:  I don't want to talk to impudent people! Get out of here! [*Pause.*] You're not going? No?

SMIRNOV:  No.

MRS. POPOV:  No?

SMIRNOV:  No!

MRS. POPOV:  We'll see about that. [*Rings.*]    90

[*Luka enters.*]

Luka, show the gentleman out!

Luka: [*Goes up to* Smirnov.] Sir, will you please leave, as you have been asked. You mustn't . . .

Smirnov: [*Jumping up.*] Shut up! Who do you think you're talking to? I'll make mincemeat out of you!

95   Luka: [*His hand to his heart.*] Oh my God! Saints above! [*Falls into chair.*] Oh, I feel ill! I can't catch my breath!

Mrs. Popov: Where's Dasha? Dasha! [*She shouts.*] Dasha! Pelagea! Dasha! [*She rings.*]

Luka: Oh! They've all gone berry picking . . . there's nobody at home . . . I'm ill! Water!

Mrs. Popov: Will you please get out!

Smirnov: Will you please be more polite?

100   Mrs. Popov: [*Clenches her fist and stamps her feet.*] You're nothing but a crude bear! A brute! A monster!

Smirnov: What? What did you say?

Mrs. Popov: I said that you were a bear, a monster!

Smirnov: [*Advancing toward her.*] Excuse me, but what right do you have to insult me?

Mrs. Popov: Yes, I am insulting you . . . so what? Do you think I'm afraid of you?

105   Smirnov: And do you think just because you're one of those romantic creations, that you have the right to insult me with impunity? Yes? I challenge you!

Luka: Lord in Heaven! Saints above! . . . Water!

Smirnov: Pistols!

Mrs. Popov: Do you think just because you have big fists and you can bellow like a bull, that I'm afraid of you? You're such a bully!

Smirnov: I challenge you! I'm not going to let anybody insult me, and I don't care if you are a woman, a delicate creature!

110   Mrs. Popov: [*Trying to get a word in edgewise.*] Bear! Bear! Bear!

Smirnov: It's about time we got rid of the prejudice that only men must pay for their insults! Devil take it, if women want to be equal, they should behave as equals! Let's fight!

Mrs. Popov: You want to fight! By all means!

Smirnov: This minute!

Mrs. Popov: This minute! My husband had some pistols . . . I'll go and get them right away. [*Goes out hurriedly and then returns.*] What pleasure I'll have putting a bullet through that thick head of yours! The hell with you! [*She goes out.*]

115   Smirnov: I'll shoot her down like a chicken! I'm not a little boy or a sentimental puppy. I don't care if she is delicate and fragile.

Luka: Kind sir! Holy father! [*Kneels.*] Have pity on a poor old man and go away from here! You've frightened her to death and now you're going to shoot her?

Smirnov: [*Not listening to him.*] If she fights, then it means she believes in equality of rights and emancipation of women. Here the sexes are equal! I'll shoot her like a chicken! But what a woman! [*Imitates her.*] "The hell with you! . . . I'll put a bullet through that thick head of yours! . . . " What a woman! How she blushed, her eyes shone . . . she accepted my challenge! To tell the truth, it was the first time in my life I've seen a woman like that. . . .

Luka: Dear sir, please go away! I'll pray to God on your behalf as long as I live!

Smirnov: That's a woman for you! A woman like that I can understand! A real woman! Not a sour-faced nincompoop but fiery, gunpowder! Fireworks! I'm even sorry to have to kill her!

120   Luka: [*Weeps.*] Dear sir . . . go away!

Smirnov: I positively like her! Positively! Even though she has dimpled cheeks, I like her! I'm almost ready to forget about the debt. . . . My fury has diminished. Wonderful woman!

MRS. POPOV: [*Enters with pistols.*] Here they are, the pistols. Before we fight, you must show me how to fire. . . . I've never had a pistol in my hands before . . .

LUKA: Oh dear Lord, for pity's sake. . . . I'll go and find the gardener and the coachman. . . . What did we do to deserve such trouble? [*Exit.*]

SMIRNOV: [*Examining the pistols.*] You see, there are several sorts of pistols . . . there are special dueling pistols, the Mortimer with primers. Then there are Smith and Wesson revolvers, triple action with extractors . . . excellent pistols! . . . they cost a minimum of ninety rubles a pair. . . . You must hold the revolver like this . . . [*Aside.*] What eyes, what eyes! A woman to set you on fire!

MRS. POPOV: Like this?

SMIRNOV: Yes, like this . . . then you cock the pistol . . . take aim . . . put your head back a little . . . stretch your arm out all the way . . . that's right . . . then with this finger press on this little piece of goods . . . and that's all there is to do . . . but the most important thing is not to get excited and aim without hurrying . . . try to keep your arm from shaking.

MRS. POPOV: Good . . . it's not comfortable to shoot indoors. Let's go into the garden.

SMIRNOV: Let's go. But I'm giving you advance notice that I'm going to fire into the air.

MRS. POPOV: That's the last straw! Why?

SMIRNOV: Why? . . . Why . . . because it's my business, that's why.                               130

MRS. POPOV: Are you afraid? Yes? Aahhh! No, sir. You're not going to get out of it that easily! Be so good as to follow me! I will not rest until I've put a hole through your forehead . . . that forehead I hate so much! Are you afraid?

SMIRNOV: Yes, I'm afraid.

MRS. POPOV: You're lying! Why don't you want to fight?

SMIRNOV: Because . . . because you . . . because I like you.

MRS. POPOV: [*Laughs angrily.*] He likes me! He dares say that he likes me! [*Points to the door.*]    135
Out!

SMIRNOV: [*Loads the revolver in silence, takes cap and goes; at the door, stops for half a minute while they look at each other in silence; then he approaches* MRS. POPOV *hesitantly.*] Listen. . . . Are you still angry? I'm extremely irritated, but, do you understand me, how can I express it . . . the fact is, that, you see, strictly speaking . . . [*He shouts.*] Is it my fault, really, for liking you? [*Grabs the back of a chair, which cracks and breaks.*] Why the hell do you have such fragile furniture! I like you! Do you understand? I . . . I'm almost in love with you!

MRS. POPOV: Get away from me—I hate you!

SMIRNOV: God, what a woman! I've never in my life seen anything like her! I'm lost! I'm done for! I'm caught like a mouse in a trap!

MRS. POPOV: Stand back or I'll shoot!

SMIRNOV: Shoot! You could never understand what happiness it would be to die under the    140
gaze of those wonderful eyes, to be shot by a revolver which was held by those little velvet hands. . . . I've gone out of my mind! Think about it and decide right away, because if I leave here, then we'll never see each other again! Decide . . . I'm a nobleman, a respectable gentleman, of good family. I have an income of ten thousand a year. . . . I can put a bullet through a coin tossed in the air . . . I have some fine horses. . . . Will you be my wife?

MRS. POPOV: [*Indignantly brandishes her revolver.*] Let's fight! I challenge you!

SMIRNOV: I'm out of my mind . . . I don't understand anything . . . [*Shouts.*] Hey, you, water!

MRS. POPOV: [*Shouts.*] Let's fight!

SMIRNOV: I've gone out of my mind. I'm in love like a boy, like an idiot! [*He grabs her hand, she screams with pain.*] I love you! [*Kneels.*] I love you as I've never loved before! I've jilted twelve women, nine women have jilted me, but I've never loved one of them as I love you. . . . I'm weak, I'm a limp rag. . . . I'm on my knees like a fool, offering you my hand. . . . Shame, shame! I haven't been in love for five years, I vowed I wouldn't; and suddenly I'm in love, like a fish out of water. I'm offering my hand in marriage. Yes or no? You don't want to? You don't need to! [*Gets up and quickly goes to the door.*]

145 Mrs. Popov: Wait!

Smirnov: [*Stops.*] Well?

Mrs. Popov: Nothing . . . you can go . . . go away . . . wait. . . . No, get out, get out! I hate you! But—don't go! Oh, if you only knew how furious I am, how angry! [*Throws revolver on table.*] My fingers are swollen from that nasty thing. . . . [*Tears her handkerchief furiously.*] What are you waiting for? Get out!

Smirnov: Farewell!

Mrs. Popov: Yes, yes, go away! [*Shouts.*] Where are you going? Stop. . . . Oh, go away! Oh, how furious I am! Don't come near me! Don't come near me!

150 Smirnov: [*Approaching her.*] How angry I am with myself! I'm in love like a student. I've been on my knees. . . . It gives me the shivers. [*Rudely.*] I love you! A lot of good it will do me to fall in love with you! Tomorrow I've got to pay the interest, begin the mowing of the hay. [*Puts his arm around her waist.*] I'll never forgive myself for this. . . .

Mrs. Popov: Get away from me! Get your hands away! I . . . hate you! I . . . challenge you!

[*Prolonged kiss. Luka enters with an ax, the Gardener with a rake, the Coachman with a pitchfork, and Workmen with cudgels.*]

Luka: [*Catches sight of the pair kissing.*] Lord in heaven! [*Pause.*]

Mrs. Popov: [*Lowering her eyes.*] Luka, tell them in the stable not to give Toby any oats today.

*CURTAIN*

## Questions

1. What was Mrs. Popov's life like with her late husband? What did she learn about him after his death? How has this knowledge affected her?

2. Who is Smirnov? What is he like, and how do you know? Why does he say what he does about women?

3. Why is Luka important? How do his responses highlight the emotions developing between Smirnov and Mrs. Popov?

4. What causes Mrs. Popov to call Smirnov a bear, a brute, a monster? What is his immediate response?

5. Why is Toby significant? How does he symbolize the shifting emotions of Mrs. Popov?

## General Questions

1. Where did you laugh in the play? Analyze those moments and try to determine the causes of your laughter.

2. From this play, what conclusions can you draw about farce as a dramatic form? Consider the breaking chairs, the shouting, the challenge, the attitude of Smirnov about being shot, the shifting of feelings, etc.

3. How does Chekhov's presentation of the characters of Smirnov and Mrs. Popov make their reversal of feelings seem normal and logical, although sudden, unexpected, and surprising?

4. What are the major ideas or themes in *The Bear*? Consider vows made by the living to the dead, the difficulty of keeping resolutions, the nature of powerful emotions, the need to maintain conventions and expectations, and so on.

## BETH HENLEY (b 1952)

Brought up in Mississippi, Beth Henley attended Southern Methodist University, where in her sophomore year she wrote *Am I Blue*, which was first produced in December 1981. She attended acting school in Illinois and went to Hollywood to take up a career as a movie actress. However, at the same time she continued to work on new plays, and it is as a writer that she has been successful. Her most notable achievement is her "Southern Gothic" play *Crimes of the Heart* (first titled *Crimes of Passion*), for which she won the Great American Play contest in 1978 and the Pulitzer Prize for Drama in 1981. She also wrote *The Wake of*  *Jamey Foster* (1983), *The Lucky Spot* (1986), *The Debutante Ball* (1991), and *Abundance* (1991). The year 1992 saw the publication of four collected plays (*Beth Henley: Four Plays*), including *The Miss Firecracker Contest*, a two-act play written in 1979 and first performed in 1984. Her play *Impossible Marriage* was produced off Broadway in 1998 at the Laura Pels Theater in New York. In addition, she has seen some of her shorter scripts produced as television plays. In 2002 she published *Three Plays by Beth Henley*, containing *Control Freaks* (1993), *L-Play* (1996), and *Sisters of the Winter Madrigal* (2001). She also did documentary in 2001 titled *Intimate Portrait: Holly Hunter*, and in 2004 her "teleplay" *It Must Be Love* appeared. *Crimes of the Heart* was made into a successful film in 1986, starring Diane Keaton, Jessica Lange, Sam Shepard, and Sissy Spacek.

In many of her plays, Henley's comedic manner develops out of the eccentricity or "kookiness" of her main female characters. The comic *donnée* is that an unusual or even disturbed action is accepted as a normal event that begins a course of dramatic action. A character in one of Henley's television plays, for example, inadvertently sets a house on fire, but the outcome turns out to be fortunate because of a lucrative home insurance policy. In *Crimes of the Heart*, one of the characters, after a failed suicide attempt, explains herself by saying that she has been having "a bad day." Even in the serious play *Abundance*, the two main female characters begin their twenty-five-year friendship after they have come west in the 1860s to become mail-order brides of men they have never seen. Ashbe of *Am I Blue* is an early original in the pattern, with her liking for hot Kool-Aid and colored marshmallows, her habit of stealing ashtrays and then donating them to a fellow tenant, and her dabbling in voodoo.

Although *Am I Blue* is an amusing play, it deals with the difficulties of adjustment to adulthood, misconceptions about social roles, unfulfilled dreams, general aimlessness and indecisiveness, and the attempt to develop individuality. The larger political and historical context of the year of the supposed events of the play, 1968, is mentioned by neither Ashbe nor John Polk, but one might connect their difficulties with some of the disturbances of that year, particularly the assassinations of Robert Kennedy and Martin Luther King, Jr.; the frustrating and seemingly endless war in Vietnam; and the many antiwar demonstrations and riots, especially during the Democratic National Convention in Chicago in the summer. Henley is very specific in dating the action of *Am I Blue* on the night of November 11, 1968—in other words, after all these disturbing and destabilizing events had taken place, and also less than a week after the election that made Richard Nixon president. One might also note the irony that November 11 had before 1954 been called Armistice Day (now Veterans Day)—a holiday dedicated to peace and stability.

*Am I Blue* thus reflects the disturbances and disruptions of the late 1960s, even though it focuses on the individual concerns and problems of John Polk and Ashbe.

Ashbe's father is an alcoholic who is absent when she needs him, and her mother has deserted the home entirely. John Polk is facing a difficult choice about his future career, and he is also trying to stay afloat in the swim of fraternity life. Unable to succeed in either situation, he seeks strength in rum instead of calling on his own inner resources. Nothing earthshaking is claimed for either John Polk or Ashbe at the play's end, but they both succeed in developing a degree of recognition—rejecting conventional behaviors and discovering their own capacities for friendship and dignity.

# Am I Blue° ((1973) 1982)

### CHARACTERS

**John Polk Richards,** seventeen

**Ashbe Williams,** sixteen

**Hilda,** a waitress, thirty-five

**Street People: Barker, Whore, Bum, Clareece**

[SCENE. *A bar, the street, the living room of a run-down apartment.*]

[TIME. *Fall 1968.*]

*The scene opens on a street in the New Orleans French Quarter on a rainy, blue bourbon night. Various people—a* WHORE, BUM, STREET BARKER, CLAREECE—*appear and disappear along the street. The scene then focuses on a bar where a piano is heard from the back room playing softly and indistinctly "Am I Blue?"° The lights go up on* JOHN POLK, *who sits alone at a table. He is seventeen, a bit overweight and awkward. He wears nice clothes, perhaps a navy sweater with large white monograms. His navy raincoat is slung over an empty chair. While drinking John Polk concentrates on the red and black card that he holds in his hand. As soon as the scene is established,* ASHBE *enters from the street. She is sixteen, wears a flowered plastic raincoat, a white plastic rain cap, red galoshes, a butterfly barrette, and jeweled cat-eye glasses. She is carrying a bag full of stolen goods. Her hair is very curly. Ashbe makes her way cautiously to John Polk's table. As he sees her coming, he puts the card into his pocket. She sits in the empty chair and pulls his raincoat over her head.*

ASHBE:  Excuse me . . . do you mind if I sit here please?

JOHN POLK:  [*Looks up at her—then down into his glass.*] What are you doing hiding under my raincoat? You're getting it all wet.

ASHBE:  Well, I'm very sorry, but after all it is a raincoat. [*He tries to pull off coat.*] It was rude of me I know, but look I just don't want them to recognize me.

JOHN POLK:  [*Looking about.*] Who to recognize you?

ASHBE:  Well, I stole these two ashtrays from the Screw Inn, ya know right down the street. [*She*
5        *pulls out two glass commercial ashtrays from her white plastic bag.*] Anyway, I'm scared the manager saw me. They'll be after me I'm afraid.

JOHN POLK:  Well, they should be. Look, do you mind giving me back my raincoat? I don't want to be found protecting any thief.

ASHBE:  [*Coming out from under coat.*] Thief—would you call Robin Hood a thief?

JOHN POLK:  Christ.

---

°The first New York City production was by the Circle Repertory Company.

°1 "*Am I Blue*?": Music by Harry Akst (1894–1963), with lyrics by Grant Clarke (1891–1931), from the film *On With the Show* (1929).

In this first production of Henley's *Am I Blue* at the Margo Jones Experimental Theater of Southern Methodist University in Dallas, Texas, in 1973, Ashbe Williams (Marcie Glaser) enters the bar where she first meets John Polk (John Tillotson). The production was directed by Jill Christine Peters, with the set designed by John Gisondi.

ASHBE: [*Back under coat.*] No, you wouldn't. He was valiant—all the time stealing from the rich and giving to the poor.

JOHN POLK: But your case isn't exactly the same, is it? You're stealing from some crummy lit- 10 tle bar and keeping the ashtrays for yourself. Now give me back my coat.

ASHBE: [*Throws coat at him.*] Sure, take your old coat. I suppose I should have explained— about Miss Marcey. [*Silence.*] Miss Marcey, this cute old lady with a little hump in her back. I always see her in her sun hat and blue print dress. Miss Marcey lives in the apart- ment building next to ours. I leave all the stolen goods, as gifts on her front steps.

JOHN POLK: Are you one of those kleptomaniacs? [*He starts checking his wallet.*]

ASHBE: You mean when people all the time steal and they can't help it?

JOHN POLK: Yeah.

ASHBE: Oh, no. I'm not a bit careless. Take my job tonight, my very first night job, if you want 15 to know. Anyway, I've been planning it for two months, trying to decipher which bar most deserved to be stolen from. I finally decided on the Screw Inn. Mainly because of the way they're so mean to Mr. Groves. He works at the magazine rack at Diver's Drugstore and is really very sweet, but he has a drinking problem. I don't think that's fair to be mean to people simply because they have a drinking problem—and, well, anyway, you see I'm not just stealing for personal gain. I mean, I don't even smoke.

JOHN POLK: Yeah, well, most infants don't, but then again, most infants don't hang around bars.

ASHBE: I don't see why not, Toulouse Lautrec did.

JOHN POLK: They'd throw me out.

ASHBE: Oh, they throw me out too, but I don't accept defeat. [*Slowly moves into him.*] Why it's the very same with my pickpocketing.

[*JOHN POLK sneers, turns away.*]

20    ASHBE: It's a very hard act to master. Why every time I've done it, I've been caught.

JOHN POLK: That's all I need, is to have some slum kid tell me how good it is to steal. Everyone knows it's not.

ASHBE: [*About his drink.*] That looks good. What is it?

JOHN POLK: Hey, would you mind leaving me alone—I just wanted to be alone.

ASHBE: Okay, I'm sorry. How about if I'm quiet?

[*JOHN POLK shrugs. He sips drink, looks around, catches her eye, she smiles and sighs.*]

25    ASHBE: I was just looking at your pin. What fraternity are you in?

JOHN POLK: S.A.E.

ASHBE: Is it a good fraternity?

JOHN POLK: Sure, it's the greatest.

ASHBE: I bet you have lots of friends.

30    JOHN POLK: Tons.

ASHBE: Are you being serious?

JOHN POLK: Yes.

ASHBE: Hmm. Do they have parties and all that?

JOHN POLK: Yeah, lots of parties, booze, honking horns, it's exactly what you would expect.

35    ASHBE: I wouldn't expect anything. Why did you join?

JOHN POLK: I don't know. Well, my brother . . . I guess it was my brother . . . he told me how great it was, how the fraternity was supposed to get you dates, make you study, solve all your problems.

ASHBE: Gee, does it?

JOHN POLK: Doesn't help you study.

ASHBE: How about dates? Do they get you a lot of dates?

40    JOHN POLK: Some.

ASHBE: What were the girls like?

JOHN POLK: I don't know—they were like girls.

ASHBE: Did you have a good time?

JOHN POLK: I had a pretty good time.

45    ASHBE: Did you make love to any of them?

JOHN POLK: [*To self.*] Oh, Christ . . .

ASHBE: I'm sorry . . . I just figured that's why you had the appointment with the whore . . . cause you didn't have anyone else . . . to make love to.

JOHN POLK: How did you know I had the, ah, the appointment?

ASHBE: I saw you put the red card in your pocket when I came up. Those red cards are pretty familiar around here. The house is only about a block or so away. It's one of the best though, really very plush. Only two murders and a knifing in its whole history. Do you go there often?

50    JOHN POLK: Yeah, I like to give myself a treat.

ASHBE: Who do you have?

JOHN POLK: What do you mean?

ASHBE: I mean which girl. [*JOHN POLK gazes into his drink.*] Look, I just thought I might know her is all.

JOHN POLK: Know her, ah, how would you know her?

ASHBE: Well, some of the girls from my high school go there to work when they get out.     55

JOHN POLK: G.G., her name is G.G.

ASHBE: G.G. . . . Hmm, well, how does she look?

JOHN POLK: I don't know.

ASHBE: Oh, you've never been with her before?

JOHN POLK: No.     60

ASHBE: [*Confidentially.*] Are you one of those kinds that likes a lot of variety?

JOHN POLK: Variety? Sure, I guess I like variety.

ASHBE: Oh, yes, now I remember.

JOHN POLK: What?

ASHBE: G.G., that's just her working name. Her real name is Myrtle Reims, she's Kay Reims'     65
older sister. Kay is in my grade at school.

JOHN POLK: Myrtle? Her name is Myrtle?

ASHBE: I never liked the name either.

JOHN POLK: Myrtle, oh, Christ. Is she pretty?

ASHBE: [*Matter of fact.*] Pretty, no she's not real pretty.

JOHN POLK: What does she look like?     70

ASHBE: Let's see . . . she's, ah, well, Myrtle had acne and there are a few scars left. It's not bad.
I think they sort of give her character. Her hair's red, only I don't think it's really red. It
sort of fizzles out all over her head. She's got a pretty good figure . . . big top . . . but the
rest of her is kind of skinny.

JOHN POLK: I wonder if she has a good personality.

ASHBE: Well, she was a senior when I was a freshman; so I never really knew her. I remember
she used to paint her fingernails lots of different colors . . . pink, orange, purple. I don't
know, but she kind of scares me. About the only time I ever saw her true personality was
around a year ago. I was over at Kay's making a health poster for school. Anyway,
Myrtle comes busting in, screaming about how she can't find her spangled bra anywhere. Kay and I just sat on the floor cutting pictures of food out of magazines while she
was storming about slamming drawers and swearing. Finally, she found it. It was pretty
garish—red with black and gold sequined G's on each cup. That's how I remember the
name—G.G.

[*As ASHBE illustrates the placement of the G's she spots HILDA, the waitress, approaching. ASHBE pulls
the raincoat over her head and hides on the floor. HILDA enters through the beaded curtains spilling her
tray. HILDA is a woman of few words.*]

HILDA: Shit, damn curtain. Nuther drink?

JOHN POLK: Mam?     75

HILDA: [*Points to drink.*] Vodka coke?

JOHN POLK: No, thank you. I'm not quite finished yet.

HILDA: Napkins clean.

[*ASHBE pulls her bag off the table. HILDA looks at ASHBE then to JOHN POLK. She walks around the table,
as ASHBE is crawling along the floor to escape. ASHBE runs into HILDA's toes.*]

ASHBE: Are those real gold?

HILDA: You again. Out.     80

ASHBE: She wants me to leave. Why should a paying customer leave? [*Back to* HILDA.] Now I'll
have a mint julip and easy on the mint.

HILDA: This pre-teen with you?

JOHN POLK: Well, I . . . No . . . I . . .

HILDA: I.D.'s.

85   ASHBE: Certainly, I always try to cooperate with the management.

HILDA: [*Looking at* JOHN POLK's *I.D.*] I.D., 11-12-50. Date: 11-11-68.

JOHN POLK: Yes, but . . . well, 11-12 is less than two hours away.

HILDA: Back in two hours.

ASHBE: I seem to have left my identification in my gold lamé bag.

90   HILDA: Well, boo-hoo. [*Motions for* ASHBE *to leave with a minimum of effort. She goes back to table.*]
No tip.

ASHBE: You didn't tip her?

JOHN POLK: I figured the drinks were so expensive . . . I just didn't . . .

HILDA: No tip!

JOHN POLK: Look, Miss, I'm sorry. [*Going through his pockets.*] Here would you like a . . . a nickel . . .
wait, wait, here's a quarter.

95   HILDA: Just move ass, sonny. You too, Barbie.

ASHBE: Ugh, I hate public rudeness. I'm sure I'll refrain from ever coming here again.

HILDA: Think I'll go in the back room and cry.

[ASHBE *and* JOHN POLK *exit.* HILDA *picks up tray and exits through the curtain, tripping again.*]

HILDA: Shit. Damn curtain.

[ASHBE *and* JOHN POLK *are now standing outside under the awning of the bar.*]

ASHBE: Gee, I didn't know it was your birthday tomorrow. Happy birthday! Don't be mad. I
thought you were at least twenty or twenty-one, really.

100   JOHN POLK: It's o.k. Forget it.

[*As they begin walking, various blues are heard coming from the nearby bars.*]

ASHBE: It's raining.

JOHN POLK: I know.

ASHBE: Are you going over to the house now?

JOHN POLK: No, not till twelve.

105   ASHBE: Yeah, the red and black cards—they mean all night. Midnight till morning.

[*At this point a street* BARKER *beckons the couple into his establishment. Perhaps he is accompanied by
a* WHORE.]

BARKER: Hey mister, bring your baby on in, buy her a few drinks, maybe tonight ya get lucky.

ASHBE: Keep walking.

JOHN POLK: What's wrong with the place?

ASHBE: The drinks are watery rot gut, and the show girls are boys . . .

110   BARKER: Up yours, punk!

JOHN POLK: [*Who has now sat down on a street bench.*] Look, just tell me where a cheap bar is. I've
got to stay drunk, but I don't have much money left.

ASHBE: Yikes, there aren't too many cheap bars around here, and a lot of them check I.D.'s.

JOHN POLK: Well, do you know of any that don't?

ASHBE: No, not for sure.

115   JOHN POLK: Oh, God, I need to get drunk.

ASHBE:  Aren't you?

JOHN POLK:  Some, but I'm losing ground fast.

[*By this time a* BUM *who has been traveling drunkenly down the street falls near the couple and begins throwing up.*]

ASHBE:  Oh, I know! You can come to my apartment. It's just down the block. We keep one bottle of rum around. I'll serve you a grand drink, three or four if you like.

JOHN POLK:  [*Fretfully.*] No, thanks.

ASHBE:  But look, we're getting all wet.                                                                120

JOHN POLK:  Sober too, wet and sober.

ASHBE:  Oh, come on! Rain's blurring my glasses.

JOHN POLK:  Well, how about your parents? What would they say?

ASHBE:  Daddy's out of town and Mama lives in Atlanta; so I'm sure they won't mind. I think
we have some cute little marshmallows. [*Pulling on him.*] Won't you really come?

JOHN POLK:  You've probably got some gang of muggers waiting to kill me. Oh, all right . . . 125
what the hell, let's go.

ASHBE:  Hurrah! Come on. It's this way. [*She starts across the stage, stops, and picks up an old hat.*]
Hey, look at this hat. Isn't something! Here, wear it to keep off the rain.

JOHN POLK:  [*Throwing hat back onto street.*] No, thanks, you don't know who's worn it before.

ASHBE:  [*Picking hat back up.*] That makes it all the more exciting. Maybe it was a butcher's who
slaughtered his wife or a silver pirate with a black bird on his throat. Who do you guess?

JOHN POLK:  I don't know. Anyway what's the good of guessing? I mean you'll never really
know.

ASHBE:  [*Trying the hat on.*] Yeah, probably not.                                                      130

[*At this point* ASHBE *and* JOHN POLK *reach the front door.*]

ASHBE:  Here we are.

[ASHBE *begins fumbling for her key.* CLAREECE, *a teeny-bopper, walks up to* JOHN POLK.]

CLAREECE:  Hey, man, got any spare change?

JOHN POLK:  [*Looking through his pockets.*] Let me see . . . I . . .

ASHBE:  [*Coming up between them, giving* CLAREECE *a shove.*] Beat it, Clareece. He's my company.

CLAREECE:  [*Walks away and sneers.*] Oh, shove it, Frizzels.                                           135

ASHBE:  A lot of jerks live around here. Come on in. [*She opens the door. Lights go up on the living
room of a run-down apartment in a run-down apartment house. Besides being merely run-down
the room is a malicious pig sty with colors, paper hats, paper dolls, masks, torn up stuffed animals,
dead flowers and leaves, dress-up clothes, etc., thrown all about.*] My bones are cold. Do you
want a towel to dry off?

JOHN POLK:  Yes, thank you.

ASHBE:  [*She picks up a towel off the floor and tosses it to him.*] Here. [*He begins drying off, as she takes
off her rain things; then she begins raking things off the sofa.*] Please do sit down. [*He sits.*] I'm
sorry the place is disheveled, but my father's been out of town. I always try to pick up and
all before he gets in. Of course, he's pretty used to messes. My mother never was too good
at keeping things clean.

JOHN POLK:  When's he coming back?

ASHBE:  Sunday, I believe. Oh, I've been meaning to say . . .                                           140

JOHN POLK:  What?

ASHBE:  My name's Ashbe Williams.

JOHN POLK:  Ashbe?

ASHBE: Yeah, Ashbe.

145 JOHN POLK: My name's John Polk Richards.

ASHBE: John Polk? They call you John Polk?

JOHN POLK: It's family.

ASHBE: [*Putting on socks.*] These are my favorite socks, the red furry ones. Well, here's some books and magazines to look at while I fix you something to drink. What do you want in your rum?

JOHN POLK: Coke's fine.

150 ASHBE: I'll see if we have any. I think I'll take some hot Kool-Aid myself.

[*She exits to the kitchen.*]

JOHN POLK: Hot Kool-Aid?

ASHBE: It's just Kool-Aid that's been heated, like hot chocolate or hot tea.

JOHN POLK: Sounds great.

ASHBE: Well, I'm used to it. You get so much for your dime, it makes it worth your while. I don't buy presweetened, of course, it's better to sugar your own.

155 JOHN POLK: I remember once I threw up a lot of grape Kool-Aid when I was a kid. I've hated it ever since. Hey, would you check on the time?

ASHBE: [*She enters carrying a tray with several bottles of food coloring, a bottle of rum, and a huge glass.*] I'm sorry we don't have Coke. I wonder if rum and Kool-Aid is good? Oh, we don't have a clock either.

[*She pours a large amount of rum into the large glass.*]

JOHN POLK: I'll just have it with water then.

ASHBE: [*She finds an almost empty glass of water somewhere in the room and dumps it in with the rum.*] Would you like food coloring in the water? It makes a drink all the more aesthetic. Of course, some people don't care for aesthetics.

JOHN POLK: No, thank you, just plain water.

160 ASHBE: Are you sure? The taste is entirely the same. I put it in all my water.

JOHN POLK: Well . . .

ASHBE: What color do you want?

JOHN POLK: I don't know.

ASHBE: What's your favorite color?

165 JOHN POLK: Blue, I guess.

[*She puts a few blue drops into the glass. As she has nothing to stir with, she blows into the glass turning the water blue.*]

JOHN POLK: Thanks.

ASHBE: [*Exits. She screams from kitchen.*] Come on, say come on, cat, eat your fresh, good milk.

JOHN POLK: You have a cat?

170 ASHBE: [*off.*] No.

JOHN POLK: Oh.

ASHBE: [*She enters carrying a tray with a cup of hot Kool-Aid and Cheerios and colored marshmallows.*] Here are some Cheerios and some cute, little, colored marshmallows to eat with your drink.

JOHN POLK: Thanks.

ASHBE: I one time smashed all the big white marshmallows in the plastic bag at the grocery store.

JOHN POLK: Why did you do that?

175 ASHBE: I was angry. Do you like ceramics?

JOHN POLK: Yes.

ASHBE: My mother makes them. It's sort of her hobby. She is very talented.

JOHN POLK: My mother never does anything. Well, I guess she can shuffle the bridge deck okay.

ASHBE: Actually, my mother is a dancer. She teaches at a school in Atlanta. She's really very talented.

JOHN POLK: [*Indicates ceramics.*] She must be to do all these.

ASHBE: Well, Madeline, my older sister, did the blue one. Madeline gets to live with Mama.      180

JOHN POLK: And you live with your father.

ASHBE: Yeah, but I get to go visit them sometimes.

JOHN POLK: You do ceramics too?

ASHBE: No, I never learned . . . but I have this great potholder set. [*Gets up to show him.*] See, I      185
make lots of multicolored potholders and send them to Mama and Madeline. I also make
paper hats. [*Gets material to show him.*] I guess they're more creative, but making potholders is more relaxing. Here, would you like to make a hat?

JOHN POLK: I don't know, I'm a little drunk.

ASHBE: It's not hard a bit. [*Hands him material.*] Just draw a real pretty design on the paper. It
really doesn't have to be pretty, just whatever you want.

JOHN POLK: It's kind of you to give my creative drives such freedom.

ASHBE: Ha, ha, ha, I'll work on my potholder set a bit.

JOHN POLK: What time is it? I've really got to check on the time.      190

ASHBE: I know. I'll call the time operator.

[*She goes to the phone.*]

JOHN POLK: How do you get along without a clock?

ASHBE: Well, I've been late for school a lot. Daddy has a watch. It's 11:03.

JOHN POLK: I've got a while yet. [*ASHBE twirls back to her chair, drops, and sighs.*] Are you a
dancer, too?

ASHBE: [*Delighted.*] I can't dance a bit, really. I practice a lot is all, at home in the afternoon. I      195
imagine you go to a lot of dances.

JOHN POLK: Not really, I'm a terrible dancer. I usually get bored or drunk.

ASHBE: You probably drink too much.

JOHN POLK: No, it's just since I've come to college. All you do there is drink more beer and
write more papers.

ASHBE: What are you studying for to be?

JOHN POLK: I don't know.

ASHBE: Why don't you become a rancher?      200

JOHN POLK: Dad wants me to help run his soybean farm.

ASHBE: Soybean farm. Yikes, that's really something. Where is it?

JOHN POLK: Well, I live in the Delta, Hollybluff, Mississippi. Anyway, Dad feels I should go to
business school first; you know, so I'll become, well, management-minded. Pass the blue.

ASHBE: Is that what you really want to do?      205

JOHN POLK: I don't know. It would probably be as good as anything else I could do. Dad
makes good money. He can take vacations whenever he wants. Sure it'll be a ball.

ASHBE: I'd hate to have to be management-minded. [*JOHN POLK shrugs.*] I don't mean to hurt
your feelings, but I would really hate to be a management mind. [*She starts walking on her
knees, twisting her fists in front of her eyes, and making clicking sounds as a management mind
would make.*]

JOHN POLK: Cut it out. Just forget it. The farm could burn down, and I wouldn't even have to
think about it.

ASHBE: [*After a pause.*] Well, what do you want to talk about?

210 JOHN POLK: I don't know.

ASHBE: When was the last dance you went to?

JOHN POLK: Dances. That's great subject. Let's see, oh, I don't really remember—it was probably some blind date. God, I hate dates.

ASHBE: Why?

JOHN POLK: Well, they always say that they don't want popcorn, and they wind up eating all of yours.

215 ASHBE: You mean, you hate dates just because they eat your popcorn? Don't you think that's kind of stingy?

JOHN POLK: It's the principle of the thing. Why can't they just say, yes, I'd like some popcorn when you ask them. But, no, they're always so damn coy.

ASHBE: I'd tell my date if I wanted popcorn. I'm not that immature.

JOHN POLK: Anyway, it's not only the popcorn. It's a lot of little things. I've finished coloring. What do I do now?

ASHBE: Now you have to fold it. Here . . . like this. [*She explains the process with relish.*] Say, that's really something.

220 JOHN POLK: It's kind of funny looking. [*Putting the hat on.*] Yeah, I like it, but you could never wear it anywhere.

ASHBE: Well, like what anyway?

JOHN POLK: Huh?

ASHBE: The things dates do to you that you don't like, the little things.

JOHN POLK: Oh, well, just the way they wear those false eyelashes and put their hand on your knee when you're trying to parallel park, and keep on giggling and going off to the bathroom with their girl friends. It's obvious they don't want to go out with me. They just want to go out so that they can wear their new clothes and won't have to sit on their ass in the dormitory. They never want to go out with me. I can never even talk to them.

225 ASHBE: Well, you can talk to me, and I'm a girl.

JOHN POLK: Well, I'm really kind of drunk, and you're a stranger . . . well, I probably wouldn't be able to talk to you tomorrow. That makes a difference.

ASHBE: Maybe it does. [*A bit of a pause and then extremely pleased by the idea she says.*] You know we're alike because I don't like dances either.

JOHN POLK: I thought you said you practiced . . . in the afternoons.

ASHBE: Well, I like dancing. I just don't like dances. At least not like . . . well, not like the one our school was having tonight . . . they're so corny.

230 JOHN POLK: Yeah, most dances are.

ASHBE: All they serve is potato chips and fruit punch, and then this stupid baby band plays and everybody dances around thinking they're so hot. I frankly wouldn't dance there. I would prefer to wait till I am invited to an exclusive ball. It doesn't really matter which ball, just one where they have huge, golden chandeliers and silver fountains, and serve delicacies of all sorts and bubble blue champagne. I'll arrive in a pink silk cape [*Laughing.*] I want to dance in pink!

JOHN POLK: You're mixed up. You're probably one of those people that live in a fantasy world.

ASHBE: I do not. I accept reality as well as anyone. Anyway, you can talk to me, remember. I know what you mean by the kind of girls it's hard to talk to. There are girls a lot that way in the small clique at my school. Really tacky and mean. They expect everyone to be as stylish as they are, and they won't even speak to you in the hall. I don't mind if they don't speak to me, but I really love the orphans, and it hurts my feelings when they are so mean to them.

JOHN POLK: What do you mean—they're mean to the "orpheens"? [*Giggles to himself at the wordplay.*]

ASHBE: Oh, well, they sometimes snicker at the orphans' dresses. The orphans usually have 235 hand-me-down, drab, ugly dresses. Once Shelly Maxwell wouldn't let Glinda borrow her pencil, even though she had two. It hurt her feelings.

JOHN POLK: Are you best friends with these orphans?

ASHBE: I hardly know them at all. They're really shy. I just like them a lot. They're the reason I put spells on the girls in the clique.

JOHN POLK: Spells, what do you mean, witch spells?

ASHBE: Witch spells? Not really, mostly just voodoo.

JOHN POLK: Are you kidding? Do you really do voodoo? 240

ASHBE: Sure, here I'll show you my doll. [*Goes to get doll, comes back with straw voodoo doll. Her air as she returns is one of frightening mystery.*] I know a lot about the subject. Cora, she used to wash dishes in the Moonlight Cafe, told me all about voodoo. She's a real expert on the subject, went to all the meetings and everything. Once she caused a man's throat to rot away and turn almost totally black. She's moved to Chicago now.

JOHN POLK: It doesn't really work. Does it?

ASHBE: Well, not always. The thing about voodoo is that both parties have to believe in it for it to work.

JOHN POLK: Do the girls in school believe in it?

ASHBE: Not really, I don't think. That's where my main problem comes in. I have to make the 245 clique believe in it, yet I have to be very subtle. Mainly, I give reports in English class or Speech.

JOHN POLK: Reports?

ASHBE: On voodoo.

JOHN POLK: That's really kind of sick, you know.

ASHBE: Not really. I don't cast spells that'll do any real harm. Mainly, just the kind of thing to make them think . . . to keep them on their toes. [*Blue-drink intoxication begins to take over and JOHN POLK begins laughing.*] What's so funny?

JOHN POLK: Nothing. I was just thinking what a mean little person you are. 250

ASHBE: Mean! I'm not mean a bit.

JOHN POLK: Yes, you are mean . . . [*Picking up color.*] . . . , and green too.

ASHBE: Green?

JOHN POLK: Yes, green with envy of those other girls; so you play all those mean little tricks.

ASHBE: Envious of those other girls, that stupid, close-minded little clique! 255

JOHN POLK: Green as this marshmallow. [*Eats marshmallow.*]

ASHBE: You think I want to be in some group . . . a sheep like you? A little sheep like you that does everything when he's supposed to do it!

JOHN POLK: Me a sheep . . . I do what I want!

ASHBE: Ha! I've known you for an hour and already I see you for the sheep you are!

JOHN POLK: Don't take your green meanness out on me. 260

ASHBE: Not only are you a sheep, you are a NORMAL sheep. Give me back my colors! [*Begins snatching colors away.*]

JOHN POLK: [*Pushing colors at her.*] Green and mean! Green and mean! Green and mean!

ASHBE: [*Throwing marshmallows at him.*] That's the reason you're in a fraternity and the reason you're going to manage your mind. And dates . . . you go out on dates merely because it's expected of you even though you have a terrible time. That's the reason you go to the whorehouse to prove you're a normal man. Well, you're much too normal for me.

JOHN POLK: Infant bitch. You think you're really cute.

ASHBE: That really wasn't food coloring in your drink, it was poison! [*She laughs, he picks up his 265 coat to go, and she stops throwing marshmallows at him.*] Are you going? I was only kidding. For Christ sake, it wasn't really poison. Come on, don't go. Can't you take a little friendly criticism?

JOHN POLK:  Look, did you have to bother me tonight? I had enough problems without . . .

[*Phone rings. Both look at phone, it rings for the third time. He stands undecided.*]

ASHBE:  Look, wait, we'll make it up. [*She goes to answer phone.*] Hello . . . Daddy. How are you? . . .
I'm fine . . . Dad, you sound funny . . . What? . . . Come on, Daddy, you know she's not
here. [*Pause.*] Look, I told you I wouldn't call anymore. You've got her number in Atlanta.
[*Pause, as she sinks to the floor.*] Why have you started again? . . . Don't say that. I can tell it. I
can. Hey, I have to go to bed now, I don't want to talk anymore, okay? [*Hangs up phone, then
softly to self.*] Goddamnit.

JOHN POLK:  [*He has heard the conversation and is taking off his coat.*] Hey, Ashbe . . . [*She looks at
him blankly, her mind far away.*] You want to talk?

ASHBE:  No, [*Slight pause.*] Why don't you look at my shell collection? I have this special shell
collection. [*She shows him collection.*]

270  JOHN POLK:  They're beautiful, I've never seen colors like this. [*ASHBE is silent, he continues to
himself.*] I used to go to Biloxi° a lot when I was a kid . . . One time my brother and I, we
camped out on the beach. The sky was purple. I remember it was really purple. We ate
pork and beans out of a can. I'd always kinda wanted to do that. Every night for about a
week after I got home, I dreamt about these waves foaming over my head and face. It was
funny. Did you find these shells or buy them?

ASHBE:  Some I found, some I bought. I've been trying to decipher their meaning. Here, listen,
do you hear that?

JOHN POLK:  Yes.

ASHBE:  That's the soul of the sea. [*She listens.*] I'm pretty sure it's the soul of the sea. Just imagine when I decipher the language. I'll know all the secrets of the world.

JOHN POLK:  Yeah, probably you will. [*Looking into the shell.*] You know, you were right.

275  ASHBE:  What do you mean?

JOHN POLK:  About me, you were right. I am a sheep, a normal one. I've been trying to get out
of it, but now I'm as big a sheep as ever.

ASHBE:  Oh, it doesn't matter. You're company. It was rude of me to say.

JOHN POLK:  No, because it was true. I really didn't want to go into a fraternity, I didn't even
want to go to college, and I sure as hell don't want to go back to Hollybluff and work the
soybean farm till I'm eighty.

ASHBE:  I still say you could work on a ranch.

JOHN POLK:  I don't know. I wanted to be a minister or something good, but I don't even know
280      if I believe in God.

ASHBE:  Yeah.

JOHN POLK:  I never used to worry about being a failure. Now I think about it all the time. It's
just I need to do something that's . . . fulfilling.

ASHBE:  Fulfilling, yes, I see what you mean. Well, how about college? Isn't it fulfilling? I mean,
you take all those wonderful classes, and you have all your very good friends.

JOHN POLK:  Friends, yeah, I have some friends.

285  ASHBE:  What do you mean?

JOHN POLK:  Nothing . . . well, I do mean something. What the hell, let me try to explain. You
see it was my "friends," the fraternity guys that set me up with G.G., excuse me, Myrtle,
as a gift for my eighteenth birthday.

ASHBE:  You mean, you didn't want the appointment?

JOHN POLK:  No, I didn't want it. Hey, ah, where did my blue drink go?

ASHBE:  [*As she hands him the drink.*] They probably thought you really wanted to go.

---

°270 *Biloxi:* city in southern Mississippi, on the Gulf of Mexico.

JOHN POLK: Yeah, I'm sure they gave a damn what I wanted. They never even asked me. Hell,   290
     I would have told them a handkerchief, a pair of argyle socks, but, no, they have to get me
     a whore just because it's a cool-ass thing to do. They make me sick. I couldn't even stay
     at the party they gave. All the sweaty T-shirts, and moron sex stories . . . . I just couldn't
     take it.

ASHBE: Is that why you were at the Blue Angel so early?

JOHN POLK: Yeah, I needed to get drunk, but not with them. They're such creeps.

ASHBE: Gosh, so you really don't want to go to Myrtle's?

JOHN POLK: No, I guess not.

ASHBE: Then are you going?                                                           295

JOHN POLK: [Pause.] Yes.

ASHBE: That's wrong. You shouldn't go just to please them.

JOHN POLK: Oh, that's not the point anymore, maybe at first it was, but it's not anymore. Now
     I have go for myself . . . to prove to myself that I'm not afraid.

ASHBE: Afraid? [Slowly, as she begins to grasp his meaning.] You mean, you've never slept with a
     girl before?

JOHN POLK: Well, I've never been in love.                                            300

ASHBE: [In amazement.] You're a virgin?

JOHN POLK: Oh, God.

ASHBE: No, don't feel bad, I am too.

JOHN POLK: I thought I should be in love . . .

ASHBE: Well, you're certainly not in love with Myrtle. I mean, you haven't even met her.   305

JOHN POLK: I know, but, God, I thought maybe I'd never fall in love. What then? You should
     experience everything . . . shouldn't you? Oh, what's it matter, everything's so screwed.

ASHBE: Screwed? Yeah, I guess it is. I mean, I always thought it would be fun to have a lot of
     friends who gave parties and go to dances all dressed up. Like the dance tonight . . . it
     might have been fun.

JOHN POLK: Well, why didn't you go?

ASHBE: I don't know. I'm not sure it would have been fun. Anyway, you can't go . . . alone.

JOHN POLK: Oh, you need a date?                                                       310

ASHBE: Yeah, or something.

JOHN POLK: Say, Ashbe, ya wanna dance here?

ASHBE: No, I think we'd better discuss your dilemma.

JOHN POLK: What dilemma?

ASHBE: Myrtle. It doesn't seem right you should . . .                                315

JOHN POLK: Let's forget Myrtle for now. I've got a while yet. Here have some more of this blue-
     moon drink.

ASHBE: You're only trying to escape through artificial means.

JOHN POLK: Yeah, you got it. Now come on. Would you like to dance? Hey, you said you liked
     to dance.

ASHBE: You're being ridiculous.

JOHN POLK: [Winking at her.] Dance?                                                  320

ASHBE: John Polk, I just thought . . .

JOHN POLK: Hmm?

ASHBE: How to solve your problem . . .

JOHN POLK: Well . . .

ASHBE: Make love to me!                                                              325

JOHN POLK: What?!

ASHBE: It all seems logical to me. It would prove you weren't scared, and you wouldn't be
     doing it just to impress others.

JOHN POLK: Look, I . . . I mean, I hardly know you . . .

ASHBE: But we've talked. It's better this way, really. I won't be so apt to point out your mistakes.

330 JOHN POLK: I'd feel great, stripping a twelve-year-old of her virginity.

ASHBE: I'm sixteen! Anyway, I'd be stripping you of yours just as well. I'll go put on some Tiger Claw perfume. [*She runs out.*]

JOHN POLK: Hey, come back! Tiger Claw perfume, Christ.

ASHBE: [*Entering.*] I think one should have different scents for different moods.

JOHN POLK: Hey, stop spraying that! You know I'm not going to . . . well, you'd get neurotic, or pregnant, or some damn thing. Stop spraying, will you!

335 ASHBE: Pregnant? You really think I could get pregnant?

JOHN POLK: Sure, it'd be a delightful possibility.

ASHBE: It really wouldn't be bad. Maybe I would get to go to Tokyo for an abortion. I've never been to the Orient.

JOHN POLK: Sure getting cut on is always a real treat.

ASHBE: Anyway, I might just want to have my dear baby. I could move to Atlanta with Mama and Madeline. It'd be wonderful fun. Why I could take him to the supermarket, put him in one of those little baby seats to stroll him about. I'd buy peach baby food and feed it to him with a tiny golden spoon. Why I could take colored pictures of him and send them to you through the mail. Come on . . . [*Starts putting pillows onto the couch.*] Well, I guess you should kiss me for a start. It's only etiquette, everyone begins with it.

340 JOHN POLK: I don't think I could even kiss you with a clear conscience. I mean, you're so small with those little cat-eye glasses and curly hair . . . I couldn't even kiss you.

ASHBE: You couldn't even kiss me? I can't help it if I have to wear glasses. I got the prettiest ones I could find.

JOHN POLK: Your glasses are fine. Let's forget it, okay?

ASHBE: I know, my lips are too purple, but if I eat carrots, the dye'll come off and they'll be orange.

JOHN POLK: I didn't say anything about your lips being too purple.

345 ASHBE: Well, what is it? You're just plain chicken, I suppose . . .

JOHN POLK: Sure, right, I'm chicken, totally chicken. Let's forget it. I don't know how, but, somehow, this is probably all my fault.

ASHBE: You're darn right it's all your fault! I want to have my dear baby or at least get to Japan. I'm so sick of school I could smash every marshmallow in sight! [*She starts smashing.*] Go on to your skinny pimple whore. I hope the skinny whore laughs in your face, which she probably will because you have an easy face to laugh in.

JOHN POLK: You're absolutely right, she'll probably hoot and howl her damn fizzle red head off. Maybe you can wait outside the door and hear her, give you lots of pleasure, you sadistic little thief.

ASHBE: Thief! Was Robin Hood . . . Oh, what's wrong with this world? I just wasn't made for it, is all. I've probably been put in the wrong world, I can see that now.

350 JOHN POLK: You're fine in this world.

ASHBE: Sure, everyone just views me as an undesirable lump.

JOHN POLK: Who?

ASHBE: You, for one.

JOHN POLK: [*Pause.*] You mean because I wouldn't make love to you?

355 ASHBE: It seems clear to me.

JOHN POLK: But you're wrong, you know.

ASHBE: [*To self, softly.*] Don't pity me.

JOHN POLK: The reason I wouldn't wasn't that . . . it's just that . . . well, I like you too much to.

ASHBE: You like me?

360 JOHN POLK: Undesirable lump, Jesus. Your cheeks they're . . . they're . . .

ASHBE: My cheeks? They're what?

JOHN POLK: They're rosy.

ASHBE: My cheeks are rosy?

JOHN POLK: Yeah, your cheeks, they're really rosy.

ASHBE: Well, they're natural, you know. Say, would you like to dance?      365

JOHN POLK: Yes.

ASHBE: I'll turn on the radio. [*She turns on radio. Ethel Waters is heard singing "Honey in the Honeycomb."*° *ASHBE begins snapping her fingers.*] Yikes, let's jazz it out.

[*They dance.*]

JOHN POLK: Hey, I'm not good or anything . . .

ASHBE: John Polk:

JOHN POLK: Yeah?      370

ASHBE: Baby, I think you dance fine!

[*They dance on, laughing, saying what they want till end of song. Then a radio announcer comes on and says the 12:00 news will be in five minutes. Billie Holiday, or Terry Pierce, begins singing, "Am I Blue?"*]

JOHN POLK: Dance?

ASHBE: News in five minutes.

JOHN POLK: Yeah.

ASHBE: That means five minutes till midnight.      375

JOHN POLK: Yeah, I know.

ASHBE: Then you're not . . .

JOHN POLK: Ashbe, I've never danced all night. Wouldn't it be something to . . . to dance all night and watch the rats come out of the gutter?

ASHBE: Rats?

JOHN POLK: Don't they come out at night? I hear New Orleans has lots of rats.      380

ASHBE: Yeah, yeah, it's got lots of rats.

JOHN POLK: Then let's dance all night and wait for them to come out.

ASHBE: All right . . . but, but how about our feet?

JOHN POLK: Feet?

ASHBE: They'll hurt.      385

JOHN POLK: Yeah.

ASHBE: [*Smiling.*] Okay, then let's dance.

[*He takes her hand, and they dance as lights black out and the music soars and continues to play.*]

*End.*

# Questions

1. What do Ashbe's actions at the start tell you about her (such as hiding under the coat, stealing and giving the stolen things away, crawling away from the waitress)? What is disclosed by her speeches?

2. Describe the circumstances of Ashbe and her family. To what degree can her character and behavior be explained by these circumstances?

---

°*"Honey in the Honeycomb"*: With music by Vernon Duke (1903–1969) and lyrics by John Latouche (1917–1956), this song was first performed in the musical *Cabin in the Sky* (1940), which starred Ethel Waters (1896–1977).

3. What is Ashbe's intention in her description of G.G., or Myrtle? What does her description tell you about her? What do you learn about her from her description of the only sort of dance she would like to go to (speech 231)?

4. What personal, occupational, and social difficulties is John Polk experiencing? Why is he trying to stay drunk before going to G.G.? What are his reactions to fraternity life and to the family business?

5. Explain the effects of the arguments between Ashbe and John Polk. How does their occasionally taunting each other influence their developing relationship?

6. Why does John Polk not take up Ashbe's invitation to make love? How does this refusal suggest the development of his character? Of Ashbe's character? What may be inferred by their concluding decision to dance the night away?

## General Questions

1. What is the plot of *Am I Blue?* Who is the protagonist (or protagonists)? Who or what is the antagonist? How is the plot resolved?

2. Describe and analyze the verbal comedy of the play, such as the "two murders and a knifing" (speech 49), Ashbe's description of Myrtle (speeches 71–73), and the inquiry about what to mix with rum (speech 148).

3. What is appealing (or not appealing) about Ashbe and John Polk? To what extent are you to consider them as realistic persons? How might they be seen as symbols, and what might they symbolize?

4. What are the major themes or ideas of the play? To what extent does the comic mode obscure these ideas? To what extent does it bring them out?

5. What is the effect of the setting in the New Orleans French Quarter and the characters to be found there? What is shown about Ashbe and John Polk by their brief interactions with the characters in the bar, especially Hilda, and on the street?

## WRITING ABOUT COMEDY

For an essay about comedy, you can choose any of the topics discussed in this chapter, such as *plot, conflict, character, point of view, setting, style, tone, symbolism,* or *theme.* You might choose one of these, or two or more; for example, how language and action define character, how character and symbol convey meaning, or how setting may influence comic structure.

Planning and prewriting strategies for each of these conventional elements are discussed at some length in Chapter 20 (pp. 912–916) and in other chapters on prose fiction and poetry. As you develop your essay on comedy, you will find it helpful to look at these suggestions.

For the most part, planning and writing about specific features of comedy are much like addressing the same topics in other forms of drama, short stories, and poetry. However, a few areas of consideration—such as plot, character, and language—are especially significant in comic drama and can be handled in a distinctive fashion.

## Questions for Discovering Ideas

PLOT, CONFLICT, STRUCTURE. What problems, adversities, or abnormal situations are in place at the comedy's opening? How is this initial situation complicated? Do the complications spring mainly from character or from situation? If from character, what aspects of behavior or personality create the problems? If from situation, what dilemmas or troubles plague the characters? What kinds of complications dominate—misunderstandings, disagreements, mistakes in identity, situational problems, or emotional entanglements? How important is coincidence?

What problems and complications occur early? Who is the comic protagonist (or protagonists) and what is the protagonist's goal (money, success, marriage, land, freedom)? How is the protagonist blocked (fathers, rivals, laws, customs, his or her own personality)? How threatening is the obstruction? What plans are hatched to overcome the blocking agents? Are the plans sensible or silly? Who initiates and executes the plans? To what extent do plans succeed (or fail)—because of chance and good luck or because of skillful planning and manipulation?

Describe the conflicts. Which conflict is central, and whom do the conflicts involve? Do they result from personality clashes or from situations? To what degree are they related to blocking activities? How does the action reach the crisis, and which characters are involved? What choices, decisions, plans, or conclusions become necessary? What events or revelations (of character, emotion, background) produce the catastrophe, and how do these affect characters, circumstances, and relationships?

In the comic resolution, to what extent are loose ends tied up and lives straightened out? Is reasonable order restored and regeneration assured or implied? Is the resolution satisfying? Disturbing? Does it leave you happy or thoughtful, or both? Are you amused by farce, pleased by romance, or disturbed by satire? If there is to be a marriage, whom will it bring together? What will the marriage settle, or whom will it divide? Most importantly, how can you account for your responses to the resolution and the play as a whole? How do they reflect the general aims of comedy?

CHARACTER. Which characters are realistic, conventional, round, flat, changing, standing still? Who is the protagonist or lover, the antagonist or blocking agent? Which characters seem excessive, eccentric, or irrational? What is the nature of their excesses? To what extent do the excesses define the characters? How do you respond to the excessive or exaggerated characters? Does the comedy provide a "cure" for the excesses? In other words, do the characters learn and change? If so, why and how? If not, why not?

From what classes are the characters derived? What class characteristics do you find? Who are the stock or stereotyped characters, and what is their significance to the protagonist? How does the playwright bring the characters to life? Who is the choric figure or *raisonneur*, if there is one? Who is the confidant? Which character can be considered a foil (or foils)?

LANGUAGE. Does the language consist of witty turns of phrase, confusions, puns, misunderstandings, or a mixture? Which characters are masters of language and which are mastered by it? Do characters use the same type of language and level of diction consistently? To what extent does language expose a character's self-interest or hypocrisy? If the language is witty and sparkling, what devices make it work effectively? If it is garbled and filled with misunderstandings, what types of errors does the playwright put into the characters' mouths? How does the language shape your response to characters, to ideas, and to the play as a whole?

## Strategies for Organizing Ideas

To develop a central idea, isolate the feature you wish to explore and consider how it affects the shape and impact of the play. For *A Midsummer Night's Dream*, for example, you might focus on Puck's character and function. You might also develop a link between Puck's conventional role as a tricky servant with his love of mischief and the chaos he creates. Remember that it is difficult to develop essays from sentences like "Puck is a comic character" or "*Am I Blue* contains dramatic satire." A more focused assertion that also reveals your thematic development is necessary, such as "Puck, modeled on the tricky servant of Roman comedy, causes most of the play's confusion," or "*Am I Blue* attacks the general indifference of people toward the situations of others."

Organize your essay by grouping related types of details together (such as observations about characters, actions, direct statements, and specific words), and choose your own order of presentation. In writing about Puck as a tricky servant and creator of chaos, for example, you might present only one kind of detail—such as direct statements—and introduce these not in their order in the play but rather as they contribute to your analysis of Puck's character.

More often than not, your supporting details will represent a variety of types of evidence—dramatic dialogue and action, individual soliloquies, special properties (such as a love potion or a disguise), or the failure or development of various plans. For example, you might support an assertion about Puck by referring to his reputation, actions, and attitudes as though each of these is equally important. Other possible strategies are to demonstrate how the topics are related according to cause and effect, to build the topics from the least to the most significant, and to trace how a common idea or image provides unity. Whatever your method of development, be sure to validate your arguments with supporting details.

A summary of key points will make your conclusion useful and effective. In addition, you can show how your conclusions in the body of the essay bear upon larger aspects of the play's meaning.

## Illustrative Student Essay

Underlined sentences in this paper *do not* conform to MLA style and are used solely as teaching tools to emphasize the central idea, thesis sentence, and topic sentences throughout the paper.

Walls 1

Suzanne Walls

Professor Tompkins

English 210

7 December 2007

### Setting as Symbol and Comic Structure in
### *A Midsummer Night's Dream*°

[1]     Shakespeare's *A Midsummer Night's Dream* might superficially be considered light and inconsequential. The changes of mind undergone by the two sets of lovers, the placing of an ass's head on one of the characters, the presence of unrealistic fairies, the acting of a silly sketch—all seem far-fetched. But the play is more serious than that. It dramatizes the accidental and arbitrary origins of love, even though it considers this serious subject in the good-natured medium of comedy.* To bring out both message and merriment, Shakespeare uses two settings—the city of Athens and the nearby forest. The play's comic structure is governed by the movements between the order and the chaos that these two locations represent.†

[2]     At the play's beginning, Athens is presented as a world of daylight, order, and law. In this setting, Duke Theseus has absolute authority, fathers are always right, and the law permits Egeus to "dispose" of Hermia "either to this gentleman [Demetrius],/Or to her death" ([1102] 1.1.43–44). The city is also the place for the exposition and the beginning of complications. Here, we meet the various groups of characters (except the fairies) and learn about the initial problem—namely, that the relationship between Hermia and Lysander is blocked by a raging father, a rival suitor, and an old law. In order to flee and then to overcome these obstructions, Lysander asks Hermia to meet him in the woods. Her agreement begins a journey from Athens to the forest that ultimately includes everyone in the play—the four lovers, Egeus, the city rulers, and the "mechanicals."

---

°See pp. 1099–1152 for this play.
*Central idea.
†Thesis sentence.

[3]        The play's second setting, the woods outside Athens, is the kingdom of Oberon and Titania, the king and queen of the fairies. It is a world of moonlight, chaos, madness, and dreams, a world that symbolizes the power of imagination and passion. The disorder in this world has many sources, including Oberon's jealousy, Titania's infatuation, and Puck's delight in mischief. When the lovers and the mechanicals enter this setting, they also become disordered and chaotic.

[4]        The woods are the setting for complication, crisis, and catastrophe. Confusion dominates the action here. Puck disrupts the mechanicals' rehearsal and transforms Bottom into a monster with the head of a jackass. In addition, the passions of the lovers are rearranged several times by Oberon and Puck through the magic of "love-in-idleness," a flower that symbolizes the irrational and overwhelming power of love. Although the first two adjustments of the lovers' feelings are done to help them in their plights, each has the effect of raising the levels of complication and disorder. Puck gleefully observes that his actions are the cause of the play's confusions ([1127] 3.2.120–21):

> those things do best please me
> That befall prepost'rously.

Puck is right; his first application of love-in-idleness causes Lysander to fall wildly in love with Helena, and his second does the same to Demetrius.

[5]        The crisis and dénouement of the main plot also occur in the woods. A crisis occurs when the two lovers challenge each other and the women attack each other. At this point, complication is at a peak, and the fairies must develop a plan to resolve the threats. Puck therefore misleads the lovers into ending their potential duel, and he adjusts their emotions one more time. The dénouement—the revelation of the newly restored emotions—occurs the next morning at the edge of the woods, in the presence of Egeus, Theseus, and Hippolyta. Thus, it ends the confusing relationships occurring in the forest and begins the regularity of relationships in the orderly world of city and society.

[6]        Resolution—the marriages and the mechanicals' production of Pyramus and Thisby—occurs in the first setting, the city, which represents law and order. But the journey to the second setting has had a significant effect on the urban world both for Theseus and for the lovers. The law has been softened and Egeus has been overruled; the young lovers have been allowed to marry as they like, and their lives have been set right. In the end, this second setting has also become the dream world of night and the

Walls 3

supernatural, and the fairy dance and blessings closing the play only emphasize the harmony and the regenerative implications of the comic resolutions.

[7]     Setting, symbolism, and comic pattern thus combine in *A Midsummer Night's Dream* to produce an intricately plotted structure. Each element reinforces the others, bringing the play toward completion though time after time there seems to be no way out. The marvel of the play is that the two settings represent, realistically, two opposed states of being, and, dramatically, two distinct stages of comic structure. The journey out of Athens, into the woods, and then back to the city is also a journey from exposition and adversity, through complication, crisis, and catastrophe, and then forward to comic resolution.

---

Walls 4

**WORK CITED**

William Shakespeare, *A Midsummer Night's Dream. Literature: An Introduction to Reading and Writing*, 4th Compact ed., Ed. Edgar V. Roberts. Upper Saddle River: Prentice Hall, 2008, 1099–1152.

## Commentary on the Essay

This essay deals with three elements of *A Midsummer Night's Dream*: setting, symbols, and comic structure. It demonstrates the way a number of different topics can be combined in a single essay. Consequently, the essay is organized to reflect the journey from the city to the woods and then back to the city.

The body of the essay takes up the settings, their symbolic meaning, and the relationship between setting and structure. Paragraph 2 deals with Athens both as a world of law and order and as the setting for exposition and the beginnings of complication. The supporting details include circumstance, actions, and dialogue.

Paragraphs 3–5 deal with the middle of the journey and of the play. Paragraph 3 discusses the symbolic implications of the forest setting, and paragraphs 4 and 5 take up the connection between the setting and comic structure, specifically, complication, crisis, and dénouement. Again, the supporting details in these paragraphs are a mixture of actions, circumstances, and direct quotations.

Paragraph 6 deals briefly with the return to the city, linking this setting with the play's comic resolution. The concluding paragraph returns to the idea about how *A Midsummer Night's Dream* connects setting, symbol, and comic pattern.

# Topics for Writing About Comedy

1. Write an essay describing Shakespeare's comic technique in *A Midsummer Night's Dream*. Consider these questions: Is the basic situation serious? How does Shakespeare keep it comic? How does the boisterousness of the low characters influence your perceptions of the lovers and the courtly characters? Would the play be as interesting without Bottom and his crowd or without the fairies and their involvement? How does the comic outcome depend on the boisterousness and colorfulness provided by the players and the fairies? For research on Shakespeare as a comic dramatist, you might wish to consult Henry B. Charlton's classic study *Shakespeare's Comedies* (rpt. 1972) and/or a more recent book by Michael Mangan, *A Preface to Shakespeare's Comedies* (1996).

2. Write an essay that analyzes the relationship of situation to comedy in *Am I Blue*. How do the eccentricity of the characters and the improbability of their circumstances produce amusement? When you finish the play, do you believe that you have been seriously engaged? Simply entertained? Explain. For comparison with other Henley plays, you might wish to take out *Beth Henley: Four Plays* (1992) from your college library.

3. *The Bear* is one of Chekhov's most popular farces. Read another Chekhov play (for example, *The Cherry Orchard, The Seagull, Three Sisters, Uncle Vanya*) and compare it to *The Bear* (characters with characters, dialogue with dialogue, situations with situations, and so on). As you make your comparison, attempt to explain the continued popularity of *The Bear*.

4. Write an essay about the nature of comedy, using *A Midsummer Night's Dream, Am I Blue*, and *The Bear* as material. Deal with issues like the following: How can comic material be defined? Does the happy outcome of a serious action qualify a play as a comedy, or should no action be serious? When is a comedy no longer comic but tragic? Are jokes necessary? Is farcical action necessary? Where are the edges between comedy and farce, on the one hand, and comedy and tragedy on the other? For a research component for this topic, you might wish to introduce materials from books by Wylie Sypher (1956, rpt. 1982, an edition of two classic essays on the comic), G. S. Amur (1963), Robert Corrigan (1965), Robert B. Heilman (1978), T. G. A. Nelson (1990), Athene Seyler (1990), Frances Teague (1994), and Janet Suzman (1995).

5. Treat the lovers in *A Midsummer Night's Dream* and *Am I Blue* as types or archetypes (see Chapter 24). What is their situation? What problems block the fulfillment of their love? How serious are these problems? What actions and ruses do they plan to make things right? How are the pairs of lovers in the two plays similar? Different?

6. Write a comic scene of your own between two people, perhaps a boy and a girl, as in *Am I Blue*; or two people who are angry with each other, as in *The Bear*; or a person under a spell and a person in normal touch with reality, as in *A Midsummer Night's Dream*. After you finish your scene, write a short essay explaining the principles on which you've written your scene, such as the reasons for your choice of material, your use of jokes (if any), straightforward dialogue, anger, outrage, amused responses, and so on.

# Chapter 23

## Four Plays for Additional Enjoyment and Study

## Henrik Ibsen, *A Dollhouse*

The Norwegian playwright Henrik Johan Ibsen (1828–1906) is the acknowledged originator—the "father"— of modern drama. He deserves this recognition because of his pioneering dramatizations of challenging and sometimes shocking private and public issues. Today there are few restrictions on dramatists except success at the box office. Plays may range freely on almost any subject, such as the drug culture, sexual inclinations, AIDS, the right to commit suicide, the problems of real-estate dealers, the life of a go-go dancer, violence, family dissension, homosexuality, the Vietnam war or the Kuwait war or the Iraq war, and the aftereffects of the atrocity of 9/11. If one includes film as drama, there is virtually no limit to the topics that dramatists currently explore. It is well to stress that writers for the stage have not always been this free, and that Ibsen was in the forefront of the struggle for unbridled dramatic expression. A brief consideration of some of his major dramatic topics shows his originality and daring: the blinding and crippling effects of congenital syphilis, a woman's renunciation of a traditional protective marriage, suicide, the manipulations of people seeking personal benefits, the sacrifices of pursuing truth, the rejection of a child by a parent, and the abandonment of personal happiness in favor of professional interests.

## Ibsen's Life and Early Work

From Ibsen's beginnings, there was little to indicate how important he was to become. He was born in Skien (SHEE-*en*), Norway, a small town just seventy miles southwest of the capital, Christiania (now Oslo). Although his parents had been prosperous, they went bankrupt when he was only seven, and in the following years the family suffered the miseries of poverty. When Ibsen was fifteen he was apprenticed to a pharmacist, and he seemed headed for an undistinguished career in this profession even though he hated it. By 1849, however, when he wrote *Catiline*, his first play in verse, it was clear that the theater was to be his life. Largely through the efforts of the famous violinist Ole Bull, a new National Theater had been established in Bergen, and Ibsen was appointed its director. He stayed in Bergen for six years

Henrik Johan Ibsen

and then went to Christiania, where for the next five years he tried to fashion a genuine Norwegian national theater. His attempts proved fruitless, for the theater went bankrupt in 1862. After writing *The Pretenders* in 1864, he secured enough governmental travel money to enable him to leave Norway. For the next twenty-seven years he lived in Germany and Italy in what has been called a self-imposed exile.

Although this first part of Ibsen's theatrical career was devoted to many practical matters—production, management, directing, and finances—he was also constantly writing. His early plays were in verse and were mainly nationalist and romantic, as a few representative titles suggest: *Lady Inger of Oestraat* (1855), *The Feast of Solhaug* (1856), *Olaf Liljekrans* (1857). In his first 10 years in Germany and Italy he finished four plays. The best known of these is *Peer Gynt* (1867), a fantasy play about a historical Norwegian hero, Peer Gynt, who is saved from spiritual emptiness by the love of the patient heroine Solveig. Today, *Peer Gynt* is best known because of the incidental music written for it by Norway's major composer, Edvard Grieg (1843–1907). Ibsen asked Grieg to compose the music for the initial performances in 1876. Grieg's response was enthusiastic and creative, and the result is still enjoyed by millions today. Ibsen also supplied the poem for which Grieg composed one of his loveliest songs, "A Swan."

## Ibsen's Major Prose Plays

During the years when Ibsen was fighting poverty and establishing his career in the theater, Europe was undergoing great political and intellectual changes. Throughout the nineteenth century, Ibsen's home country, Norway, was trying to release itself from the domination of neighboring Sweden and to establish its own territorial and national integrity. In Ibsen's twentieth year, 1848, the February Uprising in Paris resulted in the deposition of the French king and the establishment of a new French republic. This same year also saw the publication of the *Communist Manifesto* of Karl Marx (1818–1883). In 1864, the year Ibsen left Norway, Marx's first socialist International was held in London. In addition, during the time Ibsen lived in Italy and Germany, both countries were going through the tenuous political processes of becoming authentic nation states. In short, change was everywhere.

Ibsen also was changing and growing as a thinker and dramatist, driven by the idea that a forward and creative drama could bring about deeper and more permanent changes than could be effected by soldiers and politicians. To this end he developed the realistic *problem play*. Such a play posited a major personal, social, professional, or political problem that occasioned the play's dramatic conflicts and tensions. Each problem was timely, topical, and realistic, as were the characters, places, situations, and outcomes. In this vein Ibsen wrote the 12 prose plays on which his reputation rests: *The Pillars of Society* (1877), *A Dollhouse* (1879), *Ghosts* (1881), *An*

*Enemy of the People* (1882), *The Wild Duck* (1884), *Rosmersholm* (1886), *The Lady from the Sea* (1888), *Hedda Gabler* (1890), *The Master Builder* (1892), *Little Eyolf* (1894), *John Gabriel Borkman* (1896), and *When We Dead Awaken* (1899). He finished the first eight of these plays while living in Germany and Italy, the last four after returning to Norway in 1891.

In these major plays Ibsen dramatizes human beings breaking free from restrictions and inhibitions and trying to establish their individuality and freedom—freedom of self, inquiry, pursuit of truth, artistic dedication, and, above all, the freedom of love. In attempting to achieve these goals, Ibsen's dramatic characters find internal opposition in self-interest, self-indulgence, and self-denial, and external opposition in the personal and political influences and manipulations of others. Because the plays are designed to be realistic, Ibsen's characters fall short of their goals. At best they achieve a respite in their combat, as in *An Enemy of the People*, or begin a quest in new directions, as in *A Dollhouse*. They always make great sacrifices, sometimes losing life itself, as in *Hedda Gabler* and *John Gabriel Borkman*.

## *A Dollhouse*: Ibsen's Best-Known Realistic Problem Play

*A Dollhouse* (*Et Dukkehjem*, 1879)[1] is representative of Ibsen's realistic drama. Its scenes are realistic, including appropriate furniture, a piano, a Christmas tree, carpeting, and wall engravings. Its characters are in the process of realistically confronting overwhelming personal, marital, and economic problems. Realism extends also to the technique of presentation, particularly the exposition about the root causes of the problems that come to a head in the play itself. As *A Dollhouse* unfolds, we learn that years earlier, Nora Helmer had extended herself beyond her means to save Torvald from a near-fatal illness. We also learn that there had been an earlier relationship between Krogstad and Christine Linde.

## Ibsen's Symbolism in *A Dollhouse*

*A Dollhouse* is representative of Ibsen's realism, but it is also replete with contextual symbolism, like the major plays that came before and after it. At the end of the late play *John Gabriel Borkman*, for example, the major character freezes to death, an occurrence symbolic of what he had done to himself much earlier by denying love. In reference to *A Dollhouse*, the title itself symbolizes the dependent and dehumanized

---

[1]Ibsen's title *Et Dukkehjem* literally means the home (*hjem*) of a doll or puppet (*dukke*). *A Doll's House*, the traditional and most common English title of the play, is not an accurate rendering of *dukkehjem*, and, in addition, it is misleading because of some of the connotations of our word *doll*. Recent translators have used *A Doll House* as the title, but this form is not in regular use. Our English word for a toy house for dolls is listed in collegiate dictionaries as *dollhouse*, a one-word compound. *A Dollhouse* is therefore preferable to the other two titles because it accurately renders *Et Dukkehjem*, and it is also the form accepted in current dictionaries.

role of the wife within traditional middle-class marriages. In addition, the entire nation of Norway (cold, legal, male) is contrasted symbolically with Italy (warm, emotional, female). Ironically, the break in the Helmers' marriage is symbolically aligned with events that occur or have occurred in both locations. Other symbols in *A Dollhouse* are the Christmas tree, the children's presents, the death of Dr. Rank, and the mailbox.

## *A Dollhouse* as a "Well-Made Play"

The plot and structure of *A Dollhouse* show Ibsen's use of the conventions of the **well-made play** (*la pièce bien faite*), a form developed and popularized in nineteenth-century France by Eugène Scribe (1791–1861) and Victorien Sardou (1831–1908). Ibsen was familiar with well-made plays, having directed many of them himself at Bergen and Christiania. The well-made play follows a rigid and efficient structure in which the drama begins at the story's climax. Usually the plot is built on a secret known by the audience and perhaps one or two of the characters. The well-made play thus begins in suspense and offers a pattern of increasing tension produced through exposition and the timely arrivals of new characters (like Krogstad) and threatening news or props like the disclosure of Nora's earlier financial transactions. In the course of action of the well-made play, the fortunes of the protagonist go from a low point, through a *peripeteia* or reversal (Aristotle's concept), to a high point at which the protagonist confronts and defeats the villain.

Although Ibsen makes use of many of the structural elements of the well-made play, he varies and departs from the pattern to suit his realistic purposes. Thus in *A Dollhouse* his variation is that Nora's confrontation with Krogstad, who is the apparent villain, does not lead to a satisfactory resolution, but rather precipitates the more significant albeit intractable confrontation with her husband. In *A Dollhouse*, just as in many other Ibsen plays, there is not a traditionally well-made victorious outcome; rather there are provisional outcomes—adjustments—in keeping with the realistic concept that as life goes on, problems continue.

## The Timeliness and Dramatic Power of *A Dollhouse*

Ibsen's focus on real-life issues has given his plays continued timeliness and strength. Thus *A Dollhouse* vividly portrays the totally dependent position of married women in the nineteenth century. Most notably, a woman could not borrow funds legally without a man's cosignature, and Nora had been forced to violate the law to obtain the money to restore her husband's health. The mailbox, to which Torvald has the only key, symbolizes this limitation, and the ultimate disclosure of the box's contents, rather than freeing Nora and Torvald, highlights her dependency. Today's feminism has stressed the issues of female freedom and equality, together with many other issues vital to women, but the need for feminine individuality and independence has not been more originally and forcefully dramatized than in *A Dollhouse*.

# HENRIK IBSEN (1828–1906)

 # A Dollhouse (Et Dukkehjem) (1879)

*Translated by R. Farquharson Sharp*

## CHARACTERS

**Torvald Helmer,** a lawyer and bank manager
**Nora,** his wife
**Doctor Rank**
**Mrs. Christine Linde**
**Nils Krogstad,** a lawyer and bank clerk
**Ivar, Bob, and Emmy,** the Helmers' three young children
**Anne,** their nurse
**Helen,** a housemaid
**A Porter**

The action takes place in Helmer's apartment.

## ACT 1

*Scene. A room furnished comfortably and tastefully, but not extravagantly. At the back, a door to the right leads to the entrance hall, another to the left leads to Helmer's study. Between the doors stands a piano. In the middle of the left-hand wall is a door, and beyond it a window. Near the window are a round table, armchairs and a small sofa. In the right-hand wall, at the farther end, another door; and on the same side, nearer the footlights, a stove, two easy chairs and a rocking-chair; between the stove and the door, a small table. Engravings on the walls; a cabinet with china and other small objects; a small book case with well-bound books. The floors are carpeted, and a fire burns in the stove. It is winter.*

*A bell rings in the hall; shortly afterwards the door is heard to open. Enter Nora, humming a tune and in high spirits. She is in outdoor dress and carries a number of parcels; these she lays on the table to the right. She leaves the outer door open after her, and through it is seen a Porter who is carrying a Christmas Tree and a basket, which he gives to the Maid who has opened the door.*

Nora: Hide the Christmas Tree carefully, Helen. Be sure the children do not see it till this evening, when it is dressed. [*to the Porter, taking out her purse.*] How much?
Porter: Sixpence.
Nora: There is a shilling. No, keep the change. [*The Porter thanks her, and goes out. Nora shuts the door. She is laughing to herself, as she takes off her hat and coat. She takes a packet of macaroons from her pocket and eats one or two; then goes cautiously to her husband's door and listens.*] Yes, he is in.

[*Still humming, she goes to the table on the right.*]

Helmer: [*calls out from his room*] Is that my little lark twittering out there?
Nora: [*busy opening some of the parcels*] Yes, it is!
Helmer: Is my little squirrel bustling about?
Nora: Yes!
Helmer: When did my squirrel come home?

NORA: Just now. [*puts the bag of macaroons into her pocket and wipes her mouth.*] Come in here, Torvald, and see what I have bought.

10  HELMER: Don't disturb me. [*A little later, he opens the door and looks into the room, pen in hand.*] Bought, did you say? All these things? Has my little spendthrift been wasting money again?

NORA: Yes, but, Torvald, this year we really can let ourselves go a little. This is the first Christmas that we have not needed to economise.

HELMER: Still, you know, we can't spend money recklessly.

NORA: Yes, Torvald, we may be a wee bit more reckless now, mayn't we? Just a tiny wee bit! You are going to have a big salary and earn lots and lots of money.

HELMER: Yes, after the New Year; but then it will be a whole quarter before the salary is due.

15  NORA: Pooh! we can borrow till then.

HELMER: Nora! [*goes up to her and takes her playfully by the ear.*] The same little featherhead! Suppose, now, that I borrowed fifty pounds to-day, and you spent it all in the Christmas week, and then on New Year's Eve a slate fell on my head and killed me, and—

NORA: [*putting her hands over his mouth*] Oh! don't say such horrid things.

HELMER: Still, suppose that happened—what then?

NORA: If that were to happen, I don't suppose I should care whether I owed money or not.

20  HELMER: Yes, but what about the people who had lent it?

NORA: They? Who would bother about them? I should not know who they were.

HELMER: That is like a woman! But seriously, Nora, you know what I think about that. No debt, no borrowing. There can be no freedom or beauty about a home life that depends on borrowing and debt. We two have kept bravely on the straight road so far, and we will go on the same way for the short time longer that there need be any struggle.

NORA: [*moving towards the stove*] As you please, Torvald.

HELMER: [*following her*] Come, come, my little skylark must not droop her wings. What is this! Is my little squirrel out of temper? [*taking out his purse.*] Nora, what do you think I have got here?

25  NORA: [*turning around quickly*] Money!

HELMER: There you are. [*gives her some money*] Do you think I don't know what a lot is wanted for housekeeping at Christmas-time?

NORA: [*counting*] Ten shillings—a pound—two pounds! Thank you, thank you, Torvald; that will keep me going for a long time.

HELMER: Indeed it must.

NORA: Yes, yes, it will. But come here and let me show you what I have bought. And all so cheap! Look, here is a new suit for Ivar, and a sword; and a horse and a trumpet for Bob; and a doll and dolly's bedstead for Emmy—they are very plain, but anyway she will soon break them in pieces. And here are dress-lengths and handkerchiefs for the maids; old Anne ought really to have something better.

30  HELMER: And what is in this parcel?

NORA: [*crying out*] No, no! you mustn't see that till this evening.

HELMER: Very well. But now tell me, you extravagant little person, what would you like for yourself?

NORA: For myself? Oh, I am sure I don't want anything.

HELMER: Yes, but you must. Tell me something reasonable that you would particularly like to have.

35  NORA: No, I really can't think of anything—unless, Torvald—

HELMER: Well?

NORA: [*playing with his coat buttons, and without raising her eyes to his*] If you really want to give me something, you might—you might—

HELMER: Well, out with it!

NORA: [*speaking quickly*] You might give me money, Torvald. Only just as much as you can afford; and then one of these days I will buy something with it.

HELMER: But, Nora— 40

NORA: Oh, do! dear Torvald; please, please do! Then I will wrap it up in beautiful gilt paper and hang it on the Christmas Tree. Wouldn't that be fun?

HELMER: What are little people called that are always wasting money?

NORA: Spendthrifts—I know. Let us do as you suggest, Torvald, and then I shall have time to think what I am most in want of. That is a very sensible plan, isn't it?

HELMER: [*smiling*] Indeed it is—that is to say, if you were really to save out of the money I give you, and then really buy something for yourself. But if you spend it all on the housekeeping and any number of unnecessary things, then I merely have to pay up again.

NORA: Oh but, Torvald— 45

HELMER: You can't deny it, my dear little Nora. [*puts his arm round her waist*] It's a sweet little spendthrift, but she uses up a deal of money. One would hardly believe how expensive such little persons are!

NORA: It's a shame to say that. I do really save all I can.

HELMER: [*laughing*] That's very true—all you can. But you can't save anything!

NORA: [*smiling quietly and happily*] You haven't any idea how many expenses we skylarks and squirrels have, Torvald.

HELMER: You are an odd little soul. Very like your father. You always find some new way of 50 wheedling money out of me, and, as soon as you have got it, it seems to melt in your hands. You never know where it has gone. Still, one must take you as you are. It is in the blood; for indeed it is true that you can inherit these things, Nora.

NORA: Ah, I wish I had inherited many of papa's qualities.

HELMER: And I would not wish you to be anything but just what you are, my sweet little skylark. But, do you know, it strikes me that you are looking rather—what shall I say—rather uneasy to-day?

NORA: Do I?

HELMER: You do, really. Look straight at me.

NORA: [*looks at him*] Well?

HELMER: [*wagging his finger at her*] Hasn't Miss Sweet-Tooth been breaking rules in town 55 to-day?

NORA: No; what makes you think that?

HELMER: Hasn't she paid a visit to the confectioner's?

NORA: No, I assure you, Torvald—

HELMER: Not been nibbling sweets? 60

NORA: No, certainly not.

HELMER: Not even taken a bite at a macaroon or two?

NORA: No, Torvald, I assure you really—

HELMER: There, there, of course I was only joking.

NORA: [*going to the table on the right*] I should not think of going against your wishes. 65

HELMER: No, I am sure of that! besides, you gave me your word—[*going up to her*] Keep your little Christmas secrets to yourself, my darling. They will all be revealed to-night when the Christmas Tree is lit, no doubt.

NORA: Did you remember to invite Doctor Rank?

HELMER: No. But there is no need; as a matter of course he will come to dinner with us. However, I will ask him when he comes in this morning. I have ordered some good wine. Nora, you can't think how I am looking forward to this evening.

NORA: So am I! And how the children will enjoy themselves, Torvald!

70  HELMER: It is splendid to feel that one has a perfectly safe appointment, and a big enough income. It's delightful to think of, isn't it?

NORA: It's wonderful!

HELMER: Do you remember last Christmas? For a full three weeks beforehand you shut yourself up every evening till long after midnight, making ornaments for the Christmas Tree and all the other fine things that were to be a surprise to us. It was the dullest three weeks I ever spent!

NORA: I didn't find it dull.

HELMER: [*smiling*] But there was precious little result, Nora.

75  NORA: Oh, you shouldn't tease me about that again. How could I help the cat's going in and tearing everything to pieces?

HELMER: Of course you couldn't, poor little girl. You had the best of intentions to please us all, and that's the main thing. But it is a good thing that our hard times are over.

NORA: Yes, it is really wonderful.

HELMER: This time I needn't sit here and be dull all alone, and you needn't ruin your dear eyes and your pretty little hands—

NORA: [*clapping her hands*] No, Torvald, I needn't any longer, need I! It's wonderfully lovely to hear you say so! [*taking his arm*] Now I will tell you how I have been thinking we ought to arrange things, Torvald. As soon as Christmas is over—[*A bell rings in the hall.*] There's the bell. [*She tidies the room a little.*] There's someone at the door. What a nuisance!

80  HELMER: If it is a caller, remember I am not at home.

MAID: [*in the doorway*] A lady to see you, ma'am—a stranger.

NORA: Ask her to come in.

MAID: [*to* HELMER] The doctor came at the same time, sir.

HELMER: Did he go straight into my room?

85  MAID: Yes sir.

[HELMER *goes into his room. The* MAID *ushers in* MRS. LINDE, *who is in travelling dress, and shuts the door.*]

MRS. LINDE: [*in a dejected and timid voice*] How do you do, Nora?

NORA: [*doubtfully*] How do you do—

MRS. LINDE: You don't recognise me, I suppose.

NORA: No, I don't know—yes, to be sure, I seem to—[*suddenly*] Yes! Christine! Is it really you?

90  MRS. LINDE: Yes, it is I.

NORA: Christine! To think of my not recognising you! And yet how could I—[*in a gentle voice*] How you have altered, Christine!

MRS. LINDE: Yes, I have indeed. In nine, ten long years—

NORA: Is it so long since we met? I suppose it is. The last eight years have been a happy time for me, I can tell you. And so now you have come into the town, and have taken this long journey in winter—that was plucky of you.

MRS. LINDE: I arrived by steamer this morning.

95  NORA: To have some fun at Christmas-time, of course. How delightful! We will have such fun together! But take off your things. You are not cold, I hope. [*helps her*] Now we will sit down by the stove, and be cosy. No, take this arm-chair; I will sit here in the rocking-chair. [*takes her hands*] Now you look like your old self again; it was only the first moment—You are a little paler, Christine, and perhaps a little thinner.

MRS. LINDE: And much, much older, Nora.

NORA: Perhaps a little older; very, very little; certainly not much. [*stops suddenly and speaks seriously*] What a thoughtless creature I am, chattering away like this. My poor, dear Christine, do forgive me.

MRS. LINDE: What do you mean, Nora?

NORA: [*gently*] Poor Christine, you are a widow.

MRS. LINDE: Yes; it is three years ago now.    100

NORA: Yes, I knew; I saw it in the papers. I assure you, Christine, I meant ever so often to write to you at the time, but I always put it off and something always prevented me.

MRS. LINDE: I quite understand, dear.

NORA: It was very bad of me, Christine. Poor thing, how you must have suffered. And he left you nothing?

MRS. LINDE: No.

NORA: And no children?    105

MRS. LINDE: No.

NORA: Nothing at all, then?

MRS. LINDE: Not even any sorrow or grief to live upon.

NORA: [*looking incredulously at her*] But, Christine, is that possible?

MRS. LINDE: [*smiles sadly and strokes her hair*] It sometimes happens, Nora.    110

NORA: So you are quite alone. How dreadfully sad that must be. I have three lovely children. You can't see them just now, for they are out with their nurse. But now you must tell me all about it.

MRS. LINDE: No, no; I want to hear you.

NORA: No, you must begin. I mustn't be selfish to-day; to-day I must only think of your affairs. But there is one thing I must tell you. Do you know we have just had a great piece of good luck?

MRS. LINDE: No, what is it?

NORA: Just fancy, my husband has been made manager of the Bank!    115

MRS. LINDE: Your husband? What good luck!

NORA: Yes, tremendous! A barrister's profession is such an uncertain thing, especially if he won't undertake unsavoury cases; and naturally Torvald has never been willing to do that, and I quite agree with him. You may imagine how pleased we are! He is to take up his work in the Bank at the New Year, and then he will have a big salary and lots of commissions. For the future we can live quite differently—we can do just as we like. I feel so relieved and so happy, Christine! It will be splendid to have heaps of money and not need to have any anxiety, won't it?

MRS. LINDE: Yes, anyhow I think it would be delightful to have what one needs.

NORA: No, not only what one needs, but heaps and heaps of money.

MRS. LINDE: [*smiling*] Nora, Nora haven't you learnt sense yet? In our schooldays you were a    120 great spendthrift.

NORA: [*laughing*] Yes, that is what Torvald says now. [*wags her finger at her*] But "Nora, Nora" is not so silly as you think. We have not been in a position for me to waste money. We have both had to work.

MRS. LINDE: You too?

NORA: Yes; odds and ends, needlework, crochet-work, embroidery, and that kind of thing. [*dropping her voice*] And other things as well. You know Torvald left his office when we were married? There was no prospect of promotion there, and he had to try and earn more than before. But during the first year he overworked himself dreadfully. You see, he had to make money every way he could, and he worked early and late; but he couldn't stand it, and fell dreadfully ill, and the doctors said it was necessary for him to go south.

MRS. LINDE: You spent a whole year in Italy didn't you?

NORA: Yes. It was no easy matter to get away, I can tell you. It was just as Ivar was born; but    125 naturally we had to go. It was a wonderfully beautiful journey, and it saved Torvald's life. But it cost a tremendous lot of money, Christine.

MRS. LINDE: So I should think.

NORA: It cost about two hundred and fifty pounds. That's a lot, isn't it?

MRS. LINDE: Yes, and in emergencies like that it is lucky to have the money.

NORA: I ought to tell you that we had it from papa.

130 MRS. LINDE: Oh, I see. It was just about that time that he died, wasn't it?

NORA: Yes; and, just think of it, I couldn't go and nurse him. I was expecting little Ivar's birth every day and I had my poor sick Torvald to look after. My dear, kind father—I never saw him again, Christine. That was the saddest time I have known since our marriage.

MRS. LINDE: I know how fond you were of him. And then you went off to Italy?

NORA: Yes; you see we had money then, and the doctors insisted on our going, so we started a month later.

MRS. LINDE: And your husband came back quite well?

135 NORA: As sound as a bell!

MRS. LINDE: But—the doctor?

NORA: What doctor?

MRS. LINDE: I thought your maid said the gentleman who arrived here just as I did was the doctor?

NORA: Yes, that was Doctor Rank, but he doesn't come here professionally. He is our greatest friend, and comes in at least once every day. No, Torvald has not had an hour's illness since then, and our children are strong and healthy and so am I. [*jumps up and claps her hands*] Christine! Christine! it's good to be alive and happy!—But how horrid of me; I am talking of nothing but my own affairs. [*sits on a stool near her, and rests her arms on her knees*] You mustn't be angry with me. Tell me, is it really true that you did not love your husband? Why did you marry him?

140 MRS. LINDE: My mother was alive then, and was bedridden and helpless, and I had to provide for my two younger brothers; so I did not think I was justified in refusing his offer.

NORA: No, perhaps you were quite right. He was rich at that time, then?

MRS. LINDE: I believe he was quite well off. But his business was a precarious one; and, when he died, it all went to pieces and there was nothing left.

NORA: And then?—

MRS. LINDE: Well, I had to turn my hand to anything I could find—first a small shop, then a small school, and so on. The last three years have seemed like one long working-day, with no rest. Now it is at an end, Nora. My poor mother needs me no more, for she is gone; and the boys do not need me either; they have got situations and can shift for themselves.

145 NORA: What a relief you must feel it—

MRS. LINDE: No, indeed; I only feel my life unspeakably empty. No one to live for any more. [*gets up restlessly*] That was why I could not stand the life in my little backwater any longer. I hope it may be easier here to find something which will busy me and occupy my thoughts. If only I could have the good luck to get some regular work—office work of some kind—

NORA: But, Christine, that is so frightfully tiring, and you look tired out now. You had far better go away to some watering-place.

MRS. LINDE: [*walking to the window*] I have no father to give me money for a journey, Nora.

NORA: [*rising*] Oh, don't be angry with me.

150 MRS. LINDE: [*going up to her*] It is you that must not be angry with me, dear. The worst of a position like mine is that it makes one so bitter. No one to work for, and yet obliged to be always on the look-out for chances. One must live, and so one becomes selfish. When you told me of the happy turn your fortunes have taken—you will hardly believe it—I was delighted not so much on your account as on my own.

NORA: How do you mean?—Oh, I understand. You mean that perhaps Torvald could get you something to do.

MRS. LINDE: Yes, that was what I was thinking of.

NORA: He must, Christine. Just leave it to me; I will broach the subject very cleverly—I will think of something that will please him very much. It will make me so happy to be of some use to you.

MRS. LINDE: How kind you are, Nora, to be so anxious to help me! It is doubly kind in you, for you know so little of the burdens and troubles of life.

NORA: I—? I know so little of them?                                                                                  155

MRS. LINDE: [smiling] My dear! Small household cares and that sort of thing!—You are a child, Nora.

NORA: [tosses her head and crosses the stage] You ought not to be so superior.

MRS. LINDE: No?

NORA: You are just like the others. They all think that I am incapable of anything really serious—

MRS. LINDE: Come, come—                                                                                            160

NORA: —that I have gone through nothing in this world of cares.

MRS. LINDE: But, my dear Nora, you have just told me all your troubles.

NORA: Pooh!—those were trifles. [lowering her voice] I have not told you the important thing.

MRS. LINDE: The important thing? What do you mean?

NORA: You look down upon me altogether, Christine—but you ought not to. You are proud, 165 aren't you, of having worked so hard and so long for your mother?

MRS. LINDE: Indeed, I don't look down on any one. But it is true that I am both proud and glad to think that I was privileged to make the end of my mother's life almost free from care.

NORA: And you are proud to think of what you have done for your brothers.

MRS. LINDE: I think I have the right to be.

NORA: I think so, too. But now, listen to this; I too have something to be proud of and glad of.

MRS. LINDE: I have no doubt you have. But what do you refer to?                                                       170

NORA: Speak low. Suppose Torvald were to hear! He mustn't on any account—no one in the world must know, Christine, except you.

MRS. LINDE: But what is it?

NORA: Come here [pulls her down on the sofa beside her] Now I will show you that I too have something to be proud and glad of. It was I who saved Torvald's life.

MRS. LINDE: "Saved"? How?

NORA: I told you about our trip to Italy. Torvald would never have recovered if he had not 175 gone there—

MRS. LINDE: Yes, but your father gave you the necessary funds.

NORA: [smiling] Yes, that is what Torvald and all the others think, but—

MRS. LINDE: But—

NORA: Papa didn't give us a shilling. It was I who procured the money.

MR. LINDE: You? All that large sum?

NORA: Two hundred and fifty pounds. What do you think of that?                                                       180

MRS. LINDE: But, Nora, how could you possibly do it? Did you win a prize in the Lottery?

NORA: [contemptuously] In the Lottery? There would have been no credit in that.

MRS. LINDE: But where did you get it from, then?

NORA: [humming and smiling with an air of mystery] Hm, hm! Aha!

MRS. LINDE: Because you couldn't have borrowed it.                                                                  185

NORA: Couldn't I? Why not?

MRS. LINDE: No, a wife cannot borrow without her husband's consent.

NORA: [*tossing her head*] Oh, if it is a wife who has any head for business—a wife who has the wit to be a little bit clever—

190 MRS. LINDE: I don't understand it at all, Nora.

NORA: There is no need you should. I never said I had borrowed the money. I may have got it some other way. [*lies back on the sofa*] Perhaps I got it from some other admirer. When anyone is as attractive as I am—

MRS. LINDE: You are a mad creature.

NORA: Now, you know you're full of curiosity, Christine.

MRS. LINDE: Listen to me, Nora dear. Haven't you been a little bit imprudent?

195 NORA: [*sits up straight*] Is it imprudent to save your husband's life?

MRS. LINDE: It seems to me imprudent, without his knowledge, to—

NORA: But it was absolutely necessary that he should not know! My goodness, can't you understand that? It was necessary he should have no idea what a dangerous condition he was in. It was to me that the doctors came and said that his life was in danger, and that the only thing to save him was to live in the south. Do you suppose I didn't try, first of all, to get what I wanted as if it were for myself? I told him how much I should love to travel abroad like other young wives; I tried tears and entreaties with him; I told him that he ought to remember the condition I was in, and that he ought to be kind and indulgent to me; I even hinted that he might raise a loan. That nearly made him angry, Christine. He said I was thoughtless, and that it was his duty as my husband not to indulge me in my whims and caprices—as I believe he called them. Very well I thought, you must be saved—and that was how I came to devise a way out of the difficulty—

MRS. LINDE: And did your husband never get to know from your father that the money had not come from him?

NORA: No, never. Papa died just at that time. I had meant to let him into the secret and beg him never to reveal it. But he was so ill then—alas, there never was any need to tell him.

200 MRS. LINDE: And since then have you never told your secret to your husband?

NORA: Good Heavens, no! How could you think so? A man who has such strong opinions about these things! And besides, how painful and humiliating it would be for Torvald, with his manly independence, to know that he owed me anything! It would upset our mutual relations altogether; our beautiful happy home would no longer be what it is now.

MRS. LINDE: Do you mean never to tell him about it?

NORA: [*meditatively, and with a half smile*] Yes—some day, perhaps, after many years, when I am no longer as nice-looking as I am now. Don't laugh at me! I mean of course, when Torvald is no longer as devoted to me as he is now; when my dancing and dressing-up and reciting have palled on him; then it may be a good thing to have something in reserve— [*breaking off*] What nonsense! That time will never come. Now, what do you think of my great secret, Christine? Do you still think I am of no use? I can tell you, too, that this affair has caused me a lot of worry. It has been by no means easy for me to meet my engagements punctually. I may tell you that there is something that is called, in business, quarterly interest, and another thing called payment in instalments, and it is always so dreadfully difficult to manage them. I have had to save a little here and there, where I could, you understand. I have not been able to put aside much from my housekeeping money, for Torvald must have a good table. I couldn't let my children be shabbily dressed; I have felt obliged to use up all he gave me for them, the sweet little darlings!

MRS. LINDE: So it has all had to come out of your own necessaries of life, poor Nora?

205 NORA: Of course. Besides, I was the one responsible for it. Whenever Torvald has given me the money for new dresses and such things, I have never spent more than half of it; I have

always bought the simplest and cheapest things. Thank Heaven, any clothes look well on me, and so Torvald has never noticed it. But it was often very hard on me, Christine—because it is delightful to be really well dressed, isn't it?

MRS. LINDE: Quite so.

NORA: Well, then I have found other ways of earning money. Last winter I was lucky enough to get a lot of copying to do; so I locked myself up and sat writing every evening until quite late at night. Many a time I was desperately tired; but all the same it was a tremendous pleasure to sit there working and earning money. It was like being a man.

MRS. LINDE: How much have you been able to pay off in that way?

NORA: I can't tell you exactly. You see, it is very difficult to keep an account of a business matter of that kind. I only know that I have paid every penny that I could scrape together. Many a time I was at my wit's end. [*smiles*] Then I used to sit here and imagine that a rich old gentleman had fallen in love with me—

MRS. LINDE: What! Who was it? 210

NORA: Be quiet!—that he had died; and that when his will was opened it contained, written in big letters, the instruction: "The lovely Mrs. Nora Helmer is to have all I possess paid over to her at once in cash."

MRS. LINDE: But, my dear Nora—who could the man be?

NORA: Good gracious, can't you understand? There was no old gentleman at all; it was only something that I used to sit here and imagine, when I couldn't think of any way of procuring money. But it's all the same now; the tiresome old person can stay where he is, as far as I am concerned; I don't care about him or his will either, for I am free from care now. [*jumps up*] My goodness, it's delightful to think of, Christine! Free from care! To be able to be free from care, quite free from care; to be able to play and romp with the children; to be able to keep the house beautifully and have everything just as Torvald likes it! And, think of it, soon the spring will come and the big blue sky! Perhaps we shall be able to take a little trip—perhaps I shall see the sea again! Oh, it's a wonderful thing to be alive and be happy. [*A bell is heard in the hall.*]

MRS. LINDE: [*rising*] There is the bell; perhaps I had better go.

NORA: No, don't go; no one will come in here; it is sure to be for Torvald. 215

SERVANT: [*at the hall door*] Excuse me, ma'am—there is a gentleman to see the master, and as the doctor is with him—

NORA: Who is it?

KROGSTAD: [*at the door*] It is I, Mrs. Helmer. [*Mrs. Linde starts, trembles, and turns to the window.*]

NORA: [*takes a step towards him, and speaks in a strained, low voice*] You? What is it? What do you want to see my husband about?

KROGSTAD: Bank business—in a way. I have a small post in the Bank, and I hear your husband 220 is to be our chief now—

NORA: Then it is—

KROGSTAD: Nothing but dry business matters, Mrs. Helmer; absolutely nothing else.

NORA: Be so good as to go into the study, then. [*She bows indifferently to him and shuts the door into the hall; then comes back and makes up the fire in the stove.*]

MRS. LINDE: Nora—who was that man?

NORA: A lawyer, of the name of Krogstad. 225

MRS. LINDE: Then it really was he.

NORA: Do you know the man?

MRS. LINDE: I used to—many years ago. At one time he was a solicitor's clerk in our town.

NORA: Yes, he was.

MRS. LINDE: He is greatly altered. 230

NORA: He made a very unhappy marriage.

MRS. LINDE: He is a widower now, isn't he?

NORA: With several children. There now, it is burning up.

[*Shuts the door of the stove and moves the rocking-chair aside.*]

MRS. LINDE: They say he carries on various kinds of business.

235 NORA: Really! Perhaps he does; I don't know anything about it. But don't let us think of business; it is so tiresome.

DOCTOR RANK: [*comes out of HELMER'S study. Before he shuts the door he calls to him.*] No, my dear fellow, I won't disturb you; I would rather go in to your wife for a little while. [*shuts the door and sees MRS. LINDE*] I beg your pardon; I am afraid I am disturbing you too.

NORA: No, not at all. [*introducing him*] Doctor Rank, Mrs. Linde.

RANK: I have often heard Mrs. Linde's name mentioned here. I think I passed you on the stairs when I arrived, Mrs. Linde?

MRS. LINDE: Yes, I go up very slowly; I can't manage stairs well.

240 RANK: Ah! some slight internal weakness?

MRS. LINDE: No, the fact is I have been overworking myself.

RANK: Nothing more than that? Then I suppose you have come to town to amuse yourself with our entertainments?

MRS. LINDE: I have come to look for work.

RANK: Is that a good cure for overwork?

245 MRS. LINDE: One must live, Doctor Rank.

RANK: Yes, the general opinion seems to be that it is necessary.

NORA: Look here, Doctor Rank—you know you want to live.

RANK: Certainly. However wretched I may feel, I want to prolong the agony as long as possible. All my patients are like that. And so are those who are morally diseased; one of them, and a bad case too, is at this very moment with Helmer—

MRS. LINDE: [*sadly*] Ah!

250 NORA: Whom do you mean?

RANK: A lawyer of the name of Krogstad, a fellow you don't know at all. He suffers from a diseased moral character, Mrs. Helmer; but even he began talking of its being highly important that he should live.

NORA: Did he? What did he want to speak to Torvald about?

RANK: I have no idea; I only heard that it was something about the Bank.

NORA: I didn't know this—what's his name—Krogstad had anything to do with the Bank.

255 RANK: Yes, he has some sort of appointment there. [*to MRS. LINDE*] I don't know whether you find also in your part of the world that there are certain people who go zealously snuffing about to smell out moral corruption, and, as soon as they have found some, put the person concerned into some lucrative position where they can keep their eye on him. Healthy natures are left out in the cold.

MRS. LINDE: Still I think the sick are those who most need taking care of.

RANK: [*shrugging his shoulders*] Yes, there you are. That is the sentiment that is turning Society into a sickhouse.

[*NORA, who has been absorbed in her thoughts, breaks out into smothered laughter and claps her hands.*]

RANK: Why do you laugh at that? Have you any notion what Society really is?

NORA: What do I care about tiresome Society? I am laughing at something quite different, something extremely amusing. Tell me, Doctor Rank, are all the people who are employed in the Bank dependent on Torvald now?

260 RANK: Is that what you find so extremely amusing?

NORA: [*smiling and humming*] That's my affair! [*walking about the room*] It's perfectly glorious to think that we have—that Torvald has so much power over so many people. [*takes the packet from her pocket*] Doctor Rank, what do you say to a macaroon?

RANK: What, macaroons? I thought they were forbidden here.

NORA: Yes, but these are some Christine gave me.

MRS. LINDE: What! I?—

NORA: Oh, well, don't be alarmed! You couldn't know that Torvald had forbidden them. 265 I must tell you that he is afraid they will spoil my teeth. But, bah!—once in a way—That's so, isn't it, Doctor Rank? By your leave? [*puts a macaroon into his mouth*] You must have one too, Christine. And I shall have one, just a little one—or at most two. [*walking about*] I am tremendously happy. There is just one thing in the world now that I should dearly love to do.

RANK: Well, what is that?

NORA: It's something I should dearly love to say, if Torvald could hear me.

RANK: Well, why can't you say it?

NORA: No, I daren't; it's so shocking.

MRS. LINDE: Shocking? 270

RANK: Well, I should not advise you to say it. Still, with us you might. What is it you would so much like to say if Torvald could hear you?

NORA: I should just love to say—Well, I'm damned!

RANK: Are you mad?

MRS. LINDE: Nora, dear—!

RANK: Say it, here he is! 275

NORA: [*hiding the packet*] Hush! Hush! Hush!

[*HELMER comes out of his room, with his coat over his arm and his hat in his hands.*]

NORA: Well, Torvald dear, have you got rid of him?

HELMER: Yes, he has just gone.

NORA: Let me introduce you—this is Christine, who has come to town.

HELMER: Christine—? Excuse me, but I don't know— 280

NORA: Mrs. Linde, dear; Christine Linde.

HELMER: Of course. A school friend of my wife's, I presume?

MRS. LINDE: Yes, we have known each other since then.

NORA: And just think, she has taken a long journey in order to see you.

HELMER: What do you mean? 285

MRS. LINDE: No, really, I—

NORA: Christine is tremendously clever at book-keeping, and she is frightfully anxious to work under some clever man, so as to perfect herself—

HELMER: Very sensible, Mrs. Linde.

NORA: And when she heard you had been appointed manager of the Bank—the news was telegraphed, you know—she travelled here as quick as she could. Torvald, I am sure you will be able to do something for Christine, for my sake, won't you?

HELMER: Well, it is not altogether impossible. I presume you are a widow, Mrs. Linde? 290

MRS. LINDE: Yes.

HELMER: And have had some experience of book-keeping?

MRS. LINDE: Yes, a fair amount.

HELMER: Ah! well, it's very likely I may be able to find something for you—

NORA: [*clapping her hands*] What did I tell you? What did I tell you? 295

HELMER: You have just come at a fortunate moment, Mrs. Linde.

MRS. LINDE: How am I to thank you?

HELMER:  There is no need. [*puts on his coat*] But to-day you must excuse me—

RANK:  Wait a minute; I will come with you.

[*Brings his fur coat from the hall and warms it at the fire.*]

300  NORA:  Don't be long away, Torvald dear.

HELMER:  About an hour, not more.

NORA:  Are you going too, Christine?

MRS. LINDE:  [*putting on her cloak*] Yes, I must go and look for a room.

HELMER:  Oh, well then, we can walk down the street together.

305  NORA:  [*helping her*] What a pity it is we are so short of space here: I am afraid it is impossible
       for us—

MRS. LINDE:  Please don't think of it! Good-bye, Nora dear, and many thanks.

NORA:  Good-bye for the present. Of course you will come back this evening. And you too, Dr.
       Rank. What do you say? If you are well enough? Oh, you must be! Wrap yourself up well.

[*They go to the door all talking together. Children's voices are heard on the staircase.*]

NORA:  There they are. There they are! [*She runs to open the door. The NURSE comes in with the
       children.*] Come in! Come in! [*stoops and kisses them*] Oh, you sweet blessings! Look at them,
       Christine! Aren't they darlings?

RANK:  Don't let us stand here in the draught.

310  HELMER:  Come along, Mrs. Linde; the place will only be bearable for a mother now!

[*RANK, HELMER and MRS. LINDE go downstairs. The NURSE comes forward with the children; NORA
shuts the hall door.*]

NORA:  How fresh and well you look! Such red cheeks!—like apples and roses. [*The children all
       talk at once while she speaks to them.*] Have you had great fun? That's splendid! What, you
       pulled both Emmy and Bob along on the sledge?—both at once?—that was good. You are
       a clever boy, Ivar. Let me take her for a little, Anne. My sweet little baby doll! [*takes the
       baby from the MAID and dances it up and down*] Yes, yes, mother will dance with Bob too.
       What! Have you been snowballing? I wish I had been there too! No, no, I will take their
       things off, Anne; please let me do it, it is such fun. Go in now, you look half frozen. There
       is some coffee for you on the stove.

[*The NURSE goes into the room on the left. NORA takes off the children's things and throws them about,
while they all talk to her at once.*]

NORA:  Really! Did a big dog run after you? But it didn't bite you? No, dogs don't bite nice lit-
       tle dolly children. You mustn't look at the parcels, Ivar. What are they? Ah, I daresay you
       would like to know. No, no—it's something nasty! Come, let us have a game! What shall
       we play at? Hide and Seek? Yes, we'll play Hide and Seek. Bob shall hide first. Must I
       hide? Very well, I'll hide first.

[*She and the children laugh and shout, and romp in and out of the room; at last NORA hides under the
table, the children rush in and look for her, but do not see her; they hear her smothered laughter, run to
the table, lift up the cloth and find her. Shouts of laughter. She crawls forward and pretends to frighten
them. Fresh laughter. Meanwhile there has been a knock at the hall door, but none of them has noticed it.
The door is half opened, and KROGSTAD appears. He waits a little; the game goes on.*]

KROGSTAD:  Excuse me, Mrs. Helmer.

NORA:  [*with a stifled cry, turns round and gets up on to her knees*] Ah! what do you want?

315  KROGSTAD:  Excuse me, the outer door was ajar; I suppose someone forgot to shut it.

NORA: [*rising*] My husband is out, Mr. Krogstad.

KROGSTAD: I know that.

NORA: What do you want here, then?

KROGSTAD: A word with you.

NORA: With me?—[*to the children, gently*] Go in to nurse. What? No, the strange man won't do 320
mother any harm. When he has gone we will have another game. [*She takes the children
into the room on the left, and shuts the door after them.*] You want to speak to me?

KROGSTAD: Yes, I do.

NORA: To-day? It is not the first of the month yet.

KROGSTAD: No, it is Christmas Eve, and it will depend on yourself what sort of a Christmas
you will spend.

NORA: What do you want? To-day it is absolutely impossible for me—

KROGSTAD: We won't talk about that till later on. This is something different. I presume you 325
can give me a moment?

NORA: Yes—yes, I can—although—

KROGSTAD: Good. I was in Olsen's Restaurant and saw your husband going down the street—

NORA: Yes?

KROGSTAD: With a lady.

NORA: What then?

KROGSTAD: May I make so bold as to ask if it was a Mrs. Linde?    330

NORA: It was.

KROGSTAD: Just arrived in town?

NORA: Yes, to-day.

KROGSTAD: She is a great friend of yours, isn't she?    335

NORA: She is. But I don't see—

KROGSTAD: I knew her too, once upon a time.

NORA: I am aware of that.

KROGSTAD: Are you? So you know all about it; I thought as much. Then I can ask you, without
beating about the bush—is Mrs. Linde to have an appointment in the Bank?

NORA: What right have you to question me, Mr. Krogstad?—You, one of my husband's subor- 340
dinates! But since you ask, you shall know. Yes, Mrs. Linde *is* to have an appointment.
And it was I who pleaded her cause, Mr. Krogstad, let me tell you that.

KROGSTAD: I was right in what I thought, then.

NORA: [*walking up and down the stage*] Sometimes one has a tiny little bit of influence, I should
hope. Because one is a woman, it does not necessarily follow that—. When anyone is in a
subordinate position, Mr. Krogstad, they should really be careful to avoid offending anyone who—who—

KROGSTAD: Who has influence?

NORA: Exactly.

KROGSTAD: [*changing his tone*] Mrs. Helmer, you will be so good as to use your influence on my 345
behalf.

NORA: What? What do you mean?

KROGSTAD: You will be so kind as to see that I am allowed to keep my subordinate position in
the Bank.

NORA: What do you mean by that? Who proposes to take your post away from you?

KROGSTAD: Oh, there is no necessity to keep up the pretence of ignorance. I can quite understand that your friend is not very anxious to expose herself to the chance of rubbing
shoulders with me; and I quite understand, too, whom I have to thank for being turned
out.

NORA: But I assure you—

350

KROGSTAD: Very likely; but, to come to the point, the time has come when I should advise you to use your influence to prevent that.

NORA: But, Mr. Krogstad, I *have* no influence.

KROGSTAD: Haven't you? I thought you said yourself just now—

NORA: Naturally I did not mean you to put that construction on it. I! What should make you think I have any influence of that kind with my husband?

355   KROGSTAD: Oh, I have known your husband from our student days. I don't suppose he is any more unassailable than other husbands.

NORA: If you speak slightingly of my husband, I shall turn you out of the house.

KROGSTAD: You are bold, Mrs. Helmer.

NORA: I am not afraid of you any longer. As soon as the New Year comes, I shall in a very short time be free of the whole thing.

KROGSTAD: [*controlling himself*] Listen to me, Mrs. Helmer. If necessary, I am prepared to fight for my small post in the Bank as if I were fighting for my life.

360   NORA: So it seems.

KROGSTAD: It is not only for the sake of the money; indeed, that weighs least with me in the matter. There is another reason—well, I may as well tell you. My position is this. I daresay you know, like everybody else, that once, many years ago, I was guilty of an indiscretion.

NORA: I think I have heard something of the kind.

KROGSTAD: The matter never came into court; but every way seemed to be closed to me after that. So I took to the business that you know of. I had to do something; and, honestly, I don't think I've been one of the worst. But now I must cut myself free from all that. My sons are growing up; for their sake I must try and win back as much respect as I can in the town. This post in the Bank was like the first step up for me—and now your husband is going to kick me downstairs again into the mud.

NORA: But you must believe me, Mr. Krogstad; it is not in my power to help you at all.

365   KROGSTAD: Then it is because you haven't the will; but I have means to compel you.

NORA: You don't mean that you will tell my husband that I owe you money?

KROGSTAD: Hm!—suppose I were to tell him?

NORA: It would be perfectly infamous of you. [*sobbing*] To think of his learning my secret, which has been my joy and pride, in such an ugly, clumsy way—that he should learn it from you! And it would put me in a horribly disagreeable position—

KROGSTAD: Only disagreeable?

370   NORA: [*impetuously*] Well, do it, then!—and it will be the worse for you. My husband will see for himself what a blackguard you are, and you certainly won't keep your post then.

KROGSTAD: I asked you if it was only a disagreeable scene at home that you were afraid of?

NORA: If my husband does get to know of it, of course he will at once pay you what is still owing, and we shall have nothing more to do with you.

KROGSTAD: [*coming a step nearer*] Listen to me, Mrs. Helmer. Either you have a very bad memory or you know very little of business. I shall be obliged to remind you of a few details.

NORA: What do you mean?

375   KROGSTAD: When your husband was ill, you came to me to borrow two hundred and fifty pounds.

NORA: I didn't know any one else to go to.

KROGSTAD: I promised to get you that amount—

NORA: Yes, and you did so.

KROGSTAD: I promised to get you that amount, on certain conditions. Your mind was so taken up with your husband's illness, and you were so anxious to get the money for your journey, that you seem to have paid no attention to the conditions of our bargain. Therefore it will not be amiss if I remind you of them. Now, I promised to get the money on the security of a bond which I drew up.

NORA: Yes, and which I signed.     380

KROGSTAD: Good. But below your signature there were a few lines constituting your father a surety for the money; those lines your father should have signed.

NORA: Should? He did sign them.

KROGSTAD: I had left the date blank; that is to say your father should himself have inserted the date on which he signed the paper. Do you remember that?

NORA: Yes, I think I remember—

KROGSTAD: Then I gave you the bond to send by post to your father. Is that not so?     385

NORA: Yes.

KROGSTAD: And you naturally did so at once, because five or six days afterwards you brought me the bond with your father's signature. And then I gave you the money.

NORA: Well, haven't I been paying it off regularly?

KROGSTAD: Fairly so, yes. But—to come back to the matter in hand—that must have been a very trying time for you, Mrs. Helmer?

NORA: It was, indeed.     390

KROGSTAD: Your father was very ill, wasn't he?

NORA: He was very near his end.

KROGSTAD: And died soon afterwards?

NORA: Yes.

KROGSTAD: Tell me, Mrs. Helmer, can you by any chance remember what day your father     395
died?—on what day of the month, I mean.

NORA: Papa died on the 29th of September.

KROGSTAD: That is correct; I have ascertained it for myself. And, as that is so, there is a discrepancy [*taking a paper from his pocket*] which I cannot account for.

NORA: What discrepancy? I don't know—

KROGSTAD: The discrepancy consists, Mrs. Helmer, in the fact that your father signed this bond three days after his death.

NORA: What do you mean? I don't understand—     400

KROGSTAD: Your father died on the 29th of September. But, look here; your father has dated his signature the 2nd of October. It is a discrepancy, isn't it? [*NORA is silent.*] Can you explain it to me? [*NORA is still silent.*] It is a remarkable thing, too, that the words "2nd of October," as well as the year, are not written in your father's handwriting but in one that I think I know. Well, of course it can be explained; your father may have forgotten to date his signature, and someone else may have dated it haphazard before they knew of his death. There is no harm in that. It all depends on the signature of the name; and *that* is genuine, I suppose, Mrs. Helmer? It was your father himself who signed his name here?

NORA: [*after a short pause, throws her head up and looks defiantly at him*] No, it was not. It was I that wrote papa's name.

KROGSTAD: Are you aware that is a dangerous confession?

NORA: In what way? You shall have your money soon.

KROGSTAD: Let me ask you a question; why did you not send the paper to your father?     405

NORA: It was impossible; papa was so ill. If I had asked him for his signature, I should have had to tell him what the money was to be used for; and when he was so ill himself I couldn't tell him that my husband's life was in danger—it was impossible.

KROGSTAD: It would have been better for you if you had given up your trip abroad.

NORA: No, that was impossible. That trip was to save my husband's life; I couldn't give that up.

KROGSTAD: But did it never occur to you that you were committing a fraud on me?

NORA: I couldn't take that into account; I didn't trouble myself about you at all. I couldn't bear     410
you, because you put so many heartless difficulties in my way, although you knew what a dangerous condition my husband was in.

KROGSTAD: Mrs. Helmer, you evidently do not realise clearly what it is that you have been guilty of. But I can assure you that my one false step, which lost me all my reputation, was nothing more or nothing worse than what you have done.

NORA: You? Do you ask me to believe that you were brave enough to run a risk to save your wife's life?

KROGSTAD: The law cares nothing about motives.

NORA: Then it must be a very foolish law.

415 KROGSTAD: Foolish or not, it is the law by which you will be judged, if I produce this paper in court.

NORA: I don't believe it. Is a daughter not to be allowed to spare her dying father anxiety and care? Is a wife not to be allowed to save her husband's life? I don't know much about law; but I am certain that there must be laws permitting such things as that. Have you no knowledge of such laws—you who are a lawyer? You must be a very poor lawyer, Mr. Krogstad.

KROGSTAD: Maybe. But matters of business—such business as you and I have had together— do you think I don't understand that? Very well. Do as you please. But let me tell you this—if I lose my position a second time, you shall lose yours with me.

[*He bows, and goes out through the hall.*]

NORA: [*appears buried in thought for a short time, then tosses her head*] Nonsense! Trying to frighten me like that!—I am not so silly as he thinks. [*begins to busy herself putting the children's things in order*] And yet—? No, it's impossible! I did it for love's sake.

THE CHILDREN: [*in the doorway on the left*] Mother, the stranger man has gone out through the gate.

420 NORA: Yes, dears, I know. But, don't tell anyone about the stranger man. Do you hear? Not even papa.

CHILDREN: No, mother; but will you come and play again?

NORA: No, no—not now.

CHILDREN: But, mother, you promised us.

NORA: Yes, but I can't now. Run away in; I have such a lot to do. Run away in, my sweet little darlings. [*She gets them into the room by degrees and shuts the door on them; then sits down on the sofa, takes up a piece of needlework and sews a few stitches, but soon stops.*] No! [*throws down the work, gets up, goes to the hall door and calls out*] Helen! bring the Tree in. [*goes to the table on the left, opens a drawer, and stops again*] No, no! it is quite impossible!

425 MAID: [*coming in with the Tree*] Where shall I put it, ma'am?

NORA: Here, in the middle of the floor.

MAID: Shall I get you anything else?

NORA: No, thank you. I have all I want.

[*Exit MAID.*]

NORA: [*begins dressing the tree*] A candle here—and flowers here—. The horrible man! It's all nonsense—there's nothing wrong. The Tree shall be splendid! I will do everything I can think of to please you, Torvald!—I will sing for you, dance for you— [*HELMER comes in with some papers under his arm*] Oh! are you back already?

430 HELMER: Yes. Has anyone been here?

NORA: Here? No.

HELMER: That is strange. I saw Krogstad going out of the gate.

NORA: Did you? Oh yes, I forgot, Krogstad was here for a moment.

HELMER: Nora, I can see from your manner that he has been here begging you to say a good word for him.

435 NORA: Yes.

HELMER: And you were to appear to do it of your own accord; you were to conceal from me the fact of his having been here; didn't he beg that of you too?

NORA: Yes, Torvald, but—

HELMER: Nora, Nora, and you would be a party to that sort of thing? To have any talk with a man like that, and give him any sort of promise? And to tell me a lie into the bargain?

NORA: A lie—?

HELMER: Didn't you tell me no one had been here? [*shakes his finger at her*] My little song-bird 440 must never do that again. A song-bird must have a clean beak to chirp with—no false notes! [*puts his arm round her waist*] That is so, isn't it? Yes, I am sure it is. [*lets her go*] We will say no more about it. [*sits down by the stove*] How warm and snug it is here!

[*Turns over his papers.*]

NORA: [*after a short pause, during which she busies herself with the Christmas Tree*] Torvald!

HELMER: Yes.

NORA: I am looking forward tremendously to the fancy dress ball at the Stenborgs' the day after to-morrow.

HELMER: And I am tremendously curious to see what you are going to surprise me with.

NORA: It was very silly of me to want to do that.                                                        445

HELMER: What do you mean?

NORA: I can't hit upon anything that will do; everything I think of seems so silly and insignificant.

HELMER: Does my little Nora acknowledge that at last?

NORA: [*standing behind his chair with her arms on the back of it*] Are you very busy, Torvald?

HELMER: Well—                                                                                          450

NORA: What are all those papers?

HELMER: Bank business.

NORA: Already?

HELMER: I have got authority from the retiring manager to undertake the necessary changes in the staff and in the rearrangement of the work; and I must make use of the Christmas week for that, so as to have everything in order for the new year.

NORA: Then that was why this poor Krogstad—                                                          455

HELMER: Hm!

NORA: [*leans against the back of his chair and strokes his hair*] If you hadn't been so busy I should have asked you a tremendously big favour, Torvald.

HELMER: What is that? Tell me.

NORA: There is no one has such good taste as you. And I do so want to look nice at the fancy-dress ball. Torvald, couldn't you take me in hand and decide what I shall go as, and what sort of a dress I shall wear?

HELMER: Aha! so my obstinate little woman is obliged to get someone to come to her rescue? 460

NORA: Yes, Torvald, I can't get along a bit without your help.

HELMER: Very well, I will think it over, we shall manage to hit upon something.

NORA: That is nice of you. [*Goes to the Christmas Tree. A short pause.*] How pretty the red flowers look—. But, tell me, was it really something very bad that this Krogstad was guilty of?

HELMER: He forged someone's name. Have you any idea what that means?

NORA: Isn't it possible that he was driven to do it by necessity?                                       465

HELMER: Yes; or, as in so many cases, by imprudence. I am not so heartless as to condemn a man altogether because of a single false step of that kind.

NORA: No you wouldn't, would you, Torvald?

HELMER: Many a man has been able to retrieve his character, if he has openly confessed his fault and taken his punishment.

NORA: Punishment—?

470 HELMER: But Krogstad did nothing of that sort; he got himself out of it by a cunning trick, and that is why he has gone under altogether.

NORA: But do you think it would—?

HELMER: Just think how a guilty man like that has to lie and play the hypocrite with everyone, how he has to wear a mask in the presence of those near and dear to him, even before his own wife and children. And about the children—that is the most terrible part of it all, Nora.

NORA: How?

HELMER: Because such an atmosphere of lies infects and poisons the whole life of a home. Each breath the children take in such a house is full of the germs of evil.

475 NORA: [*coming nearer him*] Are you sure of that?

HELMER: My dear, I have often seen it in the course of my life as a lawyer. Almost everyone who has gone to the bad early in life has had a deceitful mother.

NORA: Why do you only say—mother?

HELMER: It seems most commonly to be the mother's influence, though naturally a bad father's would have the same result. Every lawyer is familiar with the fact. This Krogstad, now, has been persistently poisoning his own children with lies and dissimulation; that is why I say he has lost all moral character. [*holds out his hands to her*] That is why my sweet little Nora must promise me not to plead his cause. Give me your hand on it. Come, come, what is this? Give me your hand. There now, that's settled. I assure you it would be quite impossible for me to work with him; I literally feel physically ill when I am in the company of such people.

NORA: [*takes her hand out of his and goes to the opposite side of the Christmas Tree*] How hot it is in here; and I have such a lot to do.

480 HELMER: [*getting up and putting his papers in order*] Yes, and I must try and read through some of these before dinner; and I must think about your costume, too. And it is just possible I may have something ready in gold paper to hang up on the Tree. [*Puts his hand on her head.*] My precious little singing-bird!

[*He goes into his room and shuts the door after him.*]

NORA: [*after a pause, whispers*] No, no—it isn't true. It's impossible; it must be impossible.

[*The* NURSE *opens the door on the left.*]

NURSE: The little ones are begging so hard to be allowed to come in to mamma.

NORA: No, no, no! Don't let them come in to me! You stay with them, Anne.

NURSE: Very well, ma'am.

[*Shuts the door.*]

485 NORA: [*pale with terror*] Deprave my little children? Poison my home? [*a short pause. Then she tosses her head.*] It's not true. It can't possibly be true.

## ACT 2

THE SAME SCENE. *The Christmas Tree is in the corner by the piano, stripped of its ornaments and with burnt-down candle-ends on its dishevelled branches.* NORA's *cloak and hat are lying on the sofa. She is alone in the room, walking about uneasily. She stops by the sofa and takes up her cloak.*

NORA: [*drops the cloak*] Someone is coming now! [*goes to the door and listens*] No—it is no one. Of course, no one will come to-day, Christmas Day—nor tomorrow either. But, perhaps— [*opens the door and looks out*] No, nothing in the letter-box; it is quite empty. [*comes forward*]

What rubbish! of course he can't be in earnest about it. Such a thing couldn't happen; it is impossible—I have three little children.

[*Enter the* NURSE *from the room on the left, carrying a big cardboard box.*]

NURSE: At last I have found the box with the fancy dress.

NORA: Thanks; put it on the table.

NURSE: [*doing so*] But it is very much in want of mending.

NORA: I should like to tear it into a hundred thousand pieces.                                    5

NURSE: What an idea! It can easily be put in order—just a little patience.

NORA: Yes, I will go and get Mrs. Linde to come and help me with it.

NURSE: What, out again? In this horrible weather? You will catch cold, ma'am, and make yourself ill.

NORA: Well, worse than that might happen. How are the children?

NURSE: The poor little souls are playing with their Christmas presents, but—                      10

NORA: Do they ask much for me?

NURSE: You see, they are so accustomed to have their mamma with them.

NORA: Yes, but, nurse, I shall not be able to be so much with them now as I was before.

NURSE: Oh well, young children easily get accustomed to anything.

NORA: Do you think so? Do you think they would forget their mother if she went away           15
altogether?

NURSE: Good heavens!—went away altogether?

NORA: Nurse, I want you to tell me something I have often wondered about—how could you
have the heart to put your own child out among strangers?

NURSE: I was obliged to, if I wanted to be little Nora's nurse.

NORA: Yes, but how could you be willing to do it?

NURSE: What, when I was going to get such a good place by it? A poor girl who has got into     20
trouble should be glad to. Besides, that wicked man didn't do a single thing for me.

NORA: But I suppose your daughter has quite forgotten you.

NURSE: No, indeed she hasn't. She wrote to me when she was confirmed, and when she was
married.

NORA: [*putting her arms round her neck*] Dear old Anne, you were a good mother to me when
I was little.

NURSE: Little Nora, poor dear, had no other mother but me.

NORA: And if my little ones had no other mother, I am sure you would—What nonsense I am     25
talking! [*opens the box*] Go in to them. Now I must—. You will see tomorrow how charming I shall look.

NURSE: I am sure there will be no one at the ball so charming as you, ma'am.

[*Goes into the room on the left.*]

NORA: [*begins to unpack the box, but soon pushes it away from her*] If only I dared go out. If only no
one would come. If only I could be sure nothing would happen here in the meantime.
Stuff and nonsense! No one will come. Only I mustn't think about it. I will brush my muff.
What, lovely gloves! Out of my thoughts, out of my thoughts! One, two, three, four, five,
six—[*Screams.*] Ah! there is someone coming—

[*Makes a movement towards the door, but stands irresolute.*]

[*Enter* MRS. LINDE *from the hall, where she has taken off her cloak and hat.*]

NORA: Oh, it's you, Christine. There is no one else out there, is there? How good of you to
come!

Mrs. Linde: I heard you were up asking for me.

30   Nora: Yes, I was passing by. As a matter of fact, it is something you could help me with. Let us sit down here on the sofa. Look here. To-morrow evening there is to be a fancy-dress ball at the Stenborgs', who live about us; and Torvald wants me to go as a Neapolitan fisher-girl, and dance the Tarantella that I learnt at Capri.

Mrs. Linde: I see; you are going to keep up the character.

Nora: Yes, Torvald wants me to. Look, here is the dress; Torvald had it made for me there, but now it is all so torn, and I haven't any idea—

Mrs. Linde: We will easily put that right. It is only some of the trimming come unsewn here and there. Needle and thread? Now then, that's all we want.

Nora: It *is* nice of you.

35   Mrs. Linde: [*sewing*] So you are going to be dressed up to-morrow, Nora. I will tell you what— I shall come in for a moment and see you in your fine feathers. But I have completely forgotten to thank you for a delightful evening yesterday.

Nora: [*gets up, and crosses the stages*] Well I don't think yesterday was as pleasant as usual. You ought to have come to town a little earlier, Christine. Certainly Torvald does understand how to make a house dainty and attractive.

Mrs. Linde: And so do you, it seems to me; you are not your father's daughter for nothing. But tell me, is Doctor Rank always as depressed as he was yesterday?

Nora: No; yesterday it was very noticeable. I must tell you that he suffers from a very dangerous disease. He has consumption of the spine, poor creature. His father was a horrible man who committed all sorts of excesses; and that is why his son was sickly from childhood, do you understand?

Mrs. Linde: [*dropping her sewing*] But, my dearest Nora, how do you know anything about such things?

40   Nora: [*walking about*] Pooh! When you have three children, you get visits now and then from—from married women, who know something of medical matters, and they talk about one thing and another.

Mrs. Linde: [*goes on sewing. A short silence*] Does Doctor Rank come here every day?

Nora: Every day regularly. He is Torvald's most intimate friend, and a great friend of mine too. He is just like one of the family.

Mrs. Linde: But tell me this—is he perfectly sincere? I mean, isn't he the kind of man that is very anxious to make himself agreeable?

Nora: Not in the least. What makes you think that?

45   Mrs. Linde: When you introduced him to me yesterday, he declared he had often heard my name mentioned in this house; but afterwards I noticed that your husband hadn't the slightest idea who I was. So how could Doctor Rank—?

Nora: That is quite right, Christine. Torvald is so absurdly fond of me that he wants me absolutely to himself, as he says. At first he used to seem almost jealous if I mentioned any of the dear folk at home, so naturally I gave up doing so. But I often talk about such things with Doctor Rank, because he likes hearing about them.

Mrs. Linde: Listen to me, Nora. You are still very like a child in many things, and I am older than you in many ways and have a little more experience. Let me tell you this—you ought to make an end of it with Doctor Rank.

Nora: What ought I to make an end of?

Mrs. Linde: Of two things, I think. Yesterday you talked some nonsense about a rich admirer who was to leave you money—

50   Nora: An admirer who doesn't exist, unfortunately! But what then?

Mrs. Linde: Is Doctor Rank a man of means?

Nora: Yes, he is.

MRS. LINDE: And has no one to provide for?

NORA: No, no one; but—

MRS. LINDE: And comes here every day? 55

NORA: Yes, I told you so.

MRS. LINDE: But how can this well-bred man be so tactless?

NORA: I don't understand you at all.

MRS. LINDE: Don't prevaricate, Nora. Do you suppose I don't guess who lent you the two hundred and fifty pounds?

NORA: Are you out of your senses? How can you think of such a thing! A friend of ours, who 60 comes here every day! Do you realise what a horribly painful position that would be?

MRS. LINDE: Then it really isn't he?

NORA: No, certainly not. It would never have entered into my head for a moment. Besides, he had no money to lend then; he came into his money afterwards.

MRS. LINDE: Well, I think that was lucky for you, my dear Nora.

NORA: No, it would never have come into my head to ask Doctor Rank. Although I am quite sure that if I had asked him—

MRS. LINDE: But of course you won't. 65

NORA: Of course not. I have no reason to think it could possibly be necessary. But I am quite sure that if I told Doctor Rank—

MRS. LINDE: Behind your husband's back?

NORA: I *must* make an end of it with the other one, and that will be behind his back too. I *must* make an end of it with him.

MRS. LINDE: Yes, that is what I told you yesterday, but—

NORA: [*walking up and down*] A man can put a thing like that straight much easier than a 70 woman—

MRS. LINDE: One's husband, yes.

NORA: Nonsense! [*standing still*] When you pay off a debt you get your bond back, don't you?

MRS. LINDE: Yes, as a matter of course.

NORA: And can tear it into a hundred thousand pieces, and burn it up—the nasty dirty paper!

MRS. LINDE: [*looks hard at her, lays down her sewing and gets up slowly*] Nora, you are concealing 75 something from me.

NORA: Do I look as if I were?

MRS. LINDE: Something has happened to you since yesterday morning. Nora, what is it?

NORA: [*going nearer to her*] Christine! [*listens*] Hush! there's Torvald come home. Do you mind going in to the children for the present? Torvald can't bear to see dressmaking going on. Let Anne help you.

MRS. LINDE: [*gathering some of the things together*] Certainly—but I am not going away from here till we have had it out with one another.

[*She goes into the room on the left, as HELMER comes in from the hall.*]

NORA: [*going up to HELMER*] I have wanted you so much, Torvald dear. 80

HELMER: Was that the dressmaker?

NORA: No, it was Christine; she is helping me to put my dress in order. You will see I shall look quite smart.

HELMER: Wasn't that a happy thought of mine, now?

NORA: Splendid! But don't you think it is nice of me, too, to do as you wish?

HELMER: Nice?—because you do as your husband wishes? Well, well, you little rogue, I am 85 sure you did not mean it in that way. But I am not going to disturb you; you will want to be trying on your dress, I expect.

NORA: I suppose you are going to work.

HELMER: Yes. [*shows her a bundle of papers*] Look at that. I have just been into the bank. [*Turns to go into his room.*]

NORA: Torvald.

HELMER: Yes.

90 NORA: If your little squirrel were to ask you for something very, very prettily—?

HELMER: What then?

NORA: Would you do it?

HELMER: I should like to hear what it is, first.

NORA: Your squirrel would run about and do all her tricks if you would be nice, and do what she wants.

95 HELMER: Speak plainly.

NORA: Your skylark would chirp about in every room, with her song rising and falling—

HELMER: Well, my skylark does that anyhow.

NORA: I would play the fairy and dance for you in the moonlight, Torvald.

HELMER: Nora—you surely don't mean that request you made of me this morning?

100 NORA: [*going near him*] Yes, Torvald, I beg you so earnestly—

HELMER: Have you really the courage to open up that question again?

NORA: Yes, dear, you *must* do as I ask; you *must* let Krogstad keep his post in the Bank.

HELMER: My dear Nora, it is his post that I have arranged Mrs. Linde shall have.

NORA: Yes, you have been awfully kind about that; but you could just as well dismiss some other clerk instead of Krogstad.

105 HELMER: This is simply incredible obstinacy! Because you chose to give him a thoughtless promise that you would speak for him, I am expected to—

NORA: That isn't the reason, Torvald. It is for your own sake. This fellow writes in the most scurrilous newspapers; you have told me so yourself. He can do you an unspeakable amount of harm. I am frightened to death of him—

HELMER: Ah, I understand; it is recollections of the past that scare you.

NORA: What do you mean?

HELMER: Naturally you are thinking of your father.

110 NORA: Yes—yes, of course. Just recall to your mind what these malicious creatures wrote in the papers about papa, and how horribly they slandered him. I believe they would have procured his dismissal if the Department had not sent you over to inquire into it, and if you had not been so kindly disposed and helpful to him.

HELMER: My little Nora, there is an important difference between your father and me. Your father's reputation as a public official was not above suspicion. Mine is, and I hope it will continue to be so, as long as I hold my office.

NORA: You never can tell what mischief these men may contrive. We ought to be so well off, so snug and happy here in our peaceful home, and have no cares—you and I and the children, Torvald! That is why I beg you so earnestly—

HELMER: And it is just by interceding for him that you make it impossible for me to keep him. It is already known at the Bank that I mean to dismiss Krogstad. Is it to get about now that the new manager has changed his mind at his wife's bidding—

NORA: And what if it did?

115 HELMER: Of course!—if only this obstinate little person can get her way! Do you suppose I am going to make myself ridiculous before my whole staff, to let people think that I am a man to be swayed by all sorts of outside influence? I should very soon feel the consequences of it, I can tell you! And besides, there is one thing that makes it quite impossible for me to have Krogstad in the Bank as long as I am manager.

NORA: Whatever is that?

HELMER: His moral failings I might perhaps have overlooked, if necessary—

NORA: Yes, you could—couldn't you?

HELMER: And I hear he is a good worker, too. But I knew him when we were boys. It was one of those rash friendships that so often prove an incubus in after life. I may as well tell you plainly, we were once on very intimate terms with one another. But this tactless fellow lays no restraint on himself when other people are present. On the contrary, he thinks it gives him the right to adopt a familiar tone with me, and every minute it is "I say, Helmer, old fellow!" and that sort of thing. I assure you it is extremely painful for me. He would make my position in the Bank intolerable.

NORA: Torvald, I don't believe you mean that.                                                          120

HELMER: Don't you? Why not?

NORA: Because it is such a narrow-minded way of looking at things.

HELMER: What are you saying? Narrow-minded? Do you think I am narrow-minded?

NORA: No, just the opposite, dear—and it is exactly for that reason.

HELMER: It's the same thing. You say my point of view is narrow-minded, so I must be so too.   125
Narrow-minded! Very well—I must put an end to this. [*Goes to the hall-door and calls.*]
Helen!

NORA: What are you going to do?

HELMER: [*looking among his papers*] Settle it. [*Enter* MAID.] Look here; take this letter and go downstairs with it at once. Find a messenger and tell him to deliver it, and be quick. The address is on it, and here is the money.

MAID: Very well, sir.

[*Exits with the letter.*]

HELMER: [*putting his papers together*] Now then, little Miss Obstinate.

NORA: [*breathlessly*] Torvald—what was that letter?                                                  130

HELMER: Krogstad's dismissal.

NORA: Call her back, Torvald! There is still time. Oh Torvald, call her back! Do it for my sake—for your own sake—for the children's sake! Do you hear me, Torvald? Call her back!! You don't know what that letter can bring upon us.

HELMER: It's too late.

NORA: Yes, it's too late.

HELMER: My dear Nora, I can forgive the anxiety you are in, although really it is an insult to   135
me. It is, indeed. Isn't it an insult to think that I should be afraid of a starving quill-driver's vengeance? But I forgive you nevertheless, because it is such eloquent witness to your great love for me. [*takes her in his arms*] And that is as it should be, my own darling Nora. Come what will, you may be sure I shall have both courage and strength if they be needed. You will see I am man enough to take everything upon myself.

NORA: [*in a horror-stricken voice*] What do you mean by that?

HELMER: Everything, I say—

NORA: [*recovering herself*] You will never have to do that.

HELMER: That's right. Well, we will share it, Nora, as man and wife should. That is how it shall be. [*caressing her*] Are you content now? There! there!—not these frightened dove's eyes! The whole thing is only the wildest fancy!—Now, you must go and play through the Tarantella and practise with your tambourine. I shall go into the inner office and shut the door, and I shall hear nothing; you can make as much noise as you please. [*turns back at the door*] And when Rank comes, tell him where he will find me.

[*Nods to her, takes his papers and goes into his room, and shuts the door after him*]

NORA: [*bewildered with anxiety, stands as if rooted to the spot, and whispers*] He is capable of doing   140
it. He will do it. He will do it in spite of everything.—No, not that! Never, never! Anything

rather than that! Oh, for some help, some way out of it! [*The door-bell rings.*] Doctor Rank! Anything rather than that—anything, whatever it is!

[*She puts her hands over her face, pulls herself together, goes to the door and opens it.* Rank *is standing without, hanging up his coat. During the following dialogue it begins to grow dark.*]

Nora: Good-day, Doctor Rank. I knew your ring. But you mustn't go in to Torvald now; I think he is busy with something.

Rank: And you?

Nora: [*brings him in and shuts the door after him*] Oh, you know very well I always have time for you.

Rank: Thank you. I shall make use of as much of it as I can.

145 Nora: What do you mean by that? As much of it as you can?

Rank: Well, does that alarm you?

Nora:  It was such a strange way of putting it. Is anything likely to happen?

Rank: Nothing but what I have long been prepared for. But I certainly didn't expect it to happen so soon.

Nora: [*gripping him by the arm*] What have you found out? Doctor Rank, you must tell me.

150 Rank: [*sitting down by the stove*] It is all up with me. And it can't be helped.

Nora: [*with a sigh of relief*] Is it about yourself?

Rank: Who else? It is no use lying to one's self. I am the most wretched of all my patients, Mrs. Helmer. Lately I have been taking stock of my internal economy. Bankrupt! Probably within a month I shall lie rotting in the churchyard.

Nora: What an ugly thing to say!

Rank: The thing itself is cursedly ugly, and the worst of it is that I shall have to face so much more that is ugly before that. I shall only make one more examination of myself; when I have done that, I shall know pretty certainly when it will be that the horrors of dissolution will begin. There is something I want to tell you. Helmer's refined nature gives him an unconquerable disgust at everything that is ugly; I won't have him in my sick-room.

155 Nora: Oh, but, Doctor Rank—

Rank: I won't have him there. Not on any account. I bar my door to him. As soon as I am quite certain that the worst has come, I shall send you my card with a black cross on it, and then you will know that the loathsome end has begun.

Nora: You are quite absurd to-day. And I wanted you so much to be in a really good humour.

Rank: With death stalking beside me?—To have to pay this penalty for another man's sin! Is there any justice in that? And in every single family, in one way or another, some such inexorable retribution is being exacted—

Nora: [*putting her hands over her ears*] Rubbish! Do talk of something cheerful.

160 Rank: Oh, it's a mere laughing matter, the whole thing. My poor innocent spine has to suffer for my father's youthful amusements.

Nora: [*sitting at the table on the left*] I suppose you mean that he was too partial to asparagus and pâté de foie gras, don't you.

Rank: Yes, and to truffles.

Nora: Truffles, yes. And oysters too, I suppose?

Rank: Oysters, of course, that goes without saying.

165 Nora: And heaps of port and champagne. It is sad that all these nice things should take their revenge on our bones.

Rank: Especially that they should revenge themselves on the unlucky bones of those who have not had the satisfaction of enjoying them.

Nora: Yes, that's the saddest part of it all.

Rank: [*with a searching look at her*] Hm!—

NORA: [*after a short pause*] Why did you smile?

RANK: No, it was you that laughed. 170

NORA: No, it was you that smiled, Doctor Rank!

RANK: [*rising*] You are a greater rascal than I thought.

NORA: I am in a silly mood to-day.

RANK: So it seems.

NORA: [*putting her hands on his shoulders*] Dear, dear Doctor Rank, death mustn't take you 175 away from Torvald and me.

RANK: It is a loss you would easily recover from. Those who are gone are soon forgotten.

NORA: [*looking at him anxiously*] Do you believe that?

RANK: People form new ties, and then—

NORA: Who will form new ties?

RANK: Both you and Helmer, when I am gone. You yourself are already on the high road to it, 180 I think. What did that Mrs. Linde want here last night?

NORA: Oho!—you don't mean to say you are jealous of poor Christine?

RANK: Yes, I am. She will be my successor in this house. When I am done for, this woman will—

NORA: Hush! don't speak so loud. She is in that room.

RANK: To-day again. There, you see.

NORA: She has only come to sew my dress for me. Bless my soul, how unreasonable you are! 185 [*sits down on the sofa*] Be nice now, Doctor Rank, and tomorrow you will see how beautifully I shall dance, and you can imagine I am doing it all for you—and for Torvald too, of course. [*takes various things out of the box*] Doctor Rank, come and sit down here, and I will show you something.

RANK: [*sitting down*] What is it?

NORA: Just look at those!

RANK: Silk stockings.

NORA: Flesh-coloured. Aren't they lovely? It is so dark here now, but to-morrow—. No, no, no! you must only look at the feet. Oh well, you may have leave to look at the legs too.

RANK: Hm!— 190

NORA: Why are you looking so critical? Don't you think they will fit me?

RANK: I have no means of forming an opinion about that.

NORA: [*looks at him for a moment*] For shame! [*hits him lightly on the ear with the stockings*] That's to punish you. [*folds them up again*]

RANK: And what other nice things am I to be allowed to see?

NORA: Not a single thing more, for being so naughty. [*She looks among the things, humming to* 195 *herself.*]

RANK: [*after a short silence*] When I am sitting here, talking to you as intimately as this, I cannot imagine for a moment what would have become of me if I had never come into this house.

NORA: [*smiling*] I believe you do feel thoroughly at home with us.

RANK: [*in a lower voice, looking straight in front of him*] And to be obliged to leave it all—

NORA: Nonsense, you are not going to leave it.

RANK: [*as before*] And not be able to leave behind one the slightest token of one's gratitude, 200 scarcely even a fleeting regret—nothing but an empty place which the first comer can fill as well as any other.

NORA: And if I asked you now for a—? No!

RANK: For what?

NORA: For a big proof of your friendship—

RANK: Yes, yes!

NORA: I mean a tremendously big favour— 205

RANK: Would you really make me so happy for once?

NORA: Ah, but you don't know what it is yet.

RANK: No—but tell me.

NORA: I really can't, Doctor Rank. It is something out of all reason; it means advice, and help, and a favour—

210 RANK: The bigger a thing it is the better. I can't conceive what it is you mean. Do tell me. Haven't I your confidence?

NORA: More than anyone else. I know you are my truest and best friend, and so I will tell you what it is. Well, Doctor Rank, it is something you must help me to prevent. You know how devotedly, how inexpressibly deeply Torvald loves me; he would never for a moment hesitate to give his life for me.

RANK: [*leaning towards her*] Nora—do you think he is the only one—?

NORA: [*with a slight start*] The only one—?

RANK: The only one who would gladly give his life for your sake.

215 NORA: [*sadly*] Is that it?

RANK: I was determined you should know it before I went away, and there will never be a better opportunity than this. Now you know it, Nora. And now you know, too, that you can trust me as you would trust no one else.

NORA: [*rises, deliberately and quietly*] Let me pass.

RANK: [*makes room for her to pass him, but sits still*] Nora!

NORA: [*at the hall door*] Helen, bring in the lamp. [*goes over to the stove*] Dear Doctor Rank, that was really horrid of you.

220 RANK: To have loved you as much as anyone else does? Was that horrid?

NORA: No, but to go and tell me so. There was really no need—

RANK: What do you mean? Did you know—? [*MAID enters with lamp, puts it down on the table, and goes out.*] Nora—Mrs. Helmer—tell me, had you any idea of this?

NORA: Oh, how do I know whether I had or whether I hadn't? I really can't tell you—To think you could be so clumsy, Doctor Rank! We were getting on so nicely.

RANK: Well, at all events you know now that you can command me, body and soul. So won't you speak out?

225 NORA: [*looking at him*] After what happened?

RANK: I beg you to let me know what it is.

NORA: I can't tell you anything now.

RANK: Yes, yes. You mustn't punish me in that way. Let me have permission to do for you whatever a man may do.

NORA: You can do nothing for me now. Besides, I really don't need any help at all. You will find that the whole thing is merely fancy on my part. It really is so—of course it is! [*Sits down in the rocking-chair, and looks at him with a smile*] You are a nice sort of man, Doctor Rank!—don't you feel ashamed of yourself, now the lamp has come?

230 RANK: Not a bit. But perhaps I had better go—for ever?

NORA: No, indeed, you shall not. Of course you must come here just as before. You know very well Torvald can't do without you.

RANK: Yes, but you?

NORA: Oh, I am always tremendously pleased when you come.

RANK: It is just that, that put me on the wrong track. You are a riddle to me. I have often thought that you would almost as soon be in my company as in Helmer's.

235 NORA: Yes—you see there are some people one loves best, and others whom one would almost always rather have as companions.

RANK: Yes, there is something in that.

NORA: When I was at home, of course I loved papa best. But I always thought it tremendous fun if I could steal down into the maid's room, because they never moralised at all, and talked to each other about such entertaining things.

RANK: I see—it is *their* place I have taken.

NORA: [*jumping up and going to him*] Oh, dear, nice Doctor Rank, I never meant that at all. But surely you can understand that being with Torvald is a little like being with papa—

[*Enter MAID from the hall*]

MAID: If you please, ma'am. [*whispers and hands her a card*]

NORA: [*glancing at the card*] Oh! [*puts it in her pocket*]                                                   240

RANK: Is there anything wrong?

NORA: No, no, not in the least. It is only something—it is my new dress—

RANK: What? Your dress is lying there.

NORA: Oh, yes, that one; but this is another. I ordered it. Torvald mustn't know about it—        245

RANK: Oho! Then that was the great secret.

NORA: Of course. Just go in to him; he is sitting in the inner room. Keep him as long as—

RANK: Make your mind easy; I won't let him escape. [*goes into HELMER'S room*]

NORA: [*to the MAID*] And he is standing waiting in the kitchen?

MAID: Yes; he came up the back stairs.                                                                        250

NORA: But didn't you tell him no one was in?

MAID: Yes, but it was no good.

NORA: He won't go away?

MAID: No; he says he won't until he has seen you, ma'am.

NORA: Well, let him come in—but quietly. Helen, you mustn't say anything about it to anyone.   255
It is a surprise for my husband.

MAID: Yes, ma'am, I quite understand.                                                            [*Exit.*]

NORA: This dreadful thing is going to happen! It will happen in spite of me! No, no, no, it can't
happen—it shan't happen!

[*She bolts the door of HELMER'S room. The MAID opens the hall door for KROGSTAD and shuts it after
him. He is wearing a fur coat, high boots and a fur cap.*]

NORA: [*advancing towards him*] Speak low—my husband is at home.

KROGSTAD: No matter about that.

NORA: What do you want of me?

KROGSTAD: An explanation of something.                                                                     260

NORA: Make haste then. What is it?

KROGSTAD: You know, I suppose, that I have got my dismissal.

NORA: I couldn't prevent it, Mr. Krogstad. I fought as hard as I could on your side, but it was
no good.

KROGSTAD: Does your husband love you so little, then? He knows that what I can expose you   265
to, and yet he ventures—

NORA: How can you suppose that he has any knowledge of the sort?

KROGSTAD: I didn't suppose so at all. It would not be the least like our dear Torvald Helmer to
show so much courage—

NORA: Mr. Krogstad, a little respect for my husband, please.

KROGSTAD: Certainly—all the respect he deserves. But since you have kept the matter so carefully to yourself, I make bold to suppose that you have a little clearer idea, than you had
yesterday, of what it actually is that you have done?

NORA: More than you could ever teach me.                                                                   270

KROGSTAD: Yes, such a bad lawyer as I am.

NORA: What is it you want of me?

KROGSTAD: Only to see how you were, Mrs. Helmer. I have been thinking about you all day long. A mere cashier, a quill-driver, a—well, a man like me—even he has a little of what is called feeling, you know.

NORA: Show it, then; think of my little children.

275 KROGSTAD: Have you and your husband thought of mine? But never mind about that. I only wanted to tell you that you need not take this matter too seriously. In the first place there will be no accusation made on my part.

NORA: No, of course not; I was sure of that.

KROGSTAD: The whole thing can be arranged amicably; there is no reason why anyone should know anything about it. It will remain a secret between us three.

NORA: My husband must never get to know anything about it.

KROGSTAD: How will you be able to prevent it? Am I to understand that you can pay the balance that is owing?

280 NORA: No, not just at present.

KROGSTAD: Or perhaps that you have some expedient for raising the money soon?

NORA: No expedient that I mean to make use of.

KROGSTAD: Well, in any case, it would have been of no use to you now. If you stood there with ever so much money in your hand, I would never part with your bond.

NORA: Tell me what purpose you mean to put it to.

285 KROGSTAD: I shall only preserve it—keep it in my possession. No one who is not concerned in the matter shall have the slightest hint of it. So that if the thought of it has driven you to any desperate resolution—

NORA: It has.

KROGSTAD: If you had it in your mind to run away from your home—

NORA: I had.

KROGSTAD: Or even something worse—

290 NORA: How could you know that?

KROGSTAD: Give up the idea.

NORA: How did you know I had thought of *that?*

KROGSTAD: Most of us think of that at first. I did, too—but I hadn't the courage.

NORA: [*faintly*] No more had I.

295 KROGSTAD: [*in a tone of relief*] No, that's it, isn't it—you hadn't the courage either?

NORA: No, I haven't—I haven't.

KROGSTAD: Besides, it would have been a great piece of folly. Once the first storm at home is over—. I have a letter for your husband in my pocket.

NORA: Telling him everything?

KROGSTAD: In as lenient a manner as I possibly could.

300 NORA: [*quickly*] He mustn't get the letter. Tear it up. I will find some means of getting money.

KROGSTAD: Excuse me, Mrs. Helmer, but I think I told you just now—

NORA: I am not speaking of what I owe you. Tell me what sum you are asking my husband for, and I will get the money.

KROGSTAD: I am not asking your husband for a penny.

NORA: What do you want, then?

305 KROGSTAD: I will tell you. I want to rehabilitate myself, Mrs. Helmer; I want to get on; and in that your husband must help me. For the last year and a half I have not had a hand in anything dishonourable, and all that time I have been struggling in most restricted circumstances. I was content to work my way up step by step. Now I am turned out, and I am not going to be satisfied with merely being taken into favour again. I want to get on, I tell you.

I want to get into the Bank again, in a higher position. Your husband must make a place for me—

NORA: That he will never do!

KROGSTAD: He will; I know him; he dare not protest. And as soon as I am in there again with him, then you will see! Within a year I shall be the manager's right hand. It will be Nils Krogstad and not Torvald Helmer who manages the Bank.

NORA: That's a thing you will never see!

KROGSTAD: Do you mean that you will—?

NORA: I have courage enough for it now.                                                      310

KROGSTAD: Oh, you can't frighten me. A fine, spoilt lady like you—

NORA: You will see, you will see.

KROGSTAD: Under the ice, perhaps? Down into the cold, coal-black water? And then, in the spring, to float up to the surface, all horrible and unrecognisable, with your hair fallen out—

NORA: You can't frighten me.

KROGSTAD: Nor you me. People don't do such things, Mrs. Helmer. Besides, what use would it  315 be? I should have him completely in my power all the same.

NORA: Afterwards? When I am no longer—

KROGSTAD: Have you forgotten that it is I who have the keeping of your reputation? [*NORA stands speechlessly looking at him.*] Well, now, I have warned you. Do not do anything fool-ish. When Helmer has had my letter, I shall expect a message from him. And be sure you remember that it is your husband himself who has forced me into such ways as this again. I will never forgive him for that. Good-bye, Mrs. Helmer.

[*Exit through the hall*]

NORA: [*goes to the hall door, opens it slightly and listens*] He is going. He is not putting the letter in the box. Oh no, no! that's impossible! [*opens the door by degrees*] What is that? He is standing outside. He is not going downstairs. Is he hesitating? Can he—

[*A letter drops into the box; then* KROGSTAD'*s footsteps are heard, till they die away as he goes down-stairs.* NORA *utters a stifled cry and runs across the room to the table by the sofa. A short pause.*]

NORA: In the letter-box. [*steals across to the hall door*] There it lies—Torvald, Torvald, there is no hope for us now!

[MRS. LINDE *comes in from the room on the left, carrying the dress.*]

MRS. LINDE: There, I can't see anything more to mend now. Would you like to try it on—?       320

NORA: [*in a hoarse whisper*] Christine, come here.

MRS. LINDE: [*throwing the dress down on the sofa*] What is the matter with you? You look so agitated!

NORA: Come here. Do you see that letter? There, look—you can see it through the glass in the letter-box.

MRS. LINDE: Yes, I see it.

NORA: That letter is from Krogstad.                                                          325

MRS. LINDE: Nora—it was Krogstad who lent you the money!

NORA: Yes, and now Torvald will know all about it.

MRS. LINDE: Believe me, Nora, that's the best thing for both of you.

NORA: You don't know all. I forged a name.

MRS. LINDE: Good heavens—!                                                                  330

NORA: I only want to say this to you, Christine—you must be my witness.

MRS. LINDE: Your witness? What do you mean? What am I to—?

NORA: If I should go out of my mind—and it might easily happen—

MRS. LINDE: Nora!

335 NORA: Or if anything else should happen to me—anything, for instance, that might prevent my being here—

MRS. LINDE: Nora! Nora! you are quite out of your mind.

NORA: And if it should happen that there were someone who wanted to take all the responsibility, all the blame, you understand—

MRS. LINDE: Yes, yes—but how can you suppose—?

NORA: Then you must be my witness, that it is not true, Christine. I am not out of my mind at all; I am in my right senses now, and I tell you no one else has known anything about it; I, and I alone, did the whole thing. Remember that.

340 MRS. LINDE: I will, indeed. But I don't understand all this.

NORA: How should you understand it? A wonderful thing is going to happen.

MRS. LINDE: A wonderful thing?

NORA: Yes, a wonderful thing!—But it is so terrible, Christine; it *mustn't* happen, not for all the world.

MRS. LINDE: I will go at once and see Krogstad.

345 NORA: Don't go to him; he will do you some harm.

MRS. LINDE: There was a time when he would gladly do anything for my sake.

NORA: He?

MRS. LINDE: Where does he live?

NORA: How should I know—? Yes [*feeling in her pocket*] here is his card. But the letter, the letter—!

350 HELMER: [*calls from his room, knocking at the door*] Nora!

NORA: [*cries out anxiously*] Oh, what's that? What do you want?

HELMER: Don't be so frightened. We are not coming in; you have locked the door. Are you trying on your dress?

NORA: Yes, that's it. I look so nice, Torvald.

MRS. LINDE: [*who has read the card*] I see he lives at the corner here.

355 NORA: Yes, but it's no use. It is hopeless. The letter is lying there in the box.

MRS. LINDE: And your husband keeps the key?

NORA: Yes, always.

MRS. LINDE: Krogstad must ask for his letter back unread, he must find some pretence—

NORA: But it is just at this time that Torvald generally—

360 MRS. LINDE: You must delay him. Go in to him in the meantime. I will come back as soon as I can.

[*She goes out hurriedly through the hall door.*]

NORA: [*goes to HELMER'S door, opens it and peeps in*] Torvald!

HELMER: [*from the inner room*] Well? May I venture at last to come into my own room again? Come along, Rank, now you will see—[*halting in the doorway*] But what is this?

NORA: What is what, dear?

HELMER: Rank led me to expect a splendid transformation.

365 RANK: [*in the doorway*] I understood so, but evidently I was mistaken.

NORA: Yes, nobody is to have the chance of admiring me in my dress until tomorrow.

HELMER: But, my dear Nora, you look so worn out. Have you been practising too much?

NORA: No, I have not practised at all.

HELMER: But you will need to—

370 NORA: Yes, indeed I shall, Torvald. But I can't get on a bit without you to help me; I have absolutely forgotten the whole thing.

HELMER:  Oh, we will soon work it up again.

NORA:  Yes, help me, Torvald. Promise that you will! I am so nervous about it—all the people—. You must give yourself up to me entirely this evening. Not the tiniest bit of business—you mustn't even take a pen in your hand. Will you promise, Torvald dear?

HELMER:  I promise. This evening I will be wholly and absolutely at your service, you helpless little mortal. Ah, by the way, first of all I will just—

[*Goes towards the hall door*]

NORA:  What are you going to do there?

HELMER:  Only see if any letters have come.                                                                         375

NORA:  No, no! don't do that, Torvald!

HELMER:  Why not?

NORA:  Torvald, please don't. There is nothing there.

HELMER:  Well, let me look. [*Turns to go to the letter-box. NORA, at the piano, plays the first bars of the Tarantella. HELMER stops in the doorway.*] Aha!

NORA:  I can't dance to-morrow if I don't practise with you.                                                      380

HELMER:  [*going up to her*] Are you really so afraid of it, dear.

NORA:  Yes, so dreadfully afraid of it. Let me practise at once; there is time now, before we go to dinner. Sit down and play for me, Torvald dear; criticise me, and correct me as you play.

HELMER:  With great pleasure, if you wish me to.

[*Sits down at the piano.*]

NORA:  [*takes out of the box a tambourine and a long variegated shawl. She hastily drapes the shawl round her. Then she springs to the front of the stage and calls out.*] Now play for me! I am going to dance!

[*HELMER plays and NORA dances. RANK stands by the piano behind HELMER and looks on.*]

HELMER:  [*as he plays*] Slower, slower!                                                                           385

NORA:  I can't do it any other way.

HELMER:  Not so violently, Nora!

NORA:  This is the way.

HELMER:  [*stops playing*] No, no—that is not a bit right.

NORA:  [*laughing and swinging the tambourine*] Didn't I tell you so?                                           390

RANK:  Let me play for her.

HELMER:  [*getting up*] Yes, do. I can correct her better then.

[*RANK sits down at the piano and plays. NORA dances more and more wildly. HELMER has taken up a position beside the stove, and during her dance gives her frequent instructions. She does not seem to hear him; her hair comes down and falls over her shoulders; she pays no attention to it, but goes on dancing. Enter MRS. LINDE.*]

MRS. LINDE:  [*standing as if spell-bound in the doorway*] Oh!—

NORA:  [*as she dances*] Such fun, Christine!

HELMER:  My dear darling Nora, you are dancing as if your life depended on it.                                 395

NORA:  So it does.

HELMER:  Stop, Rank; this is sheer madness. Stop, I tell you! [*RANK stops playing, and NORA suddenly stands still. HELMER goes up to her.*] I could never have believed it. You have forgotten everything I taught you.

NORA:  [*throwing away the tambourine*] There, you see.

HELMER:  You will want a lot of coaching.

400 NORA: Yes, you see how much I need it. You must coach me up to the last minute. Promise me that, Torvald!

HELMER: You can depend on me.

NORA: You must not think of anything but me, either to-day or to-morrow; you mustn't open a single letter—not even open the letter-box—

HELMER: Ah, you are still afraid of that fellow—

NORA: Yes, indeed I am.

405 HELMER: Nora, I can tell from your looks that there is a letter from him lying there.

NORA: I don't know; I think there is; but you must not read anything of that kind now. Nothing horrid must come between us till this is all over.

RANK: [*whispers to* HELMER] You mustn't contradict her.

HELMER: [*taking her in his arms*] The child shall have her way. But to-morrow night, after you have danced—

NORA: Then you will be free.

[MAID *appears in the doorway to the right.*]

410 MAID: Dinner is served, ma'am.

NORA: We will have champagne, Helen.

MAID: Very good, ma'am.

[*Exit.*]

HELMER: Hullo!—are we going to have a banquet?

NORA: Yes, a champagne banquet till the small hours. [*calls out*] And a few macaroons, Helen—lots, just for once!

415 HELMER: Come, come, don't be so wild and nervous. Be my own little skylark, as you used.

NORA: Yes, dear, I will. But go in now and you too, Doctor Rank. Christine, you must help me to do up my hair.

RANK: [*whispers to* HELMER *as they go out*] I suppose there is nothing—she is not expecting anything?

HELMER: Far from it, my dear fellow; it is simply nothing more than this childish nervousness I was telling you of.

[*They go into the right-hand room.*]

NORA: Well!

420 MRS. LINDE: Gone out of town.

NORA: I could tell from your face.

MRS. LINDE: He is coming home to-morrow evening. I wrote a note for him.

NORA: You should have let it alone; you must prevent nothing. After all, it is splendid to be waiting for a wonderful thing to happen.

MRS. LINDE: What is it that you are waiting for?

425 NORA: Oh, you wouldn't understand. Go in to them, I will come in a moment. [MRS. LINDE *goes into the dining-room.* NORA *stands still for a little while, as if to compose herself. Then she looks at her watch.*] Five o'clock. Seven hours till midnight; and then four-and-twenty hours till the next midnight. Then the Tarantella will be over. Twenty-four and seven? Thirty-one hours to live.

HELMER: [*from the doorway on the right*] Where's my little skylark?

NORA: [*going to him with her arms outstretched*] Here she is!

## ACT 3

THE SAME SCENE. *The table has been placed in the middle of the stage, with chairs round it. A lamp is burning on the table. The door into the hall stands open. Dance music is heard in the room above. MRS. LINDE is sitting at the table idly turning over the leaves of a book; she tries to read, but does not seem able to collect her thoughts. Every now and then she listens intently for a sound at the outer door.*

MRS. LINDE: [*looking at her watch*] Not yet—and the time is nearly up. If only he does not—. [*listens again*] Ah, there he is. [*Goes into the hall and opens the outer door carefully. Light footsteps are heard on the stairs. She whispers.*] Come in. There is no one here.

KROGSTAD: [*in the doorway*] I found a note from you at home. What does this mean?

MRS. LINDE: It is absolutely necessary that I should have a talk with you.

KROGSTAD: Really? And is it absolutely necessary that it should be here?

MRS. LINDE: It is impossible where I live; there is no private entrance to my rooms. Come in;   5
we are quite alone. The maid is asleep, and the Helmers are at the dance upstairs.

KROGSTAD: [*coming into the room*] Are the Helmers really at a dance to-night?

MRS. LINDE: Yes, why not?

KROGSTAD: Certainly—why not?

MRS. LINDE: Now, Nils, let us have a talk.

KROGSTAD: Can we two have anything to talk about?   10

MRS. LINDE: We have a great deal to talk about.

KROGSTAD: I shouldn't have thought so.

MRS. LINDE: No, you have never properly understood me.

KROGSTAD: Was there anything else to understand except what was obvious to all the world—
a heartless woman jilts a man when a more lucrative chance turns up?

MRS. LINDE: Do you believe I am as absolutely heartless as all that? And do you believe that I   15
did it with a light heart?

KROGSTAD: Didn't you?

MRS. LINDE: Nils, did you really think that?

KROGSTAD: If it were as you say, why did you write to me as you did at the time?

MRS. LINDE: I could do nothing else. As I had to break with you, it was my duty also to put an
end to all that you felt for me.

KROGSTAD: [*wringing his hands*] So that was it, and all this—only for the sake of money!   20

MRS. LINDE: You must not forget that I had a helpless mother and two little brothers. We
couldn't wait for you, Nils; your prospects seemed hopeless then.

KROGSTAD: That may be so, but you had no right to throw me over for any one else's sake.

MRS. LINDE: Indeed I don't know. Many a time did I ask myself if I had the right to do it.

KROGSTAD: [*more gently*] When I lost you, it was as if all the solid ground went from under my
feet. Look at me now—I am a shipwrecked man clinging to a bit of wreckage.

MRS. LINDE: But help may be near.   25

KROGSTAD: It *was* near; but then you came and stood in my way.

MRS. LINDE: Unintentionally, Nils. It was only to-day that I learnt it was your place I was going
to take in the Bank.

KROGSTAD: I believe you, if you say so. But now that you know it, are you not going to give it
up to me?

MRS. LINDE: No, because that would not benefit you in the least.

KROGSTAD: Oh, benefit, benefit—I would have done it whether or no.   30

MRS. LINDE: I have learnt to act prudently. Life, and hard, bitter necessity have taught me that.

KROGSTAD: And life has taught me not to believe in fine speeches.

MRS. LINDE: Then life has taught you something very reasonable. But deeds you must believe in?

KROGSTAD: What do you mean by that?

35 MRS. LINDE: You said you were like a shipwrecked man clinging to some wreckage.

KROGSTAD: I had good reason to say so.

MRS. LINDE: Well, I am like a shipwrecked woman clinging to some wreckage—no one to mourn for, no one to care for.

KROGSTAD: It was your own choice.

MRS. LINDE: There was no other choice—then.

40 KROGSTAD: Well, what now?

MRS. LINDE: Nils, how would it be if we two shipwrecked people could join forces?

KROGSTAD: What are you saying?

MRS. LINDE: Two on the same piece of wreckage would stand a better chance than each on their own.

KROGSTAD: Christine!

45 MRS. LINDE: What do you suppose brought me to town?

KROGSTAD: Do you mean that you gave me a thought?

MRS. LINDE: I could not endure life without work. All my life, as long as I can remember, I have worked, and it has been my greatest and only pleasure. But now I am quite alone in the world—my life is so dreadfully empty and I feel so forsaken. There is not the least pleasure in working for one's self. Nils, give me someone and something to work for.

KROGSTAD: I don't trust that. It is nothing but a woman's overstrained sense of generosity that prompts you to make such an offer of yourself.

MRS. LINDE: Have you ever noticed anything of the sort in me?

50 KROGSTAD: Could you really do it? Tell me—do you know all about my past life?

MRS. LINDE: Yes.

KROGSTAD: And do you know what they think of me here?

MRS. LINDE: You seemed to me to imply that with me you might have been quite another man.

KROGSTAD: I am certain of it.

55 MRS. LINDE: Is it too late now?

KROGSTAD: Christine, are you saying this deliberately? Yes, I am sure you are. I see it in your face. Have you really the courage, then—?

MRS. LINDE: I want to be a mother to someone, and your children need a mother. We two need each other. Nils, I have faith in your real character—I can dare anything together with you.

KROGSTAD: [grasps her hands] Thanks, thanks, Christine! Now I shall find a way to clear myself in the eyes of the world. Ah, but I forgot—

MRS. LINDE: [listening] Hush! The Tarantella! Go, go!

60 KROGSTAD: Why? What is it?

MRS. LINDE: Do you hear them up there? When that is over, we may expect them back.

KROGSTAD: Yes, yes—I will go. But it is all no use. Of course you are not aware what steps I have taken in the matter of the Helmers.

MRS. LINDE: Yes. I know all about that.

KROGSTAD: And in spite of that have you the courage to—?

65 MRS. LINDE: I understand very well to what lengths a man like you might be driven by despair.

KROGSTAD: If I could only undo what I have done!

MRS. LINDE: You can. Your letter is lying in the letter-box now.

KROGSTAD:  Are you sure of that?

MRS. LINDE:  Quite sure, but—

KROGSTAD:  [*with a searching look at her*] Is that what it all means?—that you want to save your  70
friend at any cost? Tell me frankly. Is that it?

MRS. LINDE:  Nils, a woman who has once sold herself for another's sake, doesn't do it a second time.

KROGSTAD:  I will ask for my letter back.

MRS. LINDE:  No, no.

KROGSTAD:  Yes, of course I will. I will wait here till Helmer comes; I will tell him he must give
me my letter back—that it only concerns my dismissal—that he is not to read it—

MRS. LINDE:  No, Nils, you must not recall your letter.  75

KROGSTAD:  But, tell me, wasn't it for that very purpose that you asked me to meet you here?

MRS. LINDE:  In my first moment of fright, it was. But twenty-four hours have elapsed since
then, and in that time I have witnessed incredible things in this house. Helmer must know
all about it. This unhappy secret must be disclosed; they must have a complete understanding between them, which is impossible with all this concealment and falsehood
going on.

KROGSTAD:  Very well, if you will take the responsibility. But there is one thing I can do in any
case, and I shall do it at once.

MRS. LINDE:  [*listening*] You must be quick and go! The dance is over; we are not safe a moment
longer.

KROGSTAD:  I will wait for you below.  80

MRS. LINDE:  Yes, do. You must see me back to my door.

KROGSTAD:  I have never had such an amazing piece of good fortune in my life.

[*Goes out through the outer door. The door between the room and the hall remains open.*]

MRS. LINDE:  [*tidying up the room and laying her hat and cloak ready*] What a difference! what a difference! Someone to work for and live for—a home to bring comfort into. That I will do,
indeed. I wish they would be quick and come—[*listens*] Ah, there they are now. I must put
on my things.

[*Takes up her hat and cloak. HELMER'S and NORA'S voices are heard outside; a key is turned, and
HELMER brings NORA almost by force into the hall. She is in an Italian costume with a large black shawl
round her; he is in evening dress and a black domino which is flying open.*]

NORA:  [*hanging back in the doorway, and struggling with him*] No, no, no!—don't take me in. I
want to go upstairs again; I don't want to leave so early.

HELMER:  But, my dearest Nora—  85

NORA:  Please, Torvald dear—please, *please*—only an hour more.

HELMER:  Not a single minute, my sweet Nora. You know that was our agreement. Come along
into the room; you are catching cold standing there.

[*He brings her gently into the room, in spite of her resistance.*]

MRS. LINDE:  Good evening.

NORA:  Christine!

HELMER:  You here, so late, Mrs. Linde?  90

MRS. LINDE:  Yes, you must excuse me; I was so anxious to see Nora in her dress.

NORA:  Have you been sitting here waiting for me?

MRS. LINDE:  Yes, unfortunately I came too late, you had already gone upstairs; and I thought I
couldn't go away without having seen you.

HELMER: [*taking off NORA's shawl*] Yes, take a good look at her. I think she is worth looking at. Isn't she charming, Mrs. Linde?

95 MRS. LINDE: Yes, indeed she is.

HELMER: Doesn't she look remarkably pretty? Everyone thought so at the dance. But she is terribly self-willed, this sweet little person. What are we to do with her? You will hardly believe that I had almost to bring her away by force.

NORA: Torvald, you will repent not having let me stay, even if it were only for half an hour.

HELMER: Listen to her, Mrs. Linde! She had danced her Tarantella, and it had been a tremendous success, as it deserved—although possibly the performance was a trifle too realistic—a little more so, I mean, than was strictly compatible with the limitations of art. But never mind about that! The chief thing is, she had made a success—she had made a tremendous success. Do you think I was going to let her remain there after that, and spoil the effect? No indeed! I took my charming little Capri maiden—my capricious little Capri maiden, I should say—on my arm; took one quick turn round the room; a curtsey on either side, and, as they say in novels, the beautiful apparition disappeared. An exit ought always to be effective, Mrs. Linde; but that is what I cannot make Nora understand. Pooh! this room is hot. [*throws his domino on a chair and opens the door of his room*] Hullo! it's all dark in here. Oh, of course—excuse me—.

[*He goes in and lights some candles.*]

NORA: [*in a hurried and breathless whisper*] Well?

100 MRS. LINDE: [*in a low voice*] I have had a talk with him.

NORA: Yes, and—

MRS. LINDE: Nora, you must tell your husband all about it.

NORA: [*in an expressionless voice*] I knew it.

MRS. LINDE: You have nothing to be afraid of as far as Krogstad is concerned; but you must tell him.

105 NORA: I won't tell him.

MRS. LINDE: Then the letter will.

NORA: Thank you, Christine. Now I know what I must do. Hush—!

HELMER: [*coming in again*] Well, Mrs. Linde, have you admired her?

MRS. LINDE: Yes, and now I will say good-night.

110 HELMER: What already? Is this yours, this knitting?

MRS. LINDE: [*taking it*] Yes, thank you, I had very nearly forgotten it.

HELMER: So you knit?

MRS. LINDE: Of course.

HELMER: Do you know, you ought to embroider.

115 MRS. LINDE: Really? Why?

HELMER: Yes, it's far more becoming. Let me show you. You hold the embroidery thus in your left hand, and use the needle with the right—like this—with a long, easy sweep. Do you see?

MRS. LINDE: Yes, perhaps—

HELMER: But in the case of knitting—that can never be anything but ungraceful; look here—the arms close together, the knitting-needles going up and down—it has a sort of Chinese effect—. That was really excellent champagne they gave us.

MRS. LINDE: Well,—good-night, Nora, and don't be self-willed any more.

120 HELMER: That's right, Mrs. Linde.

MRS. LINDE: Good-night, Mr. Helmer.

HELMER: [*accompanying her to the door*] Good-night, good-night. I hope you will get home all right. I should be very happy to—but you haven't any great distance to go. Good-night, good-night. [*She goes out; he shuts the door after her, and comes in again.*] Ah!—at last we have got rid of her. She is a frightful bore, that woman.

NORA: Aren't you very tired, Torvald?

HELMER: No, not in the least.

NORA: Nor sleepy?                                                                                   125

HELMER: Not a bit. On the contrary, I feel extraordinarily lively. And you?—you really look both tired and sleepy.

NORA: Yes, I am very tired. I want to go to sleep at once.

HELMER: There, you see it was quite right of me not to let you stay there any longer.

NORA: Everything you do is quite right, Torvald.

HELMER: [*kissing her on the forehead*] Now my little skylark is speaking reasonably. Did you 130 notice what good spirits Rank was in this evening?

NORA: Really? Was he? I didn't speak to him at all.

HELMER: And I very little, but I have not for a long time seen him in such good form. [*looks for a while at her and then goes nearer to her*] It is delightful to be at home by ourselves again, to be all alone with you—you fascinating, charming little darling!

NORA: Don't look at me like that, Torvald.

HELMER: Why shouldn't I look at my dearest treasure?—at all the beauty that is mine, all my very own?

NORA: [*going to the other side of the table*] You mustn't say things like that to me to-night.    135

HELMER: [*following her*] You have still got the Tarantella in your blood, I see. And it makes you more captivating than ever. Listen—the guests are beginning to go now. [*in a lower voice*] Nora—soon the whole house will be quiet.

NORA: Yes, I hope so.

HELMER: Yes, my own darling Nora. Do you know, when I am out at a party with you like this, why I speak so little to you, keep away from you, and only send a stolen glance in your direction now and then?—do you know why I do that? It is because I make believe to myself that we are secretly in love, and you are my secretly promised bride, and that no one suspects there is anything between us.

NORA: Yes, yes—I know very well your thoughts are with me all the time.

HELMER: And when we are leaving, and I am putting the shawl over your beautiful young 140 shoulders—on your lovely neck—then I imagine that you are my young bride and that we have just come from the wedding, and I am bringing you for the first time into our home—to be alone with you for the first time—quite alone with my shy little darling! All this evening I have longed for nothing but you. When I watched the seductive figures of the Tarantella, my blood was on fire; I could endure it no longer, and that was why I brought you down so early—

NORA: Go away, Torvald! You must let me go. I won't—

HELMER: What's that? You're joking, my little Nora! You won't—you won't? Am I not your husband—?

[*A knock is heard at the outer door.*]

NORA: [*starting*] Did you hear—?

HELMER: [*going into the hall*] Who is it?

RANK: [*outside*] It is I. May I come in for a moment?                                              145

HELMER: [*in a fretful whisper*] Oh, what does he want now? [*aloud*] Wait a minute! [*unlocks the door*] Come, that's kind of you not to pass by our door.

RANK: I thought I heard your voice, and felt as if I should like to look in. [*with a swift glance round*] Ah, yes!—these dear familiar rooms. You are very happy and cosy in here, you two.

HELMER: It seems to me that you looked after yourself pretty well upstairs too.

RANK: Excellently. Why shouldn't I? Why shouldn't one enjoy everything in this world?—at any rate as much as one can, and as long as one can. The wine was capital—

150 HELMER: Especially the champagne.

RANK: So you noticed that too? It is almost incredible how much I managed to put away!

NORA: Torvald drank a great deal of champagne tonight, too.

RANK: Did he?

NORA: Yes, and he is always in such good spirits afterwards.

155 RANK: Well, why should one not enjoy a merry evening after a well-spent day?

HELMER: Well spent? I am afraid I can't take credit for that.

RANK: [clapping him on the back] But I can, you know!

NORA: Doctor Rank, you must have been occupied with some scientific investigation to-day.

RANK: Exactly.

160 HELMER: Just listen!—little Nora talking about scientific investigations!

NORA: And may I congratulate you on the result?

RANK: Indeed you may.

NORA: Was it favourable, then?

RANK: The best possible, for both doctor and patient—certainty.

165 NORA: [quickly and searchingly] Certainty?

RANK: Absolute certainty. So wasn't I entitled to make a merry evening of it after that?

NORA: Yes, you certainly were, Doctor Rank.

HELMER: I think so too, so long as you don't have to pay for it in the morning.

RANK: Oh well, one can't have anything in this life without paying for it.

170 NORA: Doctor Rank—are you fond of fancy-dress balls?

RANK: Yes, if there is a fine lot of pretty costumes.

NORA: Tell me—what shall we two wear at the next?

HELMER: Little featherbrain!—are you thinking of the next already?

RANK: We two? Yes, I can tell you. You shall go as a good fairy—

175 HELMER: Yes, but what do you suggest as an appropriate costume for that?

RANK: Let your wife go dressed just as she is in everyday life.

HELMER: That was really very prettily turned. But can't you tell us what you will be?

RANK: Yes, my dear friend, I have quite made up my mind about that.

HELMER: Well?

180 RANK: At the next fancy dress ball I shall be invisible.

HELMER: That's a good joke!

RANK: There is a big black hat—have you never heard of hats that make you invisible? If you put one on, no one can see you.

HELMER: [suppressing a smile] Yes, you are quite right.

RANK: But I am clean forgetting what I came for. Helmer, give me a cigar—one of the dark Havanas.

185 HELMER: With the greatest pleasure. [offers him his case]

RANK: [takes a cigar and cuts off the end] Thanks.

NORA: [striking a match] Let me give you a light.

RANK: Thank you. [She holds the match for him to light his cigar.] And now good-bye!

HELMER: Good-bye, good-bye, dear old man!

190 NORA: Sleep well, Doctor Rank.

RANK: Thank you for that wish.

NORA: Wish me the same.

RANK: You? Well, if you want me to: sleep well! And thanks for the light.

[*He nods to them both and goes out.*]

HELMER: [*in a subdued voice*] He has drunk more than he ought.

NORA: [*absently*] Maybe. [*HELMER takes a bunch of keys out of his pocket and goes into the hall.*] 195
Torvald! what are you going to do there?

HELMER: Empty the letter-box; it is quite full; there will be no room to put the newspaper in to-morrow morning.

NORA: Are you going to work to-night?

HELMER: You know quite well I'm not. What is this? Some one has been at the lock.

NORA: At the lock—?

HELMER: Yes, someone has. What can it mean? I should never have thought the maid—. Here 200
is a broken hairpin. Nora, it is one of yours.

NORA: [*quickly*] Then it must have been the children—

HELMER: Then you must get them out of those ways. There, at last I have got it open. [*Takes out
the contents of the letter-box, and calls to the kitchen.*] Helen!—Helen, put out the light over
the front door. [*Goes back into the room and shuts the door into the hall. He holds out his hand
full of letters.*] Look at that—look what a heap of them there are. [*turning them over*] What
on earth is that?

NORA: [*at the window*] The letter—No! Torvald, no!

HELMER: Two cards—of Rank's.

NORA: Of Doctor Rank's?                                                                  205

HELMER: [*looking at them*] Doctor Rank. They were on the top. He must have put them in when
he went out.

NORA: Is there anything written on them?

HELMER: There is a black cross over the name. Look there—what an uncomfortable idea! It
looks as if he were announcing his own death.

NORA: It is just what he is doing.

HELMER: What? Do you know anything about it? Has he said anything to you?              210

NORA: Yes. He told me that when the cards came it would be his leave-taking from us. He
means to shut himself up and die.

HELMER: My poor old friend. Certainly I knew we should not have him very long with us. But
so soon! And so he hides himself away like a wounded animal.

NORA: If it has to happen, it is best it should be without a word—don't you think so, Torvald?

HELMER: [*walking up and down*] He had so grown into our lives. I can't think of him as having
gone out of them. He, with his sufferings and his loneliness, was like a cloudy back-ground to our sunlit happiness. Well, perhaps it is best so. For him, anyway. [*standing still*]
And perhaps for us too, Nora. We two are thrown quite upon each other now. [*puts his
arms round her*] My darling wife, I don't feel as if I could hold you tight enough. Do you
know, Nora, I have often wished that you might be threatened by some great danger, so
that I might risk my life's blood, and everything, for your sake.

NORA: [*disengages herself, and says firmly and decidedly*] Now you must read your letters, 215
Torvald.

HELMER: No, no; not to-night. I want to be with you, my darling wife.

NORA: With the thought of your friend's death—

HELMER: You are right, it has affected us both. Something ugly has come between us—the
thought of the horrors of death. We must try and rid our minds of that. Until then—we
will each go to our own room.

NORA: [*hanging on his neck*] Good-night, Torvald—Good-night!

220  HELMER: [*kissing her on the forehead.*] Good-night, my little singing-bird. Sleep sound, Nora. Now I will read my letters through.

[*He takes his letters and goes into his room, shutting the door after him.*]

NORA: [*gropes distractedly about, seizes* HELMER'S *domino, throws it round her, while she says in quick, hoarse, spasmodic whispers*] Never to see him again. Never! Never! [*puts her shawl over her head*] Never to see my children again either—never again. Never! Never!—Ah! the icy, black water—the unfathomable depths—If only it were over! He has got it now—now he is reading it. Good-by, Torvald and my children!

[*She is about to rush out through the hall, when* HELMER *opens his door hurriedly and stands with an open letter in his hand.*]

HELMER: Nora!

NORA: Ah!—

HELMER: What is this? Do you know what is in this letter?

225  NORA: Yes, I know. Let me go! Let me get out!

HELMER: [*holding her back*] Where are you going?

NORA: [*trying to get free*] You shan't save me, Torvald!

HELMER: [*reeling*] True? Is this true, that I read here? Horrible! No, no—it is impossible that it can be true.

NORA: It is true. I have loved you above everything else in the world.

230  HELMER: Oh, don't let us have any silly excuses.

NORA: [*taking a step towards him*] Torvald—!

HELMER: Miserable creature—what have you done?

NORA: Let me go. You shall not suffer for my sake. You shall not take it upon yourself.

HELMER: No tragedy airs, please. [*locks the hall door*] Here you shall stay and give me an explanation. Do you understand what you have done? Answer me? Do you understand what you have done?

235  NORA: [*looks steadily at him and says with a growing look of coldness in her face*] Yes, now I am beginning to understand thoroughly.

HELMER: [*walking about the room*] What a horrible awakening! All these eight years—she who was my joy and pride—a hypocrite, a liar—worse, worse—a criminal! The unutterable ugliness of it all! For shame! For shame! [NORA *is silent and looks steadily at him. He stops in front of her.*] I ought to have suspected that something of the sort would happen. I ought to have foreseen it. All your father's want of principle—be silent!—all your father's want of principle has come out in you. No religion, no morality, no sense of duty—. How I am punished for having winked at what he did! I did it for your sake, and this is how you repay me.

NORA: Yes, that's just it.

HELMER: Now you have destroyed all my happiness. You have ruined all my future. It is horrible to think of! I am in the power of an unscrupulous man; he can do what he likes with me, ask anything he likes of me, give me any orders he pleases— I dare not refuse. And I must sink to such miserable depths because of a thoughtless woman!

NORA: When I am out of the way, you will be free.

240  HELMER: No fine speeches, please. Your father had always plenty of those ready, too. What good would it be to me if you were out of the way, as you say? Not the slightest. He can make the affair known everywhere; and if he does, I may be falsely suspected of having been a party to your criminal action. Very likely people will think I was behind it all— that it was I who prompted you! And I have to thank you for all this—you whom I have

cherished during the whole of our married life. Do you understand now what it is you have done for me?

NORA: [*coldly and quietly*] Yes.

HELMER: It is so incredible that I can't take it in. But we must come to some understanding. Take off that shawl. Take it off, I tell you. I must try and appease him some way or another. The matter must be hushed up at any cost. And as for you and me, it must appear as if everything between us were just as before—but naturally only in the eyes of the world. You will still remain in my house, that is a matter of course. But I shall not allow you to bring up the children; I dare not trust them to you. To think that I should be obliged to say so to one whom I have loved so dearly, and whom I still—. No, that is all over. From this moment happiness is not the question; all that concerns us is to save the remains, the fragments, the appearance—

[*A ring is heard at the front-door bell.*]

HELMER: [*with a start*] What is that? So late! Can the worst—? Can he—? Hide yourself, Nora. Say you are ill.

[*NORA stands motionless. HELMER goes and unlocks the hall door.*]

MAID: [*half-dressed, comes to the door*] A letter for the mistress.

HELMER: Give it to me. [*takes the letter, and shuts the door*] Yes, it is from him. You shall not have it; I will read it myself.                                                                                                                245

NORA: Yes, read it.

HELMER: [*standing by the lamp*] I scarcely have the courage to do it. It may mean ruin for both of us. No, I must know. [*tears open the letter, runs his eye over a few lines, looks at a paper enclosed and gives a shout of joy*] Nora! [*She looks at him questioningly.*] Nora!—No, I must read it once again—. Yes, it is true! I am saved! Nora, I am saved!

NORA: And I?

HELMER: You too, of course; we are both saved, both you and I. Look, he sends you your bond back. He says he regrets and repents—that a happy change in his life—never mind what he says! We are saved, Nora! No one can do anything to you. Oh, Nora, Nora!—no, first I must destroy these hateful things. Let me see—. [*takes a look at the bond*] No, no, I won't look at it. The whole thing shall be nothing but a bad dream to me. [*tears up the bond and both letters, throws them all into the stove, and watches them burn*] There—now it doesn't exist any longer. He says that since Christmas Eve you—. These must have been three dreadful days for you, Nora.

NORA: I have fought a hard fight these three days.                                                                               250

HELMER: And suffered agonies, and seen no way out but—. No, we won't call any of the horrors to mind. We will only shout with joy, and keep saying "It's all over! It's all over!" Listen to me, Nora. You don't seem to realise that it is all over. What is this?—such a cold, set face! My poor little Nora, I quite understand; you don't feel as if you could believe that I have forgiven you. But it is true, Nora, I swear it; I have forgiven you everything. I know that what you did, you did out of love for me.

NORA: That is true.

HELMER: You have loved me as a wife ought to love her husband. Only you had not sufficient knowledge to judge of the means you used. But do you suppose you are any the less dear to me, because you don't understand how to act on your own responsibility? No, no; only lean on me; I will advise you and direct you. I should not be a man if this womanly helplessness did not just give you a double attractiveness in my eyes. You must not think any more about the hard things I said in my first moment of consternation, when I thought everything was going to overwhelm me. I have forgiven you, Nora; I swear to you I have forgiven you.

NORA: Thank you for your forgiveness.

[*She goes out through the door to the right.*]

255 HELMER: No, don't go—. [*looks in*] What are you doing in there?

NORA: [*from within*] Taking off my fancy dress.

HELMER: [*standing at the open door*] Yes, do. Try and calm yourself, and make your mind easy again, my frightened little singing-bird. Be at rest, and feel secure; I have broad wings to shelter you under. [*walks up and down by the door*] How warm and cosy our home is, Nora. Here is shelter for you; here I will protect you like a hunted dove that I have saved from a hawk's claws. I will bring peace to your poor beating heart. It will come, little by little, Nora, believe me. Tomorrow morning you will look upon it all quite differently; soon everything will be just as it was before. Very soon you won't need me to assure you that I have forgiven you; you will yourself feel the certainty that I have done so. Can you suppose I should ever think of such a thing as repudiating you, or even reproaching you? You have no idea what a true man's heart is like, Nora. There is something so indescribably sweet and satisfying, to a man, in the knowledge that he has forgiven his wife— forgiven her freely, and with all his heart. It seems as if that had made her, as it were, doubly his own; he has given her a new life, so to speak; and she has in a way become both wife and child to him. So you shall be for me after this, my little scared, helpless darling. Have no anxiety about anything, Nora; only be frank and open with me, and I will serve as will and conscience both to you—. What is this? Not gone to bed? Have you changed your things?

NORA: [*in everyday dress*] Yes, Torvald, I have changed my things now.

HELMER: But what for?—so late as this.

260 NORA: I shall not sleep to-night.

HELMER: But, my dear Nora—

NORA: [*looking at her watch*] It is not so very late. Sit down here, Torvald. You and I have much to say to one another.

[*She sits down at one side of the table.*]

HELMER: Nora—what is this?—this cold, set face?

NORA: Sit down. it will take some time; I have a lot to talk over with you.

265 HELMER: [*sits down at the opposite side of the table*] You alarm me, Nora!—and I don't understand you.

NORA: No, that is just it. You don't understand me, and I have never understood you either— before to-night. No, you mustn't interrupt me. You must simply listen to what I say. Torvald, this is a settling of accounts.

HELMER: What do you mean by that?

NORA: [*after a short silence*] Isn't there one thing that strikes you as strange in our sitting here like this?

HELMER: What is that?

270 NORA: We have been married now eight years. Does it not occur to you that this is the first time we two, you and I, husband and wife, have had a serious conversation?

HELMER: What do you mean by serious?

NORA: In all these eight years—longer than that—from the very beginning of our acquaintance, we have never exchanged a word on any serious subject.

HELMER: Was it likely that I would be continually and for ever telling you about worries that you could not help me to bear?

NORA: I am not speaking about business matters. I say that we have never sat down in earnest together to try and get at the bottom of anything.

275 HELMER: But, dearest Nora, would it have been any good to you?

Torvald Helmer (Sam Waterston) begs Nora (Liv Ullmann) to reconsider her decision to leave home in the Joseph Papp New York Shakespeare Festival production (1995) of *A Dollhouse* (director, Tormod Skagestad).

NORA: That is just it; you have never understood me. I have been greatly wronged, Torvald—first by papa and then by you.

HELMER: What! By us two—by us two, who have loved you better than anyone else in the world?

NORA: [*shaking her head*] You have never loved me. You have only thought it pleasant to be in love with me.

HELMER: Nora, what do I hear you saying?

NORA: It is perfectly true, Torvald. When I was at home with papa, he told me his opinion    280 about everything, and so I had the same opinions; and if I differed from him I concealed the fact, because he would not have liked it. He called me his doll-child, and he played with me just as I used to play with my dolls. And when I came to live with you—

HELMER: What sort of an expression is that to use about our marriage?

NORA: [*undisturbed*] I mean that I was simply transferred from papa's hands into yours. You arranged everything according to your own taste, and so I got the same tastes as you—or else I pretended to, I am really not quite sure which—I think sometimes the one and sometimes the other. When I look back on it, it seems to me as if I had been living here like a poor woman—just from hand to mouth. I have existed merely to perform tricks for you, Torvald. But you would have it so. You and papa have committed a great sin against me. It is your fault that I have made nothing of my life.

HELMER: How unreasonable and how ungrateful you are, Nora! Have you not been happy here?

NORA: No, I have never been happy. I thought I was, but it has never really been so.

285 HELMER: Not—not happy!

NORA: No, only merry. And you have always been so kind to me. But our home has been nothing but a playroom. I have been your doll-wife, just as at home I was papa's doll-child; and here the children have been my dolls. I thought it great fun when you played with me, just as they thought it great fun when I played with them. That is what our marriage has been, Torvald.

HELMER: There is some truth in what you say—exaggerated and strained as your view of it is. But for the future it shall be different. Playtime shall be over, and lesson-time shall begin.

NORA: Whose lessons? Mine, or the children's?

HELMER: Both yours and the children's, my darling Nora.

290 NORA: Alas, Torvald, you are not the man to educate me into being a proper wife for you.

HELMER: And you can say that!

NORA: And I—how am I fitted to bring up the children?

HELMER: Nora!

NORA: Didn't you say so yourself a little while ago—that you dare not trust me to bring them up?

295 HELMER: In a moment of anger! Why do you pay any heed to that?

NORA: Indeed, you were perfectly right. I am not fit for the task. There is another task I must undertake first. I must try and educate myself—you are not the man to help me in that. I must do that for myself. And that is why I am going to leave you now.

HELMER: [springing up] What do you say?

NORA: I must stand quite alone, if I am to understand myself and everything about me. It is for that reason that I cannot remain with you any longer.

HELMER: Nora! Nora!

300 NORA: I am going away from here now, at once. I am sure Christine will take me in for the night—

HELMER: You are out of your mind! I won't allow it! I forbid you!

NORA: It is no use forbidding me anything any longer. I will take with me what belongs to myself. I will take nothing from you, either now or later.

HELMER: What sort of madness is this!

NORA: To-morrow I shall go home—I mean, to my old home. It will be easiest for me to find something to do there.

305 HELMER: You blind, foolish woman!

NORA: I must try and get some sense, Torvald.

HELMER: To desert your home, your husband and your children! And you don't consider what people will say!

NORA: I cannot consider that at all. I only know that it is necessary for me.

HELMER: It's shocking. This is how you would neglect your most sacred duties.

310 NORA: What do you consider my most sacred duties?

HELMER: Do I need to tell you that? Are they not your duties to your husband and your children?

NORA: I have other duties just as sacred.

HELMER: That you have not. What duties could those be?

NORA: Duties to myself.

HELMER: Before all else, you are a wife and a mother. 315

NORA: I don't believe that any longer. I believe that before all else I am a reasonable human being, just as you are—or, at all events, that I must try and become one. I know quite well, Torvald, that most people would think you right, and that views of that kind are to be found in books; but I can no longer content myself with what most people say, or with what is found in books. I must think over things for myself and get to understand them.

HELMER: Can you not understand your place in your own home? Have you not a reliable guide in such matters as that?—have you no religion?

NORA: I am afraid, Torvald, I do not exactly know what religion is.

HELMER: What are you saying?

NORA: I know nothing but what the clergyman said when I went to be confirmed. He told us 320 that religion was this, and that, and the other. When I am away from all this, and am alone, I will look into that matter too. I will see if what the clergyman said is true, or at all events if it is true for me.

HELMER: This is unheard of in a girl of your age! But if religion cannot lead you aright, let me try and awaken your conscience. I suppose you have some moral sense? Or—answer me—am I to think you have none?

NORA: I assure you, Torvald, that is not an easy question to answer. I really don't know. The thing perplexes me altogether. I only know that you and I look at it in quite a different light. I am learning, too, that the law is quite another thing from what I supposed; but I find it impossible to convince myself that the law is right. According to it a woman has no right to spare her old dying father, or to save her husband's life. I can't believe that.

HELMER: You talk like a child. You don't understand the conditions of the world in which you live.

NORA: No, I don't. But now I am going to try. I am going to see if I can make out who is right, the world or I.

HELMER: You are ill, Nora; you are delirious; I almost think you are out of your mind. 325

NORA: I have never felt my mind so clear and certain as to-night.

HELMER: And is it with a clear and certain mind that you forsake your husband and your children?

NORA: Yes, it is.

HELMER: Then there is only one possible explanation.

NORA: What is that? 330

HELMER: You do not love me any more.

NORA: No, that is just it.

HELMER: Nora!—and you can say that?

NORA: It gives me great pain, Torvald, for you have always been so kind to me, but I cannot help it. I do not love you any more.

HELMER: [*regaining his composure*] Is that a clear and certain conviction too? 335

NORA: Yes, absolutely clear and certain. That is the reason why I will not stay here any longer.

HELMER: And can you tell me what I have done to forfeit your love?

NORA: Yes, indeed I can. It was to-night, when the wonderful thing did not happen; then I saw you were not the man I had thought you.

HELMER: Explain yourself better—I don't understand you.

340 NORA: I have waited so patiently for eight years; for, goodness knows, I knew very well that wonderful things don't happen every day. Then this horrible misfortune came upon me; and then I felt quite certain that the wonderful thing was going to happen at last. When Krogstad's letter was lying out there, never for a moment did I imagine that you would consent to accept this man's conditions. I was so absolutely certain that you would say to him: Publish the thing to the whole world. And when that was done—

HELMER: Yes, what then?—when I had exposed my wife to shame and disgrace?

NORA: When that was done, I was so absolutely certain, you would come forward and take everything upon yourself, and say: I am the guilty one.

HELMER: Nora—!

NORA: You mean that I would never have accepted such a sacrifice on your part? No, of course not. But what would my assurances have been worth against yours? That was the wonderful thing which I hoped for and feared; and it was to prevent that, that I wanted to kill myself.

345 HELMER: I would gladly work night and day for you, Nora—bear sorrow and want for your sake. But no man would sacrifice his honour for the one he loves.

NORA: It is a thing hundreds of thousands of women have done.

HELMER: Oh, you think and talk like a heedless child.

NORA: Maybe. But you neither think nor talk like the man I could bind myself to. As soon as your fear was over—and it was not fear for what threatened me, but for what might happen to you—when the whole thing was past, as far as you were concerned it was exactly as if nothing at all had happened. Exactly as before, I was your little skylark, your doll, which you would in future treat with doubly gentle care, because it was so brittle and fragile. [getting up] Torvald—it was then it dawned upon me that for eight years I had been living here with a strange man, and had borne him three children—. Oh, I can't bear to think of it! I could tear myself into little bits!

HELMER: [sadly] I see, I see. An Abyss has opened between us—there is no denying it. But, Nora, would it not be possible to fill it up?

350 NORA: As I am now, I am no wife for you.

HELMER: I have it in me to become a different man.

NORA: Perhaps—if your doll is taken away from you.

HELMER: But to part!—to part from you! No, no, Nora, I can't understand that idea.

NORA: [going out to the right] That makes it all the more certain that it must be done.

[She comes back with her cloak and hat and a small bag which she puts on a chair by the table.]

355 HELMER: Nora, Nora, not now! Wait till to-morrow.

NORA: [putting on her cloak] I cannot spend the night in a strange man's room.

HELMER: But can't we live here like brother and sister—?

NORA: [putting on her hat] You know very well that would not last long. [puts the shawl round her] Good-bye, Torvald. I won't see the little ones. I know they are in better hands than mine. As I am now, I can be of no use to them.

HELMER: But some day, Nora—some day?

360 NORA: How can I tell? I have no idea what is going to become of me.

HELMER: But you are my wife, whatever becomes of you.

NORA: Listen, Torvald. I have heard that when a wife deserts her husband's house, as I am doing now, he is legally freed from all obligations towards her. In any case I set you free from all your obligations. You are not to feel yourself bound in the slightest way, any more than I shall. There must be perfect freedom on both sides. See here is your ring back. Give me mine.

HELMER: That too?

NORA: That too.

HELMER: Here it is.  365

NORA: That's right. Now it is all over. I have put the keys here. The maids know all about everything in the house—better than I do. To-morrow, after I have left her, Christine will come here and pack up my own things that I brought with me from home. I will have them sent after me.

HELMER: All over! All over!—Nora, shall you never think of me again?

NORA: I know I shall often think of you and the children and this house.

HELMER: May I write to you, Nora?

NORA: No—never. You must not do that.  370

HELMER: But at least let me send you—

NORA: Nothing—nothing—

HELMER: Let me help you if you are in want.

NORA: No. I can receive nothing from a stranger.

HELMER: Nora—can I never be anything more than a stranger to you?  375

NORA: [taking her bag] Ah, Torvald, the most wonderful thing of all would have to happen.

HELMER: Tell me what that would be!

NORA: Both you and I would have to be so changed that—. Oh, Torvald, I don't believe any longer in wonderful things happening.

HELMER: But I will believe in it. Tell me? So changed that—?

NORA: That our life together would be a real wedlock. Good-bye.  380

[She goes out through the hall.]

HELMER: [sinks down on a chair at the door and buries his face in his hands] Nora! Nora! [looks round, and rises] Empty. She is gone. [A hope flashes across his mind.] The most wonderful thing of all—?

[The sound of a door slamming is heard from below.]

## Questions

### Act 1

1. What does the opening stage direction reveal about the Helmer family? About the time of year?

2. Explain the ways Nora and Torvald behave toward each other.

3. What does Torvald's refusal to consider borrowing and debt tell you about him (speech 22)? Where else in the play are these characteristics important?

4. What have the Helmer finances been like in the past? How is their situation about to change?

5. How are Mrs. Linde and Nora alike? Different? Why is it ironic that Nora helps Christine get a job at the bank? How will this affect Krogstad? Nora?

6. How does Ibsen show that Krogstad is a threat when he first appears?

7. Why should Nora's scene with her children in Act 1 not be cut in production? What does it show about Nora and the household?

8. What is Nora's secret "crime"? What is the explanation and justification for it? At the end of the act, what new problems does she face?

## Act 2

9. What is symbolized by the stripped Christmas tree?

10. What is implied about Nora's self-perceptions when she calls herself "your little squirrel" and "your skylark"?

11. After sending Krogstad's dismissal, Torvald tells Nora that "You will see I am man enough to take everything upon myself" (speech 135). How does this speech conform to Nora's hopes? How is it ironic?

12. Why does Nora flirt with Dr. Rank? How and why does he distress her?

13. Why does Nora dance the Tarantella so wildly?

14. What is the "wonderful thing" that Nora is waiting for?

## Act 3

15. Explain Christine's past rejection of Krogstad. Why will she accept him now? How will their union differ from the Helmers' marriage?

16. What does Christine decide to do about Krogstad's letter? Why?

17. Explain the reactions of Torvald and Nora to the death of Dr. Rank.

18. Describe Torvald's reaction to Krogstad's first letter. How does Nora respond to Torvald? How do you respond to him? Why?

19. Explain what Nora learns about Torvald, herself, her marriage, and her identity as a woman as a result of Torvald's responses. Why does she decide to leave?

## General Questions

1. Which elements and aspects of *A Dollhouse* are most and least realistic? Explain.

2. Consider Ibsen's symbolism, with reference to Dr. Rank, macaroons, the Christmas tree, the presents, the locked mailbox, the dance, Nora's black shawl, her change of clothing in Act 3, and the door slam at the play's close.

3. Is Nora a victim of circumstances or a villain who brings about problems? What is Ibsen's view? What is yours? Why?

4. Describe the "role-playing" in the Helmer marriage. Does any evidence suggest that Nora knows she is playing a role? What degree of self-awareness, if any, characterizes Torvald's role-playing?

5. When Nora asks Torvald to restore Krogstad's job, Torvald refuses on the ground that he should not give in to his wife's pressure (Act 2, speech 113). Later, he claims that their marriage is destroyed, but that they should keep up the appearance of marital stability (Act 3, speech 242). In the light of such statements, describe Torvald's character. What concerns him most about life and marriage?

6. A major theme in the play is that weakness and corruption are passed from generation to generation. Examine this theme in connection with Krogstad and his sons, Nora and her children, Nora and her father, and Dr. Rank.

7. Discuss the ideas about individual growth, marriage, and social convention in the play. How are these ideas developed and related? Which character most closely embodies Ibsen's ideas?

8. Write an essay about any or all of the following questions:
    a. Is *A Dollhouse* a comedy, a tragedy, or something in between?
    b. How do the play's characters change for the better (or worse)?
    c. How negative, or affirmative, is the conclusion? Why?

## LANGSTON HUGHES (1902–1967)

*[For a discussion of Hughes's early life and career, and of his work in poetry, please see pages 761–764.]*

In 1931, just before he reached the age of thirty, and while he was still beginning his writing career, Hughes traveled to Russia. He spent a year there, and worked on a Soviet film about racial relations in the United States. When he returned he was filled with ideas, and his writing continued in the direction of exposing racism and inequality in America. A major result was his first collection of stories, *The Ways of White Folks*, which came out in 1934. This was a book in which he fictionalizes his disaffection with the condition of African Americans both in the South and in the North. One of these stories was "Father and Son," a version of the material that he turned into his two-act play *Mulatto*. The play was produced at the Vanderbilt Theater in New York in October 1935, and had a run of 373 performances—the record at that time for a Broadway play by an African-American dramatist.

## Hughes and the African-American Theater after 1920

At that time, the growing African-American theater was dominated by two major themes, the first being the customs and problems of Southern blacks. The most pressing problem was the cruelty and injustice of lynching. Angelina Weld Grimke's *Rachael* (1920) and James Miller's *Never No More* (1932) openly condemned the practice. Dennis Donaghue's *Legal Murder* (1934) was an attack on the false conviction for rape of nine young black men from Scottsboro, Alabama, a topic that Hughes also treated in his early drama *Scottsboro Limited: Four Poems and a Play in Verse* (1932). The second major theme concerned the adjustments that blacks needed to make after they left the South and migrated to cities in the North. Frank Wilson's *Meek Mose* was perhaps the most optimistic of these plays, in which dispossessed blacks discover oil on their new property. More typical were Garland Anderson's *Appearances* (1925), about how a black bellhop overcomes false charges of rape, and Wallace Thurman's *Harlem* (1929), about the difficulties of a black family. This theme also dominates Lorraine Hansberry's *A Raisin in the Sun* (1959), the classic drama that marked the coming of age of post-World War II African-American playwrights.

## Hughes's Career as a Dramatist

Although Hughes is not thought of principally as a dramatist, he wrote plays throughout his career. In addition to the plays already mentioned, he wrote *Little Ham* (1936) and *Soul Gone Home* (1937), a short fantasy play. As the first production for the radical Suitcase Theater, which he founded after returning as a correspondent from the Spanish Civil War, he wrote *Don't You Want to Be Free* (1938). He collaborated with Arna Bontemps in *When the Jack Hollers* (1936) and with Zora Neale Hurston in *Mule Bone* (reissued in 1991). In 1948 he wrote the lyrics for the Kurt Weill and Elmer Rice musical *Street Scene*, perhaps the best known of the plays in which he was involved. In 1951 he produced a libretto, *Just Around the Corner*, and in 1957 he wrote *Simply Heavenly*, a blues-musical play featuring the character Jesse Semple, whom he had created as a character in his weekly columns for the *Chicago Defender*. Although *Simply Heavenly* (which is a musical version of an earlier play, *Simple Takes a Wife*) concludes optimistically, one can find within it the serious theme of frustration resulting from the difficulties that African Americans experience in seeking identity and recognition. Semple says, at one point:

> I'm broke, busted, and disgusted. And just spent mighty near my last nickel for a paper— and there ain't no news in it about colored folks. Unless we commit murder, robbery or rape, or are being chased by a mob, do we get on the front page, or hardly on the back. (I.5)

Hughes's interests in the last decades of his life were in the musical theater, particularly the introduction of gospel-related music and jazz. Three of his major efforts were *Black Nativity* (1961), *The Gospel Glory* (1962), and *Jericho-Jim Crow* (1964). His output as a dramatist was indeed great, even if it may be overshadowed by his preeminence as a poet and writer of fiction.

## *Mulatto* and the Reality of the Southern Black Experience

Hughes's *Mulatto* is one of his plays dealing with life in the South during the 1930s, a time when the system of white control over blacks was absolute and uncompromisingly harsh and brutal. Hughes's first conception of the play—a troubled relationship between father and son—is a perennial one. Colonel Tom Norwood and Robert Lewis, his mulatto son, recognize their relationship but also hate and reject each other. In *Mulatto* the realistic cause of conflict is the "color line"—the symbolic line that people of different races must cross in order to accept each other as human beings. Acceptance is an ideal goal, just as the color line is an insurmountable obstacle in the society that the play depicts. The lack of ability or will to cross the line governs the pattern of action and also the violent outcome. Colonel Norwood has lived in the same house with Cora Lewis for many years, and they do well together as long as he is not confronted with the issue of his paternity or challenged about his control over the plantation. There is no way he can recognize the four "yard blacks" on his plantation as his legitimate children, however, unless he is willing to forsake his identity as a white.

There are many other marks of dramatic realism, particularly the exploitation of black women (described in Act 1, speech 61), the front entrance of the Norwood house, Robert's complaints about Miss Gray, and his speeding with the Ford. All of his so-called "uppity" actions would not be unacceptable to white society if Robert were white, but because he is black they indicate a state of revolt. In addition, Robert's identity as half white, half black—he is called "yellow" by Colonel Tom—leaves him in an anomalous position, for he is not "white" enough to be equal or "black" enough to be subservient. The reality of his situation leads him to hate both whites and blacks alike, and the sudden eruption of his seething anger leads to his violence.

*Mulatto* reflects the reality of language in the South of the 1930s. Hughes's blacks, except for Robert and Sallie, use southern black vernacular (called "darky talk" by Hughes). The introduction of such speech in literature was controversial at the time. Many black intellectuals who had also been a part of the Harlem Renaissance believed that dialect should be shunned, on the principle that it reinforced negative African-American stereotypes. However, Hughes believed using the vernacular was correct because it was truthful and realistic, enabling writers to demonstrate that blacks are not stereotypes, that they face human problems just like everyone else, and that they succeed and fail just like everyone else. Moreover, there were precedents for the realistic use of dialect that had been set by Mark Twain in *Tom Sawyer* and *Huckleberry Finn*, both of which are acknowledged classics of American literature.

*Mulatto* is one of Hughes's most important plays. In 1950 he refashioned it as a libretto, titled *The Barrier*, which was set to music by the composer Jan Meyerowitz. In addition, the play was translated into Spanish and published in South America in 1954.

# Mulatto (1935)

### CHARACTERS

**Colonel Thomas Norwood.** Plantation owner, a still vigorous man of about sixty, nervous, refined, quick-tempered, and commanding; a widower who is the father of four living mulatto children by his Negro housekeeper.

**Cora Lewis.** A brown woman in her forties who has kept the house and been the mistress of Colonel Norwood for some thirty years.

**William Lewis.** The oldest son of Cora Lewis and the Colonel; a fat, easy-going, soft looking mulatto of twenty-eight; married.

**Sallie Lewis.** The seventeen-year-old daughter, very light with sandy hair and freckles, who could pass for white.

**Robert Lewis [Bert].** Eighteen, the youngest boy; strong and well-built; a light mulatto with ivory-yellow skin and proud thin features like his father's; as tall as the Colonel, with the same gray-blue eyes, but with curly black hair instead of brown; of a fiery, impetuous temper—immature and willful—resenting his blood and the circumstances of his birth.

**Fred Higgins.** A close friend of Colonel Norwood; a county politician; fat and elderly, conventionally Southern.

**Sam.** An old Negro retainer, a personal servant of the Colonel.

**Billy.** The small son of William Lewis; a chubby brown kid about five.

**Talbot.** The overseer.

**Mose.** An elderly Negro, chauffeur for Mr. Higgins.

**A Storekeeper.**

**An Undertaker.**

**Undertaker's Helper.** Voice offstage only.

**The Mob.**

## ACT 1

*TIME. An afternoon in early fall.*

*SETTING. The same.*

*ACTION. The living room of the Big House on a plantation in Georgia. Rear center of the room, a vestibule with double doors leading to the porch; at each side of the doors, a large window with lace curtains and green shades; at left a broad flight of stairs leading to the second floor; near the stairs, downstage, a doorway leading to the dining room and kitchen; opposite at right of stage, a door to the library. The room is furnished in the long outdated horsehair and walnut style of the nineties; a crystal chandelier, a large old-fashioned rug, a marble-topped table, upholstered chairs. At the right there is a small cabinet. It is a very clean, but somewhat shabby and rather depressing room, dominated by a large oil painting of NORWOOD's wife of his youth on the center wall. The windows are raised. The afternoon sunlight streams in.*

*ACTION. As the curtain rises, the stage is empty. The door at the right opens and COLONEL NORWOOD enters, crossing the stage toward the stairs, his watch in his hand. Looking up, he shouts:.*

NORWOOD: Cora! Oh Cora!

CORA: [*Heard above*] Yes, sir, Colonel Tom.

NORWOOD: I want to know if that child of yours means to leave here this afternoon?

CORA: [*At head of steps now*] Yes, sir, she's goin' directly. I's gettin' her ready now, packin' up an' all. 'Course, she wants to tell you goodbye 'fore she leaves.

5    NORWOOD: Well, send her down here. Who's going to drive her to the railroad? The train leaves at three—and it's after two now. You ought to know you can't drive ten miles in no time.

CORA: [*Above*] Her brother's gonna drive her. Bert. He ought to be back here most any time now with the Ford.

NORWOOD: [*Stopping on his way back to the library*] Ought to be back here? Where's he gone?

CORA: [*Coming downstairs nervously*] Why, he driv in town 'fore noon, Colonel Tom. Said he were lookin' for some tubes or somethin' 'nother by de mornin' mail for de radio he's been riggin' up out in de shed.

NORWOOD: Who gave him permission to be driving off in the middle of the morning? I bought that Ford to be used when I gave orders for it to be used, not . . .

10   CORA: Yes, sir, Colonel Tom, but . . .

NORWOOD: But what? [*Pausing. Then deliberately*] Cora, if you want that hardheaded yellow son of yours to get along around here, he'd better listen to me. He's no more than any other black buck on this plantation—due to work like the rest of 'em. I don't take such a performance from nobody under me—driving off in the middle of the day to town, after I've told him to bend his back in that cotton. How's Talbot going to keep the rest of those darkies working right if that boy's allowed to set that kind of an example? Just because Bert's your son, and I've been damn fool enough to send him off to school for five or six years, he thinks he has a right to privileges, acting as if he owned this place since he's been back here this summer.

CORA: But, Colonel Tom . . .

NORWOOD: Yes, I know what you're going to say. I don't give a damn about him! There's no nigger-child of mine, yours, ours—no darkie—going to disobey me. I put him in that field to work, and he'll stay on this plantation till I get ready to let him go. I'll tell Talbot to use the whip on him, too, if he needs it. If it hadn't been that he's yours, he'd-a had a taste of it the other day. Talbot's a damn good overseer, and no saucy, lazy Nigras stay on this plantation and get away with it. [*To CORA*] Go on back upstairs and see about getting Sallie out of here. Another word from you and I won't send your [*Sarcastically*] pretty little half-white daughter anywhere, either. Schools for darkies! Huh! If you take that boy of yours for an example, they do 'em more harm than good. He's learned nothing in college but impudence, and he'll stay here on this place and work for me awhile before he gets back to any more schools. [*He starts across the room.*]

CORA: Yes, sir, Colonel Tom. [*Hesitating*] But he's just young, sir. And he was mighty broke up when you said last week he couldn't go back to de campus. [*COLONEL NORWOOD turns and looks at CORA commandingly. Understanding, she murmurs*] Yes, sir. [*She starts upstairs, but turns back.*] Can't I run and fix you a cool drink, Colonel Tom?

NORWOOD: No, damn you! Sam'll do it.                                                                                    15

CORA: [*Sweetly*] Go set down in de cool, then, Colonel. 'Taint good for you to be goin' on this way in de heat. I'll talk to Robert maself soon's he comes in. He don't mean nothing—just smart and young and kinder careless, Colonel Tom, like ma mother said you used to be when you was eighteen.

NORWOOD: Get on upstairs, Cora. Do I have to speak again? Get on! [*He pulls the cord of the servants' bell.*]

CORA: [*On the steps*] Does you still be in the mind to tell Sallie good-bye?

NORWOOD: Send her down here as I told you. [*Impatiently*] Where's Sam? Send him here first. [*Fuming*] Looks like he takes his time to answer that bell. You colored folks are running the house to suit yourself nowadays.

CORA: [*Coming downstairs again and going toward the door under the steps*] I'll get Sam for you.       20

[*CORA exits left. NORWOOD paces nervously across the floor. Goes to the window and looks out down the road. Takes a cigar from his pocket, sits in a chair with it unlighted, scowling. Rises, goes toward servants' bell and rings it again violently as SAM enters, out of breath.*]

NORWOOD: What the hell kind of a tortoise race is this? I suppose you were out in the sun somewhere sleeping?

SAM: No, sah, Colonel Norwood. Just tryin' to get Miss Sallie's valises down to de yard so's we can put 'em in de Ford, sah.

NORWOOD: [*Out of patience*] Huh! Darkies waiting on darkies! I can't get service in my own house. Very well. [*Loudly*] Bring me some whiskey and soda, and ice in a glass. Is that damn Frigidaire working right? Or is Livonia still too thickheaded to know how to run it? Any ice cubes in the thing?

SAM: Yes, sah, Colonel, yes, sah. [*Backing toward door left*] 'Scuse me, please sah, but [*As NORWOOD turns toward library*] Cora say for me to ask you is it all right to bring that big old trunk what you give Sallie down by de front steps. We ain't been able to tote it down them narrer little back steps, sah. Cora, say, can we bring it down de front way through here?

NORWOOD: No other way? [*SAM shakes his head*] Then pack it on through the back, quick. Don't       25
let me catch you carrying any of Sallie's baggage out of that front door here. You-all'll be wanting to go in and out the front way next. [*Turning away, complaining to himself*] Darkies have been getting mighty fresh in this part of the country since the war. The damn Germans should've . . . [*To SAM*] Don't take that trunk out that front door.

SAM: [*Evilly, in a cunning voice*] I's seen Robert usin' de front door—when you ain't here, and he comes up from de cabin to see his mammy. [*SALLIE, the daughter, appears at the top of the stairs, but hesitates about coming down.*]

NORWOOD: Oh, you have, have you? Let me catch him and I'll break his young neck for him. [*Yelling at SAM*] Didn't I tell you some whiskey and soda an hour ago?

[*SAM exits left. SALLIE comes shyly down the stairs and approaches her father. She is dressed in a little country-style coat-suit ready for traveling. Her features are Negroid, although her skin is very fair. COLONEL NORWOOD gazes down at her without saying a word as she comes meekly toward him, half-frightened.*]

SALLIE: I just wanted to tell you goodbye, Colonel Norwood, and thank you for letting me go back to school another year, and for letting me work here in the house all summer where mama is. [*Norwood says nothing. The girl continues in a strained voice as if making a speech*] You mighty nice to us colored folks certainly, and mama says you the best white man in Georgia. [*Still Norwood says nothing. The girl continues.*] You been mighty nice to your—I mean to us colored children, letting my sister and me go off to school. The principal says I'm doing pretty well and next year I can go to Normal and learn to be a teacher. [*Raising her eyes*] You reckon I can, Colonel Tom?

NORWOOD: Stand up straight and let me see how you look. [*Backing away*] Hum-m-m! Getting kinder grown, ain't you? Do they teach you in that school to have good manners, and not be afraid of work, *and to respect white folks*?

30  SALLIE: Yes, sir, I been taking up cooking and sewing, too.

NORWOOD: Well, that's good. As I recall it, that school turned your sister out a right smart cook. Cora tells me she's got a good job in some big hotel in Chicago. I'm thinking about you going on up North there with her in a year or two. You're getting too old to be around here, and too womanish. [*He puts his hands on her arms as if feeling her flesh*]

SALLIE: [*Drawing back slightly*] But I want to live down here with mama. I want to teach school in that there empty school house by the Cross Roads what hasn't had a teacher for five years.

[*Sam has been standing with the door cracked, overhearing the conversation. He enters with the drink and places it on the table, right. Norwood sits down, leaving the girl standing, as Sam pours out a drink.*]

NORWOOD: Don't get that into your head, now. There's been no teacher there for years—and there won't be any teacher there, either. Cotton teaches these pickaninnies enough around here. Some of 'em's too smart as it is. The only reason I did have a teacher there once was to get you young ones o' Cora's educated. I gave you all a chance and I hope you appreciate it. [*He takes a long drink.*] Don't know why I did it. No other white man in these parts ever did it, as I know of. [*To Sam*] Get out of here! [*Sam exits left*] Guess I couldn't stand to see Cora's kids working around here dumb as the rest of these no-good darkies—need a dozen of 'em to chop one row of cotton, or to keep a house clean. Or maybe I didn't want Talbot eyeing you gals. [*Taking another drink*] Anyhow, I'm glad you and Bertha turned out right well. Yes, hum-m-m! [*Straightening up*] You know I tried to do something for those brothers of yours, too, but William's stupid as an ox—good for work, though—and that Robert's just an impudent, hardheaded, yellow young fool. I'm gonna break his damn neck for him if he don't watch out. Or else put Talbot on him.

SALLIE: [*Suddenly frightened*] Please, sir, don't put the overseer on Bert, Colonel Tom. He was the smartest boy at school, Bert was. On the football team, too. Please, sir, Colonel Tom. Let brother work here in the house, or somewhere else where Talbot can't mistreat him. He ain't used . . .

35  NORWOOD: [*Rising*] Telling me what to do, heh? [*Staring at her sternly*] I'll use the back of my hand across your face if you don't hush. [*He takes another drink. The noise of a Ford is heard outside.*] That's Bert now, I reckon. He's to take you to the railroad line, and while you're riding with him, you better put some sense into his head. And tell him I want to see him as soon as he gets back here. [*Cora enters left with a bundle and an umbrella. Sam and William come downstairs with a big square trunk, and exit hurriedly, left.*]

SALLIE: Yes, sir, I'll tell him.

CORA: Colonel Tom, Sallie ain't got much time now. [*To the girl*] Come on, chile. Bert's here. Yo' big brother and Sam and Livonia and everybody's all waiting at de back door to say goodbye. And your baggage is being packed in. [*Noise of another car is heard outside.*] Who

else is that there coming up de drive? [*CORA looks out the window.*] Mr. Higgins' car,
Colonel Tom. Reckon he's coming to see you . . . Hurry up out o' this front room, Sallie.
Here, take these things of your'n [*Hands her the bundle and parasol*] while I opens de door
for Mr. Higgins. [*In a whisper*] Hurry up, chile! Get out! [*NORWOOD turns toward the front
door as CORA goes to open it*]

SALLIE: [*Shyly to her father*] Goodbye, Colonel Tom.

NORWOOD: [*His eyes on the front door, scarcely noticing the departing SALLIE, he motions.*] Yes, yes
goodbye! Get on now! [*CORA opens the front door as her daughter exits left.*] Well, well! Howdy
do, Fred. Come in, come in! [*CORA holds the outer door of the vestibule wide as FRED HIGGINS enters with rheumatic dignity, supported on the arm of his chauffeur, MOSE, a very black Negro in a
slouchy uniform. CORA closes the door and exits left hurriedly, following SALLIE.*]

NORWOOD: [*Smiling*] How's the rheumatiz today? Women or licker or heat must've made it  40
worse—from the looks of your speed!

HIGGINS: [*Testily, sitting down puffing and blowing in a big chair*] I'm in no mood for fooling, Tom,
not now. [*To MOSE*] All right. [*The CHAUFFEUR exits front. HIGGINS continues angrily.*] Norwood,
that damned yellow nigger buck of yours that drives that new Ford tried his best just now
to push my car off the road, then got in front of me and blew dust in my face for the last
mile coming down to your gate, trying to beat me in here—which he did. Such a deliberate
piece of impudence I don't know if I've ever seen out of a nigger before in all the sixty
years I've lived in this country. [*The noise of the Ford is heard going out the drive, and the cries
of the NEGROES shouting farewells to SALLIE. HIGGINS listens indignantly.*] What kind of crazy
coons have you got on your place, anyhow? Sounds like a black Baptist picnic to me.
[*Pointing to the window with his cane*] Tom, listen to that.

NORWOOD: [*Flushing*] I apologize to you, Fred, for each and every one of my darkies. [*SAM
enters with more ice and another glass.*] Permit me to offer you a drink. I realize I've got to
tighten down here.

HIGGINS: Mose tells me that was Cora's boy in that Ford—and that young black fool is what I
was coming here to talk to you about today. That boy! He's not gonna be around here
long—not the way he's acting. The white folks in town'll see to that. Knowing he's one of
your yard niggers, Norwood, I thought I ought to come and tell you. The white folks at
the Junction aren't intending to put up with him much longer. And I don't know what
good the jail would do him once he got in there.

NORWOOD: [*Tensely*] What do you mean, Fred—jail? Don't I always take care of the folks on
my plantation without any help from the Junction's police force? Talbot can do more with
an unruly black buck than your marshal.

HIGGINS: Warn't lookin' at it that way, Tom. I was thinking how weak the doors to that jail is.  45
They've broke 'em down and lynched four niggers to my memory since it's been built.
After what happened this morning, you better keep that yellow young fool out o' town
from now on. It might not be safe for him around there—today, or no other time.

NORWOOD: What the hell? [*Perturbed*] He went in just now to take his sister to the depot. Damn
it, I hope no ruffians'll break up my new Ford. What was it, Fred, about this morning?

HIGGINS: You haven't heard? Why, it's all over town already. He sassed out Miss Gray in the
post office over a box of radio tubes that come by mail.

NORWOOD: He did, heh?

HIGGINS: Seems like the stuff was sent C.O.D. and got here all smashed up, so he wouldn't
take it. Paid his money first before he saw the box was broke. Then wanted the money
order back. Seems like the post office can't give money orders back—rule against it.
Your nigger started to argue, and the girl at the window—Miss Gray—got scared and
yelled for some of the mail clerks. They threw Bert out of the office, that's all. But that's
enough. Lucky nothing more didn't happen. [*Indignantly*] That Bert needs a damn good

beating—talking back to a white woman—and I'd like to give it to him myself, the way he kicked the dust up in my eyes all the way down the road coming out here. He was mad, I reckon. That's one yellow buck don't know his place, Tom, and it's your fault he don't—sending 'em off to be educated.

50  NORWOOD: Well, by God, I'll show him. I wish I'd have known it before he left here just now.

HIGGINS: Well, he's sure got mighty aggravating ways for a buck his color to have. Drives down the main street and don't stop for nobody, white or black. Comes in my store and if he ain't waited on as quick as the white folks are, he walks out and tells the clerk his money's as good as a white man's any day. Said last week standing out on my store front that he wasn't *all* nigger no how; said his name was Norwood—not Lewis, like the rest of his family—and part of your plantation here would be his when you passed out—and all that kind of stuff, boasting to the walleyed coons listening to him.

NORWOOD: [*Astounded*] Well, I'll be damned!

HIGGINS: Now, Tom, you know that don't go 'round these parts 'o Georgia, nor nowhere else in the South. A darkie's got to keep in his place down here. Ruinous to other niggers hearing that talk, too. All this postwar propaganda on the radio about freedom and democracy— why the niggers think it's meant for them! And that Eleanor Roosevelt,° she ought to been muzzled. She's driving our niggers crazy—your boy included! Crazy! Talking about civil rights. Ain't been no race trouble in our country for three years—since the Deekin's lynch-ing—but I'm telling you, Norwood, you better see that that buck of yours goes away from here. I'm speaking on the quiet, but I can see ahead. And what happened this morning about them radio tubes wasn't none too good.

NORWOOD: [*Beside himself with rage*] A black ape! I—I . . .

55  HIGGINS: You been too decent to your darkies, Norwood. That's what's the matter with you. And then the whole country suffers from a lot of impudent bucks who take lessons from your crowd. Folks been kicking about that, too. Guess you know it. Maybe that's the rea-son you didn't get that nomination for committeeman a few years back.

NORWOOD: Maybe 'tis, Higgins. [*Rising and pacing the room*] God damn niggers! [*Furiously*] Everything turns on niggers, niggers, niggers! No wonder Yankees call this the Black Belt! [*He pours a large drink of whiskey.*]

HIGGINS: [*Soothingly*] Well, let's change the subject. Hand me my glass, there, too.

NORWOOD: Pardon me, Fred. [*He puts ice in his friend's glass and passes him the bottle.*]

HIGGINS: Tom, you get excited too easy for warm weather . . . Don't ever show black folks they got you going, though. I think sometimes that's where you make your mistake. Keep calm, keep calm—and then you command. Best plantation manager I ever had never raised his voice to a nigger—and they were scared to death of him.

60  NORWOOD: Have a smoke. [*Pushes cigars toward HIGGINS*]

HIGGINS: You ought've married again, Tom—brought a white woman out here on this damn place o' yours. A woman could help you run things. Women have soft ways, but they can keep things humming. Nothing but blacks in the house—a man gets soft like niggers are inside. [*Puffing at cigar*] And living with a colored woman! Of course, I know we all have 'em—I didn't know you could make use of a white girl till I was past twenty. Thought too much o' white women for that—but I've given many a yellow gal a baby in my time. [*Long puff at cigar*] But for a man's own house you need a wife, not a black woman.

NORWOOD: Reckon you're right, Fred, but it's too late to marry again now. [*Shrugging his shoul-ders*] Let's get off of darkies and women for awhile. How's crops? [*Sitting down*] How's politics going?

---

°53 *Eleanor Roosevelt*: Eleanor Roosevelt (1884–1962), the wife of President Franklin D. Roosevelt, was an outspoken champion of minority causes.

HIGGINS: Well, I guess you know the Republicans is trying to stir up trouble for us in Washington. I wish the South had more men like Bilbo and Rankin° there. But, say, by the way, Lawyer Hotchkiss wants to see us both about that budget money next week. He's got some real Canadian stuff at his office, in his filing case, too—brought back from his vacation last summer. Taste better'n this old mountain juice we get around here. Not meaning to insult your drinks, Tom, but just remarking. I serve the same as you myself, label and all.

NORWOOD: [*Laughing*] I'll have you know, sir, that this is prewar licker, sir!

HIGGINS: Hum-m-m! Well, it's got me feelin' better'n I did when I come in here—whatever it    65
is. [*Puffs at his cigar*] Say, how's your cotton this year?

NORWOOD: Doin' right well, specially down in the south field. Why not drive out that road when you leave and take a look at it? I'll ride down with you. I want to see Talbot, anyhow.

HIGGINS: Well, let's be starting. I got to be back at the Junction by four o'clock. Promised to let that boy of mine have the car to drive over to Thomasville for a dance tonight.

NORWOOD: One more shot before we go. [*He pours out drinks.*] The young ones must have their fling, I reckon. When you and I grew up down here it used to be a carriage and the best pair of black horses when you took the ladies out—now it's an automobile. That's a good lookin' new car of yours, too.

HIGGINS: Right nice.

NORWOOD: Been thinking about getting a new one myself, but money's been kinder tight this    70
year, and conditions are none too good yet, either. Reckon that's why everybody's so restless. [*He walks toward stairs calling.*] Cora! Oh, Cora! . . . If I didn't have a few thousand put away, I'd feel the pinch myself. [*As CORA appears on the stairs.*] Bring me my glasses up there by the side of my bed . . . Better whistle for Mose, hadn't I, Higgins? He's probably 'round back with some of his women. [*Winking*] You know I got some nice black women in this yard.

HIGGINS: Oh, no, not Mose. I got my servants trained to stay in their places—right where I want 'em—while they're working for me. Just open the door and tell him to come in here and help me out. [*NORWOOD goes to the door and calls the CHAUFFEUR. MOSE enters and assists his master out to the car. CORA appears with the glasses, goes to the vestibule and gets the COLONEL'S hat and cane which she hands him.*]

NORWOOD: [*To CORA*] I want to see that boy o' yours soon as I get back. That won't be long, either. And tell him to put up that Ford of mine and don't touch it again.

CORA: Yes, sir, I'll have him waiting here. [*In a whisper*] It's hot weather, Colonel Tom. Too much of this licker makes your heart upset. It ain't good for you, you know. [*NORWOOD pays her no attention as he exits toward the car. The noise of the departing motor is heard. Cora begins to tidy up the room. She takes a glass from a side table. She picks up a doily that was beneath the glass and looks at it long and lovingly. Suddenly she goes to the door left and calls toward the kitchen.*] William, you William! Com'ere, I want to show you something. Make haste, son. [*As CORA goes back toward the table, her eldest son, WILLIAM enters carrying a five-year-old boy.*] Look here at this purty doily yo' sister made this summer while she been here. She done learned all about sewing and making purty things at school. Ain't it nice, son?

WILLIAM: Sho' is. Sallie takes after you, I reckon. She's a smart little crittur, ma. [*Sighs*] De Lawd knows, I was dumb at school. [*To his child*] Get down, Billy, you's too heavy. [*He puts the boy on the floor*] This here sewin's really fine.

BILLY: [*Running toward the big upholstered chair and jumping up and down on the spring seat*]    75
Gityap! I's a mule driver. Haw! Gee!

CORA: You Billy, get out of that chair 'fore I skins you alive. Get on into de kitchen, sah.

---

°63 *Bilbo, Rankin*: Theodore Bilbo (1877–1947), senator from Mississippi from 1935 to 1947, and John Eliot Rankin (1882–1960), Mississippi representative to the House from 1921 to 1953, were both noted advocates of white supremacy.

BILLY: I'm playin' horsie, grandma. [*Jumps up in the chair*] Horsie! Horsie!

CORA: Get! That's de Colonel's favorite chair. If he knows any little darkie's been jumpin' on it, he raise sand. Get on, now.

BILLY: Ole Colonel's ma grandpa, ain't he? Ain' he ma white grandpa?

80  WILLIAM: [*Snatching the child out of the chair*] Boy, I'm gonna fan your hide if you don't hush!

CORA: Shs-ss-s! You Billy, hush yo' mouth! Chile, where you hear that? [*To her son*] Some o' you all been talking too much in front o' this chile. [*To the boy*] Honey, go on in de kitchen till yo' daddy come. Get a cookie from 'Vonia and set down on de back porch. [*Little* BILLY *exits left*]

WILLIAM: Ma, you know it 'twarn't me told him. Bert's the one been goin' all over de plantation since he come back from Atlanta remindin' folks right out we's Colonel Norwood's chilluns.

CORA: [*Catching her breath*] Huh!

WILLIAM: He comes down to my shack tellin' Billy and Marybell they got a white man for grandpa. He's gonna get my chilluns in trouble sho'—like he got himself in trouble when Colonel Tom whipped him.

85  CORA: Ten or 'leven years ago, warn't it?

WILLIAM: And Bert's *sho'* in trouble now. Can't go back to that college like he could-a if he'd-a had any sense. You can't fool with white folks—an de Colonel ain't never really liked Bert since that there first time he beat him, either.

CORA: No, he ain't. Leastwise, he ain't understood him. [*Musing sadly in a low voice*] Time Bert was 'bout seven, warn't it? Just a little bigger'n yo' Billy.

WILLIAM: Yes.

CORA: Went runnin' up to Colonel Tom out in de horse stables when de Colonel was showin' off his horses—I 'members so well—to fine white company from town. Lawd, that boy's always been foolish! He went runnin' up and grabbed a-holt de Colonel and yelled right in front o' de white folks' faces, "O, papa, Cora say de dinner's ready, papa!" Ain't never called him papa before, and I don't know where he got it from. And Colonel Tom knocked him right backwards under de horse's feet.

90  WILLIAM: And when de company were gone, he beat that boy unmerciful.

CORA: I thought sho' he were gonna kill ma chile that day. And he were mad at me, too, for months. Said I was teaching you chilluns who they pappy were. Up till then Bert had been his favorite little colored child round here.

WILLIAM: Sho' had.

CORA: But he never like him no more. That's why he sent him off to school so soon to stay, winter and summer, all these years. I had to beg and plead to have him home this summer—but I's sorry now I ever got that boy back here again.

WILLIAM: He's sho' growed more like de Colonel all de time, ain't he? Bert thinks he's a real white man hisself now. Look at de first thing he did when he come home, he ain't seen de Colonel in six years—and Bert sticks out his hand fo' to shake hands with him!

95  CORA: Lawd! That chile!

WILLIAM: Just like white folks! And de Colonel turns his back and walks off. Can't blame him. He ain't used to such doings from colored folks. God knows what's got into Bert since he come back. He's acting like a fool—just like he was a boss man round here. Won't even say "Yes, sir" and "No, sir" no more to de white folks. Talbot asked him warn't he gonna work in de field this mornin'. Bert say "No!" and turn and walk away. White man so mad, I could see him nearly foam at de mouth. If he warn't yo' chile, ma, he'd been knocked in de head fo' now.

CORA: You's right.

WILLIAM: And you can't talk to him. I tried to tell him something the other day, but he just laughed at me, and said we's all just scared niggers on this plantation. Says he ain't no nigger, no how. He's a Norwood. He's half-white, and he's gonna act like it. [*In amazement at his brother's daring*] And this is Georgia, too!

CORA: I's scared to death for de boy, William. I don't know what to do. De Colonel says he won't send him off to school no mo'. Says he's mo' sassy and impudent now than any nigger he ever seed. Bert never has been like you was, and de girls, quiet and sensible like you knowed you had to be. [*She sits down*] De Colonel say he's gonna make Bert stay here now and work on this plantation like de rest of his niggers. He's gonna show him what color he is. Like that time when he beat him for callin' him "papa." He say he's gwine to teach him his place and make de boy know where he belongs. Seems like me or you can't show him. Colonel Tom has to take him in hand, or these white folks'll kill him around here and then—oh, My God!

WILLIAM: A nigger's just got to know his place in de South, that's all, ain't he, ma?     100

CORA: Yes, son. That's all, I reckon.

WILLIAM: And ma brother's one damn fool nigger. Don't seems like he knows nothin'. He's gonna ruin us all round here. Makin' it bad for everybody.

CORA: Oh, Lawd, have mercy! [*Beginning to cry*] I don't know what to do. De way he's acting up can't go on. Way he's acting to de Colonel can't last. Somethin's gonna happen to ma chile. I had a bad dream last night, too, and I looked out and seed de moon all red with blood. I seed a path o' living blood across this house, I tell you, in my sleep. Oh, Lawd, have mercy! [*Sobbing*] Oh, Lawd, help me in ma troubles. [*The noise of the returning Ford is heard outside. CORA looks up, rises, and goes to the window.*] There's de chile now, William. Run out to de back door and tell him I wants to see him. Bring him in here where Sam and Livonia and de rest of 'em won't hear ever'thing we's sayin'. I got to talk to ma boy. He's ma baby boy, and he don't know de way.

[*Exit WILLIAM through the door left. CORA is wiping her eyes and pulling herself together when the front door is flung open with a bang and ROBERT enters.*]

ROBERT: [*Running to his mother and hugging her teasingly*] Hello, ma! Your daughter got off, and I've come back to keep you company in the parlor! Bring out the cookies and lemonade. *Mister* Norwood's here!

CORA: [*Beginning to sob anew*] Take yo' hands off me, boy! Why don't you mind? Why don't  105 you mind me?

ROBERT: [*Suddenly serious, backing away*] Why, mamma, what's the matter? Did I scare you? Your eyes are all wet! Has somebody been telling you 'bout this morning?

CORA: [*Not heeding his words*] Why don't you mind me, son? Ain't I told you and told you not to come in that front door, never? [*Suddenly angry*] Will somebody have to beat it into you? What's got wrong with you when you was away at that school? What am I gonna do?

ROBERT: [*Carelessly*] Oh, I knew that the Colonel wasn't here. I passed him and old man Higgins on the road down by the south patch. He wouldn't even look at me when I waved at him. [*Half playfully*] Anyhow, isn't this my old man's house? Ain't I his son and heir? [*Grandly, strutting around*] Am I not Mr. Norwood, Junior?

CORA: [*Utterly serious*] I believe you goin' crazy, Bert. I believes you wants to get us all killed or run away or something awful like that. I believes . . . [*WILLIAM enters left*]

WILLIAM: Where's Bert? He ain't come round back—[*Seeing his brother in the room*] How'd you  110 get in here?

ROBERT: [*Grinning*] Houses have front doors.

WILLIAM: Oh, usin' de front door like de white folks, heh? You gwine do that once too much.

ROBERT: Yes, like de white folks. What's a front door for, you rabbit-hearted coon?

WILLIAM: Rabbit-hearted coon's better'n a dead coon any day.

ROBERT: I wouldn't say so. Besides you and me's only half-coons, anyhow, big boy. And I'm  115 gonna act like my white half, not my black half. Get me, kid?

WILLIAM: Well, you ain't gonna act like it long here in de middle o' Georgy. And you ain't gonna act like it when de Colonel's around, either.

ROBERT: Oh, no? My stay down here'll be short and sweet, boy, short and sweet. The old man won't send me away to college no more—so you think I'm gonna stick around and work in the fields? Like fun! I might stay here awhile and teach some o' you darkies to think like men, maybe—till it gets too much for the old Colonel—but no more bowing down to white folks for me—not Robert Norwood.

CORA: Hush, son!

ROBERT: Certainly not right on my own old man's plantation—Georgia or no Georgia.

120 WILLIAM: [*Scornfully*] I hears you.

ROBERT: You can do it if you want to, but I'm ashamed of you. I've been away from here six years. [*Boasting*] I've learned something, seen people in Atlanta, and Richmond, and Washington where the football team went—real colored people who don't have to take off their hats to white folks or let 'em go to bed with their sisters—like that young Higgins boy, asking me what night Sallie was comin' to town. A damn cracker! [*To* CORA] 'Scuse me, ma. [*Continuing*] Back here in these woods maybe Sam and Livonia and you and mama and everybody's got their places fixed for 'em, but not me. [*Seriously*] Nobody's gonna fix a place for me. I'm old man Norwood's son. Nobody fixed a place for him. [*Playfully again*] Look at me. I'm a 'fay boy. [*Pretends to shake his hair back*] See these gray eyes? I got the right to everything everybody else has. [*Punching his brother in the belly*], Don't talk to me, old slavery-time Uncle Tom.

WILLIAM: [*Resentfully*] I ain't playin', boy. [*Pushes younger brother back with some force*] I ain't playin' a-tall.

CORA: All right, chilluns, stop. Stop! And William, you take Billy and go on home. 'Vonia's got to get supper and she don't like no young-uns under her feet in de kitchen. I wants to talk to Bert in here now 'fore Colonel Tom gets back. [*Exit* WILLIAM *left.* CORA *continues to* BERT] Sit down, child, right here a minute and listen.

ROBERT: [*Sitting down*] All right, ma.

125 CORA: Hard as I's worked and begged and humbled maself to get de Colonel to keep you chilluns in school, you comes home wid yo' head full o' stubbornness and yo' mouth full o' sass for me an' de white folks an' everybody. You know can't no colored boy here talk like you's been doin' to no white folks, let alone to de Colonel and that old devil of a Talbot. They ain't gonna stand fo' yo' sass. Not only you, but I 'spects we's all gwine to pay fo' it, every colored soul on this place. I was scared to death today fo' yo' sister, Sallie, scared de Colonel warn't gwine to let her go back to school, neither, 'count o' yo' doins, but he did, thank Gawd—and then you come near makin' her miss de train. Did she have time to get her ticket and all?

ROBERT: Sure! Had to drive like sin to get there with her, though. I didn't mean to be late getting back here for her, ma, but I had a little run-in about them radio tubes in town.

CORA: [*Worried*] What's that?

ROBERT: The tubes was smashed when I got 'em, and I had already made out my money order, so the woman in the post office wouldn't give the three dollars back to me. All I did was explain to her that we could send the tubes back—but she got hot because there were two or three white folks waiting behind me to get stamps, I guess. So she yells at me to move on and not give her any of my "educated nigger talk." So I said, "I'm going to finish showing you these tubes before I move on"—and then she screamed and called the mail clerk working in the back, and told him to throw me out. [*Boasting*] He didn't do it by himself, though. Had to call all the white loafers out in the square to get me through that door.

CORA: [*Fearfully*] Lawd have mercy!

ROBERT: Guess if I hadn't-a had the Ford then, they'd've beat me half-to-death, but when I saw  130
how many crackers there was, I jumped in the car and beat it on away.

CORA: Thank God for that!

ROBERT: Not even a football man[*Half-boasting*] like me could tackle the whole junction. 'Bout
a dozen colored guys standing around, too, and not one of 'em would help me—the
dumb jiggaboos! They been telling me ever since I been here, [*Imitating darky talk*] "You
can't argue wid whut folks, man. You better stay out o' this Junction. You must ain't got no
sense, nigger! You's a fool" . . . Maybe I am a fool, ma—but I didn't want to come back
here nohow.

CORA: I's sorry I sent for you.

ROBERT: Besides you, there ain't nobody in this country but a lot of evil white folks and cowardly niggers. [*Earnstly*] I'm no nigger, anyhow, am I, ma? I'm half-white. The Colonel's
my father—the richest man in the county—and I'm not going to take a lot of stuff from nobody if I do have to stay here, not from the old man either. He thinks I ought to be out
there in the sun working, with Talbot standing over me like I belonged in the chain gang.
Well, he's got another thought coming! [*Stubbornly*] I'm a Norwood—not a field-hand
nigger.

CORA: You means you ain't workin' no mo'?    135

ROBERT: [*Flaring*] No, I'm not going to work in the fields. What did he send me away to school
for—just to come back here and be his servant, or pick his hills of cotton?

CORA: He sent you away to de school because *I* asked him and begged him, and got down on
my knees to him, that's why. [*Quietly*] And now I just wants to make you see some sense,
if you can. I knows, honey, you reads in de books and de papers, and you knows a lot
more'n I do. But, chile, you's in Georgy—and I don't see how it is you don't know where
you's at. This ain't up North—and even up yonder where we hears it's so fine, yo' sister
has to pass for white to get along good.

ROBERT: [*Bitterly*] I know it.

CORA: She ain't workin' in no hotel kitchen like de Colonel thinks. She's in a office typewrit-
ing. And Sallie's studyin' de typewriter, too, at de school, but yo' pappy don't know it. I
knows we ain't s'posed to study nothin' but cookin' and hard workin' here in Georgy.
That's all I ever done, or knowed about. I been workin' on this very place all ma life—
even 'fore I come to live in this Big House. When de Colonel's wife died, I come here, and
borned you chilluns. And de Colonel's been real good to me in his way. Let you all sleep
in this house with me when you was little, and sent you all off to school when you growed
up. Ain't no white man in this county done that with his cullud chilluns before, far as I can
know. But you—Robert, be awful, awful careful! When de Colonel comes back, in a few
minutes, he wants to talk to you. Talk right to him, boy. Talk like you was colored, 'cause
you ain't white.

ROBERT: [*Angrily*] And I'm not black either. Look at me, mama. [*Rising and throwing up his arms*]  140
Don't I look like my father? Ain't I as light as he is? Ain't my eyes gray like his eyes are?
[*The noise of a car is heard outside*] Ain't this our house?

CORA: That's him now. [*Agitated*] Hurry, chile, and let's get out of this room. Come on through
yonder to the kitchen. [*She starts toward the door left.*] And I'll tell him you're here.

ROBERT: I don't want to run into the kitchen. Isn't this our house? [*As* CORA *crosses hurriedly left,*
ROBERT *goes toward the front door*] The Ford is parked out in front, anyway.

CORA: [*At the door left to the rear of the house*] Robert! Robert! [*As* ROBERT *nears the front door,*
COLONEL NORWOOD *enters, almost runs into the boy, stops at the threshold and stares unbelievingly
at his son.* CORA *backs up against the door left.*]

NORWOOD: Get out of here! [*He points toward the door to rear of the house where* CORA *is standing*].

ROBERT: [*Half-smiling*] Didn't you want to talk to me?    145

NORWOOD: Get out of here!

ROBERT: Not that way. [*THE COLONEL raises his cane to strike the boy. CORA screams. BERT draws himself up to his full height, taller than the old man and looking very much like him, pale and proud. The man and the boy face each other. NORWOOD does not strike.*]

NORWOOD: [*In a hoarse whisper*] Get out of here. [*His hand is trembling as he points.*]

CORA: Robert! Come on, son, come on! Oh, my God, come on. [*Opening the door left*]

150 ROBERT: Not that way, ma. [*ROBERT walks proudly out the front door. NORWOOD, in an impotent rage, crosses the room to a small cabinet right, opens it nervously with a key from his pocket, takes out a pistol, and starts toward the front door. CORA overtakes him, seizes his arm, stops him.*]

CORA: He's our son, Tom. [*She sinks slowly to her knees, holding his body.*] Remember, he's our son.

*Curtain*

## ACT 2

### Scene 1

TIME. *After supper. Sunset.*
SETTING. *The same.*
ACTION. *As the curtain rises, the stage is empty. Through the windows the late afternoon sun makes two bright paths toward the footlights. SAM, carrying a tray bearing a whiskey bottle and a bowl of ice, enters left and crosses toward the library. He stoops at the door right, listens a moment, knocks, then opens the door and goes in. In a moment SAM returns. As he leaves the library, he is heard replying to a request of NORWOOD's.*

SAM: Yes, sah, Colonel! Sho' will, sah! Right away, sah! Yes, sah, I'll tell him. [*He closes the door and crosses the stage muttering to himself.*] Six o'clock. Most nigh that now. Better tell Cora to get that boy right in here. Can't nobody else do notin' with that fool Bert but Cora. [*He exits left. Can be heard calling*] Cora! You, Cora . . .

[*Again the stage is empty. Off stage, outside, the bark of a dog is heard, the sound of Negroes singing down the road, the cry of a child. The breeze moves the shadows of leaves and tree limbs across the sun-lit paths from the windows. The door left opens and CORA enters, followed by ROBERT.*]

CORA: [*Softly to ROBERT behind her in the dining room*] It's all right, son. He ain't come out yet, but it's nearly six, and that's when he said he wanted you, but I was afraid maybe you was gonna be late. I sent for you to come up here to de house and eat supper with me in de kitchen. Where'd you eat yo' vittuals at, chile?

ROBERT: Down at Willie's house, ma. After the old man tried to hit me you still want me to hang around and eat up here?

CORA: I wanted you to be here on time, honey, that's all.[*She is very nervous.*] I kinder likes to have you eat with me sometimes, too, but you ain't et up here more'n once this summer. But this evenin' I just wanted you to be here when de Colonel sent word for you, 'cause we's done had enough trouble today.

5 ROBERT: He's not here on time, himself, is he?

CORA: He's in de library. Sam couldn't get him to eat no supper tonight, and I ain't seen him a-tall.

ROBERT: Maybe he wants to see me in the library, then.

CORA: You know he don't 'low no colored folks in there 'mongst his books and things 'cept Sam. Some o' his white friends goes in there, but none o' us.

ROBERT: Maybe he wants to see *me* in there, though.

10 CORA: Can't you never talk sense, Robert? This ain't no time for foolin' and jokin'. Nearly thirty years in this house and I ain't never been in there myself, not once, 'mongst de

Colonel's papers. [*The clock strikes six.*] Stand over yonder and wait till he comes out. I's gwine on upstairs now, so's he can talk to you. And don't aggravate him no mo' for' God's sake. Agree to whatever he say. I's scared fo' you, chile, de way you been actin', and de fool tricks you done today, and de trouble about de post office besides. Don't aggravate him. Fo' yo' sake, honey, 'cause I loves you—and fo' all de po' colored folks on this place what has such a hard time when his humors get on him—agree to whatever he say, will you Bert?

ROBERT:  All right, ma. [*Voice rising*] But he better not start to hit me again.

CORA:  Shs-ss-s! He'll hear you. He's right in there.

ROBERT:  [*Sullenly*] This was the day I ought to have started back to school—like my sister. I stayed my summer out here, didn't I? Why didn't he keep his promise to me? You said if I came home I could go back to college again.

CORA:  Shs-ss-s! He'll be here now. Don't say nothin', chile, I's done all I could.

ROBERT:  All right, ma.

CORA:  [*Approaching the stairs*] I'll be in ma room, honey, where I can hear you when you goes out. I'll come down to de back door and see you 'fore you goes back to de shack. Don't aggravate him, chile.

[*She ascends the stairs. The boy sits down sullenly, left, and stares at the door opposite from which his father must enter. The clock strikes the quarter after six. The shadows of the window curtains have lengthened on the carpet. The sunshine has deepened to a pale orange, and the light paths grow less distinct across the floor. The boy sits up straight in his chair. He looks at the library door. It opens. NORWOOD enters. He is bent and pale. He looks across the room and sees the boy. Suddenly he straightens up. The old commanding look comes into his face. He strides directly across the room toward his son. The boy, half afraid, half defiant, yet sure of himself, rises. Now that ROBERT is standing, the white man turns, goes back to a chair near the table, right, and seats himself. He takes out a cigar, cuts off the end and lights it, and in a voice of mixed condescension and contempt, he speaks to his son. ROBERT remains standing near the chair.*]

NORWOOD:  I don't want to have to beat you another time as I did when you were a child. The next time I might not be able to control myself. I might kill you if I touched you again. I been runnin' this plantation for thirty-five years, and I never had to beat a Nigra as old as you are. I never had to beat one of Cora's children either—but you. The rest of 'em had sense 'nough to keep out of my sight, and to speak to me like they should . . . I don't have any trouble with my colored folks. Never have trouble. They do what I say, or what Mr. Talbot says, and that's all there is to it, I give 'em a chance. If they turn in their crops they get paid. If they're workin' for wages, they get paid. If they want to spend their money on licker, or buy an old car, or fix up their cabins, they can. Do what they choose long as they know their places and it don't hinder their work. And to Cora's young ones I give all the chances any colored folks ever had in these parts. More'n many a white child's had. I sent you all off to school. Let Bertha go on up North when she got grown and educated. Intend to let Sallie do the same. Gave your brother William that house he's living in when he got married, pay him for his work, help him out if he needs it. None of my darkies suffer. Sent you to college. Would have kept on, would have sent you back today, but I don't intend to pay for no darky, or white boy either if I had one, that acts the way you've been acting. And certainly for no black fool. Now I want to know what's wrong with you? I don't usually talk about what I'm going to do with anybody on this place. It's my habit to tell people *what to do*, not to discuss it with 'em. But I want to know what's the matter with you—whether you're crazy or not. In that case, you'll have to be locked up. And if you aren't, you'll have to change your ways a damn sight or it won't be safe for you here, and you know it—venting your impudence on white women, parking the car in front of my door, driving like mad through the Junction, and going, everywhere, just as you please. Now, I'm going to let you talk to me, but I want you to talk right.

Robert: [*Still standing*] What do you mean, "talk right"?

Norwood: I mean talk like a nigger should to a white man.

20  Robert: Oh! But I'm not a nigger, Colonel Tom. I'm your son.

Norwood: [*Testily*] You're Cora's boy.

Robert: Women don't have children by themselves.

Norwood: Nigger women don't know the fathers. You're a bastard.

[*Robert clenches his fist. Norwood turns toward the drawer where the pistol is, takes it out, and lays it on the table. The wind blows the lace curtains at the windows, and sweeps the shadows of falling leaves across the paths of sunlight on the floor.*]

Robert: I've heard that before. I've heard it from Negroes, and I've heard it from white folks. Now I hear it from you. [*Slowly*] You're talking about my mother.

25  Norwood: I'm talking about Cora, yes. Her children are bastards.

Robert: [*Quickly*] And you're their father. [*Angrily*] How come I look like you, if you're not my father?

Norwood: Don't shout at me, boy. I can hear you. [*Half-smiling*] How come your skin is yellow and your elbows rusty? How come they threw you out of the post office today for talking to a white woman? How come you're the crazy young buck you are?

Robert: They had no right to throw me out. I asked for my money back when I saw the broken tubes. Just as you had no right to raise that cane today when I was standing at the door of this house where *you* live, while *I* have to sleep in a shack down the road with the field hands. [*Slowly*] But my mother sleeps with you.

Norwood: You don't like it?

30  Robert: No, I don't like it.

Norwood: What can you do about it?

Robert: [*After a pause*] I'd like to kill all the white men in the world.

Norwood: [*Starting*] Niggers like you are hung to trees.

Robert: I'm not a nigger.

35  Norwood: You don't like your own race? [*Robert is silent*] Yet you don't like white folks either?

Robert: [*Defiantly*] You think I ought to?

Norwood: You evidently don't like me.

Robert: [*Boyishly*] I used to like you, when I first knew you were my father, when I was a little kid, before that time you beat me under the feet of your horses. [*Slowly*] I liked you until then.

Norwood: [*A little pleased*] So you did, heh? [*Fingering his pistol*] A pickaninny calling me "papa." I should've broken your young neck for that first time. I should've broken your head for you today, too—since I didn't then.

40  Robert: [*Laughing scornfully*] You should've broken my head?

Norwood: Should've gotten rid of you before this. But you was Cora's child. I tried to help you. [*Aggrieved*] I treated you decent, schooled you. Paid for it. But tonight you'll get the hell off this place and stay off. Get the hell out of this county. [*Suddenly furious*] Get out of this state. Don't let me lay eyes on you again. Get out of here now. Talbot and the storekeeper are coming up here this evening to talk cotton with me. I'll tell Talbot to *see* that you go. That's all. [*Norwood motions toward the door, left.*] Tell Sam to come in here when you go out. Tell him to make a light here.

Robert: [*Impudently*] Ring for Sam—I'm not going through the kitchen. [*He starts toward the front door*] I'm not your servant. You're not going to tell me what to do. You're not going to have Talbot run me off the place like a field hand you don't want to use any more.

NORWOOD: [*Springing between his son and the front door, pistol in hand*] You black bastard! [*ROBERT goes toward him calmly, grasps his father's arm and twists it until the gun falls to the floor. The older man bends backward in startled fury and pain.*] Don't you dare put your . . .

ROBERT: [*Laughing*] Why don't you shoot, papa? [*Louder*] Why don't you shoot?

NORWOOD: [*Gasping as he struggles, fighting back*] . . . black . . . hands . . . on . . . you . . .    45

ROBERT: [*Hysterically, as he takes his father by the throat*] Why don't you shoot, papa? [*NORWOOD's hands claw the air helplessly. ROBERT chokes the struggling white man until his body grows limp*] Why don't you shoot! [*Laughing*] Why don't you shoot? Huh? Why?

[*CORA appears at the top of the stairs, hearing the commotion. She screams.*]

CORA: Oh, my God! [*She rushes down. ROBERT drops the body of his father at her feet in a path of flame from the setting sun. CORA starts and stares in horror.*]

ROBERT: [*Wildly*] Why didn't he shoot, mama? He didn't want *me* to live. Why didn't he shoot? [*Laughing*] He was the boss. Telling me what to do. Why didn't he shoot, then? He was the white man.

CORA: [*Falling on the body*] Colonel Tom! Colonel Tom! Tom! Tom! [*Gazes across the corpse at her son*] He's yo' father, Bert.

ROBERT: He's dead. The white man's dead. My father's dead. [*Laughing*] I'm living.    50

CORA: Tom! Tom! Tom!

ROBERT: Niggers are living. He's dead. [*Picks up the pistol*] This is what he wanted to kill me with, but he's dead. I can use it now. Use it on all the white men in the world, because they'll be coming looking for me now. [*Stuffs the pistol into his shirt*] They'll want me now.

CORA: [*Rising and running toward her boy*] Quick, chile, out that way, [*Pointing toward the front door*] so they won't see you in de kitchen. Make for de swamp, honey. Cross de fields fo' de swamp. Go de crick way. In runnin' water, dogs can't smell no tracks. Hurry, chile!

ROBERT: Yes, mama. I can go out the front way now, easy. But if I see they gonna get me before I can reach the swamp, I'm coming back here, mama, and [*Proudly*] let them take me out of my father's house—if they can. [*Pats the gun under his shirt*] They're not going to string me up to some roadside tree for the crackers to laugh at.

CORA: [*Moaning aloud*] Oh, O-o-o! Hurry! Hurry, chile!    55

ROBERT: I'm going, ma. [*He opens the door. The sunset streams in like a river of blood.*]

CORA: Run, chile!

ROBERT: Not out of my father's house. [*He exits slowly, tall and straight against the sun.*]

CORA: Fo' God's sake, hurry, chile! [*Glancing down the road*] Lawd have mercy! There's Talbot and de storekeeper in de drive. They sees my boy! [*Moaning*] They sees ma boy! [*Relieved*] But thank God, they's passin' him! [*CORA backs up against the wall in the vestibule. She stands as if petrified as TALBOT and the STOREKEEPER enter.*]

TALBOT: Hello, Cora. What's the matter with you? Where's that damn fool boy o' your'n goin',    60 coming out the front door like he owned the house? What's the matter with you, woman? Can't you talk? Can't you talk? Where's Norwood? Let's have some light in this dark place. [*He reaches behind the door and turns on the lights. CORA remains backed up against the wall, looking out into the twilight, watching ROBERT as he goes across the field.*] Good God, Jim! Look at this! [*The TWO WHITE MEN stop in horror before the sight of NORWOOD's body on the floor.*]

STOREKEEPER: He's blue in the face. [*Bends over the body*] That nigger we saw walking out the door! [*Rising excitedly*] That nigger bastard of Cora's . . . [*Stooping over the body again*] Why the Colonel's dead!

TALBOT: That nigger! [*Rushes toward the door*] He's running toward the swamp now . . . We'll get him . . . Telephone town—there, in the library. Telephone the sheriff. Get men, white men, after that nigger.

[*The STOREKEEPER rushes into the library. He can be heard talking excitedly on the phone.*]

STOREKEEPER: Sheriff! Sheriff! Is this the sheriff? I'm calling from Norwood's plantation. That nigger, Bert, has just killed Norwood—and run, headed for the swamp. Notify the gas station at the crossroads! Tell the boys at the sawmill to head him off at the creek. Warn everybody to be on the lookout. Call your deputies! Yes! Spread a dragnet. Get out the dogs. Meanwhile we'll start after him. [*He slams the phone down and comes back into the room.*] Cora, where's Norwood's car? In the barn? [CORA *does not answer.*]

TALBOT: Talk, you black bitch!

[*She remains silent.* TALBOT *runs, yelling and talking, out into the yard, followed by the* STOREKEEPER. *Sounds of excited shouting outside, and the roar of a motor rushing down the drive. In the sky the twilight deepens into early night.* CORA *stands looking into the darkness.*]

CORA: My boy can't get to de swamp now. They's telephoned the white folks down that way. So he'll come back home now. Maybe he'll turn into de crick and follow de branch home directly. [*Protectively*] But they shan't get him. I'll make a place for to hide him. I'll make a place upstairs down under de floor, under ma bed. In a minute ma boy'll be runnin' from de white folks with their hounds and their ropes and their guns and everything they uses to kill po' colored folks with. [*Distressed*] Ma boy'll be out there runnin'. [*Turning to the body on the floor*] Colonel Tom, you hear me? Our boy, out there runnin'. [*Fiercely*] You said he was ma boy—*ma* bastard boy. I heard you . . . but he's yours too . . . but yonder in de dark runnin'—runnin' from yo' people, from white people. [*Pleadingly*] Why don't you get up and stop 'em? He's *your* boy. His eyes is gray—like your eyes. He's tall like you's tall. He's proud like you's proud. And he's runnin'—runnin' from po' white trash what ain't worth de little finger o' nobody what's got your blood in 'em, Tom. [*Demandingly*] Why don't you get up from there and stop 'em, Colonel Tom? What's that you say? He ain't your chile? He's ma bastard chile? My yellow bastard chile? [*Proudly*] Yes, he's mine. But don't call him that. Don't you touch him. Don't you put your white hands on him. You's beat him enough, and cussed him enough. Don't you touch him now. He is *ma* boy and no white folks gonna touch him now. That's finished. I'm gonna make a place for him upstairs under ma bed. [*Backs away from the body toward the stairs*] He's ma chile. Don't you come in ma bedroom while he's up there. Don't you come to my bed no mo'. I calls you to help me now, and you just lays there. I calls you for to wake up, and you just lays there. Whenever you called me, in de night, I woke up. When you called for me to love, I always reached out ma arms fo' you. I borned you five chilluns and now one of 'em is out yonder in de dark runnin' from yo' people. Our youngest boy out yonder in de dark runnin'. [*Accusingly*] He's runnin' from you, too. You said he warn't your'n—he's just Cora's po' little yellow bastard. But he *is* your'n, Colonel Tom. [*Sadly*] And he's runnin' from you. You are out yonder in de dark, [*Points toward the door*] runnin' our chile, with de hounds and de gun in yo' hand, and Talbot's followin' 'hind you with a rope to hang Robert with. [*Confidently*] I been sleepin' with you too long, Colonel Tom, not to know that this ain't you layin' down there with yo' eyes shut on de floor. You can't fool me—you ain't never been so still like this before—you's out yonder runnin' ma boy through de fields in de dark, runnin' ma poor little helpless Bert through de fields in de dark to lynch him . . . Damn you, Colonel Norwood! [*Backing slowly up the stairs, staring at the rigid body below her*] Damn you, Thomas Norwood! God damn you!

*Curtain*

## Scene 2

TIME. *One hour later. Night.*

SETTING. *The same.*

ACTION. *As the curtain rises, the* UNDERTAKER *is talking to* SAM *at the outer door. All through this act the approaching cries of the man hunt are heard.*

UNDERTAKER:  Reckon there won't be no orders to bring his corpse back out here, Sam. None of us ain't seen Talbot or Mr. Higgins, but I'm sure they'll be having the funeral in town. The coroner told us to bring the body into the Junction. Ain't nothing' but niggers left out here now.

SAM:  [*Very frightened*] Yes, sah! Yes, sah! You's right, sah! Nothin' but us niggers, sah!

UNDERTAKER:  The Colonel didn't have no relatives far as you know, did he, Sam?

SAM:  No, sah. Ain't had none. No, sah! You's right, sah!

UNDERTAKER:  Well, you got everything o' his locked up around here, ain't you? Too bad there    5
ain't no white folks about to look after the Colonel's stuff, but every white man that's able to walk's out with the posse. They'll have that young nigger swingin' before ten.

SAM:  [*Trembling*] Yes, sah, yes, sah! I 'spects so. Yes, sah!

UNDERTAKER:  Say, where's that woman the Colonel's been living with—where's that black housekeeper, Cora, that murderin's bastard's mother?

SAM:  She here, sah! She's up in her room.

UNDERTAKER:  [*Curiously*] I'd like to see how she looks. Get her down here. Say, how about a little drink before we start that ride back to town, for me and my partner out there with the body?

SAM:  Cora got de keys to all de licker, sah!    10

UNDERTAKER:  Well, get her down here then, double quick! [SAM *goes up the stairs. The* UNDERTAKER *leans in the front doorway talking to his partner outside in the wagon*] Bad business, a white man having saucy nigger children on his hands, and his black woman living in his own house.

VOICE OUTSIDE:  Damn right, Charlie.

UNDERTAKER:  Norwood didn't have a gang o' yellow gals, though, like Higgins and some o' these other big bugs. Just this one bitch far's I know, livin' with him damn near like a wife. Didn't even have much company out here. And they tell me ain't been a white woman stayed here overnight since his wife died when I was a baby. [SAM's *shuffle is heard on the stairs*] Here comes a drink, I reckon, boy. You needn't get down off the ambulance. I'll have Sam bring it out there to you. [SAM *descends followed by* CORA *who comes down the stairs. She says nothing. The* UNDERTAKER *looks up grinning at* CORA] Well, so you're the Cora that's got these educated nigger children? Hum-m! Well, I guess you'll see one of 'em swinging full of bullet holes when you wake up in the morning. They'll probably hang him to that tree down here by the Colonel's gate—'cause they tell me he strutted right out the front gate past that tree after the murder. Or maybe they'll burn him. How'd you like to see him swinging there roasted in the morning when you wake up, girlie?

CORA:  [*Calmly*] Is that all you wanted to say to me?

UNDERTAKER:  Don't get smart! Maybe you think there's nobody to boss you now. We gonna    15
have a little drink before we go. Get out a bottle of rye.

CORA:  I takes ma orders from Colonel Norwood, sir.

UNDERTAKER:  Well, you'll take no more orders from him. He's dead out there in my wagon— so get along and get the bottle.

CORA:  He's out yonder with de mob, not in your wagon.

UNDERTAKER:  I tell you he's in my wagon!

CORA:  He's out there with de mob.    20

UNDERTAKER:  God damn! [*To his partner outside*] I believe this black woman's gone crazy in here. [*To* CORA] Get the keys out for that licker, and be quick about it! [CORA *does not move.* SAM *looks from one to the other, frightened.*]

Voice Outside: Aw, to hell with the licker, Charlie. Come on, let's start back to town. We want to get in on some of that excitement, too. They should've found that nigger by now—and I want to see 'em drag him out here.

Undertaker: All right, Jim. [*To* Cora *and* Sam] Don't you all go to bed until you see that bon-fire. You niggers are getting besides yourselves around Polk County. We'll burn a few more of you if you don't be careful. [*He exits, and the noise of the dead-wagon going down the road is heard.*]

Sam: Oh, Lawd, hab mercy on me! I prays, Lawd hab mercy! O, ma Lawd, ma Lawd, ma Lawd! Cora, is you a fool? *Is you a fool?* Why didn't you give de mens de licker, riled as these white folks is? In ma old age is I gonna be burnt by de crackers? Lawd, is I sinned? Lawd, what has I done? [*Suddenly stops moaning and becomes schemingly calm*] I don't have to stay here tonight, does I? I done locked up de Colonel's library, and he can't be wantin' nothin'. No, ma Lawd, he won't want nothin' now. He's with Jesus—or with de devil, one. [*To* Cora] I's gwine on away from here. Sam's gwine in town to his chilluns' house, and I ain't gwine by no road either. I gwine through de holler where I don't have to pass no white folks.

25   Cora: Yes, Samuel, you go on. De Colonel can get his own drinks when he comes back tonight.

Sam: [*Bucking his eyes in astonishment at* Cora] Lawd God Jesus!

[*He bolts out of the room as fast as his old legs will carry him.* Cora *comes down stairs, looks for a long moment out into the darkness, then closes the front door and draws the blinds. She looks down at the spot where the* Colonel's *body lay.*]

Cora: All de colored folks are runnin' from you tonight. Po' Colonel Tom, you too old now to be out with de mob. You got no business goin', but you had to go, I reckon. I 'members that time they hung Luke Jordon, you sent yo' dogs out to hunt him. The next day you killed all de dogs. You were kinder softhearted. Said you didn't like that kind of sport. Told me in bed one night you could hear them dogs howlin' in yo' sleep. But de time they burnt de courthouse when that po' little cullud boy was locked up in it cause they said he hugged a white girl, you was with 'em again. Said you had to go help 'em. Now you's out chasin' ma boy. [*As she stands at the window, she sees a passing figure.*] There goes yo' other woman, Colonel Tom, Livonia is runnin' from you too, now. She would've wanted you last night. Been wantin' you again ever since she got old and fat and you stopped layin' with her and put her in the kitchen to cook. Don't think I don't know, Colonel Tom. Don't think I don't remember them nights when you used to sleep in that cabin down by de spring. I knew 'Vonia was there with you. I ain't no fool, Colonel Tom. But she ain't bore you no chilluns. I'm de one that bore 'em. [*Musing*] White mens, and colored womens, and little bastard chilluns—that's de old way of de South—but it's ending now. Three of your yellow brothers yo' father had by Aunt Sallie Deal—what had to come and do your laundry to make her livin'—you got colored relatives scattered all over this county. Them de ways o' de South—mixtries, mixtries. [William *enters left, silently, as his mother talks. She is sitting in a chair now. Without looking up*] Is that you, William?

William: Yes, ma, it's me.

Cora: Is you runnin' from him, too?

30   William: [*Hesitatingly*] Well, ma, you see . . . don't you think kinder . . . well, I reckon I ought to take Libby and ma babies on down to de church house with Reverend Martin and them, or else get 'long to town if I can hitch up them mules. They's scared to be out here, my wife and her ma. All de folks done gone from de houses down yonder by de branch, and you can hear de hounds a bayin' off yonder by de swamp, and cars is tearin' up that road, and de white folks is yellin' and hollerin' and carryin' on somethin' terrible over

toward de brook. I done told Robert 'bout his foolishness. They's gonna hang him sure. Don't you think you better be comin' with us, ma. That is, do you want to? 'Course we can go by ourselves, and maybe you wants to stay here and take care o' de big house. I don't want to leave you, ma, but I . . . I . . .

CORA: Yo' brother'll be back, son, then I won't be by myself.

WILLIAM: [*Bewildered by his mother's sureness*] I thought Bert went . . . I thought he run . . . I thought . . .

CORA: No, honey. He went, but they ain't gonna get him out there. I sees him comin' back here now, to be with me. I's gwine to guard him 'till he can get away.

WILLIAM: Then de white folks'll come here, too.

CORA: Yes, de Colonel'll come back here sure.[*The deep baying of the hounds is heard at a distance through the night.*] Colonel Tom will come after his son.                                            35

WILLIAM: My God, ma! Come with us to town.

CORA: Go on, William, go on! Don't wait for them to get back. You never was much like neither one o' them—neither de Colonel or Bert—you's mo' like de field hands. Too much o' ma blood in you, I guess. You never liked Bert much, neither, and you always was afraid of de Colonel. Go on, son, and hide yo' wife and her ma and your chilluns. Ain't nothin' gonna hurt you. You never did go against nobody. Neither did I, till tonight. Tried to live right and not hurt a soul, white or colored. [*Addressing space*] I tried to live right, Lord. [*Angrily*] Tried to live right, Lord. [*Throws out her arms resentfully as if to say, "and this is what you give me."*] What's de matter, Lawd, you ain't with me?

[*The hounds are heard howling again.*]

WILLIAM: I'm gone, ma. [*He exits fearfully as his mother talks.*]

CORA: [*Bending over the spot on the floor where the* COLONEL *has lain. She calls.*] Colonel Tom! Colonel Tom! Colonel Tom! Look! Bertha and Sallie and William and Bert, all your chilluns, runnin' from you, and you layin' on de floor there, dead! [*Pointing*] Out yonder with the mob, dead. And when you come home, upstairs in my bed on top of my body, dead. [*Goes to the window, returns, sits down, and begins to speak as if remembering a far-off dream.*] Colonel Thomas Norwood! I'm just poor Cora Lewis, Colonel Norwood. Little black Cora Lewis, Colonel Norwood. I'm just fifteen years old. Thirty years ago, you put your hands on me to feel my breasts, and you say, "You a pretty little piece of flesh, ain't you? Black and sweet, ain't you?" And I lift up ma face, and you pull me to you, and we laid down under the trees that night, and I wonder if your wife'll know when you go back up the road into the big house. And I wonder if my mama'll know it, when I go back to our cabin. Mama said she nursed you when you was a baby, just like she nursed me. And I loved you in the dark, down there under that tree by de gate, afraid of you and proud of you, feelin' your gray eyes lookin' at me in de dark. Then I cried and cried and told ma mother about it, but she didn't take it hard like I thought she'd take it. She said fine white mens like de young Colonel always took good care o' their colored womens. She said it was better than marryin' some black field hand and workin' all your life in de cotton and cane. Better even than havin' a job like ma had, takin' care o' de white chilluns. Takin' care o' you, Colonel Tom. [*As* CORA *speaks the sound of the approaching mob gradually grows louder and louder. Auto horns, the howling of dogs, the far-off shouts of men, full of malignant force and power, increase in volume.*] And I was happy because I liked you, 'cause you was tall and proud, 'cause you said I was sweet to you and called me purty. And when yo' wife died—de Mrs. Norwood [*Scornfully*] that never bore you any chilluns, the pale beautiful Mrs. Norwood that was like a slender pine tree in de winter frost . . . I knowed you wanted me. I was full with child by you then—William, it was—our first boy. And ma mammy said, go up there and keep de house for Colonel Tom, sweep de floors and make de beds, and by and by, you won't have to sweep de floors and

Robert, who has been apprehended here, is confronted and taunted by members of the mob as Higgins, Talbot, and the Undertaker stand beside the body of Colonel Thomas Norwood, in the original production of Hughes's *Mulatto* at the Vanderbilt Theater in New York, October 1935, produced and directed by Martin Jones. The actors are unidentified.

make no beds. And what ma mammy said was right. It all come true. Sam and Rusus and 'Vonia and Lucy did de waitin' on you and me, and de washin' and de cleanin' and de cookin'. And all I did was a little sewin' now and then, and a little preservin' in de summer and a little makin' of pies and sweet cakes and things you like to eat on Christmas. And de years went by. And I was always ready for you when you come to me in de night. And we had them chilluns, your chilluns and mine, Tom Norwood, all of 'em! William, born dark like me, dumb like me, and then Baby John what died; then Bertha, white and smart like you; and then Bert with your eyes and your ways and your temper, and mighty nigh your color; then Sallie, nearly white, too, and smart, and purty. But Bert was yo' chile! He was always yo' child . . . Good-looking, and kind, and headstrong, and strange, and stubborn, and proud like you, and de one I could love most 'cause he needed de most lovin'. And he wanted to call you "papa," and I tried to teach him no, but he did it anyhow and [*Sternly*] you beat him, Colonel Thomas Norwood. And he growed up with de beatin' in his heart and your eyes in his head, and your ways, and your pride. And this summer he looked like you that time I first knowed you down by de road under them trees, young and fiery and proud. There was no touchin' Bert, just like there was no touchin' you. I could only love him, like I loved you. I could only love him. But I couldn't talk to him, because he hated you. He had your ways—and you beat him! After you beat that chile, then you died, Colonel Norwood. You died here in this house, and you been living dead a long time. You lived dead. [*Her voice rises above the nearing sounds of the mob.*] And when I said this evenin', "Get up! Why don't you help me?" You'd done been dead a long time—a long time before you laid down on this floor, here, with the breath choked out o' you—and Bert standin' over you living, living, living. That's why you hated him. And you want to kill him. Always, you wanted to kill him. Out there with de hounds and de torches and de cars and de guns, you want to kill ma boy. But you won't kill him! He's comin' home first. He's comin' home to me.

He's comin' home! [*Outside the noise is tremendous now, the lights of autos flash on the window curtains, there are shouts and cries. CORA sits, tense, in the middle of the room.*] He's comin' home!

A MAN'S VOICE: [*Outside*] He's somewhere on this lot.    40

ANOTHER VOICE: Don't shoot, men. We want to get him alive.

VOICE: Close in on him. He must be in them bushes by the house.

FIRST VOICE: Porch! Porch! Porch! There he is yonder—running to the door!

[*Suddenly shots are heard. The door bursts open and ROBERT enters, firing back into the darkness. The shots are returned by the mob, breaking the windows. Flares, lights, voices, curses, screams.*]

VOICES: Nigger! Nigger! Nigger! Get the nigger!

[*CORA rushes toward the door and bolts it after her son's entrance.*]

CORA: [*Leaning against the door*] I was waiting for you, honey. Yo' hiding place is all ready, up-    45
stairs, under ma bed, under de floor. I sawed a place there fo' you. They can't find you there. Hurry—before yo' father comes.

ROBERT: [*Panting*] No time to hide, ma. They're at the door now. They'll be coming up the back way, too.[*Sounds of knocking and the breaking of glass*] They'll be coming in the windows. They'll be coming in everywhere. And only one bullet left, ma. It's for me.

CORA: Yes, it's fo' you, chile. Save it. Go upstairs in mama's room. Lay on ma bed and rest.

ROBERT: [*Going slowly toward the stairs with the pistol in his hand*] Goodnight, ma. I'm awful tired of running, ma. They been chasing me for hours.

CORA: Goodnight, son.

[*CORA follows him to the foot of the steps. The door begins to give at the forcing of the mob. As ROBERT disappears above, it bursts open. A great crowd of white men pour into the room with guns, ropes, clubs, flashlights, and knives. CORA turns on the stairs, facing them quietly. TALBOT, the leader of the mob, stops.*]

TALBOT: Be careful, men. He's armed. [*To CORA*] Where is that yellow bastard of yours—    50
upstairs?

CORA: Yes, he's going to sleep. Be quiet, you all. Wait. [*She bars the way with outspread arms.*]

TALBOT: [*Harshly*] Wait, hell! Come on, boys, let's go. [*A single shot is heard upstairs.*] What's that?

CORA: [*Calmly*] My boy . . . is gone . . . to sleep!

[*TALBOT and some of the men rush up the stairway, CORA makes a final gesture of love toward the room above. Yelling and shouting, through all the doors and windows, a great crowd pours into the room. The roar of the mob fills the house, the whole night, the whole world. Suddenly TALBOT returns at the top of the steps and a hush falls over the crowd.*]

TALBOT: Too late, men. We're just a little too late.

[*A sigh of disappointment rises from the mob. TALBOT comes down the stairs, walks up to CORA and slaps her once across the face. She does not move. It is as though no human hand can touch her again.*]

*Curtain*

## Questions

### Act 1

1. Throughout the act—and the play—why are the children of Colonel Norwood and Cora referred to as just Cora's children?

2. Why does the Colonel deny permission for Sallie's bags to be carried through the front door?

3. Throughout the act, what do we learn about Robert's attitudes toward his circumstances on the plantation? What do the Colonel and Higgins say about his attitude? Once Robert appears, what does he himself say about his situation?

4. What does the Colonel say about Sallie's ambition to reopen a nearby school? What does he advise her to do instead?

5. Who is Talbot? What does he represent? Why does he not appear until late in the second act?

6. What does Higgins report about how Robert has behaved in town? What does he tell Colonel Norwood to do about it?

7. As expressed in speech 61, what is Higgins's attitude toward black women? What does this attitude disclose about his character?

8. Describe the effect on both Robert and Colonel Norwood of the childhood incident when Robert called the Colonel "papa."

9. What has the Colonel decided to do about Robert? What are Cora's fears not only for Robert but for others?

## Act 2, Scene 1

10. What are the issues in the confrontation between Robert and Colonel Norwood?

11. What is Robert's dilemma (speech 35)? What has the Colonel now determined to do about Robert?

12. What is Robert's response to the Colonel's display of the gun, and his threat to use it?

13. What do Talbot and the storekeeper do once they learn that Colonel Norwood is dead? What chance does Robert have to escape?

14. Why does Cora speak so extensively over the Colonel's body?

## Act 2, Scene 2

15. Why are the undertaker and his companion introduced at this point? What are they like?

16. According to Cora (speech 27), what was the nature of the old "ways" of the south?

17. What is the purpose of Cora's second extensive monologue (speech 39)?

18. What finally happens to Robert? Why does Talbot slap Cora at the end?

## General Questions

1. Describe *Mulatto* as a realistic play. Why is it important that the play contain many details about the plantation and the customs of the country?

2. What is the symbolism of the front door? The incident at the post office in town? Driving the Ford fast?

3. Describe Colonel Norwood. What characteristics of a Southern plantation owner does he exhibit? What is shown about him by his having sent Robert and his sisters away to school? What does Cora say about him before and after he is dead?

4. Describe the character of Robert. What are his dominant traits? How politic is he in dealing with his circumstances? To what extent does he bring about his own destruction?

5. Describe Cora. What has her life been like? To what degree has she sacrificed her individuality to stay with Colonel Norwood? How does she try to protect her children? In her two major lengthy speeches, what seems to be happening to her?

6. In light of the historical time when the play was written and produced, could there have been any other outcome?

## ARTHUR MILLER (1915–2005)

Because of his large number of important dramas, Miller can justly be considered a dominant modern American playwright, perhaps the most dominant American playwright, of the post-World War II years. He was born in New York in 1915 and received his higher education at the University of Michigan, where he won a prize for a play he had written as an undergraduate. After graduation he wrote with the Federal Theater Project (part of President Roosevelt's New Deal initiatives). When funding ran out for that project, he began writing radio plays, a novel, and, during World War II, an account of military training. He also wrote a play, *The Man Who Had All the Luck*, which met with little success on Broadway in 1944.

After the war he quickly catapulted into fame as a dramatist with *All My Sons* (1947); *Death of a Salesman* (1949); *An Enemy of the People* (1951, an adaptation of Ibsen's play); *The Crucible* (1953); and *A View from the Bridge* (1955). Many of these combine his interests in family relationships and sociopolitical issues. For instance, *All My Sons* explores the relationship between Joe Keller, an industrialist and war profiteer who had allowed faulty engines to be installed in U.S. military aircraft, and his son Chris, an army pilot returning home from World War II. The play dramatizes Joe Keller's emerging realization that the airmen who died because of his defective engines were "all" his sons. Another of Miller's most important plays, *The Crucible*, reflects the suspicions and unfounded accusations rampant in the McCarthy era early in the 1950s.

Miller's later work includes the screenplay *The Misfits* (1961), the last film in which Marilyn Monroe, who was then his wife, starred; and the plays *After the Fall* (1964), *Incident at Vichy* (1964, made into a film in 1973 and done as a radio play in 2002), *The Price* (1968), *Fame* (1970), *The Reason Why* (1972), *The Creation of the World and Other Business* (1972), *The Archbishop's Ceiling* (1976), *The American Clock* (1980), *Playing for Time* (1985), *I Can't Remember Anything* (1987), *Clara* (1987), a filmscript titled *Everybody Wins* (1990), *The Ride Down Mount Morgan* (1991, London), *Broken Glass* (1994), *Some Kind of Love Story* (1998), *Resurrection Blues* (2002, Minneapolis), and *Finishing the Picture* (2004). In 1996 *The Crucible* was revised and presented as a successful film with Daniel Day-Lewis and Winona Ryder.

## *Death of a Salesman* and the "Well-Made Play"

*Death of a Salesman*, which opened on Broadway on February 10, 1949, is similar to both *Oedipus the King* and the traditional well-made play (see p. 1190). Miller's play dramatizes the end of a much longer story. The stage action in the present (in Acts 1 and 2) covers about 24 hours, from Monday evening to Tuesday evening. The story, however, covers much of Willy Loman's life, and his memories of past events constantly impose themselves on the present. One of the play's central conflicts stems from a secret known only to Willy and his son Biff, a secret that is concealed until near the play's end. Such secrets, having a profound significance in the action, are a feature of the traditional well-made play.

## *Death of a Salesman*: Tragedy, Symbolism, and Broken Dreams

In writing a tragedy about the struggle and failure of Willy Loman, Miller effectively redefines the nature of tragedy in our modern period of democracy and belief in the significance of common people. In a *New York Times* essay published shortly after the Broadway opening, Miller argues "the common man is as apt a subject for tragedy in its highest sense as kings were."[2] He asserts that tragedy springs from the individual's quest for a proper place in the world and from his or her readiness "to lay down . . . life, if need be, to secure . . . [a] sense of personal dignity." Willy is flawed: He is self-deluded, deceitful, unfaithful, and weak; he denies the truth when he is confronted with it. But Miller links Willy's defects with the quest for dignity: "the flaw or crack in the character is really . . . his inherent unwillingness to remain passive in the face of what he conceives to be a challenge to his dignity, his image of his rightful status." It is with great justice that Linda asserts to her sons that attention must be paid to so significant a person. In this sense, Miller meets the challenge of creating a modern character worthy of tragic elevation.

Accordingly, *Death of a Salesman* is developed around the character of Willy Loman. At first, Miller wanted to call the play "The Inside of His Head," and his initial vision was of "an enormous face the height of the proscenium arch that would appear and open up, and we would see the inside of a man's head."[3] The play contains two types of time and action: real and remembered. Present events are enacted and described realistically, but such action often triggers Willy's memory of the past, which is always with him, shaping the way he reacts to the present. Sometimes past events can even occur simultaneously with present action, as in Act 1 when Willy speaks with his dead brother, whom he is remembering at the same time he is playing cards with Charley. At other times, past events take over the play completely although Willy continues to exist in the present.

Like the acting of past events, the setting of *Death of a Salesman* is symbolic and nonrealistic. The play demonstrates the degree to which Miller relies on developments in the physical theater that took place between Shakespeare's day and our own. Miller adapts both the concepts of the picture-frame proscenium stage and the apron stage. Thus the Loman house—set on the proscenium stage—is a framework with three rooms (or acting areas) on three levels: the kitchen, the sons' bedroom, and Willy's bedroom. The forestage and apron are used for all scenes away from the house and for "memory" scenes. The house is hemmed in by apartment houses and lit with an "angry glow of orange," thus suggesting that Willy's present existence is urbanized and claustrophobic. When memory takes over, however, the apartment houses

---

[2]"Tragedy and the Common Man," *New York Times,* February 27, 1949, sec. 2, p. 1.

[3]Arthur Miller, "Introduction to the Collected Plays," *Arthur Miller's Collected Plays* (New York: Viking, 1957), p. 23.

Stage set for *Death of a Salesman*.

disappear (a technique of lighting), and the orange glow gives way to pastoral colors and the shadows of leaves—the setting for dreams about past times and hopes.

*Death of a Salesman* is very much about dreams, illusions, and self-deception. Dreams pervade Willy's thoughts, conversation, family, and house, and the staging allows fluid transitions between current action and memory. Willy's central illusion is the American dream of success and wealth through the merchandizing of the self. This dream is embodied in a series of smaller dreams (illusions, lies) that Willy has created out of hope and then tried to bequeath to his sons. But reality destroys these dreams. Willy's expectation of a New York City job and a salary, for example, is wrecked by the reality of his disastrous encounter with his preoccupied and un-sympathetic boss. Only Linda escapes the tyranny of dreams. While she serves and supports Willy completely, she remains firmly planted in the reality of house payments, insurance premiums, and Willy's need for dignity and attention as his life falls apart.

At the end of the play, we are left with a number of questions about the degree to which Willy recognizes and understands the illusory nature of his dreams and his self-image. He does understand that he has run out of lies and has nothing left to sell. He also understands—according to Miller—his alienation from true values.

> Had Willy been unaware of his separation from values that endure he would have died contentedly while polishing his car. . . . But he was agonized by his awareness of being in a false position, so constantly haunted by the hollowness of all he had placed his faith in, so aware, in short, that he must somehow be filled with his spirit or fly apart, that he staked his life on the ultimate assertion.[4]

---

[4]*Ibid.*, pp. 34–35.

Yet at the end of the play, Willy is still in the grip of delusion. He imagines that his insurance money will make Biff "magnificent," and he dreams that his funeral will be massive. Both visions are delusions, for Biff has already abandoned the business world, and the funeral is attended by only five people. In the *Requiem* scene, Biff states that Willy's dreams were illusory: "He had all the wrong dreams. All, all wrong" (Requiem, speech 16). Only the character ironically named Happy retains his own unreconstructed version of Willy's dream: "He had a good dream. It's the only dream you can have—to come out number-one man" (Requiem, speech 25). Miller leaves it to the audience to evaluate the truth and validity of each character's assertions.

## 🦅 Death of a Salesman (1949)

### CHARACTERS

**Willy Loman**

**Linda**, his wife

**Biff** ⎤
            ⎬ his sons
**Happy** ⎦

**Uncle Ben**

**Charley**

**Bernard**

**The Woman**

**Howard Wagner**

**Jenny**

**Stanley**

**Miss Forsythe**

**Letta**

The action takes place in WILLY LOMAN's house and yard and in various places he visits in the New York and Boston of today.

### ACT 1

0.1   *A melody is heard, played upon a flute. It is small and fine, telling of grass and trees and the horizon. The curtain rises.*

0.2       *Before us is the Salesman's house. We are aware of towering, angular shapes behind it, surrounding it on all sides. Only the blue light of the sky falls upon the house and forestage; the surrounding area shows an angry glow of orange. As more light appears, we see a solid vault of apartment houses around the small, fragile-seeming home. An air of the dream clings to the place, a dream rising out of reality. The kitchen at center seems actual enough, for there is a kitchen table with three chairs, and a refrigerator. But no other fixtures are seen. At the back of the kitchen there is a draped entrance, which leads to the living-room. To the right of the kitchen, on a level raised two feet, is a bedroom furnished only with a brass bedstead and a straight chair. On a shelf over the bed a silver athletic trophy stands. A window opens onto the apartment house at the side.*

0.3       *Behind the kitchen, on a level raised six and a half feet, is the boys' bedroom, at present barely visible. Two beds are dimly seen, and at the back of the room a dormer window. (This bedroom is above the unseen living-room.) At the left a stairway curves up to it from the kitchen.*

0.4 *The entire setting is wholly or, in some places, partially transparent. The roof-line of the house is one-dimensional; under and over it we see the apartment buildings. Before the house lies an apron, curving beyond the forestage into the orchestra. This forward area serves as the back yard as well as the locale of all Willy's imaginings and of his city scenes. Whenever the action is in the present the actors observe the imaginary wall-lines, entering the house only through its door at the left. But in the scenes of the past these boundaries are broken, and characters enter or leave a room by stepping "through" a wall onto the forestage.*

0.5 [*From the right, WILLY LOMAN, the Salesman, enters, carrying two large sample cases. The flute plays on. He hears but is not aware of it. He is past sixty years of age, dressed quietly. Even as he crosses the stage to the doorway of the house, his exhaustion is apparent. He unlocks the door, comes into the kitchen, and thankfully lets his burden down, feeling the soreness of his palms. A word-sigh escapes his lips—it might be "Oh, boy, oh, boy." He closes the door, then carries his cases out into the living-room, through the draped kitchen doorway.*]

0.6 [*LINDA, his wife, has stirred in her bed at the right. She gets out and puts on a robe, listening. Most often jovial, she has developed an iron repression of her exceptions to WILLY's behavior—she more than loves him, she admires him, as though his mercurial nature, his temper, his massive dreams and little cruelties, served her only as sharp reminders of the turbulent longings within him, longings which she shares but lacks the temperament to utter and follow to their end.*]

LINDA: [*hearing WILLY outside the bedroom, calls with some trepidation*] Willy!
WILLY: It's all right. I came back.
LINDA: Why? What happened? [*slight pause*] Did something happen, Willy?
WILLY: No, nothing happened.
5 LINDA: You didn't smash the car, did you?
WILLY: [*with casual irritation*] I said nothing happened. Didn't you hear me?
LINDA: Don't you feel well?
WILLY: I'm tired to the death. [*The flute has faded away. He sits on the bed beside her, a little numb.*] I couldn't make it. I just couldn't make it, Linda.
LINDA: [*very carefully, delicately*] Where were you all day? You look terrible.
10 WILLY: I got as far as a little above Yonkers.° I stopped for a cup of coffee. Maybe it was the coffee.
LINDA: What?
WILLY: [*after a pause*] I suddenly couldn't drive any more. The car kept going off onto the shoulder, y'know?
LINDA: [*helpfully*] Oh. Maybe it was the steering again. I don't think Angelo knows the Studebaker.
WILLY: No, it's me, it's me. Suddenly I realize I'm goin' sixty miles an hour and I don't remember the last five minutes. I'm—I can't seem to—keep my mind to it.
15 LINDA: Maybe it's your glasses. You never went for your new glasses.
WILLY: No, I see everything. I came back ten miles an hour. It took me nearly four hours from Yonkers.
LINDA: [*resigned*] Well, you'll just have to take a rest, Willy, you can't continue this way.
WILLY: I just got back from Florida.
LINDA: But you didn't rest your mind. Your mind is overactive, and the mind is what counts, dear.
20 WILLY: I'll start out in the morning. Maybe I'll feel better in the morning. [*She is taking off his shoes.*] These goddam arch supports are killing me.

---

°10 *Yonkers:* Yonkers is immediately north of New York City, touching the city limits of the Bronx. Because Willy lives in Brooklyn, to the south, he got no more than thirty or thirty-five miles from home.

LINDA: Take an aspirin. Should I get you an aspirin? It'll soothe you.

WILLY: [*with wonder*] I was driving along, you understand? And I was fine. I was even observing the scenery. You can imagine, me looking at scenery, on the road every week of my life. But it's so beautiful up there, Linda, the trees are so thick, and the sun is warm. I opened the windshield and just let the warm air bathe over me. And then all of a sudden I'm goin' off the road! I'm tellin' ya, I absolutely forgot I was driving. If I'd've gone the other way over the white line I might've killed somebody. So I went on again—and five minutes later I'm dreamin' again, and I nearly—[*He presses two fingers against his eyes.*] I have such thoughts, I have such strange thoughts.

LINDA: Willy, dear. Talk to them again. There's no reason why you can't work in New York.

WILLY: They don't need me in New York. I'm the New England man. I'm vital in New England.

25  LINDA: But you're sixty years old. They can't expect you to keep traveling every week.

WILLY: I'll have to send a wire to Portland. I'm supposed to see Brown and Morrison tomorrow morning at ten o'clock to show the line. Goddammit, I could sell them! [*He starts putting on his jacket.*]

LINDA: [*taking the jacket from him*] Why don't you go down to the place tomorrow and tell Howard you've simply got to work in New York? You're too accommodating, dear.

WILLY: If old man Wagner was alive I'd a been in charge of New York now! That man was a prince, he was a masterful man. But that boy of his, that Howard, he don't appreciate. When I went north the first time, the Wagner Company didn't know where New England was!

LINDA: Why don't you tell those things to Howard, dear?

30  WILLY: [*encouraged*] I will, I definitely will. Is there any cheese?

LINDA: I'll make you a sandwich.

WILLY: No, go to sleep. I'll take some milk. I'll be up right away. The boys in?

LINDA: They're sleeping. Happy took Biff on a date tonight.

WILLY: [*interested*] That so?

35  LINDA: It was so nice to see them shaving together, one behind the other, in the bathroom. And going out together. You notice? The whole house smells of shaving lotion.

WILLY: Figure it out. Work a lifetime to pay off a house. You finally own it, and there's nobody to live in it.

LINDA: Well, dear, life is a casting off. It's always that way.

WILLY: No, no, some people—some people accomplish something. Did Biff say anything after I went this morning?

LINDA: You shouldn't have criticized him, Willy, especially after he just got off the train. You mustn't lose your temper with him.

40  WILLY: When the hell did I lose my temper? I simply asked him if he was making any money. Is that a criticism?

LINDA: But, dear, how could he make any money?

WILLY: [*worried and angered*] There's such an undercurrent in him. He became a moody man. Did he apologize when I left this morning?

LINDA: He was crestfallen, Willy. You know how he admires you. I think if he finds himself, then you'll both be happier and not fight any more.

WILLY: How can he find himself on a farm? Is that a life? A farmhand? In the beginning, when he was young, I thought, well, a young man, it's good for him to tramp around, take a lot of different jobs. But it's more than ten years now and he has yet to make thirty-five dollars a week!

45  LINDA: He's finding himself, Willy.

WILLY: Not finding yourself at the age of thirty-four is a disgrace!

LINDA: Shh!

WILLY: The trouble is he's lazy, goddammit!

LINDA: Willy, please!

WILLY: Biff is a lazy bum!                                                    50

LINDA: They're sleeping. Get something to eat. Go on down.

WILLY: Why did he come home? I would like to know what brought him home.

LINDA: I don't know. I think he's still lost, Willy. I think he's very lost.

WILLY: Biff Loman is lost. In the greatest country in the world a young man with such—personal attractiveness, gets lost. And such a hard worker. There's one thing about Biff—he's not lazy.

LINDA: Never.                                                                 55

WILLY: [*with pity and resolve*] I'll see him in the morning; I'll have a nice talk with him. I'll get him a job selling. He could be big in no time. My God! Remember how they used to follow him around in high school? When he smiled at one of them their faces lit up. When he walked down the street . . . [*He loses himself in reminiscences.*]

LINDA: [*trying to bring him out of it*] Willy, dear, I got a new kind of American-type cheese today. It's whipped.

WILLY: Why do you get American when I like Swiss?

LINDA: I just thought you'd like a change—

WILLY: I don't want a change! I want Swiss cheese. Why am I always being contradicted?   60

LINDA: [*with a covering laugh*] I thought it would be a surprise.

WILLY: Why don't you open a window in here, for God's sake?

LINDA: [*with infinite patience*] They're all open dear.

WILLY: The way they boxed us in here. Bricks and windows, windows and bricks.

LINDA: We should've bought the land next door.                               65

WILLY: The street is lined with cars. There's not a breath of fresh air in the neighborhood. The grass don't grow any more, you can't raise a carrot in the back yard. They should've had a law against apartment houses. Remember those two beautiful elm trees out there? When I and Biff hung the swing between them?

LINDA: Yeah, like being a million miles from the city.

WILLY: They should've arrested the builder for cutting those down. They massacred the neighborhood. [*lost*] More and more I think of those days, Linda. This time of year it was lilac and wisteria. And then the peonies would come out, and the daffodils. What fragrance in this room!

LINDA: Well, after all, people had to move somewhere.

WILLY: No, there's more people now.                                          70

LINDA: I don't think there's more people. I think—

WILLY: There's more people! That's what's ruining this country! Population is getting out of control. The competition is maddening! Smell the stink from that apartment house! And another one on the other side . . . How can they whip cheese?

[*On WILLY's last line, BIFF and HAPPY raise themselves up in their beds, listening.*]

LINDA: Go down, try it. And be quiet.

WILLY: [*turning to LINDA, guiltily*] You're not worried about me, are you, sweetheart?

BIFF: What's the matter?                                                      75

HAPPY: Listen!

LINDA: You've got too much on the ball to worry about.

WILLY: You're my foundation and my support, Linda.

LINDA: Just try to relax, dear. You make mountains out of molehills.

WILLY: I won't fight with him any more. If he wants to go back to Texas, let him go.        80

LINDA: He'll find his way.

WILLY: Sure. Certain men just don't get started till later in life. Like Thomas Edison, I think. Or B. F. Goodrich.° One of them was deaf. [*He starts for the bedroom doorway.*] I'll put my money on Biff.

LINDA: And Willy—if it's warm Sunday we'll drive in the country. And we'll open the windshield, and take lunch.

WILLY: No, the windshields don't open on the new cars.

85    LINDA: But you opened it today.

WILLY: Me? I didn't. [*He stops.*] Now isn't that peculiar! Isn't that a remarkable—[*He breaks off in amazement and fright as the flute is heard distantly.*]

LINDA: What, darling?

WILLY: That is the most remarkable thing.

LINDA: What, dear?

90    WILLY: I was thinking of the Chevvy. [*slight pause*] Nineteen twenty-eight . . . when I had that red Chevvy—[*Breaks off.*] That funny? I coulda sworn I was driving that Chevvy today.

LINDA: Well, that's nothing. Something must've reminded you.

WILLY: Remarkable. Ts. Remember those days? The way Biff used to simonize that car? The dealer refused to believe there was eighty thousand miles on it. [*He shakes his head.*] Heh! [*to LINDA*] Close your eyes, I'll be right up. [*He walks out of the bedroom.*]

HAPPY: [*to BIFF*] Jesus, maybe he smashed up the car again!

LINDA: [*calling after WILLY*] Be careful on the stairs, dear! The cheese is on the middle shelf! [*She turns, goes over to the bed, takes his jacket, and goes out of the bedroom.*]

[*Light has risen on the boys' room. Unseen, WILLY is heard talking to himself, "Eighty thousand miles," and a little laugh. BIFF gets out of bed, comes downstage a bit, and stands attentively. BIFF is two years older than his brother HAPPY, well built, but in these days bears a worn air and seems less self-assured. He has succeeded less, and his dreams are stronger and less acceptable than HAPPY's. HAPPY is tall, powerfully made. Sexuality is like a visible color on him, or a scent that many women have discovered. He, like his brother, is lost, but in a different way, for he has never allowed himself to turn his face toward defeat and is thus more confused and hard-skinned, although seemingly more content.*]

95    HAPPY: [*getting out of bed*] He's going to get his license taken away if he keeps that up. I'm getting nervous about him, y'know, Biff?

BIFF: His eyes are going.

HAPPY: No, I've driven with him. He sees all right. He just doesn't keep his mind on it. I drove into the city with him last week. He stops at a green light and then it turns red and he goes. [*He laughs.*]

BIFF: Maybe he's color-blind.

HAPPY: Pop? Why he's got the finest eye for color in the business. You know that.

100    BIFF: [*sitting down on his bed*] I'm going to sleep.

HAPPY: You're not still sour on Dad, are you, Biff?

BIFF: He's all right, I guess.

WILLY: [*underneath them, in the living-room*] Yes, sir, eighty thousand miles—eighty-two thousand!

BIFF: You smoking?

105    HAPPY: [*holding out a pack of cigarettes*] Want one?

BIFF: [*taking a cigarette*] I can never sleep when I smell it.

WILLY: What a simonizing job, heh!

HAPPY: [*with deep sentiment*] Funny, Biff y'know? Us sleeping in here again? The old beds. [*He pats his bed affectionately.*] All the talk that went across those two beds, huh? Our whole lives.

---

°82 *Thomas Edison, B. F. Goodrich*: Thomas A. Edison (1847–1931) was an American inventor who developed the electric light and the phonograph. Benjamin Franklin Goodrich (1841–1888) founded the B. F. Goodrich Rubber and Tire Company. It was Edison who suffered from deafness.

BIFF: Yeah. Lotta dreams and plans.

HAPPY: [*with a deep and masculine laugh*] About five hundred women would like to know what 110
was said in this room.

[*They share a soft laugh.*]

BIFF: Remember that big Betsy something—what the hell was her name—over on Bushwick
Avenue?

HAPPY: [*combing his hair*] With the collie dog!

BIFF: That's the one. I got you in there, remember?

HAPPY: Yeah, that was my first time—I think. Boy, there was a pig! [*They laugh, almost crudely.*]
You taught me everything I know about women. Don't forget that.

BIFF: I bet you forgot how bashful you used to be. Especially with girls.       115

HAPPY: Oh, I still am, Biff.

BIFF: Oh, go on.

HAPPY: I just control it, that's all. I think I got less bashful and you got more so. What happened, Biff? Where's the old humor, the old confidence? [*He shakes* BIFF'S *knee.* BIFF *gets up
and moves restlessly about the room.*] What's the matter?

BIFF: Why does Dad mock me all the time?

HAPPY: He's not mocking you, he—       120

BIFF: Everything I say there's a twist of mockery on his face. I can't get near him.

HAPPY: He just wants you to make good, that's all. I wanted to talk to you about Dad for a
long time, Biff. Something's—happening to him. He—talks to himself.

BIFF: I noticed that this morning. But he always mumbled.

HAPPY: But not so noticeable. It got so embarrassing I sent him to Florida. And you know
something? Most of the time he's talking to you.

BIFF: What's he say about me?       125

HAPPY: I can't make it out.

BIFF: What's he say about me?

HAPPY: I think the fact that you're not settled, that you're still kind of up in the air . . .

BIFF: There's one or two other things depressing him, Happy.

HAPPY: What do you mean?       130

BIFF: Never mind. Just don't lay it all to me.

HAPPY: But I think if you just got started—I mean—is there any future for you out there?

BIFF: I tell ya, Hap, I don't know what the future is. I don't know—what I'm supposed to want.

HAPPY: What do you mean?

BIFF: Well, I spent six or seven years after high school trying to work myself up. Shipping clerk, 135
salesman, business of one kind or another. And it's a measly manner of existence. To get on
that subway on the hot mornings in summer. To devote your whole life to keeping stock, or
making phone calls, or selling or buying. To suffer fifty weeks of the year for the sake of a
two-week vacation, when all you really desire is to be outdoors, with your shirt off. And always to have to get ahead of the next fella. And still—that's how you build a future.

HAPPY: Well, you really enjoy it on a farm? Are you content out there?

BIFF: [*with rising agitation*] Hap, I've had twenty or thirty different kinds of jobs since I left
home before the war, and it always turns out the same. I just realized it lately. In Nebraska
when I herded cattle, and the Dakotas, and Arizona, and now in Texas. It's why I came
home now, I guess, because I realized it. This farm I work on, it's spring there now, see?
And they've got about fifteen new colts. There's nothing more inspiring or—beautiful
than the sight of a mare and a new colt. And it's cool there now, see? Texas is cool now,
and it's spring. And whenever spring comes to where I am, I suddenly get the feeling, my
God, I'm not gettin' anywhere! What the hell am I doing, playing around with horses,
twenty-eight dollars a week! I'm thirty-four years old, I oughta be makin' my future.

That's when I come running home. And now, I get here, and I don't know what to do with myself. [*after a pause*] I've always made a point of not wasting my life, and everytime I come back here I know that all I've done is to waste my life.

HAPPY: You're a poet, you know that, Biff? You're a—you're an idealist!

BIFF: No, I'm mixed up very bad. Maybe I oughta get married. Maybe I oughta get stuck into something. Maybe that's my trouble. I'm like a boy. I'm not married, I'm not in business, I just—I'm like a boy. Are you content, Hap? You're a success, aren't you? Are you content?

140 HAPPY: Hell, no!

BIFF: Why? You're making money, aren't you?

HAPPY: [*moving about with energy, expressiveness*] All I can do now is wait for the merchandise manager to die. And suppose I get to be merchandise manager? He's a good friend of mine, and he just built a terrific estate on Long Island. And he lived there about two months and sold it, and now he's building another one. He can't enjoy it once it's finished. And I know that's just what I would do. I don't know what the hell I'm workin' for. Sometimes I sit in my apartment—all alone. And I think of the rent I'm paying. And it's crazy. But then, it's what I always wanted. My own apartment, a car, and plenty of women. And still, goddammit, I'm lonely.

BIFF: [*with enthusiasm*] Listen, why don't you come out West with me?

HAPPY: You and I, heh?

145 BIFF: Sure, maybe we could buy a ranch. Raise cattle, use our muscles. Men built like we are should be working out in the open.

HAPPY: [*avidly*] The Loman Brothers, heh?

BIFF: [*with vast affection*] Sure, we'd be known all over the counties!

HAPPY: [*enthralled*] That's what I dream about, Biff. Sometimes I want to just rip my clothes off in the middle of the store and outbox that goddam merchandise manager. I mean I can outbox, outrun, and outlift anybody in that store, and I have to take orders from those common, petty sons-of-bitches till I can't stand it any more.

BIFF: I'm tellin' you, kid, if you were with me I'd be happy out there.

150 HAPPY: [*enthused*] See, Biff, everybody around me is so false that I'm constantly lowering my ideals . . .

BIFF: Baby, together we'd stand up for one another, we'd have someone to trust.

HAPPY: If I were around you—

BIFF: Hap, the trouble is we weren't brought up to grub for money. I don't know how to do it.

HAPPY: Neither can I!

155 BIFF: Then let's go!

HAPPY: The only thing is—what can you make out there?

BIFF: But look at your friend. Builds an estate and then hasn't the peace of mind to live in it.

HAPPY: Yeah, but when he walks into the store the waves part in front of him. That's fifty-two thousand dollars a year coming through the revolving door, and I got more in my pinky finger than he's got in his head.

BIFF: Yeah, but you just said—

160 HAPPY: I gotta show some of those pompous, self-important executives over there that Hap Loman can make the grade. I want to walk into the store the way he walks in. Then I'll go with you, Biff. We'll be together yet, I swear. But take those two we had tonight. Now weren't they gorgeous creatures?

BIFF: Yeah, yeah, most gorgeous I've had in years.

HAPPY: I get that any time I want, Biff. Whenever I feel disgusted. The only trouble is, it gets like bowling or something. I just keep knockin' them over and it doesn't mean anything. You still run around a lot?

BIFF: Naa. I'd like to find a girl—steady, somebody with substance.

HAPPY: That's what I long for.

BIFF: Go on! You'd never come home. 165

HAPPY: I would! Somebody with character, with resistance! Like Mom, y'know? You're gonna call me a bastard when I tell you this. That girl Charlotte I was with tonight is engaged to be married in five weeks. [*He tries on his new hat.*]

BIFF: No kiddin'!

HAPPY: Sure, the guy's in line for the vice-presidency of the store. I don't know what gets into me, maybe I just have an overdeveloped sense of competition or something, but I went and ruined her, and furthermore I can't get rid of her. And he's the third executive I've done that to. Isn't that a crummy characteristic? And to top it all, I go to their weddings! [*Indignantly, but laughing*] Like I'm not supposed to take bribes. Manufacturers offer me a hundred-dollar bill now and then to throw an order their way. You know how honest I am, but it's like this girl, see. I hate myself for it. Because I don't want the girl, and, still, I take it and—I love it!

BIFF: Let's go to sleep.

HAPPY: I guess we didn't settle anything, heh? 170

BIFF: I just got one idea that I think I'm going to try.

HAPPY: What's that?

BIFF: Remember Bill Oliver?

HAPPY: Sure, Oliver is very big now. You want to work for him again?

BIFF: No, but when I quit he said something to me. He put his arm on my shoulder and he 175 said, "Biff, if you ever need anything, come to me."

HAPPY: I remember that. That sounds good.

BIFF: I think I'll go to see him. If I could get ten thousand or even seven or eight thousand dollars I could buy a beautiful ranch.

HAPPY: I bet he'd back you. 'Cause he thought highly of you, Biff. I mean, they all do. You're well liked, Biff. That's why I say to come back here, and we both have the apartment. And I'm tellin' you, Biff, any babe you want . . .

BIFF: No, with a ranch I could do the work I like and still be something. I just wonder though. I wonder if Oliver still thinks I stole that carton of basketballs.

HAPPY: Oh, he probably forgot that long ago. It's almost ten years. You're too sensitive. Any- 180 way, he didn't really fire you.

BIFF: Well, I think he was going to. I think that's why I quit. I was never sure whether he knew or not. I know he thought the world of me, though. I was the only one he'd let lock up the place.

WILLY: [*below*] You gonna wash the engine, Biff?

HAPPY: Shh!

[*BIFF looks at HAPPY, who is gazing down, listening. WILLY is mumbling in the parlor.*]

HAPPY: You hear that?

[*They listen. WILLY laughs warmly.*]

BIFF: [*growing angry*] Doesn't he know Mom can hear that? 185

WILLY: Don't get your sweater dirty, Biff!

[*A look of pain crosses BIFF's face.*]

HAPPY: Isn't that terrible! Don't leave again, will you? You'll find a job here. You gotta stick around. I don't know what to do about him, it's getting embarrassing.

WILLY: What a simonizing job!

BIFF: Mom's hearing that!

190 WILLY: No kiddin', Biff, you got a date? Wonderful!

HAPPY: Go on to sleep. But talk to him in the morning, will you?

BIFF: [*reluctantly getting into bed* ] With her in the house. Brother!

HAPPY: [*getting into bed*] I wish you'd have a good talk with him.

[*The light on their room begins to fade.*]

BIFF: [*to himself in bed*] That selfish, stupid . . .

195 HAPPY: Sh . . . Sleep, Biff.

[*Their light is out. Well before they have finished speaking, WILLY's form is dimly seen below in the darkened kitchen. He opens the refrigerator, searches in there, and takes out a bottle of milk. The apartment houses are fading out, and the entire house and surroundings become covered with leaves. Music insinuates itself as the leaves appear.*]

WILLY: Just wanna be careful with those girls, Biff, that's all. Don't make any promises. No promises of any kind. Because a girl, y'know, they always believe what you tell 'em, and you're very young, Biff, you're too young to be talking seriously to girls.

[*Light rises on the kitchen. WILLY, talking, shuts the refrigerator door and comes downstage to the kitchen table. He pours milk into a glass. He is totally immersed in himself, smiling faintly.*]

WILLY: Too young entirely, Biff. You want to watch your schooling first. Then when you're all set, there'll be plenty of girls for a boy like you. [*He smiles broadly at a kitchen chair.*] That so? The girls pay for you? [*He laughs.*] Boy, you must really be makin' a hit.

[*WILLY is gradually addressing—physically—a point offstage, speaking through the wall of the kitchen, and his voice has been rising in volume to that of a normal conversation.*]

WILLY: I been wondering why you polish the car so careful. Ha! Don't leave the hubcaps, boys. Get the chamois to the hubcaps. Happy, use newspaper on the windows, it's the easiest thing. Show him how to do it, Biff! You see, Happy? Pad it up, use it like a pad. That's it, that's it, good work. You're doin' all right, Hap. [*He pauses, then nods in approbation for a few seconds, then looks upward.*] Biff, first thing we gotta do when we get time is clip that big branch over the house. Afraid it's gonna fall in a storm and hit the roof. Tell you what. We get a rope and sling her around, and then we climb up there with a couple of saws and take her down. Soon as you finish the car, boys, I wanna see ya. I got a surprise for you, boys.

BIFF: [*offstage*] Whatta ya got, Dad?

200 WILLY: No, you finish first. Never leave a job till you're finished—remember that. [*looking toward the "big trees"*] Biff, up in Albany I saw a beautiful hammock. I think I'll buy it next trip, and we'll hang it right between those two elms. Wouldn't that be something? Just swingin' there under those branches. Boy, that would be . . .

[*YOUNG BIFF and YOUNG HAPPY appear from the direction WILLY was addressing. HAPPY carries rags and a pail of water. BIFF, wearing a sweater with a block "S," carries a football.*]

BIFF: [*pointing in the direction of the car offstage*] How's that, Pop, professional?

WILLY: Terrific. Terrific job, boys. Good work, Biff.

HAPPY: Where's the surprise, Pop?

WILLY: In the back seat of the car.

205 HAPPY: Boy! [*He runs off.*]

BIFF: What is it, Dad? Tell me, what'd you buy?

WILLY: [*laughing, cuffs him*] Never mind, something I want you to have.

BIFF: [*turns and starts off*] What is it, Hap?

HAPPY: [*offstage*] It's a punching bag!

BIFF: Oh, Pop!                                                                                     210
WILLY: It's got Gene Tunney's° signature on it!

[HAPPY *runs onstage with a punching bag.*]

BIFF: Gee, how'd you know we wanted a punching bag?
WILLY: Well, it's the finest thing for the timing.
HAPPY: [*lies down on his back and pedals with his feet*] I'm losing weight, you notice, Pop?
WILLY: [*to* HAPPY] Jumping rope is good too.                                                       215
BIFF: Did you see the new football I got?
WILLY: [*examining the ball*] Where'd you get a new ball?
BIFF: The coach told me to practice my passing.
WILLY: That so? And he gave you the ball, heh?
BIFF: Well, I borrowed it from the locker room. [*He laughs confidentially.*]                       220
WILLY: [*laughing with him at the theft*] I want you to return that.
HAPPY: I told you he wouldn't like it!
BIFF: [*angrily*] Well, I'm bringing it back!
WILLY: [*stopping the incipient argument, to* HAPPY] Sure, he's gotta practice with a regulation
    ball, doesn't he? [*to* BIFF] Coach'll probably congratulate you on your initiative!
BIFF: Oh, he keeps congratulating my initiative all the time, Pop.                                  225
WILLY: That's because he likes you. If somebody else took that ball there'd be an uproar. So
    what's the report, boys, what's the report?
BIFF: Where'd you go this time, Dad? Gee we were lonesome for you.
WILLY: [*pleased, puts an arm around each boy and they come down to the apron*] Lonesome, heh?
BIFF: Missed you every minute.
WILLY: Don't say? Tell you a secret, boys. Don't breathe it to a soul. Someday I'll have my own    230
    business, and I'll never have to leave home any more.
HAPPY: Like Uncle Charley, heh?
WILLY: Bigger than Uncle Charley! Because Charley is not—liked. He's liked, but he's not—
    well liked.
BIFF: Where'd you go this time, Dad?
WILLY: Well, I got on the road, and I went north to Providence. Met the Mayor.
BIFF: The Mayor of Providence!                                                                      235
WILLY: He was sitting in the hotel lobby.
BIFF: What'd he say?
WILLY: He said, "Morning!" And I said, "You got a fine city here, Mayor." And then he had
    coffee with me. And then I went to Waterbury. Waterbury is a fine city. Big clock city, the
    famous Waterbury clock. Sold a nice bill there. And then Boston—Boston is the cradle of
    the Revolution. A fine city. And a couple of other towns in Mass., and on to Portland and
    Bangor and straight home!
BIFF: Gee, I'd love to go with you sometime, Dad.
WILLY: Soon as summer comes.                                                                        240
HAPPY: Promise?
WILLY: You and Hap and I, and I'll show you all the towns. America is full of beautiful towns
    and fine, upstanding people. And they know me, boys, they know me up and down New
    England. The finest people. And when I bring you fellas up, there'll be open sesame for
    all of us, 'cause one thing, boys: I have friends. I can park my car in any street in New
    England, and the cops protect it like their own. This summer, heh?
BIFF AND HAPPY: [*together*] Yeah! You bet!

---

°211 *Gene Tunney*: James Joseph Tunney, a boxer who won the heavyweight championship from Jack Dempsey in 1926 and retired undefeated in 1928.

WILLY: We'll take our bathing suits.

245 HAPPY: We'll carry your bags, Pop!

WILLY: Oh, won't that be something! Me comin' into the Boston stores with you boys carryin' my bags. What a sensation!

[BIFF *is prancing around, practicing passing the ball.*]

WILLY: You nervous, Biff, about the game?

BIFF: Not if you're gonna be there.

WILLY: What do they say about you in school, now that they made you captain?

250 HAPPY: There's a crowd of girls behind him everytime the classes change.

BIFF: [*taking* WILLY's *hand*] This Saturday, Pop, this Saturday—just for you, I'm going to break through for a touchdown.

HAPPY: You're supposed to pass.

BIFF: I'm takin' one play for Pop. You watch me, Pop, and when I take off my helmet, that means I'm breakin' out. Then you watch me crash through that line!

WILLY: [*kisses* BIFF] Oh, wait'll I tell this in Boston!

[BERNARD *enters in knickers. He is younger than* BIFF, *earnest and loyal, a worried boy.*]

255 BERNARD: Biff, where are you? You're supposed to study with me today.

WILLY: Hey, looka Bernard. What're you lookin' so anemic about, Bernard?

BERNARD: He's gotta study, Uncle Willy. He's got Regents° next week.

HAPPY: [*tauntingly, spinning* BERNARD *around*] Let's box, Bernard!

BERNARD: Biff! [*He gets away from* HAPPY.] Listen, Biff, I heard Mr. Birnbaum say that if you don't start studyin' math he's gonna flunk you, and you won't graduate. I heard him!

260 WILLY: You better study with him, Biff. Go ahead now.

BERNARD: I heard him!

BIFF: Oh, Pop, you didn't see my sneakers! [*He holds up a foot* FOR WILLY *to look at.*]

WILLY: Hey, that's a beautiful job of printing!

BERNARD: [*wiping his glasses*] Just because he printed University of Virginia on his sneakers doesn't mean they've got to graduate him, Uncle Willy!

265 WILLY: [*angrily*] What're you talking about? With scholarships to three universities they're gonna flunk him?

BERNARD: But I heard Mr. Birnbaum say—

WILLY: Don't be a pest, Bernard! [*to his boys*] What an anemic!

BERNARD: Okay, I'm waiting for you in my house, Biff.

[BERNARD *goes off. The* LOMANS *laugh.*]

WILLY: Bernard is not well liked, is he?

270 BIFF: He's liked, but he's not well liked.

HAPPY: That's right, Pop.

WILLY: That's just what I mean. Bernard can get the best marks in school, y'understand, but when he gets out in the business world, y'understand, you are going to be five times ahead of him. That's why I thank Almighty God you're both built like Adonises. Because the man who makes an appearance in the business world, the man who creates personal interest, is the man who gets ahead. Be liked and you will never want. You take me, for instance. I never have to wait in line to see a buyer. "Willy Loman is here!" That's all they have to know, and I go right through.

BIFF: Did you knock them dead, Pop?

WILLY: Knocked 'em cold in Providence, slaughtered 'em in Boston.

---

°257 *Regents*: a statewide high school proficiency examination administered in New York State.

HAPPY: [*on his back, pedaling again*] I'm losing weight, you notice, Pop?                                    275

[LINDA *enters, as of old, a ribbon in her hair, carrying a basket of washing.*]

LINDA: [*with youthful energy*] Hello, dear!

WILLY: Sweetheart!

LINDA: How'd the Chevvy run?

WILLY: Chevrolet, Linda, is the greatest car ever built. [*to the boys*] Since when do you let your
    mother carry wash up the stairs?

BIFF: Grab hold there, boy!

HAPPY: Where to, Mom?                                                                                          280

LINDA: Hang them up on the line. And you better go down to your friends, Biff. The cellar is
    full of boys. They don't know what to do with themselves.

BIFF: Ah, when Pop comes home they can wait!

WILLY: [*laughs appreciatively*] You better go down and tell them what to do, Biff.

BIFF: I think I'll have them sweep out the furnace room.

WILLY: Good work, Biff.                                                                                        285

BIFF: [*goes through wall-line of kitchen to doorway at back and calls down*] Fellas! Everybody sweep
    out the furnace room! I'll be right down!

VOICES: All right! Okay, Biff.

BIFF: George and Sam and Frank, come out back! We're hangin' up the wash! Come on, Hap,
    on the double! [*He AND HAPPY carry out the basket.*]

LINDA: The way they obey him!

WILLY: Well, that's training, the training. I'm tellin' you, I was sellin' thousands and thou-            290
    sands, but I had to come home.

LINDA: Oh, the whole block'll be at that game. Did you sell anything?

WILLY: I did five hundred gross in Providence and seven hundred gross in Boston.

LINDA: No! Wait a minute, I've got a pencil. [*She pulls pencil and paper out of her apron pocket.*] That
    makes your commission . . . Two hundred—my God! Two hundred and twelve dollars!

WILLY: Well, I didn't figure it yet, but . . .                                                                295

LINDA: How much did you do?

WILLY: Well, I—I did—about a hundred and eighty gross in Providence. Well, no—it came
    to—roughly two hundred gross on the whole trip.

LINDA: [*without hesitation*] Two hundred gross. That's . . . [*She figures.*]

WILLY: The trouble was that three of the stores were half closed for inventory in Boston.
    Otherwise I woulda broke records.

LINDA: Well, it makes seventy dollars and some pennies. That's very good.                                     300

WILLY: What do we owe?

LINDA: Well, on the first there's sixteen dollars on the refrigerator—

WILLY: Why sixteen?

LINDA: Well, the fan belt broke, so it was a dollar eighty.

WILLY: But it's brand new.                                                                                    305

LINDA: Well, the man said that's the way it is. Till they work themselves in, y'know.

[*They move through the wall-line into the kitchen.*]

WILLY: I hope we didn't get stuck on that machine.

LINDA: They got the biggest ads of any of them!

WILLY: I know, it's a fine machine. What else?

LINDA: Well, there's nine-sixty for the washing machine. And for the vacuum cleaner there's    310
    three and a half due on the fifteenth. Then the roof, you got twenty-one dollars remaining.

WILLY: It don't leak, does it?

LINDA: No, they did a wonderful job. Then you owe Frank for the carburetor.

WILLY: I'm not going to pay that man! That goddam Chevrolet, they ought to prohibit the manufacture of that car!

LINDA: Well, you owe him three and a half. And odds and ends, comes to around a hundred and twenty dollars by the fifteenth.

315 WILLY: A hundred and twenty dollars! My God, if business don't pick up I don't know what I'm gonna do!

LINDA: Well, next week you'll do better.

WILLY: Oh, I'll knock 'em dead next week. I'll go to Hartford. I'm very well liked in Hartford. You know, the trouble is, Linda, people don't seem to take to me.

[*They move onto the forestage.*]

LINDA: Oh, don't be foolish.

WILLY: I know it when I walk in. They seem to laugh at me.

320 LINDA: Why? Why would they laugh at you? Don't talk that way, Willy.

[WILLY *moves to the edge of the stage.* LINDA *goes into the kitchen and starts to darn stockings.*]

WILLY: I don't know the reason for it, but they just pass me by. I'm not noticed.

LINDA: But you're doing wonderful, dear. You're making seventy to a hundred dollars a week.

WILLY: But I gotta be at it ten, twelve hours a day. Other men—I don't know—they do it easier. I don't know why—I can't stop myself—I talk too much. A man oughta come in with a few words. One thing about Charley. He's a man of few words, and they respect him.

LINDA: You don't talk too much, you're just lively.

325 WILLY: [*smiling*] Well, I figure, what the hell, life is short, a couple of jokes. [*to himself*] I joke too much! [*The smile goes.*]

LINDA: Why? You're—

WILLY: I'm fat. I'm very—foolish to look at, Linda. I didn't tell you, but Christmas time I happened to be calling on F. H. Stewarts, and a salesman I know, as I was going in to see the buyer I heard him say something about—walrus. And I—I cracked him right across the face. I won't take that. I simply will not take that. But they do laugh at me. I know that.

LINDA: Darling . . .

WILLY: I gotta overcome it. I know I gotta overcome it. I'm not dressing to advantage, maybe.

330 LINDA: Willy, darling, you're the handsomest man in the world—

WILLY: Oh, no, Linda.

LINDA: To me you are. [*slight pause*] The handsomest.

[*From the darkness is heard the laughter of a woman.* WILLY *doesn't turn to it, but it continues through* LINDA's *lines.*]

LINDA: And the boys, Willy. Few men are idolized by their children the way you are.

[*Music is heard as behind a scrim, to the left of the house,* The WOMAN, *dimly seen, is dressing.*]

WILLY: [*with great feeling*] You're the best there is, Linda, you're a pal, you know that? On the road—on the road I want to grab you sometimes and just kiss the life outa you.

[*The laughter is loud now, and he moves into a brightening area at the left, where* THE WOMAN *has come from behind the scrim and is standing, putting on her hat, looking into a "mirror" and laughing.*]

335 WILLY: Cause I get so lonely—especially when business is bad and there's nobody to talk to. I get the feeling that I'll never sell anything again, that I won't make a living for you, or a business, a business for the boys. [*He talks through* THE WOMAN's *subsiding laughter;* THE WOMAN *primps at the "mirror."*] There's so much I want to make for—

THE WOMAN: Me? You didn't make me, Willy. I picked you.

WILLY: [*pleased*] You picked me?

THE WOMAN: [*who is quite proper-looking, WILLY's age*] I did. I've been sitting at that desk watching all the salesmen go by, day in, day out. But you've got such a sense of humor, and we do have such a good time together, don't we?

WILLY: Sure, sure. [*He takes her in his arms.*] Why do you have to go now?

THE WOMAN: It's two o'clock . . .                                                      340

WILLY: No, come on in! [*He pulls her.*]

THE WOMAN: . . . my sisters'll be scandalized. When'll you be back?

WILLY: Oh, two weeks about. Will you come up again?

THE WOMAN: Sure thing. You do make me laugh. It's good for me. [*She squeezes his arm, kisses him.*] And I think you're a wonderful man.

WILLY: You picked me, heh?                                                              345

THE WOMAN: Sure. Because you're so sweet. And such a kidder.

WILLY: Well, I'll see you next time I'm in Boston.

THE WOMAN: I'll put you right through to the buyers.

WILLY: [*slapping her bottom*] Right. Well, bottoms up!

THE WOMAN: [*slaps him gently and laughs*] You just kill me, Willy. [*He suddenly grabs her and kisses*   350 *her roughly.*] You kill me. And thanks for the stockings. I love a lot of stockings. Well, good night.

WILLY: Good night. And keep your pores open!

THE WOMAN: Oh, Willy!

[*THE WOMAN bursts out laughing, and LINDA's laughter blends in. THE WOMAN disappears into the dark. Now the area at the kitchen table brightens. LINDA is sitting where she was at the kitchen table, but now is mending a pair of her silk stockings.*]

LINDA: You are, Willy. The handsomest man. You've got no reason to feel that—

WILLY: [*coming out of THE WOMAN's dimming area and going over to LINDA*] I'll make it all up to you, Linda, I'll—

LINDA: There's nothing to make up, dear. You're doing fine, better than—                355

WILLY: [*noticing her mending*] What's that?

LINDA: Just mending my stockings. They're so expensive—

WILLY: [*angrily, taking them from her*] I won't have you mending stockings in this house! Now throw them out!

[*LINDA puts the stockings in her pocket.*]

BERNARD: [*entering on the run*] Where is he? If he doesn't study!

WILLY: [*moving to the forestage, with great agitation*] You'll give him the answers!                360

BERNARD I do, but I can't on a Regents! That's state exam! They're liable to arrest me!

WILLY: Where is he? I'll whip him, I'll whip him!

LINDA: And he'd better give back that football, Willy, it's not nice.

WILLY: Biff! Where is he? Why is he taking everything?

LINDA: He's too rough with the girls, Willy. All the mothers are afraid of him!                365

WILLY: I'll whip him!

BERNARD: He's driving the car without a license!

[*THE WOMAN's laugh is heard.*]

WILLY: Shut up!

LINDA: All the mothers—

WILLY: Shut up!                                                                          370

BERNARD: [*backing quietly away and out*] Mr. Birnbaum says he's stuck up.

WILLY: Get outa here!

BERNARD: If he doesn't buckle down he'll flunk math! [*He goes off.*]

LINDA: He's right, Willy, you've gotta—

375 WILLY: [*exploding at her*] There's nothing the matter with him! You want him to be a worm like Bernard? He's got spirit, personality . . .

[*As he speaks,* LINDA, *almost in tears, exits into the living-room.* WILLY *is alone in the kitchen, wilting and staring. The leaves are gone. It is night again, and the apartment houses look down from behind.*]

WILLY: Loaded with it. Loaded! What is he stealing? He's giving it back, isn't he? Why is he stealing? What did I tell him? I never in my life told him anything but decent things.

[HAPPY *in pajamas has come down the stairs;* WILLY *suddenly becomes aware of* HAPPY's *presence.*]

HAPPY: Let's go now, come on.

WILLY: [*sitting down at the kitchen table*] Huh! Why did she have to wax the floors herself? Everytime she waxes the floors she keels over. She knows that!

HAPPY: Shh! Take it easy. What brought you back tonight?

380 WILLY: I got an awful scare. Nearly hit a kid in Yonkers. God! Why didn't I go to Alaska with my brother Ben that time! Ben! That man was a genius, that man was success incarnate! What a mistake! He begged me to go.

HAPPY: Well, there's no use in—

WILLY: You guys! There was a man started with the clothes on his back and ended up with diamond mines!

HAPPY: Boy, someday I'd like to know how he did it.

WILLY: What's the mystery? The man knew what he wanted and went out and got it! Walked into a jungle, and comes out, the age of twenty-one, and he's rich! The world is an oyster, but you don't crack it open on a mattress!

385 HAPPY: Pop, I told you I'm gonna retire you for life.

WILLY: You'll retire me for life on seventy goddam dollars a week? And your women and your car and your apartment, and you'll retire me for life! Christ's sake, I couldn't get past Yonkers today! Where are you guys, where are you? The woods are burning! I can't drive a car!

[CHARLEY *has appeared in the doorway. He is a large man, slow of speech, laconic, immovable. In all he says, despite what he says, there is pity, and now, trepidation. He has a robe over pajamas, slippers on his feet. He enters the kitchen.*]

CHARLEY: Everything all right?

HAPPY: Yeah, Charley, everything's . . .

WILLY: What's the matter?

390 CHARLEY: I heard some noise. I thought something happened. Can't we do something about the walls? You sneeze in here, and in my house hats blow off.

HAPPY: Let's go to bed, Dad. Come on.

[CHARLEY *signals to* HAPPY *to go.*]

WILLY: You go ahead, I'm not tired at the moment.

HAPPY: [*to* WILLY] Take it easy, huh? [*He exits.*]

WILLY: What're you doin' up?

395 CHARLEY: [*sitting down at the kitchen table opposite* WILLY] Couldn't sleep good. I had a heartburn.

WILLY: Well, you don't know how to eat.

CHARLEY: I eat with my mouth.

WILLY: No, you're ignorant. You gotta know about vitamins and things like that.

CHARLEY: Come on, let's shoot. Tire you out a little.

WILLY: [*hesitantly*] All right. You got cards?
CHARLEY: [*taking a deck from his pocket*] Yeah, I got them. Someplace. What is it with those vitamins?                                                                                                      400
WILLY: [*dealing*] They build up your bones. Chemistry.
CHARLEY: Yeah, but there's no bones in a heartburn.
WILLY: What are you talkin' about? Do you know the first thing about it?
CHARLEY: Don't get insulted.                                                                                                                                                                              405
WILLY: Don't talk about something you don't know anything about.

[*They are playing. Pause.*]

CHARLEY: What're you doin' home?
WILLY: A little trouble with the car.
CHARLEY: Oh, [*Pause*] I'd like to take a trip to California.
WILLY: Don't say.
CHARLEY: You want a job?                                                                                                                                                                                   410
WILLY: I got a job, I told you that. [*after a slight pause*] What the hell are you offering me a job for?
CHARLEY: Don't get insulted.
WILLY: Don't insult me.
CHARLEY: I don't see no sense in it. You don't have to go on this way.                                                                                                                                     415
WILLY: I got a good job. [*slight pause*] What do you keep comin' in for?
CHARLEY: You want me to go?
WILLY: [*after a pause, withering*] I can't understand it. He's going back to Texas again. What the hell is that?
CHARLEY: Let him go.
WILLY: I got nothin' to give him, Charley, I'm clean, I'm clean.                                                                                                                                            420
CHARLEY: He won't starve. None a them starve. Forget about him.
WILLY: Then what have I got to remember?
CHARLEY: You take it too hard. To hell with it. When a deposit bottle is broken you don't get your nickel back.
WILLY: That's easy enough for you to say.
CHARLEY: That ain't easy for me to say.
WILLY: Did you see the ceiling I put up in the living-room?                                                                                                                                                 425
CHARLEY: Yeah, that's a piece of work. To put up a ceiling is a mystery to me. How do you do it?
WILLY: What's the difference?
CHARLEY: Well, talk about it.
WILLY: You gonna put up a ceiling?
CHARLEY: How could I put up a ceiling?                                                                                                                                                                     430
WILLY: Then what the hell are you bothering me for?
CHARLEY: You're insulted again.
WILLY: A man who can't handle tools is not a man. You're disgusting.
CHARLEY: Don't call me disgusting, Willy.                                                                                                                                                                  435

[UNCLE BEN, *carrying a valise and an umbrella, enters the forestage from around the right corner of the house. He is a stolid man, in his sixties, with a mustache and an authoritative air. He is utterly certain of his destiny, and there is an aura of far places about him. He enters exactly as* WILLY *speaks.*]

WILLY: I'm getting awfully tired, Ben.
[BEN's *music is heard.* BEN *looks around at everything.*]
CHARLEY: Good, keep playing; you'll sleep better. Did you call me Ben?

[BEN *looks at his watch.*]

WILLY: That's funny. For a second there you reminded me of my brother Ben.

BEN: I only have a few minutes. [*He strolls, inspecting the place.* WILLY *and* CHARLEY *continue playing.*]

440  CHARLEY: You never heard from him again, heh? Since that time?

WILLY: Didn't Linda tell you? Couple of weeks ago we got a letter from his wife in Africa. He died.

CHARLEY: That so.

BEN: [*chuckling*] So this is Brooklyn, eh?

CHARLEY: Maybe you're in for some of his money.

445  WILLY: Naa, he had seven sons. There's just one opportunity I had with that man . . .

BEN: I must make a train, William. There are several properties I'm looking at in Alaska.

WILLY: Sure, sure! If I'd gone with him to Alaska that time, everything would've been totally different.

CHARLEY: Go on, you'd froze to death up there.

WILLY: What're you talking about?

450  BEN: Opportunity is tremendous in Alaska, William. Surprised you're not up there.

WILLY: Sure, tremendous.

CHARLEY: Heh?

WILLY: There was the only man I ever met who knew the answers.

CHARLEY: Who?

455  BEN: How are you all?

WILLY: [*taking a pot, smiling*] Fine, fine.

CHARLEY: Pretty sharp tonight.

BEN: Is Mother living with you?

WILLY: No, she died a long time ago.

460  CHARLEY: Who?

BEN: That's too bad. Fine specimen of a lady, Mother.

WILLY: [*to* CHARLEY] Heh?

BEN: I'd hoped to see the old girl.

CHARLEY: Who died?

465  BEN: Heard anything from Father, have you?

WILLY: [*unnerved*] What do you mean, who died?

CHARLEY: [*taking a pot*] What're you talkin' about?

BEN: [*looking at his watch*] William, it's half-past eight!

WILLY: [*As though to dispel his confusion he angrily stops* CHARLEY'*s hand.*] That's my build!

470  CHARLEY: I put the ace—

WILLY: If you don't know how to play the game I'm not gonna throw my money away on you!

CHARLEY: [*rising*] It was my ace, for God's sake!

WILLY: I'm through, I'm through!

BEN: When did Mother die?

475  WILLY: Long ago. Since the beginning you never knew how to play cards.

CHARLEY: [*picks up the cards and goes to the door*] All right! Next time I'll bring a deck with five aces.

WILLY: I don't play that kind of game!

CHARLEY: [*turning to him*] You ought to be ashamed of yourself!

WILLY: Yeah?

480  CHARLEY: Yeah! [*He goes out.*]

WILLY: [*slamming the door after him*] Ignoramus!

BEN: [*as* WILLY *comes toward him through the wall-line of the kitchen*] So you're William.

WILLY: [*shaking BEN's hand*] Ben! I've been waiting for you so long! What's the answer? How did you do it?

BEN: Oh, there's a story in that.

[*LINDA enters the forestage, as of old, carrying the wash basket.*]

LINDA: Is this Ben?                                                                                                485

BEN: [*gallantly*] How do you do, my dear.

LINDA: Where've you been all these years? Willy's always wondered why you—

WILLY: [*pulling BEN away from her impatiently*] Where is Dad? Didn't you follow him? How did you get started?

BEN: Well, I don't know how much you remember.

WILLY: Well, I was just a baby, of course, only three or four years old—                                         490

BEN: Three years and eleven months.

WILLY: What a memory, Ben!

BEN: I have many enterprises, William, and I have never kept books.

WILLY: I remember I was sitting under the wagon in—was it Nebraska?

BEN: It was South Dakota, and I gave you a bunch of wild flowers.                                                 495

WILLY: I remember you walking away down some open road.

BEN: [*laughing*] I was going to find Father in Alaska.

WILLY: Where is he?

BEN: At that age I had a very faulty view of geography, William. I discovered after a few days that I was heading due south, so instead of Alaska, I ended up in Africa.

LINDA: Africa!                                                                                                    500

WILLY: The Gold Coast!

BEN: Principally diamond mines.

LINDA: Diamond mines!

BEN: Yes, my dear. But I've only a few minutes—

WILLY: No! Boys! Boys! [*YOUNG BIFF and HAPPY appear.*] Listen to this. This is your Uncle Ben, a    505
great man! Tell my boys, Ben!

BEN: Why, boys, when I was seventeen I walked into the jungle, and when I was twenty-one I walked out. [*He laughs.*] And by God I was rich.

WILLY: [*to the boys*] You see what I been talking about? The greatest things can happen!

BEN: [*glancing at his watch*] I have an appointment in Ketchikan Tuesday week.

WILLY: No, Ben. Please tell about Dad. I want my boys to hear. I want them to know the kind of stock they spring from. All I remember is a man with a big beard, and I was in Mamma's lap, sitting around a fire, and some kind of high music.

BEN: His flute. He played the flute.                                                                              510

WILLY: Sure, the flute, that's right!

[*New music is heard, a high, rollicking tune.*]

BEN: Father was a very great and a very wild-hearted man. We would start in Boston, and he'd toss the whole family into the wagon, and then he'd drive the team right across the country; through Ohio, and Indiana, Michigan, Illinois, and all the Western states. And we'd stop in the towns and sell the flutes that he'd made on the way. Great inventor, Father. With one gadget he made more in a week than a man like you could make in a lifetime.

WILLY: That's just the way I'm bringing them up, Ben—rugged, well liked, all-around.

BEN: Yeah? [*to BIFF*] Hit that, boy—hard as you can. [*He pounds his stomach.*]

BIFF: Oh, no, sir!                                                                                                515

BEN: [*taking boxing stance*] Come on, get to me! [*He laughs.*]

BIFF: Okay! [*He cocks his fists and starts in.*]

WILLY: Go to it, Biff! Go ahead, show him!

LINDA: [*to* WILLY] Why must he fight, dear?

520 BEN: [*sparring with* BIFF] Good boy! Good boy!

WILLY: How's that, Ben, heh?

HAPPY: Give him the left, Biff!

LINDA: Why are you fighting?

BEN: Good boy! [*suddenly comes in, trips* BIFF, *and stands over him, the point of his umbrella poised over* BIFF's *eye.*]

525 LINDA: Look out, Biff!

BIFF: Gee!

BEN: [*patting* BIFF's *knee*] Never fight fair with a stranger, boy. You'll never get out of the jungle that way. [*taking* LINDA's *hand and bowing*] It was an honor and a pleasure to meet you, Linda.

LINDA: [*withdrawing her hand coldly, frightened*] Have a nice—trip.

BEN: [*to* WILLY] And good luck with your—what do you do?

530 WILLY: Selling.

BEN: Yes. Well . . . [*He raises his hand in farewell to all.*]

WILLY: No, Ben, I don't want you to think . . . [*He takes* BEN's *arm to show him.*] It's Brooklyn, I know, but we hunt too.

BEN: Really, now.

WILLY: Oh, sure, there's snakes and rabbits and—that's why I moved out here. Why, Biff can fell any one of these trees in no time! Boys! Go right over to where they're building the apartment house and get some sand. We're gonna rebuild the entire front stoop right now! Watch this, Ben!

535 BIFF: Yes, sir! On the double, Hap!

HAPPY: [*as he and* BIFF *run off*] I lost weight, Pop, you notice?

[CHARLEY *enters in knickers, even before the boys are gone.*]

CHARLEY: Listen, if they steal any more from that building the watchman'll put the cops on them!

LINDA: [*to* WILLY] Don't let Biff . . .

[BEN *laughs lustily.*]

WILLY: You shoulda seen the lumber they brought home last week. At least a dozen six-by-tens worth all kinds a money.

540 CHARLEY: Listen, if that watchman—

WILLY: I gave them hell, understand. But I got a couple of fearless characters there.

CHARLEY: Willy, the jails are full of fearless characters.

BEN: [*clapping* WILLY *on the back, with a laugh at* CHARLEY] And the stock exchange, friend!

WILLY: [*joining in* BEN's *laughter*] Where are the rest of your pants?

545 CHARLEY: My wife bought them.

WILLY: Now all you need is a golf club and you can go upstairs and go to sleep. [*to* BEN] Great athlete! Between him and his son Bernard they can't hammer a nail!

BERNARD: [*rushing in*] The watchman's chasing Biff!

WILLY: [*angrily*] Shut up! He's not stealing anything!

LINDA: [*alarmed, hurrying off left*] Where is he? Biff, dear! [*She exits.*]

550 WILLY: [*moving toward the left, away from* BEN] There's nothing wrong. What's the matter with you?

BEN: Nervy boy. Good!

WILLY: [*laughing*] Oh, nerves of iron, that Biff!

CHARLEY: Don't know what it is. My New England man comes back and he's bleedin', they murdered him up there.

WILLY: It's contacts, Charley, I got important contacts!

CHARLEY: [*sarcastically*] Glad to hear it, Willy. Come in later, we'll shoot a little casino. I'll take   555
some of your Portland money. [*He laughs at* WILLY *and exits.*]

WILLY: [*turning to* BEN] Business is bad, it's murderous. But not for me, of course.

BEN: I'll stop by on my way back to Africa.

WILLY: [*longingly.*] Can't you stay a few days? You're just what I need, Ben, because I—I have
a fine position here, but I—well, Dad left when I was such a baby and I never had a chance
to talk to him and I still feel—kind of temporary about myself.

BEN: I'll be late for my train.

[*They are at opposite ends of the stage.*]

WILLY: Ben, my boys—can't we talk? They'd go into the jaws of hell for me, see, but I—   560

BEN: William, you're being first-rate with your boys. Outstanding, manly chaps!

WILLY: [*hanging on to his words*] Oh, Ben, that's good to hear! Because sometimes I'm afraid
that I'm not teaching them the right kind of—Ben, how should I teach them?

BEN: [*giving great weight to each word, and with a certain vicious audacity*] William, when I walked
into the jungle, I was seventeen. When I walked out I was twenty-one. And, by God, I was
rich! [*He goes off into darkness around the right corner of the house.*]

WILLY: . . . was rich! That's just the spirit I want to imbue them with! To walk into a jungle!
I was right! I was right! I was right!

[BEN *is gone, but* WILLY *is still speaking to him as* LINDA, *in her nightgown and robe, enters the kitchen,
glances around for* WILLY, *then goes to the door of the house, looks out and sees him. Comes down to his
left. He looks at her.*]

LINDA: Willy, dear? Willy?   565

WILLY: I was right!

LINDA: Did you have some cheese? [*He can't answer.*] It's very late, darling. Come to bed, heh?

WILLY: [*looking straight up*] Gotta break your neck to see a star in this yard.

LINDA: You coming in?

WILLY: Whatever happened to that diamond watch fob? Remember? When Ben came from   570
Africa that time? Didn't he give me a watch fob with a diamond in it?

LINDA: You pawned it, dear. Twelve, thirteen years ago. For Biff's radio correspondence
course.

WILLY: Gee, that was a beautiful thing. I'll take a walk.

LINDA: But you're in your slippers.

WILLY: [*starting to go around the house at the left*] I was right! I was! [*Half to* LINDA, *as he goes, shaking his head*] What a man! There was a man worth talking to. I was right!

LINDA: [*calling after* WILLY] But in your slippers, Willy!   575

[WILLY *is almost gone when* BIFF, *in his pajamas, comes down the stairs and enters the kitchen.*]

BIFF: What is he doing out there?

LINDA: Sh!

BIFF: God Almighty, Mom, how long has he been doing this?

LINDA: Don't, he'll hear you.

BIFF: What the hell is the matter with him?   580

LINDA: It'll pass by morning.

BIFF: Shouldn't we do anything?

LINDA: Oh, my dear, you should do a lot of things, but there's nothing to do, so go to sleep.

[HAPPY *comes down the stairs and sits on the steps.*]

HAPPY: I never heard him so loud, Mom.

585 LINDA: Well, come around more often; you'll hear him. [*She sits down at the table and mends the lining of* WILLY's *jacket.*]

BIFF: Why didn't you ever write me about this, Mom?

LINDA: How would I write to you? For over three months you had no address.

BIFF: I was on the move. But you know I thought of you all the time. You know that, don't you, pal?

LINDA: I know, dear, I know. But he likes to have a letter. Just to know that there's still a possibility for better things.

590 BIFF: He's not like this all the time, is he?

LINDA: It's when you come home he's always the worst.

BIFF: When I come home?

LINDA: When you write you're coming, he's all smiles, and talks about the future, and—he's just wonderful. And then the closer you seem to come, the more shaky he gets, and then, by the time you get here, he's arguing, and he seems angry at you. I think it's just that maybe he can't bring himself to—to open up to you. Why are you so hateful to each other? Why is that?

BIFF: [*evasively*] I'm not hateful, Mom.

595 LINDA: But you no sooner come in the door than you're fighting!

BIFF: I don't know why. I mean to change. I'm tryin', Mom, you understand?

LINDA: Are you home to stay now?

BIFF: I don't know. I want to look around, see what's doin'.

LINDA: Biff, you can't look around all your life, can you?

600 BIFF: I just can't take hold, Mom. I can't take hold of some kind of a life.

LINDA: Biff, a man is not a bird, to come and go with the springtime.

BIFF: Your hair . . . [*He touches her hair.*] Your hair got so gray.

LINDA: Oh, it's been gray since you were in high school. I just stopped dyeing it, that's all.

BIFF: Dye it again, will ya? I don't want my pal looking old. [*He smiles.*]

605 LINDA: You're such a boy! You think you can go away for a year and . . . You've got to get it into your head now that one day you'll knock on this door and there'll be strange people here—

BIFF: What are you talking about? You're not even sixty, Mom.

LINDA: But what about your father?

BIFF: [*lamely*] Well, I meant him, too.

HAPPY: He admires Pop.

610 LINDA: Biff, dear, if you don't have any feeling for him, then you can't have any feeling for me.

BIFF: Sure I can, Mom.

LINDA: No. You can't just come to see me, because I love him. [*with a threat, but only a threat, of tears*] He's the dearest man in the world to me, and I won't have anyone making him feel unwanted and low and blue. You've got to make up your mind now, darling, there's no leeway any more. Either he's your father and you pay him that respect, or else you're not to come here. I know he's not easy to get along with—nobody knows that better than me—but . . .

WILLY: [*from the left, with a laugh*] Hey, hey, Biffo!

BIFF: [*starting to go out after* WILLY] What the hell is the matter with him? [HAPPY *stops him.*]

615 LINDA: Don't—don't go near him!

BIFF: Stop making excuses for him! He always, always wiped the floor with you. Never had an ounce of respect for you.

HAPPY: He's always had respect for—

BIFF: What the hell do you know about it?

HAPPY: [*surlily*] Just don't call him crazy!

BIFF: He's got no character—Charley wouldn't do this. Not in his own house—spewing out 620
that vomit from his mind.

HAPPY: Charley never had to cope with what he's got to.

BIFF: People are worse off than Willy Loman. Believe me, I've seen them!

LINDA: Then make Charley your father, Biff. You can't do that, can you? I don't say he's a great
man. Willy Loman never made a lot of money. His name was never in the paper. He's not
the finest character that ever lived. But he's a human being, and a terrible thing is happening to him. So attention must be paid. He's not to be allowed to fall into his grave like an
old dog. Attention, attention must be finally paid to such a person. You called him crazy—

BIFF: I didn't mean—

LINDA: No, a lot of people think he's lost his—balance. But you don't have to be very smart to 625
know what his trouble is. The man is exhausted.

HAPPY: Sure!

LINDA: A small man can be just as exhausted as a great man. He works for a company thirty-
six years this March, opens up unheard-of territories to their trademark, and now in his
old age they take his salary away.

HAPPY: [*indignantly*] I didn't know that, Mom.

LINDA: You never asked, my dear! Now that you get your spending money someplace else
you don't trouble your mind with him.

HAPPY: But I gave you money last— 630

LINDA: Christmas time, fifty dollars! To fix the hot water it cost ninety-seven fifty! For five
weeks he's been on straight commission,° like a beginner, an unknown!

BIFF: Those ungrateful bastards!

LINDA: Are they any worse than his sons? When he brought them business, when he was
young, they were glad to see him. But now his old friends, the old buyers that loved him
so and always found some order to hand him in a pinch—they're all dead, retired. He
used to be able to make six, seven calls a day in Boston. Now he takes his valises out of the
car and puts them back and takes them out again and he's exhausted. Instead of walking
he talks now. He drives seven hundred miles, and when he gets there no one knows him
any more, no one welcomes him. And what goes through a man's mind, driving seven
hundred miles home without having earned a cent? Why shouldn't he talk to himself?
Why? When he has to go to Charley and borrow fifty dollars a week and pretend to me
that it's his pay? How long can that go on? How long? You see what I'm sitting here and
waiting for? And you tell me he has no character? The man who never worked a day but
for your benefit? When does he get the medal for that? Is this his reward—to turn around
at the age of sixty-three and find his sons, who he loved better than his life, one a philan-
dering bum—

HAPPY: Mom!

LINDA: That's all you are, my baby! [*To BIFF*] And you! What happened to the love you had for 635
him? You were such pals! How you used to talk to him on the phone every night! How
lonely he was till he could come home to you!

BIFF: All right, Mom. I'll live here in my room, and I'll get a job. I'll keep away from him,
that's all.

LINDA: No, Biff. You can't stay here and fight all the time.

BIFF: He threw me out of this house, remember that.

LINDA: Why did he do that? I never knew why.

BIFF: Because I know he's a fake and he doesn't like anybody around who knows! 640

---

°631 *straight commission*: refers to the fact that Willy is receiving no salary, only a commission (percentage) on the sales he makes.

LINDA: Why a fake? In what way? What do you mean?

BIFF: Just don't lay it all at my feet. It's between me and him—that's all I have to say. I'll chip in from now on. He'll settle for half pay check. He'll be all right. I'm going to bed. [*He starts for the stairs.*]

LINDA: He won't be all right.

BIFF: [*turning on the stairs, furiously*] I hate this city and I'll stay here. Now what do you want?

645 LINDA: He's dying, Biff.

[*HAPPY turns quickly to her, shocked.*]

BIFF: [*after a pause*] Why is he dying?

LINDA: He's been trying to kill himself.

BIFF: [*with great horror*] How?

LINDA: I live from day to day.

650 BIFF: What're you talking about?

LINDA: Remember I wrote you that he smashed up the car again? In February?

BIFF: Well?

LINDA: The insurance inspector came. He said that they have evidence. That all these accidents in the last year—weren't—weren't—accidents.

HAPPY: How can they tell that? That's a lie.

655 LINDA: It seems there's a woman . . . [*She takes a breath as*]

BIFF: [*sharply but contained*] What woman?

LINDA: [*simultaneously*] . . . and this woman . . .

LINDA: What?

BIFF: Nothing. Go ahead.

660 LINDA: What did you say?

BIFF: Nothing. I just said what woman?

HAPPY: What about her?

LINDA: Well, it seems she was walking down the road and saw his car. She says that he wasn't driving fast at all, and that he didn't skid. She says he came to that little bridge, and then deliberately smashed into the railing, and it was only the shallowness of the water that saved him.

BIFF: Oh, no, he probably just fell asleep again.

665 LINDA: I don't think he fell asleep.

BIFF: Why not?

LINDA: Last month . . . [*with great difficulty*] Oh, boys, it's so hard to say a thing like this! He's just a big stupid man to you, but I tell you there's more good in him than in many other people. [*She chokes, wipes her eyes.*] I was looking for a fuse. The lights blew out, and I went down the cellar. And behind the fuse box—it happened to fall out—was a length of rubber pipe—just short.

HAPPY: No kidding?

LINDA: There's a little attachment on the end of it. I knew right away. And sure enough, on the bottom of the water heater there's a new little nipple on the gas pipe.

670 HAPPY: [*angrily*] That—jerk.

BIFF: Did you have it taken off?

LINDA: I'm—I'm ashamed to. How can I mention it to him? Every day I go down and take away that little rubber pipe. But, when he comes home, I put it back where it was. How can I insult him that way? I don't know what to do. I live from day to day, boys. I tell you, I know every thought in his mind. It sounds so old-fashioned and silly, but I tell you he put his whole life into you and you've turned your backs on him. [*She is bent over in the chair, weeping, her face in her hands.*] Biff, I swear to God! Biff, his life is in your hands!

HAPPY: [*to BIFF*] How do you like that damned fool!

BIFF: [*kissing her*] All right, pal, all right. It's all settled now. I've been remiss. I know that, Mom. But now I'll stay, and I swear to you, I'll apply myself. [*kneeling in front of her, in a fever of self-reproach*] It's just—you see, Mom, I don't fit in business. Not that I won't try. I'll try, and I'll make good.

HAPPY: Sure you will. The trouble with you in business was you never tried to please people. 675

BIFF: I know, I—

HAPPY: Like when you worked for Harrison's. Bob Harrison said you were tops, and then you go and do some damn fool thing like whistling whole songs in the elevator like a comedian.

BIFF: [*against HAPPY*] So what? I like to whistle sometimes.

HAPPY: You don't raise a guy to a responsible job who whistles in the elevator!

LINDA: Well, don't argue about it now.     680

HAPPY: Like when you'd go off and swim in the middle of the day instead of taking the line around.

BIFF: [*his resentment rising*] Well, don't you run off? You take off sometimes, don't you? On a nice summer day?

HAPPY: Yeah, but I cover myself!

LINDA: Boys!

HAPPY: If I'm going to take a fade the boss can call any number where I'm supposed to be and 685 they'll swear to him that I just left. I'll tell you something that I hate to say, Biff, but in the business world some of them think you're crazy.

BIFF: [*angered*] Screw the business world!

HAPPY: All right, screw it! Great, but cover yourself!

LINDA: Hap, Hap!

BIFF: I don't care what they think! They've laughed at Dad for years, and you know why? Because we don't belong in this nuthouse of a city! We should be mixing cement on some open plain, or—or carpenters. A carpenter is allowed to whistle!

[*WILLY walks in from the entrance of the house, at left.*]

WILLY: Even your grandfather was better than a carpenter. [*Pause. They watch him.*] You never 690 grew up. Bernard does not whistle in the elevator, I assure you.

BIFF: [*as though to laugh WILLY out of it*] Yeah, but you do, Pop.

WILLY: I never in my life whistled in an elevator! And who in the business world thinks I'm crazy?

BIFF: I didn't mean it like that, Pop. Now don't make a whole thing out of it, will ya?

WILLY: Go back to the West! Be a carpenter, a cowboy, enjoy yourself!

LINDA: Willy, he was just saying—     695

WILLY: I heard what he said!

HAPPY: [*trying to quiet WILLY*] Hey, Pop, come on now . . .

WILLY: [*continuing over HAPPY's line*] They laugh at me, heh? Go to Filene's, go to the Hub, go to Slattery's,° Boston. Call out the name Willy Loman and see what happens! Big shot!

BIFF: All right, Pop.

WILLY: Big!     700

BIFF: All right!

WILLY: Why do you always insult me?

BIFF: I didn't say a word! [*to LINDA*] Did I say a word?

---

°698 *Filene's, the Hub, Slattery's:* department stores in New England.

LINDA: He didn't say anything, Willy.

705 WILLY: [*going to the doorway of the living room*] All right, good night, good night.

LINDA: Willy, dear, he just decided . . .

WILLY: [*to BIFF*] If you get tired hanging around tomorrow, paint the ceiling I put up in the living-room.

BIFF: I'm leaving early tomorrow.

HAPPY: He's going to see Bill Oliver, Pop.

710 WILLY: [*interestedly*] Oliver? For what?

BIFF: [*with reserve, but trying, trying*] He always said he'd stake me. I'd like to go into business, so maybe I can take him up on it.

LINDA: Isn't that wonderful?

WILLY: Don't interrupt. What's wonderful about it? There's fifty men in the City of New York who'd stake him. [*to BIFF*] Sporting goods?

BIFF: I guess so. I know something about it and—

715 WILLY: He knows something about it! You know sporting goods better than Spalding, for God's sake! How much is he giving you?

BIFF: I don't know. I didn't even see him yet, but—

WILLY: Then what're you talkin' about?

BIFF: [*getting angry*] Well, all I said was I'm gonna see him, that's all!

WILLY: [*turning away*] Ah, you're counting your chickens again.

720 BIFF: [*starting left for the stairs*] Oh, Jesus, I'm going to sleep!

WILLY: [*calling after him*] Don't curse in this house!

BIFF: [*turning*] Since when did you get so clean?

HAPPY: [*trying to stop them*] Wait a . . .

WILLY: Don't use that language to me! I won't have it!

725 HAPPY: [*grabbing BIFF, shouts*] Wait a minute! I got an idea. I got a feasible idea. Come here, Biff, let's talk this over now, let's talk some sense here. When I was down in Florida last time, I thought of a great idea to sell sporting goods. It just came back to me. You and I, Biff—we have a line, the Loman Line. We train a couple of weeks, and put on a couple of exhibitions, see?

WILLY: That's an idea!

HAPPY: Wait! We form two basketball teams, see? Two waterpolo teams. We play each other. It's a million dollars' worth of publicity. Two brothers, see? The Loman Brothers. Displays in the Royal Palms—all the hotels. And banners over the ring and the basketball court: "Loman Brothers." Baby, we could sell sporting goods!

WILLY: That is a one-million-dollar idea!

LINDA: Marvelous!

730 BIFF: I'm in great shape as far as that's concerned.

HAPPY: And the beauty of it is, Biff, it wouldn't be like a business. We'd be out playin' ball again . . .

BIFF: [*enthused*] Yeah, that's . . .

WILLY: Million-dollar . . .

HAPPY: And you wouldn't get fed up with it, Biff. It'd be the family again. There'd be the old honor, and comradeship, and if you wanted to go off for a swim or somethin'—well, you'd do it! Without some smart cooky gettin' up ahead of you!

735 WILLY: Lick the world! You guys together could absolutely lick the civilized world.

BIFF: I'll see Oliver tomorrow. Hap, if we could work that out . . .

LINDA: Maybe things are beginning to—

WILLY: [*wildly enthused, to LINDA*] Stop interrupting! [*to BIFF*] But don't wear sport jacket and slacks when you see Oliver.

BIFF: No, I'll—

WILLY: A business suit, and talk as little as possible, and don't crack any jokes. 740

BIFF: He did like me. Always liked me.

LINDA: He loved you!

WILLY: [*to* LINDA] Will you stop! [*to* BIFF] Walk in very serious. You are not applying for a boy's job. Money is to pass. Be quiet, fine, and serious. Everybody likes a kidder, but nobody lends him money.

HAPPY: I'll try to get some myself, Biff. I'm sure I can.

WILLY: I see great things for you kids. I think your troubles are over. But remember, start big 745 and you'll end big. Ask for fifteen. How much you gonna ask for?

BIFF: Gee, I don't know—

WILLY: And don't say "Gee." "Gee" is a boy's word. A man walking in for fifteen thousand dollars does not say "Gee!"

BIFF: Ten, I think, would be top though.

WILLY: Don't be so modest. You always started too low. Walk in with a big laugh. Don't look worried. Start off with a couple of your good stories to lighten things up. It's not what you say, it's how you say it—because personality always wins the day.

LINDA: Oliver always thought the highest of him— 750

WILLY: Will you let me talk?

BIFF: Don't yell at her, Pop, will ya?

WILLY: [*angrily*] I was talking, wasn't I?

BIFF: I don't like you yelling at her all the time, and I'm tellin' you, that's all.

WILLY: What're you, takin' over this house? 755

LINDA: Willy—

WILLY: [*turning on her*] Don't take his side all the time, godammit!

BIFF: [*furiously*] Stop yelling at her!

WILLY: [*suddenly pulling on his cheek, beaten down, guilt ridden*] Give my best to Bill Oliver—he may remember me.

[*He exits through the living-room doorway.*]

LINDA: [*her voice subdued*] What'd you have to start that for? [BIFF *turns away.*] You see how 760 sweet he was as soon as you talked hopefully? [*She goes over to* BIFF.] Come up and say good night to him. Don't let him go to bed that way.

HAPPY: Come on, Biff, let's buck him up.

LINDA: Please, dear. Just say good night. It takes so little to make him happy. Come. [*She goes through the living-room doorway, calling upstairs from within the living-room.*] Your pajamas are hanging in the bathroom, Willy!

HAPPY: [*looking toward where* LINDA *went out*] What a woman! They broke the mold when they made her. You know that, Biff?

BIFF: He's off salary. My God, working on commission!

HAPPY: Well, let's face it: he's no hot-shot selling man. Except that sometimes, you have to 765 admit, he's a sweet personality.

BIFF: [*deciding*] Lend me ten bucks, will ya? I want to buy some new ties.

HAPPY: I'll take you to a place I know. Beautiful stuff. Wear one of my striped shirts tomorrow.

BIFF: She got gray. Mom got awful old. Gee, I'm gonna go in to Oliver tomorrow and knock him for a—

HAPPY: Come on up. Tell that to Dad. Let's give him a whirl. Come on.

BIFF: [*steamed up*] You know, with ten thousand bucks, boy! 770

HAPPY: [*as they go into the living-room*] That's the talk, Biff, that's the first time I've heard the old confidence out of you! [*from within the living-room, fading off*] You're gonna live with me, kid, and any babe you want just say the word . . . [*The last lines are hardly heard. They are mounting the stairs to their parents' bedroom.*]

LINDA: [*entering her bedroom and addressing* WILLY, *who is in the bathroom. She is straightening the bed for him.*] Can you do anything about the shower? It drips.

WILLY: [*from the bathroom*] All of a sudden everything falls to pieces! Goddam plumbing, oughta be sued, those people. I hardly finished putting it in and the thing . . . [*His words rumble off.*]

LINDA: I'm just wondering if Oliver will remember him. You think he might?

775 WILLY: [*coming out of the bathroom in his pajamas*] Remember him? What's the matter with you, you crazy? If he'd've stayed with Oliver he'd be on top by now! Wait'll Oliver gets a look at him. You don't know the average caliber any more. The average young man today— [*He is getting into bed*]—is got a caliber of zero. Greatest thing in the world for him was to bum around.

[BIFF *and* HAPPY *enter the bedroom. Slight pause.*]

WILLY: [*stops short, looking at* BIFF] Glad to hear it, boy.

HAPPY: He wanted to say good night to you, sport.

WILLY: [*to* BIFF] Yeah. Knock him dead, boy. What'd you want to tell me?

BIFF: Just take it easy, Pop. Good night. [*He turns to go.*]

780 WILLY: [*unable to resist*] And if anything falls off the desk while you're talking to him—like a package or something—don't you pick it up. They have office boys for that.

LINDA: I'll make a big breakfast—

WILLY: Will you let me finish? [*to* BIFF] Tell him you were in the business in the West. Not farm work.

BIFF: All right, Dad.

LINDA: I think everything—

785 WILLY: [*going right through her speech*] And don't undersell yourself. No less than fifteen thousand dollars.

BIFF: [*unable to bear him*] Okay. Good night, Mom. [*He starts moving.*]

WILLY: Because you got a greatness in you, Biff, remember that. You got all kinds a greatness . . . [*He lies back, exhausted.*]

[BIFF *walks out.*]

LINDA: [*calling after* BIFF] Sleep well, darling!

HAPPY: I'm gonna get married, Mom. I wanted to tell you.

790 LINDA: Go to sleep, dear.

HAPPY: [*going*] I just wanted to tell you.

WILLY: Keep up the good work. [HAPPY *exits.*] God . . . remember that Ebbets Field° game? The championship of the city?

LINDA: Just rest. Should I sing to you?

WILLY: Yeah. Sing to me. [LINDA *hums a soft lullaby.*] When that team came out—he was the tallest, remember?

795 LINDA: Oh, yes. And in gold.

[BIFF *enters the darkened kitchen, takes a cigarette, and leaves the house. He comes downstage into a golden pool of light. He smokes, staring at the night.*]

WILLY: Like a young god. Hercules—something like that. And the sun, the sun all around him. Remember how he waved to me? Right up from the field, with the representatives of

---

°792 *Ebbets Field*: the baseball stadium of the Brooklyn Dodgers before they moved to Los Angeles in 1958. Biff had played there in a city championship football game. See 2.210 (page 1301).

three colleges standing by? And the buyers I brought, and the cheers when he came out— Loman, Loman, Loman! God Almighty, he'll be great yet. A star like that, magnificent, can never really fade away!

[*The light on* Willy *is fading. The gas heater begins to glow through the kitchen wall, near the stairs, a blue flame beneath red coils.*]

Linda: [*timidly*] Willy dear, what has he got against you?
Willy: I'm so tired. Don't talk any more.

[Biff *slowly returns to the kitchen. He stops, stares toward the heater.*]

Linda: Will you ask Howard to let you work in New York?
Willy: First thing in the morning. Everything'll be all right.                          800

[Biff *reaches behind the heater and draws out a length of rubber tubing. He is horrified and turns his head toward* Willy's *room, still dimly lit, from which the strains of* Linda's *desperate but monotonous humming rise.*]

Willy: [*staring through the window into the moonlight*] Gee, look at the moon moving between the buildings!

[Biff *wraps the tubing around his hand and quickly goes up the stairs.*]

## ACT 2

[*Music is heard, gay and bright. The curtain rises as the music fades away.* Willy, *in shirt sleeves, is sitting at the kitchen table, sipping coffee, his hat in his lap.* Linda *is filling his cup when she can.*]

Willy: Wonderful coffee. Meal in itself.
Linda: Can I make you some eggs?
Willy: No. Take a breath.
Linda: You look so rested, dear.
Willy: I slept like a dead one. First time in months. Imagine, sleeping till ten on a Tuesday     5
  morning. Boys left nice and early, heh?
Linda: They were out of here by eight o'clock.
Willy: Good work!
Linda: It was so thrilling to see them leaving together. I can't get over the shaving lotion in
  this house!
Willy: [*smiling*] Mmm—
Linda: Biff was very changed this morning. His whole attitude seemed to be hopeful. He     10
  couldn't wait to get downtown to see Oliver.
Willy: He's heading for a change. There's no question, there simply are certain men that take
  longer to get—solidified. How did he dress?
Linda: His blue suit. He's so handsome in that suit. He could be a—anything in that suit!

[Willy *gets up from the table.* Linda *holds his jacket for him.*]

Willy: There's no question, no question at all. Gee, on the way home tonight I'd like to buy
  some seeds.
Linda: [*laughing*] That'd be wonderful. But not enough sun gets back there. Nothing'll grow
  any more.
Willy: You wait, kid, before it's all over we're gonna get a little place out in the country, and     15
  I'll raise some vegetables, a couple of chickens . . .
Linda: You'll do it yet, dear.

[WILLY *walks out of his jacket,* LINDA *follows him.*]

WILLY: And they'll get married, and come for a weekend. I'd build a little guest house. 'Cause I got so many fine tools, all I'd need would be a little lumber and some peace of mind.

LINDA: [*joyfully*] I sewed the lining . . .

WILLY: I could build two guest houses, so they'd both come. Did he decide how much he's going to ask Oliver for?

20 LINDA: [*getting him into the jacket*] He didn't mention it, but I imagine ten or fifteen thousand. You going to talk to Howard today?

WILLY: Yeah. I'll put it to him straight and simple. He'll just have to take me off the road.

LINDA: And Willy, don't forget to ask for a little advance, because we've got the insurance premium. It's the grace period now.

WILLY: That's a hundred . . . ?

LINDA: A hundred and eight, sixty-eight. Because we're a little short again.

25 WILLY: Why are we short?

LINDA: Well, you had the motor job on the car . . .

WILLY: That goddam Studebaker!

LINDA: And you got one more payment on the refrigerator . . .

WILLY: But it just broke again!

30 LINDA: Well, it's old, dear.

WILLY: I told you we should've bought a well-advertised machine. Charley bought a General Electric and it's twenty years old and it's still good, that son-of-a-bitch.

LINDA: But, Willy—

WILLY: Whoever heard of a Hastings refrigerator? Once in my life I would like to own something outright before it's broken! I'm always in a race with the junkyard! I just finished paying for the car and it's on its last legs. The refrigerator consumes belts like a goddam maniac. They time those things. They time them so when you finally paid for them, they're used up.

LINDA: [*buttoning up his jacket as he unbuttons it*] All told, about two hundred dollars would carry us, dear. But that includes the last payment on the mortgage. After this payment, Willy, the house belongs to us.

35 WILLY: It's twenty-five years!

LINDA: Biff was nine years old when we bought it.

WILLY: Well, that's a great thing. To weather a twenty-five year mortgage is—

LINDA: It's an accomplishment.

WILLY: All the cement, the lumber, the reconstruction I put in this house! There ain't a crack to be found in it any more.

40 LINDA: Well, it served its purpose.

WILLY: What purpose? Some stranger'll come along, move in, and that's that. If only Biff would take this house, and raise a family . . . [*He starts to go.*] Good-by, I'm late.

LINDA: [*suddenly remembering*] Oh, I forgot! You're supposed to meet them for dinner.

WILLY: Me?

LINDA: At Frank's Chop House on Forty-eighth near Sixth Avenue.

45 WILLY: Is that so! How about you?

LINDA: No, just the three of you. They're gonna blow you to a big meal!

WILLY: Don't say! Who thought of that?

LINDA: Biff came to me this morning, Willy, and he said, "Tell Dad, we want to blow him to a big meal." Be there six o'clock. You and your two boys are going to have dinner.

WILLY: Gee whiz! That's really somethin'. I'm gonna knock Howard for a loop, kid. I'll get an advance, and I'll come home with a New York job. Goddammit, now I'm gonna do it!

LINDA: Oh, that's the spirit, Willy!                                                50
WILLY: I will never get behind a wheel the rest of my life!
LINDA: It's changing, Willy, I can feel it changing!
WILLY: Beyond a question. G'by, I'm late. [*He starts to go again.*]
LINDA: [*calling after him as she runs to the kitchen table for a handkerchief*] You got your glasses?
WILLY: [*feels for them, then comes back in*] Yeah, yeah, got my glasses.        55
LINDA: [*giving him the handkerchief*] And a handkerchief.
WILLY: Yeah, handkerchief.
LINDA: And your saccharine?
WILLY: Yeah, my saccharine.
LINDA: Be careful on the subway stairs.                                           60

[*She kisses him, and a silk stocking is seen hanging from her hand. WILLY notices it.*]

WILLY: Will you stop mending stockings? At least while I'm in the house. It gets me nervous. I
      can't tell you. Please.

[*LINDA hides the stocking in her hand as she follows WILLY across the forestage in front of the house.*]

LINDA: Remember, Frank's Chop House.
WILLY: [*passing the apron*] Maybe beets would grow out there.
LINDA: [*laughing*] But you tried so many times.
WILLY: Yeah. Well, don't work hard today. [*He disappears around the right corner of the house.*]   65
LINDA: Be careful!

[*As WILLY vanishes, LINDA waves to him. Suddenly the phone rings. She runs across the stage and
into the kitchen and lifts it.*]

LINDA: Hello? Oh, Biff! I'm so glad you called, I just . . . Yes, sure, I just told him. Yes, he'll be
      there for dinner at six o'clock, I didn't forget. Listen, I was just dying to tell you. You know
      that little rubber pipe I told you about? That he connected to the gas heater? I finally de-
      cided to go down the cellar this morning and take it away and destroy it. But it's gone!
      Imagine? He took it away himself, it isn't there! [*She listens.*] When? Oh, then you took it.
      Oh—nothing, it's just that I'd hoped he'd taken it away himself. Oh, I'm not worried, dar-
      ling, because this morning he left in such high spirits, it was like the old days! I'm not
      afraid any more. Did Mr. Oliver see you? . . . Well, you wait there then. And make a nice
      impression on him, darling. Just don't perspire too much before you see him. And have a
      nice time with Dad. He may have big news too . . . That's right, a New York job. And be
      sweet to him tonight, dear. Be loving to him. Because he's only a little boat looking for a
      harbor. [*She is trembling with sorrow and joy.*] Oh, that's wonderful, Biff, you'll save his life.
      Thanks, darling. Just put your arm around him when he comes into the restaurant. Give
      him a smile. That's the boy . . . Good-by, dear . . . You got your comb? . . . That's fine.
      Good-by, Biff dear.

[*In the middle of her speech, HOWARD WAGNER, thirty-six, wheels in a small typewriter table on which
is a wire-recording machine and proceeds to plug it in. This is on the left forestage. Light slowly fades on
LINDA as it rises on HOWARD. HOWARD is intent on threading the machine and only glances over his
shoulder as WILLY appears.*]

WILLY: Pst! Pst!
HOWARD: Hello, Willy, come in.
WILLY: Like to have a little talk with you, Howard.                               70
HOWARD: Sorry to keep you waiting. I'll be with you in a minute.

WILLY:  What's that, Howard?

HOWARD:  Didn't you ever see one of these? Wire recorder.

WILLY:  Oh. Can we talk a minute?

75  HOWARD:  Records things. Just got delivery yesterday. Been driving me crazy, the most terrific machine I ever saw in my life. I was up all night with it.

WILLY:  What do you do with it?

HOWARD:  I bought it for dictation, but you can do anything with it. Listen to this. I had it home last night. Listen to what I picked up. The first one is my daughter. Get this. [*He flicks the switch and "Roll out the Barrel" is heard being whistled.*] Listen to that kid whistle.

WILLY:  That is lifelike, isn't it?

HOWARD:  Seven years old. Get that tone.

80  WILLY:  Ts, ts. Like to ask a little favor if you . . .

[*The whistling breaks off, and the voice of HOWARD'S DAUGHTER is heard.*]

HIS DAUGHTER:  "Now you, Daddy."

HOWARD:  She's crazy for me! [*Again the same song is whistled.*] That's me! Ha! [*He winks.*]

WILLY:  You're very good!

[*The whistling breaks off again. The machine runs silent for a moment.*]

HOWARD:  Sh! Get this now, this is my son.

85  HIS SON:  "The capital of Alabama is Montgomery; the capital of Arizona is Phoenix; the capital of Arkansas is Little Rock; the capital of California is Sacramento . . ." [*and on, and on*]

HOWARD:  [*holding up five fingers*] Five years old, Willy!

WILLY:  He'll make an announcer some day!

HIS SON:  [*continuing*] "The capital . . . "

HOWARD:  Get that—alphabetical order! [*The machine breaks off suddenly.*] Wait a minute. The maid kicked the plug out.

90  WILLY:  It certainly is a—

HOWARD:  Sh, for God's sake!

HIS SON:  "It's nine o'clock, Bulova watch time. So I have to go to sleep."

WILLY:  That really is—

HOWARD:  Wait a minute! The next is my wife.

[*They wait.*]

95  HOWARD'S VOICE:  "Go on, say something." [*pause*] "Well, you gonna talk?"

HIS WIFE:  "I can't think of anything."

HOWARD'S VOICE:  "Well, talk—it's turning."

HIS WIFE:  [*shyly, beaten*] "Hello." [*Silence*] "Oh, Howard, I can't talk into this . . . "

HOWARD:  [*snapping the machine off*] That was my wife.

100  WILLY:  That is a wonderful machine. Can we—

HOWARD:  I tell you, Willy, I'm gonna take my camera, and my bandsaw, and all my hobbies, and out they go. This is the most fascinating relaxation I ever found.

WILLY:  I think I'll get one myself.

HOWARD:  Sure, they're only a hundred and a half. You can't do without it. Supposing you wanna hear Jack Benny,° see? But you can't be at home at that hour. So you tell the maid to turn the radio on when Jack Benny comes on, and this automatically goes on with the radio . . .

---

°103 *Jack Benny*: (1894–1974), vaudeville, radio, television, and movie comedian.

WILLY: And when you come home you . . .

HOWARD: You can come home twelve o'clock, one o'clock, any time you like, and you get 105
yourself a Coke and sit yourself down, throw the switch, and there's Jack Benny's program
in the middle of the night!

WILLY: I'm definitely going to get one. Because lots of time I'm on the road, and I think to myself,
what I must be missing on the radio!

HOWARD: Don't you have a radio in the car?

WILLY: Well, yeah, but who ever thinks of turning it on?

HOWARD: Say, aren't you supposed to be in Boston?

WILLY: That's what I want to talk to you about, Howard. You got a minute?     110

[*He draws a chair in from the wing.*]

HOWARD: What happened? What're you doing here?

WILLY: Well . . .

HOWARD: You didn't crack up again, did you?

WILLY: Oh, no. No . . .

HOWARD: Geez, you had me worried there for a minute. What's the trouble?     115

WILLY: Well, tell you the truth, Howard, I've come to the decision that I'd rather not travel any
more.

HOWARD: Not travel! Well, what'll you do?

WILLY: Remember, Christmas time, when you had the party here? You said you'd try to think
of some spot for me here in town.

HOWARD: With us?

WILLY: Well, sure.

HOWARD: Oh, yeah, yeah. I remember. Well, I couldn't think of anything for you, Willy.     120

WILLY: I tell ya, Howard. The kids are all grown up, y'know. I don't need much any more. If I
could take home—well, sixty-five dollars a week, I could swing it.

HOWARD: Yeah, but Willy, see I—

WILLY: I tell ya why, Howard. Speaking frankly and between the two of us, y'know—I'm just
a little tired.

HOWARD: Oh, I could understand that, Willy. But you're a road man, Willy, and we do a road 125
business. We've only got a half-dozen salesmen on the floor here.

WILLY: God knows, Howard, I never asked a favor of any man. But I was with the firm when
your father used to carry you up here in his arms.

HOWARD: I know that, Willy, but—

WILLY: Your father came to me the day you were born and asked me what I thought of the
name of Howard, may he rest in peace.

HOWARD: I appreciate that, Willy, but there just is no spot here for you. If I had a spot I'd slam
you right in, but I just don't have a single solitary spot.

[*He looks for his lighter.* WILLY *has picked it up and gives it to him. Pause.*]

WILLY: [*with increasing anger*] Howard, all I need to set my table is fifty dollars a week.     130

HOWARD: But where am I going to put you, kid?

WILLY: Look, it isn't a question of whether I can sell merchandise, is it?

HOWARD: No, but it's a business, kid, and everybody's gotta pull his own weight.

WILLY: [*desperately*] Just let me tell you a story, Howard—

HOWARD: 'Cause you gotta admit, business is business.     135

WILLY: [*angrily*] Business in definitely business, but just listen for a minute. You don't understand this. When I was a boy—eighteen, nineteen—I was already on the road. And there

was a question in my mind as to whether selling had a future for me. Because in those days I had a yearning to go to Alaska. See, there were three gold strikes in one month in Alaska, and I felt like going out. Just for the ride, you might say.

HOWARD: [*barely interested*] Don't say.

WILLY: Oh, yeah, my father lived many years in Alaska. He was an adventurous man. We've got quite a little streak of self-reliance in our family. I thought I'd go out with my older brother and try to locate him, and maybe settle in the North with the old man. And I was almost decided to go, when I met a salesman in the Parker House.° His name was Dave Singleman. And he was eighty-four years old, and he'd drummed merchandise in thirty-one states. And old Dave, he'd go up to his room, y'understand, put on his green velvet slippers—I'll never forget—and pick up his phone and call the buyers, and without ever leaving his room, at the age of eighty-four, he made his living. And when I saw that, I realized that selling was the greatest career a man could want. 'Cause what could be more satisfying than to be able to go, at the age of eighty-four, into twenty or thirty different cities, and pick up a phone, and be remembered and loved and helped by so many different people? Do you know? when he died—and by the way he died the death of a salesman, in his green velvet slippers in the smoker of the New York, New Haven and Hartford, going into Boston—when he died, hundreds of salesmen and buyers were at his funeral. Things were sad on a lotta trains for months after that. [*He stands up. Howard has not looked at him.*] In those days there was personality in it, Howard. There was respect, and comradeship, and gratitude in it. Today, it's all cut and dried, and there's no chance for bringing friendship to bear—or personality. You see what I mean? They don't know me any more.

HOWARD: [*moving away, to the right*] That's just the thing, Willy.

140 WILLY: If I had forty dollars a week—that's all I'd need. Forty dollars, Howard.

HOWARD: Kid, I can't take blood from a stone, I—

WILLY: [*desperation is on him now*] Howard, the year Al Smith° was nominated, your father came to me and—

HOWARD: [*starting to go off*] I've got to see some people, kid.

WILLY: [*stopping him*] I'm talking about your father! There were promises made across this desk! You mustn't tell me you've got people to see—I put thirty-four years into this firm, Howard, and now I can't pay my insurance! You can't eat the orange and throw the peel away—a man is not a piece of fruit! [*after a pause*] Now pay attention. Your father—in 1928 I had a big year. I averaged a hundred and seventy dollars a week in commissions.

145 HOWARD: [*impatiently*] Now, Willy, you never averaged—

WILLY: [*banging his hand on the desk*] I averaged a hundred and seventy dollars a week in the year of 1928! And your father came to me—or rather, I was in the office here—it was right over this desk—and he put his hand on my shoulder—

HOWARD: [*getting up*] You'll have to excuse me, Willy, I gotta see some people. Pull yourself together. [*going out*] I'll be back in a little while.

[*On HOWARD's exit, the light on his chair grows very bright and strange.*]

WILLY: Pull myself together! What the hell did I say to him? My God, I was yelling at him! How could I! [*WILLY breaks off, staring at the light, which occupies the chair, animating it. He approaches this chair, standing across the desk from it.*] Frank, Frank, don't you remember what you told me that time? How you put your hand on my shoulder, and Frank . . . [*He*

---

°138 *Parker House*: a hotel in Boston.  142 *Al Smith*: Alfred E. Smith was governor of New York State (1919–1921, 1923–1929) and the Democratic presidential candidate defeated by Herbert Hoover in 1928.

*leans on the desk and as he speaks the dead man's name he accidentally switches on the recorder, and instantly*]

HOWARD'S SON: ". . . of New York is Albany. The capital of Ohio is Cincinnati, the capital of Rhode Island is . . . " [*The recitation continues.*]

WILLY: [*leaping away with fright, shouting*] Ha! Howard! Howard! Howard!                       150

HOWARD: [*rushing in*] What happened?

WILLY: [*pointing at the machine, which continues nasally, childishly, with the capital cities*] Shut it off! Shut it off!

HOWARD: [*pulling the plug out*] Look, Willy . . .

WILLY: [*pressing his hands to his eyes*] I gotta get myself some coffee. I'll get some coffee . . .

[*WILLY starts to walk out. HOWARD stops him.*]

HOWARD: [*rolling up the cord*] Willy, look . . .                                               155

WILLY: I'll go to Boston.

HOWARD: Willy, you can't go to Boston for us.

WILLY: Why can't I go?

HOWARD: I don't want you to represent us. I've been meaning to tell you for a long time now.

WILLY: Howard, are you firing me?                                                             160

HOWARD: I think you need a good long rest, Willy.

WILLY: Howard—

HOWARD: And when you feel better, come back, and we'll see if we can work something out.

WILLY: But I gotta earn money, Howard. I'm in no position to—

HOWARD: Where are your sons? Why don't your sons give you a hand?                             165

WILLY: They're working on a very big deal.

HOWARD: This is no time for false pride, Willy. You go to your sons and you tell them that you're tired. You've got two great boys, haven't you?

WILLY: Oh, no question, no question, but in the meantime . . .

HOWARD: Then that's that, heh?

WILLY: All right, I'll go to Boston tomorrow.                                                 170

HOWARD: No, no.

WILLY: I can't throw myself on my sons. I'm not a cripple!

HOWARD: Look, kid, I'm busy this morning.

WILLY: [*grasping HOWARD's arm*] Howard, you've got to let me go to Boston!

HOWARD: [*hard, keeping himself under control*] I've got a line of people to see this morning. Sit  175
down, take five minutes, and pull yourself together, and then go home, will ya? I need the
office, Willy [*He starts to go, turns, remembering the recorder, starts to push off the table holding
the recorder.*] Oh, yeah. Whenever you can this week, stop by and drop off the samples.
You'll feel better, Willy, and then come back and we'll talk. Pull yourself together, kid,
there's people outside.

[*HOWARD exits, pushing the table off left. WILLY stares into space, exhausted. Now the music is heard—
BEN's music—first distantly, then closer. As WILLY speaks, BEN enters from the right. He carries valise
and umbrella.*]

WILLY: Oh, Ben, how did you do it? What is the answer? Did you wind up the Alaska deal
already?

BEN: Doesn't take much time if you know what you're doing. Just a short business trip. Boarding
ship in an hour. Wanted to say good-by.

WILLY: Ben, I've got to talk to you.

BEN: [*glancing at his watch*] Haven't much time, William.

WILLY: [*crossing the apron to BEN*] Ben, nothing's working out. I don't know what to do.     180

BEN: Now, look here, William. I've bought timberland in Alaska and I need a man to look after things for me.

WILLY: God, timberland! Me and my boys in those grand outdoors!

BEN: You've a new continent at your doorstep, William. Get out of these cities, they're full of talk and time payments and courts of law. Screw on your fists and you can fight for a fortune up there.

WILLY: Yes, yes! Linda, Linda!

[LINDA *enters as of old, with the wash.*]

185   LINDA: Oh, you're back?

BEN: I haven't much time.

WILLY: No, wait! Linda, he's got a proposition for me in Alaska.

LINDA: But you've got—[*to* BEN] He's got a beautiful job here.

WILLY: But in Alaska, kid, I could—

190   LINDA: You're doing well enough, Willy!

BEN: [*to* LINDA] Enough for what, my dear?

LINDA: [*frightened of* BEN *and angry at him*] Don't say those things to him! Enough to be happy right here, right now. [*to* WILLY, *while* BEN *laughs*] Why must everybody conquer the world? You're well liked, and the boys love you, and someday—[*to* BEN]—why old man Wagner told him just the other day that if he keeps it up he'll be a member of the firm, didn't he, Willy?

WILLY: Sure, sure. I am building something with this firm, Ben, and if a man is building something he must be on the right track, mustn't he?

BEN: What are you building? Lay your hand on it. Where is it?

195   WILLY: [*hesitantly*] That's true, Linda, there's nothing.

LINDA: Why? [*to* BEN] There's a man eighty-four years old—

WILLY: That's right, Ben, that's right. When I look at that man I say, what is there to worry about?

BEN: Bah!

WILLY: It's true, Ben. All he has to do is go into any city, pick up the phone, and he's making his living and you know why?

200   BEN: [*picking up his valise*] I've got to go.

WILLY: [*holding* BEN *back*] Look at this boy!

[BIFF, *in his high school sweater, enters carrying suitcase.* HAPPY *carries* BIFF's *shoulder guards, gold helmet, and football pants.*]

WILLY: Without a penny to his name, three great universities are begging for him, and from there the sky's the limit, because it's not what you do, Ben. It's who you know and the smile on your face! It's contacts, Ben, contacts! The whole wealth of Alaska passes over the lunch table at the Commodore Hotel,° and that's the wonder, the wonder of this country, that a man can end with diamonds here on the basis of being liked! [*He turns to* BIFF] And that's why when you get out on that field today it's important. Because thousands of people will be rooting for you and loving you. [*to* BEN, *who has again begun to leave*] And Ben! when he walks into a business office his name will sound out like a bell and all the doors will open to him! I've seen it, Ben, I've seen it a thousand times! You can't feel it with your hand like timber, but it's there!

BEN: Good-by, William.

WILLY: Ben, am I right? Don't you think I'm right? I value your advice.

---

°202 *Commodore Hotel*: a large hotel in New York City.

BEN: There's a new continent at your doorstep, William. You could walk out rich. Rich! [*He*     205
  *is gone.*]
WILLY: We'll do it here, Ben! You hear me? We're gonna do it here!

[*YOUNG BERNARD rushes in. The gay music of the Boys is heard.*]

BERNARD: Oh, gee, I was afraid you left already!
WILLY: Why? What time is it?
BERNARD: It's half-past one!
WILLY: Well, come on, everybody! Ebbets Field next stop! Where's the pennants? [*He rushes*     210
  *through the wall-line of the kitchen and out into the dining-room.*]
LINDA: [*to BIFF*] Did you pack fresh underwear?
BIFF: [*who has been limbering up*] I want to go!
BERNARD: Biff, I'm carrying your helmet, ain't I?
HAPPY: No, I'm carrying the helmet.
BERNARD: Oh, Biff, you promised me.                                                             215
HAPPY: I'm carrying the helmet.
BERNARD: How am I going to get in the locker room?
LINDA: Let him carry the shoulder guards. [*She puts her coat and hat on in the kitchen.*]
BERNARD: Can I, Biff? 'Cause I told everybody I'm going to be in the locker room.
HAPPY: In Ebbets Field it's the clubhouse.                                                      220
BERNARD: I meant the clubhouse. Biff!
HAPPY: Biff!
BIFF: [*grandly, after a slight pause.*] Let him carry the shoulder guards.
HAPPY: [*as he gives BERNARD the shoulder guards*] Stay close to us now.

[*WILLY rushes in with the pennants.*]

WILLY: [*handing them out*] Everybody wave when Biff comes out on the field. [*HAPPY and*     225
  *BERNARD run off.*] You set now, boy?

[*The music has died away.*]

BIFF: Ready to go, Pop. Every muscle is ready.
WILLY: [*at the edge of the apron*] You realize what this means?
BIFF: That's right, Pop.
WILLY: [*feeling BIFF's muscles*] You're comin' home this afternoon captain of the All-Scholastic
  Championship Team of the City of New York.
BIFF: I got it, Pop. And remember, pal, when I take off my helmet, that touchdown is for you.     230
WILLY: Let's go! [*He is starting out, with his arm around BIFF, when CHARLEY enters, as of old, in
  knickers.*] I got no room for you, Charley.
CHARLEY: Room? For what?
WILLY: In the car.
CHARLEY: You goin' for a ride? I wanted to shoot some casino.
WILLY: [*furiously*] Casino! [*incredulously*] Don't you realize what today is?                 235
LINDA: Oh, he knows, Willy. He's just kidding you.
WILLY: That's nothing to kid about!
CHARLEY: No, Linda, what's goin' on?
LINDA: He's playing in Ebbets Field.
CHARLEY: Baseball in this weather?                                                              240
WILLY: Don't talk to him. Come on, come on! [*He is pushing them out.*]
CHARLEY: Wait a minute, didn't you hear the news?
WILLY: What?

CHARLEY: Don't you listen to the radio? Ebbets Field just blew up.

245  WILLY: You go to hell! [CHARLEY *laughs. Pushing them out.*] Come on, come on! We're late.

CHARLEY: [*as they go*] Knock a homer, Biff, knock a homer!

WILLY: [*the last to leave, turning to* CHARLEY] I don't think that was funny, Charley. This is the greatest day of his life.

CHARLEY: Willy, when are you going to grow up?

WILLY: Yeah, heh? When this game is over, Charley, you'll be laughing out the other side of your face. They'll be calling him another Red Grange.° Twenty-five thousand a year.

250  CHARLEY: [*kidding*] Is that so?

WILLY: Yeah, that's so.

CHARLEY: Well, then, I'm sorry, Willy. But tell me something.

WILLY: What?

CHARLEY: Who is Red Grange?

255  WILLY: Put up your hands. Goddam you, put up your hands!

[CHARLEY, *chuckling, shakes his head and walks away, around the left corner of the stage.* WILLY *follows him. The music rises to a mocking frenzy.*]

WILLY: Who the hell do you think you are, better than everybody else? You don't know everything, you big, ignorant, stupid. . . . Put up your hands!

[*Light rises, on the right side of the forestage, on a small table in the reception room of* CHARLEY's *office. Traffic sounds are heard.* BERNARD, *now mature, sits whistling to himself. A pair of tennis rackets and an overnight bag are on the floor beside him.*]

WILLY: [*offstage*] What are you walking away for? Don't walk away! If you're going to say something say it to my face! I know you laugh at me behind my back. You'll laugh out of the other side of your goddam face after this game. Touchdown! Touchdown! Eighty thousand people! Touchdown. Right between the goal posts.

[BERNARD *is a quiet, earnest, but self-assured young man.* WILLY's *voice is coming from right upstage now.* BERNARD *lowers his feet off the table and listens.* JENNY, *his father's secretary, enters.*]

JENNY: [*distressed*] Say, Bernard, will you go out in the hall?

BERNARD: What is that noise? Who is it?

260  JENNY: Mr. Loman. He just got off the elevator.

BERNARD: [*getting up*] Who's he arguing with?

JENNY: Nobody. There's nobody with him. I can't deal with him any more, and your father gets all upset everytime he comes. I've got a lot of typing to do, and your father's waiting to sign it. Will you see him?

WILLY: [*entering*] Touchdown! Touch—[*He sees* JENNY.] Jenny, Jenny, good to see you. How're ya? Workin'? Or still honest?

JENNY: Fine. How've you been feeling?

265  WILLY: Not much any more, Jenny. Ha, ha! [*He is surprised to see the rackets.*]

BERNARD: Hello, Uncle Willy.

WILLY: [*almost shocked*] Bernard! Well, look who's here! [*He comes quickly, guiltily, to* BERNARD *and warmly shakes his hand.*]

BERNARD: How are you? Good to see you.

---

°249 *Red Grange:* Harold Edward Grange (1903–1991), all-America halfback (1923–1925) at the University of Illinois.

WILLY: What are you doing here?

BERNARD: Oh, just stopped off to see Pop. Get off my feet till my train leaves. I'm going to 270
Washington in a few minutes.

WILLY: Is he in?

BERNARD: Yes, he's in his office with the accountants. Sit down.

WILLY: [*sitting down*] What're you going to do in Washington?

BERNARD: Oh, just a case I've got there, Willy.

WILLY: That so? [*Indicating the rackets*] You going to play tennis there? 275

BERNARD: I'm staying with a friend who's got a court.

WILLY: Don't say. His own tennis court. Must be fine people, I bet.

BERNARD: They are, very nice. Dad tells me Biff's in town.

WILLY: [*with a big smile*] Yeah, Biff's in. Working on a very big deal, Bernard.

BERNARD: What's Biff doing? 280

WILLY: Well, he's been doing very big things in the West. But he decided to establish himself
here. Very big. We're having dinner. Did I hear your wife had a boy?

BERNARD: That's right. Our second.

WILLY: Two boys! What do you know!

BERNARD: What kind of a deal has Biff got?

WILLY: Well, Bill Oliver—very big sporting-goods man—he wants Biff very badly. Called him 285
in from the West. Long distance, carte blanche, special deliveries. Your friends have their
own private tennis court?

BERNARD: You still with the old firm, Willy?

WILLY: [*after a pause*] I'm—I'm overjoyed to see how you made the grade, Bernard, overjoyed.
It's an encouraging thing to see a young man really—really—Looks very good for Biff—
very—[*He breaks off, then*] Bernard—[*He is so full of emotion, he breaks off again.*]

BERNARD: What is it, Willy?

WILLY: [*small and alone*] What—what's the secret?

BERNARD: What secret? 290

WILLY: How—how did you? Why didn't he ever catch on?

BERNARD: I wouldn't know that, Willy.

WILLY: [*confidentially, desperately*] You were his friend, his boyhood friend. There's something I
don't understand about it. His life ended after that Ebbets Field game. From the age of
seventeen nothing good ever happened to him.

BERNARD: He never trained himself for anything.

WILLY: But he did, he did. After high school he took so many correspondence courses. Radio 295
mechanics; television; God knows what, and never made the slightest mark.

BERNARD: [*taking off his glasses*] Willy, do you want to talk candidly?

WILLY: [*rising, faces* BERNARD] I regard you as a very brilliant man, Bernard. I value your
advice.

BERNARD: Oh, the hell with the advice, Willy. I couldn't advise you. There's just one thing I've
always wanted to ask you. When he was supposed to graduate, and the math teacher
flunked him—

WILLY: Oh, that son-of-a-bitch ruined his life.

BERNARD: Yeah, but, Willy, all he had to do was go to summer school and make up that subject. 300

WILLY: That's right, that's right.

BERNARD: Did you tell him not to go to summer school?

WILLY: Me? I begged him to go. I ordered him to go!

BERNARD: Then why wouldn't he go?

WILLY: Why? Why! Bernard, that question has been trailing me like a ghost for the last fifteen 305
years. He flunked the subject, and laid down and died like a hammer hit him!

BERNARD: Take it easy, kid.

WILLY: Let me talk to you—I got nobody to talk to. Bernard, Bernard, was it my fault? Y'see? It keeps going around in my mind, maybe I did something to him. I got nothing to give him.

BERNARD: Don't take it so hard.

WILLY: Why did he lay down? What is the story there? You were his friend!

310 BERNARD: Willy, I remember, it was June, and our grades came out. And he'd flunked math.

WILLY: That son-of-a-bitch!

BERNARD: No, it wasn't right then. Biff just got very angry, I remember, and he was ready to enroll in summer school.

WILLY: [*surprised*] He was?

BERNARD: He wasn't beaten by it at all. But then, Willy, he disappeared from the block for almost a month. And I got the idea that he'd gone up to New England to see you. Did he have a talk with you then?

[*WILLY stares in silence.*]

315 BERNARD: Willy?

WILLY: [*with a strong edge of resentment in his voice*] Yeah, he came to Boston. What about it?

BERNARD: Well, just that when he came back—I'll never forget this, it always mystifies me. Because I'd thought so well of Biff, even though he'd always taken advantage of me. I loved him, Willy, y'know? And he came back after that month and took his sneakers— remember the sneakers with "University of Virginia" printed on them? He was so proud of those, wore them every day. And he took them down in the cellar, and burned them up in the furnace. We had a fist fight. It lasted at least half an hour. Just the two of us, punching each other down the cellar, and crying right through it. I've often thought of how strange it was that I knew he'd given up his life. What happened in Boston, Willy?

[*WILLY looks at him as at an intruder.*]

BERNARD: I just bring it up because you asked me.

WILLY: [*angrily*] Nothing. What do you mean, "What happened?" What's that got to do with anything?

320 BERNARD: Well, don't get sore.

WILLY: What are you trying to do, blame it on me? If a boy lays down is that my fault?

BERNARD: Now, Willy, don't get—

WILLY: Well, don't—don't talk to me that way! What does that mean, "What happened?"

[*CHARLEY enters. He is in his vest, and he carries a bottle of bourbon.*]

CHARLEY: Hey, you're going to miss that train. [*He waves the bottle.*]

325 BERNARD: Yeah, I'm going. [*He takes the bottle.*] Thanks, Pop. [*He picks up his rackets and bag.*] Good-by, Willy, and don't worry about it. You know, "If at first you don't succeed . . . "

WILLY: Yes, I believe in that.

BERNARD: But sometimes, Willy, it's better for a man just to walk away.

WILLY: Walk away?

BERNARD: That's right.

330 WILLY: But if you can't walk away?

BERNARD: [*after a slight pause*] I guess that's when it's tough. [*extending his hand*] Good-by, Willy.

WILLY: [*shaking BERNARD's hand*] Good-by, boy.

CHARLEY: [*an arm on BERNARD's shoulder*] How do you like this kid? Gonna argue a case in front of the Supreme Court.

BERNARD: [*protesting*] Pop!

WILLY: [*genuinely shocked, pained, and happy*] No! The Supreme Court!     335

BERNARD: I gotta run. 'By, Dad!

CHARLEY: Knock 'em dead, Bernard!

[*BERNARD goes off.*]

WILLY: [*as CHARLEY takes out his wallet*] The Supreme Court! And he didn't even mention it!

CHARLEY: [*counting out money on the desk*] He don't have to—he's gonna do it.

WILLY: And you never told him what to do, did you? You never took any interest in him.     340

CHARLEY: My salvation is that I never took any interest in anything. There's some money— fifty dollars. I got an accountant inside.

WILLY: Charley, look . . . [*with difficulty*] I got my insurance to pay. If you can manage it—I need a hundred and ten dollars.

[*CHARLEY doesn't reply for a moment; merely stops moving.*]

WILLY: I'd draw it from my bank but Linda would know, and I . . .

CHARLEY: Sit down, Willy.

WILLY: [*moving toward the chair*] I'm keeping an account of everything, remember. I'll pay     345 every penny back. [*He sits.*]

CHARLEY: Now listen to me, Willy . . .

WILLY: I want you to know I appreciate . . .

CHARLEY: [*sitting down on the table*] Willy, what're you doin'? What the hell is goin' on in your head?

WILLY: Why? I'm simply . . .

CHARLEY: I offered you a job. You can make fifty dollars a week. And I won't send you on the     350 road.

WILLY: I've got a job.

CHARLEY: Without pay? What kind of job is a job without pay? [*He rises.*] Now, look, kid, enough is enough. I'm no genius but I know when I'm being insulted.

WILLY: Insulted!

CHARLEY: Why don't you want to work for me?

WILLY: What's the matter with you? I've got a job.     355

CHARLEY: Then what're you walkin' in here every week for?

WILLY: [*getting up*] Well, if you don't want me to walk in here—

CHARLEY: I am offering you a job.

WILLY: I don't want your goddam job!

CHARLEY: When the hell are you going to grow up?     360

WILLY: [*furiously*] You big ignoramus, if you say that to me again I'll rap you one! I don't care how big you are [*He's ready to fight.*]

[*Pause.*]

CHARLEY: [*kindly, going to him*] How much do you need, Willy?

WILLY: Charley, I'm strapped. I'm strapped. I don't know what to do. I was just fired.

CHARLEY: Howard fired you?

WILLY: That snotnose. Imagine that? I named him. I named him Howard.     365

CHARLEY: Willy, when're you gonna realize that them things don't mean anything? You named him Howard, but you can't sell that. The only thing you got in this world is what you can sell. And the funny thing is that you're a salesman, and you don't know that.

WILLY: I've tried to think otherwise, I guess. I always felt that if a man was impressive, and well liked, that nothing—

CHARLEY: Why must everybody like you? Who liked J. P. Morgan?° Was he impressive? In a Turkish bath he'd look like a butcher. But with his pockets on he was very well liked. Now listen, Willy, I know you don't like me, and nobody can say I'm in love with you, but I'll give you a job because—just for the hell of it, put it that way. Now what do you say?

WILLY: I—I just can't work for you, Charley.

370 CHARLEY: What're you, jealous of me?

WILLY: I can't work for you, that's all, don't ask me why.

CHARLEY: [*angered, takes out more bills*] You been jealous of me all your life, you damned fool! Here, pay your insurance. [*He puts the money in* WILLY's *hand.*]

WILLY: I'm keeping strict accounts.

CHARLEY: I've got some work to do. Take care of yourself. And pay your insurance.

375 WILLY: [*moving to the right*] Funny, y'know? After all the highways, and the trains, and the appointments, and the years, you end up worth more dead than alive.

CHARLEY: Willy, nobody's worth nothin' dead. [*after a slight pause*] Did you hear what I said?

[WILLY *stands still, dreaming.*]

CHARLEY: Willy!

WILLY: Apologize to Bernard for me when you see him. I didn't mean to argue with him. He's a fine boy. They're all fine boys, and they'll end up big—all of them. Someday they'll all play tennis together. Wish me luck, Charley. He saw Bill Oliver today.

CHARLEY: Good luck.

380 WILLY: [*on the verge of tears*] Charley, you're the only friend I got. Isn't that a remarkable thing? [*He goes out.*]

CHARLEY: Jesus!

[CHARLEY *stares after him a moment and follows. All light blacks out. Suddenly raucous music is heard, and a red glow rises behind the screen at right.* STANLEY, *a young waiter, appears, carrying a table, followed by* HAPPY, *who is carrying two chairs.*]

STANLEY: [*putting the table down*] That's all right, Mr. Loman. I can handle it myself. [*He turns and takes the chairs from* HAPPY *and places them at the table.*]

HAPPY: [*glancing around.*] Oh, this is better.

STANLEY: Sure, in the front there you're in the middle of all kinds a noise. Whenever you got a party, Mr. Loman, you just tell me and I'll put you back here. Y' know, there's a lotta people they don't like it private, because when they go out they like to see a lotta action around them because they're sick and tired to stay in the house by theirself. But I know you, you ain't from Hackensack.° You know what I mean?

385 HAPPY: [*sitting down*] So how's it coming, Stanley?

STANLEY: Ah, it's a dog's life. I only wish during the war they'd a took me in the Army. I coulda been dead by now.

---

°368 *J. P. Morgan:* John Pierpont Morgan (1837–1913) was the founder of U.S. Steel and the head of a gigantic family fortune that was enlarged by his son, John Pierpont Morgan (1867–1943). Charley is probably referring to the son.    384 *Hackensack:* a city in northeastern New Jersey; Stanley uses the name as a reference to unsophisticated visitors to New York City.

HAPPY:  My brother's back, Stanley.

STANLEY:  Oh, he come back, heh? From the Far West.

HAPPY:  Yeah, big cattle man, my brother, so treat him right. And my father's coming too.

STANLEY:  Oh, your father too!     390

HAPPY:  You got a couple of nice lobsters?

STANLEY:  Hundred per cent, big.

HAPPY:  I want them with claws.

STANLEY:  Don't worry. I don't give you no mice. [*HAPPY laughs.*] How about some wine? It'll put a head on the meal.

HAPPY:  No. You remember, Stanley, that recipe I brought you from overseas? With the cham-  395
pagne in it?

STANLEY:  Oh, yeah, sure. I still got it tacked up yet in the kitchen. But that'll have to cost a buck apiece anyways.

HAPPY:  That's all right.

STANLEY:  What'd you, hit a number or somethin'?

HAPPY:  No, it's a little celebration. My brother is—I think he pulled off a big deal today. I think we're going into business together.

STANLEY:  Great! That's the best for you. Because a family business, you know what I mean?—  400
that's the best.

HAPPY:  That's what I think.

STANLEY:  'Cause what's the difference? Somebody steals? It's in the family. Know what I mean? [*sotto voce°*] Like this bartender here. The boss is goin' crazy what kinda leak he's got in the cash register. You put it in but it don't come out.

HAPPY:  [*raising his head*] Sh!

STANLEY:  What?

HAPPY:  You notice I wasn't lookin' right or left, was I?

STANLEY:  No.     405

HAPPY:  And my eyes are closed.

STANLEY:  So what's the—?

HAPPY:  Strudel's comin'.

STANLEY:  [*catching on, looks around*] Ah, no, there's no—     410

[*He breaks off as a furred, lavishly dressed Girl enters and sits at the next table. Both follow her with their eyes.*]

STANLEY:  Geez, how'd ya know?

HAPPY:  I got radar or something. [*staring directly at her profile*] Oooooooo . . . Stanley.

STANLEY:  I think that's for you, Mr. Loman.

HAPPY:  Look at that mouth. Oh God. And the binoculars.

STANLEY:  Geez, you got a life, Mr. Loman.     415

HAPPY:  Wait on her.

STANLEY:  [*going to the GIRL's table*] Would you like a menu, ma'am?

GIRL:  I'm expecting someone, but I'd like a—

HAPPY:  Why don't you bring her—excuse me, miss, do you mind? I sell champagne, and I'd like you to try my brand. Bring her a champagne, Stanley.

GIRL:  That's awfully nice of you.     420

HAPPY:  Don't mention it. It's all company money. [*He laughs.*]

GIRL:  That's a charming product to be selling, isn't it?

---

°402 *sotto voce*: spoken in an undertone or "stage" whisper.

HAPPY: Oh, gets to be like everything else. Selling is selling, y'know.

GIRL: I suppose.

425 HAPPY: You don't happen to sell, do you?

GIRL: No, I don't sell.

HAPPY: Would you object to a compliment from a stranger? You ought to be on a magazine cover.

GIRL: [*looking at him a little archly*] I have been.

[*STANLEY comes in with a glass of champagne.*]

HAPPY: What'd I say before, Stanley? You see? She's a cover girl.

430 STANLEY: Oh, I could see, I could see.

HAPPY: [*to the GIRL*] What magazine?

GIRL: Oh, a lot of them [*She takes the drink.*] Thank you.

HAPPY: You know what they say in France, don't you? "Champagne is the drink of the complexion"—Hya, Biff!

[*BIFF has entered and sits with HAPPY.*]

BIFF: Hello, kid. Sorry I'm late.

435 HAPPY: I just got here. Uh, Miss—?

GIRL: Forsythe.

HAPPY: Miss Forsythe, this is my brother.

BIFF: Is Dad here?

HAPPY: His name if Biff. You might've heard of him. Great football player.

440 GIRL: Really? What team?

HAPPY: Are you familiar with football?

GIRL: No. I'm afraid I'm not.

HAPPY: Biff is quarterback with the New York Giants.

GIRL: Well, that is nice, isn't it? [*She drinks.*]

445 HAPPY: Good health.

GIRL: I'm happy to meet you.

HAPPY: That's my name. Hap. It's really Harold, but at West Point they called me Happy.

GIRL: [*now really impressed*] Oh, I see. How do you do? [*She turns her profile.*]

BIFF: Isn't Dad coming?

450 HAPPY: You want her?

BIFF: Oh, I could never make that.

HAPPY: I remember the time that idea would never come into your head. Where's the old confidence, Biff?

BIFF: I just saw Oliver—

HAPPY: Wait a minute. I've got to see that old confidence again. Do you want her? She's on call.

455 BIFF: Oh, no. [*He turns to look at the GIRL.*]

HAPPY: I'm telling you. Watch this. [*turning to the Girl*] Honey? [*She turns to him.*] Are you busy?

GIRL: Well, I am . . . but I could make a phone call.

HAPPY: Do that, will you, honey? And see if you can get a friend. We'll be here for a while. Biff is one of the greatest football players in the country.

GIRL: [*standing up*] Well, I'm certainly happy to meet you.

460 HAPPY: Come back soon.

GIRL: I'll try.

HAPPY: Don't try, honey, try hard.

[*The* GIRL *exits.* STANLEY *follows, shaking his head in bewildered admiration.*]

HAPPY: Isn't that a shame now? A beautiful girl like that? That's why I can't get married. There's not a good woman in a thousand. New York is loaded with them, kid!

BIFF: Hap, look—

HAPPY: I told you she was on call! 465

BIFF: [*strangely unnerved*] Cut it out, will ya? I want to say something to you.

HAPPY: Did you see Oliver?

BIFF: I saw him all right. Now look, I want to tell Dad a couple of things and I want you to help me.

HAPPY: What? Is he going to back you?

BIFF: Are you crazy? You're out of your goddam head, you know that? 470

HAPPY: Why? What happened?

BIFF: [*breathlessly*] I did a terrible thing today, Hap. It's been the strangest day I ever went through. I'm all numb, I swear.

HAPPY: You mean he wouldn't see you?

BIFF: Well, I waited six hours for him, see? All day. Kept sending my name in. Even tried to date his secretary so she'd get me to him, but no soap.

HAPPY: Because you're not showin' the old confidence, Biff. He remembered you, didn't he? 475

BIFF: [*stopping* HAPPY *with a gesture*] Finally, about five o'clock, he comes out. Didn't remember who I was or anything. I felt like such an idiot, Hap.

HAPPY: Did you tell him my Florida idea?

BIFF: He walked away. I saw him for one minute. I got so mad I could've torn the walls down! How the hell did I ever get the idea I was a salesman there? I even believed myself that I'd been a salesman for him! And then he gave me one look and—I realized what a ridiculous lie my whole life has been! We've been talking in a dream for fifteen years. I was a shipping clerk.

HAPPY: What'd you do?

BIFF: [*with great tension and wonder*] Well, he left, see. And the secretary went out. I was all 480 alone in the waiting-room. I don't know what came over me, Hap. The next thing I know I'm in his office—paneled walls, everything. I can't explain it. I—Hap, I took his fountain pen.

HAPPY: Geez, did he catch you?

BIFF: I ran out. I ran down all eleven flights. I ran and ran and ran.

HAPPY: That was an awful dumb—what'd you do that for?

BIFF: [*agonized*] I don't know, I just—wanted to take something. I don't know. You gotta help me, Hap, I'm gonna tell Pop.

HAPPY: You crazy? What for? 485

BIFF: Hap, he's got to understand that I'm not the man somebody lends that kind of money to. He thinks I've been spiting him all these years and it's eating him up.

HAPPY: That's just it. You tell him something nice.

BIFF: I can't.

HAPPY: Say you got a lunch date with Oliver tomorrow.

BIFF: So what do I do tomorrow? 490

HAPPY: You leave the house tomorrow and come back at night and say Oliver is thinking it over. And he thinks it over for a couple of weeks, and gradually it fades away and nobody's the worse.

BIFF: But it'll go on forever!

HAPPY: Dad is never so happy as when he's looking forward to something!

[WILLY *enters.*]

HAPPY: Hello, scout!

495 WILLY: Gee, I haven't been here in years!

[*STANLEY has followed* WILLY *in and sets a chair for him.* STANLEY *starts off but* HAPPY *stops him.*]

HAPPY: Stanley!

[*STANLEY stands by, waiting for an order.*]

BIFF: [*going to* WILLY *with guilt, as to an invalid*] Sit down, Pop. You want a drink?

WILLY: Sure, I don't mind.

BIFF: Let's get a load on.

500 WILLY: You look worried.

BIFF: N-no. [*to* STANLEY] Scotch all around. Make it doubles.

STANLEY: Doubles, right. [*He goes.*]

WILLY: You had a couple already, didn't you?

BIFF: Just a couple, yeah.

505 WILLY: Well, what happened, boy? [*nodding affirmatively, with a smile*] Everything go all right?

BIFF: [*takes a breath, then reaches out and grasps* WILLY'*s hand*] Pal . . . [*He is smiling bravely, and* WILLY *is smiling too.*] I had an experience today.

HAPPY: Terrific, Pop.

WILLY: That so? What happened?

BIFF: [*high, slightly alcoholic, above the earth*] I'm going to tell you everything from first to last. It's been a strange day. [*Silence. He looks around, composes himself as best he can, but his breath keeps breaking the rhythm of his voice.*] I had to wait quite a while for him, and—

510 WILLY: Oliver?

BIFF: Yeah, Oliver. All day, as a matter of cold fact. And a lot of—instances—facts, Pop, facts about my life came back to me. Who was it, Pop? Who ever said I was a salesman with Oliver?

WILLY: Well, you were.

BIFF: No, Dad, I was a shipping clerk.

WILLY: But you were practically—

515 BIFF: [*with determination*] Dad, I don't know who said it first, but I was never a salesman for Bill Oliver.

WILLY: What're you talking about?

BIFF: Let's hold on to the facts tonight, Pop. We're not going to get anywhere bullin' around. I was a shipping clerk.

WILLY: [*angrily*] All right, now listen to me—

BIFF: Why don't you let me finish?

520 WILLY: I'm not interested in stories about the past or any crap of that kind because the woods are burning, boys, you understand? There's a big blaze going on all around. I was fired today.

BIFF: [*shocked*] How could you be?

WILLY: I was fired, and I'm looking for a little good news to tell your mother, because the woman has waited and the woman has suffered. The gist of it is that I haven't got a story left in my head, Biff. So don't give me a lecture about facts and aspects. I am not interested. Now what've you got to say to me?

[*STANLEY enters with three drinks. They wait until he leaves.*]

WILLY: Did you see Oliver?

BIFF: Jesus, Dad!

525 WILLY: You mean you didn't go up there?

HAPPY: Sure he went up there.

BIFF: I did. I—saw him. How could they fire you?

WILLY: [*on the edge of his chair*] What kind of a welcome did he give you?

BIFF: He won't even let you work on commission?

WILLY: I'm out! [*driving*] So tell me, he gave you a warm welcome? 530

HAPPY: Sure Pop, sure!

BIFF: [*driven*] Well, it was kind of—

WILLY: I was wondering if he'd remember you. [*to* HAPPY] Imagine, man doesn't see him for ten, twelve years and gives him that kind of a welcome!

HAPPY: Damn right!

BIFF: [*trying to return to the offensive*] Pop, look— 535

WILLY: You know why he remembered you, don't you? Because you impressed him in those days.

BIFF: Let's talk quietly and get this down to the facts, huh?

WILLY: [*as though* BIFF *had been interrupting*] Well, what happened? It's great news, Biff. Did he take you into his office or'd you talk in the waiting-room?

BIFF: Well, he came in, see, and—

WILLY: [*with a big smile*] What'd he say? Betcha he threw his arm around you. 540

BIFF: Well, he kinda—

WILLY: He's a fine man. [*to* HAPPY] Very hard man to see, y'know.

HAPPY: [*agreeing*] Oh, I know.

WILLY: [*to* BIFF] Is that where you had the drinks?

BIFF: Yeah, he gave me a couple of—no, no! 545

HAPPY: [*cutting in*] He told him my Florida idea.

WILLY: Don't interrupt. [*to* BIFF] How'd he react to the Florida idea?

BIFF: Dad, will you give me a minute to explain?

WILLY: I've been waiting for you to explain since I sat down here! What happened? He took you into his office and what?

BIFF: Well—I talked. And—and he listened, see. 550

WILLY: Famous for the way he listens, y'know. What was his answer?

BIFF: His answer was—[*He breaks off, suddenly angry.*] Dad, you're not letting me tell you what I want to tell you!

WILLY: [*accusing, angered*] You didn't see him, did you?

BIFF: I did see him!

WILLY: What'd you insult him or something? You insulted him, didn't you? 555

BIFF: Listen, will you let me out of it, will you just let me out of it!

HAPPY: What the hell!

WILLY: Tell me what happened!

BIFF: [*to* HAPPY] I can't talk to him!

[*A single trumpet note jars the ear. The light of green leaves stains the house, which holds the air of night and a dream.* YOUNG BERNARD *enters and knocks on the door of the house.*]

YOUNG BERNARD: [*frantically*] Mrs. Loman, Mrs. Loman! 560

HAPPY: Tell him what happened!

BIFF: [*to* HAPPY] Shut up and leave me alone!

WILLY: No, no! You had to go and flunk math!

BIFF: What math? What're you talking about?

YOUNG BERNARD: Mrs. Loman, Mrs. Loman! 565

[LINDA *appears in the house, as of old.*]

WILLY: [*wildly*] Math, math, math!

BIFF: Take it easy, Pop!

YOUNG BERNARD: Mrs. Loman!

WILLY: [*furiously*] If you hadn't flunked you'd've been set by now!

570 BIFF: Now, look, I'm gonna tell you what happened, and you're going to listen to me.

YOUNG BERNARD: Mrs. Loman!

BIFF: I waited six hour—

HAPPY: What the hell are you saying?

BIFF: I kept sending in my name but he wouldn't see me. So finally he . . .

[*He continues unheard as light fades low on the restaurant.*]

575 YOUNG BERNARD: Biff flunked math!

LINDA: No!

YOUNG BERNARD: Birnbaum flunked him! They won't graduate him!

LINDA: But they have to. He's gotta go to the university. Where is he? Biff! Biff!

YOUNG BERNARD: No, he left. He went to Grand Central.

580 LINDA: Grand—You mean he went to Boston!

YOUNG BERNARD: Is Uncle Willy in Boston?

LINDA: Oh, maybe Willy can talk to the teacher. Oh, the poor, poor boy!

[*Light on house area snaps out.*]

BIFF: [*at the table, now audible, holding up a gold fountain pen*] . . . so I'm washed up with Oliver, you understand? Are you listening to me?

WILLY: [*at a loss*] Yeah, sure. If you hadn't flunked—

585 BIFF: Flunked what? What're you talking about?

WILLY: Don't blame everything on me! I didn't flunk math—you did! What pen?

HAPPY: That was awful dumb, Biff, a pen like that is worth—

WILLY: [*seeing the pen for the first time*] You took Oliver's pen?

BIFF: [*weakening*] Dad, I just explained it to you.

590 WILLY: You stole Bill Oliver's fountain pen!

BIFF: I didn't exactly steal it! That's just what I've been explaining to you!

HAPPY: He had it in his hand and just then Oliver walked in, so he got nervous and stuck it in his pocket!

WILLY: My God, Biff!

BIFF: I never intended to do it, Dad!

595 OPERATOR'S VOICE: Standish Arms, good evening!

WILLY: [*shouting*] I'm not in my room!

BIFF: [*frightened*] Dad, what's the matter? [*He and HAPPY stand up.*]

OPERATOR: Ringing Mr. Loman for you!

WILLY: I'm not there, stop it!

600 BIFF: [*horrified, gets down on one knee before WILLY*] Dad, I'll make good, I'll make good. [*WILLY tries to get to his feet. BIFF holds him down.*] Sit down now.

WILLY: No, you're no good, you're no good for anything.

BIFF: I am, Dad, I'll find something else, you understand? Now don't worry about anything. [*He holds up WILLY's face.*] Talk to me, Dad.

OPERATOR: Mr. Loman does not answer. Shall I page him?

WILLY: [*attempting to stand, as though to rush and silence the Operator*] No, no, no!

605 HAPPY: He'll strike something, Pop.

WILLY: No, no . . .

BIFF: [*desperately, standing over* WILLY] Pop, listen! Listen to me! I'm telling you something good. Oliver talked to his partner about the Florida idea. you listening? He—he talked to his partner, and he came to me . . . I'm going to be all right, you hear? Dad, listen to me, he said it was just a question of the amount!

WILLY: Then you . . . got it?

HAPPY: He's gonna be terrific, Pop!

WILLY: [*trying to stand*] Then you got it, haven't you? You got it! You got it!    610

BIFF: [*agonized, holds* WILLY *down*] No, no. Look, Pop. I'm supposed to have lunch with them tomorrow. I'm just telling you this so you'll know that I can still make an impression, Pop. And I'll make good somewhere, but I can't go tomorrow, see?

WILLY: Why not? You simply—

BIFF: But the pen, Pop!

WILLY: You give it to him and tell him it was an oversight!

HAPPY: Sure, have lunch tomorrow!    615

BIFF: I can't say that—

WILLY: You were doing a crossword puzzle and accidentally used his pen!

BIFF: Listen, kid, I took those balls years ago, now I walk in with his fountain pen? That clinches it, don't you see? I can't face him like that! I'll try elsewhere.

PAGE'S VOICE: Paging Mr. Loman!

WILLY: Don't you want to be anything?    620

BIFF: Pop, how can I go back?

WILLY: You don't want to be anything, is that what's behind it?

BIFF: [*now angry at* WILLY *for not crediting his sympathy*] Don't take it that way! You think it was easy walking into that office after what I'd done to him? A team of horses couldn't have dragged me back to Bill Oliver!

WILLY: Then why'd you go?

BIFF: Why did I go? Why did I go? Look at you! Look at what's become of you!    625

[*Off left*, THE WOMAN *laughs.*]

WILLY: Biff, you're going to go to that lunch tomorrow, or—

BIFF: I can't go. I've got no appointment!

HAPPY: Biff, for . . . !

WILLY: Are you spiting me?

BIFF: Don't take it that way! Goddammit!    630

WILLY: [*strikes* BIFF *and falters away from the table*] You rotten little louse! Are you spiting me?

THE WOMAN: Someone's at the door, Willy!

BIFF: I'm no good, can't you see what I am?

HAPPY: [*separating them*] Hey, you're in a restaurant! Now cut it out, both of you! [*The girls enter.*] Hello, girls, sit down.

[THE WOMAN *laughs, off left.*]

MISS FORSYTHE: I guess we might as well. This is Letta.    635

THE WOMAN: Willy, are you going to wake up?

BIFF: [*ignoring* WILLY] How're ya, miss, sit down. What do you drink?

MISS FORSYTHE: Letta might not be able to stay long.

LETTA: I gotta get up very early tomorrow. I got jury duty. I'm so excited! Were you fellows ever on a jury?

BIFF: No, but I been in front of them! [*The girls laugh.*] This is my father.    640

LETTA: Isn't he cute? Sit down with us, Pop.

Happy: Sit him down, Biff!

Biff: [*going to him*] Come on, slugger, drink us under the table. To hell with it! Come on, sit down, pal.

[*On Biff's last insistence, Willy is about to sit.*]

The Woman: [*now urgently*] Willy, are you going to answer the door!

[*The Woman's call pulls Willy back. He starts right, befuddled.*]

645 Biff: Hey, where are you going?

Willy: Open the door.

Biff: The door?

Willy: The washroom . . . the door . . . where's the door?

Biff: [*leading Willy to the left*] Just go straight down.

[*Willy moves left.*]

650 The Woman: Willy, Willy, are you going to get up, get up, get up, get up?

[*Willy exits left.*]

Letta: I think it's sweet you bring your daddy along.

Miss Forsythe: Oh, he isn't really your father!

Biff: [*at left, turning to her resentfully*] Miss Forsythe, you've just seen a prince walk by. A fine, troubled prince. A hard-working, unappreciated prince. A pal, you understand? A good companion. Always for his boys.

Letta: That's so sweet.

655 Happy: Well, girls, what's the program? We're wasting time. Come on, Biff. Gather round. Where would you like to go?

Biff: Why don't you do something for him?

Happy: Me!

Biff: Don't you give a damn for him, Hap?

Happy: What're you talking about? I'm the one who—

660 Biff: I sense it, you don't give a good goddam about him. [*He takes the rolled-up hose from his pocket and puts it on the table in front of Happy.*] Look what I found in the cellar, for Christ's sake. How can you bear to let it go on?

Happy: Me? Who goes away? Who runs off and—

Biff: Yeah, but he doesn't mean anything to you. You could help him—I can't! Don't you understand what I'm talking about? He's going to kill himself, don't you know that?

Happy: Don't I know it! Me!

Biff: Hap, help him! Jesus . . . help him . . . Help me, help me, I can't bear to look at his face! [*Ready to weep, he hurries out, up right.*]

665 Happy: [*staring after him*] Where are you going?

Miss Forsythe: What's he so mad about?

Happy: Come on, girls, we'll catch up with him.

Miss Forsythe: [*as Happy pushes her out*] Say, I don't like that temper of his!

Happy: He's just a little overstrung, he'll be all right!

670 Willy: [*off left, as The Woman laughs*] Don't answer! Don't answer!

Letta: Don't you want to tell your father—

Happy: No, that's not my father. He's just a guy. Come on, we'll catch Biff, and, honey, we're going to paint this town! Stanley, where's the check! Hey, Stanley!

[*They exit. Stanley looks toward left.*]

STANLEY: [*calling to* HAPPY *indignantly*] Mr. Loman! Mr. Loman!

[STANLEY *picks up a chair and follows them off. Knocking is heard off left.* THE WOMAN *enters, laughing.* WILLY *follows her. She is in a black slip; he is buttoning his shirt. Raw, sensuous music accompanies their speech.*]

WILLY: Will you stop laughing? Will you stop?

THE WOMAN: Aren't you going to answer the door? He'll wake the whole hotel.    675

WILLY: I'm not expecting anybody.

THE WOMAN: Whyn't you have another drink, honey, and stop being so damn self-centered?

WILLY: I'm so lonely.

THE WOMAN: You know you ruined me, Willy? From now on, whenever you come to the office, I'll see that you go right through to the buyers. No waiting at my desk any more, Willy. You ruined me.

WILLY: That's nice of you to say that.    680

THE WOMAN: Gee, you are self-centered! Why so sad? You are the saddest, self-centeredest soul I ever did see-saw. [*She laughs. He kisses her.*] Come on inside, drummer boy. It's silly to be dressing in the middle of the night. [*As knocking is heard*] Aren't you going to answer the door?

WILLY: They're knocking on the wrong door.

THE WOMAN: But I felt the knocking! And he heard us talking in here. Maybe the hotel's on fire!

WILLY: [*his terror rising*] It's a mistake.

THE WOMAN: Then tell him to go away!    685

WILLY: There's nobody there.

THE WOMAN: It's getting on my nerves, Willy. There's somebody standing out there and it's getting on my nerves!

WILLY: [*pushing her away from him*] All right, stay in the bathroom here, and don't come out. I think there's a law in Massachusetts about it, so don't come out. It may be that new room clerk. He looked very mean. So don't come out. It's a mistake, there's no fire.

[*The knocking is heard again. He takes a few steps away from her, and she vanishes into the wing. The light follows him, and now he is facing* YOUNG BIFF, *who carries a suitcase.* BIFF *steps toward him. The music is gone.*]

BIFF: Why didn't you answer?

WILLY: Biff! What are you doing in Boston?    690

BIFF: Why didn't you answer? I've been knocking for five minutes, I called you on the phone—

WILLY: I just heard you. I was in the bathroom and had the door shut. Did anything happen home?

BIFF: Dad—I let you down.

WILLY: What do you mean?

BIFF: Dad . . .    695

WILLY: Biffo, what's this about? [*putting his arm around* BIFF] Come on, let's go downstairs and get you a malted.

BIFF: Dad, I flunked math.

WILLY: Not for the term?

BIFF: The term. I haven't got enough credits to graduate.

WILLY: You mean to say Bernard wouldn't give you the answers?    700

BIFF: He did, he tried, but I only got a sixty-one.

WILLY: And they wouldn't give you four points?

BIFF: Birnbaum refused absolutely. I begged him, Pop, but he won't give me those points. You gotta talk to him before they close the school. Because if he saw the kind of man you are, and you just talked to him in your way, I'm sure he'd come through for me. The class came right before practice, see, and I didn't go enough. Would you talk to him? He'd like you, Pop. You know the way you could talk.

WILLY: You're on. We'll drive right back.

705 BIFF: Oh, Dad, good work! I'm sure he'll change it for you!

WILLY: Go downstairs and tell the clerk I'm checkin' out. Go right down.

BIFF: Yes, sir! See, the reason he hates me, Pop—one day he was late for class so I got up at the blackboard and imitated him. I crossed my eyes and talked with a lithp.

WILLY: [*laughing*] You did? The kids like it?

BIFF: They nearly died laughing!

710 WILLY: Yeah? What'd you do?

BIFF: The thquare root of thixthy twee is . . . [WILLY *bursts out laughing;* BIFF *joins him.*] And in the middle of it he walked in!

[WILLY *laughs and* THE WOMAN *joins in offstage.*]

WILLY: [*without hesitation*] Hurry downstairs and—

BIFF: Somebody in there?

WILLY: No, that was next door.

[THE WOMAN. *laughs offstage.*]

715 BIFF: Somebody got in your bathroom!

WILLY: No, it's the next room, there's a party—

THE WOMAN: [*enters, laughing. She lisps this.*] Can I come in? There's something in the bathtub, Willy, and it's moving!

[WILLY *looks at* BIFF, *who is staring open-mouthed and horrified at* THE WOMAN.]

WILLY: Ah—you better go back to your room. They must be finished painting by now. They're painting her room so I let her take a shower here. Go back, go back . . . [*He pushes her.*]

THE WOMAN: [*resisting*] But I've got to get dressed, Willy, I can't—

720 WILLY: Get out of here! Go back, go back . . . [*suddenly striving for the ordinary*] This is Miss Francis, Biff, she's a buyer. They're painting her room. Go back, Miss Francis, go back . . .

THE WOMAN: But my clothes, I can't go out naked in the hall!

WILLY: [*pushing her offstage*] Get outa here! Go back, go back!

[BIFF *slowly sits down on his suitcase as the argument continues offstage.*]

THE WOMAN: Where's my stockings? You promised me stockings, Willy!

WILLY: I have no stockings here!

725 THE WOMAN: You had two boxes of size nine sheers for me, and I want them!

WILLY: Here, for God's sake, will you get outa here!

THE WOMAN: [*enters holding a box of stockings*] I just hope there's nobody in the hall. That's all I hope. [*To* BIFF] Are you football or baseball?

BIFF: Football.

THE WOMAN: [*angry, humiliated*] That's me too. G'night. [*She snatches her clothes from* WILLY, *and walks out.*]

730 WILLY: [*after a pause*] Well, better get going. I want to get to the school first thing in the morning. Get my suits out of the closet. I'll get my valise. [BIFF *doesn't move.*] What's the matter? [BIFF *remains motionless, tears falling*] She's a buyer. Buys for J. H. Simmons. She lives down the hall—they're painting. You don't imagine—[*He breaks off. After a pause*] Now listen,

pal, she's just a buyer. She sees merchandise in her room and they have to keep it looking just so . . . [*Pause. Assuming command*] All right, get my suits. [BIFF *doesn't move.*] Now stop crying and do as I say. I gave you an order. Biff, I gave you an order! Is that what you do when I give you an order? How dare you cry! [*putting his arm around* BIFF] Now look, Biff, when you grow up you'll understand about these things. You mustn't—you mustn't overemphasize a thing like this. I'll see Birnbaum first thing in the morning.

BIFF: Never mind.

WILLY: [*getting down beside* BIFF] Never mind! He's going to give you those points. I'll see to it.

BIFF: He wouldn't listen to you.

WILLY: He certainly will listen to me. You need those points for the U. of Virginia.

BIFF: I'm not going there. 735

WILLY: Heh? If I can't get him to change that mark you'll make it up in summer school. You've got all summer to—

BIFF: [*his weeping breaking from him*] Dad . . .

WILLY: [*infected by it*] Oh, my boy . . .

BIFF: Dad . . .

WILLY: She's nothing to me, Biff. I was lonely, I was terribly lonely. 740

BIFF: You—you gave her Mama's stockings! [*His tears break through and he rises to go.*]

WILLY: [*grabbing for* BIFF] I gave you an order!

BIFF: Don't touch me, you—liar!

WILLY: Apologize for that!

BIFF: You fake! You phony little fake! [*Overcome, he turns quickly and weeping fully goes out with* 745 *his suitcase.* WILLY *is left on the floor on his knees.*]

WILLY: I gave you an order! Biff, come back here or I'll beat you! Come back here! I'll whip you!

[STANLEY *comes quickly in from the right and stands in front of* WILLY.]

WILLY: [*shouts at* STANLEY] I gave you an order . . .

STANLEY: Hey, let's pick it up, pick it up, Mr. Loman. [*He helps* WILLY *to his feet.*] Your boys left with the chippies. They said they'll see you home.

[*A* SECOND WAITER *watches some distance away.*]

WILLY: But we were supposed to have dinner together.

[*Music is heard,* WILLY's *theme.*]

STANLEY: Can you make it? 750

WILLY: I'll—sure, I can make it. [*suddenly concerned about his clothes*] Do I—I look all right?

STANLEY: Sure, you look all right. [*He flicks a speck off* WILLY's *lapel.*]

WILLY: Here—here's a dollar.

STANLEY: Oh, your son paid me. It's all right.

WILLY: [*putting it in* STANLEY's *hand*] No, take it. You're a good boy. 755

STANLEY: Oh, no, you don't have to . . .

WILLY: Here—here's some more, I don't need it any more. [*after a slight pause*] Tell me—is there a seed store in the neighborhood?

STANLEY: Seeds? You mean like to plant?

[*As* WILLY *turns,* STANLEY *slips the money back into his jacket pocket.*]

WILLY: Yes. Carrots, peas . . .

STANLEY: Well, there's hardware stores on Sixth Avenue, but it may be too late now. 760

WILLY: [*anxiously*] Oh, I'd better hurry. I've got to get some seeds. [*He starts off to the right.*] I've got to get some seeds, right away. Nothing's planted. I don't have a thing in the ground.

[WILLY *hurries out as the light goes down.* STANLEY *moves over to the right after him, watches him off. The other waiter has been staring at* WILLY.]

STANLEY: [*to the* WAITER] Well, whatta you looking at?

[*The* WAITER *picks up the chairs and moves off right.* STANLEY *takes the table and follows him. The light fades on this area. There is a long pause, the sound of the flute coming over. The light gradually rises on the kitchen, which is empty.* HAPPY *appears at the door of the house, followed by* BIFF. HAPPY *is carrying a large bunch of long-stemmed roses. He enters the kitchen, looks around for* LINDA. *Not seeing her, he turns to* BIFF, *who is just outside the house door, and makes a gesture with his hands, indicating "Not here, I guess." He looks into the living-room and freezes. Inside,* LINDA, *unseen, is seated,* WILLY'S *coat on her lap. She rises ominously and quietly and moves toward* HAPPY, *who backs up into the kitchen, afraid.*]

HAPPY: Hey, what're you doing up? [LINDA *says nothing but moves toward him implacably.*] Where's Pop? [*He keeps backing to the right, and now* LINDA *is in full view in the doorway to the living-room.*] Is he sleeping?

LINDA: Where were you?

765 HAPPY: [*trying to laugh it off*] We met two girls, Mom, very fine types. Here, we brought you some flowers. [*offering them to her*] Put them in your room, Ma.

[*She knocks them to the floor at* BIFF'S *feet. He has now come inside and closed the door behind him. She stares at* BIFF, *silent.*]

HAPPY: Now what'd you do that for? Mom, I want you to have some flowers—

LINDA: [*cutting* HAPPY *off, violently to* BIFF] Don't you care whether he lives or dies?

HAPPY: [*going to the stairs*] Come upstairs, Biff.

BIFF: [*with a flare of disgust, to* HAPPY] Go away from me! [*to* LINDA] What do you mean, lives or dies? Nobody's dying around here, pal.

770 LINDA: Get out of my sight! Get out of here!

BIFF: I wanna see the boss.

LINDA: You're not going near him!

BIFF: Where is he? [*He moves into the living-room and* LINDA *follows.*]

LINDA: [*shouting after* BIFF] You invite him for dinner. He looks forward to it all day—[BIFF *appears in his parents' bedroom, looks around, and exits.*]—and then you desert him there. There's no stranger you'd do that to!

775 HAPPY: Why? He had a swell time with us. Listen, when I—[LINDA *comes back into the kitchen.*]—desert him I hope I don't outlive the day!

LINDA: Get out of here!

HAPPY: Now look, Mom . . .

LINDA: Did you have to go to women tonight? You and your lousy rotten whores!

[BIFF *re-enters the kitchen.*]

HAPPY: Mom, all we did was follow Biff around trying to cheer him up! [*to* BIFF] Boy, what a night you gave me!

780 LINDA: Get out of here, both of you, and don't come back! I don't want you tormenting him any more. Go on now, get your things together! [*to* BIFF] You can sleep in his apartment. [*She starts to pick up the flowers and stops herself.*] Pick up this stuff, I'm not your maid any more. Pick it up, you bum, you!

[HAPPY *turns his back to her in refusal.* BIFF *slowly moves over and gets down on his knees, picking up the flowers.*]

LINDA: You're a pair of animals! Not one, not another living soul would have had the cruelty to walk out on that man in a restaurant!

BIFF: [*not looking at her*] Is that what he said?

LINDA: He didn't have to say anything. He was so humiliated he nearly limped when he came in.

HAPPY: But, Mom, he had a great time with us—

BIFF: [*cutting him off violently*] Shut up!                                                   785

[*Without another word, HAPPY goes upstairs.*]

LINDA: You! You didn't even go in to see if he was all right!

BIFF: [*still on the floor in front of LINDA, the flowers in his hand; with self-loathing*] No. Didn't. Didn't do a damned thing. How do you like that, heh? Left him babbling in a toilet.

LINDA: You louse. You . . .

BIFF: Now you hit it on the nose! [*He gets up, throws the flowers in the wastebasket.*] The scum of the earth, and you're looking at him!

LINDA: Get out of here!                                                                       790

BIFF: I gotta talk to the boss, Mom. Where is he?

LINDA: You're not going near him. Get out of his house!

BIFF: [*with absolute assurance, determination*] No. We're gonna have an abrupt conversation, him and me.

LINDA: You're not talking to him!

[*Hammering is heard from outside the house, off right. BIFF turns toward the noise.*]

LINDA: [*suddenly pleading*] Will you please leave him alone?                                   795

BIFF: What's he doing out there?

LINDA: He's planting the garden!

BIFF: [*quietly*] Now? Oh, my God!

[*BIFF moves outside, LINDA following. The light dies down on them and comes up on the center of the apron as WILLY walks into it. He is carrying a flashlight, a hoe, and a handful of seed packets. He raps the top of the hoe sharply to fix it firmly, and then moves to the left, measuring off the distance with his foot. He holds the flashlight to look at the seed packets, reading off the instructions. He is in the blue of night.*]

WILLY: Carrots . . . quarter-inch apart. Rows . . . one-foot rows. [*He measures it off.*] One foot. [*He puts down a package and measures off.*] Beets. [*He puts down another package and measures again.*] Lettuce. [*He reads the package, puts it down.*] One foot—[*He breaks off as BEN appears at the right and moves slowly down to him.*] What a proposition, ts, ts. Terrific, terrific. 'Cause she's suffered, Ben, the woman has suffered. You understand me? A man can't go out the way he came in, Ben, a man has got to add up to something. You can't, you can't—[*BEN moves toward him as though to interrupt.*] You gotta consider, now. Don't answer so quick. Remember, it's a guaranteed twenty-thousand-dollar proposition. Now look, Ben, I want you to go through the ins and outs of this thing with me. I've got nobody to talk to, Ben, and the woman has suffered, you hear me?

BEN: [*standing still, considering*] What's the proposition?                                   800

WILLY: It's twenty thousand dollars on the barrelhead. Guaranteed, gilt-edged, you understand?

BEN: You don't want to make a fool of yourself. They might not honor the policy.

WILLY: How can they dare refuse? Didn't I work like a coolie to meet every premium on the nose? And now they don't pay off? Impossible!

BEN: It's called a cowardly thing, William.

WILLY: Why? Does it take more guts to stand here the rest of my life ringing up a zero?         805

BEN: [*yielding*] That's a point, William. [*He moves, thinking, turns.*] And twenty thousand—that
     *is* something one can feel with the hand, it is there.

WILLY: [*now assured, with rising power*] Oh, Ben, that's the whole beauty of it! I see it like a dia-
     mond, shining in the dark, hard and rough, that I can pick up and touch in my hand. Not
     like—like an appointment! This would not be another damned-fool appointment, Ben,
     and it changes all the aspects. Because he thinks I'm nothing, see, and so he spites me. But
     the funeral—[*straightening up*] Ben, that funeral will be massive! They'll come from Maine,
     Massachusetts, Vermont, New Hampshire! All the old-timers with the strange license
     plates—that boy will be thunder-struck. Ben, because he never realized—I am known!
     Rhode Island, New York, New Jersey—I am known, Ben, and he'll see it with his eyes
     once and for all. He'll see what I am, Ben! He's in for a shock, that boy!

BEN: [*coming down to the edge of the garden*] He'll call you a coward.

WILLY: [*suddenly fearful*] No, that would be terrible.

810 BEN: Yes. And a damned fool.

WILLY: No, no, he mustn't, I won't have that! [*He is broken and desperate.*]

BEN: He'll hate you, William.

[*The gay music of the Boys is heard.*]

WILLY: Oh, Ben, how do we get back to all the great times? Used to be so full of light, and com-
     radeship, the sleigh-riding in winter, and the ruddiness on his cheeks. And always some
     kind of good news coming up, always something nice coming up ahead. And never even
     let me carry the valises in the house, and simonizing, simonizing that little red car! Why,
     why can't I give him something and not have him hate me?

BEN: Let me think about it. [*He glances at his watch.*] I still have a little time. Remarkable propo-
     sition, but you've got to be sure you're not making a fool of yourself.

[*BEN drifts upstage and goes out of sight. BIFF comes down from the left.*]

815 WILLY: [*suddenly conscious of BIFF, turns and looks up at him, then begins picking up the packages of
     seeds in confusion*] Where the hell is that seed? [*Indignantly*] You can't see nothing out here!
     They boxed in the whole goddam neighborhood!

BIFF: There are people all around here. Don't you realize that?

WILLY: I'm busy. Don't bother me.

BIFF: [*taking the hoe from WILLY*] I'm saying good-by to you, Pop. [*WILLY looks at him, silent, unable
     to move.*] I'm not coming back any more.

WILLY: You're not going to see Oliver tomorrow?

820 BIFF: I've got no appointment, Dad.

WILLY: He put his arm around you, and you've got no appointment?

BIFF: Pop, get this now, will you? Everytime I've left it's been a fight that sent me out of here.
     Today I realized something about myself and I tried to explain it to you and I—I think I'm
     just not smart enough to make any sense out of it for you. To hell with whose fault it is or
     anything like that. [*He takes WILLY's arm.*] Let's just wrap it up, heh? Come on in, we'll tell
     Mom. [*He gently tries to pull WILLY to left.*]

WILLY: [*frozen, immobile, with guilt in his voice*] No, I don't want to see her.

BIFF: Come on! [*He pulls again, and WILLY tries to pull away.*]

825 WILLY: [*highly nervous*] No, no, I don't want to see her.

BIFF: [*tries to look into WILLY's face, as if to find the answer there*] Why don't you want to see her?

WILLY: [*more harshly now*] Don't bother me, will you?

BIFF: What do you mean, you don't want to see her? You don't want them calling you yellow,
     do you? This isn't your fault; it's me, I'm a bum. Now come inside! [*WILLY strains to get
     away.*] Did you hear what I said to you?

[WILLY *pulls away and quickly goes by himself into the house.* BIFF *follows.*]

LINDA: [*to* WILLY] Did you plant, dear?

BIFF: [*at the door, to* LINDA] All right, we had it out. I'm going and I'm not writing any more.  830

LINDA: [*going to* WILLY *in the kitchen*] I think that's the best way, dear. 'Cause there's no use drawing it out, you'll just never get along.

[WILLY *doesn't respond.*]

BIFF: People ask where I am and what I'm doing, you don't know, and you don't care. That way it'll be off your mind and you can start brightening up again. All right? That clears it, doesn't it? [WILLY *is silent, and* BIFF *goes to him.*] You gonna wish me luck, scout? [*He extends his hand.*] What do you say?

LINDA: Shake his hand, Willy.

WILLY: [*turning to her, seething with hurt*] There's no necessity to mention the pen at all, y'know.

BIFF: [*gently*] I've got no appointment, Dad.  835

WILLY: [*erupting fiercely*] He put his arm around . . .

BIFF: Dad, you're never going to see what I am, so what's the use of arguing? If I strike oil I'll send you a check. Meantime forget I'm alive.

WILLY: [*to* LINDA] Spite, see?

BIFF: Shake hands, Dad.

WILLY: Not my hand.  840

BIFF: I was hoping not to go this way.

WILLY: Well, this is the way you're going. Good-by.

[BIFF *looks at him a moment, then turns sharply and goes to the stairs.*]

WILLY: [*stops him with*] May you rot in hell if you leave this house!

BIFF: [*turning*] Exactly what is it that you want from me?

WILLY: I want you to know, on the train, in the mountains, in the valleys, wherever you go,  845
that you cut down your life for spite!

BIFF: No, no.

WILLY: Spite, spite, is the word of your undoing! And when you're down and out, remember what did it. When you're rotting somewhere beside the railroad tracks, remember, and don't you dare blame it on me!

BIFF: I'm not blaming it on you!

WILLY: I won't take the rap for this, you hear?

[HAPPY *comes down the stairs and stands on the bottom step, watching.*]

BIFF: That's just what I'm telling you!  850

WILLY: [*sinking into a chair at the table, with full accusation*] You're trying to put a knife in me— don't think I don't know what you're doing!

BIFF: All right, phony! Then let's lay it on the line. [*He whips the rubber tube out of his pocket and puts it on the table.*]

HAPPY: You crazy—

LINDA: Biff! [*She moves to grab the hose, but* BIFF *holds it down with his hand.*]

BIFF: Leave it here! Don't move it!

WILLY: [*not looking at it*] What is that?  855

BIFF: You know goddam well what that is.

WILLY: [*caged, wanting to escape*] I never saw that.

BIFF: You saw it. The mice didn't bring it into the cellar! What is this supposed to do, make a hero out of you? This supposed to make me sorry for you?

860 WILLY: Never heard of it.

BIFF: There'll be no pity for you, you hear it? No pity!

WILLY: [*to* LINDA] You hear the spite!

BIFF: No, you're going to hear the truth—what you are and what I am!

LINDA: Stop it!

865 WILLY: Spite!

HAPPY: [*coming down toward* BIFF] You cut it now!

BIFF: [*to* HAPPY] The man don't know who we are! The man is gonna know! [*to* WILLY] We never told the truth for ten minutes in this house!

HAPPY: We always told the truth!

BIFF: [*turning on him*] You big blow, are you the assistant buyer? You're one of the two assistants to the assistant, aren't you?

870 HAPPY: Well, I'm practically—

BIFF: You're practically full of it! We all are! And I'm through with it. [*to* WILLY] Now hear this, Willy, this is me.

WILLY: I know you!

BIFF: You know why I had no address for three months? I stole a suit in Kansas City and I was in jail. [*to* LINDA, *who is sobbing*] Stop crying. I'm through with it.

[LINDA *turns from them, her hands covering her face.*]

WILLY: I suppose that's my fault!

875 BIFF: I stole myself out of every good job since high school!

WILLY: And whose fault is that?

BIFF: And I never got anywhere because you blew me so full of hot air I could never stand taking orders from anybody! That's whose fault it is!

WILLY: I hear that!

LINDA: Don't, Biff!

880 BIFF: It's goddam time you heard that! I had to be boss big shot in two weeks, and I'm through with it!

WILLY: Then hang yourself! For spite, hang yourself!

BIFF: No! Nobody's hanging himself, Willy! I ran down eleven flights with a pen in my hand today. And suddenly I stopped, you hear me? And in the middle of that office building, do you hear this? I stopped in the middle of that building and I saw—the sky. I saw the things that I love in this world. The work and the food and time to sit and smoke. And I looked at the pen and said to myself, what the hell am I grabbing this for? Why am I trying to become what I don't want to be? What am I doing in an office, making a contemptuous, begging fool of myself, when all I want is out there, waiting for me the minute I say I know who I am! Why can't I say that, Willy?

[*He tries to make* WILLY *face him, but* WILLY *pulls away and moves to the left.*]

WILLY: [*with hatred, threateningly.*] The door of your life is wide open!

BIFF: Pop! I'm a dime a dozen, and so are you!

885 WILLY: [*turning on him now in an uncontrolled outburst*] I am not a dime a dozen! I am Willy Loman, and you are Biff Loman!

[BIFF *starts for* WILLY, *but is blocked by* HAPPY. *In his fury,* BIFF *seems on the verge of attacking his father.*]

BIFF: I am not a leader of men, Willy, and neither are you. You were never anything but a hard-working drummer who landed in the ash can like all the rest of them! I'm one dollar an

Linda Loman (Mildred Dunnock) and Happy (Cameron Mitchell) restrain Biff (Arthur Kennedy) as he reproaches his father Willy (Lee J. Cobb) in the Morosco Theatre, New York City, original production of *Death of a Salesman*, staged by Elia Kazan.

hour, Willy! I tried seven states and couldn't raise it. A buck an hour! Do you gather my meaning? I'm not bringing home any prizes any more, and you're going to stop waiting for me to bring them home!

WILLY: [*directly to* BIFF] You vengeful, spiteful mutt!

[BIFF *breaks from* HAPPY. WILLY, *in fright, starts up the stairs.* BIFF *grabs him*]

BIFF: [*at the peak of his fury*] Pop I'm nothing! I'm nothing, Pop. Can't you understand that? There's no spite in it any more. I'm just what I am, that's all.

[BIFF'*s fury has spent itself, and he breaks down, sobbing, holding on to* WILLY, *who dumbly fumbles for* BIFF'*s face.*]

WILLY: [*astonished*] What're you doing? What're you doing? [*to* LINDA] Why is he crying?

BIFF: [*crying, broken*] Will you let me go, for Christ's sake? Will you take that phony dream and 890 burn it before something happens? [*Struggling to contain himself, he pulls away and moves to the stairs.*] I'll go in the morning. Put him—put him to bed. [*Exhausted,* BIFF *moves up the stairs to his room.*]

WILLY: [*after a long pause, astonished, elevated*] Isn't that—isn't that remarkable? Biff—he likes me!

LINDA: He loves you, Willy!

Happy: [*deeply moved*] Always did, Pop.

Willy: Oh, Biff! [*staring wildly*] He cried! Cried to me. [*He is choking with his love, and now cries out his promise.*] That boy—that boy is going to be magnificent!

[*Ben appears in the light just outside the kitchen.*]

895 Ben: Yes, outstanding, with twenty thousand behind him.

Linda: [*sensing the racing of his mind, fearfully, carefully*] Now come to bed, Willy. It's all settled now.

Willy: [*finding it difficult not to rush out of the house*] Yes, we'll sleep. Come on. Go to sleep, Hap.

Ben: And it does take a great kind of a man to crack the jungle.

[*In accents of dread, Ben's idyllic music starts up.*]

Happy: [*his arm around Linda*] I'm getting married, Pop, don't forget it. I'm changing everything. I'm gonna run that department before the year is up. You'll see, Mom. [*He kisses her.*]

900 Ben: The jungle is dark but full of diamonds, Willy.

[*Willy turns, moves, listening to Ben.*]

Linda: Be good. You're both good boys, just act that way, that's all.

Happy: 'Night, Pop. [*He goes upstairs.*]

Linda: [*to Willy*] Come, dear.

Ben: [*with greater force*] One must go in to fetch a diamond out.

905 Willy: [*to Linda, as he moves slowly along the edge of the kitchen, toward the door*] I just want to get settled down, Linda. Let me sit alone for a little.

Linda: [*almost uttering her fear*] I want you upstairs.

Willy: [*taking her in his arms*] In a few minutes, Linda. I couldn't sleep right now. Go on, you look awful tired. [*He kisses her.*]

Ben: Not like an appointment at all. A diamond is rough and hard to the touch.

Willy: Go on now. I'll be right up.

910 Linda: I think this is the only way, Willy.

Willy: Sure, it's the best thing.

Ben: Best thing!

Willy: The only way. Everything is gonna be—go on, kid, get to bed. You look so tired.

Linda: Come right up.

915 Willy: Two minutes.

[*Linda goes into the living-room, then reappears in her bedroom. Willy moves just outside the kitchen door.*]

Willy: Loves me. [*wonderingly*] Always loved me. Isn't that a remarkable thing? Ben, he'll worship me for it!

Ben: [*with promise*] It's dark there, but full of diamonds.

Willy: Can you imagine that magnificence with twenty thousand dollars in his pocket?

Linda: [*calling from her room*] Willy! Come up!

920 Willy: [*calling into the kitchen*] Yes! Yes. Coming! It's very smart, you realize that, don't you, sweetheart? Even Ben sees it. I gotta go, baby. 'By! 'By! [*going over to Ben, almost dancing*] Imagine? When the mail comes he'll be ahead of Bernard again!

Ben: A perfect proposition all around.

Willy: Did you see how he cried to me? Oh, if I could kiss him, Ben!

Ben: Time, William, time!

Willy: Oh, Ben, I always knew one way or another we were gonna make it, Biff and I!

BEN: [*looking at his watch*] The boat. We'll be late. [*He moves slowly off into the darkness.*]    925
WILLY: [*elegiacally, turning to the house*] Now when you kick off, boy, I want a seventy-yard
    boot, and get right down the field under the ball, and when you hit, hit low and hit hard,
    because it's important, boy. [*He swings around and faces the audience.*] There's all kinds of
    important people in the stands, and the first thing you know . . . [*suddenly realizing he is
    alone*] Ben! Ben, where do I . . . ? [*He makes a sudden movement of search.*] Ben, how do I . . . ?
LINDA: [*calling*] Willy, you coming up?
WILLY: [*uttering a gasp of fear, whirling about as if to quiet her*] Sh! [*He turns around as if to find his
    way; sounds, faces, voices, seem to be swarming in upon him and he flicks at them, crying*] Sh! Sh!
    [*Suddenly music, faint and high, stops him. It rises in intensity, almost to an unbearable scream.
    He goes up and down on his toes, and rushes off around the house.*] Shhh!
LINDA: Willy?

[*There is no answer. LINDA waits. BIFF gets up off his bed. He is still in his clothes. HAPPY sits up. BIFF
stands listening.*]

LINDA: [*with real fear*] Willy, answer me! Willy!    930

[*There is the sound of a car starting and moving away at full speed.*]

LINDA: No!
BIFF: [*rushing down the stairs*] Pop!

[*As the car speeds off, the music crashes down in a frenzy of sound, which becomes the soft pulsation of
a single cello string. BIFF slowly returns to his bedroom. He and HAPPY gravely don their jackets. LINDA
slowly walks out of her room. The music has developed into a dead march. The leaves of day are
appearing over everything. CHARLEY and BERNARD somberly dressed, appear and knock on the kitchen
door. BIFF and HAPPY slowly descend the stairs to the kitchen as CHARLEY and BERNARD enter. All stop
a moment when LINDA, in clothes of mourning, bearing a little bunch of roses, comes through the draped
doorway into the kitchen. She goes to CHARLEY and takes his arm. Now all move toward the audience,
through the wall-line of the kitchen. At the limit of the apron, LINDA lays down the flowers, kneels, and
sits back on her heels. All stare down at the grave.*]


## REQUIEM

CHARLEY: It's getting dark, Linda.

[*LINDA doesn't react. She stares at the grave.*]

BIFF: How about it, Mom? Better get some rest, heh? They'll be closing the gate soon.

[*LINDA makes no move. Pause.*]

HAPPY: [*deeply angered*] He had no right to do that. There was no necessity for it. We would've
    helped him.
CHARLEY: [*grunting*] Hmmm.
BIFF: Come along, Mom.    5
LINDA: Why didn't anybody come?
CHARLEY: It was a very nice funeral.
LINDA: But where are all the people he knew? Maybe they blame him.
CHARLEY: Naa. It's a rough world, Linda. They wouldn't blame him.
LINDA: I can't understand it. At this time especially. First time in thirty-five years we were just    10
    about free and clear. He only needed a little salary. He was even finished with the dentist.
CHARLEY: No man only needs a little salary.

LINDA: I can't understand it.

BIFF: There were a lot of nice days. When he'd come home from a trip; or on Sundays, making the stoop; finishing the cellar; putting on the new porch; when he built the extra bathroom; and put up the garage. You know something, Charley, there's more of him in that front stoop than in all the sales he ever made.

CHARLEY: Yeah. He was a happy man with a batch of cement.

15  LINDA: He was so wonderful with his hands.

BIFF: He had all the wrong dreams. All, all, wrong.

HAPPY: [*almost ready to fight BIFF*] Don't say that!

BIFF: He never knew who he was.

CHARLEY: [*stopping HAPPY's movement and reply. To BIFF*] Nobody dast blame this man. You don't understand. Willy was a salesman. And for a salesman, there is no rock bottom to the life. He don't put a bolt to a nut, he don't tell you the law or give you medicine. He's a man way out there in the blue, riding on a smile and a shoeshine. And when they start not smiling back—that's an earthquake. And then you get yourself a couple of spots on your hat, and you're finished. Nobody dast blame this man. A salesman is got to dream, boy. It comes with the territory.

20  BIFF: Charley, the man didn't know who he was.

HAPPY: [*infuriated*] Don't say that!

BIFF: Why don't you come with me, Happy?

HAPPY: I'm not licked that easily. I'm staying right in this city, and I'm gonna beat this racket! [*He looks at BIFF, his chin set.*] The Loman Brothers!

BIFF: I know who I am, kid.

25  HAPPY: All right, boy. I'm gonna show you and everybody else that Willy Loman did not die in vain. He had a good dream. It's the only dream you can have—to come out number-one man. He fought it out here, and this is where I'm gonna win it for him.

BIFF: [*with a hopeless glance at HAPPY, bends toward his mother*] Let's go, Mom.

LINDA: I'll be with you in a minute. Go on, Charley. [*He hesitates.*] I want to, just for a minute. I never had a chance to say good-by.

[*CHARLEY moves away, followed by HAPPY. BIFF remains a slight distance up and left of LINDA. She sits there, summoning herself. The flute begins, not far away, playing behind her speech.*]

LINDA: Forgive me, dear. I can't cry. I don't know what it is, but I can't cry. I don't understand it. Why did you ever do that? Help me, Willy, I can't cry. It seems to me that you're just on another trip. I keep expecting you. Willy, dear, I can't cry. Why did you do it? I search and search and I search, and I can't understand it, Willy. I made the last payment on the house today. Today, dear. And there'll be nobody home. [*A sob rises in her throat.*] We're free and clear. [*sobbing more fully, released*] We're free. [*BIFF comes slowly toward her.*] We're free . . . We're free . . .

[*BIFF lifts her to her feet and moves out up right with her in his arms. LINDA sobs quietly. BERNARD and CHARLEY come together and follow them, followed by HAPPY. Only the music of the flute is left on the darkening stage as over the house the hard towers of the apartment buildings rise into sharp focus, and The curtain falls.*]

## Questions

### Act 1

1. What do you learn about Willy from the first stage direction?

2. What instances of stealing are in the play? Why do Biff and Happy steal? Where did they learn about stealing? How is stealing related to salesmanship?

3. In Act 1 Willy claims that "I never in my life told him [Biff] anything but decent things." Is this assertion true? What does it show you about Willy?

## Act 2 and Requiem

4. What does Willy's difficulty with machines—especially his car, the refrigerator, and Howard's tape recorder—suggest about him? To what extent are these machines symbolic?

5. When Willy sees Bernard in Charley's office, he asks, "What—what's the secret?" What secret is he asking about? Does such a secret exist?

6. In Act 2 Willy buys seeds and tries to plant a garden at night. Why is Willy so disturbed that "nothing's planted" and "I don't have a thing in the ground"? What do this garden and having "things in the ground" mean to Willy?

7. In Act 2, speech 867, Biff claims that "we never told the truth for ten minutes in this house!" What does he mean? To what extent is he right?

8. Linda's last line in the play—"We're free . . . we're free"—seems to refer to the house mortgage. In what other ways, however, might you take it?

# General Questions

1. How does Miller use lighting, the set, blocking, and music to differentiate between action in the present and "memory" action?

2. The stage directions are full of information that cannot be played. In describing Happy, for example, Miller notes that "sexuality is like a color on him." What is the function of such stage directions?

3. How is Willy's suicide foreshadowed throughout the play? To what extent does this foreshadowing create tension?

4. Which characters are "real" and which are "hallucinations" that spring from Willy's memory? What are the major differences between these two groups?

5. Which characters are symbolic and what do they symbolize?

6. Describe the character of Willy Loman. What are his good qualities? In what ways does he have heroic stature? What are his bad qualities? To what extent is his "fall" the result of his flaws, and to what extent is it caused by circumstances beyond his control?

7. How is the relationship between Charley and Bernard different from the one between Willy and his sons? Why is this difference important?

8. Discuss Linda's character and role. In what ways is she supportive of Willy? In what ways does she encourage his deceptions and self-delusions?

9. What sort of person is Happy? What has he inherited from Willy? How is he a debasement of Willy? To what degree is he successful or happy?

10. Willy claims that success in business is based not on "what you do" but on "who you know and the smile on your face! It's contacts . . . a man can end up with diamonds on the basis of being well liked." How does the play support or reject this assertion?

11. Most of Willy's memories—Ben's visit, Boston, the football game—are from 1928. Why does Willy's memory return to 1928? Why is the contrast between 1928 and the present significant for Willy and for the play as a whole?

# AUGUST WILSON* (1945–2005)

To judge from the poverty of his birth and early days, one might never have supposed that August Wilson would eventually become one of America's première dramatists. His birth name was Frederick August Kittel, the fourth of six children. His father was an immigrant German, a baker, who never spent much time with the family, and by the time Wilson was five his father and mother had separated. Wilson's mother, Daisy Wilson, was an African American, and did housecleaning. It was she who taught August how to read when he was only four. When Wilson's father died, in 1965, Wilson changed his name to "August Wilson" to honor her. Daisy had remarried, and with her new husband and her family, had moved to a more prestigious neighborhood than the "Hill District" where the family had previously resided. In the new school system, Wilson, the only African-American student, experienced great hostility, both from fellow students and also from some of the teachers. He wrote a research paper about Napoleon, and his instructor accused him of plagiarising it. Because of such disparagement, Wilson left school, though still in ninth grade, and began a program of self education at a branch of Pittsburgh's Carnegie library. He educated himself so well that eventually the Library granted him a degree. It was just one of the special degrees he received, for he would later be granted two dozen honorary doctorates.

Wilson's young adulthood was also not auspicious, but he was slowly moving in the direction of becoming a writer. Three years before America became fully engaged in the Vietnam conflict, he signed up for a three-year hitch in the army, but somehow he was able to secure a discharge after a year, and he then began doing odd jobs for his subsistence. He bought a typewriter in 1965, and declared that he was a poet. At the age of 23, he co-founded the Black Horizon on the Hill Theater in Pittsburgh, and began haltingly to write a few plays, which were not distinguished or very successful. He moved to Minneapolis/St. Paul, and stayed there for a number of years. Later, he moved to Seattle, his final home, where he became one of the founders of the Seattle Repertory Theater. When living in Minnesota, he began working for the Minnesota Science Museum, and was given the duty of dramatizing Native American folk tales for visiting children. It was this rather journeyman task that confirmed his decision to follow drama as a career.

It is apparent that at some point during his years of movement from place to place, he developed the ambitious idea that would inform his major dramatic output during his lifetime career as dramatist. He planned a full cycle of 10 plays, to be called "The Pittsburgh Cycle," in which he would explore the lives and times of African Americans during the twentieth century. His aim was to dramatize the "comedy and tragedy" of blacks who were the descendents of the slaves who had been granted freedom at the time of the Civil War. Each of the plays was to deal with life during one of the decades, though Wilson did not write them in the chronological order of their topic matter. The settings of all but one of the plays is the Pittsburgh "hill district"—the location where his family had lived during the early years of his life. The 10 plays are the following:

Gem of the Ocean (1900–1910), written 2003
Joe Turner's Come and Gone (1910–20), written 1986
Ma Rainey's Black Bottom (1920–30), written 1984
The Piano Lesson (1930–40), written 1987, Pulitzer Prize
Seven Guitars (1940–50), written 1995
Fences (1957, 1965), written 1985, Pulitzer Prize

*Two Trains Running* (1960–70), written 1990
*Jitney* (1970–80), written 1982
*King Hedley, II* (1980–90), written 1999
*Radio Golf* (1990–2000), written 2005

Although Wilson's first 40 years were both an artistic and financial struggle, his later life was characterized by great recognition and praise. *Fences*, one of his best-known plays, was acclaimed for the 1987 production on Broadway, directed by Lloyd Richards and starring James Earl Jones. It won a Pulitzer Prize for Drama, and was additionally distinguished with a Tony award. For Wilson, it was also financially rewarding. His play *The Piano Lesson* received a Pulitzer Prize in 1990, along with the New York Drama Critics' Circle Award. In Wilson's final years of life, prizes and honorary degrees almost cascaded upon him. When he succumbed to cancer in 2005, he was recognized as one of America's leading dramatists.

*Fences*, written in the mid 1980s, is about a period in the 1950s during the growth of the Civil Rights Movement under Dr. Martin Luther King, but before the advent of the Black Power movement of the 1960s. Although there was progress in the 1950s, the country was still racist. It is important to recognize that major league baseball, after the Second World War, was becoming integrated, though slowly. The "Old Negro Leagues" had produced Black players with great ability, but with little public support and recognition. In the late 1940s, changes had begun to take place. Jackie Robinson became the first African-American player in the National League, and Monte Irvin led the way in the American League. By the mid 1950s, there were stalwart players like Minnie Minoso (b. 1922), Ernie Banks (b. 1931), and Elston Howard (1929–1980). The last Negro League player to move to the Big Leagues was Henry Aaron, who became almost a regular yearly member of the all-star National League teams. He went on to set the professional record of 755 home runs, which in June, 2007, was still standing.

In short, encouraging things were happening, and that is the backdrop of the world of baseball that is so much a part of the life and outlook of Troy Maxson (i.e., "maximum son"), August Wilson's protagonist in *Fences*. It is clear that Troy was a player who could hit the ball over fences, but it is also clear that circumstances prevented him from doing so. Wilson creates Troy as being too old to benefit from the integration of professional baseball, and also of American society, that were taking place at the time. Troy had spent the prime part of his youth in prison, and it was there that he was able to develop his baseball talents. The result is that with all his ability, he had become too old to be one of those to break baseball's "color line." This despite the fact that Satchel Paige had joined the Cleveland Indians in 1948, at the age of 42, almost exactly the same age that Wilson visualizes for Troy. Paige pitched for four major league teams, and did not finally retire until he was 59. Troy believes that he could have done just as well, and, as he says, "If you could play . . . then they ought to have let you play." Instead of excelling at hitting balls over the fence, however, he is in the process of retreat, and he is deeply unhappy about being no more than a garbage collector. The fence he builds around his house during the play is symbolically a fence of his own suspicion, anger, and cynicism, preventing him from glorying in the world where he might have conquered.

All this is important in considering the character of Troy. He is a special example of those whose lives were demonstrably marred by discrimination in the twentieth century. (Let us remember that *Fences* is a part of Wilson's chronicle of black life during the

10 decades from 1900 to 2000.) Wilson is careful to show that discrimination hurt Troy's family life during his boyhood. He was particularly afflicted by his father, who was "just as evil as he could be," as Troy tells his son Lyons. In 1.4 Troy describes the events of his leaving home at the age of 14. He had been raised on a cotton farm in the South, and his life was the "stoop labor" of endless cotton picking and cotton baling. Troy's father's attack on him underlies his hostility toward the dreams of his own son, Cory ("heart"), about going into professional football. Despite his negative attitude about Cory's hopes, Troy has moved beyond the narrow brutality of his own father. In 2.4, the most agitated and also the most moving scene in the play, Troy has the opportunity to swing a baseball bat at Cory, and thus he has the absolute power over Cory that his own father had exerted over him. But Troy turns away from violence, in a scene that recalls the famous "duel averted" scene in the popular eighteenth-century play *The Conscious Lovers* (1722), by Sir Richard Steele (1672–1729). Although Troy gives up his destructive power, however, he permanently alienates himself from his son.

Named after the ancient mythical city described by Homer, Troy is not only the major character of *Fences*, but he is also one of the major characters to have been created by a twentieth-century dramatist. He is a man of immense power, a leader, but by no means is he perfect. He is a drinker, he is unfaithful, and he is a man of contradictions. As he strays, he tries to justify his straying, but he is not convincing. He does not understand love, but he does understand duty, and that is his compensating strength. He somewhat resembles the Biblical patriarch Jacob, who wrestles with God (Genesis 32:24–32). Troy's perception is that he has wrestled with Death. A major theme in his story is that Death will inevitably win, but that he, Troy, is confident in himself, and defiant. He announces, as though Death is listening, "I be ready for you . . . but I ain't gonna be easy." (2.4.97). Though he is imperfect, he has great inner strength, and he is, above all, memorable.

# Fences (1985)

*for Lloyd Richards,°*
*who adds to whatever be touches*

> When the sins of our fathers visit us
> We do not have to play host.
> We can banish them with forgiveness
> As God, in His Largeness and Laws.
> —August Wilson

## CAST OF CHARACTERS

**Troy Maxson,** [fifty-three years old; a powrful man; now a garbage collector, though formerly a ballplayer and home-run hitter in the old "Negro leagues"]

**Jim Bono,** Troy's friend [of "thirty odd years"; acts as a conscience for Troy]

**Rose,** Troy's wife [of eighteen years]

**Lyons,** Troy's oldest son by a previous marriage

---

°*Lloyd Richards*: Richards (1919–2006) is perhaps best known for his having directed Lorraine Hansberry's *A Raisin in the Sun* in 1959, making him the first African American to direct a play on Broadway. Richards was a staunch friend and supportive colleague of Wilson, and eventually he directed six Broadway productions of Wilson plays, including *Fences* in 1987.

**Gabriel,** Troy's brother [severely injured in World War II]

**Cory,** Troy and Rose's son [ready to graduate from high school; an aspiring athlete]

**Raynell,** Troy's daughter [with Alberta; Raynell is seven in Act 2, Scene 5]

## SETTING

*The setting is the yard which fronts the only entrance to the Maxson household, an ancient two-story* 0.1
*brick house set back off a small alley in a big-city neighborhood. The entrance to the house is gained by*
*two or three steps leading to a wooden porch badly in need of paint.*

*A relatively recent addition to the house and running its full width, the porch lacks congruence. It* 0.2
*is a sturdy porch with a flat roof. One or two chairs of dubious value sit at one end where the kitchen*
*window opens onto the porch. An old-fashioned icebox stands silent guard at the opposite end.*

*The yard is a small dirt yard, partially fenced, except for the last scene, with a wooden saw horse, a* 0.3
*pile of lumber, and other fence-building equipment set off to the side. Opposite is a tree from which*
*hangs a ball made of rags. A baseball bat leans against the tree. Two oil drums serve as garbage recepta-*
*cles and sit near the house at right to complete the setting.*

## THE PLAY

*Near the turn of the century, the destitute of Europe sprang on the city with tenacious claws and an* 0.4
*honest and solid dream. The city devoured them. They swelled its belly until it burst into a thousand*
*furnaces and sewing machines, a thousand butcher shops and bakers' ovens, a thousand churches and*
*hospitals and funeral parlors and moneylenders.*

*The city grew. It nourished itself and offered each man a partnership limited only by his talent, his guile* 0.5
*and his willingness and capacity for hard work. For the immigrants of Europe, a dream dared and won true.*

*The descendants of African slaves were offered no such welcome or participation. They came from* 0.6
*places called the Carolinas and the Virginias, Georgia, Alabama, Mississippi, and Tennessee. They came*
*strong, eager, searching. The city rejected them and they fled and settled along the riverbanks and under*
*bridges in shallow, ramshackle houses made of sticks and tarpaper. They collected rags and wood. They*
*sold the use of their muscles and their bodies. They cleaned houses and washed clothes, they shined*
*shoes, and in quiet desperation and vengeful pride, they stole, and lived in pursuit of their own dream.*
*That they could breathe free, finally, and stand to meet life with the force of dignity and whatever elo-*
*quence the heart could call upon.*

*By 1957, the hard-won victories of the European immigrants had solidified the industrial might of* 0.7
*America. War had been confronted and won with new energies that used loyalty and patriotism as its*
*fuel. Life was rich, full, and flourishing. The Milwaukee Braves won the World Series, and the hot winds*
*of change that would make the sixties a turbulent, racing, dangerous, and provocative decade had not*
*yet begun to blow full.*

## ACT 1

### Scene 1

*It is 1957. TROY and BONO enter the yard, engaged in conversation. TROY is fifty-three years old, a large* 1.1
*man with thick, heavy hands; it is this largeness that he strives to fill out and make an accommodation with.*
*Together with his blackness, his largeness informs his sensibilities and the choices he has made in his life.*

*Of the two men, BONO is obviously the follower. His commitment to their friendship of thirty-odd* 1.2
*years is rooted in his admiration of TROY's honesty, capacity for hard work, and his strength, which*
*BONO seeks to emulate.*

*It is Friday night, payday, and the one night of the week the two men engage in a ritual of talk and* 1.3
*drink. TROY is usually the most talkative and at times he can be crude and almost vulgar, though he is*
*capable of rising to profound heights of expression. The men carry lunch buckets and wear or carry*
*burlap aprons and are dressed in clothes suitable to their jobs as garbage collectors.*

BONO: Troy, you ought to stop that lying!

TROY: I ain't lying! The nigger had a watermelon this big. [*He indicates with his hands.*] Talking about . . . "What watermelon, Mr. Rand?" I liked to fell out! "What watermelon, Mr. Rand?" . . . And it sitting there big as life.

BONO: What did Mr. Rand say?

TROY: Ain't said nothing. Figure if the nigger too dumb to know he carrying a watermelon, he wasn't gonna get much sense out of him. Trying to hide that great big old watermelon under his coat. Afraid to let the white man see him carry it home.

5   BONO: I'm like you . . . I ain't got no time for them kind of people.

TROY: Now what he look like getting mad cause he see the man from the union talking to Mr. Rand?

BONO: He come to me talking about . . . "Maxson gonna get us fired." I told him to get away from me with that. He walked away from me calling you a troublemaker. What Mr. Rand say?

TROY: Ain't said nothing. He told me to go down the Commissioner's office next Friday. They called me down there to see them.

BONO: Well, as long as you got your complaint filed, they can't fire you. That's what one of them white fellows tell me.

10   TROY: I ain't worried about them firing me. They gonna fire me cause I asked a question? That's all I did. I went to Mr. Rand and asked him, "Why? Why you got the white mens driving and the colored lifting?" Told him, "What's the matter, don't I count? You think only white fellows got sense enough to drive a truck. That ain't no paper job! Hell, any-body can drive a truck. How come you got all whites driving and the colored lifting?" He told me "take it to the union." Well, hell, that's what I done! Now they wanna come up with this pack of lies.

BONO: I told Brownie if the man come and ask him any questions . . . just tell the truth! It ain't nothing but something they done trumped up on you cause you filed a complaint on them.

TROY: Brownie don't understand nothing. All I want them to do is change the job description. Give everybody a chance to drive the truck. Brownie can't see that. He ain't got that much sense.

BONO: How you figure he be making out with that gal be up at Taylor's all the time . . . that Alberta gal?

TROY: Same as you and me. Getting just as much as we is. Which is to say nothing.

15   BONO: It is, huh? I figure you doing a little better than me . . . and I ain't saying what I'm doing.

TROY: Aw, nigger, look here . . . I know you. If you had got anywhere near that gal, twenty minutes later you be looking to tell somebody. And the first one you gonna tell . . . that you gonna want to brag to . . . is me.

BONO: I ain't saying that, I see where you be eyeing her.

TROY: I eye all the women. I don't miss nothing. Don't never let nobody tell you Troy Maxson don't eye the women.

BONO: You been doing more than eyeing her. You done bought her a drink or two.

20   TROY: Hell yeah, I bought her a drink! What that mean? I bought you one, too. What that mean cause I buy her a drink? I'm just being polite.

BONO: It's all right to buy her one drink. That's what you call being polite. But when you wanna be buying two or three . . . that's what you call eyeing her.

TROY: Look here, as long as you known me . . . you ever known me to chase after women?

BONO: Hell yeah! Long as I done known you. You forgetting I knew you when.

25   TROY: Naw, I'm talking about since I been married to Rose?

BONO: Oh, not since you been married to Rose. Now, that's the truth, there, I can say that.

TROY: All right then! Case closed.

BONO: I see you be walking up around Alberta's house. You supposed to be at Taylors' and
  you be walking up around there.

TROY: What you watching where I'm walking for? I ain't watching after you.

BONO: I seen you walking around there more than once.    30

TROY: Hell, you liable to see me walking anywhere! That don't mean nothing cause you see
  me walking around there.

BONO: Where she come from anyway? She just kinda showed up one day.

TROY: Tallahassee. You can look at her and tell she one of them Florida gals. They got some big
  healthy women down there. Grow them right up out the ground. Got a little bit of Indian
  in her. Most of them niggers down in Florida got some Indian in them.

BONO: I don't know about that Indian part. But she damn sure big and healthy. Women wear
  some big stockings. Got them great big old legs and hips as wide as the Mississippi River.

TROY: Legs don't mean nothing. You don't do nothing but push them out of the way. But them    35
  hips cushion the ride!

BONO: Troy, you ain't got no sense.

TROY: It's the truth! Like you riding on Goodyears!

*ROSE enters from the house. She is ten years younger than TROY, her devotion to him stems from her
recognition of the possibilities of her life without him: a succession of abusive men and their babies, a life of
partying and running the streets, the Church, or aloneness with its attendant pain and frustration. She
recognizes TROY'S spirit as a fine and illuminating one and she either ignores or forgives his faults, only
some of which she recognizes. Though she doesn't drink, her presence is an integral part of the Friday night
rituals. She alternates between the porch and the kitchen, where supper preparations are under way.*

ROSE: What you all out here getting into?

TROY: What you worried about what we getting into for? This is men talk, woman.

ROSE: What I care what you all talking about? Bono, you gonna stay for supper?    40

BONO: No, I thank you, Rose. But Lucille say she cooking up a pot of pigfeet.

TROY: Pigfeet! Hell, I'm going home with you! Might even stay the night if you got some
  pigfeet. You got something in there to top them pigfeet, Rose?

ROSE: I'm cooking up some chicken. I got some chicken and collard greens.

TROY: Well, go on back in the house and let me and Bono finish what we was talking about.
  This is men talk. I got some talk for you later. You know what kind of talk I mean. You go
  on and powder it up.

ROSE: Troy Maxson, don't you start that now!    45

TROY: [*puts his arm around her.*] Aw, woman . . . come here. Look here. Bono . . . when I met this
  woman . . . I got out that place, say, "Hitch up my pony, saddle up my mare . . . there's a
  woman out there for me somewhere." I looked here. Looked there. Saw Rose and latched on
  to her. I latched on to her and told her—I'm gonna tell you the truth—I told her, "Baby, I don't
  wanna marry, I just wanna be your man." Rose told me . . . tell him what you told me, Rose.

ROSE: I told him if he wasn't the marrying kind, then move out the way so the marrying kind
  could find me.

TROY: That's what she told me. "Nigger, you in my way. You blocking the view! Move out the
  way so I can find me a husband." I thought it over two or three days. Come back—

ROSE: Ain't no two or three days nothing. You was back the same night.

TROY: Come back, told her . . . "Okay, baby . . . but I'm gonna buy me a banty rooster and put    50
  him out there in the backyard . . . and when he see a stranger come, he'll flap his wings
  and crow . . . ." Look here, Bono, I could watch the front door by myself . . . it was that
  back door I was worried about.

ROSE: Troy, you ought not talk like that. Troy ain't doing nothing but telling a lie.

TROY: Only thing is . . . when we first got married . . . forget the rooster . . . we ain't had no yard!

BONO: I hear you tell it. Me and Lucille was staying down there on Logan Street. Had two rooms with the outhouse in the back. I ain't mind the outhouse none. But when that goddamn wind blow through there in the winter . . . that's what I'm talking about! To this day I wonder why in the hell I ever stayed down there for six long years. But see, I didn't know I could do no better. I thought only white folks had inside toilets and things.

ROSE: There's a lot of people don't know they can do no better than they doing now. That's just something you got to learn. A lot of folks still shop at Bella's.

55  TROY: Ain't nothing wrong with shopping at Bella's. She got fresh food.

ROSE: I ain't said nothing about if she got fresh food. I'm talking about what she charge. She charge ten cents more than the A&P.

TROY: The A&P ain't never done nothing for me. I spends my money where I'm treated right. I go down to Bella, say, "I need a loaf of bread, I'll pay you Friday." She give it to me. What sense that make when I got money to go and spend it somewhere else and ignore the person who done right by me? That ain't in the Bible.

ROSE: We ain't talking about what's in the Bible. What sense it make to shop there when she overcharge?

TROY: You shop where you want to. I'll do my shopping where the people been good to me.

60  ROSE: Well, I don't think it's right for her to overcharge. That's all I was saying.

BONO: Look here . . . I got to get on. Lucille going be raising all kind of hell.

TROY: Where you going, nigger? We ain't finished this pint. Come here, finish this pint.

BONO: Well, hell, I am . . . if you ever turn the bottle loose.

TROY: [*hands him the bottle.*] The only thing I say about the A&P is I'm glad Cory got that job down there. Help him take care of his school clothes and things. Gabe done moved out and things getting tight around here. He got that job. . . . He can start to look out for himself.

65  ROSE: Cory done went and got recruited by a college football team.

TROY: I told that boy about that football stuff. The white man ain't gonna let him get nowhere with that football. I told him when he first come to me with it. Now you come telling me he done went and got more tied up in it. He ought to go and get recruited in how to fix cars or something where he can make a living.

ROSE: He ain't talking about making no living playing football. It's just something the boys in school do. They gonna send a recruiter by to talk to you. He'll tell you he ain't talking about making no living playing football. It's a honor to be recruited.

TROY: It ain't gonna get him nowhere. Bono'll tell you that.

BONO: If he be like you in the sports . . . he's gonna be all right. Ain't but two men ever played baseball as good as you. That's Babe Ruth and Josh Gibson.° Them's the only two men ever hit more home runs than you.

70  TROY: What it ever get me? Ain't got a pot to piss in or a window to throw it out of.

ROSE: Times have changed since you was playing baseball, Troy. That was before the war. Times have changed a lot since then.

TROY: How in hell they done changed?

---

°*Babe Ruth and Josh Gibson*: George Herman Ruth, "Babe" Ruth (1895–1948), had a baseball career that lasted from 1914 to 1935. During this time he set many batting records, including his number of home runs in a season in 1927 (60) and total home runs (714). In 1957, no one had surpassed either of these records, and no one was close. Ruth was one of the first men to be made a member of the Baseball Hall of Fame. His record for a single season lasted until 1961, when Roger Maris hit 61. Joshua Gibson (1911–47), a catcher, is considered as one of the greatest home run hitters in baseball history, though he never was permitted to play in the major leagues. In seventeen seasons in the Negro Leagues, and in corrolary exhibition games, he may have batted as high as .384, and may have hit more than 800 home runs. One of the claims made about him is that he was the only batter to have hit a home run out of Yankee Stadium. He was elected posthumously to Baseball's Hall of Fame in 1972

ROSE: They got lots of colored boys playing ball now. Baseball and football.

BONO: You right about that, Rose. Times have changed, Troy. You just come along too early.

TROY: There ought not never have been no time called too early! Now you take that fellow . . .    75
What's that fellow they had playing right field for the Yankees back then? You know who
I'm talking about, Bono. Used to play right field for the Yankees.

ROSE: Selkirk?°

TROY: Selkirk! That's it! Man batting .269, understand? 269! What kind of sense that make? I
was hitting .432 with thirty-seven home runs! Man batting .269 and playing right field for
the Yankees! I saw Josh Gibson's daughter yesterday. She walking around with raggedy
shoes on her feet. Now I bet you Selkirk's daughter ain't walking around with raggedy
shoes on the feet! I bet you that!

ROSE: They got a lot of colored baseball players now. Jackie Robinson was the first. Folks had
to wait for Jackie Robinson.°

TROY: I done seen a hundred niggers play baseball better than Jackie Robinson. Hell, I know
some teams Jackie Robinson couldn't even make! What you talking about Jackie Robinson.
Jackie Robinson wasn't nobody. I'm talking about if you could play ball then they ought to
have let you play. Don't care what color you were. Come telling me I come along too early.
If you could play . . . then they ought to have let you play.

*TROY takes a long drink from the bottle.*

ROSE: You gonna drink yourself to death. You don't need to be drinking like that.    80

TROY: Death ain't nothing. I done seen him. Done wrassled with him. You can't tell me nothing about death. Death ain't nothing but a fastball on the outside corner. And you know
what I'll do to that! Lookee here, Bono . . . am I lying? You get one of them fastballs, about
waist high, over the outside corner of the plate where you can get the meat of the bat on
it . . . and good god! You can kiss it goodbye. Now, am I lying?

BONO: Naw, you telling the truth there. I seen you do it.

TROY: If I'm lying . . . that 450 feet worth of lying! [*Pause.*] That's all death is to me. A fastball
on the outside corner.

ROSE: I don't know why you want to get on talking about death.

TROY: Ain't nothing wrong with talking about death. That's part of life. Everybody gonna die.    85
You gonna die, I'm gonna die. Bono's gonna die. Hell, we all gonna die.

ROSE: But you ain't got to talk about it. I don't like to talk about it.

TROY: You the one brought it up. Me and Bono was talking about baseball . . . you tell me I'm
gonna drink myself to death. Ain't that right, Bono? You know I don't drink this but one
night out of the week. That's Friday night. I'm gonna drink just enough to where I can
handle it. Then I cuts it loose. I leave it alone. So don't you worry about me drinking myself to death. 'Cause I ain't worried about Death. I done seen him. I done wrestled with
him. Look here, Bono . . . I looked up one day and Death was marching straight at me.
Like Soldiers on Parade! The Army of Death was marching straight at me. The middle of
July, 1941. It got real cold just like it be winter. It seem like Death himself reached out and
touched me on the shoulder. He touched me just like I touch you. I got cold as ice and
Death standing there grinning at me.

ROSE: Troy, why don't you hush that talk.

---

° *Selkirk*: George Alexander ("Twinkletoes") Selkirk (1908–87), played for the Yankees for nine seasons from 1934 to 1942. When Babe Ruth retired in 1935, Selkirk became the regular Yankee right fielder. His major league lifetime batting average was .290, and he batted .269 in 1940. He hit a total of 108 home runs during his career, with 576 rbi. After 1942, he left the Yankees to serve in World War II.

° *Jackie Robinson*: Robinson (1919–72) led the way for equality in professional sports when he became the first African American to play major league baseball in 1947. He went on to have a sterling if brief major league career. He was made a member of the Baseball Hall of Fame in 1962.

TROY: I say . . . what you want, Mr. Death? You be wanting me? You done brought your army to be getting me? I looked him dead in the eye. I wasn't fearing nothing. I was ready to tangle. Just like I'm ready to tangle now. The Bible say be ever vigilant.° That's why I don't get but so drunk. I got to keep watch.

90 ROSE: Troy was right down there in Mercy Hospital. You remember he had pneumonia? Laying there with a fever talking plumb out of his head.

TROY: Death standing there staring at me . . . . carrying that sickle in his hand. Finally he say, "You want bound over for another year?" See, just like that . . . "You want bound over for another year?" I told him, "Bound over hell! Let's settle this now!" It seem like he kinda fell back when I said that, and all the cold went out of me. I reached down and grabbed that sickle and threw it just as far as I could throw it . . . and me and him commenced to wrestling. We wrestled for three days and three nights. I can't say where I found the strength from. Everytime it seemed like he was gonna get the best of me, I'd reach way down deep inside myself and find the strength to do him one better.

ROSE: Every time Troy tell that story he find different ways to tell it. Different things to make up about it.

TROY: I ain't making up nothing. I'm telling you the facts of what happened. I wrestled with Death for three days and three nights and I'm standing here to tell you about it. [*Pause.*] All right. At the end of the third night we done weakened each other to where we can't hardly move. Death stood up, throwed on his robe . . . had him a white robe with a hood on it. He throwed on that robe and went off to look for his sickle. Say, "I'll be back." Just like that. "I'll be back." I told him, say, "Yeah, but . . . you gonna have to find me!" I wasn't no fool. I wasn't going looking for him. Death ain't nothing to play with. And I know he's gonna get me. I know I got to join his army . . . his camp followers. But as long as I keep my strength and see him coming . . . as long as I keep up my vigilance . . . he's gonna have to fight to get me. I ain't going easy.

BONO: Well, look here, since you got to keep up your vigilance . . . let me have the bottle.

95 TROY: Aw hell, I shouldn't have told you that part. I should have left out that part.

ROSE: Troy be talking that stuff and half the time don't even know what he be talking about.

TROY: Bono know me better than that.

BONO: That's right. I know you. I know you got some Uncle Remus° in your blood. You got more stories than the devil got sinners.

TROY: Aw hell, I done seen him too! Done talked with the devil.

100 ROSE: Troy, don't nobody wanna be hearing all that stuff.

*LYONS enters the yard from the street. Thirty-four years old,* TROY'S *son by a previous marriage, he sports a neatly trimmed goatee, sport coat, white shirt, tieless and buttoned at the collar. Though he fancies himself a musician, he is more caught up in the rituals and "idea" of being a musician than in the actual practice of the music. He has come to borrow money from* TROY, *and while he knows he will be successful, he is uncertain as to what extent his lifestyle will be held up to scrutiny and ridicule.*

LYONS: Hey, Pop.

TROY: What you come "Hey, Popping" me for?

LYONS: How you doing, Rose? [*He kisses her.*] Mr. Bono. How you doing?

BONO: Hey, Lyons . . . how you been?

105 TROY: He must have been doing all right. I ain't seen him around here last week.

---

°*vigilant:* See I Peter, 5:8.
°*Uncle Remus:* A reference to the Uncle Remus stories (1881) of Joel Chandler Harris.

Rose: Troy, leave your boy alone. He come by to see you and you wanna start all that nonsense.

Troy: I ain't bothering Lyons. [*Offers him the bottle.*] Here . . . get you a drink. We got an understanding. I know why he come by to see me and he know I know.

Lyons: Come on, Pop . . . I just stopped by to say hi . . . see how you was doing.

Troy: You ain't stopped by yesterday.

Rose: You gonna stay for supper, Lyons? I got some chicken cooking in the oven. 110

Lyons: No, Rose . . . thanks. I was just in the neighborhood and thought I'd stop by for a minute.

Troy: You was in the neighborhood all right, nigger. You telling the truth there. You was in the neighborhood 'cause it's my payday.

Lyons: Well, hell, since you mentioned it . . . let me have ten dollars.

Troy: I'll be damned! I'll die and go to hell and play blackjack with the devil before I give you ten dollars.

Bono: That's what I wanna know about . . . that devil you done seen. 115

Lyons: What . . . Pop done seen the devil? You too much, Pops.

Troy: Yeah, I done seen him. Talked to him too!

Rose: You ain't seen no devil. I done told you that man ain't had nothing to do with the devil. Anything you can't understand, you want to call it the devil.

Troy: Look here, Bono . . . I went down to see Hertzberger about some furniture. Got three rooms for two-ninety-eight. That what it say on the radio. "Three rooms . . . two-ninety-eight." Even made up a little song about it. Go down there . . . man tell me I can't get no credit. I'm working every day and can't get no credit. What to do? I got an empty house with some raggedy furniture in it. Cory ain't got no bed. He's sleeping on a pile of rags on the floor. Working every day and can't get no credit. Come back here—Rose'll tell you— madder than hell. Sit down . . . try to figure what I'm gonna do. Come a knock on the door. Ain't been living here but three days. Who know I'm here? Open the door . . . devil standing there bigger than life. White fellow . . . got on good clothes and everything. Standing there with a clipboard in his hand. I ain't had to say nothing. First words come out of his mouth was . . . "I understand you need some furniture and can't get no credit." I liked to fell over. He say, "I'll give you all the credit you want, but you got to pay the interest on it." I told him, "Give me three rooms worth and charge whatever you want." Next day a truck pulled up here and two men unloaded them three rooms. Man what drove the truck give me a book. Say send ten dollars, first of every month to the address in the book and everything will be all right. Say if I miss a payment the devil was coming back and it'll be hell to pay. That was fifteen years ago. To this day . . . the first of the month I send my ten dollars, Rose'll tell you.

Rose: Troy lying. 120

Troy: I ain't never seen that man since. Now you tell me who else that could have been but the devil? I ain't sold my soul or nothing like that, you understand. Naw, I wouldn't have truck with the devil about nothing like that. I got my furniture and pays my ten dollars the first of the month just like clockwork.

Bono: How long you say you been paying this ten dollars a month?

Troy: Fifteen years!

Bono: Hell, ain't you finished paying for it yet? How much the man done charged you?

Troy: Ah hell, I done paid for it. I done paid for it ten times over! The fact is I'm scared to stop 125 paying it.

Rose: Troy lying. We got that furniture from Mr. Glickman. He ain't paying no ten dollars a month to nobody.

TROY:  Aw hell, woman. Bono know I ain't that big a fool.

LYONS:  I was just getting ready to say . . . I know where there's a bridge for sale.

TROY:  Look here, I'll tell you this . . . it don't matter to me if he was the devil. It don't matter if the devil give credit. Somebody has got to give it.

130  ROSE:  It ought to matter. You going around talking about having truck with the devil. . . . God's the one you gonna have to answer to. He's the one gonna be at the Judgment.

LYONS:  Yeah, well, look here, Pop . . . Let me have that ten dollars. I'll give it back to you. Bonnie got a job working at the hospital.

TROY:  What I tell you, Bono? The only time I see this nigger is when he wants something. That's the only time I see him.

LYONS:  Come on, Pop, Mr. Bono don't want to hear all that. Let me have the ten dollars. I told you Bonnie working.

TROY:  What that mean to me? "Bonnie working." I don't care if she working. Go ask her for the ten dollars if she working. Talking about "Bonnie working." Why ain't you working?

135  LYONS:  Aw, Pop, you know I can't find no decent job. Where am I gonna get a job at? You know I can't get no job.

TROY:  I told you I know some people down there. I can get you on the rubbish if you want to work. I told you that the last time you came by here asking me for something.

LYONS:  Naw, Pop . . . thanks. That ain't for me. I don't wanna be carrying nobody's rubbish. I don't wanna be punching nobody's time clock.

TROY:  What's the matter, you too good to carry people's rubbish? Where you think that ten dollars you talking about come from? I'm just supposed to haul people's rubbish and give my money to you cause you too lazy to work. You too lazy to work and wanna know why you ain't got what I got.

ROSE:  What hospital Bonnie working at? Mercy?

140  LYONS:  She's down at Passavant° working in the laundry.

TROY:  I ain't got nothing as it is. I give you that ten dollars and I got to eat beans the rest of the week. Naw . . . you ain't getting no ten dollars here.

LYONS:  You ain't got to be eating no beans. I don't know why you wanna say that.

TROY:  I ain't got no extra money. Gabe done moved over to Miss Pearl's paying her the rent and things done got tight around here. I can't afford to be giving you every payday.

LYONS:  I ain't asked you to give me nothing. I asked you to loan me ten dollars. I know you got ten dollars.

145  TROY:  Yeah, I got it. You know why I got it? 'Cause I don't throw my money away out there in the streets. You living the fast life . . . wanna be a musician . . . running around in them clubs and things . . . then, you learn to take care of yourself. You ain't gonna find me going and asking nobody for nothing. I done spent too many years without.

LYONS:  You and me is two different people, Pop.

TROY:  I done learned my mistake and learned to do what's right by it. You still trying to get something for nothing. Life don't owe you nothing. You owe it to yourself. Ask Bono. He'll tell you I'm right.

LYONS:  You got your way of dealing with the world . . . I got mine. The only thing that matters to me is the music.

TROY:  Yeah, I can see that! It don't matter how you gonna eat . . . where your next dollar is coming from. You telling the truth there.

150  LYONS:  I know I got to eat. But I got to live too. I need something that gonna help me to get out of the bed in the morning. Make me feel like I belong in the world. I don't bother nobody.

---

°*Passavant*: The University of Pittsburgh Medical Center Passavant, in Pittsburgh.

I just stay with the music cause that's the only way I can find to live in the world. Otherwise there ain't no telling what I might do. Now I don't come criticizing you and how you live. I just come by to ask you for ten dollars. I don't wanna hear all that about how I live.

TROY: Boy, your mamma did a hell of a job raising you.

LYONS: You can't change me, Pop. I'm thirty-four years old. If you wanted to change me, you should have been there when I was growing up. I come by to see you . . . ask for ten dollars and you want to talk about how I was raised. You don't know nothing about how I was raised.

ROSE: Let the boy have ten dollars, Troy.

TROY: [*to* LYONS.] What the hell you looking at me for? I ain't got no ten dollars. You know what I do with my money. [*To* ROSE.] Give him ten dollars if you want him to have it.

ROSE: I will. Just as soon as you turn it loose.                                                                    155

TROY: [*handing* ROSE *the money.*] There it is. Seventy-six dollars and forty-two cents. You see this, Bono? Now, I ain't gonna get but six of that back.

ROSE: You ought to stop telling that lie. Here, Lyons. [*She hands him the money.*]

LYONS: Thanks, Rose. Look . . . I got to run . . . I'll see you later.

TROY: Wait a minute. You gonna say, "Thanks, Rose" and ain't gonna look to see where she got that ten dollars from? See how they do me, Bono?

LYONS: I know she got it from you, Pop. Thanks. I'll give it back to you.                                          160

TROY: There he go telling another lie. Time I see that ten dollars . . . he'll be owing me thirty more.

LYONS: See you, Mr. Bono.

BONO: Take care, Lyons!

LYONS: Thanks, Pop. I'll see you again. [LYONS *exits the yard.*]

TROY: I don't know why he don't go and get him a decent job and take care of that woman    165
he got.

BONO: He'll be all right, Troy. The boy is still young.

TROY: The *boy* is thirty-four years old.

ROSE: Let's not get off into all that.

BONO: Look here . . . I got to be going. I got to be getting on. Lucille gonna be waiting.

TROY: [*puts his arm around* ROSE.] See this woman, Bono? I love this woman. I love this woman    170
so much it hurts. I love her so much . . . I done run out of ways of loving her. So I got to go back to basics. Don't you come by my house Monday morning talking about time to go to work . . . 'cause I'm still gonna be stroking!

ROSE: Troy! Stop it now!

BONO: I ain't paying him no mind, Rose. That ain't nothing but gin-talk. Go on, Troy. I'll see you Monday.

TROY: Don't you come by my house, nigger! I done told you what I'm gonna be doing.

*The lights go down to black.*

## ACT 1

## Scene 2

*The lights come up on* ROSE *hanging up clothes. She hums and sings softly to herself. It is the following morning.*

ROSE: [*sings.*]

> Jesus, be a fence all around me every day
> Jesus, I want you to protect me as I travel on my way.
> Jesus, be a fence all around me every day.

[TROY *enters from the house.*]

*Jesus, I want you to protect me*
*As I travel on my way.*

[*To* TROY.] Morning. You ready for breakfast? I can fix it soon as I finish hanging up these clothes.

TROY:  I got the coffee on. That'll be all right. I'll just drink some of that this morning.

ROSE:  That 651 hit yesterday. That's the second time this month. Miss Pearl hit for a dollar. . . . Seem like those that need the least always get lucky. Poor folks can't get nothing.

TROY:  Them numbers don't know nobody. I don't know why you fool with them. You and Lyons both.

5  ROSE:  It's something to do.

TROY:  You ain't doing nothing but throwing your money away.

ROSE:  Troy, you know I don't play foolishly. I just play a nickel here and a nickel there.

TROY:  That's two nickels you done thrown away.

ROSE:  Now I hit sometimes . . . that makes up for it. It always comes in handy when I do hit. I don't hear you complaining then.

10  TROY:  I ain't complaining now. I just say it's foolish. Trying to guess out of six hundred ways which way the number gonna come. If I had all the money niggers, these Negroes, throw away on numbers for one week—just one week—I'd be a rich man.

ROSE:  Well, you wishing and calling it foolish ain't gonna stop folks from playing numbers. That's one thing for sure. Besides . . . some good things come from playing numbers. Look where Pope done bought him that restaurant off of numbers.

TROY:  I can't stand niggers like that. Man ain't had two dimes to rub together. He walking around with his shoes all run over bumming money for cigarettes. All right. Got lucky there and hit the numbers . . .

ROSE:  Troy, I know all about it.

TROY:  Had good sense, I'll say that for him. He ain't throwed his money away. I seen niggers hit the numbers and go through two thousand dollars in four days. Man bought him that restaurant down there . . . fixed it up real nice . . . and then didn't want nobody to come in it! A Negro go in there and can't get no kind of service. I seen a white fellow come in there and order a bowl of stew. Pope picked all the meat out of the pot for him. Man ain't had nothing but a bowl of meat! Negro come behind him and ain't got nothing but the potatoes and carrots. Talking about what numbers do for people, you picked a wrong example. Ain't done nothing but make a worser fool out of him than he was before.

15  ROSE:  Troy, you ought to stop worrying about what happened at work yesterday.

TROY:  I ain't worried. Just told me to be down there at the Commissioner's office on Friday. Everybody think they gonna fire me. I ain't worried about them firing me. You ain't got to worry about that. [*Pause.*] Where's Cory? Cory in the house? [*Calls.*] Cory?

ROSE:  He gone out.

TROY:  Out, huh? He gone out 'cause he know I want him to help me with this fence. I know how he is. That boy scared of work.

*GABRIEL enters. He comes halfway down the alley and, hearing* TROY's *voice, stops.*

TROY:  [*continues.*] He ain't done a lick of work in his life.

20  ROSE:  He had to go to football practice. Coach wanted them to get in a little extra practice before the season start.

TROY:  I got his practice . . . running out of here before he get his chores done.

ROSE: Troy, what is wrong with you this morning? Don't nothing set right with you. Go on back in there and go to bed . . . get up on the other side.

TROY: Why something got to be wrong with me? I ain't said nothing wrong with me.

ROSE: You got something to say about everything. First it's the numbers . . . then it's the way the man runs his restaurant . . . then you done got on Cory. What's it gonna be next? Take a look up there and see if the weather suits you . . . or is it gonna be how you gonna put up the fence with the clothes hanging in the yard.

TROY: You hit the nail on the head then.                                                    25

ROSE: I know you like I know the back of my hand. Go on in there and get you some coffee . . . see if that straighten you up. 'Cause you ain't right this morning.

*TROY starts into the house and sees GABRIEL. GABRIEL starts singing. TROY's brother, he is seven years younger than TROY. Injured in World War II, he has a metal plate in his head. He carries an old trumpet tied around his waist and believes with every fiber of his being that he is the Archangel Gabriel. He carries a chipped basket with an assortment of discarded fruits and vegetables he has picked up in the strip district and which he attempts to sell.*

GABRIEL [*singing*].
   *Yes, ma'am I got plums*
   *You ask me how I sell them*
   *Oh ten cents apiece*
   *Three for a quarter*
   *Come and buy now*
   *'Cause I'm here today*
   *And tomorrow I'll be gone.*

*GABRIEL enters.*

GABRIEL: Hey, Rose!

ROSE: How you doing Gabe?

GABRIEL: There's Troy . . . Hey, Troy!

TROY: Hey, Gabe. [*Exit into kitchen.*]                                                    30

ROSE: [*to GABRIEL*]. What you got there?

GABRIEL: You know what I got, Rose. I got fruits and vegetables.

ROSE: [*looking in basket*]. Where's all these plums you talking about?

GABRIEL: I ain't got no plums today, Rose. I was just singing that. Have some tomorrow. Put    35
me in a big order for plums. Have enough plums tomorrow for St. Peter and everybody.

*TROY reenters from kitchen, crosses to steps.*

[*To ROSE.*] Troy's mad at me.

TROY: I ain't mad at you. What I got to be mad at you about? You ain't done nothing to me.

GABRIEL: I just moved over to Miss Pearl's to keep out from in your way. I ain't mean no harm
by it.

TROY: Who said anything about that? I ain't said anything about that.

GABRIEL: You ain't mad at me, is you?

TROY: Naw . . . I ain't mad at you, Gabe. If I was mad at you I'd tell you about it.                40

GABRIEL: Got me two rooms. In the basement. Got my own door too. Wanna see my key? [*He
holds up a key.*] That's my own key! My two rooms!

TROY: Well, that's good, Gabe. You got your own key . . . that's good.

ROSE: You hungry, Gabe? I was just fixing to cook Troy his breakfast.

GABRIEL: I'll take some biscuits. You got some biscuits? Did you know when I was in heaven . . . every morning me and St. Peter would sit down by the gate and eat some big fat biscuits? Oh, yeah! We had us a good time. We'd sit there and eat us them biscuits and then St. Peter would go off to sleep and tell me to wake him up when it's time to open the gates for the judgment.

45 ROSE: Well, come on . . . I'll make up a batch of biscuits.

*ROSE exits into the house.*

GABRIEL: Troy . . . St. Peter got your name in the book. I seen it. It say . . . Troy Maxson. I say . . . I know him! He got the same name like what I got. That's my brother!

TROY: How many times you gonna tell me that, Gabe?

GABRIEL: Ain't got my name in the book. Don't have to have my name. I done died and went to heaven. He got your name though. One morning St. Peter was looking at his book . . . marking it up for the judgment . . . and he let me see your name. Got it in there under M. Got Rose's name . . . I ain't seen it like I seen yours . . . but I know it's in there. He got a great big book. Got everybody's name what was ever been born. That's what he told me. But I seen your name. Seen it with my own eyes.

TROY: Go on in the house there. Rose going to fix you something to eat.

50 GABRIEL: Oh, I ain't hungry. I done had breakfast with Aunt Jemimah. She come by and cooked me up a whole mess of flapjacks. Remember how we used to eat them flapjacks?

TROY: Go on in the house and get you something to eat now.

GABRIEL: I got to sell my plums. I done sold some tomatoes. Got me two quarters. Wanna see? [*He shows TROY his quarters.*] I'm gonna save them and buy me a new horn so St. Peter can hear me when it's time to open the gates. [*GABRIEL stops suddenly. Listens.*] Hear that? That's the hellhounds. I got to chase them out of here. Go on get out of here! Get out! [*GABRIEL exits singing.*]

*Better get ready for the judgment*
*Better get ready for the judgment*
*My Lord is coming down*

*ROSE enters from the house.*

TROY: He's gone off somewhere.

55 GABRIEL: [*offstage.*]

*Better get ready for the judgment*
*Better get ready for the judgment morning*
*Better get ready for the judgment*
*My God is coming down.*

ROSE: He ain't eating right. Miss Pearl say she can't get him to eat nothing.

TROY: What you want me to do about it, Rose? I done did everything I can for the man. I can't make him get well. Man got half his head blown away . . . what you expect?

ROSE: Seem like something ought to be done to help him.

TROY: Man don't bother nobody. He just mixed up from that metal plate he got in his head. Ain't no sense for him to go back into the hospital.

60 ROSE: Least he be eating right. They can help him take care of himself.

TROY: Don't nobody wanna be locked up, Rose. What you wanna lock him up for? Man go over there and fight the war . . . messin' around with them Japs, get half his head blow off . . . and they give him a lousy three thousand dollars. And I had to swoop down on that.

ROSE: Is you fixing to go into that again?

TROY: That's the only way I got a roof over my head . . . cause of that metal plate.

ROSE: Ain't no sense you blaming yourself for nothing. Gabe wasn't in no condition to manage that money. You done what was right by him. Can't nobody say you ain't done what was right by him. Look how long you took care of him . . . till he wanted to have his own place and moved over there with Miss Pearl.

TROY: That ain't what I'm saying woman! I'm just stating the facts. If my brother didn't have 65 that metal plate in his head . . . I wouldn't have a pot to piss in or a window to throw it out of. And I'm fifty-three years old. Now see if you can understand that!

*TROY gets up from the porch and starts to exit the yard.*

ROSE: Where you going off to? You been running out of here every Saturday for weeks. I thought you was gonna work on this fence?

TROY: I'm gonna walk down to Taylors'. Listen to the ball game. I'll be back in a bit. I'll work on it when I get back.

*He exits the yard. The lights go to black.*

## ACT 1

## Scene 3

*The lights come up on the yard. It is four hours later. ROSE is taking down the clothes from the line. CORY enters carrying his football equipment.*

ROSE: Your daddy like to had a fit with you running out of here this morning without doing your chores.

CORY: I told you I had to go to practice.

ROSE: He say you were supposed to help him with this fence.

CORY: He been saying that the last four or five Saturdays, and then he don't never do nothing, but go down to Taylors'. Did you tell him about the recruiter?

ROSE: Yeah, I told him.                                                                                    5

CORY: What he say?

ROSE: He ain't said nothing too much. You get in there and get started on your chores before he gets back. Go on and scrub down them steps before he gets back here hollering and carrying on.

CORY: I'm hungry. What you got to eat, Mama?

ROSE: Go on and get started on your chores. I got some meat loaf in there. Go on and make you a sandwich . . . and don't leave no mess in there.

*CORY exits into the house. ROSE continues to take down the clothes. TROY enters the yard and sneaks up and grabs her from behind.*

Troy! Go on, now. You liked to scared me to death. What was the score of the game? Lucille had me on the phone and I couldn't keep up with it.

TROY: What I care about the game? Come here, woman. [*He tries to kiss her.*]                           10

ROSE: I thought you went down Taylors' to listen to the game. Go on, Troy! You supposed to be putting up this fence.

TROY: [*attempting to kiss her again.*] I'll put it up when I finish with what is at hand.

ROSE: Go on, Troy. I ain't studying you.

TROY: [*chasing after her.*] I'm studying you . . . fixing to do my homework!

ROSE: Troy, you better leave me alone.                                                                   15

TROY: Where's Cory? That boy brought his butt home yet?

ROSE: He's in the house doing his chores.

TROY: [*calling.*] Cory! Get your butt out here, boy!

ROSE *exits into the house with the laundry.* TROY *goes over to the pile of wood, picks up a board, and starts sawing.* CORY *enters from the house.*

TROY: You just now coming in here from leaving this morning?

20 CORY: Yeah, I had to go to football practice.

TROY: Yeah, what?

CORY: Yessir.

TROY: I ain't but two seconds off you noway. The garbage sitting in there overflowing . . . you ain't done none of your chores . . . and you come in here talking about "Yeah."

CORY: I was just getting ready to do my chores now, Pop . . .

25 TROY: Your first chore is to help me with this fence on Saturday. Everything else come after that. Now get that saw and cut them boards.

CORY *takes the saw and begins cutting the boards.* TROY *continues working. There is a long pause.*

CORY: Hey, Pop . . . why don't you buy a TV?

TROY: What I want with a TV? What I want one of them for?

CORY: Everybody got one. Earl, Ba Bra . . . Jesse!

TROY: I ain't asked you who had one. I say what I want with one?

30 CORY: So you can watch it. They got lots of things on TV. Baseball games and everything. We could watch the World Series.

TROY: Yeah . . . and how much this TV cost?

CORY: I don't know. They got them on sale for around two hundred dollars.

TROY: Two hundred dollars, huh?

CORY: That ain't that much, Pop.

35 TROY: Naw, it's just two hundred dollars. See that roof you got over your head at night? Let me tell you something about that roof. It's been over ten years since that roof was last tarred. See now . . . the snow come this winter and sit up there on that roof like it is . . . and it's gonna seep inside. It's just gonna be a little bit . . . ain't gonna hardly notice it. Then the next thing you know, it's gonna be leaking all over the house. Then the wood rot from all that water and you gonna need a whole new roof. Now, how much you think it cost to get that roof tarred?

CORY: I don't know.

TROY: Two hundred and sixty-four dollars . . . cash money. While you thinking about a TV, I got to be thinking about the roof . . . and whatever else go wrong here. Now if you had two hundred dollars, what would you do . . . fix the roof or buy a TV?

CORY: I'd buy a TV. Then when the roof started to leak . . . when it needed fixing . . . I'd fix it.

TROY: Where you gonna get the money from? You done spent it for a TV. You gonna sit up and watch the water run all over your brand new TV.

40 CORY: Aw, Pop. You got money. I know you do.

TROY: Where I got it at, huh?

CORY: You got it in the bank.

TROY: You wanna see my bankbook? You wanna see that seventy-three dollars and twenty-two cents I got sitting up in there?

CORY: You ain't got to pay for it all at one time. You can put a down payment on it and carry it on home with you.

45 TROY: Not me. I ain't gonna owe nobody nothing if I can help it. Miss a payment and they come and snatch it right out of your house. Then what you got? Now, soon as I get two hundred dollars clear, then I'll buy a TV. Right now, as soon as I get two hundred and sixty-four dollars, I'm gonna have this roof tarred.

CORY: Aw . . . Pop!

TROY: You go on and get you two hundred dollars and buy one if ya want it. I got better things to do with my money.

CORY: I can't get no two hundred dollars. I ain't never seen two hundred dollars.

TROY: I'll tell you what . . . you get you a hundred dollars and I'll put the other hundred with it.

CORY: All right, I'm gonna show you.                                                                    50

TROY: You gonna show me how you can cut them boards right now.

*CORY begins to cut the boards. There is a long pause.*

CORY: The Pirates won today. That makes five in a row.

TROY: I ain't thinking about the Pirates. Got an all-white team. Got that boy . . . that Puerto Rican boy . . . Clemente.° Don't even half-play him. That boy could be something if they give him a chance. Play him one day and sit him on the bench the next.

CORY: He gets a lot of chances to play.

TROY: I'm talking about playing regular. Playing every day so you can get your timing. That's   55 what I'm talking about.

CORY: They got some white guys on the team that don't play every day. You can't play everybody at the same time.

TROY: If they got a white fellow sitting on the bench . . . you can bet your last dollar he can't play! That colored guy got to be twice as good before he get on the team. That's why I don't want you to get all tied up in them sports. Man on the team and what it get him? They got colored on the team and don't use them. Same as not having them. All them teams the same.

CORY: The Braves got Hank Aaron and Wes Covington.° Hank Aaron hit two home runs today. That makes forty-three.

TROY: Hank Aaron ain't nobody. That what you supposed to do. That's how you supposed to play the game. Ain't nothing to it. It's just a matter of timing . . . getting the right followthrough. Hell, I can hit forty-three home runs right now!

CORY: Not off no major-league pitching, you couldn't.                                                  60

TROY: We had better pitching in the Negro leagues. I hit seven home runs off of Satchel Paige.° You can't get no better than that!

CORY: Sandy Koufax.° He's leading the league in strikeouts.

TROY: I ain't thinking of no Sandy Koufax.

CORY: You got Warren Spahn and Lew Burdette.° I bet you couldn't hit no home runs off of Warren Spahn.

---

°*Clemente*: Roberto Clemente (1934–72), one of the all-time best right fielders, played 18 seasons for the Pittsburgh Pirates. In 1957 he was still relatively new, and did not play full time, though Cory is correct in claiming that he was getting "lots of chances to play." Clemente eventually got 3,000 hits, and his lifetime average was .317. He was killed in a plane crash in December 1972.

°*Hank Aaron and Wes Covington*: Both were relatively new players for the Milwaukee Braves in 1957. Aaron played for the Braves for 18 seasons, and at his retirement in 1976 he was the all-time career home run champion, with 755. Covington's career was not illustrious, lasting only 10 years.

°*Satchel Paige*: Leroy Robert (Satchel) Paige (1906–82) was a legendary pitcher in the Negro Leagues for more than 20 years, and he ultimately was inducted into Baseball's Hall of Fame. He joined the Cleveland Indians in 1948 when he was already in his forties. His major league career was consequently not outstanding, though baseball fans were enthusiastic about him whenever he pitched. During the year 1957, Paige was involved in exhibition games. His last game as a pitcher took place in 1966, when he was 60 years old. He has been considered one of the alltime best pitchers.

°*Sandy Koufax*: Sandy Koufax (b. 1935), was in his third professional year in 1957, with the Brooklyn Dodgers. His best years were yet to come, in the 1960s, after the Dodgers moved to Los Angeles.

°*Warren Spahn and Lew Burdette*: Both Spahn (1921–2003) and Burdette (1926–2007) were stalwart pitchers for the Milwaukee Braves during the 1950s. Spahn won 21 games in 1957, and won the Cy Young Award. He still holds the record for the greatest number of wins by a left-handed pitcher (363). Burdette won 17 games that year, and won three games in the World Series against the Yankees.

65  TROY:  I'm through with it now. You go on and cut them boards. [*Pause.*] Your mama tell me you done got recruited by a college football team? Is that right?

CORY:  Yeah. Coach Zellman say the recruiter gonna be coming by to talk to you. Get you to sign the permission papers.

TROY:  I thought you supposed to be working down there at the A&P. Ain't you suppose to be working down there after school?

CORY:  Mr. Stawicki say he gonna hold my job for me until after the football season. Say starting next week I can work weekends.

TROY:  I thought we had an understanding about this football stuff? You suppose to keep up with your chores and hold that job down at the A&P. Ain't been around here all day on a Saturday. Ain't none of your chores done . . . and now you telling me you done quit your job.

70  CORY:  I'm going to be working weekends.

TROY:  You damn right you are! And ain't no need for nobody coming around here to talk to me about signing nothing.

CORY:  Hey, Pop . . . you can't do that. He's coming all the way from North Carolina.

TROY:  I don't care where he coming from. The white man ain't gonna let you get nowhere with that football noway. You go on and get your book-learning so you can work yourself up in that A&P or learn how to fix cars or build houses or something, get you a trade. That way you have something can't nobody take away from you. You go on and learn how to put your hands to some good use. Besides hauling people's garbage.

CORY:  I get good grades, Pop. That's why the recruiter wants to talk with you. You got to keep up your grades to get recruited. This way I'll be going to college. I'll get a chance . . .

75  TROY:  First you gonna get your butt down there to the A&P and get your job back.

CORY:  Mr. Stawicki done already hired somebody else 'cause I told him I was playing football.

TROY:  You a bigger fool than I thought . . . to let somebody take away your job so you can play some football. Where you gonna get your money to take out your girlfriend and whatnot? What kind of foolishness is that to let somebody take away your job?

CORY:  I'm still gonna be working weekends.

TROY:  Naw . . . naw. You getting your butt out of here and finding you another job.

80  CORY:  Come on, Pop! I got to practice. I can't work after school and play football too. The team needs me. That's what Coach Zellman say . . .

TROY:  I don't care what nobody else say. I'm the boss . . . you understand? I'm the boss around here. I do the only saying what counts.

CORY:  Come on, Pop!

TROY:  I asked you . . . did you understand?

CORY:  Yeah . . .

85  TROY:  What?!

CORY:  Yessir.

TROY:  You go on down there to that A&P and see if you can get your job back. If you can't do both . . . then you quit the football team. You've got to take the crookeds with the straights.

CORY:  Yessir. [*Pause.*] Can I ask you a question?

TROY:  What the hell you wanna ask me? Mr. Stawicki the one you got the questions for.

90  CORY:  How come you ain't never liked me?

TROY:  Liked you? Who the hell say I got to like you? What law is there say I got to like you? Wanna stand up in my face and ask a damn fool-ass question like that. Talking about liking somebody. Come here, boy, when I talk to you.

*CORY comes over to where TROY is working. He stands slouched over and TROY shoves him on his shoulder.*

Straighten up, goddammit! I asked you a question . . . what law is there say I got to like you?

CORY: None.

TROY: Well, all right then! Don't you eat every day? [*Pause.*] Answer me when I talk to you! Don't you eat every day?

CORY: Yeah.

TROY: Nigger, as long as you in my house, you put that sir on the end of it when you talk to me. 95

CORY: Yes . . . sir.

TROY: You eat every day.

CORY: Yessir!

TROY: Got a roof over your head.

CORY: Yessir! 100

TROY: Got clothes on your back.

CORY: Yessir.

TROY: Why you think that is?

CORY: 'Cause of you.

TROY: Ah, hell I know it's 'cause of me . . . but why do you think that is? 105

CORY: [*hesitant.*] 'Cause you like me.

TROY: Like you? I go out of here every morning . . . bust my butt . . . putting up with them crackers every day . . . 'cause I like you? You are the biggest fool I ever saw. [*Pause.*] It's my job. It's my responsibility! You understand that? A man got to take care of his family. You live in my house . . . sleep you behind on my bedclothes . . . fill you belly up with my food . . . cause you my son. You my flesh and blood. Not 'cause I like you! 'Cause it's my duty to take care of you. I owe a responsibility to you! Let's get this straight right here . . . before it go along any further . . . I ain't got to like you. Mr. Rand don't give me my money come payday 'cause he likes me. He gives me 'cause he owe me. I done give you every-thing I had to give you. I gave you your life! Me and your mama worked that out between us. And liking your black ass wasn't part of the bargain. Don't you try and go through life worrying about if somebody like you or not. You best be making sure they doing right by you. You understand what I'm saying boy?

CORY: Yes sir.

TROY: Then get the hell out of my face, and get on down to that A&P.

*ROSE has been standing behind the screen door for much of the scene. She enters as CORY exits.*

ROSE: Why don't you let the boy go ahead and play football, Troy? Ain't no harm in that. He's 110 just trying to be like you with the sports.

TROY: I don't want him to be like me! I want him to move as far away from my life as he can get. You the only decent thing that ever happened to me. I wish him that. But I don't wish him a thing else from my life. I decided seventeen years ago that boy wasn't getting involved in no sports. Not after what they did to me in the sports.

ROSE: Troy, why don't you admit you was too old to play in the major leagues? For once . . . why don't you admit that?

TROY: What do you mean too old? Don't come telling me I was too old. I just wasn't the right color. Hell, I'm fifty-three years old and can do better than Selkirk's .269 right now!

ROSE: How's was you gonna play ball when you were over forty? Sometimes I can't get no sense out of you.

TROY: I got good sense, woman. I got sense enough not to let my boy get hurt over playing no 115 sports. You been mothering that boy too much. Worried about if people like him.

ROSE: Everything that boy do . . . he do for you. He wants you to say "Good job, son." That's all.

TROY: Rose, I ain't got time for that. He's alive. He's healthy. He's got to make his own way. I made mine. Ain't nobody gonna hold his hand when he get out there in that world.

ROSE: Times have changed from when you was young, Troy. People change. The world's changing around you and you can't even see it.

TROY: [*slow, methodical.*] Woman . . . I do the best I can do. I come in here every Friday. I carry a sack of potatoes and a bucket of lard. You all line up at the door with your hands out. I give you the lint from my pockets. I give you my sweat and my blood. I ain't got no tears. I done spent them. We go upstairs in that room at night . . . and I fall down on you and try to blast a hole into forever. I get up Monday morning . . . find my lunch on the table. I go out. Make my way. Find my strength to carry me through to the next Friday. [*Pause.*] That's all I got, Rose. That's all I got to give. I can't give nothing else.

*TROY exits into the house. The lights go down to black.*

## ACT 1

### Scene 4

*It is Friday. Two weeks later. CORY starts out of the house with his football equipment. The phone rings.*

CORY: [*calling.*] I got it! [*He answers the phone and stands in the screen door talking.*] Hello? Hey, Jesse. Naw . . . I was just getting ready to leave now.

ROSE: [*calling.*] Cory!

CORY: I told you, man, them spikes is all tore up. You can use them if you want, but they ain't no good. Earl got some spikes.

ROSE: [*calling.*] Cory!

5    CORY: [*calling to ROSE.*] Mam? I'm talking to Jesse. [*Into phone.*] When she say that? [*Pause.*] Aw, you lying, man. I'm gonna tell her you said that.

ROSE: [*calling.*] Cory, don't you go nowhere!

CORY: I got to go to the game, Ma! [*Into the phone.*] Yeah, hey, look, I'll talk to you later. Yeah, I'll meet you over Earl's house. Later. Bye, Ma.

*CORY exits the house and starts out the yard.*

ROSE: Cory, where you going off to? You got that stuff all pulled out and thrown all over your room.

CORY: [*in the yard.*] I was looking for my spikes. Jesse wanted to borrow my spikes.

10    ROSE: Get up there and get that cleaned up before your daddy get back in here.

CORY: I got to go to the game! I'll clean it up *when I get back.* [*CORY exits.*]

ROSE: That's all he need to do is see that room all messed up.

*ROSE exits into the house. TROY and BONO enter the yard. TROY is dressed in clothes other than his work clothes.*

BONO: He told him the same thing he told you. Take it to the union.

TROY: Brownie ain't got that much sense. Man wasn't thinking about nothing. He wait until I confront them on it . . . then he wanna come crying seniority. [*Calls.*] Hey, Rose!

15    BONO: I wish I could have seen Mr. Rand's face when he told you.

TROY: He couldn't get it out of his mouth! Liked to bit his tongue! When they called me down there to the Commissioner's office . . . he thought they was gonna fire me. Like everybody else.

BONO: I didn't think they was gonna fire you. I thought they was gonna put you on the warning paper.

TROY: Hey, Rose! [*To BONO.*] Yeah, Mr. Rand like to bit his tongue.

*TROY breaks the seal on the bottle, takes a drink, and hands it to BONO.*

BONO: I see you run right down to Taylors' and told that Alberta gal.

TROY: [*calling.*] Hey Rose! [*To BONO.*] I told everybody. Hey, Rose! I went down there to cash  20
my check.

ROSE: [*entering from the house.*] Hush all that hollering, man! I know you out here. What they
say down there at the Commissioner's office?

TROY: You supposed to come when I call you, woman. Bono'll tell you that. [*To BONO.*] Don't
Lucille come when you call her?

ROSE: Man, hush your mouth. I ain't no dog . . . talk about "come when you call me."

BONO: [*puts his arm around ROSE.*] You hear this, Bono? I had me an old dog used to get uppity
like that. You say, "C'mere, Blue!" . . . and he just lay there and look at you. End up
getting a stick and chasing him away trying to make him come.

ROSE: I ain't studying you and your dog. I remember you used to sing that old song.  25

TROY: [*he sings.*]
Hear it ring! Hear it ring!
*I had a dog his name was Blue.*

ROSE: Don't nobody wanna hear you sing that old song.

TROY [*sings*]. You know Blue was mighty true.

ROSE: Used to have Cory running around here singing that song.

BONO: Hell, I remember that song myself.  30

TROY: [*sings.*]
*You know Blue was a good old dog*
*Blue treed a possum in a hollow log.*

That was my daddy's song. My daddy made up that song.

ROSE: I don't care who made it up. Don't nobody wanna hear you sing it.

TROY: [*makes a song like calling a dog.*] Come here, woman.

ROSE: You come in here carrying on, I reckon they ain't fired you. What they say down there at
the Commissioner's office?

TROY: Look here, Rose. . . . Mr. Rand called me into his office today when I got back from talk-  35
ing to them people down there . . . it come from up top . . . he called me in and told me
they was making me a driver.

ROSE: Troy, you kidding!

TROY: No I ain't. Ask Bono.

ROSE: Well, that's great, Troy. Now you don't have to hassle them people no more.

*LYONS enters from the street.*

TROY: Aw hell, I wasn't looking to see you today. I thought you was in jail. Got it all over the
front page of the *Courier* about them raiding Sefus's place . . . where you be hanging out
with all them thugs.

LYONS: Hey, Pop . . . that ain't got nothing to do with me. I don't go down there gambling. I go  40
down there to sit in with the band. I ain't got nothing to do with the gambling part. They
got some good music down there.

TROY: They got some rogues . . . is what they got.

LYONS: How you been, Mr. Bono? Hi, Rose.

BONO: I see where you playing down at the Crawford Grill tonight.

ROSE: How come you ain't brought Bonnie like I told you? You should have brought Bonnie
with you, she ain't been over in a month of Sundays.

LYONS: I was just in the neighborhood . . . thought I'd stop by.  45

TROY: Here he come . . .

BONO: Your daddy got a promotion on the rubbish. He's gonna be the first colored driver. Ain't got to do nothing but sit up there and read the paper like them white fellows.

LYONS: Hey, Pop . . . if you knew how to read you'd be all right.

BONO: Naw . . . naw . . . you mean if the nigger knew how to drive he'd be all right. Been fighting with them people about driving and ain't even got a license. Mr. Rand know you ain't got no driver's license?

50 TROY: Driving ain't nothing. All you do is point the truck where you want it to go. Driving ain't nothing.

BONO: Do Mr. Rand know you ain't got no driver's license? That's what I'm talking about. I ain't asked if driving was easy. I asked if Mr. Rand know you ain't got no driver's license?

TROY: He ain't got to know. The man ain't got to know my business. Time he find out, I have two or three driver's licenses.

LYONS: [*going into his pocket.*] Say, look here, Pop . . .

TROY: I knew it was coming. Didn't I tell you, Bono? I know what kind of "Look here, Pop" that was. The nigger fixing to ask me for some money. It's Friday night. It's my payday. All them rogues down there on the avenue . . . the ones that ain't in jail . . . and Lyons is hopping in his shoes to get down there with them.

55 LYONS: See, Pop . . . if you give somebody else a chance to talk sometimes, you'd see that I was fixing to pay you back your ten dollars like I told you. Here . . . I told you I'd pay you when Bonnie got paid.

TROY: Naw . . . you go ahead and keep that ten dollars. Put it in the bank. The next time you feel like you wanna come by here and ask me for something . . . you go on down there and get that.

LYONS: Here's your ten dollars, Pop. I told you I don't want you to give me nothing. I just wanted to borrow ten dollars.

TROY: Naw . . . you go on and keep that for the next time you want to ask me.

LYONS: Come on, Pop . . . here go your ten dollars.

60 ROSE: Why don't you go on and let the boy pay you back, Troy?

LYONS: Here you go, Rose. If you don't take it I'm gonna have to hear about it for the next six months. [*He hands her the money.*]

ROSE: You can hand yours over here too, Troy.

TROY: You see this, Bono. You see how they do me.

BONO: Yeah, Lucille do me the same way.

*GABRIEL is heard singing off stage. He enters.*

65 GABRIEL: Better get ready for the Judgment! Better get ready for . . . Hey! . . . Hey! . . . There's Troy's boy!

LYONS: How are you doing, Uncle Gabe?

GABRIEL: Lyons . . . The King of the Jungle! Rose . . . hey, Rose. Got a flower for you. [*He takes a rose from his pocket.*] Picked it myself. That's the same rose like you is!

ROSE: That's right nice of you, Gabe.

LYONS: What you been doing, Uncle Gabe?

70 GABRIEL: Oh, I been chasing hellhounds and waiting on the time to tell St. Peter to open the gates.

LYONS: You been chasing hellhounds, huh? Well . . . you doing the right thing, Uncle Gabe. Somebody got to chase them.

GABRIEL: Oh, yeah . . . . I know it. The devil's strong. The devil ain't no pushover. Hellhounds snipping at everybody's heels. But I got my trumpet waiting on the Judgment time.

LYONS: Waiting on the Battle of Armageddon, huh?

GABRIEL: Ain't gonna be too much of a battle when God get to waving that Judgment sword. But the people's gonna have a hell of a time trying to get into heaven if them gates ain't open.

LYONS: [*putting his arm around* GABRIEL.] You hear this, Pop. Uncle Gabe, you all right!     75

GABRIEL: [*laughing with* LYONS.] Lyons! King of the Jungle.

ROSE: You gonna stay for suppper, Gabe? Want me to fix you a plate?

GABRIEL: I'll take a sandwich, Rose. Don't want no plate. Just wanna eat with my hands. I'll take a sandwich.

ROSE: How about you, Lyons? You staying? Got some short ribs cooking.

LYONS: Naw, I won't eat nothing till after we finished playing. [*Pause.*] You ought to come     80 down and listen to me play, Pop.

TROY: I don't like that Chinese music. All that noise.

ROSE: Go on in the house and wash up, Gabe . . . I'll fix you a sandwich.

GABRIEL: [*to* LYONS, *as he exits.*] Troy's mad at me.

LYONS: What you mad at Uncle Gabe for, Pop?

ROSE: He thinks Troy's mad at him 'cause he moved over to Miss Pearl's.     85

TROY: I ain't mad at the man. He can live where he want to live at.

LYONS: What he move over there for? Miss Pearl don't like nobody.

ROSE: She don't mind him none. She treats him real nice. She just don't allow all that singing.

TROY: She don't mind that rent he be paying . . . That's what she don't mind.

ROSE: Troy, I ain't going through that with you no more. He's over there cause he want to have     90 his own place. He can come and go as he please.

TROY: Hell, he could come and go as he please here. I wasn't stopping him. I ain't put no rules on him.

ROSE: It ain't the same thing, Troy. And you know it. [GABRIEL *comes to the door.*] Now, that's the last I wanna hear about that. I don't wanna hear nothing else about Gabe and Miss Pearl. And next week . . .

GABRIEL: I'm ready for my sandwich, Rose.

ROSE: And next week . . . when that recruiter come from that school . . . I want you to sign that paper and go on and let Cory play football. Then that'll be the last I have to hear about that.

TROY: [*to* ROSE *as she exits in to the house.*] I ain't thinking about Cory nothing.     95

LYONS: What . . . Cory got recruited? What school he going to?

TROY: That boy walking around here smelling his piss . . . thinking he's grown. Thinking he's gonna do what he want, irrespective of what I say. Look here, Bono . . . I left the Commissioner's office and went down to the A&P . . . that boy ain't working down there. He lying to me. Telling me he got his job back . . . telling me he working weekends . . . telling me he working after school . . . Mr. Stawicki tell me he ain't working down there at all!

LYONS: Cory just growing up. He's just busting at the seams trying to fill out your shoes.

TROY: I don't care what he's doing. When he get to the point where he wanna disobey me . . . then it's time for him to move on. Bono'll tell you that. I bet he ain't never disobeyed his daddy without paying the consequences.

BONO: I ain't never had a chance. My daddy came on through . . . but I ain't never knew him     100 to see him . . . or what he had on his mind or where he went. Just moving on through. Searching out the New Land. That's what the old folks used to call it. See a fellow moving around from place to place . . . woman to woman . . . called it searching out the New Land. I can't say if he ever found it. I come along, didn't want no kids. Didn't know if I was gonna be in one place long enough to fix on them right as their daddy. I figured I was going searching too. As it turned out I been hooked up with Lucille near about as long as your daddy been with Rose. Going on sixteen years.

TROY: Sometimes I wish I hadn't known my daddy. He ain't cared nothing about no kids. A kid to him wasn't nothing. All he wanted was for you to learn how to walk so he could start you to working. When it come time for eating . . . he ate first. If there was anything left over, that's what you got. Man would sit down and eat two chickens and give you the wing.

LYONS: You ought to stop that, Pop. Everybody feed their kids. No matter how hard times is . . . everybody care about their kids. Make sure they have something to eat.

TROY: The only thing my daddy cared about was getting them bales of cotton in to Mr. Lubin. That's the only thing that mattered to him. Sometimes I used to wonder why he was living. Wonder why the devil hadn't come and got him. "Get them bales of cotton in to Mr. Lubin" and find out he owe him money . . .

LYONS: He should have just went on and left when he saw he couldn't get nowhere. That's what I would have done.

105  TROY: How he gonna leave with eleven kids? And where he gonna go? He ain't knew how to do nothing but farm. No, he was trapped and I think he knew it. But I'll say this for him . . . he felt a responsibility toward us. Maybe he ain't treated us the way I felt he should have . . . but without that responsibility he could have walked off and left us . . . made his own way.

BONO: A lot of them did. Back in those days what you talking about . . . they walk out their front door and just take on down one road or another and keep on walking.

LYONS: There you go! That's what I'm talking about.

BONO: Just keep on walking till you come to something else. Ain't you never heard of nobody having the walking blues? Well, that's what you call it when you just take off like that.

TROY: My daddy ain't had them walking blues! What you talking about? He stayed right there with his family. But he was just as evil as he could be. My mama couldn't stand him. Couldn't stand that evilness. She run off when I was about eight. She sneaked off one night after he had gone to sleep. Told me she was coming back for me. I ain't never seen her no more. All his women run off and left him. He wasn't good for nobody. When my turn come to head out, I was fourteen and got to sniffing around Joe Canewell's daughter. Had us an old mule we called Greyboy. My daddy sent me out to do some plowing and I tied up Greyboy and went to fooling around with Joe Canewell's daughter. We done found us a nice little spot, got real cozy with each other. She about thirteen and we done figured we was grown anyway . . . so we down there enjoying ourselves . . . ain't thinking about nothing. We didn't know Greyboy had got loose and wandered back to the house and my daddy was looking for me. We down there by the creek enjoying ourselves when my daddy come up on us. Surprised us. He had them leather straps off the mule and commenced to whupping me like there was no tomorrow. I jumped up, mad and embarrassed. I was scared of my daddy. When he commenced to whupping on me . . . quite naturally I run to get out of the way. [Pause.] Now I thought he was mad 'cause I ain't done my work. But I see where he was chasing me off so he could have the gal for himself. When I see what the matter of if was, I lost all fear of my daddy. Right there is where I become a man . . . at fourteen years of age. [Pause.] Now it was my turn to run him off. I picked up them same reins that he had used on me. I picked up them reins and commenced to whupping on him. The gal jumped up and run him off . . . and when my daddy turned to face me, I could see why the devil had never come to get him . . . 'cause he was the devil himself. I don't know what happened. When I woke up, I was laying right there by the creek, and Blue . . . this old dog we had . . . was licking my face. I thought I was blind. I couldn't see nothing. Both my eyes were swollen shut. I laid there and cried. I didn't know what I was gonna do. The only thing I knew was the time had come for me to leave my daddy's house. And right there the world suddenly got big. And it was a long time before I could cut it down to where I could handle it. Part of that cutting down was when I got to the place where I could feel him kicking in my blood and knew that the only thing that separated us was the matter of a few years.

GABRIEL *enters from the house with a sandwich.*

LYONS: What you got there, Uncle Gabe?　　　　　　　　　　　　　　　　　　　110

GABRIEL: Got me a ham sandwich. Rose gave me a ham sandwich.

TROY: I don't know what happened to him. I done lost touch with everybody except Gabriel. But I hope he's dead. I hope he found some peace.

LYONS: That's a heavy story, Pop. I didn't know you left home when you was fourteen.

TROY: And didn't know nothing. The only part of the world I knew was the forty-two acres of Mr. Lubin's land. That's all I knew about life.

LYONS: Fourteen's kinda young to be out on your own. [*Phone rings.*] I don't even think I was　115 ready to be out on my own at fourteen. I don't know what I would have done.

TROY: I got up from the creek and walked on down to Mobile. I was through with farming. Figured I could do better in the city. So I walked the two hundred miles to Mobile.

LYONS: Wait a minute . . . you ain't walked no two hundred miles, Pop. Ain't nobody gonna walk no two hundred miles. You talking about some walking there.

BONO: That's the only way you got anywhere back in them days.

LYONS: Shhh. Damn if I wouldn't have hitched a ride with someday!

TROY: Who you gonna hitch it with? They ain't had no cars and things like they got now. We　120 talking about 1918.

ROSE: [*entering.*] What you all out here getting into?

TROY: [*to ROSE.*] I'm telling Lyons how good he got it. He don't know nothing about this I'm talking.

ROSE: Lyons, that was Bonnie on the phone. She say you supposed to pick her up.

LYONS: Yeah, okay Rose.

TROY: I walked on down to Mobile and hitched up with some of them fellows that was　125 heading this way. Got up here and found out . . . not only couldn't you get a job . . . you couldn't find no place to live. I thought I was in freedom. Shhh. Colored folks living down there on the river banks in whatever kind of shelter they could find for themselves. Right down there under the Brady Street Bridge. Living in shacks made of sticks and tarpaper. Messed around there and went from bad to worse. Started stealing. First it was food. Then I figured, hell, if I steal money I can buy me some food. Buy me some shoes too! One thing led to another. Met your mama. I was young and anxious to be a man. Met your mama and had you. What I do that for? Now I got to worry about feeding you and her. Got to steal three times as much. Went out one day looking for somebody to rob . . . that's what I was, a robber. I'll tell you the truth. I'm ashamed of it today. But it's the truth. Went to rob this fellow . . . pulled out my knife . . . and he pulled out a gun. Shot me in the chest. I felt just like somebody had taken a hot branding iron and laid it on me. When he shot me I jumped at him with my knife. They told me I killed him and they put me in the penitentiary and locked me up for fifteen years. That's where I met Bono. That's where I learned how to play baseball. Got out that place and your mama had taken you and went on to make life without me. Fifteen years was a long time for her to wait. But that fifteen years cured me of that robbing stuff. Rose'll tell you. She asked me when I met her if I had gotten all that foolishness out of my system. And I told her, "Baby, it's you and baseball all what count with me." You hear me, Bono? I meant it too. She say, "Which one comes first?" I told her, "Baby, ain't no doubt it's baseball . . . but you stick and get old with me and we'll both outlive this baseball." Am I right, Rose? And it's true.

ROSE: Man, hush your mouth. You ain't said no such thing. Talking about, "Baby you know you'll always be number one with me." That's what you was talking.

TROY: You hear that, Bono. That's why I love her.

BONO: Rose'll keep you straight. You get off the track, she'll straighten you up.

ROSE: Lyons, you better get on up and get Bonnie. She waiting on you.

130   LYONS: [gets up to go.] Hey, Pop, why don't you come on down to the Grill and hear me play?

TROY: I ain't going down there. I'm too old to be sitting around in them clubs.

BONO: You got to be good to play down at the Grill.

LYONS: Come on, Pop . . .

TROY: I got to get up in the morning.

135   LYONS: You ain't got to stay long.

TROY: Naw, I'm gonna get my supper and go on to bed.

LYONS: Well, I got to go. I'll see you again.

TROY: Don't you come around my house on my payday.

ROSE: Pick up the phone and let somebody know you coming. And bring Bonnie with you. You know I'm always glad to see her.

140   LYONS: Yeah, I'll do that, Rose. You take care now. See you, Pop. See you, Mr. Bono. See you, Uncle Gabe.

GABRIEL: Lyons! King of the Jungle! [LYONS exits.]

TROY: Is supper ready, woman? Me and you got some business to take care of. I'm gonna tear it up too.

ROSE: Troy, I done told you now!

TROY: [puts his arm around BONO.] Aw hell, woman . . . this is Bono. Bono like family. I done known this nigger since . . . how long I done know you?

145   BONO: It's been a long time.

TROY: I done know this nigger since Skippy was a pup. Me and him done been through some times.

BONO: You sure right about that.

TROY: Hell, I done know him longer than I known you. And we still standing shoulder to shoulder. Hey look here, Bono . . . a man can't ask for no more than that. [Drinks to him.] I love you, nigger.

BONO: Hell, I love you too . . . I got to get home see my woman. You got yours in hand. I got to get mine.

BONO *starts to exit as* CORY *enters the yard, dressed in his football uniform. He gives* TROY *a hard, uncompromising look.*

150   CORY: What you do that for, Pop?

*He throws his helmet down in the direction of* TROY.

ROSE: What's the matter? Cory . . . . What's the matter?

CORY: Papa done went up to the school and told Coach Zellman I can't play football no more. Wouldn't even let me play the game. Told him to tell the recruiter not to come.

ROSE: Troy . . .

TROY: What you Troying me for. Yeah, I did it. And the boy know why I did it.

155   CORY: Why you wanna do that to me? That was the one chance I had.

ROSE: Ain't nothing wrong with Cory playing football, Troy.

TROY: The boy lied to me. I told the nigger if he wanna play football . . . to keep up his chores and hold down that job at the A&P. That was the conditions. Stopped down there to see Mr. Stawicki . . .

CORY: I can't work after school during the football season, Pop! I tried to tell you that Mr. Stawicki's holding my job for me. You don't never want to listen to nobody. And then you wanna go and do this to me!

TROY: I ain't done nothing to you. You done it to yourself.

CORY: Just cause you didn't have a chance! You just scared I'm gonna be better than you, 160 that's all.

TROY: Come here.

ROSE: Troy . . .

*CORY reluctantly crosses over to TROY.*

TROY: All right! See. You done made a mistake.

CORY: I didn't even do nothing!

TROY: I'm gonna tell you what your mistake was. See . . . you swung at the ball and didn't hit 165 it. That's strike one. See, you in the batter's box now. You swung and you missed. That's strike one. Don't you strike out!

*Lights fade to black.*

## ACT 2

### Scene 1

*The following morning. CORY is at the tree hitting the ball with the bat. He tries to mimic TROY, but his swing is awkward, less sure. ROSE enters from the house.*

ROSE: Cory, I want you to help me with this cupboard.

CORY: I ain't quitting the team. I don't care what Poppa say.

ROSE: I'll talk to him when he gets back. He had to go see about your Uncle Gabe. The police done arrested him. Say he was disturbing the peace. He 'll be back directly. Come on in here and help me clean out the top of this cupboard.

*CORY exits into the house. ROSE sees TROY and BONO coming down the alley.*

TROY . . . what they say down there?

TROY: Ain't said nothing. I give them fifty dollars and they let him go. I'll talk to you about it. 5 Where's Cory?

ROSE: He's in there helping me clean out these cupboards.

TROY: Tell him to get his butt out here.

> *TROY and BONO go over to the pile of wood.*
> *BONO picks up the saw and begins sawing.*

TROY: [*to BONO.*] All they want is the money. That makes six or seven times I done went down there and got him. See me coming they stick out their hands.

BONO: Yeah. I know what you mean. That's all they care about . . . that money. They don't care about what's right. [*Pause.*] Nigger, why you got to go and get some hard wood? You ain't doing nothing but building a little old fence. Get you some soft pine wood. That's all you need.

TROY: I know what I'm doing. This is outside wood. You put pine wood inside the house. Pine 10 wood is inside wood. This here is outside wood. Now you tell me where the fence is gonna be?

BONO: You don't need this wood. You can put it up with pine wood and it'll stand as long as you gonna be here looking at it.

TROY: How you know how long I'm gonna be here, nigger? Hell, I might just live forever. Live longer than old man Horsely.

BONO: That's what Magee used to say.

TROY: Magee's a damn fool. Now you tell me who you ever heard of gonna pull their own teeth with a pair of rusty pliers.

15  BONO: The old folks . . . my granddaddy used to pull his teeth with pliers. They ain't had no dentists for the colored folks back then.

TROY: Get clean pliers! You understand? Clean pliers! Sterilize them! Besides we ain't living back then. All Magee had to do was walk over to Doc Goldblum's.

BONO: I see where you and that Tallahassee gal . . . that Alberta . . . I see where you all done got tight.

TROY: What you mean "got tight"?

BONO: I see where you be laughing and joking with her all the time.

20  TROY: I laughs and jokes with all of them, Bono. You know me.

BONO: That ain't the kind of laughing and joking I'm talking about.

*CORY enters from the house.*

CORY: How you doing, Mr. Bono?

TROY: Cory? Get that saw from Bono and cut some wood. He talking about the wood's too hard to cut. Stand back there, Jim, and let that young boy show you how it's done.

BONO: He's sure welcome to it. [*CORY takes the saw and begins to cut the wood.*] Whew-e-e! Look at that. Big old strong boy. Look like Joe Louis.° Hell, must be getting old the way I'm watching that boy whip through that wood.

25  CORY: I don't see why Mama want a fence around the yard noways.

TROY: Damn if I know either. What the hell she keeping out with it? She ain't got nothing nobody want.

BONO: Some people build fences to keep people out . . . and other people build fences to keep people in. Rose wants to hold on to you all. She loves you.

TROY: Hell, nigger, I don't need nobody to tell me my wife loves me. Cory . . . go on in the house and see if you can find that other saw.

CORY: Where's it at?

30  TROY: I said find it! Look for it till you find it! [*CORY exits into the house.*] What's that supposed to mean? Wanna keep us in?

BONO: Troy . . . I done known you seem like damn near my whole life. You and Rose both. I done know both of you all for a long time. I remember when you met Rose. When you was hitting them baseball out the park. A lot of them old gals was after you then. You had the pick of the litter. When you picked Rose, I was happy for you. That was the first time I knew you had any sense. I said . . . My man Troy knows what he's doing . . . I'm gonna follow this nigger . . . he might take me somewhere. I been following you too. I done learned a whole heap of things about life watching you. I done learned how to tell where the shit lies. How to tell it from the alfalfa. You done learned me a lot of things. You showed me how to not make the same mistakes . . . to take life as it comes along and keep putting one foot in front of the other. [*Pause.*] Rose a good woman, Troy.

TROY: Hell, nigger, I know she a good woman. I been married to her for eighteen years. What you got on your mind, Bono?

BONO: I just say she a good woman. Just like I say anything. I ain't got to have nothing on my mind.

---

°*Joe Louis:* Louis (1914–81), known as the "Brown Bomber," was a dominant black heavyweight who became champion in 1937, and held the championship for 11 years. By 1957 he had long since retired from boxing, and had become a wrestler. He retired from that in 1957 because of an injury. He was proverbial for his power in the ring.

TROY: You just gonna say she a good woman and leave it hanging out there like that? Why you telling me she a good woman?

BONO: She loves you, Troy. Rose loves you. 35

TROY: You saying I don't measure up. That's what you trying to say. I don't measure up cause I'm seeing this other gal. I know what you trying to say.

BONO: I know what Rose means to you, Troy. I'm just trying to say I don't want to see you mess up.

TROY: Yeah, I appreciate that, Bono. If you was messing around on Lucille I'd be telling you the same thing.

BONO: Well, that's all I got to say. I just say that because I love you both.

TROY: Hell, you know me . . . I wasn't out there looking for nothing. You can't find a better 40 woman than Rose. I know that. But seems like this woman just stuck onto me where I can't shake her loose. I done wrestled with it, tried to throw her off me . . . but she just stuck on tighter. Now she's stuck on for good.

BONO: You's in control . . . that's what you tell me all the time. You responsible for what you do.

TROY: I ain't ducking the responsibility of it. As long as it sets right in my heart . . . then I'm okay. 'Cause that's all I listen to. It'll tell me right from wrong every time. And I ain't talking about doing Rose no bad turn. I love Rose. She done carried me a long ways and I love and respect her for that.

BONO: I know you do. That's why I don't want to see you hurt her. But what you gonna do when she find out? What you got then? If you try and juggle both of them . . . sooner or later you gonna drop one of them. That's common sense.

TROY: Yeah, I hear what you saying, Bono. I been trying to figure a way to work it out.

BONO: Work it out right, Troy. I don't want to be getting all up between you and Rose's busi- 45 ness . . . but work it so it come out right.

TROY: Ah hell, I get all up between you and Lucille's business. When you gonna get that woman that refrigerator she been wanting? Don't tell me you ain't got no money now. I know who your banker is. Mellon don't need that money bad as Lucille want that refrigerator. I'll tell you that.

BONO: Tell you what I'll do . . . when you finish building this fence for Rose . . . I'll buy lucille that refrigerator.

TROY: You done stuck your foot in your mouth now!

*TROY grabs up a board and begins to saw. BONO starts to walk out the yard.*

Hey, nigger . . . where you going?

BONO: I'm going home. I know you don't expect me to help you now. I'm protecting my money. I wanna see you put that fence up by yourself. That's what I want to see. You'll be here another six months without me.

TROY: Nigger, you ain't right. 50

BONO: When it comes to my money . . . I'm right as fireworks on the Fourth of July.

TROY: All right, we gonna see now. You better get out your bankbook.

*BONO exits, and TROY continues to work. ROSE enters from the house.*

ROSE: What they say down there? What's happening with Gabe?

TROY: I went down there and got him out. Cost me fifty dollars. Say he was disturbing the peace. Judge set up a hearing for him in three weeks. Say to show cause why he shouldn't be recommitted.

ROSE: What was he doing that cause them to arrest him? 55

TROY: Some kids was teasing him and he run them off home. Say he was howling and carrying on. Some folks seen him and called the police. That's all it was.

ROSE: Well, what's you say? What'd you tell the judge?

TROY: Told him I'd look after him. It didn't make no sense to recommit the man. He stuck out
his big greasy palm and told me to give him fifty dollars and take him on home.

ROSE: Where's he at now? Where'd he go off to?

60  TROY: He's gone about his business. He don't need nobody to hold his hand.

ROSE: Well, I don't know. Seem like that would be the best place for him if they did put him
into the hospital. I know what you're gonna say. But that's what I think would be best.

TROY: The man done had his life ruined fighting for what? And they wanna take and lock him
up. Let him be free. He don't bother nobody.

ROSE: Well, everybody got their own way of looking at it I guess. Come on and get your lunch.
I got a bowl of lima beans and some cornbread in the oven. Come and get something to
eat. Ain't no sense you fretting over Gabe.

*ROSE turns to go into the house.*

TROY: Rose . . . got something to tell you.

65  ROSE: Well, come on . . . wait till I get this food on the table.

TROY: Rose! [*She stops and turns around.*] I don't know how to say this. [*Pause.*] I can't explain it
none. It just sort of grows on you till it gets out of hand. It starts out like a little bush . . .
and the next thing you know it's a whole forest.

ROSE: Troy . . . what is you talking about?

TROY: I'm talking, woman, let me talk. I'm trying to find a way to tell you . . . I'm gonna be a
daddy. I'm gonna be somebody's daddy.

ROSE: Troy . . . you're not telling me this? You're gonna be . . . what?

70  TROY: Rose . . . now . . . see . . .

ROSE: You telling me you gonna be somebody's daddy? You telling your *wife* this?

GABRIEL [*enters from the street. He carries a rose in his hand.*] Hey, Troy! Hey, Rose!

ROSE: I have to wait eighteen years to hear something like this.

GABRIEL: Hey, Rose . . . I got a flower for you. [*He hands it to her.*] That's a rose. Same rose like
you is.

75  ROSE: Thanks, Gabe.

GABRIEL: Troy, you ain't mad at me is you? Them bad mens come and put me away. You ain't
mad at me is you?

TROY: Naw, Gabe, I ain't mad at you.

ROSE: Eighteen years and you wanna come with this.

GABRIEL [*takes a quarter out of his pocket*]. See what I got? Got a brand new quarter.

80  TROY: Rose . . . it's just . . .

ROSE: Ain't nothing you can say, Troy. Ain't no way of explaining that.

GABRIEL: Fellow that give me this quarter had a whole mess of them. I'm gonna keep this
quarter till it stop shining.

ROSE: Gabe, go on in the house there. I got some watermelon in the Frigidaire. Go on and get
you a piece.

GABRIEL: Say, Rose . . . you know I was chasing hellhounds and them bad mens come and get
me and take me away. Troy helped me. He come down there and told them they better let
me go before he beat them up. Yeah, he did!

85  ROSE: You go on and get you a piece of watermelon, Gabe. Them bad mens is gone now.

GABRIEL: Okay, Rose . . . gonna get me some watermelon. The kind with the stripes on it.
[*GABRIEL exits into the house.*]

ROSE: Why, Troy? Why? After all these years to come dragging this in to me now. It don't make no sense at your age. I could have expected this ten or fifteen years ago, but not now.

TROY: Age ain't got nothing to do with it, Rose.

ROSE: I done tried to be everything a wife should be. Everything a wife could be. Been married eighteen years and I got to live to see the day you tell me you been seeing another woman and done fathered a child by her. And you know I ain't never wanted no half nothing in my family. My whole family is half. Everybody got different fathers and mothers . . . my two sisters and my brother. Can't hardly tell who's who. Can't never sit down and talk about Papa and Mama. It's your papa and your mama and my papa and my mama . . .

TROY: Rose . . . stop it now.                                                                                        90

ROSE: I ain't never wanted that for none of my children. And now you wanna drag your behind in here and tell me something like this.

TROY: You ought to know. It's time for you to know.

ROSE: Well, I don't want to know, goddamn it!

TROY: I can't just make it go away. It's done now. I can't wish the circumstance of the thing away.

ROSE: And you don't want to either. Maybe you want to wish me and my boy away. Maybe       95 that's what you want? Well, you can't wish us away. I've got eighteen years of my life invested in you. You ought to have stayed upstairs in my bed where you belong.

TROY: Rose . . . now listen to me . . . we can get a handle on this thing. We can talk this out . . . come to an understanding.

ROSE: All of a sudden it's "we." Where was "we" at when you was down there rolling around with some godforsaken woman? "We" should have come to an understanding before you started making a damn fool of yourself. You're a day late and a dollar short when it comes to an understanding with me.

TROY: It's just . . . She gives me a different idea . . . a different understanding about myself. I can step out of this house and get away from the pressures and problems . . . be a different man. I ain't got to wonder how I'm gonna pay the bills or get the roof fixed. I can just be a part of myself that I ain't never been.

ROSE: What I want to know . . . is do you plan to continue seeing her. That's all you can say to me.

TROY: I can sit up in her house and laugh. Do you understand what I'm saying. I can laugh out     100 loud . . . and it feels good. It reaches all the way down to the bottom of my shoes. [*Pause.*] Rose, I can't give that up.

ROSE: Maybe you ought to go on and stay down there with her . . . if she's a better woman than me.

TROY: It ain't about nobody being a better woman or nothing. Rose, you ain't the blame. A man couldn't ask for no woman to be a better wife than you've been. I'm responsible for it. I done locked myself into a pattern trying to take care of you all that I forgot about myself.

ROSE: What the hell was I there for? That was my job, not somebody else's.

TROY: Rose, I done tried all my life to live decent . . . to live a clean . . . hard . . . useful life. I tried to be a good husband to you. In every way I knew how. Maybe I come into the world backwards, I don't know. But . . . you born with two strikes on you before you come to the plate. You got to guard it closely . . . always looking for the curve ball on the inside corner. You can't afford to let none get past you. You can't afford a call strike. If you going down . . . you going down swinging. Everything lined up against you. What you gonna do. I fooled them, Rose. I bunted. When I found you and Cory and a halfway decent job . . . I was safe. Couldn't nothing touch me. I wasn't gonna strike out no more. I wasn't going back to the penitentiary. I wasn't gonna lay in the streets with a bottle of wine. I was safe. I had me a family. A job. I wasn't gonna get that last strike. I was on first looking for one of them boys to knock me in. To get me home.

105 ROSE: You should have stayed in my bed, Troy.

TROY: Then when I saw that gal . . . she firmed up my backbone. And I got to thinking that if I tried . . . I just might be able to steal second. Do you understand after eighteen years I wanted to steal second.

ROSE: You should have held me tight. You should have grabbed me and held on.

TROY: I stood on first base for eighteen years and I thought . . . well, goddamn it . . . go on for it!

ROSE: We're not talking about baseball! We're talking about you going off to lay in bed with another woman . . . and then bring it home to me. That's what we're talking about. We ain't talking about no baseball.

110 TROY: Rose, you're not listening to me. I'm trying the best I can to explain it to you. It's not easy for me to admit that I been standing in the same place for eighteen years.

ROSE: I been standing with you! I been right here with you, Troy. I got a life too. I gave eighteen years of my life to stand in the same spot with you. Don't you think I ever wanted other things? Don't you think I had dreams and hopes? What about my life? What about me? Don't you think it ever crossed my mind to want to know other men? That I wanted to lay up somewhere and forget about my responsibilities? That I wanted someone to make me laugh so I could feel good? You not the only one who's got wants and needs. But I held on to you, Troy. I took all my feelings, my wants and needs, my dreams . . . and I buried them inside you. I planted a seed and watched and prayed over it. I planted myself inside you and waited to bloom. And it didn't take me no eighteen years to find out the soil was hard and rocky and it wasn't never gonna bloom. But I held on to you, Troy. I held you tighter. You was my husband. I owed you everything I had. Every part of me I could find to give you. And upstairs in that room . . . with the darkness falling in on me . . . I gave everything I had to try and erase the doubt that you wasn't the finest man in the world. And wherever you was going . . . I wanted to be there with you. 'Cause you was my husband. 'Cause that's the only way I was gonna survive as your wife. You always talking about what you give . . . and what you don't have to give. But you take too. You take . . . and don't even know nobody's giving!

*ROSE turns to exit into the house; TROY grabs her arm.*

TROY: You say I take and don't give!

ROSE: Troy! You're hurting me!

TROY: You say I take and don't give!

115 ROSE: Troy . . . you're hurting my arm! Let go!

TROY: I done give you everything I got. Don't you tell that lie on me.

ROSE: Troy!

TROY: Don't you tell that lie on me!

CORY: [*enters from the house.*] Mama!

120 ROSE: Troy. You're hurting me.

TROY: Don't you tell me about no taking and giving.

*CORY comes up behind TROY and grabs him. TROY, surprised, is thrown off balance just as CORY throws a glancing blow that catches him on the chest and knocks him down. TROY is stunned, as is CORY.*

ROSE: Troy. Troy. No! [TROY *gets to his feet and starts at* CORY.] Troy . . . no. Please! Troy!

*ROSE pulls on TROY to hold him back. TROY stops himself.*

TROY: [*to* CORY.] All right. That's strike two. You stay away from around me, boy. Don't you strike out. You living with a full count. Don't you strike out.

*TROY exits out the yard as the lights go down.*

## ACT 2

### Scene 2

*It is six months later, early afternoon.* TROY *enters from the house and starts to exit the yard.* ROSE *enters from the house.*

ROSE: Troy, I want to talk to you.

TROY: All of a sudden, after all this time, you want to talk to me, huh? You ain't wanted to talk to me for months. You ain't wanted to talk to me last night. You ain't wanted no part of me then. What you wanna talk to me about now?

ROSE: Tomorrow's Friday.

TROY: I know what day tomorrow is. You think I don't know tomorrow's Friday? My whole life I ain't done nothing but look to see Friday coming and you got to tell me it's Friday.

ROSE. I want to know if you're coming home.                                            5

TROY: I always come home, Rose. You know that. There ain't never been a night I ain't come home.

ROSE: That ain't what I mean . . . and you know it. I want to know if you're coming straight home after work.

TROY: I figure I'd cash my check . . . hang out at Taylors' with the boys . . . maybe play a game of checkers . . .

ROSE: Troy, I can't live like this. I won't live like this. You livin' on borrowed time with me. It's been going on six months now you ain't been coming home.

TROY: I be here every night. Every night of the year. That's 365 days.                  10

ROSE: I want you to come home tomorrow after work.

TROY: Rose . . . I don't mess up my pay. You know that now. I take my pay and I give it to you. I don't have no money but what you give me back. I just want to have little time to myself . . . a little time to enjoy life.

ROSE: What about me? When's my time to enjoy life?

TROY: I don't know what to tell you, Rose. I'm doing the best I can.

ROSE: You ain't been home from work but time enough to change your clothes and run out . . .   15
and you wanna call that the best you can do?

TROY: I'm going over to the hospital to see Alberta. She went into the hospital this afternoon. Look like she might have the baby early. I won't be gone long.

ROSE: Well, you ought to know. They went over to Miss Pearl's and got Gabe today. She said you told them to go ahead and lock him up.

TROY: I ain't said no such thing. Whoever told you that is telling a lie. Pearl ain't doing nothing but telling a big fat lie.

ROSE: She ain't had to tell me. I read it on the papers.

TROY: I ain't told them nothing of the kind.                                            20

ROSE: I saw it right there on the papers.

TROY: What it say, huh?

ROSE: It said you told them to take him.

TROY: Then they screwed that up, just the way they screw up everything. I ain't worried about what they got on the paper.

ROSE: Say the government sent part of his check to the hospital and the other part to you.     25

TROY: I ain't got nothing to do with that if that's the way it works. I ain't made up the rules about how it work.

ROSE: You did Gabe just like you did Cory. You wouldn't sign the paper for Cory . . . but you signed for Gabe. You signed that paper.

*The telephone is heard ringing inside the house.*

TROY: I told you I ain't signed nothing, woman! The only thing I signed was the release form. Hell, I can't read, I don't know what they had on that paper! I ain't signed nothing about sending Gabe away.

ROSE: I said send him to the hospital . . . you said let him be free . . . now you done went down there and signed him to the hospital for half his money. You went back on yourself, Troy. You gonna have to answer for that.

30   TROY: See now . . . you been over there talking to Miss Pearl. She done got mad 'cause she ain't getting Gabe's rent money. That's all it is. She's liable to say anything.

ROSE: Troy, I seen where you signed the paper.

TROY: You ain't seen nothing I signed. What she doing got papers on my brother anyway? Miss Pearl telling a big fat lie. And I'm gonna tell her about it too! You ain't seen nothing I signed. Say . . . you ain't seen nothing I signed.

*ROSE exits into the house to answer the telephone. Presently she returns.*

ROSE: Troy . . . that was the hospital. Alberta had the baby.

TROY: What she have? What is it?

35   ROSE: It's a girl.

TROY: I better get on down to the hospital to see her.

ROSE: Troy . . .

TROY: Rose . . . I got to go see her now. That's only right . . . what's the matter . . . the baby's all right, ain't it?

ROSE: Alberta died having the baby.

40   TROY: Died . . . you say she's dead? Alberta's dead?

ROSE: They said they done all they could. They couldn't do nothing for her.

TROY: The baby? How's the baby?

ROSE: They say it's healthy. I wonder who's gonna bury her.

TROY: She had family, Rose. She wasn't living in the world by herself.

45   ROSE: I know she wasn't living in the world by herself.

TROY: Next thing you gonna want to know if she had any insurance.

ROSE: Troy, you ain't got to talk like that.

TROY: That's the first thing that jumped out your mouth. "Who's gonna bury her?" Like I'm fixing to take on that task for myself.

ROSE: I am your wife. Don't push me away.

50   TROY: I ain't pushing nobody away. Just give me some space. That's all. Just give me some room to breathe.

*ROSE exits into the house. TROY walks about the yard.*

TROY [*with a quiet rage that threatens to consume him*]. All right . . . Mr. Death. See now . . . I'm gonna tell you what I'm gonna do. I'm gonna take and build me a fence around this yard. See? I'm gonna build me a fence around what belongs to me. And then I want you to stay on the other side. See? You stay over there until you're ready for me. Then you come on. Bring your army. Bring your sickle. Bring your wrestling clothes. I ain't gonna fall down on my vigilance this time. You ain't gonna sneak up on me no more. When you ready for me . . . when the top of your list say Troy Maxson . . . that's when you come around here. You come up and knock on the front door. Ain't nobody else got nothing to do with this. This is between you and me. Man to man. You stay on the other side of that fence until you ready for me. Then you come up and knock on the front door. Anytime you want. I'll be ready for you.

*The lights go down to black.*

## ACT 2

### Scene 3

*The lights come up on the porch. It is late evening three days later. ROSE sits listening to the ball game waiting for TROY. The final out of the game is made and ROSE switches off the radio. TROY enters the yard carrying an infant wrapped in blankets. He stands back from the house and calls.*

*ROSE enters and stands on the porch. There is a long, awkward silence, the weight of which grows heavier with each passing second.*

TROY: Rose . . . I'm standing here with my daughter in my arms. She ain't but a wee bittie little old thing. She don't know nothing about grownups' business. She innocent . . . and she ain't got no mama.

ROSE: What you telling me for, Troy? [*She turns and exits into the house.*]

TROY: Well . . . I guess we'll just sit out here on the porch.

*He sits down on the porch. There is an awkward indelicateness about the way be handles the body. His largeness engulfs and seems to swallow it. He speaks loud enough for ROSE to hear.*

A man's got to do what's right for him. I ain't sorry for nothing I done. It felt right in my heart. [*To the baby.*] What you smiling at? Your daddy's a big man. Got these great big old hands. But sometimes he's scared. And right now your daddy's scared cause we sitting out here and ain't got no home. Oh, I been homeless before. I ain't had no little baby with me. But I been homeless. You just be out on the road by your lonesome and you see one of them trains coming and you just kinda go like this . . . [*He sings as a lullaby.*]

> Please, Mr. Engineer let a man ride the line
> Please, Mr. Engineer let a man ride the line
> I ain't got no ticket please let me ride the blinds.

*ROSE enters from the house. TROY, hearing her steps behind him, stands and faces her.*

She's my daughter, Rose. My own flesh and blood. I can't deny her no more than I can deny them boys. [*Pause.*] You and them boys is my family. You and them and this child is all I got in the world. So I guess what I'm saying is . . . I'd appreciate it if you'd help me take care of her.

ROSE: Okay, Troy . . . you're right. I'll take care of your baby for you . . . 'cause . . . like you say . . . she's innocent . . . and you can't visit the sins of the father upon the child. A motherless child has got a hard time. [*She takes the baby from him.*] From right now . . . this child got a mother. But you a womanless man.

*ROSE turns and exits into the house with the baby. Lights go down to black.*

## ACT 2

## Scene 4

*It is two months later.* LYONS *enters the street. He knocks on the door and calls.*

LYONS: Hey, Rose! [*Pause.*] Rose!

ROSE: [*from inside the house.*] Stop that yelling. You gonna wake up Raynell. I just got her to sleep.

LYONS: I just stopped by to pay Papa this twenty dollars I owe him. Where's Papa at?

ROSE: He should be here in a minute. I'm getting ready to go down to the church. Sit down and wait on him.

5  LYONS: I got to go pick up Bonnie over her mother's house.

ROSE: Well, sit it down there on the table. He'll get it.

LYONS: [*enters the house and sets the money on the table.*] Tell Papa I said thanks. I'll see you again.

ROSE: All right, Lyons. We'll see you.

LYONS *starts to exit as* CORY *enters.*

CORY: Hey, Lyons.

10  LYONS: What's happening, Cory? Say man, I'm sorry I missed your graduation. You know I had a gig and couldn't get away. Otherwise, I would have been there, man. So what you doing?

CORY: I'm trying to find a job.

LYONS: Yeah I know how that go, man. It's rough out here. Jobs are scarce.

CORY: Yeah, I know.

LYONS: Look here, I got to run. Talk to Papa . . . he know some people. He'll be able to help get you a job. Talk to him . . . see what he say.

15  CORY: Yeah . . . all right, Lyons.

LYONS: You take care. I'll talk to you soon. We'll find some time to talk.

LYONS *exits the yard.* CORY *wanders over to the tree, picks up the bat, and assumes a batting stance. He studies an imaginary pitcher and swings. Dissatisfied with the result, he tries again.* TROY *enters. They eye each other for a beat.* CORY *puts the bat down and exits the yard.* TROY *starts into the house as* ROSE *exits with* RAYNELL. *She is carrying a cake.*

TROY: I'm coming in and everybody's going out.

ROSE: I'm taking this cake down to the church for the bake sale. Lyons was by to see you. He stopped by to pay you your twenty dollars. It's laying in there on the table.

TROY: [*going into his pocket*]. Well . . . here go this money.

20  ROSE: Put it in there on the table, Troy. I'll get it.

TROY: What time you coming back?

ROSE: Ain't no use in you studying me. It don't matter what time I come back.

TROY: I just asked you a question, woman. What's the matter . . . can't I ask you a question?

ROSE: Troy, I don't want to go into it. Your dinner's in there on the stove. All you got to do is heat it up. And don't you be eating the rest of them cakes in there. I'm coming back for them. We having a bake sale at the church tomorrow.

ROSE *exits the yard.* TROY *sits down on the steps, takes a pint bottle from his pocket, opens it, and drinks. He begins to sing.*

25  TROY.

*Hear it ring! Hear it ring!*
*Had an old dog his name was Blue*

*You know Blue was mighty true*
*You know Blue as a good old dog*
*Blue trees a possum in a hollow log*
*You know from that he was a good old dog.*

BONO: [*enters the yard.*] Hey, Troy.

TROY: Hey, what's happening, Bono?

BONO: I just thought I'd stop by to see you.

TROY: What you stop by and see me for? You ain't stopped by in a mouth of Sundays. Hell, I must owe you money or something.

BONO: Since you got your promotion I can't keep up with you. Used to see you every day.   30 Now I don't even know what route you working.

TROY: They keep switching me around. Got me out in Greentree now . . . hauling white folks' garbage.

BONO: Greentree, huh? You lucky, at least you ain't got to be lifting them barrels. Damn if they ain't getting heavier. I'm gonna put in my two years and call it quits.

TROY: I'm thinking about retiring myself.

BONO: You got it easy. You can drive for another five years.

TROY: It ain't the same, Bono. It ain't like working the back of the truck. Ain't got nobody   35 to talk to . . . feel like you working by yourself. Naw, I'm thinking about retiring. How's Lucille?

BONO: She all right. Her arthritis get to acting up on her sometime. Saw Rose on my way in. She going down to the church, huh?

TROY: Yeah, she took up going down there. All them preachers looking for somebody to fatten their pockets. [*Pause.*] Got some gin here.

BONO: Naw, thanks. I just stopped by to say hello.

TROY: Hell, nigger . . . you can take a drink. I ain't never known you to say no to a drink. You ain't got to work tomorrow.

BONO: I just stopped by. I'm fixing to go over to Skinner's. We got us a domino game going   40 over his house every Friday.

TROY: Nigger, you can't play no dominoes. I used to whup you four games out of five.

BONO: Well, that learned me. I'm getting better.

TROY: Yeah? Well, that's all right.

BONO: Look here . . . I got to be getting on. Stop by sometime, huh?

TROY: Yeah, I'll do that, Bono. Lucille told Rose you bought her a new refrigerator.   45

BONO: Yeah, Rose told Lucille you had finally built your fence . . . so I figured we'd call it even.

TROY: I knew you would.

BONO: Yeah . . . okay. I'll be talking to you.

TROY: Yeah, take care, Bono. Good to see you. I'm gonna stop over.

BONO: Yeah. Okay, Troy. [*BONO EXITS.*]   50

TROY: [*drinks from the bottle.*]

*Old Blue died and I dig his grave*
*Let him down with a golden chain*
*Every night when I hear old Blue bark*
*I know Blue treed a possum in Noah's Ark*
*Hear it ring! Hear it ring!*

*CORY enters the yard. They eye each other for a beat. TROY is sitting in the middle of the steps.*
*CORY walks over.*

CORY: I got to get by.

TROY: Say what? What's you say?

CORY: You in my way. I got to get by.

55 TROY: You got to get by where? This is my house. Bought and paid for. In full. Took me fifteen years. And if you wanna go in my house and I'm sitting on the steps . . . you say excuse me. Like your mama taught you.

CORY: Come on, Pop . . . I got to get by.

*CORY starts to maneuver his way past TROY. TROY grabs his leg and shoves him back.*

TROY: You just gonna walk over top of me?

CORY: I live here too!

TROY: [*advancing toward him.*] You just gonna walk over top of me in my own house?

60 CORY: I ain't scared of you.

TROY: I ain't asked if you was scared of me. I asked you if you was fixing to walk over top of me in my own house? That's the question. You ain't gonna say excuse me? You just gonna walk over top of me?

CORY: If you wanna put it like that.

TROY: How else am I gonna put it?

CORY: I was walking by you to go into the house cause you sitting on the steps drunk, singing to yourself. You can put it like that.

65 TROY: Without saying excuse me??? [*CORY doesn't respond.*] I asked you a question. Without saying excuse me???

CORY: I ain't got to say excuse me to you. You don't count around here no more.

TROY: Oh, I see . . . I don't count around here no more. You ain't got to say excuse me to your daddy. All of a sudden you done got so grown that your daddy don't count around here no more . . . Around here in his own house and yard that he done paid for with the sweat of his brow. You done got so grown to where you gonna take over. You gonna take over my house. Is that right? You gonna wear my pants. You gonna go in there and stretch out on my bed. You ain't got to say excuse me cause I don't count around here no more. Is that right?

CORY: That's right. You always talking this dumb stuff. Now, why don't you just get out my way?

TROY: I guess you got someplace to sleep and something to put in your belly. You got that, huh? You got that? That's what you need. You got that, huh?

70 CORY: You don't know what I got. You ain't got to worry about what I got.

TROY: You right! You one hundred percent right! I done spent the last seventeen years worrying about what you got. Now it's your turn, see? I'll tell you what to do. You grown . . . we done established that. You a man. Now, let's see you act like one. Turn your behind around and walk out this yard. And when you get out there in the alley . . . you can forget about this house. See? 'Cause this is my house. You go on and be a man and get your own house. You can forget about this. 'Cause this is mine. You go on and get yours cause I'm through with doing for you.

CORY: You talking about what you did for me . . . what'd you ever give me?

TROY: Them feet and bones! That pumping heart, nigger! I give you more than anybody else is ever gonna give you.

CORY: You ain't never gave me nothing! You ain't never done nothing but hold me back. Afraid I was gonna be better than you. All you ever did was try and make me scared of you. I used to tremeble every time you called my name. Every time I heard your footsteps in the house. Wondering all the time . . . what's Papa gonna say if I do this? . . . What's he gonna say if I do that? . . . What's Papa gonna say if I turn on the radio? And mama, too . . . she tries . . . but she's scared of you.

TROY: You leave your mama out of this. She ain't got nothing to do with this.   75

CORY: I don't know how she stand you . . . after what you did to her.

TROY: I told you to leave your mama out of this! [*He advances toward* CORY.]

CORY: What you gonna do . . . give me a whupping? You can't whup me no more. You're too old. You just an old man.

TROY: [*shoves him on his shoulder.*] Nigger! That's what you are. You just another nigger on the street to me!

CORY: You crazy! You know that?   80

TROY: Go on now! You got the devil in you. Get on away from me!

CORY: You just a crazy old man . . . talking about I got the devil in me.

TROY: Yeah, I'm crazy! If you don't get on the other side of that yard . . . I'm gonna show you how crazy I am! Go on . . . get the hell out of my yard.

CORY: It ain't your yard. You took Uncle Gabe's money he got from the army to buy this house and then you put him out.

TROY: [*advances on* CORY.] Get your black ass out of my yard! [TROY's *advance backs* CORY *up*   85 *against the tree.* CORY *grabs up the bat.*]

CORY: I ain't going nowhere! Come on . . . put me out! I ain't scared of you.

TROY: That's my bat!

CORY: Come on!

TROY: Put my bat down!

CORY: Come on, put me out. [CORY *swings at* TROY, *who backs across the yard.*] What's the matter?   90 You so bad . . . put me out! [TROY *advances toward* CORY.]

CORY: [*backing up.*] Come on! Come on!

TROY: You're gonna have to use it! You wanna draw that bat back on me . . . you're gonna have to use it.

CORY: Come on! . . . Come on!

*CORY swings the bat at* TROY *a second time. He misses.* TROY *continues to advance toward him.*

TROY: You're gonna have to kill me! You wanna draw that bat back on me. You're gonna have to kill me.

CORY, *backed up against the tree, can go no farther.* TROY *taunts him. He sticks out his head and offers him a target.*

Come on! Come on!

CORY *is unable to swing the bat.* TROY *grabs it.*

TROY: Then I'll show you.   95

CORY *and* TROY *struggle over the bat. The struggle is fierce and fully engaged.* TROY *ultimately is the stronger and takes the bat from* CORY *and stands over him ready to swing. He stops himself.*

Go on and get away from around my house.

CORY: [*stung by his defeat, picks himself up, walks slowly out of the yard and up the alley.*] Tell Mama I'll be back for my things.

TROY: They'll be on the other side of that fence. [CORY *exits.*] I can't taste nothing. Helluljah! I can't taste nothing no more. [TROY *assumes a batting posture and begins to taunt Death, the fastball on the outside corner.*] Come on! It's between you and me now! Come on! Anytime you want! Come on! I be ready for you . . . but I ain't gonna be easy.

*The lights go down on the scene.*

## ACT 2

### Scene 5

*The time is 1965. The lights come up in the yard. It is the morning of TROY's funeral. A funeral plaque with a light hangs beside the door. There is a small garden plot off to theside. There is noise and activity in the house as ROSE, LYONS, and BONO have gathered.*

 *The door opens and RAYNELL, seven years old, enters dressed in a flannel nightgown. She crosses to the garden and pokes around with a stick. ROSE calls from the house.*

ROSE: Raynell!
RAYNELL: Mam?
ROSE: What you doing out there?
RAYNELL: Nothing.
5 ROSE: [*comes to the door.*] Girl, get in here and get dressed. What you doing?
RAYNELL: Seeing if my garden growed.
ROSE: I told you it ain't gonna grow overnight. You got to wait.
RAYNELL: It don't look like it never gonna grow. Dag!
ROSE: I told you a watched pot never boils. Get in here and get dressed.
10 RAYNELL: This ain't even no pot, Mama.
ROSE: You just have to give it a chance. It'll grow. Now you come on and do what I told you.
  We got to be getting ready. This ain't no morning to be playing around. You hear me?
RAYNELL: Yes, mam.

*ROSE exits into the house. RAYNELL continues to poke at her garden with a stick. CORY enters. He is dressed in a Marine corporal's uniform, and carries a duffelbag. His posture is that of a military man, and his speech has a clipped sternness.*

CORY: [*to RAYNELL.*] Hi. [*Pause.*] I bet your name is Raynell.
RAYNELL: Uh huh.
15 CORY: Is your mama home?
RAYNELL: [*runs up on the porch and calls through the screen door.*] Mama . . . there's some man out
  here. Mama?
ROSE: [*comes to the door.*] Cory? Lord have mercy! Look here, you all!

*ROSE and CORY embrace in a tearful reunion as BONO and LYONS enters from the house dressed in funeral clothes.*

BONO: Aw, looka here . . .
ROSE: Done got all grown up!
20 CORY: Don't cry, Mama. What you crying about?
ROSE: I'm just so glad you made it.
CORY: Hey Lyons. How you doing, Mr. Bono.
LYONS: [*goes to embrace CORY.*] Look at you, man. Look at you. Don't he look good, Rose. Got
  them Corporal stripes.
ROSE: What took you so long?
25 CORY: You know how the Marines are, Mama. They got to get all their paperwork straight be-
  fore they let you do anything.
ROSE: Well, I'm sure glad you made it. They let Lyons come. Your Uncle Gabe's still in the
  hospital. They don't know if they gonna let him out or not. I just talked to them a little
  while ago.
LYONS: A Corporal in the United States Marines.
BONO: Your daddy knew you had it in you. He used to tell me all the time.
LYONS: Don't he look good, Mr. Bono?

BONO: Yeah, he remind me of Troy when I first met him. [*Pause.*] Say, Rose, Lucille's down at    30
the church with the choir. I'm gonna go down and get the pallbearers lined up. I'll be back
to get you all.

ROSE: Thanks, Jim.

CORY: See you, Mr. Bono.

LYONS. [*with his arm around* RAYNELL]. Cory . . . look at Raynell. Ain't she precious? She gonna
break a whole lot of hearts.

ROSE: Raynell, come and say hello to your brother. This is your brother, Cory. You remember
Cory.

RAYNELL: No, Mam.    35

CORY: She don't remember me, Mama.

ROSE: Well, we talk about you. She heard us talk about you. [*To* RAYNELL.] This is your brother,
Cory. Come on and say hello.

RAYNELL: Hi.

CORY: Hi. So you're Raynell. Mama told me a lot about you.

ROSE: You all come on into the house and let me fix you some breakfast. Keep up your    40
strength.

CORY: I ain't hungry, Mama.

LYONS: You can fix me something, Rose. I'll be in there in a minute.

ROSE: Cory, you sure you don't want nothing? I know they ain't feeding you right.

CORY: No, Mama . . . thanks. I don't feel like eating. I'll get something later.

ROSE: Raynell . . . get on upstairs and get that dress on like I told you.    45

*ROSE and RAYNELL exit into the house.*

LYONS: So . . . I hear you thinking about getting married.

CORY: Yeah, I done found the right one, Lyons. It's about time.

LYONS: Me and Bonnie been split up about four years now. About the time Papa retired. I
guess she just got tired of all them changes I was putting her through. [*Pause.*] I always
knew you was gonna make something out yourself. Your head was always in the right
direction. So . . . you gonna stay in . . . make it a career . . . put in your twenty years?

CORY: I don't know. I got six already, I think that's enough.

LYONS: Stick with Uncle Sam and retire early. Ain't nothing out here. I guess Rose told you    50
what happened with me. They got me down the workhouse. I thought I was being slick
cashing other people's checks.

CORY: How much time you doing?

LYONS: They give me three years. I got that beat now. I ain't got but nine more months. It ain't
so bad. You learn to deal with it like anything else. You got to take the crookeds with the
straights. That's what Papa used to say. He used to say that when he struck out. I seen him
strike out three times in a row . . . and the next time up he hit the ball over the grandstand.
Right out there in Homestead Field.° He wasn't satisfied hitting in the seats . . . he want
to hit it over everything! After the game he had two hundred people standing around
waiting to shake his hand. You got to take the crookeds with the straights. Yeah, Papa was
something else.

CORY: You still playing?

LYONS: Cory . . . you know I'm gonna do that. There's some fellows down there we got us a
band . . . we gonna try and stay together when we get out . . . but yeah, I'm still playing.

---

°*Homestead Field*: i.e., Forbes Field, the home field of the Homestead Grays of the Negro Leagues. The Grays played in the field from 1939 until
1948.

It still helps me to get out of bed in the morning. As long as it do that I'm gonna be right there playing and trying to make some sense out of it.

55  ROSE: [*calling*]. Lyons, I got these eggs in the pan.

LYONS: Let me go on and get these eggs, man. Get ready to go bury Papa. [*Pause.*] How you doing? You doing all right?

*CORY nods. LYONS touches him on the shoulder and they share a moment of silent grief. LYONS exits into the house. CORY wanders about the yard. RAYNELL enters.*

RAYNELL: Hi.

CORY: Hi.

RAYNELL: Did you used to sleep in my room?

60  CORY: Yeah . . . that used to be my room.

RAYNELL: That's what Papa call it. "Cory's room." It got your football in the closet.

ROSE [*comes to the door.*] Raynell, get in there and get them good shoes on.

RAYNELL: Mama, can't I wear these? Them other one hurt my feet.

ROSE: Well, they just gonna have to hurt your feet for a while. You ain't said they hurt your feet when you went down to the store and got them.

65  RAYNELL: They didn't hurt then. My feet done got bigger.

ROSE: Don't you give me no backtalk now. You get in there and get them shoes on. [*RAYNELL exits into the house.*] Ain't too much changed. He still got that piece of rag tied to that tree. He was out here swinging that bat. I was just ready to go back in the house. He swung that bat and then he just fell over. Seem like he swung it and stood there with this grin on his face . . . and then he just fell over. They carried him on down to the hospital, but I knew there wasn't no need . . . why don't you come on in the house?

CORY: Mama . . . I got something to tell you. I don't know how to tell you this . . . but I've got to tell you . . . I'm not going to Papa's funeral.

ROSE: Boy, hush your month. That's your daddy you talking about. I don't want hear that kind of talk this morning. I done raised you to come to this? You standing there all healthy and grown talking about you ain't going to your daddy's funeral?

CORY: Mama . . . listen . . .

70  ROSE: I don't want to hear it, Cory. You just get that thought out of your head.

CORY: I can't drag Papa with me everywhere I go. I've got to say no to him. One time in my life I've got to say no.

ROSE: Don't nobody have to listen to nothing like that. I know you and your daddy ain't seen eye to eye, but I ain't got to listen to that kind of talk this morning. Whatever was between you and your daddy . . . the time has come to put it aside. Just take it and set it over there on the shelf and forget about it. Disrespecting your daddy ain't gonna make you a man, Cory. You got to find a way to come to that on your own. Not going to your daddy's funeral ain't gonna make you a man.

CORY: The whole time I was growing up . . . living in his house . . . Papa was like a shadow that followed you everywhere. It weighted on you and sunk into your flesh. It would wrap around you and lay there until you couldn't tell which one was you anymore. That shadow digging in your flesh. Trying to crawl in. Trying to live through you. Everywhere I looked, Troy Maxson was staring back at me . . . hiding under the bed . . . in the closet. I'm just saying I've got to find a way to get rid of that shadow, Mama.

ROSE: You just like him. You got him in you good.

75  CORY: Don't tell me that, Mama.

ROSE: You Troy Maxson all over again.

CORY: I don't want to be Troy Maxson. I want to be me.

ROSE: You can't be nobody but who you are, Cory. That shadow wasn't nothing but you growing into yourself. You either got to grow into it or cut it down to fit you. But that's all you got
to make life with. That's all you got to measure yourself against that world out there. Your
daddy wanted you to be everything he wasn't . . . and at the same time he tried to make you
into everything he was. I don't know if he was right or wrong . . . but I do know he meant to
do more good than he meant to do harm. He wasn't always right. Sometimes when he
touched he bruised. And sometimes when he took me in his arms he cut. When I first met
your daddy I thought . . . Here is a man I can lay down with and make a baby. That's the first
thing I thought when I seen him. I was thirty years old and had done seen my share of men.
But when he walked up to me and said, "I can dance a waltz that'll make you dizzy," I
thought, Rose Lee, here is a man that you can open yourself up to and be filled to bursting.
Here is a man that can fill all them empty spaces you been tipping around the edges of. One
of them empty spaces was being somebody's mother. I married your daddy and settled
down to cooking his supper and keeping clean sheets on the bed. When your daddy walked
through the house he was so big he filled it up. That was my first mistake. Not to make him
leave some room for me. For my part in the matter. But at that time I wanted that. I wanted
a house that I could sing in. And that's what your daddy gave me. I didn't know to keep up
his strength I had to give up little pieces of mine. I did that. I took on his life as mine and
mixed up the pieces so that you couldn't hardly tell which was which anymore. It was my
choice. It was my life and I didn't have to live it like that. But that's what life offered me in
the way of being a woman and I took it. I grabbed hold of it with both hands. By the time
Raynell came into the house, me and your daddy had done lost touch with one another. I
didn't want to make my blessing off of nobody's misfortune . . . but I took on to Raynell like
she was all them babies I had wanted and never had.

*The phone rings.*

Like I'd been blessed to relive a part of my life. And if the Lord see fit to keep up my strength . . .
I'm gonna do her just like your daddy did you . . . I'm gonna give her the best of what's in me.

RAYNELL: [*entering, still with her old shoes.*] Mama . . . Reverend Tollivier on the phone.

*ROSE exits into the house.*

Hi.

CORY: Hi.                                                                                                    80
RAYNELL: You in the Army or the Marines?
CORY: Marines.
RAYNELL: Papa said it was the Army. Did you know Blue?
CORY: Blue? Who's Blue?
RAYNELL: Papa's dog what he sing about all the time.                                                          85
CORY: [*singing*].
    *Hear it ring! Hear it ring!*
    *I had a dog his name was Blue*
    *You know Blue was mighty true*
    *You know Blue was a good old dog*
    *Blue treed a possum in a hollow log*
    *You know from that he was a good old dog.*
    *Hear it ring! Hear it ring!*

[*RAYNELL joins in singing.*]

CORY AND RAYNELL:

> Blue treed a possum out on a limb
> Blue looked at me and I looked at him
> Grabbed that possum and put him in a sack
> Blue stayed there till I came back
> Old Blue's feets was big and round
> Never allowed a possum to touch the ground.
> Old Blue died and I dug his grave
> I dug his grave with a silver spade
> Let him down with a golden chain
> Any every night I call his name
> Go on Blue, you good dog you
> Go on Blue, you good dog you.

RAYNELL:

> Blue laid down and died like a man
> Blue laid down and died . . .

BOTH:

> Blue laid down and died like a man
> Now he's treeing possums in the Promised Land
> I'm gonna tell you this to let you know
> Blue's gone where the good dogs go
> When I hear old Blue bark
> When I hear old Blue bark
> Blue treed a possum in Noah's Ark
> Blue treed a possum in Noah's Ark.

90  ROSE: [comes to the screen door.] Cory, we gonna be ready to go in a minute.

CORY: [to RAYNELL]. You go on in the house and change them shoes like Mama told you so we can go to Papa's funeral.

RAYNELL: Okay, I'll be back.

*RAYNELL exits into the house. CORY gets up and crosses over to the tree. ROSE stands in the screen door watching him. GABRIEL enters from the alley.*

GABRIEL [calling]. Hey, Rose!

ROSE: Gabe?

95  GABRIEL: I'm here, Rose. Hey Rose, I'm here!

ROSE: [enters from the house.] Lord . . . Look here, Lyons!

LYONS: See, I told you, Rose . . . I told you they'd let him come.

CORY: How you doing, Uncle Gabe?

LYONS: How you doing, Uncle Gabe?

100  GABRIEL: Hey, Rose. It's time. It's time to tell St. Peter to open the gates. Troy, you ready? You ready, Troy. I'm gonna tell St. Peter to open the gates. You get ready now.

*GABRIEL, with great fanfare, braces himself to blow. The trumpet is without a mouthpiece. He puts the end of it into his mouth and blows with great force, like a man who has been waiting some twenty-odd years for this single moment. No sound comes out of the trumpet. He braces himself and blows again with the same results. A third time he blows. There is a weight of impossible description that falls away and leaves him bare and exposed to a frightful realization. It is a trauma that a sane and normal mind would be unable to withstand. He begins to dance. A slow, strange dance, eerie and life-giving. A dance of atavistic signature and ritual.* LYONS *attempts to embrace him.* GABRIEL *pushes* LYONS *away. He begins to howl in what is an attempt at song, or perhaps a song turning back into itself in an attempt at speech. He finishes his dance and the gates of heaven stand open as wide as God's closet.*

That's the way that go!

[BLACKOUT]

## Questions

### 1.1

1. Who is Troy Maxson? Who is Jim Bono? What are they doing as the play opens? What kind of complaint has Troy filed with commissioner? How is this complaint connected with the basic overall thought of the first scene?

2. Why does the discussion between Troy and Bono turn toward how Troy is behaving toward women other than his wife? Why does Troy deny any connections with "that Alberta gal"?

3. Describe Rose. How did Rose and Troy decide to wed? What seem to be their present feelings for each other?

4. Who is Lyons? What has Lyons come to see Troy about? Why does Troy tell the story of his having seen the devil? Whom has he actually seen? How is this story connected to the major themes of the play?

### 1.2

5. Why has Rose been playing the numbers?

6. Who is Gabriel? What has happened to him? In what way is he a symbol of Troy, his family, and his race?

### 1.3

7. Who is Cory? Whose child is he? What is his relationship to Lyons? What ambition does Cory seem to have? What does Troy want for him instead? (See also the end of 1.3.) What is the reason behind Troy's thought about Cory's athletic ability? Why is there such a conflict between the father and the son? In what way is Rose connected to Troy's discussion of how he regards his role with Cory?

8. What is the purpose of the discussion about the costs of a television set as opposed to the costs of repairing the roof?

9. Why does Troy explain his role about supporting his family? What does this explanation show about Troy? Why do Troy's words likely disappoint Cory?

### 1.4

10. Who is Alberta? What is her relationship with Troy? Why is she mentioned so early in this scene?

11. What success has Troy had with his appeal at work? What does Troy say about not having a driver's licence? Why does he disparage the act of driving a motor vehicle? What does this discussion show about his character?

12. What is significant about Gabriel's claim that he has been chasing hellhounds?

13. What forced Troy to leave home at the age of 14? What was his attitude toward his own father? What was Troy's story after he left home? How did he learn about baseball? Why does Wilson stress that Troy would have been in his twenties before he was able to develop

his baseball skills? What is the implied difference between Troy's baseball career and the careers of white players?

14. Why has Cory not been allowed to play in the football game? What is his reaction to learning that Troy has spoken to his football coach? What does Cory see as a possible outcome of this conflict?

## 2.1

15. What is the purpose of the discussion about hard and soft woods at the beginning of this scene? Why does Troy prefer hard wood instead of soft for the outside fence?

16. What has happened to Gabriel? What has Troy done to help Gabriel? What does Troy think of the judge who has been involved in Gabriel's case? In the course of the play, what do we learn about how Troy has acquired the money to pay for the house in which he and his family live? How is this detail important in the relationship between Cory and Troy?

17. Why does Bono believe that he can speak confidentially to Troy about his extramarital affair?

18. Describe the crisis scene between Troy and Rose. How does Troy explain what has happened? How does he explain his involvement with Alberta? What is Rose's response to the situation? How is Troy's attitude toward Cory affected by what happens between him and Rose?

## 2.2

19. What are relationships like in the Maxson house, six months after the events in Scene 1?

20. What has happened to Gabriel? What has Troy had to do with it?

21. What has happened to Alberta?

22. What is the significance of Troy's speech to "Mr. Death"? How is this speech echoed at the end of the play? Why does Troy, here, resolve to complete the fence that has been under construction for virtually the entire play up to this point?

## 2.3

23. What is the major action taking place in this scene?

## 2.4

24. What is the significance of the fact that Lyons is paying back Troy the 20 dollars he owes?

25. What is Troy's attitude toward ministers? What changes do you perceive have taken place in Troy's character in the course of the play?

## 2.5

26. What has happened in the eight-year interval since scene 4? What is to be the major action of scene 5? What has happened to Cory? To Lyons? Who is Raynell? What is her first response to Cory? What is happening to the family at the play's end?

## General Questions

1. Explain the importance of big-league baseball in the play. What has been Troy's connection to baseball? In what way is Troy an authority on well-known baseball stars of the 1950s? Who is Josh Gibson? How does Troy come to have known Josh Gibson? In what way is Josh Gibson's career symbolic in the play?

2. Why is this play titled *Fences*? In what way are fences used symbolically by Wilson? What fences pertain to Troy? In what way is Jesus a fence around Rose? Does Jesus separate her from others, or make her special? What fences separate Troy and Cory? What fences separate Troy and Lyons? What other meanings of fences can you think of that might apply to this play?

3. What is the significance of Troy's dog "Blue"? Why is Blue regularly mentioned in the course of the play? What is the significance of the duet, about the dog, sung by Cory and Raynell? What does their singing suggest about their attitudes toward Troy?

4. How might *Fences* be considered as a play about the relationship of fathers and sons? What is the importance of Bono's story about his father? What does Troy's account of his experience with his own father tell us about Troy? About his attitude toward his own sons? Describe the relationship between Troy and Lyons. Why does antagonism verging on hatred and outright violence between Troy and Cory develop in 2.4? What is Troy trying to establish? In what way is Troy superior to his own father, when it comes to his relationship with Cory? Why does Cory tell Troy that he is no more than "just an old man"? How does the situation escalate between Troy and Cory? How does it get resolved?

5. Explain the symbolism and meaning of Gabriel's being alone on stage at the play's end. Why is it Gabriel who is the last speaker in the play? What is the meaning of Gabriel's dance? Why does the play end as it does, with the image of Gabriel trying to blow his horn, but with no sound coming out? What is the meaning of the Gate of Heaven as the final vision? In what way is the gate also a fence?

6. What significance should one attach to the names of the play's characters: Troy, Rose, Bono, Cory, Lyons, Raynell, Gabriel? In what ways might the names be considered symbolic?

7. Describe the language, which has been called "Black English," used by the characters in *Fences*? What grammatical "rules" do the characters follow? What rules do they ignore? Is there ever any passage that is rendered obscure by the speech patterns? What difficulties, if any, does this speech offer to a modern reader? What is gained for the play by the use of this type of speech?

8. What is the relationship of the epigraph by Wilson ("As God . . . .") to the events of the play?

# Chapter 23A

# Writing Research Essays on Drama: Using Extra Resources for Understanding

At the end of the fiction section of this book, Chapter 10A (p. 428) contains a chapter on the use of research as the basis of an essay of term-paper length on fiction. Because the objects and goals of research are general, most of the materials in Chapter 10A are also essential for research projects in all the genres. It is therefore necessary to consult Chapter 10A for many relevant ways to engage in detailed research, which you can apply not only to writing about fiction, but also to writing about both poetry and drama.

Any of the essay questions following the plays in Chapters 20 to 23 can serve as the basic topic as a guide for you to find helpful research materials. Because of the general nature of research, research essays about drama are not markedly different from the research introduced in writing about fiction and poetry. As a help in such assignments with all the genres, there are suggestions for extra topics for research in Chapter 18, on the poetry of Dickinson, Frost, Hughes, and Plath.

## Topics to Discover in Research

Your goal in doing research on drama should always be to discover materials that have a meaningful bearing on the play or plays about which you are writing. As with both fiction and poetry, some things to look for might be these:

- *The period of time when the play was written, together with significant events.* In this section, Chapter 23A, the illustrative research essay on the Ghost in Shakespeare's *Hamlet* introduces sixteenth-century ideas about the nature of ghosts and the supernatural. If you look at the introductory material to Henley's *Am I Blue*, you will see that the play is dated very clearly in November, 1968, and that particular events at that time may have a bearing on our understanding of the play.

- *Social, natural, and/or political circumstances at the time of the poem or poems.* What was the dominant political situation at the time? Who were the sorts of persons in political power? What attitudes were prevalent at the time with regard to the circumstances of nature? The characters in O'Neill's *Before Breakfast* are representative of people living close to the edge in New York's Greenwich Village in the second decade of the twentieth century, with all that this way of life implied.

- *Biographical details about a dramatist.* At what time in his/her life did the dramatist write the play? What kind of work was he/she doing at the time, and which of his/her particular concerns might be relevant to our understanding of the play? Did the dramatist write anything about the play in his/her personal correspondence, if any exists? What was this? Are there any results of interviews with the dramatist that might be introduced to explain the play? What were the dramatist's aims in creating the particular play, to the degree that it is possible to discover these aims?

- *Specific or general thoughts by the dramatist that are relevant to the poem/poems.* Sometimes there might be details about a dramatist's thoughts on the thinking and reading he/she was doing, or on works of art he/she had seen, or on religious or philosophical musings in which he/she might have been engaged. Sometimes these concerns must be inferred. Langston Hughes was deeply concerned about the circumstances of African Americans in the United States, and his *Mulatto* is a deeply felt play dramatizing his concerns. It is clear from *Tea Party* that Betty Keller was acutely aware of the difficult plight of aged people who are alone and increasingly helpless.

In planning your essay, you should aim at a normal type of essay for the play you have chosen. Often, you might select an individual character and the importance of that character to the play's action, or structure. Or, you may wish to describe the character's interests, or his/her language. Much of what you may do of course depends on the nature of the play and what you discover about it. The section "Writing About the Elements of Drama" in Chapter 20, beginning on page 914, will give you ideas for how to select and develop your topic. Of greatest importance, of course, is your integration of research discoveries into the development of your essay. The following illustrative research essay indicates a full, term-paper length treatment of the Ghost, a major character in Shakespeare's *Hamlet*. You will observe that the essay treats the character of the Ghost, and also goes on to describe other aspects of the Ghost's significance in the play at large.

# Illustrative Student Essay Written with the Aid of Research

Underlined sentences in this paper *do not* conform to MLA style and are used solely as teaching tools to emphasize the central idea, thesis sentence, and topic sentences throughout the paper.

**The Ghost in *Hamlet*[1]**

**Outline**

i. Introduction

   A. The Importance of the Ghost in <u>Hamlet</u>

   B. The Ghost's Influence on the Play's Themes

ii. The Ghost's as a Spirit

iii. The Ghost's Character

iv. The Ghost's Importance in the Structure of the Play

v. The Ghost's Effect

vi. Conclusion

---

[1]See pp. 982–1080 for this play.

**Put identifying information in upper left corner, double space.**

Toni Ann Kruse

Professor Rios

English 364

10 May 2007

**Use 1/2 inch top margin, 1 inch bottom and side margin; double space throughout.**

**Center title one double space below identifying information.**

### Introduction

### A. The Importance of the Ghost in Hamlet

[1]     Even though the Ghost of Hamlet's father is present in only a few scenes of Hamlet, he is a dominating presence.* He appears twice in the first scene, and this entire scene itself is about the meaning of these and earlier appearances. He enters again in the fourth scene of Act 1, when he beckons to Hamlet and leads him offstage—in this way providing an early illustration of Hamlet's courage (Edgar 257). In the fifth scene of Act 1 he speaks for the first time, explaining how his brother Claudius murdered him, and exhorting his son, Hamlet, to kill Claudius in retribution. Because this cry for revenge directly or indirectly causes the rest of the play's action, it is clear, as Marjorie Garber puts it, that "the dead man turned Ghost is more powerful than he was when living" (304). After some words which the Ghost speaks from under the stage, he does not enter again until the fourth scene of Act 3, in the queen's closet or bedroom, when he reveals himself to Hamlet—but not to Gertrude—to reproach the Prince for not yet having killed Claudius. The Ghost is not present at the play's end, but the actions he sets in motion are concluded there, and hence his effect is always dominant in the play.

**In MLA style, put only page number in parentheses when author is named in the sentence.**

### B. The Ghost's Influence on the Play's Themes

[2]     Not only is the Ghost dominant over actions, but he is also directly linked to many of the play's themes. William Kerrigan calls the Ghost a "nightmind" who introduces the mental darkness of evil that pervades the play (42). In addition, the Ghost intensifies the play's "interior suffering" (Paris 85). This suffering is brought out in Hamlet's anguished soliloquies and also in the pain of Ophelia, Laertes, and even Claudius himself. Another theme is shown by the Ghost's commands to Hamlet—those of responsibility, whether

**In MLA style, put author and page number in parentheses when author is not named in the sentence.**

---

*Central idea.

Kruse 2

In MLA style, the header has the student's last name and page number.

personal, political, or conjugal (McFarland 15). Hamlet of course does not rush right out to kill Claudius, despite the Ghost's urgings, and hence the Ghost is indirectly responsible for the theme of hesitation—this great "Sphinx of modern Literature"—which has become one of the weaknesses cited most frequently about Hamlet's character (Jones 22). The Ghost's scary presence also poses questions about the power of superstition, terror, and fear (Campbell 211). Beyond all this, deeply within the psychological realm, the Ghost has been cited as a "confirmation" of the influence of "psychic residues in governing and shaping human life" (McFarland 34), not to mention the significance of the Oedipus complex in the development of Hamlet's character.

[3]   Because the Ghost is so important, one hardly needs to justify studying him. <u>His importance can be traced in his spirit nature, his influence on the play's structure, and his effect on Hamlet and therefore indirectly on all the major characters.</u>[†]

### II. The Ghost as a Spirit

When citing plays in MLA style, cite the act, scene, and line number.

[4]   <u>The Ghost is shown as an apparition of questionable and vague status.</u> When Hamlet first sees the Ghost, he asks whether he sees "a spirit of health, or goblin damned" (1.4.40). Horatio adds that Hamlet is "desperate with imagination" (1.4.87), thus throwing doubt on the Ghost's reality even though the vision is seen by everyone onstage. When speaking with Hamlet, the Ghost is vague about his out-of-earth location, complaining that he is suffering hellish fires but intimating that he will be compelled to do so only until his earthly sins are purged away. Although this description, according to Anthony Holden, indicates that "the Ghost . . . occupies an authentically Catholic version of Purgatory" (28), and Dobson and Wells state that "the Ghost seems to belong to a Catholic theology rather than a Protestant one" (182), Shakespeare's treatment is ambiguous. The Ghost says that he is allowed to walk the earth for a certain time—presumably, in the first act, only at night. But then, in Act 3, scene 4, the Ghost appears in the Queen's private room. Does this visit take place at night or during the day? This inconsistency about where and when the Ghost spends his time may have been deliberate on Shakespeare's part, for showing a ghost straight out of purgatory might have seemed dangerously close to Catholic doctrine. It was apparently safest for writers in the dominant Anglican culture to show the ghost only of a person who was "freshly dead or on the point of death" (O'Meara 15), and also to make the details vague and ambiguous.

---

[†]Thesis sentence.

[5]  The status and existence of Shakespeare's Ghost therefore reflects uncertainties during the Elizabethan period. Lily Campbell offers a number of ways in which Elizabethans dealt with these uncertainties. First, James VI of Scotland, who at the time *Hamlet* was first performed was soon to be James I of England, wrote about departed spirits and emphasized that the devil himself could choose the shape of loved ones to deceive and corrupt living persons. It is this danger that Hamlet specifically describes. Second, as already mentioned, a number of Elizabethan religious thinkers held it possible for souls in purgatory to return to earth for a time and speak to the living. Third, scientifically oriented thinkers interpreted ghostly appearances as a sign of madness or deep melancholia (Campbell 121), or what O'Meara calls "sorrowful imagination" (19). There were apparently a number of "tests" that might have enabled people to determine the authenticity of ghosts. Most of these required that the spirit should show goodness of character and give comfort to the living (Campbell 123).

[6]  The Ghost of Hamlet's father both passes and fails these tests. He is not totally bad (Campbell 126), but he urges Hamlet to commit murder, something that no ghost trying to reach heaven would do (McFarland 36). Although the Ghost describes the pain of a soul in purgatory, he does so to create fear, not to urge Hamlet to seek salvation. Thus he is more like the devil than a spirit on the way to redemption (Prosser 133–34; Frye 22). Another sign suggesting the Ghost's devilishness is that he withholds his appearance from Gertrude when he shows himself to Hamlet in Act 3, scene 4 (Campbell 124). Hamlet creates his own test of the Ghost by getting the touring actors to perform The Murder of Gonzago. Once he sees the King's disturbance at the play, Hamlet concludes that the Ghost is real and not just a "figment of his melancholy imagination" (Harrison 883). Perhaps the best answer to the conflicting views of the Ghost is given by Lily Campbell, who suggests that the ambiguity indicates the general uncertainty about ghosts among Shakespeare's contemporaries (127). In other words, there was no unanimity about the nature and motivation of ghosts, and Shakespeare's Ghost reflected common Elizabethan understanding and attitudes.

### III. The Ghost's Character

[7]  Uncertainty and theology aside, the Ghost is probably Shakespeare's rendering of what he thought a ghost would be like. Shakespeare inherited a tradition of noisy, bloodthirsty ghosts from his sources—what Harold Fisch calls a "Senecan ghost" (91).

There was also a tradition of "hungry ghosts," who were spirits prowling about the earth "searching for the life they were deprived of" (Austin 93). In this tradition, Shakespeare's Ghost is bloodthirsty, although ironically not as bloodthirsty as Hamlet himself becomes during the play (Gottschalk 166). The Ghost is surrounded by awe and horror (DeLuca 147) and is frightening, both to the soldiers at the beginning of the play and also to Hamlet in Act 3, scene 4 (Charney, Style 167–168). It seems that horror is the main effect that Shakespeare wanted the Ghost to achieve.

[8]  Although the Ghost is bloodthirsty and horrible, he has redeeming qualities (Alexander 30). He is toned down from a ghost in an anonymous and lost earlier play, perhaps a first version of *Hamlet* by Shakespeare himself, which was described by Shakespeare's contemporary Thomas Lodge (1558–1625) (Bloom 383). Lodge talked about "ye ghost which cried so miserally [pitifully, sorrowfully] at ye theator . . . *Hamlet, reuenge*" [sic]. Shakespeare's Ghost also cries out for vengeance, but as a former loving husband he is still concerned for the welfare of Hamlet's mother, Gertrude, directing his son to treat her kindly and help her (Kerrigan 54). Also, as a former king, he voices concern about the reputation and future of Denmark (Gottschalk 165). Paul Gottschalk points to these redeeming qualities to indicate that the Ghost is concerned with "restoration" as well as "retaliation" (166)—a view not shared by Norman Austin, who calls the Ghost "the spirit of ruin" (105).

[9]  Indeed, the Ghost has many qualities of a living human being. For example, he is witty, as Maurice Charney observes about the following interchange between the Ghost and Hamlet just at the beginning of the revelation speeches in Act 1, scene 5, lines 6–7:

> HAMLET.  Speak, I am bound to hear.
>
> GHOST.  So art thou to revenge, when thou shalt hear.

In other words, even though the Ghost may have come "with . . . airs from heaven, or blasts from hell" (1.4.41), he is still mentally alert enough to make a pun out of Hamlet's word "bound" (Charney, Style 118). To this quickness can be added his shrewd ability to judge his son's character. He knows that Hamlet may neglect duty, and hence his last words in Act 1, scene 5, are "remember me," and his first words in Act 3, scene 4 are "Do not forget." A. C. Bradley suggests that these speeches indicate Shakespeare's master touch in the development of the Ghost's character (126).

**When citing dialogue between two or more characters, indent the quotation one inch (or ten spaces) and type each character's name next to the corresponding dialogue in all caps folowed by a period.**

[10] <u>The Ghost also shows other human traits</u>. He strongly feels remorse about his lifelong crimes and "imperfections" for which his sudden death did not give him time to atone. It is this awareness that has made him bitter and vengeful. Also, he has a sense of appropriateness that extends to what he wears. Thus, at the beginning he appears on the parapets dressed in full armor. This battle uniform is in keeping with the location and also with his vengeful mission (Aldus 54). The armor is intimidating, a means of enforcing the idea that the Ghost in death has become a "spirit of hatred" (Austin 99). By contrast, in the closet scene he wears a dressing gown ["in his habit as he lived," 3.4.135], as though he is prepared for ordinary palace activities of both business and leisure (Charney, <u>Style</u> 26).

### IV. The Ghost's Importance in the Structure of the Play

[11] <u>Shakespeare's great strength as a dramatist is shown not only in his giving the Ghost such a round, full character but also in his integrating the Ghost fully within the play's structure</u>. According to Peter Alexander, the Ghost is "indispensable" in the plot as the force that sets things in motion (29). The Ghost is also a director and organizer as well as an informer—a figure who keeps the action moving until there is no stopping it (Aldus 100). A careful study of his speeches shows that he is a manipulator, playing on his son's emotions to make him hurry to kill the king. In addition, the Ghost is persistent, because his return to Hamlet in Act 3, scene 4, to "whet thy almost blunted purpose" (line 111) is the mark of a manager who nervously intervenes when his directions are being neglected or delayed.

[12] <u>The Ghost is also significant in a major structure of the play</u>. During the imagined period when the events at Elsinore are taking place, Denmark is undergoing a national preparation for war against Norway (Alexander 34). Structurally, the beginning and ending of <u>Hamlet</u> are marked by the fear of war and the political takeover by "Young Fortinbras" of Norway, who is like Hamlet because King Hamlet, now the Ghost, had killed Old Fortinbras in single combat. Young Fortinbras is therefore as much an avenger as Hamlet (Honan 283), and the cause is King Hamlet, who now as a Ghost pushes Hamlet to vengeance. So strong is the Ghost's anger against Claudius that he

insists on revenge even if it means the defeat of his country in the face of impending war. Ironically, the Ghost in death brings about the passing of the political stability he courageously promoted in life.

[13] An additional major element of structure also involves the Ghost. Maurice Charney observes that the Ghost is significant in the "symmetrical" poison plots in the play (Style 39). The first of these plots, the poisoning of King Hamlet, is described by the Ghost himself in Act 1, scene 5. The poisoning of the player king in Act 3, scene 2, is a reenactment of the first murder, and it occurs in approximately the middle of the action. The final poisonings—of Gertrude, Laertes, Claudius, and finally Hamlet himself— occur in Act 5, scene 2, the play's last scene. These actions have value as symbolic frames that measure the deterioration of the play's major characters.

### V.  The Ghost's Effect

[14] Beyond the Ghost's practical and structural importance in the action, he has profound psychological influence, mainly negative, on the characters. Roy Walker describes him as a "prologue" to the "omen" of Hamlet himself, who is the agent of the "dread purpose" of vengeance (220). Because Hamlet is already suffering depression after his father's death, this murderous mission opens the wounds of his vulnerability (Campbell 127–28). Literally, Hamlet must give up everything he has ever learned, even "the movement of existence itself," so that he can carry out the Ghost's commands (McFarland 32–33). In Harold Bloom's words, "everything in the play depends upon Hamlet's response to the Ghost" (387). Because of this malign ghostly influence, Hamlet is gripped by a melancholy that undermines his love for Ophelia, his possible friendship with Laertes, and his relationship with his mother (Kirsch 31; Kott 49). The effects are like radiating waves, with the Ghost at the center as a relentless, destructive force. No one escapes.

[15] This overwhelming ghostly force overwhelms Hamlet once the first encounter has occurred. He is possessed both literally and figuratively when the Ghost goes under the stage in Act 1, scene 5, and hears Hamlet's conversation with Horatio and the guards. The Ghost thus represents "dimensions of reality" beyond what we see on the stage, a mysterious world "elsewhere" that dominates the very souls of living persons (Charney, "Asides" 127). As a result of this ever-present force, which as far as Hamlet is

concerned might become visible at any moment, Hamlet is denied the healing that might normally occur after the death of a parent (Kirsch 26). The steady pressure to kill Claudius disrupts any movement to mental health and creates what Kirsch calls a "pathology of depression" (26) that inhibits Hamlet's actions (Bradley 123), causes his Oedipal preoccupation with the sexuality of his parents (Kirsch 22), and brings about his desire for the oblivion of suicide (Kirsch 27).

[16] It is, finally, this power over his son that gives the Ghost the greatest influence in the play. Once the Ghost has appeared, Hamlet is not and never can be the same. He loses the dignity and composure that he has assumed as his right as a prince of Denmark and as a student in quest of knowledge (McFarland 38). The Ghost's commands make it impossible for Hamlet to solve problems through negotiation—the way he would likely have chosen as prince and student. The commands force him instead into a plan requiring murder. What could be more normal than hesitation under such circumstances? Despite all Hamlet's reflections, however, the web of vengeance woven by the Ghost finally closes in on all those caught in it, both the deserving and undeserving. There is no solution but the final one—real death, which is the literal conclusion of the symbolic death represented by the Ghost when he first appears on the Elsinore battlements.

### VI. Conclusion

[17] The Ghost is real in the play's action and structure. He is seen by the characters on the stage, and when he speaks we hear him. He is made round and full by Shakespeare, and his motivation is direct and clear, even though the signs of his spirit nature are presented ambiguously. But the Ghost is more. He has been made a Ghost by the greed and envy of Claudius, and for this reason he becomes in the play either a conscious or an unwitting agent of the "unseen Fates or forces" of his own doom (Walker 220). What he brings is the horror that lurks within the depths of good, moral people, waiting to overwhelm them and destroy them. Once the horror is released, there is no restraining it, and those who are hurt cannot be rescued. The tragedy is that there is no way to win against these odds.

**WORKS CITED**

Aldus, P. J. *Mousetrap: Structure and Meaning in Hamlet*. Toronto: U of Toronto P, 1977.

Alexander, Peter. *Hamlet: Father and Son*. Oxford: Clarendon, 1955.

Austin, Norman. "Hamlet's Hungry Ghost." *Shenandoah* 37.1 (1987): 78–105.

Bloom, Harold. *Shakespeare: The Invention of the Human*. New York: Riverhead, 1998.

Bradley, A. C. *Shakespearean Tragedy*. 1904. London: Macmillan, 1950.

Campbell, Lily B. *Shakespeare's Tragic Heroes: Slaves of Passion*. New York: Barnes, 1959.

Charney, Maurice. "Asides, Soliloquies, and Offstage Speech in Hamlet." *Shakespeare and the Sense of Performance: Essays in the Tradition of Performance Criticism in Honor of Bernard Beckerman*. Ed. Marvin and Ruth Thompson. Newark: U of Delaware P, 1989. 116–31.

———. *Style in Hamlet*. Princeton: Princeton UP, 1969.

DeLuca, Diana Macintyre. "The Movements of the Ghost in Hamlet." *Shakespeare Quarterly* 24 (1973): 147–54.

Dobson, Michael, and Stanley Wells. *The Oxford Companion to Shakespeare*. Oxford: Oxford UP, 2001.

Edgar, Irving I. *Shakespeare, Medicine, and Psychiatry*. New York, Philosophical Library, 1970.

Fisch, Harold. *Hamlet and the Word*. New York: Ungar, 1971.

Frye, Roland Mushat. *The Renaissance Hamlet: Issues and Responses in 1600*. Princeton: Princeton UP, 1984.

Garber, Marjorie. "Hamlet: Giving Up the Ghost." *William Shakespeare: Hamlet*. Ed. Suzanne L. Wofford. Boston: Bedford, 1994. 297–331.

Gottschalk, Paul. "Hamlet and the Scanning of Revenge." *Shakespeare Quarterly* 24 (1973): 155–70.

Harrison, G. B., ed. *Shakespeare: The Complete Works*. 1948. New York: Harcourt.

Holden, Anthony. *William Shakespeare: The Man behind the Genius: A Biography*. Boston: Little, Brown, 1999.

Honan, Park. *Shakespeare: A Life*. Oxford: Oxford UP, 1998.

Jones, Ernest. *Hamlet and Oedipus*. 1949. New York: Doubleday, 1954.

Kerrigan, William. *Hamlet's Perfection*. Baltimore: Johns Hopkins UP, 1994.

Kirsch, Arthur. "Hamlet's Grief." *ELH* 48 (1981): 17–36.

Kott, Jan. *Shakespeare, Our Contemporary*. Trans. Boleslaw Taborski. 1967. London: Methuen, 1970.

McFarland, Thomas. *Tragic Meanings in Shakespeare*. New York: Random, 1966.

O'Meara, John. "Hamlet and the Fortunes of Sorrowful Imagination: A Re-examination of the Genesis and Fate of the Ghost." *Cahiers Elisabéthains* 35 (1989): 15–25.

Paris, Jean. *Shakespeare*. Trans. Richard Seaver. New York: Grove, 1960.

Prosser, Eleanor. *Hamlet and Revenge*. 2nd ed. Stanford: Stanford UP, 1971.

Walker, Roy. "Hamlet: The Opening Scene." *Shakespeare: Modern Essays in Criticism*. Ed. Leonard F. Dean. New York: Oxford UP, 1961.

In MLA style, the list of sources, called the Works Cited, begins a new page. Double space throughout.

List sources in alphabetical order.

## Commentary on the Essay

This essay illustrates an assignment requiring about twenty-five sources and about 2,500 words (there are actually 27 sources). The sources were located through an examination of library catalogues, the *MLA Bibliography*, library bookshelves, the Internet, and the bibliographies in some of the listed books. They represent the range of materials available in a college library with a selective, not exhaustive, set of holdings. Two of the sources (Austin and O'Meara) were obtained through Interlibrary Loan.

The writing itself is developed from the sources listed. Originality (see p. 439) is provided by the structure and development of the essay, additional observations not existing in the sources, and transitions. The topic outline is placed appropriately at the beginning, and also throughout the essay—a pattern you can follow unless your instructor asks for a more detailed outline, or, perhaps, for no outline at all.

Because the essay is concerned with only one work—and one subject about that work—it demonstrates approach 1 (p. 1376). The essay is eclectic, introducing discussions of ideas, character, style, and structure. These four topics fulfill the goal of covering the ground thoroughly within the confines of the assignment. A shorter research assignment might deal with no more than, say, the Ghost's character, ignoring other topics. A longer essay might deal further with the philosophical and theological meanings of ghosts during the Elizabethan period, or a more detailed study of all the traits of the Ghost's character, and so on.

The central idea of the essay is stressed in paragraph 1, along with an assertion that the Ghost is a major influence in the play, together with a concession that the Ghost is only a minor character in the action. The research for this paragraph is derived primarily from a reading of the play itself. Paragraph 2, continuing the exploration of the central idea, demonstrates that the Ghost figures in the major themes of *Hamlet*. Paragraph 3 is mainly functional, being used as the location of the thesis sentence.

Part II, containing paragraphs 4–6, deals with the Ghost's status as a spirit. Part III, with paragraphs 7–10 is concerned with the Ghost's human rather than spiritual characteristics. Part IV, with paragraphs 11–13, deals with the significance of the Ghost in the major structures that dominate the play. Part V, with three paragraphs, considers the Ghost's negative and overwhelming influence over the major figures of *Hamlet*, the emphasis being the character of Hamlet as the transferring agent of the Ghost's destructive revenge. The concluding paragraph (17) sums up the essay with the final idea of how the Ghost affects the tragedy of *Hamlet* as a play.

The list of works cited is the basis of all parenthetical references in the essay, in accordance with the *MLA Handbook for Writers of Research Papers*, 6th ed. Using these references, an interested reader can consult the sources for a more detailed development of the ideas in the illustrative essay. The works cited can also serve as a springboard for expanded research.

# Special Writing Topics
# about Literature

# Chapter **24**

## Critical Approaches Important in the Study of Literature

**A** number of critical theories or approaches for understanding and interpreting literture are available to critics and students alike.[1] Many of these were developed during the twentieth century to create a discipline of literary studies comparable with disciplines in the natural and social sciences. Literary critics have often borrowed liberally from other disciplines (e.g., history, psychology, politics, anthropology) but have primarily aimed at developing literature as a study in its own right.

At the heart of the various critical approaches are many fundamental questions: What is literature? What does it do? Is its concern primarily to tell stories, to divert attention, to entertain, to communicate ideas, to persuade, and to teach, or is it to describe and interpret reality, or is it to explore and explain emotions—or is it all of these? To what degree is literature an art, as opposed to a medium for imparting knowledge? What more does it do than express ideas? How does it get its ideas across? What can it contribute to intellectual, artistic, political, and social thought and history? How is literature used, and how and why is it misused? Is it private? Public? What theoretical and technical expertise may be invoked to enhance literary studies? How valuable was literature in the past, and how valuable is it now? To what degree should literature be in the vanguard of social and political change?

Questions such as these indicate that criticism is concerned not only with reading and interpreting stories, poems, and plays but also with establishing theoretical understanding. Because of such extensive aims, a full explanation and illustration of the approaches would fill the pages of a long book. The following descriptions are therefore intended as no more than brief introductions. Bear in mind that in the hands of skilled critics, the approaches are so subtle, sophisticated, and complex that they are not only critical stances but also philosophies.

Although the various approaches provide widely divergent ways to study literature and literary problems, they reflect major tendencies rather than absolute straitjacketing. Not every approach is appropriate for every work, nor are the approaches always mutually exclusive. Even the most devoted practitioners of the methods do not pursue them rigidly. In addition, some of the approaches are more "user friendly" than others for certain types of discovery. To a degree, at least, most critics therefore take a particular approach but utilize

---

[1]Some of the approaches described in this chapter are presented more simply in Chapter 1 as basic study techniques for writing about literary works.

**1390**

methods that technically belong to one or more of the other approaches. A critic stressing the topical/historical approach, for example, might introduce the close study of a work that is associated with the method of the New Criticism. Similarly, a psychoanalytical critic might include details about archetypes. In short, a great deal of criticism is *pragmatic* or *eclectic* rather than rigid.

The approaches to be considered here are these: *moral/intellectual*; *topical/historical*; *New Critical/formalist*; *structuralist*; *feminist/gender studies/queer theory*; *economic determinist/Marxist*; *psychological/psychoanalytic*; *archetypal/symbolic/mythic*; *deconstructionist*; and *reader-response*.

The object of learning about these approaches, like everything else in this book, is to help you develop your own capacities as a reader and writer. Accordingly, following each of the descriptions is a brief paragraph showing how Hawthorne's story "Young Goodman Brown" (Chapter 8) might be considered in the light of the particular approach. The illustrative paragraph following the discussion of structuralism, for example, shows an application of the structuralist approach to Goodman Brown and his story, and so also with the feminist approach, the economic determinist approach, and the others. In the Fourth Compact Edition, these paragraphs are followed by additional paragraphs illustrating the same approaches based on other literary works. Whenever you are doing your own writing about literature, you are free to use the various approaches as part or all of your assignment, if you believe the approach may help you.

# Moral/Intellectual

The **moral/intellectual critical approach** is concerned with content, ideas, and values (see also Chapter 9). The approach is as old as literature itself, for literature is a traditional mode of inculcating morality, philosophy, and religion. The concern in moral/intellectual criticism is not only to discover meaning but also to determine whether works of literature are both *true* and *significant*.

To study literature from the moral/intellectual perspective is therefore to determine whether a work conveys a lesson or a message and whether it can help readers lead better lives and improve their understanding of the world. What ideas does the work contain? How strongly does the work bring forth its ideas? What application do the ideas have to the work's characters and situations? How may the ideas be evaluated intellectually? Morally? Discussions based on such questions do not imply that literature is primarily a medium of moral and intellectual exhortation. Ideally, moral/intellectual criticism should differ from sermonizing to the degree that readers should always be left with their own decisions about whether to assimilate the ideas of a work and about whether the ideas—and values—are personally or morally acceptable.

Sophisticated critics have sometimes demeaned the moral/intellectual approach on the grounds that "message hunting" reduces a work's artistic value by treating it like a sermon or political speech; but the approach will be valuable as long as readers expect literature to be applicable to their own lives.

## Example, Hawthorne's "Young Goodman Brown"

"Young Goodman Brown" raises the issue of how an institution designed for human elevation, such as the religious system of colonial Salem, can be so ruinous. Does the failure result from the system itself or from the people who misunderstand it? Is what is true of religion as practiced by Brown also true of social and political institutions? Should any religious or political philosophy be given greater significance than good will and mutual trust? One of the major virtues of "Young Goodman Brown" is that it provokes questions like these but at the same time provides a number of satisfying answers. A particularly important one is that religious and moral beliefs should not be used to justify the condemnation of others. Another important answer is that attacks made from the refuge of a religion or group, such as Brown's Puritanism, are dangerous because the judge may condemn without thought and without personal responsibility.

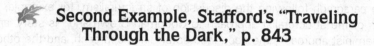 ## Second Example, Stafford's "Traveling Through the Dark," p. 843

William Stafford's "Traveling Through the Dark" presents a moral quandary. While the speaker is driving along a narrow road at night, he comes upon the carcass of a doe. Upon investigation, he finds that the doe is pregnant with a live fawn. It is customary to throw dead animals off the side of the road in order to remove the danger of having a swerving car veer off the road. But in the present situation, the speaker "hesitates." The living fawn complicates the moral option, for now life must be taken. As the speaker hesitates, he "could hear the wilderness listen," for moral decisions are not only an individual's domain but affect all of us. "I thought hard for us all," the speaker says, but then adds "my only swerving" as if uncertain if it is presumptuous for one person to think for all people. Sometimes, however, it is a human being's responsibility to make a decision, and one may argue whether the right one was made in this instance. As if to highlight the human quandary that moral situations put us in, Stafford refers to the car as aiming its headlights, as if the car were conscious. Despite that, it is only human beings who are responsible for moral action. Nature merely "listens," and objects merely "light" the path toward decision. In "Traveling Through the Dark," Stafford, through a simple situation that might confront almost anyone, probes many of the issues raised by moral action.

### READINGS

Buckley, Vincent. *Poetry and Morality: Studies in the Criticism of Matthew Arnold, T. S. Eliot, and F. R. Leavis*. London: Chato and Windus, 1959.

Else, Gerald F. *Plato and Aristotle on Poetry*. Chapel Hill: U of North Carolina P, 1986.

Farrell, James T. *Literature and Morality*. New York: Vanguard, 1947.

Foerster, Norman. *American Criticism: A Study in Literary Theory from Poe to the Present*. 1928. New York: Russell and Russell, 1962.

Gardner, John. *On Moral Fiction*. New York: Basic Books, 1978.

McCloskey, Mary A. *Kant's Aesthetic*. Basingstoke: Macmillan, 1987.

Olson, Elder. *Aristotle's Poetics and English Literature*. Chicago: U of Chicago P, 1965.

Sartre, Jean Paul. *What is Literature?* New York: Philosophical Library, 1966.

Wallis, R. T. *Neoplatonism*. London: Duckworth, 1995.

# Topical/Historical

The **topical/historical critical approach** stresses the relationship of literature to its historical period, and for this reason it has had a long life. Although much literature may be applicable to many places and times, much of it also directly reflects the intellectual and social worlds of the authors. When was the work written? What were the circumstances that produced it? What major issues does it deal with? How does it fit into the author's career? Keats's poem "On First Looking into Chapman's Homer" (p. 562), for example, is his excited response to his reading of one of the major literary works of Western civilization. Hardy's "Channel Firing" (p. 541) is an ironically acerbic response to continued armament and preparation for war in the past, in the present, and in the future.

The topical/historical approach investigates relationships of this sort, including the elucidation of words and concepts that today's readers may not immediately understand. It may also include biographical information about the author or be informed by a sociological study. For instance, knowing that William Wordsworth walked wherever he went in both England and Europe gives resonance to his "Tintern Abbey Lines" (p. 482). Obviously, the approach requires the assistance of footnotes, dictionaries, library catalogues, histories, and handbooks.

A common criticism of the topical/historical approach is that in the extreme, it deals with background knowledge rather than with literature itself. It is possible, for example, for a topical/historical critic to describe a writer's life, the period of the writer's work, and the social and intellectual ideas of the time—all without ever considering the meaning, importance, and value of any of the writers works themselves.

A reaction against such an unconnected use of historical details is the so-called **"New Historicism"**. This approach justifies the parallel reading of both literary and non-literary works in order to bring an informed understanding of the context of a literary work. The new historicist assumes that history is not a "fixed" essence but a literary construction. As such, history is a prism through which a society views itself; a work of literature is given resonance by seeing the nonobjective context in which it was produced. This approach justifies the introduction of historical knowledge by integrating it with the understanding of particular texts. Readers of Arnold's "Dover Beach" (p. 793), for example, sometimes find it difficult to follow the meaning of Arnold's statement "The Sea of Faith/Was once, too, at the full." Historical background has a definite role to play here. In Arnold's time there developed a method of treating the Bible as a historical document rather than a divinely inspired revelation. This approach has been called the Higher Criticism of the Bible, and to many thoughtful people the Higher Criticism undermined the concept that the Bible was divine, infallible, and inerrant. Therefore, Arnold's idea is that the "Sea of Faith" is no longer at full tide but is now rather at an ebb. Because the introduction of such historical material is designed to facilitate the reading of the poem—and also the reading of other literature of the period—the New Historicism represents an integration of knowledge and interpretation. As a principle, New Historicism entails the acquisition of as much historical information as possible because our knowledge of the relationship of literature to its historical period can never be complete. The practitioner of historical criticism must always seek new information on the grounds that it may prove relevant to the understanding of literature.

Cultural Study is a more recent approach which justifies the analyses of non-literary materials such as television and radio shows, movies, brochures, and advertisements. By not privileging literature over mass culture, Cultural Studies critics are able to open up new areas of interest. Langston Hughes' poem "Harlem," for example, was written in 1951 about possible resentment of African Americans when faced with constant discrimination. In 1985, August Wilson created his drama *Fences*, in which baseball has been a vital element in the life of the major character, Troy Maxson. Both works, the poem and the play, are made vital because they reflect the treatment of African Americans by the dominant white race in American society. It therefore becomes relevant that in 1948 Jackie Robinson became the first black ball player to play baseball for a major league team, and that soon after, increasing numbers of black ballplayers were joining major league clubs. Reading newspaper accounts of the problems they faced provides insights into both "Harlem" and *Fences*.

 ## Example, Hawthorne's "Young Goodman Brown"

"Young Goodman Brown" is an allegorical story by Nathaniel Hawthorne (1804–1864), the major New England writer who probed deeply into the relationship between religion and guilt. His ancestors had been involved in religious persecutions, including the Salem witch trials, and he, living 150 years afterward, wanted to analyze the weaknesses and uncertainties of the sin-dominated religion of the earlier period, a tradition of which he was a resentful heir. Not surprisingly, therefore, "Young Goodman Brown" takes place in Salem during Puritan times, and Hawthorne's implied judgments are those of a severe critic of how the harsh old religion destroyed personal and family relationships. Although the immediate concerns of the story belong to a vanished age, Hawthorne's treatment is still valuable because it is still timely.

 ## Second Example, Jarrell's *The Death of the Ball Turret Gunner*, p. 473

Juxtaposing World War II propaganda posters with Randell Jarrell's 1945 poem *The Death of the Ball Turret Gunner* gives special meaning to both. In one American 1943 poster the words "BATTLE OF GERMANY" at the top and "JOIN THE AIR CREW" at the bottom are boldly visible. In the middle is a group of bombers flying in neat formation high above a bombed German city. All that is rising from below is smoke emanating from the site of the bombing. One gets the impression that a bombing run is an orderly operation and that the bombers are high above any danger. A British poster of the same year, with the words "BACK THEM UP" at the bottom, shows a fighter plane in close up as it drops bombs on a German city. In the background other fighters can be seen in formation, apparently leaving the city after a successful bombing raid. While these posters imply a heroic struggle against an enemy, they only point obliquely to any danger. Jarrell's poem confronts the darker realities of war. The gunner of this poem is not consumed by his heroic duty. He seems to be born into his nightmarish situation, for he says "From my mother's sleep I fell into the State." His height above the action does not suggest safety but rather a remote detachment from the "dream of life." Describing his own death and how he was "washed . . . out of the turret with a hose," the speaker manifests the horrifying impersonality of war. This "dialogue" between World War II posters and Randell Jarell's poem gives the reader a richer understanding of the many motives and outcomes of an event so dangerous and complex as war.

## READINGS

During, Simon, ed. *The Cultural Studies Reader*. New York: Routledge, 1993.

Greenblatt, Stephen. *Renaissance Self-Fashioning: From More to Shakespeare*. Chicago: U of Chicago P, 1980.

Geenblatt, Stephen, ed. *Repressing the English Renaissance*. Berkeley: U of California P, 1988.

Hoggart, Richard. *The Uses of Literacy: Changing Patterns in English Mass Culture*. Harmondsworth: Penguin, 1957.

LaCapra, Dominick. *History and Criticism*. Ithaca: Cornell UP, 1985.

Lindenberger, Herbert, ed. *History in Literature: On Value, Genre, Institutions*. New York: Columbia UP, 1990.

McGann, Jerome. *The Beauty of Inflections: Literary Investigations in Historical Method and Theory*. Oxford: Clarendon P, 1985.

McGann, Jerome, ed. *Historical Studies and Literary Criticism*. Madison: U of Wisconsin P, 1985.

Said, Edward W. *Orientalism*. New York: Random House, 1978.

———.*Culture and Imperialism*. New York: Knopf, 1993.

Thomas, Brook. *The New Historicism and Other Old-Fashioned Topics*. Princeton: Princeton UP, 1991.

# New Critical/Formalist

The New Criticism (the **New Critical/formalist critical approach**) has been a dominant force in modern literary studies. It focuses on literary texts as formal works of art, and for this reason it can be seen as a reaction against the topical/historical approach. The objection raised by New Critics is that as topical/historical critics consider literary history, they evade direct contact with actual texts.

The inspiration for the New Critical/formalist approach was the French practice of *explication de texte*, a method that emphasizes detailed examination and explanation. (see "Writing a General Explication of a Poem," p. 487). The New Criticism is at its most brilliant in the formal analysis of smaller units such as entire poems and short passages. For the analysis of larger structures, the New Criticism also utilizes a number of techniques that have been selected as the basis of chapters in this book. Discussions of point of view, tone, plot, character, and structure, for example, are formal ways of looking at literature that are derived from the New Criticism.

The aim of the formalist study of literature is to provide readers not only with the means of explaining the content of works (what, specifically, does a work say?) but also with the insights needed for evaluating the artistic quality of individual works and writers (how well is it said?). A major aspect of New Critical thought is that content and form—including all ideas, ambiguities, subtleties, and even apparent contradictions—were originally within the conscious or subconscious control of the author. There are no accidents. It does not necessarily follow, however, that today's critic is able to define the author's intentions exactly, for such intentions require knowledge of biographical details that are irretrievably lost. Each literary work therefore takes on its own existence and identity, and the critic's work is to discover a reading or readings that explain the facts of the text. Note that the New Critic does not claim infallible interpretations and does not exclude the validity of multiple readings of the same work.

Dissenters from the New Criticism have noted a tendency by New Critics to ignore relevant knowledge that history and biography can bring to literary studies. In addition, the approach has been subject to the charge that stressing the explication of texts alone fails to deal with literary value and appreciation. In other words, the formalist critic, in explaining the meaning of literature, sometimes neglects the reasons for which readers find literature stimulating and valuable.

 ## Example, Hawthorne's "Young Goodman Brown"

A major aspect of Hawthorne's "Young Goodman Brown" is that the details are so vague and dreamlike that many readers are uncertain about what is happening. The action is a nighttime walk by the protagonist, Young Goodman Brown, into a deep forest where he encounters a mysterious satanic ritual that leaves him bitter and misanthropic. This much seems clear, but the precise nature of Brown's experience is not clear, nor is the identity of the stranger (father, village elder, devil) who accompanies Brown as he begins his walk. At the story's end Hawthorne's narrator states that the whole episode may have been no more than a dream or nightmare. Yet when morning comes, Brown walks back into town as though returning from an overnight trip, and he recoils in horror from his fellow villagers, including his wife Faith (p. 338). Could his attitude result from nothing more than a nightmare? Even at the story's end these uncertainties remain. For this reason one may conclude that Hawthorne deliberately creates the uncertainties to reveal how people like Brown build defensive walls of judgment around themselves. The story thus implies that the real source of Brown's anger is as vague as his nocturnal walk, but he doesn't understand it in this way. Because Brown's vision and judgment are absolute, he rejects everyone around him, even if the cost is a life of bitter suspicion and spiritual isolation.

 ## Example, Robinson's *Richard Cory*, p. 517

Edwin Arlington Robinson's *Richard Cory* is a tightly structured poem in which all the traditional elements of verse are orchestrated to form a unified and clear meaning. The four quatrains, in iambic pentameter lines, rhyme *abab cdcd efef ghgh*, forming a predictable pattern which boldly frames the ironic ending: "And Richard Cory, one calm summer night,/Went home and put a bullet through his head." The "regal" diction describing Richard Cory, contrasted with the bland circumstances of the townspeople, lets the reader know why Cory was so envied, and the diction also carries the poem forward to its shocking conclusion. The people of the town are walking on the "pavement" and "flutter" at the sight of the neighbor they envy: Richard Cory is "a gentleman from sole to crown, /... and imperially slim." Each stanza is modulated by images of Cory himself, or at least as he is perceived by those around him, along with the images of the townspeople themselves. The townspeople, including the speaker who is one of them, are so envious of Cory that they "curse" their own predicament and would rather be in his place. Yet, upon close scrutiny, the reader can see how the images describing Cory are superficial, as if only the "surface" of his personality were enough to judge him. He was "slim" and "rich" and "admirably schooled," but no reference is made to his thoughts, feelings or aspirations. By the common and unimaginative standards of the speaker, the final irony is surprising, yet by the standards of the reader it is not surprising. As in many works of art, the title of the poem is significant. Did anyone know the "core" of Richard Cory?

## READINGS

Robert Penn Warren. *Understanding Poetry.* New York: Holt, 1938.

Brooks, Cleanth. *The Well Wrought Urn: Studies in the Structure of Poetry.* New York: Reynal and Hitchcock, 1947.

Empson, William. *Seven Types of Ambiguity.* London: Chatto & Windus, 1930.

Krieger, Murray. *The New Apologists for Poetry.* Minneapolis: U of Minnesota P, 1986.

Ransom, John Crowe. *The New Criticism.* Norfolk: New Directions, 1941.

Richards, I. A. *Principles of Literary Criticism.* New York: Harcourt Brace, 1924

Wellek, Rene, and Austin Warren. *Theory of Literature.* New York: Harcourt, Brace, 1949.

Wimsatt, William K. *The Verbal Icon: Studies in the Meaning of Poetry.* Lexington: UP of Kentucky, 1954.

# Structuralist

The principle of the **stucturalist critical approach** stems from the attempt to find relationships and connections among elements that appear to be separate and unique. Just as physical science reveals unifying universal principles of matter such as gravity and the forces of electromagnetism (and is constantly searching for a "unified field theory"), the structuralist critic attempts to discover the forms unifying all literature. Thus, a structuralist description of Maupassant's "The Necklace" (p. 4) stresses that the main character, Mathilde, is an *active* protagonist who undergoes a *test* (or series of tests) and emerges with a victory, though not the kind she had originally hoped for. The same might be said of Mrs. Popov and Smirnov in Chekhov's *The Bear* (p. 1156). If this same kind of structural view is applied to Bierce's "An Occurrence at Owl Creek Bridge" (p. 70), the protagonist is defeated in the test. Generally, the structuralist approach applies such patterns to other works of literature to determine that certain protagonists are active or submissive, that they pass or fail their tests, or that they succeed or fail at other encounters. The key is that many apparently unrelated works reveal many common patterns or contain similar structures with important variations.

The structuralist approach is important because it enables critics to discuss works from widely separate cultures and historical periods. In this respect, critics have followed the leads of modern anthropologists, most notably Claude Lévi-Strauss (1908–1990). Along such lines, critics have undertaken the serious examination of folk and fairy tales. Some of the groundbreaking structuralist criticism, for example, was devoted to the structural analysis of themes, actions, and characters to be found in Russian folktales. The method also bridges popular and serious literature, making little distinction between the two insofar as the description of the structures is concerned. Indeed, structuralism furnishes an ideal approach for comparative literature, and the method also enables critics to consolidate genres such as modern romances, detective tales, soap operas, sitcoms, and film.

Like New Criticism, structuralism aims at comprehensiveness of description, and many critics would insist that the two are complementary and not separate. A distinction is that New Criticism is at its best in dealing with smaller units of literature, whereas structuralist criticism is best in the analysis of narratives and therefore larger units such as novels, myths, stories, plays, and films. Because structuralism shows how fiction is organized into various typical situations, the approach merges with the *archetypal* approach (see below, p. 1405), and at times it is difficult to find any distinctions between structuralist and archetypal criticism.

Structuralism, however, deals not just with narrative structures but also with structures of any type, wherever they occur. For example, structuralism makes considerable use of linguistics. Modern linguistic scholars have determined that there is a difference between "deep structures" and "surface structures" in language. A structuralist analysis of style, therefore, emphasizes how writers utilize such structures. The structuralist interpretation of language also perceives distinguishing types or "grammars" of language that are recurrent in various types of literature. Suppose, for example, that you encounter opening passages like the following:

1. Once upon a time a young prince fell in love with a young princess. He was so much in love that he wanted to declare his love for her, and early one morning he left his castle on his white charger, with his servants around him, riding toward her castle home high in the distant and cloud-topped mountains.

2. Early that morning, Alan found himself thinking about Anne. He had thought that she was being ambiguous when she said she loved him, and his feelings about her were not certain. His further thought left him still unsure.

The words of these two passages create different and distinct frames of reference. One is a fairy tale of the past, the other a modern internalized reflection of feeling. The passages therefore demonstrate how language itself fits into predetermined patterns or structures. Similar uses of language structures can be associated with other types of literature.

##  Example, Hawthorne's "Young Goodman Brown"

Young Goodman Brown is a hero who is passive, not active. He is a *witness*, a *receiver* rather than a *doer*. His only action—taking his trip in the forest—occurs at the story's beginning. After that point, he no longer acts but instead is acted upon, and his reactions to what he sees around him put his life's beliefs to a test. Of course, many protagonists undergo similar testing (such as rescuing victims and overcoming particularly terrible dragons), and they emerge as heroes or conquerors. Not so with Goodman Brown. He is a responder who allows himself to be victimized by his own perceptions—or misperceptions. Despite all his previous experiences with his wife and with the good people of his village, he generalizes too hastily. He lets the single disillusioning experience of his nightmare govern his entire outlook on others, and thus he fails his test and turns his entire life into darkness.

## Second Example, Jackson's "The Lottery," p. 120

Shirley Jackson's story "The Lottery" is a powerful indictment of tradition for its own sake. The narrator/resident of a small town explains how a yearly lottery is held to determine who amongst its citizens is to be stoned. Apparently, the purpose of this ritual has generally been forgotten, but the rules governing its execution are known in great detail. The plot is given resonance and predictability by following two structurally determined elements—the basic outline of a tragedy and the outlines of a contest. Like a traditional tragedy the story begins in apparent innocence and happiness and ends in definite calamity. It is a "sunny" day when the lottery is about to begin, "the flowers were blossoming profusely," and the town folk are in a jovial mood. The tension builds with the "drawing" from the black box, and the story ends with the stoning and presumed death of the victim. The horror of the story is not to be found in an individual but rather in the collective, slavish acquiescence to a shockingly anachronistic ritual. As in tragedy, the end is the inevitable outcome, for once we know that the people accept the rules of the town lottery, the end is predictable. The townspeople do not know why they must stone someone, but they know that when they partake in the lottery and follow its rules, someone will "win" the contest and meet his or her doom. Understanding the basic elements of tragedy and reading "The Lottery" as a contest or game gives the story a comprehensible and predictable form.

### READINGS

Barthes, Roland. *Writing Degree Zero.* 1953; New York: Beacon, 1970.

——. *Critical Essays.* 1964; Evanston: Northwestern UP, 1970.

——. *Mythologies.* 1957; New York: Hill and Wang, 1972.

Cassirer, Ernst. *Symbol, Myth, and Culture.* New Haven: Yale UP, 1979.

Caws, Peter. *Structuralism: The Art of the Intelligible.* Atlantic Highlands: Humanities, 1988.

Culler, Jonathan. *Structuralist Poetics.* Ithaca: Cornell UP, 1975.

Genette, Gerard. *Narrative Discourse: An Essay in Method.* Ithaca: Cornell UP, 1980.

Greimas, A. J. *Structural Semantics: An Attempt at a Method.* Lincoln: U of Nebraska P, 1984.

Lane, Michael, ed. *Structuralism: A Reader.* London: Cape, 1970.

Macksey, Richard, and Eugenio Donato, eds. *The Structuralism Controversy: The Languages of Criticism and the Sciences of Man.* Baltimore: Johns Hopkins UP, 1970.

# Feminist Criticism/Gender Studies/Queer Theory

*Feminism/gender studies/queer theory* displays divergent interests drawing insights from many disciplines. It is a still evolving and rich field of inquiry. *Feminist Criticism* had its genesis in the women's movement of the 1960s, shares many of its concerns, and has applied them to the study of literature. One of the early aims of feminist critics was to question the traditional canon and claim a place in it for neglected women writers. Writers such as Mary Shelley, Elizabeth Gaskell, Christina Rossetti, Kate Chopin, and Charlotte Perkins Gillman—three of whom are represented in this book—have been given great critical attention as a result. Feminist critics also delineate the ways both male and female characters are portrayed in literature, looking at how societal norms about sexual difference are either enforced or subverted, and focusing partly on patriarchal structures and institutions such as marriage. As early as the beginning of the twentieth century, Virginia Woolf questioned whether there was a feminine/masculine divide in writing styles, a contentious subject amongst feminist critics to this day. Feminist critics are also interested in how interpreting texts differs between the sexes. For instance, in *A Map for Rereading* (1980), critic Annette Kolodny analyzes how men and women read the same stories differently.

*Gender studies*, a more recent critical approach, brings attention to gender rather than to sexual differences. Gender studies critics see the masculine/feminine divide as socially constructed and not innate. Drawing partly on the works of the French philosopher Michel Foucault (1926–1984) such as *The History of Sexuality* and *Madness and Civilization*, which explore the way powerful institutions organize our society and way of thinking, gender studies critics apply Foucault's ideas to understanding patriarchal structures and their representations in literature. Many studies have also built on the insights of psychoanalysis and deconstruction (see below), questioning Freud's male-oriented categories and seeking insights into the way language is constructed and the way it affects our thinking. In her essay *Laugh of the Medusa* (1975), Hélène Cixous applies deconstructionist insights about binary oppositions to a study of discourse about women, showing how it disparages women. Thus, while men's discourse in relation to women's may highlight such separate ways of thinking as logic/inconsistency, it is the traditional patriarchal way of thinking that values male over female experience.

A more recent critical orientation, which came to prominence in the early 1990s is *queer theory*, which also appropriates many of the insights of deconstruction, particularly its understanding that binary oppositions are relative and that thinking about matters such as sexual orientation is partly ideological and partly social. Many queer theorists see the heterosexual/homosexual divide as less distinct than has commonly been believed. Queer theorists are interested in how homosexuals are portrayed in literature and whether they write or read literature differently than heterosexuals. Queer theory has brought attention to recent literary works, dealing explicitly with lesbian and gay themes, along with attention to sometimes "veiled" references to the same themes in writers whose works make up the standard canon. Much of queer theory is theoretical; one example, applied to reading a particular work, is Jonathan Crewe's essay, "Queering 'The Yellow Wallpaper'? Charlotte Perkins Gilman and the Politics of Form" (*Tulsa Studies in Women's Literature* 14.2 [1995]: 273–93).

## 🐿 Example, Hawthorne's "Young Goodman Brown"

At the beginning of "Young Goodman Brown," Brown's wife, Faith, is seen only peripherally. In the traditional patriarchal spirit of wife-as-adjunct, she tells her new husband of her fears, and then asks him to stay at home and take his journey at some other time. Hawthorne does not give her the intelligence or dignity, however, to let her explain her concern (or might he not have been interested in what she had to say?) and she therefore remains in the background with her pink hair ribbon as her distinguishing symbol of submissive inferiority. During the mid-forest satanic ritual she appears again and is given power, but only the power to cause her husband to go astray. Once she is led in as a novice in the practice of demonism, her husband falls right in step. Unfortunately, by following her, Brown can conveniently excuse himself from guilt by claiming that "she" had made him do it, just as Eve, in some traditional views of the fall of humankind, compelled Adam to eat the apple (Genesis 3:16–17). Hawthorne's attention to the male protagonist, in other words, permits him to neglect the independence and integrity of a female protagonist.

##  Second Example, Chopin's "The Story of an Hour," p. 287

"The Story of an Hour" by Kate Chopin is about a woman who is told that her husband has died in a train accident. Rather than feeling devastated by this news as her family and friends expect, she feels strangely free and happy to pursue a life for herself. While the story's plot suggests obvious themes of interest for feminist critics, a closer look at many details reveals how language, institutions and expected demeanor suppress the natural desires and aspirations of women. The protagonist of the story is referred to as "Mrs. Mallard," while her husband is called by his name, Brently Mallard, which has nothing to do with his marital status. Assuming that because of a heart condition Louise Mallard might not survive the bad news, she is told by her sister indirectly, "in broken sentences" of her husband's fate. At first, she reacts predictably by weeping "with sudden, wild abandonment." Soon, however, Louise finds herself resisting a feeling which is finally identified as "freedom." In moments of quiet, she imagines a life devoted only to herself, and not molded by the will of another. Her resistance is indicative of the pull of societal norms, while the abandonment to her potential liberation is a sign of her true inner self. When, at the end of the story, Louise sees her husband appear, perfectly safe and unharmed, she dies of a heart attack, which is diagnosed by attending doctors as a result "of joy that kills." Because there is no indication that Brently Mallard was anything but a good husband, we may assume that it was freedom from the bonds of marriage itself and the overpowering will of a man that turned a supposedly tragic event into a liberating one. *"The Story of an Hour"* is a powerful commentary on the institution of marriage as it suppresses the natural desires and pursuits of women.

### READINGS

Brownstein, Rachel. *Becoming a Heroine: Reading about Women in Novels.* New York: Viking, 1982.

Cameron, Deborah. *Feminism in Linguistic Theory.* London: Macmillan, 1992.

Delany, Sheila. *Writing Women: Women Writers and Women in Literature, Medieval to Modern.* New York: Schocken, 1983.

Gilbert, Sandra M., and Susan Gubar. *The Madwoman in the Attic: The Woman Writer and the Nineteenth-Century Literary Imagination.* New Haven: Yale UP, 1979.

Jacobus, Mary. *Women's Writing and Writing about Women.* New York: Barnes and Noble, 1979.

Kauffman, Linda, ed. *Gender and Theory: Dialogues on Feminist Criticism.* New York: Blackwell, 1985.

Kolodny, Annette. "Some Notes on Defining a 'Feminist Literary Criticism.'" *Critical Inquiry 2* (1975): 75–92.

Lilly, Mark, ed. *Lesbian and Gay Writing.* London: Macmillian, 1990.

Sedgwick, Eve Kosovsky. *Between Men: English Literature and Male Homosocial Desire.* New York: Columbia UP, 1985.

Showalter, Elaine. *A Literature of Their Own: British Women Novelists from Brontë to Lessing.* Princeton: Princeton UP, 1977.

Woods, Greg. *A History of Gay Literature.* New Haven: Yale UP, 1999.

## Economic Determinist/Marxist

The concept of cultural and economic determinism is one of the major political ideas of the nineteenth century. Karl Marx (1818–1883) emphasized that the primary influence on life was economic, and he saw society enmeshed in a continuous conflict between capitalist oppressors and oppressed working people. The literature that emerged from this kind of analysis often features individuals who are coping with the ill effects of economic disadvantage. Sometimes called "proletarian" literature, it focuses on persons of the lower class—the poor and oppressed who spend their lives in endless drudgery and misery, and whose attempts to rise to the top usually result in renewed oppression.

Marx's political ideas were never widely accepted in the United States and have faded still more after the political breakup of the Soviet Union, but the idea of economic determinism (and the related term *Social Darwinism*) is still credible. As a result, much literature can be judged from an economic perspective even though the economic critics may not be Marxian: What is the economic status of the characters? What happens to them as a result of this status? How do they fare against economic and political odds? What other conditions stemming from their class does the writer emphasize (e.g., poor education, poor nutrition, poor health care, inadequate opportunity)? To what extent does the work fail by overlooking the economic, social, and political implications of its material? In what other ways does economic determinism affect the work? How should readers consider the story in today's developed or underdeveloped world? Seemingly, Hawthorne's story *"Young Goodman Brown,"* which we have used for analysis in these discussions, has no major economic implications, but an **economic determinist/Marxist critical approach** might take the following turns.

 ### Example, Hawthorne's "Young Goodman Brown"

"Young Goodman Brown" is a fine story just as it is. It deals with the false values instilled by the skewed acceptance of sin-dominated religion, but it overlooks the economic implications of this situation. One might suspect that the real story in the little world of Goodman Brown's Salem should be about the disruption that an alienated member of society can produce. After Brown's condemnation and distrust of others forces him into his own shell of sick imagination, Hawthorne does not consider how such a disaffected character would injure the economic and public life of the town. Consider this, just for a moment: Why would the people from whom Brown recoils in disgust want to deal with him in business or personal matters? In town meetings, would they want to follow his opinions on crucial issues of public concern and investment? Would his preoccupation with sin and damnation make him anything more than a horror in his domestic life? Would his wife, Faith, be able to discuss household management with him, or to ask him about methods of caring for the children? All these questions of course are pointed toward another story—a story that Hawthorne did not write. They also indicate the shortcomings of Hawthorne's approach, because it is clear that the major result of Young Goodman Brown's selfish preoccupation with evil would be a serious disruption of the economic and political affairs of his small community.

## Second Example, Miller's *Death of a Salesman*, p. 1266

Arthur Miller's *Death of a Salesman* is a devastating indictment of capitalism. Willy Loman is an aging salesman who is struggling to live his later life in dignity. Although his desire to live the American dream of economic security is partly shattered by his own personal inadequacies and increasing age, much of his demise can be traced to the cruel system, which he accepts and in which he believes. As a salesman, Willy represents the purist form of capitalism. He is worth only what he sells, and he is selling less and less. The cost of fixing his car and home appliances weighs heavily on him. When he confronts his boss about a better job close to home, he is ignored and rejected, and he faces indigence and humiliation. His descent into irrationality stems from his confusion about the grimness of his economic reality. On the one hand, he professes the importance to his adult children of being well-liked, as if personality were a substitute for the harsh realities of capitalistic economic necessity. On the other hand, referring to his own "vital" role as a salesman indicates an acceptance of the values inherent in capitalism. The problem is that he is no longer productive and is therefore of no value to his employer. At the play's end, Willy kills himself for the insurance money his wife will gain, and when the last payment on his mortgage has been made, the irony only underscores how capitalism degrades life by equating human worth with economic productivity. In *Death of a Salesman*, Arthur Miller has written a powerful critique of the American economic system.

### READINGS

Adorno, Theodor. *Prisms: Cultural Criticism and Society.* 1955; London: Neville Spearman, 1967.

Althusser, Louis. *For Marx.* New York: Pantheon, 1969.

Bakhtin, Mikhail. *Between Phenomenology and Marxism.* New York: Cambridge UP, 1995.

Demetz, Peter. *Marx, Engels, and the Poets: Origins of Marxist Literary Criticism.* Chicago, U of Chicago P, 1967.

Dowling, William. *Jameson, Althusser, Marx: An Introduction to the Political Unconscious.* Ithaca: Cornel UP, 1984.

Eagleton, Terry. *Criticism and Ideology: A Study in Marxist Literary Theory.* London: New Left, 1976.

Frow, John. *Marxism and Literary History.* Ithaca: Cornell UP, 1986.

Jameson, Frederic. *Marxism and Form: Twentieth Century Dialectical Theories of Literature.* Princeton: Princeton UP, 1971.

Lukacs, Georg. *Realism in Our Time: Literature and the Class Struggle.* 1957; New York: Harper and Row, 1964.

Marcuse, Herbert. *The Aesthetic Dimension: Toward a Critique of Marxist Aesthetics.* Boston: Beacon, 1978.

# Psychological/Psychoanalytic

The scientific study of the mind is a product of psychodynamic theory as established by Sigmund Freud (1856–1939) and of the psychoanalytic method practiced by his followers. Psychoanalysis provided a new key to the understanding of character by claiming that behavior is caused by hidden and unconscious motives. It was greeted as a revelation with far-reaching implications for all intellectual pursuits. Not surprisingly, it has had a profound and continuing effect on post-Freudian literature.

In addition, its popularity produced the **psychological/psychoanalytic approach** to criticism.[2] Some critics use the approach to explain fictional characters, as in the landmark interpretation by Freud and Ernest Jones that Shakespeare's Hamlet suffers from an Oedipus complex. Still other critics use it as a way of analyzing authors and the artistic process. For example, John Livingston Lowes's study *The Road to Xanadu* presents a detailed examination of the mind, reading, and neuroses of Coleridge, the author of "Kubla Khan" (p. 536).

Critics using the psychoanalytic approach treat literature somewhat like information about patients in therapy. In the work itself, what are the obvious and hidden motives that cause a character's behavior and speech? How much background (e.g., repressed childhood trauma, adolescent memories) does the author reveal about a character? How purposeful is this information with regard to the character's psychological condition? How much is important in the analysis and understanding of the character?

In the consideration of authors, critics utilizing the psychoanalytic model consider questions like these: What particular life experiences explain characteristic subjects or preoccupations? Was the author's life happy? Miserable? Upsetting? Solitary? Social? Can the death of someone in the author's family be associated with melancholy situations in that author's work? All eleven brothers and sisters of the English poet Thomas Gray, for example, died before reaching adulthood. Gray was the only one of the twelve to survive. In his poetry, Gray often deals with death, and he is therefore considered one of the "Graveyard School" of eighteenth-century poets. A psychoanalytical critic might make much of this connection.

##  Example, Hawthorne's "Young Goodman Brown"

At the end of "Young Goodman Brown," Hawthorne's major character is no longer capable of normal existence. His nightmare should be read as a symbol of what in reality would have been lifelong mental subjection to the type of puritanical religion that emphasizes sin and guilt. Such preoccupation with sin is no hindrance to psychological health if the preoccupied people are convinced that God forgives them and grants them mercy. In their dealings with others, they remain healthy as long as they believe that other people have the same sincere trust in divine forgiveness. If their own faith is weak and uncertain, however, and if they cannot believe in forgiveness, then they are likely to transfer their own guilt—really a form of personal terror—to others. They remain conscious of their own sins, but they find it easy to claim that others are sinful—even those who are spiritually spotless, and even their own family, who should be dearest to them. When this process of projection or transference occurs, such people have created the rationale of condemning others because of their own guilt. The price that they pay is a life of gloom, a fate that Hawthorne designates for Goodman Brown after his nightmare about demons in human form.

---

[2]See also Chapter 4, "Characters: The People in Fiction."

**Example, Browning's "My Last Duchess," p. 609**

"My Last Duchess" by Robert Browning is a dramatic monologue based loosely on the real-life Duke of Ferrara, Alfonso II (1533–97). In presumably discussing a marriage proposal with an envoy, the duke reveals his jealousy, egocentrism, and greed. The duke points to a painting of his former duchess and notices her happy "countenance," which was easily aroused by strangers. From what we gather from Browning's poem about the malevolent duke, it is plausible that he had his apparently cheerful wife killed. Getting back to the business at hand, the duke escorts the envoy down the stairs, but not before pointing out a painting of Neptune "taming a seahorse." Besides indicating a love of possessions, his reference to the painting and its subject of taming also suggests a consciousness of subjugation and the desire to bend others to his will—certainly a sign of how he will treat the future duchess. While some psychological studies may point to the poet's frame of mind, *My Last Duchess* is a study of how a poem may imply a personality through a speaker's unsuspecting words.

### READINGS

Bloom, Harold. *The Anxiety of Influence*. New York: Oxford UP. 1975.

Bowie, Malcolm. *Freud, Proust and Lacan: Theory as Fiction*. New York: Cambridge UP, 1987.

Gilbert, Sandra, and Susan Gubar. *The Madwoman in the Attic*. New Haven: Yale UP, 1979.

Gilman, Sander L. ed. *Introducing Psychoanalytic Theory*. New York: Brunner/Mazel, 1982.

Holland, Norman N. *The Dynamics of Literary Response*. New York: Oxford UP, 1968.

Lacan, Jacques. *Ecrits: A Selection*. New York: Norton, 2004.

Shamdsani, Sonu, and Michael Munchow, eds. *Speculations After Freud: Psychoanalysis, Philosophy, and Culture*. New York: Routledge, 1994.

Skura, Meredith Anne. *The Literary Use of the Psychoanalytic Process*. New Haven: Yale UP, 1981.

Wright, Elizabeth. *Psychoanalytic Criticism: Theory in Practice*. New York and London: Methuen, 1984.

## Archetypal/Symbolic/Mythic

The **archetypal/symbolic/mythic critical approach**, derived from the work of the Swiss psychoanalyst Carl Jung (1875–1961), presupposes that human life is built up out of patterns, or *archetypes* ("first molds" or "first patterns") that are similar throughout various cultures and historical times.[3] The approach is similar to the structuralist analysis of literature, for both approaches stress the connections that may be discovered in literature written in different times and in vastly different locations in the world.

In literary evaluation, the archetypal approach is used to support the claim that the very best literature is grounded in archetypal patterns. The archetypal critic therefore looks for archetypes such as God's creation of human beings, the sacrifice of a hero, or the search for paradise. How does an individual story, poem, or play fit

---

[3]Symbolism also is considered in Chapters 8 and 17.

into any of the archetypal patterns? What truths does this correlation provide (particularly truths that cross historical, national, and cultural lines)? How closely does the work fit the archetype? What variations can be seen? What meaning or meanings do the connections have?

The most tenuous aspect of archetypal criticism is Jung's assertion that the recurring patterns provide evidence for a "universal human consciousness" that all of us, by virtue of our humanity, still retain in our minds and in our very blood.

Not all critics accept the hypothesis of a universal human consciousness, but they nevertheless consider the approach important for comparisons and contrasts (see Chapter 25). Many human situations, such as adolescence, dawning love, the search for success, the reconciliation with one's mother and father, and the encroachment of age and death, are similar in structure and can be analyzed as archetypes. For example, the following situations can be seen as a pattern or archetype of initiation: A young man discovers the power of literature and understanding (Keats's "On First Looking into Chapman's Homer"); a man determines the importance of truth and fidelity amidst uncertainty (Arnold's "Dover Beach"); a man and woman fall in love despite their wishes to remain independent (Chekhov's *The Bear*); a woman gains strength and integrity because of previously unrealized inner resources (Maupassant's "The Necklace"). The archetypal approach encourages the analysis of variations on the same theme, as in Glaspell's "Trifles" (p. 892) and Faulkner's "A Rose for Emily" (p. 75) when characters choose to ignore the existence of a crime (one sort of initiation) and also, as a result, assert their own individuality and freedom (another sort of initiation).

##  Example: Hawthorne's "Young Goodman Brown"

In the sense that Young Goodman Brown undergoes a change from psychological normality to rigidity, the story is a reverse archetype of the initiation ritual. According to the archetype of successful initiation, initiates seek to demonstrate their worthiness to become full-fledged members of society. Telemachus in Homer's *Odyssey*, for example, is a young man who in the course of the epic goes through the initiation rituals of travel, discussion, and battle. But in "Young Goodman Brown" we see initiation in reverse, for just as there is an archetype of successful initiation, Brown's initiation leads him into failure. In the private areas of life on which happiness depends, he falls short. He sees evil in his fellow villagers, condemns his minister, and shrinks even from his own family. His life therefore becomes filled with despair and gloom. His suspicions are those of a Puritan of long ago, but the timeliness of Hawthorne's story is that the archetype of misunderstanding and condemnation has not changed. Today's headlines of misery and war are produced by the same kind of intolerance that is exhibited by Goodman Brown.

##  Second Example: Frost's *Birches*, p. 754

Interpreting Frost's poem *Birches* symbolically gives the poem a special depth which it otherwise might not have. On the literal level the poem is about a man who describes birch trees in winter and who states his belief that a lonely boy has perhaps been swinging on them. The poem moves from the third person to the first and we come to realize that the speaker is reminiscing about his own childhood: "So I was once myself a swinger of birches." Many of the rich images of the poem are sexually suggestive. The trunks of the trees are "trailing their leaves on the ground/Like girls on hands and knees that throw their hair/Before them over their heads to dry in the sun." The speaker also describes a boy "riding" the trees "Until he took the stiffness out of them." And While hanging on the tree branches he learned "about not launching out too soon." While these images have clear suggestions about sexuality, the poem ends with the alternate yearning to ride the trees towards heaven and to return back to earth. Reading the poem symbolically thus opens up resonant avenues of interpretation. Expression is given to the dual nature of humankind—physical and spiritual release. By describing the boy swinging on birch trees, Frost is expressing the desire for sexual fulfillment and spiritual release from earthly constraints. A rich, evocative poem emerges when *Birches* is read symbolically.

READINGS

Barber, C. L. *Shakespeare's Festive Comedy: A Study of Dramatic Form and Its Relation to Social Custom*. Princeton, Princeton UP, 1972.

Bloom, Harold. *Shelley's Mythmaking*. New Haven: Yale UP, 1959.

Bodkin, Maud. *Archetypal Patterns in Poetry*. London: Oxford UP, 1934

Bush, Douglas. *Mythology and the Renaissance Tradition in English Poetry*. New York: W. W. Norton, 1963.

Chase, Richard. *Quest for Myth*. Baton Rouge: Louisiana State UP, 1949.

Frye, Northrop *Anatomy of Criticism: Four Essays. Princeton*: Princeton UP, 1957

Hyman, Stanley Edgar. *The Tangled Bank*. New York: Atheneum, 1962.

# Deconstructionist

The **deconstructionist critical approach**—which deconstructionists explain not as an approach but rather as a performance or as a strategy of reading—was developed by the French philosopher Jacques Derrida (1930–2004). In the 1970s and 1980s, it became a major mode of criticism by critiquing the "logocentric" western philosophical tradition. Logocentrism is the belief that speech is a direct expression of a speaker's intention, that it has a direct correspondence to reality, and that it is therefore the privileged arbiter of interpretation. Derrida, by exposing what he saw as the fallacious assumptions of logocentrism, sought to undermine the basis of stable meanings derivable from language. The implications for reading and therefore for literary studies were far reaching.

Deconstructionist critics begin literary analysis by assuming the instability of language and the impossibility of arriving at a fixed standard to anchor interpretation. The dictum, in Derrida's *Of Grammatology*, that "There is nothing outside the text" indicates the denial of any authoritative referent outside of words. Texts are always self-contradictory because they can always be re-read to undermine an apparently stable interpretation. In part, this is due to how meaning is derived from binary oppositions such as speech/writing, male/female, good/evil. Each word of the pair obtains its significance by contrast with the other, so that its meaning is relative, not absolute. A female may therefore be defined as lacking male features or a male as lacking female traits. In addition, each set of opposites has been arranged hierarchically; speech, for instance, is considered more immediate and therefore closer to reality than writing and therefore speech is the privileged member of the set speech/writing. These pairings are social constructs and form part of our way of thinking, even if they do not necessarily reflect reality.

Other strategies for undermining the stability of texts are to see how they have "gaps," or missing pieces of information or words with several meanings and connotations that therefore "de-center" the meaning of the texts. While a poem may seem to mean one thing when our habitual, formalistic reading strategies are applied to it, it can be shown to have a completely different meaning as well. Additional readings will yield still other meanings. The text is therefore said to "deconstruct" itself as the reading strategies applied to it are merely pointing out contradictory elements which inhere in the nature of language itself.

While formalist critics aim at resolving contradictions and ambiguities to form a unified literary work, deconstructionists aim to find disunity and disruptions in the language of a text. The typical deconstructionist strategy is to start with a standard formalistic reading of a text and then undermine that interpretation in order to yield a new one. The deconstructionist does not deny that interpretations are possible, only that there is no basis for appealing to final, absolute ones. Deconstruction has yielded some new, imaginative readings of canonical literature. Some critics of deconstruction argue that the "initial" formalistic readings of the deconstructionist strategy are the most rewarding and that often deconstructionist interpretations are incoherent.

##  Example: Hawthorne's "Young Goodman Brown"

There are many uncertainties in the details of "Young Goodman Brown." If one starts with the stranger on the path, one might conclude that he could be Brown's father, because he recognizes Brown immediately and speaks to him jovially. On the other hand, the stranger could be the devil (he is recognized as such by Goody Cloyse) because of his wriggling walking stick. After disappearing, the stranger also takes on the characteristics of an omniscient cult leader and seer, because at the satanic celebration he knows all the secret sins committed by Brown's neighbors and the community of greater New England. Additionally, he might represent a perverted conscience whose aim is to mislead and befuddle people by steering them into the holier-than-thou judgmental attitude that Brown adopts. This method would be truly diabolical—to use religion in order to bring people to their own damnation. That the stranger is an evil force is therefore clear, but the pathways of his evil are not as clear. He seems to work his mission of damnation by reaching the souls of persons like Goodman Brown through means ordinarily attributed to conscience. If the stranger represents a satanic conscience, what are we to suppose that Hawthorne is asserting about what is considered real conscience?

##  Second Example: Auden's *Musée des Beaux Arts*

*Musee des Beaux Arts* may be read as a poem about an indifferent universe in the face of human suffering. Auden posits the "old master" painters of the Renaissance as depicting this situation correctly: "About suffering they were never wrong." Suffering apparently takes place in the midst of the dull happenings of everyday life, the speaker asserts. The poem ends by focusing on a specific example—Breughel's depiction of the mythic Icarus who fell into the sea because he flew too high. No notice is apparently taken by the characters in the painting of the splash made by the falling body as it enters the water. While the poem may be read as being unified around the theme of indifference to suffering, alternate interpretations arise when the poem is deconstructed. The title of the poem indicates the museum where Breughel's painting may be seen. Museums are, in part, repositories of historical events. By referring to a painting in a specific place, Auden lets the reader know that he or she may see a depiction of Icarus' suffering. While the figures in the painting turn away from the fallen Icarus, the observer of the painting—like the reader of the poem—is made conscious of Icarus' story and his suffering. While the dichotomy-event (Icarus falling)/depiction of event (painting and poem of Icarus falling) may suggest a priority to the event itself, it is ironically Auden's poem which encourages us to think of the anguish Icarus must have felt as he fell. In describing the "white legs [of Icarus] disappearing into the green/Water," Auden focuses our attention to suffering and death. "Turns" is a key word in the poem. Auden describes how everyone in the scene "turns away/Quite leisurely from the disaster." Just as something may turn away from an event, the same motion of turning may return us to the same event, in this instance, a contemplation of suffering. While indifference to suffering may be one theme of "Musee des Beaux Arts," deconstructing the poem also shows how it "pulls" in other directions. The language of the poem itself tugs the reader in different directions.

### READINGS

Abrams, M. H. "The Deconstructive Angel." in *Doing Things with Texts*. New York and London: Norton, 1989.

Arac, Jonathan, Wlad Godzich, and Wallace Martin, eds. *The Yale Critics: Deconstruction in America*. Minneapolis: U of Minnesota P, 1983.

De Man, Paul. *Blindness and Insight*. New York: Oxford UP, 1971.

Derrida, Jacques. *Of Grammatology*. 1967; Baltimore: Johns Hopkins UP, 1976.

————. *Writing and Difference*. 1967; U of Chicago P, 1978.

Hartman, Geoffrey. *Saving the Text: Literature/Derrida/Philosophy*. Baltimore: Johns Hopkins UP, 1981.

Miller, J. Hillis. *Fiction and Repetition: Seven English Novels*. Cambridge: Harvard UP, 1982.

————. *The Linguistic Moment: From Wordsworth to Stevens*. Princeton: Princeton UP, 1985.

————. *The Ethics of Reading: Kant, de Man, Eliot, Trollope, James and Benjamin*. New York: Columbia UP, 1987.

Silverman, Hugh J., and Gary E. Aylesworth, eds. *The Textual Sublime: Deconstruction and its Differences*. Albany: State U of New York P, 1990.

# Reader-Response

The **reader-response critical approach** is rooted in *phenomenology*, a branch of philosophy that deals with the understanding of how things appear. The phenomenological idea of knowledge is based on the separation of the reality of our thoughts from the reality of the world. Our quest for truth is to be found not in the external world itself but rather in our mental *perception* and interpretation of externals. All that we human beings can know—actual *knowledge*—is our collective and personal understanding of the world and our conclusions about it.

As a consequence of the phenomenological concept, reader-response theory holds that the reader is a necessary third party in the author-text-reader relationship that constitutes the literary work. The work, in other words, is not fully created until readers make a *transaction* with it by assimilating it and *actualizing* it in the light of their own knowledge and experience. The representative questions of the theory are these: What does this work mean to me, in my present intellectual and moral make-up? How can the work improve my understanding and widen my insights? How can my increasing understanding help me understand the work more deeply? The theory is that the free interchange or transaction that such questions bring about leads toward interest and growth, so that readers can assimilate literary works and accept them as parts of their lives and as parts of the civilization in which they live.

As an initial way of reading, the reader-response method may be personal and anecdotal. In addition, by stressing response rather than interpretation, one of the leading exponents of the method (Stanley Fish) has raised the extreme question about whether texts, by themselves, have objective identity. These aspects have been cited as both a shortcoming and an inconsequentiality of the method.

It is therefore important to stress that the reader-response theory is *open*. It permits beginning readers to bring their own personal reactions to literature, but it also aims to increase their discipline and skill. The more that readers bring to literature through their interests and disciplined studies, the more "competent" and comprehensive their "transactions" will be. It is possible, for example, to explain the structure of a work not according to commonly recognized categories such as exposition and climax, but rather according to the personal reactions of representative readers. The contention is that structure, like other avenues of literary study such as tone or the comprehension of figurative language, refers to clearly definable responses that readers experience when reading and transacting with works. By such means, literature is subject not only to outward and objective analysis, but also to inward and psychological response.

The reader-response approach thus lends an additional dimension to the critical awareness of literature. If literary works imply that readers should possess special knowledge in fields such as art, politics, science, philosophy, religion, or morality, then competent readers will seek out such knowledge and utilize it in developing their responses. Also, because students experience many similar intellectual and cultural disciplines, it is logical to conclude that responses will tend not to diverge but rather to coalesce; agreements result not from personal but from cultural similarities. The reader-response theory, then, can and should be an avenue toward informed and detailed understanding of literature, but the initial emphasis is the *transaction* that readers make with literary works.

## Example, Hawthorne's "Young Goodman Brown"

"Young Goodman Brown" is worrisome because it shows so disturbingly that good intentions may cause harmful results. I think that a person with too high a set of expectations is ripe for disillusionment, just as Goodman Brown is. When people don't measure up to this person's standard of perfection, they can be thrown aside as though they are worthless. They may be good people, but whatever past mistakes they have made make it impossible for the person with high expectations to endure them. Goodman Brown makes the same kind of misjudgment, expecting perfection and turning sour when he learns about flaws. It is not that he is not a good man, because he is shown at the start as a person of belief and stability. He uncritically accepts his nightmare revelation that everyone else is evil, however (including his parents), and he finally distrusts everyone because of this baseless suspicion. He cannot look at his neighbors without avoiding them like an "anathema," and he turns away from his own wife "without a greeting" (p. 338). Brown's problem is that he equates being human with being unworthy. By such a distorted standard of judgment, all of us fail, and that is what makes the story so disturbing.

##  Second Example, Roethke's "My Papa's Waltz," p. 628

"My Papa's Waltz" by Theodore Roethke shows how complicated relationships between father and son may be. While it is the memory of a spirited "waltz" that the speaker, as a child, had with his father, the emotions it evokes are not so easy to pin down. On the one hand, the speaker recalls what might have seemed a happy time, with father and son romping "until the pans/slid from the kitchen shelf" and the boy danced off to bed "Still clinging to your [the father's] shirt." There is, however, a darker side to this memory as suggested by images that border on abuse. The whiskey on the father's breath "Could make a small boy dizzy." Also, the father "scraped a buckle" every time he missed a step of the dance and "beat time" on the boy's head; in addition, the speaker's memory is that his mother was an unhappy witness to this rough play. That her "countenance/Could not unfrown itself" suggests a disapproving uneasiness. The regular stanzas and short lines indicate the symmetry and balance of an orderly dance, but the more disturbing images imply violence. This double-edged emotion points to the complex nature of love and the ambivalent feelings we may have toward a parent. We might wish sometimes that our memories could be resolved into one overwhelming feeling, but "My Papa's Waltz," through its rich imagery, evokes the true nature of most relationships. They aren't easily categorized.

### READINGS

Altick, Richard. *The English Common Reader: A Social History of the Mass Reading Public 1800–1900.* Chicago: U of Chicago P, 1957.

Bleich, David. *Readings and Feelings: An Introduction to Subjective Criticism.* Urbana: National Council of Teachers of English, 1975.

Booth, Wayne C. *The Rhetoric of Fiction.* Chicago: U of Chicago P, 1961; 2nd ed. 1983.

Fish, Stanley. *Is There a Text in This Class? The Authority of Interpretive Communities.* Cambridge: Harvard UP, 1980.

Holland, Norman N. *The Dynamics of Literary Response.* New York: Oxford UP, 1968.

Iser, Wolfgang. *The Implied Reader: Pattern of Communication in Prose Fiction From Bunyan to Beckett.* Baltimore: Johns Hopkins UP, 1974.

Leavis, Q. D. *Fiction and the Reading Public.* London: Chatto and Windus, 1932.

Mailloux, Steven J. *Interpretive Convections.* Ithaca: Cornell UP, 1982.

Richards, I. A. *Practical Criticism: A Study of Literary Judgment.* New York: Harcourt, Brace, 1935.

Sartre, Jean-Paul. *What Is Literature?* New York: Philosophical Library, 1966.

Suleiman, Susan, and Inge Crosman, eds. *The Reader in the Text: Essays on Audience and Interpretation.* Princeton: Princeton UP, 1980.

# C h a p t e r 25

# Comparison-Contrast and Extended Comparison-Contrast: Learning by Seeing Literary Works Together

**C**omparison-contrast analysis is the act of putting things side by side—juxtaposing them, looking at them together—for a variety of purposes such as description, enhanced understanding, evaluation, and decision making. The technique underlies other important techniques, specifically (1) the analysis of causes and effects, and (2) the scientific method of constant-and-variable analysis. Significant questions of all these methods are, How is *A* both like and unlike *B*? What are the causes of *A*? How does a change in *A* affect *B*? These are all questions that call into play the technique of comparison and contrast.

The educational significance of the technique is to encourage you to make connections—*one of the most important aspects of productive thought*. As long as things *seem* different and disconnected they in fact *are* different and disconnected. In practice, they are two separate and distinct entities. But when you can demonstrate that they have similarities and connections, then you can make relationships clear. You are in a position both to stress points of likeness and also to emphasize just what makes things distinct and unique. For all these reasons, it is vital for you to find similarities and differences through the technique of comparison and contrast. In a very real sense, the language of comparison and contrast is also the language of active and creative thinking.

The immediate goal of a comparison-contrast essay on literary works is to compare and contrast different authors; two or more works by the same author; different drafts of the same work; or characters, incidents, techniques, and ideas in the same work or in a number of separate works. Developing a comparison-contrast analysis enables you to study works in perspective. No matter what works you consider together, the method helps you get at the essence of a work or writer. Similarities are brought out by comparison; differences, by contrast. In other words, you can enhance your understanding of what a thing *is* by using comparison-contrast to determine what it *is not*.

For example, our understanding of Shakespeare's Sonnet 30, "When to the Sessions of Sweet Silent Thought" (Chapter 14), can be augmented if we compare it with Denise Levertov's poem "A Time Past" (Chapter 13). Both poems treat recollections of past experiences told by a speaker to a listener, and we as readers become, as it were, witnesses to the poems. Both poems refer to persons, dead or absent, with whom the speakers were closely involved. In these respects, the poems are comparable.

In addition to these similarities, there are significant differences. Shakespeare's speaker numbers the dead persons as friends whom he laments generally. Levertov's speaker refers to a number of vanished people, but her major focus is on one person with whom she had been in love—her husband—whose sight at one time made her joyful and happy. Levertov's topics are the sorrow of past memory and lost love, the inexorable power of change, and the causes of isolation and regret. Shakespeare refers to dead friends as a way of accounting for present sorrows, but then his speaker turns to the present and asserts that thinking about the "dear friend" being addressed enables him to restore past "losses" and end all "sorrows." In Levertov's poem, there is recognition of both past and present, but no reconciliation. Instead the speaker focuses on the unpleasantness and distastefulness of the changes that time has wrought. Both poems are similarly retrospective, but they differ widely in their conclusions of how the present has been altered by the past.

# Guidelines for the Comparison-Contrast Method

The preceding example, although brief, shows how the comparison-contrast method makes it possible to identify leading similarities and distinguishing differences in two works. Frequently you can overcome the difficulties you might encounter in understanding one work by comparing and contrasting it with another work on a comparable subject. A few guidelines will help direct your efforts in writing comparison-contrast essays.

## Clarify Your Intention

When planning a comparison-contrast essay, first decide on your goal, for you can use the method in a number of ways. One objective is the equal and mutual illumination of two (or more) works. For example, an essay comparing Welty's "A Worn Path" (Chapter 2) with Hawthorne's "Young Goodman Brown" (Chapter 8) might be designed to (1) compare ideas, characters, or methods in these stories equally, without stressing or favoring either. You might also (2) emphasize "Young Goodman Brown," and therefore you would use "A Worn Path" as material for highlighting Hawthorne's story. Or, instead, you could (3) illustrate the superiority of one story over another, or (4) emphasize a method or idea that you think is especially noteworthy or appropriate.

A first task, therefore, is to decide what to emphasize. The illustrative essay on pages 1418–1421 gives "equal time" to both works being considered, without claiming the superiority of either. Unless you have a different rhetorical goal, this essay provides a suitable example for most comparisons.

## Find Common Grounds for Comparison

The second stage in preparing a comparison-contrast essay is to select and articulate a common ground for discussion. It is pointless to compare dissimilar things, for the resulting conclusions will not have much value. Instead, compare like with like: idea with idea, characterization with characterization, setting with setting, point of view with point of view, tone with tone. Nothing much can be learned from a comparison of Frost's view of individuality and Chekhov's view of love; but a comparison of the relationship of individuality with identity and character in Frost and Chekhov suggests common ground, with the promise of significant ideas to be developed through the examination of similarities and differences.

In seeking common ground, you will need to be inventive and creative. For instance, if you compare Maupassant's "The Necklace" (Chapter 1) and Chekhov's *The Bear* (Chapter 20), these two works at first may seem dissimilar. Yet common ground can be discovered, such as the treatment of self-deceit, the effects of chance on human affairs, and the authors' views of women. Although other works may seem even more dissimilar than these, it is usually possible to find a common ground for comparison and contrast. Much of your success in an essay of this type depends on your finding a workable basis—a common denominator—for comparison.

## Integrate the Bases of Comparison

Let us assume that you have decided on your rhetorical purpose and on the basis or bases of your comparison. You have done your reading and taken notes, and you have a rough idea of what you want to say. The remaining problem is the treatment of your material.

One method is to make your points first about one work and then about the other. Unfortunately, such a comparison makes your paper seem like two separate lumps. ("Work 1" takes up one half of your paper to make one lump, and "Work 2" takes up the other half to make a second lump.) Also, the method involves repetition because you must repeat many points when you treat the second subject.

Therefore, a better method is to treat the major aspects of your main idea and to refer to the two (or more) works as they support your arguments. Thus you refer constantly to *both* works, sometimes within the same sentence, and remind your reader of the point of your discussion. There are reasons for the superiority of this method: (1) You do not repeat your points needlessly, for you develop them as you raise them. (2) By constantly referring to the two works, you make your points without requiring a reader with a poor memory to reread previous sections.

As a model, here is a paragraph on "Natural References as a Basis of Comparison in Frost's 'Desert Places' and Shakespeare's Sonnet 73: 'That Time of Year Thou May'st in Me Behold'" (both poems are in Chapter 16). The virtue of the paragraph is that it uses material from each of the poems simultaneously as the substance for the development of the ideas, as nearly as the time sequence of sentences allows.

> (1) Both Shakespeare and Frost link their ideas to events occurring in the natural world. (2) Night as a parallel with death is common to both poems, with Frost speaking about it in his first line and Shakespeare introducing it in his seventh. (3) Along with night, Frost emphasizes the onset of winter and snow as a time of death and desolation. (4) With this natural description, Frost also symbolically refers to empty, secret, dead places in the inner spirit—crannies of the soul where bleak winter snowfalls correspond to selfishness and indifference. (5) By contrast, Shakespeare uses the fall season, with the yellowing and dropping of leaves and the migrations of birds, to stress the closeness of real death and therefore the need to love fully during the time remaining. (6) Both poems thus share a sense of gloom because both present death as inevitable and final, just like the emptiness of winter. (7) Because Shakespeare's sonnet is addressed to a listener who is also a loved

one, however, it is more outgoing than the more introspective poem of Frost. (8) Frost turns the snow, the night, and the emptiness of the universe inward in order to show the speaker's inner bleakness, and by extension, the bleakness of many human spirits. (9) Shakespeare instead uses the bleakness of seasons, night, and dying fires to state the need for loving "well." The poems thus use common and similar references for different purposes and effects.

This paragraph links Shakespeare's references to nature to those of Frost. Five sentences speak of both authors together; three speak of Frost alone and two of Shakespeare alone, but all the sentences are unified topically. This interweaving of references indicates that the writer has learned both poems well enough to consider them together, and it also enables the writing to be more pointed and succinct than if the works were separately treated.

You can learn from this example: If you develop your essay by putting your two subjects constantly together, you will write economically and pointedly (not only for essays but also for tests). Beyond that, if you digest the material as successfully as this method indicates, you demonstrate that you are fulfilling a major educational goal—the assimilation and *use* of material. Too often, because you learn things separately (in separate works and courses, at separate times), you tend also to compartmentalize them. Instead, you should always try to relate them, to *synthesize* them. Comparison and contrast help in this process of putting together, of seeing things not as fragments but as parts of wholes.

## Avoid the Tennis-Ball Method

As you make your comparison, do not confuse an interlocking method with a "tennisball" method, in which you bounce your subject back and forth constantly and repetitively, almost as though you were hitting observations back and forth over a net. The tennis-ball method is shown in the following example from a comparison of the characters Mathilde (Maupassant's "The Necklace") and Mrs. Popov (Chekhov's *The Bear*).

> Mathilde is a young married woman; Mrs. Popov is also young but a widow. Mathilde has a limited social life, and she doesn't have more than one friend; Mrs. Popov chooses to lead a life of solitude. Mathilde's daydreams about wealth are responsible for her misfortune, and Mrs. Popov's dedication to the memory of her husband is capable of ruining her life. Mathilde is made unhappy because of her shortcomings, but Mrs. Popov is rescued despite her shortcomings. In Mathilde's case the focus is on adversity not only causing trouble but also strengthening character. Similarly, in Mrs. Popov's case, the focus is on a strong person realizing her strength regardless of her conscious decision to weaken herself.

Imagine the effect of an entire essay written in this invariable 1, 2, 1, 2, 1, 2 order. Aside from the inflexible patterning of subjects, the tennis-ball method does not permit much illustrative development. You should not feel so constrained that you cannot take two or more sentences to develop a point about one writer or subject before you include comparative references to another. If you remember to interlock the two subjects of comparison, however, as in the paragraph about Frost and Shakespeare, your method will give you the freedom to develop your topics fully.

# The Extended Comparison-Contrast Essay

For a longer essay about a number of works—such as a limited research paper, comprehensive exam questions, and the sort of extended essay required at the end of a semester—comparison-contrast is an essential method. You may wish to compare the works on the basis of elements such as ideas, plot, language, structure, character, metaphor, point of view, or setting. Because of the larger number of works, however, you will need to modify the way in which you employ comparison-contrast. Suppose you are dealing with not just two works but with six, seven, or more. You need first to find a common ground to use as your central, unifying idea, just as you do for a comparison of only two works. Once you establish the common ground, you can classify or group your works on the basis of the similarities and differences they exemplify with regard to the topic. The idea is to get two *groups* for comparison, not just two works.

Let us assume that three or four works treat a topic in one way but that two or three do it in another (e.g., either criticism or praise of wealth and trade, the joys or sorrows of love, the enthusiasm of youth, gratitude for life, or the disillusionment of age). In writing about these works, you might treat the topic itself in a straightforward comparison-contrast method but use details from the works within the groupings as the material that you use for illustration and argument.

To make your essay as specific as possible, it is best to stress only a small number of works with each of your subpoints. Once you have established these points, there is no need to go into abundant detail with all the other works you are studying. Instead, you need to make no more than brief references to the other works, for your purpose should be to strengthen your points without creating more and more examples. Once you go to another subpoint, you should then use different works for illustration, so that by the end of your essay, you will have given due attention to each work in your assignment. In this way—by treating many works in small comparative groups—you can keep your essay reasonably brief, for there is no need to go into unproductive detail.

For illustration, the illustrative essay on pages 1422–1425 shows how this grouping may be done. In the first part of the body of this essay, six works are used comparatively to show how private needs conflict with social, public demands. The next part shows how three works can be compared and contrasted on the basis of how they treat the topic of public concerns as expressed through law.

---

## CITING REFERENCES IN A LONGER COMPARISON-CONTRAST ESSAY

For the longer comparison-contrast essay, you may find a problem in making references to many different works. Generally you do not need to repeat references. For example, if you refer to Louise of Chopin's "The Story of an Hour" (Chapter 7) or to Minnie Wright of Glaspell's *Trifles* (Chapter 20), you should make the full references only once and then refer later just to the character, story, or author, according to your needs.

When you quote lines or passages or when you cite actions or characters in special ways, you should use parenthetical line, speech, or paragraph references, as in the illustrative essay on pages 1422–1425. Be guided by the following principle: If you make a specific reference that you think your reader might want to examine in more detail, supply the line, speech, or paragraph number. If you refer to minor details that might easily be unnoticed or forgotten, also supply the appropriate number. Your intention should be to include the appropriate locating numbers whenever you are in doubt about references.

## WRITING A COMPARISON-CONTRAST ESSAY

In planning your essay, you should first narrow and simplify your topic so that you can handle it conveniently. If your subject is a comparison of two poets (as in the illustrative comparison-contrast essay on Lowell and Owen, p. 1418), choose one or two of each poet's poems on the same or a similar topic, and write your essay about these.

Once you have found an organizing principle, along with the relevant works, begin to refine and to focus the direction of your essay. As you study each work, note common or contrasting elements and use these to form your central idea. At the same time, you can select the most illustrative works and classify them according to your topic, such as war, love, work, faithfulness, or self-analysis.

### Strategies for Organizing Ideas

Begin by stating the works, authors, characters, or ideas that you are considering; then show how you have narrowed the topic. Your central idea should briefly highlight the principal grounds of comparison and contrast, such as that both works treat a common topic, exhibit a similar idea, use a similar form, or develop an identical attitude, and also that major or minor differences help make the works unique. You may also assert that one work is superior to the other, if you wish to make this judgment and defend it.

The body of your essay is governed by the works and your basis of comparison (presentations of ideas, depictions of character, uses of setting, qualities of style and tone, uses of poetic form, uses of comparable imagery or symbols, uses of point of view, and so on). For a comparison-contrast treatment on such a basis, your goal should be to shed light on both (or more) of the works you are treating. For example, you might examine stories written in the first-person point of view (see Chapter 3). An essay on this topic might compare the ways in which each author uses point of view to achieve similar or distinct effects; or it might compare poems that employ similar images, symbols, or ironic methods. Sometimes, the process can be as simple as identifying female or male protagonists and comparing the ways in which their characters are developed. Another obvious approach is to compare the *subjects*, as opposed to the *idea*. You might identify works dealing with general subjects such as love, death, youth, race, or war. Such groupings provide a basis for excellent comparisons and contrasts.

As you develop your essay, remember to keep comparison-contrast foremost. That is, your discussions of point of view, figurative language, or whatever should not so much explain these topics *as topics* but rather should explore *similarities and differences* of the works you are comparing. If your topic is an idea, for example, you need to explain the idea, but just enough to establish points of similarity or difference. As you develop such an essay, you might illustrate your arguments by referring to related uses of elements such as setting, characterization, symbolism, point of view, or metaphor. When you introduce these new subjects, you will be on target as long as you use them in the context of comparison-contrast.

In concluding, you might reflect on other ideas or techniques in the works you have compared, make observations about similar qualities, or summarize briefly the grounds of your comparison. If there is a point you have considered especially important, you might stress that point again in your conclusion. Also, your comparison might have led you to conclude that one work—or group of works—is superior to another. Stressing that point again would make an effective conclusion.

## Illustrative Student Essay (Two Works)

Underlined sentences in this paper *do not* conform to MLA style and are used solely as teaching tools to emphasize the central idea, thesis sentence, and topic sentences throughout the paper.

Mane 1

Marcelino Mane

Professor Park

English 123

6 May 2007

**The Treatment of Responses to War in Amy Lowell's**

**"Patterns" and Wilfred Owen's "Anthem for Doomed Youth"°**

[1]     Lowell's "Patterns" and Owen's "Anthem for Doomed Youth" are both powerful and unique condemnations of war.* Owen's short poem speaks broadly and generally about the ugliness of war and also about large groups of sorrowful people. Lowell's longer poem focuses on the personal grief of just one person. In a sense, Lowell's

---

°See Chapters 13 and 19 for these poems.
*Central idea.

poem begins where Owen's ends, a fact that accounts for both the similarities and the differences between the two works. <u>The anti-war themes can be compared on the basis of their subjects, their lengths, their concreteness, and their use of a common metaphor.</u>[†]

[2]     <u>"Anthem for Doomed Youth" attacks war more directly than "Patterns."</u> Owen's opening line "What passing-bells for those who die as cattle?" suggests that in war human beings are depersonalized before they are slaughtered, like so much meat, and his observations about the "monstrous" guns and the "shrill, demented" shells unambiguously condemn the horrors of war. By contrast, in "Patterns," warfare is far away, on another continent, intruding only when the messenger delivers the letter stating that the speaker's fiancé has been killed (lines 63–64). A comparable situation governs the last six lines of Owen's poem, quietly describing how those at home respond to the news that their loved ones have died in war. Thus the antiwar focus in "Patterns" is the contrast between the calm, peaceful life of the speaker's garden and the anguish of her responses. In "Anthem for Doomed Youth," the stress is more on the external horrors of war that bring about the need for ceremonies honoring the dead.

[3]     <u>Another major difference between the poems is their wide discrepancy in length</u>. "Patterns" is an interior monologue or meditation of 107 lines, but it could not be shorter and still be convincing. In the poem the speaker thinks of the past and contemplates her future loneliness. Her final outburst, "Christ! What are patterns for?" could make no sense if she did not explain her situation as extensively as she does. "Anthem for Doomed Youth," however, is brief—a 14-line sonnet—because it is more general and less personal than "Patterns." Although Owen's speaker shows great sympathy, he or she views the sorrows of others distantly, unlike Lowell, who goes right into the mind and spirit of the grieving woman. Owen's use, in his last six lines, of phrases such as "tenderness of patient minds" and "drawing down of blinds" is a powerful representation of deep grief. He gives no further details even though thousands of individual stories might be told. In contrast, Lowell tells just one of these stories as she focuses on her solitary speaker's lost hopes and dreams. Thus the contrasting lengths of the poems are determined by each poet's treatment of the topic.

[4]     <u>Despite these differences of approach and length, both poems are similarly concrete and real</u>. Owen moves from the real scenes and sounds of far-off battlefields to

---

[†]Thesis sentence.

the homes of the many soldiers who have been killed in battle, but Lowell's scene is a single place—the garden of her speaker's estate. The speaker walks on real gravel along garden paths that contain daffodils, squills, a fountain, and a lime tree. She thinks of her clothing and her ribboned shoes, and also of her fiancé's boots, sword hilts, and buttons. The images in Owen's poem are equally real but are not associated with individuals as in "Patterns." Thus Owen's images are those of cattle, bells, rifle shots, shells, bugles, candles, and window blinds. Although both poems reflect reality, Owen's details are more general and public; Lowell's are more specific and intimate.

[5]     Along with this concreteness, the poems share a major metaphor: that cultural patterns both control and frustrate human wishes and hopes. In "Patterns," this metaphor is shown in warfare itself (line 106), which is the pinnacle of organized human patterns of destruction. Further examples of the metaphor are found in details about clothing (particularly the speaker's stiff, confining gown in lines 5, 18, 21, 73, and 101, and also the lover's military boots in lines 46 and 49); the orderly, formal garden paths in which the speaker is walking (lines 1 and 93); her restraint at hearing about her lover's death; and her courtesy, despite her grief, in ordering refreshment for the messenger (line 69). Within such rigid patterns, her hopes for happiness have vanished, along with the sensuous spontaneity symbolized by her lover's hope to make love to her on a "shady seat" in the garden (lines 85–89). The metaphor of the constricting pattern is also seen in "Anthem for Doomed Youth," except that in this poem, the pattern is the funeral, not love or marriage. Owen's speaker contrasts the calm, peaceful tolling of "passing-bells" (line 1) to the frightening sounds of war represented by the "monstrous anger of the guns," "the stuttering rifles' rapid rattle," and "the demented choirs of wailing shells" (lines 2–8). Thus, while Lowell uses the metaphor to reveal the irony of hope and desire being destroyed by war, Owen uses it to reveal the irony of war's negation of peaceful ceremonies.

[6]     Though in these ways the poems share topics and some aspects of treatment, they are distinct and individual. "Patterns" includes many references to visible things, whereas "Anthem for Doomed Youth" emphasizes sound (and silence). Both poems conclude on powerfully emotional although different notes. Owen's poem dwells on the pathos and sadness that war brings to many unnamed people, and Lowell's expresses the most intimate thoughts of a woman who is alone in her first agony of grief. Although neither poem attacks the usual platitudes and justifications for war (the needs

Mane 4

to mobilize, to sacrifice, to achieve peace through fighting, and so on), the attack is there by implication, for both poems make their appeal by stressing how war destroys the relationships that make life worth living. For this reason, despite their differences, both "Patterns" and "Anthem for Doomed Youth" are parallel anti-war poems, and both are strong expressions of feeling.

Mane 5

**WORK CITED**

Amy Lowell, "Patterns," and Wilfred Owen, "Anthem for Doomed Youth." *Literature: An Introduction to Reading and Writing*. 4th Compact ed. Ed. Edgar V. Roberts. Upper Saddle River: Prentice Hall, 2008, 531, 825.

## Commentary on the Essay

This essay shows how approximately equal attention can be given to the two works being studied. Words stressing similarity are *common, share, equally, parallel, both, similar,* and *also*. Contrasts are stressed by *while, whereas, different, dissimilar, contrast, although,* and *except*. Transitions from paragraph to paragraph are not different in this type of essay from those in other essays. Thus, the phrases *despite, along with this,* and *in these ways,* which are used here, could be used anywhere for the same transitional purpose.

The central idea—that the poems mutually condemn war—is brought out in paragraph 1, together with the supporting idea that the poems blend into each other because both show responses to news of battle casualties.

Paragraph 2, the first in the body, discusses how each poem brings out its attack on warfare. Paragraph 3 explains the differing lengths of the poems as a function of differences in perspective. Because Owen's sonnet views war and its effects at a distance, it is brief; but because Lowell's interior monologue views death intimately, it needs more detail and greater length.

Paragraph 4, on the topic of concreteness and reality, shows that the two works can receive equal attention without the bouncing back and forth of the tennis-ball method. Three of the sentences in this paragraph (3, 4, and 6) are devoted exclusively to details in one poem or the other; but sentences 1, 2, 5, and 7 refer to both works, stressing points of broad or specific comparison. The scheme demonstrates that the two works are, in effect, interlocked within the paragraph.

Paragraph 5, the last in the body, considers the similar and dissimilar ways in which the poems treat the common metaphor of cultural patterns.

The conclusion, paragraph 6, summarizes the central idea, and it also stresses the ways in which the two poems, although similar, are distinct and unique.

## Illustrative Student Essay #2 (Extended Comparison-Contrast)

Underlined sentences in this paper *do not* conform to MLA style and are used solely as teaching tools to emphasize the central idea, thesis sentence, and topic sentences throughout the paper.

Mane 1

Marcelino Mane

Professor Park

English 123

6 May 2007

**Literary Treatments of the Conflicts between Private and Public Life**

[1]     The conflict between private or personal life, on the one hand, and public or civic and national life, on the other, is a topic common to many literary works.* Authors show that individuals try to maintain their personal lives and commitments even though they are tested and stressed by public and external forces. Ideally, individuals should have the freedom to follow their own wishes independently of the outside world. It is a fact, however, that living itself causes people to venture into the public world and therefore to encounter conflicts. Getting married, following a profession, observing the natural world, looking at a person's possessions, taking a walk—all these draw people into the public world in which rules, regulations, and laws override private wishes. To greater and lesser degrees, such conflicts are found in Arnold's "Dover Beach," Bierce's "An Occurrence at Owl Creek Bridge," Chekhov's *The Bear*, Glaspell's *Trifles*, Chopin's "The Story of an Hour," Hardy's "Channel Firing," Hawthorne's "Young Goodman Brown," Keats's "Bright Star," Lowell's "Patterns," and Shakespeare's Sonnet 73: "That Time of Year Thou May'st in Me Behold."[1] In these works, conflicts are shown between interests of individuals and those of the social, legal, and military public.†

[2]     One of the major private-public conflicts is created by the way in which characters respond to social conventions and expectations. In Chekhov's *The Bear*, for example, Mrs. Popov has given up her personal life to memorialize her dead husband. She wears

---

*Central idea.
[1]See Chapters 19, 2, 20, 20, 7, 13, 8, 14, 19, and 16 for these works.
†Thesis sentence.

Mane 2

black, stays in her house for a whole year, and swears eternal fidelity; and she does all this to fulfill what she considers her public role as a grieving widow. Fortunately for her, Smirnov arrives on the scene and arouses her enough to make her give up this deadly pose. Not as fortunate is Hawthorne's Goodman Brown in "Young Goodman Brown." Brown's obligation is much less public and also more philosophical than Mrs. Popov's because his religiously inspired vision of evil fills him with lifelong gloom. Although Mrs. Popov is easily moved away from her position by the prospect of immediate life and vitality, Brown's mindless distrust locks him into a fear of evil from which not even his faithful wife can shake him. The two characters therefore go in entirely different directions—one toward personal fulfillment, the other toward personal destruction.

[3]    A major idea in the various works is that philosophical or religious difficulties such as those of Goodman Brown force a crisis in an individual life. In Arnold's "Dover Beach" the speaker expresses regret about uncertainty and the loss of religious faith that symbolically wear away civilization just like surf beating on the stones of Dover Beach. This situation might be expected to make a person as dreary and depressed as Goodman Brown actually is. Arnold's speaker, however, in the lines "Ah, love, let us be true/To one another," finds power in personal fidelity and commitment (lines 29–30). In other words, the public world of "human misery" and the diminishing "Sea of Faith" is beyond control, and therefore all that is left is personal commitment. This is not to say that "Young Goodman Brown," as a story, is negative, for Hawthorne implies that a positive personal life lies in the denial of choices like those made by Brown and in the acceptance of choices like those made by Mrs. Popov and Arnold's speaker. It is only fair, however, to observe that Hawthorne does not state this idea directly.

[4]    To deny or to ignore the public world is a possible option that, under some circumstances, can be chosen. For example, "Dover Beach" reflects a conscious decision to ignore the philosophic and religious uncertainty that the speaker finds in the intellectual and public world. Even more independent of such a public world, Shakespeare's "That Time of Year" and Keats's "Bright Star" bring out their ideas as reflections on purely personal situations. Shakespeare's speaker deals with the love between himself and the listener, whereas Keats's speaker, addressing a distant star, considers his need for steadfastness in his relationship with his "fair love." Louise in Chopin's "The Story of an Hour" embodies an interesting variation on the personal matters brought up in these two sonnets. At first, Louise is crushed by the news coming from the public world that her

husband has been killed. Her first vision of herself is that of a grieving, private widow. As she thinks about things, however, she quickly begins to anticipate the liberation and freedom—to become free to explore the public world—that widowhood will give her. Ironically, it is the reappearance of her husband, who moves freely in the public world, that causes her sudden heart failure. What she looked forward to as the possibility of free choice to do what she wants and go where she wishes has suddenly been withdrawn from her by her renewed status within the publicly sanctioned system of marriage, and it is her recognition of her abrupt loss of this possibility that triggers the end of her life.

[5]     The complexity of the conflicts between private and public life is brought out in the way in which structures secure their power through law and legality. With immense power, the law often acts as an arbitrary form of public judgment that disregards personal needs and circumstances. This idea is brought out on the most personal level in Glaspell's *Trifles*, in which the two major characters, both women, urgently confront the conflict between their personal identification with the accused woman, Minnie, and their public obligation to the law. One of the women, Mrs. Peters, is reminded that she is "married to the law," but she and Mrs. Hale suppress the evidence that they know would condemn Minnie, even though technically—by law, that is—their knowledge is public property. Their way of resolving the conflict is therefore to reject public demands in favor of accepting personal concerns.

[6]     It is works about warfare that especially highlight how irreconcilable the conflicts between personal and public concerns can become. A comic but nevertheless real instance is dramatized by Hardy in "Channel Firing." In this poem, set in a church graveyard, the skeleton of "Parson Thirdly" views "gunnery practice out at sea" (line 10) as evidence that his "forty year" dedication to serving his church was a waste of time. His conclusion is that he would have been better off ignoring his public role and instead sticking "to pipes and beer." Although Thirdly is disillusioned, he has not been as deeply affected personally by warfare as the speaker of Lowell's "Patterns." Her fiancé, she learns, has been killed fighting abroad; and his death leads her to question— and by implication to doubt—the external "patterns" that destroy one's personal plans for life (line 107). Unlike both these characters, who are deeply touched by the effects of warfare, Peyton Farquhar, the main character in Bierce's "An Occurrence at Owl Creek Bridge," is actually killed by his commitment to a public concern—that of the

Mane 4

Southern forces in the Civil War. As in "Channel Firing" and "Patterns," Farquhar's situation shows the absolute power of the public world over the private.

[7]      The works examined here are in general agreement that, under ideal conditions, private life should be supreme over public life. They also demonstrate that in many ways, the public world invades the private world with a wide range of effects, from making people behave foolishly to destroying them utterly. Naturally, the tone of the works is shaped by the degree of seriousness of the conflict. Chekhov's *The Bear* is good-humored and farcical because the characters overcome the social roles in which they are cast. More sober are works such as "Dover Beach" and "Young Goodman Brown," in which characters either are overcome by public commitments or deliberately turn their backs on them. In the highest range of seriousness are works such as "Patterns," and "An Occurrence at Owl Creek Bridge," in which the individual is crushed by irresistible public forces. <u>The works compared and contrasted here show varied and powerful conflicts between public demands and personal interests</u>.

Mane 5

**WORKS CITED**

Selected Works. *Literature: An Introduction to Reading and Writing.* Ed. Edgar V. Roberts and Henry E. Jacobs. 8th ed. Upper Saddle River: Prentice Hall, 2008, Chapters 2, 7, 8, 13, 14, 16, and 19.

## Commentary on the Essay

This essay, combining for discussion the genres of fiction, poetry, and drama, is visualized as an assignment at the end of a unit of study. The expectation prompting the assignment is that a fairly large number of literary works can be profitably compared on the basis of a unifying subject, idea, or technique. For this essay, the works—five poems, three stories, and two sort plays—are compared and contrasted on the common topic of private-public conflicts. It is obviously impossible to discuss all the works in detail in every paragraph. The essay therefore demonstrates that a writer may introduce a large number of works in a straightforward comparison-contrast method without a need for detailed comparison of each work with every other work on each of the major subtopics (social, legal, military).

Thus, the first section, consisting of paragraphs 2–4, treats six of the works. In paragraph 2, however, only two works are discussed, and in paragraph 3 one of these works is carried over for comparison with only one additional work. The fourth paragraph springs out of the second, utilizing one of the works discussed there and then bringing out comparisons with three additional works.

The same technique is used in the rest of the essay. Paragraph 5 introduces only one work; paragraph 6 introduces two additional works; and paragraph 7 introduces three works for comparison and contrast. Each of the ten works is therefore discussed at least once in terms of how it contributes to the major topic. One might note that the essay concentrates on a relatively small number of the works, such as Chekhov's *The Bear* and Hawthorne's "Young Goodman Brown," but that as newer topics are introduced, the essay goes on to works that are more closely connected to these topics.

The technique of extended comparison-contrast used in this way shows how the various works can be defined and distinguished in relation to the common idea. The concluding paragraph summarizes these distinctions by suggesting a continuous line along which each of the works may be placed.

Even so, the treatment of so many texts might easily cause crowding and confusion. The division of the major topic into subtopics, as noted, is a major means of trying to make the essay easy to follow. An additional means is the introduction of transitional words and phrases such as *also, choose,* and *one of the major conflicts.*

An extended comparison-contrast essay cannot present a full treatment of each of the works. The works are unique, and there are many elements that do not yield to the comparison-contrast method. Ideas that are particularly important in Hardy's "Channel Firing," for example, are (1) that human beings need eternal rest and not eternal life, (2) that God is amused by—or indifferent to—human affairs, (3) that religious callings or vocations may be futile, and (4) that war itself is the supreme form of cruelty. All these topics could be treated in another essay, but they do not pertain to the particular goals of this particular illustrative essay. A topic compatible with the general private-public topic is needed, and the connection is readily made (paragraph 6) through the character of Hardy's Parson Thirdly. Because the essay deals with the conflicts brought out by Thirdly's comments, Hardy's poem is linked to all the other works for comparative purposes. So it is with the other works, each of which could also be the subject of analysis from many standpoints other than comparison-contrast. The effect of the comparison of all the works collectively, however, is the enhanced understanding of each of the works separately. To achieve such an understanding and to explain it are the major goals of the extended comparison-contrast method.

## Topics for Writing Comparison and Contrast Essays

1. The use of the speaker in Arnold's "Dover Beach" (p. 793) and Hardy's "Channel Firing" (p. 541).

2. The description of fidelity to love in Keats's "Bright Star" (p. 565) and Shakespeare's Sonnet 73: "That Time of Year Thou May'st in Me Behold" (p. 680), Arnold's "Dover Beach" (p. 793), or Lowell's "Patterns" (p. 825).

3. The view of women in Chekhov's *The Bear* (p. 1156) and Maupassant's "The Necklace" (p. 4) or in Glaspell's *Trifles* (p. 892) and O'Neill's "Before Breakfast" (p. 909).

4. The use of descriptive scenery in Hawthorne's "Young Goodman Brown" (p. 331) and Lowell's "Patterns" (p. 825) or in Poe's "The Masque of the Red Death" (p. 233) and Bierce's "An Occurrence at Owl Creek Bridge" (p. 69).

5. Symbols of disapproval in Hardy's "Channel Firing" (p. 541) and Frost's "Desert Places" (p. 665).

6. The treatment of loss in Lowell's "Patterns" (p. 825) and Wagner's "The Boxes" (p. 847).

7. Treatments of religion in "Spring" by Hopkins (p. 544) and "Batter My Heart" by Donne (p. 508).

8. Any of the foregoing topics applied to a number of separate works. Please consult the Topical and Thematic Table of Contents (p. xxxix) for convenient additional subjects.

# Chapter 26

# Taking Examinations
# on Literature

Succeeding on a literature examination is largely a result of intelligent and skillful preparation. Preparation means that you (1) study the material assigned, in conjunction with the comments made in class by your instructor and by fellow students in discussion; (2) develop and reinforce your own thoughts; (3) anticipate exam questions by creating and answering your own practice questions; and (4) understand the precise function of the test.

First, realize that the test is not designed either to trap you or to hold down your grade. The grade you receive is a reflection of your achievement in the course. If your grades are high, congratulations; keep doing what you have been doing. If your grades are low, however, you can improve them through diligent and systematic study. Those students who can easily do satisfactory work might do superior work if they improved their habits of study and preparation. From whatever level you begin, *you can increase your achievement by improving your study methods.*

Your instructor has three major concerns in evaluating your tests (assuming the correct use of English): (1) to assess the extent of your command over the subject material of the course (How good is your retention?); (2) to assess how well you respond to a question or deal with an issue (How well do you separate the important from the unimportant?); and (3) to assess how well you draw conclusions about the material (How well are you educating yourself?).

## Answer the Questions That Are Asked

Many elements go into writing good answers on tests, but *responsiveness* is the most important. A major cause of low exam grades is that students *often do not answer the questions asked.* Does that failure seem surprising? The problem is that some students do no more than retell a story or restate an argument, but they do not zero in on the issues in the question. This problem is not uncommon. Therefore, if you are asked, "Why does . . . ?," be sure to emphasize the *why* and use the *does* primarily to exemplify the *why.* If the question is about *organization,* focus on organization. If the question is about the *interpretation* of an idea, deal with the interpretation of the idea. In short, *always respond directly to the question or instruction.* Answer what is asked. Compare the following two answers to the same question.

**Question:** How is the setting of Ambrose Bierce's "An Occurrence at Owl Creek Bridge" (Chapter 2) important in the story's development?

## ANSWER A

The setting of Bierce's "An Occurrence at Owl Creek Bridge" is a major element in the story's development. The first scene is on a railroad bridge in northern Alabama, and the action is that a man, Peyton Farquhar, is about to be hanged. He is a southerner who has been surrounded and captured by Union soldiers. They are ready to string him up and they have the guns and power, so he cannot escape. He is so scared that his own watch seems to sound loudly and slowly, like a cannon. He also thinks about how he might escape, once he is hanged, by freeing his hands and throwing off the noose that will soon be choking and killing him. The scene shifts to the week before, at Farquhar's plantation. A Union spy deceives Farquhar, thereby tempting him to try to sabotage the Union efforts to keep the railroad open. Because the spy tells Farquhar about the punishment, the reader assumes that Farquhar had tried to sabotage the bridge, was caught, and now is going to be hanged. The third scene is also at the bridge, but it is about what Farquhar sees and thinks in his own mind: He imagines that he has been hanged and then escapes. He thinks he falls into the creek, frees himself from the ropes, and makes it to shore, from which he makes the long walk home. His final vision is of his wife coming out of the house to meet him, with everything looking beautiful in the morning sunshine. Then we find out that all this was just in his mind, because we are back on the bridge, from which Farquhar is swinging, hanged, dead, with a broken neck.

## ANSWER B

The setting of Bierce's "An Occurrence at Owl Creek Bridge" is a major element in the story's development. The railroad bridge in northern Alabama, from which the doomed Peyton Farquhar will be hanged, is a frame for the story. The bridge, which begins as a real-life bridge in the first scene, becomes the bridge that the dying man imagines in the third. In between there is a brief scene at Farquhar's home, which took place a week before. The setting thus marks the progression of Farquhar's dying vision. He begins to distort and slow down reality—at the real bridge—when he realizes that there is no escape. The first indication of this distortion is that his watch seems to be ticking as slowly as a blacksmith's hammer. Once he is dropped from the bridge to be hanged, his perceptions slow down time so much that he imagines his complete escape before his death: falling into the water, freeing himself, being shot at, getting to shore, walking through a darkening forest, and returning home in beautiful morning sunshine. The final sentence of the story brutally restores the real situation at the railroad bridge and makes clear that Farquhar is hanging from it and is actually dead despite his imaginings. In all respects, therefore, the setting is essential to the story's development.

Answer A begins well and introduces important details of the story's setting, but it does not answer the question because it does not show how the details figure into the story's development. On the other hand, answer B focuses directly on the connection between the locations and the changes in the protagonist's perceptions. Because of this emphasis, B answers the question and is also shorter than A (287 words to 221); with the focus directly on the issue, there is no need for irrelevant narrative details. Thus, A is unresponsive and unnecessarily long, whereas B is responsive and includes details only if they exemplify the major points.

# Systematic Preparation

Your challenge is how best to prepare yourself to have a knowledgeable and ready mind at examination time. If you simply cram facts into your head for the test in the hope that you can adjust to the questions, you will likely flounder. You need a systematic approach.

## Read and Reread the Material on Which You Are to Be Examined

Above all, recognize that your preparation should begin as soon as the course begins, not on the night before the exam. Complete each assignment by the date it is due, for you will understand the classroom discussion only if you know the material (see also the guides for study in Chapter 1, pp. 11–12). Then, about a week before the exam, review each assignment, preferably rereading everything completely. If particular passages were read and discussed in class, make a special point of studying the passages and referring to the notes you took at the time of the discussions. With this preparation, your study on the night before the exam will be fruitful because it is the climax of your preparation, not your entire preparation.

## Construct Your Own Questions: Go on the Attack

To prepare yourself well for an exam, read *actively*, not passively. Read with a goal, and *go on the attack* by anticipating test conditions—creating and answering your own practice questions. Don't waste time, however, in trying to guess the questions you think your instructor might ask. Guessing correctly might happen (and wouldn't you be happy if it did?) but do not turn your study into a game of chance. Instead, arrange the subject matter by asking yourself questions that help you get things straight.

How can you construct your own questions? It is not as hard as you might think. Your instructor may have announced certain topics or ideas to be tested on the exam, and you might develop questions from these, or you might apply general questions to the specifics of your assignments, as in the following examples.

**1. Ideas about a character and the interactions of characters** (see also Chapter 4). What is character *A* like? How does *A* grow or change in the work? What does *A* learn or not learn that brings about the conclusion? To what degree does *A* represent a type or an idea? How does character *B* influence *A*? Does a change in character *C* bring about any corresponding change in *A*?

**2. Ideas about technical and structural questions.** These can be broad, covering everything from point of view (Chapter 3) to poetic form (Chapter 16). The best guide here is to study those technical aspects that have been discussed in class, for it is unlikely that you will be asked to go beyond the levels considered in classroom discussion.

**3. Ideas about events or situations.** What relationship does episode *A* have to situation *B*? Does *C's* thinking about situation *D* have any influence on the outcome of event *E*?

**4. Ideas about a problem** (see also Chapter 21, pp. 1082–1089). Why is character *A* or situation *X* this way and not that way? Is the conclusion justified by the ideas and events leading up to it?

## Rephrase Your Notes as Questions

Because your classroom notes are the fullest record you have about your instructor's views, one of the best ways to construct questions is to develop them from these notes. As you select topics and phrase questions, refer to passages from the texts that were studied by the class and stressed by your instructor. If there is time, memorize as many important phrases or lines as you can from the studied works. Plan to incorporate these into your answers as evidence to support the points you make. Remember that it is useful to work not only with main ideas from your notes but also with matters such as character, setting, imagery, symbolism, ideas, and organization.

Obviously, you cannot make questions from all your notes, and you will therefore need to select from those that seem most important. As an example, here is a short note written by a student during a classroom discussion of Shakespeare's *Hamlet*: "A study in how private problems get public, how a court conspiracy can produce disastrous national and international consequences." Notice that you can devise practice questions from this note.

**1.** In what ways is *Hamlet* not only about private problems but also about public ones?

**2.** Why should the political consequences of Claudius's murder of Hamlet's father be considered disastrous?

The principle here is that most exam questions do not ask just about *what*, but rather get into the issues of *why*. Observe that the first question therefore introduces the words *in what ways* to the phrasing of the note. For the second, the word *why* has been used. Either question creates the need for you to study pointedly, and neither asks you merely to describe events from the play. Question 1 requires you to consider the wider political effects of Hamlet's hostility toward Claudius, including Hamlet's murder of Polonius and the subsequent madness of Ophelia. Question 2, with its emphasis on disaster, leads you to consider not only the ruination of the hopes and lives of those in the play but also the importance of young Fortinbras and the eventual establishment of Norwegian control over Denmark after Claudius and Hamlet have died. If you were to spend fifteen or twenty minutes writing practice answers to these questions, you could be confident in taking an examination on the material, for you could likely adapt, or even partially duplicate, your study answers to any exam question about the personal and political results of Claudius's murder of his brother.

## Make Up Your Own Questions Even When Time Is Short

Whatever your subject, spend as much study time as possible making and answering your own questions. *Writing practice answers is one of the most important things you can do in preparing for your exam.* Remember also to work with your own remarks and the ideas you develop in the notebook or journal entries that you make when doing your regular assignments (see Chapter 1, pp. 12–13). Many of these will give you additional ideas for your own questions, which you can practice along with the questions you develop from your classroom notes.

Obviously, with limited study time, you will not be able to create your own questions and answers indefinitely. Even so, don't neglect asking and answering your own questions. If time is too short for full practice answers, write out the main heads, or topics, of an answer. When the press of time (or the need for sleep) no longer permits you to make even such a brief outline answer, keep thinking of questions and their answers as you go to the exam. *Never read passively or unresponsively; always read with a creative, question-and-answer goal.* Think of studying as a preliminary step leading to writing.

The time you spend in this way will be valuable, for as you practice, you will develop control and therefore confidence. Often those who have difficulty with tests, or claim a phobia about them, prepare passively rather than actively. Your instructor's test questions compel responsiveness, organization, thought, and insight. But a passively prepared student is not ready for this challenge and therefore writes answers that are unresponsive and filled with summary. The grade for such a performance is low, and the student's fear of tests is reinforced. The best way to break such long-standing patterns of fear or uncertainty is to study actively and creatively.

## Study with a Classmate

Often the thoughts of another person can help you understand the material to be tested. Find a fellow student with whom you can work comfortably but also productively, for both of you together can help each other individually. In view of the need for steady preparation throughout a course, regular discussions about the material are a good idea. You might also make your joint study systematic by setting aside a specific evening or afternoon for work sessions. Many students have said that they encounter problems in taking examinations because they are unfamiliar with the ways in which questions are phrased. Consequently, they waste time in understanding and interpreting the questions before they begin their answers, and sometimes they lose all their time because they misunderstand the questions entirely. If you work with a fellow student, however, and trade questions, you will be gaining experience (and confidence) in dealing with this basic difficulty about exams. Working with someone else can be extremely rewarding, just as it can also be stimulating and instructive. Make the effort, and you'll never regret it.

## Two Basic Types of Questions About Literature

Generally, there are two types of questions on literature exams. Keep them in mind as you prepare. The first type is *factual*, or *mainly objective*; and the second is *general, comprehensive, broad*, or *mainly subjective*. Except for multiple-choice questions, very few questions are purely objective in a literature course.

### Anticipate the Kinds of Factual Questions That Might Be Asked

**MULTIPLE-CHOICE QUESTIONS ASK YOU TO PICK THE MOST ACCURATE AND LIKELY ANSWERS.** Multiple-choice questions are almost necessarily factual. Your instructor will most likely use them for short quizzes, usually on days when an assignment is due, to make sure that you are keeping up with the reading. Multiple-choice questions test your knowledge of facts and your ingenuity in perceiving subtleties of phrasing. On literature exams, however, this type of question is rare.

**IDENTIFICATION QUESTIONS ASK FOR ACCURACY, EXPLANATION, AND A CERTAIN AMOUNT OF INTERPRETATION.** Identification questions are interesting and challenging because they require you both to know details and also to develop thoughts about them. These types of questions are frequently used as a check on the depth and scope of your reading. In fact, an entire exam could be composed of only identification questions, each requiring perhaps five minutes for you to answer. Here are some typical examples of what you might be asked to identify.

**1. A character.** To identify a character, it is necessary to describe briefly the character's position, main activity, and significance. Let us assume that "Prince Prospero" is the character to be identified. Our answer should state that he is the prince (position) who invites a thousand followers to his castle to enjoy themselves while keeping out the plague of the Red Death in Edgar Allan Poe's "The Masque of the Red Death" (main activity). Prospero's egotism and arrogance are the major causes of the action, and he embodies the story's theme that pride is vain and that death is inescapable (significance). Under the category of "significance," of course, you might develop as many ideas as you have time for, but the short example here is a general model for most identification questions.

**2. Incidents or situations.** To identify an incident or a situation (for example, "A woman mourns the death of her husband"), first describe the circumstances and the principal character involved in them (Mrs. Popov's reaction to her widowhood in Chekhov's play *The Bear*). Then, describe the importance of this incident or situation in the work. For example, in *The Bear*, Mrs. Popov is mourning the death of her husband, and in the course of the play Chekhov uses her feelings to show amusingly that life and love with real emotion are stronger than allegiance to the dead.

**3. Things, places, and dates.** Your instructor may ask you to identify a hair ribbon (Nathaniel Hawthorne's "Young Goodman Brown") or a beach (Matthew Arnold's "Dover Beach" or Amy Clampitt's "Beach Glass"), or the date of Amy Lowell's "Patterns" (1916). For dates, you may be given a leeway of five or ten years. What is important about a date is not so much exactness as historical and intellectual perspective. The date of Lowell's "Patterns," for example, was the third year of World War I, and the poem consequently reflects a reaction against the protracted and senseless loss of life in war (even though details of the poem itself suggest an eighteenth-century war). To claim "World War I" as the date of the poem would be acceptable as an answer if it happens that you cannot remember the exact date.

**4. Quotations.** You should remember enough of the text to identify a passage taken from it, or at least to make an informed guess. Generally, you should (1) locate the quotation, if you remember it, or else describe what you think is the probable location; (2) show the ways in which the quotation is typical of the content and style of the work you have read; and (3) describe the importance of the passage. If you suffer a lapse of memory, write a reasoned and careful explanation of your guess. Even if your guess is not actually correct, the knowledge and cogency of your explanation should give you points.

**TECHNICAL AND ANALYTICAL QUESTIONS AND PROBLEMS REQUIRE YOU TO RELATE KNOWLEDGE AND TECHNICAL UNDERSTANDING TO THE ISSUE.**   In a scale of ascending importance, the third and most difficult type of factual question relates to those matters of writing with which much of this book is concerned: technique and analysis. You might be asked to analyze the *setting, images, point of view*, or *important idea* of a work; you might be asked about the *tone and style* of a story or poem; or you might be asked to *explicate* a poem that may or may not be duplicated for your benefit (if it is not duplicated, woe to students who have not studied their assignments). Questions such as these assume that you have technical knowledge, and they also ask you to examine the text within the limitations imposed by the directions.

Obviously, technical questions occur more frequently in advanced courses than in elementary ones, and the questions become more subtle as the courses become more advanced. Instructors of introductory courses may ask about ideas and problems but will likely not use many of the others unless they state their intentions to do so in advance or unless technical terms have been studied in class.

Questions of this type are fairly long, perhaps allowing from 15 to 25 minutes apiece. If you have two or more of these questions, try to space your time sensibly; do not devote eighty percent of your time to one question and leave only twenty percent for the rest.

## Understand How Your Responses Will Be Judged and Graded

**IDENTIFICATION QUESTIONS PROBE YOUR UNDERSTANDING AND APPLICATION OF FACTS.**   In all factual questions, your instructor is testing (1) your factual command and (2) your quickness in relating a part to the whole. Thus, suppose you are identifying the incident "A man kills a canary." It is correct to say that Susan Glaspell's play *Trifles* is the location of the incident, that the murdered farmer John Wright is the killer, and that the canary belonged to his wife, Minnie. Knowledge of these details clearly establishes that you know the facts. But a strong answer must go further. Even in the brief time you have for short answers, you must demonstrate your processes of thought. You should always connect the facts (1) to major causation in the work, (2) to an important idea or ideas, (3) to the development of the work, and (4) for a quotation, to the style. Time is short and you must be selective, but if you can make your answer move from facts to significance, you will always fashion superior responses. Along these lines, let us look at an answer identifying the action from *Trifles*.

> The action is from Glaspell's *Trifles*. The man who kills the bird is John Wright, the dead man, and the owner is his wife, Minnie, who, before the story begins, has been jailed on suspicion of murder. The wringing of the little bird's neck is important because it is shown as an indignity and outrage in Minnie Wright's desperate life, and it obviously has made her angry enough to put a rope around Wright's neck to strangle him in his sleep. It is thus the cause not only of the murder but also of the investigation that brings the two lawmen and their wives to the Wright kitchen. In fact, the killing of the bird makes the story possible inasmuch as it is the women who discover the dead bird's remains, and this discovery is the means by which Glaspell highlights them as the major characters of the action. Because the husband's cruelly brutal act shows how bleak the married life of Minnie Wright actually was, it dramatizes the lonely and victimized plight of women in a male-dominated way of life like that on the Wright farm. The discovery also raises the issue of legality and morality, because the women decide to conceal the evidence, therefore protecting Minnie Wright from conviction and punishment.

Any of the points in this answer could be developed as a separate essay, but the paragraph is successful as a short answer because it goes beyond fact to deal with significance. Clearly, such answers are possible at the time of an exam only if you have devoted considerable thought beforehand to the works on which you are tested. The more thinking and practicing you do before an exam, the better your answers will be. Remember this advice as an axiom: *You cannot write superior answers if you do not think extensively before the exam.* By ambitious advance study, you will be able to reduce surprise to a minimum.

**LONGER FACTUAL QUESTIONS PROBE YOUR KNOWLEDGE AND YOUR ABILITY TO ORGANIZE YOUR THOUGHTS.** More extended factual questions also require more thoroughly developed organization. Remember that for these questions your skill in writing essays is important because the thought you demonstrate in your composition will determine a major share of your instructor's evaluation of your answers. It is therefore best to take several minutes to gather your thoughts before you begin to write. Remember, *a ten-minute planned answer is preferable to a 25-minute unplanned answer.* You do not need to write every possible fact on each particular question. Of greater importance is the use to which you put the facts that you know and the organization and development of your answer. Use a sheet of scratch paper to jot down important facts and your ideas about them in relation to the question. Then, put them together, phrase a thesis sentence, and use your facts to exemplify and support your thesis.

It is always necessary to begin your answer pointedly, using key words or phrases from the question or direction if possible, so that your answer will have thematic shape. You should *never* begin an answer with "Because" and then go on from there without referring again to the question. To be most responsive during the short time available for an exam, you should use the question as your guide for your answer. Let us suppose that you have the following question on your test: "How does Glaspell use details in *Trifles* to reveal the character of Minnie Wright?" The most common way to go astray on such a question—and the easiest thing to do also—is to concentrate on Minnie Wright's character rather than on how Glaspell uses detail to bring out her character. The word *how* makes a vast difference in the nature of the final answer, and hence a good method on the exam is to duplicate key phrases in the question to ensure that you make your major points clear. Here is an opening sentence that uses the key words and phrases (italicized here) from the question to organize thought and provide focus.

> Glaspell *uses details* of setting, marital relationships, and personal habits *to reveal the char-acter of Minnie Wright* as a person of great but unfulfilled potential whom anger has finally overcome.

Because this sentence repeats the key phrases from the question and also because it promises to show *how* the details are to be focused on the character, it suggests that the answer to follow will be responsive.

## General or Comprehensive Questions Require You to Connect a Number of Works to Broader Matters of Idea and Technique

General or comprehensive questions are particularly important on final examinations, when your instructor is testing your total comprehension of the course material and your thought about it. Considerable time is usually allowed for answering this type of question, which can be phrased in a number of ways.

1. A *direct question* asking about philosophy, underlying attitudes, main ideas, characteristics of style, backgrounds, and so on. Here are some possible questions in this category.

   What use do _____, _____, and _____ make of the topic of _____?
   Define and characterize the short story as a genre of literature, using examples
      from the stories of _____, _____, and _____.
   Describe the use of dialogue by _____, _____, and _____.
   Contrast the technique of point of view as used by _____, _____, and
      _____.

2. A *"comment" question*, often based on an extensive quotation, borrowed from a critic or written by your instructor for the occasion, asking about a broad class of writers, a literary movement, or the like. Your instructor may ask you to treat this question broadly (taking in many writers) or else to apply the quotation to a specific writer.

3. A *"suppose" question*, such as "What advice might Minnie Wright of Glaspell's *Trifles* give the speakers of Elizabeth Barrett Browning's 'How Do I Love Thee'

and Keats's 'Bright Star'?" or "What might the speaker of Lowell's poem 'Patterns' say if she were told that her dead lover was actually a person like Goodman Brown of Hawthorne's 'Young Goodman Brown'?" Although "suppose" questions seem whimsical at first sight, they have a serious design and should prompt original and radical thinking. The first question, for example, might cause a test writer to bring out, from Minnie Wright's perspective, that the love expressed by both speakers overlooks the possibilities of changes in character over a long period. She would likely sympathize with the speaker of "How Do I Love Thee," a woman, but she might also say that the speaker's enthusiasm would need to be augmented by the constant exertion of kindness and mutual understanding. For the speaker of "Bright Star," a man, Mrs. Wright might say that the steadfast love he seeks should be linked to thoughtfulness and constant communication as well as passion.

Although "suppose" questions (and answers) are speculative, the need to respond to them requires a detailed consideration of the works involved, and in this respect the "suppose" question is a salutary means of learning. It is of course difficult to prepare for a "suppose" question, which you can therefore regard as a test not only of your knowledge but also of your adaptability, inventiveness, ingenuity, and power of thought.

## Understand How Your Responses to General and Comprehensive Questions Will Be Judged and Graded

When answering broad, general questions, you are dealing with an unstructured situation, and you must not only supply an answer but—equally important—also must create a *structure* within which your answer can have meaning. You might say that you make up your own specific question out of the original general question. If you were asked to consider the role of women as seen in works by Lowell, Maupassant, and Glaspell, for example, you would structure the question by focusing a number of clearly defined topics. A possible way to begin answering such a question might be this.

> Lowell, Maupassant, and Glaspell present a view of female resilience by demonstrating the inner control, endurance, and power of adaptation of their major characters.

With this sort of focus, you would be able to proceed point-by-point, introducing supporting data as you form your answer.

As a general rule, the best method for answering a comprehensive question is comparison-contrast (see also Chapter 25). The reason is that in dealing with, say, a general question on Lawrence, Chekhov, and Keats, it is too easy to write *three* separate essays rather than *one*. Thus, you should try to create a topic such as "the treatment of real or idealized love" or "the difficulties in male-female relationships" and then develop your answer point by point rather than writer by writer. By creating your answer in this way, you can bring in references to each or all of the writers as they become relevant. If you were to treat each writer separately, your comprehensive answer would lose focus and effectiveness, and it would also be repetitive.

Remember that in judging your response to a general question, your instructor is interested in seeing (1) how effectively you perceive and explain the significant issues in the question, (2) how intelligently and clearly you organize your answer, and (3) how persuasively you link your answer to materials from the work as supporting evidence.

Bear in mind that in answering comprehensive questions, you do not have the freedom or license to write about anything that crosses your mind. You must stick to the questions. The freedom you do have, however, is the freedom to create your own organization and development in response to the questions that your instructor has asked you. The underlying idea of the comprehensive, general question is that you possess special knowledge and insights that cannot be discovered by more factual questions. You must therefore demonstrate your power of thinking. You need to formulate your own responses to the material and introduce evidence that reflects your own insights and command of information.

Two final words: Good luck.

# Appendix I

# MLA Recommendations for Documenting Sources

This appendix provides general guidelines for making source citations, and therefore it is intended to augment the section titled "Documenting Your Work" in Chapter 12A. For general information on citation recommendations by the Modern Language Association (MLA), please see Joseph Gibaldi, *MLA Handbook for Writers of Reasearch Papers*, 6th ed. (New York: MLA, 2003).

The following examples show the formats you are likely to use most often, both for nonelectronic and electronic references.

## (Nonelectronic) Books, Articles, Poems, Letters, Reviews, Recordings, Programs

**For a Book by One Author**

Fitzgerald, F. Scott. *The Great Gatsby*. Upper Saddle River: Prentice Hall, 1968.

**For a Book with No Author Listed**

*The Pictorial History of the Guitar*. New York: Random, 1992.

**For a Book by Two (or Three) Authors**

Clemens, Samuel L., and Charles Dudley Warner. *The Gilded Age: A Tale of Today*. Hartford: American, 1874.

**For a Book by Four or More Authors**

Guerin, Wilfred L., Earle Labor, Lee Morgan, Jeanne C. Reesman, and John R. Willingham. *A Handbook of Critical Approaches to Literature*. New York: Oxford UP, 2004.

or

Guerin, Wilfred L., et al. *A Handbook of Critical Approaches to Literature*. New York: Oxford UP, 2004.

**For Two Books by the Same Author**

Reynolds, David S. *Beneath the American Renaissance*. Cambridge: Harvard UP, 1988.

———. *Walt Whitman's America: A Cultural Biography*. New York: Knopf, 1995.

## Citing a Book

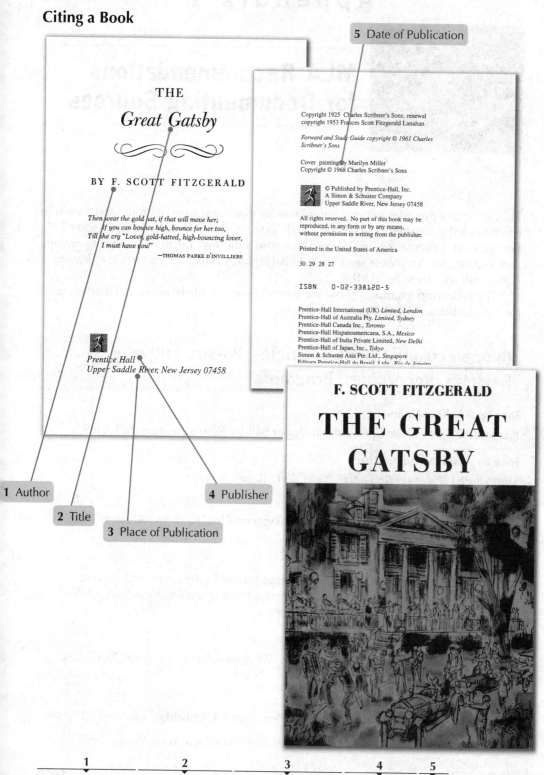

**5** Date of Publication

THE

*Great Gatsby*

BY F. SCOTT FITZGERALD

*Then wear the gold hat, if that will move her;*
  *if you can bounce high, bounce for her too,*
*Till she cry "Lover, gold-hatted, high-bouncing lover,*
  *I must have you!"*

—THOMAS PARKE D'INVILLIERS

*Prentice Hall*
*Upper Saddle River, New Jersey 07458*

Copyright 1925  Charles Scribner's Sons; renewal
copyright 1953 Frances Scott Fitzgerald Lanahan

*Forward and Study Guide copyright © 1961 Charles*
*Scribner's Sons*

Cover  painting by Marilyn Miller
Copyright © 1968 Charles Scribner's Sons

© Published by Prentice-Hall, Inc.
A Simon & Schuster Company
Upper Saddle River, New Jersey 07458

All rights reserved.  No part of this book may be
reproduced, in any form or by any means,
without permission in writing from the publisher.

Printed in the United States of America

30  29  28  27

ISBN   0-02-338120-5

Prentice-Hall International (UK) *Limited, London*
Prentice-Hall of Australia Pty. *Limited, Sydney*
Prentice-Hall Canada Inc., *Toronto*
Prentice-Hall Hispanoamericana, S.A., *Mexico*
Prentice-Hall of India Private Limited, *New Delhi*
Prentice-Hall of Japan, Inc., *Tokyo*
Simon & Schuster Asia Pte. Ltd., *Singapore*
Editora Prentice-Hall do Brasil, Ltda. *Rio de Janeiro*

F. SCOTT FITZGERALD

# THE GREAT GATSBY

**1** Author

**2** Title

**3** Place of Publication

**4** Publisher

———1———  ———2———  ———3———  ——4——  —5—
Fitzgerald, F. Scott. <u>The Great Gatsby</u>. Upper Saddle River: Prentice Hall, 1968.

**For a Book with an Editor**

Scharnhorst, Gary, ed. <u>Selected Letters of Bret Harte</u>. Norman: U of Oklahoma P, 1997.

**For a Book with Two Editors**

Dionne, Craig, and Steve Mentz, eds. <u>Rogues and Early Modern English Culture</u>. Ann Arbor: U of Michigan P, 2004.

**For a Book with an Author and an Editor**

De Quille, Dan. <u>The Fighting Horse of the Stanislaus</u>. Ed. Lawrence I. Berkove. Iowa City: U of Iowa P, 1990.

**For a Translated Book**

Cervantes Saavedra, Miguel de. <u>Don Quixote de la Mancha</u>. Trans. Charles Jarvis. New York: Oxford UP, 1999.

**For a Long Poem Published as a Book**

Homer. <u>The Odyssey</u>. Trans. Robert Fitzgerald. New York: Vintage, 1990.

**For a Collection of Poetry Published as a Book**

Mueller, Lisel. <u>Alive Together: New and Selected Poems</u>. Baton Rouge: Louisiana State UP, 1996.

**For a Literary Work in an Anthology**

Chopin, Kate, "The Story of an Hour." <u>Literature: An Introduction to Reading and Writing</u>. Ed. Edgar V. Roberts. 8th ed. Upper Saddle River: Pearson, 2007. 342–343.

**For an Introduction, Preface, Foreword, or Afterword in a Book**

Pryse, Marjorie. Introduction. <u>The Country of the Pointed Firs and Other Stories</u>. By Sarah Orne Jewett. New York: Norton, 1981. v–xix.

**For an Article in a Reference Book**

Gerber, Phillip. "Naturalism." <u>The Encyclopedia of American Literature</u>. Ed. Steven Serafin. New York: Continuum, 1999. 808–09.

**For an Article in a Journal with Continuous Paging**

Rhodes, Chip. "Satire in Romanian Literature." <u>Humor</u> 8 (1995): 275–86.

**For an Article in a Journal That Pages Each Issue Separately**

Van Tassel, Kristin. "Nineteenth-Century American Antebellum Literature: The Yeoman Becomes a Country Bumpkin. <u>American Studies</u> 43 (2002): 51–73.

**For a Signed Book Review**

Bird, John. Rev. of <u>The Singular Mark Twain</u>, by Fred Kaplan. <u>Mark Twain Annual</u> 2 (2004): 57–61.

**For an Unsigned Book Review**

Rev. of <u>Canons by Consensus: Critical Trends and American Literature Anthologies</u>, by Joseph Csicsila. <u>Essays in Arts and Sciences</u> 24 (2000): 69–74.

# Citing a Work in an Anthology

**3** Title of Anthology

**9** Pages Work Appears On in Anthology

**5** Anthology Edition Number

**1** Author of Work

**2** Title of Work

**4** Anthology Editor

**8** Anthology Copyright Year

**7** Publisher of Anthology

**6** Place of Publication of Anthology

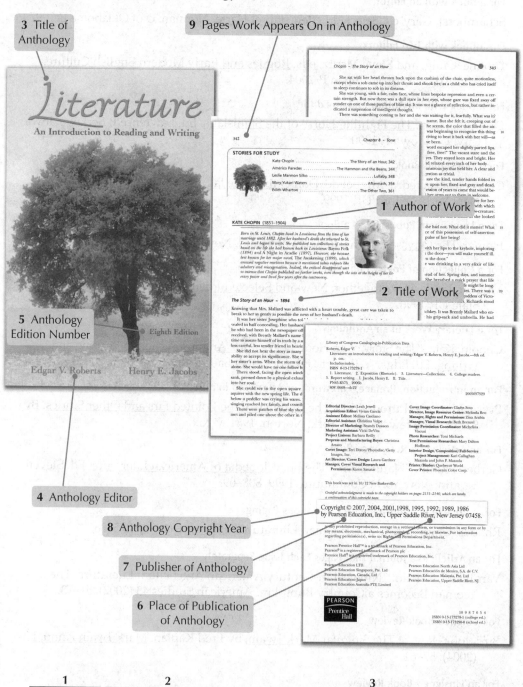

| 1 | 2 | 3 |
|---|---|---|

Chopin, Kate. "The Story of an Hour." <u>Literature: An Introduction to Reading and Writing.</u>

Ed. Edgar V. Roberts. 8th ed. Upper Saddle River: Pearson, 2007. 342–343.

| 4 | 5 | 6 | 7 | 8 | 9 |
|---|---|---|---|---|---|

# Citing an Article in a Journal

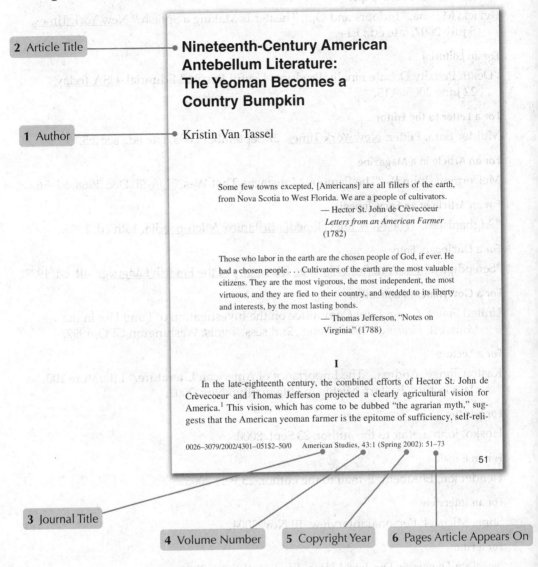

**2** Article Title

## Nineteenth-Century American Antebellum Literature: The Yeoman Becomes a Country Bumpkin

**1** Author

Kristin Van Tassel

> Some few towns excepted, [Americans] are all fillers of the earth, from Nova Scotia to West Florida. We are a people of cultivators.
> — Hector St. John de Crèvecoeur
> *Letters from an American Farmer*
> (1782)

> Those who labor in the earth are the chosen people of God, if ever. He had a chosen people . . . Cultivators of the earth are the most valuable citizens. They are the most vigorous, the most independent, the most virtuous, and they are fied to their country, and wedded to its liberty and interests, by the most lasting bonds.
> — Thomas Jefferson, "Notes on Virginia" (1788)

**I**

In the late-eighteenth century, the combined efforts of Hector St. John de Crèvecoeur and Thomas Jefferson projected a clearly agricultural vision for America.[1] This vision, which has come to be dubbed "the agrarian myth," suggests that the American yeoman farmer is the epitome of sufficiency, self-reli-

0026–3079/2002/4301–051$2–50/0　　American Studies, 43:1 (Spring 2002): 51–73

51

**3** Journal Title

**4** Volume Number　　**5** Copyright Year　　**6** Pages Article Appears On

Note: A scholarly article in printed form ordinarily provides all necessary information on its first page.

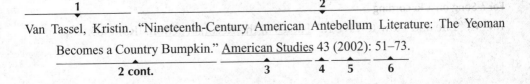

| 1 | 2 |
|---|---|

Van Tassel, Kristin. "Nineteenth-Century American Antebellum Literature: The Yeoman Becomes a Country Bumpkin." American Studies 43 (2002): 51–73.

| 2 cont. | 3 | 4 | 5 | 6 |
|---|---|---|---|---|

**For an Article in a Newspaper**

Ryzick, Melena. "Indoors and Out, Theater Is Making a Splash." <u>New York Times.</u>
    5 July 2007, late ed.: E1+.

**For an Editorial**

"Death Penalty Debate Finally Produces Useful Result." Editorial. <u>USA Today.</u>
    22 June 2005: A15.

**For a Letter to the Editor**

Mulder, Sara. Letter. <u>New York Times</u>. 27 September 2005, late ed., sec 2:5.

**For an Article in a Magazine**

McDermott, John R. "The Famous Moustache That Was." <u>Life</u> 20 Dec. 1968: 53–56.

**For an Article in an Encyclopedia**

"Afghanistan." <u>The New Encyclopedia Britanica: Micropaedia</u>. 15th ed. 1985.

**For a Dictionary Entry**

"Serendipity." <u>The American Heritage Dictionary of the English Language</u>. 4th ed. 1977.

**For a Government Publication**

United States. Cong. Joint Committee on the Investigation of Land Use in the
    Midwest. *Hearings.* 105th Cong., 2nd sess. 4 vols. Washington GPO, 1997.

**For a Lecture**

Kaston Tange, Andrea. "The Importance of American Literature." Literature 100
    class lecture. Eastern Michigan University, 5 Nov. 2002.

**For a Letter**

Hosko, John. Letter to the author. 23 Sept. 2000.

**For an E-mail**

Henderson, Elisabeth. E-mail to the author. 25 Feb. 2005.

**For an Interview**

Stipe, Michael. Personal interview. 10 Nov. 2004.

**For a Film**

*Napoleon Dynamite.* Dir. Jared Hess. Fox Searchlight, 2004.

**For a Television Program**

"The Parking Garage." <u>Seinfeld</u>. NBC. WDIV, Detroit. 23 July 1994.

**For a Sound Recording**

R.E.M. <u>Fables of the Reconstruction</u>. IRS, 1985.

**For a Song on a Recording**

R.E.M. "Life and How to Live It." <u>Fables of the Reconstruction</u>. IRS, 1985.

## Citing a Newspaper

**5** Edition

**"All the News That's Fit to Print"**

# The New York Times

**Late Edition**
New York: Today, some sun, a few storms, high 83. Tonight, early shower, low 70. Tomorrow, partly sunny and a bit less humid, high 83. Yesterday, high 71, low 65. Details, Page C10.

VOL. CLVI . . . No. 53,996    Copyright © 2007 The New York Times    NEW YORK, THURSDAY, JULY 5, 2007    ONE DOLLAR

**4** Date

**3** Newspaper Name

## THE Arts

N    E1

The New York Times    THURSDAY, JULY 5, 2007

Lauren Ambrose, as Juliet in "Romeo and Juliet," and Joseph Parks, as Orpheus in "Eurydice," are among the actors in the swim of a wet New York theater season.

Photograph by Sara Krulwich/The New York Times

## A Touching Romance, If They Just Don't Touch

**By BILL CARTER**

LOS ANGELES — In a quirky fairy tale of a mystery show called "Pushing Daisies," ABC, the network of "Lost," "Desperate Housewives" and "Ugly Betty," has yet another series that is building strong enthusiasm in advance of the fall television season.

Marked by a candy-colored palette, characters as sweet as freshly baked pie and a story line based on a touching (or in this case, no-touching) unrequited romance, "Pushing Daisies" is a dish that networks always promise but seldom serve: something completely different.

Sitting in his still-unfinished office in the Warner Brothers lot here, Bryan Fuller, the show's creator, is working on muting expectations, which are coming from advertisers

**A new TV series rides a big wave of early enthusiasm.**

and critics who have seen the pilot. "I love that it's getting this positive buzz," he said, "but I'm taking it all with a grain of salt."

Mr. Fuller, 37, has been here before. Four years ago he created another oddball early favorite, a Fox drama called "Wonderfalls." That one got a sudden cold shoulder from its own network — Mr. Fuller said he thought it was because of the show's two lesbian characters — and found itself all but abandoned after only four episodes had been filmed.

But "Pushing Daisies" is an unabashed favorite at both its studio, Warner Brothers, and its network, Peter Roth, the president of Warner Brothers Television, said, "I'd a show of this quality works, it will renew my faith in the taste of the American audience."

Steven McPherson, the president of ABC Entertainment, said: "We

## Indoors and Out, Theater Is Making a Splash

**By MELENA RYZIK**

The actors who perform in Shakespeare in the Park are used to the vagaries of outdoor theater: the inclement weather, the planes buzzing overhead, the bugs, the yowling of mating raccoons (really). But this year's production of "Romeo and Juliet" added a new difficulty: water. Lots of it, the centerpiece of this version is a 70-foot, 4,000-gallon pool.

The cast members do not shy away from diving in. They tromp and wade and paddle through the pool, which is an inch and a half to two inches deep and takes four and a half

hours to fill every day, via seven hoses, with New York City tap water. Though some of it comes from a specially constructed boiler heated to 125 degrees, the pool itself isn't heated, said Michael McGoff, the production's stage manager. By the death scenes the water temperature can dip into the 60s.

So the star-crossed lovers have another obstacle: wet suits. On cold nights Juliet (Lauren Ambrose) wears one underneath her virginal white gown. So does Romeo (Oscar Isaac) for his many splashy — literally — fight scenes. Most of the other citizens of Verona make do with Wellies and re-

hearsal Crocs, footwear that was approved as spill-safe by the actors' union. Still, Mr. McGoff said, "every night, somebody will slip or really get hit with some water where they normally don't."

And "Romeo and Juliet" is not the only piece of theater that's all wet this summer. For reasons of artistry, script or shock value a few other productions use a water effect onstage. They include the playwright Sarah Ruhl's adaptation of "Eurydice," at the Second Stage Theater, and two programs of 10-minute plays that take place in and around the rooftop pool at the Holiday

Inn Midtown, at 57th Street and Ninth Avenue. Despite the technical and practical challenges of dealing with water — from safety issues like waterproofing electrical cables to stage cleanliness to the towel supply — it's apparently worth it for the 'wow' factor.

"We can't afford pyrotechnics, we can't afford Broadway budgets, we can't even afford fly space," said Josh Sherman, the director of the Impetuous Theater Group, a two-year-old Off Off Broadway company, which is staging "Swim Shorts 3" at the

Continued on Page 5

**1** Author

**2** Article Title

**6** Section and Page Number

**1**    **2**    **3**

Ryzick, Melena. "Indoors and Out, Theater Is Making a Splash." <u>New York Times</u>

5 July 2007, late ed.: E1+.

**4**    **5**    **6**

**For a Music Video**

Outkast. "Hey Ya." <u>Speakerboxx/The Love Below</u>. La Face, 2003. Music video. Dir. Bryan Barber. MTV. 22 Aug. 2004.

# The Citation of Electronic Sources

Both students and instructors can now take advantage of the technology available to assist in research. While many libraries offer varied databases that enable researchers to locate information easily, the main thrust of technology is now the exploration of the World Wide Web. Through the use of various search engines, such as Google and Yahoo, you simply need to enter the name of an author, a title, or a topic, upon which you will be linked to a host of resources from all over the world—home pages of specific authors, literary organizations, and works on various topics by contemporary writers. You'll find a good deal of what you're searching for in only a few minutes. An important caveat is that many sources still remain in printed journals and magazines that may be or, more probably, may not be on the Web. To make your searches thorough, therefore, *you must never neglect to search for printed information.*

Because the available methods of obtaining electronic information are developing so rapidly, the printed style manuals have had difficulty keeping up with the changes. If you do a Web search looking for information on these styles, chances are that the information you discover will vary from site to site. Therefore, you need to know the basics that are required for the citation of your sources.

When recovering electronic sources, it is vital to type the letters, numbers, symbols, dots, underlines, and spaces accurately. Recovery systems are unforgiving, and mistakes or omissions of any sort will make it impossible for you to retrieve your source. The sources are often transitory because someone, somewhere, must maintain them (through the updating of information and the paying of fees). The sources are therefore not always reliable, so printing a copy of sources you plan to cite will make your citations both definite and accurate. If the Uniform Resource Locator (URL) you have used does not turn up the material for which you are searching, you may be able to locate it simply by typing in the name of the author or the name of the article. You may often rely on your search engine to turn up references for you, and autofill will often complete the entire address, with all the dots and other directions in the correct order.

By the same token, it is essential for you, when you are compiling your own list of works cited, to be absolutely accurate in reproducing the URL of your sources. You must assume that someone reading your essay and using your list will want to check out the sources themselves, and any errors in your transcription may create confusion.

The style generally accepted in the "cyber" world, and the one recommended by the MLA, places angle brackets (< >) before and after Internet addresses and URLs. If you see brackets around an address you want to use, do not include them as part of the address when you are seeking retrieval. Also, since a number of word-processing programs now support the use of italics, you can use italics as a regular practice. Some researchers, however, still prefer underlines, and if your programs (or typewriter) cannot produce italics, of course use underlines. If in doubt about which to use, consult your instructor.

## MLA Style Guidelines for Electronic Sources

Many of the guidelines the MLA has authorized for the citation of electronic sources overlap with the MLA recommendations for printed sources, but to avoid ambiguity a number of recommendations bear repetition. Electronic materials are to be documented in basically the same style as printed sources. According to the sixth edition of the *MLA Handbook*, which illustrates virtually all the situations you will ever encounter, the following items need to be included if they are available.

1. The name of the author, editor, compiler, or translator of the source (if available and relevant), last name first, followed by an abbreviation, such as *ed.*, if appropriate.

2. If there is no author listed in the source, you should list the title first: the title of a poem, short story, article, or similar short work within a scholarly project, database, or periodical (in quotation marks); or the title of a posting to a discussion list or forum (taken from the subject line and enclosed by quotation marks), concluded by the phrase "Online posting."

3. The title of a book, underlined.

4. The name of the editor, compiler, or translator of the text (if relevant and if not cited earlier), preceded by (not followed by) any necessary abbreviations, such as *Ed.*

5. Publication information for any printed version of the source.

6. The title of the scholarly project, database, periodical, or professional or personal site, underlined; or, for a professional or personal site with no title, a description such as "Home Page."

7. The name of the editor of the scholarly project or database (if available).

8. The version number of the source (if not part of the title), or, for a journal, the volume number, issue number, or other identifying number. All numbers should be in Arabic, not Roman numerals.

9. The date of publication or posting that you find in your source. Sometimes the original date is no longer available because it has been replaced with an update; if so, cite that. Dates should be arranged by (a) day of the month, (b) month (the names of longer months may be abbreviated), and (c) year.

10. For a work from a subscription service, the name of the service (and name, city, and state abbreviation if the subscriber is a library).

11. For a posting to a discussion list or forum, the name of the list or forum.

12. The number range or total number of pages, paragraphs, or other sections, if they are numbered. If you do your own numbering, include your numbers within square brackets [ ], and be sure to indicate what you have numbered.

13. The name of any institution or organization sponsoring or associated with the Web site.

14. The date when you consulted the source. If you have looked at the site a number of times, include the most recent date of use. The principle here is that the date immediately before the uniform resource locator (URL) will mark the last time you used the source.

**15.** The electronic address or URL of the source in angle brackets (< >). Many programs now automatically include the angle brackets. If the URL is too long to fit on one line, it should be divided at a slash (/) if possible—do not introduce hyphenations into the URL as these may be mistaken for actual significant characters in that address.

### For a Book

Shaw, Bernard. <u>Pygmalion</u>. 1916, 1999. Bartleby Archive. 20 Sep. 2005 <http://www.bartleby.com/138/index.html>.

### For a Poem

Carroll, Lewis. <u>The Hunting of the Snark</u>. 1876. 19 Sep. 2005 <http://www.everypoet.com/archive/poetry/Lewis_Carroll/lewis_carroll_the_hunting_of_the_snark.htm>.

### For a Play

Shakespeare, William. <u>Hamlet</u>. ca. 1601. Project Gutenberg. 20 Sep. 2005 <http://www.novelguide.com/hamlet/hamlet.txt>.

### For a Journal Article

Hewlett, Beth L. and Christa Ehmann Powers. "How Do You Ground Your Training? Sharing the Principles and Processes of Preparing Educators for Online Writing Instruction." <u>Kairos</u> 10.1 (Fall 2005). Multiple Sections. 20 September 2005 <http://english.ttu.edu/kairos/10.1/binder.html?praxis/hewett/index.htm>.

### For a Magazine Article

Jones, Kenneth. "Bill Gates and Steve Jobs Sing and Dance in New Musical, *Nerds*, Already a Hit in NYMF." <u>Playbill.com</u>. September 20, 2005. 20 September 2005 <http://www.playbill.com/news/article/95180.html>.

### Posting to a Discussion List

McElhearn, Kirk. "J. S. Bach: Oxford Composer Companion [A review]." Online posting. Google Groups. 1 Dec. 2000. 20 September 2005 <http://groups.google.com/group/alt.music.j-s-bach/browse_thread/thread/30524010237bd51a/488691878789a15d?lnk=st&q=%22Kirk+Mcelhearn%22&rnum=5#488691878789a15d>.

### For a Scholarly Project

<u>Voice of the Shuttle: Web Site for Humanities Research</u>. Ed. Alan Liu. 20 September 2005. U of California Santa Barbara. 4 Jan. 2003 <http://vos.ucsb.edu/>.

### For a Professional Site

Mann, Randall. "The Illusion of Intimacy: Discovering John Ashberry." Academy of American Poets. 2007. 20 June 2007 <http://www.poets.org/viewmedia.php/prmMID/19643>.

### For a Personal Site

Barrett, Dan. <u>The Gentle Giant Home Page</u>. 1 August 2005. 20 September 2005 <http://www.blazemonger.com/GG/index.html>.

## Citing a Professional Website

**3** Site Sponsor

**6** URL

**2** Title

**1** Author

**5** Date of Access

Note: This is the date you accessed the website. In this case, the site was used for research on June 20, 2007.

**4** Copyright

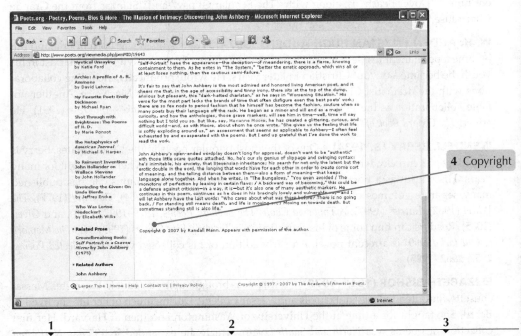

1                              2                              3

Mann, Randall. "The Illusion of Intimacy: Discovering John Ashberry." <u>Academy of American Poets</u>

2007. 20 June 2007 <http://www.poets.org/viewmedia.php/prmMID/19643>.

4      5                              6

# Appendix II

# Brief Biographies of the Poets in Part III

**JACK AGÜEROS (B. 1934)** • Agüeros, a native of New York, is a well-known Latino writer. He earned a B.A. from Brooklyn College and an M.A. from Occidental College. Not only has he written poetry, but he has also done plays, stories, and film scripts. His stories are contained in *Dominoes and Other Stories* (1993), and his poetry collections are *Correspondence Between the Stonehaulers* (1991) and *Sonnets from the Puerto Rican* (1996). "Sonnet for You, Familiar Famine" is from *Sonnets from the Puerto Rican*.

**MATTHEW ARNOLD (1822–1888)** • One of the major Victorian poets, Arnold was brought up among books and learning, and eventually (1857) became a professor of poetry at Oxford. In his Oxford lectures he described a loss of security and religious faith, and hence he stressed the need to recover absolutes—which to him was the major "function of criticism at the present time." "Dover Beach" is, along with "The Scholar Gypsy" and "Stanzas from the Grande Chartreuse," among his best-known poems.

**W. H. AUDEN (WYSTAN HUGH AUDEN, 1907–1973)** • Auden was born in England but became a permanent resident of the United States after the Spanish Civil War. A Marxist in his youth, he became a devout Christian in later years. He wrote prolifically, including collaborations with the dramatist Christopher Isherwood and the poet Louis MacNeice. Another notable collaboration is the libretto for Igor Stravinsky's opera *The Rake's Progress* (1951). He edited *The Oxford Book of Light Verse* (1938).

**WENDELL BERRY (B. 1934)** • One of the most popular poets in the United States, Berry is a resident of Kentucky, where he was brought up and educated, and where he taught for many years. His output as a poet, essayist, and novelist has been voluminous. He has published many separate volumes of poetry, including *The Broken Ground* (1964), *Clearing* (1977), *The Wheel* (1982), *Entries* (1997), *A Timbered Choir: The Sabbath Poems, 1979–1997* (1998), and *Given* (2005). Readers can find some of his short fiction in *Fidelity: Five Stories* (1993). His *The Memory of Old Jack* (1999) is a recent novel. An early edition of his collected verse is *Collected Poems, 1957–1982* (1985).

**ELIZABETH BISHOP (1911–1979)** • Bishop was brought up by an aunt in Worcester, Massachusetts. She attended private schools and Vassar College. During much of her life she lived in Brazil. She taught for a time at the University of Washington and then at Harvard. Her first collection of poems was *North and South* (1946), which she expanded in 1955 as *North and South—A Cold Spring*, for which she received the Pulitzer Prize in Poetry in 1956.

**WILLIAM BLAKE (1757–1827)** • Blake was apprenticed to an engraver in London at the age of 14. Throughout his career he published his poems with his own engravings, and these original editions are now valuable collector's items. Blake was a revolutionary at heart who thought that humanity would flower if institutions were eliminated or at least redirected. *Songs of Experience,* from which "London" is taken, is a collection of poems on this theme, published in 1794, five years after the outbreak of the French Revolution. In this same year he published *Songs of Innocence,* from which "The Lamb" is taken.

**LOUISE BOGAN (1897–1970)** • Born in Maine, Bogan spent most of her life in New York, writing regular reviews for *The New Yorker.* Her first volume of poems was *Body of This Death* (1923), in which "Women" appeared. Her *Collected Poems* (1954) was awarded the Bollingen Prize. Her major critical work was *Achievement in American Poetry, 1900–1950* (1951). *Journey Around My Room* (1980) is a posthumous autobiographical work.

**ARNA BONTEMPS (1902–1973)** • Born in Louisiana, Bontemps by profession was a librarian (at Fisk University). In addition to poetry, he published a number of novels and works of children's fiction. *One Hundred Years of Negro Freedom* (1961) is a widely heralded historical work.

**ELIZABETH BREWSTER (B. 1922)** • Elizabeth Brewster is a native of the United States but has spent her professional life largely in Canada. She received degrees from Radcliffe, Toronto, and Indiana universities. She is a Professor Emerita of the University of Saskatchewan at Saskatoon, where she taught for many years. Two of her works are *Away from Home* (1995) and *Garden of Sculpture* (1998). In 1985 she published *Selected Poems of Elizabeth Brewster,* and in 1995 she was given a Lifetime Award for Excellence in the Arts.

**EMILY BRONTË (1818–1848)** • The middle child of the Brontë sisters, Emily received no more than a minimum of formal education and was largely home taught and self-taught, although she spent some time in Belgium studying music and languages. Her unfortunately brief life was characterized by poverty and deprivation. She was deeply affected by the landscape near Haworth, the family home in Yorkshire in the Northern part of England, and her almost mystical identification of land and character pervades her best known work, the novel *Wuthering Heights* (1847). She and her sisters published a joint collection of verse in 1846, *Poems, by Currer, Ellis, and Acton Bell* (i.e., Charlotte, Emily, and Anne). "No Coward Soul Is Mine" is considered one of her best poems, along with "The Night Is Darkening Round Me" and "Remembrance."

**ELIZABETH BARRETT BROWNING (1806–1861)** • English born, Elizabeth Barrett suffered a crippling spinal injury when still a girl. Despite this adversity she had become a widely recognized poet when she married Robert Browning in 1846. Because of her condition and the English climate, the Brownings moved to Italy, where they remained until Elizabeth's death. During her lifetime, her reputation as a poet eclipsed Robert's. Her *Cry of the Children* (1843) was an early poetic protest against the industrial exploitation of children. In 1850 she published *Sonnets from the Portuguese,* which she presented as a gift to her husband.

**ROBERT BROWNING (1812–1889)** • In his twenties and early thirties, Browning wrote a number of versified plays for the stage, but these were unsuccessful, and he did not achieve fame in his native England until he was well into his fifties. Because of his experience with drama, he found his poetic voice within the medium of the dramatic monologue, which he perfected to a high degree. Both "My Last Duchess" and "Soliloquy of the Spanish Cloister" appeared in his *Dramatic Lyrics* of 1842, exactly during the time when he was also writing his plays.

**WILLIAM CULLEN BRYANT (1794–1878)** • Bryant was born in Massachusetts and spent his adult life in New York. Early in his career he practiced law, which he disliked, and after ten years of that he was pleased to take up literature and editorial work. He was a newspaper editor and owner for fifty years and at the time of his death he was one of the most beloved writers in the United States. His best known work was *Thanatopsis*, which he wrote when still a boy and published at the age of seventeen. He published many collections of poems and also did successful translations of Homer's *Iliad* and *Odyssey*. Quotations from his poem "Song of Marion's Men" (1832) may be found on p. 389.

**ROBERT BURNS (1759–1796)** • The best-known and most loved poet of Scotland, Burns gave up farming and taught himself to read and write English, French, and Latin. He published his first volume, *Scots Poems Chiefly in the Scottish Dialect*, in 1786. His use of the down-to-earth idiom of Scots peasants, together with joyous irreverence and frank lustiness, made him instantly famous.

**LEWIS CARROLL (1832–1898)** • Carroll is the pen name of the English writer Charles L. Dodgson, who is famous for *Alice's Adventures in Wonderland* and *Through the Looking-Glass*. Carroll was also a mathematician, lecturer, logician, and photographer. "Jabberwocky," from *Through the Looking-Glass*, stems out of his interest in words. The word *chortle*, which he created in this poem (a blending of *chuckle* and *snort*), is now standard English.

**HAYDEN CARRUTH (B. 1921)** • Carruth is a native of Connecticut and received degrees at the Universities of North Carolina and Chicago. In World War II he served for two years in Italy. After the war he taught, among other schools, at Syracuse and Bucknell. He has been an editor of *Poetry* and has served as poetry editor of *Harper's*. He is the author of more than two dozen poetry collections, including the recent *Doctor Jazz: Poems, 1996–2000* (2001) and *Toward The Distant Islands: New and Selected Poems* (2006). Among his many distinctions he has received the Harriet Monroe Poetry Prize, a Guggenheim Fellowship, an NEA grant, and the National Book Award of 1996 for his collection *Scrambled Eggs and Whisky: Poems: 1991–1995* (1996).

**JIMMY CARTER (B. 1924)** • James Earl Carter was born in Plains, Georgia, which is still his home. He graduated from the U.S. Naval Academy (1946), served in the Navy, became a peanut farmer, was governor of Georgia (1971–1975), and became the thirty-ninth president of the United States (1977–1981). Since his presidency he has distinguished himself in many national and international causes, such as creating the Carter Foundation, serving with the International Negotiation Network, and working closely with Habitat for Humanity. He has been the recipient of devoted recognition and many honorary degrees, but despite his national and international standing he has frequently been seen on TV house-building programs serving as a worker, along with other workers, on Habitat projects. He has sawed wood and driven many nails. His continued work for peace was recognized in 2002, when he received the Nobel Peace Prize. His varied list of published works is extensive, and he has even co-written, with his daughter Amy, a children's book. In 1995 he published *Always a Reckoning and Other Poems*, from which "I Wanted to Share My Father's World" is selected.

**AMY CLAMPITT (1920–1994)** • Clampitt was a native of Iowa, receiving her education at Grinnell College and later at Columbia University. For many years she worked in the publishing field and also for the National Audubon Society. Although she wrote poetry during most of her lifetime, she was not published until she was in her sixties, her first volume being *The Kingfisher* (1983). During the remainder of her life she published regular volumes of poems, completing *What the Light Was Like* (1985), *Archaic Figure* (1987), and *Westward* (1990). In 1994, the last year of her life, she published her final collection, *A Silence Opens*.

**LUCILLE CLIFTON (B. 1936)** • Clifton was born and educated in New York. Her productivity as a writer began in the 1970s and has been strong ever since. One of her earliest poetry collections was *An Ordinary Woman* (1974). Later she published *Next: New Poems* (1987) and *Good Woman: Poems and a Memoir, 1969–1980* (1987). In addition to her poetry, she has written a number of stories and poems for children, such as *All Us Come Cross the Water* (1973), *The Book of Light* (1993), *Everett Anderson's Christmas Coming* (1993), and *The Lucky Stone* (1999). A collection of her poems is *Blessing the Boats: New and Selected Poems, 1988–2000* (2000).

**ARTHUR HUGH CLOUGH (1819–1861)** • Clough's father was a businessman who often worked in the United States, and for a period of five years as a boy Arthur lived with his family in South Carolina. Returning to England, he attended Rugby, a famous public (i.e., private) school, and became a favorite in the household of Dr. Thomas Arnold, the headmaster. Though Clough had a good deal of academic promise, his achievement did not measure up, and he felt that he had failed in his academic goals. He was fond of giving his poems titles in foreign languages, such as "Qua Cursum Ventus" (the wind creates the course [of the ship]), "Wen Gott Betrügt, Ist Wohl Betrogen" ([the person] whom God deceives is well deceived), "Sehnsucht" (longing), and "Tò Kalón" (the beautiful). His "Say Not the Struggle Nought Availeth" is one of his famous poems, along with the satiric "The Latest Decalogue." After Clough died in Florence in 1861, his good friend Matthew Arnold commemorated his life in the monody "Thyrsis" (1866), one of the best-known elegies in the English language.

**LEONARD COHEN (B. 1934)** • Cohen is a native of Montreal, and he received his education at McGill University and also at Columbia. He traveled widely, spending years in Greece, England, New York, and California. He began writing poetry early. His first collections were *Let Us Compare Mythologies* (1956) and *The Spice Box of Earth* (1961). He also published two successful novels, *The Favorite Game* (1963) and *Beautiful Losers* (1966). Today he is best known for his featured television concerts and also for the many record albums and compact disc collections of his songs and music. Among the most recent of these are *Cohen Live* (1994) and *Ten New Songs* (2001). An anthology of his work is *The Concise Leonard Cohen* (1999).

**SAMUEL TAYLOR COLERIDGE (1772–1834)** • Coleridge was born in Devon, in southern England, and studied at Cambridge University but did not earn a degree. After a short stint as a soldier he fell into dire financial straits, from which he was rescued by the Wedgwood brothers of ceramic fame, who provided him with an annuity so that he could devote himself to poetry. Wordsworth and he together published the *Lyrical Ballads* of 1798, a collection that is the benchmark of the English Romantic movement. Coleridge contributed "The Rime of the Ancient Mariner," his most famous poem, and also "Kubla Khan." After 1802 he wrote little poetry, but his *Biographia Literaria* of 1817 is one of the major works of literary criticism of the early nineteenth century.

**BILLY COLLINS (B. 1941)** • A native of New York, Collins received degrees at Holy Cross and the University of California at Riverside. He lives in New York State and is a Distinguished Professor of English at Lehman College. Among his collections of poetry are *The Apple*

*That Astonished Paris* (1989), which includes "Schoolsville"; *Questions about Angels* (1991), a winner in the National Poetry Series competition; *The Art of Drowning* (1996); *Picnic, Lightning* (1998); *Sailing Around the Room: New and Selected Poems* (2001); *Nine Horses* (2002); and *The Trouble with Poetry and Other Poems* (2005). In 2001 he was named American Poet Laureate for 2001–2002, and the next year he was reappointed. One of his major projects as Poet Laureate was to emphasize the daily reading of poetry in the schools, and to this goal he published a significant collection of verse, *Poetry 180: A Turning Back to Poetry* (2003). He was named New York State Poet for 2004.

**FRANCES CORNFORD (1886–1960)** • Cornford, a granddaughter of Charles Darwin, lived most of her life in Cambridge, England. She published only a few volumes of verse, and her *Collected Poems* was published in 1954.

**WILLIAM COWPER (1731–1800)** • Cowper is universally recognized because of his lines "God moves in a mysterious way/His wonders to perform." He received his education at an English private ("public") school, an institution that he attacked in his *Tirocinium* in 1785. He was qualified to practice law but never made a career of it. Although throughout his life he was troubled with depression and he made at least two suicide attempts, he wrote a considerable amount of prose and much poetry. His most widely recognized long poem is *The Task* (1785), and his best lyric poems are found in the *Olney Hymns* (1775), which contain "God Moves in a Mysterious Way" and "Oh, for a Closer Walk with God."

**STEPHEN CRANE (1871–1900)** • Born in New Jersey, Crane began writing at the age of eight, and by the time he was sixteen he was helping his brothers write for newspapers. He attended a number of colleges but did not graduate. While at Syracuse University he completed his first novel, *Maggie: A Girl of the Streets*, which he published with borrowed money in 1893. During the remainder of his brief, turbulent, and cash-strapped life he worked as a writer and also as a war correspondent during the Spanish American War. He spent a year in the West, and two of his better-known stories, "The Bride Comes to Yellow Sky" and "The Blue Hotel," came out of this experience. His best-known novel, *The Red Badge of Courage*, was published in 1895. "War Is Kind" is taken from *War Is Kind*, his second volume of published verse.

**ROBERT CREELEY (1926–2005)** • A native of Massachusetts, Robert Creeley received his master's degree from the University of New Mexico. He achieved wide recognition and many honors, including a Bollingen Prize and the appointment as New York State Poet for 1989–1991. He was closely associated with the "Black Mountain Poets," a group that in the immediate post–World War II years was connected with Black Mountain College in North Carolina. This group advocated a minimalist approach to expression, and believed that poetic form should be a consequence of content. On this principle, poetry has no preconceptions, and each poem evolves freely and spontaneously as the poet writes it. Creeley authored numerous books of poetry, together with short stories, essays, correspondence, and essays. Some of his recent collections were *Thinking* (2000), *For Friends* (2000), *Just in Time: Poems, 1984–1994* (2001), and *If I Were Writing This* (2003). "Do You Think . . . " (1972) is drawn from his *Selected Poems* of 1991.

**E. E. CUMMINGS (1894–1962)** • Cummings studied at Harvard, receiving a master's degree there. During World War I, he served in the Ambulance Corps in France and, as a result of false charges of treason, was imprisoned—an experience he wrote about in his first work, *The Enormous Room* (1922). He began publishing poetry shortly thereafter and continued doing so throughout his life. His collected poetry, consisting of more than a thousand poems, was published in 1992.

**PETER DAVISON (B. 1928)** • Davison was born in New York City but grew up in Colorado. He received degrees at Harvard and Cambridge and has served as a lecturer and also as an editor with a number of leading publishers. His first poetry collection was *The Breaking of the Day and Other Poems* (1964). Among his numerous collections since then are *Praying Wrong: New and Selected Poems* (1985), *The Poems of Peter Davison, 1957–1995* (1995), and *Breathing Room: New Poems* (2000). "Delphi" is selected from *The Breaking of the Day and Other Poems.*

**CARL DENNIS (B. 1939)** • Dennis is a native of St. Louis, and received degrees from the University of Minnesota and the University of California, Berkeley. He has taught for many years at the University of Buffalo. A few of his many poetry collections are *A House of My Own* (1974), *Signs and Wonders,* (1979), and *Practical Gods* (2001). "The God Who Loves You" is from *Practical Gods,* the collection for which Dennis was awarded the Pulitzer Prize for Poetry in 2002.

**JAMES DICKEY (1923–1997)** • Dickey was a native of Georgia. He served in World War II and afterwards spent a number of years writing advertising copy. After 1969 he became a full-time writer and teacher. During the 1980s he published three volumes of poetry. Usually his poems are narratives that touch on violence and tragedy. "The Performance," for example, demonstrates, on the one hand, the violence that characterizes Dickey's well-received novel *Deliverance* (1970) and, on the other, the courageousness of a man insisting on his individuality and rights even against the greatest odds. One of his late novels was *To the White Sea,* published in 1993. A number of his works have been published posthumously in *The James Dickey Reader* (1999). His letters are included in *Crux: The Letters of James Dickey* (1999), and his poetry is collected in *James Dickey: The Selected Poems* (1998).

**EMILY DICKINSON (1830–1886)** • For a detailed biography, see pp. 733–38.

**JOHN DONNE (CA. 1572–1631)** • Donne was born into a Roman Catholic family at a time when the Protestant reign of Elizabeth I was firmly established in England. In 1591 he enrolled at Lincoln's Inn in London to study science, philosophy, law, languages, and literature. So that he might rise in English aristocratic circles, he changed his religion to Anglicanism. His hopes for preference were ended in 1601, however, because of his elopement with Ann More, whose uncle accused him of a clandestine marriage (then a crime if the woman was an heiress) and had him jailed. Although the marriage was recognized in 1602, Donne could not regain political favor, and he and Ann struggled until he took a doctorate of divinity in 1616 (Ann died in 1617). He found favor and rose quickly to become Dean of St. Paul's Cathedral in London, where his sermons were well attended by "nobility and gentry." He became widely known, publishing more than 130 of the sermons he delivered during his decade as dean. His poems, both religious and love poems, were not published during his lifetime but were circulated only privately in manuscript. They were first published two years after his death. For two centuries he was neglected, but in our times he has earned recognition as one of the greatest of English poets.

**JOHN DRYDEN (1631–1700)** • Poet Laureate from 1668 to 1688, Dryden was one of the foremost English poets and dramatists of the seventeenth century. Dr. Johnson considered him the father of English literary criticism. Dryden's major poetic achievement was to fine-tune the heroic or neoclassic couplet, which he used for "To the Memory of Mr. Oldham." He is best known for his verse satires *Mac Flecknoe* (1676, 1682) and *Absalom and Achitophel* (1681), both in rhymed couplets. Nevertheless, he used blank verse for his best play, *All for Love* (1677), which deals with the same material as Acts 4 and 5 of Shakespeare's *Antony and Cleopatra*. In 1688 he lost his official positions because he had been a supporter of King James II, who had been deposed. During the last twelve years of his life, therefore, Dryden was forced to support himself mainly with poetic translations, providing his contemporaries with versions of Virgil, Ovid, Juvenal, and Chaucer.

**PAUL LAURENCE DUNBAR (1872–1906)** • Dunbar was born in Ohio, the son of former slaves. During his brief life he rose to prominence as a poet, dramatist, and novelist. His first two collections of poems, *Oak and Ivy* (1893) and *Majors and Minors* (1895), in which "Sympathy" appeared, were favorably reviewed by William Dean Howells. His collected poems were published posthumously in 1913.

**STEPHEN DUNN (B. 1939)** • Born in New York, Dunn received a master's degree from Syracuse in 1960. He is perhaps the only Pulitzer Prize winner in Poetry to have played professional basketball. He has taught at a number of schools, including the University of Michigan and Stockton State College in New Jersey. Some of his collections are *Five Impersonations* (1971), *Looking for Holes in the Ceiling* (1974), *Between Angels* (1989), and *Loosestrife* (1996). It was for *Different Hours* (2000) that he received the Pulitzer Prize. "Hawk" is taken from *Between Angels*.

**RAY DUREM (1915–1963)** • Selected poems by Durem were printed in Dudley Randall's *The Black Poets: A New Anthology* (1971). Durem's collected verse appeared in *Take No Prisoners* (1962, 1971).

**RICHARD EBERHART (1904–2005)** • Eberhart was a man of great longevity. The recipient of many awards, including the Pulitzer Prize for Poetry in 1966, he was born in Minnesota and received his higher education at Dartmouth and Cambridge. His many works included *Maine Poems* (1988) and *Collected Poems* of 1930, 1976, and 1988. In addition, *Long Reach: Uncollected Poems, 1948–1983* appeared in 1984; *New and Selected Poems: 1930–1990*, in 1990; and *Collected Poems 1930–1976: Including 43 New Poems* in 2001. From 1959 to 1961 he was the consultant in poetry (a position now titled Poet Laureate) at the Library of Congress, and in 1982 the governor of New Hampshire, Eberhart's home state, proclaimed a Richard Eberhart Day in his honor.

**BART EDELMAN (B. 1951)** • Edelman is a native of New Jersey. He received degrees at Hofstra University and now teaches at Glendale College. In addition to his collections of poetry (*Crossing the Hackensack* [1993], *Under Damaris' Dress* [1996], *The Alphabet of Love* [1999], *The Gentle Man* [2001]), and *The Last Mojito* [2005]), he has served as the editor of *Eclipse*, has been awarded a number of significant grants and fellowships, and has done considerable research abroad. See his website at <bartedelman.com>.

**T. S. ELIOT (1888–1965)** • Born in Missouri, Thomas Stearns Eliot moved to England in 1914 and became a British citizen in 1927. With *The Waste Land* in 1922, he electrified the literary world because of his poetic use of colloquial speech and frank subject matter. Though he is considered a hyper-serious poet, his lighter side is shown in *Old Possum's Book of Practical Cats* (1939). These poems achieved popular fame in 1981 in the Broadway musical *Cats*, which then began a record run of 19 consecutive years, not closing until 2000.

**ELIZABETH TUDOR, QUEEN ELIZABETH I (1533–1603)** • Queen of England from 1558 to 1603, Elizabeth was famed for her eloquence and wit. She is perhaps best remembered today for the support she gave to Shakespeare and the acting company at the Globe Theater. She wrote a number of translations and left a small number of poems. Some other poems attributed to her are of doubtful authorship. Her works were edited and published in 1964.

**JAMES EMANUEL (B. 1921)** • Emanuel was born in Nebraska and attended Howard University. He earned his Ph.D. at Columbia in 1962 and joined the faculty of English at the City College of New York. Throughout his career, he has regularly written poetry, publishing poems in journals such as *Phylon* and *Negro Digest*. An early collection of his poems is *Panther Man (1970)*. Other collections are *Black Man Abroad: The Toulouse Poems* (1978), *A Chisel in the Dark* (1980), *The Broken Bowl* (1983), *Deadly James and Other Poems* (1987), and *Jazz: From the Haiku King* (1999). In 1967 he published a biography of Langston Hughes for the Twayne Series of American Authors.

**LYNN EMANUEL (B. 1949)** • Emanuel is a native of New York and currently is director of the University of Pittsburgh's writing program. Her first two collections of poetry are *Hotel Fiesta* and *The Dig*, which have been reprinted together by the University of Illinois Press. A recent poetry collection is *Then, Suddenly* (1999).

**RALPH WALDO EMERSON (1803–1882)** • Emerson, known in his time as the Sage of Concord, was born in Massachusetts and studied to be a minister. His first profession was indeed the ministry, but conscientiously he could not continue when he found it impossible to maintain the orthodoxy that was demanded of his chosen faith. Increasingly he turned to philosophy and became the acknowledged leader of the Transcendental movement, the ideas of which he enunciated in his seminal book *Nature* (1836). His belief in the power of the human mind led him naturally into his involvement with the equal rights of women and also with the abolitionist movement prior to the Civil War. His literary output was enormous. "The American Scholar" (1837) is one of his major essays, as is "Self Reliance" (1841). His reputation as a poet was established by *Poems* in 1846 and *May-Day* in 1867. He has been called one of the most significant of all American thinkers.

**ABBIE HUSTON EVANS (1881–1983)** • Evans was perhaps the longest-lived of all American or British poets, dying in 1983 at the age of 102. She began receiving recognition in the 1930s and was granted an honorary Litt.D. degree from Bowdoin College in 1961. Her collections of poems are *Outcrop* (1928), *The Bright North* (1938), and *Fact of Crystal* (1961). The University of Pittsburgh Press published her *Collected Poems* in 1970. "The Iceberg Seven-Eighths Under" was first published in *Fact of Crystal*.

**MARI EVANS (B. 1923)** • Evans has written fiction and criticism in addition to a major collection of poems, *I Am a Black Woman* (1970). *JD* (1975) is a collection of four stories about a young boy living in an urban housing project. Her *Black Women Writers (1950–1980): A Critical Evaluation* appeared in 1984, and *A Dark and Splendid Mass* was published in 1992. Interest in social matters prompted *Dear Corinne: Tell Somebody*, a fictional work about child abuse (1999). A collection of children's verse is *Sing My Black: Alternative Nursery Rhymes for Children* (1998).

**CAROLYN FORCHÉ (B. 1950)** • Forché is a native of Detroit. After her first volume of poems in the Yale Younger Poets series (*Gathering the Tribes* [1976]) she spent two years in El Salvador as a journalist for Amnesty International. In 1982 she translated Claribel Alegría

*Flowers for the Volcano* in an English-Spanish edition. Her next volume of poetry was *The Country Between Us* in 1982. The section of this collection entitled "In Salvador, 1978–80" contains "The Colonel." In 1993 she published *Against Forgetting: Twentieth-Century Poetry of Witness*, an anthology of poems protesting against repression and genocide. In 1995 she published a long poem, *The Angel of History*, followed in 2003 by her poetry collection *Blue Hour*.

**ROBERT C. FRANCIS (1901–1987)** • Francis received his higher education at Harvard and lived most of his life in Amherst, Massachusetts, not far from the home of Emily Dickinson. Some of his collections are *The Orb Weaver* (1980), *Come Out into the Sun* (1965), *Like Ghosts of Eagles* (1974), and *Butter Hill and Other Poems* (1984). His collected verse appeared in *Collected Poems 1936–1976* (1976). He received a number of distinctions, among them the Brandeis University Creative Arts Award in 1974.

**ROBERT FROST (1874–1963)** • For a detailed biography, see pp. 747–52.

**JOHN GAY (1685–1732)** • English poet and playwright John Gay was born and educated in Devon. As a young boy he was apprenticed to a silk mercer but freed himself to become a writer in London. For a time in the late 1720s, he was a gentleman-in-waiting to the young Duke of Cumberland, for whom he wrote his *Fables*, which were among the most popular poems in the eighteenth century. His most famous play is *The Beggar's Opera* (1728), which at a stroke created ballad opera—a form featuring spoken dialogue and songs sung to popular music. "Let Us Take the Road" is from this play, and the music is the "March" in the opera *Rinaldo* (1711) by Georg Friderich Handel.

**CHIEF DAN GEORGE (1899–1981)** • In the early part of his life, Chief Dan George took many jobs unrelated to writing. In 1947 he became chief of the Tse-lal-Watt Sioux tribe, holding this post until 1959. In the 1960s he launched himself on an acting and writing career. His greatest success as an actor was in the film *Little Big Man* (1970), for which he received an Oscar nomination as best supporting actor. After this time he appeared in a number of films and television shows, and he spent much time campaigning for more Native American involvement in the film industry. His autobiography *You Call Me Chief* appeared in 1981, the last year of his life. His poem "My Heart Soars" is from *Sannichtoni* (1974).

**ALLEN GINSBERG (1926–1997)** • One of the major voices of the "beat generation" of the 1950s and 1960s, Ginsberg was born in New Jersey and lived in San Francisco for a time. For many years he was Distinguished Professor of English at Brooklyn College. His landmark poetry collection was *Howl and Other Poems* (1956), which occasioned a court case when certain persons sued, unsuccessfully, to suppress it on the grounds of obscenity. Ironically, his collection of 1973, *The Fall of America: Poems of These States*, received a National Book Award. Among his later publications were *Cosmopolitan Greetings: Poems 1986–1992* (1994) and a four-CD/cassette box set entitled *Holy Soul Jelly Roll: Poems and Songs 1949–1993* (available from Rhino Word Beat).

**NIKKI GIOVANNI (YOLANDE CORNELIA GIOVANNI, JR., B. 1943)** • Giovanni, a poet whose reputation has coincided with the development of African-American consciousness and pride, was born in Tennessee. She has written poems for children and has also published interviews with James Baldwin and Alice Walker. Among her early collections of poetry are *Black Feeling, Black Talk* (1968), *Black Judgment* (1968), and *Cotton Candy on a Rainy Day* (1978). More recent works are *Those Who Ride the Night Winds* (1983), *Sacred Cows—and Other Edibles*

(1988), *The Selected Poems of Nikki Giovanni* (1996), *Love Poems* (1997), *Blues: For All the Changes: New Poems* (1999), and *Quilting the Black-Eyed Pea: Poems and Not Quite Poems* (2002). She currently teaches at Virginia Tech.

**LOUISE GLÜCK (B. 1943)** • A native of New York, Glück took her higher education at Sarah Lawrence and Columbia. She currently lives in Vermont and teaches at Williams College. Recent poetry collections are *Ararat* (1990), *The Wild Iris* (1992, rpt 2004), *Meadowlands* (1996), *Vita Nova: Poems* (1999), and *The Seven Ages* (2001). In 1985 she received the National Book Critics Circle Award. Her collection *The Garden* earned her the Pulitzer Prize for Poetry in 2003. She served as Poet Laureate of the United States from 2003 to 2004.

**JORIE GRAHAM (B. 1951)** • Graham is a person of international credentials. She is a native of New York but was brought up in Italy and studied in Paris. She received a degree in film from New York University. Later she studied writing at the University of Iowa, where she is a faculty member; she is also on the faculty of Harvard University. Her poetry is thoughtful—a number of critics have said difficult—as well as reflective and challenging. Among her collections are *The End of Beauty* (1987), *Region of Unlikeness* (1991), *Materialism* (1993, 1998), *The Dream of the Unified Field* (1995), *The End of Beauty* (1998), and *Swarm* (2000).

**ROBERT GRAVES (1895–1985)** • Graves fought in the British army in World War I and was badly wounded. His early autobiographical memoir, *Good-Bye to All That* (1929), deals in part with his war experiences. He became famous in the 1970s, when the BBC and PBS dramatized his historical novels about the life and times of the Roman Emperor Claudius. His studies of mythology, *The White Goddess* (1947) and *The Greek Myths* (1955), have explained the meaning of ancient religion to a generation of students.

**THOMAS GRAY (1716–1771)** • Gray was professor of history at Cambridge University. His poetic output was small, but nevertheless in 1757 he was offered the honor of the Poet Laureateship, which he refused. The "Elegy Written in a Country Churchyard" has been called one of the most often quoted poems of the English language. Another of Gray's frequently quoted poems is the "Ode on a Distant Prospect of Eton College," which concludes with the familiar lines "Where ignorance is bliss/'Tis folly to be wise."

**SUSAN GRIFFIN (B. 1943)** • Susan Griffin is a native of California, and received her B.A. and M.A. degrees from San Francisco State. During her career she has served as an editor, teacher, playwright, and writer, and she is a leading feminist critic. She received a number of grants and distinctions, and holds an honorary Ph.D. Among her poetry volumes are *Dear Sky* (1971), *Like the Iris of an Eye* (1976), *Unremembered Country: Poems* (1987), and *Bending Home: Selected and New Poems, 1967–1998* (1998). She is also the author of many volumes of nonfiction.

**MARILYN HACKER (B. 1942)** • Hacker, a native of New York City, has been the recipient of a National Book Award (1975) and a Guggenheim Fellowship. Her collections of poems include *Presentation Piece* (1974); *Separations* (1976); *Taking Notice* (1980), which includes "Sonnet Ending with a Film Subtitle"; and *Selected Poems* (1994). The year 1990 saw the publication of the collection *Going Back to the River*, and in the same year she included new and selected poems in *The Hang-Glider's Daughter*. Other collections are *Selected Poems: 1965–1990* (1995) and *Love, Death, and the Changing of the Seasons* (1995). *Squares and Courtyards* (2000) is a recent collection. In 1989 the composer Dennis Riley set five of her poems to music for soprano and chamber ensemble. In 1995 she was awarded the Lenore Marshall Poetry Prize for her eighth book of poems, *Winter Numbers* (1994). She published *Desesperanto: Poems, 1999–2002* in 2003.

**JOHN HAINES (B. 1936)** • Born in Virginia, Haines served in the Navy during World War II, receiving a number of battle stars. He lives in Alaska, where at various times he has supported himself by working as a hunter, gardener, fisherman, and trapper, in addition to writing. If any modern American writer can lay claim to being a poet of Nature and the frontier, it is Haines. He has published a number of collections, including *News from the Glacier: Selected Poems* (1982), *New Poems 1980–88* (1990), *The Owl in the Mask of the Dreamer: Collected Poems* (1996), *At the End of this Summer: Poems 1948–1954* (1997), *The Stars, the Snow, the Fire* (2000), and *From the Century's End: Poems: 1990–1999* (2001).

**DANIEL HALPERN (B. 1945)** • Halpern was born and raised in New York and is a professor in the graduate writing program of Columbia University. He has lived on both the East and West Coasts and also has a residence in Morocco. He has produced a number of poetry volumes, including *Traveling on Credit* (1972), *Seasonal Rights* (1982), *Foreign Neon* (1991), *Selected Poems* (1994), and *Something Shining: Poems* (1999). He has also done work in editing and translating and is editor of *The Art of the Story: An International Anthology of Contemporary Short Stories* (2000). Uniquely interesting about him is that he has coauthored a cookbook, *The Good Food: Soups, Stews, and Pastas* (1985). He has also written a tourist's guide, *Guide to the Essential Restaurants of Italy* (1990).

**H. S. HAMOD (B. 1936)** • Sam Hamod is a Lebanese American who was born in Indiana. He received a Ph.D. from the Writer's Workshop of the University of Iowa and has served as director of the National Communications Institute in Washington, D.C. He has published a large number of poetic volumes, including *Dying with the Wrong Name* (1980), from which "Leaves" is selected. In 1980 he received a nomination for the Pulitzer Prize for Poetry.

**THOMAS HARDY (1840–1928)** • For a brief biography, see Chapter 6, p. 256.

**JOY HARJO (B. 1951)** • Harjo, who is Creek, Cherokee, and French, was born in Oklahoma. She received her B.A. from the University of New Mexico and her M.F.A. at the University of Iowa and has taught at a number of schools, including Arizona State University. In 1990 she received the American Indian Distinguished Achievement Award, and in 1991 she received the Josephine Miles Award for excellence in literature. She enjoys playing the saxophone and has done some musical recordings. Her poetry collections are *The Last Song* (1975), *What Moon Drove Me to This?* (1980), *She Had Some Horses* (1983), *Secrets from the Center of the World* (1989), *In Mad Love and War* (1990), *The Woman Who Fell from the Sky* (1996, 1998), *A Map to the Next World: Poems and Tales* (2000), and *How We Became Human: New and Selected Poems* (2002). She was a coeditor of *Reinventing the Enemy's Language: North American Native Women's Writing* (1997).

**FRANCES E. W. HARPER (1825–1911)** • Although Harper was a native of Maryland, a slave state in 1825, she was born free. She ensured her continued freedom by eventually moving to the free state of Pennsylvania. Before the Civil War she lectured extensively against slavery and supported the Underground Railroad. Early collections of her work were *Forest Leaves* (1845), *Eventide* (1854), and *Poems on Miscellaneous Subjects* (1854), the last containing a preface by William Lloyd Garrison. Her novel, *Iola Leroy, or Shadows Uplifted* (1892), was well received and was included as part of a collection of fiction by African-American writers. One of her better-known poetry collections is *Atlanta Offering: Poems* (1895). In 1970 and 1988 her reputation as a poet was permanently secured with the publication of complete editions of her poems.

**ROBERT HASS (B. 1941)** • A native of California, Hass is one of America's most distinguished poets. He was educated at Stanford. He taught at St. Mary's College and then became Poet Resident at the University of California at Berkeley. His first collection of poems, *Field Guide* (1973), received the Yale Series of Younger Poets Award. Among his many later collections are *Praise* (1979), *Twentieth Century Pleasures* (1984), *Human Wishes* (1989), and *Sun Under Wood* (1996). He has recently published a number of translations of the work of Czeslaw Milosz. In 1995 he was appointed United States Poet Laureate.

**ROBERT HAYDEN (1913–1980)** • Born in Detroit and educated at the University of Michigan, Hayden became a professor of English at both Fisk and Michigan. His earliest collection of poems was *Heart-Shape in the Dust* (1940). He received a special prize for *A Ballad of Remembrance* at the World Festival of Negro Arts held in Senegal in 1962. His *Words in the Mourning Time* (1970) included laments for the assassinated leaders Martin Luther King and Robert Kennedy, together with poems opposing the Vietnam War.

**SEAMUS HEANEY (B. 1939)** • Heaney lives in Northern Ireland, and has written broadly on many topics. Among his collections of verse are *Wintering Out* (1972), *Field Work* (1979), *Seamus Heaney: Selected Poems, 1966–1987* (1990), *The Spirit Level* (1996) and *Opened Ground: Selected Poems 1966–1996* (1999). His verse translation (1999) of the Old English poem *Beowulf* was well accepted both critically and commercially. His *Finders Keepers: Selected Prose 1971–2001* was published in 2002. The highlight of his many awards and distinctions is the Nobel Prize in Literature in 1995.

**WILLIAM ERNEST HENLEY (1849–1903)** • Born in 1849, Henley contracted tuberculosis when still a boy. A major and lamentable result was that he suffered the amputation of a leg. During his recuperation he began writing poetry and became immediately recognized for the depth and range of his poetic vision. While still in his thirties he collaborated with Robert Louis Stevenson on four dramas, which were well received. His poetry collections were *The Song of the Sword* (1892), *London Voluntaries* (1893), *Collected Poems* (1898), and *In Hospital* (1903), in which he included his well known "Invictus." He was also a critic and editor, being one of the editors of the poetry of Robert Burns, and also of the works of Henry Fielding.

**GEORGE HERBERT (1593–1633)** • Herbert, whose brother was an English lord, became a priest in 1630 after a short career in government service. He died in 1633, leaving his poems to a friend, Nicholas Ferrar, who had them printed in 1633 as *The Temple*. The intricacy of Herbert's thought, illustrated in poems like "The Pulley" and "The Collar," has caused later critics to classify him as a "metaphysical" poet. In the twentieth and twenty-first centuries a large number of church-music composers have set many of his lyrics as choral anthems, and through this medium his works have reached untold numbers of churchgoers.

**ROBERT HERRICK (1591–1674)** • Herrick attended Cambridge and became an Anglican priest in 1627. During the English Civil War he remained loyal to King Charles I, for which he was removed from service in 1647, but he resumed his duties after the Restoration of Charles II in 1660. His major collection of poems was *Hesperides*, published in 1648. A number of people expressed disapproval because of his frank subject matter, but, as he said, though his muse was jocund, his spirit was chaste. "To the Virgins, to Make Much of Time" is one of the better-known poems in the *carpe diem* tradition.

**WILLIAM HEYEN (B. 1940)** • Heyen's father came to the United States from Germany in 1928. Two uncles who remained in Germany joined the Nazi party and were killed in combat when serving in the German army in World War II. Heyen's concern with the Holocaust is thus a complex product of his ethnic ties and his anguish over Nazi atrocities. "The Hair: Jacob Korman's Story" was published in *Erika: Poems of the Holocaust* (1984). Among his volumes of poems are *The City Parables* (1980), *Pterodactyl Rose: Poems of Ecology*, and *Ribbons: The Gulf War*. A collection of his poems titled *The Host: Selected Poems, 1965–1990* was published in 1994. This collection is also available in cassette form. A more recent collection is *Crazy Horse in Stillness: Poems* (1996). In 2002 he was the editor of *September 11, 2001: American Writers Respond*, a collection of works on the topic of the Al Qaeda attacks against the United States.

**JANE HIRSHFIELD (B. 1953)** • Jane Hirshfield was born in New York and took her undergraduate degree at Princeton. Her honors and her work in poetry have been prolific. Her collections of poetry are *Alaya* (1982), *Of Gravity and Angels* (1988), *The October Palace* (1994), *The Lives of the Heart* (1997), and *Given Sugar, Given Salt* (2001). She has also written a study of poetry and has translated and published collections of Japanese Poetry. She has taught at the University of California at Berkeley, the University of San Francisco, the University of Cincinnati, and Bennington. Among her distinctions are fellowships from the Guggenheim Foundation, the Rockefeller Foundation, the Academy of American Poets, and the NEA.

**JOHN HOLLANDER (B. 1929)** • Hollander was born in New York, received his Ph.D. from the University of Indiana, and has taught at Hunter College and Yale University. He is a remarkably energetic and diversified poet, writing shaped verse (such as "Swan and Shadow"), children's verse, and nonsense verse. His musical-critical study *The Untuning of the Sky: Ideas of Music in English Poetry, 1500–1700* appeared in 1961. In 1967 he published *Jiggery-Pokery: A Compendium of Double Dactyls*, in collaboration with Anthony Hecht. His *Rhyme's Reason* (1981) is a guide to the various forms of English verse, which he illustrates with his own examples. *Figurehead and Other Poems*, a recent collection, was published in 1999.

**A. D. HOPE (ALEC DERWENT HOPE, 1907–2000)** • Hope was an Australian whose lyrics were praised for their traditionalism, their clarity and directness, their satire, and their search for redemption in love, literature, and art. Collections are *Collected Poems* (1966), *Collected Poems, 1930–1970* (1972), *Antechinus: Poems 1975–1980* (1981), and *Selected Poems* (1992). A play, *Ladies from the Sea*, appeared in 1987. The Australian National University recognized Hope by granting him an honorary Litt.D. degree in 1972. *A. D. Hope*, a study of Hope by Robert Darling, was published in 1997 in the Twayne's English Authors Series.

**GERARD MANLEY HOPKINS (1844–1889)** • Hopkins was an English poet gifted not only in poetry but also in music and art. At the age of 22, under the pastoral care of John Henry Cardinal Newman, he converted to Roman Catholicism. He studied for the priesthood and was ordained as a priest in 1877. Although he published the long poem *The Wreck of the Deutschland* in 1875, his religious poems linking his devotion to Nature, on which his reputation now rests, were not published until early in the twentieth century. The *Poetical Works of Gerard Manley Hopkins*, edited by N. H. Mackenzie, was published in 1990.

**CAROLINA HOSPITAL (B. 1957)** • Hospital was born in Cuba in 1957 and was brought to the United States as a child of four, two years after the Castro revolution. She thus received an American education, and she earned an M.A. from the University of Florida in 1984. She included "Dear Tia" in her collection *Cuban American Writers: Los Atrevidos* (1988). Her *The Child of Exile: A Poetry Memoir* appeared in 2004. Using the *nom de plume* C. C. Medina, she published the novel *A Little Love* in 2000.

**A. E. HOUSMAN (1859–1936)** • Housman was a professor of classics at Cambridge University. He created one major book of verse, *A Shropshire Lad* (1896), a collection of poems stressing the brevity and fragility of youth and love. His major scholarly pursuit was a study of the ancient Latin writer Manilius, whose works he edited. His *More Poems* was published posthumously, and his *Complete Poems* was published in 1956.

**LANGSTON HUGHES (1902–1967)** • For a brief biography in two parts, see pp. 761–64, and also pp. 1239–41.

**JOHN HALL INGHAM (1860–CA. 1920?)** • Ingham's major work of poetry was *Pompeii of the West and Other Poems* (1903). In *An American Anthology* (1900), Clarence Steadman published "George Washington," together with two other Ingham poems, "A Summer Sanctuary" and "Genesis." In 1919, the composer Frances McCollin set Ingham's poem "The Midnight Sea" to voice with accompanying piano.

**JOSEPHINE JACOBSEN (1908–2003)** • Jacobsen, a Canadian by birth, did not receive a higher education because her parents believed that she, as a young woman, would gain no benefit from it. Despite such discouragement, she began writing poetry in 1940 with *Let Each Man Remember*, and she continued to write voluminously, both poetry and fiction, after that time. Her *The Shade-Seller: New and Selected Poems* appeared in 1974, and *In the Crevice of Time* was published in 1995. Among her many distinctions and honors were a Consultantship in Poetry (later the Poet Laureateship) to the Library of Congress and an award from the American Academy of Arts and Letters.

**RANDALL JARRELL (1914–1965)** • Jarrell was born in Tennessee. He received his B.A. and M.A. degrees from Vanderbilt University. He wrote poetry, criticism, a novel, and children's fiction. His 1945 collection of poems, *Little Friend, Little Friend*, which includes "The Death of the Ball Turret Gunner," resulted from his service in the Army Air Corps during World War II. He published a number of other verse collections, including *Selected Poems* (1955) and *The Woman at the Washington Zoo* (1960).

**ROBINSON JEFFERS (1887–1962)** • Jeffers was born in Pittsburgh and spent most of his life in California. He used negative and often brutal subject matter in his poetry, for example, fratricide in *Give Your Heart to the Hawks* (1933), betrayal in *Dear Judas, and Other Poems* (1929), and infidelity in *Thurso's Landing, and Other Poems* (1932). His adaptation of Euripides' *Medea* (1947), starring Judith Anderson in the title role, won him wide national recognition. "The Answer" and "The Purse-Seine" appeared in his *Selected Poetry* (1938).

**JOHN KEATS (1795–1821)** • Keats is one of the major English Romantic poets. Both his parents died when he was still a child, and at the age of 15 he was apprenticed to an apothecary-surgeon. In 1816 he received his license to practice medicine, but almost immediately he gave up that career in order to become a full-time poet. In the following five years he created a magnificent body of poetry. Mortally afflicted with tuberculosis, he went to Rome, where he took rooms in the building adjoining the Spanish Steps. He died in Rome at the age of 26 and is buried in the English Cemetery in Rome near the Pyramid of Sestus Sextus.

**HENRY KING (1592–1669)** • King became Bishop of Chichester in 1642 and held this position for the rest of his life. He had been a friend of John Donne and was likely one of Donne's early editors. During his lifetime he published two volumes of his own verse, one a poetic rendering of the Psalms and the other an edition of *Poems, Elegies, Paradoxes, and Sonnets* (1657). His collected poems were published in 1965.

**GALWAY KINNELL (B. 1927)** • Kinnell was born in Rhode Island and received degrees from Princeton and the University of Rochester. During his career he has taught at many schools, including the Universities of Grenoble in France, Teheran in Iran (on a Fulbright Fellowship), and Hawaii. Among his many distinctions, he was awarded the National Book Award for Poetry and the Pulitzer Prize in Poetry, both in 1983, for *Selected Poems* (1982). He was also the recipient of a prestigious MacArthur Fellowship. He has published a great number of poetry collections, such as *What a Kingdom It Was* (1960) and *A New Selected Poems* (2000). "After Making Love We Hear Footsteps" was included in *Mortal Acts, Mortal Words* (1980).

**CAROLYN KIZER (B. 1925)** • Born in Spokane, Washington, Kizer studied at the University of Washington with Theodore Roethke. During much of her life she has lived in California. One of her specialties is the adaptation of poems from China and Japan. "Night Sounds," from *Mermaids in the Basement* (1984), is an example. Since 1959 she has regularly published poetry collections, some of which are *Knock Upon Silence* (1965), *Midnight Was My Cry* (1971), *The Nearness of You* (1986), *Harping On: Poems 1985–1995* (1996), and *Cool Calm & Collected* (2000). In 1985 her collection of poems *Yin* (1984) received the Pulitzer Prize in Poetry.

**TED KOOSER (B. 1939)** • Kooser is a native of Iowa. If anyone can lay claim to being a midwest poet, it is he. He was educated at Iowa State and the University of Nebraska, and he has taught at Nebraska. In 2004 he was appointed the thirteenth Poet Laureate of the United States. Among his other honors are fellowships from the NEA, a Pushcart Prize, and the Stanley Kunitz Prize. He has published ten collections of poetry, including *Sure Signs* (1980), *One World at a Time* (1985), *Weather Central* (1994), and *Delights and Shadows* (2004).

**PHILIP LARKIN (1922–1985)** • A novelist, editor, and reviewer as well as a poet, Larkin was born in northern England and attended Oxford. His first collection of verse was *The North Ship* (1946), followed nine years later by *The Less Deceived*, in which "Next, Please" was printed. In 1964 he published *The Whitsun Weddings*, and in 1974 *High Windows*.

**DORIANNE LAUX (B. 1952)** • Laux is a native of Maine, and before receiving a degree from Mills College in 1988 she supported herself by odd jobs such as managing a gas station, cooking for a sanatorium, doing housework as a maid, and cutting holes in doughnut dough. Since then she has published four volumes of poetry: *Awake* (1990), *What We Carry* (1994), *Smoke* (2000), and *Facts About the Moon* (2005). With Kim Addonizio, she published *The Poet's Companion: A Guide to the Pleasures of Writing Poetry* (1997). She has received a fellowship from the NEA, and teaches at the University of Oregon.

**EMMA LAZARUS (1849–1887)** • Lazarus was born in New York before the Civil War, and was a member of the New York aristocracy. She began writing early, not only her own poetry but also translations of writers like Goethe and Heine. Aroused by the plight of European Jewry, she wrote articles on the need for a Jewish homeland, and also translated the poems of many Jewish writers. A few years before the dedication of the Statue of Liberty in 1886, she wrote "The New Colossus" as a celebration of immigrants coming to the United States. In 1903, sixteen years after her death, the entire sonnet was embossed on a large metal plate which was affixed to the base of the Statue. It is still there, for all visitors to read.

**DAVID LEHMAN (B. 1948)** • Lehman is a native of New York, and attended Columbia in New York and Cambridge in England. He teaches at Bennington and also the New School for Social Research. His poetry collections are *An Alternative to Speech* (1986), *Operation Memory* (1990), *Valentine Place* (1996), *The Daily Mirror: A Journal in Poetry* (2000), *The Evening Sun* (2002), and *When a Woman Loves a Man* (2005). He is a highly creative and productive writer. He originated *The Best American Poetry* series, which has been published each September since 1988. He has also written extensive criticism on the topic of poetry, and has perhaps amazed people by sustaining the habit of writing a poem a day for a number of years. He is also interested in mystery writers, and received an Edgar Award from the Mystery Writers of America for his study of detective novels, *The Perfect Murder* (1989). He has received grants from the NEA and the Guggenheim Foundation.

**DENISE LEVERTOV (1923–1997)** • Levertov was a native of England whose parents were Welsh and Jewish. She was educated at home and served as a nurse in World War II. After the war she married an American and left England to live in the United States. She began publishing poems in her twenties. Since her first poetry collection, *The Double Image*, which appeared in 1946, she published at least two collections each decade. In the 1970s she published four. Her collections ranged from personal topics to deeply political ones, particularly *Light Up the Cave* (1981), which contains a number of poems on the Vietnam War. Some of her last poetry collections were *The Double Image* (1991), *Evening Train* (1992), and *Sands of the Well* (1996). In 1995 the Academy of American Poets awarded her an Academy Fellowship. A posthumous collection of her poetry is *The Great Unknowing: Last Poems* (1999).

**ABRAHAM LINCOLN (1809–1865)** • Lincoln was the sixteenth president of the United States, serving from 1861 until his assassination in 1865. He was born in Kentucky in 1809 and with his family moved to southwestern Indiana in 1816. Because the area was still wild, Lincoln, though yet a child, was needed in helping his father clear the land and in performing the many duties needed for life on the frontier. There was virtually no time for him to attend school. Eventually, he rose to be the partner in a successful law firm in Illinois, and then he went into state politics. In 1844, before he stood for any national office and when he was campaigning for Henry Clay (1777–1852) for the presidency, he returned to Indiana, and it was then that he wrote "My Childhood's Home," one of his three surviving poems. He is perhaps the most often quoted of American presidents, but it is for his many memorable speeches, especially the Gettysburg Address, that he is best known today.

**LIZ LOCHHEAD (B. 1947)** • In addition to her poetry, Lochhead also writes plays, translations, and television scripts. She is a native of Scotland and has taught at the Glasgow School of Art and the University of Glasgow. Her poetry collection *Memo for Spring* (1972) earned her a fellowship award from the Scottish Arts Council (1973). Some of her other poetry collections are *The Grimm Sisters* (1981), *Dreaming Frankenstein and Collected Poems* (1984), and *Bagpipe Muzak* (1991). She is a featured poet in the collection *Three Scottish Poets* of 1992, and in another collection, *Four Women*

*Poets* (1996). Later works are *Perfect Days*, a play (2000); *Medea*, a translation/version of the *Medea* of Euripides (2001); and *Miseryguts/Taruffe*, translations of two Molière plays (2002).

**HENRY WADSWORTH LONGFELLOW (1807–1882)** • Longfellow was acknowledged in his own time as one of the great United States poets. He was so popular, and his poetry sold so well, that he was able to live on the proceeds of his writing. After graduating from Bowdoin College in 1825, he began mastering Spanish, French, Italian, German, and the Scandinavian languages. This mastery equipped him to accept a professorship in languages at Harvard in 1836. His translation of Dante's *Divine Comedy* appeared in 1867, and at this same time he composed a number of sonnets that he published in 1867 and 1875. Some of his best-known works are *Ballads and Other Poems* (1842), *Evangeline* (1847), *The Song of Hiawatha* (1855), *The Children's Hour* (1860), and *Paul Revere's Ride* (1863).

**AUDRE LORDE (1934–1992)** • Lorde was a New Yorker whose parents were immigrants from Jamaica. She was educated at the National University of Mexico, Hunter College, and Columbia. Some of her poetry collections are *Chosen Poems Old and New* (1982), *Our Dead Behind Us* (1986), and *Undersong* (1992). *The Marvelous Arithmetics of Distance: Poems 1987–1992* (1993) was a posthumous collection.

**AMY LOWELL (1874–1925)** • Lowell was a proponent of the Imagist school of poetry early in the twentieth century. Her earliest collection of poems was *A Dome of Many-Colored Glass* (1912). Later collections were *Sword Blades and Poppy Seed* (1914) and *Legends* (1921). "Patterns" appeared in her collection *Men, Women, and Ghosts* (1916).

**THOMAS LUX (B. 1946)** • A winner of the Kingsley Tufts Poetry Award, Lux was educated at the University of Iowa and has taught at Sarah Lawrence College for many years. His poetry has been characterized as an "ironic mingling of humor and sincerity." Some of his collections are *The Land Sighted* (1970), *The Drowned River: New Poems* (1990), *Pecked to Death by Swans* (1993), *Split Horizon* (1994), *The Blind Swimmer: Selected Early Poems, 1970–1975* (1996), *New and Selected Poems 1975–1995* (1997), and *The Street of Clocks* (2001).

**ANDREW MARVELL (1621–1678)** • Marvell, one of the major metaphysical poets of the seventeenth century, was active during the unsettled period of the English Civil Wars of 1642–1649, the Commonwealth, and the Protectorate of Oliver Cromwell. The Restoration of King Charles II (1660) ushered in a period of relative calm in Marvell's life. During his long career, which he began as a tutor in an aristocratic household, he assisted Milton (who served as Latin Secretary for the English Commonwealth), and he also was a Member of Parliament. His poems were not published until three years after his death. A modern edition of his *Poems and Letters* was published in 1971.

**JOHN MASEFIELD (1878–1967)** • The English poet John Masefield, though not an academic, was a compulsive reader and writer. In his youth he was a merchant seaman and worker at odd jobs in the United States. Eventually, he published 50 volumes of poems, together with many plays and novels, and he became Poet Laureate of England in 1930. His two best-known poems are "I Must Go Down to the Sea Again," included in *Salt-Water Ballads* (1902), and "Cargoes," which appeared in *Ballads and Poems* (1910).

**CLAUDE McKAY (1890–1948)** • McKay, one of the important voices in the Harlem Renaissance of the 1920s, was born in Jamaica, immigrated to the United States in 1912, and settled in

Harlem in 1914. He wrote a number of novels, including *Home to Harlem* (1928), and short stories, published in *Gingertown* (1932). His poems were collected in *Songs of Jamaica* (1911), *Spring in New Hampshire and Other Poems* (1920), and *Harlem Shadows* (1922), where we find "In Bondage" and "The White City."

**HERMAN MELVILLE (1819–1891)** • Melville is best known as the author of *Moby-Dick* (1851), which has been called the greatest of all American novels. He was born in New York. At the age of fifteen he left school to take up clerical work, to which he refers in his famous and long story "Bartleby the Scrivener" (1856). He spent a number of years as a seaman, which gave him the experience to write *Typee* (1846), *Omoo* (1847), *Mardi* (1849), *Redburn* (1849), *White-Jacket* (1850), and *Billy Budd* (1888, 1924), in addition to *Moby-Dick*. He wrote an extensive poem based on his visit to the Near East, *Clarel* (1876), and collected his poems in *Battle-Pieces and Aspects of the War* (1866, containing "Shiloh"), *John Marr and Other Sailors* (1888), *Timoleon* (1891), and the posthumous *Weeds and Wildings, with a Rose or Two* (1924).

**W. S. MERWIN (WILLIAM STANLEY MERWIN, B. 1927)** • Merwin was born in New York and raised in New Jersey and Pennsylvania. He currently lives in Hawaii. He published *Selected Translations 1948–1968* in 1968 and was distinguished by a PEN translation prize for this work. In 1988 he published two collections of poems: *The Rain in the Trees* and *Selected Poems*. In 1996 he published *The Vixen*, a collection of poems about people and life in the southern part of France. Also in 1996 he published *Flower & Hand: Poems 1977–1983*. Three long poems make up his *The River Sound* (1999). In 2001 he published *The Pupil: Poems*. He was awarded the Pulitzer Prize in Poetry for *The Carriers of Ladders* (1970).

**JOHN MILTON (1608–1674)** • Milton is acknowledged as one of the greatest English poets. His fame rests largely on the epic poem *Paradise Lost*, which he published in 1667, long after he became blind. He led a varied career and wrote extensively in both verse and prose, including many Latin poems. His most important political position was as Latin Secretary to Oliver Cromwell during the Interregnum (1649–1660). Latin at that time was the language of diplomacy, and a good Latinist like Milton was essential to the government. Milton's *Poems* was published in 1645, and he issued a second edition in 1673.

**JUDITH MINTY (B. 1937)** • Minty is of Finnish, Irish, and Mohawk descent. She has done a variety of things in addition to writing poetry, including working as a speech therapist, selling cosmetics, and introducing poetry to prisoners. She resides in Arcata, California, and has taught at Humboldt State University and the University of California at Santa Cruz. Among her poetry collections are *Lake Songs and Other Fears* (1974), *In the Presence of Mothers* (1981), *Counting the Losses* (1986), and *Dancing the Fault* (1991). A recent poetry collection is *Walking with the Bear* (2000).

**N. SCOTT MOMADAY (B. 1934)** • A member of the Kiowa tribe, Momaday was educated at the University of New Mexico and Stanford University. He has taught at Stanford and the University of Arizona. His reputation as a writer was gained by his *House Made of Dawn* (1968) and *The Way to Rainy Mountain* (1969). Despite his success as a novelist, he considers himself a poet. Some of his collections are *Angle of Geese and Other Poems* (1974), *The Gourd Dancer* (1976), and *In the Presence of the Sun: Stories and Poems 1961–1991* (1992).

**EUGENIO MONTALE (1896–1981)** • The poet and critic Eugenio Montale is often associated with *hermeticism*, a movement associated with other Italian poets writing in the early part of the

Twentieth century, particularly Umberto Saba, Giuseppe Ungaretti, and Salvatore Quasimodo (q.v.). Its main tenets are a deliberate obscurity, a bare style, and a deeply personal symbolism. Some have suggested that Fascist censors may have led Montale to "disguise" his meanings in difficult language and allusion, but his poetry undoubtedly has a literary rationale as well and has influenced poets outside of the Italian tradition. For many poets, the "hermetic model" reflects the complexity of modern life and the inability to reach absolute conclusions about the human condition. "English Horn" reflects the thoughts of an adolescent girl, and indeed she may be a girl from any time and place. Although the images of the wind, earth, light, and the sky resonate throughout many of Montale's poems, and have deeply personal associations for him, a careful reader of "English Horn" can understand the meanings of these major images apart from any knowledge of other Montale poems. Montale was awarded the Nobel Prize for Literature in 1975.

**LISEL MUELLER (B. 1924)** • Lisel Neumann Mueller came to this country from Germany in 1939, just as World War II was intensifying in Europe. She studied at the University of Indiana and has taught at Goddard College. Even though English is not her first language, she has mastered the craft of English poetry and has made English translations of works by Marie Luise Kaschnitz. Her poetry volumes are *Dependencies* (1965, rpt. 1998), *The Private Life* (1976), *The Need to Hold Still* (1980), *Second Language: Poems* (1986), and *Waving from Shore: Poems* (1989). Her Pulitzer Prize-winning *Alive Together: New and Selected Poems* (1996) includes poems from each of these collections and adds a number of new poems. "Hope" was originally published in *The Private Life*.

**HOWARD NEMEROV (1920–1991)** • Nemerov graduated from Harvard and served in World War II. After the war he taught at a number of colleges and began publishing his many essays, stories, plays, and poems. His poetry collections include *The Image and the Law* (1947), *The Western Approaches: Poems 1973–1975* (1975), and *Inside the Onion* (1985). The Library of Congress honored him as Poet Laureate from 1986 to 1988.

**JIM NORTHRUP (B. 1943)** • Northrup is a Chippewa Indian and lives with his family on the Fond du Lac Reservation in Minnesota. He has published a number of stories, and his poems have been published mainly in magazines and journals. His major poetry collection, which also contains stories, is *Walking the Rez Road* (1993). His *The Rez Road Follies* was published in 1997. More recently he has published poems in *Nitaawichige: Selected Poetry and Prose by Four Anishinaabe Writers* (2002). He writes a syndicated column and also works as an artist.

**NAOMI SHIHAB NYE (B. 1952)** • Nye, a Palestinian-American, is a native of Missouri but has lived for a time in Jerusalem. She is not only a poet but also a writer of children's books and, interestingly, a folk singer (with recordings to her credit). In her work as a teacher she has taught at the University of Hawaii and the University of Texas at Austin. She has published her poetry in a number of collections, including *Tattooed Feet* (1977), *Different Ways to Pray* (1980), *Hugging the Jukebox* (1982), *Yellow Glove* (1986), *Texas Poets in Concert: A Quartet* (1990, as one of four poets), *Red Suitcase* (1994), *The Words Under the Words: Selected Poems* (1995), *Fuel* (1998), *Come with Me: Poems for a Journey* (2000), and *19 Varieties of Gazelle: Poems of the Middle East* (2002). A collection of her essays, *Never in a Hurry*, was published in 1996. She published *The Space between Our Footsteps: Poems and Paintings from the Middle East* in 1998. *Habibi* (1997, 1999) is an autobiographical novel for young people.

**JOYCE CAROL OATES (B. 1938)** • For a brief biography, see p. 130.

**SHARON OLDS (B. 1942)** • Born in San Francisco, Olds received her Ph.D. from Columbia in 1972 and taught at New York University, Sarah Lawrence, Brandeis, and Columbia. In 1998 she was named New York State Poet. Her early poetry collections are *Satan Says* (1980) and *The Dead and the Living* (1984), which contains "35/10." Recent collections are *The Gold Cell* (1987), *The Father* (1992), *The Wellspring* (1996), *Blood, Tin, Straw* (1999), *The Unswept Room* (2002), and *Strike Sparks: Selected Poems 1980–2002* (2004). Although her poems are often physical and deeply personal, she remains, at heart, a private person. In a recent informal survey, members of the Academy of American Poets most often named her as their favorite contemporary American poet.

**MARY OLIVER (B. 1935)** • A native of Cleveland, Oliver took her higher education at Ohio State University and Vassar College. She is a longtime resident of Provincetown, Massachusetts, and is on the faculty of Bennington College. Her poetry collections have been regular and numerous, including *No Voyage and Other Poems* (1963), *Sleeping in the Forest* (1978), *American Primitive* (1983), *New and Selected Poems* (1992), *White Pine: Poems and Prose Poems* (1994), *Blue Pastures* (1995), *West Wind* (1997), and *Winter Hours: Poetry, Prose, and Essays* (1999). She is also the author of *A Poetry Handbook* (1994) and *Rules for the Dance: A Handbook for Writing and Reading Metrical Verse* (1998). She received the National Book Award and the Shelley Memorial Award, and in 1984 she was honored with the Pulitzer Prize in Poetry for *American Primitive*.

**MICHEAL O'SIADHAIL (B. 1941)** • Micheal O'Siadhail (pronounced "me HALL oh SHEEL") is Irish. He was born in Dublin and attended the Clongowes Wood School, the same school James Joyce had attended many years before. He received degrees from Trinity College, Dublin, and attended the University of Oslo in Norway. A noteworthy distinction is that he has performed various governmental services, one of which was his membership on the Arts Council of the Republic of Ireland. He is the author of nine collections of poetry, among which are *The Leap Year* (1978), *Springnight* (1983), *Hail! Madam Jazz: New and Selected Poems* (1992), and *The Gossamer Wall* (2002). "Abundance" is from *Poems: 1975–1995* (1999).

**WILFRED OWEN (1893–1918)** • A native of Shropshire, England, Owen became a British Army officer and was killed in France in 1918, just a week before the Armistice on November 11. He published only four poems in his lifetime, but after his death Siegfried Sassoon issued a collection of 24 poems (1920). Benjamin Britten used a number of Owen's poems, including "Anthem for Doomed Youth," as texts for his *War Requiem* (1962). The band 10,000 Maniacs recorded versions of both "Anthem for Doomed Youth" and "Dulce et Decorum Est" on their album *Hope Chest* (Elektra 9-60962-2).

**DOROTHY PARKER (1893–1967)** • Parker became legendary because of her many witty "one-liners" and also because of her often caustic book and drama reviews for *The New Yorker* in the period between the World Wars. Her first volume of poetry was *Enough Rope* (1926). "Penelope" was included in her comprehensive collection *Not So Deep as a Well* (1936). She wrote many short stories and served as a correspondent during the Spanish Civil War in the late 1930s.

**LINDA PASTAN (B. 1932)** • Pastan was born in New York. She received a B.A. from Radcliffe and an M.A. from Brandeis. Among her many volumes of verse are *A Perfect Circle of*

*Sun* (1971), *Setting the Table* (1980), *Waiting for My Life* (1981), *PM/AM: New and Selected Poems* (1983), *A Fraction of Darkness* (1985*)*, *An Early Afterlife* (1996), *Carnival Evening: New and Selected Poems 1968–1998* (1998), and *The Last Uncle* (2002).

**MOLLY PEACOCK (B. 1947)** • Peacock was born in Buffalo, New York, and received a master's degree with honors from Johns Hopkins University. The first of her many collections of poetry was *And Live Apart* (1980) Recent collections are *Paradise, Piece by Piece* (1998) and *Cornucopia: New and Collected Poems* (2002). "Desire" is selected from *Raw Heaven* (1984). She is known as a poet who deals with the "pain and joy of living," and she has been praised for her fearless and uninhibited treatment of subjects that many consider taboo, even for personal and confessional poets.

**MARGE PIERCY (B. 1936)** • A native of Detroit, Piercy received her B.A. from the University of Michigan (1957) and M.A. from Northwestern (1958). She now lives in Cape Cod. Among her novels are *Braided Lives* (1980) and *Fly Away Home* (1984). The first of her many poetry collections was *Breaking Camp* (1968). Others are *The Moon Is Always Female* (1980); *Circles on the Water: Selected Poems* (1982), including "A Work of Artifice" and "The Secretary Chant"; and *Available Light* (1988). Her most recent poetic volumes are *What Are Big Girls Made Of?* (1996), *Early Grrrl: The Early Poems of Marge Piercy* (1999), and *The Art of Blessing the Day: Poems with a Jewish Theme* (1999).

**ROBERT PINSKY (B. 1940)** • Poet, scholar, and translator, Pinsky was educated in his home state of New Jersey and also at Stanford. He has taught at the University of California, Boston University, and Harvard. Some of his poetry collections are *Sadness and Happiness* (1975), *An Explanation of America* (1979), *The Want Bone* (1990), and *The Figured Wheel: New and Collected Poems 1966–1996* (1996, 1997). His *Explanation of America* (1979) is a book-length poem. For a time he was poetry editor of *The New Republic*. In the 1990s he was Poet Laureate of the United States for three successive terms, the only person to be so honored. He has used the prestige of his position advantageously. He brought out a short book (*The Sounds of Poetry: A Brief Guide* [1998]), and he also has done much to put poetry before the public eye, appearing regularly on national television to read poems and to comment extensively on poetry. One of his important efforts for poetry has been the development of the Favorite Poem Project. The result, on which he worked in collaboration with many persons from all walks of life, is *Americans' Favorite Poems* (1999). With Maggie Dietz, he published *Poems to Read* in 2002. "Dying" is taken from his collection *History of My Heart* (1984, 1998).

**SYLVIA PLATH (1932–1963)** • For a detailed biography, see pp. 773–77.

**EDGAR ALLAN POE (1809–1849)** • For a brief biography, see p. 233.

**ALEXANDER POPE (1688–1744)** • Pope is the eminent eighteenth-century English poet, the acknowledged master of the neoclassic couplet. A childhood accident deformed his spine and retarded his physical growth, but it did not hinder his poetic gifts. Because his family was Roman Catholic, he was not sent to school but was educated at home. By the age of 23 he had completed *An Essay on Criticism* (1711), the leading English work of criticism in poetic form. After 1725 he devoted himself principally to writing satire, producing *The Dunciad* (1728, rev. 1743), the *Moral Essays* (1731–35), *An Epistle to Dr. Arbuthnot* (1735), and other satiric works, including the *Epilogues to the Satires* in dialogue form (1738). One of his life's plans was to publish a major philosophic work in poetry, but the only part he completed was *An Essay on Man* (1734).

**EZRA POUND (1885–1972)** • A native of Idaho, Pound was educated at the University of Pennsylvania and spent most of his life in Europe. He was the leading exponent of poetic imagism (see also Amy Lowell). During World War II he broadcast pro-Axis propaganda from Rome. After the war he was prosecuted for this but was exonerated on the grounds of insanity. Pound is as much known for his influence on other poets as for his own poetry (T. S. Eliot acknowledged him as "the better maker" in the dedication to *The Waste Land*). He published many poetry collections, such as *Exultations* (1909), *Canzoni* (1911), and *Cathay* (1915), which contained his versions of Chinese poems. His major work was the *Cantos*, which he worked on throughout his life after publishing the first portion in 1925.

**SALVATORE QUASÍMODO (1901–1968)** • A native of Italy, Quasímodo's early work was part of the so-called Italian "hermetic" period prior to World War II. (See *Eugenio Montale*.) That is, his poetry was highly imagistic, personal, and nonpolitical. During the war he became militantly antifascist, and for this reason Mussolini sent him to prison. After the war he became deeply concerned with the conditions of common people. In addition, he translated many works into Italian. He was the recipient of the Nobel Prize in Literature in 1959. His *Complete Poems* was published in 1984.

**DUDLEY RANDALL (1914–2000)** • A native of Washington, D.C., Randall spent five years working in the foundry at the Ford River Rouge plant in Michigan. He became a librarian after that and went on to the position of head librarian. In 1965 he founded the Broadside Press, an important and valuable publisher for African-American writers. One of the first poems from the press was "Ballad of Birmingham," which had earlier (1963) been set to music and made popular by the folk singer Jerry Moore. Randall's major poetry collections are *More to Remember: Poems of Four Decades* (1971) and *A Litany of Friends: New and Selected Poems* (1981, 1983).

**JOHN CROWE RANSOM (1888–1974)** • Along with Robert Penn Warren, Alan Tate, and Cleanth Brooks, Ransom was one of the important exponents of the New Criticism (see Chapter 24, p. 1395). He founded the *Kenyon Review* and edited it for twenty years. His major poetry collections are *Chills and Fever* (1924), *Two Gentlemen in Bonds* (1927), and *Selected Poems* (1945, revised in 1963 and 1969).

**JOHN RAVEN (B. 1936)** • Raven's poems figured importantly in Dudley Randall's collection *The Black Poets: A New Anthology* (1971). His major collection of poems is *Blues for Momma* (1970).

**HENRY REED (1914–1986)** • Reed was English and received a degree from the University of Birmingham. During the 1950s he became well known in England for his translations and radio dramas for the BBC. His major book of poems was *A Map of Verona* (1946), which contains "Naming of Parts." Five of his radio plays in verse were published as *The Streets of Pompeii* (1971), and four of his comedies in prose were published in *Hilda Tablet and Others* (1971).

**ANNE BARBARA RIDLER (1912–2001)** • Ridler was a writer not only of poems but also of plays, film plays, songs, and translations. She was an editor at the Oxford University Press, which published some of her poems, and also at Faber and Faber, where T. S. Eliot was an editor. She published her first collection of poems, *Poems*, in 1939. Following collections were *A Dream Observed and Other Poems* (1941), *The Golden Bird and Other Poems* (1951), *Selected Poems* (1961), *Some Time After and Other Poems* (1972), *New and Selected Poems* (1988), *Collected Poems* (1994), and *Anne Ridler: Collected Poems* (1997). She edited many collections, including an anthology of ghost stories. Most notable among her many other writings are English translations of the libretti of Mozart's operas *The Marriage of Figaro* and *Così fan Tutte*.

**EDWIN ARLINGTON ROBINSON (1869–1935)** • Robinson began his career inauspiciously with various jobs in New York City. The publication of *The Children of the Night* (1897) and *Captain Craig* (1902) impressed President Theodore Roosevelt, who arranged a position for him as clerk in the New York Customs House. After publication of *The Town Down the River* in 1910, he was able to support himself with his poetry. "Tilbury Town," where many of his poetic characters reside, is modeled on Gardiner, Maine, the town where he grew up. He is particularly notable because he received the first Pulitzer Prize in Poetry ever to be awarded (1922). He received the prize twice more, in 1924 and 1928. In 1976 A. R. Gurney wrote a drama, *Who Killed Richard Cory?*, which played at the Circle Repertory Theatre in New York. Simon and Garfunkel, in their early years together, created a song telling the tale of Richard Cory (available on CD).

**THEODORE ROETHKE (1908–1963)** • Roethke was born in Saginaw, Michigan, where his father operated a successful greenhouse. After graduating from the University of Michigan he taught at a number of schools, primarily at the University of Washington. His first book was *Open House* (1941), and his second was *The Lost Son and Other Poems* (1948), which included "My Papa's Waltz." His collection *The Waking* (1953) received the Pulitzer Prize in Poetry for 1954. His *Collected Poems* was published posthumously in 1966. When he died in 1963 he had achieved wide recognition and acclaim. In addition to distinguishing himself, he was also the teacher of other poets, numbering James Wright among his students at the University of Washington.

**CHRISTINA ROSSETTI (1830–1894)** • English-born Christina Rossetti's religious lyrics and ballads have made her a favorite with composers such as Gustav Holst and John Rutter. Painters of the Pre-Raphaelite Brotherhood, of whom her brother Dante Gabriel Rossetti was a leading figure, frequently called upon her to pose for their paintings. Ill health forced her to forsake a career as a governess, and after 1874 she became a virtual invalid. Some of her poetry collections are *Goblin Market and Other Poems* (1862), *The Prince's Progress and Other Poems* (1866), and *A Pageant and Other Poems* (1872). A modern edition of her *Complete Poems* was published in 1979.

**MURIEL RUKEYSER (1913–1980)** • A *poète engagée*, Rukeyser was arrested in Alabama in the 1930s for demonstrating in favor of the Scottsboro Nine (see also Chapter 23, in the introduction to *Mulatto* by Langston Hughes). Later, she wrote on behalf of an imprisoned Korean poet in *The Gates* (1976). She published many collections, including *Theory of Flight* (1935), *Beast in View* (1944), *Body of Waking* (1958), and *Collected Poems* (1979).

**GEORGE WILLIAM RUSSELL ("Æ") (1867–1935)** • Russell used the pseudonym which is rendered either as "Æ" or "A.E." He was a native of Ireland, and became an activist in the cause of Irish nationalism. For more than 25 years he was an editor, and is considered an important figure in the Irish literary renaissance of the early twentieth century. He was a friend of both Yeats and Joyce. An early collection of his verse, noted for its spiritualism, was *Homeward: Songs by the Way* (1894), and a later collection was *Selected Poems* (1935).

**LUIS OMAR SALINAS (B. 1937)** • Salinas was born in Texas. He attended Fresno State University from 1967 to 1972 and made his home in California. His first volume of poems was

*Crazy Gypsy* (1970). In 1973 he edited *From the Barrio: A Chicano Anthology,* and in 1975 he was one of four poets included (along with Gary Soto) in *Entrance: Four Chicano Poets.* Since then he has been regularly productive. One of his major volumes was *The Sadness of Days: Selected and New Poems,* which appeared in 1987.

**SONIA SANCHEZ (B. 1934)** • Sanchez was born in Alabama. She received a B.A. from Hunter College in 1955, and for a time after that she worked for the Congress of Racial Equality. Her major teaching position was at Temple University. Early volumes of poetry were *Homecoming* (1969) and *We a BaddDDD People* (1970). Later, she published *homegirls & handgrenades* (1984) and *Under a Soprano Sky* (1987), and more recently, *Does Your House Have Lions* (1997), *Wounded in the House of a Friend* (1997), *Like the Singing Coming Off the Drums: Love Poems* (1998), and *Shake Loose My Skin: New and Selected Poems* (1999, 2000).

**CARL SANDBURG (1878–1967)** • It is fair to say that Sandburg "knocked around" a good deal in his youth before working his way through Knox (then Lombard) College in Galesburg, Illinois, his hometown. He published a volume of poetry in 1904 but did not gain recognition until 1914, when *Poetry* printed some of his poems. Later he published *Chicago Poems* (1916), *Smoke and Steel* (1920), *Selected Poems* (1926), and *Good Morning, America* (1928). He received the Pulitzer Prize in History (1939) for his biography of Abraham Lincoln and the Pulitzer Prize in Poetry (1951) for his *Complete Poems* of 1950.

**SIEGFRIED SASSOON (1886–1967)** • Sassoon served as an officer in World War I, was wounded twice, and was awarded two medals for bravery (one of which he threw away). He is most widely recognized for his antiwar collections *The Old Huntsman* (1917) and *Counter-Attack and Other Poems* (1918), which contains "Dreamers." Neither of these books was well received. Later, Sassoon turned to spiritual subjects, as shown in *Vigils* (1935) and *Sequences* (1956). His *Collected Poems* was published in 1961.

**GJERTRUD SCHNACKENBERG (B. 1953)** • Originally from Washington State, Schnackenberg now lives in Boston. She achieved great critical acclaim with the publication of her first volume of poems, *Portraits and Elegies* (1982, rev. ed. 1986). She later published *The Lamplit Answer* (1985), *A Gilded Lapse of Time* (1992, 1994), and *Supernatural Love: Poems 1978–1992* (2000). She won the Rome Prize in literature for 1983–1984 and received an honorary doctorate from Mount Holyoke College, her alma mater, in 1985.

**VIRGINIA SCOTT (B. 1937)** • Canadian born, Scott received her degrees at Boston University and Wisconsin. She created, edited, and managed the Sunbury Press, a small press, and received a national award for this work in 1980. She has published poetry widely in journals. Her collected poems appear in *The Witness Box* (1985) and *Toward Appomattox* (1992). She taught at Lehman College for many years.

**ALAN SEEGER (1886–1916)** • Seeger was born in New York and was educated at Harvard. When World War I began he joined the French Foreign Legion, and he was killed in combat during the Battle of the Somme in 1916. His war poems were published in the posthumous *Poems* (1916).

**BRENDA SEROTTE (B. 1946)** • Serotte's Sephardic-Jewish grandparents came to the United States from Turkey in 1918. Born and educated in New York, Serotte worked as a secretary, but after receiving a bachelor's degree she taught English at a Bronx junior high school. She received her M.A. in literature in 1992, and then was a James A. Michener fellow in creative writing at the University of Miami, where she earned her Master of Fine Arts in 1997. She is an adjunct professor at Nova Southwestern University in Fort Lauderdale, Florida, and her first book of poetry, *The Blue Farm*, is published by Ginninderra Press (2005). Serotte's memoir, *The Fortune Teller's Kiss* (University of Nebraska Press, 2006), is about growing up Sephardic in the Bronx.

**WILLIAM SHAKESPEARE (1564–1616)** • For a brief biography, see p. 981.

**KARL SHAPIRO (1913–2000)** • Baltimore born, Shapiro lived in Nebraska and California. He was recognized early in his distinguished career as a poet and critic—his *V-Letter and Other Poems* (1944) receiving the 1945 Pulitzer Prize. Among his many poetry collections are *Essay on Rime* (1945), *Poems of a Jew* (1958), *Selected Poems* (1968), *Selected Poems: 1940–1977* (1978), and *The Wild Card: Selected Poems Early and Late* (1998). He edited *Poetry* magazine for five years, *Prairie Schooner* for ten.

**PERCY BYSSHE SHELLEY (1792–1822)** • Shelley is one of the major English Romantic poets. He was a quintessential revolutionary and suffered expulsion from Oxford as a result of an early pamphlet titled *The Necessity of Atheism*. He married before he was 20 but within three years left his wife and went to Italy with Mary Godwin (1797–1851), the author of *Frankenstein*. The two were married in 1816. Throughout these years Shelley was writing his best-known short poems. He was working on his long philosophic poem *The Triumph of Life* in 1822 when he was drowned during a storm at sea near the coast of Italy. He is buried in the English Cemetery, near the grave of Keats, in Rome. There are many excellent modern editions of his works, including the Houghton-Mifflin Cambridge edition and the Oxford edition.

**JANE SHORE (B. 1947)** • Shore was born in New Jersey and took her M.A. at the University of Iowa in 1971. Her poems have been widely circulated in journals and magazines, and the general merit of her work is shown by frequent prizes and awards, including a grant from the National Endowment for the Arts. Her poetry collections are *Lying Down in the Olive Press* (1969), *Eye Level* (1977), *The Minute Hand* (1987), *This Time, for Always* (1990), *Music Minus One: Poems* (1996, 1997), and *Happy Family* (1999, 2000).

**LESLIE MARMON SILKO (B. 1948)** • A Native American, Silko was brought up in Laguna Pueblo, New Mexico. She has taught at the University of Arizona and also at the University of New Mexico, and she has been honored with a MacArthur Foundation Fellowship. The topic in most of her works is the tradition of the Navajo people, which she treats with great love and understanding, as in "Where Mountain Lion Lay Down with Deer"(p. 842), which connects the individual with the past, the land, and Nature. A recent novel is *Gardens in the Dunes* (1999, 2000).

**STEVIE SMITH (FLORENCE MARGARET SMITH, 1902–1971)** • Smith was a native of Hull, in Yorkshire. During her life she worked in publishing, and in addition she became well known as a radio personality because of her many poetry readings for the BBC. Some of her poetry collections were *A Good Time Was Had by All* (1937) and *Not Waving But Drowning* (1957). Posthumous collections of her work are *Scorpion and Other Poems* (1972) and *Collected Poems* (1975).

**STEPHEN SPENDER (1909–1995)** • Sir Stephen Spender, along with W. H. Auden, Christopher Isherwood, and Louis MacNeice, was one of the poets known as the Oxford Poets during the late 1920s and early 1930s. After leaving Oxford, Spender lived for a time in

Germany. He believed firmly in the need for poets to be politically engaged, and he joined the Communist Party for a few weeks in the 1930s, although he later renounced this affiliation (in *The God That Failed* [1950]). Along with editing journals and writing many prose works, he, with John Lehmann, wrote a five-act poetic play *Trial of a Judge*, based on circumstances in Germany at the time of Hitler. Spender's first poems were collected in a small book titled *Twenty Poems* in 1930. Later collections were *Poems of Dedication* (1947), *Edge of Being: Poems* (1949), and *Collected Poems 1928–1953* (1955). He was knighted in 1962.

**WILLIAM E. STAFFORD (1914–1993)** • Stafford, who published more than two dozen volumes of verse, was born in Kansas. He received his Ph.D. from Iowa State in 1955. In 1975 he was named Poet Laureate of Oregon, and at his death in 1993 he was a professor emeritus at Lewis and Clark College. For *Traveling through the Dark* (1962), his second volume of poetry, he won the National Book Award for Poetry in 1963. Among his many poetry collections are *Wyoming* (1985) and *An Oregon Message* (1987). With Marvin Bell, he published *Segues* in 1983. *Down in My Heart* (1994) is his autobiography of the years he spent in an internment camp for conscientious objectors in World War II.

**GERALD STERN (B. 1925)** • Stern was born in Pittsburgh and became a faculty member of the University of Iowa's Writer's Workshop. He was honored by three grants from the National Endowment for the Arts and by a Guggenheim Fellowship. His *Lucky Life* (1977), which contains "Burying an Animal," received the Lamont Prize in Poetry in 1977. Most recently he published *Leaving Another Kingdom: Selected Poems* (1990), *Bread Without Sugar* (1992), *Odd Mercy* (1995), *This Time* (1998), and *Last Blue* (2000).

**WALLACE STEVENS (1879–1955)** • Stevens spent his professional life in business rather than academia. He wrote most of his poems after the age of 50, but he included "The Emperor of Ice-Cream" and "Disillusionment of Ten O'clock," both earlier poems, in the first edition of *Harmonium* in 1923. Some of his poetic collections are a second version of *Harmonium* (1931) and also *The Auroras of Autumn* (1950) and *Collected Poems* (1954).

**ANNE STEVENSON (B. 1933)** • Anne Stevenson, a dual citizen of the United States and England, has been living mainly in England since 1962. She received degrees from the University of Michigan in 1954 and 1962. One of her many talents is that she is an accomplished cellist and has taught cello. She is the writer of a successful biography of Sylvia Plath (1989) and has published many reviews, essays, and poetry collections. In 1996 she published *The Collected Poems of Anne Stevenson*. "The Spirit Is Too Blunt an Instrument" is taken from *Selected Poems 1956–1986* (1987).

**MARK STRAND (B. 1934)** • Strand was born in Prince Edward Island, Canada. He studied at Antioch, Yale, and the University of Iowa and taught at the University of Utah. He has received many honors, including a particularly prized MacArthur Foundation Fellowship. In 1990 he was named United States Poet Laureate. Some of his collections are *Selected Poems* (1990), *The Continuous Life* (1990, 1992), and *Blizzard of One* (1999, 2000), for which he was awarded the Pulitzer Prize in Poetry.

**MAY SWENSON (1919–1989)** • Swenson was born in Utah and was of Swedish ancestry. She experimented constantly in her poetry, not only in content but also in form, as is shown in her work with shaped verse. Her *Iconographs* (1970) was a collection of formed poetry. The formed poem "Women" was included in her collection *New and Selected Things Taking*

*Place* (1978). She also did translations from Swedish, as represented by *Windows and Stones* (1972).

**JONATHAN SWIFT (1667–1745)** • Swift was born in Ireland. He became Dean of St. Patrick's Cathedral in Dublin, a position in which he served for 31 years. His most famous prose works are *A Tale of a Tub* (1704), *Gulliver's Travels* (1726), and *A Modest Proposal* (1729). Throughout his life, however, he constantly wrote poetry, and he devoted himself almost exclusively to poetry after 1730. His poems were edited by Harold Williams and published in three volumes in 1937.

**ALFRED, LORD TENNYSON (1809–1892)** • One of the most popular of the Victorian poets, Tennyson became English Poet Laureate in 1850. His earliest verse was published in collaboration with his brother Charles in *Poems by Two Brothers* (1827). Some of his other collections were *Poems* (1842), *Locksley Hall* (1842), *The Princess* (1847), *Maud, and Other Poems* (1855), and *Idylls of the King* (1857–1891). He wrote *In Memoriam*, in which the well-known phrase "nature red in tooth and claw" appears, from 1833 to 1850. A new collected and annotated edition of his poetry was published in 1969, but there are also many other useful editions.

**ELAINE TERRANOVA (B. 1939)** • Terranova was born in Pennsylvania and received an MFA degree from Goddard College in 1977. Among her distinctions is an NEA fellowship in poetry. She has printed poems in many significant journals. Among her collections are *The Cult of the Right Hand* (1991) and *Damages* (1995, 1996), from which "Rush Hour" is selected.

**DYLAN THOMAS (1914–1953)** • A native of Wales, Thomas published his first collection, *Eighteen Poems*, in 1934. After World War II he became immensely popular in America as a speaker and lecturer because of the incantatory power with which he read his own poems. Fortunately, many of his readings survive on records and CDs. Thomas's *Collected Poems 1934–1952* was published in 1952 and was a commercial success. *The Poems of Dylan Thomas*, a definitive edition, was published in 1971. In the 1980s, the musician John Cale set "Do Not Go Gentle" to music as part of his *Falklands Suite* (found on Cale's *Words for the Dying*, Opal/Warner Bros. 9-26024-2).

**JEAN TOOMER (1894–1967)** • Toomer was born in Washington, D.C., studied at five colleges, and eventually settled in the African-American community in Sparta, Georgia. An important voice in the Harlem Renaissance, Toomer published his only book, *Cane*, a grouping of stories, poems, and a play, in 1923. A collection of his works is found in *The Wayward and the Seeking* (1980).

**JOHN UPDIKE (B. 1932)** • Updike was born in Pennsylvania, and grew up there during the Great Depression and the period of World War II. His parents were diligent about his education, and in 1950 he received a scholarship for study at Harvard, graduating in 1954. He worked for *The New Yorker* for two years before deciding to devote himself exclusively to his own writing, but since then he has remained a frequent contributor of stories and poems to that magazine. In 1959 he published his first story collection, *The Same Door*, and his first novel, *The Poorhouse Fair*. In 1960, with *Rabbit, Run*, he began his extensive *Rabbit* chronicles. In 1981 he received the Pulitzer Prize for *Rabbit Is Rich*. His collected poems were published in 1993, and he is continually productive in writing new stories and poems. Today he is considered one of the foremost American writers of fiction and poetry.

**MONA VAN DUYN (B. 1921)** • Van Duyn is a native of Iowa and received her college degrees there. She taught for a time at the University of Washington and has been considered a "Northwest" poet for this reason. Among her poetry collections are *Valentines to the Wide World* (1959), *Merciful Disguises* (1973), *Near Changes* (1990, 1992), *Firefall* (1994), and *Selected Poems* (2002).

**JUDITH VIORST (B. 1931)** • Viorst is a native of New Jersey and received her degrees from Rutgers and the Washington Psychoanalytic Institute. She is known for her wry humor. Her first major volume was *It's Hard to Be Hip over Thirty and Other Tragedies of Married Life* in 1968. Among later works are *Necessary Losses* (1986), *Forever Fifty and Other Negotiations* (1989, 1996), and *Suddenly Sixty, and Other Shocks of Later Life* (2000). She also has written a considerable amount of fiction for young people.

**SHELLY WAGNER (B. CA. 1948)** • A resident of Virginia, Wagner received her B.A. from Old Dominion University, after which she worked as an interior designer and social worker. Her younger son Andrew drowned in 1984, and it was five years later that she began her cycle of elegiac poems, *The Andrew Poems*, including "Boxes," which was published in 1994. Before this she had published poetry in publications such as *American Poetry Review* and *Poetry East*.

**DAVID WAGONER (B. 1926)** • Wagoner was born in Ohio and studied at Pennsylvania State University and the University of Indiana. In 1954 he began teaching at the University of Washington, where he was a colleague, and later an editor, of Theodore Roethke. He has been extremely productive both as poet, having published seventeen poetry collections, and writer of fiction, having published ten novels. One of his works was adapted for a film (*The Escape Artist*, 1982) produced through Francis Ford Coppolla's Zoetrope Studios. A few of Wagoner's many poetry collections are *Dry Sun, Dry Wind* (1953), *Staying Alive* (1966), *Collected Poems* (1976), *Landfall* (1981), *Through the Forest: New and Selected Poems* (1987), and *Walt Whitman Bathing* (1996).

**ALICE WALKER (B. 1944)** • Walker was born in Georgia and attended Sarah Lawrence College, graduating in 1965. In addition to teaching at Yale, Wellesley, and other schools, she has edited and published fiction, poetry, and biography, and she received a Guggenheim Fellowship in 1977. Her main hobby is gardening. For her collection of poems *Revolutionary Petunias* (1973), she received a Wall Book Award nomination. Her best-known novel, *The Color Purple* (1982), was awarded the 1983 Pulitzer Prize for Fiction, and was made into a movie that won an Academy Award for 1985. Other major works are *The Temple of My Familiar* (1989), *By the Light of My Father's Smile* (1998), *In Search of Our Mothers' Gardens* (2003, essays), *Now Is the Time to Open Your Heart: A Novel* (2004), and *We Are the Ones We Have Been Waiting For: Light in a Time of Darkness* (2006, essays).

**EDMUND WALLER (1606–1687)** • Waller, whom Dryden constantly praised for the quality and originality of his poetic couplets, was a Royalist during the English Civil Wars of 1642–1649, and for his efforts he was forced into exile. He returned in 1651 after swearing loyalty to Oliver Cromwell. During the Restoration, he supported King Charles II. His major collections of poetry were *Poems* (1645) and *Divine Poems* (1685).

**CHARLES HARPER WEBB (B. 1952)** • Webb is a native of Pennsylvania but grew up in Texas. He received degrees at Rice University, the University of Washington, and the University of Southern California. He teaches at California State University at Long Beach. Some of his books are *Everyday Outrages* (1989), *Poetry That Heals* (1991), and *A Webb for All Seasons* (1992). He has also published a novel, *The Wilderness Effect* (1982). Interestingly, before he took up teaching as a profession he had spent a decade as a rock guitarist and singer.

**PHYLLIS WEBB (B. 1927)** • Webb is a native of British Columbia. She was educated at the University of British Columbia and also at McGill University. During her career she worked with the Canadian Broadcasting Company both as a program planner and a producer; she has also taught in various Canadian colleges and universities as a guest lecturer and professor. A major concern in her poetry has been the problem of maintaining personal integrity amid a world of "hate and broken things," to quote from one of her poems in *Trio* (1954). One of her interests has been to experiment with a form of Persian poetry, the *ghazal*, which consists of five couplets. Among her poetry collections are *Wilson's Bowl* (1980), *The Vision Tree* (1982), *Selected Poems* (1982), *Water and Light: Ghazals and Anti Ghazals* (1984), and *Hanging Fire* (1990).

**BRUCE WEIGL (B. 1949)** • Weigl, who teaches at Penn State, was born in Ohio. He took his B.A. at Oberlin (1974) and his Ph.D. at the University of Utah (1979). His poetry collections include *Like a Sack Full of Old Quarrels* (1976), *Executioner* (1977), *A Romance* (1979), *The Monkey Wars* (1984), *Song of Napalm* (1988), *What Saves Us* (1992), and *Sweet Lorain* (1996). His most recent collections are *Archaeology of the Circle: New and Selected Poems* (1998, 1999), *After the Others* (1999), and *The Unraveling Strangeness* (2002).

**PHILLIS WHEATLEY (CA. 1753–1784)** • Wheatley was born in Africa. She was captured by slave traders and sold to John Wheatley, a Boston merchant, who treated her virtually as a daughter and saw to it that she was educated. When she published her *Poems on Various Subjects, Religious and Moral* (1773), however, the temper of the times made it necessary to include prefaces by Massachusetts men verifying that she was qualified to write poetry and that she had indeed written the poems in the collection. Although she wrote a second volume of poetry, she could not find a publisher for it during her lifetime. Her collected works were published in 1988.

**WALT WHITMAN (1819–1892)** • Whitman, who became a legend during his lifetime, is one of America's major poets. He was born in New York and lived with his family in both Long Island and Brooklyn. At various times he worked as a printer, teacher, reporter, and government bureaucrat. In addition, he served as a nurse during the Civil War. His major work was *Leaves of Grass*, which he first published as a collection of 12 poems in 1855, and to which he added as time went on. Many editions were published in his lifetime, the last one in 1892. *Drum Taps*, poems based on his Civil War experiences, was published in 1865; a second edition contained "When Lilacs Last in the Dooryard Bloom'd," his poem on the death of Lincoln.

**JOHN GREENLEAF WHITTIER (1807–1892)** • Whittier was born in Massachusetts of Quaker stock. He was not formally educated and was trained to be a shoemaker. However, he was a compulsive reader and at the age of 19 he wrote a poem that was accepted by William Lloyd Garrison for publication in the Newburyport *Press*. From that point Whittier went on to become one of America's best known poets and writers. Joining the abolitionist movement, he worked diligently in that cause, and for a brief period he served in the Massachusetts Legislature. The best way to describe his poetic output is that it was voluminous, and with his publication of *Snow-Bound* in 1866 and *Poetical Works* in 1869 he became financially secure. A particularly notable achievement was his being part of the group that founded the *Atlantic Monthly* in 1857.

**CORNELIUS WHUR (1782–1853)** • Whur was a Methodist minister in Suffolk, England. In 1837 he published a poetry collection, *Village Musings on Moral and Religious Subjects*, which included "The First-Rate Wife." In his obituary notice he was recognized not only as a "distinguished" poet but also as an accomplished gardener.

**RICHARD WILBUR (B. 1921)** • Wilbur was born in New York. He has published a number of poetry collections, including *New and Collected Poems* (1988, 1989), for which he was awarded the Pulitzer Prize for Poetry. He has also made a number of well-received translations of French drama and has published collections for children, such as *The Pig in the Spigot* (2000). In 1988 he was distinguished as the second United States Poet Laureate (the first being Robert Penn Warren). A recent collection is *Mayflies: New Poems and Translations* (2000).

**C. K. WILLIAMS (CHARLES KENNETH WILLIAMS, B. 1936)** • Williams is a native of New Jersey who graduated from Bucknell and the University of Pennsylvania. He taught at a number of schools and colleges and has become a permanent resident of France. He is known for his discursively long lines in the manner of Walt Whitman. Among his many volumes of poems are *Tar* (1983); *Flesh and Blood* (1987), for which he was awarded the 1987 National Book Critics Circle Award; *Poems, 1963–1983* (1988); *A Dream of the Mind* (1992); and *Repair* (1999). Recently he has undertaken translations of Greek drama. "Dimensions" is taken from *Lies*, his collection of 1969.

**WILLIAM CARLOS WILLIAMS (1883–1963)** • Williams spent his career as a practicing pediatrician, but he early became friendly with the poets Ezra Pound and Hilda Doolittle (H. D.). He developed a second career as a writer, producing poems, plays, stories, novels, and essays. At the age of thirty he began publishing poems, beginning with *Poems* (1913) and *Tempers* (1913) and ending with *Pictures from Brueghel* (1963), for which he was posthumously awarded the Pulitzer Prize.

**WILLIAM WORDSWORTH (1770–1850)** • Along with Coleridge, Wordsworth was the first of the English Romantic poets. In 1798 the two men published *Lyrical Ballads*, a landmark poetry collection that emphasizes the importance of imagination in revealing the significance of events in the lives of (mainly) ordinary people. One of Wordsworth's major ideas was that poetry grows from "emotion recollected in tranquillity," and he also believed that poetic diction should consist of everyday language that the poet chooses as a result of looking steadily at the poetic subject. Throughout much of his adult life Wordsworth wrote and revised his long poem *The Prelude*, which was intended to show how the exalted but mysterious "wisdom and spirit of the universe" reached him through his imagination and brought out his power as a poet. He became English Poet Laureate in 1843.

**JAMES WRIGHT (1927–1980)** • Wright was born in Martins Ferry, Ohio, and received his Ph.D. at the University of Washington, where he was a student of Theodore Roethke. In 1966 he began teaching at Hunter College, and he remained there until his death in 1980. His first poetry collection, *The Green Wall*, appeared in 1957, and after that he published collections regularly, receiving the 1972 Pulitzer Prize in Poetry for his *Collected Poems* (1971). *This Journey* was published posthumously in 1982, and *Above the River: The Complete Poems* appeared in 1990.

**SIR THOMAS WYATT (CA. 1503–1542)** • Wyatt was a courtier in the service of King Henry VIII. He is credited with introducing the sonnet form into English as a result of his translations of the sonnets of the Italian sonneteer Petrarch. He circulated his poems in manuscript, although a number of them were anthologized after his death in *The Court of Venus* (1542) and *Seven Penitential Psalms* (1549). Modern editions of his poems were published in 1969, 1975, and 1978.

**WILLIAM BUTLER YEATS (1865–1939)** • The foremost Irish poet of the twentieth century, Yeats was instrumental in the founding of the Abbey Theatre in Dublin in 1899. An unorthodox thinker, he developed his poems out of his vast reading and his special interest in spiritualism. He published many volumes of poems, including *The Green Helmet* (1910), *The Wild Swans at Coole* (1917), *The Winding Stair* (1929), and *The Collected Poems* (1932). He was awarded the Nobel Prize in Literature in 1923.

**PAUL ZIMMER (B. 1934)** • Zimmer, whose sister was the science-fiction writer Marion Zimmer Bradley (1930–1999), was born in Canton, Ohio, and received his B.A. from Kent State University. In the 1950s, he was among those service men who were assigned to view nuclear explosions, and his reactions were duly recorded by those who were conducting these experiments. When Zimmer became a career editor and poet he managed bookstores and university presses, including the University of Iowa Press. He now lives in retirement in Wisconsin. Among his many volumes of poems are *A Seed on the Wind* (1960), *The Ribs of Death* (1967), *Family Reunion* (1983), and *Big Blue Train* (1993). His "Zimmer" poems are collected in *The Zimmer Poems* (1976), *Earthbound Zimmer* (1983), *The American Zimmer* (1984), *The Great Bird of Love* (1989), and *Crossing to Sunlight: Selected Poems* (1996). Recently he has published *After the Fire: A Writer Finds His Place* (2002) and *Trains in the Distance* (2003).

# Glossary of Important Literary Terms

This glossary presents brief definitions of terms and concepts that are boldfaced in the text. Page references indicate where readers may find additional detail and illustration, together with discussions about how the concepts can be utilized in studying and writing about literature. Generally, words italicized as parts of various definitions are also separately glossed in their own right.

**Abstract diction**  Language describing qualities that are rarefied and theoretical (e.g., "good," "interesting," "neat," and so on); distinguished from *concrete diction*. 283

**absurd**  See *comedy of the absurd*.

**accent** or **beat**  The heavy *stresses* or accents in lines of *poetry*. Because heavy stresses are paired with *light stresses* to compose metrical *feet*, the numbers of accents or beats in a *line* usually govern the meter of the line (five beats in a *pentameter* line, four in a *tetrameter* line, etc.). 641

**accented syllable**  A syllable receiving a major, or heavy, *stress* or *accent*. 641

**actions** or **incidents**  The events or occurrences in a work. 3, 59, 100, 867

**actors**  Persons who perform as characters in a play. 872

**allegory**  A complete *narrative* that may also be applied to a parallel set of moral, philosophical, political, religious, or social situations. 69, 321–366, 323, 871

**alliteration**  The repetition of identical consonant sounds (most often the sounds beginning words) in close proximity (e.g., "*pensive poets*," "*somewhere safe to sea*," "*gracious, golden, glittering gleams*," "And *death* once *dead*, there's no more *dying* then"). 642

**allusion**  Unacknowledged references and quotations which authors make while assuming that readers will recognize the original sources and relate their meanings to the new context. Allusions are hence compliments that the author pays to readers for their perceptiveness, knowledge, and awareness. 326, 691–732, 698

**anagnorisis** or **recognition**  Aristotle's term describing that point in a play, usually the *climax*, when a character experiences understanding. 931

**analysis**  See *commentary*.

**analytical sentence outline**  A scheme or plan for an essay, arranged according to topics (A, B, C, etc.) and with the topics expressed in sentences. 32

**anapest**  A three-syllable *foot* consisting of two light *stresses* climaxed by a heavy stress, as in *ear-ly LIGHT*. The word *anapest* is sometimes spelled *anapaest*. 641

**1481**

**anaphora** ("to carry again or repeat") The repetition of the same word or phrase throughout a work or section of a work. The effect is to lend weight and emphasis. 503, 566

**ancillary characters** *Characters* in a play who set off or highlight the protagonist and who provide insight into the action. The *foil*, *choric figure*, and *raisonneur* are all ancillary characters. 866

**antagonist** The person, idea, force, or general set of circumstances opposing the *protagonist*; an essential element of *plot*. 59, 865

**anticipation** See *procatalepsis*.

**antithesis** A rhetorical device of opposition in which one idea or word is established, and then the opposite idea or word is expressed, as in "I *burn* and *freeze*" and "I *love* and *hate*." 503, 643

**antimetabole** See *chiasmus*.

**apostrophe** The addressing of a discourse to a real or imagined person who is not present; also, a speech to an abstraction. 566

**apron** or **thrust stage** A stage that projects into the auditorium area, thus increasing the space for action; a characteristic feature of Elizabethan theaters and many recent ones. 872

**archetypal/symbolic/mythic critical approach** The explanation of literature in terms of archetypal patterns (e.g., God's creation of human beings, the search for paradise, the sacrifice of a hero, the initiation or "test" of a young person). 1405

**archetype** A character, action, or situation that is a prototype or pattern of human life generally; a situation that occurs over and over again in literature, such as a quest, an initiation, or an attempt to overcome evil. Many *myths* are archetypes. 1405

**archon, eponymous** In ancient Athens, the Eponymous Archon, or Archon Eponymous, was a leading magistrate, after whom the year was named. He made arrangements for the tragedies and comedies to be performed at the yearly festivals in honor of the God Dionysus. 926

**arena stage,** or **theater-in-the-round** A theater arrangement, often outdoors, in which the audience totally surrounds a *platform stage*, with all actors entering and exiting along the same aisles used by the audience. 873

**argument** The development of a pattern of interpretation or thought with an intent to persuade. In most writing about literature, the persuasive situation is to show the validity of a particular idea or circumstance in a story, poem, or play. More broadly, the term *argument* applies to any situation about which there may be disagreement. Although sometimes argumentative discourse may become disputatious, one should never forget that true arguments should stem from the reasonable interpretation of correct and accurate data. 20

**aside** A speech, usually short and often witty or satirical, delivered by a character to the audience or to another character, the convention being that only the intended characters can hear it, along, of course, with the audience. A more extensive speech which is delivered only to the audience when the character is alone on stage is a *soliloquy*. 980

**assertion** A sentence putting an *idea* or *argument* (the subject) into operation (the predicate); necessary for both developing and understanding the idea. 367

**assonance** The repetition of identical vowel sounds in different words in close proximity, as in the d*ee*p gr*ee*n s*ea*. 642

**atmosphere** or **mood** The emotional aura invoked by a work. 67, 201

**audience** or **intended reader or listener** (1) The people attending a theatrical production. (2) The intended group of readers for whom a writer writes, such as a group of religious worshippers, or a group of rocket scientists. 874

**auditory images**   References to sounds. 535

**authorial symbol**   See *contextual symbol*.

**authorial voice**   The *voice* or *persona* used by authors when seemingly speaking for themselves. The use of the term makes it possible to discuss a narration or presentation without assuming that the ideas are necessarily those of the author in his/her own person. See also *speaker*, *point of view*, and *third-person point of view*. 112

**ballad, ballad measure**   A narrative poem, originally a popular form, composed of quatrains in *ballad measure*; that is, a pattern of iambic tetrameter alternating with iambic trimeter and rhyming *x-a-x-a*. 3, 647

**ballad opera**   An eighteenth-century comic drama, originated by John Gay (1685–1732) in *The Beggar's Opera* (1728), featuring lyrics written for existing and usually well-known tunes, such as "Greensleeves." See also *comic opera*. 1154

**beast fable**   A narrative, usually short, attributing human characteristics to animals. 325

**beat**   A *heavy stress* or *accent* in a line of poetry. The number of beats in a line dictates the *meter* of the line, such as five beats to a line of *iambic pentameter*, or three beats to a line of *trimeter*. See also *accent*. 641

**blank verse**   Unrhymed *iambic pentameter*. Most of the poetry in Shakespeare's plays is blank verse, as is the poetry of Milton's *Paradise Lost*. 642

**blocking**   In the performance of a play, the director's plan for the grouping and movement of characters on stage. 872

**blocking agent**   A person, circumstance, or attitude that obstructs the plans of various characters, such as the parental denial of permission to marry, as in Shakespeare's *A Midsummer Night's Dream*. 1093

**box set**   In the modern theater, the *realistic* setting of a single room from which the "fourth wall" is missing, so that the stage resembles a picture. 873

**brainstorming**   The exploration, discovery, and development of details to be used in a composition. 18

**business** or **stage business**   The gestures, expressions, and general activity (beyond *blocking*) of *actors* onstage. Usually, business is designed to create laughter. It is often done spontaneously by actors. 872

**buskins**   Elegantly laced boots (*kothorni* or *cothurni*) worn by actors in ancient Greek *tragedy*. Eventually the buskins became elevator shoes to stress the royal status of actors by making them seem especially tall. 937

**cadence group**   A coherent word group spoken as a single rhythmical unit, such as a prepositional phrase ("of human events") or noun phrase ("our sacred honor"). 652

**caesura,** (plural) **caesurae**   The pause(s) or juncture(s) separating words and phrases within lines of poetry, as in Pope's line "Trees, where you sit, shall crowd into a shade" (*Second Pastoral*, "Summer," line 75), in which there is a caesura after "Trees" and also after "sit." In poetic *scansion* the caesura is marked by a double *virgule* ( / / ). The control of caesurae is a vital aspect of poetic *rhythm*. 643

**catastrophe**   The "overturning" of the dramatic *plot*, the fourth stage in the structure immediately following the *climax*; the *dénouement* of a play, in which things are explained and put into place. 869

**catharsis (purgation)**   Aristotle's concept that *tragedy*, by arousing pity and fear (*eleos* and *phobos*), regularizes and shapes human emotions, and that therefore tragedy, like literature and art generally, is essential in civilized society. 929

**central idea** or **central argument**  (1) The *thesis* or main idea of an essay. (2) The *theme* of a literary work. 27

**character**  An extended verbal representation of a human being, the inner self that determines thought, speech, and behavior. 3, 58, 158–197, 865

**character, comic**  Comic characters tend to be unrealistic and sometimes exaggerated, representing classes, types, and generations. 1096

**chiasmus** or **antimetabole**  A rhetorical pattern in which words (and also ideas) are repeated in the sequence *a b b a*, as in "I lead the life I love; I love the life I lead," and "When the issue deteriorates to violence, violence becomes the issue." 503

**choragos** or **choregus**  The sponsor or financial backer of a classical Athenian dramatic production. Often the Athenians honored the choragos by selecting him to serve as the leader (*koryphaios*) of the chorus. 925

**choree**  See *trochee*.

**choric figure**  A character who remains somewhat outside the dramatic *action* and who provides commentary when appropriate. See also *raisonneur*. 866

**chorus**  In ancient Athenian drama, the chorus was composed of young men—15 in tragedies and 24 in comedies—who chanted or sang, perhaps in unison, and who performed dance movements to a flute accompaniment. The chorus was, in effect, a major (and also collective) character in the *drama*. 925

**chronology** (the **"logic of time"**)  The sequence of events in a work, with emphasis on the complex intertwining of cause and effect. 59, 867

**City Dionysia**  See *Dionysia*.

**clerihew**  A comic and often satiric closed-form poem in four lines, rhyming *a b a b*, usually on the topic of a famous real or lite⋯ person. 649

⋯ne  An overly used and ⋯ly easy rhyme, such as *moon* ⋯ *trees* and *breeze*. 644

**climax (Greek for *ladder*)**  The high point of *conflict* and tension preceding the *resolution* or *dénoument* of a *story* or *play*; the point of decision, of inevitability and no return. The climax is sometimes equated with the *crisis* in the consideration of dramatic and narrative *structure*. 245, 247, 868

**closed-form poetry**  Poetry written in specific and traditional patterns produced through control of *rhyme, meter,* line-length, and line groupings. 643

**close reading**  The detailed study of a poem or passage, designed to explain characters, motivations, similarities and contrasts of sound, situations, ideas, style, organization, word selections, settings, etc. 491

**comedy**  A literary genre which, like *tragedy*, originated in the *Dionysia* festivals of ancient Athens. Derived from the Greek *komos* songs or "songs of merrymakers," the first comedies were wildly boisterous. Later comedies became more subdued and realistic. In typical comedies today, confusions and doubts are resolved satisfactorily if not happily, and usually comedies are characterized by smiles, jokes, and laughter. 976, 1091–1186

**comedy of the absurd**  A modern form of comedy dramatizing the apparent pointlessness, ambiguity, uncertainty, and absurdity of existence. 1098, 1155

**comedy of manners**  A form of comedy, usually *regular* (five acts or three acts), in which attitudes and customs are examined and satirized in the light of high intellectual and moral standards. The *dialogue* is witty and sophisticated, and characters are often measured according to their linguistic and intellectual powers. 1097

**comic**  A pattern of action, including funny situations and language, that is solvable and correctible, and therefore satisfying. 1095

**comic opera**  An outgrowth of eighteenth-century *ballad opera*, but different because in comic opera the music is composed for the lyrics. 1154

**commedia dell'arte**  Broadly humorous farce that was developed in sixteenth-century Italy, featuring *stock characters*, stock situations, and much improvised *dialogue*. 1098

**commentary, analysis,** or **interpretation**  Passages of explanation and reflection about the meaning of actions, thoughts, dialogue, historical movements, and so on. 68, 866

**commentator**  See *raisonneur*.

**common ground of assent**  Those interests, concerns, and assumptions that the writer assumes in common with readers so that an effective and persuasive *tone* may be maintained. 604

**common measure**  A closed poetic quatrain, rhyming *a b a b*, in which lines of iambic tetrameter alternate with iambic trimeter. See also *ballad measure* and *hymnal measure*. 648

**comparison-contrast**  A technique of analyzing two or more works in order to determine similarities and differences in topic, treatment, and quality. 1412–1427

**complete, completeness**  The second element in Aristotle's definition of *tragedy*, emphasizing the logic and wholeness of the play. 931

**complication**  A stage of narrative and dramatic structure in which the major *conflicts* are brought out; the *rising action* of a *drama*. 245, 246, 868

**concrete diction**  Words that describe exact and particular conditions or qualities, such as *cold*, *sweet*, and *creamy* in reference to an ice-cream sundae. These words are *concrete*, while the application of *good* or *neat* to the sundae is *abstract*. See also *abstract diction*. 283

**concrete poetry**  See *visual poetry*.

**conflict**  The opposition or *conflict* between two characters, between large groups of people, or between *protagonists* and larger forces such as natural objects, ideas, modes of behavior, public opinion, and the like. Conflict may also be internal and psychological, involving choices facing a *protagonist*. The resolution of conflict is the essence of *plot*. 59, 101

**connotation**  The meanings that words suggest; the overtones of words beyond their bare dictionary definitions or denotations, as with "leaving," "getting away," and "turning tail," which have the same meaning, but differing connotations. 284, 504

**consonant sounds** or **consonant segments**  Consonant sounds (i.e., sounds that accompany ["con"] the [vowel] sound ["sonant"]) are produced as a result of the touching or close proximity of the tongue or the lips in relation to the teeth or palate (e.g., *m, n, p, f, sh, ch*); to be compared with *vowel sounds*. 644

**contextual, private,** or **authorial symbol**  A symbol which is derived not from common historical, cultural, or religious materials, but which is rather developed within the context of an individual work. See also *Cultural Symbol*. 68, 322, 692, 871

**convention**  An accepted feature of a genre, such as the *point of view* in a story, the *form* of a *poem* (e.g., *sonnet*, *ode*), the competence or brilliance of the detective in detective fiction, the impenetrability of disguise and concealment in a Shakespearean play, or the *chorus* in Greek *drama*. 25

**Corpus Christi play**  A type of medieval drama that enacts events from the Bible, such as the killing of Abel by Cain, the domestic problems of Noah, the jealous anger of Herod, and so on. The word is derived from the religious festival of Corpus Christi ("Christ's body"), held in the spring of each year, mainly during the fourteenth century. Also called *mystery plays* because they were performed by individual craft guilds, or *misteries*. See also *cycle*. 879

**cosmic irony (irony of fate)**  *Situational irony* that is connected to a pessimistic or fatalistic view of life. 606

**costumes**  The clothes worn by *actors*, designed to indicate historical periods, social status, economic levels, etc. 874, 937

**cothurni**  See *buskins*.

**couplet**  Two lines that may be unified by *rhyme* or, in biblical poetry, by content. 3, 643

**creative nonfiction**  A type of literature that is technically nonfiction, such as diaries journals, and news features, but which nevertheless involves high degrees of imaginative and literary skill. 3

**crisis**  The point of uncertainty and tension in a literary work—the turning point—that results from the *conflicts* and difficulties brought about through the *complications* of the plot. The crisis leads to the *climax*—that is, to the decision made by the protagonist to resolve the conflict. Sometimes the crisis and the climax are considered as two elements of the same stage of *plot* development. 246, 868

**cultural (universal) context**  See *historical context*.

**cultural** or **universal symbol**  A symbol that is recognized and shared as a result of a common political, social, and cultural heritage. See also *contextual symbol*. 68, 326, 692

**cycle**  (1) A group of closely related works. (2) In medieval religious drama, the complete set of plays performed during the *Corpus Christi* festival, from the creation of the world to the resurrection. As many as 40 plays could make up the cycle. See also *Corpus Christi plays*. 879

**dactyl**  A three-syllable foot consisting of a heavy stress followed by two lights, as in the words QUOT-*a-ble* and SYN-*the-sis*. 641

**deconstructionist critical approach**  An interpretive literary approach that rejects absolute interpretations and stresses ambigu͏ities and contradictions. 1404

The convention or expectation and subjects should be exactly —*high* or *formal* words for

serious subjects (e.g., *epic* poems, *tragedy*), and *low* or *informal* words for low subjects (e.g., *limericks, farce*). 502

**denotation**  The standard, minimal meaning of a word, without implications and connotations. See also *connotation*. 284, 504

**dénouement (untying)** or **resolution**  The final stage of *plot* development, in which mysteries are explained, characters find their destinies, lovers are united, sanity is restored, and the work is completed. Usually the dénouement is done as speedily as possible, for it occurs after all *conflicts* are ended, and little that is new can be begun to hold the interest of readers. 245, 247, 869

**description**  The exposition of scenes, actions, attitudes, and feelings. 66

**developing character**  See *round character*.

**device**  A *figure of speech*, such as a *metaphor* or a *simile*. 562

**deus ex machina ("A god out of the machine"; theos apo mechanes** in Greek, a phrase attributed to the playwright Menander)  In ancient Athenian drama, the entrance of a god to unravel the problems in a *play*. Today, the phrase *deus ex machina* refers to the artificial and illogical solution of problems. 935

**dialect**  Language characteristics—involving pronunciation, unique words, and vocal rhythms—particular to regions such as New England or the South, or to separate nations such as Britain and Australia. 500

**dialogue**  The speeches of two or more characters in a *story, play,* or *poem*. 3, 864

**diction**  Word choice, types of words, and the level of language. 281

**diction, formal** or **high**  Proper, elevated, elaborate, and often polysyllabic language. 281, 499

**diction, informal** or **low**  Relaxed, conversational, and familiar language, utilizing contractions and elisions, and sometimes employing *slang* and grammatical mistakes. 282, 499

**diction, neutral** or **middle** Correct language characterized by directness and simplicity. 281, 500

**dilemma** A situation, particularly in tragedy, presenting a character with two choices, either one of which is unacceptable, dangerous, or even lethal. 933

**dimeter** A *line* of two metrical *feet*. 641

**Dionysia**, **also City Dionysia** The religious festivals of ancient Athens held to celebrate the god Dionysus. *Tragedy* developed as part of the Great, or City Dionysia in March–April, and *comedy* developed as part of a shorter festival, the Lenaea (in February). 923

**diphthong** A meaningful vowel segment which begins with one sound and ends with another. The three diphthongs in English are those found in *house, coil,* and *fine.* 642

**director** The person in charge of guiding and instructing all persons involved in a dramatic production. 872

**discursive poetry** Non-narrative *poetry* dealing primarily with ideas and personal, social, or political commentary. 3

**discursive writing** Distinguished from imaginative writing, discursive writing is concerned with factual presentation and the development of reasonable and logical conclusions. 3

**dithyramb** An ancient Athenian poetic form sung by choruses during the earliest *Dionysia*. The first *tragedies* originated from the dithyrambs. 875, 924

**documentation** Granting recognition to the ideas and words of others, either through textual, parenthetical, or footnote references. 441

**donnée** (French for "given") The given action or set of assumptions on which a work of literature is based, such as the unpredictability of love, the bleakness and danger of a postwar world, or the inescapability of guilt. See also *postulate* or *premise.* 57

**double entendre ("double meaning")** Deliberate ambiguity, usually humorous, and often sexual. 285

**double take** A structural device whereby a concluding event or "surprise" brings about a new and more complex understanding of the previous material. 464

**drama** An individual play; also plays considered as a group; one of the three major genres of *imaginative literature.* 3, 864–922

**dramatic irony** A special kind of *situational irony* in which a character perceives his or her plight in a limited way while the audience and one or more of the other characters understand it entirely. 67, 608, 870

**dramatic monologue** A type of *poem* in which a speaker addresses an internal listener or the reader. Often the speaker includes detail reflecting the listener's unrecorded responses. The form is related to the *soliloquy* and the *aside* in drama. 609

**dramatic** or **objective point of view** A *third-person narration* reporting speech and *action*, but excluding commentary on the actions and thoughts of the *characters.* 113, 146

**dynamic character** A character who recognizes, changes with, and tries to adjust to circumstances. Such changes may be shown in (1) an action or actions, (2) the realization of new strength and therefore the affirmation of previous decisions, (3) the acceptance of new conditions and the need for making changes, (4) the discovery of unrecognized truths, or (5) the reconciliation of the character with adverse conditions. In a *short story*, there is usually only one dynamic character, whereas in a *novel* there may be many. 155, 866

**economic determinist/Marxist critical approach** An interpretive literary approach based on the theories of

Karl Marx (1818–1883), stressing that literature is to be judged from the perspective of economic and social class inequality and oppression. 1402

**elegy**    A *poem* of lamentation about a death. Often an elegy takes the form of a *pastoral*. 3, 646

**enclosing setting**    See *framing setting*.

**end-stopped line**    A poetic line ending in a full pause, usually indicated with a period or semicolon. 641

**English (Shakespearean) sonnet**    A sonnet form developed by Shakespeare, in *iambic pentameter*, composed of three *quatrains* and a *couplet*, with seven rhymes in the pattern *a b a b, c d c d, e f e f, g g*. 645

**epic**    A long *narrative poem* elevating *character*, *speech*, and *action*. 3, 54

**epigram**    A short and witty *poem*, often in *couplets*, that makes a humorous or satiric point. 3, 648

**episode** or **episodia**    (1) An acting *scene* or section of Greek tragedy. Divisions separating the episodes were called *stasima*, or sections for the chorus. (2) A self-enclosed portion of a work, such as a section, or a passage of particular narration, dialogue, or location. 69, 938

**epitaph**    A short comment or description marking someone's death. Also, a short, witty, and often satiric poem about death. 649

**essay**    A short and tightly organized written composition dealing with a topic such as a character, setting, or point of view. 16

**euphony**    Meaning "good sound," *euphony* refers to word groups containing consonants that permit an easy and pleasant flow of spoken sound. 646

**examination**    A written or oral test or inqu... esigned to discover a person's ...ding and capacity to deal with ...r topic or set of topics.

**exodos**    The final episode in a Greek tragedy, occurring after the last choral ode. 938

**explication**    A detailed analysis of a work of literature, often word by word and line by line; a close reading. 491

**exposition**    The stage of dramatic or narrative structure which introduces all things necessary for the development of the plot. 244, 245, 868

**fable**    A brief *story* illustrating a moral truth, most often associated with the ancient Greek writer Aesop. See also *beast fable*. 54, 325

**falling action**    See *catastrophe*.

**fantasy**    The creation of events that are dreamlike or fantastic, departing from ordinary understanding of *reality* because of apparently illogical *setting*, movement, causality, and *chronology*. 57

**farce**    A word derived from the Latin word *farsus*, meaning "stuffed," farce is an outlandish physical *comedy* overflowing with silly characters, improbable happenings, wild clowning, extravagant language, and bawdy jokes. 1098

**feet**    See *foot*.

**feminist critical approach (feminist critical approach, gender studies, and queer theory)**    The feminist critical approach is designed to raise consciousness about the importance and unique nature of women in literature. 1399

**fiction**    *Narratives* based in the imagination of the author, not in literal, reportorial facts; one of the three major genres of imaginative literature. 2

**figurative devices**    See *figures of speech*.

**figurative language**    See *figures of speech*.

**figures of speech**    Organized patterns of comparison that deepen, broaden, extend, illuminate, and emphasize meaning, and also that conform to particular patterns or forms such as *metaphor*, *simile*, and *parallelism*. 526–600

**first-person point of view**    The use of a first-person *speaker* or *narrator* who tells about things that he/she has seen, done, spoken, heard, thought, and also learned about in other ways. 111, 115

**flashback** A method of *narration* in which past events are introduced into a present action. Also called *selective recollection*. 246, 247

**flat character** A character, usually minor, who is not individual, but rather useful and structural, static and unchanging; distinguished from *round character*. 156, 866

**foil** A character, usually minor, designed to highlight qualities of a major character. 866

**foot, feet** A poetic foot consists of the measured combination of heavy and light *stresses*, such as the *iamb*, which contains a light stress followed by a heavy stress (e.g., "*of YEAR*"). In poetic scansion, the feet are separated by a *virgule* or single slash mark (/), as in Shakespeare's "That TIME/of YEAR/thou MAY'ST/in ME/be - HOLD." 641

**form, poetic** The various shapes and organizational modes of poetry. 641–690

**formal diction** See *diction, formal or high.*

**formalist critical approach** See *New Critical/formalist critical approach.*

**framing or enclosing setting** The same features of topic or setting used at both the beginning and ending of a work so as to "frame" or "enclose" the work. 202

**free verse** *Poetry* based on the natural *rhythms* of phrases and normal pauses, not *metrical feet*. See *open-form poetry*. 3, 650

**freewriting** See *brainstorming.*

**Freytag pyramid** A diagram graphically showing the stages of dramatic *structure*. *Complication* and emotional intensity go upward on the side of the pyramid rising to its peak or point. Once the high point is reached, intensity begins to decrease just as the other side of the pyramid descends to its base. 867

**gallery** The upper seats at the back and sides of a *theater*. 872

**general language** Words referring to broad classes of persons, objects, or phenomena; distinguished from *specific language*. 283, 498

**gender studies** A critical approach that brings attention to gender rather than to sexual differences, based on the concept that the masculine/feminine divide is socially constructed and not innate. *Feminis critical approacht, gender studies, and queer theory.* 1399

**genre** One of the types of literature, such as *fiction* and *poetry*. Also, a type of work, such as detective fiction, epic poetry, tragedy, etc. 2

**Globe Theater** The outdoor theater built at the end of the sixteenth century just south of the Thames, where many of Shakespeare's plays were originally performed. The Globe was rebuilt in the 1990s to its original appearance, and once again is a flourishing theater close to where it was at the time of Shakespeare. See Plates I–11, 12. 978

**graphic narratives, graphic novels** Graphic art that tells a continuous story. The essential quality of graphic narrative is the combination of picture and dialogue to convey a story from beginning to end. 61

**gustatory images** References to impressions of taste. 536

**haiku** A poetic form derived from Japanese, traditionally containing three lines of 5, 7, and 5 syllables, in that order, and usually treating a topic derived from Nature. 3, 648

**hamartia** The Greek word for "error or frailty" that brings about the downfall or suffering of a tragic protagonist. 932

**heavy-stress rhyme** or **rising rhyme** A *rhyme*, such as rhyming *iambs* or *anapests*, ending with a strong *stress*. The rhymes may be produced with one syllable words, like *SKY* and *FLY*, or with multisyllabic words in which the accent falls on the last syllable, such as *deCLINE* and *conFINE*. 641

**heptameter** or **the septenary** A line consisting of seven metrical *feet*. 641

**hero, heroine**   The major male and female *protagonists* in a *narrative* or *drama*. The terms are often used to describe leading characters in adventures and romances. 156

**heroic couplet**   Also called the *neoclassic couplet*. Two successive rhyming lines of *iambic pentameter*, a characteristic of much *poetry* written between 1660 and 1800. Five-stress couplets are often called "heroic" regardless of their topic matter and the period in which they were written. 643

**hexameter**   A line consisting of six metrical *feet*. 641

**high comedy**   Elegant *comedies* characterized by wit and sophistication, in which the complications grow not out of *situation* but rather out of *character*. See also *comedy of manners*. 1097

**historical critical approach**   See *topical/historical critical approach*.

**hovering accent**   See *spondee*.

**hubris** or **hybris**   Meaning "insolence, contemptuous violence," or pride, *hubris* defines the attitude/attitudes that lead tragic figures to commit their mistakes or offenses. 924

**humor**   In literature, those features of a *situation* or expression that provoke laughter and amusement. 285

**hymn, hymnal measure**   A hymn is a religious *song*, consisting of one and usually many more replicating rhythmical *stanzas*. The hymnal stanza, in iambics, consists of four lines of four stresses or else of four lines of alternating four and three stresses, rhyming *x a x a* or *a b a b*. See also *ballad measure* and *common measure*. 3, 648

**hyperbole** or **overstatement**   See *overstatement*.

**hypocrites**   (pronounced hip-pock-rih-TAYSS) Meaning "one who plays a part," *hypocrites* was the ancient Athenian word for *actor*. 925

**iamb**   A two-syllable *foot* consisting of a [light stress] followed by a heavy stress [(of WINDS, have FELT, of MAY).] [It is] the most common metrical [foot in Engli]sh poetry because it closely resembles natural speech while it also follows measured poetic accents. 641

**iambic pentameter**   A line consisting of five *iambic feet*, as in Shakespeare's "Shall I compare thee to a summer's day?" 641

**iambic rhyme**   A *heavy-stress rhyme* that is built from rhyming *iambs* such as "the WEST" and "in REST," or "adMIRE" and "deSIRE." 641

**idea** or **theme**   A concept, thought, opinion, or belief; in literature, a unifying, centralizing conception or *motif*. 367–398

**idiom**   Usage that produces unique words and phrases within regions, classes, or groups; e.g., standing *on* line or *in* line; carrying a *pail* or a *bucket*; drinking *pop* or *soda*. Also, the habits and structures of particular languages. 500

**image, imagery**   Images are references that trigger the mind to fuse together memories of sights (*visual*), sounds (*auditory*), tastes (*gustatory*), smells (*olfactory*), sensations of touch (*tactile*), and perceptions of motion (*kinetic, kinesthetic*). "Image" refers to a single mental creation. "Imagery" refers to images throughout a work or throughout the works of a writer or group of writers. Images may be *literal* (descriptive and pictorial) and *metaphorical* (figurative and suggestive). 3, 532–561, 564

**imaginative literature**   *Literature* based in the imagination of the writer; the genres of imaginative literature are *fiction, poetry*, and *drama*. 2, and *passim*

**imitation**   The theory that literature is derived from life and is an imaginative duplication of experience; closely connected to *realism* and *verisimilitude*. 57

**imperfect foot**   A *metrical foot* consisting of a single syllable, either heavily or lightly stressed, as the "er" in "a joy forever." There is nothing imperfect about an imperfect foot. It is so named because, having only one syllable, it does not fit into the patterns of the other poetic feet. Some analysts of prosody explain the absence of a syllable within an established poetic foot as a *catalexis*. 641

**incidents** See *actions*.

**incongruity** A discrepancy between what is ordinarily or normally expected and what is actually experienced. The resulting gap is usually a cause of laughter. 286

**informal diction** See *diction, informal or low*.

**intellectual critical approach** See *topical/intellectual critical approach*.

**internal rhyme** The occurrence of rhyming words within a single line of verse, as Poe's "Can ever dissever" in "Annabel Lee." 642

**interpretation** See *commentary*.

**intrigue plot** The dramatic rendering of how a young woman and her lover, often aided by a maidservant or *soubrette*, usually foil a *blocking agent* (usually a parent or guardian). 1094

**invention** The process of discovering and determining materials to be included in a composition, whether an *essay* or an imaginative work; a vital phase of prewriting. 18

**ironic comedy** A form of comedy in which characters seem to be in the grips of uncontrollable, cosmic forces. The dominant tone is therefore ironic. 1098

**irony** Broadly, a means of indirection. *Verbal irony* is language that states the opposite of what is intended. *Dramatic irony* describes the condition of characters who do not know the nature, seriousness, and extent of their circumstances. An emphasis on ineffectiveness and powerlessness is *situational irony*. 67, 201, 285, 608, 933

**irony of fate** See *cosmic irony*.

**irony of situation** See *situational Irony*.

**issue** An assertion or idea to be debated, disputed, or discussed. Sometimes the word *issue* refers to a difficult or questionable circumstance. 368

**Italian** or **Petrarchan sonnet** An *iambic pentameter* poem of fourteen lines, divided between the first eight lines (the *octave*) and the last six (the *sestet*). An Italian sonnet uses five rhymes, unlike the *Shakespearean sonnet*, which has seven rhymes. 645

**jargon** Language exclusively used by particular groups, such as doctors, lawyers, astronauts, computer operators, football players, etc. 501

**journal** A notebook or word-processor file for recording responses and observations that, for purposes of writing, may be used in the development of *essays*. 11

**kinesthetic images** Words describing human or animal motion and activity. 536

**kinetic images** Words describing general motion. 536

**kothorni** See *buskins*.

**Lenaia** The ancient Athenian early spring festival for which comedy as a form was first created. 1091

**lighting** The general word describing the many types, positions, directions, and intensities of artificial lights used in the theater. 874

**light stress** In speech and in metrical scansion, the less emphasized syllables, as in Shakespeare's "That TIME of YEAR," in which *that* and *of* are pronounced less emphatically than *TIME* and *YEAR*. 643

**limerick** A brief poem with pre-established line lengths and rhyming patterns, designed to be comic. Quite often, limericks are risqué. 3, 649

**limited point of view** or **limited third-person point of view** or **limited-omniscient point of view** A third-person narration in which the actions and thoughts of the protagonist are the primary focus of attention. 67, 113

**line** The basic poetic unit of length, appearing as a row of words on a page or else, sometimes, as a single word or even as a part of a word, and cohering grammatically through phrases and sentences. Lines in *closed-form poetry* are composed of determinable numbers of *metrical feet*; lines in *open-form poetry* are variable, depending on content and rhythmical speech patterns. 641

**listener (internal audience)**   A character or characters imagined as the audience to whom a poem or story is spoken, and as a result one of the influences on the content of the work, as in Browning's "My Last Duchess." Although the listener is usually silent, the listener's imagined reactions may affect what the speaker says and the manner in which he/she says it. Using a listener therefore enables the author to make the narrative, or poem, both personal and dramatic. 464

**literary research**   See *research.*

**literature**   Written or oral compositions that tell stories, dramatize situations, express emotions, and analyze and advocate ideas. Literature is designed to engage readers emotionally as well as intellectually, with the major genres being *fiction, poetry, drama,* and *nonfiction prose,* and with many separate sub-forms. 1, *passim*

**low comedy**   Crude, boisterous, and physical comedies and farces, characterized by sight gags, bawdy jokes, and outrageous situations. 1098

**low diction**   See *diction, informal or low.*

**lyric**   (1) A short *poem* or *song* written in a fixed stanzaic form. If the lyric is set to music for performance, each new stanza is usually sung to the original melody. (2) The Aristotelian term for the "several kinds of artistic ornament," such as strophes and antistrophes, that are to be used appropriately in a tragedy. 3, 646, 932

**magnitude**   The third element in Aristotle's definition of *tragedy,* emphasizing that a *play* should be neither too long nor too short, so that artistic balance and proportion can be maintained. 931

**main plot**   The central and major line of causality and action in a literary work. 867

**major mover**   A major participant in a ˉion who either causes things ʳor who is the subject of major ⁱe first-person narrator is also a

major mover, such as the *protagonist,* that fact gives first-hand authenticity to the narration. 108

**makeup**   The materials, such as cosmetics, wigs, and padding, applied to an actor to change appearance for a specific role, such as a youth, an aged person, or a hunchback. 874

**malapropism**   The comic use of an improperly pronounced word, so that what comes out is a real but also incorrect word. Examples are *odorous* for *odious* (Shakespeare) or *pineapple* for *pinnacle* (Sheridan). The new word must be close enough to the correct word so that the resemblance is immediately recognized, along with the error. See also *pun.* 1107, note to 1.2.2

**Marxist critical approach**   See *economic determinist/Marxist critical approach.*

**masks**   Masks were worn by ancient Athenian actors to illustrate and define dramatic characters such as youths, warriors, old men and women. 937

**meaning**   That which is to be understood in a work; the total combination of ideas, actions, descriptions, and effects. 357–398

**melodrama**   A sentimental dramatic form with an artificially happy ending. 881

**melos**   See *song.*

**metaphor ("carrying out a change")**   A *figure of speech* that describes something as though it actually is something else, thereby enhancing understanding and insight. 3, 562

**metaphorical language**   See *figures of speech.*

**meter**   The number of *feet* within a line of traditional verse, such as *iambic pentameter* referring to a line containing five *iambs.* 3, 641

**metonymy**   A *figure of speech* in which one thing is used as a substitute for another with which it is closely identified, such as when a speaker says "Dear Hearts" to refer to his/her audience. 568

**metrical foot**   See *foot.*

**metrics**   See *prosody.*

**middle comedy** The Athenian comedies written in the first two-thirds of the fourth century B.C.E. Middle comedy lessened or eliminated the *chorus*, and did away with the exaggerated costumes of the *old comedy*. No middle comedies have survived from antiquity. 876, 1093

**middle diction** See *diction, neutral or middle.*

**mimesis** or **representation** Aristotle's idea that *drama (tragedy)* represents rather than duplicates history. 930

**miracle play** A late medieval play dramatizing a miracle or miracles performed by a saint. An outgrowth of the earlier medieval *Corpus Christi* play. 880

**monologue** A long speech spoken by a single character to himself or herself, to the audience, or to an off-stage character. See also *aside, soliloquy.* 865

**monometer** A line consisting of one metrical *foot.* 641

**mood** See *atmosphere.*

**moral/intellectual critical approach** An interpretive literary approach that is concerned primarily with content and values. 1391

**morality play** A type of medieval and early Renaissance play that dramatizes how to live a pious life. The best-known morality play is the anonymous *Everyman.* 880

**motif** Meaning "something that moves," a *motif* is sometimes used in reference to a main *idea* or *theme* in a single work or in many works, such as a *carpe diem* theme, or a comparison of lovers to little worlds. See also *archetype.* 369

**motivation** The ideas and impulses that propel characters to a particular act or course of action. Motivation is the hallmark quality of *round* characters. 866

**multiple plot** or **double plot** A development in which two or more stories are both contrasted and woven together, as in Shakespeare's *A Midsummer Night's Dream.* 1100

**musical comedy** A modern prose play integrated with lyrics—and also dances—set to specially composed music. Usually, musical comedies are elaborately and expensively produced. The form is in a line of development from *ballad opera* and *comic opera.* 1154

**music of poetry** See *prosody.*

**muthos** See *myth.*

**mystery plays** See *Corpus Christi plays.*

**myth, mythology, mythos** A *myth* is a story that deals with the relationships of gods to humanity or with battles among heroes in time past. A myth may also be a set of beliefs or assumptions among societies. *Mythology* refers collectively to all the stories and beliefs, either of a single group or number of groups. A system of beliefs and religious or historical doctrines is a *mythos.* 2, 325, 930

**mythical reader** See *audience.*

**mythic critical approach** See *archetypal/symbolic/mythic critical approach.*

**mythopoeic** The propensity to create *myths* and to live in terms of them. 325

**narrative ballad** A poem in *ballad measure* telling a story and also containing dramatic speeches. 469

**narration, narrative fiction** The relating or recounting of a sequence of events or actions. Whereas a narration may be reportorial and historical, *narrative fiction* is primarily creative and imaginative. See also *prose fiction* and *creative nonfiction.* 2, 54, 61

**narrator** See *speaker.*

**naturalistic setting** A stage *setting* designed to imitate, as closely as possible, the everyday world, often to the point of emphasizing poverty and dreariness. 885

**neoclassic couplet** See *heroic couplet.*

**neutral diction** See *diction, neutral or middle.*

**new comedy** Athenian comedy that developed at the end of the fourth century B.C.E., stressing wit, romanticism.

and twists of plot. The most famous of the new comedy writers was Menander, some copies of whose plays have come to light in the last hundred years. 876, 1093

**New Critical/formalist critical approach**   An interpretive literary approach based on the French practice of *explication de texte*, stressing the form and details of literary works. 1395

**new historicism**   A type of literary criticism that emphasizes the integration of literature and historical background and culture. 1393

**nonfiction prose**   A *genre* consisting of essays, articles, and books about real as opposed to fictional occurrences and objects; one of the major *genres* of literature. 3

**nonrealistic character**   An undeveloped and often *symbolic character* without full motivation or individual identity. 866

**nonrealistic drama**   Dreamlike, fantastic, symbolic, and otherwise artificial plays that make no attempt to present an imitation of everyday reality. 873

**novel**   A long work of prose fiction. 2

**objective point of view**   See *dramatic point of view.*

**octave**   The first eight *lines* of an *Italian sonnet*, unified by topic, rhythm, and *rhyme*. 647

**ode**   A variable stanzaic poetic *form* (usually long, to contrast it with the *song*) with varying line lengths and sometimes intricate *rhyme* schemes. 3, 646

**old comedy** or **old attic comedy**   The Athenian comedies of the fifth century B.C.E., featuring song, dance, ribaldry, satire, and invective. The most famous writer of the old comedy is Aristophanes, 11 of whose plays have survived from antiquity. 876, 1092

**olfactory imagery**   *Images* referring to smel·

**·oint of view**   A *third-person* ·vhich the *speaker* or *narrator*, ·rent limitations, may

describe intentions, actions, reactions, locations, and speeches of any or all of the characters, and may also describe their innermost thoughts (when necessary for the development of the *plot*). 67, 113

**open-form poetry**   Poems that avoid traditional structural patterns, such as *rhyme* or *meter*, in favor of other methods of organization. 650

**orchestra (a part of a theater)**   (1) In ancient Greek theaters, the *orchestra*, or "dancing place," was the circular area at the base of the amphitheater where the chorus performed. (2) In modern theaters, the word "orchestra" now refers to the ground floor or first floor where the audience sits. 935

**organic unity**   The interdependence of all elements of a work, including character, actions, speeches, descriptions, thoughts, and observations. The concept of organic unity is attributed to Aristotle. 59

**outline**   See *analytical sentence outline.*

**overstatement** or **hyperbole** or **overreacher.**   A rhetorical *figure of speech* in which emphasis is achieved through exaggeration. 285, 569

**parable**   A short *allegory* designed to illustrate a religious truth, often associated with Jesus as recorded in the Gospels, primarily Luke. 2, 54, 325

*parados*   (1) A *parados* was either of the two aisles on each side of the *orchestra* in ancient Greek theaters, along which the performers could enter or exit. (2) The entry and first lyrical ode of the *chorus* in Greek tragedy, after the *prologue*. 935, 938

**paradox**   A *figure of speech* embodying a contradiction that is nevertheless true. 566

**parallelism**   A *figure of speech* in which the same grammatical forms are repeated. 503, 643

**paranomasia**   See *pun.*

**paraphrase**   A brief restatement, in one's own words, of all or part of a literary work; a *précis*. 490

**pastoral** A traditional poetic form with topic material drawn from the often idealized lives and vocabularies of rural and shepherd life. Famous English pastorals are Milton's "Lycidas," Arnold's "Thyrsis," Pope's *Pastorals*, and Spenser's *The Shepherd's Calendar*. 648

**pathos** The "scene of suffering" in tragedy, which Aristotle defines as "a destructive or painful action, such as death on the stage, bodily agony, wounds, and the like." It is the scene of suffering that is intended to evoke the response of pity (*eleos*) from the audience. 931

**pentameter** A line of five metrical *feet*. 641

**performance** An individual production of a play, either for an evening or for an extended period, comprising acting, movement, lighting, sound effects, staging and scenery, ticket sales, and the accommodation of the audience. 871

*peripeteia* or **reversal** Aristotle's term for a sudden reversal, when the action of a work, particularly a play, veers around quickly to its opposite. 930

**persona** See *speaker*.

**personification** A *figure of speech* in which human characteristics are attributed to nonhuman things or abstractions. 567

**perspective, dramatic** The *point of view* in drama, the way in which the dramatist focuses on major characters and on particular problems. 869

**Petrarchan sonnet** See *Italian sonnet*.

**phonetic, phonetics** The actual pronunciation of sounds, as distinguished from spelling or *graphics*. 641–42

**picture poetry** See *visual poetry*.

**plagiarism** A writer's use of the language and ideas of another writer or writers without proper acknowledgment. Plagiarism is a serious breach of academic conduct; some call it intellectual theft, and others call it an academic crime. 446

**platform stage** A raised stage surrounded by seats for an *arena theater* or *theater-in-the-round*. 872

**plausibility** See *probability*.

**play** See *drama*.

**plot** The plan or groundwork for a *story* or a *play*, with the *actions* resulting from believable and authentic human responses to a *conflict*. It is causality, conflict, response, opposition, and interaction that make a plot out of a series of *actions*. Aristotle's word for plot is *muthos*. 59, 100, 867

**plot of intrigue** See *intrigue plot*.

**poem, poet, poetry** A variable literary genre which is, foremost, characterized by the rhythmical qualities of language. While poems may be short (including *epigrams* and *haiku* of just a few lines) or long (*epics* of thousands of lines), the essence of poetry is compression, economy, and force, in contrast with the expansiveness and logic of prose. There is no bar to the topics that poets may consider, and poems may range from the personal and lyric to the public and discursive. A *poem* is one poetic work. A *poet* is a person who writes poems. *Poetry* may refer to the poems of one writer, to poems of a number of writers, to all poems generally, or to the aesthetics of poetry considered as an art. 2; Ch. 11, "Meeting Poetry"; Ch. 16, "From: The Shape of Poems."

**point of view** The *speaker, voice, narrator,* or *persona* of a work; the position from which details are perceived and related; a centralizing mind or intelligence; not to be confused with *opinion* or *belief*. 64, 107–150

**point-of-view character** The central figure or *protagonist* in a *limited-point-of-view narration*, the character about whom events turn, the focus of attention in the narration. 113

**postulate** or **premise** The assumption on which a work of literature is based, such as a level of absolute, literal *reality*, or as a dreamlike, fanciful set of events. See also *donnée*. 57

**private** or **contextual symbol** See *cultural symbol*.

**probability** or **plausibility** The standard that literature should be concerned with what is likely, common, normal, and usual. 157

**problem**   A question or issue about the interpretation or understanding of a work. 1082

**problem play**   A type of *play* dealing with a *problem*, whether personal, social, political, environmental, philosophical, or religious. 881, 1190, 1263

**procatalepsis** or **anticipation**   A rhetorical strategy whereby the writer raises an objection and then answers it; the goal is to strengthen an argument by dealing with possible objections before a dissenter can raise them. Procatalepsis is thus a writer's way of taking the wind out of an objector's sails. 1084

**producer**   The person in charge of practical matters connected with a stage production, such as securing finances, arranging for theater use, furnishing materials, renting or making costumes and properties, guaranteeing payments, and so on. 872

**prologue**   In ancient Athenian *tragedy*, the introductory action and speeches before the *parados*, or first entry of the *chorus*. 938

**props** or **properties**   The furniture, draperies, and the like used on stage during a play. 872

**proscenium, proscenium stage**   (1) See *proskenion*. (2) An arch that frames a box set and holds the curtain, thus creating the invisible fourth wall through which the audience sees the action of the play. 872

**prose fiction**   *Imaginative* prose narratives (*short stories* and *novels*) that focus on one or a few *characters* who undergo a change or development as they interact with other characters and deal with their problems. 2, 55

**prose poem**   A short work, laid out to look like prose, but employing the methods of verse, such as rhythm and imagery, for poetic ends. 663, 664

**prosk.....**     A raised stage built in front in ancient Greek theaters to ..... *actors* from the *chorus* and to .....ore prominent. 935

**prosody**   Metrics and versification; the *sounds*, *rhythms*, *rhymes*, and general physical qualities of *poetry*; the relationships between content and sound in poetry. 641

**protagonist**   The central *character* and focus of interest in a *narrative* or *drama*. 865

**psychological/psychoanalytic critical approach**   An interpretive literary approach stressing how psychology may be used in the explanation of both authors and literary works. 1403

**public mythology**   See *universal mythology*.

**pun,** or *paranomasia*   A witty word-play which reveals that words with different meanings have similar or even identical sounds. See also *malapropism*. 568

**purgation**   See *catharsis*.

**pyrrhic**   A *substitute* metrical *foot* consisting of two unaccented *syllables*, as in the words "on their" in this line from Pope's *Pastorals*: "Now sleeping flocks on their soft fleeces lie." 643

**quatrain**   (1) A four-line *stanza* or poetic unit. (2) In an *English* or *Shakespearean sonnet*, a group of four *lines* united by *rhyme*. 3, 645

**queer theory**   An interpretive literary approach based on the idea that sexual orientation is partly ideological and partly social. Many queer theorists see the heterosexual/homosexual divide as less distinct than has commonly been believed. 1399

**raisonneur**   A character who remains detached from the dramatic action and who provides reasoned commentary; a *choric figure*. 866

**reader-response critical approach**   An interpretive literary approach based on the proposition that literary works are not fully created until readers make *transactions* with them by *actualizing* them in the light of their particular knowledge and experience. 1409

**realism** or **verisimilitude**  The use of true, lifelike, or probable situations and concerns. Also, the theory underlying the depiction of reality in literature. 57

**realistic character**  The accurate *imitation* of individualized men and women. 866

**realistic comedy**  See *ironic comedy*.

**realistic drama**  The dramatic presentation of *action*, thoughts, and *character* that are designed to give the illusion of *reality*. 1240

**realistic setting**  A *setting* designed to resemble places that actually exist or that might exist. The setting of Wilson's *Fences* is realistic. 873

**recognition**  See *anagnorisis*.

**regular play**  A play conforming to the traditional *rules* of drama, particularly the *three unities*. Usually a regular play contains five acts (as in the Renaissance up through much of the nineteenth century). More recent regular plays contain three acts, although there is nothing hard and fast about this number. See *rules of drama*. 940

**reliable narrator**  A *speaker* who has nothing to hide by making misstatements and who is untainted by self-interest. This speaker's *narration* is therefore to be accepted at face value; contrasted with an *unreliable narrator*. 111

**repetition**  See *anaphora*.

**representation**  See *mimesis*.

**representative character**  A *flat character* with the qualities of all other members of a group (i.e., clerks, cowboys, detectives, etc.); a *stereotype*. 156

**research, literary**  The systematic use of primary and secondary sources for assistance in studying a literary *problem*. Chapters 10A, 19A, 23A

**resolution**  See *dénouement*.

**response**  A reader's intellectual and emotional reactions to a literary work. 1409

**Restoration comedy**  English *high comedies* written mainly between 1660 and 1700, dealing realistically with personal, social, and sexual issues. 1154

**revenge tragedy**  A popular type of English Renaissance drama, developed by Thomas Kyd, in which a person is called upon (often by a ghost) to avenge the murder of a loved one. Shakespeare's *Hamlet* is in the tradition of revenge tragedy. 981

**reversal**  See *peripeteia*.

**rhetoric**  The art of persuasive writing; broadly, the art of all effective writing. 503

**rhetorical figure**  See *figures of speech*.

**rhyme**  The repetition of identical or closely related sounds in the syllables of different words, almost always in concluding syllables at the ends of lines, such as Shakespeare's *DAY* and *MAY* and Swinburne's *for EVER* and *NEVER*. 641

**rhyme scheme**  A pattern of *rhyme*, usually indicated by the assignment of a letter of the alphabet to each rhyming sound, as in *a b b a a b b a* as the rhyming pattern of the octave of an *Italian* or *Petrarchan sonnet*. 642

**rhythm**  The varying speed, intensity, elevation, pitch, loudness, and expressiveness of speech, especially *poetry*. 641

**rising action**  The action in a *play* before the climax. See *Freytag Pyramid*. 868

**romance**  (1) Lengthy Spanish and French *stories* of the sixteenth and seventeenth centuries. (2) Modern formulaic *stories* describing the growth of an impulsive, passionate, and powerful love relationship. 2, 55

**romantic comedy**  Sympathetic *comedy* that presents the adventures of young lovers trying to overcome opposition and achieve a successful union. 1097

**round character**  A literary character, usually but not necessarily the *protagonist* of a story or play, who is three-dimensional, rounded, authentic, memorable, original, and true to life. A round character is the center of our attention, and is both individual and unpredictable. A round character profits from experience, and in the course of a story or play undergoes change or development. 155, 866

**rules of drama** The rules were an important concept of dramatic composition among Renaissance and eighteenth-century critics. The rules were based on ancient practice and theory, particularly the use of the five-act pyramidal (Freytag) structure and the embodiment of the *three unities* of action, place, and time. Sophocles followed the rules carefully; indeed, the rules were at least partially derived from his example. Shakespeare observed the *unity of action*, but in the interests of probability he apparently saw no reason to observe the others. See also *regular play*. 940

**satire** An attack on human follies or vices, as measured positively against a normative religious, moral, or social standard. 608

**satiric comedy** A form of *comedy* designed to correct social and individual behavior by ridiculing human vices and follies. 1097

**satyr play** A comic and burlesque *play* submitted by the ancient Athenian tragic dramatists along with their groups of three *tragedies*. On each day of tragic performances, the satyr play was performed after the three tragedies. See also *trilogy*. 926

**scan, scansion** The act of determining the prevailing *rhythm* and poetic characteristics of a *poem*. 643

**scene** In a *play*, a part or division (of an act, as in *Hamlet*, or of an entire play, as in *Fences*) in which there is a unity of subject, *setting*, and *actors*. 873

**scenery** The artificial environment created onstage to produce the illusion of a generalized place and

curtain that becomes when illuminated from

upstage, permitting action to take place under various lighting conditions. 874

**second-person point of view** A *narration* in which a second-person listener ("you") is the *protagonist* and the speaker is someone (e.g., doctor, parent, rejected lover, etc.) with knowledge that the protagonist does not possess or understand about his or her own actions. 112, 115

**selective recollection** See *flashback*.

**sentimental comedy** A type of comedy dramatizing how good nature and morality enable characters to overcome their character flaws, which otherwise seem problematic or even incorrigible. 1154

**sequence** The following of one thing upon another in time or chronology. It is the *realistic* or true-to-life basis of the cause-and-effect arrangement necessary in a *plot*. 59, 69

**seriousness** The first element in Aristotle's definition of *tragedy*, demonstrating the most elevated and significant aspects of human character. 931

**sestet** (1) A six-line stanza or unit of *poetry*. (2) The last six lines of an *Italian sonnet*. 647

**sets** The physical scenery and properties used in a theatrical production. 873

**setting** The natural, manufactured, and cultural environment in which characters live and move, including all their possessions, homes, ways of life, and assumptions. 198–243

**Shakespearean sonnet** See *English sonnet*.

**shaped verse** See *visual poetry*.

**short story** A compact, concentrated work of *narrative fiction* that may also contain description, dialogue, and commentary. Poe used the term "brief prose tale" for the short story, and emphasized that it should create a powerful and unified impact. 2, 56

**simile** A *figure of speech*, using "like" with nouns and "as" with clauses, as in "the trees were bent by the wind *like actors bowing after a performance*," 563

**sitcom**   A serial type of modern television comedy dramatizing the circumstances, assumptions, and actions of a fixed number of characters (hence "situation comedy" or "sitcom"). 1099

**situation**   The given circumstances of a *story*, *poem*, or *play*; a *donnée*. 3

**situational irony** or **irony of situation**   A type of *irony* emphasizing that human beings are enmeshed in forces beyond their comprehension and control. 67, 606, 890

*skene*   In ancient Greek theaters, the *skene* ("tent," "hut") was a building in front of the *orchestra* which contained front and side doors from which actors could make entrances and exits. It served a variety of purposes, including the storage of *costumes* and *props*. The word has given us our modern word *scene*. 935

**slang**   Informal diction and substandard vocabulary. Some slang is a permanent part of the language (e.g., phrases like "I'll be damned," "That sucks," and our many four-letter words). Other slang is spontaneous, rising within a group (*jargon*), and often then being replaced when new slang emerges. 501

**slapstick comedy**   A type of low *farce* in which the humor depends almost entirely on physical actions and sight gags. 1098

**social drama**   A type of *problem play* that deals with current social issues and the place of individuals in society. 881

**soliloquy**   A speech made by a character, alone on stage, directly to the *audience*, the convention being that the character is revealing his or her inner thoughts, feelings, hopes, and plans. A soliloquy is to be distinguished from an *aside*, which is made to the audience (or confidentially to another character) when other characters are present. 980

**song**   See *lyric*.

**sonnet**   A poem of fourteen lines (originally designed to be spoken and not sung) in *iambic pentameter*. See *Italian Sonnet* and *Shakespearean Sonnet*. 3, 645

**sound**   The phonetics of language, separately and collectively considered, See also *prosody*. 641

**speaker**   The *narrator* of a *story* or *poem*, the *point of view*, often an independent *character* who is completely imagined and consistently maintained by the author. In addition to narrating the essential events of the work (justifying the status of *narrator*), the speaker may also introduce other aspects of his or her knowledge, and may express judgments and opinions. Often the character of the speaker is of as much interest in the story as the *actions* or *incidents*. 107

**specific language**   Words referring to objects or conditions that may be perceived or imagined; distinguished from general language. 283

**speeches**   See *dialogue*.

**spondee**   A two-syllable *foot* consisting of successive, equally heavy *accents* (e.g., SLOW TIME, MEN'S EYES). 641

**stage business**   See *business*.

**stage convention**   See *convention*.

**stage directions**   A playwright's instructions concerning *blocking*, movement, *action*, tone of voice, entrances and exits, *lighting*, *scenery*, and the like. 865

**stanza**   A group of *poetic lines* corresponding to paragraphs in prose; stanzaic *meters* and *rhymes* are usually repeating and systematic. 641

**stasimon** (plural **stasima**)   A *choral ode* separating the *episodes* in Greek tragedies. Because of the word's derivation, it would seem that the chorus was sitting in the orchestra and watching during the episodes, and then stood before speaking or chanting its designated odes. 938

**static character**   A character who undergoes no change, a *flat character*; contrasted with a *dynamic character*. 156

**stereotype**   A character who is so ordinary and unoriginal that he or she seems to have been cast in a mold; a *representative* character. 866

**stichomythy**   In ancient Athenian drama, dialogue consisting of one-line speeches designed for rapid interchanges between characters. 938

**stock character**   A *flat character* in a standard role with standard *traits*, such as the irate police captain, the bored hotel clerk, the sadistic criminal, etc.; a *stereotype*. 156, 866

**story**   A *narrative*, usually fictional, and short, centering on a major character, and rendering a complete action. 56

**stress**   The emphasis given to a syllable, either strong or light. See also *accent*. 641

**structuralist critical approach**   An interpretive literary approach attempting to find relationships and similarities among elements that might originally appear to be separate and discrete. 1397

**structure**   The arrangement and placement of materials in a work. 59, 244–278, 867

**style**   The manipulation of language; the placement of words in the service of content. 280–320

**subject**   The topic that a literary work addresses, such as love, marriage, war, death, social inequality, etc. 871

**subplot**   A secondary line of action in a literary work that often comments directly or obliquely on the main plot. See also *multiple plot*. 867

**syllable**   A separately pronounced part of a word (e.g., the *sing* and *ing* parts of "singing"; the *sub*, *sti*, *tu*, and *tion* parts of "substitution"). Some words consist of only one syllable (e.g., *a, an, man, girl, the, when, screeched*), and other words have many syllables (*antidisestablishmentarianism, Aldeborontiphoscophornio*). 641

**symbol, symbolism**   A specific word, idea, or object that may stand for ideas, values, ᵖᵉ──── ʳ ways of life. 67, 201, 321–366, 6, 870

> ──acter   A character whose ──tion is symbolic, even

though the character also retains normal or *realistic* qualities. 866

**symbolic critical approach**   See *archetypal/symbolic/mythic critical approach*.

**synecdoche**   A *figure of speech* in which a part stands for a whole, or a whole for a part. 568

**synesthesia**   A *figure of speech* uniting or fusing separate sensations or feelings; the description of one type of perception or thought with words that are appropriate to another. 569

**syntax**   Word order and sentence structure. A mark of style is a writer's syntactical patterning (regular patterns and variations), depending on the rhetorical needs of the literary work. 502

**tactile imagery**   *Images* of touch and responses to touch. 536

**tenor (figures of speech)**   The ideas conveyed in a *metaphor* or *simile*. See also *vehicle*. 565

**tense**   Besides embodying reports of actions and circumstances, verbs possess altering forms—*tenses*—that signify the times when things occur, whether past, present, or future. Perfect and progressive tenses indicate completed or continuing activities. Tense is an important aspect of *point of view* because the notation of time influences the way in which events are perceived and expressed. Narratives are usually told in the past tense, but many recent writers of fiction prefer the present tense for conveying a sense of immediacy. No matter when a sequence of actions is presumed to have taken place, the introduction of *dialogue* changes the action to the present. See *point of view*. 114

**tercet** or **triplet**   A three-line unit or stanza of *poetry*, usually rhyming *a a a, b b b*, etc. 3, 644

**terza rima**   A three-line *stanza* form with the interlocking rhyming pattern *a b a, b c b, c d c*, etc. 644

**tetrameter**   A *line* of four metrical *feet*. 641

**theater**   In ancient Greece a theater was a "place for seeing." Today it is the name given to the building in which plays and other dramatic productions are performed. It is also a generic name for local or national drama in all its aspects, as in "Tonight we're going to the theater," and "This play is the best of the New York theater this year." 872, 934

**Theater of Dionysus**   The ancient Athenian outdoor amphitheater at the base of the Acropolis, where Greek drama began. 934

**theater-in-the-round**   See *arena stage* and *platform stage*.

**theme**   (1) The major or central idea of a work. (2) An essay, a short composition developing an interpretation or advancing an argument. (3) The main point or idea that a writer of an essay asserts and illustrates. 60, 367–398, 871

*theos apo mechanes*   See *deus ex machina*.

**thesis sentence** or **thesis statement**   An introductory sentence which names the topics and ideas to be developed in the body of an *essay*. 29

**third-person point of view**   A third-person method of *narration* (i.e., *she, he, it, they, them*, etc.), in which the *speaker* or *narrator* is not a part of the story, unlike the involvement of the narrator of a *first-person point of view*. Because the third-person speaker may exhibit great knowledge and understanding, together with other qualities of *character*, he or she is often virtually identified with the author, but this identification is not easily decided. See also *authorial voice, omniscient point of view*. 66, 112, 115

**third-person objective point of view**   See *dramatic point of view*.

**three unities**   Traditionally associated with Aristotle's descriptions of drama as expressed in the *Poetics*, the three unities are those of action, place, and time. The unities are a function of *verisimilitude*—the creation of literary works that are as much like reality as possible. Therefore a play should dramatize a single major *action* that takes place in a single place during the approximate time it would take for completion, from beginning to end. During the Renaissance, some critics considered the unities to be essential aspects, or *rules*, of *regular drama*. Later critics considered the unity of action important, but minimized the unities of place and time. See also *regular play*. 940

**thrust stage**   See *apron stage*.

**tiring house**   An enclosed area in an Elizabethan theater in which *actors* changed *costumes* and awaited their cues, and in which stage *properties* were kept. The word *tiring* is derived from *attire* (e.g., clothing or costumes). 979

**tone**   The techniques and modes of presentation that reveal or create attitudes. 67, 280–320, 601–624, 870

**topic sentence**   The sentence determining or introducing the subject matter of a paragraph. 29

**topical/historical critical approach**   An interpretive literary approach that stresses the relationship of literature to its historical period. 1393

**tragedy**   A drama or other literary work that recounts the fall or misfortune of an individual who, while undergoing suffering, deals responsibly with the situations and dilemmas that he or she faces, and who thus demonstrates the value of human effort and human existence. 875, 923–1090

**tragic flaw**   See *hamartia*.

**tragicomedy**   A literary work—*drama* or *story*—containing a mixture of *tragic* and *comic* elements. 880

**trait, traits**   A typical mode of behavior; the study of major traits provides a guide to the description of *character*. 151

**trilogy**   A group of three literary works, usually related or unified. For the ancient Athenian festivals of Dionysus, each competing tragic dramatist submitted a trilogy (three *tragedies*), together with a *satyr play*. 926

**trimeter**    A line of three metrical *feet*, as in "Today I went to school." 641

**triplet**    See *tercet*.

**trochaic (double) rhyme**    Rhyming trochees such as *FLOWER* and *TOWER*. 642

**trochee, trochaic**    A two-syllable *foot* consisting of a heavy *stress* followed by a light stress (e.g., *RUN-ning*, *SING-ing*, *EAT-ing*). Sometimes called a *choree*. 641

**trope**    A short dramatic dialogue inserted into the church mass during the early Middle Ages. 877

**Tudor interlude**    Tragedies, comedies, or historical plays performed by both professional actors and students during the reigns of Henry VII and Henry VIII (i.e., the first half of the sixteenth century). The Tudor interludes sometimes featured abstract and allegorical characters and provided opportunities for both music and farcical action. 978

**unaccented syllable**    A syllable receiving a *light stress*. 641

**unchanging character**    See *flat character*.

**understatement**    A *figure of speech* by which details and ideas are deliberately underplayed or undervalued in order to create emphasis—a form of *irony*. 285, 569

**unit set**    A series of platforms, rooms, stairs, and exits that form the locations for all of a play's actions. A unit set enables scenes to be changed rapidly, without the drawing of a curtain and the placement of new sets. 873

**unities**    See *three unities*.

**universal (public) mythology**    Widely known mythic systems that have been well established over a long period of time, such as Greco-Roman mythology and Germanic mythology. 58, 326

**universal symbol**    See *cultural symbol*.

**unreliable narrator**    A speaker who through ignorance, self-interest, or lack of capacity may tell lies and distort details. Locating the truth in an unreliable narrator's story requires careful judgment and not inconsiderable skepticism. 111

**unstressed syllable**    See *light stress*.

**value, values**    The attachment of worth, significance, and desirability to an *idea* so that the idea is judged not only for its significance as thought but also for its importance as a goal, ideal, or standard. 368

**vehicle**    The image or reference of figures of speech, such as a *metaphor* or *simile*; it is the vehicle that carries or embodies the *tenor*. See also *tenor*. 565

**verbal irony**    Language stressing the importance of an idea by stating the opposite of what is meant. 67, 285, 606, 870

**verisimilitude** (i.e., **"like truth"**)    A characteristic whereby the *setting*, circumstances, *characters*, *dialogue*, *actions*, and outcomes in a work are designed to seem true, lifelike, real, plausible, and probable. See also *realism*. 57, 157

**versification**    See *prosody*.

**villanelle**    A *closed-form* poem of nineteen lines, composed of five *tercets* and a concluding *quatrain*. The form requires that whole lines be repeated in a specific order and that only two rhyming sounds occur throughout. See also *tercet*. 3, 645

**visual image**    Language describing visible objects and situations. 533

**visual poetry**    Poetry written so that the lines form a recognizable shape, such as a pair of wings or a geometrical figure. Also called *concrete poetry* or *shaped verse*. 652

**voice**    See *point of view* and *speaker*.

**vowel sounds** or **vowel segments**    Meaningful continuant sounds produced by the resonation of the voice in the space between the tongue and the top of the mouth, such as the *ee* in "feel," the *eh* in "bet," and the *oo* in "cool." (641)

**well-made play (*la pièce bien faite*)**   A form developed and popularized in nineteenth-century France by Eugène Scribe (1791–1861) and Victorien Sardou (1831–1908). Typically, the well-made play is built on both secrets and the timely arrivals of new characters and threats. The protagonist faces adversity and ultimately overcomes it. Ibsen's *A Dollhouse* exhibits many characteristics of the well-made play. 1190, 1263

**words**   The spoken and written signifiers of thoughts, objects, and actions—the building blocks of language. 498–531

# AP* Practice Material

# AP* Practice Material
# Table of Contents

# AP* Introduction

This section has been designed to help students as they prepare to take the AP English Literature and Composition Exam. The general insights and suggestions contained herein will benefit any student preparing to take the exam; however, the material is specifically prepared to correlate to Roberts' *Literature: An Introduction to Reading and Writing,* Fourth Edition.

The Roberts' text provides more than 1,600 pages of literary works (fiction, poetry, and drama), commentary, analyses, and suggestions for writing. In its fourth edition, the text has established itself as a leader among those that college and university professors select for use in their literature classes—particularly literature-based composition courses as well as general introduction to literature courses. With this widespread acceptance at the college level, the text is certainly appropriate for use in an AP English class.

As a supplement to Roberts' *Literature: An Introduction to Reading and Writing,* Fourth Edition, the section you're currently reading will "connect" the literature text with the AP English Literature and Composition Exam. It begins with an overview of what to expect on the AP English Literature and Composition Exam, offers several strategies for addressing the exam's multiple-choice section and its essays, and includes a complete practice exam with detailed answers. Throughout this text, you'll also find cross-references to specific pages in the anthology where you'll find more extensive examples and explanations.

Among the best ways to prepare for the exam are to read extensively, sharpen your analytical skills, and then write extensively about your ideas and the literature. Perhaps these are among the goals that you've set for your preparation for the AP English Literature and Composition Exam. If so, then you'll find that this text works closely with the Roberts' literature text to help you achieve them.

Make the best of this opportunity to prepare for the exam and best wishes for success when you are ready to take the exam.

# What to Expect on the AP English Literature and Composition Exam

For those of us who experience a significant degree of anxiety, as we "look forward to" a visit to the dentist, the anxious moments aren't usually related to what we know about our time in the dentist's chair. No, we're most concerned about what we *don't know* about our time there. We think, "No problems since my last visit. I hope he doesn't find anything. And if he does, I sure hope he doesn't want to drill today." With these thoughts, we then grow increasingly worried about what he *might find*. It's the uncertainty that bothers us.

If your teeth are in great shape and you don't experience "dentist-chair anxiety," good for you. But perhaps you're among those who suffer from "test anxiety," especially with tests of such importance as the AP exams. If so, then maybe the unknown is what bothers you.

To help minimize the "unknown" as you prepare to take the AP English Literature and Composition Exam, let's begin with an overview of the exam itself. In the graphic that follows, you'll see a summary of what the exam involves. Then we'll proceed to the additional details about each section. Finally, we'll examine each section more thoroughly in the parts that follow.

## General Test Information

| Test Date | Early May |
|---|---|
| Total Time | 3 hours |
| Section I | Multiple Choice (60 minutes)—45% of your score on the exam<br>Total number of questions: 50–60<br>Four or five prose and/or poetry passages and a drama passage: 10–15 questions per passage |
| Section II | Essay (120 minutes)—55% of your score on the exam<br>Three essays:<br>  1. Analysis of poems<br>    Likely Options:<br>    • About a poem provided on the exam, or<br>    • Comparing two poems provided on the exam |

2. Analysis of prose
   Likely Options:
   - About a brief story provided on the exam, or
   - About an excerpt from a novel provided on the exam, or
   - About an essay provided on the exam
3. Open essay
   - About a prescribed literary topic supported by your own reading experience

# Section I of the AP English Literature and Composition Exam

## The Multiple-Choice Questions

In the multiple-choice section of the AP English Literature and Composition Exam, you're presented with four or five passages—from poetry, drama, and fiction. Each piece is followed by 10 to 15 "skill questions" in a multiple-choice format. These questions test your ability to analyze passages critically and analytically. Usually, the degree of difficulty increases as you progress numerically through the questions.

**TIP!** The questions won't expect you to recall specific facts about the complete work from which the passage has been derived. Any "fact" questions relate only to the specific passage that is given, not to the work as a whole. And these are relatively few in number.

You have 60 minutes to complete the multiple-choice section.

## Scoring the Multiple-Choice Section

The multiple-choice section is scored electronically soon after the tests are returned to Princeton, New Jersey, the home of Educational Testing Services. Points are awarded in a method similar to that used to score the SAT.

- You receive one point for each question that you answer correctly.
- You receive no points for a question left blank.
- You receive a deduction of one-fourth of a point for a question that you answer incorrectly.

## Frequently Asked Questions About the Multiple-Choice Section

### 1. Where can I obtain multiple-choice exams to use for practice?

Your AP English teacher almost certainly has a collection of multiple-choice questions similar to those you'll encounter on the exam. You can also order the complete literature exams that have been released by the College Board. To order these, visit the College Board's Web site at http://store.collegeboard.com.

### 2. Should I respond to the multiple-choice questions in the order that they appear?

You can respond in any order that makes you comfortable. If you encounter a passage that puzzles you, then feel free to move on to the next and then return later.

### 3. What if I don't finish the multiple-choice questions?

Many students don't finish the entire multiple-choice section. If you're among them, don't let it bother you. You can still earn a respectable score on the entire AP exam.

   If you notice that time is about to expire, avoid the temptation to fill in the missing answers. The odds are against your benefiting. Remember that you lose no points for the empty response, but you lose one-fourth of a point for each incorrect response.

### 4. What's the best strategy for guessing on the multiple-choice questions?

Remember, you receive no credit for an unanswered question, and you lose one-quarter point for each incorrect answer. If you can eliminate at least two of the five choices, then you've increased your odds of guessing accurately. This scenario converts the original one-in-five (20%) chance to a one-in-three (33%) chance for accuracy. If you don't feel comfortable with those odds, then don't guess, and instead move on to the next question.

   Avoid devoting too much time to a puzzling question. That time might be better spent on several less challenging questions that appear later in the exam. Just skip a puzzling question and return to it later—if time allows. (To make it easier to return, you can circle the question in the test booklet.)

### 5. How are correct responses, incorrect responses, and empty responses scored?

A correct response earns one point, an incorrect response loses one-fourth point from your score, and an omitted answer earns no points.

   Your total score on the multiple-choice section is converted to equal 45% of the exam's 150 possible points (or 67.5 of the 150 possible points).

# Section II of the AP English Literature and Composition Exam

## The Free-Response (Essay) Questions

At the conclusion of section I, you'll have a brief break and then proceed to the essay section of the AP English Literature and Composition Exam. For this section, you'll be allowed a maximum of 2 hours.

You can divide the 2 hours as you wish. Most students approach the essay section intending to allocate the remaining time equally among the three essays. Your experiences with practice exams will help you determine the approach that works best for you.

In the essay section of the AP English Literature and Composition Exam, you're presented with three essay topics. Each is intended to provide you with an opportunity to display in clear and effective prose your ability to analyze and interpret literary texts. For each of the first two, you're provided a specific passage derived from a poem or from a piece of fiction, drama, or nonfiction. The third essay topic directs you to focus on aspects, themes, and literary elements in a work that you select.

You have 120 minutes to complete the essay section.

## Scoring the Essay Section

Because of its nature, the essay section of the AP English Literature and Composition Exam requires more time for evaluation. It's read and scored by a panel of high school and college teachers who gather to read the essays in June, when these readers are available.

Each of your AP English essays is evaluated by a reader who uses a holistic approach and who "specializes" in an essay category (poetry, prose, or open). These readers can be considered specialists because of the limited number of literary pieces that serve as the basis for the poetry and prose essays. A poetry essay reader, for example, evaluates your poetry essay, but doesn't later read your prose essay. The same goes for the readers of prose essays. But because the possibilities for the literary subjects for the open essay are far more extensive, the College Board identifies a reader familiar with the work on which you base your open essay response, and then that specialist reads your open essay. None of these readers sees your responses to the multiple-choice section or knows your score on it.

Each AP English essay is scored on a scale from 0 to 9, based on criteria determined to evaluate the essay's overall quality. A high number is preferable on the essay section. The sum of your three essays' scores yields your essay section score—ranging from 0 to 27.

## Frequently Asked Questions About the Fiction and Poetry Essays

### 1. Does any essay question count more than another?

The essays are equal in value. Although you've probably spent much more time in your AP English course preparing for the open essay than for the others, the open essay counts no more than the poetry or the prose essays.

### 2. Should I respond to the essays in the order that they appear?

Respond in the order that you consider most comfortable. One of the most important decisions you might make during that time is the order in which you'll write the essays.

### 3. How long should the essay be?

Your task is to compose a thorough response to the essay topic. If your response is absolutely wonderful and triple the length of any other essay written on that essay topic, it won't receive extra credit. The reader has only 9 points to award. If, however, you write a very short essay (a single paragraph with only a few sentences), you should expect a low score. Write your best essay on the topic and then move on. Don't add sentences merely to fill up that last page.

### 4. What if I don't finish one of the essays?

Monitor the time so you can avoid such a situation. Realistically, however, you should be prepared for this possibility.

   If you write a fine essay response but you don't have time enough to include a "conclusion paragraph," your score might be affected, but only slightly—if at all.

   Your reader will give you a score based on what you've written. Even if you have time to write only half of what you'd intended, that score will be higher than if you had not responded at all.

### 5. Should I include a title?

Your reader is concerned with your essay response. If providing a title helps you write a better essay, include one. Otherwise, merely having a title won't affect an essay's score.

### 6. Should I include an outline?

The outline's value is similar to that of the title. If an outline helps you write a better essay, then you certainly should use one. As with the title, though, the outline itself won't affect your essay's score.

### 7. Should I begin my essay by rephrasing the question?

Beginning an essay by rephrasing the question is not an original method. But if doing so helps you write a better essay, do follow through. Consider, though, that the small amount of time you devote to a "non-essential" element might be better spent polishing the third essay.

### 8. Are spelling and punctuation important? What about grammar?

How many errors do you anticipate? Remember that the readers are English teachers. It's only natural for them to detect and cringe when they encounter problems in spelling, punctuation, and grammar.

Under the time constraints of the AP English Literature and Composition Exam, few writers should expect their writing to be totally free of such errors. Limiting them is the key. The litmus test might be the degree to which the errors hinder your essay's overall success.

Bottom line: Avoid allowing the errors to interfere with your reader's success in grasping your essay's intentions.

### 9. I have terrible handwriting. Is neatness important?

How troublesome is your handwriting? Those same readers/English teachers are accustomed to dealing with handwriting that would perplex even the most gifted pharmacists (who deal with the challenges of deciphering doctors' prescriptions).

Once again, the time constraints of the AP English Literature and Composition Exam virtually ensure that every writer's handwriting will diminish in quality. Limiting the effect is the key. As with the errors mentioned earlier (spelling, punctuation, and grammar), the "handwriting" litmus test might be the degree to which the errors hinder your essay's overall success.

Bottom line: Use your most legible handwriting so your readers don't encounter an unnecessary obstacle while comprehending your essay's intentions.

### 10. Do I have to use an ink pen?

As she reads the directions for the essay section, the proctor will instruct you to use an ink pen as you write your essays. If you prefer to use a pencil, you probably won't be penalized for doing so.

Realize that pencil is far more difficult to read than is ink. If you use pencil, also realize that you're placing an unnecessary burden upon your reader.

If by this point your essay's errors in spelling, punctuation, and grammar are magnified by your atrocious handwriting, this might not be the time to complicate matters further by using a difficult-to-read pencil.

## Frequently Asked Questions About the Open Essay

The questions addressed in the previous section, of course, are relevant to the open essay as well as to the fiction and poetry essays. But because the open essay topic has some distinct characteristics, a few additional questions deserve some attention.

### 1. Does this question always include a list of works that can be selected?

No, not always. Instead, you might find a list of authors. And there's the possibility that the open essay topic might not include a list at all. If that's the case, make something positive of it. Look even more closely for context clues within the topic. The most important consideration in dealing with the open essay is that you select a work (or *works*, if required) that's *appropriate to the question*.

### 2. Is there any advantage to selecting a work or author from the provided list?

No advantage. The list is provided to help illustrate the question's intentions. If you have in mind a work with which you're extremely familiar and you're convinced that it's *appropriate to the question*, then you'll almost certainly write a better response on it than if you select a work from the list.

### 3. What if I'm not sure that my choice is of "similar merit" or "comparable quality"?

If you're not confident, then don't use it. One fairly safe way to determine if your choice is of "similar merit" or "comparable quality," is to select a work that you studied in your AP English class. If your teacher included the work in the course, then you can feel fairly secure that it's *appropriate to the question*.

### 4. Is there any advantage to writing about a longer work rather than a short work?

The length of the work is not the key factor in your writing an excellent response to the topic. Whatever its length, select a work with which you're extremely familiar and you're convinced that it's *appropriate to the question*. If those two factors are in place, then you're far more likely to compose your best response.

# Your Score on the AP English Literature and Composition Exam

## The Agonizing Wait

You'll take the AP English Literature and Composition Exam in early May, and then experience what seems an incredibly long waiting period before you receive your score in early July. (Remember that the panel of readers doesn't gather until early June.) As with all Advanced Placement exams, scores are rated on a final scale of 1 to 5. Your scores on the individual sections won't reach you; the College Board doesn't report these. Don't let this bother you, though, because what you're really concerned with is the final score. Again, a high number is good.

## Interpreting your score

| Score's Meaning | Equivalent grade in first-year college course | Will you receive college credit?* |
|---|---|---|
| 5 → Extremely Well Qualified | A | Yes |
| 4 → Well Qualified | $A^-$, $B^+$ | Yes |
| 3 → Qualified | $B^-$, C | Maybe |
| 2 → Possibly Qualified | C | Rarely |
| 1 → No Recommendation | D | No |

\* N.B.: The decision to grant you college credit, of course, rests with the school in which you enroll.

# PART TWO

# Strategies for Success on the AP English Literature and Composition Exam

Your preparation for taking the AP English Literature and Composition Exam begins at least as early as your first day in the AP English Literature and Composition Exam course. But you actually began preparing years ago, as your reading skills matured and you started looking beneath the surface of what you read.

In varying degrees, we all possess these skills. The AP English Literature and Composition Exam course is intended to help you sharpen those skills. And the AP English Literature and Composition Exam is designed to measure them. Not surprisingly, though, you hold the key to determining how well you'll score on the AP English Literature and Composition Exam.

## Early Preparation

One of the most important steps involves early preparation. If you're in the midst of an AP English Literature and Composition Exam course, you have a clear idea of how consuming serious preparation can be. To perform well on the exam, you'll have to take personal responsibility for this step.

Don't assume that the few hours spent each week in the AP English classroom will assure you of a 5 on the AP English Literature and Composition Exam. Supplement the course with additional materials from a variety of sources.

Through its Web site www.apcentral.collegeboard.com, College Board provides a wide variety of resources that offer general advice about the AP English Literature and Composition Exam.

Begin your tour of the Web site by locating the AP English Literature and Composition Exam Course Home Page by searching under "subjects." Here, you'll find links to several resources, including a page devoted specifically to the exam that provides access to the actual questions that appeared on the most recent AP English Literature and Composition Exams. These authentic questions should be especially helpful as you prepare for the exam.

Also available from this Web site is the College Board's publication known as the **Acorn Book**, which provides a course description for the AP Exam in English Literature and Composition Exam (as well as the AP Exam in English Language and Composition). From the College Board Web site www.apcentral.collegeboard.com, you can download a .pdf version.

From other sources you can purchase one or more of the professionally developed preparation handbooks that are available through a good bookstore and are usually priced around $10. These are quite similar to those that help you prepare for the SAT.

Another resource, of course, is your teacher, who might provide you with a study guide for the AP English Literature and Composition Exam. Your teacher's experience with the exam can provide answers to your questions as they arise throughout these months of preparation. Don't be reluctant to ask. Your questions might also spark additional questions from your classmates.

Pearson/Longman—publisher of the text you're reading right now—sponsors a companion Web site for another of its textbooks—Roberts' *Literature: An Introduction to Reading and Writing*, Eighth Edition. At the Web site www.prenhall.com/roberts, you'll find a part-by part guide to the Roberts' *Literature: An Introduction to Reading and Writing*, Eighth Edition. You'll also find quizzes that include instant scoring. The Web site features author biographies, annotated links for further study, a literary walking tour, and an interactive timeline. There's also a wide variety of web links to research specific authors, famous works written during numerous literary periods, and online literary journals.

Here's a summary of the Web site's useful features:

- a study guide;
- online quizzes, which include instant scoring and coaching;
- built-in routing that gives students the ability to forward essay responses and graded quizzes to their instructors;
- author biographies with contextual links;
- links that provide a valuable source of supplemental information;
- an interactive timeline;
- writing activities that foster critical thinking; and
- essay questions that test students' critical thinking skills.

The Web site may be accessed at www.prenhall.com/roberts.

## Time to Get Serious

Sometime after you've returned to classes following the winter holiday break, you should intensify your preparation for the AP English Literature and Composition Exam. With over half of the AP English Course completed, you can begin your review for the exam. This portion of the process should begin in March.

Many students find it helpful to take some of the practice exams early in the review process. This provides them with a clear picture of what to expect on the exam. It often informs them of areas to concentrate on during the review. And it sets them up to detect improvement when they take other practice exams during the final week or two prior to taking the real exam.

One complete practice version of the AP English Literature and Composition Exam is available in this textbook. Most of the other preparation handbooks contain practice exams. And don't forget about the Released Exams for AP English available at the College Board's Web site.

Also in March or early April, your teacher or someone else at your school will make arrangements for you to pay the appropriate fees and file the appropriate forms so you can register to take the AP English Literature and Composition Exam. As you might expect, managing such a nationwide program requires coordination, so the College Board prescribes a series of dates as guidelines. Your teacher will help you comply.

## As Test Day Approaches

During the final days before the exam, your teacher will probably offer some specific insights related to the actual day of the exam. Listen carefully to those words of wisdom because they apply to your specific situation. To supplement those provided by your teacher, here are some points that will prove helpful.

**TIP!** If you aren't taking the exam at your school, then be certain that you're familiar with the exact location. Consider visiting the exam site a few days ahead of the actual date. If at all possible, scout the examination room for the seat where you'd feel most comfortable—in case you're allowed to choose your seat. Where's the best lighting? Notice the room temperature; this might influence what you'll wear on exam day. For example, does the air conditioner's thermostat seem set so low that you'll need a sweater or jacket?

## The Day Before Test Day

Some preparation today will help you avoid a frantic episode tomorrow morning.

- The AP English Literature and Composition Exam is usually given in the morning, lasts at least 3 hours, and might interfere with your usual lunchtime. To help you survive an attack of the munchies or to quiet your growling stomach, you might want to bring a snack. During the short break between the two major sections of the exam, you can eat the snack.

Pack the snack the day before your test so you can take it with you tomorrow.

- As you check in at the test site, you'll have to identify yourself. If you take the exam at your school, you probably won't encounter much difficulty proving that you are you. Nevertheless, bring with you photo identification (such as a driver's license or a school ID card). Also bring your social security number. (If you haven't done so already, this is a good time to memorize that number.) And you'll need to know your school code, which is available from your teacher or counselor.

Collect these items the day before the test so you can take them with you and prove your identity tomorrow.

- Bring several sharpened #2 pencils and a couple of new ink pens with dark ink. Be sure to test the ink pens. Select pens with dark-blue or black ink. Avoid writing your essays in pencil or in ink of an exotic color. In meeting these expectations, you'll help the readers of your essays. Don't make your exam memorable for the problems it poses.

Sharpen the pencils and "test drive" the ink pens the day before the test so they won't disappoint you and so you'll have them with you tomorrow.

- Beyond these pencils and pens, you won't need any additional materials, so don't bring them. In fact, you won't be allowed to take any other materials—such as correction fluid, highlighting markers, dictionaries, books, or extra paper—into the testing area. Personal laptop computers won't be allowed (except for those who have received prior permission because of established disabilities). Portable CD players, recording devices, beepers, and PDAs won't be allowed in the testing area. Even the ubiquitous cell phone is viewed with suspicion. For the duration of the exam, take a break from all connections to the outside world. You might enjoy it.

Put these items aside the day before the test so you won't be tempted to bring them with you.

- You might want to bring a watch to keep track of the time. The presence of multiple clocks in the examination room can often confuse more that help—especially if they aren't synchronized. Instead of depending on them, monitor the time yourself based on the proctor's reminders. You don't want to approach the end of the multiple-choice or essay section and discover that the wall clock near you has a weak battery. Use care to select your watch for the day. Don't bring one with a beep or an alarm. If your watch's beeper or alarm disrupts the exam, you and your watch might be escorted from the room.

Check your watch's battery the day before the test so it won't disappoint you tomorrow and now is also the time to shut off the beeper and alarm so they won't embarrass you tomorrow.

- Perhaps the most important "final day" preparation is to get a good night's sleep. Another day of cramming probably won't produce any worthwhile results. Instead, try to relax, enjoy one of your favorite activities, and get to bed at a reasonable time.

Rest and relax the day before the test so you can be alert, perform at your highest level, and capitalize on months of preparation.

## On Test Day

Here's a checklist that might prove helpful just before you depart for the testing site:

| | | | |
|---|---|---|---|
| ✓ | Snack packed? _____ | ✓ | Ink pens? _____ |
| ✓ | Driver's license? _____ | ✓ | Right color? _____ |
| ✓ | School ID? _____ | ✓ | No other items? _____ |
| ✓ | Social security number? _____ | ✓ | Not even the cell phone? _____ |
| ✓ | School code? _____ | ✓ | Quiet version of a watch? _____ |
| ✓ | Pencils? _____ | | |

Keep that snack handy. Remember that you'll have a short break (lasting approximately 10 minutes) after the multiple-choice section.

Also during the break, you'll probably be permitted to talk with fellow students, but avoid talking about the exam or the multiple-choice questions you have just completed. And to avoid any appearance of irregularity, don't talk to any AP English teachers.

Even if you're taking the exam at your school, it's wise to arrive at least 20 minutes earlier than the prescribed time so you can get comfortable before preparations for the exam begin. If you're taking the exam at an unfamiliar location, this advice is especially important. After you've taken a seat in the examination room, take several deep breaths to control your nerves and then focus on why you're there. All of those months of preparation come down to these three hours. You can tolerate anything for three hours, can't you? Yes, you can.

Now you're ready to take the exam.

## Specific Insights for Addressing the Test

### During the Test

With these thoughts in mind, you're ready to direct your attention to the AP English Literature and Composition Exam—what to expect and how to address the test itself. Turn now to Sections 3, 4, and 5, where you'll find advice for coping with the fiction, poetry, and drama that you'll encounter on the AP English Literature and Composition Exam.

# Dealing with the Fiction on the AP English Literature and Composition Exam

In the multiple-choice section of the AP English Literature and Composition Exam, you're presented with four or five passages—from poetry, drama, and fiction. Each piece is followed by 10 to 15 "skill questions" in a multiple-choice format. These questions test your ability to analyze passages critically and analytically.

To help you prepare for this section of the AP English Literature and Composition Exam, the AP English class provides large doses of careful reading and critical analysis of many pieces of literature. Through a close reading of a wide variety of texts, you'll deepen your awareness and understanding of how writers use language to achieve their goals. As you read these works, you'll examine and analyze them for insights about structure, style, themes, figurative language, imagery, symbolism, and tone.

Information in this part relates specifically to fiction. Parts Four and Five address poetry and drama, respectively. Those two parts combine with this part to help you prepare for the multiple-choice section of the AP English Literature and Composition Exam.

In the following series of boxes, you'll find insights into the types of questions that frequently appear on the multiple-choice section of the AP English Literature and Composition Exam. Accompanying each box you'll also find a connection to chapters in the anthology.

| What is its subject? | "Subject" questions you might encounter: |
| --- | --- |
| Is it intended to describe a scene? | The narrator's point in lines 22–27 is . . . . |
| Is it intended to describe a character? | In the second paragraph, the author's subject is chiefly . . . . |
| | The main subject of this passage is . . . . |

For help in evaluating a work's subject, see Chapter 2 "Fiction: An Overview" (pages 53–106—especially pages 53–69).

| Who is its narrator? | "Narrator" questions you might encounter: |
|---|---|
| Look for hints that identify the narrator, her background, and when and where she might have lived. | The narrator of passage can be best described as . . . .  The narrator is most likely a resident of . . . .  The narrator most likely lived during . . . . |

For help in evaluating a work's narrator, see Chapter 3 "Point of View: The Position of the Narrator or Speaker" (pages 107–150).

| What is its structure? | "Structure" questions you might encounter: |
|---|---|
| Look for cause/effect or comparison/contrast relationships.  Look for relationships between paragraphs—contradictions, additional support, additional questions raised.  Look for transitions—for example, "most importantly," "less vital to the discussion," and "on the contrary"—that provide hints of the author's intentions. | Which of the following pairs of paragraphs incorporates a comparison/contrast relationship?  The first and the last paragraphs are intended to contradict each other because they . . . .  Which of the following paragraphs is intended to contradict the position stated in the second paragraph? |

For help in evaluating a work's structure, see Chapter 6 "Structure: The Organization of Stories" (pages 244–279).

| Does specific diction or syntax provide insights? | "Diction/syntax" questions you might encounter: |
|---|---|
| Look for jargon or unfamiliar words.  Look for an uncommon arrangement of words. | As it is used in line 46, *ubiquitous* can be best understood to mean . . . .  The author's use of "up with which I shall not put" can be best understood to mean . . . . |

For help in evaluating a work's diction and syntax, see Chapter 7 "Tone and Style: Conveying Attitudes in Fiction" (pages 280–320).

| **What is its tone?** | **"Tone" questions you might encounter:** |
|---|---|
| Is it intended to parody or satirize?<br><br>Is it intended to be humorous?<br><br>Does it contain obvious irony? | In her discussion of her experiences with the attorney, the author incorporates a tone that is reminiscent of . . . .<br><br>This tone of this passage can be best described as . . . . |

For help in evaluating a work's tone, see Chapter 7 "Tone and Style: Conveying Attitudes in Fiction" (pages 280–320).

| **What are the most important figures of speech?** | **"Figures of speech" questions you might encounter:** |
|---|---|
| Look for these popular figures of speech: metaphor, analogy, paradox, hyperbole, and oxymoron. | The purpose of the basket metaphor in line 39 is to . . . .<br><br>The analogy in the third paragraph is intended to remind the reader of . . . .<br><br>The author's use of the phrase "less is more" is an example of . . . .<br><br>The opening paragraph's reference to the "bull in the china shop" is intended to . . . .<br><br>In the third paragraph, the author's use of "jumbo shrimp" is an example of . . . . |

For help in evaluating images and figures of speech, see Chapter 8 "Symbolism and Allegory: Keys to Extended Meaning" (pages 321–366). And, although they are intended specifically for poetry rather than for fiction, two other parts offer insights that can be transferred to fiction, so they are worth reviewing as well: Chapter 13 "Imagery: The Poem's Link to the Senses" (pages 528–559), and Chapter 14 "Figures of Speech, or Metaphorical Language: A Source of Depth and Range in Poetry" (pages 560–598).

| **What is its theme?** | **"Theme" questions you might encounter:** |
|---|---|
| Can you determine the author's intentions?<br><br>Does the author have a cause?<br><br>Does the author oppose the cause held by someone else? | With which of the following is this passage most concerned?<br><br>Which of the following best summarizes the meaning of . . . .?<br><br>The author disagrees with Johnson's position because . . . . |

For help in evaluating a work's theme, see Chapter 9 "Idea or Theme: The Meaning and the Message in Fiction" (pages 367–398).

# PART FOUR

# Dealing with the Poetry on the AP English Literature and Composition Exam

In the multiple-choice section of the AP English Literature and Composition Exam, you're presented with four or five passages—from poetry, drama, and fiction. Each piece is followed by 10 to 15 "skill questions" in a multiple-choice format. These questions test your ability to analyze passages critically and analytically.

The AP English Literature and Composition Exam course involves large doses of careful reading and critical analysis of many pieces of literature. Through a close reading of a wide variety of texts, you'll deepen your awareness and understanding of how writers use language to achieve their goals. As you read these works, you'll examine and analyze them for insights about structure, style, themes, figurative language, imagery, symbolism, and tone.

Information in this part relates specifically to poetry. Parts Three and Five address fiction and drama, respectively. Those two parts combine with this part to help you prepare for the multiple-choice section of the AP English Literature and Composition Exam.

In the following series of boxes, you'll find insights into the types of questions that frequently appear on the multiple-choice section of the AP English Literature and Composition Exam. Accompanying each box you'll also find a connection to chapters in the anthology.

| Who is its narrator? | "Narrator" questions you might encounter: |
|---|---|
| Look for hints that identify the narrator, her background, and when and where she might have lived. | The narrator of this poem can be best described as .... |
| | In this poem, "we" and "us" refer to .... |
| | At the time that the narrator is "speaking" in this poem, which of the following events could she not have experienced? |

For help in evaluating a poem's narrator, see Chapter 3 "Point of View: The Position of the Narrator or Speaker" (pages 107–150). Although this chapter is found in the section related to fiction, its message also relates to poetry.

| How are meter and rhyme used? | "Meter and Rhyme" questions you might encounter: |
| --- | --- |
| Look for patterns in rhythms that will help you identify the meter. Look for patterns in the rhyme that will help you determine the rhyme scheme. | Iambic pentameter is present in . . . . The rhyme pattern of the second stanza can be described as . . . . |

For help in evaluating a poem's structure, see Chapter 6 "Structure: The Organization of Stories" (Pages 244–279). Although this chapter is found in the section related to fiction, its message also relates to poetry.

| What is its subject? | "Subject" questions you might encounter: |
| --- | --- |
| Is it intended to describe a scene? Is it intended to describe a character? | The narrator's point in lines 6–8 is . . . . In the second stanza, the author's subject is chiefly . . . . The main subject of these lines is . . . . |

For help in evaluating a poem's subject, see Chapter 11 "Meeting Poetry: An Overview" (pages 455–493—especially page 462).

| What is its theme? | "Theme" questions you might encounter: |
| --- | --- |
| Can you determine the poet's intentions? Does the poet have a cause? Does the poet oppose the cause held by someone else? | With which of the following are these lines most concerned? Which of the following best summarizes the meaning of . . . . ? The poet's reasons for opposing are . . . . |

For help in evaluating a poem's theme, see Chapter 11 "Meeting Poetry: An Overview" (pages 455–493).

| Does specific diction or syntax provide insights? | "Diction/syntax" questions you might encounter: |
|---|---|
| Look for jargon or unfamiliar words.<br><br>Look for an uncommon arrangement of words. | As it is used in lines 10, *puddle-wonderful* can be best understood to mean . . . .<br><br>The poet's use of "Inscrutable His ways are" can be best understood to mean . . . . |

For help in evaluating a poem's diction and syntax, see Chapter 12 "Words: The Building Blocks of Poetry" (pages 494–527) and Chapter 17 "Symbolism and Allusion: Windows to Wide Expanses of Meaning" (pages 691–732).

| What are the most important figures of speech? | "Figures of speech" questions you might encounter: |
|---|---|
| Look for these popular figures of speech: metaphor, analogy, paradox, hyperbole, and oxymoron. | The purpose of the snake metaphor in line 19 is to . . . .<br><br>The analogy in the third stanza is intended to remind the reader of . . . .<br><br>The poet's use of the phrase "less is more" is an example of . . . .<br><br>The opening stanza's reference to the "higher than Everest" is intended to . . . .<br><br>In the concluding stanza, the poet's use of "bittersweet" is an example of . . . . |

For help in evaluating images and figures of speech in poetry, see Chapter 13 "Imagery: The Poem's Link to the Senses" (pages 528–559) and Chapter 14 "Figures of Speech, or Metaphorical Language: A Source of Depth and Range in Poetry" (pages 560–598).

| What is its tone? | "Tone" questions you might encounter: |
|---|---|
| Is it intended to parody or satirize?<br><br>Is it intended to be humorous? | Pertaining to the kind of behavior mentioned in lines 4–6, the poet's attitude is . . . .<br><br>This tone of lines 3–9 can be best described as . . . . |

For help in evaluating a poem's tone, see Chapter 15 "Tone: The Creation of Attitude in Poetry" (pages 599–640).

# PART FIVE

# Dealing with the Drama on the AP English Literature and Composition Exam

In the multiple-choice section of the AP English Literature and Composition Exam, you're presented with four or five passages—from poetry, drama, and fiction. Each piece is followed by 10 to 15 "skill questions" in a multiple-choice format. These questions test your ability to analyze passages critically and analytically.

To help you prepare for this section of the AP English Literature and Composition Exam, the AP English class provides large doses of careful reading and critical analyses of many pieces of literature. Through a close reading of a wide variety of texts, you'll deepen your awareness and understanding of how writers use language to achieve their goals. As you read these works, you'll examine and analyze them for insights about structure, style, themes, figurative language, imagery, symbolism, and tone.

Information in this part relates specifically to drama. Because drama can be classified as prose or as poetry, we've chosen to discuss it in a part separate from fiction (prose) and poetry. For example, Tennessee Williams' *Glass Menagerie* and Arthur Miller's *Death of a Salesman* are among the dramatic pieces commonly studied in an AP English courses. A brief glance at either of them informs us that they're written in prose.

But we can't forget that each of Shakespeare's plays is actually poetry. Remember *blank verse*? If it's verse, it's poetry.

Parts Three and Four address fiction and poetry, respectively. Those two parts combine with this part to help you prepare for the multiple-choice section of the AP English Literature and Composition Exam.

In the following series of boxes, you'll find insights into the types of questions that frequently appear on the multiple-choice section of the AP English Literature and Composition Exam. Accompanying each box you'll also find a connection to chapters in the anthology.

| What is its subject? | "Subject" questions you might encounter: |
|---|---|
| Is it intended to describe a scene? | The narrator's point in lines 22–27 is . . . . |
| Is it intended to describe a character? | In the second paragraph, the author's subject is chiefly . . . . |
| | The main subject of this passage is . . . . |

For help in evaluating a work's subject, see Chapter 20 "The Dramatic Vision: An Overview"—especially page 869.

| What is its theme? | "Theme" questions you might encounter: |
|---|---|
| Can you determine the author's intentions?<br><br>Does the author have a cause?<br><br>Does the author oppose the cause held by someone else? | With which of the following is this passage most concerned?<br><br>Which of the following best summarizes the meaning of . . . .?<br><br>The author disagrees with Johnson's position because . . . . |

For help in evaluating a work's theme, see page 869.

| What is its tone? | "Tone" questions you might encounter: |
|---|---|
| Is it intended to parody or satirize?<br><br>Is it intended to be humorous? | In her discussion of her experiences with the attorney, the author incorporates a tone that is reminiscent of . . . .<br><br>This tone of this passage can be best described as . . . . |

For help in evaluating a work's tone, see page 868.

| What is its structure? | "Structure" questions you might encounter: |
|---|---|
| Look for cause/effect or comparison/contrast relationships.<br><br>Look for relationships between paragraphs—contradictions, additional support, additional questions raised.<br><br>Look for transitions—for example, "most importantly," "less vital to the discussion," and "on the contrary"—that provide hints of the author's intentions. | Which of the following pairs of lines incorporates a comparison/contrast relationship?<br><br>Puck's words in lines 17–21 and Oberon's words in lines 32–37 are intended to contradict each other because they . . . .<br><br>Which of the following lines is intended to contradict the position stated in lines 24–32? |

For help in evaluating a work's structure, see pages 865–867.

| Who is its narrator? | "Narrator" questions you might encounter: |
|---|---|
| Look for hints that identify the narrator, her background, and when and where she might have lived. | The narrator of passage can be best described as . . . . |
| | The narrator is most likely a resident of . . . . |
| | The narrator most likely lived during . . . . |

For help in evaluating a work's narrator, see page 867.

| Does specific diction or syntax provide insights? | "Diction/syntax" questions you might encounter: |
|---|---|
| Look for jargon or unfamiliar words. | As it is used in line 46, *fishmonger* can be best understood to mean . . . . |
| Look for an uncommon arrangement of words. | "Lord, what fools these mortals be!" can be best understood to mean . . . . |

For help in evaluating a work's diction and syntax, see pages 863–864.

| What are the most important figures of speech? | "Figures of speech" questions you might encounter: |
|---|---|
| Look for these popular figures of speech: metaphor, analogy, paradox, symbol, and allegory. | The purpose of the chariot metaphor in line 39 is to . . . . |
| | The analogy in lines 17–19 is intended to remind the reader of . . . . |
| | The narrator's use of "such sweet thunder" is an example of . . . . |
| | The birdcage is best described as symbolizing . . . . |
| | The dollhouse serves as an allegorical representation of . . . . |

For help in evaluating images and figures of speech, see page 863.

# PART SIX

# Dealing with the Essays on the AP English Literature and Composition Exam

During the months of your AP English class, you'll write essay after essay, preparing for the three that count most in early May. To provide you practice that will help you develop the skills necessary to write well in May, your teacher will have a long list of topics. At some point, you might wonder how your teacher could come up with yet another topic, and another, and another. And you'll almost certainly become convinced that you've written more essays than you ever thought possible.

Supplement this writing with extensive reading. Yes, read as many other AP English essay topics as you can locate. Consider the potential resources: your teacher, the Web, other test-prep materials. But don't merely read the topic and check it off the list. Give each a thorough and careful reading—sufficient to give you enough insight to write an essay if necessary.

Despite your dilemma, doubts, and distress, there truly is a method to this madness.

The following section presents a series of recommendations intended to help you address those May essays. You'll probably find it beneficial to have these in mind during the preparation that's part of your AP English class.

## Addressing the Prose Essay Topic

- **Read the topic thoroughly and carefully.**

  1. Look for terms that indicate precisely what the topic expects you to address. Some topics instruct you to examine the *characters*, *point of view*, *tone*, or *figurative language* in a novel, play, or short story.

     A complete discussion of these literary terms is available throughout the anthology [*characters* (Chapter 4), *point of view* (Chapter 3), *tone* (Chapter 7), and *figurative language* (Chapter 8)].

  2. Look for other clues that indicate how the topic expects you to address these characteristics (e.g., *discuss*, *describe*, *define*, *explain*, *compare*, and *contrast*).

     For specific recommendations about composing a comparison and contrast analysis, see Chapter 25 "Comparison-Contrast and Extended Comparison-Contrast: Learning by Seeing Literary Works Together."

3. Some AP essay questions ask several related questions. If it is at all appropriate, address each part of the question in a separate paragraph. That method clearly conveys to your essay's reader that you've responded to each part of the question.

- **Does the topic mention required elements?**

    If the topic instructs you to compare two novels, be certain to select two novels. Don't choose two short stories, a novel and a short story, or a novel and its film version.

    Be careful to respond to each part of the question in a balanced manner. Avoid writing extensively about one required element (the first novel, for instance) followed by little or no support for another part (the second novel).

- **Consider how you'll organize your essay.**

    Pause to consider how you might best respond. How many paragraphs? Where's a useful place for a quotation? Many students handicap themselves by writing immediately, and they end up stringing together a series of brilliant but disconnected thoughts. Begin writing only after you've decided on a thesis statement.

- **Seize the moment.**

    Avoid beginning your response with a mechanical repetition of the topic. Your reader is very familiar with the topic. Get to your point. State your thesis clearly and concisely.

- **Substantiate your position.**

    Select appropriate information to incorporate as supporting evidence. Include a quotation, but only if it's clearly related to your point.

- **Maintain the focus.**

    Write in a concise manner. Avoid digressing to a related topic. If it doesn't pertain to the assigned topic, then you shouldn't include it here. Remember: There is no extra credit for the essay that goes beyond the assigned topic.

## Addressing the Poetry Essay Topic

All of the advice relating to the prose essay topic applies to the poetry essay topic as well. One section, in particular, calls for further elaboration so that you're especially aware.

- **Read the topic thoroughly and carefully.**

    The poetry essay topic is where you should anticipate a question of multiple parts. It's far more likely to appear here than in the prose essay topic. Consider the following possibilities.

1. If the topic involves a sonnet, you might be instructed to examine the question raised in the octave, and then explain how the sestet solves the problem. Such a topic encourages you to respond with an essay of two substantial paragraphs: one about the octave, the second about the sestet.

2. Another topic might instruct you to discuss the poet's attitude as it appears in the poem, and then examine the literary devices she uses to convey her opinion. Such a topic often mentions specific literary devices ("Consider the poet's diction, imagery, figurative language, and tone as she . . ."). If this is the case, be certain to address each one of these literary devices in your essay. Your essay's reader will expect to see them.

## Addressing the Open Essay Topic

Many students consider the open essay topic their favorite because it is just that: open. By its nature, the open essay topic is much less restrictive than the prose and poetry essay topics.

Yes, the open essay topic assigns a task, but it's much less restrictive about the scope of your response. The topic might mention a literary work as an example. Or it might suggest perhaps as many as a dozen works on which you might base your response. But these are merely suggestions. You're welcome to select an alternative literary work of "similar merit" or "comparable quality," and use it as the basis for your response.

As you might expect, all of the advice relating to the prose essay topic applies to the open essay topic as well (just as it does to the poetry essay topic). One section, in particular, calls for further elaboration so that you're especially aware.

- **Does the topic mention required elements?**

   The topic might instruct you to write about a novel:

   "In many novels, one of the characters is often . . . Choose a novel and write an essay that examines . . . )

   If this is the case, be certain to choose a novel. Don't hope that you can slip a play or short story past your essay's reader.

## Further Help with Writing About Literature

General insights related to writing about literature for exams are available in "Chapter 26 Taking Examinations on Literature." That chapter focuses on the types of questions that frequently appear on literature tests. Although the information is quite general in nature, many of its insights can be applied to the writing you'll do on the essay section of the AP English Literature and Composition Exam.

More specific insights about writing about literature are available throughout the anthology. The following list summarizes the topic examined in each part. For help with a specific topic, consult the appropriate part.

## Writing About Prose (Fiction)

Each of the following chapters examines its subject (for example, *plot* in Chapter Two), poses critical-thinking questions about it, offers questions for discovering ideas to help you come up with writing ideas, provides strategies for organizing ideas to help you outline, presents a student essay with commentary to help you see a completed model paper, and finally ends with special topics for writing that provide writing prompts to help you write your own paper.

---

**Chapter 2—Plot in a story**   (See especially pages 100–106.)
**Chapter 3—Point of view in a story**   (See especially pages 144–150.)
**Chapter 4—Characters in a story**   (See especially pages 190–197.)
**Chapter 5—Setting in a story**   (See especially pages 237–243.)
**Chapter 6—Structure in a story**   (See especially pages 274–279.)
**Chapter 7—Tone and style in a story**   (See especially pages 314–320.)
**Chapter 8—Symbolism and allegory in a story**   (See especially pages 354–366.)
**Chapter 9—Idea or theme in a story**   (See especially pages 392–398.)

---

## Writing About Poetry

Each of the following chapters examines its subject (for example, *tone* in Chapter 15), poses critical-thinking questions about it, offers questions for discovering ideas to help you come up with writing ideas, provides strategies for organizing ideas to help you outline, presents a student essay with commentary to help you see a completed model paper, and finally ends with special topics for writing that provide writing prompts to help you write your own paper.

---

**Chapter 11—Writing a paraphrase and an explication of a poem**   (See especially pages 486–493.)
**Chapter 12—Diction and syntax in poetry**   (See especially pages 522–527.)
**Chapter 13—Imagery in poetry**   (See especially pages 552–559.)
**Chapter 14—Figures of speech in poetry**   (See especially pages 590–598.)
**Chapter 15—Tone in poetry**   (See especially pages 634–640.)
**Chapter 16—Form in poetry**   (See especially pages 684–690.)
**Chapter 17—Symbolism and allusion in poetry**   (See especially pages 726–732.)

---

## Writing About Drama

Each of the following chapters examines its subject poses critical-thinking questions about it, offers questions for discovering ideas to help you come up with writing ideas, provides strategies for organizing ideas to help you outline, presents a student essay with commentary to help you see a completed model paper, and finally ends with special topics for writing that provide writing prompts to help you write your own paper.

Chapter 20—Writing about drama   (See especially pages 914–922.)
Chapter 21—Writing about tragedy   (See especially pages 1082–1090.)
Chapter 22—Writing about comedy   (See especially pages 1180–1186.)

# PART SEVEN

# Recommended Authors for the AP English Literature and Composition Exam

Your AP English class is designed to teach students to read literature so they can understand it and write well about it. Avoid concentrating on the exam itself. Don't let the test "wag the dog." Instead, capitalize on what the AP English class is designed to teach. Master those skills. If you boost those skills, you'll also boost your chances of performing well on the exam. And beyond the exam, those skills will pay dividends in almost every college course taken and in virtually every reading-based activity that could be encountered in the future. Bottom line: Sharpen skills and in most cases, the exam will take care of itself.

With those thoughts in mind, you shouldn't head for the exam without some idea of what to expect. One of the best ways to become familiar with the exam is to take "practice" exams that feature questions from previous exams. That method is addressed in Part Eight.

Before taking those "practice" exams, become familiar with the authors whose works have been included on previous exams and whose consistent popularity suggests that they'll appear on the exam.

## Authors Whose Works You'll Likely Encounter

Any "reading list" would artificially limit the scope of your preparation for the AP English Literature and Composition Exam. Instead, prepare for the exam by becoming familiar with as many of the writings of as many authors as time and energy permit. To help guide you to the authors whose works most frequently appear on the AP English Literature and Composition Exam, you'll find below the names of a large number of authors.

Of course, no student can reasonably be expected to undertake the colossal task of reading every work by these authors. That reality should underscore the importance of mastering those skills mentioned in this part's opening paragraph. No, you can't read everything. But you can be better prepared to read, understand, and write about any literary piece encountered.

An asterisk accompanies the name of each author who is among those found in this anthology.

## Fiction (Novel and Short Story)

Chinua Achebe
Kingsley Amis
Rudolfo Anaya
Margaret Atwood
Jane Austen
James Baldwin
Saul Bellow
Charlotte Brontë
Emily Brontë*
Raymond Carver*
Willa Cather
John Cheever
Kate Chopin*
Sandra Cisneros
Sidonie-Gabrielle Colette
Joseph Conrad*
Stephen Crane*
Anita Desai
Charles Dickens
George Eliot
Ralph Ellison*
Louise Erdrich
William Faulkner*
Henry Fielding
F. Scott Fitzgerald
Ford Madox Ford
E. M. Forster
Gabriel García Márquez
Thomas Hardy*
Nathaniel Hawthorne*
Ernest Hemingway*
Zora Neale Hurston

Kazuo Ishiguro
Henry James
James Joyce*
Maxine Hong Kingston
Joy Kogawa
Margaret Laurence
D. H. Lawrence*
Jack London
Bernard Malamud
Katherine Mansfield*
Bobbie Ann Mason
Carson McCullers
Herman Melville*
Toni Morrison
Bharati Mukherjee
Vladimir Nabokov
Flannery O'Connor*
Cynthia Ozick*
Katherine Anne Porter*
Jean Rhys
Jonathan Swift*
Leo Tolstoy
Mark Twain*
John Updike*
Luisa Valenzuela
Alice Walker*
Evelyn Waugh
Eudora Welty*
Edith Wharton
John Edgar Wideman
Virginia Woolf
Richard Wright

## Expository Prose

Joseph Addison
Gloria Anzaldúa
Matthew Arnold
James Baldwin
James Boswell
Thomas Carlyle
Jesús Colón
Ralph Waldo Emerson
John Evelyn

William Hazlitt
Samuel Johnson
Charles Lamb
Norman Mailer
Mary McCarthy
H. L. Mencken
John Stuart Mill
George Orwell
Samuel Pepys

Richard Steele
Lewis Thomas
Henry David Thoreau

Barbara Tuchman
Virginia Woolf

## Poetry

W. H. Auden*
Elizabeth Bishop*
William Blake*
Anne Bradstreet
Edward Kamau Brathwaite
Gwendolyn Brooks
Robert Browning*
George Gordon, Lord Byron
Lorna Dee Cervantes
Geoffrey Chaucer
Samuel Taylor Coleridge*
H. D. (Hilda Doolittle)
Emily Dickinson*
John Donne*
Rita Dove
T. S. Eliot*
Robert Frost*
Joy Harjo*
Seamus Heany*
George Herbert*
Garrett Hongo
Gerard Manley Hopkins*
Langston Hughes*

Ben Jonson
John Keats*
Philip Larkin
Robert Lowell
Andrew Marvell
John Milton*
Marianne Moore
Sylvia Plath*
Edgar Allan Poe*
Alexander Pope*
Adrienne Rich
Anne Sexton
William Shakespeare*
Percy Bysshe Shelley*
Leslie Marmon Silko*
Cathy Song
Alfred, Lord Tennyson*
Derek Walcott
Walt Whitman*
Richard Wilbur*
William Carlos Williams
William Wordsworth*
William Butler Yeats*

## Drama

Aeschylus
Edward Albee*
Amiri Baraka
Samuel Beckett
Anton Chekhov*
William Congreve
Oliver Goldsmith
Lorraine Hansberry
Lillian Hellman
David Henry Hwang
Henrik Ibsen*
Ben Jonson
David Mamet
Arthur Miller*
Molière

Sean O'Casey
Eugene O'Neill*
Harold Pinter
Luigi Pirandello*
William Shakespeare*
George Bernard Shaw
Sam Shepard
Richard Brinsley Sheridan
Sophocles*
Tom Stoppard
Luis Valdez
Oscar Wilde
Tennessee Williams
August Wilson*

# PART EIGHT

# Practice Multiple Choice Quizzes for Roberts' *Literature 4e*

The following quizzes match each literary element chapter in Roberts and provide additional practice for answering questions on the AP Literature and Composition Exam. These quizzes are designed for practice so all answers may be found at the end of the quiz.

## Fiction

### Chapter 2: Introduction to Fiction

*AP Practice Questions for "War, 1919"*

> The short story, with its accompanying questions, resembles closely prose and comprehension questions found on AP exams. Note the frequency of literary devices addressed within the questions. Refer to Chapter 2 (53–106) for additional information on a work's subject in fiction.

*Read the entire short story then answer the questions. "War, 1919" by Luigi Pirandello is located on pages 92–95.*

1. The setting of the passage occurs in
   A. Italy-Early 19th century
   B. France-Early 20th century
   C. Italy-Early 20th century
   D. Sicily-Early 19th century
   E. Spain-Early 19th century

2. The lines "to the amazement of everyone, broke into harrowing, heart-rending, uncontrollable sobs" appear in the story's
   A. climax
   B. resolution
   C. exposition
   D. falling action
   E. conflict

3. After reading the passage, it is evident the speaker
   A. admires parents who are willing to sacrifice their sons for country's sake
   B. believes war is necessary for the survival of a nation
   C. feels that children are not possessions of their parents
   D. affirms the loss of life supersedes feelings of patriotism and nationalism
   E. feels that war is futile in a world of powerful regimes and corruption

4. The lines "If country is a natural necessity, like bread, of which each of us must eat in order not to die of hunger . . ." contain examples of
   A. paradox
   B. simile
   C. metaphor
   D. both B and C
   E. analogy

5. The narrator implies through the motif of the "watery eyes" that the "fat traveler" has
   A. already been grieving over the loss of his son
   B. been traveling by train and is fatigued and bleary-eyed
   C. shed tears of joy because his son is a hero
   D. been trying to subdue his tears as he tries to console other parents on the train
   E. been drinking to assuage his sorrows

*Answer Key:*  1. B  2. B  3. D  4. B  5. D

## Chapter 3: Point of View

*AP Practice Questions for Point of View*

> The selected passage, with its accompanying questions, resembles closely prose and comprehension questions found on AP exams. Note the frequency of literary devices addressed within the questions. Refer to Chapter 3 (107–150) for additional information on a work's point of view in fiction.

*Read the selected passage, then answer the following questions.* "How to Become a Writer" *by Lorrie Moore may be found on pages 126–130.*

 # How to Become a Writer (1985)

First, try to be something, anything, else. A movie star/astronaut. A movie star/missionary. A movie star/kindergarten teacher. President of the World. Fail miserably. It is best if you fail at an early age—say, fourteen. Early, critical disillusionment is necessary so that at fifteen you can write long haiku sequences about thwarted desire. It is a pond, a cherry blossom, a wind brushing against sparrow wing leaving for mountain. Count the syllables. Show it to your mom. She is tough and practical. She has a son in Vietnam and a husband who may be having an affair. She believes in wearing brown because it hides spots. She'll look briefly at your writing, then back up at you with a face blank as a donut. She'll say: "How about emptying the dishwasher?" Look away. Shove the forks in the fork drawer. Accidentally break one of the freebie gas station glasses. This is the required pain and suffering. This is only for starters.

In your high school English class look only at Mr. Killian's face. Decide faces are important. Write a villanelle about pores. Struggle. Write a sonnet. Count the syllables: nine, ten, eleven, thirteen. Decide to experiment with fiction. Here you don't have to count syllables. Write a short story about an elderly man and woman who accidentally shoot each other in the head, the result of an inexplicable malfunction of a shotgun which appears mysteriously in their living room one night. Give it to Mr. Killian as your final project. When you get it back, he has written on it: "Some of your images are quite nice, but you have no sense of plot." When you are home, in the privacy of your own room, faintly scrawl in pencil beneath his black-inked comments: "Plots are for dead people, pore-face."

Take all the babysitting jobs you can get. You are great with kids. They love you. You tell them stories about old people who die idiot deaths. You sing them songs like "Blue Bells of Scotland," which is their favorite. And when they are in their pajamas and have finally stopped pinching each other, when they are fast asleep, you read every sex manual in the house, and wonder how on earth anyone could ever do those things with someone they truly loved. Fall asleep in a chair reading Mr. McMurphy's *Playboy*. When the McMurphys come home, they will tap you on the shoulder, look at the magazine in your lap, and grin. You will want to die. They will ask you if Tracey took her medicine all right. Explain, yes, she did, that you promised her a story if she would take it like a big girl and that seemed to work out just fine. "Oh, marvelous," they will exclaim.

Try to smile proudly.

5   Apply to college as a child psychology major.

As a child psychology major, you have some electives. You've always liked birds. Sign up for something called "The Ornithological Field Trip." It meets Tuesdays and Thursdays at two. When you arrive at Room 134 on the first day of class, everyone is sitting around a seminar table talking about metaphors. You've heard of these. After a short, excruciating while, raise your hand and say diffidently, "Excuse me, isn't this Bird-watching One-oh-one?" The class stops and turns to look at you. They seem to all have one face—giant and blank as a vandalized clock. Someone with a beard booms out, "No, this is Creative Writing." Say: "Oh—right," as if perhaps you knew all along. Look down at your schedule. Wonder how the hell you ended up here. The computer, apparently, has made an error. You start to get up to leave and then don't. The lines at the registrar this week are huge. Perhaps you should stick with this mistake. Perhaps your creative writing isn't all that bad. Perhaps it is fate. Perhaps this is what your dad meant when he said, "It's the age of computers, Francie, it's the age of computers."

Decide that you like college life. In your dorm you meet many nice people. Some are smarter than you. And some, you notice, are dumber than you. You will continue, unfortunately, to view the world in exactly these terms for the rest of your life.

The assignment this week in creative writing is to narrate a violent happening. Turn in a story about driving with your Uncle Gordon and another one about two old people who are accidentally electrocuted when they go to turn on a badly wired desk lamp. The teacher will hand them back to you with comments: "Much of your writing is smooth and energetic. You have, however, a ludicrous notion of plot." Write another story about a man and a woman who, in the very first paragraph, have their lower torsos accidentally blitzed away by dynamite. In the second paragraph, with the insurance money, they buy a frozen yogurt stand together. There are six more paragraphs. You read the whole thing out loud in class. No one likes it. They say your sense of plot is outrageous and incompetent. After class someone asks you if you are crazy.

Decide that perhaps you should stick to comedies. Start dating someone who is funny, someone who has what in high school you called a "really great sense of humor" and what now your creative writing class calls "self-contempt giving rise to comic form." Write down all of his jokes, but don't tell him you are doing this. Make up anagrams of his old girlfriend's name and name all of your socially handicapped characters with them. Tell him his old girlfriend is in all of your stories and then watch how funny he can be, see what a really great sense of humor he can have.

Your child psychology advisor tells you you are neglecting courses in your major. What you spend the most time on should be what you're majoring in. Say yes, you understand. 10

In creative writing seminars over the next two years, everyone continues to smoke cigarettes and ask the same things: "But does it work?" "Why should we care about this character?" "Have you earned this cliché?" These seem like important questions.

On days when it is your turn, you look at the class hopefully as they scour your mimeographs for a plot. They look back up at you, drag deeply, and then smile in a sweet sort of way.

You spend too much time slouched and demoralized. Your boyfriend suggests bicycling. Your roommate suggests a new boyfriend. You are said to be self-mutilating and losing weight, but you continue writing. The only happiness you have is writing something new, in the middle of the night, armpits damp, heart pounding, something no one has yet seen. You have only those brief, fragile, untested moments of exhilaration when you know: you are a genius. Understand what you must do. Switch majors. The kids in your nursery project will be disappointed, but you have a calling, an urge, a delusion, an unfortunate habit. You have, as your mother would say, fallen in with a bad crowd.

---

1. The narrator is alluding to which emotion in the first two paragraphs?
   A. anticipation at the prospect of becoming a successful writer
   B. frustration at having daily tasks postpone writing
   C. anger at not receiving enough positive feedback
   D. jealousy at others who are comfortable with their roles in life
   E. insecurity with the possibility of not becoming a professional writer

2. Each of the following examples from the story contribute to the narrator's authenticity of **becoming a writer** *except:*
   A. "Decide faces are important."
   B. "Apply to college as a child psychology major."
   C. "Perhaps you should stick with this mistake."
   D. "You will continue, unfortunately, to view the world in exactly these terms for the rest of your life."
   E. "On days when it is your turn, you look at the class hopefully as they scour your mimeographs for a plot."

3. All of the following examples from the story add to the narrator's comic element *except:*
   A. "[w]ith the insurance money, they buy a frozen yogurt stand together."
   B. "self-contempt giving rise to comic form."
   C. "After class someone asks you if you are crazy."
   D. "You start to get up to leave and then don't."
   E. "Start dating someone who is funn[y]"

**4.** In the story, Francie is the
   A. instructor
   B. second-person narrator
   C. first-person narrator
   D. third-person narrator
   E. the mother

**5.** Much of the excerpt is derived from the author's
   I. Creative powers
   II. Past experiences
   III. Present tense

   A. I only
   B. II only
   C. III only
   D. I and III
   E. I, II, and III

## Chapter 4: Characters: The People in Fiction

*AP Practice Questions for "Two Kinds"*

> The selected passage, with its accompanying questions, simulates prose and comprehension questions found on AP exams. Note how the questions not only pertain to character development and traits, but also the author's usage of language, dialogue, syntax, and diction. Refer to Chapter 4 (151–197) for additional information on character in fiction.

*Read the selected passage. "Two Kinds" by Amy Tan may be found on pages 180–187.*

 # Two Kinds (1989)

Three days after watching *The Ed Sullivan Show*, my mother told me what my schedule would be for piano lessons and piano practice. She had talked to Mr. Chong, who lived on the first floor of our apartment building. Mr. Chong was a retired piano teacher and my mother had traded housecleaning services for weekly lessons and a piano for me to practice on every day, two hours a day, from four until six.

When my mother told me this, I felt as though I had been sent to hell. I whined and then kicked my foot a little when I couldn't stand it anymore.

"Why don't you like me the way I am? I'm *not* a genius! I can't play the piano. And even if I could, I wouldn't go on TV if you paid me a million dollars!" I cried.

My mother slapped me. "Who ask you be genius?" she shouted. "Only ask you be your best. For you sake. You think I want you be genius? Hnnh! What for! Who ask you!"

5     "So ungrateful," I heard her mutter in Chinese. "If she had as much talent as she has temper, she would be famous now."

Mr. Chong, whom I secretly nicknamed Old Chong, was very strange, always tapping his fingers to the silent music of an invisible orchestra. He looked ancient in my eyes. He had lost most of the hair on top of his head and he wore thick glasses and had eyes that always looked tired and sleepy. But he must have been younger than I thought, since he lived with his mother and was not yet married.

I met Old Lady Chong once and that was enough. She had this peculiar smell like a baby that had done something in its pants. And her fingers felt like a dead person's, like an old peach I once found in the back of the refrigerator; the skin just slid off the meat when I picked it up.

I soon found out why Old Chong had retired from teaching piano. He was deaf. "Like Beethoven!" he shouted to me. "We're both listening only in our head!" And he would start to conduct his frantic silent sonatas.

Our lessons went like this. He would open the book and point to different things, explaining their purpose: "Key! Treble! Bass! No sharps or flats! So this is C major! Listen now and play after me!"

And then he would play the C scale a few times, a simple chord, and then, as if inspired 10 by an old, unreachable itch, he gradually added more notes and running trills and a pounding bass until the music was really something quite grand.

I would play after him, the simple scale, the simple chord, and then I just played some nonsense that sounded like a cat running up and down on top of garbage cans. Old Chong smiled and applauded and then said, "Very good! But now you must learn to keep time!"

So that's how I discovered that Old Chong's eyes were too slow to keep up with the wrong notes I was playing. He went through the motions in half-time. To help me keep rhythm, he stood behind me, pushing down on my right shoulder for every beat. He balanced pennies on top of my wrists so I would keep them still as I slowly played scales and arpeggios. He had me curve my hand around an apple and keep that shape when playing chords. He marched stiffly to show me how to make each finger dance up and down, staccato like an obedient little soldier.

He taught me all these things, and that was how I also learned I could be lazy and get away with mistakes, lots of mistakes. If I hit the wrong notes because I hadn't practiced enough, I never corrected myself. I just kept playing in rhythm. And Old Chong kept conducting his own private reverie.

So maybe I never really gave myself a fair chance. I did pick up the basics pretty quickly, and I might have become a good pianist at that young age. But I was so determined not to try, not to be anybody different that I learned to play only the most earsplitting preludes, the most discordant hymns.

Over the next year, I practiced like this, dutifully in my own way. And then one day I 15 heard my mother and her friend Lindo Jong both talking in a loud bragging tone of voice so others could hear. It was after church, and I was leaning against the brick wall wearing a dress with stiff white petticoats. Auntie Lindo's daughter, Waverly, who was about my age, was standing farther down the wall about five feet away. We had grown up together and shared all the closeness of two sisters squabbling over crayons and dolls. In other words, for the most part, we hated each other. I thought she was snotty. Waverly Jong had gained a certain amount of fame as "Chinatown's Littlest Chinese Chess Champion."

"She bring home too many trophy," lamented Auntie Lindo that Sunday. "All day she play chess. All day I have no time do nothing but dust off her winnings." She threw a scolding look at Waverly, who pretended not to see her.

"You lucky you don't have this problem," said Auntie Lindo with a sigh to my mother.

And my mother squared her shoulders and bragged: "Our problem worser than yours. If we ask Jing-Mei wash dish, she hear nothing but music. It's like you can't stop this natural talent."

And right then, I was determined to put a stop to her foolish pride.

———————————————

1. The syntax of the lines "He balanced pennies . . . staccato like an obedient little soldier" in paragraph 12 is composed primarily of a
   A. hypotaxis structure
   B. parallel structure
   C. chiasmus structure
   D. periodic sentence structure
   E. inversion structure

2. The following dialogue is an example of colloquialism:
   A. "Our problem worser than yours. If we ask Jing Mei wash dish, she hear nothing but music."
   B. "Chinatown's Littlest Chinese Chess Champion."
   C. "Key! Treble! Bass! No sharps or flats!"
   D. "Like Beethoven!" "We're both listening only in our head!"
   E. "You aren't a genius like me."

3. The interaction between the mother and the daughter in paragraphs 3–5 depicts the
   A. mother's fluency in Chinese and desire for her daughter to be bilingual
   B. daughter's ingratitude toward her mother for arranging piano lessons
   C. existentialist situation placed before the daughter
   D. willful nature of both daughter and mother
   E. determinism of the mother

4. The speaker in the passage reveals her character primarily through
   A. dialect and dialogue
   B. naturalism and determinism
   C. conflict and resolution
   D. anecdotes and stream of consciousness
   E. imagery and symbolism

5. From the passage line "And right then, I was determined to put a stop to her foolish pride" the reader can infer that the speaker is
   I. making an existential decision
   II. exerting her determinism
   III. demonstrating filial piety

   A. I only
   B. II only
   C. I and II only
   D. I and III only
   E. I, II, and III

Answer Key:  1. B  2. A  3. D  4. D  5. C

## Chapter 5: Setting: The Background of Place, Objects, and Culture in stories

*AP Practice Questions for "The Masque of the Red Death"*

> The selected passage, with its accompanying questions, resembles closely prose and comprehension questions found on AP exams. These questions focus upon the story's setting and how the environment can affect, enhance, and propel the plot. Refer to Chapter 5 (198–243) for additional information on setting in fiction.

*Read the selected passage. "The Masque of the Red Death" by Edgar Allan Poe may be found on pages 234–237.*

 ## The Masque of the Red Death (1842)

He had directed, in great part, the movable embellishments of the seven chambers, upon occasion of this great fête, and it was his own guiding taste which had given character to the masqueraders. Be sure they were grotesque. There were much glare and glitter and piquancy and phantasm—much of what has been since seen in "Hernani." There were arabesque figures with unsuited limbs and appointments. There were delirious fancies such as the madman fashions. There were much of the beautiful, much of the wanton, much of the *bizarre*, something of the terrible, and not a little of that which might have excited disgust. To and fro in the seven chambers there stalked, in fact, a multitude of dreams. And these—the dreams—writhed in and about, taking hue from the rooms, and causing the wild music of the orchestra to seem as the echo of their steps. And, anon, there strikes the ebony clock which stands in the hall of the velvet. And then, for a moment, all is still, and all is silent save the voice of the clock. The dreams are stiff-frozen as they stand. But the echoes of the chime die away—they have endured but an instant—and a light, half-subdued laughter floats after them as they depart. And now again the music swells, and the dreams live, and writhe to and fro more merrily than ever, taking hue from the many-tinted windows through which stream the rays from the tripods. But to the chamber which lies most westwardly of the seven there are now none of the maskers who venture; for the night is waning away; and there flows a ruddier light through the blood-colored panes; and the blackness of the sable drapery appalls; and to him whose foot falls upon the sable carpet, there comes from the near clock of ebony a muffled peal more solemnly emphatic than any which reaches *their* ears who indulge in the more remote gaieties of the other apartments.

But these other apartments were densely crowded, and in them beat feverishly the heart of life. And the revel went whirlingly on, until at length there commenced the sounding of midnight upon the clock. And then the music ceased, as I have told; and the evolutions of the waltzers were quieted; and there was an uneasy cessation of all things as before. But now there were twelve strokes to be sounded by the bell of the clock; and thus it happened, perhaps that more of thought crept, with more of time, into the meditations of the thoughtful among those who revelled. And thus, too, it happened, perhaps, that before the last echoes of the last chime had utterly sunk into silence, there were many individuals in the crowd who had found leisure to become aware of the presence of a masked figure which had arrested the attention of no single individual before. And the rumor of this new presence having spread itself whisperingly around, there arose at length from the whole company a buzz, or murmur, expressive of disapprobation and surprise—then, finally, of terror, of horror, and of disgust.

In an assembly of phantasms such as I have painted, it may well be supposed that no ordinary appearance could have excited such sensation. In truth the masquerade license of the night was nearly unlimited; but the figure in question had out-Heroded Herod, and gone beyond the bounds of even the prince's indefinite decorum. There are chords in the hearts of the most reckless which cannot be touched without emotion. Even with the utterly lost, to whom life and death are equally jests, there are matters of which no jest can be made. The whole company, indeed, seemed now deeply to feel that in the costume and bearing of the stranger neither wit nor propriety existed. The figure was tall and gaunt, and shrouded from head to foot in the habiliments of the grave. The mask which concealed the visage was made so nearly to resemble the countenance of a stiffened corpse that the closest scrutiny must have had difficulty in detecting the cheat. And yet all this might have been endured, if not approved, by the mad revellers around. But the mummer had gone so far as to assume the type of the Red Death. His vesture was dabbled in *blood*—and his broad brow, with all the features of the face, was besprinkled with the scarlet horror.

---

1. The lines from the first paragraph, "And anon . . . of the clock" contain an example of
   A. metaphor
   B. simile
   C. personification
   D. paradox
   E. irony

2. ". . . solemnly emphatic" is an example of
   A. oxymoron
   B. synesthesia
   C. symbolism
   D. metaphor
   E. hyperbole

3. "hall of the velvet," "sable drapery," "clock of ebony," and "blood-colored panes" are descriptions associated with
   A. classicism
   B. modernism
   C. existentialism
   D. romanticism
   E. the Gilded Age

4. All of these objects included within the setting enrich the macabre tone *except*
   A. the clock
   B. the laughter
   C. the wild music
   D. the blood-colored panes
   E. the dreams

5. On an interpretive level, the midnight chimes symbolize
   I. a death toll for the revelers
   II. the rhythm of the *fete* itself
   III. an alarm for the guests to recognize the intruder

   A. I only
   B. I and II only
   C. II and III only
   D. I and III only
   E. I, II, and III

Answer Key: 1.C 2.A 3.D 4.B 5.D

## Chapter 6: Structure

*AP Practice Questions for "Battle Royal"*

The selected passage, with its accompanying questions, resembles closely prose and comprehension questions found on AP exams. The questions focus upon the speaker's point of view and how it affects the essay's structure. Refer to Chapter 6, (244–279) for additional information on structure in fiction.

*Read the selected passage. "Battle Royal" by Ralph Ellison may be found on pages 247–256.*

## 🐦 Battle Royal (1952)

It goes a long way back, some twenty years. All my life I had been looking for something, and everywhere I turned someone tried to tell me what it was. I accepted their answers too, though they were often in contradiction and even self-contradictory. I was naïve. I was looking for myself and asking everyone except myself questions which I, and only I, could answer. It took me a long time and much painful boomeranging of my expectations to achieve a realization everyone else appears to have been born with: That I am nobody but myself. But first I had to discover that I am an invisible man!

And yet I am no freak of nature, nor of history. I was in the cards, other things having been equal (or unequal) eighty-five years ago. I am not ashamed of my grandparents for having been slaves. I am only ashamed of myself for having at one time been ashamed. About eighty-five years ago they were told that they were free, united with others of our country in everything pertaining to the common good, and, in everything social, separate like the fingers of the hand.

And they believed it. They exulted in it. They stayed in their place, worked hard, and brought up my father to do the same. But my grandfather is the one. He was an odd old guy, my grandfather, and I am told I take after him. It was he who caused the trouble. On his deathbed he called my father to him and said, "Son, after I'm gone I want you to keep up the good fight. I never told you, but our life is a war and I have been a traitor all my born days, a spy in the enemy's country ever since I gave up my gun back in the Reconstruction. Live with your head in the lion's mouth. I want you to overcome 'em with yeses, undermine 'em with grins, agree 'em to death and destruction, let 'em swoller you till they vomit or bust wide open." They thought the old man had gone out of his mind. He had been the meekest of men. The younger children were rushed from the room, the shades drawn and the flame of the lamp turned so low that it sputtered on the wick like the old man's breathing. "Learn it to the youn-guns," he whispered fiercely; then he died.

But my folks were more alarmed over his last words than over his dying. It was as though he had not died at all, his words caused so much anxiety. I was warned emphatically to forget what he had said and, indeed, this is the first time it has been mentioned outside the family circle. It had a tremendous effect upon me, however. I could never be sure of what he meant. Grandfather had been a quiet old man who never made any trouble, yet on his deathbed he had called himself a traitor and a spy, and he had spoken of his meekness as a dangerous activity. It became a constant puzzle which lay unanswered in the back of my mind. And whenever things went well for me I remembered my grandfather and felt guilty and uncomfortable. It was as though I was carrying out his advice in spite of myself. And to make it worse, everyone loved me for it. I was praised by the most lily-white men of the town. I was considered an example of desirable conduct—just as my grandfather had been. And what puzzled me was that the old man had defined it as *treachery*. When I was praised for my conduct I felt a guilt that in some way I was doing something that was really against the wishes of the white folks, that if they had understood they would have desired me to act just the opposite, that I should have been sulky and mean, and that that really would have been what they wanted, even though they were fooled and thought they wanted me to act as I did. It made me afraid that some day they would look upon me as a traitor and I would be lost. Still I was more afraid to act any other way because they didn't like that at all. The old man's words were like a curse. On my graduation day I delivered an oration in which I showed that humility was the secret, indeed, the very essence of progress. (Not that I believed this—how could I, remembering my grandfather?—I only believed that it worked.) It was a great success. Everyone praised me and I was invited to give the speech at a gathering of the town's leading white citizens. It was a triumph for our whole community.

---

1. The exposition of "Battle Royal" features the following literary device
   A. symbolism
   B. flashback
   C. imagery
   D. flash forward
   E. existentialism

2. In the first paragraph, the point-of-view narration is
   A. third-person limited
   B. third-person omniscient
   C. second-person narrative
   D. first-person narrative
   E. omniscient

3. Within the context of the passage, which of the following phrases is a paradox?
   A. ". . . ashamed of myself for having at one time been ashamed."
   B. ". . . in everything social, separate like the fingers of the hand."
   C. ". . . praised by the most lily-white men of the town."
   D. ". . . a constant puzzle which lay unanswered . . ."
   E. ". . . more afraid to act any other way because they didn't like that . . ."

4. In this excerpt, "I was in the cards . . . eighty-five years ago." (paragraph 2) can be interpreted as
   I. Laws can be mandated, but society doesn't always follow them.
   II. One can fight society's injustices by not succumbing to prejudicial expectations.
   III. Fate can predetermine a person's circumstance.

   A. I
   B. II
   C. III
   D. I and III
   E. II and III

5. The grandfather believes he has been a "traitor" and a "spy" for all of the following reasons *except*
   A. he relinquished his gun during the Reconstruction
   B. he was meek
   C. he was openly rebellious
   D. he died with a fierce admonition to "Learn it to the younguns,"
   E. silently disagreed throughout his life

Answer Key: 1.B 2.D 3.A 4.D 5.C

## Chapter 7: Tone and Style

*AP Practice Questions for "Orientation"*

The selected passage, with its accompanying questions, resembles closely prose and comprehension questions found on AP exams. Note how the author's choice of diction and syntax contribute to this excerpt's overall tone. Refer to Chapter 7 (280–320) for additional information on style in fiction.

*Read the selected passage. "Orientation" by Daniel Orozco may be found on pages 306–309.*

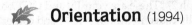 **Orientation** (1994)

Those are the offices and these are the cubicles. That's my cubicle there, and this is your cubicle. This is your phone. Never answer your phone. Let the Voicemail System answer it. This is your Voicemail System Manual. There are no personal phone calls allowed. We do, however, allow for emergencies. If you must make an emergency phone call, ask your supervisor first. If you can't find your supervisor, ask Phillip Spiers, who sits over there. He'll check with Clarissa Nicks, who sits over there. If you make an emergency phone call without asking, you may be let go.

These are your IN and OUT boxes. All the forms in your IN box must be logged in by the date shown in the upper left-hand corner, initialed by you in the upper right-hand corner, and distributed to the Processing Analyst whose name is numerically coded in the lower left-hand corner. The lower right-hand corner is left blank. Here's your Processing Analyst Numerical Code Index. And here's your Forms Processing Procedures Manual.

You must pace your work. What do I mean? I'm glad you asked that. We pace our work according to the eight-hour workday. If you have twelve hours of work in your IN box, for example, you must compress that work into the eight-hour day. If you have one hour of work in your IN box, you must expand that work to fill the eight hour day. That was a good question. Feel free to ask questions. Ask too many questions, however, and you may be let go.

That is our receptionist. She is a temp. We go through receptionists here. They quit with alarming frequency. Be polite and civil to the temps. Learn their names, and invite them to lunch occasionally. But don't get close to them, as it only makes it more difficult when they leave. And they always leave. You can be sure of that.

The men's room is over there. The women's room is over there. John LaFountaine, who    5 sits over there, uses the women's room occasionally. He says it is accidental. We know better, but we let it pass. John LaFountaine is harmless, his forays into the forbidden territory of the women's room simply a benign thrill, a faint blip on the dull flat line of his life.

Russell Nash, who sits in the cubicle to your left, is in love with Amanda Pierce, who sits in the cubicle to your right. They ride the same bus together after work. For Amanda Pierce, it is just a tedious bus ride made less tedious by the idle nattering of Russell Nash. But for Russell Nash, it is the highlight of his day. It is the highlight of his life. Russell Nash has put on forty pounds, and grows fatter with each passing month, nibbling on chips and cookies while peeking glumly over the partitions at Amanda Pierce, and gorging himself at home on cold pizza and ice cream while watching adult videos on TV.

Amanda Pierce, in the cubicle to your right, has a six-year-old son named Jamie, who is autistic. Her cubicle is plastered from top to bottom with the boy's crayon artwork—sheet after sheet of precisely drawn concentric circles and ellipses, in black and yellow. She rotates them every other Friday. Be sure to comment on them. Amanda Pierce also has a husband, who is a lawyer. He subjects her to an escalating array of painful and humiliating sex games, to which Amanda Pierce reluctantly submits. She comes to work exhausted and freshly wounded each morning, wincing from the abrasions on her breasts, or the bruises on her abdomen, or the second-degree burns on the backs of her thighs.

But we're not supposed to know any of this. Do not let on. If you let on, you may be let go.

Amanda Pierce, who tolerates Russell Nash, is in love with Albert Bosch, whose office is over there. Albert Bosch, who only dimly registers Amanda Pierce's existence, has eyes only for Ellie Tapper, who sits over there. Ellie Tapper, who hates Albert Bosch, would walk through fire for Curtis Lance. But Curtis Lance hates Ellie Tapper. Isn't the world a funny place? Not in the ha-ha sense, of course.

---

1. Beginning with paragraph 2, "These are your IN and OUT boxes" and ending with ". . . whose name is numerically coded in the lower left-hand corner" exhibits an example of
   A. verbal irony
   B. connotation
   C. denotation
   D. understatement
   E. hyperbole

2. The narrator's attitude toward the new employee can best be described as
   A. ambivalent
   B. ambiguous
   C. apathetic
   D. amicable
   E. acclimating

3. Beginning with the line in paragraph 3 "If you have twelve hours . . . ." and ending with ". . . to fill the eight hour day" the syntactical devices used are
   A. the anaphora and the aphorism
   B. synesthesia and synecdoche
   C. chiasmus and connotation
   D. the periodic sentence and parallelism
   E. anaphora and tricolon

4. ". . . a faint blip on the dull flat line of his life" is an example of
   A. simile
   B. metaphor
   C. personification
   D. synesthesia and metaphor
   E. symbolism and simile

5. During the course of the orientation, the narrator remains
   I. detached
   II. subjective
   III. objective

   A. I only
   B. II only
   C. I and II only
   D. I and III only
   E. II and III only

Answer Key: 1. C  2. C  3. D  4. D  5. D

## Chapter 7: Tone and Style

*AP Practice Questions ~ Section II*

> The selected short story, with its accompanying questions, resembles closely prose and comprehension questions found on AP exams. Please read the entire short story and note how the author's use of devices, such as irony, help contribute to this story's tone. Refer to Chapter 7 (280–320) for additional information on tone in fiction.

*Read the entire short story then answer the questions. "The Story of an Hour" by Kate Chopin may be found on pages 287–289.*

1. The passage "It was he who had been . . ." demonstrates the author's diction is primarily
   A. formal
   B. normal
   C. informal
   D. colloquial
   E. modern
   F. slang

2. All of these images evoke the antithesis of the situation except:
   A. ". . . the tops of trees that were all aquiver with the new spring life."
   B. ". . . patches of blue sky showing here and there . . ."
   C. ". . . through the clouds that had met and piled one above the other"
   D. ". . . countless sparrows twittering in the eaves."
   E. "The delicious breath of rain was in the air."

3. Mrs. Mallard is characterized primarily by her
   A. urge for solitude while mourning.
   B. determinism to feel freedom.
   C. indifference to her husband.
   D. devotion to her husband.
   E. reliance upon her sister, and others.

4. Which of the following adjectives best describe the narrator's tone?
   A. Sardonic and supercilious
   B. Affable and affectionate
   C. Sympathetic and supportive
   D. Apathetic and calculating
   E. Consoling and congratulatory

5. Each of the following conveys situational irony except:
   A. "When the doctors came they said she had died of heart disease . . ."
   B. ". . . drinking in a very elixir of life"
   C. ". . . breathed a quick prayer that life might be long."
   D. ". . . kneeling before the closed door with her lips to the keyhole . . ."
   E. ". . . carried herself unwittingly like a goddess of Victory"

Answer Key: 1.A 2.C 3.B 4.C 5.D

## Chapter 8: Symbolism and Allegory

*AP Practice Questions for "The Jilting of Granny Weatherall"*

> The selected passage, with its accompanying questions, resembles closely prose and comprehension questions found on AP exams. Note how the author's choice of symbolism and allegory further propel the story's theme. Refer to Chapter 8 (321–366) for additional information on symbolism and allegory in fiction.

*Read the entire selection. "The Jilting of Granny Weatherall" by Katherine Anne Porter may be found on pages 341–347.*

1. The shift from the opening line in paragraph 1, to the dialogue "Get along now, take your schoolbooks and go. There's nothing wrong with me" is an example of
   A. third-person narrative to first-person
   B. omniscient narrative to third-person
   C. first-person to third-person limited
   D. first-person to third-person omniscient
   E. first-person narrative to first-person

2. The allusion to the character's name, Weatherall, serves
   I. to symbolize, or suggest, the strength of the character.
   II. to draw an allegory between the character and her life events.
   III. to indicate the narrator's admiration for the character.

   A. III only
   B. I and II only
   C. I and III only
   D. II and III only
   E. I, II, and III

3. Which of the following best describes the relationship of the paragraph that begins with . . . "She lay and drowsed" to the next paragraph that begins "Tomorrow was far away . . ."
   I. Paragraph 17 that begins with "Tomorrow" is a flashback that follows the previous paragraph's example of stream of consciousness.
   II. The paragraph that begins with "She lay and drowsed" is symbolic of her life as a mother and mid-wife.
   III. The paragraph that begins with "Tomorrow" symbolically displays her meticulous household and the fallacy that life can also be orderly.

   A. I and II only
   B. III only
   C. I only
   D. I and III only
   E. I, II, and III

4. In paragraph 18, last line, "She believed she'd just plague Cornelia a little" indicates the woman
   A. intends to keep living and remain tenacious
   B. has a strained relationship with her condescending daughter
   C. wants to live so she can continue her close family bond
   D. has resigned to the fact she is dying and is cantankerous
   E. needs to continue with the security the daily chores of farm life provides

5. In the second paragraph, first sentence, "Doctor Harry spread a warm paw like a cushion on her forehead where the forked green vein danced and made her eyelids twitch" is an example of
   A. paradox and personification
   B. simile and understatement
   C. simile and personification
   D. syllogism and metaphor
   E. hyperbole and metaphor

6. The author's portrayal of Granny Weatherall is primarily
   A. a sympathetic overview of a woman who has experienced many trials in her lifetime
   B. an ironic portrayal of a woman who enjoyed a successful life
   C. a study of a woman whose adult inattentive children have left the woman with a bereft feeling of failure
   D. a pragmatic, adamant woman who reflects upon her life
   E. a comical view of the woman's predicament involving letters from two lovers

7. In paragraph 27, line 3, "The lamp was lit, they didn't have to be scared . . ." symbolizes
   A. warmth from the harsh winters on the farm
   B. security after penning in the cattle herd and another hard day's work
   C. the mother's self-reliance and how it serves as a model for her children
   D. the love the mother has for her children, and her deceased husband
   E. the cohesiveness of the familial unit and how this strengthens them

8. Which of the following sets of adjectives best describes the story's tone and use of symbolism?
   A. macabre, mysterious, and remorseful
   B. religious, pristine, and adamant
   C. humorous, candid, and insightful
   D. nostalgic, unequivocal, and spiritual
   E. passionate, loving, and forthright

9. Paragraph 61, line 1 "Again no bridegroom and the priest in the house . . ." the bridegroom symbolizes
   I. George
   II. Religious figure
   III. John

   A. II only
   B. I only
   C. I and II only
   D. I and III only
   E. I, II, and III

10. The repeated usage of the light is allegorical to
    A. Granny's own self and imminent departing soul
    B. Granny's strength despite life's disappointments
    C. her final journey as she transitions from life to death
    D. the love she has for her children and husband
    E. the love she secretly felt for George throughout the years

## Poetry

### Chapter 11: Meeting Poetry: An Overview

*AP Practice Questions for "Schoolsville"*

> The following questions simulate AP Literature and Composition exam questions. Taking the advice found on pages 461–463 of the anthology, read the poem for content, meaning, literary and rhetorical devices, and answer the following questions. Refer to Chapter 11 (455–493) for additional information regarding poetry.

*Read the entire poem then answer the questions. "Schoolsville" by Billy Collins may be found on pages 456–457.*

1. The narrator's experience in the poem can best be described as
   A. an existential awakening
   B. a realistic to surrealistic memoir of a teaching career
   C. a nostalgic look at his students' accomplishments
   D. a poignant attachment to an iconoclastic institution of learning
   E. feelings of remorse over prematurely retiring from the teaching profession

2. The following phrase, ". . . last names first and their/first names last . . ." is an example of
   A. antithesis
   B. pun
   C. polysyndeton
   D. tautology
   E. chiasmus

3. The two poetic devices used in the second stanza are, in order,
   A. personification and simile
   B. flashback and hyperbole
   C. symbolism and imagery
   D. metaphor and simile
   E. onomatopoeia and litotes

4. The poem can best be described as
   A. a villanelle
   B. an ode
   C. an epic poem
   D. a narrative
   E. an *ottava rima*

5. In lines 20–23, the grades are depicted primarily as
   A. reflections of the performance, or lack thereof, of former students
   B. a literary allusion equivalent to former students' abilities
   C. allusionary imagery of achievements
   D. universal truths of the teacher/student relationship
   E. rhetorical tools of persuasion

## Chapter 12: Words: the Building Blocks of Poetry

*AP Practice Questions for "The Lives of the Heart"*

The Chapter 12 quiz is centered upon diction, or the poet's choice of words. The following questions address diction and syntax and mirror the important role these practices play in poetry. Refer to Chapter 12 (494–527) for additional information on diction and syntax in poetry.

*Read the entire poem then answer the questions. "The Lives of the Heart" by Jane Hirshfield may be found on pages 512–513.*

1. The choice and level of diction in lines 1–5 can primarily be described as:
   A. formal and abstract
   B. informal and concrete
   C. formal and concrete
   D. informal and specific
   E. neutral and abstract

2. The line ". . . tear sweet grass with their teeth" indicates a/(an)
   A. metaphor
   B. Homeric simile
   C. personification
   D. antimetabole
   E. parallelism

3. Lines 22–23 illustrate an example of
   A. assonance
   B. consonance
   C. caesura
   D. colloquialism
   E. trochaic

4. ". . . violent, serene, consenting, suffering . . ." is an example of
   A. chiasmus
   B. onomatopoeia
   C. oxymoron
   D. omniscience
   E. overstatement

5. The most unconventional facet of the poem is its
   A. diction
   B. imagery
   C. tone
   D. syntax
   E. use of symbolism

Answer Key: 1. C 2. C 3. B 4. C 5. D

## Chapter 13: Imagery: The Poem's Link to the Senses

*AP Practice Questions for "Sonnet 130: My Mistress' Eyes Are Nothing Like the Sun"*

> The Chapter 13 quiz is centered upon imagery, or the sights the writer achieves via diction, syntax, tone, etc. The following questions address this major mode of literary expression and augment the importance of sensory experiences when explicating poetry. Refer to Chapter 13 (528–559) for additional information on imagery in poetry.

*Read the entire poem then answer the questions. "Sonnet 130: My Mistress' Eyes Are Nothing Like the Sun" by William Shakespeare may be found on page 550.*

1. Each of these classifications of senses contribute to the imagery of the sonnet except:
   A. kinesthetic
   B. sensillum
   C. olfactory
   D. visual
   E. auditory

2. The images conjured within the sonnet serve to parody
   A. the epic poem
   B. the narrative
   C. the ode
   D. the ballad
   E. the elegy

3. Lines 13–14 demonstrate the effect of the
   A. heroic couplet
   B. couplet
   C. Homeric couplet
   D. iambic couplet
   E. hyperbolic couplet

4. The order in which the synesthetic imagery progresses is attributed to the following:
   A. auditory, olfactory, kinesthetic
   B. sensillum, visual, auditory
   C. visual, auditory, kinesthetic
   D. olfactory, sensillum, auditory
   E. visual, olfactory, auditory

5. The closing lines of the sonnet can best be interpreted as
   A. an insult to the speaker's lover
   B. a diatribe on revering false goddesses
   C. an impassioned plea to the speaker's mistress
   D. a humble admission of admiration
   E. a public apology for ridiculing his lover

Answer Key: 1. B  2. C  3. A  4. E  5. D

## Chapter 14: Figures of Speech, or Metaphorical Language

*AP Practice Questions for "A Valediction Forbidding Mourning"*

> The Chapter 14 quiz is centered upon the different literary terms that belong to the classification of figurative language, or metaphorical language. The following questions address this main feature of language that lends richness and texture to the poetry itself and how metaphorical language adds dimension and meaning to a work. Refer to Chapter 14 (560–598) for additional information on figures of speech in poetry.

*Read the entire poem then answer the questions. "A Valediction: Forbidding Mourning" by John Donne may be found on pages 571–572.*

1. The tenor in quatrain one serves to emphasize that
   A. some men die silently and with dignity
   B. some men fight death
   C. some lovers can't help but mourn the passing of their love
   D. some lovers accept death and others remain in denial
   E. some men plead with their lovers to not mourn

2. The tenor of the metaphor in the third quatrain serves to emphasize
   A. though the earth trembles upon its axis, it doesn't experience the jolt of loss
   B. the lovers' relationship is ephemeral compared to the laws of planetary motion
   C. the lovers may have had trepidation in the beginning of their relationship
   D. though one lover is dying, the love itself will remain as steadfast as the earth's daily rotation
   E. those who look outwardly upon the lovers will not see the strength of their love

3. "Our two souls therefore, which are one, . . . Like gold to airy thinness beat" has which of the following metaphorical language devices?
   I. simile
   II. metaphor
   III. tenor

   A. I only
   B. II only
   C. I and II only
   D. I and III only
   E. I, II, and III

4. Which of the following lines best serve as the vehicle for quatrain six?
   A. "Our two souls therefore . . ."
   B. "Though I must go . . ."
   C. "A breach, but an expansion . . ."
   D. ". . . endure not yet . . ."
   E. ". . . gold to airy thinness beat"

5. In the eighth quatrain, the most predominant figurative language device is
   A. simile
   B. synesthesia
   C. apostrophe
   D. paronomasia
   E. paradox

Answer Key:  1.D  2.A  3.D  4.E  5.B

## Chapter 15: Tone: The Creation of Attitude in Poetry

*AP Practice Questions for "Dulce et Decorum Est"*

> The Chapter 15 quiz is centered upon tone, or the attitude, the poet gives the speaker, and how the writer achieves via diction, syntax, tone, and so on. The following questions address this major mode of literary expression and augment the importance of sensory experiences when explicating poetry. Refer to Chapter 15 (599–640) for additional information on tone in poetry.

*Read the entire poem then answer the questions. "Dulce et Decorum Est" by Wilfred Owen may be found on pages 601–602.*

1. In line 3, "haunting flares" is an example of
   A. paronomasia
   B. paradox
   C. synecdoche
   D. metonymy
   E. metaphor

2. Lines 7–8 contain an example of
   A. synecdoche
   B. metonymy
   C. synesthesia
   D. paradox
   E. paronomasia

3. The tone of the poem is primarily
   A. a poignant tribute to war veterans
   B. a deferential tribute to dead soldiers
   C. a satirical expose of the atrocities of war
   D. a caustic opposition to patriotic propaganda
   E. an inspirational overview of valor

4. The salutation "My friend" in line 25 indicates irony through
   I. connotation
   II. denotation
   III. annotation

   A. I only
   B. II only
   C. III only
   D. I and II only
   E. II and III only

5. The speaker's attitude toward war is
   A. sympathetic
   B. acrimonious
   C. apathetic
   D. sardonic
   E. sanctimonious

Answer Key: 1.E  2.C  3.D  4.A  5.B

## Chapter 16: Form: The Shape of the Poem

*AP Practice Questions for "Ozymandias"*

The following questions pertain to the elements that emphasize not only content, but the form of the poem itself. Refer to Chapter 16 (641–690) for additional information on form in poetry.

*Read the entire poem then answer the questions. "Ozymandias" by Percy Bysshe Shelley may be found on page 681.*

1. The form of this poem has been modified slightly from the
   A. Petrarchan Sonnet, closed form
   B. Elizabethan Sonnet, open form
   C. Spenserian Sonnet, closed form
   D. Shakespearean Sonnet, closed form
   E. a sonnet, closed form

2. The primary point of irony is found in
   A. the second tercet in the sestet
   B. the sestet
   C. the octet
   D. the first quatrain of the octet
   E. the second quatrain of the octet

3. A philosophical analysis of this poem would reveal
   I. Platonic ideas
   II. particulars
   III. universals

   A. II and III only
   B. I and II only
   C. I and III only
   D. I only
   E. II only

4. The versification of the following line, "And wrinkled lip and sneer of cold command" is
   A. trochaic tetrameter
   B. spondaic trimeter
   C. dactylic monometer
   D. anapestic dimeter
   E. iambic pentameter

5. The alliteration in the concluding line serves to emphasize
    A. determinism
    B. naturalism
    C. existentialism
    D. classicism
    E. romanticism

## Chapter 17: Symbolism and Allusion: Windows to Wide Expanses of Meaning

*AP Practice Questions for "Snow"*

> The selected poem, with its accompanying questions, resembles closely prose and compre-
> hension questions found on AP exams. Please read the entire poem and note how the au-
> thor's use of symbolism and allusion contribute to the overall poem. Refer to Chapter 17
> (691–732) for additional information on symbolism and allusion in poetry.

*Read the entire poem then answer the questions. "Snow" may be found on page 693.*

1. Which of the following best describes the prominent poetic device found in lines
    12–16?
    A. a metaphor emphasizing the starkness between the snow and night
    B. a simile comparing the snow to spirits passed
    C. symbolism linking the present to the past
    D. onomatopoetic words to replicate a snowfall
    E. imagery to emphasize the presences within the cottage

2. The foremost symbolic characteristic of the snow is its
    A. perpetual cycle of past and present
    B. comfort of equality among humanity
    C. urge to charter new adventures
    D. maternal instinct to protect the earth
    E. link between animals and humans

3. The snow can serve as a symbol in each of the following relationships except the
    A. old house
    B. mountains
    C. trees
    D. mother-spirit
    E. hemlock

4. The most prevailing symbol within this piece is
    A. contextual
    B. private
    C. authorial
    D. universal
    E. cultural

**5.** For the speaker, the doe is most like
  A. a deferential tribute to the cycle of life and death
  B. a link to the past and the present
  C. a reminder of the need to respect nature
  D. an object of wonderment in this wintry scene
  E. an obstacle on the road that must be avoided

# Drama

## Chapter 20: The Dramatic Vision: An Overview

*AP Practice Questions for* The Sand Box

> The selected play, with its accompanying questions, resembles closely prose and comprehension questions found on AP exams. Note the frequency of dramatic devices addressed within the questions. Refer to Chapter 20 (861–922) for additional information on the dramatic vision.

*Read the entire play then answer the questions:* The Sand Box *by Edward Albee may be found on pages 885–889.*

**1.** The play's characters derive their personalities mostly through
  A. conflict
  B. resolution
  C. determinism
  D. existentialism
  E. diction

**2.** The characters' directions to the musician and the lighting technicians add to the play's
  A. surrealism
  B. realism
  C. modernism
  D. comic relief
  E. absurdity

**3.** The most unique aspect of the play is its extensive use of
  A. stage directions
  B. dialogue
  C. introduction
  D. explanations
  E. monologue

**4.** The primary purpose of the play's sandbox is to serve as a
  A. place of recreation
  B. place of calisthenics
  C. place of respite
  D. place of burial
  E. place or resurrection

5. The denouement of *The Sandbox* reveals
    A. the ancillary character's condescending attitude toward Grandma
    B. the protagonist's shift from sarcasm to realism
    C. the antagonist's indifference and superficiality
    D. the symbolism of the musician
    E. the realistic character's sense of existentialism

Answer Key:  1. E  2. E  3. A  4. D  5. B

## Chapter 21: The Tragic Vision: Affirmation through Loss

*AP Practice Questions for* Oedipus the King

> The selected tragedy, with its accompanying questions, resembles closely prose and comprehension questions found on AP exams. Note the frequency of the elements of the Greek tragedy addressed within the questions. Refer to Chapter 21 (923–1090) for additional information on tragedy.

*Read the entire play then answer the questions.* Oedipus the King *by Sophocles may be found on pages 940–976.*

1. The term peripeteia can best be accompanied by which scene in Oedipus?
    A. when Oedipus solves the riddle of the Sphinx
    B. when Oedipus marries Jocasta
    C. when the kingdom of Thebes is bestowed upon Oedipus
    D. when Oedipus recognizes his guilt over Laius and Jocasta
    E. when Oedipus murders Laius

2. In lines 100–105 of the Prologue, the scene is best depicted as
    A. tragic irony
    B. situational irony
    C. dramatic irony
    D. cosmic irony
    E. verbal irony

3. In Episode 1, lines 305–376, Tiresius' refusal to reveal Laius' murderer stems from the following reason
    A. Tiresius knows Oedipus will deny he is the murderer
    B. Tiresius does not believe he will personally profit by revealing his knowledge of the murderer's identity
    C. Tiresius does not wish to anger the Oracle, for if he does, the Gods will withhold information
    D. Tiresius fears King Oedipus will sentence him to exile if he reveals the murderer's identity
    E. Tiresius is jealous of King Oedipus' power and prominence

4. In Episode 1, lines 385–391, the "gift" Oedipus is describing can best be interpreted as
    A. artistry
    B. kingship
    C. wealth

D. success
E. power

5. Each of the following elements constitute actions primarily featuring the chorus except the following:
   A. stasimon
   B. episode
   C. parados
   D. prologue
   E. exodos

Answer Key: 1.D 2.C 3.A 4.B 5.D

## Chapter 22: The Comic Vision: Restoring the Balance

*AP Practice Questions for* A Midsummer Night's Dream

> The selected comedy, with its accompanying questions, resembles closely prose and comprehension questions found on AP exams. Note the frequency of the elements of the comedy addressed within the questions.

*Read the entire play then answer the questions.* A Midsummer Night's Dream *by William Shakespeare may be found on pages 1100–1153.*

1. Each of the following terms are associated with the structure of a comedy according to Roman conventions *except*
   A. epilogue
   B. unity of action
   C. unity of place
   D. the five acts
   E. unity of time

2. In Act II, scene I , lines 18–31 feature couplets with the exception of lines 30–31, which is more closely associated as
   A. end rhyme
   B. free verse
   C. forced rhyme
   D. caesura
   E. blank verse

3. In Act II, scene I, from lines 60–145 the elves go into hiding because
   I.   Titania is the timid queen of the forest, and fears Oberon
   II.  They are each bringing up romances of the past
   III. Oberon and Titania quarrel at various times over the changeling boy

   A. I and III only
   B. II and III only
   C. I only
   D. III only
   E. I, II, and III only

4. Puck's dialogue in Act II, scene I, lines 18–30 is primarily written in
   A. iambic, free verse
   B. iambic, blank verse
   C. iambic pentameter
   D. iambic tetrameter
   E. iambic trimeter

5. When Oberon and Titania meet, their initial reaction is (see Act II, scene I)
   A. amiable
   B. ascetic
   C. acerbic
   D. affable
   E. argumentative

Answer Key:  1. A  2. C  3. B  4. C  5. E

# PART NINE

# Sample AP English Literature and Composition Exam

## Section I

### Multiple Choice Questions

Time—1 hour
Percent of total grade on the exam: 45%

*Instructions:* this section of the exam consists of 53 questions on the content, form, and style of all literary selections encountered in an exam session and includes prose, drama, and poetry.

*Questions 1–14.* Read the following passage carefully paragraphs 1–6 before you decide on your answers to the questions.

---

The following selection is from "An Occurrence at Owl Creek Bridge" published in 1891 by Ambrose Bierce, paragraphs 1–14.

---

 ## An Occurrence at Owl Creek Bridge (1891)

A man stood upon a railroad bridge in northern Alabama, looking down into the swift water twenty feet below. The man's hands were behind his back, the wrists bound with a cord. A rope closely encircled his neck. It was attached to a stout cross-timber above his head and the slack fell to the level of his knees. Some loose boards laid upon the sleepers supporting the metals of the railway supplied a footing for him and his executioners—two private soldiers of the Federal army, directed by a sergeant who in civil life may have been a deputy sheriff. At a short remove upon the same temporary platform was an officer in the uniform of his rank, armed. He was a captain. A sentinel at each end of the bridge stood with his rifle in the position known as "support," that is to say, vertical in front of the left shoulder, the hammer resting on the forearm thrown straight across the chest—a formal and unnatural position, enforcing an erect carriage of the body. It did not appear to be the duty of these two men to know what was occurring at the center of the bridge; they merely blockaded the two ends of the foot planking that traversed it.

Beyond one of the sentinels nobody was in sight; the railroad ran straight away into a forest for a hundred yards, then, curving, was lost to view. Doubtless there was an outpost farther along. The other bank of the stream was open ground—a gentle acclivity topped with a stockade of vertical tree trunks, loopholed for rifles, with a single embrasure through which protruded the muzzle of a brass cannon commanding the bridge. Midway of the slope between the bridge and fort were the spectators—a single company of infantry in line, at "parade rest," the butts of the rifles on the ground, the barrels inclining slightly backward against the right shoulder, the hands crossed upon the stock. A lieutenant stood at the right of the line, the point of his sword upon the ground, his left hand resting upon his right. Excepting the group of four at the center of the bridge, not a man moved. The company faced the bridge, staring stonily, motionless. The sentinels, facing the banks of the stream, might have been statues to adorn the bridge. The captain stood with folded arms, silent, observing the work of his subordinates, but making no sign. Death is a dignitary who when he comes announced is to be received with formal manifestations of respect, even by those most familiar with him. In the code of military etiquette silence and fixity are forms of deference.

The man who was engaged in being hanged was apparently about thirty-five years of age. He was a civilian, if one might judge from his habit, which was that of a planter. His features were good—a straight nose, firm mouth, broad forehead, from which his long, dark hair was combed straight back, falling behind his ears to the collar of his well-fitting frock coat. He wore a mustache and pointed beard, but no whiskers; his eyes were large and dark gray, and had a kindly expression which one would hardly have expected in one whose neck was in the hemp. Evidently this was no vulgar assassin. The liberal military code makes provision for hanging many kinds of persons, and gentlemen are not excluded.

The preparations being complete, the two private soldiers stepped aside and each drew away the plank upon which he had been standing. The sergeant turned to the captain, saluted and placed himself immediately behind that officer, who in turn moved apart one pace. These movements left the condemned man and the sergeant standing on the two ends of the same plank, which spanned three of the cross-ties of the bridge. The end upon which the civilian stood almost, but not quite, reached a fourth. This plank had been held in place by the weight of the captain; it was now held by that of the sergeant. At a signal from the former the latter would step aside, the plank would tilt and the condemned man go down between two ties. The arrangement commended itself to his judgment as simple and effective. His face had not been covered nor his eyes bandaged. He looked a moment at his "unsteadfast footing," then let his gaze wander to the swirling water of the stream racing madly beneath his feet. A piece of dancing driftwood caught his attention and his eyes followed it down the current. How slowly it appeared to move! What a sluggish stream!

5    He closed his eyes in order to fix his last thoughts upon his wife and children. The water, touched to gold by the early sun, the brooding mists under the banks at some distance down the stream, the fort, the soldiers, the piece of driftwood—all had distracted him. And now he became conscious of a new disturbance. Striking through the thought of his dear ones was a sound which he could neither ignore nor understand, a sharp, distinct, metallic percussion like the stroke of a blacksmith's hammer upon the anvil; it had the same ringing quality. He wondered what it was, and whether immeasurably distant or near by—it seemed both. Its recurrence was regular, but as slow as the tolling of a death knell. He awaited each stroke with impatience and—he knew not why—apprehension. The intervals of silence grew progressively longer; the delays became maddening. With their greater infrequency the sounds increased in strength and sharpness. They hurt his ear like the thrust of a knife; he feared he would shriek. What he heard was the ticking of his watch.

He unclosed his eyes and saw again the water below him. "If I could free my hands," he thought, "I might throw off the noose and spring into the stream. By diving I could evade the bullets and, swimming vigorously, reach the bank, take to the woods and get away home. My home, thank God, is as yet outside their lines; my wife and little ones are still beyond the invader's farthest advance."

As these thoughts, which have here to be set down in words, were flashed into the doomed man's brain rather than evolved from it the captain nodded to the sergeant. The sergeant stepped aside.

## II

Peyton Farquhar was a well-to-do planter, of an old and highly respected Alabama family. Being a slave owner and like other slave owners a politician he was naturally an original secessionist and ardently devoted to the Southern cause. Circumstances of an imperious nature, which it is unnecessary to relate here, had prevented him from taking service with the gallant army that had fought the disastrous campaigns ending with the fall of Corinth, and he chafed under the inglorious restraint, longing for the release of his energies, the larger life of the soldier, the opportunity for distinction. That opportunity, he felt, would come, as it comes to all in war time. Meanwhile he did what he could. No service was too humble for him to perform in aid of the South, no adventure too perilous for him to undertake if consistent with the character of a civilian who was at heart a soldier, and who in good faith and without too much qualification assented to at least a part of the frankly villainous dictum that all is fair in love and war.

One evening while Farquhar and his wife were sitting on a rustic bench near the entrance to his grounds, a gray-clad soldier rode up to the gate and asked for a drink of water. Mrs. Farquhar was only too happy to serve him with her own white hands. While she was fetching the water her husband approached the dusty horseman and inquired eagerly for news from the front.

"The Yanks are repairing the railroads," said the man, "and are getting ready for another     10 advance. They have reached the Owl Creek bridge, put it in order and built a stockade on the north bank. The commandant has issued an order, which is posted everywhere, declaring that any civilian caught interfering with the railroad, its bridges, tunnels or trains will be summarily hanged. I saw the order."

"How far is it to the Owl Creek bridge?" Farquhar asked.

"About thirty miles."

"Is there no force on this side of the creek?"

"Only a picket post half a mile out, on the railroad, and a single sentinel at this end of the bridge."

_____

1. Peyton Farquhar is a
   A. Federal scout
   B. Sergeant in the Confederate Army
   C. Captain in the Union Army
   D. Union civilian
   E. Confederate civilian

2. The narrator's point of view is
   A. limited omniscient third-person
   B. first-person
   C. second-person
   D. omniscient
   E. dramatic third-person

3. The contextual structure of paragraph five is primarily composed of
    A. flashbacks
    B. flash forwards
    C. dramatic irony
    D. stream of consciousness
    E. expose

4. In paragraph two, line three, the word "acclivity" can best be interpreted as
    A. a mountain peak
    B. a gorge
    C. a berm
    D. an uprising hill
    E. a virgule

5. The syntactical arrangement in lines 7–9 of paragraph 4, "At a signal from . . . between two ties" includes primarily
    A. the periodic sentence
    B. a compound sentence
    C. a parallelism
    D. compound-complex sentence
    E. antithesis

6. The primary effect of the line "The sergeant stepped aside" with regard to the passage, is to convey
    A. the beginning of the civilian's dream sequence
    B. the ending of the civilian's dream sequence
    C. a heightened sense of surrealism
    D. the civilian's death
    E. the civilian's escape

7. The main conflict within the provided passage lies within the character's
    A. identity
    B. values
    C. existentialism
    D. sense of realism
    E. loyalty

8. The passage indicates that the character believes which of the following to be true?
    A. He has escaped and is swimming downstream
    B. He is having trouble removing the bindings
    C. He will valiantly sacrifice his life for the cause
    D. He is anxious, to the point his perception of reality is altered
    E. He feels a surge of energy, and is willing to stab, or harm the enemy

9. The civilian didn't serve in the war because of
    A. age
    B. mental disorders
    C. he would place his family in peril
    D. previous injury
    E. wealth and attainment

10. Paragraph five of the passage is marked by a series of
    A. rhetorical questions to enhance a sense of confidentiality
    B. a series of flashbacks to indicate the speaker's nostalgia

    C. shifts from reality to fantasy to emphasize the speaker's conflict

    D. periodic sentences to emphasize the main points

    E. flash forwards to illustrate the speaker's restlessness

**11.** The sentence, "Death is a dignitary who when he comes announced is to be received with formal manifestations of respect, even by those most familiar with him" contains which of the following literary devices?

    I. metaphor

    II. personification

    III. metonymy

    A. I only

    B. II only

    C. I and II

    D. I and III

    E. I, II, and III

**12.** The function of the narrator can best be described as

    A. an active participant

    B. an uninterested observer

    C. a disinterested narrator

    D. an omniscient observer

    E. an uninvolved spectator

**13.** In paragraph 9, the words ". . . with her own white hands . . ." implies all of the following *except:*

    A. supercilious

    B. adroit

    C. coddled

    D. pampered

    E. indulged

**14.** The causal theme of the passage implies

    A. the arrogance and gullibility of Southern plantation owners

    B. the universality of war by only naming the main character

    C. the ageless military tactic of utilizing the spy

    D. the deference and hierarchy of soldiers in rank

    E. the futility of war

*Questions 15–29.* Read the following passage carefully before you decide on your answers to the questions.

---

The selection is from "Luck" by Mark Twain, published in 1891. Lines 1–50 are used.

---

 **Luck** (1891)

It was at a banquet in London in honor of one of the two or three conspicuously illustrious English military names of this generation. For reasons which will presently appear, I will withhold his real name and titles and call him Lieutenant-General Lord Arthur Scoresby, Y.C., K.C.B., etc., etc. What a fascination there is in a renowned name! There sat the man, in actual flesh, whom I had heard of so many thousands of times since that day, thirty years before, when his name shot suddenly to the zenith from a Crimean battlefield, to remain forever celebrated. It was food and drink to me to look, and look, and look at that demi-god; scanning, searching, noting: the quietness, the reserve, the noble gravity of his countenance; the simple honesty that expressed itself all over him; the sweet unconsciousness of his greatness—unconsciousness of the hundreds of admiring eyes fastened upon him, unconsciousness of the deep, loving, sincere worship welling out of the breasts of those people and flowing toward him.

The clergyman at my left was an old acquaintance of mine—clergyman now, but had spent the first half of his life in the camp and field and as an instructor in the military school at Woolwich. Just at the moment I have been talking about a veiled and singular light glimmered in his eyes and he leaned down and muttered confidentially to me—indicating the hero of the banquet with a gesture:

"Privately—he's an absolute fool."

This verdict was a great surprise to me. If its subject had been Napoleon, or Socrates, or Solomon, my astonishment could not have been greater. Two things I was well aware of: that the Reverend was a man of strict veracity and that his judgment of men was good. Therefore I knew, beyond doubt or question, that the world was mistaken about this hero: he *was* a fool. So I meant to find out, at a convenient moment, how the Reverend, all solitary and alone, had discovered the secret.

5      Some days later the opportunity came, and this is what the Reverend told me:

About forty years ago I was an instructor in the military academy at Woolwich. I was present in one of the sections when young Scoresby underwent his preliminary examination. I was touched to the quick with pity, for the rest of the class answered up brightly and handsomely, while he—why, dear me, he didn't know *anything*, so to speak. He was evidently good, and sweet, and lovable, and guileless; and so it was exceedingly painful to see him stand there, as serene as a graven image, and deliver himself of answers which were veritably miraculous for stupidity and ignorance. All the compassion in me was aroused in his behalf. I said to myself, when he comes to be examined again he will be flung over, of course; so it will be simply a harmless act of charity to ease his fall as much as I can. I took him aside and found that he knew a little of Caesar's history; and as he didn't know anything else, I went to work and drilled him like a galley-slave on a certain line of stock questions concerning Caesar which I knew would be used. If you'll believe me, he went through with flying colors on examination day! He went through on that purely superficial "cram," and got compliments too, while others, who knew a thousand times more than he, got plucked. By some strangely lucky accident—an accident not likely to happen twice in a century—he was asked no question outside of the narrow limits of his drill.

It was stupefying. Well, all through his course I stood by him, with something of the sentiment which a mother feels for a crippled child; and he always saved himself—just by miracle, apparently.

Now, of course, the thing that would expose him and kill him at last was mathematics. I resolved to make his death as easy as I could; so I drilled him and crammed him, and crammed him and drilled him, just on the line of questions which the examiners would be most likely to use, and then launched him on his fate. Well, sir, try to conceive of the result: to my consternation, he took the first prize! And with it he got a perfect ovation in the way of compliments.

Sleep? There was no more sleep for me for a week. My conscience tortured me day and night. What I had done I had done purely through charity, and only to ease the poor youth's fall. I never had dreamed of any such preposterous results as the thing that had happened. I felt as guilty and miserable as Frankenstein. Here was a wooden-head whom I had put in the way of glittering promotions and prodigious responsibilities, and but one thing could happen: he and his responsibilities would all go to ruin together at the first opportunity.

———————————————

15. The speaker's tone in paragraph one is intended to convey
    A. reverence for English military officers
    B. mock exaltation
    C. disdain for blundering officers
    D. awe for altruistic Englishmen
    E. deference for the officer's unassuming attitude

16. In line 6 the word "zenith" can best be interpreted to mean
    A. the press
    B. forefront
    C. battlefield
    D. heavenward
    E. ranks

17. In paragraph 4, the allusion to "Napoleon, or Socrates, or Solomon" is used to
    I. universalize the officer's popularity
    II. satirize this officer's fame
    III. parallel the officer's wisdom to other noble historical figures

    A. I only
    B. I and II only
    C. II only
    D. III only
    E. II and III only

18. The shift of the speaker's attitude from paragraphs 1 and 2 to 3 and 4 emphasizes the speaker's
    A. gullibility
    B. incredulity
    C. inquisitiveness
    D. veracity
    E. impudence

19. The second speaker's attitude toward Scoresby could best be described as
    A. pitying
    B. humble
    C. charitable
    D. arrogant
    E. dogmatic

20. In paragraph 6, the speaker attributes Scoresby's success on the first exam to
    A. pluck
    B. luck
    C. the drills
    D. accident
    E. perseverance

21. In lines 2–3 of paragraph 8, the following rhetorical device is being used
    A. antithesis
    B. epistrophe
    C. anaphora
    D. tautology
    E. chiasmus

22. The grammatical function of the phrase "[b]eyond doubt or questio[n]" serves as
    A. a prepositional phrase
    B. an appositive phrase
    C. a pronoun antecedent
    D. an adverb phrase
    E. a comparison

23. Paragraph 8 serves mainly to show that the narrator
    A. remains compassionate toward Scoresby
    B. is incredulous at Scoresby's test results
    C. reveres Scoresby's ability to triumph
    D. feigns surprise at his prowess at teaching
    E. is pleased with the ovations for Scoresby

24. In paragraph 6, "He was evidently . . . for stupidity and ignorance" the writer uses all of
    the following stylistic devices *except*
    A. polysyndeton
    B. simile
    C. biblical allusion
    D. tautology
    E. oxymoron

25. In its context, "consternation" (line 5, paragraph 7) can best be interpreted to mean
    A. confusion
    B. surprise
    C. deliberate
    D. enigma
    E. hindrance

26. In sentence starting in paragraph 4, "Therefore I knew" serves to
    A. contradict the sentence preceding it
    B. develop the assertions in the sentence preceding it
    C. emphasize the competency of Scoresby
    D. transition and gives a call to action for the first speaker
    E. introduce the second speaker

27. In paragraphs 6–8, the narrator is alluding to
    A. the reverend's intellect
    B. Scoresby's ability to be a quick study
    C. the luck that accompanies Scoresby
    D. the cursory training methods of the military
    E. the gullibility of the public

28. The shift in the narrator's rhetorical stance between paragraph 8 and lines 1–2 of para-
    graph 8 can best be described as one from
    A. objective to subjective
    B. active to passive
    C. nurturing to critical

    D. assertive to judgmental
    E. intrepid to trepidation

**29.** In line 3 of paragraph 8, the word "crammed" is meant to be defined as
    A. stuffed
    B. stowed
    C. condensed
    D. contracted
    E. packed

*Questions 30–40.* Read the following dialogue carefully before you decide on your answers to the questions.

> The following selection is from "A Dollhouse (Et Dukkehjem)" by Henrik Ibsen, published in 1879. Lines 194–205 are used.

 ## A Dollhouse (Et Dukkehjem) (1879)

MRS. LINDE: Listen to me, Nora dear. Haven't you been a little bit imprudent?

NORA: [*sits up straight*] Is it imprudent to save your husband's life?

MRS. LINDE: It seems to me imprudent, without his knowledge, to—

NORA: But it was absolutely necessary that he should not know! My goodness, can't you understand that? It was necessary he should have no idea what a dangerous condition he  5 was in. It was to me that the doctors came and said that his life was in danger, and that the only thing to save him was to live in the south. Do you suppose I didn't try, first of all, to get what I wanted as if it were for myself? I told him how much I should love to travel abroad like other young wives; I tried tears and entreaties with him; I told him that he ought to remember the condition I was in, and that he ought to be kind and indulgent to  10 me; I even hinted that he might raise a loan. That nearly made him angry, Christine. He said I was thoughtless, and that it was his duty as my husband not to indulge me in my whims and caprices—as I believe he called them. Very well I thought, you must be saved—and that was how I came to devise a way out of the difficulty—

MRS. LINDE: And did your husband never get to know from your father that the money had  15 not come from him?

NORA: No, never. Papa died just at that time. I had meant to let him into the secret and beg him never to reveal it. But he was so ill then—alas, there never was any need to tell him.

MRS. LINDE: And since then have you never told your secret to your husband?

NORA: Good Heavens, no! How could you think so? A man who has such strong opinions  20 about these things! And besides, how painful and humiliating it would be for Torvald, with his manly independence, to know that he owed me anything! It would upset our mutual relations altogether; our beautiful happy home would no longer be what it is now.

MRS. LINDE: Do you mean never to tell him about it?

NORA: [*meditatively, and with a half smile*] Yes—some day, perhaps, after many years, when I am  25 no longer as nice-looking as I am now. Don't laugh at me! I mean of course, when Torvald is no longer as devoted to me as he is now; when my dancing and dressing-up and reciting have palled on him; then it may be a good thing to have something in reserve— [*breaking off*] What nonsense! That time will never come. Now, what do you think of my great secret, Christine? Do you still think I am of no use? I can tell you, too, that this affair  30 has caused me a lot of worry. It has been by no means easy for me to meet my engagements punctually. I may tell you that there is something that is called, in business, quarterly interest, and another thing called payment in instalments, and it is always so

dreadfully difficult to manage them. I have had to save a little here and there, where I
35 could, you understand. I have not been able to put aside much from my housekeeping
money, for Torvald must have a good table. I couldn't let my children be shabbily dressed;
I have felt obliged to use up all he gave me for them, the sweet little darlings!

MRS. LINDE: So it has all had to come out of your own necessaries of life, poor Nora?

NORA: Of course. Besides, I was the one responsible for it. Whenever Torvald has given me the
40 money for new dresses and such things, I have never spent more than half of it; I have
always bought the simplest and cheapest things. Thank Heaven, any clothes look well on
me, and so Torvald has never noticed it. But it was often very hard on me, Christine—
because it is delightful to be really well dressed, isn't it?

MRS. LINDE: Quite so.

45 NORA: Well, then I have found other ways of earning money. Last winter I was lucky enough
to get a lot of copying to do; so I locked myself up and sat writing every evening until
quite late at night. Many a time I was desperately tired; but all the same it was a tremendous pleasure to sit there working and earning money. It was like being a man.

---

**30.** Which of the following adjectives best describes the tone of the conversation?
   A. Impudent
   B. Arrogant
   C. Confiding
   D. Capricious
   E. Indulgent

**31.** Lines 25–26 ("Yes . . . don't laugh at me!") indicate Mrs. Linde's opinion of Nora is
   A. condescending
   B. admirable
   C. dubious
   D. disdainful
   E. reserved

**32.** Upon hearing of her father's terminal health condition, Nora seems
   A. stricken
   B. in denial
   C. relieved
   D. melancholy
   E. nostalgic

**33.** In the beginning, Nora's character is
   A. self-effacing
   B. possessive
   C. insecure
   D. manipulative
   E. insincere

**34.** The sentiment expressed in line 21, "And besides, . . . be for . . ." is an example of which
of the following?
   A. antithesis
   B. paradox
   C. synchises
   D. tautology
   E. oxymoron

**35.** The repeated use of the first person pronoun in lines 4–14 reflects Nora's
- A.  omniscient view of life
- B.  determinism
- C.  delicate condition
- D.  myopic focus
- E.  lackadaisical indifference

**36.** Nora's reference to "I tried tears and entreaties to him" (line 9) does which of the following?
-   I.  reveals Nora's ingenuity
-  II.  exposes the vast difference between Nora and Torvald
- III.  demonstrates nineteenth century feminine ideology

- A.  I only
- B.  III only
- C.  II only
- D.  I and III only
- E.  I, II, and III only

**37.** In line 30, the word "affair" can best be associated with
- A.  a romantic tryst
- B.  a social engagement
- C.  a business transaction
- D.  Torvald's occupation
- E.  Torvald's condition

**38.** The simile in line 50 serves to emphasize the
- A.  gullibility of Nora
- B.  hopelessness of the situation
- C.  limitations of women in the 19th century
- D.  expectations of women in the 19th century
- E.  Nora's satisfaction of performing an occupation

**39.** In line 38, the addition of the phrase "poor Nora" serves to
- A.  emphasize Mrs. Linde's admiration
- B.  reveal Mrs. Linde's contempt
- C.  illustrate Mrs. Linde's sardonic attitude
- D.  allude to Mrs. Linde's subservience
- E.  idealize Mrs. Linde's camaraderie with Nora

**40.** The rhetorical question in line 43 illustrates
- A.  a transition in Nora's attitude
- B.  Nora's materialism
- C.  Mrs. Linde's determinism
- D.  Nora's optimism
- E.  Mrs. Linde's humorous side

*Questions 41–53.* Read the following poem carefully before you decide on your answers to the questions.

---

The poem selected is "Preludes" by T.S. Eliot (1910)

---

# 🖋 Preludes (1910)

**I**

The winter evening settles down
With smell of steaks in passageways.
Six o'clock.
The burnt-out ends of smoky days.
5  And now a gusty shower wraps
The grimy scraps
Of withered leaves about your feet
And newspapers from vacant lots;
The showers beat
10 On broken blinds and chimney-pots,
And at the corner of the street
A lonely cab-horse steams and stamps.
And then the lighting of the lamps.

**II**

The morning comes to consciousness
15 Of faint stale smells of beer
From the sawdust-trampled street
With all its muddy feet that press
To early coffee-stands.
With the other masquerades
20 That time resumes,
One thinks of all the hands
That are raising dingy shades
In a thousand furnished rooms.

**III**

You tossed a blanket from the bed,
25 You lay upon your back, and waited;
You dozed, and watched the night revealing
The thousand sordid images
Of which your soul was constituted;
They flickered against the ceiling.
30 And when all the world came back
And the light crept up between the shutters
And you heard the sparrows in the gutters,
You had such a vision of the street,
As the street hardly understands;
35 Sitting along the bed's edge, where
You curled the papers from your hair,
Or clasped the yellow soles of feet
In the palms of both soiled hands.

IV

His soul stretched tight across the skies
That fade behind a city block,                                     40
Or trampled by insistent feet
At four and five and six o'clock;
And short square fingers stuffing pipes,
And evening newspapers, and eyes
Assured of certain certainties,                                    45
The conscience of a blackened street
Impatient to assume the world.
　I am moved by fancies that are curled
Around these images, and cling:
The notion of some infinitely gentle                               50
Infinitely suffering thing.

　Wipe your hand across your mouth, and laugh;
The worlds revolve like ancient women
Gathering fuel in vacant lots.

─────────────────

41. In stanza I, lines 1–7, the following classical tool of rhetoric is being used
    A. imagery
    B. simile
    C. oxymoron
    D. synesthesia
    E. tautology

42. The narrator's view in stanzas II and III shifts from
    A. omniscient to second person
    B. third person, limited to second person
    C. omniscient to third person
    D. formal to informal
    E. informal to formal

43. In line 14, the literary device being used is
    A. symbolism
    B. metaphor
    C. simile
    D. personification
    E. imagery

44. In line 19, the word "masquerades" is best described as
    A. routine
    B. holidays
    C. balls
    D. commutes
    E. work

45. Stanza I derives its images primarily from what kind of setting?
    A. suburban
    B. urban
    C. agrarian
    D. pastoral
    E. desert

**46.** Which of the following best summarizes the meaning of lines 43–45
   A. There can be comfort in a daily ritual, in a little indulgence
   B. The daily newspaper can be depressing
   C. Modern life makes people feel anonymous
   D. Daily rituals can make life monotonous
   E. Despite the insecurities of modern life, routine can give comfort

**47.** The most significant shift in narration occurs between
   A. Stanzas I and II
   B. Stanzas II and III
   C. Stanzas III and IV
   D. Stanzas I and III
   E. Stanzas II and IV

**48.** Which of the following literary techniques most significantly contributes to the poem's unity?
   A. its rhythmic patterns
   B. the use of figurative language
   C. the blend of setting and mood
   D. the conflict and resolution
   E. the repetition of sounds

**49.** Lines 53–54 suggest
   A. spirits move beyond time and place
   B. the constancy and necessity of work
   C. the emptiness of human life
   D. the shallowness of modernism
   E. the enigma of existentialism

**50.** The tone of the poem can best be described as all of the following except
   A. Existential
   B. Ethereal
   C. Desperate
   D. Eternal
   E. Euphoric

**51.** Lines 48–51 serve to offer
   A. despair
   B. hope
   C. salvation
   D. emulation
   E. personification

**52.** By setting the poem in the city the poet
   I. draws a parallel between the setting and the times
   II. establishes a mood of anonymity
   III. establishes a mood of solemnity

   A. I only
   B. II only
   C. III only
   D. I and II only
   E. I, II, and III

**53.** The repeated use of the second person pronoun in Stanza III serves primarily to
A. allude to a sense of respect
B. elicit a sense of voyeurism
C. suggest a feeling of disdain
D. illustrate irony
E. mock the hopelessness of the situation

## ENGLISH LITERATURE AND COMPOSITION
### Section II
### Question 1

(*Suggested time*—40 minutes. This question counts as one-third of the total essay score.)

*Instructions:* The following passage is an excerpt from "The Lottery" written by Shirley Jackson. After reading the passage, discuss in a well-organized essay the various literary devices Jackson uses, and how these techniques enhance the story's suspense.

### The Lottery (1948)

"Remember," Mr. Summers said, "take the slips and keep them folded until each person has taken one. Harry, you help little Dave." Mr. Graves took the hand of the little boy, who came willingly with him up to the box. "Take a paper out of the box, Davy," Mr. Summers said. Davy put his hand into the box and laughed. "Take just *one* paper," Mr. Summers said. "Harry, you hold it for him." Mr. Graves took the child's hand and removed the folded paper from the tight fist and held it while little Dave stood next to him and looked up at him wonderingly.

"Nancy next," Mr. Summers said. Nancy was twelve, and her school friends breathed heavily as she went forward, switching her skirt, and took a slip daintily from the box. "Bill, Jr.," Mr. Summers said, and Billy, his face red and his feet over-large, nearly knocked the box over as he got a paper out. "Tessie," Mr. Summers said. She hesitated for a minute, looking around defiantly, and then set her lips and went up to the box. She snatched a paper out and held it behind her.

"Bill," Mr. Summers said, and Bill Hutchinson reached into the box and felt around, bringing his hand out at last with the slip of paper in it.

The crowd was quiet. A girl whispered, "I hope it's not Nancy," and the sound of the whisper reached the edges of the crowd.

"It's not the way it used to be," Old Man Warner said clearly. "People ain't the way they used to be." 5

"All right," Mr. Summers said. "Open the papers. Harry, you open little Dave's."

Mr. Graves opened the slip of paper and there was a general sigh through the crowd as he held it up and everyone could see that it was blank. Nancy and Bill, Jr., opened theirs at the same time, and both beamed and laughed, turning around to the crowd and holding their slips of paper above their heads.

"Tessie," Mr. Summers said. There was a pause, and then Mr. Summers looked at Bill Hutchinson, and Bill unfolded his paper and showed it. It was blank.

"It's Tessie," Mr. Summers said, and his voice was hushed. "Show us her paper, Bill."

Bill Hutchinson went over to his wife and forced the slip of paper out of her hand. It had 10 a black spot on it, the black spot Mr. Summers had made the night before with the heavy pencil in the coal-company office. Bill Hutchinson held it up, and there was a stir in the crowd.

"All right, folks," Mr. Summers said. "Let's finish quickly."

Although the villagers had forgotten the ritual and lost the original black box, they still remembered to use stones. The pile of stones the boys had made earlier was ready; there were stones on the ground with the blowing scraps of paper that had come out of the box. Mrs. Delacroix selected a stone so large she had to pick it up with both hands and turned to Mrs. Dunbar. "Come on," she said. "Hurry up."

Mrs. Dunbar had small stones in both hands, and she said, gasping for breath, "I can't run at all. You'll have to go ahead and I'll catch up with you."

The children had stones already, and someone gave little Davy Hutchinson a few pebbles.

15     Tessie Hutchinson was in the center of a cleared space by now, and she held her hands out desperately as the villagers moved in on her. "It isn't fair," she said. A stone hit her on the side of the head.

Old Man Warner was saying, "Come on, come on, everyone." Steve Adams was in the front of the crowd of villagers with Mrs. Graves beside him.

"It isn't fair, it isn't right," Mrs. Hutchinson screamed, and then they were upon her.

---

## Question 2

(*Suggested time*—40 minutes. This question counts as one-third of the total essay score.)

> *Instructions:* Read the following poem carefully (the poem can also be found on page 681). In a well-organized essay express how the language of each stanza reveals the perceptions and feelings of the narrator.

 ## Do Not Go Gentle into That Good Night (1951)

Do not go gentle into that good night,
Old age should burn and rave at close of day;
Rage, rage against the dying of the light.

Though wise men at their end know dark is right,
5   Because their words had forked no lightning they
Do not go gentle into that good night.

Good men, the last wave by, crying how bright
Their frail deeds might have danced in a green bay,
Rage, rage against the dying of the light.
10   Wild men who caught and sang the sun in flight,
And learn, too late, they grieved it on its way,
Do not go gentle into that good night.

Grave men, near death, who see with blinding sight
Blind eyes could blaze like meteors and be gay,
15   Rage, rage against the dying of the light.

And you, my father, there on the sad height,
Curse, bless, me now with your fierce tears, I pray.
Do not go gentle into that good night.
Rage, rage against the dying of the light.

## Question 3

(*Suggested time*—40 minutes. This question counts as one-third of the total essay score.)

"Call me Ishmael. Some years ago—never mind how long precisely—having little or no money in my purse, and nothing particular to interest me on shore, I thought I would sail about a little and see the watery part of the world. "

—Herman Melville
*Moby Dick*

*Instructions:* Throughout many works of literature, the main protagonist feels a certain restlessness, a yearning, to explore new realms of the world, and in doing so, discovers new facets of his or her character during the process of this journey. Write an essay in which you explain the character's sojourn to self-identity and how this journey is essential to the novel's main theme.

You can select a work from the list below, or *feel free to choose another work you have read* that is commensurate in literary worth to the provided titles.

*The Adventures of Huckleberry Finn*
*The Grapes of Wrath*
*I Know Why the Caged Bird Sings*
*Heart of Darkness*
*Catch-22*
*Their Eyes Were Watching God*
*Long Day's Journey Into Night*
*Of Mice and Men*
*Great Expectations*
*The Sun Also Rises*
*Lord Jim*
*Lord of the Flies*
*The Call of the Wild*
*The Great Gatsby*
*The Catcher in the Rye*
*The Good Earth*
*The Poisonwood Bible*
*The Existentialist Journey to Self-Identity*

## Answer Key for the AP Literature and Composition Practice Exam

## Annotated Answers to Section I: Multiple Choice Answers 1–53

1. **E.** He is a Southern plantation owner eager to help the Confederacy. All other answers indicate either an officer or a civilian for the Union side.

2. **A.** The narrator focuses upon the main character, Peyton Farquhar; therefore, the point of view is limited, omniscient third person. B is incorrect, because first person addresses "I," whereas C, second person, addresses "you." D, omniscient, lets the narrator expose other characters besides the main character, and E, dramatic third person, addresses only what is said and what happens.

3. **D.** Stream of consciousness. Note how Farquhar's thoughts are random; they shift from the objects around him, to the macabre sound of his watch, to his imminent anxiety.

A is incorrect because the action is current, and B is incorrect because the action remains in the present. C is incorrect because irony is not a principle element in this paragraph. E also is incorrect because it is not an expose.

4. **D.** The acclivity is defined as a slope or uprising. A is incorrect, because acclivity is linked to verticalness, but not its zenith as a peak denotes. B is incorrect because a gorge is more closely associated to a canyon. C, a berm, is a path, and E, a virgule, is defined as a diagonal.

5. **A.** In the periodic sentence, the most important element is placed last. B is incorrect because the sentence does not have two independent clauses that are linked by either the coordinating conjunction, or the semicolon followed by the adverb. C is incorrect because the grammatical structure is not identical, and D is incorrect because the sentence does not contain two independent clauses and at least one subordinate clause.

6. **C.** A heightened sense of surrealism. The ticking of the clock, "seeing" his family all indicate Farquhar's imagination is heightened, lending a surreal element to his final seconds of life. It isn't exactly a dream, so A and B are both incorrect. Once the sergeant steps aside, there still is another second or so until Farquhar is actually dead, so D is incorrect, and no mention of an escape occurs, so E is incorrect.

7. **D.** The surreal ticking of the clock, his dream-like visions of his family all are centered upon fantasy as a defense mechanism against the horror of being executed. There are no conflicts with his identity; Farquhar is proud of his Southern heritage, so A is incorrect, and his values entail his involvement with the Confederacy, so B is incorrect. C is incorrect because he feels his responsibility for being was to defend the Confederacy, and E also is incorrect because he is willing to die for the cause.

8. **D.** There is a line that denotes Farquhar's agitation, especially as the "delays became maddening" and this is what causes his anxiety. The "escape" scene does not appear until later in the story, so A is incorrect, and B is incorrect because he merely is contemplating removing the bindings. C is incorrect because he doesn't think about being valiant while on the bridge, and E is incorrect because only the pain feels like a stab. It is not an action he is considering.

9. **E.** The key word is "imperious," which means attainment that is used in paragraph 8. Farquhar didn't serve because of his wealth. The other factors are not considered part of Farquhar's character that would preclude him from fighting.

10. **C.** Standing on the bridge, waiting to be executed are what heighten the character's sense of imminent death, and this is what causes him to hallucinate, to become anxious. There are no rhetorical questions asked so A is incorrect. B is incorrect because the action is current, and D is incorrect because there aren't numerous periodic sentences, and the events do not shift forward until later in the story.

11. **E.** This contains all three literary devices, or uses of figurative language. "Death is . . . ." indicates the metaphor, but is also is a metonymy because it compares death to something of great meaning, rather than just the "dignitary" comparison. Personification also is present because it refers to death as a dignitary, and addresses death with the pronoun him.

12. **D.** The narrator never tries to evoke sympathy from the reader, rather, the narrator merely retells the events, while also letting the reader get a glimpse of the character's inner thoughts.

13. **B.** Adroit denotes dexterity, or accomplishment. Here, the narrator is emphasizing the words "white hands," which has a connotation of the stereotypical Romanticized Southern

belle with delicate hands that have not experienced hard work. All other choices, A supercilious, C coddled, D pampered, and E indulged allude to the "imperious" class of Southern plantation mistresses.

14. **C.** Note the word causal. The entire action of the story revolves around the fact Peyton Farquhar was duped by the "Federal Scout." Had he not been cajoled by the scout's trap about the bridge, he would not have been caught, and later executed.

*Questions 15–29 from "Luck" by Mark Twain.*

15. **B.** The diction gets flowery and idealized to indicate a mockery of the officer being feted. Since it is a satirical piece, reverence in A, and selections D and E, indicating awe and deference respectively, are incorrect. The disdain doesn't get revealed until later in the selection, *after* paragraph one, so C is incorrect.

16. The word zenith means at the highest point, so the correct answer is heavenward, or D. All other supplied answers/definitions reveal aspects of a battle.

17. **B.** Diction such as "fascination" and "renowned name" indicate Scoresby's exalted appeal, and with just one remark by the reverend, the speaker's opinion shifts dramatically. Granted, the narrator does credit the reverend with veracity, but the swiftness of the shift from admiration to derision does reveal the speaker's fickleness.

18. The first speaker shifts from one belief to another, without ever questioning, so B is incorrect. The first speaker doesn't ask the reverend why the officer is a fool; he merely listens to the information, so C is incorrect. The first speaker's trustworthiness is never addressed, so D is incorrect, nor is the first speaker ever rude or obtuse, so D is incorrect.

19. **C.** The reverend wishes to assist Scoresby by tutoring him. A is incorrect because the reverend acts upon Scoresby's ignorance; he doesn't merely pity him. The reverend is pompous during his narration of his admirable teaching prowess, so B is incorrect. Although the reverend does at times convey a certain arrogance with diction such as "drilled him like a galley slave" and "launched him on his fate" he does offer the officer free tutoring. The reverend is a taskmaster, but punctuated throughout the lessons, he also conveys a sense of compassion for Scoresby, so E is incorrect, although close to being correct.

20. **C.** This correct answer stems from a cause-and-effect pattern. The numerous drills are what enable Scoresby to pass. Luck (choice B) does play a role, but only because there were no other questions outside of the drills. Pluck means to have courage, so A is incorrect. The answer D is incorrect because the drills, which enabled him to pass, were deliberate, and not accidental. The fact the questions did not extend beyond the parameters of the reverend's tutoring does indicate a lucky or accidental occurrence; nonetheless, the officer would not have passed without the drills.

21. **E.** A chiasmus is the repetition of a phrase or words, except the second grouping is the reverse of the first. The other rhetorical devices are A, antithesis, which is a pairing of two opposites. B, the epistrophe, is the repetition of words at the end of a phrase; and C, the anaphora, is the repetition of words or phrases at the beginning. D, tautology is a repetition of similar words in a sentence, such as "It is altogether fitting and proper."

22. **D.** Here, the verb knew is being modified; therefore, even though "beyond" is a preposition, in this case, the preposition is now an adverb phrase. A is incorrect, prepositional phrases modify nouns, in this sentence, it is the verb knew that is being modified. An appositive phrase merely adds additional information about a noun, so B is incorrect. A pronoun antecedent occurs in the beginning of a sentence, so C is incorrect. There is no comparison in this sentence, so E is incorrect.

23. **D.** It is evident the second speaker has a sense of egoism; therefore, when Scoresby wins, he "acts" surprised, but the victory also means he is quite accomplished as well. The narrator does show compassion, but soon, with the teaching style, and so on, the compassion subsides, so A is incorrect. The shock at the test results is not ingenuous, so B is incorrect. There is no reverence associated with the test results, only "surprise." The narration never mentions how pleased the reverend is, so E is incorrect.

24. **E.** An oxymoron features two words, placed side by side, yet they oppose each other. For example, professional jealousy can be considered an oxymoron because if a person is being professional, she'll put petty jealousies aside. In lines 4–9 of paragraph 6, all other rhetorical devices are used: the polysyndeton (choice A) with the abundance of coordinating conjunctions; the simile (choice B) is used with the "serene as a graven image" phrase, and the biblical allusion (choice C) to the "graven image" connotation to false worship also works well. A tautology is the usage of two similar words; the phrase "stupidity and ignorance" demonstrates the tautology, or the answer D.

25. **B.** The *primary* definition of consternation is amazement, or surprise, that can be *followed by* manifestations of confusion (choice A) and hindrance (choice E). The award of first prize has no deliberateness (choice C) involved, and it was not a mystery, or enigma (choice D).

26. **B.** Remember to only focus upon the one sentence in lines 3–4 of paragraph 6. This sentence does add more detail to the reverend, and why the speaker believes the assertions in the previous sentence. There is no contradiction, just development, so A is incorrect. According to the reverend, Scoresby is a fool, so C is incorrect. The call to action (choice D) does not appear until line 5 of paragraph 4. E is incorrect because the reverend has already spoken by paragraph 3.

27. **D.** The haunting allusion is the military's lack of adequate training for its soldiers, and how quickly they are rewarded for doing little. The reverend merely drills; he is not a mathematician, so A is incorrect, and Scoresby isn't a quick study because the reverend had to "drill and cram" as earlier learned in the passage. C is incorrect because although it was luck at having the same questions as the drills, it is the underlying message that is being sought. The gullibility of the public, choice E, refers to the first scene, not in paragraphs 6–8, even though the military is gullible in thinking someone like Scoresby could be a mighty leader.

28. **C.** The reverend's interest in "standing by" indicates a nurturing stance. The emotional appeal, counters any objectivity, so A is incorrect. The reverend's surprise, and subsequent inner pride, are contrary to passivity, so B is incorrect. The reverend is not judgmental as much as he is surprised and critical of the outcome, so D is incorrect. The reverend is never shy, so E is incorrect.

29. **C.** The reverend was on a strict timeline to get as much data into Scoresby's mind as possible. A is incorrect, because stuffed is not as succinct to the task at hand; neither is stowed (choice B), contracted (choice D) or packed (choice E).

30. **C.** Nora is confiding to Mrs. Linde about her husband's condition. A is incorrect because impudent means rude; B also is a synonym for rude, or haughty; and capricious (choice D) is incorrect because capricious is defined as impulsive, and Nora is actually plotting how to help her husband, and although Nora isn't the most mature of characters, she is not indulgent here in the conversation, so E is incorrect.

31. **A.** Mrs. Linde's tone remains matronly, with an air of sarcasm, which exposes her condescending nature, as if she is underestimating Nora. B is incorrect because Mrs. Linde is

anything but in awe of Nora, whereas Mrs. Linde does doubt Nora's capabilities, her tone is more sardonic. Mrs. Linde does not judge or stigmatize Nora's actions, and she is free with her comments so E is incorrect.

32. **C.** The fact Nora needs some finances to help her ailing husband, and she needs her father's wealth indicate her father's death could prove to be actually helpful. Nora displays no outward signs of grief, so A is incorrect; she confronts her father's terminal condition, so B is incorrect. Nora's incandescent character is not altered into a state of malaise, so D is incorrect, and she does no reminiscing over her father's condition, so E is incorrect.

33. **A.** Despite the fact she is a 19th-century woman with few financial resources, she is trying to obtain funds to help her husband. Nora is not possessive, so B is incorrect, and the fact she reveals her immature personality reveals she is not as insecure as Mrs. Linde would like to believe. Nora is not as much manipulative (D) as she is striving to assist her husband, and although Nora does appear shallow at times, she sincerely wants her husband well, so E is incorrect.

34. **D.** "painful and humiliating" is a pairing of synonymous words, which is an example of a tautology. Antithesis (choice A) is an arrangement of opposites with one sentence, and paradox (choice B) is a statement that, at first, appears untrue but upon further consideration is actually true. The synchises (choice C) is not apparent, and there are no side-by-side opposing terms.

35. **B.** This paragraph is paradoxical, for upon a first reading, Nora appears myopic (choice D), but after a close reading, Nora is only referring to how she has tried to mask her efforts by deliberately acting in her normal indulgent ways. Nora is actually trying to secure funds, and by focusing upon herself, her husband won't suspect Nora's original intentions: that of aiding Torvald. A is incorrect because Nora is primarily telling Mrs. Linde about herself, although there is a small reference to Torvald's reaction, but only from Nora's point of view. Nora actually shows strength in this paragraph as she "devise[s] a way out of the difficulty" so choice C is incorrect. Although the pronoun "I" is used extensively, it is not to secure Nora's own interests, so D is incorrect, and she is definitely interested in her husband's fate, so E is incorrect.

36. **E.** All three elements of female behavior, as oftentimes portrayed during the 19th century, are revealed via Nora's character.

37. **E.** Torvald's condition is what has prompted Nora into action and determinism to secure funds to help her ailing husband. Nora is not involved with anyone else, so A is incorrect. No social engagements are mentioned, so B is incorrect. The business of acquiring the funds does occupy her time, but that is not referred to as "affair," and Torvald's occupation is not the chief topic as she confides in Mrs. Linde, so D is incorrect.

38. **C.** The 19th-century ideology posited that if a woman did an outstanding job, she still was compared to a man, instead of giving credit to the woman herself. A is incorrect because it doesn't reflect Nora's naiveté; it's more about the sociological, or ideological aspect. Nora feels accomplishment, not hopelessness, so B is incorrect. During the 19th century, women's expectations were confined to homemaking, or traditional occupations such as a teacher, or nurse, so D is incorrect. While Nora is pleased (choice E) with her accomplishments, it is the ideology that prevails in this dialogue.

39. **C.** Mrs. Linde has a sarcastic attitude toward Nora, with no admiration (choice A). Mrs. Linde does not feel inadequate, or a person of lesser importance (choice D) and she is not a close friend of Nora's (choice E).

40. **B.** Nora emphasizes several times in her conversation with Mrs. Linde material objects such as clothes and furniture. Nora's attitude remains relatively constant as she explains her predicament to Nora. Mrs. Linde is merely a listener, so C is incorrect. The question serves only to ponder the importance of clothes, nothing as noble as optimism is presented here, so D is incorrect. E is incorrect, because Nora is the speaker.

41. **D.** Synesthesia is when perceptions of the senses are realized via diction. For example, the "smell of steaks," and "withered leaves about your feet." These two phrases elicit the senses of smell and touch. Imagery is incorrect because it is a literary tool, and is not primarily associated with a classical tool of rhetoric. There are no comparisons using like or as, so B is incorrect. No side-by-side comparisons are made, so C is incorrect, and there are not synonymous comparisons within the same line, so E is incorrect.

42. **A.** There is a feeling of an all-knowing narrator, and then it immediately in the third stanza shifts to "you." B is incorrect, because stanza two is not limited by a third person, and C is incorrect, because stanza three has a preponderance of "You," the second-person pronoun. The tone does not shift that much from formal to informal or vice versa, so D and E are both incorrect.

43. **D.** As the morning reaches a "consciousness" it indicates a human, or living being, function. The morning can symbolize (A) a new beginning, but it is the humanlike attribute that makes D the best choice. The morning is not being compared to anything else, so B is incorrect, and there are no comparisons using like or as, so C is incorrect. Imagery usually contains color, textures, and that is not present in line 14, so E is incorrect.

44. **A.** The "masquerades" is a metaphor for the daily grinds, or the routine that is performed day in, day out. Holidays and balls, (choices B and C, respectively) indicate gala occasions. The commutes (choice D) themselves, the act of going to and fro is a good choice, but it does not indicate if the people are actually going to work, so E also is incorrect.

45. **B.** This is a quintessential urban, or city, setting. A is incorrect because that would be a subdivision outside of a city, and agrarian, (choice C) is referring to a farm. Choice D indicates a country setting, and E, the desert, is incorrect.

46. **A.** The daily reading of a newspaper, and the assurance of something tangible like a newspaper, and having a smoke, gives assurance. There is no reference if the news is good or bad, so B is incorrect. The allusion to anonymity is found within the poem, but not with lines 43–45, so C is incorrect. The word "assurance" makes the term monotonous, incongruous with lines 43–45, so D is incorrect. Although choice E, with the comfort of routine aspect does seem like a valid answer, there is no reference to any other daily ritual, but the smoking of the pipe, usually associated with an action that promotes a small pleasurable sensation, is not a part of this answer.

47. **B.** The omniscience of the urban cityscape and this intimate portrait of a woman arising from sleep indicate the greatest shift. A is incorrect, and although there is one reference of "you," the general tone is omniscient, and stanza two also is omniscient. C is incorrect because the point of view has little shift. Due to the one reference of the second-person pronoun in stanza one, and the second-person pronoun in stanza three, it doesn't shift as dramatically, so D is incorrect, and E also.

48. **C.** Eliot's tone creates a mood that is inescapable from the images produced by the urban setting. The flow is rhythmic, but not definitive such as an iambic pentameter pattern, so A is incorrect. The images (choice B) are pronounced, but it does not overcome the mood of isolation in a modern world. D is incorrect because no resolution is reached,

and although there is consonance and a few rhymes, they are not pronounced so as to override the mood.

49. **B.** The term "fuel" is meant to convey wood-a necessary element for fires, for cooking, for daily life in ancient times. This simple act emphasizes the timelessness of work. A is incorrect because it is a comparison, not a definitive action of the women, and C is incorrect because there's a call to action, and therefore optimism that the call will be heeded. Existentialism requires a choice, but no choice is being made, only a suggestion, in lines 53–54, so E is incorrect.

50. **E.** Euphoric is to indicate a happy, elated mood. Its main tone does not convey a happy, joyful mood.

51. **B.** A sliver of hope is offered here with the verb "cling" to an idea, or notion, that something else out there suffers right along with another. A is incorrect because there is an element of companionship, albeit slight. There is no religious overtone of redemption in lines 48–51, so C is incorrect, and there is no sense of one being trying to be like another, so D is incorrect. E is incorrect because personification is applying inanimate objects with humanlike characteristics, and the use of the pronoun "I" precludes this.

52. **E.** One of the aspects of setting is also the time, and this modern view of life, with its anonymous inhabitants, and with the lack of noise, or of people's emotions indicates a solemn mood.

53. **A.** The speaker relates a sense of awe at the person who, daily, despite what confronts that person, gets up and begins anew. B is incorrect because although the reader gets the sense the person in the room is being watched, there is still a sense of wonder. Voyeurism is confined to satisfying curiosity. The scene is merely displayed, no feelings of negative judgment are present, and so C is incorrect. There is no element of irony, the person in the room could be anyone, and this lifestyle may be exactly how this person thought his or her life would be, so D is incorrect. There is no sense of impending doom, or disaster, just a sense of the situation itself, so E is incorrect.

## Question 1:   Shirley Jackson's "The Lottery"

The question calls for a reading of Shirley Jackson's "The Lottery" followed by a discussion of the various literary devices, and also how these devices add to the story's suspense. Note the plural form of "various literary devices." This means the essayist is prompted to discuss more than one. This is, in fact, another example of the typical essay prompt that asks the student to discuss "X" and further evaluate how the "X," in this case, the literary devices, add to the "Y," or more specifically, here, the suspense. An essay of three well-developed paragraphs that discusses the literary devices and then addresses how these devices add to the suspense by the third paragraph will marshal evidence of a full command of not only the prompt, but critical analyses as well.

Patent literary devices at work within the short story are foreshadowing and the theme of time should be addressed within the student essay. The most obvious passage is that which focuses upon the "black dot" upon the paper, and how tense the mood becomes.

The following essay is a timed student response. The student had 40 minutes to write this essay. After reading the essay, please see the comments immediately following.

## Essay Response to Question 1

"Strange is it not? That of the myriads who/before us passed the door of Darkness through,/not one returns to tell us of the Road,/Which to discover we must travel too." Omar

Khayyam's macabre poem *Rubaiyat*, written between the 11th and 12th centuries, presents the immense wonder that envelops the daunting subject of the end of human life. Yet despite the almost playful treatment of the subject that Khayyam employs in his writing, his fascination with the manner that death has been treated, not only through literature but also by society, reveals obscure wonder concerning the subject. It is this wonder, which is displayed by not merely Khayyam but nearly all of society, which constitutes the greatest suspense that human life has ever experienced—that of the end of their being.

Suspense is one of the hardest subjects to identify, and moreover, define. It lurks within that region of feeling not consciously triggered or mentally extinguishable, but rather that autonomic nervous response inherently in our being that makes us hold our breath, grit our teeth, and merely brace for the climax. The qualities of suspense and the construction of such rely heavily on the unknown, foreshadowing, helplessness, and time. It is these four qualities that Shirley Jackson utilizes in her short story "The Lottery," to construct the tension and apprehension necessary to invoke suspense.

Jackson uses a variety of methods to bolster the suspenseful atmosphere of the ending of her story, the first of which being an appeal to emotion. "'Harry, you help little Dave.' Mr. Graves took the hand of the little boy, who came willingly with him up to the box. 'Take a paper out of the box, Davy'" (Jackson 213). Through the incorporation of a child in her lottery for a stoning, Jackson creates a sense of the aforementioned helplessness as well as eliciting the protective instincts of the reader—that of a mammal nurturing its young. The use of not only an adult audience allows the writer to expand the scope of her helplessness not only to the reader but also the subject, only strengthening her connection to suspense and emotion by involving the audience of her story with the audience in her story.

The greatest factor in Jackson's construction of suspense is that of foreshadowing. "It had a black spot on it, the black spot Mr. Summers had made the night before with the heavy pencil in the coal-company office"(213). Black and darkness have long been a symbol of death and the unknown, and can even be seen in Khayyam's aforementioned poem. This societal use of black as a symbol for death introduces—for the first time in the passage—the fate of the victim and foreshadows the happenings later of Mrs. Hutchinson. However, the spot does more than simply foreshadow and wherefore bolster Jackson's suspense. The subject with the spot presents the factor of mystery and fear into the work, wherefore creating another pillar of suspense. However, this symbol of death is strengthened with a great allusion found in the black spot. The actual symbol of the black spot, not only the color, has long been used to mark death. Such a symbol gained its great popularity and lore through its rumored use in the 14th through 18th centuries among privateers, or hired ships, as a manner to indicate death and frighten others. It is through this historical allusion that the reader can draw such strong parallels between its presentation and the eventual fate of Mrs. Hutchinson and wherefore does Jackson add to the suspense in her story.

The greatest of Jackson's tools and manner of writing that promotes suspense is that of delay. Time, and the delay of such, forces the reader's mind to dwell on that of the characters and their fates. Through Jackson's description of her character's appearances and reaction as they approach the box and her delay to reveal the meaning and possessor of the marked slip creates such suspense through the reader's own creative mind. Suspense lies in the reaction of the reader, the content of the story can only hope to stir that reaction. By creating a needless delay in the outcome of her story does Jackson create the only window in the reading of her story for suspense to build. Without the incorporation of such an element and the lengthening of her work, Jackson would have essentially a textbook rendition of a trail of events. It is through embellishment and the reader's interpretation that Jackson creates as she does and avoids a mere drawling tale of atrocity.

Stoning—this symbol of punishment—contains the greatest and most powerfully emotional allusion brought to bear. From its use as a form of public punishment and sadistic entertainment by the Romans and Jews, to its more modern use in Wyoming against Matt Shepard in 1998 that created the modern judicial precedent for gay hate crimes, stoning has elicited fear, hate, and emotion throughout its history. With its eventual ending in death, stoning introduces the strongest aspect of Jackson's suspense—the unknown. This incorporation of death allows the reader to connect on a personal level with the dilemma presented at the conclusion of the work. In the words of a Jewish proverb taken from *A Treasury of Jewish Folklore*, "For dying, you always have time." The conclusion of Jackson's story presents the reader with the conclusion of their own life, their thoughts, and the greatest suspense of all.

Essay by Miles VanKopp

## Comments on the Student Essay

The introduction alludes to Omar Khayyam's classic poem and it immediately commands the reader's attention because the essayist is beginning the classic "global and noble" introduction. Furthermore, this literary allusion establishes a mature tone and indicates the student's intellectual repertoire. By initially referring to the end of one's existence it establishes the parallel between the short story, and the timeless conflict of approaching death the poem expresses. With this parallel, immediately, the reader knows the theme of death is apparent in this short story.

Note how in the second paragraph the student addresses suspense, and each sentence builds upon the following to introduce the clear, salient thesis: "The qualities of suspense and the construction of such rely heavily on the unknown, foreshadowing, helplessness, and time. It is these four qualities, which Shirley Jackson utilizes in her short story, "The Lottery," to construct the tension and apprehension necessary to invoke suspense." The student has created an excellent point of attack—that of tension and apprehension—within the thesis.

In paragraph three the essay displays a sound structure of thesis defense by visiting the element of the unknown, and incorporates the dichotomy of child and adult within the setting. The analysis of "[a] mammal nurturing its young" serves to help ease the tension felt by the children, and also serves to heighten the suspense within the story itself.

Literary devices such as foreshadowing when Mrs. Hutchinson draws the paper with the black spot have been addressed. In paragraph four, the student makes a strong case for not only foreshadowing, but also of symbolism to add to the mounting suspense. The incorporation of quotes from the short story continually adds credence to specific literary analytical sentences. Also, the historical references indicate, like the literary reference in the introductory paragraph, that this student is well read, and has material ready to be synthesized into a cohesive, salient analytical essay.

In paragraph five, the essayist further defends the thesis of "tension and apprehension" by analyzing how the delay of time also invites the reader to ponder this outmoded, bizarre ritual. The student closes with a contemporary connection, that of a modern tragedy involving a young man in mid-west America, and further extrapolates and eloquently expresses how the inhumanness of prejudice and hate are factors in forms of punishment.

This essay would earn nothing less than a nine on a nine-point essay scale.

## Question 2

This essay prompt stems from a poem, a villanelle, to be exact. The literary devices found in the short story such as foreshadowing will not be addressed in this student essay; rather, it is the use of language that will be addressed. Language can encompass anything from literary devices to rhetoric and this student chooses, wisely, the rhetorical tools that also elicit the "perceptions and feelings" of the poem's speaker.

When reading this essay, ask yourself, "What are this essay's strengths?" Also, how does this essay differ in content from the first essay that addresses the short story excerpt? Could you write a better response than the following student example? Also, remember this is a student-written essay performed in 40 minutes.

## Essay Response to Question 2

Of all the forms of art that mankind has developed over the millennia, poetry is, perhaps, the one with the most potential to convey human thought and emotion. Because of the creative images, verbiage, and rhetoric that so frequently form the basis of good verse, deducing an author's feelings and perceptions on a topic given in the form of poetry as opposed to prose, while not always easier, will often yield more fruitful results. Such is the case in the poetic work "Do Not Go Gentle into That Good Night," by Dylan Thomas. Throughout six stanzas, Thomas employs significant images, words, and ideas to show how four different categories of men exemplify a commonality that all men share (or at least, should share) when faced with their mortal ends.

As with any good written work, Thomas built his poetic message around powerful and poignant images; when first reading his poem, one's senses are completely and utterly overwhelmed with stimuli. While it affects all of the five senses to some extent, however, this synesthesia mainly exploits and affects one's sense of sight, as images crop up continually that are comprised of forms of light. Thomas discusses constantly the "dying of the light," which refers to the life of a man when it comes to an end, and also mentions "forked lightning," and how "old age should burn and rave at the close of day." The link between the images is no accident; in fact, it serves a very distinct purpose. By creating a running allegory that describes life as day, or daylight, Thomas establishes the first of his most important perceptions about life: Life, like day, and daylight, does not last forever.

Images alone, however, are not enough to express the entirety of Thomas' message. The specific words and phrases he uses also play a crucial role in expanding upon his overall meaning. Through his use of repetition and potent words and phrases, Thomas takes the initial comparison of life to daylight, and uses it to give the most basic form of his overall premise. Four of the six stanzas, for instance, end with the phrase "Rage, rage against the dying of the light," and two end with "Do not go gentle into that good night." None of these stanzas, however, begin in the same way; each describes a unique classification of man. From "wise men" to "good men," and from "wild men" to "grave men," or, in other words, serious men, Thomas uses his four interior stanzas to point out different types of man, but then links them all together using the repetition at the closing of each verse. By repeating those specific, powerful lines numerous times, Thomas first establishes that life is as temporary as light, and then shows that this concept applies to all strata of mankind, no matter how different they may be.

What clinches his meaning, however, are neither the images nor the wording contained in his poem, but the ideas they create that at first seem counterintuitive to his overall message. By first establishing the unavoidable mortality of mankind, Thomas' urge to "rage, rage against the dying of the light" at first seems unfitting towards reality. This instance of opposition, however, is what truly crystallizes Thomas' message to his readers. Despite the inevitable reality of mortality, Thomas urges men of all kinds and backgrounds to "not go gentle into that good night." Thomas' assertion that "old age should burn and rage at the close of day" shows that although Thomas knows "rage" is truly ineffectual in the face of death, he truly believes that it is no excuse for man to go down without a fight. Even if death is inevitable, it is no reason for man to give up his passions and his life to go weakly to his grave. In other words, knowing that dusk is approaching is no reason for one to simply lie down and wait for it.

Ergo, Thomas' images and composition are both essential to lay down the basis of the message that Thomas is trying to convey; without them, he would have no means through which to reveal his personal perceptions and feelings to the readers. It is his oppositional ideas, however, that truly communicate his meaning best. By establishing a truth and then instantly championing the futile fight against it, Thomas effectively expresses his views and perceptions on death to his readers. Without all three of these linguistic techniques, "Do Not Go Gentle into That Good Night" would merely be a confusing collection of ideas. However, Thomas' mastery of images, composition, and conceptual opposition synthesize perfectly to create a work that denotes an undeniable universal truth; even "though wise men at their ends know dark is right, / . . . do not go gentle into that good night."

Essay written by Emily Barber

## Comments on Essay 2

Like the first essay, the introduction begins with the "global, noble" introduction that commands attention and wisely **qualifies** the assertion of poetry's efficacy in conveying emotion. The thesis statement is strong with a salient point of attack: a "commonality" when confronted with death.

The second paragraph illustrates the poignant images, and her knowledge of synesthesia, a rhetorical tool, is deftly used here. The essayist then swirls in quotes betwixt and between analyses to bolster the assertion of the strong images conveyed. The use of the "running allegory" also gives further evidence of the speaker's perceptions, and treatment of light in this stanza.

Note the specificity in paragraph three when the student is cognizant of the speaker's comparison of "life to daylight" and it is this perception that is stressed in this poem. A linguistic approach is then addressesd, as the student does a stanza count, and how "four of the six stanzas . . . end with the phrase 'Rage, rage against the dying of the light,'" This kind of emphasis upon word placement denotes a sophisticated, mature control of not only literary analysis, but also a command of essay writing.

Moving from specifics, the essayist then elevates the essay with enhanced diction by addressing how Thomas makes this villanelle cohesive by 'linking' the "repetition at the closing of each verse." Succinctly locating the most effective linguistic devices, coupled with Thomas' usage of technique makes this essay an outstanding example.

For its saliency and thesis defense, this essay would earn nothing less than an eight in a nine-point essay scale.

## Essay Response to Question 3

As one progresses through life, it is often difficult not also to journey toward knowledge of the world and the way in which it functions. In turn, as one acquires knowledge, one's character is fundamentally changed as the goal of self-identity is finally reached. Until that point, however, people are habitually filled with a sense of restlessness and longing that cannot be sated. Mark Twain's *The Adventures of Huckleberry Finn* begins as a scathing social commentary of "civilized society" before specifically addressing problems inherent within the institutions of slavery and racism. As Huck Finn journeys on his raft, he comes to an existential conclusion about not only himself, but also about society in general.

As the novel begins, Huck Finn petulantly refuses any attempts to civilize him. As he dislikes regular bathing, attending school and church, and rules in general, Huck has a difficult time adjusting to the sometimes bureaucratic regulations others seem keen to follow—for example, he does not understand the point of religion or its true meaning, as he receives mixed messages on the subject. However, with the reappearance of his abusive father, and Huck's subsequent captivity under him, the need to escape becomes quite clear. On the other hand, escaping back to civilized life doesn't quite suit Huck, so he plans to run away to an island after faking his own death. It is on this island that he coincidentally meets another runaway, Jim, who is the escaped slave of Huck's adopted aunt. On the island the two find paradise—there is an abundant supply of food, they can act in whichever manner pleases them most, and they find real peace. The island serves as an example of Locke's state of nature—there are no rules, and the natural rights of the people are being protected, whereas in "civilized" society, Jim would be property and Huck would be abused. Unfortunately, fear of being discovered eventually drives the pair to leave the island on a raft.

It is on this raft that Jim and Huck attempt to travel north, which represents freedom, so that Jim can shed his fugitive identity and Huck, can start a new life. However, circumstances eventually go awry and they end up traveling south. Along the way, the boys have several adventures that lead both to personal growth and a mutual understanding. In one case, a particularly scary adventure is worsened by Huck, who feels obligated to apologize to Jim, a vast social gaffe. At one point, Jim is nearly caught by a pair of boatmen who ask to look aboard the raft, as their initial suspicion is exacerbated by the reward offered in return for Jim's retrieval. Huck, battling with issues of morality, eventually decides to protect Jim by lying to the men. As Huck fights the urge to call out after the men to confess his "sin," he reaches a pre-existentialist questioning of right and wrong—despite his southern upbringing, Huck sees clear problems with racism and slavery. The decision to protect Jim, however, marks the beginnings of Huck's disregarding of conventional morality.

Throughout the rest of the novel, such issues as racism continually rear their ugly heads, although isolated incidents serve to further the existential method. Rather than engage in the familial feuds exhibited by people who would otherwise have been perfectly gracious hosts, Huck finds Jim and escapes yet again. In addition, he forges his own moralistic path when confronted with the duke and the dauphin. Huck chooses to neither reveal them nor make a big deal out of their scams. Only when he worries that truly innocent bystanders may get hurt does he intervene. Woven throughout these ethical dilemmas is the true focus of the novel— the integrity, or lack thereof, of slavery and its byproducts. At the conclusion of the novel, Huck chooses his own moral path as he declares "All right then, I'll go to Hell!" as he chooses to save Jim rather than leave him in captivity.

Just as the raft represents the vehicle with which Huck is able to complete his goal of self-identity, the journey itself represents his forging of his own path. The necessity of the journey, of his experiences, of the fulfillment of his longing for freedom is great, as they serve to form the core of his being and enables him to make key decisions for the rest of his life.

Essay Written by Megan Dunphy

## Comments on Essay 3

The essay begins with a universal dilemma: social injustices. Note the thesis and how it goes from specific, knowledge of Huck, and then it shifts to a general theme as well: society. The following paragraphs defend this main point of attack with not only examples, but also punctuated by sophisticated vocabulary such as "sated" and "petulantly" to enhance the sophistication of diction and control of the language.

In paragraph two, the essayist begins defending the thesis with insights into Huck's existential dilemma. Note the historical reference to Locke, and the natural state of society. This inclusion further emphasizes the student's repertoire of knowledge of global issues and how they can connect to the world of fiction.

While there is a dangling modifier error in paragraph three with the "social gaffe" the message, and the specific example of Huck playing a trick on Jim to further introduce Huck's journey from ignorance to awareness helps offset the grammatical error.

The essayist's treatment of Huck's moral dilemma, and of also recalling one of the most famous lines of Twain's classic, "All right, I'll go to Hell!" further emphasize the student's complete command of the prompt's address to discover the restlessness and the "sojourn of self identity."

For reasons of verbal command, diction, style, this essay would earn nothing less than an eight in a nine-point essay scale.

# AP* CORRELATION CHART

## Literature: An Introduction to Reading and Writing Correlated to the AP English Literature and Composition Exam

All references to CB are to the College Board's publication known as the Acorn Book, which provides a course description for the AP Exam in English Literature and Composition Exam (as well as the AP Exam in English Language and Composition). From the College Board Web site http://apcentral.collegeboard.com, you can download a .pdf version.

### I. The Literature

| Fiction | |
|---|---|
| **Abundance** | Roberts includes 41 short stories—one in an introductory part on "The Process of Reading, Responding to, and Writing About Literature" (1–47); 36 in a nine-chapter section on the various facets of fiction (54–398); and four in "Four Stories for Additional Enjoyment and Study" (399–454). |
| **Quality of Selections: "Recognized Literary Merit" (CB 45)** | The College Board provides a list of fiction authors (48) to indicate the possible "range and quality of reading" (47–48) expected in an AP course. A similar list is provided in Part Eight of this AP help text. Of the 46 authors on this list, 22 are featured in this anthology. |
| | Emily Bronte (699) |
| | Raymond Carver (116) |
| | Kate Chopin (287) |
| | Joseph Conrad (202) |
| | Stephen Crane (802) |
| | Ralph Ellison (247) |
| | William Faulkner (75) |
| | Thomas Hardy (256) |
| | Nathaniel Hawthorne (331) |
| | Ernest Hemingway (289) |
| | James Joyce (226) |
| | D. H. Lawrence (378) |

Katherine Mansfield (176)
Herman Melville (674)
Flannery O'Connor (418)
Cynthia Ozick (230)
Katherine Anne Porter (341)
Jonathan Swift (630)
Mark Twain (187)
John Updike (309)
Alice Walker (848)
Eudora Welty (95)

The College Board's list is neither prescriptive nor exhaustive. This anthology includes numerous other fiction writers of "comparable literary merit" (a College Board term that encourages teachers and students to read not only widely but well). Among these other fiction writers:

Ambrose Bierce (69)
Anton Chekhov (1156)
Charlotte Perkins Gilman (408)
Shirley Jackson (120)
John Steinbeck (347)

Note also the large number of authors cited under the remaining fiction topics below.

| **Emphasis on works written in English, with representative British and American authors (CB 46)** | Roberts' text includes **short stories** by these classic American authors. |
|---|---|

Kate Chopin (287)
Stephen Crane (802)
William Faulkner (75)
Nathaniel Hawthorne (331)
Ernest Hemingway (289)
Flannery O'Connor (418)
Katherine Anne Porter (341)
Mark Twain (187)
John Updike (309)
Alice Walker (848)
Eudora Welty (95)

The text also includes short stories by several classic British authors.

Joseph Conrad (202)
James Joyce (226)
D. H. Lawrence (378)
Frank O'Connor (300)
Jonathan Swift (630)

| Inclusion of representative periods and literary movements: 16th–20th century (CB 45) | Because of the genre's historical development, the editors concentrate on short stories from the 19th and 20th centuries. |
|---|---|
| | Roberts' anthology offers a wide variety of choices for the AP teacher and student— |
| | • The high style of Hawthorne ("Young Goodman Brown," 331) |
| | • The simple, clean style pioneered by Hemingway ("Hills Like White Elephants," 289) |
| | • The introspective convolutions of Faulkner ("A Rose for Emily," 75); |
| | • The unassuming realism of Steinbeck ("The Chrysanthemums," 347) |
| | • Recent experiments in fiction by Cynthia Ozick ("The Shawl," 230), and Tim O'Brien ("The Things They Carried," 81). |
| | In total, 242 authors are represented here in the anthology, including four anonymous authors. Slightly more than 58 percent of the authors—142— were born after 1900. Of the 63 writers born since 1935, 32 are women. |
| **Authorial diversity: geographic, cultural, ethnic, stylistic, gender (CB 46)** | Among the fiction offerings, Roberts includes "The Myth of Atalanta" (327), from the classical civilizations of Greece and Rome. To sample the diversity of the fictional offerings, consider the following authors: |
| | Aesop (326) |
| | Toni Cade Bambara (373) |
| | Kate Chopin (287) |
| | Anita Scott Coleman (328) |
| | Ralph Ellison (247) |
| | Ernest J. Gaines (158) |
| | Charlotte Perkins Gilman (408) |
| | Katherine Mansfield (176) |
| | Lorrie Moore (126) |
| | Alice Munro (293) |
| | Daniel Orozco (305) |
| | Cynthia Ozick (230) |
| | Americo Parédes (388) |
| | Leslie Marmon Silko (842) |
| | Amy Tan (180) |
| | Alice Walker (848) |
| | Eudora Welty (95) |
| | Tom Whitecloud (269) |

| Poetry | |
|---|---|
| Abundance | Of the textbook's 1,600+ pages, Roberts devotes most of it to literature, 405 of which the editors allot to poetry (456–860). The poetry section comprises nine chapters; a typical part includes several poems in the early pages of instruction and commentary on a particular aspect of poetry, followed by a group of "Poems for Study," each of which is followed by questions that guide the student to examine it in the light of the part focus. |
| | For example, Chapter 15 "Tone: The Creation of Attitude in Poetry" (599–640), opens with five poems that illustrate the editors' comments about tone, followed by 24 "Poems for Study." The poetry section closes with Chapter 19, "Eighty-Four Poems for Additional Enjoyment and Study" (791–860), offering 84 poems by 79 poets. |
| **Quality of Selections: "Recognized Literary Merit" (CB 45)** | The College Board provides a list of poets (48) to indicate the possible "range and quality of reading" (47–48) expected in an AP course. Of the 47 poets on this list, 27 appear in Roberts' anthology: |
| | W. H. Auden (794)<br>Elizabeth Bishop (533)<br>William Blake (608)<br>Robert Browning (609)<br>Samuel Taylor Coleridge (536)<br>Emily Dickinson (733)<br>John Donne (807)<br>T. S. Eliot (539)<br>Robert Frost (752)<br>Joy Harjo (472)<br>Seamus Heaney (618)<br>George Herbert (654)<br>Gerard Manley Hopkins (669)<br>Langston Hughes (764)<br>John Keats (818)<br>John Milton (674)<br>Sylvia Plath (788)<br>Edgar Allan Poe (233)<br>Alexander Pope (607)<br>William Shakespeare (649)<br>Percy Bysshe Shelley (681)<br>Leslie Marmon Silko (842) |

| | Alfred, Lord Tennyson (644)<br>Walt Whitman (723)<br>Richard Wilbur (723)<br>William Wordsworth (588)<br>William Butler Yeats (725) |
| --- | --- |
| | As a further service to both students and teachers, the editors include a brief biographical sketch of each poet in the anthology. The information is found in Appendix II "Brief Biographies of the Poets in Part III" (1450–1480). |
| **Inclusion of representative periods and literary movements: 16th–20th centuries (CB 45)** | Roberts' anthology offers a rich mixture of poets, primarily British and American. In addition, Chapter 18, "Four Major American Poets" (733–790), focuses on four distinct and significant voices in the poetry of the English language: William Wordsworth, a giant of the early Romantic period in British poetry; Emily Dickinson, a 19th-century Transcendentalist with a voice so spare and modern as to enjoy international stature at the beginning of the 21st century; Robert Frost, whose New England colloquialism transcends regional and national boundaries four decades after his death; and Sylvia Plath, a confessional poet whose works, which earned her a posthumous Pulitzer Prize, were inextricably tied to her personal experiences. |
| | This chapter features 15 poems by Hughes (764–773) who is known for the variety in his works and his employment of various voices. The 19 Dickinson poems (738–747) can best be described as terse, intense, and acerbic. Frost's classic understatement and his simple, unobtrusive form are on display in 16 poems (752–760). In addition, the 13 Plath poems contribute lyric poems that represent a combination of the personal self and an imagined self composed by the poet. |
| | With a part on "Form: The Shape of the Poem" (641–689), the editors present poems in a wide range of forms, both open and closed. |
| | Finally—with parts such as "Words: The Building Blocks of Poetry" (494–527), "Symbolism and Allusion: Windows to Wide Expanses of Meaning" (691–731)—this textbook allows AP courses to examine poetry in its many facets. |

| Authorial diversity: geographic, cultural, ethnic, stylistic, gender (CB 46) | In addition to the great names in poetry, the anthology includes a rich variety of poets who have made a more recent contribution to the genre. Consider the following: |
|---|---|
| | Lucille Clifton (612)<br>Mari Evans (575)<br>Nikki Giovanni (667)<br>Louise Gluck (708)<br>Audre Lorde (824)<br>W. S. Merwin (828)<br>Liesel Mueller (458)<br>Sharon Olds (622)<br>Marge Piercy (833)<br>Robert Pinsky (623)<br>Luis Omar Salinas (836)<br>Sonia Sanchez (836)<br>Gertrude Schnackenberg (838)<br>Mark Strand (519)<br>Jean Toomer (682)<br>Alice Walker (848)<br>Paul Zimmer (854) |

## Drama

| Abundance | Roberts' textbook includes 14 complete plays over four chapters (875–1375). |
|---|---|
| Quality of Selections: "Recognized Literary Merit" (CB 45) | The College Board provides a list of dramatists (48) to "indicate the possible range and quality of reading" (47–48) in an AP course. Of the 29 authors on this list, 10 appear among the offerings in Roberts' anthology.<br><br>Edward Albee<br>   *The Sandbox* (884)<br><br>Anton Chekhov<br>   *The Bear* (1156)<br><br>Henrik Ibsen<br>   *A Dollhouse* (1191)<br><br>Arthur Miller<br>   *Death of a Salesman* (1263) |

Eugene O'Neill
*Before Breakfast* (909)

William Shakespeare
*Hamlet* (981)
*A Midsummer Night's Dream* (1099)

Sophocles
*Oedipus the King* (939)

August Wilson
*Fences* (1330)

All eight of these playwrights appear regularly on the open question section of the AP English Literature and Composition Exam. One of three essays featured yearly on the exam, the open question presents a phenomenon characteristic of numerous great works of literature, with a prompt directing the examinee to write an essay using a single work to illuminate the phenomenon in question. The question usually includes a list of appropriate works, along with the proviso that examinees may choose another work of comparable literary merit. That the eight dramatists listed above appear frequently on this list attests to the issue here of "recognized literary merit."

| | |
|---|---|
| **Inclusion of representative periods and literary movements: 16th–20th centuries (CB 45)** | Because drama originates with the ancient Greeks and because AP courses pay homage to the roots of drama, it is fitting that Roberts' anthology includes *Oedipus the King* as the first play in Chapter 21, "The Tragic Vision: Affirmation Through Loss" (923–1090)—and that the text illustrates the evolution of the tragedy by anthologizing *Hamlet* to represent Renaissance tragedy and *Death of a Salesman* to represent tragedy for the 20th century. From the realism of Ibsen to the neoclassicism of O'Neill and the 20th-century lyricism of Miller—this textbook admirably represents the richness of the genre. (Page numbers for individual playwrights are listed under preceding topic.) |
| **Authorial diversity: geographic, cultural, ethnic, stylistic, gender (CB 46)** | With the 14 full-length works, Roberts' text does an admirable job of addressing the diversity inherent in this genre—including Ancient Greece, Renaissance England, late 19th-century Norway, and 20th-century America. With Edward Albee (883), Susan Glaspell |

| | |
|---|---|
| | (891), August Wilson (1328), Beth Henley (1165), Langston Hughes (619), and Betty Keller (904), the editors further exemplify the diverse expressions of the genre. |
| **Essay/Nonfiction** | Because AP literature courses—much like introductory literature courses at the college level—focus on fiction, poetry, and drama, Roberts' anthology does the same. The textbook does not include a separate section devoted to the study of nonfiction/the essay. |

## II. Support materials for instruction in reading and writing

| | |
|---|---|
| **Organization and sequencing of contents: to support instruction in "the experience of literature, the interpretation of literature, and the evaluation of literature" (CB 45)** | Roberts' anthology begins with an "Introduction: The Process of Reading, Responding to, and Writing About Literature" (Chapter 1, pages 1–51). Here the editors offer advice and instruction in how students can increase their awareness of what they experience as they read and how they can articulate their experience of literature, expand the ways in which they experience literature, and begin to analyze their experience of literature. To model this kind of experience, the editors reprint Guy de Maupassant's seminal short story, "The Necklace" (4–15)—annotated in the margins with the kind of reader-response observations that can increase readers' awareness of their experience of literature and develop the rudiments of analysis and evaluation. The introductory part continues, with explicit instructions and examples of student entries in "Reading and Responding in a Notebook or Computer File" (11–16), followed by detailed instructions on the "how-to" of writing a first essay about literature (16–51).

With the introductory cornerstone in place, the editors begin each major section—fiction, poetry, and drama—with an overview of the genre, guiding students through a conscious experience of their reading and moving toward a piece of writing that articulates the essence of the reading experience. Subsequent parts offer guidance in the analysis of |

discrete elements of the genre in question. The textbook is explicit and thorough on the subject of analysis, although it does not address evaluation *per se*. It should be noted, however, that analysis—"the interpretation of literature"—is the cornerstone of an AP literature course.

The fiction section begins with "Fiction: An Overview" (1–51), including student essays that illustrate and provide examples of responding to literature (43–45). Subsequent parts guide students through recognition and analysis of the elements of short fiction with representative stories to serve as examples: point of view (107–150), character (151–197), setting (198–243), structure (244–279), tone and style (280–320), symbolism and allegory (321–366), and idea or theme (367–398).

The poetry section begins with "Meeting Poetry: An Overview" (456–493), including direct instruction in how to read a poem (461–463) paraphrasing a poem (486–487) and writing an explication (487–493). The following nine chapters guide students through analysis of such elements as diction and syntax (494–527), imagery (528–559), figures of speech (560–598), tone (599–640), form (641–690), and symbolism and allusion (691–732).

The drama section begins with "The Dramatic Vision: An Overview" (862–922), with direct instruction in writing (862–873). Subsequent parts address analysis of tragedy (873–883), comedy (873–883), dramatic reality and non-reality (873–883). To provide students with further practice in "the experience of literature, the interpretation of literature, and the evaluation of literature," Roberts' text culminates each genre section with parts designed to build on the skills covered thus far. The fiction section ends with "Four Stories for Additional Enjoyment and Study" (399–427). Similarly, the poetry section closes with "Four Major American Poets: Emily Dickinson, Robert Frost, Langston Hughes, and Sylvia Plath" (733–790) and "Eighty Poems for Additional Enjoyment and Study" (791–860). The drama section concludes with "Four Plays for Additional Enjoyment and Study" (1187–1375).

| | |
|---|---|
| **Direct instruction in writing in these three modes** | Roberts' anthology begins with direct instruction in the basics of writing about literature. (See the first paragraph above, under "Organization and sequencing of contents.") In addition, each chapter offers concise instruction in writing about the literary element in question. Finally, Chapter 25 offers guided instruction in a literary essay of comparison-contrast (1412–1427). |
| **Writing assignments that direct students in the practice of these three modes** | Parts typically close by focusing on a particular writing activity, arranged by the editors in three logical steps:<br><br>• Brief instruction on the activity in question.<br><br>• A sample student essay to model the focal activity, including the editors' comments on the essay.<br><br>• A list of writing topics that ask the student to practice examining literature from the perspective of the part in question.<br><br>Chapter 9, for example, examines "Idea or Theme: The Meaning and the Message in Fiction" (367–398). As the chapter closes, the editors offer instruction in "Writing about a Major Idea in Fiction" (392–398), followed by a student essay examining meaning in a D.H. Lawrence short story (394–397), with the editors' commentary on the student essay (397–398)—and, finally, five "Special Topics for Writing and Argument About Ideas" (398). |
| **Student-written essays that model these three modes** | Chapters that focus on a particular facet of the genre in question include one or two student-written essays that examine a piece of literature from the perspective under examination. Each student essay takes its place in this structure, and is provided under the heading of "Writing About . . ." assignments. The introductory chapter offers two student essays. Chapters 2–9 and 10A, on fiction—as well as Chapters 11–17 and 19A, on poetry, and Chapters 20–22 and 23A, on drama—offer additional student essays. Chapter 25, on comparison-contrast, also provides a student essay. |
| **A discrete writing handbook section suitable for the AP student** | The introductory chapter (1–51)—discussed in detail above—offers the kind of structure and instruction worthy of a good writing handbook. |

| | The closing section of the textbook—"Special Writing Topics About Literature" (1390–1438)—offers three parts of useful information for the student writer in an AP literature course. |
|---|---|
| | • In Chapter 24 (1389–1411), Roberts offers thumbnail sketches of ten "Critical Approaches Important in the Study of Literature"—providing a genuine service to the AP teacher and student. |
| | • Chapter 25 (1412–1427) offers explicit instruction in the comparison-contrast essay. |
| | • Chapter 26 (1428–1438) offers brief and useful advice on "Writing Examinations on Literature." |
| **A glossary and/or index of literary terms** | Roberts' text offers a "Glossary of Literary Terms" (1481–1503)—handy and accessible definitions suitable for the AP student. The terms themselves are discussed in context; in addition, page numbers are provided for reference—making them all the more useful for instruction in an AP course. |
| **Instruction and support materials for the teaching of research** | Three parts offer guidance in research:<br><br>• Chapter 10A (428–454) about fiction<br>• Chapter 19A (855–860) about poetry<br>• Chapter 23A (1376–1387) about drama<br><br>Appendix I (1439–1449) offers concise and useful information in documenting sources. |

## III. Miscellaneous features

| | |
|---|---|
| **Table of contents** | Roberts' text offers two variations on the table of contents:<br><br>• The standard table of contents (iii–xxxviii) showcases the editors' genre approach. By using variations in typeface (boldface, italics, all-caps, varying font sizes) and by using white space judiciously, the editors make the various contents accessible at a rapid glance.<br><br>• A thematic table of contents (xl–l) assists teachers and students who prefer a thematic approach to literature. Each theme is subdivided by genre—stories, poems, plays and art. |

| Index | The textbook includes an "Index of Authors, Titles, and First Lines" (1512–1530) as well as a subject index (2). |
|---|---|
| **Instructor's Manual** | Like the textbook itself, the instructor's manual is composed of three major sections and a fourth shorter section: "Fiction" (1–455), "Poetry" (456–860), "Drama" (861–1389), and "Special Writing Topics About Literature" (1390–1438). The manual itself is paginated on the bottom outer page corners; top outer page corners are annotated with the correlating page numbers of the textbook itself. |
| | The fiction section follows the order of the textbook, with the editors offering comments on the stories, answers to the study questions, and comments on the writing topics. Showing considerable thought for the literature teacher, the editors close their handling of each story with a list of works for comparison by author, title, and page number. |
| | The poetry section also follows the order of the textbook, with similar offerings for the anthologized poems. AP teachers will discover a real boon to their teaching with "Using Extra Resources for Understanding" (855–860), an extensive listing of Web site listings and audio resources for many of the textbook's anthologized poets. |
| | The drama section offers commentary on each author and each play, as well as discussion of questions and writing topics. |
| | The editors offer brief comments on the parts of the writing section. |
| | The companion Web site, an online study guide to accompany Roberts' series, offers AP students valuable supplemental information and activities directly related to the contents of the text book, and serves as a gateway to electronic literary research and a chance to communicate with other students of literature. This resource may be found at www.prenhall.com/roberts and is available at no additional cost. |
| | After logging on, students will arrive at a home page offering a quick, accessible overview of the |

site, with two options available for instruction and enrichment:

- Selecting an author for further study.

  - Selecting a chapter from the textbook—for guided commentary and further study.

Selecting an author takes students to a page that offers:

- A brief biography.

- Links to a "Comprehension Quiz" and "Essay Questions" for the relevant story, poem, or play included in Roberts' text.

- Links to reliable Web sites offering further biographical and bibliographical information as well as pertinent literary criticism. These Web sites, of course, offer further links to the research-minded student.

**Selecting a chapter** takes students to a page that offers:

- Timeline

  This option takes students to a colorful, dynamic timeline covering the most recent 500 years of British and U.S. history. Students may view the timeline from three perspectives: Politics, International Affairs, or Society and Culture. With each choice, the timeline is marked by a number of significant events. Clicking on a particular event typically links students to a page offering a thumbnail sketch, relevant images, and numerous links for further research. This timeline offers invaluable enrichment for the AP student.

- Part Authors

  This option is discussed above.

- Writing About . . .

  This option offers students guided instruction linked to one of four introductory parts in Roberts' text: Chapter 1, with its introduction to literature; Chapter 2, with its overview of fiction; Chapter 11, poetry; and Chapter 20, drama. Each part web page offers several textboxes allowing students to compose as they follow guided advice on writing.

| | |
|---|---|
| | Students can print these textboxes or—with participating classes—send them to their teachers for feedback. |
| | • Writing Workshops |
| | This option offers three student essays: one on fiction, one on poetry, one on drama. A photograph and thumbnail biography of the student author accompany each essay. In addition, the student can see each essay in three versions: a first draft, a second draft, and the final paper. Each draft is presented in a facsimile, with instructor's comments marked in red. Further, the first and second drafts are linked to a detailed commentary by the instructor. Finally, students with sophisticated computers can hear the student writer's thoughts on the original writing assignment. |
| **Companion Web site** | For students struggling to adjust to the demands of an AP environment, the Web site offers the kind of basic guidance, support, and practice in analytical thinking and writing skills that can lead to genuine academic success. Further, the Web site serves as a vehicle that can take students to a broader, deeper understanding of literature and its vital role in our world. |

# Text Credits

**Agüeros, Jack** "Sonnet for You, Familiar Famine" from SONNETS FROM THE PUERTO RICAN. Copyright © 1996 by Jack Agüeros. Reprinted with the permission of Hanging Loose Press.

**Albee, Edward** "THE SANDBOX." Copyright © 1959, renewed 1987 by Edward Albee. Reprinted with the permission of William Morris Agency, Inc. on behalf of the author.

**Auden, W. H.** "The Unknown Citizen" from COLLECTED POEMS. Copyright © 1940 and renewed © 1968 by W. H. Auden. Reprinted with the permission of Random House, Inc.

**Bambara, Toni Cade** "The Lesson" from GORILLA, MY LOVE. Copyright © 1972 by Toni Cade Bambara. Reprinted with the permission of Random House, Inc.

**Berry, Wendell** "Another Descent" from COLLECTED POEMS: 1957–1982. Copyright © 1985 by Wendell Berry. Reprinted with the permission of North Point Press, a division of Farrar, Straus and Giroux, LLC.

**Bishop, Elizabeth** "The Fish" and "One Art" from COMPLETE POEMS: 1927–1979 by Elizabeth Bishop. Copyright © 1979, 1983 by Alice Helen Methfessell. Reprinted with the permission of Farrar, Straus and Giroux, LLC.

**Bogan, Louise** "Women" from THE BLUE ESTUARIES: POEMS 1923–1968. Copyright © 1968 by Louise Bogan, renewed © 1996 by Ruth Limmer. Reprinted with the permission of Farrar, Straus and Giroux, LLC.

**Bontemps, Arna** "A Black Man Talks of Reaping" from PERSONALS. Copyright © 1963 by Arna Bontemps. Reprinted with the permission of Harold Ober Associates, Incorporated.

**Brewster, Elizabeth** "Where I Come From" from SELECTED POEMS OF ELIZABETH BREWSTER, 1944–84 by Elizabeth Brewster. Reprinted with the permission of Oberon Press.

**Carruth, Hayden** "An Apology for Using the Word 'Heart' in Too Many Poems" from COLLECTED SHORTER POEMS 1946–1991. Copyright © 1992 by Hayden Carruth. Reprinted with the permission of Copper Canyon Press.

**Carter, Jimmy** "I Wanted to Share My Father's World" from ALWAYS A RECKONING AND OTHER POEMS. Copyright © 1995 by Jimmy Carter. Reprinted with the permission of Times Books, a division of Random House, Inc.

**Carver, Raymond** "Neighbors" from WILL YOU PLEASE BE QUIET, PLEASE. Copyright © 1989 by Tess Gallagher. Reprinted with the permission of International Creative Management, Inc.

**Chioles, John** "Before the Firing Squad." Copyright 1983 by John Chioles; first printed in The Available Press/PEN Short Story Collection (Ballantine, 1985) by permission of the PEN Syndicated Fiction Project. Reprinted with the permission of the author.

**Clampitt, Amy** "Beach Glass" from THE KINGFISHER. Copyright © 1983 by Amy Clampitt. Reprinted with the permission of Alfred A. Knopf, a division of Random House, Inc.

**Clifton, Lucille** "Homage to My Hips" from TWO-HEADED WOMAN (first published by University of Massachusetts). Copyright © 1980 by Lucille Clifton. Reprinted with the permission of Curtis Brown, Ltd.

**Cohen, Leonard** "The Killers" from STRANGER MUSIC by Leonard Cohen. Reprinted with the permission of McClelland & Stewart Ltd.

**Coleman, Anita Scott** "Unfinished Masterpieces" from THE CRISIS, March 1927. The editor wishes to thank The Crisis Publishing Co., Inc., the publisher of the magazine of the National Association for the Advancement of Colored People, for authorizing the use of this work.

**Collins, Billy** "Schoolsville" from THE APPLE THAT ASTONISHED PARIS. Copyright © 1988 by Billy Collins. Reprinted with the permission of University of Arkansas Press; "The Names" reprinted with the

# Index of Authors, Titles, and First Lines

The names of authors are printed in **bold type**, *titles in italic type*, and first lines in Roman type.

# Photo Credits

Chapter 2: pg 63 © Dan Piraro. King Features Syndicate; pg 65 From MAUS II: A SURVIVOR'S TALE/AND HERE MY TROUBLE BEGAN by Art Spiegelman, copyright © 1986, 1989, 1990, 1991, by Art Spiegelman. Reprinted by the permission of Pantheon Books, a division of Random House, Inc.; pg 69 Culver Pictures, Inc.; pg 75 Corbis/Bettmann; pg 81 Jerry Bauer; pg 95 AP Wide World Photos. Chapter 3: pg 116 Marion Ettlinger; pg 120 Erich Hartmann/Magnum Photos, Inc.; pg 126 Joyce Ravid; pg 130 © McLeod Murdo/CORBIS. Chapter 4: pg 152 *Bust of Lorenzo de' Medici*, Florentine, 15th or 16th century, probably after a model by Andrea del Verocchio and O. Benintendi. Photograph © Board of Trustees, National Gallery of Art, Washington, D.C. Samuel H. Kress Collection; pg 158 Mercer University; pg 176 Getty Images Inc.—Hulton Archive Photos; pg 180 © Reuters NewMedia Inc./CORBIS; pg 187 Corbis/ Bettmann. Chapter 5: pg 202 Alvin Langdon Coburn/Getty Images Inc.—Hulton Archive Photos; pg 226 Corbis/Bettmann; pg 230 Julius Ozick/Raines and Raines; pg 233 Corbis/Bettmann. Chapter 6: pg 247 Ben Martin/Getty Images/Time Life Pictures; pg 256 © Bettmann/CORBIS; pg 269 © National Archives/ CORBIS, All Rights Reserved. Chapter 7: pg 287 Missouri Historical Society; pg 289 UPI/Corbis/ Bettmann; pg 293 Jerry Bauer; pg 300 Dublin Writers Museum and Shaw Birthplace; pg 309 AP Wide World Photos. Chapter 8: pg 326 Joseph Martin/Picture Desk, Inc./Kobal Collection; pg 331 Corbis/ Bettmann; pg 339 The Granger Collection, New York; pg 341 UPI/Corbis/Bettmann; pg 347 Library of Congress. Chapter 9: pg 378 Corbis/Bettmann; pg 388 Benson Latin American Collection. Chapter 10: pg 404 AP Wide World Photos; pg 408 Culver Pictures, Inc.; pg 418 Corbis/Bettmann. Chapter 11: pg 456 AP Wide World Photo; pg 471 © Bettmann/CORBIS; pg 472 *Remember* from the book SHE HAD SOME HORS-ES by Joy Harjo. Copyright © 1983, 1987 Thunder's Mouth Press. Appears by permission of the publisher, Thunder's Mouth Press, a member of Perseus Books Group; pg 473 © Bettmann/CORBIS; pg 478 © 1998 James McGoon. Chapter 12: pg 503 © Stapleton Collection/CORBIS; pg 504 © Bettmann/CORBIS; pg 505 The New York Public Library; pg 506 American Poetry Review Records, Rare Book & Manuscript Library, University of Pennsylvania; pg 507 © Bettmann/CORBIS; pg 508 Michael Nicholson/Corbis/Bettmann; pg 509 Susan Cisco; pg 510 Courtesy of the Library of Congress; pg 513 © E. O. Hoppe/Corbis; pg 514 © Christopher Felver/CORBIS; pg 515 AP Wide World Photos; pg 517 Colby College Special Collections, Waterville, ME; pg 519 © Bettmann/CORBIS; pg 521 Thomas Victor/University of Pennsylvania. Chapter 13: pg 536 © Bettmann/CORBIS; pg 539 © Bettmann/CORBIS; pg 544 Getty Images, Inc.; pg 549 © E. O. Hoppe/CORBIS. Chapter 14: pg 562 © Bettmann/CORBIS; pg 583 AP Wide World Photo; pg 584 © Oscar White/CORBIS; pg 587 © CORBIS; pg 588 Culver Pictures, Inc. Chapter 15: pg 609 © Bettmann/CORBIS; pg 612 © Christopher Felver/CORBIS; pg 622 © Christopher Felver/CORBIS; pg 624 Courtesy of the Library of Congress; pg 625 Getty Images Inc.—Hulton Archive Photos; pg 630 The Granger Collection, New York; pg 633 North Wind Picture Archives. Chapter 16: pg 658 © Oscar White/CORBIS; pg 666 © Hulton-Deutsch Collection/CORBIS; pg 667 By permission of author/subject, Nikki Giovanni; pg 674 © Bettmann/CORBIS; pg 681 © Hulton-Deutsch Collection/CORBIS; pg 682 © Bettmann/CORBIS; pg 683 © Pach Brothers/CORBIS. Chapter 17: pg 707 Bettmann/CORBIS; pg 708 AP Wide World Photos; pg 708 AP Wide World Photos; pg 713 Bettmann/CORBIS; pg 718 Getty Images, Inc.; pg 722 Milton Viorst, c/o Lescher & Lescher Ltd.; pg 723 © CORBIS. Chapter 18: pg 734 Amherst College Archives and Special Collections, by permission of the Trustees of Amherst College; pg 748 Courtesy of the Herbert H. Lamson Library, Plymouth State College, Plymouth, New Hampshire; pg 761 UPI/Corbis/Bettmann; pg 773 © Bettmann/CORBIS. Chapter 19: pg 793 © Bettmann/CORBIS; pg 819 The Krater of Thanagra. Wedding Procession and Musicians. 4th BCE. National Archeological Museum, Athens, Greece. Alinari/Art Resource, NY; pg 824 © Bettmann/CORBIS; pg 837 Corbis/Bettmann. Chapter 20: pg 882 Larry Riley/ Miramax/Picture Desk, Inc./Kobal Collection; pg 883 © Universal International Pictures/Photofest; pg 891 AP Wide World Photos; pg 893 Billy Rose Theatre Collection, The New York Public Library for the Performing Arts, Astor, Lenox and Tilden Foundations; pg 903 Joel Johnstone/Betty C. Keller; pg 905 Meriwether Publishing Ltd.; pg 907 UPI/Corbis/Bettmann; pg 910 Playwrights Theater production of

Eugene O'Neill's "Before Breakfast." Provincetown Playhouse, New York City, August 2001. Directed by Stephen Kennedy Murphy, Set Design by Roger Hanna, Costume Design by Adrienne K. Wheeler, Lighting Design by Matthew E. Adelson; pg 936 (TOP) © Vanni/Art Resource, NY; (BOTTOM) Benaki Museum, Athens-Photographic Archive. **Chapter 21:** pg 981 Stock Montage, Inc./Historical Pictures Collection; pg 1030 Nancy LeVine/Photofest. **Chapter 22:** pg 1136 Photofest; pg 1156 Corbis/Bettmann; pg 1165 © Neal Preston/CORBIS; pg 1167 Southern Reflective Methodist University/Meadows School of the Arts Division of Theatre. **Chapter 23:** pg 1188 Corbis/Bettmann; pg 1233 Photofest; pg 1239 UPI/Corbis/Bettmann; pg 1260 Billy Rose Theatre Collection, The New York Public Library for the Performing Arts, Astor, Lenox and Tilden Foundations; pg 1263 AP Wide World Photos; pg 1265 Billy Rose Theatre Collection, The New York Public Library for the Performing Arts, Astor, Lenox and Tilden Foundations/Art Resource, NY.; pg 1323 Photofest. **Color Insert:** pg I–1 Martin Johnson Heade (American, 1819–1904), *Approaching Storm: Beach Near Newport*, c. 1861–1862. Oil on canvas, 28 x 58 3/8 in. (71.12 x 148.27 cm). Courtesy Museum of Fine Arts, Boston. Gift of Maxim Karolik for the M. and M. Karolik Collection of American Paintings, 1815–1865. 45.889. Reproduced with permission. (© 2003 Museum of Fine Arts, Boston. All rights reserved.); pg I–2 Joseph Mallord William Turner (1775–1851), *Keelmen Heaving In Coals by Moonlight*, 1942. Oil on Canvas, 36 1/4 x 48 1/4 in. National Gallery of Art, Washington, D.C., Widener Collection; pg I–3 (TOP) Fernand Leger (1881–1955), *The City*, 1919. Oil on canvas, 91 x 177 1/2 in. The Philadelphia Museum of Art, Philadelphia. A. E. Gallatin Collection. (© 2004 Artists Rights Society [ARS], New York/ADAGP, Paris); pg I–3 (BOTTOM) Edward Hopper (1882–1967), *Automat*, 1927. Oil on canvas, 28 1/8 x 36 in. Des Moines Art Center Permanent Collections; purchased with funds from the Edmundson Art Foundation, Inc. 1958.2. (Photograph by Michael Tropea, Chicago); pg I–4 (TOP) Thomas Cole (1801–1848), *View from Mount Holyoke, Northampton, Massachusetts, After a Thunderstorm (The Oxbow)*, 1836. Oil on canvas, 51 1/2 in. high x 76 in. wide (130.8 x 193 cm). Signed and dated: T. Cole 1836 (lower left). The Metropolitan Museum of Art, New York. Gift of Mrs. Russell Sage, 1908 (08.228). (Photograph © 1995 The Metropolitan Museum of Art); pg I–4 (BOTTOM) Albert Bierstadt (1830–1902), *Among the Sierra Nevada Mountains, California*, 1868. Oil on canvas, 71 x 120 in. (183 x 305 cm). (© Smithsonian American Art Museum, Washington, DC/Art Resource, New York); pg I–5 (TOP) Sir Hubert von Herkomer (1849–1914), *Hard Times*, 1885. (© Manchester City Art Gallery); pg I–5 (BOTTOM) Pieter Brueghel the Elder (c. 1525–1569), *Landscape with the Fall of Icarus*, c. 1554–1555. Musées Royaux des Beaux-Arts, Brussels. (© Scala/Art Resource, New York); pg I–6 (TOP) Pablo Picasso (1881–1973), *Guernica*, 1937. Oil on canvas, 350 x 782 cm. Museo Nacional Centro de Arte Reina Sofia, Madrid. (© Estate of Pablo Picasso/Artists Rights Society [ARS], New York); pg I–6 (BOTTOM) Claude Lorrain (1600–1682), *Harbour at Sunset (Seaport at Sunset)*, 1639. Oil on canvas. Louvre, Paris. (© Erich Lessing/Art Resource, New York); pg I–7 (TOP) Pieter Brueghel the Elder (c. 1525–1569), *Peasants' Dance*, 1568. Oil on oak wood, 114 x 164 cm. Kunsthistorisches Museum, Vienna. (© Erich Lessing/Art Resource, New York); pg I–7 (BOTTOM) Jacques-Louis David (1748–1825), *The Death of Socrates*, 1787. Oil on canvas, 51 x 77.25 in. (129.5 x 196.2 cm). Signed and dated: L. David (on bench at right); L.D./MDCCLXXXVII (lower left). The Metropolitan Museum of Art, New York. Catherine Lorillard Wolfe Collection, Wolfe Fund, 1931. 31.45. (Photograph © 1995 The Metropolitan Museum of Art); pg I–8 (LEFT) August Renoir (1841–1919), *The Umbrellas (Les Parapluies)*, c. 1881–1886. National Gallery, London. (© Art Resource, New York); pg I–8 (RIGHT) François Boucher (1703–1770), *Madame de Pompadour*. Paper on canvas, 60 x 45.5 cm. Louvre, Paris. (© Erich Lessing/Art Resource, New York); pg I–9 (LEFT) James Abbott McNeill Whistler (1834–1903), *The Little White Girl, Symphony in White, No. 2*, 1864. Oil on canvas, 76.5 x 51.1 cm. (© Tate Gallery, London/Art Resource, New York); pg I–9 (RIGHT) Francisco de Goya y Lucientes (1746–1828), *The Colossus*, 1808–1810. Oil on canvas, 116 x 105 cm. Museo del Prado, Madrid. (© Erich Lessing/Art Resource, New York); pg I–10 (TOP) *Hercules and the Infant Telephus*. A Roman fresco from Herculaneum. Museo Archeologico Nazionale, Naples. (© Scala/Art Resource, New York); pg I–11 (TOP) *Interior of the Globe Theatre*. London. (Photograph by April Roberts); pg I–11 (BOTTOM) *Exterior of the Globe Theatre*. Authentic reconstruction based on sixteenth-century drawings and archaeological research, opening 1996. London. (Photograph by April Roberts); pg I–12 *Stage of the Globe Theater*. London. (Photograph by April Roberts).